Blue Book
Electric Guitars™
9th Edition

Text by Zachary R. Fjestad
Edited by S.P. Fjestad

$29.95
Publisher's Softcover
Suggested List Price

Publisher's Limited
Edition Hardcover
Suggested List Price - $49.95

Publisher's Note: This book is the result of continual guitar research accomplished by attending guitar shows, receiving contributing editor's updates, communicating with guitar dealers and collectors throughout the country each year, and staying on top of trends as they occur. This book represents an analysis of prices and information on currently manufactured, recently manufactured, and vintage/collectible guitars.

Although every reasonable effort has been made to compile an accurate and reliable guide, guitar prices may vary significantly depending on such factors as the locality of the sale, the number of sales we were able to consider, famous musician endorsement of certain makes/models, regional economic conditions, and other critical factors.

Accordingly, no representation can be made that the guitars listed may be bought or sold at prices indicated, nor shall the editor or publisher be responsible for any error made in compiling and recording such prices.

Blue Book Publications, Inc.
8009 34th Avenue South, Suite 175
Minneapolis, MN 55425 U.S.A.
Phone: 800-877-4867 (USA and Canada orders only)
Phone: 952-854-5229
Fax: 952-853-1486
Email: guitars@bluebookinc.com
Website: http://www.bluebookinc.com

Published and printed in the United States of America
ISBN 1-886768-57-9
Library of Congress ISSN - Pending

Distributed in part by Music Sales Corporation and Omnibus Press
257 Park Avenue South, New York, NY 10010 USA
Phone: 212-254-2100 • Fax: 212-254-2013
www.musicsales.com

9th Edition *Blue Book of Electric Guitars* Credits:

Production Manager & Art Director - Clint H. Schmidt
Assistant Art Director - Zachary R. Fjestad
Cover Layout & Design - Clint H. Schmidt
Copyeditor - Stacy M. Knutson
Executive Assistant Editor - Cassandra Faulkner
Cover Photography & Design - Clint H. Schmidt and Zachary R. Fjestad
Cover Instruments & Credits - Please refer to "About the Cover" on page 12.
Printer - Bang Printing, Brainerd, MN

This publication was conceived, written, photographed, edited, published, and printed in the United States of America.

CONTENTS

GENERAL INFORMATION

Many of you have probably purchased products from Blue Book Publications, Inc. over the years, and it may be helpful for you to know more about the company operation and what we are currently publishing, both in books and software. We are also the leaders in online informational services in various fields of collectibles, including guns and pool cues. As this edition goes to press, the following titles, products, and services are currently available. All pricing is in U.S. dollars, and does not include any shipping charges. Many of these softcover editions are also available in hardcover deluxe editions. Please check our website for more information, including the most current availablility, pricing, and S/H charges on all titles.

9th Edition *Blue Book of Electric Guitars* by Zachary R. Fjestad, edited by S.P. Fjestad - $29.95

9th Edition *Blue Book of Acoustic Guitars* by Zachary R. Fjestad, edited by S.P. Fjestad - $24.95

2nd Edition *Blue Book of Guitar Amplifiers* by Zachary R. Fjestad, edited by S.P. Fjestad - $24.95

9th Editions *Blue Book of Guitars* CD-ROM (includes information from both books) with inventory program - $19.95

1st Edition *Blue Book of Guitars and Guitar Amplifiers Condensed* by Zachary R. Fjestad, edited by S.P. Fjestad - $19.95

The Nethercutt Collection - The Cars of San Sylmar, 3rd Edition by Dennis Adler (deluxe hardcover with slipcase) - $65.00

26th Edition *Blue Book of Gun Values* by S.P. Fjestad (also available on CD-ROM) - $39.95

5th Edition *Blue Book of Airguns* by John Allen & Dr. Robert Beeman, edited by S.P. Fjestad - $24.95

4th Edition *Blue Book of Modern Black Powder Values* by John Allen - $24.95

Parker Gun Identification & Serialization compiled by Charlie Price & S.P. Fjestad - $34.95

3rd Edition *Blue Book of Pool Cues* by Brad Simpson (to be published soon)

Online Guitar, Gun, and Pool Cue Services: www.bluebookinc.com

If you would like to order or get more information about any of the above publications/products, simply contact us at:

Blue Book Publications, Inc.
8009 34th Avenue South, Suite 175
Minneapolis, MN 55425 USA
www.bluebookinc.com
800-877-4867 (toll free domestic)
952-854-5229 (non-domestic) • Fax: 952-853-1486

Since our phone system has been updated to auto-attendant technology, please follow the prompts and use the following extension numbers when contacting our staff:

Extension 10 - Beth Marthaler	bethm@bluebookinc.com	Extension 17 - Zachary R. Fjestad	zachf@bluebookinc.com
Extension 11 - Katie Sandin	katies@bluebookinc.com	Extension 18 - Tom Stock	toms@bluebookinc.com
Extension 12 - John Andraschko	johnand@bluebookinc.com	Extension 19 - Cassandra Faulkner	cassandraf@bluebookinc.com
Extension 13 - S.P. Fjestad	stevef@bluebookinc.com	Extension 22 - Stacy Knutson	stacyk@bluebookinc.com
Extension 15 - Clint Schmidt	clints@bluebookinc.com	Extension 27 - Shipping	
Extension 16 - John Allen	johna@bluebookinc.com		

Office hours are: 8:30 a.m. - 5:00 p.m. CST, Monday - Friday.
Orders only: 800-877-4867 • Phone: 952-854-5229
Additionally, an automated message service is available for both ordering and leaving messages.
Fax: 952-853-1486 (available 24 hours a day)
Email: guitars@bluebookinc.com (checked several times daily)
Website: http://www.bluebookinc.com

We would like to thank all of you for your business in the past – you are the reason(s) we are successful. Our goal remains the same – to give you the best products, the most accurate and up-to-date information for the money, and the highest level of customer service available in today's marketplace. If something's right, tell the world over time. If something's wrong, please tell us immediately.

ACKNOWLEDGMENTS

Whenever possible, the *Blue Book of Electric Guitars* has listed proper reference sources within a section (see "Guitar References" & "Periodicals Listings" for complete sources). These books are invaluable resources for gaining additional knowledge within separate fields and cover the wide variety of today's guitar marketplace.

CONTRIBUTING EDITORS

The editor and publisher extends a special thanks to those Contributing Editors listed below who took their valuable time to make important revisions, corrections, and additions – all making this a better publication. We couldn't have done it without them.

Dave Rogers, Eddy Thurston, and the rest of the crew at Dave's Guitar Shop
Michael Jones
John Beeson - The Music Shoppe
Keith Smart - Zematis Guitar Owners Club
Jay Pilzer
Jim Fisch
Walter Carter

Gurney Brown
Larry Meiners
Dave Hinson - Killer Vintage
Stan Slubowski
Rick Wilkiewicz
Jack Wadsworth - Ft. Worth, TX
Jay Wolfe - Wolfe Guitars
Doug Tulloch

Scott Sanders
Kwinn Kastrosky
David Newell
Walter Murray - Frankenstein Fretworks
R. Steven Graves

FACTORY SUPPORT & ASSISTANCE

The following factory people really went out of their way (as if they're not busy enough already) to either give us or track down the information we requested. A special thanks to all of you for your unselfishness – there's no greater gift than someone's time.

Paul Jernigan - Fender
Thom Fowle, Vic Russelavage, David Rohrer, Sam Catalona, Rick Gembar, Cindy Bowker, David Schenk, and **Kevin Young** - Gibson
Paul Reed Smith, Larry Urie, Jim Cullen, Debra Wolstein, and **Laura Rausch** - PRS Guitars
Robert & Cindy Benedetto - Benedetto Archtop Guitars

Will Jones - Epiphone
Andreas Pichler - Andreas Guitars
Tom Wayne & David Brown - Yamaha
Steve Helgeson - Moonstone
The Dean Girls
Jason Scheuner - Timeless Timber
Andy Robinson - Taylor

Jim Donahue - Ibanez
Tommy Thomasson - Rickenbacker International Corp.
Frank Rindone - Hamer
Tom Anderson & Laurie Berg - Tom Anderson Guitarworks
Hill Custom Guitars - Tobin Northrup

ADVISORY BOARD

In addition to the above listed contributing editors and factory support and assistance personnel, the Advisory Board members listed below are generally people who let us pick their sometimes overworked and twisted brains. We highly value their range of attitudes and opinions (no shortage there) - very little idle chit chat or 9-5 mentality here! These elite, card-carrying members pretty much span the humanitarian gamut in guitar intelligence (guitarded?). Occasionally, you might even see some cocktails exchanged among various members of this group, sometimes disguised as rogues lurking in dark shadows, boisterously discussing their next move on the ever-changing guitar chessboard! Thanks to the following, you really helped us out!

Dave Rogers, Eddy Thurston, and cheddarheads at Dave's Guitar Shop
Trent Salter - Musician's Hotline
Jimmy Wallace & Mark Pollock - Dallas Guitar Show
Don & Jeff Lace (Travel Trailer Kings) - Lace Music Products
Rick Powell - Guitar Center
Hartley Peavey - Peavey Electronics Corporation
Robert and Cindy Benedetto - Benedetto Archtop Guitars
Rick Turner - Renaissance Guitars
John and Rhonda Kinnemire - JK Lutherie
Henry Lowenstein
Nate Westgor - Willie's American Guitars
Texas Amigos & staff - John Brinkmann, Dave Crocker, & Eugene Robertson

Chad Speck - Encore Music
Joe Lamond & Larry Linkin - NAMM
Seymour Duncan - Seymour Duncan Pickups
Willie G. Moseley
Paul Day
Dave Hinson - Killer Vintage
George Gruhn - Gruhn's Guitars
Rick Vito
Yasuhiko Iwanade
Charles "Duke" Kramer
Jimmy "The Wilbur" and Ryan "Lil' Wilbur" Triggs - Triggs Guitars
Marco Nobili - *Guitar Club* magazine, Italy
Larry Briggs - Strings West
Art Wiggs - Wings Guitar Products
Paul Riario - *Guitar World* magazine
Doug Chandler
Pierpaolo Adda - Soave Guitar Festival, Italy

David Nordscow
Greg Rich
Chris Trider
Zebuelon Cash-Lane (and Dumpmaster)
Ray Matusa, Lawrence & James Acunto - *20th Century Guitar* magazine
Gregg Hopkins - Vintage Amp Restoration
Norm Harris - Norman's Rare Guitars
Tom "Murphdog" Murphy - Guitar Preservation
Dave Amato - lead guitarist, REO Speedwagon
Joe Naylor - Reverend Guitars
Lisa Sharken - *Guitar Shop* magazine
Kent Armstrong - Kent Armstrong Pickups
Rick Nielsen - Cheap Trick
Jeff "Skunk" Baxter - Steely Dan

Steve Cropper - Booker T & the MGs
Ray Kennedy
Barry Clark
Jimmy Gravity - Gravity Strings
Pete Wagener - LaVonne Wagener Music
Gerald Weber - Kendrick Amplifiers
The gang at Solid Body Guitars
The Podium - Minneapolis, MN
Ari Latella - Toys From the Attic
The crew at Elderly Instruments
Rock and Roll Hall of Fame Museum, Cleveland, OH
Steven A. Wilson - Music Sales Corp.

PHOTO ACKNOWLEDGEMENTS

The following people/companies provided instruments and advice for this edition's Photo Grading System (pages 33-48). Thanks again!

Dave Rogers - Dave's Guitar Shop
John Beeson - The Music Shoppe
Willie's American Guitars

Dale Hanson
Glenn Wetterland
S.P. Fjestad

George McGuire
Clint Schmidt
Zachary Fjestad

And thanks to all the dealers, collectors, and individuals who have been nice enough to let the digital "drive by catch & release" photo crew from Blue Book Publications, Inc. photograph their guitar(s) that have been included in the A-Z sections. We haven't lost/damaged an instrument yet!

Blue Book Publications would also like to send out a special thanks to John Beeson and Erick Johnson from The Music Shoppe for substantial help to our photos in the book. Without Erick, Clint and Zach would still be putting stuff away in Terre Haute! We would also like to thank the good folk in LaCrosse at Dave's Guitar Shop for letting us set up shop. Thanks again guys!

INTRODUCTION

Author Zachary R. Fjestad (r) with legendary Rock 'N Roll Hoochie Koo, Rick Derringer at the 2004 Arlington Guitar Show.

Welcome to the new Ninth Edition *Blue Book of Electric Guitars*. This publication represents all of the ongoing research and data entry that we do at Blue Book Publications every day. Many people think we only update our books once a year, but this occurs more frequently. Even though a new book is not released every time the database is updated, new information is always available through our electronic subscriptions.

What's new and improved over the eighth editions? First of all, all of the new models for 2005 are included. Most companies debut their new products at the Winter NAMM show, which is most helpful for the rest of the year. Second, all vintage guitar prices have been updated. Once again, prices on Les Pauls, Stratocasters, Telecasters, and Jazz and Precision Basses have continued to climb at exponential rates. Just when we thought there might have been a ceiling on prices in sight, consumers continued to buy guitars at higher prices. We have to change our database quarterly to keep up with the ever-changing vintage market, which makes it wise to check our online subscriptions for the most current prices.

Several sections were completely overhauled, including B.C. Rich, Dean, Epiphone, Fender, Rickenbacker, and Serialization. B.C. Rich has changed the way they do business several times in the past years, but we have included many of the models from these transitions. Fender is always difficult to organize effectively. This year, we tried to make the Stratocaster and Telecaster sections as easy to understand as possible. We also paid attention to many of the "House Brand" companies. In previous editions, individual models were never listed. These guitars show up frequently on the used market, and even though they typically do not bring a high premium, there is a demand for them. Whenever possible, we include pricing on the House Brand instruments. Serialization was completely revised as well.

We experimented with a new product called The *Blue Book of Guitars and Guitar Amps Condensed,* first Edition. This book was published in September 2004, but contained all three of our large publications, and was condensed down to a 384-page book. We did this by omitting all manufacturer descriptions, category descriptions, model and sub-model descriptions, as well as model notes. What we ended up with was a book with models, production years, and prices in two columns per page. This book received mixed criticism, because most people know us for our extensive information along with prices. What we wanted to provide was a book that could be easily transported and used at guitar shows, pawn shops, etc. We are always looking for advice, and if anybody has any recommendations about this product, our current large books, or any other ventures, by all means let us know.

We are always trying to put the best product on the market. Even though not every model is listed, we try to include as much information as possible. Certain models and one-of-a-kind instruments may not make it into this publication. However, we do our best to include as many as we can. This job cannot be completed by just myself and an editor; several people behind the scenes make this book available every year. Please see page five for acknowledgments. Unfortunately, there are always people who are omitted for one reason or another who contributed to this book. For these people, you are just as important as every one else who contributes! Of course, without any family or friends, I would have no support to complete this project. I must also thank everyone who encouraged me to complete my college degree in technical writing. Even though means of communication has never been better, people are communicating less and less. Knowing how to communicate and write is an ever-important skill.

I hope you enjoy the new Ninth Edition *Blue Book of Electric Guitars*.

Sincerely,

Zachary R. Fjestad
Author
Blue Book of Electric Guitars

FOREWORD

The 6th edition cover, cover instrument, and the man whose company made it! Paul Reed Smith (r) & S.P. Fjestad take a little time to enjoy one of his guitar clinics at Dave's Guitar Shop in LaCrosse, WI. These PRS clinics bring out the best in Paul Reed Smith and those fortunate enough to attend.

Welcome to this newest 9th edition to the *Blue Book of Electric Guitars*. No other single publication comes close to giving you this amount of information and up-to-date pricing on both current and vintage electric guitars. Now with over 1,000 pages, this publication has become the guitar industry's standard reference work on almost all electric instruments made during the past seventy-five years.

As in the past, this new edition not only contains all the new domestic makes and models, but also includes the ever increasing amount of imported instruments coming in from the Pacific Rim. Asian importation has grown to the point that it now impacts the domestic guitar marketplace significantly. Many consumers and industry personnel originally dismissed these non-major trademark instruments as low/poor quality, made-for-a-price-point entry level instruments. If Johnny/Susie decided he/she didn't want to become the next Eric Clapton or Sheryl Crow, Mom and Dad weren't out a lot of dough. This has changed considerably. Most of the instruments coming in from Asia today are high quality, with many companies how having accumulated over a decade of guitar building experience. This enables today's consumer to have the best choice of good quality instruments, regardless of price point.

The vintage guitar marketplace continues to rack up unprecedented values on desirable and original condition major trademarks and models. How high can these prices go? Several dealers have indicated they are basically paying today's retail prices for top quality, original Les Pauls, Strats, Teles, early PRS, and other favorites because the runaway vintage marketplace is going up so fast that next year they'll be able to resell them at a nice profit. It's almost like there is no wholesale on the really good stuff, which continues to get harder and harder to find.

While there can be no question that today's vintage marketplace is being fueled by the disproportionate number of baby boomers who have most of the disposable dollars, it remains to be seen whether values will continue to skyrocket as the baby boomers get older and start to liquidate their vintage guitars, Harleys, Hemi Cudas, etc. Will Generations X and Y, who are growing up playing Jacksons, Charvels, Ibanez, Deans, etc., take a second mortgage on their homes to buy a crispy blonde '50s Tele or plunk down the $300K it now takes to buy a really nice '59 'Burst? Maybe, but maybe not. If not, the vintage marketplace will undergo a lot of changes in the next several decades.

We feel fortunate to include a feature article and chronology on the 20th Anniversary of PRS guitars. Paul Reed Smith's long and hard climb to become America's third largest electric guitar maker is a fascinating story, and PRS is unequaled in today's corporate-run guitar conglomerates. Every PRS player, collector, and admirer knows why PRS has achieved such a great reputation. Make sure you read both the interview, originally conducted by Trent Salter and published in Musician's Hotline, plus the entire chronology of Paul Reed Smith and his achievements on pages 13-18.

Well-known vintage author Larry Meiners, who has written *The Flying V* and *Gibson Shipment Totals*, has provided us with a concise and up-to-date report on the vintage guitar marketplace (see pages 19-21), based on his years of experience as both a collector and dealer. You'll find his commentary on how vintage guitars have performed against traditional investments (i.e, the stock market) fascinating, and he leaves you with more than a few important guidelines on what the crystal ball holds for this important segment of collectables.

And last, but certainly not least, a fresh perspective is provided from a young musician who couldn't care less about vintage LPs. Sixteen-year-old Tegan Godfrey of Cannon Falls, MN, feels fortunate to be able to bend the strings of his inexpensive Jackson, and doesn't expect his parents to spend $3,000-$4,000 for a big brand name guitar. His tale describes how he went from being a hip-hop kid to a player who has now been seduced by the call of rock, blues, and Motown in only five years! Tegan's story is one about learning and enjoying music, not concentrating on how cool his guitar is (see pages 22-23). After all, Stevie Ray Vaughan seemed to do OK with a beat up, second hand guitar from a music store!

As in the previous editions, the informational format remains the same. Please read the "How To Use" section for a complete explanation on how to get all the information out of this 9th edition. Whenever possible, the last MSR of a discontinued guitar has been provided as a reference point. Years of manufacture have also been provided, and don't forget the "Serialization" section in the back of the book, which allows you to determine the year of manufacture of your instrument(s). An expanded and updated "Trademark Index" will also give you the current contact information for most of the manufacturers/trademarks.

In closing, I would really like to thank my nephew, Zachary Fjestad, now a legitimate college graduate (something his uncle never achieved), who now does most of the data entry and research on both this book and the *Blue Book of Acoustic Guitars*. It's a big job, and sucks more time than he ever believed possible. He has also written the *Blue Book of Guitar Amplifiers*, now in its 2nd edition - it's the perfect complement to these 9th editions. Making it worthwhile is knowing this publication of this type is the best in its field, in addition to going to the various guitar/trade shows and exchanging comments/ideas with the wide variety of human personalities and the instruments they represent.

Thanks again for your help and support in the past, and we look forward to continuing to provide you with the best information possible.

Sincerely,

S.P. Fjestad
Editor & Publisher
Blue Book of Electric Guitars

PS - Don't forget that this book is also available on CD-ROM, by individual download, or by online subscription. Good information never sleeps!

HOW TO USE THIS BOOK

This new Ninth Edition of the *Blue Book of Electric Guitars™*, when used properly, will provide you with more up-to-date electric guitar information and pricing than any other single source. Now with almost 900 pages of specific guitar models and pricing, this publication continues to be more of a complete informational source than a simple "hold-your-hand" pricing guide. In theory, you should be able to identify the trademark/name off the guitar's headstock (whenever applicable), and be able to find out the country of origin, date(s) produced, and other company/model-related facts for that guitar. **Many smaller, out-of-production trademarks and/or companies which are only infrequently encountered in the secondary marketplace are intentionally not priced in this text, as it is pretty hard to pin the tail on a donkey that is nowhere to be seen.** Unfortunately, this lack of information can be a disadvantage to sellers, who may find buyers saying "Would you take any less? After all, nobody seems to know anything about it." In other words, don't confuse rarity with desirability when it comes to these informational voids. As in the past, if you own this current Ninth Edition of the *Blue Book of Electric Guitars™* and still have questions, we will try to assist you in identifying/pricing your guitar(s). Please refer to page 23 for this service.

The prices listed in the Ninth Edition *Blue Book of Electric Guitars™* are based on average national retail prices for both vintage and, currently manufactured guitars. This is NOT a wholesale pricing guide – prices reflect the numbers you typically see on a guitar's price tag. More importantly, do not expect to walk into a music store, guitar shop, or pawn shop and think that the proprietor should pay you the retail price listed within this text for your instrument(s). Dealer offers on most models could be 20%-50% less than values listed, depending upon desirability, locality, and profitability.

In other words, if you want to receive 100% of the price (retail value), then you have to do 100% of the work (become the retailer, which also includes assuming 100% of the risk). Suceeding in business usually means making a profit, and is essential in today's tough retail environment.

Currently manufactured guitars are typically listed with condition factors ranging from 60% to 100%, since condition below 60% is seldom encountered and obviously, less desirable. A few older vintage instruments may only have the 20%-90% condition factors listed, since 95%+ condition factors are seldom encountered and are difficult to price accurately. Please consult the revised fourteen-page, digital color **Photo Grading System™** (pages 33-48) to learn more about the condition of your electric guitar(s). The *Blue Book of Electric Guitars™* will continue using selected photos to illustrate real world condition factors. Guitar porno, it isn't. Since condition is the overriding factor in price evaluation, study these photos carefully to learn more about the condition of your instrument(s). **Remember, the price will be wrong if the condition factor isn't right.**

For your convenience, an explanation of guitar grading systems, how to convert them, and descriptions of individual conditions appear on pages 31-32 (Explanation & Converting Guitar Grading Systems) to assist you in learning more about guitar grading systems and individual condition factors. Please read these pages carefully, as the values in this publication are based on the grading/condition factors listed. This will be especially helpful when evaluating older vintage instruments.

All values within this text assume original condition. From the vintage marketplace or (especially) a collector's point of view, any repairs, alterations, modifications, "enhancements," "improvements," "professionally modified to a more desirable configuration," or any other non-factory changes usually detract from an instrument's value. Please refer to page 31 for an explanation on finishes, repairs, alterations/modifications, and other elements which have to be factored in before determining the correct condition. Depending on the seriousness of the modification/alteration, you may have to go down one-to-three condition factors when re-computing the price for these alterations. Determining values for damaged and/or previously repaired instruments will usually depend on the parts and labor costs necessary to return them to playable and/or original specifications.

You may note that this new Ninth Edition contains many new black-and-white photos of individual electric models/variations to assist you with more visual identification. **Remember, the photos may not necessarily be on the same page as the model listing/descriptions.**

The Ninth Edition *Blue Book of Electric Guitars™* provides many company histories, notes on influential luthiers and designers, and other bits of knowledge as a supplement to the pricing text. Hopefully, this information will alleviate those "grey areas" of the unknown, and shed light on the efforts of those new luthiers/companies who keep pushing the envelope.

We have designed an easy-to-use (and consistent) text format throughout this publication to assist you in quickly finding specific information and there is a lot of it!

1. Trademark, manufacturer, company name (if luthier or individual, last name will appear first), brand name, or importer is listed in bold face type and will appear alphabetically as follows:

ARIA/ARIA PRO II, DEAN, SAMICK, WASHBURN

2. **Manufacturer Status:** Trademark, manufacturer, or other company/luthier information, and production dates (if possible), are listed directly beneath the trademark heading:

   Current trademark owned by Dean Guitar Co., with headquarters located in Clearwater, FL. Instruments currently produced in Plant City, FL (Custom Shop and all the USA series) and Korea (the American Spirit series). Distributed by Armadillo Enterprises of Clearwater, FL. Dean guitars with the set-neck design were previously built in Evanston, IL from 1977 to 1986. In 1985, Dean began production of some models in Japan and Korea. Dean production from 1986 to 1993 was based in Asia.

3. **Manufacturer Description:** A company overview, model information recap, and/or other relatively useful information may follow within a smaller block of text. If the section is small enough, limited model and pricing information is included here. This section will vary in length due to the amount of information available:

   Australian luthier Stephen Gilchrist is known for his high qualilty mandolins, mandolas and mandocellos. Gilchrist began building instruments in 1976, and spent 1980 in the U.S. working in Nashville, Tennessee at Gruhn Guitars. After 1980, Gilchrist returned to Australia and continues to produce guitars and mandolins. For further information regarding current model specifications and pricing, contact the Carmel Music Company directly (see Trademark Index). Gilchrist has built a number of acoustic and electric guitars; most of the electric guitars were built between 1987 to 1988. To make identification of these guitars a bit difficult, some models do not have the Gilchrist name anywhere on the instrument and none of them have a serial number.

4. **Category Name:** The next major classification under a heading name may include a category name which appears in upper-case, is flush left, and is inside a darkly shaded box. Category names refer mostly to the guitar's primary configuration, which are typically listed in order as Electric, and Electric Bass:

ELECTRIC

ELECTRIC BASS

Many trademarks have several series within the category name. These series are divided with a colon after the Electric or Electric Bass category name and will look like this:

ELECTRIC: ARTISAN SERIES

When a proper model-by-model listing is not available (due to space considerations), a small paragraph may follow with the company history and related production data. These paragraphs may also include current retail prices. The following example is from Goya:

ELECTRIC

While Goya mainly offered acoustic guitars, the first electrics debuted in the late 1950s. The first series of electrics were built by Hagstrom, and feature a sparkly plastic covering. A later series of electrics such as the Range Masters, were produced from 1967-1969 (by EKO of Italy) and featured pushbutton controls. Other Eko/Goya creations include the Panther, P-26, and P-46. Goya also offered a number of electric guitar amplifiers in the 1950s and 1960s.

Category names may be used for general information also. Certain trademarks will have an overview of their guitars, listing of finishes, or other general information that does not fit in the other listed areas. In this case, the information is located as a category name in the beginning of the section. A section of information may look like this:

PRODUCTION MODEL CODES

Godin is currently using a system similar to the original Gretsch system, in that the company is assigning both a model name and a four-digit number that indicates the color finish specific to that guitar model. Thus, the four-digit code will indicate which model and color from just one number. References in this text will list the four-digit variances for color finish within the model designations.

5. **Sub-category:** A sub-classification of the category name (upper- and lower-case description inside a shaded box) is used on some of the larger series (Stratocaster, Telecaster, Les Paul, etc.) This makes it easier to group specific series inside of a general series:

Telecaster: American Series (2000-Current Mfg.)

Les Paul: Early Mfg. & Standard Models

6. **Category Note:** A category note may follow either a category or subcategory heading, and contains information specific to that category. Category notes may also list general pricing for models covered within that category (typically bold face). An example would be:

Firebird guitars were offered in custom colors as well as standard Gibson finishes. The Firebirds were available in these Custom Colors: Amber Red, Cardinal Red, Frost Blue, Golden Mist, Heather, Inverness Green, Kelly Green, Pelham Blue, Polaris Blue, and Silver Mist finishes.

7. **Model names** appear flush left, are in bold, uppercase lettering, and appear in alpha-numerical (normally) sequence which are grouped under the various subheadings:

DC135, SPECIAL (U.S. MFG.), TORONADO (MEX. MFG., NO. 013-0700), LES PAUL CLASSIC (LPCS)

Parentheses after a model or submodel name refer to either a previous model name, factory family code/number, or production years of certain models to assist in proper identification. In some cases, it may include a combination of all three.

8. **Sub-Model:** Sub-models are listed when there are different variations of the same model. The most common sub-models are cutaways, different wood types, 12-string guitars, left-handed models, and five- or six-string basses. Variations within a model appear as sub-models, are indented, italicized, and appear in both upper and lower case type:

DC135T, EVO Special 7, Les Paul Classic Plus, Chaparral 5-String Bass, GRX20 L,

Model sub-variations follow in the text under the description/pricing of the main model(s).

9. **Model/sub-model descriptions** appear directly under model/sub-model names and appear as follows:

- ash or alder body, rosewood fingerboard with dot position markers, hand-rolled fingerboard edges, 3 custom staggered single coil pickups, 5-way switch, two-point synchronized tremolo, staggered tuners, 22 medium-jumbo frets, 1 Volume/2 tone controls, currently available in 3-Color Sunburst, Hot Rod Red, black, Olympic White, Chrome Red, Chrome Blue, Butterscotch Blonde, or Sky Blue finishes, case included, mfg. 2001-present.

Model/submodel descriptions are where most of the critical information regarding that model or submodel is located. Typically, these descriptions list configuration first, type of wood(s), fretboard description, bridge/tuner specifications, other important features, pickup(s)/electronics, and factory finish descriptions. If possible, years of production are listed last. In many cases, this allows the last MSR and the dates of manufacture to be known. Whenever possible, black and white photos have been provided on the right-hand pages, even though they may not appear on the same page as the model name/description.

10. **Pricing/Price Line:** Typically, pricing is located directly underneath the model description. The primary pricing line example in this book is listed below. **When this price line is encountered,**

GRADING		100% MINT	98% NEAR MINT	95% EXC+	90% EXC	80% VG+	70% VG	60% G
MSR	$1,799		$1,250	$1,125	$950	$825	$725	$575	$450

it automatically indicates that the guitar is currently manufactured and the manufacturer's suggested retail price (MSR) is shown left of the 100% column. The 100% price on a currently manufactured instrument is what you can typically expect to pay for that model, and may reflect a discount off the MSR. Musical instruments, like other consumer goods, may be discounted to promote consumer spending. Discounting is generally used as a sales tool within the music industry, and users of this method include many music/guitar establishments, chain stores, mail-order companies, eBay, and other retailers to help move merchandise. Discounted prices depend on the manufacturers and dealers (if any). Some companies/ dealers may not discount at all, but offer quality service and support/advice after your purchase. With the advent of manufacturer MAPs (minimum advertised prices), discounting seems to become more manageable than it was in the 1990s. 20%-40% off of the retail is typical for most manufacturer's MAPs.

The 100% condition factor (mint), when encountered in a currently manufactured guitar, assumes the guitar has not been previously sold at retail and includes a factory warranty. A currently manufactured new instrument must include EVERYTHING the factory originally provided with the instrument – including the case (if originally included), warranty card, instruction manual (if any), hang tags (if any), etc. Because of this, a slightly used instrument that appears new no longer qualifies for 100%, and may be worth only 50%-90% of its current MSR, depending on the overall desirability factor. The values for the remaining 98%-60% condition factors represent actual selling prices for instruments in various conditions. Simply refer to the correct condition column of the instrument in question and refer to the price listed directly underneath.

Please consult the Photo Grading System™ on pages 33-48 to learn more about how to visually determine electric guitar condition factors accurately. Also, please read pages 31-32 thoroughly to understand and convert the various guitar grading systems – individual grades are also explained in detail. An "N/A" instead of a price means that either that model hasn't been produced long enough for wear to occur, or the rarity factor precludes accurate pricing.

A price line with seven values listed (as the first example below demonstrates) indicates a discontinued, out of production model with values shown for 100%-60% conditions.

GRADING	100% MINT	98% NEAR MINT	95% EXC+	90% EXC	80% VG+	70% VG	60% G
	$550	$475	$400	$335	$275	$250	$225
1954-57	N/A	$7,000	$6,250	$5,700	$5,250	$4,400	$4,000

Obviously, "MSR" will not appear in the left margin, but a model note may appear below the price line indicating the last MSR. In this edition, 1996 has typically been used for the cutoff on some 100% values (i.e., Gibson, Gretsch, Guild). **An N/A (Not Available) may appear in place of pricing for these older instruments which are not normally encountered in 100%, 98%, and lower condition factor(s). The longer an instrument has been discontinued, the less likely you will find it in 100% condition.** Some instruments that are only ten years old and have never been taken out of the case (unplayed) may not be 100% (new), as the finish may have slightly cracked, tarnished, faded, or deteriorated. **100% is new – no excuses, period.**

The following price line indicates that either

MSR $1,995

this model is produced in small enough quantities and is not discounted (perhaps consumer direct sales only), or has only been in production for a short time, and used guitars simply do not exist yet. As time goes on, these slots will need to be filled in.

11. While the Manufacturer's Suggested Retail (MSR) price is included in the regular pricing line of currently manufactured instruments, the last MSR for discontinued, out of production models may appear in smaller typeface to the right:

Last MSR was $699.

12. Extra cost features/special orders and other value added/subtracted items (add-ons for currently manufactured guitars reflect an option's retail price), are placed directly under individual price lines, and appear bolder than other descriptive typeface:

Add $25 for 3-Color Sunburst finish. Add $75 for 2-Color Sunburst, White Blonde, and Natural finishes (disc.).

On many electric guitars that are less than fifteen years old, these add/subtract items will be the last factory retail price for that option.

13. Manufacturer's notes, model information, and available options appear in smaller type, typically following price lines, and are significant since they contain both important model changes and other related information:

Natural, Aqua Marine Metallic, 2-Color Sunburst, and White Blonde finishes were discontinued in 2002. Olympic White, Chrome Red, Chrome Blue, and Sky Blue finishes were introduced in 2002. Butterscotch Blonde new 2003. Also available with maple neck (Model 011-7402). Also available in Hard Tail Model (no tremolo unit) with rosewood fingerboard (Model 011-7430) and Hard Tail Model with maple neck (Model 011-7432). The Hard Tail models are only available in 3-Color Sunburst, Olympic White, Black, or Chrome Red finishes.

14. Grading lines will appear at the top of each page where applicable or wherever pricing lines change. The most commonly encountered grading line (with corresponding price line for currently manufactured instruments) in this text is 100%-60%:

GRADING	100% MINT	98% NEAR MINT	95% EXC+	90% EXC	80% VG+	70% VG	60% G
MSR $1,400	$975	$800	$725	$625	$550	$425	$325

Values are listed for 90%-20% condition factors only since condition over 90% is seldom encountered and almost impossible to accurately value. To find a particular electric guitar in this book, first try to identify the name/trademark on the headstock. This will usually identify the manufacturer, trademark, importer, or possible brand/trade name. Then refer to this listing within the correct alphabetical section. Next, locate the correct category name, Electric, Electric Basses, etc. Models will be grouped either alphanumerically (i.e., LB75, LB76, LB76A, etc.), or alphabetically (i.e., Chet Atkins, Clipper, Convertible, etc.), or in some cases, chronological sequence, starting with the oldest model to the newest.

Once you find the correct model or sub-model under its respective subheading, determine that particular electric guitar's percentage of original condition (see the Photo Grading System™ on pages 33-48), and simply find the corresponding grading column to ascertain price. Special/limited editions usually appear last under a manufacturer's heading. When using serialization charts (pages 883-896), make sure your model is listed, and find the serial number within the yearly range listings. However, do not date your instrument on serial number information alone! Double check parts/finish variations in the text accompanying the model, or reference the coding on your instrument's potentiometers (tone and volume controls), if applicable.

In order to save time when looking up a particular model(s), you may want to look first at our revised and expanded Index on pages 989-1007. Also, an up-to-date Trademark Index is located on pages 972-988– this is the only up-to-date and comprehensive listing of current electric manufacturers and luthiers in print. Another Trademark Index on Strings and Pickups is also provided on pages 968-969. Once again, the Glossary (pages 26-30) and Anatomy of a Guitar (page 11) sections have been updated – there's a lot of information in both.

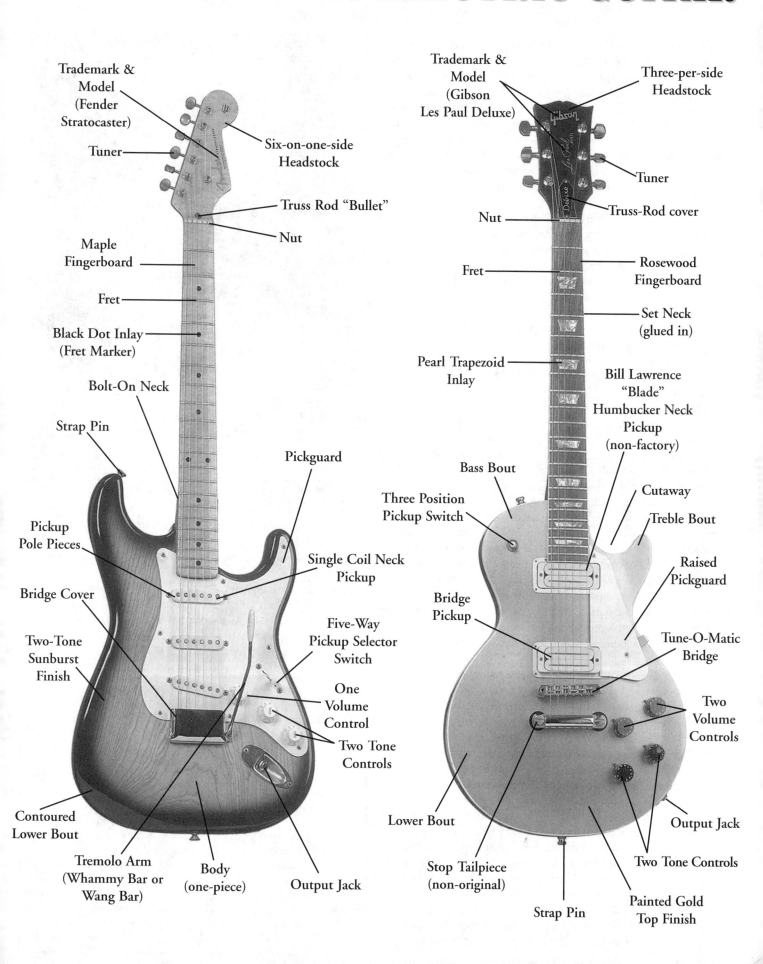

ABOUT THE COVER

by S.P. Fjestad

I know what you're thinking, and it's wrong. The unusual instrument on the 9th edition cover is not a leftover prop from a musical scene in "Star Wars," it's not a do-it-yourself kit guitar gone wrong, nor is it a rare vintage model from a '60s Erector set. And yes, it's also not supposed to have a conventional body. So how does the cover guitar, a Teuffel Guitars Birdfish, actually work, and how could anyone ever come up with such an unusual design? The answer to the first question is somewhat complex, but if you know Ulrich Teuffel from New Ulm, Germany, the second answer is easy.

Teuffel explains his theory on guitars in his own inimitable manner and dialogue:

Despite their simple construction, guitars are subject to special acoustic and electro-acoustic rules. The fundamental character of the sound is formed by the resonant properties of the body wood. Underneath the strings are the pickups, which, according to their position between the bridge and the neck, convert string movements to electrical signals comprised of various frequencies and harmonics. The composition of the pickups is made out of copper wire and magnets and is tonally significant. These three fundamental principles form the character of the instrument. If one were to make them variable, then one could thereby change the character of the instrument.

This is the theme of the Birdfish. The body, as a source of tone, is reduced to two cylindrical resonators, which are available in different materials, including swamp ash and maple. They are easily interchangeable by means of a screw connection. The resonators define the fundamental sound. They are easily exchangeable. Two blue resonators made of swamp ash are supplied, which are very responsive, yielding clear lows and highs. Two red maple resonators are also included in the set. They sound more powerful and forceful.

The two aluminum sculptures, "bird" and "fish," assume the connection of all the components. They are bridges of vibration-transfer, and establish contact to the body of the player. The bird piece (attached to neck) is one of the two central elements that connect the components. This part's tonal function is crucial. It requires an extraordinarily careful manufacture. The fish piece is the second of the two central elements that connect components, including the bridge and electronics box. For this element, a particularly neutral-sounding aluminum alloy is used. The casting process for this fish element occurs in a vacuum. Afterwards, the sculpture is hand-polished to a high gloss and chrome-plated.

The adjustable pickups are arranged on a rail with linear markings and therefore pick up the overtones variably. Additionally, five pickups with different characteristics are at one's disposal. One can very easily go through all the variations, since these pickups are shiftable and twistable. In addition, they can be easily exchanged by means of a screw connection. That way, the strings can remain in their tuning. Two single coils and three humbuckers are included. They can be adjusted into any position. Naturally, all the pickups are hand-wound with great care.

The neck has a 25-1/2 inch scale length (650 mm). Like the fingerboard, it is made of bird's-eye maple. The neck is connected to the bird element with a metrical screw connection. The frets are narrow and tall. The string clamp serves as the string attachment to the neck. You can use regular strings, without double-ball ends. The strings are easily secured with the small levers. Headless hardware, with which you tune the guitar. The strings are easily installed by the ball-ends. The instrument is tuned by turning the tuning knobs. Normal strings can be used.

The electronics box pod is adjustable, in order for the fade-in control to conform to your playing position. The five-way selector corresponds

No one else on the planet builds/designs guitars like Uli Teuffel, shown at a recent NAMM show with his famous Birdfish model. Does it actually work, and what does it sound like? The Reverend Billy Gibbons claims that it is second only to his 1959 Les Paul Sunburst Standard, affectionately known as the "Pearly Gates." Any other questions?

to that of a Stratocaster. An optional Midi version with RMC Piezo bridge and Poly-drive controller is also available, and coupled with an interchangeable tune-o-matic bridge, enables the quick change into a Midi-Birdfish.

Completing the set is a heavily padded gig bag made out of the finest Nubuck leather, with four external pockets, which contains the two extra pickups and sound resonators. A shoulder strap is also included. Only five hundred of these instruments will be manufactured, and each one is individually hand serial numbered. ∎

About his guitar building and design philosophy, Ulrich Teuffel says the following:

"I have been building guitars since 1984, only electric guitars since 1988. During my studies of Product-Design from 1992 until 1997, I had the opportunity to get to know my work from a standpoint other than that of traditional craftsmanship. Alongside completely other projects, at this time, the first thoughts about instruments like the Birdfish and the Tesla emerged."

"Every good luthier knows with which construction and materials a certain sound is obtained. The artistry lies in giving the instrument a very distinct appearance or effect along with the sound. I see my instruments as absolute. This means that every instrument has a certain symbolic meaning and function in the pop complex. One can compare this to the clothing that we wear. We select clothing according to function, e.g. job, sport, winter clothing, etc., as well as according to an expression of fashion with which we then distinguish ourselves. So will one, as a musician, decide which statement he wants to achieve with his choice of instrument."

For more information on Teuffel guitars, please visit: www.teuffel.com.

PRS Guitars' 20th Anniversary

Introduction by S.P. Fjestad and Interview by Trent Salter

Paul Reed Smith only comes as a package. If he could be personified as one of his instruments, he would definitely qualify as a quilted double ten top with dragon neck inlay, and finished in Tiger Eye. Either you take the entire contents of his package the way it is, or forget about it. Smaller, individual portions/segments of him are not available - it's all or nothing. It's not a bad thing, and anyone exposed to him for the first time will quickly understand how intense the package is, and perhaps even how much it encompasses. If you are petty by nature, enjoy talking about the weather, and/or like engaging in idle chit-chat, Paul is not the person you want to talk to.

Because of what he's done, how he's done it, and what he's constantly doing to improve it, Paul Reed Smith's ears are probably worth an easy $2 million. When you hook them up to his musically powered brain, you can double that. And when you factor in his guitar playing skills, and what he knows and has sacrificed for his most sacred word - TONE - he should probably be a salary level equal to that of many of today's top professional athletes.

While he can be very easy going, whimsical, and downright comical at times (his clinics bring this out), when the word tone comes up, you better be deadly serious, and you better know what you're talking about. Paul is very fussy about everything between his guitar strings and speaker cone, and his guitar knowledge is very extensive after decades of repairing and building instruments. Nothing gets taken for granted. We feel fortunate to provide you with this feature article for the 20th Anniversary of PRS Guitars.

The following interview was conducted by Trent Salter of Musician's Hotline magazine. The publisher wishes to thank both Trent Salter and MHL for allowing this interview to be included in the 9th edition Blue Book of Electric Guitars.

Q: Paul, congratulations on the company's twenty-year anniversary. The evolution of PRS is an incredible success story. Let's start with the early days. Tell us about the official opening of the company and the very first instruments that were offered.

PRS: The official opening of the company was the closing of a sales period for our Limited Partnership. We actually got all the investors to invest a half a million dollars to start the company. The sales period was to open April 1st 1985, and was to go for six months. We closed it one week after it opened. We were shipping guitars by late August of '85.

As far as our early instruments, there were two models. One was the Custom and the other was the PRS. The PRS was the mahogany version of the guitar. We had a Custom 24, and a Standard (PRS) 24. We still make those guitars today. We had some prototypes: we built five or six for one trade show and then twenty for the next trade show. One month after that, we were shipping guitars.

The first instruments were not quilted. We were buying all our woods from Michigan. I was hopping in a rental car and driving around Michigan to get wood. I believe we used curly maple and mahogany. My favorite is actually Brazilian rose-

wood. It rings more beautifully and longer in my opinion. The second would be mahogany, because it is remarkable in a way. I like the woods that instrument makers have used over time: Brazilian rosewood, mahogany, maple, ebony, spruce, curly maple, quilted maple, East Indian rosewood. There are two that I really like that aren't on the list: American walnut, and Queensland maple.

Q: How did things proceed during the first couple of years? What was the vision and the branding of PRS Guitars early on?

PRS: You remember MXR, Fender, and Gretsch. There are so many words out there with brand name recognition. The first thing we did was spend ten years just showing pictures of the guitars and putting the logo up. My vision was that in two or three years, everybody in the guitar industry would know who we were. That didn't happen for fifteen to sixteen years. It took four or five times longer than I thought. Another vision I had was survival. Keeping the company alive was key. Hap Kuffner,

During the summer of 1975, Paul Reed Smith shows off one of his early apprentice instruments, an all-mahogany double cutaway, patterned after Gibson's post-1958 Les Paul Special. Except for a little "salt," his hair hasn't changed!

(he is pretty famous in our industry. He helped start Steinberger, as well as helped get EMG off the ground) said to me "So you're going in the bucket. You'll be out of your mind for ten years. In ten years when you get your mind back, I'll come talk to you." Sure enough, ten years later, to the day, he showed up. He was so right on it. Basically, we started our company in survival mode, and when we came out the other side, we were sane enough for him to talk to us. Getting over that ten-year mark was not easy.

Q: There are instruments referred to in the collectables market as "Pre-'85" PRS's. The familiar bird inlay on the actual headstock identifies these guitars. Tell us a bit about those early guitars, and how they differ from the guitars built today.

PRS: They have been scooped up pretty well, and they are going for an alarming amount of money. The curly maple ones are going for $40,000 apiece, and a few are worth double that.

Q: As a long-time guitar player yourself, Paul, who's luthiering experience seemed to influence you the most, and why?

PRS: Well, everything that Gibson and Fender did in the '50s and early '60s are teachers. Everything that Martin did prior to about 1972 is a teacher. Everything that Collins is doing now is a teacher. I would say a lot of things that Tom Anderson has done in his career would be teachers. I would say that all the instruments that were in my repair shop, the ones with problems as well as the ones without, would be teachers. All the magic guitars that came in my repair shop were teachers. I'd say Ren Ferguson, who built the doubleneck for John McLaughlin, had a fundamental impact on me. I would say Ren Ferguson, Randy Curly, all the guys at Hamer—Joel, and Frank, and Paul Hamer, the guys at Oasis Guitars, Rick Turner at Alembic, Harvey Citron. I would say all the guys who were trying to get it done early on. Anyone I am missing? Ted McCarty, Dean Zelinsky.

Q: Was there any particular break or development, such as an endorser or dealer, that seemed to really propel the brand equity of your guitars, and please supply us with a time frame.

PRS: No particular break, but there were little things that made a difference. The different artists playing the guitar really helped, such as Carlos Santana, Al Dimeola, and Howard Leese; Rick Turner doing the first review for *Guitar Player*; Carlos playing the guitar on Tom Snyder or at the Olympics, or at

Nobody does colors better than PRS Guitars, and this Modern Eagle in Faded Blue Jean proves it. Introduced in 2004, this model features a spectacular, highly figured maple top, and a solid Brazilian rosewood neck/fretboard with rippled abalone bird inlays, a PRS trademark.

Double-digit Grammy winner and recent performer at the Academy Awards, Carlos Santana, with 36 albums, is shown performing with his signature Santana model at the 2005 winter NAMM show. Paul Reed Smith made the first guitar for Carlos in 1980, and Carlos has been playing PRS instruments ever since!

Live-Aid in Philadelphia; stuff like that really got the name out there. Just this year, Carlos played one at the Academy Awards; that was a big deal.

Washington Music Center was our first dealer. They said they would take three or four or five. If they sold, they would buy a lot more. That was an amazing order. They now have 180 in stock and sell one every day. Just unbelievable.

Q: In 1995, PRS built the most advanced guitar manufacturing facility in history. PRS is still located there today in Stevensville, MD. Tell us about some of the revolutionary technological advances you felt this factory brought to the industry, and, more importantly, how this factory enhanced the products, as well as taking PRS to an entirely new level.

PRS: I think it is a state-of-the-art, humidity controlled facility that would be remarkable even if it were built today. I don't think it has been copied. The reason we did it was because we didn't think we could make great guitars if we didn't. We didn't build it to prove something to our peers or to the industry or anything like that.

In our experience, if you don't build a guitar in 50% relative humidity at 72 degrees, either the necks will bow forward or backwards, depending on where you send it out in the world. If you do not have humidity-controlled spray rooms in the summer, the wood absorbs too much moisture, and in the winter, it dries out too much. You have to have the air going through the spray rooms be exactly that, but you don't want to suck the air out of the factory, otherwise you are sucking dust into the spray rooms.

When we say state-of-the-art, we are talking about in-depth dust collection, and humidity and temperature control, even in the spray rooms. Plus, we are insulated. There was a lot of arguing and fussing, but the bottom line is, it works. There have been a lot of other companies that have visited here, but there has never been anybody that has sat me down and asked specifically about the humidity control, how we do that in our place.

Another state-of-the-art thing is the very sophisticated spray rooms, drying rooms, and CNC equipment; all are very important. We were the first to do robotic buffing of guitars.

Q: Can you supply us, in somewhat chronological order, what you personally feel were key developments for PRS over the past twenty years and the time frames associated with these developments?

PRS: Coming out with the first guitars, having them play in tune and basically stay in tune, generally without Floyd Roses; the changing of the neck to a 22-fret; that new stoptail piece we came out with; changing the pickups away from the original pickups; getting rid of the sweet switch; using animals for inlays and getting away with it; the tuning peg thing, then changing the tuning peg thing to the new screw pegs. I don't know, you are asking a complicated question. We have about four hundred things we've changed in the last ten years. We sign off on them and write about them. The Modern Eagle is a big deal. You need to play a Modern Eagle and a 513. We have a doubleneck Dragon, Private Stock guitars, Brazilian Rosewood neck guitars and production guitars. Not a year goes by when we don't try to push the envelope.

A showstopper! During the 2000 summer NAMM show, Paul is shown with the late Ted McCarty. Ted's visionary accomplishments while president of Gibson (1950-1966) included overseeing such legendary models/designs as the Les Paul, ES-335, Flying V, Explorer, Firebird, SG, Byrdland, tune-o-matic bridge, and the humbucking pickup.

The dragon came about when I had somebody named Eric Chamberlain draw the first dragon on a piece of paper when I was in early high school. I knew I wanted to do it a long time ago. I always like the English water dragons and not so much the Chinese dragons.

Q: I have always felt personally that your guitars and the courage to introduce them to the marketplace was the catalyst to opening the door for many talented grass roots builders of today. How do you feel about the higher-end (boutique) guitar market in general, and how it continues to improve and evolve?

PRS: Well, thanks for the courage comment, it was scary. There are so many boutique builders that are trying to fight the fight.

I think it is good for the industry and I think it is good for guitars. I think it is part of the deal, but it is very hard to make a living as a builder. My tax returns for the first couple years were $8,000. I'm not saying what I think their tax returns are, but it is very hard to make a living as a builder in a single shop unless you are getting a lot of money for the instruments and you are heavily back ordered.

Overall, I think it is good for the industry, good for guitar making, and God bless them for doing it.

Q: During 2000, PRS introduced the Singlecut model. Gibson filed suit against PRS, alleging this particular design was an infringement on their trademark Les Paul design. What is your personal opinion on this matter, and how has the company responded to this development?

PRS: I regret that the industry had to be dragged through this. I don't believe we have done anything wrong. There is not a shred of evidence in this case that anybody ever bought a PRS thinking they were buying something else. I've never tried to confuse the customer, ever. There are so many differences between the two guitars. For example: the position and shape of the logo on the headstock: our logo is ninety degrees turned. They have a black headstock. Our headstocks are the color of the guitars. Our headstock is much smaller. Those are just a few examples.

I don't think there is any part of the guitars that are interchangeable. As a matter of fact, a Singlecut will not fit into a Les Paul case. So the shape is pretty different.

I don't think it is cool to take somebody else's body shape. I don't think it is cool to take someone else's headstock. But come on, you've been to NAMM, there are single cut-away guitars in hundreds of booths; how come I'm not allowed in? This is the equivalent of not being allowed into the minivan business.

As a matter of fact, we got a MIPA award (Music International Press Award). They gave us an award for the Singlecut as the best new electric guitar in 2000. They didn't do that for what they thought was a copy instrument; they did that for what they thought was advancement.

Q: PRS just celebrated the twenty-year anniversary in typical NAMM Show style. Tell us about the celebration and the current new products that were unveiled at the NAMM Show.

PRS: We had a meeting a while ago and talked about taking all the archived guitars on the road. We decided instead to display them at the show. I went through our entire history with the press. Even doing this interview now, it reminds me that being around twenty

The PRS 20th Anniversary celebration at the 2005 winter NAMM show. This serious axe grinder roll call includes (left to right): David Grissom, Howard Leese (Heart), Al Dimeola, Paul Reed Smith, Dave Navarro, Carlos Santana, and Sergio Vallin.

years and surviving and standing in the same circles as the icons is a big deal. They had a thing in *Guitar Player* magazine the other day where they rated my making one of the prototypes as one of the top one hundred things in the guitar industry.

For me, all these artists showing up and agreeing to play the party dropped my jaw. All three original endorsers were involved. Carlos Santana played, Dave Navarro played, Mark Tremoni played. David Grissom played, Bugs Henderson played. Some new, some old, but almost all the original endorsers, even if they went to another company, they were there and played. That just blew me away.

Q: Paul, in closing, you must be (and rightfully so) very proud of the company's accomplishments as you celebrate this twenty-year anniversary. Tell us what you feel are the most unique aspects of your guitars, your commitment of excellence, and what you feel has attributed to your over whelming success?

PRS: Fender went out of business with the Stratocaster in the mid-'60s. There wasn't a Les Paul made between 1961 and 1968. I'd say the first thing is there are people who are picking the guitars up, and are getting a sound out of them [that] is the same kind of thing that gave those instruments life again. When Hendrix picked up a Strat, that breathed life back into that model forever.

One of the things I am proud of is we haven't had to go out of production to breathe life into our product. I'm always reminded that sometimes things take a lot longer to catch on than anybody would ever think. Another thing I am proud of is that children here have benefited greatly from the health insurance that we carry here at our company. I think that kind of employee protection commitment has a great impact and has given back to the people that work here. When your kid is sick, and he's got strep, and you don't want to go to the doctor because you don't think you can afford the visit, [that] is just not cool.

I'm proud that when it has gotten really ugly on many occasions, people buckle down and work through it. I'm proud that some musicians find a home in our instruments and make really good music with them. I'm proud of the care that the people who actually build the guitars put into them. People comment all the time that you can tell the love and care the employees have for the guitars. I'm proud that I play one of our guitars. If there were another guitar that was better than ours, I'd play it. People would want to kill me for it, but I'm a musician, and I pick up the best thing that I know to use. Right now, the best instrument I have is a char-

coal Modern Eagle right off the line. Before that, I was playing the first Private Stock Guitar and a CE Bolt-on, right off the line.

Of course, I am proud of how pretty the guitars are, and how well they sound. Sometimes you get one that comes off the line with a voice; that is when I love it.

Q: Any closing statements that you would like to leave our readers with?

PRS: You cannot make it in this business without the support of the other companies. If you've got the big boys against you, you're dead. The amount of support we have gotten from our peers is overwhelming. I'm very thankful for all the support we've gotten from within the industry. ∎

Paul Reed Smith, at his best, which means a guitar in hands. In this case, it's a Santana SE model. PRS Guitars currently has close to two hundred highly-skilled employees, and their quality control standards are second to none.

THE PRS CHRONOLOGY

by S.P. Fjestad

Feb. 18, 1956 - Paul Reed Smith is born in Bethesda, MD, a suburb of Washington, D.C. He is one of four boys - Charles, Jim, and Robert - and one sister - Anne Marie. His father, Jack, was originally a big band director, and later gave up the baton to become a mathematician. His guitar-playing and vocalist mother, Ernestine, helps raise the children, while both parents encourage and nurture a musical home environment.

Circa 1968 - Smith tries to play the Beatles' "Daytripper" on his mother's Hi-Lo classical guitar. He also starts playing the bass, and during his formulative high school years, gigs with numerous, short-lived bands.

Circa 1970 - The fourteen-year-old finally saves enough money from odd jobs to buy a Gibson Melody Maker, but is still disappointed, since the Fender Telecaster he really wanted and lusted after has just been sold from a local music store. After the purchase, he decides the guitar is "his way out."

Circa 1972 - While in high school wood shop, Smith becomes interested in guitar building and constructs a new mahogany solid body for a Japanese copy of a Hofner Beatle Bass after taking the neck off. Recognizing his newfound interest and skill, he gets a job half-days as a guitar repairman while finishing high school during the other half.

Circa 1974 - Smith enrolls at St. Mary's College of Maryland as a math major, and after putting in eighteen months of drudgery, decides that $C^2 = A^2 + B^2$ really isn't for him, knowing that becoming a luthier is now his priority.

Mid-1975 - After leaving college, Smith returns home and turns his brother's bedroom into a guitar workshop, with his brother helping him build single and double cutaway solid bodies.

Late 1975 - After another brief stint at St. Mary's College, Smith drops out, and decides to move to 33 West Street in Annapolis. At the same time, many of the best rock bands have concerts scheduled in the Washington/Baltimore area. During one of these concerts, Smith meets Ted Nugent, and the hard rocker gives the nineteen-year-old an order for a solid body guitar patterned after a Gibson Byrdland.

1976 - A pivotal year for the young luthier. Smith delivers Ted Nugent's guitar in February, and also meets Peter Frampton, fresh off his 1975 multi-platinum album, *Frampton Comes Alive*. Frampton buys Smith's tenth guitar for $500, complete with birds-in-flight fretboard inlays copied from his mother's bird watching guide. The headstock features a landing eagle inlay that has been Xeroxed from one of Paul's T-shirts. Al Dimeola also buys a twelve-string with built-in phase shifter, and, maybe most importantly, Smith gets to jam with his guitar idol, Carlos Santana, backstage at the Capitol Center.

1977 - Smith now has completed seventeen instruments, and locals Steve Hildebrand and Bonni Lloyd decide to help Paul and his fledgling enterprise. Most of the tight money supply comes from repairing instruments, and Smith both works at the small shop and sleeps in the cubbyhole-sized attic at 33 West Street.

1978 - Roy Buchanan orders an instrument, and Smith makes his first guitar with a dragon inlay on the body.

Late 1978-1979 - Tired of being broke, constantly hungry (he has lived on macaroni and cheese for years, since the food budget is $2/day), Smith realizes that he can't make ends meet, and takes a job as a repairman at Veneman Music in Rockville, MD. By year's end, he's back in Annapolis making and repairing guitars at his small shop on West 33rd Street.

1980 - A new decade, and Smith finally starts making a name for himself. John Ingram becomes Smith's assistant. A friend's mom has a wood dresser with full-figured curly maple drawer fronts. Smith replaces the maple with cherry, and uses it to make his first maple-top guitar (all previous instruments had mahogany tops). Howard Leese of Heart eventually buys this stunning flame top for $2,000, and it quickly becomes his primary instrument. This guitar's killer tone is heard on millions of Heart albums, and Leese dubs it his "Golden Eagle." Nancy Wilson also buys a twelve-string. Carlos Santana plays one of Smith's mahogany-topped guitars, but orders a maple flame top like Leese's, and specifies a vibrato unit that won't go out of tune. It takes Smith a month to build this ultra-critical and important instrument, and, after playing it, Carlos Santana calls it "an accident of God" because of its killer feedback tone. And last, but certainly not least, Smith meets his future wife, Barbara, who will help him immensely in the years to come.

1981 - Neil Schon buys a guitar. Smith continues to gig with several bands on the side, including Kite.

1982 - The 27-fret "Sorcerer's Apprentice" is designed/created by Smith with Eric Pritchard, an important new addition to the small crew. Thinking he's finally onto something big, Smith flies to Japan and meets with Yamaha honchos to potentially sell/license this new design, but Yamaha's offer wouldn't pay for his hotel bill.

1984 - A new body shape incorporating the best features and designs from both the Fender Stratocaster and Gibson Les Paul is designed, and a mahogany prototype is built. Smith appears in *Musicians* magazine with this new guitar, and later tries to sell it to most of the larger guitar companies. Everyone tells him no. Later that year, Smith embarks on an East Coast road trip to get enough orders to start a company and build a factory. Things go well. Smith sees Ritchie Ash of Sam Ash in NYC, who immediately gives him a good order for six stores, and then tells Smith to double it every month! This thirty-guitar order, plus orders from another ten stores, totals over $300K! To finance a new factory to fill the delivery of these instruments, investor Warren Esann creates a limited partnership financial agreement, where investors will become part owners and Smith will be the managing director. Smith has two models to sell - the mahogany PRS guitar, and the PRS Custom with curly maple top.

1985 - PRS shows up at NAMM with eight instruments, and, as John Ingram would later recall, "We went to that NAMM '85 show on a wing and a prayer." A successful NAMM show, coupled with the new limited partnership finances, enables the small crew (a staff of six, plus Smith and his wife Barbara) to move into a new location on Virginia Avenue. Twenty guitars, including a new Custom Model with killer maple top, moon inlays, and sweet switch, are made for the summer NAMM show, and the staff now totals eighteen dedicated, underpaid souls. The first serial numbered PRS is built in August. In December, Smith's first child, a boy named Sam, is born.

1986 - The 1,000th PRS guitar rolls off the production line. A fully optioned Custom with bird inlays and Brazilian rosewood fingerboard has a MSR of $1,550. Rick Turner sums up a PRS Custom in his review in the April 1986 *Guitar Player* magazine by saying "It may well become a new standard against which other guitars are judged." Four- and five-string basses are introduced, and the Metal Model introduced last year is quickly discontinued due to lack of sales. A Signature Model is added, with only the finest quality curly maple top and bird inlays - all 1,000 have hand-signed headstocks.

1987 - The PRS guitar model name is changed to the Standard Model (mahogany body/neck), and a Special Model is introduced with a MSR of $1,640. PRS is now making six different pickups for its models, which are also sold separately at $90 each. The numeral "10" is added to the back of the headstock, indicating 10-top wood. Smith's second child, a daughter named Sarah, is born.

1988 - Several new models are introduced, including the Studio and Classic Electric with bolt-on neck. Forty-five employees are now making approxroximately fifteen guitars a day. More custom colors continue to be introduced.

1989 - Limited editions are unveiled with hollow tone chambers and a non-vibrato, tune-o-matic bridge and gold-plated stud tailpiece. Top woods include cedar, redwood, and even lacewood. The Classic Electric's name is changed to CE, since Hartley Peavey already has a guitar called the Classic.

1990 - CE basses introduced. Smith's second son, William, is born.

1991 - Bass models are discontinued, and the EG (Electric Guitar) model is introduced. The PRS factory now has seventy employees, and is making approximately four hundred guitars a month. An Artist I Model is also released, with a retail of $3,780.

1992 - Two solid-state amps are introduced - the HG-70 Head and HG-212 Combo (HG designates Harmonic Generator). Only 350 are shipped before the project is dropped. An acoustic guitar, co-developed with Dana Bourgeois, is also released. While the prototypes sound good, only eleven are manufactured. The big news this year is the introduction of the Dragon I ($7,000 MSR) - an instrument with elaborate dragon fingerboard inlays (201 pieces of abalone, turquoise, and mother-of-pearl) which Smith had dreamed about since he was sixteen.

1993 - Dragon II Model is released for a list price of $13,000 - only one hundred are built.

1994 - The McCarty Model is introduced, sporting the first covered humbuckers on a production PRS instrument. The Dragon III Model is released, with a retail of $16,000. One hundred are manufactured.

1995 - Santana I is introduced with a MSR of $8,000. PRS moves to new state-of-the art factory in Stevensville, MD. On December 22, the last PRS is shipped from the Virginia Avenue facility. Robotics are now incorporated into some operations, including buffing. A tenth anniversary model

becomes the most recent limited edition, with a MSR of $6,600.

1996 - Production resumes at the new 25,000-square-foot PRS facility on Kent Island in Stevensville, just across the Chesapeake bridge. The first Private Stock instrument is completed on April 19, 1996 - each instrument is a one-of-a-kind.

1997 - PRS Guitars grosses over $10 million.

1998 - McCarty Archtop and Hollowbody Models are released, and Ted McCarty, former president of Gibson between 1950 and 1966, is recognized for his consultancy work. Production increases to 110 employees producing seven hundred guitars per month.

1999 - The PRS Piezo bridge system pickup is introduced at the winter NAMM show.

2000 - The Singlecut model makes its debut at the winter NAMM show in January. Also, the outrageously designed Dragon 2000 Model is launched, with a MSR of $20,000 (dragon inlays are on body only). Later in the year, Gibson Guitar Corp. files suit against PRS Guitars regarding copyright infringement on the Singlecut Model.

2001 - PRS posts a 50% sales gain. The Santana SE Model (Student Edition), manufactured in South Korea, is released with a $738 MSR.

2002 - PRS manufactures 13,000 instruments, a new record.

2003 - 180 dedicated employees are now working together to make the best instruments possible.

2004 - March 11 - Gibson Guitar Corp. wins the first round of a trademark infringement case against PRS. This case declared that the PRS Singlecut model infringed on Gibson's valid Les Paul trademark design. During November, Smith gives a clinic at the Beijing Music Festival in China.

2005 - 20th anniversary of PRS Guitars. The company continues to expand and work on new innovative designs. Approximately 845 Private Stock instruments have been constructed during the last nine years, with orders for two hundred more. Smith continues to conduct his unique guitar clinics in various domestic and international locations, averaging one a month. Faded Blue Jean debuts, and PRS colors continue to be the best in the industry. When asked why, Smith comments, "Lots of time, effort, and research, going to different manufacturers for unique colors and combinations. Our in-depth stain process and Dupont's Clear Coat is a glossy finish which makes every color jump out more." PRS argues trademark infringement case in federal appeals court.

Sources:

Burrluck, Dave; *The PRS Guitar Book - A Complete History of Paul Reed Smith Guitars*, 2002, Backbeat Books, San Francisco, CA.

Dragon Electric Guitar by Paul Reed Smith; Jan. 2000, National Museum of American History, Smithsonian.org

Gibson Guitar Wins Legal Battle; Aug. 13, 2004, Gibson.com

Innovative Lives; March 3, 2005, Smithsonian Institution, Smithsonian.org

Lyden, Jackie; *At PRS Guitars, A Second Golden Age*; All Things Considered, Aug. 30, 2003, National Public Radio.

Salter, Trent; 20 Year Anniversary Profile - PRS Guitars, *Musician's Hotline*, April/May, 2005, Heartland Communications Group, Fort Dodge, IA.

Smith, Paul; various interviews and conversations, May, 2005.

Suttle, Cliff; *The Man, the Company, & His Guitars - An interview with Paul Reed Smith*, 1998, Harmony-Central.com

THE VINTAGE GUITAR MARKET UPDATE

By Larry Meiners

Blue Book Publication's 9th Edition *Blue Book of Electric Guitars* provides guitar aficionados everywhere the ability to peruse well-researched information and stay current with vintage guitar prices and values for recently released and used instruments. For a modest fee, we get to enjoy the fruits of their labor and experience the most complete and detailed value guide available for electric guitars.

The availability of this edition is well-timed. Quantum leaps in vintage guitar values have been logged during the last eighteen months. Tier-1 models have increased the most, with other desirable models not far behind. Particular guitars have more than doubled in value while other models have increased in price far above the market average and the rate of inflation.

More people than at any time I can recall are buying old guitars. I am hearing about car-trunk dealers, regional brokers, and guitar store owners keeping the finest of their acquisitions. This is certainly a change in behavior for some of these treasure hunters. With prices increasing at the current rate, many of these sellers feel they will be "leaving money on the table" by selling at this time. This 'buy and hold' mentality fuels additional price increases due to the finite quantity of great vintage instruments available for sale. Some people feel they must buy that special guitar now or risk being priced out of the market. Some tier-1 models are already out of the price range of many buyers. Basically, it's high-net-worth individuals buying expensive guitars. The average working person who is facing college expenses for dependant children is not spending a hundred thousand dollars or more for nice Bursts or other rare guitars.

It is difficult to discuss vintage guitars without mentioning baby boomers. Baby boomers have had the greatest generational effect on vintage guitar prices over the last twenty years. In addition, the great bull market for stocks began in 1982 and may have ended in 2000 (the jury is still out on that one). The stock bull market was driven in part by baby boomers during their peak-earnings years with disposable income. Although the S&P Small and Mid-cap indices have reached new all-time highs early in 2005, the major indices (Dow Jones Industrial Average, S&P 500 and the NASDAQ Composite) have failed to eclipse their 2000 highs. Baby boomers have

experienced one of the greatest stock bull markets in history and are still witnessing the ongoing bull market in vintage guitars. What happens if or when baby boomers sell their cherished guitar collections? Large collectors, foreign buyers, and boomer children will probably be required to step up and buy these guitars for the market to remain robust. Will any of this happen? No one knows.

As a follow-up to my article published March, 2003 entitled, "Money Flows from Wall Street's Bear to Vintage Guitars' Bull," I am addressing the market's current performance. At the time the article appeared in print, the multi-year bear market that had started in 2000 had bottomed. A rally began elevating the major averages in 2003 and 2004. The Dow, S&P 500 and the NASDAQ Composite gained 28%, 35%, and 59%, respectively, over the last two years after giving up 27%, 40%, and 67% the previous two years.

During the fifteen-year period leading up to the NASDAQ 5000 'bubble' peak during the year 2000, many top-tier vintage guitars manufactured by Gibson, Fender, and Martin performed, in general, below the aggregate average of the Dow Jones Industrial Average, S&P 500 and the NASDAQ Composite. Since the bursting of the stock market bubble, including the last two-year double-digit stock rally, many top-tier vintage guitars manufactured by Gibson, Fender, and Martin have, in general, significantly outperformed the Dow Jones Industrial Average, the S&P 500, and the NASDAQ Composite. Over the last nineteen years, it's been no contest; the best vintage guitars have outperformed the major stock averages by a wide mark. During the last five years, the major averages lost ground while old guitar prices increased, and stocks ran into a vicious bear while old guitars rode the musical bull. In general, key vintage solid-body guitars outperformed acoustic guitars during the last five years. Prior to 2000, important acoustic guitar models from the flat-top golden-era period outperformed many solid-body models.

How did the two major U.S. stock market averages perform over the period from October, 1982 to the end of 2004 versus a number of guitar models? Let's look at the estimates for guitars versus these well-known stock indices:

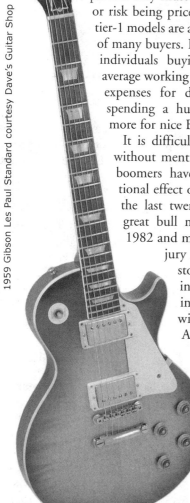

1959 Gibson Les Paul Standard courtesy Dave's Guitar Shop

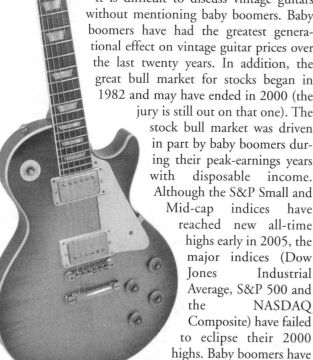

PERFORMANCE OF STOCKS & VINTAGE GUITARS FROM OCT. 1982-2004

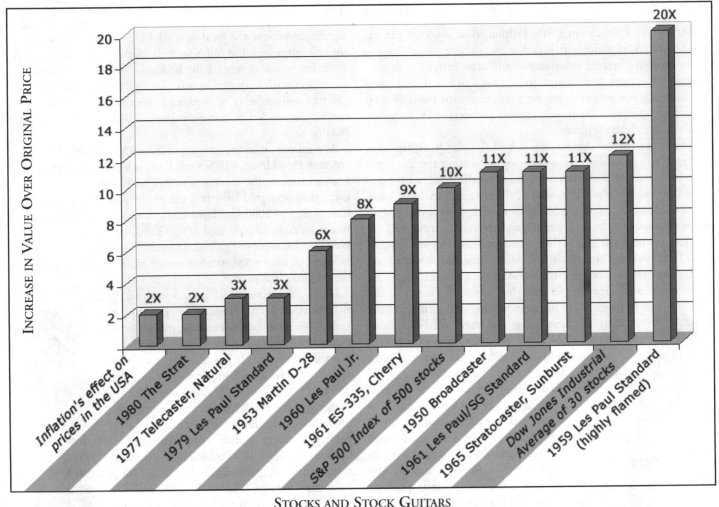

STOCKS AND STOCK GUITARS

* Source Larry Meiners (X = times original value)

We infer from the Stocks and Stock Guitars chart above that the tier-1 vintage Burst model outperformed the two large stock indices and most other vintage models by a large margin. Tier-2 vintage models performed inline with the S&P 500 and DJIA. The remaining models performed below these two stock indices. The 1970s-1980s guitars in this example increased at or above the inflation rate.

Some vintage guitars have been a great investment over the last twenty-five years. However, some influential vintage guitar collectors say you should buy a guitar because you have an emotional attachment to these musical icons versus buying them strictly for investment purposes. Stock and guitar market future performance is unknown and it is possible that vintage guitar values could level off or even decrease in the future. Unlike stocks, there is no future stream of earnings to help value guitars. The intrinsic value of classic vintage guitars is far less than their current market value.

Along with increased demand for old guitars, and therefore prices, many people ask: Why are vintage guitars so expensive? The same people scratching their collective heads about guitar prices are not happy about $2.00+/gallon gasoline either. Are guitar prices high? When I hear a question like this, I look for hard data that will help answer the question. Please remember that prices are set by market dynamics, not a group of dealers.

Prices are ultimately set by supply and demand. The supply is rather limited for the best examples and the demand seems to be growing. These conditions help explain the higher prices the market has experienced.

Looking at my historic database of recent and vintage guitar prices, I picked a few instruments of interest and will attempt to shed some light on our subject. I also consulted the website of the Federal Reserve Bank of Minneapolis (Alan Greenspan is their boss) that displays a formula to calculate the worth of a dollar over time accounting for inflation. For example: What is an item or service purchased in 19XX worth in current dollars? The Federal Reserve Bank uses the CPI (Consumer Price Index) to calculate the value.

Let's start with the price of gasoline and work up to guitars since everyone is familiar with that. In 1978, gas was about $0.60 per gallon. Using the Fed model, the equivalent price today would be about $1.80. Therefore, we are paying about 22% more for gas relative to 1978 (assuming gas is $2.20 per gallon). Yes, gas is more expensive than in 1978, even when accounting for inflation. It looks as if gas prices may increase even more in the coming years. The known supply is sold against an increasing demand and, similar to vintage guitar pricing, historically, gas prices may increase from current levels.

Next, let's look at the Gibson Flying V (finished white like Michael Schenker's guitar from his UFO days), which I bought new in 1978. The list price for the guitar and case was about $900 with an 'A mark' dealer cost of about $450. A Chicagoland dealer marked it up 33% from cost and sold it to me for about $600. The Fed says the equivalent price in today's dollars would be almost $1800. Checking the sites of large online dealers, the street price for a new white Gibson Flying V is about $1000. It seems a new Flying V is about 40% less expensive than in 1978.

Please keep in mind that the USA's home version of 'spend your money before it's worth almost nothing' (aka hyper-inflation combined with low growth, or stagflation) was creeping into the American economy at that time, which affected the cost of domestic products. Interest rates hit a staggering 19% in 1981. Still, you could say that new Flying V guitars are cheaper today than in 1978, and that gas is more expensive (if you account for inflation). On the other hand, an excellent condition 1978 white Flying V is worth about 40-50% more today than in 1978, solely in terms of current dollars (and not accounting for inflation). More new Flying V guitars can be made, but the same isn't true for oil underground or classic vintage guitars aboveground.

Now, let's look at an old guitar example from 1978. An excellent condition 1967 ES-335-12 (twelve-string) guitar sold for about $400 in 1978. The Fed says the price in today's dollars is close to $1200. But buying one today would set you back about $2000. So, this vintage model is selling for about 70% more than in 1978. However, as an investment, the ES-335-12 lags far behind major stock indices and all tier-1 vintage models.

What may we conclude from this exercise? Prices are established by supply and demand. Vintage guitars are neither intrinsically expensive nor intrinsically cheap at prevailing market prices. They may be viewed as expensive or cheap from your relative point of view, since current prices reflect the buyers' and sellers' perception of value for these instruments.

My opinion is that gas is a bit more expensive than we have been accustomed to paying (even accounting for inflation) and some standard model new guitars are less expen-

Gibson ES-335 courtesy Dave's Guitar Shop

sive. Also, buying the 'right' vintage guitar has been a great investment, but not all old guitars are great investments. Certain vintage guitar models go in and out of favor while others stand the test of time and always seem to be the popular choice.

Compare vintage guitars to other collectables, and current prices may not seem so high-priced. Baseball cards have sold for $100,000 or even more than $600,000. You have to love baseball to pay half a million dollars for a piece of cardboard. How about someone paying $71,000 for an old bottle of wine? How about an individual purchasing a dress worn by an actress for $1,150,000? That's more than a million dollars for a used dress! How about a collector purchasing a toy car for $3,000? Personally, I'd rather have a '62 Jaguar (the guitar, not the car). Speaking of cars, how about an Italian sports car from the 1950s that sold for $2,500,000? That amounts to two and one-half million dollars for a car with lousy gas mileage. Wow! In comparison, vintage guitars seem (Dare I say?) … "cheap."

One of the maxims of vintage guitar collecting is: "Buy the best examples of the best models you can afford." In 1978, the most expensive models were the Gibson Lloyd Loar F-5 mandolin (1920s), Gibson's 1958 Flying V and Explorer, the Gibson Burst (1958-1960) and the pre-war Martin D-45. Those models have historically proven to be great financial performers, far exceeding most other investment options. I'll stick by my statement that, with few exceptions, certain pre-1966 electric guitars and basses, pre-1946 flat-top guitars and Loar-era Gibson mandolins are true vintage classics and the best models ever produced. ■

Gibson Flying V courtesy Dave's Guitar Shop

Larry Meiners writes articles as well as a monthly column about vintage and collectible guitars and is the author of the *Gibson Flying "V"* and *Gibson Shipment Totals* books, as well as the audio CD book for instrument collectors, *Live! At The Guitar Show.*

For more information, please visit www.flyingvintage.com.

Larry can be reached by email at flyingvintage@aol.com.

TALES FROM A BEGINNING STRING BENDER

by Tegan Godfrey

Getting a guitar for Christmas 2003 was a giant highlight in my life. It opened me up to a wide variety of music. Before I got my Jackson FR 5 Dinky Reverse I used to listen to a lot of rap and hip-hop. That changed in about twenty seconds. Rock was the number one priority in my life from then on.

For me to rock I needed to join the rock persona. Before I knew it, my hair started to reach my shoulders and weird and funny hand gestures snatched my attention. With Maiden and Priest now my gods I started to learn as many heavy metal songs as I could. There was only one teeny tiny problem. I couldn't read music. What was I going to do? How was I to learn the beautiful symphonies of the rock-and-roll way?

I started to go down the path of darkness, but it wasn't all dark, because at the end of this tunnel there was light. Almighty beautiful light. And that light was Jake Davisson. This man was to teach me the way, and it was the way I must learn. With me at my knees begging for help he said two words that I shall never forget. "Power Chords," he said to me with his mighty rock voice. And thus I learned these power chords until my fingertips bled.

I started to think I was getting good, but I needed a test. Battle of the bands was the test I must pass, but for that I needed a band. So, together, some fellow musicians and I formed Deep Cycle. Dylan Olson, Caleb Smith, Matt Lindell, Tommy Quinn, Ryan Lee and I were to be the greatest band Cannon Falls had ever seen. It was around April and the battle was to be set for July 3 at the Cannon Valley Fair. We were to play against five other bands. Luckily, my friends had been playing their instruments for quite a while. We practiced in Caleb's basement. He had been playing the drums since he was a little kid, and his sister was also a musician, so they had a pretty nice setup at their house.

There we started to act like a real band. We argued and fought over which songs we were going to play and who would be playing which part. After a couple of weeks of arguing, we decided to play three songs. We were going to cover "Meant to Live" by Switchfoot, "Down on the Corner" by CCR, and our own little version of "Wild Thing." We practiced our hearts out and put on a little show for our families to see if we were any good.

Then July 3 came and we were to play second to last. There ended up being a total of four bands in the battle. The first band went, and they were not bad. The second band came and they were awesome. They had written their own music, and they didn't sing but they were really good with their instruments. Now it was our turn. We played "Meant to Live" first because it was in drop d-tuning. After that song our drummer did a little solo, so we had time to tune back up to E. We then played "Down on the Corner" and "Wild Thing." The crowd loved us! They screamed and cheered as we got off the stage. Then the last band played and it was all over. We ended up taking second place, right under the band that had played all the instrumentals. One of the members of that band came up to us and said "Well, we might have won the battle, but you guys won all the girls."

After that I thought that we were going to keep practicing and keep looking for some more gigs. But I was wrong. The rest of the summer none of us got together to practice. I would see some of my band members around and ask when we were going to practice again, and all they ever said was "I don't know." That's when I started to write my own stuff. It wasn't much; it was basically comedy music. I would write the music, and then some of my friends would come over and we would work on the lyrics together. We recorded the songs on my sister's karaoke machine and then passed the tapes out to our friends. The singer of our band and I got together and started listening to some music one day. He said that he wanted to make a rap song into a rock song. So we started looking for songs that would be pretty cool. We ended up with nothing because most of the rap songs sounded exactly the same, so we gave up on that idea.

School started up again and my friends and I kept writing comedy songs. To my surprise, there was another battle of the bands coming up for homecoming. I jumped on the idea and I went to go tell the band. To my disbelief, they all said they didn't want to do it. They told me they didn't have enough time to practice and there weren't going to be many bands signing up. I looked at them and said "Well, I guess I will just do an acoustic then!" So I got some other friends together and we wrote a

song about the homecoming football game and the homecoming queen. We sang the song at the pep fest and it was a hit! Even the teachers liked it. They said we showed a ton of school spirit and they hadn't heard a song like ours in a long time. My friends really started getting into music after that. A lot of them started playing the guitar and asked me to teach them. I said that I had only two words for them: "Power Chords!" I was reliving the moment when Jake had said those words to me.

One day, I watched a movie called *Spinal Tap*. If you've never heard of it, it's a big spoof on the way rock stars live. Anyways, there is a solo in there where Nigel plays Mozart. It was really cool, and I thought that it would be cool if I kind of mixed classical with modern day music. So I learned that solo, and started to play some hard rock with it. To my surprise, it actually sounded pretty cool. So I started playing these classical and rock mixes and am still improving on them to this day. My parents started to get annoyed that I always used my amp when I played. After that I didn't use my amp much, but then they would get annoyed at me because they couldn't hear me. Go figure!

I went onto the Internet and started looking at acoustic guitars. There was no way I had the money to pay for another guitar. Hope came to me at last when my friend Chad Stauffer said he needed his guitar tuned. He came over, and I found that it was an acoustic guitar. He left my house later, forgetting his guitar. I started playing it and my parents loved the sound of it. I came up with a routine to help me get better with the guitar. I practiced on the acoustic and then played on my electric guitar. What was great about that was that when I played the acoustic guitar my fingertips hurt so badly that they started to bleed, and that built up more and more calluses so my fingertips got stronger and stronger. Pretty soon, when I played again it felt pretty good and I wanted to never let go of the guitar.

After a month Chad still had not come to pick up his guitar. I felt kind of guilty because I never told him to come over and get it since I really liked playing it. I finally decided to call him up and tell him to pick it up before I wore it out. He said he would pick it up, but another month went by and he still did not stop over. I stopped feeling guilty because I knew I had done all I could and it was his responsibility.

I found out recently that there is another musician in our family. My great uncle Tim also plays the guitar. I talked to him about guitar playing and found out that he had started playing around the same age I had. He said he only plays one form of music and that is the blues. He says that it is the only music worth playing, but harder than hell to play. I started thinking that the blues would sound really sweet. At about that same time, Jake Davisson gave me a CD called *The Best of Otis Redding*. After listening to him I got really into the blues.

To break it down, I love every form of music there is. If there is a way to play it on the guitar, I will play it. If there isn't, I will find a way to make it work! ∎

Images courtesy Cassandra Faulkner, Alison Godfrey, and Matt Young.

INTERESTED IN CONTRIBUTING

The good thing about publishing a book on an annual basis is that you will find out what you don't know yearly. Each new edition should be an improvement on the last. Even though you can't do it all in one, ten, or even twenty editions, accumulating the new information is an ongoing process, with the results being published in each new edition.

The *Blue Book of Electric Guitars*™ has been the result of non-stop and continual guitar research carried out by obtaining relevant information from both manufacturers and luthiers (this research also involves visiting their production facilities whenever the opportunity arises). Also of major importance is speaking directly with experts (both published and unpublished), reading books, catalogs, and company promo materials, gathering critical and up-to-date manufacturer/luthier information obtained from the NAMM Shows and the makers themselves, and observing and analyzing market trends by following major vintage dealer and collector pricing and trends.

We also have a great batch of contributing editors and advisory board members that pump out a lot of good information annually – including vintage pricing updates. Going to a lot of guitar and trade shows, in addition to visiting a variety of music stores, guitar shops, pawn shops, and second-hand stores, also hones our chops.

If you feel that you can contribute in any way to the materials published herein, you are encouraged to submit hard copy regarding your potential additions, revisions, corrections, or any other pertinent information that you feel would enhance the benefits this book provides to its readers. Unfortunately, we are unable to take your information over the phone (this protects both of us)! Earn your way into the ranks of the truly twisted, join the motley crew of contributing editors, and see that your information can make a difference! We thank you in advance for taking the time to make this a better publication.

All materials sent in for possible inclusion into upcoming editions of the *Blue Book of Electric Guitars*™ should be either mailed, faxed, or emailed to us at the address listed below.

Blue Book Publications, Inc.
Attn: Guitar Contributions
8009 34th Avenue South, Ste. 175
Minneapolis, MN 55425 USA
Fax: 952-853-1486
Email: guitars@bluebookinc.com (please include "Blue Book" in the subject line)
Website: http://www.bluebookinc.com
If you're emailing us an image, please make sure it is in TIF or JPEG format on a simple white background.
Poor quality images cannot be used for publication.

CORRESPONDENCE INQUIRIES

Can't find your guitar in the book? No one's ever seen or heard of this make/model? Color or feature not listed? What's this thing worth? When was it manufactured? These are the most common type of questions we get when conducting research. This type of researching is a big job, and to do it properly, you must have a good working knowledge of instruments and their values, an up-to-date reference library, the right contacts (huge), keep going to guitar/trade shows, and actually read the guitar mags. We have helped out hundreds of people in the past, and hope to maintain this service in the future as well.

As with any ongoing publication, certain makes and models will not be included within the scope of the text. As expanded research uncovers model variations and new companies, the book's body of text will always have some unlisted instruments. Not believing in ivory towers and one-way traffic, this editor/publisher offers a mechanism for the consumer to get further information about makes and models not listed in these pages. For those reasons, we are offering correspondence inquiries to help you obtain additional information on items not listed, or even questions you may have regarding values and other related information.

Answering your correspondence (including letters, faxes, and email) under normal circumstances takes us between ten and fourteen working days. On hard-to-research items, more time is necessary. To make sure we can assist you with any correspondence, please include good quality photos of the specimen in question, any information available about that particular specimen – including manufacturer/trademark, model, body style, color/finish, unusual or other discernible features (if any) – that will assist us with identifying your guitar(s). If you're emailing us an image, please make sure it is in TIF or JPEG format. Poor quality images cannot be properly used for determining value. The charge for this comprehensive research program is $20.00 per instrument. In addition to payment, be sure to include both your address and phone number, giving us an option of how to contact you for best service. To keep up with this constant onslaught of correspondence, we have a large network of both dealers and collectors who can assist us (if necessary) to answer most of your questions within this time frame.

Remember, the charge for this research service is $20.00 per guitar, and payment must accompany your correspondence. Your inquiry will be answered in the order it was received. Thank you for your patience. Sometimes proper research can't be hurried.

You may also want to check our website for additional guitar information, including the Photo Grading System™ for ascertaining guitar condition factors. Good information never sleeps!

All correspondence regarding information and appraisals (not potential contributions or buying/selling guitars) should be directed to:

Blue Book Publications, Inc.
Attn: Guitar Research
8009 34th Avenue South, Ste. 175
Minneapolis, MN 55425 USA
Toll-free (U.S. & Canada): 800-877-4867 (voicemail only)
Fax: 952-853-1486
Email: guitars@bluebookinc.com (please include "Blue Book" in the subject line)
Website: http://www.bluebookinc.com
SORRY - No order or request for research paid by credit card will be processed without a credit card expiration date.

BUYING, SELLING, or TRADING

Interested in buying or selling a particular guitar? Not sure about eBay, or perhaps another risky alternative? Does consigning scare you? Or maybe you're just hesitating because you're not sure what a fair market price is? To be sure that you are getting a fair price or getting what you paid for, a buy/sell referral contact will be made, typically based on your interest(s) and geographical location. This referral service is designed to help all those people who are worried or scared about purchasing a potentially "bad guitar" or getting "ripped off" when selling. There is no charge for this referral service – we are simply connecting you with the best person(s) possible within your interest(s), making sure that you get a fair deal. This sort of matchmaking (no easy task) can make a world of difference on potentially buying or selling a guitar. Please contact the *Blue Book of Electric Guitars*™ with your request (email or fax preferred). If selling or trading, please mail or email (TIF or JPEG format) us a good quality image(s). On a buy request, please as specific as possible. All replies are treated strictly confidentially, and should be directed to:

Blue Book Publications, Inc.
Attn: Guitars B/S/T
8009 34th Ave. S., Ste. 175
Minneapolis, MN 55425 USA
Email: guitars@bluebookinc.com (please include "Blue Book" in the subject line)
Website: http://www.bluebookinc.com
Fax: 952-853-1486
Toll-free (U.S. & Canada): 800-877-4867
Non-domestic: 952-854-5229

COMMON GUITAR ABBREVIATIONS

The abbreviations listed below may be found as prefixes and suffixes with a company's model names, and may indicate a special quality about that particular designation. This list should be viewed as being a guide only; abbreviations specifically relating to individual trademarks (i.e., Fender, Gibson, Martin) are listed separately within their sections.

A	-Ash	H	-Herringbone	MSR	-Manufacturer's Suggested Retail	RSH	-Round Soundhole
AE	-Acoustic Electric	HB	-Humbucker	N, NAT	-Natural	S	-Spanish, Solid Body, Special or Super
B	-Bass, Brazilian Rosewood, or Blue (finish)	HC	-Hard Case	N/A	-Not Applicable/ Not Available	SB, S/B	-Sunburst
BLK, BK, BL	-Black (finish)	HDWR	-Hardware	NAMM	-National Association of Musical Merchants	Ser. No.	-Serial Number
		HH	-Two humbucker pickup configuration			SG	-Solid Guitar
B&S	-Back & Sides	HS	-Headstock	NOS	-New Old Stock	SGL	-Single
C	-Cutaway	HSH	-Two humbucker and one single coil pickup in the middle configuration	OEM	-Original Equipment Manufacture	SN	-Serial Number
CH	-Channel					SSS	-Three single coil pickup configuration
C.I.T.E.S.	-Convention for International Trade of Endangered Species (July 1,1975)	HSS	-One humbucker and two single coil pickup configuration	OH	-Original Hardshell	STD	-Standard
				OHSC	-Original Hardshell Case	SWD	-Smartwood
D	-Dreadnought or Double	J	-Jumbo	OM	-Orchestra Model	T	-Tremolo or Thinline
		K	-Koa	OSC	-Original Soft Case	TOB	-Tobacco
DC	-Double Cutaway	L, LH	-Left Handed	OTRA	-On The Road Again	TREM	-Tremolo
E	-Electric	LE	-Limited Edition	PG	-Pickguard	TV	-TV Color Finish
EQ	-Equalizer	M	-Mahogany or Maple	PU (P.U.)	-Pickup	V	-V shaped Neck, Venetian, Vibrato or Vintage Series
ES	-Electric (Electro) Spanish	MFG.	-Manufactured	R	-Reverse (headstock) Red (finish), or Rosewood		
		MENG	-MENG!			VIB	-Vibrato
F	-Fretless or Florentine	MH	-Mahogany	REFIN	-Refinished	W/	-With
		MPL	-Maple	REFRET	-Refretted	W/O	-Without
FB	-Fingerboard			REPRO	-Reproduction	WOB	-Wood Out Binding

GLOSSARY

This glossary is divided into four sections: General Glossary, Hardware: Bridges, Pegs, Tailpieces, and Tuners, Pickups/Electronics, and Book Terminology. If you are looking for something and can't find it in one section, please check the others. You may also want to refer to Anatomy of An Electric Guitar (page 11) for visual identification on many of the terms listed below. For wood terminology, please see the Know Your Woods section.

GENERAL GLOSSARY

Abalone - Shellfish material used in instrument ornamentation.

Action - Action is the height the strings are off of the fingerboard, stretched between the nut and bridge.

Arch/Arched Top - The top of an instrument that has been carved or pressed to have a "rounded" top.

Avoidire - Blonde mahogany.

Back Plate - Refers to the cover plate on the back of an instrument allowing access into the body cavity for repair/alterations.

Bass Bout - Upper left hand part of body (left side of lower fingerboard on right-hand guitars).

Bell - Truss Rod cover located directly above nut. Most are bell shaped, and may have model/make information on the outside.

Binding (bound) - Trim that goes along the outer edge of the body, neck or headstock. It is made out of many different materials, natural and synthetic.

"Black Beauty" - This term is generally used in reference to early (1955-1960) Gibson Les Paul Customs, due to their glossy black finish.

Body - The main bulk of the instrument, usually. It is where the bridge, tailpiece and pickguard are located. On electrics, it is where the pickups are routed into and the electronics housing is stored. It is what the player cradles.

Bolt On/Bolt On Neck - Construction technique that involves attaching the neck to the body by means of bolts or screws. Bolt-on necks are generally built and finished separately from the guitar body, and parts are assembled together later.

Bookmatched - Refers to the process where a single wood block is cut in half, and both pieces are carefully aligned and glued in the middle, matching the grain from left to right. Very popular on instruments with maple backs and a lot of flame.

Bound - See BINDING.

Bout/Bouts - Also see BASS BOUT, LOWER BOUT, and TREBLE BOUT. The rounded, generally, side/sides on the top and bottom of an instrument's body.

Bridge - Component that rests on the top of the instrument and transfers vibrations from string to body. It is usually attached by glue or screws but is also found to be held in place by string tension, the same as a violin.

Carved Top - See ARCHTOP.

Cello Tail Adjuster - The Cello tail adjuster is a 1/8 inches diameter black nylon-type material that attaches to the tailpiece and loops around an endpin jack (or ebony endpin). Nylon, of course, replaced the real (if unstable) gut material several years ago. This tail adjuster is used on virtually every cello tailpiece in the world, and figures prominently in a number of archtop guitar designs.

Cutaway - An area that has been cut away on the treble bout, or both bouts, to allow access to the higher frets. See FLORENTINE and VENETIAN.

Ding - Small mark or dent on a guitar. Also the noise you swear you hear when your guitar hits another object, thus causing the mark.

Ebonized - A process by which the wood has been stained dark to appear to be ebony; alternatively, also referring to something black in color (such as bridge adjuster wheels) made to blend in with ebony fittings on an archtop guitar.

Ebonol - A synthetic material that is used as replacement for wood (generally as a fingerboard).

F-Hole - Stylized f-shaped soundhole that is carved into the top of various instruments, most commonly acoustic. It usually comes in pairs.

Fingerboard - An area on top of the neck that the string is pressed against to create the desired note (frequency).

Finish - The outer coat of an instrument. The sealant of the wood. The protector of the instrument. Finishes include Gloss, Satin, Nitrocellulose, Matte, Spar, Polyurethane, Tongue Oil, etc.

Florentine - sharp point on the treble forward horn of a body cutaway. See also VENETIAN.

Fret - A strip of metal that is embedded at specific intervals into the fingerboard.

Fretboard - Another way of saying fingerboard and specifying that it has frets embedded into it.

Fretless Fingerboard - Commonly found on bass instruments, this fingerboard is smooth, with no frets.

Graphite - Used in various forms of instrument construction because of its rigidity and weight, this type of synthetic material may be used in the body, neck, nut, saddle, etc.

Hardware - Generic term typically used for the bridge, tailpiece, tuners, and/or vibrato system.

Headless - This means the instrument has no headstock.

Headstock - Top portion of the neck assembly where the tuning machines are located. Headstock design is a field unto itself, and many makes and models can be instantly identified by simply looking at an instrument's headstock design or configuration. Additional information about the instrument, such as serialization (typically on back side or top), model number, and/or distinctive logo/trademark may also be part of the headstock.

Heel - On the backside of an instrument, the heel is located at the base of the lower neck where the neck meets the body. May be bound, inlaid, or carved as well.

Inlay - Decoration or identifying marks on an instrument that are inlaid into one of the surface areas. They are made of a number of materials, though abalone, pearl and wood are the most common.

Locking Tuners - These tuners are manufactured with a locking mechanism built right into them, thus preventing string slippage.

Logo - An identifying feature on an instrument: it could be a symbol or a name; and it could appear as a decal, an inlay, or painted on (and it could be missing).

Lower Bout(s) - Refers to the lower part of an instrument's contour(s). A lower bout measurement is the maximum distance between an instrument's two lower bouts.

Mortise - Wood construction procedure where one piece of wood is carefully fitted to join another.

Mother-of-Pearl - A shellfish (oyster/clam) material used for inlay.

Nato - A lower grade or quality of mahogany, sometimes referred to as "lumberyard" mahogany.

Neck - The area that the strings of the instrument are stretched along, the headstock sits at the top, and the body lies below the last fret.

Neck Angle - The angle at which the neck joins the body (more common on set neck instruments). Different neck angles can affect both tone and volume, especially on acoustic guitars.

Octave - In Western Notation, every 12 frets on a stringed instrument is an octave in the musical scale.

Pearl - Short for mother-of-pearl, the inside shell from a shellfish. See MOTHER-OF-PEARL.

Pearloid - A synthetic material made of plastic and pearl dust.

Peghead - See HEADSTOCK. Originally used to describe the pegs/tuners extruding from the guitar head.

Phenolic - A synthetic material that is used as fingerboard wood replacement.

Pickguard - A piece of material used to protect the instrument's top or finish from gouges that are caused by the pick or your fingers.

Pickup - An electronic device utilizing magnetic induction to transform string vibrations into electronic signals needed for sound amplification. Pickups can either be high (most popular) or low (less output) impedance.

Position Marker - Usually, some form of decorative inlay which is inlaid into the neck to help the player identify fret position.

"Pre-CBS" - Collector's terminology that refers to the CBS purchase of Fender Instruments in 1965. A "Pre-CBS" instrument is one built by Leo Fender's original company.

Purfling - Decorative trim that is found running along the inside of the binding.

Relief - The upward slope of the fingerboard that keeps the strings off the frets.

Reverse Headstock - On this instrument the headstock has been flipped over from the normal configuration and the tuners are all on the highest note side of the instrument (tuners are all located on one side).

Rims - also referred to as Sides – refers to the sides of an instrument, typically between 1½ -5 inches deep.

Saddle - A natural or synthetic component generally attached to the bridge on which the strings rest, enabling the strings to resonate properly through the bridge and instrument top, and to assist in intonation.

Scale Length - The length measured in inches between the nut and the bridge/saddle/tailpiece.

Scalloped - This is what the area on the fingerboard between the frets is called when it has been scooped out, creating a dip between the frets.

Scratch Plate - Slang for Pickguard. - See PICKGUARD.

Semi-Acoustic - Term used to describe a shallow bodied instrument that is constructed with a solid piece of wood running the length of the center of the body.

Sides - Also referred to as Rims – refers to the sides of an instrument, typically between 1½ -5 inches deep.

Slotted Headstock - A headstock design usually associated with acoustic guitars, featuring 2 internal "slotted" areas where the strings are guided and the tuning machines spindles are placed horizontally.

Strings - Typically made from gut (older), nylon, steel, or bronze. Metal strings may or may not be coated also. They range in a variety of sizes, both in diameter and length. The weight of the string is what determines the range of frequencies it will cover.

Sunburst (Sunburst Finish) - Typically, either a 2 or 3 color finish that is applied around the outside of the body (may include rims, back, and neck also), leaving the inside a lighter, unstained natural color.

Thinline - Original Gibson terminology referring to a hollow bodied instrument that has a shallow depth of body.

Through Body (Thru Body; Neck Through) - Type of construction that consists of the neck wood extending through the entire length of the instrument and the pieces of wood that make up the body being attached to the sides of the neck wood (called "wings").

Treble Bout - Upper right hand part of body (right side of lower fingerboard on right hand guitars).

Tremolo - An increase of decrease in the frequency of a tone. Tremolo in relation to guitars usually refers to a tremolo unit, or tremolo effects. Please refer to individual listings.

Truss Rod - Typically, an adjustable rod (usually metal) placed in an instrument's neck, adding stability, and allowing for a neck adjustment in the case of a warped/curved neck.

Venetian - Rounded point on the treble forward horn of a body cutaway. See also FLORENTINE.

Vibrato - The act of physically lengthening or shortening the medium (in this case, it will be strings) to produce a fluctuation in frequency. The pitch altering mechanism on your guitar is a vibrato, not a tremolo!

Volute (also Neck Volute) - Additional protruding wood used as a strengthening support where an angled back of the headstock is spliced to the end of the neck. This carved (or shaped) piece of the neck is also referred to as a "handstop".

Warpage - Generally refers to a neck that becomes bowed or warped, making playability difficult/impossible. On necks with truss rods, the neck may be adjusted to become straight again. On instruments with set necks, often times the neck must be taken off and repaired, or needs to be replaced.

Wings - The body pieces attached to the sides of a through body neck blank, thus forming a complete body.

Zero Fret - The zero fret is a length of fret wire fitted into a fret slot which is cut at the exact location as that of a conventional nut. The fingerboard is generally cut off 1/8" longer than usual, at which point the nut is fitted. When used in conjunction with the zero fret, the nut serves as a string guide. The fret wire used on the zero fret is usually slightly larger than that used on the fingerboard itself - the slightly higher zero fret establishes the open string's height above the fingerboard.

HARDWARE: BRIDGES, PEGS, TAILPIECES AND TUNERS

Banjo Tuners - Tuners that are perpendicular to the headstock and pass through it, as opposed to being mounted on the side of the headstock, (like classic style headstock tuners).

Bigsby Vibrato - A vibrato system that involves a roller bar with little pegs that run in a perpendicular line, around which you hook

GLOSSARY

the string balls. One end of the bar has an arm coming off of it, a spring is located under the arm, and the entire apparatus is connected to a trapeze tailpiece. The bridge is separate from the vibrato system. This vibrato was designed by Paul Bigsby.

Bridge - Component that connects the strings to the body of the instrument. Bridge materials may be wood, metal, alloy, synthetic, or even a combination. It is usually attached to the top of an instrument's body by glue or screws but can also be held in place by string tension, the same as a violin. Bridge placement is determined by the instrument's scale length.

Bridge Pins - Pins or dowels used to secure string to bridge. These pins usually utilize friction to seat properly, and are typically made from hard wood, synthetic materials (ivoroid is popular), or ivory. Also referred to as Pegs.

Double Locking Vibrato - A vibrato system that locks the strings into place by tightening down screws on each string, thus stopping the string's ability to slip. There is also a clamp at the top of the fingerboard that holds the strings from the tuners. These more modern designs were formulated separately by Floyd Rose and the Kahler Company. As guitarist Billy Gibbons (ZZ Top) is fond of saying, the locking vibratos give you the ability to "turn Steel into Rubber, and have 'er bounce back on a dime". - See VIBRATO.

Fixed Bridge - Body hardware component that typically contains the saddles, bridge, and tailpiece in one integrated unit, and is usually mounted utilizing screws/studs.

Headless - Term meaning that the instrument's headstock is missing (example: Steinberger). The top of the neck is capped with a piece of hardware that acts like a regular tailpiece on the instrument body.

Locking Tuners - These tuners are manufactured with a locking mechanism built into them, thus preventing string slippage.

Nut - Device located at the top of the fingerboard (opposite from the bridge) that determines the action and spacing of the strings.

Pegs - Can refer to either the small pegs used to secure the strings in the bridge or older tuners used on some vintage instruments (hence the term peghead).

Pins - Pegs that are used to anchor the strings in place on the bridge.

Roller Bridge - This is a Gretsch trademark feature. It is an adjustable metal bridge that sits on a wooden base, the saddles of this unit sit on a threaded bar and are easily moved back and forth to allow personal string spacing.

Saddle/Saddles - A part of the bridge that holds the string/strings in place, helps transfer vibrations to the instrument body and helps in setting the action.

Set- In Neck - Guitar construction that involves attaching the neck to the body by gluing a joint (such as a dovetail). Set necks cannot be adjusted by shims as their angle of attachment to the body is pre-set in the design.

Sideways Vibrato - Built off the trapeze tailpiece concept, this unit has a lever that pulls the string attachment bar back along a pair of poles that have springs attached them to push the bar back into place. This is all covered by a plate with a design on it.

Single Locking Vibrato - A vibrato system that locks the strings on the unit to keep them from going out of tune during heavy arm use. This style of vibrato does not employ a clamping system at the top of the fingerboard.

Standard Vibrato - Usually associated with the Fender Stratocaster, this unit has the saddles on top and an arm off to one side. The arm allows you to bend the strings, making the frequencies (notes) rise or drop. All of this sits on a metal plate that rocks back and forth. Strings may have an area to attach to on top or they may pass through the body and have holding cups on the back side. A block of metal, usually called the Inertia Block, is generally located under the saddles to allow for increased sustain. The block travels through the instrument's body and has springs attached to it to create the tension necessary to keep the strings in tune. - See VIBRATO SYSTEM.

Steinberger Bridge - A bridge designed by Ned Steinberger, it combines the instrument bridge and tuners all in one unit. It is used with headless instruments.

Steinberger Vibrato - A vibrato system that has the instrument's bridge, vibrato and tuners all in one unit. Like the Steinberger Bridge, this was also designed by Ned Steinberger. It is also used with headless instruments.

Stop Tailpiece - Machined metal part attached to lower body by screws, which is usually slotted to hold the string balls. Generally used with a tune-o-matic bridge.

Strap button - Typically refers to oversized metal buttons on the outside of an instrument allowing the player to attach a strap to the instrument.

String Through Anchor Block - Refers to a steel block located in a tremolo unit to help sustain and anchor strings.

Strings Through Body (Anchoring) - A tailpiece that involves the strings passing through an instrument's body and the string balls are held in place by recessed cups on the back side.

Stud Tailpiece – See STOP TAILPIECE.

Tailpiece - The device that holds and typically positions (along with a possible bridge) the strings at the lower body. It may be all in one unit that contains the saddle/saddles also, or stands alone. Electric tailpieces are mostly metal construction, although metal, wood, alloy, synthetic or other materials have also been used.

Trapeze Tailpiece - A type of tailpiece that is hinged, has one end attached to either the lower bout or bottom rim of the instrument, and the top portion has internal grooves to hold the string balls.

Tremolo Unit – Refers to a mechanical device typically incorporated into the bridge of an instrument utilizing a tremolo (whammy) bar to produce changes in frequencies.

Truss Rod - Refers to a metal truss rod fitted into the back of an instrument's neck, adding stability, and allowing for a neck adjustment in the case of a warped/curved neck. Gibson invented this solution for neck adjusting in the mid 1920s.

Tuner(s)/Tuning Machine(s) - Mechanical device that is used to stretch the strings to the right tension for adjustable tuning. These are typically located on the headstock.

Tunable Stop Tailpiece - A tailpiece that rests on a pair of posts and has small fine-tuning machines mounted on top of it.

Tune-o-matic Bridge - A bridge that is attached to the instrument's top by two metal posts and has adjustable small moving saddles allowing for the intonation of individual strings. Tune-o-matic was originally a proprietary Gibson trademark that was designed by the late Ted McCarty in 1952, and introduced in 1954 on the Gibson Les Paul Custom.

GLOSSARY

Vibrato - Generic term used to describe Vibrato System.

Vibrato System - A device that increases or decreases the string tension by using a lever (whammy bar) and a fulcrum (typically pivot pins or blades).

Wang Bar - Slang term used for Vibrato System.

Whammy (Whammy Bar) - Slang term used for Vibrato System.

Wraparound Tailpiece – Design allowing strings to be wrapped around the tailpiece, then secured.

Wrapover Bridge - A self contained bridge/tailpiece bar device that is attached to the body, with the strings wrapping over the bar.

Wrapunder Bridge - The same as above except the strings wrap under the bar.

PICKUPS/ELECTRONICS

The Pickup Principle follows this idea: your instrument's pickup is composed of a magnetic core that has wire wrapped about it. This creates a magnetic field that the strings pass through. As the string is plucked it vibrates in this field and creates fluctuations. These fluctuations are then translated into electronic pulses by induction; the magic of having electrons excited into activity by being wrapped next to each other via the wire coils. Once the fluctuations are in electron form they move along the wires in groups called waveforms, which move to an amplifier and get enlarged. The rest is up to you.

Active Electronics - A form of electronic circuitry that involves some power source, usually a 9-volt battery. Most of the time the circuit is an amplification circuit, though it may also be onboard effects circuitry.

Alnico Pickup - A pickup utilizing an alloy magnet consisting of Aluminum, Nickel and Cobalt.

Amplify/Amplification - To increase, in this case to increase the volume of the instrument.

Blade - A pickup that uses a blade or rail instead of polepieces.

Bobbin - The structure, usually plastic, that the coil wires are wound around. See COILS.

Ceramic - A substance used in pickup magnets that consists of magnetic particles mixed with a clay-like base.

Coils - Insulated wire wrapped around a nonconductive material.

Coil Split - A switch and a term that means you are splitting the coils in a humbucker and turning it into two single coil pickups. - See SPLIT PICKUP.

Coil Tap - A term and a switch that refers to accessing a coil tap in a pickup. - See TAPPED.

Control/Controls - See POT and POTENTIOMETERS

Decade Switch - Typically, a switch or potentiometer involved in the tone circuitry that changes an instrument's sound by altering resistance levels.

Dirty Fingers - Coverless humbucker pickups that have black and white bobbins.

Equalizer - An effect that allows you to boost or cut certain frequencies.

'Floating' pickup - A magnetic pickup that is suspended over (versus being built into) the top of the guitar, just below the fingerboard. This enables the guitar to be used acoustically or electrically. Examples include the Benedetto pickup, the DeArmond #1100G, or the Gibson Johnny Smith pickup.

Hex Pickup - A device that has six individual pickups, one for each string, housed in a single unit. This unit is used to provide the signals for synth (synthesizer) instruments.

'Horseshoe' Pickup - Generally refers to Rickenbacker's original "frying pan" design pickups that resemble a horseshoe. The pickup "wings" extend up and back over the strings, but do not meet in the middle (split).

Humbucker - Consists of two single coil pickups being placed side by side and wired together in such a fashion that the hum is canceled out of the single coils.

J- Style - A single coil pickup, though some are humbucker pickups, designed for electric bass and usually placed near the bridge. It is largely associated with the Fender Jazz Bass.

"Jazz" Pickup - A pickup, suspended ('floating') or built- in on an archtop guitar that gives the instrument a traditional, mainstream jazz sound.

Lace Sensor - A pickup developed by Don Lace that takes a single bobbin and windings and places it inside a magnetic housing with an open top. This creates an electromagnetic shielding effect and allows only the area directly over the pickup to sense string vibration. As a result, the magnetic force ("string pull") on the string is lessened.

Lipstick (or Lipstick Tube) Pickup - Term coined in the vintage guitar market to describe the chrome single coil pickups found in Danelectro guitar models. The wound single coil pickups were actually placed in two chromed halves of lipstick casings (Danelectro bought the casings from a manufacturer who serviced the cosmetic industry). Since then, the 'Lipstick Tube' term has been applied to any similar single coil pickup in a chromed tube cover.

Mini-humbucker – similar to humbucker, except is smaller in size.

Onboard - Usually referencing effects, it means built into the instrument.

Out Of Phase - When a signal from two pickups are run through a switch that puts their respective signals 180 degrees out of phase with each other.

P-90 - original Gibson terminology for single coil pickup (also referred to as Soapbar).

P- Style - An offset pickup with two magnets per half. They are usually located near the neck and are associated with the Fender Precision Bass.

P.A.F. (Patent Applied For) - Common term used to mean the pickup that Seth Lover designed for Gibson in 1955. The patent was not awarded till 1959, so pickups used in the meantime had the P.A.F. stickers underneath the housing.

Parametric Equalizer - An equalizer that allows you to specifically choose which range of frequencies you wish to affect.

Passive Electronics - Electronic circuitry that has no power supply. Usually it consists of filter circuitry.

Phase Switch - A switch used to accomplish the feat of putting the signal out of phase. - See OUT OF PHASE.

Pickup - An electronic device utilizing magnetic induction to transform string vibrations into electronic signals needed for sound amplification. Pickups can either be high (most popular) or low (less output) impedance.

Pickup Trim Ring – A trim ring that goes around the outside of the pickup. Typically used w/o pickguard, and may be recessed into body.

GLOSSARY

Piezo (piezoelectric) - A crystalline substance that induces an electrical current caused by pressure or vibrations.

Polepiece/Polepieces - Small magnetic rods that are found inside the pickup coils and, usually, situated under the instrument's strings. Some of these polepieces are adjustable.

Pot - Short for "potentiometer," or so they say.

Potentiometer - A variable resistor that is typically used to make tone and volume adjustments on an instrument.

Preamp - An electronic circuit that amplifies the signal from the pickup/s and preps it for the amplifier.

Rail Pickup - See BLADE.

Shielding - Term used to describe materials (usually copper) used to protect the signal in electronic instruments from outside electrical interference.

Single Coil - See opening paragraph for this section, it applies to this term.

Soap Bar - Term used to describe a specific Gibson single coil pickup, model number: P-90.

Split Pickup - A humbucker that has been wired so it has the capability of being split into two single coil pickups.

Stacked Coil - A form of humbucker pickup that is in a stacked configuration so it can be installed as a replacement for a single coil.

Tapped - The process of taking a wire out of the midst of the windings in a pickup and leaving it open for hookup to a switch. This can be done a number of times in one pickup. "Tapping" the pickup allows access to a different amount of winding (a percentage of the full winding) and thus different sounds from the same pickup.

Transducer/Transducer Pickup - A device that converts energy from one form to another, in this instance it is the vibrations caused by the strings, moving along the wood and being converted into electrical energy for amplification.

BOOK TERMINOLOGY

This glossary section should help you understand the jargon used in the model descriptions of the instruments in this text.

3-per-side - Three tuners on each side of the headstock on a six string instrument.

3/2-per-side - This is in reference to a 5-string instrument with three tuners on one side of the headstock and two tuners on the other.

335 Style - Refers to an instrument that has a semi-hollowbody cutaway body style similar to that of the Gibson 335.

4-on-one-side - Four tuners on one side of the headstock on a 4-string instrument.

4-per-side - Four tuners on each side of the headstock an eight-string instrument.

4/1-per-side - On an instrument with five strings this would mean four tuners are on one side of the headstock, and one is on the other.

4/2-per-side - Four tuners on one side and two on the other side of a headstock.

4/3-per-side - This instrument has seven strings with four of the tuners located on one side of the headstock and three on the other side.

5-on-one-side - All the tuners on one side of the headstock on a 5-string instrument.

6-on-one-side - All six tuners on one side of the headstock on a 6-string instrument.

6-per-side - Six tuners on each side of the headstock on an twelve string instrument.

6/1-per-side - A seven string instrument with six tuners on one side and one on the other.

7-on-one-side - A term referring to a seven-string instrument with all the tuners on the headstock are on one side.

14/20-Fret - Term in which the first number describes the fret at which the neck joins the body, and the second number is the total number of frets on the fingerboard.

Contoured Body - A body design that features some carved sections that fit easier to the player's body (a good example is the Fender Stratocaster).

Dual Cutaway - Guitar design with two forward horns, both extending forward an equal amount (see OFFSET DOUBLE CUTAWAY, SINGLE CUTAWAY).

Explorer style - The instrument's body shape, a unique 'hourglass' shape, is similar to the original Gibson Explorer model.

Jazz Style - A body shape similar to the traditional jazz archtop or semi-hollowbody design, or some parts/designs of a traditional jazz archtop.

Les Paul (LP) Body Style - Typically refers to original Gibson Les Paul style body.

Offset Double Cutaway - Guitar design with two forward horns, the top (bass side) horn more prominent of the two (see DUAL CUTAWAY, SINGLE CUTAWAY).

Point Fingerboard - A fingerboard that has a "V-ed" section on it at the body end of the fingerboard.

Point(y) Headstock - Tip of the headstock narrows (i.e. Charvel/Jackson or Kramer models).

Precision Style (P-Style) - A bass guitar body shape similar to the original Fender Precision Bass; also refers to the split single coil design of the pickup.

Single Cutaway - Guitar design with a single curve into the body, allowing the player access to the upper frets of the fretboard (See DUAL CUTAWAY, OFFSET DOUBLE CUTAWAY).

Sleek - A more modern body style, perhaps having longer forward horns, more contoured body, or a certain aerodynamic flair (!).

Strat Style - Typically refers to a Fender Stratocaster body style.

Tele Style - A single cutaway 'plank' body similar to the original Fender Telecaster; also refers to the style of fixed bridge.

Through Body (Neck-Through Construction) - Type of construction that consists of the neck wood extending through the entire length of the instrument and the pieces of wood that make up the body being attached to the sides of the neck wood.

Tune-o-matic Stop Tailpiece - This unit is a combination bridge/tailpiece that has adjustable (tune-o-matic) saddles mounted on a wrap around tailpiece.

V Style - The instrument's body shape, a unique 'V' shape, is similar to the original Gibson Flying V model.

Volume/Tone Control - When encountered, refers to an instrument which has a volume and/or tone control. A numerical prefix (2 or 3) preceding the term indicates the amount of volume/tone controls.

Rating the condition factor of a guitar is, at best, subjective, while at worst, totally misrepresentative. We've attempted to give a few examples of things that may affect the pricing and desirability of vintage electric guitars, but it's almost impossible to accurately ascertain the correct condition factor (especially true on older instruments) without knowing what to look for - which means having the instrument in your hands (or someone else's whose checked out). Even then, three different experienced sources will probably come up with slightly different grades, not to mention different values based on different reasons. Listed below are major factors to consider when determining both the condition and value of any used electric instrument. Also, please study the PGS digital color photographs carefully on pages 33-48 to learn more about the factors described below.

Finish (read that original finish) - Original finish in good shape is, of course, the most desirable, and is the Holy Grail for collectors when hooked up with a major trademark and desirable model. A light professional overspray will negatively affect the value of a guitar somewhat. Professionally refinished instruments are typically worth 50% of the value of an original, and a poor refin is below that. An exception might be a case where there's only one or two examples of a highly desirable item, and condition may take a back seat to rarity.

Major repairs - Many older guitars have had repairs, of course. A well-done neck reset won't affect the overall value that much. Replaced bridges will have an affect, but the better the work, the better the resale value. A replaced neck, fingerboard, part of a side, top or back will cause the price to drop noticeably. Again, if it's an especially rare item, the rarity factor might negate the major repair(s).

Modifications - Any non-factory modification on an original guitar is going to hurt the value. Deciding to refinish the top of your 1959 LP Standard for example, will cost you the price of refinishing, plus another $15,000-$40,000 for non-originality! Modifications on pickups, tailpieces, and even installing a tremelo unit will also subtract from a guitars value. Think really really hard before you do any of these things to your vintage guitar. You won't get a second chance to make it original.

Replacement Tuners and other non-original parts - Many older guitars have been fitted with new tuners at some point. These days, there are good replacement tuners available that fit the original holes, etc. There are also sleeves that will make an oversized hole into the correct size for original style tuners. Even a good, appropriate replacement set will have a negative affect on value, even though it constitutes a playing improvement over what was available when the instrument was manufactured.

Cracks - Electric guitars are made of wood and cracks do happen. Unfortunately, unattended cracks tend to get bigger and usually do not go back together perfectly. Any crack will affect value, but a small, professionally well repaired crack will take much less of a bite out of the price than a large gaping crack that wouldn't go together properly.

Frets - A good analogy for frets would be found in the vintage car market: you rarely find a vintage car with original tires. Guitars were made to be played and frets do wear out. A good professional fret job using factory spec parts should not affect the value of your instrument. Again, this question won't come up with a mint, unplayed guitar.

Cosmetics - The cleaner an instrument, the more it's worth. Don't ever underestimate the value of eye appeal. A mint, unplayed, original condition guitar with tags will always bring more than the prices for "excellent" condition. On the other hand, an instrument with most of the finish worn off from years of use might bring less than the average shown here.

General Guitar Maintenance & Tips - Airplanes are meant to be flown, cars are meant to be driven, and guitars are meant to be played. Since instrument construction is typically wood, and wood expands/contracts like many other natural materials, don't allow instruments to go from one extreme temp./humidity factor to another (i.e., don't ship your Gibson Super 400 CES from Ft. Meyers, FL to Thief River Falls, MN in Jan.). Try to maintain a stable temp. and humidity level. Also, use good quality, professional products to clean, polish, and maintain (Virtuoso is recommended, www.virtuosopolish.com) your instruments (investments). Remember, maintaining a fine guitar requires some common sense and TLC.

Guitars, even vintage ones, are meant to be played. Enjoy yours, take proper care of it, play it once in awhile, and don't let temperature and/or humidity factors get to extremes.

Explanation & Converting Guitar Grading Systems

Since the 9th Edition *Blue Book of Electric Guitars*™ continues to use the **Photo Grading System**™ (PPGS) to describe condition, please study the color electric guitar condition photos on the following pages carefully to help understand and identify each electric guitar's unique condition factor. These photos, with condition factors, serve as a guideline, not an absolute. Remember, if the condition factor isn't right, the price is wrong!

The conversion chart listed below has been provided to help you convert the **Photo Grading System**™ to several other grading systems. All percentage descriptions and/or possible conversions made thereof, are based on original condition – alterations, repairs, refinishing work, and any other non-original alterations that have changed the condition of an instrument must be listed additionally, and typically subtracted from the values based on condition throughout this text (please refer to page 31 for an explanation of these critical factors affecting both condition and price).

Electric Guitar PGS Condition Factors with Explanations & Conversions

100% - New - Factory new with all factory materials, including warranty card, owner's manual, case, and other items that were originally included by the manufacturer. On currently manufactured instruments, the 100% price refers to an instrument not previously sold at retail. Even if a new instrument was played only twice, and traded in a week later, it no longer qualifies at 100%. On out-of-production instruments (including dealer "new, old stock," or NOS), the longer a guitar has been discontinued, the less likely you will find it in 100% condition. Some instruments that are less than 20 years old and have never been taken out-of-the-case (unplayed) may not be 100% (new), as the finish may have slightly cracked, tarnished, faded, or deteriorated. **Remember, there are no excuses in 100% condition.**

98% - Near Mint, Excellent++, 9.8 - Only very slightly used and/or played very little – may have minor "case" wear or light dings on exterior finish only, without finish cracking, very close to new condition, also refers to a currently manufactured instrument that has previously sold at retail, even though it may not have been played. May have a slight scratch – otherwise as new. Also, should have original case.

95% - Excellent+ (Exc.+), 9.5 - Very light observable wear, perhaps some very light plating deterioration on metal parts, extremely light finish scratching, may have slight neck wear.

90% - Excellent (Exc.), 9.0 - Light exterior finish wear with a few minor dings, no paint chips down to the wood, normal nicks and scratches, light observable neck wear in most cases.

80% - Very Good+ (VG+), Above Average, approx. 8.0 - More exterior finish wear (20% of the original finish is gone) that may include minor chips that extend down to the wood, body wear, but nothing real serious, nice shape overall, with mostly honest player wear.

70% - Very Good (VG), Average, approx. 7.0 - More serious exterior finish wear that could include some major gauges and nicks, player arm wear, and/or fret deterioration.

60% - Good (G), Sub-average, approx. 6.0 - Noticeable wear on most areas - normally this consists of some major belt buckle wear and finish deterioration, may include cracking, possible repairs or alterations. When this condition factor is encountered, normally an instrument should have all logos intact, original pickups, minor headstock damage, and perhaps a few non-serious alterations, with or without original case.

40% - Fair (F), Below Average, approx. 3.0 to 5.0 - Major features are still discernible, major parts missing, probably either refinished or repaired, structurally sound, though many times encountered with non-factory alterations.

20% - Poor (P), approx. 2.0 - Ending a life sentence of hard labor, must still be playable, most of the licks have left, family members should be notified immediately, normally not worthy unless the ad also mentions first year Tele. May have to double as kindling if in a tight spot on a cold night.

2004 Paul Reed Smith McCarty Model - Ser. no. 4 84685, Cherry Sunburst finish, 100% new condition. The McCarty model was built as a tribute to Ted McCarty, who was the president of Gibson during the 1950s. Gibson introduced many innovative ideas during his tenure, including the Explorer, Flying V, and humbucker pickups. 100% condition assumes the guitar has not previously sold at retail. There should be no visible wear on the guitar anywhere, and all original parts should be intact. Vintage guitars are often not valued at the 100% condition because they have been played. Once a guitar is purchased and played, it moves down to the 98% category. 100% condition only applies to new guitars. There are no exceptions for 100% condition. Courtesy John Beeson/The Music Shoppe.

2001 Hamer Sunburst - Ser. no. 151415, Cherry Sunburst finish, 98%, near mint condition. Hamer is one of the few guitar companies that survived the guitar market crash of the early 1980s. The Sunburst was the second model introduced, and, with a lower price than a Gibson Les Paul, it created a lot of demand from players who wanted a quality instrument without paying a premium for a favorite traditional. Good quality guitars with low price points became very popular during the 1980s. This guitar is virtually flawless, but has a condition of 98% because it has been played. Just like a car, when you drive it off the lot it loses a substantial amount of value. Almost all vintage guitars that are mint appear in this category. Courtesy George McGuire.

1957 Gibson Les Paul Model - Ser. no. 7 6122, Gold Top finish, 95% excellent plus condition. 1957 was the first year for humbucker pickups in the Gibson Les Paul. This was also the last year before the Standard was introduced. The Les Pauls from this era increase in value daily, and original '57s like this are now over $45,000! There is minimal wear on the bass bout top, but the rest of the guitar is virtually flawless with no wear on the neck. 95% condition allows for some minor cosmetic flaws, but it should still represent a guitar almost entirely intact. Courtesy Dave Rogers/Dave's Guitar Shop.

1966 Fender Telecaster With Bigsby Tailpiece - Ser. no. N/A, Dakota Red finish, 90% excellent condition. The Telecaster was Leo Fender's second production electric guitar design. In the 1960s, a Bigsby vibrato tailpiece became an option. Even though the Bigsby was a price add-on, original models without the Bigsby command a premium. This guitar has noticeable nicks and wear on the bass bout on the front side and on the treble bout on the back. A 90% guitar is still in good shape, but it will have a few more dings and wear. There is also minimal neck wear, which is normal for a guitar of this age. Courtesy Dave Rogers/Dave's Guitar Shop.

1957 Fender MusicMaster - Ser. no. 22273, Black finish, approx. 85% refinished condition with replaced pickup. During 1957, Fender was enjoying unprecedented success with its Stratocaster model (released in 1954), and Telecaster (released in 1951). This MusicMaster has been refinished, and the pickup is not original – in this case, reducing value by 50%. Whenever possible, Fender collectors and players would rather have a 60% original guitar than a 95%+ refinished model with non-original parts. MusicMaster models have not received the attention or obtained the collectibility of Strats and Teles, possibly making original instruments a good value in today's guitar marketplace. Courtesy John Beeson/The Music Shoppe.

Circa 1963 Magnatone Typhoon - Ser. no. 200301, Sunburst finish, 80% condition. It's no secret that after the success of the Fender Stratocaster, many companies (domestic and foreign) copied the body style and offered these competitive models with different appointments and hardware. Note this instrument's pickguard, slide pickup switches, pickups, bridge, and tailpiece with tremolo. Normal player wear on this instrument is not serious, nor does it suffer from any major gouges, nicks, scratches or dents. Many Strat players like this type of inexpensive clone as it offers them a different sound and feel. Magnatone had show offices in both NY and CA during this time period. Courtesy George McGuire.

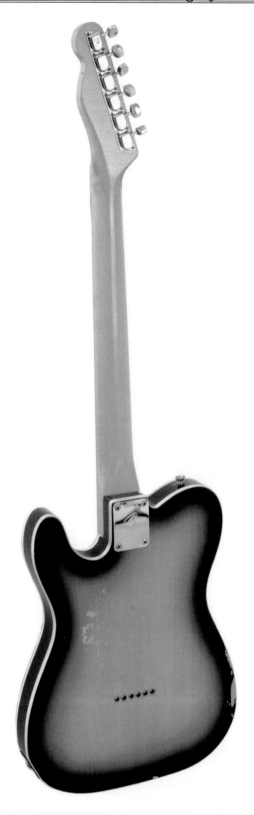

1967 Fender Esquire Custom - Ser. no. 208410, Two-Tone Sunburst finish, 80% condition. Note the visible wear on the front and back, as well as the cracked binding. Neck and fretboard are in good condition, probably indicating that this Fender has been handled more than played. This instrument's chrome hardware is in excellent condition, with no freckling (light rust), scratches, or flaking. This Esquire Custom was produced after CBS Broadcasting Company bought Fender Musical Instruments during early 1965. Pre-CBS manufactured instruments are more sought after in today's secondary marketplace, with prices typically 50% more than post-1965 guitars. Courtesy Dave Rogers/Dave's Guitar Shop.

1990 G&L Model L2000 Bass - Ser. no. B022040, Two-Tone Sunburst finish, 70% condition. Nothing too special here. Average condition bass guitar – note "Leo Fender" stenciled signature on upper bass bout. Maybe the most important thing to consider is the chunk of wood missing from the lower bass bout, indicating that this G&L bass guitar was probably dropped. Also note wear around the pickups. Unfortunately, the nice back on this instrument does not offset the damage/wear done on the front. Overall, bass guitars are not as collectible as other electric instruments, mainly because bass players tend to have fewer working instruments than guitar players. Courtesy John Beeson/The Music Shoppe.

1981 Gibson Sonex 180 Deluxe - Ser. no. 82611776, 70% very good condition. How is this model different than a Les Paul? It features a wood core with a resin outer layer and a bolt-on neck. It may have been an innovative idea at the time, but it did not catch on. Gibson tried several projects like this during the late 1970s, and early 1980s, and most died within a few years of inception. The good news is most of these U.S.-made guitars can be purchased for under $500, which is unheard of for a Gibson in today's vintage marketplace. Note the considerable wear on the back, neck, and headstock. With this much finish missing, the guitar falls into the 70% condition factor. More good news about this guitar: finish wear does not affect the value very much (after all, 20% of nothing is still nothing). Courtesy Freedom Guitar Inc.

1958 Gretsch White Falcon Model 6136 - Ser. no. 26356, White Finish, 70%, very good condition. Besides the ultra-rare White Penguin model, the White Falcon is the most collectible Gretsch electric. Gretsch produced many high-quality guitars before the introduction of the White Falcon, but none had been so eye-catching. The white finish complemented with gold sparkle binding, mother-of-pearl inlays, and 24-karat gold plated hardware, set a standard that many other builders at the time hadn't dreamed of. This guitar has extreme wear on the neck, but most of the body is fairly clean. However, the neck wear brings the overall condition down to 80%. A guitar does not have to be worn in many areas to bring the overall condition factor down. Courtesy Dave Rogers/Dave's Guitar Shop.

1957 Danelectro U-1 - Ser. no. N/A, Yellow finish, 70%, very good condition. Nathan Daniels began building amplifiers in the 1930s and moved on to building guitars in the 1950s. He built guitars under the Danelectro name, but sold a majority (85%) with the Silvertone trademark for Sears & Roebuck. Danelectro guitars were priced very reasonably in the 1950s, and '60s, and because of high demand the company produced thousands of instruments. Most of these guitars are still reasonably priced, but because of their coolness, some models are worth substantially more. This yellow model has seen its share of playing. There is considerable wear on the top, back, and neck. 75% is not listed specifically in the book, but this guitar falls somewhere in between 70% and 80%. Courtesy Piney Woods, Old Guitar Shop.

1979 Fender Stratocaster - Ser. no. S934889, Black finish, 60% condition. This Strat's condition factor is somewhat deceiving, since the original finish on the neck (good) does not match the body. In this case, the extreme body wear is due to the wood not being dry when the Black finish was originally applied, and, eventually, moisture soaked through the finish. This explains its current condition, including the bubbling around the upper and lower bouts. This instrument doesn't have much collector interest left, due partly to this period of Fender manufacture in the late '70s (not as desirable as the '50s and '60s), and its finish problems. Courtesy John Beeson/The Music Shoppe.

1965 Gibson Melody Maker - Ser. no. 336880, Cherry finish, 60% condition. This is another example of an instrument that has a much better back than top. Note three exposed non-factory screw holes below bridge (indicating someone put on a different bridge at some point), scratches, and normal body wear around the edges. Even though this instrument has lost most of its collectible value due to a major alteration, many guitar dealers would rather have an average original condition instrument with this type of problem than a refinished guitar in excellent condition. Whenever possible, collectors prefer original condition, even if there are some problems. Courtesy John Beeson/The Music Shoppe.

1957 Fender MusicMaster - No ser. no., Three-Tone Sunburst finish, 50% condition. If this Fender had any more holes drilled into it, it would be Swiss cheese! Close observation reveals four non-original small holes above the nut in the headstock, and another two below the bridge. Also note cracks in pickguard and player wear around body edges. Typically, 25%-40% of the value must be subtracted for these types of major, non-factory alterations on major trademark instruments. Always check the headstock carefully where it joins the neck for previous breaks and/or repairs/cracking on instruments that show a lot of use and abuse. Courtesy John Beeson/The Music Shoppe.

Circa 1970s Anderbilt - No model or ser. no., Sunburst finish, 50% condition. So you like weird and kinky instruments with a few problems, especially if the hanging tag's price has been lowered several times? As seen in the insert, there is a half-inch gap between the neck and body, while the neck is physically loose. This used axe has bottomed out in value (and interest), and other no-name instruments similar to this are usually seen priced in the $125-$250 range, depending on playability, repair costs, and the cool factor (if any). Even if in mint original condition, this model may only hit $350-450, mostly because it's a novelty item. Courtesy Dave Rogers/Dave's Guitar Shop.

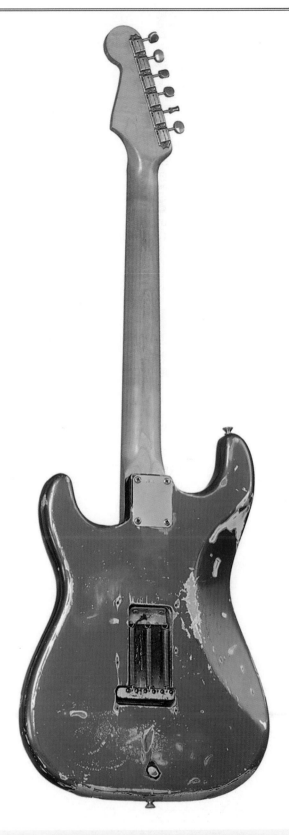

1964 Fender Stratocaster - Ser. no. L50558, Red finish, 40% condition. So you like your Strats well-worn, but can't afford to have the Fender Custom Shop beat a Relic up for you? The body of this rough Strat has been resprayed twice, once with black and once with custom graphics. What is seen here is the attempt to get it back to the original condition, and it is in very tough shape. Since Fender collectors are typically more concerned about originality than condition, especially on rare colors, there is almost no collector value left in this instrument. Also note natural player wear on the back of the neck. Courtesy Glen Wetterland.

Section A

A

See chapter on House Brands.

This trademark has been identified as a House Brand of the Alden department store chain. One of the models shares similarities with the Harmony-built Stratotone of the 1960s, while a previously identified model dates back to the 1950s (source: Willie G. Moseley, *Stellas & Stratocasters*).

A BASSES

Instruments previously built in Waltham-Boston, Massachusetts.

A Basses was founded in 1976 by Albey Balgochian. In 1985, working with high profile bassist Darryl Jones (sideman to the Rolling Stones), they came up with the Darryl Jones Signature bass. By 2002 they were producing only the **World Bass**, **Jade Bass**, and **Upright Bass** models. These models are similar in shape to the Fender Jazz Bass. As of January 1st, 2003, A Basses will no longer be taking orders. There will be a few basses available here and there on the website (see Trademark Index), but no more custom orders. Pricing is tough to pinpoint because of the low second hand marketplace of these guitars and the fact that they stopped producing new models.

GRADING	100% MINT	98% NEAR MINT	95% EXC+	90% EXC	80% VG+	70% VG	60% G

ELECTRIC BASS: DARRYL JONES SERIES

All three models are offered in active or passive versions.

DARRYL JONES STANDARD EDITION - offset double cutaway alder body, bolt-on maple neck, 21-fret rosewood fingerboard with dot inlay, bridge, 4-on-a-side tuners, 2 Seymour Duncan pickups (see specs below), 2 volume/tone controls, passive electronics, disc.

Last MSR was $1,595.

Add $150 for active electronics (Lightning Rod Pickups/slap contour/3-band EQ).

DARRYL JONES SIGNATURE MODEL - similar to Darryl Jones Standard Edition, except has Aero pickups, optional Aguilar preamp, current mfg.

$1,750	$1,500	$1,350	$1,200	$1,100	$950	$800

Last MSR was $1,995.

A Basses Darryl Jones
courtesy A Basses

DARRYL JONES DELUXE EDITION - similar to the Darryl Jones Standard, except features a Quilted maple laminate top, available in 3-Color Sunburst finish, disc.

Last MSR was $1,795.

Add $150 for active electronics (Lightning Rod Pickups/slap contour/3-band EQ).

DARRYL JONES 5-STRING - similar to the Darryl Jones Standard, except features a 5-string configuration, disc.

Last MSR was $1,795.

Add $150 for active electronics (Lightning Rod Pickups/slap contour/3-band EQ).

ELECTRIC BASS: JADE BASS SERIES

JADE BASS SERIES - alder or Swamp ash body, maple neck, choice of fingerboards, fretted or fretless, optional figured maple top and/or Aguilar preamp, disc. 2003.

Last MSR was $1,995.

ELECTRIC BASS: WORLD BASS SERIES

The World Bass has an alder or Swamp ash body with figured top, extra long ebony fingerboard, Aero pickups, optional Aguilar preamp. Last list price was $2,695.

ELECTRIC BASS: UPRIGHT BASS SERIES

The Upright bass features a hand carved body that is not like any of the other A Bass models. This is an upright bass that is quite narrow and has a scroll-type feature towards the top of the body. The last list price on this was $4,995.

A Basses Jade Bass
courtesy A Basses

APP

Instruments previously built in the early 1940s in Burlington, Iowa; later models were built in the early 1960s.

Guitar instructor/inventor O.W. Appleton was another contributor of the electric solid body guitar concept. In the early 1940s, Appleton built a carved top solid body guitar that featured a single cutaway design, raised bridge/trapeze tailpiece, and single coil pickup. Appleton even went so far as to put a Gibson neck on his design, but received no interest from the Gibson company. Comparing an APP to the later 1952 Gibson Les Paul is somewhat akin to comparing a Bigsby guitar to a Fender's Telecaster model (it's deja vu all over again!).

GRADING	100% MINT	98% NEAR MINT	95% EXC+	90% EXC	80% VG+	70% VG	60% G

Of course, Rickenbacker in Los Angeles had marketed the solid body lap steel since the 1930s; Lloyd Loar's Vivi-Tone company had attempted to market an electric Spanish guitar. In 1941, guitar marvel Les Paul had begun work on **The Log**, a solid 4 in. x 4 in. neck-through design with pickups. Les Paul attached body wings from an Epiphone archtop guitar to the sides of the neck (The Log was constructed after hours at the original Epiphone facilities in New York). It is interesting now to look back and view how many people were working towards the invention of the solid body electric guitar (source: Tom Wheeler, *American Guitars*).

Guitars bearing the APP trademark appeared in the early 1960s. One such model appeared in Teisco Del Rey's column in Guitar Player magazine (June 1985), and featured an offset double cutaway body that was shaped like an inverted "V". Appleton later retired to Arizona, but the 1960s models are still a mystery.

ASI
Also AUDIO SOUND INTERNATIONAL. Instruments previously built in Korea. Previously distributed in the U.S. market by Audio Sound International, Inc. of Indianapolis, Indiana.

ASI, the company that also supplied Quantum amplifiers and Rackmaster gear, developed a number of solid body guitars to market the Sustainiac pickup system.

The Sustainiac system as developed by Maniac Music features on-board magnetic circuitry to create real string sustain. Similar to the system that Kaman/Hamer put in the Chaparral Elite, ASI used both the GA2 and GA4 in a number of Taiwan-, Korean-, and Japanese-built guitars in an effort to bring the system down to a more affordable price in the guitar market. The AE 7S was an earlier model from 1990, and was followed by the AS-121 in 1991. Two more maple-bodied models followed (the AS 100 and AS 85).

Used prices must be weighed from the pickup system against the quality of the guitar it is installed in. Average prices run from $150 up to $250.

ABEL AXE
Instruments currently built in Evanston, Wyoming since 1992. Distributed by Abel Axe of Evanston, Wyoming.

Designer/inventor Jeff Abel spent two years in research and development refining his aluminum body/wood neck concept. Due to the nature of the dense body material, the sustain and harmonics produced are markedly different compared to traditional wood technologies. The Abel Axe body is CNC machined from a solid slab of aircraft grade aluminum and the finished guitar weighs in at only 8 pounds. The colors offered are then anodized to the body, and become part of the aluminum during the process. Assisted by his brother, Jim Abel, Jeff Abel currently produces limited/custom orders. Abel estimates that over 250 guitars have been produced to date.

ELECTRIC: PRO SERIES

Pro Series guitars are offered factory direct from Abel Axe. Abel Axe also offers the aluminum body separately (with strap buttons and back plate) directly from the factory for those players interested in creating their own custom instrument. The tuning machines can be anodized to match body color.

ABEL AXE - offset double cutaway aluminum body, circular body hollows, bolt-on maple neck, 22-fret rosewood (or maple) fingerboard with dot inlay, strings through bridge, 6-on-a-side Sperzel tuners, black hardware, 2 Kent Armstrong humbucker pickups, volume control, 3-position switch, available in Red, Black, Blue, Teal, Violet, and Aluminum (Silver) anodized finishes, mfg. 1994-96.

$1,000	$850	$750	$650	$575	$500	$425

Last MSR was $1,000.

This model is available with optional locking tremolo (Abel Axe T).

ABEL AXE 211 - offset double cutaway aluminum body, slot-style body hollows, bolt-on maple neck, 22-fret rosewood fingerboard with dot inlay, string through tailpiece, 6-on-a-side Sperzel tuners, black hardware, Kent Armstrong humbucker pickup(s), volume control, available in Red, Black, Blue, Teal, Violet, and Aluminum (Silver) anodized finishes, mfg. 1996-present.

N/A	$425	$375	$300	$250	$200	$150

Last MSR was $490.

ELECTRIC BASS

ABEL AXE BASS - offset double cutaway body, bolt-on maple neck, 22-fret rosewood (or maple) fingerboard with dot inlay, 34" scale, fixed brass bridge, 4-on-a-side Gotoh tuners, black hardware, Kent Armstrong pickup, volume control, available in Red, Black, Blue, Teal, Violet, and Aluminum (Silver) anodized finishes, mfg. 1995-96.

$1,100	$900	$800	$700	$600	$500	$400

Last MSR was $1,100.

ABILENE
Instruments currently produced in Korea by Samick. Distributed in the U.S. by Advantage Worldwide.

The Abilene trademark is distributed in the U.S. by Advantage Worldwide. The Abilene trademark is offered on a range of acoustic, acoustic/electric, and solid body electric guitars and practice amplifiers. The guitars are built by Samick of Korea, and the electric guitar models feature designs based on popular American models.

ELECTRIC & ELECTRIC BASS

Abilene builds guitars based on popular American designs. The **AS10** series are based off of Fender Stratocaster designs. The **ALK35** series are also Stratocaster shaped but of the Showmaster caliber. For the cheap-o who likes Gibson, Abilene has "LP" models as well: the **ASL 21 GS** (slab body, 2 humbuckers), the **ALSE 450 HS** (arched top, raised pickguard), and the **ASL22**. Abilene is also responsible for an SG-based design, a telecaster, a 335 Gibson style, and various other models.

Abilene also got their feet wet with bass guitars as well. The **AB-11** series are based on the Fender Precision bass. They have the **AYBE5** series as well, which aren't really based on anything and feature 5-strings. There are other various models as well.

ABYSS
Instruments currently built in Forest City, Iowa, beginning 1997.

Kevin L. Pederson constructs each Abyss Guitar by hand. Each guitar is a custom made model. The NSII and NSC models start with a $2,800 deposit to get the ball rolling. The sky is literally the limit when it comes to what the customer can dream of in a guitar. Most guitars sell for a lot more than the $2,800 base price.

Abyss guitars feature handpicked tops and neck woods, alder bodies, and quartersawn hard maple necks. Al Stokka, who helped with the website said, "Although prices and woods may vary, meticulous construction techniques do not - which ensures a great sounding, stable guitar." Contact the Abyss Guitar Company for a current price quote and specifications (see Trademark Index).

ACACIA
Instruments currently built in Southampton, Pennsylvania since 1986.

Luthier Matt Friedman has been designing and building high quality custom instruments actively for the past seven years. Friedman began carving bodies back in 1980, and spent a number of years doing repair work for local music stores. In 1989, he began full-time production of instruments.

ELECTRIC BASS

All Acacia bass body contours are hand carved. The 24-fret neck is available in any scale lengths at no additional charge. Hardware is available in gold or black. Basses can be ordered with electronics by Lane Poor, Bartolini, Aero, and John East. Friedman also offers choices of bookmatched tops such as striped ebony, tulipwood, leopardwood, kingwood, or pink ivory (call for pricing).

Add $500 for Novax Fanned Fret fretboard (licensed by Ralph Novak). Add $225 for Bartolini pickups/preamp/3-band EQ. Add $270 for John East preamp/3-band EQ with mid-sweep. Add $300 for left-handed configuration. Add Light-wave Optical Bridge System - Call for price.

**Acoustic Black Widow
courtesy The Music Shoppe**

CUSTOM - sleek offset double cutaway mahogany body, bookmatched exotic wood top/back, through-body multilaminated neck (4- and 5-string basses feature a 9-piece design while the 6- and 7-string models feature a 13-piece neck) of Wenge, Mahogany, and other exotic woods with graphite epoxy reinforcement, 24-fret ebony or snakewood fingerboard, customer's choice of electronics/preamp/EQ, available in Natural Oil finish, new 1986.

Custom 4-string
  MSR $3,800

Custom 5-string
  MSR $4,000

Custom 6-string
  MSR $4,200

Custom 7-string
  MSR $4,400

EMOTION - sleek offset double cutaway body, bookmatched exotic wood top/back, through-body multilaminated Wenge or zebrawood neck, ebony fretless fingerboard, ebony bridge, Aero twin coil pickup, RMC bridge-mounted piezo pickup, volume/blend/EQ controls, John East preamp, available in Natural Oil finish, new 1995.

Emotion 4-string
  MSR $4,200

Emotion 5-string
  MSR $4,400

Emotion 6-string
  MSR $4,600

Emotion 7-string
  MSR $4,800

THE GRUV (GLB) - sleek offset double cutaway swamp ash body, bolt-on 5-piece neck, 24-fret ebony fingerboard with sterling silver side dot inlay, Ebony bridge, Hipshot Ultralite tuners, 2 Custom Aero pickups, volume/blend/tone controls, available in Natural finish, new 1996.

Gruv 4-string
  MSR $3,600

Gruv 5-string
  MSR $3,800

  This model has an optional bookmatched figured maple top, a set-in neck, and numerous different transparent finishes.

ACOUSTIC
Instruments previously produced in Japan during the early 1970s. Distributed by the Acoustic amplifier company of California.

While the Acoustic company was going strong in the amplifier business with models like the 360, they decided to add a guitar and bass model to the product line. The first Black Widows were produced in Japan, and distributed through the Acoustic company. Towards the end of the run of the guitar, production actually switched to Semie Moseley of Mosrite (model neck dimensions correspond to the Mosrite feel). There has been some indication that Paul Barth's Bartell company may have built some as well.

The most striking feature of the Acoustic Black Widow is the finish. The darkened rosewood fingerboard and deep black maple body, combined with the red pad in the back, supposedly resembles the markings of a black widow spider.

GRADING	100% MINT	98% NEAR MINT	95% EXC+	90% EXC	80% VG+	70% VG	60% G

ELECTRIC

BLACK WIDOW - double cutaway semi-hollow maple body, maple neck, 24-fret rosewood fingerboard, bridge/stop tailpiece, 3-per-side Grover Rotomatic tuners, chrome hardware, 2 humbucker pickups, volume/tone controls, 3-position selector, available in Black lacquer finish, mfg. circa 1972-74.

	N/A	$850	$750	$650	$550	$475	$375

Last MSR was $415.

This model has a red pad attached to the back of the instrument.

ELECTRIC BASS

BLACK WIDOW BASS - double cutaway semi-hollow maple body, maple neck, 20-fret rosewood fingerboard, bridge/stop tailpiece, 2-per-side Grover Rotomatic tuners, chrome hardware, humbucker pickups volume/tone controls, available in Black lacquer finish, mfg. circa 1972-74.

	N/A	$750	$650	$550	$475	$400	$350

Last MSR was $415.

This model has a red pad attached to the back of the instrument.

ADLER CUSTOM GUITARS

Instruments currently built in Southern California.

Adler Guitars was started as a true custom shop about four years ago by Michael Adler in an effort to bring genuinely custom instruments to those who couldn't previously afford them. Adler basses are hand built to order, but there are select dealers now with some basses in stock. Previously, Adler was factory direct only. Custom scale lengths, hardware, pickups, and preamps are all available at no extra cost. Custom body shapes and inlays are also available. All basses include a lifetime warranty. Contact Adler directly for more information (see Trademark Index).

ELECTRIC BASS

Adler currently produces the ACG series of bass guitars. These guitars are available in 4-11 string variations. The neck is built out of five pieces of maple and purpleheart that goes through the body. The body is made out of the customer's choice of wood. Groth tuners, Schaller bridges, Bartolini pickups, and Aguilar onboard preamps are all standard equipment. The 4-string starts at $2,550, the 5-string is $2,750, and the 6-string lists for $2,950. On the 7-string and larger basses, the neck is a seven-piece maple and purpleheart. Pricing is custom on guitars with seven strings and larger.

Adler has also released a Sub-Contra Bass at the 2004 NAMM show. Adler is a true custom shop with several options that are available. Because of this, every guitar has a different price tag. Contact Adler to get a list of all available options (see Trademark Index).

AELITA

Instruments previously built in Russia during the 1970s (headstock lettering in Cyrillic may appear as a capital A, backwards e, r, u, m, or a; we have anglicized the brand name).

These solid bodied guitars were produced by the Rostov-on-Don accordion factory, and the design may strike the casual observer as favoring classic Italian designs of the 1960s (source: Tony Bacon, *The Ultimate Guitar Book*).

AIRCRAFT

Instruments currently built in Japan.

Guitars carrying the Aircraft logo are actually manufactured by the Morris company, which also builds instruments for such brand names as their own Morris trademark and the Hurricane logo.

AIRLINE

See Supro. Instruments previously manufactured by Valco in Chicago, Illinois during the 1960s. See chapter on House Brands.

This trademark has been identified as a House Brand of the Montgomery Wards department store chain. These guitars were produced by Kay and were basically variations of what Kay had already built. There are several models just like there are in Kay; therefore, it is almost impossible to list them all. Author/researcher Willie G. Moseley indicates that the unique body design is proprietary to the Airline brand. Models can be found constructed of both Res-O-Glas (a hollow fiberglass body) and wood.

Valco began building solid body wood instruments in 1952, and built fiberglass body electric guitars from 1962 to 1966. The top of Airline headstocks, just like the Nationals, ran low-to-high from the left to the right. Not that it matters with regard to playability and tone, but Supros dipped the headstock in the opposite way (sources: Willie G. Moseley, *Stellas & Stratocasters* and Michael Wright, *Guitar Stories*, Vol II).

ELECTRIC GUITARS

Due to the large number of guitar models, they have been broken down into the different pickup types. Within each type, there will be guitars with various features and finishes, but they will generally follow the same pricing line.

RES-O-GLAS - double cutaway fiberglass body, three pickups, raised black pickguard, pickup selector switch, six knobs on the bass side of body, one on treble side, Bigsby tremolo, available in white finish, mfg. 1960s.

	N/A	$800	$700	$600	$525	$450	$350

The neck was sometimes made out of fiberglass as well. There are rumors that this guitar was found in other pickup configurations.

SOLID BODY SINGLE PICKUP - solid body, various features, single pickup, basic controls, mfg. late 1950s-1960s.

	N/A	$350	$275	$225	$175	$125	$75

SOLID BODY DOUBLE PICKUP - solid body, various features, two pickups, more advanced controls, usually four knobs, mfg. late 1950s-1960s.

	N/A	$550	$475	$400	$325	$250	$175

GRADING	100% MINT	98% NEAR MINT	95% EXC+	90% EXC	80% VG+	70% VG	60% G

HOLLOW BODY DOUBLE PICKUP - hollow electric body, usually f-holes, tremolo, two pickups, four knobs, mfg. 1960s.

	N/A	$450	$375	$325	$275	$225	$150

HOLLOW BODY TRIPLE PICKUP - hollow electric body, usually f-holes, tremolo, three pickups, six knobs, mfg. 1960s.

	N/A	$600	$500	$425	$350	$275	$200

ELECTRIC BASS

Like guitars, there have been several Airline basses made. They can be broken down into two categories for the most part. We have listed them as either one or two pickup models and they will each have their own features and finishes.

SINGLE PICKUP MODELS - double cutaway, single pickup, two knobs typically, mfg. 1960s.

	N/A	$300	$250	$200	$150	$100	$50

DOUBLE PICKUP MODELS - double cutaway, two pickups, two or four knobs typically, mfg. 1960s.

	N/A	$400	$350	$300	$250	$175	$100

AK ADMIRAL
Instruments previously produced in Russia in the early 1980s.

These guitars were built in Leningrad as part of a project to mass-produce good quality electrics. While the styling and hardware seem more modern in design, the project unfortunately failed. The *Blue Book of Electric Guitars* welcomes any information on Russian-built guitars in our attempt to document trademarks and brands of the world (source: Tony Bacon, *The Ultimate Guitar Book*).

ALAMO
Instruments previously manufactured in San Antonio, Texas from 1960 to 1970. Distributed in part by C. Bruno & Sons.

In 1947, Charles Eilenberg was recruited by Milton Fink to manufacture electronic gear in San Antonio, Texas. Fink, the owner of Southern Music company, was a publisher and music wholesaler. By 1950, the company was producing instrument cases, tube amplifiers, and lap steel guitars (as well as radios and phonographs).

The company continued to expand, and in 1960 introduced its first electric Spanish guitar. Alamo offered both solid body and semi-hollow electrics that were generally entry-level quality, and designed with the student or beginner player in mind. Outside of a few Valco-produced models, all Alamo guitars were built in San Antonio during the ten-year period. The company also continued to produce tube amplifiers until 1970, when solid state models began to be produced. Alamo went out of business in 1982 (source: Michael Wright, *Vintage Guitar Magazine*).

Used electric solid and hollow body models can be found usually between $100 and $300.

**Airline Electric
courtesy Dave Rogers
Dave's Guitar Shop**

ALAMO GUITARS
Instruments currently made in Houston, Texas. Distributed by Alamo Music Products.

Alamo produces guitars in the heart of Texas, and these guitarss feature some unique designs. Please contact the company directly for more information (see Trademark Index).

ELECTRIC GUITARS

Alamo Guitars manufactures several models, including the **Tonemonger** (MSR $1,860), **Tonemonger Custom** (MSR $1,970), **Tonemonger Custom with exotic top** (MSR $2,195), and the **Tonemonger Custom 5** (MSR $2,070). Features include a Strat style body from Swamp ash or African Fakimba, nitrocellulose lacquer finish, maple neck, with choice of maple or rosewood fingerboard, custom center point tremolo system, master volume and tone control, with 5-way selector switch, includes hardshell case. Alamo also offers a model called the **Surfmaster** (MSR $1,860), which features two Rio Grande Surfmaster pickups.

ALCIVAR
Instruments previously produced.

Alcivar is a trademark for which little information is known. It appears that these are Japanese instruments that were produced in the 1980s. They are often copies of popular American copies (i.e. Les Paul, ES-335, etc.). There have been instruments found with DiMarzio pickups and active electronics. These appear to be fairly well-built guitars; however, they do not command a lot of money like most people think. This is because very little information is known about them, and 99 out of 100 Asian guitar manufacturers have produced very cheap guitars. These guitars are often found in pawn shops and online. Serial numbers and model information are often nonexistent, and if they were ever available, this information was once on a sticker that fell off long ago. Do not expect to pay too much or receive too much when you sell them. Anyone with any information on Alcivar guitars can submit information directly to the publisher.

ALDEN
Instruments currently produced in Korea.

Alden makes several electric guitar and bass models as well as other musical instruments. Alden has some original designs as well as the typical American styles. Most Alden models are the typical copy of popular American designs, including the Stratocaster, Telecaster, Les Paul, and Precision Basses. They also make acoustic guitars and guitar amplifiers.

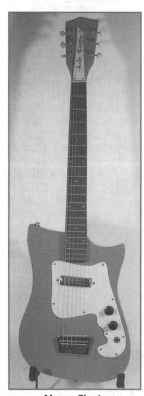

**Alamo Fiesta
courtesy Austin Thomerson**

ALEMBIC

Instruments currently built in Santa Rosa, CA. Previous production was centered in San Francisco, CA. Distribution is handled by Alembic, Inc. of Santa Rosa, CA.

The Alembic company was founded in San Francisco in 1969, primarily to incorporate new ways to clarify and amplify the sound of the rock group "Grateful Dead." The Alembic workshop covered three main areas: a recording studio, PA/sound reinforcement, and guitar electronics. Wickersham was developing a low impedance pickup coupled with active electronics. Up until this point all electronics in production guitars and basses were passive systems. Artists using these "Alembicized" instruments early on include David Crosby (a Guild 12-string), Jack Casady (Guild bass), and Phil Lesh (SG and Guild basses). Both Bob Weir's and Jerry Garcia's guitars were converted as well. Wickersham found that mounting the active circuitry in the instrument itself gave the player a greater degree of control over his tone than ever before.

The new company turned from customizing existing instruments in 1970 to building new ones in 1971. Founder Ron Wickersham, an electronics expert, was joined by luthier/designer Rick Turner, Bob Matthews (a recording engineer), and Jim Furman (later to start his own Furman Sound Company), among others. When Alembic incorporated in 1970, Wickersham, Turner, and Matthews were the principal shareholders. In addition to running a state-of-the-art 16-track recording studio on Brady Street, Alembic opened a music store in 1971 that sold their own guitars and basses, as well as cabinets (with tie-dyed speaker cloth) and PA gear. Alembic continued to work with the Grateful Dead for taping and PA requirements, and in 1972 also produced a monthly critique column for *Guitar Player Magazine* (*The Alembic Report*).

In 1973, Alembic received a distribution offer from the L.D. Heater company, a subsidiary of Norlin. Wickersham and Turner then began tooling up for production in earnest. Turner's choices in exotic woods and laminated bodies gained attention for the craftsmanship involved. The right combination of a new distributor and a new jazz talent named Stanley Clarke actively playing an Alembic bass propelled the company into the spotlight in the mid-1970s.

In 1974, Alembic began to focus on the manufacturing side of their high-end instruments. The company sold off the assets of the recording studio, and sold the music store to Stars Guitars (Stars Guitars' Ron Armstrong later wrote the Product Profile column for *Guitar Player* magazine after *The Alembic Report* was discontinued). Bob Matthews' shares were bought out by Alembic. A new distribution deal was started with Rothchild Musical Instruments (San Francisco) in 1976, after the original L.D. Heater/Norlin distribution deal.

Geoff Gould, an aerospace engineer and bass player, was intrigued by an Alembic-customized bass he saw at a Grateful Dead concert. Assuming that the all-wood construction was a heavy proposition, he fashioned some samples of carbon graphite and presented them to Alembic. An experimental model with a graphite neck was displayed in 1977, and a patent issued in 1978. Gould formed the Modulus Graphite company with other ex-aerospace partners to provide necks for Alembic, and also build necks for Music Man's Cutlass bass model as well as their own Modulus Graphite guitars.

Rick Turner left Alembic to form Turner Guitars in 1978, the same year that Alembic decided to forego future distribution deals and fulfill distribution themselves. As the company expanded, the workshop continued to move, from San Francisco to Cotati to Santa Rosa. In addition to guitar and bass production, the 1980s saw expansion in F2B preamp demand as well as the production of modular-based (no soldering) Activator pickups and active electronics. In 1989 Alembic settled into a larger facility in Santa Rosa, and currently has a twenty-six person staff, (company history courtesy Mica and Susan Wickersham, Alembic).

The tops of Alembic instruments are bookmatched and the wood types vary widely, though the most consistently used woods are as follows: bocate, bubinga, cocobola, figured (bird's eye, burl, flame, quilted) maple, figured (burl and flame) walnut, flame koa, lacewood, rosewood (and burl rosewood), tulipwood, vermillion and zebrawood.

MODEL IDENTIFICATION & GENERAL INFORMATION

Alembic models can be identified in the serial number: The first two digits indicate the year built, and the letter codes directly after the first two digits indicate the model. As the body style, peghead style, and electronic/hardware configurations and combinations may vary from instrument to instrument due to Alembic's numerous options, identification can be most easily made from this letter coding.

Furthermore, all series between 1972 and 1976 carry either an AE (Alembic Export General) or AC (Alembic Export Canada) stamp.

On new instruments, the serial number is stamped on the truss rod cover and also in the electronics cavity (Epic and Orion models have the number stamped in the back of the peghead and in the electronics cavity). On older instruments, the serial number is stamped directly on the ebony fingerboard below the 24th fret. Earliest Alembic models have serial numbers stamped on top of the headstock (for further dating of Alembic instruments, see the Serialization section in the back of this edition).

If an Alembic model is noted as "disc." (as in discontinued), it does not mean that the company will not build any more instruments to those specifications. It may mean that the model is not carried on the current price sheet. 7-, 8-, 10-, 12-string, and doubleneck configurations are currently available on some models as a "Call for Price Quote" listing. Even though certain models or configurations may not be currently offered by Alembic, the design templates are on storage for a customer's special order. Alembic is really close to a true custom shop for guitars and basses. This means that every guitar is usually custom ordered with its own options. This also means every guitar has a different price point. When looking up a value on an Alembic, keep in mind the price shown is for the basic equipment. Options are going to add to the value. Every instrument needs to be treated seperately when determining value.

20th Anniversary - AM	**Europa - U**	**Series I - (Blank)**
Custom - C	**Mark King Deluxe - MK**	**Series II - (Blank)**
Distillate - D	**Mark King Standard - MJ**	**Spectrum - BG (or M)**
Elan - H	**Orion (Bass) - OW**	**Spoiler - S**
Electrum - E	**Orior (Guitar) - O**	**Spoiler (3/4 size) - R**
Epic - W	**Persuader - P (or V or F)**	**Stanley Clarke Deluxe - SC**
Essence - K	**Roque - Q**	**Standard - SJ**

Add $1,800 for burl amboyna. Add $1,500 for burl buckeye. Add $1,200 for burl maple. Add $1,200 for burl walnut. Add $1,200 for burl madrone. Add $800 for coco bolo. Add $1,000 for flamed koa. Add $1,200 for macassar ebony. Add $500 for AAA grade quilted maple. Add $1,000 for AAAAA quilted maple. Add $800 for Indian rosewood. Add $600 superb flame walnut. Add $800 for spalted English beech. Add $800 for spalted maple. Add $800 for tulipwood. Add $1,200 for ziricote. Add $800 for F-1X, F-2B, or SF-2 preamp effects. Add $500 for bass control activators (various configurations).

ELECTRIC

CALIFORNIA SPECIAL (CSLG6) - offset double cutaway maple body, through-body maple neck, brass truss rod cover plate, 24-fret ebony fingerboard with pearl oval inlay, double locking vibrato, brass nut, body matching peghead with bronze logo, 6-on-a-side tuners, chrome hardware, 2 single coil/1 humbucker Alembic pickups, volume/tone control, 3 mini switches, available in Natural, Metal Ruby Red, Metal Sapphire Blue, Trans. Ruby Red, or Trans. Sapphire Blue finishes, disc.

$3,200	$2,750	$2,350	$1,950	N/A	N/A	N/A

Last MSR was $3,900.

GRADING	100% MINT	98% NEAR MINT	95% EXC+	90% EXC	80% VG+	70% VG	60% G

Add 15% for 12-string configuration (CSLSG12, last MSR $4,400).

Also available in baritone configuration (CSBSG6, last MSR $3,900).

FURTHER - double cutaway, semi-hollow purpleheart body with either purpleheart maple, quilted maple, or flamed maple sandwich, AAA quilted maple top, 5-piece flamed maple neck with purpleheart and cherry, ebony with MOP oval inlay fingerboard, 3 Alembic STR, HG, and HG pickups, four knobs, four switches, effects loop, 3-per-side gold tuners, brass hardware, available in natural finish, 8 lbs., current mfg.

	MSR $7,500		$6,000	$5,200	$4,500	$3,800	N/A	N/A	N/A

Add $200 for baritone configuration (MSR $7,700). Add $700 for 12-string configuration (MSR $8,200).

ORION (OLSB6) - offset sweeping double cutaway mahogany body, flame maple (or Flame California Walnut, Bird's-Eye Maple, Wenge, Zebrawood, Bocate, Bubinga, or Vermillion) top, walnut accent veneer, 3-piece maple set neck, 25.75 in. scale, 24-fret ebony fingerboard with pearl oval inlay, six-on-a-side Alembic-Gotoh tuners, brass nut, gold hardware, 2 Alembic HG humbucking pickups, volume/treble/bass controls, pickup selector switch, available in a satin polyurethane finish, mfg. 1996-present.

	MSR $3,700		$3,200	$2,700	$2,200	$1,900	N/A	N/A	N/A

Add $200 for baritone configuration (OBSC6, MSR $3,900). Add $700 for 12-string configuration (MSR $4,400).

SERIES I (LSGI-6) - similar to California Special, except has treble/bass volume/tone control, treble Q/bass Q/pickup switch, 5-pin stereo output jack, current mfg.

	MSR $11,200		$10,000	$9,000	$8,200	$7,500	N/A	N/A	N/A

Add $200 for baritone configuration (BSGI-6, MSR $11,400). Add $700 for 12-string configuration (LSGI-12, MSR $11,900).

SERIES II (LSGII-6) - similar to California Special, except has master/treble/bass volume control, treble/bass tone control, treble CVQ/bass CVQ/pickup switch, 5-pin stereo output jack, current mfg.

	MSR $15,000		$13,000	$11,500	$10,500	$9,500	N/A	N/A	N/A

Add $200 for baritone configuration (BSG6-II, MSR $15,200). Add $700 for 12-string configuration (LSG12-II, MSR $15,700).

**Alembic Series II Guitar
courtesy Alembic**

SKYLARK - double cutaway, semi-hollow mahogany body, double thick flamed maple, 3-piece maple neck with 2 walnut stripes, ebony with MOP inlay fingerboard, 2 Alembic HG 4 pickups, four knobs, two switches, mono output, 3-per-side gold tuners, brass hardware, available in natural finish, 8 lbs., current mfg.

	MSR $4,000		$3,500	$2,900	$2,500	$2,100	N/A	N/A	N/A

Add $200 for baritone configuration (MSR $4,200). Add $700 for 12-string configuration (MSR $4,700).

SPECTRUM (MLSG6) - offset double cutaway mahogany body, figured maple (or Bocate, Bubinga, Walnut, or Zebrawood) top, 25.75 in. scale, through-body maple/purpleheart laminate neck, 24-fret ebony fingerboard with pearl oval inlay, fixed solid brass bridge/string retainer, brass nut, body matching peghead with bronze logo, 6-on-a-side Alembic-Gotoh tuners, gold hardware, 2 single coil/1 humbucker Alembic pickups, volume/pan/low pass filter (with q switch) controls, 5-way selector, available in natural gloss polyester finish, current mfg.

	MSR $6,300		$5,500	$4,700	$4,000	$3,500	N/A	N/A	N/A

Add $200 for baritone configuration (MBSG6, MSR $6,500). Add $700 for 12-string configuration (MLSG12, MSR $7,000).

The Spectrum guitar model is the complement to the Europa bass.

TRIBUTE - double cutaway, semi-hollow flamed maple body with either cocobola, maple, vermilion, or flamed maple sandwich, double thick cocobola top, 5-piece flamed maple neck with purpleheart and cherry, ebony with MOP inlay fingerboard, Alembic STR, HG, and HG pickups (3), four knobs, effects loop, 3-per-side gold tuners, brass hardware, available in natural finish, 8.5 lbs., current mfg.

	MSR $8,700		$7,500	$6,500	$5,700	$5,000	N/A	N/A	N/A

Add $200 for baritone configuration (MSR $8,900). Add $700 for 12-string configuration (MSR $9,400).

ELECTRIC BASS

All models have through-body maple, or maple/mahogany laminate neck construction, dual truss rods, 24-fret ebony fingerboard with pearl oval inlay (unless otherwise listed), adjustable brass saddles/bridge/tailpiece/nut (these items may be chrome or gold plated), active electronics, ebony fingerboard and clear gloss finish.

A number of the earlier instruments were custom ordered, so there are variations that may be found that are not standard items. The Omega Cut refers to the stylish rounded cut in the lower bout sometimes found on Series I and II models - it´s a custom option.

20TH ANNIVERSARY - slightly offset double cutaway body with Omega Cut on lower bout, maple core Quilted maple top and back with Purpleheart accents or walnut core/Burl walnut top and back with vermilion accents, through-body maple/purpleheart laminated neck, 24-fret ebony fingerboard with oval inlays, 4-on-a-side tuners, brass hardware, 2 Alembic AXY pickups, 2 volume/2 filter (with q switch) controls, 4-position selector switch, mono/stereo switch, active electronics, available in Natural finish, mfg. 1989 only.

		$2,500	$2,250	$2,000	$1,600	$1,300	N/A	N/A

Last MSR was $3,630.

Only 200 instruments were built. The 25th Anniversary Edition is limited to only 25 pieces.

**Alembic Elan 5-String
courtesy Dave Rogers
Dave's Guitar Shop**

GRADING	100% MINT	98% NEAR MINT	95% EXC+	90% EXC	80% VG+	70% VG	60% G

CLASSICO UPRIGHT - updated upright bass-shaped semi-hollow mahogany body, figured maple top, 41.5 in. scale, 3-piece maple neck, rosewood fingerboard, ebony nut, 2+2 open headstock, maple bridge, rosewood tailpiece, Alembic Magnetic CS-2 pickups, volume/bass/treble controls, available in hand-rubbed satin polyester finish, mfg. 1994-present.

	MSR $15,000		$13,000	$11,000	$9,500	$8,500	N/A	N/A	N/A

Add $600 for 5-String configuration (MSR $15,200). Add $1,200 for 12-string configuration (MSR $15,700).

ELAN - offset double cutaway asymmetrical body, Honduras mahogany back, brass truss rod plate, body matching peghead with bronze logo, 4-on-a-side tuners, gold Alembic-Gotoh tuners, 2 P-style Alembic pickups, volume/tone/balance control, active electronics switch, mfg. 1985-1997.

	$2,000	$1,600	$1,400	$1,200	$1,000	$850	$700

Last MSR was $2,770.

Add 15% for 5-string configuration (last MSR $3,090). Add 25% for 6-string configuration (last MSR $3,415). Add 40% for 7-string configuration (last MSR $5,220). Add 50% for 8-string configuration (last MSR $3,570). Add 60% for 10-string configuration (last MSR $4,325).

EPIC (WLB4) - offset double cutaway mahogany body, standard woods top, 34 in. scale, 3-piece maple set neck, 24-fret ebony fingerboard, brass truss rod plate, body matching peghead with brass logo, chrome Alembic-Gotoh tuners, 2 Alembic MXY pickups, 2-per-side tuners, volume/pan/treble/bass controls, active electronics, satin polyurethane finish, mfg. 1994-present.

	MSR $3,700		$3,200	$2,800	$2,400	$2,000	N/A	N/A	N/A

Add $400 for 5-String configuration (MSR $4,200). Add $950 for 6-String configuration (MSR $5,000).

ESSENCE (KLB4) - offset double cutaway body, flame maple top, rock maple back, brass truss rod plate, body matching peghead with bronze logo, chrome Alembic-Gotoh tuners, 2 Alembic MXY pickups, 2-per-side tuners, volume/tone/balance control, mfg. 1991-present.

	MSR $4,400		$3,800	$3,300	$2,900	$2,600	N/A	N/A	N/A

Add $500 for 5-string configuration (MSR $4,900). Add $1,300 for 6-string configuration (MSR $5,700). Add $1,000 for 8-string configuration (last MSR $3,950).

EUROPA (ULB4) - offset double cutaway asymmetrical Honduras mahogany body, brass truss rod plate, body matching peghead with bronze logo, gold Alembic-Gotoh tuners, 2 Alembic MXY pickups, 4-on-a-side tuners, volume/tone/balance control, bass/treble/Q switches, mfg. 1986-present.

	MSR $6,300		$5,500	$4,800	$4,300	$3,800	N/A	N/A	N/A

Add $500 for 5-string configuration (MSR $6,800). Add $1,300 for 6-string configuration (MSR $7,600). Add 20% for 7-string configuration (disc. 1998, last MSR $5,850). Add 30% for 8-string configuration (disc. 1998, last MSR $5,150). Add 35% for 10-string configuration (disc. 1998, last MSR $6,050).

7-, 8-, and 10-string configurations currently available by special order only.

EXCEL - double cutaway with long bass bout, 3-piece ash body, 3-piece maple neck with 2 walnut stripes, pau ferro fingerboard, single Alembic Fat-Boy 4 pickup, three knobs, 2-per-side gold tuners, brass hardware, natural finish, current mfg.

	MSR $3,700		$3,200	$2,800	$2,400	$2,000	N/A	N/A	N/A

Add $500 for 5-String configuration (MSR $4,200). Add $1,300 for 6-String configuration (MSR $5,000).

MARK KING DELUXE SERIES (MKLB4) - offset double cutaway body with bottom bout point, long scale length, 5-piece mahogany body and exotic top, Mark King signature on peghead with gold-plated sterling silver logo, 2-per-side gold Alembic-Gotoh tuners, mfg. 1989-present.

	MSR $6,300		$5,050	$4,300	$3,600	$3,100	N/A	N/A	N/A

Mark King Deluxe 5 (MKLB5) - 5-piece body with mahogany core/exotic woods top, 2/3-per-side tuners, mfg. 1989-present.

	MSR $5,100		$4,100	$3,575	$3,300	$2,800	N/A	N/A	N/A

MARK KING STANDARD 4 (MJLB4) - offset double cutaway body with bottom bout point, long scale length, 3-piece mahogany body and exotic top, Mark King signature on peghead with gold plated sterling silver logo, 2-per-side gold Alembic-Gotoh tuners, mfg. 1990-present.

	MSR $4,900		$3,995	$3,300	$2,900	$2,500	$2,100	$1,700	$1,300

Mark King Standard 5 (MJLB5) - similar to the Mark King Standard 4, except in 5-string configuration, 2/3-per-side tuners, mfg. 1990-present.

	MSR $5,400		$4,400	$3,700	$3,200	$2,800	$2,400	$1,900	$1,400

ORION (OLB4) - offset double cutaway mahogany body, walnut top with maple veneer, maple/walnut laminated neck, 4-on-a-side tuners, active electronics, mfg. 1996-present.

	MSR $3,700		$3,200	$2,800	$2,400	$2,000	N/A	N/A	N/A

Add $500 for 5-string configuration (MSR $4,200). Add $1,300 for 6-string configuration (MSR $5,000).

ROGUE (QLB4) - sleek offset double cutaway mahogany body, vermillion top with maple accents, 2-per-side tuners, maple/walnut laminated neck, active electronics, mfg. 1996-present.

	MSR $5,400		$4,600	$4,000	$3,500	$3,100	N/A	N/A	N/A

Add $500 for 5-string configuration (MSR $5,900). Add $1,300 for 6-string configuration (MSR $6,700). Add 20% for 7-string configuration (disc. 1998, last MSR $4,700). Add 15% for 8-string configuration (disc. 1998, last MSR $4,000). Add 25% for 10-string configuration (disc. 1998, last MSR $4,900).

7-, 8-, and 10-string configurations currently available by special order only.

SERIES I (LBI4) - offset double cutaway mahogany core body with bottom bout point, figured wood top/back, brass truss rod plate, body matching peghead with sterling silver logo, chrome Schaller tuners, chrome plated hardware, single coil/dummy humbucker/single coil pickups, 2-per-side tuners, treble/bass volume/tone control, treble Q/bass Q/pickup switch, 5-pin stereo output jack, mfg. 1971-present.

	MSR $11,200		$10,000	$9,000	$8,200	$7,500	N/A	N/A	N/A

Add $500 for 5-string configuration (MSR $11,700). Add $1,300 for 6-string configuration (MSR $12,500). Add 20% for 7-string configuration (disc. 1998, last MSR $8,800). Add 15% for 8-string configuration (disc. 1998, last MSR $8,100). Add 25% for 10-string configuration (disc. 1998, last MSR $9,000).

GRADING	100% MINT	98% NEAR MINT	95% EXC+	90% EXC	80% VG+	70% VG	60% G

SERIES II (LBII4) - offset double cutaway mahogany core body, figured wood top/back, 34 in. scale, 7-piece neck, brass truss rod plate, body matching peghead with gold-plated sterling silver logo, gold Schaller tuners, gold plated hardware, single coil/dummy humbucker/single coil pickups, 2-per-side tuners, master/treble/bass volume control, treble/bass tone control, treble CVQ/bass CVQ/pickup switch, 5-pin stereo output jack, side position LED fret markers, mfg. 1971-present.

MSR $15,000		$13,000	$11,500	$10,500	$9,500	N/A	N/A	N/A

Add $400 for 5-string configuration (MSR $15,500). Add $1,300 for 6-string configuration (MSR $16,300). Add 20% for 7-string configuration (disc. 1998, last MSR $10,500). Add 15% for 8-string configuration (disc. 1998, last MSR $9,800). Add 25% for 10-string configuration (disc. 1998, last MSR $10,700).

7-, 8-, and 10-string configurations currently available by special order only.

SPOILER - offset double cutaway Honduras mahogany body, brass truss rod plate, body matching peghead with bronze logo, chrome Alembic-Gotoh tuners, 2 humbucker pickups, 2-per-side tuners, volume/tone control, pickup/Q switch, mfg. 1980-1999.

		$2,500	$2,200	$1,900	$1,600	$1,350	$1,150	$900

Last MSR was $3,200.

Add 15% for 5-string configuration (last MSR $3,500). Add 25% for 6-string configuration (last MSR $3,800).

The Spoiler was also offered in a 3/4 size model between 1986 to 1996.

STANLEY CLARKE DELUXE (SCSB4) - offset double cutaway body with rounded bottom bout, 5-piece body with exotic wood top, short scale length, Stanley Clarke signature on peghead with gold plated sterling silver logo, 2-per-side gold Alembic-Gotoh tuners, mfg. 1986-present.

MSR $6,300		$5,050	$4,300	$3,600	$3,100	N/A	N/A	N/A

Stanley Clarke Deluxe 5 (SCSB5) - 5-piece body with mahogany core/exotic woods top, 2/3-per-side tuners, mfg. 1986-present.

MSR $6,800		$5,500	$4,800	$4,300	$3,800	N/A	N/A	N/A

STANLEY CLARKE STANDARD 4 (SJSB4) - offset double cutaway body with rounded bottom bout, 3-piece body with exotic wood top, short scale length, Stanley Clarke signature on peghead with gold-plated sterling silver logo, 2-per-side gold Alembic-Gotoh tuners, mfg. 1990-present.

MSR $4,900		$3,995	$3,300	$2,900	$2,500	$2,100	$1,700	$1,300

Stanley Clarke Standard 5 (SJSC5) - similar to the Stanley Clarke Standard 4, except in 5-string configuration, 2/3-per-side tuners, mfg. 1990-present.

MSR $5,400		$4,400	$3,700	$3,200	$2,800	$2,400	$1,900	$1,400

**Alembic Epic 5-String
courtesy Rick Wilkiewicz**

ELECTRIC BASS: ARTIST SIGNATURE SERIES

Originally, both Stanley Clarke and Mark King had specific signature models. These models lead to the individual Stanley Clarke Series and Mark King Series models.

SIGNATURE SERIES - brass truss rod plate, body matching peghead with gold-plated sterling silver logo, brass hardware, 2 humbucker pickups, volume/2 tone/balance controls, 2 Q switches, 5-pin stereo output jack.

Mark King (MKLSB) - offset double cutaway mahogany core body with bottom bout point, long scale length, Mark King signature on peghead with gold-plated sterling silver logo, 2-per-side gold Alembic-Gotoh tuners, disc. 1993.

		$1,975	$1,700	$1,400	$1,125	N/A	N/A	N/A

Last MSR was $2,815.

See Mark King Series for current models.

Stanley Clarke (SCSSB) - offset double cutaway mahogany core body with rounded bottom bout, short scale length, Stanley Clarke signature on peghead with gold-plated sterling silver logo, 2-per-side gold Alembic-Gotoh tuners, disc. 1993.

		$2,000	$1,750	$1,500	$1,200	N/A	N/A	N/A

Last MSR was $2,815.

See Stanley Clarke Series for current models.

ALLEN, RICHARD C.

Instruments currently built in Almonte, California.

Luthier R.C. Allen has been playing the guitar since his high school days in the late 1940s. Allen has been playing, collecting, repairing, and building guitars for a great number of years. After working sixteen years as a warehouseman for a paper company, Allen began doing repair work for West Coast guitar wholesaler/distributors like C. Bruno and Pacific Music. In 1972, Allen began building guitars full time.

Allen's designs focus on hollowbody and semi-hollowbody guitars. While he has built some electric guitars, the design was semi-hollow (similar to the Rickenbacker idea) with a flattop/back and f-holes. Currently, Allen focuses on jazz-style archtops. Now in his 50th year of building guitars, he is building 15 in., 16 in., 17 in., and 18 in. wide guitars. He is also building a series of commemorative guitars honoring country singer Hank Thompson.

ALLEN, ROB

Instruments currently built in Santa Monica, California since 1996. Distributed by Rob Allen Guitars (Santa Monica), LA Bass Exchange (San Fernando Valley), and Rudy's Music (New York).

Luthier Rob Allen has a background as both a musical artist and a fine craftsman. It is a culmination of his experiences that make his instruments distinctly musical, organic in concept, and naturally appealing to the player. As a musician, Allen has played guitar with Melissa Etheridge (World Tour '92-'93), Ceremony (Geffen Records), and Kindred Spirit

**Alembic Europa 6-String
courtesy Alembic**

GRADING	100% MINT	98% NEAR MINT	95% EXC+	90% EXC	80% VG+	70% VG	60% G

(I.R.S.). Allen has taught guitar at UCLA, and has recorded his own solo album (*Mysterious Measures*, released on the Suppletone label).

Allen built his first electric guitar from raw materials at the age of seventeen, and shortly thereafter served as an apprentice to Seymour Duncan (Seymour Duncan Pickups) for three years. Allen has also had an apprenticeship with luthier Rick Turner, the well-known co-founder of Alembic and now Rick Turner Guitars. In addition to working on his own designs, Allen has drawn from both of these modern pioneers. Since 1996, Allen has been handcrafting 4- and 5-string basses that feature internal hollow tone chambers, and Fishman piezo electronics (no magnetic pickups). Allen also custom builds his RA series guitars and BB series Baritone guitars.

ELECTRIC GUITAR

Hot on the heels of Allen´s **MB** series basses are the **BB** series Baritone guitars. The **BB** model Baritone has a semi-hollow offset double cutaway body, 4/2-per-side headstock, 2 lipstick tube pickups, and a fixed bridge. The **BB-1** Baritone has ultra-premium grade woods, bound headstock, and gloss lacquer finish (list $2,000); the **BB-2** Baritone has premium grade woods and an oil finish (list $1,500).

ELECTRIC BASS

The **MB-2** features a sleek offset double cutaway swamp ash body with internal tone chambers, quilted maple top, bolt-on bird's-eye maple neck, fretless cocobola fingerboard, through-body stringing, carved cocobola bridge, 2-per-side Hipshot Ultralite tuners, Fishman Acoustic Matrix Natural transducer, volume control (mounted on bridge), trim pot (in controls area in back), Fishman electronics, and is available in Tung Oil/Carnuba Wax finish. 4-string fretless bass starts at $1,899 and the 5-string $2,299. These are available in fretted versions that start at $1,949 and $2,349, respectively. The **Mouse 30**, is a shorter scale bass and retails for $1,750 in the fretless version and $1,949 in the fretted version. The **Deep 4** and **Deep 5** are semi-hollow basses. They start at $3,749 for the 4-string version and $3,949 for the 5-string. There are several options available as far as wood. Contact Rob Allen for more information and pricing options.

Add 15% for left-hand configuration.

MB-1 (SERIES 1) - similar to the MB-2, except features ultra premium wood selection, bound headstock, available in Natural, Plum, Red, Sunburst, or Vintage Amber gloss finishes, disc.

	$2,000	$1,500	$1,300	$1,150	$950	$800	$650
					Last MSR was $2,000.		

MB-1 (SERIES 1) 5-string - disc.

	$2,200	$1,750	$1,550	$1,300	$1,100	$900	$700
					Last MSR was $2,200.		

Retail list price includes a deluxe padded gig bag.

ALLIGATOR
Instruments previously built in England in 1983.

In celebration of Alligator Amplifications´ first anniversary, Reeve Guitars (UK) built a number of instruments designed by Pete Tulett (source: Tony Bacon and Paul Day, *The Guru's Guitar Guide*).

ALOHA
Instruments previously built in San Antonio, Texas, and Chicago, Illinois. Distributed by the Aloha Publishing and Musical Instrument Company of Chicago, Illinois.

The Aloha company was founded in 1935 by J.M. Raleigh. True to the nature of a House Brand distributor, Raleigh´s company distributed both Aloha instruments and amplifiers and Raleigh brand instruments through his Chicago office. Acoustic guitars were supplied by Harmony, and initial amplifiers and guitars were supplied by the Alamo company of San Antonio. By the mid-1950s, Aloha was producing its own amps, but continued using Alamo products (source: Michael Wright, *Vintage Guitar Magazine*). Aloha guitars typically sell for $50-$150 in the used market.

ALRAY
Instruments previously built in Neodesha, Kansas circa 1967. Distributed by Holman-Woodell, Inc. of Neodesha, Kansas.

The Holman-Woodell company built guitars during the late 1960s in Neodesha, Kansas (around 60 miles due south from Topeka). After they had produced guitars for Wurlitzer, they also built guitars under the trademark names of Holman, Alray, and 21st Century. The Holman-Woodell company is also famous for building the La Baye 2 x 4 guitars for Wisconsin-based designer Dan Helland (source: Michael Wright, *Guitar Stories* Volume One).

ALVAREZ
Instruments previously manufactured in either Japan or Korea. Distributed by St. Louis Music of St. Louis, Missouri.

The St. Louis Music Supply Company was originally founded in 1922 by Bernard Kornblum as a violin shop. In 1957, Bernard´s son, Gene Kornblum, joined the family business.

The Alvarez trademark was established in 1965, and the company was the earliest of Asian producers to feature laminate-body guitars with solid wood tops. Initially, Alvarez guitars were built in Japan during the late 1960s, and distributed through St. Louis Music.

St. Louis Music also distributed the Electra and Westone brands of solid body electrics. St. Louis Music currently manufactures Crate and Ampeg amplifiers in the U.S., while Alvarez instruments are designed in St. Louis and produced overseas.

Alvarez does not currently produce electric guitars. There are several other series that have been produced in past years that include the Classic, the Dana Scoop, the Dana Signature, the Regulator, the Trevor Rabin Signature, and the Villain Series.

St. Louis Music now has the Austin line of guitars that produce about the same quality of electric guitars that Alvarez did. This allows Alvarez to focus entirely on acoustic guitars.

ELECTRIC: ASG SERIES

ASG1 - double cutaway solid basswood body, bolt-on maple neck, 6-on-a-side tuners, rosewood fingerboard with 12th-fret diagonal inlay, 25.5 in. scale, 2 Humbucker pickups, 1 volume/1 tone knobs, 5-position switch, Floyd Rose Locking bridge, black pearl hardware, available in Deep Purple, Red Metallic, or Blue Metallic finishes, mfg. 2002 only.

	$450	$400	$350	$300	$275	$250	$225
					Last MSR was $589.		

GRADING	100% MINT	98% NEAR MINT	95% EXC+	90% EXC	80% VG+	70% VG	60% G

ASG2 - contoured double cutaway solid alder body, quilted maple top with transparent colors, bolt-on maple neck, 6-on-a-side tuners, rosewood fingerboard with dot position markers, 25.5 in. scale, 2 Alnico SC single coil pickups and 1 Alnico HB Humbucker pickup, 1 volume/2 tone switches, 5-position switch, Wilkinson vibrato, Kluson-style locking tuners, nickel hardware, available in Surf Green and Purple Hayes and Black Cherry and Amber Burst on quilted maple tops, mfg. 2000-02.

		$350	$300	$250	$200	$175	$150	$120

Last MSR was $459.

Add $30 for Black Cherry and Amber Burst finishes.

ASG3 - contoured double cutaway solid alder body, bolt-on one-piece maple neck and fingerboard, 6-on-a-side tuners, black dot position markers, 25.5 in. scale, 3 Alnico SC single coil pickups, 1 volume/2 tone controls, 5-position switch, vintage vibrato, Kluson-style tuners, nickel hardware, available in 3-Tone Sunburst, Vintage White, Gold Metallic, or Burgundy Metallic finishes, mfg. 2000-01.

		$275	$245	$210	$180	$150	$125	$100

Last MSR was $379.

ASG4 - contoured single cutaway solid alder body, bolt-on one piece maple neck and fingerboard, 6-on-one-side tuners, black dot position markers, 25.5 in. scale, 3 Alnico SC single coil pickups, 1 volume/2 tone switches, 5-position switch, vintage fixed bridge, Kluson-style tuners, nickel hardware, available in Gold Metallic, Red Metallic, Cherry Sunburst, or black finishes, mfg. 2000-02.

		$275	$245	$210	$180	$150	$125	$100

Last MSR was $379.

Add $50 for Cherry Sunburst finish.

Black finish was discontinued in 2001.

ELECTRIC: CLASSIC SERIES

AE 10 BK CLASSIC I - single cutaway solid alder body, bolt-on maple neck, 21-fret maple fingerboard with black dot inlay, fixed bridge, 6-on-a-side die-cast tuners, chrome hardware, white pickguard, 2 single coil pickups, volume/tone controls on metal plate, 3-way selector, available in Gloss Black finish, mfg. 1994-99.

		$275	$250	$225	$195	$160	$125	$100

Last MSR was $379.

AE 15 BK CLASSIC II (AE 15 SB) - offset double cutaway solid alder body, bolt-on maple neck, 21-fret rosewood fingerboard with white dot inlay, vintage tremolo, 6-on-a-side Alvarez tuners, chrome hardware, white pickguard, 2 single coil/1 humbucker pickups, volume/2 tone controls, 5-position switch, available in Gloss Black (Model AE 15 BK) or Sunburst (Model AE 15 SB) finishes, disc. 1999.

		$275	$250	$225	$195	$160	$125	$100

Last MSR was $379.

AE 20 CLASSIC II - offset double cutaway alder body, bolt-on maple neck, 21-fret maple fingerboard with black dot inlay, standard vibrato, 3-per-side tuners, chrome hardware, pearloid pickguard, 2 single coil/1 humbucker pickups, volume/2 tone controls, 5-position switch, available in Black or Sunburst finishes, mfg. 1994-97.

	$250	$200	$175	$150	$125	$100	$85

Last MSR was $350.

In 1995, Black finish was introduced.

AE 25 BK CLASSIC STANDARD (AE 25 NA) - offset double cutaway solid alder body, bolt-on maple neck, 22-fret rosewood fingerboard with white dot inlay, vintage-style tremolo, 6-on-a-side Alvarez tuners, chrome hardware, black pickguard, 2 single coil/1 humbucker pickups, volume/tone controls, 5-position switch, available in Gloss Black (Model AE 25 BK) or Natural Satin (Model AE 25 NA) finishes, disc. 1999.

		$325	$285	$250	$215	$180	$145	$110

Last MSR was $439.

Subtract $10 for Satin Natural finish (Model AE 25 NA), last MSR was $429.

AE 30 BK CLASSIC III (AE 30 SB, AE 30 TB, AE 30 TR) - offset double cutaway solid alder body, bolt-on maple neck, 22-fret rosewood fingerboard with white dot inlay, Accutune II tremolo, 6-on-a-side Alvarez die-cast tuners, chrome hardware, white pickguard, 2 single coil/1 humbucker pickups, volume/2 tone controls, 5-position switch, available in Gloss Black (Model AE 30 BK), Sunburst (Model AE 30 TB), Trans. Blue (Model AE 30 TB), or Trans. Red (Model AE 30 TR) finishes, disc. 1999.

		$350	$300	$265	$225	$195	$160	$120

Last MSR was $469.

AE 40 FB CLASSIC DELUXE (AE 40 SB) - offset double cutaway alder body, bolt-on maple neck, 22-fret rosewood fingerboard with pearl dot inlay, fixed bridge, 6-on-a-side Alvarez die-cast tuners, chrome hardware, white pearloid pickguard, 2 single coil/1 humbucker pickups, volume/tone controls, 5-position switch, available in Tobacco Sunburst or Walnut finishes, mfg. 1994-99.

		$450	$395	$350	$295	$250	$195	$150

Last MSR was $599.

In 1996, Faded Blue (Model AE 40 FB) and Sunburst (Model AE 40 SB) finishes replaced Tobacco Sunburst and Walnut finishes, and vintage-style tremolo and gold hardware replaced original parts/design.

**Alvarez AE 10 BK Classic I
courtesy Alvarez**

**Alvarez AE 30 BK Classic III
courtesy Alvarez**

GRADING	100% MINT	98% NEAR MINT	95% EXC+	90% EXC	80% VG+	70% VG	60% G

AE 50 CLASSIC V - similar to AE 40 Classic Deluxe, except has standard tremolo, roller nut, gold hardware, available in Ivory or Vintage Sunburst finishes, mfg. 1994-96.

	$400	$350	$300	$275	$225	$185	$150

Last MSR was $575.

In 1995, Ivory finish was introduced.

AE 60 FB CLASSIC (AE 60 SB) - similar to AE 40 Classic Deluxe, except has Wilkinson tremolo, Sperzel locking tuners, pearloid pickguard, volume/tone controls, available in Faded Blue (Model AE 60 FB) or Sunburst (Model AE 60 SB) finishes, disc. 1999.

	$700	$625	$550	$465	$385	$300	$225

Last MSR was $949.

ELECTRIC: DANA SCOOP SERIES

The Scoop guitar model was designed by luthier Dana Sutcliffe in 1988, and won the *Music and Sound Retailer* magazine´s "Most Innovative Guitar of the Year Award" in 1992. Produced between 1992 and 1995, the scoop-shaped slot in the guitar body´s design reinforces and channels neck vibrations into a single point where the neck and body meet.

AE 600 - offset double cutaway maple body with a "scoop" cutaway, bolt-on maple neck, 22-fret rosewood fingerboard with pearl block inlay, double locking vibrato, 6-on-a-side tuners, black hardware, single coil/humbucker pickups, volume/tone control, 3-position switch, available in Dark Metallic Blue or Fire Red finishes, disc. 1995.

	$550	$500	$425	$350	$300	$250	$225

Last MSR was $850.

In 1994, active electronics and Blue Pearl and Red Glow finishes were added.

AE 600 MA - similar to AE 600, except has figured maple top, maple fingerboard, available in Honey Burst finish, mfg. 1994 only.

	$725	$650	$550	$425	$395	$350	$325

Last MSR was $1,090.

AE 6001 - similar to AE 600, except has Modulus Graphite neck/fingerboard, available in Black finish, disc. 1993.

	$600	$550	$450	$350	$300	$250	$200

Last MSR was $900.

AE 650 - offset double cutaway maple body with a "scoop" cutaway, bolt-on maple neck, 22-fret rosewood fingerboard with pearl dot inlay, double locking vibrato, 6-on-a-side tuners, black hardware, single coil/triple Dana pickups, volume/tone control, 5-position switch, available in Black or Trans. White finishes, mfg. 1994 only.

	$525	$475	$400	$325	$295	$250	$225

Last MSR was $800.

This model was also available with a maple fingerboard with black dot inlay.

AE 655 - similar to AE 650, except has maple fingerboard with black dot inlay, gold hardware, disc.

	$600	$550	$450	$350	$315	$275	$250

Last MSR was $900.

AE 3000 - offset double cutaway alder body with a "scoop" cutaway, bolt-on maple neck, 22-fret rosewood fingerboard with pearl dot inlay, double locking vibrato, 3-per-side tuners, smoked chrome hardware, 2 single coil/1 humbucker Dana pickups, volume/tone control, 5-position switch, active electronics, available in Ivory finish, mfg. 1994 only.

	$525	$475	$400	$325	$275	$250	$225

Last MSR was $800.

AE 5000 - similar to AE 3000, except has fixed bridge, disc.

	$450	$400	$350	$280	$250	$225	$200

Last MSR was $700.

ELECTRIC: DANA SIGNATURE SERIES

Designer/luthier Dana Sutcliffe has over twenty years experience in the music industry. Combining his experiences as a practicing musician, Sutcliffe has been designing quality forward-thinking guitars and amplifiers. In 1990, Sutcliffe co-designed the Alvarez Electric Guitar line for St. Louis Music. Innovative designs include the "Tri-Force" pickups, the Dana "Scoop" slotted body design, and the Dana "Off Set" bass design.

AED 100 - offset double cutaway alder body, bolt-on maple neck, 22-fret rosewood fingerboard with pearl block inlay, tune-o-matic bridge/stop tailpiece, 6-on-a-side tuners, chrome hardware, 2 DSR humbucker pickups, volume/2 tone controls, 3-position and coil tap switches, available in Black finish, disc. 1995.

	$350	$300	$250	$200	$180	$165	$150

Last MSR was $500.

AED 200 - offset double cutaway hardwood body, bolt-on maple neck, 22-fret maple fingerboard with black dot inlay, standard vibrato, 6-on-a-side tuners, chrome hardware, 2 single coil/1 humbucker Alvarez pickups, volume/tone control, 5-position switch, available in Black and White finishes, mfg. 1994 only.

	$250	$225	$195	$150	$135	$100	$95

Last MSR was $375.

AED 250 - similar to the AED 200, except features 22-fret rosewood fingerboard with pearl dot inlay, fixed bridge, 3-per-side tuners, single coil/triple Dana pickup, available in Red finish, mfg. 1994 only.

	$265	$235	$200	$160	$140	$115	$100

Last MSR was $390.

GRADING	100% MINT	98% NEAR MINT	95% EXC+	90% EXC	80% VG+	70% VG	60% G

AED 260 - similar to AED 250, except has alder body, figured maple top, transparent pickguard, maple fingerboard with black dot inlay, gold hardware, available in Trans. Red finish, mfg. 1994-96.

	$400	$325	$275	$225	$185	$140	$100

Last MSR was $550.

AED 275 - offset double cutaway alder body, transparent pickguard, bolt-on maple neck, 22-fret rosewood fingerboard with pearl dot inlay, double locking vibrato, 3-per-side tuners, chrome hardware, single coil/triple Dana pickup, 1 volume/2 tone controls, 5-position switch, available in Red or White finishes, mfg. 1994-96.

	$425	$350	$300	$250	$200	$150	$115

Last MSR was $575.

Add $50 for Blue Pearl/Transparent Red finish (AED 275 VR).

AED 280 - similar to AED 275, except has humbucker/single coil/humbucker pickups, available in Blue Pearl finish, mfg. 1994-96.

	$450	$365	$325	$275	$225	$165	$125

Last MSR was $635.

AED 300 - offset double cutaway alder body, bolt-on maple neck, 22-fret rosewood fingerboard with pearl dot inlay, double locking vibrato, 6-on-a-side tuners, black hardware, 2 single coil/1 humbucker DSR pickups, volume/2 tone controls, 5-position switch, available in Fire Red or White finishes, disc. 1995.

	$325	$300	$250	$200	$175	$145	$125

Last MSR was $500.

In 1994, White finish became available.

ELECTRIC: REGULATOR SERIES

AE 100 - offset double cutaway alder body, black pickguard, bolt-on maple neck, 22-fret maple fingerboard with black dot inlay, standard vibrato, 6-on-a-side tuners, chrome hardware, 2 single coil/1 humbucker EMG pickups, volume/2 tone controls, 5-position switch, available in Trans. Blue or Trans. Red finishes, disc. 1993.

	$325	$275	$225	$200	$180	$150	$115

Last MSR was $450.

AE 200 - similar to AE 100, except has maple body, rosewood fingerboard with pearl dot inlay, gold hardware and humbucker/single coil/humbucker EMG pickups, available in Cherry Sunburst finish, disc. 1995.

	$450	$395	$325	$260	$200	$175	$135

Last MSR was $650.

AE 300 - similar to AE 100, except has maple body, Modulus Graphite neck/fingerboard, gold hardware and humbucker/single coil/humbucker EMG pickups, available in Black finish, disc. 1993.

	$350	$300	$250	$200	$180	$165	$135

Last MSR was $500.

AE 400 - offset double cutaway alder body, black pickguard, bolt-on maple neck, 22-fret maple fingerboard with black dot inlay, double locking vibrato, 3-per-side tuners, chrome hardware, 1 single coil/1 triple Alvarez pickups, volume/tone control, 5-position switch, available in Black finish, mfg. 1994 only.

	$425	$375	$300	$250	$225	$185	$145

Last MSR was $600.

AE 500 - similar to the AE 400, except has black hardware and single coil/humbucker Dan Armstrong pickups, mfg. 1994 only.

	$400	$360	$300	$240	$200	$165	$125

Last MSR was $600.

ELECTRIC: TREVOR RABIN SIGNATURE SERIES

This series was designed in conjunction with guitarist Trevor Rabin of the band Yes.

AER 100 - offset double cutaway alder body, arched maple top, maple neck, 24-fret ebony fingerboard with slanted abalone inlay, double locking Kahler vibrato, 6-on-a-side tuners, black hardware, 2 Alnico humbucker pickups, volume/2 tone controls, 3-position switch, available in Black or White finishes, disc. 1995.

	$600	$550	$475	$395	$325	$275	$240

Last MSR was $925.

In 1993, Black finish was disc.

AER 200 - similar to AER 100, except has fixed bridge, gold hardware and 1 tone control, available in White finish, disc. 1993.

	$825	$750	$650	$525	$475	$400	$350

Last MSR was $1,300.

AER 300 - similar to AER 100, except has bolt-on maple neck, rosewood fingerboard with pearl dot inlay, standard vibrato, chrome hardware, 2 single coil/1 humbucker pickups and 5-position switch, available in Red finish, disc. 1993.

	$650	$575	$500	$400	$350	$300	$250

Last MSR was $1,000.

Alvarez AEB 250 TRD
courtesy Alvarez

Alvarez AEB 260 WA
courtesy Alvarez

GRADING	100% MINT	98% NEAR MINT	95% EXC+	90% EXC	80% VG+	70% VG	60% G

ELECTRIC: VILLAIN SERIES

Some models may have Select by EMG pickups.

AEV 410 - offset double cutaway alder body, bolt-on maple neck, 22-fret rosewood fingerboard with pearl dot inlay, double locking Kahler vibrato, 6-on-a-side tuners, chrome hardware, 2 single coil/1 humbucker Dan Armstrong pickups, volume/tone controls, 5-position switch, available in Black, Red, or White finishes, disc. 1993.

| | N/A | $400 | $350 | $275 | $225 | $200 | $175 |

Last MSR was $650.

AEV 425 - similar to AEV 410, except has Modulus Graphite neck/fingerboard and black hardware, available in Dark Grey Metallic or Red Pearl finishes, disc. 1993.

| | N/A | $500 | $425 | $350 | $275 | $225 | $195 |

Last MSR was $800.

AEV 520 - similar to AEV 410, except has maple body, black hardware and humbucker/single coil/humbucker Dan Armstrong pickups, available in Cherry Sunburst finish, disc. 1993.

| | N/A | $550 | $450 | $375 | $325 | $275 | $215 |

Last MSR was $900.

ELECTRIC BASS: AEB SERIES

In 2001, the AEB4, 5, and 6 bass guitars were available with a translucent finish as the AEB400, 500, and 600, respectively. These finishes will add a 5-10% premium, typically.

AEB4 - contoured double cutaway solid alder body with quilted maple top, bolt-on maple neck, rosewood fingerboard with dot position markers, 34 in. scale, 2 custom Alvarez HB Humbucker pickups, 2 volume/1 tone control, high mass die-cast bridge, Alvarez custom die-cast tuners, 2-per-side tuners, chrome hardware, available in Amber Burst, Black Cherry, or Purple Burst on Quilted Maple, mfg. 2000-02.

| | $400 | $375 | $350 | $300 | $275 | $250 | $200 |

Last MSR was $539.

AEB5 - similar to the AEB4 except in 5-string configuration, mfg. 2000-02.

| | $490 | $450 | $425 | $375 | $325 | $275 | $225 |

Last MSR was $649.

AEB6 - similar to the AEB4 except in 6-string configuration, available in Purple Burst finish only, mfg. 2000-02.

| | $675 | $600 | $550 | $475 | $425 | $375 | $325 |

Last MSR was $899.

AEB4000 - double cutaway solid mahogany body with bubinga top, neck-through body maple/walnut neck, rosewood fingerboard with 12th-fret diagonal inlay, 35 in. scale, 2 custom Alvarez HB Humbucker pickups, 2 volume/2 tone control, active electronics, high mass die-cast bridge, Alvarez custom die-cast tuners, 2-per-side tuners, satin chrome hardware, available in Natural finish, mfg. 2002 only.

| | $600 | $550 | $500 | $450 | $400 | $350 | $275 |

Last MSR was $799.

AEB5000 - similar to the AEB4000 except in 5-string configuration, 3/2-per side tuners, mfg. 2002 only.

| | $675 | $600 | $550 | $475 | $425 | $375 | $325 |

Last MSR was $899.

ELECTRIC BASS: DANA SIGNATURE SERIES

The Alvarez Dana "Off Set" Bass design, designed by Dana Sutcliffe, was nominated for the 1992 "Most Innovative Bass of the Year" award during its first year of production.

AE 700 - offset double cutaway asymmetrical alder body, bolt-on maple neck, 24-fret rosewood fingerboard with pearl block inlay, fixed bridge, 4-on-a-side tuners, black hardware, P/J-style pickups, volume/2 tone controls, 3-way switch, available in Black or Dark Blue Metallic finishes, disc. 1993.

| | N/A | $500 | $425 | $350 | $275 | $225 | $175 |

Last MSR was $700.

ELECTRIC BASS: PANTERA SERIES

AEB P 1 - offset double cutaway alder body, bolt-on maple neck, 24-fret ebony fingerboard with abalone slant inlay, fixed bridge, 2-per-side tuners, gold hardware, 2 pickups, volume/2 tone controls, 3-position switch, available in Black or White finishes, disc. 1995.

| | $475 | $425 | $375 | $325 | $275 | $225 | $175 |

Last MSR was $750.

In 1993, Black finish was disc.

AEB P 2 - similar to AEB P 1, except has rosewood fingerboard with pearl dot inlay and chrome hardware, available in Black finish, disc. 1993.

| | $575 | $500 | $450 | $350 | $325 | $275 | $225 |

Last MSR was $900.

ELECTRIC BASS: VILLAIN SERIES

AE 800 - offset double cutaway alder body, bolt-on maple neck, 24-fret rosewood fingerboard with pearl dot inlay, fixed bridge, 2-per-side tuners, black hardware, P/J-style EMG pickups, 2 volume/1 tone controls, available in Black, Red Pearl, Trans. Black, or Trans. Red finishes, disc. 1995.

| | $425 | $375 | $325 | $250 | $225 | $175 | $150 |

Last MSR was $685.

GRADING	100% MINT	98% NEAR MINT	95% EXC+	90% EXC	80% VG+	70% VG	60% G

AE 800 CS - similar to AE 800, except has maple body, disc. 1993.

	$525	$450	$375	$300	$275	$245	$225

Last MSR was $750.

AE 800 WA - similar to AE 800, except has Natural finish, mfg. 1994 only.

	$475	$425	$350	$295	$250	$225	$200

Last MSR was $725.

AE 900 5-STRING - similar to AE 800, except has 5 strings, 3/2-per-side tuners, disc. 1993.

	$450	$395	$325	$275	$225	$195	$175

Last MSR was $650.

AE 7000 - offset double cutaway asymmetrical alder body, bolt-on maple neck, 24-fret rosewood fingerboard with pearl dot inlay, brass fixed bridge, 2-per-side tuners, chrome hardware, J/P/J-style Dana pickups, volume/treble/mid/bass controls, 3-position switch, available in Trans. Black or Trans. Red finishes, mfg. 1994 only.

	$525	$450	$375	$300	$275	$245	$225

Last MSR was $750.

AE 7050 - similar to AE 7000, except has fretless ceramic fingerboard, available in Trans. White finish, mfg. 1994 only.

	$475	$425	$350	$275	$250	$225	$200

Last MSR was $775.

AEB 200 NA VILLAIN BASS (AEB 200 TBK, AEB 200 TRD) - offset double cutaway solid alder body, bolt-on maple neck, 22-fret rosewood fingerboard with offset pearl dot inlay, die-cast fixed bridge, 2-per-side Alvarez die-cast tuners, chrome hardware, P/J-style pickups, 2 volume/1 tone controls, available in Natural (Model AEB 200 NA), Trans. Black (Model AEB 200 TBK), or Trans. Red (Model AEB 200 TRD) finishes, mfg. 1994-99.

	$400	$350	$300	$265	$225	$175	$135

Last MSR was $539.

AEB 250 NA VILLAIN 5-STRING (AEB 250 TRD) - similar to AEB 200, except has 5-string configuration, 3/2-per-side tuners, active electronics, available in Natural (Model AEB 250 NA) and Trans. Red (Model AEB 250 TRD) finishes, mfg. 1995-99.

	$475	$425	$375	$325	$265	$215	$160

Last MSR was $639.

AEB 260 WA VILLAIN 6-STRING - similar to AEB 200, except has 6-string configuration, 3-per-side tuners, 2 Alvarez custom J-style pickups, active electronics, available in Natural Walnut finish, mfg. 1995-99.

	$675	$585	$525	$450	$375	$295	$225

Last MSR was $899.

AMBUSH CUSTOM BASSES
Instruments currently built in Frederick, Maryland.

Luthier/bassist Scott Ambush has been playing bass for 26 years, and professionally with the jazz group Spyro Gyra for the past 6 years. Ambush has been building basses as a hobby for the past ten years, and decided to offer them to players in 1998.

ELECTRIC BASS

The **Ambush Custom 4-String** bass (ACB-4, retail list $2,395) features an asymmetrical deep double cutaway ash or alder body, choice of (.25 in. thick) exotic wood top, 34 in. or 35 in. scale, graphite reinforced composite constructed neck, 22-fret resin impregnated wood fingerboard, Hipshot tuners/´B´ bridge, Bartolini J-style or double humbucker pickups, volume/blend controls, and treble/mid/mid position/bass cut and boost controls. Ambush basses are optionally available with 24-fret bird's-eye maple, rosewood, or ebony fingerboards; and black, gold, and silver hardware.

The **Ambush Custom 5-String** bass (ACB-5, retail list $2,695) has the same features as the four string except with the addition of a fifth string. The **Ambush Custom 6-String** bass (ACB-6, retail list $2,995) has the same features as the five string except with the addition of a sixth string.

Contact Scott for more information (see Trademark Index).

Add $150 for LT suffix (Laminated Top, not Lawrence Taylor).

AMERICAN SHOWSTER
Instruments currently built in Bayville, New Jersey since 1995.

The American Showster company first debuted the tailfin-bodied AS-57 solid body guitar at the NAMM show in the late 1980s. In addition to the original model, Bill Meeker, David Seal, and Richard Haines are continuing to debut new exciting guitar designs. American Showster guitars are also available with custom graphics (call for price quote).

ELECTRIC: CUSTOM SERIES

The tailfin brake light on the AS-57 model is fully functional. The brake light is activated by either the push-pull tone pot on the fixed-bridge model or by depressing the vibrola on the Floyd Rose-equipped model.

AS-57 CLASSIC (MODEL AS-57-FX) - alder body shaped like the tailfin of a '57 Chevy, operational chromed tailfin brake-light assembly, 6-bolt maple neck, 25.5 in. scale, 22-fret rosewood or maple fingerboard with dot inlay, 6-on-a-side Schaller tuners, tune-o-matic bridge/custom through-body bolt chevron V stop tailpiece, chrome hardware, 3 ER single coil pickups, master volume/master treble-cut tone controls, 5-way selector switch, available in Black, Red, Turquoise, or Yellow finishes, mfg. 1987-present.

MSR $2,400	$2,200	$1,500	$1,350	$1,200	$1,000	$800	$600

Add $100 for Wilkinson VSV tremolo (Model AS-57-VT). Add $200 for Floyd Rose tremolo (Model AS-57-FR).

BIKER - alder body shaped like gas tank on a motorcycle, 6-bolt maple neck, 25.5 in. scale, 22-fret rosewood or maple fingerboard with dot inlay, 6-on-a-side Schaller tuners, Wilkinson VSV tremolo, 3 Lace Sensor single coil pickups, master volume/master treble-cut tone controls, 5-way selector switch, available in Black Flame, Red Flame, or Yellow Flame finishes, mfg. 1997-present.

MSR $1,795	$1,500	$1,200	$1,050	$950	$800	$600	$400

HOT ROD 327 - alder body, bolt-on maple neck, rosewood fingerboard, chrome hardware, volume/tone controls, 5-way selector, 3 DiMarzio single coil pickups, Wilkinson VSV tremolo, available in Flame Fade finish, mfg. 1997-present.

MSR $1,795	$1,500	$1,200	$1,050	$950	$800	$600	$400

HOT ROD 409 - similar to the Hot Rod 327, except features korina body, tune-o-matic bridge/stop tailpiece, 2 DiMarzio humbucking pickups, mfg. 1997-present.

MSR $1,650	$1,300	$1,050	$950	$850	$700	$500	$350

ELECTRIC: STANDARD SERIES

The Standard Series is produced in Czechoslovakia.

AS-57 - alder body shaped like the tailfin of a '57 Chevy, operational chromed tailfin brake-light assembly, 6-bolt maple neck, 25.5 in. scale, 22-fret rosewood fingerboard with dot inlay, 6-on-a-side Schaller tuners, Schaller tune-o-matic bridge/V-shaped stop tailpiece, chrome hardware, 3 Showster single coil pickups, volume/tone controls, 5-way selector switch, available in Black, Red, or Turquoise finishes, mfg. 1997-present.

MSR $1,399	$1,100	$900	$825	$700	$575	$450	$325

BIKER-FM - alder body shaped like a gas tank on a motorcycle, 6-bolt maple neck, 25.5 in. scale, 22-fret rosewood fingerboard with dot inlay, 6-on-a-side Schaller tuners, chrome hardware, Schaller tune-o-matic bridge/V-shaped stop tailpiece, 3 Showster single coil pickups, volume/tone controls, 5-way selector switch, available in Black with Hot 3-Tone Flame finish, mfg. 1997-present.

MSR $1,199	$800	$700	$625	$550	$475	$350	$275

This model is also available with 2 Showster Humbucking pickups (with individual splitters).

Biker-TD - similar to the Biker-FM, available in Black, Red, and Turquoise Two-Tone Tear Drop finishes, mfg. 1997-present.

MSR $999	$700	$600	$525	$450	$350	$250	$150

This model is also available with 2 Showster Humbucking pickups (with individual splitters).

ICE PICK - offset double cutaway alder body, bolt-on neck, 25.5 in. scale, 22-fret fingerboard with dot inlay, Schaller tune-o-matic bridge/V-shaped stop tailpiece, 6-on-a-side Schaller tuners, 3 Showster single coil pickups, chrome hardware, volume/tone controls, 5-way selector, available in Black, Sea Foam (Green), Trans. Green, or Trans. Red finishes, mfg. 1997-present.

MSR $799	$550	$450	$375	$325	$275	$225	$150

This model is also available with 2 single coil/humbucker (with splitter) pickups.

ELECTRIC BASS

AS-57 BASS (MODEL AS-57-B) - alder body shaped like the tailfin of a '57 Chevy, operational chromed tailfin brake-light assembly, 6-bolt maple neck, 22-fret rosewood or maple fingerboard with dot inlay, 4-on-a-side Schaller tuners, BadAss II bridge, chrome hardware, P/J-style EMG pickups, volume/tone controls, pickup selector switch, available in Black, Red, Turquoise, or Yellow finishes, mfg. 1996-present.

MSR $2,600	$2,400	$1,900	$1,700	$1,500	$1,200	$900	$600

AMKA

Instruments previously built in Holland.

Amka instruments were produced by the Veneman family. Later, Kope Veneman moved to the U.S. and opened a music store in Maryland. In the 1960s, Kope Veneman introduced the Kapa instrument line, and his crown shield logo was similar to his father's Amka logo (source: Michael Wright, *Guitar Stories* Volume One).

AMPEG/DAN ARMSTRONG AMPEG

See also Armstrong, Dan. Instruments previously built in the U.S. from the early 1960s through the early 1970s. Burns by Ampeg instruments were imported from Britain between 1963 and 1964. Some Ampeg AEB-1 style models with magnetic pickups were built in Japan, and distributed by both Ampeg and Selmer (circa 1970s). Current models are built in the U.S., and distributed by St. Louis Music, Inc. of St. Louis, Missouri.

The Ampeg company was founded in late 1940s by Everett Hull and Jess Oliver. While this company is perhaps better known for its **B-15** "flip top" **Portaflex** or **SVT** bass amplifiers, the company did build various electric guitar and bass designs during the 1960s. As both Hull and Oliver came from jazz music traditions (and were musicians), the first Ampeg bass offered was an electric upright-styled **Baby Bass**. Constructed of fiberglass bodies and wood necks, a forerunner to the Baby Bass was produced by the Dopyera Brothers (See DOBRO and VALCO) as an electric pickup-equipped upright mini-bass under the **Zorko** trademark. In 1962, Everett Hull from Ampeg acquired the rights to the design. Hull and others improved the design, and Jess Oliver devised a new 'diaphragm-style' pickup.

During the early 1960s, Ampeg imported Burns-built electric guitars and basses from England. Burns instruments had been available in the U.S. market under their own trademark prior to the distribution deal. Five models were briefly distributed by Ampeg, and bear the "Ampeg by Burns of London" designation on the pickguard.

With the relative success of the Ampeg electric upright and their tube bass amps among jazz and studio musicians, Ampeg launched their first production solid body electric bass in 1966. Named the **AEB-1** (Ampeg Electric Bass), this model was designed by Dennis Kager. Ampeg also offered the **AUB-1**

GRADING	100% MINT	98% NEAR MINT	95% EXC+	90% EXC	80% VG+	70% VG	60% G

(Ampeg Unfretted Bass) in late 1966. Conversely, the Fender Instrument company did not release a fretless model until 1970, and even then Fender's first model was a fretless Precision (which is ironic considering the name and Leo Fender's design intention back in 1951). Both instruments featured the Ampeg scroll headstock, and a pair of f-holes that were designed through the body. A third model, the ASB-1/AUSB-1, was designed by Mike Roman.

Both the fretted and fretless models feature exaggerated body horns, which have been nicknamed "devil horns" by vintage guitar collectors.

Everett Hull sold the Ampeg company to a group of investors in 1967. Unimusic, lead by Al Dauray, John Forbes, and Ray Mucci, continued to offer the inventively shaped Ampeg basses through 1970. Ampeg introduced the SVT bass amplifier and V-4 guitar amp stack in 1968, again making their mark in the music business.

In 1969, luthier/designer Dan Armstrong devised a guitar that had a wood neck and a plastic lucite body. The purpose of the lucite was to increase sustain, and was not intended as a gimmick. Nevertheless, the guitars and basses gained the nickname see-through, and were produced from 1969 to 1971. The instruments featured formica pickguards that read "Dan Armstrong Ampeg" and clear acrylic bodies (although a small number were cast in black acrylic as well).

Ampeg continued to offer guitars and basses during the mid-1970s. The Stud series of guitar and bass models were produced in Asia. In the late 1970s, Ampeg teamed up with the Swedish Hagstrom company to design an early guitar synthesizer. Dubbed the Patch 2000, the system consisted of a guitar and a footpedal-controlled box which generated the synthesizer sounds. While advertising included both guitar and bass models, it is unlikely that any of the bass systems ever got beyond the prototype stage.

In 1997, Ampeg released a number of updated designs and reissue models. Both the AEB-2 and AUB-2 combine modern pickup design and construction with the looks of their 1960s counterparts, the Baby Bass was re-introduced, and even the Dan Armstrong-approved Lucite guitars were reproduced (source: Tony Bacon and Barry Moorhouse, *The Bass Book*, and Paul Day, *The Burns Book*).

In 1966, Jess Oliver left Ampeg to form Oliver Sound, and released a number of his own musical products. Oliver is still offering electronic services of repairs and modifications through the Oliver Sound company: 225 Avoca Avenue, Massapequa Park, NY 11762. Phone 516.799.5267.

MODEL DATING IDENTIFICATION

Due to various corporate purchases of Ampeg, production records have been lost or accidentally destroyed. Model productions are estimates based on incomplete records.

1962: Ampeg debuts the Baby Bass.

1963-1964: Importation of electric guitars and basses built by Burns; the five models are identical to the Burns models, except feature a pickguard inscribed "Ampeg by Burns of London".

1966-1970: Production of Ampeg's Horizontal bass models (AEB-1/AUB-1, ASB-1/AUSB-1, SSB-1/SSUB-1).

1969-1971: Dan Armstrong invents the Lucite-bodied guitar, nicknamed the See-Through.

Mid 1970s: The Stud series is imported in from Japan.

Late 1970s: Introduction of the Hagstrom-built Patch 2000 guitar synthesizer system.

1997: The Baby Bass is re-released, the Scroll Bass is released.

1998: The new Dan Armstrong series is released in bass and guitar format (based on the original design).

2001: The AMG1 guitar is released for "serious rock n´ roll" players. It was discontinued along with all other Ampeg instruments by 2002.

**Ampeg ASB-1 Devil Bass
courtesy Alvarez**

ELECTRIC: AMPEG BY BURNS OF LONDON SERIES

Between 1963 and 1964, Ampeg made an agreement with Burns of London to import in five models built in England. All five are directly identical to the Burns version, with the exception that the pickguard´s logo read "Ampeg by Burns of London." All five models were renamed for the U.S. market.

SONIC SIX (MODEL EGSS) - offset double cutaway hardwood body with short horns, 23.375 in. scale, bolt-on neck, 22-fret rosewood fingerboard with white dot inlay, 6-on-a-side tuners, chrome hardware, black inscribed pickguard, 2 Burns ´Nu-Sonic´ single coil pickups, bridge/tremolo tailpiece, volume/2 tone controls, 3-way selector switch, available in Cherry finish, mfg. 1963-64.

N/A	$450	$375	$300	$250	$200	$150

This model was built by the Burns Guitar company, and basically is a renamed Nu-Sonic.

THINLINE (MODEL EGT-1) - offset double cutaway semi-solid body (solid center section), 2 f-holes, white body binding, bolt-on neck, 24.75 in. scale, 22-fret bound rosewood fingerboard with white dot inlay, 3-per-side tuners, bound headstock, bridge/tremolo tailpiece, 2 Burns ´Ultra-Sonic´ pickups, raised black inscribed pickguard with volume/bass/treble roller controls mounted underneath, 3-way selector switch, available in Red Sunburst finish, mfg. 1963-64.

N/A	$450	$375	$300	$250	$200	$150

This instrument was built by the Burns Guitar company, and basically is a renamed TR 2 (originally "TRansistorized 2 Pickup" designation).

WILD DOG (MODEL EG1-S) - offset double cutaway hardwood body with inward curving horns, 23.375 in. scale, bolt-on neck, 22-fret rosewood fingerboard with white dot inlay, 6-on-a-side tuners, chrome hardware, black inscribed pickguard, 3 Burns ´Split-Sonic´ pickups, bridge/tremolo tailpiece, volume/tone controls, 4-way selector switch, available in Red Sunburst finish, mfg. 1963-64.

N/A	$450	$375	$300	$250	$200	$150

This instrument was built by the Burns Guitar company, and basically is a renamed Jazz Split Sound. The four notable tone settings on this model include Treble, Bass, Split-Sound, and mondo-popular Wild Dog.

**Ampeg ARMB-2
Dan Armstrong Bass
Blue Book Publications**

GRADING	100% MINT	98% NEAR MINT	95% EXC+	90% EXC	80% VG+	70% VG	60% G

Deluxe Wild Dog (Model EG-3) - similar to the Wild Dog, except has a shorter horn double cutaway body, 24.75 in. scale, available in Red Sunburst finish, mfg. 1963-64.

	N/A	$500	$425	$350	$275	$225	$175

This instrument was built by the Burns Guitar company, and basically is a renamed Split Sonic.

ELECTRIC: DAN ARMSTRONG & AMG SERIES (RECENT MFG.)

In 2001, Ampeg released the infamous Dan Armstrong guitars and basses. These new reissue models were based on the same design as the old models along with a new guitar with AAA grade maple, the AMG1. By 2002, the whole line of guitars and basses were discontinued in the Ampeg line.

ADAG1 - double cutaway clear acrylic style body, maple neck with 24-fret rosewood fingerboard, 24.75 in. scale, rosewood bridge, RT and MD pickups by Keng Armstrong, 3-on-a-side tuners, chrome hardware, brown woodgrain removable pickguard, wood-grain headstock, volume and tone knobs, 3-position switch, available in clear, see-through finish only, mfg. 1998-2001.

	$1,000	$850	$775	$725	$650	$575	$500

Last MSR was $1,499.

ADAG2 - similar to the ADAG1 except has a smoked black acrylic body, mfg. 1998-2001.

	$1,050	$875	$800	$725	$650	$575	$500

Last MSR was $1,549.

AMG1 - double cutaway clear mahogany body with quilted top, maple neck with 22-fret rosewood fingerboard, 24.75 in. scale, Wilkinson wraparound bridge, 2 Seymour Duncan SP-90 pickups, 3-on-a-side tuners, chrome hardware, black pickguard, matching color headstock, volume and tone knobs, 3-position switch, available in Amber Burst, Purple Burst, Black Cherry, and Trans. Black, mfg. 2001 only.

	$750	$675	$625	$575	$500	$425	$375

Last MSR was $1,099.

ELECTRIC: ORIGINAL DAN ARMSTRONG SERIES

ARMG-2 DAN ARMSTRONG - clear lucite body, bolt-on maple neck, 24.5 in. scale, 24-fret rosewood fingerboard, Schaller (or Grover) tuners, adjustable straight bar bridge, 1 (interchangeable) pickup, volume/tone controls, mfg. 1969-1971.

	N/A	$1,600	$1,350	$1,150	$950	$750	$600

Last MSR was $340.

Add 20% for Black lucite bodies (end of production).

This model is nicknamed the See-Through guitar; Ampeg later had this title copy written for the model.

ELECTRIC: STUD SERIES (JAPAN)

STUD (GE-100) - double sharp cutaway body (SG style), bolt-on neck, 21-fret maple fingerboard with white block inlay, 3-per-side tuners, chrome hardware, Bigsby-style bridge (Model GET-100), black pickguard, 2 covered humbucker pickups, four volume/tone controls, 3-way pickup selector, mfg. 1973-75.

	N/A	$250	$210	$180	$150	$125	$95

HEAVY STUD (GE-150) - single cutaway body, bolt-on maple neck, 21-fret maple fingerboard with white block inlay, 3-per-side tuners, chrome hardware, Bigsby-style bridge (GEH-150), white pickguard, covered humbucker/single coil pickups, volume/tone controls, 3-way pickup selector, controls mounted on metal plate, mfg. 1973-75.

	N/A	$325	$275	$245	$225	$175	$125

SUPER STUD (GE-500) - double sharp cutaway body (SG style), bolt-on neck, 21-fret fingerboard with white block inlay, 3-per-side tuners, chrome hardware, Bigsby-style bridge, black pickguard, 2 covered humbucker pickups, four volume/tone controls, 3-way pickup selector, mfg. 1973-75.

	N/A	$350	$300	$275	$250	$200	$150

ELECTRIC BASS: HORIZONTAL BASS (AEB-1, AUB-1, & ASB-1) SERIES

AEB-1 - single smooth cutaway, cutaway f-holes, black pickguard covering most of the body with Ampeg on bass side, 20-fret rosewood or blonde fingerboard with dot inlay, open scroll style headstock, "myserious" hidden pickup under bridge, two knobs, bridge extending past body, available in white, sunburst, or red finishes, mfg. 1966-69.

	N/A	$1,500	$1,300	$1,100	$950	$750	$500

The "mysterious" pickup was a variation of the pickup used on the Baby Bass. This is a different type of arrangement in the pickup that allows for non-magnetic strings to be used.

AUB-1 - similar to the AEB-1, except has a fretless fingerboard, mfg. 1966-69.

	N/A	$1,600	$1,400	$1,200	$1,000	$750	$500

ASB-1 DEVIL BASS - double cutaway "long-horned" body, triangle cutouts, black pickguard covering most of body, 20-fret fingerboard with dot inlay, open scroll style headstock, two knobs, single hidden pickup under the bridge, mfg. 1967-68.

	N/A	$2,800	$2,500	$2,200	$1,800	$1,300	$800

These basses were produced very few at a time and they are very rare. The horns are designed to allow access to the higher fingerboard easily.

ASUB-1 Devil Bass - similar to the ASB-1 Bass, except has a fretless fingerboard, mfg. 1967-68.

	N/A	$3,000	$2,600	$2,200	$1,800	$1,400	$950

GRADING	100% MINT	98% NEAR MINT	95% EXC+	90% EXC	80% VG+	70% VG	60% G

ELECTRIC BASS: ORIGINAL BABY BASS SERIES

BABY BASS 4-STRING (BB-4) - 3/4 sized upright-bass style, similar to a violin or cello shape, fiberglass body and later made of Uvex, 41 in. scale length, f-holes, retractable end pin, open-style headstock, fretless fingerboard, available in Mahogany Wood Grain, White, Red, Black, or Turquoise finishes, mfg. 1962-1972.

	N/A	$2,000	$1,700	$1,400	$1,000	$700	$500

Add $300 for red, white, or black finish. Add $500 for turquoise finish.

BABY BASS 5-STRING (BB-5) - similar to the BB-4, except in five-string configuration, available mfg. 1964-1971.

	N/A	$2,200	$1,800	$1,400	$1,000	$700	$500

Add $300 for Red, White, or Black finish. Add $500 for turquoise finish.

ELECTRIC BASS: ORIGINAL DAN ARMSTRONG SERIES

ARMB-2 DAN ARMSTRONG BASS - clear lucite body, bolt-on maple neck, 30 1/2" scale, 24-fret rosewood fingerboard, Schaller tuners, adjustable straight bar bridge, 2 (stacked) pickups, volume/tone controls, pickup selector switch, mfg. 1970-71.

	N/A	$1,350	$1,150	$1,000	$850	$725	$600

Last MSR was $340.

This model was available with a fretless fingerboard.

WILD DOG BASS (MODEL EB-3) - offset double (almost dual) cutaway hardwood body with short horns, 31.5 in. scale, bolt-on neck, 20 fret rosewood fingerboard with white dot inlay, 4-on-a-side tuners, chrome hardware, black inscribed pickguard, 3 Burns 'Tri-Sonic' pickups, bridge/tailpiece, volume/tone controls, 4-way selector switch, available in Red Sunburst finish, mfg. 1963-64.

	N/A	$500	$425	$350	$275	$225	$175

This instrument was built by the Burns Guitar company, and basically is a renamed Vista Sonic.

ARMG-2 DAN ARMSTRONG
courtesy Dave Rogers
Dave's Guitar Shop

ELECTRIC BASS: SCROLL BASS REISSUE SERIES

In 1997, Ampeg offered the **AEB-2** and the **AUB-2**. Designed and developed by Bruce Johnson (Johnson's Extremely Strange Musical Instrument Company of Burbank, California) in cooperation with Ampeg beginning in 1995, the first prototypes were completed in November, 1996. Rather than just release a historic reissue, Johnson sought to marry the eye-catching original body design to state-of-the-art electronics and neck construction.

AEB-2 (FRETTED) - offset double cutaway western ash body, bolt-on rock maple neck, 35 in. scale, 20-fret ebony fingerboard with white dot inlay, scroll headstock, aluminum bridge, brass tailpiece and nut, 2-per-side Schaller tuners, chrome hardware, humbucking magnetic pickup, bridge-mounted piezo pickups, 2 volume/tone controls, 3-position tone select switch, available in Solid Black (Model AEB-2 BL), Black with Natural Neck (Model AEB-2 BT), Natural (Model AEB-2 NT), and Sunburst (Model AEB-2 SB) finishes, mfg. 1997-2000.

$1,750	$1,500	$1,300	$1,100	$950	$800	$650

Last MSR was $2,000.

Add $100 for Solid Black (Model AEB-2 BL) and Sunburst (Model AEB-2 SB) finishes. Add $100 for gold hardware: Solid Black (Model AEB-2 BL G), Black with Natural Neck (Model AEB-2 BT G), Natural (Model AEB-2 NT G), and Sunburst (Model AEB-2 SB G) finishes.

The pickup/on-board 18-volt preamp system was developed by Rick Turner.

AUB-2 (Fretless) - similar to the AEB-2, except has fretless fingerboard, available in Solid Black (Model AUB-2 BL), Black with Natural Neck (Model AUB-2 BT), Natural (Model AUB-2 NT), and Sunburst (Model AUB-2 SB) finishes, mfg. 1997-2000.

$1,750	$1,500	$1,300	$1,100	$950	$800	$650

Last MSR was $2,000.

Add $100 for left-handed configuration ("L" code designation). Add $100 for Solid Black (Model AUB-2 BL) and Sunburst (Model AUB-2 SB) finishes. Add $100 for gold hardware: Solid Black (Model AUB-2 BL G), Black with Natural Neck (Model AUB-2 BT G), Natural (Model AUB-2 NT G), and Sunburst (Model AUB-2 SB G) finishes.

ABB-1 BABY BASS - upright sloped shoulder urethane foam/fiberglass body with internal aluminum structure, bolt-on tilt-adjustable hard rock maple neck, 41.5 in. scale, fretless Macassar ebony fingerboard, open slot scroll headstock, 2-per-side chrome tuners, rock maple bridge, black finished aluminum tailpiece, dual coil Alnico magnetic diaphragm pickup, dual piezo-electric element pickups, Master volume/active blend/tone controls, available in Solid Black (Model ABB-1 BK), Solid Red (Model ABB-1 RD), Solid White (Model ABB-1 WH), or Sunburst (Model ABB-1 SB) finishes, mfg. 1997-2000.

$2,600	$2,200	$1,900	$1,600	$1,300	$1,050	$800

Last MSR was $3,600.

Add $100 for Sunburst (Model ABB-1 SB) finish.

ADAB1 - double cutaway clear acrylic style body, 4-string, maple neck with 24-fret rosewood fingerboard, brown removable pickguard, brown headstock, 30 in. scale, carved rosewood bridge, BB and DB pickups by Kent Armstrong, volume and tone knobs, two-position switch, available in clear finish only, mfg. 1997-2001.

$1,000	$825	$750	$700	$625	$525	$450

Last MSR was $1,499.

Ampeg AEB-2 (Fretted)
courtesy Bass Palace

GRADING	100% MINT	98% NEAR MINT	95% EXC+	90% EXC	80% VG+	70% VG	60% G

ADAB2 - similar to the ADAB1 except has smoked black acrylic body, mfg. 1997-2001.

| | $1,050 | $850 | $775 | $725 | $625 | $525 | $450 |

Last MSR was $1,549.

AMB1 - double cutaway basswood body, 4-string, maple neck with 24-fret rosewood fingerboard, black pickguard, matching color headstock, 30 in. scale, carved rosewood bridge, 1 Seymour Duncan SMD-4 Basslines pickup, volume and tone knobs, two-position switch, available in Blue Pearl, Black Pearl, or Purple Metallic, mfg. 2001 only.

| | $635 | $550 | $475 | $425 | $375 | $325 | $275 |

Last MSR was $899.

Add $50 for Quilted top with Black Cherry, Amber Burst, or Purple Burst colors.

ELECTRIC BASS: STUD SERIES (JAPAN)

GEB-101 LITTLE STUD - double cutaway P-Bass style, 20-fret neck with block inlay, black pickguard, metal cover over pickup and cover over bridge, two knobs, single input, 2-per-side tuners, available in various colors, mfg. 1973-75.

| | N/A | $350 | $300 | $250 | $200 | $150 | $100 |

GEB-750 BIG STUD - double cutaway early 50s P-Bass style, 20-fret neck, pearl pickguard, exposed single pickup and cover over bridge, two knobs, single input, 2-per-side tuners, available natural and possibly other various colors, mfg. 1973-75.

| | N/A | $400 | $350 | $300 | $250 | $200 | $150 |

ANDERBILT

Instruments previously built in Corpus Christi or Brownsville, Texas during the mid- to late 1960s.

With the help of repairman Gene Warner of Meteor Music (San Antonio), Teisco Del Rey attempted to track down the origins of the Anderbilt (also possibly Andertone) guitars. The builder was rumored to be a Baptist minster and the educated guess was made that his last name was Anderson.

The most striking feature of Anderbilt guitars is the vibrato: rather than being located on the bridge or tailpiece, the neck is the mechanism! Built in the style of a pump shotgun, the entire neck has to be pushed in toward the body and pulled away to raise or lower the pitch. Features on the guitar include a six-on-a-side headstock, 2 pickups, a "coat-of-arms" body design, and separate volume and tone knobs for each pickup. Anyone with further information to share on the Anderbilt guitars is invited to write to the *Blue Book of Electric Guitars* (source: Teisco Del Rey, *Guitar Player Magazine*, October 1988).

ANDERSON STRINGED INSTRUMENTS

Please refer to the *Blue Book of Acoustic Guitars.*

ANDREAS

Instruments previously manufactured in Dollach, Austria 1995-2004. During 2003, Andreas Guitars became a part of Thomastik-Infeld, established and located in Vienna, Austria since the early 1920s. Even though production has stopped (approx. 300 were manufactured total), some Andreas dealers may still have unsold new instruments in their inventory. Previously distributed by Connolly & Co, located in East Northport, NY.

ELECTRIC GUITARS

On recent production Andreas models, standard features include: a bolt-on maple neck/fingerboard with red stripe, custom-made single coil and humbucking pickups by Harry Haüssel, wood headstock, and unique softcoating finish. Approx. 400 Andreas guitars (electric and bass) have been manufactured to date.

On models manufactured before 2002, standard features included: brushed galvanized aluminum fingerboards glued to maple necks, 22 or 24 frets, graphite nut, 4-bolt necks, ergonomically contoured bodies, Gotoh Side Adjuster truss rod, matte chrome finish Schaller hardware and matte-finished bodies. In 2002 the only available colors were black, yellow, and green.

SHARK GUITAR - single cutaway ergonomically contoured body, maple (disc. 2002), mahogany (H-type, new 2003), or red alder (S-type, new 2003) body, maple (new 2003) or aluminum (disc. 2002) fingerboard and headstock, 22 jumbo frets, 6-on-a-side tuners, available with custom made Harry Haussel pickups (single coil or humbucker, new 2003), or EMG/Seymour Duncan pickups (disc. 2002), Gotch (new 2003) or Schaller (disc. 2002) locking tuners, Wilkinson (new 2003) or Schaller 2000 (disc. 2002) tremolo/tailpiece, unique softcoating finish, Blue, Red, Black, Yellow (disc. 2002), Green (disc. 2002) or Nature Sunburst White (Gray Shark, disc. 2002) finishes.

| | $2,995 | $2,500 | $2,200 | $1,650 | $1,350 | $975 | $750 |

Last MSR was $3,900.

FIERCE SHARK - similar to Shark, except body is constructed of Western Larch, then sandblasted, stained, and literally burned to give it its 3-D layered appearance, available in Sandblasted, Stained, Burnt finish, disc. 2002.

| | $1,450 | $1,175 | $995 | $850 | $725 | $600 | $500 |

Last MSR was $2,005 - $2,615.

SILVERTIP SHARK - similar to other Shark models except has two single coil pickups and 1 humbucker pickup, available in Nature White Sunburst, Nature Black Sunburst, and stained Black Matte finishes, disc. 2002.

| | $975 | $850 | $775 | $700 | $625 | $550 | $475 |

Last MSR was $1,425.

ANDREAS INFELD GUITAR - asymmetrical body design, red alder body, bolt-on maple neck with red stripe, Wilkinson bridge/tremolo, 18/22 frets, 3 custom Harry Haussel single coil pickups, Gotch tuners, 25.59 in. scale, unique soft coating finish, available in Red or Black, new 2003.

| | $2,350 | $2,000 | $1,700 | $1,450 | $1,200 | $995 | $750 |

Last MSR was $3,350.

GRADING	100% MINT	98% NEAR MINT	95% EXC+	90% EXC	80% VG+	70% VG	60% G

ELECTRIC BASS

BASKING SHARK - choice of maple or ash body, 5 strings, balanced ergonomically designed body, aluminum fingerboard, Schaller BM Light tuners, Schaller 2000 Series 3 dimensionally adjustable bridge, 2 Alembic AE-3 Soapbar pickups with active circuitry, volume, balance, bass and high controls, handmade Thomastik-Infeld strings, also available in 4-string and fretless configurations, available in Stained Sunburst, Sunburst Orange, Sunburst Blue, and Nature Sunburst matte finishes, limited mfg., disc. 2002.

	$2,150	$1,875	$1,600	$1,400	$1,200	$995	$850

Last MSR was $2,905-$3,055.

BULL SHARK - similar to Basking Shark except has Tobacco Sunburst Matte finish, also available in 4-string and fretless configurations, limited mfg., disc. 2002.

	$2,100	$1,825	$1,600	$1,400	$1,200	$995	$850

Last MSR was $2,800-$2,940.

SHARK BASS - body shape similar to Basking Shark, 4- or 5-string, red alder body, bolt-on 24-fret maple neck, two Bartollini pickups, Schaller tuners, unique softcoating finish, available in Red or Black, new 2003.

	$2,995	$2,500	$2,200	$1,650	$1,350	$975	$750

Last MSR was $3,900.

Anderbilt Electric courtesy Dave Rogers Dave's Guitar Shop

ANGELICA
Instruments previously built in Japan from circa 1967 to 1975.

The Angelica trademark is a brand name used by UK importers Boosey & Hawkes on these entry-level guitars and basses based on classic American designs. Some of the original designs produced for Angelica are actually better in quality (source: Tony Bacon and Paul Day, *The Guru's Guitar Guide*).

Angelica instruments were not distributed to the U.S. market. Some models may be encountered in the U.S., but the average price for these guitars ranges around $100 to $150.

ANGELO
Instruments currently produced in Thailand. Distributed by T. Angelo Industrial Co., Ltd., of Bangkok, Thailand.

Don't let the Thailand address fool you - the T. Angelo Industrial company is building credible acoustic and electric guitar models based on classic American designs. The prices are in the entry to intermediate players range, with acoustic retailing between $185 and $260, and acoustic/electrics ranging from $499 to $595. The A'50 and A'60 Vintage Strat-ish models fall between $450 to $545. Hot-rodded modern designs with locking tremolo systems run a bit higher ($540 to $675).

ANTORIA
See GUYATONE. Instruments previously built in Japan in the 1950s, later switching to Korean-built models.

The ANTORIA trademark was a brand name used by a UK importer for guitars produced by Guyatone. Guyatone began building guitars in 1933, and started producing solid body electrics in the late 1950s. While the original Antorias were cheap entry-level models, the quality level rose when production switched to the same factory that was producing Ibanez guitars. Currently, the trademark has been applied to solid and semi-hollowbody guitars built in Korea (source: Tony Bacon and Paul Day, *The Guru's Guitar Guide*).

APOLLO
Instruments previously produced in Japan from early to mid-1970s. Distributed in the U.S. by St. Louis Music of St. Louis, Missouri.

Apollo instruments were generally entry-level to student-quality guitars that featured original designs which incorporated some American design ideas as well as some Burns-inspired pointy body shapes. St. Louis Music, the American distributors, switched from Valco-built Custom Craft models to the Japanese-produced instruments in the 1970s when domestic sources dried up. This product line included thinline hollow body electric archtops as well as solid body guitars and basses.

Most of the Apollo instruments were built by Kawai, who also produced Teisco guitars during this time period. St. Louis Music also introduced their Electra trademark in 1971 (classic American-based designs), and phased out Apollo instruments sometime in the mid-1970s. Apollo was St. Louis Music's budget line brand (source: Michael Wright, *Vintage Guitar Magazine*).

While technically a vintage instrument (based on date of production), market desirability dictates the prices found for Apollo guitars. Examine the construction quality of the hollowbody models (especially the neck pocket) before spending the big bucks! Prices should range between $75 and $125, depending on condition and playability.

ARBITER
Instruments previously built in Japan during the mid-1960s to late-1970s.

The ARBITER trademark is the brand of a UK importer. Original models are of entry level quality, later models are good quality copy designs and some original designs (source: Tony Bacon and Paul Day, *The Guru's Guitar Guide*).

Andreas Shark courtesy Andreas

GRADING	100% MINT	98% NEAR MINT	95% EXC+	90% EXC	80% VG+	70% VG	60% G

ARBOR

Instruments currently manufactured in Asia. Distributed in the U.S. by Midco International of Effingham, Illinois.

Arbor guitars are aimed at the entry-level student to the intermediate player. The Midco International company imported and distributed both acoustic and solid body guitars to the U.S. market for a good number of years. Musicorp is now the distributor and they only sell acoustic models. For more information, see the *Blue Book of Acoustic Guitars*.

ELECTRIC

Electric Arbor solid body guitars feature a range of designs based on classic American designs. Again, hardware and pickup options are geared towards the entry-level and student players. Most models feature bolt-on neck designs, laminate bodies and solid finishes, and adjustable truss rods. "Superstrat" models built in the early 1990s had new retail list prices ranging from $319 to $399. 4-string bass models with P/J pickups ranged from $369 to $429.

ARCH KRAFT

Instruments previously built by the Kay Musical Instrument Company of Chicago, Illinois during the early 1930s.

These entry level acoustic flattop and archtop guitars were built by Kay (one of the three U.S. jobber guitar companies), and distributed through various outlets. Arch Kraft developed a tilt-neck adjustment for the Venetian Kay Kraft models around the 1920s. Arch Kraft produced guitars between the 1920s and the 1960s. Used models in excellent condition can be priced between $150 and $300 (source: Michael Wright, *Vintage Guitar Magazine*).

ARDSLEYS

Instruments previously built in Japan during the mid-1960s.

These entry level instruments can also be found with "Elite" or "Canora" on the headstock, depending on the U.S. importer. A fine example of a matching set can be found on the cover of The Shaggs "Philosophy of the World" LP (reissued by Rounder Records).

ARIA/ARIA PRO II

Instruments currently produced in Japan since 1956. Current models are produced in the U.S., Japan, Korea, China, Indonesia, and Spain. Distributed in the U.S. market by Aria USA/NHF Musical Merchandise Inc. of Pennsauken, NJ.

ARIA is the trademark of the Aria Company of Japan, which began producing guitars in 1956. Prior to 1975, the trademark was either Aria or Aria Diamond.

Original designs in the 1960s gave way to a greater emphasis on replicas of American designs in the late 1970s. Ironically, the recognition of these well-produced replicas led to success in later years as the company returned to producing original designs. The Aria trademark has always reflected high production quality, and currently there has been more emphasis on stylish designs (such as the Fullerton guitar series, or in bass designs such as the AVB-SB). The Aria company has produced instruments under their Aria/Aria Diamond/Aria Pro II trademark for a number of years. They have also built instruments distributed under the Univox and Cameo labels as well. Aria also offers the Ariana line of acoustic steel-string and nylon-string models.

ELECTRIC: GENERAL INFORMATION

Aria has been producing guitars since 1956 and they have not been shy about introducing, changing, discontinuing, and reintroducing guitars. Therefore, there are literally hundreds of different Aria models out there. It is next to impossible to try to get every one listed in the book. However, we have tried to take the most popular ones and get them listed. Keep looking in future editions for updated listings, as more information surfaces daily.

ELECTRIC: 615 SERIES

This series has bolt-on maple necks (with 5 bolts), pearloid pickguard with 3-Tone Sunburst and Red finishes, and red pickguard with White finish.

5 615 CST (U.S. MFG.) - single sharp cutaway alder body, pickguard, metal controls plate, 22-fret rosewood fingerboard with pearl dot inlay, strings through Wilkinson bridge, screened peghead logo, 6-on-a-side tuners with pearloid buttons, chrome hardware, 3 single coil Seymour Duncan pickups, volume/tone controls, one 5-position/1 mini-rhythm switches, available in 3-Tone Sunburst, See-Through Red, or Off-White finishes, mfg. 1995-98.

	$700	$600	$500	$425	$350	$325	$275
					Last MSR was $999.		

5 615 DLX (U.S. MFG.) - similar to 5 615 CST, except has 3 Don Lace single coil pickups, mfg. 1995-98.

	$600	$500	$425	$350	$300	$275	$250
					Last MSR was $850.		

5 615 SPL - similar to 5 615 CST, except has 2 single coil Aria pickups, available in 3-Tone Sunburst, Red, or White finishes, mfg. 1995-98.

	$295	$250	$225	$200	$175	$150	$125
					Last MSR was $399.		

5 615 STD - similar to 5 615 CST, except has 3 Aria single coil pickups, available in 3-Tone Sunburst, See-Through Red, or Off White finishes, mfg. 1995-98.

	$475	$425	$375	$325	$295	$250	$200
					Last MSR was $679.		

ELECTRIC: AQUANOTE SERIES

CR 60 - offset double cutaway alder body, bolt-on maple neck, 24-fret rosewood fingerboard with pearl dot inlay, standard vibrato, 6-on-a-side locking tuners, chrome hardware, 2 single coil/1 humbucker pickups, volume/tone control, 5-position switch, coil split on tone control, available in Black, Midnight Cherry, Navy Blue, or Pearl White finishes, disc. 1993.

	N/A	$550	$475	$425	$375	$325	$250
					Last MSR was $850.		

GRADING	100% MINT	98% NEAR MINT	95% EXC+	90% EXC	80% VG+	70% VG	60% G

CR 65 - similar to CR 60, except has black hardware, single coil/humbucker pickups, 3-position and separate coil split switches, available in Amber Natural, Dark Red Shade, or Purple Shade finishes, disc. 1993.

	N/A	$600	$525	$475	$425	$350	$275

Last MSR was $950.

CR 65/12 - similar to CR 60, except has 12 strings, fixed bridge, disc. 1993.

	N/A	$575	$500	$425	$375	$325	$275

Last MSR was $850.

CR 80 - offset double cutaway carved top alder body, set-in maple neck, 24-fret rosewood fingerboard with pearl dot inlay, non-locking vibrato, 6-on-a-side locking tuners, black hardware, CS-2AL single coil/humbucker pickups, volume/tone control, 3-position switch, coil split in tone control, available in Black, Midnight Cherry, or Pearl White finishes, disc. 1993.

	N/A	$675	$600	$525	$475	$425	$350

Last MSR was $1,000.

CR 100 - offset double cutaway carved top ash body, set-in maple neck, 24-fret rosewood fingerboard with pearl oval inlay, non-locking vibrato, 6-on-a-side locking tuners, silver black hardware, Seymour Duncan single coil/humbucker pickups, volume/tone control, 3-position switch, coil split in tone control, available in Blue Shade, Dark Red Shade, Purple Shade, or Vintage Sunburst finishes, disc. 1993.

	N/A	$900	$800	$700	$600	$500	$400

Last MSR was $1,500.

**Aria Pro II XL STD 3
courtesy Aria Pro II**

ELECTRIC: BLACK 'N GOLD LIMITED EDITION SERIES

In 1983, Aria released a number of guitar and bass models under the **Black 'N Gold Limited Editions**, which featured a Gloss Black finish and gold hardware. Guitar models included the **CS-400**, **PE-60**, **PE-R 80**, **TA-60**, and **TS-500**; Bass models included the **CSB-450** and **SB-R 80**. The Black 'N Gold models were applied to other models that were already in the Aria line. This option will add 10%-20% to the value of the original model.

ELECTRIC: EXCEL SERIES

XL STD 3 - offset double cutaway hardwood body, bolt-on maple neck, 22-fret bound rosewood fingerboard with pearl wedge inlay, standard vibrato, 6-on-a-side tuners, black hardware, 2 single coil/1 humbucker pickups, volume/tone control, 5-position switch, coil split in tone control, available in Black, Candy Apple, Midnight Blue, or White finishes, disc. 1995.

	$280	$240	$200	$160	$145	$130	$120

Last MSR was $400.

XL SPT 3 - similar to XL STD 3, except has KKT-2 double-locking vibrato, disc. 1991.

	$350	$300	$250	$200	$185	$165	$150

Last MSR was $500.

XL DLX 3 - similar to XL STD 3, except has ART-10 double-locking vibrato, disc. 1995.

	$360	$275	$260	$220	$200	$180	$165

Last MSR was $500.

XL CST 3 - similar to XL STD 3, except has curly maple top/back, ART-10 double locking vibrato, gold hardware, available in Trans. Black, Trans. Blue, or Trans. Red finishes, disc. 1994.

	$420	$360	$300	$240	$215	$195	$180

Last MSR was $600.

ELECTRIC: FULL ACOUSTIC (FA) SERIES

FA 50 E(BS) - all mahogany non-cutaway arched top with single floating mini-humbucker, vintage tuners, volume and tone controls mounted on pickguard, available in Brown Sunburst finish, mfg. 1999-present.

MSR $595		$450	$400	$350	$325	$295	$250	$200

FA 65 - single round cutaway hollow body, arched maple top/back/sides, bound body/f-holes, maple neck, 20-fret bound rosewood fingerboard with pearl block inlay, rosewood bridge, trapeze tailpiece, bound peghead with 3-per-side tuners, raised black pickguard, 2 humbucker pickups, 4 knobs, 3-position switch, chrome hardware, available in Brown Sunburst or Black finishes, mfg. 2004-present.

MSR $440		$330	$275	$240	$210	$180	$150	$120

FA 70 (JOHNNY SMITH) - single round cutaway hollow style, arched maple top/back/sides, bound body/f-holes, raised black pickguard, maple neck, 20-fret bound rosewood fingerboard with pearl split block inlay, rosewood bridge, trapeze tailpiece, bound peghead with pearl Aria Pro II logo and dove inlay, 3-per-side tuners, gold hardware, 2 humbucker pickups, 2 volume/tone controls, 3-position switch, available in Brown Sunburst and Vintage Sunburst finishes, mfg. 1991-present.

MSR $795		$600	$525	$450	$375	$325	$275	$225

In 1993, Brown Sunburst finish was disc. A similar model, the FA 70 TR was offered until 1992. This model had a tremolo tailpiece and the same construction. Later superseded by the FA 75 TR model. This model is also known as the Johnny Smith model.

FA 71 - similar to 5 FA 70, except has deeper body, one humbucking pickup and two knobs, mfg. 2001-present.

MSR $795		$600	$525	$450	$375	$325	$275	$225

GRADING	100% MINT	98% NEAR MINT	95% EXC+	90% EXC	80% VG+	70% VG	60% G

FA 75 TR - similar to 5 FA 70 VS, except has rosewood/metal bridge, vibrato tailpiece, mfg. 1992-93, reintroduced 2003-present.

	MSR	$895		$675	$600	$525	$450	$375	$300	$250

Last MSR was $800.

5 FA 80 - similar to the 5 FA 70 guitar except has maple carved top, and a VBT-2 Vibrato tailpiece (similar to a Bigsby), available in Orange, Wine Red, or Walnut finishes, mfg. 2001-present.

	MSR	$895		$675	$600	$550	$475	$400	$325	$275

ELECTRIC: FULLERTON SERIES

5 FL 05 - offset double cutaway alder body, white pickguard, bolt-on maple neck, 22-fret maple fingerboard with black dot inlay, stop tailpiece, screened peghead logo, 6-on-a-side tuners, chrome hardware, 3 single coil pickups, 1 volume/2 tone controls, 5-position switch, available in 3-Tone Sunburst, Black, Blue, or Red finishes, mfg. 1995-99.

$225	$195	$170	$150	$125	$100	$75

Last MSR was $299.

5 FL 10 S - similar to 5 FL 05, except has vintage tremolo, available in 3-Tone Sunburst, Black, Blue, or Red finishes, mfg. 1995-99.

$250	$215	$190	$165	$140	$115	$85

Last MSR was $329.

5 FL 10 SL - similar to 5 FL 10 S, except in left-handed configuration, available in 3-Tone Sunburst or Black finishes, mfg. 1995-99.

$270	$240	$215	$180	$150	$120	$90

Last MSR was $359.

5 FL 10 H - similar to 5 FL 05, except has standard vibrato, 2 single coil/1 humbucker pickups, coil tap, available in 3-Tone Sunburst, Black, or Red, mfg. 1995-99.

$260	$220	$195	$170	$140	$115	$85

Last MSR was $339.

5 FL 10 HL - similar to 5 FL 10 H, except in left-handed configuration, available in 3-Tone Sunburst or Black finishes, mfg. 1995-99.

$275	$240	$215	$185	$150	$125	$95

Last MSR was $369.

5 FL 20 S - offset double cutaway alder body, white pickguard, bolt-on maple neck, 22-fret rosewood fingerboard with pearl dot inlay, vintage tremolo, screened peghead logo, 6-on-a-side tuners, chrome hardware, 3 single coil pickups, 1 volume/2 tone controls, 5-position switch, available in 3-Tone Sunburst, See-Through Blue, or See-Through Red finishes, mfg. 1995-99.

$325	$280	$250	$215	$180	$145	$110

Last MSR was $429.

5 FL 20 H - similar to 5 FL 20 S, except has 2 single coil/1 humbucker pickups, 1 volume/1 tone controls, 5-position switch, 1 coil tap switch, mfg. 1995-99.

$340	$290	$255	$220	$185	$150	$115

Last MSR was $449.

5 FL 21 HSDW - offset double cutaway alder body, flamed tiger maple top, pearl pickguard, bolt-on maple neck, 22-fret rosewood fingerboard with pearl dot inlay, Wilkinson VS-50 tremolo, screened peghead logo, 6-on-a-side Gotoh tuners, chrome hardware, 2 Duncan Designed SC-101 single coil/1 Duncan Designed HB-103 humbucker pickups, 1 volume/1 tone controls, 5-position switch, coil tap switch, available in 3-Tone Sunburst, or See-Through Blue finishes, mfg. 1996-99.

$575	$520	$460	$395	$330	$265	$200

Last MSR was $799.

5 FL 30 H - offset double cutaway ash body, pearloid pickguard, bolt-on maple neck, 22-fret rosewood fingerboard with pearl dot inlay, knife edge tremolo system, screened peghead logo, 6-on-a-side Gotoh tuners, black hardware, 2 single coil/1 humbucker pickups, coil tap switch, 5-way selector switch, available in See-Through Black, See-Through Blue, or See-Through Red finishes, mfg. 1995-99.

$405	$325	$275	$240	$215	$190	$145

Last MSR was $579.

5 FL 30 HSDW - similar to the 5 FL 30 H, except features a Wilkinson VS-50 tremolo and 2 Duncan Designed SC-101 single coil/1 Duncan Designed HB-103 humbucking pickups, 1 volume/1 tone controls, 5-position switch, coil tap switch, available in See-Through Black, See-Through Blue, or See-Through Red finishes, mfg. 1995-99.

$625	$545	$480	$415	$350	$280	$215

Last MSR was $839.

5 FL 40 W - offset double cutaway ash body, black pearl pickguard, bolt-on maple neck, 22-fret rosewood fingerboard with pearl dot inlay, Wilkinson VS-50 tremolo, screened peghead logo, 6-on-a-side Gotoh tuners, chrome hardware, humbucker/single coil/humbucker pickups, bridge pickup coil tap switch, 5-way selector switch, available in Natural or See-Through Red finishes, mfg. 1995-99.

$575	$520	$460	$395	$330	$265	$200

Last MSR was $799.

5 FL 50 S (5 FL 50 SSDW, U.S. MFG.) - offset double cutaway alder body, white pickguard, bolt-on (5-bolt neck joint) maple neck, 22-fret rosewood fingerboard with pearl dot inlay, Wilkinson VS-50 vibrato, screened peghead logo, 6-on-a-side Sperzel locking tuners, chrome hardware, 3 single coil Don Lace pickups, volume/tone controls, available in 3-Tone Sunburst, Blue, Candy Apple Red, or White finishes, mfg. 1995-99.

$700	$600	$500	$425	$350	$300	$250

Last MSR was $999.

In 1996, Blue, Candy Apple Red, and White finishes were disc.; See-Through Red finish was introduced.

GRADING	100% MINT	98% NEAR MINT	95% EXC+	90% EXC	80% VG+	70% VG	60% G

5 FL 60 H (5 FL 60 HSDW, U.S. Mfg.) - similar to 5 FL 50, except has a pearloid pickguard, Wilkinson VS-100 tremolo, 2 single coil/1 mini humbucker Seymour Duncan pickups, available in See-Through Red or White finishes, mfg. 1995-99.

	$950	$800	$675	$550	$475	$400	$350

Last MSR was $1,299.

This instrument has white pearloid pickguard with Red finish, red pearloid pickguard with White finish. In 1996, 3-Tone Sunburst finish was introduced. In 1998, White finish was disc.; See-Through Black finish was introduced.

FL MID - offset double cutaway alder body, flamed maple or ash top, bolt-on maple neck, 22-fret rosewood fingerboard with pearl dot inlay, bridge/stop tailpiece, screened peghead logo, 6-on-a-side tuners, gold hardware, 2 single coil/1 humbucking Duncan Designed pickups, piezo bridge pickups, magnetic pickup volume/tone controls, synth volume/piezo volume controls, magnetic pickup selector switch, magnetic/piezo selector switch, S1/S2 controller switches. 1/4 in. phono output and 13-pin DIN connector jack mounted on side, available in See-Through Black, See-Through Red, or Tobacco Sunburst finishes, disc. 1994.

	N/A	$525	$475	$425	$375	$300	$250

Headstock may read "Aria Custom Shop/Fullerton" (model series). This model was designed to interface with a Roland GR-09 MIDI device.

ELECTRIC: M SERIES

M-28 - double rounded cutaway, agatis body, maple bolt-on neck, 3-per-side tuners, white pickguard, rosewood fretboard with pearl dot inlay, 24 frets, 25.5 in. scale, single coil pickup, volume/tone knobs, VGB-1 bridge/tailpiece, chrome hardware, available in black finish, mfg. 1999-2002.

	$325	$275	$250	$200	$170	$145	$120

Last MSR was $430.

M-38 - double rounded cutaway, agatis body, maple bolt-on neck, 3-per-side tuners, white pickguard, rosewood fretboard with pearl dot inlay, 24 frets, 25.5 in. scale, 3 lipstick pickups, volume/tone knobs, 5-way selector switch, VGB-1 bridge/tailpiece, chrome hardware, available in Metallic Mint finish, mfg. 1999-2002.

	$400	$350	$300	$250	$195	$160	$140

Last MSR was $540.

M-48V - double rounded cutaway, agatis semi-hollow body, maple bolt-on neck, 3-per-side tuners, tortise pickguard, rosewood fretboard with pearl dot inlay, 24 frets, 25.5 in. scale, 2 APS-9 single coil pickups, volume/tone knobs, 5-way selector switch, VGB-1 bridge, VVT-1 Virbato unit, chrome hardware, available in Off-White finish, mfg. 1999-2002.

	$500	$450	$400	$350	$305	$260	$210

Last MSR was $680.

M-650 - double rounded cutaway, agatis body, maple bolt-on neck, 3-per-side tuners, white sparkle pickguard, rosewood fretboard with block dot inlay, 24 frets, 25.5 in. scale, 2 MH-1A Metal Humbucker pickups, 2 volume 2 tone knobs, 5-way selector switch, GSB-1 bridge, GST-1 tailpiece unit, chrome hardware, available in Metallic Blue, Pearl Orange, or Candy Apple Red finishes, mfg. 1999-2002.

	$525	$465	$400	$350	$305	$260	$210

Last MSR was $700.

M-650T - similar to the M-650 except has a VVT-1 Vibrato unit, available in Silver Sparkle, Gold Sparkle, or Red Sparkle finishes, mfg. 1999-2002.

	$575	$500	$450	$400	$350	$300	$250

Last MSR was $790.

ELECTRIC: MAC SERIES

MAC-30 - double cutaway, alder carved top, maple bolt-on neck, rosewood fingerboard with pearl dot inlay, 24 frets, matching color headstock, two single coil/one humbucker pickups, five way selector and coil tap switches, two knobs (v, tone), VFT-1 Tremolo unit, Matte Silver hardware, available in Black, Metallic Dark Red, or Metallic Navy Blue finishes, 25.5 in. scale, mfg. 2004-present.

MSR $300		$225	$175	$140	$110	$90	$75	$60

MAC-35 - double cutaway, alder carved top, maple bolt-on neck, rosewood fingerboard with pearl dot inlay, 24 frets, 25.5 in. scale, matching color headstock, two single coil/one humbucker pickups, five-way selector and coil tap switches, two knobs (v, tone), VFT-1 Tremolo unit, chrome hardware, available in Matte Metallic Black, Metallic Blue, Metallic Burgandy, or Gun Metal finishes, mfg. 2003-present.

MSR $375		$285	$235	$190	$165	$140	$120	$95

MAC-40 - double cutaway, alder carved top, maple bolt-on neck, rosewood fingerboard with pearl dot inlay, 24 frets, matching color headstock, one single coil and two humbucker pickups, five way selector and coil tap switches, two knobs (v, tone), double locking Tremolo unit, Matte Silver hardware, available in Black, Metallic Dark Red, or Metallic Navy Blue finishes, 25.5 in. scale, mfg. 2004-present.

MSR $420		$315	$260	$220	$190	$160	$130	$100

MAC-50Q - double cutaway, alder carved top, flamed gravure body, maple bolt-on neck, rosewood fingerboard with pearl dot inlay, 24 frets, 25.5 in. scale, matching color headstock, two single coil/one humbucker pickups, five-way selector and coil tap switches, two knobs (v, tone), VFT-1 Tremolo unit, chrome hardware, available in See-Through Blue, Green, or Red, mfg. 2000-present.

MSR $395		$300	$250	$200	$175	$150	$125	$100

Aria Pro II 5 FL 10
courtesy Aria Pro II

GRADING	100% MINT	98% NEAR MINT	95% EXC+	90% EXC	80% VG+	70% VG	60% G

MAC-55 - similar to the MAC-50Q except has two humbucker pickup and a hardtail bridge, mfg. 2003-present.

MSR $450	$340	$275	$225	$190	$165	$135	$115

MAC-50/7 - similar to the MAC-50Q except has seven strings, no flamed gravure finish, two humbucker pickups, KKT-C tremolo unit, and black hardware, available in black finish, mfg. 2000-present.

MSR $495	$375	$325	$275	$235	$195	$160	$130

MAC-60 - double cutaway, flamed maple carved top, alder body, maple bolt-on neck, rosewood fingerboard with pearl dot inlay, 24 frets, 25.5 in. scale, matching color headstock, two single coil/one humbucker Seymour Duncan pickups, five-way selector and coil tap switches, two knobs (v, tone), VS-50K Tremolo unit, chrome hardware, available in Amber Natural or See-Through Blue, mfg. 2000-present.

MSR $695	$525	$475	$425	$375	$325	$275	$225

ELECTRIC: MAGNA SERIES

Instruments in this series had "crystal shape" carved tops.

MA 09 - offset double cutaway hardwood body, bolt-on maple neck, 24-fret maple fingerboard with black dot inlay, standard vibrato, 6-on-a-side tuners, chrome hardware, 2 single coil/1 humbucker pickups, volume/tone controls, 5-position switch, available in Black, Blue, or Red finishes, mfg. 1994 only.

	N/A	$250	$220	$190	$160	$130	$100

Last MSR was $370.

MA 10 - offset double cutaway alder body, bolt-on maple neck, 22-fret rosewood fingerboard with pearl dot inlay, standard vibrato, roller nut, 6-on-a-side tuners, black hardware, 2 single coil/1 humbucker pickups, volume control, push-pull tone control with humbucker coil tap, 5-position switch, available in Black, Fiero Red, Metallic Red Shade, Metallic Blue Shade, or White finishes, disc. 1996.

	$295	$250	$215	$180	$160	$140	$120

Last MSR was $400.

In 1993, Fiero Red finish was disc.

MA 15 - similar to MA 10, except has sen body, available in Trans. Black, Trans. Blue, or Trans. Red finishes, mfg. 1994-96.

	$350	$300	$250	$200	$175	$150	$125

Last MSR was $500.

MA 15 ST - similar to MA 10, except has sen body, fixed strings through bridge, available in Trans. Blue or Trans. Red finishes, mfg. 1994-96.

	$305	$250	$225	$200	$175	$150	$125

Last MSR was $430.

MA 22 (MA 20) - similar to MA 10, except has double locking vibrato, chrome hardware, available in Metallic Red Shade, Purple Pearl Burst, or Silver Metallic finishes, disc. 1996.

	$375	$300	$250	$200	$175	$150	$135

Last MSR was $550.

MA 28 - similar to MA 10, except has flamed maple top/alder body, double locking vibrato, available in Trans. finishes, disc. 1996.

	$400	$325	$275	$225	$200	$175	$150

Last MSR was $600.

MA 28 G - similar to MA 28, except has gold hardware, available in Brown sunburst, Dark Blue shade, or Dark Red shade finishes, disc. 1994.

	$425	$350	$300	$250	$200	$175	$150

MA 29 - similar to MA 10, except has ash carved top body, single coil/humbucker pickups, available in Natural and Paduak Red semi-gloss finishes, disc. 1994.

	N/A	$400	$350	$300	$250	$200	$150

MA 30 - similar to MA 10, except has 24-fret fingerboard, double locking vibrato, available in Black, Navy Blue, Purple Cherry, or Pearl White finishes, disc. 1996.

	$550	$475	$400	$325	$275	$250	$225

Last MSR was $900.

MA 35 - offset double cutaway alder body, bolt-on maple neck, 24-fret rosewood fingerboard with pearl dot inlay, double locking vibrato, roller nut, 6-on-a-side tuners, black hardware, single coil/humbucker pickups, volume/tone control, 3-position switch, coil split in tone control, available in Metallic Blue, Metallic Burgundy, or Metallic Violet finishes, mfg. 1991 only.

	N/A	$600	$525	$450	$375	$325	$275

Last MSR was $900.

MA 40 - offset double cutaway alder body, bolt-on maple neck, 24-fret rosewood fingerboard with pearl dot inlay, double locking vibrato, roller nut, 6-on-a-side tuners, black hardware, 2 single coil/1 humbucker pickups, volume/2 EQ controls, 3-position and 2 EQ switches, active electronics, available in Black, Metallic Blue, Metallic Burgundy, Metallic Violet, Navy Blue, Pearl White, or Purple Cherry finishes, mfg. 1991 only.

	N/A	$625	$550	$475	$400	$350	$300

Last MSR was $960.

MA 45 - similar to MA 40, except has bound fingerboard with pearl oval inlay, tune-o-matic bridge/stop tailpiece, gold hardware, disc. 1992.

	N/A	$650	$575	$500	$425	$375	$325

Last MSR was $1,025.

MA 50 - offset double cutaway alder body, bolt-on maple neck, 24-fret rosewood fingerboard with pearl dot inlay, standard vibrato, roller nut, 6-on-a-side tuners, gold hardware, 2 single coil/1 humbucker pickups, volume/tone control, three 3-position switches, coil split in tone control, available in Black, Metallic Blue, Metallic Burgundy, Metallic Violet, Navy Blue, Pearl White, or Purple Cherry finishes, disc. 1993.

	N/A	$625	$550	$475	$400	$350	$300

Last MSR was $1,000.

GRADING	100% MINT	98% NEAR MINT	95% EXC+	90% EXC	80% VG+	70% VG	60% G

MA 55 - offset double cutaway sen body, bolt-on maple neck, 24-fret rosewood fingerboard with pearl dot inlay, standard vibrato, roller nut, 6-on-a-side locking tuners, 2 single coil/1 humbucker pickups, volume/tone control, 5-way & coil split switches, available in Amber Natural, Blue Shade, or Dark Red Shade finishes, mfg. 1992 only.

	N/A	$650	$575	$500	$425	$375	$325

Last MSR was $1,050.

MA 60 - offset double cutaway alder body, maple neck, 24-fret bound rosewood fingerboard with pearl oval inlay, double locking vibrato, roller nut, 6-on-a-side tuners, gold hardware, 2 single coil/1 humbucker pickups, volume/ 2 EQ controls, 3-position and 2 EQ switches, active electronics, available in Black, Metallic Blue, Metallic Burgundy, Metallic Violet, Navy Blue, Pearl White, or Purple Cherry finishes, mfg. 1991-92.

	N/A	$675	$600	$525	$450	$375	$325

Last MSR was $1,100.

MA 75 - offset double cutaway sen body, bolt-on maple neck, 22-fret rosewood fingerboard with pearl oval inlay, double locking vibrato, 6-on-a-side tuners, gold hardware, humbucker/single coil/humbucker pickups, volume/ tone control, 5-position and coil split switches, available in Amber Natural, Cherry Sunburst, Purple Shade, or Vintage Sunburst finishes, mfg. 1992 only.

	N/A	$675	$600	$525	$450	$400	$350

Last MSR was $1,150.

MA 90 - offset double cutaway alder body, bolt-on maple neck, 24-fret bound rosewood neck with pearl oval inlay, double locking vibrato, 6-on-a-side tuners, silver black hardware, 2 single coil/Seymour Duncan humbucker pickups, volume/tone control, 5-position switch, coil split in tone control, available in Emerald Green Sunburst, Gun metal Grey, Navy Blue Sunburst, or Rose Red Sunburst finishes, mfg. 1991-92.

	N/A	$750	$675	$600	$525	$450	$375

Last MSR was $1,295.

MA 100 - similar to MA-90, except has set neck, available in Gun Metal Grey finish, mfg. 1991-92.

	N/A	$800	$725	$625	$525	$450	$400

Last MSR was $1,400.

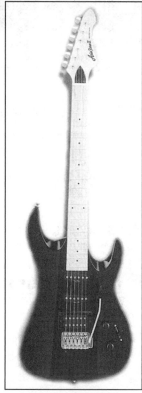

Aria Pro II MA 09
courtesy Aria Pro II

ELECTRIC: NEO SERIES

5 NEO X 10 - small, lightweight alder body with bolt-on neck, two single coil and one humbucker pickup, 24-frets, VFT-1C tremolo, 5-position selector switch, chrome hardware, available in Antique Violin Color, See-Through Blue Shade, Cherry Sunburst, or Vintage Sunburst finishes, mfg. 1999 only.

	$250	$225	$200	$175	$150	$100	$75

Last MSR was $359.

ELECTRIC: NEXTAR SERIES

NX-20 - double cutaway, alder body, maple bolt-on neck, rosewood fingerboard with pearl dot inlay, 22 frets, matching color headstock, 6-on-one-side tuners, three single coil pickups, two knobs (v, tone), five-way selector switch, white pickguard, VFT-1 tremolo unit, chrome hardware, available in Creamy Blue, Creamy Orange, Creamy Green, or Creamy Red finishes, mfg. 2000-02.

	$200	$175	$150	$130	$110	$90	$70

Last MSR was $280.

NX-20H - similar to the NX-20 except has a single humbucker pickup in bridge position, mfg. 2000-02.

	$210	$185	$160	$140	$120	$100	$80

Last MSR was $300.

ELECTRIC: PRO ELECTRIC SERIES

PE ANNIV - single sharp cutaway, quilted maple carved top, mahogany back, maple set neck, rosewood fingerboard with block inlay, three-per-side tuners, matching headstock, elaborate binding, two Seymour Duncan Humbucker pickups, three way toggle switch, 2 volume, 2 tone knobs, gold hardware, available in Antique Violin finish, mfg. 2001-present.

MSR $995	$750	$695	$650	$575	$500	$425	$350

PE F30 - single sharp cutaway, alder body, maple bolt-on neck, rosewood fingerboard with pearl dot inlay, three-per-side tuners, painted headstock, white pickguard, two single coil/single humbucker pickups, five-way toggle switch, selector and coil tap switches, volume/tone knobs, VFT-1 tremolo, chrome hardware, available in Candy Apple Red, Midnight Blue, or black finishes, mfg. 2001-03.

	$225	$200	$185	$160	$135	$115	$90

Last MSR was $300.

5 PE 40 LIMITED EDITION 40TH ANNIVERSARY MODEL - single sharp cutaway mahogany body, bound quilted maple top, set-in maple neck, 22-fret bound ebony fingerboard with fancy abalone inlays, tune-o-matic bridge/stop tailpiece, 3-per-side locking tuners, gold hardware, 2 humbucker pickups, 2 volume/2 tone controls, 1 selector switch, available in Antique Violin Shade finish only, mfg. 1996-99.

	$875	$780	$685	$590	$495	$395	$300

Last MSR was $1,199.

Aria Pro II MA 29
courtesy Aria Pro II

GRADING	100% MINT	98% NEAR MINT	95% EXC+	90% EXC	80% VG+	70% VG	60% G

PE F120R - single sharp cutaway, maple carved top and back, mahogany center body, maple set neck heel-less, rosewood fingerboard with pearl dot inlay, three-per-side tuners, matching headstock, binding, two Infinity humbucker pickups, three-way toggle switch, dual sound switches, 2 volume, 2 tone knobs, chrome hardware, available in Antique Violin finish, mfg. 2001-03.

	$1,875	$1,750	$1,600	$1,400	$1,200	$1,000	$850

Last MSR was $2,500.

PE 1000 - single sharp cutaway mahogany body, bound curly maple top, set-in maple neck, 22-fret bound rosewood fingerboard with abalone/pearl block inlay, bridge/stop tail piece, 3-per-side tuners, gold hardware, 2 humbucker pickups, 2 volume/2 tone controls, available in See-Through Blue, See-Through Red, or Vintage Sunburst, mfg. 1991-92.

	N/A	$800	$700	$600	$500	$400	$300

Last MSR was $1,200.

PE 1000 TR - similar to the PE 1000, except has abalone/pearl split block inlay, non-locking tremolo system, 3-per-side locking tuners, volume/tone controls, 3-way pickup selector switch, available in Blondy Natural, Trans. Scarlet, or Twilight Black finishes, mfg. 1991-92.

	N/A	$850	$750	$650	$550	$450	$350

Last MSR was $1,300.

PE 1500 - similar to the PE 1000, except has mahogany body, carved maple top and back, 2 Seymour Duncan humbuckers, abalone/pearl snowflake inlay, available in Antique Violin finish, mfg. 1991-92.

	N/A	$900	$800	$700	$600	$500	$375

Last MSR was $1,400.

PE-1500R '76 REISSUE - single sharp cutaway, maple carved top and back with a chamber block body, maple set neck, 22-fret rosewood fingerboard with dot inlay, matching headstock with three-per-side tuners, elaborate binding, Super Matic bridge, two DiMarzio Humbucker pickups, three-way toggle switch, 2 knobs, chrome hardware, available in Stained Brown finish, mfg. 2004-present.

MSR $3,330	$2,500	$2,200	$1,950	$1,750	$1,550	$1,350	$1,150

PE JR 600 - single sharp cutaway maple body, bolt-on maple neck, 22-fret rosewood fingerboard with pearl dot inlay, tune-o-matic bridge/stop tailpiece, 3-per-side tuners, chrome hardware, 2 single coil pickups, 2 volume/tone controls, 3-position switch, available in Black, Metallic Blue Shade, or Metallic Violet Shade finishes, disc. 1992.

	N/A	$525	$450	$375	$300	$250	$200

Last MSR was $775.

PE JR 750 - similar to PE JR 600, except has bound body, vibrato tailpiece, gold hardware, volume/tone control, available in Cherry Sunburst, Pearl White, or Vintage Sunburst finishes, disc. 1992.

	N/A	$625	$550	$475	$400	$350	$300

Last MSR was $1,000.

5 PE CLS - single sharp cutaway semi-hollow alder body, bound flame maple top, set in maple neck, 25.5 in. scale, four wave-shaped soundholes, 24-fret bound rosewood fingerboard with abalone/pearl block inlay, string through rosewood tailpiece, 3-per-side tuners with pearl button pegs, slotted headstock, gold hardware, Fishman AG-125 piezo system, volume/active treble/middle/bass controls, available in Rose Natural finish, mfg. 1994-99.

	$925	$850	$775	$650	$550	$450	$325

Last MSR was $1,299.

5 PE DLX - single sharp cutaway alder body, bound flamed maple top, bolt-on maple neck, 22-fret bound rosewood fingerboard with pearl block inlay, tune-o-matic bridge/stop tailpiece, 3-per-side locking tuners, gold hardware, 2 humbucker pickups, 2 volume/2 tone controls, 1 selector switch, available in See-Through Black, See-Through Blue, See-Through Green, See-Through Purple, Violin Shade, or See-Through Wine Red finishes, current mfg.

MSR $660	$495	$425	$375	$345	$290	$230	$175

5 PE STD - similar to the 5 PE DLX, except has a maple top, chrome hardware, bolt-on neck, available in Violin Shade finish only, mfg. 1997-present.

MSR $395	$300	$250	$200	$160	$130	$105	$85

5 PE PRO - similar to 5 PE DLX except has gold hardware, available in black, Vintage Sunburst, or Wine Red finishes, mfg. 1999-2000.

	$475	$425	$375	$325	$275	$225	$200

Last MSR was $649.

5 PE SPL - similar to 5 PE DLX, except features a set-in neck, available in Natural Violin Shade finish only, mfg. 1994-present.

MSR $650	$490	$425	$375	$325	$275	$225	$175

PE DLX MID - single sharp cutaway mahogany body, flamed maple carved top, set-in maple neck, 22-fret rosewood fingerboard with pearl block inlay, bridge/stop tailpiece, screened peghead logo, 3+3 tuners, gold hardware, 2 humbucker Duncan Designed pickups, piezo bridge pickups, magnetic pickup volume/tone controls, synth volume/piezo volume controls, magnetic pickup selector switch, magnetic/piezo selector switch, S1/S2 controller switches. 1/4 in. phono output and 13-pin DIN connector jack mounted on side, available in Vintage Sunburst finish only, disc. 1994.

	N/A	$525	$450	$375	$325	$290	$235

Headstock may read "Aria Custom Shop". This model was designed to interface with a Roland GR-09 MIDI device. Aria also offered a PE CLS MID model (a MIDI version of the PE CLS).

PE INSPIRE - single sharp cutaway, mahogany back, quilted maple carved top, mahogany set neck, 22-fret rosewood fingerboard with block inlay, three-per-side tuners, black headstock, elaborate binding, two Seymour Duncan Humbucker pickups, three-way toggle switch, 2 knobs, gold hardware, available in Ink Blue, Natural Oak, See-Thru Wine Red, or Vintage Sunburst finishes, mfg. 2004-present.

MSR $2,995	$2,300	$2,000	$1,800	$1,600	$1,400	$1,200	$1,000

PE ELITE - single sharp cutaway mahogany body with flame-carved maple top, set maple neck, 22-fret rosewood fingerboard with oval inlays, original bridge and stop tailpiece, two humbucker pickups, four knobs, three-way switch, chrome hardware, available in Brown Sunburst, Honey Burst, or Wine Red finishes, mfg. 2004-present.

MSR $400	$300	$250	$200	$170	$140	$110	$90

A

GRADING	100% MINT	98% NEAR MINT	95% EXC+	90% EXC	80% VG+	70% VG	60% G

Aria Pro II PE DLX MID
courtesy Aria Pro II

PE EXTREME - single sharp cutaway mahogany body with flame maple top, mahogany neck, 22-fret rosewood fingerboard with oval inlays, original bridge and stop tailpiece, two Joe Barden humbucker pickups with no mounting rings, two knobs, three-way switch, mini-switch, chrome hardware, available in Ink Blue, Natural Oak, or See-Thru Wine Red finishes, mfg. 2004-present.

MSR $4,000	$3,000	$2,600	$2,300	$2,000	$1,750	$1,500	$1,250

PE STUDIO - single sharp cutaway carved maple top, bolt-on maple neck, 22-fret rosewood fingerboard with oval inlays, original bridge and stop tailpiece, two humbucker pickups, four knobs, three-way switch, chrome hardware, available in Brown Sunburst, Honey Burst, or Wine Red finishes, mfg. 2004-present.

MSR $320	$240	$200	$170	$140	$120	$100	$80

ELECTRIC: STG SERIES

5 STG 002 - similar to 5 STG 003, except has maple fingerboard, available in Black, Blue, Red, and White finishes, mfg. 1998-2000.

	$210	$180	$160	$135	$110	$90	$65

Last MSR was $279.

5 STG 003 - offset double cutaway hardwood body, white pickguard, bolt-on maple neck, 22-fret rosewood fingerboard with white dot inlay, vintage style tremolo, 6-on-a-side tuners, chrome hardware, 3 single coil pickups, volume/2 tone controls, 5-position switch, available in 2-Tone Sunburst, 3-Tone Sunburst, Aged Sunburst, Black, Blue, Candy Apple Red, Metallic Blue, Metallic Gold, Metallic Silver, Red, Salmon Pink, Sonic Blue, Surf Green, or White finishes, 25.5 in. scale, mfg. 1996-present.

MSR $280	$210	$180	$160	$135	$110	$90	$65

Add $75 for active electronics (STG 003DX).

In 1997, 3-Tone Sunburst finish was disc. and Blue and Green finishes were introduced.

5 STG 003 L - similar to 5 STG 003, except in left-handed configuration, available in Black finish only, mfg. 1996-present.

MSR $300	$225	$195	$170	$145	$120	$95	$70

5 STG 004 - similar to 5 STG 003, except features 2 single coil/humbucker pickups, vintage-style VFT-1M tremolo, available in 3-Tone Sunburst, Natural, See-Through Blue, See-Through Green, or See-Through Wine Red finishes, mfg. 1998-present.

MSR $300	$225	$195	$170	$145	$120	$95	$70

Add $75 for active electronics (STG 004DX).

In 1998, Midnight Blue, Metallic Black, Metallic Green, Metallic Lavender, and Metallic Silver finishes were introduced.

5 STG 004/7 - similar to the 5 STG 004 except is in 7-string configuration, has diagonal pickups, and is available in Black or Three Tone Sunburst, mfg. 2001-02.

	$250	$220	$185	$150	$120	$95	$75

Last MSR was $340.

5 STG 005 - similar to the 5 STG 004 except has two Humbucker pickups, black pickguard and knobs, available in Black or Candy Apple Red, mfg. 2001-present.

MSR $300	$225	$195	$170	$145	$120	$95	$70

5 STG 006 - similar to the 5 STG 004 except has two Humbucker pickups and one single coil pickup, available in black, Metallic Blue, Candy Apple Red, Metallic Silver, or Natural finishes, mfg. 2003-present.

MSR $300	$225	$195	$170	$145	$120	$95	$70

5 STG 012 S - offset double cutaway hardwood body, white pickguard, bolt-on maple neck, 22-fret maple fingerboard with black dot inlay, fixed bridge, 6-on-a-side tuners, chrome hardware, 2 single coil pickups, volume/tone control, 3-position switch, available in Black, Blue, or 3-Tone Sunburst finishes, mfg. 1994-97.

	$200	$150	$125	$95	$85	$80	$75

Last MSR was $279.

5 STG 013 S - offset double cutaway hardwood body, white pickguard, bolt-on maple neck, 22-fret maple fingerboard with black dot inlay, strings through bridge, 6-on-a-side tuners, chrome hardware, 3 single coil pickups, volume/tone controls, 5-position switch, available in Black, Blue and 3-Tone sunburst finishes, mfg. 1994-97.

	$250	$210	$180	$150	$130	$110	$90

Last MSR was $349.

STG 013 X - similar to STG 013 S, except has standard vibrato, 2 single coil/1 humbucker pickup, mfg. 1994-97.

	$275	$225	$180	$160	$140	$120	$110

Last MSR was $360.

STG 023 C - offset double cutaway figured maple body, black pickguard, bolt-on maple neck, 22-fret rosewood fingerboard with pearl dot inlay, double locking vibrato, 6-on-a-side tuners, chrome hardware, 2 single coil pickups and 1 humbucker pickup, volume/tone control, 5-position switch, available in Dark Blue Shade, Dark Red Shade, or Tobacco Sunburst finishes, mfg. 1994-96.

	$350	$275	$225	$175	$150	$135	$125

Last MSR was $440.

GRADING	100% MINT	98% NEAR MINT	95% EXC+	90% EXC	80% VG+	70% VG	60% G

STG 023 X - similar to STG 023 C, except had gold hardware, mfg. 1994-96.

	$450	$325	$275	$225	$200	$175	$150

Last MSR was $550.

ELECTRIC: THIN ACOUSTIC (TA) SERIES

TA 40 - double rounded cutaway semi-hollow style, mahogany arched top/back/sides, bolt-on mahogany neck, 24.75 in. scale, bound body, bound f-holes, raised black pickguard, 22-fret bound rosewood fingerboard with pearl dot inlay, tune-o-matic bridge/stop tailpiece, 3-per-side tuners, chrome hardware, 2 MH-1C humbucker pickup, 2 volume/tone controls, 3-position switch, available in Walnut or Wine Red finishes, current mfg.

MSR $550	$425	$370	$325	$280	$235	$190	$145

In 1999, black finish was added.

5 TA 40/12 - similar to the 5 TA 40 except in 12-string configuration, mfg. 2000-02.

	$450	$385	$335	$290	$235	$190	$145

Last MSR was $600.

5 TA 60 - similar to 5 TA 40, except features block inlay on fingerboard, gold hardware, 2 MH-1G humbucker pickup, available in Pearl Black, Walnut, and Wine Red finishes, disc. 1999.

	$550	$450	$375	$325	$275	$225	$175

Last MSR was $799.

In 1993, Walnut finish was disc.

5 TA 61 - similar to TA 60, except has maple arched top/back/sides, transparent pickguard, bound peghead, tone selector switch, available in Amber Natural, Cherry, and Vintage Sunburst finishes, disc. 2001.

	$600	$525	$475	$425	$350	$275	$225

Last MSR was $800.

In 1993, Cherry finish was disc. In 1996, Wine Red finish was introduced.

5 TA 62 - similar to the 5 TA 60, except has maple arched top/back/sides, set-in maple neck, available in Amber Natural, Wine Red, or Vintage Sunburst finishes, mfg. 1998-99.

	$600	$525	$455	$395	$325	$265	$200

Last MSR was $799.

TA 65 TR - similar to TA 60, except has vibrato tailpiece, available in Amber Natural, Cherry, Vintage Sunburst, Walnut, or Wine Red finishes, disc. 1991.

	N/A	$475	$400	$325	$275	$240	$200

Last MSR was $700.

TA 70 - double cutaway semi-hollow body, spruce arched top, mahogany arched back/sides, f-holes, bound body, raised black pickguard, maple set-neck, 22-fret bound rosewood fingerboard with pearl dot inlay, bridge/stop tailpiece, unbound peghead, 3-per-side tuners, chrome hardware, 2 humbucker pickups, 2 volume/tone controls, 3-position switch, available in Vintage Sunburst or Wine Red finishes, disc. 1995, reintroduced 2000-02.

	$600	$525	$450	$400	$350	$300	$250

Last MSR was $820.

TA 80 - double cutaway semi-hollow body, flamed maple arched top/back/sides, f-holes, bound body, raised tortoiseshell pickguard, maple set-neck, 22-fret bound rosewood fingerboard with pearl dot inlay, bridge/stop tailpiece, bound peghead, 3-per-side tuners, gold hardware, 2 humbucker pickups, 2 volume/tone controls, 3-position switch, available in Antique Sunburst or Antique Violin color finishes, disc. 1995, reintroduced 2003-present.

MSR $850	$625	$575	$500	$425	$350	$300	$250

TA 80 TR - similar to TA 80, except has vibrato tailpiece, available in Antique Sunburst and Antique Violin color finishes, disc. 1995, reintroduced 2000-02.

	$650	$595	$545	$485	$435	$375	$300

Last MSR was $870.

TA 900 (TA STD) - double cutaway semi-hollow body, maple arched top/back/sides, f-holes, bound body, raised black pickguard, mahogany neck, 22-fret bound rosewood fingerboard with pearl dot inlay, bridge/stop tailpiece, unbound peghead, 3-per-side tuners, chrome hardware, 2 humbucker pickups, 2 volume/tone controls, 3-position switch, available in Black, Brown Sunburst, or Trans. Red finishes, mfg. 1991-92.

	$875	$750	$625	$500	$450	$415	$375

Last MSR was $1,250.

TA 1300 (TA DLX) - double rounded cutaway semi-hollow style, sycamore top/back/sides, bound body, bound f-holes, raised bound tortoise pickguard, mahogany neck, 22-fret bound ebony fingerboard with abalone/pearl split block inlay, tune-o-matic bridge/stop tailpiece, bound peghead with pearl Aria Pro II logo and dove inlay, 3-per-side tuners, gold hardware, 2 humbucker pickups, 2 volume/tone controls, 3-position switch, available in Brown Sunburst or Vintage Sunburst finishes, mfg. 1991-92.

	N/A	$1,200	$1,050	$900	$750	$650	$525

Last MSR was $1,750.

TA 50 - double rounded cutaway semi-hollow style, maple top/back/sides, set maple neck, bound body, bound f-holes, raised black pickguard, 22-fret bound rosewood fingerboard with parallelogram inlay, SPT/QH bridge/stop tailpiece, 3-per-side tuners, 2 MH humbucker pickups, 2 volume/tone controls, 3-position switch, chrome hardware, available in Black, Brown Sunburst, or Wine Red finishes, mfg. 2004-present.

MSR $420	$315	$260	$220	$190	$160	$130	$100

ELECTRIC: VIPER SERIES

VP-30 - offset double cutaway maple body, bolt-on maple neck, 22-fret rosewood fingerboard with pearl dot inlay, standard vibrato, roller nut, 6-on-a-side tuners, chrome hardware, 2 single coil/1 humbucker pickups, volume/tone control, 5-position switch, available in Black, Fiero Red, or White finishes, mfg. 1991 only.

	N/A	$275	$230	$195	$160	$130	$110

Last MSR was $390.

GRADING	100% MINT	98% NEAR MINT	95% EXC+	90% EXC	80% VG+	70% VG	60% G

VP-40 - offset double cutaway alder body, pearloid pickguard, bolt-on maple neck, 22-fret rosewood fingerboard with pearl wedge inlay, locking vibrato, 6-on-a-side tuners, black hardware, 2 single coil/1 humbucker pickup, volume/tone control, 5-position switch, available in Black, Fiero Red, Navy Blue, Pearl White, or White finishes, mfg. 1991 only.

	N/A	$325	$275	$235	$200	$175	$150

Last MSR was $500.

VP-50 - similar to VP-40, except has coil split switch, available in Black, Candy Apple, Navy Blue, Midnight Cherry, or Pearl White finishes, disc. 1995.

	$650	$540	$420	$300	$270	$245	$225

Last MSR was $1,000.

VP-65 - similar to VP-40, except has pearloid pickguard, humbucker/single coil/humbucker pickups, coil split switch, available in Black, Metallic Lavender Shade, or Pearl Blue finishes, disc. 1993.

	N/A	$650	$575	$500	$425	$375	$325

Last MSR was $995.

VP-90 - semi-solid offset double cutaway maple body, figured maple top, wedge soundhole, bound body and soundhole, maple neck, 22-fret bound rosewood fingerboard with pearl dot inlay, standard vibrato, 6-on-a-side locking tuners, chrome hardware, volume/tone control, 3-position and coil split switch, available in Cherry Sunburst or Natural finishes, disc. 1993.

	N/A	$150	$130	$110	$90	$75	$60

Last MSR was $240.

ELECTRIC BASS: AVANTE BASS SERIES

6 AVB 20 - offset double cutaway alder body, bolt-on maple neck, 24-fret rosewood fingerboard with dot inlay, fixed bridge, 4-on-a-side tuners, chrome hardware, P/J-style pickups, 2 volume/1 tone controls, available in Black finish only, mfg. 1995-2002.

	$395	$350	$315	$270	$225	$185	$140

Last MSR was $549.

Aria Pro II TA 80
courtesy Aria Pro II

AVB 30 - offset double cutaway hardwood body, bolt-on maple neck, 24-fret rosewood fingerboard with dot inlay, fixed bridge, 4-on-a-side tuners, chrome hardware, P/J-style pickups, 2 volume/1 tone controls, available in Black, Blue, Red, and White finishes, disc. 1996.

	$290	$250	$220	$195	$165	$120	$95

Last MSR was $400.

6 AVB 40 - offset double cutaway alder body, bolt-on maple neck, 24-fret rosewood fingerboard with dot inlay, fixed bridge, 4-on-a-side tuners, chrome hardware, P/J-style pickups, 2 volume/1 tone controls, available in Natural, See-Through Blue, See-Through Green, See-Through Purple, or See-Through Red finishes, mfg. 1994-2002.

	$450	$375	$325	$275	$225	$190	$150

Last MSR was $599.

6 AVB 40 FL - similar to 6 AVB 40, except in fretless configuration, available in Natural finish only, mfg. 1996-2002.

	$450	$375	$325	$275	$225	$190	$150

Last MSR was $599.

6 AVB 40 LN - similar to 6 AVB 40, except in left-handed configuration, available in Natural finish only, mfg. 1996-2002.

	$475	$395	$350	$300	$250	$200	$150

Last MSR was $649.

6 AVB 45 - offset double cutaway alder body, bolt-on maple neck, 24-fret rosewood fingerboard with pearl oval inlay, fixed bridge, 4-on-a-side tuners, black hardware, P/J-style pickups, volume/treble/bass/balance controls, active electronics, available in Natural, See-Through Blue, or See-Through Red finishes, mfg. 1994-2002.

	$600	$525	$475	$400	$350	$275	$200

Last MSR was $849.

6 AVB 45/5 5-String - similar to AVB 45, except has 5-string configuration, 4/1 per side tuners, 2 J-style pickups, mfg. 1994-2002.

	$650	$575	$500	$425	$350	$275	$225

Last MSR was $899.

AVB 50 - offset double cutaway alder body, bolt-on maple neck, 24-fret rosewood fingerboard with pearl dot inlay, fixed bridge, 4-on-a-side tuners, chrome hardware, P-style/J-style pickups, 2 volume/1 tone controls, available in Black, Fiero Red, or White finishes, mfg. 1991-2002.

	$345	$290	$245	$195	$175	$160	$150

Last MSR was $490.

AVB 55 - similar to AVB 50, except has carved top and black hardware, available in Alsace Red, Black, Navy Blue, or Pearl White finishes, disc. 1993.

	N/A	$550	$475	$400	$325	$275	$225

Last MSR was $850.

Aria Pro II TA 80 TR
courtesy Aria Pro II

GRADING	100% MINT	98% NEAR MINT	95% EXC+	90% EXC	80% VG+	70% VG	60% G

AVB 80 - similar to AVB 50, except has carved top, gold hardware and active electronics, available in Black, Navy Blue Sunburst, Pearl White, or Rose Red Sunburst, disc. 1993.

	N/A	$700	$625	$550	$475	$400	$325

Last MSR was $1,100.

AVB 95 - offset double cutaway mahogany body, walnut carved top/back, bolt-on maple neck, 24-fret rosewood fingerboard with pearl dot inlay, fixed bridge, 4-on-a-side tuners, gun metal hardware, 2 Seymour Duncan humbucker pickups, volume/balance/bass/treble active controls, bypass switch, available in Natural Walnut finish, disc. 1996.

	$1,000	$875	$750	$600	$525	$450	$400

Last MSR was $1,600.

AVB MID 4 - offset double cutaway alder body, flamed maple carved top, bolt-on maple neck, 24-fret rosewood fingerboard with pearl dot inlay, BST-4 bass bridge, screened peghead logo, 4-on-a-side tuners, black hardware, 2 single coil SJS-04 pickups, piezo bridge pickups, magnetic pickup volume/magnetic pickup balance stacked controls, synth volume/magnetic pickup active bass EQ stacked controls, piezo pickup volume/magnetic pickup active treble EQ stacked controls, magnetic/piezo selector switch, S1/S2 controller switches. 1/4 in. phono output and 13-pin DIN connector jack mounted on side, available in Tobacco Sunburst finish only, disc. 1994.

	N/A	$525	$450	$375	$300	$250	$200

Headstock may read "Aria Custom Shop". This model was designed to interface with a Roland GI-10 MIDI device. Aria also offered AVB MID 5 (5-string model), and the AVB MID 6 (6-string model).

ELECTRIC BASS: AVB STEVE BAILEY SERIES

These AVB models were designed in collaboration with bassist Steve Bailey and Trev Wilkinson. Steve Bailey AVB bass models debuted in 1994.

6 AVB SB 4 D - offset double cutaway ash body, tortoiseshell pickguard, bolt-on maple neck, 24-fret rosewood fingerboard with pearl dot inlay, fixed bridge, 4-on-a-side tuners, pearl black hardware, 2 J-style Basslines by Seymour Duncan pickups, volume/concentric treble/bass controls, USA Seymour Duncan active electronics, available in 3-Tone Sunburst finish, mfg. 1994-2002.

	$1,050	$950	$850	$725	$600	$500	$400

Last MSR was $1,499.

See-Through Black finish added in 1999. This model has an optional fretless ebony fingerboard (AVB SB 4 FL).

6 AVB SB 5 D - similar to 6 AVB SB 4 D, except in 5-string configuration, 4/1-per side tuners, available in Three Tone Sunburst finish, mfg. 1994-2002.

	$1,200	$1,050	$950	$825	$700	$575	$425

Last MSR was $1,699.

This model has an optional fretless ebony fingerboard (AVB SB 5 FL).

6 AVB SB 6 D - similar to 6 AVB SB 4 D, except in 6-string configuration, 4/2-per-side tuners, black hardware, 2 humbucker pickups, available in Three Tone Sunburst finish, mfg. 1994-2002.

	$1,400	$1,200	$1,050	$975	$825	$650	$500

Last MSR was $1,999.

This model has an optional fretless ebony fingerboard (AVB SB 6 FL).

ELECTRIC BASS: AVB TN SERIES

The AVB TN series features a maple neck-through design and alder body.

6 AVB TN 4 - offset double cutaway alder body, through-body maple neck, 24-fret rosewood fingerboard with pearl oval inlay, fixed bridge, 4-on-a-side tuners, black hardware, 2 J-style pickups, 2 volume/1 tone controls, active electronics, available in Natural or Walnut finishes, mfg. 1994-99.

	$800	$725	$650	$575	$475	$400	$300

Last MSR was $1,149.

6 AVB TN 5 - similar to AVB TN 4, except has 5-string configuration, 4/1-per-side-tuners, mfg. 1994-99.

	$850	$750	$675	$600	$525	$425	$325

Last MSR was $1,199.

6 AVB TN 6 - similar to AVB TN 4, except has 6-string configuration, 4/2-per-side tuners, mfg. 1994-99.

	$900	$800	$725	$650	$550	$450	$350

Last MSR was $1,299.

ELECTRIC BASS: INTEGRA (IGB) SERIES

Integra basses have a carved top and slightly elongated top horn.

IGB 30 - offset double cutaway alder body, bolt-on maple neck, 24-fret rosewood fingerboard with pearl dot inlay, fixed bridge, 2-per-side tuners, chrome hardware, P/J-style pickups, 2 volume/1 tone controls, available in Black and Brown Sunburst finishes, disc. 1994, reintroduced 1999 only, in Black, Stained Natural, or Stained Walnut finishes.

	$450	$375	$315	$250	$225	$205	$190

Last MSR was $599.

IGB 35 - offset double cutaway carved alder body, bolt-on maple neck, 24-fret rosewood fingerboard with pearl dot inlay, fixed bridge, two-per-side tuners, two Double Coil pickups, four knobs, Matte Silver hardware, available in Black, Metallic Navy Blue, or Metallic Red Shade, mfg. 2004-present.

MSR $400		$300	$260	$230	$200	$170	$140	$110

IGB 35/5 - similar to the IGB 35, except in five-string configuration, 3/2-per-side tuners, mfg. 2004-present.

MSR $450		$340	$290	$250	$220	$190	$160	$130

GRADING	100% MINT	98% NEAR MINT	95% EXC+	90% EXC	80% VG+	70% VG	60% G

IGB 40 - offset double cutaway alder body, bolt-on maple neck, 24-fret rosewood fingerboard with pearl dot inlay, fixed bridge, 2-per-side tuners, chrome hardware, P/J-style pickups, 2 volume/1 tone controls, available in Black, Blue Shade, Metallic Red Shade,or Dark Red Shade, mfg. 1999-present.

	MSR $375		$285	$250	$225	$200	$175	$150	$125

This model is also available as a medium scale sized guitar (820mm) for the same price, and a short scale sized guitar for a retail of $350.

IGB 48 - offset double cutaway alder body, bolt-on maple neck, 24-fret rosewood fingerboard with pearl dot inlay, fixed bridge, two-per-side tuners, one single coil pickups and one humbucker pickup, four knobs, black hardware, available in Matte Black, Matte Blue Metallic, or Matte Gun Metal finishes, mfg. 2003-present.

	MSR $450		$340	$290	$250	$220	$190	$160	$130

IGB 50 - similar to IGB 30, except has mahogany body, Infinity double coil and single pickups, matte chrome hardware, volume/balance/active treble/active bass controls, available in Dark Oak and Natural Mahogany finishes, disc. 1994, reintroduced 1999-present.

	MSR $650		$490	$450	$400	$350	$300	$250	$225

IGB 50/5 - similar to the 6 IGB 50 except in 5-string configuration, current mfg.

	MSR $750		$575	$525	$475	$425	$375	$325	$275

IGB 55 - Double cutaway ash carved body, maple bolt-on neck, 24 fret rosewood fingerboard w/ pearl dot inlay, 34 in. scale, matching headstock, two-per-side tuners, single humbucker pickup, two knobs (v, tone), coil tap switch, matte chrome hardware, available in Stainded Nato, Stained Black, or See-Through Blue, mfg. 2000-03.

		$560	$500	$460	$410	$350	$310	$275

Last MSR was $740.

**Aria Pro II AVB 45
courtesy Aria Pro II**

IGB 58 - ash carved top with rosewood fingerboard, 24-frets, one MBH-4 bass humbucker pickup, active treble, middle and bass controls, coil tap switch, bypass switch, matte chrome hardware, available in See-Through Blue and Stained Natural finishes, mfg. 1999 only.

		$650	$450	$400	$325	$275	$225	$200

Last MSR was $859.

IGB 60 - similar to IGB 30, except has mahogany body, maple neck-through-body design, black hardware, volume/balance/active treble/active bass controls, available in Dark Oak or Natural Mahogany finishes, disc. 1994.

		N/A	$550	$475	$425	$375	$325	$275

IGB 65 - double cutaway ash carved body, maple bolt-on neck, 24 fret rosewood fingerboard with pearl dot inlay, 34 in. scale, matching headstock, two-per-side tuners, one single coil/one twin coil pickups, five knobs, Matte Chrome hardware, available in Stainded Nato, Stained Black, Dark Red Shade, or See-Through Blue, mfg. 2000-present.

	MSR $850		$650	$575	$500	$425	$350	$300	$250

IGB 68 - double cutaway ash carved body, maple bolt-on neck, 24 fret rosewood fingerboard with pearl dot inlay, 34 in. scale, matching headstock, two-per-side tuners, one humbucker pickup, four knobs (v, b, m, t), matte chrome hardware, coil-tap and bypass swithces, available in Stained Nato, Stained Black, Dark Red Shade, or See-Through Blue, mfg. 2000-present.

	MSR $750		$575	$500	$450	$400	$350	$275	$225

IGB 68/5 - similar to the IGB-68 except is in five-string configuration, mfg. 2000-present.

	MSR $895		$675	$625	$575	$525	$475	$400	$325

IGB SPT - jazz style maple body, bolt-on maple neck, 24-fret rosewood fingerboard with pearl dot inlay, fixed bridge, 2-per-side tuners, black hardware, P-style/J-style pickups, 2 volume/1 tone controls, available in Alsace Red, Black, Navy Blue, or White finishes, disc. 1992.

		N/A	$425	$375	$325	$275	$225	$175

Last MSR was $630.

IGB STD - similar to IGB-SPT, except has chrome hardware, disc. 1996.

		$650	$550	$475	$400	$325	$275	$225

Last MSR was $900.

IGB CST - similar to IGB SPT, except has sen body, gold hardware and volume/bass/treble/mix controls, available in Blue Shade, Dark Red Shade, Trans. Black, or Trans. White finishes, disc. 1993.

		N/A	$625	$550	$475	$425	$375	$325

Last MSR was $1,000.

IGB DLX - similar to IGB SPT, except has black hardware, volume/bass/treble/mix controls, disc. 1996.

		$700	$600	$525	$450	$375	$325	$275

Last MSR was $1,000.

IGB DLX/5 - similar to IGB DLX, except has 5 strings, 4/1-per-side-tuners, black hardware, volume/bass/treble/mix controls, disc. 1996.

		$725	$625	$550	$475	$400	$350	$300

Last MSR was $1,100.

**Aria Pro II AVB MID 4
courtesy Aria Pro II**

GRADING	100% MINT	98% NEAR MINT	95% EXC+	90% EXC	80% VG+	70% VG	60% G

ELECTRIC BASS: MAGNA SERIES

MAB 09 - offset double cutaway hardwood body, bolt-on maple neck, 22-fret maple fingerboard with black dot inlay, fixed bridge, 4-on-a-side tuners, chrome hardware, P/J-style pickups, 1 volume/2 tone controls, available in Black, Blue and Red finishes, mfg. 1994 -96, reintroduced 1999-2002.

	$300	$250	$200	$160	$145	$130	$120

Last MSR was $400.

This model is also available as a fretless (MAB-09FL) at no extra charge.

MAB 09A - similar to the MAB 09 except is an active version, mfg. 1999-2002.

	$425	$375	$335	$290	$240	$180	$145

Last MSR was $590.

MAB 09/5 - similar to the MAB 09 except in 5-string configuration, available in Black, Metallic Blue or Metallic Red finishes, mfg. 2000-02.

	$400	$350	$290	$250	$200	$150	$110

Last MSR was $550.

MAB 09/6 - similar to the MAB 09 except in 6-string configuration, available in black, Metallic Blue or Metallic Red finishes, mfg. 2000-02.

	$550	$500	$450	$400	$350	$295	$250

Last MSR was $760.

MAB 20 - offset double cutaway alder body, bolt-on maple neck, 22-fret rosewood fingerboard with pearl dot inlay, fixed bridge, 4-on-a-side tuners, black hardware, P/J-style pickups, 2 volume/1 tone controls, available in Apple Red, Black, Midnight Blue, or White finishes, disc. 1996.

	$375	$300	$250	$200	$180	$165	$150

Last MSR was $500.

MAB 20/5 - similar to MAB 20, except has 5 strings, 24 frets and 2 J-style pickups, available in Apple Red, Black or White finishes, disc. 1996.

	$395	$265	$250	$200	$180	$165	$150

Last MSR was $540.

MAB 25 - similar to MAB 20, except has P/J-style pickups, chrome hardware, available in Dark Oak, Natural, or See-Through Red semi-gloss finishes, disc. 1994.

	N/A	$425	$375	$325	$275	$225	$175

MAB 40 - similar to MAB 20, except has active EQ in tone control, 3-position and bypass switch, available in Black, Midnight Cherry, Navy Blue, Pearl Black, Pearl White, or White finishes, disc. 1996.

	$475	$400	$325	$275	$225	$175	$150

Last MSR was $700.

MAB 50 - similar to MAB 20, except has 24 frets, gold hardware, volume/bass/treble/mix controls, active electronics, available in Midnight Cherry, Pearl Black, or Pearl White finishes, disc. 1996.

	$675	$600	$525	$450	$400	$350	$300

Last MSR was $995.

MAB 60 - offset double cutaway sen body, bolt-on maple neck, 24-fret rosewood fingerboard with pearl dot inlay, fixed bridge, 4-on-a-side tuners, gold hardware, 2 J-style pickups, volume/bass/treble/mix controls, available in Blue Shade, Dark Red Shade, Purple Shade, or Vintage Sunburst finishes, disc. 1992.

	N/A	$750	$650	$550	$475	$400	$350

Last MSR was $1,195.

MAB 60/5 - similar to MAB-60, except has 5 strings, ebony fingerboard, black hardware and 2 double coil pickups, available in Midnight Cherry, Navy Blue, Pearl Black, or Pearl White finishes, disc. 1992.

	N/A	$800	$700	$600	$525	$450	$375

Last MSR was $1,195.

ELECTRIC BASS: SUPER BASS (SB) SERIES

SB 40 - offset double cutaway alder body, bolt-on maple neck, 24-fret rosewood fingerboard with dot inlay, two-per-side tuners, standard bridge, two double coil pickups, three knobs, chrome hardware, available in Black, Candy Apple Red, Midnight Blue, or White finishes, mfg. 2003-present.

MSR $395	$300	$250	$210	$180	$150	$120	$95

Add $40 for active electronics (Model SB40-A). Also available in fretless configuration for no additional cost (Model SB40-FL).

SB 40/5 - similar to the SB 40, except in five-string configuration, 3/2-per-side tuners, mfg. 2003-present.

MSR $450	$340	$290	$250	$220	$190	$160	$130

SB 40 LIMITED EDITION 40TH ANNIVERSARY - jazz style, alder body, bolt-on maple neck, 24-fret rosewood fingerboard with pearl dot inlay, fixed bridge, 2-per-side tuners, gold hardware, P/J-style active pickups, 2 volume/1 tone controls, available in Walnut finish only, mfg. 1997-99.

	$650	$575	$500	$450	$375	$300	$225

Last MSR was $899.

SB 404 - offset double cutaway ovankol body, five-piece maple/nato neck-thru body, 24-fret rosewood fingerboard with oval inlays, two-per-side tuners, standard bridge, two double coil pickups, four knobs, black hardware, available in Stained Natural finish, mfg. 2004-present.

MSR $900	$675	$575	$500	$425	$375	$325	$275

SB 404/5 - similar to the SB 404, except in five-string configuration, 3/2-per-side tuners, mfg. 2004-present.

MSR $1,000	$750	$650	$575	$500	$425	$375	$325

GRADING	100% MINT	98% NEAR MINT	95% EXC+	90% EXC	80% VG+	70% VG	60% G

SB 1000 - jazz style, sen body, maple/walnut through-body neck, 24-fret rosewood fingerboard with pearl dot inlay, fixed bridge, 2-per-side tuners, gold hardware, 2 humbucker pickups, 2 volume/1 tone controls, active electronics, available in Black, Light Oak, Trans. Black, or Trans. Red finishes, disc. 1993.

	$975	$850	$700	$550	$500	$450	$400

Last MSR was $1,400.

SB 1000-RI - offset double cutaway ash body, five-piece maple/walnut neck-thru body, heel-less, 24-fret ebony fingerboard with dot inlay, matching headstock with two-per-side tuners, standard bridge, single double coil pickup, three knobs, single mini-switch, gold hardware, available in Oak finish, mfg. 2004-present.

MSR $2,500	$1,900	$1,650	$1,450	$1,250	$1,050	$900	$750

SB LTD - similar to SB 1000, except has ebony fingerboard with pearl oval inlay and Alembic pickups, available in Trans. Black or Trans. Red finishes, disc. 1994.

	$1,250	$1,100	$900	$795	$675	$595	$525

Last MSR was $1,800.

SB JR 600 - jazz style, alder body, bolt-on maple neck, 24-fret rosewood fingerboard with pearl dot inlay, fixed bridge, 2-per-side tuners, black hardware, P/J-style pickup, 2 volume/1 tone controls, available in Midnight Cherry, Navy Blue, Pearl Black, or Pearl White finishes, disc. 1992.

	N/A	$550	$475	$400	$350	$300	$250

Last MSR was $850.

SB JR 750 - similar to SB JR600, except has maple/walnut/sen body, gold hardware and volume/bass/treble and mixed controls, available in Amber Natural, Deep Blue, or Dark Cherry Shade finishes, disc. 1992.

	N/A	$750	$650	$550	$475	$400	$350

Last MSR was $1,100.

ELECTRIC BASS: STB SERIES

6 STB PB 01 - offset double cutaway hardwood body, black pickguard, bolt-on maple neck, 20-fret maple fingerboard with black dot inlay, fixed bridge, 4-on-a-side tuners, chrome hardware, P/J-style pickups, volume/tone controls, 3-position switch, available in Black, Blue, or 3-Tone Sunburst finishes, mfg. 1994-99.

	$325	$275	$250	$220	$185	$150	$115

Last MSR was $449.

6 STB PB 02 X - offset double cutaway hardwood body, flamed maple top and back, black pickguard, bolt-on maple neck, 20-fret rosewood fingerboard with white dot inlay, fixed bridge, 4-on-a-side tuners, gold hardware, P/J-style pickups, 2 volume/1 tone controls, 3-position switch, available in Dark Blue shade or Dark Red shade finishes, disc. 1995.

	$325	$275	$225	$200	$180	$140	$100

Last MSR was $450.

6 STB PJ - offset double cutaway hardwood body, bolt-on maple neck, 20-fret rosewood fingerboard with pearl dot inlay, fixed bridge, 4-on-a-side tuners, chrome hardware, P/J-style pickups, volume/tone controls, 3-position switch, available in Black, Red, White, or 3-Tone Sunburst finishes, mfg. 1995-present.

MSR $350	$260	$225	$200	$170	$145	$115	$90

6 STB PJ L - similar to the 6 STB PJ, except in left-handed configuration, available in Black finish only, mfg. 1995-2003.

	$285	$250	$220	$190	$160	$125	$95

Last MSR was $380.

6 STB PB - similar to 6 STB PJ but with maple neck and fingerboard, one split pickup, volume and tone controls, available in Black, Blue, Red, and White finishes, current mfg.

MSR $330	$250	$175	$150	$125	$100	$75	$50

Add $10 for active electronics (STB PB DX).

6 STB JB - similar to the STB bass series except is in a Jazz bass shape, mfg. 2000-present.

MSR $370	$275	$235	$210	$175	$145	$115	$95

Add $10 for active electronics (STB JB DX).

ELECTRIC BASS: SWB SERIES

SWB basses were compact electric upright instruments equipped with Fishman pickups and Aria electronics. Original production was handled by the Aria Pro Custom Shop.

SWB 01 - sleek upright alder body, bolt-on neck, 41 1/3 in. scale, darkened maple fingerboard, 2-per-side slotted rounded headstock, maple bridge, Aria piezo pickup, chrome hardware, available in Black finish, disc. 1994.

	N/A	$1,500	$1,250	$1,000	$800	$650	$500

Last MSR was $2,899.

SWB 02 - sleek upright alder body, bolt-on neck, 41 1/3 in. scale, darkened maple fingerboard, 2-per-side slotted scroll headstock, maple bridge, Fishman BP-100 pickup, chrome hardware, available in Antique Violin color finish, disc. 1994.

	N/A	$1,500	$1,250	$1,000	$800	$650	$500

Last MSR was $2,999.

Aria Pro II MAB 50
courtesy Aria Pro II

GRADING	100% MINT	98% NEAR MINT	95% EXC+	90% EXC	80% VG+	70% VG	60% G

SWB 02/5 - similar to SWB 02, except has 5-string configuration, 2/3-per-side slotted scroll headstock, both Fishman BP-100 and BIR individual pickups, volume/active treble/active bass controls, pickup selector switch, disc. 1994.

	N/A	$1,600	$1,300	$1,050	$900	$750	$600

SWB 04 - similar to SWB 02, except has alder back, maple carved top, ebony fingerboard, both Fishman BP-100 and BIS individual pickups, 2 f-holes, volume/attack/active treble/active bass controls, BIS and piezo on/off switches, BIS and piezo sensing controls, available in Brown Sunburst or Vintage Sunburst finishes, current mfg.

MSR $3,550	$2,850	$2,485	$2,250	$1,975	$1,700	$1,450	$1,100

ELECTRIC BASS: TA SERIES

TAB-60 - double rounded cutaway, mahogany hollow-body, maple bolt-on neck, 20-fret rosewood fingerboard, black headstock, 2-per-side tuners, black pickguard, 2 humbucker pickups, four knobs (2v, 2tone), pickup selector switch, chrome hardware, available in Brown Sunburst or Wine Red finishes, mfg. 2000-03.

	$495	$425	$375	$335	$290	$250	$200

Last MSR was $660.

TAB-66 - double rounded cutaway hollowbody, laminated maple top/back/sides, set maple neck, 20 fret rosewood fingerboard with dot inlay, black headstock with two-per-side tuners, black pickguard, 2 humbucker pickups, two knobs, three-way switch, chrome hardware, available in Black, Brown Sunburst, or Wine Red finishes, mfg. 2004-present.

MSR $750	$575	$500	$450	$400	$350	$300	$250

ARIANA

Instruments currently built in Asia. Distributed in the U.S. market by Aria USA/NHF of Pennsauken, New Jersey.

Ariana is one of the trademarks of the Aria Company of Japan, and Aria began producing guitars in 1957. Ariana is the budget line of Aria. These guitars are generally low quality and meant for the student or entry-level guitar player. Most guitars retail for around $100 and sell for considerably less. Contact Aria for more information on the Ariana line.

ARIRANG

Instruments previously built in Korea during the early 1980s.

This trademark consists of entry level copies of American designs, and some original designs (source: Tony Bacon and Paul Day, *The Guru's Guitar Guide*).

ARISTONE

See FRAMUS & BESSON. Instruments previously built in West Germany during the late 1950s through the early 1960s.

While ARISTONE was the brandname for a UK importer, these guitars were made by, and identical to, certain FRAMUS models. Research also indicates that the trademark BESSON was utilized as well (source: Tony Bacon and Paul Day, *The Guru's Guitar Guide*).

ARITA

Instruments previously manufactured in Japan.

Arita instruments were distributed in the U.S. market by the Newark Musical Merchandise Company of Newark, New Jersey (source: Michael Wright, *Guitar Stories*, Volume One).

ARMSTRONG, DAN

See AMPEG. Instruments previously produced in England between 1973 and 1975.

Luthier/designer Dan Armstrong has been involved in the music industry for over thirty years. Armstrong originally was a musician involved with studio recording in New York, and rented equipment from a music shop called Caroll's. The owner noticed that his rental instruments were coming back in better shape than when they went out, and began using Armstrong to repair guitars. In 1965, Armstrong opened his own luthier/repair shop on 48th Street across from Manny's Music, and one of his first customers was John Sebastian (Loving Spoonful). As his new business grew, his studio calls for standby work also had him working with numerous artists. Armstrong's shop was open from 1966 to 1968 (which was then demolished to make room for the Rockefeller building), and then he moved locations to a shop in Laguardia Place in the Village.

Armstrong's shop sold new instruments as well. Armstrong used to stabilize Danelectros by changing the factory tuners for after-market Klusons, and by replacing the factory bridges. Nat Daniels (Danelectro) once visited his shop, and, upon discovering Armstrong's stabilizing techniques, got mad and left. Armstrong met William C. Herring at a swap meet in New Jersey a year after MCA folded the Danelectro company in 1968. Herring had bought the company from MCA in late 1968 or early 1969, and Armstrong acquired some interest in the trademark. The facilities produced some 650 to 700 single cutaway models that had one humbucker, no peghead logo, and Dan Armstrong Modified Danelectro on the pickguard.

During the same time period, Armstrong was contracted by Ampeg to produce solid body guitars and basses. Prototypes of the lucite-bodied instruments were produced in 1969, and production ran from 1970 to 1971. Lucite was chosen for its sustaining properties, but the novelty of a transparent body led to the nickname See-Throughs (which Ampeg later copyrighted). The clear-bodied guitars featured interchangeable pickups designed by Bill Lawrence; however, the plastic was prone to expanding when the body warmed up. While most of the production was clear lucite, a number of instruments were also cast in black lucite. In 1973, Armstrong moved to England and produced wood body guitars based on the lucite designs. These guitars had the same sliding pickup design and an anodized aluminum pickguard. The English wood body instruments were produced between 1973 and 1975.

Armstrong produced a number of non-guitar designs as well. Armstrong assisted in some designs for Ampeg's SVT bass amp and the V-4 guitar amplifiers. Musictronics produced the Dan Armstrong Boxes in the mid-1970s, while Armstrong was still living in England. These six small boxes of circuitry plugged into the guitar directly, and then a cable was attached to the amplifier. Modules included the Red Ranger (EQ), Blue Clipper (distortion), Purple Peaker (EQ), Green Ringer (ring modulator), Yellow Humper (EQ) and the acclaimed Orange Squeezer (compression). Armstrong also had a hand in devising the Mutron Octave divider, Volume Wah, and Gizmo.

Dan Armstrong stayed busy in the early to mid-1980s inventing circuit designs and building prototypes of amplifiers in a consulting fashion. Armstrong was featured in numerous *Guitar Player* magazine articles on aftermarket rewiring schematics that expanded the potential voicings of Fender and Gibson production guitar models. Armstrong built some guitar prototypes for the Westone product line in the late 1980s, and his most recent projects were the Hot Cabs instrument speaker line for Cerwin Vega and overseeing St. Louis Music/Ampeg's Reissue guitar models, (biographical information courtesy Dan Armstrong) May/June 1996. Dan died in June, 2004 of a stroke.

GRADING	100% MINT	98% NEAR MINT	95% EXC+	90% EXC	80% VG+	70% VG	60% G

ARMSTRONG, ROB
Instruments currently built in England since the late 1970s.

Luthier Rob Armstrong is known for his custom guitar building. He makes custom flattop guitars, mandolins, parlor guitars, and other instruments. One of his more famous jobs appears to be a Kellogg's Corn Flakes box-turned-guitar for Simon Nicol (Fairport Convention) (source: Tony Bacon, *The Ultimate Guitar Book*).

ARPEGGIO KORINA
Instruments currently built in Pennsylvania since 1995. Distributed by the Arpeggio Korina Guitar Company, a division of Arpeggio Music, Inc.

Ron and Marsha Kayfield have been running Arpeggio Music, Inc. since 1992. Their music shop deals in new, used, and vintage guitars and amplifiers. Arpeggio Music also offers new and vintage refinishing, as well as restoration and repairs.

In 1995, Ron introduced the Korina model, which combines the best features of earlier guitar models in one new versatile package. Guitar players may note the stingray-shaped 3+3 headstock design and arrow-shaped truss rod cover. The access to the truss rod has been moved back away from the nut to avoid the potential weak neck syndrome inherent in other designs. Headstocks are tilted back 17 degrees, and the neck has custom-shaped '50s or '60s neck profiles. The Arpeggio Korina Guitar company also offers custom inlay in both abalone and mother-of-pearl (call for price quote) on their handmade guitars. Arpeggio also sells factory direct on their website.

ELECTRIC: ARPEGGIO KORINA SERIES

All Korina electronics feature Seymour Duncan pickups and custom wiring by Rusty Gray of Musician's Electronic Service. Both the volume and tone controls feature push/push potentiometers: The volume pot controls both the overall volume of the instrument, as well as controlling the pickups phase/out of phase while the selector is in the middle position; the tone pot controls both the overall tone of the instrument as well as coil tapping mode.

ARPEGGIO KORINA CUSTOM - single cutaway korina body, wood binding, hand-carved premium tiger maple book-matched top, korina set neck, Brazilian rosewood fingerboard with abalone diamond snowflake inlay, brass string-through V-shaped tailpiece/trapeze bridge, 3+3 stingray-shaped headstock, gold hardware, 2 Seymour Duncan '59 humbucking pickups, volume/tone push/push controls, 3-way selector switch, available in Chestnut Burst, Ice Tea Burst, Natural, Tequila Sunrise, Vintage Amber Burst, Vintage Natural, and other trans. nitrocellulose finishes, current mfg.

Arpeggio Korina Custom
courtesy Ron & Marsha Kayfield

MSR	N/A	$4,000	$3,500	$3,100	$2,600	$2,200	$1,800	$1,400

Retail price includes a fitted hardshell case. Flamed tiger maple or tiger Koa fingerboards are options.

ARPEGGIO KORINA PLAYER - similar to the Korina Custom, except has an ebony or rosewood fingerboard, abalone or mother-of-pearl dot inlays, nickel hardware and custom brass V-shaped tailpiece, and no maple top, current mfg.

MSR	N/A	$3,400	$2,900	$2,600	$2,300	$1,900	$1,400	$950

Retail price includes a fitted hardshell case.

Arpeggio Korina Player Special - similar to the Korina Player, except has a nickel or gold with brass plate hardware, and a see-through top, current mfg.

MSR	N/A	$3,800	$3,300	$2,900	$2,500	$2,000	$1,600	$1,200

ARTISAN
Instruments previously produced in Japan.

Artisan instruments were distributed in the U.S. market by the Barth-Feinberg company of New York (source: Michael Wright, *Guitar Stories*, Volume One).

ARTISAN (RECENT MFG.)
Instruments previously manufactured by Eikosha Musical Instrument Co., Inc. of Nagoya, Japan. Distributed in the U.S. by V.J. Rendano, located in Boardman, OH.

Artisan electric instruments include good quality archtop models.

ASAMA
Instruments previously built in Japan during the early 1980s.

Guitars with this trademark are generally medium to good quality copies of American design as well as some original designs (source: Tony Bacon and Paul Day, *The Guru's Guitar Guide*).

ASLIN DANE
Instruments distributed by David Burns Musical Instruments Inc., located in West Islip, NY.

Aslin Dane produces many styles of electric guitars and basses. There are various configurations that include both original and popular American designs. Please contact the distributor directly for more information on Aslin Dane instruments (see Trademark Index). Most models retail for $500-$800.

ASTRO (U.S. MFG.)
Instruments previously produced in California circa 1963.

Astro guitars were kit (ready to assemble) guitars produced in the Rickenbacker factory around 1963. There was no reference whatsoever to Rickenbacker (for obvious reasons). Research continues on Astro Guitars for upcoming editions of the *Blue Book of Electric Guitars*, (Astro information courtesy John Hall, Rickenbacker International Corporation).

Arpeggio Korina PLayer
courtesy Ron & Marsha Kayfield

ASTRO (GERMANY MFG.)
Instruments previously built in Nuremberg, Germany.

The Astro guitar company was founded by luthier August Strohmer. He produced guitars under the name Astro (A from August and Stro from Strohmer to make Astro!), during the 1960s and early 1970s. This company never became very large, with only a five-employee workforce even during the 1960s guitar boom. Astro produced mainly entry to medium level solid bodies, semi-acoustics, and archtops. They usually featured Schaller pickups and hardware. Used Astro electric guitars are found in the price range between $100-$300 (Information courtesy Gerold Schulz, Germany).

ASTRO (ITALY MFG.)
Instruments previously built in Italy during the mid- to late 1960s. The U.S. distributor is currently unknown.

Astro guitars are entry-level instruments, similar to other late 1960s strat-y import/exports. According to owner Randy Varrone, his two pickup model has a bolt-on neck (four bolts and a plate), a ply body, six-on-a-side headstock, and a white pickguard with 2 pickups and controls mounted on it. The electronic controls feature a pickup selector marked "B/ALL/T," a volume knob, and two tone knobs marked "B" and "G."

As these instruments were entry level to begin with, used models are generally priced between $79 and $119 (Information courtesy Randy Varrone, Pulse Music of Logansport, Indiana).

ATELIER Z
Instruments currently produced in Japan. Distributed by the Day's Corporation of Tokyo, Japan.

Atelier Z instruments are high quality guitars and basses that have been produced since 1988. They are produced in Japan and imported by Day's Corporation.

ELECTRIC

Progressive series guitars featured a Strat-ish sort of design, with a shorter rounded bass horn, alder body, Gotoh (or Schaller tuners) and 635 mm scale (25 in.). The **AG-STD** Standard (last retail was $1,320 in 1998) has 3 Atelier Z single coil pickups, while the **AG-DLX** Deluxe (last retail was $1,633 in 1998) has 2 single coils and a humbucker in the bridge position. The current Atelier Z guitars are The **Lower East Side**, which is based of a Strat, The **Villlage**, a Strat with different pickup configurations, and the **Manhattan**, a Showmaster style. All current prices are only in Yen.

ELECTRIC BASS

M Standard model basses are similar to Jazz basses, except feature 2 volume/treble/bass controls and matching headstock finishes. The **MZ-188** Basic 4-string (disc. last retail $1,400) has a 2-piece ash body and BadAss II bridge; the **M-245** 4-string ($2,100), the **M-265** ($2,250), and the **M-285** ($2,600). Standard basses have a Bartolini XTCT preamp.

The more modern and sleek design of the **US Series** feature a 2-piece ash body and maple neck/maple fingerboard. The **ZX-500** 5-string (disc. last retail was $2,000) has Bartolini FN5W pickups, Bartolini NTMB preamp and volume/balancer/3-band EQ controls; the **ZAP-600** 6-string (list $2,600) has Bartolini FN6W pickups and a Demeter BEQP-1 preamp.

In 1999, the CLB and JS series were introduced. The **CLB-4** features a maple top with four strings and retails for $1,900. The **CLB-5** is the same version in 5-string configuration for $2,100. The **JS-4** is an ash top four string model that retails for $1,900. The **JS-5** is a five string variation of the JS-4 listing for $2,100. Atelier Z has apparently renamed some of its basses. These basses come in a variety of features, but are only listed in Yen prices.

ATHELETE
Instruments previously built in New York, New York.

Luthier Fumi Nozawa created these high quality 4-, 5-, or 6-string acoustic basses, as well as acoustic guitars for several years.

ATLANSIA
Instruments currently built in Matsumoto (Nagano), Japan. Distributed by Atlansia Instrumental Technology, Ltd. of Matsumoto, Japan.

The best way to describe instruments designed and built by luthier N. Hayashi is sleek. Every curve on any model seems aerodynamic, and the instruments have a nice balance to them. During the early 1980s, models like the Concorde, Stealth, and Galaxie were offered in the U.S. market (the U.S. distributor was based in Texas). These models, and many more, are still available through the manufacturer in Japan.

Atlansia guitars and basses are readily identifiable by the Atlansia logo on the headstock (or body). Models will feature either covered single coil or humbucker pickups; Atlansia also produces the ARS individual round pickups (generally one per string) which are the size of dimes. These pickups are similar to the individual round Bunker designs in that each one contains its own pole piece and winding.

ELECTRIC

While bass models seem to "rule the roost" at Atlansia, there are at least five guitar models regularly produced. The **Century** is a semi-hollow design with a single cutaway body and two f-holes. The **Stroke** is an offset double cutaway solid body, with either a single or two single coil pickups. The **Pentagon**, **Victoria**, and **Stealth** guitar models have matching bass model conterparts.

ELECTRIC BASS

The **Pentagon** bass model has a sleek, single cutaway body. The **Garland** model has a slightly offset double cutaway shape, with extra shaping in the lower bout. **Concord** models have an extended bass horn, and mild cutaway on the treble side. The **Stealth** model has a similar body shape, but features a slim 4-in-line tuning machine profile (as opposed to the Concord's 3/1-per-side headstock). **Victoria** basses have a scrolled bass horn; **Galaxy** and **Pegasus** models have a very extended bass horn and sloped treble bout (no treble side horn). The **Solitaire** featured a body shaped like a pool cue with a single string, bridge unit, and one pickup (you would think that a single string bass model would appeal to 'heavy metal' bass players in the mid-1980s!). The other models are not that extreme; any of the 4-, 5-, or 6-string models are well-balanced and eminently playable.

ATLAS
See chapter on House Brands.

This trademark has been identified as a House Brand of the RCA Victor Records Stores (source: Willie G. Moseley, *Stellas & Stratocasters*).

AUDITION

See chapter on House Brands.

This trademark has been identified by researcher Willie G. Moseley as a House Brand of the F. W. Woolworth (Woolco) department stores.

Further information from authors Tony Bacon and Paul Day indicate that guitars with this trademark originated in Japan (later Korea) during the 1960s and 1970s (source: Tony Bacon and Paul Day, *The Guru's Guitar Guide*).

AUERSWALD

Instruments currently built in Konstanz, Germany since the early 1990s.

Luthier Jerry Auerswald builds high quality original design solid body guitars and basses that are visually exciting as well. Auerswald hand crafts all his instruments, so production is based on his output alone. For further information regarding specifications and pricing, please contact Auerswald through the Index of Current Manufacturers located in the back of this book.

Auerswald electrics are easily identified by the unique body/neck design, the additional sustain bow on three of the models, and the Auerswald logo on the truss rod cover and bridge hardware. All models feature Auerswald hardware (bridge, string rider, tremolo). Contact the company directly via their website to order or for more information (see Trademark Index).

Austin AU731 Standard
Courtesy Austin

ELECTRIC

Auerswald models feature maple bodies, cherry/wenge necks, EMG pickups, Sperzel hardware, and Auerswald custom tremolo and EQ systems. The **Anastasia** and **Chico Hablas** guitar models both feature a sustain bow (a body arm that attaches to the headstock and provides extra stiffening support to the upper end of the neck). Anastasia models feature wenge bodies, cherry necks, 33-fret ebony fingerboards (66 cm scale), 2 EMG single coil/humbucker (model 81) pickups, and volume/2 tone controls.

Both the **Diva** and **Gloria** models feature angular semi-hollow bodies and reverse headstock designs as well as V-shaped f-holes. The **Naomi** and **Viva** solid body electrics have reverse headstocks, and exaggerated top horns to accentuate the sleek body contours. The Naomi Power Slam model has a maple body, glued-in cherry/wenge neck, 27-fret ebony finger-board (66 cm scale), 2 EMG 89 humbuckers, and Sperzel tuners.

The **Venus** 8-string model has a pair of sustain bows on either side of the neck, culminating in an open triangular head-piece. This model features reverse stringing, and the tuning knobs are cleverly concealed on the back of the lower bout. The **Aliki** acoustic/electric model has three cat's-eye-shaped f-holes, a 3+3 slotted headstock, and controls mounted on the side of the upper bout. This model is also offered in a 4-string acoustic/electric bass, with a 2+2 solid headstock.

Auerswald also offers the **Shinjun**, **Symbol**, and the **Lolly/TA**.

ELECTRIC BASS

The **Hammer** bass model has a cherry wood body with extended bass and treble horns, glued-in neck, 25-fret ebony finger-board (86.4 cm scale), and reverse stringing (tuners near bridge). Electronics consist of a set of EMG P/J pickups, 2 vol-ume/one tone controls. Auerswald also offers the **Cleo** bass model, which features a sustain bow: a body arm that attaches to the headstock and provides extra stiffening support to the upper end of the neck. Cleo basses feature wenge bodies, cherry wood necks, 24-fret ebony fingerboards (86.4 cm scale), 2 Auerswald (or EMG) humbuckers, and 2 volume/one tone controls. Auerswald also offers the **Aliki**, **Lolly/TA**, and the **A. Clayton** models.

AUROC

Instruments previously built in England from 1988-late 1990s/early 2000s.

Luthier Pat Luckett built guitars with a 'strat'-styled synthetic marble body coupled with a graphite neck, a promising design that may eliminate the "tweakage" phenomenon of wood necks. The *Blue Book of Electric Guitars* encourages anyone with further information to contact us for future edition updates.

AUSTIN

Instruments currently built in Korea and China. Distributed by St. Louis Music of St. Louis, Missouri.

Asian-produced Austin instruments are good quality entry- or student-level acoustic and electric guitars.

ELECTRIC

Austin AU754 Rock Standard
Courtesy Austin

The **AU731 Era Standard** (retail $199) has a 'Strat'-style body, with three single coil pickups; add $10 for Metallic finish. The **Era Deluxe** (last retail $249) has a rosewood fingerboard and 2 single coil/humbucker pickups. The Era Deluxe is also available in a left-handed configuration. The **AU766 Vintage Rock** has a 'Les Paul' style body and retails for $299. The AU786 Custom Vintage Rock is the same guitar with gold hardware (retail $399) and flamed or quilted top (retail $449).

The **AU754 Rock Standard**, **AU758 Rock Pro**, and the **AU792 Tour Pro** all feature 'PRS' style bodies. The Standard retails for $289, the Rock Pro has a tremolo and retails for $389, and the Tour Pro has a quilted top for $469.

The **Austin Mini Era** (retail list $149) is a scaled-down electric with one single coil pickup, volume control, and adjustable bridge; the **Mini Era Deluxe** (list $179) has 3 single coils, volume and tone controls, and a traditional tremolo. The **Vintage Rock** (list $329) is an archtop model with multi-layer celluloid body binding, 2 humbuckers, and a tune-o-matic bridge.

Austin also produces a variety of ES-335 styled guitars. Used pricing on all Austin electric guitars are typically 50%-75% off of the retail price.

ELECTRIC BASS

Austin bass models feature hardwood bodies, bolt-on maple necks, and fixed bridges. The **AU 759** P-style bass (list $269) has a split P-style pickup; this model has an optional left-handed configuration (**Model AU 770**), or in Black, Red, Sunburst, or Transparent Blue finishes. The **AU 769** PJ-style bass has P/J-style pickups and a rosewood fingerboard (list $299). The

AU 779 Intruder Bass has 2 J-style pickups, rosewood fingerboard, and chrome hardware. In 2004, the P-Style basses were renumbered as **AU829** and retail for $249.

The Eclipse Bass Series are higher end models with fine wood finishes. The **AU850 Standard 4-String** retails for $299, and the **AU855 5-String** retails for $349. The **AU860 Custom 4-String** retails for $499 and the **AU865 5-String** retails for $599. The Eclipse Pro is the top of the line and feature bubinga tops. The **AU870 4-String** retails for $749 and the **AU875 5-String** retails for $849.

Used prices on Austin bass guitars are typically 50%-75% off of the retail.

AUSTIN HATCHET
Trademark of instruments previously distributed by Targ and Dinner of Chicago, Illinois circa mid-1970s to early-1980s. Instrument production location unknown.

The Austin Hatchet was one of the first travel guitars (along with Erlewine's Chiquita model) available for the "musician on the move."

ELECTRIC

The **Austin Hatchet** is a scaled-down electric with a wedge-shaped body, 22-fret fingerboard, 3-per-side arrowhead headstock, 2 humbuckers, fixed bridge, 2 volume/1 tone knobs, pickup selector switch, and phase switch.

The company also offered a **Flying V**-style model, with gold hardware, brass nut, 2 humbuckers, and a "lead" switch. TheFlying V model was 43 in. long, and 17 in. across the bottom "V" wings.

Austin Hatchet models in good condition range between $150 and $200.

AVALON
See Wandre.

Instruments such as Avalon's Rock Oval model were produced in Italy during the 1960s.

AVANTI
Instruments previously produced in Europe during the 1960s.

Research continues into this trademark. Most models that are encountered seem to have a resounding feel of 1960s entry level Italian production. Further information will be updated in future editions of the *Blue Book of Electric Guitars* (source: Rittor Books, *60s Bizarre Guitars*). Used Avanti guitars typically range from $100 to $200 in excellent condition.

AVON
Instruments previously built in Japan during the early to late 1970s.

The AVON trademark is the brandname of a UK importer. Avons are generally low to medium quality copies of American designs (source: Tony Bacon and Paul Day, *The Guru's Guitar Guide*).

AW SHADOWS GUITARS
Instruments currently built in Princeton, Minnesota.

In 1998, AW Shadows introduced a new take on guitar body shapes: curved! The **CRS Curve** guitar incorporates a traditional single cutaway body design with an ergonomic vertical curve in the lower bout, beginning after the bridge/stop tailpiece. This patent-pending design lets players keep their arms in a natural position close to the body, eliminating "playing-related maladies such as tendinitis, carpal tunnel syndrome, muscle strain, and back pain," as the company claims.

The CRS Curve model features a cherry wood body with walnut accents, maple neck-through design, 24.5 in. scale, rosewood or ebony fingerboards, custom made ebony saddle, 3-per-side tuners, 2 humbuckers, 2 volume/2 tone controls, and 3-way toggle switch.

AW Shadows specializes in custom wine barrels, and it is unlikely that they still produce their guitar.

AXE
Instruments previously built in Korea from 1988 to 1989.

Entry level two pickup guitar that came in a "starter pack." Although we're not familiar with the guitar, the idea of a package containing all sorts of guitar paraphernalia (how-to booklet, strings, tuner of some sort, strap, etc.) actually sounds like a novel idea if coupled with lessons (source: Tony Bacon and Paul Day, *The Guru's Guitar Guide*).

AXELSON
Instruments currently built in Duluth, Minnesota.

Luthier Randy Axelson has been providing top-notch guitar repair, restoration, and custom guitar building on a regular basis. For information, pricing, and availability contact luthier Axelson (see Trademark Index).

AXEMAN
Instruments previously built in Japan during the late 1970s.

The AXEMAN trademark is the brand name of a UK importer. The guitars are generally medium quality copies of American designs (source: Tony Bacon and Paul Day, *The Guru's Guitar Guide*).

AXIS
Instruments previously built in Korea circa 1989.

The AXIS trademark is the brand name of a UK importer. Axis guitars are entry level to medium quality solid body copies of American designs (source: Tony Bacon and Paul Day, *The Guru's Guitar Guide*).

AXL
Instruments currently built overseas. Distributed by the Music Link.

The Axl trademark was introduced in 2001 as a line of electric and acoustic guitars as well as a line of amplifiers. These instruments are produced with modern equipment and the best available material to create a quality line of guitars at affordable prices. Electric models are mainly based on popular American designs (Stratocaster, Telecaster). For more information on Axl refer to The Music Link's website (see Trademark Index).

AXTECH
Instruments currently built in Korea.

Axtech instruments are generally entry level to medium quality solid body and acoustic guitars based on Classic American designs.

AXTRA
Instruments currently built in Kenosha, Wisconsin since 1985. Distributed by Axtra Guitars, Inc. of Kenosha, Wisconsin.

Axtra Guitars, Inc. was founded in 1985 by Bill Michaelis, who heads the organization. His tremendous creativity, experience, innovativeness, and commitment to the highest standards of manufacturing excellence have been the keys to the great satisfaction of guitar players who own Axtra instruments.

This company is not a huge, impersonal organization, but a custom specialty shop that also manufactures a standard line of guitars and basses. Personally run by Bill, dedication to the finest quality products, service, and customer satisfaction is the basic aim. The result is a modern, progressive company dedicated to meeting the needs of every musician: great sound - versatility - reliability - durability - individual custom features. Everyone at Axtra takes great pride in producing the highest quality guitars and basses (source: Bill Michaelis, Axtra Guitars).

ELECTRIC: GENERAL INFORMATION

Michaelis offers a number of body designs, as well as the flexibility of a custom design (hardware, pickups, and other options are at the customer´s choice). Some of the Axtra standard designs include bolt-on or set-neck designs; quartersawn maple or mahogany necks; maple, rosewood, ebony, pau ferro, bubinga, or wenge fingerboards; figured maple or curly birch tops; ash, mahogany, basswood, and maple bodies; locking or non-locking tremolos, or tune-o-matic bridges; Sperzel tuners; and Seymour Duncan pickups. Instruments are finished in transparent or solid colors, or custom graphics.

ELECTRIC: BOLT-ON NECK MODELS

The Axtra "Strat"-style guitar model (suggested list price starts at $1,200) features a choice of basswood or maple or mahogany body, maple bolt-on neck, maple fretboard, Seymour Duncan pickups, and Wilkinson hardware. A "Tele"-style guitar model had a single cutaway body design, but similar construction details as the ´Strat.´ The list price starts at $1,600 and up, depending on options.

ELECTRIC: DESIGNER MODELS

Axtra offers a number of specialty models based on the "strat" or "super strat" configuration. The 7/8 Strat has a flame maple top/basswood body, maple neck, 22-fret rosewood fingerboard, 25.5 in. scale, Wilkinson bridge, and many options to explore at a list price of $1,800. A full sized mahogany body with curly birch top is offered beginning at $2,000; the same mahogany body can be matched with a carved curly birch top for $2,400.

A custom 7-string semi-hollow "Tele" is available with a flamed maple body, special Seymour Duncan pickups, custom bridge, and ebony fingerboard at $2,400.

**Axtra 7-String Semi-Acoustic
courtesy Axtra**

ELECTRIC: STYLIST SERIES

The Axtra Stylist (suggested list price starts at $1,800 and up) features a flame maple top, basswood body, maple set-in neck, 25.5 in. scale, 24-fret bound pau ferro fingerboard with musical note inlay, and Gotoh bridge. Also offered in a 24-fret bolt-on neck design for $2,000.

ELECTRIC BASS

Axtra offers both a P-style and a P/J-styled model bass in 4-, 5-, and 6-string configurations. The suggested list price begins at $1,500. Many options (like a Northern Ash body, bubinga fingerboard, and quartersawn maple neck) are available on the bass models. Axtra also has their own sleek bass design in a maple body and Bartolini soapbar pickups that starts at $2,400.

AZOLA BASSES
Instruments currently built in Ramona, CA. Previously built in San Marcos, CA.

Azola´s line of electric uprights has grown dramatically since bringing the Baby Bass (Ampeg-like) back to life and giving it their own twist and modern versatility. In 1997, the evolution of the Baby Bass came full circle when Ampeg contracted Azola to manufacture the official reissue Ampeg Baby Bass with its fiberglass body and magnetic diaphragm pickup system. Piezo bridge pickups are also available.

Azola is owned by Steve and Jill Azola, and offers Baby Basses under their own name in a hardwood hollow body version available with any of their various pickup options (and they still offer replacement parts and accessories for vintage Ampeg and Zorko Baby Basses). Other instruments include the Acoustic Baby Bass and the EuroCoustic Baby Bass.

Many aspects of this design have either been incorporated into the current models, or have become options available to all models. Azola also has a custom shop that produces instruments on a special order only basis directly from the factory. For more information please contact the manufacturer directly (see Trademark Index).

ELECTRIC BASS: UPRIGHT SERIES

Azola offers three different models in either **Standard** or **Floating Top** configuration, and a large number of options to choose from. The **Standard Series** bass configuration shares these features: ash bodies, 2-piece maple tilt-adjust neck, bubinga fingerboard, 41.5 in. scale, piezo bridge pickups with passive volume control, adjustable endpin and bout, black hardware, LaBella strings, and are finished in a natural semi-gloss finish.

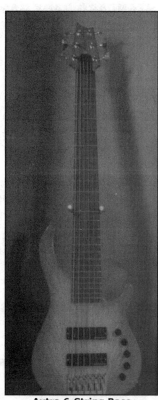

**Axtra 6-String Bass
courtesy Axtra**

GRADING	100% MINT	98% NEAR MINT	95% EXC+	90% EXC	80% VG+	70% VG	60% G

The semi-hollow **Floating Top** configuration features an arched spruce top on an ash body (a design concept from Martin Clevinger), a bass bar and sound post, passive bass boost/arco sensitive control, Thomastik strings, and an ebony fingerboard.

For a two-year period, Azola offered an upright, violin-shaped Mahogany body **StradiBass** model, which featured a Clevinger-designed Floating spruce Top, figured maple laminated neck, ebony fingerboard, 41.5 in. scale, maple bridge, gold hardware, and a multi-piezo bridge pickup system with 3-band active EQ at a retail price of $4,995.

Options, upgrades and accessories available for all the listed models include six different types of pickup systems, such as the Clevinger-design bridge/dual piezo system, multi-piezo bridge pickup system, and the Latin (and Latin+) pickup system. Custom color high gloss finishes are also available on all three models.

Add $75 for position markers. Add $100 for "Iced Tea" sunburst semi-gloss finish. Add $250 for ebony fingerboard. Add $300 for on-board preamp with active EQ. Add $500 for 5-string configuration.

ACOUSTIC BABY BASS
- hollow body, arched laminated maple top and back, ash sides, f-holes, maple tilt-adjust neck, rosewood fingerboard, 39-41.5 in. scale, adjustable endpin and bout, Grover tuners, black hardware, Vintage Honey Blonde Satin finish, 15 lbs., mfg. 2004-present.
MSR $3,295

EUROCOUSTIC BUG BASS
- hollow body, hand-carved Spruce top, arched maple back and bent maple sides, maple neck, ebony fingerboard, 41.5 in. scale, scroll-style headstock, bass bar with soundpost, Azola piezo bridge and pickup, available in Dark, Medium, or Blonde Satin Violin finishes, 11 lbs., new 2004.
MSR $2,995

The Eurocoustic series is built in Europe with craftsmen that have the same high standards of Azola. Instruments are all inspected by Steve in the U.S. before being shipped to the consumer.

Eurocoustic Mini Bass - similar to the Bug Bass, except has a "Azola Mini-Style" body, new 2004.
MSR $3,295

Eurocoustic Baby Bass - similar to the Bug Bass, except has a "Azola Baby-Style" body, 14 lbs., new 2004.
MSR $3,495

LIGHTNING BUG
- slender solid ash body, maple tilt-adjust neck, rosewood fingerboard, 41 in. scale, Grover tuners, dual piezo pickup system, adjustable bout & endpin, 11 lbs., natural finish, mfg. 2002-present.
MSR $1,995

Lightning Bug Latin Version - similar to the Lightning Bug except has Ampeg Baby Bass style magnetic diaphragm pickup system, mfg. 2002-present.
MSR $2,495

Lightning Bug Floating Top - similar to the Lightning Bug except has an arched spruce top, mfg. 2002-present.
MSR $2,995

MINI BABY BASS
- sculpted ash body, maple tilt-adjust neck, rosewood fingerboard, maple bridge, 39-41.5 in. scale, adjustable bout and endpin, Azola Tru-Acoustic piezo pickup and on-board active EQ, Grover tuners, black hardware, available in Natural Satin finish, 15 lbs., new 2004.
MSR $2,495

STANDARD BABY BASS
- classical shape, ash body, 2-piece maple tilt-adjust neck, bubinga fingerboard, 41.5 in. scale, 2-per-side tuners on slotted headstock, scroll headpiece, piezo bridge pickups with passive volume control, adjustable endpin and bout, black hardware, LaBella strings, available in Natural semi-gloss finish, disc. 2003.

Last MSR was $3,495.

Floating Top Baby Bass - similar to the Standard Baby Bass, except features semi-hollow body construction, arched spruce top, ebony fingerboard, bass bar, soundpost, mfg. 1998-2003.

Last MSR was $4,495.

STANDARD BUGBASS
- ultra compact upright body style, ash body, 2-piece maple tilt-adjust neck, bubinga fingerboard, 41.5 in. scale, 2-per-side tuners on slotted headstock, rounded headpiece, piezo bridge pickups with passive volume control, adjustable endpin and bout, black hardware, LaBella strings, available in Natural semi-gloss finish, disc.

$1,300	$1,150	$1,000	$850	$750	$650	$500

Last MSR was $1,495.

Floating Top BugBass - similar to the Standard BugBass, except features semi-hollow body construction, arched spruce top, ebony fingerboard, bass bar, sound post, mfg. 1998-2003.

$2,000	$1,750	$1,500	$1,300	$1,100	$900	$700

Last MSR was $2,495.

STANDARD BUGBASS II
- Solid Ash body, maple tilt-adjust neck, rosewood fingerboard, 41.5 in. scale, Grover tuners, adjustable endpin and bout, several options at added cost, mfg. 2002-present.
MSR $1,995

SCARAB BASS
- similar to the Bugbass II except is an internally braced hollow body, with a spruce top, and electronics, mfg. 2002-present.
MSR $2,995

STANDARD MINIBASS
- sleek contoured violin-shaped upright body, ash body, 2-piece maple tilt-adjust neck, bubinga fingerboard, 41.5 in. scale, 2-per-side tuners on slotted headstock, scroll headpiece, piezo bridge pickups with passive volume control, adjustable endpin and bout, black hardware, LaBella strings, available in Natural semi-gloss finish, disc. 2003.

Last MSR was $2,295.

Floating Top MiniBass - similar to the Standard MiniBass, except features semi-hollow body construction, arched spruce top, ebony fingerboard, bass bar, sound post, mfg. 1998-2003.

Last MSR was $3,495.

ELECTRIC BASS: AZOLA CUSTOM SHOP

The Azola Custom Shop´s special **Deco Bass** model (list price from $4,995 laminated, and $5,995 for fully carved) features an arched spruce top over a hollow body, maple neck, upright-style fingerboard, 34 in. scale, and multi-piezo bridge pickup system. Contact Azola for further specifications.

The **Nouveau** is a semi-hollow ash body bass guitar that features a modern retro design. This model starts at $1,995, and the Acoustic/Electric model starts at $2,495.

A **Vintage Style Baby Bass**, which is sort of a reissue in tribute to the Ampeg Baby Bass, is a fiberglass body with a "Latin" pickup system, and prices start at $3,295.

Other custom shop models have been produced over the years. Azola is also open to Signature Special Projects. Since most of these instruments are one-offs and other rarities, it is difficult to put a market value on them. Contact the Azola Custom Shop for more information.

ELECTRIC BASS: JAZZMAN SERIES

Azola´s Jazzman Series was a part of their Custom Shop operations. The **Jazzman I** features an offset double cutaway body, J-style neck and fingerboard/4-on-a-side tuners, one Basslines humbuckering pickup, 3-band active EQ, and a semi-gloss finish. Prices begin at $1,295. The **Jazzman II** (prices start at $1,295) is similar in design, but features 2 Bassline humbuckers (with coil switching), and passive volume and tone controls. The semi-hollow **Jazzman III** has a spruce top, upright style fingerboard, magnetic or piezo pickup, and passive volume and tone controls. The Jazzman III´s list price begins at $1,995.

Jazzman model Upgrades include exotic woods (call for prices), a figured top (add $250), custom color or sunburst gloss finish (add $250), the "Vintage Package" of pickguard and control plate (add $100), and an active EQ (add $250). These models are no longer offered by Azola.

AZUMI
See LEW CHASE. Instruments previously built in Japan during the early 1980s.

Azumi guitars were generally medium quality solidbodys of original design. Research continues to document these body designs (source: Tony Bacon and Paul Day, *The Guru's Guitar Guide*).

NOTES

Section B

B & G

See chapter on House Brands.

B & G instruments were built by Danelectro in Neptune City, New Jersey in the late 1950s/early 1960s (source: Willie G. Moseley, *Stellas & Stratocasters*).

B & J

See chapter on House Brands.

This trademark has been identified as a House Brand of the B & J company (source: Willie G. Moseley, *Stellas & Stratocasters*).

B.C. RICH

Instruments currently built in Hesperia, CA (American Handmade series) and Asia (N.J., Platinum and Bronze series). Distributed by B.C. Rich Guitars International, Inc. of San Bernadino, CA and B.C. Rich Guitars USA. Import models (N.J., Platinum, and Bronze Series) distributed by Davitt & Hanser Music of Cincinnati, OH.

Luthier Bernardo Chavez Rico used to build classical and flamenco guitars at Bernardo's Valencian Guitar Shop, the family's business in Los Angeles. During the mid-1960s folk music boom (and boom in guitar sales), a distributor suggested a name change - and B.C. Rich guitars was born. Between 1966 and 1968, Rico continued to build acoustic guitars, then changed to solid body electrics. The company began producing custom guitars based on Fender and Gibson designs, but Rico wanted to produce designs that represented his tastes and ideals. The Seagull solid body (first produced in 1971) was sleek, curvy, and made for rock 'n roll. Possessing a fast neck, hot-rodded circuitry and pickups, and a unique body profile, this was (and still is) an eye-catching design.

In 1974, Neal Mosher joined the company. Mosher also had a hand in some of the guitars designed, and further explored other designs with models like the Mockingbird, Eagle, Ironbird, and the provocatively-named Bich. The first 6-tuners-on-a-side headstocks began to appear in 1981. In the mid-1980s, B.C. Rich moved from Los Angeles to El Monte, California.

The company began to import models in the **U.S. Production Series**, Korean-produced kits that were assembled in the U.S. between 1984 and 1986. In 1984, the Japanese-built **N.J. Series** line of B.C. Rich designs were introduced, and was built by the Terada company for two years. Production of the N.J. series was moved to Korea in 1986 (models were built in the Cort factory).

In 1988, Rico licensed the Korean-built, lower priced **Platinum** and entry level **Rave** Series to the Class Axe company, and later licensed the B.C. Rich name and designs in 1989. Class Axe moved production of the U.S.-built guitars to a facility in Warren, New Jersey, and stepped up importation of the N.J. (named after Nagoya, Japan - not New Jersey), Platinum, and Rave Series models.

Unfortunately, the lower priced series soon began to show a marked drop in quality. In 1994, Rico came back out of semi-retirement, retook control over his trademark, and began to rebuild the company. Rico became partners with Bill Shapiro, and the two divided up areas of responsibility. Rico once more began building acoustic and high end electrics at his Hesperia facilities, and Shapiro began maintaining quality control over the imported N.J., Platinum, and U.S. series in San Bernadino. In 1998, Davitt & Hanser Music of Cincinnati, Ohio began distributing the import models (N.J., Platinum, and Bronze Series). Additional model commentary courtesy Bernie Rich, President/Founder of B.C. Rich International, May 1997.

MODEL SERIES IDENTIFICATION

B.C. Rich models all have different body profiles. However, this distinct model profile may be offered in one of five different series, and those different series have different price levels based on construction and distinctions.

Acrylic Series: These guitars feature acrylic (see-through) clear or colored bodies.

American Production: Any American-built neck-through guitar or bass with B.C. Rich, Rico, or R logos.

Bronze Series: Entry level instruments that are produced overseas with basic features.

N.J. Series: Mid-level quality instruments. In 2004, this series started using the Floyd Rose Speedloader tremolo bridge. The N.J. Series also features Classic models, which are based on the famous designs of the 1970s, and the Signature Series, which are guitars produced with famous names in the music industry.

Platinum Series: The next step up from the Bronze Series, but below the N.J. Series.

Platinum Pro Series: Similar to the Platinum Series, except features a Floyd Rose tremolo.

Rave Series: At one time, this was the entry level line of guitars.

B.C. RICH ACTIVE ELECTRONICS

B.C. Rich has a long history of offering on-board active electronic packages. Here's a short guide to all those extra switches and knobs: The **Active Electronic** package available on Mockingbird Supreme and Eagle Supreme (guitar and bass models) consists of (listed top to bottom, as if the guitar was held by the neck): Master Volume knob, Pickup Selector Switch, PreAmp Volume Knob, PreAmp On/Off switch, a 6-position Vari-Tone chicken head knob, phase mini-switch, Rhythm pickup coil tap switch, Lead pickup coil tap switch, Master Tone knob. Due to space constraints, the **Full Active Electronic** package is only available on the Bich models. This package consists of (listed top to bottom): Master Volume knob, Pickup Selector Switch, PreAmp #1 On/Off mini-switch, PreAmp #2 On/Off mini-switch, phase mini-switch, PreAmp #1 Volume

B

Knob, Pre-Amp #2 Volume Knob, Rhythm pickup Volume, a 6-position Vari-Tone chicken head knob, Master Tone knob, Rhythm pickup coil tap switch, Lead pickup coil tap switch. Now that´s tonal variety!

GENERAL INFORMATION

B.C. Rich offers numerous options for the current instrument line through their Custom Shop. There is no additional charge for left-handed configuration. For information and pricing on custom inlays, graphic paint jobs, and exotic woods, please contact the B.C. Rich Custom Shop. B.C. Rich also offers a Combo Pack with a B.C. Rich Bronze Series Warlock guitar and a B.C. Rich 12W amplifier. Listings within this section are alphabetized by series.

Add $40 for black hardware. Add $40 for coil tap switch. Add $40 for phase switch. Add $40 for rosewood fingerboard. Add $50 for paint matching headstock. Add $75 for headstock binding. Add $75 for fingerboard binding. Add $75 for ebony fingerboard. Add $100 for gold hardware. Add $125 for Sunburst finish. Add $125 for Pearl or Candy finishes. Add $150 for Marble finish (this option was discontinued in 1998). Add $150 for active electronics (Mockingbird Supreme and Eagle Supreme, Guitars and Basses). Add $250 for full active electronics (due to space constraints, Bich models only). Add $200 for Floyd Rose tremolo. Add $200 for full active electronics. Add $225 for urethane Transparent finish. Add $250 for Nitrocellulose Lacquer finish.

ELECTRIC: ASSASSIN SERIES

The Assassin model was introduced in 1986, and phased out by 2002.

ASM 1 (U.S. NECK-THROUGH-BODY) - offset double cutaway body, mahogany body wings, figured maple top, maple neck-through design, 25 1/2" scale, 24-fret bound ebony fingerboard with diamond insert inlays, locking Floyd Rose vibrato, 6-on-a-side tuners, chrome hardware, 2 Seymour Duncan humbucker pickups, volume/tone controls, 3-way selector switch, available in Amber Burst, Cherry Sunburst, Trans. Black, Trans. Blue, or Trans. Red finishes, mfg. 1998-99.

$1,525	$1,325	$1,125	$925	$825	$700	$575

Last MSR was $1,899.

ASM 2 (U.S. Neck-through-body) - similar to the ASM 1, except features pearl diamond fingerboard inlay, black hardware, unbound fingerboard/headstock, pickup selector mini-switches, mfg. 1998-99.

$1,275	$1,075	$875	$775	$675	$575	$475

Last MSR was $1,699.

ASM 3 (U.S. Bolt-On Neck) - similar to the ASM 1, except features basswood body, bolt-on maple neck, pearl teardrop fingerboard inlay, unbound fingerboard/headstock, mfg. 1998-99.

$1,175	$1,050	$850	$750	$650	$550	$450

Last MSR was $1,549.

ASM B (U.S. Bolt-On Neck) - similar to the ASM 1, except features basswood body, figured maple top, bolt-on maple neck, available in Amber Burst, Cherry Sunburst, Trans. Blue, or Trans. Magenta finish, mfg. 1998-99.

$1,175	$1,050	$850	$750	$650	$550	$450

Last MSR was $1,549.

ASSASSIN (NJ SERIES) - Assassin body style, NJ Series appointments, available in black, Trans. Red, Trans. Blue, or Blood Red finishes, mfg. 2000-02.

$375	$325	$275	$235	$185	$145	$105

Last MSR was $549.

Add $50 for Trans. Red or Trans. Blue finishes.

ASSASSIN (NJ NECK-THRU SERIES) - Assassin body style, NJ Series appointments, neck-thru body design, available in Black, Trans. Amber, or Trans. Red, finish, mfg. 2000 only.

$550	$475	$425	$375	$325	$275	$225

Last MSR was $775.

Add $50 for Trans. Red or Trans. Amber finishes.

ASSASSIN (PLATINUM) - Assassin body style, lower end appointments, available in Black, Metallic Red, Metallic Blue, or Blood Red finishes, mfg. 2000-02.

$300	$250	$215	$185	$150	$110	$70

Last MSR was $419.

ASSASSIN (U.S. NECK-THROUGH-BODY) - offset double cutaway body, alder body wings/maple neck-thru design, 24 5/8 in. scale, 24-fret ebony fingerboard with diamond-shaped inlays, double locking Floyd Rose vibrato, blackface peghead with screened logo, 6-on-a-side Sperzel tuners, black hardware, 2 Seymour Duncan humbucker pickups, 2 volume/1 tone controls, 3-way selector, available in Black, Blue, Emerald Green, Golden Yellow, Magenta, Red, or Tangerine translucent finish, mfg. 1986-1998.

$1,000	$900	$800	$675	$575	$450	$325

Last MSR was $1,399.

In 1994, Black, Purple, Red, and White finishes replaced previous item. In 1995, rosewood fingerboard, fixed bridge replaced previous item. This model was previously available with other pickup configurations: 3 single coil pickups (with 3 mini switches), single coil/humbucker pickups (with mini switches).

Assassin MMT (Maple Molded Top-U.S. Neck-through-body) - similar to the Assassin model, except has offset double cutaway mahogany body, figured maple top, 2 DiMarzio humbucker pickups, 2 volume/1 tone controls, 3-position switch, available in Emerald Green, Red Tangerine, Trans. Blue, Trans. Gold, or Trans. Purple finish, disc. 1995.

$1,050	$900	$795	$695	$575	$475	$375

Last MSR was $1,499.

This model had an optional B.C. Rich stop bridge/tailpiece or standard Wilkinson vibrato. In 1995, pearl blade fingerboard inlay, Trans. Blue, Trans. Cherry Red, Trans. Emerald Green and Trans. Pagon Gold finishes were introduced. Emerald Green, Red Tangerine, Trans. Blue, Trans. Gold and Trans. Purple finishes were discontinued.

B

GRADING	100% MINT	98% NEAR MINT	95% EXC+	90% EXC	80% VG+	70% VG	60% G

Assassin Hollow (U.S. Neck-through-body) - offset double cutaway semi hollow mahogany body, figured maple top, f-holes, set maple neck, 24-fret ebony fingerboard, B.C. Rich stop bridge/tailpiece, blackface peghead with screened logo, 6-on-a-side tuners, black hardware, 2 humbucker DiMarzio pickups, 2 volume/1 tone controls, 3-position switch, available in Emerald Green, Trans. Blue, Trans.Pagan Gold or Trans. Cherry Red finish, disc. 1995.

	$1,100	$950	$825	$725	$625	$525	$425

Last MSR was $1,499.

ASSASSIN STANDARD (U.S. BOLT-ON-NECK) - offset double cutaway alder body, bolt-on maple neck, 24-fret ebony fingerboard with abalone blade inlay at 12th fret, double locking Floyd Rose vibrato, blackface peghead with screened logo, 6-on-a-side Sperzel tuners, black hardware, Seymour Duncan single coil/humbucker pickups, 2 volume/1 tone controls, 3-position switch, available in Black, Candy Blue, Candy Red, Deep Metallic Purple, Pearl Emerald, Red, or various trans. colors finishes, disc. 1998.

	$800	$725	$650	$550	$475	$375	$300

Last MSR was $1,199.

In 1995, Blue, Purple, Turquoise and White finishes were introduced, Candy Color finishes became options, Deep Metallic Purple, Pear Emerald and Trans. Color finishes were discontinued. In 1996, Cobalt Blue finish was introduced, and Turquoise finish was discontinued.

Assassin MMT (Maple Molded Top U.S. Bolt-On Neck) - similar to Assassin Standard, except has mahogany body, quilted maple top, chrome hardware, no Blade inlay at 12th fret, available in Translucent Black, Translucent Blue, Translucent Emerald Green, Trans. Golden Yellow, Trans. Magenta, Trans. Red, or Trans. Tangerine, disc. 1998.

	$1,050	$900	$800	$675	$575	$450	$350

Last MSR was $1,399.

In 1995, Translucent Pagan Gold and Translucent Purple finishes were introduced; Trans. Black, Trans. Golden Yellow, Trans. Magenta, and Trans. Tangerine finishes were discontinued.

MB 1 (MASON BERNARD, U.S. BOLT-ON-NECK) - offset double cutaway alder (or poplar) body, bolt-on maple neck, 25 1/2 " scale, 24-fret ebony fingerboard, locking Floyd Rose vibrato, blackface peghead with screened logo, 6-on-a-side tuners, chrome hardware, Seymour Duncan single coil/humbucker pickups, volume/tone controls, 3-position switch, available in Black, Gunmetal Grey, Metallic Red, Wine Purple, and White finishes, mfg. 1998-99.

	$900	$775	$675	$575	$475	$375	$250

Last MSR was $1,199.

MB 2 (Mason Bernard, U.S. Bolt-On Neck) - similar to the MB 1, except features 2 Seymour Duncan humbucking pickups, mfg. 1998 only.

	$925	$800	$700	$600	$500	$400	$275

Last MSR was $1,249.

ELECTRIC: BEAST SERIES

BEAST STANDARD - double sharp cutaway 4-point body, alder or poplar body, maple neck-thru body, 24-fret ebony fingerboard with diamond inlays, 2 DiMarzio humbucker pickups, Beast style headstock, available in Black, White, Red, or Blue finish, mfg. 1999 only.

	$1,275	$1,150	$1,025	$900	$750	$625	$500

Last MSR was $1,799.

Beast Deluxe - similar to the Beast Standard, except has a mahogany body with quilt/flamed top, mahogany neck-thru body, ebony fingerboard with crown inlay, and quad bridge, available in Trans. Red, Trans. Green, Trans. Blue, or Black finish, mfg. 1999 only.

	$1,695	$1,450	$1,300	$1,150	$1,000	$850	$700

Last MSR was $2,399.

Beast 7-String - similar to the Beast Standard, except in 7-String configuration, mfg. 1999 only.

	$1,350	$1,175	$1,025	$925	$825	$700	$600

Last MSR was $1,899.

BEAST (NJ SERIES) - Beast style, mahogany body, bolt-on maple neck, matching color neck and headstock, ebony fingerboard with diamond inlays, Floyd Rose SpeedLoader tremolo, 2 BDSM humbucker pickups, black hardware, available in Black, Trans. Blue, or Trans. Red finish, mfg. 2001-present.

MSR $950	$675	$600	$525	$475	$425	$375	$325

Beast Floyd Rose (NJ Series) - similar to the Beast NJ, except has a Floyd Rose tremolo bridge, available in Trans. Black or Trans. Red finishes, new 2005.

MSR $900	$630	$575	$525	$475	$425	$350	$300

BEAST (PLATINUM SERIES) - Beast style, agathis body, bolt-on maple neck, 24-fret rosewood fingerboard with dot inlays, adjustable bridge, 2 BDSM humbucker pickups, chrome hardware, available in Black or Metallic Red finish, mfg. 2003-present.

MSR $600	$425	$375	$325	$275	$225	$175	$125

Beast (Platinum Pro Series) - similar to the Beast Platinum, except has a matching color neck and headstock, and a Floyd Rose tremolo, available in Black, Tombstone, or Metallic Red finish, mfg. 2003-present.

MSR $760	$535	$475	$425	$375	$325	$275	$225

B.C. Rich Beast NJ Series courtesy B.C. Rich

GRADING	100% MINT	98% NEAR MINT	95% EXC+	90% EXC	80% VG+	70% VG	60% G

ELECTRIC: BICH SERIES

The Bich model was introduced in 1976. The first bolt-on neck versions were offered in 1977.

BICH STANDARD (U.S. NECK-THROUGH-BODY) - offset double cutaway body with bottom bout cutaways, through-body mahogany neck, alder (or poplar) wings, 24 5/8 in. scale, 24-fret rosewood fingerboard with pearl diamond inlay, Quadmatic stop bridge/tailpiece, blackface peghead with screened logo, 3-per-side tuners, chrome hardware, 2 DiMarzio humbucker pickups, 2 volume/1 tone controls, 3-position switch, available in Black, Blue, Red, White, or Yellow finish, mfg. 1976-1999.

	$1,125	$975	$850	$750	$650	$500	$400

Last MSR was $1,599.

In 1995, maple neck, black hardware, Seymour Duncan humbuckers replaced previous items. Purple finish was introduced; Blue and Yellow finishes were discontinued. In 1998, maple neck replaced the mahogany neck; DiMarzio pickups and Blue finish re-introduced.

Bich Doubleneck (U.S. Neck-through-body) - similar to the Bich Standard, except has mahogany body wings, maple through-body necks in 6- and 12-string configurations, abalone cloud inlays, Imperial-style tuning machines, full active electronics on 6-string neck, 2 volume/1 tone controls on 12-string neck, available in Trans. Blue, Trans. Emerald Green, Trans. Oriental Blue, Trans. Pagan Gold, or Trans. Red finish, mfg. circa 1978-1999.

	$3,000	$2,600	$2,300	$2,000	$1,700	$1,400	$1,000

Last MSR was $6,399.

Bich Deluxe (U.S. Neck-through-body) - similar to the Bich Standard, except features mahogany/maple body, mahogany neck-through design, ebony fingerboard, Imperial-style tuning machines, available in Natural, Trans. Black, Trans. Blue, Trans. Green, or Trans. Red finish, mfg. 1998-99.

	$1,275	$1,150	$1,050	$950	$850	$750	$650

Last MSR was $1,799.

Bich Special (U.S. Neck-through-body) - offset double cutaway maple (or koa) body with bottom bout cutaways, through-body maple neck, 24-fret ebony fingerboard with abalone diamond inlay, Quadmatic fixed bridge, blackface peghead with pearl logo inlay, chrome hardware, 3-per-side Imperial-style tuning machines, 2 DiMarzio humbucker pickups, 2 volume/1 tone controls, 3-position switch, available in Natural, Trans. Blue, Trans. Emerald Green, Trans. Purple, Trans. Tangerine, or Trans. Red finish, disc. 1998.

	$1,100	$950	$850	$750	$625	$525	$400

Last MSR was $1,599.

In 1995, koa body became an option, Trans. Black, Trans. Cherry Red, Trans. Emerald, and Trans. Orange finishes were introduced; Trans. Tangerine finish was discontinued. In 1996, Trans. Cherry Red, Trans. Emerald, and Trans. Orange finishes were discontinued.

Bich Supreme (U.S. Neck-through-body) - similar to the Bich Deluxe, except has quilted maple or koa body, bound fingerboard with abalone cloud inlay, bound peghead, Imperial-style tuning machines, active electronics (2 coil tap/1 phase mini switches, 6-position rotary Vari-tone switch, on-board preamp switch, volume control), available in Natural finish, disc. 1999.

	$1,625	$1,475	$1,250	$1,100	$900	$700	$500

Last MSR was $2,299.

In 1998, Trans. Black, Trans. Blue, and Trans. Red finishes were introduced.

Bich 10 String (U.S. Neck-through-body) - similar to the Bich Standard, except features 10-String configuration, mahogany/maple body, ebony fingerboard, 3-per-side headstock/4 tuners on bass bout, Imperial-style tuning machines, available in Natural, Trans. Black, Trans. Blue, Trans. Green, or Trans. Red finish, mfg. 1976-1999.

	$1,700	$1,550	$1,400	$1,300	$1,200	$1,050	$900

Last MSR was $2,399.

BICH BOLT-ON (U.S. BOLT-ON-NECK) - offset double cutaway alder (or poplar) body, bottom bout cutaways, maple bolt-on neck, 25.5 in. scale, 24-fret rosewood fingerboard with pearl dot inlay, Floyd Rose tremolo, 6-on-a-side tuners, black hardware, 2 humbucker pickups, 2 volume/1 tone controls, 3-position switch, available in Black, Purple, Red, White or Yellow finish, disc. 1999.

	$950	$850	$750	$625	$525	$400	$295

Last MSR was $1,399.

In 1998, Blue finish was introduced; Purple and Yellow finishes were disc. This model is available with a Quadmatic stop tailpiece/bridge.

Bich (N.J. Series) - similar to the Bich U.S.: Bolt-on, except has 24.75 in. scale, B.C. Rich angled headstock with N.J. logo, die-cast tuners, additional toggle switch, available in Black, Metallic Red, Trans. Black, Trans. Purple, or White finish, current mfg.

MSR	$900		$630	$575	$525	$475	$425	$375	$325

Add $20 for Blue Burst finish.

In 1998, Trans. Blue and Trans. Purple finishes were discontinued and Blood Red finish was introduced; Metallic Red finish was disc. In 2000, Trans. Red was disc.; Blue Burst finish was introduced. In 2005, a Floyd Rose tremolo bridge, nato body, and Trans. Black and Trans. Purple finishes were introduced.

Bich (Platinum Series) - similar to the Bich U.S.: Bolt-on, except has 24.75 in. scale, B.C. Rich 3-per-side headstock with Platinum logo, die-cast tuners, additional toggle switch, available in Black, Metallic Red, or White finish, current mfg.

MSR	$559		$395	$325	$275	$240	$210	$180	$140

Add $20 for Metallic Red or Metallic Blue finish. Add $25 for Transparent Purple or Transparent Red finish (Transparent Purple finish was discontinued in 1998). Add $20 for Blue Burst finish. Add $200 for Acrylic Green and Acrylic Red finishes.

In 1998, Blood Red finish was introduced; Metallic Red finish was disc. In 1999, Trans. Red and white finishes were disc. In 2000, Blue Burst, Acrylic Green and Acrylic Red finishes were introduced.

Bich Archtop (SEBGAO) - similar to the Bich, except has an arched top, no inlays, black hardware, available in Onyx finish, new 2005.

MSR	$500		$350	$300	$250	$210	$180	$150	$120

Bich Baritone (SEBBAO) - similar to the Bich, except in baritone configuration, available in Onyx finish, 30 in. scale, new 2005.

MSR	$550		$390	$325	$275	$235	$190	$160	$130

GRADING	100% MINT	98% NEAR MINT	95% EXC+	90% EXC	80% VG+	70% VG	60% G

ELECTRIC: BLASTER & OUTLAW SERIES

BLASTER (U.S. SERIES) - single cutaway alder laminated body, bolt-on hard maple neck, 25.5 in. scale, 21-fret maple fingerboard with black dot inlay, 6-saddle tele-style bridge, B.C. Rich vintage headstock, 6-on-a-side tuners, white pickguard, chrome hardware, 2 humbucker pickups, volume/tone controls, 3-position switch, control plate, available in Black, Bright Green, Creme, Red, or White finish, disc. 1998.

	$225	$200	$175	$150	$125	$100	$75

Last MSR was $329.

Outlaw Blaster (U.S. Series) - similar to the Blaster, except has 6-on-a-side B.C. Rich angled headstock, disc. 1998.

	$250	$225	$175	$150	$125	$100	$75

Last MSR was $359.

OUTLAW (U.S. SERIES) - offset double cutaway alder laminated body, bolt-on maple neck, 25.5 in. scale, 21-fret maple fingerboard with black position dots, ST-style tremolo, B.C. Rich angled headstock, 6-on-a-side tuners, chrome hardware, 2 humbucker pickups, volume/tone controls, 3-position switch, available in Black, Blue, Purple, Red, or White finishes, mfg. 1987-1998.

	$250	$225	$175	$150	$125	$100	$75

Last MSR was $349.

ELECTRIC: CONDOR SERIES

The first **Condor** was designed and made in 1983. The Condor was of archtop design with a 24 5/8 in. scale. As with all B.C. Rich guitars of that period, it was of neck-through construction with a mahogany neck and body, and a maple con-toured top. Basically, the **Eagle Arch Top Supreme** is the predecessor to the Condor.

ELECTRIC: ROBERT CONTI SERIES

In the mid-1980s, guitarist Robert Conti also inspired B.C. Rich to build archtop jazz guitar models such as the **RTJG** and **RTSG**.

ROBERT CONTI 8 STRING JAZZ (CONTOURED TOP, U.S. NECK-THROUGH-BODY) - single rounded cutaway mahogany body, bound carved maple top, through-body multi-laminated maple neck, 25.5 in. scale, 24-fret bound ebony fingerboard with abalone block inlay, trapeze bridge/stop tailpiece, gold hardware, bound peghead with rosewood veneer and pearl logo inlay, 4-per-side tuners, Bartolini custom wound humbucker pickup, volume/tone controls, available in Burgundy Pearl, Cream, Emerald Green, Gold, Metallic Blue, Pearl White, Porsche Red, Solid Black, Solid White, Tropical Blue, Trans. Red or Violet finish, disc. 1999.

	$1,750	$1,500	$1,350	$1,200	$1,050	$900	$750

Last MSR was $2,499.

This model is also available in a 7-string configuration.

Conti 6 String (U.S. Neck-through-body) - similar to the Robert Conti 8 String Jazz (Contoured Top), except has extra select figured maple top, 3-per-side headstock, 2 Seymour Duncan Jazz pickups, 2 volume/2-Tone controls, 3-way selector, available in Trans. Black, Trans. Blue, Trans. Root Beer, or Solid Black finish, disc. 1999.

	$1,550	$1,400	$1,250	$1,100	$950	$800	$650

Last MSR was $2,199.

This model is available with chrome hardware.

ELECTRIC: DAGGER SERIES

SE DAGGER - double pointed cutaway semi-hollow body, solid maple center block, black or white body binding, two f-dagger shaped holes, 22-fret ebony fingerboard with triangle inlays, three-per-side tuners, tune-o-matic bridge, stop tailpiece, two humbucker pickups, three knobs, three-way switch, black hardware, available in Blood (red), Gun Metal Gray, Onyx, or Shadow (matte black), 24.75 in. scale, new 2005.

MSR $600	$420	$350	$300	$250	$210	$180	$150

ELECTRIC: EAGLE SERIES

The Eagle model was introduced in 1994.

EAGLE STANDARD (U.S. NECK-THROUGH-BODY) - offset double cutaway poplar body, through-body maple neck, 24 5/8 in. scale, 24-fret rosewood fingerboard with abalone diamond inlay, tune-o-matic bridge/stop tailpiece, chrome hardware, 3-per-side tuners, 2 DiMarzio humbucker pickups, 2 volume/1 tone controls, 3-position switch, available in Black, Blue, Red, or White finish, mfg. 1998-99.

	$1,125	$1,000	$875	$750	$625	$500	$375

Last MSR was $1,599.

Eagle Deluxe (U.S. Neck-through-body) - similar to the Eagle Standard, except has mahogany body, mahogany through-body neck, bound ebony fingerboard with pearl triangle inlay, bound headstock, available in Natural, Trans. Black, Trans. Blue, Trans. Green, or Trans. Red finishes, mfg. 1998-99.

	$1,275	$1,075	$950	$850	$750	$650	$525

Last MSR was $1,799.

B.C. Rich Bich Platinum Series courtesy B.C. Rich

B.C. Rich Outlaw Blaster courtesy B.C. Rich

GRADING	100% MINT	98% NEAR MINT	95% EXC+	90% EXC	80% VG+	70% VG	60% G

Eagle Special (U.S. Neck-through-body) - similar to the Eagle Standard, except has maple or koa body, ebony fingerboard with abalone diamond inlay, Quadmatic bridge/stop tailpiece, blackface peghead with pearl logo inlay, available in Natural, Trans. Blue, Trans. Emerald Green, Trans. Purple, Trans. Tangerine, or Trans. Red finishes, disc. 1998.

	$1,100	$950	$850	$750	$625	$525	$400

Last MSR was $1,599.

In 1995, koa body became an option, Trans. Black, Trans. Cherry Red, Trans. Emerald, and Trans. Orange finishes were introduced; Trans. Tangerine finish was discontinued. In 1996, Trans. Cherry Red, Trans. Emerald, and Trans. Orange finishes were discontinued.

Eagle Supreme (U.S. Neck-through-body) - similar to the Eagle Special, except has maple/mahogany body, mahogany through-body neck, bound ebony fingerboard with abalone cloud inlay, bound peghead, active electronics (2 coil tap/1 phase mini switches, 6-position rotary Vari-tone switch, on-board preamp switch, volume control), available in Natural finish, mfg. 1977-1999.

	$1,675	$1,450	$1,275	$1,100	$925	$725	$550

Last MSR was $2,299.

In 1998, Trans. Black, Trans. Blue, Trans. Green, and Trans. Red finishes were introduced.

Eagle Arch Top Supreme (U.S. Neck-through-body) - similar to the Eagle Special, except has mahogany body, carved quilted or flame maple top, through-body mahogany neck, 24 5/8 in. scale, white body binding, bound fingerboard with green abalone cloud inlay, bound peghead, 2 Seymour Duncan custom (or DiMarzio) humbuckers, available in Gold Top, Trans. Blue, Trans. (Emerald) Green, Trans. Purple, Trans. Tangerine, and Trans. Red finishes, mfg. 1994-99.

	$1,675	$1,450	$1,275	$1,100	$925	$725	$550

Last MSR was $2,299.

In 1995, Gold Top and Trans. Tangerine finishes were disc. In 1998, Butterscotch Sun, Cherry Sunburst, Magenta Burst, and Trans. Black finishes were introduced; Trans. Blue and Trans. Purple finishes were disc.

Eagle (Platinum Series) - offset double cutaway solid alder body, bolt-on hard maple neck, 24.75 in. scale, 22-fret rosewood fingerboard with white dot inlay, tune-o-matic bridge, 6-on-a-side headstock, die-cast tuners, chrome hardware, 2 humbucker pickups, 2 volume/1 tone controls, 1 toggle switch, 3-position selector, available in Black, Metallic Red, or White finish, disc. 1997.

	$350	$295	$250	$225	$200	$175	$125

Last MSR was $489.

Add $25 for Trans. Purple and Trans. Red finishes.

ELECTRIC: EXCLUSIVE SERIES

Exclusive Series models feature neck-through construction, and were hand crafted in the U.S.

EXCLUSIVE MODEL ACT (ABALONE ARCH TOP) - slightly offset double cutaway mahogany body, bound highly figured carved maple top, abalone body binding, through-body mahogany neck, 24 5/8 in. scale, 24-fret bound ebony fingerboard with abalone oval inlay, tune-o-matic bridge/stop tailpiece, chrome hardware, bound blackface peghead with pearl logo inlay, 3-per-side tuners, 2 Seymour Duncan Alnico Pro humbucker pickups, 2 volume/1 tone controls, 3-position switch, available in Butterscotch Sun, Cherry Sunburst, Trans. Black, Trans. Magenta, or Trans. Red finish, current mfg.

	$2,200	$2,000	$1,800	$1,600	$1,300	$1,050	$750

Last MSR was $3,100.

This model was originally available in Burgundy Pearl, Cream, Emerald Green, Gold, Metallic Blue, Pearl White, Porsche Red, Solid Black, Solid White, Tropical Blue, and Violet finishes (current colors were introduced in 1998). This model was briefly available with an unbound fingerboard and headstock (this option, discontinued in 1998, originally had a retail list price of $2,150).

Exclusive Model ACT Premier (Abalone Bound Top) - similar to the Exclusive ACT, except has abalone binding on the neck, mfg. 1999 only.

	$2,700	$2,400	$2,200	$1,950	$1,600	$1,300	$1,000

Last MSR was $3,900.

Exclusive Model CT (Arch Top) - similar to the Exclusive Model ACT, except does not feature the abalone inlay on the top, available in Black, Butterscotch Sun, Cherry Sunburst, Gold Top Pearl, Trans. Magenta, or White finish, disc. 1999.

	$1,675	$1,475	$1,275	$1,100	$925	$750	$525

Last MSR was $2,199.

Exclusive Model FT 1 (Flat Top) - similar to the Exclusive Model ACT, except does not feature the carved arched top, available in Cherry Sunburst, Trans. Green, Trans. Magenta, or Trans. Pagan Gold finish, disc. 1999.

	$1,275	$1,100	$950	$825	$675	$550	$400

Last MSR was $1,699.

This model was briefly available without the abalone inlay on top (this option was disc. in 1998).

Exclusive Model FT 2 (Flat Top) - similar to the Exclusive Model FT 1, except features an alder or poplar body, rosewood fingerboard, available in Black, Blue, Gun Metal Gray, or White finish, disc. 1999.

	$1,000	$900	$775	$675	$550	$450	$325

Last MSR was $1,299.

EXCLUSIVE DOUBLENECK 6/12 - offset double cutaway mahogany body, white bound figured carved maple top, through-body mahogany necks, 24-fret rosewood fingerboards w/ abalone block inlay, trapeze bridge/stop tailpiece, chrome hardware, blackface peghead with pearl logo inlay, 3-per-side tuners (6 string), 6-per-side tuners (12 string), both necks each feature 2 humbucker pickups, 2 volume/1 tone controls, 3-way switch, plus master neck selector switch, available in Acapulco Blue, Black, White, or Wine Purple finish, disc. 1998.

	$2,500	$2,200	$1,900	$1,650	$1,400	$1,200	$1,000

Last MSR was $3,499.

Add $225 for Trans. Emerald Green, Trans. Oriental Blue, Trans. Pagan Gold, Trans. Purple, and Trans. Red finishes.

B

GRADING	100% MINT	98% NEAR MINT	95% EXC+	90% EXC	80% VG+	70% VG	60% G

EXCLUSIVE EM1 - offset double cutaway nato body with an arched maple top, five-ply body binding, neck-thru body, 24-fret fingerboard with diamond inlay, matching headstock with three-per-side tuners, tune-o-matic bridge, stop tailpiece, two humbucker pickups, four knobs, three-way switch, chrome hardware, available in Cherry Sunburst or Trans. Amber Burst finish, new 2005.

MSR $1,200		$850	$750	$675	$600	$525	$450	$375

VICTOR SMITH COMMEMORATIVE EXCLUSIVE - slightly offset double cutaway mahogany body, bound highly figured carved maple top, through-body mahogany neck, 24 5/8 in. scale, 24-fret bound ebony fingerboard with abalone block inlay, tune-o-matic bridge/stop tailpiece, gold hardware, bound blackface peghead with pearl B.C. Rich logo inlay, 3-per-side tuners, 2 Seymour Duncan Seth Lover humbucker pickups, 2 volume/2-Tone controls, 3-position switch, available in Butterscotch Sun, Cherry Sunburst, or Magenta Burst finish, mfg. 1998-99.

	$2,200	$2,000	$1,800	$1,600	$1,400	$1,200	$1,000

Last MSR was $3,100.

The Victor Smith model is available in two different body weights: SL (Slim Line) and HV (Heavier Weight, for those players who want a chunkier sound). The Victor Smith Commemorative is named after the early guitar pickup designer. In 1929, Smith introduced the first commercial Spanish-style electric guitar while working at the Dobro Guitar company.

B.C. Rich Eagle Archtop Supreme
courtesy B.C. Rich

ELECTRIC: EXCLUSIVE EM SERIES

Exclusive EM Series models feature bolt-on neck construction, and are imported to the U.S. market.

EM I (PLATINUM SERIES, EXCLUSIVE EM I) - slightly offset double cutaway solid alder body, bolt-on maple neck, 24.75 in. scale, multiple layer bound body, 24-fret rosewood fingerboard with pearloid rectangular position markers, tune-o-matic bridge, chrome hardware, blackface peghead with logo inlay, 3-per-side tuners, Exclusive-style headstock, 2 humbucker pickups, 2 volume/1 tone controls, 3-way selector, available in Trans. Blue, Trans. Natural, Trans. Purple, or Trans. Orange finishes, mfg. 1996-2004.

	$525	$450	$400	$350	$300	$250	$200

Last MSR was $750.

In 1998, Black, Trans. Red, and White finishes were introduced; Trans. Natural, Trans. Purple, and Trans. Orange finishes were discontinued. In 1999, Black, White and Trans. Red finishes were discontinued. In 2000, Trans. Black was introduced.

EM I Archtop - similar to the Exclusive EM I, except has carved arched top, available in Trans. Blue, Trans. Natural, Trans. Purple, and Translucent Orange finishes, mfg. 1996-98.

	$500	$450	$400	$350	$300	$250	$175

Last MSR was $699.

EM II - similar to the Exclusive EM I, except has single layer body binding, available in Black, Purple, Red, and White finishes, mfg. 1996-2000.

	$280	$250	$210	$180	$150	$120	$90

Last MSR was $399.

EM 3 (Platinum Series, Exclusive EM III) - similar to the Exclusive EM I, except has single coil/humbucker pickups, tele-style bridge, dot position markers, and 6-on-a-side Exclusive-style headstock, available in Black, Gun Metal Gray, Red, or White finishes, mfg. 1996-98.

	$350	$300	$250	$210	$180	$150	$120

Last MSR was $499.

In 1998, Red finish was discontinued.

ELECTRIC: EXCLUSIVE BOLT-ON SERIES

Exclusive Bolt-On Series models have the similar body design as the Exclusive series models, but feature bolt-on necks. Constructed in the U.S.

EXCLUSIVE MODEL TBH - slightly offset double cutaway mahogany body, highly figured carved maple top, bolt-on maple neck, 24 5/8 in. scale 24-fret ebony fingerboard with abalone dot inlay, tele-ish bridge, chrome hardware, blackface peghead with pearl logo inlay, 3-per-side tuners, single coil/humbucker pickups, volume/tone controls, 5-way selector, control plate, available in Burgundy Pearl, Cream, Emerald Green, Gold, Metallic Blue, Pearl White, Porsche Red, Solid Black, Solid White, Tropical Blue, Trans. Red and Violet finish, disc. 1999.

	$925	$825	$750	$675	$575	$450	$350

Last MSR was $1,299.

Later production models may feature an alder or poplar body and rosewood fingerboard. This model was also available with 2 humbucker pickups, volume/tone controls, and 3-way selector switch as the Model EXB O.

Exclusive Model TBS - similar to the Exclusive Model TBH, except has single coil pickup in bridge position, disc. 1999.

	$900	$825	$750	$675	$575	$450	$350

Last MSR was $1,399.

ELECTRIC: FAT BOB & G STRING SERIES

FAT BOB - motorcycle gas tank style alder body, bolt-on maple neck, 25 1/2" scale, 22-fret rosewood fingerboard with pearl flames inlay, tremolo, 6-on-a-side tuners, chrome hardware, humbucker pickup, volume control, available in Black with Red/White/Yellow flames finish, mfg. 1984-86.

	N/A	$900	$800	$700	$600	$500	$400

B.C. Rich Exclusive EM1
courtesy B.C. Rich

GRADING	100% MINT	98% NEAR MINT	95% EXC+	90% EXC	80% VG+	70% VG	60% G
G STRING - mfg. mid-1980s.							
	N/A	$350	$300	$250	$210	$170	$130

ELECTRIC: GUNSLINGER SERIES

The Gunslinger model was introduced in 1987.

GUNSLINGER (U.S. BOLT-ON-NECK) - offset double cutaway alder body, bolt-on maple neck, 25.5 in. scale, 22-fret maple fingerboard with black dot inlay, standard Wilkinson vibrato, reverse blackface peghead with screened logo, 6-on-a-side tuners, black hardware, humbucker pickup, volume control, dual sound switch, available in Black, Cobalt Blue, Emerald Green, Purple, Red, White, or Yellow finish, mfg. 1994-99.

	$900	$775	$675	$600	$500	$400	$300

Last MSR was $1,299.

Add $125 for optional Candy Color finishes.

In 1995, double locking Floyd Rose vibrato replaced original part/design; Candy Color finishes became optional, Powder Blue finish was briefly introduced (1 year), Emerald Green and Yellow finishes were discontinued.

Gunslinger 2 (U.S. Bolt-On Neck) - similar to Gunslinger, except has alder or poplar body, 24-fret rosewood fingerboard, 2 Seymour Duncan humbuckers, 2 volume/1 tone controls, 3-way selector, available in Black, Gun Metal Gray, Red, or White finish, mfg. 1994-present.

	$975	$825	$725	$600	$500	$400	$300

Last MSR was $1,399.

ELECTRIC: JEFF COOK SIGNATURE ALABAMA SERIES

These models were designed in conjunction with guitarist Jeff Cook (Alabama).

JEFF COOK MODEL 1 (U.S. BOLT-ON-NECK) - offset double cutaway alder body, bolt-on maple neck, maple fingerboard with abalone dot inlay, tele-style bridge, chrome hardware, 6-on-a-side tuners, 2 single coil pickups, volume/tone controls, 3-way selector, available in Black, Blue Metallic, Emerald Green, Glitter Rock White, Purple, Red, or White finish, disc. 1999.

	$1,050	$900	$800	$675	$575	$450	$350

Last MSR was $1,499.

Add $225 for optional transparent finish.

Jeff Cook Model 2 (U.S. Bolt-On Neck) - similar to the Jeff Cook Model 1, except has humbucker in the bridge position, disc. 1998.

	$1,000	$900	$800	$695	$595	$475	$375

Last MSR was $1,399.

ELECTRIC: JUNIOR V SERIES

JUNIOR V BOLT-ON (U.S. BOLT-ON-NECK) - flying V-shaped alder body, bolt-on maple neck, 25 1/2" scale, 24-fret rosewood fingerboard with dot inlays, fixed bridge, chrome hardware, 6-on-a-side tuners, 2 humbuckers, 2 volume/1 tone controls, 3-way selector, available in Black, (Cobalt) Blue, Red, or White finish, disc. 1999.

	$975	$875	$750	$650	$550	$425	$300

Last MSR was $1,399.

In 1998, poplar body replaced the alder body.

Jr. V (Platinum Series) - flying V-shaped solid alder body, bolt-on hard maple neck, 24.75 in. scale, 22-fret rosewood fingerboard with white dot inlay, tune-o-matic bridge, 6-on-a-side headstock, die-cast tuners, chrome hardware, 2 humbucker pickups, 2 volume/1 tone controls, 1 toggle switch, 3-position selector, available in Black, Metallic Red, Metallic Blue, or White finish, disc. 2002.

	$375	$325	$275	$225	$175	$125	$90

Last MSR was $529.

Add $25 for Trans. Purple, Trans. Red, Metallic Red, or Metallic Blue finish (trans. finishes were disc. in 1998).

In 1998, Gunmetal Grey finish was introduced; Metallic Red finish was disc. In 1999, Metallic Red and White finishes were disc.

JUNIOR V STANDARD (U.S. NECK-THROUGH-BODY) - flying V-shaped body, alder body wings, through-body maple neck, 24 5/8 in. scale, 24-fret rosewood fingerboard with diamond inlays at 12th fret, tune-o-matic fixed bridge, 6-on-the-other-side tuners, reverse blackface headstock with logo, black (or chrome) hardware, 2 Seymour Duncan custom humbuckers, volume/tone controls, 3-way selector, available in Black, Purple, Red, or White finish, disc. 1999.

	$1,125	$1,000	$875	$750	$625	$500	$375

Last MSR was $1,599.

In 1998, poplar body wings replaced the alder body wings; DiMarzio humbuckers replaced the Seymour Duncan humbuckers; Blue finish was introduced; Purple finish was discontinued.

Junior V Supreme (U.S. Neck-through-body) - similar to the Junior V Standard, except has mahogany body wings, mahogany neck, bound figured maple top, bound ebony fingerboard with abalone 'V' inlays, bound unreversed headstock, locking Floyd Rose tremolo or fixed bridge, available in Trans. Sunburst Emerald Green, Trans. Sunburst Gold, Trans. Sunburst Pagan Blue, or Trans. Sunburst Red finish, disc. 1999.

	$1,675	$1,500	$1,350	$1,100	$950	$800	$650

Last MSR was $2,399.

In 1998, the figured maple top was discontinued (all mahogany body). In 1998, Trans. Black, Trans. Blue, Trans. Magenta, and Trans. Red finishes were introduced; Trans. Sunburst Emerald Green, Trans. Sunburst Gold, Trans. Sunburst Pagan Blue, and Trans. Sunburst Red finishes were discontinued.

GRADING	100% MINT	98% NEAR MINT	95% EXC+	90% EXC	80% VG+	70% VG	60% G

JUNIOR V (NJ SERIES) - Flying V shaped mahogany body, maple bolt-on neck, 24-fret ebony fingerboard with diamond inlay, Floyd Rose Speedloader tremolo bridge, 2 BDSM humbucking pickups, two knobs, one switch, black hardware, available in black, Trans. Blue, or Trans. Red finishes, mfg. 2000-02.

	$490	$425	$375	$325	$275	$225	$175

Last MSR was $700.

Add $75 for trans. finishes (veneer top).

JUNIOR V (PLATINUM PRO SERIES) - Flying V shaped agathis body, maple bolt-on neck, 24-fret rosewood fingerboard with dot inlay, Floyd Rose tremolo bridge, 2 BDSM humbucking pickups, two knobs, one switch, black hardware, available in black finish, mfg. 2004-present.

MSR $700		$490	$425	$375	$325	$275	$225	$175

KKV KERRY KING SIGNATURE JUNIOR V (U.S. NECK-THROUGH-BODY) - similar to the Junior V Standard, except has mahogany body wings, mahogany neck, figured maple top, ebony fingerboard with abalone diamond inlays, blackface reverse headstock with Kerry King/B.C. Rich logos, locking Floyd Rose or Kahler tremolo, available in Trans. Black Sunburst, Trans. Blue, or Trans. Magenta finishes, mfg. 1998-99.

	$1,750	$1,575	$1,450	$1,275	$1,075	$875	$650

Last MSR was $2,499.

Add $150 for Tribal graphic finishes.

ELECTRIC: IGNITOR SERIES

IGNITOR STANDARD (U.S. NECK-THROUGH-BODY) - offset double cutaway alder (or poplar) body, pointed forward horns, scooped lower bout cutaway, bolt-on maple neck, 24 5/8 in. scale, 24-fret rosewood fingerboard with inlay at 12th fret, blackface headstock with silk-screened logo, Quadmatic fixed bridge, chrome hardware, 6-on-a-side tuners, 2 DiMarzio humbuckers, volume/tone controls, 3-way selector, available in Black, Blood Red, Gun Metal Gray, or White finish, mfg. 1998-99.

	$1,125	$1,050	$925	$775	$650	$500	$375

Last MSR was $1,599.

Ignitor Supreme (U.S. Neck-through-body) - similar to Ignitor Standard, except has a maple/mahogany body, mahogany through-body neck, 24-fret ebony fingerboard, locking Floyd Rose or Quadmatic fixed bridge, available in Blue Sunburst, Trans. Black, or Trans. Pagan Gold finish, mfg. 1998-99.

	$1,500	$1,325	$1,150	$975	$825	$650	$475

Last MSR was $1,899.

Ignitor 7-String - similar to the Ignitor Standard, except in 7-string configuration, maple body, mfg. 1999 only.

	$1,195	$1,025	$950	$875	$750	$625	$500

Last MSR was $1,699.

B.C. Rich Ignitor
courtesy B.C. Rich

IGNITOR BOLT-ON (U.S. BOLT-ON-NECK) - offset double cutaway alder (or poplar) body, pointed forward horns, scooped lower bout cutaway, bolt-on maple neck, 25.5 in. scale, 24-fret rosewood fingerboard with inlay at 12th fret, blackface headstock with silk-screened logo, Quadmatic fixed bridge, chrome hardware, 6-on-a-side tuners, 2 DiMarzio humbuckers, volume/tone controls, 3-way selector, available in Black, Blood Red, Cobalt Blue, or White finish, disc. 1999.

	$975	$900	$775	$650	$525	$425	$325

Last MSR was $1,399.

In 1998, Cobalt Blue finish was discontinued.

ELECTRIC: IRONBIRD SERIES

The Ironbird model was introduced in 1983.

IRONBIRD STANDARD (U.S. NECK-THROUGH-BODY) - angular offset cutaway body, pointed treble bout/rear body bouts, alder body wings, 24 5/8 in. scale, through-body maple neck, 24-fret rosewood fingerboard with pearl diamond inlay, fixed bridge, blackface peghead with screened logo, 3-per-side tuners, black hardware, 2 Seymour Duncan custom humbucker pickups, 2 volume/1 tone controls, 3-position switch, available in Black, Blue, Red, White, or Yellow finish, disc. 1999.

	$1,125	$975	$850	$750	$600	$475	$350

Last MSR was $1,599.

In 1995, Purple finish was introduced, Blue and Yellow finishes were disc.

Ironbird (U.S. Bolt-On Neck) - angular offset double cutaway alder body with pointed treble bout/rear body bouts, bolt-on maple neck, 25.5 in. scale, 22-fret rosewood fingerboard with white dot inlay, double locking Floyd Rose vibrato, 6-on-a-side tuners, black hardware, 2 humbucker pickups, 2 volume/1 tone controls, 3-position switch, available in Black, Blue, Emerald Green, Red, White, or Yellow finish, disc. 1999.

	$975	$900	$825	$725	$625	$500	$400

Last MSR was $1,399.

Add $125 for optional Candy Color finish.

In 1995, Candy Color finishes became optional, Purple finish was introduced, Blue and Emerald Green finishes were disc.

B.C. Rich Junior V
Platinum Pro Series
courtesy B.C. Rich

B

GRADING	100% MINT	98% NEAR MINT	95% EXC+	90% EXC	80% VG+	70% VG	60% G

Ironbird (N.J. Series) - similar to the Ironbird [U.S.: Bolt-On Neck], except has 24.75 in. scale, diamond inlays, N.J. logo on headstock, die-cast tuners, additional toggle switch, available in Black, Metallic Red, Trans. Red, Trans. Blue, or White finish, disc. 1998, 2000-02.

	$490	$450	$400	$350	$300	$250	$200

Last MSR was $699.

Add $25 for Trans Blue or Trans Red finish. In 1998, Metallic Red and white finishes were disc.

Ironbird Deluxe (U.S. Neck-Through-Body) - similar to the Ironbird Standard, except has a mahogany body with a quilted/flamed maple, maple neck-thru body, rosewood fingerboard, and quad bridge, available in Trans. Red, Trans. Green, Trans. Blue, or black finish, mfg. 1999 only.

	$1,275	$1,125	$1,000	$900	$800	$700	$600

Last MSR was $1,799.

Ironbird 7-String - similar to the Ironbird Standard, except has a maple body in 7-String configuration, mfg. 1999 only.

	$1,195	$1,075	$950	$850	$750	$650	$550

Last MSR was $1,699.

IRONBIRD (PLATINUM SERIES) - Ironbird-shaped agathis body, bolt-on maple neck, 24-fret rosewood fingerboard with dot inlay, adjustable bridge, 2 BDSM humbucking pickups, silver hardware, available in Black, Metallic Blue, or Metallic Red finish, mfg. 2000-04.

	$395	$350	$310	$270	$230	$190	$150

Last MSR was $560.

IRONBIRD (PLATINUM PRO SERIES) - Ironbird-shaped agathis body, bolt-on maple neck, 24-fret rosewood fingerboard with dot inlay, Floyd Rose tremolo, 2 BDSM humbucking pickups, black hardware, available in Shadow finish, mfg. 2004 only.

	$490	$450	$400	$350	$300	$250	$200

Last MSR was $700.

ELECTRIC: MOCKINGBIRD SERIES

The Mockingbird model was introduced in 1976.

MOCKINGBIRD ARCH TOP (U.S. NECK-THROUGH-BODY) - offset double cutaway mahogany body, extended pointed treble bout/rounded lower bout, carved highly figured quilted maple top, white body binding, through-body mahogany neck, 24 5/8 in. scale, 24-fret bound ebony fingerboard with green abalone cloud inlay, Quadmatic fixed bridge, 3-per-side tuners, chrome hardware, 2 DiMarzio (or Seymour Duncan Alnico Pro) humbucker pickups, 2 volume/1 tone controls, 3-way selector, available in Trans. Black, Trans. Blue, Trans. (Emerald) Green, Trans. Purple, or Trans. Red finish, mfg. 1995-99.

	$1,625	$1,450	$1,250	$1,100	$895	$700	$525

Last MSR was $2,299.

This model was designed for Slash (Guns 'N Roses). In 1998, Butterscotch Sun, Cherry Sunburst, and Magenta Burst finishes were introduced; Trans. Blue and Trans. Purple finishes were disc.

MOCKINGBIRD STANDARD (U.S. NECK-THROUGH-BODY) - offset double cutaway body, extended pointed treble bout/rounded lower bout, alder (or poplar) body wings, through-body maple neck, 24 5/8 in. scale, 24-fret rosewood fingerboard with pearl diamond inlay, Quadmatic fixed bridge, blackface peghead with logo, 3-per-side tuners, black hardware, 2 Seymour Duncan custom humbucker pickups, 2 volume/1 tone controls, 3-position switch, available in Black, Blue, Red, White, or Yellow finish, mfg. 1976-1999.

	100%	98%	95%	90%	80%	70%	60%
1995-1999	$1,125	$1,000	$875	$750	$625	$500	$375
1976-1979	N/A	$1,750	$1,500	$1,300	$1,100	$900	$700
1980-1994	N/A	$1,500	$1,250	$1,050	$900	$750	$600

Last MSR was $1,599.

In 1995, Purple finish was introduced, Blue and Yellow finishes were disc. In 1998, DiMarzio humbuckers replaced Seymour Duncan humbuckers; Blue finish reintroduced; Purple finish was disc.

Mockingbird Deluxe (U.S. Neck-through-body) - similar to the Mockingbird Standard, except features mahogany body wings, figured maple top, mahogany through-body neck, ebony fingerboard, 2 DiMarzio humbuckers, available in Natural, Trans. Black, Trans. Blue, Trans. Green, or Trans. Red finishes, mfg. 1998-99.

	$1,275	$1,150	$1,000	$875	$725	$575	$425

Last MSR was $1,799.

Mockingbird Special (U.S. Neck-through-body) - offset double cutaway body, extended pointed treble bout/rounded lower bout, maple or koa body wings, through-body maple neck, 24 5/8 in. scale, 24-fret ebony fingerboard with abalone diamond inlay, Quadmatic bridge/stop tailpiece, blackface peghead with pearl logo inlay, 3-per-side tuners, 2 DiMarzio humbucker pickups, 2 volume/1 tone controls, 3-position switch, available in Natural, Trans. Blue, Trans. Emerald Green, Trans. Purple, Trans. Tangerine, or Trans. Red finish, disc. 1998.

	$1,125	$1,000	$850	$750	$625	$525	$400

Last MSR was $1,599.

In 1995, koa body became optional, Trans. Black, Trans. Cherry Red, Trans. Emerald, and Trans. Orange finishes were introduced; Trans. Tangerine finish was disc. In 1996, Trans. Cherry Red, Trans. Emerald, and Trans. Orange finishes were disc.

Mockingbird Supreme (U.S. Neck-through-body) - similar to the Mockingbird Special, except has quilted maple or koa body, bound fingerboard with abalone cloud inlay, bound peghead, active electronics (2 coil tap/1 phase mini switches, 6-position rotary Vari-tone switch, on-board preamp switch, volume control), available in Natural finish, disc. 1999.

	$1,625	$1,450	$1,250	$1,100	$895	$700	$525

Last MSR was $2,299.

In 1998, the koa body was disc.; Trans. Black, Trans. Blue, Trans. Green, and Trans. Red finishes were introduced.

GRADING	100% MINT	98% NEAR MINT	95% EXC+	90% EXC	80% VG+	70% VG	60% G

Mockingbird SL (Slash Limited Edition) (U.S. Neck-through-body) - similar to the Mockingbird Special, except features a mahogany body/neck, quilted maple top, locking Floyd Rose 2 Tremolo, 2 DiMarzio (or Seymour Duncan Alnico Pro) humbuckers, black hardware, available in Trans. Red finish, disc. 1999.

	$1,350	$1,200	$1,075	$950	$775	$600	$450

Last MSR was $1,899.

In 1998, Trans. Black, Trans. Blue, and Trans. Green finishes were introduced.

Mockingbird SLP (U.S. Neck-through-body) - similar to the Mockingbird SL, except features bound body/neck/peghead, abalone cloud fingerboard inlays, tune-o-matic bridge, 2 DiMarzio humbuckers, chrome hardware, 2 volume/2-Tone controls, available in Butterscotch Sun, Cherry Sunburst, Magenta Burst, Trans. Black, Trans. Green, or Trans. Red finishes, mfg. 1998-99.

	$1,675	$1,450	$1,250	$1,100	$895	$700	$525

Last MSR was $2,399.

Mockingbird 7-String - similar to the Mockingbird, except has maple body with a maple neck-thru body, 7-string configuration, available in Black, White, Red, or Blue finishes, mfg. 1999 only.

	$1,195	$1,050	$950	$825	$725	$625	$500

Last MSR was $1,699.

MOCKINGBIRD BOLT-ON (U.S. BOLT-ON-NECK) - offset double cutaway alder (or poplar) body, extended pointed treble bout/rounded lower bout, bolt-on maple neck, 25.5 in. scale, 24-fret rosewood fingerboard with pearl dot inlay, locking Floyd Rose 2 tremolo, 6-on-a-side tuners, black hardware, 2 DiMarzio humbucker pickups, 2 volume/1 tone controls, 3-way selector, available in Black, Purple, Red, White, or Yellow finishes, disc. 1999.

	$975	$850	$750	$625	$525	$400	$300

Last MSR was $1,399.

Add $125 for optional Candy Color finish.

In 1998, Blood Red and Blue finishes were introduced; Purple, Red, and Yellow finishes were disc.

Mockingbird (Bronze Series) - similar to the Mockingbird [U.S.: Bolt-On Neck], except has laminated alder body, headstock with B.C. Rich/Bronze logos, covered machine heads, chrome hardware, available in Black, Red, or White finishes, mfg. 1998-present.

MSR $320		$225	$185	$150	$120	$95	$75	$55

Mockingbird (Evil Edge) - similar to the Mockingbird Platinum, except has a brass bridge, tailpiece, and pickguard, available in Onyx finish, 25.5 in. scale, current mfg.

MSR $500		$350	$300	$250	$210	$180	$150	$120

Add $20 for left-handed configuration. Add $25 for Trans. Blue and Trans. Red finishes (Trans. Blue finish was discontinued in 1998). Add $20 for Blue Burst or Tombstone finish. Add $200 for Acrylic Red and Acrylic Green finishes.

In 1998, Metallic Red finish was disc. In 1999, white finish was disc. In 2000, Blue Burst, Acrylic Green and Acrylic Red finishes were introduced.

Mockingbird (N.J. Series) - similar to the Mockingbird [U.S.: Bolt-On Neck], except has 24.75 in. scale, diamond inlays, N.J. logo on headstock, die-cast tuners, additional toggle switch, available in Black, Metallic Red, Trans. Black, Trans. Red, or White finishes, current mfg.

MSR $900		$630	$575	$525	$475	$425	$350	$300

In 1998, Blood Red finish was introduced; Metallic Red finish was disc. In 1999, Trans. Red and White finishes were disc. In 2000, Blue Burst finish was introduced. In 2005, a Floyd Rose tremolo bridge, nato body, and Trans. Black and Trans. Red finishes were introduced.

Mockingbird (N.J. Neck-Thru Series) - Mockingbird style, soft maple body with rosewood stringers, 3-piece neck-thru body maple neck, 24-fret rosewood fingerboard with cloud inlays, 2 BDSM humbucker pickups, Floyd Rose tremolo, black hardware, available in black, natural or Trans. Red finishes, mfg. 2000-02.

	$675	$600	$550	$500	$450	$400	$325

Last MSR was $969.

Mockingbird (N.J. Classic Series) - Mockingbird style, mahogany body with quilted maple top, bolt-on maple neck, 24-fret ebony fingerboard with cloud inlays, 2 humbucker pickups, adjustable bridge, chrome hardware, available in natural finish, mfg. 2003-04.

	$630	$575	$525	$475	$425	$375	$300

Last MSR was $900.

Mockingbird (Platinum Series) - similar to the Mockingbird [U.S.: Bolt-On Neck], except has 24.75 in. scale, white inlay dots, B.C. Rich 3-per-side headstock with Platinum logo, fixed bridge, die-cast tuners, chrome hardware, additional toggle switch, available in Black, Blood Red, Metallic Red, or White finishes, current mfg.

MSR $560		$395	$350	$300	$250	$200	$160	$120

Add $20 for left-handed configuration. Add $25 for Trans. Blue and Trans. Red finishes (Trans. Blue finish was discontinued in 1998). Add $20 for Blue Burst or Tombstone finish. Add $200 for Acrylic Red and Acrylic Green finishes.

In 1998, Metallic Red finish was disc. In 1999, White finish was disc. In 2000, Blue Burst, Acrylic Green and Acrylic Red finishes were introduced.

Mockingbird (Platinum Pro Series) - Mockingbird-shaped agathis body, bolt-on maple neck, 24-fret rosewood fingerboard with dot inlay, Floyd Rose tremolo, 2 BDSM humbucker pickups, black hardware, available in Black or Metallic Blue finish, mfg. 2003-present.

MSR $700		$490	$450	$400	$350	$300	$250	$200

Add $20 for Trans. Blue finish.

B.C. Rich Ironbird courtesy B.C. Rich

B.C. Rich Mockingbird Archtop courtesy John Beeson The Music Shoppe

B

GRADING	100% MINT	98% NEAR MINT	95% EXC+	90% EXC	80% VG+	70% VG	60% G

Mockingbird Acrylic - similar to the Mockingbird Platinum Pro, except has an acrylic see-through body, available in Green or Ice finishes, mfg. 2004-present.

MSR $760	$530	$450	$400	$350	$300	$250	$200

Add $20 for Trans. Blue finish.

ELECTRIC: NIGHTHAWK/PHOENIX SERIES

The **NightHawk** was the first attempt for a bolt-on neck guitar for B.C. Rich. It was introduced around 1979. This model, along with the **Phoenix**, was made as an affordable B.C. Rich guitar for those times. The NightHawk was in the Eagle shape and the Phoenix was in the Mockingbird shape.

NIGHTHAWK - Eagle style mahogany body, maple neck, 25.5 in. scale, rosewood fingerboard with dot inlays, 2 Dimarzio Super Distortion pickups, mfg. 1978-1982.

	N/A	$600	$525	$450	$350	$250	$150

PHOENIX - Mockingbird style mahogany body, maple neck, 25.5 in. scale, rosewood fingerboard with dot inlays, 2 Dimarzio Super Distortion pickups, mfg. 1978-1982.

	N/A	$600	$525	$450	$350	$250	$150

ELECTRIC: SEAGULL SERIES

The Seagull model was first introduced in 1971. "These models were the first production B.C. Rich electric guitars. To my knowledge, the Seagull Guitar and Bass were the first guitars to offer the neck-through design featuring total access with the heel-less neck-through concept," writes Bernie Rico.

Earlier Seagull models from the 1970s are generally priced between $1,000-$1,500.

SEAGULL - sculpted single cutaway body, neck-thru body, 24-fret fingerboard with diamond inlays, two exposed humbucker pickups, black pickguard on treble bout only, 3-per-side tuners, four knobs, three switches, available in Suburst and possibly other finishes, mfg. 1971-76.

	N/A	$1,500	$1,350	$1,200	$1,000	$800	$600

SEAGULL WOODIE JR (U.S. NECK-THROUGH-BODY) - sculpted single cutaway mahogany body, maple set neck, 22-fret rosewood fingerboard with pearl dot inlay, B.C. Rich bridge/stop tailpiece, blackface peghead with pearl logo inlay, 3-per-side Grover Imperial tuners, chrome hardware, 2 DiMarzio humbucker pickups, 2 volume/1 tone controls, 3-position switch, available in Black, Blue, DiMarzio Creme, Porsche Red, Translucent Blue, or White finishes, mfg. 1995-96.

	$800	$600	$525	$450	$395	$325	$250

Last MSR was $1,000.

ELECTRIC: ST SERIES

The ST (Strat) model was introduced in 1987.

ST MSS (MAPLE MOLDED TOP, U.S. NECK-THROUGH-BODY) - offset double cutaway mahogany body, contoured quilted maple top, through-body maple neck, 24-fret ebony fingerboard with tear-drop inlay, double locking Floyd Rose tremolo, 6-on-a-side tuners, chrome hardware, 2 Seymour Duncan custom humbucker pickups, 2 volume/1 tone controls, 3-way selector, available in Trans. Blue, Trans. Pagan Gold, Trans. Purple, or Trans. Red finishes, mfg. 1995-98.

	$1,125	$950	$850	$750	$625	$525	$400

Last MSR was $1,599.

This model was part of the Tony MacAlpine Signature series.

ST MSS (U.S. BOLT-ON-NECK) - offset double cutaway alder body, contoured quilted maple top, bolt-on maple neck, 25.5 in. scale, 24-fret ebony fingerboard with tear-drop inlay, locking Floyd Rose tremolo, 6-on-a-side tuners, chrome hardware, 2 Seymour Duncan custom humbucking pickups, 2 volume/1 tone controls, 3-way selector, available in Trans. Black, Trans. (Oriental) Blue, Trans. Magenta, Trans. Purple, or Trans. Red finishes, current mfg.

	$1,125	$1,075	$950	$825	$675	$550	$400

Last MSR was $1,599.

In 1998, basswood body replaced the alder body; Trans. Root Beer finish was introduced; Trans. Purple finish was disc. This model was previously available with 2 single coil/1 humbucker pickup configuration.

ST 2001 (U.S. Bolt-On Neck) - similar to the ST MSS [U.S.: Bolt-On Neck], except has mahogany body, non-contoured quilted maple top, 22-fret maple fingerboard with black dot inlay, double locking Floyd Rose or Wilkinson fixed bridge, reverse headstock, available in Trans. Blue, Trans. Emerald Green, Trans. Pagan Gold, or Trans. Red finishes, mfg. 1994-98.

	$900	$775	$695	$600	$500	$425	$325

Last MSR was $1,299.

ST (PLATINUM SERIES) - offset double cutaway solid alder body, bolt-on hard maple neck, 24.75 in. scale, 22-fret rosewood fingerboard with white inlay dots, B.C. Rich vintage-style 6-on-a-side headstock with Platinum logo, accutune tremolo, die-cast tuners, chrome hardware, 2 single coil/1 humbucker pickups, volume/tone controls, additional mini toggle switch, 5-way selector, available in Black, Metallic Red, or White finishes, disc. 1998.

	$350	$295	$250	$225	$195	$150	$125

Last MSR was $489.

Add $25 for Transparent Blue and Transparent Red finishes.

ST (BRONZE SERIES, U.S. SERIES) - offset double cutaway laminated alder body, bolt-on hard maple neck, 25.5 in. scale, 21-fret maple fingerboard with black inlay dots, B.C. Rich vintage-style 6-on-a-side headstock, ST-style tremolo, covered machine heads, chrome hardware, 2 humbucker pickups, 2 volume/1 tone controls, 3-way selector, available in Black, Red, Blue, Purple, or White finishes, disc. 1998.

	$250	$225	$200	$175	$150	$125	$95

Last MSR was $349.

ST (U.S. Series) models were available in Black, Blue, Purple, Red, and White finishes (until model transition in 1998).

B

GRADING	100% MINT	98% NEAR MINT	95% EXC+	90% EXC	80% VG+	70% VG	60% G

ST III (U.S. Series) - similar to the ST (U.S. Series), except features 3 single coil pickups, 5-way selector switch, disc. 1998.

	$225	$195	$175	$150	$125	$95	$75

Last MSR was $299.

ST B1 (U.S. Series) - similar to the ST (U.S. Series), except has a bound laminated alder body, single coil/humbucker pickups, disc. 1998.

	$235	$200	$175	$150	$125	$100	$75

Last MSR was $329.

ST-1 (Rave Series) - similar to the ST III (U.S. Series), except has only 1 pickup, disc. 1993.

	N/A	$200	$175	$150	$125	$100	$75

Last MSR was $279.

ST-3 (Rave Series) - similar to the ST III (U.S. Series), and features 3 single coil pickups, disc. 1993.

	N/A	$225	$200	$175	$150	$125	$100

Last MSR was $339.

ELECTRIC: STEALTH SERIES

The Stealth model was introduced in 1983. "The Stealth was designed in collaboration with Rick Derringer and Bernie Rich. Due to trend changes and slow sales, production was discontinued in 1989 and was only made through the Custom Shop." The Stealth model was briefly offered again as a production model in the late 1990s, then returned to its Custom Shop niche in 1998.

STEALTH STANDARD (U.S. NECK-THROUGH-BODY) - offset double cutaway body, alder body wings, through-body maple neck, 24 5/8 in. scale, 24-fret rosewood fingerboard with pearl diamond inlay, fixed bridge, blackface peghead with logo, 3-per-side tuners, black hardware, 2 Seymour Duncan custom humbucker pickups, 2 volume/1 tone controls, 3-position switch, available in Black, Purple Red, or White finish, disc. 1999.

	$1,125	$975	$850	$750	$650	$550	$450

Last MSR was $1,599.

B.C. Rich Seagull
courtesy Jeff Mikols

Stealth (U.S. Bolt-On Neck) - similar to the Stealth Standard, except has alder body, bolt-on maple neck, 25.5 in. scale, 22-fret fingerboard with dot inlay, 2 DiMarzio custom humbuckers, available in Black, Cobalt Blue, Red, and White finishes, disc. 1999.

	$975	$850	$750	$650	$550	$450	$350

Last MSR was $1,399.

STEALTH DELUXE - similar to the Stealth Standard, except has a mahogany body with a quilt/flamed top, mahogany neck, rosewood fingerboard, and quad style bridge, available in Trans. Red, Trans. Green, Trans. Blue, or black finishes, mfg. 1999 only.

	$1,275	$1,150	$1,000	$875	$750	$600	$450

Last MSR was $1,799.

STEALTH 7-STRING - similar to the Stealth Standard, except has a maple body, and in 7-string configuration, mfg. 1999 only.

	$1,195	$1,075	$950	$825	$700	$575	$450

Last MSR was $1,699.

ELECTRIC: TS SERIES

TS series models were produced in the U.S. during the mid 1980s. The two models (**TS-100** and **TS-200**) both featured a tele-style design, and a bolt-on maple neck.

ELECTRIC: VIRGIN SERIES

The Virgin model was introduced in 1987.

VIRGIN (U.S. NECK-THROUGH-BODY) - offset double cutaway body, pointed forward horns, rounded bottom bout, Honduran mahogany body wings, through-body maple neck, 22-fret rosewood fingerboard with pearl diamond inlay, Kahler Steeler tremolo, blackface peghead with logo, 3-per-side Sperzel tuners, black hardware, 2 Seymour Duncan humbucker pickups, volume/tone controls, 3-way selector, available in Black, Gun Metal Gray, Natural, Pearl Blue, Pearl Purple, Pearl White, Pearl Violet, Red, or Yellow finishes, mfg. 1987-1993.

	N/A	$1,500	$1,300	$1,100	$900	$700	$500

Last MSR was $2,099.

Add $100 for optional Candy Color finishes. Add $150 for optional translucent finishes.

Virgin (U.S. Bolt-On Neck) - similar to the Virgin [U.S.: Neck-through-body], except has mahogany body, bolt-on maple neck, mfg. 1987-1993.

	N/A	$950	$850	$750	$650	$525	$400

Last MSR was $1,299.

Virgin (N.J. Series) - similar to the Virgin [U.S. Bolt-On Neck], except has diamond position markers, double locking Floyd Rose tremolo, EMG Select pickups, available in Black, Trans. Red, Trans. Blue, or Red finishes, mfg. 1987-1993, 2000-02.

	$495	$425	$375	$325	$275	$225	$175

Last MSR was $699.

Add $20 for reverse headstock. Add $75 for optional Trans. finishes. Red finish discontinued in 1993.

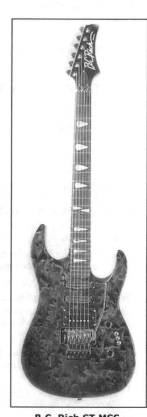

B.C. Rich ST MSS
courtesy B.C. Rich

GRADING	100% MINT	98% NEAR MINT	95% EXC+	90% EXC	80% VG+	70% VG	60% G

B

Virgin (Platinum Series) - similar to the Virgin [U.S. Bolt-On Neck], except has dot position markers, double locking Floyd Rose tremolo, available in Black, Metallic Blue, Metallic Red, Satin Black, or Red finishes, mfg. 1987-1993, 2000-present.

MSR $560	$395	$350	$310	$275	$225	$175	$125

Last MSR was $469.

Virgin (Platinum Pro Series) - Virgin body style, agathis body, bolt-on maple neck, rosewood fingerboard with dot inlay, 2 BDSM humbucker pickups, Floyd Rose tremolo, black hardware, available in black finish, mfg. 2003-present.

MSR $700	$490	$425	$375	$325	$275	$225	$175

ELECTRIC: VIRGO SERIES

The Virgo is a combination of the Virgin and Warlock shapes.

VIRGO - symmetrical double cutaway nato beveled body, bolt-on neck, 24-fret ebony fingerboard with skull inlays, matching headstock with three-per-side tuners, STB, one humbucker and one rail pickup, two knobs, three-way switch, black hardware, available in Black with white bevels or White with black bevels, 25.5 in. scale, new 2005.

MSR $640	$450	$375	$325	$275	$235	$195	$160

ELECTRIC: WARLOCK SERIES

The Warlock model was introduced in 1981.

WARLOCK STANDARD (U.S. NECK-THROUGH-BODY) - offset double cutaway body, pointed forward horns, centered large "V" cutaway in bottom bout, alder (or poplar) body wings, through-body maple neck, 24 5/8 in. scale, 24-fret rosewood fingerboard with pearl diamond inlay, fixed bridge, blackface peghead with logo, 6-on-a-side tuners, black hardware, 2 Seymour Duncan custom humbucker pickups, 2 volume/1 tone controls, 3-way selector, available in Black, Purple, Red, or White finishes, mfg. 1981-1999.

1981-1993	N/A	$1,300	$1,150	$1,000	$850	$700	$550
1994-1999	$1,125	$1,000	$875	$750	$625	$525	$425

Last MSR was $1,599.

In 1998, Floyd Rose 2 tremolo replaced the fixed bridge; Blood Red and Blue finishes were introduced; Purple and Red finishes were disc.

Warlock Supreme (U.S. Neck-through-body) - similar to the Warlock Standard, except has mahogany body wings, mahogany neck, bound figured maple top, bound ebony fingerboard with abalone blade inlays, 3-per-side tuners, bound headstock, Floyd Rose tremolo or Quadmatic fixed bridge, 2 DiMarzio humbuckers, available in Trans. Sunburst Emerald Green, Trans. Sunburst Gold, Trans. Sunburst Pagan Blue, or Trans. Sunburst Red finishes, disc. 1999.

	$1,400	$1,200	$1,050	$950	$825	$650	$500

Last MSR was $1,999.

In 1998, Blue Sunburst, Trans. Black, Trans. Green, and Trans. Red finishes were introduced; Trans. Sunburst Emerald Green, Trans. Sunburst Gold, Trans. Sunburst Pagan Blue, and Trans. Sunburst Red finishes were disc.

Warlock Deluxe - similar to the Warlock, except has a mahogany body with a quilt/flamed top, mahogany neck, rosewood fingerboard, and a quad style bridge, available in Trans. Red, Trans. Green, Trans. Blue, or Black finish, mfg. 1999 only.

	$1,275	$1,150	$1,000	$875	$750	$625	$500

Warlock 7-String - similar to the Warlock, except has a maple body and neck (thru-body), and in 7-String configuration, mfg. 1999 only.

	$1,400	$1,200	$1,050	$950	$825	$700	$575

Last MSR was $1,999.

WARLOCK BOLT-ON (U.S. BOLT-ON-NECK) - offset double cutaway alder body, pointed forward horns, centered large V cutaway in bottom bout, bolt-on maple neck, 25.5 in. scale, 24-fret rosewood fingerboard with white dot inlay, locking Floyd Rose 2 tremolo, 6-on-the-other-side tuners, reverse headstock, black hardware, 2 DiMarzio humbucker pickups, 2 volume/1 tone controls, 3-way selector, available in Black, Blue, Emerald Green, Red, White, or Yellow finish, disc. 1999.

	$975	$875	$800	$700	$600	$500	$375

Last MSR was $1,399.

Add $125 for optional Candy Color finish.

In 1995, Candy Color finishes became optional, Purple finish was introduced, and Blue, Emerald Green, and Yellow finishes were disc. In 1998, poplar body replaced the alder body; Blue finish was reintroduced; Purple and White finishes were disc.

Warlock (N.J. Series) - similar to the Warlock [U.S. Bolt-On Neck], except has 24.75 in. scale, diamond inlays, N.J. logo on headstock, die-cast tuners, additional toggle switch, available in Black, Metallic Red, Trans. Black, Trans. Blue, Trans. Purple, Trans. Red, or White finish, current mfg.

MSR $900	$630	$550	$500	$450	$400	$350	$300

Add $25 for Trans. Blue or Trans. Red finish (Trans. Blue finish was discontinued in 1998). Add $20 for Blue Burst finish. Add $100 for Supreme Black finish. Add $25 for left-hand model with Black finish. Add $35 for left-handed configuration.

In 2005, a Floyd Rose tremolo bridge was an option, and Trans. Black and Trans. Purple finishes were introduced.

Warlock (Platinum Series) - similar to the Warlock [U.S. Bolt-On Neck], except has 24.75 in. scale, white inlay dots, B.C. Rich angled headstock with Platinum logo, 6-on-a-side die-cast tuners, chrome hardware, accu-tune tremolo, additional toggle switch, available in Black, Metallic Red, or White finish, current mfg.

MSR $560	$395	$350	$310	$275	$225	$175	$125

Add $25 for Trans. Blue, Trans. Purple, and Trans. Red finishes (Trans. Blue and Trans. Purple finishes were discontinued in 1998). Add $20 for Blue Burst finish. Add $100 for Supreme Black finish. Add $200 for Acrylic Red and Acrylic Green finishes. Add $25 for left-hand model with Black finish. Add $35 for 7-string configuration.

In 1998, Blood Red finish was introduced; Metallic Red finish was discontinued. In 2000, Blue Burst, Supreme Black, Acrylic Green and Acrylic Red finishes were introduced.

B

GRADING	100% MINT	98% NEAR MINT	95% EXC+	90% EXC	80% VG+	70% VG	60% G

Warlock (Platinum Pro Series) - Warlock style, agathis body, bolt-on maple neck, 24-fret rosewood fingerboard with dot inlay, 2 BDSM humbucker pickups, 3-per-side tuners, black hardware, available in black or tombstone finishes, mfg. 2003-present.

MSR $700	$490	$425	$375	$325	$275	$225	$175

Add $20 for Tombstone finish. Add $25 for left-hand configuration. Add $50 for 7-String configuration.

Warlock (Bronze Series, Warlock WG-5T) - similar to the Warlock [U.S.: Bolt-On Neck], except has laminated body, 24.75 in. scale, dot position markers, B.C. Rich angled headstock, 6-on-a-side covered tuners, chrome hardware, tremolo, available in Black, Red, or White finishes, current mfg.

MSR $320	$225	$185	$150	$125	$100	$80	$60

Warlock Acrylic - similar to the Warlock Platinum, except has an acrylic see-through body, available in Ice or Red finishes, mfg. 2004-present.

MSR $760	$530	$450	$400	$350	$300	$250	$200

Add $20 for Tombstone finish. Add $25 for left-hand configuration. Add $50 for 7-String configuration.

Warlock WG-1 (Rave Series) - similar to the Warlock WG-5T, except has only 1 pickup, disc. 1993.

	N/A	$225	$200	$175	$150	$125	$95

Last MSR was $309.

Warlock WG-2 (Rave Series) - similar to the Warlock WG-5T, and features 2 pickups, disc. 1993.

	N/A	$250	$225	$200	$175	$150	$125

Last MSR was $339.

ELECTRIC: WAVE SERIES

The Wave model was introduced in 1983.

WAVE (U.S. NECK-THROUGH-BODY) - offset double cutaway body with curled bottom bout cutaway, ash/mahogany body wings, through-body rock maple neck, 24.75 in. scale, 22-fret rosewood (or ebony) fingerboard with pearl diamond inlay, Kahler Steeler tremolo, blackface peghead with pearl logo inlay, 3-per-side tuners, chrome hardware, 2 DiMarzio humbucker pickups, 2 volume/1 tone controls, 3-position switch, available in Black, Gun Metal Gray, Natural, Pearl Blue, Pearl Purple, Pearl White, Pearl Violet, Red, or Yellow finishes, mfg. 1983-1993.

	N/A	$1,500	$1,300	$1,100	$900	$700	$500

Last MSR was $2,099.

Add $100 for optional Candy Color finishes. Add $150 for optional translucent finishes.

Wave Supreme (U.S. Neck-through-body) - similar to the Wave, except has figured maple body, 24-fret bound ebony fingerboard with pearl cloud inlay, Leo Quan wraparound bridge, 2 volume/2-Tone controls, 4 mini switches, on-board preamp, available in Trans. Blue, Trans. Emerald Green, Natural, Trans. Pagan Gold, or Trans. Red finishes, mfg. 1983-89.

	N/A	$1,600	$1,400	$1,200	$1,000	$800	$600

Wave (U.S. Bolt-On Neck) - similar to the Wave Bass [U.S. Neck-through-body], except has Honduran mahogany body, bolt-on maple neck, mfg. 1983-1993.

	N/A	$1,000	$850	$700	$575	$450	$350

Last MSR was $1,299.

WAVE STANDARD - Wave style, alder or poplar body, maple neck-thru body, 24-fret ebony fingerboard with diamond inlays, 2 DiMarzio humbucker pickups, fixed or Floyd Rose tremolo, 3-per-side tuners, available in Blue, White, Red, or Black finishes, mfg. 1999 only.

	$1,125	$975	$850	$750	$650	$550	$450

Last MSR was $1,599.

Wave Deluxe - similar to the Wave, except has a mahogany top with a quilt/flamed top, mahogany neck-thru body, rosewood fingerboard, and a quad style bridge, available in Trans. Red, Trans. Blue, Trans. Green, or Black finishes, mfg. 1999 only.

	$1,275	$1,150	$1,000	$875	$750	$625	$500

Last MSR was $1,799.

Wave Supreme - similar to the Wave Deluxe, except has an ebony fingerboard with cloud inlays, mfg. 1999 only.

	$1,625	$1,425	$1,300	$1,150	$1,025	$900	$750

Last MSR was $2,299.

Wave 7-String - similar to the Wave Standard, except in 7-String configuration and maple body, mfg. 1999 only.

	$1,195	$1,050	$950	$850	$750	$650	$550

Last MSR was $1,699.

ELECTRIC: WIDOW SERIES

The Widow model was introduced in 1983. "The Widow was designed in collaboration with Blackie Lawless (W.A.S.P.). The Widow was made in a guitar and bass configuration. This model was never part of our production lineup; however, we did make quite a few Widow guitars and basses in the Custom Shop." In 1999, B.C. Rich did list the Widow as a standard production model. This was made as a Standard (Neck-thru), bolt-on, Deluxe, and a 7-String. Pricing followed that of the other production models of the same time period.

B.C. Rich Warlock Platinum Pro Series courtesy B.C. Rich

B.C. Rich Wave courtesy B.C. Rich

GRADING	100% MINT	98% NEAR MINT	95% EXC+	90% EXC	80% VG+	70% VG	60% G

ELECTRIC: WRATH SERIES

WRATH (U.S. NECK-THROUGH-BODY) - offset double cutaway body, pointed forward horns, asymmetrical waist/rounded bottom bout, Honduran mahogany body wings, through-body maple neck, 22-fret rosewood fingerboard with pearl diamond inlay, Kahler Steeler tremolo, blackface peghead with logo, 3-per-side Sperzel tuners, black hardware, 2 Seymour Duncan humbucker pickups, volume/tone controls, 3-way selector, available in Black, Gun Metal Gray, Natural, Pearl Blue, Pearl Purple, Pearl White, Pearl Violet, Red, or Yellow finishes, disc. 1993.

	N/A	$1,500	$1,300	$1,100	$900	$700	$500

Last MSR was $2,099.

Add $100 for optional Candy Color finishes. Add $150 for optional translucent finishes.

Wrath (U.S. Bolt-On Neck) - similar to the Wrath [U.S.: Neck-through-body], except has mahogany body, bolt-on maple neck, disc. 1993.

	N/A	$1,000	$850	$700	$600	$500	$400

Last MSR was $1,299.

ELECTRIC: ZOMBIE SERIES

ZOMBIE (PLATINUM PRO SERIES) - offset double cutaway body with distinct pointed horns and bottom bouts, agathis body, bolt-on neck, 24-fret rosewood fingerboard with dot inlay, matching headstock with three-per-side tuners, Floyd Rose licensed tremolo bridge, two humbucker pickups, three knobs, three-way switch, black hardware, available in Tombstone and Shadow (matte black) finishes, 25.5 in. scale, new 2005.

MSR $700	$490	$425	$375	$325	$275	$225	$175

ELECTRIC BASS: BEAST SERIES

BEAST BASS (U.S. NECK-THRU-BODY) - double sharp cutaway, 4-point body, alder or poplar body, maple neck-thru-body, 24-fret ebony fingerboard with diamond inlays, 2 P-style DiMarzio pickups, Badass 2 style bridge, available in Black, White, Red, or Blue finishes, mfg. 1999 only.

	$1,275	$1,125	$1,000	$875	$750	$625	$500

Last MSR was $1,799.

BEAST BASS (PLATINUM SERIES) - double sharp cutaway, 4-point body, agathis body, maple bolt-on neck, 24-fret rosewood fingerboard with dot inlays, 2 P-style pickups, adjustable bridge, chrome hardware, available in black finish, mfg. 2003-present.

MSR $650	$455	$395	$350	$300	$250	$200	$150

BEAST BASS (N.J. SERIES) - double sharp cutaway, 4-point body, mahogany body, maple bolt-on neck, 24-fret rosewood fingerboard with diamond inlays, 2 P-style pickups, active EQ, adjustable bridge, black hardware, available in black or Trans. Red finish, mfg. 2001-present.

MSR $850	$595	$525	$475	$375	$325	$275	$225

Add $35 for Trans. Red finish (quilted maple top).

ELECTRIC BASS: BERNARDO SERIES

In 1999, they produced the Bernardo Recording model. This was a less-expensive version of the Bernardo Deluxe that had a mahogany top with solid colors for finishes. It retailed for $1,899, $1,999, and $2,199, respectively for the 4-, 5-, and 6-string configurations.

BERNARDO DELUXE (U.S. NECK-THRU-BODY, BERNARDO ARTIST) - offset double cutaway maple/purpleheart body, through-body maple neck, 34 in. scale, 24-fret ebony fingerboard with abalone oval inlays, black peghead with logo, 2-per-side tuners, black hardware, 2 Seymour Duncan Bassline soapbar pickups, volume/blend/stacked bass/mid/treble controls, active electronics, available in Black, Natural Gloss, Trans. Black, Trans. Red, White, or Natural Hand-Rubbed Oil finishes, disc. 1999.

	$1,625	$1,475	$1,350	$1,100	$950	$750	$550

Last MSR was $2,299.

Bernardo 5-string configuration - 3/2-per-side tuners.

	$1,695	$1,525	$1,375	$1,175	$975	$775	$575

Last MSR was $2,399.

Bernardo 6-string configuration - 3-per-side tuners.

	$1,825	$1,675	$1,500	$1,300	$1,075	$850	$625

Last MSR was $2,599.

BERNARDO STANDARD (U.S. NECK-THRU-BODY) - similar to the Bernardo Deluxe, except featured less figured woods, pau ferro fingerboard, chrome hardware, available in Acapulco Blue, Black, Cream, White, or Wine Purple solid finishes, disc. 1998.

	$1,195	$1,050	$925	$800	$675	$550	$425

Last MSR was $1,699.

Standard 5-string configuration

	$1,275	$1,100	$975	$825	$700	$575	$450

Last MSR was $1,799.

Standard 6-string configuration

	$1,350	$1,150	$1,025	$875	$725	$600	$475

Last MSR was $1,899.

GRADING	100% MINT	98% NEAR MINT	95% EXC+	90% EXC	80% VG+	70% VG	60% G

ELECTRIC BASS: BICH BASS SERIES

BICH BASS STANDARD (U.S NECK-THRU-BODY) - offset double cutaway body, asymmetrical bottom bout cutaways, maple body wings, through-body maple neck, 34 in. scale, 24-fret rosewood fingerboard with pearl diamond inlay, fixed Wilkinson bridge, blackface peghead with pearl logo inlay, 2-per-side tuners, black hardware, P/J-style DiMarzio pickups, 2 volume/1 tone controls, 3-way selector, available in Black, Porsche Red, White or Wine Purple finish, disc. 1999.

| $1,195 | $1,050 | $900 | $750 | $650 | $550 | $450 |

Last MSR was $1,699.

Bich Bass Special (U.S. Neck-through-body) - similar to the Bich Standard, except has hard rock maple neck, quilted or flame maple body wings, ebony fingerboard with abalone cloud inlays, active electronics, available in Natural, Trans. Blue, Trans. Emerald Green, Trans. Purple, or Trans. Red finish, disc. 1998.

| $1,125 | $975 | $850 | $750 | $625 | $525 | $400 |

Last MSR was $1,599.

Bich Bass Supreme (U.S.: Neck-through-body) - similar to the Bich Standard, except has hard rock maple neck, AAA select quilted or flame maple body wings, bound ebony fingerboard and headstock, abalone cloud inlays, 2 DiMarzio P-style pickups, full active electronics, available in Natural, Trans. Blue, Trans. Emerald Green, Trans. Purple, or Trans. Red finish, disc. 1999.

| $1,675 | $1,475 | $1,275 | $1,100 | $950 | $800 | $650 |

Last MSR was $2,399.

Bich 8 String Bass (U.S.: Neck-through-body) - similar to the Bich Supreme, except in an 8-string configuration, 30 in. scale, 4-per-side tuners, disc. 1999.

| $1,895 | $1,600 | $1,400 | $1,200 | $1,050 | $900 | $750 |

Last MSR was $2,699.

Bich Bass Deluxe (U.S. Neck-Thru-Body) - similar to the Bich Bass Supreme, except has an ebony fingerboard with diamond inlays, mfg. 1999 only.

| $1,350 | $1,175 | $1,100 | $950 | $800 | $675 | $550 |

Last MSR was $1,899.

BICH BASS BOLT-ON (U.S. BOLT-ON-NECK) - offset double cutaway maple body with asymmetrical bottom bout cutaways, bolt-on maple neck, 34 in. scale, 22-fret rosewood fingerboard with pearl diamond inlay, fixed bridge, blackface peghead with logo inlay, 2-per-side tuners, black hardware, P/J-style DiMarzio pickups, 2 volume/1 tone controls, 3-way selector, available in Black, Red, White, or Wine Purple finish, disc. 1998.

| $900 | $775 | $700 | $600 | $525 | $450 | $350 |

Last MSR was $1,299.

Add $125 for Candy Color finish.

B.C. Rich Beast Bass Platinum Series courtesy B.C. Rich

ELECTRIC BASS: EAGLE BASS SERIES

The Eagle Bass model was introduced in 1977.

EAGLE STANDARD (U.S. NECK-THRU-BODY) - offset double cutaway figured maple, alder, or poplar body, through-body maple neck with koa stringers, 24-fret ebony fingerboard with diamond inlay, fixed Wilkinson bridge, blackface peghead with pearl logo inlay, 2-per-side tuners, black hardware, P/J-style pickups, 2 volume/1 tone controls, available in Natural, black, white, red, or blue finish, mfg. 1977-1996.

| 1979-1994 | N/A | $1,500 | $1,300 | $1,100 | $900 | $700 | $500 |
| 1995-1999 | $1,195 | $1,050 | $900 | $775 | $650 | $525 | $400 |

Last MSR was $1,899.

This model had an optional koa body/neck. In 1995, active electronics were introduced and bound fingerboard/peghead replaced original part/designs.

EAGLE DELUXE (U.S. NECK-THRU-BODY) - similar to the Eagle Standard, except has a mahogany body with quilt/flamed top, mahogany neck-thru-body, available in Trans. Red, Trans. Green, Trans. Blue, or Black finish, mfg. 1999 only.

| $1,350 | $1,200 | $1,050 | $950 | $825 | $700 | $575 |

Last MSR was $1,899.

EAGLE SUPREME (U.S. NECK-THRU-BODY) - similar to the Eagle Deluxe, except has a cloud inlay on fingerboard, disc. 1999.

| $1,675 | $1,500 | $1,300 | $1,100 | $950 | $800 | $675 |

Last MSR was $2,399.

EAGLE (PLATINUM SERIES) - Eagle style offset double cutaway agathis body with quilt maple top on Natural, bolt-on maple neck, 24-fret rosewood fingerboard with dot inlay, two-per-side tuners, standard bridge, two P-style pickups, three knobs, three-way switch, chrome hardware, available in Onyx or Natural finish, 34 in. scale, new 2005.

| MSR $650 | $460 | $400 | $350 | $300 | $250 | $200 | $150 |

B

GRADING	100% MINT	98% NEAR MINT	95% EXC+	90% EXC	80% VG+	70% VG	60% G

ELECTRIC BASS: EXCLUSIVE ARCH TOP SERIES

EXCLUSIVE ARCH TOP BASS (U.S. NECK-THRU-BODY) - offset double cutaway mahogany body, bound figured maple top, through-body maple neck, 34 in. scale, 24-fret bound ebony fingerboard with pearl block inlay, fixed bridge, blackface peghead with pearl 'R' inlay, 2-per-side tuners, chrome hardware, P/J-style Bassline pickups, 2 volume/1 tone controls, 3-way selector, available in Cherry Sunburst, Natural, Trans. Black, Trans. Magenta, or Trans. Red finish, mfg. 1998 only.

	$1,675	$1,525	$1,375	$1,200	$1,025	$900	$750

Last MSR was $2,400.

EXCLUSIVE BASS "THUNDERER" - offset double cutaway mahogany body, maple neck-thru-body, no fingerboard inlays, Duncan SMB-4A pickup, Mighty Mite bridge, available in Black, White, Red, or Blue finish, mfg. 1999 only.

	$1,275	$1,100	$975	$850	$750	$650	$550

Last MSR was $1,799.

ELECTRIC BASS: GUNSLINGER SERIES

GUNSLINGER BASS (U.S. BOLT-ON NECK) - offset double cutaway swamp ash body, bolt-on maple neck, 34 in. scale, 22-fret rosewood fingerboard with pearl dot inlay, fixed bridge, blackface peghead with logo, 4-on-a-side tuners, chrome hardware, DiMarzio High Output P-style pickup, volume/tone controls, available in Black, Creme, Porsche Red, or White finish, disc. 1998.

	$850	$725	$650	$550	$475	$395	$325

Last MSR was $1,199.

Add $40 for optional black hardware.

ELECTRIC BASS: IGNITOR SERIES

IGNITOR BASS (U.S. BOLT-ON NECK) - offset double cutaway maple body, pointed forward horns, scooped lower bout cutaway, bolt-on maple neck, 34 in. scale, 22-fret rosewood fingerboard with dot inlays, fixed bridge, black hardware, 4-on-a-side tuners, P/J-style DiMarzio pickups, 2 volume/1 tone controls, 3-way selector, available in Black, Red, White, or Wine Purple finish, disc. 1998.

	$900	$775	$700	$600	$500	$425	$325

Last MSR was $1,299.

ELECTRIC BASS: INNOVATOR SERIES

The Innovator Bass model was introduced in 1987.

INNOVATOR BASS 4 (U.S. NECK-THRU-BODY) - offset double cutaway maple/purpleheart body, maple through-body neck, 34 in. scale, 24-fret ebony fingerboard with abalone block inlay, fixed bridge, 4-on-a-side tuners, chrome hardware, 2 Seymour Duncan Bassline soapbar pickups, 2 volume/blend/tone controls, active electronics, available in Natural Hand-Rubbed Oil finish, mfg. 1987-1998.

	$1,200	$1,075	$975	$850	$725	$575	$425

Last MSR was $1,699.

Add $200 for optional transparent color Urethane finish.

Innovator Bass 5 (U.S. Neck-through-body) - similar to Innovator Bass 4, except has 5-string configuration, 3/2-per-side tuners, disc. 1998.

	$1,150	$1,075	$975	$850	$725	$575	$450

Last MSR was $1,599.

Innovator Bass 6 (U.S. Neck-through-body) - similar to Innovator Bass 4, except has 6-string configuration, through-body maple neck with rosewood stringers, ebony fingerboard with pearl cloud inlay, 3-per-side tuners, 2 humbucker Bartolini pickups, disc. 1997.

	$1,400	$1,200	$1,000	$925	$775	$650	$475

Last MSR was $2,000.

INNOVATOR (U.S. BOLT-ON NECK) - offset double cutaway swamp ash body, bolt-on maple neck, 34 in. scale, 22-fret pau ferro fingerboard with pearl dot inlay, fixed bridge, blackface peghead with logo, 4-on-a-side tuners, chrome hardware, Seymour Duncan Bassline soapbar pickup, volume/tone controls, active electronics, available in Black, Creme, Porsche Red, or White finish, disc. 1998.

	$900	$775	$695	$600	$500	$425	$325

Last MSR was $1,299.

Add $100 for optional gold hardware.

INB-104 INNOVATOR BASS 4 STRING - offset double cutaway solid ash and maple body, bolt-on maple neck, 34 in. scale, 22-fret rosewood fingerboard with dot inlay, fixed bridge, 4-on-a-side tuners, chrome hardware, 2 active soapbar pickups, 2 volume/1 tone controls, 3-way selector, available in Black, Natural, Red, or White finish, disc. 1998.

	$475	$395	$350	$300	$250	$200	$150

Last MSR was $649.

Add $25 for Trans. Blue, Trans. Purple, or Trans. Red finish.

INB-105 Innovator Bass 5 String - similar to the INB-104 Innovator Bass, except in a 5-string configuration, disc. 1998.

	$495	$425	$375	$325	$275	$225	$175

Last MSR was $699.

INNOVATOR (NJ SERIES) - offset double cutaway chesswood body with AAA quilted maple top, five-ply maple/walnut neck, 24-fret rosewood fingerboard with diamond inlays, matching headstock with two-per-side tuners, standard bridge, two EMG pickups, four knobs, active electronics, gold hardware, available in Natural or Trans. Aqua finish, mfg. 2003-present.

MSR	$1,000	$700	$625	$550	$475	$400	$350	$300

GRADING	100% MINT	98% NEAR MINT	95% EXC+	90% EXC	80% VG+	70% VG	60% G

Innovator 5-String (NJ Series) - similar to the Innovator, except in five-string configuration with 3/2-per-side tuners, mfg. 2003-present.

MSR $1,200	$850	$750	$675	$600	$525	$450	$375

ELECTRIC BASS: IRONBIRD SERIES

IRONBIRD STANDARD (U.S. NECK-THRU-BODY) - angular offset cutaway body, pointed treble bout/rear body bouts, maple body wings, through-body maple neck, 34 in. scale, 24-fret rosewood fingerboard with pearl diamond inlay, fixed bridge, blackface peghead with logo, 4-on-a-side tuners, black hardware, P/J-style DiMarzio pickups, 2 volume/1 tone controls, 3-way selector, available in Black, Porsche Red, White, or Wine Purple finish, mfg. 1984-1998.

	$1,050	$900	$800	$700	$575	$475	$350

Last MSR was $1,499.

Ironbird (U.S. Bolt-On Neck) - angular offset cutaway maple body, pointed treble bout/rear body bouts, bolt-on maple neck, 34 in. scale, 22-fret rosewood fingerboard with pearl dot inlay, fixed bridge, 4-on-a-side tuners, black hardware, P/J-style DiMarzio pickups, 2 volume/1 tone controls, 3-way selector, available in Black, Red, or White finish, disc. 1998.

	$900	$775	$695	$600	$500	$425	$325

Last MSR was $1,299.

Add $125 for optional Candy Color finishes.

ELECTRIC BASS: MOCKINGBIRD SERIES

MOCKINGBIRD BASS STANDARD (U.S. NECK-THRU-BODY) - offset double cutaway asymmetrical body, maple body wings, through-body maple neck, 34 in. scale, 24-fret rosewood fingerboard with pearl diamond inlay, fixed bridge, blackface peghead with pearl logo inlay, 2-per-side tuners, black hardware, P/J-style DiMarzio pickups, 2 volume/1 tone controls, 3-position switch, available in Black, Porsche Red, White, Blue, or Wine Purple finish, mfg. 1976-1999.

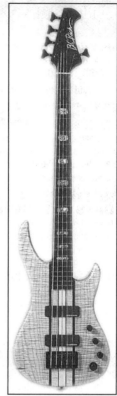

B.C. Rich Innovator Bass courtesy B.C. Rich

1976-1993	N/A	$1,500	$1,300	$1,100	$900	$700	$500
1994-1999	$1,195	$1,050	$900	$750	$650	$550	$450

Last MSR was $1,699.

In 1998, Porsche Red and Wine Purple finishes were discontinued; Blood Red and Metallic Red finishes were introduced.

Mockingbird Arch Top Bass (U.S. Neck-through-body) - similar to the Mockingbird Standard, except has mahogany body wings, carved maple top, mahogany through-body neck, chrome hardware, available in Black, Oriental Blue, Purple, Red, or White finish, disc. 1998.

	$1,350	$1,175	$1,025	$875	$725	$575	$425

Last MSR was $1,699.

Mockingbird Bass Special (U.S. Neck-through-body) - similar to the Mockingbird Standard, except has quilted or flame maple body wings, hard rock maple neck-through-body, ebony fingerboard with abalone cloud inlays, 2 P-style DiMarzio pickups, active electronics, available in Natural, Trans. Blue, Trans. Emerald Green, Trans. Purple, or Trans. Red finish, disc. 1998.

	$1,125	$1,000	$875	$750	$625	$525	$400

Last MSR was $1,599.

Mockingbird Bass Supreme (U.S. Neck-through-body) - similar to the Mockingbird Standard, except has AAA select quilted or flame maple body wings, hard rock maple neck-through-body, bound ebony fingerboard with abalone cloud inlays, bound headstock, 2 P-style DiMarzio pickups, full active electronics, available in Natural, Trans. Blue, Trans. Emerald Green, Trans. Purple, or Trans. Red finish, disc. 1999.

	$1,675	$1,450	$1,250	$1,100	$950	$800	$600

Last MSR was $2,399.

Mockingbird Bass Deluxe (U.S. Neck-Thru-Body) - similar to the Mockingbird Bass Supreme, except has diamond fingerboard inlays, mfg. 1999 only.

	$1,350	$1,175	$1,050	$925	$800	$700	$600

Last MSR was $1,899.

MOCKINGBIRD BASS BOLT-ON (U.S. BOLT-ON NECK) - offset double cutaway asymmetrical maple body, bolt-on maple neck, 34 in. scale, 22-fret rosewood fingerboard with pearl dot inlay, fixed bridge, 2-per-side tuners, black hardware, P/J-style DiMarzio pickups, 2 volume/1 tone controls, 3-position switch, available in Black, Red, White, or Wine Purple finish, disc. 1998.

	$900	$775	$700	$600	$500	$425	$325

Last MSR was $1,299.

Add $125 for optional Candy Color finishes.

Mockingbird 4 String (Platinum Series) - similar to the Mockingbird (U.S. Bolt-On Neck), except has solid maple body, dot position markers, 2-per-side headstock with Platinum logo, chrome hardware, 2 P-style pickups, available in Black, Red, Natural, Tombstone, Metallic Blue, or White finish, disc. 1998, 2000-present.

MSR $600	$425	$350	$325	$275	$225	$195	$175

Add $20 for Trans. Blue, Trans. Green, Trans. Purple, Metallic Blue, Natural, or Tombstone finishes.

B.C. Rich Mockingbird Bass Bolt-on courtesy B.C. Rich

GRADING	100% MINT	98% NEAR MINT	95% EXC+	90% EXC	80% VG+	70% VG	60% G

Mockingbird Bass (N.J. Series) - similar to the Mockingbird, except has solid mahogany body with a AA+ quilted maple top, matching neck and headstock finish, and diamond fingerboard inlays, available in Black, Natural, or Trans. Red finishes, mfg. 2001-present.

MSR $800	$560	$495	$450	$400	$350	$300	$250

Add $25 for Natural finish.

ELECTRIC BASS: SEAGULL SERIES

The Seagull model was introduced in 1972. "The **Eagle Bass** was formerly called the Bodine Bass. It was named after a very good friend named Bill Bodine, who, at the time, was the bass player for Olivia Newton-John. After the Seagull was redesigned slightly, it was renamed the Bodine Bass. The original Seagull featured a shorter upper horn and the Bodine/Eagle featured a longer upper horn. The upper horn was modified to give the bass better balance.

ELECTRIC BASS: ST & TBB SERIES

ST BASS (U.S. SERIES) - offset double cutaway laminated alder body, bolt-on hard maple neck, 34 in. scale, 21-fret maple fingerboard with black dot inlay, vintage-style fixed bridge, 4-on-a-side vintage-style headstock, open gear tuners, chrome hardware, P-style pickup, volume/tone controls, available in Black, Bright Green, Creme, Red, or White finishes, disc. 1998.

	$280	$250	$200	$175	$150	$125	$100

Last MSR was $399.

TBB BASS (U.S. NECK-THRU-BODY) - offset double cutaway body, mahogany body wings, through-body maple neck, 34 in. scale, 22-fret rosewood fingerboard with pearl diamond inlay, fixed bridge, 2-per-side tuners, chrome hardware, P/J-style DiMarzio pickups, 2 volume/2-Tone controls, 3-way selector, available in Black, Creme, Red, or White finishes, disc. 1998.

	$1,050	$900	$800	$700	$575	$475	$350

Last MSR was $1,499.

ELECTRIC BASS: VIRGIN SERIES

VIRGIN BASS (U.S. NECK-THRU-BODY) - offset double cutaway body, pointed forward horns, rounded bottom bout, Honduran mahogany body wings, through-body maple neck, 34 in. scale, 22-fret rosewood fingerboard with pearl diamond inlay, fixed bridge, blackface peghead with logo, 4-on-a-side tuners, black hardware, P/J-style Seymour Duncan pickups, volume/tone controls, 3-way selector, available in Black, Gun Metal Gray, Natural, Pearl Blue, Pearl Purple, Pearl White, Pearl Violet, Red, or Yellow finishes, disc. 1993.

	N/A	$1,475	$1,250	$1,050	$900	$750	$600

Last MSR was $2,099.

Add $100 for optional Candy Color finishes. Add $150 for optional translucent finishes.

Virgin Bass (U.S. Bolt-On Neck) - similar to the Virgin Bass [U.S. Neck-through-body], except has mahogany body, bolt-on maple neck, disc. 1993.

	N/A	$900	$800	$725	$650	$550	$450

Last MSR was $1,299.

Virgin Bass 4 String (N.J. Series) - similar to the Virgin Bass [U.S. Bolt-On Neck], except has diamond position markers, EMG Select pickups, available in Black or Red finishes, disc. 1993.

	N/A	$450	$375	$325	$275	$225	$175

Last MSR was $629.

Add $20 for reverse headstock. Add $50 for optional translucent finishes.

Virgin Bass 4 String (Platinum Series) - similar to the Virgin Bass [U.S. Bolt-On Neck], except has dot position markers, available in Black or Red finishes, disc. 1993.

	N/A	$325	$275	$225	$175	$150	$125

Last MSR was $469.

ELECTRIC BASS: WARLOCK SERIES

WARLOCK BASS STANDARD (U.S. NECK-THRU-BODY) - offset double cutaway body, pointed forward horns, centered large "V" cutaway in bottom bout, maple body wings, through-body maple neck, 34 in. scale, 24-fret rosewood fingerboard with pearl diamond inlay, fixed bridge, blackface peghead with pearl logo inlay, 2-per-side tuners, black hardware, P/J-style DiMarzio pickups, 2 volume/1 tone controls, 3-position switch, available in Black, Porsche Red, White, or Wine Purple finishes, mfg. 1981-1999.

1981-1993	N/A	$1,200	$1,050	$900	$750	$600	$450
1994-1999	$1,195	$1,050	$925	$775	$650	$500	$375

Last MSR was $1,699.

In 1998, Porsche Red and Wine Purple finishes were discontinued; Blood Red and Metallic Red finishes were introduced.

WARLOCK (U.S. BOLT-ON NECK) - offset double cutaway maple body, pointed forward horns, centered large "V" cutaway in bottom bout, bolt-on maple neck, 34 in. scale, 22-fret rosewood fingerboard with pearl dot inlay, fixed bridge, 2-per-side tuners, black hardware, P/J-style DiMarzio pickups, 2 volume/1 tone controls, 3-position switch, available in Black, Red, White, or Wine Purple finishes, disc. 1997.

	$900	$775	$700	$600	$500	$425	$325

Last MSR was $1,299.

This model had optional Candy Color finishes.

Warlock Bass (Platinum Series) - similar to the Warlock [U.S.: Bolt-On Neck], except has solid maple body, dot position markers, 2-per-side headstock with Platinum logo, P/J-style pickups, available in Black, Red, Metallic Blue, or White finishes, current mfg.

MSR $600	$425	$375	$325	$275	$225	$195	$150

Add $20 for Trans. Blue, Trans. Green, Trans. Purple, or Metallic Blue finishes. Add $20 for left-hand configuration.

B

GRADING	100% MINT	98% NEAR MINT	95% EXC+	90% EXC	80% VG+	70% VG	60% G

Warlock Bass (N.J. Series) - similar to the Warlock, except has solid mahogany body, matching neck and headstock finish, diamond fingerboard inlays, available in Black, Natural, or Trans. Red finishes, current mfg.

MSR $800		$560	$495	$450	$400	$350	$300	$250

Add $50 for Trans. Red finishes. Add $50 for 5-string configuration.

Warlock Bass (N.J. Neck-Thru Series) - similar to the Warlock N.J. Series, except has a neck-thru-body, available in Black or Trans. Black finishes, mfg. 2000-02.

		$675	$600	$550	$500	$450	$400	$325

Last MSR was $950.

Add $20 for Trans. Black finishes.

Warlock Bass (Bronze Series) - similar to the Warlock N.J. Series, except is entry level model with an agathis body and bolt-on maple neck, available in Black or Trans. Red finishes, mfg. 2003-present.

MSR $330		$235	$190	$160	$130	$105	$80	$65

ELECTRIC BASS: WAVE SERIES

WAVE BASS STANDARD (U.S. NECK-THRU-BODY) - offset double cutaway body with curled bottom bout cutaway, maple (ash or mahogany) body wings, through-body rock maple neck, 34 in. scale, 22-fret rosewood (or ebony) fingerboard with pearl diamond inlay, fixed bridge, blackface peghead with pearl logo inlay, 2-per-side tuners, black hardware, P/J-style DiMarzio pickups, 2 volume/2-Tone controls, 3-position switch, available in Black, Blood Red, Metallic Red, Natural, Trans. Blue, Trans. Emerald Green, Trans. Pagan Gold, Trans. Red, and White finishes, disc. 1995, reintroduced 1999 only.

		$1,195	$1,050	$900	$775	$650	$525	$425

Last MSR was $1,699.

Add $100 for optional Candy Color finishes. Add $150 for optional translucent finishes.

Wave Bass Supreme (U.S. Neck-through-body) - similar to the Wave Bass, except has figured maple body, 24-fret bound ebony fingerboard with pearl cloud inlay, 2 volume/2-Tone controls, on-board preamp, available in Trans. Blue, Trans. Emerald Green, Natural, Trans. Pagan Gold, or Trans. Red finishes, disc. 1999.

		$1,695	$1,450	$1,250	$1,100	$950	$800	$650

Last MSR was $2,399.

Wave Bass Deluxe (U.S. Neck-Thru-Body) - similar to the Wave Bass Supreme, except has diamond fingerboard inlays, mfg. 1999 only.

		$1,350	$1,150	$1,000	$875	$750	$650	$550

Last MSR was $1,899.

B.C. Rich Mockingbrid Bass
NJ Series
courtesy B.C. Rich

Wave Bass (U.S. Bolt-On Neck) - similar to the Wave Bass [U.S. Neck-through-body], except has ash body, bolt-on maple neck, rosewood fingerboard, 2 volume/1 tone controls, available in Black, Sunburst, Turquoise, or White finishes, disc. 1995.

		$900	$775	$650	$525	$475	$425	$375

Last MSR was $1,299.

ELECTRIC BASS: WRATH SERIES

WRATH BASS (U.S. NECK-THRU-BODY) - offset double cutaway body, pointed forward horns, asymmetrical waist/rounded bottom bout, Honduran mahogany body wings, through-body maple neck, 34 in. scale, 22-fret rosewood fingerboard with pearl diamond inlay, fixed bridge, blackface peghead with logo, 4-on-a-side tuners, black hardware, P/J-style pickups, volume/tone controls, 3-way selector, available in Black, Gun Metal Gray, Natural, Pearl Blue, Pearl Purple, Pearl White, Pearl Violet, Red, and Yellow finishes, disc. 1993.

	N/A	$1,400	$1,200	$1,000	$850	$700	$550

Last MSR was $2,099.

Add $100 for optional Candy Color finishes. Add $150 for optional translucent finishes.

Wrath Bass (U.S.: Bolt-On Neck) - similar to the Wrath Bass [U.S.: Neck-through-body], except has mahogany body, bolt-on maple neck, disc. 1993.

	N/A	$850	$750	$650	$550	$450	$350

Last MSR was $1,299.

BD DEY

Instruments previously built in the Czech Republic. Previously distributed by BD Dey Musical Instruments of the Czech Republic.

The Czech Republic is the popular place for companies looking for an alternative to Asian guitar production. Various areas in the Czech Republic have a reputation for excellent instrument craftsmanship, evolving from the earlier days of violin and viola production. BD Dey offered five different electric guitar models, and a 6- and 12-string jumbo acoustic guitar model.

ELECTRIC

All BD Dey electric guitar models feature Gotoh hardware, Kent Armstrong or Porizta pickups, and S I T strings. The **Dey 01** has a double cutaway mahogany body with sharp forward horns, mahogany neck, 24-fret ebony fingerboard, 6-per-side tun-

B.C. Rich Warlock Bass
NJ Series
courtesy B.C. Rich

ers, and 2 humbucking pickups. The **Dey 02** has a similar design, with slimmed down maple body, maple neck, and rosewood fingerboard; the **Dey 03** features a semi-hollow walnut body, mahogany neck, and 3 Kent Armstrong single coils. The **Dey 04** is more of a superstrat style, with basswood body, maple neck, ebony fingerboard, 6-on-a-side tuners, and 2 humbuckers. The **Dey 05** is a throwback to the 1980s heavy metal guitar years, and features a chopped explorer-style alder body and maple neck.

BM

Instruments previously built in both Japan and Britain during the early 1960s through the mid-1980s.

The BM trademark was utilized by the UK importer Barnes & Mullins. While the company did import some entry level to medium quality guitars from Japan, they also distributed some British-built SHERGOLD originals under their trademark (source: Tony Bacon and Paul Day, *The Guru's Guitar Guide*).

BSX BASS, INC.

Instruments currently built in Aliquippa, Pennsylvania since 1989.

BSX currently produces upright basses that are easily portable. BSX produces traditional instruments as well as innovative narrow styles. BSX basses fit the niche when you want that upright feel and sound, but can't put an upright acoustic bass in the back seat of your economy car! For more information and photos, refer to the BSX website (see Trademark Index).

BSX briefly offered the BSX Traveler, which featured a detachable neck and a piezo bridge pickup. These innovations have been incorporated into the T Series model.

ELECTRIC BASS

There are several options available on almost every model. Each option differs per model and style. Refer to the BSX website for all available options.

BSX ALLEGRO 4 SB - violin shaped poplar solid body, rock maple neck, ebony fingerboard, 41.5 in. scale, 2-per-side tuners, Piezo-bridge system, active Bartolini electronics, 3-band EQ, individual volume control per string, rotating tummy rest, detachable neck, classical violin color with satin finish, 15 lbs, current mfg.

    MSR $2,900

BSX ALLEGRO 5 SB - similar to the BSX Allegro 4 SB except in five-string configuration, current mfg.

    MSR $3,050

BSX ALLEGRO 6 SB - similar to the BSX Allegro 4 SB except in six-string configuration, current mfg.

    MSR $3,350

BSX ALLEGRO 4 A - violin shaped acoustic body, spruce or cedar top with f-holes, maple back, rock maple neck, ebony fingerboard, 41.5 in. scale, 2-per-side tuners, Piezo-bridge system, active Bartolini electronics, 3-band EQ, individual volume control per string, rotating tummy rest, detachable neck, classical violin color with satin finish, 15 lb, current mfg.

    MSR $3,200

BSX ALLEGRO 5 A - similar to the BSX Allegro 4 A except in five-string configuration, current mfg.

    MSR $3,350

BSX ALLEGRO 6 A - similar to the BSX Allegro 4 A except in six-string configuration, current mfg.

    MSR $3,650

BSX SM 4 - student model of the standup bass, same scale as the ST Series, 3 in. high bridge, current mfg.

    MSR $1,095

BSX SM 5 - similar to the BSX SM 4 except in five-string configuration, current mfg.

    MSR $1,195

        Add the electronic package to the BSX SM4 and SM5 guitar for $375 or $400, respectively.

BSX T 4 - slim upright poplar body, detachable tilting rock maple neck, 41.5 in. scale, fretless ebony fingerboard, 5 in. tall wood bridge, 2-per-side Hipshot tuners, open center peghead, rotating tummy rest, adjustable endpin, multi-sensor piezo bridge pickup, volume control per string, treble/mid/bass EQ controls, active Bartolini electronics, available in Burgundy or Tobacco gloss (or satin) finishes, body length - 55 inches, body width - 5.5 inches, weight - 12 lbs., current mfg.

    MSR $2,500

BSX T 5 - similar to the T 4, except features 5-string configuration, 3/2-per-side tuners, current mfg.

    MSR $2,600

BSX T 6 - similar to the T 4, except features 6-string configuration, 3-per-side tuners, current mfg.

    MSR $2,700

BSX ST 4 - similar to the BSX T 4, except features non-removable neck, 3 in. tall wood bridge, 39 in. to 41.5 in. scale (specify when ordering), solid "paddle" headstock, available in Burgundy or Tobacco gloss (or satin) finishes, body length - 50 inches, body width - 5 inches, weight - 9 lbs, current mfg.

    MSR $1,600

BSX ST 5 - similar to the ST 4, except features 5-string configuration, 3/2-per-side tuners, current mfg.

    MSR $1,800

BSX ST 6 - similar to the ST 4, except features 6-string configuration, 3-per-side tuners, current mfg.

    MSR $1,900

BSX FLIP 4 - slim poplar body, set-in rock maple neck, 34 in. scale, fretless ebony fingerboard, wood bridge, 2-per-side Hipshot tuners, solid peghead, multi-sensor piezo bridge pickup, volume control per string, treble/mid/bass EQ controls, active Bartolini electronics, available in Burgundy or Tobacco gloss (or satin) finishes, body length - 43 inches, body width - 5 1/2 inches, weight - 7 lbs, current mfg.

    MSR $1,100

    The BSX Flip model is not available with a tummy rest, thigh rest, or end pin. The BSX Flip can be played upright or strapped on like a conventional electric bass.

BSX Flip 5 - similar to the Flip 4, except features 5-string configuration, 3/2-per-side tuners, current mfg.

    MSR $1,250

GRADING	100% MINT	98% NEAR MINT	95% EXC+	90% EXC	80% VG+	70% VG	60% G

BSX J 4 - offset double cutaway body with elongated bass horn, through-body maple neck, 34 in. scale, 24-fret ebony fingerboard with pearl dot inlay, Hipshot fixed bridge, 2-per-side Hipshot tuners, black chrome hardware, 2 J-style Bartolini pickups, volume/tone controls, Bartolini electronics, available in Natural satin or gloss finishes, disc.

	$1,100	$975	$900	$825	$750	$650	$575

Last MSR was $1,500.

BSX J 5 - similar to the J 4, except features 5-string configuration, 3/2-per-side tuners, disc.

	$1,200	$1,025	$950	$850	$775	$650	$575

Last MSR was $1,700.

BACHMANN

Instruments currently built in Antholz-Mittertal, Germany.

This independent luthier is currently building a number of high quality guitars. Bachmann built his first prototype in 1993, and has been producing ever since. They make acoustic, electric, and electric bass guitars. For further information regarding specifications and pricing, please contact Bachmann Guitars directly (see Trademark Index).

BAKER

Instruments currently built in Riverside, California. Distributed in the U.S. by Baker Guitars U.S.A. and Intertune, Inc. in Japan.

Gene Baker began playing guitar at age eleven, and honed his woodworking skills in Junior High preparing for his guitar-building career. Baker attended the Guitar Institute of Technology (G.I.T.) to further his playing abilities. After graduation, Baker served as a teacher/repairman for various stores, and briefly worked at Ernie Ball/Music Man. Baker built a number of guitars in a limited partnership under the Mean Gene trademark between 1989 and 1991.

Baker then took a Masters apprentice job at the Gibson West Custom Shop, serving under Roger Griffin. His duties included warranty repairs, vintage restorations, and custom building guitars. After Gibson closed down the shop, Baker moved to the Fender Custom Shop in Corona. Baker's first production work at Fender included working on the Robben Ford Signature Series, as well as the Carved Top Strat. In 1995, Baker was promoted to Master Builder (at age 28), and continued to produce around 60 custom Fender guitars a year.

In his spare time, Baker produces a limited amount of Baker guitars in his own workshop. Baker guitars strive to meld Gibson and Fender designs while keeping as much individuality and vintage values in the instrument.

BSX Allegro 5SB
courtesy BSX Bass Inc.

ELECTRIC

Baker offers a number of custom options on his models, such as a Bigsby tailpiece, Korina bodies, or gold hardware (call for pricing). Suggested list prices include hardshell case.

B1 - single white bound mahogany body, figured maple top, set-in mahogany neck, 25.5 in. scale, 22-fret bound rosewood fingerboard with custom side block inlays, Grover tuners, nickel hardware, Tune-o-matic bridge/stop tailpiece, 2 Seymour Duncan humbuckers, 2 volume/2-Tone controls, pickup selector, available in 2-Tone Sunburst, Cherry Burst, Gold Top with Natural or Trans. Brown back, Honey Burst, Trans. Amber, Trans. Bing Cherry, Trans. Blue, Trans. Blue Burst, or Trans. Red finishes, mfg. 1997-present.

MSR $3,698	$2,700	$2,450	$2,195	$1,995	$1,795	$1,595	$1,395

This model is available with optional Bigsby tailpiece and gold hardware.

B1 Chambered (B1C) - similar to the B1H, except does not have Talon f-hole, carved flamed maple top, available in Watermelon, Aged Cherry Burst, Cherry Sun Burst, Tequila Sunrise, Antique Burst, Two-Tone Sun Burst, Binge Cherry and Ice Tea Burst finishes, current mfg.

MSR $3,998	$2,850	$2,550	$2,200	$1,800	$1,500	$1,200	$999

B1 Hollow (B1H) - similar to the B1, except has single white bound mahogany neck/headstock/body, 3/4 chambered body, carved undertop with bound f-hole, mfg. 1997-present.

MSR $4,298	$3,100	$2,750	$2,400	$2,050	$1,750	$1,450	$1,150

This model is available with optional Bigsby tailpiece and gold hardware.

B1 Seven String - similar to the B1, except in a 7-string configuration, top bound solid mahogany body, highly figured carved maple top, mahogany set neck, 22-fret rosewood fingerboard with custom side block position markers, medium jumbo frets, 2 DiMarzio Custom Humbucker pickups, Tone Pros/Baker Nashville Tune-O-Matic bridge, 1 volume/2-Tone controls, 5-way pickup selector, Schaller tuners, nickel hardware, available in Watermelon, Aged Cherry Burst, Chery Sun Burst, Tequila Sunrise, Antique Burst, Two-Tone Sunburst, Binge Cherry and Ice Tea Burst finishes, disc.

	$2,850	$2,550	$2,250	$1,950	$1,650	$1,350	$999

Last MSR was $3,780.

BJ - mahogany body, set-in mahogany neck, 24 5/8 in. scale, 22-fret rosewood fingerboard with pearl dot inlays, Grover tuners, nickel hardware, Wilkinson wrap around/stop tailpiece, 2 P-90 pickups, volume/tone controls, pickup selector, available in 2-Tone Sunburst, Trans. Amber, Trans. Red, or TV Yellow finishes, mfg. 1997-present.

MSR $2,698	$1,995	$1,775	$1,550	$1,350	$1,150	$950	$750

This model is available with optional Korina neck and body.

BJ Hollow - similar to the BJ, except has hollow mahogany body, highly figured maple top, medium jumbo frets, available with two P-90 or 2 humbucker pickups, Schaller Nashville Tune-O-Matic bridge, 2 volume/1 tone control, 3-way pickup selector, Schaller tuners, nickel hardware, available in Watermelon, Aged Cherry Burst, Cherry Sun Burst, Tequila Sunrise, Antique Burst, Two-tone Sunburst, Binge Cherry, or Ice tea Burst finishes, current mfg.

MSR $3,025	$2,275	$2,075	$1,875	$1,675	$1,450	$1,250	$1,050

Baker Electric Guitar
courtesy Baker

B

BNT - mahogany body, figured maple top, mahogany neck-through-body, 25.5 in. scale, 22-fret bound rosewood fingerboard with custom side block inlays, Grover tuners, nickel hardware, Wilkinson tremolo, 2 Seymour Duncan humbuckers, volume/tone (push/pull) controls, pickup selector, available in 2-Tone Sunburst, Cherry Burst, Honey Burst, Transparent Amber, Trans. Bing Cherry, Trans. Blue, Trans. Blue Burst, or Trans. Red finishes, mfg. 1997-2000.

$2,550	$2,350	$2,150	$1,950	$1,750	$1,550	$1,350

Last MSR was $3,400.

ELECTRIC BASS

B1 BASS - single white bound mahogany body, figured maple carved top, set-in mahogany neck, 34 in. scale, 21-fret bound rosewood fingerboard with custom side block inlays, Grover tuners, nickel hardware, Badass fixed bridge, 2 Seymour Duncan pickups, active controls, available in 2-Tone Sunburst, Cherry Burst, Gold Top with Natural or Trans. Brown back, Honey Burst, Trans. Bing Cherry, Trans. Blue, Trans. Blue Burst, or Trans. Red finishes, mfg. 1997-2002.

$3,300	$2,995	$2,695	$2,395	$1,995	$1,695	$1,395

Last MSR was $4,400.

BAKER, JAMES R.
Instruments currently built in Shoreham, New York.

Luthier James R. Baker builds conventional archtop guitars as well as experimental archtop designs that enhance the electric capabilities of the guitar. While his **Classic** features traditionally placed f-holes, Baker's innovative **Legend** and **Special** models have teardrop-shaped soundholes in the lower bout, and a patented structure which eliminates feedback and increases sustain. All models now feature Kent Armstrong pickups. All Baker guitars need to be priced individually according to the options. Contact Baker directly for more information (see Trademark Index).

ELECTRIC

THE CLASSIC - single rounded cutaway body design, bookmatched spruce and bookmatched flame maple materials, 3 in. depth, 17 in. width across the lower bout, 25.5 in. scale, antiqued ivoroid body/f-hole binding, ebony fingerboard, matching maple pickguard/violin style bridge/wood fingerjointed hinge tailpiece, 3-per-side headstock with note design, Schaller or Grover tuning machines, Kent Armstrong or EMG floating pickup, pickguard-mounted volume control, available in Honey Blond Lacquer finish, case included, current mfg.
MSR $4,900 + Options

The Legend - similar to the Classic, except has Spanish cedar top, bookmatched African mahogany neck and sides, African Sapele with inlaid art work of rosewood/ebony/zebrawood, 2 lower bout teardrop soundholes, 2 upper bout smaller teardrop soundholes, EMG 91 active/passive floating pickup, available in Clear Natural Lacquer finish, case included, current mfg.
MSR $4,900+ Options

The Special - similar to the Classic, except has 2 teardrop soundholes in lower bout instead of f-holes, ebony or maple pickguard, available in Clear Natural or Black Burst Lacquer finish, case included, current mfg.
MSR $4,900+ Options

ONE-PIECE HOLLOW BODY MODEL - carved from a single book matched billet of tonewood, single cutaway design, Kent Armstrong pickups, "Equal Space" TM neck profile, available in a large quantity of exotic tonewoods and finishes, current mfg.
MSR $3,950 + Options

BAKES GUITARS
Instruments currently built in Elgin, Illinois since 1983. Distributed by Bakes Guitars of Elgin, Illinois.

Luthier Robert Bakes has been handcrafting fine guitars since 1983. Since 1983, Bakes has been performing repairs and custom building instruments out of the Bakes Guitars shop in Elgin, Illinois. Ably assisted by his wife Beverly, Bakes also produces the classic vintage instrument show, "Guitar Madness." This show is held yearly in September. For information regarding either the guitars or the guitar show, please contact Bakes Guitars directly (see Trademark Index).

BALDWIN
Instruments previously produced between 1965 and 1970. Baldwin guitars and basses were initially built in England by Burns; later models were shipped by components and assembled in Booneville, Arkansas. Distributed by the Baldwin Piano Company of Cinncinati, Ohio.

In 1962, as Leo Fender's health was faltering, he discussed the idea of selling Fender Electric Instruments company to Don Randall (head of Fender Sales). While Randall toyed with the idea even as late as the summer of 1963, they eventually concluded to sell to a third party who had money. Negotiations began with the Baldwin Piano Company in April of 1964, who offered $5 million (minus Fender's liabilities). When talks bogged down over acoustic guitar and electric piano operations, Randall met with representatives of the Columbia Broadcasting System (CBS). An agreement with CBS was signed in October, 1964, for $13 million that took effect in January of 1965.

Baldwin, outbid by CBS but still looking to diversify its product lines, then bought the Burns manufacturing facilities from Jim Burns (regarded as "the British Leo Fender") in September, 1965. U.S. distributed models bore the Baldwin trademark. During Baldwin's first year of ownership, only the logos were changed on the imported guitars. In 1966, the Burns-style scroll headstock was redesigned; and in 1967 the 700 series was debuted. The Baldwin company then began assembling the imported Burns parts in Booneville, Arkansas.

Baldwin acquired the Gretsch trademark when Fred Gretsch, Jr. sold the company in 1967. As part of a business consolidation, the New York Gretsch operation was moved to the Arkansas facility in 1970. Baldwin then concentrated its corporate interests in the Gretsch product line, discontinuing further Baldwin/Burns models. However, it is interesting to note that many Burns-style features (like the bridge vibrato) began to turn up on Gretsch models after 1967. For further Baldwin/Gretsch history, see Gretsch (source: Paul Day, *The Burns Book*; and Michael Wright, *Vintage Guitar Magazine*).

GRADING	100% MINT	98% NEAR MINT	95% EXC+	90% EXC	80% VG+	70% VG	60% G

ELECTRIC

706 MODEL - double cutaway hollow ES-335 style body, white body binding, f-holes, 22-fret rosewood fingerboard with dot inlays, raised black pickguard, 2 "Double Pole" pickups, double trapeze tailpiece with "B" in the middle, four knobs, one switch, scroll style headstock, 3-per-side tuners, available in Golden Sunburst or Red finishes, mfg. 1967-1970.

	N/A	$650	$550	$450	$350	$250	$150

706V MODEL - similar to the Model 706, except has a Bigsby-style vibrato unit.

	N/A	$700	$600	$500	$400	$300	$175

712R MODEL - 12-string configuration, double cutaway hollow ES-335 style body, white body binding, f-holes, 22-fret rosewood fingerboard with dot inlays, raised black pickguard, 2 "Double Pole" pickups, double trapeze tailpiece with "B" in the middle, four knobs, one switch, scroll style headstock, 6-per-side tuners, available in Golden Sunburst or Red finishes, mfg. 1967-1970.

	N/A	$650	$550	$450	$350	$250	$150

712T MODEL - similar to the Model 712R, except has a thinner neck, mfg. 1967-1970.

	N/A	$650	$550	$450	$350	$250	$150

BABY BISON - sharp pointed double cutaway solidbody, 24.75 in. scale length, bolt-on maple neck, 22-fret rosewood fingerboard with dot inlay, 3 seperate black pickguards, 2 "bar magnet" pickups, tremolo bridge, scroll style headstock, 3-per-side tuners, 3 knobs, 1 switch, available in Golden Sunburst, Red, or White finish, mfg. 1966-1970.

	N/A	$1,000	$850	$700	$600	$500	$400

Some models may have a painted headstock and neck.

BISON - sharp pointed double cutaway solidbody, bolt-on maple neck, 22-fret rosewood fingerboard with dot inlay, 3 seperate tortoiseshell pickguards, 3 single coil pickups, tremolo bridge, scroll style headstock, 3-per-side tuners, 3 knobs, 2 switches, available in Black or White finish, mfg. 1965-1970.

	N/A	$1,250	$1,100	$950	$800	$650	$500

In 1966, the headstock was redesigned. Some models may have a painted headstock and neck.

Baldwin Virginian
courtesy Dave Rogers
Dave's Guitar Shop

DOUBLE SIX - 12-string configuration, offset double cutaway solidbody, bolt-on maple neck, 21-fret rosewood fingerboard with dot inlay, 3 seperate black pickguards, 3 diagonal single coil pickups, tremolo bridge, scroll style headstock, 6-per-side tuners, 3 knobs, 1 switches, available in Red, White, Black, Red Sunburst, or Green Sunburst finishes, mfg. 1965-1970.

	N/A	$1,100	$950	$800	$700	$600	$500

In 1966, the headstock was redesigned. Some models may have matching headstock and neck finish.

G.B. 65 - single cutaway hollow body acoustic, vertical soundholes similar to f-holes, bolt-on maple neck, 21-fret rosewood fingerboard with dot inlay, 2 pickguards (one for switches), 2 "bar magnet" pickups, double trapeze tailpiece, regular style headstock, 3-per-side tuners, 2 knobs, 1 switch, available in natural finish, mfg. circa 1965.

	N/A	$700	$600	$500	$400	$300	$200

G.B. 66/G.B. 66 DELUXE - single cutaway hollow body, f-holes, bolt-on maple neck, 22-fret rosewood fingerboard with dot inlay, black pickguard with "Baldwin" engraved, 2 "bar magnet" pickups, double trapeze tailpiece bridge, regular style headstock, 3-per-side tuners, 3 knobs, 1 switch, available in Golden sunburst and other color finishes, mfg. 1965-1970.

	N/A	$800	$650	$550	$450	$350	$250

The difference between the Standard and the Deluxe models were an added density control on the treble bout.

JAZZ SPLIT SOUND - offset double cutaway solidbody, bolt-on maple neck, 22-fret rosewood fingerboard with dot inlay, black pickguard, 3 single coil pickups, tremolo bridge, scroll style headstock, 3-per-side tuners, 3 knobs, available in Red, Red Sunburst or Green Sunburst finishes, mfg. 1965-1970.

	N/A	$1,000	$850	$750	$650	$525	$400

In 1966, the headstock was redesigned. Some models may have a painted headstock and neck.

MARVIN - offset double cutaway solidbody, bolt-on maple neck, 21-fret rosewood fingerboard with dot inlay, 3 seperate blue/gray tortoise or brown pickguards, 3 diagonal single coil pickups, tremolo bridge, scroll style headstock, 3-per-side tuners, 3 knobs, 1 switches, available in White finish, mfg. 1965-1970.

	N/A	$900	$750	$650	$550	$450	$350

In 1966, the headstock was redesigned. Some later models may have the "bar magnet" pickups.

VIBRASLIM - double cutaway arched hollowbody, f-holes, bolt-on maple neck, 22-fret rosewood fingerboard with dot inlay, small, clear pickguard, 2 "bar magnet" pickups, "Rezo-tube" tremolo bridge, scroll style headstock, 3-per-side tuners, 3 knobs, single switch, available in Natural, Brown, Red Sunburst, or Golden Sunburst finishes, mfg. 1966-1970.

	N/A	$1,000	$850	$750	$650	$525	$400

In 1966, the headstock was redesigned. Some models may have a painted headstock and neck.

VIRGINIAN - single cutaway hollow body acoustic, round soundhole, bolt-on maple neck, 22-fret rosewood fingerboard with dot inlay, black, clear, or tortoise pickguard, 2 "bar magnet" pickups on either side of soundhole, moustache bridge, scroll style headstock, 3-per-side tuners, 3 knobs, 1 switch, available in Natural finish, mfg. 1965-1970.

	N/A	$1,200	$1,050	$900	$800	$700	$600

Add $100 for Rezo-tube vibrato unit.

In 1966, the headstock was redesigned. Later models feature a Rezo-tune bridge and vibrato unit.

Baldwin Marvin
courtesy Encore Music

GRADING	100% MINT	98% NEAR MINT	95% EXC+	90% EXC	80% VG+	70% VG	60% G

ELECTRIC BASS

704 MODEL BASS - double cutaway hollow ES-335 style body, white body binding, f-holes, 20-fret rosewood fingerboard with dot inlays, raised black pickguard, 2 "Double Pole" pickups, double trapeze tailpiece with "B" in the middle, four knobs, one switch, scroll style headstock, 2-per-side offset tuners, available in Golden Sunburst or Red finishes, mfg. 1967-1970.

	N/A	$600	$525	$450	$350	$250	$150

BABY BISON BASS - sharp pointed double cutaway solidbody, 30 in. scale length, bolt-on maple neck, 22-fret rosewood fingerboard with dot inlay, 3 seperate black pickguards, 2 "bar magnet" pickups, tremolo bridge, scroll style headstock, 3-per-side tuners, 3 knobs, 1 3-way switch, available in Golden Sunburst, Red, or White finish, mfg. 1966-1970.

	N/A	$950	$800	$650	$550	$450	$350

BISON BASS - sharp pointed double cutaway solidbody, bolt-on maple neck, 22-fret rosewood fingerboard with dot inlay, 3 seperate tortoiseshell pickguards, 3 single coil pickups, cover over second pickup, scroll style headstock, 32-per-side offset tuners, 3 knobs, 1 switch, available in Black or White finish, mfg. 1965-1970.

	N/A	$1,400	$1,200	$1,050	$900	$750	$600

G.B. 66 BASS - single cutaway hollow body, f-holes, bolt-on maple neck, 22-fret rosewood fingerboard with dot inlay, black pickguard with "Baldwin" engraved, 2 "bar magnet" pickups, double trapeze tailpiece bridge, regular style headstock, 2-per-side tuners, 3 knobs, 1 switch, available in Golden Sunburst and other color finishes, mfg. 1965-1970.

	N/A	$700	$600	$500	$400	$300	$200

JAZZ BASS - offset double cutaway solidbody, 30 in. scale, bolt-on maple neck, 22-fret rosewood fingerboard with dot inlay, black pickguard, 3 single coil pickups, bridge with cover, scroll style headstock, 2-per-side offset tuners, 3 knobs, available in Red, Red Sunburst or Green Sunburst finishes, mfg. 1965-1970.

	N/A	$1,200	$1,000	$900	$800	$700	$600

SHADOWS BASS - offset double cutaway solidbody, bolt-on maple neck, 22-fret rosewood fingerboard with dot inlay, 3 seperate blue/gray tortoise or brown pickguards, 3 diagonal single coil pickups, cover over middle pickup, scroll style headstock, 3-per-side tuners, 3 knobs, 1 switches, available in White finish, mfg. 1965-1970.

	N/A	$850	$700	$600	$500	$400	$300

Some models feature the "Bar Magnet" style pickups.

VIBRASLIM BASS - double cutaway arched hollowbody, f-holes, bolt-on maple neck, 22-fret rosewood fingerboard with dot inlay, black pickguard, 2 "bar magnet" pickups, regular style headstock, 3-per-side tuners, 4 knobs mounted under pickguard, single switch, available in Natural, Brown, Red Sunburst, or Golden Sunburst finishes, mfg. 1965-1970.

	N/A	$1,000	$850	$750	$650	$525	$400

Subtract $200 for the later version (knobs on body).

In 1966, the headstock changed to the scroll style, the pickguard was smaller, and the controls were mounted on the body instead of under the pickguard.

BALEANI
Instruments previously built in Italy during the mid-1960s.

These solid body guitars are generally entry level quality, but the sparkle/pearloid plastic finish says "Las Vegas" every time! (source: Tony Bacon and Paul Day, *The Guru's Guitar Guide*).

BAMBU
Instruments previously built in Japan in the late 1970s.

The model CB625 was a solid body built by the Maya company, and featured a laminated bamboo neck, two humbuckers and active circuitry (source: Tony Bacon and Paul Day, *The Guru's Guitar Guide*).

BARCLAY
See chapter on House Brands. Instruments previously produced in Japan during the 1960s, and produced as a House Brand in the United States.

Barclay instruments were generally entry level, quality guitars with shorter scale necks that appealed to beginners. These guitars were built in Japan, and the American distributor is unknown. The product line included thinline hollow body electric archtop as well as solid body guitars and basses. Some models appear to be built by Kawai/Teisco, although this has not yet been confirmed.

Models that were produced in the United States were possibly built by Harmony. Pickups on some of these Barclays (Gibson copies) are the same that were featured in Harmony Rockets (source: Michael Wright, *Vintage Guitar Magazine*, U.S.A. information courtesy Mark Watson). Most Barclay electric guitars are priced between $150 and $250.

BARKER GUITARS, LTD.
Instruments currently built in Rockford, Illinois.

Dwayne Barker is currently producing custom guitars in Rockford, Illinois. For further information, please contact Barker Guitars, Ltd. directly (see Trademark Index).

BARON (JAPAN MFG.)
See Domino. Instruments previously manufactured in Japan circa mid- to late 1960s. Distributed by Maurice Lipsky Music Company, Inc., of New York, New York.

Baron solid body guitars were advertised as "Perfect for the Beginner," and featured an offset double cutaway body, 6-on-a-side headstock, Jaguar-ish tremolo bridge, and one large pickguard with an individual on/off pickup switch (per pickup), volume/tone knobs, and a phase on/off switch. The **Model 401** was offered with one pickup (retail list $57), two pickups (retail list $69), three pickups (retail list $85), or four pickups (retail list $97). These guitars were all finished in solid colors, no doubt in order to cover the plywood nature of the body (Domino catalog courtesy John Kinnemeyer, JK Lutherie).

BARON (U.S. MFG.)

See chapter on House Brands.

This trademark has been identified as a House Brand of the RCA Victor Records Store; furthermore, KAY exported guitars bearing this trademark to the Thibouville-Lamy company of France (source: Willie G. Moseley, *Stellas & Stratocasters*).

BARRINGTON

Instruments previously produced in Japan during the late 1980s. Distribution in the U.S. market was handled by Barrington Guitars of Barrington, Illinois.

Barrington Guitars offered both solid body electric guitars and basses during the late 1980s, as well as acoustic and acoustic/electric models. The guitar models were produced in Japan by Terada. The company now specializes in brass instruments as the L.A. Sax Company of Barrington, Illinois.

ELECTRIC

Barrington solid body guitars were styled after the superstrat design prevalent in the late 1980s, and were built in Japan (possibly by the Terada company). Generally good-playing and good-looking guitars.

While the vintage/used market is currently focusing on vintage-style designs, models like these are generally overlooked, and as a result are generally inexpensive. Used prices on the electrics range between $200 to $400, $250 to $450 on the semi-hollow body models, and $250 to $500 on the acoustic models.

BARTELL

See Barth. Instruments previously built in Riverside, California between 1964 and 1969.

The Bartell company was formed by Paul Barth (engineer) and Ted Peckles (owner and company president) in the mid-1960s after Barth returned from Magnatone's facilities on the East Coast. One of Barth's co-workers at Rickenbacker was Roger Rossmeisel, who introduced the German Carve (a beveled ridge around the top of a guitar) to Rickenbacker, and later Fender designs. The same German Carve can be found on both Bartell and Mosrite guitars. Bartells were produced from 1964 to 1969, and former owner Peckles estimates that around 2,000 instruments were produced. The Bartell company also built instruments for rebranding for **Hohner**, **St. George**, and later edition Acoustic **Black Widow** models.

Bartell guitars feature a strat-style offset double cutaway body, a Mosrite-inspired headstock, German Carve ridge, and two single coil pickups. Electronics include a volume and tone knob, two on/off pickup selector switches, and a third switch for in/out of phase between the two pickups. There is also mention of a semi-hollowbody that features a design that is a cross between the above model and an ES-335 (source: Teisco Del Rey, *Guitar Player magazine*).

BARTH

Instruments previously built in Southern California during the mid- to late 1950s.

Luthier/designer Paul Barth, nephew to National's John Dopyera, was one of the three men responsible for Rickenbacker's "Frying Pan" solid body electric steel guitar (along with George Beauchamp and Adolph Rickenbacker). Barth left Rickenbacker in 1956, and formed his own company briefly to build and market guitars with the Barth trademark. One of Paul Barth's employees at Rickenbacker in the early 1950s was Semie Moseley, and when Moseley later formed his own company, Barth briefly used Moseley's finishing skills to complete an order of guitars. Barth later went to work for Magnatone in the early 1960s, designing models at Magnatone's Torrance, California facilities. For further biographical information, see Bartell. (source: Teisco Del Rey, *Guitar Player Magazine*).

BARTOLINI (ITALIAN MFG.)

Instruments previously built in Italy during the 1960s.

Author Tony Bacon, *The Ultimate Guitar Book*, notes that Italy, like many other European countries, experienced the 1960s pop music popularity that led to a larger demand for electric guitars. However, many electric guitar builders were also manufacturers of accordions. As a result, many guitars ended up with accordion-style finishes. Wacky or not, Leo Fender was using this same sort of heat-molded acetate finish on some of his lap steel models in the early 1950s. What Leo wasn't using was the accordion-style push buttons, however.

BARTOLINI, BILL (U.S. MFG.)

Instruments previously built in 1960s. Bartolini now produces a line of high quality guitar pickups in Livermore, California.

Luthier Bill Bartolini used to build classical guitars in California during the 1960s. Bartolini estimates that perhaps only a dozen guitars were built. Research on resonances produced during this time formed the basis for his pickup designs, and his clear, high quality pickups are standard features on numerous luthiers' creations, (information courtesy Bill Bartolini).

BASS COLLECTION

Instruments previously manufactured in Japan from 1985 to 1992. Distributed by Meisel Music, Inc. of Springfield, New Jersey.

Bass Collection (and Guitar Collection) instruments are medium grade instruments with good hardware, and a modern, rounded body design. Their current appeal may fall in the range of the novice to intermediate player looking for a solid-feeling instrument.

Bass Collection instruments were originally distributed by Meisel Music, Inc. for a number of years between 1985 and 1992. Their on-hand stock was purchased by the Sam Ash music store chain of New York in 1994 and sold through the Sam Ash stores.

B

GRADING	100% MINT	98% NEAR MINT	95% EXC+	90% EXC	80% VG+	70% VG	60% G

ELECTRIC BASS: 300 SERIES

These models had an optional ash body with Trans. Red finish.

SB301 - offset double cutaway alder body, bolt-on maple neck, 24-fret rosewood fingerboard, fixed bridge, 2-per-side Gotoh tuners, black hardware, P/J-style pickups, 2 volume/2-Tone controls, available in Black, Magenta, Metallic Grey, or Sunburst finishes, mfg. 1985-1992.

	N/A	$400	$325	$275	$225	$175	$125

Last MSR was $700.

SB302 - similar to SB301, except has fretless fingerboard, available in Black, Magenta, or Metallic Grey finishes, mfg. 1985-1992.

	N/A	$400	$325	$275	$225	$175	$125

Last MSR was $700.

SB305 - similar to SB301, except has 5 strings, 2 J-style pickups, mfg. 1985-1992.

	N/A	$425	$350	$300	$250	$200	$150

Last MSR was $670.

SB305FL - similar to SB301, except has 5-string configuration, fretless fingerboard, 2 J-style pickups, mfg. 1985-1992.

	N/A	$450	$375	$325	$275	$225	$175

Last MSR was $800.

ELECTRIC BASS: 400 SERIES

SB401 - offset double cutaway basswood body, bolt-on maple neck, 24-fret rosewood fingerboard, fixed bridge, 2-per-side Gotoh tuners, black hardware, P/J-style pickups, 2 volume/2-tone controls, active electronics, 2-band EQ, available in Black, Metallic Red, or Pearl White finishes, mfg. 1985-1992.

	N/A	$575	$500	$425	$375	$325	$275

Last MSR was $995.

SB402 - similar to SB401, except has fretless fingerboard, mfg. 1985-1992.

	N/A	$575	$500	$425	$375	$325	$275

Last MSR was $995.

SB405 - similar to SB401, except has 5-string configuration, 2 J-style pickups, mfg. 1985-1992.

	N/A	$650	$575	$500	$425	$350	$300

Last MSR was $1,195.

ELECTRIC BASS: 500 SERIES

SB501 - offset double cutaway alder body, bolt-on 3-piece maple neck, 24-fret ebony fingerboard, fixed bridge, 2-per-side tuners, black hardware, P/J-style pickups, 2 volume/2-Tone controls, active electronics with 2-band EQ, available in Black, Natural, or Pearl White finishes, mfg. 1985-1992.

	N/A	$650	$575	$500	$425	$350	$300

Last MSR was $1,195.

Add $75 for left-handed version.

SB502 - similar to SB501, except has fretless fingerboard, mfg. 1985-1992.

	N/A	$650	$575	$500	$425	$375	$300

Last MSR was $1,195.

Add $150 for left-handed version.

SB505 - similar to SB501, except has 5-string configuration, mfg. 1985-1992.

	N/A	$700	$625	$550	$475	$400	$325

Last MSR was $1,395.

This model had an optional ash body with Trans. Red finish.

ELECTRIC BASS: 600 SERIES

SB611 - offset double cutaway asymmetrical maple body with padauk or walnut top, bolt-on maple neck, 24-fret ebony fingerboard, fixed bridge, 2-per-side Gotoh tuners, gold hardware, P/J-style pickups, 2 volume/2-Tone controls, active electronics with 2-band EQ, available in Oil finishes, mfg. 1985-1992.

	N/A	$750	$675	$600	$525	$450	$375

Last MSR was $1,495.

This model had an optional fretless fingerboard (Model SB612).

SB615 - similar to SB611, except has 5-string configuration, mfg. 1985-1992.

	N/A	$800	$725	$650	$575	$500	$425

Last MSR was $1,650.

ELECTRIC BASS: DB SERIES

DB41R - asymmetrical double cutaway ash body, bolt-on maple neck, 24-fret rosewood fingerboard with abalone dot inlay, fixed bridge, 2-per-side tuners, chrome hardware, 2 J-style pickups, 2 volume/2-Tone controls, available in Trans. Black or Trans. Red finishes, mfg. 1991-92.

	N/A	$625	$550	$475	$400	$350	$300

Last MSR was $1,150.

B

GRADING	100% MINT	98% NEAR MINT	95% EXC+	90% EXC	80% VG+	70% VG	60% G

DB43E - similar to DB41R, except has padauk/maple/mahogany laminated or walnut/maple/mahogany laminated body, ebony fingerboard, gold hardware, 2 humbucker pickups, available in Oil finishes, mfg. 1991-92.

	N/A	$800	$725	$650	$575	$500	$425

Last MSR was $1,630.

DB51R - similar to DB41R, except has 5-string configuration, mfg. 1991-92.

	N/A	$750	$675	$600	$525	$450	$375

Last MSR was $1,560.

DB53E - similar to DB41R, except has 5 strings, padauk/maple/mahogany laminated or walnut/maple/mahogany laminated body, ebony fingerboard, gold hardware, 2 humbucker pickups, available in Oil finishes, mfg. 1991-92.

	N/A	$850	$775	$700	$625	$550	$475

Last MSR was $2,000.

BASS O LIN

Instruments currently built in New York, New York since 1994. Distributed by Bass O Lin (Dan Agostino) of Lanoka Harbor, New Jersey.

Designer Danny Agostino is currently offering "the world's most versatile electric bass." Inspired in the early 1970s by Jimmy Page's explorations of a Les Paul and a violin bow, Agostino developed a bass design in the early 1980s that could be played by tapping, plucking, or bowing. The Bass O Lin's bridge is constructed similarly to an upright bass's bridge, with different string planes for bowing access.

The bass's unique design allows 10 different playing positions: 3 different strap configurations - standing, or on either leg in a sitting position; and five different positions seated or standing with the optional quick-release playing stand. This stand features non-dampening rubber mounts that allow the instrument to vibrate freely.

ELECTRIC BASS

While compact, the instrument has a 34 in. scale. Models are offered with 3-piece curly maple necks, African Mahogany or Quilted Maple bodies, fretted or fretless Rosewood or Ebony fingerboards, Sperzel locking tuners, High Resolution Micro U pickup, and gold-plated brass tailpiece and electronics rear cover. The custom designed Agostino radiused pickup combines with an RMC Pizz-Arco piezo bridge, and active preamp circuitry featuring a master volume and master pickup blend controls. The rear of the body has the locking strap/playing stand jacks and a knee pad for bowing leverage and comfort.

Bass Collection SB501 AN courtesy Bass Collection

BASSLINE

Instruments currently built in Krefeld, Germany. Previously distributed in the U.S. by Salwender International of Trabuco Canyon, California.

The Bassline Custom Shop currently offers both electric upright models as well as 4-, 5-, and 6-string electric bass guitars. Salwender International is currently offering the **Universal** model in the U.S. Market.

The Buster Art-Line models are set-neck, while the Buster Bolt-On is a bolt-neck design. Both versions feature Gotoh/ETS tuners, and EMG or Seymour Duncan pickups. Models are available in 4-, 5-, and 6-string versions, and are currently available in Europe.

ELECTRIC BASS

After 10 years of research and development, Bassline introduced the **Universal** electric upright model. The Universal (retail list price $5,659) has an enlarged neck for stability and tone. Equipped with piezo and magnetic pickups, this 36 in. scale instrument is constructed of one-piece flamed maple body and curved ebony fingerboard, and flamed maple bridge/ebony string holders. Models are available in 4- and 5-string configurations, and can be played both arco or pizz-style upright. There are also other models available. Visit their website for more information (see Trademark Index).

BATMAN

See C & R GUITARS.

BELIGER GUITARS

Instruments currently built in Garden City, Michigan.

Luthier Lemon James is handcrafting a line of Foxey electric guitars, which share a unique and original flowing, curved body shape. Two current eye-catching models include a Burl Maple body and the Transparent (lucite material) body with clear headstock and 8 super bright red LEDs that illuminate the body in the dark. For further information regarding these handcrafted custom guitars, contact luthier James directly (see Trademark Index).

BELLA

Instruments previously built in Chalmette, Louisiana.

Bella Guitars used to offer the Bella Deluxe model (last MSR $2,400), which features a mahogany body, curly maple or quilted maple (or other exotic tops), rosewood fingerboard, Schaller tuners, Seymour Duncan or DiMarzio pickups, and a 25.5 in. scale.

BELLTONE

Instruments previously manufactured in Japan, or constructed of Japanese-produced parts during the late 1960s.

Belltone was the brand name of the Peter Sorkin Music Company. The Sorkin company distributed Premier guitars, which were built at the Multivox company of New York. Other guitars built or distributed (possibly as rebrands) were ROYCE, STRAD-O-LIN, BELLTONE, and MARVEL. Parts varied, as pickups were Japanese, while the roller bridges may have been Italian or Japanese (source: Michael Wright, *Guitar Stories*, Volume One).

Bass Collection SB611 WOS courtesy Bass Collection

GRADING	100% MINT	98% NEAR MINT	95% EXC+	90% EXC	80% VG+	70% VG	60% G

BELTONE
See chapter on House Brands.

This trademark has been identified as a House Brand of the Monroe Catalog House. Various Beltone instruments appear to be rebranded Zen-On instruments. Zen-On guitars were produced in Japan during the 1960s (source: Willie G. Moseley, *Vintage Guitar Magazine*).

BENAVENTE
Instruments currently built in Grants Pass, Oregon.

Luthier Chris Benavente is currently producing custom built guitars. Each instrument is completely handcrafted, and features exotic woods and multiple piece laminated neck-through design. Custom instruments are also available on request. For more information contact Benavente directly (see Trademark Index).

ELECTRIC

Benavente offers a variety of models: The **100 Series** (disc. last retail $1,899), the **200 Series** (disc. last MSR starting at $650), and the **2K**, **2K DC**, & **2K Archtop Series** (prices start at $3,000, $5,000 for the Archtop). All models feature customer´s choice of body wood, 5-piece neck-through-body design, rosewood fingerboard, EMG active electronics, and chrome (or black or gold) hardware. A wide variety of endless options are available on all Benavente Guitars - limited only by the customer´s imagination.

ELECTRIC BASS

Benavente´s bass models follow the sleek offset lines of the the **219 Bass Series** (prices start at $1,800 for bolt-on, $2,200 for set neck, and $2,500 for through neck), **219B** (prices start at $2,300 for bolt-on, $2,500 for set neck, and $2,800 for through neck), the **Standard Series** (last MSR prices started at $2,100), the **Custom Bolt-on Series** (last MSR prices started at $875), and the **Singlecut Bass Series** (prices start at $2,350 for bolt-on, $2,600 for set neck, and $3,200 for through neck). The Singlecut series is available in an A, B, and J Style. Standard construction is similar to the guitar models, except feature a 21-fret fingerboard, 34 in. scale, and a Schaller roller bridge. Benavente offered the **J 150** model, which is a classic J-styled bass with a maple neck, ebony fingerboard, and EMG pickups (last MSR was $2,100). Benavente also offers the **51**, which has a P-Bass design from the early 50s, with the Benavente touch (MSR $1,700). They also offer the **Vortex**, which has a little J-Bass influence, but is mostly an original design (prices start at $1,800 for bolt-on, $2,200 for set neck, and $2,500 for through neck). The **Vintage Vortex** is similar to the Vortex, except it has a black pickguard and chrome control plate (prices start at $1,800 bolt-on only). Most basses are offered with either a bolt-on, set, or thru-body neck. The factory recommends calling your local Benavente dealer for a price and delivery time.

BENEDETTO, ROBERT
Instruments currently built in Corona, California by the Guild Custom Shop (select models only) beginning in 2000, through a licensing agreement with the Fender Musical Instrument Corporation (FMIC).

Master Luthier Robert Benedetto has been handcrafting fine archtop guitars since 1968. Benedetto was born in New York in 1946. Both his father and grandfather were master cabinetmakers, and Benedetto´s uncles were musicians. While growing up in New Jersey, Benedetto began playing the guitar professionally at age thirteen. Being near the New York/New Jersey jazz music scene, Benedetto had numerous opportunities to perform repair and restoration work on other classic archtops. Benedetto built his first archtop in 1968, and his pre-eminence in the field is evidenced by his having made archtop guitars longer than any living builders and has a growing list of endorsers. Current endorsers range from Jimmy Bruno and Kenny Burrell to Earl Klugh and Andy Summers.

Benedetto moved to Homosassa, Florida in 1976. Three years later, he relocated to Clearwater, Florida. A veteran innovator, Benedetto began concentrating on the acoustic properties of the guitar designs, and started a movement to strip away unnecessary adornment (inlays, bindings) in 1982. While continuing his regular work on archtop building, Benedetto also built violins between 1983-1987. Violinist extraordinaire Stephane Grappelli purchased one of his violins in 1993. Benedetto even built a small number of electric solid body guitars and basses (which debuted at the 1987 NAMM show) in addition to his regular archtop production schedule. After 10 years in East Stroudsburg, PA, Benedetto relocated back to Florida during 2000. His endorsers span three generations of jazz guitarists. Not since John D´Angelico has anyone made as many archtop guitars nor had as many well-known players endorsing and recording with his guitars. Closer scrutiny reveals nuances found only from a maker of his stature. His minimalist delicate inlay motif has become a trademark as have his novel use of black, rather than gold, tuning machines, black bridge height adjustment wheels, and an ebony nut (versus bone), all of which harmonize with the ebony fittings throughout the guitar. He is the originator of the solid ebony tailpiece, uniquely fastened to the guitar with cello tail adjustor. Likewise, he was the first to use exotic and natural wood veneers on the headstock and pioneered the use of violin pigments to shade his guitars. His Honey Blonde finish is now widely used within the guitar industry. Benedetto is also well-known for refining the 7-string archtop and is that unique model´s most prolific maker.

Benedetto is the Archtop Guitar Construction Editor and "Guitar Maintenance" columnist for "Just Jazz Guitar" magazine, and is the author of *Making an Archtop Guitar* (Center stream Publishing, 1994). He released his 9 1/2 hour instructional video, *Archtop Guitar Design & Construction*, in November 1996. He is currently at work on a second book tentatively entitled *Anecdotes, Insights, and Facts about Archtop Guitar Construction*. His forthcoming biography is being written by eminent jazz guitar historian Adrian Ingram. He also markets the Benedetto "floating" pickup, a standard size humbucking pickup, and solid ebony tailpiece for his (and other) archtop acoustic guitars.

In March 1999, through a licensing agreement with the Fender Musical Instrument Corporation (FMIC), Benedetto licensed the Benny & Bambino series to be made at the Guild custom shop in Nashville, TN, beginning in 2000, and now in Corona, California. As of March 1, 1999, Robert Benedetto stopped making standard Models.

Benedetto pickups were licensed in late 1999 to be sold exclusively by Seymour Duncan.

As of spring 2003, Benedetto has built over 750 musical instruments. While the majority (475) are archtop guitars, he has produced 157 electric solid body guitars, 52 electric basses, 48 violins, 5 violas, 2 mandolins and 1 cello. Benedetto currently schedules his production to 6 archtop guitar instruments per year, as well as a few violins, (biographical information courtesy Cindy Benedetto).

ELECTRIC ARCHTOP

FRATELLO (NO. 395-9500) - single smooth cutaway hollow body, carved hand-graduated spruce top, carved hand-graduated flamed maple back and sides, two bound f-holes, body and neck binding, three-piece flamed maple neck, 21-fret ebony fingerboard with large MOP block inlays, three-per-side Schaller mini tuners with ebony buttons, adjustable ebony bridge, ebony pickguard, single Benedetto S-6 humbucker pickup, two knobs (v, tone), gold hardware, available in Antique Burst, Claret, Honey Blonde, or Opulent Brown finishes, 25 in. scale, current mfg.

MSR $21,000	N/A	N/A	N/A	N/A	N/A	N/A	N/A

B

GRADING	100% MINT	98% NEAR MINT	95% EXC+	90% EXC	80% VG+	70% VG	60% G

LA VENEZIA (NO. 395-9800) - single smooth cutaway hollow body, carved hand-graduated spruce top, carved hand-graduated flamed maple back and sides, two f-holes, three-piece flamed maple neck, 21-fret ebony fingerboard, three-per-side Schaller mini tuners with ebony buttons, adjustable ebony bridge, ebony pickguard, single Benedetto S-6 humbucker pickup, two knobs (v, tone), black hardware, available in Claret, Honey Blonde, or Violin Burst finishes, 17 in. width, 3 in. depth, 25 in. scale, current mfg.

MSR $26,250	N/A	N/A	N/A	N/A	N/A	N/A	N/A

MANHATTAN (NO. 395-9600) - single smooth cutaway hollow body, carved hand-graduated spruce top, carved hand-graduated flamed maple back and sides, two f-holes, body and neck binding, three-piece flamed maple neck, 21-fret ebony fingerboard with 12th fret ebony inlay, three-per-side Schaller mini tuners with ebony buttons, adjustable ebony bridge, ebony pickguard, single Benedetto S-6 humbucker pickup, two knobs (v, tone), gold hardware, available in Antique Burst, Claret, Honey Blonde, or Opulent Brown finishes, 25 in. scale, current mfg.

MSR $22,500	N/A	N/A	N/A	N/A	N/A	N/A	N/A

Manhattan 7 (No. 395-9700) - similar to the Manhattan, except in 7-string configuration, mfg. 2004-present.

MSR $24,000	N/A	N/A	N/A	N/A	N/A	N/A	N/A

ELECTRIC: SEMI-HOLLOW

During his archtop building career, Benedetto built 8 semi-hollowbody electric guitars (6 of which were built between 1982 and 1983 and have been dubbed Semi-dettos by author Adrian Ingram). These versatile guitars feature a carved top, dual cutaway body design with two separate tone chambers and a solid center block. Each model was crafted to the original owner´s needs and specifications, resulting in slight differences between the models. The other two semi-hollowbody electric guitars were prototypes built by Benedetto in 1997.

ELECTRIC: BAMBINO SERIES

The **Bambino** model was introduced in 2000, and was manufactured under license by the Guild Custom Shop, located in Nashville, TN. This model features a 14.5 in. lower body, 2.25 in. body depth, single florentine cutaway, carved two-piece Sitka spruce top, carved two-piece American Maple back with matching maple sides, three-piece American Maple neck, solid ebony fingerboard, nut, saddle, bridge, trussrod cover, and tailpiece and narrow finger rest. Black Schaller M6 mini tuning machines with ebony buttons, one Benedetto B-6 built-in pickup with volume/tone controls, and abalone "Benedetto" logo inlaid in serpentine headstock (same size and shape as Benny model). Retail price was $10,000. This model is no longer produced.

ELECTRIC: BENNY SERIES

Bob Benedetto stopped individually making his standard Benny model in mid-1999. In March of 1999, Benedetto licensed his name to the Fender Musical Instruments Corp. (FMIC) for his standard models (including the Benny Series) to be made by Guild Guitars in their custom shop located in Corona, CA.

BENNY (NO. 360-9000) single cutaway mahogany body with routed tone chambers, carved spruce top, set-in mahogany neck, ebony fingerboard with a single abalone inlay at the 12th fret, 3-per-side tuners, gold plated hardware, Leo Quan Badass bridge, 2 custom Kent Armstrong (1998 and earlier) or Benedetto (new 1999) humbucking pickups, volume/push-pull tone controls, 3-way selector switch, available in Honey Blonde or Sunburst top with Wine back/sides/neck finishes, 25 in. scale, current mfg.

MSR $6,000	N/A	N/A	N/A	N/A	N/A	N/A	N/A

BENNY 7 (NO. 360-9100) - similar to Benny model, except has 7 strings, current mfg.

MSR $7,000	N/A	N/A	N/A	N/A	N/A	N/A	N/A

ELECTRIC: BRAVO SERIES

BRAVO (NO. 360-9400) - single smooth cutaway hollow body, laminated spruce top, laminated flamed maple back and sides, two f-holes, body and neck binding, three-piece flamed maple neck, 22-fret ebony fingerboard with 12th fret ebony inlay, three-per-side Schaller mini tuners with ebony buttons, adjustable ebony bridge, black pickguard, single Benedetto A-6 humbucker pickup, two knobs (v, tone), gold hardware, available in Antique Burst, Claret, or Honey Blond finishes, mfg. 2004-present.

MSR $5,000	N/A	N/A	N/A	N/A	N/A	N/A	N/A

ELECTRIC: BUCKY PIZZARELLI SERIES

BUCKY PIZZARELLI 7-STRING (NO. 360-9300) - 7-string configuration, single smooth cutaway hollow body, laminated spruce top, laminated flamed maple back and sides, two f-holes, body and neck binding, three-piece flamed maple neck, 22-fret ebony fingerboard with 12th fret ebony inlay, three-per-side Schaller mini tuners with ebony buttons, adjustable ebony bridge, black pickguard, single Benedetto B-7 humbucker pickup, two knobs (v, tone), gold hardware, available in Antique Burst, Bucky Burst, Claret, Honey Blonde, or Opulent Brown finishes, 25 in. scale, new 2005.

MSR $6,000	N/A	N/A	N/A	N/A	N/A	N/A	N/A

Benedetto Limited courtesy Robert and Cindy Benedetto

Benedetto Benny courtesy Robert and Cindy Benedetto

B

ELECTRIC: 1000 SERIES

Originally a joint venture between Robert Benedetto and John Buscarino, these solid body electric instruments were made in Clearwater, Florida between May, 1986 and April, 1987. All instruments were completely handmade on the premises, without using premade necks or bodies. Buscarino focused on the electronics, while Benedetto brought the feel of his jazz guitar necks to the models. Following the electric line's debut at the January 1987 NAMM show, the partnership was dissolved. Benedetto continued working alone through April, 1987. While the instruments were well received, he could not produce them fast enough. The line was discontinued and Benedetto resumed making archtop guitars full-time.

A separate serial number was maintained, starting at #1001. A decal (in black or white), with the name "Benedetto" in all lowercase letters, was used on all models. 157 electric guitars and 52 electric basses were produced.

1000S - offset double cutaway poplar body, bolt-on rock maple neck, 25 1/2" scale, 22-fret rosewood fingerboard, graphite/teflon nut, 6-on-a-side Grover mini tuners, chrome hardware, Gotoh GE-1055T fulcrum tremolo, 3 Select by EMG single coil pickups, volume/tone controls, 5-way selector switch, available in Black, Red, and White Durocoat finishes, mfg. 1986-87.

Model has not traded sufficiently to quote pricing. For historical interest, the 1987 retail list price was $469.

1000T - similar to the 1000S, except features a single cutaway poplar body, Gotoh GTC-301C bridge, single coil/humbucker Select by EMG pickups, 3-way selector switch.

Model has not traded sufficiently to quote pricing. For historical interest, the 1987 retail list price was $439.

ELECTRIC: 3000 SERIES

3000S - offset double cutaway poplar body, bolt-on rock maple neck, 25.5 in. scale, 22-fret rosewood fingerboard, graphite/teflon nut, 6-on-a-side Grover mini tuners, black headstock, black chrome hardware, Gotoh GE-1055T fulcrum tremolo, 3 Select by EMG single coil pickups, volume/tone controls, 5-way selector switch, available in Black, Red, Taxi Yellow, or White Durocoat finishes, mfg.1986-87.

Model has not traded sufficiently to quote pricing. This model had an optional a 2-piece alder body with Prussian Blue Sunburst or Brown Maple Sunburst finishes (an additional $120), or Black neck finish (an additional $40). For historical interest, the 1987 retail list price was $569.

3000T - similar to the 3000S, except features a single cutaway poplar body, Gotoh GTC-301B bridge, single coil/humbucker Select by EMG pickups, 3-way selector switch.

Model has not traded sufficiently to quote pricing. For historical interest, the 1987 retail list price was $539.

ELECTRIC: WAVE SERIES

The Wave Series was the top of the Benedetto 1986-1987 electric solid body line, and featured one guitar model and one bass guitar model. The specifications are similar to the 3000 Series instruments, except featured a choice of exotic wood (quilted and highly figured curly maple, burl, etc.), ebony fingerboard, EMG active electronics, and upgraded hardware. A limited number of the custom Wave instruments were produced. The base retail list price in 1987 was $999.

ELECTRIC BASS

1000B - offset double cutaway poplar body, bolt-on rock maple neck, 34 in. scale, 22-fret rosewood fingerboard, graphite/teflon nut, 4-on-a-side Grover mini tuners, chrome hardware, Gotoh GEB-204C bridge, P/J-style Select by EMG pickups, volume/tone controls, 3-way selector switch, available in Black, Red, or White Durocoat finishes, mfg. 1986-87.

Model has not traded sufficiently to quote pricing. This model had an optional fretless fingerboard (an additional $60). For historical interest, the 1987 retail list price was $399.

3000B - similar to the 1000B, except features black headstock, black chrome hardware, available in Black, Red, Taxi Yellow, and White Durocoat finishes, mfg. 1986-87.

Model has not traded sufficiently to quote pricing. This model had an optional 2-piece alder body with Prussian Blue Sunburst or Brown Maple Sunburst finishes (an additional $120), or Black neck finish (an additional $40). For historical interest, the 1987 retail list price was $499.

BENEDICT GUITARS
Instruments currently built in Cedar, Minnesota since 1981. Distributed by the Benedict Guitar Company of Cedar, Minnesota.

Luthier Roger Benedict began building guitars back in 1974 in Elizabethtown, New York. Benedict moved to Minneapolis, Minnesota in 1981, and continued to build custom guitars. In 1988, he unveiled the Groovemaster model (as named by Jackson Browne, who owns two), a Strat-styled semi-hollowbody design. Unfortunately, Benedict passed away in 1994. He was remembered all over Minneapolis by musicians as a generous man who was easy-going and a great luthier.

In late 1995, Bill Hager purchased the rights to the trademark and designs from the estate, and continues to produce Benedict guitars. Hager, a printer and luthier, was apprenticed to Roger Benedict for five years. Hager continues to offer the Groovemaster, as well as a baritone guitar, and an acoustic/electric, and continues to build custom models. For more information, contact Benedict directly (see Trademark Index).

BENTLY
Instruments previously manufactured in Asia. Previously imported by St. Louis Music.

Bently instruments are entry-level to medium-quality solid body guitars and basses that feature designs based on classic American favorites. They are usually found priced between $50 and $100 on the used market.

BERT WEEDON
Please refer to the W section in this text.

BESSON
See Framus & Aristone. Instruments previously built in West Germany during the late 1950s through the early 1960s.

While Besson was the brand name for a UK importer, these guitars were made by and identical to certain Framus models. Research also indicates that the trademark Aristone was utilized as well (source: Tony Bacon and Paul Day, *The Guru's Guitar Guide*).

BEVERLY
See chapter on House Brands.

This trademark has been identified as a House Brand of Selmer UK in England (source: Willie G. Moseley, *Stellas & Stratocasters*).

BIAXE
Instruments previously built in Stamford, Connecticut from 1978 to 1985.

The original Biaxe Guitar company manufactured instruments for roughly eight years. When the company briefly reformed, they focused on retrofit devices that yielded the sound of a fretless bass on a fretted neck bass guitar. Dubbed "The Fretless Wizard", the kits were produced for 4-, 5-, and 6-string basses, and included an instructional cassette (these retrofit devices are no longer offered).

BIGSBY, PAUL
Instruments previously built in Downey, California from 1947 to 1965.

Paul Arthur Bigsby was a pattern-maker who was fond of motorcycle repair and racing. During the 1940s, Bigsby was contacted by country music star Merle Travis to repair a worn-out Vibrola on his Gibson L-10. Rather than just repair it, Bigsby produced a better vibrato tailpiece. The Bigsby vibrato was marketed for a number of years after he finished the first prototype. In 1965, Ted McCarty (ex-Gibson president) bought Bigsby's vibrato company, and produced Bigsby vibrato models until Fred Gretsch purchased the company in 1999.

In 1947-1948, Travis and Bigsby collaborated on a solid body electric which featured a 6-on-a-side headstock, single cutaway, neck-through-body construction, and a string-through-body bridge and tailpiece. Bigsby produced solid body guitars like this in small numbers on a custom order basis. Bigsby also had success with his electric pedal steel guitar beginning in the late 1940s. In 1956, Bigsby designed Magnatone's Mark IV (one pickup/trapeze tailpiece), and Mark V (two pickups/Bigsby tremolo) model electric guitars. These guitars were produced in Magnatone's factory. Paul Bigsby passed away in 1968. In 2002, they made a reissue of the original lap pedal steel of Bigsby.

Bigsby serialization can be found on the guitars stamped down by the lower strap button, and on pedal steels near the leg attachment. Serialization corresponds with the date produced (month/day/year).

ELECTRIC

While Bigsby's instruments were built on a custom order basis, there is some overall uniformity to the differences in models. One model was based on Merle Travis' neck-through/semi-hollowbody/single Florentine cutaway original design. The **Electric Standard** was similar, except had different scroll appointments and adjustable pole pieces on the pickups. A model built for Jack Parsons again had a single pointed cutaway, but a 3 in. deep body. Bigsby's last design had a double cutaway body.

In his workshop, Bigsby built Spanish guitars, mandolins, electric guitars, pedal steel guitars, and neck replacements on other company's acoustic guitars. It is estimated that there were only 25 to 50 electric Spanish guitars built (and only 3 or 4 doublenecks), 6 mandolins, around 150 pedal steel guitars, and perhaps a dozen or so Bigsby neck replacements (source: Michael Wright, *Vintage Guitar Magazine*; and Tom Wheeler, *American Guitars*).

These guitars are very rare, and when one is encountered, we suggest having several professional appraisals done on it before determining a value. These guitars have been seen priced anywhere between $5,000 and $25,000.

BILL LAWRENCE
Instruments previously produced in Korea by the Moriadara Guitar company.

These entry level quality solid body guitars feature designs based on classic American favorites. While they do bear his name, Bill Lawrence (Bill Lawrence Guitar Company, Keystone Pickups) is not associated with these models.

ELECTRIC

Bill Lawrence guitars feature designs based on American designs. The **MB-120** features an offset cut body, 3+3 headstock, 2 humbucker pickups, and a stop tailpiece. The **BLIR-150** features more of a Strat-style design, and has two humbuckers, a volume knob, and a pickup selector switch.

These models are available primarily in Japan. Instruments may turn up in the western states in the U.S. market. Estimated prices may run from $250 to $450, depending on condition.

BILL LAWRENCE GUITAR COMPANY LLC
Instruments currently built in California.

Bill Lawrence, a legend in the field of guitar and pickup design, also had a career as a well-known jazz guitarist in Germany. Born Willi Lorenz Stich in Wahn-Heide, Germany (eight miles southeast of Cologne) on March 24, 1931, Lawrence began violin lessons and the study of counterpoint at the age of eight. Five years later, he suffered a childhood accident that fractured his left hand and ended his violin-playing career. At age 14, Lawrence became an interpreter for the American and British armies after World War II. After being exposed to recordings of the Les Paul Trio, King Cole Trio, Glenn Miller, Lionel Hampton, and Benny Goodman, Lawrence became interested in the guitar playing styles of such notables as Charlie Christian, Barney Kessel, Oscar Moore, and Les Paul.

In 1946, Lawrence began learning to play the guitar - and by 1947 was performing in Cologne at the Hot Club '47. By 1951, Lawrence was established as a well-known guitarist in Germany. Two years later, he met Frederick Wilfer, president of the Framus Guitar Company. After complaining about the level of quality in contemporary guitar models, Wilfer created a prototype of a guitar based on Lawrence's ideas. When the decision was made to market this new guitar model, Lawrence (nee' Stich) changed his performing name to Billy Lorento. This performing name was applied to Framus' top-of-the-line model, and Lawrence used the Lorento name over the next ten years while performing publicly.

During that time, Lawrence was working for Framus as a consultant. His main job was to improve the sound and playability of their guitars. In 1962, Lawrence left Framus and changed his name to Bill Lawrence to endorse Fender guitars in Germany (the 'Billy Lorento' name was owned by Framus). In 1965, he started his first pickup company

**Benedetto Wave
courtesy Robert and
Cindy Benedetto**

and came to the United States to meet designer Dan Armstrong. The two spent a couple of years discussing guitar design aspects, and later collaborated on Armstrong's Dan Armstrong Lucite guitar (Lawrence built the prototypes for the pickups).

After working with Armstrong, Lawrence worked as a designer with the Gibson Guitar Company during the early 1970s. After a brief return to Framus, Lawrence came back to Gibson and helped design features for models like the S-1, L6-S, and Howard Roberts model guitars as well as the G-3 and Ripper bass. While designing other products at Gibson, Lawrence came up with a prototype for a flattop pickup. When people at Gibson suggested he market it on his own, Lawrence founded the Lawrence Sound Research in 1975. Lawrence currently produces Keystone pickups, and is debuting the new high quality Wilde USA guitar design that feature his own pickups. In 2003, Bill Lawrence relocated to Corona, California.

Lawrence's Keystone series of pickups are available in single coil and humbucker models for guitars as well as 'P', 'J', and 'Soapbar' styles for basses. These models are designed for aftermarket installation and as OEM-based parts for guitar companies.

WILDE GUITAR SERIES

Lawrence is currently offering his guitar design that features Lawrence's own special noise-free pickups. Wilde guitar models have an offset, double cutaway alder body, flamed maple top, bolt-on rock maple neck with 22-fret rosewood fretboard (25.5 in. scale) or solid rock maple neck/no fingerboard, fixed bridge, pickguard, 2 single coil/humbucker pickup configuration, volume and tone controls, and a 2 position, Series to Parallel, Selector-switch to change the inductance of the lead pickup from 4.8 to 1.2 Henry (high to medium impedance). The guitar is also available with different pickup combinations. The pickup systems are interchangeable. The **Standard** model (suggested list $1,500) features popular classic colors, while the **Deluxe** (suggested retail $1,650) features a selected flame maple top and translucent finishes. All models are hand finished with thin coats of high impact varnish. Lawrence's Wilde guitars are available through direct dealers only.

BISCAYNE
See also PALMER. Instruments currently produced in Asia. Distributed by Tropical Music Corporation of Miami, Florida.

Biscayne electric guitars and basses are entry level instruments based on traditional American designs. Biscayne models are distributed by Tropical Music Corporation, which has been servicing customers throughout Central and South America, the Caribbean, and the West Indies since 1975. Biscayne instruments are also available in the U.S. market through various wholesale catalogs. For more information on new Biscayne models contact the Tropical Music Corporation (see Trademark Index). Biscayne electric guitars and basses are usually priced in used condition from $75 up to $250.

BLACK HILLS
See chapter on House Brands.

This trademark has been identified as a House Brand of the Wall Drug stores (source: Willie G. Moseley, *Stellas & Stratocasters*).

BLACKHURST
Instruments currently built in Roseville, California.

Luthier Dave Blackhurst is presently building high quality custom designed guitars and basses that feature numerous options. Retail prices listed below are the base price; other customer-chosen options are priced extra.

ELECTRIC

In 1996, Blackhurst introduced a new custom model that was called **The Big One** (retail list $2,000 and up). The Big One is a playable hand-carved guitar or bass shaped like a fish - bluegill, halibut, bass (you name it). This fully functional instrument can also be mounted on your wall, like the trophy catch that it is! Other models offered in the past include the more traditional **STX** and **TLX** that feature deeper body cutaways.

The **Tigershark** series has a sleek double cutaway body design. The **Tigershark I/II F** has an alder body with cutaway neck heel, maple neck, ebony fingerboard, fixed bridge, and Seymour Duncan pickups (retail list $1,295 and up).

The **Tigershark I/II NL** is the non-locking tremolo version (list $1,350 and up), while the **Tigershark I/II-12** is the 12-string version. The **Tigershark I/II-12** has 6 tuners on the lower bout, and 6 tuners on the headstock (list $1,350 and up). The limited production **Tigershark II C/F** features a highly flamed maple carved top and an alder body (list $2,250 and up). Prices range from $1,295 up to $2,250.

ELECTRIC BASS

Blackhurst's **Home Bass** is a headless model constructed of koa or light ash, and has a 24-fret ebony fingerboard (list price $1,495 and up). This model is available in a fretless fingerboard configuration.

The **Tigershark Bass** is styled after the Tigershark guitar model, and is available in 4-, 5-, and 6-string configurations in customer's choice of woods (list $1,150 and up). Both bass models are available in a variety of pickup configurations.

BLACKJACK
Instruments previously produced in Japan circa 1960s.

The Blackjack brand name appears on these electric hollowbody guitars and basses. Neither the Japanese manufacturer (some models may have been built by Aria) nor the U.S. distributor have not been identified.

Violin-shaped Blackjack instruments are generally entry level to medium quality, and hold little fascination in the vintage market. Prices should range between $75 and $150 in excellent or 90% condition (source: Michael Wright, *Vintage Guitar Magazine*).

BLADE
Instruments currently produced in England and Japan. Distributed in the U.S. & Canada exclusively by Lasar Music Corporation, located in Brentwood, Tennessee. Previously distributed by Musician's Friend of Medford, Oregon through 1998. Distributed internationally by L-TEK International of Allschwil, Switzerland.

Designer Gary Levinson began building guitars in Illinois in 1964. In 1971, he moved to Basel, Switzerland on a scholarship to study geology. The idea and prototypes for the first Blade guitars came about in 1982 and the first guitars were introduced in 1987.

Levinson approaches his guitar building from an analytical standpoint based on his multiple university degrees in applied and natural sciences. As a result, Blade guitars combine traditional designs with quality craftsmanship and modern updated hardware, on-board electronics, and pickup combinations. The resulting instruments have more tonal options than older vintage models, but still maintain the feel that players are familiar with.

Levinson's design headquarters and Custom Shop are located in Allschwil (near Basel), Switzerland. The Custom Shop is the driving force in product development, derived in part from the input received from working musicians.

GRADING	100% MINT	98% NEAR MINT	95% EXC+	90% EXC	80% VG+	70% VG	60% G

The on-board **Variable Spectrum Control** electronics devised by Levinson give the Blade guitar player additional control over the guitar´s tone. Trim pots on the VSC (accessed through the back of the guitar) preset tone controls, and were activated through the VSC mini-switch (or push/pull pot) mounted near the volume and tone controls. It is estimated that Blade sold over 27,000 instruments worldwide between 1987 and 1997.

GENERAL INFORMATION

The Guitar VSC package offered a midrange boost (0 to 12 dB at 650 Hz) in the mini-switch´s up (1) position, VSC bypass in middle (2) position, and treble and bass boost/cut in down (3) position. The treble control ranged from -4 dB to +12 db at 7500 Hz, and the bass control ranged from -4 dB to +12 db at 160 Hz.

The Bass VSC package offered two preset EQ curves and two separate **hum trimmer** controls. In the mini-switch´s up (2) position, the VSC went to the user´s preset EQ curve, and in the down (1) position defaulted to the factory setting. Both EQ presets offered a three band (treble, mid, bass) separate cut/boost switch.

ELECTRIC: DISC. MODELS (R3, R4, ABILENE, & AUSTIN SERIES)

Blade California Standard Model CS Courtesy Blade

R 3 (MODEL R3-MB) - offset double cutaway soft maple body, white pickguard, bolt-on maple neck, 22-fret maple fingerboard with black dot inlay, Falcon tremolo system, graphite nut, 6-on-a-side Sperzel Trimlock tuners, black hardware, 3 SS-1 single coil pickups, volume/tone control, 5-position pickup selector switch, VSC switch, Variable Spectrum Control electronics, available in Black, Ice Blue, Iridescent White, or Purple Rain opaque finishes, mfg. 1988-1992.

N/A	$1,000	$875	$775	$700	$600	$500

Last MSR was $1,675.

Add $75 for ebony fingerboard with pearl dot inlay (R3-EB).

This model was available with chrome hardware.

RH 3 (Model RH3-MB) - similar to R 3 (R3-MB), except has 2 SS-1 single coil/1 LH-4 humbucker pickups, mfg. 1988-1992.

N/A	$1,025	$900	$800	$725	$625	$500

Last MSR was $1,700.

Add $100 for ebony fingerboard with pearl dot inlay (RH3-EB).

R 4 (MODEL R4-MB) - offset double cutaway light ash body, black pickguard, bolt-on maple neck, 22-fret maple fingerboard with black dot inlay, Falcon tremolo system, graphite nut, 6-per-side Sperzel Trimlock tuners, black hardware, 3 SS-1 single coil pickups, volume/tone control, 5-position pickup selector switch, VSC switch, Variable Spectrum Control active electronics, available in Ocean Blue and See-Through Red Translucent finishes, mfg. 1988-1992.

N/A	$1,100	$950	$850	$750	$650	$550

Last MSR was $1,800.

Add $100 for ebony fingerboard with pearl dot inlay (R4-EB).

R4-MG - similar to R4-MB, except has gold hardware, available in Honey, Misty Violet, Nightwood and 2-Tone Sunburst Translucent finishes, mfg. 1988-1992.

N/A	$1,125	$975	$875	$775	$675	$575

Last MSR was $1,870.

Add $100 for ebony fingerboard with pearl dot inlay (R4-EG).

ABILENE - offset double cutaway sen ash body, white pearloid pickguard, bolt-on maple neck, 22-fret maple fingerboard with black dot inlay, FT-3 Vint-Edge tremolo, graphite nut, 6-on-a-side Sperzel Trimlock tuners, chrome hardware, white knobs and pickup covers, 3 V-1 humcancelling single coil pickups, volume/tone control, 5-position pickup selector switch, VSC-Gain boost electronics, available in Harvest Gold and 2-Tone Sunburst Translucent finish, mfg. 1993 only.

N/A	$1,000	$875	$775	$695	$600	$525

This model was also available with a rosewood fingerboard and pearl dot inlays.

AUSTIN - similar to the Abilene, except has rosewood fingerboard, black pearloid pickguard, black hardware, 2 V-1 single coil/1 LM humbucker pickups, black knobs and pickup covers, available in Harvest Gold, Nightwood, and Ocean Blue translucent finishes, mfg. 1993 only.

N/A	$1,100	$950	$850	$750	$650	$550

ELECTRIC: CALIFONIA MODELS

CALIFORNIA STANDARD (MODEL CS) - offset double cutaway swamp ash body, bolt-on hard rock maple neck, 22-fret rosewood fingerboard with pearl dot inlay, Wilkinson VS-50K tremolo, graphite nut, 6-on-a-side die-cast tuners, chrome hardware, white pearloid pickguard, 2 VS-1 single coil/HD-4 humbucker pickups, volume/tone (push-pull coil tap) control, 5-position selector switch, VSC mini-switch, Variable Spectrum Control electronics, available in Black, Sparkling Blue, and Sparkling Purple finishes, mfg. 1994-present.

MSR $1,080		$875	$775	$700	$625	$550	$475	$400

Some early models may have an alder body instead of swamp ash. In 1996, Black, Sparkling Blue, and Sparkling Purple finishes were discontinued; Aegean (Adriatic) Blue Burst, Cherry Sunburst, and Honey Burst finishes were introduced.

B

GRADING	100% MINT	98% NEAR MINT	95% EXC+	90% EXC	80% VG+	70% VG	60% G

California Deluxe - similar to the California Standard, except featured a mahogany body, figured maple top, Levinson FT-4 tremolo, Sperzel Trimlock tuners, VSC-2 electronics, available in Natural Silk satin finish, mfg. 1994-95.

	$1,100	$975	$900	$825	$725	$595	$500

This model had 3 VS-3 single coils as a pickup configuration option.

California Hybrid - similar to the California Standard, except features a hexaphonic piezo bridge pickup system, EA (electric/acoustic) mix control, EA system switch, available in Aegean Blue Burst, Cherry Sunburst, or Honey Burst finishes, mfg. 1998-2003.

	$1,150	$1,000	$875	$750	$625	$525	$400

Last MSR was $1,699.

CALIFORNIA CUSTOM (MODEL CC) - similar to the California Standard, except features a swamp ash body/figured maple top, ebony fingerboard, Levinson Falcon FT-4 tremolo, chrome Sperzel Trimlock tuners, translucent pickguard, 2 V-1 Humcanceller single coil/LH-55 humbucker pickups, available in Aegean Blue Burst, Cherry Sunburst, Honey Burst, or Violet Burst finishes, mfg. 1994-present.

MSR $3,040	$2,500	$2,100	$1,800	$1,500	$1,300	$1,100	$900

This model is custom built in Switzerland.

ELECTRIC: CLASSIC MODELS

DELTA T 2 (MODEL T2/DET2) - single cutaway sen ash body, bolt-on hard rock maple neck, 22-fret rosewood fingerboard with pearl dot inlay, black pickguard, fixed bridge, graphite nut, 6-on-a-side Levinson SG-36 tuners, gold hardware, 2 single coil Levinson T 4/2 Calibrated pickups, volume/tone control, 3-position selector switch, VSC switch, chrome controls plate, Variable Spectrum Control electronics, available in Honey, Ocean Blue, or Sunset Purple See-Through finishes, disc. 2003.

	$1,150	$1,000	$875	$775	$650	$550	$425

Last MSR was $1,699.

This model is also available with a one-piece maple neck (limited quantities). In 1998, 3-Tone Sunburst and Fire Red finishes were introduced.

Delta Standard T 1 (Model T1) - similar to the Delta T 2, except features hardwood body, chrome hardware, available in Black, Candy Apple Red, Lake Placid Blue, or Vintage White finishes, mfg. 1998-present.

MSR $690	$575	$500	$450	$400	$350	$300	$250

RH 4 STANDARD (MODEL RS4) - offset double cutaway sen ash body, bolt-on hard rock maple neck, 22-fret rosewood fingerboard with pearl dot inlay, Levinson Vint-Edge FT-3 tremolo, graphite nut, 6-per-side Gotoh MG7 Magnum Lock tuners, chrome hardware, sepia mirror pickguard, 2 V-3 stacked coil/1 LH-55 humbucker pickups, volume/push-pull tone (humbucker coil tap) controls, 5-position selector switch, VSC switch, Variable Spectrum Control active electronics, available in Honey, Misty Violet, Ocean Blue, or See-Through Red finishes, mfg. 1996-present.

MSR $1,995	$1,350	$1,150	$950	$800	$700	$600	$500

This model is available with a one-piece maple neck (limited quantities), or 3 single coil pickups. Early versions of this model may have black pickguards.

RH 4 Classic (Model RH4) - similar to the RH 4 Standard, except features an ebony or flamed maple fingerboard, Levinson Falcon tremolo, Sperzel Trimlock tuners, and gold hardware, mfg. 1996-present.

MSR $2,425	$2,000	$1,700	$1,450	$1,250	$1,050	$900	$750

Add $150 for maple neck.

This model is available with a one-piece flamed maple neck (limited quantities), or 3 single coil pickups.

T 2 (MODEL T2-MG) - single cutaway light ash body, bolt-on maple neck, 22-fret maple fingerboard with black dot inlay, fixed bridge, graphite nut, 6-on-a-side tuners, gold hardware, 2 single coil pickups, volume/tone control, 3-position switch, VSC switch, Variable Spectrum Control electronics, available in Harvest Gold, Misty Violet, Ocean Blue, or See-Through Red Translucent finishes, mfg. 1991-92.

	N/A	$750	$675	$600	$525	$450	$375

Last MSR was $1,290.

Add $40 for rosewood fingerboard with pearl dot inlay (T2-RG).

TEXAS (MODEL TE) - offset double cutaway alder body, bolt-on maple neck, 22-fret rosewood fingerboard with pearl dot inlay, Levinson Vint-Edge FT-2 tremolo, graphite nut, 6-on-a-side Levinson Staggered tuners, chrome hardware, white pearloid pickguard, 3 single coil pickups, volume/tone control, 5-position pickup selector switch, bypass mini-switch, gain boost electronics, available in Black and 3-Tone Sunburst finishes, mfg. 1994-97.

	$800	$700	$625	$550	$475	$400	$325

Last MSR was $1,299.

This model was available with a one piece maple neck, and/or a black pickguard with 2 single coil/humbucker pickups.

TEXAS DELUXE - similar to the Texas Standard, except had alder body with maple top, 2 single coil/1 humbucker pickups, gold tuners, available in Fire Red, Ocean Blue, Purple, Cherry Sunburst, Honey, Misty Violet, or 2-Tone Sunburst finishes, mfg. 1994-95, 2003-present.

MSR $975	$800	$700	$625	$550	$475	$375	$325

This model was reintroduced in 2003. Previously it featured a sen ash body.

TEXAS JR - similar to the Texas TE, except had sen ash body, 2 single coil/1 humbucker pickups, Levinson FT- 3 tremolo, Sperzel Trimlock tuners, variable mid-boost electronics (push/pull tone knob), available in Blue Oil, Purple Oil, or Red Oil finishes, mfg. 1994-95.

	$975	$875	$800	$725	$650	$550	$450

TEXAS STANDARD (MODEL TE-2) - offset double cutaway North American alder body, bolt-on hard rock maple neck, 22-fret maple fingerboard with black dot inlay, Levinson FT-3 tremolo, graphite nut, 6-on-a-side Staggered SG-36 tuners, chrome hardware, white pickguard, 3 VS-1 single coil pickups, volume/tone controls, 5-position selector switch, gain boost mini-switch, gain boost electronics, available in 3-Tone Sunburst, Black, Candy Apple Red, Lake Placid Blue, Sea Foam Green, Sonic Blue, or Olympic White finishes, mfg. 1998-present.

MSR $865	$700	$625	$550	$475	$400	$350	$300

This model has an optional rosewood fingerboard with pearl dot inlay.

GRADING	100% MINT	98% NEAR MINT	95% EXC+	90% EXC	80% VG+	70% VG	60% G

TEXAS SPECIAL (MODEL TS) - similar to the Texas Standard (TE-2), except has sen ash body, and an LH-55 humbucker (bridge position), available in Fire Red, Honey, Ocean Blue, and Sunset Purple See-Through finishes, mfg. 1994-2003.

	$850	$725	$650	$575	$500	$425	$350

Last MSR was $1,399.

This model has an optional rosewood fingerboard with pearl dot inlay, or one-piece maple neck (limited quantities).

TEXAS VINTAGE CUSTOM (MOD. TV) - similar to the Texas TE, except has sen ash body, available in 3-Tone Sunburst, Black, Candy Apple Red, Indian Turquoise, Sea Foam Green, Sonic Blue, Mary Kay Blonde, or Tobacco Sunburst finishes, mfg. 1998-present.

MSR $1,750		$1,200	$1,050	$925	$800	$675	$550	$425

This model has an optional one-piece maple neck (Tobacco Sunburst finish only).

TEXAS VINTAGE 62 - similar to the Texas Vintage Custom except is modeled like the '62 Strat, disc. 2004.

	$1,100	$950	$825	$750	$625	$525	$400

Last MSR was $1,595.

TEXAS VINTAGE 57 - similar to the Texas Vintage Custom except is modeled like the '57 Strat, disc. 2004.

	$1,100	$950	$825	$750	$625	$525	$400

Last MSR was $1,595.

THINLINE THS (MODEL THS/DTHS) - similar to the Delta T 2, except features a semi-solid sen ash body, unbound f-hole, rounded white pearl pickguard, no chrome controls plate, available in Honey, Ocean Blue, and Sunset Purple translucent finishes, mfg. 1994-2004.

	$1,395	$1,175	$1,000	$875	$725	$600	$475

Last MSR was $1,995.

This model is also available with a one-piece maple neck (limited quantities). In 1998, 3-Tone Sunburst and Fire Red finishes were introduced.

Thinline THH (Model THH/DTHH) - similar to the Thinline (Model THS), except features an LH-55 humbucker/T 4 Bridge single coil pickups, push/pull tone (humbucker coil tap) control, available in 3-Tone Sunburst, Fire Red, Honey Burst, Ocean Blue, and Sunset Purple finishes, mfg. 1993-2004.

	$1,425	$1,200	$1,025	$875	$725	$600	$475

Last MSR was $2,045.

This model was originally listed as the Delta Queen (1993-1994), and was offered in Harvest Gold, Misty Violet, Ocean Blue, and 3-Tone Sunburst finishes.

Blade Texas Standard
Courtesy Blade

ELECTRIC: DURANGO MODELS

The Durango T Classic was scheduled for release in Spring, 2004, but there is no current MSR.

DURANGO (MODEL DU) - offset double cutaway alder body, bolt-on maple neck, 22-fret rosewood fingerboard with pearl dot inlay, Wilkinson HT100T tremolo, graphite nut, 6-on-a-side Sperzel non-locking tuners, chrome hardware, white pearloid pickguard, 1 single coil/1 humbucker pickups, volume/tone control, 3-position pickup selector switch, bypass mini-switch, gain boost electronics, available in Amber, Black, Candy Apple Red, Purple, or Turquoise finishes, mfg. 1994-97.

	$900	$775	$695	$625	$525	$450	$375

Last MSR was $1,499.

DURANGO STANDARD (MODEL DS) - offset double cutaway mahogany body, bolt-on hard rock maple neck, 25.5 in. scale, 22-fret rosewood fingerboard with pearl dot inlay, Wilkinson VS-50K tremolo, graphite nut, 6-on-a-side die-cast tuners, chrome hardware, white pearloid pickguard, 2 VS-1 single coil/LH-55 humbucker pickups, volume/tone controls, 5-position pickup selector switch, available in Blue Metallic, Cherry, or Natural Oil finishes, mfg. 1996-present.

MSR $830		$675	$575	$500	$425	$375	$325	$275

In 1997, Black and Matte Stained Mahogany finishes were introduced; Blue Metallic, Cherry, and Natural Oil finishes were disc.

DURANGO DELUXE (MODEL DD) - similar to the Durango Standard, except features North American alder body, Levinson FT-4 tremolo, chrome Sperzel Trimlock tuners, and Seymour Duncan L'il 59 mini-humbucker/HD-4 humbucker pickups, volume/push/pull tone (humbucker coil tap) controls, gain boost electronics, available in Amber, Black, Candy Apple Red, Cherry, Purple, or Turquoise finishes, mfg. 1994-2003.

	$1,325	$1,100	$925	$800	$650	$550	$425

Last MSR was $1,999.

Add $150 for 2 single coil/humbucker pickups with VSC electronics configuration.

This model is custom built in Switzerland. In 1997, Ice Blue finish was introduced; Amber, Cherry, Purple, and Turquoise finishes were discontinued.

DURANGO MAGNUM (MODEL DM) - similar to the Durango Standard, available in Black, See-Through Cherry, Blue Metallic, or See-Through Matte Stained Mahogany finishes, mfg. 1998-2003.

	$625	$550	$475	$425	$350	$295	$225

Last MSR was $799.

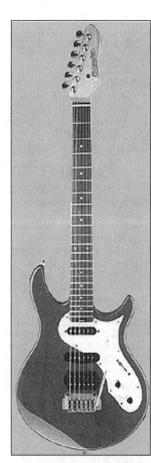

Blade Durango Standard
Courtesy Blade

B

GRADING	100% MINT	98% NEAR MINT	95% EXC+	90% EXC	80% VG+	70% VG	60% G

DURANGO T (MODEL DT) - similar to the Durango Standard, except features set-in mahogany neck, 24.75 in. scale, tune-o-matic bridge/stop tailpiece, 2 LP-90 oversized single coil pickups, volume/tone push/pull (gain boost on/off) controls, 3-way selector switch, available in See-Through Cherry or Tobacco Sunburst finishes, mfg. 1997-2003.

	$625	$550	$475	$425	$350	$295	$225

Last MSR was $759.

DURANGO T HYBRID (MODEL DTH) - offset single cutaway mahogany body, hard rock maple neck, 25.5 in. scale, 22-fret rosewood fingerboard with pearl dot inlay, hexaphonic piezo bridge/stop tailpiece, graphite nut, 6-on-a-side SG-36 tuners, chrome hardware, curved white pearloid pickguard, 2 single coil/humbucker magnetic pickups, master volume/tone/EA (electric/acoustic) mix controls, 5-position magnetic pickup selector switch, EA system switch, "hideaway" push-in piezo treble/bass boost controls (on bass bout), available in Sunburst finish only, mfg. 1997-2003.

	$975	$800	$700	$600	$525	$425	$325

Last MSR was $1,399.

ELECTRIC BASS

Blade basses were offered with a fretted or fretless fingerboard.

B-1 TETRA STANDARD - offset double cutaway contoured alder body, bolt-on hard rock maple neck, 20-fret rosewood fingerboard with pearl dot inlay, fixed bridge, 4-on-a-side tuners, 2 JS-1 Alnico single coil pickups, chrome hardware, 3 knobs, BMB-1 electronics with midrange boost, available in black, Olympic White, or 3-Tone Sunburst finishes, mfg. 2003-present.

MSR $899	$725	$625	$550	$475	$425	$375	$325

B-2 (TETRA 4) - offset double cutaway contoured sen ash body, bolt-on maple neck, 4-string configuration, 21-fret rosewood fingerboard with pearl dot inlay, fixed bridge, 4-on-a-side Gotoh tuners, 2 JHB-2 J-style pickups, gold hardware, master volume/pickup balance/Treble boost/Bass boost controls, Variable Bass Spectrum Control 2 (VSC 2) active electronics, available in Honey, Misty Violet, Nightwood, Ocean Blue, or See-Through Red Translucent finishes, mfg. 1993, 2003-present.

MSR $2,138	$1,750	$1,500	$1,300	$1,100	$950	$825	$700

The Bass push/pull control activates the VSC 2 setting. Trim pots in the back of the Tetra 4 are pre-set to a different EQ setting.

B 3 - offset double cutaway contoured soft maple body, bolt-on maple neck, 21-fret ebony fingerboard with pearl dot inlay, fixed bridge, 4-on-a-side Gotoh tuners, 2 J-style pickups, black hardware, volume/pickup balance/tone controls, VSC switch, Variable Bass Spectrum Control II electronics, available in Black, Ice Blue, Purple Rain, or Snow White opaque finishes, mfg. 1991-92.

	N/A	$1,100	$895	$800	$695	$625	$500

Last MSR was $1,740.

B 4 - similar to B 3, except has light ash body, and gold hardware, available in Honey, Misty Violet, Ocean Blue, and See-Through Red translucent finishes, mfg. 1991-92.

	N/A	$1,100	$950	$825	$700	$600	$500

Last MSR was $1,970.

B 4 Custom - similar to the B 4, except featured mahogany body, mfg. 1991-92.

	N/A	$1,100	$950	$825	$700	$600	$500

Last MSR was $1,970.

B-25 (PENTA 5) - offset double cutaway contoured sen ash body, bolt-on maple neck, 5-string configuration, 21-fret rosewood fingerboard with pearl dot inlay, fixed bridge, 4/1 per side Gotoh tuners, 2 JHB-25 J-style pickups, gold hardware, master volume/pickup balance/Treble boost/Bass boost controls, Variable Bass Spectrum Control 2 (VSC 2) active electronics, available in Honey, Misty Violet, Nightwood, Ocean Blue, and See-Through Red translucent finishes, mfg. 1993, 2003-present.

MSR $2,297	$1,850	$1,600	$1,350	$1,150	$1,000	$875	$750

The Bass push/pull control activates the VSC 2 setting. Trim pots in the back of the Penta 5 pre-set a different EQ setting.

BLAIR GUITARS LTD.
Instruments previously built in Ellington, Connecticut.

Designer Douglas Blair has over twenty years experience in the music field, and has been building his own guitars since his teens. Blair has recorded 3 independent EP/LPs, and toured with acts like Run 21 and W.A.S.P. Throughout his professional playing career, Blair found himself constantly switching between his electric guitar and an Ovation acoustic on a stand for live performances. In 1990, Blair conceived of the **Mutant Twin** guitar model as a way to solve the problem, which combined a solid body half with an "acoustic" half (with hollow tuned sound chamber and Fishman preamp). Prototypes were developed with the aid of Ovation R & D designer Don Johnson in 1990, and the guitar debuted in Boston in 1991. Blair Guitars Ltd. debuted at the 1994 NAMM winter show.

In 1997, Blair's design was licensed to Guild (FMIC) as the new Slash signature Crossroads custom design doubleneck guitar. This model came in Black or Crimson Transparent finishes (Guild last MSR was $4,000).

ELECTRIC

Doug Blair's **Blair Guitars Ltd.** produced the **Mutant Twin Standard 6**, which last retailed for $2,299. The doubleneck guitar had a solid mahogany "common" body and a solid cedar or spruce braced soundboard (on the acoustic half) over a tuned acoustic sound chamber in the body. The two Warmouth necks had Graph Tech nuts and Schaller tuning machines. The acoustic side of the guitar had a custom 'pinless' rosewood bridge and Fishman piezo bridge pickup (and preamp); the electric side had Gibson humbuckers and either a Schaller or Wilkinson locking tremolo.

The **Mutant Twin Standard 12** (last MSR $2,799) is the 6-string electric/12-string acoustic doubleneck configuration. Other variations include the **Mutant Twin Memphis Belle 6** (last MSR $2,799), which has 6-string electric/6-string dobro resophonic Tele-style downsized alder body, tricone resonator, biscuit bridge, Fishman pickup and preamp, maple necks with maple or rosewood fingerboards, DiMarzio pickups (electric half), and a nitrocellulose finish. The **Mutant Twin Madrid Eyes 6** (last MSR $2,799) is similar to the Standard 6 but pairs the electric side's two Gibson '57 humbuckers with a nylon string half, along with an ebony fingerboard and an X-braced cedar top. The **Mutant Twin Bristol Shores 6** (last MSR $2,299) is also similar to the Standard 6, but has 3 Dimarzio "Class of '55" single coil pickups, a 5-way selector, and a Wilkinson non-locking tremolo bridge. The Bristol Shores also came in a 12-string/6-string configuration (last MSR $2,799).

B

ELECTRIC BASS

Blair also produced the **Generation X 8** bass model which has a Les Paul Jr.-style body, Dual Format 8-string configuration with P/J-style pickups and Fishman piezo bridge pickups (on octave strings only), active tone/EQ controls, discrete outputs, and a 3-way magnetic/piezo pickup selector (last MSR $1,999).

BLUE SAGE
See MELODY.

The Italian-built Blue Sage series debuted in 1982, and was part of the overall Melody guitar line. The Blue Sage series of original designs was of higher quality than the traditional offerings of the company (source: Tony Bacon, *Ultimate Guitar Book*).

BLUE STAR GUITAR COMPANY
Instruments currently built in Fennville, Michigan since 1981. Distributed by Elderly Instruments of Lansing, Michigan.

Luthier Bruce Herron has been building guitars since 1979. The first Blue Star electric guitar was built in 1984. Herron´s initial production model, the Travelcaster (a travel-sized 6-string electric) was introduced in 1990. In his one-man shop, Herron now offers a range of electric stringed instruments distributed both in his hometown near Holland, Michigan, as well as through Elderly Instruments.

ELECTRIC

Blue Star instruments feature solid wood construction topped with an eye-catching, psychedelic Phenolic burst top. This durable reflective material is occasionally found on drum sets (Herron admits that his inspiration began with ´50s Gretsch drum sets and guitars). All models have a chip-resistant finish on the sides and back, chrome hardware, and a limited lifetime warranty from Herron, available in Blueburst, Chromeburst, Goldburst, Redburst, and Silverburst. The **Travelcaster** (Model BS-1) has a 22 in. scale, one humbucker, double cutaway body, 3-per-side headstock, rosewood fingerboard, adjustable truss rod, and a tune-o-matic type bridge. Last MSR was $550 factory direct,(retail price at Elderly is $385). The left-handed Travelcaster (Model BS-1L) last retailed at $420.

Herron´s full scale guitar, the **Psychocaster (Model PC)**, is a Telecaster-style design that features two single coil pickups, string through-body bridge, adjustable truss rod, volume/tone controls, 3-way pickup selector switch, and choice of maple or rosewood fingerboards. The **PC** last retailed at $560 factory direct (retail price at Elderly is $462); the left-handed **PCL**´s last retail price was $504. Currently, there are no electric guitars offered for sale at Elderly.

Another stringed instrument produced by Herron is the **Mandoblaster** (Model BSMB), a 4- or 5-string electric solid body mandolin. Mandoblasters have been the most popular since introduced and feature one single coil pickup, double cutaway body, adjustable truss rod, volume/tone controls, and choice of maple or rosewood fingerboards. The retail list for the BSMB-4 (4-string) or the BSMB (5-string) is $750 factory direct (retail price at Elderly is $563). Herron´s **Lapmaster** is a electric lap steel with one humbucker, volume and tone controls, and carpeted (like amplifier covering) back and sides (retail list is $400 factory direct - list price at Elderly is $300).

In 1997, Herron introduced the **Banjocaster**. A 5-string double cutaway electric banjo with 2-lipstick pickups, 4-on-a-side peghead and Schaller-geared 5th peg, string through-body bridge, adjustable truss rod, volume/tone controls, 3-way pickup selector switch, and choice of maple or rosewood, and scalloped or radius options for the fingerboard. Last MSR was $850, and factory or Elderly price was $595.

The "**Otis Taylor-Bluesman**" model Banjocaster was introduced in 1998. This model featured a cool body shape with 3 mini-lipstick pickups and was personally autographed by Otis Taylor. Last MSR was $995 factory direct, or $696.50 at Elderly Instruments. The Otis Taylor Bluesman model was also available at Otis´ favorite hometown music store, the Denver Folklore Center.

Herron´s **Konablaster** Ukulele has a pineapple-shaped body, Pacific Blue top/non-slip Ozite carpeted back and sides, one single coil pickup, and a nickel plated "thirty-aught-six" shell casing tailpiece! The headstock on this model is personally signed by Allan Woody (Allman Brothers, Gov´t Mule). List price is $400 and $300 at Elderly.

BLUE STAR MUSIC
Instruments currently built in Lovingston, Virginia since 1995.

Luthier Joe Madison began operating Blue Star Music in 1988. He thought he had "seen it all" until artist Willie Kirschbaum brought in a hand-sculpted guitar body that featured a beautifully carved face with long flowing hair. Originally the bodies were displayed at art shows and galleries, and sparked a lot of interest. Jack Roy, an electronics specialist and vintage Fender aficionado, was also impressed. The three combined their talents to create these uniquely beautiful guitars, with hand carved headstocks that echo the body design.

Each guitar has a unique figure carved into the wood, be it a dragon, a face, a snake, or almost any design. Custom guitars can be standard shape or radical designs with many wood choices and unlimited electronic configurations. Prices range from $1,000 to $4,500, depending on the intricacy of the sculpting and design. All are outfitted with top quality hardware.

BLUESOUTH
Instruments previously built in Muscle Shoals, Alabama.

Ronnie Knight began Bluesouth Guitars in 1991 with the idea of building stringed musical instruments which celebrate the musical heritage of the American South. Blues, jazz, country, rock, and spiritual music were all created in the southern American states. This small area from Texas to the Carolinas, and from Kentucky to Florida, has been the hotbed of the world´s musical culture in the twentieth century. Several small towns within the southeast have had a huge impact on today´s popular music: Muscle Shoals, Alabama; Macon, Georgia; and Clarksdale, Mississippi. The results of this project have been unique, light-bodied guitars with large, comfortable necks. Bluesouth contends that "fierce individualism" is the key ingredient in their guitar making operation. Starting in a small shop over a record store in early 1992, Bluesouth moved to a much larger industrial facility in the spring of 1995. In the late 1990s, the company offered seven models, including two electric basses. Bluesouth also built its own cases and pickups in-house (company history courtesy Ronnie Knight, April 17, 1996).

Blade B-2 Tetra 4 Bass
Courtesy Blade

Blade B-25 Penta 5 Bass
Courtesy Blade

B

ELECTRIC

All Bluesouth instruments feature mahogany or swamp ash bodies in sleek ergonomic designs, a mahogany set-neck with 22-fret fingerboard, 24.75 in. scale, Sperzel tuners, Wilkinson or Gotoh hardware, and Bluesouth´s own pickups. Models run from the **Clarksdale** (last MSR $1,295), which has a mahogany body, rosewood fingerboard, 2 Bluesouth soapbar pickups, and a tune-o-matic bridge; to the **Macon** (last MSR $1,895), which has a carved top mahogany body, ebony fingerboard, Schaller humbuckers, and an ivoroid bound body. The **Jimmy Johnson** "Original Swamper" (last MSR $1,895) has a single cutaway Tele-style swamp ash body, bolt-on maple neck, and 2 single coil pickups. The **Muscle Shoals** (last MSR $1,495) model has a swamp ash body, rosewood fingerboard, 3 Bluesouth single coil pickups, and a Wilkinson HT-100C bridge; the **Muscle Shoals DLX** (last MSR $2,095) has a carved top ivoroid bound mahogany body, 2 Bluesouth soapbar pickups, and rosewood fingerboard.

ELECTRIC BASS

The **Clarksdale** 4-string bass (30 in. or 34 in. scale) last retailed at $1,895 and also came in 5-string. The **Clarksdale** has a mahogany body, set-in mahogany neck, rosewood or ebony fingerboard (21-, 22-, or 24-fret), and 2 EMG J-style pickups.

BLUNDELL
Instruments previously built in England during the early 1980s.

These British-built solid body guitars were patterned after the Explorer and Flying V designs (source: Tony Bacon and Paul Day, *The Guru's Guitar Guide*).

BOGART
Instruments currently built in Germany since 1991. Previously distributed by Salwender. Currently there is no U.S. distributor.

Bogart has been producing high quality basses since 1991. Models feature a patented Blackstone material for the bodies and bolt-on graphite necks. Bogart basses have Bartolini pickups, solid brass bridge (with fine tuners) and Schaller tuning machines.

The Blackstone material consists of a wood core surrounded by epoxy foam. However, the neck, pickups, and hardware all bolt to the wood core.

ELECTRIC BASS: BASIC SERIES

Basic model options include black or black nickel hardware, and Bartolini J-Bass pickups. The **Basic Classic 4** features an offset double cutaway Blackstone body, bolt-on graphite neck, 86.4 cm scale, 24-fret graphite fingerboard, 3/1 per side Schaller tuners, chrome hardware, Bartolini humbucker, bridge/stop tailpiece with fine tuners, volume/tone control, passive electronics, available in Black, Pink, Red, Sky Blue, White, or Yellow Struktur finishes, and retails for $2,795. 5- and 6-string configurations are available for $3,064 and $3,656, respectively.

The **Basic II/4** is a lower-end version that has a simple hardwood body and retails for $1,695. A 5-string version retails for $1,895.

> **Add $75 for fretless Phenolic fingerboard.**

ELECTRIC BASS: CUSTOM BASIC SERIES

Custom Basic model options include gold hardware, and custom Multicolor painting. The **Collier Bogart 4** features an offset double cutaway mahogany or European maple body, set-in graphite neck, 86.4 cm scale, 24-fret phenolic fingerboard, 3/1 per side Schaller tuners, black hardware, Bartolini soapbar humbucker, ETS bridge, volume control, 2- or 3-band EQ controls, available in Natural satin-like polyester finish, mfg. 1997-current, and retails for $2,881. 5- and 6-string configurations are available for $3,156 and $3,504, respectively.

The **Custom Basic 4** features an offset double cutaway mahogany or European maple body, set-in graphite neck, 86.4 cm scale, 24-fret phenolic fingerboard, 3/1 per side Schaller tuners, black hardware, Bartolini soapbar humbucker, ETS bridge, volume control, 2- or 3-band EQ controls, available in Natural satin-like polyester finish, mfg. 1997-present, and retails for $2,617. 5- and 6-string configurations are available for $2,881 and $3,504 respectively.

> **Add $75 for fretless Phenolic fingerboard.**

COLLIER BOGART 4 - offset double cutaway mahogany or European maple body, set-in graphite neck, 86.4 cm scale, 24-fret phenolic fingerboard, 3/1 per side Schaller tuners, black hardware, Bartolini soapbar humbucker, ETS bridge, volume control, 2 or 3-band EQ controls, available in Natural satin-like polyester finish, mfg. 1997-present.

> **MSR $2,881**

Collier Bogart 5 - similar to the Collier Bogart 4, except has 4/1-per-side-headstock and 5-string configuration, mfg. 1997-present.

> **MSR $3,156**

Collier Bogart 6 - similar to the Collier Bogart 4, except has 4/2-per-side headstock and 6-string configuration, current mfg.

> **MSR $3,504**

CUSTOM BASIC 4 - offset double cutaway Blackstone body, bolt-on graphite neck, 86.4 cm scale, 24-fret graphite fingerboard, 3/1 per side Schaller tuners, black or blacknickel hardware, Bartolini soapbar humbucker, bridge/stop tailpiece with fine tuners, volume control, treble/mid/bass EQ controls, BBA3 active EQ, available in Black, Burgundy, Green, Light Red, Light Green, Midnight Blue, White, or Yellow Blackstone finishes, current mfg.

> **MSR $2,617**

Custom Basic 5 - similar to the Custom Basic 4, except has 4/1 per side headstock and 5-string configuration, current mfg.

> **MSR $2,881**

Custom Basic 6 - similar to the Custom Basic 4, except has 4/2-per-side headstock and 6-string configuration, current mfg.

> **MSR $3,504**

BOGUE, REX
Instruments previously built in San Gabriel, California circa early 1970s. Previously distributed by Rex Bogue Guitars of San Gabriel, California.

Designer Rex Bogue was an independent luthier perhaps best known for his association with jazz guitarist Mahavishnu John McLaughlin, and the heavily inlaid doubleneck Double Rainbow guitar that Bogue created for him. Bogue credited the inlay work from S.S. Stewart banjo inlays and the French art nouveau painted Alphonse Mucha as inspiration for the "Tree of Life" fingerboard inlay design on McLaughlin´s guitar.

GRADING	100% MINT	98% NEAR MINT	95% EXC+	90% EXC	80% VG+	70% VG	60% G

Luthier Bogue was associated with the Ren Ferguson Guitar Company in Venice, California when the Double Rainbow was created; he later formed his own Rex Bogue Guitars in San Gabriel. Bogue created a number of other custom inlay commissioned works during the early 1970s, including a 4-string bass/6-string guitar doubleneck for bassist Miraslav Vitous (ex-Weather Report).

McLaughlin's doubleneck also attracted the attention of Jeff Hasselberger at Ibanez, who received Bogue's permission to duplicate the look of the guitar. Ibanez' vaguely SG-shaped doubleneck recreation debuted in the 1975 Ibanez catalog as the model 2670, under the **Professional** or **Artist** Autograph series. While the model 2670 was available from 1975 through 1980, it is estimated that only a dozen were actually produced and the 1970s retail list was $1,500, (Ibanez connection information courtesy Michael Wright, *Guitar Stories*, Vol. 1).

BOND
Instruments previously built in England between 1984 and 1986.

Advanced design Bond guitars were designed by Scotland's Andrew Bond. The Electraglide model featured such innovations as a graphite body, stepped ridges instead of a conventional fretted neck, and a digital LED readout. Despite interest in the innovations and feel of the guitar, production lagged and the retail cost climbed. The company eventually closed in 1986, despite considerable financial investment and endorsements by The Edge (U2's guitarist). Production amounts are limited, understandably (source: Greg Smith).

ELECTRIC

ELECTRAGLIDE - dual cutaway graphite body, synthetic stepped ridges fingerboard with dot inlay, 3+3 headstock, bridge/stop tailpiece, raised pickguard, 3 single coil pickups, 5 pushbutton-type pickup selectors, 3 rocker switches, digital LED preset control, available in Black finish, mfg. 1984-86.

N/A	$1,000	$850	$750	$650	$550	$450

This model was available with an optional vibrato.

BOOGALOO
Instruments currently built in Britain since 1986.

The Boogaloo trademark is used by luthier Frank Lemaux on his original designed high quality solid body guitars (source: Tony Bacon and Paul Day, *The Guru's Guitar Guide*).

BOOGIE BODY
Instruments currently built in Gig Harbor, Washington.

Over twenty years ago, Lynn Ellsworth and Wayne Charvel founded Boogie Body guitars, a two-man company that produced electric guitar bodies of exotic woods. During the 1970s, Boogie Body had an impressive client roster of Eddie Van Halen (the red- and white-striped guitars), The Who, and Steppenwolf. Ellsworth closed Boogie Body in 1982, but reopened the company later in Gig Harbor, Washington.

Ellsworth recently developed the 2TEK bridge, an innovative through-body bridge system that improves the overall sound of guitars and basses. Boogie Body/VVT Technologies is also building Speedster hand-crafted amplifiers, an innovative design that features front panel control over the tube amp's biasing. In addition to the Mayan Gold series basses, Boogie Body also offers the BC-1 guitar model.

The current **Mayan Gold Series** basses feature an offset cocobola body design with lengthened bass horn. Designed by Bishop Cochran, these handcrafted instruments feature a deep cutaway on the upper bout to provide full access to all 24 frets. Other features include a six-bolt aluminum plate joining the neck to the body with machine screws and threaded brass inserts, EMG or Seymour Duncan pickups, and a 2TEK bridge. The **BC-1** bass has a list price of $1,995, the **BC-20** bass retails at $1,695, and the **BC Standard** bass retails at $1,495.

BORJES, RALF
Instruments currently built in Bad Zwischenahn, Germany. Distributed by Dacapo Musik of Bad Zwischenahn, Germany, and Ralf Schulte of Palm Beach, Florida.

Designer Ralf Borjes offers three guitar and three bass models, as well as Dacapo Basstronic on-board preamp/EQs and other bass-related electronics. All instruments are very good quality, and have transparent finishes.

ELECTRIC

Borjes' **Hunter** model has a superstrat body, 2 Seymour Duncan humbuckers, special 5-way switch, 24-fret neck, double locking Floyd Rose bridge, and 6-on-a-side tuners. The **ST-Maniac** features a strat-styled body, 3 Seymour Duncan single coils or 2 singles/1 humbucker, vintage tremolo or locking Floyd Rose, and 22-fret neck. The third design, the T-Master, is a tele-shaped guitar with 2 Seymour Duncan or Joe Barden single coils, fixed bridge, and 22-fret neck. Retail prices start at $1,995.

ELECTRIC BASS

The JB-Custom bass has a Jazz-style alder (or alder with maple top) body, bolt-on maple neck, 21-fret rosewood or maple fingerboard, 2 Kent Armstrong single coil or humbucker pickups, and is available in 4- and 5-string configurations. Borjes' Groover model features an original body design with extended bass horn and narrow waist in cherry or flamed maple, bolt-on 3-piece maple neck, 24-fret ebony fingerboard, 2 Kent Armstrong soapbar pickups with single coil switch, and can be had in a 4-, 5-, or 6-string configuration. Basses in 4-string configuration have a 34 in. scale, while the 5- and 6-string models have a 36 in. scale. Retail prices start at $2,100.

GRADING	100% MINT	98% NEAR MINT	95% EXC+	90% EXC	80% VG+	70% VG	60% G

BORN TO ROCK
Instruments currently built in New York, NY.

Designer Robert Kunstadt came up with a new way to answer the age-old problem of neck warpage by redesigning the nature of the neck/body/headstock interface, and by building the resulting innovative design out of aluminum tubing. The hollow aluminum tubing adds a new dimension to the instrument's sustain, and the neck joint assures that the neck will always line up straight with the strings. Both the 6-string guitar (Model F4c) and 4-string bass (Model F4b) carry a new retail price of $3,380 each. T-shirts and guitar picks are also available!

BORYS
Instruments currently built in Burlington, VT beginning in the mid-1970s.

Luthier Roger Borys began guitar repair work in the early 1970s, and completed building his first guitar in 1976. Borys has concentrated on building versatile, high quality instruments designed for the jazz guitarist. In 1980, Borys united with James D'Aquisto and musician Barry Galbraith to design the BG 100 Jazz electric. This instrument, later labeled the **Model B 120**, was co-built between Borys and Chip Wilson. Other instruments have included the **B 222 Jazz Solid**, which has a solid jazz voice, but can be used in playing other forms of music. Used guitars by Borys should be valued individually, because each guitar has its own features and options.

BOSS AXE
Instruments previously produced in Japan.

Boss Axe instruments are built in Japan by the Shimokura company. The U.S. distributor is unknown and we are unsure if there ever was one.

BOSSA
Instruments previously built in Japan. Previously distributed by Soniq Trading, Inc. of North Hollywood, CA.

Luthier Toshio Setozaki hand crafts exquisite looking and sounding basses and guitars.

ELECTRIC: OG SERIES

OG models are available in Natural Hand Rubbed Oil, Walnut Hand Rubbed Oil, Trans. Black, Trans. Blue, Trans. Red, Trans. Violet, Honey Sunburst, Turquoise Sunburst, 2-Tone Sunburst, and Snow White finishes.

Add $200 for Spalted maple top/Honduras mahogany back.

OG-1 JAY GRAYDON SIGNATURE - offset double cutaway asymmetrical Honduras mahogany body, quilted maple top, 24.75 in. scale, hardrock maple neck, 24-fret ebony (or maple) fingerboard with pearl dot inlays, 6-on-a-side Gotoh tuners, Floyd Rose locking tremolo, chrome hardware, 2 Bossa/Jay Graydon custom Dimarzio humbuckers, master volume/master tone controls, 3-way pickup selector switch, 2 coil tap switches, mfg. 1996-disc.

$2,000	$1,700	$1,450	$1,250	$1,000	$800	$600

Last MSR was $2,550.

This model was designed in conjunction with guitarist Jay Graydon. This model comes standard with a hardshell case.

OG-2 JAY GRAYDON STANDARD - similar to the OG-1 Jay Graydon, except features a light ash body, mfg. 1996-disc.

$1,500	$1,250	$1,050	$900	$750	$600	$500

Last MSR was $2,000.

OG-3 - offset double cutaway contoured body, 25.5 in. scale, hardrock maple neck, 22-fret ebony (or maple) fingerboards with pearl dot inlay, Wilkinson VS-100 tremolo by Gotoh, 6-on-a-side Gotoh tuners, logo peghead decal, chrome hardware, 2 Bossa custom Dimarzio humbucker pickups, 1 Bossa custom single coil, master volume/master tone controls, 3-position pickup selector switch, coil tap switches, center single coil on/off switch, mfg. 1997-disc.

$1,400	$1,200	$1,050	$900	$750	$625	$500

Last MSR was $1,950.

OG-3 Mahogany Body And Quilted Maple Top - disc.

$1,700	$1,400	$1,200	$1,050	$900	$750	$600

Last MSR was $2,350.

OG-5 - similar to the OG-3, except features a quilted maple top, Honduras mahogany body, stop tailpiece, mfg. 1998-disc.

$1,950	$1,600	$1,400	$1,200	$1,000	$800	$600

Last MSR was $2,550.

This model comes standard with a hardshell case.

ELECTRIC BASS: PRICING OPTIONS

Bossa basses are available in Natural Hand Rubbed Oil, Walnut Hand Rubbed Oil, Transparent Black, Transparent Blue, Transparent Red, Transparent Violet, Honey Sunburst, Turquoise Sunburst, 2-Tone Sunburst, and Snow White finishes (Antique White was offered on the OB series until 1995). Pau Ferro fingerboards were offered on both bass models until 1998.

OB and **OBJ** models have an optional on-board 18-volt active circuit, C.A.T. (Convertible Action Tremolo) system, and black or gold hardware.

Add $40 for a clear pickguard. Add $80 for quilted maple wood Pickup Fence (string cover). Add $100 for fretless fingerboard. Add $400 for 4-string custom C.A.T. tremolo bridge. Add $500 for 5-string custom C.A.T. tremolo bridge. Add $600 for 6-string custom C.A.T. tremolo bridge. Add 20% for left-handed configuration.

ELECTRIC BASS: OB SERIES

Add $50 for Coil Tap Balancer Switch. Add $200 for solid walnut body. Add $500 for Quilted maple top/Light ash back body.

GRADING	100% MINT	98% NEAR MINT	95% EXC+	90% EXC	80% VG+	70% VG	60% G

OB-4 - offset double cutaway asymmetrical solid Light ash body, 3-piece hardrock maple neck, 34 in. scale, 25-fret Maple (or ebony) fingerboards with pearl dot inlay, fixed bridge, 2-per-side Gotoh tuners, logo peghead decal, chrome hardware, 2 humbucker pickups, volume/pickup balance controls, treble/mid/bass EQ controls, disc.

	$1,500	$1,250	$1,050	$900	$750	$600	$500

Last MSR was $2,000.

OB-5 - similar to the OB-4, except features 5-string configuration, 3/2-per-side tuners, disc.

	$1,700	$1,400	$1,200	$1,000	$850	$700	$575

Last MSR was $2,300.

OB-6 - similar to the OB-4, except features 6-string configuration, 3-per-side tuners, disc.

	$1,900	$1,550	$1,300	$1,100	$950	$800	$650

Last MSR was $2,600.

ELECTRIC BASS: OBJ SERIES

Add $200 for solid walnut body. Add $500 for Quilted maple top/light ash back body.

OBJ-4 - offset double cutaway solid Light ash contoured body, 3-piece hardrock maple neck, 34 in. scale, 24-fret Maple (or ebony) fingerboards with pearl dot inlay, fixed bridge, 2-per-side Gotoh tuners, logo peghead decal, chrome hardware, 2 humbucker pickups, volume/pickup balance controls, coil tap balancer switch, treble/mid/bass EQ controls, mfg. 1997-disc.

	$1,600	$1,350	$1,150	$1,000	$850	$700	$550

Last MSR was $2,100.

OBJ-5 - similar to the OBJ-4, except features 5-string configuration, 3/2-per-side tuners, disc.

	$1,800	$1,500	$1,250	$1,050	$900	$750	$600

Last MSR was $2,400.

OBJ-6 - similar to the OBJ-4, except features 6-string configuration, 3-per-side tuners, disc.

	$2,000	$1,650	$1,350	$1,100	$950	$800	$650

Last MSR was $2,700.

BOUVIER

Instruments previously built in Ocean Gate, New Jersey.

Dennis Bouvier Bourke, a professional guitarist and recording studio owner, debuted a new guitar design in 1997 that mates a mahogany body with a DuPont Corian top as a way to deliver a consistent, rich sound. The DuPont Corian is available in over sixty colors, and is guaranteed to never fade or discolor.

The **Bouvier Guitar - Revolution #1** is available in 2 models. The **Custom** (last MSR $1,600 to $2,000) features a choice mahogany body, .25 in. Corian top, maple neck, maple or rosewood fingerboard, .5 in. Corian forearm rest, 2 humbucker pickups, and chrome (or black or gold) hardware. The **Deluxe** (last MSR $1,900 to $2,500) is similar in design, but features 2 soapbar P-90 pickups, Bigsby tremolo, Schaller roller saddle, and vintage-style locking tuners. Both models' retail price varies according to choices of Corian color, pickups, and hardware.

Bouvier also offers the **Coritone** electric bass, designed by Michael Tobias. Construction details are similar to the guitar models, and also feature passive P/J-style pickups. The last MSR was from $1,600 to $2,000.

BOWN, RALPH S.

Instruments currently built in Walmgate, England.

This independent luthier is currently building high quality guitars. Bown used to be located in York, England. He produces guitars and other instruments such as harp guitars.

BOY LONDON

Instruments currently produced. On You Co., Ltd., is the exclusive agent located in Osaka, Japan.

The Boy London trademark was introduced in 1976. Boy London guitars include both acoustic, acoustic electric, and electric guitars and basses. There are a wide variety of configurations, styles, colors, and features. Boy London also includes a line of amplifiers. It is unknown if they are available in the U.S.

BRADFORD

See chapter on House Brands.

This trademark has been identified as a House Brand of the W.T. Grant company, one of the old style Five and Dime retail stores. W. T. Grant offered the Bradford trademarked guitars during the mid-1960s. Many of the instruments have been identified as produced by Guyatone in Japan. Bradford models ranged from flattop acoustics to thinline hollowbody and solidbody electric guitars and basses (source: Michael Wright, *Vintage Guitar Magazine*). Used prices on these guitars are typically between $100 and $200 for guitars in excellent condition.

BRADLEY

Instruments previously produced in Japan.

The American distributor for this trademark was Veneman Music of Bethesda, Maryland (source: Michael Wright, *Guitar Stories*, Vol. 1).

BRANDONI

Instruments currently produced in Wembley, England.

Roberto Brandoni was born and raised in Castelfidardo, Italy's premier musical instrument production area. By age six, he was already helping out in his father's accordion factory. In 1972, Brandoni resettled in England and has become part of the British music industry. After working for UK distributor Dallas-Arbiter, Brandoni started his own firm specializing in music-related accessories like Quik-Lok stands and cases.

Brandoni became involved in guitar production after buying out leftover Vox and Hayman spare parts. Setting up workshops in Wembley, he produced and customized a number of instruments over the years (such as Graffiti of London). In 1987, Brandoni acquired the remaining inventory of EKO parts after the company closed down. Brandoni also purchased the contents of the Welson factory (another leading Italian guitar builder). Brandoni is currently offering guitars built of parts from decommissioned EKO, Vox, and Welson factories. Models and parts can come from bodies, necks, bridges, tailpieces, pickups, accessories, and strings. All prices, as well as more information on the parts, are listed on their website (see Trademark Index).

BRAWLEY

Instruments currently produced both in the U.S.A. and overseas.

Brawley guitars offers a wide range of solid body guitars and basses. For more information, contact the company directly (see Trademark Index).

BRIAN EASTWOOD GUITARS

Instruments currently built in England.

Brian Eastwood has been making guitars since childhood. He builds, repairs and restores all types of electric and acoustic guitars. Custom instruments made to individual specifications are a specialty. Standard models include the Distortorcaster, Jellycaster, Burnt Marvel, and Collision Bass. Brian's "Blue Moon" is featured in Tony Bacon's, *The Ultimate Guitar Book,* and is possibly the most photographed guitar in the world. Brian's latest model is the Rocket, which features a standard 6-string neck, mandolin neck, single bass string, and a detachable electric violin. His creations are something that words cannot describe, and need to be seen to be appreciated. Check out his website for more information and pictures (see Trademark Index).

BRIAN MOORE CUSTOM GUITARS

Instruments produced in Brewster, NY since 1994. Distributed by Brian Moore Custom Guitars of Brewster, NY.

Pat Cummings and Brian Moore teamed up with Kevin Kalagher in 1992 to begin prototype designs on the MC/1. Both Cummings and Moore had prior experience in producing guitars for another company, but elected to stay in New York when their division was moved south by headquarters. Moore designed the composite body shapes and incorporated the tonewood tops while Cummings arranged the electronics and pickup configurations. After testing seven prototypes, the MC (Moore/Cummings) 1 debuted in 1993.

After continued success both in the U.S. and Japan, the company expanded the product line with the **C Series**. Designed similar to the MC/1, the different models featured all wood bodies and bolt-on necks. The MC/1 was also offered with elaborate fretboard inlays (the Art Guitars), or with built-in MIDI equipment.

Brian Moore Art Guitars feature custom inlay work, and this is available on any of the models (call for details). Brian Moore guitars are available with an installed MIDI system. The RMC MIDI Ready System is currently the featured product, and is compatible with all 13-pin guitar synthesizer inputs. The RMC system uses piezo saddles as the MIDI pickup, and all hardware and electronics are mounted internally. As a result, there are full blending capabilities between MIDI, piezo pickups, and magnetic pickups.

TRANSITIONAL MODELS

Brian Moore Custom guitars briefly produced a number of models that lead to the expansion of the C Series guitars. These transition models are referred to in the catalogs, but not widely produced:

The **C-50** had a contoured alder body, bolt-on maple neck, Wilkinson tremolo, and 2 Seymour Duncan humbuckers. The suggested retail price was $1,695 ($1,850 with additional piezo bridge pickup).

The **C-70** model was similar in construction, but featured a swamp ash body and 2 single coil/1 humbucker Seymour Duncan pickups. Announced retail list price was $1,995, or $2,150 with the optional piezo bridge. Again, these were transition models only, and they are not listed only to avoid any confusion with older catalogs. In 1997, Brian Moore Custom Guitars offered a pair of models in the **C Series** that were the entry level models to the entire product line (these models were discontinued in 1998):

The **C-10** model featured the Brian Moore-style offset double cutaway contoured basswood body, a bolt-on maple neck, a 22-fret rosewood fingerboard with pearl dot inlays, Wilkinson standard vibrato, chrome hardware, 2 Duncan Design humbucker pickups, volume/tone controls, and a 3-way selector switch. C-10 models were available in solid color finishes. The listed retail price was $795, and the **C-10 P** model with the additional piezo bridge pickup was $1,045.

The **C-30** model was similar to the C-10, except featured an ash body, 2 Duncan Design single coils/1 Duncan Design humbucker pickups, volume/tone controls, and 5-way selector switch. The C-30 was available in transparent finishes. The suggested retail list price was $995 (the **C-30 P** model had an additional piezo bridge pickup, and a retail price of $1,245).

CUSTOM SHOP MODELS

The Brian Moore Custom Shop offers some very high-quality guitars with almost endless options. At Brian Moore they can specially coustom design any guitar and turn it into a piece of art. For custom designed inlay work, refer to the company to see what they can create for you. Brian Moore also offers a Mandolin from the custom shop with an available 13-pin synth.

The Brian Moore Custom Shop consists of The C Series, which is the entrance line, if you can call it that, to the Custom Shop. The DC/1 Series is a step up from that and the MC/1 series goes way above and beyond that.

ELECTRIC: C SERIES

In 1996, the company offered variations in the C-series design, but with solid wood bodies and no synthetic backs. The C- series originally offered different pickup configurations and tonewood tops. Every model is available as a left-handed configuration. The price includes a hardshell case.

C-55 - offset double cutaway contoured mahogany body, figured maple top, bolt-on maple neck, 25.5 in. scale, 22-fret rosewood fingerboard with pearl dot inlays, 2/4-per-side sculpted headstock with Sperzel tuners, Wilkinson standard vibrato, chrome hardware, 2 Seymour Duncan humbucker pickups, volume/tone controls, 5-way selector switch, available in Transparent colors and Sunburst finishes, mfg. 1997-2002.

$1,400	$1,200	$1,050	$925	$800	$700	$575

Last MSR was $1,895.

GRADING	100% MINT	98% NEAR MINT	95% EXC+	90% EXC	80% VG+	70% VG	60% G

C-55 P - similar to the C-55, except features an additional piezo bridge pickup, mfg. 1997-2002.

		$1,600	$1,400	$1,250	$1,100	$975	$850	$700

Last MSR was $2,145.

C-90 - offset double cutaway contoured mahogany body, figured maple top, bolt-on figured maple neck, 25.5 in. scale, 22-fret rosewood fingerboard with pearl dot inlays, 2/4-per-side sculpted headstock with Sperzel tuners, Wilkinson standard vibrato, gold hardware, Seymour Duncan humbucker/single coil/humbucker pickups, volume/tone controls, 5-way selector switch. Available in Blue, Gray, Green, Natural, Purple, Red, or Yellow Trans. finish, and Sunburst-style finish, mfg. 1996-present.

MSR $3,395		$2,550	$2,200	$2,000	$1,800	$1,500	$1,200	$950

Add $100 for Tone Pros-Tunamatic Bridge (Suffix T). Add $150 for fixed bridge (Model C-90FB).

This model was briefly offered with a swamp ash body/figured maple top. All the C-90 models are available with a fixed bridge at the same cost as the Wilkinson Vibrato.

**Brian Moore C-90
Courtesy Brian Moore
Custom Guitars**

C-90F - similar to the C-90 except has a Floyd Rose-Original tremolo system, current mfg.

MSR $3,595		$2,700	$2,300	$2,100	$1,850	$1,550	$1,250	$1,025

C-90P - similar to the C-90, except features an additional piezo bridge pickup, mfg. 1997-present.

MSR $3,695		$2,775	$2,350	$2,150	$1,900	$1,600	$1,300	$1,000

Add $100 for Tone Pros-Tunamatic Bridge (Suffix T). Add $150 for fixed bridge (Model C-90PFB).

C-90P-13 - similar to the C-90P excet has a 13 Pin synth output, current mfg.

MSR $4,295		$3,225	$2,900	$2,600	$2,300	$1,950	$1,600	$1,250

Add $100 for Tone Pros-Tunamatic Bridge (Suffix T). Add $150 for fixed bridge (Model C-90P-13FB).

C-907 - similar to the C-90 except is in 7-string configuration, current mfg.

MSR $3,895		$2,925	$2,600	$2,300	$2,000	$1,700	$1,400	$1,100

C-907P - similar to the C-907 except has an RMC Piezo pickup, current mfg.

MSR $4,295		$3,250	$2,850	$2,450	$2,100	N/A	N/A	N/A

ELECTRIC: DC/1 SERIES

The DC/1 model was a joint design with luthier/sound engineer Tom Doyle and Patrick Cummings (DC = Doyle/Cummings).

DC/1 - single cutaway contoured mahogany body, figured maple top, set-in mahogany neck, 24.75 in. scale, 22-fret bound rosewood fingerboard with pearl dot inlays, 2/4-per-side sculpted headstock with Sperzel tuners, tune-o-matic bridge/stop tailpiece, gold hardware, 2 Seymour Duncan Seth Lover model humbucker pickups, volume/tone controls, 3-way selector switch, available in Blue, Gray, Green, Natural, Purple, Red, or Yellow Trans. finish, or Sunburst-style finish, mfg. 1997-present.

MSR $3,995		$3,000	$2,700	$2,400	$2,000	N/A	N/A	N/A

This model is available with the T.W. Doyle pickup system.

DC/1P - similar to the DC/1, except features an additional piezo bridge pickup, mfg. 1998-present.

MSR $4,295		$3,250	$2,850	$2,500	$2,100	N/A	N/A	N/A

DC/1P-13 - similar to the DC/1P except has a 13-pin synth onboard, current mfg.

MSR $4,895		$3,700	$3,300	$3,000	$2,500	N/A	N/A	N/A

ELECTRIC: MC/1 SERIES

MC/1 guitars feature an offset double cutaway body and neck of one solid piece of composite material, and a variety of figured wood tops with natural binding. Various pickup and electronic configurations are optionally offered along with choice of hardware. These guitars are available as a Special Limited Edition. Only 12 MC series instruments are produced a year. Visit the website for more information.

MC/1 - offset double cutaway neck-through contoured composite body, arched figured maple top with wood binding, 25.5 in. scale, 24-fret ebony or rosewood fingerboard with pearl dot inlays, chrome or gold hardware, 2/4-per-side sculpted headstock, Wilkinson or Floyd Rose tremolo, 2 humbucking pickups, volume/tone controls, custom 5-way pickup selector switch, mfg. 1993-present.

MSR $7,995		$6,000	N/A	N/A	N/A	N/A	N/A	N/A

MC/1 P - similar to the MC/1, except features an additional piezo bridge pickup, mfg. 1998-present.

MSR $8,295		$6,300	N/A	N/A	N/A	N/A	N/A	N/A

MC/1 P-13 - similar to the MC/1P, except features an onboard 13-pin synth, mfg. 1998-present.

MSR $8,995		$6,750	N/A	N/A	N/A	N/A	N/A	N/A

ELECTRIC: iGUITAR SERIES: OVERVIEW

What does the "i" stand for in the iGuitar series? Brian Moore Guitars offers such phrases as imagination, inspiration and innovation. Essentially, the "i" stands for fun, as in the possiblities that Brain Moore Guitars offers. The iGuitar features the 13-pin output, which allows the guitarist to plug the guitar into a number of mediums, including digital applications, mixers, and other 13-point sound devices.

**Brian Moore DC1 P13
Courtesy Brian Moore
Custom Guitars**

GRADING	100% MINT	98% NEAR MINT	95% EXC+	90% EXC	80% VG+	70% VG	60% G

ELECTRIC: iGUITAR & i2000 SERIES

The iGuitar and i2000 Series are the same except for the 13-pin RMC system for electronic systems. These series are listed together because they are the same except for the addition of the electronics. The iGuitar includes the 13-pin system and is indicated by the suffix, "-13". EMG pickups were available on the i2 and i8 models for a short while between 2002-03. These command a slight premium.

i1 - double sharp cutaway, contoured Kalantas Mahogany body and neck, highly figured maple top, matching maple headstock with 2/4-per-side tuners, 22-fret rosewood fingerboard, Ivoroid binding, 25.5 in. scale, 3 Seymour Duncan pickups (two humbucker, one single), coil tapping, volume and tone knobs, five-way switch, standard vibrato, gold hardware, available in Cherry Sunburst, Emerald Green, or Natural finish, current mfg.

MSR $1,795	$1,350	$1,200	$1,050	$900	$750	$625	$525

i1f - similar to the i1 except has a Floyd Rose Tremolo with locking nut, and 24-fret fingerboard, available in Trans. Red, Vintage Sunburst, or Trans. Purple finish, current mfg.

MSR $1,795	$1,350	$1,200	$1,050	$900	$750	$625	$525

i1p - similar to the i1 except the vibrato has an RMC piezo pickup, added knob, same finishes as the i1, current mfg.

MSR $2,095	$1,575	$1,350	$1,150	$1,000	$850	$750	$650

iGuitar1p-13 - similar to the i1 except has 13-pin RMC system onboard electronics, available in Vintage Yellow, Charcoal Gray, or Cherry Sunburst finishes, current mfg.

MSR $2,195	$1,650	$1,450	$1,250	$1,100	$950	$800	$675

i2 - single sharp cutaway, contoured Kalantas Mahogany body and bolt-on neck, highly figured maple top, matching figured maple headstock with 2/4-per-side-tuners, 22 fret rosewood fingerboard, Ivoroid binding, 24.75 in. scale, 2 gold covered Seymour Duncan humbucking pickups, coil tapping, volume and tone knobs, pickup switch, tunomatic bridge, gold hardware, available in Cherry Sunburst, Tobacco Sunburst, or Natural finish, current mfg.

MSR $1,695	$1,275	$1,125	$1,000	$875	$750	$650	$550

i2p - similar to the i2 except has the vibrato has an RMC piezo pickup, added knob, current mfg.

MSR $1,995	$1,500	$1,300	$1,150	$1,000	$900	$750	$625

iGuitar2p-13 - similar to the i2 except has 13-pin RMC system onboard electronics, current mfg.

MSR $2,095	$1,575	$1,350	$1,150	$1,000	$875	$750	$650

i8 - double sharp cutaway, Kalantas Mahogany body, highly figured maple top, unique sculpted headstock with 2/4-per-side-tuners, maple bolt-on neck, 22-fret rosewood fingerboard, 25.5 in. scale, 2 Seymour Duncan humbucking pickups, coil tapping, volume and tone knobs, pickup switch, fixed bridge, chrome hardware, available in Vintage Sunburst, Transparent Red, or Natural finish, current mfg.

MSR $1,295	$975	$875	$775	$700	$600	$500	$400

i8p - similar to the i8 except has a fixed bridge RMC piezo pickup, available in Tobacco Sunburst, Cherry Sunburst, or Natural, current mfg.

MSR $1,595	$1,200	$1,075	$975	$875	$750	$625	$500

iGuitar8p-13 - similar to the i8 except has 13-pin RMC system onboard electronics, two added knobs and switches, available in Vintage Sunburst, Transparent, or Natural finish, current mfg.

MSR $1,795	$1,350	$1,200	$1,050	$900	$750	$625	$500

i9 - double sharp cutaway, contoured Kalantas Mahogany body, highly figured maple top, unique sculpted headstock with 2/4-per-side-tuners, bolt-on maple neck, 22-fret rosewood fingerboard, Ivoroid binding, 25.5 in. scale, 3 Seymour Duncan pickups (two humbucker, one single), coil tapping, volume and tone knobs, five-way switch, standard vibrato, gold hardware, available in Chocolate, Vintage Yellow, or Tobacco Sunburst finish, current mfg.

MSR $1,495	$1,150	$1,025	$900	$775	$650	$550	$450

i9f - similar to the i9 except has a Floyd Rose Tremolo with locking nut, and 24-fret fingerboard on a 3-piece maple neck, chrome hardware, available in Trans. Red, Charcoal Gray, or Trans. Blue finishes, current mfg.

MSR $1,495	$1,150	$1,025	$900	$775	$650	$550	$450

i9p - similar to the i9 except the vibrato has an RMC piezo pickup, added knob, available in Tobacco Sunburst, Natural, or Cherry Sunburst finish, current mfg.

MSR $1,795	$1,350	$1,200	$1,050	$900	$750	$625	$500

iGuitar9p-13 - similar to the i9 except has 13-pin RMC system onboard electronics, two added knobs and switches, available in Trans. Blue, Charcoal Gray, or Emerald Green finish, current mfg.

MSR $1,895	$1,425	$1,250	$1,100	$950	$800	$700	$600

i9-7 - similar to the i9 except is in 7-string configuration, available in Vintage Yellow, Charcoal Gray, or Trans. Purple finish, disc. 2003.

	$900	$800	$725	$650	$575	$500	$425

Last MSR was $1,195.

ELECTRIC: i1000 SERIES

The i1000 series is similar to the other Brian Moore guitars in applications, but they are offered at a competitive price. All guitars come with a gig bag.

i21 - single sharp cutaway, contoured mahogany body, figured and bookmatched maple top, 3-piece mahognay set neck, 22-fret rosewood fingerboard with pearl dot inlays, unique sculpted headstock with 2/4-per-side-tuners, 24.75 in. scale, Ivoroid binding, two covered Classic "iM" Alnico humbucking pickups, volume and tone knobs, pickup switch, tunomatic bridge, rear output jack, chrome hardware, available in Charcoal Gray, Cinnamon, Emerald Green, Natural, Purple, or Turquoise finishes, current mfg.

MSR $795	$600	$525	$475	$400	$325	$250	$175

i21-13 - similar to the i21 except has 13-pin RMC system synth electronics, two added knobs and switches, current mfg.

MSR $1,195	$900	$800	$725	$650	$575	$500	$425

GRADING	100% MINT	98% NEAR MINT	95% EXC+	90% EXC	80% VG+	70% VG	60% G

i81 - double sharp cutaway, contoured mahogany body, mahognay bolt-on neck, figured and bookmatched maple top, 22-fret rosewood fingerboard with pearl dot inlays, unique sculpted headstock with 2/4-per-side-tuners, 25.5 in. scale, Ivoroid binding, two Classic "iM" Alnico humbucking pickups, volume and tone knobs, pickup switch, fixed bridge, chrome hardware, available in Charcoal Gray, Cinnamon, Emerald Green, Natural, Purple, or Turquoise finish, current mfg.

MSR $595	$450	$375	$325	$275	$235	$190	$150

i81-13 - similar to the i81 except has 13-pin RMC system synth electronics, two added knobs and switches, current mfg.

MSR $995	$750	$675	$625	$575	$500	$425	$350

i91 - double sharp cutaway, contoured mahogany body, mahognay bolt-on neck, figured and bookmatched maple top, 22-fret rosewood fingerboard with pearl dot inlays, unique sculpted headstock with 2/4-per-side-tuners, 25.5 in. scale, Ivoroid binding, two Classic "iM" Alnico humbucker and one single coil pickups, volume and tone knobs, pickup switch, standard vibrato, chrome hardware, available in Charcoal Gray, Cinnamon, Emerald Green, Natural, Purple, or Turquoise finish, current mfg.

MSR $695	$525	$450	$400	$350	$300	$250	$200

i91-13 - similar to the i91 except has 13-pin RMC system synth electronics, two added knobs and switches, current mfg.

MSR $1,095	$825	$750	$675	$600	$525	$450	$375

ELECTRIC BASS: TC SERIES

Brian Moore makes two different bass configurations, a four-string and a five-string. The current series is the i2000 application, and the older models are in the TC Series.

Brian Moore TC Bass models are a joint design with Michael Tobias (MTD/Michael Tobias Design) and Patrick Cummings. All TC Series bass models are optionally available with a piezo bridge pickup system.

TC/4 - offset double cutaway contoured swamp ash body, bolt-on maple neck, 34 in. scale, 21-fret rosewood fingerboard with pearl dot inlays, 1/3 per side sculpted headstock with Sperzel tuners, Wilkinson bridge, gold or chrome hardware, Seymour Duncan Bassline passive pickups, volume/blend/tone controls, available in Transparent colors and Sunburst-style finish, mfg. 1997-2002.

$1,500	$1,300	$1,150	$1,000	$875	$700	$575

Last MSR was $1,995.

This model is available with Bartolini pickups.

TC/4+ - similar to the TC/4, except features highly figured wood top and Seymour Duncan Bassline active electronics, mfg. 1997-2002.

$1,850	$1,625	$1,450	$1,250	$1,100	$950	$800

Last MSR was $2,495.

TC/5 - offset double cutaway contoured swamp ash body, bolt-on maple neck, 34 in. scale, 21-fret rosewood fingerboard with pearl dot inlays, 2/3-per-side sculpted headstock with Sperzel tuners, Wilkinson bridge, gold or chrome hardware, Seymour Duncan Bassline passive pickups, volume/blend/tone controls, available in Transparent colors and Sunburst-style finish, mfg. 1997-2002.

$1,650	$1,450	$1,250	$1,100	$950	$800	$650

Last MSR was $2,195.

This model is available with Bartolini pickups.

TC/5+ - similar to the TC/5, except features highly figured wood top and Seymour Duncan Bassline active electronics, mfg. 1997-2002.

$2,000	$1,750	$1,550	$1,350	$1,150	$1,000	$850

Last MSR was $2,695.

ELECTRIC BASS: i2000 SERIES

i4 - double offset sharp cutaway, contoured ash body, highly figured maple top with matching headstock, three-piece maple/padouk/maple neck-thru body, 24-fret rosewood fingerboard, 34 in. scale, two black soapbar pickups, five knobs, slap switch, active electronics, standard bridge, gold hardware, available in Tobacco Sunburst, Cherry Sunburst or Natural finish, current mfg.

MSR $1,495	$1,150	$1,025	$900	$775	$650	$550	$450

i4P - similar to the i4 bass except has a piezo pickup in the bridge, current mfg.

MSR $1,895	$1,425	$1,250	$1,100	$950	$800	$700	$600

i4-f - similar to the i4 bass except is in fretless configuration, current mfg.

MSR $1,695	$1,275	$1,125	$1,000	$900	$775	$650	$525

i4p-f - similar to the i4 bass except is in fretless configuration and has a piezo pickup in the bridge, current mfg.

MSR $1,895	$1,425	$1,250	$1,100	$950	$800	$675	$550

i4B - similar to the i4 bass except has Bartolini active electronics, mfg. 2002-present.

MSR $1,695	$1,275	$1,100	$950	$800	$675	$600	$500

i4Bp - similar to the i4 bass except has Bartolini active electronics and piezo pickup in the bridge, mfg. 2002-present.

MSR $2,195	$1,650	$1,350	$1,200	$1,050	$900	$750	$625

Brian Moore i1
Courtesy Brian Moore
Custom Guitars

Brian Moore iGuitar2p-13
courtesy Rich Gasciato

GRADING	100% MINT	98% NEAR MINT	95% EXC+	90% EXC	80% VG+	70% VG	60% G

i4B-f - similar to the i4 bass except is in fretless configuraiton, and has Bartolini active electronics, mfg. 2002-present.

| MSR $2,095 | $1,575 | $1,300 | $1,150 | $1,000 | $850 | $725 | $600 |

i4Bp-f - similar to the i4 bass except is in fretless configuration, has Bartolini active electronics, and a piezo pickup in the bridge, mfg. 2002-present.

| MSR $2,395 | $1,800 | $1,450 | $1,250 | $1,100 | $950 | $825 | $700 |

i4-13 - similar to the i4 bass except has 13-pin system syntch onboard, Bartolini active electronics, and a piezo pickup in the bridge, mfg. 2002-present.

| MSR $2,495 | $1,875 | $1,500 | $1,300 | $1,150 | $1,000 | $850 | $750 |

i5 - Double offset sharp cutaway, 5-string configuration, contoured ash body, highly figured maple top with matching headstock, three piece maple/padouk/maple neck-thru body, 24-fret rosewood fingerboard, 34 in. scale, two black soapbar pickups, five knobs, slap switch, active electronics, standard bridge, gold hardware, available in Tobacco Sunburst, Cherry Sunburst or Natural finish, current mfg.

| MSR $1,695 | $1,275 | $1,100 | $950 | $800 | $675 | $600 | $500 |

i5P - similar to the i5 bass except has a piezo pickup in the bridge, current mfg.

| MSR $2,095 | $1,575 | $1,300 | $1,150 | $1,000 | $850 | $725 | $600 |

i5-f - similar to the i5 bass except is in fretless configuration, current mfg.

| MSR $1,895 | $1,425 | $1,200 | $1,050 | $900 | $750 | $650 | $550 |

i5p-f - similar to the i5 bass except is in fretless configuration and has a piezo pickup in the bridge, current mfg.

| MSR $2,295 | $1,725 | $1,400 | $1,200 | $1,050 | $900 | $775 | $650 |

i5B - similar to the i5 bass except has Bartolini active electronics, mfg. 2002-present.

| MSR $2,095 | $1,575 | $1,300 | $1,150 | $1,000 | $850 | $725 | $600 |

i5Bp - similar to the i5 bass except has Bartolini active electronics and piezo pickup in the bridge, mfg. 2002-present.

| MSR $2,395 | $1,800 | $1,450 | $1,250 | $1,100 | $950 | $825 | $700 |

i5B-f - similar to the i5 bass except is in fretless configuraiton, and has Bartolini active electronics, mfg. 2002-present.

| MSR $2,295 | $1,725 | $1,400 | $1,200 | $1,050 | $900 | $775 | $650 |

i5Bp-f - similar to the i5 bass except is in fretless configuration, has Bartolini active electronics, and a piezo pickup in the bridge, mfg. 2002-present.

| MSR $2,595 | $1,950 | $1,600 | $1,350 | $1,150 | $1,000 | $850 | $750 |

i5-13 - similar to the i5 bass except has 13-pin system syntch onboard, Bartolini active electronics, and a piezo pickup in the bridge, mfg. 2002-present.

| MSR $2,695 | $2,025 | $1,650 | $1,400 | $1,200 | $1,050 | $900 | $800 |

BRIDWELL WORKSHOP
Instruments previously produced in Palatine, Illinois.

The Bridwell Workshop built high quality guitars during the 1990s.

BROADWAY
Instruments previously built in Britain, Japan, and West Germany in the early to late 1960s.

The Broadway trademark is the brand name of a UK importer. The solid and semi-hollowbody guitars were of original design, but entry level quality (source: Tony Bacon and Paul Day, *The Guru's Guitar Guide*).

BROCK, A. R.
Instruments previously built in Brooklyn, NY, unknown production date.

An example of an A.R. Brock Harp Guitar surfaced at a Texas Guitar show in 1996. The instrument's only company clue appears on the headstock, and reads "Brooklyn, New York." The guitar was decently built, and sounded okay when plugged into an amp.

BRONSON
See chapter on House Brands.

George Bronson was a guitar teacher in Detroit, MI during the 1930s and 1940s. He specialized in steel guitars and many of the Bronsons are square neck guitars made by the National/Valco company. There are also regular Bronson guitars made by the Harmony company. George ran the "Bronson Music & Sales Company" in the Kerr Building in Detroit, MI, where he sold and distributed sheet music and guitars. There was also a popular model electric lap steel that National/Valco made for Bronson, which was sold under the name "Bronson Singing Electric" (source: Walter Murray).

BRUBAKER
Instruments currently built in Reisterstown, Maryland.

Brubaker has been producing guitars and basses since 1993. While his instruments always featured carved flame or quilt maple tops and innovations such as his smooth sculpted heel, this new line offers colored, figured maple fingerboards, natural bindings, and the best available hardware and electronics. Brubaker instruments have tonal qualities of both a set neck and a bolt-on, thanks to this unique neck-through-bolt-on joint. The neck goes 8 inches into the body (7 inches for the guitar), giving lateral stability and sustain.

Unfortunately, Brubaker suffered a fire in 2003, but they are once again producing guitars. Howeve,r they have relocated from Westminster to Reisterstown. All Brubaker guitars come with a hardshell case included in the price. There are also numerous possible upgrades such as different types of woods, bindings, and hardware. Check with Brubaker for availability and pricing (see Trademark Index).

ELECTRIC

B2 STANDARD - lightweight ash or mahogany body, maple neck and fingerboard, 2 Seymour Duncan humbucking pickups, 1-volume/1 tone, 3-way switch, Hipshot chrome hardtail bridge, chrome Grover tuners, available in Black, White, Seafoam Green, Royal Blue, Platinum and Viper Red finish. Hardshell case included, current mfg.

| MSR $2,600 | $2,600 | $2,400 | $2,100 | $1,800 | N/A | N/A | N/A |

B

GRADING	100% MINT	98% NEAR MINT	95% EXC+	90% EXC	80% VG+	70% VG	60% G

B2 Standard Upgrade - similar to the B2 Standard except has Sperzel locking tuners, coil tap switch, and rosewood fingerboard, available in Translucent Amber, Mahogany Red, Sapphire Blue, Purple/Violet, or Natural finish, current mfg.

MSR $2,900	$2,900	$2,600	$2,300	$1,950	N/A	N/A	N/A

B2 NC CUSTOM - similar to B2 Standard, except has AAAAA Flame Maple Top with matching headstock, maple or mahogany neck with mahogany or ash body, Satin or Gloss finish, maple, Birdseye maple or rosewood fingerboard, chrome Point Technologies Tremolo Bridge, available in Translucent Amber, Cherry Red, Sapphire Blue, Purple/Violet, Black, Emerald Green and Natural finish, current mfg.

MSR $3,900	$3,900	$3,500	$3,200	$2,800	N/A	N/A	N/A

B2 NX XTREME - similar to B2 Custom, except choice of lightweight ash, mahogany, swamp ash or paulownia body material, hard maple neck, available in Custom colors, current mfg.

MSR $8,300	$8,300	N/A	N/A	N/A	N/A	N/A	N/A

K-4 STANDARD - single cutaway, lightweight ash or mahogany body, maple neck and fingerboard, 2 Seymour Duncan Humbucker pickups, Hipshot Chrome fixed bridge, two knobs (v, tone), 3-way switch, chrome hardware, available in black, white, Seafoam Green, Royal Blue, Viper Red, or Platinum finish, current mfg.

MSR $2,600	$2,600	$2,400	$2,100	$1,800	N/A	N/A	N/A

K-4 Standard Upgrade - similar to the K-4 Standard except has Sperzel locking tuners, coil tap switch, and rosewood fingerboard, available in Translucent Amber, Mahogany Red, Sapphire Blue, Purple/Violet, or Natural finish, current mfg.

MSR $2,900	$2,900	$2,600	$2,300	$1,950	N/A	N/A	N/A

K-4 CUSTOM - similar to K4 Standard, except has AAAAA Flame Maple Top with matching headstock, maple or mahogany neck with mahogany or ash body, Satin or Gloss finish, maple, Birdseye maple or rosewood fingerboard, chrome Point Technologies Tremolo Bridge, available in Translucent Amber, Cherry Red, Sapphire Blue, Purple/Violet, Black, Emerald Green and Natural finish, current mfg.

MSR $3,900	$3,900	$3,500	$3,200	$2,800	N/A	N/A	N/A

K-4 XTREME - similar to K4 Custom, except choice of lightweight ash, mahogany, swamp ash or paulownia body material, hard maple neck, available in Custom colors, current mfg.

MSR $8,300	$8,300	N/A	N/A	N/A	N/A	N/A	N/A

Brian Moore i5 Bass
Courtesy Brian Moore
Custom Guitars

ELECTRIC BASS

In the summer of 1996, Brubaker introduced the Bo Axe, a slim-bodied upright bass with 35 in. scale. The Bo Axe mounts to a support stand, and can be played both in an upright stance, and sideways, by re-adjusting the stand. Disc.

K4-B - the K4-B is a bass guitar that has an extended single cutaway with a larger bass bout. This bass is available in all the same configurations that the NBS series are in and they also follow the same pricing. At this point in time you can use the NBS basses to price the K4-B.

LEXA - maple body, purpleheart or padauk with curly maple top, 4-string, bolt-on one-piece hard maple neck with 24-fret fingerboard, passive or active Seymour Duncan pickups, Gotoh tuners, 2TEK bridge, available in Natural, Cherry Red, Scarlett Red, Rose Red, Juniper Green, Forest Green, Sapphire Blue, or Indigo Waterborne finish, mfg. 1996-disc.

	$2,000	$1,750	$1,500	$1,300	$1,150	$1,000	$850

Lexa 5-string

	$2,200	$1,900	$1,650	$1,425	$1,200	$1,050	$900

Lexa 6-string

	$2,400	$2,100	$1,800	$1,600	$1,350	$1,125	$950

NBS 22-FRET STANDARD - Ash body, 4-string, maple neck and fingerboard, single Bartolini Humbucker style pickup or Jazz pickups with a volume and tone control, chrome Hipshot B style bridge, chrome Hipshot tuners, available in Black, White, Seafoam Green, Royal Blue, Platinum or Viper Red finish, current mfg.

MSR $2,990	$2,990	$2,700	$2,400	$2,100	N/A	N/A	N/A

5-string

MSR $3,270	$3,270	$2,950	$2,600	$2,300	N/A	N/A	N/A

6-string

MSR $3,840	$3,840	$3,500	$3,100	$2,700	N/A	N/A	N/A

Add $200 for Standard Upgrade Package consisting of rosewood fingerboard, AAA maple top, 3-band preamp, available in Translucent Amber, Cherry Red, Sapphire Blue, Purple/Violet, Black, Emerald Green or Natural finish.

NBS 24-FRET CUSTOM - similar to NBS 22-fret Standard, except has 24-fret neck, AAAAA flame maple or quilted maple top with matching headstock, hard maple neck, Cocobola or Birdseye Maple fingerboard, Bartolini P25 Soapbar pickups (quadcoil), with NTMB pre-amp, chrome Hipshot A Style bridge and chrome Hipshot tuners, available in Translucent Amber, Cherry Red, Sapphire Blue, Purple/Violet, Black or Emerald Green finish, current mfg.

MSR $3,990	$3,990	$3,550	$3,100	$2,750	N/A	N/A	N/A

5-String

MSR $4,270	$4,270	$3,700	$3,300	$2,950	N/A	N/A	N/A

6-String

MSR $4,840	$4,840	$4,500	$4,100	$3,600	N/A	N/A	N/A

Brubaker K-4 Custom
Courtesy Brubaker

B

NBS 24-FRET XTREME - similar to NBS 24-fret Custom, except has choice of lightweight ash, Swamp ash, alder or Paulownia body and custom colors, current mfg.

MSR $7,100	$7,100	N/A	N/A	N/A	N/A	N/A	N/A

5-String

MSR $7,370	$7,370	N/A	N/A	N/A	N/A	N/A	N/A

6-String

MSR $7,500	$7,500	N/A	N/A	N/A	N/A	N/A	N/A

BUNKER GUITARS

Also Bunker Instruments. Instruments currently built in Sequim, Washington. Distributed by Bunker Guitars, LLC, of Mill Creek, Washington. Guitars were previously built in Tacoma, Washington between circa early 1960s to mid 1960s (Astral Series), 1976 to 1982 (Pro-Line), and in Mill Creek circa late 1990s.

Luthier/designer and musician David Bunker has been building guitars and basses for more than 40 years. In 1955, Bunker built his first doubleneck Touch Guitar with his father, Joe Bunker. This model was named the Duo-Lectar. Bunker later received input from Irby Mandrell (Barbara Mandrell's father) regarding scale length. Bunker was granted his first patent in June of 1961. Bunker and his Touch Guitar was the foundation for *The Dave Bunker Show*, which was very popular in Las Vegas at the Golden Nugget between 1965 and 1974. Bunker also built other guitar models for his fellow performers in the band.

The *Astral Series* models, often described as "radically designed," debuted in the early 1960s. The advertising for Bunker guitars proclaimed them to be "The Guitars of Tomorrow!" Of course, the same advertising also had a favorite catchphrase: "It Looks Like No Other Guitar - Because It Is Like No Other Guitar!" Rather than be different for different's sake, Bunker's Astral Series models were designed to solve certain inherent solid body design flaws. Bunker instruments are completely modular - you can change out any piece (neck or headstock or body or electronics, etc.) rather than repair the guitar, if you so chose. These detachable body and headstock pieces bolted to the center neck/minimalist body. Pickups and bridge hardware were also directly attached to the center frame.

In 1976, Bunker built a small number of Pro-Line models (12, actually). These models are identifiable by their headless (reverse tuning) headstock, upswept lower bout with reverse tuners, and Bunker pickups. Even the cases were custom-made, and built by Case's Inc. of Seattle, Washington.

After the Bunker company, David Bunker was later involved with **PBC Guitar Technology, Inc.** in Pennsylvania, which had noticeable success with the "Tension-Free" neck design and the Wishbone hollowbody series (see **PBC**). PBC was in business from 1989 to 1996, and produced a number of high quality bass and guitar models with innovative ideas.

After PBC closed their doors, Bunker relocated to Mill Creek, Washington. In 1998, Bunker was back to building the same quality PBC-style models, as well as the Through-body Bridges, a new Touch Guitar model, a new full body acoustic model, and Tension Free neck modifications. Bunker and a number of the key employees from PBC will be debuting the "new" Bunker models in the near future, but information and purchasing news is currently available at the company's website. So, for current information regarding the new Bunker instruments, contact Bunker Guitars directly (see Trademark Index), (Bunker model information courtesy Ryland Fitchett of Rockohaulix).

MODEL CONSTRUCTION NOTES

Bunker instruments do have many similar innovative features. The Bunker Split Bridge bypassed the conventional single bridge piece for an individual bridge piece for each string. Each individual bridge was fully adjustable, and separated to prevent electrical or acoustical cross-feed. Bunker's **Magnum** round pickups featured a 1/4" diameter Alnico V magnet with its own vertically wrapped wire coil. Instead of a common coil and magnets/pole pieces, the Magnum was an individual pickup per string. All Bunker models feature the "Floating Neck" design that was later utilized on various PBC and Treker models (as well as some high end Ibanez USA Prestige models).

Bunker instruments are strung in reverse, so tuning keys are on the end of the body similar to the Steinberger bridge. **Nova** and **Supernova** models featured Peg Tuning, in which the string passed through the end of the body and was tuned by tightening a peg with a drum key (similar to autoharp stringing). After the primary tuning was completed, further tuning was accomplished by the Fine Tuner, an additional piece between the bridge and tuning machines that used adjustment screws to deliver a "finer, more precise tuning of strings."

ELECTRIC: PREVIOUS MFG.

All Bunker models were available in Fixed (wings attached) or the optional Snap-On/Quick Change kit that allowed interchangeable wings to be attached to the body. As the catalog pointed out, "This invaluable device permits a performer to have many guitars in one - an advantage loved by the Pros." In addition to Eastern maple and Black Walnut, other Snap-On bodies include Satin Black, Silverflake vinyl, leather bound Blue Denim, Fire (Red and Black swirled) Naugahyde, Earth (Brown with Gold flecks) Naugahyde, and Charcoal (Black with Silver Flecks) Naugahyde.

Optional Body Sets for the guitar models had a new retail price of $85 for **Fabric** (vinyl), $90 for **Wood**, and $110 for **Denim** (leather bound Denim).

HELLBENDER (MODEL HB-25-10) - minimalist neck-through eastern hard maple or black walnut body with 2 attached wings, 25 in. scale, bolt-on neck, 23-fret fingerboard with dot inlay, metal Bunker logo on headstock, 3-per-side tuners on end of body, 6 individual string brass bridge pieces, chrome hardware, 10 round Magnum pickups (in a dual bank), black 'roll' volume control, volume control/tone filter on/off switches, stainless steel controls plate, available in Natural finish, mfg. circa 1960s.

$1,000	$900	$800	$700	$600	$500	$400

Last MSR was $830.

Hellbender (Model HB-25-10-FT) - similar to the Hellbender, except also features the Bunker Fine Tuner adjustable tuning system.

$1,200	$1,050	$900	$800	$700	$600	$500

Last MSR was $860.

Hellbender (Model HB-25-10-CK) - similar to the Hellbender, except features the Quick Change kit for interchangeable bodies.

$1,200	$1,050	$900	$800	$700	$600	$500

Last MSR was $860.

Hellbender (Model HB-25-10-FT-CK) - similar to the Hellbender, except features both the Bunker Fine Tuner and Quick Change kit.

$1,250	$1,100	$950	$825	$700	$600	$500

Last MSR was $810.

B

GRADING	100% MINT	98% NEAR MINT	95% EXC+	90% EXC	80% VG+	70% VG	60% G

NOVA (MODEL N-25-6-FT) - minimalist neck-through eastern hard maple or black walnut body with 2 attached wings, 25 in. scale, bolt-on neck, 23-fret fingerboard with dot inlay, metal Bunker logo on headstock, 6-in-a-row brass Bunker Peg Tuner pegs/Delrin Brake Block/chrome string guard on end of body, 6 individual string brass bridge pieces, Bunker Fine Tuner, chrome hardware, 6 round Magnum pickups, black roll volume control, volume control/tone filter on/off switches, stainless steel controls plate, available in Natural finish, mfg. circa 1960s.

	$950	$850	$750	$650	$550	$450	$350

Last MSR was $720.

Nova (Model N-25-6-FT-CK) - similar to the Nova, except features both the Bunker Fine Tuner and Quick Change kit.

	$1,150	$1,000	$875	$775	$675	$575	$450

Last MSR was $750.

STARDUSTER (MODEL SD-25-6) - similar to the Nova, except features 3-per-side chromed solid brass tuners (in place of the Bunker Peg Tuner pegs, Fine Tuner adjustable tuning system), available in Natural finish, mfg. circa 1960s.

	$1,000	$900	$800	$700	$600	$500	$400

Last MSR was $740.

Starduster (Model SD-25-6-FT) - similar to the Starduster, except also features the Bunker Fine Tuner adjustable tuning system.

	$1,200	$1,050	$900	$800	$700	$600	$500

Last MSR was $780.

Starduster (Model SD-25-6-CK) - similar to the Starduster, except features the Quick Change kit for interchangeable bodies.

	$1,200	$1,050	$900	$800	$700	$600	$500

Last MSR was $770.

Starduster (Model SD-25-6-FT-CK) - similar to the Starduster, except features both the Bunker Fine Tuner and Quick Change kit.

	$1,200	$1,050	$900	$800	$700	$600	$500

Last MSR was $810.

SUPERNOVA (MODEL SN-265-12-FT) - minimalist neck-through eastern hard maple or black walnut body with 2 attached wings, 26.5 in. scale, bolt-on neck, 24-fret fingerboard with dot inlay, metal Bunker logo on headstock, 6 in a row brass Bunker Peg Tuner pegs/Delrin Brake Block/chrome string guard on end of body, 6 individual string brass bridge pieces, Bunker Fine Tuner, chrome hardware, 12 round Magnum pickups (2 banks of 6), black roll volume control, 2 volume control/2-Tone filter on/off/2 pickup on/off switches, hi-lo switch, stainless steel controls plate, available in Natural finish, mfg. circa 1960s.

	$1,200	$1,050	$900	$800	$700	$600	$500

Last MSR was $925.

Supernova (Model SN-265-12-FT-CK) - similar to the Supernova, except features both the Bunker Fine Tuner and Quick Change kit.

	$1,300	$1,150	$1,000	$850	$700	$600	$500

Last MSR was $955.

SUNSTAR (MODEL SS-265-12) - similar to the Supernova, except features 3-per-side tuners (in place of the Bunker Peg Tuner pegs, Fine Tuner adjustable tuning system), available in Natural finish, mfg. circa 1960s.

	$1,100	$950	$850	$750	$650	$550	$450

Last MSR was $945.

Sunstar (Model SS-265-12-FT) - similar to the Sunstar, except also features the Bunker Fine Tuner adjustable tuning system.

	$1,300	$1,150	$1,000	$850	$700	$600	$500

Last MSR was $975.

Sunstar (Model SS-265-12-CK) - similar to the Sunstar, except features the Quick Change kit for interchangeable bodies.

	$1,300	$1,150	$1,000	$850	$700	$600	$500

Last MSR was $965.

Sunstar (Model SS-265-12-FT-CK) - similar to the Sunstar, except features both the Bunker Fine Tuner and Quick Change kit.

	$1,300	$1,150	$1,000	$850	$700	$600	$500

Last MSR was $995.

ELECTRIC: CURRENT MFG.

There are options on almost every model. These need to be considered when determining the value of the guitar. The prices listed here are strictly for the base model.

AT 100 - single cutaway hollow-body archtop, figured maple top with f-holes, alder back and sides, maple neck, 22-fret rosewood fingerboard, 2 pickups either Seymour Duncan or Bill Lawrence Keystone's, ebony or Brazillian rosewood bridge, 3-per-side tuners, 3 knobs, Natural Quilt, Amberburst, or Jewel Top Transparent finish, current mfg.

MSR $1,995		$1,530	$1,375	$1,200	$1,075	$950	$800	$650

B

GRADING	100% MINT	98% NEAR MINT	95% EXC+	90% EXC	80% VG+	70% VG	60% G

AT 200 - similar to the AT 100 except has a matched maple back, available in same finish, current mfg.

	MSR $2,195		$1,600	$1,425	$1,250	$1,100	$975	$825	$700

AT 300 - similar to the AT 200 except features a 3 in. thick body with pickguard, current mfg.

	MSR $2,495		$1,800	$1,550	$1,300	$1,150	$1,000	$850	$700

BAT 375 - single cutaway hollow body Jazz Fusion archtop, exotic maple top and back, alder sides, maple neck with choice of fingerboard, 22 frets, 2 Seymour Duncan or Bill Lawrence Keystone pickups, 3-per-side tuners, bridge with tailpiece, four knobs, gold or chrome hardware, available in Natural, Amberburst, or Jewel Top Transparent finishes, current mfg.

	MSR $3,295		$2,300	$2,000	$1,750	$1,450	$1,275	$1,050	$875

BG-2000S - offset double cutaway (Showmaster style) body, different types of body tonewoods, figured maple top, hard-rock maple neck, 22-fret fingerboard with dot inlay, reverse headstock 6-on-one-side tuners, Magnum bridge, available in Sunburst finish, current mfg.

	MSR $1,495		$1,000	$850	$750	$650	$550	$450	$350

ELECTRIC BASS: PREVIOUS MFG.

Optional Body Sets for the bass models had a new retail price of $89 for Fabric (vinyl), $100 for Wood, and $114 for Denim (leather bound Denim).

GALAXY I (MODEL GL-305-4) - minimalist neck-through eastern hard maple or black walnut body with 2 attached wings, 30.5 in. scale, bolt-on neck, 23-fret fingerboard with dotted circle inlay, metal Bunker logo on headstock, 2-per-side tuners on end of body, 4 individual string brass bridge pieces, chrome hardware, 4 round Magnum pickups, volume control/tone filter on/off switches, stainless steel controls plate, available in Natural finish, mfg. circa 1960s.

$1,000	$900	$800	$700	$600	$500	$400

Last MSR was $740.

Galaxy I (Model GL-305-4-CK) - similar to the Galaxy I, except features the Quick Change kit for interchangeable bodies.

$1,200	$1,050	$900	$800	$700	$600	$500

Last MSR was $820.

GALAXY II (MODEL GL-305-8) - similar to the Galaxy I, except features 8 round Magnum pickups (2 sets of 4), pickup bank selector switch, mfg. circa 1960s.

$1,200	$1,050	$900	$800	$700	$600	$500

Last MSR was $860.

Galaxy II (Model GL-305-8-CK) - similar to the Galaxy II, except features the Quick Change kit for interchangeable bodies.

$1,400	$1,200	$1,050	$900	$750	$650	$550

Last MSR was $890.

ELECTRIC BASS: CURRENT MFG.

GALAXY BTX400 - double offset cutaway, figured maple top, alder back, 5-piece quartersawn maple necks, 22 frets, through-body bridge, rosewood fingerboard, 2-per-side tuners, EMG dual coils or Bill Lawrence Keystone pickups, 3 knobs, thumb rest with pickup changer, chrome hardware, available in natural, Brazilian/Exotic, Amberburst, or Vintageburst finish, current mfg.

	MSR $2,295		$1,600	$1,450	$1,325	$1,150	$1,000	$850	$700

Galaxy BTX500 - similar to the Galaxy BTX400 except is in five-string configuration, current mfg.

	MSR $2,495		$1,750	$1,575	$1,450	$1,250	$1,100	$900	$750

SUNSTAR GTB354 - double offset cutaway, figured maple top, alder back, 5-piece quartersawn maple necks, 24 frets, through-body bridge, rosewood fingerboard, 2-per-side tuners, EMG dual coils or Bill Lawrence Keystone pickups, 3 knobs, thumb rest with pickup changer, chrome hardware, available in Natural, Exotic Maple, Amberburst, or Vintageburst finish, current mfg.

	MSR $2,495		$1,750	$1,575	$1,450	$1,250	$1,125	$950	$775

Sunstar GTB355 - similar to the Sunstar GTB355 except is in five-string configuration, current mfg.

	MSR $2,695		$1,999	$1,750	$1,575	$1,350	$1,225	$1,000	$800

Sunstar GTB356 - similar to the Sunstar GTB354 except is in six-string configuration, current mfg.

	MSR $2,995		$2,300	$2,000	$1,750	$1,450	$1,275	$1,050	$875

ASTRAL ATB400 - double offset cutaway hollow body, figured maple top, alder back, 5-piece quartersawn maple necks, 22 frets, gold or chrome bridge, rosewood fingerboard, 2-per-side tuners, EMG dual coils or Bill Lawrence Keystone pickups, 2 knobs, thumb rest with pickup changer, chrome hardware, available in natural, Amberburst, or Vintageburst finish, current mfg.

	MSR $2,595		$1,850	$1,675	$1,525	$1,350	$1,175	$1,000	$800

Astral ATB500 - similar to the Alstar ATB400 except is in five-string configuration, current mfg.

	MSR $2,895		$2,000	$1,800	$1,600	$1,375	$1,225	$1,000	$800

BURNS LONDON LTD./BURNS U.S.A.

Instruments previously built in Britain during the late 1950s. The exception being Baldwin-built Burns from 1965 to 1972, which were U.S. produced by assembling imported parts in Booneville, Arkansas. Current production is based in Surrey, England by Burns London Ltd. Current Burns products are distributed in the U.S.A. by Codel Enterprises of Bethel, CT.

Jim Burns has been hailed as the British Leo Fender due to his continual electric guitar designs and innovations. Widely accepted in England and Europe, Burns guitars never really caught on in the U.S. market.

James Ormsted Burns was born in 1925. Burns built his first lap steel while still serving in the Royal Air Force in 1944. By 1952, he completed his first solid body electric, and, along with partner Alan Wooten, Burns built his first twenty guitars under the Supersound name in 1958. Burns' first production guitars were built with Henry Weill in 1959 under the Burns-Weill trademark, then later under the Burns logo. The Burns, London company (1960 to 1965) was the watermark of Jim Burns' career, as the company stayed very successful producing guitars, basses, amplifiers, and accessories. Even while many popular British artists used Burns instruments, Jim Burns turned to exporting his instruments to the U.S. market briefly under both the Ampeg and Burns trademarks.

In 1965, the Baldwin company lost to CBS in its bid to acquire Fender. Searching for another proven winner, Baldwin bought Burns and began importing the instruments under the Baldwin or Baldwin/Burns trademarks. Jim Burns stayed on as managing director and "idea man" through 1966, then left to pursue other projects. Baldwin eventually began assembling imported parts in Booneville, Arkansas. By 1970, Baldwin decided to concentrate on production of Gretsch guitars and drums (acquired in 1967, the Gretsch operation was also moved down to Arkansas).

In 1969, Jim Burns returned to the musical instrument world as a design consultant to Dallas-Arbiter's Hayman trademark. Along with ex-Vox employee Bob Pearson, Burns was reunited with Jack Golder (ex-Burns mainstay) but only continued his affiliation until 1971. A new Burns organization arose in 1973 as Burns, U.K., but this company met with less success than intended and folded in 1977. A later stab at affairs continued as the Jim Burns Company from 1979 to 1983.

Jim Burns died in 1998, and also served as an acting consultant at Burns, London Ltd. This Surrey, England-based company was established in 1992, and is currently producing authentic reproductions of the desirable 1960s-style Burns models (source: Paul Day, *The Burns Book*).

The most collectible Burns instruments would be from the company's heyday between 1960 and 1965. The Burns-Weill models are relatively scarce, and the Ampeg by Burns of London models were only distributed from 1963 to 1964. Baldwin models, while not plentiful, do surface in the U.S. vintage market - and some examples pop up in Elvis Presley's 1960s movies! A Double-Six 12-string model is currently on display in Graceland. Later, Burns' companies probably contributed to smaller guitar productions, although the Burns U.K. Flyte model has a pretty cool jet plane-shaped body design. Jim Burns was the first to pioneer a number of distinct design ideas that are accepted worldwide in guitar production. Burns originated interesting features like the 24-fret fingerboard, the heel-less glued-in neck joint, knife-edge bearing vibrato unit, active electronics, and stacked-coil pickups.

TRADEMARK DATING INFORMATION

Jim Burns' career spanned from 1958 through 1984. Along the way, Burns founded a number of production companies and company trademarks. The following is an overview of his companies:

1958: Supersound, with Alan Wooten.

1959: Burns-Weill, with Henry Weill. These models were Jim Burns' first production guitars.

1960-1965: Burns London.

1965-1970: Baldwin, Baldwin/Burns, importation by Baldwin to the U.S. market. Jim Burns stayed on with the company through 1966.

1973, 1974-1977: Burns, U.K.

1979-1984: Jim Burns company.

1992: Burns London formed by Barry Gibson, Jim Burns acts as consultant.

1998: Jim Burns passed away.

2002: Burns USA formed in the U.S.A. as exclusive distributor in North America.

ELECTRIC: LIMITED EDITIONS

The Custom model **Burns Cobra**, introduced in 1998, has vintage body styling, a scroll headstock, and Wilkinson tremolo unit. The 30/50 Anniversary limited edition model built in 1994 celebrates the 30th anniversary of the Shadows' changeover to Burns guitars, and the 50th anniversary of the building of James Ormston Burns' first guitar.

ELECTRIC: LEGEND SERIES

The **Legend Standard** has a double cutaway body, glued-in maple neck, 25.5 in. scale, 21-fret rosewood fingerboard with pearl dot inlay, 3-per-side tuners, scrolled headstock, 3-piece tortoiseshell pickguard, chrome hardware, 3 pickups, Rez-O-Tube tail piece, volume/rotary tone selector/push-pull tone controls, 5-way pickup selector. The **Deluxe** (Shadows Model) is similar, except features a slimline body and figured maple neck; the **Custom Deluxe** (Shadows Model) also features gold-plated hardware, a bound body, and unbound highly figured maple neck. Legend Series models are available in a white finish, but are also available in optional Green or Blue Sunburst finishes.

The **Legend 'S' Type** is a hollowed body version of the Standard. The guitar body is Brazilian mahogany with a Sycamore ripple top, and the glued-in beech neck has a rosewood fingerboard. The Legend 'S' Type is standard with a Green finish and white pearloid 3-piece pickguard.

ELECTRIC: 1960s-1970s MFG.

The **Nu Sonic model GB/98** features a single cutaway magnolia or mahogany body, glued-in maple neck, 25.5 in. scale, 22-fret rosewood fingerboard with pearl dot inlay, 3-per-side tuners, scrolled headstock, chrome hardware, black (or white) pickguard, 2 pickups, Rez-O-Tube tail piece, volume/rotary tone selector/push-pull tone controls, 3-way pickup selector. Model **GB/98 B** is similar in design, and features 3 pickups, a piezo transducer system, and a 5-way pickup selector; model **GB/98 B** Custom has a similar layout and gold-plated hardware. The **Steve Howe Signature** model has two pickups (which includes a split coil humbucker at the neck position). Nu-Sonic models are available in Black, White, or Fiesta Red; custom colors include Blue Sunburst and Green Sunburst. Body binding is optional.

ARTIST - double cutaway body, 24-fret maple fingerboard with dot inlay, cream pickguard, 3 Tri-Sonic pickups, 6 knobs, 2 switches, available in Cherry finish, mfg. 1960 only.

	N/A	$800	$700	$600	$500	$400	$300

Vibra-Artist - similar to the Artist, except has a tremolo unit, mfg. 1960-62.

	N/A	$1,000	$850	$725	$600	$500	$400

Later models have rosewood fingerboards and black pickguards. There are several variations of this guitar in dimensions and options.

GRADING	100% MINT	98% NEAR MINT	95% EXC+	90% EXC	80% VG+	70% VG	60% G

Vibra Artist De Luxe - simliar to the Vibra Artist, except has an ivorine-bound rosewood fingerboard, MOP tuner buttons, laminated black pickguard with controls in it, 3 knobs, 3 switches, available in Cherry finish, mfg. 1961-62.

	N/A	$1,500	$1,250	$1,000	$850	$700	$550

Very few of these guitars were ever produced.

BISON - double cutaway, 22-fret rosewood fingerboard, gray tortoise pickguard, 3 "Rez-o-Matik" pickups, tremolo unit, 3 knobs, 2 switches, scroll style headstock, 3-per-side tuners, black or white finish, mfg. 1964-65.

	N/A	$1,250	$1,000	$800	$700	$600	$500

Black Bison 3 Pickup - similar to the Bison, except has 3 "Ultra-Sonic" pickups, regular style headstock, 6-per-side tuners, four knobs, available in black finish only, mfg. 1962-64.

	N/A	$1,600	$1,350	$1,100	$950	$800	$650

Black Bison 4 Pickup - similar to the Black Bison 3 Pickup, except has 4 "Ultra-Sonic" pickups, one volume knob, and two pickup selector knobs, available in black finish only, mfg. 1961-62.

	N/A	$2,000	$1,750	$1,500	$1,250	N/A	N/A

Only 49 of these instruments were ever produced.

DOUBLE SIX - 12-string configuration, offset double cutaway solidbody, bolt-on maple neck, 21-fret rosewood fingerboard with dot inlay, 3 seperate black pickguards, 3 diagonal single coil pickups, tremolo bridge, scroll style headstock, 6-per-side tuners, 3 knobs, 1 switch, available in White, Black, Red Sunburst, or Green Sunburst finish, mfg. 1964-65.

	N/A	$1,100	$950	$800	$700	$600	$500

JAZZ - offset double cutaway hardwood body with inward curving horns, 23 3/8 in. scale, bolt-on neck, 22-fret rosewood fingerboard with white dot inlay, 6-on-a-side tuners, chrome hardware, black inscribed pickguard, 2 Burns Tri-Sonic pickups, bridge/tremolo tailpiece, 2 knobs, 1 switch, available in Red Sunburst finish, mfg. 1962-65.

	N/A	$850	$750	$650	$550	$450	$350

JAZZ SPLIT SOUND - offset double cutaway hardwood body with inward curving horns, 23 3/8" scale, bolt-on neck, 22-fret rosewood fingerboard with white dot inlay, 6-on-a-side tuners, chrome hardware, black inscribed pickguard, 3 Burns Split-Sonic pickups, bridge/tremolo tailpiece, volume/tone controls, 4-way tone selector switch (Treble, Jazz, Split-Sound, and Wild Dog), available in Red Sunburst finish, mfg. 1962-65.

	N/A	$1,000	$850	$700	$600	$500	$400

MARVIN - offset double cutaway solidbody, bolt-on maple neck, 21-fret rosewood fingerboard with dot inlay, 3 seperate blue/gray tortoise or brown pickguards, 3 diaganol Rez-o-Matik pickups, tremolo bridge, scroll style headstock, 3-per-side tuners, 3 knobs, 1 switch, available in White finish, mfg. 1964-65.

	N/A	$1,200	$1,000	$850	$700	$600	$500

NU-SONIC - offset double cutaway hardwood body with short horns, 23 3/8 in. scale, bolt-on neck, 22-fret rosewood fingerboard with white dot inlay, 6-on-a-side tuners, chrome hardware, black inscribed pickguard, 2 Burns Nu-Sonic pickups, bridge/tremolo tailpiece, volume/2-Tone controls, 3-way selector switch, available in Black or Cherry finish, mfg. 1964-65.

	N/A	$400	$350	$300	$265	$225	$175

SONIC - double cutaway body, 23.385 in. scale, 21-fret maple or rosewood fingerboard with dot inlay, 2 Tri-Sonic pickups, 3 knobs, 2 switches, black pickguard, tremolo bridge, 6-on-one side tuners, available in Cherry finish, mfg. 1960-64.

	N/A	$400	$350	$300	$250	$200	$150

Add $50 for maple fingerboard.

SPLIT SONIC - offset double cutaway hardwood body with short horns, 24.75 in. scale, bolt-on neck, 22-fret rosewood fingerboard with white dot inlay, 6-on-a-side tuners, chrome hardware, black inscribed pickguard, 3 Burns Split-Sonic pickups, bridge/tremolo tailpiece, volume/2-Tone controls, 4-way tone selector switch (Treble, Bass, Split-Sound, and Wild Dog), available in Red Sunburst and Custom Color finish, mfg. 1962-64.

	N/A	$700	$600	$525	$450	$375	$300

Add 10% for a bound fingerboard. Add 20% for Custom Color finish. Add 25% for White finish/inscribed White pickguard.

TR 2 - offset double cutaway semi-solid body (solid center section), 2 f-holes, white body binding, bolt-on neck, 24.75 in. scale, 22-fret bound rosewood fingerboard with white dot inlay, 3-per-side tuners, bound headstock, bridge/Mk. 9 tremolo tailpiece, 2 Burns Ultra-Sonic covered pickups, raised black inscribed pickguard with volume/bass/treble roller controls mounted underneath, 3-way selector switch, battery powered on-board preamp, available in Cherry, Natural, and Red Sunburst finish, mfg. 1963-64.

	N/A	$425	$350	$300	$265	$225	$175

Add 20% for Cherry and Natural finishes.

The TR 2 name stood for Transistorized 2 Pickup model.

VIBRASLIM - offset double cutaway semi-hollow body, 2 f-holes, white body binding, bolt-on neck, 22-fret rosewood fingerboard with dot inlay, 2 Ultra-Sonic pickups, tremolo tailpiece, black pickguard with controls mounted underneath, 4 knobs, 1 switch, available in Red Sunburst finish, mfg. 1964-65.

	N/A	$500	$425	$350	$300	$250	$175

VISTA SONIC - offset double cutaway, 22-fret rosewood fingerboard with dot inlay, black pickguard with Burns London engraved, 3 "Tri-Sonic" pickups, 2 knobs, 1 switch, tremolo unit, available in Red Sunburst finish, mfg. 1962-64.

	N/A	$600	$500	$425	$350	$275	$200

ELECTRIC: CLUB-CLASSIC SERIES (RECENT MFG.)

The Club Classic Series are guitars that are essentially reissues of models from the 1960s and 1970s. Most of these are built to the exact specifications of their older counterparts.

GRADING	100% MINT	98% NEAR MINT	95% EXC+	90% EXC	80% VG+	70% VG	60% G

BRIAN MAY SIGNATURE - double offset cutaway, solid mahogany body and neck, ebony 24-fret fingerboard with pearl dot inlays and zero fret, matching headstock, 3-per-side tuners, black pickguard, three Burns Tri-Sonic pickups wired in series, switches for each pickup, two knobs (v, tone), chrome hardware, tremolo bridge, signed by Brian May, available in Vintage Red, Blue, Green, Black, or Three-Tone Sunburst finish, mfg. 2002-present.

MSR $1,125	$800	$725	$650	$575	$500	$450	$400

Brian May Signature Left-Handed - similar to the Brian May Signature except is in left-hand configuration, mfg. 2002-present.

MSR $1,225	$850	$775	$700	$600	$525	$450	$400

Brian May Special - similar to the Brian May Signature, except has gold hardware, MOP body and neck bindings, and is available in Black finish, new 2004.

MSR $1,395	$995	$900	$800	$700	$625	$550	$450

MARQUEE GUITAR - double offset cutaway, solid alder body, maple neck, maple or rosewood 22-fret fingerboard with dot inlays and zero fret, classic scrolled headstock, 3-per-side tuners, 3-piece pickguard, three single coil Rez-o-matic pickups, five-way switch, push/pull pickup system for a possible 7 pickup selections, three knobs (v, 2 tones), gold hardware, Burns twin-pivot tremolo bridge, available in Greenburst, Red, Redburst, Silver or White finish, current mfg.

MSR $739	$525	$475	$400	$350	$300	$250	$215

This guitar is a reproduction of the 1960s model.

Marquee Left-Handed - similar to the Marquee except is in left-hand configuration, current mfg.

MSR $775	$550	$495	$425	$350	$300	$260	$220

Marquee Special - similar to the Marquee guitar except has a flat top with body bindings on the top and a photo-flame finish, available in Trans. Green, Red, or Blue finish, current mfg.

MSR $775	$550	$495	$425	$350	$300	$275	$235

THE BISON - double offset cutaway with pointed horns, solid alder body, maple neck, rosewood 22-fret fingerboard with dot inlays, matching color "bat-wing" headstock, 6-on-a-side tuners, black pickguard with Burns inscription, three Tri-sonic pickups, four knobs (v, 2 tones, pickup selector), chrome hardware, Burns knife-edge tremolo bridge, available in Red, Red Sunburst, Black, Satin Black, or White finish, current mfg.

MSR $775	$550	$495	$425	$350	$300	$275	$235

This model features gold hardware on the white finish.

Burns Marquee Guitar courtesy Blue Book Archive

THE DOUBLE SIX - double cutaway 12-string, alder body, hard-rock maple neck, 21-fret rosewood fingerboard, classic Burns matching finish headstock, three-piece black pickguard with Burns logo, 6-per-side tuners, three chrome Tri-Sonic pickups, three knobs (v, 2 tones), five-way switch plus push/pull, Gotoh bridge with stop tailpiece, chrome hardware, available in Green, Red Sunburst, or Solid White finish, current mfg.

MSR $849	$675	$600	$550	$475	$400	$350	$275

THE FLYTE - update version of the classic Flyte, arrowhead-shaped body with contours, alder body, bolt-on rock maple neck, 22-fret rosewood MOP bound fingerboard with dot inlay, two seperate pickguards, 2 Burns split humbucker pickups, stop tailpiece, 3 knobs, single switch, 3-per-side tuners, black hardware, available in "Gothic" Satin Black or Metallic Silver finish, mfg. 2003-present.

MSR $775	$550	$475	$425	$375	$325	$275	$225

Add $50 for Floyd Rose tremolo unit.

THE SCORPION - updated version of the 1980s Scorpion, double cutaway, alder body, bolt-on rock maple neck, 24-fret MOP bound fingerboard with dot inlay, 2 Burns split humbucker pickups, two pickguards, three knobs, two switches, 3-per-side tuners, Scorpion headstock, black hardware, available in "Gothic" satin black, mfg. 2003-present.

MSR $879	$625	$550	$475	$400	$350	$300	$250

Add $50 for Floyd Rose tremolo unit.

THE STEER - semi-hollow alder body with acoustic chambers, hard rock maple neck and 22-fret fingerboard, black plate that goes around the soundhole and pickups, two pickups (single coil, humbucker), black pickguard with Burns inscription, classic Burns pointed headstock with string guides, coil-tap switch with pickup selector, three knobs, chrome hardware, available in Greenburst finish, current mfg.

MSR $775	$550	$495	$425	$350	$300	$275	$235

The Steer Cutaway - similar to the Steer except has a single cutaway, available in Green Sunburst or Red finish, mfg. 2003-present.

MSR $845	$675	$600	$550	$475	$400	$350	$285

The Steer Cutaway Deluxe - similar to the Steer except has a single cutaway with a curly maple top and gold hardware, available in Honey Sunburst, new 2004.

MSR $845	$675	$600	$550	$475	$400	$350	$285

ELECTRIC BASS: 1960S MFG.

VISTA SONIC BASS - offset double (almost dual) cutaway hardwood body with short horns, 31.5 in. scale, bolt-on neck, 20-fret rosewood fingerboard with white dot inlay, 4-on-a-side tuners, chrome hardware, black inscribed pickguard, 3 Burns Tri-Sonic pickups, bridge/tailpiece, volume/tone controls, 4-way tone selector switch (Treble, Bass, Contra-Bass, Wild Dog), available in Red Sunburst finish, mfg. 1962-64.

	N/A	$500	$450	$400	$325	$250	$200

Add 20% for a bound fingerboard.

Burns Bison courtesy Steve Krueger

B

GRADING	100% MINT	98% NEAR MINT	95% EXC+	90% EXC	80% VG+	70% VG	60% G

ELECTRIC BASS/BARITONE: CURRENT MFG.

BARRACUDA BARITONE - baritone configuration, Marquee body style, alder body, maple neck, 23-fret rosewood MOP bound fingerboard with dot inlay, 3 Burns Tri-Sonic pickups, 3 seperate pickguards, 3 knobs, 5-way switch, push/pull control for 7 possible pickup combinations, stop tailpiece, scroll style headstock, 3-per-side tuners, chrome hardware, available in Trans. Blue or red finish, mfg. 2003-present.

MSR $949	$675	$600	$550	$500	$450	$400	$350

BISON BASS - double sharp cutaway alder body, hard-rock maple neck, 20-fret rosewood fingerboard, matching headstock, 4-on-one-side tuners, black pickguard, three Tri-Sonic pickups, four knobs (v, 2 tones, pickup selector), chrome hardware, available in White, Black, or Transparent Red finish, current mfg.

MSR $849	$675	$600	$550	$475	$400	$350	$285

Early models featured Rez-O-Matic pickups.

MARQUEE BASS - double cutaway select alder body, rock maple neck, 20-fret rosewood fingerboard 32 in. scale, matching headstock, 4-on-one-side tuners, three piece black pickguard, three Tri-Sonic pickups, two knobs (v, tone), five-way switch, gold hardware, available in White, Red Sunburst, or Green Sunburst finish, current mfg.

MSR $775	$550	$475	$425	$350	$300	$275	$225

SCORPION BASS - double cutaway Scorpion bass alder body, bolt-on rock maple neck, 22-fret rosewood MOP fingerboard with dot inlays, P/J style pickups, 3 black pickguards, 3 knobs, 3-way switch, 2-per-side tuners, available in "Gothic" Satin Black finish, mfg. 2003-present.

MSR $899	$575	$500	$450	$400	$350	$300	$250

BURNSIDE
See Guild. Instruments previously built in Korea during the late 1980s.

Between 1987 and 1988, Guild introduced a line of imported entry level instruments to augment their sales line. The headstock trademark reads "Burnside by Guild" and consisted of four solid body guitar models and two bass models (source: Michael Wright, *Vintage Guitar Magazine*). Prices on these strat-styled instruments may range from $150 up to $250, depending on hardware/pickup packages.

BUSCARINO, JOHN
Instruments currently built in Franklin, N.C. Distributed by the Buscarino Guitar Company of Franklin, N.C.

Luthier John Buscarino apprenticed with Master acoustic guitar builder Augustino LoPrinzi for over a year in 1978, and with Bob Benedetto of archtop lutherie fame from 1979 to 1981. Later that year, Buscarino formed **Nova U.S.A.**, which built high quality solid body electrics and acoustic/electric instruments. In 1990, Buscarino changed the company name to Buscarino Guitars to reflect the change to building acoustic instruments. Buscarino continues to produce limited production custom guitars, and is currently focusing on archtop guitar building. Circa 2002, they relocated to Franklin NC, from Largo, FL. Buscarino no longer produces electric guitars.

For current information on John Buscarino's acoustic and acoustic archtop models, please refer to the *Blue Book of Acoustic Guitars*.

ELECTRIC: DELUXE SERIES

Buscarino also built a number of solid body designs. Deluxe Series instruments featured bolt-on rock maple necks, rosewood fingerboards, chrome hardware, and Sperzel tuners. All models were available in Antique Cherry Sunburst, Black, Caribbean Blue Sunburst, Eggshell White, Tobacco Brown Sunburst, Transparent Blue, Transparent Red polyester finish.

The **Classic** featured a Wilkinson tremolo, white pickguard, 3 EMG or Duncan SSL-2 single coil pickups, while the **Telstar** had a Gotoh Tele Tailpiece, no pickguard, and 2 single coil pickups. The **Nashville St.** featured a single cutaway body (with or without pickguard) and 3 Van Zant single coil pickups. The **Pro Bass** model had active EMJ P/J-style pickups, poplar or alder body, and 4 Sperzel Tuners. Retail prices ran from $1,245 up to $1,445.

ELECTRIC: SUPREME SERIES

Instruments in the Supreme Series had highly figured exotic wood bodies with decorative binding/pinstriping, the Buscarino patented Dead Bolt releaseable bolt-on rock maple necks. The semi-acoustic **Hybrid** model allowed players to change from piezo to magnetic pickups. The upgraded TeleStar was available with numerous pickup and tone wood choices, while the **Mira** featured a flame or quilt maple top over alder or basswood body. Retail prices listed from $2,195 to $2,495.

ELECTRIC: MONARCH SERIES

Monarch Series instruments are custom carved archtop electric guitars with bookmatched flame or quilt maple over mahogany or alder/basswood bodies. All models featured glued-in purpleheart/ebony/flame maple necks, contoured bodies, and gold hardware. List prices ranged from $2,995 to $3,995.

BYRD GUITAR CO.
Instruments currently built in Seattle, Washington.

Byrd guitars are built by the Byrd Guitar Co. and completely designed by James Bird. The Super Avianti model with Balance Compensated Wing design is a combination of Byrd's favorites, the Stratocaster and Flying V. Features of this guitar include a balanced headstock and a seven-way pickup selector. Please contact the company directly for more information and current pricing on this model (see Trademark Index).

Section C

C & R GUITARS

Instruments previously built in Tulsa, Oklahoma circa 1989 to 1991.

Luthier/designer John Bolin and Bill Rich are the men behind those spectacular and rather rare **Batman** and **Joker** custom electric guitars. Bolin, who has created custom guitars for such players as Billy Gibbons, Rick Nielsen, and Albert King, teamed up with Rich and received full licensing rights from DC Comics to produce the guitars. The Batman model was introduced in 1989, the same year that director Tim Burton released the movie **Batman** (starring Jack Nicholson and Michael Keaton -- more importantly, featuring music by Danny Elfman and Prince). Coincidence or savvy business practices?

The Batman model was produced in a limited run of fifty pieces. The Joker model was scheduled to be a limited run of one hundred pieces, but only forty-two were actually built. Rumors abound that there were models for the Penguin and Riddler to follow, but the licensing fee took an astronomical jump and put the ki-bosh on future plans. Ka-Blam! Quick, Robin, to the Batpole! (Information courtesy Mitch Walters.)

ELECTRIC

The **Batman** model has an SG-ish body shape with the Caped Crusader´s face on the headstock, Batman chest logo in yellow, and an overall black finish. The 3-piece laminated mahogany neck runs through the body, and has mystery Batwood wings (the overall weight is pretty light - hmmm...) and a maple fingerboard with no inlay. All hardware is black, of course, and the guitar has a single humbucker pickup and one volume knob, 3-per-side tuners, and a bridge/stop tailpiece combination. The Batman guitar came in its own Bat gigbag, with a Bat strap and certificate of authenticity. There were only 50 Batman guitars produced in this limited edition.

A year later, the team of Rich and Bolin struck again with the limited edition **Joker** guitar (and Joker gigbag). The Joker featured more of an explorer winged shape, with similar mahogany neck-through design and mysterywood wings. The guitar´s body featured a pinstriped purple finish, with a green neck and Joker face graphic on the headstock. C & R Guitars announced that there would be 100 instruments made in the limited edition - but only 42 were actually built. The first 41 were numbered similar to their matching Batman counterpart, but the 42nd guitar was numbered #100.

No matter how you slice it, there are only 41 sets of Batman and Joker guitars. There is "#100" Joker, and 9 additional Batman models swinging loose in Gotham City right now. The last recorded asking price for the set of two was $5,000. Given the nature of the guitars themselves, it´s a safe bet that it will be a seller´s market when they are available for sale.

C. Hall PME-B
Courtesy C. Hall Guitars

C. HALL GUITARS

Instruments currently produced in Pine Mountain Club, CA.

C. Hall guitars was founded in 2002 and debuted at the Winter 2002 NAMM show. These guitars are built by the founder, Charlie Hall. These guitars are built with weight in mind, trying to keep guitars as light as possible. There is no plastic used on these guitars where even the pickguard, coverplates, and knobs are all made of wood! For more information and model updates refer to their website (see Trademark Index).

ELECTRIC

The Model **PME-B** is a semi-solid body model with two pickups that retails for $5,500. The Model **PME-J** is a small jazz archtop with a single pickup that retails for $5,500. The **SS-1** is a semi-solid body with two Lace Sensor pickups. The **SH-2** is a hollowbody with a double coil and two single coil Lace Sensor pickups, and features two output jacks. The **SB-2** is a solidbody made out of solid quilted maple that features a carved top and has three single coil Lace Sensor pickups. Pricing on the other models will be listed in future editions.

CMI

Cleartone Musical Instruments - see Ned Callan. Instruments previously produced in England, later imports were built in Japan during the 1970s and 1980s.

The CMI trademark was used by UK importer/distributor Cleartone Musical Instruments. Early instruments were built by Ned Callan in England, but were later joined by Japanese-built copies (source: Tony Bacon and Paul Day, *The Guru's Guitar Guide*).

CSL

Instruments previously built in Japan during the 1970s through the late 1980s.

The CSL trademark was used by UK importer C. Summerfield Ltd. The 1970s copies of American designs were built at the same source as Ibanez (and Ibanez copies were good enough for a lawsuit from Norlin!); later solid body designs in the 1980s look vaguely Fender-ish. CSL owners who want to testify about the quality of their instruments are invited to write to the *Blue Book of Electric Guitars* (source: Tony Bacon and Paul Day, *The Guru's Guitar Guide*). Tim Swain was nice enough to share some information about his CSL guitars he has found in his journeys. The two examples he has found include a Les Paul style and a Strat style. Both guitars are very strong and built well with bolton necks. The Les Paul has "Deluxe '59er Model" on the headstock, and includes two humbucker style pickups, fixed bridge, adjustable saddle, gold hardware, and black finish. The other features follow those of the real Les Paul. The Strat copy also is very similar to real Stratocasters with three single coil pickups, three knobs, and five-way switch, (courtesey Tim Swain). Prices on these guitars can usually be found between $75 and $200.

C. Hall SB2
Courtesy C. Hall Guitars

C

CAIRNES
Also see Colt. Instruments previously built in Britain during the 1980s.

Company featured high quality and original designs on models named Solo, Stud, Starguard, and Colt Peacemaker. These solid body guitars also came equipped with luthier Jim Cairnes' own pickups and hardware (source: Tony Bacon and Paul Day, *The Guru's Guitar Guide*).

CALLAHAM VINTAGE GUITARS
Instruments currently built in Winchester, Virginia.

Callaham Vintage Guitars creates vintage reproduction solid body electric guitars and amplifiers. Callaham feels that only a small number of guitars from the 1950s and 1960s are in proper playing condition - the majority are worn excessively, have replaced parts (or swapped parts), or have been rendered un-playable by incompetent repairmen through the years. With a large number of historical books on the market, it can be demonstrated that the large manufacturers' vintage reproductions are rough approximations. Rather than pay extreme prices on the vintage market, Callaham figures to offer reproductions of the vintage guitars that players are searching for, and to offer them at prices that players are prepared to pay.

Callaham manufactures all of their own bodies and necks, and is concentrating on their own line of guitars which have many custom features (they are not interested in making one-of-a-kind or replica guitars). While they do offer some of the parts (hardware and electronics) used on their guitars, they do not sell the necks and bodies separately. The also make custom amplifiers; please refer to the *Blue Book of Guitar Amplifiers* for more information.

ELECTRIC

Callaham Vintage Guitars' reproductions are based on Fender-style solid body electrics. Callaham's **S Model**, which is a Strat design, features either a one-piece alder (solid color finishes) or one-piece Swamp ash (for Sunburst and Blonde finishes) offset double cutaway bodies, with bolt-on curly maple necks and rosewood fingerboards. The necks are available in four different contours (like Fender) including the 54 Club, 57 Vee, 58 Soft Vee, and 60 Flat Round. Lindy Fralin single coil Vintage Pickups are used on all S Models, combined with a 5-way selector switch and volume/2 tone controls. S Models feature nickel vintage reproduction parts, and are available in 2-Tone or 3-Tone Sunbursts, Blonde, Black, Burgundy Purple Mist, Firemist Gold Metallic, Lake Placid Blue, Ocean Turquoise, and Shoreline Gold nitrocellulose, among other custom lacquer finishes. Retail list price is $2,550 and case is included.

The S Model has optional gold parts (add $80), Base Plate/Blender Pot combo (add $10), and matching painted headstock in solid colors (add $50). The Base Plate is located on the lead pickup, and helps boost the lows and mid-range frequencies; the Blend Pot blends the neck and bridge pickups together. The S Model is also available in left-hand configuration (add $100).

The **T Model** (retail list $2,425) is a single cutaway body with similar construction to the S Model. This model is similar to a Telecaster. However, 2 Seymour Duncan Alnico II single coil pickups are standard. There are three different bridge configurations: an original 3-saddle vintage-style bridge, a 6-saddle bridge, or an angled 3-saddle bridge. The angled 3-saddle bridge is an additional $25. Add $50 for matching painted headstock and $100 for left-hand configuration.

CAMP, MICHAEL
Instruments previously built in Plymouth, Michigan.

Luthier Michael Camp handcrafted high quality electric guitars. These instruments feature single piece mahogany necks, offset double cutaway mahogany bodies with flame maple tops, Wilkinson fixed bridges or tremolo systems, Schaller tuners, 3-per-side headstocks, Seymour Duncan humbucker pickups, and nitrocellulose lacquer finishes. The **Master Series** models feature ebony fingerboards, gold hardware, and matching headstock finishes, while the **Players Series** models have rosewood fingerboards, chrome hardware, and black headstocks. The **Bolt-On Series** features the 'zing' delivered by bolt-on necks, maple or rosewood fingerboards, 2 or 3 single coil pickups, and natural wood headstocks.

CANORA
See Ardsleys.

CARLO ROBELLI
Please refer to the R section of this text.

CARLSON GUITAR COMPANY
Instruments currently built in St. Joseph, Missouri.

In addition to handcrafting his own custom-built instruments, Jim Carlson is the owner and operator of a lutherie shop where he currently performs repair and refinishing work for some of the St. Joseph and Kansas City area music stores.

As Jim explains, "My earliest recollection of my love for stringed instruments (especially the guitar) was around the age of five or six." All of Carlson's family members play stringed instruments of some kind, "Even my Grandmother, who can play just about anything on anything - a very gifted woman. My father used to play his guitar around the house in his spare time, and I found myself glued to the floor right in front of his chair in total amazement of the sounds being produced by the movement of his fingers on the fretboard. So as far back as I can recall music and the instruments that create it have been my life."

"I began playing at the age of eight, and have thoroughly enjoyed it for the last twenty-seven years. But the intrigue didn't stop with just the sounds that musical instruments produce - I also found myself very fascinated with the instruments themselves: the beauty of the finish, the way they felt, and the various woods that were being used to make them. By the age of fifteen, I was tinkering with my guitars and adjusting the action to try and get it as low as possible - after all, at age fifteen I was bound to be the world's next David Gilmour or Eric Clapton! Well, at least that's how most of us young musicians felt when we were fifteen."

"My parents didn't take things nearly as serious as I had, so needless to say they wouldn't pay for my expensive refins or buy me the beautiful Les Paul Custom that I had my eye on. I began a self-taught quest to build guitars (my own guitars) with the help of a few good pointers from books to auto body shops - believe it or not, there is some good information that you can pick up from paint and body mechanics concerning finish work. My first guitar was a success, in fact I have used it on a CD where I was invited to do some guitar playing. Some twenty years have come and gone since I first started seriously tinkering with my old Univox and Stratocaster, and I have continued to build custom guitars. Oh, and by the way, I did finally get that 1978 Les Paul Custom that I had my eye on!" (Biography courtesy Jim and Pam Carlson).

ELECTRIC

Carlson offers 4 distinct models, and the hardware and finish can be altered upon request at the time of commission. The **Elite** has a single cutaway body, maple neck-through design, flamed maple carved arched top, 22-fret ebony fingerboard with dot inlay, 3-per-side tuners, tune-o-matic/stop tailpiece bridge, 2 Gibson '57 Classic humbuckers, volume and tone controls, 3-way toggle, and top-mounted cord jack. The **Retro** model has similar construction features, but has a sloped shoulder/cutaway body, bookmatched zebrawood top, PRS-style tremolo, 3-per-side Sperzel locking tuners, and 2 DiMarzio **Super Distortion** humbuckers. The **Signature** model has a through-body mahogany neck/mahogany top, bound single cutaway body, bound ebony fingerboard, gold-plated hardware, Schaller bridge, 3-per-side Grover tuners, and 2 Gibson '57 Classic humbuckers.

For all the single coil pickup fans, Carlson offers an almost-dual cutaway model called the **Honeymoon**. The Honeymoon features a laminated maple/mahogany neck-through design, maple core/mahogany top body, 22-fret ebony fingerboard, PRS-style tremolo, 3-per-side Grover tuners, 3 active EMG SA single coil pickups (with SPC control), volume and 2 tone controls, and a 5-way selector switch.

In addition to his custom instruments, Carlson continues to offer repair work for the professional and semi-professional players in his area. For questions regarding specifications and pricing, contact Jim Carlson at Carlson Lutherie directly (see Trademark Index).

CARMINE STREET GUITARS
Instruments currently built in New York City, New York.

Carmine Street Guitars is located in the heart of New York City, in a truly old-fashioned shop that, at one time, may have been a speakeasy. In addition to their guitar sales and repair work, Carmine Street Guitars offers good quality custom-built instruments.

ELECTRIC

The **Kellycaster** model is offered in a solid body or sound chambered version, with carved tops and one-piece necks. The suggested retail price is $1,500 and features different pickup and bridge options. **Kelly Kustoms** begin at a retail price of $1,000 for custom-shaped, one-of-a-kind designs that are customer specified, or one of the over 20 ideas from the shop. For further information regarding pricing and specifications, contact Carmine Street Guitars directly (see Trademark Index).

CARRIVEAU
Instruments previously built in Phoenix, Arizona.

Carriveau custom-built instruments have been described as high quality, well-built guitars. However, we never recieved any more information on this manufacturer and people with any knowledge of this trademark are welcome to submit information directly to the publisher.

CARRUTHERS, JOHN
Instruments currently built in Venice, California.

Luthier/designer John Carruthers is currently offering a number of custom-built guitars and an "S-U-B-1" Upright Bass. Carruthers has been a consultant and subcontractor for the Fender, Ibanez, and Yamaha guitar companies. He has also written numerous articles and reviews for *Guitar Player* magazine for a ten-year period.

ELECTRIC

Carruthers is currently offering a wide range of custom-built solidbody and acoustic electric semi-hollow steel string guitars. All models are built with high quality hardware and pickups, and range in price from $1,895 up to $2,995. Model descriptions and specifications are available from Carruthers Guitars.

ELECTRIC BASS

Carruthers bass models all feature an alder body and EMG pickups. The **CB 4C** (list $1,795) has a bolt-on maple neck, striped ebony fingerboard, and active electronics; the **CB 4B** (list $2,095) has similar construction but features a figured maple top. The **CB 4A** (list $2,595) has a set-in maple neck, figured maple top, and striped ebony fingerboard.

Carruthers 5-string models all have a 34.5 in. scale. The **CB 5C** (list $1,995) has a bolt-on maple neck, striped ebony fingerboard, and active electronics; the **CB 5B** (list $2,295) has similar construction but features a figured maple top. The **CB 4A** (list $2,795) has a set-in maple neck, figured maple top, and striped ebony fingerboard.

The Carruthers electric Stand-Up Bass (SUB-1) has a retail price of $2,795. This model is a high quality, portable electric upright 4-string bass guitar. It is constructed with an alder body, detachable maple neck, ebony fingerboard, and features piezo electric pickups. For further information, please contact Carruthers Guitars directly (see Trademark Index).

CARVIN
Instruments currently produced in Escondido, CA since 1969. Previous production was located in Covina, CA from 1949 to 1969. Carvin instruments are sold through direct catalog sales, as well as through their four factory stores in CA: Covina, Hollywood, San Diego, and Santa Ana.

In 1946, Lowell Kiesel founded Kiesel Electronics in Los Angeles, California. Three years later, the Kiesel family settled in Covina, California, and began the original catalog business of manufacturing and distributing lap steel guitars, small tube amps, and pickups. The Carvin trademark was derived from Kiesel's two oldest sons, Carson and Gavin. Guitars were originally offered in kit form, or by parts since 1949; Carvin began building complete guitars in 1956. By 1978, the glued set-neck design replaced the bolt-on necks. The majority of the current guitar and bass models currently feature a neck-through design.

Carvin has always been a mail-order-only company, and offers players a wide range of options on the individual models. Even though they can't be tried out before they're bought, Carvin offers a ten-day money-back guarantee. Because Carvin sells factory direct, these guitars are not stocked in music stores. It is suggested that a current copy of their catalog be requested (free of charge) to find out more about the company's current models and pricing. Carvin also used to have a factory store in Sherman Oaks.

Carvin offers a full range of guitar and bass replacement parts in their full line catalog. The Carvin company also offers mixing boards, power amplifiers, power mixers, P.A. speakers, monitor speakers, guitar combo amps/heads/cabinets, and bass amps/cabinets.

Carlson Elite
courtesy Carlson Guitar Co.

Carlson Retro
courtesy Carlson Guitar Co.

C

GRADING	100% MINT	98% NEAR MINT	95% EXC+	90% EXC	80% VG+	70% VG	60% G

GENERAL INFORMATION & OPTIONS

Every Carvin guitar is available with custom options. These options include color finishes, wood construction, hardware, inlays, pickups, and other items. Each of these have an added up charge. Most small upgrades (i.e. other pickups) command a $10-$15 premium. For other options that are not listed below, please refer to Carvin directly, as their prices change on all options, and each instrument´s options needs to be addressed separately.

Add $40 for Custom Translucent finish. Add $200 for a translucent color over a .5 in. thick AAA flamed maple top. Add $300 for a translucent color over a .5 in. thick AAA quilted maple top. For other wood options please inquire.

ELECTRIC: AE SERIES

AE150 - offset double cutaway poplar body, through-body maple neck, 24-fret ebony fingerboard with pearl dot inlay, fixed bridge, blackface peghead with screened logo, 6-on-a-side locking Sperzel tuners, 2 humbucker/1 acoustic bridge Carvin pickups, 1 volume/2 tone/1 mix controls, 3-position switch, mfg. 1994-96.

	$800	$600	$550	$500	$450	$400	$350

Last MSR was $1,600.

AE160 - single cutaway poplar body, through-body maple neck, 24-fret ebony fingerboard with pearl dot inlay, fixed bridge, blackface peghead with screened logo, 6-on-a-side locking Sperzel tuners, 2 humbucker/1 acoustic bridge Carvin pickups, 1 volume/2 tone/1 mix controls, 3-position switch, mfg. 1994-96.

	$800	$600	$550	$500	$450	$400	$350

Last MSR was $1,600.

AE185 - single cutaway mahogany body, internal acoustic chambers, AAA Englemann spruce top, through-body mahogany neck, 24-fret ebony fingerboard with pearl dot inlay, fixed bridge, blackface peghead with screened logo, 3-per-side tuners, 2 Carvin humbuckers (C22N and C22T), Carvin F60 acoustic bridge pickup, master volume control, tone (electric)/tone (acoustic)/blend controls, 3-position selector (electric) switch, dual output jacks, mfg. 1996-present.

MSR $2,199	$925	$825	$725	$625	$550	$500	$450

AE185-12 - similar the AE185, except in 12-string configuration, 6-per-side headstock, mfg. 1997-present.

MSR $2,379	$1,000	$850	$750	$650	$595	$525	$475

ELECTRIC: BOLT SERIES

Carvin´s Bolt Series models feature a bolt-on maple neck.

THE BOLT - offset double cutaway alder body, bolt-on graphite reinforced maple neck, 25.5 in. scale, 22-fret ebony fingerboard with pearl dot inlay, maple headstock veneer, fixed bridge, graphite nut, 6-on-a-side Carvin tuners, chrome hardware, white multi-layer pickguard, 3 Carvin AP11 single coil pickups, volume/tone control, 5-way selector switch, available in Black, Natural (Tung Oil), Pearl Blue, Pearl Red, Pearl White, Red, White and Clear Gloss standard finishes, mfg. 1997-present.

MSR $1,299	$625	$550	$475	$400	$350	$300	$275

Add $20 for 2 direct mount C22 Humbucking pickups. Add $50 for Wilkinson tremolo. Add $100 for Floyd Rose Tremolo.

Left-handed configuration is optional at no extra charge.

Bolt-T - similar to the Bolt, except features a Wilkinson tremolo system, mfg. 1997-present.

MSR $1,399	$675	$600	$525	$450	$400	$350	$300

Add $20 for 2 direct mount C22 Humbucking pickups. Add $50 for Wilkinson tremolo. Add $100 for Floyd Rose Tremolo.

ELECTRIC: CALIFORNIA CARVED TOP

CT3M - offset double cutaway contoured mahogany body, set Honduras mahogany neck, 22-fret ebony fingerboard with dot inlay, matching color headstock with three-per-side tuners, STB, two Classic humbucker pickups, two knobs, three-way switch, available in various finishes, mfg. 2004-present.

MSR $1,999	$900	$800	$725	$650	$575	$500	$450

CT3C - similar to the CT3M, except has a Floyd Rose tremolo unit, mfg. 2004-present.

MSR $2,199	$975	$875	$800	$725	$650	$575	$500

CT3T - similar to the CT3M, except has a Wilkinson tremolo unit, mfg. 2004-present.

MSR $2,049	$925	$825	$750	$675	$600	$525	$475

CT4M - offset double cutaway contoured mahogany body with an Eastern maple top, set Honduras mahogany neck, 22-fret ebony fingerboard with dot inlay, matching color headstock with three-per-side tuners, STB, two Classic humbucker pickups, two knobs, three-way switch, available in Natural Gloss on back and sides with various finishes on top, mfg. 2004-present.

MSR $2,099	$950	$850	$775	$700	$625	$550	$475

CT4C - similar to the CT3M, except has a Floyd Rose tremolo unit, mfg. 2004-present.

MSR $2,299	$1,025	$925	$825	$750	$675	$600	$525

CT4T - similar to the CT4M, except has a Wilkinson tremolo unit, mfg. 2004-present.

MSR $2,149	$975	$875	$800	$725	$650	$575	$500

CT6M - offset double cutaway contoured mahogany body with a 20mm thick flamed curly maple top, set Honduras mahogany neck, 22-fret ebony fingerboard with pearl block inlay, matching maple headstock with 24kt gold plated logo and three-per-side tuners, STB, two Classic humbucker pickups, two knobs, three-way switch, gold hardware, available in triple step stained color finishes on top, 25 in. scale, mfg. 2004-present.

MSR $3,599	$1,300	$1,150	$1,000	$900	$800	$700	$600

C

GRADING	100% MINT	98% NEAR MINT	95% EXC+	90% EXC	80% VG+	70% VG	60% G

CT6C - similar to the CT3M, except has a Floyd Rose tremolo unit, mfg. 2004-present.

MSR $3,799		$1,400	$1,250	$1,100	$950	$850	$750	$650

CT6T - similar to the CT3M, except has a Wilkinson tremolo unit, mfg. 2004-present.

MSR $3,649		$1,350	$1,200	$1,050	$925	$825	$725	$625

ELECTRIC: CONTOUR SERIES

CONTOUR 66 (C66) - offset double cutaway alder body, flamed maple top and headstock, graphite neck with dual action truss-rod, 22-fret ebony fingerboard with pearl dot inlay, 6-on-a-side tuners, 2 C22 Humbucking pickups, five-way switch, volume and tone knobs, fixed bridge, chrome hardware, available in various colors, mfg. 2003-present.

MSR $2,179		$875	$775	$700	$625	$550	$500	$450

C66T - similar to the C66 except has Wilkinson Tremolo unit, mfg. 2003-present.

MSR $2,279		$900	$800	$700	$625	$550	$475	$425

C66C - similar to the C66 except has Floyd Rose Tremolo unit, mfg. 2003-present.

MSR $2,379		$975	$875	$800	$725	$650	$575	$500

ELECTRIC: DC SERIES

Carvin AE185
courtesy Carvin

DC120 - offset double cutaway poplar body, 12-string, through-body maple neck, 24-fret ebony fingerboard with pearl block inlay, fixed bridge, graphite nut, 6-per-side locking Sperzel tuners, chrome hardware, 2 Carvin C22 humbucker pickups, volume/treble/bass and mix controls, bright boost, phase/coil split switches, active electronics, current mfg.

MSR $2,049		$925	$825	$750	$675	$600	$525	$450

DC125 - offset double cutaway poplar body, through-body maple neck, 24-fret ebony fingerboard with pearl dot inlay, fixed bridge, graphite nut, 6-on-a-side locking Sperzel tuners, chrome hardware, 1 Carvin humbucker pickup, volume control, one coil split switch, mfg. 1991-96.

		$525	$425	$375	$325	$275	$200	$150

Last MSR was $1,050.

DC125T - similar to DC125, except has standard Carvin vibrato, mfg. 1991-96.

		$600	$450	$395	$350	$275	$225	$175

Last MSR was $1,200.

DC127 - offset double cutaway alder body, through-body maple neck, 24-fret ebony fingerboard with pearl dot inlay, fixed bridge, graphite nut, 6-on-a-side locking Sperzel tuners, chrome hardware, 2 Carvin C22 humbucker pickups, volume/tone control, 3-position/2-coil split switches, mfg. 1991-present.

MSR $1,699		$725	$625	$550	$475	$425	$375	$325

DC127C - similar to DC127, except has double locking Floyd Rose vibrato, mfg. 1993-present.

MSR $1,899		$825	$725	$650	$575	$500	$450	$400

DC127M - similar to DC127, except has string-thru-body bridge, mfg. 2003-present.

MSR $1,749		$750	$650	$575	$500	$450	$400	$350

DC127T - similar to DC127, except has standard Carvin/Wilkinson vibrato, current mfg.

MSR $1,799		$775	$675	$600	$525	$475	$425	$375

DC135 - offset double cutaway poplar body, through-body maple neck, 24-fret ebony fingerboard with pearl dot inlay, fixed bridge, graphite nut, 6-on-a-side locking Sperzel tuners, chrome hardware, 2 Carvin S60 single coil/1 Carvin C22 humbucker pickups, volume/tone control, 3 pickup mini switches, mfg. 1991-present.

MSR $1,699		$725	$625	$550	$475	$425	$375	$325

DC135C - similar to DC135, except has double locking Floyd Rose vibrato, current mfg.

MSR $1,899		$825	$725	$650	$575	$500	$450	$400

DC135M - similar to DC135, except has strings-thru-body bridge, mfg. 2003-present.

MSR $1,749		$750	$650	$575	$500	$450	$400	$350

DC135T - similar to DC135, except has standard Carvin/Wilkinson vibrato, current mfg.

MSR $1,799		$775	$675	$600	$525	$475	$425	$375

DC145 - offset double cutaway poplar body, through-body maple neck, 24-fret ebony fingerboard with pearl dot inlay, fixed bridge, graphite nut, reverse peghead, 6-on-a-side locking Sperzel tuners, chrome hardware, 2 humbuckers/single coil Carvin pickups, volume/tone controls, 5-position/coil split switches, mfg. 1991-93, reintroduced 2004-present.

MSR $1,779		$750	$650	$575	$500	$425	$375	$325

DC145C - similar to DC145, except has a Floyd Rose tremolo, mfg. 2004-present.

MSR $1,979		$850	$750	$675	$600	$525	$450	$375

Last MSR was $1,370.

DC145T - similar to DC145, except has standard Carvin/Wilkinson vibrato, mfg. 1991-93, reintroduced 2004-present.

MSR $1,849		$800	$700	$625	$550	$475	$400	$350

Last MSR was $1,370.

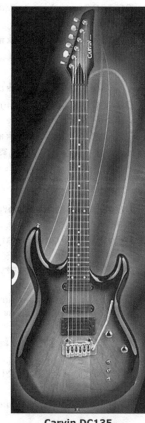

Carvin DC135
courtesy Carvin

C

GRADING	100% MINT	98% NEAR MINT	95% EXC+	90% EXC	80% VG+	70% VG	60% G

DC150 - double cutaway maple body, through-body maple neck, 24-fret maple fingerboard with black dot inlay, tune-o-matic bridge/stop tailpiece, 3-per-side tuners, black pickguard, chrome hardware, 2 Carvin M22 humbuckers, volume/tone controls, 3-position switch, 2-coil tap/1 phase mini switches, available in Classic White, Clear Maple, Ferrari Red, Jet Black, Pearl Blue, Pearl Red and Pearl White finishes, mfg. 1977-1991, reintroduced 2002-03.

1977-1991	N/A	$600	$500	$450	$425	$375	$325
2002-2003	$769	$675	$600	$525	$450	$395	$350

Last MSR was $1,499.

This model was available with an ebony fingerboard with pearl dot inlays.

DC150C - similar to DC150, except has double locking Floyd Rose vibrato, disc. 1991.

	N/A	$550	$475	$425	$375	$300	$250

Last MSR was $1,200.

DC200 - offset double cutaway poplar body, through-body maple neck, 24-fret ebony fingerboard with pearl block inlay, fixed bridge, graphite nut, 3-per-side locking Sperzel tuners, chrome hardware, 2 Carvin humbucker pickups, volume/treble/bass and mix controls, bright boost, phase and coil split switches, active electronics, current mfg.

MSR $1,899	$825	$725	$650	$575	$525	$475	$425

DC200C - similar to DC200, except has double locking Floyd Rose vibrato, mfg. 1994-present.

MSR $2,099	$925	$825	$750	$675	$600	$550	$500

DC200 Koa - similar to DC200, except has Koa body/neck, brass nut/bridge/tailpiece, Schaller M6 mini tuners, available in Black or Natural finishes, mfg. 1981-86.

	N/A	$850	$750	$650	$550	$450	$350

Last MSR was $560.

DC200M - similar to DC200, except has strings-thru-body bridge, mfg. 2003-present.

MSR $1,949	$850	$750	$675	$600	$525	$475	$425

DC200T - similar to DC200, except has standard Carvin/Wilkinson vibrato, current mfg.

MSR $1,999	$875	$775	$700	$625	$575	$525	$475

DC400 - offset double cutaway koa body, AAA bookmatched flamed maple top, koa through-body neck, 24-fret ebony fingerboard with abalone block inlay, fixed bridge, body matching headstock, graphite nut, 6-on-a-side locking Sperzel tuners, chrome hardware, 2 Carvin humbucker pickups, volume/treble/bass and mix controls, bright boost, phase and coil tap switches, available in Blueburst, Cherry Sunburst, Classic Sunburst, Clear finish, Crimson Red, Deep Purple, Emerald Green, Greenburst, Sapphire Blue, Tobacco Sunburst, or Vintage Yellow translucent finish, current mfg.

MSR $2,499	$1,025	$925	$825	$750	$675	$600	$525

Add $200 for AAAA book matched Claro Walnut top. Add $200 for Anniversary model upgrades.

In 1993, poplar body, through-body maple neck replaced original part/designs. In 1996, alder body replaced poplar body.

DC400C - similar to DC400, except has double locking Floyd Rose vibrato, mfg. 1994-present.

MSR $2,699	$1,125	$1,000	$900	$825	$750	$675	$600

Add $200 for AAAA book matched Claro Walnut top. Add $200 for Anniversary model upgrades.

DC400M - similar to DC400, except has string-thru-body bridge, mfg. 2003-present.

MSR $2,549	$1,050	$950	$850	$775	$700	$625	$550

Add $200 for AAAA book matched Claro Walnut top. Add $200 for Anniversary model upgrades.

DC400T - similar to DC400, except has standard Carvin/Wilkinson vibrato, current mfg.

MSR $2,599	$1,050	$950	$875	$800	$725	$650	$575

Add $200 for AAAA book matched Claro Walnut top.

DC400A ANNIVERSARY - similar to the DC400 except is an anniversary model that celebrates Carvin's 50th year (1946-1996), features a highly figured flamed maple top and headstock, five-piece maple and walnut laminated through-neck, three piece laminated body with fully rounded edges, available in various colors, mfg. 1996-present.

MSR $2,999	$1,200	$1,050	$950	$875	$800	$725	$650

DC400CA Anniversary - similar to DC400, except has double locking Floyd Rose vibrato, current mfg.

MSR $3,199	$1,300	$1,150	$1,050	$950	$875	$800	$725

DC400MA Anniversary - similar to DC400, except has string-thru-body bridge, mfg. 2003-present.

MSR $3,049	$1,250	$1,125	$1,000	$900	$825	$750	$675

DC400TA Anniversary - similar to DC400, except has standard Carvin/Wilkinson vibrato, current mfg.

MSR $3,099	$1,275	$1,125	$1,025	$925	$850	$775	$700

DC727 - 7-string configuration, offset double cutaway alder body, maple neck-thru-body, ebony fingerboard with dot inlays, 2 C26 humbucker pickups, 2 knobs, 3 switches, standard bridge, 4/3-per-side tuners, available in various colors, mfg. 2003-present.

MSR $1,849	$800	$700	$625	$550	$475	$425	$375

Add $70 for Floyd Rose Tremolo (Model DC727C). Add $70 for active/passive electronics.

DC747 - 7-string configuration, offset double cutaway alder body, maple neck-thru-body, ebony fingerboard with dot inlays, 2 C26 humbucker and 1 AP13 single coil pickups, 2 knobs, 3 switches, standard bridge, 4/3-per-side tuners, available in various colors, mfg. 2003-present.

MSR $1,899	$825	$725	$650	$575	$525	$475	$425

Add $70 for Floyd Rose Tremolo (Model DC727C). Add $30 for two coil tap switches.

C

GRADING	100% MINT	98% NEAR MINT	95% EXC+	90% EXC	80% VG+	70% VG	60% G

ELECTRIC: DN & DT SERIES

DN612 - offset sharp double cutaway poplar body, 2 maple through-body necks in a 12/6 configuration, 24-fret ebony fingerboards with pearl dot inlays, fixed bridges, graphite nut, 6-per-side on 12-string neck, 3-per-side on 6-string neck, locking Sperzel tuners, chrome hardware, 2 Carvin humbucker pickups, volume/tone control, two 3-way pickup selector/1 neck selector switches, 2 separate output jacks, disc. 1996.

	$1,600	$1,475	$1,325	$1,200	$1,000	$925	$800

Last MSR was $3,200.

This model was also available with a 4-string bass neck instead of a 12-string neck as the DN640, or with two bass necks (fretted and unfretted) as the DN440.

DN612 Koa - similar to the DN612, except has natural Koa body, mfg. 1981-86.

N/A	$1,800	$1,600	$1,450	$1,300	$1,100	$900

DT650 - offset single cutaway hard rock maple body, 2 maple through-body necks in a 12/6 configuration, 22-fret ebony fingerboards with pearl block inlays, bridge/stop tailpieces, 6-per-side on 12-string neck, 3-per-side on 6-string neck, Schaller M6 tuners, chrome hardware, black pickguards, 2 Carvin APH-6S humbucker pickups, volume/tone control (per neck), 3-way pickup selector (per neck), 2-coil tap/1 phase mini switches (per neck), neck selector switch, 2 separate output jacks, mfg. circa late 1970s.

N/A	$1,200	$1,000	$850	$700	$550	$400

Last MSR was $599.

This model was also available with a 4-string bass neck instead of a 12-string neck as the DB630.

ELECTRIC: HOLDSWORTH, ALLAN SIGNATURE (H1 & H2) SERIES

These models were developed in conjunction with guitarist Allan Holdsworth.

H1 - single rounded cutaway alder body, internal acoustic chambers, alder top, set-in alder neck, 25.5 in. scale, 24-fret ebony fingerboard with pearl dot inlays, graphite nut, 2/4 headstock design, locking Sperzel tuners, chrome hardware, tune-o-matic bridge and tailpiece, one Carvin H22 humbucker, volume/tone controls, mfg. 1996-2001.

	$750	$675	$625	$575	$525	$475	$425

Last MSR was $1,699.

Carvin DC400A Anniversary courtesy Carvin

H1T - similar to the H1, except features a Carvin/Wilkinson tremolo, mfg. 1996-2001.

	$800	$725	$675	$625	$575	$525	$475

Last MSR was $1,849.

H2 HOLDSWORTH - single rounded cutaway alder body, internal acoustic chambers, alder top, set-in alder neck, 25.5 in. scale, 24-fret ebony fingerboard with pearl dot inlays, graphite nut, 2/4 headstock design, locking Sperzel tuners, chrome hardware, tune-o-matic bridge and tailpiece, two Carvin H22 humbucker pickups, volume/tone controls, mfg. 1996-present.

MSR $2,199	$925	$850	$750	$675	$600	$550	$500

H2T Holdsworth - similar to the H2, except features a Carvin/Wilkinson tremolo, mfg. 1996-present.

MSR $2,299	$975	$875	$775	$700	$625	$575	$525

HF2 Fatboy - similar to the H2, except features a set neck, thicker body (2.375 in.), floating twin beam suspension, white birch top and back, optional flame maple top, mfg. 2001-present.

MSR $2,449	$1,025	$900	$800	$725	$650	$600	$550

ELECTRIC: LS SERIES

LS175 - offset double cutaway poplar body, through-body maple neck, 22-fret ebony fingerboard with pearl dot inlay, tune-o-matic bridge/stop tailpiece, 6-on-a-side tuners, chrome hardware, 3 stacked humbucker Carvin pickups, volume/tone controls, 5-position switch, available in Classic White, Ferrari Red, Jet Blue, Natural, Pearl Blue, Pearl Red, or Pearl White finishes, disc. 1991.

N/A	$600	$525	$475	$425	$375	$300

Last MSR was $1,140.

LS175C - similar to LS175, except has double locking Floyd Rose vibrato, disc. 1991.

N/A	$650	$575	$525	$475	$400	$325

Last MSR was $1,340.

ELECTRIC: SC SERIES

SC90 - single rounded cutaway alder body, through-body maple neck, 24-fret ebony fingerboard with pearl dot inlay, fixed bridge, graphite nut, 3-per-side locking Sperzel tuners, chrome hardware, 2 Carvin humbucker pickups, 2 volume/2 tone controls, 3-position switch, disc. 1996.

	$625	$550	$500	$450	$400	$350	$295

Last MSR was $1,199.

SC90C - similar to SC90, except has double locking Floyd Rose vibrato, current mfg.

MSR $1,899	$825	$725	$650	$575	$525	$450	$375

SC90M - similar to SC90, except has string-thru-body bridge, mfg. 2003-present.

MSR $1,749	$750	$650	$575	$500	$425	$375	$325

Carvin SC90S courtesy Carvin

GRADING	100% MINT	98% NEAR MINT	95% EXC+	90% EXC	80% VG+	70% VG	60% G
SC90S - similar to the SC90, except features a tune-o-matic bridge/stop tailpiece, current mfg.							
MSR $1,699	$725	$625	$550	$475	$400	$350	$300
SC90T - similar to SC90, except has standard Carvin/Wilkinson vibrato, current mfg.							
MSR $1,799	$775	$675	$600	$525	$450	$400	$350

ELECTRIC: TL SERIES

TL60 - single cutaway poplar body, through-body maple neck, 24-fret ebony fingerboard with pearl dot inlay, fixed bridge, graphite nut, 6-per-side locking Sperzel tuners, chrome hardware, 2 Carvin S60 single coil pickups, volume/tone control, series/parallel mini switch, 3-position switch, mfg. 1993-present.

MSR $1,699	$725	$625	$550	$475	$425	$350	$300

In 1996, alder body replaced poplar body.

TL60T - similar to TL60, except has standard Carvin/Wilkinson vibrato, current mfg.

MSR $1,769	$750	$650	$575	$500	$425	$375	$325

ELECTRIC: ULTRA V SERIES

ULTRA V - V-shape poplar body, maple through-body neck, 24-fret ebony fingerboard with pearl dot inlay, fixed bridge, graphite nut, 6-on-a-side locking Sperzel tuners, chrome hardware, 2 humbucker pickups, volume/tone control, 3-way switch, mfg. 1991-94.

	N/A	$550	$475	$425	$375	$325	$275
				Last MSR was $1,060.			

Ultra VT - similar to Ultra V, except has standard Carvin/Wilkinson vibrato, mfg. 1991-94.

	N/A	$600	$525	$475	$425	$375	$325
				Last MSR was $1,220.			

ELECTRIC: X SERIES

X220 - offset double cutaway V-shaped poplar body, maple through-body neck, 24-fret ebony fingerboard with pearl dot inlay, fixed bridge, graphite nut, 6-on-a-side locking Sperzel tuners, chrome hardware, 2 humbucker pickups, volume/tone control, 3-way/2-coil split switches, mfg. 1991-92.

	N/A	$575	$500	$450	$400	$350	$300
				Last MSR was $1,140.			

X220C - similar to X220, except has standard Carvin/Wilkinson vibrato, mfg. 1991-92.

	N/A	$625	$550	$500	$450	$395	$350
				Last MSR was $1,340.			

ELECTRIC BASS: GENERAL INFORMATION & OPTIONS

In 1996, Carvin´s combination bass bridge/tailpiece unit by Hipshot became standard on all Carvin bass models. This new design can be strung through the back of the bridge or through the body using string ferrules. Carvin briefly offered (1996-1997) the 2-Tek bridge (add $150) as a custom option; the 2-Tek was not available on left-handed configurations.

The standard features on all neck-through-body bass models are: 34 in. scale, graphite-reinforced maple neck, 24-fret ebony fingerboard, graphite nut, and chrome hardware. Carvin bass models are available in these standard colors: Classic White, Ferrari Red, Jet Black, Pearl Blue, Pearl Red, and Pearl White. The Natural Tung Oil finish was discontinued in 1998.

Add $20 for fretless fingerboard with white inlaid lines. Add $30 for fretless fingerboard with white inlaid lines and dot position markers. Add $60 for factory installed Hipshot bass detuner.

ELECTRIC BASS: B (BOLT-ON) SERIES

B 4 - offset double cutaway alder body, bolt-on graphite-reinforced maple neck, 22-fret ebony fingerboard with offset pearl dot inlay, Hipshot fixed bridge, graphite nut, 4-on-a-side tuners, chrome hardware, 2 J-style H50N humbucking pickups, 2 volume/1 tone controls, available in Black, Pearl Blue, Pearl White, Red, White, or Natural Tung Oil finish, mfg. 1997-present.

MSR $1,299	$625	$550	$475	$400	$350	$300	$200

Add $70 for Passive/Active electronics package (master volume, pickup blend, active bass/mid/treble controls).

This model has an optional fretless fingerboard (B 4F) at no extra charge.

B 5 - similar to the B 4, except features 5-string configuration, 3/2-per-side tuners, mfg. 1997-present.

MSR $1,499	$725	$625	$550	$475	$400	$350	$300

Add $70 for Passive/Active electronics package (master volume, pickup blend, active bass/mid/treble controls).

This model has an optional fretless fingerboard (B 5F) at no extra charge.

ELECTRIC BASS: BB (BUNNY BRUNEL) SERIES

BB Series basses were designed in conjunction with bassist Bunny Brunel. BB Series basses differ from the LB75 model with a slightly wider body, longer tapered bass horn, asymmetrical neck design, .25 in. wider at the 24th fret, and position dots are centered between the first four strings.

BB70 - offset double cutaway poplar body, through-body maple neck, 24-fret ebony fingerboard with offset pearl dot inlay, fixed bridge, graphite nut, 2-per-side tuners, chrome hardware, 2 J-style pickups, volume/treble/bass/mix controls, active electronics, mfg. 1994-present.

MSR $2,099	$900	$800	$725	$650	$575	$525	$475

Add $120 for P-Series electronics.

This model has an optional fretless fingerboard (BB70F).

GRADING	100% MINT	98% NEAR MINT	95% EXC+	90% EXC	80% VG+	70% VG	60% G

BB75 - offset double cutaway poplar body, 5-string, through-body maple neck, 24-fret ebony fingerboard with off-set pearl dot inlay, fixed bridge, graphite nut, 3/2-per-side tuners, chrome hardware, 2 J-style pickups, volume/treble/bass and mix controls, active electronics, current mfg.

MSR $2,199		$950	$850	$750	$675	$600	$550	$500

Add $120 for P-Series electronics.

This model has an optional fretless fingerboard (BB75F).

BB76 - offset double cutaway poplar body, 6-string, through-body maple neck, 24-fret ebony fingerboard with off-set pearl dot inlay, fixed bridge, graphite nut, 3-per-side tuners, chrome hardware, 2 J-style pickups, volume/treble/bass and mix controls, active electronics, current mfg.

MSR $2,399		$1,050	$925	$825	$750	$675	$600	$525

Add $120 for P-Series electronics.

This model has an optional fretless fingerboard (BB75F).

ELECTRIC BASS: LB SERIES

LB20 - offset double cutaway poplar body, through-body maple neck, 24-fret ebony fingerboard with pearl dot inlay, fixed bridge, graphite nut, 4-on-a-side locking Sperzel tuners, chrome hardware, 2 J-style H50N passive pickups, 2 volume/1 tone controls, mfg. 1991-present.

MSR $1,599		$725	$625	$550	$475	$400	$350	$300

In 1996, alder body replaced poplar body. This model has an optional fretless fingerboard (LB20F).

LB70 - offset double cutaway poplar body, through-body maple neck, 24-fret ebony fingerboard with pearl dot inlay, fixed bridge, graphite nut, 4-on-a-side locking Sperzel tuners, chrome hardware, 2 J-style pickups, volume/blend/bass/mid/treble controls, passive/active electronics, mfg. 1991-present.

MSR $1,799		$800	$700	$625	$550	$475	$400	$350

Add $120 for P-Series electronics.

In 1996, alder body replaced poplar body. This model has an optional fretless fingerboard (LB70F).

LB70A - similar to the LB70 except is 50th anniversary edition, features flamed maple top, 5 piece maple/walnut neck-through body, 3-piece maple/walnut/alder body, rounded body edges, current mfg. 1996-present.

MSR $3,499		$1,250	$1,100	$950	$850	$750	$675	$600

Add $100 for quilted maple top and matching headstock veneer. Add $120 for abalone block inlays.

This model has an optional fretless fingerboard (LB70AF).

Carvin TL60
courtesy Carvin

LB70W - similar to the LB70 except has California Claro Walnut top, five piece neck-through construction, three piece body, fully rounded edges, available in Natural finish, mfg. 1997-present.

MSR $3,499		$1,250	$1,100	$950	$850	$750	$675	$600

Add $120 for P-Series electronics.

LB75 - similar to LB70, except has 5-string configuration, and 3/2-per-side tuners, current mfg.

MSR $1,899		$850	$750	$675	$600	$525	$450	$375

Add $120 for P-Series electronics.

This model has an optional fretless fingerboard (LB75F). Before 1992, 5-on-a-side tuners were used.

LB75A - similar to the LB75 except is 50th anniversary edition, features flamed maple top, 5 piece maple/walnut neck-through body, 3-piece maple/walnut/alder body, rounded body edges, current mfg. 1996-present.

MSR $3,649		$1,300	$1,150	$1,000	$900	$800	$725	$650

Add $100 for quilted maple top and matching headstock veneer. Add $120 for abalone block inlays. Add $120 for P-Series electronics.

This model has an optional fretless fingerboard (LB75AF).

LB75W - similar to the LB75 except has California Claro Walnut top, five piece neck-through construction, three piece body, fully rounded edges, available in natural finish, mfg. 1997-present.

MSR $3,649		$1,300	$1,150	$1,000	$900	$800	$725	$650

Add $120 for P-Series electronics.

LB76 - similar to LB70, except has 6-string configuration, 3-per-side headstock, mfg. 1992-present.

MSR $2,099		$950	$850	$775	$700	$625	$550	$475

Add $120 for P-Series electronics.

This model has an optional fretless fingerboard (LB76F).

LB76A - similar to the LB76 except is 50th anniversary edition, features flamed maple top, 5 piece maple/walnut neck-through body, 3-piece maple/walnut/alder body, rounded body edges, current mfg. 1996-present.

MSR $3,899		$1,400	$1,200	$1,050	$950	$850	$750	$675

Add $100 for quilted maple top and matching headstock veneer. Add $120 for abalone block inlays. Add $120 for P-Series electronics.

This model has an optional fretless fingerboard (LB76AF).

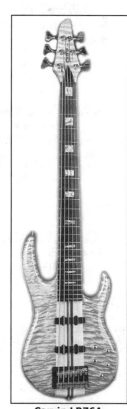

Carvin LB76A
courtesy Carvin

GRADING	100% MINT	98% NEAR MINT	95% EXC+	90% EXC	80% VG+	70% VG	60% G

LB76W - similar to the LB76 except has California Claro Walnut top, five piece neck-through construction, three piece body, fully rounded edges, available in natural finish, mfg. 1997-present.

	MSR $3,899	$1,400	$1,200	$1,050	$950	$850	$750	$675

Add $120 for P-Series electronics.

ELECTRIC BASS: TBS (TIMOTHY B. SCHMIT) SERIES

TBS4 - offset double cutaway alder body, Eastern hard-rock maple neck-through design, 24-fret ebony fingerboard, two pickups, one volume knob, chrome hardware, 4-per-side tuners, various color finishes, mfg. 2003-present.

	MSR $2,099	$950	$850	$775	$700	$625	$550	$475

ELECTRIC BASS: X SERIES

XB75 - offset double cutaway alder body, 5-string, maple neck-through design, 22-fret ebony fingerboard, two J-99 single coil pickups, six knobs, chrome hardware, 2/3-on-a-side tuners, various color finishes, 34 in. scale, mfg. 2002-present.

	MSR $2,049	$925	$825	$750	$675	$600	$525	$475

Add $120 for P-Series electronics.

This model is also available in a 31.25 in. scale.

XB76 - offset double cutaway alder body, 6-string, maple neck-through design, 22-fret ebony fingerboard, two J-99 single coil pickups, six knobs, chrome hardware, 3-per-side tuners, various color finishes, mfg. 2002-present.

	MSR $2,149	$1,025	$900	$800	$725	$650	$575	$500

Add $120 for P-Series electronics.

This model is also available in 31.25 in. scale.

CASIO
Instruments previously produced in Japan by Fuji Gen Gakki from 1987 to 1988.

The Casio company of Tokyo, Japan began producing keyboards in 1980. By the late 1980s, Casio unveiled the angular model **MG-500** and vaguely Fenderish **MG-510** electric guitars that could also be used as controllers by sending MIDI information. In 1988, Casio introduced the **PG-380**, a strat-styled guitar with an on-board synthesizer as well as a MIDI port. The PG-380 also has a companion module that takes up two rack spaces, and offers extra processing facilities. These guitars are usually priced between $100 and $300.

Casio also produced a number of guitar-shaped "Digital Guitars" in 1987. The **DG10** is more self-contained, while the **DG20** can send processing information to an external synthesizer. Both models have plastic bodies, plastic strings and a number of buttons and built-in features. These may appeal more to keyboard players, or entry level guitar synthesist enthusiasts. The plastic body models usually price under $150.

CASTELFIDARDO
Instruments previously built in Italy, production date unknown.

Castelfidardo guitars are associated with Italian luthier Alfredo Bugari (see also **Stonehenge II**), but the distributor (if any) to the U.S. market is still unknown.

David Pavlick is the current owner of this "mystery guitar." The 3-per-side headstock features a decal which reads "Castelfidardo - Excelsior - New York," and features a 15 5/16 in. archtop body, two pickups, bound 22-fret neck, 2 volume/2 tone controls, 3-way pickup selector on the upper bass bout, and trapeze tailpiece. Inside both f-holes there is "1 52" stamped into the back wood (source: David J. Pavlick, Woodbury, Connecticut).

CATALINA
See chapter on House Brands.

This trademark has been identified as a House Brand of the Abercrombie & Fitch company (source: Willie G. Moseley, *Stellas & Stratocasters*).

CATALYST INSTRUMENTS USA
Instruments currently manufactured in West Islip, New York.

Catalyst Instruments currently manufactures a **Panther** (Strat style configuration), **Tigress Bass** (Jazz bass style), the **Jakkerman** (Les Paul style, introduced 1999), and the **NXT** (new design). For current information and prices regarding these models, please contact the company directly (see Trademark Index).

CELINDER
Instruments currently produced in Copenhagen, Denmark.

Chris Celinder, founder of Celinder guitars, started business in 1987 as the Basslab, which is not to be confused with the Basslab in Germany. He worked with electronics wizard Henrik Thomsen until 1990 when he went on his own and started Celinder basses. They relocated within the city of Copenhagen in 1992 when space ran out, and this is where instruments are currently produced. Celinder basses are based off of the popular American Fender design of the Jazz and Precision basses. Celinder takes the original design of Leo Fender and incorporates modern-day knowledge to produce some of the finest bass guitars on the market. For more information or to locate an American dealer, refer to the Celinder website (see Trademark Index).

BASS GUITARS

Celinder focused mainly on the J-Series until the year 2000. Since then, they have several new series out. On the J and P Series there are several options that are available. Left-hand and Fretless models are all available at no cost. Other options such as wood choices, electronics, etc. are available at additional costs. Please refer to the Celinder website for all options (see Trademark Index).

The **J Series** are models that are based off of Fender Jazz Bass. The **J Classic 4** is a string bass that is a standard model bassed on the 1960 J bass and retails for $2,795. The **J Vintage 4 and 5** are early 1960s designs and retail at $2,850 for the four-string and $3,050 for the five-string. The **J Update** is based around the late '70s Jazz Bass and retails for $2,950 for the four-string and $3,150 for the five-string. The **J Miller Tribute** is a model based on Marcus Miller's '77 Jazz

GRADING	100% MINT	98% NEAR MINT	95% EXC+	90% EXC	80% VG+	70% VG	60% G

C

Bass. This model comes in four-string for $3,850 and $4,050 for the five-string. The **J Graham Tribute** is inspired by Mr. Graham´s White Moon bass. This also comes in four- and five-string variations retailing for $3,950 and $4,150, respectively.

After the success of the **J Series** basses, Celinder released the P Series, which are models that are based on the Fender Precision Bass. This series starts with the **P Classic 4**, which is a standard P-Bass from around 1957. This model lists for $2,695. The **P Vintage 4** and **5** are based on early 1960s Fender Precision basses and retail for $2,650 and $2,850, respectively. The **P Update 4** and **5** are P-Basses that are based on the mid to late 1970s models. These retail for $2,750 and $2,950, respectively.

The **AURA** series are models that are built with some higher quality woods. The AURA comes in four, five, and six string models. The body of these guitars are made out of Brazilian mahogany. They retail for $4,200, $4,550, and $4,700 respectively.

The Custom Series are high-end instrument where the customer is invited to use his/her creative processess and create a guitar that is truly unique to the player. This concept is the original idea that dates back to 1985, even before the company was started. The customer is the one who comes up with all the options on the guitar. The base price starts out at $4,300 for a four string (disc.), $4,600 for a five-string, and $4,900 for a six-string or the **octa8** (disc.).

Add approx. 5-10% per option depending on grade.

CHANDLER

Instruments currently built in Chico, CA since circa 2002. Previously built in Burlingame, CA, from 1982-2000.

Chandler was located in Burlingame, California 1980-2000. The company originally focused on providing high quality replacement guitar parts, and then expanded to include guitar production beginning in 1985. Chandler´s high quality models definitely feature some original design innovations!

In 1996, Chandler began offering a line of lap steels. The **RH-2** features a solid mahogany body, while the **RH-4** is a hollow body of mahogany or koa. The **RH-7** is a baritone model lap steel (30 in. scale length). Last retail list prices for the lap steel models was $399.

The company offered a line of guitar accessories such as the Super 60 hand wound pickups, Chandler vintage-style replacement pickups, the CC-90 soap bar pickup, replacement pickguards, as well as other related components. Chandler´s electrical components featured the Stereo Digital Echo, an analog/digital rack unit that emulates a tape-driven echo effect; the Dynamo tube preamp, Tone-X active mid-boost circuit, and others.

Circa 2002, Chandler started producing guitars again. Some models are based on previous designs while others are new. For more information, contact Chandler directly (see Trademark Index).

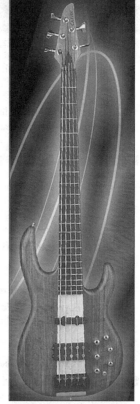

Carvin XB75 Bass
courtesy Carvin

ELECTRIC: 555 SERIES

555 CLASSIC (MODEL 5552) - double sharp cutaway alder body, set-in maple neck, 25.5 in. scale, white pickguard, 22-fret rosewood fingerboard with pearl dot inlay, fixed bridge, slotted peghead, 3-per-side tuners, chrome hardware, pearl or tortoiseshell pickguard, 3 mini humbucker Chandler pickups, volume/tone control, 5-position switch, available in Gloss Black (**Model 5552**), Crimson Red (**Model 5554**), Surf Green (**Model 5558**), Trans. Vintage Blonde, or Trans. Wine Red finishes, mfg. 1992-2000.

$1,200	$1,050	$925	$800	$675	$550	$425

Last MSR was $1,598.

Add $100 for figured maple top (Model 5550).

In 1993, Crimson Red finish was added and Transparent Wine Red finish was discontinued.

555 Twin (Model 5560) - similar to the 555 Classic, except has two mini humbucker pickups, Vintage Blond finish, mfg. 1993-98.

$1,250	$1,100	$975	$850	$725	$600	$475

Last MSR was $1,849.

ELECTRIC: AUSTIN SPECIAL & FUTURAMA SERIES

AUSTIN SPECIAL - single offset sharp cutaway bound alder body, bolt-on maple neck, 25.5 in. scale, 22-fret rosewood fingerboard with pearl dot inlay, fixed bridge, 6-on-a-side tuners, chrome hardware, 1 single coil (neck)/ 2 dual single coils (bridge) lipstick tube pickups, volume and push/pull tone chickenhead control knobs, 3-position switch, available in Black finish, mfg. 1992-96, 1998-2000.

$1,150	$1,000	$900	$775	$650	$500	$375

Last MSR was $1,499.

In 1993, White finish became available. This model was developed by Ted Newman-Jones with input from Keith Richards (Rolling Stones).

Austin Special 5 - similar to Austin Special, except has 5-string configuration, mfg. 1993-95.

$1,200	$1,050	$925	$800	$675	$550	$425

Last MSR was $1,700.

Austin Special R - similar to Austin Special, except has traditional tele-style single coil in bridge position, mfg. 1993 only.

N/A	$900	$800	$700	$600	$500	$400

Last MSR was $998.

Austin Baritone - similar to Austin Special, except has 30 in. scale (longer neck), 2 single coil lipstick tube pickups, tremolo bridge, available in Gold Super Sparkle, Red Super Sparkle, or Surf Green finishes, mfg. 1993-95.

$1,450	$1,250	$1,050	$900	$750	$650	$575

Last MSR was $1,900.

Chandler Austin Special
courtesy Chandler

GRADING	100% MINT	98% NEAR MINT	95% EXC+	90% EXC	80% VG+	70% VG	60% G

FUTURAMA (MODEL 1512) - offset double cutaway alder body, bolt-on maple neck, 25.5 in. scale, 22-fret rosewood fingerboard with dot inlay, custom tremolo, 6-on-a-side tuners, chrome hardware, 2-tone pickguard, 3 Chandler Super 60 pickups, volume/tone controls, 5-position switch, available in 3-Tone Sunburst, Black, Coral Pink, Fiesta Red, Olympic White, Surf Green, mfg. 1996-2000.

	$950	$850	$750	$625	$525	$400	$300

Last MSR was $1,199.

Add $40 for metallic finish (Model 1514). Add $50 for Wilkinson tremolo.

ELECTRIC: METRO & SPITFIRE SERIES

METRO (MODEL 2010) - offset double cutaway alder body, bolt-on bird's-eye maple neck, 25.5 in. scale, 22-fret rosewood or maple fingerboard with dot inlay, fixed bridge, 6-on-a-side tuners, chrome hardware, pearl or tortoiseshell pickguard, P-90 style (neck)/humbucker (bridge) pickups, volume/tone control, 3-position switch, chrome controls plate, available in Fiesta Red, mfg. 1995-2000.

	$900	$800	$700	$600	$500	$400	$300

Last MSR was $1,139.

Add $50 for Wilkinson tremolo.

Metro Deluxe (Model 2100) - similar to Metro, except has sparkle finish and ivory (or shell or pearl) bound body, mfg. 1995-98.

	$1,100	$1,000	$900	$775	$595	$475	$375

Last MSR was $1,449.

Add $100 for figured maple top (Model 2140).

Metro Baritone (Model 8522) - similar to the Metro, except features a 30 in. scale, 24-fret rosewood fingerboard with pearl dot inlay, tremolo bridge, 2 single coil lipstick pickups, available in Black, Surf Green, or White finishes, mfg. 1995-2000.

	$1,100	$1,000	$900	$775	$600	$475	$375

Last MSR was $1,499.

Add $100 for ivory, shell, or pearl body binding (Model 8520). Add $200 for sparkle finish and body binding (Model 8500).

SPITFIRE (MODEL 1210, PATHOCASTER) - offset double cutaway alder (or swamp ash or mahogany) body, bolt-on maple neck, 25.5 in. scale, 22-fret rosewood or maple fingerboard with dot inlay, fixed bridge, 6-on-a-side tuners, chrome hardware, pearl or tortoiseshell pickguard, 3 Chandler single coil pickups, volume/2 tone controls, 5-position switch, available in Natural finish, mfg. 1995-2000.

	$650	$575	$500	$450	$375	$300	$225

Last MSR was $899.

Add $50 for Wilkinson tremolo. Add $180 for vintage finish (Model 1214): 2-Tone Sunburst, 3-Tone Sunburst, Black, Olympic White, or Surf Green. Add $240 for vintage finish and 3 Chandler Super 60 pickups (Model 1220). Add $340 for vintage finish and 3 Chandler Lipstick tube pickups (Model 1222).

ELECTRIC: TELEPATHIC SERIES

TELEPATHIC BASIC (MODEL 1110) - single round cutaway alder body, pearloid pickguard, bolt-on maple neck, 25.5 in. scale, 22-fret maple or rosewood fingerboard with dot inlays, fixed bridge, 6-on-a-side Gotoh tuners, pearl or tortoiseshell pickguard, chrome hardware, Chandler single coil pickup, volume/tone control, available in Natural finish, mfg. 1994-2000.

	$500	$450	$400	$350	$300	$250	$175

Last MSR was $649.

When the Telepathic model debuted in 1994, it was available in a wide range of finishes: 2-Tone Sunburst, 3-Tone Sunburst, Chandler Super sparkle, Cherry Sunburst, Gloss Black, Olympic White, Surf Green and Vintage Blonde. As the model's popularity grew, these finishes were designated to specific variations.

Telepathic Standard (Model 1114) - similar to Telepathic Basic, except has 2 Chandler single coil pickups, available in 2-Tone Sunburst finish, mfg. 1994-98.

	$900	$800	$675	$550	$450	$375	$295

Last MSR was $1,149.

Telepathic Deluxe (Model 1122) - similar to Telepathic Basic, except has ivory (or shell or pearl) body binding, 2 Chandler single coil pickups, available in 2-Tone Sunburst, mfg. 1994-98.

	$975	$875	$750	$695	$550	$450	$325

Last MSR was $1,249.

Add $100 for Chandler Super Sparkle finish (Model 1130).

TELEPATHIC THINLINE TV (MODEL 1132) - similar to Telepathic, except has semi-hollow mahogany body, f-hole, and Seymour Duncan mini 59 pickup, available in TV Blond or SG Red finishes, mfg. 1995-2000.

	$1,000	$900	$775	$675	$550	$450	$325

Last MSR was $1,299.

Telepathic Thinline (Model 1150) - similar to Telepathic Basic, except has semi-hollow mahogany body, figured maple top, f-hole, and 2 single coil pickups, mfg. 1995-98.

	$1,200	$1,000	$875	$725	$600	$525	$395

Last MSR was $1,549.

GRADING	100% MINT	98% NEAR MINT	95% EXC+	90% EXC	80% VG+	70% VG	60% G

ELECTRIC BASS

HI FIDELITY (MODEL 1610) - offset double cutaway P-bass-style alder body, bolt-on maple neck, 34 in. scale, 21-fret maple or rosewood fingerboard with dot inlay, chrome hardware, 4-on-a-side tuners, fixed bridge (with optional through-body stringing), tortoiseshell pickguard, 2 Chandler Super 60 single coil pickups, 2 volume/1 tone controls, available in vintage finishes, mfg. 1996-2000.

	$1,150	**$1,000**	**$825**	**$700**	**$575**	**$495**	**$350**

Last MSR was $1,449.

Add $40 for Metallic finish (Model 1612).

OFFSET CONTOUR BASS (MODEL 1622) - offset double cutaway J-bass-style alder body, bolt-on maple neck, 34 in. scale, 21-fret maple or rosewood fingerboard with dot inlay, chrome hardware, 4-on-a-side tuners, fixed bridge, tortoiseshell pickguard, 2 Chandler single coil pickups, 2 volume/1 tone controls, available in Natural finish, mfg. 1996-2000

	$1,000	**$875**	**$750**	**$695**	**$550**	**$450**	**$325**

Last MSR was $1,249.

Add $200 for Vintage finish (Model 1620).

ROYALE 12-STRING BASS (MODEL 1630) - single cutaway Honduran mahogany body, bolt-on graphite-reinforced maple neck, 21-fret rosewood fingerboard with pearl dot inlays, retro-designed layered plastic headstock, tortoise (or pearl or ivory) body binding with matching pickguard, 6-per-side tuners, chrome hardware, 1 split coil/2 soap bar Super 60 pickups, 3 volume controls, 3 on/off pickup selector switches, mfg. 1996-2000.

	N/A	**N/A**	**N/A**	**N/A**	**N/A**	**N/A**	**N/A**

Last MSR was $3,500.

This specialty model was designed in conjunction with Tom Petersson (Cheap Trick). Too few models exist for adequate secondary market information.

Chandler Spitfire courtesy Chandler

CHAPIN

Instruments currently built in San Jose, California.

Handcrafted Chapin guitars feature carefully thought out designs that provide ergonomic comfort and a wide palette of tones. All Chapin guitars are handcrafted by luthiers Bill Chapin and Fred Campbell; all guitars feature the Campbell/Chapin locking dovetail set-in neck joint.

The Chapin Insight guitar inspection camera features a small-bodied camera on a flexible mount that allows the luthier/repairman an inside view of the acoustic guitar to help solve internal problems. This low-light camera features a 3.6 mm lens for ultra-close crack inspection, and has an RCA output that feeds directly into a VCR or camcorder for video documentation. The Insight (list $349) operates on a 9-volt battery - so it is mobile as well. The importance to collectors? Now there is a tool for proper guitar authentication: the internal signatures and dates of an acoustic (or semihollow body) guitar can be read in seconds - and right at the guitar show, if necessary!

For current information on Chapin´s acoustic electric models, please refer to the *Blue Book of Acoustic Guitars*.

ELECTRIC

The main Chapin electric design is based on the single cutaway body of a tele. This model was previously called the Falcon, but was renamed the T-Bird in 2003. The **T-Bird** (list $2,275 + options) has an alder or swamp ash body, maple neck with Campbell/Chapin locking dovetail joint, maple or rosewood fingerboard, 25.5 in. scale, 2 Van Zandt single coil pickups, volume/tone controls, 3-way selector, and a thin nitrocellulose lacquer finish. The **T-Bird Special** (list $2,475 + options) has Velvet Hammer pickups, custom wiring, and a 5-way switch; the **T-Bird Deluxe** has a 24.9 in. scale, 2 Tom Holmes PAF or Filtertron style humbuckers, hardtail bridge, and gold hardware - with a Bigsby or tune-o-matic bridge/stop tailpiece as custom options (list $2,475 + options).

The **Hawk** is a cross between the Tele and SG body designs. This model was originally designed for Billy Johnson (John Lee Hooker´s band), and features a beveled mahogany or alder body, mahogany or maple neck, ebony or rosewood fingerboard, single coil/P-90-style or Tom Holmes humbucker pickups, 3-way switch, 25.5 in. scale, and a bolt-on or set neck (list $2,200 + options). A Cherry nitrocellulose finish is standard.

The semi-hollow **Fatline** ($3,275 + options) has a mahogany body with three different internal tuned chamber designs. The set-in figured maple neck is available in a 24.9" in. or 25.5 in. scale, with a bound 22-fret rosewood or African blackwood fingerboard. The 2 Velvet Hammer humbuckers are set into an AAAA grade figured maple or redwood top, and feature custom wiring. The all-out **Fatline TV** (list $4,875 + options) was designed originally for guitarist Tim Volpicella, and features private stock aged tonewoods, quilted or flame maple top, koa pickguard/headstock plate/back plates, Brazilian rosewood fingerboard, vibrato bridge, gold hardware (call for more description of this model – these specs don´t do it justice).

ELECTRIC BASS

The **Phoenix** (last MSR $2,675) has a double cutaway one-piece alder body, quilted or flame maple top, set-in graphite-reinforced wenge neck, 34 in. scale, striped ebony fingerboard, Bartolini pickups (P/J, JJ, or soap bar), active TBT electronics, Mann Made bridge, Hipshot Ultralite tuners, and a nitrocellulose finish. The Phoenix has an optional 35 in. scale 5-string (last MSR $2,975), 35 in. scale 6-string (last MSR $3,195), with a fretless fingerboard, and multi-laminated body or choice of woods. This model was disc. circa 2003.

Chapin T-Bird Courtesy Chapin

C

CHAPPELL
Instruments currently built in Richmond, California since 1969.

Luthier Sean Chappell has been building custom guitars and repairing musical instruments in the San Francisco Bay Area for the past twenty=eight years. Chappell's partial list of clients includes John Lee Hooker, Tom Waits, Elvin Bishop, and David Newman. Recently, Chappell collaborated with guitarist Roy Rogers on a custom double neck dubbed Duo Chops, a blues guitar from hell.

CHARVEL
Instruments currently produced overseas and distributed by the Fender Musical Instrument Corporation. Trademark previously produced in Korea. The Charvel trademark was established in 1978 by the Charvel Manufacturing Company. Distributed by Jackson/Charvel Guitar Company (Akai Musical Instruments) of Fort Worth, TX. Charvel instruments were previously manufactured in the U.S. between 1978 and 1985. Later (post-1985) production was in U.S., Japan, and Korea.

In the late 1970s, Wayne Charvel's Guitar Repair shop in Azusa, California acquired a reputation for making custom, high-quality bodies and necks. Grover Jackson began working at the shop in 1977, and a year later bought out Charvel and moved the company to San Dimas. Jackson debuted the Charvel custom guitars at the 1979 NAMM show, and the first catalog depicting the bolt-neck beauties and custom options arrived in 1981.

The standard models from Charvel Manufacturing carried a list price between $880 and $955, and the amount of custom options was staggering. In 1983, the Charvel company began offering neck-through models under the Jackson trademark.

Grover Jackson licensed the Charvel trademark to the International Music Corporation (IMC) in 1985; the company was sold to them a year later. In late 1986, production facilities were moved to Ontario, California. Distribution eventually switched from Charvel/Jackson to the Jackson/Charvel Guitar company, currently a branch of the Akai Musical Instruments company. As the years went by and the Charvel line expanded, its upper end models were phased out and moved into the Jackson line (which had been the Charvel/Jackson Company's line of custom made instruments) and were gaining more popularity. For example, the **Charvel Avenger** (Mfg. 1991 to 1992), became the **Jackson Rhoads EX Pro** (mfg. 1992-recent). For further details, see the Jackson guitars section in this edition.

In 1988, Charvel sent a crew of luthiers to Japan for a year or so to crosstrain the Japanese builders on building methods for custom-built guitars. The resulting custom instruments had a retail list price between $1,000 and $1,300. U.S. custom-built guitars have a four-digit serial number and the Japanese custom-built models have a six-digit serial number. Numbers may be prefaced with a "C," which may stand for "custom-made" (this point has not been completely verified).

By the early 1990s, the only Charvel models left were entry level 'Strat'-style electrics and dreadnought and jumbo-style (full-bodied and cutaways) acoustic guitars. In the late 1990s, even the electrics were phased out in favor of the acoustic and acoustic/electric models. During 1999, instruments with the Charvel trademark had ceased production, and Wayne Charvel began building a new line of instruments utilizing the Wayne Guitars trademark.

Jackson purchased the rights to Charvel and by 2002 were producing guitars once again. In the fall of 2002, Fender (FMIC) purchased the Jackson/Charvel corporation. Currently Jackson/Charvel still produces guitars in their manufacturing facilities and these are distributed by FMIC, (early Charvel history courtesy Baker Rorick, Guitar Shop magazine; additional information courtesy Roland Lozier, Lozier Piano & Music).

MODEL IDENTIFICATION

As a general rule of thumb, you can identify the country of origin on earlier instruments that have the guitar-shaped **Charvel** logo by the color of the logo. The early model guitars with black or gold logos were manufactured in the U.S., and the ones with white logos were manufactured overseas. Early guitar-shaped logos have a '3-per-side headstock' in the graphic; current models have a 6-on-a-side headstock in the graphic.

Another way to determine the origin of manufacture is manufacturer's retail price point. In most cases, the lower the retail price (last retail price on discontinued models) the more likely the instrument was manufactured overseas. Charvel **San Dimas** and **Charvel USA** guitars were built in California. Other production models are built in Japan; **CHS** series electrics were built in Korea.

The only production models under the Charvel trademark currently produced are the **550** and **625** series Acoustic models. These acoustics are built in Korea.

Charvel has produced guitars throughout the years and has different series that have run in different years. Currently they have a custom shop that produces guitars with different options and body woods. Prices for a bolt-on guitar star at $2,500. Prices for a bolt-on bass start at $2,000.

On standard models there are several color options available at an upcharge.

ELECTRIC: CHS SERIES

CHS 1 - offset double cutaway alder body, white pickguard, bolt-on maple neck, 22-fret rosewood fingerboard with pearl dot inlay, standard vibrato, screened peghead logo, 6-on-a-side tuners, black chrome hardware, 3 single coil exposed pickups, volume/tone controls, 5-position switch, available in Black, Bright Red, Metallic Blue, and Snow White finishes, mfg. 1995-97.

$225	$200	$175	$150	$125	$100	$85

Last MSR was $345.

CHS 2 - similar to CHS 1, except has 2 single coil/humbucker pickups, available in Black, Bright Red, Metallic Blue, and Snow White finishes, mfg. 1995-97.

$225	$200	$175	$150	$125	$100	$85

Last MSR was $345.

CHS 3 - similar to CHS 1, except has no pickguard, 24-fret fingerboard, 2 exposed humbucker pickups, available in Black, Bright Red, Metallic Blue, and Snow White finishes. Mfg. 1995 to 1997.

$275	$225	$195	$150	$125	$100	$90

Last MSR was $395.

ELECTRIC: CLASSIC SERIES

STX CUSTOM - offset double cutaway basswood body, pearloid pickguard, bolt-on maple neck, 22-fret rosewood fingerboard with pearl dot inlay, double locking vibrato, 6-on-a-side tuners, chrome hardware, 2 single coil/1 humbucker Jackson pickups, volume/tone control, 5-position switch, available in Black and Deep Metallic Blue finishes, mfg. 1991-94.

$625	$525	$450	$350	$325	$300	$275

Last MSR was $895.

GRADING	**100% MINT**	**98% NEAR MINT**	**95% EXC+**	**90% EXC**	**80% VG+**	**70% VG**	**60% G**

STX Custom (Trans) - similar to STX Custom, except has ash body, available in Tobacco Sunburst, Trans. Blue or Trans. Red finishes, mfg. 1991-94.

	$695	$595	$500	$400	$350	$325	$300

Last MSR was $995.

STX DELUXE - similar to STX Custom, except has standard vibrato, available in Black, Deep Metallic Blue, Dark Metallic Red, Pearl White and Turquoise finishes, mfg. 1991-94.

	$475	$425	$350	$275	$250	$225	$200

Last MSR was $695.

TX CUSTOM (TE CUSTOM) - single cutaway basswood body, pearloid pickguard, bolt-on maple neck, 22-fret maple fingerboard with black dot inlay, fixed bridge, 6-on-a-side tuners, chrome hardware, volume/tone control, 5-position switch, available in Black, Dark Metallic Red, Tobacco Sunburst, or Turquoise finishes, mfg. 1992-96.

	$525	$400	$350	$275	$250	$200	$175

Last MSR was $795.

This model was also available with a rosewood fingerboard with pearl dot inlay.

TX Custom (Trans) - similar to TX Custom, except has ash body, available in Tobacco Sunburst finish, disc. 1996.

	$525	$400	$350	$295	$250	$225	$195

Last MSR was $795.

This model was also available with a rosewood fingerboard with pearl dot inlay.

TTX - single cutaway basswood body, pearloid pickguard, bolt-on maple neck, 24-fret maple fingerboard with black dot inlay, standard vibrato, 6-on-a-side locking tuners, chrome hardware, single coil/humbucker Jackson pickup, 3-position/mini switches, available in Black, Deep Metallic Blue, Deep Metallic Red, or Metallic Purple finishes, mfg. 1993 only.

	$400	$350	$300	$250	$225	$195	$150

Last MSR was $595.

TTX (Trans) - similar to TTX, except has ash body, available in Trans. Black, Trans. Blue, or Trans. Red finishes, mfg. 1993 only.

	$425	$375	$325	$250	$225	$200	$175

Last MSR was $645.

Charvel CHS-2
courtesy Charvel

ELECTRIC: CONTEMPORARY SERIES

275 DELUXE CLASSIC - offset double cutaway hardwood body, white pickguard, bolt-on maple neck, 22-fret maple fingerboard with black dot inlay, double locking vibrato, 6-on-a-side tuners, chrome hardware, single coil/humbucker pickups, volume control, 5-position switch, available in Candy Blue, Ferrari Red, Midnight Black, or Snow White finishes, mfg. 1991-92.

	$395	$350	$300	$250	$225	$175	$150

Last MSR was $600.

275 Deluxe Contemporary - similar to 275 Deluxe Classic, except has rosewood fingerboard with pearl dot inlay, black hardware, 3 stacked coil pickups (2 side by side at the bridge), mfg. 1988-1991.

	$450	$395	$350	$275	$250	$225	$200

Last MSR was $695.

375 DELUXE CLASSIC - offset double cutaway hardwood body, white pickguard, bolt-on maple neck, 22-fret maple fingerboard with black dot inlay, double locking vibrato, 6-on-a-side tuners, chrome hardware, 2 single coil/1 humbucker pickups, volume/tone controls, 5-position switch, available in Candy Red, Desert Crackle, Magenta, Metallic Black, Pearl Blue, Pearl White, or Platinum finishes, mfg. 1988-1991.

	$495	$425	$350	$275	$250	$225	$200

Last MSR was $700.

Add 10% for figured wood body with Natural finish.

375 Deluxe Contemporary - similar to 375 Deluxe Classic, except has rosewood fingerboard with pearl dot inlay, available in Candy Red, Magenta, Metallic Black, Pearl Blue, or Pearl White finishes, mfg. 1991-92.

	$525	$475	$395	$325	$275	$250	$225

Last MSR was $795.

Add 10% for figured wood body with Natural finish.

This model has an optional maple fingerboard with black dot inlay.

475 SPECIAL CLASSIC - offset double cutaway hardwood body, white pickguard, bolt-on maple neck, 22-fret maple fingerboard with black dot inlay, double locking vibrato, 6-on-a-side tuners, chrome hardware, 2 stacked coil/1 Jackson humbucker pickups, volume/2 tone controls, 5-position switch, available in Candy Red, Desert Crackle, Magenta, Metallic Black, Pearl Blue, or Pearl White finishes, mfg. 1988-1991.

	$495	$425	$350	$275	$250	$225	$200

Last MSR was $700.

Add 10% for figured wood body with Natural finish.

Charvel TX Custom
courtesy Charvel

GRADING	100% MINT	98% NEAR MINT	95% EXC+	90% EXC	80% VG+	70% VG	60% G

475 Special Contemporary - similar to 475 Special Classic, except has bound rosewood fingerboard with pearl shark fin inlay, bound peg-head, black hardware, active electronics, available in Candy Red, Magenta, Metallic Black, Pearl Blue, or Pearl White finishes, mfg. 1991-92.

	$695	$595	$500	$400	$375	$325	$275

Last MSR was $995.

Add 10% for figured wood body with Natural finish.

550 XL PROFESSIONAL - offset double cutaway hardwood body, through-body maple neck, 22-fret bound rosewood fingerboard with pearl shark fin inlay, double locking vibrato, 6-on-a-side tuners, black hardware, Jackson humbucker pickup, volume control, available in Candy Red, Metallic Black, Pearl White, Platinum, or Snow White finishes, mfg. 1988-1991.

	$675	$575	$475	$395	$350	$325	$275

Last MSR was $970.

650 XL CONTEMPORARY - offset double cutaway hardwood body, through-body maple neck, 22-fret bound rosewood fingerboard with pearl shark fin inlay, double locking vibrato, 6-on-a-side tuners, gold hardware, 2 stacked coil pickups and 1 Jackson humbucker pickup, volume/2 tone controls, 5-position switch, active electronics, available in Candy Red, Metallic Black, Pearl White, or Snow White finishes, mfg. 1991-92.

	$850	$775	$650	$525	$475	$425	$375

Last MSR was $1,295.

650 XL Professional - similar to 650 XL Contemporary, except has 2 single coil/1 humbucker pickups, available in Candy Red, Desert Crackle, Metallic Black, Pearl White, Platinum, or Snow White finishes, mfg. 1988-1991.

	$775	$650	$550	$450	$395	$350	$300

Last MSR was $1,100.

750 XL PROFESSIONAL - offset double cutaway hardwood body, bolt-on maple neck, 22-fret bound rosewood fingerboard with pearl shark fin inlay, double locking vibrato, 6-on-a-side tuners, gold hardware, 2 Jackson humbucker pickups, volume/tone controls, 5-position switch, active electronics, available in Candy Red, Desert Crackle, Metallic Black, Pearl White, Platinum, or Snow White finishes, mfg. 1988-1991.

	$795	$700	$575	$475	$425	$375	$325

Last MSR was $1,170.

Add 10% for figured maple top with Natural finish.

AVENGER - shark fin style hardwood body, bolt-on maple neck, 22-fret rosewood fingerboard with white dot inlay, double locking vibrato, 6-on-a-side Gotoh tuners, black hardware, 3 stacked coil Charvel pickups (2 side by side at the bridge), volume control, 5-position switch, available in Candy Blue, Ferrari Red, Midnight Black, or Snow White finishes, mfg. 1991-92.

	$475	$425	$350	$275	$250	$225	$200

Last MSR was $695.

PREDATOR - offset double cutaway hardwood body, bolt-on maple neck, 22-fret rosewood fingerboard with white dot inlay, double locking vibrato, reverse headstock, 6-on-a-side tuners, black hardware, blade stacked coil/humbucker Jackson pickups, volume control, 5-position switch, available in Candy Blue, Candy Red, Magenta, Midnight Black, or Pearl White finishes, mfg. 1991 only.

	$550	$475	$395	$325	$275	$225	$200

Last MSR was $795.

SPECTRUM - similar to Predator, except has white pickguard, chrome hardware, 3 stacked coil Jackson pickups, active electronics with switch, available in Candy Red, Midnight Black, Sea Green and Tobacco Sunburst finishes, mfg. 1991 only.

	$625	$525	$450	$350	$325	$275	$250

Last MSR was $895.

This model was also available with maple fingerboard with black dot inlay.

ELECTRIC: CS SERIES

CS Series models were produced in Korea.

CS 10 - offset double cutaway alder body, bolt-on maple neck, 22-fret rosewood fingerboard with dot inlay, GR-6 steel fulcrum vibrato, 6-per-side tuners, chrome hardware, pickguard, 3 single coil pickups, volume/tone controls, 5-way switch, available in Black, Bright Red, Blue, or White finishes, disc. 1998.

		$225	$175	$150	$125	$115	$95	$75

Last MSR was $289.

CS 20 - similar to the CS 10, except features 2 single coil/humbucker pickups, disc. 1998.

		$225	$175	$150	$125	$115	$95	$75

Last MSR was $289.

ELECTRIC: CX SERIES

This series was manufactured in Korea.

CX290 - strat-style basswood body, white pickguard, bolt-on maple neck, 22-fret rosewood fingerboard with pearl dot inlay, standard vibrato, 6-per-side tuners, chrome hardware, 3 single coil Jackson pickups, volume/tone control, 5-position switch, available in Black, Bright Red, Deep Metallic Blue, and Snow White finishes, mfg. 1992-96.

		$250	$195	$175	$150	$125	$100	$95

Last MSR was $395.

This model also available with 2 single coil/humbucker pickup configuration (Model CX291).

C

CX390 - strat-style basswood body, black pickguard, bolt-on maple neck, 22-fret rosewood fingerboard with pearl dot inlay, double locking vibrato, 6-on-a-side tuners, chrome hardware, 2 single coil/1 Jackson humbucker pick-ups, volume/tone control, 5-position switch, available in Black, Bright Red, Deep Metallic Blue, or Snow White finishes, mfg. 1992-96.

	$275	$225	$200	$175	$150	$125	$100

Last MSR was $495.

This model also available with humbucker/single coil/humbucker pickup configuration (Model CX391).

ELECTRIC: FUSION SERIES

FUSION CUSTOM - offset double cutaway poplar body, bolt-on maple neck, 24-fret rosewood fingerboard with white dot inlay, double locking vibrato, 6-on-a-side tuners, black hardware, 2 rail stacked coil/1 Jackson humbucker pickups, volume/tone control, 5-position switch, available in Candy Blue, Candy Red, Metallic Black, or Snow White finishes, mfg. 1991 only.

	$625	$525	$450	$350	$325	$295	$275

Last MSR was $895.

FUSION DELUXE - similar to Fusion Custom, except has chrome hardware, rail stacked coil/humbucker Jackson pickups, volume control, mfg. 1991 only.

	$550	$475	$395	$325	$275	$250	$225

Last MSR was $795.

This model was also available with maple fingerboard with black dot inlay.

FUSION PLUS - offset double cutaway ash body, bolt-on maple neck, 24-fret rosewood fingerboard with offset white dot inlay, double locking vibrato, 6-on-a-side tuners, black hardware, 2 humbucker Jackson pickups, volume/tone control, 5-position switch with coil split, available in Tobacco Sunburst, Trans. Amber, Trans. Red, Trans. Violet, or Trans. White finishes, disc. 1992.

	$625	$525	$450	$350	$325	$300	$275

Last MSR was $895.

FUSION SPECIAL - offset double cutaway poplar body, through-body maple neck, 24-fret rosewood fingerboard with white dot inlay, double locking vibrato, 6-on-a-side tuners, black hardware, 3 stacked coil Charvel pickups (2 side by side at the bridge), volume control, 5-position switch, available in Candy Blue, Ferrari Red, Midnight Black, or Snow White finishes, mfg. 1991 only.

	$485	$425	$350	$275	$250	$225	$200

Last MSR was $695.

Charvel LS-1
courtesy Charvel

ELECTRIC: LS SERIES

LS-1 - offset double cutaway asymmetrical bound carved mahogany body, mahogany neck, 22-fret bound rosewood fingerboard with pearl dot inlay, tune-o-matic bridge, string through-body tailpiece, bound blackface peghead with screened logo, 3-per-side tuners, chrome hardware, 2 humbucker Jackson pickups, volume/tone control, 3-position switch, available in Black, Deep Metallic Blue, or Gold finishes, mfg. 1993-96.

	$650	$595	$500	$425	$350	$325	$250

Last MSR was $995.

LSX-I - offset double cutaway asymmetrical ash body, figured maple top, mahogany neck, 22-fret rosewood fingerboard with pearl dot inlay, Wilkinson vibrato, roller nut, blackface peghead with screened logo, 3-per-side tuners, black hardware, 2 humbucker Jackson pickups, volume/tone control, 3-position switch, available in Natural Green Sunburst, Natural Purple Sunburst, or Natural Red Sunburst finishes, mfg. 1994-96.

	$575	$495	$450	$350	$325	$275	$225

Last MSR was $895.

LSX-II - offset double cutaway asymmetrical mahogany body, mahogany neck, 22-fret rosewood fingerboard with pearl dot inlay, double locking vibrato, blackface peghead with screened logo, 3-per-side tuners, black hardware, 2 humbucker Jackson pickups, volume/tone control, 3-position switch, available in Black or Trans. Red finishes, mfg. 1994-96.

	$525	$450	$395	$325	$275	$250	$200

Last MSR was $795.

LSX-III - offset double cutaway asymmetrical ash body, mahogany neck, 22-fret rosewood fingerboard with pearl dot inlay, string through-body bridge, blackface peghead with screened logo, 3-per-side tuners, black hardware, 2 humbucker Jackson pickups, volume/tone control, 3-position switch, available in Tobacco Sunburst, Trans. Blue, or Trans. Red finishes, mfg. 1994-96.

	$450	$425	$350	$275	$250	$225	$175

Last MSR was $695.

ELECTRIC: MODEL SERIES

MODEL 1 - offset double cutaway hardwood body, white pickguard, bolt-on maple neck, 22-fret maple fingerboard with black dot inlay, fixed bridge, 6-on-a-side tuners, chrome hardware, J90-C humbucker pickup, volume control, available in Ferrari Red, Midnight Black, Royal Blue, or Snow White finishes, mfg. 1987-89.

	$325	$275	$225	$195	$150	$125	$100

Last MSR was $400.

Charvel LSX-1
courtesy Charvel

C

GRADING	100% MINT	98% NEAR MINT	95% EXC+	90% EXC	80% VG+	70% VG	60% G

Model 1A - similar to Model 1, except has 3 single coil pickups, tone control, 5-position switch.

	$350	$275	$225	$195	$150	$125	$100

Last MSR was $450.

MODEL 2 - similar to Model 1, except has standard vibrato, mfg. 1986-89.

	$425	$325	$275	$225	$200	$175	$150

Last MSR was $550.

MODEL 3 - similar Model 1, except has 2 single coil/1 humbucker pickups, tone control, 5-position switch, mfg. 1986-89.

	$450	$395	$325	$250	$225	$200	$175

Last MSR was $650.

Model 3A - similar to Model 3, except has 2 humbucker pickups, standard vibrato, mfg. 1986-88.

	$425	$350	$300	$250	$225	$175	$150

Last MSR was $600.

MODEL 4 - similar to Model 1, except has standard vibrato, 2 humbucker pickups, tone control, 5-position switch, active electronics, mfg. 1986-89.

	$595	$500	$425	$375	$325	$295	$275

Last MSR was $850.

MODEL 5 - similar to Model 1, except has through-body neck, standard vibrato, 2 humbucker pickups, tone control, 5-position switch, mfg. 1986-89.

	$675	$575	$475	$375	$325	$300	$275

Last MSR was $950.

MODEL 6 - similar to Model 5, except has standard vibrato, 2 single coil/1 humbucker pickups, tone control, 5-position switch, active electronics, mfg. 1986-89.

	$725	$625	$550	$450	$395	$350	$300

Last MSR was $1,050.

ELECTRIC: PRO SERIES (2002-03 MFG.)

JOURNEYMAN (NO. 292-0100) - double cutaway alder body, bolt-on quartersawn maple neck, 24-fret rosewood fingerboard with pearl dot inlay, single Seymour Duncan humbucking pickup, coil-tap switch, two knobs (v, tone), six-on-one-side tuners, vintage-style bridge with tremolo, black hardware, available in Black, Cobalt Blue, Electric Blue, Faded Tobacco, Sunburst, Faded Cherry Sunburst, Natural, Blue, or Wine Red finishes, mfg. 2002-03.

	$525	$450	$395	$350	$300	$250	$200

Last MSR was $748.

Journeyman Rising Sun - similar to the Journeyman except features a "rising sun" graphic finish, mfg. 2002-03.

	$595	$525	$450	$400	$350	$275	$225

Last MSR was $851.

MODEL A (NO. 292-0200) - double cutaway mahogany body, bolt-on quartersawn maple neck, 24-fret ebony fingerboard with pearl dot inlay, 2 Live Wire Metal Seymour Duncan pickups, 3-way switch, 2 knobs (v, tone), six-on-one-side tuners, black hardware, JT580LP Double Locking Tremolo, available in Black, Cobalt Blue, or Electric Blue finishes, mfg. 2002-03.

	$850	$775	$700	$650	$575	$500	$425

Last MSR was $1,194.

Model A Quilted Maple - similar to the Model A except features a quilted maple top, available in Faded Tobacco, Sunburst, Faded Cherry Sunburst, Natural, Blue, or Wine Red, all translucent, mfg. 2002-03.

	$1,125	$1,025	$950	$850	$750	$625	$500

Last MSR was $1,594.

MODEL A PLUS (NO. 292-0205) - similar to the Model A except features a bird's-eye maple neck and has 3 Seymour Duncan pickups (2 Li'l Screamin' Demon single coils, plus one Pearly Gates in the bridge), available in Black, Cobalt Blue, or Electric Blue finishes, mfg. 2002-03.

	$950	$875	$775	$700	$625	$575	$475

Last MSR was $1,346.

Model A Plus Quilted Maple - similar to the Model A Plus except features a quilted maple top, available in Faded Tobacco, Sunburst, Faded Cherry Sunburst, Natural, Blue, or Wine Red, all translucent, mfg. 2002-03.

	$1,225	$1,100	$1,000	$925	$850	$725	$600

Last MSR was $1,744.

Model A PlusK - Similar to the Model A Plus except features a Hawaiian Koa Top, available in Natural Koa or Transparent Red finishes, mfg. 2002-03.

	$1,225	$1,100	$1,000	$925	$850	$725	$600

Last MSR was $1,744.

STANDARD (NO. 292-0300) - double cutaway alder body, bolt-on quartersawn maple neck, 24-fret maple fingerboard with black dot inlay, 2 Seymour Duncan humbuckers, 3-way switch, 2 knobs (v, tone), vintage style tremolo, six-on-a-side tuners, black hardware, available in Black, Cobalt Blue, or Electric Blue finishes, mfg. 2002-03.

	$575	$500	$450	$400	$350	$275	$215

Last MSR was $794.

Standard Quilted Maple - similar to the Standard except features a quilted maple top, available in Faded Tobacco, Sunburst, Faded Cherry Sunburst, Natural, Blue, or Wine Red, all translucent, mfg. 2002-03.

	$850	$775	$700	$650	$575	$500	$425

Last MSR was $1,194.

C

GRADING	100% MINT	98% NEAR MINT	95% EXC+	90% EXC	80% VG+	70% VG	60% G

TRADITIONAL (NO. 292-0500) - double cutaway alder body, bolt-on quartersawn maple neck, 22-fret rosewood fingerboard with pearl dot inlays, 3 Seymour Duncan pickups (humbucker, 2 single coils), 5-way switch, two knobs (v, tone), JT580LP Double Locking Tremolo, six-on-a-side tuners, black hardware, available in Black, Cobalt Blue, or Electric Blue finishes, mfg. 2002-03.

	$805	$725	$650	$575	$500	$425	$375

Last MSR was $1,144.

Traditional Quilted Maple - similar to the Traditional except features a quilted maple top, available in Faded Tobacco, Sunburst, Faded Cherry Sunburst, Natural, Blue, or Wine Red, all translucent, mfg. 2002-03.

	$1,099	$1,000	$925	$850	$750	$625	$500

Last MSR was $1,544.

ELECTRIC: SAN DIMAS SERIES

This series was entirely handmade at the Jackson Custom Shop located in Ontario, California.

SAN DIMAS I - offset double cutaway lacewood (or mahogany) body, bolt-on bird's-eye maple neck, 24-fret rosewood fingerboard with pearl dot inlay, double locking Floyd Rose vibrato, screened peghead logo, 6-on-a-side Gotoh tuners, gold hardware, 2 exposed humbucker DiMarzio pickups, volume control, 3-position switch, available in Natural Oil finish, mfg. 1995-97.

	$925	$850	$725	$575	$525	$450	$350

Last MSR was $1,395.

Add $100 for koa body.

San Dimas II - similar to San Dimas I, except has standard Wilkinson vibrato, locking Sperzel tuners, black hardware, available in Natural Oil finish, mfg. 1995-97.

	$850	$695	$650	$525	$475	$425	$325

Last MSR was $1,295.

Add $100 for koa body.

SAN DIMAS III - offset double cutaway mahogany body, quilted maple top, bolt-on bird's-eye maple neck, 24-fret pau ferro fingerboard with pearl dot inlay, double locking Floyd Rose vibrato, screened peghead logo, 6-on-a-side Gotoh tuners, black hardware, 2 single coil rail/1 exposed DiMarzio pickups, volume/tone controls, 5-position/coil tap switches, available in Trans. Green, Trans. Purple, Trans. Red, or Vintage Sunburst finishes, mfg. 1995-97.

	$975	$900	$750	$600	$550	$495	$375

Last MSR was $1,495.

San Dimas IV - similar to San Dimas III, except has koa body, bound quilted maple top, body matching peghead with screened logo, gold hardware, no coil tap, available in Trans. Green, Trans. Purple, Trans. Red, or Vintage Sunburst finishes, mfg. 1995-97.

	$1,100	$950	$850	$675	$600	$550	$425

Last MSR was $1,695.

SAN DIMAS STANDARD - offset double cutaway alder body, bolt-on maple neck, 24-fret rosewood fingerboard with pearl dot inlay, standard vibrato, screened peghead logo, 6-on-a-side locking Sperzel tuners, chrome hardware, 2 single coil/humbucker exposed DiMarzio pickups, volume/tone controls, 5-position switch, available in Black, Forest Green, Garnet Red, Sapphire Blue, or Snow White finishes, mfg. 1995-97.

	$650	$595	$500	$400	$350	$300	$250

Last MSR was $995.

SAN DIMAS TRADITIONAL - offset double cutaway alder body, pearloid pickguard, bolt-on maple neck, 22-fret rosewood fingerboard with pearl dot inlay, standard Wilkinson vibrato, string tree, screened peghead logo, 6-on-a-side locking Sperzel tuners, black hardware, 3 single coil exposed DiMarzio pickups, volume/tone controls, 5-position switch, available in Black, Forest Green, Garnet Red, Sapphire Blue, or Snow White finishes, mfg. 1995-97.

	$650	$595	$500	$400	$350	$300	$250

Last MSR was $995.

ELECTRIC: STANDARD SERIES

STANDARD 1 - offset double cutaway hardwood body, white pickguard, bolt-on maple neck, 22-fret maple fingerboard with black dot inlay, standard vibrato, 6-on-a-side tuners, chrome hardware, 1 DiMarzio humbucker pickup, volume control, available in Black, Blue, Red, or White finish, mfg. 1983-85.

	N/A	$675	$550	$450	$375	$325	$275

Last MSR was $960.

STANDARD 2 - similar to Standard 1, except has 2 DiMarzio humbucker pickups, 3-position switch, mfg. 1985 only.

	N/A	$725	$575	$475	$400	$350	$300

Last MSR was $1,030.

STANDARD 3 - similar to Standard 1, except has 3 DiMarzio single coil pickups, 3 mini switches, mfg. 1983-85.

	$750	$600	$500	$375	$350	$300	$275

Last MSR was $1,040.

C

GRADING	100% MINT	98% NEAR MINT	95% EXC+	90% EXC	80% VG+	70% VG	60% G

ELECTRIC: SURFCASTER SERIES

SURFCASTER - offset double rounded cutaway asymmetrical semihollow basswood body, offset wedge soundhole, bound body and soundhole, pearloid pickguard, bolt-on maple neck, 24-fret bound rosewood fingerboard with pearl shark fin inlay, standard vibrato, bound peghead, roller nut, 3-per-side tuners, chrome hardware, 2 single coil lipstick pickups, volume/tone control, 3-position switch, phase reversal in tone control, available in Black, Magenta, or Turquoise finishes, mfg. 1992-94.

	$695	$595	$500	$400	$350	$295	$275

Last MSR was $995.

Surfcaster (Trans) - similar to Surfcaster, except has figured maple top/mahogany body, available in Star Glo, Trans. Orange, or Trans. Red finishes, mfg. 1992-94.

	$775	$650	$550	$425	$395	$350	$300

Last MSR was $1,095.

SC1 (SURFCASTER HT) - offset double round cutaway asymmetrical semihollow basswood body, bound wedge soundhole, bound body, pearloid pickguard, bolt-on maple neck, 24-fret bound rosewood fingerboard with pearl shark fin inlay, tune-o-matic bridge/trapeze tailpiece with stylized C, bound peghead with screened logo, 3-per-side tuners, chrome hardware, 2 single coil lipstick pickups, volume/tone control, 3-position switch, phase reversal in tone control, available in Black, Metallic Violet, or Turquoise finishes, mfg. 1992-96.

	$655	$575	$475	$400	$350	$300	$275

Last MSR was $895.

In early 1994, single coil/humbucker pickups configuration replaced original part/design. The phase reversal switch was discontinued in 1996.

Surfcaster HT (Trans) - similar to SC1 (Surfcaster HT), except has figured maple top/mahogany body, available in Natural Green Burst, Natural Red Burst, Star Glo, Tobacco Sunburst, Trans. Orange, or Trans.Red finishes, mfg. 1992-94.

	$725	$625	$525	$425	$375	$325	$275

Last MSR was $995.

In early 1994, Natural Green Burst, Natural Red Burst and Tobacco Sunburst finishes were introduced, single coil/humbuckers pickup configuration replaced original part/design, Star Glo, Transparent Orange and Trans. Red finishes were discontinued.

SURFCASTER 12 - offset double round cutaway asymmetrical semi-hollow basswood body, bound wedge soundhole, bound body, pearloid pickguard, bolt-on maple neck, 24-fret bound ebony fingerboard with pearl shark fin inlay, fixed bridge, bound peghead with screened logo, roller nut, 6-per-side tuners, chrome hardware, 2 single coil lipstick pickups, volume/tone control, 3-position switch, phase reversal in tone control, available in Black, Magenta, or Turquoise finishes, mfg. 1992-94.

	$795	$675	$575	$475	$425	$375	$325

Last MSR was $1,050.

In early 1994, bound rosewood fingerboard replaced original part/design.

Surfcaster 12 (Trans) - similar to Surfcaster 12, except has figured maple top/mahogany body, available in Star Glo, Trans. Orange, or Trans. Red finishes, mfg. 1992-94.

	$850	$725	$615	$515	$465	$425	$385

Last MSR was $1,150.

ELECTRIC: USA STANDARD SERIES

EVH ART SERIES (NO. 282-7801/7802/7803) - offset double cutaway basswood body, bolt-on quartersawn eastern hard rock maple neck, 22-fret maple fingerboard, six-on-one-side tuners, Floyd Rose tremolo and locking nut, black pickguard, single EVH custom wound humbucker pickup, EVH D-Tuna, single knob, chrome hardware, available in White with Black stripes, Black with Yellow stripes, or Red with White and Black stripes, mfg. 2004-present.

MSR $3,300		$2,500	$2,200	$1,950	$1,750	$1,550	$1,350	$1,150

SAN DIMAS (NO. 282-1000/1010/1020) - offset double cutaway alder body, bolt-on quartersawn Eastern hard rock maple neck, 22-fret ebony, maple, or rosewood fingerboard with dot inlay, six-on-one-side tuners, Seymour Duncan pickups in a variety of configurations (H, HH, H/S/S, H/S), brass tremolo, single knob, black hardware, available in Black, Candy Blue, Ferrari Red, or Snow White finishes, mfg. 2004-present.

MSR $2,000		$1,500	$1,300	$1,150	$1,000	$850	$700	$600

Add $100 for HH, H/S/S, or H/S pickup configuration. Add $100 for Floyd Rose tremolo.

STAR (NO. 282-1001/1011/1021) - star-shaped body with extended upper treble and lower bass horns, bolt-on quartersawn Eastern hard rock maple neck, 22-fret ebony, maple, or rosewood fingerboard with dot inlay, six-on-one-side tuners, brass tremolo, Seymour Duncan pickups in a variety of configurations (H, HH, H/S/S, H/S), single knob, black hardware, available in Black, Candy Blue, Ferrari Red, or Snow White finishes, mfg. 2004-present.

MSR $2,000		$1,500	$1,300	$1,150	$1,000	$850	$700	$600

Add $100 for HH, H/S/S, or H/S pickup configuration. Add $100 for Floyd Rose tremolo.

ELECTRIC BASS: CONTEMPORARY SERIES

There are no current bass models produced by Charvel.

575 DELUXE CLASSIC - offset double cutaway hardwood body, bolt-on maple neck, 21-fret rosewood fingerboard with white dot inlay, fixed bridge, 4-on-a-side tuners, chrome hardware, P/J-style pickups, 2 volume/2 tone controls, available in Candy Blue, Ferrari Red, Midnight Black, Platinum, or Snow White finishes, mfg. 1988-1991.

	$425	$350	$300	$250	$225	$175	$150

Last MSR was $600.

C

GRADING	100% MINT	98% NEAR MINT	95% EXC+	90% EXC	80% VG+	70% VG	60% G

575 Deluxe Contemporary - similar to 575 Deluxe Classic, except has rosewood fingerboard with pearl dot inlay, volume/tone control, 3-position switch, available in Candy Blue, Candy Red, Metallic Black, or Snow White finishes, mfg. 1991-92.

	$475	$425	$350	$275	$250	$225	$200

Last MSR was $695.

850 XL PROFESSIONAL - offset double cutaway hardwood body, bolt-on maple neck, 21-fret rosewood fingerboard with white dot inlay, fixed bridge, 4-on-a-side tuners, chrome hardware, P/J-style pickups, volume/treble/bass/mix controls, available in Candy Blue, Ferrari Red, Midnight Black, Platinum, or Snow White finishes, mfg. 1988-1991.

	$700	$600	$500	$400	$350	$300	$250

Last MSR was $1,000.

ELECTRIC BASS: CONTEMPORARY SERIES

CX490 - offset double cutaway poplar body, bolt-on maple neck, 22-fret rosewood fingerboard with pearl dot inlay, fixed bridge, 4-on-a-side tuners, chrome hardware, P/J-style Jackson pickups, volume/tone and mix controls, available in Black, Bright Red, Deep Metallic Blue, or Snow White finishes, mfg. 1992-95.

	$325	$295	$250	$195	$175	$150	$125

Last MSR was $495.

ELECTRIC BASS: FUSION SERIES

FUSION IV - offset double cutaway hardwood body, bolt-on maple neck, 24-fret rosewood fingerboard with off-set pearl dot inlay, pearl Charvel block inlay at 12th fret, fixed bridge, 4-on-a-side tuners, black hardware, P/J-style Charvel pickups, volume/treble/bass and mix controls, active electronics, available in Candy Blue, Ferrari Red, Magenta, Metallic Black, or Pearl White finishes, mfg. 1991 only.

	$525	$475	$395	$325	$275	$250	$225

Last MSR was $795.

FUSION V - similar to Fusion IV, except has 5-string configuration, 3/2-per-side tuners, mfg. 1991 only.

	$650	$595	$500	$400	$375	$325	$275

Last MSR was $995.

Charvel Surfcaster Standard
courtesy Charvel

ELECTRIC BASS: LS SERIES

LS-1 BASS - offset double cutaway asymmetrical bound mahogany body, mahogany neck, 21-fret bound rosewood fingerboard with pearl dot inlay, tune-o-matic bridge, through-body ring and ball holder tailpiece, 2 Jackson pickups, volume/treble/bass/mix control, available in Black, Deep Metallic Blue, or Gold finishes, mfg. 1993-96.

	$775	$650	$600	$525	$450	$395	$300

Last MSR was $1,195.

ELECTRIC BASS: MISC. MODELS

STANDARD 1 - offset double cutaway hardwood body, white pickguard, bolt-on maple neck, 21-fret maple fingerboard with black dot inlay, fixed bridge, 4-on-a-side tuners, chrome hardware, P-style Charvel pickups, volume/tone controls, available in Black, Red, or White finishes, mfg. 1985 only.

	N/A	$675	$575	$475	$375	$325	$275

Last MSR was $960.

STANDARD 2 - offset double cutaway asymmetrical hardwood body, bolt-on maple neck, 21-fret maple fingerboard with black dot inlay, fixed bridge, 4-on-a-side tuners, chrome hardware, 2 J-style Charvel pickups, 2 volume/1 tone controls, available in Black, Red, or White finishes, mfg. 1983-85.

	N/A	$725	$625	$500	$425	$375	$325

Last MSR was $1,030.

ELIMINATOR - offset double cutaway hardwood body, bolt-on maple neck, 24-fret rosewood fingerboard with white dot inlay, fixed bridge, 4-on-a-side tuners, black hardware, P/J-style Charvel pickups, volume/treble/bass and mix controls, active electronics, available in Candy Blue, Ferrari Red, Midnight Black, or Snow White finishes, mfg. 1991 only.

	$495	$425	$350	$295	$250	$225	$200

Last MSR was $695.

JX BASS - offset double cutaway asymmetrical poplar body, bolt-on maple neck, 22-fret rosewood fingerboard with pearl dot inlay, fixed bridge, 4-on-a-side tuners, chrome hardware, P/J-style Jackson pickups, volume/tone/mix controls, available in Black, Deep Metallic Blue, Dark Metallic Red, Snow White, or Turquoise finishes, mfg. 1992-94.

	$475	$425	$350	$295	$250	$225	$210

Last MSR was $695.

Charvel Surfcaster HT
courtesy Charvel

GRADING	100% MINT	98% NEAR MINT	95% EXC+	90% EXC	80% VG+	70% VG	60% G

ELECTRIC BASS: MODEL SERIES

MODEL 1B - offset double cutaway hardwood body, bolt-on maple neck, 21-fret rosewood fingerboard with pearl dot inlay, fixed bridge, 4-on-a-side tuners, chrome hardware, P-style Charvel pickup, volume/tone controls, available in Black, Red, or White finishes, mfg. 1986-89.

	$325	$275	$225	$175	$150	$125	$100

Last MSR was $450.

MODEL 2B - similar to Model 1B, except has P/J-style pickups, 2 volume/2 tone controls, mfg. 1986-89.

	$425	$350	$300	$250	$225	$175	$150

Last MSR was $600.

MODEL 3B - similar to Model 1B, except has through-body neck, 2 J-style pickups, 2 volume/2 tone controls, mfg. 1986-89.

	$595	$525	$425	$350	$300	$275	$225

Last MSR was $850.

ELECTRIC BASS: SURFCASTER SERIES

SURFCASTER BASS - sleek offset double rounded cutaway basswood body, pearloid pickguard, bolt-on maple neck, 21-fret bound rosewood fingerboard with offset pearl inlay, fixed bridge, bound peghead, 2-per-side tuners, chrome hardware, 2 single coil lipstick pickups, volume/tone control, 3-position switch, phase reversal in tone control, available in Black, Magenta, or Turquoise finishes, mfg. 1992-94.

	$700	$600	$500	$400	$360	$330	$300

Last MSR was $995.

Surfcaster Bass (Trans) - similar to Surfcaster Bass, except has figured maple top/mahogany body, available in Star Glo, Trans. Orange or Trans. Red finishes, mfg. 1992-94.

	$765	$655	$545	$435	$395	$360	$330

Last MSR was $1,095.

ELECTRIC BASS: USA STANDARD SERIES

SAN DIMAS BASS (NO. 282-1002/1012/1022) - offset double cutway (P-Style) alder body, bolt-on quartersawn eastern hard rock maple neck, 21-fret ebony, maple, or rosewood fingerboard with dot inlay, four-on-one-side tuners, Badass Bass II bridge, P/J Bassline pickups, three knobs, black hardware, available in Black, Candy Blue, Ferrari Red, or Snow White finishes, mfg. 2004-present.

MSR $1,700		$1,300	$1,150	$1,000	$850	$750	$650	$550

Add $75 for P/P or J/J pickup configurations.

STAR BASS (NO. 282-1003/1013/1023) - star-shaped body with extended upper treble and lower bass horns, bolt-on quartersawn eastern hard rock maple neck, 21-fret ebony, maple, or rosewood fingerboard with dot inlay, four-on-one-side tuners, Badass Bass II bridge, P/J Bassline pickups, three knobs, black hardware, available in Black, Candy Blue, Ferrari Red, or Snow White finishes, mfg. 2004-present.

MSR $1,700		$1,300	$1,150	$1,000	$850	$750	$650	$550

Add $75 for P/P or J/J pickup configurations.

CHARVETTE

Instruments previously produced in Korea from 1989 to 1994. Charvette, an entry level line to Charvel, was distributed by the International Music Corporation of Ft. Worth, Texas.

The Charvette trademark was distributed by the Charvel/Jackson company as a good quality entry level guitar based on their original Jackson USA superstrat designs. Where the Charvel and Jackson models may sport Jackson pickups, Charvettes invariably had Charvel pickups to support a company/product unity.

ELECTRIC

All models in this series were available in Ferrari Red, Midnight Black, Royal Blue, Snow White, and Splatter finishes, unless otherwise listed.

100 - offset double cutaway hardwood body, bolt-on maple neck, 22-fret rosewood fingerboard with white dot inlay, standard vibrato, reverse peghead, 6-on-a-side tuners, black hardware, stacked coil/humbucker Charvel pickup, volume/tone control, 3-position switch, mfg. 1989-1992.

	N/A	$225	$175	$150	$125	$100	$75

Last MSR was $365.

150 - similar to 100, except has locking vibrato, standard peghead, mfg. 1989-1992.

	N/A	$250	$225	$175	$150	$125	$100

Last MSR was $395.

170 - similar to 100, except has double locking vibrato, standard peghead, no tone control, mfg. 1991-92.

	N/A	$275	$250	$215	$180	$150	$120

Last MSR was $495.

175 - similar to 100, except has 24-fret fingerboard, standard peghead, no tone control, mfg. 1989-1991.

	N/A	$250	$225	$175	$150	$125	$100

Last MSR was $420.

200 - similar to 100, except has 2 single coil/1 Charvel humbucker pickups, mfg. 1989-1992.

	N/A	$225	$200	$175	$150	$125	$100

Last MSR was $375.

GRADING	100% MINT	98% NEAR MINT	95% EXC+	90% EXC	80% VG+	70% VG	60% G

250 - similar to 100, except has locking vibrato, standard peghead, stacked coil/single coil/humbucker Charvel pickups, mfg. 1989-1992.

	N/A	$250	$220	$175	$150	$125	$100

Last MSR was $425.

270 - similar to 100, except has double locking vibrato, standard peghead, stacked coil/single coil/humbucker Charvel pickups, no tone control, mfg. 1991-92.

	N/A	$300	$250	$200	$175	$150	$125

Last MSR was $525.

275 - similar to 100, except has 24-fret fingerboard, standard peghead, locking vibrato, stacked coil/single coil/humbucker pickups, no tone control, mfg. 1989-1991.

	$300	$250	$220	$175	$150	$125	$100

Last MSR was $430.

300 - similar to 100, except has 3 single coil Charvel pickups, mfg. 1989-1992.

	N/A	$275	$250	$215	$180	$150	$120

Last MSR was $495.

ELECTRIC BASS

400 - offset double cutaway hardwood body, bolt-on maple neck, 21-fret rosewood fingerboard with pearl dot inlay, fixed bridge, 4-on-a-side tuners, chrome hardware, P-style Charvel pickup, volume/tone control, mfg. 1989-1992.

	N/A	$250	$225	$175	$150	$125	$100

Last MSR was $425.

450 - similar to 400, except has P/J-style pickups, 2 volume/2 tone controls, mfg. 1991-92.

	N/A	$275	$250	$215	$180	$150	$120

Last MSR was $495.

**Charvel CHS 4 Bass
courtesy Charvel**

CHATWORTH
Instruments previously built in England.

Luthier Andy Smith previously built high quality guitars in England.

CHRIS
See chapter on House Brands.

This trademark has been identified as a separate budget line of guitars from the Jackson-Guldan company of Columbus, Ohio (source: Willie G. Moseley, *Stellas & Stratocasters*).

CHRIS LARKIN CUSTOM GUITARS
Instruments currently built in Ireland since 1979.

Since 1977, Chris Larkin Custom Guitars have been based at Castlegregory, County Kerry, on the west coast of Ireland. Chris Larkin works alone, hand building a range of original designs to custom order with a very high level of quality from the finest available materials. The range is wide ("it stops me from becoming bored!") including acoustic, electric, archtop, and semi-acoustic guitars; acoustic, electric, semi-acoustic, and upright ´stick´ basses; and archtop mandolins. ´One-off´ designs are also built and Chris admits to having made some very high spec copies when offered enough money! Company information courtesy Chris Larkin, Chris Larkin Custom Guitars.

As each instrument is handmade to order, the customer has a wide choice of woods, colors, fret type, fingerboard radius, neck profile, and dimensions within the design to enable the finished instrument to better suit the player. All Larkin instruments from 1980 on have a shamrock as the headstock inlay. Sales are worldwide through distributors in some areas, or direct from the maker.

SERIALIZATION

Since 1982, a simple-six digit system has been used. The first two digits indicate the year, the next two the month, and the final two the sequence in that month. For example, 970103 was the third instrument in January 1997. Before 1982 the numbers are a bit chaotic! Chris Larkin has full documentation for almost every instrument that he has ever built, so he can supply a history from the serial number in most cases.

ELECTRIC

Larkin´s **ASAD** model is a solid body electric guitar with set-in neck, mahogany body, and bookmatched exotic wood overlays. This model is available in **Standard** (flat topped with contours), and **Custom** (carved arched top). Guitars start at 1,780 Euro.

ELECTRIC BASS

Reactor basses are similar in body style to the ASAD guitars, and feature laminated set-in necks, mahogany bodies, and bookmatched exotic wood tops. Reactor basses are available in 4- and 5-string configurations, and as a **Standard** (flat topped) and **Custom** (carved arched top). Prices start at 1,600 euro. The Bassix 6-string prices start at 1,600 euro; the **Basseven** 7-string (Larkin built one model as early as 1968) prices also start at 1,600 euro. In addition to the high quality solid body basses, Larkin also builds minimalist body electric semi-hollow upright basses. The **Blen** Upright Electric Bass is available in 4-, 5-, and 6-string configurations. Prices start at 2,430 euro.

**Clevinger Basic
courtesy Martin Clevinger**

CIMAR
Instruments previously built in Japan during the 1970s and 1980s.

Cimar produced good- to medium-quality guitars that featured similar versions of classic American designs, as well as some original and thinline hollowbody designs (source: Tony Bacon and Paul Day, *The Guru's Guitar Guide*).

CIPHER
Instruments previously produced in Japan circa 1960s.

Cipher guitars were distributed in the U.S. market by Inter-Mark, and featured oddly-shaped body designs (source: Michael Wright, *Guitar Stories*, Volume One). Used guitars are typically priced between $75 and $150.

CITATION
Instruments previously produced in Japan.

The U.S. distributor of Citation guitars was the Grossman company of Cleveland, Ohio (source: Michael Wright, *Guitar Stories*, Volume One).

CITRON
Instruments currently built in Woodstock, NY since 1983.

Luthier Harvey Citron has been building high quality, innovative, solid body guitars since the early 1970s. Citron, a noted guitarist and singer, co-founded the Veillette-Citron company in 1975. During the partnership's eight years, they were well-known for the quality of their handcrafted electric guitars, basses, and baritone guitars. Citron also designed the **X-92 Breakaway** model for Guild and was a regular contributing writer for several guitar magazines.

Citron instruments are available direct from Harvey Citron, or through a limited number of dealers. Citron maintains a current price list and descriptions of his models at his website. His Basic Guitar Set-Up and Repair instructional video is available from Homespun Tapes; and Citron's cleverly designed Guitar Stand has a list price of $399.

CITRON INSTRUMENT SPECIFICATIONS

All Citron instruments are topped with figured/exotic woods such as curly or quilted maple, swamp ash, korina, purple heart, wenge, macassar ebony, and rosewood. bodies without the figured/exotic woods are available at a lower price (call for price quote). Necks are constructed from hard rock maple and mahogany, and fingerboards feature materials such as ebony, rosewood, pau ferro, wenge, and maple.

Citron welcomes custom orders, and offers choices in woods, colors, finish, electronics, hardware, and other specifications (call for price quote). Citron instruments feature custom blended Citron pickups or pickups built by other custom pickup makers. The standard finish on a Citron body is a hand rubbed oil finish. All retail prices include a hardshell case.

Add $350 for a gloss polyester finish (bolt-on style models).

ELECTRIC

All Electric guitar models feature a 25 1/2 in. scale. A chambered guitar model was introduced in 2005. Look for more information in upcoming editions.

CC1 - offset double cutaway body, internal hollowed chambers, bolt-on neck, 6-on-a-side headstock, tremolo, 3 pickups, volume/tone controls, 5-way selector switch, current mfg.
MSR $3,400

    CC2 - similar to the CC1, except features 2 humbucker pickups, bridge/stop tailpiece, mfg. 1998-present.
    MSR $3,200

CF1 - sleek, balanced reverse Firebird-style body, bolt-on neck, 6-on-a-side reverse headstock, fixed bridge, 2 pickups, volume/tone controls, 3-way selector switch, current mfg.
MSR $3,100

CS1 - offset double cutaway body, bolt-on neck, 6-on-a-side headstock, tremolo, 3 pickups, volume/tone controls, 5-way selector switch, current mfg.
MSR $3,200

CT1 - single cutaway body, bolt-on neck, 6-on-a-side headstock, fixed bridge, 3 pickups, volume/tone controls, 3- way selector switch, current mfg.
MSR $3,000

ELECTRIC BASS

All bass models feature active electronics. Fingerboards available in fretless configuration at no additional cost. A chambered bass model was introduced in 2005. Look for more information in upcoming editions.

BO4 - offset double cutaway body, 34 in. scale, bolt-on neck, four on a side headstock, 2 pickups, fixed bridge, active electronics, volume/blend/tone controls, current mfg.
MSR $3,200

    Subtract $250 for passive electronics.

    BO5 - Similar to the BO4, except has 35 in. scale, 5-string configuration, current mfg.
    MSR $3,400

    BO6 - Similar to the BO4, except has 35 in. scale, 6-string configuration, current mfg.
    MSR $3,600

NT4 - Offset double cutaway body, 34 in. scale, neck-through-body construction, four-on-a-side headstock, 2 pickups, fixed bridge, active electronics, volume/blend/tone controls, current mfg.
MSR $3,800

    NT5 - Similar to the NT4, except has 35 in. scale, 5-string configuration, current mfg.
    MSR $4,000

    NT6 - Similar to the NT4, except has 35 in. scale, 6-string configuration, current mfg.
    MSR $4,200

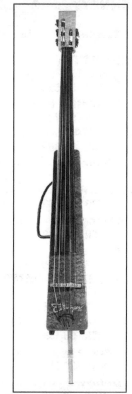

CLEARSOUND
Instruments previously built in Japan during the 1970s.

Shades of Dan Armstrong! The Clearsound Strat model of the late 1970s was built of see-through plastic with a wood neck and three single coil pickups. If you begin the tally with the original Dan Armstrong/Ampeg lucite See-Throughs, Renaissance company's original designs, the Univox and Ibanez "Dan Armstrong" copies, as well as the models currently built by George Fedden, this brings the total count of companies who produced these type of lucite guitars to six! Source for Clearsound: Tony Bacon, *The Ultimate Guitar Book*.

CLEVINGER
Instruments currently built in Oakland, CA, since 1982.

Martin Clevinger has been building solid body electric double basses since the early 1980s. As a working bassist on both the acoustic and bass guitar for many years, Clevinger knew that a more durable double bass could be built that would help lessen the wear and tear on a bassist's more expensive older upright, and at the same time be more adaptable in modern musical situations. The first Clevinger was released in 1982. Clevinger originally purchased and was dissatisfied with a Framus Triumph and a Zorko. He then set out to build prototypes that overcame their shortcomings. After building a few basses and playing them on his gigs, other bassists became interested and wanted Clevinger to build instruments for them (company history and information courtesy Martin Clevinger).

Clevinger has reissued the original Clevinger Bass. These vintage models are faithful reproductions of the 1984 models. They retain the keyhole body shape, the cut scroll head with deep neck heel. The pickup system and controls have been updated (Clevinger Near Field pickup). Each is custom-built on demand, and carries a retail price of $3,595. This model has a choice of Vintage Gold Transparent, Vintage Black with Gold Transparent neck, or custom colors.

MODEL DATING IDENTIFICATION

Here is information concerning production as well as the various brand names found on Clevinger upright basses:

1982-1984: First Clevinger basses produced by Ace Industries in San Francisco, California.

1985-1987: Incorporation of Ace Industries in 1985 resulted in the removal of the Clevinger name from basses produced by Able Tech, Inc. These instruments were identical to the original Clevinger basses but were labeled Solid Acoustic. Several hundred were produced. Able Tech, Inc. was dissolved by 1989.

1986-1995: New Clevinger bass models resulted from Martin Clevinger licensing all new Clevinger designs to Robert Lee Guitars. Instruments built during this time period bore the trademark Clevinger by Robert Lee. A joint design project between Clevinger, Azola Basses, and Robert Lee, dubbed the **C.A.L.** bass were briefly produced in 1995. Both companies currently offer a version or similar design options in their separate product lines, each incorporating Clevinger and Azola designs.

1996: Martin Clevinger takes sales in-house, producing instruments with the name Clevinger. The curvaceous Clevinger Opus models with elegant scrolled headstock were unveiled at the 1996 NAMM trade show.

Clevinger Deluxe 5-String
courtesy Martin Clevinger

ELECTRIC BASS

Clevinger Basses are offered in a Black highly polished polyurethane or Honey transparent urethane. Other custom colors, such as Golden Brown, Reddish Brown, Sunbursts, or solid colors are available. Clevinger also offers custom woods and different pickup options (call for price quotes). In 1997, the Clevinger Near Field pickup was introduced.

Clevinger basses weigh between 15 and 19 pounds, and range between 53 in. and 57 in. length. These slim body basses are constructed of poplar, while the neck is rock maple and features an ebony fingerboard. The solid body instruments have a scale length of 41.5 in., have a telescoping endpin, and a black metal tubular (detachable) right bout (the left bout is an added accessory). Pickups technology is designed by Clevinger, and the tuners are by Hipshot. Clevinger basses featuring acoustic floating spruce tops are available for acoustic purists.

Add $100 (per string) for Clevinger Near Field pickup (standard equipment on Opus and Deluxe models). Add $125 (per string) for RMC string saddle sensors. Add $575 for Barbera pickup in Clevinger bridge (4-string only).

1983 CLEVINGER BASS - a reissue of the original Clevinger bass circa 1983, 4-string only, mfg. 2003-04.
Last MSR was $3,599.

1985 CLEVINGER BASS - a reissue of the original Clevinger bass, 4-string only, disc. 2004.
Last MSR was $3,599.

AZOLA VIRTUOSO - custom Azola violin body, floating spruce top, scrolled headstock, 2-per-side tuners, ebony fittings, Clevinger Near Field pickup, available in Tuscan Red Sunburst high gloss finish, mfg. 1995-2000.
Last MSR was $4,295.

Clevinger also offered 5-string and 6-string configurations of this model. The Clevinger/Azola Virtuoso 5 had a 3/2-per-side headstock (MSR of $4,495), and the Clevinger/Azola Virtuoso 6 had a 3-per-side headstock (MSR of $4,695). These models may be custom options at this date.

BASS BOY X-FORMER - 36.5 in. scale, Clevinger Arco Virtuoso pickup, rounded headstock, 2-per-side tuners, mfg. 1997-2000.
Last MSR was $1,295.

The Clevinger Jr., first introduced in 1987, was one of the first instruments to bridge the gap between the guitar-type basses and classical string bass. The 5-pound Bass Boy model is the current interpretation of the Clevinger Jr. This model may be played in an upright position, or may be strapped on for horizontal playing.

BASSBOY POQUITO - 23.25 in. scale, trapezoid body, 2-per-side tuners, mfg. 2000-present.
MSR $3,199

BASSIC - rounded headstock, 4-string only, no custom options, 2-per-side tuners, current mfg.
MSR $2,599

Clevinger Opus 5
courtesy Martin Clevinger

C

BENNETT - acoustic hollowed body, floating spruce top, modified scroll headstock, 2-per-side tuners, mfg. 1996-2004.

Last MSR was $4,399.

Bennett 5 - similar to the Bennett except in 5-string configuration, disc. 2004.

Last MSR was $4,599.

BENNETT II - similar to the Bennett except is lighter, more compact, better tone, and enhanced durability, scroll head optional, flame maple top option, Honey or Tucson Red finish, current mfg.

MSR $4,599

Bennett II 5 - similar to the Bennett except in 5-string configuration, current mfg.

MSR $4,799

CHIMERA - cello style shaped body, scroll headstock, 2-per-side tuners, mfg. 2002-present.

MSR $4,899

Chimera 5 - similar to the Chimera except in 5-string configuration, 3/2-per-side tuners, disc. 2004.

Last MSR was $4,899.

CONCERTO - violin shaped body, scrolled headstock, 2-per-side tuners, current mfg.

MSR $3,399

Concerto 5 - similar to the Concerto except in 5-string configuration, 3/2-per-side tuners, current mfg.

MSR $3,599

Concerto 6 - similar to the Concerto except in 6-string configuration, 3-per-side tuners, current mfg.

MSR $3,799

CONCERTO GRANDE - similar to the Concerto, except has a solid arched spruce top, solid maple back and sides, and graceful f-holes, mfg. 2004-present.

MSR $5,499

DELUXE 4 - squared headstock, 2-per-side tuners, mfg. 1996-present.

MSR $3,199

Deluxe 5 - similar to the Deluxe 4, except has 5 strings and a 3/2 headstock, current mfg.

MSR $3,399

Deluxe 6 - similar to the Deluxe 4, except has 6 strings and a 3-per-side headstock, current mfg.

MSR $3,599

IMPERION MIDI BASS - Opus shaped body, 6-string, features MIDI electronics, current mfg.

MSR $5,799

This model is also available in 4- or 5-string configurations. Contact the company for pricing.

MJ WIDE BASS GUITAR - offset double cutaway poplar body with neural crest styling, through-body laminated neck, 25.75 in. fingerboard with full-width spacing, one humbucker and one J-style pickups, available in various finishes, new 2005.

MSR $5,499

MJ Wide Bass Guitar 5 - similar to the MJ Wide Bass Guitar, except in 5-string configuration, new 2005.

MSR $5,699

MJ Wide Bass Guitar 6 - similar to the MJ Wide Bass Guitar, except in 6-string configuration, new 2005.

MSR $5,899

OPUS 4 - contoured body, scrolled headstock, available in black or honey transparent, mfg. 1996-present.

MSR $3,299

Opus 5 - similar to the Opus 4, except in 5-string configuration, 3/2-per-side headstock, mfg. 1996-present.

MSR $3,499

Opus 6 - similar to the Opus 4, except in 6-string configuration, 3-per-side headstock, mfg. 1996-present.

MSR $3,699

SOLID ACOUSTIC CONCERTO - semi-acoustic, similar to the Concerto, mfg. 2004-present.

MSR $3,899

Solid Acoustic Concerto 5 - similar to the Solid Acoustic Concerto, except in 5-string configuration, mfg. 2004-present.

MSR $4,099

Solid Acoustic Concerto 6 - similar to the Solid Acoustic Concerto, except in 6-string configuration, mfg. 2004-present.

MSR $4,299

SOLID ACOUSTIC (DELUXE) - semi-acoustic, violin shape body, scroll headstock, mfg. 2003-present.

MSR $3,599

Add $100 for trapezoid shaped body with square flat headstock.

Solid Acoustic (Deluxe) 5 - similar to the Solid Acoustic except in 5-string configuration, current mfg.

MSR $3,799

Add $100 for trapezoid shaped body with square flat headstock.

Solid Acoustic (Deluxe) 6 - similar to the Solid Acoustic except in 6-string configuration, current mfg.

MSR $3,999

Add $200 for trapezoid shaped body with square flat headstock.

CLIFTON
Instruments currently built in Blackheath, England since 1986.

Luthier Mo Clifton became involved in instrument design as a result of shoulder problems incurred from playing a bass guitar with a heavy headstock. As a result, Clifton basses have a balanced body design and no headstock (guitar and upright models do feature headstocks). Clifton also offers full luthier services, but asks that visits are by appointment only.

ELECTRIC BASS

Clifton´s **Downright** Bass derives its name from the New York jazz bassists who often refer to their electric bass guitar as the downright as opposed to their Upright (or double bass). The 5-string model has a solid mahogany body and select hardwood top, and a choice of 34 in. or 36 in. scale. The two octave ebony fingerboard has side dot position markers, and is available fretless (with or without lines). The headless neck is reverse strung to an ABM bridge, and the customer has a choice between Bartolini or EMG pickups (and one or two).

Clifton also offers a 5-string **Piccolo Bass** model. The original inspiration began from a repaired jumbo acoustic that was restrung with five strings tuned one octave above the strings on a bass. The resulting model has a single cutaway mahogany body that is partially hollowed to form an acoustic chamber, and either a spruce or cedar top. The neck is rock maple, and the fingerboard and bridge are ebony. The Piccolo Bass has a 24 in. scale, and is available in 4-, 5-, and 6-string configurations. A 6-string guitar model also grew out of this project, and features a choice of Kent Armstrong single coil or humbucker pickups, and Schaller hardware.

Other Clifton stringed instruments include the **Clifton Upright**, a solid body electric upright bass with scroll headstock; the **Electric Cello**, a solid body cello outfitted with a Fishman transducer; an **Alibatta Cello**, Clifton´s aluminum-bodied copy of the Stradivarius Batta cello; and the 6- or 7-string **Clifton Jazz Guitar**, a semi-acoustic jazz box with a custom designed humbucker pickup.

CLOVER
Instruments currently built in Recklinghausen, Germany. Distributed in the U.S. by Clover.

Clover handcrafts custom basses in Germany, and the company prefers to build-to-order to fully satisfy all serious bassists. Clover basses are high quality instruments that feature non-endangered tone wood bodies, graphite necks, and Bartolini pickups. All prices from Clover are now in Euros.

ELECTRIC BASS: AVENGER SERIES

Avenger Basses are available in both 4- and 5-string configurations. Models have a maple body, bolt-on graphite neck, 21-fret ebony fingerboard (86.4 cm scale), Clover tuning machines and Quick Change bridge, two Bartolini soapbar pickups, two-band active EQ circuit, and volume/balance/treble/bass controls. Avenger models (last MSR $2,695) are finished in a durable urethane finish that feature custom colors such as simulated marble stone.

ELECTRIC BASS: BASS-TARD SERIES

The **Bass-Tard 4** (last MSR $3,195) is constructed with a solid Flame Maple body, bolt-on graphite neck (86.4 cm scale), 24-fret ebony fingerboard, Gotoh tuning machines, Clover Special Design bridge, two Bartolini soapbar pickups, three band active EQ circuit, and volume/balance/treble/mid/bass controls. Bass-Tard models are wood-stained then finished in a high gloss.

The **Bass-Tard 5** (last MSR $3,595) has a 5-string configuration, and is available with the 24-fret (86.4 cm scale) or the 25-fret (91.5 cm scale) neck. Either model also comes in an Alder body with an opaque finish.

ELECTRIC BASS: SLAPPER SERIES

Clover´s Slapper Series features two models: The **Giant Five** 5-string (last MSR $3,795) and the **Beelzebub** 6-string (last MSR $3,995). Both models sport a reverse strung (no headstock) graphite neck-through body design with select tops and backs, and the 25-fret super long scale 91.6 cm necks. Hardware is Schaller tuners and bridge, and Bartolini dual coil humbuckers. The on-board active/passive EQ is either a 2-band optimized or 3-band with parametric mid control. The **Giant 5 Bolt-On** model features a bolt-on neck, and a last MSR price of $3,395.

ELECTRIC BASS: XPRESSION SERIES

In 1998, Clover debuted the **Xpression** model. The Xpression has an offset double cutaway red alder or Swamp ash body, Canadian rock maple neck, 24-fret ebony or maple fingerboard (86.4 cm scale), 2-per-side tuners, fixed bridge, Bartolini humbucker pickup, volume/2-band EQ controls, and a white pickguard (the first Clover model to do so). The base model is the Xpression Classic, which lists for 1,059 euro. There are several other Xpression models available that each have individual configurations.

COBRA
See John Birch. Instruments previously built in England during the early 1980s.

Luthier John Birch, known for his custom guitar building, teamed up with Barry Kirby to create models under this trademark (source: Tony Bacon and Paul Day, *The Guru's Guitar Guide*).

CODE
Instruments previously manufactured in New Jersey during the 1950s.

Luthier John D´Angelico supplied finished necks to the Code (pronounced ko-day) company for a series of plywood body guitars (Model G-7) that bear the D´Angelico trademark. The D´Angelico/Code guitars were similar in appearance to Gibson's ES-175 (source: Paul William Schmidt, *Acquired of the Angels*).

Clover Paragon Studio
courtesy Clover

Clover Paragon Custom
courtesy Clover

C

COLLIER QUALITY BASSES
Instruments previously built in Belgium.

Ed Collier started offering a number of high quality, low quantity bass guitars in 1988 and continued to offer them through the late 1990s/early 2000s.

ELECTRIC BASS

The **Collier Graphite** series feature a set-in Graphite neck, 24-fret phenol fingerboard (or fretless), Basstec or Bartolini soapbar pickups, solid ETS hardware and a 2- or 3-band EQ. Wood choices include Olive Ash, figured Sycamore (Euopean Maple), different Mahoganies (also Pomele) or Red Alder together with a large choice of exotic or 5A selected wood for tops. These basses are available in 4-, 5-, and 6-string left/right versions. The **Standard** model features black hardware and a satin-like Polyester finish. The **Exclusive** model is the top of the line, and features rare and exotic woods, as well as the best bass components.

The **Collier Power** series are identical with the **Graphite** series, but with a wooden core and shell in and around the graphite neck (4EVER neck). This creates a wooden look and sound with the stability of graphite. The **Collier Vintage** series are available in 4- or 5-string configurations and feels like a ´62 Jazz Bass. Prices ranged from $2,000 to $3,000.

COLLOPY
Instruments currently built in San Francisco, California.

Luthier Rich Collopy has been building and performing repairs on guitars for the past 25 years. In the last year, Collopy also opened a retail musical instrument shop. For further information concerning specifications and pricing, please contact Collopy directly (see Trademark Index).

COLT
See also Cairnes. Instruments previously built in England in the late 1970s.

These solidbody guitars from the Guitarzan company were shaped like guns, and featured 2 pickups (source: Tony Bacon and Paul Day, *The Guru's Guitar Guide*).

COLUMBUS
Instruments previously built in Japan, then manufacturing switched to Korea during the late 1960s.

The Columbus trademark was the brand name of a UK importer. Although the first models were cheap entry level guitars, subsequent Japanese-built guitars raised up to medium quality copies of American designs. The manufacturer then switched to Korean production (source: Tony Bacon and Paul Day, *The Guru's Guitar Guide*).

COMMODORE
Instruments previously built in Japan during the late 1960s through the 1970s.

The Commodore trademark was the brand name of a UK importer. In an unusual switch, the Japanese-built guitars started out as cheap entry-level instruments of original design and then progressed into copying American designs. To further this twist, one of the models copied was the Dan Armstrong See-Through lucite design! (source: Tony Bacon and Paul Day, *The Guru's Guitar Guide*).

CONCERTONE
See chapter on House Brands.

This trademark has been identified as a House Brand of Montgomery Wards. Instruments were built by either Kay or Harmony (source: Michael Wright, *Guitar Stories*, Volume One).

CONKLIN
Instruments currently built in Springfield, Missouri since 1984. Distributed by Conklin Guitars of Springfield, Missouri.

Bill Conklin began producing one-of-a-kind custom instruments in 1984 after designing the Quick Co-Necked Double Neck; a guitar and bass component system in which the individual instruments can be played separately or in their doubleneck configuration.

Early Conklin models incorporate traditional body styles as well as more outlandish signature models like the **Boomerang**, **Elec-trick**, or the **Shadow**. Conklin guitars were offered with many custom options, such as custom finishes and graphics, electronic packages, and fingerboard inlays.

In 1991, Conklin offered an entirely new guitar construction technique called Melted Tops. These 3-piece and 5-piece tops differ from the standard bookmatched variety in that they consist of different species of wood joined with virtually flawless joints. Each Melted Top is unique in its species selection, orientation, and grain patterns - which ensures a limitless combination of exotic tops. The Melted Top configuration is offered on all Session Model versions of Conklin instruments.

The Sidewinder 7-string bass was introduced in 1992, and offered such features as full stereo panning, pickup splitting, an on-board parametric EQ, and the full range and versatility of up to a three-octave fingerboard. Tuned from the low B to high F, the Sidewinder 7-string is perfect for chording, soloing, slap and funk styles. Currently, the Sidewinder body design is the basis for the New Century Bass series, and is available in 4-, 5-, 6-, and 7-string configurations.

Another innovative addition to the Conklin product line is the **M.E.U.** or Mobile Electric Upright bass. Introduced in 1995, this electric upright bass is strapped on like an electric bass but hangs on the body in an upright position. The M.E.U. can be plucked or bowed, and is fully mobile and easily transported. It´s even small enough to fit the overhead compartment of most airplanes.

The past 15 years have shown tremendous growth from Bill Conklin and the staff from Conklin Guitars. Conklin credits a large part of his success to the practice of listening and catering to the wants and needs of each individual customer.

Conklin still offers handcrafted instruments with numerous custom options. Custom instruments start at $3,600; prices vary by nature of the custom work involved. All Conklin instruments carry a limited lifetime warranty.

ELECTRIC: NEW CENTURY SERIES

Currently, the Sidewinder and Crossover Guitar series are offered in three basic models. The **Club Model** has a solid Cherry or swamp ash body and no pickguard. At the next level, the **Tour Model** features a figured Maple top or a figured Maple pickguard over the Cherry or swamp ash body. Both Club and Tour models are available in Cellophane Blue, Cellophane Green, Cellophane Purple, Cellophane Red, and Natural in hand-rubbed oil or Clearcoat finish. At the **Session Model** level, the instruments have a 3-piece Melted Top of Maple, Purpleheart, and Walnut over the cherry or swamp ash body, and are only available in a Natural finish. Prices include an Ultralite case from Modern Case Company.

Add $500 for piezo bridge, gold hardware, Seymour Duncan preamp and 3-band EQ (Pro Package). Add $500 for neck-through body construction (Premium Package).

GRADING	100% MINT	98% NEAR MINT	95% EXC+	90% EXC	80% VG+	70% VG	60% G

C

CROSSOVER 6-STRING CLUB MODEL
- rounded single cutaway cherry body, bolt-on muti-laminated neck with tilt-back 3-per-side headstock, 25.5 in. scale, 24-fret rosewood or purpleheart fingerboard with off-sides dot inlays, Gotoh tuners, tele-style bridge, 2 Seymour Duncan pickups, volume/tone controls, 3-way switch, chrome or black hardware, straplock hardware, locking input jack, current mfg.

MSR $1,999	$1,999	$1,800	$1,600	$1,400	$1,200	$1,000	$800

Add $100 for Model 202 options, which include a tune-o-matic bridge, arched top, and Seymour Duncan pickups.

Also available in Model 111, which includes a vintage-style fixed bridge and 3 Seymour Duncan single coil pickups.

Crossover 6-String Tour Model
- similar to the Club Model, except has Tour model appointments, current mfg.

MSR $2,299	$2,299	$2,050	$1,800	$1,600	$1,400	$1,200	$1,000

Add $100 for Model 202 options, which include a tune-o-matic bridge, arched top, and Seymour Duncan pickups.

Also available in Model 111, which includes a vintage-style fixed bridge and 3 Seymour Duncan single coil pickups.

Crossover 6-String Session Model
- similar to the Club Model, except has Session model appointments, current mfg.

MSR $2,499	$2,499	$2,200	$1,950	$1,750	$1,550	$1,350	$1,150

Add $100 for Model 202 options, which include a tune-o-matic bridge, arched top, and Seymour Duncan pickups.

Also available in Model 111, which includes a vintage-style fixed bridge and 3 Seymour Duncan single coil pickups.

CROSSOVER 7-STRING CLUB MODEL
- similar to the Crossover 6-string, except has a 7-string configuration, 4/3-per-side headstock, 5-piece Maple/Purpleheart laminated neck, vintage-style fixed bridge, 3 Seymour Duncan single coil pickups, volume/tone controls, 5-way switch, current mfg.

MSR $2,399	$2,399	$2,100	$1,800	$1,550	$1,300	$1,100	$900

Also available in Model 202 configuration with tune-o-matic bridge and 2 Seymour Duncan humbucker pickups.

Crossover 7-String Tour Model
- similar to the Club model, except has Tour model appointments, current mfg.

MSR $2,699	$2,699	$2,400	$2,100	$1,850	$1,500	$1,300	$1,100

Also available in Model 202 configuration with tune-o-matic bridge and 2 Seymour Duncan humbucker pickups.

Crossover 7-String Session Model
- similar to the Club model, except has Session model appointments, current mfg.

MSR $2,899	$2,899	$2,600	$2,300	$2,000	$1,750	$1,500	$1,250

Also available in Model 202 configuration with tune-o-matic bridge and 2 Seymour Duncan humbucker pickups.

CROSSOVER 8-STRING CLUB MODEL
- similar to the Crossover 6-string, except has an 8-string configuration, 4-per-side headstock, 5-piece Maple/Purpleheart laminated neck, vintage-style fixed bridge, 3 Seymour Duncan single coil pickups, volume/tone controls, 5-way switch, current mfg.

MSR $2,799	$2,799	$2,450	$2,150	$1,850	$1,550	$1,300	$1,050

Add $100 for Model 202 options, which include a tune-o-matic bridge, arched top, and 2 Seymour Duncan humbucker pickups.

Crossover 8-String Tour Model
- similar to the Club model, except has Tour model appointments, current mfg.

MSR $3,099	$3,099	$2,650	$2,300	$2,000	$1,700	$1,400	$1,150

Add $100 for Model 202 options, which include a tune-o-matic bridge, arched top, and 2 Seymour Duncan humbucker pickups.

Crossover 8-String Session Model
- similar to the Club model, except has Session model appointments, current mfg.

MSR $3,299	$3,299	$2,850	$2,500	$2,200	$1,900	$1,550	$1,200

Add $100 for Model 202 options, which include a tune-o-matic bridge, arched top, and 2 Seymour Duncan humbucker pickups.

SIDEWINDER 6-STRING CLUB MODEL
- offset double cutaway asymmetrical cherry body, bolt-on muti-laminated neck with tilt-back 3-per-side headstock, 25.5 in. scale, 24-fret rosewood or purpleheart fingerboard with off-sides dot inlays, Gotoh tuners, chrome or black hardware, straplock hardware, tele-style bridge, 2 Seymour Duncan pickups, volume/tone controls, 3-way switch, locking input jack, current mfg.

MSR $1,999	$1,999	$1,800	$1,600	$1,400	$1,200	$1,000	$800

Add $100 for Model 202 options, which include a tune-o-matic bridge, arched top, and 2 Seymour Duncan humbucker pickups.

Also available in Model 111, which includes a vintage-style fixed bridge and 3 Seymour Duncan single coil pickups.

C

GRADING	100% MINT	98% NEAR MINT	95% EXC+	90% EXC	80% VG+	70% VG	60% G

Sidewinder 6-String Tour Model - similar to the Club Model, except has Tour model appointments, current mfg.

MSR $2,299	$2,299	$2,050	$1,800	$1,600	$1,400	$1,200	$1,000

Add $100 for Model 202 options, which include a tune-o-matic bridge, arched top, and 2 Seymour Duncan humbucker pickups.

Also available in Model 111, which includes a vintage-style fixed bridge and 3 Seymour Duncan single coil pickups.

Sidewinder 6-String Session Model - similar to the Club Model, except has Session model appointments, current mfg.

MSR $2,499	$2,499	$2,200	$2,000	$1,800	$1,600	$1,400	$1,200

Add $100 for Model 202 options, which include a tune-o-matic bridge, arched top, and 2 Seymour Duncan humbucker pickups.

Also available in Model 111, which includes a vintage-style fixed bridge and 3 Seymour Duncan single coil pickups.

SIDEWINDER 7-STRING CLUB MODEL - similar to the Sidewinder 6-string, except has a 7-string configuration, 4/3-per-side headstock, 5-piece Maple/Purpleheart laminated neck, vintage-style fixed bridge, 3 Seymour Duncan single coil pickups, volume/tone controls, 5-way switch, current mfg.

MSR $2,399	$2,399	$2,100	$1,800	$1,550	$1,300	$1,100	$900

Also available in Model 202 configuration with tune-o-matic bridge and 2 Seymour Duncan humbucker pickups.

Sidewinder 7-String Tour Model - similar to the Club Model, except has Tour model appointments, current mfg.

MSR $2,699	$2,699	$2,400	$2,100	$1,850	$1,500	$1,300	$1,100

Also available in Model 202 configuration with tune-o-matic bridge and 2 Seymour Duncan humbucker pickups.

Sidewinder 7-String Session Model - similar to the Club model, except has Session model appointments, current mfg.

MSR $2,899	$2,899	$2,600	$2,300	$2,000	$1,750	$1,500	$1,250

Also available in Model 202 configuration with tune-o-matic bridge and 2 Seymour Duncan humbucker pickups.

SIDEWINDER 8-STRING CLUB MODEL - similar to the Sidewinder 6-string, except has an 8-string configuration, 4-per-side headstock, 5-piece Maple/Purpleheart laminated neck, vintage-style fixed bridge, 3 Seymour Duncan single coil pickups, volume/tone controls, 5-way switch, current mfg.

MSR $2,799	$2,799	$2,450	$2,150	$1,850	$1,550	$1,300	$1,050

Add $100 for Model 202 options, which include a tune-o-matic bridge, arched top, and 2 Seymour Duncan humbucker pickups.

Sidewinder 8-String Tour Model - similar to the Club model, except has Tour model appointments, current mfg.

MSR $3,099	$3,099	$2,650	$2,300	$2,000	$1,700	$1,400	$1,150

Add $100 for Model 202 options, which include a tune-o-matic bridge, arched top, and 2 Seymour Duncan humbucker pickups.

Sidewinder 8-String Session Model - similar to the Club model, except has Session model appointments, current mfg.

MSR $3,299	$3,299	$2,850	$2,500	$2,200	$1,900	$1,550	$1,200

Add $100 for Model 202 options, which include a tune-o-matic bridge, arched top, and 2 Seymour Duncan humbucker pickups.

ELECTRIC: GROOVE TOOLS SERIES

CGTG-7 - string, offset double cutaway solid cherry body, arched top and back, 5-piece maple/purpleheart laminated neck, 24-fret rosewood fingerboard, fixed bridge, string through-body, 2 custom humbucker pickups, 4/3 headstock configuration, 1 vol/1 push/pull tone control and coil tap switch, available in Cherry and Black finishes, current mfg.

MSR $679	$600	$525	$450	$400	$350	$300	$250

CGTG-7T - similar to CGTG-7, except has a non-locking tremolo and Sperzel locking tuners, available in Cherry and Black finishes, current mfg.

MSR $779	$650	$575	$500	$450	$400	$350	$300

ELECTRIC BASS: NEW CENTURY SERIES

Currently, the Sidewinder Bass is offered in three different models. The **Club Model** has a solid cherry body. At the next configuration, the **Tour Model** features a figured maple top over the Cherry body. Both Club and Tour models are available in Cellophane Blue, Cellophane Green, Cellophane Purple, Cellophane Red, and Natural in hand-rubbed oil or Clearcoat finish. At the **Session Model** level, the instruments have a 3-piece Melted Top of maple, purpleheart, and walnut over the cherry body, and are only available in a Natural finish. Prices include an Ultralite case from Modern Case Company.

Add $200 for Seymour Duncan 3-band EQ (Plus Package). Add $500 for gold hardware, piezo bridge, and Bartolini preamp and EQ (Pro Package). Add $500 for neck-through body construction (Premium Package).

SIDEWINDER BASS 4 CLUB MODEL - offset double cutaway asymmetrical cherry body, bolt-on muti-laminated neck with tilt-back 2-per-side headstock, 34 in. scale, 24-fret rosewood or purpleheart fingerboard with off-sides dot inlays, fixed bridge, Gotoh tuners, chrome or black hardware, 2 Seymour Duncan soapbar pickups, volume/blend/tone controls, straplock hardware, locking input jack, current mfg.

MSR $2,199	$2,199	$2,000	$1,800	$1,600	$1,400	$1,200	$1,000

Sidewinder Bass Tour Model - similar to the Club model, except has Tour model appointments, current mfg.

MSR $2,499	$2,499	$2,200	$2,000	$1,800	$1,600	$1,400	$1,200

Sidewinder Bass Session Model - similar to the Club model, except has Session model appointments, current mfg.

MSR $2,699	$2,699	$2,400	$2,100	$1,850	$1,500	$1,300	$1,100

SIDEWINDER BASS 5 CLUB MODEL - similar to the Sidewinder Bass 4, except has 5-string configuration, 3/2 headstock, 5-piece laminated Maple/Purpleheart necks, current mfg.

MSR $2,399	$2,399	$2,100	$1,800	$1,550	$1,300	$1,100	$900

Sidewinder Bass 5 Tour Model - similar to the Club model, except has Tour model appointments, current mfg.

MSR $2,699	$2,699	$2,400	$2,100	$1,850	$1,500	$1,300	$1,100

C

GRADING	100% MINT	98% NEAR MINT	95% EXC+	90% EXC	80% VG+	70% VG	60% G

Sidewinder Bass 5 Session Model - similar to the Club model, except has Session model appointments, current mfg.

MSR $2,899	$2,899	$2,600	$2,300	$2,000	$1,750	$1,500	$1,250

SIDEWINDER BASS 6 CLUB MODEL - similar to the Sidewinder Bass 4, except has 6-string configuration, 3-per-side headstock, 7-piece laminated Maple/Purpleheart necks, current mfg.

MSR $2,799	$2,799	$2,450	$2,150	$1,850	$1,550	$1,300	$1,050

Sidewinder Bass 6 Tour Model - similar to the Club model, except has Tour model appointments, current mfg.

MSR $3,099	$3,099	$2,650	$2,300	$2,000	$1,700	$1,400	$1,150

Sidewinder Bass 6 Session Model - similar to the Club model, except has Session model appointments, current mfg.

MSR $3,299	$3,299	$2,850	$2,500	$2,200	$1,900	$1,550	$1,200

SIDEWINDER BASS 7 CLUB MODEL - similar to the Sidewinder Bass 4, except has 7-string configuration, 4/3 headstock, 7-piece laminated Maple/Purpleheart necks, mfg. 1992-present.

MSR $2,799	$2,799	$2,450	$2,150	$1,850	$1,550	$1,300	$1,050

Sidewinder Bass 7 Tour Model - similar to the Club model, except has Tour model appointments, current mfg.

MSR $3,099	$3,099	$2,650	$2,300	$2,000	$1,700	$1,400	$1,150

Sidewinder Bass 7 Session Model - similar to the Club model, except has Session model appointments, current mfg.

MSR $3,299	$3,299	$2,850	$2,500	$2,200	$1,900	$1,550	$1,200

Conklin 4-String
courtesy Bill Conklin

ELECTRIC BASS: GROOVE TOOLS SERIES

GT-4 - offset double cutaway Swamp ash body with figured maple top, 5-piece Wenge/Purpleheart laminated bolt-on neck, Purpleheart fingerboard, 2-per-side tuners, 34 in. scale, 24 medium/jumbo frets, Conklin active pickups, black hardware, available in Cellophane Wine or Clear Hard finishes, current mfg.

MSR $995	$650	$575	$500	$425	$375	$325	$275

Add $100 for fretless fingerboard (Model GT-4FL).

GTRP-4 - co-designed with Rocco Prestia, 4-string special, 21-fret bolt-on neck, Sidewinder body style with bird's-eye maple pickguard, Bartolini P/J style pickups, mfg. 2001-present.

MSR $1,395	$975	$900	$825	$750	$675	$600	$500

GT-5 - similar to GT-4, except in a 5-string configuration, available in Cellophane Wine or Clear Hard finishes, current mfg.

MSR $1,095	$750	$675	$600	$525	$450	$400	$350

Add $100 for fretless configuration (Model GT-5FL).

GT-7 - similar to GT-4, except in a 7-string configuration, 7-piece Wenge/Purpleheart laminated neck, Bartolini active pickups, available in Cellophane Wine or Clear Hard finishes, current mfg.

MSR $1,695	$1,250	$1,100	$950	$850	$750	$650	$550

Add $100 for fretless configuration (Model GT-6FL).

GTBD-7 Bill Dickens Signature Model - similar to GT-7, except has 7-piece maple/Purpleheart neck-through body construction, gold hardware, custom bartolini pickups and electronics, available in Cellophane Purpleburst finish, current mfg.

MSR $2,395	$1,500	$1,350	$1,200	$1,050	$900	$800	$700

ELECTRIC BASS: MEU SERIES

M.E.U. (MOBILE ELECTRIC UPRIGHT) - cello-styled hollow swamp ash body, cherry top, bolt-on muti-laminated neck with tilt-back 2-per-side headstock, 34 in. scale, rosewood or ebony fingerboard, solid wood bridge and tailpiece, Gotoh tuners, removable balance block, chrome or black hardware, bridge mounted piezo pickups, volume/tone controls, straplock hardware. Includes custom case, mfg. 1995-present.

MSR $3,200	N/A	N/A	N/A	N/A	N/A	N/A	N/A

M.E.U. 5-String - similar to the M.E.U., except in five-string configuration, current mfg.

MSR $3,500	N/A	N/A	N/A	N/A	N/A	N/A	N/A

This electric upright bass is strapped on like an electric bass but hangs on the body in an upright position. Overall length is 52 inches.

CONRAD

Instruments previously produced in Japan circa 1972 to 1978.

The Conrad trademark was a brand name used by U.S. importers David Wexler and Company of Chicago, Illinois. The Conrad product line consisted of 6- and 12-string acoustic guitars, thinline hollowbody electrics, solid body electric guitars and basses, mandolins, and banjos. Conrad instruments were produced by Kasuga International (Kasuga and Tokai USA, Inc.), and featured good quality designs specifically based on popular American designs (source: Michael Wright, *Guitar Stories*, Volume One). Used guitars are found typically priced between $200 and $300 in excellent condition.

Conklin Groove Tools GT-4
courtesy Conklin

C

GRADING	100% MINT	98% NEAR MINT	95% EXC+	90% EXC	80% VG+	70% VG	60% G

CONTINENTAL
See also Conn. Instruments previously produced in Japan.

As well as distributing the Conn guitars, the Continental Music Company of Chicago, Illinois also distributed their own brand name guitars under the Continental logo in the U.S (source: Michael Wright, *Guitar Stories*, Volume One).

COOG INSTRUMENTS
Instruments currently built in Santa Cruz, California.

Luthier Ronald Cook runs Coog Instruments as a hobby/semi-business. Cook's primary focus is on handcrafted folk instruments such as guitars and dulcimers, but has also constructed various electric guitars, hurdy-gurdies, and harpsichords through the years. Cook also performs repair work on antique or vintage stringed instruments.

Cook's building and repairs are conducted in his spare time; thus, the lead time on a custom guitar or dulcimer order is a bit longer than running down to your local "guitar club mega-gigantic store" and buying one off the wall. If patience and a custom-built folk instrument is what you're into, then please call Cook directly (see Trademark Index).

CORAL
Instruments and amplifiers previously produced in Neptune City, New Jersey from 1967 to 1968 by the Danelectro Corporation. Distributed by MCA, after buying the Danelectro company and trademark.

In 1967, after MCA purchased the Danelectro Corporation, the Coral trademark was introduced. The Coral line was MCA's marketing strategy for direct wholesale selling to individual dealers, instead of selling to Sears & Roebuck. Once the company went that route, however, they came up against competition from the larger guitar manufacturers at the dealer level. The Coral line of guitars and amplifiers was only produced for about one year.

CORT
Instruments currently produced in Inchon and Taejon, Korea and Surabuya, Indonesia. Distributed in the U.S. by Cort Musical Instrument Company, Ltd. of Northbrook, IL.

Since 1960, Cort has been providing students, beginners and mid-level guitar players with quality acoustic, semihollow body, and solid body guitars and basses. All Cort instruments are produced in Asia in Cort company facilities, which were established in 1973. Cort is one of the few U.S. companies that owns their overseas production facilities. Cort also produces most of their own electronics (pickups, circuit boards, and other guitar parts); additional parts and custom pieces are available under the Mightymite trademark.

The Cort engineering and design center is located in Northbrook, Illinois. Wood is bought from the U.S. and Canada and shipped to their production facilities in Korea. Cort instruments are then produced and assembled in the main Cort factories in Korea. After shipping the finished instruments back to the U.S., all instruments are checked in the Illinois facilities as part of quality control prior to shipping to the dealer.

In addition to their traditional designs, Cort also offers a large number of their own designs, as well as featured designs by other luthiers. Beginning in 1996, Cort began commissioning designs from noted luthier Jerry Auerswald; this lead to other designs from such noted U.S. luthiers as Jim Triggs, Bill Conklin, and Greg Curbow. Cort has also worked with guitarists Larry Coryell and Matt "Guitar" Murphy on their respective signature series models (the **LCS-1** and the **MGM-1**).

In the mid-1980s, Cort licensed the Steinberger bridge/reverse tuner and double ball end string design for their minimalist body/headless instrument design. These Steinberger-derived models were available in both a guitar and bass model (either had a retail list price of $349). Both models featured neck-through construction, and were available in black or white finishes. The bass model had Powersound P/J-style pickups, and 2 volumes/1 tone control.

Cort's left-handed models are generally a special order, and produced in limited quantities. There is an additional $30 charge for left-handed configuration models in the current production line-up.

ELECTRIC: CL SERIES

CL 200 - similar to CL 1000, except has mahogany body and mahogany bolt-on neck. Power Sound open pickups with Zebra bobbins, no binding, chrome hardware, available in Black, Trans. Blue, or Trans. Red finishes, mfg. 1999-2001.

$250	$195	$175	$150	$125	$95	$65

Last MSR was $350.

CL 1000 - similar to CL 1500, except does not have f-hole or chambered body, available in Trans. Blue, Trans. Red, Natural, or Cherry Red Sunburst finishes, mfg. 1999-present.

$425	$350	$315	$275	$240	$210	$175

Last MSR was $595.

CL 1400 - similar to CL1500, except has mahogany body with flamed maple top, mahogany neck, rosewood fingerboard with split block position markers, 24.75 in. scale, 2 Mightymite covered vintage alnico humbucker pickups, 3-per-side tuners, FK-1 combination bridge, chrome hardware, available in Cherry Red Sunburst, Trans. Teal or Trans. Black finishes, mfg. 2000-01.

$625	$550	$495	$450	$395	$350	$295

Last MSR was $895.

CL 1500 - Double cutaway (one sharp, one smooth) carved body design, mahogany body with quilted maple top, chamber body with f-hole, mahogany neck with rosewood fingerboard with floral inlay pattern, set neck, 1 volume and 1 tone control, coil tap, Mightymite covered alnico humbuckers, toggle switch, ivoroid binding, FK-1 combination bridge, gold hardware, available in Black, Cherry Sunburst, 3-Tone Sunburst or Vintage Burst finishes, mfg. 1999-2003.

$675	$595	$550	$495	$450	$395	$350

Last MSR was $950.

ELECTRIC: G SERIES

G Series guitars have a offset double cutaway body, satin finished hard rock maple neck, various pickup combinations, 1-Volume/1-Tone control, 5-way switch.

GRADING	100% MINT	98% NEAR MINT	95% EXC+	90% EXC	80% VG+	70% VG	60% G

G200 - agathis body, rosewood fingerboard, 3 single coil Powersound pickups, die-cast tuners, Full-Action II tremolo, available in Black, Blue, Red, Trans. Red, Trans. Blue, or 2-Toneburst finishes, mfg. 2001-present.

MSR $199		$150	$125	$110	$95	$80	$65	$50

Add $10 for transparent finishes and 2-Toneburst finish. Add $35 for left-hand model (G200L).

G205 - similar to G200 except, has maple fingerboard, available in Red, Trans. Red, or Blue finishes, mfg. 2001-03.

		$150	$125	$110	$95	$80	$65	$50

G210 - similar to G200 except, has 1 Powersound humbucker pickup and 2 Powersound single coil pickups, available in Black, Blue, Red, Trans. Blue, Trans. Red, or 2-Toneburst finishes, mfg. 2001-03, 2005-present.

MSR $249		$175	$140	$120	$100	$85	$70	$55

G250 - similar to G200 except, has basswood body, 1 Mighty mite humbucker pickup and 2 Mighty mite single coil pickups, Wilkinson VS50 II bridge, available in 2-Toneburst, Trans. Red or Trans. Blue finishes, mfg. 2001-present.

MSR $299		$225	$185	$150	$125	$105	$85	$65

G250P - similar to the G250 except has a Fishman Power Bridge pickup with piezo controls, available in 2-Tone Burst finish, mfg. 2002-04.

		$425	$350	$325	$300	$260	$235	$190

Last MSR was $595.

G254 - similar to G250 except has no pickguard, available in Black Metallic or Walnut Satin finishes, new 2005.

MSR $299		$225	$185	$150	$125	$105	$85	$65

G255 - similar to G250 except has Select by EMG pickups, available in Amber Stain, Walnut Stain, Bordeaux Red Metallic and Grey Nickel finishes, mfg. 2001.

G260 - similar to G200 except has light swamp ash body, 3 Duncan Designed Hot Rail pickups, Wilkinson VS50 II bridge, available in Transparent Black, Natural and Honeyburst finishes, mfg. 2001 only.

G270 - similar to G200 except, has light swamp ash body with flamed maple top, 1 Duncan Designed humbucker pickup and 2 Duncan Designed single coil pickups. Wilkinson VS50 II bridge, available in 3-Toneburst and Vintageburst finishes, mfg. 2001-03.

		$425	$375	$350	$295	$250	$225	$195

Last MSR was $595.

G285 - offset double cutaway basswood body with flame maple top, bolt-on maple neck, 22-fret rosewood fingerboard with offset dot inlay, six-on-one-side tuners, CFA III bridge, white pickguard, Seymour Duncan S/S/H pickups, three knobs, chrome hardware, available in Shadow Blue Burst finish, new 2005.

MSR $1,095		$750	$650	$575	$500	$425	$350	$300

G290 - similar to G200 except, has light swamp ash body with quilted maple top, carved top, Seymour Duncan JB and Vintage staggered pickups, Sperzel Trim-Lok tuners, Wilkinson VS50 II bridge, available in Antique Violinburst and Cherry Red Sunburst finishes, mfg. 2001-present.

MSR $1,095		$750	$650	$575	$500	$425	$350	$300

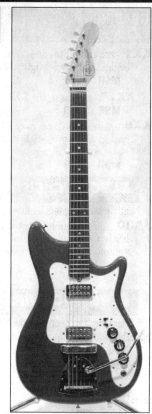

**Continental
Blue Book Publications**

ELECTRIC: JC SERIES

The three JC Series guitar models were introduced in 1998 and discontinued in 2001. Models include the **JC 2** (last MSR was $269), **JC 3** (last MSR was $259), and the **JC 4** (last MSR was $279).

ELECTRIC: JIM TRIGGS SERIES

The Cort **TRG** model was designed in conjunction with luthier/designer Jim Triggs. Triggs has been building handcrafted instruments in his Nashville, Tennessee shop and now Kansas Shop, for the past 25 years.

TRG-1 - single sharp cutaway semi-hollow bound body, maple top, maple back/sides, 2 cat's-eye f-holes, set-in maple neck, 24 3/4" scale, 22-fret bound rosewood fingerboard, bound headstock with Triggs signature imprint inlay, gold hardware, 3-per-side tuners with white buttons, rosewood bridge/trapeze tailpiece, Mightymite humbucker pickup, volume/tone controls, available in Robin's Egg Blue or See-Through Orange finishes, mfg. 1998-2004.

		$500	$450	$395	$350	$275	$225	$175

Last MSR was $699.

TRG-2 - similar to TRG-1 except in a two pickup configuration, maple top, sides and back, 24.75 in. scale, maple neck, 2 Mightymite covered vintage alnico humbucker pickups, 2 cat's eye f-holes, "C" vibrato bridge, gold hardware, 3-per-side tuners, available in Black or Trans. Orange finishes, mfg. 2000-present.

MSR $895		$625	$550	$475	$395	$325	$250	$195

Also available as the TRG-2A at no additional charge.

TRG-CHAMBER - Offset double cutaway, agathis top, back and sides, maple neck, rosewood fingerboard with dot position markers, 3-per-side tuners, 24.75 in. scale, 2 Powersound pickups, Tune-O-Matic bridge, chrome hardware, available in Black and Robin's Egg Blue finishes, mfg. 2000-02.

		$250	$205	$175	$140	$110	$90	$65

Last MSR was $350.

**Cort Solo (Ash)
courtesy Cort**

ELECTRIC: KATANA (KX) SERIES

The KX Series features Mighty Mite Motherbucker pickups, STB, and a TonePros licensed locking bridge system.

C

GRADING	100% MINT	98% NEAR MINT	95% EXC+	90% EXC	80% VG+	70% VG	60% G

KX1 - offset double cutaway mahogany body, set-mahogany neck, 24-fret rosewood fingerboard with dot inlay, three-per-side tuners, TonePros licensed bridge, STB, two Mighty Mite Motherbucker pickups, two knobs, three-way switch, chrome hardware, Black finish, new 2005.

	MSR $575	$400	$325	$275	$230	$195	$165	$135

KX1F - similar to the KX1, except has a flame maple top, available in Shadow Blue Burst or Trans. Charcoal Gray finishes, new 2005.

	MSR $650	$450	$375	$325	$275	$235	$195	$160

KX5 - offset double cutaway basswood body, bolt-on maple neck, 24-fret rosewood fingerboard with dot inlay, three-per-side tuners, TonePros licensed bridge, STB, two Mighty Mite Motherbucker pickups, two knobs, three-way switch, chrome hardware, available in Black or Canon Blue Satin finishes, new 2005.

	MSR $349	$250	$200	$170	$140	$120	$100	$80

ELECTRIC: LUTHITE (EF) SERIES

Luthite series guitars feature Cort´s patented Environmentally Friendly body material. The **JA 30** model is designed by Jerry Auerswald (Auerswald Guitars).

JA30 - offset double cutaway EF (Luthite) body, bolt-on hard maple neck, 25.5 in. scale, 22-fret rosewood fingerboard with offset dot inlays, chrome hardware, reverse headstock, 6-on-the-other-side side chrome tuners, Accutune II tremolo bridge, 2 single coil/1 humbucker Mightymite pickups, volume/tone controls, 5-way position switch, available in Atlantic Blue Metallic, or Black finishes, mfg. 1997-99.

	$325	$275	$250	$225	$175	$150	$125
					Last MSR was $450.		

ELECTRIC: MIRAGE SERIES

There has also been a model M100 and M700, but they were never offered in the price list.

M200 - offset double cutaway agathis body, arched top, maple bolt-on neck, 22-fret rosewood fingerboard, two Powersound pickup humbuckers, two knobs, 3-per-side die-cast tuners, chrome hardware, available in Black, Bordeaux Red Metallic, or Deep Blue Metallic, mfg. 2002-present.

	MSR $289	$210	$175	$150	$125	$105	$90	$75

Add $20 for left-hand configuration.

M500 - offset double cutaway mahogany body, mahogany neck, 24.75 in. scale, rosewood fingerboard with dot position markers, 3-per-side tuners, 2 Mightymite covered vintage alnico humbucker pickups, 1 Volume/1-Tone control, 3-way switch, Tune-O-Matic bridge, chrome hardware, available in Bordeaux Red Metallic and Deep Blue Metallic finishes, mfg. 2000-01.

	$275	$250	$225	$195	$175	$150	$125
					Last MSR was $395.		

M520 - offset double cutaway mahogany body, set mahogany neck, 22-fret rosewood fingerboard with dot inlays, three-per-side tuners, TonePros licensed locking bridge, two MMLP covered humbucker pickups, two knobs, three-way switch, chrome hardware, available in Black and Tobacco Burst finishes, new 2005.

	MSR $550	$390	$325	$275	$230	$195	$160	$130

M600 - similar to Mirage 500, except has bound top, available in Honeyburst and Antique Violin Dark finishes, mfg. 2001-present.

	MSR $629	$450	$385	$345	$305	$260	$235	$195

M700 - similar to Mirage 500 except, has Wilkinson VS50 II Tremolo bridge, gold hardware, available in Cherry Red Sunburst finish, mfg. 2000-01.

	$595	$495	$450	$425	$395	$350	$295
					Last MSR was $850.		

M800 - similar to the M600, except has a chambered body with f-holes, available in Light Vintage Burst finish, mfg. 2003-present.

	MSR $850	$595	$525	$475	$425	$350	$295	$250

M1200 - similar to the M600, except has a vine inlaid fingerboard and 2 Seymour Duncan humbucker pickups, available in Antique Sunburst finish, mfg. 2003-04.

	$700	$625	$550	$500	$450	$400	$350
					Last MSR was $999.		

ELECTRIC: PERFORMER SERIES

IMPALA - offset double cutaway Agathis body, bolt-on hard rock maple neck, 25.5 in. scale, 22-fret maple fingerboard with black dot inlay, vintage style tremolo, 6-on-a-side natural wood headstock, chrome hardware, white pickguard, 3 single coil Mightymite pickups, volume/2 tone controls, 5-way selector switch, available in 2-Tone Burst, Black, Gold Metallic, or Ivory finishes, disc. 1999.

	$225	$195	$175	$150	$125	$100	$75
					Last MSR was $299.		

STATURE - similar to the Impala, except has rosewood fingerboard with white dot inlays, Accutune II tremolo, roller nut, black pickguard, 2 single coil/1 humbucker Mightymite pickups, available in Amber Burst, Black, See-Through Black, or See-Through Blue finishes, disc. 1999.

	$325	$275	$250	$225	$175	$150	$125
					Last MSR was $450.		

Stature Gold - similar to the Stature, except has Wilkinson VS-50K tremolo, pearloid pickguard, and gold hardware, available in See-Through Black or Vintage Burst finishes, disc. 1999.

	$350	$295	$275	$225	$195	$175	$125
					Last MSR was $450.		

In 1998, Amber Glossy and Black finishes were introduced; See-Through Black and Vintage Burst finishes were discontinued.

GRADING	100% MINT	98% NEAR MINT	95% EXC+	90% EXC	80% VG+	70% VG	60% G

MEGA STANDARD - similar to the Stature, except features flamed maple top, white pickguard, gold hardware, 2 single coil/1 humbucker Select by EMG pickups, available in Amber Glossy, Blue Burst, Crimson Burst, or See-Through Black finishes, disc. 1999.

| | $400 | $325 | $295 | $250 | $225 | $175 | $150 |

Last MSR was $550.

JC 65 - offset double cutaway slim-waisted Agathis body, bolt-on hard rock maple neck, 25.5 in. scale, 21-fret rosewood fingerboard with white dot inlay, bigsby-style JC tremolo, 6-on-a-side natural wood headstock, chrome hardware, white pickguard, 3 single coil Mightymite pickups, volume/2 tone controls, 5-way selector switch, available in Black, Foam Green, Shell Pink, or 2-Tone Burst finishes, mfg. 1997-98.

| | $350 | $300 | $275 | $225 | $195 | $150 | $125 |

Last MSR was $500.

JC 67 - similar to the JC 65, available in Pink Sparkle and Silver Sparkle finishes, mfg. 1998-99.

| | $275 | $250 | $225 | $195 | $150 | $125 | $100 |

Last MSR was $399.

VIVA GOLD - offset double cutaway contoured maple body, bolt-on hard rock maple neck, 25.5 in. scale, 24-fret rosewood fingerboard with offset white dot inlay, Lo-Pro Floyd Rose licensed tremolo, 6-on-a-side black headstock, chrome hardware, Mightymite humbucker/single coil/humbucker pickups, volume/tone controls, 5-way selector switch, available in Black, Natural Satin, Red Metallic, or Vintage Burst finishes, disc. 1998.

| | $525 | $450 | $395 | $350 | $275 | $225 | $195 |

Last MSR was $750.

Viva Gold II - similar to the Viva Gold, except features white silver hardware, available in Natural Stain or Walnut Stain finishes, mfg. 1998-disc.

| | $500 | $425 | $375 | $325 | $275 | $225 | $175 |

Last MSR was $650.

Viva 7 - similar to the Viva Gold except in 7-string configuration, disc. 2002.

| | $475 | $425 | $375 | $325 | $275 | $225 | $175 |

Last MSR was $650.

Cort Mega Standard
courtesy Cort

ELECTRIC: S SERIES

Prior **S Series** models may be designated as **Sterling** or **Starlite** on the headstock.

S400 - sleek offset double cutaway Agathis body, bolt-on hard rock maple neck, 25.5 in. scale, 22-fret rosewood fingerboard with offset dot inlay, vintage style Full Action II tremolo, 3-per-side natural wood headstock, chrome hardware, white pickguard, 3 single coil Power Sound pickups, volume/2 tone controls, 5-way selector switch, available in Black, Foam Green, See-Through Red, or Shell Pink finishes, mfg. 1997-2001.

| | $195 | $175 | $150 | $125 | $110 | $95 | $75 |

Last MSR was $270.

In 1998, See-Through Blue finish was introduced.

S500 - similar to the S400, except has 2 single coil/humbucker Powersound pickups, volume/tone controls, available in Black, Foam Green, See-Through Blue, or See-Through Red finishes, mfg. 1998-2000.

| | $200 | $175 | $150 | $125 | $110 | $95 | $75 |

Last MSR was $279.

S1000 - similar to the S400, except has mahogany body, black headstock with silk screened logo, fixed bridge, no pickguard, 2 Mightymite humbuckers, volume/tone controls, 3-way selector, available in Black or Cherry Red Sunburst finishes, disc. 1999.

| | $250 | $225 | $200 | $175 | $150 | $125 | $95 |

Last MSR was $359.

S2000 - similar to the S1000, except has maple fingerboard, natural wood headstock, Full Action II tremolo, 2 single coil/humbucker Mightymite pickups, 5-way selector switch, available in Black, Crimson Burst, or Walnut Satin finishes, disc. 1998.

| | $275 | $250 | $200 | $175 | $150 | $125 | $100 |

Last MSR was $399.

S2100 - similar to the S400, except has black headstock with silk screened logo, 2 single coil/1 humbucker Mightymite pickups, volume/tone controls, available in Black, Red Metallic, or White finishes, mfg. 1997-98.

| | $275 | $250 | $200 | $175 | $150 | $125 | $100 |

Last MSR was $399.

S2500 - similar to the S1000, except has maple body, Wilkinson VS-50K tremolo, 2 single coil/1 humbucker Mightymite pickups, 5-way selector switch, available in Amber Satin, Black, Cherry Red, or Oil Satin finishes, mfg. 1996-99.

| | $325 | $275 | $250 | $225 | $195 | $150 | $125 |

Last MSR was $449.

S2500 M - similar to the S2500, except has mahogany body, available in Cherry Red or Oil Satin finishes, mfg. 1996-98.

| | $350 | $300 | $275 | $225 | $200 | $175 | $125 |

Last MSR was $499.

Cort S2000
courtesy Cort

C

GRADING	100% MINT	98% NEAR MINT	95% EXC+	90% EXC	80% VG+	70% VG	60% G

S2550 - similar to S2500, except has soft maple body, hard maple neck, Mighty Mite pickups, one volume and one tone control, coil tap, 5-way switch, Wilkinson VS50K tremolo, available in Amber Satin, Walnut Satin, or Vintage Burst finishes, disc. 2000.

	$300	$250	$225	$200	$175	$150	$100

Last MSR was $429.

S2600 - similar to S2500, except has soft maple body, hard maple neck, Dincan designed hot rails, one volume and one tone switch, coil tap, 5-way switch, Wilkinson VS50K tremolo, available in Trans. Blue, Trans.Red, or Vintage Burst finishes, disc. 2000.

	$375	$325	$300	$250	$200	$175	$125

Last MSR was $499.

S2800 - similar to the S2500, except has maple body/quilted maple top, white pearloid pickguard, 2 single coil/humbucker Seymour Duncan pickups, satin gold hardware, available in Amber Satin, Walnut Stain, and Vintage Burst finishes, mfg. 1998-2000.

	$575	$495	$450	$375	$300	$250	$200

Last MSR was $795.

S2900 - similar to S2500, except has quilted maple top, arched body top, hard maple neck, has Seymour Duncan SSL-1 and TB-4 pickups, one volume control and one tone control with coil tap. Wilkinson VS50K tremolo and Sperzel Trimlok tuners, available in Cherry Red Sunburst or Blue Burst finishes, mfg. 1999-2000.

	$600	$525	$475	$425	$375	$325	$250

Last MSR was $850.

S3000 - similar to the S2500, except has basswood body, Lo-Pro licensed Floyd Rose double locking tremolo system, Mightymite humbucker/single coil/humbucker pickups, available in Black, Blue Metallic, and See-Through Red finishes, disc. 1998.

	$425	$350	$300	$275	$225	$175	$150

Last MSR was $590.

In 1997, See-Through Red finish was discontinued.

ELECTRIC: SIGNATURE SERIES

BECK-ALTO - single cutaway, semihollow body design with spruce top and flamed maple back and sides, maple neck with rosewood fingerboard and white dot inlays, 24 3/4" scale, custom-made bass/treble split pickup, 2 volume and 1 tone control, toggle switch, dual jacks, special string gauge tuned A to A and incorporating a split signal allowing one to chord and play an accompanying bass line simultaneously, available in Natural Glossy and Vintage Sunburst finishes, mfg. 1999-2002.

	$825	$750	$650	$550	$450	$395	$350

Last MSR was $1,195.

The Joe Beck Alto and Beck-6 were designed in conjunction with guitarist Joe Beck.

BECK-6 - Joe Beck Signature Standard Model, single cutaway design, spruce top, maple back and sides, maple neck, Mightymite covered alnico pickups, 1 volume and 1-tone control, 2 uniquely shaped soundholes, available in Natural Glossy and Vintage Sunburst finishes, mfg. 1999-present.

MSR $695	$490	$400	$350	$300	$250	$200	$150

The Joe Beck Alto and Beck-6 were designed in conjunction with guitarist Joe Beck.

HIRAM BULLOCK HBS - offset double cutaway light swamp ash body, bird's-eye hard maple neck, 6-on-a-side tuners, rosewood fingerboard with dot position markers, 2 Mightymite humbucker pickups and 1 Mightymite single coil pickup, 1 volume/1 tone control, 5-way switch, Wilkinson VS50 II Tremolo bridge, chrome hardware, available in 3-Tone Sunburst or Black finish, white pickguard, 25.5 in. scale, current mfg.

MSR $795	$560	$475	$400	$350	$300	$250	$200

The Cort HBS model was designed in conjunction with guitarist Hiram Bullock who was the first guitarist on Saturday Night Live.

LARRY CORYELL LCS-1 - single cutaway semi-hollow bound body, spruce top, flamed maple back/sides, maple neck, 21-fret bound rosewood fingerboard with block inlays, bound headstock with Larry Coryell signature imprint inlay, raised pickguard, gold hardware, 3-per-side tuners, rosewood bridge/C trapeze tailpiece, 2 Duncan Designed humbucker pickups, 2 volume/2 tone controls, 3-way selector switch located on lower treble bout, available in Natural Glossy and Vintage Burst finishes, 24.75 in. scale, current mfg.

MSR $1,695	$1,200	$1,050	$900	$800	$700	$600	$500

Natural Glossy finish was disc. in 1999. The Cort LCS-1 model was designed in conjunction with guitarist Larry Coryell.

LARRY CORYELL LCS-2 - similar to LCS-1 except has maple back and sides, Duncan designed pickups, available in Vintageburst, Natural, or Black finishes, mfg. 2001-present.

MSR $995	$700	$600	$525	$450	$400	$350	$300

MATT GUITAR MURPHY MGM-1 - slightly offset double cutaway Agathis body, quilted maple top, set-in maple neck, 22-fret bound rosewood fingerboard with block inlays, bound headstock with abalone design inlay, gold hardware, 3-per-side tuners with white buttons, tun-o-matic bridge/stop tailpiece, 2 Mightymite humbucker pickups, volume/tone controls, 3-way selector switch, available in Amber Glossy, 3-Tone Sunburst or Trans. Purple finishes, 24.75 in. scale, current mfg.

MSR $895	$625	$550	$475	$400	$350	$300	$250

3-Tone Burst finish added in 1999. The Cort MGM-1 model was designed in conjunction with guitarist Matt "Guitar" Murphy (Blues Brothers).

NEIL ZAZA NZS-1 - offset double cutaway American basswood body with a quilted maple top, bolt-on three-piece maple neck, 24-fret ebony fingerboard with dot and 12th fret inlays, three-per-side tuners, TonePros T3BT bridge, STB, two Seymour Duncan humbucker pickups, two knobs, three-way switch, chrome hardware, Deep Sea Blue finish, new 2005.

MSR $1,295	$950	$850	$750	$675	$600	$525	$450

This guitar was designed with Neil Zaza and includes features such as an asymmetrical neck shape and fret treatment.

PAGELLI PAG-1 - single cutaway body with unique points, mahogany body with flame maple top, set mahogany neck, 22-fret rosewood fingerboard, three-per-side tuners, TonePros licensed bridge, CT1 tailpiece, two Mighty Mite humbucker pickups, two knobs, three-way switch, chrome hardware, Light Chocolate Burst finish, new 2005.

MSR $750	$525	$450	$400	$350	$300	$250	$200

This model was designed by Claudio Pagelli from Switzerland.

GRADING	100% MINT	98% NEAR MINT	95% EXC+	90% EXC	80% VG+	70% VG	60% G

Cort Solid G100
courtesy Cort

ELECTRIC: SOLO SERIES

The Solo Series models feature a sleek superstrat style body, and slightly more exaggerated horns than the Performer Series models.

SOLO FA - offset double cutaway Agathis body, bolt-on hard rock maple neck, 25.5 in. scale, 24-fret rosewood fingerboard with offset white dot inlay, Full Action II tremolo, 6-on-a-side black headstock, chrome hardware, 2 single coil/1 humbucker Power Sound pickups, volume/tone controls, 5-way selector switch, available in Black, Blue Metallic, or Red Metallic finishes, mfg. 1997-99.

	$225	$175	$150	$125	$115	$95	$75

Last MSR was $289.

SOLO WK - similar to the Solo FA, except has Wilkinson VS-50K tremolo, 2 Mightymite humbuckers, 3-way pickup selector, available in Black or Crimson Burst finishes, mfg. 1997-99.

	$300	$275	$250	$200	$175	$150	$100

Last MSR was $429.

SOLO QM - similar to Solo FA, except has quilted mahogany top, Mightymite pickups, one volume switch, one tone switch with coil tap, 5-position switch, Floyd Rose licensed LO-PRO tremolo, available in Transparent Red or Transparent Blue finishes, mfg. 1999-2001.

	$450	$375	$350	$325	$300	$275	$225

Last MSR was $599.

SOLO SL - similar to the Solo FA, except has a maple fingerboard, FR III-S licensed Floyd Rose double locking tremolo, 2 Mightymite humbuckers, 3-way pickup selector, available in Black, Blue Metallic, or Red Metallic finishes, disc. 2000.

	$325	$275	$250	$225	$195	$150	$125

Last MSR was $479.

SOLO VS - similar to Solo FA, except has Wilkinson VS10 bridge, available in black, Blue Metallic or Red Metallic finishes, mfg. 2001 only.

	$200	$165	$145	$115	$90	$70	$50

Last MSR was $289.

SOLO FR - similar to the Solo FA, except has Lo-Pro licensed Floyd Rose double locking tremolo, Mightymite humbucker/single coil/humbucker pickups, 5-way pickup selector, available in Black or Blue Metallic finishes, disc. 1998.

	$450	$395	$350	$300	$250	$200	$150

Last MSR was $650.

ELECTRIC: SPACE SERIES

G3T - Headless design licensed by Steinberger, maple body, hard maple neck, rosewood fingerboard, EMG Select pickups, one volume and one tone control, three mini toggles, available in black, disc. 1999.

	$425	$400	$350	$325	$300	$250	$200

Last MSR was $599.

ELECTRIC: STANDARD SERIES

SOLID G100 - single cutaway arched Agathis body, bolt-on hard rock maple neck, 24 3/4" scale, 22-fret rosewood fingerboard with white dot inlay, tune-o-matic bridge/stop tailpiece, 3-per-side black headstock, raised black pickguard, chrome hardware, 2 Power Sound humbucker pickups, 2 volume/2 tone controls, 3-way pickup selector, available in Black and Cherry Red finishes, disc. 2000.

	$250	$200	$175	$150	$125	$110	$95

Last MSR was $349.

Solid G100 LH - similar to the Solid G100, except in left-handed configuration, available in Black or Cherry Red Sunburst finishes, disc. 1999.

	$275	$225	$195	$175	$150	$125	$95

Last MSR was $379.

Solid G50 - details of this model unknown, mfg. 1999-2000.

	$175	$150	$125	$95	$75	$65	$50

Last MSR was $250.

STAT 2T - offset double cutaway Agathis body, bolt-on hard rock maple neck, 25.5 in. scale, 22-fret maple fingerboard with black dot inlay, vintage style Full Action II tremolo, 6-on-a-side natural wood headstock, chrome hardware, white pickguard, 3 Power Sound single coil pickups, volume/2 tone controls, 5-way selector switch, available in 2-Tone Burst, Black, Foam Green, Ivory, Red, or Shell Pink finishes, disc. 1999, reintroduced 2003-present.

MSR $179	$140	$110	$90	$70	$55	$40	$25

STAT 2T LH - similar to the Stat 2T, except in left-handed configuration, available in Black finish only, disc. 1999.

	$195	$175	$155	$135	$115	$95	$75

Last MSR was $269.

Cort Matt Guitar Murphy
MGM-1
courtesy Cort

GRADING	100% MINT	98% NEAR MINT	95% EXC+	90% EXC	80% VG+	70% VG	60% G

STAT 3T - similar to the Stat 2T, except has rosewood fingerboard with white dot inlay, 2 single coil/humbucker Power Sound pickups, available in 2-Tone Burst, Black, Ivory, or Red finishes, disc. 1999.

	$175	$150	$135	$115	$100	$85	$65

Last MSR was $259.

In 1998, See-Through Red finish was introduced; Ivory and Red finishes were discontinued.

TC CUSTOM - single cutaway Agathis body, bolt-on hard rock maple neck, 25.5 in. scale, 22-fret maple fingerboard with black dot inlay, 6-saddle tele-style bridge, 6-on-a-side natural wood headstock, chrome hardware, white pickguard, 2 Power Sound single coil pickups, volume/tone controls, 3-way pickup selector, chrome control plate, available in Black and Ivory finishes, disc. 1998.

	$195	$175	$150	$125	$115	$95	$75

Last MSR was $280.

VS 2R - offset double cutaway Agathis body, bolt-on hard rock maple neck, 25.5 in. scale, 22-fret rosewood fingerboard with black dot inlay, vintage standard tremolo, 6-on-a-side natural wood headstock, chrome hardware, white pickguard, 3 Power Sound single coil pickups, volume/2 tone controls, 5-way pickup selector, available in 2-Tone Burst, Black, or Ivory finishes, mfg. 1998 only.

	$195	$150	$135	$115	$100	$85	$65

Last MSR was $269.

ELECTRIC: TRADITIONAL & JAZZBOX SERIES

CLASSIC - single cutaway mahogany body, arched maple top, set-in mahogany neck, 24 3/4" scale, 22-fret rosewood fingerboard with white block inlay, tune-o-matic bridge/stop tailpiece, 3-per-side black headstock, gold hardware, raised pickguard, 2 covered Mightymite humbucker pickups, 2 volume/2 tone controls, 3-way pickup selector, available in Black or Cherry Red Sunburst finishes, disc. 1999.

	$495	$425	$375	$325	$275	$225	$175

Last MSR was $695.

Classic II - similar to the Classic, except has 2 exposed Mightymite humbuckers and chrome hardware, available in Cherry Red Sunburst finish only, disc. 1998.

	$495	$425	$375	$325	$275	$225	$175

Last MSR was $699.

SOURCE - dual cutaway semi-hollow bound body, maple top, maple back/sides, maple neck, 24 3/4" scale, 20-fret bound rosewood fingerboard with block inlays, fleur-de-lis/Source headstock inlay, raised pickguard, gold hardware, 3-per-side tuners, tune-o-matic bridge/stop tailpiece, 2 covered Mightymite humbucker pickups, 2 volume/2 tone controls, 3-way selector switch, available in Black and Vintage Burst finishes, disc. 1998, reintroduced 2002-present.

MSR $750	$525	$450	$375	$325	$275	$225	$175

YORKTOWN - single cutaway semi-hollow bound body, spruce top, flamed maple back/sides, maple neck, 24 3/4" scale, 20-fret bound rosewood fingerboard with block inlays, fleur-de-lis/Yorktown headstock inlay, raised black pickguard, gold hardware, 3-per-side tuners, rosewood bridge/C trapeze tailpiece, 2 covered Mightymite humbucker pickups, 2 volume/2 tone controls, 3-way selector switch located on lower treble bout, available in Natural Glossy and Vintage Burst finishes, disc. 1998, reintroduced 2002-present.

MSR $795	$560	$475	$400	$350	$300	$250	$200

ELECTRIC: X SERIES

X GUITAR - dual cutaway Agathis body, bolt-on hard rock maple neck, 24 3/4" scale, 22-fret rosewood fingerboard with white dot inlay, wrap-around stop tailpiece, blackface headstock, 3-per-side tuners, chrome hardware, 2 Power Sound Humbucker pickups, 2 volume/2 tone controls, 3-way pickup selector, available in Black, Cherry Red Sunburst, and Ivory finishes, mfg. 1998-99.

	$190	$160	$135	$115	$100	$85	$65

Last MSR was $269.

X-2 - offset double cutaway basswood body, bolt-on hard rock maple neck, 2 Powersound humbucking pickups, 6-on-a-side die-cast tuners, Full-Action II tremolo bridge, available in Black, Red Metallic and Blue Metallic finishes, mfg. 2001-present.

MSR $259	$185	$150	$125	$95	$75	$50	$30

Add $25 for left-handed configuration (X2-LH).

X-6 - similar to X-2 except, has 2 Mightymite humbucker pickups and 1 Mightymite single coil pickup, Floyd Rose Licensed SL tremolo bridge, available in Black, Iron Pruple Metallic, or Blue Violet Metallic finishes, mfg. 2001-present.

MSR $369	$260	$220	$190	$175	$150	$125	$95

X-7 - similar to X-2 except, in a 7-string configuration, 3-piece hard maple neck, 2 Mightymite 7 humbucking pickups, Full-Action II-7 tremolo bridge, available in Black and Iron Purple Metallic finishes, mfg. 2001-02.

	$245	$215	$175	$150	$125	$95	$65

Last MSR was $350.

X-9 - similar to X-2 except, has 2 Mightymite humbucker pickups and 1 Mightymite single coil pickup, Floyd Rose Licensed Lo-Pro tremolo bridge, available in Black, Iron Purple Metallic and Blue Violet Metallic finishes, mfg. 2001 only.

	$415	$350	$295	$250	$225	$195	$165

Last MSR was $590.

X-CUSTOM - similar to X-2 except, has American Basswood body, custom-made neck, bolt-on hard rock maple neck, Seymour Duncan JB and Jazz pickups, Floyd Rose Licensed Lo-Pro tremolo bridge, available in Black Metallic finish, mfg. 2001-present.

MSR $995	$700	$600	$525	$450	$400	$350	$300

GRADING	100% MINT	98% NEAR MINT	95% EXC+	90% EXC	80% VG+	70% VG	60% G

ELECTRIC: ZENOX (Z) SERIES

Z22 - offset double cutaway contoured agathis body with tapered armrest, bolt-on maple neck, 22-fret rosewood fingerboard with dot inlay, three-per-side tuners, Tune-O-Matic bridge, STB, small pickguard, two Power Sound humbucker pickups, two knobs, three-way switch, chrome hardware, available in Black, Black Satin, or Silver Metallic finishes, new 2005.

MSR $279	$199	$160	$130	$100	$80	$60	$40

Add $10 for Black Satin or Silver Metallic finishes.

Z42 - single cutaway contoured mahogany body with tapered armrest, bolt-on maple neck, 22-fret rosewood fingerboard with dot inlay, three-per-side tuners, TonePros licensed bridge, STB, two Power Sound humbucker pickups, three knobs, three-way switch, chrome hardware, available in Trans. Black or Wine Red finishes, new 2005.

MSR $325	$230	$190	$160	$130	$110	$90	$70

Z44 - single cutaway contoured mahogany body with tapered armrest, set mahogany neck, 22-fret rosewood fingerboard with 12th-fret design inlay, three-per-side tuners, TonePros licensed bridge, STB, two covered Mighty Mite Motherbucker humbucker pickups, three knobs, three-way switch, chrome hardware, available in Black or Gray Nickel finishes, new 2005.

MSR $499	$350	$290	$250	$220	$190	$160	$130

ELECTRIC BASS: ACTION BASS SERIES

ACTION BASS - offset double cutaway Agathis body, bolt-on hard rock maple neck, 24-fret rosewood fingerboard with offset dot inlays, black squared headstock, fixed bridge, chrome hardware, 2-per-side tuners, 2 Power Sound P/J-style pickups, volume/blend/tone controls, available in Black, See-Through Blue, and See-Through Red finishes, 34 in. scale, current mfg.

MSR $299	$225	$190	$165	$145	$125	$95	$75

In 2000, Walnut Stain finish was introduced.

Action Bass LH - similar to Action Bass, only in a left-handed version, available in Walnut Stain finish, current mfg.

MSR $339	$250	$220	$190	$175	$150	$125	$100

ACTION BASS V (ALSO ACTION BASS 5) - similar to the Action Bass, except in 5-string configuration, 2/3-per-side tuners, 2 Power Sound J-style pickups, available in Black or See-Through Red finishes, current mfg.

MSR $359	$260	$225	$195	$175	$150	$125	$100

In 2000, Walnut Stain finish was introduced.

ACTION BASS ASH - similar to the Action Bass, except features a swamp ash body, gold hardware, available in Natural Satin and Padauk Satin finishes, disc. 1998.

$425	$375	$325	$275	$225	$195	$150

Last MSR was $600.

ELECTRIC BASS: ARTISAN SERIES

The **Artisan Bass** Series models are very similar to prior **C M Artist** Series models (the block inlay at 12th fret on those models read "C M Artist"). In 2001, Cort changed the model designation of the Artisan series from A to NA. This lasted for a year when it was turned back to A.

A4 (NA4) - offset double cutaway select maple body, through-body wenge/maple laminated neck, 34 in. scale, 24-fret rosewood fingerboard with offset dot inlays, Artisan block inlay on 24th fret, black headstock, fixed bridge, gold hardware, squared headstock, 2-per-side tuners, 2 Mightymite soapbar pickups, 2 volume/2 tone controls, active electronics, available in Natural Satin, See-Through Red, or Walnut Stain finishes, mfg. 1996-present.

MSR $1,195	$850	$750	$675	$600	$525	$450	$400

A5 (NA5) - similar to the Artisan A4, except in 5-string configuration and 2/3-per-side headstock, available in Amber Glossy, Natural Satin, or See-Through Red finishes, mfg. 1996-present.

MSR $1,295	$925	$825	$725	$650	$575	$500	$450

A6 (NA6) - similar to the Artisan A4, except in 6-string configuration and 3-per-side headstock, available in Natural Satin and See-Through Blue finishes, mfg. 1996-present.

MSR $1,395	$999	$900	$800	$700	$625	$550	$475

In 1998, See-Through Red finish was introduced; See-Through Blue finish was discontinued.

B4 (NA4) - similar to the Artisan A4, except features a bolt-on wenge neck, natural wenge headstock, and black hardware, available in Amber Glossy, Natural Satin, Vintage Burst, or Walnut Satin finishes, current mfg.

MSR $795	$560	$500	$425	$350	$300	$250	$200

B4 FL (NB4 FL) - similar to the B4, except has fretless fingerboard, available in Amber Satin, or Vintage Burst finishes, mfg. 1997-2002, 2005-present.

MSR $850	$595	$525	$450	$400	$350	$300	$250

In 1998, Walnut Stain finish was introduced; Amber Satin and Vintage Burst finishes were discontinued.

Cort Custom TC
courtesy Cort

Cort Action Bass
courtesy Cort

C

GRADING	100% MINT	98% NEAR MINT	95% EXC+	90% EXC	80% VG+	70% VG	60% G

B5 - similar to the Artisan B4, except in 5-string configuration, 2/3-per-side tuners, available in Natural Satin, Vintage Burst, or Walnut Satin finishes, current mfg.

MSR $895	$650	$575	$500	$425	$350	$300	$250

In 1998, Amber Satin and Vintage Burst finishes were introduced; Natural Satin, Vintage Burst, and Walnut Satin finishes were discontinued.

B5 FL - similar to the Artisan B5, except has fretless fingerboard, available in Amber Satin or Vintage Burst finishes, mfg. 1997-2000.

	$625	$550	$475	$425	$350	$295	$225

Last MSR was $895.

In 1998, Natural Satin and Walnut Satin were introduced; Amber Satin finish was discontinued.

B6 - similar to the Artisan B4, except in 6-string configuration, 3-per-side tuners, available in Oil Satin, or Walnut Satin finishes, disc.1999.

	$695	$575	$500	$450	$375	$325	$250

Last MSR was $950.

In 1998, Vintage Burst finish was introduced; Walnut Satin finish was discontinued.

C4 - offset double cutaway agathis body, bolt-on hard rock maple neck, 24-fret rosewood fingerboard with offset dot inlays, black squared headstock, fixed bridge, chrome hardware, 2-per-side tuners, 2 Mightymite soapbar pickups, volume/blend/tone controls, available in Amber Satin, Gray Nickel, Lake Placid Blue, or Black finishes, 34 in. scale, current mfg.

MSR $595	$425	$350	$300	$250	$210	$180	$150

In 1998, Blue Metallic and See-Through Red finishes were introduced; Amber Satin finish was discontinued.

C4P - similar to the C4 bass except features a Fishman power bridge pickup with added Piezo control, available in Black or Walnut Satin finishes, mfg. 2002-04.

	$575	$500	$450	$400	$350	$300	$250

Last MSR was $795.

C5 - similar to the Artisan C4, except in a 5-string configuration, 2/3-per-side tuners, available in Black finish only, current mfg.

MSR $695	$490	$425	$375	$325	$275	$235	$195

The C5 was also available in left-handed configuration.

C5P - Similar to the C5 bass except features a Fishman power bridge pickup with added Piezo control, available in Black or Walnut Satin finishes, mfg. 2002-04.

	$595	$525	$450	$400	$350	$300	$250

Last MSR was $850.

ELECTRIC BASS: BILLY COX SERIES

BILLY COX FREEDOM BASS - Offset double cutaway ashwood body, maple neck, 34 in. scale, rosewood fingerboard with block position markers, 4-on-a-side tuners, 3 custom made single coil pickups, stacked volume and tone knobs, active to passive control, EB74 bridge, chrome hardware, available in 3-Tone Sunburst, white and black finishes, current mfg.

MSR $750	$525	$450	$395	$350	$295	$250	$175

ELECTRIC BASS: GB SERIES

Besides the models listed, there also exists a GB64 and GB65. These models were never listed in either the catalog or price list.

GB24 - offset double cutaway agathis body, hard rock maple neck, 22-fret rosewood fingerboard, single powersound humbucking pickup, two knobs, white pickguard, 4-on-one-side tuners, available in black, Walnut Satin, Amber Satin, Trans. Red, or Trans. Blue finishes, mfg. 2001-02.

	$195	$170	$150	$125	$100	$80	$65

Last MSR was $270.

GB25 - similar to the GB24 except in five-string configuration, 5-on-one side tuners, mfg. 2001-03.

	$235	$200	$175	$150	$130	$105	$85

Last MSR was $330.

GB34(A) - offset double cutaway agathis body, maple neck, 22-fret rosewood fingerboard, Powersound Jazz & MB4 pickups, three knobs, white pickguard, 4-on-one-side tuners, available in Black, Walnut Satin, Lake Placid Blue, or Red Metallic finishes, mfg. 2003-present.

MSR $339	$240	$200	$170	$140	$110	$90	$70

GB35 - similar to the GB34, except in five-string configuration, 3/2-per-side tuners, available in Black or Walnut Satin finish, mfg. 2003-04.

	$250	$220	$190	$160	$130	$100	$70

Last MSR was $350.

GB44 - offset double cutaway basswood body, hard rock maple neck, 22-fret rosewood fingerboard, Mightymite Alnico pickups, four knobs, white pickguard, 4-on-one-side tuners, available in Amber, Walnut Satin, Trans. Red, or Trans. Blue finishes, mfg. 2001-02.

	$315	$275	$235	$205	$175	$145	$110

Last MSR was $450.

GB45 - similar to the GB44 except in five-string configuration, 5-on-one side tuners, mfg. 2001-03.

	$340	$290	$250	$225	$195	$170	$145

Last MSR was $480.

ELECTRIC BASS: GARY CURBOW SERIES

Gary Curbow has developed this series from a synthetic composite called luthite. These were originally the Luthite Series (see Luthite Series).

GRADING	100% MINT	98% NEAR MINT	95% EXC+	90% EXC	80% VG+	70% VG	60% G

CURBOW 4 - slimmed down offset double cutaway luthite body, bolt-on hard rock maple neck, 24-fret ebanol fingerboard with white dot inlays, 2-per-side die-cast tuners, fixed bridge, chrome hardware, Mightymite humbucker pickup, volume/treble/mid/bass controls, available in Lake Placid Blue, or Red Metallic finishes, 34 in. scale, mfg. 1998-present.

	MSR $550		$390	$325	$275	$235	$195	$160	$130

Curbow 4FL - similar to the Curbow 4 except is in fretless configuration, available in Lake Placid Blue, Red Metallic, or Black finishes, current mfg.

	MSR $595		$425	$375	$325	$275	$225	$175	$140

CURBOW 5 - similar to the Curbow 4, except features a 5-string configuration, 3/2-per-side tuners, mfg. 1998-present.

	MSR $650		$475	$400	$350	$300	$250	$200	$150

Curbow 5FL - similar to the Curbow 5 except is in fretless configuration, available in Lake Placid Blue, Red Metallic, or black finishes, disc. 2003.

	$525	$450	$400	$350	$300	$250	$200

Last MSR was $750.

CURBOW 6 - similar to the Curbow 5, except features a 6-string configuration, 3-per-side tuners, available in Burled Walnut finish, mfg. 1998-present.

	MSR $795		$525	$475	$425	$375	$320	$265	$220

CURBOW RETRO - similar to the Curbow 4, except has an agathis body and Powersound pickups, available in 2-Tone Sunburst, or Black finishes, mfg. 2003-present.

	MSR $350		$245	$210	$180	$150	$130	$100	$70

ELECTRIC BASS: JOSH PAUL SERIES

JPS5 - offset double cutaway light swamp ash body, figured maple top, maple neck, 24-fret fingerboard, 2 Bartolini MK-1 pickups, MK-1 EQ, five knobs, active electronics, 3/2-per-side tuners, black hardware, available in Emerald Green, Cherry Red, or Natural finishes, mfg. 2003-04.

	$850	$775	$700	$625	$575	$525	$450

Last MSR was $1,195.

ELECTRIC BASS: LUTHITE (EF) SERIES

Luthite series basses feature Cort´s patented Environmentally Friendly body material. Luthite series basses are designed in conjunction with Jerry Auerswald (Auerswald Guitars) and Greg Curbow (Curbow Custom Basses). The following models were developed by Gary Auerswald. See Gary Curbow series for current Gary Curbow lucite models.

EFVB1 - violin-shaped EF (luthite) body, bolt-on hard rock maple neck, 32 in. scale, 22-fret rosewood fingerboard with dot inlay, fixed bridge, chrome hardware, 2 on a side squared headstock, chrome tuners, 2 Mightymite pickups, volume/blend/tone controls on black control plate, available in Black finish only, mfg. 1997-98.

	$300	$250	$225	$190	$150	$125	$100

Last MSR was $399.

JAB 70 - offset double cutaway EF (luthite) body, bolt-on hard rock maple neck, 34 in. scale, 24-fret rosewood fingerboard with offset dot inlays, fixed bridge, chrome hardware, reverse headstock, 4-on-the-other-side chrome tuners, P/J-style Select by EMG pickups, volume/blend/tone controls, available in Atlantic Blue Metallic and Black finishes, mfg. 1997-98.

	$350	$300	$250	$225	$190	$150	$125

Last MSR was $450.

ELECTRIC BASS: S SERIES

SB10 - sleek offset double cutaway Agathis body, bolt-on hard rock maple neck, 34 in. scale, 22-fret rosewood fingerboard with white dot inlay, vintage style fixed bridge, natural wood headstock, 2-per-side tuners, chrome hardware, white pickguard, Mightymite humbucker pickup, volume/tone controls, available in Black, Foam Green, or See-Through Red finishes, mfg. 1998-2001.

	$225	$195	$175	$150	$125	$100	$75

Last MSR was $300.

SB70 - similar to SB10 except, has soft maple body, alnico bass humbucker pickup, active EQ, black hardware, available in Amber Stain, Walnut Stain, or Vintage Burst finishes, disc. 2000.

	$385	$350	$295	$250	$225	$195	$150

Last MSR was $550.

ELECTRIC BASS: SPACE SERIES

B2A - headless bass design licensed by Steinberger, maple body, hard maple neck, rosewood fingerboard, 34 in. scale, EMG/Select pickups, two volume and one tone control with active EQ, one mini-toggle switch, available in Black finish, disc. 1999.

	$450	$375	$325	$300	$275	$225	$195

Last MSR was $599.

GRADING	100% MINT	98% NEAR MINT	95% EXC+	90% EXC	80% VG+	70% VG	60% G

B2AV - similar to B2A, only in a 5-string model with Mightymite bass humbucker pickups, Steinberger 5-String bridge, available in Black finish, disc. 1999.

	$525	$475	$425	$400	$375	$325	$295

Last MSR was $695.

ELECTRIC BASS: STANDARD SERIES

JJ BASS - offset double cutaway slim-waisted Agathis body, bolt-on hard rock maple neck, 34 in. scale, 20-fret rosewood fingerboard with white dot inlays, natural wood headstock, fixed bridge, chrome hardware, 4-on-a-side tuners, 2 Power Sound J-style pickups, 2 volume/1 tone controls, available in Black or 2-Tone Burst finishes, disc. 1998.

	$225	$195	$175	$150	$125	$100	$75

Last MSR was $325.

ELECTRIC BASS: T.M. STEVENS SERIES

FUNK MACHINE-S-1 - offset double cutaway body, 3-piece hard maple thru-neck, 24-fret fingerboard with 3 "sailboat" inlays per fret, Bartolini active mk-1 pickups, five knobs, two switches, built-in "Funk-wah" circuitry, Fortress bridge, 2-per-side tuners, chrome hardware, available in Black finish with elaborate airbrushing graphics including red, yellow, or green colors, mfg. 2001-present.

MSR $2,500	$1,750	$1,500	$1,300	$1,100	$950	$850	$750

FUNK MACHINE II - similar to the Funk Machine-S-1 except features basswood body, bolt-on neck, and no airbrushing, mfg. 2001-present.

MSR $995	$699	$625	$550	$500	$425	$350	$295

ELECTRIC BASS: TRADITIONAL SERIES

PB 1L - offset double cutaway Agathis body, bolt-on hard rock maple neck, 20-fret maple fingerboard with black dot inlays, natural wood headstock, fixed bridge, chrome hardware, 4-on-a-side tuners, Power Sound P bass-style pickup, volume/tone controls, available in 2-Tone Burst, Black, Ivory, Tobaccoburst, or Red finishes, 34 in. scale, current mfg.

MSR $239	$180	$150	$125	$100	$80	$60	$45

In 1998, Ivory finish was discontinued.

PJ Bass - similar to the PB 1L, except has rosewood fingerboard with white dot inlays and Power Sound P/J-style pickups, available in 2-Tone Burst, Black, and Red finishes, disc. 1999.

	$200	$175	$150	$125	$100	$75	$50

Last MSR was $279.

PJ Bass LH - similar to the PJ Bass, except in left-handed configuration, disc. 1999.

	$215	$185	$165	$145	$125	$100	$75

Last MSR was $309.

ELECTRIC BASS: VIVA SERIES

VIVA ACTIVE - offset double cutaway contoured maple body, bolt-on hard rock maple neck, 34 in. scale, 24-fret rosewood fingerboard with offset dot inlays, black squared headstock, fixed bridge, chrome hardware, 2-per-side tuners, P/J-style Select by EMG pickups, volume/blend/treble/bass controls, active EQ, available in Black, See-Through Black, See-Through Red, or Walnut Satin finishes, disc. 1999.

	$375	$300	$275	$225	$195	$150	$125

Last MSR was $495.

Viva Active 5 - similar to the Viva Active, except has a 5-string configuration, 3/2-per-side tuners, and 2 J-style Select by EMG pickups, available in Black or Natural Satin finishes, disc. 1999.

	$425	$375	$325	$275	$250	$195	$150

Last MSR was $595.

CORTEZ

Instruments previously built in Japan circa 1969 to 1988. Distributed in the U.S. market by Westheimer Musical Industries of Chicago, Illinois.

Cortez acoustics were produced in Japan, and imported to the U.S. market as an affordable alternative in the acoustic guitar market. Westheimer's Cortez company and trademark could be viewed as a stepping stone towards his current Cort company (See Cort).

COTE´

Instruments currently built in Largo, Florida. Previously based in St. Petersburg, Florida.

Charles Cote´ Basses is a family owned business that was founded in Atlanta, Georgia in 1992. Cote´ began building guitars in 1987, and worked as a guitar builder from 1989 to 1991 at John Buscarino's Nova Guitar Company. A professional bassist for a number of years, Cote´ brings his player's experience to his designs, and each instrument features a hand carved neck and body. It it unknown if Cote' basses are still available.

ELECTRIC BASS

The initial body design of the R series was inspired by a drawing by graphic artist Cris Rosario. List price includes a deluxe hardshell case.

Add $240 for figured maple top. Add $240 for lacquer finish. Add $275 for 35 in. scale length.

GRADING	100% MINT	98% NEAR MINT	95% EXC+	90% EXC	80% VG+	70% VG	60% G

R4 4-STRING - offset double cutaway alder (or Southern ash or korina) body, bolt-on graphite reinforced rock maple neck, 34 in. scale, 24-fret morado or maple fingerboard, 2-per-side headstock, black hardware, BadAss II fixed bridge, 2 Kent Armstrong-wound Cote´ humbucker pickups, volume/blend/tone controls, active electronics, available in Emerald Green, Amber, Natural, Ocean, or Scarlet hand-rubbed oil finishes, disc.

	$2,000	$1,800	$1,600	$1,400	$1,200	$1,000	$800

Last MSR was $1,820.

R5 5 String - similar to the R4 4-string, except features a 5-string configuration, 2/3-per-side headstock, BadAss Bass V bridge, disc.

	$2,300	$2,050	$1,850	$1,600	$1,400	$1,200	$1,000

Last MSR was $1,953.

R6 6-String - similar to the R4 4-string, except features a 6-string configuration, 3-per-side headstock, custom Cote´ bridge, disc.

	$2,500	$2,250	$2,000	$1,800	$1,600	$1,400	$1,200

Last MSR was $2,310.

CONTINUUM BASIC 4 - similar to the R4 4-string, except has an ash body, bolt-on rock maple neck, 22-fret rosewood or maple fingerboard with pearl dot inlay, tortoiseshell pickguard, 2 Lindy Fralin single coil pickups, 2 volume/tone controls, disc.

	$1,500	$1,350	$1,200	$1,050	$900	$750	$600

Last MSR was $1,659.

This model is available with a fretless fingerboard and maple line marker inlays.

Continuum Standard 4 - similar to the Continuum Basic 4, except features alder or southern ash body, available in a variety of color lacquer finishes, disc.

	$1,700	$1,500	$1,350	$1,200	$1,050	$900	$750

Last MSR was $1,899.

Continuum Deluxe 4 - similar to the Continuum Basic 4, except features alder or southern ash body, figured maple top, available in a variety of color lacquer finishes, disc.

	$1,800	$1,600	$1,400	$1,200	$1,050	$900	$750

Last MSR was $1,999.

**Cort Viva Active Bass
courtesy Cort**

CRAFTSMAN

Instruments previously produced in Japan during the late 1970s through the mid-1980s.

Craftsman built entry level to medium quality copies of American designs (source: Tony Bacon and Paul Day, *The Guru's Guitar Guide*).

CRATE

Also Crate/Electra. Instruments currently produced in Korea. Distributed by St. Louis Music of St. Louis, Missouri.

St. Louis Music's Crate amplifier line featured a "Starter Pack" in 1997, which featured a Crate GX15 amp, cable, strap, and a Crate (or Crate/Electra) *Nashville Standard* model LP-style guitar.

ELECTRIC

CALIFORNIA CLASSIC - Strat-style body, bolt-on maple neck, 2 single coil/1 humbucker pickups, 6-per-side tuners, available in black, 3-Tone Tobacco Sunburst, or Metallic Red finishes, mfg. late 1990s.

	$175	$150	$125	$100	$70	$50	$30

Last MSR was $230.

NASHVILLE STANDARD - LP style body, set-in neck, 2 humbucker pickups, bound body/fingerboard, available in Black or 2-Tone Tobacco Sunburst finish, mfg. late 1990s.

	$200	$160	$130	$100	$70	$50	$30

CRESTLINE

Instruments previously built in Japan circa mid- to late 1970s. Distributed by the Grossman Music Corporation of Cleveland, Ohio.

These entry level to intermediate solid body guitars featured designs based on classic American favorites. Crestline offered a wide range of stringed instruments, including classical, folk, dreadnought, and 12-string acoustics; solid body electric guitars and basses; amplifiers; banjos, mandolins, and ukuleles. Considering the amount of instruments available, the Crestline trademark was probably used on guitars built by one of the bigger Japanese guitar producers and rebranded for the U.S. market. One model reviewed at a vintage guitar show was based on Gibson's Les Paul design, and had Grover tuners, 2 Japanese covered humbuckers, and decent wood.

CRIPE, STEVE

Instruments previously built in Trilby, Florida from 1990 to 1996.

Although he is best known for building the **Lightning Bolt** and **Top Hat** guitars for Jerry Garcia, Stephen R. Cripe also built a number of guitars for other players across the country. A self-taught luthier, Cripe's guitar designs were based on photos and video footage of Jerry Garcia's performances, not actual guitar templates.

Steve Cripe was born and raised in southern Michigan, and spent his high school years in Elkhart, Indiana. In 1972, he moved with his parents to Marathon, Florida and purchased a boat for his living quarters. After developing his talents fixing up his boat, he turned to hand-building ornate wood interiors for sailboats.

GRADING	100% MINT	98% NEAR MINT	95% EXC+	90% EXC	80% VG+	70% VG	60% G

In 1983, Cripe moved to North Carolina for a year, then later to Miami, Florida. While continuing to work on boats, he began to study guitars and their construction. Cripe started hand building guitars in 1990 mainly to learn to play, but found he enjoyed building them instead. Cripe selected and used exotic woods in his guitar building, and always finished them naturally (adding no stain or color).

A self-described Dead Head, Cripe studied photographs and videos of Jerry Garcia (Grateful Dead). Inspired by the Doug Irwin-built model that Garcia played, Cripe decided to create his own guitar for Garcia. "I figured that the building of the instrument would be easy, but getting it to him would be a challenge," Cripe said, "Once the guitar was finished, I contacted numerous music magazines requesting an address to which to send the guitar. No such luck."

Through a series of intermediaries, Cripe sent the guitar to Garcia. After five weeks of waiting, Cripe received a message on his answering machine that Garcia was fiddling around with the guitar and was intrigued by it. A relationship developed between Cripe and Garcia, and Cripe began building a few more guitars for him. After completing the Top Hat-named guitar, Cripe shipped it to Garcia. Garcia began playing it immediately, and continued using them up until his death.

Steve Cripe completed commissions for a number of anxious buyers, and found time to build a new workshop for guitar production. Unfortunately, Cripe died in a devastating explosion in his workshop on June 18, 1996 (source: Hal Hammer).

CROWN
Instruments previously produced in Japan during the mid-1960s.

The U.S. distributor for the Crown trademark is still currently unknown; the Japanese manufacturer is also unknown. The Crown logo has been spotted on violin-shaped hollow body electric guitars and basses, as well as solid body electrics. The solid body guitars are reported as being generally cheap entry level instruments (source: Tony Bacon and Paul Day, *The Guru's Guitar Guide*; and Michael Wright, *Vintage Guitar Magazine*).

Most electric instruments can be found priced between $100 and $200. However there is a Barney Kessel model known to exist that could bring as much as $400 or $500.

CRUCIANELLI
See Elite. Instruments previously produced in Italy during the 1960s.

Author Tony Bacon notes in his book, *The Ultimate Guitar Book*, that Italy, like many other European countries, experienced the 1960s pop music popularity that led to a larger demand for electric guitars. However, many electric guitar builders were also manufacturers of accordions. As a result, many guitars ended up with accordion-style finishes. Wacky or not, Leo Fender was using this same sort of heat-molded acetate finish on some of his early lap steel models in the early 1950s.

CURBOW
Instruments currently built in Morgantown, Georgia.

Luthier Greg Curbow offers a line of high quality stringed instruments that feature **Rockwood** necks. The Rockwood material is a composite of birch and phenolic based resins formed under pressure and heat, which produces a neck unaffected by changes in temperature and humidity. Curbow basses and guitars are handcrafted directly at the Curbow workshop in the North Georgia mountains.

For current information on Curbow acoustic electric basses, please refer to the *Blue Book of Acoustic Guitars*.

ELECTRIC

INTERNATIONAL EXOTIC PETITE CARVED TOP (SIX STRING) - offset double cutaway mahogany body, wenge (or zebra or bubinga, rock maple, figured maple, walnut or cherry) top, bolt-on Rockwood neck, 25.5 in. scale, 24-fret Rockwood fingerboard, 3-per-side headstock, chrome hardware, tune-o-matic bridge/stop tailpiece, 2 single coil/humbucker Bartolini or Seymour Duncan pickups, volume/2 band EQ controls, pickup selector switch, mfg. 1994-present.

	100%	98%	95%	90%	80%	70%	60%
MSR $6,095	N/A	N/A	N/A	N/A	N/A	N/A	N/A

Price includes a custom hardshell case. This model is available with a tremolo bridge. This model is available with a semi-hollow body (International Exotic Petite Carved Top Semihollow).

INTERNATIONAL EXOTIC PETITE CARVED TOP (SEVEN STRING) - similar to the Petite Six, except features a 7-string configuration and 3/4-per-side headstock, mfg. 1997-present.

	100%	98%	95%	90%	80%	70%	60%
MSR $6,395	N/A	N/A	N/A	N/A	N/A	N/A	N/A

This model is available with a semihollow body (International Exotic Petite Carved Top Semihollow Seven String).

ELECTRIC BASS: ELITE SERIES

Both the Grande and International Elite Series basses feature a handcarved top of cherry, figured maple, rock maple, walnut, wenge, or zebra wood. Custom colors and other woods are available (please call for price quote).

AMERICAN ELITE - offset double cutaway maple or swamp ash body, bolt-on Rockwood neck, 34 in. scale, 24-fret Rockwood fingerboard with white dot inlays, 2-per-side headstock, brass bridge, Sperzel tuners, Bartolini Split Coil pickup, volume/3-band EQ controls, variable mid switch, available in Black Pearl, Ice Blue Pearl, Purple Pearl, Red Pearl, or White Pearl finishes, mfg. 1997-present.

American Elite 4-string
	100%	98%	95%	90%	80%	70%	60%
MSR $2,995	N/A	N/A	N/A	N/A	N/A	N/A	N/A

American Elite 5-string
	100%	98%	95%	90%	80%	70%	60%
MSR $3,195	N/A	N/A	N/A	N/A	N/A	N/A	N/A

American Elite 6-string
	100%	98%	95%	90%	80%	70%	60%
MSR $3,395	N/A	N/A	N/A	N/A	N/A	N/A	N/A

American Elite 7-string
	100%	98%	95%	90%	80%	70%	60%
MSR $3,595	N/A	N/A	N/A	N/A	N/A	N/A	N/A

Fretless (with or without lines) fingerboards are available at no additional cost. Retail price includes a gig bag.

INTERNATIONAL ELITE - offset double cutaway mahogany body, hand-carved exotic wood top, bolt-on Rockwood neck, 34 in. scale, 24-fret Rockwood fingerboard with white dot inlays, 2-per-side headstock, quick release bridge, Sperzel tuners, Bartolini Split-Coil pickup, volume/blend/3-

C

GRADING	100% MINT	98% NEAR MINT	95% EXC+	90% EXC	80% VG+	70% VG	60% G

band EQ controls, variable Midrange switch, slap contour switch, available in Amethyst Glow, Cocoa Burst, Grape Burst, Honey Burst, Scarlet Glow, and Turquoise Glow finishes. Also available in a Clear Coat or Oil and Wax finishes, current mfg.

International Elite 4-string
MSR $4,895	N/A	N/A	N/A	N/A	N/A	N/A	N/A

International Elite 5-string
MSR $5,195	N/A	N/A	N/A	N/A	N/A	N/A	N/A

International Elite 6-string
MSR $5,495	N/A	N/A	N/A	N/A	N/A	N/A	N/A

International Elite 7-string
MSR $5,795	N/A	N/A	N/A	N/A	N/A	N/A	N/A

Add $195 for semi-hollow body.

This model has optional choice of woods, gold hardware, and fretless (with or without lines) fingerboards are available at no additional cost. Retail price includes a lined hardshell case.

GRANDE ELITE - similar to the International Elite, except features an 18-volt 3-band EQ system, available in Amethyst Glow, Cocoa Burst, Grape Burst, Honey Burst, Scarlet Glow, and Turquoise Glow finishes, also available in a Clear Coat or Oil and Wax finishes, current mfg.

Grande Elite 4-string
MSR $3,495	N/A	N/A	N/A	N/A	N/A	N/A	N/A

Grande Elite 5-string
MSR $3,795	N/A	N/A	N/A	N/A	N/A	N/A	N/A

Grande Elite 6-string
MSR $4,095	N/A	N/A	N/A	N/A	N/A	N/A	N/A

Grande Elite 7-string
MSR $4,395	N/A	N/A	N/A	N/A	N/A	N/A	N/A

Add $195 for semi-hollow body.

This model has optional choice of woods, gold hardware, and fretless (with or without lines) fingerboards are available at no additional cost. Retail price includes a lined hardshell case.

ELECTRIC BASS: RETRO SERIES

RETRO - offset double cutaway maple or Swamp ash body, bolt-on Rockwood Lite neck, 34 in. scale, 24-fret Rockwood neck with white dot inlays, 2-per-side headstock, brass bridge, Sperzel tuners, Black Pearl or White Pearl pickguard, Bartolini Dual-Coil pickup, volume/treble/mid/bass controls, active 9-volt 3-band parametric EQ system, available in Black Pearl, Ice Blue Pearl, Red Pearl, and White Pearl finishes, mfg. 1997-present.

Retro 4-string
MSR $3,895	N/A	N/A	N/A	N/A	N/A	N/A	N/A

Retro 5-string
MSR $4,095	N/A	N/A	N/A	N/A	N/A	N/A	N/A

Retro 6-string
MSR $4,295	N/A	N/A	N/A	N/A	N/A	N/A	N/A

Fretless (with or without lines) fingerboards are available at no additional cost. Retail price includes a gig bag.

RETRO II - similar to the Retro, except features 2 Bartolini J-style pickups, 2 volume/tone controls, current mfg.

Retro II 4-string
MSR $4,095	N/A	N/A	N/A	N/A	N/A	N/A	N/A

Retro II 5-string
MSR $4,295	N/A	N/A	N/A	N/A	N/A	N/A	N/A

Retro II 6-string
MSR $4,595	N/A	N/A	N/A	N/A	N/A	N/A	N/A

Add $200 for active 3-band EQ with variable mid switch.

Fretless (with or without lines) fingerboards are available at no additional cost. Retail price includes a gig bag.

ELECTRIC BASS: XT SERIES

XT-33 - offset double cutaway mahogany body, handcarved exotic wood top, bolt-on Rockwood neck, 34 in. scale, extended 33-fret Rockwood fingerboard with white dot inlays, 2-per-side headstock, brass bridge, Sperzel tuners, Bartolini Quad-Coil pickup, volume/blend controls, Bartolini 3-band EQ, 18-volt electronics, variable midrange switch, slap contour switch, available in Amethyst Glow, Cocoa Burst, Grape Burst, Honey Burst, Scarlet Glow, and Turquoise Glow finishes, also available in a Clear Coat or Oil and Wax finishes, current mfg.

XT-33 4-string
MSR $5,295	N/A	N/A	N/A	N/A	N/A	N/A	N/A

GRADING	100% MINT	98% NEAR MINT	95% EXC+	90% EXC	80% VG+	70% VG	60% G
XT-33 5-string							
MSR $5,595	N/A	N/A	N/A	N/A	N/A	N/A	N/A
XT-33 6-string							
MSR $5,895	N/A	N/A	N/A	N/A	N/A	N/A	N/A
XT-33 7-string							
MSR $6,195	N/A	N/A	N/A	N/A	N/A	N/A	N/A
XT-33 8-string							
MSR $6,495	N/A	N/A	N/A	N/A	N/A	N/A	N/A

Add $195 for semi-hollow body.

This model has optional choice of woods, gold hardware, and lined or unlined fretless fingerboard.

CUSTOM GUITAR COMPANY
Instruments currently built in Sunnyvale, CA, and previously built in Santa Clara, CA.

These quality custom instruments are built in Southern California.

CUSTOM KRAFT
See chapter on House Brands.

This trademark has been identified as a House Brand of St. Louis Music. The St. Louis Music Supply Company was founded in 1922 by Bernard Kornblum, originally as an importer of German violins. The St. Louis, Missouri-based company has been a distributor, importer, and manufacturer of musical instruments over the past seventy-five years.

In the mid-1950s, St. Louis Music distributed amplifiers and guitars from other producers such as Alamo, Harmony, Kay, Magnatone, Rickenbacker, and Supro. By 1960, the focus was on Harmony, Kay, and Supro: all built "upstream" in Chicago, Illinois. 1960 was also the year that St. Louis Music began carrying Kay's **Thinline** single cutaway electric guitar.

Custom Kraft was launched in 1961 as St. Louis Music's own House Brand. The first series of semi-hollowbody Custom Kraft **Color Dynamic** Electric guitars were built by **Kay**, and appear to be Thinline models in Black, Red, and White finishes. In 1963, a line of solid body double cutaway electrics built by **Valco** were added to the catalog under the Custom Kraft moniker, as well as Kay-built archtop and flattop acoustic.

In 1967, Valco purchased Kay, a deal that managed to sink both companies by 1968. St. Louis Music continued advertising both companies models through 1970, perhaps NOS supplies from their warehouse. St. Louis Music continued to offer Custom Kraft guitars into the early 1970s, but as their sources had dried up so did the trademark name. St. Louis Music's next trademark guitar line was **Electra** (then followed by **Westone**, and **Alvarez**).

Custom Kraft models are generally priced according to the weirdness/coolness factor, so don't be surprised to see the range of prices from $125 up to $400! The uncertainty indicates a buyer-directed market, so if you find one that you like, don't be afraid to haggle over the price. The earlier KAY and VALCO built guitars date from the 1960s, while later models were probably built in Japan (source: Michael Wright, *Vintage Guitar Magazine*).

CYCLONE
Instruments previously produced in Japan.

Cyclone guitars were distributed in the U.S. market by Leban Imports of Baltimore, Maryland (source: Michael Wright, *Guitar Stories*, Volume One).

Section D

D. C. HILDER BUILDER

Instruments currently built in Guelph (Ontario), Canada.

David Hilder has been building instruments for over 20 years. The acoustic stand-up basses are what they mainly produce. These models include the **Doghouse** and **Cathouse** and they are over six feet tall. Current retail is $750 for the Cathouse and $1,200 for the Doghouse. Hilder´s Garcia´s Guitar model features seven laminated layers of hard wood, which are then hand carved for the top and back contouring. These guitars range in price between $900 and $2,000, depending upon options. For more information contact Hilder directly (see Trademark Index).

D´AGOSTINO

Instruments previously produced in Italy by the EKO company between 1978 and 1982. Instrument production was contracted to the EKO Custom Shop in Milwaukee, Wisconsin, and distributed by PMS Music of New York, New York. After 1982, instruments were produced in Japan.

Pat D´Agostino (ex-Gibson/Maestro Effects) began his own instrument importing company in 1975. The D´Agostino Corporation of New Jersey began importing acoustic dreadnoughts, then introduced the Italian-built **Benchmark Series** of guitars in 1977. These models featured laminated neck-through designs, two humbuckers, and a 3+3 headstock. Production then moved to Korea in the early 1980s, although some better models were built in Japan in the 1990s. Pat, assisted by Steven D´Agostino and Mike Confortti, have always maintained a high quality control level and limited quantities. Used guitars are typically found priced between $150 and $300.

D´ANGELICO

Instruments previously built in New York, NY between 1932 and 1964.

Master Luthier John D´Angelico (1905-1964) was born and raised in New York City, New York. In 1914, he apprenticed to his great-uncle, and learned the luthier trade of building and repairing stringed instruments. After 18 years of working on stringed instruments, he opened his own shop on Kenmare Street (D´Angelico was 27). D´Angelico guitars were entirely handcrafted by D´Angelico with assistance by shop employees such as Vincent DiSerio (assistant/apprentice from 1932 to 1959). In the early 1950s, D´Angelico´s workshop had a bench and counter for guitar work, and a showcase with new United or Favilla guitars, used "trade-ins" and a few amplifiers from Nat Daniel´s Danelectro or Everett Hull´s Ampeg company. A very young James D´Aquisto became the second assistant to the shop in 1953.

In 1959, the building where D´Angelico worked and lived was condemned by the city due to an unsafe foundation. While scouting out new locations, D´Angelico and DiSerio had a serious argument over finances. DiSerio left and accepted work at the Favilla guitar plant. After a number of months went by, D´Angelico and D´Aquisto finally reopened the guitar shop at its new location. Unfortunately, D´Angelico´s health began to take a turn for the worse. John D´Angelico passed away in his sleep in September of 1964.

John D´Angelico created 1,164 serialized acoustic guitars (electric models were not part of the serialization ledgers), as well as unnumbered mandolins and novelty instruments (source: Paul William Schmidt, *Acquired of the Angels*). For complete model listings, refer to the *Blue Book of Acoustic Guitars*.

**D'Angelico New Yorker
courtesy Dr. Tom Van Hoose**

ELECTRIC MODELS

Although John D´Angelico prided himself on producing the finest acoustic archtop guitars, many of his customers ultimately outfitted them with DeArmond floating pickups as the guitar´s role in modern music changed. Though he did make a few acoustic instruments with built-in pickups, D´Angelico electric guitars - sometimes referred to as the model "G-7" after the numbers stamped inside their bodies - were the luthier´s concession to those clients wanting a non-carved, utilitarian guitar with built-in pickups. The plywood, maple cutaway bodies were obtained from either the United or Code companies, both located in New Jersey. To these, he affixed his hand-fashioned maple neck, replete with ebony fingerboard, block inlays, adjustable truss rod, and a distinctive 5-point, flared headstock. As was typical of most of his instruments, the pearl D´Angelico script inlay adorned the headstock. Pickups vary from model to model, and they often reflected the requests of a particular customer. It is common to see non-original pickups in these electric guitars, as it reflected the working musician´s desire to keep up with the latest electronic technology. Both single and double pickup, blonde, and sunburst models were produced. Body size was typically 16-16.5 in. wide, and body depth varied from 2.25-275 in. One seldom sees two identical D´Angelico electric guitars. In addition to all of the above, pickguards, tailpieces, knobs, and decorative headstock inlays changed according to what the luthier seems to have had on hand. Electric guitars are not recorded as part of the serialization in the D´Angelico ledgers. These guitars bring significantly less on the vintage market than comparable acoustic models. The publisher wishes to express his thanks to Mr. Jim Fisch for the above information. D´Angelico electric pricing: Prices for original instruments with no modifications/alterations are currently in the $7,500-$10,000 range, assuming excellent condition. It is highly recommended that several professional appraisals be secured before buying/selling/trading any D´Angelico electric instrument.

D´ANGELICO II

Instruments previously built in the U.S during the 1990s. Distributed by Archtop Enterprises, Inc. of Merrick, NY.

The D´Angelico II company offered high quality reproductions of John D´Angelico´s New Yorker and Excel models. Models share similar construction features such as spruce tops, figured maple back and sides, ebony fingerboard with mother-of-pearl inlays, and gold-plated Grover tuners and tailpiece. All guitars are individually handcrafted and hand engraved.

ELECTRIC

The 18 in. New Yorker is offered in cutaway (last MSR $12,000) and non-cutaway (last MSR $11,750) versions, and in a Sunburst or Antique Natural finish. The Excel cutaway model (last MSR $11,500), Style B non-cutaway (last MSR $9,500), and Jazz Classic (last MSR $7,250) share a 17 in. body (measured across the lower bout). A smaller single pickup electric model called the Jazz Artist (last MSR $4,650) has a 16 in. body. A semi-hollowbody electric archtop called the Fusion (last MSR $3,750) is offered in Antique Natural, New Yorker Sunburst, or Flaming Red nitrocellulose lacquer finish.

D'ANGELICO GUITARS OF AMERICA (VESTAX)

Instruments currently built in Japan, since 1988. Distributed by D'Angelico Guitars of America in Colts Neck, NJ.

In 1988 Mr. Jerry Berberine signed a deal with Mr. Hidesato Shino to re-launch the D'Angelico line of guitars that were to be made in Japan. These new instruments are built with the same quality that the vintage models were, as well as any improvements. Since 1997, more models have been introduced and they are now available in the U.S. market. Refer to their website for more information (see Trademark Index). For other guitars produced by Vestax, refer to the Vestax section.

ELECTRIC ARCHTOP

The New Yorker Series are the current line of electric archtops produced by D'Angelico. They are available in a number of different variations. In 2005, the Excel line of guitars was introduced and are modeled after the vintage Excel models.

The **NYL-1** (MSR $12,600) is the original New Yorker (17 in.) with a German spruce top, maple back and sides, a single dual-coiled pickup with two knobs, and comes in Natural, Sunburst, Blue Sunburst, See-Through Black, Natural Yellow, and Vintage Blue. The **NYS-1** (MSR $12,600) is the small version (14.5 in.) of the New Yorker. The **NYL-7** (disc.) is also a full-sized New-Yorker (17 in.) with all the same specifications of the NYL-1 except in seven-string configuration. The **NYL-3** (MSR $13,200) an 18 in. size body with a solid German spruce top with maple back and sides. Controls are the same as the NYL-1. The NYL-3 has an ebony tailpiece and is available in Sunburst or Natural Yellow, both of which are all-lacquer coating. The **NYL-4** (MSR $4,950) is similar to the NYL-3 except has the original New Yorker style brass tailpiece and is available in the same colors as the NYL-4. The **NYL-5** (MSR $4,500) is a 17 in. full-size body with 5-ply maple back and sides. Other features are simlar to the NYL-1. The **NYL-6** (MSR $3,795) has even more simplified appointments.

The **NYL-2** has several models within this number designation. The NYL-2 (MSR $4,750) is very similar to the NYL-1 except costs about 1/3 less and features these changes. The NYL-2 has a press curved solid spruce top with 5-ply maple back and sides, a original style New Yorker pickguard, New Yorker brass trapeze tailpiece, and is available in all the same colors. This model is then broken down into different sub-models including the **NYS-2** (MSR $4,500), a small-body version (14.5 in.), the **NYL-2 Custom** (MSR $6,450), which has better quality woods, the **NYL-2 Lefty** (MSR $4,950) in left-hand configuration (the only one in the collection), and the **NYL-2FH** (disc.), which features an Alnico humbucker pickup. The **NYL-2DH** (MSR $4,950) features two humbucker pickups. Plenty of guitars for all young and old!

There is also a New Yorker Semi-Acoustic body (similar to the ES-Series by Gibson). The **NYSS-3** (MSR $4,390, also known as the NY22-3) has a New Yorker body (14.5 in.) with a solid spruce top and 5-ply maple back and sides, two original dual coil pickups, tune-o-matic bridge, four knobs, and is available in all the standard colors. This model is also available as the **NYSS-3B N** (MSR $4,390), which features a New Yorker trapeze tailpiece.

ELECTRIC SOLID-BODY

Unlike the archtop D'Angelico's, there is only one solid-body model. The **NYSD-9** (MSR $4,200) is a single-cutaway and in some strange way is reminiscent of the original New Yorker design. The body is made out of mahogany with a maple arched top, the neck is mahogany with a 22-fret ebony fingerboard with pearl zig-zag position inlays, multiple body, neck, and headstock binding, two original dual coiled pickups, four knobs, stop-bar tailpiece, gold hardware, and comes in Natural Yellow, Big Apple Red, or Walnut finishes.

D'AQUISTO

Instruments previously built in Huntington, NY, and Greenport, NY, 1965-1995.

Master luthier James L. D'Aquisto (1935-1995) met John D'Angelico around 1953. At the early age of 17, D'Aquisto became D'Angelico's apprentice, and by 1959 was handling the decorative procedures and other lutherie jobs. When D'Angelico had a falling out with another member of the shop during the move of the business, D'Aquisto began doing actual building and shaping work. This lutherie work continued until the time of D'Angelico's death in 1964. The loss of D'Angelico in 1964 affected D'Aquisto both personally and professionally. Although he took over the business and shop with the encouragement of D'Angelico's brother, business under his own trademark started slowly. D'Aquisto continued to work in D'Angelico's shop repairing instruments at the last address - 37 Kenmare Street, New York City, New York. Finally, one year after D'Angelico's death, D'Aquisto summoned the nerve to build a guitar with the D'Aquisto inlay on the headpiece.

In 1965, D'Aquisto moved his shop to Huntington, New York, and sold his first instrument, styled after a D'Angelico New Yorker. Most of D'Aquisto's traditional design instruments are styled after John D'Angelico's Excel and New Yorker, with D'Aquisto adding refinements and improvements. D'Aquisto set up a deal with the Swedish-based Hagstrom company to produce guitars based on his designs in 1968, and the Ampeg company was one of the U.S. distributors. In 1973, D'Aquisto relocated his business once again, this time setting up shop in Farmingdale, New York. He produced his first flattop guitar in 1975, and his first solid body electric one year later. The Fender Musical Instrument Corporation produced a number of D'Aquisto-designed guitars beginning in the 1980s, and two models in the Designer series (D'Aquisto Ultra and Deluxe) were hand-made in small quantities at the Fender Custom Shop by Stephen Stern, who was trained by D'Aquisto himself. These guitars were discontinued during 2002. In the late 1980s, D'Aquisto again moved his shop to Greenport, New York, and continued to produce instruments from that location. In 1987, D'Aquisto broke away from archtop design tradition when he debuted the **Avant Garde**. The Excel and New Yorker style models were disc in 1991, as D'Aquisto concentrated on creating more forward-looking and advanced archtops. In 1994, models such as the **Solo** with four soundholes (only nine built), and Centura models were introduced. James L. D'Aquisto passed away in April, 1995.

Since D'Aquisto's death in 1995, a line of D'Aquisto reproductions are now available. These models use the old design, with new technology to produce some decent guitars (source: Paul William Schmidt, *Acquired of the Angels*).

ELECTRIC

James D'Aquisto built several hundred instruments, from archtops to flattops to solid body electrics. Even thouogh D'Aquisto is more famous for his acoustic archtops, his electric guitars are also very special. D'Aquisto electric instruments typically range between $7,500 and $20,000, depending on the desirability of the configuration and embellishments/special orders. Like D'Angelico, most of D'Aquisto's instruments were made to order and varied in dimensions and details. When buying/selling/appraising a D'Aquisto, it is the recommendation of the *Blue Book of Electric Guitars* that two or three professional appraisals be obtained.

GRADING	100% MINT	98% NEAR MINT	95% EXC+	90% EXC	80% VG+	70% VG	60% G

D'AQUISTO (CURRENT MFG.)

Instruments currently produced in Japan by Aria since 2002. Distributed by Aria USA in Pennsauken, NJ.

In 2002, D'Aquisto licensed their designs to be built by Aria of Japan. Designs are based off of the popular models that D'Aquisto produced during his lifetime. For more information contact Aria or D'Aquisto directly (see Trademark Index).

D'HAITRE

Instruments previously built in Maple Falls, WA during the early 1990s.

Luthier Andy Beech offered several quality solid body guitar and bass models that featured a neck-through-body design. Beech, with 18 years experience playing and building guitars, offered handcrafted work and select hardwoods in his constructions. The *Blue Book of Electric Guitars* will continue to research luthier Beech and the D'Haitre trademark for future editions. Anyone with any information on Beech and D'Haitre is welcome to submit it directly to the publisher.

D'LECO

Instruments currently built in Oklahoma City, OK starting in 1992. Distributed by the D'Leco company of Oklahoma City, OK.

James Dale, Jr., like his father, had a background in cabinet making that the two shared since 1953. Recently, Dale decided to begin building guitars full time. It was the love of jazz guitars that sparked the desire to build archtops. In the summer of 1992, Dale met a young jazz guitarist and entrepreneur named Maurice Johnson. After seeing one of Dale's archtops, Maurice was impressed and proposed a collaboration to build and market D'Leco guitars. In 1994, D'Leco acquired the rights to produce the **Charlie Christian Tribute** model. In 1995, Samick/Valley Arts began backing the proposed tribute model, and signed an exclusive agreement to build three unique production models based on the original guitars that were designed by D'Leco (source: Hal Hammer).

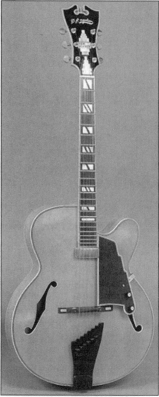

D'Angelico NYL-1 Archtop courtesy D'Angelico Guitars of America (Vestax)

ELECTRIC

D'Leco offers the Charlie Christian Tribute model. The **Solo Flight S-15** (last MSR $5,000) electric hollowbody has a hand carved top, 15 in. bout, 17th fret neck joint, 5-layer binding, gold plated humbuckers, ebony or cocobola fretboard, bridge and pickguard. The **Solo Flight S-16** has a hand carved spruce top, curly maple back and sides, 16 in. bout, 15th fret neck joint, bound fretboard, Charlie Christian Straight Bar floating pickup, and hand-rubbed lacquer. Portions of the sales proceeds went to the Christian family.

D'Leco also offered electric solid body bass guitars custom built by a young Oklahoma City luthier named David Stys. Stys was discovered by James Dale while he was building basses, and accepted the opportunity to join the D'Leco company and further his skills and development. D'Leco/Stys basses feature exotic wood tops, through-body neck, hand-contoured body shaping, and the player's choice of electronics package. D'Leco/Stys basses were built on a custom order basis, and had a last MSR of $4,000. Infomation is unavailable on other models.

DAIMARU

Instruments previously produced in Japan.

Daimaru guitars were distributed in the U.S. by the Daimaru New York Corporation of New York, NY (source: Michael Wright, *Guitar Stories*, Volume One).

DAION

Instruments previously built in Japan from the late 1970s through the mid-1980s. Some guitars may also carry the trademark of Joodee or Yamaki. Distributed by MCI, Inc. of Waco, TX.

Originally, these Japanese-produced high quality guitars were based on popular U.S. designs in the 1970s, but turned to original designs in the 1980s. The Daion logo was applied to a range of acoustic, semihollow body, and solid body guitars and basses. Some Daion headstocks also feature a stylized tuning fork logo.

ELECTRIC

Within the trends of the late 1970s, the electric guitar models had brass nuts and brass hardware, set-neck construction, and generally good finishes that seemed to concentrate on light and dark brown and translucent green. Other electric models had new prices ranging from $600 to $800.

HEADHUNTER HH-555 - ES 335 style, semi-hollowbody, dip in the lower bout by strap peg, various finishes, mfg. late 1970s to mid-1980s.

	N/A	$800	$700	$625	$550	$475	$350

Last MSR was $695.

ELECTRIC BASS

POWER SERIES BASS - various designs, set or multi-laminated thru-body necks, brass hardware, available in various finishes, mfg. late 1970s-mid 1980s.

SET NECK	N/A	$500	$425	$350	$275	$200	$150
THRU-BODY NECK	N/A	$750	$650	$550	$450	$350	$250

Last MSR was $675-$895.

D'Angelico NYSD-9 Solidbody courtesy D'Angelico Guitars of America (Vestax)

GRADING	100% MINT	98% NEAR MINT	95% EXC+	90% EXC	80% VG+	70% VG	60% G

DAISY ROCK

Instruments currently produced overseas. Daisy Rock guitars are distributed by Alfred Publishing.

Daisy Rock was founded by Tish Ciravolo in October, 2000. Tish created Daisy Rock to make guitars that appealed to girls specifically. In a male-dominated rock 'n roll world, guitars that were sculpted to the female player just didn't exist. Being the mother of two girls and playing guitar for many years, she was inspired to create this company. Guitars feature slimmer necks for smaller hands, more lightweight and smaller bodies, and visual features appealing to women. Early in existence, Daisy Rock was a division of Schecter Guitar Research. Daisy Rock is now co-owned by Alfred Publishing, which distributes the line exclusively. Hardshell cases and custom guitars are also available. For more information on Daisy Rock or Alfred Publishing, refer to the website (see Trademark Index).

ELECTRIC: ARTIST, HEARTBREAKER & ROCK SERIES

BUTTERFLY - butterfly-shaped basswood body, rock maple neck, 22-fret rosewood fingerboard with daisy inlays, single Duncan design humbucker pickup, two knobs, 3-way switch, chrome hardware, available in Fantasy or Monarch finishes, mfg. 2004-present.

MSR $459	$345	$300	$265	$230	$195	$160	$115

Butterfly Short Scale - similar to the Butterfly, except in 22.5 in. scale and a deluxe humbucker pickup, mfg. 2004-present.

MSR $299	$225	$195	$175	$150	$125	$100	$75

DAISY ARTIST - petal-shaped basswood body, rock maple neck, rosewood 22-fret fingerboard, 24.75 in. scale, pearloid daisy inlays, white headstock with 3-per-side tuners, two pickups (Duncan Design humbucker and single coil), two knobs (volume, tone), 3-way switch, circle pickguard, hardtail bridge, chrome hardware, available in Pepper Mint, Dreamy Daisy (Yellow), Daisy White, or Awesome Blue finishes with white accents, gig bag included, mfg. 2000-present.

MSR $429	$325	$275	$250	$220	$190	$150	$100

Add $20 for left-handed configuration.

Daisy Short-Scale - similar to the Daisy Artist except features a 22.5 in. scale, one deluxe Humbucker pickup, and one knob, mfg. 2000-present.

MSR $279	$220	$190	$175	$150	$125	$100	$75

Add $20 for left-hand configuration.

DAISY HEARTBREAKER - heart-shaped basswood body, bolt-on rock maple neck, 24.75 in. scale, rosewood 22-fret fingerboard with pearloid heart inlay, matching color painted headstock with 3-per-side tuners, two pickups (Duncan Design humbucker & single coil), two knobs (volume, tone), 3-way switch, heart-shaped pickguard, hardtail bridge, chrome hardware, available in Red Hot Red, Princess Purple, Pink Heart, or Blackheart finishes, mfg. 2002-present.

MSR $429		$325	$275	$250	$220	$190	$150	$100

Add $20 for left-hand configuration.

Daisy Heartbreaker Short-Scale - similar to the Daisy Heartbreaker except features a 22 1/2" scale, one deluxe Humbucker pickup, and one knob, mfg. 2000-present.

MSR $279	$220	$190	$175	$150	$125	$100	$75

Add $20 for left-hand configuration.

DAISY ROCK STAR - Double cutaway basswood body, bolt-on maple neck, 22 fret rosewood fingerboard, two humbucker pickups two knobs (volume, tone) 3-way switch, features built-in amplifier and speaker just below bridge, 9-volt powered, chrome hardware, available in Super Nova Red or Super Sonic Silver finishes, mfg. 2001 only.

	$225	$190	$175	$150	$125	$100	$75

Last MSR was $269.

ROCK CANDY - single cutaway mahogany body w/ contoured top, bolt-on rock maple neck, rosewood 22-fret fingerboard with star inlay, matching color painted headstock with 3-per-side tuners, two Duncan Design humbucker pickups, two knobs (volume, tone), 3-way switch, hardtail bridge, chrome hardware, available in Atomic Pink or Champagne Sparkle finishes, 24.75 in. scale, mfg. 2004-present.

MSR $499	$375	$325	$280	$250	$200	$160	$125

Add $20 for left-handed configuration.

Rock Candy Special - similar to the Rock Candy, except has a quilted maple top, and Tune-O-Matic bridge with string-thru-body, available in Pink Metro or Blue Shimmer finishes, mfg. 2004-present.

MSR $599	$450	$375	$325	$275	$240	$210	$175

Add $20 for left-handed configuration.

ELECTRIC: STARDUST SERIES

Add $20 for left-hand configuration on all models.

ELITE - double cutaway mahogany body, rock maple set neck, rosewood 22-fret fingerboard with piano key inlays, matching headstock with 3-per-side tuners, two covered high output humbucker pickups, two knobs (volume, tone), three-way switch with coil-tapping, body binding, combination bridge, chrome hardware (Black or Crimson Burst finish), available in Violet Burst, Emerald Burst, Golden Pearl, or Crimson Burst finishes, 24.75 in. scale, mfg. 2003-present.

MSR $499	$375	$325	$280	$250	$200	$160	$125

Elite Special - similar to the Elite, except has a full mahogany body, no pearloid binding, and Duncan Designed humbucker pickups, available in Blue Mermaid finish, new 2005.

MSR $699	$525	$450	$400	$350	$300	$250	$200

GRADING	100% MINT	98% NEAR MINT	95% EXC+	90% EXC	80% VG+	70% VG	60% G

RETRO-H - double cutaway basswood semi-hollow body, single f-hole, rock maple bolt-on neck, rosewood 22-fret fingerboard with dot inlays, 24.75 in. scale, black headstock with 3-per-side tuners, two covered mini humbucker pickups, two knobs (volume, tone), three-way switch, body binding, comination bridge, chrome hardware, available in White Pearl, Ice Blue, Metallic Pink, or Black finishes, mfg. 2003-present.

MSR $429	$325	$295	$265	$230	$190	$150	$120

Retro-H 12-String - similar to the Retro-H, except in 12-string configuration, available in Metallic Pink or White Pearl finishes, mfg. 2003-present.

MSR $499	$375	$325	$275	$250	$225	$175	$125

Retro-H Special - similar to the Elite, except has a TonePros bridge and Duncan Design mini-humbucker pickups, available in Purple Passion or Stormy Blue finishes, new 2005.

MSR $629	$475	$400	$350	$300	$250	$210	$170

VENUS - double cutaway mahogany body, mahogany set neck, rosewood 22 fret fingerboard with vines and flowers inlay, 24.75 in. scale, matching headstock with 3-per-side tuners, two covered high output humbucker pickups, two knobs (volume, tone), three-way switch with coil-tapping, abalone body binding, tune-o-matic w/stop bar bridge, chrome hardware, available in Vintage Ivory Pearl finish, mfg. 2003-present.

MSR $549	$425	$375	$335	$295	$250	$200	$150

ELECTRIC: TOM BOY SERIES

TOM BOY - single cutaway Telecaster-ish design, agathis body, maple bolt-on neck, 22-fret maple fingerboard with dot inlay, three-per-side tuners, Telecaster-style bridge, white narrow pickguard, Duncan designed single coil and humbucker pickups, three knobs, two slider switches, chrome hardware, available in Blue Fire, White Lightning, or Wild Orchid finishes, new 2005.

MSR $569	$425	$375	$325	$275	$235	$195	$160

Add $20 for left-handed configuration.

ELECTRIC BASS MODELS

BUTTERFLY BASS - butterfly-shaped basswood body, rock maple neck, 22-fret rosewood fingerboard with daisy inlays, single Duncan Design P Style pickup, two knobs, chrome hardware, available in Fantasy finish, mfg. 2004-present.

MSR $459	$345	$300	$265	$230	$195	$150	$115

Daisy Rock
Daisy Heartbreaker
Courtesy Daisy Rock

DAISY ARTIST BASS - petal-shaped basswood body, bolt-on rock maple neck, 22-fret rosewood neck with pearloid daisy inlay, 30" scale, white painted headstock with 2-per-side tuners, circle pickguard, Duncan Design P Style pickup, two knobs (volume, tone), vintage style bridge, available in Pepper Mint, Dreamy Daisy (Yellow), Daisy White, or Awesome Blue finishes, mfg. 2000-present.

MSR $429	$325	$275	$250	$220	$190	$150	$100

Add $20 for left-handed configuration.

DAISY HEARTBREAKER BASS - heart-shaped basswood body, bolt-on rock maple neck, 22-fret rosewood neck with pearloid heart inlay, 30 in. scale, matching color headstock with 2-per-side tuners, circle pickguard, Duncan Design P Style pickup, two knobs (volume, tone), vintage style bridge, available in Red Hot Red, Princess Purple, Pink Heart, or Blackheart finishes, mfg. 2002-present.

MSR $429	$325	$275	$250	$220	$190	$150	$100

Add $20 for left-handed configuration.

ELITE BASS - double cutaway mahogany body with pearloid top, mahogany set neck, rosewood 21 fret fingerboard with piano key inlays, 31 in. scale, matching headstock with 2-per-side tuners, two covered humbucker pickups, four knobs, active electronics, body binding, combination bridge, chrome hardware, available in Violet Burst or Crimson Burst finishes, mfg. 2003-present.

MSR $549	$425	$375	$325	$275	$235	$195	$160

Add $20 for left-handed configuration.

RETRO-H BASS - double cutaway basswood semi-hollow body with pearloid top, rock maple set neck, 22-fret rosewood fingerboard with dot inlays, matching headstock with 2-per-side tuners, two mini-humbucker pickups, four knobs, active electronics, body binding, combination bridge, chrome hardware, available in Stormy Blue or White Pearl finishes, 30 in. scale, new 2005.

MSR $499	$375	$325	$275	$235	$195	$160	$130

Add $20 for left-handed configuration.

ROCK CANDY BASS - single cutaway basswood body w/ glitter top, bolt-on rock maple neck, 34 in. scale, rosewood 22-fret fingerboard with star inlay, matching color painted headstock with 2-per-side tuners, two EMG select pickups, four knobs, combination bridge, chrome hardware, available in Atomic Pink or Champagne Sparkle finishes, mfg. 2004-present.

MSR $549	$425	$375	$325	$275	$235	$195	$160

Add $20 for left-handed configuration.

Daisy Rock Retro H
Courtesy Daisy Rock

DALLAS

Instruments previously made in England, West Germany, and Japan during the early to mid-1960s. Some guitars may also carry the trademark of Tuxedo.

The Dallas and Tuxedo trademarks are the brand names used by a UK importer/distributor. Early solid body guitars were supplied by either Fenton-Weill or Vox in Britain, with entry level German and Japanese original design guitars imported (source: Tony Bacon and Paul Day, *The Guru's Guitar Guide*).

DANELECTRO (1954-1969 MFG.)

Instruments originally manufactured in Red Bank, NJ from 1953 to mid-1958, then production moved to Neptune, NJ until the company's demise in 1969. Between roughly 1956 and 1967, distribution was handled by the Danelectro Corporation of Neptune, NJ. However, the majority of instruments were sold or distributed through the Sears & Roebuck chain. From 1967 to 1969, distribution was handled by the MCA Corporation after they purchased Danelectro.

Nathan I. Daniels (1912-1994) was a New York electronics buff who began assembling amplifiers at home in 1934. In the mid 1930s, he was contracted by Epiphone (NYC) to build Electar amps, and successfully created a reputation and finances to start the Danelectro Corporation in 1948. Daniels' new company had offices and a factory in Red Bank, New Jersey.

By 1953, the first guitar was designed, and it was introduced in 1954. It has been hypothesized/assumed that Daniels had consulted his long time friend John D'Angelico for assistance in the fret spacing and bridge placement. While most people believe the body frame under the masonite is pine, Paul Bechtoldt confirmed that the body is poplar (and his source was Vinnie Bell!). In 1959 or 1960, the company moved to 207 West Sylvania Avenue in Neptune City, New Jersey, where it remained until its demise in 1968.

All models were assembled in the Neptune City factory, and the majority were sold to Sears, Roebuck under their Silvertone trademark. Many of the popular designs should be considered semi-hollowbodies, for they have a masonite top and back mounted on a pine frame. The renowned Lipstick Tube pickups are exactly that: Danelectro bought the lipstick casings from a manufacturer who serviced the cosmetics industry, and then sent them to another contractor for plating before the pickup was installed inside.

The company grew during the 1960s guitar boom from under 100 employees to a peak of 503. George Wooster, Danelectro's production manager, estimated that the company produced 150 to 200 guitars a day during peak periods.

In late 1967, MCA (the entertainment conglomerate) bought Danelectro. In the same year, they introduced the Coral line. While 85% of Danelectro's output (guitars and amps) was for Sears, the Coral line was Danelectro's catalog line. The bodies for the Coral series were built in Japan, but the parts and assembly were done in the New Jersey plant. After MCA purchased the company, they began to do business with individual music shops instead of the big distributors - which brought them into competition with Fender and Gibson. Rather than point out the problem with that corporate thinking, let history do the talking: MCA folded Danelectro in 1968.

William C. Herring bought Danelectro's factory from MCA for $20,000 in late 1968 or 1969. Herring met Dan Armstrong (ex-Ampeg) and the pair visited the empty facilities and found numerous partially completed guitars and machinery. Armstrong contracted to build Danelectros for Ampeg, but by then the amplifier company was in financial straits and couldn't pay for them. These models have the single cutaway bodies, and Dan Armstrong modified Danelectro on the pickguard.

In the late 1980s, the rights to the Danelectro name were acquired by Anthony Marks, who set about building "new" Danelectros with Asian-built bodies and NOS Danelectro necks. While the *Blue Book of Electric Guitars* has heard of this project, there have been no guitars witnessed to date. It is unknown how extensive this undertaking was.

The rights to license the Danelectro name was purchased by the Evets company in late 1995. The "new" Danelectro company debuted three different effects pedals at the NAMM industry trade show in January, 1997. The new Danelectro effects pedals included the **Daddy O** overdrive ($79), the **Fab Tone** distortion ($79), and the **Cool Cat** chorus ($99). In 1998, the company debuted the **Dan-O-Matic** on-stage tuner ($79), and the **Dan-Echo** tape echo-style pedal ($129).

But the important news to the guitar community was that the Danelectro company began offering guitars! The Danelectro reissue **56-U2** is based on the popular U2 model that originated in 1956. Produced in Asia, the 56-U2 has a retail price of $299 - another nod to the original Danelectro concept (source: Paul Bechtoldt and Doug Tulloch, *Guitars From Neptune*; and Mark Wollerman, Wollerman Guitars).

The vintage market is stronger now on Danelectros and Silvertones than in the past. With the arrival of a solid reference book to help differentiate between the models produced (Bechtoldt and Tulloch's *Guitars from Neptune*), and a time frame indicated for model production, dealers are more confident in displaying model names. Danelectros have a different tone, feel, and vibe from Fenders, Gibsons, and Rickenbackers.

Keep in mind, a Danelectro guitar was a modern production-built instrument, and the company made quite a few of them (and quite a few is an understatement). But as in any marketplace, when the demand/supply ratio changes, prices can go up.

The publisher would like to thank Mr. Doug Tulloch for his significant contributions to this Danelectro section.

ELECTRIC: FIRST MODEL, C, U, & DOUBLE NECK SERIES

1954 FIRST MODEL - single cutaway poplar wood body w/ vinyl edging, neck reinforcement consisted of a .75 in. square aluminum rod which ran from nut to bridge, "Bell"-shaped headstock with large rear volute and angled stenciled logo with "curly-cue" design soon changed to vertical stenciled logo. Early versions had one or two pre-Lipstick tube pickups concealed under a thin single-ply white plastic pickguard, soon changed to lipstick tube pickups w/ clear pickguard with stenciled "D" logo and perimeter stripe, available in a variety of finishes and textured coverings including Black, Red, Bronze, Blue, and Yellow, extremely rare model, introduced 1954, phased out 1955.

ONE PICKUP	N/A	$900	$800	$700	$600	$500	$400
TWO PICKUPS	N/A	$1,200	$1,050	$950	$850	$750	$650

"C" SERIES (SINGLE CUTAWAY) - single cutaway wood smaller 11.25 in. "Peanut" size body w/vinyl edging, one or two pickups, early versions have brown vinyl tape wrapped pickups then lipstick covers, clear pickguard w/ contrasting underlay, input jack on lower body edge, available in a ginger colored vinyl rare model, introduced 1955, phased out 1956.

ONE PICKUP	N/A	$500	$425	$375	$325	$275	$225
TWO PICKUPS	N/A	$700	$625	$550	$475	$400	$350

D

GRADING	100% MINT	98% NEAR MINT	95% EXC+	90% EXC	80% VG+	70% VG	60% G

"U" SERIES - single cutaway Masonite body w/ vinyl edging, one or two pickups three pickups avail. in 1957, stenciled "D" logo and perimeter stripe on clear pickguard, input jack on lower body edge, "Coke bottle" headstock, two- and three- pickup models have stacked concentric knobs, available in Gleaming Black, Antique Bronze, Grained Ivory Leatherette, Jade Green, Bermuda Coral, and Lagoon Aqua, introduced 1956, phased out 1958.

U-1	N/A	$350	$300	$250	$200	$150	$100
U-2	N/A	$800	$700	$600	$500	$400	$300
U-3	N/A	$1,200	$1,050	$950	$850	$750	$650
UB-2 BASS	N/A	$1,100	$1,000	$900	$800	$700	$600

Add 25%-50% for custom colors.

LONGHORN - "lyre"-shaped Masonite body w/ vinyl edging, two pickups, wooden pointer concentric knobs, clear pickguard, input jack on lower body edge, "Coke bottle" headstock, pickups on early versions are mounted close together in the neck position as with the Guitarlin, later versions had wide pickup spacing neck and bridge. Bronze and White Sunburst only, introduced 1958, available through 1969.

#4423 4 String Bass

1958-1962	N/A	$1,500	$1,300	$1,100	$950	$800	$650
1963-1969	N/A	$1,200	$1,050	$900	$800	$700	$600

#4623 6 String Bass

	N/A	$1,200	$1,050	$900	$800	$700	$600

#4123 Guitarlin

	N/A	$1,500	$1,300	$1,100	$950	$800	$650

DOUBLENECK #3923 - 4-string bass/6-string guitar, "Shorthorn" style Masonite body w/vinyl edging, two pickups, concentric knobs, clear pickguards, input jack on lower body edge, "Coke bottle" headstocks, Bronze and White Sunburst only, introduced 1958, phased out 1969.

	N/A	$1,600	$1,400	$1,200	$1,050	$900	$750

Danelectro "U" Series U-1
courtesy Piney Woods
Old Guitar Shop

ELECTRIC: SHORTHORN SERIES

SHORTHORN STANDARD - double cutaway Masonite body w/ vinyl edging, one or two pickups, "Coke bottle" headstock, early versions had a clear "Kidney"-shaped pickguard with a separate white vinyl underlay and the input jack mounted on the lower body edge. This was soon changed to the input jack mounted on a white painted "Seal" shaped pickguard. Available in Black, Bronze, and Blonde, introduced 1958, phased out 1966.

1 P/U #3011/3012	N/A	$400	$350	$300	$250	$200	$150
2 P/U BLACK #3021	N/A	$1,000	$850	$750	$650	$550	$450
2 P/U BRONZE #3022	N/A	$750	$650	$575	$500	$425	$350
2 P/U BLONDE #3025	N/A	$850	$750	$650	$550	$450	$350

Note: The above model #3021 is closely associated with Led Zeppelin guitarist Jimmy Page and has strong collector appeal. Specs. MUST be as follows: Black finish, two pickups, "Coke bottle" headstock, concentric knobs, "Seal"-shaped pickguard, NO tremolo.

SHORTHORN DELUXE - double cutaway Masonite body w/vinyl edging, one, two, or three pickups, "Coke bottle" headstock, available in White w/ brown body binding or Walnut w/ white body binding, input jack on lower body edge, headstock and back of neck painted white, glued on pickguard, Kluson Deluxe tuners. Two and three pickup models have wooden pointer style concentric knobs, introduced 1958, phased out 1966.

1 P/U #6016/6017	N/A	$500	$450	$400	$350	$300	$250
2 P/U #6026/6027	N/A	$750	$675	$600	$525	$450	$350
3 P/U #6036/6037	N/A	$1,000	$850	$750	$650	$550	$450

SHORTHORN BASS - double cutaway Masonite body w/ vinyl edging, one pickup, white painted "Seal" shaped pickguard, "Coke bottle" headstock, pickguard mounted input jack, four- and six- string versions, available in Bronze finish only, introduced 1958, phased out 1966.

4 STRING #3412	N/A	$600	$525	$475	$425	$375	$325
6 STRING # 3612	N/A	$900	$800	$700	$600	$500	$400

ELECTRIC: HAND VIBRATO, CONVERTIBLE & BELLZOUKI SERIES

HAND VIBRATO GUITAR - double cutaway Masonite body w/ vinyl edging, one or two pickups, Batwing headstock w/ raised chrome script logo, all equipped with "vibrato" bridge, large white painted pickguard which surrounds pickups, pickguard mounted input jack, Gleaming Black finish only, introduced 1965, phased out 1967.

1 P/U #4011	N/A	$500	$450	$400	$350	$300	$250
2 P/U #4021	N/A	$700	$625	$550	$475	$400	$325

GRADING	100% MINT	98% NEAR MINT	95% EXC+	90% EXC	80% VG+	70% VG	60% G

CONVERTIBLE - double cutaway Masonite body w/ vinyl edging and round soundhole, floating bridge, NO pickguard, body mounted input jack, "Coke bottle" headstock with decal logo through 1967, then 6-in-line headstock w/ raised chrome script logo through 1969. Offered with or without electronics hence the name Convertible. If without electronics, chrome "decorative" inserts are fitted in the control holes. Early versions have a single screw mounting the tailpiece and only two Allen screws on the rosewood bridge, later versions have two screws mounting the tailpiece with three Allen screws on the rosewood bridge, available in Blonde, Red, or Blue finishes, introduced 1958 and available through 1969.

NO ELECT. #5005	N/A	$400	$350	$300	$250	$200	$150
W/ ELECT. #5015	N/A	$500	$450	$400	$350	$300	$250
COMPANION #5025	N/A	$750	$675	$600	$525	$450	$375

Add 25% for Red or Blue finish.

BELLZOUKI - three body variations centered around a masonite teardrop shaped body, one or two pickups, body mounted input jack, tortoiseshell pickguard and pickup surround, "Batwing" headstock, raised chrome script logo, Tobacco Brown Sunburst only, introduced 1961, phased out 1967.

1 P/U #7010	N/A	$750	$675	$600	$525	$450	$375
2 P/U #7020	N/A	$1,000	$850	$750	$650	$550	$450

Coral Sitar Two Pickup #7021 - "Coral Sitar"-style body w/ treble horn, white "reflective stylized" pickguard (rare model), mfg. circa 1967-69.

	N/A	$1,200	$1,050	$950	$850	$750	$650

ELECTRIC: PRO, SITAR, HAWAIIAN, HAWK, & SLIMLINE SERIES

PRO 1 - square-ish offset masonite body w/ vinyl edging, one pickup, white baked melamine triangular pickguard, Brown w/ sparkle accents only, introduced in 1963, phased out in 1964.

	N/A	$500	$450	$400	$350	$300	$250

SITAR - oval-shaped wood body, keyhole shaped headstock, one pickup w/ chrome surround, "Reflective Stylized" pickguard w/ stenciled border design, chrome plated lap mount, "Sitarmatic" bridge, NO drone strings as on Coral version, very rare model, introduced 1968 through 1969.

	N/A	$1,200	$1,050	$900	$800	$700	$600

HAWAIIAN GUITAR - staggered three piece natural wood body w/ brown felt backing, one pickup, 36-fret stenciled pattern on fingerboard, stenciled logo on Rosewood slab mounted to headstock, extremely rare model, introduced 1958 through 1959.

	N/A	$600	$525	$450	$375	$300	$225

HAWK - guitar, bass, and twelve-string versions, offset solid wood body w textured finish, six-in-line matching headstock twelve string resembles "Batwing" headstock, one or two pickups on two-pickup models, the lower half of the concentric knobs are painted to match body color, raised chrome script logo, optional "Flexbridge" vibrato, white painted pickguard, available in Brilliant Red, Baby Blue, or Panther Black textured finishes, introduced 1967 through 1968.

1N	N/A	$400	$350	$300	$250	$200	$150
1V FLEXBRIDGE	N/A	$450	$400	$350	$300	$250	$200
1N12	N/A	$450	$400	$350	$300	$250	$200
1B4 BASS	N/A	$450	$400	$350	$300	$250	$200
2N	N/A	$500	$450	$400	$350	$300	$250
2V FLEXBRIDGE	N/A	$525	$475	$425	$375	$325	$275
2N12	N/A	$550	$500	$450	$400	$350	$300

SLIMLINE - six- and twelve-string guitar, offset masonite semi-solid body w/ vinyl edging, six-in-line matching headstock twelve string resembles "Batwing" headstock w/ raised chrome script logo, two or three pickups two for twelve string, optional vibrato on six-string models, rear painted plastic pickguard w/perimeter stripe and pickguard mounted input jack, two volume/two tone with twin slider switches, available in White w/ Black trim, Midnite Green w/White trim, Black and Yellow Sunburst w/ White trim, introduced 1967 through 1969.

2N	N/A	$425	$375	$325	$275	$225	$175
2V VIBRATO	N/A	$450	$400	$350	$300	$250	$200
2N12	N/A	$475	$425	$375	$325	$275	$225
3N	N/A	$750	$675	$600	$525	$450	$350
3V VIBRATO	N/A	$750	$675	$600	$525	$450	$350

ELECTRIC: DANE A, B, C, & D SERIES

Models in this category are named after their configuration. The first letter stands for the model series, the number indicates the number of pickups, the third letter indicates wheter it is a vibrato or bass, and the last numbers indicate how many strings it has other than six. For example a C2N12 would be a model C 12-string guitar with 2 pickups.

DANE "A" SERIES - guitar, bass, and twelve-string versions. Offset solid wood body, six-in-line matching headstock twelve-string resembles "Batwing" headstock} w/raised chrome script logo, one or two pickups one for bass, optional "Flexbridge" vibrato on six-string models, white painted pickguard w/ pickguard mounted input jack, two pickup models have stacked concentric knobs, standard textured finish is Brown, textured custom colors were Red, Black, and Blue, introduced 1967 through 1969.

A1N	N/A	$300	$250	$200	$175	$150	$125
A2N	N/A	$350	$300	$250	$225	$200	$175
A1V	N/A	$300	$250	$200	$175	$150	$125
A2V	N/A	$350	$300	$250	$225	$200	$175
A1N12	N/A	$325	$275	$225	$200	$175	$150
A2N12	N/A	$375	$325	$275	$250	$225	$200
A1B4	N/A	$350	$300	$250	$200	$175	$150

GRADING	100% MINT	98% NEAR MINT	95% EXC+	90% EXC	80% VG+	70% VG	60% G

"B" SERIES - guitar and twelve-string versions, offset semi-solid "Durabody" w/ vinyl edging, six-in-line matching headstock twelve-string resembles "Batwing" headstock w/ raised chrome script logo, two or three pickups w/ chrome surrounds, optional vibrato on six-string models, black or white rear painted plastic pickguard w/ contrasting perimeter stripe and pickguard mounted input jack, two volume/two tone with three slider switches three pickup model has additional master volume control, standard finish is White w/ Black trim, custom finish is Green w/ White trim.

B2N	N/A	$400	$350	$300	$250	$200	$150
B3N	N/A	$600	$550	$500	$450	$400	$350
B2V	N/A	$425	$375	$325	$275	$225	$175
B3V	N/A	$625	$550	$500	$450	$400	$350
B2N12	N/A	$450	$400	$350	$300	$250	$200
B3N12	N/A	$650	$575	$525	$475	$425	$375

"C" SERIES - guitar, bass four- and six-string, twelve-string, offset semi-solid "Durabody" w/ vinyl edging, six-in-line matching headstock twelve-string resembles "Batwing" headstock w/ raised chrome script logo, two or three pickups w/ chrome surrounds, optional vibrato on six-string models, black or white rear painted plastic pickguard w/contrasting perimeter stripe and pickguard mounted input jack, two volume/two tone with two slider switches three-pickup model has three slider switches and additional master volume control}, standard "Gator" textured finish is Gator Black w/ Red trim, custom finishes are Gator Black w/ Blue trim, and Gator Black w/ Beige trim.

C2N	N/A	$400	$350	$300	$250	$200	$150
C3N	N/A	$600	$550	$500	$450	$400	$350
C2V	N/A	$425	$375	$325	$275	$225	$175
C3V	N/A	$625	$550	$500	$450	$400	$350
C2N12	N/A	$450	$400	$350	$300	$250	$200
C3N12	N/A	$650	$600	$550	$500	$450	$375
C2B4	N/A	$450	$400	$350	$300	$250	$200
C2B6	N/A	$650	$575	$500	$425	$350	$275

Danelectro Doubleneck courtesy Atomic Guitars

"D" SERIES - guitar, bass four- and six-string, twelve-string, offset sculpted solid wood body, six-in-line matching headstock twelve string resembles "Batwing" headstock w/raised chrome script logo, two or three pickups w/ chrome surrounds, optional vibrato on six-string models, "Reflective Stylized" pickguard w/ perimeter stripe, stainless control panel, two pickup model has individual volume for each pickup and master volume w/ 4 slider switches, three pickup model has individual volume for each pickup and master volume w/ 3 slider switches, available in Red, White, Black, Natural Black, Natural.

D2N	N/A	$400	$350	$300	$250	$200	$150
D3N	N/A	$600	$550	$500	$450	$400	$350
D2V	N/A	$425	$375	$325	$275	$225	$175
D3V	N/A	$625	$550	$500	$450	$400	$350
D2N12	N/A	$450	$400	$350	$300	$250	$200
D3N12	N/A	$650	$600	$550	$500	$450	$375
D2B4	N/A	$450	$400	$350	$300	$250	$200
D2B6	N/A	$650	$575	$500	$425	$350	$275

DANELECTRO (CURRENT MFG.)

Instruments currently produced in Asia since 1998. Distributed by Danelectro Corporation of Laguna Hills, California.

Danelectro's cool guitars have become so popular in recent years, that they decided to revive the name with a new line of guitars based on old designs as well as new designs. Along with guitars, they also produce amplifiers, effect pedals, and a number of accessories.

They have recently focused on effects pedals and a new pedal named the Wasabi.

ELECTRIC

56-U1 REISSUE - single cutaway semi-hollow body, masonite top and bottom, bolt-on maple neck, adjustable truss rod, 21-fret rosewood fingerboard with white dot inlays, rosewood/metal stop tailpiece, "coke bottle" peghead with screened logo, 3-per-side sealed tuners, chrome hardware, 1 lipstick tube style single coil pickup, single stacked volume/tone control, available in Nifty Aqua, Limo Black, Daddy-O Yellow, Beatnik Burgundy, Commie Red, and Retro Purple, mfg. 1998-99.

	$160	$135	$110	$90	$75	$60	$50

Last MSR was $199.

56-U2 REISSUE - same as 56-U1 except has 2 lipstick tube-style single coil pickups, 2 sets stacked volume/tone controls, 3-way selector switch, available in Aqua Burst, Beatnik Burgundy, Blue Burst, Blue Suede, Commie Red, Cool Copper, Copper Burst, Daddy-O Yellow, Limo Black, Malt Shop Creme, or Nifty Aqua finishes, mfg. 1998-present.

MSR $299	$240	$200	$175	$150	$125	$100	$75

In 1999, Beatnick Burgundy finish was disc. In 2000, Black Burst finish was introduced.

Danelectro DC Bass courtesy Dave Rogers Dave's Guitar Shop

GRADING	100% MINT	98% NEAR MINT	95% EXC+	90% EXC	80% VG+	70% VG	60% G

56-U2 Lefthanded Reissue - similar to the 56-U2 except is mirrored for the left-handed musician, available in Nifty Aqua, Limo Black, Daddy-O Yellow, Commie Red, Aqua Burst or Copper Burst, mfg. 1998-present.

MSR $399	$319	$275	$250	$200	$150	$125	$100

56-U3 REISSUE - same as the 56-U2 but has three lipstick tube single coil pickups. Features Select-O-Matic switching allowing for seven different tone settings. Override switch allows for activation of all three pickups regardless of tone setting. Gotoh tuners and individual string saddles, available in Limo Black, Commie Red, Burgundy Burst, Black Metal Flake, Silver Metalflake, or Turquoise Metalflake, mfg. 1999-present.

MSR $399	$325	$275	$250	$200	$150	$125	$100

In 1999, Commie Red, Burgundy Burst and Black Metalflake finishes were disc.

59-DC REISSUE - similar to the 56-U2 except has double cutaway body style. Two lipstick tube style single coil pickups and two stacked volume/tone controls. 3-way selector switch, available in Daddy-O Yellow, Commie Red, Limo Black, Peachy Keen, Beatnik Burgundy, Cool Copper or Retro Purple, mfg. 1998-99.

	$240	$200	$175	$150	$125	$100	$75

Last MSR was $299.

´59 DC Pro - similar to 59 DC Reissue, except has adjustable bridge, Gotoh tuners, available in Silver Metalflake, Black/Gold Pearl, or Deep Blue Pearl finishes, mfg. 2000-present.

MSR $349	$279	$250	$200	$150	$125	$100	$75

DC-3 REISSUE - same as the 56-U3 except has double cutaway body style, available in Blue Suede, Limo Black, Commie Red, Black Metalflake, Silver Metalflake, or Turquoise Metalflake, mfg. 1999-present.

MSR $399	$325	$275	$250	$200	$150	$125	$100

In 1999, Blue Suede and Commie Red finishes were disc.

12-STRING - 12-string variation of the 59-DC. Two single coil Lipstick Tube pickups and two stacked volume/tone controls. Has Gotoh tuners and adjustable bridge, available in Limo Black, White Pearl, Dark Blue Metalflake, Deep Purple Metalflake, or Red Pearl, mfg. 1999-present.

MSR $399	$319	$275	$225	$195	$175	$150	$95

BARITONE REISSUE - 56 body style with 24-fret rosewood fingerboard with white dot inlays. Dual Lipstick Tube single coil pickups and two stacked volume/tone controls, 3-way selector switch, available in Nifty Aqua, Limo Black, Daddy-O Yellow, Commie Red, Aqua Burst, or Copper Burst, mfg. 1999-present.

MSR $399	$325	$275	$250	$200	$150	$125	$100

In 1999, Daddy-O Yellow, Aqua Burst and Copper Burst finishes were disc.

CONVERTIBLE REISSUE - acoustic/electric, double cutaway design with a single lipstick tube style single coil pickup and stacked volume/tone control. Can be used as an acoustic or an electric guitar, available in Nifty Aqua, Limo Black, Beatnik Burgundy, Malt Shop Creme, Blue Burst, or Copper Burst, mfg. 1999 only.

	$239	$200	$175	$150	$125	$100	$75

Last MSR was $299.

Convertible Pro - similar to Convertible Reissue, except has Gotoh tuners, available in Dark Blue Metalflake, Deep Purple Metalflake, Beep Blue Pearl, or White Pearl finishes, mfg. 2000-present.

MSR $349	$279	$250	$195	$175	$150	$125	$95

DOUBLENECK REISSUE - available as either a 6-string/12-string combo or a 6-string/baritone combo. two lipstick tube single coil pickups per neck with separate stacked volume/tone controls for each. Selector switch. Gotoh tuners, available in Light Blue Pearl, White Pearl, or Black Burst, mfg. 1999-present.

MSR $599	$480	$425	$375	$325	$275	$250	$225

GUITAR/MANDOLIN REISSUE - longhorn double cutaway styling with 31-fret neck, lower frets used for normal guitar sounds. Upper frets are used for mandolin-like effect. two lipstick tube single coil pickups and two stacked volume/tone controls. Selector switch, available in Commie Red, Black Metalflake, or Black Burst, mfg. 1999-present.

MSR $399	$325	$275	$250	$200	$150	$125	$100

HEARSAY - offset double cutaway body, Hard Maple neck with rosewood fingerboard, dot position markers, 21 frets, 3 single coil Dano Tuned pickups with middle pickup reverse wound, volume, tone, built-in distortion, distortion sweep, stereo jacks (1 bypass and 1 effects), fulcrum-style tremolo, available in Red Sparkle Burst, Black Sparkle, or Blue Sparkle Burst finishes, mfg. 2001-present.

MSR $219	$175	$145	$125	$95	$75	$60	$45

HODAD - double cutaway model with offset waist, has 4 lipstick tube single coil pickups wired like two Humbuckers, pull-on tone knobs for out of phase and coil-tap on each pickup set. Twelve tone variations, available with or without whammy bar. Dual tone and volume controls. Gotoh tuners, available in Black/Gold Pearl, Violet Pearl, Deep Blue Pearl, White/Violet Pearl, Red Pearl, or Light Blue Metalflake, mfg. 1999-present.

MSR $399	$325	$275	$250	$200	$150	$125	$100
(w/ Whammy) $499	$400	$375	$350	$300	$250	$200	$150

Hodad Baritone - similar to Hodad, except long scale, 3 Lipstick pickups, 7-tone Select-O-Matic switching, available in Black Metal Flake, Black/Gold Pearl and White/Violet Pearl finishes, mfg. 2000-present.

MSR $499	$399	$350	$295	$250	$195	$150	$95

Hodad 12-String - similar to Hodad, except in a 12-string configuration, 3 lipstick pickups, 7-tone Select-O-Matic switching. 6-per-side tuners, available in Black/Gold Pearl, Deep Blue Pearl and White/Violet Pearl finishes, mfg. 2000-present.

MSR $499	$399	$350	$295	$250	$195	$150	$95

INNUENDO - offset double cutaway solid body, 3 single coil Dano-Tuned pickups with the middle pickup reverse wound, 4 built-in effects, push-button Distortion, Chorus, Tremolo and Echo, volume, tone, distortion control and tremolo speed, pearloid pickguard, fulcrum style tremolo, 3-per-side tuners, graphite nut, stereo jacks (1 bypass, 1 effects), available in Limo Black, Gold Sparkle Burst, or Blue/Silver Sparkle Burst finishes, mfg. 2001-present.

MSR $299	$240	$190	$160	$130	$95	$75	$55

D

GRADING	100% MINT	98% NEAR MINT	95% EXC+	90% EXC	80% VG+	70% VG	60% G

Innuendo 12-String - similar to Innuendo, except in a 12-string configuration, 4 built-in effects, available in Black Sunburst, Red Sunburst and Blue Burst finishes, mfg. 2001-present.

MSR $349		$280	$225	$185	$155	$125	$95	$70

Innuendo Baritone - similar to Innuendo, exept has a long scale neck, 22 frets, 4 built-in effects, available in Red Sunburst, Black Sunburst, or Blue Burst finishes, mfg. 2001-present.

MSR $349		$280	$225	$185	$155	$125	$95	$70

MOD 6 & 7 - single cutaway body style, 2 single coil lipstick pickups and 1 humbucker pickup, Select-O-Matic switching, coil tap, 11 tone variations, pearloid pickguard, available in 6- and 7-string sub-models, available in Black/Gold Pearl, White/Violet Pearl, Aqua Pearl, or Violet Pearl finishes, mfg. 2000-present.

MSR $599		$479	$395	$350	$295	$250	$195	$150

Violet Purple is available on the 6-string version only.

ELECTRIC BASS

58-LONGHORN BASS REISSUE - double cutaway with extended Horns, two lipstick tube single coil pickups and two stacked volume/tone controls, 24-fret rosewood fingerboard with white dot inlays, available in Nifty Aqua, Blue Suede, Limo Black, Daddy-O Yellow, Beatnik Burgundy, Commie Red, Aqua Burst, Blue Burst, Copper Burst, Black Burst, or Burgundy Burst, mfg. 1998-99.

		$275	$250	$225	$200	$175	$150	$125

Last MSR was $349.

Longhorn Pro - similar to '58 Longhorn Bass Reissue, except has adjustable bridge and upgraded tuners, available in Deep Blue Pearl and Black/White Pearl Burst finishes, mfg. 2000-present.

MSR $399		$319	$250	$225	$195	$150	$125	$95

DC BASS - electronically similar to the 58-Longhorn Bass Reissue, except has normal double cutaway body style, long scale rosewood neck with white dot inlays, dual tone and volume controls, available in Cool Copper, Limo Black, Daddy-O Yellow, Commie Red, Black, or Silver Metalflake, mfg. 1999-present.

MSR $349		$280	$250	$225	$200	$175	$150	$125

In 1999, Cool Copper and Daddy-O Yellow finishes were disc.

DC Lefthanded Bass - similar to the DC Bass except in left-handed configuration, available in Limo Black, or Silver Metalflake, mfg. 1999-present.

MSR $449		$359	$299	$275	$250	$225	$175	$150

HODAD BASS - similar to Hodad in design, long scale, 3 single coil lipstick pickups, 7-tone Select-O-Matic switching, available in Black/Gold Pearl, Deep Blue Pearl, or White/Violet Pearl finishes, mfg. 2000-present.

MSR $499		$399	$350	$295	$250	$195	$150	$95

RUMOR BASS - offset double cutaway solid body, hard maple neck with rosewood fingerboard, 34 in. scale, 20 frets, Dano-Tuned bass pickups, built-in Chorus, adjustable bridge, 2-per-side tuners, available in Red Sparkle Burst, Blue Burst, or Black Sparkle finishes, mfg. 2001-present.

MSR $199		$159	$139	$120	$95	$75	$55	$40

6-STRING BASS REISSUE - 56 body style in a 6-string bass version, two lipstick tube style single coil pickups and stacked volume/tone controls, selector switch, upgraded tuners, available in Limo Black, or Turquoise Metalflake, mfg. 1999-present.

MSR $449		$359	$299	$275	$250	$225	$175	$150

DAVID ANDREW DESIGN RESEARCH
Instruments previously built in CA during the mid-1980s.

David Andrew Design Research was founded in 1984 by David W. Newelll and Andrew Derosiers of Choes, NY. They received their first two U.S. patents two years later. Newell & Derosiers designed the first "Crusader" (later called Bladerunner by Guild guitars) prototype in the summer of 1984, and was featured in several guitar magazines later that year. The first guitars made their debut at Alex Music on 48th St. in NY during the fall of 1985. Newell & Derosiers met J.J. French of Twisted Sister later that year, which bore their relationship with Mark Dronge of Guild Guitars. Guild adopted the Crusader guitar and bass design, and renamed it the Bladerunner in early 1986. The Bladerunner made its debut on the world market at the 1986 summer NAMM Show in New Orleans. The Bladerunner was in production through 1988, until Mark Dronge sold the company. The Bladerunner made its video debut in the Aerosmith/Run D.M.C. video, "Walk this Way." The Bladerunner was played by several top guitar players of the 1980s, including Joe Perry of Aerosmith, Howarde Leese of Heart, Eddie O'Jeda of Twisted Sister, and Ben Orr of The Cars.

The David Andrew Crusader/Bladerunner was an explorer-style solid body guitar with triangular cut-outs, a poplar body, dovetail glued in neck, 24-fret ebony fingerboard, Grover tuners, EMG pickups and electronics and lacquer finish and graphics, and came with a hardshell case. The last MSR was $1,500. Production continued through 1988. The publisher would like to thank Mr. David W. Newell for the information.

DAVID THOMAS MCNAUGHT GUITARS
See McNAUGHT GUITARS.

DAVIDSON STRINGED INSTRUMENTS
Instruments currently built in Lakewood, Colorado.

The Davidson Stringed Instrument company offers handcrafted electric guitars and basses with a wide selection of pickups and hardware options to choose from. There are two models of guitars to choose from. The **Vintage Classic** (list price $2,395) features a slightly offset double cutaway walnut body with a carved flame maple top, 5-piece maple/walnut neck which runs through the body, 24-fret rosewood fingerboard, stop tailpiece, and gold hardware (a Wilkinson tremolo is an additional $150). The Vintage Classic is available in Natural Clear or Transparent finishes. The **Vintage Classic Sunburst** (list price $2,795) features similar construction, and has a 25-piece abalone/pearl inlay on the ebony fingerboard, flame maple binding, and choice of Sunburst finish. Davidson bass guitar models are available in 4-, 5-, and 6-string configurations in a neck-through-body design.

DAVIS, J. THOMAS
Instruments currently built in Columbus, OH.

Luthier Tom Davis estimates that while he builds a handful of custom guitars each year, his primary focus is on repair work. Davis has over twenty years experience in guitar building and repair. He began working on guitars while working on a music degree in the 1970s. The company moved to a store front in 1977 and relocated again in 1993. Now the company repairs both electric and acoustic guitars as well as builds acoustic models. For further information about repair work or custom guitar pricing, please contact luthier Tom Davis directly (see Trademark Index).

DAVIS, K.D. GUITARS
Instruments currently built in Sonoma, CA.

Luthier Kevin D. Davis is currently building handcrafted custom guitars.

DAVIS, WILLIAM
Instruments currently built in Boxford, ME.

William Davis´ hand-built guitars are available through his Boxford, Maine lutherie.

DAVOLI
See also Wandre, Gherson, and Krundaal. Instruments previously built in Italy from the early 1960s through the early 1970s.

The Davoli company built Wandre and Krundaal guitars in the 1960s, and progressed towards the Gherson trademark in the 1970s (source: Tony Bacon and Paul Day, *The Guru's Guitar Guide*).

DELACUGO GUITARS/DELACUGO, TONY
See TDL Guitar Works.

DE WHALLEY
Instruments previously built in England during the mid-1980s.

This original design solid body was available in Standard, Deluxe, and Custom. Anyone with further information on the CV model is invited to write to the *Blue Book of Electric Guitars*. We will update future editions as the information becomes available (source: Tony Bacon and Paul Day, *The Guru's Guitar Guide*).

DEAKON ROADS GUITARS
Instruments currently manufactured in Saskatoon, Saskatchewan, Canada beginning 1999.

Veteran Canadian guitar designer Glen McDougall was commissioned to design professional guitars for Deakon Roads Guitars. These guitars are original designs with many different optional parts and finishes.

ELECTRIC

INTRUDER - offset double cutaway body constructed of soft maple, Eastern rock maple neck with walnut fingerboard (optional Eastern rock maple fingerboard), dot position markers, 25 in. scale, 22 frets, adjustable high-mass bridge, Grover Mini Roto-Matic tuners, chrome plated brass hardware, 3 single coil highly shielded pickups, black pickguard, 1 volume/1 tone control, 5-way switch, available in Electric Blue Metallic, Emerald Green Metallic, Teal Metallic, Pewter Metallic, Burgundy Metallic, Silver Metallic, Charcoal Metallic, Candy Apple Red, Midnight Black, Trans. Blue, Trans. Red, Trans. Green, Trans. Teal, Trans. Amber, or Trans. Burgundy finishes, current mfg.

MSR $995		$925	$875	$825	$750	$675	$550	$475

DEAN
Current trademark owned by Dean Guitar Co., with headquarters located in Clearwater, FL. Instruments currently produced in Plant City, FL (Custom Shop and all the USA series) and Korea (the American Spirit series). Distributed by Armadillo Enterprises of Clearwater, FL. Dean guitars with the set-neck design were previously built in Evanston, IL from 1977 to 1986. In 1985, Dean began production of some models in Japan and Korea. Dean production from 1986 to 1993 was based in Asia.

The original Evanston, Illinois-based company was founded by Dean Zelinsky in 1977 after he graduated from high school in 1976. Zelinsky, fond of classic Gibson designs, began building high quality electric solid body instruments and eventually started developing his own designs. Originally, there were three models: The V (similar to the Flying V), The Z (Explorer body shape), and the ML (sort of a cross between the V and an Explorer, and named after the initials of Matt Lynn, Zelinsky's best friend growing up). As the company's guitars gained popularity, production facilities were moved to Chicago in 1980.

Zelinsky originally got into the guitar building business to fill a void he felt the larger companies had: a high-quality, set-neck, eye-catching stage guitar. Though new designs continued to be developed, manufacturing of these instruments was shifted more and more to overseas builders. In 1986, Dean closed the USA Shop, leaving all construction to be completed overseas. The U.S. market had shifted towards the then-popular bolt neck super-strat design, and Zelinsky's personal taste leaned in the opposite direction.

Zelinsky sold Dean Guitars in 1990 to Oscar Medros, founder and owner of Tropical Music (based in Miami, Florida). The Dean Guitars facility in Plant City, Florida is currently run by Tracy Hoeft and Jon Hill, and new guitars are distributed to markets in the U.S., Japan, Korea, and Europe.

IDENTIFYING FEATURES

Zelinsky has estimated that between 6,000 and 7,000 (possibly 8,000) guitars were built in the U.S. between 1977 and 1986. It has been estimated by various Dean collectors that the Japanese Dean models were built by the ESP Guitar company in Japan (circa 1986 to 1989). In 1998, the Dean Guitar company introduced the Dean Stack in the Box (retail new $44.95), a stereo headphone amp that can be hooked up to home stereos; and the Dean Mean 16 (list $109.95), a 16-watt solid state amp with overdrive. There are other features about the guitar to help identify it.

Listed below are standard configurations of instruments. However, being a highly handcrafted product though, instruments can be found with numerous options. Several finishes were used throughout this trademark´s early life, including Cheetah, Tiger, and Zebra Graphic finishes, and models are not necessarily limited to finishes listed.

HEADSTOCK VARIATIONS

1977-1982: Guitars built between 1977 and 1982 had the large forked ´Dean´ headstock.

1983-On: In 1983, the smaller headstock (nicknamed the shrimp fork) was introduced for models with a tremolo; then all of U.S. made instruments were shifted over to the smaller forked peghead. Korean-built bolt neck superstrat guitars have a pointy 6-on-a-side drooped design.

SERIALIZATION

The serial numbers for U.S. produced Dean guitars were stamped into the back of the headstock, and have the year of production within the number. Imported Dean models do not carry the stamped and year-coded serial numbers. See the Serialization section in this book for more information.

MODEL DATING IDENTIFICATION

Author/researcher Michael Wright briefly discussed Dean guitar history in his book, *Guitar Stories*, Volume One (Vintage Guitar Books, 1995). In the course of the Dean chapter, Wright provided some key developments in the company´s history that helps date the various series offered.

1976-1978: Zelinsky opens his first factory in Evanston, Illinois; Introduction of the **ML**, **V**, and **Z** models.

1979-1980: Introduction of the Cadillac and E´Lite models; the company moves to a larger factory in Chicago.

1982: The downsized-body Baby models are introduced. This series began production with the large V-shaped peghead, but shortly after switched to the small fork style peghead that is the most commonly found (the large V-shaped peghead was offered optionally). The Baby configuration has an unbound fingerboard and dot inlays, while the Baby Deluxe has a bound fingerboard and block inlays.

1983-1984: Bolt-neck Bel Aire superstrat models were produced.

1985: The Japanese-built Hollywood models were introduced.

1985-1987: Korean bolt-neck Signature superstrat models were produced.

1987-1990: More Korean bolt-neck designs arrive: the Eighty-Eight (perhaps a year early?), Jammer, and Playmate models.

1990: Zelinsky sells Dean Guitar Company to Tropical Music.

1991: The six-screw bolt-neck superstrat 90E, 91E, and 92E are introduced.

1993-1994: The U.S.-built Reissue Series of the classic 1977 designs are briefly built in Northern California.

1994: American Custom ML, US Cadillac, and SL models first built in Cleveland, Ohio.

1995: New Dean facilities opened in Plant City, Florida. American Custom instruments are completely built in the U.S., while the U.S. Series instruments feature Dean USA necks, Korean bodies, and assembly in the U.S. The D Series is produced in Korea.

1997: U.S.-built guitars are offered in the Coupe, Deluxe, LTD, and Korina Series; similar-styled imported Dean models fall under the various American Spirit series.

1998: The American Spirit terminology is disc. but the models retain their respective tiered pricing and quality levels. U.S.-built guitars fall under the USA Custom Shop: Coupe and LTD Series are still maintained; Flame, Ultima, and U.S. Phantom Series are added; and the Deluxe (basically an Original Floyd Rose tremolo option) is disc. European Custom and European Premium Series are added; the European Custom Series takes over korina (V and Z) models from the U.S. Korina models (a U.S. korina model would now be a USA Custom Shop model). Even more important, Dean acoustic guitars, acoustic/electric guitars, and even resonator models are introduced.

1999: The ML Platinum guitar is introduced. Some of the Edge basses are produced in Europe. The new Playmate series was introduced around this time.

2000: The Dean Tonic series debuts. Two new bass series emerged the Rhapsody and the Razor, and a new Jeff Berlin Signature Bass is available.

2002: Dean celebrated their 25th Anniversary and celebrated with only one new electric model, the Stylist Phantom, and other models received new features. Several new models were released in the acoustic lineup.

2003: The Custom Series added the Custom 450 and the Custom Zone. The ML Series welcomed a reissue of the 1979, with the ML79. This model is also available in a lefty. A new Sarasota guitar is revealed. New models were also added to the Edge Bass series. The new Dean "Rack" program was offered for dealers using provocative marketing; anyone who has visited the Dean booth at NAMM will know what I'm talking about. Hardtail bridges are introduced.

ELECTRIC: 90S SERIES

The series of 90E, 91E, and 92E models was manufactured from 1991 to 1993 in Korea. All instruments in this series had a six-bolt neck plate, and were available in Black, Blueburst, Grayburst, Red, and White finishes (unless otherwise listed).

**Dean Icon Standard
courtesy Armadillo Enterprises**

GRADING	100% MINT	98% NEAR MINT	95% EXC+	90% EXC	80% VG+	70% VG	60% G

D

90E - offset double cutaway alder body, bolt-on maple neck, 24-fret rosewood fingerboard with pearl wings inlay, standard vibrato, blackface peghead with screened logo, 6-on-one-side tuners, chrome hardware, 2 single coil/1 humbucker pickups, 1 volume/2 tone controls, 5-position switch, mfg. 1991-93.

| | N/A | $275 | $240 | $205 | $175 | $150 | $125 |

Last MSR was $400.

91E - similar to 90E, except has bound arched top, double locking Floyd Rose vibrato, humbucker/single coil/humbucker pickups, black hardware. mfg. 1991-93.

| | N/A | $400 | $350 | $300 | $250 | $200 | $150 |

Last MSR was $620.

92E - similar to 90E, except has carved maple top, double locking Floyd Rose vibrato, gold hardware, available in Sunburst finish, mfg. 1991-93.

| | N/A | $400 | $350 | $300 | $250 | $200 | $150 |

Last MSR was $620.

ELECTRIC: AVALANCHE SERIES

AVALANCHE ZONE H (AVZH) - double cutaway Strat-style basswood body, bolt-on maple neck, 22-fret rosewood fingerboard with dot inlays, 3-per-side tuners with straight string pull headstock, white pickguard, two black humbucker pickups, two black knobs (volume, tone), switch, vintage tremolo bridge, available in Classic Black or Classic Red finishes, mfg. 2000-present.

| MSR $275 | | $179 | $150 | $130 | $110 | $85 | $65 | $45 |

AVALANCHE ZONE S (AVZS) - similar to the Avalanche Zone H, except has 3 single coil white pickups and 3 knobs, available in Classic Black or Antique White finishes, mfg. 2000-present.

| MSR $275 | | $179 | $150 | $130 | $110 | $85 | $65 | $45 |

AVALANCHE ZONE ONE (AV1) - similar to the Avalanche Zone H, except has 2 single coil and 1 humbucker pickups, has floating tremolo bridge, 3 knobs, available in Classic Black, Trans. Red, Trans. Blue, or Trans. Braziliaburst finishes, mfg. 1999-present.

| MSR $375 | | $250 | $220 | $195 | $175 | $150 | $120 | $90 |

Add $30 for left-handed configuration.

AVALANCHE ZONE MQ (AVMQ) - similar to the Avalanche Zone One, except has a quilt maple top and maple fingerboard, available in Transparent Amber, Trans. Red, Trans. Blue, or Trans. Power Purple finishes, mfg. 1999-2004.

| | $325 | $275 | $240 | $205 | $170 | $135 | $100 |

Last MSR was $500.

Add $50 for left-handed configuration.

AVALANCHE 7 - similar to the Avalanche Zone H, except is in 7-string configuration, no pickguard, 4/3-per-side tuners, available in Metallic Black, Metallic Charcoal, or Trans. Red finishes, mfg. 2000-02.

| | $300 | $250 | $220 | $185 | $155 | $125 | $95 |

Last MSR was $399.

A left-handed version was available in Classic Black finish.

AVALANCHE 7 ULTRA - similar to the Avalanche 7, except has Floyd Rose tremolo, available in Classic Black or Metallic Charcoal finishes, mfg. 2000-02.

| | $375 | $325 | $275 | $240 | $205 | $165 | $115 |

Last MSR was $499.

ELECTRIC: BABY SERIES

The Baby series are scaled-down models of Dean´s popular line. They have produced the Baby Z in past years and they now introduced the V and ML series.

BABY ML - downsized Flying V-style with treble horn poplar body, poplar neck, 22-fret rosewood fingerboard with pearl dot inlay, tunable wrap over tailpiece, body matching peghead with screened logo, 3-per-side tuners, chrome hardware, exposed Dimarzio humbucker pickups, volume/tone controls, available in Black, Blueburst, Pearl Blue, Pearl Pink, Pearl Red, Pearl White, Red, or White finishes, mfg. 1982-86.

| | N/A | $600 | $525 | $450 | $375 | $325 | $250 |

Last MSR was $660.

This model had an optional 24-fret fingerboard.

BABY ML (CURRENT MFG. BML) - ML style 3/4 size body, basswood body with contoured top, maple bolt-on neck, 22-fret rosewood fingerboard with dot inlay, two Dean humbucker pickups, black hardware, available in Metallic Silver or Powder Black finishes, mfg. 2000-present.

| MSR $315 | | $205 | $175 | $150 | $125 | $100 | $75 | $50 |

BABY V - downsized Flying V-shaped poplar body, poplar neck, 22-fret rosewood fingerboard with pearl dot inlay, tunable wrap over tailpiece, body matching peghead with screened logo, 3-per-side tuners, chrome hardware, exposed humbucker DiMarzio pickup, volume/tone controls, available in Black, Blueburst, Pearl Blue, Pearl Pink, Pearl Red, Pearl White, Red, or White finishes, mfg. 1982-86.

| | N/A | $500 | $425 | $350 | $300 | $250 | $200 |

Last MSR was $660.

This model has an optional 24-fret fingerboard.

BABY V (CURRENT MFG. BV) - V style 3/4 size body, basswood body with contoured top, maple bolt-on neck, 22-fret rosewood fingerboard with dot inlay, two Dean humbucker pickups, black hardware, available in Metallic Copper or Powder Black finishes, mfg. 2000-present.

| MSR $315 | | $205 | $175 | $150 | $125 | $100 | $75 | $50 |

D

GRADING	100% MINT	98% NEAR MINT	95% EXC+	90% EXC	80% VG+	70% VG	60% G

BABY Z - downsized Explorer-style poplar body, poplar neck, 22-fret rosewood fingerboard with pearl dot inlay, tunable wrap over tailpiece, 3-per-side tuners, chrome hardware, exposed humbucker DiMarzio pickup, volume/tone controls, available in Black, Blueburst, Pearl Blue, Pearl Pink, Pearl Red, Pearl White, Red or White finishes, mfg. 1982-86.

	N/A	$500	$425	$375	$325	$275	$225

Last MSR was $660.

This model has an optional 24-fret fingerboard.

BABY Z (CURRENT MFG. BZ) - Z style 3/4 size body, basswood body with contoured top, maple bolt-on neck, 22-fret rosewood fingerboard with dot inlay, two Dean humbucker pickups, black hardware, available in Metallic Red or Powder Black finishes, mfg. 2000-present.

MSR $315	$205	$175	$150	$125	$100	$75	$50

BABY Z COUPE (USA CUSTOM SHOP) - downsized Explorer-style mahogany body, set-in mahogany neck, 22-fret ebony fingerboard with dot inlay, tune-o-matic bridge/V-shaped stop tailpiece, V-shaped peghead with screened logo, 3-per-side Grover tuners, chrome hardware, 2 Seymour Duncan humbucker pickups, volume/2 tone controls, 3-position switch, available in Brite Blue, Canary Yellow, Cherry Sunburst, Classic Black, or Lipstick Red solid finishes, mfg. 1997-98.

	$1,050	$950	$850	$750	$625	$500	$400

Last MSR was $1,599.

Baby Z Deluxe - similar to the Baby Z Coupe, except has Original Floyd Rose tremolo, available in Braziliaburst, Brite Blue, Canary Yellow, Classic Black, or Lipstick Red solid finishes, mfg. 1997-98.

	$950	$850	$750	$650	$550	$450	$350

Last MSR was $1,499.

Baby Z LTD - similar to the Baby Z Coupe, except has bound body/fingerboard/headstock, available in Braziliaburst, Cherry Sunburst, Classic Black, Trans. Blue, or Trans. Red finishes, mfg. 1997-98.

	$1,250	$1,100	$975	$850	$750	$625	$475

Last MSR was $1,899.

Korina Baby Z (U.S. Mfg.) - similar to the Baby Z Coupe, except has korina body, available in Braziliaburst, Cherry Sunburst, Gloss Natural, Trans. Amber, or Trans. Red finishes, mfg. 1997-98.

	$1,150	$1,025	$950	$850	$750	$600	$450

Last MSR was $1,899.

**Dean Baby Z Standard
courtesy Armadillo Enterprises**

BABY Z STANDARD (MODEL DGK-BZST, AMERICAN SPIRIT BABY Z STANDARD) - downsized Explorer-style mahogany body, set-in mahogany neck, 22-fret rosewood fingerboard with dot inlay, tune-o-matic bridge/strings-through-body, chrome hardware, large V-shaped headstock, 3-per-side Grover tuners, 2 "Zebra" humbuckers, volume/tone controls, 3-way selector, available in Classic Black, Trans. Blue, Trans. Braziliaburst, or Trans. Red finishes, mfg. 1998 only.

	$425	$375	$325	$275	$250	$195	$150

Last MSR was $599.

American Spirit Baby Z Ultra - similar to the American Spirit Baby Z Standard, except has Floyd Rose tremolo, mfg. 1997-98.

	$500	$450	$400	$350	$300	$250	$195

Last MSR was $749.

BABY Z X (MODEL DGK-BZX, AMERICAN SPIRIT BABY Z X) - downsized Explorer-style basswood body, bolt-on maple neck, 22-fret rosewood fingerboard with dot inlays, tune-o-matic bridge/strings-through-body, large V-shape peghead with screened logo, 3-per-side Grover tuners, chrome hardware, 2 "Zebra" humbuckers, volume/tone controls, 3-position switch, available in Trans. Braziliaburst, Classic Black, Trans. Blue, or Trans. Red finishes, mfg. 1997-99.

	$275	$250	$225	$195	$175	$150	$125

Last MSR was $349.

BABY Z XT (Model DGK-BZXT, American Spirit Baby Z XT) - similar to the Baby Z X, except has licensed Floyd Rose tremolo, available in Trans. Braziliaburst, Classic Black, Trans. Blue, or Trans. Red finishes, mfg. 1997-98.

	$325	$295	$275	$225	$195	$165	$125

Last MSR was $449.

ELECTRIC: BEL AIRE SERIES

The bodies for the Bel Aire models were produced and instruments were assembled in the USA by Dean (the serial numbers were stamped under the neck plate area), with the remaining parts being made in Japan by ESP. By 1985, total production had moved to Japan. Revived in 1987, the Bel Aire models were entirely produced in Korea through 1989.

BEL AIRE - offset double cutaway maple body, bolt-on maple neck, 22-fret rosewood fingerboard with pearl dot inlay, standard vibrato, 3-per-side tuners, chrome hardware, 2 single coil/1 humbucker pickups, 2 volume/tone controls, 5-position switch, available in Black, Blueburst, Pearl, Pinkburst, or White finishes, mfg. 1983-84, 1987-89.

	N/A	$600	$525	$450	$375	$300	$225

Last MSR was $1,050.

This model had an optional maple fingerboard. In 1984, double locking Kahler vibrato became an option. In 1985, 6-on-one-side tuners replaced original part/design.

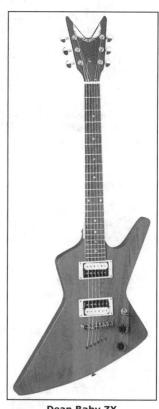

**Dean Baby ZX
courtesy Armadillo Enterprises**

GRADING	100% MINT	98% NEAR MINT	95% EXC+	90% EXC	80% VG+	70% VG	60% G

HOLLYWOOD BEL AIRE - downsized offset double cutaway hardwood body, bolt-on maple neck, 24-fret rosewood fingerboard with pearl dot inlay, tune-o-matic bridge/stop tailpiece, shrimp fork peghead with screened logo, 3-per-side tuners, chrome hardware, 2 humbucker pickups, volume/tone control, 3-position switch, available in Black, Blueburst, Bolt, Flames, Pearl Blue, Pearl Pink, Pearl Red, Pearl White, Red, Wedge, White, and Zebra Graphic finishes, mfg. 1985-87.

| | N/A | $300 | $250 | $200 | $160 | $130 | $95 |

Last MSR was $350.

Hollywood Bel Aire V - similar to Hollywood Bel Aire, except has double locking vibrato, mfg. 1985-87.

| | N/A | $350 | $275 | $225 | $175 | $135 | $95 |

Last MSR was $450.

ELECTRIC: CADILLAC SERIES

The body design looks like a cross between a Les Paul and an Explorer with the rounded lower bout and Explorer-ish treble horn. The Cadillac version originally featured three pickups (versus the E´lite´s two) but now the Cadillac name designates the body style.

The Cadillac series recently released the 25th Anniversary Cadillac at a retail of $2,899. There are other Cadillac models as well. Since these are sold individually between different dealers, accurate pricing is yet to develop on most of these.

CADILLAC - single horn cutaway round bottom bound mahogany body, mahogany neck, 22-fret bound ebony fingerboard with pearl block inlay, tune-o-matic bridge/stop tailpiece, blackface peghead with logo, 3-per-side tuners, gold hardware, 3 humbucker pickups, 2 volume/2 tone controls, 3-position switch, available in Braziliaburst, Caine White, Cherry, Cherryburst, Opaque Black, or Walnut finishes, mfg. 1979-1985.

| | N/A | $700 | $600 | $525 | $450 | $375 | $300 |

Last MSR was $1,600.

This model had optional 2 humbucker pickups.

CADILLAC RESISSUE - single horn cutaway hardwood body, bound figured maple top, through-body mahogany neck, 24-fret bound rosewood fingerboard with pearl block inlay, tune-o-matic bridge/stop tailpiece, bound rosewood veneered peghead with screened logo, 3-per-side tuners, gold hardware, 2 covered humbucker pickups, 2 volume/2 tone controls, 3-position switch, available in Cherry Sunburst, Natural, Trans. Blue and Trans. Red finishes, mfg. 1992-94.

| | N/A | $450 | $375 | $325 | $275 | $225 | $175 |

Last MSR was $790.

The Reissue models were produced in Korea.

CADILLAC DELUXE - single horn cutaway round bottom mahogany body, bound arched mahogany top, set-in mahogany neck, 22-fret bound ebony fingerboard with pearl dot inlay, tune-o-matic bridge/stop tailpiece, bound V-shape peghead with screened logo, 3-per-side tuners, chrome hardware, 2 exposed Seymour Duncan humbuckers, 2 volume/2 tone controls, 3-position switch, available in Classic Black, Classic Red, Torrid Teal, and Wine Red finishes, mfg. 1996-97.

| | $1,100 | $1,000 | $900 | $800 | $675 | $550 | $425 |

Last MSR was $1,650.

Add $100 for flame maple top, mahogany body, available in Flame Black, Flame Blue, Flame Braziliaburst, Flame Cherry, Flame Cherry Sunburst, Flame Green, Flame Purple, Flame Teal, and Flame Vintage Sunburst finishes. Add $125 for gold hardware and covered Seymour Duncan humbuckers (Model Cadillac DX GH).

CADILLAC STANDARD - similar to the Cadillac Deluxe, except has a flat (non-arched) alder top, alder body, rosewood fingerboard, mfg. 1996-97.

| | $600 | $525 | $450 | $375 | $325 | $275 | $225 |

Last MSR was $875.

Add $20 for flame maple top, alder body, available in Flame Black, Flame Blue, Flame Braziliaburst, Flame Cherry, Flame Cherry Sunburst, Flame Green, Flame Purple, Flame Teal, and Flame Vintage Sunburst finishes. Add $125 for gold hardware and covered Seymour Duncan humbuckers (Model Cadillac ST GH).

CADILLAC ARCH - single horn cutaway round bottom mahogany body, arched top, set-in mahogany neck, 22-fret ebony fingerboard with pearl dot inlay, tune-o-matic bridge/stop tailpiece, V-shape peghead with screened logo, 3-per-side Grover tuners, chrome hardware, 2 Seymour Duncan humbuckers, 2 volume/2 tone controls, 3-position switch, available in Braziliaburst, Cherry Sunburst, Classic Black, Trans. Blue, or Trans. Candy Red finishes, mfg. 1997-98.

| | $1,000 | $900 | $800 | $725 | $600 | $475 | $350 |

Last MSR was $1,399.

Cadillac Flame (USA Custom Shop) - similar to the Cadillac Arch, except has arched flame maple top, wood body binding, available in Trans. Amber, Trans. Black, Trans. Blue, Trans. Candy Red, Trans. Green, Trans. Power Purple, or Trans. Root Beer finishes, mfg. 1997-1998.

| | $1,250 | $1,100 | $975 | $850 | $750 | $625 | $475 |

Last MSR was $1,899.

Cadillac Ultima (USA Custom Shop) - similar to the Cadillac Flame, except has bound body/neck/peghead, block fingerboard inlays, gold hardware, mfg. 1997-99.

| | $1,750 | $1,600 | $1,425 | $1,250 | $1,000 | $850 | $695 |

Last MSR was $2,649.

CADILLAC COUPE (USA CUSTOM SHOP) - similar to the Cadillac Arch, except has flat (non-arched) mahogany body, available in Brite Blue, Canary Yellow, Cherry Sunburst, Classic Black, and Lipstick Red solid finishes, mfg. 1997-98.

| | $1,050 | $950 | $850 | $750 | $625 | $500 | $395 |

Last MSR was $1,599.

Korina Cadillac (U.S. Mfg.) - similar to the Cadillac Arch, except has flat (non-arched) korina body, available in Braziliaburst, Cherry Sunburst, Gloss Natural, Trans. Amber, or Trans. Red high gloss finishes, mfg. 1997-98.

| | $1,150 | $1,025 | $950 | $850 | $750 | $650 | $495 |

Last MSR was $1,899.

GRADING	100% MINT	98% NEAR MINT	95% EXC+	90% EXC	80% VG+	70% VG	60% G

D

CADILLAC LTD (USA CUSTOM SHOP) - similar to the Cadillac Arch, except has flat (non-arched) mahogany body, bound body/fingerboard/headstock, gold hardware, available in Braziliaburst, Cherry Sunburst, Classic Black, Trans. Blue, or Trans. Candy Red finishes, mfg. 1997-98.

	$1,250	$1,100	$975	$850	$750	$625	$475

Last MSR was $1,899.

Cadillac LTD 3 - similar to the Cadillac LTD, except has 3 Seymour Duncan humbuckers, custom fingerboard inlay, mfg. 1997-98.

	$1,300	$1,150	$1,025	$875	$750	$650	$495

Last MSR was $1,899.

CADILLAC JUNIOR - similar to the Cadillac Arch, except has flat (non-arched) hardwood body, bolt-on maple neck, 22-fret rosewood fingerboard with dot inlays, fixed bridge, available in Classic Black, Classic Red, and Vintage Sunburst finishes, mfg. 1997-98.

	$250	$225	$200	$175	$150	$125	$95

Last MSR was $349.

Dean Cadillac Standard
courtesy Armadillo Enterprises

CADILLAC X (MODEL DGK-CADIX) - single horn cutaway round bottom basswood body, bolt-on maple neck, 22-fret rosewood fingerboard with dot inlays, tune-o-matic bridge/stop tailpiece, large V-shape peghead with screened logo, 3-per-side Grover tuners, chrome hardware, 2 "Zebra" humbuckers, 2 volume/2 tone controls, 3-position switch, available in (Trans.) Braziliaburst, Classic Black, Trans. Blue, or Trans. Red finishes, mfg. 1997-present.

MSR $375	$250	$220	$195	$175	$150	$120	$95

Add $20 for left-handed configuration (Model DGK-CADIXL), available in Classic Black and Trans. Red finishes.

CADILLAC STANDARD (MODEL DGK-CADIST) - similar to the Cadillac X, except has mahogany body, set-in mahogany neck, available in Classic Black, Trans. Blue, Trans. Braziliaburst, or Trans. Red finishes, mfg. 1998-99.

	$425	$375	$325	$275	$250	$195	$150

Last MSR was $599.

CADILLAC SELECT (MODEL DGK-CADISEL) - similar to the Cadillac X, except has mahogany body, triple bound arched flame maple top, set-in mahogany neck, triple bound headstock, block fingerboard inlays, gold hardware, available in Flame Amberburst, Flame Black, Flame Cherry Sunburst, Flame Purple, or Flame Red finishes, mfg. 1998-present.

MSR $750	$495	$425	$375	$325	$275	$225	$175

CADILLAC 3 ULTRA (MODEL DGK-CADI3, AMERICAN SPIRIT CADILLAC ULTRA) - similar to the Cadillac X, except has mahogany body, set-in mahogany neck, bound body/fingerboard/headstock, fingerboard block inlays, 3 covered humbuckers, gold hardware, available in Cherry Sunburst, Classic Black, or Trans. Red finishes, mfg. 1997-99.

	$500	$425	$375	$325	$275	$225	$175

Last MSR was $699.

Earlier models may have 3 "Zebra" humbuckers, or a Metallic Red finish.

CADILLAC ULTIMA EUROPEAN CUSTOM (MODEL DGE-CAUL) - single horn cutaway round bottom mahogany body, arched flame top, set-in mahogany neck, 22-fret rosewood fingerboard with pearl block inlay, tune-o-matic bridge/stop tailpiece, large V-shape peghead with screened logo, 3-per-side Schaller tuners, chrome hardware, 2 "Zebra" humbuckers, 2 volume/2 tone controls, 3-position switch, available in Flame Amber, Flame Blue, Flame Green, Flame Red, 24K Gold Sparkle, Ruby Sparkle, or Silver Sparkle finishes, mfg. 1998-99.

	$750	$675	$600	$525	$425	$350	$275

Last MSR was $1,099.

This model was produced in Europe.

European Premium Cadillac Premium Ultima (DGE-PR-CU) - similar to the Cadillac Ultima European Custom, except features highly figured maple top, celluloid bound body/neck/headstock, gold hardware, 2 Seymour Duncan humbuckers, available in Flame Amber, Flame Amberburst, Flame Black, Flame Blue, Flame Cherry Sunburst, Flame Green, Flame Purple, or Flame Red finishes, disc.

	$900	$800	$700	$600	$525	$425	$325

Last MSR was $1,299.

This model was manufactured in Europe.

CADILLAC USA PROFESSIONAL - Cadillac body style, mahogany body, mahogany set-neck, 22-fret rosewood fingerboard with dot inlay, traditional Dean headstock with three-per-side tuners, hardtail bridge, two humbucker pickups, four knobs, three-way switch, chrome hardware, available in Dark Cherry, Natural, Rosewood, or Walnut finishes, mfg. 2004-present.

MSR $2,000	$1,300	$1,150	$1,000	$900	$800	$700	$600

U.S.A. SERIES CADILLAC-92 - single horn cutaway round bottom mahogany body, bound carved figured maple top, through-body mahogany neck, 22-fret bound ebony fingerboard with pearl dot inlay, Schaller tune-o-matic bridge/stop tailpiece, bound V-shape peghead with screened logo, 3-per-side tuners, chrome hardware, 3 exposed humbucker pickups, 2 volume/2 tone controls, 3-position switch, available in Cherry Sunburst, Natural, Trans. Blue, or Trans. Red finishes, mfg. 1992-93.

	N/A	$950	$850	$775	$650	$525	$400

Last MSR was $1,600.

The U.S.A. series were produced in Northern California.

Dean Cadillac Select
courtesy Armadillo Enterprises

GRADING	100% MINT	98% NEAR MINT	95% EXC+	90% EXC	80% VG+	70% VG	60% G

D

ELECTRIC: CUSTOM SERIES

The Custom Series featured four special airbrushed color graphics.

BEAR METAL - offset double cutaway hardwood body, bolt-on maple neck, 22-fret rosewood fingerboard with pearl dot inlay, Floyd Rose tremolo, 6-on-a-side pointy headstock with screened logo, chrome hardware, EMG Select humbucker, volume/tone control, available in airbrushed claw/metal custom finish, mfg. 1989-1991.

	N/A	$350	$300	$250	$200	$150	$100

Last MSR was $799.

DERRI-AIR - similar to the Bear Metal, except features airbrushed view of a butt in a bikini bottom custom finish, mfg. 1989-1991.

	N/A	$450	$400	$350	$300	$250	$200

Last MSR was $799.

PIZZA FACE - similar to the Bear Metal, except features airbrushed likeness of Freddy Krueger (*Nightmare on Elm Street*) custom finish, mfg. 1989-1991.

	N/A	$400	$350	$300	$250	$200	$150

Last MSR was $799.

SPACE ANGELS - similar to the Bear Metal, except features airbrushed scene of two female angels in space custom finish, mfg. 1989-1991.

	N/A	$350	$300	$250	$200	$150	$100

Last MSR was $799.

CUSTOM 450 (C450) - double cutaway body, neck-thru body construction, 24-fret rosewood fingerboard with pearl dot inlay, black headstock with 6-on-one-side tuners, locking nut, Floyd Rose tremolo, two EMG Humbucker pickups, two knobs, one switch, black hardware, available in Tiger Eye, Metallic Charcoal, or Pearl Black, mfg. 2003-04.

	$600	$525	$450	$375	$325	$275	$225

Last MSR was $925.

CUSTOM ZONE (CZ) - double cutaway rounded body, bolt-on neck, 22-fret rosewood fingerboard with dot inlay, 2 black Humbucker pickups, two knobs labeled volume and tone, one switch, Vintage tremolo bridge, available in Classic Black, Fluorescent Pink, or Metallic Red, mfg. 2003-present.

MSR $340		$225	$195	$160	$130	$105	$75	$55

The Custom Zone is available with a matching color fingerboard, and we suggest the pink.

ELECTRIC: D SERIES

The D Series/DS model guitars were produced in Korea from 1994 to 1996. Their body designs were similar to the 1990s Series models, except they reverted to the 3-per-side shrimp fork type headstock instead of 6-per-side tuners. D Series models have 4-bolt neckplates.

DS 87 - similar to the DS 90, except has 3 single coil pickups, 6-on-a-side headstock, chrome hardware, white pickguard, available in Classic Black, Classic Red, or Vintage Sunburst finishes, mfg. 1996-97.

	$225	$175	$150	$125	$100	$90	$75

Last MSR was $285.

DS 90 - offset double cutaway hardwood body, bolt-on maple neck, 24-fret rosewood fingerboard with pearl wings inlay, standard vibrato, blackface peghead with screened logo, 3-per-side tuners, black hardware, 2 single coil/1 humbucker pickups, 1 volume/2 tone controls, 5-position switch, available in Black, Red, or White finishes, mfg. 1994-96.

	$300	$250	$225	$175	$150	$125	$95

Last MSR was $375.

This model was offered in a left-handed configuration as the DS 90 L.

DS 91 - similar to DS 90, except has alder body, bound carved top, double locking Floyd Rose vibrato, humbucker/single coil/humbucker pickups, available in Black Flame Maple, Burgundy Flame Maple, Metallic Black, or Vintage Sunburst finishes, mfg. 1994-96.

	$425	$350	$300	$250	$225	$175	$150

Last MSR was $555.

DS 92 - similar to DS 90, except has carved maple top, double locking Floyd Rose vibrato, gold hardware, six-on-a-side tuners, available in Black Flame Maple, Burgundy Flame Maple, Metallic Black, or Vintage Sunburst finishes, mfg. 1994-96.

	$450	$375	$325	$275	$250	$200	$150

Last MSR was $595.

This model was offered in a left-handed configuration as the DS 92 L.

ELECTRIC: DIMEBAG DARREL TRIBUTE SERIES

Darrel "Dimebag" Abbott signed an endorsement deal with Dean in fall, 2004. Dimebag previously endorsed Washburn guitars from 1998 to 2004. Dimebag recieved a Dean guitar for Christmas from his dad in the late 1970s. He has played Dean guitars for several years and is known for the original Blue Lightning Bolt model that has been customized. Dimebag was fatally shot on stage at a Damage Plan concert on December 8, 2004, just a few weeks after announcing that he would be at the Winter NAMM show 2005 to promote the new line of Dimebag guitars. At the request of Dime's family, Dean went ahead with the new line of guitars and they debuted at NAMM. Dean also had the finest memorial/tribute at the show with a giant TV screen and a few of Dime's original guitars.

DBD TRIBUTE ML - ML star-style body with four points with the upper bass horn being short, basswood body, bolt-on maple neck, 22-fret rosewood fingerboard with dot inlay, traditional Dean headstock with tribute crest and three-per-side tuners, Tune-O-Matic bridge, Flying V-style tailpiece, two Zebra humbucker pickups, three knobs, three-way switch, chrome hardware, Classic Black finish with Dimebag Quad Sticker, new 2005.

MSR $500		$325	$275	$240	$210	$180	$150	$120

Dime-O-Flage ML - similar to the DBD Tribute ML, except features Dime-O-Flage finish, new 2005.

MSR $500		$325	$275	$240	$210	$180	$150	$120

GRADING	100% MINT	98% NEAR MINT	95% EXC+	90% EXC	80% VG+	70% VG	60% G

DIME-O-FLAME ML - ML star-style body with four points with the upper bass horn being short, mahogany body, mahogany neck, 22-fret rosewood fingerboard with dot inlay, traditional matching Dean headstock with tribute crest and three-per-side tuners, Floyd Rose licensed tremolo, one Dimebucker and one Seymour Duncan humbucker pickups, three knobs, three-way switch, chrome hardware, Custom Fire Finish with Dimebag Quad Sticker, new 2005.

	MSR $1,376		$899	$800	$725	$650	$575	$500	$425

FBD TRIBUTE ML - ML star-style body with four points with the upper bass horn being short, mahogany body with flame maple top, mahogany neck, cream body and neck binding, 22-fret rosewood fingerboard with dot inlay, traditional matching Dean headstock with tribute crest and three-per-side tuners, Floyd Rose licensed tremolo, one Dimebucker and one Seymour Duncan humbucker pickups, three knobs, three-way switch, chrome hardware, Vintage Braziliaburst Finish with Dimebag Quad Sticker, hardshell case included, new 2005.

	MSR $1,539		$1,000	$900	$800	$725	$650	$575	$500

RAZORBACK - ML inspired body with juttison edges that look slightly like lightning bolts, mahogany body, mahogany neck, cream body and neck binding, 22-fret rosewood fingerboard with dot inlay, matching Dean headstock with tribute crest and three-per-side tuners, Floyd Rose licensed tremolo, one zebra and one Dimebucker humbucker pickups, three knobs, three-way switch, black hardware, available in Black and Silver Two-Tone, Shard Bone, or Slime Green Bumblebee finish, new 2005.

	MSR $1,690		$1,100	$950	$850	$750	$675	$600	$525

This model is very similar to the ML series in the configuration. However, the body has slightly different modifications and was designed by Dimebag Darrel.

USA RAZORBACK TRIBUTE - ML inspired body with juttison edges that look slightly like lightning bolts, mahogany body, mahogany neck, cream body and neck binding, 22-fret rosewood fingerboard with pearl razor inlay, Dean headstock with tribute crest and three-per-side Grover tuners, Floyd Rose tremolo, one DiMarzio and one Dimebucker humbucker pickups, three knobs, three-way switch, black hardware, hand-airbrushed rusted metal finish, new 2005.

	MSR $5,550		$4,000	$3,500	$3,000	N/A	N/A	N/A	N/A

This model is very similar to the ML series in the configuration. However, the body has slightly different modifications and was designed by Dimebag Darrel. This model is produced in the U.S. and only 333 instruments are scheduled to be produced.

ELECTRIC: E´LITE SERIES

The body design looks like a cross between a Les Paul and an Explorer with the rounded lower bout and Explorer-ish treble horn. The Cadillac version of the E´lite originally featured three pickups while the E´lite model had two, but now the Cadillac name is used to designate the body style on current models.

E´LITE - single horn cutaway round bottom mahogany body, mahogany neck, 22-fret bound rosewood fingerboard with pearl dot inlay, tune-o-matic bridge/stop tailpiece, blackface peghead with logo, 3-per-side tuners, chrome hardware, 2 DiMarzio exposed humbucker pickups, 2 volume/2 tone controls, 3-position switch, available in Braziliaburst, Caine White, Cherry, Cherryburst, Opaque Black, or Walnut finish, mfg. 1978-1985.

		N/A	$900	$825	$750	$650	$550	$450
					Last MSR was $1,030.			

E´lite Deluxe - similar to E´lite, except has bound body, bound ebony fingerboard, available in Bursts or Natural finish, mfg. 1981-85.

		N/A	$950	$850	$775	$675	$575	$475
					Last MSR was $1,230.			

E´lite Special Edition - similar to E´lite, except has bound curly maple top, bound ebony fingerboard with abalone dot inlay, gold hardware, covered pickups, available in Natural finish, mfg. 1982-84.

		N/A	$950	$850	$750	$650	$550	$450
					Last MSR was $1,200.			

Golden E´lite - similar to E´lite, except has bound body, bound ebony fingerboard with abalone dot inlay, gold hardware, covered pickups, available in Walnut finish, mfg. 1979-1981.

		N/A	$950	$850	$750	$650	$550	$450
					Last MSR was $1,200.			

U.S.A. SERIES ELITE-92 - single horn cutaway mahogany body, bound carved figured maple top, through-body mahogany neck, 22-fret bound ebony fingerboard with pearl dot inlay, Schaller tune-o-matic bridge/stop tailpiece, bound V-shape peghead with screened logo, 3-per-side tuners, chrome hardware, 2 exposed humbucker pickups, 2 volume/2 tone controls, 3-position switch, available in Cherry Sunburst, Natural, Trans. Blue, or Trans. Red finish, mfg. 1992-93.

		N/A	$1,100	$950	$850	$750	$625	$495
					Last MSR was $1,600.			

The U.S.A. series were produced in Northern California.

ELITE REISSUE - single horn cutaway hardwood body, through-body mahogany neck, 22-fret rosewood fingerboard with pearl dot inlay, double locking vibrato, body matching peghead with screened logo, 3-per-side tuners, chrome hardware, 2 exposed humbucker pickups, 2 volume/2 tone controls, 3-position switch, available in Black, Blueburst, Grayburst, Red, or White finish, mfg. 1992-94.

		N/A	$600	$525	$450	$375	$300	$225
					Last MSR was $790.			

The Reissue models were produced in Korea.

Dean Dimebag Darrel Tribute Series DBD Tribute ML Courtesy Dean

Dean Dimebag Darrel Tribute Series Razorback Courtesy Dean

GRADING	100% MINT	98% NEAR MINT	95% EXC+	90% EXC	80% VG+	70% VG	60% G

ELITE HOLLOW BODY - semi-hollow single horn cutaway mahogany body, bound arched mahogany top, set-in mahogany neck, 22-fret bound ebony fingerboard with pearl dot inlay, tune-o-matic bridge/stop tailpiece, bound V-shape peghead with screened logo, 3-per-side tuners, chrome hardware, 2 exposed Seymour Duncan humbuckers, 2 volume/2 tone controls, 3-position switch, available in Classic Black, Classic Red, Torrid Teal, or Wine Red finish, mfg. 1996-97.

	$1,200	$1,100	$950	$800	$675	$550	$425

Last MSR was $1,650.

Add $100 for flame maple top, mahogany body, available in Flame Black, Flame Blue, Flame Braziliaburst, Flame Cherry, Flame Cherry Sunburst, Flame Green, Flame Purple, Flame Teal, and Flame Vintage Sunburst finish. Add $125 for gold hardware and covered Seymour Duncan humbuckers (Model Elite GH).

ELITE X (MODEL DGK-ELX) - single horn cutaway round bottom basswood body, bolt-on maple neck, 22-fret rosewood fingerboard with dot inlays, tune-o-matic bridge/stop tailpiece, small offset V-shape peghead with screened logo, 3-per-side Grover tuners, chrome hardware, 2 "Zebra" humbuckers, 2 volume/2 tone controls, 3-position switch, available in (Trans.) Braziliaburst, Classic Black, Trans. Blue, or Trans. Red finish, mfg. 1998-99.

	$275	$250	$225	$195	$175	$150	$125

Last MSR was $349.

ELITE SELECT (MODEL DGK-ELSE) - similar to the Elite X, except has mahogany body, triple bound arched flame maple top, set-in mahogany neck, triple bound headstock, block fingerboard inlays, gold hardware, available in Flame Amberburst, Flame Black, Flame Cherry Sunburst, Flame Purple, or Flame Red finish, mfg. 1998 only.

	$495	$425	$375	$325	$275	$225	$175

Last MSR was $699.

ELITE AX (MODEL DGK-ELAX) - similar to the Elite X, except features mahogany body, bound arched flame maple top, available in Flame Amberburst, Flame Black, Flame Blue, Flame Cherry Sunburst, or Flame Red finish, mfg. 1998 only.

	$350	$300	$275	$225	$195	$150	$125

Last MSR was $499.

Elite AXV (Model DGK-ELAXV) - similar to the Elite AX, except features a 2-point floating tremolo, available in Flame Amberburst, Flame Black, Flame Blue, Flame Cherry Sunburst, or Flame Red finish, mfg. 1998 only.

	$350	$300	$275	$225	$195	$150	$125

Last MSR was $499.

ELITE FLAME EUROPEAN CUSTOM (MODEL DGE-ELFL) - single horn cutaway round bottom mahogany body, arched flame top, set-in mahogany neck, 22-fret rosewood fingerboard with pearl dot inlay, tune-o-matic bridge/stop tailpiece, small offset V-shape peghead with screened logo, 3-per-side Schaller tuners, chrome hardware, 2 "Zebra" humbuckers, 2 volume/2 tone controls, 3-position switch, available in Flame Amber, Flame Amberburst, Flame Green, Flame Purple, or Flame Red finish, mfg. 1998 only.

	$695	$595	$525	$450	$375	$325	$250

Last MSR was $999.

This model was produced in Europe.

ELECTRIC: EIGHTY EIGHT SERIES

EIGHTY EIGHT - offset double cutaway maple body, bolt-on maple neck, 22-fret ebanol fingerboard with dot inlay, Floyd Rose tremolo, blackface peghead with screened logo, black pickguard, 6-on-a-side tuners, black hardware, 2 single coil/humbucker EMG Select pickups, volume/tone controls, 3 pickup selector mini-switches, available in Black, Blue Purpleburst, Gun Metal Grey, Pearl Purpleburst, Pearl Red, Pink, or White finish, mfg. 1987-89.

	N/A	$350	$300	$260	$230	$195	$150

Last MSR was $649.

ELECTRIC: EVO SERIES

For the EVOcoustic see the *Blue Book of Acoustic Guitars*.

EVO 60 - similar to EVO FT, except has 2 soapbar pickups, arched mahogany top, single-ply binding, available in 24K Gold, Classic Black, Powder Blue or Silver Sparkle finish, disc. 2003.

	$410	$375	$350	$295	$250	$195	$150

Last MSR was $549.

Add $80 for left-hand configuration.

EVO DN76 - similar to EVO Special, except is not an archtop and is not bound, available in Metallic Charcoal finish, disc. 2002.

	$575	$500	$450	$400	$350	$300	$250

Last MSR was $789.

EVO DELUXE - similar to EVO Special, except has Schaller tuners, 2 Zebra humbucking pickups, ebony fingerboard, available in Flame Amberburst, Flame Amber, Flame Cherry Sunburst, or Flame Red finish, disc. 2003.

	$675	$600	$550	$500	$450	$375	$325

Last MSR was $899.

EVO DRAGSTER (EVODSTER) - EVO style, custom flame finish, mfg. 2004-present.

MSR $550	$360	$310	$275	$240	$200	$160	$125

EVO EBONY - similar to the EVO Special, except has gold hardware and block inlays, available in Classic Black finish, disc. 2003.

	$825	$750	$700	$640	$575	$500	$425

Last MSR was $1,099.

GRADING	100% MINT	98% NEAR MINT	95% EXC+	90% EXC	80% VG+	70% VG	60% G

EVO FTX (EVOFTX) - similar to EVO X, except has exposed zebra-coil humbucking pickups and Grover tuners, available in Antique White, Trans. Amber, Trans. Black, Trans. Red, or Trans. Braziliaburst finish, disc. 2004.

	$305	$260	$230	$195	$160	$130	$105

Last MSR was $465.

EVO FT (EVOFT) - similar to EVO FTX, except has mahogany set neck, mahogany body, flame maple top, available in Antique White, Trans. Amber, Trans. Black, Trans. Green, or Trans. Braziliaburst finish, disc. 2004.

	$375	$330	$295	$260	$230	$195	$150

Last MSR was $565.

EVO MILLENIUM - similar to EVO Premium, except has V Schaller tuners, Honduras mahogany body, 5 Star Figured Maple top, Flame Maple neck, Wood binding, EVO Mother-of-Pearl inlay at the 12th fret, available in Flame Amber Burst finish, disc. 2001.

	$2,350	$2,150	$1,850	$1,600	$1,350	$1,100	$850

Last MSR was $3,299.

EVO NOIR (EVON) - similar to the EVO Special except has triple black hardware, no inlays, and is available in Classic Black finish, mfg. 2002-present.

MSR $750	$495	$425	$375	$325	$275	$225	$175

EVO PHANTOM - similar to EVO Special, except has triple black hardware, 2 Blade pickups, arched mahogany top, no binding, available in Classic Black finish, mfg. 2001-02.

	$450	$399	$375	$325	$275	$225	$165

Last MSR was $599.

EVO PREMIUM - similar to EVO Deluxe, except has gold hardware, 2 Seymour Duncan "Pearly Gates" humbucker pickups, block position markers, available in Flame Amber Burst, Flame Amber, or Flame Cherry Sunburst finish, disc. 2003.

	$900	$825	$750	$675	$600	$525	$450

Last MSR was $1,199.

EVO SPECIAL (EVOSP) - similar to EVO 60, except has 2 Dean humbucker pickups, arched Figured Maple top, fully bound, available in Classic Black or Quilt Amber finish, current mfg.

MSR $690	$450	$400	$350	$300	$250	$200	$150

EVO Special 7 - similar to EVO Special except in a 7-string configuration, mini Grover tuners, arched maple top, available in Flame Blue, Flame Red, Quilt Amberburst or Quilt Black finish, disc. 2002.

	$450	$399	$375	$325	$275	$225	$165

Last MSR was $599.

EVO Special Select (EVOSS) - similar to the EVO Special except features Zebra humbucker pickups and hourglass inlays, available in Quilt Vintage Sunburst, Tiger Eye, or Vintage Sunburst finish, mfg. 2000-present.

MSR $790	$525	$450	$375	$325	$275	$225	$175

Add $50 for left-handed configuration.

EVO TEVO (EVOTEVO) - EVO style body, all mahogany construction, set-neck, natural finish, new 2004.

MSR $375	$250	$220	$195	$175	$150	$125	$95

EVO X (EVOX) - single cutaway basswood body, bolt-on maple neck, rosewood fingerboard with dot position markers, 24.75 in. scale, 22-frets, Tune-O-Matic bridge, chrome hardware sealed tuners, 2 humbucker pickups, available in Classic White or Classic Black finish, current mfg.

MSR $375	$250	$220	$195	$175	$150	$125	$95

EVO XM (EVOXM) - similar to the EVO X, except has a solid mahogany body and neck, natural finish, new 2004.

MSR $190	$125	$105	$90	$75	$60	$45	$30

ELECTRIC: FLORIDA SERIES

BOCA - double cutaway semi-hollow mahogany body, maple top, bolt-on maple neck, rosewood fingerboard with abalone dot position markers, 22 frets, 3-per-side chrome Grover tuners, 2 Dean humbucker pickups, Tune-O-Matic bridge, 1 volume/1 tone control, 3-way switch, chrome hardware, available in Classic Black, Metallic Charcoal and Metallic Red finish, disc. 2004.

	$350	$300	$265	$235	$205	$170	$130

Last MSR was $525.

SARASOTA - similar to Boca, except has mahogany set neck, 2 Zebra humbucker pickups, Flame Maple top, single-ply binding, available in Trans. Amber, Trans. Braziliaburst, or Trans. red finish, disc. 2004.

	$465	$425	$375	$325	$275	$225	$175

Last MSR was $715.

Sarasota Standard - similar to the Sarasota except has a solid body, gold hardware, available in Trans. Amber or Trans. Braziliburst, mfg. 2003-04.

	$510	$450	$400	$350	$300	$250	$200

Last MSR was $775.

Sarasota 12 - similar to the Sarasota except in 12-string configuration, 6-per-side tuners, available in Trans. Red or Trans. Amber finish, current mfg.

MSR $865	$575	$500	$425	$375	$325	$275	$225

Dean Elite X
courtesy Armadillo Enterprises

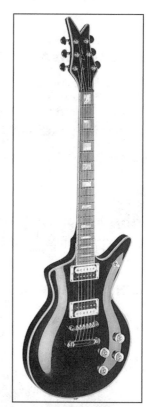

Dean Elite Select
courtesy Armadillo Enterprises

D

GRADING	100% MINT	98% NEAR MINT	95% EXC+	90% EXC	80% VG+	70% VG	60% G

DEL SOL - similar to Sarasota Model, except has gold hardware, gold covered pickups, multi-ply binding, mother-of-pearl Sun position markers, available in Classic White, Trans. Amber, Trans. Blue, or Trans. Red finish, disc. 2004.

$650	$575	$500	$425	$375	$325	$275

Last MSR was $1,000.

ELECTRIC: HARDTAIL SERIES

HARDTAIL - offset double cutaway mahogany body with maple carved top, set quartersawn mahogany neck, 22-fret ebony fingerboard with custom abalone inlays, wood binding, 3-per-side Grover tuners, two Seymour Duncan humbucker pickups, TonePros bridge, four knobs, one switch, nickel hardware, available in jet black finish, mfg. 2003 only.

$2,150	$1,700	$1,450	$1,200	$1,050	$900	$800

Last MSR was $2,799.

Hardtail Flame USA - similar to the Hardtail except has a flamed maple top, available in Indian Turquoise, Vintage Cherry Sunburst, Emerald Green, Dark Cherry, Midnight Blue, Deep Purple, Transparent Amberburst, Faded Denim, Transparent Brazilburst, Transparent Black, Transparent Cherry Sunburst, Powder Black, Tiger Eye, or Gloss Natural finish, mfg. 2003 only.

$2,275	$1,800	$1,500	$1,250	$1,075	$925	$800

Last MSR was $2,999.

Add $150 for the Hardtail Quilt top.

HARDTAIL STANDARD - offset double cutaway with slightly longer bass horn, mahogany body, set mahogany neck, 22-fret rosewood fingerboard with dot inlay and 12th fret design, Hardtail headstock with three-per-side tuners, hardtail bridge and tailpiece, two covered humbucker pickups, four knobs, three-way switch, chrome hardware, available in Classic Black, Copper Orange, or Flip Pearl, mfg. 2004-present.

MSR $750	$495	$425	$375	$325	$275	$225	$175

HARDTAIL SELECT - offset double cutaway with slightly longer bass horn, mahogany body with flame maple top, set mahogany neck, 22-fret rosewood fingerboard with dot and 12th fret abalone Hardtail inlay, Hardtail headstock with three-per-side tuners, hardtail bridge and tailpiece, two covered humbucker pickups, four knobs, three-way switch, nickel hardware, available in Tiger Eye, Trans. Amber, Trans. Blue, Trans. Brazilliaburst, or Trans. Red finish, mfg. 2004-present.

MSR $1,000	$650	$575	$500	$450	$400	$350	$300

Hardtail Select Vibrato - similar to the Select, except has a floating tremolo and Trim-Lock tuning machines, new 2005.

MSR $1,250	$825	$725	$650	$575	$500	$425	$350

HARDTAIL COLLECTOR'S EDITION - similar to the Hardtail except has features for a Collector's edition, which includes original design V-neck with binding, sterling silver inlays, master grade maple top, champagne pearl finished hardware, first 150 are hand signed by Dean B. Zelinsky himself, and comes with an embossed leather hardtail jacket and black leatherette plush lined case, available in Indian Turquoise, Vintage Cherry Sunburst, Emerald Green, Dark Cherry, Midnight Blue, Deep Purple, Trans. Amberburst, Faded Denim, Trans. Brazilburst, Trans. Black, Trans. Cherry Sunburst, Powder Black, Tiger Eye, or Gloss Natural finish, mfg. 2003 only.

$2,875	$2,350	$2,150	$1,850	$1,600	$1,350	$1,100

Last MSR was $3,799.

Add $150 for the Hardtail Quilt top.

HARDTAIL USA PROFESSIONAL - Hardtail body style, mahogany body, mahogany set-neck, 22-fret rosewood fingerboard with dot and 12th fret inlay, headstock with three-per-side tuners, hardtail bridge, two humbucker pickups, four knobs, three-way switch, chrome hardware, available in Dark Cherry, Natural, Rosewood, or Walnut finish, mfg. 2004-present.

MSR $2,000	$1,300	$1,150	$1,000	$900	$800	$700	$600

ELECTRIC: ICON SERIES

The Icon was introduced in 1997. The Icon resembles a cross between a Les Paul and a PRS, and has a new 3-per-side offset 'V' headstock design.

ICON CONTOUR - offset double cutaway round bottom mahogany body, carved top, set-in mahogany neck, 22-fret ebony fingerboard with dot inlay, fixed bridge, chrome hardware, small offset V-shaped headstock, 3-per-side Grover tuners, 2 Seymour Duncan humbuckers, volume/tone controls, 3-way selector, available in Braziliaburst, Cherry Sunburst, Classic Black, Trans. Blue, or Trans. Candy Red finish, mfg. 1997-98.

$1,000	$900	$825	$725	$600	$495	$350

Last MSR was $1,399.

ICON FLAME (USA CUSTOM SHOP, ICON EXOTIC) - similar to the Icon Contour, except has carved flame maple top, available in Transparent Amber, Transparent Black, Transparent Blue, Transparent Candy Red, Transparent Green, Transparent Power Purple, or Transparent Root Beer finish, mfg. 1997-99.

$1,250	$1,100	$975	$850	$750	$625	$475

Last MSR was $1,899.

ICON EXOTIC PLUS - similar to the Icon Exotic, except has a piezo mounted tremolo bridge, mfg. 1997-98.

$1,250	$1,100	$975	$850	$750	$625	$475

Last MSR was $1,899.

ICON ULTIMA (USA CUSTOM SHOP) - similar to the Icon Exotic, except has carved quilted maple top, block fingerboard inlays, gold hardware, mfg. 1997-98.

$1,750	$1,600	$1,425	$1,250	$1,000	$850	$695

Last MSR was $2,649.

Early models may have a piezo mounted tremolo bridge.

GRADING	100% MINT	98% NEAR MINT	95% EXC+	90% EXC	80% VG+	70% VG	60% G

KORINA ICON (U.S. MFG.) - similar to the Icon Contour, except has korina body, piezo mounted tremolo bridge, available in Braziliaburst, Cherry Sunburst, Gloss Natural, Trans. Amber, or Trans. Red high gloss finish, mfg. 1997-98.

	$1,300	$1,150	$1,000	$950	$800	$700	$525

Last MSR was $2,099.

ICON AX (MODEL DGK-ICAX) - offset double cutaway round bottom mahogany body, bound arched flame maple top, bolt-on maple neck, 22-fret rosewood fingerboard with dot inlay, Tune-O-Matic bridge/stop tailpiece, chrome hardware, offset V-shaped headstock, 3-per-side Grover tuners, 2 "Zebra" humbuckers, volume/tone controls, 3-way selector, available in Flame Black, Flame Blue, Flame Cherry Sunburst, or Flame Red finish, mfg. 1998 only.

	$350	$300	$275	$225	$195	$150	$125

Last MSR was $499.

Icon AXV (Model DGK-ICAXV) - similar to the Icon AX, except features a 2-point floating tremolo, available in Flame Black, Flame Blue, Flame Cherry Sunburst, or Flame Red finish, mfg. 1998 only.

	$350	$300	$275	$225	$195	$150	$125

Last MSR was $499.

ICON STANDARD (MODEL DGK-ICST) - offset double cutaway round bottom mahogany body, set-in mahogany neck, 22-fret rosewood fingerboard with dot inlay, Tune-O-Matic bridge/strings-through Icon wood bridge, chrome hardware, offset V-shaped headstock, 3-per-side Grover tuners, 2 "Zebra" humbuckers, volume/tone controls, 3-way selector, available in Cherry Sunburst, Classic Black, Trans. Blue, Trans. Braziliaburst, Trans. Purple, or Trans. Red finish, mfg. 1998-2003.

	$350	$300	$275	$250	$195	$150	$110

Last MSR was $499.

ICON SELECT (MODEL DGK-ICSE) - similar to the Icon Standard, except has triple bound arched flame maple top, triple bound headstock, block fingerboard inlays, gold hardware, available in Flame Amberburst, Flame Black, Flame Cherry Sunburst, Flame Purple, or Flame Red finish, mfg. 1998-2002.

	$425	$350	$325	$275	$225	$175	$135

Last MSR was $599.

ICON SPECIAL SELECT - similar to the Icon Special Select except has hourglass inlays, wood binding, and nickel hardware, available in Quilt Amberburst, Quilt Black, or Quilt Blue finish, mfg. 2002-03.

	$490	$425	$375	$325	$250	$200	$150

Last MSR was $649.

ICON NOIR - similar to the Icon Special Select except has all black hardware, available in Classic Black finish, mfg. 2003 only.

	$425	$350	$325	$275	$225	$175	$135

Last MSR was $599.

**Dean Icon Ultima
courtesy Armadillo Enterprises**

ICON PZ (MODEL DGK-ICPZ, AMERICAN SPIRIT ICON PZ) - offset double cutaway round bottom mahogany body, arched flame maple top, set-in mahogany neck, 22-fret rosewood fingerboard with dot inlay, 2-point floating tremolo, chrome hardware, offset V-shaped headstock, 3-per-side Grover tuners, 2 "Zebra" humbuckers, bridge-mounted piezo pickup, 2 volume/1 tone controls, 3-way magnetic pickup selector, 3-way magnetic/piezo pickups selector, available in Flame Cherry Sunburst, Flame Blue, Flame Purple, or Flame Red finish, mfg. 1997-99.

	$625	$550	$475	$400	$325	$275	$225

Last MSR was $799.

Earlier versions of this model were available in Trans. Cherry Sunburst, Trans. Blue, Trans. Purple, and Trans. Red high gloss finish.

ICON FLAME EUROPEAN CUSTOM (MODEL DGE-ICFL) - offset double cutaway round bottom mahogany body, arched flame top, set-in mahogany neck, 22-fret rosewood fingerboard with pearl dot inlay, tune-o-matic bridge/stop tailpiece, small offset V-shape peghead with screened logo, 3-per-side Schaller tuners, chrome hardware, 2 "Zebra" humbuckers, volume/tone controls, 3-position switch, available in Flame Amber, Flame Amberburst, Flame Green, Flame Purple, or Flame Red finish, mfg. 1998-99.

	$700	$600	$525	$450	$375	$325	$250

Last MSR was $999.

This model was produced in Europe.

European Premium Icon Premium Flame (DGE-PR-IC) - similar to the Icon Flame European Custom, except features highly figured maple top, wood bound body, pearl block fingerboard inlays, gold hardware, 2 Seymour Duncan humbuckers, available in Flame Amber, Flame Amberburst, Flame Black, Flame Blue, Flame Cherry Sunburst, Flame Green, Flame Purple, or Flame Red finish, mfg. 1998-99.

	$850	$775	$700	$600	$525	$425	$325

Last MSR was $1,299.

This model is produced in Europe.

ELECTRIC: JAMMER SERIES

JAMMER - offset double cutaway hardwood body, bolt-on maple neck, 22-fret rosewood fingerboard with dot inlay, locking tremolo, blackface peghead with screened logo, black pickguard, 6-on-a-side tuners, chrome hardware, 2 single coil/1 humbucker exposed pole piece pickups, volume/tone controls, 5-way pickup selector, available in Black, Blue Purpleburst, Gun Metal Grey, Pearl Purpleburst, Pearl Red, Pink, or White finish, mfg. 1987-89.

	N/A	$250	$225	$200	$175	$150	$125

Last MSR was $549.

**Dean Icon AX
courtesy Armadillo Enterprises**

GRADING	100% MINT	98% NEAR MINT	95% EXC+	90% EXC	80% VG+	70% VG	60% G

ELECTRIC: ML SERIES

The ML is a cross between the Flying V and the Explorer - designed like a Flying V with the treble horn of the Explorer up front.

ML FLAME - Flying V-style with treble horn mahogany body, 'V'-shaped strings plate, mahogany neck, 22-fret bound rosewood fingerboard with pearl dot inlay, Tune-O-Matic bridge/strings through-body tailpiece, Dean wing peghead with screened logo, 3-per-side Kluson tuners, chrome hardware, 2 DiMarzio humbucker pickups, 2 volume/1 tone controls, 3-position switch, available in Black, Braziliaburst, Cherry, Cherryburst, Metallic or White finish, mfg. 1978-1985.

	N/A	$1,200	$1,050	$950	$825	$700	$550

Last MSR was $1,100.

In 1981, Blueburst, Pearl and Pinkburst finish were introduced.

ML STANDARD - similar to ML Flame, except has bound maple top, ebony fingerboard, Grover tuners, available in Black, Braziliaburst, Cherry, Cherryburst, Metallic, or White finish, mfg. 1977-1986.

	N/A	$1,250	$1,100	$950	$825	$700	$550

Last MSR was $1,190.

This model had optional Black, Cream, Multiple, and White body binding. In 1981, Blueburst, Pearl and Pinkburst finishes were introduced.

U.S.A. SERIES ML-92 - single horn cutaway V-shape mahogany body, carved figured maple top, V-shape strings plate, Through-body mahogany neck, 22-fret bound ebony fingerboard with pearl dot inlay, Schaller tune-o-matic bridge/strings through-body tailpiece, V-shape peghead with screened logo, 3-per-side tuners, chrome hardware, 2 exposed humbucker pickups, 2 volume/1 tone controls, 3-position switch, available in Cherry Sunburst, Natural, Trans. Blue, or Trans. Red finish, mfg. 1992-93.

	N/A	$1,100	$950	$850	$725	$625	$475

Last MSR was $1,600.

The U.S.A. series was manufactured in Northern California.

ML REISSUE - single horn cutaway V-shape hardwood body, through-body mahogany neck, 22 bound rosewood fingerboard with pearl dot inlay, double locking vibrato, V-shape peghead with screened logo, 3-per-side tuners, chrome hardware, 2 exposed humbucker pickups, 2 volume/1 tone controls, 3-position switch, available in Black finish, mfg. 1992-94.

	N/A	$475	$400	$350	$300	$250	$200

Last MSR was $800.

Add $50 for Lightning Graphic finish.

The Reissue series was manufactured in Korea.

ML NECK-THROUGH (MODEL ACML) - single horn cutaway V-shape alder body, V-shape strings plate, through-body maple neck, 22-fret bound rosewood fingerboard with pearl dot inlay, fixed bridge, V-shape peghead with screened logo, 3-per-side tuners, chrome hardware, 2 Seymour Duncan humbucker pickups, volume/2 tone controls, 3-position switch, available in Classic Black, Classic Red, Torrid Teal, or Wine Red finish, mfg. 1996-97.

$950	$825	$700	$600	$525	$425	$325

Last MSR was $1,345.

Add $30 for Floyd Rose tremolo.

ML BOLT-ON (MODEL ACXML) - similar to the ML Neck-Through, except has a bolt-on maple neck, 2 Bill Lawrence humbuckers, mfg. 1996-97.

$675	$600	$525	$450	$375	$300	$225

Last MSR was $925.

Add $30 for Floyd Rose tremolo.

USX ML - single horn cutaway V-shape alder body, bolt-on maple neck, 22-fret rosewood fingerboard with dot inlay, Floyd Rose licensed tremolo, blackface peghead with screened logo, 3-per-side tuners, chrome hardware, 2 Duncan-designed humbuckers, 1 volume/2 tone controls, 3-way switch, available in Cherry Sunburst, Classic Black, Metallic Red, or Vintage Sunburst finish, mfg. 1996-97.

$525	$450	$395	$350	$275	$225	$175

Last MSR was $689.

USX ML Pro - similar to the USX ML, except has ash body, Sperzel tuners, 2 Bill Lawrence L500 humbuckers, available in Trans. Black, Trans. Blue, Trans. Cherry, or Vintage Sunburst finish, mfg. 1996-97.

$575	$525	$450	$395	$325	$275	$200

Last MSR was $789.

ML COUPE (USA CUSTOM SHOP) - single horn cutaway V-shaped mahogany body, set-in mahogany neck, 22-fret ebony fingerboard with dot inlay, Tune-O-Matic bridge/V-shaped stop tailpiece, V-shaped peghead with screened logo, 3-per-side Grover tuners, chrome hardware, 2 Seymour Duncan humbucker pickups, volume/2 tone controls, 3-position switch, available in Brite Blue, Canary Yellow, Cherry Sunburst, Classic Black, or Lipstick Red solid finish, mfg. 1997-98.

$1,050	$950	$850	$750	$625	$500	$395

Last MSR was $1,599.

ML Deluxe - similar to the ML Coupe, except has Original Floyd Rose tremolo, available in Braziliaburst, Brite Blue, Canary Yellow, Classic Black, or Lipstick Red solid finish, mfg. 1997-98.

$1,000	$900	$800	$725	$650	$500	$375

Last MSR was $1,499.

ML LTD (USA Custom Shop) - similar to the ML Coupe, except has bound body/fingerboard/headstock, available in Braziliaburst, Cherry Sunburst, Classic Black, Trans. Blue, or Trans. Red finish, mfg. 1997-98.

$1,300	$1,150	$1,025	$875	$750	$625	$475

Last MSR was $1,899.

GRADING	100% MINT	98% NEAR MINT	95% EXC+	90% EXC	80% VG+	70% VG	60% G

U.S. PHANTOM ML (USA CUSTOM SHOP) - single horn cutaway V-shaped mahogany body, set-in mahogany neck, 22-fret ebony fingerboard (no inlay), large V-shaped peghead with screened logo, 3-per-side Grover tuners, Original Floyd Rose tremolo, all black hardware, 2 Seymour Duncan humbucker pickups, 2 volume/1 tone controls, 3-position switch, available in Classic Black finish only, mfg. 1996-98.

	$1,400	$1,200	$1,000	$925	$775	$650	$500

Last MSR was $1,999.

ML Phantom X (Model DGK-MLPX) - similar to the U.S. Phantom ML, except has a basswood body, bolt-on maple neck, 22-fret rosewood fingerboard, tune-o-matic bridge/V-shaped stop tailpiece, 2 Dean Phantom Rail humbuckers, available in Classic Black finish only, mfg. 1998-2003.

	$295	$270	$245	$215	$160	$135	$100

Last MSR was $429.

ML Phantom XT (Model DGK-MLPXT) - similar to the U.S. Phantom ML, except has a basswood body, bolt-on maple neck, 22-fret rosewood fingerboard, licensed Floyd Rose tremolo, 2 Dean Phantom Rail humbuckers, available in Classic Black finish only, mfg. 1998-2002.

	$375	$322	$275	$245	$210	$160	$135

Last MSR was $529.

ML Phantom Standard (Model DGK-MLPST) - similar to the U.S. Phantom ML, except has 22-fret rosewood fingerboard, tune-o-matic bridge/V-shaped stop tailpiece, 2 Dean Phantom Rail humbuckers, available in Classic Black finish only, mfg. 1998-2002.

	$395	$365	$335	$295	$250	$200	$150

Last MSR was $549.

ML (PHANTOM) STANDARD (MODEL DGK-MLST, AMERICAN SPIRIT ML STANDARD) - single horn cutaway V-shaped mahogany body, set-in mahogany neck, 22-fret rosewood fingerboard with dot inlay, tune-o-matic bridge/V-shaped stop tailpiece, chrome hardware, large V-shaped headstock, 3-per-side Grover tuners, 2 "Zebra" humbuckers, 2 volume/1 tone controls, 3-way selector, available in Classic Black, Trans. Blue, Trans. Braziliaburst, or Trans. Red finish, mfg. 1997-2002.

	$395	$365	$335	$295	$250	$200	$150

Last MSR was $549.

Dean ML Standard
courtesy Armadillo Enterprises

ML SELECT (MODEL DGK-MLSE) - similar to the ML Standard, except has triple bound flame maple top, triple bound headstock, block fingerboard inlays, gold hardware, available in Flame Blue, Flame Braziliaburst, Flame Cherry Sunburst, Flame Red, Metallic Black, or Metallic Red finish, mfg. 1998-2002.

	$425	$375	$325	$275	$225	$175	$125

Last MSR was $599.

ML ULTRA (MODEL DGK-MLUL, AMERICAN SPIRIT ML ULTRA) - similar to the ML Standard, except has licensed Floyd Rose tremolo, available in Classic Black, Trans. Blue, Trans. Braziliaburst, or Trans. Red finish, mfg. 1997-99.

	$600	$525	$450	$375	$325	$250	$195

Last MSR was $749.

Add $20 for left-handed configuration (Model DGK-MLUL-L), available in Classic Black and Trans. Red finishes.

ML X (MODEL DGK-MLX, AMERICAN SPIRIT ML X) - single horn cutaway V-shaped basswood body, bolt-on maple neck, 22-fret rosewood fingerboard with dot inlays, tune-o-matic bridge/V-shaped stop tailpiece, large V-shape peghead with screened logo, 3-per-side Grover tuners, chrome hardware, 2 "Zebra" humbuckers, 2 volume/1 tone controls, 3-position switch, available in (Trans.) Braziliaburst, Classic Black, Transparent Blue, or Trans. Red finish, mfg. 1997-present.

MSR $375		$250	$220	$195	$175	$150	$125	$95

Add $50 for left-handed configuration (Model DGK-MLXL), available in Classic Black and Trans. Braziliaburst (disc.) finishes.

ML XT (Model DGK-MLXT, American Spirit ML XT) - similar to the ML X, except has licensed Floyd Rose tremolo, available in (Trans.) Braziliaburst, Classic Black, Trans. Blue, or Trans. Red finish, mfg. 1997-2003.

	$325	$285	$265	$225	$195	$165	$125

Last MSR was $429.

Add $20 for left-handed configuration (Model DGK-MLXTL), available in Classic Black and Transparent Braziliaburst finishes

ML Noir XT (MLPXT) - similar to the ML XT except has triple black finish, Blade pickups, is available in Classic Black finish, mfg. 2003-present.

MSR $665		$440	$390	$350	$300	$250	$200	$150

ML '79 (79ML) - reissue of the 1979 ML model with a Floyd Rose Tremolo, Grover tuners, available in classic black, Classic White, Trans. Braziliaburst, or Trans. Cherry Sunburst, mfg. 2003-present.

MSR $750		$495	$425	$375	$325	$275	$225	$175

Add $80 for left-handed configuration.

ML '79F - similar to the ML '79 except has flamed maple top, available in Trans. Braziliaburst or Classic Black finish, mfg. 2003-present.

MSR $940		$615	$550	$475	$425	$375	$325	$275

Dean ML Ultra
courtesy Armadillo Enterprises

GRADING	100% MINT	98% NEAR MINT	95% EXC+	90% EXC	80% VG+	70% VG	60% G

ML USA PROFESSIONAL - ML body style, mahogany body, mahogany set-neck, 22-fret rosewood fingerboard with dot inlay, traditional Dean headstock with three-per-side tuners, Tune-O-Matic bridge, V style tailpiece, two humbucker pickups, four knobs, three-way switch, chrome hardware, available in Dark Cherry, Natural, Rosewood, or Walnut finish, mfg. 2004-present.

MSR $2,000	$1,300	$1,150	$1,000	$900	$800	$700	$600

ML USA TIME CAPSULE - ML body shape, mahogany body with maple top, DiMarzio custom pickups, other features similar to the original, available in Classic Black, Trans. Amberburst, Trans. Brazilburst, Trans. Cherry Sunburst, or Trans. Red, mfg. 2000-03.

	$1,950	$1,625	$1,350	$1,150	$1,000	$850	$700

Last MSR was $2,599.

ELECTRIC: MACH SERIES

Both the Mach I and Mach V models were designed in 1985, and had a very limited production run in Korea. The Mach VII was designed the same year, but produced in the U.S. There are very few of the Mach Series instruments in circulation.

MACH V - single cutaway hardwood body, exaggerated treble horn/extended lower bout, bolt-on maple necks, 24-fret rosewood fingerboard with dot inlays, 3-per-side shrimp fork headstock, traditional vibrato, chrome hardware, 2 humbuckers, volume/tone controls, available in Jet Black, Pearl Blueburst, Pearl Red, or Pearl White finish, mfg. 1985-86.

	N/A	$300	$260	$230	$195	$160	$130

Last MSR was $499.

Mach I - Similar to the Mach V, except has a 6-on-a-side headstock, mfg. 1985-86.

	N/A	$300	$260	$230	$195	$160	$130

Last MSR was $499.

Mach VII - similar to the Mach V construction (U.S. built), available in special Leopard, Tiger, and other exotic finish, mfg. 1985-86.

	N/A	$1,200	$1,050	$900	$800	$700	$600

Last MSR was $1,999.

It is estimated that only a handful were built

MACH V (REISSUE) - reissue of the original Mach V, available in Classic Black or Metallic White finish, mfg. 2001-02.

	$325	$275	$235	$185	$150	$125	$100

Last MSR was $439.

Mach 5X (Reissue) - Similar to the Mach V, available in Classic Black finish only, mfg. 2001-02.

	$485	$450	$405	$360	$325	$275	$200

Last MSR was $679.

ELECTRIC: MICHAEL SCHENKER SERIES

MICHAEL SCHENKER STANDARD - V-style guitar, basswood body, bolt-on maple neck, 22-fret rosewood fingerboard with dot inlay, matching traditional Dean headstock with three-per-side tuners, two humbucker pickups, three knobs, three-way switch, chrome hardware, Schenker Classic Black and White finish, new 2005.

MSR $500	$325	$275	$240	$210	$180	$150	$120

MICHAEL SCHENKER CUSTOM - V-style guitar, mahogany body, mahogany neck, body and neck binding, 22-fret rosewood fingerboard with dot inlay, matching traditional Dean headstock with three-per-side tuners, two zebra Schenker custom would humbucker pickups, three knobs, three-way switch, chrome hardware, Schenker Classic Black and White finish, case included, new 2005.

MSR $1,375	$900	$800	$725	$650	$575	$500	$425

MICHAEL SCHENKER USA - V-style guitar, mahogany body, mahogany neck, custom black and white opposing body and neck binding, 22-fret rosewood fingerboard with pearl block inlay, matching traditional Dean headstock with three-per-side tuners, two zebra Schenker custom wound humbucker pickups, three knobs, three-way switch, chrome hardware, hand-painted Schenker Classic Black and White finish, case included, new 2005.

MSR $3,800	$2,500	$2,200	$1,950	$1,700	$1,500	$1,300	$1,100

ELECTRIC: PALOMINO/PSYCHOBILLY

PALOMINO - single cutaway ES-5 style hollow body archtop, 2 f-holes, 21-fret rosewood fingerboard with pearl block inlays, three-per-side tuners, Tune-O-Matic bridge with music staff tailpiece, black pickguard, three P-90 pickups, two knobs, five-way switch, available in Classic Black, Natural, Florida Orange, Sea Green, or Vintage Sunburst finish, 16 in. width, 24.75 in. scale, mfg. summer 2004-present.

MSR $690	$450	$390	$350	$300	$250	$200	$150

PSYCHOBILLY - single smooth cutaway Jazz style hollow body archtop, 2 f-holes, 22-fret rosewood fingerboard with pearl block inlays, three-per-side tuners, classic tremolo system, black pickguard, two humbucker pickups, four knobs, three-way switch, black hardware, available in Cabbie (Yellow with white and black checkered sides), Natural, or Picasso finish, 16 in. width, 24.75 in. scale, mfg. summer 2004-present.

MSR $690	$450	$390	$350	$300	$250	$200	$150

Subtract $50 for Natural finish.

ELECTRIC: PLAYMATE SERIES

For the current Playmate series, refer to Playmate in the P section.

PLAYMATE - Offset double cutaway hardwood body, bolt-on maple neck, 22-fret rosewood fingerboard with dot inlay, traditional vibrato, blackface peghead with screened logo, black pickguard, 6-on-a-side tuners, chrome hardware, 3 single coil exposed pole piece pickups, volume/tone controls, 5-way pickup selector, available in Black, Red, and White finish, mfg. 1987-89.

	N/A	$200	$160	$130	$105	$80	$55

Last MSR was $349.

D

GRADING	100% MINT	98% NEAR MINT	95% EXC+	90% EXC	80% VG+	70% VG	60% G

ELECTRIC: SS SERIES

The SS model was introduced in 1998, and features an offset double cutaway body similar to a superstrat design. Dean´s Practice Pack (Model DGP-GPP1) is an all-in-one starter system that includes an SS-One electric guitar, a Stack in the Box headphone amp, a guitar strap, Dean picks, and a guitar tuner. This complete package retails for $349. The Stagecoach (Model DGP-GSP2) is a similar all-in-one starter system that includes an SS-One electric guitar, a Dean Mean 16 guitar amp, a guitar strap, Dean picks, and a guitar tuner. This complete package retails for $449.

SS-ONE (MODEL DGK-SS1) - offset double cutaway basswood body, bolt-on maple neck, 22-fret rosewood fingerboard with dot inlays, 2-point floating tremolo, graphite nut, small offset V-shaped wood peghead with screened logo, 3-per-side Grover tuners, chrome hardware, white pearloid pickguard, 2 single coil/humbucker pickups, volume/2 tone controls, 5-position switch, available in Classic Black, Trans. Blue, or Trans. Red finish, mfg. 1998-99.

	$225	$175	$150	$130	$110	$90	$70

Last MSR was $299.

Add $20 for left-handed configuration (Model DGK-SS1L), available in Classic Black and Transparent Red finishes.

SS PLUS (MODEL DGK-SS+) - similar to the SS-One, except features flame maple top, available in Flame Black, Flame Blue, Flame Braziliaburst, Flame Cherry Sunburst, Flame Red, Metallic Black, Metallic Charcoal, or Metallic Red finish with matching headstock, mfg. 1998-99.

	$275	$250	$225	$195	$150	$125	$100

Last MSR was $399.

Add $20 for left-handed configuration (Model DGK-SS+L), available in Flame Blue and Flame Braziliaburst finishes.

SS ULTRA (MODEL DGK-SSUL) - similar to the SS-One, except features 24-fret fingerboard, no pickguard, licensed Floyd Rose tremolo, available in Metallic Black, Metallic Green, Metallic Purple, or Metallic Red finish with matching headstock, mfg. 1998-99.

	$425	$375	$325	$275	$250	$195	$150

Last MSR was $599.

ELECTRIC: SIGNATURE SERIES

The Signature Series was Dean´s first Korean production guitar series, and was introduced in 1985.

DEAN Z AUTOGRAPH - offset double cutaway hardwood body, bolt-on maple neck, 22-fret white painted fingerboard with dot inlay, double locking tremolo, blackface peghead with screened logo, mirror pickguard, 6-on-a-side tuners, chrome hardware, 2 single coil/1 humbucker exposed pole piece pickups, volume/tone controls, 5-way pickup selector, available in Electric Blue, Hot Flamingo, Ice White, Jet Black, Lemon-Lime, or Rock-It Red fluorescent finish, mfg. 1985-87.

	N/A	$300	$260	$220	$180	$140	$100

Last MSR was $349.

ELECTRIC: STYLISH JAZZ SERIES

STYLISH STANDARD (STY STD) - single cutaway hollow body archtop, flame maple top, mahogany back/sides, set mahogany neck, 20-fret rosewood fingerboard with dot inlay, f-holes, two covered humbucker pickups, Tune-o-matic bridge, trapeze tailpiece, two knobs, one switch, 3-per-side Grover tuners, gold hardware, available in Gloss Natural, Trans. Red, or Vintage Sunburst finish, mfg. 2001-04.

	$450	$400	$350	$300	$250	$200	$150

Last MSR was $690.

STYLISH PHANTOM (NOIR STYN) - similar to the Stylish Standard except has triple black hardware in Black finish only, disc. 2004.

	$450	$400	$350	$300	$250	$200	$150

Last MSR was $690.

STYLISH DELUXE (STY DLX) - similar to the Stylish Standard except has spruce top, flamed maple back and sides, block inlays, and abalone multi-ply binding, available in Gloss Natural or Vintage Sunburst finish, mfg. 2001-04.

	$600	$525	$475	$425	$375	$325	$250

Last MSR was $925.

ELECTRIC: V SERIES

The Dean V was Zelinsky´s variation of a ´58 Flying V.

V FLAME - Flying V-shaped mahogany body, V-shaped strings plate, mahogany neck, 22-fret bound rosewood fingerboard with pearl dot inlay, tune-o-matic bridge/strings Through-body tailpiece, V-shape peghead with screened logo, 3-per-side Kluson tuners, chrome hardware, 2 humbucker DiMarzio pickups, 2 volume/1 tone controls, 3-position switch, available in Black, Braziliaburst, Cherry, Cherryburst, Metallic, or White finish, mfg. 1978-1985.

	N/A	$1,200	$1,050	$900	$750	$600	$450

Last MSR was $1,100.

In 1981, Blueburst, Pearl and Pinkburst finishes were introduced.

Dean SS-One
courtesy Armadillo Enterprises

Dean V Standard
courtesy Armadillo Enterprises

GRADING	100% MINT	98% NEAR MINT	95% EXC+	90% EXC	80% VG+	70% VG	60% G

V STANDARD - similar to V Flame, except has bound maple top, ebony fingerboard, Grover tuners, available in Black, Braziliaburst, Cherry, Cherryburst, Metallic, or White finish, mfg. 1977-1986.

	N/A	$1,250	$1,100	$900	$750	$600	$450

Last MSR was $1,190.

This model had an optional black, cream and white body binding. In 1981, Blueburst, Pearl and Pinkburst finish were introduced.

HOLLYWOOD V - Flying V-shaped hardwood body, bolt-on maple neck, 24-fret rosewood fingerboard with pearl dot inlay, tune-o-matic bridge/stop tailpiece, body matching small fork peghead with screened logo, 3-per-side tuners, chrome hardware, 2 humbucker pickups, volume/tone controls, 3-position switch, available in Black, Blueburst, Bolt, Flames, Pearl Blue, Pearl Pink, Pearl Red, Pearl White, Red, Wedge, White, or Zebra Graphic finish, mfg. 1985-87.

	N/A	$300	$270	$230	$195	$160	$130

Last MSR was $500.

Hollywood V V - similar to Hollywood V, except has double locking vibrato, mfg. 1985-87.

	N/A	$350	$300	$250	$210	$170	$140

Last MSR was $600.

V NECK-THROUGH (MODEL ACDV) - Flying V-shaped alder body, V-shaped strings plate, through-body maple neck, 22-fret bound rosewood fingerboard with pearl dot inlay, fixed bridge, V-shape peghead with screened logo, 3-per-side tuners, chrome hardware, 2 Seymour Duncan humbucker pickups, volume/2 tone controls, 3-position switch, available in Classic Black, Classic Red, Torrid Teal, or Wine Red finish, mfg. 1996-97.

	$950	$825	$700	$600	$525	$425	$325

Last MSR was $1,345.

Add $30 for Floyd Rose tremolo.

V PHANTOM (MODEL PHXDV) - similar to the V Neck-Through, except has no fingerboard inlays, black hardware, 2 Bill Lawrence humbuckers, available in Gloss Black finish only, mfg. 1996-97.

$675	$600	$525	$475	$425	$350	$275

Last MSR was $995.

Add $50 for Floyd Rose tremolo.

V BOLT-ON (MODEL ACXDV) - similar to the V Neck-Through, except has a bolt-on maple neck, 2 Bill Lawrence humbuckers, mfg. 1996-97.

$575	$500	$425	$350	$300	$275	$225

Last MSR was $925.

Add $30 for Floyd Rose tremolo.

V COUPE (USA CUSTOM SHOP) - Flying V-shaped mahogany body, set-in mahogany neck, 22-fret ebony fingerboard with dot inlay, Tune-O-Matic bridge/V-shaped stop tailpiece, V-shaped peghead with screened logo, 3-per-side Grover tuners, chrome hardware, 2 Seymour Duncan humbucker pickups, volume/2 tone controls, 3-position switch, available in Brite Blue, Canary Yellow, Cherry Sunburst, Classic Black, or Lipstick Red solid finish, mfg. 1997-98.

$1,050	$950	$850	$750	$625	$500	$375

Last MSR was $1,599.

V Deluxe - similar to the V Coupe, except has Original Floyd Rose tremolo, available in Braziliaburst, Brite Blue, Canary Yellow, Classic Black, or Lipstick Red solid finish, mfg. 1997-98.

$1,000	$900	$800	$725	$650	$500	$375

Last MSR was $1,499.

V LTD (USA Custom Shop) - similar to the V Coupe, except has bound body/fingerboard/headstock, available in Braziliaburst, Cherry Sunburst, Classic Black, Trans. Blue, or Trans. Red finish, mfg. 1997-98.

$1,300	$1,150	$1,025	$875	$750	$625	$475

Last MSR was $1,899.

Korina V (U.S. Mfg.) - similar to the V Coupe, except has korina body, available in Braziliaburst, Cherry Sunburst, Gloss Natural, Trans. Amber, or Trans. Red high gloss finish, mfg. 1997-98.

$1,200	$1,050	$950	$850	$750	$650	$495

Last MSR was $1,899.

U.S. PHANTOM V (USA CUSTOM SHOP) - Flying V-shaped mahogany body, set-in mahogany neck, 22-fret ebony fingerboard (no inlay), large V-shaped peghead with screened logo, 3-per-side Grover tuners, Original Floyd Rose tremolo, all black hardware, 2 Seymour Duncan humbucker pickups, 2 volume/1 tone controls, 3-position switch, available in Classic Black finish only, mfg. 1998 only.

$1,400	$1,200	$1,000	$925	$775	$650	$500

Last MSR was $1,999.

V STANDARD (MODEL DGK-VST) - Flying V-shaped mahogany body, set-in mahogany neck, 22-fret rosewood fingerboard with dot inlay, tune-o-matic bridge/V-shaped stop tailpiece, chrome hardware, large V-shaped headstock, 3-per-side Grover tuners, 2 Zebra humbuckers, 2 volume/1 tone controls, 3-way selector, available in Classic Black, Trans. Blue, Trans. Braziliaburst, or Trans. Red finish, mfg. 1998-99.

$425	$375	$325	$275	$250	$195	$150

Last MSR was $599.

V PLATINUM (MO. DGK-VPLA) - similar to the V Standard except has a fully bound body, block fingerboard inlays, grover tuners, available in Classic Black, Metallic Red, or Metallic Charcoal finish, mfg. 1998-2001.

$295	$250	$215	$190	$150	$125	$100

Last MSR was $399.

GRADING	100% MINT	98% NEAR MINT	95% EXC+	90% EXC	80% VG+	70% VG	60% G

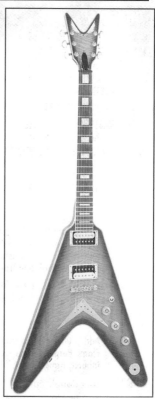

V SELECT (MODEL DGK-VSE) - similar to the V Standard, except has triple bound flame maple top, triple bound headstock, block fingerboard inlays, gold hardware, available in Flame Blue, Flame Braziliaburst, Flame Cherry Sunburst, Flame Red, Metallic Black, or Metallic Red finish, mfg. 1998-2001.

	$425	$375	$325	$275	$225	$175	$125

Last MSR was $599.

V ULTRA (MODEL DGK-VUL) - similar to the V Standard, except has licensed Floyd Rose tremolo, available in Classic Black, Trans. Blue, Trans. Braziliaburst, or Trans. Red finish, mfg. 1998 only.

	$600	$525	$450	$375	$325	$250	$195

Last MSR was $749.

V X (MODEL DGK-VX, AMERICAN SPIRIT V X) - Flying V-shaped basswood body, bolt-on maple neck, 22-fret rosewood fingerboard with dot inlays, tune-o-matic bridge/V-shaped stop tailpiece, large V-shape peghead with screened logo, 3-per-side Grover tuners, chrome hardware, 2 "Zebra" humbuckers, 2 volume/1 tone controls, 3-position switch, available in (Trans.) Braziliaburst, Classic Black, Trans. Blue, or Trans. Red finish, mfg. 1997-present.

MSR $375		$250	$220	$195	$175	$150	$125	$95

Add $50 for left-handed configuration (Model DGK-VXL), available in Classic Black finish only.

V XT (Model DGK-VXT) - similar to the V X, except has licensed Floyd Rose tremolo, available in (Trans.) Braziliaburst, Classic Black, Trans. Blue, or Trans. Red finish, mfg. 1998-2003.

	$300	$275	$225	$195	$165	$125	$95

Last MSR was $419.

Add $20 for left-handed configuration (Model DGK-VXTL), available in Classic Black and Transparent Braziliaburst finishes (disc.).

V Noir XT - similar to the V X except has a mahogany body with maple top, triple black hardware, blade pickups, available in Classic Black finish, mfg. 2002-03.

	$375	$335	$280	$240	$205	$175	$135

Last MSR was $519.

Dean V Select
courtesy Armadillo Enterprises

V '79 (79V) - reissue based off of the 1979 model V, available in Classic Black, Classic White, Trans. Braziliaburst, or Trans. Cherry Sunburst, mfg. 2003-present.

MSR $750		$495	$425	$375	$325	$275	$225	$175

KORINA V EUROPEAN CUSTOM (MODEL DGE-KV) - Flying V-shaped korina body, set-in korina neck, 22-fret rosewood fingerboard with pearl dot inlay, tune-o-matic bridge/V-shaped stop tailpiece, large V-shape peghead with screened logo, 3-per-side Schaller tuners, gold hardware, 2 "Zebra" humbuckers, 2 volume/1-tone controls, 3-position switch, available in Gloss Natural, Trans. Amber, Trans. Braziliaburst, or Trans. Red finish, mfg. 1998-99.

	$675	$600	$525	$450	$375	$325	$250

Last MSR was $999.

V USA PROFESSIONAL - V body style, mahogany body, mahogany set-neck, 22-fret rosewood fingerboard with dot inlay, traditional Dean headstock with three-per-side tuners, Tune-O-Matic bridge, V style tailpiece, two humbucker pickups, four knobs, three-way switch, chrome hardware, available in Dark Cherry, Natural, Rosewood, or Walnut finish, mfg. 2004-present.

MSR $2,000		$1,300	$1,150	$1,000	$900	$800	$700	$600

V USA TIME CAPSULE - V body shape, mahogany body with maple top, DiMarzio custom pickups, other features similar to the original, available in Classic Black, Trans. Amberburst, Trans. Brazilburst, Trans. Cherry Sunburst, or Trans. Red, mfg. 2000-03.

	$1,950	$1,625	$1,350	$1,150	$1,000	$850	$700

Last MSR was $2,599.

ELECTRIC: VENDETTA SERIES

VENDETTA 1.0 - offset double cutawawy Showmaster style, mahogany body, bolt-on maple neck, 24-fret rosewood fingerboard with dot inlay, three-per-side tuners, Tune-O-Matic bridge, STB, two exposed humbucker pickups, two knobs, three-way switch, black hardware, available in Classic Black or Natural finish, 25.5 in. scale, mfg. 2004-present.

MSR $375		$250	$210	$180	$160	$140	$120	$100

VENDETTA 2.0 - offset double cutawawy Showmaster style, mahogany body with flame maple top, bolt-on maple neck, 24-fret rosewood fingerboard with dot inlay, three-per-side tuners, Tune-O-Matic bridge, STB, two covered humbucker pickups, two knobs, three-way switch, nickel hardware, available in Tiger Eye, Trans. Amber, Trans. Black, or Trans. Red finish, 25.5 in. scale, mfg. 2004-present.

MSR $550		$360	$310	$270	$230	$190	$160	$130

VENDETTA 3.0 - offset double cutawawy Showmaster style, mahogany body, set maple neck, 24-fret rosewood fingerboard with razor wire inlay, three-per-side tuners, Tune-O-Matic bridge, STB, two covered humbucker pickups, two knobs, three-way switch, black hardware, available in Classic Black, Copper Orange, or Flip Pearl finish, 25.5 in. scale, mfg. 2004-present.

MSR $701		$460	$400	$350	$300	$260	$220	$180

Dean V XT
courtesy Armadillo Enterprises

GRADING	100% MINT	98% NEAR MINT	95% EXC+	90% EXC	80% VG+	70% VG	60% G

VENDETTA 4.0 - offset double cutawawy Showmaster style, mahogany body with quilted maple top and back, set maple neck, 24-fret rosewood fingerboard with razor wire inlay, three-per-side tuners, Tune-O-Matic bridge, STB, two covered humbucker pickups, two knobs, three-way switch, nickel hardware, available in Tiger Eye, Trans. Amber, or Trans. Blue finish, 25.5 in. scale, mfg. 2004-present.

	MSR	$800		$525	$450	$400	$350	$300	$250	$200

ELECTRIC: X SERIES

The X model body design was a newer model to the 1990s, and had an offset double cutaway body that is reminiscent of a sleek superstrat design.

AMERICAN CUSTOM ACX (BOLT-ON) - offset double cutaway alder body, bolt-on maple neck, 24-fret rosewood fingerboard with pearl dot inlay, fixed or Wilkinson bridge (or Floyd Rose tremolo), 'shrimp fork' blackface peghead with screened logo, 3-per-side tuners, chrome hardware, 2 slanted single coil/humbucker Seymour Duncan pickups, 1 volume/2 tone controls, 5-position switch, available in Classic Black, Classic Red, Torrid Teal, or Wine Red finish, mfg. 1996-97.

	$600	$550	$500	$450	$350	$250	$200

Last MSR was $885.

Add $30 for Big V headstock (in Black). Add $50 for Big V headstock (color matched). Add $50 for flame maple top, alder body, available in Flame Black, Flame Blue, Flame Braziliaburst, Flame Cherry, Flame Cherry Sunburst, Flame Green, Flame Purple, Flame Teal, and Flame Vintage Sunburst finish. Add $60 for ash body and translucent finish, available in Trans. Black, Trans. Blue, Trans. Braziliaburst, Trans. Cherry, Trans. Cherry Sunburst, Trans. Green, Trans. Purple, Trans. Teal, and Trans. Vintage Sunburst finishes.

American Custom ACSL (Neck-Through) - similar to the American Custom ACX, except features a maple through-neck design, Floyd Rose tremolo, mfg. 1996-97.

	$800	$700	$625	$550	$500	$400	$325

Last MSR was $1,299.

Add $100 for flame maple top, alder body, available in Flame Black, Flame Blue, Flame Braziliaburst, Flame Cherry, Flame Cherry Sunburst, Flame Green, Flame Purple, Flame Teal, and Flame Vintage Sunburst finishes. Add $100 for ash body and trans. finish, available in Trans. Black, Trans. Blue, Trans. Braziliaburst, Trans. Cherry, Trans. Cherry Sunburst, Trans. Green, Trans. Purple, Trans. Teal, or Trans. Vintage Sunburst finishes.

USX - offset double cutaway alder body, bolt-on maple neck, 24-fret rosewood fingerboard with dot inlay, Wilkinson VS10 bridge, blackface peghead with screened logo, 6-on-a-side tuners, chrome hardware, 2 slanted single coil/1 humbucker Duncan Designed pickups, 1 volume/2 tone controls, 5-position switch, available in Cherry Sunburst, Classic Black, Metallic Red, or Vintage Sunburst finish, mfg. 1996-97.

	$350	$300	$275	$225	$195	$150	$125

Last MSR was $489.

USX Pro - similar to the USX, except has ash body, available in Trans. Black, Trans. Blue, Trans. Cherry, or Vintage Sunburst finish, mfg. 1996-98.

	$400	$350	$325	$295	$250	$195	$150

Last MSR was $589.

USXL - similar to the USX, except has Floyd Rose tremolo, available in Cherry Sunburst, Classic Black, Metallic Red, or Vintage Sunburst finish, mfg. 1996-98.

	$425	$375	$350	$325	$275	$225	$175

Last MSR was $589.

USXL Pro - similar to the USXL, except has ash body, available in Trans. Black, Trans. Blue, Trans. Cherry, or Vintage Sunburst finish, mfg. 1996-98.

	$450	$400	$375	$350	$300	$250	$200

Last MSR was $689.

ELECTRIC: Z SERIES

The Z was the first Dean model announced, and the body design resembles an Explorer.

Z FLAME - Explorer-style mahogany body, mahogany neck, 22-fret bound rosewood fingerboard with pearl dot inlay, tune-o-matic bridge/stop tailpiece, V-shape peghead with screened logo, 3-per-side Kluson tuners, chrome hardware, 2 humbucker DiMarzio pickups, 2 volume/1 tone controls, 3-position switch, available in Black, Braziliaburst, Cherry, Cherryburst, Metallic or White finish, mfg. 1978-1985.

	N/A	$1,200	$1,050	$900	$750	$600	$450

Last MSR was $1,100.

In 1981, Blueburst, Pearl and Pinkburst finishes were introduced.

Z STANDARD - similar to Z Flame, except has bound maple top, ebony fingerboard, Grover tuners, available in Black, Braziliaburst, Cherry, Cherryburst, Metallic or White finish, mfg. 1977-1986.

	N/A	$1,250	$1,100	$900	$750	$600	$450

Last MSR was $1,190.

This model had an optional black, cream and white body binding. In 1981, Blueburst, Pearl and Pinkburst finishes were introduced.

HOLLYWOOD Z - Explorer-style hardwood body, bolt-on maple neck, 24-fret rosewood fingerboard with pearl dot inlay, tune-o-matic bridge/stop tailpiece, body matching small fork peghead with screened logo, 3-per-side tuners, chrome hardware, 2 humbucker pickups, volume/tone controls, 3-position switch, available in Black, Blueburst, Bolt, Flames, Pearl Blue, Pearl Pink, Pearl Red, Pearl White, Red, Wedge, White, or Zebra Graphic finish, mfg. 1985-87.

	N/A	$300	$270	$230	$195	$160	$130

Last MSR was $350.

Hollywood Z V - similar to Hollywood Z, except has double locking vibrato, mfg. 1985-87.

	N/A	$350	$300	$250	$210	$170	$140

Last MSR was $450.

GRADING	100% MINT	98% NEAR MINT	95% EXC+	90% EXC	80% VG+	70% VG	60% G

D

Z COUPE (USA CUSTOM SHOP) - Explorer-style mahogany body, set-in mahogany neck, 22-fret ebony fingerboard with dot inlay, Tune-O-Matic bridge/V-shaped stop tailpiece, V-shaped peghead with screened logo, 3-per-side Grover tuners, chrome hardware, 2 Seymour Duncan humbucker pickups, volume/2 tone controls, 3-position switch, available in Brite Blue, Canary Yellow, Cherry Sunburst, Classic Black, or Lipstick Red solid finish, mfg. 1997-98.

	$1,050	$950	$850	$750	$625	$500	$375

Last MSR was $1,599.

Z Deluxe - similar to the Z Coupe, except has Original Floyd Rose tremolo, available in Braziliaburst, Brite Blue, Canary Yellow, Classic Black, or Lipstick Red solid finish, mfg. 1997-98.

	$1,000	$900	$800	$725	$650	$500	$375

Last MSR was $1,499.

Z LTD (USA Custom Shop) - similar to the Z Coupe, except has bound body/fingerboard/headstock, available in Braziliaburst, Cherry Sunburst, Classic Black, Trans. Blue, or Trans. Red finish, mfg. 1997-98.

	$1,300	$1,150	$1,025	$875	$750	$625	$475

Last MSR was $1,899.

Korina Z (U.S. Mfg.) - similar to the Z Coupe, except has korina body, available in Braziliaburst, Cherry Sunburst, Gloss Natural, Trans. Amber, or Trans. Red high gloss finish, mfg. 1997-98.

	$1,200	$1,050	$950	$850	$750	$650	$495

Last MSR was $1,899.

U.S. PHANTOM Z (USA CUSTOM SHOP) - Explorer-style mahogany body, set-in mahogany neck, 22-fret ebony fingerboard (no inlay), large V-shaped peghead with screened logo, 3-per-side Grover tuners, Original Floyd Rose tremolo, all black hardware, 2 Seymour Duncan humbucker pickups, 2 volume/1 tone controls, 3-position switch, available in Classic Black finish only, mfg. 1998 only.

	$1,400	$1,200	$1,000	$925	$775	$650	$500

Last MSR was $1,999.

Z STANDARD (MODEL DGK-ZST, AMERICAN SPIRIT Z STANDARD) - Explorer-style mahogany body, set-in mahogany neck, 22-fret rosewood fingerboard with dot inlay, tune-o-matic bridge/V-shaped stop tailpiece, chrome hardware, large V-shaped headstock, 3-per-side Grover tuners, 2 "Zebra" humbuckers, 2 volume/1 tone controls, 3-way selector, available in Classic Black, Trans. Blue, Trans. Braziliaburst, or Trans. Red finish, mfg. 1998 only.

	$425	$375	$325	$275	$250	$195	$150

Last MSR was $599.

Dean Z Standard courtesy Armadillo Enterprises

Z PLATINUM - similar to the Z Standard except has a fully bound body, block fingerboard inlays, grover tuners, available in Classic Black, Metallic Red, or Metallic Charcoal finish, mfg. 1998-2001.

	$295	$250	$215	$190	$150	$125	$100

Last MSR was $399.

Z SELECT (MODEL DGK-ZSE) - similar to the Z Standard, except has triple bound flame maple top, triple bound headstock, block fingerboard inlays, gold hardware, available in Flame Blue, Flame Braziliaburst, Flame Cherry Sunburst, Flame Red, Metallic Black, or Metallic Red finish, mfg. 1998-2001.

	$425	$375	$325	$275	$225	$175	$125

Last MSR was $599.

Z ULTRA (MODEL DGK-ZUL, AMERICAN SPIRIT Z ULTRA) - similar to the Z Standard, except has licensed Floyd Rose tremolo, available in Classic Black, Trans. Blue, Trans. Braziliaburst, or Trans. Red finish, mfg. 1997-98.

	$600	$525	$450	$375	$325	$250	$175

Last MSR was $749.

Z X (MODEL DGK-ZX, AMERICAN SPIRIT Z X) - Explorer-style basswood body, bolt-on maple neck, 22-fret rosewood fingerboard with dot inlays, tune-o-matic bridge/V-shaped stop tailpiece, large V-shape peghead with screened logo, 3-per-side Grover tuners, chrome hardware, 2 "Zebra" humbuckers, 2 volume/1 tone controls, 3-position switch, available in (Trans.) Braziliaburst, Classic Black, Trans. Blue, or Trans. Red finish, mfg. 1997-present.

MSR $375	$250	$220	$195	$175	$150	$125	$95

Add $20 for left-handed configuration (Model DGK-ZXL), available in Trans. Red finish only.

Z XT (Model DGK-ZXT, American Spirit Z XT) - similar to the Z X, except has licensed Floyd Rose tremolo, available in (Trans.) Braziliaburst, Classic Black, Trans. Blue, or Trans. Red finish, mfg. 1997-98.

	$325	$295	$275	$225	$195	$165	$125

Last MSR was $449.

Z Noir XT - similar to the Z XT except has triple black hardware, and Blade pickups, available in Classic Black finish only, mfg. 2002-03.

	$375	$335	$280	$240	$205	$175	$135

Last MSR was $519.

Z '79 - reissue based off of the original model Z in 1979, available in Classic Black, Classic White, Trans. Braziliburst, or Trans. Cherry Sunburst, mfg. 2003-present.

MSR $750	$495	$425	$375	$325	$275	$225	$175

Dean Z X courtesy Armadillo Enterprises

D

GRADING	100% MINT	98% NEAR MINT	95% EXC+	90% EXC	80% VG+	70% VG	60% G

KORINA Z EUROPEAN CUSTOM (MODEL DGE-KZ) - Explorer-style korina body, set-in korina neck, 22-fret rosewood fingerboard with pearl dot inlay, tune-o-matic bridge/V-shaped stop tailpiece, large V-shape peghead with screened logo, 3-per-side Schaller tuners, gold hardware, 2 "Zebra" humbuckers, 2 volume/1 tone controls, 3-position switch, available in Gloss Natural, Trans. Amber, Trans. Braziliaburst, or Trans. Red finish, mfg. 1998 only.

	$675	$600	$525	$450	$375	$325	$250

Last MSR was $999.

Z USA PROFESSIONAL - V body style, mahogany body, mahogany set-neck, 22-fret rosewood fingerboard with dot inlay, traditional Dean headstock with three-per-side tuners, Tune-O-Matic bridge, V-style tailpiece, two humbucker pickups, four knobs, three-way switch, chrome hardware, available in Dark Cherry, Natural, Rosewood, or Walnut finish, mfg. 2004-present.

MSR $2,000	$1,300	$1,150	$1,000	$900	$800	$700	$600

Z USA TIME CAPSULE - Z body shape, mahogany body with maple top, DiMarzio custom pickups, other features similar to the original, available in Classic Black, Trans. Amberburst, Trans. Brazilburst, Trans. Cherry Sunburst, or Trans. Red, mfg. 2000-03.

	$1,950	$1,625	$1,350	$1,150	$1,000	$850	$700

Last MSR was $2,599.

ELECTRIC BASS: 90'S SERIES

The DB series of electric bass models were produced in Korea from 1991 to 1996. All instruments in this series were available in Black, Blueburst, Grayburst, Red, and White finishes (unless otherwise listed).

DB 91 - offset double cutaway alder body with slap contour area (pop slot) on lower bout, bolt-on maple neck, 24-fret rosewood with pearl wings inlay, fixed bridge, 2-per-side tuners, chrome hardware, P/J-style pickups, 2 volume/1 tone controls, 3-position switch, mfg. 1991-96.

	$300	$250	$210	$180	$150	$120	$90

Last MSR was $425.

> **Add $20 for fretless fingerboard (Model DB 91 F).**

This model was offered in a left-handed configuration as the DB 91 L. In 1995, Grayburst and Red finish were disc; Flame Cherry Sunburst finish was introduced.

DB 94 - similar to DB 91, except has black hardware, volume/treble/bass/blend controls, no 3-position switch, active electronics, mfg. 1991-96.

	$400	$350	$300	$260	$230	$200	$150

Last MSR was $595.

In 1995, Black, Grayburst, Red, and White finishes were disc; Black Flame Maple and Vintage Sunburst finishes were introduced.

DB 95 - similar to DB 91, except has 5-string configuration, 3/2-per-side tuners, gold hardware, volume/treble/bass/blend controls, no 3-position switch, active electronics, mfg. 1991-96.

	$450	$400	$350	$300	$250	$200	$150

Last MSR was $630.

DB 6X - Similar to DB 95, except has 6-string configuration, 3-per-side tuners, mfg. 1995-96.

	$475	$425	$350	$300	$250	$200	$150

Last MSR was $640.

ELECTRIC BASS: BRIAN BROMBERG SERIES

There are Brian Bromberg Signature Series to be produced in the U.S. later in 2003. There are no retail prices or specs on these yet.

B SQUARED 4 - offset double cutaway basswood body with quilted maple top, maple/rosewood neck-thru design, 24-fret rosewood fingerboard with 12th fret inlay, 2 Custom Dean pickups, 3-band EQ, Piezo pickups under each string with seperate volume and EQ, matching color headstock, 4-on-one-side Grover tuners, black hardware, available in Trans. Amber, Trans. Black, Trans Teal, or Trans. Amberburst, mfg. 2002-present.

MSR $1,250	$825	$725	$650	$575	$500	$425	$350

B SQUARED 5 - similar to the B Squared 4 except in five-string configuration, 3/2-per-side tuners, same colors as the 4-string version, mfg. 2002-present.

MSR $1,375	$895	$825	$750	$675	$600	$525	$450

ELECTRIC BASS: EDGE SERIES

The entire range of Edge bass models debuted in 1998. The Bespeak (Model DGP-BP) is an all-in-one starter system that includes an Edge One electric bass, a Dean bass amp, a guitar strap, Dean picks, and a guitar tuner. This complete package retails for $469.

EDGE ONE (NO. DGB-E1) - offset double cutaway basswood body, bolt-on maple neck, 24-fret rosewood fingerboard with white dot inlay, fixed bridge, small offset V-shaped peghead with screened logo, 2-per-side die-cast tuners, chrome hardware, 2 soapbar pickups, 2 volume/1 tone controls, available in Classic Black, Trans. Amberburst, Trans. Red, or Classic White finish, mfg. 1998-present.

MSR $375	$250	$220	$195	$175	$150	$125	$95

> **Add $30 for left-handed configuration.**

Edge One-5 - similar to the Edge One except in five-string configuration, available in Classic Black, Metallic Red, or Trans. Amberburst, mfg. 2001-present.

MSR $465	$300	$250	$220	$195	$165	$135	$105

EDGE 4 (NO. DGB-EDGE4) - offset double cutaway basswood body, bolt-on laminated maple neck, 34 in. scale, 24-fret rosewood fingerboard with white dot inlay, fixed bridge, small offset V-shaped peghead with screened logo, 2-per-side die-cast tuners, black hardware, 2 EMG-HZ soapbar pickups, 2 volume/1 tone controls, available in Classic Black, Powder Silver, Trans. Amberburst, Trans. Black, Trans. Blue, Trans. Goldenburst, Trans. Purple, or Trans. Red finish, mfg. 1998-present.

MSR $525	$350	$300	$260	$220	$190	$160	$130

> **Add $50 for left-handed configuration (No. DGB-EDGE4L), available in Trans. Black or Trans. Red finishes.**

GRADING	100% MINT	98% NEAR MINT	95% EXC+	90% EXC	80% VG+	70% VG	60% G

Edge 5 (No. DGB-EDGE5) - similar to the Edge 4, except features 5-string configuration, 35 in. scale, 3/2-per-side tuners, available in Classic Black, Powder Silver, Trans. Black, Trans. Blue, Trans. Goldenburst, Trans. Purple, Trans. Amberburst, or Trans. Red finish, mfg. 1998-present.

MSR $625	$410	$350	$300	$250	$200	$170	$135

Add $50 for left-handed configuration (No. DGB-EDGE5L), available in Trans. Black or Trans. Red finish.

Edge 6 (No. DGB-EDGE6) - similar to the Edge 4, except features 6-string configuration, 35 in. scale, 3-per-side tuners, available in Classic Black, Trans. Black, Trans. Blue, Trans. Goldenburst, Trans. Purple, or Trans. Red finish, mfg. 1998-present.

MSR $750	$495	$425	$375	$325	$275	$225	$175

Add $20 for left-handed configuration (Model DGB-EDGE6L), available in Transparent Black finish only.

Edge 8 - similar to the Edge 4 except in 8-string configuration, 4-per-side tuners, available in Classic Black finish, mfg. 2003-present.

MSR $800	$525	$450	$400	$350	$300	$250	$200

EDGE 4 FRETLESS (NO. DGB-E4FRLS) - similar to the Edge 4, except has a fretless fingerboard, available in Trans. Black, Trans. Goldenburst, or Trans. Red finish, mfg. 1998-present.

MSR $565	$375	$325	$285	$245	$205	$165	$125

Edge 5 Fretless (No. DGB-E5FRLS) - similar to the Edge 4 Fretless, except features 5-string configuration, 35 in. scale, 3/2-per-side tuners, available in Trans. Black, Trans. Goldenburst, or Trans. Red finish, mfg. 1998-present.

MSR $665	$435	$390	$350	$300	$250	$200	$150

Edge 6 Fretless (No. DGB-E6FRLS) - similar to the Edge 4 Fretless except features 6-string configuration, 3-per-side tuners, available in Classic Black finish only, mfg. 1999-present.

MSR $800	$525	$450	$400	$350	$300	$250	$200

EDGE HAMMER - similar to the Edge 4 except has a mahogany body, active electronics, available in natural oil finish only, mfg. 2003-present.

MSR $750	$495	$425	$375	$325	$275	$225	$175

Edge Hammer 5 - similar to the Edge Hammer, except in five-string configuration, mfg. 2003-present.

MSR $875	$575	$500	$425	$375	$325	$275	$225

Edge Hammer 10 - similar to the Edge Hammer, except in ten-string configuration, mfg. 2004-present.

MSR $940	$615	$550	$475	$400	$350	$300	$250

EDGE PRO - similar to the Edge 4 except has neck-thru construction, Dean 3D Preamp, Bass Clef inlay, gold hardware, available in Tiger Eye, Trans. Black, Trans. Amberburst, or Trans. Braziliaburst finish, mfg. 2003-present.

MSR $875	$575	$500	$425	$375	$325	$275	$225

Edge Pro 5 - similar to the Edge Pro, except in five-string configuration, mfg. 2003-present.

MSR $1,000	$650	$575	$500	$425	$375	$325	$275

Dean Edge 4
courtesy Dave Rogers
Dave's Guitar Shop

EDGE 4 CUSTOM (NO. DGB-EC4) - offset double cutaway mahogany body, flame maple top, bolt-on laminated maple neck, 34 in. scale, 24-fret rosewood fingerboard with white dot inlay, fixed bridge, small offset V-shaped peghead with screened logo, 2-per-side die-cast tuners, black hardware, 2 EMG-HZ soapbar pickups, 2 volume/1 tone controls, active electronics, available in Flame Amber, Flame Black, Flame Blue, Flame Goldenburst, or Flame Red finish, mfg. 1998-2002.

$440	$385	$335	$295	$260	$195	$150

Last MSR was $619.

Add $20 for left-handed configuration (Model DGB-EC4L), available in Flame Amber finish only.

Edge 5 Custom (No. DGB-EC5) - similar to the Edge 4 Custom, except features 5-string configuration, 35 in. scale, 3/2-per-side tuners, available in Flame Amber, Flame Black, Flame Blue, Flame Goldenburst, or Flame Red finish, mfg. 1998-2002.

$530	$425	$375	$325	$295	$250	$195

Last MSR was $699.

Add $20 for left-handed configuration (Model DGB-EC5L), available in Flame Amber finish only.

Edge 6 Custom (No. DGB-EC6) - similar to the Edge 4 Custom, except features 6-string configuration, 35 in. scale, 3-per-side tuners, available in Flame Amber, Flame Black, Flame Blue, Flame Goldenburst, or Flame Red finish, mfg. 1998 only.

$525	$450	$400	$350	$300	$250	$195

Last MSR was $699.

EDGE 4 CUSTOM PZ (NO. DGB-EC4PZ) - similar to the Edge 4 Custom, except has 2 EMG-HZ soapbar pickups/Shadow piezo bridge pickup, 2 volume/2 tone controls, active electronics, available in Flame Black, Flame Blue, Flame Goldenburst, Flame Purple, or Flame Red finish, mfg. 1998-99.

$500	$425	$375	$325	$275	$225	$175

Last MSR was $699.

Edge 5 Custom PZ (No. DGB-EC5PZ) - similar to the Edge 4 Custom PZ, except features 5-string configuration, 35 in. scale, 3/2-per-side tuners, available in Flame Black, Flame Blue, Flame Goldenburst, Flame Purple, or Flame Red finish, mfg. 1998-99.

$575	$500	$425	$375	$325	$275	$225

Last MSR was $799.

Dean Edge 5 Custom
courtesy Armadillo Enterprises

D

GRADING	100% MINT	98% NEAR MINT	95% EXC+	90% EXC	80% VG+	70% VG	60% G

EDGE SELECT 4 (NO. DGB-ES4) - offset double cutaway mahogany body, flame maple top, through-body laminated maple neck, 34 in. scale, 24-fret rosewood fingerboard with white dot inlay, fixed bridge, small offset V-shaped peghead with screened logo, 2-per-side die-cast tuners, black hardware, 2 EMG-HZ soapbar pickups, 2 volume/2 tone controls, active electronics, available in Flame Amber, Flame Black, Flame Blue, Flame Goldenburst, or Flame Red finish, mfg. 1998-2002.

	$575	$500	$425	$375	$325	$275	$225

Last MSR was $799.

Edge Select 5 (No. DGB-ES5) - similar to the Edge Select 4, except features 5-string configuration, 35 in. scale, 3/2-per-side tuners, available in Flame Amber, Flame Black, Flame Blue, Flame Goldenburst, or Flame Red finish, mfg. 1998-2002.

	$625	$550	$475	$400	$350	$300	$225

Last MSR was $869.

Edge Select 6 (Model DGB-ES6) - similar to the Edge Select 4, except features 6-string configuration, 35 in. scale, 3-per-side tuners, available in Flame Amber, Flame Black, Flame Blue, Flame Goldenburst, or Flame Red finish, mfg. 1998 only.

	N/A	$600	$525	$450	$375	$325	$250

Last MSR was $799.

EDGE EXCEL 4 (MODEL DGB-EE4) - Offset double cutaway mahogany body, flame maple top, through-body laminated maple neck, 34 in. scale, 24-fret rosewood fingerboard with white block inlay, fixed bridge, small offset V-shaped peghead with screened logo, 2-per-side Grover tuners, gold hardware, 2 EMG pickups, 2 volume/2 tone controls, EMG active electronics, available in Flame Amber, Flame Black, Flame Blue, Flame Goldenburst, or Flame Red finish, mfg. 1998 only.

	$695	$600	$525	$450	$375	$325	$250

Last MSR was $999.

Edge Excel 5 (Model DGB-EE5) - similar to the Edge Excel 4, except features 5-string configuration, 35 in. scale, 3/2-per-side tuners, available in Flame Amber, Flame Black, Flame Blue, Flame Goldenburst, or Flame Red finish, mfg. 1998 only.

	$750	$650	$575	$500	$425	$350	$275

Last MSR was $1,049.

Edge Excel 6 (Model DGB-EE6) - similar to the Edge Excel 4, except features 6-string configuration, 35 in. scale, 3-per-side tuners, available in Flame Amber, Flame Black, Flame Blue, Flame Goldenburst, or Flame Red finish, mfg. 1998 only.

	$795	$675	$595	$525	$450	$375	$295

Last MSR was $1,099.

EDGE IMPROV 4 (MODEL DGB-EI4) - offset double cutaway alder body, flame maple top, through-body laminated maple neck, 34 in. scale, 24-fret rosewood fingerboard with white block inlay, fixed bridge, small offset V-shaped peghead with screened logo, 2-per-side Schaller tuners, gold hardware, 2 EMG pickups, 2 volume/2 tone controls, active electronics, available in Flame Amber, Flame Blue, Flame Honeyburst, Flame Purple, Flame Red, or Satin Natural finish, mfg. 1998-2002.

	$775	$675	$575	$495	$395	$350	$275

Last MSR was $1,299.

Edge Improv 5 (Model DGB-EI5) - similar to the Edge Improv 4, except features 5-string configuration, 35 in. scale, 3/2-per-side tuners, available in Flame Amber, Flame Black, Flame Blue, Flame Goldenburst, or Flame Red finish, mfg. 1998-2002.

	$875	$775	$675	$575	$495	$395	$315

Last MSR was $1,450.

EDGE Q4 - similar to the Edge 4 Series basses, except have a quilted maple top (hence the Q prefix), lighter basswood body, and a smoother neck, available in Quilt Amberburst, Quilt Black, Quilt Blue, or Quilt Red, mfg. 1999-present.

MSR $690	$450	$375	$325	$275	$225	$175	$140

Add $40 for Trans. finish. Add $80 for Bartolini pickups.

Edge Q5 - Similar to the Edge Q4 except in five-string configuration, available in the same finishes as the Q4, mfg. 1999-present.

MSR $815	$530	$450	$375	$325	$275	$225	$175

Add $15 for Trans. finishes.

Edge Q6 - Similar to the Edge Q4 except in six-string configuration, available in the same finishes as the Q4, mfg. 1999-present.

MSR $875	$575	$500	$425	$350	$300	$250	$200

ELECTRIC BASS: EIGHTY EIGHT SERIES

EIGHTY EIGHT BASS - offset double cutaway maple body, bolt-on maple neck, 20-fret ebanol fingerboard with dot inlay, fixed bridge, black-face peghead with screened logo, black pickguard, 4-on-a-side tuners, chrome hardware, P-style EMG Select pickup, volume/tone controls, available in Black, Blue Purpleburst, Gun Metal Grey, Pearl Purpleburst, Pearl Red, Pink, or White finish, mfg. 1987-89.

	N/A	$300	$260	$230	$195	$160	$130

ELECTRIC BASS: JEFF BERLIN SERIES

JEFF BERLIN STANDARD - offset double cutaway alder body, bolt-on 3-piece maple neck with ebony fingerboard, 21 frets, dot position markers, 34 in. scale, Schaller tuners, gold hardware, Custom Bartolini pickups, available in Trans. Amberburst, Trans. Green or Trans. Red finish, disc. 2003.

	$750	$675	$625	$575	$500	$450	$375

Last MSR was $999.

JEFF BERLIN EXOTIC - similar to Jeff Berlin Standard, except has choice of redwood burl, zebrawood or quilted maple top, available in Natural finish, disc. 2003.

	$1,125	$1,025	$925	$825	$725	$625	$525

Last MSR was $1,499.

GRADING	100% MINT	98% NEAR MINT	95% EXC+	90% EXC	80% VG+	70% VG	60% G

D

ELECTRIC BASS: ML SERIES

ML BASS I - Flying V-style with treble horn mahogany body, maple neck, 22-fret bound rosewood fingerboard with pearl dot inlay, fixed bridge, wing shaped peghead with screened logo, 2-per-side Kluson tuners, chrome hardware, humbucker coil pickup, volume/tone controls, active electronics, available in Black, Blueburst, Pearl Blue, Pearl Pink, Pearl Red, Pearl White, Red, or White finish, mfg. 1980-85.

	N/A	$850	$775	$700	$625	$550	$450

Last MSR was $1,050.

ML BASS II - similar to ML I, except has bound figured maple top, 2 humbucker pickups, 2 volume/1 tone controls, mfg. 1980-85.

	N/A	$1,000	$875	$800	$700	$600	$500

Last MSR was $1,200.

ML VINTAGE BASS (MODEL DGB-MLBX) - Flying V-style with treble horn basswood body, bolt-on maple neck, 24-fret rosewood fingerboard with white dot inlay, fixed bridge, V-shaped peghead with screened logo, 2-per-side tuners, chrome hardware, P/J-style pickups, 2 volume/1 tone controls, available in Classic Black, Trans. Blue, Trans. Braziliaburst, or Trans. Red finish, mfg. 1998-present.

MSR $465		$300	$250	$220	$195	$165	$135	$105

BABY ML BASS - down-sized Flying V-style with treble horn poplar body, poplar neck, 22-fret rosewood fingerboard with pearl dot inlay, fixed bridge, body matching peghead with screened logo, 2-per-side tuners, chrome hardware, single coil pickup, volume/tone controls, available in Black, Blueburst, Pearl Blue, Pearl Pink, Pearl Red, Pearl White, Red or White finish, mfg. 1983-85.

	N/A	$500	$425	$350	$275	$200	$125

ELECTRIC BASS: MACH SERIES

These models were designed in 1985, and had very limited production runs. There are very few of either Mach bass guitar models in circulation.

MACH V BASS - single cutaway hardwood body, exaggerated treble horn/extended lower bout, bolt-on maple necks, 24-fret rosewood fingerboard with dot inlays, 2-per-side shrimp fork headstock, fixed bridge, chrome hardware, P/J-style pickups, volume/tone controls, available in Jet Black, Pearl Blueburst, Pearl Red, or Pearl White finish, mfg. 1985-86.

	N/A	$600	$525	$450	$375	$300	$225

Last MSR was $499.

MACH VII BASS - similar to the Mach V construction (U.S. built), available in special Leopard, Tiger, and other exotic finishes, mfg. 1985-86.

	N/A	$1,300	$1,150	$1,000	$850	$750	$650

Last MSR was $1,999.

ELECTRIC BASS: MISC. SERIES

CADILLAC BASS (CADIB) - Cadillac body style, set-neck, P/J pickups, active electronics, available in Classic Black finish, mfg. 2004-present.

MSR $750		$495	$425	$375	$325	$275	$225	$175

DEMONATOR - offset double cutaway explorer style mahogany body, neck-thru design, Traditional V-style Dean headstock, MOP hourglass inlays, two active soapbar pickups, 3 knobs, 2-per-side Grover tuners, black hardware, available in Black finish only, mfg. 2003-present.

MSR $750		$495	$425	$375	$325	$275	$225	$175

This model was design with the Genitorturers bass player Evil D Vincent. According to Evil D, "You can get the guitar in any color ...as long as it's black."

EVO XM - single cutaway all wood body, bolt-on maple neck, 24-fret rosewood fingerboard with dot inlay, two-per-side tuners, two humbucker pickups, three knobs, black hardware, Natural finish, 30 in. scale, mfg. summer 2004-present.

MSR $276		$180	$150	$125	$100	$80	$60	$40

PLAYMATE BASS - offset double cutaway hardwood body, bolt-on maple neck, 20-fret rosewood fingerboard with dot inlay, fixed bridge, blackface peghead with screened logo, black pickguard, 4-on-a-side tuners, chrome hardware, P-style pickups, volume/tone controls, available in Black, Red, or White finish, mfg. 1987-89.

	N/A	$200	$160	$130	$105	$80	$55

Last MSR was $359.

SB BASS - offset double cutaway alder or mahogany body, maple neck-through design, 34 in. scale, 24-fret rosewood with pearl dot inlay (wings inlay at 12th fret), fixed bridge, 2-per-side tuners, black hardware, 2 J-style pickups, volume/treble/bass/blend controls, active electronics, mfg. 1995-96.

	$1,000	$925	$825	$725	$625	$525	$400

Last MSR was $1,695.

This model had an optional curly maple top.

Dean Edge Q4 Bass
Courtesy Dean

Dean ML Bass
courtesy Armadillo Enterprises

GRADING	100% MINT	98% NEAR MINT	95% EXC+	90% EXC	80% VG+	70% VG	60% G

SLEDGEHAMMER 4 (SLHAM4) - offset double cutaway, all mahogany body and neck, bolt-on neck, rosewood fingerboard, single high output pickup, active electronics, Grover tuners, available in Satin Natural finish, mfg. 2004-present.

MSR $790	$525	$450	$400	$350	$300	$250	$195

Sledgehammer 4 Ash (SLHAMA4) - similar to the Sledgehammer, except has a solid swamp ash body, maple neck with maple fingerboard and 12th fret Dean D inlay, Natural finish, new 2005.

MSR $839	$550	$475	$425	$375	$325	$275	$225

Sledgehammer 5 (SLHAM5) - similar to the Sledgehammer 4, except in 5-string configuration, new 2004.

MSR $870	$575	$500	$425	$375	$325	$275	$225

Sledgehammer 5 Ash (SLHAMA5) - similar to the Sledgehammer 5, except has a solid swamp ash body, maple neck with maple fingerboard and 12th fret Dean D inlay, Natural finish, new 2005.

MSR $924	$600	$525	$450	$400	$350	$300	$250

STYLIST B1 (STYB) - single cutaway hollow archtop body, floating Tune-O-Matic bridge, trapeze tailpiece, cat's-eye sound holes, two pickups, available in Pearl Black or Vintage Sunburst finish, mfg. 2004-present.

MSR $626	$425	$375	$325	$275	$225	$175	$125

ELECTRIC BASS: PACE SERIES

PACE 4 - stand-up thin bodied bass (similar to Clevinger, etc.), solid maple thru-neck body, fretless rosewood fingerboard, open-style headstock with two-per-side tuners, piezo bridge with Buffer preamp, single knob on side, black chrome hardware, avaialble in Classic Black, Metallic Red, Natural, or IBL finish, mfg. summer 2004-present.

MSR $1,000	$650	$575	$500	$450	$400	$350	$300

PACE 5 - similar to the Pace 4, except in five-string configuration with 3/2-per-side tuners, mfg. summer 2004-present.

MSR $1,251	$825	$725	$650	$575	$500	$450	$400

ELECTRIC BASS: RAZOR SERIES

RAZOR 1 - offset double cutaway basswood body, bolt-on maple neck, 24-fret rosewood fingerboard with dot inlay, 2 Dean Session pickups, 3 silver knobs, 2-per-side die-cast tuners, chrome hardware, available in Cranberry, Metallic Charcoal, or Powder Silver finish, mfg. 2000-03.

			$285	$235	$195	$160	$135	$115	$95

Last MSR was $399.

Razor 1-5 - similar to the Razor 1 except in five-string configuration with 3/2-per-side tuners, available in Metallic Charcoal or Powder Silver finish, mfg. 2002-03.

			$335	$260	$225	$195	$150	$125	$105

Last MSR was $469.

RAZOR STANDARD - offset double cutaway ash body, bolt-on maple and walnut neck, 24-fret rosewood fingerboard with abalone dot inlay, 2 Dean Session pickups, Dean 3D preamp, five silver knobs, black headstock, 2-per-side Grover tuners, brushed chrome hardware, available in natural oil, mfg. 2000-03.

			$425	$375	$325	$260	$210	$150	$125

Last MSR was $599.

This model was also available in Trans. Black and Trans. Purple finishes prior to 2002.

RAZOR PHANTOM - similar to the Razor Standard except features all black hardware, available in Powder Black finish only, mfg. 2000-02.

			$465	$405	$345	$290	$250	$200	$145

Last MSR was $649.

RAZOR NT - offset double cutaway alder body with quilted maple top, maple and walnut neck, neck-thru construction, 24-fret rosewood fingerboard with abalone dot inlays, 2 Dean Session pickups, Dean 3D preamp, five silver knobs, black headstock, 2-per-side Grover tuners, gold hardware, available in natural oil, Trans. Amberburst, or Trans. Red finish, mfg. 2000-03.

			$575	$500	$450	$395	$350	$275	$225

Last MSR was $799.

Razor NT-5 - similar to the Razor NT except in five-string configuration, available in Quilted Amberburst finish, mfg. 2002-03.

			$635	$550	$495	$440	$375	$295	$250

Last MSR was $899.

ELECTRIC BASS: RHAPSODY SERIES

RHAPSODY 1 - scroll-shaped double cutaway basswood body, bolt-on maple neck, 24-fret rosewood fingerboard with abalone dot inlays, 1 Soapbar pickup, black headstock, 2-per-side Die-cast tuners, 2 knobs, black hardware, available in Classic Black finish only, mfg. 2000-03.

			$260	$225	$175	$150	$125	$95	$75

Last MSR was $369.

RHAPSODY HB - scroll-shaped double cutaway semi-hollow mahogany body, bolt-on maple and walnut neck, 24-fret rosewood fingerboard with abalone dot inlays, 1 soap bar pickup, black headstock, 2-per-side Die-cast tuners, 2 knobs, black hardware, available in Trans. Amberburst finish only, mfg. 2000-present.

MSR $625	$410	$350	$300	$250	$200	$170	$135

This model is also available in a fretless version (Rhapsody HBF) with an Ebinol fingerboard for no additional cost.

RHAPSODY 4BB - scroll-shaped double cutaway mahogany body with a bubinga top, bolt-on maple and walnut neck, 24-fret rosewood fingerboard with abalone dot inlays, 2 EMG-HZ pickups, Dean 3D preamp, Dean 2-piece anchor bridge system, five knobs, black headstock, 2-per-side tuners, black hardware, available in bubinga finish, mfg. 2002-03.

			$425	$375	$325	$275	$225	$175	$150

Last MSR was $599.

GRADING	100% MINT	98% NEAR MINT	95% EXC+	90% EXC	80% VG+	70% VG	60% G

RHAPSODY Q4 - similar to the Rhapsody 4BB except has a quilted maple top, available in Trans. Amberburst, Trans. Black, Trans. Purple, or Trans. Red, mfg. 2000-03.

	$425	$375	$325	$275	$225	$175	$150

Last MSR was $599.

RHAPSODY 5BB - similar to the Rhapsody 4BB except in five-string configuration, 3/2-per-side tuners, available in bubinga finish only, mfg. 2002-03.

	$495	$425	$375	$325	$275	$225	$175

Last MSR was $699.

RHAPSODY Q5 - similar to the Rhapsody Q4 except in five-string configuration, 3/2-per-side tuners, available in same finish as the Q4, mfg. 2000-03.

	$495	$425	$375	$325	$275	$225	$175

Last MSR was $699.

RHAPSODY 8 - similar to the Rhapsody 4BB except is in 8-string configuration, 4-per-side tuners, available in bubinga or Trans. Black (disc.) finish, mfg. 2000-present.

MSR $865	$575	$500	$425	$375	$325	$275	$225

RHAPSODY 12 - similar to the Rhapsody 4BB except is in 12-string configuration, 6-per-side tuners, available in Trans. Black finish only, mfg. 2000-present.

MSR $990	$650	$575	$500	$425	$375	$325	$275

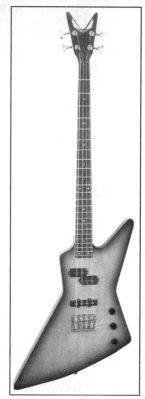

Dean Z Bass
courtesy Armadillo Enterprises

ELECTRIC BASS: VENDETTA SERIES

VENDETTA 4 - double offset body with flame maple top, bolt-on five-piece maple neck, rosewood fingerboard with razer wire inlay, two-per-side tuners, two Dean pickups, active two-band electronics, four knobs, black hardware, available in Tiger Eye, Trans. Amber, Trans. Black, or Trans. Red finish, mfg. summer 2004-present.

MSR $746	$490	$425	$375	$325	$275	$225	$175

VENDETTA 5 - similar to the Vendetta 4, except in five-string configuration and 3/2-per-side tuners, mfg. summer 2004-present.

MSR $840	$550	$475	$425	$375	$325	$275	$225

ELECTRIC BASS: X SERIES

The X Bass model body design had a sleek, offset double cutaway body. For selected models the following applies:

Add $30 for flame maple top, alder body, available in Flame Black, Flame Blue, Flame Braziliaburst, Flame Cherry, Flame Cherry Sunburst, Flame Green, Flame Purple, Flame Teal, and Flame Vintage Sunburst finishes. Add $100 for ash body and translucent finish, available in Trans. Black, Trans. Blue, Trans. Braziliaburst, Trans. Cherry, Trans. Cherry Sunburst, Trans. Green, Trans. Purple, Trans. Teal, and Trans. Vintage Sunburst finishes.

AMERICAN CUSTOM ACX B4 (BOLT-ON) - offset double cutaway alder body, bolt-on maple neck, 34 in. scale, 24-fret rosewood fingerboard with pearl dot inlay, Dean fixed bridge, shrimp fork peghead with screened logo, 2-per-side tuners, chrome hardware, 2 Seymour Duncan pickups, 2 volume/tone controls, available in Classic Black, Classic Red, Torrid Teal, or Wine Red finish, mfg. 1996-97.

	$675	$625	$550	$475	$395	$325	$250

Last MSR was $965.

AMERICAN CUSTOM ACX B5 (BOLT-ON) - similar to the American Custom ACX B4, except in a 5-string configuration, 3/2-per-side headstock, mfg. 1996-97.

	$700	$650	$595	$525	$425	$350	$250

Last MSR was $1,050.

AMERICAN CUSTOM ACS B4 (NECK-THROUGH) - similar to the American Custom ACX B4, except features a maple through-neck design, 2 Seymour Duncan soapbar pickups, mfg. 1996-97.

	$1,000	$900	$825	$750	$650	$575	$450

Last MSR was $1,550.

AMERICAN CUSTOM ACS B5 (NECK-THROUGH) - similar to the American Custom ACS B4, except in a 5-string configuration, 3/2-per-side headstock, mfg. 1996-97.

	$1,100	$950	$875	$800	$695	$600	$475

Last MSR was $1,650.

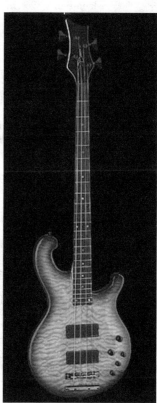

ELECTRIC BASS: Z SERIES

Z BASS I - Explorer-style mahogany body, maple neck, 22-fret bound rosewood fingerboard with pearl dot inlay, fixed bridge, V-shaped peghead with screened logo, 2-per-side Kluson tuners, chrome hardware, humbucker pickup, volume/tone control, active electronics, available in Black, Blueburst, Pearl Blue, Pearl Pink, Pearl Red, Pearl White, Red, or White finish, mfg. 1982-85.

	N/A	$650	$575	$500	$425	$350	$275

Last MSR was $1,050.

Z BASS II - similar to Z I, except has bound figured maple top, 2 humbucker pickups, 2 volume/1 tone controls, mfg. 1982-85.

	N/A	$750	$675	$600	$525	$450	$375

Last MSR was $1,200.

Dean Rhapsody Q4 Bass
Courtesy Dean

GRADING	100% MINT	98% NEAR MINT	95% EXC+	90% EXC	80% VG+	70% VG	60% G

Z VINTAGE BASS (MODEL DGB-ZBX) - Explorer-style basswood body, bolt-on maple neck, 24-fret rosewood fingerboard with white dot inlay, fixed bridge, V-shaped peghead with screened logo, 2-per-side tuners, chrome hardware, P/J-style pickups, 2 volume/1 tone controls, available in Classic Black, Trans. Blue, Trans. Braziliaburst, or Trans. Red finish, mfg. 1998-present.

MSR $465		$300	$250	$220	$195	$165	$135	$105

BABY Z BASS - Explorer-style poplar body, poplar neck, 22-fret bound rosewood fingerboard with pearl dot inlay, fixed bridge, 2-per-side tuners, chrome hardware, single coil pickup, volume/tone controls, available in Black, Blueburst, Pearl Blue, Pearl Pink, Pearl Red, Pearl White, Red, or White finish, mfg. 1983-85.

N/A		$500	$425	$375	$325	$250	$175

Last MSR was $800.

This model is not sold in the U.S., and has no current domestic MSR.

DE ARMOND BY GUILD
Instruments currently produced in Korea. DeArmond by Guild instruments are not available in the U.S. market. Distributed in Europe by Fender Musical Instruments GmbH of Dusseldorf, Germany.

Another European conundrum! The DeArmond (DeArmond by Guild) trademark is applied to a series of Guild style instruments on a product line not available in the U.S. These instruments have the DeArmond logo across the headstock.

Fender Musical Instruments Corporation products are identified by a part number that consists of a three-digit location/facility code, a four-digit model code, and a hyphen that separates the two parts (there are additional digits that continue to identify the model). In the overall scheme, a "0" designates a Fender product without a Floyd Rose tremolo, a "1" indicates a Fender product with a Floyd Rose tremolo, and a "3" indicates a Guild product (see Fender Production Model Codes).

A Rhode Island Guild product would thus be designated 3 50 - XXXX (X indicates the four-digit model code). However, the DeArmond by Guild models carry a 0 35 - XXXX production code. Internal coding would thus indicate a Fender (non-Guild) product from the Korean (33 versus 35) facility code; a "33" facility code is used for Korean-built Fender and Squire instruments. By the Fender production codes, the *Blue Book of Electric Guitars* has deduced that the following instruments are Korean products. All models listed below do not have a U.S. retail list price. There are several other models out there as well, but the whole site is in German and that makes about as much sense as Gibson's serialization!

ELECTRIC

DE ARMOND JET-STAR (MODEL 035-0200) - offset double slightly cutaway mahogany body, set-in mahogany neck, 24.625 in. scale, 22-fret bound palisander fingerboard with white block inlay, adjustable metal bridge/stop tailpiece, 3-per-side tuners, chrome hardware, black pickguard, 2 DeArmond humbucking pickups, 2 volume/2 tone controls, 3-way switch, available in Black (-506), Crimson Red Transparent (-538), Moon Blue (-596), or Tyrian Purple (-582), current mfg.

This model is not sold in the U.S., and has no current domestic MSR.

DE ARMOND M 75 (MODEL 035-7500) - single round cutaway bound Agathis solid body, maple top, raised black pickguard, set-in maple neck, 24.625 in. scale, 22-fret bound palisander fingerboard with white block inlay, tune-o-matic bridge/metal Harp tailpiece, 3-per-side tuners, chrome hardware, 2 DeArmond humbucker pickups, 2 volume/2 tone controls, 3-position switch, available in Antique Burst (-537), Black (-506), Moon Blue (-596), or Tyrian Purple (-582), current mfg.

This model is not sold in the U.S., and has no current domestic MSR.

De Armond M 75 T (Model 035-7600) - similar to the M 75, except features 2 DeArmond 2K single coil pickups, tune-o-matic bridge/Bigsby-style DeArmond tremolo, available in Antique Burst (-537), Black (-506), Blue Sparkle (-513), or Champagne Sparkle (-517). Current Mfg.

This model is not sold in the U.S., and has no current domestic MSR.

DE ARMOND STARFIRE II SPECIAL (MODEL 035-3000) - single Florentine cutaway laminated maple body, 2 f-holes, set-in maple neck, 24.625 in. scale, 22-fret bound palisander fingerboard with white dot inlay, tune-o-matic bridge/Bigsby-styled DeArmond tremolo, 3-per-side tuners, chrome hardware, raised black pickguard, 2 DeArmond 2K single coil pickups, 2 volume/2 tone controls, 3-position switch, available in Antique Burst (-537), Black (-506), or Crimson Red Trans. (-538), current mfg.

This model is not sold in the U.S., and has no current domestic MSR.

De Armond Starfire IV (Model 035-4000) - similar to the Starfire II Special, except features dual rounded cutaway semi-hollow bound laminated maple body, tune-o-matic bridge/metal Harp tailpiece, 2 DeArmond humbucker pickups, available in Antique Burst (-537), Black (-506), Crimson Red Transparent (-538), or Natural (-521), current mfg.

DE ARMOND X-155 (MODEL 035-1700) - single round cutaway semi-hollow body, bound laminated maple top, 2 bound f-holes, raised black pickguard, laminated maple back/sides, set-in neck, 24.625 in. scale, 20-fret palisander fingerboard with white block inlay, adjustable rosewood bridge/metal Harp tailpiece, 3-per-side tuners, chrome hardware, 2 DeArmond humbucker pickups, 2 volume/2 tone controls, 3-position switch, available in Antique Burst (-537), or Natural (-521), current mfg.

This model is not sold in the U.S., and has no current domestic MSR.

ELECTRIC BASS

DE ARMOND JET-STAR BASS (MODEL 035-0500) - offset double slightly cutaway mahogany body, set-in maple neck, 30.75 in. scale, 21-fret palisander fingerboard with white dot inlay, fixed bridge, 2-per-side tuners, chrome hardware, 2 DeArmond 1B single coil pickups, volume/tone controls, 3-way switch, available in Black (-506), Crimson Red Transparent (-538), Moon Blue (-596), or Tyrian Purple (-582), current mfg.

This model is not sold in the U.S., and has no current domestic MSR.

DE ARMOND STARFIRE II BASS (MODEL 035-6000) - dual rounded cutaway semi-hollow bound laminated maple body, 2 f-holes, set-in maple neck, 30.75 in. scale, 21-fret bound palisander fingerboard with white dot inlay, fixed bridge, 2-per-side tuners, chrome hardware, 2 DeArmond 2B dual-coil pickups, 2 volume/2 tone controls, 3-position switch, available in Antique Burst (-537), Black (-506), or Crimson Red Transparent (-538), current mfg.

DECCA
Instruments previously produced in Japan.

The Decca trademark was a brand name used by U.S. importers Decca Records (source: Michael Wright, *Guitar Stories*, Volume One).

DEERING BANJO COMPANY INC.
Instruments (guitar models) previously built in Lemon Grove, CA from 1989 to 1991.
Deering has produced high quality banjos in Lemon Grove since 1975.

In 1975, Greg and Janet Deering began producing the quality banjos for which the company is known. While continuing to offer innovative banjo designs, the Deerings also offer several models from entry level to professional play. Deering offers a banjo model that is tuned and played like a guitar. The **MB-6** is designed for the guitar player who doesn't have to learn banjo to play banjo. The MB-6 is also available in a 12-string configuration.

In the late 1980s, Deering offered four different solid body guitar models in two variations that carried a retail price between $1,498-$2,850. The guitar models were also offered with some custom options, but were only produced for little over one year.

For more information on Deering banjos, contact the company directly (see Trademark Index).

DEFIL
Instruments currently built in Poland.

The long-established DEFIL company is the only mass producer of guitars in Poland. DEFIL stands for Dolnoslaska Fabryka Instrumentow Lutniczyc, and have been producing guitars since the 1970s. DEFIL has been in existence since 1896. DEFIL has a wide range of solid body and semi-hollow body designs (source: Tony Bacon, *The Ultimate Guitar Book*).

DEMARINO
Instruments previously built in Copiague, NY 1973-2000.

Deeply rooted in music, Ronald J. DeMarino's career spanned four decades. DeMarino was playing New York clubs in 1956, when he had his first meeting with John D'Angelico (DeMarino was having his 1948 Gibson L-5 repaired!). D'Angelico took a liking to him, and after spending a great deal of time in his shop, DeMarino was fascinated with the idea of guitar building. DeMarino experimented for years, and finally launched his own shop. DeMarino Guitars was established in 1967, and was in continuous operation since the inception of the business. DeMarino was a second generation, family-owned business, and for 27 years specialized in the restoration of fine instruments, as well as custom building special order guitars and basses (source: Hal Hammer).

ADDITONAL INFORMATION

In addition to the quality standard model configurations, DeMarino also offered custom options such as flame maple or big leaf quilt maple tops, ebony fingerboards, abalone or MOP inlays, and other exotic woods (spalted or burled maple, burled walnut, or lacewood).

**Demarino Black Guard
courtesy Ronald J. Demarino**

ELECTRIC: CONTOUR SERIES

The **Contour Standard** (last retail was $2,715) offerd a cutaway alder or ash body, a maple set-in neck, rosewood fingerboard, Sperzel tuners, EMG pickups, and either a DeMarino custom bridge or Wilkinson tremolo system.

The **Contour Custom** (last retail was $3,240) upgraded the body woods to a Honduran mahogany body and set-in neck, as well as a figured maple top and an ebony fingerboard. A DeMarino fixed bridge and a hand rubbed nitrocellulose finish completed the package.

On a slightly different note, the **Contour Pro** (last retail was $2,400) consisted of an alder body, a maple bolt-on neck with rosewood fingerboard, and a Wilkinson tremolo combined with locking Sperzel tuners (a Floyd Rose locking tremolo system is optional).

ELECTRIC: THIN-LINE SERIES

Four models comprised the Thin-Line Series. The primary models **Pro-1** (last retail was $1,900) and **Pro-2** (last retail was $1,900) both featured an alder body, custom color lacquer finishes, and a flat-mount Wilkinson bridge. The Pro-1 had 2 single coil pickups, and the Pro-2 had 2 EMG humbuckers. The **Thin-Line Standard** (last retail was $2,300) offered a swamp ash body topped with a figured maple top, rosewood fingerboard, EMG-T pickups, and a Wilkinson Tele-bridge. The top of the line **Custom** (last retail was $2,500) had a Honduran mahogany body under the maple top, an ebony fingerboard, and two EMG humbuckers.

ELECTRIC: VINTAGE SERIES

The **Vintage** models offered a sleek single cutaway body design with finishes and parts that seem right at home in the vintage guitar market. The **TV Contour** was offered with either one single coil pickup (**Single**, last retail was $2,250) or two (**Double**, last retail was $2,350). Both models had a Honduran mahogany body and neck, a Vintage limed mahogany finish, rosewood fingerboard, and a wrap-around stud tailpiece.

The **Mary K.** (last retail was $2,250) combined a swamp ash body with a maple bolt-on neck, gold hardware, a See-Through Blonde finish, and three EMG-SV single coils.

Change the finish to a butterscotch lacquer, substitute a pair of EMG-T pickups and a black vintage-styled pickguard, and the results would be the Black Guard model (last retail was $2,150).

DEVON GUITARS
Instruments currently built in Pewaukee, WI.

Devon Guitars manufactures custom hand crafted bass instruments featuring unidirectional-fiber graphite necks. Devon uses the saying "Never settle for anything but the best." For more information contact the website or company directly (see Trademark Index).

ELECTRIC BASS

Models include the **Diamond D** ($2,395.95 for 4-string, $2,595.95 for 5-string), **Diamond J** ($2,295.95 for 4-string, $2,495.95 for 5-string), **Diamond P** ($2,195.95 for 4-string, $2,395.95 for 5-string), the **Lightwave** series ($2,695.95 for 4-string, $2,895.95 for the 5-string), and the **Grace** Series ($2,199.95 for 4-string, $2,399.95 for 5-string, $2,999.95 for 6-string, $3,399.95 for 7-string, add $200 for neck-through construction).

**Demarino Mary Kay
courtesy Ronald J. Demarino**

D

DEY
See BD Dey.

DEYOE
Instruments currently built in Denver, CO.

Luthier Eric Deyoe worked at the Colfax Guitar Shop in Denver, Colorado, before he opened up his own shop in the same town.

IMPERIAL - 18 in. wide hollow maple body with a single cutaway, f-holes, arched top and back, 4 in. body depth, 3-piece set maple neck, 24.75 in. scale, 22-fret bound ebony fingerboard, single layer cream body binding, Bigsby tremolo, gold or chrome hardware, 2 'soapbar' pickups, volume and tone controls, 3-way toggle switch, available in Apricot, Blue, Cherry, Green, Gold, Plum, Silver, and Teal sparkle finishes; and Black and Tobacco Sunburst finishes, current mfg.

MSR $5,000

This model is also available in a Thin Line model with 2 in. body depth.

DIAMOND
See ARIA. Instruments previously built in Korea during the 1980s.

These entry level instruments were originally distributed by the Pennino Musical Corporation, and later by Aria USA. Designs mostly fell in the strat or superstrat guitar configuration, and a pointy headstock/sleek curves P-Bass bass guitar. The trademark on the headstock generally read "DIAMOND by Aria".

DIAMOND-S
Instruments previously built in Independence, VA during the 1970s.

When Micro-Frets closed operations in Maryland in either 1974 or 1975, the company assets were purchased by David Sturgill. Sturgill, who served as the company president of Grammer Guitars for three years, let his sons John and Danny gain access to leftover Micro-Frets parts. In addition to those parts, they had also purchased the remains of New Jersey's Harptone guitar company. The two assembled a number of solid body guitars which were then sold under the Diamond-S trademark. Unfortunately, that business venture did not catch on, and dissipated sometime in 1976.

DIEGO
Instruments previously built in Hannover, Germany. Distributed by Goldo Music of Hannover, Germany.

Diego brand Deluxe Guitars were offered by Dieter Golsdorf of Goldo Music. Diego instruments are vintage reproductions of late '50s Strats.

Diego instruments feature American alder bodies (shaped similar to a '59 strat), 22 jumbo fret slab-cut rosewood fingerboard, bolt-on maple necks, 3 '59 Grand Vintage single coil pickups, vintage-style tremolo, Gotoh Kluson Replica tuners, and aged-color pickguard/knobs/pickup covers, available in vintage-style finishes.

DILLON
Instruments currently built in Bloomsburg, PA.

John Dillon started building guitars in New Mexico in 1975. Dillon now produces guitars in Pennsylvania. Dillon Guitars offers quality custom built instruments.

DINGWALL DESIGNER GUITARS
Instruments currently built in Saskatoon, Canada.

Luthier Sheldon Dingwall founded Dingwall Designer Guitars in the mid-1980s, after years of actively playing music and doing guitar repair work. Dingwall moved from designing guitar models to bass models, specifically concentrating on fanned fretboard designs pioneered by Ralph Novak. Bass notables such as Lee Sklar, Michael Rhodes, Mike Brignardello, Mark Fain, and Hank Insell are all currently playing and recording with Dingwall basses.

Disaster struck on October 8, 1996, when the warehouse where the Dingwall factory was located caught fire. The fire eventually consumed the entire building, including the tooling and construction tools. When Dingwall began rebuilding the company, he received help from other Canadian luthiers such as Glenn MacDougall of Fury Guitars (see Fury) and Byron Olsen of Olsen Audio (a contract manufacturer of musical and audio equipment). As a result, the combined manufacturing experience totalled over 50 years! Local musicians and businesses held a benefit to raise funds for the re-tooling of the bass line. Dingwall basses were back to production 12 months later.

While Dingwall is concentrating on bass guitars, he used to offer several high quality electric guitar models. All models featured bolt-on necks, 3-per-side headstock with Sperzel or Gotoh tuners, and passive pickups. The Roadster featured a single cutaway body, stop tailpiece, mini-humbucker (neck position) and single coil (bridge). The ATV had an offset double cutaway body, tremolo bridge, and three single coils wired to a custom switching harness that delivered 10 distinct tones! The LVQ (Low Volume Resonance) model offered similar stylings to the ATV, except the design featured tone chambers (semi-hollowbody) and a stop tailpiece. Contact Dingwall Designer Guitars for availability.

All VooDoo series custom basses feature the Novax fanned fret system on the fingerboards. This system is licensed from famed inventor/luthier Ralph Novak, and contributes a more accurate intonation and harmonic system to the staggered bridge design developed by Dingwall.

Dingwall basses all have an innovative bridge design that allows each string the proper scale length to achieve optimum tone. Thus, the scale length is staggered from the low B string (37 in.) up to the G string (34 in.) on a five string bass.

Basses built prior to the fire featured 9-ply laminated necks and Kahler/Dingwall custom bridges. Since the fire and re-tooling, basses now feature a 5-ply laminated maple neck, a new 3 band switchable EQ, and Dingwall bridge.

There are several options available to every basic model. Each option carries a different price for each model and each model needs to be assessed individually. Contact the company directly for prices to each option as they change frequently.

For the most part, Dingwall basses sell close to the actual retail price. They haven't circulated enough to set a used price all of them.

Here are some of the most common features:

Add $150 for lined fretless fingerboard. Add $180 for 3 active/passive band EQ with switchable midrange. Add $100 for Basslines pickups and electronics. Add $100 for 2-Tone Sunburst finish. Add $150 for 3-Tone Sunburst finish. Add $200 for Hipshot Xtender key.

ELECTRIC BASS: AFTERBURNER SERIES

AFTERBURNER I 4-STRING - double cutaway maple body, maple bolt-on neck, 24-fret Novax Fanned Fret System fingerboard, 2-per-side tuners, 2 Dingwall pickups, Passive Plus electronics, 3 knobs, black hardware, available in black or blueberry, current mfg.

MSR $1,300

Afterburner I Flame 4-String - similar to the Afterburner I except has a flamed maple top, available in Honeyburst finish, current mfg.

MSR $1,650

AFTERBURNER I 5-STRING - double cutaway maple body, maple bolt-on neck, 24-fret Novax Fanned Fret System fingerboard, 3/2-per-side tuners, 2 Dingwall pickups, Passive Plus electronics, 3 knobs, black hardware, available in black or blueberry, current mfg.

MSR $1,550

Afterburner I Flame 5-String - similar to the Afterburner I except has a flamed maple top, available in Honeyburst finish, current mfg.

MSR $1,900

Afterburner I Flame 6-String - similar to the Afterburner I except has a flamed maple top in 6-string configuration, available in Honeyburst finish, current mfg.

MSR $2,150

ELECTRIC BASS: PRIMA BASS SERIES

Add $1,300 for the Artist package that includes matching knobs, pickup covers, control covers, and contrasting laminates.

PRIMA 4-STRING - offset double cutaway American Black walnut body core, padauk bookmatched top/back, carbon fiber reinforced 5-ply laminated rock maple bolt-on neck, 24-fret pau ferro fingerboard, 2-per-side Gotoh tuners, 2 Bartolini custom soapbar pickups, black hardware, Dingwall custom aircraft aluminum bridge, volume/blend/2-band EQ controls, available in Oil finishes, current mfg.

MSR $3,600

Prima 5-String - similar to the Prima 4-string, except has 5-string configuration, 2/3-per-side tuners, current mfg.

MSR $4,000

Prima 6-String - similar to the Prima 4-string, except has 6-string configuration, 3-per-side tuners, current mfg.

MSR $4,300

**DiPinto Belvedere
courtesy DiPinto Guitars**

ELECTRIC BASS: Z-SERIES (ZEBRA OR Z2)

Add $1,150 for the Artist package that includes matching knobs, pickup covers, control covers, and contrasting laminates.

ZEBRA 4-STRING - similar to Prima, except features a solid Northern Ash body, available in Black Cherry Burst (BB), Colaburst (CB), Marylin's Lipstick Red (ML), Sticky Fingers Warm Caramel (SF), Stormy Monday Blue (SM), Sunlight through a Cola Deep Red/Brown (SC), and Whalepool Blue (WP) Transparent color finishes, current mfg.

MSR $3,400

The Zebra name is derived from the Transparent color finishes which highlight the wood's grain pattern.

Zebra 5-string - similar to the Zebra 4-string, except in 5-string configuration, 2/3-per-side tuners, current mfg.

MSR $3,800

Zebra 6-string - similar to the Zebra 4-string, except in 6-string configuration, 3-per-side tuners, current mfg.

MSR $4,100

DINOSAUR

Instruments and other products currently produced in China. Distributed by Eleca International Inc. in Walnut, CA.

Dinosaur makes a wide variety of products including guitars, amplifiers, and other accessories in the music industry. They are built in China and sold throughout the United States. Among the products that they produce include combo packs that have a guitar, amp, and other accessories for the starting guitar player. For more information refer to the distributors website (see Trademark Index).

ELECTRIC & ELECTRIC BASSES

Dinosaur's guitars are mainly based off of popular American designs such as the Fender Stratocaster, Precision Bass, and Jazz Bass. These guitars have expected options and are offered at a competitive price.

DIPINTO

Instruments currently built in Korea. Instruments previously produced in the U.S.

Luthier Chris DiPinto handcrafts solid body electric guitars that recall the wackier side of the 1960s while still being solid, playable instruments (which sometimes can't be said for those 1960s inspirations!). Currently DiPinto guitars are manufactured in Korea then shipped to Philadelphia for final set-up and assembly.

DiPinto maintains a stock of colored sparkle and pearl materials for customized pickguards, as well as the more traditional tortoiseshell material. All models are available in a left-handed configuration at no additional charge.

Earlier versions of the Custom Series models featured 3-piece maple body, adjustable rosewood bridge/sparkle finish stop tailpiece, and 2 EMG single coil pickups.

**DiPinto Galaxie 4
courtesy DiPinto Guitars**

GRADING	100% MINT	98% NEAR MINT	95% EXC+	90% EXC	80% VG+	70% VG	60% G

ELECTRIC

All DiPinto **Custom Series** models feature neck-through construction, 24.75 in. scale, volume and tone controls, 2 on/off rocker pickup selectors, and a pre-set volume control stomp switch.

BELVEDERE - single cutaway poplar body, textured lizard skin top/sparkle plastic back overlays, through-body maple neck, 24.75 in. scale, 22-fret rosewood fingerboard with thumbnail sparkle inlay, 3-per-side tuners, 2 Wilde mini-humbucker pickups, chrome hardware, silver sparkle fixtures, adjustable tune-o-matic bridge/metal tailpiece, volume/tone controls, 2 pickup on/off rocker switches, preset volume control stomp switch, available in Black, Blue, and Red finishes, disc.

	N/A	$1,500	$1,300	$1,100	$950	$800	$650

Last MSR was $2,150.

Add $250 for gold hardware/gold sparkle fixtures/Beige finish.

Belvedere (Korean Mfg.) - similar to Belvedere, except has bolt-on neck, 2 Vintage Twang Humbucker pickups, available in Black and White or Blue Sparkle finishes, current mfg.

MSR $699		$500	$450	$400	$350	$300	$250	$200

Add $75 for tremolo.

Also available in left-hand configuration at no extra charge. Also available in a Deluxe version with a sparkle pickguard and star inlays.

GALAXIE - offset double cutaway (pointy horns) poplar body, through-body maple neck, 24 in. scale, 22-fret rosewood fingerboard with V-wedge inlay, 6-on-a-side vintage style chrome button tuners, 2 Wilde Noiseless single coil pickups, chrome hardware, pearloid pickguard/chrome metal controls plate, Schaller roller bridge/pearloid finish Vibro*Star tremolo, volume/tone controls, 2 pickup on/off rocker switches, preset volume control stomp switch, available in Black (with Purple pickguard); Black, Navy, or Red (with White pickguard); and Dark Green and Light Blue (with Gold pickguard) finishes, disc.

	N/A	$1,200	$1,050	$900	$750	$625	$500

Last MSR was $1,600.

Add $50 for locking tuners.

Galaxie 2 (Korean Mfg.) - offset double cutaway, poplar body with bolt-on maple neck, 25.5 in. scale, rosewood fingerboard with dot or star inlays, six on a side pearl button tuners, two humbuckers with a three-position switch, available in Red, Sunburst, Black, Silver Sparkle, Green Sunburst, or Pink Sparkle, mfg. 1999-present.

MSR $649		$450	$400	$350	$300	$250	$200	$150

Also available in a Los Straitjackets model which has a silver sparkle with a gold pickguard.
Also available in left-handed models.

Galaxie 4 (Korean Mfg.) - offset double cutaway, poplar body with bolt-on maple neck, 25.5 in. scale, rosewood fingerboard with dot or star inlays, six on a side pearl button tuners, four single coil pickups, five position selector switch, available in Red, Sunburst, Black, Silver Sparkle, Green Sunburst, or Pink Sparkle, mfg. 1999-present.

MSR $749		$550	$500	$450	$400	$350	$300	$250

Also available in a Los Straitjackets model which has a silver sparkle with a gold pickguard.
Also available in left-handed models.

MACH IV - offset double cutaway (Mosrite-ish) poplar body, through-body maple neck, 24.75 in. scale, 22-fret bound rosewood fingerboard with star inlay, 3-per-side tuners, 2 Wilde Noiseless single coil pickups, chrome hardware, white pickguard, Schaller roller bridge/sparkle covered stop tailpiece, volume/tone controls, 2 pickup on/off rocker switches, preset volume control stomp switch, available in Candy Apple Red and Hard Candy Blue finishes with a sporty White racing stripe, disc.

	N/A	$1,200	$1,050	$900	$750	$625	$500

Last MSR was $1,600.

Add $250 for Vibro*Star tremolo.

Mach IV (Korean Mfg.) - similar to Mach IV, except has bolt-on neck, 1 DiPinto single coil pickup, 1 DiPinto "Dual Single" humbucker pickup, Tune-O-Matic bridge with stop tailpiece, available in Candy Apple Red, Hard Candy Blue, Black, Gold, Bubble Gum, or Sedated White finishes, current mfg.

MSR $699		$500	$450	$400	$350	$300	$250	$190

Left-hand configuration available in Candy Apple Red at no extra charge.

Mach IV 12-String (Korean Mfg.) - similar to Mack IV, except in 12-string configuration, available in Candy Apple Red or Hardy Candy Blue with white stripes, new 2005.

MSR $799		$600	$525	$475	$425	$375	$325	$275

ELECTRIC BASS

In 1998, DiPinto teamed up with jazz bassist Jamaladeen Tacuma to design the 4-string Belvedere Bass.

BELVEDERE BASS STANDARD - single cutaway poplar body, through-body maple neck, 34 in. scale, 24-fret rosewood fingerboard with dot inlay, 2-per-side tuners, 2 Wilde pickups, chrome hardware, white pickguard, fixed bridge, volume/tone controls, 3-way toggle switch, available in a variety of color combinations, disc.

	N/A	$900	$775	$650	$550	$450	$350

Last MSR was $1,200.

GRADING	100% MINT	98% NEAR MINT	95% EXC+	90% EXC	80% VG+	70% VG	60% G

Belvedere Bass (Korean Mfg.) - similar to Belvedere Bass Standard, except has bolt-on neck, 2 mini-humbucker pickups, available in Black and White and Green Sparkle finishes, current mfg.

MSR $749		$550	$500	$450	$400	$350	$300	$225

Add $150 for custom pickguard.

Also available in a Deluxe version with a sparkle pickguard and star inlays.

CUSTOM - similar to the Belvedere Bass Standard, except features a white textured lizard skin top/laminated sparkle plastic back, 24-fret bound ebony fingerboard with thumbnail sparkle inlay, chrome hardware, 2 chrome covered mini-humbucker pickups, rosewood bridge/sparkle covered stop tailpiece, silver sparkle fixtures, volume/tone controls, 2 on/off pickup rocker switches, available in Black, Blue, or Red finishes, disc.

N/A	$1,500	$1,300	$1,100	$950	$800	$650

Last MSR was $2,150.

Add $250 for gold hardware/gold sparkle fixtures/Beige finish.

GALAXIE BASS - double cutaway poplar body, through-body maple neck, 34 in. scale, 22-fret rosewood fingerboard with dot inlay, 4-on-a-side tuners, split coil pickup, chrome hardware, gold pearl pickguard, fixed bridge, volume/tone controls, available in Silver Sparkle finish, mfg. 2004-present.

MSR	$699	$500	$450	$400	$350	$300	$250	$200

Add $35 for Los Straitjackets model with silver finish.

DiPinto Mach IV
courtesy DiPinto Guitars

DOBRO

Current trademark of instruments currently built by Original Acoustic Instruments (OAI), located in Nashville, TN. Original Acoustic Instruments is a division of the Gibson Guitar Corporation. Previously manufactured by Original Musical Instruments Company, located in Huntington Beach, CA. In 1997, production was moved to Nashville, TN. Distributed by the Gibson Guitar Corporation of Nashville, TN. The original Dobro company was formed in 1928 in Los Angeles, CA.

The Dopyera family emigrated from the Austro-Hungary area to Southern California in 1908. In the early 1920s, John and Rudy Dopyera began producing banjos in Southern California. They were approached by guitarist George Beauchamp to help solve his volume (or lack thereof) problem with other instruments in the vaudeville orchestra. In the course of their conversation, the idea of placing aluminum resonators in a guitar body for amplification purposes was developed. John Dopyera and his four brothers (plus some associates, like George Beauchamp) formed National in 1925. The initial partnership between Dopyera and Beauchamp lasted for about two years, and then John Dopyera left National to form the Dobro company. The Dobro name was chosen as a contraction of the *Do*pyera *Bro*thers (and it also means good in Slavic languages).

The Dobro and National companies were later remerged by Louis Dopyera in 1931 or 1932. The company moved to Chicago, Illinois in 1936, and a year later granted Regal the rights to manufacture Dobros. The revised company changed its name to Valco in 1943, and worked on war materials during World War II. In 1959, Valco transferred the Dobro name and tools to Emil Dopyera. Between 1966 and 1967, the Dobro trademark was sold to Semie Moseley, of Mosrite fame. Moseley constructed the first Dobros out of parts from Emil's California plant, and later built his own necks and bodies. Moseley also built Mobros, a Mosrite-inspired Dobro design. After Mosrite collapsed, the name was still held by Moseley; so in the late 1960s, Emil's company produced resonator guitars under the trade name of Hound Dog and Dopera (note the missing 'y') Originals. When the Dobro name finally became available again, Emil and new associates founded the Original Musical Instruments Company, Inc. (OMI) in 1970. OMI has been producing Dobros ever since.

In 1985, Chester and Mary Lizak purchased OMI from Gabriela and Ron Lazar; and eight years later in 1993, OMI was purchased by the Gibson Guitar Corporation, and production continued to be centered in California. The production of Dobro instruments was moved to Nashville, Tennessee in the Spring of 1997, (early company history courtesy Bob Brozman, *The History and Artistry of National Resonator Instruments*).

For further information regarding Dobro acoustic guitars, please refer to the *Blue Book of Acoustic Guitars*.

ELECTRIC

BLUESMAKER (MODEL DEBLU) - available in Black Burst, Blue Burst, Cherry Burst, Green Burst, Purple Burst, Vintage Burst, or Wine Burst finishes, mfg. 1996-2000.

		$1,125	$975	$850	$725	$600	$475	$350

Last MSR was $1,399.

BluesMaker Deluxe (Model DEBLU DLX) - similar to the Bluesmaker, except has fancier appointments, mfg. 1996-2000.

		$1,275	$1,100	$950	$800	$675	$550	$425

Last MSR was $1,599.

DOBROLEKTRIC - figured maple single cutaway body, single upper body f-hole, single body binding, biscuit style resonator, poinsetta cover plate, two pickups (nickel bridge transducer and black P-90 neck), 3 knobs, available in Vintage Sunburst finish, slimline deluxe hardshell case included, disc. 2003.

		$1,720	$1,500	$1,250	$1,050	$925	$750	$575

Last MSR was $2,142.

The Dobrolektric was also available in Blackburst and Wine Red finishes for a short time.

DiPinto Mach IV
courtesy DiPinto Guitars

GRADING	100% MINT	98% NEAR MINT	95% EXC+	90% EXC	80% VG+	70% VG	60% G

VALPRO (MODEL DEVAL) - available in Black, Coral Pink, Cream, Light Sky Blue, and Seafoam Green finishes, mfg. 1996-2000.

	$1,200	$1,050	$900	$750	$625	$500	$375

Last MSR was $1,499.

ValPro Jr. (Model DEVJR) - mfg. 1996-2000.

	$1,200	$1,050	$900	$750	$675	$500	$375

Last MSR was $1,499.

DODGE

Instruments currently built in Tallahassee, FL since 1996. Distributed by Dodge Guitars of Pompano Beach, FL.

Rick Dodge apprenticed to master stringed instrument maker Paris Bancetti in the mid-1970s, and has been a luthier for over 20 years, making both acoustic and electric guitars for personal use and for friends and family. Each guitar was carefully crafted from fine woods, and guitars made by Dodge achieved high quality aesthetics and sound. After building many electric guitars and experimenting with different electronic configurations, Dodge was struck with the idea of making a modular guitar that could completely exchange the electronics without sacrificing the high quality sound or beauty of a fine instrument. Dodge then developed the idea of a rear-mounted modular system: the pickups and electronics would be mounted on a section that could be inserted into the body area. Rick Dodge formed the Dodge Guitar Company in the spring of 1996. Production of the modular guitars began in September, 1996, (Company information courtesy Janice Dodge, July, 1996).

ELECTRIC

Dodge guitar models with interchangeable pickup modules are known as the Convertible series. These are available in two body styles, the **DC-Classic** and the **SC-Classic**. The DC-Classic, also known as the Standard model, has an offset, short-horned, double cutaway body while the SC-Classic, also known as the Blue Pearl, has a rounded single cutaway body. Standard features on both models include a select maple body, figured birds-eye maple neck, 22-fret Brazilian rosewood fingerboard with dot inlay, 25.5 in. scale, MannMade hardtail brass bridge, locking Sperzel tuners, and a high gloss polyester finish. Dodge guitars have optional tremolo system, and Sunburst and Translucent finishes.

The standard package includes one electric guitar with three differently configured electronics-containing modules (pickup configurations similar to a Strat, Tele, and Les Paul). Other modules are available for the customer´s own choice of pickups and configurations. Prices will vary considerably depending on what features are included and which brands and designs of electronics are installed. The current package is the "Triple Play," which includes a Dodge Convertible (standard model) guitar, three electronics modules, and a gig bag for holding everything for $1,749. The Blue Pearl (single cutaway) is available in the same package for $1,949.

ELECTRIC BASS

The **Standard Convertible Bass**, also known as the **DC Classic Bass**, (list $1,150) has a double cutaway maple body, bird's-eye maple neck, rosewood fingerboard, Sperzel Trim Lok tuners, and a brass fixed bridge. The three bass modules feature Bassline pickups that retail for different prices each. Like the electric guitars, the bass is available in single-cutaway version as the Blue Pearl "Big Bang" model, which retails for $1,350. Electronics are sold seperately on all bass guitars. Contact luthier Dodge directly for prices and customizing options (see Trademark Index).

DOLCE

See chapter on House Brands.

This trademark has been identified as the House Brand used by such stores as Marshall Fields, Macy´s, and Gimbles (source: Willie G. Moseley, *Stellas & Stratocasters*).

DOMINO

Instruments previously manufactured in Japan circa mid- to late 1960s. Distributed by Maurice Lipsky Music Company, Inc., of New York, NY.

These Japanese-produced guitars and basses were imported to the U.S. market by the Maurice Lipsky company of New York, New York (Domino was a division of The Orpheum Manufacturing Company). Domino offered a wide range of Vox- and Fender-derived solid body models, and Gibson-esque 335 semi-hollow (or perhaps completely hollow) models. In 1967, the Domino design focus spotlighted copies of Fender´s Jazzmaster/Jaguar and Mustang models renamed the **Spartan** and the **Olympic**. You just know that these guitars are the product of the 1960s, as the Domino catalog claimed that their guitars had "Lightning Fast Action - Psychedelic Sounds - Elegant Mod Styling." As they say on late night commercials, "Now how much will you pay? But Wait!" The entire Domino product line featured Japanese hardware and pickups. Domino´s Thunder-Matic line of drums featured six-ply shells, and internal adjustable mufflers (source: Michael Wright, Guitar Stories Volume One; Domino catalog courtesy John Kinnemeyer, JK Lutherie).

ELECTRIC

Here are some more "Features built into Every Domino:" 1) Mallory Full Range adjustable pickups. 2) Mark Steel "Lightning Fast" Speed Scale Jazz Neck - the shorter distances between frets permits easier fingering and, naturally, faster handling. 3) Mark Steel 3 ounce tremolo/micrometric roller bridge, 6 coats of gloss lacquer. 4) extra value(!) $400 worth of dramatic sound, features, superb styling, handling - yet Domino prices start as low as $22.50 - Compare and You'll Agree!

Domino guitars may look cool from a distance, but up close they're a tough tone nut to crack. Prices in the vintage market range from $100 to $300 (in excellent condition) as many players bypass the wacky 1960s models to look for a newer model entry level guitar.

All Domino electric models were offered with 1, 2, or 3 pickups, with a corresponding change in the model's designation number. For example, the Californian model was offered with 1 pickup (**Model 501**), 2 pickups (**Model 502**), or 3 pickups (**Model 503**). Models were also offered in a 12-string configuration: A **Californian Model 513** was a 12-string with 3 pickups. However, not all models follow this fairly simple system!

The model (# BB62) **Beatle Guitar** was basically a Hofner design ripoff, with a single f-hole, raised pickguard, adjustable bridge/metal tailpiece, 2 pickups, volume/tone controls, and a 3-way toggle. Retail list price was $110.

The (# 502) **Californian** is frequently encountered at guitar shows. This model is based on the Vox Phantom, and features a 5-sided hardwood body, 21-fret fingerboard, 24.75 in. scale, 6-per-side tuners, a (big) richly grained rosewood pickguard, covered bridge/tremolo tailpiece, mallory pickups, pickup on/off switches, individual mute/solo/rhythm switches per pickup, and volume and tone controls. **Californian** models were available in Metallic Blue, Sunburst Red, Sunburst Yellow, White, and Yellow Mist finishes. The Californian model was offered as the 1 pickup Model 501 (retail list $60), 2 pickup Model 502 (list $75), and 3 pickup Model 503 (list $90). The Californian Model 513 (list $125) has a 12-string configuration and 3 pickups.

The (# **80E2**) **Californian Rebel** looks like an expanded, floppy Californian model, and has single f-hole, pickup on/off switches, and volume and tone controls. The Californian Rebel model was offered as the 2 pickup **Model 80E2** (list $90), and 3 pickup **Model 80E3** (list $105). The **Californian Rebel 12-string** model had a retail list price of $140.

The Vox "teardrop" copy (# **15E2**) **Fireball** model had a rounded hardwood body, single f-hole, 6-per-side headstock, volume and tone controls, and a 3-way switch. The Fireball model was offered with 2 pickups (list $90), and 3 pickups (list $105). The Californian Rebel 12-string model had a retail list price of $140.

The (# **302**) **Spartan** model was a Fender Jaguar copy, with an unbound fingerboard with dot inlay, tremolo bridge, 6-on-a-side tuners, tortoiseshell pickguard, metal controls plate, volume and 2 tone controls. The **Spartan** was offered as the 2 pickup **Model 302** (list $99.50), and the 3 pickup **Model 303** (list $110). The **Spartan 12-string** model had a retail list price of $125. An upscale version, the (# **D302**) Spartan Deluxe was the same as the Spartan, except featured block inlays, a bound fingerboard, and Mallory alnico pickups. The **Spartan Deluxe** was offered as the 2 pickup **Model D302** (list $149.95), and the 3 pickup **Model D303** (list $147.95). The **Model D313** Spartan Deluxe 12-string model had a retail list price of $174.95. At the top of the list, the (# **DC302**) **Spartan Custom** was similar to the Spartan Deluxe, except had custom colors.

Dodge Guitar DC Classic courtesy Rick Dodge

These colors include (**A**) Sunset Red, (**B**) Sunburst Yellow, (**C**) Metallic Blue, (**D**) Palamino White, (**E**) Desert, and (**F**) Diamond Blue. There was a $50 upcharge for exotic Starfire wood grain finish. The **Spartan Custom** was offered as the 2 pickup **Model DC302** (list $174.95), and the 3 pickup **Model DC30** (list $199.95). The Model **DC313 Spartan Custom 12-string** model had a retail list price of $189.95.

From the Jaguar copy to the Music master copy! The (# **202**) **Olympic** model had an offset double cutaway hardwood body, 24.75 in. scale, 21-fret unbound fingerboard with dot inlay, tremolo bridge, 6-on-a-side tuners, and volume/2 tone controls (all controls were mounted on the pickguard). The Olympic model was offered as the 2 pickup **Model 202** (list $99.95), and as the 3 pickup **Model 203** (list $110). The **Olympic 12-string** model had a retail list price of $125. The **Olympic Deluxe** model is the same as the Olympic, except features block inlays, bound fingerboard, and Mallory alnico pickups. The Olympic Deluxe model was offered as the 2 pickup model. **Model D202** (list $124.95), and as the 3 pickup **Model D203** (list $149.95). The **Model D212 Olympic Deluxe 12-string** model had a retail list price of $174.95.

The **Olympic Custom** model was similar to the Olympic Deluxe, except featured such custom colors as (**A**) Sunset Red, (**B**) Sunburst Yellow, (**C**) Metallic Blue, (**D**) Palamino White, (**E**) Desert Sand, and (**F**) Diamond Blue. The Olympic Custom model was offered as the 2 pickup **Model DC202** (list $149.95), and as the 3 pickup **Model DC203** (list $174.95). The **Model DC212 Olympic Custom 12-string** had a retail list price of $199.95. There was a $50 upcharge for the exotic "Starfire" wood grain finish.

The Domino (# **40E2**) **Dawson** was a 335-style guitar, but fully hollow. This model had 2 f-holes, 24.75 in. scale, 21-fret bound fingerboard with white block inlay, raised black pickguard, bridge/attached tailpiece tremolo, chrome hardware, six-per-side headstock, volume/tone controls, 3-way pickup selector toggle switch. The Dawson model was available in Gunmetal Red, Yellow Sunburst, Sunburst Walnut, Silver-Red, and Golden-Mist finishes. The Dawson model was offered as the 1 pickup **Model 40E1** (retail list $90), 2 pickup **Model 40E2** (list $110), and 3 pickup **Model 40E3** (list $120). The Dawson **Model 40E12** (list $150) has a 12-string configuration and 3 pickups.

Domino's (# **22E2**) **Silverhawk** was similar to the Dawson, except featured unbound fingerboard with dot inlay, metal bridge with wood feet/tremolo tailpiece, 3-per-side tuners, chrome hardware, 2 pickups, volume and tone controls, and 2 toggle switches (one on bass bout, one on treble bout, both have an individual pickguard). Silverhawk models were available in White, Sunburst Red, Metallic Blue, Black, and Deep Red finishes. The Silverhawk model was offered as the 1 pickup **Model 22E1** (retail list $85) with tremolo, 2 pickup **Model 22E2** (list $110) with tremolo, and 3 pickup **Model 22E3** (list $130) with tremolo. The Dawson **Model 22E12** (list $150) has a 12-string configuration and 2 pickups.

The (# **7E1**) **Hawk** model has a single cutaway hollow body, 2 f-holes, same bridge/tremolo as the **Silverhawk**, raised black pickguard, 3-per-side tuners, one pickup, volume and tone controls, and a jack mounted on a metal controls plate, available in White finish only (retail list $75).

ELECTRIC BASS

The model (#**BB62**) **Beatle Bass** was basically a Hofner design ripoff, with a single f-hole, raised pickguard, adjustable bridge/metal tailpiece, 2 pickups, volume/tone controls, and a 3-way toggle. Retail list price was $129.95.

The **Californian Bass** model has a 5-sided hardwood body, 4-per-side tuners, a big, richly grained rosewood pickguard, Mallory pickups, pickup on/off switches, and volume and tone controls. **Californian** models were available in Metallic Blue, Sunburst Red, Sunburst Yellow, White, and Yellow Mist finishes. The **Californian Bass** model was offered as the 1 pickup **Model 551** (retail list $100), and 2 pickup **Model 552** (list $115). The **Californian Rebel Bass** model had a retail list price of $105.

The Vox "teardrop" copy Fireball Bass model had a rounded hardwood body, single f-hole, 4-per-side headstock, 2 pickups, volume and tone controls, 3-way selector.(list $105).

The **Spartan Bass** model had an unbound fingerboard with dot inlay, 4-on-a-side tuners, tortoiseshell pickguard, metal controls plate, volume and tone controls (list $115). The slightly upscale version **Spartan Deluxe Bass** was the same as the Spartan, except featured block inlays, a bound fingerboard, and Mallory alnico pickups. The **Spartan Deluxe Bass** was offered as the 2 pickup **Model D362** (list $154.95), and the 3 pickup **Model D363** (list $169.95). At the top of the list, the **Spartan Custom Bass** was similar to the Spartan Deluxe, except had custom colors like (**A**) Sunset Red, (**B**) Sunburst Yellow, (**C**) Metallic Blue, (**D**) Palamino White, (**E**) Desert Sand, and (**F**) Diamond Blue. The **Spartan Custom Bass** was offered as the 2 pickup **Model DC362** (list $179.95), and the 3 pickup **Model DC363** (list $189.95). There was a $50 upcharge for exotic Starfire wood grain finish.

The **Olympic Bass** Music master copy had an offset double cutaway hardwood body, unbound fingerboard with dot inlay, 4-on-a-side tuners, volume/tone controls (all controls were mounted on the pickguard). The Olympic Bass model had a retail list price of $115. The **Olympic Deluxe Bass** model is the same as the Olympic, except features block inlays, bound fingerboard, and 2 Mallory alnico pickups. The **Model D262 Olympic Deluxe Bass** model had a retail list price of $129.95. The **Olympic Custom Bass** model was similar to the Olympic Deluxe, except featured such custom colors as (**A**) Sunset Red, (**B**) Sunburst Yellow, (**C**) Metallic Blue, (**D**) Palamino White, (**E**) Desert Sand, and (**F**) Diamond Blue. The **Model DC262 Olympic Custom Bass** model had a retail list price of $154.95. There was a $50 upcharge for the exotic Starfire wood grain finish.

The **Dawson Bass** (**Model 40E62**) was a hollow, 335-style model (retail list $130). This model had 2 f-holes, bound fingerboard with white block inlay, fixed bridge, chrome hardware, 4-on-a-side headstock, 2 pickups, volume/tone controls, 3-way pickup selector toggle switch. The **Dawson Bass** was available in Gunmetal Red, Yellow Sunburst, Sunburst Walnut, Silver, Red, and Golden-Mist finishes.

Domino´s **Silverhawk Bass** was similar to the **Dawson Bass**, except featured unbound fingerboard with dot inlay, metal bridge with wood feet/metal tailpiece, 2-per-side tuners, chrome hardware, volume and tone controls, and 2 toggle switches (one on bass bout, one on treble bout, both have an individual pickguard). Silverhawk models were available in White, Sunburst Red, Metallic Blue, Black, and Deep Red finishes. The Silverhawk Bass model was offered as the 1 pickup **Model 22E61** (retail list $110) and the 2 pickup **Model 22E62** (list $130).

DORADO
Instruments previously produced in Japan circa early 1970s. Distributed in the U.S. by the Baldwin Piano and Organ Company of Cincinnati, OH.

The Dorado trademark was briefly used by Baldwin (during its Gretsch ownership) on a product line of Japanese-built acoustics and electric guitars and basses. Dorado instruments are of decent quality, but are often found at slightly inflated asking prices due to the attachment of the Gretsch name. Remember, these are 1970s Japanese guitars imported in by Gretsch during their phase of Baldwin ownership! Dorados are sometimes rightly priced between $125 and $200; but many times they are tagged at prices double that. Of course, what a guitar is tagged at and what it sells at (cash talks, baby!) are always two different animals (source: Walter Murray, *Frankenstein Fretworks*; and Michael Wright, *Vintage Guitar Magazine*).

DOUBLE EAGLE
Guitar parts previously produced in Japan.

As companies like Mighty Mite, Schecter, and DiMarzio pioneered the availability of high quality guitar components for the do-it-yourself builders, other companies joined in. Japan´s Double Eagle company provided a wide range of quality parts.

DRAGONFLY
Instruments currently produced in Japan by Harry's Co. Inc.

Dragonfly guitars are built in Japan by Harry's Co. Inc. They currently produce several models, the **Hi Sta** (High Standard), the **Standard**, the **Zone B**, the **Custom Made**, the **Hitee**, and the **B6**. What sets this company from the rest is the model B6, which has a 27 fret neck. The guitar is tuned down to B but still has the accesability that a regular E guitar would have. There bodies are made out of fine woods and are based around Fender designs. They also have a line of bass guitars. For more information, refer to their website (see Trademark Index).

DRAJAS
Instruments currently built in Hamburg, Germany.

Drajas is currently offering high quality guitar models.

ELECTRIC

Options for the Drajas guitar models include a mahogany body, bird's-eye or curly maple neck, ebony or pau ferro fingerboard, a bone nut, 25.5 in. or 24.75 in. scale length, Floyd Rose tremolo, and nitrocellulose or oil/wax finishes. There are additional charges for these options.

All Drajas solid body guitars feature offset double cutaway alder bodies, bolt-on maple necks, 24-fret rosewood fingerboards with dot inlays, a 25.2 in. scale, graphite nut, 3-per-side Gotoh Magnum Lock tuners, Gotoh G510 tremolo, Drajas pickups, volume and tone controls, and a polyurethane finish. The three Drajas models are offered in three different top styles: a Flat top, Round top (arched), and Violin shape. The Hornet has a locking tremolo system and humbucker/single coil/humbucker pickups; the **Hornet S** is similar save for a Floyd Rose tremolo system. The **Hornet V** has a fixed bridge and 2 humbucking pickups.

DRISKILL GUITARS
Instruments currently built in Fort Worth, TX. Distributed by Driskill Guitars of Fort Worth, TX.

The Driskill Diablo and Diablo Blues are handcrafted in Fort Worth, Texas by Joe Driskill. These are high quality electric guitars with exceptional tonewoods.

ELECTRIC

The Driskill **Diablo** features a sleek offset double cutaway and has a carved mahogany body with highly figured flame or quilted maple top. The neck is laminated mahogany with carbon fibre and double action truss rods, rosewood or ebony 24-fret rosewood fingerboard, fat or thin 25 in. scale, Schaller locking tuners, Schaller fixed bridge, custom wound Van Zandt pickups, volume and tone controls, 5-position selector switch, gold or chrome hardware. The Diablo model is available in custom finishes and colors. Form-fitted hardshell case included. Retail price $2,800-$4,000 depending on options.

The **Diablo Blues** features a carved solid ash highly figured body, set laminated hard maple neck, 22-fret fingerboard with paua abalone or Mother-of-Pearl dot inlay, fat or thin 25" scale, Schaller locking tuners, Schaller fixed bridge, single coil/humbucker (or 2 single coil/humbucker or 3 single coil) pickups, volume and tone controls, 5-position selector switch, custom inlays available, no-heel neck joint, chrome hardware, gold hardware option, optional piezo bridge. Form fitted hardshell case included. Retail price $2,200-$2,800 depending on options.

MIDI control is available. Driskill is using new and different woods on the guitars. For further information regarding specifications and pricing, please contact luthier Driskill directly (see Trademark Index).

DRIVE
Instruments currently produced. Distributed by Switchmusic.com, Inc. of Ontario, CA.

Drive is a trademark of the Switchmusic.com, Inc. company. They produce entry level guitars at competitive prices. Their products include the Traditional Series of guitars that are similar to popular American models (Stratocaster, Les Paul, Jazz Bass), and they also have original designs such as the Wild Fire models. For more information consult their website (see Trademark Index).

DUBREUILLE, PHILIPPE
Instruments currently built in London, England. Previously built and distributed in Europe by Philippe Dubreuille of Bonnatrait, France.

Luthier/Designer Philippe Dubreuille custom crafts guitars that are playable works of art. He has been building guitars since the early 1980s. Dubreuille´s creations are played by a number of top guitarists, such as Iggy Pop, Joe Perry and Brad Whitford (Aerosmith), Robert Smith and Porl Thomson (The Cure), Dave Stewart, and Vernon Reid. All of Dubreuille´s guitars are unique designs that need to be seen and played to be appreciated, let alone trying to describe what they look like! As most of his creations were custom commissioned, specifications and pricing will vary by nature of the finished guitar. For information and photos of the guitars refer to their website (see Trademark Index).

DUESENBERG

Instruments currently built in Hannover, Germany. Previously distributed in the U.S. by Salwender International of Orange, CA. Currently distributed by 3 Sons Specialized Music.

Duesenburg guitars were designed by Dieter Golsdorf, and these semi-hollowbody and solid body guitars combine a stylish retro look with modern electronic options. Dieter Golsdorf is also the designer and producer of Diego guitars (see Diego).

ELECTRIC

Duesenberg reports that 120 guitars were built in 1996. In 1998, the TV version of the Starplayer model was introduced, which features a sparkle finish on the guitars´ tops, or sparkle finish on the guitars´ headstocks. Hardly any models have been circulated in the market in the USA. Due to this, no fair market prices have been established on these guitars.

CARL CARLTON SIGNATURE - single cutaway semi-hollow body, arched spruce top, flame maple arched back, single f-hole, hard rock maple neck, 22-fret Indian rosewood fingerboard with dot inlay, three-per-side tuners, vintage style bridge and tremolo, pickguard, one P-90 and one humbucker pickups, two knobs, three-way switch, nickel plated hardware, CC emblem on body, available in Trans. Black, Trans. Orange, or Trans. Sunburst finishes, current mfg.

MSR $2,489

DOUBLE CAT - double cutaway semi-hollow alder body with maple top, hard rock maple neck, 22-fret rosewood neck with dot inlays, wrap-around fixed bridge or vintage style tremolo, 3-per-side Grover tuners, black or white pickguard, P-99 single coil/humbucker pickups, volume/tone controls, 5-way selector switch, nickel hardware, available in Fire Burst, Red Burst, Surf Green, Silver Sparkle, or Trans. Orange finishes, mfg. 1997-present.

MSR $2,308

Double Cat 12-String - similar to the Double Cat, except in 12-string configuration and six-per-side tuners, available in Black or Fire Burst finishes, current mfg.

MSR $2,548

IMPERIAL - single cutaway semi-hollow thick body, arched spruce top, flame maple arched back, two f-holes, hard rock maple neck, 22-fret Indian rosewood fingerboard with dot inlay, three-per-side tuners, vintage style bridge and tremolo, clear pickguard, one P-90 and one humbucker pickups, three knobs, three-way switch, nickel plated hardware, available in Trans. Light Orange, or Trans. Red Burst finishes, current mfg.

MSR $3,398

STARPLAYER I - single cutaway semi-hollow mahogany body, laminated maple/spruce top, hard rock maple neck, 25.5 in. scale, 22-fret rosewood neck with dot inlays, 3-per-side Grover tuners, wrap-around fixed bridge, chrome hardware, tortoiseshell or black pickguard, 2 Alnico humbuckers (or 2 P-99 single coil pickups), volume/tone controls, 5-way selector switch, available in Surf Green (Model DSP-SG), Silver Sparkle, and Transparent Orange (Model DSP-TO) finishes, mfg. 1996-2000.

Last MSR was $2,229.

Starplayer II - similar to the Starplayer I, except features a tune-o-matic bridge/Bigsby tremolo tailpiece.

Last MSR was $2,229.

STARPLAYER SPECIAL - single cutaway solid alder body with arched maple top, rock maple neck, 22-fret Indian rosewood fingerboard with dot inlay, three-per-side tuners, tune-o-matic style bridge, stop tailpiece, white pickguard, two humbucker pickups, two knobs, three-way switch, nickel hardware, available in Blue Sparkle, Fiesta Red, Silver Sparkle, Surf Green, Trans. Black, Trans. Orange, or Vintage White finishes, current mfg.

MSR $1,596

Add $30 for Sparkle finishes.

STARPLAYER TV - single cutaway semi-hollow body, arched spruce top, flame maple arched back, single f-hole, hard rock maple neck, 22-fret Indian rosewood fingerboard with dot inlay, three-per-side tuners, vintage style bridge and tremolo, pickguard, one P-90 and one humbucker pickups, two knobs, three-way switch, nickel plated hardware, available in 2-Tone Sunburst, Black, Blue Sparkle, Silver Sparkle, Surf Green, Trans. Orange, or Vintage White finishes, current mfg.

MSR $2,198

ROCKET - Flying V-style solid alder body with arched maple top, rock maple neck, 22-fret Indian rosewood fingerboard with dot inlay, three-per-side tuners, tune-o-matic style bridge, stop tailpiece, white pickguard, two humbucker pickups, two knobs, three-way switch, nickel hardware, available in split Black/White finish, current mfg.

MSR $1,958

Add $100 for tremolo unit.

V-CASTER - single cutaway solid alder body, rock maple neck, 22-fret Indian rosewood fingerboard with dot inlay, three-per-side tuners, tune-o-matic style bridge, stop tailpiece, white pickguard, three single coil pickups, two knobs, three-way switch, nickel hardware, available in Blue Sparkle, Red Sparkle, Sunburst, Surf Green, Trans. Black, or Vintage White finishes, current mfg.

MSR $1,758

Add $100 for tremolo unit.

**Driskill Diablo
courtesy Driskill**

ELECTRIC BASS

STAR BASS - single cutaway semi-hollow body, arched spruce top, arched flame maple back, single f-hole, maple neck, 22-fret Indian rosewood with dot inlay, two-per-side tuners, fully adjustable bridge, trapeze tailpiece, white pickguard, single humbucker pickup, three knobs, nickel hardware, available in Sunburst, Trans. Black, or Trans. Orange finishes, current mfg.

    MSR $2,230

VIOLIN BASS - Hofner style violin semi-hollow body, arched spruce top, arched flame maple back, maple neck, 22-fret Indian rosewood with dot inlay, two-per-side tuners, fully adjustable bridge, trapeze tailpiece, single humbucker pickup, three knobs, nickel hardware, available in Sunburst or Trans. Black finishes, current mfg.

    MSR $2,230

DWIGHT

See chapter on House Brands. Instruments previously produced by Valco of Chicago, Illinois (circa 1950s), and Epiphone of Kalamazoo, Michigan (circa 1963 to 1968). Distributed by the Sunny Shields Music Shop of East St. Louis, Illinois.

This trademark has been identified as a House Brand of the Sunny Shields Music Shop of East St. Louis, Illinois. The Dwight name was for the owner of Sunny Shields, Mr. Charles "Dwight" Shields.

The Sunny Shields Music Shop marketed some Supro (Valco-built) guitars. In addition, Shields also marketed a rebranded Epiphone Coronet model between 1963 and 1968. According to Bob Vail, a retired employee from the Sunny Shields Music Shop, the Chicago Musical Instrument (C.M.I.) company always sold the rebranded Epiphones on a per dozen basis to the store (which, of course, reinforces the notion of a House Brand instrument). Vail feels that before Gibson "bastardized" the Epiphone name, they made some pretty good guitars - the Dwight models are counted among the good ones.

In addition to the Supro and Epiphone Dwight model guitars, Shields also offered Dwight steel guitars and accordions. Vail estimates that there are probably plenty of Dwight instruments in basements and attics throughout southwestern Illinois.

The Epiphone-built Dwight Coronet model has Dwight on the headstock and a D in the center of the pickguard. Epiphone guitars were built during this time period at the Gibson facilities in Kalamazoo, Michigan (American Epiphone production ran from 1961 to 1969), and were distributed by the Chicago Musical Instrument (C.M.I.) company (source: Bob Vail, Sunny Shields Music Shop employee from 1949 to 1951, and 1955 to 1958; and Michael Wright, *Vintage Guitar Magazine*).

DYNELECTRON

Instruments previously built in Italy between 1974 and 1976.

This company specialized in reproducing the Danelectro ´Guitarlin´ model. Like Jerry Jones, they took an existing model - and built it better! However, vintage Danelectro models are still more valuable to collectors (source: Tony Bacon and Paul Day, *The Guru´s Guitar Guide*).

Section E

ESH

Instruments currently produced in Trier, Germany. North/South American Distribution is by Sound Elite Productions Ltd. Co. in Murphy TX.

Esh currently offers a range of neck-through and bolt-on model basses with original design double cutaway bodies (like a redesigned Jazz Bass). Other custom Esh features include Esh electronics, Bartolini pickups, 24-fret rosewood fingerboards, rock maple or 5-piece rock maple/mahogany necks, Teflon wiring harnesses. Distribution was previously handled by Esh USA/MTC of New York, NY.

ELECTRIC BASS AND GUITAR

ESH basses and guitars are available with many different options. Most models are available in either 4-, 5-, and 6-string configurations and other options at additional prices. Check the website for availability on all options and what value those may add to various models, as well as other information (see Trademark Index). The J-Bass is discontinued.

The **Hero** is the entry level model in the ESH series. It has basic features including 2 single coil pickups and retails at $789 for the 4-string and $889 for the 5-string. The **Various**, **Impact**, and **Stinger** are all available in the same configurations at the same prices. The four-string lists for $1,639, the five-string at $1,799, and the six-string goes for $1,899.

The **Notorious I** bass has a Music Man-style offset double cutaway body, while the **Notorious II** model is a Jazz bass-style body. Both models feature a select Hungarian ash body, maple neck, maple or rosewood fingerboard with 21 frets and dot inlay, soapbar (or 2 J-style or J/soapbar) pickups, volume and tone controls, and an oil/wax finish. Prices are $1,549 for the four-string, and $1,649 for the five string on both the Notorious I & II models.

The **Sovereigns** are higher-end basses that are built out of Hungarian ash. Their basic features are fairly elaborate and has Kent Armstrong pickups. The four string retails for $2,299.99, the five string for $2,499.99, and the six string at $2,699. The **Genuine** moves you to an even higher price point. This model also has Hungarian ash as well as other features. The four-string starts at $3,399.99, five-string for $3,699.99, and the six-string at $3,899.99. The **Serious** series of models are available at the same price as the Genuine´s except that the four-string costs $100 more than its Genuine counterpart ($3,499.99).

The **Genuine** guitar is now available in a six-string version for $1,279.99, and a seven string for $1,495.

**ESP Screaming Skull
courtesy ESP**

ESP

Instruments currently produced in Tokyo, Japan since the early 1980s. Distributed in the U.S. by the ESP Guitar Company of Hollywood, CA.

ESP was originally known as a source for high quality guitar components and replacement parts. In the early 1980s the company focused on building Fender- and Gibson-derived designs, evolving to high quality "superstrat" models. Currently, ESP is offering newer designs that combine vintage tastes with modern designs.

The ESP Guitar Company was formed in 1985 as the USA distribution point (and custom work shop) for ESP guitars. These U.S. custom instruments are offered as custom option-outfitted equipment.

ESP is also responsible for the LTD line of guitars. LTD guitars have been produced since at least 1995. They are based off of the ESP designs but are offered for a cheaper price. LTD has replaced all the lower-end ESP models, and ESP focuses on the higher-end models now.

In the mid-1990s, ESP opened a USA Custom Shop, in California. This is where the majority of ESP (if not all) ESP guitars have been produced since the inception of the LTD line. For LTD guitars, see the L section.

In 2003, ESP introduced the XTone trademark, which introduced ESP into the hollow body electric market. For more information see XTone in the X section.

GRADING	100% MINT	98% NEAR MINT	95% EXC+	90% EXC	80% VG+	70% VG	60% G

ELECTRIC: ECLIPSE SERIES

ECLIPSE CUSTOM (FIRST VERSION) - single cutaway bound mahogany body, bolt-on maple neck, 22-fret ebony fingerboard with pearl dot inlay, strings though bridge, blackface peghead with screened logo, 6-on-a-side tuners, black hardware, 2 exposed humbucker pickups, volume/tone controls, 3-position switch, available in Baby Blue, Black, Bubble Gum Pink, Candy Apple Blue, Fiesta Red, Metallic Blue, Metallic Red, Midnight Black, Mint Green, Snow White, Trans. Cherry Red, or Trans. Blue finishes, mfg. 1986-87.

N/A	$650	$575	$500	$425	$350	$275

Last MSR was $1,150.

Eclipse Custom (Second Version) - similar to the Eclipse Custom (First Version), except has through-body maple neck, bound fingerboard, offset pearl block fingerboard inlay, redesigned bound peghead, chrome hardware, available in Cherry Sunburst, Pearl Gold, Pearl Pink, Pearl White, or Turquoise finishes, mfg. 1987-88.

N/A	$700	$625	$550	$475	$400	$325

Last MSR was $1,150.

**ESP Eclipse
courtesy ESP**

GRADING	100% MINT	98% NEAR MINT	95% EXC+	90% EXC	80% VG+	70% VG	60% G

Eclipse Custom T - similar to Eclipse Custom (Second Edition), except has double locking tremolo, available in Black, Cherry Sunburst, Pearl Gold, Pearl Pink, Pearl White, or Turquoise finishes, mfg. 1987-88.

	N/A	$725	$650	$575	$500	$425	$350

Last MSR was $1,750.

In 1988, Black, Cherry Sunburst, Pearl Gold and Pearl Pink finishes were disc; Burgundy Mist, Brite Red, Midnight Black and Pearl Silver finishes were introduced.

Eclipse Deluxe - similar to Eclipse Custom, except has standard vibrato, mfg. 1986-88.

	N/A	$675	$600	$525	$450	$375	$300

Last MSR was $1,450.

In 1988, Black, Cherry Sunburst, Pearl Gold and Pearl Pink finishes were disc, double locking vibrato replaced original part/design, Burgundy Mist, Brite Red, Midnight Black and Pearl Silver finishes were introduced.

ECLIPSE (SOLID BODY) - single cutaway mahogany body, bolt-on maple neck, 24-fret bound rosewood fingerboard with pearl dot inlay (logo block inlay at 12th fret), tune-o-matic bridge/stop tailpiece, 3-per-side tuners, bound headstock, chrome hardware, 2 ESP LH-200 humbucker pickups with nickel covers, volume/2-Tone controls, 3-position switch, available in Black, Gunmetal Blue, Metallic Gold, or Pearl White finishes, disc. 2000.

	$900	$825	$725	$625	$525	$400	$300

Last MSR was $1,199.

Add $300 for Original Floyd Rose locking tremolo (Model Eclipse with Floyd Rose).

In 1998, See-Through Blue, See-Through Green, See-Through Purple, and See-Through Red finishes were introduced as regular production finishes (these finishes were previously a $100 optional upgrade); Gunmetal Blue and Pearl White finishes were disc.

Eclipse Arch Top - similar to the Eclipse Solid Body, except features a bound arched top semi-hollow mahogany body, cat's-eye f-hole, 22-fret bound fingerboard, tune-o-matic bridge/trapeze tailpiece, available in Black, Metallic Gold, Pearl White, or Turquoise finishes, mfg. 1996-2000.

	$1,150	$1,000	$875	$750	$625	$500	$375

Last MSR was $1,429.

In 1998, See-Through Blue, See-Through Green, See-Through Purple, and See-Through Red finishes were introduced as regular production finishes (these finishes were previously a $100 optional upgrade); Pearl White and Turquoise finishes were disc.

Eclipse Semi-Acoustic (Steel String) - similar to the Eclipse Arch Top, except has rosewood bridge, bound maple top, piezo pickup, volume/tone controls, on-board active EQ system, available in Honey Sunburst, See-Through Black, See-Through Blue, See-Through Green, See-Through Purple, or See-Through Red finishes, mfg. 1996-2000.

	$1,050	$925	$800	$675	$550	$425	$350

Last MSR was $1,349.

Eclipse Semi-Acoustic (Nylon String) - similar to the steel string semi-acoustic except has nylon strings, spruce top, and a slotted headstock, available in Natural finish, disc. 1999.

	$1,050	$900	$775	$675	$550	$425	$350

Last MSR was $1,349.

ECLIPSE CUSTOM (USA CUSTOM SERIES) - single cutaway mahogany body, bound figured maple top, bolt-on maple neck, 24-fret bound rosewood fingerboard with mother-of-pearl dot inlay (logo block inlay at 12th fret), tune-o-matic bridge/stop tailpiece, 3-per-side Sperzel locking tuners, bound headstock, black hardware, 2 EMG-81 humbucker pickups with nickel covers, 2 volume/tone controls, 3-position switch, available in Amber, Natural Satin, See-Through Blue, See-Through Green, See-Through Purple, or See-Through Red finishes, mfg. 1998-2000.

	$1,5500	$1,350	$1,150	$975	$825	$650	$500

Last MSR was $1,999.

ECLIPSE CUSTOM (ESP CUSTOM SERIES) - single cutaway mahogany body with quilted maple top, 3-piece maple neck, 24-fret ebony fingerboard with flag inlays and 12th fret ESP logo, 2 EMG-81 Humbucker pickups, 3-per-side tuners, TonePros System II locking bridge, white with abalone neck binding, natural body binding, three black knobs, switch, black hardware, available in See-Through Black or See-Through Black Cherry finishes, mfg. 2003-present.

MSR	$4,329	$3,250	$2,950	$2,650	$2,350	$2,100	$1,650	$1,275

ECLIPSE II (STANDARD SERIES) - single cutaway mahogany body with quilted maple top, mahogany neck, 22-fret rosewood fingerboard with flag inlays and 12th fret ESP logo, two EMG-81 or two Duncan Humbucker pickups, 3-per-side tuners, Gotoh tune-o-matic bridge, white B/N/H binding, four knobs, switch, black or chrome hardware, available in Amber Cherry Sunburst or See-Through Black Cherry finishes, 24.75 in. scale, mfg. 2004-present.

MSR	$1,899	$1,425	$1,250	$1,100	$950	$800	$650	$500

Subtract $75 for Duncan pickups (introduced in 2005).

ELECTRIC: E X P & ULTRATONE SERIES

E.X.P. (EXPLORER) - radical offset hourglass mahogany body, bolt-on maple neck, 22-fret rosewood fingerboard with pearl dot inlay, tune-o-matic bridge/stop tailpiece, black drooping peghead with screened logo, 6-on-a-side tuners, black hardware, 2 EMG-81 humbucker pickups, volume/tone controls, 3-position switch, available in Black or Olympic White finishes, case included, mfg. 1996-2000.

	$1,500	$1,350	$1,150	$975	$825	$650	$500

Last MSR was $1,999.

ULTRATONE - offset double cutaway alder body, bolt-on maple neck, rosewood fingerboard with dot inlays, 22 XJ frets, white neck binding, tune-o-matic bridge, stop tailpiece, 3 Duncan Mini-Hum with Coil Split, 3-per-side tuners, pearloid pickguard, chrome hardware, available in 3-Tone Sunburst, Black or Pearl White finishes, mfg. 2000 only.

	$1,150	$1,025	$925	$825	$700	$550	$400

Last MSR was $1,499.

GRADING	100% MINT	98% NEAR MINT	95% EXC+	90% EXC	80% VG+	70% VG	60% G

ELECTRIC: HORIZON SERIES

HORIZON (FIRST VERSION) - offset double cutaway bound ash body, bolt-on maple neck, 22-fret maple fingerboard with black dot inlay, standard vibrato, maple peghead with screened logo, 6-on-a-side tuners, chrome hardware, 3 single coil pickups, 1 volume/2-Tone controls, 5-position switch, available in Baby Blue, Black, Bubblegum Pink, Candy Apple Blue, Fiesta Red, Metallic Blue, Metallic Red, Midnight Black, Mint Green, Snow White, Trans. Cherry Red or Trans. Blue finishes, disc. 1986.

	N/A	$450	$375	$325	$275	$225	$175

Horizon (Second Version) - offset double cutaway arched top alder or ash body, natural binding, bolt-on maple neck, 24-fret rosewood fingerboard, tune-o-matic bridge/stop tailpiece, curved point peghead, 3-per-side tuners, chrome hardware, 2 ESP LH-200 humbuckers, volume/tone controls (with coil tap switching capability), pickup selector switch, available in Black, Gunmetal Blue, Metallic Gold, or Pearl White finishes, mfg. 1996-2000.

$1,075	$950	$850	$750	$625	$500	$375

Last MSR was $1,429.

Add $200 for Original Floyd Rose tremolo (disc. in 1998).

In 1998, Honey Sunburst, See-Through Blue, See-Through Green, See-Through Purple, and See-Through Red finishes were introduced as regular production finishes (these finishes were previously a $100 optional upgrade); Gunmetal Blue, Metallic Gold, and Pearl White finishes were disc.

HORIZON CUSTOM (USA CUSTOM SERIES) - offset double cutaway one-piece mahogany body, figured maple top, bolt-on maple neck, 24-fret bound rosewood fingerboard with mother-of-pearl dot inlay (logo block inlay at 12th fret), tune-o-matic bridge/stop tailpiece, 3-per-side Sperzel locking tuners, headstock, black hardware, 2 Seymour Duncan humbucker pickups (JB and '59 models), volume/tone controls, 3-position switch, available in Amber, Natural Satin, See-Through Blue, See-Through Green, See-Through Purple, or See-Through Red finishes, mfg. 1998-2001.

$1,500	$1,350	$1,150	$975	$825	$650	$500

Last MSR was $1,999.

**ESP E.X.P.
courtesy ESP**

HORIZON CUSTOM (JAPAN MFG.) - offset double cutaway arched top ash body, through-body maple neck, 24-fret bound ebony fingerboard, double locking vibrato, bound peghead, 6-on-a-side tuners, chrome hardware, single coil/humbucker EMG pickups, 1 volume/2-Tone controls, 3-position switch, available in Black, Fiesta Red, Magenta, Pearl Rose, or Pearl White finishes, mfg. 1987-1993.

	N/A	$1,000	$875	$750	$650	$550	$450

Last MSR was $2,195.

In 1988, Brite Red, Burgundy Mist, Gunmetal Blue, and Midnight Black finishes were introduced; Fiesta Red and Pearl Rose finishes were disc. In 1990, Candy Apple Red and Dark Metallic Blue finishes were introduced; black hardware replaced original part/design; Brite Red, Burgundy Mist, Magenta and Midnight Blue finishes were disc. In 1991, Dark Metallic Purple finish was introduced; bound fingerboard with 12th fret pearl logo block inlay, redesigned peghead, 3-per-side tuners replaced original part/designs. In 1992, Dark Metallic Green finish was introduced; Dark Metallic Blue finish was disc.

HORIZON DELUXE - similar to Horizon Custom, except has bolt-on neck, 22-fret rosewood fingerboard with pearl dot inlay, gold hardware, available in Black, Brite Red, Burgundy Mist, Gunmetal Blue, Magenta, or Pearl White finishes, mfg. 1989-1992.

	N/A	$800	$725	$650	$575	$500	$425

Last MSR was $1,695.

In 1990, Candy Apple Red and Dark Metallic Blue finishes were introduced; black hardware replaced original part/design; Brite Red, Burgundy Mist and Magenta finishes were disc. In 1991, Trans. Blue, Trans. Purple and Trans. Red finishes were introduced; bound fingerboard with 12th fret pearl logo block inlay, tune-o-matic bridge/stop tailpiece, redesigned peghead, 3-per-side tuners replaced original part/designs; Candy Apple Red, Dark Metallic Blue and Gunmetal Blue finishes were disc. In 1992, Transparent Green finish was introduced; 24-fret fingerboard replaced original part/design; Cherry Sunburst finish was disc.

Horizon Deluxe T - similar to Horizon Custom, except has bolt-on neck, 24-fret bound rosewood fingerboard with offset pearl dot inlay/12th fret block logo inlay, black hardware, available in Black, Pearl White, Trans. Blue, Trans. Green, Trans. Purple, or Trans. Red finishes, mfg. 1992-93.

	N/A	$850	$750	$675	$600	$525	$450

Last MSR was $1,895.

HORIZON CLASSIC (U.S. MFG.) - similar to the Horizon Custom, except had offset double cutaway carved mahogany body, set-in mahogany neck, pearl dot fingerboard inlay/12th fret logo block inlay, available in Cherry Sunburst, Honey Sunburst, See-Through Black, See-Through Blue, See-Through Green, See-Through Purple, or See-Through Red finishes, mfg. 1993-95.

	N/A	$1,750	$1,500	$1,250	$1,100	$950	$800

Last MSR was $2,795.

Add $500 for mahogany body with figured maple top/matching headstock.

Horizon Classic instruments were all handcrafted in the USA to customer specifications.

**ESP Eclipse II
Standard Series
courtesy ESP**

GRADING	100% MINT	98% NEAR MINT	95% EXC+	90% EXC	80% VG+	70% VG	60% G

HORIZON CUSTOM (ESP CUSTOM SERIES) - double cutaway mahogany body with quilted maple top, 3-piece maple set neck, 24 XJ fret ebony fingerboard with pearl offset blocks with ESP at 12th fret, matching headstock with Horizon Custom on it, 3-per-side tuners, 2 Seymour Duncan JB/59 humbucker pickups, 3-way-switch, two knobs (v, tone), TonePros locking bridge with string-thru body, white neck and natural body binding, available in Amber Sunburst or See-Through Aqua finishes, mfg. 2003-present.

MSR	$3,999		$3,000	$2,700	$2,400	$2,100	$1,850	$1,600	$1,350

Horizon 3 Custom - similar to the Horizon Custom, except has a different shaped body, pearl dot inlays, no body binding, and stop tailpiece bridge, available in Amber Sunburst or See-Through Aqua finishes, mfg. 2003-present.

MSR	$3,999		$3,000	$2,700	$2,400	$2,100	$1,850	$1,600	$1,350

HORIZON NT-II (STANDARD SERIES) - double cutaway mahogany body with quilted maple top, 3-piece maple set neck, 24 XJ fret ebony fingerboard with pearl offset blocks with ESP at 12th fret, matching headstock with Horizon Custom on it, 3-per-side tuners, 2 Seymour Duncan JB/59 humbucker pickups, 3-way-switch, two knobs (v, tone), Gotoh tune-o-matic STB, white B/N/H binding, available in Dark Brown Sunburst finish, mfg. 2004-present.

MSR	$1,899		$1,425	$1,250	$1,100	$950	$800	$650	$500

ELECTRIC: HYBRID SERIES

HYBRID - offset double cutaway alder or mahogany body, maple neck, 22-fret rosewood fingerboard with pearl dot inlay, strings-through fixed bridge, 6-on-a-side tuners, chrome hardware, shell (or black) pickguard, TS-120 single coil/LH-200 humbucker ESP pickups, 3-way switch (on treble bout), volume/tone controls mounted on chrome control plate, available in Black, Metallic Gold, Pearl White, or Turquoise finishes, mfg. 1993, 1996-98.

		$950	$825	$700	$600	$500	$425	$350

Last MSR was $1,395.

Add $100 for See-Through Blue, See-Through Green, See-Through Purple, or See-Through Red finishes. Add $200 for Sparkle finishes, available in Blue Sparkle, Gold Sparkle, Purple Sparkle, Red Sparkle, and Silver Sparkle.

This model was first offered with a single ESP humbucker pickup, and additional finishes: Burgundy Mist, Fiesta Red, Lake Placid Blue, and Olympic White.

HYBRID I - offset double cutaway hardwood body, bolt-on maple neck, 22-fret rosewood fingerboard with pearl dot inlay, standard vibrato, 6-on-a-side tuners, chrome hardware, 2 single coil pickups, volume/tone control, 3-position switch, metal control plate, available in Baby Blue, Black, Blonde, Fiesta Red, Lake Placid Blue, Metallic Blue, Metallic Red, Natural, Olympic White, Salmon Pink, Two Tone Sunburst, or 3-Tone Sunburst finishes, disc. 1986.

	N/A	$375	$325	$275	$225	$175	$125

HYBRID II - similar to Hybrid I, except has 3 single coil pickups, disc. 1986.

	N/A	$400	$350	$300	$250	$200	$150

ELECTRIC: M-I SERIES

M-I CUSTOM - offset double cutaway alder body, through-body maple neck, 24-fret bound rosewood fingerboard with pearl offset block inlay/logo block inlay at 12th fret, double locking vibrato, body matching bound peghead with screened logo, 6-on-a-side tuners, chrome hardware, ESP humbucker pickup, volume control, coil tap switch, available in Black, Fiesta Red, Snow White or Turquoise finishes, mfg. 1987-1994.

	N/A	$600	$525	$450	$375	$300	$225

In 1988, Magenta, Metallic Black, Midnight Black, and Pearl Yellow were introduced; Bright Yellow and Cherry Sunburst finishes were disc. In 1989, Dark Metallic Blue, Candy Apple Red, and Pearl White finishes were introduced; Fiesta Red, Metallic Black, Midnight Black, Snow White, and Turquoise finishes were disc.

M-I DELUXE - similar to the M-I Custom, except has bolt-on maple neck, 22-fret maple fingerboard with black dot inlay (or rosewood fingerboard with pearl dot inlay), black pickguard, 2 single coil/1 humbucker ESP pickups, 1 volume/2-Tone controls, 5-position switch, available in Bright Yellow, Candy Apple Red, Cherry Sunburst, Dark Metallic Blue, Pearl Pink Sunburst, or Pearl White finishes, mfg. 1987-89.

	N/A	$550	$475	$400	$325	$275	$225

In 1988, Magenta, Metallic Black, Midnight Black, and Pearl Yellow finishes were introduced; Bright Yellow and Cherry Sunburst finishes were disc.

M-I STANDARD - similar to the M-I Custom, except has hardwood body, bolt-on maple neck, 22-fret rosewood fingerboard with pearl dot inlay, standard vibrato, available in Bright Yellow, Candy Apple Red, Cherry Sunburst, Dark Metallic Blue, Pearl Pink Sunburst, or Pearl White finishes, mfg. 1987-1990.

	N/A	$500	$425	$375	$325	$275	$225

In 1988, Magenta, Metallic Black, Midnight Black, and Pearl Yellow were introduced; Bright Yellow and Cherry Sunburst finishes were disc. In 1990, Black and Snow White finishes were introduced; black hardware, single coil/humbucker pickups replaced original designs; Dark Metallic Blue, Magenta, Metallic Black, Midnight Black, Pearl Pink Sunburst, Pearl White, and Pearl Yellow finishes were disc.

ELECTRIC: M-II SERIES

M-II - offset double cutaway alder or ash body, bolt-on maple neck, 24-fret maple or rosewood fingerboard with dot inlay (logo block inlay at 12th fret), Original Floyd Rose tremolo, reverse pointy blackface peghead with screened logo, 6-on-the-other-side tuners, black hardware, 2 ESP LH-200 humbucker pickups, volume control, 3-position switch, available in Black, Brite Red, or Snow White finishes, mfg. 1989-1994, 1996-2000.

	$975	$875	$775	$675	$550	$450	$325

Last MSR was $1,299.

Add $100 for See-Through Blue, See-Through Green, See-Through Purple, or See-Through Red finishes (this option was disc. in 1998).

Earlier versions of this model may have 22-fret maple or rosewood fingerboards with offset dot inlays; and ESP single coil/humbucker pickups. In 1990, Candy Apple Red finish was introduced; Brite Red finish was disc. In 1996, Candy Apple Red and Snow White finishes were disc; Gunmetal Blue, Honey Sunburst, Metallic Purple, and Pearl White finishes were introduced. In 1997, Metallic Purple finish was disc; Metallic Gold finish was introduced. In 1998, ash body was disc; Metallic Purple finish was reintroduced.

GRADING	100% MINT	98% NEAR MINT	95% EXC+	90% EXC	80% VG+	70% VG	60% G

M-II CUSTOM - similar to the M-II, except has offset double cutaway alder body, through-body maple neck, 24-fret bound rosewood fingerboard with pearl offset block inlay (logo block inlay at 12th fret), reverse bound peghead, available in Black, Candy Apple Red, Gunmetal Blue, Magenta, or Pearl White finishes, mfg. 1990-1994, 2001.

	$1,650	$1,400	$1,200	$1,050	$900	$750	$600

Last MSR was $2,199.

In 1991, Dark Metallic Blue and Dark Metallic Purple finishes were introduced; Magenta finish was disc. In 1992, Metallic Green finish was introduced; Dark Metallic Blue was disc. In 1993, pearl dot fingerboard inlay replaced original part/design.

M-II DELUXE - similar to M-II Custom, except has bolt-on neck, unbound fingerboard with pearl dot inlay/12th fret logo block inlay, unbound peghead with screened logo/model, available in Black, Pearl White, Trans. Blue, Trans. Green, Trans. Purple, or Trans. Red finishes, mfg. 1992-96, 2000.

	$1,275	$1,100	$975	$850	$725	$600	$450

Last MSR was $1,699.

Add $300 for Seymour Duncan Cool Rail/JB humbucker pickups.

This model has an optional maple fingerboard. From 1995 to 1996, a Koa wood body/oil finish replaced original part/design.

M-II (STANDARD SERIES) - offset double cutaway alder body, maple neck, 24 XJ fret maple or rosewood fingerboard with dot inlays and ESP at 12th fret, matching headstock with M-II on it, 6-on-a-side tuners, 2 Seymour Duncan JB/59 humbucker pickups, 3-way-switch, one volume knobs, Original Floyd Rose tremolo, available in Black finish, 25.5 in. scale, mfg. 2004-present.

MSR	$1,699	$1,275	$1,100	$950	$825	$700	$575	$450

M-II Urban Camo - similar to the M-II Standard, except has EMG 81 pickups and Urban Camo finish, new 2005.

MSR	$2,199	$1,650	$1,450	$1,250	$1,100	$950	$800	$650

ELECTRIC: M-III SERIES

M-III - offset double cutaway alder body, bolt-on maple neck, 22-fret rosewood (or maple) fingerboard with pearl dot inlay (logo block inlay at 12th fret), Original Floyd Rose tremolo, reverse blackface peghead with screened logo, 6-on-the-other-side tuners, black hardware, 2 ESP SH-100 single coil/LH-200 humbucker pickups, volume/tone controls, 5-position switch, available in Black, Metallic Purple, or Pearl White finishes, mfg. 1989-1994, 1998-2000.

	$1,050	$900	$800	$700	$575	$450	$350

Last MSR was $1,349.

Early models (1989-1994) had pearl offset block inlay (or maple fingerboard with black offset dot inlay) and Black, Brite Red, and Snow White finishes.

M-III CUSTOM W/WILKINSON BRIDGE (USA CUSTOM SERIES) - offset double cutaway one-piece mahogany body, walnut veneer top, bolt-on maple neck, 22-fret ebony fingerboard with pearl dot inlay (logo block inlay at 12th fret), Wilkinson VS-100 tremolo, matching peghead veneer, 6-on-a-side tuners, black hardware, white pickguard, EMG-81 humbucker/EMG-SA single coil/EMG-89R humbucker pickups, volume/tone controls, 5-position switch, available in Amber, Natural Satin, See-Through Blue, See-Through Green, See-Through Purple, or See-Through Red finishes, mfg. 1998-99.

	$1,500	$1,350	$1,150	$975	$825	$650	$500

Last MSR was $1,999.

M-III Custom Reverse (USA Custom Series) - similar to M-III Custom except has reverse headstock and EMG 81/SA/81 pickup combination, mfg. 2000 only.

	$1,650	$1,450	$1,200	$1,000	$850	$700	$550

Last MSR was $2,199.

M-III Custom W/Original Floyd Rose Bridge (USA Custom Series) - similar to the M-III Custom w/ Wilkinson Bridge, except features an Original Floyd Rose tremolo, mfg. 1998-99.

	$1,500	$1,350	$1,150	$975	$825	$650	$500

Last MSR was $1,999.

ELECTRIC: MH & MV SERIES

MH CUSTOM (USA CUSTOM SERIES) - offset double cutaway mahogany body with figured maple top, bolt-on maple neck with ebony fingerboard, dot inlays, 6-on-a-side tuners, black hardware and black Sperzel tuners, Original Floyd Rose bridge, 24 XJ frets, two EMG-81 pickups, available in Amber Sunburst, See-Through Black Cherry, See-Through Aqua, Amber, Natural Stain, See-Through Blue, See-Through Green, See-Through Purple, or See-Through Red finishes, mfg. 2000-01.

	$1,650	$1,450	$1,200	$1,000	$850	$700	$550

Last MSR wsa $2,199.

MH DELUXE (USA DELUXE SERIES) - similar to MH Custom except has alder body with maple neck, rosewood fingerboard with dot position markers with "Deluxe" at the 12th fret, Seymour Duncan TB-4 and SH-1 pickups, mfg. 2001 only.

	$1,275	$1,100	$975	$850	$725	$600	$450

Last MSR was $1,699.

ESP Horizon Custom
courtesy ESP

ESP M-II Deluxe
courtesy ESP

E

GRADING	100% MINT	98% NEAR MINT	95% EXC+	90% EXC	80% VG+	70% VG	60% G

MV CUSTOM (USA CUSTOM SERIES) - offset double cutaway design, mahogany body with flamed maple top, bolt-on maple neck with ebony fingerboard, abalone purfling, dot position markers with "Custom" at the 12th fret, black hardware and Sperzel locking tuners, tune-o-matic bridge with string-through-body, white top and neck binding, 24 XJ frets, Seymour Duncan SH-4 and SSL-1 pickups, 1 volume/1 tone control, 3-way toggle, available in See-Through Aqua, or See-Through Orange finishes, mfg. 2001 only.

	$1,500	$1,300	$1,150	$975	$825	$650	$500

Last MSR was $1,999.

MV DELUXE (USA DELUXE SERIES) - similar to MV Custom except has alder body, maple neck with rosewood fingerboard, dot inlays with "Deluxe" at the 12th fret, available in Black Gold, Metallic Gold, or Ice Blue finishes, mfg. 2001 only.

	$1,125	$1,000	$875	$750	$650	$500	$425

Last MSR was $1,499.

ELECTRIC: MAVERICK SERIES

MAVERICK - offset double cutaway hardwood body, bolt-on maple neck, 24-fret maple fingerboard with black offset dot inlay (or rosewood fingerboard with pearl dot inlay), double locking vibrato, blackface peghead with screened logo, 6-on-a-side tuners, black hardware, single coil/humbucker ESP pickups, volume control, 3-position switch, available in Black, Brite Yellow, Candy Apple Red, Dark Metallic Blue, Fluorescent Pink, or Snow White finishes, mfg. 1989-1991.

	N/A	$375	$325	$275	$225	$175	$125

In 1990, Pearl White and Turquoise finishes were introduced; Brite Yellow, Fluorescent Pink, and Snow White finishes were disc. In 1991, Dark Metallic Purple and Gunmetal Blue finishes were introduced; Turquoise finish was disc.

MAVERICK DELUXE (1988) - similar to the Maverick, except has ash body, 24-fret rosewood fingerboard with pearl dot inlay, 2 ESP humbucker pickups, available in Brite Red, Brite Yellow, Flour. Pink, Flour. White, Gunmetal Blue, or Midnight Black finishes, mfg. 1988 only.

	N/A	$400	$350	$300	$250	$200	$150

The neck position pickup was a stacked humbucker.

MAVERICK DELUXE (1992) - similar to the Maverick, except has ash body, pearloid pickguard, 24-fret rosewood fingerboard with pearl dot inlay/12th fret logo block inlay, maple peghead with screened logo, 2 single coil/1 humbucker ESP pickups, volume/tone controls, 5-position switch, available in Black, Pearl White, Trans. Blue, Trans. Green, Trans. Purple, and Trans. Red finishes, mfg. 1992 only.

	N/A	$700	$625	$550	$475	$400	$325

Last MSR was $1,495.

ELECTRIC: METAL SERIES

METAL I - offset double cutaway alder body, bolt-on maple neck, 22-fret rosewood fingerboard with pearl dot inlay, standard vibrato, maple peghead with screened logo, 6-on-a-side tuners, gold hardware, exposed humbucker pickup, volume/tone control, available in Pearl Blue, Pearl Green, Pearl Pink, Pearl White, or Metallic Purple, mfg. 1986 only.

	N/A	$350	$300	$250	$200	$150	$100

METAL II - similar to Metal I, except has single horn cutaway V-shape body, mfg. 1986 only.

	N/A	$350	$300	$250	$200	$150	$100

METAL III - reverse offset double cutaway asymmetrical alder body, bolt-on maple neck, 22-fret maple fingerboard with black dot inlay, standard vibrato, maple peghead with screened logo, 6-on-a-side tuners, gold hardware, exposed humbucker pickup, volume control, mfg. 1986 only.

	N/A	$400	$350	$300	$250	$200	$150

ELECTRIC: MIRAGE SERIES

MIRAGE (FIRST EDITION) - offset double cutaway hardwood body, bolt-on maple neck, 22-fret bound rosewood fingerboard with pearl offset block inlay/logo block inlay at 12th fret, double locking vibrato, bound blackface peghead with screened logo, 6-on-a-side tuners, black hardware, 2 single coil/1 humbucker ESP pickups, volume/tone control, 5-position switch, available in Black, Candy Apple Red, Dark Metallic Blue, Dark Metallic Purple, Gunmetal Blue, or Pearl White finishes, mfg. 1991 only.

	N/A	$900	$825	$750	$675	$600	$500

Last MSR was $1,695.

MIRAGE (SECOND EDITION) - offset double cutaway alder or ash body, maple neck, 22-fret rosewood fingerboard with pearl dot inlay (logo block inlay at 12th fret), Wilkinson VS-100 tremolo, reverse peghead, 6-on-a-side Sperzel locking tuners, black hardware, 2 SS-100 single coil/1 LH-200 humbucker ESP pickups, volume/tone control, 5-position switch, available in Black, Gunmetal Blue, Metallic Gold, or Pearl White finishes, mfg. 1994-98.

	N/A	$800	$725	$650	$575	$500	$425

Last MSR was $1,495.

Add $100 for See-Through Blue, See-Through Green, See-Through Purple, or See-Through Red finishes.

MIRAGE STANDARD - offset double cutaway mahogany body, bolt-on maple neck, 22-fret rosewood fingerboard with pearl dot inlay, strings through bridge, blackface peghead with screened logo, 6-on-a-side tuners, black hardware, exposed humbucker pickup, volume/tone controls, available in Baby Blue, Black, Bubblegum Pink, Candy Apple Blue, Fiesta Red, Metallic Blue, Metallic Red, Midnight Black, Mint Green, Snow White, Trans. Cherry Red, or Trans. Blue finishes, mfg. 1986 only.

	N/A	$450	$400	$350	$300	$250	$200

MIRAGE CUSTOM - similar to Mirage Standard, except has 2 exposed humbucker pickups, 3-position switch, mfg. 1986-1990.

	N/A	$550	$475	$425	$375	$324	$275

In 1987, Pearl Gold, Pearl Pink, Pearl White, and Turquoise finishes were introduced, through-body maple neck, 24-fret bound ebony fingerboard with offset pearl block inlay/logo block inlay at 12th fret, double locking vibrato, redesigned bound peghead, 2 single coil/1 humbucker pickups, 5-position switch replaced original part/designs, Baby Blue, Bubblegum Pink, Candy Apple Blue, Metallic Blue, Metallic Red, Mint Green, Snow White, Transparent Cherry Red, and Transparent Blue finishes were disc. In 1988, Brite Red, Gunmetal Blue,

E

GRADING	100% MINT	98% NEAR MINT	95% EXC+	90% EXC	80% VG+	70% VG	60% G

Magenta, Mediterranean Blue, and Pearl Silver finishes were introduced; Fiesta Red, Pearl Gold, and Pearl Pink finishes were disc. In 1989, Candy Apple Red and Lake Placid Blue finishes were introduced, 2 stacked coil/1 humbuckers replaced respective item, Brite Red, Mediterranean Blue, and Pearl Silver finishes were disc. In 1990, Magenta and Turquoise finishes were disc.

MIRAGE DELUXE - similar to Mirage Custom, except has bound rosewood fingerboard with pearl offset block inlay, double locking vibrato, stacked coil/humbucker pickups, available in Black, Fiesta Red, Pearl Gold, Pearl Pink, Pearl White, or Turquoise finishes, mfg. 1987-1990.

	N/A	$500	$450	$400	$350	$300	$250

Finish colors from 1988 to 1990 follow the same changes as the Mirage Custom.

ELECTRIC: PHOENIX SERIES

PHOENIX - asymmetrical hourglass style mahogany body, white pickguard, through-body mahogany neck, 22-fret bound rosewood fingerboard with pearl dot inlay, double locking vibrato, bound blackface peghead with screened logo, 6-on-a-side tuners, black hardware, 2 covered humbucker pickups, 2 volume/2-Tone controls, 3-position switch, available in Black, Fiesta Red, Snow White, or Turquoise finishes, mfg. 1987 only.

	N/A	$650	$575	$500	$425	$350	$275

Last MSR was $1,550.

ELECTRIC: S SERIES

S-454 - offset double cutaway alder body, white pickguard, bolt-on maple neck, 22-fret maple fingerboard with black dot inlay, standard vibrato, maple peghead with screened logo, 6-on-a-side tuners, chrome hardware, 3 single coil exposed pickups, 1 volume/2-Tone controls, 5-position switch, available in Baby Blue, Black, Blonde, Fiesta Red, Lake Placid Blue, Metallic Blue, Metallic Red, Natural, Olympic White, Salmon Pink, 2-Tone Sunburst, or 3-Tone Sunburst finishes, mfg. 1986-87.

	N/A	$450	$400	$350	$300	$250	$200

S-465 - similar to S-454, except has rosewood fingerboard with pearl dot inlay, mfg. 1986-87.

	N/A	$450	$400	$350	$300	$250	$200

S-487 DELUXE - offset double cutaway hardwood body, black lam pickguard, bolt-on maple neck, 22-fret rosewood fingerboard with pearl dot inlay, double locking vibrato, maple peghead with screened logo, 6-on-a-side tuners, chrome hardware, 3 single coil exposed pickups, 1 volume/2-Tone controls, 5-position switch, available in Black, Brite Red, Burgundy Mist, Cherry Sunburst, Mediterranean Blue, or Snow White finishes, mfg. 1987-88.

	N/A	$500	$425	$375	$325	$275	$225

S-487 Standard - similar to S-487 Deluxe, except has black pickguard, standard vibrato, black hardware, mfg. 1987-88.

	N/A	$400	$350	$300	$250	$200	$150

This model had an optional maple fingerboard with black dot inlay.

S-500 - offset double cutaway ash body, bolt-on maple neck, 22-fret rosewood fingerboard with pearl dot inlay, vintage vibrato, graphite nut, 6-on-a-side locking Sperzel tuners, gold hardware, 2 single coil/1 humbucker ESP pickups, volume/tone control, 5-position switch, available in Black, Pearl White, Trans. Blue, Trans. Green, Trans. Purple, or Trans. Red finishes, mfg. 1991-93.

	N/A	$900	$800	$725	$650	$575	$475

Last MSR was $1,495.

S-500 T - similar to S-500, except has double locking vibrato, mfg. 1992 only.

	N/A	$950	$850	$750	$650	$575	$475

Last MSR was $1,695.

ELECTRIC: SIGNATURE SERIES

All models in this series are built to their namesakes´ specifications. The retail list price for Signature Series models include a hardshell case.

BRUCE KULICK (BOLT-ON) - offset waist/double cutaway mahogany body with pointed horns, mahogany neck, 22-fret bound rosewood fingerboard with pearl parallelogram inlays, 3-per-side headstock with screened signature/logo, chrome hardware, shell pickguard, tune-o-matic bridge/stop tailpiece, 2 ESP LH-200 humbuckers with nickel covers/black retaining rings, volume/tone control, 3-way pickup toggle switch, available in Black finish, mfg. 1996-99.

$1,275	$1,100	$975	$850	$725	$600	$450

Last MSR was $1,699.

Bruce Kulick (Neck-Through) - similar to the Bruce Kulick (Bolt-On), except features neck-through-body design, 2 Seymour Duncan humbuckers with nickel covers, mfg. 1996-99.

$1,500	$1,300	$1,150	$975	$825	$650	$500

Last MSR was $1,999.

DAVE MUSTAINE AXXION - double cutaway X-shaped body with slightly extended lower bass bout, mahogany body, set three-piece mahogany neck, 24-fret ebony fingerboard with XX inlays, three-per-side tuners, TonePros locking bridge, STB, two Seymour Duncan humbucker pickups, three knobs, three-way switch, black hardware, available in Black finish, 25.5 in. scale, new 2005.

MSR	$3,999		$3,000	$2,700	$2,400	$2,100	$1,850	$1,600	$1,350

**ESP Mirage
courtesy ESP**

**ESP Mirage Custom
courtesy ESP**

GRADING	100% MINT	98% NEAR MINT	95% EXC+	90% EXC	80% VG+	70% VG	60% G

DAVE MUSTAINE DV8 - Flying V-style with sharp points, mahogany body, 3-piece mahogany neck-thru body, 24 jumbo ebony fingerboard with dot inlay and 8 Ball 1st fret inlay, 25.5 in. scale, 2 Seymour Duncan JB/Jazz humbucker pickups, black pickguard, 3 knobs (v, v, tone) 3-way switch, Tone Pros bridge with STB, white N/H binding, available in Black, Metallic Silver, or Snow White finishes, mfg. 2003-present.

MSR	$3,299	$2,475	$2,200	$1,900	$1,600	$1,300	$1,050	$800

GEORGE LYNCH - all instruments in this group have the following items; offset double cutaway alder body, bolt-on maple neck, 22-fret fingerboard, double locking vibrato, reverse headstock, 6-on-a-side tuners, black hardware, single coil/humbucker pickups, pan control.

Kamikaze (Kamikaze I, II, III) - rosewood fingerboard with pearl dot inlay, available in black/brown/red camouflage Kamikaze graphic finishes, mfg. 1990-present.

MSR	$2,599	$1,950	$1,700	$1,500	$1,300	$1,100	$900	$700

Different Kamikaze models have different color camouflage graphic.

Kamikaze (4) Ltd. - maple fingerboard with black dropping bomb inlay, reverse sawtooth peghead, available in green/yellow/red Kamikaze graphic finish, mfg. 1992-95, 2001-present.

MSR	$2,899	$2,175	$1,900	$1,700	$1,500	$1,300	$1,050	$850

This model was originally just the Kamikaze Limited, but was reintroduced in 2001 as the Kamikaze 4.

Flamed Baritone - George Lynch model in baritone configuration, mfg. 2003-04.

	$2,475	$2,200	$1,900	$1,600	$1,300	$1,050	$800

Last MSR was $3,299.

Serpent - rosewood fingerboard with pearl dot inlay/ESP logo block inlay at 12th fret, peghead has screened logo/initial, available in Black/White Serpent graphic finish, mfg. 1993-2003.

	$1,900	$1,650	$1,450	$1,250	$1,050	$850	$650

Last MSR was $2,499.

Serpent Custom - similar to the Serpent configuration, available in Black/Brown Serpent graphic finish with Turquoise and white highlights, mfg. 1994-98.

	$1,700	$1,500	$1,300	$1,100	$975	$795	$575

Last MSR was $2,295.

Skull & Bones - hand carved maple body, maple bolt-on neck with ebony fingerboard, white dot inlays, 22 XJ frets, Original Floyd Rose bridge, Duncan Screamin' Demon pickup, vibrato bar, limited production, available in Bone finish, mfg. 1999 only.

	$3,200	$2,700	$2,300	$2,000	$1,700	$1,400	$1,200

Last MSR was $3,999.

Skull & Snakes (Skull and Snakes Ltd) - rosewood fingerboard with pearl skull/swords inlay, available in Skulls and Snake graphic finish, mfg. 1990-present.

MSR	$2,499	$1,875	$1,650	$1,500	$1,350	$1,200	$1,050	$850

Sunburst Tiger - rosewood fingerboard with pearl dot inlay, 6-on-a-side droopy headstock, available in Purple/Red/Yellow Tiger Sunburst finish, mfg. 1990-present.

MSR	$2,499	$1,875	$1,650	$1,500	$1,350	$1,200	$1,050	$850

M-1 Tiger - similar to the Sunburst Tiger, except has M-I body design, 22-fret maple fingerboard with black dot inlay, exposed ESP humbucker, volume knob, available in Yellow/Black Tiger Stripe Graphic finish with matching headstock, mfg. 1996-present.

MSR	$2,199	$1,650	$1,450	$1,250	$1,050	$900	$750	$600

GL-56 - pre-aged offset double cutaway basswood body, bolt-on maple neck, 22-fret maple fingerboard with dot inlay, 6-on-a-side Sperzel locking tuners, 2-point tremolo bridge, chrome hardware, white pickguard, 3 Seymour Duncan Classic Stack pickups, 2 volume/tone controls, available in distressed Natural finish, mfg. 1998-2002.

	$1,500	$1,300	$1,150	$1,000	$850	$675	$500

Last MSR was $1,999.

Ultra Tone - bound rosewood fingerboard with pearl dot inlay, 3-per-side vintage-style tuners, screened logo/Ultra Tone/graphic on headstock, 3 Seymour Duncan covered mini-humbuckers, tune-o-matic bridge/stop tailpiece, chrome hardware, black/white marblized pickguard, 3 control knobs, available in 3-Tone Sunburst, Black, or Pearl White finishes, mfg. 1995-2000.

	$1,200	$1,050	$900	$775	$650	$500	$375

Last MSR was $1,499.

JAKE E. LEE - offset double cutaway alder body, bolt-on maple neck, 24.75 in. scale, 22-fret maple or rosewood fingerboard with dot inlay, strings-through fixed bridge, screened peghead signature/logo, 6-on-a-side tuners, chrome hardware, white pickguard, 2 slanted single coil/1 humbucker ESP pickups, volume/tone controls, 5-position switch, available in Black, Metallic Purple, or Snow White finishes, mfg. 1994-96.

	$895	$825	$725	$600	$500	$400	$295

Last MSR was $1,395.

This model has an optional rosewood fingerboard with pearl dot inlay.

JAMES HETFIELD JH-1 - Flying V-style mahogany body, 22-fret rosewood fingerboard with abalone custom inlay, 3-per-side headstock, fixed bridge, black hardware, 2 EMG humbuckers, volume/tone controls, 3-way selector, available in Hot Rod flame graphic finish (body and matching headstock) only, mfg. 1997 only.

	$2,200	$2,000	$1,750	$1,500	$1,250	$1,050	$850

Last MSR was $2,695.

Production of this model was limited to 200 pieces.

GRADING	100% MINT	98% NEAR MINT	95% EXC+	90% EXC	80% VG+	70% VG	60% G

JAMES HETFIELD JH-2 - Explorer-style mahogany body, black Diamond-plate metal top, bolt-on maple neck, 22-fret rosewood fingerboard with pearl diamond custom inlay, 6-on-a-side headstock, tune-o-matic bridge/stop tailpiece, black hardware, 2 EMG (models 81/60) humbuckers, volume/tone controls, 3-way selector, available in Black finish with matching headstock, mfg. 1998 only.

	$2,200	$2,000	$1,750	$1,500	$1,250	$1,050	$850

Last MSR was $2,699.

This is a limited production model.

JAMES HETFIELD JH-3 - single cutaway mahogany body, maple-set neck with rosewood fingerboard, 22 XJ frets with custom flag inlays, Creme body and neck binding, tune-o-matic bridge, two EMG (models 81/60) humbucker pickups, gold hardware, two volume and two tone controls, limited production, available in Black finish with pinstripes, mfg. 1999 only.

	$2,200	$2,000	$1,750	$1,500	$1,250	$1,050	$850

Last MSR was $2,699.

JAMES HETFIELD "TRUCKSTER" SIGNATURE - single cutaway Les Paul style mahogany body, set three-piece mahogany neck, 22-fret rosewood fingerboard with flag and 12th fret ESP inlays, matching headstock with JH initial and three-per-side tuners, Tone Pros Locking bridge, stop tailpiece, two EMG active pickups, three knobs, three-way switch, chrome hardware, finished in Aged Primer Grey with custom black, white, and red wear marks, 24.75 in. scale, new 2005.

MSR	$2,499	$1,875	$1,600	$1,400	$1,200	$1,000	$800	$650

JEFF HANNEMAN SIGNATURE - double cutaway maple neck-through body with Alder sides, maple neck with rosewood fingerboard, white dot inlays with "Slayer" logo at 12th fret, 24 XJ frets, two EMG-81 humbucker pickups with SPC control, white neck binding, black hardware, Kahler Pro bridge, available in Black finish, mfg. 1999-present.

MSR	$2,999	$2,250	$2,000	$1,750	$1,500	$1,300	$1,100	$900

KELLY HAYES SIGNATURE - single cutaway mahogany body (similar to a Les Paul), maple neck, 24-fret ebony figerboard with cold spiders inlays and "13" at 12th fret, 2 EMG-81 humbucker pickups, TonePros locking bridge with string-thru body, two knobs (v, tone), 3-way switch, available in black with large white cold spider graphic, mfg. 2002-present.

MSR	$3,599	$2,700	$2,450	$2,100	$1,900	$1,700	$1,500	$1,200

KERRY KING KK STANDARD - Flying V-style mahogany body, set-in mahogany neck, 24-fret rosewood fingerboard with pearl diamond inlay, reverse curved headstock with screened signature/logo, 6-on-a-side tuners, Kahler Pro tremolo, black hardware, 2 EMG-81 humbuckers, volume/tone controls, 3-way selector, EMG PA-2 preamp, available in Black finish only, disc. 1998.

	$1,800	$1,600	$1,400	$1,200	$1,000	$800	$650

Last MSR was $2,395.

Kerry King KK Custom - similar to the Kerry King KK Standard, except features neck-through-body construction, pearl eagle fingerboard inlays, available in Red/Black Crackle finish, disc. 1998.

	$3,000	$2,700	$2,400	$2,100	$1,800	$1,500	$1,200

Last MSR was $3,995.

KIRK HAMMETT KH-1 - Flying V-style mahogany body, 22-fret rosewood fingerboard with pearl custom 'devil' inlay, 3-per-side headstock, Floyd Rose tremolo, black hardware, white pickguard, EMG-81 humbucker, volume controls, available in Black finish only, disc. 1998.

	$2,000	$1,800	$1,650	$1,400	$1,150	$950	$695

Last MSR was $2,695.

KIRK HAMMETT KH-2 (CUSTOM M-II) - offset double cutaway alder body, bolt-on maple neck, 24-fret rosewood fingerboard with pearl skull and crossbones inlay, Floyd Rose tremolo, reverse pointed peghead with screened logo/initials, 6-on-a-side tuners, black hardware, 2 EMG-81 humbuckers, 1 volume/2-Tone controls, 5-position switch, available in Black finish only, current mfg.

MSR	$2,399	$1,800	$1,550	$1,350	$1,150	$950	$800	$650

Kirk Hammett KH-2 (Custom M-II with Ouija Graphic) - similar to the Kirk Hammett KH-2, except has a custom Ouija graphic finish, mfg. 1996-99.

	$1,875	$1,650	$1,450	$1,250	$1,050	$850	$650

Last MSR was $2,499.

Kirk Hammett KH-2 Vintage (Relic) - similar to the Kirk Hammett KH-2 except has a distressed Black finish with graphics, limited production (custom shop), mfg. 2001-present.

MSR	$4,299	$3,225	$2,850	$2,500	N/A	N/A	N/A	N/A

KIRK HAMMETT KH-3 - single cutaway alder body, mahogany neck, 24-fret rosewood fingerboard with pearl skull and spider inlay, Floyd Rose tremolo, blackface peghead with screened signature/logo, 3-per-side tuners, black hardware, 2 EMG-81 humbuckers, 1 volume/2-Tone controls, 3-position switch, available in Black with Spider/Web graphic finish, mfg. 1994-present.

MSR	$2,699	$2,025	$1,800	$1,600	$1,400	$1,150	$950	$750

KIRK HAMMETT KH-4 - offset double cutaway body, alder wings, through-body maple neck, 24-fret rosewood fingerboard with pearl dot inlay, Original Floyd Rose tremolo, reverse pointed peghead with screened logo/initials, 6-on-the-other-side tuners, black hardware, white pearloid pickguard, 2 EMG-81 humbuckers, 2 volume/tone controls, 5-position switch, available in Black finish only, disc. 1999.

	$2,200	$1,850	$1,600	$1,400	$1,150	$900	$675

Last MSR was $2,699.

ESP Kirk Hammett 2 w/Ouija Graphic courtesy ESP

E

ESP James Hetfield Truckster courtesy ESP

GRADING	100% MINT	98% NEAR MINT	95% EXC+	90% EXC	80% VG+	70% VG	60% G

LOW G SIGNATURE - offset double cutaway Alder body, bolt-on maple neck with rosewood fingerboard, white dot inlays, white neck binding, 22 XJ frets, one EMG-81 pickup, tune-o-matic bridge, stop tailpiece, chrome hardware, available in Black and White Pearloid finish, mfg. 1999 only.

	$2,750	$2,400	$2,025	$1,725	$1,475	$1,250	$995

Last MSR was $3,499.

MAX CAVALERA - offset double cutaway design similar to an SG, alder body, maple neck, ebony fingerboard, soulfly logo position markers, XXX at 12-fet, Tune-O-Matic bridge, string-through-body, white neck binding, 24 XJ frets, one Seymour Duncan SH-6 pickup, volume knob, available in Brazil Green with yellow graphic around the pickup, mfg. 2001-present.

MSR	$3,299	$2,475	$2,200	$1,900	$1,650	$1,400	$1,150	$900

RON WOOD - single round cutaway bound alder body, bolt-on maple neck, 22-fret maple fingerboard with black dot inlay, strings-through fixed bridge, 6-on-a-side tuners, natural headstock with screened signature/logo, chrome hardware, white pickguard, humbucker/single coil ESP pickups, volume/tone control on metal plate, 3-position switch, available in Black, Fiesta Red, or Metallic Blue finishes, current mfg.

MSR	$1,399	$1,050	$950	$850	$725	$600	$475	$350

Ron Wood with Stringbender - similar to Ron Wood, except has pearloid pickguard, 2 humbucker pickups, Parsons-White Stringbender, disc. 1995.

	$1,250	$1,100	$1,000	$900	$800	$700	$575

Last MSR was $2,095.

STEPHEN CARPENTER SIGNATURE - double cutaway maple neck-through-body with alder sides, maple neck with ebony fingerboard, no inlays, white neck binding, 24 XJ frets, one Duncan TB-4 pickup, one ESP LH-200 and one ESP SS-120 pickup, tune-o-matic bridge, chrome hardware, available in See-Through Green, Snow White, or Sonic Blue finishes, mfg. 1999-present.

MSR	$2,499	$1,875	$1,600	$1,400	$1,200	$1,000	$800	$650

Stephen Carpenter 7 - similar to Stephen Carpenter Signature Model except in a 7-string configuration, tune-o-matic 7 bridge, Duncan JB-7, '59-7, and SSL-7 pickups, available in Black finish with pearl binding, mfg. 2000 only.

	$2,150	$1,950	$1,750	$1,550	$1.350	$1,150	$950

Last MSR was $2,699.

ELECTRIC: T SERIES

T-454 - single cutaway alder body, white pickguard, metal control plate, bolt-on maple neck, 22-fret maple fingerboard with black dot inlay, strings through bridge, maple peghead with screened logo, 6-on-a-side tuners, chrome hardware, 2 single coil pickups, volume/tone controls, 3-position switch, available in Baby Blue, Black, Blonde, Fiesta Red, Lake Placid Blue, Metallic Blue, Metallic Red, Natural, Olympic White, Salmon Pink, Two-Tone Sunburst, or 3-Tone Sunburst finishes, mfg. 1986-87.

	N/A	$400	$350	$300	$250	$200	$150

T-465 (T-463) - similar to T-454, except has bound body, rosewood fingerboard with pearl dot inlay, mfg. 1986-87.

	N/A	$400	$350	$300	$250	$200	$150

TRADITIONAL - offset double cutaway alder body, bolt-on maple neck, 21-fret rosewood fingerboard with pearl dot inlay, standard vibrato, maple peghead with screened logo, 6-on-a-side tuners, chrome hardware, 3 single coil ESP pickups, 1 volume/2 tone controls, 5-position switch, available in Black, Candy Apple Red, Lake Placid Blue, Olympic White, Two-Tone Sunburst, or Three-Tone Sunburst finishes, mfg. 1989-1990.

	N/A	$700	$600	$525	$450	$375	$300

Last MSR was $1,295.

This model had an optional maple fingerboard with black dot inlay.

TRADITIONAL REISSUE - similar to Traditional, except has pearloid pickguard, 22-fret fingerboard with pearl dot inlay, locking tuners, available in Black, Burgundy, Candy Apple Red, Gunmetal Blue, Metallic Blue, Metallic Purple, Pearl Yellow, or Pearl White finishes, mfg. 1993 only.

	N/A	$700	$600	$525	$450	$375	$300

Last MSR was $1,295.

ELECTRIC: VINTAGE PLUS SERIES

VINTAGE - offset double cutaway alder body, white lam pickguard, bolt-on maple neck, 22-fret maple or rosewood fingerboard with dot inlay, standard vibrato, 6-on-a-side tuners, chrome hardware, 3 single coil ESP pickups, 1 volume/2-Tone controls, 5-position switch, available in Black, Burgundy Mist, Candy Apple Red, Olympic White, 2-Tone Sunburst, 3-Tone Sunburst, or Turquoise finishes, mfg. 1994-95.

	$825	$750	$675	$600	$525	$450	$375

Last MSR was $1,095.

VINTAGE PLUS S - offset double cutaway alder or ash body, bolt-on maple neck, 22-fret maple or rosewood fingerboard with dot inlay (logo block inlay at 12th fret), 2-point tremolo, 6-on-a-side Sperzel locking tuners, chrome hardware, pearloid pickguard, 3 Vintage Rail Seymour Duncan single coil pickups, 1 volume/2 tone controls, 5-position switch, available in 2-Tone Sunburst, 3-Tone Sunburst, Black, Metallic Gold, Pearl White, or Turquoise finishes, mfg. 1995-2000.

	$950	$850	$775	$650	$575	$450	$425

Last MSR was $1,249.

In 1998, 3 ESP SS-120 single coil pickups replaced the 3 Vintage Rail Seymour Duncan pickups; Honey Sunburst, Trans. Blue, Transparent Green, Transparent Purple, and Transparent Red finishes were introduced (these finishes were previously a $100 optional upgrade); Metallic Gold, Pearl White, and Turquoise finishes were disc.

Vintage Plus S with Floyd Rose - similar to Vintage Plus S, except has double locking Floyd Rose vibrato, 2 single coil/1 humbucker ESP pickups, volume/tone control, mfg. 1995-98.

	$1,200	$1,050	$925	$800	$650	$525	$400

Last MSR was $1,595.

E

GRADING	100% MINT	98% NEAR MINT	95% EXC+	90% EXC	80% VG+	70% VG	60% G

VINTAGE PLUS T - single cutaway bound alder or ash body, bolt-on maple neck, 22-fret maple or rosewood fingerboard with dot inlay (logo block inlay at 12th fret), string-through fixed bridge, 6-on-a-side tuners, chrome hardware, pearloid pickguard, 2 single coil Seymour Duncan Vintage '54 pickups, volume/tone control, 3-position switch, controls mounted on a chrome plate, available in 2-Tone Sunburst, 3-Tone Sunburst, Black, Metallic Gold, Pearl White, or Turquoise finishes, mfg. 1994-2000.

	$1,100	$975	$850	$750	$625	$500	$375

Last MSR was $1,449.

In 1998, 2 ESP TS-120 single coil pickups replaced the 2 Seymour Duncan Vintage '54 single coil pickups; Honey Sunburst, Trans. Blue, Trans. Purple, and Trans. Red finishes were introduced (these finishes were previously a $100 optional upgrade); Metallic Gold, Pearl White, Trans. Green, and Turquoise finishes were disc.

ELECTRIC: VIPER & XJ SERIES

VIPER - offset waist/double cutaway mahogany body with pointed horns, bolt-on maple neck, 24-fret bound rosewood fingerboard, 3-per-side bound headstock, chrome hardware, tune-o-matic bridge/stop tailpiece, 2 ESP LH-200 humbuckers with nickel covers/black retaining rings, volume/tone control, 3-way pickup toggle switch, available in Black, Metallic Gold, Pearl White, or Turquoise finishes, mfg. 1997-99.

	$900	$825	$750	$675	$600	$525	$450

Last MSR was $1,199.

In 1998, See-Through Blue, See-Through Green, See-Through Purple, and See-Through Red finishes were introduced (these finishes were previously a $100 optional upgrade); Metallic Gold and Turquoise finishes were disc.

ESP Vintage Plus Custom
courtesy ESP

VIPER CUSTOM (ESP CUSTOM SHOP) - offset double cutaway (similar to an SG) mahogany body with flamed maple top, 3-piece maple neck, 24-fret ebony fingerboard with flag inlays and ESP logo at 12th fret, matching headstock with 3-per-side tuners, 2 EMG-81 Humbucker pickups, TonePros locking bridge/tailpiece, two knobs (v, tone), 3-way switch, black hardware, available in See-Through Black Cherry or See-Through Black finishes, mfg. 2003-present.

MSR	$4,299		$3,225	$2,850	$2,500	$2,250	$2,000	$1,700	$1,400

VIPER (STANDARD SERIES) - offset double cutaway (similar to an SG) mahogany body, mahogany neck, 24-fret ebony fingerboard with dot inlays and ESP logo at 12th fret, 3-per-side tuners, 2 EMG-81 humbucker pickups, Gotoh tune-o-matic with stop tailpiece, two knobs (v, tone), 3-way switch, black hardware, available in Black or Camo finishes, mfg. 2004-present.

MSR	$1,799		$1,350	$1,175	$1,025	$900	$775	$650	$500

Add $75 for Camo finish.

XJ-6 - offset double cutaway alder or ash body with pointed bass bout/rounded treble bout, maple neck, 22-fret maple or rosewood neck with dot inlay, 6-on-a-side reverse headstock, shell pickguard, chrome hardware, fixed bridge, 2 Seymour Duncan mini-humbuckers, volume/tone control, 3-way pickup toggle switch (on treble bout), 3-way split/series/parallel mini-switch, available in 2-Tone Sunburst, 3-Tone Sunburst, Black, Metallic Gold, Pearl White, or Turquoise finishes, mfg. 1996-98.

	$1,050	$900	$800	$725	$625	$495	$395

Last MSR was $1,495.

Add $100 for See-Through Blue, See-Through Green, See-Through Purple, or See-Through Red finishes.

XJ-12 - similar to the XJ-6, except has 12-string configuration, 4/8 reverse headstock, 2 ESP LH-200 humbuckers, mfg. 1996-98.

	$1,150	$1,000	$850	$750	$675	$550	$425

Last MSR was $1,595.

ELECTRIC BASS: B SERIES

The only current models that ESP makes for bass are the signature series. All other basses are made under the LTD name.

Add $250 for Seymour Duncan bass pickup set on models where the Seymour Duncans are not standard. Add $300 for 2-Tek bridge.

B-1 - offset double cutaway alder body, maple neck, 21-fret maple or rosewood fingerboard with dot inlay, 2-per-side headstock, fixed tailpiece, black hardware, Seymour Duncan MusicMan Basslines humbucker, volume/treble/bass controls, active EQ, available in Black, Candy Apple Red, Metallic Gold, or Pearl White, mfg. 1997-2000.

	$950	$850	$750	$650	$575	$450	$350

Last MSR was $1,349.

B-FIVE - sleek offset double cutaway ash body, maple neck, 24-fret rosewood fingerboard with pearl dot inlay, 3/2-per-side headstock, fixed bridge, black hardware, 2 ESP single coil pickups, 2 volume/blend/tone controls, 2 pickup selector switches, active CIR-1 EQ circuit, available in Black, Natural, See-Through Blue, See-Through Green, See-Through Purple, or See-Through Red finishes, mfg. 1995-97.

	$1,400	$1,150	$1,025	$900	$775	$650	$500

Last MSR was $1,895.

B-FOUR - similar to the B-5, except in a 4-string configuration, 2-per-side headstock, mfg. 1996-97.

	$1,250	$1,050	$950	$850	$725	$600	$450

Last MSR was $1,695.

ESP B-Four
courtesy ESP

GRADING	100% MINT	98% NEAR MINT	95% EXC+	90% EXC	80% VG+	70% VG	60% G

ELECTRIC BASS: J SERIES

J-FOUR - offset double cutaway asymmetrical alder or ash body, bolt-on maple neck, 21-fret rosewood fingerboard with pearl dot inlay (logo block inlay at 12th fret), fixed bridge, 4-on-a-side tuners, chrome hardware, pearloid pickguard, 2 J-style ESP pickups, 2 volume/1 tone controls mounted on metal plate, available in 2-Tone Sunburst, 3-Tone Sunburst, Black, Candy Apple Red, Gunmetal Blue, or Pearl White finishes, mfg. 1994-2000.

	$825	$750	$650	$550	$450	$375	$275

Last MSR was $1,079.

In 1997, Candy Apple Red, Gunmetal Blue, 2-Tone Sunburst finishes were disc; Metallic Gold and Turquoise finishes were introduced. In 1998, See-Through Blue, See-Through Green, See-Through Purple, and See-Through Red finishes were introduced; Metallic Gold and Turquoise finishes were disc.

J-Five - similar to J-Four, except has 5-string configuration, 5-on-one-side tuners, mfg. 1994-2000.

	$875	$800	$700	$600	$500	$400	$295

Last MSR was $1,179.

J-464 - Offset double cutaway asymmetrical hardwood body, bolt-on maple neck, 21-fret rosewood fingerboard with pearl dot inlay, fixed bridge, 4-on-a-side tuners, chrome hardware, white pickguard, 2 J-style pickups, 2 volume/1 tone controls, available in 2-Tone Sunburst, 3-Tone Sunburst, Baby Blue, Black, Blonde, Fiesta Red, Lake Placid Blue, Metallic Blue, Metallic Red, Natural, Olympic White, or Salmon Pink finishes, mfg. 1986 only.

	N/A	$350	$300	$250	$200	$150	$100

This model has an optional tortoiseshell pickguard.

ELECTRIC BASS: HORIZON SERIES

HORIZON - offset double cutaway mahogany body, bolt-on maple neck, 21-fret maple fingerboard with black dot inlay, fixed bridge, 4-on-a-side tuners, black hardware, P-style pickup, volume/tone control, available in Baby Blue, Black, Bubblegum Pink, Candy Apple Blue, Fiesta Red, Metallic Blue, Metallic Red, Midnight Black, Mint Green, Snow White, Transparent Cherry Red, or Trans. Blue finishes, mfg. 1986 only.

	N/A	$450	$400	$350	$300	$250	$200

HORIZON PJ - similar to Horizon, except has rosewood fingerboard with pearl dot inlay, P/J-style pickups, 2 volume/1 tone controls, mfg. 1986 only.

	N/A	$450	$400	$350	$300	$250	$200

HORIZON-4 - offset double cutaway maple body, bolt-on maple neck, 24-fret ebony fingerboard, fixed bridge, blackface peghead with screened logo, 2-per-side tuners, chrome hardware, P/J-style EMG pickups, volume/bass/treble/mix controls, active electronics, available in Black, Bright Red, Snow White, or Turquoise finishes, mfg. 1987-1993.

	N/A	$1,500	$1,300	$1,150	$1,000	$850	$700

Last MSR was $2,195.

In 1988, Gunmetal Blue, Mediterranean Blue, Midnight Black, Pearl Pink and Pearl Yellow finishes were introduced. In 1989, Burgundy Mist, Cherry Sunburst were introduced, through-body maple neck, bound fingerboard with offset pearl dot inlay, bound peghead, black hardware, replaced original part/designs, Mediterranean Blue, Midnight Black, Pearl Pink and Pearl Yellow finishes were disc. In 1990, Candy Apple Red, Dark Metallic Blue and Pearl White finishes were introduced, offset pearl dot fingerboard inlay/12th logo block inlay replaced respective items, Bright Red, Burgundy Mist, Cherry Sunburst, Snow White and Turquoise finishes were disc. In 1991, Dark Metallic Purple finish was introduced. In 1992, Metallic Green finish was introduced, Dark Metallic Blue finish was disc.

HORIZON-5 - similar to Horizon-4, except has 5-string configuration, 3/2-per-side tuners, mfg. 1987-1993.

	N/A	$1,600	$1,400	$1,200	$1,050	$900	$750

Last MSR was $2,395.

ELECTRIC BASS: M-4 SERIES

M-4 STANDARD - offset double cutaway alder body, bolt-on maple neck, 21-fret maple fingerboard with black dot inlay, fixed bridge, 4-on-a-side tuners, black hardware, P/J-style pickups, volume/tone controls, 3-position switch, available in Fiesta Red, Flip Flop Pearl Blue, Flip Flop Pearl Red, Pearl White, or Turquoise finishes, mfg. 1987-1993.

	N/A	$900	$825	$750	$650	$500	$350

Last MSR was $1,295.

In 1989, Black, Brite Red and Snow White finishes were introduced, rosewood fingerboard replaced original part/design, Fiesta Red, Flip Flop Pearl Blue, Flip Flop Pearl Red, Pearl White and Turquoise finishes were disc. In 1990, Candy Apple Red finish was introduced, and Brite Red was disc. From 1990 to 1992, model was disc. In 1992, model was reintroduced, available in Black, Candy Apple Red, Gunmetal Blue, Metallic Green, Metallic Purple and Pearl White finishes.

M-4 CUSTOM - offset double cutaway asymmetrical ash body, bolt-on maple neck, 21-fret rosewood fingerboard with pearl dot inlay, fixed bridge, 4-on-a-side tuners, black hardware, P/J-style pickups, 2 volume/1 tone controls, available in Black, Cherry Sunburst, Pearl White, Trans. Blue, Trans. Purple, or Trans. Red finishes, mfg. 1991 only.

	N/A	$1,000	$875	$750	$650	$525	$375

Last MSR was $1,595.

M-4 DELUXE - similar to M-4 Standard, except has rosewood fingerboard with pearl dot inlay, available in Brite Red, Gunmetal Blue, Midnight Black, Pearl Yellow, Pearl White, or Turquoise finishes, mfg. 1988-1990.

	N/A	$850	$775	$700	$625	$500	$350

Last MSR was $1,195.

In 1989, Black, Candy Apple Red and Magenta finishes were introduced, redesigned bound peghead, P/J-style stacked coil pickups replaced original part/designs, Brite Red, Midnight Black and Turquoise finishes were disc. In 1990, Pearl Yellow finish was disc.

GRADING	100% MINT	98% NEAR MINT	95% EXC+	90% EXC	80% VG+	70% VG	60% G

ELECTRIC BASS: M-5 SERIES

M-5 STANDARD - offset double cutaway asymmetrical hardwood body, bolt-on maple neck, 21-fret rosewood fingerboard with pearl dot inlay, fixed bridge, 5-on-one-side tuners, chrome hardware, 2 J-style pickups, 2 volume/1 tone controls, available in Black, Dark Metallic Blue, Flip Flop Pearl Red, or Pearl White finishes, mfg. 1987 only.

	N/A	$350	$300	$250	$200	$150	$100

M-5 CUSTOM - offset double cutaway asymmetrical ash body, bolt-on maple neck, 21-fret rosewood fingerboard with pearl dot inlay, fixed bridge, 5-on-one-side tuners, black hardware, P/J-style pickups, 2 volume/1 tone controls, available in Black, Candy Apple Red, Dark Metallic Blue, Dark Metallic Purple, Gunmetal Blue and Pearl White finishes, mfg. 1991 only.

	N/A	$800	$700	$600	$500	$400	$300

Last MSR was $1,695.

M-5 DELUXE - similar to M-5 Standard, except has rosewood fingerboard with pearl dot inlay, available in Brite Red, Gunmetal Blue, Midnight Black, Pearl Yellow, Pearl White, or Turquoise finishes, mfg. 1988 only.

	$400	$350	$250	$300	$250	$200	$150

ELECTRIC BASS: MISC. MODELS

ECLIPSE BASS - single cutaway alder body, maple neck, 21-fret bound rosewood fingerboard with pearl dot inlay/logo block inlay at 12th fret, 2-per-side bound headstock, fixed bridge, chrome hardware, 2 ESP exposed humbucker pickups, volume/blend/tone controls, available in Black, Gunmetal Blue, Honey Sunburst, Metallic Gold, or Pearl White finishes, mfg. 1996-97.

	$1,200	$1,050	$900	$750	$650	$550	$450

Last MSR was $1,595.

Add $300 for Transparent finish and EMG pickups (Available in See-Through Black, See-Through Blue, See-Through Green, See-Through Purple, and See-Through Red finishes).

This model has an optional mahogany body.

METAL IV - Offset double cutaway hardwood body, bolt-on maple neck, 21-fret maple fingerboard with black dot inlay, fixed bridge, 4-on-a-side tuners, gold hardware, P/J-style pickups, 2 volume/1 tone controls, available in Pearl Blue, Pearl Green, Pearl Pink, Pearl White, or Metallic Purple, mfg. 1986 only.

	N/A	$350	$300	$250	$200	$150	$100

ELECTRIC BASS: P SERIES

P-457 - offset double cutaway hardwood body, white pickguard, bolt-on maple neck, 21-fret maple fingerboard with black dot inlay, fixed bridge, 4-on-a-side tuners, chrome hardware, P-style pickup, 2 volume/1 tone controls, available in Baby Blue, Black, Blonde, Fiesta Red, Lake Placid Blue, Metallic Blue, Metallic Red, Natural, Olympic White, Salmon Pink, Two-Tone Sunburst, or Three-Tone Sunburst finishes, mfg. 1986 only.

	N/A	$350	$300	$250	$200	$150	$100

P-464 - similar to P-457, except has tortoiseshell pickguard, rosewood fingerboard with pearl dot inlay, mfg. 1986 only.

	N/A	$350	$300	$250	$200	$150	$100

ESP Tom Araya courtesy ESP

ELECTRIC BASS: SIGNATURE SERIES

TOM ARAYA BASS - offset double cutaway gothic look, alder body and maple neck, ebony gingerboard with pentagram position markers, Slayer logo at 12th fret, black hardware, 2-per-side tuners, Gotoh 206 bridge, 24 XJ frets, two EMG-35-DC pickups, volume, pan, EMG-BQS, Active EQ, available in Black finish, mfg. 2001-present.

MSR	$3,499		$2,625	$2,300	$2,100	$1,850	$1,600	$1,400	$1,200

MARCELO DIAS - double cutaway alder body, maple neck, 22-fret ebony fingerboard with symbol inlays, singature on headstock with 2-per-side tuners, 2 Basslines SMB-4D pickups, Seymour Duncan STC-3M3 active EQ with slap control, four knobs, Gotoh Deluxe Bass bridge, black hardware, Gray Satin finish with "9" graphic, mfg. 2002-03.

	$2,475	$2,200	$1,950	$1,700	$1,500	$1,300	$1,100

Last MSR was $3,299.

JEREMY MARSHALL - offset double cutaway ash body, 5-piece maple and walnut neck, 24-fret ebony fingerboard with cold spider inlays, 5-string configuration, signature on headstock with 3/2-per-side tuners, 2 EMG 40-DC pickups, EMG BQS active EQ, five knobs, Gotoh bridge, chrome hardware, available in Black Satin finish, mfg. 2002-03.

	$2,625	$2,350	$2,100	$1,850	$1,600	$1,400	$1,200

Last MSR was $3,499.

ESP Surveyor II Standard courtesy ESP

GRADING	100% MINT	98% NEAR MINT	95% EXC+	90% EXC	80% VG+	70% VG	60% G

ELECTRIC BASS: SURVEYOR SERIES

SURVEYOR - offset double cutaway mahogany body, black pickguard, bolt-on maple neck, 21-fret ebony fingerboard with pearl dot inlay, fixed bridge, 4-on-a-side tuners, black hardware, P/J-style pickups, 2 volume/1 tone controls, available in Black, Bright Yellow, Snow White, or Trans. Cherry Red finishes, mfg. 1987 only.

	N/A	$400	$350	$300	$250	$200	$150

SURVEYOR CUSTOM - offset double cutaway mahogany body, black pickguard, bolt-on maple neck, 21-fret ebony fingerboard, fixed bridge, 4-on-a-side tuners, black hardware, P/J-style pickups, volume/tone control, 3-way switch, available in Baby Blue, Black, Bubblegum Pink, Candy Apple Blue, Fiesta Red, Metallic Blue, Metallic Red, Midnight Black, Mint Green, Snow White, Trans. Cherry Red and Trans. Blue finishes, mfg. 1986-89.

	N/A	$450	$400	$350	$300	$250	$200

In 1988, Brite Red, Gunmetal Blue, Mediterranean Blue, Pearl Yellow, Pearl White and Turquoise finishes were introduced, redesigned body/bound peghead, through-body maple neck, 24-fret bound fingerboard with offset pearl block inlay/logo block inlay at 12th fret replaced original part/designs, Baby Blue, Bubblegum Pink, Candy Apple Blue, Fiesta Red, Metallic Blue, Metallic Red, Mint Green, Trans. Cherry Red and Trans. Blue finishes were disc. In 1989, Candy Apple Red and Magenta finishes were introduced, Brite Red, Mediterranean Blue, Snow White and Turquoise finishes were disc.

SURVEYOR DELUXE - similar to Surveyor Custom, except has pearl dot fingerboard inlay, mfg. 1986 only.

	N/A	$450	$400	$350	$300	$250	$200

This model had an optional rosewood fingerboard with black dot inlay.

SURVEYOR II (STANDARD SERIES) - offset double cutaway (P-Bass style), ash body, bolt-on maple neck, 21 XJ fret maple or ebony fingerboard with dot inlay and ESP logo in 12th fret, EMG MMTW/35-P4 pickups, four knobs, matching headstock, 4-on-a-side tuners, Wikinson bridge, chrome hardware, available in Natural or Black finishes, mfg. 2004-present.

MSR	$1,549		$1,175	$1,025	$925	$800	$675	$550	$425

Add $35 for Black finish.

EYB GUITARS

Instruments currently built in Leonberg, Germany.

Luthier Gunter Eyb handcrafts custom electric guitar and bass models. Models are constructed using a wide range of clever designs based on classic configurations, and utilize additional piezo pickups and sustainer pickups. For further information concerning specifications and pricing, contact luthier Gunter Eyb directly (see Trademark Index).

EAGLE (GERMANY)

Instruments currently built in Murr, Germany.

Eagle Country Instruments produces the smallest full-size electric bass guitar (34 in. scale, 36 in. overall length). This innovative design features a padauk/maple/mahogany construction, reverse stringing/no headstock. Retail prices run from $1,480 (4-string) to $1,620 (5-string). No new information was available at time of publication.

EAGLE (SWEDEN)

Instruments currently produced in Korea under the name Sweagle. See Sweagle.

ECCLESHALL

Instruments currently built in England since the early 1970s.

Luthier Christopher J. Eccleshall is known for the high quality guitars that he produces. Eccleshall also builds violins, mandolins, and banjos. Some of his original designs carry such model designations as **Excalibur**, **EQ**, and **Craftsman**. Eccleshall was also the first UK maker to have Japanese-built solid body guitars. Eccleshall also is an authorized repairer of Gibson, Guild, and Martin guitars (source: Tony Bacon and Paul Day, *The Guru's Guitar Guide*).

ECHEVERRIA GUITARS

Instruments currently built in Tucson, AZ, beginning 1984.

Luthier Richard Echeverria designed, built, restored and sold guitars for over twenty years. He has been a member of both G.A.L. (since 1980) and A.S.I.A. (since 1989) lutherie groups, and introduced his formalized line of guitars after years of building custom one-of-a-kind instruments. He used to build in Morrow, Georgia.

Mahogany was one of Echeverria's favorite woods that he used extensively to create his original design electrics. All models had a tongue-and-groove set-in neck design, and were finished in a nitrocellulose lacquer finish. Echeverria uses a wide range of quality (and some custom) pickups from Tom Holmes, Joe Barden, Van Zandt, Seymour Duncan, and DiMarzio.

ELECTRIC

The **Aztore** model is a hybrid of design ideas from Gibson's Firebird and Explorer models, combined with an original modernistic body design. Echeverria favors Korina and mahogany in the construction, a 24.625 in. scale, 6-on-a-side reverse banjo style tuners with pearloid buttons, a tune-o-matic stop tailpiece, and 2 humbuckers.

The **Magnolia** (list $3,200) shares a similar 24.625 in. scale and Gibson-esque vibe, but this model has a single rounded/Florentine cutaway mahogany body and an arched flame maple top. Body, fingerboard, and headstock are all bound, and the fingerboard has block inlays. 2 humbuckers and a tune-o-matic bridge/stop tailpiece wrap up this classicly designed model, thus proving that "Les" is more!

The **Echo** has a Fender-y Jazzmaster feel to the offset double cutaway mahogany (or alder or swamp ash) body. The 25.5 in. scale is combined with a 3-per-side headstock, 2 humbuckers, and a tune-o-matic bridge/stop tailpiece - offering a different tonal feel to a Fender-scale guitar. This model is also available with a flame maple top.

ECLECTIC "GUITARS BY DESIGN"

Instruments currently built in Duncan, SC.

Luthier Brad Armstrong offers custom-crafted, custom-designed electric guitars. Armstrong offers a wide range of exotic woods such as Lacewood, Purpleheart, and Zebrawood in his creations. Eclectic guitars are entirely built on the customers requests. The guitars start at $850 and take about three months to finish.

ED CLARK GUITARS, INC.

Instruments currently built in Ronkonkoma, NY.

Luthier and repairman Ed Clark specializes in all phases of guitar repair work, fretwork, and bridge installations, and he also custom builds guitars and basses. Clark is also a contributing editor in *20th Century Guitar* magazine.

EGMOND

See Rosetti and Lion. Instruments previously built in Holland between 1960 and 1972.

In response to the pop music boom of the 1960s, guitar companies kept turning out instruments to try to meet the generated demand. These entry level guitars were aimed at the novice guitar player, and featured a line of Dutch-built solid and semi-hollow body designs (source: Tony Bacon and Paul Day, *The Guru's Guitar Guide*). Used models are typically are found between $200 and $400.

EGYPT

Instruments previously produced in England between 1985 and 1987.

The Egypt trademark was utilized by Scottish builders Maurice Bellando and James Cannell in the mid- to late 1980s. These high quality, strikingly original solid body designs also featured Egyptian names. The luthiers also produced a range of Fender/Gibson-style models as well (source: Tony Bacon and Paul Day, *The Guru's Guitar Guide*).

EKO

Trademark of instruments currently built the Czech Republic, Asia, Spain (classical), and Italy. EKO is now part of the E Group, which is split into EKO (Italian distributor of musical instruments), Esound (Italian distributor of musical instruments), Etek (professional audio producer and world wide musical instruments distributor), and Res (service society). Instruments were formerly built in Italy from the early 1960s through 1987. Distribution in the U.S. market by the LoDuca Bros. of Milwaukee, WI.

**Edmon Eletric
courtesy John Beeson
The Music Shoppe**

The LoDuca Bros. musical distribution company was formed in 1941 by brothers Tom and Guy LoDuca. Capitalizing on money made through their accordion-based vaudevillian act, lessons, and accordion repair, the LoDucas began importing and selling Italian accordions. Throughout the 1940s and 1950s, the LoDucas built up a musical distributorship with accordions and sheet music. By the late 1950s, they were handling Magnatone amplifiers and guitars.

In 1961, the LoDucas teamed up with Italy-based Oliviero Pigini & Company to import guitars. Pigini, one of the LoDuca's accordion manufacturers, had formed the EKO company in anticipation of the boom in the guitar market. The LoDucas acted as technical designers and gave input on EKO designs (as well as being the exclusive U.S. dealers), and EKO built guitars for their dealers. Some of the sparkle finishes were no doubt inspired by the accordions produced in the past. In fact, the various on/off switches and tone settings are down right reminiscent of accordion voice settings! The plastic-covered guitars lasted through the mid 1960s, when more conventional finishes were offered. EKO also built a number of guitars for Vox, Goya, and Thomas companies.

By 1967, EKO had established dealers in 57 countries around the world. During the late 1960s and early 1970s, the guitar market began to get soft, and many guitar builders began to go out of business. EKO continued on, but cut back the number of models offered. In the late 1970s, EKO introduced a custom shop branch that built neck-through designed guitars for other trademarks. Once such company was D'Agostino, and EKO produced the **Bench Mark** models from 1978 to 1982.

The EKO company kept producing models until 1985. By the mid-1980s, the LoDuca Bros. company had begun concentrating on guitar case production, and stopped importing the final Alembic-styled set-neck guitars that were being produced. The original EKO company's holdings were liquidated in 1987.

Currently, the EKO trademark has again been revived in Italy, and appears on entry level solid body guitars built in various countries. The revived company is offering a wide range of acoustic, classical, and solid body electric guitars and amplifiers - all with contemporary market designs (EKO history source: Michael Wright, *Guitar Stories*, Volume One).

ELECTRIC

EKO produced a number of different models, like the semi-hollowbody 335-ish **Barracuda** series; or electric/acoustic cutaway models like the **Escort**, **Commander**, and **Mascot**. EKO offered violin-shaped guitars and basses; and solid body guitars like the double offset cutaway **Lancer** series, or the rocket ship-shaped **Roke** guitars and basses. More traditional were the **Kadett** and **Cobra** lines. A number of EKO designs were based on Fender's Jazzmaster model.

Current models are Gibson- and Fender-based electric guitar designs, and dreadnought style acoustics.

Prices on vintage EKO models typically range $200-$400 - some of the more elaborate models may be priced as high as $500-$700, depending on condition, appeal, and relative coolness of the piece.

**EKO 500-3V
courtesy J.R. Guitars**

GRADING	100% MINT	98% NEAR MINT	95% EXC+	90% EXC	80% VG+	70% VG	60% G

EKO's new models consist of the **Camaro**, **Manta**, and the **Cobra II** for electric guitars. They make a **Manta** and a **Cobra** in bass form as well. These models are based off of the popular '60s style guitars. For more information on the new models refer to their website (see Trademark Index).

MODEL 500/1 - offset double cutaway assymetrical body (Jazzmaster style), small tortoiseshell pickguard, 1 single coil pickup, two knobs, available in various sparkle plastic finishes (Red, Blue, Yellow, etc.), mfg. circa early 1960s.

	N/A	$400	$325	$275	$225	$175	$125

MODEL 500/2 - offset double cutaway assymetrical body (Jazzmaster style), large tortoiseshell pickguard with EKO logo, 2 single coil pickups, two knobs, 4 pickup slide switches, available in various sparkle plastic finishes (Red, Blue, Yellow, etc.), mfg. circa early 1960s.

	N/A	$500	$425	$350	$275	$225	$175

MODEL 500/3 - offset double cutaway assymetrical body (Jazzmaster style), large tortoiseshell pickguard with EKO logo, 3 single coil pickups, two knobs, 6 pickup slide switches, available in various sparkle plastic finishes (Red, Blue, Yellow, etc.), mfg. circa early 1960s.

	N/A	$600	$525	$450	$375	$300	$225

Model 500/3V - similar to the Model 500/3, except has a vibrato arm, mfg. circa early 1960s.

	N/A	$650	$575	$500	$425	$350	$275

MODEL 500/4 - offset double cutaway assymetrical body (Jazzmaster style), large tortoiseshell pickguard with EKO logo, 4 single coil pickups in humbucker placement, two knobs, 6 pickup slide switches, available in various sparkle plastic finishes (Red, Blue, Yellow, etc.), mfg. circa early 1960s.

	N/A	$700	$625	$550	$450	$350	$250

Model 500/4V - similar to the Model 500/4, except has a vibrato tailpiece, mfg. circa early 1960s.

	N/A	$750	$675	$600	$500	$400	$300

MODEL 700/4V - offset double cutaway assymetrical body (Jazzmaster style) with lower bout cutout ("tulip body"), large tortoiseshell pickguard with EKO logo, 4 single coil pickups in humbucker placement, two knobs, 6 pickup slide switches, vibrato tailpiece, available in various sparkle plastic finishes (Red, Blue, Yellow, etc.), mfg. circa early 1960s.

	N/A	$1,200	$1,050	$900	$750	$600	$450

EL MAYA

See Maya. Instruments previously built in Japan from the mid-1970s to the mid-1980s.

The El Maya instruments were generally good quality solid body guitars featuring original designs and some based on Fender styles. The El Maya trademark was part of range offered by the Maya guitar producer (source: Tony Bacon and Paul Day, *The Guru's Guitar Guide*).

ELECA

Instruments currently produced in China. Distributed by Eleca International Inc. of Walnut, CA.

Eleca instruments are produced in China and distributed throughout the United States. They produce a variety of electric and acoustic guitars. Most electric guitars are based off of popular American designs, such as the Les Paul, Telecaster, and the Flying V. Most of their products are offered at a competitive price. For more information please refer to the website (see Trademark Index).

ELECTRA

Instruments previously built in Japan circa 1971 to 1983/1984. Distributed by the St. Louis Music Supply Company of St. Louis, MO.

Electra guitars, like Alvarez, was a brand name used by the St. Louis Music Supply company. The Electra and Apollo brands were introduced in 1971 as a replacement for the U.S.-built Custom Kraft instruments (Apollo was the budget brand line). Many models were bolt-neck versions of popular American instruments.

Tom Presley was hired by St. Louis Music in 1975 to work on the Modular Powered Circuits (MPC) program. The MPC line of guitars (mostly a Les Paul-ish style) featured cavities in the back of the instrument where 2 battery-powered effects modules could be plugged in. Thus, the guitarists' effects would be mounted in the instrument instead of located on the floor like stomp box effects. The effect modules had controls that could be preset after being plugged in; the guitar face had on/off toggle switches. The MPC idea is actually pretty clever! The distortion MPC modules also led to the development of SLM's Crate guitar amplifiers.

In 1983, St. Louis Music noticed that a west coast dealer had begun selling low-end imported guitars using the Electra trademark. Although prior use belonged to St. Louis Music, it was felt that there would be some confusion with dealers and the public sorting out the differing levels of quality. Right off, the trademark switched to Electra/Phoenix. Then, in 1984, St. Louis Music announced that the Electra trademark would be merged with another Japanese-built brand, Westone. Models were sold under the Electra/Westone imprint for a year, then finally Westone only as the Electra aspect was disc. (early trademark history courtesy Michael Wright, *Vintage Guitar Magazine*).

MODEL IDENTIFICATION

1971-1975: All models have bolt-on necks, and resemble models offered by Univox during the same time period. By 1975, a wide range of Fender-ish/Gibson-esque models were offered.

1975: Joint venture agreement signed with a guitar company in Matsumoku, Japan; Tom Presley hired to oversee guitar design.

1976-1977: Les Paul-styled guitars switch to glued (set-in) necks. MPC guitar models introduced.

1983-1985: Electra trademark phased out in favor of Westone name.

ELECTRIC: AVENGER, ROCK, & TREE OF LIFE SERIES

AVENGER - offset double cutaway hardwood body, bolt-on maple neck, 22-fret maple fingerboard with black dot inlays, tremolo bridge, chrome hardware, 6-on-a-side tuners, white pickguard, 3 single coil pickups, volume/tone controls, available in Cream, Jet Black, or Sunburst finishes, mfg. 1972-79.

	N/A	$350	$300	$250	$200	$150	$100

GRADING	100% MINT	98% NEAR MINT	95% EXC+	90% EXC	80% VG+	70% VG	60% G

ELECTRA ROCK - single cutaway bound mahogany body, bird's-eye maple (or jacaranda) top, bolt-on maple neck, 22-fret maple fingerboard with black trapezoidal inlays, chrome or gold hardware, 3-per-side headstock, bridge/stop tailpiece, white raised pickguard, 2 humbucker pickups, 2 volume/2 tone controls, 3-way selector, available in Apple Red, Black, Goldtop, or Sunburst finishes, mfg. 1972-75.

	N/A	$375	$325	$275	$225	$175	$125

SUPER ROCK (MODEL 2245) - single cutaway bound mahogany body, maple top, bolt-on maple neck, 22-fret rosewood fingerboard with pearl crown inlays, chrome or gold hardware, 3-per-side headstock, bridge/stop tailpiece, white raised pickguard, 2 humbucker pickups, 2 volume/2-Tone controls, 3-way selector, available in Apple Red, Black, Goldtop, or Sunburst finishes, mfg. 1972-77.

	N/A	$350	$300	$250	$200	$150	$100

Magnum II - similar to the Super Rock, except has black body binding, black bound maple fingerboard with black crown inlay, clear pickguard, available in Natural finish only, mfg. 1974-77.

	N/A	$300	$250	$220	$185	$150	$120

Omega - similar to the Super Rock, except has Tone Spectrum Circuit: 5-way rotary pickup selector switch on upper bass bout, mfg. 1976-78.

	N/A	$325	$275	$225	$175	$150	$125

TREE OF LIFE - single cutaway bound mahogany body, leaf-design carved maple top, bolt-on maple neck, 22-fret maple fingerboard with vine design inlay, chrome hardware, 3-per-side headstock, tune-o-matic bridge/stop tailpiece, raised transparent pickguard, 2 humbucker pickups (1 covered, 1 exposed coils), 2 volume/2 tone controls, 3-way selector, available in Natural finish, mfg. circa 1973-75.

	N/A	$500	$425	$375	$325	$275	$225

ELECTRIC: MPC SERIES

Modular Powered Circuit (MPC) model guitars were introduced in 1976. The purpose of the design was to place effects typically found in pedals directly on-board the guitar itself. MPC models were available in 11 different types of effects: The Phase Shifter and Booster modules were included with the MPC instrument. Other modules available were the Power Overdrive, Treble/Bass Expander, Electronic Fuzz, Tank Tone, Frog Nose, Triggered Filter, Auto Wah, Tube Sound, Octave Splitter, and Flanger.

MPC - single cutaway mahogany body, maple top, set-in maple neck, 22-fret rosewood fingerboard with abalone block inlays, chrome hardware, 3-per-side headstock, bridge/stop tailpiece, white raised pickguard, 2 covered Magnaflux humbucker pickups, volume/tone controls, 2 effects control knobs, 2 effects on/off switches, 5-way pickup selector switch on upper bass bout, available in Natural or Sunburst finishes, mfg. 1976-77.

	N/A	$450	$375	$325	$275	$225	$175

Last MSR was $599.

This model has a hinged cover on the back of the instruments that allows access to MPC modules. This cavity holds two MPC modules, and is powered by a 9-volt battery.

MPC STANDARD - similar to the MPC, except has redesigned headstock, available in Antique Sunburst, Jet Black, Trans. Apple Red, Satin Jacaranda, or Sunburst Curly Maple finishes, mfg. 1978-1984.

	N/A	$475	$400	$350	$300	$250	$200

Last MSR was $695.

After 1978, fancier versions such as the MPC Custom, Ultima MPC (special back/heel contour), and double cutaway Leslie West MPC were also offered.

MPC OUTLAW - similar to the MPC Standard, except had a dual cutaway body, mahogany neck-through design, black pickguard, available in Charcoal Grey Sunburst, Natural Mahogany, or Tobacco Sunburst finishes, mfg. 1978-1984.

	N/A	$500	$425	$375	$325	$275	$225

Last MSR was $775.

ELECTRIC: ELECTRA/PHOENIX MFG.

In 1983, the Electra trademark was changed to Electra/Phoenix. These guitars were only produced until 1984, and were made in Japan. These guitars featured an active EQ and custom paint jobs.

PEARL CLOUD (MODEL X155) - offset double cutaway body, bolt-on rock maple neck, 21-fret rosewood fingerboard with white dot inlay, 6-on-a-side headstock, chrome hardware, fixed bridge/through-body stringing, blackface peghead, 2 Magnaflux humbuckers, 2 volume/2 tone push/pull controls, available in Pearl Cloud White finish, mfg 1982-83.

	N/A	$250	$220	$190	$160	$130	$100

Last MSR was $379.

This was a limited edition production instrument. The push/pull controls allowed access to pickup coil tapping and phase reversal.

EKO 500-4V
courtesy J.R. Guitars

Electra Tree-of-Life
courtesy John Boyer

GRADING	100% MINT	98% NEAR MINT	95% EXC+	90% EXC	80% VG+	70% VG	60% G

ELECTRIC BASS: MPC SERIES

MPC OUTLAW BASS - dual cutaway body, neck-through-body construction, 20-fret rosewood fingerboard with bowtie abalone inlays, brass nut, chrome hardware, 2-on-a-side headstock, fixed bridge, black pickguard, covered Magnaflux humbucker (neck position)/P-style pickup, volume/tone controls, 2 effects control knobs, 2 effects on/off switches, 5-way pickup selector switch on upper bass bout, available in Antique Sunburst, or Charcoal Sunburst finishes, mfg. 1978-1984.

	N/A	$450	$375	$325	$275	$225	$175

Last MSR was $695.

This model has a hinged cover on the back of the instrument that allows access to MPC modules. This cavity holds two MPC modules, and is powered by a 9-volt battery.

ELECTRA/PHOENIX

See Electra, Electric: Electra/Phoenix Mfg.

ELECTRA BY WESTONE

See Electra and Westone.

In the late 1970s, the Matsumoku factory in Japan was beginning to build and market Westone guitars. The majority of these instruments were high quality, innovative design instruments with limited (not mass) production. Westone guitars were first introduced to the U.K. market by 1981.

After changing the Electra brandname to Electra/Phoenix in 1984, St. Louis Music announced that the Electra trademark would be merged with Westone in the U.S. market. From 1984 to 1985, models were sold under the Electra by Westone, or Electra/Westone, imprint.

ELECTRO

Instruments previously produced by Electro String Instruments. Distributed by Radio-Tel. See Rickenbacker.

ELGER

Instruments previously produced in Ardmore, PA from 1959 to 1965. Elger began importing instruments produced in Japan during the early 1960s.

Elger instruments were distributed in the U.S. by the Elger Company of Ardmore, Pennsylvania. The roots of the Elger company were founded in 1954 by Harry Rosenbloom when he opened Medley Music in Bryn Mawr, Pennsylvania. In 1959, Rosenbloom decided to produce his own acoustic guitars as the Elger Company (named after his children, Ellen and Gerson). Rosenbloom soon turned from U.S. production to Japanese when the Elger company became partners with Hoshino Gakki Gen, and introduced the **Ibanez** trademark to the U.S. market. Elger did maintain the Pennsylvania facilities to check incoming shipments and correct any flaws prior to shipping merchandise out to their dealers. For further company history, see Ibanez (source: Michael Wright, *Guitar Stories*, Volume One).

ELITE

See Crucianelli. Also see Ardsleys. Instruments previously built in Italy during the mid-1960s.

Entry level solid body guitars that featured similar accordion-style finishes. Many Italian instrument producers were building accordions before the worldwide explosion of guitar popularity in the 1960s, and pearloid finishes are the direct result. Elite´s semi-hollowbody guitars were more normal in appearance (source: Tony Bacon and Paul Day, *The Guru´s Guitar Guide*).

ELK

Instruments previously produced in Japan during the 1960s.

Elk instruments were mid-quality solid body guitars that featured some designs based on classic American favorites. Elk also produced a line of amplifiers with circuitry and cosmetics similar to Fender amps (source: Rittor Books, *60s Bizarre Guitars*).

ELRICK

Instruments currently built in Chicago, IL.

Luthier Robert Elrick handcrafts custom bass guitars. All instruments are constructed with bodies of koa or swamp ash, and feature bookmatched exotic wood tops and backs. Elrick favors Bartolini pickups and 3-band active/passive EQ preamps.

ELECTRIC BASS

The **Elrick Bass Guitar** (thru-neck) has a neck-through design that features either hard maple or wenge necks reinforced with graphite stiffening rods. A 24-fret phenolic fingerboard is standard at a 35 in. scale, however, both 34 in. and 36 in. scale lengths are offered. The **Elrick Bass 4-String** retail lists at $3,600, the **Elrick Bass 5-string** at $3,800, **Elrick Bass 6-string** at $4,000, and the **Elrick Bass 7-String** at $4,200.

Elrick´s **Empire** bolt-on neck bass guitar has similar construction to the neck-through model, except has a heel-less design and 5 bolts attaching the neck to the swamp ash or white ash body. The Empire is available in 4 different string configurations as the **Empire 4-String** ($2,700), **Empire 5-string** ($2,900), **Empire 6-string** ($3,100), and the **Empire 7-String** ($3,300). The Empire Series became the Deluxe series in 1999.

The **Foundation** bolt-on neck bass guitar model has a solid swamp ash body, bolt-on quarter sawn wenge neck, wenge (or bubinga) fingerboard, Bartolini pickups, and 3-band active/passive preamp. The Foundation bass is available in 3 different string configurations as the **Foundation 4-String** ($1,995), **Foundation 5-string** ($2,295), and the **Foundation 6-string** ($2,595). The Foundation series became the Standard Series in 1999.

A **Piccolo Bass Guitar** with a 28.625 in. scale (tuned one octave higher than regular bass) is offered as a custom instrument in 4-, 5-, 6-, 7-, and 8-string configurations. For further information regarding prices and specifications, contact Elrick directly (see Trademark Index).

The **New Jazz Standard** is available as a four-string and a five-string only. These guitars feature 24 frets and the zero fret. The four-string is $2,400 and five-string $2,600.

Elrick now has a new line of basses that are known as the Platinum Series. The thru-neck, which is also the Elrick Bass Guitar, is also part of this series. The **Single Cut** series is priced at $4,100 for a 4-string, $4,300 for a 5-string, $4,500 for a 6-string, and $4,700 for a 7-string. The **Hybrid** Series runs $3,200 for a 4-string, $3,400 for a 5-string, $3,600 for a 6-string, and $3,800 for a 7-string. The Hybrid Series is also available as the **Hybrid Semi-Hollow**. Prices are as follows: $4,400 for a 4-string, $4,600 for a 5-string, $4,800 for a 6-string, and $5,000 for a 7-string.

The **Gold Series** is the entry level line of basses for Elrick. The bolt-on model is available in four-string ($2,400), five-string ($2,600), six-string ($2,800), and seven-string ($3,000). The New Jazz Standard is available in four-string ($2,400) and five-string ($2,600).

Encore P100
courtesy John Horn
by Skewe & Co.

EMERY

Instruments currently built in Britt, MN. Distributed by Resound Vintage Guitars of Britt, MN.

Luthier Jean-Paul Emery has been customizing and building guitars as well as performing restoration work on vintage instruments for several years. For further information, contact luthier Emery directly (see Trademark Index).

EMINENCE

Distributed by G. Edward Lutherie, Inc.

G. Edward Lutherie, Inc. is currently offering a portable upright bass that has a fully acoustic body (that's right, it's hollow). Current models include 4 and 5 strings with removable or non-removable neck and an electric violin. The laminated arched spruce top is mated to laminated arched curly maple back, and combined with piezo pickups and an L.R. Baggs Para Acoustic D.I. This bass has an overall length of 63 in., and total weight of 11 pounds. Retail list price is $3,290. The 4-string retails for $2,800 and the 5-string for $3,050. The removable neck 4-string retails for $3,200, and the 5-string for $2,450. The electric violin retails for $890. For further information, please contact G. Edward Lutherie, Inc. directly (see Trademark Index).

EMMONS

Instruments previously built in Burlington, NC early 1970s. Distributed by the Emmons Guitar Company, Inc. of Burlington, NC.

The Emmons Guitar Company, Inc., perhaps more well-known for their steel guitars produced between the early 1970s and the early 1980s, constructed four different bass models in the early 1970s.

ELECTRIC BASS

It has been estimated that the initials of the bass models correspond with the description of the bass models: For example, does the **LSB-U** model stand for Long Scale Bass Unfretted? Because that's exactly what the model is.

LS-B - offset double cutaway (solid) body, 34 in. scale, 21-fret rosewood fingerboard, 2-per-side Kluson tuners, adjustable bridge, chrome hardware, black pickguard, one Emmons pickup, volume/tone controls, length 46 in., body width 13 in., mfg. circa early 1970s.

N/A	$500	$425	$350	$300	$250	$200

Last MSR was $325.

LSB-U - similar to the LS-B, except has a fretless rosewood fingerboard, length 46 in., body width 13 in., mfg. early 1970s.

N/A	$500	$425	$350	$300	$250	$200

Last MSR was $315.

SS-B - offset double cutaway (solid) body, 30 in. scale, 22-fret rosewood fingerboard, 2-per-side Kluson tuners, adjustable bridge, chrome hardware, black pickguard, one Emmons pickup, volume/tone controls, length 43.5 in., body width 13 in., mfg. circa early 1970s.

N/A	$450	$375	$325	$275	$225	$175

Last MSR was $325.

EMPERADOR

Instruments previously built in Japan by the Kasuga company circa 1966 to 1992. Distributed by Westheimer Musical Instruments of Chicago, IL.

The Emperador trademark was a brand name used in the U.S. market by the Westheimer Musical Instruments of Chicago, Illinois. The Emperador trademark was the Westheimer company's entry level line to their Cort products line through the years. Emperador models are usually shorter-scaled entry level instruments, and the trademark can be found on both jazz-style thinline acoustic/electric archtops and solid body electric guitars and basses. Solid body Emperadors are typically priced between $150 and $250.

EMPIRE GUITARS

Instruments currently built in Glendora, CA. Built by GMW Guitarworks.

Empire guitars are built by GMW Guitarworks. They are mainly upper-end instruments that have many custom options that are available and prices start at around $1,625. For more information regarding Empire guitars, refer to the GMW Guitarworks website (see Trademark Index).

Encore E 83 B Bass
courtesy John Horn
by Skewe & Co.

GRADING	100% MINT	98% NEAR MINT	95% EXC+	90% EXC	80% VG+	70% VG	60% G

ENCORE

Instruments currently produced in Asia. Distributed by John Hornby Skewes & Co., Ltd. of Garforth (Leeds), England.

The Encore trademark is the brand name of UK importer John Hornby Skewes & Co., Ltd. The company was founded in 1965 by its namesake, Mr. John Hornby Skewes. The Encore line consists of solidly built guitars and basses that feature designs based on popular American favorites. Encore instruments are of medium to good quality, and their model E83 bass was named "Most Popular U.K. Bass Guitar" in from 1992 to 1995.

In addition to the Encore line, the John Hornby Skewes company distributes the Vintage instruments line (see Vintage).

ELECTRIC

Though not available in the U.S. market, Encore´s **RK** series is based on popular Rickenbacker stylings. There are also Stratocaster, Les Paul, and Precision Bass copies. For a listing of current Encore models and pricing (in English pounds), please visit John Hornby´s website (see Trademark Index).

ENGLISH GUITARS

Instruments currently built in Jamul, CA since 1993.

English Guitars was founded in 1993 by Jim English. English, disappointed at the quality, price, and playability of current new guitars, decided to offer an alternative with his handcrafted Gretsch-ish guitar models. These models definitely catch the vibe of the 1950s and 1960s, and offer the guitarist the smooth, warm Nashville sound, similar to those that Chuck Berry, Duane Eddy, and Brian Setzer have, according to the catalog.

ELECTRIC

The English guitar model has a single cutaway laminated maple (plain, flame, or quilted) body, 2 bound f-holes, set-in rock maple neck, multiple-ply binding on body/neck/headstock, ebony fingerboard with gold or white mother-of-pearl inlays, 3-per-side Grover Imperial tuners, 2 Filtertron pickups, gold or chrome hardware, Bigsby vibrato tailpiece, 23 karat white or yellow gold leaf under raised pickguard/truss rod cover/pickup rings, master volume/individual pickup volumes/tone controls, and a pickup selector switch. The body width is 17 in. and the body depth is 3 in. English guitars are available in Black, Blue, Country Orange, Fire Orange, Honey Blonde, Sunburst, Walnut, and White finishes.

The **Guitar Model #1** is made of full maple and prices at $3,750. The **Esquire** model has a thinner body (2.3125 in.) and lists for $3,750. English´s **Jazz King** model is similar in construction, except features a 3.25 in. body depth and a solid tailpiece. This model is priced at $4,100.

Prices will vary from model to model. For further information regarding prices and specifications, please contact Jim English directly (see Trademark Index).

ENSENADA

Instruments previously produced in Japan, circa 1970s. Distributed by Strum & Drum of Chicago, IL.

The Ensenada trademark was a brand name of U.S. importers Strum & Drum of Chicago, Illinois. Strum and Drum were later owners of the National trademark, acquired when Valco´s holdings were auctioned off. Ensenada instruments were distributed between roughly 1973 and 1974 (source: Michael Wright, *Guitar Stories*, Volume One).

EPCORE

See Bill Gruggett.

EPI

Instruments produced in China or Indonesia. Distributed by Epiphone (Gibson Musical Instruments) of Nashville, TN.

Epi stringed instruments are the entry level line to the current Epiphone range of guitars and basses.

ELECTRIC

ES-200 (MODEL ES20) - offset double cutaway plywood body, bolt-on maple neck, maple fingerboard, 6-on-a-side tuners, chrome hardware, standard tremolo, two pickups, volume/tone controls, 3-way switch, available in Ebony, Red, Vintage Sunburst, or White finishes, disc.

$145	$130	$115	$100	$85	$70	$55

Last MSR was $249.

ES-300 (MODEL ES30) - similar to ES-200, except has three pickups, available in Ebony, Red, Vintage Sunburst, or White finishes, disc.

$160	$135	$120	$105	$90	$75	$60

Last MSR was $259.

ELECTRIC BASS

EB-100 (MODEL EB10) - offset double cutaway plywood body, bolt-on maple neck, maple fingerboard, 4-on-a-side tuners, chrome hardware, P-style pickup, volume/tone controls, available in Ebony, Red, Vintage Sunburst, or White finishes, disc.

$165	$140	$120	$105	$90	$75	$60

Last MSR was $289.

EPIPHONE

Trademark of instruments currently produced in Korea since 1983. Epiphone is a division of and distributed by Gibson Musical Instruments of Nashville, TN. The original Epiphone company was based in New York, NY from 1930 to 1953, and later in Philadelphia, PA from 1954 to 1957. When Epiphone was purchased by Gibson, production moved to Kalamazoo, MI from 1958 to 1969; then to Japan from 1970 to 1983. Some specialty models were built in Nashville, TN in 1982 to 1983, also from 1989 to 1994.

According to family history, Anastasios Stathopoulo (b. 1863) began constructing musical instruments in his home town of Sparta, Greece in 1873. He moved to the U.S. with his family is 1903, settling in New York City, where he produced a full range of stringed instruments bearing his own name up until the time of his death in 1915. The company, which soon became known as The House of Stathopoulo, continued under the direction and ownership of his wife, Marianthe (b. 1875) and eldest son, Epaminondas (Epi [b. 1893]).

Following Marianthe's death in 1923, The House of Stathopoulo was incorporated with Epi as president and majority shareholder, his sister Alkminie (Minnie [1897-1984]) as treasurer, and brother Orpheus (Orphie [1899-1973]) as secretary. They immediately announced that "the new policy of business [would be] the production of banjos, tenor banjos, banjo mandolins, banjo guitars, and banjo ukuleles under the registered trademark of Epiphone.

The name "Epiphone" was a combination of Epi's nickname with "phone," the Greek word for sound. Their elegant Recording line of tenor banjos was considered to be among the finest ever made. These were joined in the late 1920s by a full line of Recording model guitars. In 1928, the company's name was changed to The Epiphone Banjo Co.

The **Masterbilt** series of guitars was introduced in 1931 and marked Epiphone's entrance into the production of modern, carved, f-hole archtop guitars, based on violin construction principles. Indeed, at the time of their introduction, the Masterbilt guitar line was the most complete selection of "f"-hole guitars available from any instrument maker in the world. Complementary Spanish and Hawaiian flattop models and carved-top mandolins were likewise included under the Masterbilt Aegis. Soon, Epiphone advertisements would claim that it was "The World's Largest Producer of First Grade Fretted Instruments." Whether this was an accurate boast or not, it set the stage for a two-decade rivalry between Epiphone and its largest competitor, Gibson.

By 1935, the company was now known simply as Epiphone, Inc., and was producing its Electar brand of electric Hawaiian and Spanish guitars, as well as amplifiers which were designed by electronics pioneer and Danelectro founder, Nat Daniels (1912-1994). That same year marked the introduction of the flagship 18.375 in. **Emperor** model archtop guitar and signaled the redesign and enlargement of the company's entire Masterbilt archtop line.

Notable Epiphone innovations in this era included the first patented electronic pickup with individual pole pieces and the distinctive Frequensator tailpiece. Both were designed by salesman and acknowledged jack-of-all-trades, Herb Sunshine (1906-1988), and in production by 1937. In 1940, the company also introduced a full line of well-respected bass violins produced under the watchful eye of the youngest of the Stathopoulo brothers, Frixo (1905-1957), who had joined the firm in the early 1930s.

During this period, Epiphone's growing product line was considered to be second to none, and could boast such endorsers as George Van Eps (with the Ray Noble Orchestra), Carmen Mastren (with Tommy Dorsey), Allan Reuss (with Benny Goodman's band), and many, many more.

Epi Stathopoulo died from leukemia in 1943 at the age of 49, and this, combined with the many hardships incurred during World War II, set the company on a downward spiral. Orphie Stathopoulo, who took over as president, was unable to recapture the momentum of the prewar years, and constant friction between he and his brother Frixo (now vice-president) began to pull the company apart at the seams.

In 1951, simmering labor problems resulted in a strike which shut down the New York plant for several months. During this time, Orphie sold a stake in the business to the large distribution company, Continental Music. Continental moved production to Philadelphia, and most instruments manufactured from 1952 to 1957 were made there. It is doubtful, however, if much was produced in the final two years, as Epiphone was rapidly being overtaken by new entrants into the guitar market, notably Fender and Guild, the later of which had ironically been started by many former Epiphone employees under the leadership of Alfred Dronge and former Epiphone executive George Mann.

It had become increasingly apparent that Epiphone was no longer capable of developing the new products necessary to capture the imagination of the guitar-buying public and its financial viability had come to an end. Following Frixo's sudden death in 1957, Orphie, now the company's sole owner, approached Gibson president Ted McCarty, who had previously expressed interest in buying Epiphone's bass violin production. A deal was signed and trucks were dispatched from Kalamazoo to New York and Philadelphia to make the move. Records during this time period indicate that the out-of-work ex-Epiphone workers in New Berlin, New York "celebrated" by hosting a bonfire behind the plant with any available lumber (both finished and unfinished!). When the vans returned to the Gibson warehouse in Michigan, McCarty realized (much to his surprise) that not only had he received the bass-making operation, but all the jigs, fixtures, and machinery necessary for making guitars, plus much of the work in progress. For the sum of $20,000, Gibson had acquired its once mighty rival (including what would become the most profitable trademark) lock, stock, and barrel.

It was decided that Epiphone would be re-established as a first rate guitar manufacturer, so that Gibson's parent company CMI (Chicago Musical Instruments) could offer a product comparable in every way to Gibson. This was done primarily as a way of offering music stores which, due to existing contractual obligations in a particular sales area, were not allowed to carry the exclusive Gibson line. The Epiphone brand could now be offered to competing retailers who were also carrying many of the other well-known brands which were distributed by the giant CMI. Though Epiphone was set up as an autonomous company, in a separate part of the Gibson complex, parallel product lines were soon established, and Gibson was (in effect) competing with itself.

After Epiphone was moved to Kalamazoo, instruments were built in the U.S through 1969. In 1970, production was moved overseas. Instruments were originally built in Japan (1970-1983), but during the early 1980s, Japanese production costs became pricey due to the changing ratio of the dollar/yen.

Since 1984, the majority of guitars have been produced in Korea. However, there have been a number of models like the Spirit, Special, USA Pro, and USA Coronet that were produced in Nashville, Tennessee. These models are the exception to the rule. Epiphone currently offers a very wide range of acoustic, semi-hollow, and solid body electric guitars.

In 1998, Epiphone offered the new EZ-Bender, a detachable "B" string bender that can be installed on any guitar equipped with a stop bar tailpiece. The EZ-Bender can be installed with no modifications whatsoever to the guitar (source: N.Y. Epiphone information by L.B. Fred and Jim Fisch, *Epiphone: The House of Stathopoulo*, additional Epiphone history courtesy Walter Carter, *Epiphone: The Complete History*).

**Epiphone Alleykat
courtesy Epiphone**

**Epiphone Broadway
courtesy Epiphone**

GRADING	100% MINT	98% NEAR MINT	95% EXC+	90% EXC	80% VG+	70% VG	60% G

EPIPHONE PRODUCTION LOCATION

Epiphone guitars have been produced in a wide range of places. The following list gives a rough approximation to production facilities by year. Guitars produced from the late 1920s up to the time of Gibson´s purchase of the company are known by collectors as New York Epiphones

New York, NY:	Late 1920s to 1952.
Philadelphia, PA:	1952 to 1957.

GIBSON PRODUCTION LOCATION

For further information on Epiphone acoustic models, please refer to the *Blue Book of Acoustic Guitars*. The Epiphone Chet Atkins Series models will be found in the Acoustic edition.

Japan	1970-1983	Japan	1988-1989 (Spotlights, Thinlines)
Taiwan	1979-1981	Nashville, TN	1989-1994 (USA Pro) (USA Coronet)
Nashville, TN	1982-1983 (Spirit, Special, U.S. Map)	China	1997-Current
Korea	1983-Current	Indonesia	1997-Current

ELECTRIC ARCHTOP: ALLEYKAT, FLAMEKAT, & WILDCAT SERIES

ALLEYKAT LIMITED EDITION (MODEL ETAK) - single cutaway semi-hollow body design, mahogany body, flame maple top, maple set neck, rosewood fingerboard with pearl block inlays, 3-per-side tuners, f-holes, chrome hardware, 1 New York mini humbucker in the neck position and 1 ´57 classic humbucker in the bridge position, Tune-O-Matic bridge, stop tailpiece, master volume, available in Heritage Cherry Sunburst, Trans. Black, or Vintage Sunburst finishes, mfg. 2000-present.

	MSR	$831		$500	$425	$375	$325	$275	$225	$175

FLAMEKAT LIMITED EDITION (HELLKAT, MODEL ETA1) - single cutaway design, laminated maple top, mahogany body, maple set neck with rosewood fingeboard, dice inlays, f-holes, chrome hardware, 2 "New York" mini-humbucker pickups, Vibratone tailpiece (Bigsby tailpiece new in 2003), dice knobs, Ebony finish with yellow and red flames, mfg. 1999-present.

	MSR	$999		$600	$525	$475	$425	$375	$325	$275

WILDKAT LIMITED EDITION (MODEL ETBK) - single cutaway semi-hollow body design, mahogany body, flame maple top, maple set neck, rosewood fingerboard with dot inlays, 3-per-side tuners, f-holes, chrome hardware, 2 Alnico-V P-90 pickups, Vibratone tailpiece (Bigsby tailpiece new in 2003), master volume, available in Trans. Black, Turquoise, or Antique Natural finishes, mfg. 2000-present.

	MSR	$831		$500	$425	$375	$325	$275	$225	$175

ELECTRIC ARCHTOP: B.B. KING SERIES

B.B. KING LUCILLE (MODEL ETBB) - dual cutaway semi-hollow body, 22-fret rosewood fingerboard with block inlay, gold hardware, 2 covered humbuckers, 2 volume/2 tone controls, 3-way toggle switch, 6-position Vari-Phase switch, available in Ebony finish, current mfg.

	MSR	$1,332		$800	$700	$625	$575	$525	$475	$400

ELECTRIC ARCHTOP: BROADWAY SERIES

BROADWAY - single round cutaway hollow style, spruce top, f-holes, raised bound black pickguard, bound body, maple back/sides/neck, 20-fret bound rosewood fingerboard with pearl block inlay, adjustable rosewood bridge/Frequensator tailpiece, bound blackface peghead with pearl column/logo inlay, 3-per-side nickel tuners with plastic buttons, 2 single coil pickups, volume/tone control, 3-position switch, available in Natural, Cherry, or Sunburst finishes, mfg. 1958-1970.

1958-1962	N/A	$3,200	$2,800	$2,500	$2,200	$1,900	$1,600
1963-1970	N/A	$2,700	$2,400	$2,100	$1,800	$1,500	$1,200

Add 25% for Natural finish.

In 1961, mini humbucker pickups replaced original part/designs. In 1963, tune-o-matic bridge replaced original part/design. In 1967 only, Cherry finish became an option. In 1968, Natural finish became an option.

BROADWAY (MODEL ETBW) - contempoprary re-issue, available in Antique Sunburst, Ebony, Natural, or Vintage Cherry Sunburst, mfg. 1997-present.

	MSR	$1,332		$800	$725	$650	$575	$500	$425	$350

In 2000, Ebony and Vintage Cherry Sunburst finishes were disc.

BROADWAY ELITIST (MODEL ELBR, JAPAN) - solid spruce top, AAA Flame Maple back and sides, 5-piece maple and rosewood set neck, Ebony fingerboard and bridge, 50SR and 50ST USA Humbuckers, 24Kt. gold hardware, Grover tuners with Imperial buttons, 2 volume, 2 tone and 3-way pickup selector, available in Natural or Vintage Sunburst finishes, 25.5 in. scale, mfg. 2003-present.

	MSR	$3,075		$2,000	$1,700	$1,450	$1,250	$1,100	$950	$800

ELECTRIC ARCHTOP: BYRDLAND SERIES

BYRDLAND ELITIST (MODEL ELBY, JAPAN) - solid Spruce top, AAA Flame Maple back and sides, 5-piece maple and rosewood set neck with ebony fingerboard, 50SR and 50ST USA humbuckers, 2 volume, 2 tone and 3-way pickup selector, 24Kt. gold hardware, Grover tuners with Imperial buttons, available in Vintage Sunburst and Natural finishes, 23.5 in. scale, mfg. 2003-present.

	MSR	$3,075		$2,000	$1,700	$1,450	$1,250	$1,100	$950	$800

GRADING	100% MINT	98% NEAR MINT	95% EXC+	90% EXC	80% VG+	70% VG	60% G

ELECTRIC ARCHTOP: CASINO SERIES

CASINO (TWO PICKUPS) - thin double rounded cutaway hollow body, bound laminate body, bound fingerboard with dot inlay, tune-o-matic bridge/trapeze tailpiece, white 3-ply pickguard, 2 P-90 pickups, volume/tone controls, pickup selector switch, available in Royal Tan or Sunburst finishes, 24.75 in. scale, 16 in. body width, mfg. 1962-69.

1961-1965	N/A	$3,750	$3,250	$2,800	$2,500	$2,200	$1,900
1966-1969	N/A	$3,500	$3,000	$2,600	$2,300	$2,000	$1,700

In 1962, the Tremotone Vibrato tailpiece became optional, and a single parallelogram inlay was introduced. In 1963, chrome pickup covers were introduced. In 1967, Cherry finish became available.

Casino (One Pickup) - similar to the Casino except has only one pickup, mfg. 1962-69.

1961-1965	N/A	$2,000	$1,750	$1,500	$1,250	$1,000	$750
1966-1969	N/A	$1,700	$1,450	$1,250	$1,050	$850	$650

CASINO (MODEL ETCA) - contemporary re-issue, available in Cherry, Ebony, Natural, or Vintage Cherry Sunburst finishes, current mfg.

MSR	$999	$599	$525	$450	$400	$350	$300	$250

Add $150 for metallic finishes: Black Metallic, Metallic Light Blue, Metallic Burgundy Mist, and Turquoise finishes. Add $250 for metal flake finishes: Gold Flake and Silver Flake finishes.

Vintage Cherry Sunburst finish disc. All metallic finishes disc except turquoise, which is now included without the premium. All metal flake finishes disc.

Casino Reissue with Vibrotone (Model ETCA) - available in Ebony, Gold Flake, Natural, Silver Flake, Turquoise, or Vintage Cherry Sunburst, mfg. 1997-99.

	$875	$800	$725	$650	$550	$450	$350

Last MSR was $1,249.

Casino Left-Handed (Model ETCAL) - Similar to the Casino except in left-handed configuration, available in Vintage Cherry Sunburst (disc 1999) or Natural finishes, mfg. 1997-99, 2003-present.

MSR	$1,032	$619	$550	$475	$425	$375	$325	$275

**Epiphone Casino
courtesy Epiphone**

1965 CASINO ELITIST (MODEL ELCS, JAPAN) - 5-ply maple top, back, and sides, 1-piece mahogany set neck with rosewood fingerboard and 22 frets, bone nut, P90R and P90T USA single coil pickups, nickel hardware, Grover tuners, 2 volume, 2 tone and 3-way pickup selector, available in Vintage Sunburst or Natural finishes, 24.75 in. scale, mfg. 2003-present.

MSR	$2,075	$1,350	$1,150	$1,000	$850	$750	$650	$550

JOHN LENNON "1965" CASINO (MODEL USC5) - assembled in the USA, original body shape, mid-60s Kalamazoo tooling specs, five-layer body of maple and birch, top contour bracing, one piece mahogany neck with 14 degree grain orientation, rosewood fingerboard with pearloid parallelogram fret markers, neck joint at 17th fret, neck binding covers fret ends, Corian nut, mother-of-pearl headstock logo, Gibson-factory electronics, nickel plated P-90 pickup covers, Switchcraft 3-way toggle switch with old style black washer, nickel ABR bridge with nylon saddles, 3-ply pickguard, nickel Gibson-factory hardware with nickel Gotoh Kluson style machine heads, available in Vintage Sunburst nitrocellulose finish, vintage style case with shroud included, mfg. 1999-present.

MSR	$3,194	$2,575	$2,200	$1,900	$1,650	$1,400	$1,200	$1,000

JOHN LENNON "REVOLUTION" CASINO (MODEL USCR) - similar to John Lennon "1965" Casino, except has "Stripped" Vintage Natural nitrocellulose finish as John's original guitar appeared after being refinished. Also features gold Grover tuners and dents, holes from original Kluson tuners for authenticity. Vintage style case with shroud included, mfg. 1999-present.

MSR	$3,194	$2,575	$2,200	$1,900	$1,650	$1,400	$1,200	$1,000

ELECTRIC ARCHTOP: CENTURY SERIES

CENTURY (1939-1957 MFG.) - single bound laminated mahogany body, 14/20-fret bound rosewood fingerboard with dot inlays, single (non-adjustable) pickup with handrest, bakelite pickguard, trapeze tailpiece, individual tuners with plastic buttons, metal peghead logo plate, volume/tone controls (octagon knobs), available in Sunburst finish, 14.75 in. body width, mfg. 1939-1957.

1939-1949	N/A	$900	$800	$700	$600	$500	$400
1950-1957	N/A	$1,000	$900	$800	$700	$600	$500

In 1941, 15 1/4 in. body, the f-holes were moved even with the pickup and the hand rest was removed. In the mid-1940s, a 16 3/8 in. maple body, Tone Spectrum oblong pickup, square control plates, and an unbound fingerboard were introduced, and the back access plate was removed. In 1949, a large rectangular pickup with unadjustable poles, knobs with lines, and a Stylized E on the pickguard were introduced. In 1950, a New York pickup with no poles was introduced. In 1953, DeArmond pickup, clear barrel knobs, and Blonde finish was optional.

**Epiphone 1965 Casino Elitist
courtesy Epiphone**

GRADING	100% MINT	98% NEAR MINT	95% EXC+	90% EXC	80% VG+	70% VG	60% G

CENTURY (1958-1970 MFG.) - 16 3/8 in. body width, thin hollow body, 25.5 in. scale, dot fingerboard inlay, rosewood bridge/trapeze tailpiece, tortoise pickguard, metal peghead logo plate, P-90 pickup, volume/tone controls, available in Sunburst finish, mfg. 1958-1970.

	N/A	$900	$800	$700	$600	$500	$400

In 1959, a P-90 pickup was introduced. In 1961, Royal Burgundy finish became available. In 1963, the peghead plate was removed. From 1968-1970, only Sunburst finish was available. A 3/4 size Century in 22 inch scale was available from 1961-67.

ELECTRIC ARCHTOP: CIAOLA SERIES

CAIOLA, CAIOLA CUSTOM - 16 in. body width, thin double cutaway body, laminated top, multiple body binding, 25.5 in. scale, bound rosewood fingerboard with block inlay and "Custom" on end of neck, zero fret, ebony adjustable bridge/trapeze tailpiece with Caiola Model inlaid in trapeze insert, bound peghead, peghead inlay, 2 mini-humbucker pickups, 2 volume controls, 5 switches, pickup selector switch, available in Black, Walnut, or Yellow Sunburst finishes, mfg. 1963-1970.

	N/A	$2,500	$2,200	$1,900	$1,600	$1,300	$950

In 1965, Tune-O-Matic bridge replaced old bridge. In 1966, Ciaola was renamed the Ciaola Custom. From 1968-1970, Walnut finish was only available.

Caiola Standard - similar to Caiola Custom, except features single body binding, dot fingerboard inlay, unbound peghead, no peghead inlay, 2 P-90 pickups, mfg. 1966-1970.

	N/A	$2,000	$1,750	$1,500	$1,250	$1,000	$750

In 1968, Cherry and Sunburst finishes were introduced.

ELECTRIC ARCHTOP: CORONET SERIES

CORONET - Non-adjustable single body binding, dot fingerboard inlay, trapeze tailpiece, metal peghead logo plate, volume/tone controls, available in Brown Sunburst finish, 14 3/8" body width, mfg. 1939-1949.

	N/A	$800	$700	$600	$500	$400	$300

In 1941, the top of the f-holes were even with the pickup, the jack was on the side of the guitar, and the knobs were closer to the edge. This name would later be evolved into an electric solid body in 1958.

ELECTRIC ARCHTOP: DOT & ES SERIES

DOT (MODEL ETDT) - 335-style double cutaway design, semihollow body archtop, 22-fret rosewood fingerboard with dot position markers, 2 covered humbucker pickups, 2 volume, 2 tone and 3-way pickup selector, nickel hardware, available in Cherry, Ebony, Natural, and Vintage Sunburst finishes, current mfg.

MSR	$665	$400	$325	$275	$230	$195	$160	$130

Add $20 for left-handed configuration (Model EDTDL).

DOT STUDIO (MODEL EDTS) - 335-style double cutaway design, semihollow laminated maple body archtop, f-holes, 22 fret rosewood fingerboard, 2 Alnico humbucker pickups, 2 knobs and 3-way pickup selector, black hardware, available in Black, Ice Blue, Alpine White, Lemon, Tomato, or Dolphin Gray finishes, new 2004.

MSR	$499	$300	$250	$220	$190	$160	$130	$100

Add $20 for left-handed configuration (Model EDTDL).

1963 ELITIST DOT (MODEL ELDT, JAPAN) - 5-ply maple top, back, and sides, one-piece mahogany set neck with rosewood fingerboard and 22 frets, 50SR and 50ST USA humbuckers, nickel hardware, Grover tuners, 2 volume, 2 tone and 3-way pickup selector, available in Cherry, Vintage Sunburst, or Natural finishes, 24.75 in. scale, mfg. 2003-present.

MSR	$1,999	$1,300	$1,150	$1,000	$875	$750	$650	$550

ES-295 (MODEL ET29) - design based on the Gibson ES-295, hollow body design with single Florentine cutaway, laminated maple top, back, and sides, mahogany set neck with split parallelograms, bound body and neck, 24.75 in. scale, 2 Alnico P-90 pickups, 2 volume, 2 tone, and 3-way pickup selector, chrome hardware, licensed Bigsby tailpiece, mfg. 1998-2000, 2003-present.

MSR	$1,249	$750	$675	$625	$575	$525	$475	$425

Models produced between 1998-2000 featured a Vibrotone tailpiece.

ELECTRIC ARCHTOP: ELECTAR SERIES

ELECTAR MODEL C - Spanish style, 13.5 in. wide, laminated maple body, flat back, single bound body, extended rosewood fingerboard with dot inlay, oblong blade pickup, two knobs, jack on top of guitar, Electar logo on peghead with point at top, Sunburst top with brown back/sides, mfg. 1935-39.

	N/A	$900	$750	$650	$550	$450	$350

Some early models may have only had a single knob. In 1937, a rhythm control was added for a total of three knobs. A tenor and plectrum version were also available.

ELECTAR MODEL M - Spanish style, 14.75 in. wide, laminated maple body, flat back, single bound body, extended single bound rosewood fingerboard with dot inlay, "horseshoe" pickup, two knobs, jack on top of guitar, Electar logo on peghead with point at top, Sunburst top with brown back/sides, mfg. 1935-39.

	N/A	$1,000	$875	$750	$650	$550	$450

Some early models may have only had a single knob. In 1937, a rhythm control was added for a total of three knobs. In late 1937, an oblong pickup with poles was introduced and the next extension was raised off of the top. A tenor and plectrum version were also available.

GRADING	100% MINT	98% NEAR MINT	95% EXC+	90% EXC	80% VG+	70% VG	60% G

E

ELECTRIC ARCHTOP: EMPEROR SERIES

The Emperor contemporary re-issue model was introduced in 1982, as the Emperor (F) and the Emperor (T) models (available in Antique Sunburst). In 1992, Natural finish was introduced; in 1993, the Emperor II (Model ETE2) preempted the Emperor. Two years later, jazz guitar great Joe Pass "adopted" the Emperor II as his signature model. The silk-screened signature on the pickguard would began on models produced in 1995 (models but produced from 1992 to 1994 would not have this silk-screened logo on the pickguard). Epiphone´s "Imperial Collection" model Emperor 1930s (Model EIEM) was introduced in 1993. This premium model was built in Japan. The Emperor 1930s was renamed Emperor Re-Issue in 1994, but did not last into 1995 (last retail list was $3,100).

EMPEROR - single rounded cutaway thin body, 18.5 in. wide, f-holes, multiple body binding, 20-fret fingerboard with V pearl block inlay, raised pickguard, 3 New York pickups, double trapeze tailpieces, four knobs, vine peghead inlay, "stairstep" tuning pegs, gold hardware, available in Natural or Sunburst finish, mfg. 1958-1969.

	100%	98%	95%	90%	80%	70%	60%
1958-1963	N/A	$7,500	$6,800	$6,000	$5,200	$4,400	$3,500
1964-1969	N/A	$8,500	$7,500	$6,500	$5,500	$4,500	$3,500

In 1961, mini-humbucker pickups were introduced. Starting in 1963, this model was only available as a special order. After 1965, Sunburst was the only available finish.

JOE PASS EMPEROR II (MODEL ETE2, EMPEROR II, EMPEROR) - single round cutaway hollow style, arched bound laminated maple top, 2 f-holes, bound tortoiseshell pickguard with stylized E logo, laminated maple back/sides, 3-piece maple neck, 24.75 in. scale, 20-fret bound rosewood fingerboard with pearl block inlay, adjustable rosewood bridge/stylized trapeze tailpiece, bound peghead with pearl vine/logo inlay, 3-per-side tuners, gold hardware, 2 covered humbucker pickups with exposed screws, 2 volume/tone controls, 3-position switch, available in Natural or Vintage Sunburst finishes, mfg. 1982-1992 (as Emperor), 1993-94 (as Emperor II), 1995-current (Joe Pass Emperor II).

	100%	98%	95%	90%	80%	70%	60%
1982-1992	N/A	$525	$450	$400	$350	$300	$250
1993-1994	N/A	$500	$425	$350	$300	$250	$200
1995-2003	$800	$700	$625	$525	$450	$350	$275
2004-MSR $999	$600	$525	$450	$400	$350	$300	$250

In 1994, Heritage Cherry Sunburst finish was introduced. In 1995, silk-screened Joe Pass signature added to pickguard. In 1996, select spruce top replaced laminated maple top; Metallic Gold and Wine Red finishes were introduced. In 2000, Metallic Gold and Wine Red finishes disc.

Emperor II Left-Handed (Model ETE2L) - available in Natural finish, current mfg.

		98%	95%	90%	80%	70%	60%
MSR	$1,032	$619	$550	$475	$425	$375	$325	$275

EMPEROR REGENT (MODEL ETEM) - single round hollow cutaway, arched bound spruce top, bound f-holes, raised bound black pickguard with stylized E logo, maple back/sides/neck, 20-fret bound rosewood fingerboard with pearl block/abalone triangle inlay, adjustable rosewood bridge/Frequensator tailpiece, bound peghead with pearl vine/logo inlay, 3-per-side tuners, gold hardware, covered humbucker pickup with exposed screws, pickguard mounted volume/tone controls, available in Antique Sunburst, Natural, or Vintage Cherry Sunburst finishes, mfg. 1994-present.

		98%	95%	90%	80%	70%	60%
MSR	$1,249	$750	$675	$600	$525	$475	$425	$375

Add $150 for metallic finishes: Black Metallic, Metallic Light Blue, Metallic Burgundy Mist, and Turquoise finishes. Disc. 1998. Add $225 for metallic flake finishes: Gold Flake and Silver Flake finishes. Disc. 1998.

Epiphone Emperor
Courtesy: Dave Rogers
Dave's Guitar Shop

ELECTRIC ARCHTOP: GRANADA SERIES

GRANADA - 16.25 in. body width, thin hollow body, dot fingerboard inlay, one f-hole, rosewood bridge/trapeze tailpiece, one Melody Maker pickup, volume/tone controls, available in Sunburst finish, mfg. 1962-1970.

			98%	95%	90%	80%	70%	60%
		N/A	$750	$675	$600	$500	$400	$300

GRANADA CUTAWAY - similar to the Granada, except features a single pointed cutaway, mfg. 1965-1970.

			98%	95%	90%	80%	70%	60%
		N/A	$850	$750	$650	$550	$450	$350

ELECTRIC ARCHTOP: HARRY VOLPE & KENT SERIES

HARRY VOLPE - bound body, dot fingerboard inlay, trapeze tailpiece, metal peghead logo plate, non-adjustable DeArmond pickup, volume/tone controls, available in Sunburst finish 15.25 in. body width, mfg. 1955-57.

			98%	95%	90%	80%	70%	60%
		N/A	$800	$725	$650	$575	$500	$400

KENT - single bound laminated arched mahogany body (with flat back), 14/20-fret rosewood fingerboard with dot inlays, single large (non-adjustable) Tone Spectrum pickup, tortoiseshell pickguard, trapeze tailpiece, 3-on-a-strip tuners with plastic buttons, metal peghead logo plate, volume/tone controls (octagon knobs), available in Sunburst finish 15.375 in. body width, mfg. 1949-1954.

			98%	95%	90%	80%	70%	60%
		N/A	$700	$625	$550	$475	$400	$325

ELECTRIC ARCHTOP: HOWARD ROBERTS SERIES

For the Howard Roberts Custom, see the *Blue Book of Acoustic Guitars*.

Epiphone Joe Pass Emperor II
courtesy Epiphone

GRADING	100% MINT	98% NEAR MINT	95% EXC+	90% EXC	80% VG+	70% VG	60% G

HOWARD ROBERTS STANDARD - single sharp cutaway hollow style, arched spruce top, bound oval soundhole/body, mahogany back/sides/neck, 20-fret bound rosewood fingerboard with pearl slotted block inlay, adjustable rosewood bridge/trapeze tailpiece, blackface peghead with pearl cloud/logo inlay, 3-per-side tuners, nickel tuners, mini humbucker pickup, volume/tone control, available in Cherry finish, mfg. 1964-1970.

	N/A	$3,000	$2,600	$2,300	$2,000	$1,700	$1,300

This instrument was co-designed by Howard Roberts. In 1965, 3-stripe purfling was introduced, Natural and Sunburst finishes became optional. In 1967, tune-o-matic/rosewood base bridge replaced original part/design. In 1968, Natural and Sunburst finishes became standard, Cherry finish was disc.

HOWARD ROBERTS (MODEL ETHR) - contemporary re-issue, available in Translucent Black or Wine Red finishes, disc. 2000.

	$775	$675	$600	$525	$425	$350	$275

Last MSR was $1,099.

ELECTRIC ARCHTOP: NOEL GALLAGHER SUPERNOVA SERIES

NOEL GALLAGHER SUPERNOVA (MODEL ETSN) - available in Ebony, Cherry, Metallic Light Blue, and Vintage Sunburst finishes, current mfg.

MSR	$1,099	$660	$575	$525	$475	$425	$375	$325

This model was developed in conjunction with Noel Gallagher (Oasis). In 1999, Ebony, Cherry and Vintage Sunburst finishes were disc.

NOEL GALLAGHER UNION JACK SUPERNOVA - similar to the Noel Gallagher Supernova, except has a Red, White, and Blue finish like the British flag, mfg. 1999-present.

MSR	$1,199	$719	$650	$575	$500	$450	$400	$350

ELECTRIC ARCHTOP: PROFESSIONAL SERIES

PROFESSIONAL - 16 in. body width, thin double rounded cutaway bound body, tune-o-matic bridge, Frequensator tailpiece, single parallelogram fingerboard inlay, mini-humbucker, 2 knobs (treble side), 3 knobs and multiple switches (bass side), multi-prong jack, 1/4 in. jack, available in Mahogany finish, mfg. 1962-66.

WITH AMP	N/A	$2,000	$1,750	$1,500	$1,250	$1,000	$750
WITHOUT AMP	N/A	$1,500	$1,250	$1,000	$800	$650	$500

This guitar model was paired with the Professional model amp, which had no control knobs on the faceplate. All controls were mounted on the front of the guitar, and controlled the amp through the cable attached to the multiprong jack. The amp was rated at 15 watts, and had a 12 in. speaker. When this combination was introduced in the 1963 Epiphone catalog as the Professional Outfit (Model EA7P), the original retail price was $495. This model was also available with a large amp with a 15 in. speaker, tremolo, and reverb (Model EA8P).

ELECTRIC ARCHTOP: RIVIERA SERIES

RIVIERA - thin double cutaway body, bound fingerboard with single parallelogram inlay, bound body, tune-o-matic bridge/trapeze tailpiece, bound tortoiseshell pickguard, 2 mini-humbucker pickups, volume/tone controls, available in Royal Tan finish, 16 in. body width, mfg. 1962-1970.

	N/A	$3,200	$2,800	$2,500	$2,200	$1,900	$1,500

In 1965, Sunburst finish became standard. In 1966, a white 3-ply pickguard was introduced and Cherry finish became option. In 1967, a vibrato tailpiece became optional. There was a limited edition produced in Nashville between 1993 and 1994. There were 250 of these made.

RIVIERA (MODEL ETRI) - contemporary re-issue, available in Cherry, Ebony, Natural, or Vintage Cherry Sunburst finishes, current mfg.

MSR	$999	$600	$525	$475	$425	$375	$325	$275

Add $150 for metallic finishes: Black Metallic, Metallic Light Blue, Metallic Burgundy Mist, and Turquoise finishes. Disc 1998. Add $250 for metallic flake finishes: Gold Flake and Silver Flake finishes, disc 1998.

In 2000, Natural and Vintage Cherry Sunburst finishes were disc.

Riviera with Vibrotone (Model ETRI) - similar to the Riviera, except features a Bigsby-derived Vibrotone tremolo, available in Cherry, Gold Flake, Silver Flake, or Turquoise finishes, mfg. 1997-98.

	$1,000	$900	$800	$700	$600	$500	$400

Last MSR was $1,499.

Riviera 12-String (Model ETR2) - available in Cherry, Ebony, Natural, or Vintage Cherry Sunburst finishes, mfg. 1997-2000.

	$800	$725	$650	$550	$475	$375	$300

Last MSR was $1,199.

RIVIERA ELITIST (MODEL ELRI, JAPAN) - 5-ply maple top, back, and sides, 1-piece mahogany set neck with rosewood fingerboard and 22 frets, 24.75 in. scale, 60NYR and 60NYT NY Mini-humbuckers, nickel hardware, Grover tuners, 2 volume, 2 tone and 3-way pickup selector, available in Cherry or Vintage Sunburst finishes, mfg. 2003-present.

MSR	$2,229	$1,450	$1,250	$1,100	$950	$825	$725	$625

Riviera Elitist 12 (Model ELR12, Japan) - 12-string version of the Riviera, five-ply maple top, back, and sides, 1-piece mahogany set neck with rosewood fingerboard and 22 frets, 60NYR and 60NYT NY mini-humbuckers, Nickel hardware, Grover tuners, 2 volume, 2 tone and 3-way pickup selector, available in Cherry finish only, 24.75 in. scale, mfg. 2003-present.

MSR	$2,306	$1,500	$1,300	$1,150	$1,000	$900	$800	$700

JORMA KAUKONEN RIVIERA DELUXE (MODEL ETJK) - similar to Model ETRI except has gold hardware, laminated maple body, gold Vibratone tailpiece (Bigsby new 2003), Grover machine heads, 2 Epiphone '57 Classic Alnico-V pickups, available in Cherry finish, mfg. 2000-present.

MSR	$1,165	$700	$625	$550	$500	$450	$400	$350

GRADING		100% MINT	98% NEAR MINT	95% EXC+	90% EXC	80% VG+	70% VG	60% G

ELECTRIC ARCHTOP: SHERATON SERIES

SHERATON - double rounded cutaway, arched bound maple top, f-holes, raised bound tortoiseshell pickguard with stylized E logo, maple back/sides, center block maple neck, 22-fret bound rosewood fingerboard with pearl/abalone block/triangle inlay, tune-o-matic bridge/stop tailpiece, Frequensater, or gold-plated Tremotone bridge/tailpiece, bound peghead with pearl vine/logo inlay, 3-per-side tuners, gold hardware, 2 humbucker covered pickups with exposed screws, 2 volume/tone controls, 3-position switch, available in Cherry, Natural, or Sunburst finishes, mfg. 1958-1970, 1980-81, and 1993-94.

1958-1960	N/A	$8,500	$7,500	$6,500	$5,500	$4,500	$3,500
1961-1963	N/A	$7,000	$6,200	$5,400	$4,600	$3,800	$3,000
1964-1966	N/A	$5,000	$4,400	$3,800	$3,300	$2,800	$2,400
1967-1970	N/A	$4,000	$3,500	$3,000	$2,500	$2,000	$1,500
1980-1981	N/A	$750	$675	$600	$525	$450	$325
1993-1994	N/A	$600	$525	$450	$400	$350	$300

Add 20% for Natural finish on models produced between 1958 and 1970.

In 1961, mini-humbucker pickups were introduced and a vibrato tailpiece became standard. In 1965, Cherry finish was an option. This model was reissued from 1980-81 and produced in Japan/Korea. It was reintroduced again in 1993-94 as a limited edition of 250 instruments produced from the Nashville factory.

SHERATON II (MODEL ETS2) - contemporary re-issue, available in Ebony, Natural, Pearl White, or Vintage Sunburst finishes, mfg. 1997-present.

MSR	$998	$599	$525	$450	$400	$350	$300	$250

In 2000, Pearl White finish was disc.

Sheraton II Left-Handed (Model ETS2L) - available in Vintage Sunburst finish, mfg. 1997-present.

MSR	$1,032	$620	$550	$475	$425	$375	$325	$275

ELITIST SHERATON (MODEL ELSH, JAPAN) - 5-ply maple top, back, and sides, 1-piece mahogany set neck with rosewood fingerboard and 22 frets, 60NYR and 60NYT USA NY mini-humbuckers, 24K gold hardware, Grover tuners with Imperial buttons, 2 volume, 2 tone and 3-way pickup selector, available in Vintage Sunburst or Natural finishes, 24.75 in. scale, mfg. 2003-present.

MSR	$2,460	$1,600	$1,400	$1,250	$1,100	$950	$850	$750

JOHN LEE HOOKER 1964 SHERATON (MODEL USS1) - faithful reproduction of John Lee Hooker's original 1964 Sheraton, multi-bound original body shape and materials, larger original style headstock, 17 degree angle, top contour bracing, spruce/maple/spruce, original relief cut and spacing, solid center block construction, 1-piece mahogany neck with 14 degree grain orientation, neck joint at 19th fret, rosewood fingerboard with original mother-of-pearl and Abalone block and triangle inlays, 2 gold plated "New York" mini humbucker pickups, 5-layer bound pickguard, gold plated Gibson hardware, Grover machine heads, Switchcraft 3-way toggle, Frequensator tailpiece, Antique Natural or Vintage Sunburst finishes, mfg. 2000-present.

MSR	$3,194	$2,575	$2,200	$1,900	$1,650	$1,400	$1,200	$1,000

JOHN LEE HOOKER 1964 SHERATON II (MODEL USS2) - similar to Model USS1 except has stop tailpiece and is available in Antique Natural or Vintage Sunburst finishes, mfg. 2000-present.

MSR	$3,194	$2,575	$2,200	$1,900	$1,650	$1,400	$1,200	$1,000

Epiphone Rivera courtesy George McGuire

ELECTRIC ARCHTOP: SORRENTO SERIES

SORRENTO (ONE PICKUP) - thin single pointed cutaway body, dot fingerboard inlay, tune-o-matic bridge/trapeze tailpiece, tortoiseshell pickguard, metal peghead logo plate, nickel hardware, mini-humbucker pickup, volume/tone controls, pickup selector switch, available in Natural, Sunburst, or Royal Tan finish, 16.25 in. body width, 24.75 in. scale, mfg. 1960-1970.

	N/A	$1,750	$1,500	$1,250	$1,000	$800	$600

In 1962, oval inlays were introduced and the vibrato tailpiece was discontinued. In 1963, the peghead plate was removed. In 1968, Cherry and Sunburst finishes were introduced. This model was also available as a 3/4 size with a 22 in. scale from 1961-62.

Sorrento (Two Pickups) - similar to the the Sorrento except has two mini-humbucker pickups, mfg. 1960-1970.

	N/A	$1,950	$1,650	$1,400	$1,200	$1,000	$800

This model was also available in a 3/4 size (22 in. scale) configuration (mfg. 1961 to 1962).

SORRENTO (MODEL ETSO) - contemporary re-issue, available in Antique Sunburst, Cherry, Ebony, Orange, or Vintage Cherry Sunburst finishes, disc. 2000.

	$700	$600	$525	$450	$375	$300	$225

Last MSR was $999.

Add $150 for metallic finishes: Black Metallic, Metallic Light Blue, Metallic Burgundy Mist, and Turquoise finishes. Add $250 for metallic flake finishes: Gold Flake and Silver Flake finishes.

Sorrento with Vibrotone (Model ETSO) - similar to Sorrento, except features a Bigsby-derived Vibrotone tremolo, available in Gold Flake, Orange, Silver Flake, or Turquoise finishes, mfg. 1997-98.

	$950	$875	$800	$700	$600	$500	$400

Last MSR was $1,499.

Epiphone Sorrento courtesy George McGuire

GRADING	100% MINT	98% NEAR MINT	95% EXC+	90% EXC	80% VG+	70% VG	60% G

Sorrento Left-Handed (Model ETSOL) - similar to Sorrento, except in a left-handed configuration, available in Orange finish, mfg. 1997-99.

	$750	$650	$550	$475	$400	$325	$250

Last MSR was $1,099.

ELECTRIC ARCHTOP: WINDSOR SERIES

WINDSOR - single pointed cutaway thin body, 16 3/8 in. body width, tortoiseshell pickguard, oval fingerboard inlay, 1 or 2 New York pickups, rosewood bridge, trapeze tailpiece, metal peghead plate with logo, gold hardware, available in Sunburst or Natural finishes, mfg. 1959-1962.

	N/A	$1,500	$1,300	$1,150	$1,000	$850	$700

Add 10% for 2 pickup model.

In 1960, the peghead plate was removed. In 1961 mini-humbucker pickups were introduced.

ELECTRIC ARCHTOP: ZEPHYR SERIES

ZEPHYR - maple top, multiple body binding, bound fingerboard with block inlay, bound body, trapeze tailpiece, metal peghead logo plate, 2 knobs on round Mastervoicer plate, single oblong pickup, available in Blonde finish 16 3/8 in. body width, mfg. 1939-1957.

1939-1943	N/A	$1,500	$1,300	$1,100	$950	$800	$650
1944-1957	N/A	$1,300	$1,150	$1,000	$850	$700	$550

In 1941, the f-holes were placed even with the pickup, the hand rest was removed, the jack was on the side of the guitar, and the knobs were moved closer to the edge. In 1943, the cutout for the pickup was longer. In 1944, single body binding was introduced, the top mounted pickup was in the middle position, and some intruments appeared with Sunburst finish and laminated spruce tops. By 1947, a 17 3/8 in. body width, and a large metal pickup with poles was introduced. In 1949, laminated spruce tops no longer appeared, a New York pickup was introduced, and a 3-piece cherry/maple neck replaced the earlier neck. In 1950, a Frequensator tailpiece and knobs on a line were introduced, and Sunburst and Blonde finishes were available. In 1953, clear barrel knobs were introduced and some models had De Armond pickups. In 1954, the model was changed to the Zephyr Electric in both cutaway and non-cutaway versions. A tenor version was also available in 1954.

ZEPHYR (GIBSON MADE) - single rounded cutaway, thin-body, 17 3/8 in. body width, tortoiseshell pickguard, slotted-block fingerboard inlay, 2 New York Pickups, metal peghead plate with logo, avialable in Natural or Sunburst finishes, mfg. 1958-1964.

	N/A	$2,200	$1,950	$1,700	$1,450	$1,200	$950

In 1960, the peghead plate was removed. In 1961, mini-humbucker pickups were introduced.

ZEPHYR BLUES DELUXE (MODEL ETA3) - based on the 1949 Gibson ES-5, Flame Maple top, Flame maple body, maple set neck, rosewood fingerboard with block inlays, bound body and neck, f-holes, 3 Alnico-V P-90 pickups, 3 volume controls and 1 master tone control, gold hardware, available in Natural or Vintage Sunburst finishes, mfg. 1999-present.

MSR	$1,415	$850	$775	$700	$625	$550	$475	$400

ZEPHYR DE LUXE - spruce top, bound rosewood fingerboard with cloud inlay, multiple body binding, bound pickguard, bound peghead with vine inlay, Frequensator tailpiece, gold hardware, oblong pickup with slot head screw poles, volume/tone controls on shared shaft with Mastervoicer control plate, available in Blonde finish, 17 3/8 in. body width, mfg. 1941-1954.

1941-1949	N/A	$2,800	$2,500	$2,200	$1,900	$1,600	$1,300
1950-1954	N/A	$2,200	$1,950	$1,700	$1,450	$1,200	$950

In 1942, the knobs were mounted on the "Mastervoicer" plate. In 1947, the pickup was moved to the middle position and some appeared with Sunburst finish. In 1948, a large metal covered pickup was introduced. In 1949, the pickup was moved to the neck position. In 1950, New York pickups were introduced, 2 pickups were optional with a 3-way switch, and Sunburst and Blonde finishes were available. In 1951, the knobs were moved to be parallel to the strings.

ZEPHYR DE LUXE REGENT - rounded cutaway, laminated spruce top, bound rosewood fingerboard with V-block inlay, multiple body binding, bound pickguard, bound peghead with vine inlay, Frequensator tailpiece, gold hardware, 2 rectangular pickups, 2 knobs, Mastervoicer control plates, available in Blonde or Sunburst finishes, 17 3/8 in. body width, mfg. 1949-1958.

1949-1953	N/A	$3,000	$2,700	$2,400	$2,100	$1,800	$1,500
1954-1958	N/A	$4,000	$3,500	$3,000	$2,600	$2,200	$1,800

Add 15% for Natural finish.

In 1949, 2 pickups were optional with a 3-way switch and knobs parallel to the strings. In 1950, the single-pickup was discontinued, and New York pickups were introduced. In 1951, 5-ply body binding and a triple bound pickguard was introduced. In 1953, knobs were moved to cross the strings. In 1954, this model was re-designated the De Luxe Electric, with a laminated maple top, and some had a single flower peghead inlay. In the mid-1950s, some models appeared with an 18.5 in. wide body, single bound f-holes, and nickel hardware.

ZEPHYR EMPEROR REGENT - rounded cutaway, laminated spruce top, bound rosewood fingerboard with V-block inlay, multiple body binding, bound peghead, Frequensator tailpiece, gold hardware, 3 pickups, 2 knobs, 6 push buttons on control plate, available in Blonde or Sunburst finishes, 18.5 in. body width, mfg. 1950-58.

1950-1953	N/A	$4,800	$4,300	$3,900	$3,500	$3,000	$2,500
1954-1958	N/A	$5,800	$5,300	$4,800	$4,300	$3,800	$3,000

This model was also known as the Zephyr Emperor Vari Tone. Some models between 1953 and 1957 had DeArmond pickups. In 1954, this model was re-designated the Emperor Electric. In 1958, this model was changed to the Gibson-Epiphone Emperor (see Emperor series).

ZEPHYR REGENT - rounded cutaway, laminate maple top, 20-fret bound rosewood fingerboard with notched rectangle inlay, single body binding, tortoiseshell pickguard, trapeze tailpiece, nickel hardware, one pickup, volume/tone controls, available in Natural or Sunburst finishes, 17 3/8 in. body width, mfg. 1950-1964.

1950-1953	N/A	$2,200	$1,950	$1,750	$1,550	$1,300	$1,050
1954-1958	N/A	$1,800	$1,600	$1,400	$1,200	$1,000	$800

Starting in 1953, some models were available with DeArmond pickups, and clear plastic barrel knobs and Sunburst and Blonde finishes were introduced. In 1954, this model was re-designated the Zephyr Electric as a cutaway or non-cutaway. In 1958, this model was renamed the Gibson-Epiphone Zephyr.

GRADING		100% MINT	98% NEAR MINT	95% EXC+	90% EXC	80% VG+	70% VG	60% G

ZEPHYR REGENT (MODEL ETA2) - Florentine body style, laminated maple top, mahogany body, maple set neck, rosewood fingerboard with split parallelogram inlays, bound body and neck, f-holes, 1 humbucker pickup, gold hardware, white pickguard, available in Ebony (disc. 2000), Natural, or Vintage Sunburst finishes, mfg. 1999-present.

MSR	$832	$500	$425	$375	$325	$275	$225	$175

ELECTRIC: 31 SERIES (435, 635, 935, & PRO)

435i (KOREA MFG.) - offset double cutaway body, bolt-on maple neck, 22-fret rosewood fingerboard with offset dot inlays, Bennder tremolo system, black hardware, 2 single coil and one humbucker pickups, two knobs, 5-way selector switch, available in Black, Red, or White finishes, mfg. 1989-1992.

	N/A	$300	$250	$220	$190	$160	$130	

Last MSR was $399.

635i (KOREA MFG.) - similar to the 435i, except has a carved poplar body with a cambered top and a Floyd Rose tremolo, available in Black Metallic, Pearl White, or Red Metallic finishes, mfg. 1989-1992.

	N/A	$350	$300	$250	$220	$190	$160	

Last MSR was $599.

935i (KOREA MFG.) - similar to the 435i, except features a carved poplar body with a cambered top, one single coil Gibson SC-2 and one Gibson L-8 humbucker pickups, and a Floyd Rose tremolo, available in Black Metallic or Magenta finishes, mfg. 1989-1992.

	N/A	$375	$325	$275	$235	$205	$175	

Last MSR was $769.

PRO - offset double cutaway carved poplar body, bolt-on maple neck, 24-fret diagonal rosewood fingerboard with offset dot inlay, six-on-one-side tuners, Floyd Rose licensed tremolo bridge, one Gibson SC-2 single coil and one Gibson L-8 humbucker pickups, two knobs, three-way switch, black hardware, 25.5 in. scale, available in Alpine White, Black, or Candy Apple Red finishes, mfg. 1989-1992.

	N/A	$400	$325	$275	$235	$195	$160	

ELECTRIC: CORONET SERIES

CORONET (U.S. MFG.) - symmetrical dual cutaway body, bass bout slightly longer than treble, glue-in neck, dot fingerboard inlay, bridge/tailpiece combination, metal peghead logo plate, one New York pickup, large white pickguard, 2 knobs, available in Cherry, Black, Silver Fox, Sunset Yellow, California Coral, or Pacific Blue finishes, mfg. 1958-1970.

1958-1962	N/A	$2,000	$1,700	$1,500	$1,200	$1,000	$800	
1963-1964	N/A	$1,800	$1,550	$1,350	$1,150	$850	$700	
1965-1970	N/A	$1,500	$1,300	$1,100	$950	$800	$650	

In 1959, P-90 pickups were introduced. In 1960, the body depth was changed to 1 3/8 in. with rounded body edges, and a symmetrical pickguard was introduced. In 1962, a Maestro vibrato tailpiece became optional. In 1963, a covered P-90 pickup was introduced and Silver Fox finish was optional. In 1966, the vibrato tailpiece was discontinued. This model originally was a single pickup Crestwood model.

CORONET (MODEL EECO) - contemporary reissue, available in Black Metallic, Metallic Blue, Metallic Green, Metallic Purple, or Red Metallic finishes, mfg. 1995-2000.

	$350	$300	$275	$225	$195	$150	$125	

Last MSR was $499.

Coronet with Vibrotone (Model EECO) - similar to the Coronet, but equipped with a Bigsby-style Vibrotone tremolo bridge, available in Black Metallic, Metallic Blue, Metallic Green, Metallic Purple, or Red Metallic finishes, mfg. 1997-99.

	$425	$375	$325	$275	$225	$175	$125	

Last MSR was $599.

CORONET (U.S. 1991-94 MFG.) - offset double cutaway mahogany body, white pickguard, mahogany neck, 24-fret bound rosewood fingerboard with pearl block inlay, tune-o-matic bridge/stop tailpiece, black face reverse peghead with logo/USA inscription, 6-on-a-side tuners, gold hardware, single coil/humbucker exposed pickups, volume/tone control, 5-position switch control, active electronics, available in Black, California Coral, Cherry, Pacific Blue, Sunburst, Sunset Yellow, or White finishes, mfg. 1991-94.

	N/A	$650	$575	$500	$425	$350	$275	

Last MSR was $900.

Add $100 for double locking Floyd Rose vibrato, black hardware.

ELECTRIC: CRESTWOOD SERIES

CRESTWOOD (U.S. MFG.) - double cutaway body, set-in neck, 24.75 in. scale, rosewood fingerboard with dot inlay, tune-o-matic bridge, gold hardware, pickguard with stylized 'E', metal logo peghead plate, 2 pickups, volume/tone controls, 3-way switch, available in Cherry finish, mfg. 1958-59.

	N/A	$2,500	$2,200	$1,900	$1,650	$1,400	$1,150	

In 1959, this model was renamed the Crestwood Custom (see Crestwood Custom listing).

Epiphone Zephyr Blues Deluxe
courtesy Epiphone

Epiphone Coronet
courtesy George McGuire

GRADING	100% MINT	98% NEAR MINT	95% EXC+	90% EXC	80% VG+	70% VG	60% G

CRESTWOOD CUSTOM (U.S. MFG.) - similar to the Crestwood, except features 2 mini humbuckers, no pickguard logo, no peghead plate, oval fingerboard inlay, mfg. 1959-1969.

1959-1964	N/A	$2,300	$2,000	$1,700	$1,400	$1,100	$800
1965-1969	N/A	$1,700	$1,400	$1,150	$900	$725	$550

Add 15% for Pacific Blue, Sunset Yellow, or California Coral (White) finishes.

In 1961, mini-humbucker pickups, oval inlays, Tremotone vibrato, no pickguard logo, and a pearl peghead logo was introduced. In 1962, White finish became available. In 1963, the body was changed with an asymmetrical pickguard. In 1965, vibrato became standard.

CRESTWOOD DELUXE - offset double cutaway body, set-in neck, bound ebony fingerboard with block inlay, tune-o-matic bridge, Tremotone vibrato, 6-on-a-side tuners, bound peghead, pickguard, 3 mini-humbucker pickups, volume/tone controls, pickup selector switch, available in Cherry or White finishes, mfg. 1963-69.

	N/A	$2,400	$2,100	$1,800	$1,400	$1,200	$1,000

ELECTRIC: E SERIES

BASHER - Les Paul style laminated alder/maple body, bolt-on hard maple neck, rosewood fingerboard with dot position markers, 22-frets, 2 open coil humbucker pickups, chrome hardware, 3-per-side tuners, available in Vintage Sunburst, Just Black, Heritage Cherry Sunburst, Blood Stain, or Bruise Purple finishes, mfg. 2001-02.

	$210	$175	$150	$125	$95	$75	$50

Last MSR was $299.

Add $30 for Blood Stain and Bruise Purple finishes.

BEAST - Explorer-style body, solid tonewood, bolt-on hard maple neck, select grade Indian Rosewood fingerboard with dot position markers, 6-on-a-side tuners, 22-frets, string through body, 2 covered humbucker pickups, chrome hardware, 1 volume/1 tone control, 3-way switch, available in Black Metallic, Red Metallic, or Light Blue Metallic, mfg. 2001-02.

	$299	$270	$245	$225	$195	$150	$125

Last MSR was $499.

Beast FX (Model EXFX) - similar to the Beast, except has on-board effects package to inlcude 2 "Ultra Hot" exposed coil humbucker pickups, chorus and distortion effects, mfg. 2002 only.

	$425	$375	$325	$275	$225	$175	$125

Last MSR was $599.

BULLY - double cutaway solid body with G-style design (SG), laminated alder/maple body, bolt-on hard maple neck, 22-fret rosewood fingerboard with dot position markers, 3-per-side tuners, 2 open coil humbucker pickups, chrome plated hardware, 1 Volume/1 Tone control, 3-way switch, available in Just Black, Blood Stain, or Bruise Purple finishes, mfg. 2001 only.

	$189	$165	$145	$125	$100	$85	$75

Last MSR was $315.

DEMON - Modified V-shaped tonewood body, hard rock maple neck, select grade Indian Rosewood fingerboard with dot position markers, 22-frets, 2 covered humbucker pickups, 6-on-a-side tuners, 1 volume/1 tone control, 3-way switch, string-through-body construction, chrome plated hardware, available in Black Metallic, Metallic Red, or Metallic Light Blue finishes, mfg. 2001-02.

	$299	$270	$245	$225	$195	$150	$125

Last MSR was $499.

Demon FX (Model EVFX) - similar to the Demon, except has on-board effects package to inlcude 2 "Ultra Hot" exposed coil humbucker pickups, chorus and distortion effects, mfg. 2002 only.

	$425	$375	$325	$275	$225	$175	$125

Last MSR was $599.

EVOLUTION - modified Explorer body style, solid tonewood body, bolt-on hard maple neck, 22-fret select Indian Rosewood fingerboard with dot inlays, string through body, 2 "Ultra-Hot" covered humbucker pickups, two knobs (volume, tone), 3-way switch, chrome hardware, available in Metallic Black, Metallic Red, or Metallic Light Blue finishes, mfg. 2002 only.

	$199	$150	$125	$100	$75	$60	$50

Last MSR was $499.

LP XTREME - Les Paul style solid tonewood body, carved top, select grade Indian Rosewood fingerboard with dot position markers, 22 frets, 3-per-side tuners, 2 exposed coil humbucker pickup, chrome hardware, available in Black/White Crackle, Blue/Yellow Crackle, Green/Yellow Crackle, or Red/Yellow Crackle finishes, mfg. 2001 only.

	$599	$475	$400	$350	$300	$250	$225

Last MSR was $999.

PIERCED "SG" (MODEL ESGX) - G-400 (SG) body style, solid tonewood body, bolt-on hard maple neck, rosewood fingerboard with dot inlays, 2 exposed coil humbucker pickups, large "X"-shaped hole completely penetrates the body, two knobs (v, tone), 3-way switch, black satin hardware, available in distressed Pitch Black finish, mfg. 2002 only.

	$239	$195	$175	$150	$125	$95	$65

Last MSR was $399.

SLASHER - double cutaway solid body similar to the Firebird design, solid tonewood body, bolt-on hard maple neck, 22-fret select grade Indian Rosewood fingerboard with dot position markers, 6-on-a-side tuners, string-through-body design, 2 covered humbucker pickups, chrome plated hardware, available in Metallic Red, Light Blue Metallic, or Black Metallic finishes, mfg. 2001 only.

	$299	$265	$240	$215	$190	$165	$125

Last MSR was $499.

GRADING	100% MINT	98% NEAR MINT	95% EXC+	90% EXC	80% VG+	70% VG	60% G

ELECTRIC: E "POLY" SERIES

POLY MOD (MODEL EPOM) - modified V body style, solid tonewood body with flame maple veneer top, 2 "Ultra Hot" exposed coil humbucker pickups, metal speed knobs, die-cast tuners, Floyd Rose tremolo and locking nut, "Smooth Tone" pots, chrome hardware, available in Translucent Blue or Translucent Black finishes, mfg. 2001 only.

	$475	$395	$350	$300	$240	$190	$150

Last MSR was $665.

POLY V (MODEL EPOV) - modified V body style, solid tonewood body with flame maple veneer top, hard maple bolt-on neck, select Indian Rosewood fingerboard, 2 "Ultra Hot" exposed coil humbucker pickups, metal speed knobs, die-cast tuners, Floyd Rose tremolo and locking nut, "Smooth Tone" pots, chrome hardware, available in Translucent Blue or Translucent Black finishes, mfg. 2001 only.

	$475	$395	$350	$300	$240	$190	$150

Last MSR was $665.

POLY X (MODEL EPOX) - Explorer body style, solid tonewood body with flame maple veneer top, hard maple bolt-on neck, select Indian Rosewood fingerboard, 2 "Ultra Hot" exposed coil humbucker pickups, metal speed knobs, die-cast tuners, Floyd Rose tremolo and locking nut, "Smooth Tone" pots, chrome hardware, available in Trans. Red or Trans. Black finishes, mfg. 2001 only.

	$475	$395	$350	$300	$240	$190	$150

Last MSR was $665.

ELECTRIC: E "GOTHIC" SERIES

Add $40 for Floyd Rose Tremolo on the Explorer, Flying V, and Les Paul Studio Gothics.

1958 GOTHIC EXPLORER (MODEL EXP2) - Explorer body style, mahogany body and set neck, ebony fingerboard with side markers, XII inlay at 12th fret, 2 exposed coil humbucker pickups, black pickguard, black hardware, available in Black Satin finish, mfg. 2002-present.

MSR	$749		$450	$400	$350	$300	$250	$200	$150

1958 GOTHIC FLYING V (MODEL EGV2) - Flying V body style, mahogany body and set neck, ebony fingerboard with side markers, XII inlay at 12th fret, 2 exposed coil humbucker pickups, black pickguard, black hardware, available in Black Satin finish, mfg. 2002-present.

MSR	$749		$450	$400	$350	$300	$250	$200	$150

GOTHIC LES PAUL STUDIO (MODEL ENL1) - Les Paul body style, mahogany body and set neck, ebony fingerboard with side markers, XII inlay at 12th fret, 2 Alnico V exposed coil humbucker pickups, black pickguard, black hardware, available in Black Satin finish, mfg. 2002-present.

MSR	$749		$450	$400	$350	$300	$250	$200	$150

GOTHIC G-400 (MODEL EGG4) - G-400 (SG) body style, mahogany body and set neck, ebony fingerboard with side markers, XII inlay at 12th fret, 2 exposed coil humbucker pickups, black pickguard, black hardware, available in Black Satin finish, mfg. 2002-present.

MSR	$665		$400	$325	$275	$225	$190	$155	$120

Gothic G-400 Xtreme-FR (Model EGXT) - similar to the Gothic G-400 except has a Floyd Rose tremolo, mfg. 2002-present.

MSR	$749		$450	$400	$350	$300	$250	$200	$150

ELECTRIC: E (U.S.A.) SERIES

APOLLO (MODEL USOV) - modified Flying V style, solid tonewood body, bound top, hard maple bolt-on neck, select Indian Rosewood fingerboard, 2 covered PAF humbucker pickups, Gotoh wraparound tailpiece, white recessed guard, Grover mini-tuners, chrome hardware, available in Baby Blue, poduced in the USA in limited quantities, mfg. 2001 only.

	$1,165	$1,050	$975	$850	$750	$675	$600

Last MSR was $1,665.

COMET (MODEL USCO) - trapezoidal body design, solid tonewood body, ivory color top binding, hard maple bolt-on neck, select Indian Rosewood fingerboard, 3 covered mini-humbucker pickups, Vibrotone tremolo, ivory colored recessed guard, Grover mini-tuners, chrome hardware, available in Gold Metallic Nitrocellulose finished top, walnut back, produced in the USA in limited quantities, mfg. 2001 only.

	$1,165	$1,050	$975	$850	$750	$675	$600

Last MSR was $1,665.

FUTURA (MODEL USEX) - modified Explorer body style, solid tonewood body, white color top binding, hard maple bolt-on neck, select Indian Rosewood fingerboard, 2 covered PAF humbucker pickups, Floyd Rose tremolo, white colored recessed guard, Grover mini-tuners, chrome hardware, available in Pink Nitrocellulose finished top, black satin back, produced in the USA in limited quantities, mfg. 2001 only.

	$1,165	$1,050	$975	$850	$750	$675	$600

Last MSR was $1,665.

Epiphone Crestwood Deluxe courtesy George McGuire

Epiphone Demon courtesy Epiphone

GRADING	100% MINT	98% NEAR MINT	95% EXC+	90% EXC	80% VG+	70% VG	60% G

MODERNE (MODEL USEX) - moderne body style, solid tonewood body, ivory color top binding, hard maple bolt-on neck, select Indian Rosewood fingerboard, 2 covered PAF humbucker pickups, Floyd Rose tremolo, ivory colored recessed guard, Grover mini-tuners, chrome hardware, available in Copper Top finish, produced in the USA in limited quantities, mfg. 2001 only.

	$1,165	$1,050	$975	$850	$750	$675	$600

Last MSR was $1,665.

ELECTRIC: EM SERIES

Epiphone´s EM series is based on the Gibson M-III model.

EM-1 (EM-1 REBEL STANDARD) - offset sweeping double cutaway alder body, bolt-on maple neck, 24-fret rosewood fingerboard with pearl trapezoid inlay, standard vibrato, reverse peghead, 6-on-a-side tuners, gold hardware, humbucker/single coil/humbucker covered pickups, volume/tone control, 5-position/mini switches, available in Black, Red, Sunburst, or White finishes, mfg. 1991-98.

	$325	$275	$225	$175	$150	$125	$100

Last MSR was $450.

EM-2 (EM-2 Rebel Custom) - similar to EM-1, except has double locking Floyd Rose vibrato, mfg. 1991-95.

	$400	$325	$275	$225	$200	$175	$150

Last MSR was $550.

EM-3 Rebel Custom - similar to EM-1, except features limba body and Jam-Trem locking tremolo, mfg. 1994-95.

	$425	$350	$300	$250	$225	$195	$175

ELECTRIC: ET SERIES

In 1970, prior to the takeover of CMI (Epiphone/Gibson´s parent company) by the ECL investment group (later Norlin), the decision was made to close down Kalamazoo production of Epiphones in favor of building them overseas in Japan. Ephiphone reviewed a number of models trademarked **Lyle** (built by Matsumoku of Japan), and decided to offer a "new" line of Japanese-built Epiphones that had more in common with other Japanese copies than previous Epiphone products! Japanese-built Epiphones generally sport a blue label that reads "Epiphone, Inc. Kalamazoo, Michigan" but rarely sport a "Made in Japan" sticker.

ET-270 (JAPAN MFG.) - Strat-style double cutaway body, bolt-on hardwood neck, rosewood fingerboard with dot inlay, vibrola tremolo, chrome hardware, 2 single coil pickups, volume/tone controls, pickup selector toggle switch, available in Cherry Red finish, mfg. 1971-75.

	N/A	$300	$250	$220	$190	$160	$130

ET-275 (JAPAN MFG.) - Crestwood custom-style double cutaway hardwood body, bolt-on hardwood neck, rosewood fingerboard with dot inlay, vibrato bridge, chrome hardware, 2 pickups, volume/tone controls, pickup selector switch, available in Sunburst finish, mfg. 1971-75.

	N/A	$325	$275	$225	$195	$165	$135

ET-276 (JAPAN MFG.) - Crestwood custom-style double cutaway hardwood body, bolt-on hardwood neck, rosewood fingerboard with dot inlay, stop tailpiece, chrome hardware, 2 pickups, volume/tone controls, pickup selector switch, available in Mahogany finish, mfg. 1976 to 1979.

	N/A	$325	$275	$225	$195	$165	$135

ET-278 (JAPAN MFG.) - Crestwood custom-style body, bolt-on hardwood neck, bound rosewood fingerboard with dot inlay, chrome hardware, 2 pickups, 2 volume/tone controls, pickup selector toggle switch, available in Ebony finish, mfg. 1971-75.

	N/A	$350	$300	$250	$200	$170	$140

ET-290 (JAPAN MFG.) - Crestwood custom-style double cutaway maple body, set-in maple neck, rosewood fingerboard with block inlay, stop tailpiece, gold hardware, 2 pickups, volume/tone controls, pickup selector switch, available in Cherry Sunburst finish, mfg. 1976-79.

	N/A	$350	$300	$250	$200	$170	$140

ET-290 N (Japan Mfg.) - similar to the ET-290, except features bound maple fingerboard with black dot inlay, available in Natural finish, mfg. 1976-79.

	N/A	$375	$325	$275	$225	$175	$145

ELECTRIC: EXPLORER SERIES

EXPLORER (MODEL EXP1) - Explorer-style body, chrome hardware, white pickguard, 2 humbuckers, available in Alpine White, Ebony, or Red finishes, mfg. 1986-89, 1994-98.

	$375	$325	$295	$250	$225	$175	$150

Last MSR was $549.

"1958" KORINA EXPLORER (MODEL EXP2) - Explorer-style korina body, set-in mahogany neck, rosewood fingerboard with dot inlay, gold hardware, white pickguard, 2 covered humbuckers, available in Ebony or Natural finishes, mfg. 1998-present.

MSR	$749		$450	$375	$325	$275	$225	$175	$125

ELECTRIC: FLYING V SERIES

"1967" FLYING V (MODEL EGV1) - Flying V-style mahogany body, similar to the 1958 Flying V except has a stop tailpiece and open coil humbucker pickups, available in Alpine White, Ebony, or Red finishes, mfg. 1989-1999, 2003-present.

MSR	$582		$350	$300	$260	$230	$200	$165	$130

In 1998, Vintage White finish replaced the Alpine White finish.

"1958" KORINA FLYING V (MODEL EGV2) - Flying V-style korina body, set-in mahogany neck, rosewood fingerboard with dot inlay, gold hardware, white pickguard, 2 covered humbuckers, available in Ebony or Korina finishes, mfg. 1998-present.

MSR	$749		$450	$375	$325	$275	$225	$190	$165

GRADING	100% MINT	98% NEAR MINT	95% EXC+	90% EXC	80% VG+	70% VG	60% G

"Popa Chubby" Flying V (Model EGV3) - similar to the "1958" Flying V except is based on Popa Chubby's own custom Flying V, two P-90 pickups, tortiseshell pickguard, and gold Grover tuners and hardware, available in Natural (Korina) finish, mfg. 2002-03.

		$490	$375	$325	$275	$225	$200	$175

Last MSR was $729.

WAYNE STATIC FLYING V (MODEL EGVX) - Flying V-style mahogany body, set maple neck, ebonal fingerboard with no inlay, STB, single knob and switch, black hardware, Plain Black finish, mfg. 2004-present.

MSR	$832	$499	$425	$350	$300	$250	$220	$180

ELECTRIC: FIREBIRD SERIES

FIREBIRD (MODEL EGFB) - available in Ebony, Red, Vintage Sunburst, and White finishes, mfg. 1995-2000.

		$475	$425	$375	$325	$275	$225	$175

Last MSR was $649.

´63 FIREBIRD-VII (MODEL EGF7) - reverse body and headstock, mahogany body and neck, block inlays, 6-on-a-side tuners, 3 Alnico-V Mini-Humbucker pickups, 3 volume, 1 tone, toggle switch, original style Maestro tremolo, white pickguard, gold hardware, available in Antique Ivory, Red, Vintage Sunburst or Black finishes, mfg. 2000-present.

MSR	$831	$499	$425	$350	$300	$275	$250	$225

In 2003, this model was renamed simply the Firebird-VII and Vintage Sunburst finish was introduced.

FIREBIRD 300 (KOREA MFG.) - reverse firebird-style body, laminated mahogany neck-through-body, 25.5 in. scale, 22-fret ebanol fingerboard with dot inlay, Steinberger KB locking tremolo, white pickguard with red firebird graphic, black hardware, single coil/humbucker EMG Select pickups, volume/tone controls, pickup selector switch, mfg. 1986-88.

		N/A	$325	$275	$225	$175	$135	$95

FIREBIRD 500 (KOREA MFG.) - similar to the Firebird 300, except has 2 EMG Select humbuckers, mfg. 1986-88.

		N/A	$350	$300	$250	$200	$150	$100

ELECTRIC: G SERIES

The G Series is essentially Epiphone's version of Gibson's SG and the Gibson Doubleneck.

G-310 (MODEL EGG1) - double sharp cutaway alder body, bolt-on mahogany neck, 22-fret rosewood fingerboard with pearl dot inlay, tune-o-matic bridge/stop tailpiece, blackface peghead with logo, 3-per-side tuners, chrome hardware, 2 exposed coil humbucker pickups, 2 volume/2 tone controls, 3-position switch, available in Ebony, Red, or Vintage White finishes, mfg. 1989-present.

MSR	$331	$200	$170	$140	$120	$105	$85	$65

G-310 Left-Handed (Model EGG1L) - similar to G-310, except in left-handed configuration, available in Ebony finish, current mfg.

MSR	$349	$210	$180	$150	$130	$110	$85	$65

G-310 Junior (Model EGGJ) - similar to G-310, except has a laminated alder/maple SG-style body, available in Ebony, Cherry, or TV Yellow finishes, disc. 2000.

		$160	$140	$120	$100	$80	$70	$50

Last MSR was $229.

G-310 "Emily the Strange" (Model EGG1) - G-310 body style with Emily the Strange graphics, includes strap and gig bag, mfg. 2003-present.

MSR	$499	$299	$260	$230	$200	$170	$140	$110

G-400 (MODEL EGG4) - similar to G-310, except has mahogany body, set-in mahogany neck, trapezoid fingerboard inlays, 3-per-side vintage-style tuners, smaller pickguard, 2 covered humbucker pickups, available in Cherry or Ebony finishes, mfg. 1989-present.

MSR	$665	$400	$325	$275	$235	$200	$165	$130

This model is based on Gibson's SG model, circa 1962. In 1998, Ebony finish was introduced.

G-400 Left-Handed (Model EGG4L) - similar to the G-400 except in left-handed configuration, available in Cherry finish, mfg. 2003-present.

MSR	$699	$420	$350	$300	$250	$210	$170	$140

G-400 Deluxe (Model EGF4) - similar to the G-400 except has a flame maple top, available in Vintage Sunburst finish, mfg. 1999-present.

MSR	$832	$500	$425	$375	$325	$275	$235	$190

G-400 with Vibrotone (Model EGG4) - similar to G-400, except has Bigsby-derived tremolo bridge, available in Cherry finish, mfg. 1997-99.

		$475	$425	$375	$325	$275	$225	$175

Last MSR was $699.

Epiphone Moderne
courtesy Epiphone

Epiphone G-400
courtesy Epiphone

GRADING	100% MINT	98% NEAR MINT	95% EXC+	90% EXC	80% VG+	70% VG	60% G

G-400 Custom (Model EGG5) - similar to G-400, except has 3 covered humbuckers, white pickguard, gold hardware, fingerboard block inlays, bound neck and headstock, available in Antique Ivory finish, mfg. 1998-2000, reintroduced 2003-present.

MSR	$832	$500	$425	$375	$325	$275	$235	$190

G-400 Korina (Model EGG4) - similar to G-400, except has korina body, white pickguard, gold hardware, fingerboard block inlays, bound neck and headstock, available in Natural finish, mfg. 1998-2000.

		$500	$450	$400	$350	$300	$250	$190

Last MSR was $729.

Vintage G-400 - similar to the G-400 except has either a Worn Cherry or Worn Black finish, mfg. 2003-present.

MSR	$665	$400	$325	$275	$235	$190	$160	$130

TONY IOMMI SIGNATURE G-400 (MODEL EGGI) - G-400 style guitar that is based on the 1962 Gibson SG, 24-fret Slim-Taper neck, Gibson USA Tony Iommi Humbuckers, Tony Iommi's cross inlays, Tony Iommi signature on truss-rod cover, black chrome hardware, available in Ebony finish, mfg. 2003-present.

MSR	$1,082	$650	$575	$500	$425	$375	$325	$275

Tony Iommi Signature G-400 Left-Handed (Model EGGIL) - similar to the Tony Iommi signature except in left-handed configuration, available in Ebony finish, mfg. 2003-present.

MSR	$1,115	$670	$600	$525	$450	$400	$350	$295

G-1275 STANDARD DOUBLENECK (MODEL EGDS) - SG-style body, 2 bolt-on necks (12-string configuration, 6-per-side tuners; 6-string configuration, 3-per-side tuners), available in Cherry finish, disc. 1998.

		$1,000	$850	$750	$650	$550	$450	$350

Last MSR was $1,399.

G-1275 Custom Doubleneck (Model EGDC) - similar to the G-1275 Standard, except features set-in necks, available in Cherry finish, disc. 2000 reintroduced 2002-present.

MSR	$1,299	$780	$700	$625	$550	$475	$425	$375

ELECTRIC: GENESIS SERIES

Genesis series guitars were produced in Taiwan from 1979 to 1981.

GENESIS STANDARD - dual cutaway mahogany body, set-in neck, rosewood fingerboard with dot inlay, 3-per-side tuners, chrome hardware, 2 humbucker pickups, volume/tone control, pickup selector switch, coil tap switch, mfg. 1979-1981.

		N/A	$350	$300	$250	$220	$190	$160

GENESIS CUSTOM - similar to the Genesis Standard, except features bound rosewood fingerboard with crown inlay, mfg. 1979-1981.

		N/A	$400	$350	$300	$250	$220	$190

GENESIS DELUXE - similar to the Genesis Standard, except features bound rosewood fingerboard with block inlay, gold hardware, mfg. 1979-1981.

		N/A	$450	$400	$350	$300	$250	$210

ELECTRIC: LES PAUL SERIES

LES PAUL 1 (KOREA MFG.) - Les Paul-style basswood body, bolt-on maple neck, 25.5 in. scale, 22-fret rosewood fingerboard with small block inlays, split diamond peghead inlay, black hardware, double locking Steinberger KB tremolo, humbucker pickup, volume control, available in Black, Red, or White finishes, mfg. 1986-89.

		N/A	$350	$300	$260	$230	$200	$165

Les Paul 2 (Korea Mfg.) - similar to the Les Paul I, except has 2 humbuckers, 2 volume/2 tone controls, 3-way switch, mfg. 1986-89.

		N/A	$375	$325	$275	$240	$210	$175

Les Paul 3 (Korea Mfg.) - similar to the Les Paul I, except has 2 single coils/Gibson humbucker pickups, volume/tone controls, 3 mini-switches, mfg. 1986-89.

		N/A	$400	$350	$300	$250	$220	$190

LES PAUL SIGNATURE (MODEL ENL 5) - offset double cutaway laminated maple semi-hollow body, laminated maple top, raised creme pickguard, set-in maple neck, 24.75 in. scale, 22-fret bound rosewood fingerboard with trapezoid fingerboard inlay, tune-o-matic bridge/stop tailpiece, unbound peghead, 3-per-side tuners, chrome hardware, 2 low impedance humbuckers, volume/tone controls, 3-way selector toggle switch, varigain selector switch, phase switch, available in Ebony, Metallic Gold, or Vintage Sunburst finishes, mfg. 1998-2000.

		$700	$625	$550	$500	$450	$400	$325

Last MSR was $1,299.

LES PAUL STANDARD (MODEL ENS-) - Les Paul-style single cutaway mahogany body, figured maple top, raised white pickguard, set-in mahogany neck, 22-fret bound rosewood fingerboard with trapezoid fingerboard inlay, tune-o-matic bridge/stop tailpiece, unbound peghead, 3-per-side tuners, chrome hardware, 2 humbuckers, 2 volume/2 tone controls, 3-way toggle switch, available in Ebony finish, mfg. 1989-present.

MSR	$831	$499	$425	$350	$300	$250	$220	$180

Add $50 for Heritage Cherry Sunburst and Honey Burst finishes.

Les Paul Standard with Vibrotone (Model ENS-) - similar to the Les Paul Standard, except has Bigsby-styled tremolo system, available in Ebony finish, mfg. 1997 only.

		$700	$625	$550	$475	$400	$325	$275

Last MSR was $949.

Add $75 for Heritage Cherry Sunburst and Honey Burst finishes.

GRADING	100% MINT	98% NEAR MINT	95% EXC+	90% EXC	80% VG+	70% VG	60% G

E

Les Paul Standard Left-Handed (Model ENSL) - similar to the Les Paul Standard, except in left-handed configuration, available in Heritage Cherry Sunburst or Ebony finishes, mfg. 1996-present.

MSR	$865	$520	$450	$400	$350	$300	$250	$200

Les Paul Standard Plus (Model ENS-) - similar to the Les Paul Standard except has a flamed maple top, available in Honey Burst, Heritage Cherry Sunburst, Trans. Amber, Trans. Blue, Vintage Sunburst, or Wine Red finishes, mfg 2003-present.

MSR	$999	$600	$525	$475	$425	$375	$325	$275

Les Paul Standard Plus Left-Handed (Model ENSL) - similar to the Les Paul Standard Plus except in left-handed configuration, available in Heritage Cherry Sunburst or Vintage Sunburst finishes, mfg. 2003-present.

MSR	$1,024	$615	$540	$490	$440	$390	$340	$290

Les Paul Standard Goldtop (Model ENS-MG) - similar to the Les Paul Standard, available in Metallic Gold finish, mfg. 1995-98.

		$650	$575	$500	$450	$400	$325	$250

Last MSR was $979.

Les Paul ´56 Goldtop (Model EN56) - similar to the Les Paul Standard, except features 2 creme-colored P-90-style single coil pickups, creme-colored pickguard, available in Metallic Gold finish, mfg. 1998-present.

MSR	$999	$599	$525	$450	$400	$350	$300	$250

Les Paul Standard Translucent Edition (Model ENST) - available in Trans. Amber, Trans. Black, Trans. Blue, Trans. Purple, Trans. Red, Trans. Green, or Wine Red finishes, disc. 2000.

		$650	$575	$500	$425	$350	$300	$250

Last MSR was $959.

Les Paul Standard Translucent Edition with VibroTone (Model ENST) - equipped with Bigsby-derived tremolo bridge, available in Trans. Amber, Trans. Black, Trans. Blue, Trans. Purple, Trans. Red, Trans. Green, or Wine Red finishes, mfg. 1997 only.

		$700	$625	$550	$475	$400	$325	$275

Last MSR was $1,099.

Epiphone Les Paul Standard
courtesy Epiphone

Les Paul Standard Metal Edition (Model ENSM) - available in Gold Flake, Blue Flake, Green Flake, Purple Flake, Red Flake, or Silver Flake finishes, disc. 2000.

		$625	$550	$475	$400	$325	$275	$225

Last MSR was $929.

Les Paul Standard Metal Edition with VibroTone (Model ENSM) - equipped with Bigsby-derived tremolo bridge, available in Gold Flake, Blue Flake, Green Flake, Purple Flake, Red Flake, or Silver Flake finishes, mfg. 1997 only.

		$800	$725	$650	$575	$500	$425	$350

Last MSR was $1,269.

Les Paul Standard P-90 Deluxe - similar to other Les Paul models except has carved alder top, bound mahogany body, set neck, bound rosewood fingerboard, trapezoid neck inlays, 2 P-90 single coil pickups, Bigsby vibrato tailpiece, chrome hardware, available in Ebony finish, mfg. 2002-03.

		$525	$450	$400	$350	$300	$225	$150

Last MSR was $1,099.

Les Paul Standard Baritone (Model ENLB) - similar to the Standard Les Paul, except is in baritone configuration, has black hardware, and is available in Alpine White, Iron Cross, Red Oval, Worn Brown, or Plain Black finishes, mfg. 2004-present.

MSR	$831	$499	$425	$350	$300	$260	$230	$200

LES PAUL STANDARD ELITIST (MODEL ELLPS, JAPAN) - book-matched African mahogany back and book-matched maple top, one-piece mahogany set neck with rosewood fingerboard and 22 frets, 50SR and 60ST USA humbuckers, nickel hardware, Grover tuners, 2 volume, 2 tone and 3-way pickup selector, available in Faded Cherryburst, Ebony, Honeyburst, or Vintage Sunburst finishes, 24.75 in. scale, mfg. 2003-present.

MSR	$1,614	$1,050	$900	$800	$700	$625	$550	$475

Add $50 for left-handed configuration.

LES PAUL STANDARD PLUS ELITIST (MODEL ELLPF, JAPAN) - book-matched African mahogany back and book-matched Flame Maple top, one-piece mahogany set neck with rosewood fingerboard and 22 frets, 50SR and 60ST USA humbuckers, nickel hardware, Grover tuners, 2 volume, 2 tone and 3-way pickup selector, available in Faded Cherryburst, Honeyburst, or Vintage Sunburst finishes, 24.75 in. scale, mfg. 2003-present.

MSR	$1,767	$1,150	$1,000	$900	$800	$725	$650	$550

LES PAUL BLACK BEAUTY 3 (MODEL ENBB) - similar to the Les Paul Standard, except has gold hardware, 3 humbucker pickups, available in Ebony finish only, current mfg.

MSR	$1,165	$700	$625	$550	$475	$400	$350	$300

Les Paul Black Beauty with Vibrotone (Model ENS-EB) - similar to the Les Paul Black Beauty, except has Bigsby-styled tremolo system, gold hardware, available in Ebony finish, mfg. 1997-99.

	N/A	$600	$525	$450	$400	$325	$250

Last MSR was $899.

Epiphone Les Paul
Black Beauty
courtesy Epiphone

GRADING	100% MINT	98% NEAR MINT	95% EXC+	90% EXC	80% VG+	70% VG	60% G

Les Paul Black Beauty 3 with VibroTone (Model ENBB) - similar to the Les Paul Black Beauty, except has Bigsby-styled tremolo system, gold hardware, 3 humbucker pickups, available in Ebony finish, mfg. 1997-99.

		$750	$625	$550	$475	$425	$350	$275

Last MSR was $1,049.

LES PAUL CLASSIC (MODEL ENCS) - Les Paul Style mahogany/alder body with a flamed maple top, chrome hardware, available in Ebony finish, mfg. 2003-present.

MSR	$831	$499	$425	$375	$325	$275	$225	$175

Les Paul Classic Plus (Model ENCP) - similar to the Les Paul Classic except has open coil Alnico-V Humbucker pickups, available Heritage Cherry Sunburst, Metallic Gold, or Vintage Sunburst finishes, mfg. 2003-present.

MSR	$999	$600	$525	$450	$400	$350	$300	$250

Les Paul Classic-7 (Model ENC7) - mahogany body with flamed maple top, mahogany set neck, rosewood fingerboard with pearl trapezoid inlays, 4/3 tuners, 2 open coil humbucker pickups, bound body and neck, white pickguard, chrome hardare, available in Vintage Sunburst or Trans. Black finishes, mfg. 2000-present.

		$650	$475	$425	$375	$325	$275	$225

Last MSR was $929.

Les Paul Classic-12 (12-String) (Model ENL 4) - similar to the Les Paul Standard, except features bound flame maple top, 12-string configuration, 6-per-side tuners, 2 open coil humbuckers, available in Heritage Cherry Sunburst, or Vintage Sunburst finishes, mfg. 1998-2000.

		$625	$550	$475	$425	$375	$325	$250

Last MSR was $899.

Les Paul Classic Birdseye (Model ENSB) - available in Amber, Heritage Cherry Sunburst, or Natural finishes, mfg. 1996-99.

		$600	$525	$475	$400	$350	$275	$225

Last MSR was $869.

LES PAUL CUSTOM (MODEL ENC-) - similar to Les Paul Standard, except has arched bound maple top, raised black pickguard, 22-fret bound rosewood fingerboard with pearl block inlay, bound peghead with pearl split diamond/logo inlay, gold hardware, available in Black or White finishes, mfg. 1989-present.

MSR	$999	$599	$525	$450	$400	$350	$300	$250

Les Paul Custom Left-Handed (Model ENCL) - similar to the Les Paul Custom, except in left-handed configuration, available in Ebony finish, mfg. 2003-present.

MSR	$1,049	$630	$550	$475	$425	$350	$300	$250

Les Paul Custom Plus (Model ENC-) - similar to the Les Paul Custom, except features highly figured maple top, available in Heritage Cherry Sunburst and Vintage Sunburst finishes, mfg. 1998-present.

MSR	$1,165	$700	$625	$550	$475	$400	$350	$300

50th Anniversary Ltd. Ed. Les Paul Custom (Model ENC5) - similar to the Les Paul Custom except has 50th Anniversary features, available in Ebony finish, mfg. 2003 only.

		$599	$525	$450	$400	$350	$300	$250

Last MSR was $999.

LES PAUL CUSTOM ELITIST (JAPAN) - book-matched African mahogany back and book-matched maple top, one-piece mahogany neck with rosewood fingerboard and 22 frets, 50SR and 60ST USA humbuckers, 24Kt. Gold hardware, Grover tuners, 2 volume, 2 tone and 3-way pickup selector, available in Ebony, Vintage White, or Wine Red finishes, 24.75 in. scale, mfg. 2003-present.

MSR	$1,690	$1,100	$950	$825	$750	$675	$600	$525

LES PAUL DOUBLE CUTAWAY (MODEL ELPS) (LES PAUL SPECIAL DC) - dual cutaway body, available in Cherry, Ebony, and TV Yellow finishes, mfg. 1995-2000.

		$500	$425	$375	$325	$275	$240	$195

Last MSR was $729.

LES PAUL DELUXE (MODEL ENL3) - available in Ebony finish, mfg. 1998-2000.

		$575	$525	$475	$425	$375	$300	$200

Last MSR was $819.

LES PAUL ELITE (MODEL ENSE) - semi-hollowbody body, single f-hole, gold hardware, available in Ebony finish, disc. 1999.

		$725	$625	$550	$475	$425	$350	$275

Last MSR was $1,029.

LES PAUL ES (MODEL ENL7) - ES style semi-hollow body, Flame Maple top, mahogany body, maple set neck, rosewood fingerboard with trapezoid inlays, bound body and neck, gold hardware, 2 humbucker pickups, available in Amber, Heritage Cherry Sunburst, Vintage Sunburst, or Wine Red finishes, mfg. 1999-2000.

		$625	$550	$475	$425	$375	$325	$250

Last MSR was $899.

LES PAUL STUDIO (MODEL ENL1) - similar to the Les Paul Standard except has a black pickguard and no binding, available in Ebony, Heritage Cherry Sunburst, Wine Red, or Vintage Sunburst finishes, mfg. 1998-present.

MSR	$665	$400	$325	$275	$235	$190	$160	$130

Les Paul Studio Pearl (Model ENL2) - similar to the Les Paul Studio except has a white pearloid pickguard/truss rod cover/toggle switch ring, black hardware, available in Trans. Black finish, mfg. 1998-99.

		$480	$440	$390	$340	$290	$240	$190

Last MSR was $689.

GRADING	100% MINT	98% NEAR MINT	95% EXC+	90% EXC	80% VG+	70% VG	60% G

E

Les Paul Studio Standard (Model ELSB) - available in Heritage Cherry Sunburst, Honey Burst, or Metallic Gold finishes, disc. 1998.

		$500	$450	$400	$350	$300	$250	$195

Last MSR was $769.

LES PAUL STUDIO ELITIST (MODEL ELLPD) - Les Paul body, mahogany body with book-matched maple top, 1 piece mahogany neck, 22-fret rosewood fingerboard with dot inlays, raised black pickguard, 2 humbucker pickups, four knobs, 3-way switch, nickel hardware, available in Ebony, Antique White, Wine Red, or Vintage Sunburst finishes, mfg. 2003-present.

MSR	$999	$650	$550	$475	$425	$375	$325	$275

Add $50 for Vintage Sunburst or Wine Red finishes.

LES PAUL '57 GOLDTOP ELITIST (MODEL ELLPS) - Les Paul body, book-matched mahogany body with hard maple top, 1 piece mahogany neck, 22-fret rosewood fingerboard with trapezoid inlays, raised white pickguard, 2 humbucker pickups, four knobs, 3-way switch, nickel hardware, Gold Top finish only, mfg. 2003-present.

MSR	$1,690	$1,100	$975	$850	$750	$650	$575	$500

LES PAUL COLLEGIATE GUITAR (MODEL EECG) - Les Paul model with the top 50 NCAA Division 1-A schools available for decals, available 2004, with models released staggered through the year.

MSR	$500	$300	$260	$230	$200	$170	$140	$110

Add 20% for University of Minnesota model.

LES PAUL ULTRA (MODEL ENSU) - Les Paul-style single cutaway chambered mahogany body, quilt maple top, raised white pickguard, set-in mahogany neck, 22-fret bound rosewood fingerboard with trapezoid fingerboard inlay, tune-o-matic bridge/stop tailpiece, unbound peghead, 3-per-side tuners, gold hardware, 2 Alnico humbucker pickups, 2 volume/2 tone controls, 3-way toggle switch, available in Faded Cherry finish, 24.75 in. scale, new 2005.

MSR	$831	$499	$425	$350	$300	$250	$220	$180

ACE FREHLEY LES PAUL CLASSIC (MODEL ENAC) - multi-bound, premium flamed maple top, rosewood fingerboard with lightning bolt inlays, chrome plated hardware, three Dimarzio USA Super Distortion Humbucker pickups, inlay of Ace's face on the headstock, available in Heritage Cherry Sunburst or Translucent Black finishes, mfg. 1999-present.

MSR	$1,332	$800	$700	$625	$550	$475	$400	$350

Epiphone Ace Frehley Les Paul Classic courtesy Epiphone

BOB MARLEY LP SPECIAL (MODEL ENMS) - Les Paul body shape, mahogany body, rosewood fingerboard with red/yellow/green block inlays, 2 Alnico humbucker pickups, chrome hardware, "One Love" inlay in headstock, available in Natural finish with Bob Marley portrait, comes with a hemp gig bag as well, mfg. 2004-present.

MSR	$749	$450	$375	$325	$275	$225	$190	$165

Look for this model to be very popular around college dorms, Dave Matthews concerts, and your local bodega.

JOE PERRY BONEYARD LP (MODEL ENSA) - Les Paul style guitar, mahogany back with flamed maple top, mahogany set neck, 22-fret rosewood fingerboard with trapezoid pearl inlays, 2 U.S.A. Burstbucker Pickups, chrome hardware, headstock with Joe's "Boneyard" logo, available in aged yellow-green tiger finish, mfg. 2004-present.

MSR	$1,332	$800	$725	$625	$550	$475	$400	$325

JOHN CONNOLLY SIGNATURE LES PAUL (MODEL ENJC) - Les Paul style guitar, John Connolly signature, available in Translucent Black finish, mfg. 2003-present.

MSR	$1,332	$800	$700	$625	$550	$475	$400	$350

LYNYRD SKYNYRD 30TH ANNIVERSARY (MODEL ENS-) - Les Paul body shape, mahogany with maple top body, rosewood fingerboard with LYNYRD SKYNYRD inlay, 2 Alnico humbucker pickups, chrome hardware, available in Gold Top finish with Lynyrd Skynyrd logo on back, mfg. 2004-present.

MSR	$999	$600	$525	$450	$400	$350	$300	$250

SLASH LES PAUL CLASSIC (MODEL ENSH) - Slash Snake graphic on lower bout, flamed maple top, black hardware, no raised pickguard, 2 exposed polepiece humbucker pickups, available in Transparent Red finish, mfg. 1997-2000.

		$700	$600	$525	$450	$375	$325	$250

Last MSR was $999.

TAK MATSUMOTO LES PAUL STANDARD ELITIST (MODEL ELLPT) - Les Paul body, book-matched mahogany body with book-matched quilted maple top, one-piece mahogany neck, 22-fret rosewood fingerboard with abalone trapezoid inlays, 2 Burst bucker pickups, four knobs, 3-way switch, nickel hardware, TakBurst finish only, new 2004.

MSR	$1,999	$1,350	$1,150	$1,025	$900	$775	$675	$575

ZAKK WYLDE SIGNATURE LES PAUL (MODEL ENCZ) - Les Paul style guitar, mahogany back with maple top body, hard maple set neck, 22-fret rosewood fingerboard Zakk Wylde signature, 2 U.S.A. EMG-HZ H4 Pickups, gold hardware, available in Zakk's signature bull's-eye black and white finish, Buzzsaw, or Camo finishes, mfg. 2003-present.

MSR	$1,332	$800	$700	$625	$550	$475	$400	$325

In 2005, Buzzsaw and Camo finishes were introduced.

Epiphone Les Paul Studio courtesy Epiphone

GRADING	100% MINT	98% NEAR MINT	95% EXC+	90% EXC	80% VG+	70% VG	60% G

ELECTRIC: LP (LES PAUL) SERIES

The bolt-on neck LP Series models are produced in Korea.

LP-100 (MODEL ENB-) - Les Paul-style alder/mahogany body, alder/maple top, bolt-on mahogany neck, 2 exposed coil humbucker pickups, available in Ebony, Red, Heritage Sunburst, Vintage Sunburst, Antique Sunburst, or Pearl White finishes, mfg. 1994-present.

	MSR	$415	$250	$210	$180	$150	$120	$90	$60

Add $50 for Antique Sunburst, Heritage Cherry Sunburst, and Vintage Sunburst finishes.

In 1998, Antique Sunburst finish was disc. Pearl White finish was disc in 2000.

LP-100 LEFT HANDED (MODEL ENBL) - similar to the LP-100, except features left-handed configuration, available in Ebony or Heritage Cherry Sunburst finishes, current mfg.

	MSR	$515	$310	$275	$245	$200	$150	$125	$100

LP-100 PLUS (MODEL ENBP) - available in Ebony, Red, or White finishes, mfg. 1997-98.

		$425	$350	$300	$260	$220	$180	$140

Last MSR was $589.

Add $30 for Heritage Cherry Sunburst and Vintage Sunburst finishes.

LP-300 (KOREA MFG.) - Les Paul-style body, bolt-on neck, bound fingerboard with block inlays, mfg. 1989-1992.

	N/A	$350	$300	$250	$210	$170	$130

ELECTRIC: MISC. MODELS

For space consideration, all models that are not listed under other categories are listed here.

DEL REY STANDARD (MODEL EEXC) - double cutaway mahogany body with flamed maple top, mahogany bolt-on neck, 24-fret rosewood fingerboard with dot inlay, 2 OBL humbucker pickups, tune-o-matic bridge, two knobs, one switch, coil-tapping, 3-per-side tuners, gold hardware, available in Amber, Heritage Cherry Sunburst, Trans. Black, or Wine Red finishes, mfg. 1995-2000.

	$525	$450	$400	$350	$300	$250	$195

Last MSR was $749.

ELP 2 (KOREA MFG.) - similar to the Epiphone Les Paul design, but featured a bolt-on neck, mfg. 1988-89.

	N/A	$300	$250	$220	$190	$160	$130

FAT-210 (MODEL EGF2) - Offset double cutaway (Stratocaster style) laminated alder body, maple neck, 22-fret maple or rosewood fingerboard with dot inlay, 3 pickups (2 single coil, 1 humbucker), tremolo, chrome hardware, available in Ebony, Vintage Sunburst, or Vintage White finishes, disc. 2004.

	$140	$125	$110	$95	$80	$65	$50

Last MSR was $232.

JUNIOR SC (MODEL EGJR) - Single cutaway laminated alder/maple body, bolt-on mahogany neck, 22-fret rosewood fingerboard with pearl dot inlay, wraparound tune-o-matic bridge, blackface peghead with screened logo, 3-per-side tuners, chrome hardware, black pickguard, dog-ear P-90-style single coil pickup, volume/tone controls, available in Ebony, Cherry, Heritage Cherry Sunburst, TV Yellow, and Vintage Sunburst finishes, mfg. 1997-2000.

	$150	$130	$115	$100	$80	$60	$45

Last MSR was $215.

Epiphone Junior Series models are based on Gibson's Melody Maker instruments.

Junior DC (Model EGJC) - similar to Junior SC, except has an offset double cutaway body, available in Ebony, Cherry, or TV Yellow finishes, mfg. 1997-2000.

	$160	$140	$120	$100	$80	$60	$50

Last MSR was $229.

SG '61 STANDARD ELITIST (MODEL ELSGS, JAPAN) - double cutaway solid body, book-matched African mahogany top, one-piece mahogany set neck with Rosewood fingerboard, 22 frets, 24.75 in. scale, 50SR and 60ST USA humbuckers, Grover tuners, nickel hardware, 2 volume, 2 tone and 3-way pickup selector, available in Cherry or Ebony finishes, mfg. 2003-present.

	MSR	$1,229	$799	$725	$650	$575	$500	$425	$350

SG SPECIAL (MODEL ESGS) - double sharp cutaway (SG) laminated alder/maple body, maple neck, rosewood fingerboard with dot inlay, 2 Epi open coil humbucker pickups, chrome hardware available in Cherry or Ebony finishes, current mfg.

	MSR	$249	$150	$125	$105	$85	$70	$55	$40

SPECIAL (U.S. MFG.) - SG-style body, set-in neck, rosewood fingerboard with dot inlay, chrome hardware, stop tailpiece, 1 (or 2) humbucker pickups, has Epiphone U.S.A. on headstock, mfg. 1982-83.

	N/A	$650	$575	$500	$450	$400	$350

SPECIAL II (MODEL ENJR) - single cutaway body, bolt-on neck, 2 exposed coil pickups, tune-o-matic bridge/stop tailpiece, volume/tone controls, 3-way selector, available in Ebony, Red, Heritage Cherry Sunburst, Vintage Sunburst, Wine Red, or White finishes, mfg. 1996-present.

	MSR	$249	$150	$125	$105	$85	$70	$55	$40

Add $50 for Heritage Cherry Sunburst, Vintage Sunburst, and Wine Red finishes.

Special II Left-Handed (Model ENJRL) - similar to the Special II, except in a left-handed configuration, available in Vintage Sunburst or Heritage Sunburst finish, mfg. 1997-present.

	MSR	$349	$210	$180	$160	$140	$120	$100	$80

GRADING	100% MINT	98% NEAR MINT	95% EXC+	90% EXC	80% VG+	70% VG	60% G

SPECIAL II PLUS (MODEL ENJRP) - similar to the Special II, except features die-cast tuners, 2 OBL humbuckers, coil tap capabilities, available in Ebony, Red, Heritage Cherry Sunburst, Vintage Sunburst, or White finishes, mfg. 1997-99.

	$275	$225	$195	$175	$150	$125	$95

Last MSR was $379.

Add $30 for Heritage Cherry Sunburst and Vintage Sunburst finishes.

SPIRIT (U.S. MFG.) - Les Paul-style double cutaway body, set-in neck, bound rosewood fingerboard with dot inlay, stoptail bridge, chrome hardware, 3-per-side tuners, 1 (or 2) humbucker pickups, volume/tone controls, has Epiphone U.S.A. on headstock, mfg. 1982-83.

	N/A	$1,000	$875	$750	$650	$550	$450

This model is similar to the Gibson version Spirit model. Some of the Epiphone models may have bound, figured maple tops.

SPOTLIGHT (JAPAN MFG.) - slightly offset double cutaway body, set-in neck, rosewood fingerboard with chevron inlays, 3-per-side headstock, 2 humbucker pickups, available in Metallic Black, Metallic Red, Pearl White, and PRS/Alembic type walnut, mfg. 1986-89.

	N/A	$500	$425	$350	$300	$250	$200

In 1988, a Steinberger KB tremolo was introduced with a coil tap switch on one of the knobs.

T-310 (MODEL EGT1) - single cutaway body, fixed bridge, 6-on-a-side tuners, 2 single coil pickups, available in Ebony, French Cream, Red, Vintage Sunburst, or Vintage White finishes, mfg. 1989-2000.

	$225	$195	$170	$150	$125	$100	$75

Last MSR was $309.

T-310 Custom - similar to T-310, except featured a chrome-covered humbucker in neck position, mfg. 1995-97.

	$225	$195	$170	$150	$125	$100	$75

Last MSR was $339.

TRAILER PARK TROUBADOUR AIRSCREAMER (MODEL EEAS) - limited edition guitar shaped like the Airstream trailer, mahogany body, hard maple bolt-on neck, 22-fret rosewood fingerboard with dot inlay, 2 EMG pickups, chrome hardware, Airstream silver finish, mfg. 2003-present.

MSR	$915	$550	$475	$425	$375	$325	$275	$225

Epiphone Special II courtesy Epiphone

U.S.A. MAP GUITAR (U.S. MFG.) - map-shaped mahogany body, set-in neck, chrome hardware, tune-o-matic bridge/stop tailpiece, 2 covered humbucker pickups, 2 volume/2 tone controls, 3-way selector switch, mfg. 1983 only.

	N/A	$1,750	$1,500	$1,250	$1,000	$800	$600

Map guitar models were part of the final production runs at the original Kalamazoo plant prior to its closure in 1984. The Epiphone version of the Map guitar was introduced before the Gibson version, and some Epiphone models "became" Gibson models towards the end of the production run to meet demand.

V 2 (KOREA MFG.) - Flying V-style body, bolt-on neck, rosewood fingerboard with dot inlay, 6-on-a-side tuners, chrome hardware, standard tremolo, 2 humbucker pickups, volume/tone controls, 3-way switch, mfg. 1986-89.

	N/A	$350	$275	$235	$205	$175	$135

X-1000 (KOREA MFG.) - offset double cutaway body, laminated maple neck-through-body, 25.5 in. scale, 24-fret bound ebanol fingerboard with white chevron inlay, 6-on-a-side and 3-per-side tuners, bound rounded point headstock, black hardware, tremolo, 2 single coil/humbucker EMG Select pickups, volume/tone controls, 3 mini-switches, mfg. 1986-89.

	N/A	$350	$300	$250	$200	$150	$100

In 1988, a Steinberger KB tremolo was introduced with a coil tap switch on one of the knobs.

ELECTRIC: NIGHTHAWK SERIES

Epiphone Nighthawk models are based on the popular Gibson Nighthawk Series.

NIGHTHAWK STANDARD (MODEL ENHS) - available in Heritage Cherry Sunburst, Trans. Amber, or Vintage Sunburst finishes, mfg. 1995-2000.

	$500	$450	$400	$350	$300	$250	$195

Last MSR was $729.

NIGHTHAWK STANDARD WITH TREMOLO (MODEL ENHST) - similar to Nighthawk Standard, except features tremolo bridge, available in Heritage Cherry Sunburst, Trans. Amber, or Vintage Sunburst finishes, disc. 1998.

	$550	$500	$450	$400	$325	$275	$225

Last MSR was $849.

NIGHTHAWK SPECIAL (MODEL ENHP) - available in Ebony or Red finishes, mfg. 1995-98.

	$525	$475	$425	$375	$325	$275	$225

Last MSR was $759.

NIGHTHAWK SPECIAL WITH TREMOLO (MODEL ENHPT) - similar to Nighthawk Special, except features tremolo bridge, available in Ebony or Red finishes, disc. 1998.

	$550	$500	$450	$400	$325	$275	$225

Last MSR was $779.

Epiphone T-310 courtesy Epiphone

GRADING	100% MINT	98% NEAR MINT	95% EXC+	90% EXC	80% VG+	70% VG	60% G

ELECTRIC: OLYMPIC SERIES

OLYMPIC SINGLE - single cutaway body, set-in neck, rosewood fingerboard with dot inlay, combination bridge/tailpiece, 3-per-side tuners, chrome hardware, one pickup, volume/tone controls, available in Sunburst finish, mfg. 1960-69, 1977-79.

1960-1969 (USA MFG.)	N/A	$900	$750	$650	$550	$450	$350
1977-1979 (JAPAN MFG.)	N/A	$500	$425	$350	$300	$250	$200

In 1963, the body style changed to an offset double cutaway design. In 1964, 6-on-a-side headstock was introduced and a Maestro vibrato became optional. In 1965, vibrato became standard. This model was also available in a two pickup configuration.

OLYMPIC DOUBLE (U.S. MFG.) - similar to the Olympic, except features 2 pickups, 3-way selector switch, mfg. 1960-69.

	N/A	$1,000	$850	$750	$650	$550	$450

OLYMPIC 3/4 SIZE (U.S. MFG.) - similar to Olympic, except features 3/4 size body, mfg. 1960-64.

	N/A	$700	$625	$550	$475	$400	$325

OLYMPIC CUSTOM (JAPAN MFG.) - similar to Olympic, except features bound neck, mfg.1977-79.

	N/A	$750	$625	$500	$400	$300	$200

OLYMPIC SPECIAL (U.S. MFG.) - similar to the Olympic, except features sharper cutaways, one Melody Maker pickup, mfg. 1962-69.

	N/A	$850	$725	$600	$500	$400	$300

ELECTRIC: PLAYER PACKS

The **Special II Gig Rig** package (list $399, 100% $239) includes a Special II electric guitar, Studio 10 amplifier, cord, Qwik-Tune quartz tuner, black gig bag, strap, picks, and a 30-minute Guitar Essentials Hal Leonard video tape. The **Fat-210 Gig Rig** package (list $399, 100% $239) is similar but substitutes a Fat-210 electric guitar. For guitarists on the move, Epiphone also offers the **LP PeeWee Rave Rig** package (list $299, 100% $179) that features a Les Paul mini electric guitar, 9-volt Mini-Tweed amplifier, strap, cord, and gig bag. This is also available as a **Flying-VeeWee**, for the same price.

ELECTRIC: PRO SERIES

(USA) PRO (U.S. MFG.) - offset double cutaway carved poplar body, bolt-on maple neck, 24-fret diagonal rosewood fingerboard with offset dot inlay, six-on-one-side tuners, Floyd Rose licensed tremolo bridge, one Gibson SC-2 single coil and one Gibson L-8 humbucker pickups, two knobs, three-way switch, black hardware, 25.5 in. scale, available in Alpine White, Black, California Coral, Candy Apple Red, Cherry, Pacific Blue, Sunburst, Sunset Yellow, or White finishes, mfg. 1989-1994.

	N/A	$375	$325	$275	$225	$175	$125

Last MSR was $600.

PRO-1 - offset double cutaway body, bolt on neck, mfg. 1995-97.

	N/A	$400	$350	$300	$250	$200	$150

Last MSR was $749.

PRO-2 (MODEL EPR2) - Similar to Pro-1, except features a Jam-Trem vibrato, 2 slanted humbucker pickups, available in Black Metallic, Metallic Blue, Pearl White, or Red Metallic finishes, mfg. 1995-98.

	N/A	$450	$400	$350	$300	$250	$200

Last MSR was $779.

ELECTRIC: S SERIES

S Series instruments were produced in Korea.

S-210 (MODEL EGSO) - offset double cutaway body, tremolo bridge, available in Ebony, Red, Vintage Sunburst, or Vintage White finishes, mfg. 1998-99.

	$180	$160	$140	$120	$100	$80	$50

Last MSR was $259.

S-310 (MODEL EGS1) - offset double cutaway maple body, black pickguard, bolt-on maple neck, 22-fret maple fingerboard with black dot inlay, standard vibrato, 6-on-a-side tuners, chrome hardware, 3 single coil exposed pickups, volume/2 tone controls, 5-way selector switch, available in Black, Red, or White finishes, mfg. 1986-1999.

	$225	$195	$175	$150	$125	$100	$75

Last MSR was $309.

S-310 Left-Handed (Model EGS1L) - similar to S-310, except features left-handed configuration, available in Black Metallic finish, disc. 1999.

	$230	$200	$175	$150	$125	$100	$75

Last MSR was $334.

S-310 Custom - similar to S-310, except features 2 single coil/humbucker pickups, mfg. 1995-96.

	$250	$200	$175	$150	$125	$100	$90

Last MSR was $349.

S-400 - similar to S-310, except features rosewood fingerboard with shark tooth inlays, Bennder tremolo, and 2 single coil/humbucker pickups, mfg. 1986-89.

	N/A	$250	$210	$170	$140	$110	$80

S-600 - offset double cutaway hardwood body, bolt-on maple neck, 25.5 in. scale, 21-fret rosewood fingerboard with white sharktooth inlay, 6-on-a-side tuners, rounded point headstock, black hardware, Bennder tremolo, 2 single coil/humbucker exposed pole piece pickups, volume/2 tone controls, 5-way selector, mfg. 1986-89.

	N/A	$300	$250	$210	$170	$130	$95

In 1988, a Steinberger KB tremolo was introduced with a coil tap on one of the knobs, and the headstock changed from the sharp pointed style to a smooth curve.

GRADING	100% MINT	98% NEAR MINT	95% EXC+	90% EXC	80% VG+	70% VG	60% G

S-800 - similar to S-600, except features a basswood body with a carved cambered top, 2 single coil/humbucker covered pickups, volume/tone controls, and 3 mini-switches, mfg. 1986-89.

	N/A	$350	$300	$250	$200	$150	$110

In 1988, a Steinberger KB tremolo was introduced with a coil tap on one of the knobs, and the headstock changed from the sharp pointed style to a smooth curve.

S-900 - similar to the S-600, except features a bound body with a smoothly cambered top, maple neck-through-body design, 2 single coil/humbucker covered pickups, volume/tone controls, 3 mini-switches, mfg. 1986-89.

	N/A	$425	$375	$325	$275	$225	$150

In 1988, a Steinberger KB tremolo was introduced with a coil tap on one of the knobs, and the headstock changed from the sharp pointed style to a smooth curve.

**Epiphone Accu Bass Junio
courtesy Epiphone**

ELECTRIC: SC (SCROLL) SERIES

The SC, or Scroll series guitars have a distinct scroll on the upper bass bout, and a carved edge along the top. This series was produced in Japan.

SC-350 - offset double cutaway mahogany body with scrolled bass bout, 3-piece bolt-on mahogany neck, 24-fret ebonized maple fingerboard with white dot inlay, 3-per-side tuners, chrome hardware, wraparound bridge, 2 chrome-covered humbuckers, volume/tone controls, 3-way selector, available in Mahogany finish, mfg. 1976-79.

	N/A	$350	$300	$250	$200	$150	$100

SC-450 - similar to SC-350, except features maple body, set neck, rosewood fingerboard, available in Natural or Mahogany finishes, mfg. 1976-79.

	N/A	$400	$325	$275	$225	$175	$125

SC-550 - similar to SC-350, except features maple body, set-in 3-piece maple neck, ebony fingerboard with block inlay, gold hardware, coil tap mini-switch, available in Natural (SC550N) or Ebony (SC550B) finishes, mfg. 1976-79.

	N/A	$450	$375	$300	$250	$200	$150

ELECTRIC: WILSHIRE SERIES

WILSHIRE - dual cutaway body, set-in neck, rosewood fingerboard with dot inlay, 3-per-side tuners, chrome hardware, tune-o-matic bridge, 2 white P-90 soapbar pickups, volume/tone controls, 3-way selector, mfg. 1959-1969, 1977-79.

	100% MINT	98% NEAR MINT	95% EXC+	90% EXC	80% VG+	70% VG	60% G
1959-1962 (U.S. MFG.)	N/A	$3,500	$3,000	$2,700	$2,400	$2,100	$1,800
1963-1969 (U.S. MFG.)	N/A	$3,000	$2,500	$2,200	$1,900	$1,600	$1,300
1977-1979 (JAPAN MFG.)	N/A	$600	$525	$450	$375	$325	$275

In 1961, black P-90 soapbar pickups replaced original parts/design. In 1963, an offset double cutaway body, 2 mini-humbuckers, and 6-on-a-side tuners replaced original parts/design.

Wilshire 12-string (U.S. Mfg.) - similar to the Wilshire, except features a 12-string configuration, 6-per-side-tuners, mfg. 1966-68.

	N/A	$2,500	$2,000	$1,700	$1,400	$1,200	$1,000

ELECTRIC BASS: GENERAL INFORMATION/PLAYER PACKS

On many models, the Epiphone family model name is listed after the model name/number in parentheses. Also, any older nomenclature may appear within the parentheses. The Accu-Bass Jr. Gig Rig package (list $429, 100% $260) includes an Accu-Bass Jr. electric bass, Studio Bass 10 amplifier, cord, Qwik-Tune quartz tuner, black gig bag, strap, picks, and a 30-minute Guitar Essentials Hal Leonard video tape. An EB-0 Bass is also available (list $449, 100% $270).

ELECTRIC BASS: ACCU SERIES

ACCU BASS (MODEL EBAC) - offset double cutaway maple body, black pickguard with thumb rest, bolt-on maple neck, 20-fret maple fingerboard with black dot inlay, fixed bridge, body matching peghead with logo inscription, 4-on-a-side tuners, chrome hardware, P-style exposed pickup, volume/tone control, available in Black, Red, Vintage Sunburst or White finishes, disc. 2002.

	$230	$185	$165	$150	$135	$120	$100

Last MSR was $359.

Accu Bass Left-Handed (Model EBACL) - similar to Accu-Bass, except features left-handed configuration, available in Ebony finish, disc. 2002.

	$250	$200	$180	$165	$150	$135	$120

Last MSR was $384.

Accu Bass Junior (Model EBAJ) - available in Ebony, Red, Vintage Sunburst, or White finishes, disc. 2004.

	$149	$125	$105	$85	$70	$55	$40

Last MSR was $249.

GRADING	100% MINT	98% NEAR MINT	95% EXC+	90% EXC	80% VG+	70% VG	60% G

ELECTRIC BASS: EB SERIES

EB-0 (MODEL EBGO, SG-1) - offset double cutaway mahogany body with pointy forward horns, bolt-on mahogany neck, 20-fret rosewood fingerboard with pearl dot inlay, fixed bridge, blackface peghead with screened logo, 2-per-side tuners, chrome hardware, black pickguard, chrome-covered Sidewinder humbucker pickup, volume/tone controls, available in Cherry or Ebony finishes, 30 in. scale, mfg. 1998-present.

	MSR	$415		$250	$210	$180	$150	$130	$110	$90

EB-1 (MODEL EBB1) - viola-shaped mahogany body, bolt-on mahogany neck, painted on f-hole, 32 in. scale, 20-fret rosewood fingerboard with pearl dot inlay, fixed bridge, blackface peghead with screened logo, 2-per-side tuners, chrome hardware, raised black pickguard, chrome-covered Sidewinder humbucker pickup, volume/tone controls, available in Red Brown Mahogany finish, mfg. 1998-2000.

	$420	$375	$325	$275	$225	$200	$150

Last MSR was $599.

This model is equipped with a floor stand (for upright playing).

EB-1 Fretless (Model EBB 1F) - same as Model EBB1, but in a fretless configuration, disc. 2000.

	$425	$350	$300	$260	$220	$185	$155

Last MSR was $599.

EB-3 (MODEL EBG3) - SG body style, 1 Sidewinder humbucker pickup and 1 mini humbucker pickup, mahogany body and set neck, rosewood fingerboard with trapezoid inlays, two volume and two tone controls, selector switch, 34 in. scale, chrome hardware, available in Cherry or Ebony finishes, mfg. 1999-present.

	MSR	$665		$400	$350	$300	$260	$230	$190	$160

EB-3 5-STRING (MODEL EBG5) - SG body style, 3/2 headstock configuration, set neck, trapezoid inlays, 2 DualRail pickups, 5-way rotary tone selector switch, stop tailpiece, chrome hardware, available in Cherry or Ebony finishes, mfg. 2000-01.

	$550	$425	$375	$335	$300	$265	$235

Last MSR was $799.

EB-3 ELITIST (MODEL ELBSG, JAPAN) - book-matched African mahogany top, 1 piece mahogany set neck with rosewood fingerboard and 20 frets, bone nut, EGBR USA Humbucker and EGBT USA mini humbucker, 2 volume, 2 tone and 4-way rotary switch, nickel hardware, Gotoh tuners, available in Cherry or Ebony finishes, 30.5 in. scale, mfg. 2003-present.

	MSR	$1,537		$1,000	$875	$800	$25	$650	$575	$500

ELECTRIC BASS: EBM SERIES

EBM-4 (MODEL EBM4, EBM-4 REBEL STANDARD) - offset sweeping double cutaway basswood body, bolt-on maple neck, 24-fret rosewood fingerboard with pearl offset dot inlay, fixed bridge, blackface reverse peghead, 4-on-a-side tuners, chrome hardware, P/J-style covered pickups, 2 volume/tone controls, available in Cherry, Black, Frost Blue, Pearl White, or Vintage Sunburst finishes, mfg. 1991-99.

	$375	$325	$295	$250	$225	$175	$150

Last MSR was $559.

EBM-5 (MODEL EBM5, EBM-5 REBEL STANDARD) - similar to EBM-4, except has 5-string configuration, 5-per-side tuners, available in Cherry, Black, Frost Blue, Pearl White, ot Vintage Sunburst finishes, mfg. 1991-99.

	$375	$325	$295	$250	$225	$175	$150

Last MSR was $559.

EBM-5 Fretless (Model EBM5F) - similar to EBM-5, except features fretless fingerboard, available in Ebony finish, disc. 1999.

	$400	$350	$300	$250	$225	$195	$150

Last MSR was $599.

ELECTRIC BASS: EMBASSY SERIES

EMBASSY DELUXE - offset double cutaway body, set-in neck, rosewood fingerboard with dot inlay, tune-o-matic bridge chrome hardware, 4-on-a-side tuners, metal hand rest (over strings), 2 Thunderbird-style pickups, volume/tone controls, available in Cherry finish, 34 in. scale, mfg. 1962-68.

	N/A	$1,500	$1,250	$1,050	$900	$750	$600

EMBASSY SPECIAL BASS (MODEL EBEP) - offset double cutaway body, laminated maple body, bolt-on maple neck, 22-fret rosewood fingerboard with dot inlay, single split humbucker pickup, two knobs, chrome hardware, available in Alpine White, Blue, Ebony, or Red finishes, mfg. 2004-present.

	MSR	$249		$149	$125	$105	$85	$70	$55	$40

EMBASSY STANDARD BASS IV (MODEL EBES) - offset double cutaway body, swamp ash body, bolt-on maple neck, 22-fret rosewood fingerboard with dot inlay, two bass humbucker pickups, three knobs, black hardware, available in Natural, Trans. Black, Trans. Blue, or Walnut finishes, mfg. 2004-present.

	MSR	$415		$250	$210	$180	$150	$120	$90	$60

Embassy Standard Bass V (Model EBS5) - similar to the Embassy Standard IV, except is in five-string configuration, mfg. 2004-present.

	MSR	$499		$299	$250	$220	$190	$160	$130	$95

ELECTRIC BASS: KORINA EXPLORER & FLYING V SERIES

1958 KORINA EXPLORER BASS (MODEL EBEX) - Korina body, mahogany set neck, rosewood fingerboard with white dot inlays, 34 in. scale, gold hardware, two humbucker pickups, available in Natural Korina (disc. 2000) or Ebony finishes, mfg. 1999-present.

	MSR	$729		$440	$375	$325	$285	$245	$205	$175

GRADING	100% MINT	98% NEAR MINT	95% EXC+	90% EXC	80% VG+	70% VG	60% G

1958 KORINA FLYING V BASS (MODEL EBFV) - Flying V-shaped korina body, mahogany neck, 21-fret rosewood fingerboard with pearl dot inlay, fixed bridge, blackface peghead with screened logo, 2-per-side tuners, gold hardware, white pickguard, 2 humbucker pickups, 2 volume/1 tone controls, 3-way selector toggle, available in Ebony or Korina finishes, 30.5 in. scale, mfg. 1998-2004.

	$425	$360	$320	$280	$240	$200	$160

Last MSR was $699.

Korina finish was disc. in 2000.

Epiphone EB-1 Fretless
courtesy Epiphone

ELECTRIC BASS: LES PAUL SERIES

LES PAUL SPECIAL BASS (MODEL EBLP) - Available in Heritage Cherry Sunburst or Vintage Sunburst finishes, disc 2002.

	$350	$295	$250	$225	$195	$150	$125

Last MSR was $499.

LES PAUL STANDARD BASS (MODEL EBB5) - Flame maple top, 2 chrome covered humbuckers, trapezoid fingerboard inlay, available in Ebony, Heritage Cherry Sunburst, or Vintage Sunburst finishes, mfg. 1998-present.

MSR	$749	$450	$375	$325	$275	$235	$195	$160

LES PAUL STANDARD 5-STRING BASS (MODEL EBL5) - mahogany body with flame maple top, maple neck, rosewood fingerboard with trapezoid inlays, 3/2 headstock configuration, 2 DualRail humbucker pickups, 5-way rotary tone switch, stop tailpiece, chrome hardware, available in Trans. Black or Vintage Sunburst finishes, mfg. 2000 only.

	$500	$450	$400	$365	$335	$300	$275

Last MSR was $699.

ELECTRIC BASS: NEWPORT SERIES

NEWPORT BASS - offset double cutaway body, set-in neck, 30.5 in. scale, rosewood fingerboard with dot inlay, chrome hardware, 2-per-side tuners, combination bridge/tailpiece, chrome hand rest (over strings), rectangular pickup with pole pieces, available in Cherry finish, mfg. 1961-68, 1977-79.

1961-68 (USA MFG.)	N/A	$950	$825	$700	$600	$500	$400
1977-79 (JAPAN MFG.)	N/A	$350	$300	$250	$200	$150	$100

Add 20% for custom colors. Add 20% for 2 pickups.

In 1963, 4-on-a-side tuners replaced original part/design.

ELECTRIC BASS: POWER & RIPPER SERIES

POWER BASS - offset double cutaway maple body, bolt-on maple neck, 20-fret rosewood fingerboard with pearl dot inlay, fixed bridge, body matching peghead with logo inscription, 4-on-a-side tuners, black hardware, P/J-style exposed pickups, 2 volume/1 tone controls, available in Black, Red, or White finishes, disc. 1998.

	$300	$250	$200	$175	$150	$125	$100

Last MSR was $420.

RIPPER (MODEL EBR2) - slightly offset double cutaway maple body, bolt-on maple neck, 34 in. scale, 20-fret maple fingerboard with dot inlay, large black pickguard, available in Ebony or Natural finishes, mfg. 1998-2000.

	$350	$275	$225	$200	$175	$150	$125

Last MSR was $499.

This model is based on Gibson's Ripper electric bass.

ELECTRIC BASS: RIVOLI SERIES

RIVOLI - thin double cutaway body, 2 f-holes, set-in neck, rosewood fingerboard with dot inlay, chrome hardware, 2-per-side banjo style tuners, oval peghead inlay, one rectangular pickup with pole pieces, volume/tone controls, available in Natural or Sunburst finishes, mfg. 1959-1970.

SINGLE P/U	N/A	$950	$825	$700	$600	$500	$400
DOUBLE P/U	N/A	$1,500	$1,250	$1,050	$900	$750	$600

In 1960, right angle tuners replaced original parts/design. 2 pickups became standard in 1970 only.

RIVOLI BASS (MODEL EBR1) - contemporary reissue, available in Cherry, Ebony, Natural, or Vintage Cherry Sunburst, disc. 2000.

	$695	$600	$525	$450	$395	$325	$250

Last MSR was $999.

RIVOLI-II BASS (MODEL EBB6) - Thin double cutaway body, set neck, rosewood fingerboard with dot inlays, 2-per-side tuners, 1 Sidewinder humbucker pickup and 1 mini-humbucker pickup, 2 volume, 2-Tone, toggle switch, black pickguard, available in Sunburst finish, disc. 2000.

	$775	$675	$600	$525	$450	$375	$300

Last MSR was $1,099.

Epiphone Rivoli Bass
courtesy Dave Rogers
Dave's Guitar Shop

GRADING	100% MINT	98% NEAR MINT	95% EXC+	90% EXC	80% VG+	70% VG	60% G

ELECTRIC BASS: ROCK SERIES

ROCK BASS (MODEL EBRO) - offset double cutaway maple body, bolt-on maple neck, 20-fret rosewood fingerboard with pearl dot inlay, fixed bridge, body matching peghead with logo inscription, 4-on-a-side tuners, black hardware, black pickguard with thumb rest and chrome controls plate, chrome hardware, 2 J-style exposed pickups, 2 volume/1 tone controls, available in Black, Red, or White finishes, disc. 2000.

		$275	$225	$200	$175	$150	$125	$100

Last MSR was $389.

ELECTRIC BASS: SIGNATURE SERIES

ALLEN WOODY LTD. ED. RUMBLEKAT (MODEL EBAK) - Woody's signature model, single cutaway, semi-hollow body archtop, 30 inch scale, 2 tuners per side, 2 mini-humbucker pickups, gold hardware, available in Wine Red finish, mfg. 2003-present.

MSR	$799	$480	$400	$350	$300	$260	$220	$190

JACK CASADY BASS (MODEL EBJC) - offset double cutaway semi-hollow laminated maple body, 2 f-holes, set-in mahogany neck, 20-fret rosewood fingerboard with pearl trapezoid inlay, 2-per-side tuners, fixed bridge, creme-colored raised pickguard, chrome hardware, creme-colored low impedance humbucker pickup, volume/tone controls, 3-way impedance boost knob, available in Ebony or Metallic Gold finish, mfg. 1997-present.

MSR	$1,199	$725	$625	$550	$475	$425	$375	$325

V HORNSBY LP STD BASS (MODEL EBVH) - V Hornsby's signature model, available in Trans. Black finish, mfg. 2003-present.

MSR	$1,399	$850	$750	$675	$600	$525	$450	$375

ELECTRIC BASS: THUNDERBIRD SERIES

THUNDERBIRD IV BASS (REVERSE, MODEL EBTB) - reverse Thunderbird body, available in Vintage Sunburst or Goth Black finishes, current mfg.

MSR	$599	$375	$325	$275	$245	$215	$190	$170

Subtract $25 for Goth Black finish.

THUNDERBIRD ELITIST (MODEL ELBTB, JAPAN) - book-matched African mahogany top, mahogany wings, 1-piece mahogany neck with rosewood fingerboard, 20 frets, 34 inch scale, bone nut, ETBR and ETBT USA humbuckers, 2 volume, and 1 tone control, nickel hardware, Gotoh tuners, available in Vintage Sunburst finish, mfg. 2003-present.

MSR	$1,767	$1,150	$1,000	$875	$775	$700	$625	$550

THUNDERBIRD 4 BASS (MODEL EBT4) - available in Frost Blue, Sea Foam Green, or Vintage Sunburst finishes, disc. 1998.

		$500	$450	$395	$350	$295	$250	$195

Last MSR was $719.

Thunderbird 5 Bass (Model EBT5) - similar to Thunderbird 4, except features 5-string configuration, 5-on-a-side tuners, available in Frost Blue, Sea Foam Green, or Vintage Sunburst finishes, disc. 1998.

		$525	$450	$425	$375	$325	$250	$200

Last MSR was $799.

ELECTRIC BASS: VIOLA SERIES

VIOLA BASS (MODEL EBV1) - violin-shaped bound laminated maple body, flame maple top, set-in maple neck, 22-fret rosewood fingerboard with dot inlay, 2-per-side tuners, 2 chrome-covered mini-humbuckers, rosewood bridge/chrome tailpiece, chrome hardware, 2 volume/tone controls, pearloid controls plate, available in Vintage Sunburst finish, current mfg.

MSR	$781	$480	$400	$350	$300	$260	$220	$190

Viola Bass Left-Handed (Model EBVL) - similar to Viola Bass, except features left-handed configuration, available in Vintage Sunburst finish, disc. 1999.

		N/A	$495	$425	$375	$325	$250	$200

Last MSR was $804.

ELECTRIC BASS: XTREME SERIES

XTREME BASS (MODEL EBGX) - double offset four-point body mahogany body, thru-body hard maple neck, 24-fret ebonal fingerboard with 12th fret bat inlays, diamond plate pickguard, 2 U.S.A. EMG 35HZ pickups, three knobs, 2-per-side tuners, black hardware, Goth Black finish only, mfg. 2004 only.

		$499	$425	$375	$325	$275	$235	$200

Last MSR was $831.

ERLEWINE GUITARS

Instruments currently built in Austin, TX since 1973.

Luthier Mark Erlewine began building guitars and basses with his cousin Dan (noted repairman/columnist for *Guitar Player* magazine) in Ypsilanti, Michigan in 1970. Three years later, Mark moved to Austin, Texas and continued building guitars as well as performing repairs and custom work. Erlewine Custom Guitars is still based in Austin, Texas.

GRADING	100% MINT	98% NEAR MINT	95% EXC+	90% EXC	80% VG+	70% VG	60% G

ELECTRIC

Luthier Erlewine produces three models. In 1979, Erlewine and Billy Gibbons (ZZ Top) developed the **Chiquita Travel Guitar**, a 27 in. long playable guitar that fits in an airplane overhead storage. The Chiquita features a solid hardwood body and one humbucker. Later, the two developed the **Erlewine Automatic**, a cross between the best features of a Strat and a Les Paul. The Automatic is currently offered as a custom-built guitar, and the price is reflected in the customer´s choice of options. In 1982, Erlewine developed the **Lazer**, a headless guitar with a reverse tuning bridge and minimal body. The Lazer model is highly favored by Johnny Winter. For more information on these guitars, contact Erlewine directly.

Erlewine licensed the Chiquita and Lazer model designs to the Hondo Guitar company in the early 1980s. The licensed models do not have Erlewine´s logo on them. Erlewine also offers guitar repair work.

ERNIE BALL/MUSIC MAN

Instruments currently produced in San Luis Obispo, CA under the Ernie Ball/Music Man trademark since 1984. Earlier Music Man models were produced in Fullerton, CA between 1976 and 1979. Current manufacture and distribution by Ernie Ball/Music Man.

Ernie Ball was born in Cleveland, Ohio in 1930. The American Depression pressured the family to move to Santa Monica, California in 1932. By age nine, Ball was practicing guitar, and this interest in music led to a twenty-year career as a professional steel guitarist, music teacher, and retailer.

During the 1950s, the steel guitar was a popular instrument to play - but there was some difficulty in obtaining a matched set of strings. Early electric guitar players were also turning to mixing sets of strings to get the desired string gauges, but at a waste of the other strings. Ball found great success in marketing prepackaged string sets in custom gauges, and the initial mail order business expanded into a nationwide wholesale operation of strings, picks, and other accessories.

In the early 1970s Ball founded the Earthwood company, and produced both electric guitars and acoustic basses for a number of years. After some production disagreements between the original Music Man company and Leo Fender´s CLF Research in 1978 (see Music Man), Fender stopped building instruments exclusively for Music Man, and began designs and production for his final company (G & L). In 1984 Ernie Ball acquired the trademark and design rights to Music Man. Ball set up production in the factory that previously had built the Earthwood instruments. Ernie Ball/Music Man instruments have been in production at that location since 1984.

The first instruments that returned to production were Music Man basses, due to their popularity in the market. By 1987, the first guitar by Ernie Ball/Music Man was released. The Silhouette model was then followed by the Steve Morse model later in that year. Ernie Ball/Music Man has retained the high level of quality from original Fender/CLF designs, and has introduced some innovative designs to their current line. Ernie Ball passed away in 2004

ELECTRIC

Add $200 for 2005 Limited Edition options, including Buttercream finish, matching headstock, shell pickguard, burgundy silk-screened logo with 2005 logo, and vintage Palamino Brown case.

ALBERT LEE (MODEL 920/930) - angular offset double cutaway ash body, aluminum-lined pickguard, bolt-on maple neck, 22-fret maple fingerboard with black dot inlay, strings-through fixed bridge, 4/2-per-side Schaller M6-IND locking tuners, chrome hardware, 3 single coil Seymour Duncan or MM90 pickups, volume/tone control, 5-position switch, available in Black, Pearl Blue, Pearl Red, or Translucent Pinkburst finishes, mfg. 1994-present.

MSR	$1,715		$1,350	$1,150	$1,000	$875	$750	$650	$550

Add $100 for 3-Tone Sunburst finish with shell pickguard. Add $250 for piezo bridge (Model 921/931).

In 1998, Black, Pearl Red, and Translucent Pinkburst finishes were disc. The Albert Lee model was designed in conjunction with guitarist Albert Lee.

Albert Lee with Tremolo (Model 925/935) - similar to the Albert Lee, except has Music Man vintage tremolo, mfg. 1994-present.

MSR	$1,815		$1,400	$1,200	$1,050	$925	$800	$700	$600

Add $250 for Piezo bridge (Model 926/936).

AXIS - single cutaway basswood body, bound figured maple top, bolt-on maple neck, 22-fret maple or rosewood fingerboard with black dot inlay, strings through bridge, 4/2-per-side Schaller tuners with pearl buttons, chrome hardware, 2 humbucker DiMarzio pickups, volume control, 3-position switch, available in Trans. Gold, Trans. Purple, Trans. Red, Trans. Sunburst, or Opaque Blacktop finishes, mfg. 1996-disc.

			$1,295	$1,150	$995	$850	$700	$550	$425

Last MSR was $1,600.

In 1998, Trans. Purple, Trans. Red, Trans. Sunburst, and Opaque Blacktop finishes were disc. This model was formerly known as the Edward Van Halen model. Refer to Edward Van Halen listing.

Axis with Tremolo (Model 300) - similar to Axis, except has Floyd Rose tremolo, available in Trans. Black, Trans. Blue, Trans. Gold, Trans. Natural, Trans. Pink, Trans. Purple, Trans. Red, or Trans. Sunburst finishes, current mfg.

MSR	$1,945		$1,525	$1,300	$1,125	$975	$825	$725	$625

In 1998, Trans. Black and Trans. Pink finishes were disc.

**Epiphone Allen Woody Ltd.
Ed. Rumblekat
courtesy Epiphone**

**Epiphone Thunderbird IV
Bass
courtesy: Epiphone**

GRADING	100% MINT	98% NEAR MINT	95% EXC+	90% EXC	80% VG+	70% VG	60% G

AXIS SPORT - similar to Axis, except features ash body, Schaller M6-IND locking tuners, choice of 2 humbuckers, 3 single coils, or 2 single coil/humbucker configuration, volume and tone controls, 5-way switch, patented Silent Circuit noise reduction electronics, available in Black, Ivory, Trans. Blue, Trans. Gold, Trans. Green, Trans. Purple, Trans. Red, or Vintage Sunburst finishes, mfg. 1997-present.

	$1,225	$975	$900	$750	$575	$500	$400

Last MSR was $1,545.

Add $100 for 3-Tone Vintage Sunburst finish.

In 1998, Opaque Black finish was introduced; Black, Ivory, Trans. Blue, Trans. Gold, Trans. Green, Trans. Purple, and Trans. Red were disc. The Axis sport is available with either HH or MM90 pickups at the same price.

Axis Sport with Tremolo - similar to the Axis Sport, except features Music Man vintage style non-locking tremolo, available in Trans. Blue, Trans. Gold, Trans. Purple, or Trans. Red finishes, mfg. 1997-present.

	$1,275	$1,075	$950	$850	$675	$525	$425

Last MSR was $1,645.

AXIS SUPER SPORT (MODEL 310/330) - similar to the Axis sport except has a basswood or ash body, pearl tuners, 2 Custom DiMarzio humbucker pickups or 2 Music Man MM90's, available in various colors, current mfg.

MSR	$1,775	$1,325	$1,125	$975	$850	$725	$625	$525

Add $250 for Piezo bridge (Model 311/331). Add $80 for left-handed configuration (Model 410/420/430/440).

Axis Super Sport with Tremolo (Model 320/340) - similar to the Axis Super Sport, except has a tremolo unit, current mfg.

MSR	$1,875	$1,475	$1,250	$1,100	$975	$825	$725	$625

Add $250 for Piezo bridge (Model 321/341).

EDWARD VAN HALEN - single cutaway basswood body, bound figured maple top, bolt-on maple neck, 22-fret maple fingerboard with black dot inlay, strings through bridge, 4/2-per-side Schaller tuners with pearl buttons, chrome hardware, 2 humbucker DiMarzio pickups, volume control (with tone knob!), 3-position switch, available in Trans. Gold, Trans. Purple, or Trans. Red finishes, mfg. 1991-95.

	N/A	$2,300	$1,900	$1,600	$1,300	$1,000	$700

Last MSR was $1,600.

The Edward Van Halen model was co-designed with Edward Van Halen, and introduced in 1991. Upon dissolution of the endorsement deal, this model was renamed the Axis.

Edward Van Halen with Tremolo - similar to Edward Van Halen, except has Floyd Rose double locking vibrato, available in Black, Metallic Gold, Natural, Sunburst, Trans. Black, Trans. Blue, Trans. Gold, Trans. Pink, Trans. Purple, or Trans. Red finishes, mfg. 1991-95.

	N/A	$2,500	$2,100	$1,700	$1,400	$1,100	$800

Last MSR was $1,750.

JOHN PETRUCCI (MODEL 960) - offset double cutaway basswood body, maple neck, 24 fret rosewood fingerboard with optional custom inlays, 2 custom DiMarzio humbucking pickups, custom John Petrucci Music Man tremolo bridge, three black knobs, 3-way switch, 4/2-per-side tuners, chrome hardware, available in various colors, current mfg.

MSR	$1,875	$1,475	$1,250	$1,100	$975	$825	$725	$625

Add $250 for Piezo bridge (Model 961). Add $300 for Mystic Dream finish.

John Petrucci 7-String (Model 970) - similar to the John Petrucci except in seven -tring configuration, 4/3-per-side tuners, current mfg.

MSR	$2,075	$1,650	$1,350	$1,200	$1,025	$900	$775	$675

Add $250 for Piezo bridge (Model 971).

LUKE (MODEL 915) - offset double cutaway alder body, bolt-on maple neck, 25.5 in. scale, 22-fret rosewood fingerboard with pearl dot inlay, Floyd Rose vibrato, 4/2-per-side Schaller tuners, chrome hardware, 2 single coil/1 humbucker EMG pickups, volume control, 5-position switch, active electronics, available in Pearl Blue or Pearl Red finishes, mfg. 1994-present.

1994-1997		N/A	$1,100	$950	$850	$750	$650	$550
1998-MSR $1,875		$1,475	$1,250	$1,100	$975	$825	$725	$625

Add $250 for Piezo bridge (Model 916).

In 1998, the Luke model was reconfigured Luke II to feature a Music Man vintage-style tremolo, Schaller M6-IND, locking tuners, custom wound EMG-SLV single coil pickups, volume and tone controls. Luke Blue (Light Pearl Blue) finish was introduced; Pearl Blue and Pearl Red finishes were disc. The Luke model was designed with artist Steve Lukather (Toto, Los Lobotomys).

SILHOUETTE (MODEL 510) - offset double cutaway alder, ash or poplar body, aluminum-lined pickguard, bolt-on maple neck, 24-fret maple or rosewood fingerboard with dot inlay, strings-through bridge, 4/2-per-side Schaller tuners, chrome hardware, 2 single coil/1 humbucker DiMarzio pickups, volume/tone control, 5-position switch, available in Black, Natural, Sunburst, Trans. Blueburst, Trans. Teal, Trans. Red, or White finishes, mfg. 1987-present.

MSR	$1,530	$1,199	$1,050	$925	$775	$650	$550	$450

Add $250 for 3 single coil pickups (this option was disc in 1998). Add $250 for 2 humbucker pickups (this option was disc in 1998). Add $250 for Piezo bridge (Model 511).

In 1996, Natural and Trans. Blueburst finishes were disc. In 1998, humbucker/single coil/humbucker pickup configuration replaced the 2 single coil/humbucker pickup configuration; Trans. Teal and Trans. Red finishes were disc. The Silhouette was the first Ernie Ball/Music Man production guitar. Designed by Dudley Gimpel, and developed in part by guitarist Albert Lee, this design was influenced by earlier CLF Research models but a number of modern refinements added.

Silhouette with Tremolo - similar to Silhouette, except has Floyd Rose tremolo, disc. 1998, 2001-present.

MSR	$1,630	$1,275	$1,100	$975	$825	$700	$600	$500

Last MSR was $1,200.

Add $25 for humbucker/single coil/humbucker pickups. Add $250 for Piezo bridge (Model 521).

GRADING		100% MINT	98% NEAR MINT	95% EXC+	90% EXC	80% VG+	70% VG	60% G

SILHOUETTE SPECIAL (MODEL 530/535) - similar to Silhouette, except has alder body, 22-fret fingerboard, Schaller M6-IND locking tuners, 3 single coil (or 2 single coil/1 humbucker) DiMarzio pickups, patented Silent Circuit noise reduction electronics, available in Candy Red, Pearl Blue, Pearl Green, or Pearl Purple finishes, current mfg.

MSR	$1,565	$1,250	$1,075	$950	$800	$675	$575	$475

Add $100 for 3-Tone Vintage Sunburst finish. Add $250 for Piezo bridge (Model 531/536). Add $80 for left-handed configuration (Model 630/635).

In 1998, Pearl Blue and Pearl Green finishes were disc.

Silhouette Special with Tremolo (Model 540/545) - similar to Silhouette Special, except has a Music Man vintage-style tremolo, current mfg.

MSR	$1,665	$1,350	$1,150	$1,000	$850	$725	$600	$500

Add $250 for Piezo bridge (Model 541/546). Add $80 for left-handed configuration (Model 640/645).

Early models may feature a Wilkinson VSV tremolo.

STEVE MORSE (MODEL 900) - offset double cutaway poplar body, black shielded pickguard, bolt-on maple neck, 22-fret rosewood fingerboard with pearl dot inlay, tune-o-matic bridge/stop tailpiece, 4/2-per-side Schaller tuners, chrome hardware, humbucker/slanted single coil/single coil/humbucker DiMarzio pickups, volume/tone control, 3-position selector, and 2 mini switches, available in Trans. Blueburst finish, mfg. 1988-present.

MSR	$1,765	$1,399	$1,200	$1,050	$925	$800	$675	$575

Steve Morse with Tremolo - similar to Steve Morse, except has Floyd Rose tremolo, current mfg.

MSR	$1,915	$1,525	$1,250	$1,100	$950	$825	$700	$600

STEVE MORSE Y2D (MODEL 901) - offset double cutaway poplar body, bolt-on maple neck, 22-fret rosewood fingerboard with dot inlay, 4/2-per-side tuners, standard bridge, MusicMan stop tailpiece, various pickguards, two DiMarzio humbucker and two DiMarzio single coil pickups in H/S/S/H configuration, two knobs, three-way switch, two mini-switches, chrome hardware, available in various finishes, 25.5 in. scale, new 2005.

MSR	$2,095	$1,675	$1,425	$1,250	$1,075	$925	$800	$675

Steve Morse Y2D Floyd Rose (Model 906) - similar to the Steve Morse, except has a Floyd Rose tremolo bridge and locking tuners, new 2005.

MSR	$2,245	$1,800	$1,550	$1,350	$1,150	$1,000	$850	$700

SUB 1 GUITAR (X50) - offset double cutaway poplar body, maple neck, 22-fret rosewood fingerboard with dot inlay, diamond plate or matte black pickguard, single humbucker pickup (others optional), STB, 4/2-per-side tuners, two knobs, chrome hardware, available in Black, White, Teal, Red, Blue, Graphite, or Cinnamon finishes, new 2004.

MSR	N/A	$595	$525	$450	$400	$350	$300	$250

Add $50 for two humbucker pickups (Model X51). Add $50 for tremolo unit (Model X60/X61).

Ernie Ball Axis Sport
courtesy Ernie Ball

ELECTRIC BASS

Add $300 for a bridge with piezo pickup. Add $100 for left-handed configuration.

BONGO 4-STRING (MODEL 140) - offset double cutaway, extended bass horn with square edges, basswood body, selected maple neck, 24-fret rosewood fingerboard with dot inlays or fretless pau ferro fingerboard, single humbucker pickup (more available), various pickguards, 3/1-per-side tuners, four knobs, various finishes, mfg. 2003-present.

MSR	$1,495	$1,200	$1,050	$925	$800	$675	$550	$425

Add $80 for two humbucker pickups (Model 142) or single/humbucker pickup (Model 144). Add $280 for Piezo bridge (Model 141/143/145).

Bongo 5-String (Model 160) - similar to the Bongo 4-String, except in five-string configuration, 4/1-per-side tuners, mfg. 2003-present.

MSR	$1,725	$1,395	$1,200	$1,050	$925	$800	$675	$550

Add $80 for two humbucker pickups (Model 162) or single/humbucker pickup (Model 164). Add $280 for Piezo bridge (Model 161/163/165).

SABRE - offset double cutaway alder, ash, or poplar body, 34 in. scale, bolt-on maple neck, 21-fret maple or rosewood fingerboard with dot inlay, fixed bridge, 3/1 per side Schaller tuners, chrome hardware, 2 Ernie Ball humbucker pickups, volume/treble/mid controls, 5-way selector switch, active electronics, available in Black, Natural, Sunburst, Trans. Blueburst, Trans. Red, and Trans. Teal finishes, mfg. 1988-1991.

	N/A	$900	$750	$650	$550	$450	$350	

Last MSR was $1,095.

Add $50 for 3-band EQ (volume/treble/mid/bass controls). Add $50 for 3-Tone Vintage Sunburst finish. Add $75 for Butterscotch finish with shell pickguard. Add $75 for Trans. White finish with shell pickguard.

This model had an optional fretless pau ferro fingerboard (with or without inlaid fretlines).

Ernie Ball Steve Morse Y2D
courtesy Ernie Ball

GRADING	100% MINT	98% NEAR MINT	95% EXC+	90% EXC	80% VG+	70% VG	60% G

SILHOUETTE (MODEL 580/590) - offset double cutaway poplar body, bolt-on maple neck, 29.625 in. scale, 22-fret maple fingerboard with black dot inlay, strings through fixed bridge, 4/2-per-side Schaller tuners, chrome hardware, 2 DiMarzio humbucker pickups, volume/tone/series-parallel control, 5-way position switch, available in Black finish, mfg. 1993-present.

	MSR	$2,105		$1,675	$1,425	$1,225	$1,075	$925	$775	$625

STERLING (MODEL 170) - offset double cutaway ash body, pickguard, 34 in. scale, bolt-on maple neck, 22-fret maple or rosewood fingerboard with dot inlay, fixed bridge, 3/1 per side Schaller tuners, chrome hardware, Ernie Ball humbucker/phantom coil pickups, volume/treble/mid/bass controls, 3-way selector switch, active electronics, available in Black, Pearl Blue, Sunburst, or Trans. Red finishes, mfg. 1994-present.

	MSR	$1,725		$1,350	$1,150	$1,000	$875	$750	$650	$550

Add $150 for Natural Ash Velvet finished body/black pickguard (this option disc. in 1998). Add $280 for Piezo bridge (Model 171). Add $80 for left-handed configuration (Model 270).

This model had an optional fretless pau ferro fingerboard (with or without inlaid fretlines). The 3-way selector switch has three different pickup selections: both coils, series; single coil; both coils, parallel.

STING RAY (MODEL 110) - offset double cutaway ash body, pickguard, bolt-on maple neck, 34 in. scale, 21-fret maple or rosewood fingerboard with dot inlay, fixed bridge, 3/1 per side Schaller tuners, chrome hardware, humbucker pickup, volume/2-band EQ controls, active electronics, chrome plated brass control cover, available in Black, Sunburst, Trans. Teal, Trans. Red, or White finishes, current mfg.

	MSR	$1,615		$1,275	$1,100	$975	$825	$700	$600	$500

Add $50 for 3-band EQ (volume/treble/mid/bass controls, Model 130). Add $100 for 3-Tone Vintage Sunburst with black pickguard. Add $150 for Natural and Natural ash velvet finished body/black pickguard (this option disc in 1998). Add $280 for Piezo bridge (Model 111). Add $80 for left-handed configuration (Model 210).

In 1998, White finish was disc. This model has an optional fretless pau ferro fingerboard (with or without inlaid fretlines). The Sting Ray model with 3-band EQ is available in a left-handed configuration.

20th Anniversary Sting Ray (1976-1996) - similar to Sting Ray, except has bookmatched figured maple top, black/white/black wood laminate layer, ash body, tortoiseshell pickguard, Ernie Ball custom humbucker, volume/treble/mid/bass controls, available in Natural Top/Trans. Red Back finish, mfg. 1996 only.

				$1,700	$1,500	$1,300	$1,150	$1,000	$850	$700

Last MSR was $1,996.

Only 2,000 models were produced. This model had an optional fretless pau ferro fingerboard (with or without inlaid fretlines).

Sting Ray 5 (Model 150) - similar to Sting Ray, except has 5-strings, 4/1 per side tuners, volume/3-band EQ controls, 3-position switch, current mfg.

	MSR	$1,885		$1,475	$1,250	$1,100	$975	$825	$725	$625

Add $100 for 3-Tone Vintage Sunburst with black pickguard. Add $150 for Natural and Natural ash velvet finished body/black pickguard (this option was disc. in 1998). Add $320 for Piezo bridge (Model 151). Add $80 for left-handed configuration (Model 250).

This model is available in a left-handed configuration. This model has an optional fretless pau ferro fingerboard (with or without inlaid fretlines). The 3-way selector switch has three different pickup selections: both coils, series; single coil; both coils, parallel.

SUB BASS (MODEL X01) - Sting Ray-style poplar body, maple neck painted black, 22-fret rosewood or fretless pau ferro fingerboards, diamond plate or matte black pickguard, single humbucker, 3 knobs on a plate, chrome hardware, available in Black, White, Teal, Red, Blue, Graphite, or Cinnamon finishes, mfg. 2003-present.

	MSR	N/A		$645	$575	$500	$450	$400	$350	$300

Add $50 for active electronics (Model X02).

Sub Bass 5 (Model X03) - similar to the Sub, except in five-string configuration, 4/1-per-side tuners, mfg. 2003-present.

	MSR	N/A		$695	$625	$550	$500	$450	$400	$350

Add $50 for active electronics (Model X04).

SUB STERLING (MODEL X07) - Sterling style poplar body, maple neck painted black, 22-fret rosewood or fretless pau ferro fingerboards, diamond plate or matte black pickguard, single humbucker pickup, 4 knobs, chrome hardware, available in Black, White, Teal, Red, Blue, Graphite, or Cinnamon finishes, mfg. 2003-present.

	MSR	N/A		$695	$625	$550	$500	$450	$400	$350

Add $50 for active electronics (Model X02).

ERNIE BALL'S EARTHWOOD

Instruments previously produced in San Luis Obispo, CA in the early to mid-1970s.

After finding great success with prepackaged string sets and custom gauges, Ernie Ball founded the Earthwood company to produce a four-string acoustic bass guitar. George Fullerton built the prototype, as well as helping with other work before moving to Leo Fender's CLF Research company in 1974. Earthwood offered both the acoustic bass guitar and a lacquer finished solid body guitar with large sound chambers in 1972, but production was short lived (through February 1973). In April of 1975, bass guitar operations resumed on a limited basis for a number of years.

EROS

Instruments previously produced in Japan between the early 1970s through the early 1980s.

The EROS trademark is the brand name of a UK importer. These guitars were generally entry level copies of American designs (source: Tony Bacon and Paul Day, The Guru's Guitar Guide).

ERRINGTON
Instruments currently produced in North Yorks, England.

Errington offers models in the Herald line such as the Deluxe or the Artizan with a single cutaway routed body, a cat's-eye-shaped f-hole, bolt-on neck, six-per-side Gotoh tuners, chrome hardware, volume/tone controls, and a five-way selector switch.

ESTEY
See Magnatone. Instruments previously built in Italy during the late 1960s. Distributed in the U.S. market by Magnatone (Estey Electronics).

Estey thinline electric guitars were offered by Magnatone (Estey Electronics) during the late 1960s. These guitars were imported in from Italy (source: Michael Wright, *Vintage Guitar Magazine*).

EUGEN
Instruments currently built in Bergen, Norway.

Luthier Henry Eugen began playing guitar in Norway during his teenage years, and built up a guitar collection by age twenty. Customizing existing models led to designing his own guitars, and then learning to build the electric models. In 1979, Eugen began offering his handcrafted solid body electrics. Eugen custom guitars are still produced by him in a one man shop.

Ernie Ball Bass Silhouette courtesy Ernie Ball

ELECTRIC & ELECTRIC BASS

Eugen currently offers 7 distinct body designs in four different models. The **Basic** (#1) model has a 2-piece laminated body, while the **Paragon** (#2) has an additional maple top, Wood Out Binding or plastic-bound body. The **Paramount's** (#3) maple top is arched instead of flat with the W.O.B., and the **Mr. Eugen** (#4) is the Paramount model with select neck and body wood. The following body designs will indicate model availability.

The **Eugen** model (1-2-3-4) has a slightly offset dual cutaway model with curved forward horns and round lower bout. The set-in neck has a 22-fret fingerboard and 3+3 headstock. Pickups, configuration, and hardware are options discussed with the customer. The **Eugen 10/8** (3-4) is similar to the Eugen, except has 2 large/2 small internal tone chambers.

Eugen's **Little Wing** (1-2) is based on a Gibson Explorer, except the extended upper wing has been caved down to a rounded lower bout, and this model has a 6-on-a-side headstock. The **Classic T** (1-2) is a single cutaway model based on the Tele, while the **Classic S** (1-2-3) is a double cutaway Strat-style guitar (the **Classic S 7/8** has a slightly smaller body).

The **Eugen Bass** is available in 4-, 5-, and 6-string configurations, and in the Basic or Paragon model construction.

For prices and more information on Eugen guitars visit their website (see Trademark Index). The pricelist is in Krona (Norway's currency).

EUROPA
Instruments previously built in France in the mid-1980s.

This company built high quality Fender-style solid body guitars, and offered both hardware options and choice of a graphite neck (source: Tony Bacon and Paul Day, *The Guru's Guitar Guide*).

EXCETRO
Instruments previously built in Japan during the mid-1970s.

The Excetro company featured a range of medium quality semi-hollowbody guitars based on Rickenbacher-derived designs (source: Tony Bacon and Paul Day, *The Guru's Guitar Guide*).

Ernie Ball Sterling courtesy Dave Rogers Dave's Guitar Shop

NOTES

Section F

F BASS

Previously F Guitars. Instruments currently built in Hamilton, Ontario (Canada).

F Guitars was founded by George Furlanetto (luthier/bassist) and Froc Filipetti (musician) in 1976. Their high quality basses and guitars are the result of their custom building and designing backgrounds. The two designers have over 20 years of collective experience in guitar customizing, and they applied that knowledge in designing "the classic vintage sound without the noise, and an even response through the extended range of modern 5- and 6-string basses." F Guitars winds their own pickups, and then matches them to the different wood combinations to achieve specific tonal characteristics. The company is now called F Basses and focuses directly on bass guitars.

ELECTRIC BASS

F Bass models are available in Natural Satin, Sunburst, Transparent Electric Blue, Transparent Royal Purple, and Transparent Wine Red finishes. Prices include a high quality Cordura nylon bag with "F" logo. The **BN-5 5-String** (retail list $3,399) features a solid ash, swamp ash, or alder body, 3-piece bolt-on maple neck, 22-fret maple fingerboard, lightweight Hipshot bridge, 2 humcancelling single coil pickups in wooden shells that match the body wood and finish, and a 3-band EQ preamp system with active/passive bypass switch. The **BN-6 6-String** has similar construction except for the 24-fret fingerboard (list $3,899). The **BN-4 4-String** is similar also, but has a 21-fret fingerboard (disc. 2004, last MSR $3,199).

The extended range **BNF-5 5-String** has an alder body, 3-piece maple bolt-on neck, 28-fret ebony fingerboard, ebony bridge, black hardware, and 2 humcancelling single coil pickups (list $4,199). The **BNF-6 6-String** has the same construction features (list $4,799).

The 5-string fretted **Studio Model** bass has a 20-fret maple or rosewood fingerboard, bolt-on maple neck, lightweight Hipshot bridge, and 3-band active EQ (last MSR was $3,199). This model is now discontinued.

F Guitars also offers the **Alain Caron Model 6-String Fretless Bass**, known as the "king" of basses. This top-of-the-line model has an acoustically chambered figured maple body, spruce top, bolt-on 3-piece maple neck with oil finish, extended range (28-fret) ebony fingerboard, ebony bridge, black hardware, one magnetic pickup, RMC piezo bridge pickups. The Alain Caron model is available in Sunburst finish with matching headstock (retail list $6,299). An **Alain Caron** 5-string version is also available (list $5,999). For further information regarding specifications and pricing, please contact F Bass directly (see Trademark Index).

> **Add 10% for left-handed configuration. Add $120 for gold or black hardware. Add $150 for Sunburst finish. Add $250 for ebony fingerboard. Add $250 for fret lines on fretless models. Add $395 for preamp. Add $500 for figured maple top. Add $500 for "Ceruse" finish (Black and White, Magenta and Black, Turquoise and Black). Add $500 for neck-through or set-neck construction. Custom orders start at an additional $700. Add $395 for preamp with 3-band EQ.**

**F Bass BN-6
courtesy F Bass**

FM

Instruments currently built in Austin, TX.

Luthier Fred Murray has been building custom guitars, and repairing or modifying guitars around Austin for a number of years.

FMO

See Factory Music Outlet.

FABREGUES BASSES

Basses currently built in San Juan, Puerto Rico.

Pepe Fabregues currently builds basses in 4-, 5-, or 6-string configurations. They have ash or swamp ash bodies, with maple neck, and ebony, pau ferro, or maple fretboards. All hardware and electronics are custom made for Fabregues instruments. Please contact the company directly for current model information and pricing (see Trademark Index).

FACTORY MUSIC OUTLET

Instruments previously built in Kenmore, NY 1981-2000.

Factory Music Outlet was founded in 1981 by Carol Lund. Lund had worked in California with the late Harry Wake. The business began as a hobby, and became a full time business as the need for quality repairs required more of her time. The repair business expanded to include violins, cellos, and all forms of stringed instruments.

As the repair business expanded, Lund realized the need for high quality, one-of-a-kind instruments. Each individual player seemed to have an idea of what their instrument should be. This evolved into a custom building segment of the business. FMO took pride in providing cutting edge innovations for customers. FMO employed the use of graphite and graphite composites for structural integrity as well as tonal quality. They featured graphite-reinforced wood necks, bridge plates, cello and violin boards as well as all-graphite necks. FMO used the 2-TEK bridge in many of their custom guitars and basses. The Sabine tuner was also an innovation that FMO used frequently, in both the on-board and removable format.

Factory Music Outlet's mission plan was simple: develop and build instruments that are one-of-a-kind. These instruments must be functional and durable as well as aesthetically pleasing.

The model name Black Widow is derived from the use of graphite components and American Black Walnut wood. The graphite is black, as is the Walnut when refinished using their See-Through Black finish. While FMO's original guitars and basses were made exclusively of these materials, they built guitar models using a variety of woods and combinations of wood types.

**F Bass Alain Caron Model
6-String Fretless Bass
courtesy F Bass**

GRADING	100% MINT	98% NEAR MINT	95% EXC+	90% EXC	80% VG+	70% VG	60% G

Factory Music Outlet's other custom built guitar model was the Tribute to Jerry Guitar (last retail list $3,000). This model was composed of exotic woods, brass, abalone, and graphite components. It was available as a custom order only, and had many unique features. Price included a deluxe Bullhyde case.

FARMER, SIMON

Instruments currently built in East Sussex, Britian.

In November 1991, a source close to Blue Book Publications Inc. sent in a fax containing a picture and write up of a prototype guitar built by Simon Farmer. The Guitube, as the prototype was named, featured a routed Canadian rock maple fingerboard, a Kent Armstrong humbucker pickup, a gas-spring dampened tremolo system, and steel tubing that formed the bouts of the guitar body. The pointed headstock has six-on-a-side tuners. As of this date, the *Blue Book of Electric Guitars* has not heard nor seen this prototype or any production designs approaching this model. In 1997, Farmer displayed a handcrafted carbon fiber guitar at the January NAMM show. Farmer's current workshop is located in East Sussex, England.

FARNELL GUITARS, INC.

Previously Farnell Custom Guitars. Instruments currently built in Ontario, CA and overseas. Previous production was based in Pomona and Rancho Cucamonga, CA in the early 1990s.

Designer Al Farnell has been producing guitars that feature synthetic bodies of fiberglass for the past several years. The Farnell guitar is very light and features a patent-pending for body that is built of a closed-cell polyfoam material with a mahogany insert called the Sound Reservoir.

ELECTRIC

EXP-K - double cutaway Endever body style, 2 EMG SAV single coil pickups, EMG 81 or 85 humbucker in the bridge position, Gotoh H.A.P. tuners, pearl pickguard, fixed bridge and tailpiece, 6-on-a-side tuners, Graph-Tech graphite nut, 1 vol/1 tone control, 5-way switch, available in Ultra Black, Ultra Green, Ultra Purple, Ultra Blue, or Ultra Red finishes, disc.

	N/A	$600	$525	$450	$375	$300	$225

Last MSR was $799.

EXG-K - similar to EXP, except EMG 89 pickup in the neck position and EMG 85 or 81 pickup in the bridge position, push/pull splitter on the volume control, 1 volume/1 tone, 3-way switch, available in Black Tiger, Purple Tiger, Amber Tiger, Cherry Tiger, Honey Tiger, Burgundy Tiger, or Blue Tiger finishes, disc.

	N/A	$600	$525	$450	$375	$300	$225

Last MSR was $799.

EXG-PRO (U.S.A.) - similar to EXG, except has Graph-Tech Graphite saddles, After Burner 20 DB Booster and SPC Mid Booster, available in Brown Tiger, Black Tiger, Burgundy Tiger, Purple Tiger, Cherry Tiger, or Amber Tiger finishes, current mfg.

MSR $1,500

EXP-PRO (U.S.A.) - similar to EXP-K, except has push/pull splitter, quartersawn rock maple neck, slab rosewood fingerboard, gold hardware, EMG 89 humbucker pickup in the bridge position, EMG Afterburner, graphite bridge saddles, available in Ultra Black, Ultra Green, Ultra Purple, Ultra Blue, or Ultra Red finishes, current mfg.

MSR $1,500

EXT-USA - similar to the EXP-Pro except has a vintage tremolo system, current mfg.

MSR $1,500

MILLENIUM PRO (U.S.A.) - millennium body, EMG 85 humbucker pickup in the neck position, EMG 89 humbucker pickup in the bridge position, push/pull splitter, GoToh H.A.P. tuners, quartersawn rock maple neck, 1 volume/1 tone, 3-way switch, slab rosewood fingerboard, stop tailpiece, gold hardware, EMG Afterburner, graphite bridge saddles, available in Black Tiger, Brown Tiger, Burgundy Tiger, Purple Tiger, Cherry Tiger and Amber Tiger finishes, disc.

MSR $1,499

Millenium Standard - similar to the Millenium Pro except is produced not in the U.S., current mfg.

MSR	$499		$350	$300	$250	$200	$170	$140	$100

STANDARD EXP-C - unique double cutaway body style, two humbucker pickups, available in Ultra Blue, Cherry Tiger, Ultra Red, Natural Honey Tiger, Ultra Black, or Ultra White finishes, current mfg.

MSR	$499		$350	$300	$250	$200	$170	$140	$100

Standard EXG-C - similar to the Standard EXP-C except has one humbucker and two single coil pickups, current mfg.

MSR	$499		$350	$300	$250	$200	$170	$140	$100

Standard EXT-C - similar to the Standard EXG-C except has a vintage tremolo system, current mfg.

MSR	$499		$350	$300	$250	$200	$170	$140	$100

ELECTRIC BASS

EXPJ BASS - oversized double cutaway Endever body style, EMG P/J pickup combination, 4-on-a-side GoToh H.A.P. mini-tuners, 2 volume/1 tone controls, Graph-Tech graphite nut, available in same colors as EXP, disc.

EXB-4 BASS-USA - double cutaway Endever body style, 2 EMG Soapbar pickups, GoToh mini-tuners, 3-piece quartersawn rock maple neck, rosewood fingerboard, 2 volume/1 tone controls, gold hardware, available in Black Tiger, Brown Tiger, Burgundy Tiger, Purple Tiger, Cherry Tiger, or Amber Tiger finishes, current mfg.

MSR $1,550

EXB-5 Bass-USA - similar to the EXB-4 Bass except in five-string configuration, current mfg.

MSR $1,650

GRADING		100% MINT	98% NEAR MINT	95% EXC+	90% EXC	80% VG+	70% VG	60% G

EXB-4K BASS - similar to EXB-4, except has Farnell Ultralight body design, 2 Farnell active soapbar pickups, GoToh Farnell bridge, available in same colors as EXB-4, current mfg.

MSR	$549		$375	$325	$275	$225	$185	$150	$125

EXB-5 Bass - similar to the EXB-4 Bass except in five-string configuration, current mfg.

MSR	$589		$400	$350	$295	$250	$200	$160	$135

Farnell EXG PRO USA
courtesy Farnell

FEDDEN

Instruments currently built in Comack, NY, beginning 1999. Previously built in Port Washington, New York.

Luthier George Fedden is currently producing acrylic see-through guitar bodies that feature colored inlays inside the body for a stunning effect. Designs are based on classic American favorites, and feature wood bolt-on necks, gold hardware, and gold-plated Kent Armstrong pickups. Their clarity and clean wiring harnesses will definitely make you take a second look. The overall feel and body weight will make you want to play them! Fedden instruments are available directly from the builder.

FENDER

Instruments currently produced in Corona, CA (U.S.), Mexico, Japan, Tianjin (China), and Korea. Distributed by the Fender Musical Instruments Corporation of Scottsdale, AZ. The Fender trademark established circa 1948 in Fullerton, CA.

Clarence Leonidas Fender was born in 1909, and was raised in Fullerton, California. As a teenager, he developed an interest in electronics, and soon was building and repairing radios for fellow classmates. After high school, Leo Fender held a bookkeeping position while he still did radio repair at home. After holding a series of jobs, Fender opened up a full-scale radio repair shop in 1939. In addition to service work, the Fender Radio Service store soon became a general electronics retail outlet. However, the forerunner to the Fender Electric Instruments company was a smaller two-man operation that was originally started as the K & F company in 1945. Leo Fender began modestly building small amplifiers and electric lap steels with his partner, Clayton Orr Doc Kaufman. After K & F dissolved, Fender formed the Fender Electric Instrument company in 1946, located on South Pomona Avenue in Fullerton, California. The company sales, though slow at first, began to expand as his amplifiers and lap steel began meeting acceptance among West Coast musicians. In 1950, Fender successfully developed the first production solid body electric guitar. Originally the Broadcaster, the name was quickly changed to the Telecaster after the Gretsch company objected to the infringement of their Broadkaster drum sets.

Soon Fender´s inventive genius began designing new models through the early 1950s and early 1960s. The Fender Precision Bass guitar was unveiled in 1951. While there is some kind of an existing background for the development of an electric solid body guitar, the notion of a 34 in. scale instrument with a fretted neck that could replace an upright acoustic doublebass was completely new to the music industry. The Precision bass (so named because players could fret the note precisely) coupled with a Fender Bassman amplifier gave the bass player more sonic projection. Fender then followed with another design in 1954, the Stratocaster. The simplicity in design, added to the popular sounds and playability, makes this design the most copied world wide. Other popular models of guitars, basses, and amplifiers soon followed.

By 1964, Fender´s line of products included electric guitars, basses, steel guitars, effects units, acoustic guitars, electric pianos, and a variety of accessories. Leo´s faltering health was a factor in putting the company up for sale, and he first offered it to Don Randall (the head of Fender Sales) for a million and a half dollars. Randall opened negotiations with the Baldwin Piano & Organ company, but when those negotiations fell through, offered it to the conglomerate CBS (who was looking to diversify the company holdings). Fender (FEIC) was purchased by CBS on January 5, 1965 (actually in December of 1964) for thirteen million dollars. Leo Fender was kept on as a special consultant for five years, and then left when then contract was up in 1970. Due to a ten-year, no compete clause, the next Leo Fender-designed guitars did not show up in the music industry until 1976 (Music Man).

While Fender was just another division of CBS, a number of key figures left the company. Forrest White, the production manager, left in 1967 after a dispute in producing solid state amplifiers. Don Randall left in 1969, disenchanted with corporate life. George Fullerton, one of the people involved with the Stratocaster design, left in 1970. Obviously, the quality in Fender products did not drop the day Leo Fender sold the company. Dale Hyatt, another veteran of the early Fender days, figured that the quality on the products stayed relatively stable until around 1968 (Hyatt left in 1972). But a number of cost-cutting strategies, and attempts to produce more products, had a deteriorating effect. This reputation leads right to the classic phrase heard at vintage guitar shows, "Pre-CBS?"

In the early 1980s, the Fender guitar empire began to crumble. Many cost-cutting factors and management problems forced CBS to try various last ditch efforts to salvage the instrument line. In March of 1982, Fender (with CBS´ blessing) negotiated with Kanda Shokai and Yamano Music to establish Fender Japan. After discussions with Tokai (who built a great Fender Strat replica, among other nice guitars), Kawai, and others, Fender finally chose Fuji Gen Gakki (based in Matsumoto, about 130 miles northwest of Tokyo). In 1983 the Squier series was built in Japan, earmarked for European distribution. The Squier trademark came from a string-making company in Michigan (V.C. Squier) that CBS had acquired in 1965.

In 1984 CBS decided to sell Fender. Offers came in from IMC (Hondo, Charvel/Jackson), and the Kaman Music Corporation (Ovation). Finally, CBS sold Fender to an investment group led by William Schultz in March for twelve and a half million dollars. This investment group formally became the Fender Musical Instruments Corporation (FMIC). As the sale did not include production facilities, USA guitar production ceased for most of 1985. It has been estimated that 80% of the guitars sold between late 1984 and mid-1986 were made in Japan. Soon after, a new factory was built in Corona, California, and USA production was restored in 1986 and continues to this day. FMIC expanded their company by purchasing Sunn amplifiers in 1987.

In 1990, the Fender (FMIC) company built an assembly facility in Mexico to offset rising costs of oriental production due to the weakening of the American dollar in the international market. Fender also experimented with

F

production based in India from 1989 to 1990. The Fender (FMIC) company currently manufactures instruments in China, Japan, Korea, Mexico, and the U.S. In 1991, Fender relocated its headquarters from Corona, California to Scottsdale, Arizona. This is where they are today. In 1992, the amplifier custom shop was opened.

As FMIC began to expand in the 1990s, they also started to buy into other interests. The Guild guitar company has been making high-quality instruments since 1952, but the company went up for the sale in the early 90s. Fender completed the sale in 1995 and began building instruments in the Custom Shop in Nashville, Tennessee in 1996. Fender also picked up Manuel Rodriguez guitars for classical guitars hand-crafted in Spain.

As reported in the March 1998 edition of MMR, Fender CEO Schultz sent out a letter to Fender dealers (dated January 9, 1998) which discussed the company establishing a "limited number" of Fender mail-order catalog dealers. Fender has announced specific guidelines as to what is allowed in mail-order catalog sales. Most importantly, Fender "announced a minimum advertised price (MAP) policy applicable to mail-order catalogs only," stated Schultz, "The MAP for mail-order catalogs is set at a maximum 30 percent off the Fender suggested retail price, and will be enforced unilaterally by Fender." What this does to the Fender retail price overall is basically lower the bar - but the impact on regular guitar stores has not been fully realized. While it's one thing to buy because of a discounted price through a catalog, it's a different situation to walk into a dealer's shop and be able to "test drive" a guitar before it is purchased. Retail music stores have to be aware that there is now an outside source (not under their control) that dictates minimum sales prices - the national catalogs. Of course, retail shops still control the maximum sale price applied to an instrument. Readers familiar to the *Blue Book of Electric Guitars* will note both the manufacturer's suggested retail price and the appropriate discounted price (100% listing) under currently produced models.

In 1998, Fender opened up a new 177,000-square-foot manufacturing facility in Corona, California. This is a state-of-the-art facility that can pump out 350 guitars a day and produces 95% clean air that comes from the factory. In Summer 2002, Fender announced the purchase of the Gretsch guitar line. Gretsch has been making guitars and other instruments since the 1900s! The sale went in effect on January 1, 2003. Fender also owns SWR, and Jackson/Charvel (source for earlier Fender history: Richard R. Smith, *Fender: The Sound Heard 'Round the World*).

VISUAL IDENTIFICATION FEATURES

When trying to determine the date of an instrument's production, it is useful to know a few things about feature changes that have occurred over the years. The following information may help you to determine the approximate date of manufacture of a Fender instrument by visual observation, without having to handle (or disassemble) the instrument for serial number verification. This is a list indicating what features were available for different years on fingerboards:

1950-1959: All necks were made out of a solid piece of maple with the frets being driven right into the neck. This is the standard design for maple necks.

1959-1962: The maple neck was planed flat and a rosewood fingerboard with frets and inlay was glued to the top of the neck. This is known as the slab top, or slab fingerboard.

1962-1983: The maple necks were rounded to the neck's radius and a thinner piece of rosewood was glued to the neck area. This design is called the veneer fingerboard.

1983-date: Fender returned to the slab top fingerboard design of the 1959 to 1962 era. This is a list indicating what features were available for different years on the neckplate:

1950 to 1971: The neck was attached to the body by means of a 4-screw neckplate.

1971 to 1981: The neckplate was changed to 3-screws, and a micro neck adjustment device was added.

In 1981: A transition from the 3-screw design back to the 4-screw design began to occur.

By 1983: The 4-screw neckplate was back in standard production, with the micro neck adjuster remaining.

PRODUCTION MODEL CODES

Current Fender instruments are identified by a part number that consists of a three-digit location/facility code and a four-digit model code (the two codes are separated by a hyphen). An example of this would be:

010 - 9200

(The 010-9200 part number is the California-built Stevie Ray Vaughn model.) As Fender guitars are built in a number of locations worldwide, the three-digit code will indicate where production took place (this does not indicate where the parts originated, however; just assembly of components). The first digit differentiates between Fender bridges and Floyd Rose tremolos:

0	**Fender Product, non-Floyd Rose/Orpheum/Olympia/Manual Rodriguez/Tacoma**
1	**Floyd Rose Bridge**
2	**Gretsch/Charvel/Jackson Product**
3	**Guild/Benedetto/ Product**

The second/third digit combination designates the production location:

10	**U.S., Guitar (Corona)**	26	**Korea**	50	**Guild Product Acoustic and**
13	**Mexico, Guitar and Bass**	27	**Japan, Guitar/Bass**		**Electric (Rhode Island)**
19	**U.S., Bass (Corona)**	33	**Korea, Guitar/Bass**	94	**Spain, Acoustic**
	Bass (Ensenada)	33	**China, Guitar/Bass**		**Guitar (Classical)**
25	**Japan, Guitar/Bass**	33	**Indonesia, Guitar and Bass**		

The four digits on the other side of the hyphen continue defining the model. The fourth/fifth digit combination is the product designation. The sixth digit defines left-handedness, or key parts inherent to that product. The final seventh digit indicates which type of wood fingerboard. The eighth digit indicates what type of case the guitar comes with. An eighth digit of "3" indicates a gig bag, a "5" means the guitar comes with no case, a "7" indicates that the guitar comes with a standard case, and an "8" means it comes with a deluxe case. The last numbers (ninth and tenth) indicate the finish/color. A chart follows on the next page.

Unless otherwise noted, most Series models are produced in the same country of origin. For further information on Fender acoustic models, please refer to the *Blue Book of Acoustic Guitars*.

GRADING					100% MINT	98% NEAR MINT	95% EXC+	90% EXC	80% VG+	70% VG	60% G

00	3 Color Sunburst	29	Blue Agave	66	Burgundy Mist Metallic
01	White Blonde	31	Aged Cherry	67	Honey Blonde
02	Lake Placid Blue	32	Brown Sunburst	71	Candy Green
03	2-Color Sunburst	34	Aged Natural	72	Sonic Blue
04	Daphne Blue	38	Crimson Trans.	74	Aqua Marine Metallic
05	Olympic White	40	Fiesta Red	75	Midnight Wine
06	Black	41	Vintage White	76	Midnight Purple
07	Vintage Blonde	43	Pewter	77	Frost Red
08	Ocean Turquoise	44	Shorline Gold	80	Arctic White
09	Candy Apple Red	45	Teal Green Metallic	81	Surf Pearl
10	Black W/ Gold Paisley	46	Sherwood Metallic	82	Candy Tangerine
11	Black W/ White Paisley	47	Sienna Sunburst	83	Ice Blue Metallic
15	Hot Rod Red	48	Teal Green Trans.	85	Bright Amber Metallic
19	Sage Green Metallic	50	Butterscotch Blonde	86	Bright Sapphire Metallic
20	Amber	51	Sky Blue		
21	Natural	52	Tobacco Sunburst	91	Chrome Silver
22	Sunset Orange Trans.	54	Dakota Red	92	Walnut
23	Pearl White	55	Frost White	95	Chrome Blue
24	Inca Silver	56	Shell Pink	96	Orange
25	Chrome Red	57	Surf Green	98	Green
26	Violet	58	Torino Red	99	Bronze
27	Sapphire Blue Trans.	63	Graffiti Yellow		

**Fender Cyclone
courtesy Fender**

GENERAL INFORMATION

In late 1997, Fender began marketing the StratPak (Model 013-4600-011), an all-in-one package that included a Mexican production Fender Standard Stratocaster, a gig bag, Fender Frontman 15R amplifier (with reverb), tuner, cable, strings, and picks (retail list $650). This all-in-one set helps the guitar student get into an electric guitar package in "one-stop shopping."

In the late 1970s, instrument bodies generally became heavier and less desirable due to their weight. With the higher prices of 1950s and 1960s Stratocasters and Telecasters on today´s vintage market (and less access to the average player), however, the 1970s models are beginning to climb in price.

Here´s a bit of revisionist history: The 1970s were Fender´s "Dark Ages," which lead to players and dealers looking for the models from the ´50s and ´60s (and the formation of today´s vintage guitar market). Now that the source of the sought-after models is drying up or getting "too spendy," those 1970s models aren´t looking too bad!

The most common Fender custom color finishes from the 1950s/1960s found are Candy Apple Red, Lake Placid Blue and Olympic White. These custom colors may not be as highly sought-after as other custom color finishes, and therefore will not be as highly valued as rarer custom colors such as Burgundy Mist.

Fender also produced a number of other electric stringed instruments. In early 1956, Fender debuted the solid body Electric Mandolin. This four-stringed model originally had a slab cut body, but became more contoured like a Stratocaster in 1959. The Electric Mandolin had a four on a side Fender headstock, single coil pickup, volume/tone control, and a 2-screw shared-saddle bridge, available in Blond or Sunburst finishes, the Electric Mandolin was in production from 1956 to 1976.

Fender´s Electric Violin was first introduced (briefly) in 1958. The first production model had a violin-shaped solid body, single coil pickup, volume/tone controls, and a slotted peghead with four-on-a-side tuners. A revised edition with a scrolled headstock and ebony tuning pegs was produced from 1969 to 1975.

Add 20%-50% to the price of those vintage Fenders with an original factory custom color finish, depending on the rarity of color and original condition. An original custom color Fender's price tag will depend on both the rarity of the finish/model, and the original condition factor.

As a rule, professional refinished guitars are worth approximately 50% less than an original model, if the refinish is in the original color/finish.

ELECTRIC: BULLET SERIES

The Bullet model was introduced in 1983, and was designed by John Page (now with the Fender Custom shop). Originally built in Korea, production was switched back to the U.S. facilities after six months and remained there through 1983. The original design featured a Telecaster-ish body design and slim headstock, a 25.5 in. scale, and two pickups that were "leftovers" from the Mustang production line. The Bullet had a suggested list price of $189, although this amount changed as more models were introduced to the series.

Models in this series have offset double cutaway alder body, white pickguard, bolt-on maple neck, 22-fret maple fingerboard with black dot inlay, fixed bridge, telecaster style peghead, 6-on-one-side tuners, chrome hardware, volume/tone control (unless otherwise listed), available in Ivory, Red, Metallic Red, Sunburst, Walnut, and White finishes.

BULLET (FIRST VERSION) - single cutaway body, 22-fret rosewood fingerboard with pearl dot inlay, 2 single coil covered pickups, 3-position switch, mfg. 1981-83.

N/A	$350	$300	$250	$200	$150	$100

This model was also available with black pickguard. In 1983, the body was changed to offset double cutaway alder body, known as the Second Version of the Bullet.

**Fender Electric XII
courtesy Rod and Hanks
Vintage Guitars**

GRADING	100% MINT	98% NEAR MINT	95% EXC+	90% EXC	80% VG+	70% VG	60% G

Bullet Deluxe - single cutaway mahogany body, 22-fret rosewood fingerboard with pearl dot inlay, strings through bridge, 2 single coil covered pickups, 3-position switch.

	N/A	$350	$300	$250	$200	$150	$100

This model was also available with black pickguard.

BULLET H-1 - covered humbucker pickup, push button coil split switch, mfg. 1983 only.

	N/A	$300	$250	$210	$170	$130	$95

BULLET H-2 - strings through bridge, 2 covered humbucker pickups, 3-position switch, 2 push button coil split switches, mfg. 1983 only.

	N/A	$350	$300	$250	$200	$150	$100

BULLET S-2 - laminated plastic pickguard, strings through bridge, 2 single coil covered pickups, 3-position switch, mfg. 1983 only.

	N/A	$350	$300	$250	$200	$150	$100

BULLET S-3 - strings through bridge, 3 single coil covered pickups, 5-position switch, mfg. 1983 only.

	N/A	$400	$350	$300	$250	$200	$150

ELECTRIC: CORONADO SERIES

CORONADO (U.S. MFG.) - double rounded cutaway semi-hollow bound beech body, arched top, f-holes, raised white pickguard, bolt-on maple neck, 21-fret rosewood fingerboard with pearl dot inlay, adjustable rosewood bridge/trapeze tailpiece, 6-on-one-side tuners, chrome hardware, single coil covered pickup, volume/tone control, available in Cherry, Custom Colors, or Sunburst finishes, mfg. 1966-1970.

	N/A	$800	$700	$600	$500	$400	$300

Add 50% for custom colors.

This model was also offered with these options: checkered binding, gold pickguard, and tune-o-matic bridge/vibrato tailpiece.

CORONADO II (U.S. MFG.) - similar to the Coronado, except has 2 pickups, bound f-holes and fingerboard, block inlays, and some featured a tremolo and checkered binding, mfg. 1966-1970.

	N/A	$900	$775	$650	$550	$450	$350

Add 50% for custom colors.

Coronado II Wildwood (U.S. Mfg.) - similar to Coronado, except has dye-injected beechwood body, bound f-holes, white pickguard with engraved Wildwood/I-VI, bound fingerboard with block inlay, tune-o-matic bridge/vibrato trapeze tailpiece, pearl tuner buttons, 2 single coil covered pickups, 2 volume/2 tone controls, 3-position switch, available in Wildwood finishes, mfg. 1967-1970.

	N/A	$1,300	$1,150	$1,000	$850	$700	$550

The Wildwood finish was the result of a seven-year process in Germany where dye was injected into growing beech trees. After the trees were harvested, veneers were cut and laminated to the guitar tops. Pickguard numbers (I-VI) refer to the dye color (primary color of green, blue, and gold) and the applied finish.

CORONADO XII (U.S. MFG.) - similar to Coronado, except has 12-string configuration, dye-injected beechwood body, bound f-holes, white pickguard with engraved Wildwood/I-VI, bound fingerboard with block inlay, tune-o-matic bridge/trapeze tailpiece, ebony tailpiece insert with pearl 'F' inlay, 6-per-side tuners with pearl buttons, 2 single coil covered pickups, 2 volume/2 tone controls, 3-position switch, available in Natural finish, mfg. 1967-1970.

	N/A	$1,000	$875	$750	$650	$550	$450

Add 50% for custom colors.

Coronado XII Wildwood (U.S.MFG.) - similar to the Coronado XII, except has the Wildwood injected dye finish, mfg. 1967-1970.

	N/A	$1,400	$1,200	$1,050	$900	$750	$600

ELECTRIC: CUSTOM SERIES

CUSTOM (U.S. MFG.) - offset double cutaway asymmetrical body with point on bottom bout, tortoiseshell pickguard, bolt-on maple neck, 21-fret bound rosewood fingerboard with pearl block inlay, floating bridge/vibrato with bridge cover, droopy peghead, 3-per-side tuners, chrome hardware, 2 split covered pickups, volume/tone control, 4-position rotary switch, available in Sunburst top/Black back finish, mfg. 1969-1971.

	N/A	$2,000	$1,750	$1,500	$1,250	$1,000	$750

The Custom model was devised by long time Fender employee Virgilio "Babe" Simoni as a method to use up necks and bodies left over from the Electrix XII model. The twelve-string peghead was refitted to six strings, and the body was recarved into a different design. The Custom model was originally to be named the "Maverick," which appears on some pegheads. Simoni estimated production to be around 600 to 800 completed pieces.

ELECTRIC: CYCLONE SERIES

CYCLONE (MEX. MFG., NO. 013-0500) - slightly offset double cutaway poplar body, bolt-on maple neck, 24.75" scale, 22-fret rosewood neck with dot inlay, synchronized tremolo, 6-on-a-side tuners, chrome hardware, brown or white shell pickguard, Tex-Mex single coil/Atomic humbucker pickups, volume/tone controls, 3-position toggle switch, chrome metal controls plate, available in Black, Candy Apple Red, Caramel Metallic, Chrome Red, Graffiti Yellow, or Orange finishes, mfg. 1998-present.

MSR	$700	$490	$425	$375	$325	$275	$225	$175

Add $25 for Brown Sunburst finish.

Arctic White and Brown Sunburst finishes were discontinued in 2001. Graffiti Yellow and Orange finishes were introduced in 2001. In 2005, Chrome Red and Caramel Metallic finishes were introduced. This model is also available with two humbuckers (Cyclone HH, No. 013-0400, available in Black, Pewter, Blizzard Pearl, or Orange finishes).

GRADING	100% MINT	98% NEAR MINT	95% EXC+	90% EXC	80% VG+	70% VG	60% G

CYCLONE II (MEX. MFG., NO. 013-0600) - slightly offset double cutaway poplar body, bolt-on maple neck, 24.75 in. scale, 22-fret rosewood neck with dot inlay, synchronized tremolo, 6-on-a-side tuners, chrome hardware, white shell pickguard, 3 Jaguar single coil pickups with switching for each pickup, volume/tone controls, chrome metal control plate, available in Daphne Blue or Candy Apple Red finishes, finish includes competition stripe like the Fender Mustang, mfg. 2002-present.

MSR	$785		$550	$475	$425	$375	$325	$275	$225

ELECTRIC: JAMES D´AQUISTO SERIES

James D´Aquisto Signature models were designed by Master Luthier James D´Aquisto, following his initial designs for the Master Series (1984-1985). James D´Aquisto Signature Series models were handcrafted in Fender´s Custom Shop.

In 1984, Fender contacted D´Aquisto to design three arch top guitar models to be produced in Japan under the Master Series designation. The top-of-the-line Ultra was an acoustic model with a 17 in. body width, carved spruce top, carved figured maple back and sides, 25.5 in. scale, and an optional floating pickup attached to the raised pickguard. The Elite has a 16 in. body width, 24.75 in. scale, arched spruce top, one humbucker, and ebony tailpiece/bridge/fingerboard/pickguard. The Standard model has a laminated maple top and back, and features 2 humbuckers and rosewood instead of ebony. All Japanese-built Master Series models feature a "Designed by D´Aquisto" headstock engraving. It is estimated that only 30 (+/-) Ultra models were built, and 1,000 Elites and Standards. For the D'Aquisto Ultra model see the *Blue Book of Acoustic Guitars.*

D´AQUISTO STANDARD (JAPAN MFG.) - single round cutaway laminated maple body, laminated maple top, f-holes, maple neck, raised bound solid rosewood pickguard, 20-fret bound rosewood fingerboard with pearl block inlay, adjustable rosewood bridge/rosewood trapeze tailpiece, bound peghead with pearl fan/logo inlay, 3-per-side tuners with ebony buttons, gold hardware, two humbucker pickups, 2 volume/2 tone controls, available in Black, Natural, or Violin Sunburst finish, mfg. 1984 only.

	N/A	$1,500	$1,300	$1,100	$950	$800	$650

Last MSR was $899.

Fender Coronado II Antiqua
courtesy Dave Rogers
Dave's Guitar Shop

D´AQUISTO CLASSIC ROCKER - aditional hollow body jazz design, 17 in. laminated maple hollow body with black and white "Checkerboard" multi-bound top, set three-piece figured maple neck, rosewood fingerboard with special "diamond" inlays, multiple binding, two Custom DeArmond 2000 single coil pickups, Bigsby vibrato tailpiece, chrome hardware, 3-per-side tuners, available in Amber, Black, or Crimson Trans. finishes, disc. 2001.

$2,800	$2,500	$2,200	$1,900	$1,600	$1,300	$1,000

Last MSR was $4,000.

D´AQUISTO DELUXE (U.S. MFG., NO. 010-2030) - single round cutaway laminated figured maple body (15.75 in. width), f-holes, maple neck, raised black pickguard, 22-fret bound ebony fingerboard with pearl block inlay, adjustable rosewood bridge/rosewood trapeze tailpiece, black peghead with pearl fan/logo inlay, 3-per-side tuners, chrome hardware, humbucker pickup, volume/tone controls, available in Antique Burst, Black, Natural, or Crimson Red Transparent finishes, mfg. 1994-2002.

$2,300	$2,000	$1,750	$1,550	$1,250	$1,050	$895

Last MSR was $3,280.

Black finish was discontinued in 2001.

D´AQUISTO ELITE (JAPAN/U.S. MFG., NO. 010-4050) - single round cutaway hollow figured maple body, arched bound spruce top, bound f-holes, maple neck, raised bound ebony pickguard, 22-fret bound ebony fingerboard with pearl block inlay, adjustable ebony bridge/ebony trapeze tailpiece, bound peghead with pearl fan/logo inlay, 3-per-side tuners with ebony buttons, gold hardware, humbucker pickup, volume/tone controls, available in Natural finish, mfg. 1984, 1989-1994, 1999-2001.

1984	N/A	$2,500	$2,200	$1,900	$1,600	$1,300	$1,000
1989-1994	N/A	$2,000	$1,750	$1,500	$1,250	$1,000	$750
1999-2001	$5,700	$5,000	$4,300	$3,700	$3,100	$2,500	$1,900

Last MSR was $8,030.

This model was produced in Japan in 1984 and again from 1989-1994. In 1999, it was reintroduced and produced in the Custom Shop in the U.S.

ELECTRIC: DUO-SONIC SERIES

DUO-SONIC (U.S. MFG.) - offset double cutaway hardwood 3/4 size body, metal pickguard, bolt-on maple neck, 21-fret rosewood fingerboard with pearl dot inlay, fixed bridge with cover, 6-on-one-side tuners with plastic buttons, chrome hardware, 2 single coil pickups, volume/tone control, 3-position switch, available in Desert Sand, Sunburst, or Custom Color finishes, mfg. 1956-1964.

1956-1959 LONG SCALE	N/A	$1,400	$1,200	$1,050	$900	$750	$600
1956-1959 SHORT SCALE	N/A	$1,200	$1,000	$850	$700	$600	$500
1960-1964	N/A	$1,000	$800	$650	$550	$450	$350

In 1964 Red, Blue, and White finishes were introduced. This model was released as a student model. In 1960, tortoiseshell or white plastic pickguard replaced metal pickguard.

Duo-Sonic II (U.S. Mfg.) - similar to Duo-Sonic, except has asymmetrical waist body, restyled plastic/metal pickguard, 22-fret fingerboard, enlarged peghead, 2 pickup selector slide switches, available in Blue, Red, or White finishes, mfg. 1965-69.

	N/A	$1,000	$850	$700	$600	$500	$400

This instrument had a longer scale length than its predecessor.

Fender Custom
courtesy John Beeson
The Music Shoppe

GRADING	100% MINT	98% NEAR MINT	95% EXC+	90% EXC	80% VG+	70% VG	60% G

DUO-SONIC (MEX MFG., NO. 013-0202) - offset double cutaway poplar body, bolt-on maple neck, 22.7 in. scale, 21-fret maple neck with black dot inlay, fixed bridge, 6-on-a-side tuners, chrome hardware, white pickguard, 2 single coil pickups, volume/tone controls, 3-position switch, available in Arctic White, Black, or Torino Red finishes, mfg. 1994-98.

	$200	$175	$150	$135	$115	$95	$75

Last MSR was $289.

ELECTRIC: ESQUIRE SERIES

ESQUIRE (U.S. MFG.) - single cutaway ash body, black pickguard, bolt-on maple neck, 21-fret maple fingerboard with black dot inlay, strings through bridge with cover, 6-on-one-side tuners, chrome hardware, single coil pickup, volume/tone control, 2-position switch, controls mounted on metal plate, available in Butterscotch Blonde, Sunburst, or Custom Color finishes, mfg. 1950-1970.

1950-1954 (BLACK PG)	N/A	$17,000	$14,000	$12,000	$10,000	$8,500	$7,500
1955	N/A	$12,000	$9,500	$8,000	$7,000	$6,000	$5,000
1956-1958	N/A	$9,000	$7,500	$6,500	$6,000	$5,500	$5,000
1959-1961 (SLAB BOARD)	N/A	$7,000	$6,250	$5,500	$5,000	$4,500	$4,000
1962-1964	N/A	$6,500	$5,750	$5,000	$4,250	$3,500	$2,750
1965-1967	N/A	$4,500	$3,800	$3,200	$2,600	$2,000	$1,500
1968-1970	N/A	$3,500	$2,900	$2,500	$2,100	$1,700	$1,300

Add 50% for Candy Apple Red, Lake Placid Blue, or Olympic White finishes. Add 100% for Burgundy Mist finish.

A few models in 1950 were produced with 2 single coil pickups and a 3-way switch. First runs on this series were sparse and no instruments were made between fall 1950 and January, 1951. In late 1954, a routing channel was introduced between pickups. In late 1954, white pickguard replaced black pickguard. In 1955, level pole piece pickups were standard. In summer 1956, the logo was placed above the string guide. In 1959, rosewood fingerboard with pearl dot inlay replaced the all maple neck. In 1967, maple fingerboard was an option. In 1969, maple fingerboard became standard.

Esquire Custom (U.S. Mfg.) - similar to Esquire, except has bound body, white pickguard, rosewood fingerboard with pearl dot inlay, available in Sunburst finish, mfg. 1959-1970.

1959-1960	N/A	$15,000	$12,000	$10,000	$8,500	$7,000	$6,000
1961-1962 (SLAB BOARD)	N/A	$12,000	$9,500	$8,000	$7,000	$6,000	$5,000
1963-1964	N/A	$10,000	$8,000	$6,500	$5,500	$4,500	$3,500
1965-1970	N/A	$7,500	$6,000	$5,000	$4,000	$3,200	$2,500

In 1960, a 3-ply pickguard was introduced.

'50s ESQUIRE - ash body, maple neck, 21-fret maple fingerboard with black dot inlay, vintage bridge, chrome hardware, white pickguard, 1 single coil pickup, 2 knobs (v, tone), available in 2-Tone Sunburst, Black, or White finishes, gig bag included, new 2005.

MSR	$900	$630	$550	$475	$425	$375	$325	$275

'54 ESQUIRE REISSUE (JAP. MFG.) - single cutaway ash body, black pickguard, bolt-on maple neck, 21-fret maple fingerboard with black dot inlay, strings through bridge with cover, 6-on-one-side tuners, chrome hardware, single coil pickup, volume/tone control, 3-position switch, controls mounted metal plate, available in Blonde and 2-Tone Sunburst finishes, disc. 1994.

	N/A	$400	$325	$275	$235	$195	$160

Last MSR was $570.

This model was a limited edition instrument available by custom order.

'62 Esquire Custom (Jap. Mfg.) - similar to '54 Esquire, except has bound body, white pickguard, rosewood fingerboard with pearl dot inlay, available in Candy Apple Red and 3-Tone Sunburst finishes, disc. 1994.

	N/A	$425	$350	$300	$250	$210	$170

Last MSR was $580.

This model was a limited edition instrument available by custom order.

'59 ESQUIRE NOS (NEW OLD STOCK, U.S. MFG. NO. 015-3002) - single cutaway premium ash body, '50s C-Shaped neck, 20-fret rosewood fingerboard with dot inlay, single Tele single coil pickup, Vintage top load 3 saddle bridge, two knobs (v, tone), 3-way switch chrome hardware, available in White Blonde or Black N.O.S. finishes, mfg. 2003-present.

MSR	$3,125	$2,200	$2,000	$1,800	$1,600	$1,400	$1,200	$1,000

'59 Esquire Closet Classic (U.S. Mfg. No. 015-3102) - similar to the '59 Esquire N.O.S. except has Closet Classic finish, mfg. 2003-present.

MSR	$3,435	$2,450	$2,200	$1,950	$1,750	$1,550	$1,350	$1,150

'59 Esquire Relic (U.S. Mfg. No. 015-3202) - similar to the '59 Esquire N.O.S. except has Relic finish, mfg. 2003-present.

MSR	$3,595	$2,550	$2,300	$2,050	$1,800	$1,600	$1,400	$1,200

ESQUIRE CUSTOM CELTIC (NO. 026-1200) - single cutaway contoured mahogany body, modified C-Shaped set-in mahogany neck, 22-fret rosewood fingerboard with 12th fret Celtic inlay, single Atomic II Humbucker pickup, 6 saddle S-T-B bridge, volume knob, black hardware, available in Silver finish, mfg. 2003 only.

	$630	$575	$500	$450	$400	$350	$275

Last MSR was $900.

ESQUIRE CUSTOM SCORPION (NO. 026-1600) - single cutaway contoured mahogany body, modified C-Shaped set-in mahogany neck, 22-fret rosewood fingerboard with 12th fret Scorpion inlay, single Atomic II Humbucker pickup, 6 saddle S-T-B bridge, volume knob, black hardware, available in Black finish, mfg. 2003 only.

	$630	$575	$500	$450	$400	$350	$275

Last MSR was $900.

F

GRADING	100% MINT	98% NEAR MINT	95% EXC+	90% EXC	80% VG+	70% VG	60% G

ESQUIRE CUSTOM GT (NO. 026-2200) - single cutaway contoured mahogany body, modified C-Shaped set-in mahogany neck, 22-fret rosewood fingerboard with dot inlay, single Atomic II Humbucker pickup, 6 saddle S-T-B bridge, volume knob, black/chrome hardware, racing stipe down the middle, available in Crimson Red Metallic or Chrome Blue finish, mfg. 2003 only.

	$630	$575	$500	$450	$400	$350	$275

Last MSR was $900.

SEYMOUR DUNCAN ARTIST ESQUIRE (U.S. MFG. NO. 015-0060) - single cutaway premium ash body, C-Shaped maple neck, 21-fret maple fingerboard, white pickguard, single tapped custom Seymour Duncan pickup, vintage bridge with 3 saddles, 2 knobs (v, tone), 3-way switch, chrome hardware, signature on headstock, available in 2-Color Sunburst, mfg. 2003-present.

MSR	$3,980	$2,800	$2,500	$2,200	$1,950	$1,700	$1,450	$1,200

ELECTRIC: ESPRIT AND FLAME (MASTER SERIES) MODELS

In 1984, Fender offered two models under the Master Series. The Master Series models were produced in Japan. The Esprit and Flame models are dual cutaway, semi-hollow (tone chambered bodies) alder bodies with spruce or maple tops, set-in maple necks, ebony or rosewood fingerboards, 3-on-a-side tuners, and 2 humbucker pickups.

ESPRIT STANDARD (JAPAN MFG.) - double cutaway body, carved maple top, maple set neck, rosewood fingerboard, fully bound body and neck, two humbucker pickups with exposed poles, individual string bridge and tailpiece, 2 knobs, 3-way switch, 3-per-side tuners, available in Black or Sunburst finishes, mfg. 1984 only.

	N/A	$700	$625	$550	$450	$350	$250

Esprit Elite (Japan Mfg.) - similar to the Esprit Standard, except has Snowflake fingerboard inlays, pearl tuners, fine tuner tailpiece, four knobs, and a coil-tap switch, available in Sunburst or other colors, mfg. 1984 only.

	N/A	$900	$800	$700	$600	$500	$400

Esprit Ultra (Japan Mfg.) - similar to the Esprit Standard, except has a bound ebony fingerboard with split block inlays, carved spruce top, ebony tuners, fine tuner tailpiece, four knobs, coil-tap switch, and gold hardware, available in Sunburst or other colors, mfg. 1984 only.

	N/A	$1,100	$950	$825	$700	$600	$500

FLAME STANDARD (JAPAN MFG.) - double cutaway body, carved maple top, maple set neck, rosewood fingerboard, fully bound body and neck, two humbucker pickups with exposed poles, individual string bridge and tailpiece, 2 knobs, 3-way switch, 3-per-side tuners, available in Black or Sunburst finishes, mfg. 1984 only.

	N/A	$600	$525	$450	$375	$300	$225

This model is the same as the Esprit in a smaller configuration.

Flame Elite (Japan Mfg.) - similar to the Flame Standard, except has Snowflake fingerboard inlays, pearl tuners, fine tuner tailpiece, four knobs, and a coil-tap switch, available in Sunburst or other colors, mfg. 1984 only.

	N/A	$800	$700	$600	$500	$400	$300

This model is the same as the Esprit Elite in a smaller configuration.

Flame Ultra (Japan Mfg.) - similar to the Flame Standard, except has a bound ebony fingerboard with split block inlays, carved spruce top, ebony tuners, fine tuner tailpiece, four knobs, coil-tap switch, and gold hardware, available in Sunburst or other colors, mfg. 1984 only.

	N/A	$1,000	$850	$725	$600	$500	$400

This model is the same as the Esprit Ultra in a smaller configuration.

ELECTRIC: JAG-STANG SERIES

JAG-STANG (JAP MFG. NO. 025-4200) - offset double cutaway asymmetrical basswood body, bolt-on maple neck, oversized ('60s Strat) headstock, 22-fret rosewood fingerboard with white dot inlay, 24 in. scale, floating bridge/Fender Dynamic vibrato tailpiece, 6-on-a-side tuners, chrome hardware, white pickguard, Vintage Strat single coil/humbucker pickups, volume/tone controls, 2 3-position selector switches, available in Fiesta Red or Sonic Blue, disc. 1999, reintroduced 2003-04.

	$540	$475	$400	$325	$250	$200	$150

Last MSR was $757.

This model was developed in conjunction with Kurt Cobain, who was front-man of the former band, Nirvana. The used model was so popular, Fender decided to reintroduce this guitar. Used models in excellent condition were selling for $600+.

Jag-Stang Left Hand (Mexico Mfg. No. 013-4220) - similar to the Jag-Stang, except in a left-handed configuration, disc. 1998.

	N/A	$500	$425	$350	$300	$250	$200

Last MSR was $689.

1952 Fender Esquire courtesy Dave Rogers Dave's Guitar Shop

Fender Esquire Custom courtesy Dave Rogers Dave's Guitar Shop

GRADING	100% MINT	98% NEAR MINT	95% EXC+	90% EXC	80% VG+	70% VG	60% G

ELECTRIC: JAGUAR SERIES

JAGUAR (U.S. MFG.) - offset double cutaway asymmetrical alder body, metal/plastic pickguard, bolt-on maple neck, 22-fret rosewood fingerboard with pearl dot inlay, string mute, floating bridge/vibrato, bridge cover plate, 6-on-one-side tuners, chrome hardware, 2 single coil exposed pickups, volume/tone control, volume/tone roller control, preset slide switch, 3 preset slide switches, available in Sunburst, Black, Blonde, or custom colors finishes, mfg. 1962-1975.

1962	N/A	$3,000	$2,600	$2,300	$2,000	$1,700	$1,400
1963-65	N/A	$2,700	$2,300	$2,000	$1,700	$1,400	$1,100
1966-1967	N/A	$2,500	$2,100	$1,800	$1,500	$1,200	$900
1968-1969	N/A	$2,200	$1,900	$1,600	$1,350	$1,100	$850
1970-1975	N/A	$1,600	$1,350	$1,100	$950	$800	$650

Add 20% for Dakota Red, Fiesta Red, Daphne Blue, Sonic Blue, Sherwood Green, or Gold finishes. Add 50% for Burgundy Mist, Surf Green, Shell Pink, or Inca Silver finishes.

In 1965, the fingerboard was bound. In 1966, block fingerboard inlay replaced dot inlay.

´62 JAGUAR (U.S. MFG., NO. 010-0900) - alder body with '60s styling, maple neck with rosewood fingerboard, 22 vintage size frets, 24 in. scale, vintage style tuners, 2 US Jaguar Special Design single-coil pickups, Lead circuit has 2-position tone switch, volume, tone. Rhythm circuit has volume, tone, and circuit selector, brown shell or aged white/black/white pickguard, vintage stlye floating tremolo with tremolo lock button, contoured body with offset waist, currently available in 3-Color Sunburst, Olympic White, Black, Ocean Turquoise, Surf Green, Ice Blue Metallic, or Inca Silver finishes, case included, mfg. 1999-present.

MSR	$2,000	$1,400	$1,200	$1,050	$900	$800	$700	$600

Add $35 for Sunburst color option.

In 2001, Inca Silver, Dakota Red, and Ice Blue Metallic (-833) finishes were introduced, and Candy Apple Red, Fiesta Red and Sherwood Metallic finishes were discontinued. In 2002 Ocean Turquoise, Surf Green were introduced, and Dakota Red was discontinued.

´62 JAGUAR (JAP. MFG. NO. 027-7700) - offset double cutaway asymmetrical basswood body, bolt-on maple neck, 24 in. scale, 21-fret rosewood fingerboard with white dot inlay, string mute, floating bridge/vibrato with tremolo lock, bridge cover plate, 6-on-a-side tuners, chrome hardware, metal and plastic pickguard, 2 single coil pickups, volume/tone control, volume/tone roller control, circuit selector slide switch, 3 preset slide switches, available in 3-Tone Sunburst, Candy Apple Red, or Vintage White finishes, disc. 1998.

	$550	$475	$425	$375	$325	$250	$200

Last MSR was $799.

Jaguar Left Hand (Jap. Mfg., No. 027-7720) - similar to the Jaguar, except in a left-handed configuration, available in 3-Tone Sunburst finish, mfg. 1995-98.

	$600	$525	$450	$400	$350	$275	$225

Last MSR was $869.

JAGUAR BARITONE CUSTOM (NO. 025-9400) - Jaguar body style strung for Baritone, available in 3-Color Sunburst finish, new 2004.

MSR	$1,000	$700	$625	$550	$475	$425	$375	$325

This model was released in popular response of the Bass VI. However this only has 2 single coil pickups, whereas the Bass VI had 3.

ELECTRIC: JAZZMASTER SERIES

JAZZMASTER (U.S. MFG.) - offset double cutaway asymmetrical alder body, gold metal (or tortoiseshell) pickguard, bolt-on maple neck, 21-fret rosewood fingerboard with pearl dot inlay, floating bridge/vibrato, bridge cover plate, 6-on-one-side tuners, chrome hardware, 2 single coil exposed pickups, volume/tone control, volume/tone roller control, 3-position switch, preset selector slide switch, available in custom colors and Sunburst finishes, mfg. 1958-1980.

1958	N/A	$5,000	$4,300	$3,600	$3,000	$2,400	$1,900
1959	N/A	$4,500	$3,800	$3,200	$2,600	$2,100	$1,600
1960-1961	N/A	$3,500	$3,000	$2,600	$2,200	$1,800	$1,500
1962-1964	N/A	$3,000	$2,600	$2,300	$2,000	$1,700	$1,400
1965-1966	N/A	$2,500	$2,100	$1,800	$1,500	$1,300	$1,100
1967-1969	N/A	$2,000	$1,750	$1,500	$1,250	$1,000	$800
1970-1972	N/A	$1,750	$1,500	$1,250	$1,000	$800	$600
1973-1980	N/A	$1,500	$1,250	$1,050	$900	$750	$600

Add 20% for Dakota Red, Fiesta Red, Candy Apple Red, Olympic White, Sonic Blue, Lake Placid Blue, or Gold Metallic finishes. Add 50% for Burgundy Mist, Surf Green, Fire Mist Silver, or Shell Pink finishes.

In 1960, tortoiseshell pickguard replaced metal pickguard. In 1965, the fingerboard was bound. In 1966, block fingerboard inlay replaced dot inlay. In 1976, black pickguard replaced tortoiseshell pickguard.

´62 JAZZMASTER (U.S. MFG. NO. 010-0800) - alder body with '60s styling, maple neck with rosewood fingerboard, 21 vintage size frets, 25.5 in. scale, vintage style tuners, 2 US Jazzmaster pickups, 3-way switch, lead circuit has volume and tone, rhythm circuit has volume, tone and circuit selector, brown tortoiseshell or aged white/black/white pickguard, vintage style floating tremolo with tremolo lock button, contoured body with offset waist, available in 3-Color Sunburst, Olympic White, Black, Candy Apple Red, Fiesta Red, Ocean Turquoise, Surf Green, Ice Blue Metallic, or Sherwood Metallic finishes, mfg. 1999-present.

MSR	$2,000	$1,400	$1,200	$1,050	$900	$800	$700	$600

Add $35 for Sunburst color option.

In 2001, Inca Silver, Dakota Red, and Ice Blue Metallic finishes were introduced, and Candy Apple Red, Fiesta Red and Sherwood Metallic finishes were discontinued. In 2002, Inca Silver and Dakota Red finishes were discontinued, and Surf Green and Ocean Turquoise were introduced.

GRADING	100% MINT	98% NEAR MINT	95% EXC+	90% EXC	80% VG+	70% VG	60% G

´62 JAZZMASTER (JAP. MFG. NO. 027-7800) - offset double cutaway asymmetrical basswood body, bolt-on maple neck, 21-fret rosewood fingerboard with pearl dot inlay, floating bridge/vibrato with tremolo lock, bridge cover plate, 6-on-one-side tuners, chrome hardware, tortoiseshell pickguard, 2 single coil pickups, volume/tone control, volume/tone roller control, 3-position switch, preset selector slide switch, available in 3-Tone Sunburst, Candy Apple Red, or Vintage White finishes, disc. 1999.

	$550	$475	$425	$375	$325	$275	$225

Last MSR was $799.

Jazzmaster Left Hand (Jap. Mfg., No. 027-7820) - similar to the ´62 Jazzmaster, except in a left-handed configuration, available in 3-Tone Sunburst finish, mfg. 1995-98.

	$600	$525	$450	$400	$350	$300	$250

Last MSR was $869.

VENTURES LIMITED EDITION JAZZMASTER (JAP. MFG., NO. 027-8200) - offset double cutaway asymmetrical light ash body, bolt-on maple neck, 22-fret rosewood fingerboard with white block inlay, floating bridge/vibrato, bridge cover plate, 6-on-one-side tuners, white shell pickguard, gold hardware, 2 Seymour Duncan JM single coil pickups, volume/tone control, volume/tone roller control, 3-position switch, preset selector slide switch, available in Midnight Black Trans. finish, mfg. 1996 only.

	N/A	$1,000	$850	$750	$650	$550	$450

Last MSR was $1,344.

ELECTRIC: MISC. MODELS

Fender Jaguar
courtesy Dave Rogers
Dave's Guitar Shop

BRONCO (U.S. MFG.) - offset double cutaway poplar body, white pickguard, bolt-on maple neck, 22-fret rosewood fingerboard with pearl dot inlay, standard vibrato, covered single coil pickup, volume/tone control, available in Black, Red, or White finishes, mfg. 1967-1980.

1967-1969	N/A	$650	$575	$500	$425	$375	$325
1970-1974	N/A	$550	$475	$400	$350	$300	$250
1975-1980	N/A	$500	$425	$375	$325	$275	$225

ELECTRIC XII (U.S. MFG.) - offset double cutaway asymmetrical body, tortoiseshell pickguard, bolt-on maple neck, 21-fret rosewood fingerboard with pearl dot inlay, strings through bridge, droopy peghead, 6-per-side tuners, chrome hardware, 2 split covered pickups, volume/tone controls, 4-position rotary switch, available in Sunburst or custom color finishes, mfg. 1965-69.

1965-1966	N/A	$2,300	$1,900	$1,600	$1,300	$1,050	$850
1967-1969	N/A	$1,600	$1,350	$1,150	$950	$800	$700

Add 20% for Dakota Red, Fiesta Red, Daphne Blue, Sonic Blue, Sherwood Green, or Gold Metallic finishes. Add 50% for Burgundy Mist, Surf Green, Shell Pink, or Inca Silver finishes.

In 1965, the fingerboard was bound. In 1966, block fingerboard inlay replaced dot inlay.

KATANA (JAPAN MFG.) - wedge-shaped body, maple set neck with rosewood fingerboard, offset triangle position markers, 22 frets, arrow-head shaped headstock, 2 black exposed-coil humbucking pickups, 1 volume/1 tone control, 3-way switch, 2 pivot bridge with vibrato, available in white, yellow frost, blue sparkle, and black finishes, mfg. 1985-86.

	N/A	$350	$300	$250	$200	$150	$100

LEAD I (U.S. MFG.) - offset double cutaway alder body, black pickguard, bolt-on maple neck, 21-fret maple fingerboard with black dot inlay, strings through bridge, 6-on-one-side tuners, chrome hardware, humbucker exposed pickup, 2 two-position switches, available in Black or Brown finishes, mfg. 1979-1982.

	N/A	$350	$300	$250	$200	$150	$100

In 1981, custom colors became optional, including Olympic White.

LEAD II (U.S. MFG.) - similar to Lead I, except has 2 single coil exposed pickups, mfg. 1979-1982.

	N/A	$400	$350	$300	$250	$200	$150

LEAD III (U.S. MFG.) - similar to Lead I, except has 2 humbuckers, mfg. 1981-82.

	N/A	$450	$375	$325	$275	$225	$175

LTD (U.S. MFG.) - single round cutaway hollow figured maple body, 17 in. wide, arched bound spruce top, unbound f-holes, raised tortoiseshell pickguard, bolt-on maple neck, 20-fret bound ebony fingerboard with pearl "diamond-in-block" inlay, adjustable ebony bridge/metal trapeze tailpiece, ebony tailpiece insert with pearl F inlay, bound peghead with pearl "mirrored F"/logo inlay, 3-per-side tuners with pearl buttons, gold hardware, covered humbucker pickup, volume/tone control, available in Sunburst finish, mfg. 1969-1975.

	N/A	$4,800	$4,100	$3,500	$3,000	$2,500	$2,000

This model was designed by luthier Roger Rossmeisel, and is very rare.

Fender Jazzmaster
courtesy George McGuire

GRADING	100% MINT	98% NEAR MINT	95% EXC+	90% EXC	80% VG+	70% VG	60% G

MARAUDER (U.S. MFG.) - offset double cutaway asymmetrical alder body, white pickguard, 3 control mounted metal plates, bolt-on maple neck, 21-fret bound rosewood fingerboard with pearl block inlay, strings through bridge with metal cover, 6-on-one-side tuners, chrome hardware, 4 pickups, volume/tone controls on lower treble bout, volume/tone controls, slide switch on upper bass bout, 4 push switches on upper treble bout, available in custom colors and Sunburst finishes, mfg. 1965-66, approx. 8 mfg.

	N/A	N/A	N/A	N/A	N/A	N/A	N/A

Extreme rarity precludes accurate pricing on this model. If and when one surfaces, the asking price could be in the $7,500 and up range. The pickups on this instrument were set under the pickguard, making the guitar appear to have no pickups. Due to unknown circumstances, this model never went into full production. There are few of these instruments to be found, and though they were featured in 1965 sales brochures, they would have to be considered prototypes. Most seasoned Fender dealers have never seen a Marauder. In the 1965-1966 catalog, the newly introduced Marauder carried a list price of $479. Compare this to the then-current list price of the Stratocaster's $281! This model had an optional standard vibrato. In 1966, the "second generation" Marauder featured 3 exposed pickups (which replaced original hidden pickups). According to Gene Fields, who was in the Fender R & D section at the time, 8 prototypes were built: 4 with regular frets and 4 with slanted frets.

Again, the Marauder was not put into full production.

From 1954-1958, some models were made with aluminum pickguards - Black and Blonde finishes were special order items. In 1956, gold hardware became an option. In 1956, an alder body replaced the original ash body. Ash wood was used on custom color models, as well as models finished in Blonde. In 1956, Fender offered custom colors in DuPont Ducco finish. Black, Dakota Red, Desert Sand, Fiesta Red, Lake Placid Blue, Olympic White and Shoreline Gold finishes became an option.

MAVERICK (U.S. MFG.) - refer to the Custom Model.

MONTEGO I (U.S. MFG.) - single round cutaway hollow figured maple body, arched bound spruce top, bound f-holes, raised black pickguard, bolt-on maple neck, 20-fret bound ebony fingerboard with pearl "diamond-in-block" inlay, adjustable ebony bridge/metal trapeze tailpiece, ebony tailpiece insert with pearl F inlay, bound peghead with pearl fan/logo inlay, 3-per-side tuners with pearl buttons, chrome hardware, covered humbucker pickup, volume/tone control, available in Natural or Sunburst finishes, mfg. 1968-1974.

	N/A	$2,200	$1,900	$1,600	$1,300	$1,000	$700

Montego II (U.S. Mfg.) - similar to Montego I, except has 2 humbucker pickups, 2 volume/2 tone controls, and 3-position switch, mfg. 1968-1974.

	N/A	$2,500	$2,200	$1,900	$1,600	$1,300	$950

MUSICLANDER/SWINGER/ARROW (U.S. MFG.) - offset double cutaway asymmetrical alder body with cutaway on bottom bout, pearloid pickguard, bolt-on maple neck, 21-fret rosewood fingerboard with pearl dot inlay, fixed bridge, pointed peghead, 6-on-one-side tuners, chrome hardware, single coil covered pickup, volume/tone control, available in White, Black, Blue, Green, or Red finishes, mfg. 1969-1972.

	N/A	$1,500	$1,250	$1,050	$900	$750	$600

Fender's Mustang model was initially offered in both the full-scale or 3/4-scale neck. While the Mustangs were in great demand, both necks were produced; but many of the 3/4-scale models were returned from the field due to lack of popularity as compared to the full-scale neck. To salvage leftover parts, Virgilio "Babe" Simoni then redesigned the headstock (which then began to resemble a spear) while another worker redesigned the body. These changes are purely cosmetic; the Musiclander model is basically a Mustang with the 3/4-scale neck and a single pickup. Simoni estimates that, all in all, perhaps 250 to 300 were built, and even some of these were renamed into the Arrow or Swinger.

MUSICMASTER (U.S. MFG.) - offset double cutaway poplar body, metal pickguard, bolt-on maple neck, 21-fret maple fingerboard with black dot inlay, fixed bridge with cover, 6-on-one-side tuners, chrome hardware, single coil covered pickup, volume/tone control, available in Blonde, custom colors and Sunburst finishes, mfg. 1956-1980.

1956-1958	N/A	$850	$750	$650	$550	$450	$350
1959-1964	N/A	$750	$650	$550	$450	$375	$300
1965-1969	N/A	$650	$575	$500	$425	$350	$275
1970-1980	N/A	$500	$425	$375	$325	$275	$225

In 1959, rosewood fingerboard with pearl dot inlay replaced maple fingerboard. In 1960, pickguard was changed to plastic: tortoiseshell or white. In 1964, Red, White, or Blue finishes were introduced and the model was offered in 24 in. scale for this year before it became the Musicmaster II. In 1965, the Musicmaster II was introduced, which was 24 in. scale. In 1969, the Musicmaster II was disc. and the regular Musicmaster was offered in 22.5 or 24 in. scales. In 1975, 24 in. scale was standard, and 22-fret fingerboard and Black or White finish was introduced. Models produced after 1975 are also available in alder or ash bodies.

Musicmaster II (U.S. Mfg.) - similar to Musicmaster, except in 24 in. scale, mfg. 1965-69.

	N/A	$605	$575	$500	$425	$350	$275

In 1969, 24-fret fingerboard replaced 21-fret fingerboard.

PERFORMER (JAP. MFG.) - offset double cutaway body, maple neck with rosewood fingerboard, arrowhead shaped headstock, string clamp, 24 frets, 6-on-a-side tuners, 1 volume/1 tone control, 3-way switch, 2 angled white pickups, 2 pivot bridge with vibrato, mfg. 1985-86.

	N/A	$850	$750	$650	$550	$450	$350

PRODIGY (U.S. MFG.) - offset double cutaway asymmetrical poplar body, black pickguard, bolt-on maple neck, 22-fret rosewood fingerboard with pearl dot inlay, standard vibrato, 6-on-one-side tuners, 2 single coil/1 humbucker exposed pickups, volume/tone controls, 5-position switch, available in Arctic White, Black, Crimson Red Metallic, or Lake Placid Blue finishes, mfg. 1991-95.

	N/A	$375	$325	$275	$225	$175	$125

Last MSR was $570.

This model is also available with maple fingerboard with black dot inlay.

STARCASTER (U.S. MFG.) - offset double cutaway asymmetrical semi-hollow maple body, bound arched top, f-holes, raised black pickguard, bolt-on maple neck, 22-fret maple fingerboard with black dot inlay, fixed bridge, 6-on-one-side tuners, chrome hardware, 2 covered humbucker pickups, master volume plus 2 volume and 2 tone controls, 3-position switch, available in Black, Blonde, Natural, Tobacco Sunburst, Walnut, or White finishes, mfg. 1976-1980.

	N/A	$1,850	$1,600	$1,400	$1,200	$1,000	$800

The Starcaster was Fender's answer to Gibson's popular ES-335, designed by Gene Fields.

GRADING	100% MINT	98% NEAR MINT	95% EXC+	90% EXC	80% VG+	70% VG	60% G

F

ELECTRIC: MUSTANG SERIES

MUSTANG (U.S. MFG.) - offset double cutaway asymmetrical ash body, pearloid or shell pickguard, bolt-on maple neck, 21- or 22-fret rosewood fingerboard with pearl dot inlay, floating bridge/vibrato with bridge cover, 6-on-one-side tuners with plastic buttons, chrome hardware, 2 single coil covered pickups, volume/tone control, 2 selector slide switches, available in Black, Blonde, Blue, Natural, Sunburst, Red, Walnut, or White finishes, mfg. 1964-1982.

1964	N/A	$1,500	$1,250	$1,050	$900	$750	$600
1965-1969	N/A	$1,250	$1,050	$850	$700	$600	$500
1970-1974	N/A	$1,000	$850	$700	$600	$500	$400
1975-1982	N/A	$800	$700	$600	$500	$400	$300

Fender offered the Mustang model in both the full-scale or a student-sized 3/4-scale neck. The Mustang model stayed popular for a number of years with the full-scale neck, but many of the 3/4-scale models were returned from dealers due to lack of acceptance (See Musiclander). As a result, the number of 3/4-scale Mustangs available in the vintage market is small. In 1969, 22-fret fingerboard became standard. In the 1970s, Black, Blonde, Natural, Sunburst and Walnut were the standard finishes. In 1975, tuner buttons became metal; black pickguard replaced original parts/design.

Competition Mustang (U.S. Mfg.) - similar to Mustang, except has Competition finishes (finishes with 3 racing stripes on front), available in Blue, Burgundy, Orange, or Red finishes, mfg. 1969-1973.

	N/A	$1,100	$950	$800	$700	$600	$500

'69 MUSTANG (JAPAN MFG. NO. 027-3700/3705) - offset double cutaway slimmed basswood body, bolt-on maple neck, 22-fret rosewood fingerboard with white dot inlay, floating bridge/Fender Dynamic vibrato, 6-on-one-side tuners, chrome hardware, tortoiseshell-style pickguard, 2 covered single coil pickups, volume/tone controls, 2 pickup selector on/off slide switches, available in Sonic Blue or Vintage White finishes, 24 in. scale, mfg. 1995-99, reintroduced 2005-present.

MSR	$900	$630	$550	$475	$425	$375	$325	$275

Mustang Left Hand (Japan Mfg. No. 027-3720) - similar to the Mustang, except in a left-handed configuration, mfg. 1995-98.

	$500	$425	$375	$325	$275	$225	$175

Last MSR was $719.

COMPETITION MUSTANG (JAP MFG. NO. 025-3700) - offset double cutaway alder body, maple neck with rosewood fingerboard, 24 in. scale, 22 frets with white dot inlays, vibrato tailpiece, 6-on-a-side tuners, chrome hardware, tortiseshell pickguard, 2 single coil covered black pickups with switches, volume/tone control, available in Lake Placid Blue and Candy Apple Red with appropriate competition stripe, mfg. 2002 only.

	$500	$425	$350	$300	$260	$220	$180

Last MSR was $700.

Fender Marauder courtesy Dave Rogers Dave's Guitar Shop

ELECTRIC: ROBBEN FORD SIGNATURE SERIES

The Robben Ford models were designed with Ford´s input and specifications, and built in the Fender Custom Shop.

ROBBEN FORD - double cutaway alder body, hollowed tone chambers, arched bound spruce top, maple neck, 22 jumbo fret bound ebony fingerboard with pearl split block inlay, Robben Ford´s signature on the truss rod cover, tune-o-matic bridge/stop tailpiece, bound peghead with pearl stylized fan/logo inlay, 3-per-side tuners with ebony buttons gold hardware, 2 exposed polepiece humbucker pickups, 2 volume/tone controls, 3-position/coil tap switches, available in Antique Burst, Autumn Gold, or Black finishes, mfg. 1989-1994.

	N/A	$1,250	$1,050	$900	$775	$650	$550

Last MSR was $1,750.

ROBBEN FORD ELITE FM (U.S. MFG. NO. 010-3040) - double cutaway mahogany body, arched figured maple top, set-in mahogany neck, 22-fret pau ferro fingerboard with abalone dot inlay, adjustable bridge/tunable tailpiece, blackface peghead with logo inlay, 3-per-side tuners, chrome hardware, 2 Seymour Duncan humbuckers, 2 volume/2 tone controls, 3-position selector, coil tap switch, active electronics, available in Three-Color Sunburst or Crimson Red Trans. finishes, mfg. 1994-2001.

$1,850	$1,625	$1,475	$1,300	$1,150	$1,000	$850

Last MSR was $2,630.

ROBBEN FORD ULTRA FM (U.S. MFG. NO. 010-3060) - similar to Robben Ford Elite, except has internal tone chambers (semi-hollow design), carved flame maple top, multibound ebony fingerboard with pearl block inlay, gold (or nickel) hardware, available in Three-Color Sunburst and Crimson Red Trans. finishes, mfg. 1994-2001.

$4,250	$3,800	$3,200	$2,800	$2,400	N/A	N/A

Last MSR was $6,030.

ROBBEN FORD ULTRA SP (U.S. MFG. NO. 010-3050) - similar to Robben Ford Elite, except has internal tone chambers (semi-hollow design), carved solid spruce top, multibound ebony fingerboard with pearl block inlay, gold hardware, available in Black, Three-Color Sunburst, or Crimson Red Trans. finishes, mfg. 1994-2001.

$4,225	$3,800	$3,200	$2,800	$2,400	N/A	N/A

Last MSR was $6,030.

Fender Musicmaster courtesy Dave Rogers Dave's Guitar Shop

GRADING	100% MINT	98% NEAR MINT	95% EXC+	90% EXC	80% VG+	70% VG	60% G

ELECTRIC: SHOWMASTER SERIES

SHOWMASTER STANDARD (U.S. MFG. NO. 010-4202) - downsized alder body, carved maple top, maple neck, 22-fret maple fingerboard with abalone dot inlay, LSR nut, Fender Deluxe tremolo, Sperzel Trim-Lok tuners, chrome hardware, 2 Custom Shop Fat '50s single coil/Seymour Duncan '59 Trembucker humbucker pickups, volume/2 tone controls, special switching, available in Black, Crimson Trans., Frost Gold, Bright Sapphire Metallic, Aged Cherry Sunburst, Bing Cherry Trans., or Cobalt Blue Trans. finishes, mfg. 1998-present.

MSR	$2,472	$1,750	$1,500	$1,300	$1,100	$900	$750	$600

This model is optional with rosewood neck with abalone dot inlays (Model 010-4200).

Showmaster with Deluxe Locking Tremolo (U.S. Mfg. No. 010-4292) - similar to the Showmaster with Deluxe Tremolo, except features a Fender Deluxe locking tremolo, available in Aged Cherry Sunburst, Bing Cherry Trans., or Cobalt Blue Trans. finishes, mfg. 1998 only.

$2,100	$1,800	$1,550	$1,300	$1,100	$900	$750

Last MSR was $2,999.

This model is optional with rosewood neck with abalone dot inlays (Model 010-4290).

SHOWMASTER CELTIC H (NO. 026-1400) - double cutaway basswood body, modified C-shaped maple neck, 24-fret rosewood fingerboard with celtic inlay, single Atomic II Humbucker pickup, S-T-B bridge, volume knob, black/chrome hardware, available in Silver finish, mfg. 2003 only.

$630	$575	$500	$450	$400	$350	$275

Last MSR was $900.

Also available with a tremolo unit (No. 026-1500).

SHOWMASTER ELITE (U.S. MFG. NO. 015-6870/6880) - Showmaster style, flame, quilt, spalted, or lacewood top, set mahogany neck, 22-fret ebony fingerboard with tribal sun inlays, 6-on-a-side tuners, 2 Seymour Duncan humbucker pickups, 5-way switch, 2 knobs, with either tremolo or hard tail bridge, available in Amber, Cherry Sunburst, or Honey Burst finishes, mfg. summer 2004-present.

MSR	$2,880	$2,050	$1,800	$1,550	$1,300	$1,100	$950	$800

Subtract $25 for Spalted Maple or Lacewood tops (Models 015-7000/7100/7200/7300).

This model is available in many different configurations and they each have a different stocking number.

SHOWMASTER FA/QB (NO. 026-3170/3180) - Showmaster style, flame ash or quilted bubinga top, set maple neck, 24-fret rosewood fingerboard with dot inlays, 3 single coil or 2 humbucker Seymour Duncan pickups, Strat-style headstock, tremolo bridge, 2 knobs, 5-way switch, chrome hardware, available in Cherry Sunburst (flame ash top) or Brown Trans. (quilt bubinga), mfg. 2004-present.

MSR	$900	$630	$550	$475	$425	$325	$275	$225

There is also a Blackout Showmaster available that features black hardware and is available in Black or Atlantic Blue Metallic finishes (MSR $900, No. 026-3000).

SHOWMASTER FMT/QMT (NO. 026-3270/3280) - Showmaster style, basswood body, flame maple or quilt maple top, set maple neck, 24-fret rosewood fingerboard with dot inlays, two humbucker Seymour Duncan pickups, Strat-style headstock, tremolo bridge, 2 knobs, 5-way switch, chrome hardware, available in Cherry Sunburst or Natural in flame maple and Tobacco Sunburst or Black Cherry Burst in quilt maple, 25.5 in. scale, new 2005.

MSR	$900	$630	$550	$475	$425	$325	$275	$225

SHOWMASTER FMT (U.S. MFG. NO. 010-4270) - similar to Showmaster except with figured maple top and Deluxe 2-point synchronized tremolo with pop-in arm, rosewood fingerboard, available in Aged Cherry Sunburst, Antique Burst, Teal Green Trans., Bing Cherry Trans., or Cobalt Blue Trans. finishes, current mfg.

MSR	$2,639	$1,850	$1,600	$1,350	$1,150	$950	$800	$650

This model is also available with a maple fingerboard (No. 010-4272).

Showmaster FMT Set Neck (U.S. Mfg. No. 010-4300) - Similar to the Showmaster FMT except has a set neck, no tremolo, same colors as Showmaster FMT, current mfg.

MSR	$2,851	$2,000	$1,700	$1,450	$1,200	$1,000	$850	$700

Add $35 for Tremolo bridge (No. 010-4390).

SHOWMASTER SCORPION HH (NO. 026-1800) - double cutaway basswood body, modified C-shaped maple neck, 24-fret rosewood fingerboard with scorpion inlay, two Atomic II Humbucker pickups, S-T-B bridge, two knobs (v, tone), 5-way switch, black/chrome hardware, available in Black finish, mfg. 2003 only.

$630	$575	$500	$450	$400	$350	$275

Last MSR was $900.

Also available with a tremolo unit (No. 026-1900).

SHOWMASTER 7-STRING HH (U.S. MFG. NO. 015-4430) - similar to Showmaster except in a 7-string configuration, rosewood fingerboard, 2 humbucker pickups, hard-tail, available in Black, Antique Burst, Teal Green Trans., Bing Cherry Trans., or Cobalt Blue Trans. finishes, disc. 2001.

$1,775	$1,550	$1,350	$1,150	$950	$850	$695

Last MSR was $2,500.

Add $150 for Teal Green Trans. and Bing Cherry Trans. finishes. Add $100 for Fender Deluxe Locking Tremolo (Model 015-4490).

FLATHEAD SHOWMASTER (U.S. MFG. NO. 015-4300) - Showmaster body style, flat alder body, contoured back and neck heel, maple neck, 22-fret ebony fingerboard with 12th fret crossed piston inlay, 2 EMG humbucker pickups, single knob, 3-way switch, black hardware, available in Light Gray, Dark Gray, Black, or Mustard finishes, mfg. 2003-current

MSR	$2,000	$1,450	$1,200	$1,050	$950	$750	$600	$500

GRADING	100% MINT	98% NEAR MINT	95% EXC+	90% EXC	80% VG+	70% VG	60% G

F

HIGHWAY 1 SHOWMASTER HH (U.S. MFG. NO. 111-1900)
- double cutaway alder body, bolt-on modified C-shaped neck, 24-fret rosewood fingerboard with dot inlay, 2 Enforcer Humbucker pickups, no pickguard, Floyd Rose double locking tremolo, special 3-way switch, two volume knobs, chrome hardware, available in Black, Pewter, or Chrome Silver finishes, mfg. 2003 only.

$799	$725	$650	$575	$500	$425	$375

Last MSR was $1,142.

Also available as the Highway 1 Showmaster HSS (No. 111-1800), which has one humbucker and two single coils.

ELECTRIC: STRATOCASTER SERIES

Leo Fender´s Stratocaster was his second guitar design after the Telecaster. The Stratocaster was designed in 1953, with actual production beginning in early 1954 (a Fender ad mentioned that "Shipments are expected to begin May 15"). The model went through a series of changes (detailed below) and various permutation through the years.

Here´s some additional dates to remember to aid in dating those late 1970s and 1980s Strat variants: Fender´s three-way selector switch was updated to the 5-way in 1977. In the mid-1970s, the "Thick Skin" high gloss all-polyester finish was introduced. After CBS sold Fender in 1985, there was no production of Fender guitars in the U.S. from February, 1985 to October, 1985. When the Corona plant was started up, only the Vintage Reissue Stratocaster models were produced between late 1985 and 1986.

Finally, the Fender-Lace Sensor was introduced in early 1987. The Lace Sensor was offered in 4 models: the Gold (classic late ´50s sound), Silver (more mid-range punch), Blue (a late ´50s humbucker sort of sound), and Red (a high output humbucker-ish sound). A "Dually" was created when two Lace Sensors were placed side-by-side, looking like a humbucker but were actually two independent pickups.

For further detailing of the history of the Stratocaster, see A.R. Duchossoir´s book *The Fender Stratocaster*, a fact-filled overview of the Stratocaster from 1953 to 1993.

Stratocaster: Standard (1954-1985 Mfg.)

This series has an offset double cutaway body, bolt-on maple neck, 6-on-a-side tuners, 3 single coil pickups (unless otherwise listed).

Fender Showmaster Elite courtesy Fender

STRATOCASTER (PRE-CBS, MFG. 1954-1959)
- ash body, single-ply white pickguard, 4-screw bolt-on maple neck, 21-fret maple fingerboard with black dot inlay, nickel-plated Kluson tuners, strings through bridge, nickel hardware, 3 single coil exposed pickups, 1 volume/2 tone controls, 3-position switch, available in 3-Tone Sunburst nitro-cellulose lacquer finish, mfg. 1954-59.

1954	N/A	$40,000	$35,000	$30,000	$26,000	$23,000	$20,000
1955	N/A	$35,000	$30,000	$25,000	$21,000	$18,000	$15,000
1956	N/A	$32,000	$27,000	$22,000	$19,000	$16,000	$13,000
1957	N/A	$30,000	$25,000	$20,000	$16,000	$13,000	$10,000
1958	N/A	$25,000	$20,000	$17,000	$14,000	$11,000	$8,000
1959	N/A	$20,000	$15,000	$13,000	$11,000	$9,000	$7,500

Add $10,000 for Blonde/Mary Kaye Blonde finish. Add $10,000 for custom colors.

During 1954, the standard vibrato back cover had round string holes. During 1955, the standard vibrato back cover had oval string holes.

From 1954-1958, some models were made with aluminum pickguards - Black and Blonde finishes were special order items. In 1956, gold hardware became an option. In 1956, an alder body replaced the original ash body. Ash wood was used on custom color models, as well as models finished in Blonde. In 1956, Fender offered custom colors in DuPont Ducco finish. Black, Dakota Red, Desert Sand, Fiesta Red, Lake Placid Blue, Olympic White and Shoreline Gold finishes became an option.

In 1957, Fender offered a "deluxe" version with 14 karat gold-plated parts and Blonde (a creamy off-white) finish. This model is unofficially nicknamed the "Mary Kaye" model, due to entertainer Mary Kaye posing with the deluxe model in the 1957 catalog supplement. While Blonde was a standard finish for Telecaster models, it was a custom finish for Stratocasters in the early years. In 1959, 3-layer pickguard replaced original parts/design, rosewood fingerboard became an option.

STRATOCASTER WITH ROSEWOOD FINGERBOARD (PRE-CBS, MFG. 1959-1964)
- similar to Stratocaster, except has rosewood fingerboard with pearl dot inlay, 3-ply white pickguard, mfg. 1959-1964.

1959	N/A	$20,000	$16,000	$13,000	$11,000	$9,000	$7,000
1960	N/A	$20,000	$16,000	$13,000	$11,000	$9,000	$7,000
1961	N/A	$18,000	$14,500	$12,000	$10,000	$8,000	$6,500
1962	N/A	$17,000	$13,500	$11,000	$9,000	$7,500	$6,000
1963	N/A	$15,000	$12,500	$10,500	$8,500	$7,000	$5,500
1964	N/A	$15,000	$12,500	$10,500	$8,500	$7,000	$5,500

Add $8,000 - $10,000 for custom colors.

In 1960, some models were issued with tortoiseshell pickguards, but this was not a standard practice, and Burgundy Mist, Candy Apple Red, Daphne Blue, Foam Green, Inca Silver, Shell Pink, Sonic Blue and Surf Green finishes became an option. In July, 1962, rosewood veneer fingerboard replaced original parts/design.

1954 Fender Stratocaster courtesy Dave Rogers Dave's Guitar Shop

GRADING	100% MINT	98% NEAR MINT	95% EXC+	90% EXC	80% VG+	70% VG	60% G

STRATOCASTER W/O TILTED NECK (CBS MFG. 1965-1971) - similar to Stratocaster, except has smaller body contours,
large headstock, rosewood fingerboard with pearl dot inlay, mfg. 1965-1971.

1965	N/A	$12,000	$9,500	$7,500	$6,000	$5,000	$4,000
1966	N/A	$10,000	$7,500	$5,500	$4,500	$3,800	$3,000
1967	N/A	$10,000	$7,500	$5,500	$4,500	$3,800	$3,000
1968	N/A	$10,000	$7,500	$5,500	$4,500	$3,800	$3,000
1969	N/A	$12,000	$9,500	$7,500	$6,000	$5,000	$4,000
1970	N/A	$8,000	$6,000	$4,800	$3,800	$3,000	$2,500
1971	N/A	$6,000	$4,500	$3,500	$2,900	$2,300	$1,600

Add $2,500 - $5,000 for custom colors.

The 1969 Model Stratocaster is worth more than earlier models because of the Jimi Hendrix model, which was a 1969.

"CBS Mfg." notation refers to the sale of Fender Electric Instruments Company to the CBS Broadcasting Co. in January, 1965. In 1965, Blue Ice, Charcoal Frost, Firemist Gold, Firemist Silver, Ocean Turquoise and Teal Green finishes became options. In December of 1965, enlarged peghead became standard. In 1967, the maple fingerboard became an option (the one-piece maple neck was optional after 1970). The Stratocaster was also available with a bound fingerboard from roughly 1965 to 1968, but most examples found today are fairly rare.

In 1967, Fender chrome-plated tuning keys (F stamped) replaced the original nickel-plated Kluson tuners. In 1968, Polyester finish replaced the original nitro-cellulose finish. In 1970, Blonde, Black, Candy Apple Red, Firemist Gold, Firemist Silver, Lake Placid Blue, Ocean Turquoise, Olympic White, and Sonic Blue finishes became options.

STRATOCASTER WITH TILTED NECK AND BULLET HEADSTOCK (CBS MFG. 1971-1980) - similar to Stratocaster, except has alder or ash body, 3-bolt neck plate with neck adjustment ("Tilt Neck"), large peghead with truss rod adjustment, black logo, maple fingerboard with black dot or rosewood fingerboard with pearl dot inlay, gloss polyester finish, mfg. 1971-1980.

1972	N/A	$3,500	$2,700	$2,300	$1,900	$1,700	$1,500
1973	N/A	$3,000	$2,500	$2,100	$1,750	$1,550	$1,350
1974	N/A	$2,500	$2,100	$1,800	$1,500	$1,300	$1,100
1975	N/A	$2,000	$1,700	$1,400	$1,200	$1,000	$800
1976	N/A	$1,800	$1,500	$1,250	$1,050	$850	$750
1977	N/A	$1,650	$1,400	$1,200	$1,000	$800	$650
1978-1980	N/A	$1,500	$1,300	$1,100	$950	$800	$650

During Leo Fender's five-year consultant contract with CBS/Fender, he developed a neck adjustment system in 1970 that corrected the pitch of the neck in the neck pocket with a micro adjustment in the neckplate (rather than the old-fashioned method of using shims). This device, along with the 3-bolt neck plate, were installed on Stratocasters beginning in mid-1971. In 1972, Natural finish became a standard item. Ash bodies became more predominent in guitar production. In late 1974, flush polepieces replaced staggered polepieces in the pickups. In 1975, pickups were installed that had flat pole pieces along the bobbin top. A 3-ply black pickguard became available. In 1977, the 5-way selector switch replaced the 3-way switch. In 1980, the Fender X-1 lead pickup (hotter output) replaced original parts/design.

STANDARD STRATOCASTER ("SMITH STRAT," CBS MFG., 1981-83) - alder body, 21-fret maple fingerboard with black dot or rosewood fingerboard with pearl dot inlay, 4-bolt neckplate, small peghead with black logo, vibrato tailpiece, 3-ply white pickguard, chrome hardware, 3 single coil exposed pickups, volume/2 tone control, 3-position switch, polyurethane finishes, mfg. 1981-83.

	N/A	$1,050	$900	$775	$675	$575	$475

Last MSR was $895.

In 1981, Fender hired Dan Smith as Director of Marketing. Smith revised the Standard Stratocaster back to the 4-bolt neckplate, and returned to the smaller (pre-CBS) style headstock.

STANDARD STRATOCASTER (CBS MFG. 1983-85) - alder body, 21-fret maple fingerboard with black dot or rosewood fingerboard with pearl dot inlay, 4-bolt neckplate, small peghead with silver logo, chrome-plated die-cast tuners, "Freeflyte" vibrato tailpiece, single-ply white pickguard, chrome hardware, 3 single coil exposed pickups, volume/tone control, 3-position switch, available in Black, Brown Sunburst, Ivory, or Sienna Sunburst polyurethane finishes, mfg. 1983-85.

	N/A	$850	$700	$600	$500	$425	$350

Last MSR was $699.

This model also featured a vibrato system that was surface mounted and without a vibrato back cavity. The cord receptor was mounted through the pickguard at a right angle.

MARBLE FINISH STANDARD STRATOCASTER ("BOWLING BALL" STRAT) - similar to the Standard Stratocaster (mfg. 1983-1984), except featured a novel swirled finish, mfg. 1984 only.

	N/A	$3,000	$2,500	$2,100	$1,700	$1,400	$1,100

Last MSR was $799.

Approximately 225 of these instruments were produced. The unique finish is the result of dipping the (white) primer coated bodies into an oil-based finish that floated on water. After dipping, the guitar received a top coat of polyurethane. Fender produced three dominant colors. The Red finish had black and white swirled in (sometimes resulting in gray areas as well). The Blue finish was mixed with yellow and black, and the Yellow finish was combined with white and silver (sometimes resulting in gold patches).

Stratocaster: American Standard Series (1986-2000 Mfg.)

AMERICAN STANDARD STRATOCASTER (U.S. MFG. NO. 010-7402) - alder body, 22-fret maple fingerboard with black dot inlay, 4-bolt neck plate, chrome-plated die-cast tuners, standard vibrato with 2 pivot point design, chrome hardware, 3-ply white pickguard, 3 single coil exposed polepiece pickups, 5-position switch, available in Arctic White, Black, Brown Sunburst, Caribbean Mist, Lipstick Red, Midnight Blue, or Midnight Wine polyurethane finishes, mfg. late 1986-2000.

1986-89	N/A	$850	$750	$675	$600	$525	$450
1990-97	N/A	$800	$700	$600	$525	$450	$375
1998-2000	$700	$600	$525	$475	$425	$350	$325

Last MSR was $999.

GRADING	100% MINT	98% NEAR MINT	95% EXC+	90% EXC	80% VG+	70% VG	60% G

Add $100 for Natural Ash finish (1998-2000).

This model is also available with rosewood fingerboard with pearl dot inlay (Model 010-7400). In 1997, Candy Apple Red, Inca Silver, Sonic Blue, and Vintage White finishes were introduced; Arctic White, Caribbean Mist, Lipstick Red, Midnight Blue and Midnight Wine finishes were discontinued. In 1998, the DeltaTone system (high output bridge pickup and special "no-load" tone control) electronics was introduced; 3-Color Sunburst, Lake Placid Blue, and Olympic White finishes were introduced; Sonic Blue and Vintage White finishes were discontinued.

American Standard Stratocaster Hard Tail (U.S. Mfg. No. 010-7432) - similar to the American Standard Stratocaster, except features a fixed bridge/strings through-body (w/ ferrules), available in 3-Color Sunburst, Black, Candy Apple Red, Inca Silver, Lake Placid Blue, or Olympic White finishes, mfg. 1998-2000.

	$725	$625	$550	$450	$375	$300	$225

Last MSR was $999.

Add $100 for Natural Ash finish (1998 to 2000).

This model is also available with rosewood fingerboard with pearl dot inlay (Model 010-7430).

American Standard Stratocaster Left Hand (U.S. Mfg. No. 010-7422) - similar to the American Standard Stratocaster, except in a left-handed configuration, available in Black, Brown Sunburst, Candy Apple Red, or Vintage White finishes, disc. 2000.

	$775	$650	$575	$500	$425	$350	$275

Last MSR was $1,099.

This model is also available with rosewood fingerboard with pearl dot inlay (Model 010-7420). In 1998, 3-Color Sunburst and Olympic White finishes were introduced and Brown Sunburst and Vintage White finishes were discontinued.

Deluxe American Standard Stratocaster (U.S. Mfg.) - similar to the American Standard Stratocaster, except features 3 Gold Lace Sensor pickups, mfg. 1989-1990.

	N/A	$900	$775	$650	$525	$450	$375

Last MSR was $799.

This model was also available with rosewood fingerboard with pearl dot inlay.

American Standard Stratocaster Aluminum Body (U.S. Mfg.) - similar to American Standard Stratocaster, except has a hollow aluminum body, available in Blue Marble, Purple Marble, or Red/Silver/Blue Flag graphic anodized finish, mfg. 1994 only.

	N/A	$1,800	$1,550	$1,300	$1,100	$900	$700

It is estimated that only 400 instruments were produced.

AMERICAN STANDARD STRATOCASTER GR ROLAND READY (U.S. MFG., NO. 010-7462)
- similar to American Standard Stratocaster, except has a Roland GK-2A synth driver mounted behind bridge pickup, 3 synth control knobs, available in Black, Brown Sunburst, Candy Apple Red, or Vintage White finishes, mfg. 1995-98.

	$800	$725	$650	$575	$500	$425	$350

Last MSR was $1,299.

1965 Fender Stratocaster courtesy Dave Rogers Dave's Guitar Shop

This model was also available with rosewood fingerboard with pearl dot inlay (Model 010-7460). This model is built pre-wired to drive the Roland GR series guitar synthesizer, as well as perform like a Stratocaster. Roland's GK-2A pickup system can interface with Roland's GR-1, GR-09, and GR-50 synthesizers; as well as the VG-8 guitar system and GI-10 guitar/MIDI interface.

Stratocaster: American Series (2001-Current Mfg.)

AMERICAN SERIES STRATOCASTER (U.S. MFG., NO. 011-7400) - ash or alder body, rosewood fingerboard with dot position markers, hand-rolled fingerboard edges, 3 custom staggered single coil pickups, 5-way switch, two-point synchronized tremolo, staggered tuners, 22 Medium-Jumbo frets, 1 Volume/2 tone controls, currently available in 3-Color Sunburst, Hot Rod Red, black, Olympic White, Chrome Red, Chrome Blue, Butterscotch Blonde, or Sky Blue finishes, case included, mfg. 2001-present.

MSR	$1,328		$930	$825	$725	$650	$575	$500	$425

Add $25 for 3-Color Sunburst finish. Add $75 for 2-Color Sunburst, White Blonde, and Natural finishes (disc.).

Natural, Aqua Marine Metallic, 2-Color Sunburst, and White Blonde finishes were discontinued in 2002. Olympic White, Chrome Red, Chrome Blue, and Sky Blue finishes were introduced in 2002. Butterscotch Blonde new 2003. Also available with maple neck (Model 011-7402). Also available in Hard Tail Model (no tremolo unit) with rosewood fingerboard (Model 011-7430) and Hard Tail Model with maple neck (Model 011-7432). The Hard Tail models are only available in 3-Color Sunburst, Olympic White, Black, or Chrome Red finishes.

American Series Stratocaster Left Hand (U.S. Mfg., No. 011-7420) - similar to the American Strat except in left-hand configuration, currently available in 3-Color Sunburst, Olympic White, Black, and Chrome Red finishes, mfg. 2001-present.

MSR	$1,328		$930	$825	$725	$650	$575	$500	$425

This model is also available with a maple neck (No. 011-7422).

1972 Fender Stratocaster courtesy John Beeson The Music Shoppe

GRADING	100% MINT	98% NEAR MINT	95% EXC+	90% EXC	80% VG+	70% VG	60% G

American Series Stratocaster HSS/HH (U.S. Mfg., No. 011-7000/7100) - similar to the American Strat except has HSS or HH pickup configuration, S-1 switching, available in 3-Color Sunburst, Olympic White, Black, Chrome Silver, Chrome Blue, Butterscotch Blonde, Sienna Sunburst, or Chrome Red finishes, mfg. 2003-present.

	MSR	$1,357	$950	$850	$750	$675	$600	$525	$450

The American Strat HSS is avaiable with a maple neck (No. 011-7002). The American Strat HH is available with a hard tail bridge (No. 011-7130).

Stratocaster: American Deluxe Series

This series represents the ultimate in high performance, classically contoured solid "Tone-Wood" bodies with distinctive neck shapes.

Add $100 for Natural, White Blonde, and Purple Transparent finishes.

AMERICAN DELUXE STRATOCASTER (U.S. MFG., NO. 010-1000) - premium alder or ash body, one-piece maple neck, rosewwod fingerboard, 25.5 in. scale, Bi-Flex truss rod, Micro-Tilt neck adjustment, Fender Deluxe locking tuners, 22 medium-jumbo frets, Fender Vintage Noiseless pickups, 5-way switch, Deluxe 2-point synchronized tremolo, Schaller Straplock ready, available in 3-Color Sunburst, Chrome Red, Candy Tangerine, Aged Cherry Burst, Natural, Purple Trans., White Blonde, Crimson Trans., Black, or Teal Green Trans. finishes, disc. 2004.

			$1,125	$950	$895	$850	$795	$750	$650

Last MSR was $1,600.

Also available with maple neck (Model 010-1002). Purple Trans. finish was disc. in 2001.

American Deluxe Stratocaster Left-Hand (U.S. Mfg., 010-1020) - Similar to the American Deluxe Stratocaster except in left-hand configuration, available in Three-Color Sunburst, White Blonde, Black, Chrome Red, Aged Cherry Sunburst, or Crimson Trans. finishes, disc. 2004.

			$1,150	$975	$900	$850	$795	$750	$650

Last MSR was $1,650.

Also available with maple neck (No. 010-1022). White Blonde finish was disc. in 2002.

AMERICAN DELUXE FAT STRAT HSS (U.S. MFG., NO. 010-1100) - similar to American Deluxe Stratocaster, except has Fender DH-1 Humbucker in the bridge position. The two single coil pickups are wound extra hot for proper balance with the DH-1 Humbucker, LSR roller nut, rosewood fingerboard, available in the same colors as the American Deluxe Stratocaster, disc. 2004.

			$1,125	$975	$900	$850	$795	$750	$650

Last MSR was $1,600.

Also available with maple fingerboard (Model 010-1102).

American Deluxe Fat Strat HSS With Locking Tremolo (U.S. Mfg., No. 010-1190) - Similar to American Deluxe Fat Stratocaster HSS, except has a deluxe locking tremolo unit, disc. 2004.

			$1,200	$1,050	$950	$875	$825	$775	$675

Last MSR was $1,700.

Also available with maple fingerboard (Model 010-1192).

AMERICAN DELUXE STRATOCASTER (U.S. MFG. NO. 010-1200) - select alder body, maple C-shape neck, 22-fret rosewood fingerboard with dot inlay, 3 single coil Noiseless pickups, various pickguards, 3 knobs, 5-way switch, S-1 switching, Deluxe tremolo, chrome hardware, available in 3-Color Sunburst, Amber, Montego Black, Candy Tangerine, or Chrome Silver, mfg. 2004-present.

	MSR	$1,500	$1,050	$925	$825	$700	$625	$550	$475

Add $50 for Deluxe Locking Tremolo (No. 010-1590/1592).

Also available with a maple fingerboard (No. 010-1202). Also available with a HSS pickup configuration (No. 010-1500/1502). Also available in left-handed configuration (No. 010-1220/1222, 3-Color Sunburst, Chrome Silver, or Montego Black finishes only). Also available in a V-Shape neck (No. 010-1302, 3-Color Sunburst, Black, Candy Apple Red, or Honey Blonde finishes only). All Deluxe models have different colored pickguards for various finishes. This model replaces the American Deluxe Stratocaster that was disc. in late 2003/early 2004.

American Deluxe Strat Ash (No. 010-1400) - similar to the American Deluxe Stratocaster, except has a premium ash body, available in Aged Cherry Burst, Butterscotch Blonde, or Tobacco Sunburst finishes, mfg. 2004-present.

	MSR	$1,657	$1,175	$1,050	$900	$800	$700	$600	$500

Also available with maple neck (No. 010-1402). Also available in left-handed configuration (No. 010-1420/1422).

American Deluxe Strat FMT/QMT HSS (No. 010-1570/1580) - similar to the American Deluxe Stratocaster, except has a flamed or quilted maple top, rosewood fingerboard, and HSS pickup configuration, available in Tobacco Sunburst, Bing Cherry Trans., Cobalt Blue Trans., or Amber finishes, new 2004.

	MSR	$1,800	$1,300	$1,150	$1,025	$900	$800	$700	$600

AMERICAN DELUXE 50th ANNIVERSARY STRATOCASTER (NO. 011-2004) - select alder body, maple C-shape neck, 22-fret maple fingerboard with abalone dot inlays, single ply white pickguard, 3 Noiseless single coil pickups, 3 knobs, 5-way switch, S-1 switching, deluxe tremolo, 50th Anniversary logo on pickguard and neckplate, gold hardware, available in 2-Color Sunburst, mfg. 2004 only.

			$1,250	$1,050	$900	$775	$650	$550	$450

Last MSR was $1,714.

Stratocaster: Anniversary Series

Anniversay Stratocaster models celebrate the introduction of the Stratocaster model in 1954.

25th ANNIVERSARY STRATOCASTER (U.S. MFG.) - alder body, black pickguard, black Anniversary logo on bass bout, 21-fret maple fingerboard with black dot inlay, Sperzel tuners, 4-bolt neckplate with "1954 - 1979 25th Anniversary" logo, standard vibrato, chrome hardware, 3 single coil pickups, volume/2 tone controls, 5-position switch, available in Metallic Silver finish, mfg. 1979-1980.

		N/A	$1,350	$1,100	$950	$800	$650	$500

Last MSR was $800.

Approximately 10,000 of these instruments were produced. List price included a hardshell case. Anniversary Stratocaster 6-digit serial numbers begin with a 25. Early models (estimated to be around 500) of this series were finished in a Pearl White finish, which checked and cracked very badly. Most models were returned to the factory to be refinished.

GRADING	100% MINT	98% NEAR MINT	95% EXC+	90% EXC	80% VG+	70% VG	60% G

35th ANNIVERSARY STRATOCASTER (U.S. MFG.)
- quilted maple top/alder body, white pickguard, bird's-eye maple neck, 22-fret ebony fingerboard with abalone dot inlay, standard vibrato, locking tuners, chrome hardware, 3 single coil Silver Fender Lace Sensors, 5-position selector/mini switches, active electronics, available in 3-Tone Sunburst finish, mfg. 1989-1991.

	N/A	$2,500	$2,100	$1,800	$1,500	$1,200	$900

This model was a Custom Shop Limited Edition, based in part on the Strat Plus model. Only 500 instruments were made.

40th ANNIVERSARY STRATOCASTER (U.S. MFG.)
- bolt-on maple neck, 3 single coil pickups, volume/tone controls, 5-way switch, stamped neckplate with serial number (# out of 1,954), mfg. 1994 only.

	N/A	$1,600	$1,350	$1,150	$1,000	$850	$700

Last MSR was $1,800.

Fender supposedly produced 1,954 of the American Standard edition 40th Anniversary Stratocasters.

40th Anniversary Stratocaster (Fender Diamond Dealer Edition U.S. Mfg.)
- ash body, flamed maple top, bolt-on bird's-eye maple neck, fancy fingerboard inlay with "1954 - 1994" at 12th fret, gold hardware, gold pickguard, 3 single coil pickups, 5-position switch, mfg. 1994 only.

	N/A	$5,000	$4,000	$3,300	$2,500	N/A	N/A

Last MSR was $6,999.

This model was equipped with a tweed gig bag and flight case. It is estimated that Fender only produced 50 of the Diamond Dealer edition 40th Anniversary Stratocasters.

50th ANNIVERSARY AMERICAN STRATOCASTER (NO. 010-2004)
- ash body, maple C-shape neck, 22-fret maple fingerboard with abalone dot inlays, single-ply white pickguard, 3 Custom Shop Vintage 1954 Strat single coil pickups, 3 knobs, 5-way switch, American 2 point tremolo, 50th Anniversary logo on neckplate, chrome hardware, available in 2-Color Sunburst, mfg. 2004 only.

	$1,100	$975	$875	$800	$725	$650	$575

Last MSR was $1,500.

FENDER'S 50th ANNIVERSARY MODEL STRATOCASTER (U.S. MFG.)
- flame maple top, 3 Vintage Style pickups, gold 50th Anniversary coin on back of headstock, mfg. 1996 only.

	N/A	$1,200	$1,050	$900	$800	$700	$600

Last MSR was $1,299.

Only 2,500 instruments were produced.

Fender American Deluxe Stratocaster courtesy Fender

Stratocaster: American Special Series

JIMI HENDRIX VOODOO STRATOCASTER (U.S. MFG. NO. 010-6602)
- right-handed alder body, (left-handed) bolt-on maple neck, 25.5 in. scale, 21-fret maple fingerboard with black dot inlay, vintage-style tremolo, Fender/Schaller vintage F tuners, chrome hardware, white pickguard, 3 Vintage Strat single coil pickups, volume/2 tone controls, VooDoo Strat engraved neckplate, available in 3-Color Sunburst, Black, or Olympic White finishes, mfg. 1998-99.

	$1,250	$1,100	$950	$800	$700	$600	$500

Last MSR was $1,349.

This model is available with a rosewood fingerboard (Model 010-6600).

'68 REVERSE STRATOCASTER SPECIAL (U.S. MFG. NO. 011-6602)
- similar to Jimi Hendrix model, available in Three-Color Sunburst, Olympic White, or black, mfg. 2001-02.

	$1,150	$1,100	$950	$800	$700	$600	$500

Last MSR was $1,428.

Add $35 for 3-color Sunburst.

SUB-SONIC STRATOCASTER HSS (U.S. MFG. NO. 011-4530)
- alder body, 27 in. scale, rosewood fingerboard, tuned B-E-A-D-G-B, string through body, hardtail bridge, 1 humbucker pickup and 2 single coil pickups, deluxe die-cast sealed tuners, 22 medium-jumbo frets, 1 volume/2 tone controls, Special 5-Way switch, available in 3-Color Sunburst, Black, Hot Rod Red, or Aqua Marine Metallic finishes, mfg. 2001 only.

	$1,000	$850	$750	$675	$600	$525	$450

Last MSR was $1,430.

Add $35 for 3-Color Sunburst finish.

Also available with maple fingerboard (Model 011-4532). Also available with 2 humbucker pickups and rosewood fingerboard, Sub-Sonic Stratocaster HH (Model 015-4630) and with 2 humbucker pickups and maple fingerboard (Model 015-4632). The Sub-Sonic is meant to sound like the seven-string guitars with the feel of a six-string. The high E string is eliminated. This model was previously only available from the custom shop.

STRAT-O-SONIC DOVE I (NO. 011-4600)
- Stratocaster style Honduran Mahogany body with five tone chambers, maple C-shaped neck, 22-fret rosewood fingerboard with dot inlay, black pickguard, 6-on-a-side tuners, black headstock, single DE-9000 Black Dove pickup, two knobs, Tech-Tonic™ bridge, chrome hardware, available in Brown Sunburst, Crimson Trans., or Butterscotch Blonde, mfg. 2003-04.

	$980	$875	$750	$650	$575	$500	$425

Last MSR was $1,400.

Strat-o-Sonic Dove II
- similar to the Strat-o-Sonic Dove I except has two pickups and a 3-way switch, mfg. 2003-present.

MSR	$1,571		$1,100	$950	$800	$700	$625	$550	$475

Fender Strat-O-Sonic Dove II courtesy Fender

GRADING	100% MINT	98% NEAR MINT	95% EXC+	90% EXC	80% VG+	70% VG	60% G

Stratocaster: California Series

The California Strat series was introduced in 1997. The production of this model is a joint effort between Fender's U.S. and Mexican plants.

CALIFORNIA STRAT (U.S. MFG. NO. 010-1402) - alder body, tinted maple neck, 21-fret maple fingerboard with black dot inlay, vintage-style tremolo, chrome hardware, white pickguard, 3 Tex-Mex Trio single coil pickups, volume/2 tone controls, available in Black, Brown Sunburst, Candy Apple Red, Fiesta Red, or Vintage White finishes, mfg. 1997-99.

$600	$525	$450	$375	$300	$250	$200

Last MSR was $799.

This model is also available with a rosewood fingerboard and white dot inlay (Model 010-1400).

California Fat Strat (U.S. Mfg. No. 010-1502) - similar to the California Strat, except has 2 single coil/humbucker pickups, mfg. 1997-99.

$650	$575	$500	$425	$350	$275	$225

Last MSR was $849.

This model is also available with a rosewood fingerboard and white dot inlay (Model 010-1500).

Stratocaster: Classic Series

The Classic Series is very similar to the California Series.

'50s STRATOCASTER (MEX. MFG., NO. 013-1002) - poplar or alder body, '50s style "V" neck, 21-fret maple fingerboard with black dot inlay, synchronized tremolo bridge, chrome hardware, white pickguard, 3 single coil pickups, 3 knobs (v, 2 tones), available in Black, Dakota Red, Fiesta Red, 2-Color Sunburst, Daphne Blue, Surf Green, Shoreline Gold, or Olympic White, gig bag included, current mfg.

MSR	$900		$630	$525	$475	$425	$375	$325	$275

Add $35 for 2-Color Sunburst finish.

In 2001, Surf Green finish was introduced.

'60s STRATOCASTER (MEX. MFG., NO. 013-1000) - poplar or alder body, '60s style "C" neck, 21-fret rosewood fingerboard with white dot inlay, synchronized tremolo bridge, chrome hardware, white pickguard, 3 single coil pickups, 3 knobs (v, 2 tones), available in Black, Candy Apple Red, Inca Silver, Lake Placid Blue, 3-Color Sunburst, Shell Pink, Burgundy Mist, or Olympic White, gig bag included, current mfg.

MSR	$900		$630	$525	$475	$425	$375	$325	$275

Add $35 for 3-Color Sunburst finish.

In 2001, Lake Placid Blue finish was introduced.

'70s STRATOCASTER (MEX. MFG., NO. 013-7000) - ash body, "U"-shaped neck, large headstock, bullet truss rod, solid ash body, one-piece maple neck, rosewood neck and fingerboard, 25.5 in. scale, Schaller vintage F tuners, 21 frets, 3 vintage strat pickups, 1 volume control, 2 tone controls, 5-way switch, synchronized tremolo, available in 3-Color Sunburst, Olympic White, black, or Natural finishes, gig bag included, current mfg.

MSR	$957		$675	$575	$500	$450	$400	$350	$300

This model is also available with a maple neck and fingerboard (Model 013-7002).

50th ANNIVERSARY GOLDEN STRATOCASTER (NO. 013-2004) - alder body, maple neck, 21-fret maple fingerboard with black dot inlays, 3 single coil vintage style pickups, gold pickguard, gold plated hardware, available in Aztec Gold finish, mfg. 2004 only.

$700	$625	$550	$475	$400	$350	$300

Last MSR was $1,000.

Stratocaster: Collectibles Series

Earlier models of the '50s Stratocaster and '60s Stratocaster featured Fender's Foto-Flame finish, which simulated the look of a 'flame' top (i.e., heavily figured maple). Current versions now strive to be a vintage replica. This series has offset double cutaway basswood body, white pickguard, bolt-on maple neck, 21-fret fingerboard, standard vibrato, 6-on-one-side tuners, nickel hardware, 3 single coil pickups, volume/2 tone controls with aged knobs, and 5-position switch (unless otherwise listed).

'50s STRATOCASTER (JAPAN MFG. NO. 027-1002) - maple fingerboard with black dot inlay, available in 2-Tone Sunburst, Black, Candy Apple Red, Olympic White, Shell Pink, or Sonic Blue finishes, mfg. 1992-98.

$450	$375	$325	$275	$225	$195	$150

Last MSR was $599.

Earlier models may have a stop tailpiece. Blue and Crimson Foto Flame finishes were discontinued in 1995.

'50s Stratocaster Left Handed (Japan Mfg. No. 027-1022) - similar to '50s Stratocaster, except in a left-handed configuration, available in 2-Tone Sunburst finish, disc. 1998.

$475	$400	$350	$300	$250	$210	$160

Last MSR was $669.

'60s STRATOCASTER (JAPAN MFG. NO. 027-1000) - rosewood fingerboard with pearl dot inlay, available in 3-Tone Sunburst, Black, Blue Foto Flame, Candy Apple Red, Crimson Foto Flame, Olympic White, Shell Pink, or Sonic Blue finishes, mfg. 1992-98.

$450	$375	$325	$275	$225	$195	$150

Last MSR was $599.

In 1995, Blue and Crimson Foto Flame finishes were discontinued.

'60s Stratocaster Left-Hand (Jap. Mfg. No. 027-1020) - similar to the '60s Stratocaster, except in a left-handed configuration, available in 3-Tone Sunburst finish, disc. 1998.

$475	$400	$350	$300	$250	$210	$160

Last MSR was $669.

GRADING	100% MINT	98% NEAR MINT	95% EXC+	90% EXC	80% VG+	70% VG	60% G

'60s Strat Natural - similar to '60s Stratocaster, except had an alder body, basswood top, available in Natural Foto-Flame finish, mfg. 1994-95.

	N/A	$500	$475	$350	$300	$250	$200

Last MSR was $790.

'68 STRATOCASTER (JAPAN MFG., NO. 027-9202) - ash body, 21-fret maple fingerboard with black dot inlay, oversized (mid '60s) headstock, available in 3-Tone Sunburst, Natural, or Vintage White finishes, disc. 1999.

	$500	$425	$375	$325	$275	$225	$175

Last MSR was $699.

'68 Stratocaster Left Hand (Japan Mfg., No. 027-9222) - similar to the '68 Stratocaster, except in a left-handed configuration, disc. 1998.

	$525	$450	$375	$325	$295	$250	$195

Last MSR was $749.

FOTO FLAME STRATOCASTER (JAPAN MFG.) - alder body with basswood top and Foto Flame finish, rosewood fingerboard with pearl dot inlay, white shell pickguard, available in Aged Cherry Sunburst, Autumn Burst, Natural, or Tri-Color Transparent, disc. 1995.

	$500	$425	$350	$300	$275	$250	$195

Last MSR was $799.

Fender '50s Stratocaster (Classic Series) courtesy Fender

Stratocaster: Custom Shop

Prior to the formation of the Custom Shop, the Research and Development section used to construct custom guitars requested by artists. In 1987, Fender brought in Michael Stevens and John Page to start what was envisioned as a boutique lutherie shop - building an estimated 5 or 6 guitars a month. When work orders for the first opening month almost totaled 600, the operation was expanded, and more master builders were added to the Custom Shop. Michael Stevens later left the Custom Shop in the Fall of 1990.

The Custom Shop quickly began a liaison between artists requesting specific building ideas and Fender´s production models. Page eventually became manager of both the Custom Shop and the R & D area, and some model ideas/designs that started on custom pieces eventually worked their way into regular production pieces.

In addition to the custom guitars and Limited Edition runs, the Custom Shop also produces a number of models in smaller production runs. The following models have a Stratocaster offset double cutaway body, bolt-on neck, 6-on-a-side headstock, three single coil pickups, and volume/2 tone controls (unless otherwise specified).

'57 LEFT-HAND STRATOCASTER (U.S. MFG. NO. 010-5722) - alder body, white pickguard, 21-fret maple fingerboard with black dot inlay, vintage-style tremolo, chrome hardware, 3 Texas Special single coil pickups, 3-position switch, available in Black or Olympic White finishes, disc. 1998.

	$1,750	$1,525	$1,350	$1,200	$1,050	$850	$650

Last MSR was $2,499.

'62 Left-Hand Stratocaster (U.S. Mfg. No. 010-6220) - similar to '57 Left-Hand Stratocaster, except has rosewood fingerboard, aged pickguard/knobs, available in Black or Olympic White finishes, disc. 1998.

	$1,750	$1,550	$1,350	$1,200	$1,000	$850	$650

Last MSR was $2,499.

'58 STRATOCASTER (U.S. MFG. NO. 010-0802) - ash body, 21-fret maple neck with black dot inlays, vintage-style tremolo, 3 Fat '50s single coil pickups, aged pickguard/knobs, available in 3-Tone Sunburst, Black, or Blonde finishes, disc. 1998.

	N/A	$1,750	$1,500	$1,300	$1,100	$900	$700

Last MSR was $2,299.

This model was available with gold hardware (Model 010-0812).

CARVED TOP STRATOCASTER (U.S. MFG. NO. 010-9700) - ash body, carved figured maple top, figured maple neck, rosewood fingerboard, deluxe tremolo, chrome hardware, 2 Texas Special single coil/Seymour Duncan JB humbucker pickups, volume/tone controls, 5-way selector, available in Aged Cherry Sunburst, Antique Burst, Crimson Transparent, Natural, or Teal Green Trans. finishes, disc. 1998.

$2,350	$2,100	$1,800	$1,550	$1,350	$1,100	$850

Last MSR was $3,299.

This model was available with maple neck with black dot inlays (Model 010-9702).

CONTEMPORARY STRATOCASTER (U.S. MFG. NO. 010-9900) - down-sized alder body, 22-fret rosewood fingerboard with pearl dot inlay, Deluxe tremolo, chrome hardware, white pickguard, 2 Texas Special single coil/Seymour Duncan JB humbucker pickups, volume/tone controls, 5-way selector, available in Aged Cherry Sunburst, Natural, Shoreline Gold Metallic, or Teal Green Trans. finishes, mfg. 1989-1998.

$1,650	$1,450	$1,250	$1,100	$950	$800	$650

Last MSR was $2,299.

This model was available with optional maple neck with black dot inlays (Model 010-9902), Floyd Rose tremolo, flame maple top (Model 010-9970), and maple neck/flame maple top (Model 010-9972). The U.S.-built Contemporary Stratocaster first debuted circa 1989/1990.

Fender '57 Left-Hand Stratocaster courtesy Fender

GRADING	100% MINT	98% NEAR MINT	95% EXC+	90% EXC	80% VG+	70% VG	60% G

Stratocaster: Custom Shop Contemporary Series

CARVED TOP STRAT HSS (U.S. MFG. NO. 010-2802) - swamp ash body, carved highly figured book-matched maple top, maple neck, 22-fret maple fingerboard with dot inlay, LSR nut, Fender Deluxe tremolo, locking tuners, chrome hardware, 2 Texas Special single coil/Seymour Duncan JB humbucker pickups, volume/2 tone controls, special switching, available in Antique Burst, Aged Cherry Sunburst, Crimson Trans., Natural, or Teal Green Trans. finishes, mfg. 1998.

	$2,350	$2,100	$1,900	$1,700	$1,450	$1,275	$1,100

Last MSR was $3,299.

Add $100 for Natural finish.

This model is optional with rosewood neck with pearl dot inlays (Model 010-2800).

Carved Top Strat Dual Humbuckers (U.S. Mfg. No. 010-2902) - similar to the Carved Top Strat HSS, except features 2 Seymour Duncan humbucker pickups, available in Antique Burst, Aged Cherry Sunburst, Crimson Trans., Natural, or Teal Green Trans. finishes, mfg. 1998.

	$2,350	$2,100	$1,900	$1,650	$1,400	$1,250	$1,075

Last MSR was $3,299.

Add $100 for Natural finish.

This model is optional with rosewood neck with pearl dot inlays (Model 010-2900).

SET NECK STRATOCASTER (U.S. MFG. NO. 010-2700) - ash body, highly figured book-matched maple top, set-in maple neck, 22-fret ebony fingerboard with pearl dot inlay, Fender Deluxe vibrato, LSR roller nut, locking tuners, chrome hardware, 2 Texas Special single coil/Seymour Duncan JB humbucker pickups, volume/2 tone controls, 5-position switch, available in Antique Burst or Natural finishes, mfg.1992-98.

	$1,700	$1,450	$1,250	$1,100	$950	$800	$650

Last MSR was $2,399.

In 1998, rosewood fingerboard replaced the ebony fingerboard. In 1995 mahogany body replaced ash. There are different pickup variations available such as Lace pickups. This model has an optional gold hardware with Brite White finish.

Set Neck Floyd Rose Strat (U.S. Mfg.) - similar to Set Neck Stratocaster, except has double locking Floyd Rose vibrato, 2 single coil/1 humbucker pickups, mfg. 1992-95.

	N/A	$1,500	$1,300	$1,100	$950	$800	$650

Last MSR was $2,150.

Stratocaster: Custom Shop Custom Classic Series

'54 STRATOCASTER (U.S. MFG. NO. 010-5402) - swamp ash body, lightly figured maple neck, 21-fret maple fingerboard with black dot inlay, vintage-style tremolo, white pickguard, nickel hardware, 3 Custom '50s single coil pickups, 3-position switch, available in Aztec Gold, 2-Tone Sunburst, or Vintage Blonde finishes, disc. 1998.

	$1,650	$1,450	$1,250	$1,100	$950	$800	$650

Last MSR was $2,299.

Add $200 for gold hardware (Model 010-5412).

'54 Stratocaster FMT (U.S. Mfg. No. 010-5472) - similar to the '54 Stratocaster, except features a highly figured flame maple top, available in 2-Tone Sunburst, Aged Cherry Sunburst, or Natural finishes, disc. 1998.

	$1,800	$1,550	$1,350	$1,150	$1,000	$850	$700

Last MSR was $2,499.

Add $200 for gold hardware (Model 010-5482).

1960 STRATOCASTER (U.S. MFG. NO. 010-6000) - similar to '54 Stratocaster, except has alder body, rosewood fingerboard with pearl dot inlay, 3 Texas Special single coil pickups with aged covers, available in 3-Tone Sunburst, Black, or Olympic White finishes, disc. 1998.

	$1,650	$1,400	$1,250	$1,100	$950	$800	$650

Last MSR was $2,299.

Add $150 for custom color finishes. Add $200 for gold hardware (Model 010-6010).

Instruments with Olympic White finish have tortoiseshell pickguards and body-matching pegheads.

1960 Stratocaster FMT (U.S. Mfg. No. 010-6070) - similar to the 1960 Stratocaster, except features a highly figured flame maple top, available in 3-Tone Sunburst, Aged Cherry Sunburst, or Natural finishes, disc. 1998.

	$1,800	$1,550	$1,350	$1,150	$1,000	$850	$700

Last MSR was $2,499.

Add $200 for gold hardware (Model 010-6080).

'69 STRATOCASTER (U.S. MFG. NO. 010-6900) - alder body, maple neck, 21-fret rosewood fingerboard with dot inlay, oversized (late '60s) headstock, chrome hardware, 3 Custom '69 single coil pickups, available in 3-Tone Sunburst, Black, or Olympic White finishes, disc. 1998.

	$1,850	$1,650	$1,450	$1,250	$1,050	$900	$750

Last MSR was $2,599.

This model was available with maple neck with black dot inlays (Model 010-6902).

F

GRADING	100% MINT	98% NEAR MINT	95% EXC+	90% EXC	80% VG+	70% VG	60% G

AMERICAN CLASSIC STRATOCASTER (U.S. MFG. NO. 010-4702) -
alder body, lightly figured maple neck, 22-fret maple fingerboard, chrome American Standard hardware, American Standard tremolo, 3 Texas Special single coil pickups, custom detailing, available in 3-Tone Sunburst, 2-Tone Sunburst, or White Blonde finishes, disc. 1998.

	$1,250	$1,075	$950	$825	$700	$575	$450

Last MSR was $1,699.

This model was available with a rosewood fingerboard (Model 010-4700). In 1998, the option for gold hardware (Model 010-4712), or rosewood fingerboard/gold hardware (Model 010-4710) was discontinued. Instruments with Olympic White finish have tortoiseshell pickguard. Some early models may have Black Holo-Flake finishes with pearloid pickguards, Olympic White, or custom finishes.

CLASSIC PLAYER STRAT C-NECK (U.S. MFG NO. 010-0702) -
alder or ash body, rounded "C"-shaped maple neck, 22-fret maple fingerboard, chrome hardware, Sperzel Trim-Lok tuners, 2-point vintage-style tremolo, 3 Custom Shop Noiseless single coil pickups, available in Aged Cherry Sunburst, Black, or Teal Green Trans. finishes, mfg. 1998-2000.

	$1,400	$1,200	$1,000	$850	$725	$600	$500

Last MSR was $2,000.

Add $150 for custom color finishes.

This model is available with a rosewood fingerboard (Model 010-0700). The Black finish features a gold anodized pickguard; the Aged Cherry Sunburst and Teal Green Trans. finishes each feature a parchment pickguard.

Classic Player Strat V-Neck (U.S. Mfg., No. 010-0602) -
similar to the Classic Player Strat C-Neck, except features a soft "V"-shaped maple neck, available in Aged Cherry Sunburst, Black, or Teal Green Trans. finishes, mfg. 1998 only.

	$1,400	$1,200	$1,000	$850	$725	$600	$500

Last MSR was $2,000.

Add $150 for custom color finishes.

This model is available with a rosewood fingerboard (Model 010-0600). The Black finish features a gold anodized pickguard; the Aged Cherry Sunburst and Teal Green Trans. finishes each feature a parchment pickguard.

**Fender Classic Player Strat
courtesy Fender**

CLASSIC PLAYER STRAT (NO. 015-6600) -
thin lacquer-finished alder or ash body, lightly figured maple neck, rosewood fingerboard with abalone dot position markers, lightly figured "V"-shaped neck, 22 Medium-Jumbo frets, Sperzel Trim-Loc tuners, 3 Custom Shop "Vintage-Noiseless" pickups, gold anodized pickguard, aged white plastic parts, custom vintage two-point synchronized tremolo, available in 3-Color Sunburst, 2-Color Sunburst, Black, Bing Cherry Trans., Cobalt Blue Trans., Honey Blonde, Midnight Blue, or Midnight Wine finishes, mfg. 2001-present.

MSR	$2,515	$1,800	$1,550	$1,350	$1,200	$1,050	$900	$750

Add $100 for 2-Color Sunburst, Bing Cherry Transparent, Cobalt Blue Transparent, and Honey Blonde finishes.

Also available in "V" neck with maple fingerboard (Model 015-6602). Also available with "C" neck with rosewood fingerboard (Model 015-6700) and "C" neck with maple fingerboard (Model 015-6702).

CUSTOM CLASSIC STRATOCASTER (NO. 015-6200) -
Custom Shop version of the American Series Stratocaster, thin lacquer-finished alder or ash body, lightly figured "V"-shaped neck, rosewood fingerboard, 22 Medium-Jumbo frets, Fender Deluxe cast/sealed tuners, 3 Modern Classic single coil pickups including the Hot Classic bridge pickup with custom steel inductance plate, 3-ply parchment pickguard, aged white plastic parts, Custom Classic two-point synchronized tremolo with milled solid stainless steel saddles, solid steel spring block, pop-in tremolo arm, available in 3-Color Sunburst, Daphne Blue, Black, Honey Blonde, Cobalt Blue Trans., or Bing Cherry Trans. finishes, mfg 2001-present.

MSR	$2,258	$1,600	$1,400	$1,250	$1,100	$950	$800	$650

Add $100 for 2-Color Sunburst, Bing Cherry Transparent, Cobalt Blue Transparent, and Honey Blonde finishes.

Also available with "V" neck with maple fingerboard (Model 015-6202). Also available with "C" neck with rosewood fingerboard (Model 015-6300) and "C" neck with maple fingerboard (Model 015-6302).

N.O.S. (NEW OLD STOCK) STRATOCASTER (U.S. MFG. NO. 010-0502) -
alder body, maple neck, 21-fret maple fingerboard, chrome hardware, vintage-style tremolo, 3 Custom '65 (replica) single coil pickups, available in Black, Bleached 3-Color Sunburst, or Olympic White "Thinskin" finishes, mfg. 1998 only.

	$2,000	$1,700	$1,450	$1,200	$1,000	$850	$700

Last MSR was $2,800.

Add $150 for custom color finishes.

This model was available with a rosewood fingerboard (Model 010-0500). This model is "a detailed recreation of a mid-1960s Strat," built by using the original tooling and production techniques. There are no N.O.S. parts on this reproduction model. This model is now part of the Custom Shop.

Stratocaster: Custom Shop Limited Edition

The Limited Edition Stratocasters are produced in very limited production runs by Fender's Custom Shop. These models are generally labeled # instrument/total amount, and are offered to Fender Diamond level dealers to broker to the public. As such, there is no announced retail price per model - only availability. The following models have a Stratocaster offset double cutaway body, three single coil pickups, bolt-on neck, and 6-on-a-side headstock (unless otherwise specified).

**Fender Custom Classic
Stratocaster
courtesy Fender**

GRADING	100% MINT	98% NEAR MINT	95% EXC+	90% EXC	80% VG+	70% VG	60% G

50th ANNIVERSARY 1954 STRATOCASTER (NO. 015-1954)
- premium ash body, maple U-Shape neck, 21-fret maple fingerboard with abalone dot inlays, single ply white pickguard, 3 Custom Shop Vintage 1954 Strat single coil pickups, 3 knobs, 3-way switch, vintage tremolo, nickel/chrome hardware, 50th Anniversary case included, available in 2-Color Sunburst Closet Classic finish, mfg. 2004 only.

	100%	98%	95%	90%	80%	70%	60%
	$4,000	$3,500	$3,200	$2,900	N/A	N/A	N/A

Last MSR was $5,400.

ALUMINUM BODY STRATOCASTER (U.S. MFG.)
- hollow aluminum body, available in Chrome (with Black Custom Shop pickguard/headstock), Green with Black and Gold swirls, or Jet Black (with chrome pickguard) anodized finishes, mfg. 1994 only.

	100%	98%	95%	90%	80%	70%	60%
	N/A	$2,500	$2,200	$1,900	$1,600	$1,300	$1,000

BILL CARSON STRATOCASTER (U.S. MFG.)
- similar to the 1957 Reissue, except has neck shaped to Bill Carson's specifications, available in Cimarron Red, mfg. 1992 only.

	100%	98%	95%	90%	80%	70%	60%
	N/A	$2,000	$1,700	$1,400	$1,200	$1,000	$800

Only 100 instruments were built. The first 41 were built for Music Trader and have documentation (non-Music Trader models do not have this paperwork). Package includes tweed hardshell case. Guitarist Bill Carson gave advice on the design of the original Stratocaster.

FREDDY TAVARES ALOHA STRATOCASTER (U.S. MFG. NO. 010-4404)
- hollow aluminum body, available with Hawaiian scene anodized finish, mfg. 1993-94.

	100%	98%	95%	90%	80%	70%	60%
	N/A	$4,000	$3,500	$3,000	$2,500	$2,000	$1,500

Only 153 instuments were built.

HANK MARVIN SIGNATURE LIMITED EDITION (U.S. MFG.)
- available in Fiesta Red finish, mfg. 1995-96.

	100%	98%	95%	90%	80%	70%	60%
	N/A	$2,000	$1,700	$1,400	$1,200	$1,000	$800

Only 164 instruments were built for European distribution.

HARLEY DAVIDSON STRATOCASTER (U.S. MFG. NO. 010-4401)
- hollow aluminum body, chrome inscribed pickguard, available in Chrome finish only, mfg. 1993 only.

	100%	98%	95%	90%	80%	70%	60%
	N/A	$20,000	$17,000	$14,000	N/A	N/A	N/A

Only 109 instruments were built. The 60 models made available to Diamond Edition dealers carry a Diamond emblem on the headstock. The 40 models available for export, and the 9 that were delivered to the Harley Davidson company, do not carry this emblem.

HOMER HAYNES LIMITED EDITION (HLE/HLE REISSUE '88, U.S. MFG.)
- gold anodized pickguard, gold hardware, available in Gold finish only, mfg. 1988 only.

	100%	98%	95%	90%	80%	70%	60%
	N/A	$2,000	$1,700	$1,400	$1,200	$1,000	$800

Only 500 instruments were built. This model was one of the early Custom Shop limited edition runs, and was based on a 1957 model Stratocaster.

JIMI HENDRIX MONTEREY (U.S. MFG.)
- reverse headstock, white pickguard, available in red/green psychadelic-style finish with backstage pass sticker on lower bout, mfg. 1997 only.

	100%	98%	95%	90%	80%	70%	60%
	N/A	$7,000	$6,200	$5,500	$4,800	$4,000	$3,200

Last MSR was $6,999.

Only 210 instruments were built. Sources have written in to indicate that there was possibly another Hendrix Custom Shop model built circa 1993. This yet-uncomfirmed model was similar to the 1980 Hendrix model, except the '93 version had a maple cap neck and Transition style logo on the headstock.

PLAYBOY 40TH ANNIVERSARY STRATOCASTER (U.S. MFG. NO. 010-4402)
- gold hardware, maple fingerboard with black pearl bunny inlays, available with custom Marilyn Monroe graphic finish, mfg. 1994 only.

	100%	98%	95%	90%	80%	70%	60%
	N/A	$6,000	$5,200	$4,500	$3,700	$2,900	$2,100

Last MSR was $8,000.

Only 175 instruments were built. Package includes red Playboy leather strap, red gig bag, and hardshell case.

STEVENS LJ STRATOCASTER (U.S. MFG. NO. 010-3500)
- set-in neck, highly figured top, Brazilian rosewood fingerboard, 2 special design humbuckers, available in Autumn Gold, Antique Burst, Crimson Stain, or Ebony Stain, mfg. 1987 only.

	100%	98%	95%	90%	80%	70%	60%
	N/A	$2,800	$2,400	$2,000	$1,700	$1,400	$1,100

Last MSR was $2,799.

The Stevens LJ was the first Custom Shop model released. It is estimated that only 35 to 40 instruments were built. Only 4 additional prototypes of the Stevens LJ II and Stevens LJ III (2 each) were constructed.

STEVIE RAY VAUGHN NUMBER ONE LIMITED EDITION
- a limited edition reproduction of SRV's number one guitar, built to every last aspect of SRV's guitar, mfg. 2004 only.

	100%	98%	95%	90%	80%	70%	60%
	N/A	N/A	N/A	N/A	N/A	N/A	N/A

Only 100 instruments built. These guitars retailed for $10,000 new, but quickly sold out and sold for or close to the retail price. Not enough have shown up on the second-hand market to accurately value these instruments.

Stratocaster: Custom Shop "Relic" Series

"Relic" series instruments were cosmetically aged by the Fender Custom Shop. Instruments are stamped on the headstock and into the body (under the pickguard) with the Custom Shop logo to avoid future cases of "mistaken identity" in the Vintage Guitar market. Died-in-the-wool Strat players/collectors don't seem to be satisfied with a 100% "fresh paint" finish, explaining why this series was initially offered. The Relic Series was discontinued in 2000.

'50s "RELIC" STRATOCASTER (U.S. MFG. NO. 010-5802)
- light ash body, maple neck, 21-fret maple fingerboard with black dot inlay, vintage-style tremolo, aged white pickguard/nickel hardware/knobs/pickup covers/etc., 3 Custom '54 single coil pickups, volume/2 tone controls, available in 2-Color Sunburst or Vintage Blonde finishes, disc. 2000.

	100%	98%	95%	90%	80%	70%	60%
	$1,850	$1,600	$1,400	$1,200	$1,000	$875	$750

Last MSR was $2,599.

Add $200 for aged gold hardware (Model 010-5812).

GRADING	100% MINT	98% NEAR MINT	95% EXC+	90% EXC	80% VG+	70% VG	60% G

'60s "Relic" Stratocaster (U.S. Mfg. No. 010-6400) - similar to the '50s Relic Stratocaster, except features an alder body, rosewood 'slab' fingerboard, 3 Custom '60s single coil pickups, similar distressed aging, available in 3-Color Sunburst or Olympic White finishes, disc. 2000.

	$1,850	$1,600	$1,400	$1,200	$1,000	$875	$750

Last MSR was $2,599.

Add $200 for aged gold hardware (Model 010-6410). Add $150 for custom color finish: Burgundy Mist, Daphne Blue, Fiesta Red, and Lake Placid Blue.

"RELIC" FLOYD ROSE STRATOCASTER (U.S. MFG. NO. 010-6802) - alder body, maple neck, 21-fret maple fingerboard with black dot inlay, Original Floyd Rose tremolo, aged white pickguard/ chrome hardware/knobs/pickup covers/etc., 2 custom '69 single coil/Seymour Duncan '59 humbucker pickups, volume/2 tone controls, available in Black or Olympic White finishes, mfg. 1998 only.

	$1,950	$1,700	$1,500	$1,300	$1,100	$950	$800

Last MSR was $2,799.

This model is available with a rosewood fingerboard (Model 110-6800).

**Fender Deluxe
Powerhouse Strat
courtesy Fender**

Stratocaster: Deluxe Series (Mex. 1998-Current Mfg.)

DELUXE FAT STRAT HSS (MEX. MFG., NO. 013-3100) - poplar body, 21-fret rosewood fingerboard with dot inlay, large headstock, synchronized tremolo, chrome hardware, black pickguard, 2 Tex-Mex single coil, 1 Tex-Mex humbucker pickups, volume/2 tone controls, 5-way selector, available in Black or Pewter finishes, gig bag included, mfg. 1998-present.

MSR	$700	$499	$450	$400	$350	$300	$250	$200

Arctic White finish was discontinued in 2001.

Double Fat Strat (Mex. Mfg., No. 013-3300) - similar to the Deluxe Fat Strat, except features 2 Tex-Mex humbucker pickups, mfg. 1998-present.

MSR	$700	$515	$450	$400	$350	$325	$275	$250

FAT STRAT FLOYD ROSE (MEX. MFG., NO. 113-3100) - poplar body, 21-fret rosewood fingerboard with dot inlay, large headstock, Floyd Rose locking tremolo, chrome hardware, black pickguard, 2 Tex-Mex single coil/Tex-Mex humbucker pickups, volume/2 tone controls, 5-way selector, available in Black or Pewter finishes, gig bag included, mfg. 1998-2004.

	$575	$475	$450	$425	$395	$360	$325

Last MSR was $770.

Arctic White finish was disc. in 2001.

Double Fat Strat Floyd Rose (Mex. Mfg., No. 113-3300) - Similar to the Fat Strat Floyd Rose, except features 2 Tex-Mex humbucker pickups, available in Black or Pewter finishes, mfg. 1998-2004.

	$595	$495	$475	$450	$395	$365	$325

Last MSR was $800.

DELUXE POWERHOUSE STRAT (MEX. MFG., NO. 013-9500) - poplar body, 21-fret rosewood fingerboard with black dot inlay, vintage-style tremolo, chrome hardware, white shell pickguard, 3 Powerhouse (ultra quiet) single coil pickups (with hum-cancelling slave coil), master volume/master "no-load" tone/ active 12 dB mid-range boost controls, available in Black, Blizzard Pearl, Caramel Metallic, Chrome Red, Navy Blue Metallic, Lake Placid Blue, Candy Apple Red, Pewter, Graffiti Yellow, or Arctic White finishes, gig bag included, mfg. 1998-present.

MSR	$842	$599	$525	$450	$400	$350	$300	$250

This model is also available with a maple fingerboard and white dot inlay (Model 013-9502). In 2005, Blizzard Pearl, Caramel Metallic, Chrome Red, and Navy Blue Metallic finishes were introduced.

DELUXE SUPER STRAT (MEX. MFG., NO. 013-9400) - ash body, tinted maple neck, 21-fret rosewood fingerboard with black dot inlay, vintage-style tremolo, gold-plated hardware, brown shell pickguard, 3 Super Fat Strat single coil pickups, volume/tone (neck)/tone (middle) controls, push/push switch (bridge pickup activation), available in Black, Brown Sunburst, Crimson Transparent, or Honey Blonde finishes, gig-bag included, mfg. 1998-present.

MSR	$800	$575	$495	$425	$375	$325	$275	$225

Add $35 for the Brown Sunburst finish.

This model is also available with a maple fingerboard and white dot inlay (Model 013-9402). This model is equipped with "Super Switching," an additional push/push switch for activating the bridge pickup independent of the 5-way selector switch.

ACOUSTASONIC STRATOCASTER (MEX. MFG. NO. 013-9700) - alder hollowed-out body, oval oblong soundhole, maple M-Shaped neck, 22-fret rosewood fingerboard with dot inlay, 3 in-bridge Piezo pickups, no pickguard, 3 knobs, rosewood bridge, chrome hardware, available in Sapphire Blue Trans., Crimson Red Trans., Ebony Trans., or Pewter finishes, mfg. 2004-present.

MSR	$1,042	$730	$650	$575	$500	$425	$350	$275

DELUXE PLAYERS STRAT (MEX. MFG. NO. 013-3000) - ash body, maple C-Shaped neck, 21-fret rosewood fingerboard with dot inlay, 3 single coil Noiseless pickups, tortoiseshell pickguard, 3 knobs, 5-way switch, vintage style tremolo, gold plated hardware, available in 3-Color Sunburst, Saphire Blue Trans., Crimson Red Trans., or Honey Blonde finishes, mfg. summer 2004-present.

MSR	$842	$599	$525	$450	$400	$350	$300	$250

Also available with a maple fingerboard (No. 013-3002).

**Fender Custom Classic
Stratocaster
courtesy Fender**

GRADING	100% MINT	98% NEAR MINT	95% EXC+	90% EXC	80% VG+	70% VG	60% G

Stratocaster: Elite Series

The Elite series instruments were Fender´s attempt to combine the classic Stratocaster design with active electronics and a revised tremolo system with "drop-in" string loading.

ELITE STRATOCASTER (U.S. MFG.) - alder body, 21-fret maple fingerboard with black dot inlay, Freeflyte vibrato, chrome hardware, white pickgard, 3 single coil covered Alnico II pickups, volume/2 tone controls, 3 push-button pickup selectors, active MDX (mid-range) and TBX (high-range) electronics, available in Aztec Gold, Candy Apple Green, Emerald Green, Mocha Brown, Pewter, Ruby Red, Sapphire Blue, or Stratoburst finishes, mfg. 1983-84.

N/A	$950	$825	$700	$600	$500	$400

Last MSR was $799.

This instrument was also available with rosewood fingerboard with pearl dot inlay. The output jack was located on the side of the body (instead of the top), and had no rear cover for the drop-in tremolo bridge. There was a backplate for access to the 9-volt battery (required for the active electronics).

Gold Elite Stratocaster (U.S. Mfg.) - similar to Elite Stratocaster, except has pearloid tuner buttons, gold hardware, mfg. 1983-84.

N/A	$1,000	$850	$750	$625	$525	$425

Last MSR was $899.

Walnut Elite Stratocaster (U.S. Mfg.) - similar to Elite Stratocaster, except has American black walnut body/neck, ebony fingerboard, pearloid tuner buttons, gold hardware, mfg. 1983-84.

N/A	$1,500	$1,250	$1,050	$900	$750	$600

Last MSR was $999.

Stratocaster: Fender Japan Limited Edition Series

The following models were limited edition instruments produced by Fender Japan, and available through custom order.

PAISLEY STRAT (JAPAN MFG.) - offset double cutaway ash body, bolt-on maple neck, 21-fret maple fingerboard with black dot inlay, standard vibrato, 6-on-one-side tuners, Paisley pickguard, chrome hardware, 3 single coil pickups, 2 volume/1 tone controls, 5-position switch, available in a Pink Paisley finish, disc. 1994.

N/A	$1,100	$950	$800	$700	$600	$500

Last MSR was $820.

Blue Flower Strat (Japan Mfg.) - similar to Paisley Strat, except has Blue Flower pickguard/finish, disc. 1994.

N/A	$1,100	$950	$800	$700	$600	$500

Last MSR was $720.

´72 STRATOCASTER (JAPAN MFG.) - offset double cutaway ash body, bolt-on maple neck, 21-fret maple fingerboard with black dot inlay, ´70s oversized headstock, standard vibrato, 6-on-one-side tuners, white pickguard, chrome hardware, 3 single coil pickups, volume/2 tone controls, 5-position switch, available in Natural or Vintage White finishes, disc. 1995.

N/A	$600	$525	$450	$375	$325	$275

Last MSR was $710.

Stratocaster: Floyd Rose Series

Floyd Rose, the inventor of the double-locking tremolo, entered into an agreement with Fender in 1991. The Floyd Rose Classic Stratocaster debuted in 1992.

FLOYD ROSE CLASSIC STRATOCASTER (U.S. MFG. NO. 110-6000) - alder body, 22-fret rosewood fingerboard with pearl dot inlay, Original Floyd Rose tremolo, chrome hardware, 2 American Standard single coil/1 DiMarzio humbucker pickups, volume/2 tone controls, 5-position switch, available in 3-Tone Sunburst, Black, Candy Apple Red, or Vintage White finishes, mfg. 1992-99.

$950	$825	$725	$625	$525	$425	$325

Last MSR was $1,379.

This model had an optional maple fingerboard with black dot inlay (Model 110-6002).

FLOYD ROSE STANDARD STRATOCASTER (MEX. MFG. NO. 110-6002) - similar to Floyd Rose Classic, except has poplar body, 21-fret fingerboard, Floyd Rose II locking tremolo, 2 single coil/humbucker pickups, available in Arctic White or Black, mfg. 1994-98.

$375	$325	$275	$235	$195	$160	$130

Last MSR was $529.

This model had an optional maple fingerboard with black dot inlay (Model 113-1102).

Floyd Rose Standard Stratocaster Foto Flame - Similar to Floyd Rose Standard, except has basswood body, 21-fret rosewood fingerboard, Floyd Rose II locking tremolo, available in Antique Foto Flame, Blue Foto Flame, or Crimson Foto Flame finishes, disc. 1995.

N/A	$375	$325	$275	$235	$195	$160

Last MSR was $639.

FLOYD ROSE STRAT SPECIAL HSS (U.S. MFG., NO. 110-6500) - alder body, 22-fret rosewood fingerboard with pearl dot inlay, Original Floyd Rose double locking tremolo, 3-ply white pickguard, chrome hardware, 2 American Standard single coil/1 Fender DH-1 humbucker pickups, volume/2 tone controls, 5-position switch, available in 3-Color Sunburst, black, Candy Apple Red, and Vintage White finishes, includes case, mfg. 1998-2003.

$1,050	$900	$750	$650	$575	$500	$425

Last MSR was $1,500.

Add $35 for 3-Color Sunburst finish.

This model has an optional maple fingerboard with black dot inlay (Model 110-6502).

GRADING	100% MINT	98% NEAR MINT	95% EXC+	90% EXC	80% VG+	70% VG	60% G

Floyd Rose Strat Special HH (U.S. Mfg., No. 110-6700) - similar to the Floyd Rose Classic Strat HSS, except features 2 Fender DH-1 humbucker pickups, available in 3-Color Sunburst, Black, Candy Apple Red, or Vintage White finishes, includes case, mfg. 1998-2002.

	$1,075	$925	$775	$675	$600	$525	$450

Last MSR was $1,550.

Add $35 for 3-Color Sunburst finish.

This model has an optional maple fingerboard with black dot inlay (Model 110-6702).

Stratocaster: H.M. ('Heavy Metal') Series

Originally produced overseas. In 1988, the H.M. Strat series moved to U.S. production from 1989 through 1992. H.M. Series Strats feature a sharply contoured basswood body, 24-fret fingerboard, black headstock finish, and various pickup combinations of DiMarzio humbuckers/American Standard single coils/Fender-Lace Sensor pickups.

H.M. STRAT (JAPAN, U.S. MFG.) - basswood body, 24-fret maple fingerboard with black dot inlay, double locking Kahler vibrato, black face peghead with STRAT logo, black hardware, various pickup configurations (see above), pickup selector switch, volume/2 tone controls (where applicable), coil tap, available in Black, Blue, Red, or White finishes, mfg. 1988-1990.

	N/A	$350	$300	$260	$230	$200	$170

This instrument was also available with rosewood fingerboard with pearl dot inlay. U.S.-produced H.M. Strats were available with the following pickup configurations: 1 Silver Fender-Lace Sensor single coil/1 DiMarzio humbucker (Model 10-2200), 2 DiMarzio humbuckers (Model 10-2300), 2 American Standard single coils/1 DiMarzio humbucker pickups (Models 10-2100, 10-2102).

H.M. STRAT ULTRA (U.S. MFG. NO. 010-2000) - similar to H.M. Strat, except has figured maple top/back, ebony fingerboard with pearl triangle inlay, mother-of-pearl headstock logo, Blue single coil/ Gold single coil/2 Red single coil ("Dually" configuration) Fender-Lace Sensor pickups, volume/2 tone controls, 5-position/mini switches, mfg. 1990-92.

	N/A	$450	$400	$350	$300	$250	$200

Stratocaster: "HRR" (Hot-Rodded Reissue) Series

"HRR" Stratocaster models feature a double-locking Floyd Rose tremolo and a humbucker in the bridge position. These Japanese-produced models were available from 1990 to 1995.

"HRR" '50s STRATOCASTER (JAPAN MFG. NO. 025-1002) - basswood body, 22-fret maple fingerboard with black dot inlay, double locking Floyd Rose vibrato, 2 single coil/1 DiMarzio humbucker pickups, volume/2 tone controls, 5-position/coil split switches, available in Black, Blue Foto Flame, Crimson Foto Flame, Olympic White, or 2-Tone Sunburst finishes, mfg. 1990-95.

	N/A	$450	$400	$350	$300	$250	$200

Last MSR was $900.

"HRR" '60s STRATOCASTER (JAPAN MFG. NO. 025-1000) - similar to "HRR" '50s Stratocaster, except has rosewood fingerboard with pearl dot inlay, available in Black, Blue Foto Flame, Crimson Foto Flame, Olympic White, or 3-Tone Sunburst finishes, mfg. 1990-94.

	N/A	$450	$400	$350	$300	$250	$200

Last MSR was $900.

Stratocaster: Highway 1 Series (2002-Current Mfg.)

The U.S. Special Highway 1 Stratocaster series was released at the Summer 2002 NAMM show. This is an American Stratocaster brought back to the basics. It retails low enough so it can be purchased at $600 by Fender´s MAP price!

HIGHWAY 1 STRATOCASTER (NO. 011-1100) - alder body, maple neck, rosewood fretboard, 22 medium jumbo, Fender Cast/sealed tuning machines, 3 single coil Alnico pickups, Fender Synchronized tremolo, satin lacquer finish, available in 3-Color Sunburst, Sapphire Blue Trans., Crimson Red Trans., Cocoa Trans., Teal Green Trans., or Honey Blonde Trans., gig bag included, mfg. 2002-present.

MSR	$900	$630	$550	$475	$425	$375	$325	$275

This model is also available with a maple neck (No. 011-1102). In 2003, the Highway 1 Stratocaster was introduced as a left-handed model (No. 011-1120) and the HSS with a special Fender Atomic II Humbucker pickup and an enlarged headstock. Both models have the same retail as the Hiway 1 Strat.

Stratocaster: Hot Rodded American Series & Other Hot Rodded Models

AMERICAN STRAT TEXAS SPECIAL (NO. 011-7300) - alder or ash body, rosewood fingerboard with dot position markers, deluxe staggered die-cast sealed tuners, 22 medium-jumbo frets, 3 Texas Special single coil pickups, 1 volume/2 tone controls, super 5-way switch, two-point synchronized tremolo, available in 3-Color Sunburst, White Blonde, black, Candy Apple Red, Shoreline Gold, Teal Green Metallic, Chrome Silver, Surf Pearl, or Sienna Sunburst finishes, case included, mfg. 2001-03.

	$950	$850	$750	$650	$575	$500	$425

Last MSR was $1,350.

Add $35 for 3-Color Sunburst finish and $100 for Sienna Sunburst and White Blonde finish.

Also available with maple neck (Model 011-7302). Candy Apple Red and White Blonde were discontinued in 2002. Chrome Silver and Surf Pearl were introduced in 2002.

Fender Gold Elite Stratocaster courtesy Robert Keeley

Fender Floyd Rose Strat Special HSS Stratocaster courtesy Fender

GRADING	100% MINT	98% NEAR MINT	95% EXC+	90% EXC	80% VG+	70% VG	60% G

American Fat Strat Texas Special (No. 011-7900)
similar to American Strat Texas Special except has Seymour Duncan "Pearly Gates Plus" humbucker pickup in the bridge position rosewood fingerboard, case included, mfg. 2001-03.

	$950	$850	$750	$650	$575	$500	$425

Last MSR was $1,350.

Add $35 for 3-Color Sunburst finish and $100 for Sienna Sunburst and White Blonde finish.

Also available with maple neck (Model 011-7902). The American Fat Strat is not available in Shoreline Gold finish.

American Double Fat Strat (No. 011-7200)
similar to American Fat Strat Texas Special except has two Seymour Duncan humbucker pickups, rosewood fingerboard with dot position markers, case included, mfg. 2001-03.

	$1,000	$875	$775	$675	$600	$525	$450

Last MSR was $1,428.

Add $35 for 3-Color Sunburst finish and $100 for Sienna Sunburst and White Blonde finish.

Also available in a Hard Tail model (Model 011-7230). Sienna Sunburst finish not available for this model.

BIG APPLE STRAT (U.S. MFG. NO. 010-7202)
alder body, 22-fret maple fingerboard with black dot inlay, standard vibrato, chrome hardware, brown or white shell pickguard, 2 Seymour Duncan ('59 and Pearly Gates Plus) pickups, 5-position switch, available in Black, Candy Apple Red, Olympic White, Shoreline Gold, or Teal Green Metallic finishes, mfg. 1997-2000.

	$850	$750	$650	$575	$500	$425	$350

Last MSR was $1,249.

Add $80 for 3-Tone Sunburst finish. Add $150 for BAS-Special w/ ash body & rosewood fingerboard & Sienna Sunburst finish (Model 010-7200-822).

This model was also available with a rosewood fingerboard and white dot inlay (Model 010-7200).

Big Apple Strat Hard Tail (U.S. Mfg. No. 010-7232)
similar to the Big Apple Strat, except features a fixed bridge/strings through-body (with ferrules), available in Black, Candy Apple Red, Olympic White, Shoreline Gold, and Teal Green Metallic finishes, mfg. 1998-2000.

	$850	$750	$650	$575	$500	$425	$350

Last MSR was $1,249.

Add $80 for 3-Tone Sunburst finish.

This model is also available with a rosewood fingerboard and white dot inlay (Model 010-7230).

LONE STAR STRAT (U.S. MFG. NO. 010-7902)
alder body, 22-fret maple fingerboard with black dot inlay, standard tremolo, chrome hardware, white (or brown) shell pickguard, 2 Texas Special single coil/1 Seymour Duncan Pearly Gates Plus humbucker pickups, volume/2 tone controls, 5-position switch, available in Black, Candy Apple Red, Olympic White, Shoreline Gold, or Teal Green Metallic finishes, mfg. 1996-2000.

	$800	$700	$625	$550	$475	$400	$325

Last MSR was $1,199.

Add $80 for 3-Tone Sunburst finish. Add $150 for LSS-Special, ash body with maple neck & Sienna Sunburst finish (Model 010-7902-847).

This model is also available with a rosewood fingerboard and white dot inlay (Model 010-7900).

ROADHOUSE STRAT (U.S. MFG. NO. 010-7302)
poplar body, tortoiseshell pickguard, 22-fret maple fingerboard with black dot inlay, tremolo bridge, chrome hardware, 3 Texas Special single coil pickups, 5-position switch, available in Black, Blue, Red, Silver, or White finishes, mfg. 1997-2000.

	$750	$675	$600	$525	$450	$375	$300

Last MSR was $1,159.

Add $80 for 3-Tone Sunburst finish.

This model is also available with a rosewood fingerboard and white dot inlay (Model 010-7300)

Stratocaster: Model Variations

The models below represent variations not categorized in the other subcategories.

1997 COLLECTOR'S EDITION STRATOCASTER (U.S. MFG., NO. 010-1997)
alder body, tinted maple neck, 21-fret rosewood fingerboard with pearl dot inlay/oval-shaped 1997 pearl inlay at 12th fret, vintage-style vibrato, gold hardware, tortoiseshell pickguard, 3 Texas Special single coil pickups, volume/2 tone controls with white knobs, 5-position switch, available in 3-Tone Sunburst nitrocellulose finish, mfg. 1997 only.

	$1,275	$1,100	$950	$800	$700	$600	$500

Last MSR was $1,799.

Production was scheduled for only 1,997 instruments. List price included brown tolex hardshell case.

CONTEMPORARY STRATOCASTER (JAPAN MFG.)
alder body, white pickguard, 22-fret rosewood fingerboard with pearl dot inlay, double locking vibrato, black face peghead, chrome hardware, single exposed polepiece humbucker pickup, volume control, mfg. 1985-89.

	N/A	$300	$250	$220	$190	$160	$130

Add 10-15% for two humbucker or two single-coil and one humbucker pickups.

This model was also available with black pickguard, 2 humbucker pickups, volume/tone control, 3-position switch, coil tap configuration; or 2 single coil/1 humbucker pickups, volume/tone control, 5-position switch, coil tap configurations. The Japan Mfg. Contemporary Stratocaster is not to be confused with the U.S. Mfg. Contemporary Strat (available between 1989 to 1991). Please refer to the Stratocaster: Fender Custom Shop for the U.S. Mfg. Contemporary Strat.

GOLD STRATOCASTER (U.S. MFG. 1981-83)
alder body, 21-fret maple fingerboard with black dot inlay, 4-bolt neckplate, standard brass vibrato, brass tuners, gold-plated brass hardware, 3-ply white pickguard, 3 single coil exposed pickups, volume/2 tone controls, 5-position switch, available in Metallic Gold finish, mfg. 1981-83.

	N/A	$1,250	$1,100	$950	$800	$700	$600

Last MSR was $975.

This model has been nicknamed the "Gold/Gold" Stratocaster. In 1981, it was offered as a limited edition in the Collector's Series.

GRADING	100% MINT	98% NEAR MINT	95% EXC+	90% EXC	80% VG+	70% VG	60% G

"SHORT SCALE" STRAT (JAPAN MFG.) - offset double cutaway ash body, white pickguard, bolt-on maple neck, 22-fret maple fingerboard with black dot inlay, standard vibrato, 6-on-a-side tuners, chrome hardware, 3 single coil pickups, volume/2 tone controls, 5-position switch, available in Arctic White, Black, Frost Red, or 3-Tone Sunburst finishes, mfg. 1989-1994.

	N/A	$450	$375	$325	$275	$225	$175

Last MSR was $550.

This model had an optional rosewood fingerboard with pearl dot inlay and was a limited edition model available through custom order.

STRATOCASTER SPECIAL (MEX. MFG. NO. 013-5602) - ash veneer body, 21-fret maple fingerboard with black dot inlay, vintage-style tremolo, chrome hardware, 2 single coil/humbucker pickups, volume/2 tone controls, 5-position switch, available in Black, Brown Sunburst, Crimson Transparent, or Vintage Blond Transparent finishes, disc. 1995.

	N/A	$375	$325	$275	$225	$175	$125

Last MSR was $559.

This model is also available with a rosewood fingerboard and white dot inlay (Model 013-5600).

STRATOCASTER XII (JAPAN MFG. NO. 027-8900) - alder body, white pickguard, 22-fret rosewood fingerboard with pearl dot inlay, strings through bridge, 6-per-side tuners, chrome hardware, 3 single coil pickups, volume/2 tone controls, 5-position switch, available in Candy Apple Red finish, mfg. 1988-1995.

	N/A	$700	$600	$500	$400	$300	$200

Last MSR was $919.

TEX-MEX STRAT (MEX. MFG. NO. 013-7602) - poplar body, maple neck, 21-fret maple fingerboard with black dot inlay, vintage-style tremolo, chrome hardware, white pickguard, 3 Tex-Mex Trio single coil pickups, volume/2 tone controls, 5-position switch, available in Black, Brown Sunburst, Candy Apple Red, Sonic Blue, or Vintage White finishes, mfg. 1996-98.

$425	$375	$325	$275	$225	$195	$150

Last MSR was $599.

This model is also available with a rosewood fingerboard and white dot inlay (Model 013-7600).

Tex-Mex Strat Special (Mex. Mfg., No. 013-7802) - similar to the Tex-Mex Strat, except has 2 single coil/1 humbucker Tex-Mex pickups, mfg. 1997-98.

$450	$395	$350	$300	$250	$200	$175

Last MSR was $649.

Fender Buddy Guy Polka Dot courtesy Fender

This model is also available with a rosewood fingerboard and white dot inlay (Model 013-7800).

THE STRAT (CBS MFG. 1980-83) - alder body, white pickguard, 21-fret maple fingerboard with black dot inlay, 4-bolt neck plate, standard brass vibrato, body matching smaller peghead with Strat logo, brass tuners, gold hardware, 3 single coil pickups, volume/tone/rotary controls, 5-position switch, available in Candy Apple Red, or Lake Placid Blue finishes, mfg. 1980-83.

	N/A	$1,000	$850	$700	$600	$500	$400

Last MSR was $1,095.

The redesigned wiring of the Strat offers 9 basic and different sounds. The Fender X-1 lead pickup had a hotter output than standard Fender single coil pickups. In 1981, Artic White finish became available.

Walnut Strat (Super Strat, U.S. Mfg.) - similar to The Strat, except has American black walnut body, 1-piece walnut neck, black pickguard/pickup covers, gold hardware, available in Natural finish, mfg. 1981-83.

	N/A	$1,100	$950	$800	$700	$600	$500

Last MSR was $1,195.

A few of these instruments have ebony fingerboards.

TRADITIONAL STRATOCASTER (MEX. MFG. NO. 013-3602) - poplar body, maple neck, 21-fret maple fingerboard with black dot inlay, vintage-style tremolo, chrome hardware, 3-ply white pickguard, 3 single coil pickups, volume/2 tone controls, 5-position switch, available in Arctic White, Black, or Torino Red finishes, disc. 1998.

$200	$180	$160	$140	$120	$100	$80

Last MSR was $329.

This model is also available with a rosewood fingerboard and white dot inlay (Model 013-3600).

Traditional Stratocaster Left-Hand (Mex. Mfg. No. 013-3620) - similar to the Traditional Stratocaster, except in left-handed configuration, rosewood fingerboard only, available in Arctic White or Black finishes, disc. 1998.

$225	$200	$175	$150	$130	$110	$95

Last MSR was $379.

Traditional Fat Strat (Mex. Mfg. No. 013-3700) - similar to the Traditional Stratocaster, except has a humbucker pickup in the bridge position, disc. 1998.

$220	$195	$170	$150	$125	$105	$90

Last MSR was $349.

Stratocaster: Signature Series

Artist Signature Series Stratocasters are designed in collaboration with the artist whose name appears on the headstock. The nature of the Signature Series is to present an instrument that contains the idiosyncrasies similar to the artist's personal guitar.

Fender Signature Series Eric Johnson courtesy Fender

GRADING	100% MINT	98% NEAR MINT	95% EXC+	90% EXC	80% VG+	70% VG	60% G

BONNIE RAITT (U.S. MFG NO. 010-9300) - alder body, 22-fret rosewood fingerboard with white dot inlay, larger (1960s-style) headstock, vintage-style vibrato, Bonnie Raitt's signature on peghead, chrome hardware, white shell pickguard, 3 Texas Special single coil pickups, available in 3-Tone Sunburst or Desert Sunburst finishes, mfg. 1996-2001.

		$1,325	$1,150	$975	$850	$750	$650	$550

Last MSR was $1,850.

BUDDY GUY (U.S. MFG. NO. 010-7802) - alder body, 22-fret maple fingerboard with black dot inlay, standard vibrato, Buddy Guy's signature on headstock, chrome hardware, 3 single coil Lace Sensor Gold pickups, active electronics, available in 2-Tone Sunburst (white shell pickguard) or Honey Brown (brown shell pickguard) finishes, mfg. 1995-present.

MSR	$2,000	$1,400	$1,200	$1,050	$900	$750	$650	$550

BUDDY GUY POLKA DOT (MEX. MFG. NO. 013-8802-306) - alder Body, maple neck and fingerboard with black dot inlay, 21 frets, "V"-shaped neck, Buddy Guy's signature on headstock, chrome hardware, black pickguard, 3 black single coil pickups, black knobs and switch, Fender/Gotoh vintage-style tuning machines, synchronized tremolo, available in black with white polka dots finish only, mfg. 2002-present.

MSR	$828	$580	$500	$425	$350	$300	$250	$200

DICK DALE (U.S. MFG. NO. 010-6100) - alder body, rosewood fingerboard with pearl dot inlay, standard vibrato, Dick Dale's signature on reverse peghead, chrome hardware, 3 Custom '50s single coil pickups, special switching, available in Chartreuse Sparkle finish, mfg. 1992-present.

MSR	$3,266	$2,350	$2,050	$1,800	$1,550	$1,200	$1,000	$800

ERIC CLAPTON (U.S. MFG. NO. 010-7602) - alder body, 22-fret maple fingerboard with black dot inlay, vintage-style vibrato, Eric Clapton's signature on headstock, chrome hardware, 3 single coil Vintage Noiseless pickups (Lace Sensors prior 2001), active electronics, available in Black, Candy Green, Olympic White, Pewter, or Torino Red finishes, case included, mfg. 1988-present.

MSR	$2,000	$1,400	$1,200	$1,050	$900	$750	$650	$550

In 2002, this model was revised by replacing the Lace Sensor pickups with new Fender Vintage Noiseless pickups, a "V" neck, and new active mid-boost and TBX circuits.

Eric Clapton Custom Shop Signature (No. 015-0082) - similar to the Eric Clapton Signature, except made in the Custom Shop, available in Mercedes Blue, Midnight Blue, or Black finishes, mfg. summer 2004-present.

MSR	$2,931	$2,150	$1,850	$1,650	$1,450	$1,250	$1,100	$950

ERIC JOHNSON (U.S. MFG. NO. 011-7702) - alder '57 body, maple custom V-shape neck, 21-fret maple fingerboard with dot inlay, 3 special design Eric Johnson single coil pickups, vintage tremolo bridge, chrome hardware, available in Two-Color Sunburst, Black, Candy Apple Red, or White Blonde finishes, new 2005.

MSR	$2,300	$1,625	$1,400	$1,250	$1,100	$950	$800	$700

HENDRIX MODEL (1980 U.S. MFG.) - alder body, 21-fret maple fingerboard with black dot inlay, standard vibrato, reverse headstock, 4-bolt neckplate, chrome hardware, white pickguard, 3 single coil pickups, volume/2 tone controls, 5-way selector switch, available in White polyester finish, mfg. 1980 only.

	N/A	$1,250	$1,100	$950	$850	$750	$650

Last MSR was $1,500.

It is estimated that only 25 instruments were produced. The Hendrix model featured construction similar to the 25th Anniversary model, except had a reverse headstock and an additional body contour on the front.

IRON MAIDEN STRATOCASTER (JAPAN MFG. NO. 025-2502) - basswood body, maple neck and fingerboard, vintage-style tuning machines, 22 Super Jumbo nickel silver frets, 3 pickups (2 Seymour Duncan Hot Rails, 1 Seymour Duncan JB Jr. humbucker in bridge position), three knobs (v, tone, tone) five-way switch, Floyd Rose original bridge, available in Black finish, mfg. 2001 only.

		$800	$700	$625	$550	$475	$400	$325

Last MSR was $1,140.

JEFF BECK (U.S. MFG. NO. 010-9600) - alder body, 22-fret rosewood fingerboard with pearl dot inlay, standard vibrato, LSR roller nut, Jeff Beck's signature on peghead, locking tuners, chrome hardware, 4 single coil Lace Sensor Gold pickups (2 in humbucker configuration), coil tap switch, available in Surf Green or Olympic White finishes, case included, mfg. 1991-present.

MSR	$2,000	$1,400	$1,200	$1,050	$900	$750	$650	$550

Midnight Purple finish was discontinued in 2001. This model was revised for 2002 with a "C"-shaped neck, contoured heel, and the new Fender Special Design "Noiseless" pickups.

Jeff Beck Custom Shop Signature (No. 015-0083) - similar to the Jeff Beck Signature, except made in the Custom Shop, available in Olympic White or Surf Green finishes, mfg. summer 2004-present.

MSR	$2,931	$2,150	$1,850	$1,650	$1,450	$1,250	$1,100	$950

JERRY DONAHUE LIMITED EDITION (JAPAN MFG. NO. 025-8900) - basswood body, 21-fret maple fingerboard with dot inlay, LSR nut, midnight blue sparkle pickguard, 3 Seymour Duncan single coil pickups, volume/tone controls, 2-position rotary switch, 5-way selector, available in Trans. Blue Sapphire finish, mfg. 1997-98.

		$850	$725	$625	$525	$450	$375	$300

Last MSR was $1,150.

JIMI HENDRIX TRIBUTE (U.S. MFG. NO. 010-6822) - alder body, 21-fret maple fingerboard with black dot inlay, reverse oversized (late '60s) headstock, vintage-style vibrato, reverse logo/headstock information, chrome hardware, F tuning keys, 3 reverse staggered single coil pickups, available in Olympic White finish, mfg. 1997-2000.

		$1,150	$1,000	$850	$775	$700	$625	$550

Last MSR was $1,600.

This model is essentially a left-handed guitar strung right-handed.

JIMMY VAUGHN TEX-MEX (MEX. MFG. NO. 013-9202) - poplar body, 21-fret maple fingerboard with black dot inlay, vintage-style vibrato, Jimmy Vaughn's signature on peghead, nickel hardware, single-ply white pickguard, 3 Tex-Mex single coil pickups, volume/2 tone

GRADING	100% MINT	98% NEAR MINT	95% EXC+	90% EXC	80% VG+	70% VG	60% G

controls, 5-position switch, special wiring, available in Olympic White, Black, Candy Apple Red, or 2-Tone Sunburst finishes, mfg. 1997-present.

| MSR | $828 | $580 | $500 | $425 | $350 | $300 | $250 | $200 |

Add $35 for 2-Tone Sunburst finish.

In 1999, Black, and Candy Apple Red finishes were introduced.

JOHN JORGENSEN LIMITED EDITION HELLECASTER (JAPAN MFG. NO. 025-8800) - maple body, maple neck, large reversed Strat headstock, 22-fret rosewood fingerboard with gold sparkle dot inlays, Schaller locking tuners, two pivot point tremolo, gold hardware, gold sparkle pickguard, 3 split Seymour Duncan single coil pickups, custom wired 5-way selector switch, available in Black Sparkle finish, mfg. 1997-98.

| | $925 | $825 | $750 | $675 | $600 | $525 | $450 |

Last MSR was $1,300.

MARK KNOPFLER (U.S. MFG. NO. 011-7800) - 57 style ash body, C-shaped 62 maple neck, 21-fret rosewood fingerboard, 3 Texas Special single coil pickups, five-way switch, available in Hot Rod Red finish, mfg. 2003-present.

| MSR | $2,000 | $1,400 | $1,200 | $1,050 | $900 | $750 | $650 | $550 |

MATTHIAS JABS (JAPAN MFG. NO. 025-7400) - alder body, maple neck, 22-fret rosewood fingerboard with custom Saturn planet inlays, custom shape small headstock, Gotoh vintage locking tuners, vintage tremolo, nickel hardware, single-ply white pickguard, 2 Custom Shop '50s single coil/Seymour Duncan JB humbucker pickups, TBX circuitry, available in Candy Apple Red finish, mfg. 1998 only.

| | $775 | $700 | $625 | $550 | $475 | $400 | $325 |

Last MSR was $1,099.

RICHIE SAMBORA (U.S. MFG. NO. 010-2602/010-2702) - alder body, 22-fret maple fingerboard with abalone star inlay, Original Floyd Rose vibrato, Richie Sambora's signature on peghead, pearl tuner buttons, chrome hardware, 2 Texas Special single coil/1 DiMarzio PAF Pro humbucker pickups, active electronics, currently available in 3-Color Sunburst, Fiesta Red, or Vintage White finishes, mfg. 1993-2002.

| | $1,350 | $1,175 | $1,025 | $895 | $775 | $625 | $495 |

Last MSR was $1,900.

**Fender Eric Clapton
Stratocaster
courtesy Fender**

In 1999, 3-Color Sunburst, Fiesta Red & Vintage White finishes were introduced; Arctic White & Cherry Sunburst finishes were discontinued.

Richie Sambora Standard (Mex. Mfg. No. 113-2700) - poplar body, 21-fret rosewood fingerboard with pearl dot inlay, Floyd Rose II vibrato, chrome hardware, 2 single coil/1 DiMarzio PAF Pro humbucker pickup, available in Arctic White, Black, Candy Apple Red, or Lake Placid Blue finishes, mfg. 1994-2002.

| | $575 | $500 | $425 | $375 | $325 | $275 | $225 |

Last MSR was $800.

In 1999, Candy Apple Red finish was introduced and Crimson Red Metallic finish was discontinued.

Richie Sambora Limited Edition Black Paisley (Japan Mfg. No. 125-2702) - similar to the Richie Sambora Signature model, except features 2 RS Special single coil/custom wound humbucking pickups, available in Black Paisley finish, mfg. 1996 only.

| | N/A | $1,000 | $850 | $725 | $600 | $500 | $400 |

Last MSR was $1,369.

RITCHIE BLACKMORE LIMITED EDITION (JAPAN MFG. NO. 025-8400) - basswood body, oversized headstock, partially scalloped 21-fret rosewood fingerboard with dot inlay, chrome/nickel hardware, white pickguard, 2 Seymour Duncan Quarter Pounder single coils (no middle pickup - cover only), 3-bolt neckplate, black control knobs, available in Olympic White, case included, mfg. 1997 only.

| | N/A | $750 | $675 | $600 | $525 | $450 | $375 |

Last MSR was $1,000.

RITCHIE BLACKMORE (U.S. MFG NO. 010-2400) - ash body, set maple neck, scalloped rosewood fingerboard with dot position markers, 22 jumbo frets, 70s large headstock, deluxe locking tuners, two Gold Fender-Lace Sensor pickups, 1 Volume/2 tone controls, two-point synchronized tremolo, Dunlop flush-mount straplock system, available in Olmypic White, case included, current mfg.

| MSR | $5,573 | $4,000 | $3,500 | $3,200 | $2,900 | $2,600 | $2,300 | $2,000 |

Add $300 for Roland GK-2 pickup system (Roland Ready, Model 010-2460).

ROBERT CRAY (U.S. MFG. NO. 010-9100) - alder body, 21-fret rosewood fingerboard with pearl dot inlay, strings through bridge, Robert Cray's signature on peghead, chrome hardware, 3 single coil exposed pickups, available in Inca Silver, 3-Tone Sunburst or Violet finishes, mfg. 1990-present.

| MSR | $2,997 | $2,150 | $1,900 | $1,650 | $1,400 | $1,150 | $900 | $700 |

This model is available by custom order only. In 1998, gold hardware replaced chrome hardware.

Robert Cray (Mex Mfg. No. 013-9100) - alder body, 21 fret maple '61 C-Shape neck, rosewood fingerboard with dot inlay, 3 Custom Vintage Strat pickups, 3-ply white pickguard, Vintage HT tremolo bridge, 5-way switch, 3 knobs (v, 2 tones), chrome hardware, signature on headstock, available in 3-Color Sunburst, Inca Silver, or Violet finishes, mfg. 2003-present.

| MSR | $828 | $580 | $500 | $425 | $350 | $300 | $250 | $200 |

Add $35 for 3-Color Sunburst.

**Fender Signature Series
Stevie Ray Vaughn
courtesy Fender**

GRADING	100% MINT	98% NEAR MINT	95% EXC+	90% EXC	80% VG+	70% VG	60% G

ROBIN TROWER (NO. 015-5102) - alder body, maple custom C-shape neck, 21-fret maple fingerboard with dot inlay, 2 Custom '50s single coil pickups, and 1 Tex Mex single coil in bridge position, large 70s style headstock, vintage tremolo bridge, chrome hardware, available in Arctic White, Midnight Wine Burst, or Black finishes, mfg. summer 2004-present.

	MSR	$3,280		$2,400	$2,050	$1,800	$1,600	$1,400	$1,200	$1,000

RORY GALLAGHER (NO. 015-0080) - select alder body, maple '60s C-Shape neck, 21-fret rosewood fingerboard with dot inlay, 3 custom single coil '60s pickups, 3 knobs, 5-way switch, Tremolo bridge, nickel/chrome hardware, available in 3-Color Sunburst, which most of is worn off to reveal a mainly wood-only guitar, mfg. summer 2004-present.

	MSR	$3,930		$2,850	$2,500	$2,200	$1,900	$1,700	$1,500	$1,300

One of the12th fret inlays is replaced with white plastic instead of the original clay; talk about reproduction!

STEVIE RAY VAUGHN (U.S. MFG. NO. 010-9200) - alder body, 21-fret rosewood fingerboard with clay dot inlay, left-handed vintage-style vibrato, Stevie Ray Vaughn's signature on peghead, gold hardware, black pickguard with SRV logo, 3 Texas Special single coil pickups, volume/2 tone controls, 5-position switch, available in 3-Tone Sunburst finish, mfg. 1992-present.

	MSR	$2,000		$1,400	$1,200	$1,050	$900	$750	$650	$550

TOM DELONGE STRATOCASTER (MEX. MFG. NO. 013-8200) - alder body, rosewood fingerboard, vintage style tuning machines, 21 medium/jumbo frets, Seymour Duncan Invader pickup, one volume control, white speckled pickguard, hardtail bridge, available Daphne Blue, Black, Sea Foam Green, or Graffiti Yellow, gig bag included, mfg. 2001-03.

				$525	$450	$375	$350	$300	$250	$200

Last MSR was $750.

VENTURE'S LIMITED EDITION (JAPAN MFG. NO. 025-8100) - light ash body, 22-fret rosewood fingerboard with white block inlay, vintage-style vibrato, white shell pickguard, gold hardware, 3 Lace Sensor Gold single coil pickups, active electronics, available in Midnight Black Trans. finish, mfg. 1996 only.

				$1,100	$950	$825	$700	$600	$500	$400

Last MSR was $1,489.

YNGWIE MALMSTEEN (U.S. MFG. NO. 010-7702) - alder body, 22-fret scalloped maple fingerboard with black dot inlay, American Standard vibrato, brass nut, Yngwie Malmsteen's signature on peghead, chrome hardware, 2 DiMarzio HS-3/1 American Standard Stratocaster single coil pickups, active electronics, available in Candy Apple Red, Sonic Blue, or Vintage White finishes, mfg. 1988-1998.

		N/A		$1,150	$1,000	$850	$750	$650	$550

Last MSR was $1,599.

This model was also available with rosewood fingerboard and pearl dot inlays (Model 010-7700).

Yngwie Malmsteen Standard (Japan Mfg. No. 027-2702) - similar to Yngwie Malmsteen model, except has basswood body, '70s style headstock, no active electronics, available in Black, Sonic Blue, or Vintage White finishes, mfg. 1991-94.

		N/A		$700	$625	$550	$475	$400	$325

Last MSR was $960.

YNGWIE MALMSTEEN CURRENT MFG. (U.S. MFG. NO. 010-7100) - alder body, 21-fret scalloped rosewood fingerboard with black dot inlay, large headstock, vintage vibrato, brass nut, Yngwie Malmsteen's signature on peghead, Schaller F tuners, pre-aged chrome hardware, mint green pickguard, 2 DiMarzio YJM single coil/DiMarzio HS-3 single coil pickups, 3-way selector switch, available in Candy Apple Red, Sonic Blue, or Vintage White finishes, mfg. 1998-present.

	MSR	$2,000		$1,400	$1,200	$1,050	$900	$750	$650	$550

This model is also available with maple fingerboard and pearl dot inlays (Model 010-7102).

Stratocaster: Special Edition Series

AERODYNE STRATOCASTER (JAPAN MFG. NO. 025-6505) - basswood body with unique carved top, maple neck, 21-fret rosewood fingerboard with dot inlay, matching color headstock, 6-on-a-side tuner, vintage style tremolo bridge, no pickguard, three single coil pickups, three knobs (v, t, t), five-way switch, chrome hardware, Black finish, new 2005.

	MSR	$900		$630	$550	$475	$425	$375	$325	$275

LITE ASH STRATOCASTER (JAP. MFG. NO. 026-5002) - lightweight ash body, bird's-eye maple C-Shaped neck, 22-fret bird's-eye maple neck with dot abalone inlay, single ply black pickguard, 3 Seymour Duncan single coil pickups, black pickup covers and knobs (3), 5-way switch, tremolo bridge, chrome hardware, available in Black, Vintage White, or Natural finishes, mfg. 2004-present.

	MSR	$900		$630	$550	$475	$425	$375	$325	$275

Stratocaster: Strat Plus Series

The American-built Strat Plus Series models are the upscale versions of the American Standard Series Stratocasters. Current models all feature Fender-Lace Sensor pickups, LSR roller nuts, and locking tuners.

STRAT PLUS (U.S. MFG. NO. 010-7502) - Alder body, 22-fret maple fingerboard with black dot inlay, vibrato bridge, LSR roller nut, Sperzel or Schaller locking tuners, chrome hardware, white shell pickguard, 3 single coil Lace Sensor Gold pickups, volume/2 tone controls, 5-position switch, available in Arctic White, Black, Black Pearl Dust, Blue Pearl Dust, Brown Sunburst, Caribbean Mist, Grafitti Yellow, Lipstick Red, Midnight Blue, or Midnight Wine finishes, mfg. 1987-1999.

				$850	$750	$650	$550	$475	$400	$325

Last MSR was $1,199.

Add $35 for 3-Color Sunburst finish.

This model also available with rosewood fingerboard with pearl dot inlay (Model 010-7500). This was the first model to feature Fender Lace sensors. In 1997, Candy Apple Red, Inca Silver, Sonic Blue, and Vintage White finishes were introduced; Arctic White, Black Pearl Dust, Blue Pearl Dust, Caribbean Mist, Lipstick Red, Midnight Blue, and Midnight Wine finishes were discontinued.

GRADING	100% MINT	98% NEAR MINT	95% EXC+	90% EXC	80% VG+	70% VG	60% G

DELUXE STRAT PLUS (U.S. MFG. NO. 110-9502) similar to Strat Plus, except has ash top/back, alder body, 2 Silver/1 Blue Lace Sensor single coil pickups, available in Antique Burst, Black, Blue Burst, Crimson Burst, Mystic Black, Natural, or Shoreline Gold finishes, mfg. 1989-1999.

		$1,000	$850	$750	$650	$550	$450	$350

Last MSR was $1,499.

This model also available with rosewood fingerboard with pearl dot inlay (Model 110-9500). In 1990, this model was released with an alternative set of Lace Sensors: Silver/Blue/Red. Some models may have a Floyd Rose tremolo bridge.

STRAT ULTRA (U.S. MFG. NO. 110-9800) - similar to Strat Plus, except has figured maple top/back, alder body, ebony fingerboard with abalone dot inlay, Floyd Rose vibrato, 4 Lace Sensor single coil pickups Blue/Silver/2 Red (Dually configuration), mini switch, available in Antique Burst, Black, Blue Burst, or Crimson Burst finishes, mfg. 1990-99.

		$1,250	$1,100	$950	$825	$700	$575	$450

Last MSR was $1,799.

Stratocaster: Standard Series (Mex. Current Mfg.)

STANDARD STRATOCASTER (MEX. MFG. NO. 013-4600) - poplar body, white pickguard, 22-fret rosewood fingerboard with black dot inlay, vintage-style tremolo, chrome hardware, 6-on-a-side die-cast tuners, 3 single coil pickups, volume/tone contols, 5-position switch, available in Arctic White, Black, Blue Agave, Brown Sunburst, Lake Placid Blue, Midnight Blue, Midnight Wine, or Sage Green Metallic finishes, mfg. 1991-present.

MSR	$528		$370	$320	$270	$235	$200	$175	$150

Add $35 for Brown Sunburst finish.

This model also available with optional maple fingerboard with pearl dot inlay (Model 013-4602). Crimson Red Metallic and Lake Placid Blue finishes were disc. in 2001, and Blue Agave, Midnight Blue, and Midnight Wine were introduced.

Standard Stratocaster Satin (Mex. Mfg. No. 013-4400) - similar to the Standard Stratocaster except has satin finish, black pickguard, and black pickups, available in Candy Apple Red, Gun Metal Blue, Midnight Blue, or Midnight Wine, mfg. 2003-present.

MSR	$528		$370	$320	$275	$235	$200	$175	$150

This model is also available with optional maple fingerboard (No. 013-4402).

Standard Stratocaster Left-Hand (Jap. Mfg., No. 027-4620) - similar to the Standard Stratocaster, except in a left-handed configuration with rosewood fingerboard, available in Black finish, disc. 1997.

		N/A	$320	$275	$230	$200	$175	$150

Last MSR was $439.

Also available with maple fingerboard (013-4622).

Standard Stratocaster Left-Hand (Mex. Mfg., No. 013-4620) - similar to Standard Stratocaster Japanese Mfg. except mfg. in Mexico, mfg. 1997-present.

MSR	$528		$370	$320	$275	$235	$200	$175	$150

Also available with maple neck (Model 013-4622), current mfg.

STANDARD FAT STRAT HSS (MEX. MFG. NO. 013-4700) - similar to Standard Stratocaster, except has 2 single coil pickups and 1 humbucker pickup, rosewood fingerboard, available in Black, Sage Green Metallic, Brown Sunburst, Midnight Blue, Blue Agave, Midnight Wine, or Arctic White finishes, current mfg.

MSR	$528		$370	$320	$275	$235	$200	$175	$150

Add $35 for Brown Sunburst finish.

Also available with maple neck and fingerboard (Model 013-4702). Midnight Blue finish was discontinued in 2002. Sage Green Metallic and Blue Agave finishes were introduced in 2002. Also available with 2 humbucker pickups as the HH model (Model 013-4800, new 2004).

Standard Fat Strat Floyd Rose (Mex. Mfg. No. 113-4700) - similar to Standard Fat Strat, except has Floyd Rose licensed double locking tremolo, rosewood fingerboard, current mfg.

MSR	$700		$490	$400	$350	$300	$260	$230	$190

STANDARD "ROLAND READY" STRATOCASTER (MEX. MFG. NO. 013-4660) - similar to the American Standard Stratocaster GR Ready, except features poplar body, 21-fret rosewood fingerboard, Standard hardware, available in Artic White, Black, or Brown Sunburst finishes, mfg. 1998-present.

MSR	$900		$630	$550	$475	$425	$375	$325	$275

Add $35 for Brown Sunburst finish.

This model has a built-in Roland GK-2A pickup and controls, which is pre-wired to drive the Roland GR series guitar synthesizer, as well as perform like a Stratocaster. Roland's GK-2A pickup system can interface with Roland's GR-1, GR-09, and GR-50 synthesizers; as well as the VG-8 guitar system and GI-10 guitar/MIDI interface.

STRATOCASTER JR. (MEX. MFG. NO. 013-3800) - mini version of the Standard Stratocaster, 22.72 in. length, 2 knobs, available in Black or Torino Red finishes, mfg. 2004-present.

MSR	$500		$350	$300	$275	$235	$195	$165	$135

**Fender Stratocaster Plus
courtesy George McGuire**

**Fender Standard
Stratocaster
courtesy Fender**

GRADING	100% MINT	98% NEAR MINT	95% EXC+	90% EXC	80% VG+	70% VG	60% G

Stratocaster: Time Machine Series (Custom Shop)

Built to exacting specifications of their respective vintages, body contours and radii, neck shape, fingerboard radius, pickups, electronics and hardware. Original materials, tooling and production techniques are employed whenever possible, available in three distinct finish packages: NOS (New-Old Stock), as if the guitar was bought new in its respective year and brought forward to the present day; Closet Classic, as if guitar was bought new in its respective year, played perhaps a dozen times a year and then put carefully away (has a few slight dings, lightly checked finish, oxidized hardware and aged plastic parts) Relic (shows natural wear and tear of years of heavy use - nicks, scratches, worn finish, rusty hardware and aged plastic parts).

'56 STRATOCASTER NOS (NO. 015-0402) - alder or ash body, 10/56 shaped maple neck, single-ply white pickguard and original spec pickups, available in White Blonde, 2-Color Sunburst, Black, or Fiesta Red finishes, mfg. 2001-present.

	MSR	$3,011		$2,150	$1,900	$1,650	$1,450	$1,250	$1,050	$850

Add $150 for gold hardware (Model 015-0412).

'56 Stratocaster Closet Classic (No. 015-0502) - similar to '56 Stratocaster NOS except in Closet Classic finish, available in 2-Color Sunburst, black, Fiesta Red and Vintage Blonde finishes, mfg. 2001-present.

	MSR	$3,231		$2,300	$2,000	$1,750	$1,500	$1,300	$1,100	$900

Add $150 for gold hardware (Model 015-0512).

'56 Stratocaster Relic (No. 015-0602) - similar to '56 Stratocaster NOS except in Relic finish, available in 2-Color Sunburst, Black, Vintage Blonde, or Fiesta Red finishes, mfg. 2001-present.

	MSR	$3,481		$2,450	$2,150	$1,850	$1,600	$1,400	$1,200	$1,000

Add $150 for gold hardware (Model 015-0612).

'60 STRATOCASTER NOS (NO. 015-0700) - alder body, "C" shaped neck with rosewood fingerboard, white/black/white pickguard, original specification pickups, available in 3-Color Sunburst, Daphne Blue, Olympic White, or Fiesta Red finishes, mfg. 2001-present.

	MSR	$3,000		$2,100	$1,850	$1,600	$1,400	$1,200	$1,000	$800

Add $150 for gold hardware (Model 015-0710).

'60 Stratocaster Closet Classic (No. 015-0800) - similar to '60 Stratocaster NOS except in Closet Classic finish, available in 3-Color Sunburst, Daphne Blue, Olympic White, or Fiesta Red., mfg. 2001-present.

	MSR	$3,310		$2,350	$2,050	$1,800	$1,550	$1,350	$1,150	$950

Add $150 for gold hardware (Model 015-0810).

'60 Stratocaster Relic (No. 015-0900) - similar to '60 Stratocaster NOS except in Relic finish, available in 3-Color Sunburst, Daphne Blue, Olympic White, or Fiesta Red finishes, mfg. 2001-present.

	MSR	$3,470		$2,450	$2,150	$1,850	$1,600	$1,400	$1,200	$1,000

Add $150 for gold hardware (Model 015-0910).

'65 STRATOCASTER NOS (NO. 015-2700) - alder body, "C" shaped maple neck, 21-fret round-lam rosewood fingerboard with dot inlay, white pickguard, 3 Custom '65 S-C pickups, American Vintage Style tremolo, 3-way switch, 3 knobs (v, 2 tones), chrome hardware, available in 3-Color Sunburst, Lake Placid Blue, Olympic White, or Charcoal Forst Metallic, mfg. 2003-present.

	MSR	$3,221		$2,300	$2,000	$1,750	$1,500	$1,300	$1,100	$900

'65 Stratocaster Closet Classic (No. 015-2800) - similar to the '65 Strat NOS except has Closet Classic finish, mfg. 2003-present.

	MSR	$3,531		$2,500	$2,200	$1,900	$1,600	$1,350	$1,150	$925

'65 Stratocaster Relic (No. 015-2900) - similar to the '65 Strat NOS except has Relic finish, mfg. 2003-present.

	MSR	$3,691		$2,600	$2,300	$2,000	$1,700	$1,450	$1,200	$950

'66 STRATOCASTER NOS (NO. 150-6600) - alder body, "U"-shaped maple neck, large headstock, round-lam fingerboard rosewood fingerboard, white/black/white pickguard, original specification pickups, available in Candy Apple Red, Teal Green Metallic, or Firemist Gold Metallic finishes, mfg. summer 2004-present.

	MSR	$3,227		$2,300	$2,000	$1,750	$1,500	$1,300	$1,100	$900

Also available with maple fingerboard (Model 150-6602).

'66 Stratocaster Closet Classic (No. 151-6600) - similar to '66 Stratocaster NOS except in Closet Classic finish, mfg. summer 2004-present.

	MSR	$3,537		$2,500	$2,200	$1,900	$1,650	$1,400	$1,150	$950

Also available with maple fingerboard (Model 151-6602).

'66 Stratocaster Relic (No. 152-6600) - similar to '66 Stratocaster NOS except in Relic finish, mfg. summer 2004-present.

	MSR	$3,697		$2,600	$2,300	$2,000	$1,750	$1,500	$1,250	$1,000

Also available with maple fingerboard (Model 152-6602).

'69 STRATOCASTER NOS (NO. 015-1700) - alder body, "U"-shaped maple neck, large headstock, round-lam fingerboard rosewood fingerboard, white/black/white pickguard, original specification pickups, available in 3-Color Sunburst, Olympic White, or Black finishes, mfg. 2001-present.

	MSR	$3,227		$2,300	$2,000	$1,750	$1,500	$1,300	$1,100	$900

Also available with maple fingerboard (Model 015-1702).

'69 Stratocaster Closet Classic (No. 015-1800) - similar to '69 Stratocaster NOS except in Closet Classic finish, rosewood fingerboard. Available in 3-Color Sunburst, Olympic White and Fiesta Red finishes, mfg. 2001-present.

	MSR	$3,537		$2,500	$2,200	$1,900	$1,650	$1,400	$1,150	$950

Also available with maple fingerboard (Model 015-1802).

GRADING		100% MINT	98% NEAR MINT	95% EXC+	90% EXC	80% VG+	70% VG	60% G

´69 Stratocaster Relic (No. 015-1900) - Similar to ´69 Stratocaster NOS except in Relic finish, rosewood fingerboard, available in 3-Color Sunburst, Olympic White, or Fiesta Red finishes, mfg. 2001-present.

	MSR	$3,697	$2,600	$2,300	$2,000	$1,750	$1,500	$1,250	$1,000

Also available with maple fingerboard (Model 015-1902).

Stratocaster: U.S. Vintage Reissue Series

The ´57 and ´62 Vintage Reissue models were originally produced at the CBS/Fender Fullerton facility (1982-1985). These models were the first Stratocasters of the post-CBS era to be made in the U.S. at the Corona, California production facility.

´57 STRATOCASTER (U.S. MFG. NO. 010-0102/010-0908) - alder body, white pickguard, 21-fret maple fingerboard with black dot inlay, vintage-style vibrato, nickel hardware, 3 American Vintage single coil pickups, volume/2 tone controls, 3-position switch, available in 2-Tone Sunburst, Black, Candy Apple Red, Fiesta Red, Ocean Turquoise, Shoreline Gold, or Vintage White finishes, mfg. 1982-85 (Fullerton, CA), 1985-present (Corona, CA).

1982-1985		N/A	$1,400	$1,200	$1,000	$850	$700	$550
1985-1994		N/A	$1,200	$1,050	$900	$750	$600	$450
1995-MSR	$1,900	$1,350	$1,150	$950	$800	$700	$600	$500

Add $35 for 2-Color Sunburst finish (1998-current). Add $100 for White Blonde finish.

In 1997, Shoreline Gold finish was introduced. In 1999, White Blonde & Aztec Gold finishes were introduced; Shoreline Gold & Vintage White finishes were discontinued. In 2001, Inca Silver, Dakota Red and Ice Blue Metallic finishes were introduced.

´57 Stratocaster Left-Hand (U.S. Mfg., No. 010-0122) - similar to the ´57 Stratocaster except in left-hand configuration, available in 2-Color Sunburst, mfg. 1998-present.

	MSR	$1,957	$1,375	$1,150	$1,000	$850	$700	$600	$500

´62 STRATOCASTER (U.S. MFG. NO. 010-0100/010-0909) - alder body, white pickguard, 21-fret rosewood fingerboard with pearl dot inlay, vintage-style vibrato, nickel hardware, 3 American Vintage single coil pickups, volume/2 tone controls, 3-position switch, available in 3-Tone Sunburst, Black, Candy Apple Red, Fiesta Red, Ocean Turquoise, Shoreline Gold, Ice Blue Metallic, and Vintage White finishes, mfg. 1982-85 (Fullerton, CA), 1985-present (Corona, CA).

1982-1985		N/A	$1,400	$1,200	$1,000	$850	$700	$550
1985-1994		N/A	$1,200	$1,050	$900	$750	$600	$450
1995-MSR	$1,900	$1,350	$1,150	$950	$800	$700	$600	$500

Add $35 for 3-Color Sunburst finish (1998-current).

In 1997, Shoreline Gold finish was introduced, Ocean Turquoise finish was discontinued. In 1999, Olympic White and Sherwood Metallic finishes were introduced and Vintage White and Shoreline gold finishes were discontinued. In 2000, Sherwood Metallic finish was discontinued. In 2001, Inca Silver, Dakota Red and Ice Blue Metallic finishes were introduced. In 2003, Inca Silver and Dakota Red were disc.

´62 Stratocaster Left-Hand (U.S. Mfg. No. 010-0120) - similar to the ´62 Stratocaster except in left-hand configuration, available in 3-Color Sunburst, mfg. 1998-present.

	MSR	$1,957	$1,375	$1,150	$1,000	$850	$700	$600	$500

Fender ´69 Stratocaster Relic
courtesy Fender

TELECASTER SERIES

All instruments in this series have a single cutaway body, bolt-on maple neck, 6-on-one-side tuners, unless otherwise listed. There were no American-made Telecasters made between 1986 and 1987.

Telecaster: Broadcaster & "No"Caster Models

BROADCASTER (MFG. 1950) - ash body, black pickguard, 21-fret maple fingerboard with black dot inlay, fixed bridge with cover, chrome hardware, 2 single coil pickups, 3-position switch, volume/tone control, available in Translucent Butterscotch finish, mfg. 1950 only.

	N/A	$50,000	$42,000	$35,000	$30,000	$25,000	$20,000

This model's value should be determined on a piece-by-piece basis as opposed to the usual market. Prototypes and custom models existed before 1948. After Fender released the Broadcaster model, the Fred Gretsch company objected to the similarity of the name to their Broadkaster trademark used on Gretsch drums. Fender, the new kids on the block (at that time), complied with the request. In 1951, the Broadcaster name was changed to Telecaster.

"NO"CASTER - similar to Broadcaster, except has Fender name only, no model, on the headstock, mfg. 1950-51.

	N/A	$37,000	$32,000	$28,000	$24,000	$19,000	$15,000

In the transition period between the Broadcaster and Telecaster model names, Fender continued producing guitars. Leo Fender, never one to throw money away, simply clipped the Broadcaster name off of the labels already in stock. Therefore, the guitars produced between the Broadcaster and Telecaster name changeover have been nicknamed the "No"caster by collectors due to lack of model name after the Fender logo on the headstock.

1950 Fender "No"Caster
Courtesy: Dave Rogers
Dave's Guitar Shop

GRADING	100% MINT	98% NEAR MINT	95% EXC+	90% EXC	80% VG+	70% VG	60% G

Telecaster: Early Models (1950-1985 Mfg.)

TELECASTER (FENDER MFG. 1951-1964) - ash body, black pickguard, 21-fret maple fingerboard with black dot inlay, strings through bridge, chrome hardware, 2 single coil pickups, volume/tone controls, 3-position switch, controls mounted metal plate, available in Blonde finish, mfg. 1951-1964.

	100%	98%	95%	90%	80%	70%	60%
1951	N/A	$25,000	$22,000	$19,000	$16,000	$14,000	$12,000
1952	N/A	$23,000	$20,000	$17,000	$14,000	$12,000	$10,000
1953	N/A	$21,000	$18,000	$15,000	$13,000	$11,000	$9,000
1954 BLACK P/G	N/A	$19,000	$16,000	$14,000	$12,000	$10,000	$8,000
1954-55 WHITE P/G	N/A	$17,000	$14,000	$12,000	$10,000	$8,500	$7,000
1956	N/A	$15,000	$12,500	$10,500	$9,000	$7,500	$6,000
1957	N/A	$13,000	$11,000	$9,000	$7,500	$6,500	$5,500
1958	N/A	$11,000	$9,000	$7,500	$6,500	$5,500	$4,500
1959	N/A	$10,000	$8,500	$7,000	$6,000	$5,000	$4,000
1960	N/A	$9,500	$8,000	$6,700	$5,700	$4,700	$3,700
1961	N/A	$9,000	$7,500	$6,500	$5,500	$4,500	$3,500
1962	N/A	$8,500	$7,000	$6,200	$5,200	$4,200	$3,200
1963	N/A	$8,000	$6,700	$5,800	$5,000	$4,000	$3,000
1964	N/A	$7,500	$6,500	$5,500	$4,800	$3,900	$3,000

Add 25% for Sunburst finish. Add 75%-100% for custom colors.

In late 1954, white pickguard replaced the black pickguard. In 1955, level pole piece pickups became standard. In 1956, the logo was moved above the string guide on the headstock. In 1957, custom colors became available, and alder bodies were used with those finishes. In 1958, a strings-through-bridge replaced the fixed bridge. In 1959, rosewood fingerboard with pearl dot inlay replaced maple fingerboard and the pickguard design was changed to 8 screws. In 1963, a laminated pickguard was introduced.

TELECASTER (CBS MFG. 1965-1983) - similar to original Telecaster, except has "F" stamp on back of neck plates, mfg. 1965-1982.

	100%	98%	95%	90%	80%	70%	60%
1965	N/A	$7,000	$5,800	$5,000	$4,300	$3,700	$3,000
1966	N/A	$6,500	$5,500	$4,500	$3,800	$3,300	$2,700
1967	N/A	$5,500	$4,500	$3,500	$3,000	$2,500	$2,000
1968	N/A	$5,000	$4,000	$3,200	$2,600	$2,200	$1,800
1969	N/A	$4,500	$3,500	$2,800	$2,200	$1,750	$1,500
1970	N/A	$4,000	$3,200	$2,600	$2,000	$1,700	$1,400
1971	N/A	$3,500	$2,700	$2,200	$1,800	$1,500	$1,300
1972	N/A	$3,000	$2,500	$2,100	$1,700	$1,400	$1,200
1973	N/A	$2,500	$2,100	$1,800	$1,500	$1,300	$1,100
1974	N/A	$2,250	$1,850	$1,600	$1,400	$1,200	$1,000
1975-1979	N/A	$1,800	$1,500	$1,250	$1,050	$850	$700
1980-1982	N/A	$1,500	$1,250	$1,050	$900	$750	$600

Add 15% for Sunburst finish. Add 25%-50% for custom color finishes.

This model is referred to as CBS Mfg. because of the sale of Fender Musical Instruments Corp. to the CBS Broadcasting Co. in early 1965. From 1967-1974, Bigsby vibrato tailpiece was an option. From 1967-1969, maple fingerboard was an option. In 1969, maple fingerboard with black dot inlay replaced rosewood fingerboard. In 1972, 2 string guides were introduced on the headstock. In 1975, black pickguard replaced white pickguard. In 1981, white pickguard replaced the black pickguard. In 1982, this model was changed to the Standard Telecaster.

TELECASTER WITH BIGSBY VIBRATO (CBS MFG. 1967-1975) - similar to original Telecaster, except has Bigsby vibrato unit, mfg. 1967-1975.

	100%	98%	95%	90%	80%	70%	60%
1967	N/A	$4,500	$3,700	$3,200	$2,700	$2,400	$2,100
1968	N/A	$4,000	$3,200	$2,500	$2,000	$1,700	$1,400
1969	N/A	$3,500	$2,800	$2,300	$1,900	$1,600	$1,300
1970	N/A	$3,000	$2,400	$2,000	$1,700	$1,400	$1,100
1971	N/A	$2,500	$2,100	$1,800	$1,500	$1,200	$1,000
1972	N/A	$2,000	$1,700	$1,400	$1,200	$1,000	$800
1973-1975	N/A	$1,500	$1,300	$1,100	$950	$800	$650

Telecasters with a maple cap fingerboard bring a higher premium.

STANDARD TELECASTER (U.S. MFG., 1982-85) - similar to the original Telecaster except with different name, available in various finishes, mfg. 1982-85.

	100%	98%	95%	90%	80%	70%	60%
	N/A	$1,000	$850	$750	$650	$550	$450

In 1983, a 6-saddle bridge with top loading strings, and a single-ply pickguard with 5 screws was introduced. This Standard Stratocaster is not to be confused with the Mexican-made Standard that was introduced in 1991, and is still in production.

GRADING	100% MINT	98% NEAR MINT	95% EXC+	90% EXC	80% VG+	70% VG	60% G

Telecaster: Elite & Marble Series (1983-85 Mfg.)

ELITE TELECASTER (U.S. MFG. 1983-85) - bound alder body, 21-fret fingerboard with black dot inlay, fixed bridge, chrome hardware, 2 covered humbuckers, 2 volume/2 tone controls, 3-position switch, active electronics, available in Natural or Sunburst finishes, mfg. 1983-85.

	N/A	$950	$800	$700	$600	$500	$400

This model came with a white pickguard that could be applied with the supplied adhesive backing. This model was also available with rosewood fingerboard with pearl dot inlay.

Elite Telecaster Gold (U.S. Mfg.) - similar to Elite Telecaster, except has pearloid button tuners, gold hardware, mfg. 1983-85.

	N/A	$1,000	$850	$750	$650	$550	$450

Elite Telecaster Walnut (U.S. Mfg.) - similar to Elite Telecaster, except has walnut body/neck, ebony fingerboard with pearl dot inlay, pearloid button tuners, gold hardware, available in Natural finish, mfg. 1983-85.

	N/A	$1,000	$850	$750	$650	$550	$450

MARBLE FINISH TELECASTER ("BOWLING BALL") - similar to the 1983-1984 Telecaster, except featured a novel swirled finish, mfg. 1984 only.

	N/A	$3,200	$2,500	$2,000	$1,700	$1,400	$1,100

Last MSR was $799.

Approximately 75 of these instruments were produced. The unique finish is the result of dipping the (white) primer coated bodies into an oil-based finish that floated on water. After dipping, the guitar received a top coat of polyurethane. Fender produced three dominant colors. The Red finish had black and white swirled in (sometimes resulting in gray areas as well). The Blue finish was mixed with yellow and black, and the Yellow finish was combined with white and silver (sometimes resulting in gold patches).

Telecaster: American Standard Series (1988-2000 Mfg.)

AMERICAN STANDARD (U.S. MFG. 1988-2000, NO. 010-8402) - alder body, bolt-on maple neck, 22-fret maple fingerboard with black dot inlay, fixed bridge, chrome hardware, 2 American Standard Telecaster single coil pickups, volume/tone control, 3-position switch, controls mounted metal plate, available in Black, Caribbean Mist, Lipstick Red, Midnight Blue, Midnight Wine, Sunburst, or Vintage White finishes, mfg. 1988-2000.

1988-1993	N/A	$850	$700	$600	$500	$400	$300
1994-2000	N/A	$750	$650	$550	$450	$350	$250

Last MSR was $999.

Add $50 for 3-Color Sunburst (1999). Add $100 for Natural and White Blonde finishes.

This model also available with rosewood fingerboard with pearl dot inlay (Model 010-8400). These were the first Telecasters of the post-CBS era to be made in the U.S. (at the Corona, California production facility). Only the vintage series Telecasters were available between 1986 and 1987. In 1997, Brown Sunburst, Candy Apple Red, Inca Silver, and Sonic Blue finishes were introduced; Caribbean Mist, Lipstick Red, Midnight Blue, Midnight Wine, and Sunburst finishes were discontinued. In 1999, Aqua Marine Metallic, Metallic Purple, Natural, and White Blonde finishes were introduced. This model is not to be confused with the American Standard that was introduced in Summer, 2000.

American Standard Left Hand (U.S. Mfg., No. 010-8422) - similar to the American Standard Telecaster, except in a left-handed configuration, available in Black, 3-Color Sunburst, Candy Apple Red, or Vintage White finishes, disc. 2000.

	N/A	$750	$650	$550	$450	$350	$250

Last MSR was $1,099.

Add $50 for 3-Color Sunburst finish (1999).

In 1999, Metallic Purple and 3-Color Sunburst finishes were introduced and Brown Sunburst and Candy Apple Red finishes were discontinued.

AMERICAN STANDARD TELECASTER ALUMINUM BODY (U.S. MFG.) - similar to American Standard Telecaster, except has a hollow aluminum body, available in Blue Marble, Purple Marble, or Red/Silver/Blue Flag graphic anodized finish, mfg. 1994 only.

	N/A	$2,500	$2,100	$1,800	$1,500	$1,200	$900

It is estimated that only 100 instruments were produced.

AMERICAN STANDARD B-BENDER (U.S. MFG. NO. 010-8442) - similar to the American Standard Telecaster, except has custom designed Parsons/White B-Bender system installed, available in Black, Brown Sunburst, Candy Apple Red, or Vintage White finishes, mfg. 1995-99.

	$800	$700	$600	$525	$450	$375	$300

Last MSR was $1,129.

1952 Fender Telecaster
courtesy Dave Rogers
Dave's Guitar Shop

Fender Telecaster With Bigsby
courtesy Dave Rogers
Dave's Guitar Shop

GRADING	100% MINT	98% NEAR MINT	95% EXC+	90% EXC	80% VG+	70% VG	60% G

Telecaster: American Series (2000-Current Mfg.)

AMERICAN TELECASTER (U.S. MFG. NO. 011-8400) - alder or ash body, rosewood fingerboard, deluxe staggered cast/sealed tuners, 22 medium-jumbo frets, American Tele pickups, 1 volume/1 tone control, 3-way switch, 6-saddle STB bridge, case included, available in 3-Color Sunburst, Olympic White, Vintage White, Black, Natural, Chrome Red, or 2-Color Sunburst finishes, mfg. 2000-present.

| MSR | $1,328 | $930 | $825 | $725 | $650 | $575 | $500 | $425 |

Add $25 for S-1 Switching. Add $35 for 3-Color Sunburst finish. Add $100 for White Blonde, Natural, and 2-Color Sunburst finishes.

Also available with maple fingerboard (Model 011-8402). In 2002 White Blonde, Hot Rod Red, and Aqua Marine Metallic finishes were discontinued, and Olympic White and Chrome Red were introduced. In 2003 the Telecaster HS and HH were introduced at no extra cost. The HS (No. 011-8600/8602) has a humbucker and a Single Coil pickup and the HH (No. 011-8700/8702) has two humbuckers. They are available in Black, Pewter, Chrome Red or Chrome Blue finishes. In 2004, the HS and HH models were equipped with the new S-1 Switching, for more pickup options. These models retail for $1,357 (HS No. 011-8662, HH No. 011-8760).

American Telecaster Left Hand (U.S. Mfg., No. 011-8422) - similar to the American Telecaster except in left-hand configuration, available in 3-Color Sunburst and Black finishes, mfg. 2001-present.

| MSR | $1,328 | $930 | $825 | $725 | $650 | $575 | $500 | $425 |

Hot Rod Red finish was disc. in 2002.

American Telecaster Ash (U.S. Mfg., No. 011-8502) - similar to the American Telecaster except has an ash body, available in 2-Color Sunburst (Parchment P/G) or Honey Blonde (black P/G) finishes, mfg. 2003-present.

| MSR | $1,471 | $1,030 | $925 | $825 | $725 | $650 | $575 | $500 |

Telecaster: American Deluxe & Deluxe Series

AMERICAN DELUXE (U.S. MFG. NO. 010-4600) - premium ash or alder body with bound top and contoured back, special shape maple neck, rosewood fingerboard, abalone dot inlays, 25.5 in. scale, 22 medium-jumbo frets, deluxe Fender die-cast tuners, 2 Vintage Tele Noiseless pickups, master tone, master volume, 3-ply aged white or Brown shell pickguard, Fender Deluxe Tele bridge, Bi-flex truss rod, Micro-tilt neck adjustment, Schaller Strap-Lock ready, currently available in 3-Color Sunburst, White Blonde, Black, Teal Green Trans., Aged Cherry Burst, Chrome Red, or Candy Tangerine finishes, disc. 2004.

| | | $1,225 | $1,075 | $950 | $850 | $750 | $575 | $475 |

Last MSR was $1,750.

Add $150 for Natural, White Blonde, and Purple Transparent finishes.

Also available with maple fingerboard (Model 010-4602). Purple Trans. finish was disc. in 2001. In 2002, Natural, Crimson Trans. finishes were disc. and Aged Cherry Burst, Chrome Red, and Candy Tangerine were introduced.

American Deluxe Power Tele (U.S. Mfg. No. 010-5700) - similar to American Deluxe Telecaster, except has rosewood fingerboard, Fender/Fishman Power Bridge, 6-Piezo pickup, 3-way mini toggle for Power Bridge, dual concentric volume and tone controls, available in 3-Color Sunburst, Black, White Blonde, Natural, Crimson Trans. and Teal Green Trans. finishes, mfg. 1999-2001.

| | | $1,600 | $1,400 | $1,200 | $1,050 | $925 | $850 | $750 |

Last MSR was $2,280.

Also available with maple fingerboard (Model 010-5702).

AMERICAN DELUXE TELECASTER (NO. 010-1600) - select alder body, maple C-shape neck, 22-fret rosewood fingerboard with dot inlay, 2 single coil Noiseless pickups, various pickguards, 2 knobs, 3-way switch, S-1 switching, American Tele bridge, chrome hardware, available in 3-Color Sunburst, Montego Black, Candy Tangerine, or Aged Cherry Burst finishes, mfg. 2004-present.

| MSR | $1,571 | $1,100 | $950 | $850 | $750 | $650 | $575 | $500 |

Also available with a maple fingerboard (No. 010-1602).

American Deluxe Telecaster Ash (No. 010-1702) - similar to the American Deluxe Telecaster, except has a premium ash body, available in Butterscotch Blonde or 2-Color Sunburst finishes, mfg. 2004-present.

| MSR | $1,714 | $1,200 | $1,050 | $950 | $850 | $750 | $650 | $575 |

American Deluxe Telecaster FMT/QMT HH (No. 010-1670/1680) - similar to the American Deluxe Telecaster, except has a flamed or quilted maple top, rosewood fingerboard, and 2 Enforcer humbucker pickups, available in Tobacco Sunburst, Bing Cherry Trans., Cobalt Blue Trans., or Amber finishes, mfg. 2004-present.

| MSR | $1,900 | $1,350 | $1,150 | $1,000 | $900 | $800 | $700 | $600 |

TELECASTER DELUXE (MFG. 1972-1982) - similar to the Telecaster except has two humbucking pickups, Stratocaster style neck and large headstock, 6-piece bridge, featured a back contoured like a Stratcoaster, black pickguard, 3-way switch, four knobs, available in Blonde, Sunburst, Olympic White, Black, Walnut, Antigua, or Natural finishes, mfg. 1972-1982.

| | 1972-1974 | N/A | $2,000 | $1,700 | $1,400 | $1,200 | $1,000 | $800 |
| | 1975-1982 | N/A | $1,500 | $1,250 | $1,050 | $900 | $750 | $600 |

Add 15% for Antigua finish.

This model was basically a "Stratocasterized Telly with Humbuckers." From 1977-79, Antigua finish was available with matching pickguard.

DELUXE NASHVILLE TELE (MEX. MFG. NO. 013-5300) - alder body, rosewood neck, 21-fret maple fingerboard with black dot inlay, 6-saddle bridge, chrome hardware, brown shell pickguard, Tex-Mex Tele/Tex-Mex Strat/Tex-Mex Tele single coil pickups, volume/tone control, 5-position "Strat-o-Tone" switch, controls mounted metal plate, available in Black, Brown Sunburst, Candy Apple Red, Amber, Honey Blonde, or Arctic White finishes, mfg. 1998-present.

| MSR | $742 | $525 | $450 | $400 | $350 | $300 | $250 | $200 |

Add $35 for Brown Sunburst finish.

This model also available with maple fingerboard with pearl dot inlay (Model 013-5302).

GRADING		100% MINT	98% NEAR MINT	95% EXC+	90% EXC	80% VG+	70% VG	60% G

Deluxe Power Tele (Mex. Mfg. No. 013-5000) - similar to Nashville Tele, except has Fender/Fishman Power Bridge, available in 2-Color Sunburst, Black, Arctic White, Candy Apple Red, Honey Blonde, or Brown Sunburst finishes, mfg. 1999-present.

MSR	$957		$675	$600	$525	$475	$425	$375	$325

In 2005, 2-Color Sunburst and Honey Blonde finishes were introduced.

'90s TELE DELUXE (JAPAN MFG. NO. 025-9000) - similar to the '90s Tele Custom, except has Strat body contours, alder body, white shell pickguard, 2 Strat/1 Tele single coil pickups, 5-way selector, available in 3-Tone Sunburst, Black, Candy Apple Red, Sonic Blue, or Vintage White finishes, disc. 1998.

		$575	$500	$425	$375	$325	$275	$225

Last MSR was $819.

Fender Telecaster Custom
courtesy Dave Rogers
Dave's Guitar Shop

Telecaster: Custom Series

TELECASTER CUSTOM (MFG. 1959-1972) - bound alder body, white pickguard, 21-fret maple fingerboard with pearl dot inlay, strings through bridge, chrome hardware, 2 single coil pickups, volume/tone controls, 3-position switch, controls mounted metal plate, available in custom colors finish, mfg. 1959-1972.

Year		100%	98%	95%	90%	80%	70%	60%
1959	N/A		$20,000	$17,000	$14,000	$12,000	$10,000	$8,000
1960	N/A		$16,000	$13,000	$11,000	$9,000	$7,500	$6,000
1961	N/A		$14,000	$12,000	$10,000	$8,500	$7,000	$5,800
1962	N/A		$12,000	$10,000	$8,500	$7,500	$6,500	$5,500
1963	N/A		$11,000	$9,500	$8,200	$7,000	$6,200	$5,300
1964	N/A		$10,000	$8,500	$7,200	$6,300	$5,500	$4,800
1965	N/A		$9,000	$7,500	$6,500	$5,500	$5,000	$4,500
1966	N/A		$8,000	$6,700	$5,900	$5,000	$4,500	$4,000
1967	N/A		$7,000	$6,000	$5,200	$4,500	$3,800	$3,400
1968	N/A		$6,000	$5,200	$4,500	$3,800	$3,200	$2,700
1969	N/A		$5,500	$4,700	$4,000	$3,300	$2,800	$2,400
1970	N/A		$5,000	$4,200	$3,500	$3,000	$2,500	$2,000
1971	N/A		$4,500	$3,700	$3,000	$2,500	$2,100	$1,700
1972	N/A		$4,000	$3,200	$2,500	$2,100	$1,700	$1,300

Add 50%-75% for custom colors. Add 50% for slab boards.

This model is also available with an ash body.

Telecaster Custom II (Mfg. 1972-78) - similar to the Telecaster Custom except has a humbucker and single coil pickup configuration, mfg. 1972-78.

		100%	98%	95%	90%	80%	70%	60%
1972-1974	N/A		$2,000	$1,700	$1,400	$1,200	$1,000	$800
1975-1978	N/A		$1,500	$1,250	$1,050	$900	$750	$600

'90s TELE CUSTOM (JAPAN MFG. NO. 025-2500) - double bound basswood body, pearloid binding, maple neck, 21-fret rosewood fingerboard with pearl dot inlay, STB bridge, gold hardware, color-matched (to body binding) pearloid pickguard, 2 Vintage Tele single coil pickups, volume/tone controls, 3-way selector, controls mounted metal plate, available in Black or Olympic White finishes, mfg. 1995-98.

	$500	$425	$375	$325	$275	$235	$195

Last MSR was $749.

Telecaster: Highway 1 Series

HIGHWAY 1 TELECASTER (NO. 011-1200) - alder body, modified C-shaped maple neck, 22-fret rosewood fingerboard with dot inlay, 2 standard vintage Tele single coil pickups, white pickguard, vintage 3 saddle bridge, 3-way switch, two knobs (v, tone), chrome hardware, available in 3-Color Sunburst, Daphne Blue Trans., Crimson Red Trans., or Honey Blonde Trans., mfg. 2003-present.

MSR	$900		$630	$525	$475	$425	$375	$325	$275

Also available with a maple fingerboard (No. 011-1202).

HIGHWAY 1 TEXAS TELECASTER (NO. 011-3502) - similar to the Highway 1 Telecaster, except has an ash body and Texas pickups, available in 2-Color Sunburst or Honey Blonde Trans. finishes, mfg. 2003-present.

MSR	$1,200		$850	$750	$650	$575	$500	$425	$350

Telecaster: Paisley Series

PINK PAISLEY, BLUE FLORAL TELECASTER (U.S. MFG.) - ash body, floral/paisley pickguard, 21-fret maple fingerboard with black dot inlay, strings through bridge, chrome hardware, 2 single coil pickups, volume/tone controls, 3-position switch, controls mounted metal plate, available in Blue Floral or Pink Paisley finishes, mfg. 1968-1970.

		100%	98%	95%	90%	80%	70%	60%
PINK	N/A		$8,000	$6,800	$5,800	$5,000	$4,300	$3,500
BLUE	N/A		$7,500	$6,000	$5,000	$4,200	$3,300	$2,700

Fender Paisley Telecaster
courtesy Dave Rogers
Dave's Guitar Shop

GRADING	100% MINT	98% NEAR MINT	95% EXC+	90% EXC	80% VG+	70% VG	60% G

PAISLEY TELECASTER (JAPAN MFG. NO. 027-4902) - single cutaway ash body, paisley pickguard, bolt-on maple neck, 21-fret maple fingerboard with black dot inlay, strings through bridge, 6-on-one-side tuners, chrome hardware, 2 single coil pickups, volume/tone controls, 3-position switch, controls mounted metal plate, available in Paisley finish, disc. 1998.

	N/A	$800	$700	$625	$550	$475	$400

Last MSR was $759.

This model was a limited edition instrument available by custom order. Later models have a basswood body.

Blue Flower Telecaster (Japan Mfg.) - similar to Paisley Tele, except has Blue Floral pickguard/finish, disc. 1994.

	N/A	$750	$675	$600	$525	$450	$375

Last MSR was $720.

This model was a limited edition instrument available by custom order.

Telecaster: Rosewood Series

ROSEWOOD TELECASTER (U.S. MFG.) - rosewood body, black pickguard, bolt-on rosewood neck, 21-fret rosewood fingerboard with pearl dot inlay, strings through bridge with cover, chrome hardware, 2 single coil pickups, volume/tone control, 3-position switch, controls mounted metal plate, available in Natural finish, mfg. 1969-1972.

	N/A	$6,000	$5,200	$4,500	$3,800	$3,200	$2,700

The Rosewood Telecaster was also offered with a hollowed (3 chambers) body between 1971-72.

ROSEWOOD TELECASTER (JAPAN MFG.) - single cutaway rosewood body, black pickguard, bolt-on rosewood neck, 21-fret rosewood fingerboard with pearl dot inlay, strings through bridge with cover, chrome hardware, 2 single coil pickups, volume/tone control, 3-position switch, controls mounted metal plate, available in Natural finish, disc. 1995.

	N/A	$1,200	$1,050	$900	$750	$600	$500

Last MSR was $1,230.

This model was a limited edition instrument available by custom order.

Telecaster: Thinline Series

TELECASTER THINLINE (MFG. 1968-1971) - similar to the Telecaster except has a hollow mahogany or ash body with an f-hole, an enlarged pickguard, rearranged knobs and switch, available in Blonde and custom colors, mfg. 1968-1971.

1968	N/A	$4,500	$3,700	$3,200	$2,700	$2,300	$2,000
1969	N/A	$4,000	$3,300	$2,700	$2,300	$2,000	$1,700
1970	N/A	$3,500	$2,900	$2,300	$1,900	$1,600	$1,300
1971	N/A	$3,000	$2,500	$2,100	$1,800	$1,500	$1,200

Telecaster Thinline with Humbuckers (Mfg. 1972-78) - similar to the Telecaster Thinline except has two humbucking pickups, available in Blonde and custom colors, mfg. 1972-78.

1972-1974	N/A	$3,200	$2,600	$2,200	$1,900	$1,600	$1,350
1975-1978	N/A	$2,200	$1,900	$1,600	$1,350	$1,100	$850

´90s TELE THINLINE (U.S. MFG. NO. 010-8202) - double bound semi-hollow ash body, f-hole, bolt-on maple neck, 22-fret maple fingerboard with black dot inlay, STB bridge, white or brown shell pickguard, chrome hardware, 2 American Standard Telecaster single coil pickups, volume/tone control, 3-position switch, controls mounted metal plate, DeltaTone system (high output bridge pickup and special "no-load" tone control) electronics, available in 3-Color Sunburst, Black, Crimson Trans., Natural, Sunset Orange Trans., and Olympic White finishes, mfg. 1988-2001.

	$1,350	$1,200	$1,050	$875	$725	$600	$475

Last MSR was $1,950.

This model also available with rosewood fingerboard with pearl dot inlay (Model 010-8200). Models with Natural or Olympic White finishes have brown shell pickguards and matching binding. Sunset Orange Transparent was introduced in 2001.

Telecaster: Model Variations

1998 COLLECTOR´S EDITION TELECASTER (U.S. MFG NO. 010-1998) - ash body, maple neck, 21-fret rosewood fingerboard with abalone dot inlay and special 12th fret inlay, fixed bridge, gold vintage-style hardware, single-ply white pickguard, 2 vintage-style single coil pickups, volume/tone controls, 3-way selector, controls mounted metal plate, engraved neckplate, available in 2-Color Sunburst finish, mfg. 1998 only.

	$1,200	$1,050	$900	$800	$700	$600	$500

Last MSR was $1,699.

Production is scheduled for only 1,998 instruments. List price includes brown Tolex hardshell case.

40TH ANNIVERSARY TELECASTER (U.S. MFG.) - ash body, bound figured maple top, cream pickguard, 22-fret maple fingerboard with black dot inlay, fixed bridge, pearl tuner buttons, gold hardware, 2 single coil pickups, volume/tone control, 3-position switch, available in Antique Two-Tone, Natural, or Trans. Red finishes, mfg. 1988-1990.

	N/A	$2,000	$1,700	$1,400	$1,200	$1,000	$800

Last MSR was $1,299.

Approximately 300 of these instruments were produced.

50TH ANNIVERSARY TELECASTER (U.S. MFG.) - flamed maple top and back, two vintage style pickups, gold hardware, gold 50th Anniversary coin on back of headstock, available in Sunburst finish, mfg. 1996 only.

	$1,600	$1,400	$1,200	$1,050	$900	$750	$600

There were 1250 of these produced.

GRADING	100% MINT	98% NEAR MINT	95% EXC+	90% EXC	80% VG+	70% VG	60% G

AMERICAN FAT TELE (U.S. MFG. NO. 011-8000) - solid alder body, one-piece maple neck, Micro-Tilt neck adjustment, rosewood fingerboard, deluxe Fender die-cast tuners, 22 medium-jumbo frets, 1 American Standard Tele pickup and 1 Fender DH-1 Humbucker pickup, master volume, master tone, 6-saddle string-through-body bridge, white shell pickguard, Schaller Straplock ready, available in 3-Color Sunburst, Black, Sienna Sunburst, or Chrome Silver finishes, disc. 2002.

	$1,000	**$850**	**$750**	**$650**	**$550**	**$450**	**$350**

Last MSR was $1,400.

Add $35 for 3-Color Sunburst finish. Add $100 for White Blonde finish which was availlable only in 2001.

Also available with maple fingerboard (Model 010-8002, disc. 2000). White Blonde, Candy Apple Red, and Olympic White were discontinued in 2002, and Black, Sienna Sunburst, and Chrome Silver were introduced.

AMERICAN NASHVILLE B-BENDER TELE (U.S. MFG. NO. 011-8342) - allows for country bends, steel guitar glisses and wild special effects, poplar body, maple fingerboard with black dot position markers, Deluxe cast/sealed tuners, 22 Medium-Jumbo frets, 2 American Tele pickups and 1 Texas Special Strat pickup, 1 Volume/1Tone control, Super 5-way Strat-o-Tele switch, 6-saddle string through body, case included, available in 3-Color Sunburst, Olympic White, black and Candy Apple Red finishes, current mfg.

MSR	**$1,657**	**$1,200**	**$1,050**	**$900**	**$800**	**$700**	**$600**	**$525**

In 2002, Olympic White and Candy Apple Red finishes were discontinued.

BLACK & GOLD TELECASTER (U.S. MFG.) - hardwood body, black pickguard, 21-fret maple fingerboard with black dot inlay, brass strings through bridge, blackface peghead with logo, gold hardware, 2 single coil pickups, volume/tone control, 3-position switch, controls mounted metal plate, available in Black finish, mfg. 1981-83.

	N/A	**$1,400**	**$1,200**	**$1,050**	**$900**	**$750**	**$600**

This model was also available with rosewood fingerboard with pearl dot inlay.

CALIFORNIA TELE (U.S. MFG. NO. 010-1602) - alder body, maple neck, 21-fret maple fingerboard with black dot inlay, 6-saddle bridge, chrome hardware, 3-ply white pickguard, Tex-Mex Strat/Tex-Mex Tele single coil pickups, volume/tone control, 3-position switch, controls mounted metal plate, available in Black, Brown Sunburst, Candy Apple Red, Fiesta Red, or Vintage White finishes, mfg. 1998 only.

	N/A	**$600**	**$525**	**$450**	**$400**	**$350**	**$300**

Last MSR was $799.

This model also available with rosewood fingerboard with pearl dot inlay (Model 010-1600).

California Fat Tele (U.S. Mfg. No. 010-1702) - similar to the California Tele, except features Tex-Mex humbucker/Tex-Mex Tele single coil pickups, special switching, available in Black, Brown Sunburst, Candy Apple Red, Fiesta Red, or Vintage White finishes, mfg. 1997-98.

	N/A	**$650**	**$575**	**$500**	**$425**	**$375**	**$325**

Last MSR was $849.

CONTEMPORARY TELECASTER (JAPAN MFG.) - hardwood body, 22-fret rosewood fingerboard with pearl dot inlay, standard vibrato, black hardware, 2 single coil/1 humbucker pickup, volume/tone controls, 3 mini switches, mfg. 1985-87.

	N/A	**$350**	**$300**	**$250**	**$220**	**$190**	**$160**

This model was also available with 2 humbucker pickups, 3-position/coil tap switches.

SPARKLE TELECASTER - poplar body, white pickguard, figured maple neck, 21-fret maple fingerboard with black dot inlay, strings through bridge with brass saddles, nickel hardware, 2 single coil pickups, volume/tone control, 3-position switch, available in Champagne Sparkle, Gold Sparkle, or Silver Sparkle finishes, mfg. 1993-95.

	N/A	**$1,550**	**$1,350**	**$1,150**	**$1,000**	**$850**	**$700**

Last MSR was $2,150.

This model was available by custom order only.

TELE-SONIC (U.S. MFG. NO. 010-1800) - chambered mahogany body, maple neck, 24.75 in. scale, 22-fret rosewood fingerboard with dot inlay, Wilkinson stop tailpiece, die-cast tuners, chrome hardware, black pickguard, 2 DeArmond 2K single coil pickups, 2 volume/2 tone control, 3-position toggle switch, available in Brown Sunburst, Butterscotch Blonde, or Crimson Trans. finishes, mfg. 1998-2004.

	$1,000	**$850**	**$750**	**$675**	**$600**	**$525**	**$475**

Last MSR was $1,430.

Butterscotch Blonde was introduced in 2003.

TELECASTER ACOUSTIC/ELECTRIC (JAPAN MFG. NO. 025-2400) - single round cutaway semi-hollow basswood body, bound solid spruce top, f-hole, maple neck, 22-fret rosewood fingerboard with pearl dot inlay, rosewood bridge, 6-on-one-side die-cast tuners, chrome hardware, single coil/piezo bridge pickups, volume/pan/tone controls, available in 3-Tone Sunburst or Black finishes, mfg. 1995-98.

	$450	**$400**	**$350**	**$300**	**$250**	**$200**	**$150**

Last MSR was $699.

Telecaster Classical Thinline (Jap. Mfg. 025-2800) - similar to the Telecaster Acoustic/Electric, except in a nylon string configuration, 21-fret rosewood fingerboard, piezo bridge pickup (only), volume/tone controls, active electronics, available in 3-Tone Sunburst or Black finishes, mfg. 1995-98.

	$450	**$400**	**$350**	**$300**	**$250**	**$200**	**$150**

Last MSR was $699.

Fender Telecaster Thinline With Humbuckers courtesy Dave Rogers Dave's Guitar Shop

1996 Fender Telecaster 50th Anniversary courtesy Barry Clark

GRADING	100% MINT	98% NEAR MINT	95% EXC+	90% EXC	80% VG+	70% VG	60% G

TELECASTER PLUS (U.S. MFG. NO. 010-8500) - alder body, bound ash veneer top/back, maple neck, 22-fret rosewood fingerboard with pearl dot inlay, fixed bridge, chrome hardware, white pickguard, 3 single coil Lace Sensor pickups, volume/tone control, 3-position switch, controls mounted metal plate, available in Antique Burst, Black, Blue Burst, Crimson Burst, or Teal Green Metallic finishes, mfg. 1995-98.

	$925	$800	$700	$625	$550	$475	$400

Last MSR was $1,299.

Add $100 for solid ash body with Natural finish.

This model also available with maple fingerboard with black dot inlay (Model 010-8502).

TELECASTER SPECIAL (MEX. MFG. NO. 013-5502) - poplar body, ash top, 22-fret maple fingerboard with black dot inlay, fixed strings through bridge, chrome hardware, humbucker/single coil pickups, volume/tone controls, 3-position switch, available in Natural finish, mfg. 1994-98.

	$350	$300	$250	$200	$175	$150	$125

Last MSR was $510.

TEX-MEX TELE SPECIAL (MEX. MFG. NO. 013-7302) - poplar body, bolt-on maple neck, 21-fret maple fingerboard with black dot inlay, vintage-style bridge, chrome hardware, white pickguard, Tex-Mex humbucker/Tex-Mex single coil pickups, volume/tone control, 3-way switch, controls mounted metal plate, available in Black, Brown Sunburst, Candy Apple Red, Sonic Blue, or Vintage White finishes, mfg. 1997-98.

	$475	$400	$350	$300	$250	$200	$150

Last MSR was $649.

TRADITIONAL TELECASTER (MEX. MFG. NO. 013-3202) - poplar body, bolt-on maple neck, 21-fret maple fingerboard with black dot inlay, fixed bridge, chrome hardware, 3-ply white pickguard, 2 single coil pickups, volume/tone control, 3-position switch, controls mounted metal plate, available in Arctic White, Black, or Torino Red finishes, disc. 1998.

	$235	$200	$175	$150	$125	$100	$75

Last MSR was $329.

Telecaster: Special Edition Series

AERODYNE TELECASTER (JAPAN MFG. NO. 025-6605) - basswood body with unique carved top, maple neck, 21-fret rosewood fingerboard with dot inlay, matching color headstock, 6-on-a-side tuner, standardbridge, no pickguard, one single coil and one soapbar pickups, two knobs (v, t), three-way switch, chrome hardware, Black finish, new 2005.

MSR	$900		$630	$550	$475	$425	$375	$325	$275

CUSTOM TELECASTER HH FMT (NO. 026-2000) - mahogany back with flamed maple top, C-shaped set-in maple neck, 22-fret rosewood fingerboard with dot inlay, matching headstock, two humbucking pickups (Atomic II & Black Canyon), 6-saddle S-T-B, 3-way switch, 3 knobs (v, tone, coil-tap), chrome/black hardware, available in Crimson Trans., Ebony Trans., or Brown Trans., mfg. 2003-present.

MSR	$900		$630	$550	$475	$425	$375	$325	$275

This model is also available as a special model (No. 026-2100). Also available as a Blackout model available in Black or Atlantic Blue Metallic (No. 026-2400).

LITE ASH TELECASTER (JAP. MFG. NO. 026-5102) - lightweight ash body, bird's-eye maple C-shaped neck, 22-fret fingerboard with dot abalone inlay, single ply black pickguard, 2 Seymour Duncan single coil pickups, 2 knobs, 5-way switch, vintage style bridge, chrome hardware, available in Black, Vintage White, or Natural finishes, mfg. 2004-present.

MSR	$900		$630	$550	$475	$425	$375	$325	$275

TELECASTER TC-90 THINLINE (JAP. MFG. NO. 026-2300) - symmetrical double cutaway ash body, single f-hole in bass bout, set maple C-shape neck, 22-fret rosewood fingerboard with abalone dot inlays, unique shaped black pickguard, matching color headstock, 2 Seymour Duncan P-90 single coil pickups, 2 knobs, 3-way switch, Adjusto-Matic bridge, chrome hardware, available in Vintage White or Black Cherry Burst finishes, mfg. 2004-present.

MSR	$900		$630	$550	$475	$425	$375	$325	$275

Telecaster: Standard Series (Current Mfg.)

STANDARD TELECASTER (MEX. MFG. NO. 013-5102/013-5202) - poplar body, bolt-on maple neck, 21-fret maple fingerboard with black dot inlay, fixed bridge, chrome hardware, 3-ply white pickguard, 2 single coil pickups, volume/tone control, 3-position switch, controls mounted metal plate, available in Arctic White, Black, Brown Sunburst, Midnight Wine, Blue Agave, or Sage Green Metallic finishes, current mfg.

MSR	$528		$370	$320	$275	$235	$200	$175	$150

Add $35 for Brown Sunburst finish.

In 1998, Midnight Blue and Midnight Wine finishes were introduced; Crimson Red Metallic, and Lake Placid Blue finishes were discontinued. In 2001 Blue Agave was introduced.

Standard Telecaster Left-Hand (Mex. Mfg. No. 013-5122) - Similar to the Standard Telecaster except in left-hand configuration, available in Black, Brown Sunburst, Midnight Wine, or Blue Agave, current mfg.

MSR	$528		$370	$320	$275	$235	$200	$175	$150

Add $35 for Brown Sunburst finish.

Telecaster: H.M.T. Series

H.M.T. TELECASTER - Telecaster shape, basswood body, maple top, single f-hole in bass bout, top body binding, no pickguard, 2 DiMarzio humbucker pickups, 2 knobs, black hardware, available in Black finish, mfg. 1990-93.

	N/A	$325	$275	$235	$195	$160	$135

H.M.T. stands for Heavy Metal Telecasters. Models also include the 2 DiMarzio humbucker Model 025-2100, Blue Fender-Lace Sensor single coil Model 025-2200, and piezo bridge/Silver Fender-Lace Sensor Model 025-2300.

GRADING		100% MINT	98% NEAR MINT	95% EXC+	90% EXC	80% VG+	70% VG	60% G

F

Telecaster: American Vintage Reissue Series

´52 TELECASTER (U.S. MFG. NO. 010-0202/010-1303) - light ash body, maple neck, 21-fret maple fingerboard with black dot inlay, vintage-style fixed bridge, chrome hardware, black pickguard, 2 American Vintage single coil pickups, volume/tone control, 3-position switch, controls mounted metal plate, available in Black, Butterscotch Blonde, or Copper finishes, current mfg.

MSR	$1,900		$1,350	$1,150	$1,000	$850	$750	$650	$550

In 2000, Copper finish was discontinued. In 2001, Black finish was discontinued.

´52 Telecaster Left Hand (U.S. Mfg., No. 010-0222) - similar to the ´52 Telecaster except in left-hand configuration, available in Butterscotch Blonde finish only, current mfg.

MSR	$1,900		$1,350	$1,150	$1,000	$850	$750	$650	$550

´52 TELE SPECIAL (U.S. Mfg., No. 010-0212-803/010-0212) - premuim ash body, one-piece "U"-shape maple neck with truss rod, maple fingerboard, 25.5 in. scale, 21 frets, gold hardware, gold vintage style tuners, gold original style Tele bridge with gold "ash tray" bridge cover, 1-ply white pickguard, 2 New American Vintage Tele pickups, 3-position switch, master tone, master volume, available in 2-Color Sunburst or Black finish, case included, disc. 2001.

		$1,300	$1,150	$975	$875	$775	$675	$575

Last MSR was $1,855.

In 2000, Black finish was discontinued.

´62 CUSTOM TELECASTER (U.S. MFG. NO. 010-6200) - alder body with maple "C" shape neck, bound top and back, rosewood fingerboard, 25.5" scale, 21 vintage style frets, vintage style tuners, ´62 Tele pickups, 3-way switch, master volume, master tone, aged 3-ply pickguard, vintage Tele bridge, available in 3-Color Sunburst, Black, Ocean Turquoise, Surf Green, or Ice Blue Metallic finishes, mfg. 1999-present.

MSR	$2,000		$1,400	$1,200	$1,050	$900	$800	$700	$600

Add $35 for 3-Color Sunburst.

In 2001, Dakota Red, Inca Silver and Ice Blue Metallic finishes were introduced. In 2002 Candy Apple Red, Dakota Red, and Inca Silver finishes were discontinued, and Ocean Turquoise and Surf Green finishes were introduced.

Telecaster: Classic/Collectible Series

The following models have a Telecaster single cutaway body, two single coil pickups, bolt-on neck, and six-on-a-side headstock (unless otherwise specified).

´50s TELECASTER (JAPAN MFG. NO. 027-1202) - basswood body, maple neck, 21-fret maple fingerboard with black dot inlay, vintage-style bridge, chrome hardware, black pickguard, 2 single coil pickups, volume/tone control, 3-position switch, controls mounted metal plate, available in 2-Tone Sunburst, Black, Blonde, Candy Apple Red, Shell Pink, or Sonic Blue finishes, disc. 1998.

		N/A	$550	$475	$400	$350	$300	$250

Last MSR was $599.

´50s Telecaster Left-Hand (Japan Mfg. No. 027-1222). - similar to the ´50s Telecaster, except in left-handed configuration, available in Blonde finish only, disc. 1998.

		N/A	$550	$475	$400	$350	$300	$250

Last MSR was $669.

´50s TELECASTER (MEX. MFG. NO. 013-1202) - solid ash body, one-piece maple neck, Fender vintage style tuners, 25.5 in. scale, 21 nickel silver frets, single-ply white pickguard, 2 Vintage Tele pickups, master tone, master volume, 3-way switch, 3-saddle string-through-body bridge, available in White Blonde, 2-Color Sunburst, or Black finishes, current mfg.

MSR	$957		$675	$575	$500	$450	$400	$350	$300

´60s TELECASTER (MEX. MFG. NO. 013-1600) - alder body, rosewood fingerboard, Fender Vintage tuners, 21 Vintage frets, 2 Mexican-made Vintage-style pickups, 2 control knobs (v, tone), 3-way switch, vintage-style 3-saddle bridge, available in Olympic White, Black, or Candy Apple Red, mfg. 2001-present.

MSR	$957		$675	$575	$500	$450	$400	$350	$300

´62 CUSTOM TELECASTER (JAPAN MFG. NO. 027-5100) - double bound basswood body, maple neck, 21-fret rosewood fingerboard with white dot inlay, vintage-style bridge, chrome hardware, white pickguard, 2 single coil pickups, volume/tone control, 3-position switch, controls mounted metal plate, available in 3-Tone Sunburst or Candy Apple Red finishes, disc. 1999.

		$525	$450	$375	$325	$275	$225	$175

Last MSR was $669.

´62 Custom Telecaster Left Hand (Japan Mfg. No. 027-5120) - similar to the ´62 Custom Telecaster, except in left-handed configuration, available in 3-Tone Sunburst or Candy Apple Red finishes, disc. 1998.

		$550	$450	$375	$325	$275	$225	$175

Last MSR was $739.

Fender '52 Telecaster courtesy Fender

Fender '62 Telecaster Custom courtesy Fender

GRADING	100% MINT	98% NEAR MINT	95% EXC+	90% EXC	80% VG+	70% VG	60% G

´69 TELECASTER THINLINE (JAPAN MFG. NO. 027-7702) - semi-hollow mahogany body, f-hole, maple neck, 21-fret rosewood fingerboard with white dot inlay, vintage-style bridge, chrome hardware, white shell pickguard, 2 single coil pickups, volume/tone control, 3-position switch, available in Natural finish, disc. 1998.

	$600	$525	$450	$375	$325	$275	$225

Last MSR was $749.

´69 Telecaster Thinline (Mex Mfg. No. 013-6902) - semi-hollow mahogany or ash body, one-piece maple neck, 25.5 in. scale Schaller vintage "F" tuners, 21 nickel silver frets, white shell pickguard, 2 Vintage Tele pickups, master tone, master volume, 3-way switch, 3-saddle string-through-body bridge, available in 3-Color Sunburst, 2-Color Sunburst, Black, or Natural finishes, current mfg.

MSR	$985	$699	$600	$525	$475	$425	$375	$325

´72 TELECASTER CUSTOM (JAPAN MFG. NO. 027-7602) - basswood body, maple neck, 21-fret maple fingerboard with black dot inlay, vintage-style bridge, chrome hardware, 3-ply black pickguard, covered humbucker/single coil pickups, 2 volume/2 tone controls, 3-position switch, available in 3-Tone Sunburst or Black finishes, disc. 1999.

	$550	$475	$400	$325	$250	$225	$175

Last MSR was $659.

´72 Telecaster Custom (Mex. Mfg. No. 013-7500) - poplar or alder body, maple "U"-shaped neck, Micro-Tilt neck adjustment, rosewood fingerboard, 25.5 in. scale, 21 frets, Bullet truss rod, Fender/Schaller "F" style tuners, 1 Fender "Wide Range" Humbucker pickup and 1 single coil Tele pickup, 3-way switch, 2 volume controls, 2 tone controls, 3-ply pickguard, vintage style 6-saddle Tele bridge, available in 3-Color Sunburst or Black finishes, mfg. 1999-present.

MSR	$985	$699	$600	$525	$475	$425	$375	$325

Add $35 for 3-Color Sunburst finish.

Also available with maple fingerboard (Model 013-7502).

'72 TELECASTER DELUXE (MEX. MFG. NO. 013-7702) - alder body, maple C-shaped neck, 21-fret maple fingerboard with black dot inlay, 3-ply black pickguard, '70s Strat-style headstock, 2 wide-range humbucker pickups, four knobs (2 v, 2 tone), 3-way switch, Vintage Strat style S-T-B hardtail bridge, chrome hardware, available in 3-Color Sunburst, Walnut Satin, or Black finishes, mfg. 2004-present.

MSR	$985	$699	$600	$525	$475	$425	$375	$325

´72 TELECASTER THINLINE (MEX. MFG. NO. 013-7402) - semi-hollow ash body, f-hole, maple neck and fingerboard, 25.5 in. scale, Bullet truss rod, Fender/Schaller "F" style tuners, 2 Fender Reissue Wide Range humbucker pickups, 3-way switch, master tone, master volume, white Pearloid pickguard, '70s Strat non-tremolo bridge, available in 3-Color Sunburst or Natural finishes, mfg. 1999-present.

MSR	$942	$675	$600	$525	$475	$425	$375	$325

´72 Telecaster Thinline (Japan Mfg. No. 027-3202) - similar to the '72 Telecaster Thinline, except was produced in Japan, available in Natural finish, disc. 1999.

	$600	$525	$450	$375	$325	$275	$225

Last MSR was $799.

Telecaster: Fender Custom Shop Contemporary Series

In addition to specialty custom guitars and Limited Edition runs, the Custom Shop also produces a number of models in smaller production runs as Contemporary Models and Custom Classics.

SET NECK TELE JR. (U.S. MFG. NO. 010-3400) - mahogany body with 11 tone chambers (semi-hollow design), set-in mahogany neck, 22-fret pau ferro fingerboard with white dot inlay, chrome hardware, tortoiseshell pickguard, 6-on-a-side tuners, American Standard (Strat) bridge, 2 Seymour Duncan P-90 pickups, volume/tone controls, 3-way selector, controls mounted metal plate, available in Antique Burst, Crimson Red Trans., Natural, or Vintage White finishes, mfg. 1997-2000.

	$1,825	$1,550	$1,350	$1,250	$1,150	$1,000	$850

Last MSR was $2,599.

SET NECK TELECASTER (U.S. MFG.) - mahogany body, bound figured maple top, mahogany neck, 22-fret rosewood fingerboard with pearl dot inlay, strings through bridge, locking tuners, 2 DiMarzio humbucker pickups, volume/tone control, 3-position/coil tap switches, available in Antique Burst, Autumn Gold, Trans. Crimson, Trans. Ebony, and Trans Sapphire Blue finishes, mfg. 1990-95.

	N/A	$1,400	$1,200	$1,050	$900	$750	$600

Last MSR was $2,150.

This model is also available with double locking Floyd Rose vibrato, roller nut. In 1993, pau ferro fingerboard became standard.

Set Neck Telecaster C/A (U.S. Mfg.) - similar to Set Neck Telecaster, except has tortoiseshell pickguard, pau ferro fingerboard, gold hardware, humbucker/single coil pickups, available in Gold Sparkle, Natural, Silver Sparkle, or Trans. Sunset Orange finishes, mfg. 1991-95.

	N/A	$1,400	$1,200	$1,050	$900	$750	$600

Last MSR was $2,150.

Telecaster: Fender Custom Shop Custom Classic Series

The following Custom Shop production models have a Telecaster single cutaway body, two single coil pickups, bolt-on neck, and six-on-a-side headstock (unless otherwise specified).

´50s TELECASTER (U.S. MFG. NO. 010-5002) - light ash body, figured maple neck, 21-fret maple fingerboard with black dot inlay, vintage-style bridge, nickel hardware, single-ply white pickguard, 2 American Vintage single coil pickups, volume/tone controls, 3-position switch, available in 2-Tone Sunburst, Black, or (White) Blonde finishes, disc. 1998.

	$1,650	$1,400	$1,200	$1,000	$850	$700	$550

Last MSR was $2,299.

Add $200 for gold hardware (Model 010-5012).

GRADING	100% MINT	98% NEAR MINT	95% EXC+	90% EXC	80% VG+	70% VG	60% G

'60s TELECASTER CUSTOM (U.S. MFG. NO. 010-6300) - similar to the '50s Telecaster, except has double bound alder body, 21-fret rosewood fingerboard with white dot inlay, 2 Texas Special Tele single coil pickups, available in custom colors, 3-Tone Sunburst, or Black finishes, mfg. 1997-98.

	$1,900	$1,650	$1,400	$1,200	$1,000	$850	$700

Last MSR was $2,699.

Add $150 for custom color finishes. Add $200 for gold hardware (Model 010-6310).

'52 TELE CUSTOM CLASSIC LEFT HAND (U.S. MFG. NO. 010-5222) - alder body, figured maple neck, 21-fret maple fingerboard with black dot inlay, vintage-style bridge, chrome hardware, black pickguard, 2 Texas Special Tele single coil pickups, volume/tone controls, 3-position switch, available in 2-Tone Sunburst or Honey Blonde finishes, disc. 1998.

	$1,750	$1,500	$1,300	$1,100	$950	$800	$650

Last MSR was $2,499.

AMERICAN CLASSIC TELECASTER (U.S. MFG. NO. 010-4802) - alder body, figured maple neck, 22-fret maple fingerboard with black dot inlay, American Standard Tele bridge, chrome hardware, brown or white shell pickguard, 2 Texas Special Strat/Texas Tele bridge single coil pickups, volume/tone controls, 3-position switch, available in custom colors and 2-Tone Sunburst, 3-Tone Sunburst, Blonde, or Olympic White finishes, disc. 1998.

	$1,200	$1,050	$900	$800	$700	$600	$500

Last MSR was $1,699.

This model is available with rosewood fingerboard (Model 010-4800). In 1998, gold hardware (Model 010-4812), or rosewood fingerboard/gold hardware (Model 010-4810) option was discontinued; Blonde and Olympic White finishes were discontinued; White Blonde finish was introduced. The Sunburst finishes feature a white shell pickguard; the White Blonde finish has a brown shell pickguard.

BAJO SEXTO TELECASTER (U.S. MFG. NO. 010-4002) - swamp ash body, 30.2 in. scale, 24-fret maple fingerboard with black dot inlay, strings through bridge with brass saddles, nickel hardware, black pickguard, 2 Texas Special single coil pickups, volume/tone control, 3-position switch, series wiring, available in Honey Blonde and 2-Tone Sunburst finishes, mfg. 1993-98.

	$1,400	$1,200	$1,050	$900	$750	$625	$500

Last MSR was $1,999.

*Fender '72 Telecaster Custom
courtesy Fender*

This instrument is a longer scaled (baritone) instrument.

TELECASTER XII (U.S. MFG. NO. 010-4100) - swamp ash body, bolt-on figured maple neck, 22-fret rosewood fingerboard with white dot inlay, chrome hardware, white (or black) pickguard, 6-per-side tuners, vintage-style 12-string bridge, 2 Texas Special single coil pickups, series wiring, volume/tone controls, 3-way selector, controls mounted metal plate, available in 2-Tone Sunburst, 3-Tone Sunburst, Sea Foam Green, or Vintage Blonde finishes, disc. 1998.

	$1,750	$1,500	$1,300	$1,100	$950	$800	$650

Last MSR was $2,499.

This model is available with a maple fingerboard with black dot inlay (Model 010-4102).

CUSTOM CLASSIC TELECASTER (NO. 015-6400) - this guitar is the Custom Shop version of the American Series Telecaster. Thin lacquer-finished premium ash body, lightly figured maple neck, rosewood fingerboard, 22 medium-jumbo frets, Fender Deluxe cast/sealed tuners, new "Twisted Tele" neck pickup and new Classic Tele bridge pickup, reverse control plate with 3-way switch towards rear, three-ply parchment pickguard, new Custom Classic bridge with solid steel bridge plate and chrome-plated solid milled brass saddles, available in 3-Color Sunburst, Bing Cherry Trans., Cobalt Blue Trans., or Honey Blonde finishes, mfg. 2001-present.

MSR	$2,484		$1,800	$1,550	$1,300	$1,100	$950	$800	$700

Also available with maple fingerboard (Model 015-6402).

FLATHEAD TELECASTER (U.S. MFG. NO. 015-4900) - Telecaster body style, flat alder body, contoured back and neck heel, maple neck, 22-fret ebony fingerboard with 12th fret crossed piston inlay, 2 EMG humbucker pickups, single knob, 3-way switch, black hardware, available in Light Gray, Dark Gray, or Black finishes, mfg. summer 2004-present.

MSR	$2,000		$1,450	$1,200	$1,050	$950	$750	$600	$500

SUB-SONIC TELECASTER (NO. 015-4732) - tuned B-E-A-D-G-B to provide the low growl of a 7-string guitar, 27 in. scale, maple fingerboard, thin lacquer-finished alder body, available in White Blonde, 2-Color Sunburst, Black, or Butterscotch Blonde finishes, mfg. 2001-present.

MSR	$2,600		$1,850	$1,600	$1,350	$1,150	$1,000	$850	$750

Telecaster: Relic Series

Relic series instruments are cosmetically aged by the Fender Custom Shop. Instruments are stamped on the headstock and into the body (under the pickguard) with the Custom Shop logo to avoid future cases of "mistaken identity" in the Vintage Guitar market.

Some debate has begun in regards to grading Relic series instruments. Is proper degradation of the instrument as it occurs at the Fender factory the only damage allowed, or do the dents and chips that occur at a dealer's shop (pre-sale) count? If a Relic series model gets further abused in the hands of a player, does the value go up? How does a dealer determine if the damage was "factory" versus aftermarket in the secondary guitar market? The *Blue Book of Electric Guitars* will continue to report on this debate in future editions.

*Fender Sub-Sonic Telecaster
courtesy Fender*

GRADING	100% MINT	98% NEAR MINT	95% EXC+	90% EXC	80% VG+	70% VG	60% G

'50s RELIC NO-CASTER (U.S. MFG. NO. 010-5102) - light ash body, maple neck, 21-fret maple fingerboard with black dot inlay, strings through vintage bridge with 3 Gatton saddles, aged nickel hardware, 2 Custom '50s single coil pickups, volume/tone control, 3-position switch, controls mounted on metal plate, available in Honey Blonde finish, disc. 1998.

	$1,900	$1,650	$1,450	$1,250	$1,100	$950	$800

Last MSR was $2,599.

Telecaster: Signature Series

Signature Series Telecasters are designed in collaboration with the artist whose name appears on the headstock. The intent of the Signature Series is to present an instrument that contains the idiosyncrasies similar to the artist´s guitar.

ALBERT COLLINS (U.S. MFG. NO. 010-8800) - bound ash body, white pickguard, bolt-on maple neck, 21-fret maple fingerboard with black dot inlay, strings through bridge with cover, 6-on-one-side tuners, chrome hardware, humbucker/single coil pickups, volume/tone control, 3-position switch, controls mounted on a metal plate, available in Natural finish, mfg. 1990-present.

MSR	$3,950	$2,900	$2,600	$2,300	$2,000	$1,700	$1,500	$1,300

BUCK OWENS LIMITED EDITION (JAPAN MFG. NO. 025-7500) - basswood body, maple neck, 22-fret rosewood fingerboard with dot inlay, 3-saddle fixed bridge, gold-plated vintage hardware, gold pickguard, 2 Vintage Tele pickups with Alnico magnets, volume/tone controls, 3-way switch, gold-plated metal controls plate, available in Red/Silver/Blue Sparkle finish, mfg. 1998-2001.

	$850	$700	$600	$500	$425	$375	$325

Last MSR was $999.

CLARENCE WHITE (U.S. MFG. NO. 010-5602) - ash body, tortoiseshell pickguard, figured maple neck, 21-fret maple fingerboard with black dot inlay, strings through bridge, Parsons-White stringbender, 2 Texas Tele/'54 Strat single coil pickups, volume/tone control, 3-position switch, available in 2-Tone Sunburst finish, mfg. 1994-2001.

	$3,750	$3,250	$2,750	$2,300	$1,950	$1,550	$1,350

Last MSR was $5,330.

This instrument has Scruggs banjo tuners on the E strings.

DANNY GATTON (U.S. MFG. NO. 010-8700) - swamp ash body, white pickguard, bolt-on maple neck, 22-fret maple fingerboard with black dot inlay/cubic zirconium side markers, strings through stainless steel bridge, 2 twin blade Joe Barden single coil pickups, volume/tone control, 3-position switch, available in Frost Gold or Honey Blonde finishes, part of the Custom Shop, current mfg.

MSR	$4,052	$3,000	$2,700	$2,400	$2,100	$1,800	$1,500	$1,200

JAMES BURTON (U.S. MFG. NO. 010-8602) - light ash body, 21-fret maple fingerboard with black dot inlay, strings through bridge, gold hardware, 3 single coil Lace Sensor pickups, volume/tone control, 5-position switch, available in Black with Candy Red Paisley, Black with Gold Paisley, Frost Red, or Pearl White finishes, mfg. 1990-present.

MSR	$2,000	$1,400	$1,200	$1,050	$900	$750	$650	$550

This model features black chrome hardware on the Black with Gold Paisley and Frost Red finishes.

James Burton Standard (Mex. Mfg. No. 013-8602) - similar to the James Burton, except has poplar body, white pickguard, chrome hardware, 2 Texas Special Tele pickups, available in 2-Tone Sunburst, Black, Candy Apple Red, or Vintage Blonde finishes, mfg. 1995-present.

MSR	$828	$580	$500	$425	$350	$300	$250	$200

In 1999, 2-Tone Sunburst, Black, and Vintage Blonde finishes were discontinued. In 2000, Vintage White finish was introduced. In 2002, Candy Apple Red was the only finish available.

JERRY DONAHUE TELECASTER (U.S. MFG. NO. 010-8902) - ash body, bird's-eye maple top/back, black pickguard, bird's-eye maple neck, 21-fret maple fingerboard with black dot inlay, strings through bridge, 6-on-one-side tuners, Jerry Donahue´s signature on peghead, gold hardware, 2 Seymour Duncan single coil pickups, volume/tone control, 5-position switch, controls mounted metal plate, available in 3-Tone Sunburst, Crimson Red Trans., and Sapphire Blue Trans. finishes, mfg. 1992-2001.

	$2,300	$2,000	$1,800	$1,600	$1,400	$1,200	$1,000

Last MSR was $3,180.

J.D. Telecaster (Jap. Mfg. No. 027-9702) - similar to the Jerry Donahue Telecaster, except features bound basswood body, 2 single coil pickups, 5-way switch, special wiring, available in 3-Color Sunburst, Black, Crimson Red Trans., and Sapphire Blue Trans. finishes, mfg. 1992-99.

	$500	$425	$375	$325	$275	$225	$175

Last MSR was $709.

JIMMY BRYANT (U.S. MFG. NO. 015-0062) - premium ash body, maple C-shape neck, 21-fret maple fingerboard with dot inlays, single-ply black pickguard with leather overlay, 2 Custom '51 Nocaster single coil pickups, two knobs, 3-way switch, vintage style bridge, nickel/chrome hardware, available in White Blonde finish, mfg. summer 2004-present.

MSR	$3,200	$2,300	$2,000	$1,750	$1,550	$1,350	$1,150	$950

JOHN 5 (NO. 015-5000-806) - Telecaster style, white double bound ash body, enlonged headstock, 3-per-side tuners, chrome pickguard, Custom Shop Humbucker and single coil pickups, two knobs, 3-way switch, available in Black finish, mfg. 2003-present.

MSR	$3,296	$2,400	$2,100	$1,850	$1,500	$1,300	$1,100	$900

John 5 Bigsby (No. 015-5500-806) - similar to the John 5, except has a Bigsby tailpiece and a Seymour Duncan single coil pickup in the bridge position, mfg. 2003-present.

MSR	$3,635	$2,600	$2,300	$2,050	$1,850	$1,550	$1,300	$1,100

John 5 Standard (Mex. Mfg., No. 013-9000) - standard version of the John 5 Telecaster with an Enforcer humbucker and Custom Shop Twisted Tele neck pickup, available in Black finish, mfg. summer 2004-present.

MSR	$1,042	$730	$650	$575	$500	$425	$350	$275

GRADING	100% MINT	98% NEAR MINT	95% EXC+	90% EXC	80% VG+	70% VG	60% G

JOHN JORGENSON TELECASTER (U.S. MFG. NO. 010-4400) - Korina body, maple neck, 22-fret African rosewood fingerboard with pearloid dot inlay, Sperzel TrimLok tuners, vintage-style bridge, chrome hardware, matching sparkle pickguard, 2 custom vintage-looking humbucking pickups, volume/tone controls, 3-position switch, chrome metal controls plate, available in Black, Champagne Sparkle, or Silver Sparkle tops with Natural body finishes, mfg. 1998-2001.

	$2,500	$2,250	$2,000	$1,800	$1,600	$1,400	$1,200

Last MSR was $4,030.

Both the Champagne and Silver Sparkle finishes feature white pearloid binding. The Black finish model has gold sparkle binding and ebony fingerboard with gold sparkle dot inlay. In 2000, Natural finish was discontinued.

MERLE HAGGARD TRIBUTE (U.S. MFG. NO. 010-0402) - laminated figured maple top, ivoroid body binding, set-in maple neck, 22-fret maple fingerboard with dot inlay, abalone "Tuff Dog Tele" headstock inlay, gold hardware, white ivoroid pickguard, 2 Texas Tele pickups, custom 4-way switching, available in 2-Color Sunburst finish, mfg. 1998-present.

MSR	$6,257	$4,500	$4,100	$3,800	$3,500	$3,200	$2,900	$2,500

MUDDY WATERS TRIBUTE TELECASTER 2000 (U.S. MFG.) - exact replica of the late '50s Telecaster that was Muddy's signature guitar, every ding, scratch and gouge is present along with amplifier knobs on the controls, mfg. 2000 only.

	$2,500	$2,200	$1,900	$1,650	$1,400	$1,150	$850

MUDDY WATERS (MEX. MFG. NO. 013-8500) - ash body, rosewood fingerboard with dot position markers, vintage machine heads, 21 medium-jumbo frets, 2 U.S. Special Vintage Tele pickups, 1 volume/1 tone control, 3-way switch, American vintage '52 Tele bridge, available in Candy Apple Red finish only, mfg. 2001-present.

MSR	$828	$580	$500	$425	$350	$300	$250	$200

NOKIE EDWARDS LIMITED EDITION (JAPAN MFG. NO. 025-8500) - laminated ash/basswood/rock maple body with flame maple top (strat-style) back and arm contours, bolt-on 3-ply maple neck, 22-fret ebony fingerboard with pearloid dot inlay and zero fret, tilt back headstock, 6-on-one-side tuners, gold hardware, 2 Seymour Duncan humbucking pickups, volume/push-pull tone (for coil tapping) controls, 3-position switch, available in Natural finish, mfg. 1996 only.

	N/A	$1,700	$1,400	$1,200	$1,000	$800	$600

Last MSR was $1,959.

It is estimated that only 35 instruments were produced.

Fender Albert Collins Telecaster courtesy Fender

WAYLON JENNINGS TRIBUTE (U.S. MFG. NO. 010-0302) - bound top/back light ash body, 21-fret maple fingerboard with dot inlay/Flying W at 12th fret, Scruggs tuner on low 'E' string, Elite tuning keys with pearloid buttons, chrome hardware, 3-ply white pickguard, 2 Texas Tele pickups, available in Black finish with leather White Rose inlay, mfg. 1995-2003.

	$3,175	$2,650	$2,325	$2,000	$1,850	$1,700	$1,550

Last MSR was $4,530.

WILL RAY LIMITED EDITION JAZZ-A-CASTER (JAPAN MFG. NO. 025-8700) - basswood body, satin-finished maple neck, small Strat headstock, 22-fret rosewood fingerboard with white pearloid triangle inlay, Schaller tuners, Hipshot B-Bender, chrome hardware, white shell pickguard, 2 Seymour Duncan Jazzmaster pickups, volume/tone controls, 4-position switch, available in Gold Foil finish, mfg. 1997-98.

	$1,100	$950	$800	$700	$600	$500	$400

Last MSR was $1,550.

WILL RAY SIGNATURE MOJO TELE (U.S. MFG. NO. 010-4500) - ash body, maple neck, Strat headstock, 22-fret rosewood fingerboard with pearl VooDoo Skulls inlay, Sperzel TrimLok tuners, custom Tele bridge with 3-string saddles, chrome hardware, white shell pickguard, 2 Custom Shop Jazzmaster pickups, volume/tone select/tone controls, 3-position switch, available in Cadmium Orange, Lime Green, or Ultra Marine Blue finishes with 23 Kt. Gold Foil Leaf applique, mfg. 1998-2001.

	$3,100	$2,700	$2,400	$2,100	$1,800	$1,500	$1,200

Last MSR was $4,330.

Add $250 for Hipshot String Bending system (Model 010-4540).

Telecaster: Time Machine Custom Shop Series

Time Machine Series Telecasters are built to exacting specifications of their respective vintages, including: body contours and radii, neck shape, fingerboard radius, pickups, electronics and hardware. Original materials, tooling and production techniques are employed whenever possible.

Each model is available in three distinct finish packages: NOS (New Old Stock), as if the guitar was bought new in its respective year and brought forward in time to the present day; Closet Classic, as if the guitar was bought new in its respective year, played perhaps a dozen times a year and then carefully put away - has a few small dings, lightly checked finish, oxidized hardware and aged plastic parts; Relic, shows natural wear and tear of years of heavy use - nicks, dings, scratches, worn finish, rusty hardware, and aged plastic parts.

'51 "NOCASTER" NOS (NO. 015-0102) - ash body, "U"-shaped maple neck, single-ply black pickguard and original specification pickups, available in Vintage Blonde finish, mfg. 2001-present.

MSR	$3,110	$2,200	$1,850	$1,650	$1,450	$1,250	$1,050	$850

Fender James Burton Telecaster courtesy Fender

GRADING	100% MINT	98% NEAR MINT	95% EXC+	90% EXC	80% VG+	70% VG	60% G

'51 "Nocaster" Closet Classic (No. 015-0202) - similar to '51 "Nocaster" (NOS) except in Closet Classic finish, available in Honey Blonde finish, mfg. 2001-present.

MSR	$3,420	$2,450	$2,200	$1,950	$1,700	$1,450	$1,200	$950

'51 "Nocaster" Relic (No. 015-0302) - similar to '51 "Nocaster" (NOS) except in Relic finish, available in Honey Blonde finish, mfg. 2001-present.

MSR	$3,580	$2,600	$2,300	$2,000	$1,750	$1,500	$1,250	$1,000

'60 TELE CUSTOM NOS (NO. 015-3300) - alder body, "C"-shaped maple neck, 21-fret rosewood fingerboard with dot inlay, 2 Custom '60s single coil pickups, vintage style bridge with three saddles, 3-way switch, 2 knobs (v, tone), nickel/chrome hardware, available in 3-Color Sunburst, Candy Apple Red, or Sonic Blue finishes, mfg. 2003-04.

		$2,750	$2,450	$2,150	$1,850	$1,500	$1,250	$1,050

Last MSR was $3,795.

'60 Tele Custom Closet Classic (No. 015-3400) - similar to the NOS Tele Custom except has Closet Classic finish, mfg. 2003-04.

		$2,950	$2,650	$2,350	$2,100	$1,850	$1,600	$1,350

Last MSR was $4,105.

'60 Tele Custom Relic (No. 015-3500) - similar to the NOS Tele Custom except has Relic finish, mfg. 2003-04.

		$3,050	$2,700	$2,400	$2,100	$1,800	$1,500	$1,250

Last MSR was $4,265.

'63 TELECASTER NOS (NO. 015-1000) - alder body, "C"-shaped maple neck with round-lam rosewood fingerboard, white/black/white pickguard and original specification pickups, available in White Blonde finish, mfg. 2001-present.

MSR	$3,276	$2,325	$2,000	$1,750	$1,500	$1,300	$1,100	$900

'63 Telecaster Closet Classic (No. 015-1100) - similar to '63 Telecaster (NOS) except in Closet Classic finish, available in Lake Placid Blue, Candy Apple Red, or Vintage Blonde finishes, mfg. 2001-present.

MSR	$3,586	$2,600	$2,300	$2,000	$1,700	$1,450	$1,200	$950

Add $100 for Vintage Blonde finish.

'63 Telecaster Relic (No. 015-1200) - similar to '63 Telecaster (NOS) except in Relic finish, available in Lake Placid Blue, Candy Apple Red, or Vintage Blonde finishes, mfg. 2001-present.

MSR	$3,746	$2,700	$2,350	$2,050	$1,750	$1,500	$1,250	$1,000

Add $100 for Vintage Blonde finish.

'67 TELECASTER NOS (NO. 155-6700) - alder body, maple C-shape neck, 21-fret rosewood fingerboard, original style Tele bridge, available in White Blonde, Black, or Shorline Gold finishes, mfg. summer 2004-present.

MSR	$3,276	$2,325	$2,000	$1,750	$1,500	$1,300	$1,100	$900

Also available with a maple fingerboard (No. 155-6702).

'67 Telecaster Closet Classic (No. 156-6700) - similar to the '67 Telecaster NOS, except in Closet Classic finish, mfg. summer 2004-present.

MSR	$3,586	$2,600	$2,300	$2,000	$1,700	$1,450	$1,200	$950

Also available with a maple fingerboard (No. 155-6702).

'67 Telecaster Relic (No. 157-6700) - similar to the '67 Telecaster NOS, except in Relic finish, mfg. summer 2004-present.

MSR	$3,746	$2,700	$2,350	$2,050	$1,750	$1,500	$1,250	$1,000

Also available with a maple fingerboard (No. 157-6702).

ELECTRIC: TORONADO SERIES

TORONADO (MEX. MFG., NO. 013-0700/0900) - offset cutaway/sloped shoulder poplar body, bolt-on maple neck, 24.75 in. scale, 22-fret rosewood neck with dot inlay, strings-through hard tail bridge, 6-on-a-side tuners, chrome hardware, brown shell pickguard, 2 chrome covered Atomic humbucker pickups, 2 volume/2 tone controls, 3-position toggle switch, available in Black, Candy Apple Red, Caramel Metallic, Brown Sunburst, Chrome Red, Pewter, Graffiti Yellow, Orange, Navy Blue Metallic, or Arctic White finishes, mfg. 1998-present.

MSR	$742	$525	$450	$400	$350	$300	$250	$200

Add $35 for Brown Sunburst finish.

In 2002, Candy Apple Red, Brown Sunburst and Arctic White finishes were discontinued, and Pewter, Graffiti Yellow, and Orange finishes were introduced. In 2005, this model was revised and renumbered to 013-0900.

TORONADO GT HH (JAP. MFG. NO. 026-0700) - similar to the Toronado HH, except has two Seymour Duncan humbucker pickups and a white or black racing stripe, available in Blue (white), Bronze (black), Green (black), or Red (white) finishes, new 2005.

MSR	$900	$630	$550	$475	$425	$375	$325	$275

AMERICAN SPECIAL TORONADO DE-9000 (U.S. MFG. NO. 011-0600) - offset cutaway/sloped shoulder Alder body, bolt-on neck, 24 in. scale, 22-fret rosewood neck with dot inlay, strings through hard tail bridge, 6-on-a-side tuners, chrome hardware, black pickguard, 2 Fender DE-9000 Black Dove pickups, 2 volume/2 tone controls, 3-position toggle switch, available in Butterscotch or Crimson Trans. finishes, mfg. 2002-04.

		$900	$800	$725	$650	$575	$500	$425

Last MSR was $1,285.

American Special Toronado HH (U.S. Mfg., No. 011-0700) - Similar to the American Special Toronado DE-9000 except has 2 Atomic II Humbucker pickups, mfg. 2002-04.

		$900	$825	$725	$650	$575	$500	$425

Last MSR was $1,285.

GRADING	100% MINT	98% NEAR MINT	95% EXC+	90% EXC	80% VG+	70% VG	60% G

HIGHWAY 1 TORONADO (U.S. MFG. NO. 011-0800) - Offset cutaway/sloped shoulder alder body, bolt-on modified C-shaped maple neck, 22-fret rosewood fingerboard with dot inlay, 2 Atomic II Humbucker pickups, black pickguard, Adjusto-Matic bridge, 3-way switch, two knobs (v, tone), chrome hardware, available in Black, Pewter, or Chrome Silver, mfg. 2003-04.

	$800	$725	$650	$575	$500	$425	$375

Last MSR was $1,142.

ELECTRIC BASS: BASS V, BASS VI, & BASS VI REISSUE SERIES

BASS V (U.S. MFG.) - offset double cutaway elongated ash body, bolt-on maple neck, 15-fret rosewood fingerboard with pearl dot inlay, strings through bridge, coverplate with F logo, 5-on-one-side tuners, chrome hardware, white plastic/metal pickguard, thumb rest, single coil split covered pickup, pickup coverplate, volume/tone control, available in custom colors or Sunburst finishes, mfg. 1965-1970.

	N/A	$2,000	$1,750	$1,550	$1,350	$1,150	$950

Add $100 for left-hand version. Add 25%-50% for custom colors.

In 1966, bound fingerboard with black inlay became standard.

BASS VI (U.S. MFG.) - offset double cutaway asymmetrical ash body, bolt-on maple neck, 21-fret rosewood fingerboard with pearl dot inlay, floating bridge/vibrato with bridge cover, 6-on-one-side tuners, chrome hardware, tortoise/metal or white pickguard, 3 single coil exposed pickups with metal rings, volume/tone control, 3 on/off pickup selector switches, low cut switch, available in custom colors or Sunburst finishes, mfg. 1961-1975.

1961-1962	N/A	$4,500	$4,000	$3,600	$3,200	$2,800	$2,400
1963-1964	N/A	$4,000	$3,500	$3,100	$2,700	$2,300	$1,900
1965-1966	N/A	$3,500	$3,000	$2,600	$2,200	$1,800	$1,500
1967-1969	N/A	$3,000	$2,600	$2,300	$2,000	$1,700	$1,400
1970-1972	N/A	$2,500	$2,100	$1,800	$1,600	$1,400	$1,200
1973-1975	N/A	$2,100	$1,800	$1,600	$1,400	$1,200	$1,000

Add 25%-50% for custom colors.

In 1963, strings mute and another 2-position switch were added, a maple fingerboard with black dot inlay was made available. In 1965, bound fingerboard with dot inlays became standard. In 1966, bound fingerboard with block inlay became standard. In 1969, Fender locking vibrato was optionally offered. In 1974, a black pickguard became standard.

BASS VI REISSUE (JAPAN MFG. NO. 027-7600) - offset double cutaway asymmetrical alder body, bolt-on maple neck, 30.3 in. scale, 21-fret rosewood fingerboard with pearl dot inlay, floating tremolo with trem-lock, 6-on-one-side tuners, chrome hardware, red shell pickguard, 3 single coil pickups, master volume/master tone controls, 3 pickup selector switches, low cut (strangle) switch, available in 3-Tone Sunburst finish, mfg. 1995-98.

	$750	$650	$575	$500	$425	$350	$275

Last MSR was $1,000.

**Fender Bass VI
courtesy Dave Rogers
Dave's Guitar Shop**

ELECTRIC BASS: BULLET SERIES

BULLET B30 - offset double cutaway alder body, white pickguard, bolt-on maple neck, 19-fret maple fingerboard with black dot inlay, fixed bridge, tele-style peghead, chrome hardware, 1 split covered pickup, volume/tone control, available in Brown Sunburst, Custom Colors, Ivory, Red, or Walnut finishes, mfg. 1982-83.

	N/A	$400	$325	$275	$225	$175	$140

BULLET B34 - similar to Bullet B30, except has a long scale length, mfg. 1982-83.

	N/A	$425	$350	$300	$250	$200	$160

BULLET B40 - similar to Bullet B30, except has 20-fret fingerboard, mfg. 1982-83.

	N/A	$450	$375	$325	$275	$225	$175

ELECTRIC BASS: CORONADO SERIES

CORONADO BASS I (U.S. MFG.) - double rounded cutaway semi-hollow bound maple body, arched top, f-holes, 2 finger rests, bolt-on maple neck, 21-fret rosewood fingerboard with pearl dot inlay, adjustable aluminum bridge/trapeze tailpiece, ebony tailpiece insert with pearl F inlay, 4-on-one-side tuners, chrome hardware, single coil covered pickup, volume/tone control, available in Cherry or Sunburst finishes, mfg. 1966-1970.

	N/A	$1,100	$950	$800	$700	$600	$500

A wide variety of bridge styles was available on this model.

CORONADO BASS II (U.S. MFG.) - similar to Coronado Bass I, except has bound f-holes/fingerboard with block inlay, tune-o-matic bridge, string mutes, 2 single coil covered pickups, 2 volume/2 tone controls, 3-position switch, mfg. 1967-1970.

	N/A	$1,200	$1,050	$900	$750	$650	$550

Add 20% for Wildwood finish.

Wildwood finishes were optional. The Wildwood finish was the result of a seven-year process in Germany where dye was injected into growing beech trees. After the trees were harvested, veneers were cut and laminated to the guitar tops. Pickguard numbers (I-VI) refer to the dye color (primary color of green, blue, and gold) and the applied finish.

**Fender Bullet B34
courtesy George McGuire**

GRADING	100% MINT	98% NEAR MINT	95% EXC+	90% EXC	80% VG+	70% VG	60% G

Coronado Bass II Antigua (U.S. Mfg.) - similar to Coronado Bass II, except has Antigua (Black to Silver Sunburst) finish, mfg. 1970-72.

| | N/A | $1,500 | $1,250 | $1,100 | $950 | $800 | $650 |

ELECTRIC BASS: DIMENSION SERIES

DIMENSION BASS IV (MEX. MFG. NO. 013-8000) - offset double cutaway alder body, maple C-shaped neck, 24-fret pao-ferro fingerboard with dot inlays, 1 split single coil P-style and 1 Noiseless J-style pickup, five black knobs, 2-per-side tuners, black headstock, standard bridge, chrome hardware, available Amber, Pewter, Sienna Sunburst, or Black finishes, mfg. 2004-present.

| MSR | $1,000 | $700 | $625 | $550 | $475 | $425 | $375 | $325 |

Add $35 for Sienna Sunburst finish.

Dimension Bass V (Mex. Mfg. No. 013-8005) - similar to the Dimension IV, except in 5-string configuration, and 3/2-per-side tuners, mfg. 2004-present.

| MSR | $1,100 | $775 | $700 | $625 | $550 | $475 | $400 | $350 |

ELECTRIC BASS: H.M./H.M.T SERIES

The H.M. Series more than likely stood for Heavy Metal.

H.M. BASS ULTRA (U.S. MFG.) - basswood body, figured maple top/back, rosewood fingerboard, 3 pickups in different configurations, 2 knobs, 5-way switch, black hardware, available in various finishes, mfg. late 1980s-early 1990s.

| | N/A | $500 | $425 | $375 | $325 | $275 | $225 |

The different pickup configurations include the 3 Silver Fender-Lace Sensor Model 19-4600, 3 Jazz Bass single coil pickups Models 19-4500, 19-4400, and piezo bridge/Silver Fender-Lace Sensor Model 25-9600.

H.M. BASS (JAPAN MFG.) - similar to the U.S. made H.M. bass, mfg. early 1990s.

| | N/A | $400 | $350 | $300 | $250 | $200 | $250 |

H.M. BASS V (JAPAN MFG.) - similar to the H.M. Bass, except in 5-string configuration, mfg. early 1990s.

| | N/A | $450 | $375 | $325 | $275 | $225 | $175 |

ELECTRIC BASS: JP & MB SERIES

JP-90 (NO. 014-4100) - offset double cutaway asymmetrical poplar body, black pickguard, bolt-on maple neck, 20-fret rosewood fingerboard with pearl dot inlay, fixed bridge, 4-on-one-side tuners, chrome hardware, P/J-style pickups, volume/tone control, 3-position switch, available in Arctic White, Black, or Torino Red finishes, mfg. 1990-94.

| | N/A | $550 | $475 | $400 | $350 | $300 | $250 |

Last MSR was $530.

MB-4 - offset double cutaway asymmetrical basswood body, black pickguard, bolt-on maple neck, 22-fret rosewood fingerboard with pearl dot inlay, fixed bridge, 4-on-one-side tuners, chrome hardware, P/J-style pickups, concentric volume/treble/bass/mix controls, 3-position switch, available in Black, Red, or White finishes, mfg. 1994-95.

| | N/A | $400 | $350 | $300 | $250 | $200 | $150 |

Last MSR was $550.

MB-5 - similar to MB-4, except has 5-string configuration, 5-on-one-side tuners, mfg. 1994-95.

| | N/A | $450 | $375 | $325 | $275 | $225 | $175 |

Last MSR was $620.

This model has an optional poplar body.

ELECTRIC BASS: MUSICMASTER & PERFORMER SERIES

MUSICMASTER (U.S. MFG.) - offset double cutaway asymmetrical ash body, black pickguard, thumb rest, bolt-on maple neck, 19-fret rosewood fingerboard with pearl dot inlay, fixed bridge, 4-on-one-side tuners, chrome hardware, single coil covered pickup, volume/tone control, available in Black, Blue, Red, or White finishes, mfg. 1970-1983.

| 1970-1978 | N/A | $650 | $575 | $500 | $425 | $375 | $325 |
| 1979-1983 | N/A | $550 | $475 | $400 | $350 | $300 | $250 |

PERFORMER - Offset dual cutaway asymmetrical hardwood body, white pickguard, bolt-on maple neck, 24-fret rosewood fingerboard with pearl dot inlay, fixed bridge, 4-on-one-side tuners, chrome hardware, 2 single coil covered pickups, 2 volume/1 tone controls, active electronics, available in Sunburst finish, mfg. 1987-88.

| | N/A | $700 | $625 | $550 | $475 | $400 | $325 |

ELECTRIC BASS: MUSTANG SERIES

MUSTANG (U.S. MFG.) - offset double cutaway poplar body, plastic/metal pickguard, thumb rest, bolt-on maple neck, 19-fret rosewood fingerboard with pearl dot inlay, fixed bridge, 4-on-one-side tuners, chrome hardware, P-style pickup, volume/tone control, available in Antigua, Black, Blonde, Blue, Natural, Red, Sunburst, Walnut, White, or Wine finishes, mfg. 1966-1983.

1966-1969	N/A	$1,350	$1,150	$1,000	$850	$700	$550
1970-1978	N/A	$1,100	$950	$800	$650	$550	$450
1979-1983	N/A	$900	$750	$650	$550	$450	$350

Add $45 for left-hand version. Add $100 for Competition finishes.

In 1969, Competition finishes were introduced. These finishes consist of solid colors (blue, burgundy, orange and red) with racing stripes. The instrument was also referred to as Competition Mustang Bass with these finishes.

GRADING	100% MINT	98% NEAR MINT	95% EXC+	90% EXC	80% VG+	70% VG	60% G

MUSTANG BASS (JAPAN MFG. NO. 025-3900) - offset double cutaway Alder body, maple neck, rosewood fingerboard with white dot inlays, 30 in. scale, 19 nickel silver frets, one single-coil split pickup, tortiseshell (red finish) or brown shell (white finish) pickguard, volume and tone control on metal plate, available in Vintage White or Fiesta Red, mfg. 2002-present.

	MSR	$800	$575	$500	$425	$375	$325	$275	$225

ELECTRIC BASS: PRODIGY SERIES

PRODIGY ACTIVE BASS - offset double cutaway poplar body, bolt-on maple neck, 20-fret rosewood fingerboard with pearl dot inlay, fixed bridge, 4-on-one-side tuners, chrome hardware, P/J-style pickups, concentric volume-pan/treble-bass controls, active electronics, available in Arctic White, Black, Crimson Red Metallic, or Lake Placid Blue finishes, mfg. 1992-95.

N/A	$450	$375	$300	$250	$200	$150

Last MSR was $600.

ELECTRIC BASS: PROPHECY SERIES

PROPHECY I - offset double cutaway asymmetrical basswood body, bolt-on maple neck, 22-fret rosewood fingerboard with pearl dot inlay, fixed bridge, 2-per-side tuners, chrome hardware, P/J-style pickups, volume/treble/bass/mix controls, available in Sunburst finish, disc. 1995.

N/A	$550	$475	$400	$325	$275	$225

Last MSR was $770.

PROPHECY II - similar to Prophecy I, except has ash body, gold hardware, active electronics, disc. 1995.

N/A	$600	$525	$475	$400	$350	$300

Last MSR was $870.

PROPHECY III - similar to Prophecy I, except has alder/walnut/bubinga body, through body maple neck, gold hardware, active electronics, disc. 1995.

N/A	$950	$875	$800	$725	$650	$575

Last MSR was $1,330.

Fender Dimension Bass IV courtesy Fender

ELECTRIC BASS: SIGNATURE SERIES

MARK HOPPUS SIGNATURE BASS (MEX. MFG. NO. 013-8300) - alder Jazz-shaped body, maple Precision bass neck, rosewood fingerboard with white dot inlays, 34 in. scale, 20 medium/jumbo frets, 4-ply White Pearloid pickguard, single Seymour Duncan Quarter Pound P Bass pickup, volume control, available in Daphne Blue, Olympic White, Black, Shell Pink, and Surf Green, mfg. 2002-present.

MSR	$800	$575	$500	$425	$375	$325	$275	$225

Mark Hoppus is the bass player for the band Blink-182. This guitar features a Jazz Bass body fitted with a Precision Bass neck and a Seymour Duncan pickup.

ROSCOE BECK IV BASS (U.S. MFG. NO. 019-6400/6402) - offset double cutaway alder body, bolt-on maple neck with graphite reinforcement, 22-fret rosewood or maple fingerboard with pearl dot inlay, strings through body bridge, Roscoe Beck's signature on peghead, chrome hardware, mint white (or brown shell) pickguard, 2 Special J Humbucker pickups, volume/tone controls, 3 3-way switches, available in 2-Color Sunburst, Lake Placid Blue, Crimson Red Trans., or Honey Burst finishes, mfg. 2004-present.

MSR	$1,900	$1,350	$1,150	$1,000	$850	$725	$600	$500

ROSCOE BECK V BASS (U.S. MFG. NO. 019-6500) - offset double cutaway alder body, bolt-on maple neck with graphite reinforcement, 22-fret pau ferro fingerboard with pearl dot inlay, strings through body bridge, Roscoe Beck's signature on peghead, chrome hardware, mint white (or brown shell) pickguard, 2 Dual Jazz 5 pickups, volume/tone controls pickup selector switch, 2 mini-switches, available in 3-Tone Sunburst, Candy Apple Red, Shoreline Gold, or Teal Green Metallic finishes, mfg. 1997-present.

MSR	$1,942	$1,375	$1,175	$1,025	$875	$750	$625	$525

STU HAMM URGE BASS (U.S. MFG. NO. 019-1400) - down-sized offset double cutaway alder body, bolt-on maple neck, 32 in. scale, 24-fret pau ferro fingerboard, strings through body gold plated bridge, Stu Hamm's signature on peghead, 4-on-one-side black chrome tuners, white pearloid pickguard, J/P/J-style pickups, volume/pan, treble/bass concentric ('stacked') controls, 3-position mini/rotary switches, active electronics, available in Burgundy Mist, Lake Placid Blue, Montego Black, or Sherwood Green Metallic finishes, mfg. 1993-99.

$1,125	$950	$875	$800	$725	$650	$575

Last MSR was $1,599.

This instrument was designed in collaboration with bassist Stu Hamm, and debuted in 1993.

STU HAMM URGE BASS II (U.S. MFG. NO. 019-1500) - poplar body, rosewood fingerboard, matching painted headstock, deluxe lightweight tuning machines, 24 frets, 3 pickups (2 Noiseless jazz, 1 Custom P-Bass), white pickguard, four black knobs (v, blend, 3 band EQ, 3-way switching, combo S-T-B top load bridge, available in 3-Color Sunburst, Black, Bright Amber Metallic, or Bright Saphire Metallic, current mfg.

MSR	$2,000	$1,400	$1,200	$1,050	$900	$800	$700	$600

Stu Hamm Urge Standard Bass (Mex. Mfg., No. 013-1400) - similar to Stu Hamm Urge Bass, except has poplar body, rosewood fingerboard, 2 J-style pickups, volume/tone controls, pickup selector mini-switch, active electronics, available in Arctic White, Black, Crimson Red Metallic, or Lake Placid Blue finishes, mfg. 1994-99.

$425	$375	$325	$290	$250	$215	$175

Last MSR was $599.

Fender Stu Hamm Urge Bass II courtesy Fender

GRADING	100% MINT	98% NEAR MINT	95% EXC+	90% EXC	80% VG+	70% VG	60% G

ELECTRIC BASS: TELECASTER SERIES

TELECASTER BASS (1ST VERSION, U.S. MFG.) - offset double cutaway ash body, white pickguard, finger rest, bolt-on maple neck, 20-fret maple fingerboard with black dot inlay, fixed bridge with cover, 4-on-one-side tuners, chrome hardware, single coil exposed pickup with cover, volume/tone control, available in Blonde and Custom Colors finishes, mfg. 1968-1972.

	100%	98%	95%	90%	80%	70%	60%
1968-1969	N/A	$2,750	$2,300	$2,000	$1,700	$1,400	$1,200
1970-1972	N/A	$2,400	$2,000	$1,700	$1,500	$1,300	$1,100

In 1970, a fretless fingerboard became optional.

Telecaster Bass (2nd Version, U.S. Mfg.) - similar to Telecaster, except has redesigned pickguard, thumb rest, 2-section bridge, covered humbucker pickup with no separate cover, available in Blonde or Sunburst finishes, mfg. 1972-79.

	100%	98%	95%	90%	80%	70%	60%
1972-1973	N/A	$1,700	$1,450	$1,250	$1,050	$850	$700
1974-1976	N/A	$1,500	$1,300	$1,100	$950	$800	$650
1977-1979	N/A	$1,200	$1,050	$900	$750	$600	$450

Between 1977 to 1979, a 4-section single string groove bridge was available.

Telecaster Bass Paisley, Telecaster Bass Blue Floral (U.S. Mfg.) - similar to Telecaster Bass, except available in Blue Floral or Pink Paisley finishes and had a single coil pickup, mfg. 1968-1970.

	100%	98%	95%	90%	80%	70%	60%
	N/A	$4,000	$3,250	$2,750	$2,250	$1,900	$1,750

ELECTRIC BASS: ZONE SERIES

AMERICAN DELUXE ZONE BASS (U.S. MFG. NO. 019-9500) - figured maple over alder or walnut over mahogany body, maple neck with rosewood fingerboard, deluxe lightweight tuning machines, 2 Humbucking pickups, five control knobs (v, blend, 3-band EQ), blend switching, deluxe chrome-plated bridge, available in Amber or Walnut finishes, mfg. 2001-present.

		98%	95%	90%	80%	70%	60%
MSR	$2,085	$1,475	$1,250	$1,100	$950	$850	$750	$650

DELUXE ZONE BASS (MEX MFG. NO. 013-5800) - alder Precision-shaped body, rosewood fingerboard, chome mini tuning machines, 22 medium Jumbo frets, 2 special design JP pickups, five black control knobs (v, blend, 3 band EQ), blend switching, deluxe chrome-plated steel bridge, available in Sage Metallic, Pewter, Sienna Sunburst, or Black finishes, mfg. 2001-present.

		98%	95%	90%	80%	70%	60%
MSR	$900	$630	$550	$475	$425	$375	$325	$275

Add $35 for Sienna Sunburst finish.

Deluxe Zone Bass 5-String (Mex. Mfg. No. 013-5900) - similar to the Deluxe Zone Bass, except in 5-String configuration, mfg. 2003-present.

		98%	95%	90%	80%	70%	60%
MSR	$957	$675	$600	$525	$450	$400	$350	$300

JAZZ BASS SERIES

Instruments in this series have an offset double cutaway (slim waist) body, bolt-on maple neck, 4-on-one-side tuners (unless otherwise specified). Currently, Jazz basses are more popular and desirable than the P Bass.

Jazz Bass: Early Models (1960-1984 Mfg.)

JAZZ BASS (FENDER MFG. 1960-64) - alder body, tortoiseshell/metal pickguard with finger rest, 20-fret rosewood fingerboard with pearl dot inlay, fixed bridge with string mutes, F logo bridge cover, chrome hardware, 2 J-style pickups, 2 concentric (volume/tone) controls, available in Blonde, Custom Colors, or 3-Tone Sunburst finishes, mfg. 1960-64.

	100%	98%	95%	90%	80%	70%	60%
1960	N/A	$18,000	$15,000	$12,000	$10,000	$8,500	$7,000
1961	N/A	$16,000	$13,000	$11,000	$9,500	$8,000	$6,500
1962 (Stacked)	N/A	$14,000	$12,000	$10,000	$8,500	$7,000	$6,000
1962 (3 Knobs)	N/A	$13,000	$11,000	$9,500	$8,000	$6,500	$5,500
1963	N/A	$11,000	$9,500	$8,000	$7,000	$6,000	$5,000
1964	N/A	$10,000	$8,500	$7,200	$6,000	$5,000	$4,000

Add 25% for Dakota Red, Fiesta Red, Candy Apple Red, Olympic White, Sonic Blue, Lake Placid Blue, or Gold Metallic finishes. Add 50% for Burgundy Mist, Surf Green, Fire Mist Silver, or Shell Pink finishes.

Instruments from 1960 and 1961 to mid-1962 have concentric stacked volume and tone knobs. After mid-1962, 2 volume and 1 tone controls replaced the stacked control knobs. In 1962, Blonde and custom color finishes were introduced, Blonde finish instruments have ash body. Custom Color finishes have white pickguards. In 1963, string mutes were removed.

GRADING	100% MINT	98% NEAR MINT	95% EXC+	90% EXC	80% VG+	70% VG	60% G

F

JAZZ BASS (CBS MFG. 1965-1974)
- Alder body, tortoise/metal pickguard with finger rest, 20-fret rosewood fingerboard with pearl dot inlay, fixed bridge with string mutes, F logo bridge cover, chrome hardware, 2 J-style pickups, 2 concentric (volume/tone) controls, available in Blonde, Black, Custom Colors, or 3-Tone Sunburst finishes, mfg. 1965-1974.

Year	100%	98%	95%	90%	80%	70%	60%
1965	N/A	$7,500	$6,000	$5,000	$4,000	$3,100	$2,500
1966	N/A	$6,500	$5,000	$4,300	$3,600	$3,000	$2,300
1967	N/A	$5,500	$4,500	$3,700	$3,100	$2,500	$2,000
1968	N/A	$4,500	$3,700	$3,000	$2,500	$2,100	$1,700
1969	N/A	$4,000	$3,200	$2,700	$2,300	$1,900	$1,500
1970	N/A	$3,500	$2,800	$2,400	$2,000	$1,700	$1,400
1971	N/A	$3,000	$2,500	$2,200	$1,900	$1,600	$1,300
1972	N/A	$2,700	$2,300	$2,000	$1,700	$1,400	$1,200
1973	N/A	$2,500	$2,100	$1,800	$1,500	$1,300	$1,100
1974	N/A	$2,200	$1,900	$1,650	$1,400	$1,200	$1,000

Add 25% for Dakota Red, Fiesta Red, Candy Apple Red, Olympic White, Sonic Blue, Lake Placid Blue, or Gold Metallic finishes. Add 50% for Burgundy Mist, Surf Green, Fire Mist Silver, Sherwood Green, or Shell Pink finishes.

In 1965, bound fingerboard was added. In 1966, block fingerboard inlay replaced dot inlay. In 1969, black bound maple fingerboard with black block inlay was made optional.

JAZZ BASS (3-BOLT NECK, CBS MFG. 1975-1980)
- similar to Jazz, except has a 3-bolt neck, mfg. 1975-1981.

Year	100%	98%	95%	90%	80%	70%	60%
1975-1976	N/A	$2,000	$1,700	$1,500	$1,300	$1,100	$900
1977-1980	N/A	$1,500	$1,300	$1,100	$950	$800	$650

JAZZ BASS GOLD (U.S. MFG.)
- similar to Jazz, except has gold hardware, available in Gold finish, mfg. 1981-84.

	100%	98%	95%	90%	80%	70%	60%
	N/A	$1,100	$950	$800	$700	$600	$500

JAZZ BASS (ONE PIECE PICKGUARD, CBS MFG. 1983-84)
- similar to Jazz, except has a one-piece white pickguard (no chrome metal controls plate), mfg. 1983-84.

	100%	98%	95%	90%	80%	70%	60%
	N/A	$1,000	$850	$750	$650	$550	$450

**Fender Telecaster Bass
courtesy Dr. Paul McCombs**

Jazz Bass: American Series (Current Mfg.)

AMERICAN JAZZ BASS (U.S. MFG. NO. 019-3400/3460/019-2400) - alder body, bolt-on maple neck with graphite reinforcement, 20-fret rosewood fingerboard with pearl dot inlay, strings through body bridge, chrome hardware, white/metal pickguard, 2 J-style American Vintage Jazz pickups, 2 volume/1 tone controls, currently available in 3-Color Sunburst, 2-Color Sunburst, Black, Sunset Orange Trans., Chrome Red, Sky Blue, Hot Rod Red, or Aqua Marine Metallic finishes, current mfg.

MSR	$1,500	$1,050	$900	$800	$700	$625	$550	$475

Add $80 for 3-Color Sunburst finish. Add $100 for Natural Ash finish.

This model is also available with a maple neck (No. 019-3400). In 1996, Arctic White, Carribbean Mist, Lipstick Red, Midnight Blue, and Midnight Wine colors were discontinued; Candy Apple Red, Vintage White, Crimson burst, and Sonic Blue finishes were introduced. In 1998, Vintage White, Crimson burst, and Sonic Blue finishes were discontinued; 3-Color Sunburst, Inca Silver, Lake Placid Blue, Natural Ash, and Olympic White finishes were introduced. In 1999, Aqua Marine Metallic, & White Blonde finishes were introduced; Lake Placid Blue finish was discontinued. In 2000, Inca Silver finish was discontinued. In 2003, a new model was introduced (No. 019-3460) with the new S-1 pickup switching.

American Jazz Bass Fretless (U.S. Mfg. No. 019-3408/3468/019-2408) - similar to American Standard Jazz Bass, except in a fretless configuration, rosewood fingerboard, available in 3-Color Sunburst, Olympic White, Black, or Purple Metallic finishes, current mfg.

MSR	$1,500	$1,050	$900	$800	$725	$625	$550	$475

Add $80 for 3-Color Sunburst finish.

In 2002, Olympic White and Purple Metallic finishes were discontinued. In 2003, a new model was introduced (No. 019-3468) with the new S-1 pickup switching.

American Jazz Bass V (U.S. Mfg. No. 019-3500/3560/019-2500) - similar to the American Standard Jazz, except has 20-fret pao ferro fingerboard, 2 J-style American Vintage Jazz 5 pickups, currently available in Black, 3-Color Sunburst, 2-Color Sunburst, Sunset Orange Transparent, Chrome Red, or Sky Blue finishes, current mfg.

MSR	$1,614	$1,150	$1,000	$900	$800	$725	$650	$575

Add $80 for 3-Color Sunburst finish.

In 1998, Brown Sunburst finish was discontinued; 3-Color Sunburst finish was introduced. In 1999, Aqua Marine Metallic, and White Blonde finishes were introduced; Lake Placid Blue finish was discontinued. In 2000, Hot Rod Red finish was introduced. Candy Apple Red, Olympic White, Inca Silver, and Brown Sunburst finishes were discontinued. In 2003, a new model was introduced (No. 019-3560) with the new S-1 pickup switching.

**Fender Jazz Bass
courtesy Dr. Paul McCombs**

GRADING	100% MINT	98% NEAR MINT	95% EXC+	90% EXC	80% VG+	70% VG	60% G

Jazz Bass: American Deluxe & Deluxe Series

Add $100 for Natural, White Blonde, and Purple Trans. finishes.

AMERICAN DELUXE JAZZ BASS (U.S. MFG. NO. 019-5860) - premium ash or alder body, rosewood neck with 22 American Standard frets, graphite reinforced neck, rosewood fingerboard with abalone dot inlays, 34 in. scale, American Deluxe tuners, Fender Noiseless Jazz Bass pickups, pan pot, master volume, 3-band active EQ with treble boost/cut, Mid-boost/cut, and Bass-boost/cut, aged white or brown shell pickguard, deluxe top-load or S-T-B bridge, currently available in 3-Color Sunburst, Aged Cherry Burst, black, Teal Green Trans., Candy Tangerine, Chrome Red, mfg. 1999-present.

MSR	$1,750		$1,225	$1,050	$950	$850	$750	$600	$500

Add $50 for the left-hand model (No. 019-5820), mfg. 1999-2001.

American Deluxe Jazz Bass V (U.S. Mfg. No. 019-5960) - similar to the American Deluxe Jazz Bass except has five strings with a 4/1-per-side tuners, and a pau ferro neck, mfg. 1999-present.

MSR	$1,800		$1,275	$1,075	$975	$850	$750	$600	$500

This model is also available with a maple fingerboard (No. 019-5962).

American Deluxe Jazz Bass Fretless (U.S. Mfg. No. 019-5808) - similar to the American Deluxe Jazz Bass except has a fretless neck, mfg. 1999-2001.

			$1,200	$1,025	$950	$850	$750	$600	$500

Last MSR was $1,700.

Also available with maple fingerboard (Model 019-5802).

AMERICAN DELUXE JAZZ BASS (NO. 019-4460) - select alder body, maple C-shaped neck with graphite reinforcements, 22-fret rosewood fingerboard with dot inlay, brown shell, gold vinyl, silver shell, or M/B/M pickguard, 2 single coil Noiseless pickups, four knobs, Top-load or S-T-B bridge, chrome hardware, available in 3-Color Sunburst, Amber, Montego Black, or Candy Tangerine finishes, mfg. 2004-present.

MSR	$1,685		$1,200	$1,050	$900	$800	$700	$600	$500

Also available with maple fingerboard (No. 019-4462). This model replaced the earlier American Deluxe Jazz Bass. Also availble in left-handed configuration (No. 019-4490, in 3-Color Sunburst or Montego Black finish). Also available in fretless configuration (No. 019-4468, in 3-Color Sunburst or Monetgo Black finish).

American Deluxe Jazz Bass V (No. 019-4760) - similar to the American Deluxe Jazz Bass, except in 5-string configuration, 4/1-per-side tuners, and pau-ferro fingerboard, mfg. 2004-present.

MSR	$1,785		$1,275	$1,125	$975	$850	$750	$650	$550

Also available with maple fingerboard (No. 019-4662).

American Deluxe Jazz Bass Ash (No. 019-4560) - similar to the American Deluxe Jazz Bass, except has a premium ash body, available in Tobacco Sunburst, Aged Cherry Sunburst, or Butterscotch Blonde finishes, new 2004.

MSR	$1,828		$1,300	$1,150	$1,000	$875	$775	$675	$575

Also available with maple fingerboard (No. 019-4562).

American Deluxe Jazz Bass Ash V (No. 019-4760) - similar to the American Deluxe Jazz Bass Ash, except in 5-string configuration, 4/1-per-side tuners, pau-ferro fingerboard, mfg. 2004-present.

MSR	$1,942		$1,375	$1,175	$1,025	$900	$800	$700	$600

Also available with maple fingerboard (No. 019-4762).

AMERICAN DELUXE JAZZ BASS FMT/QMT (U.S. MFG NO. 019-4470/4480) - similar to the American Deluxe Jazz Bass except has a figured maple or quilted maple top over an alder body, available in Amber, Crimson Trans., Tobacco Sunburst, Bing Cherry Trans., or Aged Cherry Sunburst, mfg. 2001-present.

MSR	$2,357		$1,650	$1,450	$1,250	$1,100	$950	$800	$700

This model is also available with a rosewood fingerboard (No. 019-4472/4482).

American Deluxe Jazz Bass V FMT/QMT (U.S. Mfg., No. 019-4670/4680) - similar to the American Deluxe Jazz Bass FMT excpet has five strings and a pao ferro neck, mfg. 2001-present.

MSR	$2,428		$1,750	$1,550	$1,350	$1,150	$1,000	$850	$750

DELUXE ACTIVE JAZZ BASS (MEX. MFG. NO. 013-6700/6760) - poplar body, bolt-on maple neck, 20-fret rosewood fingerboard with dot inlay, fixed bridge, chrome hardware, brown shell and metal pickguard, 2 American Deluxe J-Bass pickups, volume/blend/bass/mid/treble controls, active electronics, available in Arctic White, Black, Brown Sunburst, Vintage White, or Candy Apple Red finishes, mfg. 1998-present.

MSR	$842		$600	$525	$450	$375	$325	$275	$225

Add $35 for Brown Sunburst Color finish.

In 2004, this model was upgraded and changed to No. 013-6760, and Vintage White finish was introduced.

Deluxe Active Jazz Bass V (Mex. Mfg., No. 013-6800/6860) - similar to the Active Jazz Bass, except has 5-string configuration, 5-on-a-side tuners, 20-fret pau ferro fingerboard, 2 American Deluxe J-Bass V pickups, available in Arctic White, Black, Brown Sunburst, or Candy Apple Red finishes, mfg. 1998-present.

MSR	$900		$630	$550	$475	$425	$375	$325	$275

Add $35 for Brown Sunburst Color finish.

In 2004, this model was upgraded and changed to No. 013-6860, and Vintage White finish was introduced.

JAZZ BASS DELUXE (U.S. MFG NO. 019-4400) - down-sized alder body, ash veneer top/back, bolt-on tinted maple neck with graphite reinforcement, 22-fret rosewood fingerboard with pearl dot inlay, strings through body bridge, chrome hardware, white (or brown) shell/metal pickguard, 2 J-style Jazz Bass humbucking pickups, 2 volume/3-band EQ controls, active electronics, available in Antique Burst, Black, Blue Burst, Crimson Burst, Shoreline Gold, or Teal Green Metallic finishes, disc. 1998.

			$875	$750	$675	$600	$525	$450	$375

Last MSR was $1,249.

GRADING	100% MINT	98% NEAR MINT	95% EXC+	90% EXC	80% VG+	70% VG	60% G

Jazz Bass Deluxe w/Maple Neck (U.S. Mfg., No. Model 019-4402) - similar to the Jazz Bass Deluxe, except has maple fingerboard with black dot inlay, available in Antique Burst, Black, Blue Burst, Crimson Burst, Shoreline Gold, or Teal Green Metallic finishes, mfg. 1997-98.

		$875	$750	$675	$600	$525	$450	$375

Last MSR was $1,249.

Jazz Bass Deluxe Fretless (U.S. Mfg., No. 019-4408) - similar to the Jazz Bass Deluxe, except has fretless rosewood fingerboard, available in Antique Burst, Black, Shoreline Gold, or Teal Green Metallic finishes, disc. 1998.

	$925	$800	$700	$625	$550	$475	$400

Last MSR was $1,299.

Jazz Bass Deluxe V String (U.S. Mfg., No. 019-4500) - similar to the Jazz Bass Deluxe, except has 5-string configuration, 20-fret pau ferro fingerboard, 2 J-style American Vintage Jazz 5 pickups, available in Antique Burst, Black, Blue Burst, Crimson Burst, Shoreline Gold, or Teal Green Metallic finishes, disc. 1998.

	$925	$800	$700	$625	$550	$475	$400

Last MSR was $1,299.

AERODYNE JAZZ BASS (JAPAN MFG. NO. 025-4500) - lightweight design bound basswood body, maple neck, 20-fret rosewood fingerboard, matching color headstock, four-on-one-side tuners, standard 4-saddle bridge, two pickups (precision, jazz), 3 knobs (v, v, tone), black/chrome hardware, available in Black finish only, mfg. 2003-present.

MSR	$900	$630	$575	$525	$450	$400	$350	$300

Fender American Deluxe Jazz Bass FMT courtesy Fender

Jazz Bass: Highway 1 Series

HIGHWAY 1 JAZZ BASS (U.S. MFG. NO. 011-1400) - alder body, modified C-shaped maple neck, 20-fret rosewood fingerboard with dot inlay, 2 Standard Vintage Single Coil pickups, white pickguard, standard 4-on-one-side tuners, standard vintage bridge, 3 knobs (v, v, tone), available in 3-Color Sunburst, Daphne Blue Trans., Crimson Red Trans., or Honey Blonde Trans., mfg. 2003-present.

MSR	$957	$675	$600	$525	$450	$400	$350	$300

Jazz Bass: Misc. Models

JAZZ SPECIAL - precision style basswood body, Jazz Bass style neck, no pickguard, graphite nut, black hardware, P/J pickup configuration, mfg. late 1980s-early 1990s.

	N/A	$400	$325	$275	$225	$175	$125

Jazz "Power" Special - similar to Jazz Special, except has triple laminated maple/rosewood/graphite neck, active circuitry, mfg. late 1980s-early 1990s.

	N/A	$450	$375	$325	$275	$225	$175

JAZZ PLUS (U.S. MFG. NO. 019-8402) - alder body, 22-fret rosewood fingerboard with pearl dot inlay, fixed bridge, chrome hardware, 2 J-style Lace Sensor pickups, volume/pan control, concentric treble/bass control, active electronics, available in Arctic White, Black, Black Pearl Burst, Blue Pearl Burst, Brown Sunburst, Caribbean Mist, Lipstick Red, Midnight Blue, Midnight Wine, or Natural finishes, mfg. 1990-94.

		N/A	$650	$575	$500	$450	$400	$350

Last MSR was $1,120.

This model was available with a maple fingerboard (Model 19-8400). This model was optional with an ash body and maple fingerboard with black dot inlay (Model 19-8500).

Jazz Plus V (U.S. Mfg.) - similar to Jazz Plus, except has 5 strings, 5-on-one-side tuners, mfg. 1990-94.

	N/A	$700	$625	$550	$500	$450	$400

Last MSR was $1,190.

CONTEMPORARY JAZZ BASS (JAPAN MFG. NO. 027-9000) - ash body, 20-fret rosewood fingerboard with pearl dot inlay, carbon graphite nut, fixed bridge, chrome hardware, Fender/Gotoh tuners, P/J-style pickups, volume/tone/frequency sweep controls, mfg. 1987 only.

	N/A	$400	$350	$300	$250	$200	$150

This model was also available in a fretless configuration.

TRADITIONAL JAZZ BASS (MEX. MFG. NO. 013-3500) - poplar body, bolt-on maple neck, 20-fret rosewood fingerboard w/ white dot inlay, fixed bridge, chrome hardware, 3-ply white/metal pickguard, 2 J-style pickups, 2 volume/1 tone controls, available in Arctic White, Black, or Torino Red finishes, disc. 1998.

	$235	$205	$175	$150	$125	$100	$75

Last MSR was $339.

Jazz Bass: Standard Series

STANDARD JAZZ BASS (MEX. MFG. NO. 013-6200) - poplar body, bolt-on maple neck, 20-fret rosewood fingerboard with white dot inlay, fixed bridge, chrome hardware, 3-ply white/metal pickguard, 2 J-style pickups, 2 volume/1 tone controls, available in Arctic White, Black, Brown Sunburst, Crimson Red Metallic, Blue Agave, Sage Green Metallic, Midnight Wine, or Lake Placid Blue finishes, mfg. 1998-present.

MSR	$628	$440	$360	$300	$250	$220	$190	$160

In 1998, Midnight Blue and Midnight Wine finishes were introduced; Crimson Red Metallic and Lake Placid Blue finishes were discontinued. Before 2001 this model had an SKU of 013-6500. Blue Agave was introduced in 2001. Sage Green Metallic and Midnight Wine finishes were introduced in 2002.

Fender Aerodyne Jazz Bass courtesy Fender

GRADING		100% MINT	98% NEAR MINT	95% EXC+	90% EXC	80% VG+	70% VG	60% G

Standard Jazz Bass Left Hand (Mex. Mfg. No. 013-6520) - similar to Standard Jazz Bass, except has left-handed configuration, mfg. 1998-present.

MSR	$628	$440	$360	$300	$250	$220	$190	$160

Add $35 for Brown Sunburst finish.

Standard Jazz Bass Fretless (Mex. Mfg. No. 013-6508) - similar to Standard Jazz Bass, except has left-handed configuration, mfg. 1998-present.

MSR	$628	$440	$360	$300	$250	$220	$190	$160

Add $35 for Brown Sunburst finish.

This model was previously produced in Japan before 1998.

Standard Jazz Bass Left Hand (Japan Mfg. No. 027-6720) - similar to Standard Jazz Bass, except has basswood body, left-handed configuration, available in 3-Color Sunburst or Vintage White finishes, disc. 1998.

		N/A	$375	$325	$275	$235	$200	$170
						Last MSR was $769.		

Standard Jazz Bass V (U.S. Mfg. No. 013-6600) - similar to Standard Jazz Bass, except has 5-string configuration, 5-on-a-side tuners, 20-fret pau ferro fingerboard, mfg. 1998-present.

MSR	$685	$480	$400	$350	$300	$250	$210	$170

Add $35 for Brown Sunburst finish.

Jazz Bass: U.S. Vintage Reissue Series

´62 JAZZ BASS (U.S. MFG. NO. 019-0209) - alder body, bolt-on maple neck, 34 in. scale, 20-fret rosewood fingerboard with pearl dot inlay, fixed bridge, chrome hardware, white (or black or tortoiseshell)/metal pickguard with finger rest, 2 J-style American Vintage Jazz pickups, 2 volume/tone concentric (´stacked´) controls, available in 3-Color Sunburst, Black, or Olympic White finishes, mfg. 1982-present.

MSR	$2,000	$1,400	$1,200	$1,050	$900	$800	$700	$600

Add $35 for 3-Color Sunburst finish.

In 1996, Vintage White finish was discontinued. In 1999, Lake Placid Blue and Olympic White finishes were introduced. In 2001, Inca Silver, Dakota Red, and Ice Blue Metallic finishes were introduced. In 2002, Lake Placid Blue, Dakota Red, Inca Silver, and Ice Blue Metallic finishes were discontinued.

´75 JAZZ BASS (U.S. MFG. NO. 019-0302) - ash body, bound maple fingerboard, block position markers, black/white/black pickguard, "bullet" truss rod, 3-bolt "micro-tilt" neck, 2 vintage bi-pole pickups, 20 frets, 2 volume/1 tone control, Vintage-4 Saddle bridge, case included, available in 3-Color Sunburst, Black, or Natural finishes, mfg. 1982-present.

MSR	$2,042	$1,450	$1,250	$1,100	$950	$825	$700	$600

Also available with rosewood fingerboard and white/black/white pickguard (Model 019-3000). In 2002, all finishes except natural were discontinued.

Jazz Bass: Classic/Collectible Series

´60s JAZZ BASS - basswood body, white/metal pickguard with finger rest, 20-fret rosewood fingerboard with pearl dot inlay, fixed bridge, chrome hardware, 2 J-style pickups, 2 volume/1 tone controls, available in Black, Candy Apple Red, Olympic White, Sonic Blue or 3-Color Sunburst finishes, disc. 1995.

		N/A	$500	$425	$375	$325	$275	$225
						Last MSR was $700.		

´60s Jazz Natural - similar to Reissue 60s Jazz, except has Foto-Flame finish, mfg. 1994-95.

		N/A	$550	$475	$400	$350	$300	$250
						Last MSR was $800.		

´60s JAZZ BASS (MEX. MFG. NO. 013-1800) - alder body, rosewood fingerboard, vintage reverse tuning machines, 20 vintage frets, 2 vintage-style Bi-pole pickups, three black knobs (v, v, tone), Vintage 4-saddle bridge, available in 3-Color sunburst, Olympic White, or Black, mfg. 2001-present.

MSR	$957	$675	$600	$525	$450	$400	$350	$300

´75 JAZZ (JAPAN MFG. NO. 027-3500) - ash body, bolt-on maple neck, 20-fret rosewood fingerboard with white block inlay, bullet truss rod adjustment, fixed bridge with string mutes, ´F´ logo bridge cover, chrome hardware, white/metal pickguard with finger rest, 2 J-style Jazz Bass pickups, 2 volume/1 tone controls, available in 3-Color Sunburst or Natural finishes, disc. 1999.

		$575	$500	$425	$375	$325	$275	$225
						Last MSR was $799.		

This model also available with maple fingerboard (Model 027-3502).

Jazz Bass: Fender Custom Shop Production

´62 JAZZ BASS LEFT HAND (U.S. MFG. NO. 019-6120) - left-handed configuration, alder body, bolt-on maple neck, 34 in. scale, 20-fret rosewood fingerboard with pearl dot inlay, fixed bridge, chrome hardware, tortoiseshell/metal pickguard with finger rest, 2 J-style Vintage Jazz pickups, 2 volume/tone controls, available in Black or Olympic White finishes, disc. 1998.

		$2,100	$1,850	$1,650	$1,450	$1,250	$1,050	$850
						Last MSR was $2,899.		

GRADING	100% MINT	98% NEAR MINT	95% EXC+	90% EXC	80% VG+	70% VG	60% G

AMERICAN CLASSIC JAZZ BASS (U.S. MFG. NO. 019-7200) - bound down-sized swamp ash body, graphite reinforced bolt-on maple neck, 34 in. scale, 22-fret rosewood fingerboard with white shell block inlay, strings through bridge, chrome hardware, tortoiseshell/metal pickguard with finger rest, 2 J-style American Jazz pickups, volume/3-band EQ controls, active electronics, available in (Tri) 3-Color Sunburst or Natural finishes, disc. 1998.

	$1,825	$1,600	$1,400	$1,200	$1,050	$900	$750

Last MSR was $2,599.

This model was also available with optional flame maple top (American Classic Jazz Bass FMT).

Jazz Bass: Artist Signature

The Artist Signature Jazz Basses are produced in smaller production runs by Fender's Custom Shop. The following models have a Jazz Bass sleek offset double cutaway body, two single coil pickups, bolt-on neck, and four-on-a-side headstock (unless otherwise specified).

GEDDY LEE LIMITED EDITION (JAPAN MFG. NO. 025-7702) - alder body, maple neck, 20-fret black bound maple fingerboard with black block inlay, chrome hardware, BadAss II bridge, 3-ply white pickguard, Fender/Schaller tuners, 2 '62 U.S. Jazz Bass single coil pickups, bakelite knobs, metal controls plate, available in Black finish, mfg. 1998-present.

MSR	$1,000	$700	$600	$525	$450	$400	$350	$300

JACO PASTORIUS TRIBUTE (U.S. MFG. NO. 019-6200) - Alder body, special shaped maple neck, epoxy coated fretless rosewood fingerboard, replacement P-Bass control knobs, Vintage reversed tuners, 20 fret lines, 2 volume/1 tone control, Vintage-4 Saddle bridge, distressed finish, available in 3-Color Sunburst finish, disc 2002.

	$1,300	$1,150	$1,000	$900	$800	$700	$600

Last MSR was $1,850.

Jaco Pastorius Jazz Bass Fretless (U.S. Mfg., No. 019-6208) - similar to the Jaco Pastorius Jazz Bass excpet has a fretless pao ferro fingerboard with fret lines, current mfg.

MSR	$2,000	$1,400	$1,200	$1,050	$900	$800	$700	$600

MARCUS MILLER LIMITED EDITION (JAPAN MFG. NO. 025-7802) - ash body, maple neck, 20-fret white bound maple fingerboard with pearloid block inlay, chrome hardware, BadAss II bridge, oversized black pickguard, vintage-style tuners, chrome pickup cover, 2 Vintage Jazz Bass single coil pickups, 2 volume/treble/bass controls, 2-band active EQ with bypass switch, available in 3-Color Sunburst, Natural, or Olympic White finishes, mfg. 1998-present.

MSR	$1,200	$850	$725	$650	$575	$500	$425	$375

MARCUS MILLER V JAZZ BASS (U.S. MFG. NO. 019-7802) - similar to the Marcus Miller Jazz Bass except made in the U.S., has five strings with 4/1-per-side tuners, available in 3-Color Sunburst, Black, Aged Natural, Vintage White, or Shoreline Gold finish, mfg. 2003-present.

MSR	$2,400	$1,750	$1,550	$1,350	$1,150	$1,000	$850	$700

NOEL REDDING LIMITED EDITION (JAPAN MFG. NO. 025-8600) - alder body, maple neck, 20-fret rosewood fingerboard with dot inlay, chrome/nickel hardware, tortoiseshell pickguard, available in 3-Tone Sunburst finish, mfg. 1997 only.

	$700	$625	$550	$500	$450	$400	$350

Last MSR was $900.

THE VENTURES LIMITED (JAP. MFG. NO. 025-8300) - light ash body, white shell/metal pickguard with finger rest, 20-fret rosewood fingerboard with white block inlay, fixed bridge, gold hardware, 2 J-style Fender USA pickups, volume/tone controls, available in Midnight Black Transparent finish, mfg. 1996 only.

	$1,050	$925	$825	$725	$625	$550	$475

Last MSR was $1,439.

VICTOR BAILEY J-BASS (U.S. MFG. NO. 019-6800) - koa/rosewood/mahogany body, maple neck, rosewood fingerboard, deluxe lightweight tuning keys, 22 medium/jumbo frets, 2 noiseless pickups, four control knobs (v, blend, 3-band equalizer, switch), combo S-T-B top load bridge, available in Natural finish, mfg. 2001-present.

MSR	$2,100	$1,500	$1,300	$1,100	$950	$850	$750	$650

Jazz Bass: Artist Signature Custom Shop

JACO PASTORIUS RELIC JAZZ BASS (U.S. MFG. NO. 019-6108) - select alder body, special shaped maple neck, rosewood fingerboard, Vintage reversed tuners, 20 frets, 2 volume/1 tone control, Vintage-4 Saddle bridge, available in 3-Color Sunburst finish, current mfg.

MSR	$4,329	$3,100	$2,800	$2,500	$2,200	$1,900	$1,600	$1,300

REGGIE HAMILTON JAZZ BASS (U.S. MFG. NO. 015-8400) - alder body, quarter-sawn maple neck, rosewood fretboard, 21 vintage frets, '70s stamped open tuners, 4-ply black, white, or tortiseshell pickguard, 2 pickups (one American P-series, one Noiseless J), four black control knobs, chrome plate steel bridge with nickle plated saddles, available in 3-Color Sunburst and Black finishes, mfg. 2002-present.

MSR	$3,290	$2,350	$2,100	$1,900	$1,700	$1,500	$1,300	$1,100

Reggie Hamilton Jazz Bass V (U.S. Mfg. 015-8500) - similar to the Reggie Hamilton Jazz Bass except has five strings with 4/1-per-side tuners, and has a Custom revers American P Bass pickup instead of American, mfg. 2002-present.

MSR	$3,382	$2,450	$2,150	$1,950	$1,750	$1,550	$1,350	$1,150

GRADING	100% MINT	98% NEAR MINT	95% EXC+	90% EXC	80% VG+	70% VG	60% G

Jazz Bass: Time Machine Series (Custom Shop)

Built to exacting specifications of their respective vintages, including: body contours and radii, neck shape, fingerboard radius, pickups, electronics and hardware. Original materials, tooling, and production techniques are employed whenever possible. 3 finish packages are available-NOS (New Old Stock): as if the guitar was bought new in its respective year and brought forward in time to the present day, Closet Classic: as if the guitar was bought new in its respective year, played perhaps a dozen times each year and then put carefully away, has small dings, lightly checked finish, oxidized hardware, and aged plastic parts. Relic: shows natural wear and tear of years of heavy use - nicks, scratches, worn finish, rusty hardware and aged plastic parts.

´64 JAZZ BASS NOS (NEW OLD STOCK, NO. 015-1300) - alder body, maple neck with round-lam rosewood fingerboard, brown shell pickguard, original specification pickups, Vintage Reversed tuners, 20 frets, 2 volume/1 tone control, Vintage-4 Saddle bridge, available in 3-Color Sunburst or Olympic White finishes, mfg. 2001-present.

	MSR	$3,045		$2,200	$1,950	$1,700	$1,500	$1,300	$1,100	$900

´64 Jazz Bass Closet Classic (No. 015-1400) - similar to ´64 Jazz Bass NOS except with Closet Classic finish, available in 3-Color Sunburst and Olympic White finishes, mfg 2001-present.

	MSR	$3,355		$2,400	$2,100	$1,850	$1,600	$1,400	$1,200	$1,000

´64 Jazz Bass Relic (No. 015-1500) - similar to ´64 Jazz Bass NOS except with Relic finish, available in 3-Color Sunburst and Olympic White finishes, mfg 2001-present.

	MSR	$3,515		$2,500	$2,200	$1,900	$1,650	$1,450	$1,250	$1,050

Jazz Bass: Custom Classic Series (Custom Shop)

CUSTOM CLASSIC JAZZ BASS (U.S. MFG. NO. 015-7400) - alder or ash body, rosewood fingerboard, deluxe lightweight tuning machines, 21 medium-jumbo frets, 2 Custom Noiseless pickups, four black control knobs (v, blend, 3-band EQ, switching blend), string-thru-body bridge, available in Three-Color Sunburst, Olympic White, black, Aged Cherry Sunburst, Ebony Trans., Bing Cherry Trans., Cobalt Blue Trans., or Ice Blue Metallic, mfg. 2001-present.

	MSR	$2,693		$1,950	$1,700	$1,500	$1,300	$1,100	$950	$800

Add $100 for Aged Cherry Sunburst, Ebony Transparent, Bing Cherry Trans., and Cobalt Blue Trans. finishes.

This model is also available with a maple fingerboard (No. 015-7402).

Custom Classic Jazz Bass V (U.S. Mfg. No. 015-7500) - similar to the Custom Classic Jazz Bass except has five strings and a pao ferro fingerboard, mfg. 2001-present.

	MSR	$2,782		$2,000	$1,750	$1,550	$1,350	$1,150	$1,000	$850

Add $100 for Aged Cherry Sunburst, Ebony Trans., Bing Cherry Trans., and Cobalt Blue Trans. finishes.

This model is also available with a maple fingerboard (No. 015-7502).

Jazz Bass: Relic Custom Shop Series

Relic series instruments were cosmetically aged by the Fender Custom Shop. Instruments are stamped on the headstock and into the body (under the pickguard) with the Custom Shop logo to avoid future cases of "mistaken identity" in the Vintage Guitar market.

´60s "RELIC" JAZZ BASS (U.S. MFG. NO. 019-6300) - alder body, maple neck, 20-fret rosewood fingerboard with dot inlay, aged nickel hardware, 2 Vintage Jazz single coil pickups, tortoiseshell pickguard, available in 3-Tone Sunburst or Olympic White finishes, disc. 1998.

				$1,850	$1,650	$1,450	$1,300	$1,150	$900	$750

Last MSR was $2,599.

PRECISION BASS SERIES

All instruments in this series have an offset double cutaway body, bolt-on maple neck, 4-on-one-side tuners, unless otherwise listed.

Precision Bass: Early Models (1951-1984 Mfg.)

PRECISION BASS (MFG. 1951-54) - ash body, black pickguard, 20-fret maple fingerboard with black dot inlay, strings-through bridge, chrome bridge cover, chrome hardware, single coil exposed pickup with cover, volume/tone controls on metal plate, available in Blonde finish, mfg. 1951-54.

1951	N/A	$11,000	$9,500	$8,000	$7,000	$6,100	$5,500
1952	N/A	$10,000	$8,500	$7,200	$6,300	$5,600	$4,900
1953	N/A	$9,500	$8,000	$6,800	$5,800	$5,100	$4,500
1954	N/A	$9,000	$7,500	$6,300	$5,300	$4,600	$3,900

The Precision bass was the first production electric bass with a fretted fingerboard. Early Precision basses have a similar design to Fender´s Telecaster guitar (and similar slimmer headstocks). In 1957, the classic Precision design (wider headstock, split pickup, controls/pickup/1/4 in. socket all mounted on the pickguard) debuted.

PRECISION BASS (FENDER MFG. 1954-1964) - similar to original design Precision, except has white pickguard and contoured body (similar to the contour of a Fender Stratocaster), available in Blonde, Custom Colors, 2-Tone Sunburst, or 3-Tone Sunburst finishes, mfg. 1954-1964.

1954 CONTOUR	N/A	$8,000	$6,500	$5,600	$4,900	$4,300	$3,600
1955	N/A	$7,500	$6,200	$5,000	$4,100	$3,300	$2,700
1956	N/A	$7,000	$5,800	$4,700	$3,900	$3,400	$2,900
1957	N/A	$7,000	$5,800	$4,700	$3,900	$3,400	$2,700

GRADING	100% MINT	98% NEAR MINT	95% EXC+	90% EXC	80% VG+	70% VG	60% G
1958	N/A	$7,000	$5,800	$4,700	$3,900	$3,200	$2,600
1959	N/A	$7,000	$5,800	$4,700	$3,800	$3,100	$2,500
1960	N/A	$7,000	$5,800	$4,700	$3,700	$3,000	$2,400
1961	N/A	$7,000	$5,500	$4,500	$3,600	$2,900	$2,300
1962	N/A	$6,500	$5,300	$4,400	$3,500	$2,800	$2,200
1963	N/A	$6,000	$4,500	$3,700	$3,000	$2,600	$2,100
1964	N/A	$5,500	$4,200	$3,500	$2,900	$2,400	$2,000

Add 25% for Dakota Red, Fiesta Red, Candy Apple Red, Olympic White, Sonic Blue, Lake Placid Blue, or Gold Metallic finishes. Add 50% for Burgundy Mist, Surf Green, Fire Mist Silver, Sherwood Green, or Shell Pink finishes.

Black pickguard with Blonde finish was an option. During 1957, a redesigned aluminum pickguard, fixed bridge, strat style peghead and split pickup replaced the original parts/designs. In 1959, rosewood fingerboard with pearl dot inlay replaced maple.

PRECISION BASS (CBS MFG. 1965-1981) - similar to the 1957 Precision, available in Blonde, Custom Colors, 2-Tone Sunburst, or 3-Tone Sunburst finishes, mfg. 1965-1981.

	100%	98%	95%	90%	80%	70%	60%
1965	N/A	$4,500	$3,700	$3,200	$2,700	$2,300	$1,900
1966	N/A	$4,000	$3,200	$2,600	$2,300	$2,000	$1,700
1967	N/A	$3,700	$3,000	$2,500	$2,100	$1,800	$1,500
1968	N/A	$3,000	$2,500	$2,100	$1,800	$1,500	$1,300
1969	N/A	$2,750	$2,300	$2,000	$1,700	$1,400	$1,200
1970	N/A	$2,500	$2,100	$1,800	$1,500	$1,300	$1,100
1971	N/A	$2,200	$1,900	$1,600	$1,400	$1,200	$1,000
1972-1974	N/A	$2,000	$1,700	$1,500	$1,300	$1,100	$900
1975-1978	N/A	$1,750	$1,500	$1,300	$1,100	$900	$750
1979-1981	N/A	$1,400	$1,200	$1,050	$900	$750	$600

Add 25% for Dakota Red, Fiesta Red, Candy Apple Red, Olympic White, Sonic Blue, Lake Placid Blue, or Gold Metallic finishes. Add 50% for Burgundy Mist, Surf Green, Fire Mist Silver, Sherwood Green, or Shell Pink finishes.

In 1968, maple fingerboard was an option. In 1970, fretless fingerboard was an option. By 1976, thumb rest on pickguard was standard.

Fender Precision Bass courtesy Gary Schaeffer

Precision Bass: Elite Series (1983-85 Mfg.)

PRECISION ELITE I - ash body, white pickguard, 20-fret maple fingerboard with black dot inlay, fixed bridge with tuners, die-cast tuners, chrome hardware, P-style covered pickup, volume/tone control, active electronics, mfg. 1983-85.

	N/A	$700	$625	$550	$475	$400	$325

PRECISION ELITE II - similar to Precision Elite I, except has 2 P-style pickups, 2 volume/1 tone controls, 3-way mini switch, mfg. 1983-85.

	N/A	$800	$700	$625	$550	$475	$400

PRECISION GOLD ELITE I - similar to Precision Elite I, except has gold hardware, mfg. 1983-85.

	N/A	$725	$625	$550	$475	$400	$325

PRECISION GOLD ELITE II - similar to Precision Elite I, except has gold hardware, 2 P-style pickups, 2 volume/1 tone controls, 3-position mini switch, mfg. 1983-85.

	N/A	$825	$725	$625	$550	$475	$400

PRECISION WALNUT ELITE I - similar to Precision Elite I, except has walnut body/neck, black pickguard, ebony fingerboard with pearl dot inlay, strings through bridge, gold hardware, P-style exposed pickup, volume/treble/bass controls, series/parallel switch, available in Natural finish, mfg. 1983-85.

	N/A	$700	$625	$550	$475	$400	$325

PRECISION WALNUT ELITE II - similar to Precision Elite I, except has walnut body/neck, black pickguard, ebony fingerboard with pearl dot inlay, strings through bridge, gold hardware, 2 P-style exposed pickups, volume/treble/bass controls, series/parallel switch, available in Natural finish, mfg. 1983-85.

	N/A	$800	$700	$625	$550	$475	$400

Precision Bass: 1985-1995 Mfg.

PRECISION BASS (FMIC MFG. 1985-1995) - similar to the 1957 Precision, available in Blonde, Custom Colors, 2-Tone Sunburst, or 3-Tone Sunburst finishes, mfg. 1985-1995.

	$750	$675	$600	$525	$450	$400	$375

PRECISION CONTEMPORARY - similar to Precision, except has no pickguard and a rosewood fingerboard, mfg. 1987 only.

	N/A	$400	$350	$300	$250	$200	$150

Fender Precision Bass courtesy Willie's American Guitars

GRADING	100% MINT	98% NEAR MINT	95% EXC+	90% EXC	80% VG+	70% VG	60% G

Precision Bass: American Series (1996-Current Mfg.)

AMERICAN PRECISION BASS (U.S. MFG. NO. 019-3200/3260/019-2200) - alder body, graphite reinforced rosewood neck with vintage decal, 34 in. scale, 20-fret rosewood fingerboard with pearl dot inlay, strings-through-body bridge, chrome hardware, white pickguard, P-style American Vintage Precision pickup, volume/tone controls, currently available in 3-Color Sunburst, 2-Color Sunburst, Sunset Orange Trans., Chrome Red, Sky Blue, Natural, Black, or Aqua Marine Metallic finishes, mfg. 1996-present.

	MSR	$1,428		$1,000	$850	$750	$675	$600	$525	$450

Add $35 for 3-Color Sunburst finish. Add $100 for Natural (Ash) finish.

Also available with maple neck (Model 019-3202), formerly Model 019-2202). In 1999, 3-Color Sunburst, Aqua Marine Metallic, White Blonde, Natural, Purple Metallic, and Olympic White finishes were introduced. Brown Sunburst, Candy Apple Red, Sonic Blue, and Vintage White finishes were discontinued. In 2003, a new model was introduced (No. 019-3260) with the new S-1 pickup switching. In 2005, a left-handed model was introduced (No. 019-3290, in 3-Color Sunburst or Black finishes).

American Standard Precision Left-Hand (U.S. Mfg. No. 019-2220) - similar to the American Standard Precision, except in left-handed configuration, available in Black, Brown Sunburst, Candy Apple Red, or Vintage White finishes, mfg. 1996-99.

			$775	$700	$625	$550	$475	$400	$325

Last MSR was $1,079.

American Standard Precision Fretless (U.S. Mfg. No. 019-2208) - similar to the American Standard Precision, except with fretless neck, available in Black, Brown Sunburst, Candy Apple Red, or Vintage White, mfg. 1996-98.

		N/A	$700	$625	$550	$475	$400	$325

Last MSR was $1,029.

Precision Bass: Classic Series

´51 PRECISION BASS (JAPAN MFG. NO. 027-1902) - ash body, thick C-shape maple neck, 20-fret maple fingerboard with dot inlay, 4-on-one side vintage reverse tuners, single original single coil pickup, vintage 2-saddle bridge, two knobs (v, tone), chrome hardware, available in 2-Color Sunburst or Butterscotch Blonde, mfg. 2003-present.

	MSR	$900		$630	$550	$475	$425	$375	$325	$275

Precision Bass: American Deluxe & Deluxe Series

AMERICAN DELUXE PRECISION BASS (U.S. MFG. NO. 019-5200) - premium ash or alder body, maple neck with 22 American Standard frets, graphite reinforced neck, rosewood fingerboard, 34 in. scale, American Deluxe tuners, 1 Vintage Spec Split Single-Coil pickup, 1 New Special Design Humbucker pickup, master volume, pan pot, 3-band active EQ with treble boost/cut, mid-boost/cut, bass-boost/cut, aged white or brown shell pickguard, deluxe top-load or string-through-body bridge, available in 3-Color Sunburst, Aged Cherry Burst, Candy Tangerine, Chrome Red, White Blonde, Black, Natural, Crimson Trans., Teal Green Trans., or Purple Trans. finishes, disc. 2004.

		$1,225	$1,050	$975	$850	$750	$650	$525

Last MSR was $1,750.

Add $100 for Natural, White Blonde, and Purple Trans. finishes.

Also available with maple fingerboard (Model 019-5202). Purple Trans. was discontinued in 2001. In, 2002 Natural, White Blonde, and Crimson Trans. finishes were discontinued.

American Deluxe Precision Bass V (U.S. Mfg., No. 019-5300) - similar to American Deluxe Precision Bass, except in a 5-string configuration, pao ferro fingerboard, mfg. 1999-2004.

		$1,275	$1,100	$975	$875	$750	$650	$475

Last MSR was $1,800.

Add $100 for Natural, White Blonde, and Purple Trans. finishes.

Also available with maple fingerboard (Model 019-5302).

AMERICAN DELUXE PRECISION BASS (NO. 019-4060) - select alder body, maple C-shaped neck with graphite reinforcements, 22-fret rosewood fingerboard with dot inlay, brown shell, gold vinyl, silver shell, or M/B/M pickguard, 1 split P-Style pickup and 1 Humbucker J-Style pickup, four knobs, Topload or S-T-B bridge, chrome hardware, available in 3-Color Sunburst, Amber, Montego Black, or Chrome Silver finishes, mfg. 2004-present.

	MSR	$1,685		$1,200	$1,050	$900	$800	$700	$600	$500

Also available with maple fingerboard (No. 019-4062). This model replaced the earlier American Deluxe Precision Bass.

American Deluxe Precision Bass V (No. 019-4260) - similar to the American Deluxe Precision Bass, except in 5-string configuration, 4/1-per-side tuners, pao-ferro fingerboard, available in 3-Color Sunburst, Amber, or Montego Black finishes, mfg. 2004-present.

	MSR	$1,785		$1,275	$1,125	$975	$850	$750	$650	$550

Also available with maple fingerboard (No. 019-4262).

American Deluxe Precision Bass Ash (No. 019-4160) - similar to the American Deluxe Precision Bass, except has a premium ash body, available in Tobacco Sunburst, Aged Cherry Sunburst, or Butterscotch Blonde finishes, mfg. 2004-present.

	MSR	$1,828		$1,300	$1,150	$1,000	$875	$775	$675	$575

Also available with maple fingerboard (No. 019-4162).

American Deluxe Precision Bass Ash V (No. 019-4360) - similar to the American Deluxe Precision Bass Ash, except in 5-string configuration, 4/1-per-side tuners, pau-ferro fingerboard, mfg. 2004-present.

	MSR	$1,942		$1,375	$1,175	$1,025	$900	$800	$700	$600

Also available with maple fingerboard (No. 019-4362).

GRADING	100% MINT	98% NEAR MINT	95% EXC+	90% EXC	80% VG+	70% VG	60% G

DELUXE P-BASS SPECIAL (MEX. MFG. NO. 013-5700)
alder P-Bass body, maple Jazz Bass neck with standard truss rod, rosewood fingerboard, 20 medium-jumbo frets, 34 in. scale, chrome hardware, standard tuners, US Vintage P-Bass bridge, gold anodized pickguard, 1 Vintage Special P-Bass pickup, 1 Vintage Special Jazz Bass pickup 2 volume controls, master tone control, side-mounted jack, US electronic components, available in Arctic White, Black, Blizzard Pearl, Brown Sunburst, Candy Apple Red, Chrome Red, or Navy Blue Metallic finishes, disc. 2003, reintroduced 2005.

	MSR	$800		$575	$500	$425	$350	$300	$250	$200

Add $35 for Brown Sunburst finish.

Also available with maple fingerboard (Model 013-5702/5762). This model was reintroduced in 2005 with minor revisions and finishes include: Black, Blizzard Pearl, Chrome Red, and Navy Blue Metallic.

PRECISION BASS DELUXE (U.S. MFG. NO. 019-4200)
down-sized alder body, ash veneer top/back, graphite reinforced tinted maple neck, 34 in. scale, 22-fret rosewood fingerboard with pearl dot inlay, fixed bridge, chrome hardware, white (or brown) shell pickguard, P-style American Vintage Precision/humbucker pickups, volume/3-band EQ controls, available in Antique Burst, Black, Blue Burst, Crimson Burst, Shoreline Gold, or Teal Green Metallic finishes, disc. 1998.

			$875	$775	$675	$575	$500	$425	$350

Last MSR was $1,249.

This model is also available with a maple fingerboard with black dot inlay (Model 019-4202).

Precision Bass: Highway 1 Series

HIGHWAY 1 PRECISION BASS (U.S. MFG. NO. 011-1300)
alder body, modified C-shaped maple neck, 20-fret rosewood fingerboard with dot inlay, four-on-a-side tuners, single standard Vintage Split Coil pickup, white pickguard, Vintage bridge, chrome hardware, two knobs (v, tone), available in 3-Color Sunburst, Daphne Blue Trans., Crimson Red Trans., or Honey Blonde Trans., mfg. 2003-present.

	MSR	$957		$675	$600	$525	$450	$400	$350	$300

Precision Bass: Variations (Misc. Models)

HOT ROD P-BASS (U.S. MFG NO. 019-4800/019-1900)
alder or ash body, maple neck, 20 American Standard frets, rosewood fingerboard, graphite-reinforced neck, 34 in. scale, American Standard tuners, 1 New "Hot-Vintage P-Bass pickup, 1 New "Hot -Vintage" Jazz Bass pickup, 2 volume controls, master tone, brown shell pickguard, deluxe top-load or S-T-B, available in 3-Color Sunburst, Olympic White, Black, Natural, or Sunset Orange finishes, mfg. 1999-2001.

		$1,025	$900	$800	$700	$600	$500	$400

Last MSR was $1,430.

Add $100 for LH configuration (Model 019-4820, retail $1,550, formerly Model 019-1920). Add $80 for 3-Color Sunburst finish. Add $100 for Natural and Sunset Orange Transparent finishes.

Also available with maple fingerboard (Model 019-4802, formerly model 019-1902).

50th ANNIVERSARY AMERICAN SERIES P-BASS (U.S. MFG. NO. 019-2001)
ash body, maple neck and fingerboard, cast/open back tuning machines, 20 medium/jumbo frets, single split-coil pickup, two control knobs (v, tone), string-thru body bridge, available in Butterscotch Blonde finish, mfg. 2001 only.

		$1,075	$925	$825	$750	$675	$600	$525

Last MSR was $1,500.

This is a limited edition model for the 50th Anniversary of the Fender Bass.

PRECISION ACOUSTIC/ELECTRIC (JAPAN MFG. NO. 027-9608)
hollowed basswood body, bound solid spruce top, f-hole, fretless rosewood fingerboard, strings through acoustic style rosewood bridge, chrome hardware, P-style Silver Fender-Lace Sensor/piezo bridge pickups, volume/tone/pan controls, active electronics, available in Antique Burst or Natural finishes, disc. 1995.

		N/A	$800	$700	$625	$550	$475	$400

Last MSR was $1,230.

This model is also available with 20-fret fingerboard.

PRECISION BASS SPECIAL (MEX. MFG. NO. 013-5400)
poplar body, ash veneer top, maple neck, 20-fret rosewood fingerboard with white dot inlay, fixed bridge, chrome hardware, black pickguard, P/J-Style covered pickups, volume/pan/tone controls, available in Black, Brown Sunburst, Crimson Burst, or Vintage Blonde finishes, disc. 1998.

		$400	$350	$300	$260	$220	$180	$140

Last MSR was $569.

PRECISION BASS LYTE STANDARD (JAPAN MFG. NO. 025-9500)
down-sized basswood body, bolt-on maple neck, 22-fret rosewood fingerboard with pearl dot inlay, fixed bridge, chrome hardware, P/J-style covered pickups, volume/treble/bass/pan controls, active electronics, available in Antique Burst, Fiesta Red, Frost White, or Montego Black finishes, disc. 2001.

		$550	$475	$400	$350	$300	$250	$200

Last MSR was $756.

Earlier models may have Lace Sensor pickups, and Blue Foto Flame, Crimson Foto Flame, or Frost Red finishes. In 1999, Frost Red was introduced and Fiesta Red was discontinued.

Fender American Deluxe Precision Bass courtesy Fender

Fender Highway 1 Precision Bass courtesy Fender

GRADING	100% MINT	98% NEAR MINT	95% EXC+	90% EXC	80% VG+	70% VG	60% G

Precision Bass Lyte Deluxe (Japan Mfg. No. 025-9800) - similar to the Precision Bass Lyte Standard, except has down-sized mahogany body, gold hardware, P-Style/humbucking covered pickups, volume/pan/treble/mid/bass controls, available in Natural finish, disc 2001.

	$650	$575	$500	$425	$350	$300	$250

Last MSR was $899.

CALIFORNIA P-BASS SPECIAL (U.S. MFG. NO 019-1802) - alder Precision body, bolt-on satin-finished Jazz-style maple neck, 20-fret maple fingerboard with dot inlay, vintage-style bridge, creme pickguard, chrome hardware, Vintage spec P/J-Bass pickups, 2 volume/1 tone controls, available in Black, Brown Sunburst, Candy Apple Red, or Vintage White finishes, disc. 1998.

	$600	$425	$375	$325	$275	$225	$175

Last MSR was $849.

This model is available with a rosewood fingerboard (Model 019-1800)

PRECISION BASS PLUS (U.S. MFG. NO. 019-7502) - alder body, 22-fret rosewood fingerboard with pearl dot inlay, fixed bridge with tuners, chrome hardware, P/J-style Silver Lace Sensor pickups, volume/tone control, 3-position switch, series/parallel push button, TBX active electronics, available in Arctic White, Black, Black Pearl Burst, Blue Pearl Burst, Brown Sunburst, Caribbean Mist, Lipstick Red, Midnight Blue, Midnight Wine, or Natural finishes, mfg. 1990-94.

	N/A	$850	$750	$650	$550	$450	$350

Last MSR was $1,000.

Add $100 for ash body with Natural finish.

This model was also available with maple fingerboard with black dot inlay (Model 19-7500).

Precision Plus Deluxe (U.S. Mfg.) - similar to Precision Plus, except has down-sized body style, volume/treble/bass/pan controls, redesigned active electronics, mfg. 1990-94.

	N/A	$950	$850	$750	$650	$550	$450

Last MSR was $1,200.

PRECISION SPECIAL (U.S. MFG.) - alder body, white pickguard, 20-fret maple fingerboard with black dot inlay, fixed bridge, gold-plated brass hardware, P-style exposed pickup, volume/treble/bass controls, on/off mini switch, active electronics, available in Candy Apple Red, Lake Placid Blue, or White finishes with matching headstock finish, mfg. 1980-83.

	N/A	$800	$700	$600	$500	$400	$300

The Precision Special functioned in two modes: Active and Passive. In both modes, the volume control remains the same; in Passive mode the second control is the master tone control; in Active mode the second and third controls become the bass/treble controls.

Precision Special Walnut (U.S. Mfg.) - similar to Precision Special, except has walnut body/neck, available in Natural finish, mfg. 1982-83.

	N/A	$1,000	$850	$700	$600	$500	$400

TRADITIONAL PRECISION BASS (MEX. MFG. NO. 013-3400) - poplar body, bolt-on maple neck, 20-fret rosewood fingerboard with white dot inlay, fixed bridge, chrome hardware, 3-ply white pickguard, P-style pickup, volume/tone control, available in Arctic White, Black, and Torino Red finishes, disc. 1998.

	$240	$210	$175	$150	$125	$100	$75

Last MSR was $339.

Precision Bass: Standard Series

STANDARD PRECISION BASS (MEX. MFG. NO. 013-6100) - poplar body, bolt-on maple neck, 20-fret rosewood fingerboard with white dot inlay, fixed bridge, chrome hardware, 3-ply white pickguard, P-style pickup, volume/tone control, available in Arctic White, Black, Brown Sunburst, Sage Green Metallic, Blue Agave, or Midnight Wine finishes, mfg. 1987-present.

MSR	$571		$400	$335	$280	$240	$210	$180	$150

Add $35 for Brown Sunburst finish.

In 1998, Midnight Blue and Midnight Wine finishes were introduced; Crimson Red Metallic, and Lake Placid Blue finishes were discontinued. Blue Agave was introduced in 2001. This model was fomerly No. 013-6000, before 2001.

STANDARD PRECISION BASS JR. (MEX. MFG. NO. 013-4000) - similar to the Standard Precision Bass, except in a smaller 28.59 in. scale, available in Torino Red or Black finishes, mfg. 2004-present.

MSR	$571		$400	$335	$280	$240	$210	$180	$150

Precision Bass: Time Machine Series (Custom Shop)

Built to exacting specifications of their respective vintage including body contours and radii, neck shape, fingerboard radius, pickups, electronics and hardware. Original materials, tooling and production techniques are employed whenever possible. Three distinct finish packages are avalable: NOS (New Old Stock) as if the instrument was bought new in its respective year and brought forward in time to the present day; Closet Classic, as if the instrument was bought new in its respective year, played perhaps a dozen times each year and then put carefull away - small dings, lightly checked finish, oxidized hardware and aged plastic parts; Relic, shows natural wear and tear of years of heavy use - nicks, scratches, worn finish, rusty hardware and aged plastic parts.

Add $100 for White Blonde finish. Add $100 for Vintage Blonde finish.

'55 PRECISION BASS NOS (NEW OLD STOCK, U.S. MFG. NO. 015-2402) - lightweight ash body, C-shaped maple neck, 20-fret rosewood fingerboard with dot position markers, early white pickguard, Vintage Reversed tuners, 20 frets, Vintage split-coil pickups, 1 volume/1tone control, Vintage bridge, available in 2-Color Sunburst, Black, or White Blonde finishes, mfg. 2003-present.

MSR	$3,146		$2,300	$2,000	$1,750	$1,500	$1,250	$1,050	$900

'55 Precision Bass Closet Classic (No. 015-2502) - similar to '59 Precision Bass NOS except with Closet Classic finish, available in 2-Color Sunburst, Black, or Vintage Blonde finishes, mfg. 2003-present.

MSR	$3,456		$2,500	$2,200	$1,900	$1,650	$1,400	$1,200	$1,000

GRADING		100% MINT	98% NEAR MINT	95% EXC+	90% EXC	80% VG+	70% VG	60% G

'55 Precision Bass Relic (No. 015-2602) - similar to '59 Precision Bass NOS except with Relic finish, available in 2-Color Sunburst, Black, or Vintage Blonde finishes, mfg. 2003-present.

	MSR	$3,616		$2,600	$2,300	$2,000	$1,750	$1,500	$1,250	$1,050

'59 PRECISION BASS NOS (NEW OLD STOCK, U.S. MFG. NO. 015-2100) - alder or ash body, rosewood fingerboard with dot position markers, Vintage Reversed tuners, 20-frets, Vintage split-coil pickups, 1 volume/1 tone control, Vintage-4 Saddle bridge, available in 3-Color Sunburst or White Blonde finishes, mfg. 2001-present.

	MSR	$2,998		$2,150	$1,900	$1,650	$1,450	$1,250	$1,050	$850

'59 Precision Bass Closet Classic (No. 015-2200) - similar to '59 Precision Bass NOS except with Closet Classic finish, available in 3-Color Sunburst or Vintage Blonde finishes, mfg. 2001-present.

	MSR	$3,308		$2,400	$2,100	$1,800	$1,650	$1,400	$1,150	$950

'59 Precision Bass Relic (No. 015-2300) - similar to '59 Precision Bass NOS except with Relic finish, available in 3-Color Sunburst and Vintage Blonde finishes, mfg. 2001-present.

	MSR	$3,468		$2,500	$2,220	$1,900	$1,650	$1,450	$1,200	$1,000

Precision Bass: U.S. Vintage Reissue Series

'57 PRECISION (U.S. MFG. NO. 019-0115) - ash body, bolt-on maple neck, 20-fret maple fingerboard with black dot inlay, fixed bridge, gold hardware, gold anodized pickguard with thumb rest, P-style pickup, volume/tone control, currently available in 2-Color Sunburst, White Blonde, or Black finishes, mfg. 1982-present.

	MSR	$1,828		$1,300	$1,100	$950	$800	$700	$600	$500

Add $35 for 2-Color Sunburst. Add $100 for White Blonde finish.

In 1989, alder body and chrome hardware replaced original parts/designs. In 1994, Blond and Vintage White finishes were discontinued. In 1999, Candy Apple Red and White Blonde finishes were introduced. In 2001, Inca Silver, Dakota Red and Ice Blue Metallic finishes were introduced.

'62 PRECISION (U.S. MFG. NO. 019-0116) - alder body, bolt-on maple neck, 20-fret rosewood fingerboard with pearl dot inlay, fixed bridge, chrome hardware, tortoiseshell pickguard with thumb rest, P-style pickup, volume/tone control, currently available in 3-Tone Sunburst, Black, and Olympic White finishes, mfg. 1982-present.

	MSR	$1,900		$1,350	$1,150	$1,000	$850	$725	$625	$525

Add $35 for 3-Color Sunburst finish.

Fender Standard Precision Bass courtesy Fender

In 1994, Blonde and Vintage White finishes were discontinued. In 1999, Fiesta Red and Olympic White finishes were introduced. In 2000, Inca Silver, Dakota Red and Ice Blue Metallic finishes were introduced.

'62 Precision Left-Hand (U.S. Mfg.) - similar to (U.S. Vintage) '62 Precision, except in a left-handed configuration, available in Black or Olympic white finishes, disc. 1994.

		N/A		$1,150	$1,000	$850	$725	$600	$500

Last MSR was $2,200.

Precision Bass: Fender Japan Limited Edition Series

This model was a limited edition that was produced by Fender Japan, and was available by custom order.

'75 PRECISION (JAPAN MFG.) - ash body, bolt-on maple neck, 20-fret maple fingerboard with black dot inlay, strings-through bridge, chrome hardware, P-style pickup, volume/tone controls on metal plate, available in Natural finish, disc. 1995.

		N/A		$550	$475	$400	$325	$275	$225

Last MSR was $720.

This model also available with rosewood fingerboard with pearl dot inlay.

Precision Bass: Collectible Series

'51 P-BASS REISSUE (JAPAN MFG NO. 027-1902) - offset double cutaway ash body, bolt-on maple neck, 20-fret maple fingerboard with black dot inlay, vintage 2-saddle bridge, chrome hardware, black pickguard, single coil exposed pole piece pickup, volume/tone controls on metal plate, available in 2-Tone Sunburst or Blonde finishes, disc. 1998.

		N/A		$550	$475	$400	$350	$300	$250

Last MSR was $739.

Custom Shop '51 Precision (U.S. Mfg.) - similar to the '51 P-Bass Reissue, these models were part of a Custom Shop Limited run.

		N/A		$1,500	$1,300	$1,100	$950	$800	$650

'50s PRECISION - basswood body, white pickguard, 20-fret maple fingerboard with black dot inlay, fixed bridge, chrome hardware, P-style exposed pickup, volume/tone control, available in Black, Candy Apple Red, Olympic White, Sonic Blue, or 3-Tone Sunburst finishes, mfg. 1994-95.

		N/A		$475	$400	$350	$300	$250	$200

Last MSR was $690.

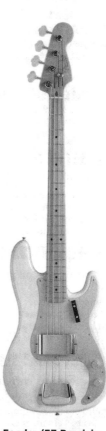

Fender '57 Precision Bass (U.S. Series) courtesy Fender

GRADING	100% MINT	98% NEAR MINT	95% EXC+	90% EXC	80% VG+	70% VG	60% G

´60s PRECISION - similar to Precision Reissue ´50s, except has tortoiseshell pickguard, rosewood fingerboard with pearl dot inlay, mfg. 1994-95.

	N/A	$475	$400	$350	$300	$250	$200

Last MSR was $690.

This model also available with white pickguard.

´60s *Precision Natural* - similar to Precision Reissue ´50s, except has tortoiseshell pickguard, rosewood fingerboard with pearl dot inlay, available in Foto-Flame finish, mfg. 1994-95.

	N/A	$575	$500	$450	$400	$350	$300

Last MSR was $800.

Precision Bass: Custom Shop Production

´57 PRECISION BASS LEFT HAND (U.S. MFG. NO. 019-5722) - left-handed configurtion, alder body, bolt-on maple neck, 20-fret maple fingerboard with black dot inlay, fixed bridge, chrome hardware, gold anodized pickguard with thumb rest, P-style pickup, volume/tone control, available in Black and Olympic white finishes, disc. 1998.

	$1,750	$1,550	$1,400	$1,250	$1,100	$950	$800

Last MSR was $2,499.

VINTAGE PRECISION BASS CUSTOM (U.S. MFG. NO. 019-5602) - swamp ash body, bolt-on figured maple neck, 20-fret maple fingerboard with black dot inlay, fixed bridge, nickel hardware, black pickguard, P/J-style Vintage pickups, volume/tone controls mounted on metal plate, available in 2-Tone Sunburst or Honey Blonde finishes, mfg. 1993-2000.

	$1,625	$1,450	$1,250	$1,100	$950	$800	$650

Last MSR was $2,299.

Precision Bass: Limited Editions & Signature Series

DONALD "DUCK" DUNN (JAPAN MFG. NO. 025-7602) - alder body, bolt-on ´50s-shaped maple neck, 20-fret maple fingerboard with black dot inlay, Donald "Duck" Dunn signature on headstock, vintage 4-post bridge, vintage-style tuners, chrome-plated nickel hardware, gold anodized pickguard, Vintage P-Bass pickup, volume/tone controls, available in Candy Apple Red finish, mfg. 1998 only.

	$575	$500	$450	$400	$350	$300	$250

Last MSR was $799.

MIKE DIRNT (MEX. MFG. NO. 013-4800) - ash body, maple thick C-shaped neck, 20-fret rosewood fingerboard with dot inlay, 1 Custom Vintage ´59 Split single coil P-bass pickup, white or Parchment pickguard style like the early 1950s P-Bass, two knobs mounted on metal plate, Bad Ass II bridge, chrome hardware, available in 2-Color Sunburst, Vintage White, or Black finishes, mfg. 2004-present.

MSR	$900		$630	$550	$475	$425	$375	$325	$275

Add $35 for 2-Color Sunburst finish.

Mike Dirnt is the bass player for the band Green Day.

STEVE HARRIS PRECISION BASS (JAPAN MFG. NO. 025-2602) - basswood body, maple neck and fingerboard, vintage-style tuning machines, 20 medium/jumbo frets, Seymour Duncan Basslines Quarter Pound pickup, black pickguard, two black knobs (v, tone), Bad Ass II bridge, available in Lake Placid Blue finish, mfg. 2001 only.

	$575	$500	$450	$400	$350	$300	$250

Last MSR was $800.

STING PRECISION BASS (JAPAN MFG. NO. 025-1902) - ash body, maple neck and fingerboard, vintage-style tuning machines, 20 frets, one vintage single coil pickup, white pickguard on upper-half, Sting signature in 12th fret pearl inlay, two silver control knobs (v, tone), vintage 2-saddle, S-T-B, available in 2-Color Sunburst, mfg. 2001-present.

MSR	$900		$630	$550	$475	$425	$375	$275	$275

FENIX

Instruments previously built in Korea circa 1989 to 1992, and 1996 to late 1990s.

The Fenix trademark was used by instrument manufacturer Young Chang (Korea). Fenix guitars were built at the same time that the factory was producing Squier models for Fender. As a result, models with the Fenix brand name tend to be derived from Fender-based designs. Fenix guitars and basses were popular for a four-year run in England due to their decent quality at a relatively low price. In 1996, U.K. distributors Barnes & Mullins reintroduced the product line, for a short while.

FENTON-WEILL

Instruments previously built in England from 1959 through the mid-1960s.

Henry Weill´s company after collaboration with Jim Burns (Burns-weill trademark) produced a decent range of distinctive solid body designs. While earlier models may seem similar to Burns-Weill models, they were soon restyled and other models of "similar character" were added. Fenton-Weill also produced fiberglass bodied guitars under the trademark of FIBRATONE. As author Tony Bacon has noted, "although UK-made guitars have often offered better value and quality, they apparently lack the mystique of leading USA instruments." Most English-built guitars were destined for English consumption. Few have shown up in the United States (source: Tony Bacon, *The Ultimate Guitar Book*).

FERNANDES

Instruments currently produced in Tokyo, Japan since 1969. Distributed in the U.S. by Fernandes Guitars U.S.A. Inc., of North Hollywood, CA.

In 1969, Fernandes Company Ltd. (based in Tokyo, Japan) was established to produce quality classical guitars at an affordable price. Over the next twenty years, Fernandes expanded the line and became one of the largest selling guitar manufacturers in the world. Fernandes is the number one selling guitar in Japan, and at times has held as much as 40% of the Japanese market.

GRADING	100% MINT	98% NEAR MINT	95% EXC+	90% EXC	80% VG+	70% VG	60% G

In late 1992, Fernandes Company Ltd. began distributing their entire line of guitars to the U.S. market as Fernandes Guitars U.S.A., Inc. Fernandes Company Ltd. uses only the top facilities located in Japan, Taiwan, China, and Korea to produce their guitars. Once the factory is done manufacturing the guitars, they are shipped to the United States where they are inspected and set up again.

In 1998, Fernandes renamed their instruments. For example, the eye-catching H-80 art-deco-style guitar model became the Vertigo Deluxe. In addition to their RetroRocket and Retrospect series, Fernandes is concentrating on the newer additions to their line like the P-Project, Native, Dragonfly, and Lexington series. Fernandes also offers amplifiers for guitars and basses. For more information on Fernandes amps see the *Blue Book of Guitar Amplifiers*. Company history courtesy Bryan Wresinski, Fernandes Guitars U.S.A.

Fernandes guitars now represent one of the most diverse groups of guitars in the market today. Since its inception, the Fernandes company has consistently raised the bar for the entire industry to follow. No product typifies this more than the Fernandes Sustainer System. The Sustainer is a specially designed neck pickup and circuit that allows the guitar to sustain chords or single notes indefinitely, giving the player complete control of sustain and feedback without the excessive volume from an amplifier. The Sustainer operates in three modes: Standard (sustains fundamental pitch or pitches), Harmonic (creates various 3rd and 5th harmonics of the note being sustained), and Mix (a combination of the first two modes).

ELECTRIC: AFR SERIES

AFR-35 - offset double cutaway alder body, bolt-on maple neck, 25.5 in. scale, 24-fret rosewood fingerboard with dot inlay, standard tremolo, 6-on-a-side tuners, black hardware, black pickguard, 2 single coil/humbucker pickups, volume/tone controls, 5-way switch, available in Black, Metallic Blue, or Metallic Red finishes, disc. 1998.

	$375	$325	$275	$235	$195	$165	$130

Last MSR was $499.

Add $200 for Sustainer Standard pickup system. Add $225 for Sustainer Custom pickup system.

AFR-45 - offset double cutaway basswood body, bolt-on maple neck, 24-fret rosewood fingerboard with dot inlay, standard tremolo, 6-on-a-side tuners, chrome hardware, 2 single coil/humbucker pickups, volume/tone control, 5-way switch, available in Black, Metallic Red, or Metallic Blue finishes, disc. 1996.

	$300	$250	$225	$200	$175	$150	$125

Last MSR was $459.

AFR-55 - similar to the AFR-45, except features gold hardware, available in Black Burst, Blue Burst, and Red Burst finishes, disc. 1996.

	$325	$250	$225	$200	$175	$150	$125

Last MSR was $499.

AFR-55GF - similar to the AFR-35, except features a basswood body, gold hardware, no pickguard, available in Black Burst, Blue Burst, or Red Burst finishes, disc. 1998.

	$525	$475	$425	$375	$325	$275	$225

Last MSR was $739.

Add $200 for Sustainer Standard pickup system. Add $225 for Sustainer Custom pickup system.

Fender Sting
Precision Bass
courtesy Fender

AFR-65 - similar to the AFR-55, except features black hardware, Fernandes double locking tremolo, available in Black, Turquoise Metallic, or Wine Red Metallic finishes, disc. 1996.

	$400	$350	$300	$250	$215	$180	$145

Last MSR was $599.

AFR-65X - similar to the AFR-55, except features humbucker/single coil/humbucker pickups, 3-way switch, available in Gun Metal Blue, Metallic Black, or Metallic Red finishes, disc. 1996.

	$400	$350	$300	$260	$220	$180	$140

Last MSR was $599.

AFR-70S - similar to the AFR-45, except features 22-fret fingerboard, black hardware, Fernandes Sustainer/single coil/humbucker pickups, volume/tone/sustainer volume controls, available in Black or Cobalt Blue finishes, disc. 1996.

	$450	$375	$325	$275	$235	$195	$165

Last MSR was $699.

AFR-75A - similar to the AFR-35, except features a basswood body, gold hardware, no pickguard, available in Black Burst, Blue Burst, or Red Burst finishes, disc. 1998.

	$575	$500	$450	$400	$350	$300	$250

Last MSR was $869.

Add $200 for Sustainer Standard pickup system.

AFR-80 - offset double cutaway maple (or ash) body, bolt-on maple neck, 24-fret rosewood fingerboard with pearl dot inlay, double locking vibrato, 6-on-a-side tuners, black hardware, 2 stacked coil/humbucker pickups, volume/tone controls, 5-way switch, available in Candy Apple Red, Metallic Blue, Pearl Black, or Pearl White finishes, mfg. 1991-92.

	N/A	$500	$425	$350	$300	$250	$200

Last MSR was $750.

AFR-80S - similar to the AFR-70S, except features ash body, maple fingerboard, chrome hardware, Fernandes Sustainer/2 single coil pickups, available in Natural finish, disc. 1996.

	$500	$450	$375	$325	$275	$230	$195

Last MSR was $799.

Fender Mike Dirnt
courtesy Fender

GRADING	100% MINT	98% NEAR MINT	95% EXC+	90% EXC	80% VG+	70% VG	60% G

AFR-85 - similar to AFR-80, except has humbucker/stacked coil/humbucker pickups, disc. 1992.

| | N/A | $550 | $475 | $400 | $350 | $300 | $250 |

Last MSR was $800.

AFR-90S - similar to the AFR-70S, except features gold hardware, double locking tremolo system, available in Black, Summer Green Metallic, or Wine Red Metallic finishes, disc. 1996.

| | $575 | $500 | $425 | $375 | $325 | $275 | $225 |

Last MSR was $899.

AFR-120S - similar to the AFR-75A, except features Monkey Pod body, gold hardware, 22-fret fingerboard, Fernandes Sustainer Custom/single coil/humbucker pickups, volume/tone/sustainer volume controls, 5-way switch, available in Natural finish, disc. 1998.

| | $1,000 | $850 | $750 | $650 | $550 | $450 | $350 |

Last MSR was $1,799.

AFR-150S - similar to the AFR-90S, except features mahogany body, flame maple top, ebony fingerboard, Fernandes Sustainer/single coil/humbucker, available in Natural finish, disc. 1996.

| | $1,100 | $950 | $800 | $700 | $600 | $500 | $400 |

Last MSR was $1,899.

ELECTRIC: AMG SERIES

AMG-60 - double cutaway basswood body, set-in maple neck, 24-fret maple fingerboard with black dot inlay, standard vibrato, 3-per-side tuners, gold hardware, 2 humbucker pickups, volume/tone control, 3-position switch, available in Fire Red, Navy Blue, Screaming Yellow, or Snow White finishes, mfg. 1991-92.

| | N/A | $450 | $375 | $325 | $275 | $225 | $175 |

Last MSR was $730.

AMG-70 - similar to AMG-60, except has ash body, rosewood fingerboard with white dot inlay, black hardware, 2 stacked coil/humbucker pickups, available in Trans. Black, Trans. Green, Trans. Purple, and Trans. Red finishes, disc. 1993.

| | N/A | $500 | $425 | $350 | $300 | $250 | $200 |

Last MSR was $750.

This model was available with gold hardware (Model AMG-70G).

ELECTRIC: DECADE SERIES

The Decade Series was introduced in 1997.

DECADE-S1 - 7/8 size sleek offset double cutaway basswood body, bolt-on maple neck, 25.5 in. scale, 21-fret rosewood fingerboard with dot inlay, standard tremolo, 6-on-a-side tuners, chrome hardware, white pickguard, 3 single coil pickups, volume/tone controls, 5-way switch, available in Black, Pewter or Vintage Metallic Blue finishes, mfg. 1997-98.

| | $300 | $260 | $230 | $200 | $175 | $150 | $125 |

Last MSR was $429.

DECADE STANDARD (DECADE-A1) - sleek slightly offset double cutaway alder body, bolt-on maple neck, 25.5 in. scale, 21-fret rosewood fingerboard with dot inlay, vintage tremolo, 6-on-a-side tuners, chrome hardware, white pearloid pickguard, 3 single coil pickups, volume/tone controls, 5-way switch, available in Black, Cream White, or Sea Foam Green finishes, disc. 1999.

| | $350 | $300 | $270 | $235 | $200 | $165 | $130 |

Last MSR was $479.

DECADE CUSTOM (DECADE-A2) - similar to the Decade Standard, except features a fixed bridge, 2 chrome covered humbucker pickups, 3-way switch, available in Black, Cream White, or Sea Foam Green finishes, mfg. 1997-99.

| | $400 | $350 | $300 | $250 | $220 | $190 | $160 |

Last MSR was $549.

Add $200 for Sustainer Standard pickup system (available 1997 only).

In 1998, Silver and Vintage Metallic Blue finishes were introduced; Cream White and Sea Foam Green finishes were discontinued.

DECADE DELUXE (DECADE-J1) - similar to the Decade Standard, except Gotoh tuners, 1 volume/2 tone controls, available in Black or 3-Tone Sunburst finishes, mfg. 1997-99.

| | $575 | $500 | $425 | $375 | $325 | $275 | $225 |

Last MSR was $849.

In 1998, Sea Foam Green finish replaced Black finish.

DECADE PRO - sleek slightly offset double cutaway alder body, bolt-on maple neck, 25.5 in. scale, 21-fret rosewood fingerboard with dot inlay, vintage-style tremolo, 6-on-a-side tuners, pearloid pickguard, chrome hardware, Sustainer Transducer/exposed coil humbucker pickups, volume/tone magnetic controls, Sustainer volume control, 3-way pickup selector switch, Sustainer on/off/Sustainer mode selector mini-switches, available in Vintage Metallic Blue finish, mfg. 1998-99.

| | $575 | $500 | $425 | $375 | $325 | $275 | $225 |

Last MSR was $849.

DECADE ELITE - similar to Decade Pro, except features mahogany body, maple top, 22-fret fingerboard, black Gotoh hardware, black or pearloid pickguard, available in Black Satin, 3-Tone Sunburst, or Rust finishes, mfg. 1998-2000.

| | $900 | $800 | $700 | $600 | $500 | $400 | $300 |

Last MSR was $1,299.

In 1999, Black Satin and Rust finishes were discontinued.

GRADING	100% MINT	98% NEAR MINT	95% EXC+	90% EXC	80% VG+	70% VG	60% G

ELECTRIC: DEUCE SERIES (WS SERIES)

The Deuce Series was introduced in 1997. Early (WS) models were optional with the Sustainer Standard pickup system.

Add $200 for Sustainer Standard pickup system (available 1997 only).

DEUCE STANDARD (WS-500) - dual cutaway alder body, bolt-on maple neck, 24.75 in. scale, 22-fret rosewood fingerboard with dot inlay, stop tailpiece, 3-per-side tuners, chrome hardware, pearloid pickguard, 2 chrome covered humbucker pickups, volume/tone controls, 3-way switch, available in Black or Cream White finishes, mfg. 1997-99.

		$350	$300	$260	$225	$195	$160	$130

Last MSR was $479.

DEUCE DELUXE (WS-1000) - similar to the Deuce Standard, except features mahogany body/neck, Tune-O-Matic bridge/stop tailpiece, Gotoh tuners, available in Mahogany Brown or Wine Red finishes, mfg. 1997-99.

		$675	$600	$525	$450	$375	$325	$275

Last MSR was $999.

ELECTRIC: DRAGONFLY SERIES (APG SERIES)

Early versions of the APG-50, APG-95GF, and APG-145 were optional with the Sustainer Standard pickup system.

Add $200 for Sustainer Standard pickup system.

DRAGONFLY STANDARD (APG-50) - slightly double cutaway alder body, bolt-on maple neck, 25.5 in. scale, 22-fret rosewood fingerboard with dot inlay, stop tailpiece, 3-per-side tuners, chrome hardware, 2 chrome covered humbucker pickups, volume/tone controls, 3-way switch, available in Black, Dark Red, or Gold finishes, disc. 2000.

		$325	$290	$260	$230	$190	$160	$130

Last MSR was $449.

DRAGONFLY CUSTOM (APG-95GF) - similar to APG-50, except has a basswood body, carved maple Gravure top, 24.75 in. scale, tune-o-matic bridge/stop tailpiece, Gotoh tuners, available in Black Burst, Cherry Sunburst or Tobacco Sunburst finishes, disc. 1999.

		$700	$600	$525	$450	$375	$300	$225

Last MSR was $999.

DRAGONFLY DELUXE (APG-145) - similar to APG-50, except has mahogany body, carved maple top, set-in maple neck, 24.75 in. scale, bound body, bound headstock, tune-o-matic bridge/stop tailpiece, Gotoh tuners, coil tap capability, available in Black, Gold, Lemon Drop, See-Thru Amber, See-Thru Black, or See-Thru Green finishes, disc. 1999, reintroduced 2005-present.

MSR	$1,100	$900	$800	$700	$625	$550	$475	$400

In 1998, Honey Burst finish replaced Lemon Drop finish. When this model was reintroduced it featured See-Thru Amber, See-Thru Black, and See-Thru Green finishes.

DRAGONFLY PRO - slightly double cutaway basswood body, bolt-on maple neck, 25.5 in. scale, 24-fret rosewood fingerboard with dot inlay, vintage-style tremolo, 3-per-side tuners, gold Gotoh hardware, Sustainer Transducer/single coil/humbucker pickups, volume/tone magnetic controls, Sustainer volume control, 5-way pickup selector switch, Sustainer on/off/Sustainer mode selector mini-switches, available in Lava Burst or Ocean Burst finishes, mfg. 1998-present.

MSR	$650	$525	$450	$400	$350	$300	$250	$200

In 1999, Ocean Burst finish was discontinued. In 2000, Metallic Black and Gun Metal Blue finishes were introduced.

DRAGONFLY ELITE - similar to Dragonfly Pro, except features mahogany body, licensed Floyd Rose locking tremolo, available in Black Metallic Satin, Dark Green Metallic Satin, Lava Burst, Gun Metal Blue, or Silver finishes, mfg. 1998-2003, 2005-present.

MSR	$1,300	$1,050	$900	$800	$700	$600	$500	$400

In 1999, Gun Metal Blue and Siver finishes were discontinued. In 2000, Black Metallic Satin, Dark Green Metallic Satin and Lava Burst finishes were introduced. In 2002, Lava Burst was disc.

DRAGONFLY X - similar to Dragonfly Pro, except has alder body, 2 high output single coil pickups and 1 high output single coil pickup in the bridge position, black tuners, black hardtail bridge, available in Black Burst, Blue Burst, or Red Burst finishes, mfg. 2000-present.

MSR	$360	$290	$250	$210	$180	$150	$120	$90

In 2001, Metallic Black, Ocean Burst and Lava Burst finishes were introduced. Black Burst and Blue Burst finishes were discontinued.

APG-65S - double cutaway basswood body, bolt-on maple neck, 24-fret rosewood fingerboard with dot inlay, standard tremolo, 3-per-side tuners, black hardware, Fernandes Sustainer/humbucker pickups, volume/tone/sustainer volume controls, 3-way switch, available in Black or Cobalt Blue finishes, disc. 1996.

		$450	$375	$325	$275	$225	$175	$125

Last MSR was $699.

APG-80 - double cutaway bound mahogany body, maple top, set-in maple neck, 24-fret rosewood fingerboard with pearl dot inlay, double locking vibrato, bound peghead, 3-per-side tuners, gold hardware, stacked coil/hum-

GRADING	100% MINT	98% NEAR MINT	95% EXC+	90% EXC	80% VG+	70% VG	60% G

bucker pickups, volume/tone control, 3-position switch, available in Lemon Drop, Trans. Blue, Trans. Purple, or Trans. Red finishes, mfg. 1991-92.

| | N/A | $600 | $525 | $450 | $400 | $350 | $300 |

Last MSR was $900.

APG-85S - similar to APG-65S, except has mahogany body, gold hardware, double locking tremolo, Fernandes Sustainer/single coil/humbucker pickups, available in Black, Deep Metallic Red, or Wine Red Metallic finishes, disc. 1996.

| | $600 | $525 | $450 | $400 | $350 | $300 | $250 |

Last MSR was $899.

APG-90FS - similar to APG-80, except has arched maple top, tune-o-matic bridge/stop tailpiece, 2 humbucker pickups, mini switch, active electronics, available in Lemon Drop, Trans. Black, and Trans. Red finishes, disc. 1993.

| | N/A | $700 | $625 | $550 | $475 | $425 | $375 |

Last MSR was $1,200.

APG-100 - similar to APG-80, except has arched maple top, tune-o-matic bridge/stop tailpiece and 2 humbucker pickups, available in Cherry Sunburst, Lemon Drop, Trans. Black, and Trans. Red finishes, mfg. 1991-96.

| | N/A | $700 | $625 | $550 | $475 | $400 | $325 |

Last MSR was $1,200.

ELECTRIC: FSG SERIES

FSG-60 - offset double cutaway basswood body, bolt-on maple neck, 22-fret rosewood fingerboard with pearl dot inlay, standard vibrato, 6-on-a-side tuners, black hardware, 2 single coil/humbucker pickups, 2 volume/tone control, 3-way switch, 2 mini switches, active electronics, available in Black, Cobalt Blue, or Cream White finishes, mfg. 1993-94.

| | N/A | $500 | $425 | $350 | $300 | $250 | $200 |

Last MSR was $800.

FSG-80 - similar to FSG-60, except has ash body, available in Tobacco Sunburst, Trans. Black, Trans. Purple, or Trans. Red finishes, disc. 1994.

| | N/A | $550 | $475 | $400 | $350 | $300 | $250 |

Last MSR was $900.

FSG-100 - similar to FSG-60, except has ash body, double locking vibrato, gold hardware, available in Trans. Black, Trans. Purple, Trans. Red, or Tobacco Sunburst finishes, disc. 1994.

| | N/A | $600 | $525 | $450 | $400 | $350 | $300 |

Last MSR was $1,100.

ELECTRIC: LE SERIES

LE-1X - classic offset double cutaway alder body, bolt-on maple neck, 25.5 in. scale, 21-fret rosewood fingerboard with dot inlay, standard tremolo, 6-on-a-side tuners, chrome hardware, white pickguard, 3 single coil pickups, volume/2 tone controls, 5-way switch, available in Black, Cream White, Red, 2-Tone Sunburst, and 3-Tone Sunburst finishes, disc. 1998.

| | $215 | $180 | $155 | $135 | $115 | $95 | $75 |

Last MSR was $299.

LE-1 - similar to the LE-1X, except features a basswood body, rosewood or maple fingerboard, available in Black, Cream White, Pewter, Red, Sea Foam Green, Vintage Metallic Blue, or 3-Tone Sunburst finishes, mfg. 1993-98.

| | $350 | $300 | $250 | $220 | $180 | $150 | $120 |

Last MSR was $499.

LE-1G - similar to the LE-1, except features gold hardware, available in Gold finish, disc. 1998.

| | $375 | $325 | $275 | $235 | $200 | $160 | $130 |

Last MSR was $549.

LE-2 - similar to the LE-1, except features 7.25 in. vintage radius on neck, antique finish on neck, available in Black, Cream White, Candy Apple Red, Sonic Blue, Pewter, Sea Foam Green, Vintage Metallic Blue, 2-Tone Sunburst, or 3-Tone Sunburst finishes, mfg. 1991-98.

| | $500 | $425 | $375 | $325 | $275 | $225 | $175 |

Last MSR was $699.

LE-2FS - similar to LE-2, except has active electronics, disc. 1993.

| | N/A | $500 | $425 | $350 | $275 | $225 | $175 |

Last MSR was $710.

LE-2G - similar to LE-2, except has gold hardware, available in Candy Apple Red, Cream White, Gold, Vintage Metallic Blue, or 3-Tone Sunburst finishes, disc. 1998.

| | $525 | $450 | $400 | $350 | $300 | $250 | $200 |

Last MSR was $749.

LE-2L - similar to LE-2, except in left-handed configuration, available in Black, Candy Apple Red, Cream White, Sonic Blue, Vintage Metallic Blue, 2-Tone Sunburst, or 3-Tone Sunburst finishes, disc. 1998.

| | $575 | $500 | $450 | $400 | $350 | $300 | $250 |

Last MSR was $849.

LE-2N - similar to LE-2, except has an ash body, fixed bridge, tortoiseshell pickguard, available in Black, Candy Apple Red, Cream White, Sonic Blue, Vintage Metallic Blue, 2-Tone Sunburst, or 3-Tone Sunburst finishes, disc. 1998.

| | $575 | $500 | $450 | $400 | $350 | $300 | $250 |

Last MSR was $849.

GRADING	100% MINT	98% NEAR MINT	95% EXC+	90% EXC	80% VG+	70% VG	60% G

LE-2X - similar to LE-2, except has double locking vibrato, 2 single coil/humbucker pickups, available in Black, Candy Apple Red, Cream, Sonic Blue, or 3-Tone Sunburst finishes, disc. 1993.

	N/A	$350	$300	$250	$220	$180	$140

Last MSR was $600.

This model has optional reverse peghead and gold hardware.

LE-3 - offset double cutaway basswood body, white pickguard, bolt-on maple neck, 21-fret maple fingerboard with black dot inlay, standard vibrato, roller nut, 6-on-one-side tuners, chrome hardware, 3 single coil pickups, volume/2 tone controls, 5-position switch, available in Black, Cream White, or Red finishes, disc. 1993.

	N/A	$450	$375	$325	$275	$225	$175

Last MSR was $700.

LE-3FS - similar to LE-3, except has active electronics, disc. 1993.

	N/A	$550	$475	$400	$325	$250	$200

Last MSR was $1,000.

ELECTRIC: LEXINGTON SERIES

LEXINGTON STANDARD (BSA-100) - slightly offset double cutaway hollow body, arched maple top, maple back/sides, single layer body binding, set-in mahogany neck, 24.75 in. scale, 22-fret ebony fingerboard with dot inlay, bound neck/headstock, tune-o-matic bridge/stop tailpiece, 3-per-side Gotoh tuners, chrome hardware, 2 covered humbucker pickups, 2 volume/2 tone controls, 3-way switch, available in Black or Wine Red finishes, disc. 1999.

$1,350	$1,200	$1,050	$900	$750	$600	$500

Last MSR was $1,899.

LEXINGTON DELUXE (BSA-135) - similar to the BSA-100, except features gold hardware, gold covered humbuckers, multi-layered body binding, bound neck/headstock/soundholes, triangle trapezoid fingerboard inlays, available in Black finish, disc. 1999.

$1,500	$1,350	$1,200	$1,050	$900	$750	$600

Last MSR was $2,199.

ELECTRIC: MONTEREY SERIES (LS SERIES)

Earlier LS Series models were optional with a Sustainer Standard pickup system. Add $200 if it is an option.

LS-50 - single cutaway basswood body, bolt-on maple neck, 25.5 in. scale, 22-fret rosewood fingerboard with dot inlay, stop tailpiece, 3-per-side tuners, chrome hardware, 2 humbucker pickups, volume/tone controls, 3-way switch, available in Black, Dark Red, or Pewter finishes, disc. 1998.

$300	$260	$230	$210	$190	$170	$150

Last MSR was $429.

MONTEREY STANDARD (LS-75) - single cutaway alder body, bolt-on maple neck, 24.75 in. scale, 22-fret rosewood fingerboard with dot inlay, stop tailpiece, 3-per-side tuners, black pickguard, chrome hardware, 2 chrome covered humbucker pickups, 2 volume/2 tone controls, 3-way switch, available in Black, Tobacco Sunburst, or TV Yellow finishes, disc. 1999.

$325	$275	$240	$215	$190	$160	$130

Last MSR was $449.

In 1998, Dark Red and Silver finishes were introduced. Earlier LS-75 models may have a 25.5 in. scale.

MONTEREY PRO - similar to Monterey Standard, except has Sustainer Driver/Humbucker pickup in the neck position and a high ouput humbucker pickup in the bridge position, volume/tone controls, Suatainer Mode Selector, Sustainer on/off, Sustainer Intensity, available in Metallic Black, Wine Red, or Tobacco Sunburst finishes, new specs for 2000, current mfg.

MSR	$600		$500	$425	$375	$325	$275	$225	$175

Add $50 for left-hand configuration, available in Metallic Black, Pewter, and Wine Red finishes.

MONTEREY X - similar to Monterey Pro, except has 2 high output humbucking pickups, volume/tone controls, 3-way selector switch, available in Black, Dark Green, or Tobacco Sunburst finishes, disc. 2004, still available as part of the X pack.

$250	$220	$190	$160	$130	$100	$70

Last MSR was $300.

In 2000, Dark Green and Tobacco Sunburst finishes were discontinued. In 2001, Lava Flame and Tobacco Flames finishes were introduced.

MONTEREY CUSTOM (LS-80) - similar to the LS-75, except features mahogany body, set-in mahogany neck, 2 chrome covered mini humbuckers, pearloid pickguard, Gotoh tuners, available in Wine Red finish, disc. 1999.

$900	$800	$700	$600	$525	$450	$375

Last MSR was $1,299.

MONTEREY DELUXE (LS-135) - single cutaway mahogany core body, carved quilted maple top and back, set-in mahogany neck, multi-layered body binding, 24.75 in. scale, 22-fret bound ebony fingerboard with triangle trapezoid inlay, bound headstock, stop tailpiece, 3-per-side Gotoh tuners, gold hardware, 2 covered humbucker pickups, 2 volume/2 tone controls, 3-way switch, available in Cherry Sunburst finish, disc. 1999.

$1,250	$1,100	$950	$800	$700	$600	$500

Last MSR was $1,849.

GRADING	100% MINT	98% NEAR MINT	95% EXC+	90% EXC	80% VG+	70% VG	60% G

Monterey Deluxe (Current Mfg.) - similar to the old style Monterey Deluxe except has a maple/mahogany body, Seymour Duncan pick-ups, available Metallic Black Satin or Honey Burst finish, mfg. 2002-present.

MSR	$1,000	$825	$725	$625	$550	$475	$400	$325

MONTEREY ELITE - similar to the Monterey Deluxe except has a carved maple top, Fernandes sustainer, and has three knobs, available in Metallic Black Satin, Wine Red, or Honey Burst finishes, current mfg.

MSR	$1,200	$975	$825	$725	$625	$525	$450	$375

MONTEREY MAGNACOUSTIC (LSA-50 ELECTRIC/ACOUSTIC) - single cutaway alder body, bolt-on maple neck, 24.75 in. scale, 22-fret rosewood fingerboard with dot inlay, Indian rosewood bridge, 3-per-side tuners, chrome hardware, double-bladed humbucker pickup, Shadow bridge piezo pickup, 2 volume/treble/bass controls, 3-way switch, active preamp, available in Black or Dark Red finishes, disc. 1999.

		$675	$600	$525	$450	$375	$300	$225

Last MSR was $899.

Monterey Elecoustic (LSA-65 Electric/Acoustic) - similar to the LSA-50, except features basswood body, flame maple gravure top, single layer binding, triangle trapezoid inlays, 3-per-side gold Gotoh tuners with tortoise buttons, wood knobs, bridge mounted Shadow piezo pickup, volume/treble/bass controls, Fishman preamp, available in Black, See-Through Blue, See-Through Red, Tobacco Sunburst, and Vintage Natural finishes, disc. mfg.

		$850	$750	$650	$550	$450	$375	$300

Last MSR was $1,199.

MONTEREY X-PACK - includes a Monterey X guitar, 10-Watt Fernandes Guitar Amplifier, gig bag, cable strap, tuner, picks, and a CD-ROM for lessons, guitar available in Black, Blue or Red finish, current mfg.

MSR	$350	$280	$240	$210	$180	$150	$120	$90

ELECTRIC: NATIVE SERIES

The Native model was designed in 1996 at the Fernandes Custom Shop in North Hollywood, California. Early models from 1996-1997 were optional with the Sustainer Standard pickup system.

Add $240 for Sustainer Standard pickup system (1996-1997).

NATIVE STANDARD (NATIVE-A1) - rounded shoulder single cutaway alder body, bolt-on maple neck, 25.5 in. scale, 22-fret rosewood fingerboard with dot inlay, vintage-style tremolo, 3-per-side tuners, pearloid pickguard, chrome hardware, 2 chrome covered humbucker pickups, 2 volume/1 tone controls, 3-way switch, available in Black, Cream White, or Sea Foam Green finishes, disc. 1999.

		$375	$325	$275	$235	$195	$155	$120

Last MSR was $499.

NATIVE CUSTOM (NATIVE-A2) - similar to Native Standard, except features 2 black Fernandes FP-90 single coil pickups, available in Black, Cream White, or Sea Foam Green finishes, disc. 1999.

		$425	$375	$325	$275	$235	$195	$160

Last MSR was $599.

NATIVE PRO - rounded shoulder single cutaway alder body, bolt-on maple neck, 22-fret rosewood fingerboard with dot inlay, vintage-style tremolo, 3-per-side tuners, pearloid pickguard, chrome hardware, Sustainer Transducer/exposed coil humbucker pickups, volume/tone magnetic controls, Sustainer volume control, 3-way pickup selector switch, Sustainer on/off/sustainer mode selector mini-switches, available in Sea Foam Green finish, 25.5 in. scale, mfg. 1998-2003, 2005-present.

MSR	$650	$525	$450	$375	$325	$275	$225	$175

In 1999, Sea Foam Green finish was discontinued. In 2000, Metallic Black and Dark Green Metallic finishes were introduced.

NATIVE ELITE - similar to Native Pro, except features basswood body, flame maple gravure top, Gotoh hardware, licensed Floyd Rose locking tremolo, available in Black Burst finish, mfg. 1998-2003.

		$700	$625	$550	$475	$425	$375	$325

Last MSR was $999.

In 2000, Lava Burst and Ocean Burst finishes were introduced. In 2001, Lava Burst and Ocean Burst finishes were discontinued and See-Through Red and See-Through Blue finishes were introduced.

NATIVE X - similar to Native Pro, except has 2 high output humbucker pickups, black pickguard, available in Metallic Black, Blue Sparkle, Red Sparkle, Silver Sparkle, white pickguard optional, disc. 2003, reintroduced 2005-present.

MSR	$360	$290	$240	$210	$180	$150	$120	$90

Last MSR was $349.

ELECTRIC: NOMAD SERIES

The Nomad has a body shape that is described as a "standing elephant." These guitars are meant to be portable as they have smaller bodies and onboard amplifiers and a speaker. The amp is run by a battery.

NOMAD STANDARD (ZO-3 TRAVEL GUITAR) - hardwood body, bolt-on maple neck, 22-fret rosewood fingerboard with dot inlay, fixed bridge, 6-on-a-side tuners, chrome hardware, humbucker pickup, built-in 3.5 in. speaker, volume control, LED light, on/off switch, available in Black, Cream White, Gold, Red, Silver, or Vintage Metallic Blue finishes, 24 in. scale, current mfg.

MSR	$400	$325	$275	$230	$195	$160	$125	$95

The built-in 5 watt amplifier is powered by a 9-volt battery. Early versions of this model may have Blue, Green, Pewter, Pink, or Yellow finishes. In 1999, Cream White, Gold, Silver and Vintage Metallic Blue finishes were discontinued. In 2000, Blue and Sunburst finishes were introduced. In 2001, Vintage Metallic Blue finish was reintroduced and 3-Tone Sunburst finish was introduced. In 2002, all finishes except for Black were discontinued. In 2004, Red finish was reintroduced.

NOMAD CUSTOM - similar to the Nomad Standard, available in UK Flag or USA Flag graphic finishes, disc. 1999.

		$260	$230	$210	$185	$150	$125	$95

Last MSR was $369.

GRADING		100% MINT	98% NEAR MINT	95% EXC+	90% EXC	80% VG+	70% VG	60% G

NOMAD DELUXE - similar to Nomad Standard, except has effects processor controls, available in Metallic Black, Candy Apple Red, Silver, Hot Rod Flame, USA Flag and UK flag, current mfg.

MSR	$650	$525	$450	$375	$325	$275	$225	$175

NOMAD STAR WARS - Nomad style guitar with Star Wars graphics of Darth Vadar, Stormtrooper, or Boba Fett, disc. 2003.

		$225	$200	$180	$160	$140	$120	$100

Last MSR was $320.

These guitars feature Star Wars characters on the body for graphics; sorry, no Jar-Jar Binks model.

ELECTRIC: P-PROJECT SERIES

P-PROJECT - single cutaway hollowed body, spruce top, mahogany back, bolt-on mahogany neck, 25.5 in. scale, 22-fret ebony fingerboard, wenge bridge, 6-on-a-side gold Gotoh tuners with tortoise buttons, Fishman bridge piezo pickup, volume control (mounted on bridge), bass/treble tone controls (mounted inside back panel), Fishman preamp, available in Natural finish, mfg. 1997 (special order), 1998-99.

	$2,100	$1,750	$1,500	$1,300	$1,100	$900	$700

Last MSR was $2,999.

ELECTRIC: RAVELLE SERIES

RAVELLE DELUXE - single cutaway maple/mahogany body, mahogany set neck, 22-fret rosewood fingerboard with split block inlays, two Seymour Duncan humbucker pickups, pickguard, two knobs (v, tone) push/pull pickup split, Tune-O-Matic style bridge, chrome hardware, available in Wine Red, Black, Ivory, or Honey Burst finishes, mfg. 2002-present.

MSR	$1,000	$825	$725	$625	$550	$475	$400	$325

RAVELLE ELITE - single cutaway carved maple top, mahogany body, mahogany set neck, 22-fret rosewood fingerboard with split block inlays, two Seymour Duncan humbucker pickups, pickguard, two knobs (v, tone) push/pull pickup split, Tune-O-Matic style bridge, chrome hardware, available in Wine Red Flame, Black, Ivory, or Honey Burst finishes, mfg. 2004-present.

MSR	$1,200	$975	$825	$725	$625	$525	$450	$375

RAVELLE ELITE DAVE KUSHNER SIGNATURE - single cutaway carved maple top, mahogany body, mahogany set neck, 22-fret rosewood fingerboard with split trapezoid inlays, two Seymour Duncan humbucker pickups, pickguard, two knobs (v, tone) push/pull pickup split, Tune-O-Matic style bridge, chrome hardware, available in Forest Green Metallic finish, new 2005.

MSR	$1,400	$1,125	$975	$850	$750	$650	$550	$475

RAVELLE AMERICAN CUSTOM - single cutaway mahogany body with carved maple top, mahogany set neck, 22-fret rosewood fingerboard with split trapezoid inlays, body binding, 2 Seymour Duncan humbucker pickups, 3-per-side tuners, 3-way switch, two knobs (v, tone), Tune-O-Matic style bridge, chrome hardware, available in Vintage Burst finish, mfg. 2003 only.

	$2,500	$2,200	$1,950	$1,750	$1,550	$1,350	$1,150

Last MSR was $3,499.

ELECTRIC: RAVEN SERIES

RAVEN ELITE - offset double cutaway maple/mahogany body, bolt-on maple neck, 24.75 in. scale, rosewood fingerboard with dot position markers, 24 large frets, Sustainer Driver/Single Coil pickup in the neck position and high output humbucker in the bridge position, volume/tone controls, Sustainer on/off, Sustainer Intensity and Sustainer Mode Selector switches, black Gotoh tuners, black Wilkinson tremolo bridge, available in Metallic Black Satin, Dark Green Metallic, or Black Burst finish, disc. 2003.

			$750	$675	$600	$525	$450	$375	$300

Last MSR was $1,060.

RAVEN STANDARD - similar to Raven Elite, except has alder body, 2 high output humbucking pickups, volume. 3-way selector switch, available in Metallic Black or Metallic Blue finishes, mfg. 2000 only.

		$350	$300	$250	$210	$170	$140	$110

Last MSR was $499.

RAVEN X - similar to the Raven except has alder body, bolt-on maple neck, standard pickups, and Tune-O-Matic style bridge, available in Metallic Black or Gun Metal Blue finishes, disc. 2003.

		$220	$195	$175	$150	$125	$100	$75

Last MSR was $339.

ELECTRIC: REEVES GABRELS SERIES

RG-13 REEVES GABRLES SIGNATURE - single sharp cutaway mahogany body with carved top, set mahogany neck, 22 narrow/tall fret rosewood fingerboard with split trapezoid and 12th fret signature inlays, 2 Dimarzio Megadrive pickups, 3-per-side tuners, Tune-O-Matic bridge, 3-way switch, 3 knobs, chrome hardware, available in Gold Top finish, disc. 2003.

	$1,500	$1,350	$1,100	$975	$900	$825	$750

Last MSR was $2,000.

GRADING	100% MINT	98% NEAR MINT	95% EXC+	90% EXC	80% VG+	70% VG	60% G

ELECTRIC: RETROROCKET SERIES

RETROROCKET ELITE - offset double cutaway basswood body, bolt-on maple neck, 25.5 in. scale, 22-fret rosewood fingerboard with dot inlay, Wilkinson tremolo, 6-on-a-side satin chrome Gotoh tuners, mint green pickguard, Sustainer Transducer/2 double blade stacked humbucker pickups (looks like three single coil pickups from a distance), volume/tone magnetic controls, Sustainer volume control, 5-way pickup selector switch, Sustainer on/off/Sustainer mode selector mini-switches, available in 3-Tone Sunburst or Vintage Metallic Blue finishes, mfg. 1998-present.

MSR	$1,400	$1,125	$975	$850	$750	$650	$550	$475

In 2000, 2-Tone Sunburst/maple finish was introduced. In 2001, 3-Tone Sunburst, Vintage Metallic Blue and 2-Tone Sunburst/maple finishes were discontinued and See-Through Red, See-Through Blue and Tobacco Sunburst finishes were introduced.

RETROROCKET PRO - similar to Retrorocket Elite, except has alder body, 1 Sustainer Driver/Single Coil pickup, 1 high output single coil pickup and 1 high output humbucker pickup in the bridge position, chrome tuners, chrome vintage tremolo, available in Black, Candy Apple Red, Vintage Metallic Blue or 3-Tone Sunburst finishes, current mfg.

MSR	$550	$450	$375	$325	$275	$235	$190	$160

Add $30 for left-handed configuration.

RETROROCKET X - similar to Retrorocket Pro, except has 2 high output single coil pickups and 1 high output humbucking pickup in the bridge position, volume/tone controls, 5-way switch, available in Black, Dark Red, Dark Green, Sonic Blue, or 3-Tone Sunburst finishes, current mfg.

MSR	$260	$210	$180	$150	$130	$110	$90	$70

Add $30 for left-handed configuration.

In 2000, Sonic Blue finish was discontinued. In 2001, Lava Flame and Blue Flame finishes were introduced. In 2002, Tobacco Flame and new specs were introduced.

RETROROCKET X ONE - similar to Retrorocket X, except has 3 single coil high output pickups, available in Black, Cream White, Dark Red, or 3-Tone Sunburst finishes, mfg. 2000-present.

MSR	$250	$200	$175	$150	$130	$110	$90	$70

RETROROCKET STAR WARS - Retrorocket style alder body with Star Wars graphics of Darth Vadar or Stormtrooper, two single coil pickups/one humbucker, Star Wars case included, disc. 2003.

		$925	$850	$750	$650	$575	$500	$425

Last MSR was $1,300.

ELECTRIC: REVOLVER SERIES

REVOLVER PRO - offset double cutaway basswood body, bolt-on maple neck, 25.5 in. scale, 22-fret rosewood fingerboard with dot inlay, vintage-style tremolo, 6-on-a-side tuners, black Gotoh hardware, Sustainer Transducer/single coil/humbucker exposed pole piece pickups, volume/tone magnetic controls, Sustainer volume control, 5-way pickup selector switch, Sustainer on/off/Sustainer mode selector mini-switches, available in Black or Cobalt Blue finishes, mfg. 1998-present.

MSR	$650	$525	$450	$400	$350	$300	$250	$200

In 1999, Black and Cobalt Blue finishes were discontinued. In 2000, Metallic Black, Dark Green Metallic and Silver finishes were introduced. In 2003, Metallic Blue was introduced.

Revolver Pro 7 - similar to Revolver Pro, except in a 7-string configuration, available in Metallic Black finish, mfg. 2000-03.

	$675	$600	$525	$475	$425	$375	$325

Last MSR was $949.

Revolver Pro Hardtail - similar to the Revolver Pro except has no tremolo, available in Metallic Black finish, disc. 2003.

	$575	$500	$450	$400	$350	$300	$250

Last MSR was $809.

Revolver Pro Left-Hand - similar to the Revolver Pro except in left-hand configuration, available in Metallic Black finish, disc. 2002, reintroduced 2005-present.

MSR	$750	$600	$525	$450	$400	$350	$300	$250

Last MSR was $929.

REVOLVER X - similar to Revolver Proo, except has 2 high output humbucker pickups, volume/tone controls, 3-way switch, available in Black, Dark Blue, or Dark Red finishes, mfg. 2000-03, 2005-present.

MSR	$400	$320	$275	$230	$195	$160	$125	$95

REVOLVER STANDARD - similar to Revolver Pro, except has basswood body, graphite nut, 2 high output single coil pickups and 1 high output humbucker pickup in the bridge position, volume/tone control, 5-way switch, chrome Gotoh tuners, chrome vintage tremolo, available in Black, Metallic Blue, Metallic Red, or Tobacco Sunburst finishes, mfg. 2000 only.

	$450	$400	$350	$300	$250	$200	$150

Last MSR was $649.

Add $100 for left-hand configuration (Model Revolver Standard LH).

REVOLVER DELUXE - similar to Revolver Standard, except has Fernandes/Floyd Rose Licensed Tremolo bridge, available in Gun Metal Blue, Mava Burst, Ocean Burst, or White Pearl finishes, mfg. 2000 only.

	$625	$550	$475	$425	$375	$325	$275

Last MSR was $849.

Revolver Deluxe (Set-Neck) - similar to the Revolver Deluxe except has a neck-thru body, and Seymour Duncan pickups, available in Black or Metallic Red, mfg. 2002-03.

	$1,000	$875	$800	$725	$650	$575	$500

Last MSR was $1,440.

GRADING	100% MINT	98% NEAR MINT	95% EXC+	90% EXC	80% VG+	70% VG	60% G

REVOLVER ELITE - similar to Revolver Pro, except chrome Gotoh hardware, licensed Floyd Rose locking tremolo, available in Metallic Black, Metallic Red, Gun Metal Blue, or Silver finishes, mfg. 1998-2004.

	$1,150	$1,000	$875	$750	$650	$550	$450

Last MSR was $1,400.

In 1999, Black and Silver finishes were discontinued. In 2000, Metallic Black, Metallic Blue and Metallic Red finishes were introduced.

ELECTRIC: TE SERIES

TE-1 - classic single cutaway alder body, white pickguard, bolt-on maple neck, 25.5 in. scale, 21-fret rosewood or maple fingerboard with dot inlay, fixed bridge, 6-on-a-side tuners, chrome hardware, black pickguard, 2 single coil pickups, volume/tone control, 3-way switch, available in Black, Candy Apple Red, Cream White, or Three Tone Sunburst finishes, mfg. 1993-98.

	$325	$290	$260	$230	$190	$160	$130

Last MSR was $449.

TE-1N - similar to the TE-1, except features an ash body, 7.25 in. vintage radius on neck, antique finish on neck, available in Blonde or Vintage Natural finishes, disc. 1998.

	$525	$450	$400	$350	$300	$250	$200

Last MSR was $799.

TE-2 - similar to TE-1N, except has a bound basswood body, white pickguard, available in Black, Candy Apple Red, Vintage Metallic Blue, or 3-Tone Sunburst finishes, disc. 1998.

	$500	$450	$400	$350	$300	$250	$200

Last MSR was $749.

TE-3 - similar to TE-1N, except has semi-hollow ash body, pearloid pickguard, available in Black, Candy Apple Red, Natural, or 3-Tone Sunburst finishes, disc. 1998.

	$650	$575	$500	$450	$400	$350	$300

Last MSR was $949.

ELECTRIC: VERTIGO SERIES (H SERIES)

VERTIGO STANDARD (H-65) - original ("art deco coffee table") style alder body, bolt-on maple neck, 24.75 in. scale, 22-fret rosewood fingerboard with dot inlay, stop tailpiece, 3-per-side tuners, chrome hardware, upside-down 'U' pearloid pickguard, 2 chrome covered humbucker pickups, volume/tone controls, 3-way switch, available in Black, Pale Cobalt, or Vivid Orange finishes, disc. 2000.

	$395	$325	$275	$235	$195	$165	$135

Last MSR was $499.

In 1998, Dark Red and Vintage Metallic Blue finishes were introduced. In 1999, pale Cobalt, Vivid Orange, Dark Red and Vintage Metallic Blue Finishes were discontinued. In 2000, 3-Tone Sunburst and Dark Green Metallic finishes were introduced.

VERTIGO X - similar to Vertigo Standard, except has 1 high output humbucker pickup in the bridge position, volume control, available in Black, Dark Green, or Dark Red finishes, current mfg.

MSR	$360	$290	$250	$210	$180	$150	$130	$110

Add $30 for left-handed configuration.

VERTIGO FX - similar to the Vertigo except has 24 on-board effects, and 3 outputs, available in Metallic Black, Gun Metal Blue, or Metallic Red finishes, disc. 2003.

	$550	$475	$425	$375	$325	$275	$225

Last MSR was $769.

VERTIGO ELITE - similar to Vertigo Deluxe, except has maple bolt-on neck, Sustainer driver/humbucker pickup in the neck position and high output humbucker in the bridge position, Sustainer mode selector, Sustainer Intensity and Sustainer on/off, black pickguard, available in Metallic Black, Wine Red, Dark Green Metallic, or Matte Black finish, current mfg.

MSR	$1,200	$975	$825	$725	$625	$525	$450	$375

VERTIGO DELUXE (H-80) - similar to the H-65, except features mahogany body/neck, bound neck/headstock, forward-pointing pearloid pickguard, Gotoh chrome hardware, 2 mini humbuckers, triangle trapezoid inlays, available in Mahogany Brown or Pewter finishes, current mfg.

MSR	$1,000	$825	$725	$625	$550	$475	$400	$325

In 1998, Silver finish replaced Pewter finish. In 1999, Mahogany Brown and Silver finishes discontinued. In 2000, Black Sunburst and Red Burst finishes introduced.

VERTIGO CUSTOM X-RIGGS SIGNATURE - Vertigo style body, neck-thru construction, maple body/neck, single Seymour Duncan Full Shred pickup, X inlays, large guitar strap hooks, available in Black Satin finish, disc. 2004.

	$750	$675	$600	$525	$450	$375	$300

Last MSR was $900.

H-85 - original (art deco coffee table) style alder body, bolt-on maple neck, 22-fret rosewood fingerboard with dot inlay, double locking vibrato, 3-per-side tuners, black hardware, 2 humbucker pickups, volume/tone controls, 3-way switch, available in Shining Green or Neon Pink finishes, disc. 1996.

	$625	$550	$475	$425	$375	$325	$275

Last MSR was $999.

**Fernandes TE-1
courtesy Blue Book
Publications**

F

GRADING	100% MINT	98% NEAR MINT	95% EXC+	90% EXC	80% VG+	70% VG	60% G

ELECTRIC: VORTEX SERIES

VORTEX ELITE - modified "V"-shaped alder body, bolt-on maple neck, 24.75 in. scale, rosewood fingerboard with split trapezoid position markers, Sustainer Driver/Humbucker pickup in the neck position and high output humbucker pickup in the bridge position, volume control, Sustainer Mode Selector, Sustainer Intensity and Sustainer on/off controls, black Gotoh tuners, black double locking Fernandes/Floyd Rose Licensed Tremolo bridge, available in Metallic Black finish, disc. 2003.

	$775	$700	$625	$575	$525	$450	$350

Last MSR was $1,099.

ELECTRIC BASS: AMB SERIES

AMB-4 - offset double cutaway alder body, bolt-on maple neck, 34 in. scale, 24-fret rosewood fingerboard with dot inlay, fixed bridge, 2-per-side tuners, chrome hardware, P/J-style passive pickups, 2 volume/tone control, available in Black, Metallic Blue, or Metallic Red finishes, disc. 1998.

	$350	$300	$275	$225	$195	$160	$130

Last MSR was $469.

AMB-4GF - similar to the AMB-4, except features basswood body, graphic finishes, available in Black Burst, Blue Burst, or Red Burst finishes, disc. 1998.

	$550	$475	$425	$375	$325	$250	$200

Last MSR was $799.

AMB-40 - offset double cutaway basswood body, bolt-on maple neck, 24-fret rosewood fingerboard with pearl dot inlay, fixed bridge, 2-per-side tuners, chrome hardware, P/J-style Fernandes pickups, 2 volume/tone control, available in Black, Blue Sunburst, Fire Red, or Snow White finishes, mfg. 1991-93.

	N/A	$400	$325	$275	$225	$175	$125

Last MSR was $570.

Add $80 for left-handed configuration (Model AMB-40L).

AMB-45 - similar to AMB-40, except has black hardware, available in Black, Metallic Blue, or Metallic Red finishes, disc. 1996.

	$325	$275	$235	$195	$160	$130	$100

Last MSR was $499.

Add $100 for left-handed configuration (Model AMB-45L).

AMB-55 - similar to AMB-45, available in Black Burst, Blue Burst, or Red Burst finishes, disc. 1996.

	$400	$325	$275	$225	$190	$160	$130

Last MSR was $599.

AMB-60 - similar to AMB-40, except has black hardware, disc. 1994.

	$400	$325	$275	$225	$190	$160	$130

Last MSR was $600.

AMB-70 - similar to AMB-40, except has ash body, active pickups, and gold hardware, available in Trans. Black, Trans. Purple, Trans. White, or Vintage Natural finishes, disc. 1992.

	N/A	$500	$425	$350	$300	$250	$200

Last MSR was $800.

ELECTRIC BASS: APB (GRAVITY) SERIES

The Gravity bass model debuted in 1993.

GRAVITY 4 DELUXE (APB-4) - offset double cutaway ash body, bolt-on 3-piece maple neck, 34 in. scale, 24-fret rosewood fingerboard with dot inlay, fixed bridge, 2-per-side tuners, gold Gotoh hardware, active P/J-style pickups, volume/blend/treble/bass controls, active pre-amp, available in Black, Emerald Green, See-Through Purple, or Oil Natural finishes, disc. 1999, reintroduced 2002-present.

MSR	$1,300		$1,050	$900	$800	$700	$600	$500	$400

This model is also available with a maple fingerboard (Gravity 4M, APB-4M), available in the same colors. This model was reintroduced in 2003 as the Gravity Deluxe.

Gravity 4 Standard - similar to Gravity 4, except has basswood body, 2 volume/1 tone control, available in Black, Metallic Blue, Silver or Tobacco Sunburst finish, mfg. 2000 only.

	$525	$475	$425	$375	$325	$275	$225

Last MSR was $749.

Add $20 for Flame top (Model Gravity 4 Standard GF), available in See-Through Black Burst, Blue Burst and Red Burst finishes. Add $50 for Quilt top (Model Gravity 4 Standard GQ), available in Ocean Burst, Lava Burst and Purple Burst finishes.

GRAVITY 5 DELUXE (APB-5) - similar to the APB-4, except has 5-string configuration, 3/2-per-side tuners, 2 active J-style pickups, available in Black, Emerald Green, See-Through Purple, and Vintage Natural finishes, disc. 1999, reintroduced 2002-present.

MSR	$1,400		$1,125	$975	$850	$750	$650	$550	$450

This model is also available with a maple fingerboard (Gravity 5M, APB-5M), available in the same colors. This model was reintroduced in 2003 as the Gravity Deluxe.

GRAVITY 6 (APB-6) - similar to the APB-5, except has 6-string configuration, 3-per-side tuners, 2 J-style passive pickups, available in Black, Emerald Green, See-Through Purple, or Vintage Natural finishes, disc. 2000.

	$1,125	$1,000	$875	$750	$650	$550	$450

Last MSR was $1,599.

In 1999, Emerald Green and Vintage Natural finishes were discontinued. In 2000, See-Through Blue finish was introduced.

GRADING	100% MINT	98% NEAR MINT	95% EXC+	90% EXC	80% VG+	70% VG	60% G

GRAVITY 8 (APB-8) - similar to the APB-4, except has 8-string configuration (4 pairs of strings), 4-per-side tuners, Schaller bridge, active P/J-style pickups, available in Black finish, disc. 2000.

	$1,075	$925	$825	$725	$600	$500	$400

Last MSR was $1,549.

GRAVITY 4X - double offset cutaway alder body, bolt-on maple neck, 24-large fret rosewood fingerboard with dot inlay, 2-per-side tuners, 2 pickups: p-style, j-style, three knobs, vintage style bridge, chrome hardware, available in Black, Metallic Blue, or Dark Green Metallic finishes, current mfg.

MSR	$300	$250	$220	$190	$170	$150	$130	$110

Gravity 5X - similar to the Gravity 4X, except in 5-string configuration, mfg. 2004-present.

MSR	$400	$320	$275	$235	$200	$170	$150	$130

APB-80 - offset double cutaway ash body, bolt-on maple neck, 24-fret rosewood fingerboard with pearl dot inlay, fixed bridge, 2-per-side tuners, gold hardware, P/J-style pickups, 2 volume/tone control, available in Black, Fire Red, Metallic Blue, or Snow White finishes, disc. 1993.

	N/A	$500	$425	$350	$300	$250	$200

Last MSR was $700.

APB-90 - similar to APB-80, except has active pickups, volume/treble/bass/mix controls, available in Trans. Black, Trans. Blue, Trans. Purple, Trans. Red, Trans. White, Tobacco Sunburst, or Vintage Natural finishes, disc. 1996.

	$625	$500	$475	$400	$350	$300	$250

Last MSR was $959.

This model has an optional fretless fingerboard. This model also available with maple fingerboard with black dot inlay, 2 J-style pickups (Model APB-90M).

APB-100 - similar to APB-80, except has 5-string configuration, 3/2-per-side tuners, 2 active J-style pickups, available in Trans. Black, Trans. Purple, Trans. White, Tobacco Sunburst, or Vintage Natural finishes, disc. 1996.

	$700	$625	$550	$475	$400	$350	$300

Last MSR was $1,049.

This model has an optional fretless fingerboard.

ELECTRIC BASS: LEB SERIES

LEB-J4 - offset double cutaway alder body, bolt-on maple neck, 34 in. scale, 20-fret rosewood fingerboard with dot inlay, fixed bridge, 4-on-a-side tuners, chrome hardware, white pickguard, 2 J-style passive pickups, 2 volume/tone controls, available in Black, Cream White, Candy Apple Red, Vintage Metallic Blue, or 3-Tone Sunburst, disc. 1998.

	$350	$300	$260	$230	$200	$160	$130

Last MSR was $479.

LEB-J5 - similar to J4-C, except features a 5-string configuration, 4/1 per side tuners, available in Black, Cream White, Candy Apple Red, Vintage Metallic Blue, or 3-Tone Sunburst, disc. 1998.

	$650	$575	$500	$425	$350	$275	$200

Last MSR was $999.

LEB-P4 - offset double cutaway alder body, bolt-on maple neck, 34 in. scale, 20-fret rosewood fingerboard with dot inlay, fixed bridge, 4-on-a-side tuners, chrome hardware, white pickguard, passive P-style pickups, volume/tone controls, available in Black, Cream White, Candy Apple Red, Vintage Metallic Blue, or 3-Tone Sunburst, disc. 1998.

	$350	$300	$260	$230	$200	$160	$130

Last MSR was $479.

LSB-65 - Single cutaway basswood body, bolt-on maple neck, 24-fret rosewood fingerboard with dot inlay, fixed bridge, 2-per-side tuners, humbucker pickup, volume/tone controls, available in Black or 3-Tone Sunburst finishes, disc. 1996.

	$425	$375	$325	$275	$225	$175	$125

Last MSR was $699.

ELECTRIC BASS: MISC MODELS

ASB-100 - mahogany body, bolt-on maple neck, 24-fret rosewood fingerboard with dot inlay, fixed bridge, 2-per-side tuners, Fernandes Sustainer/humbucker pickups, volume/tone controls, available in Black finish, disc. 1996.

	$800	$725	$650	$575	$500	$425	$350

Last MSR was $1,299.

This model has an optional fretless fingerboard.

ATLAS 4 STANDARD/4X - offset double cutaway alder body, bolt-on maple neck, 21-fret maple neck with dot inlays, 4-on-one-side tuners, single FSB humbucking pickup, vintage style bridge, two knobs, one switch, chrome hardware, available in Candy Apple Red, Metallic Black, Gun Metal Blue, or Metallic Red finishes, mfg. 2001-03, reintroduced as the 4X 2005-present.

MSR	$300	$250	$210	$180	$150	$130	$110	$90

HB-65 - basswood body, bolt-on maple neck, 24-fret rosewood fingerboard with dot inlay, fixed bridge, 2-per-side tuners, humbucker pickup, volume/tone controls, available in Black and 3-Tone Sunburst finishes, disc. 1996.

	$495	$450	$400	$350	$300	$250	$200

Last MSR was $799.

GRADING	100% MINT	98% NEAR MINT	95% EXC+	90% EXC	80% VG+	70% VG	60% G

J4-C - offset double cutaway basswood body, bolt-on maple neck, 34 in. scale, 20-fret rosewood fingerboard with dot inlay, fixed bridge, 4-on-a-side tuners, chrome hardware, white pickguard, 2 J-style passive pickups, 2 volume/tone controls, available in Black, Cream White, Red, and 3-Tone Sunburst, disc. 1998.

		$300	$250	$225	$200	$175	$135	$100

Last MSR was $399.

NOMAD BASS (PIEZO BASS TRAVEL GUITAR) - "Standing elephant"-shaped basswood body, bolt-on maple neck, 25.5 in. scale, 20-fret rosewood fingerboard with dot inlay, rosewood bridge, 4-on-a-side tuners, chrome hardware, Shadow piezo bridge pickup, built-in (9 Volt) amp and 4 in. speaker, volume control, LED light, on/off switch, available in Black, Candy Apple Red, Metallic Blue, or 3-Tone Sunburst, current mfg.

MSR	$500	$400	$325	$275	$235	$195	$160	$130

P4-C - offset double cutaway basswood body, bolt-on maple neck, 34 in. scale, 20-fret rosewood fingerboard with dot inlay, fixed bridge, 4-on-a-side tuners, chrome hardware, white pickguard, passive P-style pickups, volume/tone controls, available in Black, Cream White, Red, or 3-Tone Sunburst, disc. 1998.

		$290	$250	$225	$200	$175	$135	$100

Last MSR was $399.

TEB-1 - single cutaway basswood body, black pickguard, bolt-on maple neck, 21-fret rosewood or maple fingerboard with dot inlay, fixed bridge, 4-on-one-side tuners, gold hardware, P/J-style pickups, 2 volume/tone controls, available in Black or Cream White finishes, mfg. 1993-96.

		$475	$425	$375	$325	$275	$225	$175

Last MSR was $779.

VERTIGO BASS - original ("art deco coffee table") style alder body, bolt-on maple neck, 34 in. scale, 22-fret rosewood fingerboard with dot inlay, fixed bridge, 2-per-side tuners, chrome hardware, upside down 'U' white pickguard, 2 J-style pickups, 2 volume/1 tone controls, available in Black or Three Tone Sunburst finishes, mfg. 1998-99.

		$395	$325	$275	$235	$195	$165	$135

Last MSR was $549.

ELECTRIC BASS: RETROSPECT SERIES

RETROSPECT 4 STANDARD - offset double cutaway alder body, bolt-on maple neck, 34 in. scale, 22-fret rosewood fingerboard with dot inlay, fixed bridge, 4-on-a-side tuners, chrome hardware, white pearloid pickguard, 2 J-style single coil pickups, 2 volume/1 tone controls, series/parallel switch, available in Black, Vintage Metallic Blue, or 3-Tone Sunburst finishes, disc. 2000.

		$395	$350	$300	$260	$230	$200	$160

Last MSR was $549.

Retrospect 4X - similar to Retrospect 4 Standard, except has passive P-style split-coil pickup mounted mid-body, available in Black, Dark Blue, or Red finishes, disc. 2000.

		$290	$250	$225	$200	$175	$150	$120

Last MSR was $399.

RETROSPECT 5 STANDARD - similar to Retrospect 4 Standard, except features a 5-string configuration, 4/1-per-side tuners, available in Black, Vintage Metallic Blue, or 3-Tone Sunburst finishes, disc. 2000.

		$525	$450	$400	$350	$300	$250	$200

Last MSR was $749.

In 1999, Black finish was discontinued.

RETROSPECT 4 DELUXE - similar to Retrospect 4 Standard, except features a basswood body, flame maple gravure top, 2 passive J-style pickups, Gotoh tuners, mint green pickguard, volume/bass/treble/blend controls, active preamp, available in 3-Tone Sunburst finish with Antique finish on neck, disc. 2000.

		$775	$675	$600	$525	$450	$375	$300

Last MSR was $1,099.

In 1999, 3-Tone Sunburst finish was discontinued. In 2000, Red Burst and Tobacco Sunburst finishes were introduced.

RETROSPECT 5 DELUXE - similar to Retrospect 4 Deluxe, except features a 5-string configuration, 4/1-per-side tuners, available in 3-Tone Sunburst finish with antique finish on neck, disc. 2000.

		$900	$750	$675	$600	$525	$450	$375

Last MSR was $1,249.

In 1999, 3-Tone Sunburst finish was discontinued. In 2000, Red Burst and Tobacco Sunburst finishes were introduced.

RETROSPECT 4X - double offset cutaway alder body, bolt-on maple neck, 22-fret rosewood fingerboard with dot inlay, 4-on-one-side tuners, 2 pickups: J-style, P-style, white pickguard, three knobs, vintage style bridge, chrome hardware, available in Black or Dark Blue finishes, disc. 2004.

		$250	$220	$190	$170	$150	$130	$110

Last MSR was $300.

RETROSPECT 5X - similar to the Retrospect 4X except in five-string configuration, 4/1-on-a-side tuners, available in Black or 3-Tone Sunburst finishes, disc. 2003.

		$350	$325	$290	$250	$210	$175	$125

Last MSR was $519.

ELECTRIC BASS: TREMOR SERIES

TREMOR 4 - offset double cutaway alder body with rounded cutaway in lower bout, bolt-on maple neck, 34 in. scale, 24-fret rosewood fingerboard with dot inlay, fixed bridge, 2-per-side tuners, chrome hardware, P/J-style pickups, 2 volume/1 tone controls, series/parallel switch, available in Black, Dark Green Metallic, or Metallic Blue finishes, mfg. 1998-99.

		$395	$325	$295	$250	$225	$175	$150

Last MSR was $549.

GRADING	100% MINT	98% NEAR MINT	95% EXC+	90% EXC	80% VG+	70% VG	60% G

Tremor 4 Standard - similar to Tremor 4, except has black tuners, black traditional bridge, available in Metallic Black, Dark Green Metallic, or Metallic Blue finishes, new specs for 2000, disc. 2003.

		100%	98%	95%	90%	80%	70%	60%
		$350	$325	$275	$225	$195	$175	$150

Last MSR was $489.

Tremor 4X - similar to Tremor 4 Standard, except has passive P-style pickup mounted mid-body, chrome tuners, chrome traditional bridge, available in Black, Dark Blue, or Red finishes, mfg. 2000-present.

MSR	$300	$250	$220	$190	$170	$150	$130	$110

Tremor 4 Deluxe - similar to Tremor 4 Standard, except has bass wood body, 2 Active FGI Technology Soapbar pickups, volume, bass, treble and blend controls, black Gotoh bridge, available in Metallic Black or Dark Red Metallic finishes, current mfg.

MSR	$1,200	$975	$825	$725	$625	$525	$450	$375

TREMOR 5 STANDARD - similar to Tremor 4 Standard except in a 5-string configuration, available in Metallic Black or Dark Green Metallic finishes, new specs for 2000, disc. 2003.

		$425	$375	$325	$275	$225	$175	$125

Last MSR was $599.

Tremor 5 - similar to Tremor 5, except features older specs, available in Black and Dark Green Metallic finishes, mfg. 1998-99.

		$595	$500	$425	$375	$325	$275	$225

Last MSR was $849.

Tremor 5X - similar to Tremor 5 Standard, except has passive P-style pickup mounted mid body, chrome tuners, chrome traditional bridge, available in Ocean Burst, Lava Burst, or Black finishes, mfg. 2004-present.

MSR	$400	$320	$275	$235	$200	$170	$150	$130

Tremor 5 Deluxe - similar to Tremor 4 deluxe, exccept in a 5-string configuration, available in Metallic Black or Dark Metallic Red finishes, current mfg.

MSR	$1,300	$1,050	$900	$800	$700	$600	$500	$400

TREMOR 4X X-PACK - includes a Tremor 4X bass, 15-Watt Fernandes Guitar Amplifier, gig bag, cable strap, tuner, picks, and a CD-ROM for lessons, guitar available in Black, Blue or Red, current mfg.

MSR	$400	$320	$275	$235	$200	$170	$150	$130

FERRINGTON, DANNY

Instruments currently built in Santa Monica, CA since 1980.

Luthier Danny Ferrington was born and raised in Louisiana. Ferrington's father, Lloyd, was a cabinet maker who had previously played guitar and bass in a local country western combo. Ferrington's first experiences with woodworking were in his father's shop in Monroe, Louisiana. Ferrington accepted an apprenticeship in 1975 at the Old Time Pickin' Parlour in Nashville, Tennessee. He spent the next five years working with noted acoustic guitar builder Randy Woods. Ferrington's first acoustic was built in 1977, and he continued to hone his craft. In 1980, Ferrington moved to Los Angeles, California. Ferrington spent a number of years experimenting with different designs, and tones from instruments, and continued building custom guitars. Many of the features on the custom guitars are developed through discussions with the musician commissioning the piece. It is estimated that by 1992, Ferrington had constructed over one hundred custom instruments (source: Kate Geil, et al, the *Ferrington Guitars Book*).

GENERAL INFORMATION

In the late 1980s, the Kramer guitar company was offering several models designed by Ferrington. After Kramer went under, the Ferrington Guitar Company of Long Branch, New Jersey (phone number was previously listed at 908.870.3800) offered essentially the same models (KFS-1, KFT-1, and KFB-1) with Ferrington on the headstock. These models featured a maple neck, rosewood fingerboard, acoustic body, 3-band EQ, and a thinline bridge transducer.

FIBRATONE

See Fenton-Weill. Instruments previously produced in the 1960s.

These semi-hollow body guitars were built of fiberglass, and produced by the Fenton-Weill company of England in the 1960s.

FICHTER

Instruments currently built in Germany since 1988.

Fichter has been building modern electric upright basses since 1988. The Fichter electric upright bass is minimally larger than an electric bass guitar, and can easily fit in the back seat of a mid-sized car. Fichter estimates that his annual production is now at about fifty instruments a year.

ELECTRIC BASS

Fichter's electric bass is constructed of maple and mahogany, has a 41 in. contrabass scale, and weighs only 13 pounds. The model features an ebony fingerboard, active preamp and coaxial or magnetic pickup system, and custom Schaller tuners. 4 and 5-string configurations (strung with either high C or low B) are available. A deluxe custom-made bag comes with every bass. Check the Fichter website (see Trademark Index) for current prices in U.S. dollars (prices are computed in Euros and vary with the exchange rate).

F

FINGERBONE

Instruments previously built in England from 1986 to 1989.

The Fastback model was a high quality solid body guitar with an original design and different hardware options (source: Tony Bacon and Paul Day, *The Guru's Guitar Guide*).

FIREFOX

Instruments previously built in Japan since late 1980s.

These medium quality solid body guitars were based on American designs, and produced in either full size or "mini" versions (source: Tony Bacon and Paul Day, *The Guru's Guitar Guide*).

FIRST ACT

Instruments currently produced in Newton, MA and China since 1997. Distributed by First Act of Newton, MA.

First Act produces a line of custom made electric guitars in MA as well as a mass-market line of guitars in China. Most electrics feature Kent Armstrong pickups. For more information refer to their website (see Trademark Index).

ELECTRIC GUITARS

First Act produces both high-end and low-end instruments. The custom shop models built in the U.S. include the Athena (MSR $4,000), the Loki (MSR $4,000), the Persephon (MSR MSR $4,000), the Venus (MSR $4,000), and the Overtone (MSR $3,000). The mass market electric models include the ME201 (MSR $238), the ME952 (MSR $148), the ME962 (MSR $186), the ME300, the ME301, the ME401, the ME501, and the ME601. First Act also has a line of bass guitars.

FISCHER FINE INSTRUMENTS

Instruments currently produced in Lake Stevens, WA.

Kenneth F. Kraft produces Fischer instruments. These guitars are unique in that the back and neck are made of carbon fiber. Carbon fiber is used because it produces rich sound and powerful projection. The tops of the guitars are hand-rubbed and not veneered. For more information, refer to their website (see Trademark Index).

FISHER

Instruments previously built in Coalport, PA in the early 1990s.

Fisher guitars offered two models of solid body electric guitars that featured American components (hardware and pickups). Any information about Fisher guitars would be appreciated and can be submitted directly to the publisher.

FISHER, ROGER

Instruments previously built in Bellevue, WA during the late 1980s.

Guitarist Roger Fisher was part of the original line-up in the rock group Heart. Fisher left Heart in October 1979. Soon after he departed Heart, he founded the Roger Fisher Band, and later Ten Bulls. In the late 1980s, Fisher became a guitar designer/manufacturer. Known for upgrading and re-working his guitars as early as his Heart playing days, Fisher's Trout guitar featured a variety of non-standard features. The Fisher Trout model features a double cutaway custom-shaped body, an on-board speaker, and amp that also doubles as a sustain/feedback device. The guitar also has a 7-band graphic EQ, a headphone output that also doubled as a line-out to mixers or monitor system, a piezo bridge pickup and magnetic pickups, fiber optic position markers, and an asymmetrical neck shaping. It is estimated that a number of these custom guitars are still in the hands of their original owners, as they rarely show up in the secondary market. The original retail price is currently unknown.

FITZPATRICK JAZZ GUITARS

Instruments currently built in Wickford, RI.

Luthier Charles Fitzpatrick builds acoustic, acoustic electric, and semi-hollow body electric archtop guitars in 15 in., 16 in., 17 in., and 18 in. body widths. The Jazz Box Select features single cutaway body consisting of fancy quilted or flamed maple with matching rim and neck, solid carved top of North American spruce, fine line black and white body binding, mother-of-pearl block fingerboard inlays, gold tune-o-matic tailpiece, bound tortoiseshell finger rest, and a suspended jazz pickup. List prices range from $3,270 (16 in.), $3,800 (17 in.), and $4,500 (18 in). The list price includes a hardshell case, and Fitzpatrick offers a range of options and custom inlays.

FIVE STAR

See chapter on House Brands.

This trademark has been identified as a House Brand, but the retailer or distributor has not yet been identified (source: Willie G. Moseley, *Stellas & Stratocasters*).

FLEISHMAN

Instruments currently built in Sebastopol, CA since 1975. Instruments were previously produced in Boulder, CO.

Luthier Harry Fleishman has been designing and building high quality guitars and basses since 1975. In addition to the electric solid body models that Fleishman is known for, he also builds a small number of acoustic guitars on a yearly basis. Fleishman is also the director of the LSI (Luthiers School International). Fleishman designed the Flash model for Hondo during the 1980s, a minimalist body reverse-tuned bass with a number of innovative design features.

ELECTRIC BASS

Fleishman currently offers a new upright electric bass model, which is available in 4-, 5-, and 6-string configuration. The 35 in. (or 42 in.) scale instrument features a neck and body of curly maple, an aged ebony fingerboard, and a combination of electronics to produce a "clear, woody tone". Other models include the **Anti-Gravity Bass**, a hollow body bass with floating tone board; the 4-, 5-, and 6-string **Scroll Bass** with hand carved scroll headstock and ebony fingerboard; and the headless **Jayne** bass, which features an exotic wood body. For more information regarding pricing and model specifications, please contact luthier Fleishman directly (see Trademark Index).

FLOYD ROSE

Instruments currently produced since 2003.

Floyd Rose introduced his original locking tremolo bridge in 1977. This was a huge change in the way people played the guitar. Floyd Rose set out to change the guitar world again with the introduction of the Floyd Rose guitar. These guitars are built to meet the uncompromising demands of professional musicians. The guitars are produced with the finest tonal wood bodies with incomparable necks, the Speedloader Bridge system, and Floyd Rose pickups. The most identifying feature may be the headstock that is of a typical Stratocaster but the middle is hollowed out since no strings are attached to the headstock. For more information refer to their website (see Trademark Index).

ELECTRIC

The line of Floyd Rose guitars is known as the Redmond Series. Models include the Model 1, Model 2, Model 3, Model 4, Model 5, and Model K. Prices start at $2,400. The discovery series are the budget models based on the Redmond Series. Prices start at $529 for these guitars.

FOCUS

See Kramer. Instruments previously built in Japan circa mid- to late 1980s.

The Focus series of guitars were built overseas in the ESP factory for Kramer in the mid to late 1980s to supplement the higher end American models. The Kramer company could then offer a wider price range of models to consumers, and still maintain design and quality control over their product. The Focus series of guitars is not to be confused with the actual Kramer Focus model (1000, 2000, etc.).

FODERA

Instruments currently built in Brooklyn, NY since 1983.

Luthiers Vinnie Fodera and Joseph Lauricella founded Fodera Guitars in 1983. Fodera, who had previously worked with Stuart Spector and Ned Steinberger in the late 1970s, focused directly on bass building. Bassists such as Anthony Jackson, Victor Wooten, Lincoln Goines, and Matthew Garrison all swear by their Fodera basses. All Fodera models feature select aged woods and water-based lacquer finishes (a penetrating oil finish is available on request). The Diamond Series Bass Strings are hand wound at the Fodera workshop. Fodera stainless steel and nickel round wound strings are available in 4-, 5-, and 6-string sets in Light to Heavy sizes. "You will Hear and Feel the Difference!"

ELECTRIC BASS: GENERAL INFORMATION

Fodera models are offered in three different construction designs: Bolt-On (the neck is bolted on), Deluxe (set-in neck), and Elite (through-body neck). Fodera basses are offered with a number of pickup options, as well as custom inlay (call for pricing). All retail prices include a hard case.

The Anthony Jackson Contrabass, designed in conjunction with bassist supreme Anthony Jackson, has a single cutaway alder body, AAA top, 24-fret rosewood fingerboard, 6-string configuration, 3-per-side tuners, Bartolini or Lane Poor pickups (call for retail list price).

Add 15% for left-handed configuration. Add $250 for fretless fingerboard with inlaid lines. Add $250 for 5-piece laminated neck. Add $250 for High Gloss custom color. Add $300 for maple fingerboard. Add $500 for AAA grade top.

ELECTRIC BASS: EMPEROR SERIES

Imperial Series basses are similar in design to the Anthony Jackson contrabass. Imperial models are only available in the Elite through-body neck configuration.

EMPEROR 4-STRING - offset double cutaway alder (or ash or mahogany) body, flamed (or quilted) maple top, 3-piece bolt-on neck, 34 in. scale, 21-fret ebony (or rosewood) fingerboard with dot inlay, solid brass nut, 2-per-side tuners, Fodera bridge, Bartolini (or EMG or Lane Poor) pickups, volume/tone controls, Fodera circuitry, available in hand-rubbed clear satin finish, current mfg.

MSR $4,864

Emperor 4-String Deluxe - similar to the Emperor 4-String, except in Deluxe version with a set-neck, current mfg.

MSR $5,274

Emperor 4-String Elite - similar to the Emperor Deluxe, except in Elite configuration, current mfg.

MSR $5,884

EMPEROR 5-STRING - offset double cutaway alder (or ash or mahogany) body, 5-string configuration, flamed (or quilted) maple top, 3-piece bolt-on neck, 35 in. scale, 22-fret ebony (or rosewood) fingerboard with dot inlay, solid brass nut, 3/2-per-side tuners, Fodera bridge, Bartolini (or EMG or Lane Poor) pickups, volume/tone controls, Fodera circuitry, available in hand-rubbed clear satin finish, current mfg.

MSR $5,365

Emperor 5-String Deluxe - similar to the Emperor 5-String, except in Deluxe version with a set-neck, current mfg.

MSR $5,775

Emperor 5-String Elite - similar to the Emperor 5-String, except in Elite version with a set-neck, current mfg.

MSR $6,385

EMPEROR 6-STRING - similar to the Emperor, except in six-string configuration, current mfg.

MSR $5,866

Emperor 6-String Deluxe - similar to the Emperor 5-String, except in Elite version with a set-neck, current mfg.

MSR $6,886

ELECTRIC BASS: IMPERIAL SERIES

IMPERIAL 4-STRING ELITE - single cutaway alder (or ash or mahogany) body, flamed (or quilted) maple top, through-body 3-piece neck, 35 in. scale, 21-fret ebony (or rosewood) fingerboard with dot inlay, solid brass nut, 2-per-side tuners, Fodera bridge, Bartolini (or EMG or Lane Poor) pickups, volume/tone controls, Fodera circuitry, available in Hand Rubbed Clear Satin finish, current mfg.

MSR $5,894

IMPERIAL 5-STRING ELITE - single cutaway alder (or ash or mahogany) body, flamed (or quilted) maple top, through-body 3-piece neck, 35 in. scale, 21-fret ebony (or rosewood) fingerboard with dot inlay, solid brass nut, 3/2-per-side tuners, Fodera bridge, Bartolini (or EMG or Lane Poor) pickups, volume/tone controls, Fodera circuitry, available in Hand Rubbed Clear Satin finish, current mfg.

MSR $6,395

IMPERIAL 6-STRING ELITE - single cutaway alder (or ash or mahogany) body, 6-string configuration, flamed (or quilted) maple top, through-body 3-piece neck, 36 in. scale, 24-fret ebony (or rosewood) fingerboard with dot inlay, solid brass nut, 3-per-side tuners, Fodera bridge, Bartolini (or EMG or Lane Poor) pickups, volume/tone controls, Fodera circuitry, available in Hand Rubbed Clear Satin finish, current mfg.

MSR $6,896

ELECTRIC BASS: MONARCH SERIES

Monarch Series basses are similar to the Emperor body design, except have a sleeker profile and slightly further extended horns.

MONARCH 4-STRING DELUXE - sleek offset double cutaway alder (or ash or mahogany) body, flamed (or quilted) maple top, 3-piece neck, 34 in. scale, 21-fret ebony (or rosewood) fingerboard with dot inlay, solid brass nut, 2-per-side tuners, Fodera bridge, Bartolini (or EMG or Lane Poor) pickups, volume/tone controls, Fodera circuitry, available in Hand Rubbed Clear Satin finish, current mfg.

MSR $5,274

Monarch 4-String Elite - similar to the Monarch 4-String, except in Elite configuration, current mfg.

MSR $5,884

MONARCH 5-STRING DELUXE - sleek offset double cutaway alder (or ash or mahogany) body, 5-string configuration, flamed (or quilted) maple top, 3-piece neck, 35 in. scale, 21-fret ebony (or rosewood) fingerboard with dot inlay, solid brass nut, 3/2-per-side tuners, Fodera bridge, Bartolini (or EMG or Lane Poor) pickups, volume/tone controls, Fodera circuitry, available in Hand Rubbed Clear Satin finish, current mfg.

MSR $5,775

Monarch 5-String Elite - similar to the Monarch 5-String, except in Elite configuration, current mfg.

MSR $6,385

FOSTER

Instruments currently built in Covington, LA, since the late 1960s/early 1970s.

Luthier Jimmy Foster offers repair and restoration work in addition to his current guitar designs, and has been working in the New Orleans area for over many years. He has been doing luthier work for over 30 years. In addition to his standard models (listed below), Foster also offers custom orders available with choice of woods, inlays, and trim. For further information, contact luthier Foster directly (see Trademark Index).

ELECTRIC: ARCH-TOP MODELS

AT 1 - carved spruce top with beveled f-holes, carved mahogany back, bound body, mahogany neck, ebony fingerboard and pickguard, 25.5 in. scale, Armstrong Humbucker pickup, gold hardware, disc. 2003.

Last MSR was $4,750.

AT 2 - carved spruce top with beveled f-holes, carved mahogany back, Lesser multi-bound body, maple neck, bound ebony fingerboard and pickguard, inlaid bound headstock, 25.5 in. scale, Armstrong Humbucker pickup, gold tailpiece and hardware, disc. mfg.

Last MSR was $4,950.

Add $250 for ebony tailpiece. Add $250 for bound f-holes.

AT 3 - carved spruce top with beveled f-holes, carved maple back, Lesser multi-bound body, maple neck, inlaid bound headstock, bound ebony fingerboard and pickguard, 25.5 in. scale, Armstrong Humbucking pickup, gold tailpiece and hardware, disc. 2003.

Last MSR was $5,950.

Add $300 for inlaid ebony tailpiece. Add $250 for bound f-holes.

AT 4 - similar to AT 3, except has mahogany back, sides, and neck rather than maple, disc. mfg.

Last MSR was $6,250.

AT 5 - master-grade woods, carved spruce top, carved maple back, maple sides, 5-piece maple neck, multibound ebony fingerboard, headstock, and pickguard, bound f-holes, Abalone inlaid ebony tailpiece, bridge, and headstock, 25.5 in. scale, Armstrong Humbucking pickup, gold hardware, disc. 2003.

Last MSR was $7,650.

Add $500 for quilted maple top. Add $500 for left-handed configuration. Add $60 each for tone control and coil tap under pickguard.

BASIN STREET - 6- or 7-string configuration, single Venetian cutaway, 15 in. body, f-holes, carved cedar top, mahogany back and sides, 1-piece mahogany neck, ebony fingerboard, small fleur-de-lis inlays in the headstock, tailpiece, truss rod cover, bridge base, and heel cap, single ply black body bindings, floating Kent Armstrong pickup, black pickguard with two knobs, gold hardware, natural finish, current mfg.

MSR $3,995

Add $1,000 for left-handed configuration.

CRESCENT CITY - 6- or 7-string configuration, single Venetian cutaway, 17 in. body, f-holes, carved Sitka Spruce top, select mahogany back and sides, 1-piece laminated maple neck, ebony fingerboard, multi-piece abalone fleur-de-lis inlays in the headstock, tailpiece, truss rod cover, bridge base, and heel cap, single-ply white body bindings, floating Kent Armstrong pickup, black pickguard with two knobs, gold hardware, natural finish, current mfg.

MSR $5,500

Add $1,000 for left-handed configuration.

Crescent City Classic - similar to the Crescent City, except has figured maple back/sides/neck and 5-ply body binding, current mfg.
MSR $6,700

Crescent City Elite - similar to the Crescent City Classic, except has Big Leaf maple back/sides/neck, 9-ply body binding, and fancier inlays, current mfg.
MSR $8,500

FLEUR DE LIS ELITE
- 6- or 7-string configuration, single Venetian cutaway, 17 in. body, f-holes, Master Grade Select Sitka Spruce top, book matched master grade Big Leaf Maple Back and sides, 7-piece laminated maple neck with walnut center stripes, ebony fingerboard with abalone fleur-de-lis inlays, multi piece abalone fleur-de-lis inlays in the headstock, tailpiece, truss rod cover, bridge base, and heel cap, multi-ply wood body bindings, floating Kent Armstrong pickup, black pickguard with two knobs, gold hardware, natural finish, current mfg.
MSR $10,500

> Add $1,000 for 18 in. body. Add $1,000 for left-handed configuration.

ROYALE
- 6- or 7-string configuration, single smooth cutaway, 17 in. body, f-holes, Master Grade European Spruce top, book matched master grade European or Quilted Maple Back and sides, 7-piece laminated maple neck with walnut center stripes, ebony fingerboard with abalone fleur-de-lis inlays, multi piece abalone fleur-de-lis inlays in the headstock, tailpiece, truss rod cover, bridge base, and heel cap, multi-ply wood body bindings, floating Kent Armstrong pickup, black pickguard with two knobs, natural finish, current mfg.
MSR $18,000

> Add $1,000 for 18 in. body. Add $1,000 for left-handed configuration.

SAINT CHARLES AVENUE
- 6- or 7-string configuration, single Venetian cutaway, 15 in. body, f-holes, carved cedar top, mahogany back and sides, 1-piece mahogany neck, ebony fingerboard, tailpiece, truss rod cover, bridge base, and heel cap, single ply white body bindings, Kent Armstrong pickup, black pickguard with two knobs, gold hardware, natural finish, current mfg.
MSR $3,600

> Add $1,000 for left-handed configuration.

**Foster AT-5
courtesy Jimmy Foster**

ELECTRIC: SOLID BODY MODELS

The T Series models all feature basswood bodies, maple necks, ebony fingerboards, Armstrong humbucker pickup with split coil wiring, 25.5 in. scale, and volume and tone controls. The T 1 lists for $1,750. The T 3 has a bound curly maple top (list $1,950); and the T 5 has a bound highly figured maple top (list $2,250).

PERFORMER
- single cutaway Telecaster style, basswood body with a highly figured maple top, bolt-on figured maple neck, single Kent Armstrong humbucker pickup, 6-on-a-side tuners, two knobs, chrome hardware, available in Natural finish, current mfg.
MSR $2,900

Performer Custom - similar to the Performer, except has 5-ply body binding and fancy side purflings, current mfg.
MSR $3,300

FRAMUS

Instruments currently produced in Markneukirchen, Germany. Distributed by Warwick GmbH & Co. Music Equipment Kg of Markneukirchen, Germany. Instruments were previously produced in Germany from the late 1940s through the mid-1970s. In 1996, the trademark was reintroduced and is distributed by Dana B. Goods in the U.S.

When Frederick Wilfer returned to his home town of Walthersgrun at the end of World War II, he realized that the American-controlled Sudetenland area was soon to fall under control of the Russian forces. With the help of the Americans, Wilfer succeeded in resettling a number of violin makers from Schonbach to Franconia (later in the district of Erlangen). Between 1945 and 1947, Wilfer continued to find homes and employment for the Schonbach violin makers.

In 1946, Wilfer founded the Framus production company, the company name an acronym for Franconian Musical instruments. As the company established itself in 1946, Wilfer drew on the knowledge of his violin builder from Schonbach to produce a range of musical instruments including violins and cellos. The new Framus company expanded out of its first couple of production buildings, eventually building a new factory in Bubenreuth in 1955.

The first Framus electric guitars appeared in the 1950s. Due to the presence of American servicemen stationed there, the influence of rock 'n roll surfaced earlier in Germany than other European countries. As a result, German guitar builders had a headstart on answering the demand caused by the proliferation of pop groups during the 1960s. Furthermore, as the German production increased, they began exporting their guitars to other countries (including the U.S.). The Framus company stayed active in producing acoustic and electric guitars, and electric basses until the mid 1970s.

In the 1970s, increased competition and serious price undercutting from firms in the Asian market had a serious effect on established companies. Unfortunately, one aspect was to force a number of firms into bankruptcy - and Framus was one of those companies in 1975. However, Wilfer did have the opportunity to watch his son, Hans-Peter Wilfer, establish his own company in 1982 (see Warwick). Warwick's success allowed Hans-Peter to re-introduce the Framus trademark to the European musical market in 1996. In honor of his father Frederick, Hans-Peter chose to use the world famous Framus trademark when he began offering guitar models in 1996 (source: Hans Peter Wilfer, Warwick GmbH & Co. Music Equipment Kg; and Tony Bacon and Paul Day, *The Guru's Guitar Guide*).

Current Framus instruments (including the electric guitars, acoustics, and hand wired tube guitar amps) are produced at the Warwick facility. Currently, Framus instruments are available in England, Germany, Sweden, and Switzerland, and the United States by Dana B. Goods of Ventura, California.

GRADING	100% MINT	98% NEAR MINT	95% EXC+	90% EXC	80% VG+	70% VG	60% G

ELECTRIC (1946-1975 MFG.)

While the original Hollywood series was Gibson-influenced, the later Strato series of guitars were strikingly Fender-ish. However, the company did pioneer their own designs such as the Big 6 double neck model, the Melodie 9-string guitar, and the Billy Lorento signature model (see Bill Lawrence). Research still continues on early Framus models for upcoming editions of the *Blue Book of Electric Guitars*.

Current high quality solid body Framus models include the single cutaway arched top Panthera and double cutaway Diablo models. Both models feature the easily recognizable Framus headstock and 3-per-side tuners, good quality woods, pickups, and hardware. For further information regarding the Framus line of instruments, please contact the Framus company directly (see Trademark Index).

JAN AKKERMAN MODEL - single sharp hollow cutaway, two-piece bookmatched flamed maple top, single f-hole, flamed sycamore set neck, 24-fret ebony fingerboard with custom inlays, 3-per-side tuners, two humbucker pickups, two knobs (v, tone) and 6-way rotary switch, gold hardware, available in Black, Cherry Sunburst, or Vintage Sunburst finishes, mfg. mid-1970s.

	N/A	$900	$750	$650	$550	$475	$400

STRATO - offset double cutaway, several variations, one, two, or three pickups, bolt-on neck, tremolo, various finishes, mfg. early 1960s-1972.

	N/A	$450	$375	$325	$275	$225	$175

This model came in several variations. These variations include, pickups, string number, knobs, switches, colors, etc.

ELECTRIC (1996-CURRENT MFG.)

AZ1974 - single sharp hollow cutaway, two-piece flamed maple body, 2-piece bookmatched flamed maple top, single f-hole, flamed sycamore set neck, 22-fret ebony fingerboard with cross and diamond inlays, 3-per-side tuners, Framus Tunomatic bridge and stop tailpiece, two Seymour Duncan HH pickups, two knobs (v, tone) and 6-way rotary switch, gold hardware, available in Black, Cherry Sunburst, or Creme gloss finishes, current mfg.

MSR	$3,199		$2,400	$2,150	$1,950	$1,750	$1,600	$1,450	$1,300

This is based off of the Jan Akkerman model of the 1970s.

CAMARILLO CUSTOM - double offset cutaway, two-piece swamp ash body, 2-piece boomatched flame maple top, bolt-on ovangkol neck, 22-fret ebony fingerboard with cross and diamond inlay, 3-per-side tuners, Framus Tunomatic bridge and stop tailpiece, 2 Seymour Duncan HH pickups, two knobs (v, tone), three-way switch, chrome or gold hardware, available in Almond, Cherry, French Violet, Honey Violin, Natural Oil, Nirvana Black, Ocean Blue, or Sunburst Satin Oil finishes, current mfg.

MSR	$1,899		$1,425	$1,300	$1,150	$1,050	$950	$850	$750

DIABLO CUSTOM - double offset cutaway, two-piece swamp ash body, 2-piece boomatched flame maple top, bolt-on ovangkol neck, 22-fret ebony fingerboard with cross and diamond inlay, 3-per-side tuners, Wilkinson tremolo, 3 Seymour Duncan SSH pickups, two knobs (v, tone), five-way switch, chrome hardware, available in Almond, Cherry, French Violet, Honey Violin, Natural Oil, Nirvana Black, Ocean Blue, or Sunburst Satin Oil finishes, current mfg.

MSR	$1,999		$1,500	$1,350	$1,200	$1,100	$1,000	$900	$800

DIABLO PRO - double offset cutaway, two-piece swamp ash body, bolt-on ovangkol neck, 22-fret rosewood fingerboard with dot inlay, 3-per-side tuners, MOP celluloid pickguard, Wilkinson tremolo, 3 Seymour Duncan SSH pickups, two knobs (v, tone), five-way switch, chrome hardware, available in French Violet, Honey Violin, Natural Oil, Nirvana Black, or Ocean Blue Satin Oil finishes, current mfg.

MSR	$1,399		$1,050	$950	$850	$750	$675	$600	$525

Add $75 for French Violet, Honey Violin, Nirvana Black, or Ocean Blue Satin Oil finishes.

HOLLYWOOD CUSTOM - single cutaway Explorer/Charvel design, hollow Honduras mahogany body, two-piece bookmatched flamed maple top, two f-holes, wood body binding, bolt-on ovangkol neck, 22-fret ebony fingerboard with cross and diamond inlay, 3-per-side tuners, two MOP celluloid pickguards, Framus Bigsby tremolo bridge, 2 Seymour Duncan P-90 pickups, two knobs (v, tone), three-way switch, chrome hardware, available in Almond, Cherry, French Violet, Honey Violin, Natural Oil, Nirvana Black, Ocean Blue, or Sunburst Satin Oil finishes, current mfg.

MSR	$2,599		$1,950	$1,750	$1,550	$1,400	$1,250	$1,100	$950

PANTHERA CUSTOM - single cutaway, Honduras mahogany body, two-piece bookmatched flamed maple top, bolt-on ovangkol neck, 22-fret ebony fingerboard with cross and diamond inlay, 3-per-side tuners, one-piece fixed bridge, 2 Seymour Duncan HH pickups, two knobs (v, tone), three-way switch, chrome hardware, available in Almond, Cherry, French Violet, Honey Violin, Natural Oil, Nirvana Black, Ocean Blue, or Sunburst gloss finishes, current mfg.

MSR	$2,199		$1,650	$1,500	$1,350	$1,200	$1,075	$950	$850

PANTHERA PRO - single cutaway, Honduras mahogany body, two-piece flamed maple top, bolt-on ovangkol neck, 22-fret rosewood fingerboard with dot inlay, 3-per-side tuners, Framus Tunomatic bridge and stop tailpiece, 2 Seymour Duncan HH pickups, two knobs (v, tone), three-way switch, chrome hardware, available in French Violet, Honey Violin, Natural Oil, Nirvana Black, or Ocean Blue Satin Oil finishes, current mfg.

MSR	$1,599		$1,200	$1,050	$950	$850	$775	$700	$625

Add $75 for French Violet, Honey Violin, Nirvana Black, or Ocean Blue Satin Oil finishes.

PANTHERA STUDIO CUSTOM - single cutaway, Honduras mahogany body, two-piece bookmatched flamed maple top, bolt-on ovangkol neck, 22-fret ebony fingerboard with cross and diamond inlay, 3-per-side tuners, one-piece fixed bridge, 3 Seymour Duncan HSH pickups, three knobs (v, blend, tone), two switches, chrome hardware, available in Almond, Cherry, French Violet, Honey Violin, Natural Oil, Nirvana Black, Ocean Blue, or Sunburst gloss finishes, current mfg.

MSR	$2,399		$1,800	$1,600	$1,450	$1,300	$1,150	$1,000	$875

PANTHERA STUDIO PRO - single cutaway, Honduras mahogany body, two-piece flamed maple top, bolt-on ovangkol neck, 22-fret rosewood fingerboard with dot inlay, 3-per-side tuners, Framus Tunomatic bridge and stop tailpiece, 3 Seymour Duncan HSH pickups, three knobs (v, blend, tone), two switches, chrome hardware, available in French Violet, Honey Violin, Natural Oil, Nirvana Black, or Ocean Blue Satin Oil finishes, current mfg.

MSR	$1,799		$1,350	$1,200	$1,050	$925	$800	$725	$650

Add $75 for French Violet, Honey Violin, Nirvana Black, or Ocean Blue Satin Oil finishes.

GRADING	100% MINT	98% NEAR MINT	95% EXC+	90% EXC	80% VG+	70% VG	60% G

RENEGADE CUSTOM - single cutaway, two-piece swamp ash body, bolt-on ovangkol neck, 22-fret ebony fingerboard with cross and diamond inlay, 3-per-side tuners, one-piece fixed bridge, 2 Seymour Duncan HH pickups, two knobs (v, tone), three-way switch, chrome hardware, available in Almond, Cherry, French Violet, Honey Violin, Natural Oil, Nirvana Black, Ocean Blue, or Sunburst Satin Oil finishes, current mfg.

MSR	$1,899	$1,425	$1,300	$1,150	$1,050	$950	$850	$750

RENEGADE PRO - single cutaway, two-piece swamp ash body, bolt-on ovangkol neck, 22-fret rosewood fingerboard with dot inlay, 3-per-side tuners, STB bridge, 2 Seymour Duncan HH pickups, two knobs (v, tone), three-way switch, chrome hardware, available in French Violet, Honey Violin, Natural Oil, Nirvana Black, or Ocean Blue Satin Oil finishes, current mfg.

MSR	$1,299	$975	$875	$800	$700	$625	$550	$475

Add $75 for French Violet, Honey Violin, Nirvana Black, or Ocean Blue Satin Oil finishes.

TENNESSEE CUSTOM - single cutaway, hollow Honduras mahogany body, two-piece bookmatched flamed maple top, single f-hole, bolt-on ovangkol neck, 22-fret ebony fingerboard with cross and diamond inlay, 3-per-side tuners, MOP celluloid pickguard, Framus Tunomatic bridge and stop tailpiece, 2 Seymour Duncan HH pickups, two knobs (v, tone), three-way switch, chrome hardware, available in Almond, Cherry, French Violet, Honey Violin, Natural Oil, Nirvana Black, Ocean Blue, or Sunburst Satin Oil finishes, current mfg.

MSR	$2,599	$1,950	$1,750	$1,550	$1,400	$1,250	$1,100	$950

TENNESSEE PRO - single cutaway, hollow Honduras mahogany body, two-piece bookmatched flamed maple top, single f-hole, bolt-on ovangkol neck, 22-fret rosewood fingerboard with dot inlay, 3-per-side tuners, MOP celluloid pickguard, Framus Tunomatic bridge and stop tailpiece, 2 Seymour Duncan HH pickups, two knobs (v, tone), three-way switch, chrome hardware, available in French Violet, Honey Violin, Natural Oil, Nirvana Black, or Ocean Blue Satin Oil finishes, current mfg.

MSR	$1,999	$1,500	$1,350	$1,200	$1,100	$1,00	$900	$800

Framus Strato
courtesy John Beeson
The Music Shoppe

FRANCONIA

Instruments previously built in Japan between 1980-85.

The Franconina trademark was a brand name used by a UK importer. The guitars were generally entry level to mid-quality copies of American designs (source: Tony Bacon and Paul Day, *The Guru's Guitar Guide*).

FREDDY´S FRETS

Instruments currently built in Welland (Ontario), Canada.

Luthier Freddy Gabrsek is currently offfering a number of handcrafted acoustic and electric guitar models. The Gabrsek Jumbo Steel String is a concert quality acoustic guitar made from the finest materials. (Priced from $3,500). Electric guitars include the Deluxe Model (last MSR $2,450) featuring mahogany set neck, mahogany body, spectacularly figured maple top with the highest quality hardware. The Standard Model (last MSR $1,950) features a swamp ash or alder body with a bolt-on quartered maple neck. Models currently produced are all custom order and every part of the guitar can be chosen by the customer. For further information regarding specifications and complete pricing, contact Freddy´s Frets directly (see Trademark Index).

FRENZ

Instruments previously built in Columbus, OH in the late 1990s-early 2000s.

Frenz guitars are higher-end models with several features. Frenz worked directly with the customer specifying the guitar model to insure the proper custom built guitar.

ELECTRIC

The Rapier CT 26 (last MSR was $2,200) is a radical Strat-shaped model with either a mahogany or padauk carved top body, set-in maple neck, 26-fret rosewood fingerboard, and single coil/humbucker pickups. Frenz also built the custom-built Ultimate Custom, which allows the customer choice of scale length, number of frets (up to 40), and any combination of suitable materials. "Your Design or Ours" was Frenz´ motto (price quote is based on factors such as design, materials, and hardware).

ELECTRIC BASS

The Morpheus bass features a neck-through construction, 34 in., 35 in., or 36 in. scale, 2 through 12-string configurations, and choice of woods and electronics. Headless models are offered in 4-, 5-, and 6-string configurations.

FRESHER

Instruments previously produced in Japan from the late 1970s to the early 1980s.

Fresher solid body and semi-hollow body guitars were generally medium quality copies of American designs. However, viewing the "Fresher" logo on a strat-style guitar from a distance will make you check your eyesight - and finding a Fresher "Straighter" with built-in effects will make you check your blood pressure! (source: Michael Wright, *Guitar Stories,* Volume One). Fesher guitars were never imported into the U.S., however guitars do show up on the second-hand market and at guitar shows. Guitars are typically priced between $150 and $300 depending upon the features. The Straighter model may bring $250 - $350.

FRESHMAN

Instruments previously built in Japan in the mid-1960s.

As an inexpensive, entry level guitar, the Freshman trademark is quite apt, however, a Senior, it isn't. In fact, it's not even close to a Sophomore (source: Tony Bacon and Paul Day, *The Guru's Guitar Guide*). These guitars sold new for under $100 and are worth even less today.

FRITZ BROTHERS

Instruments currently built in Albion, CA. Previously built in Mobile, AL circa 1988.

Luthier Roger Fritz met Marc Fisher in Nashville in 1987. Together with guitarist Roy Buchanan they formed Fritz Brothers guitars, which was relocated to Alabama a year later. During 1988, the Fritz Brothers began building the Roy Buchanan Bluesmaster model; Buchanan died later that year (portion of the sales goes to Buchanan's estate) (source: Tom Wheeler, *American Guitars*). Roger is now making guitars and other instruments out of his new shop in Albion, California.

FRONTIER

Instruments previously produced in Japan during the early 1980s.

Frontier guitars feature good quality original designs as well as copies of American designs. One puzzling model is the signature model of Norris Fant. Guitar collectors or Fan club members who wish to enlighten us on Mr. Fant are invited to write to the *Blue Book of Electric Guitars* (source: Tony Bacon and Paul Day, *The Guru's Guitar Guide*).

FRONTLINE

Instruments previously produced in Korea in the late 1980s.

Guitars under this trademark are medium quality vaguely Fender-ish solid body designs (source: Tony Bacon and Paul Day, *The Guru's Guitar Guide*).

FRUDUA GUITAR WORKS

Instruments currently built in Imola, Italy.

The Frudua Guitar Works is currently offering a number of Strat-style electric guitars featuring alder bodies and figured maple tops (as well as lacewood bodies). Frudua Guitar Works models also feature high quality pickups and hardware. Most Frudua bass models feature a Jazz Bass-style body, graphite-reinforced wood necks, laminated maple/purpleheart necks or hard rock maple necks, and figured maple or spruce tops. However, they also offer their own innovative designs. For further information regarding specifications and pricing, contact the Frudua Guitar Works directly (see Trademark Index).

FRYE

Instruments previously built in Green Bay, WI from 1987-late 1990s.

Luthier/repairman Ben Frye has been repairing guitars in the Green Bay area for almost 12 years, and building custom guitars for the past 10 years. Frye estimates that he has built a total of 700 guitars to date (100 built in the last year), and looks forward to a higher production amount this year.

Frye guitars are constructed at The String Instrument Workshop, a shop Ben shares with his father. Lawrence Frye, a repairman and luthier for the past 25 years, was the former teacher at Redwing College's Violin and Guitar Making course between 1974 to 1980. The Workshop, a former bar restored to its turn-of-the-century appearance in Green Bay's downtown area, is the central area to the Fryes' stringed instrument repair.

ELECTRIC

Ben Frye attended the Redwing College Guitar course in 1994, but grew up learning and experimenting under his father's supervision. Frye's guitar models feature bolt-on neck construction, Red Rhodes' Velvet Hammer or Lindy Fralin pickups, different electronic packages and hardware, and other customer specified options. Frye turns the necks, and carves and routs out the guitar bodies with templates and power tools instead of using CNC machines. The El Pique (last MSR was $1,300) is a double cutaway, strat-style solid body with a 25.5 in. scale. A single cutaway model, named the Over Easy (last MSR was $1,200 and up) is closer to a Tele-influenced model. The Over Easy is also offered with a carved maple top as the Extra Crispy model (last MSR was $1,800 and up), or as the Scully hollowbody (last MSR was $1,200). The Scully (named after the first person who ordered one, not the X-Files character) is fully hollow, with a solid back/sides and carved out top. Scully models feature a single f-hole, and are constructed of solid spruce, redwood, or cedar. The Epiphany (last MSR was $1,700) is a wide/thin (2 in. body depth) electric/acoustic model with a "No Tension Top," and offset soundhole. The Epiphany model has a bound top, 3-per-side tuners, and Fishman Matrix pickup. Frye also offers a double cutaway solid body named the Top Tone, that features a 24.75 in. scale and a 3-per-side headstock design (last MSR starting at $1,200). The Top Tone body shape is reminiscent of a LP Junior or a Rickenbacker. The Top Tone Ultra (last MSR was $1,900) has a bird's-eye maple neck, ebony fingerboard, wood binding, abalone inlay, and exotic wood top. Any guitar model could be converted to a 30 in. scale Baritone for an additional $250. Frye also offered his models with hollowed out tone chambers which accentuate acoustic properties (dubbed Fat Free) for an extra $100.

ELECTRIC BASS

Frye offered a bolt-on bass model in 4- or 5-string configurations, as well as a set neck version in 4, 5, and 6-string models. The Big Ben bass has a smaller, balanced offset waist and extended bass horn. Models range in last MSR price from $1,400 to $1,500 (bolt-on), and $1,600 to $2,000 for the set neck models. The options range from wood and pickup types, as well as others.

FULLERTON

Instruments currently produced in Asia since 2003. Fullerton is distributed by NHF Musical Merchandise, Inc. in Pennsauken, NJ.

Fullerton are another brand name labeled on guitars by the Aria company. The Fullertone line are based off of popular American designs including the Stratocaster, Les Paul, Telecaster, ES-5, ES-335, Jazz Bass, and Precision Bass. Guitars are produced overseas and adjusted in the USA shop for final inspection. Prices are very competitive with most guitars retailing between $200 and $400. However, the actual selling price is much lower. For more information contact the Aria company directly (see Trademark Index).

FURY

Instruments currently built in Saskatoon (Saskatchewan), Canada since 1962.

Glenn McDougal was born in Wadena (Saskatchewan), Canada on February 13, 1937. In the mid-to-late 50s McDougal played guitar in a rock and roll band called Blue Cadillac which toured Canada and the United States. In 1958, a car accident ended McDougal's career as a player and he turned to guitar design.

The Fury Guitar Company was founded in 1962. The purpose of the new company was to expand upon the design of specific components that would improve both sound and performance. The objective was to create a distinctive character that would set Fury apart from other makes, yet stay within the boundaries of traditional guitar design. During 1962, McDougal launched the Fireball, the first model of his new company.

Throughout the history of the company, numerous cutting edge inventions emerged, and continue today, helping to make Fury instruments unique. The decision was made early on to keep the company small, so quality could always be assured. The company is still fully owned and operated by Glenn and Janet McDougall.

Now in its 42th year of operation, Fury is Canada's oldest electric guitar manufacturer, and continues to design and develop instruments with advanced features, making their products desirable to serious players. Fury Guitars introduced solid body 6-string and 12-string guitars, as well as doubleneck models, hollow bodies, and electric bass throughout the 1960s. A new factory was built in the mid 1970s, and the company experienced a major breakthrough in the early 1980s with the development of their ZP pickup.

In 1998, Fury Guitars made their first U.S. show "debut" at the January NAMM industry show. In addition to their new Tornado Bass, McDougall also showcased his limited edition 35th Anniversary Fireball guitar model (source: Sanford Greve, Fury Historian).

GENERAL INFORMATION

Currently, Fury makes 4 models of 6-strings, a 12-string, baritone and a bass with an optional drop D bridge. Since 1962 McDougal has built over 7,000 guitars and basses. 8 models are still in production, and these high quality Fury guitars are still produced in Saskatoon, Canada.

Add $75 for a colored neck. Add $75 for a colored headstock. Add $100 for a metallic pickguard. Add $100 for a Transparent or Natural Blonde finish. Add $125 for a moderately flamed maple body. Add $250 for a highly flamed maple body. Add $325 for a 24kt triple plated gold hardware.

ELECTRIC: EARLY MODELS

20TH CENTURY ARTIST - double cutaway hollowbody 6-string, Honduras mahogany back and sides carved from one solid piece, maple back with tuned reflex chamber, 3-piece rock maple neck with rosewood overlay on angled headstock, 2 stylized f-holes, 22-fret Brazilian rosewood fingerboard with small dot markers on the bass side, 23.75 in. scale length, 3-per-side Grover Roto-matic tuners, two angled black Fury piggyback humbucking pickups, Fury vibrato with pop-out lever, black pinline pickguard, master volume/2 tone controls, 3-position toggle switch, available in a wide variety of lacquer finishes, including Tobacco Sunburst, Cherry Red, Blonde, or White, mfg. 1968-1989.

CONCORD - double cutaway hollowbody 6-string, Honduras mahogany back and sides carved from one solid piece, maple back with tuned reflex chamber, 3-piece maple neck with rosewood overlay on angled headstock, 2 stylized f-holes, 22-fret African ebony fingerboard with small dot markers on bass side, 23.75 in. or 25 in. scale length, 3-per-side Grover Roto-matic tuners, two angled black Fury piggyback humbucker pickups, black pinline pickguard, 2 volume/2 tone controls, 3-position toggle switch, Fury trapeze tailpiece, available in a wide variety of lacquer finishes, including Tobacco Sunburst and Blonde, mfg. 1974-1988.

F12 - double rounded cut-a-way 12-string, solid Honduras mahogany body, rock maple neck, 20-fret maple or Brazilian rosewood fingerboard with small dot markers on bass side, 25.064 in. scale length, 6-per-side Kluson Deluxe tuners, two Fury piggyback humbucker pickups, master volume/master tone controls, 3-position toggle switch, available in a wide variety of lacquer finishes, including Tobacco Sunburst and Cherry Red, mfg. 1966-1992.

F22 - double cutaway 6-string, solid Honduras mahogany body, maple neck, 22-fret maple or Brazilian rosewood fingerboard with small dot markers on bass side, 25.064 in. scale length, 3-per-side Kluson Deluxe tuners, 2 black Fury piggyback humbucking pickups (early models had white pickups), 2 volume/1 tone controls, tone bypass switch, 3-position toggle switch, available in a wide variety of lacquer finishes, including Cherry Red and California Red, mfg. 1967-1981.

ELECTRIC: BANDIT SERIES

BANDIT - single rounded cutaway 6-string, solid basswood or Honduras mahogany body, maple neck, 22-fret Brazilian rosewood fingerboard with small dot markers on bass side, 25.064 in. scale length, 3-per-side Kluson tuners, 2 black Fury single coil pickups, master volume/master tone controls, 3-position toggle switch, available in a wide variety of lacquer finishes, mfg. 1967-1971.

BANDIT REISSUE (3S, 2H, HSS) - single rounded cutaway body, 6-string, maple body/neck, 22-fret maple or pau ferro fingerboard with small dot markers on bass side, 25.064 in. scale length, 6-in-a-line grover mini roto-matic tuners, 3 Fury ZP single coil pickups, master volume/tone controls, 3-position level switch, and rim jack, available in a wide variety of lacquer finishes, mfg. 1999-present.

MSR   **$1,395 & Up**

BBM - similar to the BBM (2S), except has two ZP5S single coil pickups/ZP20 bridge humbucker pickup, 5-position lever switch, coil tap switch, master volume control, mfg.1985-present.

MSR   **$1,550 & Up**

BBM 12 12-STRING - similar to the BBM (2S), except features two Fury piggyback humbucker pickups, Fury high-mass 12-string bridge, 6-per-side Schaller mini-tuners, price includes hard case, mfg. 1989-present.

MSR   **$1,650 & Up**

ELECTRIC: FIREBALL SERIES

The original Fireball model was built from 1963 to 1966. In 1990, Fury began offering the Fireball Reissue model, based on the original design.

FIREBALL - offset double cutaway Honduras mahogany body, maple neck, 20-fret rosewood fingerboard with pearl block inlays, 25.064 in. scale length, 6-in-line Kluson tuners, 2 white Fury single coil pickups, black pinline pickguard, volume control on bass side upper bout, 2 tone controls, tone bypass switch, 3-position toggle switch, available in a wide variety of DuPont Duco lacquer finishes, mfg. 1962-66.

FIREBALL (CURRENT MFG.) - offset rounded double cutaway 6-string, solid soft maple body with rock maple center core, rock maple neck, 22-fret maple or pau ferro fingerboard with small dot markers on bass side, 25.064 in. scale length, 6-in-line Schaller mini-tuners, Fury ZP8 neck and ZP20's bridge humbucker pickups, master volume and tone control, rim-mount jack, 2 coil tap switches, 3-position toggle switch, no pickguard, Fury high-mass bridge/tailpiece or high-mass vibrato, available in a wide variety of lacquer finishes, price includes hard case, mfg. 1989-present.

   MSR   **$1,550 & Up**

FIREBALL BARITONE - offset rounded double cutaway 6-string baritone guitar tuned A to A (a fifth below standard pitch), solid soft maple body with rock maple center core, rock maple neck, 22-fret maple or pau ferro fingerboard with small dot markers on bass side, 29.858 in. scale length, 4+2 Schaller mini-tuners, Fury ZP8 neck and ZP20's bridge humbucker pickups, master volume & tone control, 2 coil tap switches, 3-position toggle switch, no pickguard, Fury high-mass bridge/tailpiece, available in a wide variety of lacquer finishes, price includes hard case, mfg. 1984-present.

   MSR   **$1,550 & Up**

ELECTRIC BASS MODELS

ANTHEM BASS - double cutaway 4-string bass, soft solid maple body with rock maple center core, 24-fret maple or pau ferro fingerboard, 31.640 in. scale length, 4-in-line Grover Titan tuners, Fury ZP9B neck and ZP11B bridge humbucker pickups, two volume and one master tone control, 3-position toggle switch, Fury high-mass bridge or Drop-D bridge, available in a wide variety of lacquer finishes, mfg. 1988-1997.

TORNADO BASS - same as Anthem Bass, except with deep cutaway on treble side allowing easy access to 24th fret, master volume/master tone controls, 3-position coil tap switch (for single, humbucker, and modified humbucker tones) Fury ZP9B neck pickup, and Fury ZP6B bridge pickup, Hipshot Ultra light tuners and rim-mount jack, current mfg.

   MSR   **$1,885 & Up**

LS4 BASS - double cutaway with long sharp horns, 4-string fretted or fretless, solid Honduras mahogany body, maple neck, 20-fret maple or Brazilian rosewood fingerboard, maple fret inlays on fretless model, 31.625 in. scale length, stepped upright-style headstock with 4-in-line Kluson tuners, 1 Fury piggyback humbucking pickup (later models available with 2 pickups), master volume/master tone controls, available in a wide variety of lacquer finishes, the most popular being Whiskey, White, and Midnight Green, mfg. 1967-1988.

FUTURAMA

Some guitars may also carry the trademark of Grazioso. Instruments previosuly built in Czechoslovakia, then Sweden, and finally in Japan between 1958 and 1967.

The Futurama trademark is the brand name of the British importer/distributor Selmer (UK). However, you can also find the Grazioso trademark on some of the real early Czech-built instruments. Production of this line of solid body guitars continued in Eastern Europe until supplanted by some strat-styled models built by Hagstrom in Sweden. Finally, the Futurama world tour ended on production of small-body model versions built in Japan (source: Tony Bacon, *The Ultimate Guitar Book*).

Section G

G & L

Instruments currently produced in Fullerton, CA since 1980. Distributed by BBE Sound of Huntington Beach, CA.

In the late 1970s, the controlling interest at (pre-Ernie Ball) Music Man was making offers to purchase Leo Fender's CLF guitar production facility. Fender and George Fullerton turned down repeated offers, and Music Man began cutting production orders. The controversy settled as CLF Research stopped manufacturing instruments for Music Man in late 1979. In April of 1980, Fender and Fullerton started a new company, G & L (for George & Leo), to continue producing Leo Fender's ongoing design ideas and models. As Fender once again handled R & D in his office/workshop, George Fullerton maintained production management and Dale Hyatt (another ex-Fender company man) was in charge of administrative management and sales.

Between 1980 and 1991, Leo Fender continued to refine his vision of his Fender guitar. Where other people saw individual models, Fender saw an ongoing project that kept refining his ideas about the electric guitar. Clarence L. Fender passed away in March, 1991. As researcher/collector Paul Bechtoldt has noted, "during the eleven years that Fender owned G & L, less than 27,000 guitars were produced. That is less than most companies make in half a year! With monthly production totals less than 800, Leo was making more guitars at his old company in the 1950s than at G & L!"

The G & L company was purchased on December 5, 1991, by John McLaren of BBE Sound, and continues to produce the affordable, quality solid body guitars based on Leo Fender's designs. Leo's wife, Phyllis, remains as Honorary Chairman of G & L, and George Fullerton remains as a permanent consultant. In 1998, G & L opened their Custom Creations Department, a custom shop area for the company (source: Paul Bechtoldt, G&L: *Leo's Legacy*).

GRADING	100% MINT	98% NEAR MINT	95% EXC+	90% EXC	80% VG+	70% VG	60% G

**G & L ASAT
courtesy John Beeson
The Music Shoppe**

PRODUCTION MODEL & GENERAL INFORMATION

In addition to the G & L bridges, both the Kahler tremolo system (1984-1986) and the Wilkinson roller nut were options on certain models. In 1998, G & L instruments underwent a major change. All models are now produced with a 4-bolt neck-plate, and the serial numbers are applied decals. Unless otherwise listed, G & L guitars are available with 22-fret maple fingerboard with black dot inlay or rosewood fingerboard with pearl dot inlay. Current models are available in left-handed configurations at no extra charge. The following listed models are available in these **Standard** finishes: Belair Green, Black, Black Silver Swirl (disc.), Blue Swirl (disc.), Candy Apple Red, Cherryburst, Cobalt Blue, Electric Blue, Emerald Blue, Fullerton Red, Gold Metallic, Gold Metallicburst (disc.), Green Swirl (disc.), Lake Placid Blue, Pearl White (new 1998), Red Swirl (disc.), Silver Metallic, Sparkle Black (disc.), Sparkle Purple (disc.), Sparkle Red (disc.), Sunburst, Three-Tone Sunburst, Tobacco Sunburst, Two-Tone Sunburst, Vintage White, and White. G & L also offers a number of **Premier** finishes on certain models. These finishes include: Blonde, Blue Burst, Butterscotch Blonde, Clear Blue, Clear Forest Green, Clear Orange, Clear Red, Honey, Honeyburst, Natural Ash, Natural Satin, and Red Burst. Premier finishes are also available on the Legacy, ASAT, and ASAT Special (contact dealer for availability). **Metal Flake** finishes include, Blue Metal Flake, Gold Metal Flake, Green Metal Flake, Red Metal Flake, and Silver Metal Flake.

ELECTRIC: ASAT SERIES

In 1998, Bigsby tremolos became optional on ASAT models: **ASAT Special**, **ASAT Deluxe**, **ASAT Semi-Hollow**, and **ASAT Deluxe Semi-Hollow**.

ASAT - single cutaway maple body, bolt-on maple neck, 22-fret maple or rosewood fingerboard, 25.5 in. scale, black pickguard, fixed bridge with locking saddles, 6-on-a-side tuners, black hardware, 2 single coil pickups, volume/tone control, 3-position switch, mfg. 1986-1998.

	$1,000	$850	$750	$650	$550	$450	$350

Last MSR was $1,300.

In 1992, alder body replaced maple body.

ASAT III - similar to ASAT, except has three magnetic field single coil pickups, chrome hardware, 3-ply white pickguard, and 5-position switch, mfg. 1995-98.

	$1,000	$850	$750	$650	$550	$450	$350

Last MSR was $1,300.

ASAT CLASSIC - similar to ASAT, except has ash body, white pickguard, vintage style fixed bridge, 3-ply white pickguard, chrome hardware, mfg. 1990-present.

MSR	$1,550		$1,200	$1,050	$900	$775	$650	$550	$450

This model is currently available in Premier and Standard finishes.

ASAT Bound Classic - similar to ASAT, except has bound ash body, white pickguard, mfg. 1994-98.

	N/A	$900	$750	$650	$575	$500	$425

Last MSR was $900.

ASAT Classic Custom - similar to ASAT, except has bookmatched swamp ash top, alder body, top wood binding, 2 magnetic field single coil pickups, vintage style fixed bridge, chrome hardware, and pearl pickguard, mfg. 1995-98, reintroduced 2002-and still produced.

MSR	$1,780		$1,375	$1,150	$1,000	$850	$750	$650	$550

**G & L ASAT Classic
courtesy George McGuire**

GRADING	100% MINT	98% NEAR MINT	95% EXC+	90% EXC	80% VG+	70% VG	60% G

ASAT Classic "Blues Boy" - similar to ASAT, has alder body on Standard finishes and all solid finishes, swamp ash on all Premier finishes, hard rock maple neck with rosewood or maple fingerboard, dot position markers, Schaller non-locking tuners, traditional "Boxed" steel bridge with six saddles, Seymour Duncan "Seth Lover" 1955 humbucker neck pickup and G&L Magnetic Field single coil pickup, 1 volume/1 tone control, 3-way switch, available in Standard and Premier finishes, current mfg.

ASAT SPECIAL DELUXE - similar to ASAT, has maple top on American Tilla back, hard rock maple neck with rosewood or maple fingerboard, dot position markers, 2 large rectangular G&L Magnetic Field high output single coil pickups, Schaller non-locking tuners, G&L patented "Saddle Lock" fixed bridge, 1 volume/1 tone control, 3-way switch, rear mounted controls, no pickguard, chrome hardware, available in Standard finishes, molded hard case included, current mfg.

ASAT DELUXE - similar to ASAT, except has bound flamed maple top, mahogany body, 2 Seymour Duncan humbuckers, rear loaded controls, no pickguard, chrome hardware, and fixed bridge with saddle lock, mfg. 1995-present.

MSR	$1,950	$1,450	$1,100	$875	$725	$650	$595	$525

This model is currently available in See-Through finishes only, and comes with deluxe Tolex case.

ASAT SPECIAL - similar to ASAT, except has 3-ply white pickguard, and chrome hardware, mfg. 1994-present.

MSR	$1,300	$1,050	$900	$775	$660	$550	$435	$325

ASAT JUNIOR LIMITED EDITION - single cutaway chambered (semi-hollow) mahogany body, mahogany neck, 22-fret ebony fingerboard, black pickguard, Tune-O-Matic bridge/stop tailpiece, 6-on-a-side tuners, chrome hardware, 2 black Custom ASAT Special single coil pickups, volume/tone control, 3-way toggle switch, mfg. 1998-99.

	$1,350	$1,100	$950	$825	$700	$600	$500

Last MSR was $1,950.

Only 250 instruments are scheduled in this Limited Edition.

ASAT SEMI-HOLLOW - single cutaway swamp ash body with 2 voice chambers (semi-hollow), f-hole, bolt-on maple neck, 22-fret maple or rosewood fingerboard, 25.5 in. scale, pearl (black, white, tortoiseshell, or vintage) pickguard, fixed bridge with locking saddles, 6-on-a-side tuners, chrome hardware, 2 magnetic field single coil pickups, volume/tone control, 3-position switch, controls mounted on metal plate, mfg. 1997-present.

MSR	$1,450	$1,025	$875	$775	$670	$570	$465	$365

This model is currently available in Premier and Standard finishes. All three semi-hollow guitar models are available with or without the f-hole.

ASAT Classic Semi-Hollow - similar to the ASAT semi-hollow, except features Schaller vintage-style fixed bridge, bird's-eye maple neck, mfg. 1997-present.

MSR	$1,450	$1,025	$875	$775	$670	$570	$465	$365

ASAT Classic "Blues Boy" Semi-Hollow - similar to ASAT Classic semi-hollow, has swamp ash body with twin Voice Chambers, hard rock maple neck with roswood or maple fingerboard, dot position markers, Schaller non-locking tuners, Traditional "Boxed" steel bridge with six saddles, 3-way switch, 1 volume/1 tone control, chrome hardware, 3-ply black or white pickguard, with or without f-hole, available in Standard and Premier finishes, current mfg.

ASAT Deluxe Semi-Hollow - similar to the ASAT semi-hollow, except bound mahogany body, curly maple top, features G & L fixed bridge, 2 Seymour Duncan humbuckers, rear-loaded controls, mfg. 1997-present.

MSR	$1,950	$1,350	$1,175	$1,050	$900	$770	$635	$500

This model is currently available in See-Through finishes only, and comes with deluxe Tolex case.

ASAT S 3 - single cutaway swamp ash or alder body, hard rock maple neck with rosewood or maple fingerboard, 22 frets, Schaller locking tuners, G&L "Saddle Lock" fixed bridge, volume and tone controls, five-way pickup selector, three large rectangular G&L Magnetic Field high output single coil pickups, chrome hardware, three-ply white pickguard, available in Standard and Premiere finishes, G&L molded hard case included, mfg. 1998-2000.

	$1,050	$900	$775	$650	$550	$450	$350

Last MSR was $1,500.

ASAT Z 3 - single cutaway swamp ash or alder body, bolt-on hard rock maple neck, 22-fret maple or rosewood fingerboard, 25.5 in. scale, pearl pickguard, fixed bridge with locking saddles, 6-on-a-side Schaller tuners, chrome hardware, 3 "Z-Coil" magnetic field single coil pickups, volume/tone control, 5-position switch, controls mounted on metal plate, mfg. 1998-present.

MSR	$2,050	$1,550	$1,350	$1,200	$1,050	$900	$750	$600

This model is available in Premier or Standard Finishes. Black, White, Tortoiseshell, or Creme pickguards are optional.

ASAT Z 3 Semi-Hollow - similar to the ASAT Z 3, except features with 2 voice chambers (semi-hollow), f-hole, mfg. 1998-present.

MSR	$1,700	$1,200	$1,045	$930	$790	$665	$545	$425

ELECTRIC: BROADCASTER SERIES

BROADCASTER - single cutaway alder body, black pickguard, bolt-on maple neck, fixed bridge with locking saddles, body color matching peghead, 6-on-a-side tuners, black hardware, 2 single coil pickups, volume/tone control, 3-position switch, available in Black finish, mfg. 1985-86.

MAPLE FB	N/A	$2,000	$1,750	$1,500	$1,200	$950	$700
EBONY FB	N/A	$1,800	$1,600	$1,400	$1,100	$900	$650

Last MSR was $706.

A Certificate of Authenticity was issued with each instrument. This model had an optional ebony fingerboard with pearl dot inlay. 42 of these instruments have double locking Kahler vibratos. Two of these instruments are left handed. These instruments returned as an embellishment to Leo Fender's original Telecaster design. In 1948, Leo Fender designed a guitar, named it the Broadcaster, and put it into production. After shipping a number of instruments, he was notified that another company had the rights to the name. Fender then changed the Broadcaster to the Telecaster, and the rest is solid body guitar history. In 1985, believing that the Broadcaster name had been abandoned, Fender once again named a production model the Broadcaster. Once again, another company stepped in and informed G & L that the Broadcaster name was taken. Leo's policy was to honor all trademarks, and decided to cease using the Broadcaster name within a reasonable amount of time (and after a reasonable number of guitars were sold!). G & L produced this instrument for one year, with all instruments being signed and dated by Leo in the neck pocket of the body. Broadcasters carry their own unique serial number prefix (BC). G & L decided to manufacture a limited number of instruments. The total number produced was 869. Of these, 308 have maple fingerboards. In late 1986, the Broadcaster was renamed the ASAT.

GRADING	100% MINT	98% NEAR MINT	95% EXC+	90% EXC	80% VG+	70% VG	60% G

**G & L ASAT Special
courtesy G & L**

ELECTRIC: CAVALIER SERIES

CAVALIER - offset double cutaway ash body, bolt-on maple neck, 25.5 in. scale, black pickguard, standard vibrato, 6-on-a-side tuners, chrome hardware, 2 slanted humbucker pickups, 1 volume/2 tone control, 5-position switch, mfg. 1983-86.

	N/A	$850	$725	$600	$500	$400	$300

It is estimated that 1,400 Cavaliers were produced.

ELECTRIC: CLIMAX SERIES

CLIMAX - offset double cutaway ash body, bolt-on maple neck, double locking vibrato, 6-on-a-side tuners, black hardware, 2 single coil/humbucker pickups, volume/tone control, 5-position switch, mfg. 1993-95.

	N/A	$800	$700	$625	$550	$475	$400

Last MSR was $1,150.

CLIMAX PLUS - similar to Climax, except has humbucker/single coil/humbucker pickups, mfg. 1993-95.

	N/A	$900	$800	$700	$600	$525	$450

Last MSR was $1,250.

CLIMAX XL - similar to Climax, except has 2 humbucker pickups, 3-position switch, mfg. 1993-95.

	N/A	$850	$750	$675	$600	$525	$450

Last MSR was $1,180.

ELECTRIC: COMANCHE SERIES

COMANCHE V - offset double cutaway maple body, black pickguard, bolt-on maple neck, 22-fret maple fingerboard with black dot inlay, standard vibrato, 6-on-a-side tuners, chrome hardware, 3 Z-shaped single coil pickups, volume/2 tone controls, 5-position switch, available in Black, Blonde, Cherryburst and Natural finishes, mfg. 1990-91.

	N/A	$950	$825	$725	$625	$550	$475

Last MSR was $1,325.

Add $50 for Leo Fender vibrato.

This model also had an optional ebony fingerboard with pearl dot inlays.

Comanche VI - similar to Comanche V, except has 6 mini switches, not the 5-position switch, mfg. 1990-91.

	N/A	$1,100	$950	$850	$750	$650	$550

Last MSR was $1,325.

Add $50 for Leo Fender vibrato.

The six mini switches offered over 40 different pickup/tone combinations.

COMANCHE REISSUE - offset double cutaway swamp ash or alder body, bolt-on hard rock maple neck, 22-fret maple or rosewood fingerboard with dot inlay, Dual Fulcrum vibrato, 3-ply pickguard, 6-on-a-side Schaller locking tuners, chrome hardware, 3 Z-Coil magnetic field single coil pickups, volume/tone controls, 5-position switch, mini-toggle switch, mfg. 1998-present.

MSR	$2,200	$1,650	$1,450	$1,250	$1,100	$950	$800	$650

This model is available with Premium and Standard finishes.

ELECTRIC: COMMEMORATIVE SERIES

COMMEMORATIVE - single cutaway maple body, bolt-on maple neck, 22-fret maple fingerboard with black dot inlays, 25.5 in. scale, white pickguard, Leo Fender/1909-1991 with rose inlay on upper bass bout, vintage style bridge, 6-on-a-side tuners, gold hardware, 2 single coil pickups, volume/tone control, 3-position switch, mfg. 1992-97.

	N/A	$2,500	$2,100	$1,800	$1,550	$1,300	$1,100

Last MSR was $3,200.

ELECTRIC: F-100 SERIES

The F-100 series was the first model offered from the G & L company in 1980. The only difference between a model I and a model II is the radius of the fretboard (7.5 in. versus 12 in.).

F-100-I - offset double cutaway mahogany body, bolt-on maple neck, 22-fret maple fingerboard (12 in. radius) with black dot inlay, fixed bridge, 6-on-a-side tuners, chrome hardware, 2 humbucker pickups, volume/tone control, 3-position selector switch, available in Natural or Sunburst finishes, mfg. 1980-85.

	N/A	$750	$675	$600	$525	$450	$375

This model was available with a G & L vibrato. This model may have an ash, maple, or mahogany body, and a maple or ebony fingerboard.

F-100-IE - similar to the F-100-I, except has on-board preamp and additional coil tap/preamp switches, mfg. 1980-85.

	N/A	$800	$725	$650	$575	$500	$425

**G & L Comanche
courtesy Buffalo Bros.
Guitars**

GRADING	100% MINT	98% NEAR MINT	95% EXC+	90% EXC	80% VG+	70% VG	60% G

F-100-II - similar to the F-100-I, except has a 7.5 in. radius fretboard, mfg. 1980-85.

	N/A	$750	$675	$600	$525	$450	$400

F-100-IIE - similar to the F-100-II, except has on-board preamp and additional coil tap/preamp switches, mfg. 1980-85.

	N/A	$800	$725	$650	$575	$500	$425

ELECTRIC: G-200 SERIES

G-200 - offset double cutaway mahogany body, bolt-on maple neck, 22-fret maple fingerboard with black dot inlay, 24.75 in. scale, fixed bridge, 6-on-a-side tuners, chrome hardware, 2 humbucker pickups, 2 volume/2 tone controls and jack mounted on black plate on lower bout, 3-position selector switch, available in Natural or Sunburst finishes, mfg. 1981-82.

	N/A	$1,000	$850	$750	$650	$550	$450

It is estimated that around 200 instruments were produced. Between 12 and 20 of the later instruments have rear loaded controls. This model was also available with an ebony fingerboard with pearl dot inlays.

ELECTRIC: GEORGE FULLERTON SIGNATURE MODEL

GEORGE FULLERTON SIGNATURE MODEL - offset double cutaway maple body, bolt-on maple neck, 22-fret maple fingerboard with black dot inlay, single ply white pickguard, standard vibrato, 6-on-a-side tuners, chrome hardware, 3 G & L vintage alnico single coil pickups, 1 volume/2 tone controls, 5-position selector switch, mfg. 1994-present.

MSR	$1,600		$1,300	$1,125	$1,000	$825	$695	$550	$395

This model comes with an autographed copy of George Fullerton's *Guitar Legends* book. This model was also available with a rosewood fingerboard with pearl dot inlays. This model is currently available in Premier and Standard finishes.

ELECTRIC: HG SERIES

HG series guitars were only built in 1982. An estimated 1,000 instruments were produced, and more HG-1 models were made than HG-2 models. HG series guitars are similar in design to the SC series, except have one or two G & L Magnetic Field humbucking pickups (depending on the model).

HG-1 - offset double cutaway maple body, bolt-on maple neck, 22-fret maple fingerboard with black dot inlay, standard vibrato, 6-on-a-side tuners, chrome hardware, 1 humbucker pickup, volume/tone controls and jack mounted on black quarter moon-shaped panel, mfg. 1982-83.

	N/A	$1,200	$1,050	$900	$750	$600	$450

HG-2 - similar to the HG-1, except has two humbucker pickups, and a pickup selector switch mounted on control panel near volume and tone controls, mfg. 1982-83.

	N/A	$1,500	$1,300	$1,100	$950	$800	$650

ELECTRIC: INTERCEPTOR SERIES

INTERCEPTOR (1ST DESIGN) - radical offset double cutaway ash body, additional shaped armrest on lower bout, bolt-on maple neck, 22-fret maple fingerboard with black dot inlay, 25.5 in. scale, standard vibrato, 6-on-a-side tuners, chrome hardware, 2 humbucker pickups, volume/tone controls and jack mounted on black panel, mfg. 1983-85.

	N/A	$1,500	$1,300	$1,100	$950	$800	$650

The first design Interceptors have more triangular-pointed horns. Also, pickup configuration can and does vary (i.e., 3 single coils). This model may have ash, maple, or mahogany bodies, and maple or rosewood fingerboards.

INTERCEPTOR (2ND DESIGN) - similar to the first Interceptor design, except the horns are slimmer and rounded; controls are rear loaded, and the jack is on the side of the body, mfg. 1985-86.

	N/A	$1,300	$1,150	$1,000	$850	$700	$550

It is estimated that a total of 67 Interceptors (first and second design) were built.

INTERCEPTOR (3RD DESIGN) - offset double cutaway ash body, bolt-on maple neck, 22-fret rosewood fingerboard, standard vibrato, 6-on-a-side tuners, chrome hardware, 2 single coil/humbucker pickups, volume/tone controls, 5-position switch, mfg. 1987-89.

	N/A	$1,000	$900	$800	$700	$600	$500

The third Interceptor design is more traditional than the previous two incarnations. The controls are rear loaded, and the top has a carved sloped ledge along the bass side.

ELECTRIC: INVADER SERIES

INVADER (1ST DESIGN) - offset double cutaway poplar body, bolt-on maple neck, 25.5 in. scale, 22-fret rosewood fingerboard with pearl dot inlays, double locking vibrato, 6-on-a-side tuners, chrome hardware, 2 single coil/humbucker pickups, 1 volume/2 tone control, 3 pickup selector mini-switches, mfg. 1984-88.

	N/A	$750	$675	$600	$525	$450	$375

This model may have ash, maple, or poplar bodies, and maple or rosewood fingerboards.

INVADER (CURRENT MFG.) - offset double cutaway body, bolt-on maple neck, 25.5 in. scale, 22-fret maple or rosewood fingerboard with dot inlays, double locking Original Floyd Rose vibrato, 6-on-a-side tuners, black or chrome hardware, 2 dual blade/1 TB4 humbucker Seymour Duncan pickups, 1 volume/tone control, 5-way selector, coil tap mini-switch, mfg. 1997-present.

MSR	$1,900		$1,425	$1,250	$1,100	$950	$775	$625	$475

This model is available in both the Standard and Premier finishes, and comes complete with deluxe Tolex case.

INVADER DELUXE - similar to the Invader, except has figured maple top, mahogany body, woodgrain edges around top, bird's-eye maple, rosewood, or ebony fingerboards, mfg. 1997-99.

	$1,600	$1,400	$1,225	$1,050	$900	$750	$600

Last MSR was $2,150.

GRADING		100% MINT	98% NEAR MINT	95% EXC+	90% EXC	80% VG+	70% VG	60% G

INVADER PLUS - similar to the Invader, except has humbucker/single coil blade/humbucker Seymour Duncan pickups, mfg. 1997-present.

MSR	$2,000		$1,500	$1,300	$1,150	$995	$825	$650	$500

Invader Plus Deluxe - similar to the Invader Plus, except has figured maple top, mahogany body, woodgrain edges around top, bird's-eye maple, rosewood, or ebony fingerboards, mfg. 1997-99.

			$1,700	$1,450	$1,300	$1,100	$925	$750	$575

Last MSR was $2,250.

INVADER XL - similar to the Invader, except has 2 Seymour Duncan humbuckers, mfg. 1997-present.

MSR	$1,950		$1,475	$1,300	$1,125	$950	$800	$650	$495

Invader XL Deluxe - similar to the Invader XL, except has figured maple top, mahogany body, woodgrain edges around top, bird's-eye maple, rosewood, or ebony fingerboards, mfg. 1997-99.

			$1,650	$1,425	$1,250	$1,100	$900	$725	$550

Last MSR was $2,200.

ELECTRIC: LEGACY SERIES

LEGACY - offset double cutaway body, white pickguard, bolt-on maple neck, standard vibrato, 6-on-a-side tuners, chrome hardware, 3 vintage Alnico single coil pickups, volume/treble/bass controls, 5-position switch, mfg. 1992-present.

MSR	$1,300		$975	$875	$775	$675	$575	$475	$375

Legacy Deluxe - similar to Legacy, has maple top on American Tilla back, hardrock maple neck with rosewood or maple fingerboard, dot position markers, 2 G&L Vintage style Alnico V single coil pickups and a Seymour Duncan TB4 Humbucker pickup in the bridge position, Schaller non-locking tuners, G&L patented Dual Fulcrum tremolo, 5-way selector switch, rear mounted controls, chrome hardware, no pickguard, G&L molded hard case included, available in standard finishes, current mfg.

Legacy HB - similar to Legacy, has alder body on all standard and solid finishes, swamp ash body on all Premier finishes, Hard Rock Maple neck with rosewood or maple fingerboard, dot position markers, Schaller non-locking tuners, G&L patented "Dual Fulcrum" tremolo, 2 G&L vintage style Alnico V single coil pickups and a Seymour Duncan TB4 Humbucking pickup in the bridge position. 5-way selector switch, mini-toggle allows the humbucker to be split, volume control, chrome hardware, 3-ply white pickguard, G&L molded case included, available in Standard finishes, current mfg.

Legacy 2HB - similar to Legacy HB, except a Seymour Duncan 58N humbucking pickup in the neck position and a Seymour Duncan JB humbucker pickup in the bridge position, available in Standard finishes, current mfg.

Legacy Special - similar to Legacy, except has graphite nut, locking Sperzel tuners, 2 dual blade/1 humbucking power blade pickups, available in Premier and Standard finishes, mfg. 1993-present.

MSR	$1,300		$1,050	$900	$795	$675	$550	$450	$325

ELECTRIC: RAMPAGE SERIES

RAMPAGE - offset double cutaway maple body, bolt-on hardrock maple neck, 25.5 in. scale, 22-fret rosewood fingerboard (12 in. radius) with pearl dot inlays, double locking vibrato, 6-on-a-side tuners, chrome hardware, 1 humbucker pickup, volume control, mfg. 1984-88.

		N/A	$750	$675	$600	$525	$450	$375

This model may have ash, maple, or poplar bodies; and maple or rosewood fingerboards.

ELECTRIC: S SERIES

S-500 - offset double cutaway body, white pickguard, bolt-on maple neck, 25.5 in. scale, standard vibrato, 6-on-a-side locking Sperzel tuners, chrome hardware, 3-ply white pickguard, 3 vintage Alnico-V single coil pickups, volume/treble/bass control, 5-position/mini switch, mfg. 1982-1996.

1982-1991		N/A	$800	$700	$625	$550	$475	$400
1992-1996		N/A	$700	$625	$550	$475	$400	$325

S-500 (CURRENT) - similar to S-500, except has alder or swamp ash body depending on finish, hard Rock Maple neck with rosewood or maple fingerboard, Schaller locking tuners, G&L patented "Dual Fulcrum" tremolo, chrome hardware, 3 G&L Magnetic Field single coil pickups, available in Standard finishes, current mfg.

MSR	$1,300		$1,050	$900	$795	$675	$550	$450	$325

Early models may have ash, maple, or mahogany bodies, and maple or ebony fingerboards. This model is currently available in Premier and Standard finishes.

S-500 Deluxe - similar to S-500, except has maple top on American tilla back, standard finishes available, current mfg.

MSR	$1,750		$1,350	$1,150	$1,000	$850	$750	$650	$550

ELECTRIC: SC SERIES

The SC series was produced over a period of eighteen months, beginning in 1982. An estimated 1,200 instruments total were produced. SC series guitars have one, two, or three G & L Magnetic Field single coil pickups (depending on the model).

SC-1 - offset double cutaway maple body, bolt-on maple neck, 22-fret maple fingerboard with black dot inlay, standard vibrato, 6-on-a-side tuners, chrome hardware, 1 single coil pickup, volume/tone controls and jack mounted on black quarter moon-shaped panel, mfg. 1982-84.

		N/A	$600	$525	$450	$400	$350	$300

Less than 250 SC-1 models were built.

G & L F-100-II
courtesy Dale Hanson

G

G & L Legacy Special
courtesy G & L

GRADING	100% MINT	98% NEAR MINT	95% EXC+	90% EXC	80% VG+	70% VG	60% G

SC-2 - similar to the SC-1, except has two single coil pickups, and a pickup selector switch mounted on control panel near volume and tone controls, mfg. 1982-84.

	N/A	$650	$575	$500	$425	$375	$325

SC-3 - similar to the SC-1, except has three single coil pickups, and a pickup selector switch mounted on control panel near volume and tone controls, mfg. 1982-84.

	N/A	$700	$625	$550	$475	$400	$350

ELECTRIC: SKYHAWK, NIGHTHAWK, & SUPERHAWK SERIES

SKYHAWK (NIGHTHAWK) - offset double cutaway ash body, white pickguard, 22-fret bolt-on maple neck, 25.5 in. scale, standard vibrato, 6-on-a-side tuners, chrome hardware, 3 single coil pickups, 1 volume/2 tone control, 5-position switch, mfg. 1983-85.

	N/A	$750	$675	$600	$525	$450	$400

The Skyhawk model debuted in 1983 as the Nighthawk. Due to a conflict with a Washington D.C. band of the same name, the name was changed in 1984. It is estimated that 269 Nighthawk-labeled instruments were produced. Early models may have ash, maple, or mahogany bodies, and maple or ebony fingerboards.

SUPERHAWK - offset double cutaway maple body, bolt-on maple neck, 25.5 in. scale, 22-fret rosewood fingerboard with pearl dot inlays, double locking vibrato, 6-on-a-side tuners, chrome hardware, 2 humbucker pickups, 1 volume/2 tone control, 3-position switch, mfg. 1984-89.

	N/A	$700	$625	$550	$475	$400	$325

This model may have ash, maple, or mahogany bodies, and maple or rosewood fingerboards.

ELECTRIC BASS

G & L basses are available with 21-fret maple fingerboard with black dot inlay or rosewood fingerboard with pearl dot inlay, or ebony fretless (with or without "Ghostlines"), and feature a fixed bridge with locking saddles.

The following listed models are available in these **Standard** finishes: Belair Green, Black, Black Silver Swirl, Blue Swirl, Candy Apple Red, Cherryburst, Cobalt Blue, Electric Blue, Emerald Blue, Fullerton Red, Gold Metallic, Gold Metallicburst, Green Swirl, Lake Placid Blue, Pearl White, Red Swirl, Silver Metallic, Sparkle Black, Sparkle Purple, Sparkle Red, Sunburst, Tobacco Sunburst, and White.

G & L also offers a number of **Premier** finishes on certain models. These finishes include: Blonde, Blueburst, Clear Blue, Clear Forest Green, Clear Orange, Clear Red, Honey, Honeyburst, Natural Satin, and Natural Ash. Premier finishes are also available on the LB-100, SB-1, and SB-2 (contact dealer for availability).

ASAT BASS - single cutaway ash (or maple) body, bolt-on maple neck, 34 in. scale, 21-fret maple fingerboard, 4-on-a-side tuners, chrome hardware, 2 dual coil pickups, volume/treble/bass controls, pickup/series-parallel/preamp switches, active electronics, mfg. 1989-present.

MSR	$1,850	$1,425	$1,200	$1,050	$900	$750	$650	$550

This model is currently available in Premier and Standard finishes.

ASAT Bass Semi-Hollow - similar to ASAT Bass, except has swamp ash body with twin Voice Chambers, 2 G&L Magnetic Field humbucking pickups, Custom G&L "Ultra-Lite" tuners, G&L patented "Saddle Lock" bridge, G&L Tri-Tone active/passive electronics, series/parallel mini-toggle, pre-amp control mini-toggle, available in Standard finishes.

MSR	$1,750	$1,350	$1,150	$1,000	$850	$700	$600	$500

CLIMAX BASS - offset double cutaway ash body, bolt-on maple neck, 4-on-a-side ultralite tuners, no pickguard/rear loaded controls, chrome hardware, 1 humbucker pickup, volume/treble/bass controls, bypass/preamp switches, mfg. 1993-95.

	N/A	$800	$700	$625	$550	$475	$400

Last MSR was $1,100.

EL TORO - offset double cutaway ash body, bolt-on maple neck, 34 in. scale, 21-fret maple fingerboard with black dot inlays, fixed bridge, 4-on-a-side tuners, 2 bi-pole smaller humbucker pickups, volume/treble/bass controls, pickup selector switch, mfg. 1983-85.

	N/A	$750	$675	$600	$525	$450	$375

This model may have ash, maple, or mahogany bodies; and ebony, maple, or rosewood fingerboards.

INTERCEPTOR BASS - offset double cutaway maple body, bolt-on maple neck, 34 in. scale, 21-fret maple fingerboard with black dot inlays, 4-on-a-side tuners, 2 bi-pole smaller humbucker pickups, volume/treble/bass controls, pickup selector switch, mfg. 1984-89.

	N/A	$950	$850	$750	$650	$550	$450

The Interceptor Bass shared similar design lines of the third model Interceptor guitar, and the same electronics as the El Toro model bass. This model may have ash, maple, or mahogany bodies, and ebony, maple, or rosewood fingerboards.

JB-2 BASS - offset double cutaway alder body (swamp ash body on Premier finishes), hard rock maple neck with rosewood or maple fingerboard, dot position markers, Custom G&L "Ultra-Lite" tuners, G&L patented "Saddle-Lock" bridge, 2 volume/1 tone control, chrome hardware, no pickguard, available in Standard colors, current mfg.

MSR	$1,600	$1,225	$1,050	$900	$750	$650	$550	$450

LB-100 (LEGACY BASS) - offset double cutaway alder body, bolt-on maple neck, 21-fret maple or rosewood fingerboard, 4-on-a-side ultra-lite tuners, white pickguard, chrome hardware, fixed bridge with locking saddles, P-Bass-style split-coil pickup, volume/tone control, passive electronics, mfg. 1993-2001.

	$900	$800	$700	$600	$525	$450	$375

Last MSR was $1,200.

In late 1993, the Legacy Bass was renamed the LB-100. This model is available in Standard finishes.

L-1000 - offset double cutaway maple body, bolt-on maple neck, 34 in. scale, 21-fret maple fingerboard with black dot inlays, 4-on-a-side tuners, humbucker pickup, volume/treble/bass controls, series-parallel switch, available in Natural and Sunburst finishes, mfg. 1980-1994.

	N/A	$700	$625	$550	$475	$400	$325

Last MSR was $950.

This model may have ash, maple, or mahogany bodies, and ebony, maple, or rosewood fingerboards.

L-1000 F - similar to the L-1000, except has fretless neck.

	N/A	$700	$625	$550	$475	$400	$325

GRADING	100% MINT	98% NEAR MINT	95% EXC+	90% EXC	80% VG+	70% VG	60% G

L-1500 - similar to L-1000, except has 5 strings, alder body, no pickguard, rear loaded controls, 3/2-per-side tuners, chrome hardware, G & L magnetic field humbucker, preamp on/off switch, series/parallel switch, volume/treble/bass controls, active/passive electronics, mfg. 1995-present.

MSR	$1,300	$925	$850	$750	$675	$550	$450	$325

This model is currently available in Premier and Standard finishes.

L-1500 Custom - similar to the L-1500, except has bookmatched ash top, alder body, wood binding, and no contour on top, mfg. 1996-98.

	$1,100	$950	$800	$700	$600	$500	$400

Last MSR was $1,449.

This model is currently available in See-Through finishes only, and comes complete with a deluxe Tolex case.

L-1505 - offset double cutaway American tilia body, swamp ash top, bolt-on maple neck, 21-fret maple or rosewood fingerboard, rear loaded controls, 3/2-per-side tuners, chrome hardware, G & L magnetic field humbucker, preamp on/off switch, series/parallel switch, volume/treble/bass controls, active/passive electronics, available in premier and standard finishes, mfg. 1997-present.

MSR	$1,500	$1,050	$975	$850	$775	$650	$500	$375

L-1505 Custom - similar to the L-1505, except has bookmatched ash top, alder body, bird's-eye maple neck, wood binding, mfg. 1997-98.

	$1,150	$1,000	$850	$750	$650	$550	$450

Last MSR was $1,649.

This model is currently available in See-Through finishes only, and comes complete with a deluxe Tolex case. In 1998, STB option was introduced; 3/2-per-side headstock was redesigned, eliminating the string retainer.

L-2000 (L-2000 E) - similar to L-1000, except has 2 humbucker pickups, pickup/series-parallel/preamp/treble boost switches, active electronics, available in premier and standard finishes, mfg. 1980-present.

MSR	$1,600	$1,225	$1,050	$900	$750	$650	$550	$450

The L-2000 was originally introduced with passive electronics and the L-2000E was introduced in 1981 with active electronics.

L-2000 Custom - similar to the L-2000, except has bookmatched ash top, alder body, wood binding, no top contour, mfg. 1996-98.

	$1,150	$1,000	$850	$750	$650	$550	$450

Last MSR was $1,549.

This model is currently available in See-Through finishes only, and comes with deluxe Tolex case.

L-2000 F - similar to the L-2000, except has fretless neck and passive tone circuitry, disc. 1998.

	N/A	1,050	$900	$750	$650	$550	$450

Last MSR was $1,250.

L-2000 FE - similar to the L-2000 E, except has fretless neck, disc. 1998.

	N/A	$1,050	$900	$750	$650	$550	$450

Last MSR was $1,250.

L-2500 - similar to L-1000, except has 5 strings, no pickguard, rear loaded controls, 3/2-per-side tuners, chrome hardware, 2 magnetic field humbucker pickups, preamp switch, coil tap switch, pickup selector, volume/treble/bass controls, Tri-tone active/passive electronics, available in premier and standard finishes, mfg. 1994-present.

MSR	$1,600	$1,150	$1,050	$925	$825	$695	$550	$400

In 1998, STB option was introduced; 3/2-per-side headstock was redesigned, eliminating the string retainer.

L-2500 Custom - similar to the L-2500, except has bookmatched ash top, alder body, wood binding, and no contour on top, available in See-Through finishes, deluxe tolex case include, mfg. 1996-98.

	$1,225	$1,100	$975	$875	$750	$600	$450

Last MSR was $1,749.

L-5000 - similar to L-1000, except has 5 strings, alder body, black pickguard, 4/1 per side tuners, volume/tone control, passive electronics, mfg. 1987-1994.

	N/A	$850	$750	$650	$550	$475	$400

Last MSR was $950.

This model may have an ash, maple, or poplar body, and a maple or rosewood fingerboards.

L-5500 - similar to L-1000, except has 5 strings, alder body, no pickguard, rear loaded controls, 4/1 per side tuners, black hardware, 2 EMG 40 DC humbucker pickups, volume/concentric treble-bass/pan control, EMG BTC electronics, available in premier and standard finishes, mfg. 1994-97.

	N/A	$950	$850	$750	$650	$550	$450

Last MSR was $1,550.

L-5500 Custom - similar to the L-5500, except has bookmatched ash top, alder body, wood binding, and no contour on top, available in See-Through finishes, mfg. 1996-98.

	N/A	$1,200	$1,050	$900	$750	$650	$550

Last MSR was $2,100.

LYNX - offset double cutaway maple body, bolt-on hard rock maple neck, 34 in. scale, 21-fret maple fingerboard with black dot inlays, black pickguard, 4-on-a-side tuners, chrome hardware, 2 single coil pickups, volume/tone control, pickup selector, mfg. 1984-86.

	N/A	$600	$525	$450	$400	$350	$300

This model may have ash, maple, or mahogany body, and an ebony, maple, or rosewood fingerboard.

G & L SC-3
courtesy George McGuire

G

G & L L-2000
courtesy G & L

GRADING	100% MINT	98% NEAR MINT	95% EXC+	90% EXC	80% VG+	70% VG	60% G

SB-1 - offset double cutaway maple body, bolt-on hardrock maple neck, 34 in. scale, 21-fret maple fingerboard with black dot inlays, black pickguard, 4-on-a-side tuners, chrome hardware, split coil pickup, volume/tone control, mfg. 1982-2001.

			$850	$750	$675	$600	$525	$450	$375

Last MSR was $1,200.

SB-2 - similar to SB-1, except has split coil/single coil pickups, 2 volume controls, mfg. 1981-present.

MSR	$1,250		$875	$800	$725	$650	$550	$425	$325

This model has an optional rosewood fingerboard with pearl dot inlays.

G. GOULD MUSIC
Instruments currently built in San Francisco, CA. Distributed by G.Gould Music of San Francisco, CA.

Bassist/designer Geoff Gould was the founder and president of Modulus Graphite for almost two decades (see Modulus). While at Modulus, Gould was responsible for the development of the stringed instrument graphite neck and pioneered the use of the 35 in. scale length on production bass instruments that featured a low 'B' string. In addition to his new bass and guitar models, Gould is offering extra long scale (35 in. scale) 5-string bass string sets in Standard and Taper-Core. For more information regarding the string sets or the G. Gould guitar and bass instruments, please contact Geoff Gould directly (see Trademark Index).

ELECTRIC

Gould's Slant T guitar model is available by special order only. This single cutaway model has either specially made OEM Modulus necks or a maple/graphite composite neck (call for pricing and availability).

ELECTRIC BASS

The **GGJ4 4-String Bass** features a sleek offset double cutaway ash body, graphite-reinforced hardwood neck, 34 in. scale, 24-fret rosewood fingerboard with dot inlay, 4-on-a-side tuners, angled back headstock, 2 EMG-JV pickups, volume/tone controls, EMG-BQCS active bass/mid/treble controls, and is available with a maple top. This guitar retails for $2,495. The **GGJ5 5-String Bass** features a sleek offset double cutaway alder body, figured maple top, graphite-reinforced hardwood neck, 35 in. scale, 24-fret rosewood fingerboard with dot inlay, 4/1 per side tuners, angled back headstock, 2 custom EMG soapbar pickups, volume/tone controls, EMG-BQCS active bass/mid/treble controls, has an optional 17 or 17.5 mm string spacing, and retails for $2,995. The **GGJ6** has a six-string configuration, has EMG-45DC pickups, is available with a figured maple top and cocabola is optional, and retails for $3,495.

There is also a Vintage Series. These basses are available as the **Vintage J 4-String** for $1,595 and the **Vintage J 5-String** for $1,995.

Add $100 for lightweight ash body (Vintage Series only). Add $160 for hardshell case. Add $200 for primo quilt top. Add $300 for cocabola top.

G.H. RENO
Please refer to this listing in the R section.

GLF
Instruments currently built in Rogers, MN. Distributed by the GLF Custom Shop of Rogers, MN.

Luthier Kevin Smith has been building and messing around with guitars since his high school days. He was born in Fosston, Minnesota in 1961 and later attended Red Wing Technical College. He spent a number of years as a lighting and guitar tech for the regional band Encounter, which was based out of Chicago, Illinois.

Smith opened the GLF Custom Shop in 1984. Although the original focus was on both lighting and guitars, he soon focused directly on guitar repair and custom building. A custom ordered guitar may range between $1,200 and $1,500 (depending on hardware and pickups), but for further details on models and components contact the GLF shop. In addition to his busy schedule, he also provides custom finishes for the Benedict Guitar company. Smith also introduced his ToneSmith line of guitars in 1997 (see Tonesmith). Smith holds the patent on the Combo Rack, a guitar stand that attaches to the player's amplifier and holds the instrument when not in use.

GMP GUITARS
Instruments currently built in San Dimas, CA since 1990. Distributed by G M Precision Products, Inc. of San Dimas, CA.

GMP has been producing high quality guitars since 1990 (first prototypes were built in 1989). GMP has always favored the latest in technology in their designs, including the use of Sperzal locking tuners, Wilkinson vibratos and roller nuts, and other techniques. GMP uses Honduran mahogony, quilted and flamed maple, and select Western alder. Options include Seymour Duncan or Tom Holmes pickups, transparent colors, and special wiring. For further information and specifications, contact GM Precision Products directly (see Trademark Index).

ELECTRIC

All guitar models feature the GMP center dipped 3-per-side headstock, Seymour Duncan pickups, Sperzel locking tuners, Schaller roller bridges or Wilkinson vibratos, Schaller strap locks, hardware choices (color and type), and numerous color finishes. All models are equipped with a hardshell case. Options include Tom Holmes humbuckers and Van Zandt pickups (call for pricing).

Add $300 for Flame or Quilted Maple top.

CLASSIC - similar to the Custom, except features an alder or basswood body, maple neck, 24-fret rosewood or maple fingerboard with dot inlay, pickguard, pickguard-mounted electronics, choice of pickup configuration, available in (unlimited) solid color finishes, current mfg.

MSR	$2,050		$1,650	$1,350	$1,200	$1,050	$900	$775	$650

CUSTOM - sleek offset double cutaway mahogany body with pointy forward horns, flame (or quilted) maple top, mahogany neck, 24-fret rosewood or ebony fingerboard with abalone diamond inlay, Wilkinson tremolo or Tune-O-Matic bridge/STB ferrules, 3-per-side tuners, gold hardware, 2 humbucker pickups, volume/tone controls, 3-way toggle switch, available in (unlimited) Transparent Color finishes, current mfg.

MSR	$2,650		$2,125	$1,950	$1,750	$1,500	$1,200	$950	$750

ELITE - offset double cutaway mahogany body, flame (or quilted) maple top, mahogany neck, 22-fret rosewood or ebony fingerboard with abalone diamond inlay, Wilkinso tremolo or Tune-O-Matic bridge/STB ferrules, 3-per-side tuners, gold hardware, 2 humbucker pickups, volume/tone controls, 3-way toggle switch, available in (unlimited) Transparent Color finishes, disc. 2003.

			$2,850	$2,500	$2,150	$1,850	$1,600	$1,350	$1,100

Last MSR was $3,550.

GRADING	100% MINT	98% NEAR MINT	95% EXC+	90% EXC	80% VG+	70% VG	60% G

Elite Deluxe - similar to the Elite, except has a mahogany body with a maple top, set mahogany neck, ebony fingerboard with abalone diamond inlays, two Duncan '59N pickups, Tone Pros tunamatic bridge, available in Classic White, Ebony, Gun Metal Gray, Midnight Blue, or Wine Red Metallic finishes, mfg. 2003-present.

	MSR	$3,250		$2,600	$2,250	$1,950	$1,650	$1,350	$1,100	$900

Elite Doubleneck - 6/12 doubleneck version of the Elite, offset double cutaway mahogany body, premium grade quilted or flamed maple tops, mahogany necks, rosewood or ebony 22-fret fingerboards, diamond-shaped abalone position markers, STB on 12-string side, Wilkinson vibrato tailpiece on 6-string side, 2 exposed zebra coil humbucker pickups, (unlimited) transparent colors, disc. 2003.

	$4,800	$4,300	$3,800	$3,500	$3,000	$2,500	$2,000

Last MSR was $6,000.

Elite Special - similar to the Elite, except has an alder body, set maple neck, rosewood fingerboard, two Duncan '59N pickups, and CC bridge, available in Classic White, Ebony, Gun Metal Gray, Midnight Blue, or Wine Red Metallic finishes, mfg. 2003-present.

	MSR	$2,050		$1,650	$1,350	$1,200	$1,050	$900	$775	$650

INLAY TOP - similar to the Custom, except features an exotic wood (bird's-eye, flame, or quilted maple) top inlay (on the top of the body), available in (unlimited) Transparent Color finishes, current mfg.

	MSR	$2,950		$2,375	$2,100	$1,850	$1,500	$1,250	$1,050	$850

PAWN SHOP ORIGINAL - offset single cutaway basswood or alder body, maple neck, 22-fret rosewood fingerboard with abalone dot inlay, Tune-O-Matic bridge/strings through-body ferrules, 3-per-side tuners, black chrome or chrome hardware, 2 humbucker pickups, 2 volume/2 tone controls, 3-way toggle switch, available in Black, Classic White, Ebony, Gun Metal Gray, Metallic Blue, Midnight Blue, Red, or White finishes, current mfg.

	MSR	$1,650		$1,325	$1,100	$950	$825	$700	$600	$500

This model is available in other optional colors (call for availability and pricing).

Pawn Shop Special - similar to the Pawn Shop, except features a creme bound mahogany or alder body, bound f-hole, mahogany neck, bound ebony fingerboard with abalone dot position markers/abalone diamond inlay at 12th fret, bound headstock, chrome or gold hardware, available in (unlimited) Solid Color finishes, current mfg.

	MSR	$3,050		$2,450	$2,100	$1,850	$1,550	$1,250	$1,050	$850

Pawn Shop Deluxe - similar to the Pawn Shop, except has a mahogany body with western maple top, available in unlimited solid colors, current mfg.

	MSR	$3,250		$2,600	$2,250	$1,950	$1,650	$1,350	$1,100	$900

GMP "V" - V-shaped mahogany body, mahogany neck, rosewood or ebony 22-fret fingerboard, 3-per-side tuners, abalone diamond shaped position markers, STB or stop tailpiece, available in (unlimited) solid colors, disc. 2003.

	$2,250	$2,000	$1,800	$1,500	$1,250	$1,050	$850

Last MSR was $2,800.

GMP Original - similar to the GMP, excet has an alder body, set maple neck, rosewood fingerboard, 2 Kent Armstrong pickups, and is available in various colors, mfg. 2003-present.

	MSR	$1,650		$1,325	$1,100	$950	$825	$700	$600	$500

GMP Standard - similar to the GMP, excet has an alder body, set maple neck, rosewood fingerboard, 2 Kent Armstrong pickups, and is available in various colors, mfg. 2003-present.

	MSR	$1,650		$1,325	$1,100	$950	$825	$700	$600	$500

ROXIE SS - offset single rounded cutaway mahogany body, creme bound Western maple top, mahogany neck, 22-fret bound rosewood fingerboard with matching metal flake finish color diamond inlay, Tune-O-Matic bridge/trapeze tailpiece, 3-per-side tuners, bound headstock, chrome hardware, 2 humbucker pickups, volume/tone controls, 3-way toggle switch, available in (unlimited) Metal Flake finishes, current mfg.

	MSR	$3,250		$2,600	$2,300	$2,050	$1,800	$1,500	$1,300	$1,050

Add $100 for Bigsby tremolo/Schaller roller bridge.

Roxie II - similar to the Roxie SS except has a completely chambered body available with or without an f-hole, available in unlimited metal flake finishes, current mfg.

	MSR	$3,250		$2,600	$2,300	$2,050	$1,800	$1,500	$1,300	$1,050

ELECTRIC BASS

Options include Bartolini and EMG pickups (call for pricing).

ROXIE SS 4/5 BASS - offset dual cutaway body, 4- or 5-string configuration, creme body binding, alder or mahogany body wings, through-body maple neck, 34 in. scale, 22-fret bound ebony fingerboard with matching metal flake finish color diamond inlay, fixed bridge, 2- or 2/3-per-side tuners, bound headstock, chrome hardware, 2 Seymour Duncan Basslines pickups, volume/tone controls, available in Metal Flake finishes, current mfg.

	MSR	$2,950		$2,375	$2,100	$1,850	$1,550	$1,300	$1,050	$900

ELITE BASS - offset double cutaway maple and exotic hardwood multi-laminate neck through-body construction, 4-, 5-, or 6-string, carved quilted or flame maple top, mahogany, alder, or ash sides, ebony or pau ferro 24-fret fingerboards, EMG or Bartolini pickups available, 34 in. scale. Oil, Wax, or Polyurethane finishes available, current mfg.

	MSR	$3,050		$2,450	$2,200	$1,950	$1,650	$1,350	$1,100	$950

Add $100 for 6-string model.

G & L SB-2
courtesy G & L

G

GMP Pawn Shop Deluxe
courtesy GMP

GRADING	100% MINT	98% NEAR MINT	95% EXC+	90% EXC	80% VG+	70% VG	60% G

STANDARD BASS - offset double cutaway body, alder or mahogany body wings, flame or quilted maple top, through-body maple neck, 34 in. scale, 24-fret rosewood or ebony fingerboard, 4-, 5-, or 6-string configuration, fixed bridge, 2, 3/2, or 3 per-side-tuners, black hardware, P/J-style Seymour Duncan Basslines pickups, 2 volume/1 tone controls, available in (unlimited) Transparent Colors, Oil & Wax, or Polyurethane finishes, disc.

4/5 String	$1,880	$1,450	$1,250	$1,150	$995	$850	$750
6 String	$1,975	$1,500	$1,300	$1,175	$1,000	$875	$750

Last MSR was $2,350.

GR BASSES
Instruments currently built in San Marcos, CA.

GR Basses feature an electric solid body design with an open headstock with sideways mounted tuners (inspired by upright basses) for ideal string tension; other features include a curved heel with five bolts holding the neck stable, and a custom GR bridge with large radius saddles for increased resonance. As if the open headstock isn't enough of an identification clue, all models have the "GR" logo on the tip of the headstock. For further information regarding pricing and specifications, please contact GR Basses directly (see Trademark Index).

ELECTRIC BASS

GR Basses are also available with alder or poplar body woods.

Add $50 for a fretless fingerboard. Add $50 for pearloid box inlays. Add $50 for pearloid or tortoiseshell pickguard. Add $50 for active/passive switch. Add $50 for colored oil finish. Add $75 for 2 single coil pickups (Jazz only). Add $150 for 5-string configuration. Add $150 for dual Bassline Music Man pickups. Add $150 for figured ash or maple top. Add $150 for active 3-band equalizer. Add $200 for Basslines 2-band active EQ (with slap contour). Add $200 for left-handed configuration. Add $200 for solid color finish. Add $250 for High Gloss finish.

CLASSIC SERIES (GRP/GRJ/GRT) 4-STRING - offset double cutaway (GRP) or single cutaway body (GRT) solid ash body, bolt-on maple neck, 34 in. scale, 22-fret rosewood (or ebony or maple) fingerboard with pearl (or abalone or black inlays), 2-per-side open headstock, chrome or black hardware (seymour Duncan) Bassline Music Man pickup, volume/tone controls, available in Oil finish, current mfg.

MSR	$1,349		$950	$850	$750	$675	$600	$525	$450

ROAD SERIES (RSP4/RSJ4/RST4) - production version of the Classic series, maple neck, open headstock, curved heel, lacquer finish, Music-Man style pickup, available in Gloss Black, Vintage Sunburst, Trans. Green, or Trans. Burgundy, current mfg.

MSR	$949 - 999	$700	$625	$550	$500	$450	$400	$350

GRD (GUITAR RESEARCH AND DESIGN)
Instruments previously built in South Strafford, VT between 1978 and 1982. Distributed initially by United Marketing International of Grapevine, TX; distribution was later retained by Guitar Reseach and Design.

GRD (Guitar Reseach and Design) was founded in 1978 by luthier/designer Charles Fox. The Guitar Reseach and Design company grew out of the School of Guitar Research and Design Center, which was founded by Fox in South Strafford, Vermont in 1973. The GRD Center was the first guitar building school in North American. The GRD company workforce consisted of graduates from the school.

GRD first advertised in *Guitar Player* magazine in October of 1978, and their guitars were distributed by United Marketing International of Grapevine, Texas. This same issue also featured pictures of their Chicago NAMM booth on page 23, while page 24 showed a picture of then-GP columnist and vintage guitar expert George Gruhn holding one of their double cutaway models. The ads in the November and December 1978 issues of *Guitar Player* announced that they were available direct to the musician and to select professional sound shops around the country. A letter to customers during this time period who had requested the company's brochures announced that GRD had broken ties with their distributor.

George Gruhn's January 1979 Guitar Player column featured GRD instruments. Gruhn called them "one of the most interesting guitars I saw at the entire (NAMM) show and are capable of producing almost any type of sound. The instruments are beautifully crafted, and while modernistic in design, they were tasteful, reserved, and elegant. It is a significant instrument that demonstrates the future potential in both electrical and physical design." The last mention of GRD was in the January 1981 issue of Guitar Player magazine, in which Jim Nollman stated that Charles Fox was designing him a 3/4-size guitar to use in playing slide guitar in Jim's attempt to communicate with whales. And you thought that slide guitar playing only perked up the ears of dogs in the neighborhood! GRD closed its doors in 1982, and Fox moved to San Francisco to pursue other interests. Fox became a biofeedback therapist, yoga instructor, and professional gambler as he stayed out of the guitar business. However, the lure of teaching and the world of lutherie beckoned, and Fox started the American School of Luthiery in Healdsburg, California. In 1998, Fox also returned to guitar manufacturing as he founded the CFOX guitar company (see CFOX) which is currently building high quality acoustic guitars (source: Vincent Motel, G R D Historian).

GRD DESIGN FEATURES

Guitar Reseach and Design was an innovative company during the late 1970s. Some of the company's ideas include the thin body acoustic guitar, brass nuts, hexaphonic pickups, and active electronics that featured on-board compression, distortion, and wireless broadcasters. GRD electric guitars utilized fade/mix controls (instead of the usual toggle switches) to blend the pickups' outputs; and featured coil tap (coil split) and phase switches. GRD electric guitars were also available with built-in 6 band graphic equalizers that offered 18 dB of cut or boost, and parametric equalizers with selectable frequency centers and cut or boost controls (these features are usually associated with P.A. mixing boards).

GRD hardware was manufactured in house, and the pickups used on the electric models were specially wound and potted by DiMarzio. What appears to be binding on the solid body models is actually two laminated layers of maple sandwiching a layer of ebonized maple in the center. GRD instruments all feature the highly noticeable "Omega" headstock cutaway.

ELECTRIC: STANDARD GRD SERIES

The 1978 GRD brochure illustrated 3 different solid body styles that had 2 different electronic systems. These two different electronic systems were comprised of the **PF** models, which have wide range parametric variable filters with stacked frequenct "Q" controls which could be set in hi-pass, lo-pass, or band-pass modes. The **EQ** models have 2 modified MXR 6 band graphic equalizers with 18 dB of cut or boost.

All necks and bodies were pattern grade Honduran mahogany, and each body had a thick solid rosewood overlay. Often mistaken for a "really nice piece of ebony," the fingerboards were phenolic resin! GRD electrics feature a unique heel-less neck/body joint, and the head and arm are cut from separate pieces which are spliced rather than being bandsawn from one piece of wood. The 3-per-side headstocks feature gold-plated Schaller tuners.

The nut is 1/4" wide solid brass, and each string has its own separate 1" deep brass bridge block (each block is individually adjustable for height and length). The tailpiece is solid brass, and the rear cover plates are solid brass too. Instead of a toggle switch, there is a fader (mixer) which allows the guitarist to blend the pickups in varying amounts. The magnetic pickups are specially wound and potted DiMarzio units, and there is a transducer pickup mounted in the neck. Pickups have no mounting rings, and are mounted through the back of the instrument. GRD electric models were optionally offered with dual distortion circuits, compressor sustainer units, and hexaphonic pickups.

GRD offered three different solid body models, all of which feature a 645 mm scale and 24-fret fingerboard. The **DC** model has a dual cutaway body reminiscent of the Hamer Artist model (or Gibson Les Paul Double Cutaway). The **SC** model is a single cutaway model similar to a Les Paul; and the unique **M 1** model (featured in Wheeler´s American Guitars book) has a rectangular (or wedge) body with large "O" or "Omega" cutaway in its lower bout. Outside of the Bo Diddly- approved **M 1**, all GRD models feature rather traditional body designs.

All 1987 models have active electronics; but instead of on-board batteries, the guitars use a single three conductor cord that runs through a small power supply box between the guitar and the amplifier. Early GRD guitars have a built-in NiCad battery which is always charging when the guitar is played through, or simply plugged into its normal power supply. If the guitar is played without its normal power supply, it is ready with a fully charged battery.

ELECTRIC: GRD AX SERIES

The **AX Series** was introduced in early 1979 as a more affordable alternative to the standard series. The **AX Series** was available in all four electric body styles (DC, SC, M 1, and Bass). While the neck/body construction was the same as the **Standard Series**, the hardware was different. Bodies and necks were Honduran Mahogany, and the face woods were Jet Black maple (or Fancy Flamed maple, or rosewood) with fancy interface laminates. There were two different control set-ups available, but the pickups were the same DiMarzio custom design used on all the other guitars. One DiMarzio was a PAF design, while the second model had a hotter output. Active models were powered with a 9-volt battery.

The **Standard AX** had a master volume and 2 tone controls, slide type pickup selector (mixer), 2 Dual Sound switches (one per pickup).

The **Active AX** had a master volume and master tone controls, slide type pickup selector (mixer), 2 Dual Sound switches (one per pickup), EQ/preamp switch, and 6 band graphic equalizer (with 18 dB cut or boost).

ELECTRIC: GRD PASSIVE PICKUP SERIES

GRD offered passive pickup models starting in 1979 (there was no catalog featuring these particular guitar models). These models were available in either an Explorer or Flying V body shapes. The customer could choose any pickup configuration, although GRD recommended using different pickups for the neck and bridge positions (for example, a DiMarzio SDHP in the neck position and a DiMarzio X2N in the bridge position). The pickups were mounted with standard mounting rings made of brass, and were also available with the rear mounted specially potted DiMarzio pickups. The pickups also had coil taps for humbucker or single coil operation as well as a phase switch when both pickups were selected. These guitars still featured brass nuts, Schaller tuners, and featured Schaller wrap-around bridges. Gold-plated hardware was standard, but chrome hardware was available as an option (that´s certainly a switch from today´s marketplace!). Fine tuners were also optional.

The **Passive** models had the same two piece headstock/neck configuration, and heel-less body joint as the **Active** models. They also had the same mahogany neck/body woods as well as rosewood or maple tops.

Passive models feature the same 24-fret phenolic fingerboard and scale length as the Active models.

ELECTRIC BASS

The electric bass model from 1978 has an 865 mm scale and 24-fret fingerboard. The **B** Bass Guitar was also offered with a fretless fingerboard. All other construction techniques were similar to the electric guitars.

GTX

Instruments previously produced in Korea. Distributed by the Kaman Music Corporation of Bloomfield, CT from 1988-1994.

The GTX trademark was a brandname of the Kaman Corporation. These guitars are based on several electric American designs such as Strats and Les Pauls. Some models featured a hybrid locking tremolo and some had a feedback sustain unit. Kaman Music aquired Hamar guitars in the late 1980s, and when this line became larger and more important, Kaman decided to drop the GTX brand.

GADOW GUITARS

Instruments currently produced in Durham, NC since 1994.

Ryan Gadow is the president and luthier of Gadow Guitars. He founded the company in 1994 based on the principle of bringing rock and making music back to what it used to be. Gadow Guitars are instruments built and priced for musicians, and not for an investment or to be put out for display. Ryan uses high-quality workmanship with clean tone. The guitars feature original designs that are yet simple and stylish. All guitars are built in the USA. For more information refer to their website (see Trademark Index).

ELECTRIC

There are several models available from Gadow. List prices are what the guitars start at, but there are options for every instrument that will up the price. All guitars are based on the same Custom design. The **Classic** is the "entry level" guitar for Gadow, and starts at $1,695. The **Custom Single** is their first design, has a single cutaway, and starts at $1,895. A set-neck version is available for $2,495. The **Custom Double**, is a double cutaway, which has a slightly different design than the single, and starts at $1,895. A set-neck version is available for $3,195. The **Custom Hollow** is a single cutaway Custom semi-hollow body that starts at $2,095. The **Nashville** is a single cutaway design that is geared towards country music and starts at $2,095. The **Jazz** model is a double cutaway design in a traditional hollow body with f-holes and starts at $3,295.

GR Basses GRJ 4-STring courtesy GR Basses

Gadow Classic courtesy Gadow

G

ELECTRIC BASS

The Gadow bases are available in a Classic and Custom series. The **Classic Bass Series** is a double-cutaway with an extended bass bout, alder body, and starts at $1,495 for the four-string, and $1,895 for the five-string. The **Custom Bass Series** has the same design as the Classic series but features an alder or swamp ash body with a highly figured maple top, maple neck, wide variety of fretboard woods, and starts at $1,795 for the four-string, $2,095 for the five-string, and $2,495 for the six-string.

GALANTI
Instruments previously built in Italy during the early 1960s through the early 1970s.

The Galanti company focused on fairly straightforward original designs on their solid and semi-hollowbody guitars. It is possible that these guitars were produced by either Goya or Eko. One known model is similar to the Goya Rangemaster and features a double cutaway with a sharp bass bout, two pickups, tremolo bridge, two knobs, and four black slider switches on the bass bout. The company also offered a number of amp designs. Prices are relatively unknonw in the second-hand market due to lack of activity. (Source: Tony Bacon, *The Ultimate Guitar Book*). Any information regarding Galanti can be submitted directly to the publisher.

GALE, GEOFF
Instruments previously built in England through the 1970s.

Original designs were featured on these solid body guitars, and they carried model designations such as the Magnum, Quasar, Cobra, and Phasar (source: Tony Bacon and Paul Day, *The Guru's Guitar Guide*).

GEMELLI
Instruments previously produced in Italy during the 1960s.

Guitars bearing this trademark were built by Benito & Umberto Cingolani in Recanti, Italy. Like many other European countries, Italy experienced the 1960s pop music popularity that led to a larger demand for electric guitars. However, many electric guitar builders were also manufacturers of accordions. As a result, many guitars ended up with accordion-style finishes and touches, such as a barrage of buttons for pickup or tone selection. It is up to the individual guitar player to make the choice: play 'em or pose with 'em! (Source: Tony Bacon, *The Ultimate Guitar Book*).

GHERSON
Instruments previously produced in Italy from the mid-1970s to early 1980s.

The Gherson company produced a number of good quality copies of American designs in the solid body format. Some examples are of a Les Paul, SG, and Rickenbacker 4001 Bass. (Source: Tony Bacon and Paul Day, *The Guru's Guitar Guide*).

GIBSON
Current trademark established circa 1896, and manufactured by the Gibson Guitar Corp., with production facilities located in Nashville, TN (beginning 1974), Bozeman, MT (beginning 1989, and Memphis, TN (beginning 2001). Custom shops are located in both Nashville, TN and Bozeman, MT. All Gibson instruments are currently distributed by the Gibson Guitar Corporation located in Nashville, TN.

Gibson instruments were previously produced in Kalamazoo, MI, from 1896 to 1984. The Gibson Mandolin-Guitar Manufacturing Company, Limited (which evolved into the Gibson Guitar Corporation) produced both electric and acoustic instruments in Kalamazoo, MI from 1902 to 1984. Gibson's first electric guitar, the ES-150 (also known as the Charlie Christian model) was manufactured during 1936.

Most acoustic instruments are currently produced in the Bozeman, MT plant - for more information, please refer to the *Blue Book of Acoustic Guitars.*

Luthier Orville H. Gibson was born in Chateaugay, New York. In 1856, he moved west to Kalamazoo, Michigan. City records from 1896-1897 indicate a business address of 114 South Burdick for O.H. Gibson, Manufacturer, Musical Instruments. By 1899-1902, the city directories indicate a change to the Second Floor of 104 East Main.

The Gibson Mandolin-Guitar Manufacturing Company, Limited was established at 2:55 p.m. on October 11, 1902. The agreement was formed by John W. Adams (president), Samuel H. Van Horn (treasurer), Sylvo Reams (secretary and also production manager), Lewis Williams (later secretary and General Manager), and Leroy Hornbeck. Orville Gibson was not one of the founding partners, but had a separate contract to be a consultant and trainer. Gibson was also the first to purchase 500 shares of the new company's stock. In 1915, Gibson and the company negotiated a new agreement in which Orville was to be paid a monthly salary for the rest of his life. Orville, who had some troubles with his health back in 1911, was treated in 1916 at the pyschiatric center of St. Lawrence State hospital in Ogdensburg, New York. Orville Gibson died of endocarditis on August 21, 1918.

In 1906 the company moved to 116 East Exchange Place, and the name was changed to Gibson Mandolin Guitar Company. In 1917, production facilities were opened at Parsons Street (the first of a total of five buildings at that location). Chicago Musical Instruments (CMI) acquired controlling interest in Gibson, Inc. in 1944. Maurice H. Berlin (president of CMI) became general secretary and treasurer of Gibson. From this date, the Gibson Sales Department became located in Chicago while the Kalamazoo plant concentrated on production.

In 1935, Gibson began investigating into a prototype electric pickup. Musician Alvino Rey started research with engineers at the Lyon & Healy company (see Washburn) in Chicago, and a year later the research was moved in-house to Kalamazoo. In late 1935, Gibson debuted the hexagonal pickup on a lap steel model; this same pickup was applied to an archtop guitar and offered as the ES (Electric Spanish) 150 in 1936. The ES-150 was used by jazz guitarist Charlie Christian, and this model is still known as the "Charlie Christian" model.

After the release of Leo Fender's Broadcaster (later Telecaster) model, Gibson and guitarist Les Paul collaborated in the release of the solid body Gibson Les Paul in 1952. This model was refined with the introduction of the Tune-O-Matic bridge/stop tailpiece combination, and P.A.F. humbuckers through the 1950s. Under the direction of then Gibson president Ted McCarty, the Gibson company attempted to throw off the tag of being "stodgy" and old-fashioned when they introduced the Flying V and Explorer models in the late 1950s. In this case, they pre-judged the public's tastes by about 10 years! As guitar players' tastes changed in the late 1950s, Gibson discontinued the single cutaway Les Paul model in favor of the double cutaway SG in 1960. As the popularity of the electric blues (as championed by Eric Clapton and Michael Bloomfield) grew during the 1960s, Gibson reissued the Les Paul in 1968.

Gibson acquired Epiphone in 1957, and production of Gibson-made Epiphones began in 1959, and lasted until 1969. In 1970, production moved to Japan (or, the Epiphone name was then applied to imported instruments).

In December of 1969, E.C.L. Industries, Inc. took control of CMI. Gibson, Inc. stayed under control of CMI until 1974, when it became a subsidiary of Norlin Industries (Norlin is named after H. Norton Stevens, president of E.C.L. and Maurice H. Berlin, president of CMI). A new factory was opened in Nashville, Tennessee the same year.

In 1980, Norlin decided to sell Gibson. Norlin also relocated some of the sales, marketing, administration, and finance personnel from Chicago to the Nashville plant. Main Gibson production was then handled in Nashville, and Kalamazoo became a specialist factory for custom orders. In 1983, then-

Gibson president Marty Locke informed plant manager Jim Deurloo that the Kalamazoo plant would close. Final production was June 1984, and the plant closed three months later. On a side note: Rather than give up on the 65-year-old facilities, Jim Deurloo, Marv Lamb, and J.P. Moats started the Heritage Guitar Company in April of 1985. The company is located in the original 1917 building.

In January of 1986, Henry Juszkiewicz (pres), David Berryman (VP of finance and accounting), and Gary Zebrowski (electronics business) bought Gibson for five million dollars. Since the purchase in 1986, the revived Gibson USA company has been at work to return to the level of quality the company had reached earlier. Expansion of the acoustic guitar production began at the Bozeman, Montana facilities. Many hard rock bands and guitarists began playing (and posing) with Gibson guitars, again fueling desire among the players.

Gibson's Historic Collection models were introduced in 1991, and custom pieces built at Gibson's Custom Shop began sporting their own Gibson Custom Art Historic logo on the headstock in 1996. This new division is responsible for producing Historic Collection models, commemorative guitars, custom-ordered and special edition guitars, as well as restoration and repair of vintage models.

In the tail end of 1996, both the Dobro production facilities in California and the Montana mandolin guitar facilities were closed down. New production facilities for both named Original Musical Instruments (O.M.I.) opened in Nashville, TN in late 1998.

In 1998, Gibson opened up a new dealer level for specialty guitars. The Gibson Historic Collection Award models are only available through the (estimated) 50 Award Level dealers, and feature specific year/model designated instruments at an upscale price. As noted elsewhere, the antique and vintage firearm market has authentic reproductions of especially prized models. Whether or not Gibson is building "reproductions" with these designated models, the bottom line is that they are damn fine instruments that any Gibson fan would be honored to own (and play).

During 1999, Gibson once again released a large number of new models and finishes, further filling out their electric guitar lineup. In the *Blue Book of Electric Guitars*, both the Custom Collection and Historic Series Models from the Custom Shop have been grouped in the back of the Gibson section for easier lookup. Since Gibson continues to change their model lineup on a regular basis, it is suggested that a trip to their website is in order to learn more on what's current, and, just as important, what has been discontinued.

Gibson started the new millennium in perhaps its best shape for a long time. With the Montana plant now producing consistently high quality acoustic instruments (perhaps their best ever), and the electric models being led by the extensive offerings from the Gibson Custom, Art, and Historic Division, this legendary American guitar company seems to be in great shape for the next century of guitar manufacturing. Additionally, Gibson recently opened up a new archtop production facility in Memphis, TN during 2001.

During 2001, Gibson opened up a new production facility in Memphis, TN, primarily manufacturing ES-335 electric instruments and variations. At the end of 2001, Gibson Guitar Corp. purchased Baldwin, longtime manufacturer of pianos and organs.

At the 2002 Nashville summer NAMM Show, Gibson celebrated the 50th anniversary of the Les Paul by announcing the world's first truly digital guitar - a digital LP. Gibson's abbreviated terminology for this new technology is called MaGIC (Media Accelerated Global Information Carrier). This technology converts an analog signal to a high quality digital signal inside the guitar, utilizing Gibson's patented HEX pickup, which measures both up and down and side to side motions on each string. Also, since each string is individually recorded and converted, MaGIC allows tonal/EQ adjustments on each string. Guitar output is via a RJ-45 connector, and standard Cat 5 ethernet cable. This new MaGIC technology also is 100% compatible with existing equipment. Gibson has announced that production models will be available during 2003.

During 2002, Gibson purchased long time guitar retailer Valley Arts Guitars, and opened up a separate retail store in downtown Nashville.

During the Nashville summer NAMM Show in 2003, Gibson celebrated the 10th anniversary of its Custom Shop, which was relocated in a separate production facility on Massman Drive during 1993.

Source: Walter Carter, *Gibson Guitars: 100 Years of an American Icon*; Tom Wheeler, *American Guitars*, and www.gibson.com.

**Gibson Flying V II
courtesy Dale Hanson**

G

ELECTRIC IDENTIFYING FEATURES: HEADSTOCK LOGO

The most consistent and easily found feature that goes across all models of Gibson production is the logo, or lack of one, found on the peghead. The very earliest instruments made are generally found with a star inside a crescent design, or a blank peghead, and labels inside the body. This lasted until approximately 1902.

From 1902 to the late 1920s, "The Gibson," inlaid in pearl and placed at a slant, is found on the peghead. In the late 1920s, this style of logo was changed to having "The Gibson" read straight across the peghead as opposed to being slanted. Flattop acoustics production began at approximately this time and these instruments generally do not have "The" on the inlay. They just have "Gibson" in script writing. By 1933, this was the established peghead logo for Gibson. Just before WWII, Gibson began making the lettering on the logo thicker and this became standard on most prewar instruments. Right after WWII, the styling of the logo remained but it became slanted once again.

In 1947, the logo that is still in use today made its debut. This logo has a block styling with the "G" having a tail, the "i" dot is touching the "G", the "b" and "o" are open and the "n" is connected at the bottom. The logo is still slanted. By 1951, the dot on the "i" was no longer connected to the "G." In 1967, the logo styling became even more squared (pentographed) with the "b" and "o" becoming closed and the "i" dot being removed.

In 1970, Gibson replaced the black tinted piece of wood that had been used on the peghead face with a black fiber that the logo and other peghead inlay were placed into. With the change in peghead facing came a slightly smaller logo lettering. In 1972, the "i" dot reappeared on the peghead logo. In 1981, the "n" is connected at the top of the "o." There are a few models through the years that do not follow this timeline, such as: reissues and limited editions, but most of the production instruments can be found with the above feature changes.

ELECTRIC IDENTIFYING FEATURES: TUNERS & HARDWARE

The configuration of the Kluson tuners used on Gibson instruments can be used to date an instrument. Before 1959, all Kluson tuners with plastic buttons had a single ring around the stem end of the button. In 1960, this was changed to a double ring configuration. Early 1950s tuners have no writing in the center line. Mid- to late 1950s production features Kluson deluxe tuners with single line marking. By the mid-1960s, a two-line marking states "Kluson Deluxe."

**Gibson EDS-1275
courtesy Gibson**

ELECTRIC IDENTIFYING FEATURES: PEGHEAD & VOLUTE

"Made in USA" stamped into wood in back of peghead beginning 1969. Another dating feature of Gibsons is the use of a peghead volute found on instruments between 1970 and 1973. Also, in 1965 Gibson switched from 17 degrees to 14 degrees on the tilt of the peghead. Before 1950, peghead thickness varied, getting narrower towards the top of the peghead. After 1950, pegheads all became one uniform thickness, from bottom to top.

ELECTRIC SERIALIZATION

For more information on Gibson electric serialization, please refer to the Gibson listing under the Serialization section in the back of this text. Please read this section carefully, as Gibson has changed the format of its serialization a lot over the decades.

GIBSON COMMON ABBREVIATIONS

The abbreviations listed below may also be used in sequence (i.e., and ES-150DC is an Electric Spanish model with cutaway and double pickups).

C	Cutaway	J	Jumbo	T	Tremolo or Thinline
D	Dreadnought or Double Pickup	LE	Limited Edition	V	Venetian or Vibrato
E	Electric	S	Spanish, Solid Body, Special or Super	V	Venetian or Vibrato
ES	Electric (Electro) Spanish	SG	Solid Guitar		

GIBSON FINISH ABBREVIATIONS/HARDWARE

AB	Ambay Guasu (Smartwood only)	EB	Ebony	PE	Peroba (Smartwood only)
AC	Aged Cherry	ED	Emerald Burst (Green)	PM	Pewter Metallic
AG	Antique Gold	ES	Ebony Stain	PR	Pacific Reef
AN	Antique Natural	FI	Fireburst	PT	Pewter or Platinum
AW	Alpine White	FC	Faded Cherry	R1	Red Metallic
B1	Blue Metallic	FT	Faded Tobacco	RB	Lavaburst (red)
BA	Banara (Smartwood only)	G1	Green Metallic	RD	Translucent Red (Faded Cherry)
BC	Black Chrome or Brown with Creme stripes	GE	Gecko	RO	Root Beer
BE	Beale Street Blue	GH	Gold Hardware	SB	Saddle Brown
BF	Flat Black/Gothic	GT	Gold Top	SC	Satin Cherry
BG	Bigsby Gold	HB	Honeyburst	SE	Satin Ebony
BG	Bullion Gold	HC	Heritage Cherry	SL	Silver
BL	Translucent Black	HE	Black	SO	Sunrise Orange
BM	Blue Mist	HS	Heritage Cherry Sunburst	SP	Special
BR	Trans Brown or Cremona Brown	IT	Ice Tea	SS	Sante Fe Sunrise
BS	Black Sparkle	JB	Oxblood	SY	Satin Yellow
BT	Blue Teal Flip-flop	JJ	JuJu	TA	Translucent Amber
BU	Translucent Blue	LB	Light Burst	TB	Triburst
BZ	Blues Burst	LC	Latte Creme	TE	Iced Tea Burst
C1	Copper	LC	Lyre Vibrola Chrome	TP	Translucent Purple
CA	Candy Apple Red or Cayenne	LG	Lyre Vibrola Chrome	TR	Translucent Red
CB	Chicago Blue	LM	Lemonburst	TS	Tobacco Sunburst
CG	Country Gentleman Brown	MC	Vibrola Chrome	TV	TV Yellow
CH	Cherry	MD	Midnightburst (Blue)	TVW	TV White
CH	Chrome Hardware	MM	Manhattan Midnight	VB	Viceroy Brown Sunburst
C1	Copper Metallic	MR	Mahogany Red	VS	Vintage Sunburst
CN	Cinnamon	MU	Muricatiara	WB	Worn Brown
CN	Copper Natural	NA	Natural	WC	Worn Cherry or Washed Cherry
CR	Crème	NB	Natural Burst	WE	Worn Ebony
CU	Curupay (Smartwood only)	NH	Nickel Hardware	WR	Wine Red
CW	Classic White	NS	Natural Satin	WY	Worn Yellow
DB	Desert Burst (Brown)	OR	Sunrise Orange	Y1	Yellow Metallic
		PB	Pelham Blue		

GIBSON SHIPMENT TOTALS & MODEL/FAMILY CODES

For ease in identifying current Gibson production guitar models, the Gibson Family Code (in parenthesis) follows the model's name (in some cases, only the alphabetical prefix is listed, as the individual finishes and/or colors will result in the rest of the code). This also is true when brackets are encountered within a family code.

For anyone who is interested in individual Gibson model production totals from 1937 to 1979 (including guitars, basses, artist models, custom models, mandolins, banjos, ukuleles, steel guitars, effects, and amps), please look at *Gibson Shipment Totals 1937-1979* by Larry Meiners.

GIBSON ACOUSTIC/ACOUSTIC ELECTRIC

For further information regarding Gibson acoustic and acoustic electric models, please refer to the *Blue Book of Acoustic Guitars*. Gibson Chet Atkins and the J-160 Series acoustic electric models will be found in the Gibson Acoustic Electric section in the *Blue Book of Acoustic Guitars*.

GIBSON ELECTRIC MODEL CATEGORIES & LAYOUT

For organizational consideration, the following category names and variations for standard production models have been listed in the following sequence: B.B. King Series, Barney Kessel Series, Byrdland Series, Centennial & Guitar of the Month Series, Challenger Series, Chet Atkins Series, Corvus Series, Doubleneck Series, ES Series, Electric Models: Miscellaneous, Explorer Series, Firebird Reverse Series, Firebird Series, Flying V Series, Howard Roberts Series, Johnny Smith Series, L-4, L-5, L-6, Super V CES & Le Grande Series, Les Paul Series: Standard Mfg., M Series, Marauder Series, Melody Maker Series, Moderne Series, Night-

GRADING	100% MINT	98% NEAR MINT	95% EXC+	90% EXC	80% VG+	70% VG	60% G

hawk, Blueshawk, & Hawk Series, RD Series, SG Series, Sonex Series, Spirit Series, Super 400 CES Series, Tal Farlow Series, and Trini Lopez Series. Depending on the amount of variations and models under these major category headings, there also may be subcategories (i.e., Les Paul and Variations), which further define individual listings. Musician´s models are alphabetized by their first names.

Following the above standard production listings, the Gibson Custom Shop & Historic Collection Model information is listed in the following sequence: Custom Shop: General Information, Custom Shop: Custom Collection Abbreviations, Custom Shop: Historic Collection Abbreviations, Custom Shop: Carved Top Series, Custom Shop: ES Series, Custom Shop: Designer Series, Custom Shop: SG Series, Custom Shop: Historic Collection Les Paul Series, Custom Shop: Custom Collection Les Paul Series, and Custom Shop: Les Paul Limited Editions.

Following these Custom Shop/Historic Collection listings, Electric basses will appear in the following sequence: Electric Bass: EB Series, Electric Bass: Misc. Models, Electric Bass: Les Paul Bass Series, Electric Bass: LPB (Les Paul Bass) Series, and Electric Bass: Thunderbird Series.

Add 15%-30% for original Natural Blonde finish (depending on rarity) on all non-current Gibson electrics listed below which were manufactured with this finish option.

Subtract approx. 50% for refinishing on all models listed below.

Typically subtract 10%-20% for Gibson electric guitars with factory fitted Kahler or Floyd Rose locking tremolos, as they are not as desirable as those instruments without.

Gibson B.B. King Lucille
courtesy Gibson

ELECTRIC: B.B KING SERIES

For further information on the Little Lucille (introduced 1999), please refer to the Nighthawk Series section later in this text.

B.B. KING STANDARD - double round cutaway semi-hollow bound body, arched maple top, raised layered black pickguard, maple back/sides/neck, 22-fret bound rosewood fingerboard with pearl dot inlay, Tune-O-Matic bridge/tunable stop tailpiece, blackface peghead with pearl Lucille/logo inlay, 3-per-side tuners, chrome hardware, 2 covered humbucker pickups, 2 volume/2 tone controls, 3-position switch, stereo output. Available in Cherry and Ebony finishes, mfg. 1980-85.

	N/A	$1,350	$1,175	$925	$750	$650	$575

B.B. King Lucille (ARLC) - similar to B.B. King Standard, except has bound pickguard, bound ebony fingerboard with pearl block inlay, bound peghead, gold hardware, Vari-tone switch. Available in Cherry, Ebony, and Beale Street Blue (BE, mfg. 2002-2004) finishes, mfg. 1980-current, current mfg. is in Memphis.

MSR	$3,678	$2,450	$1,775	$1,525	$1,225	$1,025	$875	$750

Add $1,148 for "Lucille" fretboard inlay (disc. 2005).

From 1980 to 1988, this model was named the B.B. King Custom. Early production models had "Lucille" inlaid into the fretboard. Beginning in 2002, this model again became available with an optional signature in fretboard.

B.B. King Super Lucille (ARLS) - similar to B.B. King Lucille, except available in Black Sparkle finish, mfg. in Memphis 2002-2004.

	$2,650	$2,050	$1,700	$1,350	$1,100	$925	$800

Last MSR was $4,000.

ELECTRIC: BARNEY KESSEL SERIES

BARNEY KESSEL REGULAR - double sharp cutaway semi-hollow bound body, arched maple top, bound f-holes, raised layered black pickguard, maple back/sides, mahogany neck, 22-fret bound rosewood fingerboard with pearl block inlay, adjustable rosewood bridge/trapeze tailpiece, wood tailpiece insert with pearl model name inlay, bound blackface peghead with pearl crown/logo inlay, 3-per-side tuners, nickel hardware, 2 covered humbucker pickups, 2 volume/2 tone controls, 3-position switch, available in Cherry Sunburst finish, approx. 1,100 mfg. 1961-1973.

	N/A	$3,000	$2,650	$2,250	$1,950	$1,600	$1,295

Barney Kessel Custom - similar to Barney Kessel Regular, except has bowtie fingerboard inlay, musical note peghead inlay, gold hardware. Aprrox. 740 mfg. 1961-1973.

	N/A	$3,650	$3,150	$2,750	$2,400	$2,000	$1,750

ELECTRIC: BYRDLAND SERIES

Please refer to the Custom Shop/Historic Collection section for current Byrdland production information.

BYRDLAND - single round cutaway multi-bound hollow body, 17 in. wide by 21 in. long by 2.25 in. deep, 23.5 in. scale, solid spruce top, raised bound tortoiseshell pickguard, bound f-holes, maple back/sides/neck, 14/22-fret multi-bound ebony pointed fingerboard with pearl block inlay, Tune-O-Matic bridge/rosewood base, trapeze tailpiece, multi-bound blackface peghead with pearl flowerpot/logo inlay, 3-per-side tuners, gold hardware, 2 single coil Alnico pickups, 2 volume/2 tone controls, 3-position switch, available in Natural and Sunburst (most common) finishes, mfg. 1955-1985.

1955-1961	N/A	$9,000	$7,750	$6,500	$5,650	$5,000	$4,500
1962-1968	N/A	$4,500	$3,800	$3,375	$3,150	$2,850	$2,600
1969-1985	N/A	$4,000	$3,350	$2,800	$2,500	$2,300	$2,050

Highly flamed maple will add a premium to the above prices.

The Byrdland model was designed in conjunction with Billy Byrd and Hank Garland. In 1958, 2 covered P.A.F. humbucker pickups replaced original part/design. In 1959, Stereo-Varitone electronics were optionally offered. In 1960, single sharp cutaway replaced original part/design. In 1962, Patent Number humbucker pickups replaced the previous P.A.F. humbuckers. In mid-1968, single round cutaway replaced previous part/design. During 1976 only, a Byrdland 12-string was offered - less than 20 were mfg.

Gibson Byrdland
courtesy Dave Rogers
Dave's Guitar Shop

GRADING	100% MINT	98% NEAR MINT	95% EXC+	90% EXC	80% VG+	70% VG	60% G

ELECTRIC: CENTENNIAL & GUITAR OF THE MONTH SERIES

During 1988, Gibson started a "Guitar of the Month" program. These guitars were special runs with non-standard colors and utilized EMG pickups. Only 200 of each model were manufactured per month. Instruments included: Les Paul Custom with Ruby finish - March, SG ´62 with Blue finish - April, ES-335 with Beige finish - May, LP Standard with Silverburst finish - June, Chet Atkins CEw with Vintage Sunburst finish - July, Les Paul Custom Lite with Gold Top finish - Aug., WRC SR-71 with White finish - Sept., SG Custom with Ferrari Red finish - Oct., and U2 - Nov. There were no guitars produced in this series during Jan., Feb. or Dec. Individual Guitar of the Month models in excellent to average condition will be priced similarly to their respective standard models with similar features. NIC examples may be worth a slight premium, depending on the overall desirability of the configuration.

During 1994, Gibson began offering the electric Centennial series models to celebrate Gibson´s 100-year anniversary (1894 to 1994). There were 12 models in the program - and were released at the rate of one new model per month. No more than 101 instruments of each model were produced. Gibson´s plan was to have 100 dealers that year, with each one committed to a package of 12 guitars. Those dealers received a custom made oak and glass humidfied display cabinet at no charge to display each new model. Since the Custom Shop opened in 1994, the only Custom Shop Centennial model was the L-5 CES. The other 11 models were built by Gibson USA, and include the Firebird VII in Vintage Sunburst (Sept.), Flying V in Antique Gold (July), Les Paul Double Cutaway in Heritage Cherry (Jan.), Les Paul Classic Gold Top (Feb.), ES 350T (March), Explorer in Antique Gold (April), EDS 1275 in Ebony (May), ES 335 in Cherry (June), 1957 Black Beauty with 3 pickups (Nov.), L5 in Ebony (Dec.), and a Les Paul Standard in Vintage Sunburst (Oct.). Each instrument in the series retailed for $10,000. The serial numbers run from #1894 to #1994.

All Centennial models feature gold-plated hardware, gold control knobs with raised Centennial logo, a diamond dot over the "i" in the Gibson logo, serial number on tailpiece with numeral ´1´ in diamonds, medallion on the back of peghead with the image of Orville Gibson, an engraved 100th Anniversary banner inlay on the 12th fret, and a Centennial logo on the pickguard. Centennial models came with a black leather-covered case, a gold signet ring with Centennial logo, and a framed 16 x 20 photograph. The Centennial Series was discontinued in 1999.

Original MSR on most of the folowing Centennial models was $9,000. Current values for new in case Centennial Series models can vary somewhat, but the Gibson dealers we polled came up with the following price ranges:
LP Special Double Cutaway - $1,500 - $2,000. LP Classic Gold Top - $2,500 - 3,000. ES 350T - $3,000 - 3,500. Explorer - $3,000 - 3,500. EDS 1275 - $2,000 - 2,500. ES 335 - $3,000 - 3,500. Flying V - $2,000 - 2,500. Firebird VII - $3,000 - 3,500. LP Standard - $1,750 - 2,250. 1957 Black Beauty - $2,000 - 2,500. L5 CES (Custom Shop) - $3,750 - 4,500

ELECTRIC: CHALLENGER SERIES

CHALLENGER I - single cutaway mahogany body, black pickguard, bolt-on maple neck, 22-fret rosewood fingerboard with pearl dot inlay, Tune-O-Matic stud tailpiece, 3-per-side tuners, chrome (and silver) hardware, humbucker pickup, volume/tone control, available in Cherry Red finish, mfg. 1983-85.

	N/A	$300	$250	$200	$175	$150	$125

Challenger II - similar to Challenger I, except has 2 humbucker pickups, 2 volume controls, mfg. 1983-85.

	N/A	$325	$275	$250	$215	$175	$150

ELECTRIC: CHET ATKINS SERIES

CHET ATKINS COUNTRY GENTLEMAN (ARCF) - single round cutaway semi-hollow bound maple body, bound f-holes, raised bound tortoiseshell pickguard, bound arm rest on bottom bass bout, 3-piece maple neck, 22-fret rosewood fingerboard with offset red block inlay, Tune-O-Matic bridge with or w/o Bigsby vibrato tailpiece, blackface peghead with pearl plant/logo inlay, 3-per-side tuners, gold hardware, 2 covered humbucker pickups, master volume on upper treble bout, 2 volume/1 tone controls, 3-position switch, available in Country Gentleman Brown (CG), Ebony (EB), Sunrise Orange (OR), or Wine Red (WR) finishes, mfg. 1987-present.

MSR	$4,702		$3,100	$2,100	$1,850	$1,575	$1,325	$1,150	$975

Add $800 for Bigsby tailpiece (ARCA, mfg. 2002-2004).

In 1994, Ebony finish was discontinued.

CHET ATKINS TENNESSEAN (ARCT) - single round cutaway semi-hollow bound maple body, f-holes, raised pickguard with engraved "Tennessean," arm rest on bottom bass bout, 3-piece maple neck, 22-fret rosewood fingerboard with offset pearl dot inlay, Tune-O-Matic bridge/stop tailpiece, blackface peghead with signature/pearl logo inlay, 3-per-side tuners with pearl buttons, chrome hardware, 2 covered humbucker pickups, master volume on upper treble bout, 2 volume/1 tone controls, 3-position switch, available in Country Gentleman Brown (CG, disc.), Faded Cherry (RD), Sunrise Orange (OR), Ebony (EB, disc.), Pelham Blue (mfg. 2004) or Wine Red (WR).

MSR	$3,040		$2,050	$1,575	$1,250	$1,025	$925	$850	$750

In 1994, Country Gentleman Brown (CG), Sunrise Orange (OR) and Wine Red (WR) finishes became standard, Ebony finish was discontinued.

CHET ATKINS SUPER 4000 - single rounded cutaway hollow body (Super 400 size), bound carved Sitka spruce top, bound f-holes, raised multi-bound tortoiseshell pickguard, carved bookmatched maple back/sides, multiple bound body, 5-piece curly maple neck, 20-fret bound ebony fingerboard, pearl split block fingerboard inlay, adjustable ebony bridge base/gold Tune-O-Matic bridge, gold trapeze tailpiece with ebony inserts and abalone fleur-de-lis inlay, multi-bound blackface peghead with pearl 5-piece split diamond/logo inlay, 3-per-side gold Kluson tuners with mother-of-pearl buttons, floating pickup and linear sliding volume control with ebony knob (under raised pickguard), includes authenticity certificate signed by Chet Atkins, available in Sunburst or Natural finishes, mfg. 1997 only.

	N/A	$17,500	$12,500	N/A	N/A	N/A	N/A

Last MSR was $40,000.

It is estimated that only 25 Super 4000 models were built. Only 20 instruments were available to the public.

ELECTRIC: CORVUS SERIES

CORVUS I - can opener style hardwood body, black pickguard, bolt-on maple neck, 22-fret rosewood fingerboard with white dot inlay, Tune-O-Matic stud tailpiece, 6-on-a-side tuners, chrome hardware, covered humbucker pickup, volume/tone control, available in Silver finish, mfg. 1982-84.

	N/A	$400	$325	$275	$225	$195	$150

GRADING	100% MINT	98% NEAR MINT	95% EXC+	90% EXC	80% VG+	70% VG	60% G

Corvus II - similar to Corvus I, except has 2 covered humbucker pickups, 3-position switch, mfg. 1982-84.

	N/A	$495	$350	$295	$250	$225	$175

Corvus III - similar to Corvus I, except has 3 exposed single coil pickups, 5-position switch, mfg. 1982-84.

	N/A	$550	$500	$395	$325	$295	$225

ELECTRIC: DOUBLENECK SERIES

DOUBLE TWELVE - double cutaway hollow maple body, carved spruce top, 2-stripe bound body, double neck configuration with 12- and 6-string necks, 2 bound black pickguards, 3-position neck selector switch, each mahogany neck has 20-fret bound rosewood fingerboard with pearloid parallelogram inlay, Tune-O-Matic bridge/fixed tailpiece, 6-per-side/3-per-side tuners with pearl buttons, chrome hardware, 2 covered humbucker pickups, volume/tone control, 3-position switch, available in Black, Sunburst, or White finishes, mfg. 1958-1962.

	N/A	$24,000	$20,000	$16,500	$13,500	$11,000	$8,750

EMS 1235 - similar to EDS 1275, except has octave 6 plus 6-string necks, hollow body 1958-1961, solid body beginning 1962, mfg. 1958-1967.

1958-1961	N/A	$9,250	$8,500	$7,500	$6,500	$6,000	$5,650
1962-1967	N/A	$7,000	$6,500	$6,000	$5,500	$5,000	$4,500

EBS 1250 - similar to EDS 1275, except has bass configuration instead of 12-string configuration on upper neck, built-in fuzztone, mfg. 1962-67, and 1977-78.

	N/A	$5,500	$4,950	$4,500	$4,150	$3,950	$3,750

EDS 1275 (1963-68 MFG.) - double cutaway mahogany body, double neck configuration, 2 black 3-ply laminated pickguards, 3-position neck/pickup selector switches, 2 volume/2 tone controls, each mahogany neck has 20-fret bound rosewood fingerboard with pearl parallelogram inlay, Tune-O-Matic bridge/fixed tailpiece, 6-per-side/3-per-side tuners with pearl buttons, chrome hardware, 2 covered humbucker pickups, available in Jet Black, Sunburst, or White finishes, mfg. 1963-68.

	N/A	$7,000	$6,500	$6,000	$5,600	$5,200	$4,800

EDS 1275 (1977-CURRENT MFG.) - similar to EDS 1275, except available in Alpine White, Cherry, Heritage Cherry, Cherry Sunburst, Sunburst, Walnut, or White finishes, mfg. 1974-present.

1974-1986	N/A	$2,150	$1,850	$1,650	$1,450	$1,325	$1,200
1987-1989	N/A	$1,575	$1,250	$1,100	$925	$825	$725
1990-1998	$2,100	$1,600	$1,375	$1,175	$950	$750	$525

Add 10% for Alpine White finish with gold hardware.

In 1984, Cherry Sunburst, Walnut and White finishes became standard part/design. In 1987, Cherry finish became an option. In 1990, Alpine White (with gold hardware) and Heritage Cherry (with chrome hardware) finishes became standard part/design.

EDS 1275 Alpine White (DSED-AW) - gold hardware, available in Alpine White finish, current mfg.

MSR	$4,332	$2,900	$1,750	$1,450	$1,200	$975	$775	$550

This model was manufactured by Gibson USA until 2003.

EDS 1275 Heritage Cherry (DSED-HC) - chrome hardware, available in Heritage Cherry Sunburst finish, current mfg.

MSR	$4,097	$2,775	$2,400	$1,950	$1,850	$1,625	$1,450	$1,200

This model was manufactured by Gibson USA until 2003.

Gibson Chet Atkins Country Gentleman courtesy Gibson

G

ELECTRIC: ES-SERIES

The standard production ES models listed below are listed in numerical sequence, with the ES Artist appearing at the end. Custom Shop ES Series intruments are located under the Gibson Custom Shop category.

Add approx. $350 for left-hand on current models.

ES-5 & ES-5 SWITCHMASTER - single round cutaway hollow body, 17 in. wide by 21 in. long, by 3.375 in. deep, 25.5 in. scale, arched figured maple top, bound f-holes, raised layered black pickguard, 3-stripe bound body, figured maple back/sides/neck, 14/20-fret multi-bound pointed fingerboard with pearl block inlay, adjustable ebony bridge/trapeze tailpiece, bound blackface peghead with pearl crown/logo inlay, 3-per-side tuners with plastic buttons, gold hardware, 3 black single coil pickups until 1957, after which humbuckers became standard, tone control on cutaway bout, 3 volume controls, available in Natural and Sunburst (more common) finishes, mfg. 1949-1961.

1949-1955 (ES-5)	N/A	$5,500	$4,950	$4,450	$4,100	$3,875	$3,600
1955-1956 (ES-5 SWITCH)	N/A	$8,250	$7,500	$6,500	$5,500	$4,950	$4,450
1957-1961 (ES-5 SWITCH)	N/A	$12,000	$10,000	$8,950	$7,850	$6,850	$5,900

A few early models can be found with unbound f-holes. In 1955, the ES-5 model was renamed ES-5 Switchmaster, and a Tune-O-Matic bridge, 3 volume/3 tone controls, 4 position switch replaced previous part/design. In 1957, humbucker pickups replaced single coil P-90s. In 1960, sharp cutaway replaced rounded treble bout.

Gibson Chet Atkins Super 4000 courtesy Dave Rogers Dave's Guitar Shop

GRADING	100% MINT	98% NEAR MINT	95% EXC+	90% EXC	80% VG+	70% VG	60% G

ES-100 - arched maple top, f-holes, raised black pickguard, bound body, maple back, mahogany sides/neck, 14/20-fret rosewood fingerboard with pearl dot inlay, adjustable rosewood bridge/trapeze tailpiece, blackface peghead with pearl logo inlay, 3-per-side tuners, nickel hardware, single coil pickup, volume/tone control, available in Sunburst finish, mfg. 1938-1941.

1938-1939	N/A	$1,250	$975	$850	$725	$600	$500
1940-1941	N/A	$800	$700	$600	$475	$350	$300

ES-120 T - arched maple top, molded black pickguard, f-hole, maple back, mahogany sides/neck, 14/20-fret rosewood fingerboard with pearl dot inlay, adjustable rosewood bridge/trapeze tailpiece, 3-per-side tuners with plastic buttons, chrome hardware, single coil pickup, volume/tone control, available in Sunburst finish, mfg. 1961-1970.

	N/A	$600	$525	$450	$375	$350	$325

Add $100 for 2 pickup versions (ES-120 TD).

ES-125 - arched maple top, f-holes, 16.25 in. by 20.25 in. by 3.375 in., raised black pickguard, bound body, maple back, mahogany sides/neck, 14/19-fret rosewood fingerboard with pearl dot inlay, adjustable rosewood bridge/trapeze tailpiece, blackface peghead with pearl logo inlay, 3-per-side tuners, nickel hardware, single coil pickup, volume/tone control, available in Sunburst finish, variations mfg. 1941-1970.

	N/A	$1,000	$850	$750	$675	$600	$550

Some production occurred in 1941, though the majority of production was post-World War II. In 1946, a few models were produced with an all mahogany body. In 1950, a standard P-90 pickup was introduced. In 1955, a 14/19-fret fingerboard was introduced.

ES-125 C - similar to ES-125, except has a cutaway body, mfg. 1965-1970.

	N/A	$1,250	$1,100	$925	$800	$700	$600

ES-125 CD - similar to ES-125, except has cutaway body and double pickups, mfg. 1965-1970.

	N/A	$1,500	$1,300	$1,075	$950	$850	$725

ES-125 T - similar to ES-125, except has a thin body, 16.25 in. by 20.25 in. by 1.75 in. deep, 24.75 in. scale, mfg. 1956-1969.

	N/A	$1,000	$875	$700	$600	$500	$450

ES-125 T 3/4 - similar to ES-125 T, except has a 3/4 size body, 22.75 in. scale, mfg. 1957-1970.

	N/A	$725	$650	$575	$500	$425	$365

ES-125 TC - similar to ES-125 T, except has thin body and cutaway, mfg. 1960-1970.

	N/A	$1,000	$750	$675	$600	$600	$550

ES-125 TD - similar to ES-125, except has a thin body and double pickups, mfg. 1957-1963.

	N/A	$1,000	$850	$750	$675	$600	$550

ES-125 TCD/TDC - similar to ES-125, except has a thin body, cutaway, and double pickups, available in Cherry Sunburst, and Tobacco Sunburst during 1960 only (ES-125 TCD), mfg. 1960-1970, ES-125 TCD mfg. circa 1960 only, followed by the TDC suffix 1961-1970.

	N/A	$2,000	$1,750	$1,500	$1,250	$1,000	$875

This model is the most desirable of the ES-125 Series, mostly because it has been made popular by George Thorogood.

ES-130 - same body size as ES-125, arched maple top, layered black pickguard, f-hole, maple back, mahogany sides/neck, 14/20-fret bound rosewood fingerboard with pearl block inlay, adjustable rosewood bridge/trapeze tailpiece, 3-per-side tuners with plastic buttons, nickel hardware, one P-90 single coil pickup, volume/tone control, available in Sunburst finish, mfg. 1954-58.

	N/A	$1,150	$975	$850	$750	$675	$600

This model was renamed the ES-135 in 1956.

ES-135 (MFG. 1954-58) - archtop, bound maple body, single bound top/back and fingerboard, f-holes, laminated raised black pickguard, mahogany neck, 22-fret rosewood fingerboard with pearl trapezoid inlays, trapeze tailpiece, decal logo on headstock, 3-per-side tuners with pearl buttons, chrome hardware, one P-90 single coil pickup mounted one inch from fingerboard, volume/tone controls, 16.25 in. wide, 24.75 in. scale. Available in Sunburst finish, mfg. 1954-58.

	N/A	$1,750	$1,475	$1,250	$1,050	$900	$800

ES-135 (MFG. 1991-2002) - single sharp cutaway semi-hollow bound maple body, f-holes, raised black pickguard, maple neck, 22-fret rosewood fingerboard with pearl dot inlay, Tune-O-Matic bridge/trapeze tailpiece, 3-per-side tuners with pearl buttons, chrome hardware, two P-90 single coil pickups, 2 volume/2 tone controls, 3-position switch. Available in various finishes (including Gothic, 100% Satin Black finish, black chrome hardware, and 12th fret moon and star inlay), hardshell case became standard in 1998, mfg. in Memphis, disc. 2002.

	$1,075	$900	$775	$650	$550	$450	$395

Last MSR was $1,537.

Subtract approx. 10% for Gothic finish (matte black, mfg. 1999 only).

ES-135 w/Humbuckers (ES3H) - similar to ES-135, except has 2 humbucker pickups, satin finish, chrome or gold hardware. Available in Ebony, Cherry, Vintage Sunburst, Natural, Blues Burst (BZ, new 2002), or Wine Red finish, mfg.1999-2004.

	$1,095	$900	$775	$650	$550	$450	$395

Last MSR was $1,656.

ES-137 CUSTOM (ES3) - figured maple/poplar laminate top/back, maple neck with ebony fingerboard and pearloid split diamond inlays, available with either two P-90 single coil (disc. 2002) or '57 Classic humbucker pickups, available in Metallic Blue (disc. 2004), Bullion Gold (P-90 only, disc. 2004), Copper (disc. 2004), Metallic Green (P-90 only, disc. 2004), Candy Apple Red (humbucker only), Heritage Cherry Sunburst (new 2005), Light Burst (new 2005), Triburst (new 2005), or Silver (disc. 2004, humbucker only) finish. New 2002, current mfg in Memphis.

MSR	$3,375	$2,250	$1,575	$1,275	$1,075	$950	$850	$750

ES-137 Classic C/CU - similar to ES-137, except has rosewood fingerboard with pearloid trapezoid inlays, white top/body binding, gold hardware, C is inlaid between 11th and 12th fret, CU model is Smartwood, available in Blues Burst, Heritage Cherry Sunburst, Silver, Trans. Black, Candy Apple Red (disc. 2004), Light Burst (Smartwood only, disc. 2004), or Triburst (Smartwood only until 2005) finish, new 2002.

MSR	$2,410	$1,550	$1,125	$975	$850	$750	$650	$550

Add $500 for ES-137CU (Smartwood, disc. 2005).

GRADING	100% MINT	98% NEAR MINT	95% EXC+	90% EXC	80% VG+	70% VG	60% G

ES-140 3/4 - single sharp cutaway body, 3.25 in. deep, arched maple top, raised black pickguard, f-holes, bound body, maple back/sides, mahogany neck, 19-fret rosewood fingerboard with pearl dot inlay, adjustable rosewood bridge/trapeze tailpiece, 3-per-side tuners with plastic buttons, nickel hardware, P-90 single coil pickup, volume/tone control, available in Natural or Sunburst finishes, mfg. 1950-57.

	N/A	$1,150	$1,000	$925	$850	$750	$650

ES-140 T 3/4 - similar to ES-140 3/4, except had a thin body, 12.75 in. wide, 17.25 in. long, and 1.75 in. deep, 22.75 in. scale, 13/19-fret fingerboard, mfg. 1956-1970.

	N/A	$975	$750	$650	$575	$500	$450

ES-150 (1936-1942 MFG.) - spruce top, f-holes, bound black pickguard, bound body, flat maple back, mahogany sides/neck, 14/19-fret bound rosewood fingerboard with pearl dot inlay, adjustable rosewood bridge/trapeze tailpiece, pearl peghead logo inlay, 3-per-side tuners, nickel hardware, single coil pickup, volume/tone control, available in Sunburst finish, mfg. 1936-1942.

	N/A	$4,000	$3,500	$3,150	$2,750	$2,400	$2,100

This guitar was informally known as the Charlie Christian model. In 1940, arched back and unbound fingerboard replaced original part/design. In 1941, a different pickup was introduced.

ES-150 (1946-1956 MFG.) - similar to ES-150 (pre-war model), except has slightly larger body, layered black pickguard, silkscreen peghead logo, mfg. 1946-1956.

	N/A	$1,950	$1,700	$1,500	$1,250	$1,100	$1,000

In 1950, bound fingerboard with trapezoid inlay replaced original part/design.

ES-150 DC - double cutaway semi-hollow style, arched maple top, f-holes, raised layered black pickguard, bound body, maple back/sides, mahogany neck, 22-fret rosewood fingerboard with pearl block inlay, Tune-O-Matic bridge/trapeze tailpiece, 3-per-side tuners, chrome hardware, 2 covered humbucker pickups, master volume control on upper treble bout, 2 volume/2 tone controls, 3-position switch, available in Cherry, Natural, or Walnut finishes, mfg. 1970-1975.

1970	N/A	$1,700	$1,500	$1,450	$1,350	$1,200	$1,100
1971-1975	N/A	$1,200	$1,100	$995	$875	$825	$795

ES-165 HERB ELLIS (ARHE) - single sharp cutaway hollow bound maple body, f-holes, raised black pickguard, mahogany neck, 20-fret bound rosewood fingerboard with pearl parallelogram inlay, Tune-O-Matic metal/rosewood bridge/trapeze tailpiece, peghead with pearl plant/logo inlay, 3-per-side tuners with pearl buttons, gold hardware, 2 covered humbucker pickups, 2 volume/2 tone controls, 3-position switch, available in Cherry (CH, disc. 2001), Light Burst (new 2004), Wine Red, Ebony (EB), or Vintage Sunburst (VS) finishes, current mfg.

MSR	$3,363	$2,250	$1,700	$1,425	$1,175	$950	$875	$750

ES-165 Herb Ellis Plus (ARHE+) - includes f-hole mutes, available in Light Burst, Vintage Sunburst, Wine Red, or Bullion Gold. Mfg. 2002-2004.

	$2,900	$2,100	$1,775	$1,500	$1,325	$1,100	$950

Last MSR was $4,100.

Add $616 for Bullion Gold finish.

ES-175 (W/ SINGLE PICKUP, ES75) - single sharp cutaway body, 16.25 in. wide by 20.25 in. long, and 3 3/8 in. deep, 24 3/4 in. scale, arched maple top, f-holes, raised layered black pickguard, bound body, maple back/sides, mahogany neck, 14/20-fret bound rosewood fingerboard with pearl parallelogram inlay, adjustable rosewood bridge/trapeze tailpiece, black face peghead with pearl crown/logo inlay, nickel hardware, one single coil or humbucker pickup, volume/tone control, available in Natural or Sunburst finishes, mfg. 1949-1979.

1949-1956 (P90 PICKUP)	N/A	$4,000	$3,250	$2,650	$2,300	$1,850	$1,600
1957-1962 (PAF PICKUP)	N/A	$8,000	$7,000	$6,000	$5,200	$4,000	$2,750
1963-1979	N/A	$2,500	$2,150	$1,750	$1,500	$1,250	$1,000

In 1957, PAF humbucker pickup replaced original part/design. In 1962, Pat. No. humbucker pickups replaced previous part/design. This model was also produced in a thinline body, ES-175 T, mfg. 1976-79. Further research continues on this configuration for future editions.

ES-175 CC - similar to ES-175, except has Charlie Christian single coil pickup. Mfg. 1979-disc.

	N/A	$2,250	$1,975	$1,500	$1,300	$995	$875

ES-175 D (W/ TWO PICKUPS) - similar to ES-175, except has 2 single coil (disc.) or humbucker pickups (current pickups are '57 Classic humbuckers), current dimensions are 16 in. wide, 20.5 in. long, and 3.5 in. thick, current mfg. utilizes curly maple/poplar/maple laminate top, sides, and back with mahogany neck and rosewood fretboard, 2 volume/2 tone controls, 3-position switch, currently available in Vintage Sunburst, Wine Red, or Natural finish, mfg. 1953-present.

1953-1956	N/A	$4,500	$4,000	$3,350	$2,500	$2,150	$1,750
1957-1962	N/A	$9,500	$8,500	$7,250	$6,000	$5,100	$3,750
1962-1969	N/A	$3,500	$3,000	$2,500	$2,100	$1,775	$1,500
1970-1997	N/A	$2,000	$1,850	$1,375	$1,250	$995	$875
1998-MSR $4,563	$3,075	$2,350	$1,675	$1,650	$1,450	$1,100	$975

Add $529 for Natural finish on current mfg. Add $523 for Aged finish, including antique hardware, worn neck and body, and old style wire tailpiece (2003-2004).

Current production instruments (except for Aged finishes) are produced in either a Wine Red (WR), Vintage Sunburst (VS) or Natural (AN) finish with nickel or gold hardware. In 1957, P.A.F. humbucker pickups replaced original part/design. In 1962, Pat. No. humbucker pickups replaced previous part/design. In 1974, neck volute was introduced. By 1977, Tune-O-Matic bridge replaced original part/

**Gibson ES-140
courtesy George McGuire**

**Gibson ES-150
courtesy Dave Hull**

GRADING	100% MINT	98% NEAR MINT	95% EXC+	90% EXC	80% VG+	70% VG	60% G

design. In 1981, neck volute was discontinued. In 1983, mahogany back/sides replaced original part/design. In 1990, maple back/sides replaced previous part/design. Guitars are currently produced in Memphis, Tennessee.

ES-175 D-AN (ES75-AN) - similar to ES-175 D, except has 2 single coil pickups, 2 volume/2 tone controls, 3-position switch, available in Antique Natural finish and nickel hardware, disc. 2000.

	$3,625	$2,850	$2,475	$2,100	$1,700	$1,350	$1,100

Last MSR was $5,589.

ES-175T - similar to the ES-175D, except has a thinline body, available in Natural, Sunburst, or Wine Red finishes, mfg. 1976-79

	N/A	$2,200	$1,900	$1,600	$1,400	$1,200	$1,000

ES-175 Steve Howe Signature - exact copy of Steve's Howe's favorite guitar, a 1964 ES-175, includes signature case, trapeze tailpiece, Vintage Sunburst finish, mfg. 2001-present.

MSR	$4,629	$3,075	$2,300	$1,875	$1,600	N/A	N/A	N/A

ES-225 T - single sharp cutaway thin body, 16.25 in. wide by 20.25 in. long by 1.75 in. deep, 24.75 in. scale, arched maple top, f-holes, raised layered black pickguard, bound body, maple back/sides, mahogany neck, 14/20-fret bound rosewood fingerboard with pearl dot inlay, trapeze wrapover tailpiece, blackface peghead with pearl logo inlay, single coil pickup, volume/tone control, available in Sunburst finish, mfg. 1955-59.

	N/A	$1,300	$1,200	$1,100	$925	$800	$750

Extreme rarity factor precludes accurate price evaluation.

ES-225 TD - similar to ES-225T, except has 2 pickups, 2 volume/2 tone controls, mfg. 1956-59.

	N/A	$1,875	$1,625	$1,450	$1,250	$1,050	$925

ES-240 - very rare model, only 3 are known to exist, mfg. 1977-78.

ES-250 - jumbo style, spruce top, raised bound black pickguard, 3-stripe bound body, maple back/sides/neck, 14/20-fret bound rosewood fingerboard with pearl open book inlay, adjustable rosewood bridge/trapeze tailpiece, blackface stairstep peghead with pearl logo inlay, 3-per-side tuners, nickel hardware, single coil Charlie Christian pickup, volume/tone control, available in Natural or Sunburst finishes, mfg. 1938-1940.

	N/A	N/A	$7,500	$6,200	$5,750	$4,400	$3,650

In 1940, standard style peghead, split half circle fingerboard inlay replaced original part/design.

ES-295 - single sharp cutaway body, similar body size/scale specs as ES-175, multi-bound maple top, f-holes, raised white pickguard with etched flowers, maple back/sides/neck, 19- or 20-fret bound rosewood fingerboard with pearl parallelogram inlay, trapeze wrapover tailpiece, blackface peghead with pearl plant/logo inlay, 3-per-side tuners with pearl buttons, gold hardware, 2 single coil pickups until 1958, when humbuckers became standard, 2 volume/2 tone controls, 3-position switch, available in Gold finish, mfg. 1952-58.

	N/A	$6,500	$5,500	$4,750	$3,750	$3,200	$2,950

In 1955, 20-fret fingerboard replaced original part/design. In 1958, humbucker pickups replaced original part/design. Current production instruments are part of the Historic Collection Series, found at the end of this section.

ES-300 (1940-42 MFG.) - spruce top, bound black pickguard, multi-bound body, maple back/sides/neck, 14/20-fret rosewood fingerboard with pearl parallelogram inlay, adjustable rosewood bridge/trapeze tailpiece, bound peghead with pearl crown/logo inlay, 3-per-side tuners, nickel hardware, diagonally mounted single coil pickup, volume/tone control, available in Natural or Sunburst finishes, mfg. 1940-42.

	N/A	N/A	N/A	$2,400	$2,100	$1,500	$1,250

This model was also manufactured with a split diamond peghead inlay.

ES-300 (1946-1953 Mfg.) - similar to ES-300 Prewar, except has layered black pickguard, bound fingerboard, mfg. 1946-1953.

	N/A	$2,100	$1,650	$1,450	$1,200	$1,000	$925

In 1948, 2 single coil pickups, 2 volume controls replaced original part/design. Tone control moved to upper treble bout.

ES-320 TD - double round cutaway semi-hollow bound body, arched maple top, f-holes, raised black pickguard, maple back/sides/neck, 22-fret rosewood fingerboard with pearl dot inlay, fixed Tune-O-Matic bridge with logo engraved cover, 3-per-side tuners, nickel hardware, 2 single coil pickups, volume/tone control, 2 slide switches, available in Cherry, Natural, or Walnut finishes, mfg. 1971-75.

	N/A	$750	$625	$500	$425	$350	$295

ES-325 TD - double round cutaway semi-hollow bound body, arched maple top, f-hole, raised layered black pickguard, maple back/sides/neck, 22-fret rosewood fingerboard with pearl dot inlay, Tune-O-Matic bridge/trapeze tailpiece, 3-per-side tuners with plastic buttons, nickel hardware, 2 mini humbucker pickups, 2 volume/2 tone controls, 3-position switch, control mounted on black plastic plate, available in Cherry, Walnut, or Wine Red finishes, mfg. 1972-79.

	$850	$750	$650	$550	$475	$375	$325

ES-330 T - double round cutaway semi-hollow bound body, arched maple top, raised bound black pickguard, f-holes, maple back/sides, mahogany neck, 22-fret bound rosewood fingerboard with pearl dot inlay, Tune-O-Matic bridge/trapeze tailpiece, blackface peghead with pearl logo inlay, 3-per-side tuners with plastic buttons, nickel hardware, single coil pickup, volume/tone control, available in Cherry (ES-330 TC) Natural, or Sunburst finishes, mfg. 1959-1963.

	N/A	$3,000	$2,600	$2,200	$1,850	$1,500	$1,200

In 1962, block fingerboard inlays replaced dot inlays and chrome covered pickups replaced black plastic pickups, Cherry finish became an option, Natural finish was discontinued.

ES-330 TD - similar to ES-330 T, except has 2 single coil pickups, 2 volume/2 tone controls, 3-position switch, mfg. 1959-1975.

		100%	98%	95%	90%	80%	70%	60%
1959-1962		N/A	$4,000	$3,500	$3,000	$2,450	$1,900	$1,500
1963-1975		N/A	$2,500	$2,150	$1,750	$1,400	$1,100	$850

In 1960, Cherry finish became an option (Model ES-330 TDC). In 1962, pearl block fingerboard inlay replaced original part/design, and Natural finish was discontinued. Between 1967 and 1969, Sparkling Burgundy finish was an option. In 1968, Walnut finish was an option.

ES-333 - same body size/style as ES-335, maple/poplar laminate top and back, 2 exposed black humbucker pickups, mahogany neck with 10/22-fret rosewood fingerboard with pearloid dot inlays, no pickguard, nickel hardware, electronics similar to ES-335, Trans. Brown, Trans. Red, and Natural finish, includes gig bag. Mfg. in Memphis, new 2003.

MSR	$1,599	$1,275	$850	$750	$675	$600	$550	$500

GRADING	100% MINT	98% NEAR MINT	95% EXC+	90% EXC	80% VG+	70% VG	60% G

ES-335 TD (1958-1982 MFG.)

- double round cutaway semi-hollow bound body, arched maple top, interior maple block runs down the middle of body between tailpiece and endpin, unbound f-holes, raised layered black or tortoiseshell pickguard, maple back/sides, mahogany neck, 22-fret rosewood fingerboard with pearl dot (originally mfg. 1958-1962) or block (became standard 1962) inlays, Tune-O-Matic bridge, stop, trapeze, or Bigsby tailpiece, blackface peghead with pearl crown/logo inlay, 3-per-side tuners, nickel hardware, 2 covered humbucker PAF pickups, 2 volume/2 tone controls, 3-position switch, available in various finishes, including Ebony (1974-79, ES-335 TD), Wine Red (1975-79, ES-335 TD), Walnut, Cherry, Natural, Sunburst (1958-1970, and 1974), or Tobacco Sunburst (mfg. 1974 only), 16 in. wide by 1.675 in. deep, 24.75 in. scale, mfg. 1958-1982.

	100%	98%	95%	90%	80%	70%	60%
1958-1959	N/A	$28,000	$25,000	$21,000	$17,000	$15,000	$13,000
1960-1961	N/A	$17,500	$15,000	$13,500	$11,000	$9,250	$8,000
1962-1964	N/A	$10,000	$8,750	$7,500	$6,500	$5,500	$4,750
1965-1969	N/A	$3,500	$3,000	$2,650	$2,250	$1,850	$1,425
1970-1982	N/A	$2,200	$1,950	$1,600	$1,400	$1,200	$1,000

Subtract approx. 25% if w/ Bigsby tailpiece.

In 1958, some instruments were unbound. In 1960, Cherry finish became an option. In 1960, the name changed to ES-335 TD, and a smaller pickguard replaced original part/design. In 1962, block fingerboard inlays became standard, and Pat. No. pickups replaced original part/design. In 1964, trapeze tailpiece replaced original stop tailpiece. In 1970, Walnut finish became an option - some instruments included a slanted block fingerboard inlay. From 1969 to 1970, a neck volute was available. From 1971-79, approx. 130 left-hand ES-335 TD models were manufactured. In 1977, a coil tap switch was added. In 1982, this original version was discontinued in favor of the ES-335 Dot (a return to the 1960 style with dot fingerboard markers). The ES-335 TD Dot is currently known as the ES-335 TD (ESDT).

Gibson ES-330 TD courtesy Dave Rogers Dave's Guitar Shop

ES-335 PRO

- bound fingerboard, dot inlays, crown peghead inlay, two Dirty Finger humbucker pickups with exposed coils, Tune-O-Matic bridge, stop tailpiece, available in Antique Sunburst or Cherry Red finish, mfg. 1979-1981.

	N/A	$2,200	$1,950	$1,600	$1,400	$1,200	$1,000

ES-335 S STANDARD (ES-335 SOLID BODY)

- double round cutaway maple body, black pickguard, mahogany neck, 22-fret rosewood fingerboard with pearl dot inlay, Tune-O-Matic bridge/stop tailpiece, 3-per-side tuners, nickel hardware, 2 "exposed" humbucker pickups, 2 volume/2 tone controls, mini switch (for coil tapping), 3-way selector switch, available in Natural or Sunburst finishes, mfg. 1980-83.

	N/A	$800	$725	$650	$550	$475	$400

This model was clearly based on the popular ES-335 semi-hollow model; the width of the solid body is narrower than the semi-hollow model it is based on.

ES-335 S Custom

- similar to the ES-335 S Standard, except features a mahogany body, 2 Gibson Dirty Finger humbucker pickups, mfg. 1981 only.

	N/A	$850	$775	$675	$600	$525	$475

ES-335 S Deluxe

- similar to the ES-335 S Standard, except features a mahogany body, bound ebony fingerboard, brass nut, TP-6 Fine Tuning tailpiece/Tune-O-Matic bridge, 2 Gibson Dirty Finger humbucker pickups, mfg. 1980-83.

	N/A	$850	$775	$675	$600	$525	$475

ES-335 TD REISSUE (ESDT)

- double round cutaway semi-hollow bound maple body, f-holes, raised black pickguard, mahogany neck, 22-fret bound rosewood fingerboard with pearl dot inlay, Tune-O-Matic bridge/stop tailpiece, blackface peghead with pearl plant/logo inlay, 3-per-side tuners, nickel hardware, 2 covered humbucker pickups, 2 volume/2 tone controls, 3-position switch. Available in Natural, Cherry (CH), Trans Brown. (BR, disc. 2005), Vintage Sunburst (VS), Trans. Purple (TP, disc. 2004), Wine Red (WR, disc. 2005), Light Burst (new 2004), Triburst (new 2004), Beale Street Blue (BE, disc. 2005), or Gothic (100% satin black finish, black chrome hardware, and 12th fret moon and star inlay, disc.) finishes, mfg. 1982-present, current mfg. is in Memphis.

	100%	98%	95%	90%	80%	70%	60%
1982-1997	N/A	$2,000	$1,875	$1,750	$1,650	$1,575	$1,500
MSR	$3,683	$2,450	$1,850	$1,575	$1,350	$1,150	$950	$825

Subtract approx. 35% for Gothic finish (matte black, mfg. 1999 only).

In 1994, Ebony finish was discontinued.

ES-335 TD-AN

- similar to the ES-335 TD, available in Antique Natural finish (with nickel hardware), current mfg.

MSR	$4,212	$2,825	$2,300	$1,875	$1,625	$1,400	$1,200	$1,000

ES-335 TD Plain Wood (ESBP/ESDP)

- similar to the ES-335 TD, except has plain wood top, and choice of block (ESBP, disc. 2001) or dot (ESDP) neck inlays, available in Trans. Blue (disc. 2001), Natural (disc. 2001), Trans. Red (disc. 2001, reintroduced 2005), Trans Black (TBK, new 2005), Bullion Gold (mfg. 2002-2004), Cinnamon Burst (new 2004) or Ebony (dot neck only, gloss finish) finish. New 1999.

MSR	$3,153	$2,100	$1,600	$1,375	$1,175	$975	$850	$700

Subtract $524 for RD or TBK finish.

ES-335 TD-12

- similar to the ES-335 TD, except in 12-string configuration, fingerboard block inlay, triangular peghead inlay, available in Sunburst or Cherry finish only, mfg. 1965-1970.

	N/A	$1,500	$1,300	$1,100	$900	$825	$750

ES-335 Studio

- similar to ES-335 TD, except has no f-holes, mfg. 1987-1994.

	N/A	$800	$700	$600	$550	$475	$400

Last MSR was $900.

Gibson ES-335 courtesy Dave Rogers Dave's Guitar Shop

GRADING		100% MINT	98% NEAR MINT	95% EXC+	90% EXC	80% VG+	70% VG	60% G

ES-335 LARRY CARLTON SIGNATURE (ESLC) - nickel hardware, available in Heritage Cherry Sunburst, Pelham Blue, or Vintage Sunburst, mfg. in Memphis. Mfg. 2002 only, reintroduced 2005.

	MSR	$4,688	$3,100	$2,200	$1,850	$1,725	$1,450	$1,300	$1,175

ES-335 ALVIN LEE SIGNATURE - copy of Alvin Lee's original ES-335, Cherry finish. New 2005.

	MSR	$5,137	$3,425	$2,650	$2,350	$1,925	$1,600	$1,400	$1,175

ES-340 TD - double round cutaway semi-hollow bound body, arched maple top, f-holes, raised layered black pickguard, maple back/sides/neck, 22-fret rosewood fingerboard with pearl dot inlay, Tune-O-Matic bridge/stop tailpiece, blackface peghead with pearl crown/logo inlay, 3-per-side tuners, nickel hardware, 2 covered humbucker pickups, volume/mixer/2 tone controls, 3-position switch, available in Natural or Walnut finishes, mfg. 1969-1974 and 1978.

	N/A	$2,000	$1,775	$1,525	$1,250	$1,000	$900

ES-345 TD - double rounded cutaway semi-hollow bound body, arched maple top, unbound f-holes, raised layered black or tortoiseshell pickguard, maple back/sides, mahogany neck, 22-fret bound rosewood fingerboard with pearl parallelogram inlay, Tune-O-Matic bridge, stop, trapeze, or Bigsby tailpiece, blackface peghead with pearl crown/logo inlay, 3-per-side tuners with plastic buttons, gold hardware, 2 covered humbucker pickups, 2 volume/2 tone controls, 3-position/Vari-tone switches, stereo output, available in Ebony (1974 mfg. only), Wine Red (introduced 1976), Cherry (introduced 1960), Natural (very rare in 1959), Tobacco Sunburst (1974 mfg. only), Sunburst, or Walnut (introduced 1970) finishes, mfg. 1959-1982.

1959-1962	N/A	$18,000	$15,000	$13,500	$10,750	$9,500	$8,250
1963-1964	N/A	$8,000	$7,350	$6,450	$5,750	$4,850	$4,200
1965-1969	N/A	$4,000	$3,500	$3,000	$2,500	$2,100	$1,850
1970-1982	N/A	$2,500	$2,100	$1,850	$1,500	$1,200	$1,150

Add 200% for Natural finish (1959 mfg. only).

Subtract 25% for Bigsby.

During 1959-1964 and 1982, this model had a stop tailpiece, and a trapeze tailpiece from 1965-1982.

ES-345 REISSUE (ES45) - reproduction of B.B. King's original ES-345, gold hardware, available in Trans. Brown, Trans. Red, Triburst, or Vintage Sunburst. New 2002, mfg. in Memphis.

	MSR	$4,603	$3,100	$2,425	$1,975	$1,725	$1,500	$1,350	$1,100

ES-347 TD - double rounded cutaway semi-hollow bound body, arched figured maple top, f-holes, raised layered black pickguard, maple back/sides/neck, 22-fret bound ebony fingerboard with pearl block inlay, Tune-O-Matic bridge/tunable stop tailpiece, bound blackface peghead with pearl crown/logo inlay, 3-per-side tuners, gold hardware, 2 covered humbucker pickups, 2 volume/2 tone controls, 3-position/coil tap switches, available in Sunburst finish, mfg. 1978-1991.

	N/A	$2,000	$1,825	$1,575	$1,325	$1,075	$1,000

ES-350 - single rounded cutaway hollow bound body, arched figured maple top, bound f-holes, raised layered black pickguard, maple back/sides/neck, 22-fret bound rosewood fingerboard with pearl parallelogram inlay, adjustable rosewood bridge/trapeze tailpiece, bound blackface peghead with pearl crown/logo inlay, 3-per-side tuners with plastic buttons, gold hardware, covered single coil pickup, volume/tone controls, available in Natural and Sunburst finishes, mfg. 1947-1956.

1947-1956 (1 PICKUP)	N/A	$3,500	$3,150	$2,800	$2,350	$2,000	$1,750
1948-1956 (2 PICKUPS)	N/A	$4,000	$3,400	$3,000	$2,600	$2,300	$2,000

In 1948, 2 P-90 pickups became an option, tone control was placed on cutaway bout, and 2 volume controls were introduced. In 1952, 2 volume/2 tone controls and 3-position switch replaced previous part/design. In 1956, Tune-O-Matic bridge replaced original part/design.

ES-350 T/TD - similar to ES-350, except has thin body, 17 in. wide by 21 in. long, and 2.25 in. deep, 23.5 in. scale length, mfg. 1955-1963, and 1977-1981.

1955-1956	N/A	$4,350	$3,850	$3,250	$2,750	$2,250	$1,850
1957-1963	N/A	$7,500	$6,850	$5,750	$4,650	$3,500	$2,500
1977-1981	N/A	$2,500	$2,250	$1,875	$1,500	$1,250	$1,000

ES-350 T models with PAF pickups and/or a Blonde finish command a premium.

In 1957, P.A.F. humbucker pickups replaced original part/design. In 1960, sharp cutaway replaced original part/design.

ES-355 TD/ES-335 TDSV - double rounded cutaway semi-hollow bound body, arched maple top, unbound f-holes, raised layered black or tortoiseshell pickguard, maple back/sides, mahogany neck, 22-fret bound ebony fingerboard with pearl block inlay, Tune-O-Matic bridge, stop or Bigsby vibrato tailpiece, bound blackface peghead with pearl split diamond/logo inlay, 3-per-side tuners, gold hardware, 2 covered P.A.F. humbucker pickups, 2 volume/2 tone controls, Model ES-335 TDSV has stereo output and 3-position/Vari-tone switch, available in Cherry or Walnut (introduced 1971) finishes, Model ES-355 TD mfg. 1958-1970, ES-335 TDSV mfg. 1959-1982.

1958-1962	N/A	$15,000	$12,500	$11,000	$9,250	$8,000	$7,000
1963-1969	N/A	$4,500	$4,000	$3,350	$2,750	$2,350	$1,950
1970-1974	N/A	$2,500	$2,250	$2,150	$1,950	$1,900	$1,750
1975-1982	N/A	$2,500	$2,200	$1,800	$1,550	$1,350	$1,200

Add 20% for ES-355 TDSV with stereo output and Vari-tone.

This model with mono PAFs and stop tailpiece is the most desirable. In 1961, side-pull vibrato replaced original part/design. In 1962, Pat. No. humbucker pickups replaced original part/design. In 1963, Vibrola tailpiece with engraved lyre/logo replaced previous part/design. In 1969, Bigsby vibrato replaced previous part/design. In 1974, neck volute was introduced. In 1981, neck volute was discontinued.

ES-369 - double rounded cutaway semi-hollow bound body, arched maple top, f-holes, raised cream pickguard, maple back/sides, mahogany neck, 22-fret bound rosewood fingerboard with pearl trapezoid inlay, Tune-O-Matic bridge/tunable stop tailpiece, blackface peghead with pearl logo inlay, 3-per-side tuners, chrome hardware, 2 exposed humbucker pickups, 2 volume/2 tone controls, 3-position/coil tap switches, available in Cherry, Natural, Sunburst, or Walnut finishes, mfg. 1982 only.

	N/A	$1,500	$1,200	$1,100	$950	$775	$725

GRADING	100% MINT	98% NEAR MINT	95% EXC+	90% EXC	80% VG+	70% VG	60% G

ES-775 - single sharp cutaway hollow bound maple body, f-holes, raised bound black pickguard, 3-piece figured maple neck, 20-fret bound ebony fingerboard with pearl block inlay, Tune-O-Matic metal/ebony bridge/trapeze tailpiece, ebony block tailpiece insert, bound peghead with pearl stylized bird/logo inlay, 3-per-side Grover Imperial tuners, gold hardware, 2 covered humbucker pickups, 2 volume/2 tone controls, 3-position switch, available in Ebony finish, disc. 1996.

$2,250	$2,000	$1,650	$1,450	$1,250	$1,075	$900

Last MSR was $2,400.

Add $400 for Antique Natural or Vintage Sunburst finishes.

ES ARTIST ACTIVE - double rounded cutaway semi-hollow bound body, arched maple top, raised layered black pickguard, maple back/sides, mahogany neck, 22-fret bound ebony fingerboard with pearl offset dot inlay, Tune-O-Matic bridge/tunable stop tailpiece, blackface peghead with pearl winged-f/logo inlay, 3-per-side tuners, gold hardware, 2 covered humbucker pickups, 2 volume/1 tone controls, 3-position switch, 3 mini switches, active electronics, stereo output. Available in Cherry, Natural, Sunburst, or Walnut finishes, mfg. 1979-1986.

$1,750	$1,550	$1,275	$1,150	$925	$800	$675

A few ES Artist models were produced with a unique ES Artist trapeze tailpiece, 3-Tone Sunburst finish, stereo output, and unusual fretboard inlays. This variation is rare, and prices are typically in the $3,250-$4,500 range.

ELECTRIC: MISCELLANEOUS MODELS

Since the following models do not fit into any other subcategories, they have been placed under this miscellaneous subheading. Models include: the Tom Delonge Signature, ETG-150 Tenor, GK-55, KZ II, Midnight Special, SR-71, U-2, US-1, All American II, Futura, Invader, Victory MV-2, Victory MV-10, United States Map, and the S-1.

TOM DELONGE SIGNATURE - ES-335 body style with maple/poplar/maple laminate back and top, maple sides, mahogany neck with rosewood fingerboard and pearloid dot inlays, single ply binding on neck and body, two exposed Dirty Fingers humbucker pickups, one volume control, Tune-O-Matic bridge with locking sperzel tuners, brown body color with three creme stripes through center, mfg. 2004-present.

MSR	$3,443		$2,250	$1,625	$1,450	$1,275	$1,100	$975	$850

Gibson ES-340 TD
courtesy Sam J. Maggio

CITATION - please refer to the Acoustic Electric section in the *Blue Book of Acoustic Guitars*.

EST-150/ETG-150 TENOR - tenor version of the ES-150, 16.25 in. wide, arched back, jack on side, EST-150 introduced 1937, reintroduced as the ETG-150 in 1940. EST-150 Mfg. 1937-1940, and ETG 150 mfg. 1940, 1942-1971.

N/A	$1,500	$1,250	$1,125	$950	$800	$750

Production on the ETG-150 ceased for WWII in 1942. It was reintroduced in 1947 with one P-90 pickup, laminated beveled edge pickguard, bound fingerbaord with dot inlay, and plain peghead.

GK-55 - single cutaway mahogany body, bolt-on mahogany neck, 22-fret rosewood fingerboard with pearl dot inlay, Tune-O-Matic bridge/stop tailpiece, 3-per-side tuners, chrome hardware, 2 exposed humbucker pickups, 2 volume/2 tone controls, 3-position switch, available in Tobacco Sunburst finish, 828 mfg. 1979 only.

$375	$325	$275	$240	$200	$170	$130

According to sources contacted at Gibson, the KZ II was a project at Kalamazoo to use up "leftover parts and pieces." The design was later sold to another company, which produced the model as the Spirit. Jimmy KcKenzie, a current owner of one of these guitar models, describes the guitar as "having a Les Paul neck affixed to a Melody Maker body." More research continues into this model. The relative rarity and scarity of information about this late Kalamazoo era solid body makes pricing difficult.

KALAMAZOO AWARD - please refer to the Acoustic Electric section in the *Blue Book of Acoustic Guitars*.

KZ II - dual cutaway body, mahogany neck, rosewood fingerboard, 3-per-side tuners, truss rod cover with engraved KZ II logo, mfg. 1980 only.

MIDNIGHT SPECIAL - same body shape as the L-6S, non-beveled top around bass side, two humbucker pickups with metal covers and no polepieces, two knobs, two-way tone switch, large Tune-O-Matic bridge, bolt-on maple neck, maple fingerboard, decal logo, metal tuner buttons, chrome plated hardware, finishes include Ebony, Natural Maple Gloss (most common), White (least common), and Wine Red, mfg. 1974-79.

N/A	$500	$450	$400	$350	$325	$275

SR-71 - offset double cutaway, 2 single coil/1 humbucker pickups, Wayne Charvel design, mfg. 1989 only.

N/A	$360	$325	$295	$275	$250	$225

While Lockheed Martin made this model famous, Gibson's attempt ended up in a tailspin.

U-2 - offset double cutaway basswood body, maple neck, rosewood fingerboard, Kahler vibrato, 6-on-a-side tuners, black hardware, 2 single coil/humbucker pickups, mfg. 1987-1994.

$450	$400	$360	$330	$300	$275	$250

Last MSR was $949.

US-1 - offset double cutaway basswood body, bound maple top/back, balsa wood core, ebony fingerboard, 6-on-a-side tuners, 1 humbucker/2 stacked coil humbuckers, with or w/o tremolo, three mini-switches, black hardware, available in Natural top finish, mfg. 1987-1994.

$500	$450	$400	$350	$300	$275	$250

Last MSR was $1,575.

In 1988, a Steinberger KB tremolo was introduced with a coil tap switch on one of the knobs. This model was designed by Wayne Charvel.

Gibson ES Artist
courtesy S.P. Fjestad

GRADING	100% MINT	98% NEAR MINT	95% EXC+	90% EXC	80% VG+	70% VG	60% G

ALL AMERICAN II - dual cutaway (Melody Maker-style) solid mahogany body, mahogany neck, 24.75 in. scale, 22-fret rosewood fingerboard with dot inlay, vibrola (tremolo) bridge, blackface peghead with silkscreened logo, engraved "All American II" on truss rod cover, 3-per-side tuners, chrome hardware, 2 exposed polepiece single coil pickups, volume/tone controls, 3-way toggle switch, available in Ebony (EB), or Dark Wineburst (DW) finishes, mfg. 1996-98.

	$450	$395	$350	$300	$275	$225	$175

Last MSR was $649.

FUTURA - can opener style hardwood body, black tri-laminated pickguard, through-body maple neck, 22-fret rosewood fingerboard with white dot inlay, Tune-O-Matic bridge/stop tailpiece, 6-on-a-side tuners, chrome hardware, 2 covered humbucker pickups, 2 volume/1 tone controls, 3-position/rotary coil tap switches, available in Ebony, Ultraviolet, or White finishes, mfg. 1983-85.

	$325	$275	$225	$195	$165	$135	$100

INVADER - single cutaway mahogany body/neck, 22-fret ebony fingerboard with dot inlay, double locking vibrato, 6-on-a-side tuners, black hardware, 2 exposed Dirty Finger humbucker pickups, 2 volume/2 tone controls, 3-position switch, available in Black finish, some were also mfg. with a red/white/blue Confederate flag motif on the top and headstock, mfg. 1983-89.

	$350	$300	$250	$200	$175	$125	$100

VICTORY MV-2 - offset double cutaway, rosewood fingerboard, 6-on-a-side tuners, 2 humbuckers, available in Antique Sunburst or Candy Apple Red finishes, mfg. 1981-84.

	$325	$275	$225	$195	$175	$150	$125

Victory MV-10 - similar to Victory MV-2, except has an ebony fingerboard, stacked coil pickup, coil tap switch, available in Apple Red or Twilight Blue finishes.

	$350	$295	$225	$175	$150	$125	$100

MAP - mahogany body shaped like United States, 3-piece maple neck, 22-fret bound rosewood fingerboard with pearl dot or star inlay, Tune-O-Matic bridge/stop tailpiece, blackface peghead with pearl logo inlay, chrome hardware, 2 covered humbucker pickups, 2 volume/2 tone controls, 3-position switch, available in Natural finish or with red, white and blue flag painted finish, mfg. 1983 only.

	N/A	$1,250	$800	$700	$500	$400	$350

S-1 - single cutaway alder body, black tri-lam pickguard, bolt-on maple neck, 22-fret rosewood or maple fingerboard with pearl dot inlay, Tune-O-Matic bridge/stop tailpiece, 3-per-side tuners, chrome hardware, 3 single coil bar pickups, volume/tone control, 3-position/rotary switches, available in Ebony, Natural, Natural Satin, or Tobacco Sunburst finish, mfg. 1975-1980.

	N/A	$400	$350	$295	$225	$200	$175

This model was previously endorsed by Ron Wood.

Q-SERIES - body shape similar to Victory/MV Series, bolt-on neck, available in 4 models, limited mfg. 1985-87.

Q-100 - one Dirty Fingers humbucking pickup, Tune-O-Matic bridge, optional Kahler Flyer vibrato, ebony fingerboard, dot inlay, 6-on-a-side tuners, chrome-plated or black-plated hardware, Ebony or Panther Pink finish, mfg. 1985-86.

	N/A	$375	$325	$275	$225	$175	$150

Q-200/Q-2000 - one HP-90 single coil pickup in neck position, one Dirty Fingers humbucking pickup in bridge position, coil tap, Kahler Flyer vibrato, ebony fingerboard, dot inlays, 6-on-a-side tuners, black chrome or chrome-plated hardware, Ebony or Alpine White finish, mfg. 1985-86.

	N/A	$395	$350	$300	$250	$200	$175

During late 1985, this model was renamed the Q-2000, and was available in Ebony, Ferrari Red, or Panther Pink finish.

Q-300/Q-3000 - three HP-90 single coil pickups, two knobs, selector switch, Kahler Flyer vibrato, no pickguard, ebony fingerboard, dot inlays, 6-on-a-side tuners, black chrome or chrome-plated hardware, Ebony or Wine Red finish, mfg. 1985-86.

	N/A	$450	$400	$350	$300	$250	$200

During late 1985, this model was renamed the Q-3000, and was available with a rosewood fingerboard, three mini-switches, in Ebony, Ferrari Red, or Panther Pink finish.

Q-400/Q-4000 - one humbucking pickup, one Dirty Fingers humbucking pickup and two single coil pickups, master tone and volume knobs, three mini-switches, Kahler Flyer vibrato, ebony fingerboard, dot inlays, black hardware, decal logo, Ebony, Ferrari Red, or Panther Pink finish, mfg. 1985-87.

	N/A	$375	$325	$275	$225	$200	$175

During late 1985, this model was renamed the Q-400, and was available in Ebony finish.

ELECTRIC: EXPLORER SERIES

EXPLORER (KORINA) - offset hourglass korina (African limba wood) body, white pickguard, korina neck, 22-fret rosewood fingerboard with pearl dot inlay, Tune-O-Matic bridge/stop tailpiece, blackface peghead with pearl logo inlay, 6-on-a-side tuners, gold (1958-59) or nickel (1962-63) hardware, 2 P.A.F. (1958-59) or patent number (1962-63) humbucker pickups, 2 volume/1 tone controls, 3-position switch, available in Natural finish, approx. 22 mfg. 1958-1959, parts clean-up during 1962-1963 (brown case 1958-59, black case 1962-63).

A few early specimens were produced with a V-shaped peghead and a raised plastic logo. The first prototype was dubbed the Futura. The Explorer model was introduced shortly after the Flying V and had a 1958 retail price of $247.50. A modernistic concept guitar from Gibson, this model had very limited manufacture (estimated to be under 100 instruments). Original Explorers exhibiting some wear and no problems are currently priced in the $55,000-85,000 range, and really nice examples may go all the way up to $135,000. Even though the 1962-1963 period of manufacture was mostly a clean-up of earlier bodies and related parts that were never finished during the first production run, values seem to be the same for both periods. Until someone finds and documents a Moderne, the Explorer (Korina) will continue to be Gibson's most desirable and rarest electric instrument.

Explorer Reissue - similar to Explorer (Korina), except has mahogany body/neck, available in Black, Natural (most common), or White finishes, mfg. 1975-1980.

	N/A	$1,500	$1,295	$1,100	$950	$850	$750

GRADING	100% MINT	98% NEAR MINT	95% EXC+	90% EXC	80% VG+	70% VG	60% G

Explorer II (E2) - similar to Explorer (Korina), except has 5-piece laminated walnut/maple body, maple neck, ebony fingerboard with dot inlay, E 2 engraved truss rod cover, tunable TP-6 stop tailpiece, gold hardware, 2 exposed coil humbucker pickups, available in Natural finish, mfg. 1979-1984.

	N/A	$1,250	$1,100	$1,000	$900	$825	$775

This model was also available with maple neck. Body woods on this model were interchangeable (i.e. walnut or maple used on top). Models with a bound curly maple top may be an Explorer CMT (see model below).

Explorer (I) - similar to Explorer II, except has mahogany body, rosewood fingerboard with dot inlay, decal headstock logo, Tune-O-Matic bridge/stop tailpiece or black Kahler Flyer tremolo, 2 uncovered humbuckers, available in Black or White finishes, mfg. 1981-89.

	N/A	$900	$850	$795	$750	$700	$675

Subtract 35% if w/ Kahler tremolo.

In 1987, ebony fingerboard replaced rosewood fingerboard; tremolo bridge was discontinued. This model was also available in a left-handed configuration (Explorer left hand), available 1984 to 1987.

EXPLORER KORINA REISSUE (1984 MFG.)
- offset hourglass korina body, black pickguard, korina neck, 22-fret rosewood fingerboard with pearl dot inlay, Tune-O-Matic bridge/stop tailpiece, blackface peghead with pearl logo inlay, stamped serial number on peghead, 6-on-a-side Schaller tuners, gold hardware, 2 humbucker pickups, 2 volume/1 tone controls, 3-position switch, available in Antique Natural, Candy Apple Red, Ebony, or Ivory finishes, mfg. 1984 only.

	N/A	$3,000	$2,650	$2,250	$1,950	$1,650	$1,450

Subtract $1,000 for non-Natural finishes.

This was Gibson's first Explorer Korina reissue model. In 1984, this Limited Edition was designed as a reissue of 1958 Explorer. It is estimated that only 1,000 instruments were produced. Current production instruments (1958 Korina Explorer) are part of the Historic Collection Series, found at the end of this section.

Explorer Heritage (Limited Edition) - similar to Explorer Korina Reissue, except has inked serial number on peghead, pearloid buttons, black control knobs, available in Antique Natural, Ebony, or Ivory finishes, mfg. 1983 only.

	N/A	$3,500	$3,000	$2,500	$2,000	$1,800	$1,650

It is estimated that 100 of these instruments were manufactured. Serial numbers on the Explorer Heritage models consist of a single letter followed by 3 digits.

Explorer Heritage (Custom Shop) - similar to Explorer Korina Reissue, except has stamped serial number on peghead, black pickguard, gold hardware, available in Antique Natural, Ebony, or Ivory finishes, mfg. 1983 only.

	N/A	$3,000	$2,650	$2,250	$1,950	$1,650	$1,450

It is estimated that 500 of these instruments were manufactured.

EXPLORER 83 (EXPLORER)
- offset hourglass body, mahogany neck, 22-fret rosewood fingerboard with pearl dot inlay, tremolo tailpiece (Kahler and Floyd Rose systems), 6-on-a-side tuners, chrome hardware, 2 exposed coil humbucker pickups, 2 volume/tone controls, 3-position switch, available in Black and White finishes, mfg. 1984 to 1989.

	N/A	$750	$675	$595	$525	$450	$425

In 1984, alder wood replaced Korina for the body. When the name was changed from the Explorer 83 to Explorer, this model was offered with optional custom graphics and original artist finishes.

Explorer w/Black Hardware - similar to Explorer 83, except has Kahler tremolo system and black hardware, mfg. 1985 only.

	N/A	$750	$675	$595	$525	$450	$425

Explorer CMT - similar to Explorer 83, except has bound curly maple top, mfg. 1984 only.

	N/A	$1,000	$850	$750	$675	$600	$525

Some models may have "E 2" engraved on the truss rod cover.

EXPLORER III
- offset hourglass alder body, white pickguard, korina neck, 22-fret rosewood fingerboard with pearl dot inlay, Tune-O-Matic bridge/stop tailpiece, peghead logo decal, 6-on-a-side tuners, chrome hardware, 3 soapbar P-90 pickups, volume/tone controls, 3-position switch, available in Natural finish, mfg. 1984-85.

	N/A	$750	$675	$600	$550	$500	$450

Explorer III w/Black Hardware - similar to Explorer III, except has Kahler tremolo system and black hardware, mfg. 1985 only.

	N/A	$625	$575	$550	$500	$475	$450

EXPLORER 425
- offset hourglass mahogany body, set-in mahogany neck, white pickguard, 22-fret ebony fingerboard with pearl dot inlay, Kahler vibrato, blackface peghead with pearl logo inlay, 6-on-a-side tuners, black hardware, 2 uncovered single coil/humbucker pickups, volume/tone controls, 3 mini switches, available in Natural finish, mfg. 1986 only.

	N/A	$600	$550	$500	$475	$425	$400

XLP CUSTOM
- similar to Explorer 425, except has bound top, sharply pointed horns, rounded cutout on lower treble bout, 2 Dirty Fingers exposed coil humbuckers, double locking tremolo system, mfg. 1985-87.

	N/A	$975	$850	$695	$650	$595	$485

Gibson Map courtesy Dave Rogers Dave's Guitar Shop

Gibson Explorer courtesy Dave Hinson Killer Vintage

G

GRADING	100% MINT	98% NEAR MINT	95% EXC+	90% EXC	80% VG+	70% VG	60% G

X-PLORER (DSXR, EXPLORER '76 REISSUE) - offset hourglass mahogany body/neck, white or mirror (new 2002) pickguard, 22-fret rosewood fingerboard with pearl dot inlay, Tune-O-Matic bridge/stop tailpiece, blackface peghead with pearl logo inlay, 6-on-a-side tuners, chrome hardware, 2 ceramic (496R and 500T) magnet humbuckers, 2 volume/1 tone controls, 3-position switch, available in Cherry (CH), Classic White (CW), Ebony (EB), Natural, Natural Burst, Vintage Sunburst (VS, disc. 1994), or Gothic (Satin Black finish, black chrome hardware, and 12th fret moon and star inlay, disc.) finishes, mfg. 1990-present.

MSR	$1,388	$995	$825	$725	$625	$525	$425	$350

> **Add $270 for Classic White finish (with or w/o mirror pickguard). Add $270 for Natural. Add $90 for Natural Burst finish (disc.). Subtract $150 for Gothic finish (disc.).**

X-PLORER PRO (DSX+) - similar to Explorer '76 Reissue, except has AA maple single bound top, ebony fingerboard with pearl block inlays, chrome hardware, available in Trans. Amber or Trans. Black finish, mfg. 2002-04.

		$1,450	$1,050	$925	$800	$725	$625	$525

> Last MSR was $2,098.

EXPLORER 90 DOUBLE - offset hourglass mahogany body/neck, 25.5 in. scale, white pickguard, 22-fret rosewood fingerboard with pearl dot inlay, Tune-O-Matic bridge/stop tailpiece, blackface peghead with pearl split diamond/logo inlay, 6-on-a-side tuners, gold hardware, 2 humbucker pickups, 2 volume/1 tone controls, 3-position switch, available in Natural finish, mfg. 1989-1991.

		N/A	$900	$825	$675	$550	$495	$450

EXPLORER VOODOO (DSXV) - features JuJu (JJ) finish and bright chrome hardware. Mfg. 2002.

		$995	$875	$750	$625	$500	$400	$325

> Last MSR was $1,899.

X-PLORER STUDIO (DSXS) - smaller poplar or swamp ash Explorer body size (90%), mahogany neck with rosewood fingerboard, pearloid dot inlays, two high output ceramic mini humbucker pickups, Tune-O-Matic bridge with stopbar tailpiece, 24.75 in. scale, available in Studio Copper, Metallic Blue, Studio Blue (disc. 2004), Studio Red (disc. 2004), Studio Yellow (disc. 2004) Metallic Green (available 2004 only), Metallic Yellow (available 2004 only) or FSC certified swamp ash body with satin finish, mfg. 2003-04.

		$775	$575	$500	$450	$400	$350	$300

> Last MSR was $1,098.

ELECTRIC: FIREBIRD SERIES

Firebird guitars were offered in custom colors as well as standard Gibson finishes. The Firebirds were available in these Custom Colors: Amber Red, Cardinal Red, Frost Blue, Golden Mist, Heather, Inverness Green, Kelly Green, Pelham Blue, Polaris Blue, and Silver Mist finishes.

> **Add 25% - 50% for custom colors (depending on rarity of the custom color).**

Firebird: Reverse Models

The Reverse Series Firebirds were designed by automotive stylist Ray Dietrich, and first released in 1963. They are called Reverse models, since the asymmetrical body shape is characterized by a longer/pronounced lower treble bout and an extended upper rear bout. Additionally, the headstocks resemble a backwards Fender design, with the tuners located on the right side of the headstock.

FIREBIRD - available in Ebony, Natural, Tobacco Sunburst (most common) or White (rare) finish, mfg. 1976-79.

		N/A	$1,250	$1,075	$875	$750	$650	$550

FIREBIRD I - asymmetrical hourglass style mahogany body, layered white pickguard, 4-inch through-body mahogany neck, 22-fret Brazilian rosewood fingerboard with pearl dot inlay, wrapover stop tailpiece, partial blackface reverse peghead with pearl logo inlay, 6-on-a-side banjo tuners, nickel hardware, covered mini-humbucker pickup, volume/tone control, available in Sunburst finish, mfg. 1963-69.

		N/A	$4,500	$4,000	$3,500	$3,000	$2,500	$2,200

> A few of these guitars were produced with vibratos. In 1965, peghead design changed to bass side tuner array. In 1965, some models found with perpendicular to peghead tuners, single coil pickups.

FIREBIRD III - similar to Firebird I, except has bound fingerboard with dot inlays, Tune-O-Matic bridge/vibrato tailpiece, wrap-around bridge with raised integral saddles, 2 humbucker pickups, 2 volume/2 tone controls, 3-position switch, mfg. 1963-69.

		N/A	$4,500	$4,000	$3,500	$3,000	$2,500	$2,200

> In 1965, peghead design changed to bass side tuner array, some models found with perpendicular to peghead tuners, single coil pickups.

FIREBIRD V - similar to Firebird I, except has bound fingerboard with trapezoid inlay, Tune-O-Matic bridge/vibrato with engraved cover, 2 humbucker pickups, 2 volume/2 tone controls, 3-position switch, mfg. 1963-69.

		N/A	$6,000	$5,350	$4,750	$4,150	$3,650	$3,150

> In 1965, peghead design changed to bass side tuner array.

Firebird V Medallion Limited Edition - similar to original Firebird V model, except has medallion and "Gibson" is stamped on the pickup covers. 366 mfg. 1972-73 only.

		N/A	$6,000	$5,350	$4,750	$4,150	$3,650	$3,150

FIREBIRD V (DSFR, REISSUE) - asymmetrical hourglass style mahogany body, white pickguard with engraved Firebird symbol, through-body 9-piece mahogany/walnut neck, 22-fret rosewood fingerboard with pearl trapezoid inlay, Tune-O-Matic bridge/stop tailpiece, partial blackface peghead with pearl logo inlay, 6-on-a-side banjo tuners, chrome hardware, 2 covered regular or ceramic mini-humbucker (current mfg.) pickups, 2 volume/2 tone controls, 3-position switch, available in Cardinal Red (disc.), Desert Burst, Cherry (CH), Classic White (CW), Ebony (EB, disc.), Heritage Cherry (HC, disc.), or Vintage Sunburst finishes, mfg. 1990-present.

MSR	$2,498	$1,700	$1,175	$995	$850	$750	$675	$575

> In 1994, Cardinal Red, Classic White, Ebony and Heritage Cherry finishes were discontinued. Circa 1975, a Firebird V "Reissue" (call it the 1st Reissue?) was briefly offered in a gold coil finish - these older reissues are currently selling in the $2,775 range.

GRADING	100% MINT	98% NEAR MINT	95% EXC+	90% EXC	80% VG+	70% VG	60% G

FIREBIRD VII - asymmetrical hourglass-style mahogany body, layered white pickguard, through-body mahogany neck, 22-fret bound ebony fingerboard with pearl block inlay, Tune-O-Matic bridge/vibrato tailpiece with engraved cover, partial blackface reverse peghead with pearl logo inlay, 6-on-a-side banjo tuners, gold hardware, 3 covered humbucker pickups, 2 volume/2 tone controls, 3-position switch, available in Sunburst finish, mfg. 1963-69.

	N/A	$9,500	$8,500	$7,750	$7,000	$6,250	$5,500

In 1965, peghead design changed to bass side tuner array.

FIREBIRD VII REISSUE (DSF7) - similar design as original Firebird VII, available in Blue Mist (BM, disc. 2004), Copper Metallic (C1, disc. 2004), Vintage Sunburst (VS, disc. 2004), Cherry (CH), or Red Metallic (R1) finish, mfg. 2002-present.

MSR	$2,849		$1,925	$1,375	$1,125	$950	$825	$700	$600

FIREBIRD '76 - similar to Firebird V, except has red/white/blue Firebird emblem on pickguard, pearl dot fingerboard inlay, 2 humbucker pickups, available in Black, Mahogany, Sunburst or White finishes, mfg. 1976 only.

	N/A	$1,500	$1,350	$1,200	$1,050	$950	$895

FIREBIRD STUDIO (DSFS) - features reverse mahogany body two Alnico humbucking pickups (490R and 498T), similar controls as Firebird V, rosewood fingerboard with pearloid dot inlays, chrome or gold hardware, six-on-a-side mini-Grover tuners, available in Ebony (EB) or Cherry (CH) finishes, mfg. 2004-present.

MSR	$1,658		$1,125	$925	$800	$700	$600	$500	$450

Firebird: Non-Reverse Models

Non-Reverse Firebirds had traditional bout designs where the upper treble bout extended below the lower treble bout, and tuners were on the upper left side of headstock.

FIREBIRD I - asymmetrical hourglass style mahogany body, layered white pickguard with engraved Firebird logo, mahogany neck, 22-fret Brazilian rosewood fingerboard with pearl dot inlay, compensated bridge/vibrato tailpiece, 6-on-a-side tuners, chrome hardware, 2 single coil P-90 pickups, 2 volume/2 tone controls, 3-position switch, available in Custom Color and Sunburst finishes, mfg. 1966-69.

	N/A	$1,500	$1,350	$1,175	$995	$875	$775

FIREBIRD III - similar to Firebird I, except has 3 black soapbar P-90 pickups, mfg. 1965-69.

	N/A	$1,750	$1,575	$1,350	$1,150	$1,025	$950

**Gibson Firebird III
courtesy Dave Rogers
Dave's Guitar Shop**

FIREBIRD V - similar to Firebird I, except has Tune-O-Matic bridge/vibrato tailpiece with engraved cover, 2 covered original style Firebird humbucker pickups, mfg. 1965-69.

	N/A	$3,250	$2,875	$2,400	$2,000	$1,650	$1,350

FIREBIRD V-12 - similar to Firebird I, except has 12 strings, blackface peghead with pearl split diamond inlay, Tune-O-Matic bridge/fixed tailpiece, 6-on-a-side tuners, mfg. 1966-67.

	N/A	$1,500	$1,325	$1,100	$975	$850	$725

It is estimated that only 272 instruments were produced.

FIREBIRD VII - similar to Firebird I, except has Tune-O-Matic bridge/vibrato tailpiece with engraved cover, gold hardware, 3 original style Firebird humbucker pickups, mfg. 1966-69.

	N/A	$2,500	$2,300	$1,950	$1,775	$1,550	$1,375

ELECTRIC: FLYING "V" SERIES

For complete information on this unusual Gibson model, please read *Flying V - An Illustrated History of the Modernistic Guitar* by Larry Meiners.

FLYING V (KORINA) - Korina body in V-shape, layered white pickguard, rubber strip on treble side of body, Korina neck, 22-fret rosewood fingerboard with pearl dot inlay, ABR-1 Tune-O-Matic bridge, strings through anchoring with V-shaped metal plate, raised plastic lettering on peghead, 3-per-side tuners with amber buttons, gold (1958-59) or nickel (1962-63) hardware, 2 PAF (1958-59) or patent number (1962-63) humbucker pickups, 2 volume/1 tone controls, available in Natural finish, brown case 1958-59, black case 1962-63, approx. 98 mfg. 1958-59, parts clean-up 1962-63.

A few models had black pickguards. The Flying V model was introduced in 1958 and had an original retail price of $247.50 plus $75 for the case. A modernistic concept guitar (along with the Explorer and Moderne) from Gibson, this model had very limited manufacture (98 instruments were produced during 1958-59, no records are available for 1960-63). Original Flying Vs exhibiting some wear and no problems are currently priced in the $75,000-$125,000 range, and up to $150,000 for a really clean specimen (even more with a famous musician premium attached). Original Flying V cases have sold for as much as $10,000! The 1962-1963 period of manufacture was mostly a clean-up of earlier bodies and related parts that were never finished during the first production run, and values seem to be less than the 1958 models.

Flying V (1st Reissue) - similar to Flying V, except has mahogany body/neck, no rubber strip on body, Tune-O-Matic bridge/stud tailpiece (and Gibson vibrato), embossed logo on truss rod cover, redesigned (shorter and rounder) peghead, available in Cherry or Sunburst finishes, approx. 175 mfg. 1966-1970.

	N/A	$16,500	$13,000	$11,000	$9,500	$8,000	$7,500

Flying V Medallion - similar to Flying V (1st Reissue), except has Limited Edition medallion on top, redesigned (shorter) peghead, approx. 350 mfg. 1971 only.

	N/A	$7,000	$5,500	$4,500	$3,950	$3,500	$3,250

Flying V (2nd Reissue) - similar to Flying V (1st Reissue). Available in Ebony, Natural (most common), Tobacco Sunburst (rare), or White finishes, mfg. 1975-1980.

	N/A	$2,800	$2,400	$2,100	$1,800	$1,600	$1,400

**Gibson Flying V
courtesy Dave Rogers
Dave's Guitar Shop**

GRADING	100% MINT	98% NEAR MINT	95% EXC+	90% EXC	80% VG+	70% VG	60% G

FLYING V II (V2) - 5-piece laminated V-shaped walnut/maple body, layered black pickguard, walnut neck, 22-fret ebony fingerboard with pearl dot inlay, Tune-O-Matic bridge, strings through anchoring with V-shaped metal plate, blackface peghead with pearl logo, "V 2" engraved on truss rod cover, 3-per-side tuners, gold hardware, 2 V-shaped humbucker pickups, 2 volume/tone controls, 3-position switch, available in Natural finish, mfg. 1979-1982.

	N/A	$1,800	$1,500	$1,250	$1,050	$900	$825

This model was also available with maple neck. Body woods on this model were interchangeable, i.e. walnut or maple were used for top. Towards the end of the production run, rectangular humbuckers were substituted for the V-shaped original pickups. Models with a bound curly maple top may be a Flying V CMT (see model below).

FLYING V HERITAGE (LIMITED REISSUE, FLYING V 3RD REISSUE) - korina V-shaped body, layered white pickguard, rubber strip on treble side of body, korina neck, 22-fret rosewood fingerboard with pearl dot inlay, Tune-O-Matic bridge, strings through anchoring with V-shaped metal plate, raised plastic lettering on peghead, 3-per-side tuners with plastic single ring buttons, gold hardware, 2 humbucker PAF pickups, 2 volume/1 tone gold controls, available in Antique Natural, Candy Apple Red, Ebony, or White finishes, mfg. 1981-82 (Flying V Heritage), 1983-84 (Flying V 3rd Edition).

	N/A	$3,000	$2,500	$2,150	$1,900	$1,825	$1,675

> Subtract 10% for White finish. Add 30% for Candy Apple Red finish.

Serial numbers for the Flying V Heritage consisted of the letter A followed by 3 digits. In 1983, renamed Flying V (3rd Reissue); black control knobs replaced original part/design. It is estimated that only 1,000 instruments were produced between 1983 and 1984. Current production instruments (1958 Korina Flying V) are part of the Historic Collection Series, found at the end of this section.

THE V (1983 MFG.) - mahogany V-shaped body, bound curly maple top, mahogany neck, 22-fret ebony fingerboard with pearl dot inlay, Tune-O-Matic bridge/stop tailpiece, 3-per-side tuners, chrome hardware, 2 humbucker pickups, 2 volume/1 tone controls, 3-position switch, available in Antique Natural, Antique Sunburst, or Vintage Cherry Sunburst finishes, mfg. 1983 only.

	N/A	$900	$750	$650	$575	$500	$425

FLYING V 83 (FLYING V) - alder V-shaped body, mahogany neck, 22-fret rosewood fingerboard with pearl dot inlay, tremolo tailpiece (Kahler or Floyd Rose), 3-per-side tuners, chrome hardware, peghead logo decal, 2 exposed coil humbucker pickups, 2 volume/1 tone controls, 3-position switch. Available in Ebony and Ivory finishes, mfg. 1983 (Flying V 83), 1984-89 (Flying V).

	N/A	$650	$525	$450	$395	$350	$300

In 1984, renamed Flying V, 2 Dirty Fingers humbuckers and Tune-O-Matic bridge replaced original part/design. Ivory finish discontinued, Alpine White and Red finishes were introduced. In 1984, tremolo and locking nut system were options. In 1984, Custom and Designer finishes were options. This model was also available in a left-handed configuration (Flying V left-hand), available 1984 to 1989.

Flying V CMT - similar to Flying V, except has bound curly maple top. Available in Antique Sunburst or Vintage Cherry Sunburst finishes, mfg. 1984 only.

	N/A	$900	$750	$650	$575	$500	$425

This model had an optional tremolo bridge. Some models may have a V 2 engraved on the truss rod cover.

Flying V w/Black Hardware - similar to Flying V (circa 1984), except has Kahler locking tremolo, black hardware, available in Alpine White, Ebony, or Red finishes, mfg. 1985 only.

	N/A	$650	$600	$500	$400	$360	$330

FLYING V XPL - mahogany V-shaped body, layered white pickguard, set-in mahogany neck, 22-fret rosewood fingerboard with pearl dot inlay, Tune-O-Matic bridge/stop tailpiece, 6-on-a-side tuners, black hardware, 2 humbucker pickups, 2 volume/1 tone controls. Available in Night Violet and Plum Wineburst finishes, mfg. 1984-87.

	N/A	$750	$650	$575	$500	$425	$350

This model had an optional Kahler tremolo system.

Flying V XPL w/Black Hardware - similar to Flying V XPL, except has locking Kahler tremolo system, black hardware, available in Alpine White, Ebony, or Red finishes, mfg. 1985 only.

	N/A	$750	$650	$575	$500	$425	$350

Flying V 90 Double - similar to Flying V XPL, except has 24-fret ebony fingerboard with pearl split diamond inlay, 25.5 in. scale, strings through anchoring with V-shaped metal plate, blackface peghead with pearl logo inlay, single coil/humbucker pickups, volume/tone control, 3-position switch, available in Black finish, mfg. 1989-1992.

	N/A	$1,000	$850	$725	$600	$500	$425

FLYING V (1988-89 MFG.) - similar to original Flying V, except has a 24-fret ebony fingerboard, Steinberger KB-X vibrato or string through-body design, double coil pickup, mfg. 1988-89.

	N/A	$550	$475	$400	$350	$300	$250

FLYING V FACTOR X ('67, DSVR, FLYING V REISSUE) - mahogany V-shaped body, white or mirror (new 2002) pickguard, mahogany neck, 22-fret rosewood fingerboard with pearl dot inlay, Tune-O-Matic bridge/stop tailpiece, arrow style peghead, 3-per-side tuners with pearl buttons, chrome hardware, 2 exposed humbucker pickups, 2 volume/1 tone controls, 3-position switch., available in Cherry (CH), Classic White (CW), Ebony (EB), Natural (disc. 2004), Vintage Sunburst (VS, disc. 2004), Translucent Purple (Mfg. 1999-2001), Natural Burst (Mfg. 1999-2001), or Gothic (mfg. 1999-2002, Satin Black finish, black chrome hardware, and 12th fret moon and star inlay) finishes, mfg. 1990-present.

MSR	$1,388	$995	$825	$675	$550	$500	$465	$435

> Add $270 for Natural or Classic White finish.

In 1994, Vintage Sunburst finish was discontinued.

FLYING V '98 - mahogany body and neck, 2 ceramic (496R and 500T) magnet humbuckers, rosewood fingerboard, Tune-O-Matic bridge with stop tailpiece, chrome or gold hardware, finishes include Gothic (100% satin black finish, black chrome hardware, and 12th fret moon and star inlay), Natural Burst, Translucent Purple, Natural, and Classic White (Disc. 2001), 40th Anniversary Limited Edition, mfg. 1998-2002.

	N/A	$1,050	$900	$875	$750	$650	$575

Last MSR was $1,845.

> Add $153 for Natural finish.

GRADING	100% MINT	98% NEAR MINT	95% EXC+	90% EXC	80% VG+	70% VG	60% G

FLYING V VOODOO (DSVV) - features JuJu (JJ) finish and bright chrome hardware, mfg. 2002 only.

| | | $1,275 | $925 | $825 | $700 | $650 | $575 | $500 |

Last MSR was $1,700.

FLYING V FADED - similar to Flying V, except has one coat finish, available in Worn Cherry finish, includes gig bag, mfg. 2002-present.

| MSR | $998 | $660 | $525 | $450 | $400 | $350 | $325 | $300 |

ELECTRIC: HOWARD ROBERTS SERIES

HOWARD ROBERTS ARTIST - single sharp cutaway body, arched maple top, oval soundhole, raised multi-bound tortoiseshell pickguard, 3-stripe bound body/rosette, maple back/sides/neck, 22-fret bound ebony fingerboard with pearl slot block inlay, adjustable ebony bridge/trapeze tailpiece, wood tailpiece insert with pearl model name inlay, bound peghead with pearl flower/logo inlay, 3-per-side tuners, gold hardware, humbucker pickup, volume/treble/mid controls, available in Natural, Red Wine, or Sunburst finishes, mfg. 1976-1981.

| | N/A | $2,200 | $1,950 | $1,675 | $1,450 | $1,250 | $1,000 |

In 1979, two pickups became an option.

Howard Roberts Custom - similar to Howard Roberts Artist, except has rosewood fingerboard, chrome hardware, available in Cherry, Sunburst and Wine Red finishes, mfg. 1973-1981.

| | N/A | $2,000 | $1,775 | $1,525 | $1,250 | $1,000 | $825 |

Gibson also made a few Howard Roberts HR instruments in 1970 only. These guitars were available in 4 different configurations - the HR-CE (Custom Electric), HR-DE (Double Pickup), HR-S (Standard), and the HR-SE (Standard Electric).

HOWARD ROBERTS FUSION III (ARFU) - single sharp cutaway semi-hollow bound maple body, f-holes, raised black pickguard, maple neck, 20-fret bound rosewood fingerboard with pearl dot inlay, Tune-O-Matic bridge/adjustable tailpiece, peghead with pearl plant/logo inlay, 3-per-side tuners, gold hardware, 2 covered humbucker pickups, 2 volume/2 tone controls, 3-position switch, available in Ebony (EB), Natural (new 2002), Vintage Sunburst, Cherry, or Fireburst (disc. 1994) finishes, mfg. 1979-2003, reintroduced 2005 and is still produced.

| MSR | $3,125 | $2,075 | $1,500 | $1,200 | $1,075 | $875 | $750 | $650 |

In 1990, 6-finger tailpiece replaced original part/design.

Gibson Howard Roberts Fusion III courtesy Gibson

ELECTRIC: JOHNNY SMITH SERIES

JOHNNY SMITH - single rounded cutaway bound hollow body, carved spruce top, bound f-holes, raised bound tortoise pickguard, figured maple back/sides/neck, 20-fret bound ebony fingerboard with pearl split block inlay, adjustable rosewood bridge/trapeze tailpiece, multi-bound peghead with split diamond/logo inlay, 3-per-side tuners, gold hardware, one or two (introduced 1963 - model name is Johnny Smith D) mini humbucker pickups, pickguard mounted volume control, available in Natural or Sunburst (most common) finishes, mfg. 1961-1989.

1961-1968	N/A	$7,500	$6,900	$5,750	$5,225	$4,775	$4,100
1969-1973	N/A	$6,000	$5,500	$5,150	$4,500	$4,250	$3,500
1974-1989	N/A	$4,500	$4,200	$4,100	$3,750	$3,250	$2,850

In 1963, the two pickup model (Johnny Smith D) was introduced, and is more desirable than a single pickup. By 1979, 6-finger tailpiece replaced original part/design.

ELECTRIC: L-4, L-5, L-6, SUPER V CES & LE GRANDE SERIES

L-4 CES - solid spruce top, bound rosewood fingerboard, double paralellogram inlays, 16.25 in. wide, pointed cutaway, Charlie Christian pickup. Very limited mfg., available by special order beginning 1958, only 9 shipped during 1969.

| | N/A | $3,250 | $2,850 | $2,500 | $2,250 | $2,000 | $1,850 |

For current manufacture, please refer to the listing under Custom Shop: Carved Top Series.

L-5 CES - single rounded cutaway bound hollow body, 17 in. wide by 21 in. long by 3.375 in. deep, 25.5 in. scale, carved spruce top, layered tortoiseshell pickguard, bound f-holes, maple back/sides/neck, 14/20-fret bound pointed ebony fingerboard with pearl block inlay, ebony bridge with pearl inlay on wings, model name engraved trapeze tailpiece with chrome insert, multibound blackface peghead with pearl flame/logo inlay, 3-per-side tuners, gold hardware, 2 single coil pickups, 2 volume/2 tone controls, 3-position switch, available in Natural or Sunburst (most common) finishes, mfg. 1951-present.

1951-1959	N/A	$20,000	$15,000	$12,000	$8,575	$7,750	$7,100
1960-1964	N/A	$14,000	$12,000	$10,000	$6,500	$5,850	$5,375
1965-1968	N/A	$8,500	$7,500	$6,500	$4,295	$3,850	$3,550
1969-RECENT	$6,000	$5,500	$5,000	$4,000	$2,350	$2,150	$1,950

Between 1951 and 1953, P90 pickups were standard, and between 1953 and 1957, Alnico pickups were standard. In 1957, humbucker pickups replaced Alnico pickups. In 1960, sharp cutaway replaced original part/design. In 1962, Pat. No. humbucker pickups replaced P.A.F. humbuckers. In 1969, round cutaway replaced previous part/design. During 1973-76, the L-5 CES Custom Model was also offered, with a Super 400 neck - less than 20 were mfg. In 1974, neck volute was introduced. In 1981, neck volute was discontinued. Current production instruments (L-4 CES and L-5 CES models) are now part of the Historic Collection Series, found at the end of this section.

Gibson L-5 CES courtesy Leonard Shapiro

GRADING	100% MINT	98% NEAR MINT	95% EXC+	90% EXC	80% VG+	70% VG	60% G

L-5 S - single sharp cutaway multi-bound maple body, carved figured maple top, maple neck, 22-fret bound ebony pointed-end fingerboard with abalone block inlay, Tune-O-Matic bridge/trapeze tailpiece, silver center tailpiece insert with engraved model name, multi-bound blackface peghead vase/logo inlay, 3-per-side tuners, gold hardware, 2 covered low impedance (one diagonal) or regular humbucker pickups, 2 volume/2 tone controls, 3-position switch, available in Natural, Vintage Sunburst, or Cherry Sunburst finish, mfg. 1973-1985.

HIGH IMPEDANCE PICKUPS	N/A	$3,000	$2,650	$2,350	$2,000	$1,750	$1,500
LOW IMPEDANCE PICKUPS	N/A	$2,500	$2,225	$2,000	$1,800	$1,600	$1,400

This model is most desirable with 2 humbuckers and stop tailpiece. In 1974, covered humbucker pickups replaced original low impedance pickups (bridge pickup is diagonal). In 1975, stop tailpiece replaced the original trapeze tailpiece. In 1976, tunable stop tailpiece replaced the stop tailpiece.

SUPER V CES - similar to L-5 CES, except has Super 400 neck and peghead, 6-finger tailpiece, available in Antique Sunburst, Vintage Sunburst, Ebony, Wine Red, or Natural finish, mfg. 1978-1993.

	N/A	$5,500	$5,000	$4,500	$4,000	$3,800	$3,650

This model was also manufactured with one pickup. The model name was the Super V BJB.

L-5 STUDIO (CSL5[ ]NH) - please refer to the Custom/Historic Collection Series listing.

L-6 S/L-6 CUSTOM - single sharp cutaway maple body, black pickguard, maple neck, 24-fret maple fingerboard with pearl block inlay, tunable bridge/stop tailpiece, blackface peghead, 3-per-side tuners, chrome hardware, 2 covered humbucker pickups, 2 volume/1 tone controls, rotary switch, available in Ebony (common), Tobacco Sunburst, Wine Red (25 mfg. 1975-77), Cherry (16 mfg. 1975 only) or Natural Maple gloss (most common) finishes, mfg. 1973-1980.

	N/A	$650	$575	$500	$425	$350	$275

This model was available with ebony fingerboard in Tobacco Sunburst finish. In 1975, pearl dot inlay replaced block inlay, instrument renamed L-6 S Custom.

L-6 S Deluxe - similar to L-6 S, except has bolt-on maple neck, pearl dot fingerboard inlay, strings through anchoring, volume/tone control, 3-position switch, Ebony, Tobacco Sunburst, Natural Satin (most common), and Wine Red finishes, mfg. 1975-1980.

	N/A	$500	$450	$395	$335	$260	$225

A few of these models have set necks. This instrument was also available with rosewood fingerboard.

LE GRAND - single round cutaway body, spruce top, bound f-holes, raised bound tortoise pickguard, figured maple back/sides/neck, 19-fret bound ebony fingerboard with abalone/pearl split block inlay, adjustable ebony bridge with pearl inlay/finger tailpiece, bound blackface peghead with pearl split diamond/logo inlay, 3-per-side tuners, gold hardware, floating single coil pickup, available in Chablis, Sunrise Orange, or Translucent Amber finishes, mfg. 1994-96.

$4,500	$4,000	$3,750	$3,200	$2,500	$2,300	$2,050
				Last MSR was $6,300.		

LE GRANDE (HSLGGH) - please refer to listing in the Custom/Historic Collection Series.

ELECTRIC: LES PAUL SERIES

Les Paul (regular production, non-Custom Shop) subcategories have been arranged in the following sequence: Les Paul - Early Mfg. & Standard Models, Les Paul Custom Series, Les Paul Deluxe Models, Les Paul Low-Impedance Series, The Paul Series, Les Paul Variations - Misc., Les Paul Anniversary Models, Les Paul Signature Series, Les Paul Classic Premium Plus vs. Les Paul Reissue: Evolution of the Les Paul (An Overview), Les Paul Classic Series, Les Paul - XR Series, Les Paul Double Cutaway (DC) Series, Les Paul Studio Series, Les Paul Special Series, and Les Paul Junior Series. The Les Paul model debuted in 1952, and was Gibson´s first production solid body electric guitar. Because of the almost endless variations that have been produced over the years, this model has become a field unto itself.

Early models are without binding around the fingerboard and do not have a plastic ring around the selector switch. It has been noted that some of the early models have the Gold finish continuing on the sides and back in addition to the top. The original Gold Top finish is prone to a greenish hue around the lower bouts of the instrument where the player´s arm(s) rubbed off the clear and/or color coat. Because the color coat was originally mixed with bronze powder, the exposure of the bronze with air will produce a green oxidation (the same type of oxidation that occurs on the metal parts occasionally when the finish is rubbed off). Horizontal weather checking striations are also normal on original Gold Top finishes.

Les Paul: Early Mfg. & Standard Models

LES PAUL STANDARD GOLD TOP MODEL (1952-58 MFG.) - single sharp cutaway solid mahogany body, 13 in. wide, 17.25 in. long and 2 in. deep, 24.75 in. scale, bound carved maple top, raised cream pickguard, one piece mahogany neck, 16/22-fret bound rosewood fingerboard with pearl trapezoid inlays, trapeze bridge/tailpiece, blackface peghead with holly veneer/pearl logo inlay, silkscreen model name on peghead, 3-per-side Kluson tuners with plastic single ring buttons, nickel hardware, 2 single coil P-90 pickups, 2 volume/2 tone controls, with or w/o Bigsby vibrato, 3-position switch, available in Gold Top/Natural back finish, mfg. 1952-58.

1952	N/A	$10,000	$7,750	$5,750	$5,000	$4,500	$4,000
1953 TRAPEZE TAILPIECE	N/A	$9,000	$7,000	$5,500	$4,750	$4,250	$3,750
1953 STOP TAILPIECE	N/A	$15,000	$12,000	$10,000	$8,500	$7,000	$6,000
1954-1955	N/A	$20,000	$15,000	$12,000	$10,000	$8,500	$7,000
1956 S/C PICKUPS	N/A	$22,500	$17,500	$15,000	$13,000	$11,000	$9,000
1956 P-90 PICKUPS	N/A	$30,000	$25,000	$20,000	$17,000	$14,500	$12,500
1957 P-90 PICKUPS	N/A	$30,000	$25,000	$20,000	$17,000	$14,500	$12,500
1957 HUM PICKUPS	N/A	$55,000	$50,000	$42,000	$36,000	$31,000	$27,000
1958	N/A	$80,000	$65,000	$55,000	$47,000	$42,000	$37,000

Originally, bridge tailpieces were used with the strings traveling under the bar of the bridge. During 1952 and through most of 1953, the strings were changed to travel over the bridge bar. Special order instruments have Dark Brown back finish. In 1952, these models were not serialized. In 1953, ink stamped serial numbers on back of peghead were introduced. In 1953, wrapover bridge/tailpiece replaced original part/design. In 1955, Tune-O-Matic bridge/stop tailpiece replaced previous part/design. In 1957, humbucker PAF pickups replaced original part/design - these humbucker supplied Gold Tops came standard with cream colored pickup rings. Since they are the same color style as the most common ones used on the LP Standard Sunburst instruments, many Gold Top cream pickup rings have been taken off and used on the Standard Sunburst model.

GRADING	100% MINT	98% NEAR MINT	95% EXC+	90% EXC	80% VG+	70% VG	60% G

LES PAUL STANDARD SUNBURST (1958-1960 MFG.)

 - single sharp cutaway mahogany body, bound carved plain or flame maple top, raised cream pickguard, one-piece mahogany neck, 22-fret rosewood fingerboard with pearl trapezoid inlay, Tune-O-Matic bridge, stop or Bigsby tailpiece, blackface peghead with holly veneer/pearl logo inlay, 3-per-side Kluson tuners with single ring plastic buttons, nickel hardware, two covered (1959-1960) or uncovered (1958-1959) humbucker PAF pickups, 2 volume/2 tone controls, 3-position switch, inked serialization, available in Cherry Sunburst or Cherry (very rare) finish, approx. 400 mfg. 1958, 640 mfg. 1959, and 635 mfg. 1960.

There are three major considerations when determining value of 1958-1960 'Bursts - they are: original condition, amount of flame, and how much the color on top has faded. Original 'Bursts in average (60%-80%) original condition without much flame or color start in the $65,000 - $90,000 range. 80%-90% original condition guitars with some flame are currently trading in the $125,000-$175,000 range. Recent original Sunburst flametop sales/asking prices on strong instruments with nice flame are selling between $225,000 and 300,000+, depending on the amount of color remaining and degree of flame. Subtract approx. 10%-20% if Bigsby has been removed. 1959 mfg. is the most desirable.

Double black exposed humbucker pickups (circa 1958-59) are the most common, Zebra (black and white humbuckers) are less common (1959-1960 mfg.), and the double cream colored pickups (circa 1959-1960) are the most desirable. In 1959, large frets replaced original part/design. In 1960, thin neck, double ring tuner buttons replaced original part/design.

It is estimated that Gibson built 1,700 of these beauties between 1958 and 1960; and perhaps only 1,500 have still survived to today. In 1959, they retailed for $279 - the value of a flame top Gibson Les Paul Standard today depends on two factors: the degree of flame (figuring) in the maple top and the degree of original condition. It's hard to believe that two good bookmatched pieces of figured maple that no one paid much attention to in 1959 will cost you $100,000+ today. Not bad price appreciation, considering that George Gruhn remembers a time in the 1960s when they were under $1,000!

This particular model has achieved legendary status among guitar collectors, players, and investors throughout the world. The original LP 'Burst, more than any other electric guitar, proves what turbo-charged desirability can do to an instrument's price tag. Needless to say, the *Blue Book of Electric Guitars* fully recommends that several professional appraisals be secured before purchasing a collectible guitar of this magnitude. After Jimmy Page, Eric Clapton, and Mike Bloomfield made the 'Burst popular back in the late 1960s, some musicians were having their gold-tops stripped and refinished to join the craze! Given the magnitude of this particular portion of this nitch market place, some fakes and re-topped or refinished guitars have surfaced.

1953 Gibson Les Paul Standard courtesy Dave Rogers Dave's Guitar Shop

LES PAUL (SG BODY STYLE 1960-63 MFG.)

 - double sharp cutaway mahogany body, layered black pickguard, mahogany neck, 22-fret bound rosewood fingerboard with pearl trapezoid inlay, Tune-O-Matic bridge/side-pull vibrato, blackface peghead with pearl logo inlay, 3-per-side Kluson tuners with double ring plastic tuners, nickel hardware, 2 covered humbucker pickups, 2 volume/2 tone controls, 3-position switch, available in Cherry finish, mfg. 1960-63.

	N/A	$8,000	$6,750	$5,500	$4,750	$4,000	$3,400

In late 1960, the body style was changed to what is now known as the SG (solid guitar) body style. The Les Paul logo was still applied on the peghead (see submodel description directly below). In 1961, the Les Paul name was put on truss rod cover, and did not have a model name on the peghead. Pearl crown peghead inlay. In 1962, some models were produced with ebony tailblock and pearl inlay. In 1963, the Les Paul was renamed SG Standard. See SG Series later in text.

LES PAUL STANDARD GOLD TOP (1968-69 MFG.)

 - single sharp cutaway solid mahogany body, deeper cutaway binding, bound carved maple top, raised cream pickguard, mahogany neck, 22-fret bound rosewood fingerboard with pearl trapezoid inlay, Tune-O-Matic bridge/stop tailpiece, blackface peghead with pearl logo inlay, 3-per-side Kluson tuners with double ring plastic buttons, nickel hardware, 2 single coil P-90 pickups, 2 volume/2 tone controls, with or w/o Bigsby vibrato, 3-position switch, available in Gold Top/Natural Back finish, mfg. 1968-69.

1968	N/A	$7,500	$6,500	$5,500	$4,650	$3,950	$3,400
1969	N/A	$6,000	$5,200	$4,600	$3,800	$3,000	$2,450

This was Gibson's first Gold Top reissue.

LES PAUL STANDARD GOLD TOP (1971-73 MFG.)

 - single sharp cutaway solid mahogany body, bound carved maple top, raised cream pickguard, mahogany neck, 22-fret bound rosewood fingerboard with pearl trapezoid inlay, wrapover bridge tailpiece, blackface peghead with pearl logo inlay, 3-per-side Kluson tuners with plastic double ring buttons, nickel hardware, 2 single coil P-90 pickups, 2 volume/2 tone controls, 3-position switch, available in Gold Top finish, mfg. 1971-73.

	N/A	$3,000	$2,400	$1,800	$1,400	$1,100	$800

This model did not have a neck volute. This model was a reissue of the 1954 Les Paul.

LES PAUL STANDARD (1974-1997 MFG., LPS)

 - single cutaway mahogany body, set-in mahogany (or maple) neck, bound carved 3-piece maple top, 22-fret bound rosewood fingerboard with pearl trapezoid inlay, Tune-O-Matic bridge/stop tailpiece, blackface peghead with pearl logo inlay, "Standard" engraved on truss rod cover, 3-per-side tuners with pearloid buttons, chrome hardware, cream pickguard, 2 covered humbucker pickups, 2 volume/2 tone controls, 3-position switch, available in Cherry Sunburst, Dark Sunburst, Ebony (EB), Gold Top, Heritage Sunburst, Honey Burst, Natural, Tobacco Sunburst, TV Yellow, Vintage Sunburst and Wine Red (WR) finishes, mfg. 1974-1997.

1972-1973	N/A	$3,750	$2,800	$2,300	$1,900	$1,600	$1,400
1974-1975	N/A	$2,850	$2,500	$2,100	$1,800	$1,500	$1,300
1976-1981	N/A	$2,000	$1,800	$1,500	$1,300	$1,100	$950
1982-1989	N/A	$1,900	$1,700	$1,450	$1,250	$1,050	$900
1990-1997	N/A	$1,800	$1,600	$1,350	$1,150	$1,000	$850

Add $100 for Wine Red finish (LPS-WR). Add $300 for Heritage Cherry Sunburst (LPS-HS), Honey Burst (LPS-HB), and Vintage Sunburst (LPS-VS) finishes. Add $225 for left-handed configuration (production models 1990 to 1997).

In 1974, neck volute was introduced, slab cut body replaced original part/design. In 1978, one-piece body replaced original part/design. In 1981, carved top replaced previous part/design, neck volute was discontinued. Gibson's Les Paul Standards made between 1974 and 1981 often have maple necks and three-piece maple tops. These models are viewed as less desirable in the vintage guitar market. In 1990, TV Yellow finish became standard. In 1994, Cherry

1959 Gibson Les Paul Standard courtesy Dave Rogers Dave's Guitar Shop

GRADING	100% MINT	98% NEAR MINT	95% EXC+	90% EXC	80% VG+	70% VG	60% G

Sunburst, Dark Sunburst, Gold Top, Heritage Sunburst, Natural, Tobacco Sunburst and TV Yellow finishes were discontinued. In 1998, the Les Paul Standard was redesignated the LPS8, and reduced to only 4 finishes (choice of chrome or gold hardware). See listing below.

Gibson has offered a twelve-string version of the Les Paul in the past. However, these instruments have either been very, very low production batches, specialty productions, or custom shop orders.

Current Specialty versions of classic Les Paul configurations (Les Paul '56 Gold Top Reissue, Les Paul '59 Flametop Reissue, Les Paul '60 Flametop Reissue) are part of the Historic Collection Series, and can be found at the end of this section.

LES PAUL STANDARD REISSUE (1982 MFG.) - limited mfg. in Kalamazoo before plant closes, also refer to Kalamazoo Custom
Order '59 Reissue model listing under Les Paul: Variations - Misc.

	N/A	$3,000	$2,600	$2,200	$1,850	$1,500	$1,250

LES PAUL SUNBURST '59 REISSUE (1983-85) - first Gibson reissue of the famous '59 Sunburst, specs based on original '59 LP Sunburst, figured flame two-piece maple top, nickel plated hardware, Sunburst finish, original mfg. in Kalamazoo (rare), later mfg. was in Nashville, mfg. 1983-85.

	N/A	$3,500	$3,000	$2,500	$2,000	$1,650	$1,350

LES PAUL STANDARD (1998-CURRENT, LP PREFIX) - single cutaway mahogany body, set-in mahogany neck, bound carved maple or mahogany (new 2002) top, 24.75 in. scale, 22-fret bound rosewood fingerboard with pearl trapezoid inlay, Tune-O-Matic bridge/stop tailpiece, blackface peghead with pearl logo inlay, "Standard" engraved on truss rod cover, 3-per-side tuners, chrome hardware, cream pickguard, 2 or 3 (new 2002, HC finish and mahogany top only) covered humbucker (490R/498T) pickups, 2 volume/2 tone controls, 3-way toggle switch, available in Bullion Gold (BG, mfg. 2001), Cayenne (CA, new 2004), Darkburst (new 2002), Light Burst (new 2002), Trans. Amber (new 2002), Gecko (GE, new 2004), Heritage Cherry Sunburst (HS), Honey Burst (HB), Wine Red (WR) Vintage Sunburst (new 1999), Frost and Crimson Sparkle (disc. 2000), Ice Tea (IT, new 2004), Latte Creme (LC, new 2004), Root Beer (RO, new 2004), Green, Blue, and Diamond Sparkle (disc. 2001) finishes, mfg. 1998-2004.

	$2,100	$1,525	$1,375	$1,150	$925	$800	$650

Last MSR was $3,098.

Add $300 for mahogany top with 3 pickups (LPS3, mfg.2002-2004). Add approx. $300 for Bullion Gold finish (disc. 2001). Add $100 for gold hardware (disc.). Add approx. $200 for left-handed configuration.

In 1998, the Les Paul Standard was redesignated LPS-8, and was introduced in 3 finishes, and a choice of chrome or gold (disc. 1999) hardware. This was discontinued during 2003, and the prefix is now LPS. Base price is for Faded 50s/60s

Les Paul Standard w/50s or 60s Neck - similar to Les Paul Standard, except has a 50s/60s neck with nickel hardware, available in Ebony (EB), Gold Top (GT), or custom colors, mfg. 2002-present.

MSR	$3,248		$2,100	$1,475	$1,275	$1,050	$950	$825	$750

Add $220 for custom colors (new 2004). Add $220 for Gold Top. Add approx. $350 (different for the 50s and 60s neck) for Manhatten Midnight Blue, Pacific Reef, or Santa Fe Sunrise finishes.

Les Paul Standard Faded 50s/60s Neck (LP) - similar to the Les Paul Standard with 50s/60s neck, except has faded neck, available in Honey Burst (HB), Heritage Cherry Sunburst (HS), or Tobacco Burst (TB) finishes, new 2005.

MSR	$3,008		$1,950	$1,525	$1,200	$925	$850	$775	$675

Les Paul Standard Raw Power - similar to Les Paul Standard, except has Natural Satin finish, mfg. 2001-02.

	$1,950	$1,425	$1,275	$1,075	$900	$800	$700

Last MSR was $2,845.

Les Paul Standard Lite (LPLI) - double cutaway design, carved maple top, mahogany back, 24.75 in. scale, includes treble '57 Classic Plus humbucker and rythmn 492R Alnico magnet humbucker pickups, gold hardware, available in Translucent Amber, Translucent Black, or Translucent Blue finish, mfg. 1999-2001.

	$1,575	$1,250	$1,050	$900	$800	$700	$625

Last MSR was $2,399

Les Paul Standard Bird's-eye - similar to Les Paul Standard (LPS-), except has bird's-eye maple top. Available in Heritage Sunburst, Honey Burst, or Vintage Sunburst finishes, mfg. 1993-95.

	$1,950	$1,350	$1,140	$860	$775	$710	$645

Last MSR was $2,699.

Les Paul Standard Plus (LPS+) - available in Heritage Cherry Sunburst (HS), Honey Burst (HB), Light Burst (LB, new 2001), or Vintage Sunburst (VS), disc. 1997, reintroduced 2001 only.

	$2,450	$1,325	$1,100	$975	$875	$800	$725

Last MSR was $3,614.

Les Paul Standard Premium Plus (LPPP) - available in Heritage Cherry Sunburst (HS), Honey Burst (HB), Light Burst (LB), or Vintage Sunburst (VS, disc. 2004), Desert Burst (DB), Trans. Black (BL), Trans Amber (TA), or Wine Red (WR, disc. 2004), mfg. 2001-present.

MSR	$3,688		$2,500	$1,700	$1,250	$1,000	$900	$825	$750

Les Paul Standard Digital (LPDG) - similar to the Les Paul Standard design, except features Hex pickups (seperate signal for individual strings) that are capable of either analog (Classic) or digital output, signal goes to the onboard digital converter utilizing Gibson's patented Magic Digital Transport Technology to send the signal out of the guitar by Cat-5 Ethernet cable (can be up to 100m long), the Ethernet Cable is then plugged into outboard breakout box (BoB), which converts the digital information back to analog and outputs it into SUM, stereo, or Hex configuration, includes headphone jack with volume control, available in Blue Mist finish, mfg. 2004-present.

MSR	$5,618		$3,850	$2,750	$2,350	$2,050	$1,800	$1,550	$1,225

Les Paul: Custom Series

LES PAUL CUSTOM (1954-57 MFG.) - single sharp cutaway multi-bound mahogany body with carved top, 13 in. wide, 17.25 in. long and 2 in. deep, 24.75 in. scale, raised bound black pickguard, mahogany neck, 22-fret bound ebony fingerboard with pearl block inlay, "Les Paul Custom" engraved on truss rod cover, Tune-O-Matic bridge/stop tailpiece, multi-bound peghead with pearl split diamond/logo inlay, 3-per-side Deluxe Kluson tuners with plastic single ring buttons, gold hardware, 2 single coil pickups with plastic covers (neck pickup has oblong polepieces, bridge pickup has round polepieces, 2 volume/2 tone controls, with or w/o Bigsby vibrato, 3-position switch, available in Black finish, mfg. 1954-57.

	N/A	$11,500	$10,000	$8,750	$7,500	$6,750	$5,950

This guitar was nicknamed the "Black Beauty" and also the "Fretless Wonder."

GRADING	100% MINT	98% NEAR MINT	95% EXC+	90% EXC	80% VG+	70% VG	60% G

LES PAUL CUSTOM '54 REISSUE - reissue of '54 Les Paul Custom, Alnico V neck pickup, P-90 bridge pickup, standard 6 digit ser. no. with "LE" prefix, mfg. 1972-73.

	N/A	$2,500	$2,250	$1,875	$1,650	$1,400	$1,250

Gibson shipping records indicate 3 instruments were shipped in 1975, and one was shipped in 1977.

LES PAUL CUSTOM (1957-1960 MFG.) - similar to earlier models, except most have 3 humbucker pickups with metal covers, mfg. 1957-1960.

	N/A	$22,000	$18,500	$15,000	$12,500	$10,000	$8,500

This guitar was nicknamed the "Black Beauty" and also the "Fretless Wonder."

In 1959, Grover tuners replaced original part/design. Current production instruments (Les Paul Custom Black Beauty ´54 Reissue, Les Paul Custom Black Beauty ´57 Reissue) are part of the Historic Collection Series, and can be found in the Historic Series.

LES PAUL CUSTOM (SG BODY STYLE 1961-63 MFG.) - double sharp cutaway mahogany body, white layered pickguard, mahogany neck, 22-fret bound ebony fingerboard with pearl block inlay, Tune-O-Matic bridge/side-pull gold plated Gibson vibrato, multi-bound peghead with pearl split diamond inlay, 3-per-side tuners, gold hardware, 3 covered humbucker pickups, 2 volume/2 tone controls, 3-position switch, available in Black or White finishes, mfg. 1961-63.

	N/A	$8,250	$7,250	$6,000	$5,250	$4,500	$3,750

Models in black finish are very rare. In 1962, some models were produced with pearl inlaid ebony tail-piece insert. In 1963, renamed SG Custom (see SG Series later in text). Current production instruments (SG Les Paul Custom) are part of the Historic Collection Series, found at the end of this section.

LES PAUL CUSTOM 1968 REISSUE - single sharp cutaway mahogany body, multi-bound carved maple top, raised bound black pickguard, one piece mahogany neck, 22 small fret bound ebony fingerboard with pearl block inlay, Tune-O-Matic bridge/stop tailpiece, multi-bound peghead with pearl split diamond/logo inlay, no neck volute, 3-per-side Grover tuners, gold hardware, 2 humbucker Pat. No. pickups, 2 volume/2 tone controls, 3-position switch, available in Black finish, 433 mfg. 1968 only.

	N/A	$3,500	$3,150	$2,750	$2,450	$2,150	$1,900

This instrument was a reissue of 1957 version of the Les Paul Custom.

LES PAUL CUSTOM 1969 REISSUE (LPC-) - similar to Les Paul Custom 1968 Reissue, except has 3-piece mahogany/maple body, 3-piece neck. Available in Alpine White (AW, current), Black, Cherry, Cherry Sunburst (common), Ebony (EB, most common, current), Heritage Sunburst, Heritage Cherry Sunburst (current), Honeyburst, Natural, Tobacco Sunburst, Vintage Sunburst, Walnut, White, and Wine Red (WR, current) finishes. Mfg. 1969-2003.

1969	N/A	$3,500	$3,150	$2,750	$2,450	$2,050	$1,600
1970-1975	N/A	$2,000	$1,750	$1,500	$1,250	$1,000	$850
1976-2003	$2,000	$1,800	$1,600	$1,450	$1,175	$950	$825

Last MSR was $3,948.

Recent production models were available in a left-handed configuration at $200 retail upcharge.

During 1970-1981, the Les Paul Custom had neck volute and Made in U.S.A. on back of headstock. Left-handed models were introduced during 1971. In 1971, Cherry and Cherry Sunburst finishes became options. From 1971 to 1973 and in 1978, 3 humbucker pickup configuration was an option (163 were mfg.). In 1972, Tobacco Sunburst became an option. In 1975, jumbo frets was an option - only 26 were mfg. Natural and White finishes became an option. In 1976, Wine Red finish became available. In 1977, one piece mahogany body replaced original part/design, and Walnut finish became available. Also during 1977, a maple fingerboard became available, and in 1979, a solid maple fingerboard became available. In 1988, Alpine White, Ebony, Heritage Sunburst and Vintage Sunburst finishes became available; in addition to gold hardware. In 1990, Honey Burst finish became available. In 1994, Black, Cherry, Cherry Sunburst, Heritage Sunburst, Honeyburst, Tobacco Sunburst, Vintage Sunburst, Walnut and White finishes were discontinued.

Les Paul Custom Plus (LPCC) - similar to Les Paul Custom, except has bound figured maple top and gold hardware, available in Dark Wineburst, Honey Burst (HB), Heritage Cherry Sunburst (HS), or Vintage Sunburst (VS) finishes, disc. 1996.

	$1,995	$1,750	$1,500	$1,250	$1,050	$925	$800

Last MSR was $4,439.

In 1994, Dark Wineburst finish was discontinued.

Les Paul Custom Premium Plus - similar to Les Paul Custom, except has highest quality bound figured maple top, available in Dark Wineburst, Honey Burst, Heritage Cherry Sunburst, or Vintage Sunburst finishes, disc. 1994.

	$2,095	$1,800	$1,500	$1,200	$1,100	$995	$900

Last MSR was $3,000.

LES PAUL CUSTOM LITE - single sharp cutaway multi-bound mahogany body with carved top, raised bound black pickguard, mahogany neck, 22-fret bound ebony fingerboard with pearl block inlay, Tune-O-Matic bridge/stop tailpiece, multi-bound peghead with pearl split diamond/logo inlay, 3-per-side tuners with chrome buttons, gold hardware, 2 covered humbucker pickups, volume/tone control, 3-position switch, mini coil tap switch, available in Black finish, mfg. 1987-1990.

	N/A	$1,250	$1,050	$875	$775	$650	$525

This model was also available with double locking vibrato.

Les Paul Custom Lite Showcase Edition - similar to original Les Paul Custom Lite, except has lighter body with Gold Top finish, all black hardware, EMG pickups, triple top body binding, no pickguard. Limited edition, 200 mfg. 1988 only.

	N/A	$1,575	$1,325	$1,150	$950	$850	$725

2000 Gibson Les Paul Standard courtesy Gibson

Gibson Les Paul Custom courtesy Gibson

GRADING	100% MINT	98% NEAR MINT	95% EXC+	90% EXC	80% VG+	70% VG	60% G

Les Paul: Deluxe Series

LES PAUL DELUXE (1969-1985 MFG.) - single sharp cutaway 3-piece mahogany/maple body, 13 in. wide, 17.25 in. long and 2 in. deep, 24.75 in. scale, deeper cutaway binding, bound carved maple top, raised cream pickguard, mahogany neck, 22-fret bound rosewood fingerboard with pearl trapezoid inlay, "Deluxe" engraved on truss rod cover, Tune-O-Matic bridge/stop tailpiece, widened blackface peghead with pearl logo inlay, 3-per-side Kluson tuners with plastic double ring buttons, nickel hardware, 2 mini humbucker pickups, 2 volume/2 tone controls, 3-position switch, available in Blue Sparkle Top (approx. 230 mfg. 1975-77), Cherry (mfg. 1971-75), Cherry Sunburst, Gold Top (introduced 1970), Red Sparkle Top (rare, approx. 125 mfg. 1975 only), Tobacco Sunburst, Walnut (approx. 112 mfg. 1971-72), Natural or Wine Red finishes, mfg. 1969-1985.

	100%	98%	95%	90%	80%	70%	60%
1969-1970	N/A	$3,400	$3,000	$2,500	$2,100	$1,650	$1,400
1971-1985	N/A	$1,500	$1,325	$1,100	$900	$800	$700

Add 50%-100% for Blue or Red Sparkle finishes.

A few of these models between 1969 and 1971 were produced with 2 single coil P-90 pickups. In 1971, neck volute was introduced, and Cherry, Cherry Sunburst and Walnut finishes became standard. Also during 1971, a left-hand model was introduced. In 1972, the Walnut finish was discontinued, the Tobacco Sunburst finish became standard, and standard humbucker pickups were optional with standard on truss rod cover. In 1975, Natural and Wine Red finishes became options. In 1976, standard humbucker option was discontinued. In 1977, 2-piece mahogany body replaced original part/design. In 1981, neck volute was discontinued.

LES PAUL PRO DELUXE (1976-1982 MFG.) - similar to Les Paul Deluxe, except has ebony fingerboard with crown inlays, chrome hardware, and P-90 pickups, marked "PRO" on truss-rod cover, "Les Paul Model" on headstock, cream colored plastic pickguard, available in Black, Cherry Sunburst, Gold Top, or Tobacco Sunburst finishes, mfg. 1976-1982.

	N/A	$1,500	$1,250	$1,000	$875	$750	$650

LES PAUL DELUXE GOLDTOP - similar to Les Paul Deluxe, except has mini-humbucker pickups only, "Hall of Fame" decal on neck bend, and Gold finish, mfg. 1991 only.

	N/A	$1,500	$1,200	$995	$850	$725	$650

Les Paul: Low-Impedance Series

LES PAUL PERSONAL - single cutaway multi-bound mahogany body, carved top, raised bound pickguard, mahogany neck, 22-fret bound ebony fingerboard with pearl block inlay, Tune-O-Matic bridge/stop tailpiece, multi-bound blackface peghead with pearl diamond/logo inlay, 3-per-side tuners with plastic buttons, gold hardware, 2 low impedance pickups, mic volume control on upper bass bout, volume/decade/treble/bass controls, two 3-position switches, phase slide switch, available in Walnut finish, approx. 370 mfg. 1969-1973.

	N/A	$1,500	$1,250	$1,100	$895	$725	$650

This instrument had an optional Bigsby vibrato.

LES PAUL PROFESSIONAL - single cutaway bound mahogany body, raised black pickguard, mahogany neck, 22-fret rosewood fingerboard with pearl trapezoid inlay, Tune-O-Matic bridge/stop tailpiece, blackface peghead with pearl logo inlay, 3-per-side tuners, nickel hardware, 2 low impedance pickups, volume/decade/treble/bass controls, two 3-position switches, phase slide switch, available in Walnut finish, approx. 2,300 mfg. 1969-1979.

	N/A	$1,500	$1,250	$1,100	$895	$750	$650

This instrument had an optional Bigsby vibrato.

LES PAUL RECORDING - single cutaway bound mahogany body, carved top, raised multi-layer pickguard, mahogany neck, 22-fret bound rosewood fingerboard with pearl block inlay, Tune-O-Matic bridge/stop tailpiece, multi-bound peghead with pearl split diamond/logo inlay, 2 covered low impedance pickups, "Gibson" formed on pickup covers, volume/decade/treble/bass controls, two 3-position switches, impedance/phase slide switches, built-in transformer, available in Walnut finish, approx. 5,400 mfg. 1971-1980.

	N/A	$1,350	$1,100	$950	$850	$750	$650

In 1975, White finish became an option. In 1978, Ebony and Cherry Sunburst finishes became an option.

LES PAUL SIGNATURE - offset double cutaway, arched maple top, raised cream pickguard, f-holes, maple back/sides, mahogany neck, 22-fret bound rosewood fingerboard with pearl trapezoid inlay, Tune-O-Matic bridge/stop tailpiece, blackface peghead with pearl logo inlay, 3-per-side tuners with plastic buttons, chrome hardware, 2 low impedance humbucker pickups, plastic pickup covers with stamped logo, volume/tone control, 3-position/phase/level switches, available in Gold Top (approx. 1,400 mfg.) or Tobacco Sunburst (rare, approx. 85 mfg.) finishes, mfg. 1973-79.

	N/A	$2,600	$2,200	$2,000	$1,750	$1,600	$1,400

This model has walnut back/sides with Gold Top finish. After 1976, high and low impedance humbuckers became available.

Les Paul: The Paul Series

THE PAUL STANDARD (FIREBRAND) - single sharp cutaway walnut body/neck, 22-fret ebony fingerboard with pearl dot inlay, Tune-O-Matic bridge/stop tailpiece, 3-per-side tuners, chrome hardware, 2 exposed humbucker pickups, 2 volume/2 tone controls, 3-position switch, available in Natural satin nitrocellulose finish, mfg. 1979-1982.

	N/A	$495	$425	$325	$275	$225	$200

In 1980, this guitar was renamed Firebrand, with the Firebrand logo burned into the peghead.

The Paul Deluxe - similar to original The Paul Standard, except has mahogany body/neck. Available in Antique Natural, Ebony, Natural or Wine Red finishes, mfg. 1980-86.

	N/A	$550	$475	$350	$300	$250	$200

In 1985, Ebony and Wine Red finishes replaced original part/design.

THE PAUL II - single cutaway solid mahogany body, mahogany neck, 24.75 scale, 22-fret rosewood fingerboard with dot inlay, Tune-O-Matic bridge/stop tailpiece, blackface peghead with silkscreened logo, engraved "The Paul II" on truss rod cover, 3-per-side tuners, chrome hardware, 2 exposed pole piece humbucker pickups (490R/498T), 2 volume/2 tone controls, 3-way toggle switch, available in Ebony (EB), or Wine Red (WR) finishes, mfg. 1996-98.

$495	$425	$350	$300	$275	$225	$175

Last MSR was $849.

GRADING	100% MINT	98% NEAR MINT	95% EXC+	90% EXC	80% VG+	70% VG	60% G

THE PAUL SL (LPTP) - single cutaway solid mahogany body with carved top, mahogany neck, 24.75" scale, 22-fret rosewood fingerboard with pearl dot inlay, Tune-O-Matic bridge/stop tailpiece, blackface peghead with silkscreened logo, 3-per-side vintage-style tuners, chrome hardware, 2 exposed polepiece humbucker pickups (490R/498T), 2 volume/2 tone controls, 3-way toggle switch, available in UV-Cured Ebony (EB), Emerald (EX), or Ruby (RX) finishes, mfg. 1996-99.

	$650	$475	$425	$375	$325	$300	$275

The engraved truss rod cover may (incorrectly) read "The Paul II."

Les Paul: Variations - Misc.

Since the following Les Paul Variations do not fit into any other subcategories, they have been placed under this miscellaneous subheading. Models include: The Les Paul, Les Paul Artisan, Les Paul Artist, Kalamazoo Custom Order ´59 Reissue LP, Les Paul Kalamazoo, Les Paul Heritage Series Standard 80, Les Paul Spotlight Special, Les Paul CMT, Les Paul ´59 Sunburst Reissue, LP-XPL, LP 1985 Reissue, Les Paul Smartwood, Les Paul Smartwood Exotic, and Les Paul Voodoo.

THE LES PAUL - single sharp cutaway body, rosewood bound carved 2-piece bookmatched flame maple top/back/sides, mahogany core, raised rosewood pickguard, maple neck, 22-fret bound 3-piece ebony/rosewood/ebony fingerboard with abalone block inlay, Tune-O-Matic bridge/stop tailpiece, pearl split diamond/logo peghead inlay, 3-per-side Schaller tuners with pearl buttons, serial number engraved pearl plate on peghead back, gold hardware, 2 Super humbucker pickups with rosewood surrounds, 2 volume/2 tone rosewood control knobs, 3-position switch, rosewood control plate on back, available in Natural (approx. 70 mfg.) or Wine Red (18 mfg.) finishes, mfg. 1976-1980.

Last MSR was $3,000.

Due to extreme rarity (ser. nos. #61-#68 were made without their rosewood parts), accurate price evaluation is difficult for this model. Since this variation, at the time, was perhaps Gibson's most elaborate and ornate (not to mention most expensive) LP, most of these instruments were not played. As a result, remaining specimens are usually in 95%+ condition. Current asking prices for this condition factor are presently in the $10,000 to $15,000 price range, depending on the condition. Later mfg. w/o rosewood parts are not as desirable and are worth approx. 25% less. A few early models had solid figured maple bodies. In 1978, Schaller Tune-O-Matic bridge/tunable stop tailpiece replaced original part/design. In 1979, Wine Red finish was discontinued.

Gibson Les Paul Deluxe Goldtop Series George McGuire

LES PAUL ARTISAN - single sharp cutaway mahogany body, multi-bound carved maple top, raised bound black pickguard, mahogany neck, 22-fret bound ebony fingerboard with pearl flowers/heart inlay, Tune-O-Matic bridge/tunable stop tailpiece, multi-bound peghead with pearl split flowers/heart/logo inlay, 3-per-side tuners, gold hardware, 2 single coil pickups, 2 volume/2 tone controls, 3-position switch, available in Ebony, Tobacco Sunburst or Walnut finishes, mfg. 1976-1982.

	N/A	$2,450	$2,000	$1,675	$1,475	$1,125	$900

Originally offered with 3 optional humbuckers pickups - the 3 humbucker configuration became standard in 1979. In 1980, larger Tune-O-Matic bridge replaced original part/design.

LES PAUL ARTIST - single cutaway mahogany body, multi-bound carved maple top, raised black pickguard, mahogany neck, 22-fret bound ebony fingerboard with pearl block inlay, Tune-O-Matic bridge/tunable stop tailpiece, multibound blackface peghead with pearl script LP/logo, 3-per-side tuners, gold hardware, 2 covered humbucker pickups, volume/treble/bass controls, 3-position selector/3 mini switches, active electronics, available in Sunburst finish, less than 500 mfg. 1979-1981.

	N/A	$2,000	$1,650	$1,350	$1,075	$925	$800

In 1980, Ebony and Fireburst finishes became optional.

KALAMAZOO CUSTOM ORDER ´59 REISSUE LES PAUL - ´59 LP Standard style appointments, highly figured (flame or quilted) maple tops, ebonized holly veneered pegheads, original inked serialization, other ´59 Standard features, approx. 1,500 mfg. circa 1978-79.

These instruments are considered desirable because Gibson (unofficially) duplicated an original 1959 Les Paul Standard almost exactly for a few companies, including Leo's in California (approx. 800 mfg., 400 were exported to Japan), The Guitar Trader in New Jersey (approx. 47 mfg.), and Jimmy Wallace (approx. several hundred) through Arnold and Morgan Music in Texas. These companies custom ordered Les Paul models that were patterned exactly after an original Gibson 1959 Standard Model and feature individualized truss rod covers. Currently, pricing on the Guitar Trader model can range from $4,000 to $7,500, the larger amount if with original PAF humbuckers installed by Guitar Trader. Mfg. for Leo's and Jimmy Wallace are currently selling in the $3,500 - $4,500 range, assuming excellent original condition.

LES PAUL KALAMAZOO (LES PAUL KM) - single sharp cutaway solid mahogany body, bound carved maple top, raised cream pickguard, mahogany neck, 22-fret bound rosewood fingerboard with pearl trapezoid inlay, Nashville Tune-O-Matic bridge/stop tailpiece, large blackface peghead with pearl logo inlay, "Les Paul K.M." engraved on truss cover, 3-per-side Grover tuners, nickel hardware, 2 cream colored covered humbucker pickups, 2 volume/2 tone controls, 3-position switch, available in Antique Sunburst, Cherry Sunburst, or Natural finishes, approx. 1,050 mfg. 1979 only.

	N/A	$2,000	$1,775	$1,525	$1,300	$1,100	$900

This was Gibson's first nationally distributed flame top reissue. The first production run of these instruments exhibited a metal plate with engraved custom-made logo below the tailpiece.

Gibson Kalamazoo Custom Order ´59 Reissue Les Paul courtesy Jimmy Wallace

GRADING	100% MINT	98% NEAR MINT	95% EXC+	90% EXC	80% VG+	70% VG	60% G

LES PAUL HERITAGE SERIES STANDARD 80 - single sharp cutaway mahogany body, bound carved flame maple top, raised cream pickguard, 3-piece mahogany neck, 22-fret rosewood fingerboard with pearl trapezoid inlay, Tune-O-Matic bridge/stop tailpiece, blackface peghead with pearl logo inlay, "Heritage 80" on truss cover, 3-per-side Grover tuners, nickel hardware, 2 covered humbucker pickups, 2 volume/2 tone controls, 3-position switch, available in Cherry Sunburst or Honey Sunburst finishes, mfg. 1980-82.

	N/A	$3,000	$2,570	$2,150	$1,725	$1,550	$1,400

This was Gibson's first attempt at recreating a Les Paul that was similar in performance and specs to those instruments the company produced in the late 1950s. A few of these instruments were produced with Ebony finish and are very rare.

Les Paul Heritage 80 Elite - similar to the Les Paul Heritage 80, except has quilted maple top, one piece neck, and ebony fingerboard, mfg. 1980-82.

	N/A	$3,000	$2,575	$2,150	$1,750	$1,550	$1,425

LES PAUL SPOTLIGHT SPECIAL - single sharp cutaway mahogany body, bound carved 3-piece maple/mahogany/maple top, no pickguard, features central block of walnut on figured maple sides, mahogany neck, 22-fret rosewood fingerboard with pearl trapezoid inlay, Tune-O-Matic bridge/stop tailpiece, blackface peghead with pearl logo inlay, 3-per-side tuners with plastic buttons, gold plated hardware, 2 covered humbucker pickups, 2 volume/2 tone controls, 3-position switch, custom shop edition logo on back of headstock, special serialization with "83" followed by special 3-digit serial number, available in Natural finish, mfg. 1980-85.

	N/A	$2,500	$2,250	$1,950	$1,600	$1,295	$1,150

LES PAUL CMT - similar to Les Paul Spotlight Special, except has maple/walnut/maple body, curly maple top, mfg. 1986-89.

	N/A	$2,500	$2,150	$1,795	$1,450	$1,295	$1,200

LES PAUL LP-XPL - single sharp cutaway solid mahogany body, bound carved maple top, raised cream pickguard, mahogany neck, 22-fret bound ebony fingerboard with pearl dot inlay, Tune-O-Matic bridge/stop tailpiece, blackface peghead with pearl logo inlay, 6-on-a-side tuners, chrome hardware, 2 single coil pickups, 2 volume/2 tone controls, 3-position switch, available in Cherry Sunburst finish, mfg. 1984-87.

	N/A	$800	$675	$575	$475	$425	$350

This model was also available with a double cutaway body and a model with 2 single coil/1 humbucker pickups configuration.

LES PAUL SUPREME - features AAAA flame maple top/back, multi-bound top, gold hardware, Supreme inlayed in headstock, available in pearl split block inlays on ebony fingerboard, standard finishes include Alpine White (AW, new 2004), Ebony (EB), or Wine Red (WR), mfg. 2003-present.

MSR	$4,268	$2,950	$2,400	$1,800	$1,400	$1,150	$925	$800

Add $420 for Trans Black (BL, new 2004), Desert Burst (DB, new 2004), Heritage Cherry Sunburt (HS), Translucent Amber (TA), or Root Beer (RO).

LES PAUL SMARTWOOD STANDARD (LPSW) - single cutaway mahogany body, (Alternative wood project Les Paul model), carved top, 22-fret fingerboard with pearl dot inlay, Tune-O-Matic bridge/stop tailpiece, blackface peghead with pearl logo inlay, "SmartWood" engraved on truss rod cover, 3-per-side tuners, gold hardware, 2 covered humbucker pickups, 2 volume/2 tone controls, 3-position switch, available in Antique Natural (AN) finish, mfg. 1995-2001.

	$2,000	$1,550	$1,300	$1,100	$975	$850	$750

Last MSR was $3,299.

SmartWood is a program of the Rainforest Alliances, an international non-profit conservation organization that certifies if certain woods are harvested in a sustainable manner.

LES PAUL SMARTWOOD EXOTIC - single cutaway mahogany body, carved Ambay Guasu, Banara, Cancharana (disc. 2001), Curupay, Peroba, or Taperyva Guasu (disc. 2001) top, 22-fret Curupay fingerboard with pearloid dot inlay, Tune-O-Matic bridge/stop tailpiece, blackface peghead with pearl logo inlay, "Exotic Wood" engraved on truss rod cover, 3-per-side tuners with plastic buttons, gold hardware, 2 covered humbucker (490R/498T) pickups, 2 volume/2 tone controls, 3-position switch, includes gig bag, available in UV-Cured Matte finish, mfg. 1998-2002.

	$975	$825	$725	$625	$525	$425	$350

Last MSR was $1,537.

LES PAUL VOODOO (LPSV) - available in JuJu finish (JJ), bright chrome hardware, mfg. 2002 only.

	$1,250	$925	$825	$725	$625	$550	$500

Last MSR was $1,948.

Les Paul: Anniversary Models

LES PAUL CUSTOM TWENTIETH ANNIVERSARY - single sharp cutaway multi-bound mahogany body with carved top, raised bound black pickguard, mahogany neck, 22-fret bound ebony fingerboard with pearl block inlay, Twentieth Anniversary engraved into block inlay at 15th fret, Tune-O-Matic bridge/stop tailpiece, multi-bound peghead with pearl split diamond/logo inlay, 3-per-side tuners with plastic buttons, gold hardware, 2 humbucker pickups, 2 volume/2 tone controls, 3-position switch, available in Black, White, or Cherry Sunburst finishes, 60 mfg. 1974-75.

	N/A	$2,500	$2,150	$1,875	$1,600	$1,400	$1,150

LES PAUL 25/50 ANNIVERSARY - mahogany body, carved maple top, slashed block fingerboard inlay, "Les Paul 25 50" peghead inlay, 2 humbuckers, approx. 3,400 mfg. 1978-79 only.

	N/A	$2,150	$1,850	$1,600	$1,350	$1,200	$1,000

Last MSR was $1,250.

Add 10% for Natural finish.

This guitar commemorated 25 years of the Les Paul model, and 50 years of Les Paul's continuing career.

LES PAUL STANDARD THIRTIETH ANNIVERSARY - single sharp cutaway mahogany body, bound carved maple top, raised cream pickguard, mahogany neck, 22-fret rosewood fingerboard with pearl trapezoid inlay, pearl Thirtieth Anniversary inlay at 15th fret, Tune-O-Matic bridge/stop tailpiece, blackface peghead with pearl logo inlay, 3-per-side tuners with plastic buttons, nickel hardware, 2 covered humbucker pickups, 2 volume/2 tone controls, 3-position switch, available in Gold Top finish, mfg. 1982-84.

	N/A	$2,150	$1,850	$1,600	$1,350	$1,200	$1,000

GRADING	100% MINT	98% NEAR MINT	95% EXC+	90% EXC	80% VG+	70% VG	60% G

LES PAUL DELUXE THIRTIETH ANNIVERSARY - similar to Les Paul Deluxe, except has mini-humbucker pickups, chrome hardware, standard pearloid trapezoid inlays (w/o anniversary markings), available in Ebony, Wine Red, or Bullion Gold (mfg. 2001-02) finish, mfg. 1999-2002.

	$1,950	$1,700	$1,450	$1,175	$950	$850	$775

Last MSR was $2,922.

Add approx. 10% for Bullion Gold finish, original MSR was $531 for this option.

LES PAUL CUSTOM THIRTY-FIFTH ANNIVERSARY - similar to original Les Paul Custom Twentieth Anniversary, except has Thirty-Fifth Anniversary etched on peghead inlay, 3 humbucker pickups, black finish only, mfg. 1989 only.

	N/A	$1,875	$1,600	$1,400	$1,250	$950	$850

LES PAUL STANDARD FORTIETH ANNIVERSARY - similar to Les Paul Standard Thirtieth Anniversary, except has ebony fingerboard, gold hardware, 2 stacked P-100 humbucker pickups, mfg. 1992 only.

	N/A	$1,650	$1,425	$1,150	$875	$775	$700

LES PAUL FIFTIETH ANNIVERSARY - features carved koa top, figured maple back, 3-piece flamed maple neck with koa strips, gold hardware, two '57 classic humbucker pickups, ebony control knobs, abalone cloud inlays, gold Grover Imperial tuners, includes limited edition hardshell case with embroidered case cover, available in Antique Natural finish, limited run mfg. by Custom Shop 2002-2003.

	$7,950	$6,150	$4,500	$3,900	$3,300	$2,750	$2,250

Last MSR was $13,728.

Les Paul: Signature Series

GARY MOORE SIGNATURE LES PAUL - features AA carved maple top with Lemon Burst finish, exposed Burst-Bucker pickups, Gary Moore signature engraved on truss rod cover. Mfg. 2001-2002.

	$2,000	$1,750	$1,500	$1,200	$1,000	$875	$750

Last MSR was $2,922.

This model was a standard production model, not manufactured by the Custom Shop.

Les Paul: Custom Shop Models

Please refer to the listings in the Custom Shop/Historic Collection sections at the end of this section. For more information on the Les Paul Custom Shop Signature Series, including the Ace Frehley, Jimmy Page, Joe Perry, Zack Wylde, and Peter Frampton models, please refer to the Custom Shop section later in this text.

The Les Paul Classic Premium Plus Versus the Les Paul Reissue: The Evolution of the Les Paul Reissue

The origin of the Les Paul Reissue dates back to the mid-1970s when a few vintage-oriented dealers began requesting reproductions of the increasingly precious late 1950s Les Paul Standards. In the early 1980s Gibson added a variation of the model to the product line. At the time, merely applying a figured maple top to the current stock model seemed to suffice. Although it received minor cosmetic and hardware changes through the 1980s, it was not based on accurate 1950s design and detail until 1993. The Les Paul Reissue had been distinguishable because of its figured maple top, inked serial number, ABR bridge, etc. until the appearance of the Les Paul Classic in the early 1990s.

Designed by J.T. Ribiloff of Gibson R & D, the Classic featured a noticeably thinner 1960 neck profile as well as features previously exclusively found on the Reissue. To enhance the vintage look, Ribiloff redesigned a smaller headstock with push-in bushing tuners and aged fingerboard inlays. Of course, these features soon made their way to the Reissue. It was at this point that the Reissue and the Classic were structurally very similar.

Originally, the Classic was not to have a figured maple top, but the grading standards for the figuring in the tops for the Reissues became so high that the tops that did not qualify as Reissue quality were applied to the Classic, thus creating the Les Paul Classic Plus. Some of these "Plus" tops would turn out to be more figured than others, and thus became "Premium Plus" tops - and introduced the Les Paul Classic Premium Plus.

By 1992, there existed the Les Paul Classic, the Classic Plus, the Classic Premium Plus, and the Les Paul Reissue - and one more! The thin profile 1960 "classic" neck was offered on the Reissue, creating the 1960 Reissue.

At this point, there was some confusion between the 1960 Classic and the 1960 Reissue. Gibson actually began addressing the problem as early as 1991, and began blueprinting original instruments in 1992. By the winter NAMM show in 1993, the redesigned '59 Reissue (Model LPR9) was introduced.

In the spring of 1993, Gibson changed the model decal on the headstock face of the Classic to read Les Paul Classic. Reissue Les Paul models in 1993 retained the silkscreened logo (just like the originals). The Historic Reissue line can be identified by the "R" plus the model year (R9 = '59 Reissue, R7 = '57 Reissue, R6 = '56 Reissue) stamped into the ledge in the bottom of the control cavity. From 1993 until the spring of 1994 all Reissues received a Historic decal on the back of the headstock (some early 1993 models may have the Custom Shop decal instead). Reissue Information courtesy Gibson Guitar Corporation.

The various grades of this series can be determined by the handwritten initials indicating grade underneath the rythmn pickup (i.e., LPPP refers to Les Paul Premium Plus).

Gibson Les Paul Heritage Series Standard 80 courtesy Dale Hanson

Gibson Les Paul Smartwood Standard courtesy Gibson

GRADING	100% MINT	98% NEAR MINT	95% EXC+	90% EXC	80% VG+	70% VG	60% G

Les Paul: Classic Series

LES PAUL CLASSIC (LPCS) - single sharp cutaway mahogany body, bound carved maple top, bound rosewood fingerboard with pearl trapezoid inlay, Tune-O-Matic bridge/stop tailpiece, blackface peghead with pearl logo inlay, pearloid button tuners, nickel hardware, cream pickguard with engraved "1960," 2 exposed humbucker pickups, 2 volume/2 tone controls, 3-way toggle selector, available in Ebony (EB), Honey Burst (HB), Heritage Cherry Sunburst (HS), Translucent Amber (TA), and Vintage Sunburst (VS, disc. 2003) finishes from 1990-98, Wine Red (WR, new 2004), Light Burst (LB, new 2004), Copper Natural (CN, new 2004), or Bullion Gold (mfg. 1998-2001), current mfg. is in Memphis.

	MSR	$2,618	$1,825	$1,375	$1,125	$975	$850	$775	$700

Add approx. $900 for Bullion Gold finish. Add $500 for Honey Burst (HB), Vintage Sunburst (VS), or Wine Red (WR) finishes.

This Les Paul Classic model is unique in that it has a 6-digit serial number. In 1994, Ebony (EB) and Vintage Sunburst (VS) finishes were discontinued. In 1998, Honey Burst (HB) and Heritage Cherry Sunburst (HS) finishes were discontinued. In 2001, all finishes except Ebony were reintroduced, Ebony was reintroduced during 2003 and became the standard finish.

Les Paul Classic Plus - similar to Les Paul Classic, except has curly maple top. Available in Honey Burst (disc.), Heritage Cherry Sunburst (disc.), Translucent Amber, Translucent Purple (disc.), Translucent Red and Vintage Sunburst (disc.) finishes. Disc. 1995, retintroduced 1999-2001.

	$1,900	$1,650	$1,450	$1,300	$1,175	$950	$875

Last MSR was $3,837.

In 1994, Translucent Purple, Translucent Red and Vintage Sunburst finishes were discontinued.

Les Paul Classic Premium Plus (LPPP) - similar to Les Paul Classic, except has higher quality curly maple top, available in Honey Burst (HB), Heritage Cherry Sunburst (HS), Trans. Amber (TA), Trans. Purple, Trans. Red and Vintage Sunburst finishes, disc. 1996.

	$2,400	$2,150	$1,850	$1,650	$1,450	$1,250	$1,050

Last MSR was $5,099.

In 1994, Translucent Purple, Translucent Red and Vintage Sunburst finishes were discontinued.

Les Paul Classic Bird´s-eye - similar to Les Paul Classic, except has bird´s-eye maple top, available in Honey Burst, Heritage Cherry Sunburst, Trans. Amber, Trans. Purple, Trans. Red, or Vintage Sunburst finishes, disc. 1994.

	$1,900	$1,650	$1,450	$1,300	$1,175	$950	$875

Last MSR was $2,600.

Les Paul Classic Premium Bird´s-eye - similar to Les Paul Classic, except has highest quality bird´s-eye maple top, available in Honey Burst, Heritage Cherry Sunburst, Trans. Amber, Trans. Purple, Trans. Red, or Vintage Sunburst finishes, disc. 1994.

	$2,250	$1,850	$1,650	$1,450	$1,250	$1,050	$900

Last MSR was $4,700.

Les Paul: XR Series

LES PAUL XR-I - single cutaway mahogany body, carved maple top, 22-fret rosewood fingerboard with pearl dot inlay, Tune-O-Matic bridge/stop tailpiece, 3-per-side tuners with pearloid buttons, chrome hardware, 2 exposed humbucker pickups, 2 volume/2 tone controls, 3-position/coil tap switches, available in Cherry Sunburst, Goldburst, or Tobacco Sunburst finishes, mfg. 1981-83.

	N/A	$695	$625	$550	$475	$400	$350

Les Paul XR-II - similar to Les Paul XR-I, except has bound figured maple top, "Gibson" embossed pickup covers, available in Honey Sunburst finish.

	N/A	$800	$700	$575	$495	$425	$375

Les Paul: DC (Double Cutaway) Series

LES PAUL DC PRO (CSDC4TH[ ]NH) - offset double cutaway mahogany back, bound AAA flamed maple top, set-in mahogany neck, 24.75 in. scale, 24-fret ebony fingerboard with pearl dot inlay, Tune-O-Matic bridge/stop tailpiece, 3-per-side Schaller mini-tuners, black slimmed peghead with pearl logo inlay, nickel hardware, 2 covered humbuckers ('57 Classic/'97 Classic), master volume/master tone controls, 3-way toggle. Available in Butterscotch (BS), Faded Cherry (FC), Trans. Black (TB), and Trans. Indigo (TI) finishes, mfg. by the Custom Shop 1997-2001.

	$2,200	$1,875	$1,625	$1,400	$1,200	$850	$700

Last MSR was $4,195.

The DC Pro is a Gibson Custom Shop model and will have the Custom Shop logo on the back of the headstock. This model had an optional 25 in. scale length by special order.

Les Paul DC Pro w/WrapAround Bridge (CSDC4WH[ ]NH) - similar to the Les Paul DC Pro, except features a wraparound bridge. Available in Butterscotch (BS), Faded Cherry (FC), Translucent Black (TB), or Translucent Indigo (TI) finishes, mfg. 1997-2001.

	$2,200	$1,875	$1,625	$1,400	$1,200	$1,000	$850

Last MSR was $4,195.

Les Paul DC Pro w/WrapAround Bridge/P-90s (CSDC4WP[ ]NH) - similar to the Les Paul DC Pro, except features a wraparound bridge, 2 P-90 single coil pickups. Available in Butterscotch (BS), Faded Cherry (FC), Trans. Black (TB), and Trans. Indigo (TI) finishes, mfg. 1997-2001.

	$2,100	$1,825	$1,600	$1,350	$1,200	$1,000	$850

Last MSR was $3,950.

LES PAUL CLASSIC DOUBLE CUTAWAY (LPCD) - double cutaway body, 19/24-fret rosewood fretboard, choice of two P-90 or humbucker pickups, nickel hardware, Bullion Gold finish, mfg. 2003-04.

	$1,550	$1,125	$950	$875	$800	$700	$600

Last MSR was $2,298.

LES PAUL FADED DOUBLE CUTAWAY (LPFD) - double cutaway body, features faded Worn Yellow (WY), Worn Cherry (WC), or Satin Ebony (SE) finishes, includes gig bag, mfg. 2003-present.

	MSR	$1,118	$725	$575	$475	$400	$350	$300	$265

GRADING	100% MINT	98% NEAR MINT	95% EXC+	90% EXC	80% VG+	70% VG	60% G

LES PAUL DC STANDARD (LPS2) - offset double cutaway mahogany back, AAA flamed maple top, set-in mahogany neck, 24.75 in. scale, 24-fret bound rosewood fingerboard with pearloid trapezoid inlay, Tune-O-Matic bridge/stop tailpiece, 3-per-side tuners, black peghead, chrome hardware, 2 covered (490R/498T) humbuckers, volume/tone controls, 3-way toggle, available in Trans Red (TR), Translucent Amber (TA), Trans Black (BL), Midnight Burst (MD, disc.), Amber Serrano (AS, disc.), Blue Diamond (BD, disc.), Black Pepper (BP, disc.), Green Jalapeno (GJ, disc.), and Red Hot Tamale (RT, disc.) lacquer translucent finishes, standard production, mfg. 1998-99, reintroduced 2001-present.

MSR	$2,278		$1,600	$1,150	$975	$875	$800	$700	$600

Add $100 for gold hardware (disc.).

Les Paul DC Standard Sunburst Limited Edition (LPS2) - available in either Tangerineburst with gold hardware or Lemonburst with chrome hardware, disc. 2000.

		$1,625	$1,300	$1,000	$875	$800	$700	$600

Last MSR was $2,409.

Add approx. $100 for Tangerine (LPS2-TN) finish.

Les Paul: Studio Series

LES PAUL DOUBLE CUTAWAY STUDIO (LPDS) - offset double cutaway mahogany back, carved maple top, set-in mahogany neck, 24-fret rosewood fingerboard with dot inlay, wrap-around stop tailpiece, 3-per-side tuners, chrome hardware, 2 covered humbuckers, volume/tone controls, 3-way toggle, available in Ebony (EB), Heritage Cherry Sunburst (HS), Emerald Green, Ruby, or Wine Red (WR) finishes, mfg. 1997-99.

		$825	$750	$625	$550	$475	$400	$325

Last MSR was $1,378.

Add $125 for Heritage Cherry Sunburst finish.

In 1998, Emerald Green (EZ) and Ruby (RZ) finishes were introduced; Wine Red (WR) finish was discontinued.

LES PAUL STUDIO (LPST) - single sharp cutaway mahogany or swamp ash (new 2003) body, carved maple top, raised black pickguard, 22-fret rosewood fingerboard with pearl dot inlay, Tune-O-Matic bridge/stop tailpiece, 3-per-side tuners, chrome hardware, 2 covered humbucker pickups, 2 volume/2 tone controls, 3-position switch. Available in Alpine White (AW), Classic White, Fireburst, Platinum (new 2003), Pewter (PT, mfg. 2002) Gothic (disc.), Ebony (EB), Blue Teal Flip-Flop (BT), White (disc. 1994), or Wine Red (WR) finishes, mfg. 1984-1998, reintroduced 2001- and is currently produced.

MSR	$1,718		$1,200	$925	$825	$725	$675	$600	$550

Add $150 for Classic White, Alpine White, Fireburst, or Platinum finishes. Add $150 for Gothic (disc.) finish. Subtract $170 for swamp ash model (LPSA).

In 1987, ebony fingerboard replaced rosewood fingerboard. In 1990, trapezoid fingerboard inlay replaced dot inlay.

Les Paul Studio Limited Colors - similar to Les Paul Studio, available in Blue Metallic, Copper Metallic, Studio Green Metallic (new 2004), Metallic Red, or Yellow Metallic, mfg. 2002-04.

		$1,150	$825	$700	$600	$525	$450	$400

Last MSR was $1,648.

Les Paul Studio Voodoo - similar to Les Paul Studio, except has Juju (JJ) finish and swamp ash body, two-tone red/back humbucker pickups, features Voodoo skull inlay in red pearl acrylic in ebony fretboard, mfg. 2003-04.

		$1,350	$1,025	$900	$800	$700	$600	$550

Last MSR was $1,998.

Les Paul Studio Smartwood - similar to Les Paul Studio, except is Smartwood, with Muricatiara (MU) finish, includes signature case, mfg. 2003-present.

MSR	$1,448		$1,100	$825	$700	$600	$525	$450	$400

Les Paul Studio Baritone - similar to Les Paul Studio, except is baritone with 28 in. scale, two Alnico humbucker pickups (490R and 498T), Tune-O-Matic bridge/stop tailpiece, brushed platinum finished hardware, ebony fingerboard, available in Bluemist (BM), Black (HE), Pewter Metallic (PM), or Sunrise Orange (SO), mfg. 2004-present.

MSR	$1,808		$1,300	$1,025	$900	$800	$700	$600	$550

Les Paul Studio (LPSO) - similar to Les Paul Studio, gold or chrome hardware, available in Amber (AZ, disc. 1999), Ebony (EB), Emerald (EZ), or Ruby (RZ) finishes, mfg. 1996-99.

		$900	$775	$675	$575	$500	$450	$425

Last MSR was $1,700

Add $100 for gold hardware. Add $150 for Amber finish with gold hardware.

Les Paul Studio Custom - similar to Les Paul Studio, except has multi-bound body, bound fingerboard, multi-bound peghead, available in Cherry Sunburst, Ebony, or Sunburst finishes, mfg. 1984-87.

		N/A	$750	$675	$600	$525	$440	$380

Les Paul Studio Gem Limited Edition (LPGS) - similar to the Les Paul Studio, except features 2 creme P-90 pickups, cream pickguard, trapezoid fingerboard inlay, and gold hardware, available in Amethyst (AM), Emerald (EM), Ruby (RU), Sapphire (SP), or Topaz (TO) finishes, mfg. 1996-98.

		$950	$850	$750	$650	$500	$425	$375

Last MSR was $1,639.

Gibson Les Paul DC Pro courtesy George McGuire

Gibson Les Paul Studio courtesy Gibson

GRADING	100% MINT	98% NEAR MINT	95% EXC+	90% EXC	80% VG+	70% VG	60% G

Les Paul Studio Standard - similar to Les Paul Studio, except has bound body, available in Cherry Sunburst, Sunburst, or White finishes, mfg. 1984-87.

	N/A	$675	$595	$495	$395	$350	$325

Les Paul Studio Lite (LPLT) - similar to Les Paul Studio, except has no pickguard, ebony fingerboard with trapezoid inlay, black chrome hardware, exposed pickups, available in Trans. Black, Trans. Blue (BU) and Trans. Red finishes, disc. 1998.

	$995	$900	$800	$695	$575	$450	$400

Last MSR was $1,749.

Add $150 for gold hardware with Heritage Cherry Sunburst (LPLT-HS) and Vintage Sunburst (LPLT-VS) finishes.

In 1994, Translucent Black and Translucent Red finishes were discontinued.

Les Paul Studio Lite/M III - similar to Les Paul Studio, except has no pickguard, exposed humbucker/single coil/humbucker pickups, volume/tone control, 5-position switch, disc. 1995.

	$950	$775	$700	$595	$425	$350	$250

Last MSR was $1,350.

LES PAUL STUDIO PLUS (LPO+) - similar to Les Paul Studio, except is available in Desert Burst (DB), Trans Black (BL, new 2004), or Trans Red (TR, disc. 2003) finish, gold hardware, mfg. 2001-present.

MSR	$2,198	$1,550	$1,125	$975	$875	$800	$700	$600

G

Les Paul: Special Series

LES PAUL SPECIAL (MFG. 1955-1960) - single cutaway mahogany body, 13 in. wide, 17.25 in. long, and 1.875 in. deep, 24.75 in. scale, multi-layer black pickguard, mahogany neck, 16/22-fret bound rosewood fingerboard with dot inlay, wrapover stop tailpiece, 3-per-side tuners with plastic buttons, nickel hardware, 2 single coil pickups, 2 volume/2 tone controls, 3-position switch, available in TV (Limed Mahogany, introduced 1955), Cherry, and Cherry Red finish. Approx. 7,330 mfg. 1955-1960.

CHERRY	N/A	$5,000	$4,500	$4,000	$3,500	$3,000	$2,500
TV SPECIAL	N/A	$8,750	$7,500	$6,500	$5,800	$4,800	$4,200

In 1959, double round cutaway body replaced original part/design, Cherry finish became available. A few instruments were also made in double cutaway with 2 black soapbar pickups and Cherry Red finish.

LES PAUL SPECIAL (SG BODY STYLE) - double cutaway mahogany body, black pickguard, mahogany neck, 22-fret rosewood fingerboard with pearl dot inlay, Tune-O-Matic bridge/stop tailpiece, silkscreened model name on peghead, 3-per-side tuners with plastic buttons, nickel hardware, single coil pickup, volume/tone control, available in Cherry (most common), TV, or White finish, mfg. 1961-63.

CHERRY/WHITE FINISH	N/A	$3,100	$2,750	$2,400	$2,125	$1,800	$1,500
TV FINISH	N/A	$4,250	$3,750	$3,350	$2,800	$2,350	$1,925

In 1962, Maestro vibrato became an option. In 1963, renamed SG Special. See SG Series later in text.

Les Paul Special 3/4 - similar to Les Paul Special, except has a 3/4 size body, shorter neck, available in Cherry Red finish, approx. 100 mfg. 1959-1961.

	N/A	$2,000	$1,675	$1,400	$1,200	$1,000	$850

LES PAUL SPECIAL SINGLE CUTAWAY REISSUE (LES PAUL 55) - similar to Les Paul Special single cutaway, except has Tune-O-Matic bridge/stop tailpiece, stacked humbucker pickups, nickel hardware, available in Ebony, Heritage Cherry (HC), Tobacco Sunburst (TS), or T.V. Yellow (TV) finishes, mfg. 1974-1981.

	N/A	$750	$650	$550	$500	$425	$375

In 1977, Sunburst or Limed Mahogany finishes were introduced. In 1979, Wine Red finish was optional.

Les Paul Special Double Cutaway - reissue of the double cutaway Les Paul Special, rounded horns, two black soapbar P-90 pickups, 22-fret bound rosewood fingerboard, 24.75 in. scale, mahogany neck, Tune-O-Matic bridge, dot inlays, metal tuner buttons and chrome hardware, available in Ebony, Cherry (new 1979), Limed Mahogany (new 1979), Tobacco Sunburst, Sunburst, or Wine Red finishes, mfg. 1976-1988.

	N/A	$1,200	$1,050	$950	$850	$750	$650

In 1988, model was changed to Les Paul Junior Double Cutaway Special.

LES PAUL SPECIAL (LPJ2) - similar to Les Paul Special, except has Tune-O-Matic bridge/stop tailpiece, stacked humbucker pickups, nickel hardware, available in Ebony, Heritage Cherry (HC), Tobacco Sunburst (TS), or T.V. Yellow (TV) finishes, mfg. 1989-1998.

	$875	$750	$650	$550	$500	$450	$400

Last MSR was $1,239.

Add $400 for TV Yellow finish (last LPJ2-TV retail list price was $1,639).

Les Paul Special Double Cutaway (LPJD) - similar to Les Paul Special (LPJ2), except has double cutaway body design instead of single cutaway, available in Heritage Cherry (HC), or TV Yellow (TV) finishes, mfg. 1993-1995.

	$925	$800	$700	$600	$500	$400	$350

Last MSR was $1,339.

Add $400 for TV Yellow finish (last LPJD-TV retail list price was $1,739).

In 1998, this model was reintroduced as the Custom Shop 1960 Les Paul Special Double Cutaway (see Custom Shop listing).

LES PAUL SPECIAL SL (LPJSH) - single cutaway solid mahogany body, set-in mahogany neck, 24.75 in. scale, 22-fret rosewood fingerboard with pearl dot inlay, Tune-O-Matic bridge/stop tailpiece, blackface peghead with silkscreened logo, 3-per-side vintage-style tuners, chrome hardware, pearloid pickguard, 2 P-100 stacked humbucker (looks like a black P-90) pickups, 2 volume/2 tone controls, 3-way toggle switch, available in UV-cured Worn Cherry (WC), Worn Ebony (WE, disc.), Worn Yellow (WY, disc.) Ebony (EB, disc.), Emerald (EX, disc.), or Ruby (RX, disc.) finishes, mfg. 1996-99, reintroduced 2001-and is currently produced.

MSR	$1,118	$750	$625	$550	$475	$425	$375	$335

GRADING	100% MINT	98% NEAR MINT	95% EXC+	90% EXC	80% VG+	70% VG	60% G

Les Paul: Junior Series

LES PAUL JUNIOR - single cutaway mahogany body, 13 in. wide, 17.25 in. long, 1.875 in. deep, 24.75 in. scale, black pickguard, mahogany neck, 16/22-fret rosewood fingerboard with dot inlay, wrapover stop tailpiece, 3-per-side tuners with plastic buttons, nickel hardware, single P-90 coil pickup, volume/tone control. Available in Brown Sunburst or Cherry finishes, approx. 19,000 mfg. 1954-1960.

	N/A	$4,000	$3,500	$3,000	$2,500	$2,100	$1,750

Some Les Paul Jr. models were produced with 3/4 scale necks on the full size bodies (approx. 785 mfg. 1956-1961). In 1958, double round cutaway body, tortoise pickguard replaced original part/design, Cherry finish became available, Sunburst finish was discontinued. In 1961, the body switched to the SG design, with laminated pickguard and Les Paul Jr. peghead logo (available in a Cherry finish). See Les Paul Jr. (SG Body Style) model below.

Les Paul Junior (LPJ-) - similar to Les Paul Jr., except has chrome hardware, includes gig bag, available in Vintage Sunburst (VS) or Ebony (EB) finish, limited mfg. 2001-2002.

	$850	$600	$550	$500	$465	$435	$400

Last MSR was $1,152.

LES PAUL JUNIOR TV - similar to the single cutaway Les Paul Jr., except has Limed Mahogany TV finish, mfg. 1954-1960.

	N/A	$9,500	$8,500	$7250	$6,000	$5,000	$4,000

A few of these guitars were made with a 3/4 size body. In 1958, double round cutaway body and multi-layer pickguard replaced original part/design. In 1959, the double rounded cutaway horns was renamed the SG TV (see SG Series later in text).

LES PAUL JUNIOR SPECIAL (LPJS) - single cutaway mahogany body, mahogany neck, 2 black P-100 stacked humbucker pickups, 22-fret rosewood fingerboard, chrome hardware, choice of Ebony (disc.), Cinnamon (disc.), or Natural finish, includes gig bag, mfg. 1999-2003.

	$950	$700	$600	$500	$465	$435	$400

Last MSR was $1,348.

LES PAUL JUNIOR SPECIAL PLUS (LPJ+) - similar to Les Paul Junior Special, except has AA figured maple top, 2 covered Alnico humbucker pickups, and choice of Trans. Amber (TA) or Trans. Red (TR) finish, mfg. 2001-04.

	$1,125	$825	$700	$600	$525	$450	$400

Last MSR was $1,648.

LES PAUL JUNIOR (SG BODY STYLE) - double cutaway mahogany body, black pickguard, mahogany neck, 22-fret rosewood fingerboard with pearl dot inlay, Tune-O-Matic bridge/stop tailpiece, silkscreened model name on peghead, 3-per-side tuners with plastic buttons, nickel hardware, P-90 single coil pickup, volume/tone control, available in Cherry finish, mfg. 1961-63.

	N/A	$1,750	$1,500	$1,250	$1,075	$875	$750

In 1962, Maestro vibrato became an option. In 1963, renamed the SG Jr. (see SG Series later in text).

Les Paul Junior 3/4 - similar to Les Paul Junior, except has 3/4 size body, shorter neck, approx. 1,075 mfg. 1956-1961.

	N/A	$1,500	$1,300	$1,050	$850	$725	$650

Les Paul Junior II - similar to Les Paul Junior, except has two P-100 pickups, mfg. 1989 only.

	N/A	$800	$695	$575	$450	$400	$375

This model was also available in a dual cutaway version.

Les Paul Junior (Reissue) - similar to Les Paul Junior. Available in Cherry, Tobacco Sunburst, TV Yellow, or White finishes, mfg. 1986-1996.

	$725	$550	$450	$350	$325	$300	$275

Last MSR was $900.

In 1988, a Steinberger KB tremolo was introduced with a coil tap switch on one of the knobs.

LES PAUL JUNIOR LITE (LPJL) - similar to Les Paul Junior (SG Body Style), except has 2 P-100 pickups, 22-fret rosewood fingerboard, chrome hardware, choice of Ebony, Natural, or Cinnamon finish, includes gig bag, mfg. 1999-2002.

	$725	$500	$450	$415	$385	$360	$340

Last MSR was $998.

Add $77 for Natural finish.

ELECTRIC: M SERIES

M III DELUXE - offset double cutaway poplar/maple/walnut body, tortoise pickguard with engraved "M III" logo, maple neck, 24-fret maple fingerboard with wood arrow inlay, double locking Floyd Rose vibrato, reverse blackface peghead with screened logo, 6-on-a-side tuners, black chrome hardware, exposed humbucker/single coil/humbucker pickups, volume/tone control, 5-position/tone selector switches, available in Antique Natural finish, disc. 1994.

	$500	$450	$400	$350	$300	$250	$200

Last MSR was $1,300.

**Gibson Les Paul Junior TV
courtesy Dave Rogers
Dave's Guitar Shop**

**Gibson Les Paul Jr.
courtesy Rick Wilkiewicz**

GRADING	100% MINT	98% NEAR MINT	95% EXC+	90% EXC	80% VG+	70% VG	60% G

M III Standard - similar to M III Deluxe, except has solid poplar body. Available in Alpine White, Candy Apple Red, or Ebony finishes, disc. 1994.

	$500	$425	$375	$325	$300	$250	$200

Last MSR was $1,080.

Add $55 for Translucent Amber and Translucent Red finishes, no pickguard.

M IV S DELUXE - offset double cutaway black limba body, maple neck, 24-fret ebony fingerboard with pearl arrow inlay, Steinberger vibrato, reverse blackface peghead with screened logo, 6-on-a-side Steinberger locking tuners, black chrome hardware, exposed humbucker/single coil/humbucker pickups, volume/tone control, 5-position/tone selector switches, available in Natural finish, mfg. 1994-96.

	$800	$725	$650	$575	$500	$425	$350

Last MSR was $2,375.

M IV S Standard - similar to M IV S Deluxe, except has poplar body, pearl dot fingerboard inlay, available in Ebony finish, mfg. 1994-96.

	$800	$725	$650	$575	$500	$425	$350

Last MSR was $2,100.

ELECTRIC: MARAUDER SERIES

MARAUDER - single cutaway alder body, white pickguard, bolt-on maple neck, 22-fret rosewood fingerboard with pearl dot inlay, Tune-O-Matic bridge/stop tailpiece, 3-per-side tuners, chrome hardware, humbucker/single coil pickups, volume/tone control, rotary switch, available in Ebony, Natural Satin (most common), Wine Red, Tobacco Sunburst (rare, approx. 240 mfg.), or Natural (ultra rare, 1 mfg. 1974 only) finishes, mfg. 1975-1982.

	N/A	$600	$500	$425	$350	$275	$200

Black pickguards were also available on this instrument. In 1978, maple fingerboard replaced original part/design, and some had pickup switch on the treble bout.

Marauder Custom - similar to Marauder, except has bound fingerboard with block inlay, 3-position switch, no rotary switch, available in Tobacco Sunburst finish, approx. 80 mfg. 1976-78.

	N/A	$625	$525	$425	$350	$275	$200

ELECTRIC: MELODY MAKER SERIES

Melody Maker notes apply to all variations in this section, unless otherwise noted.

MELODY MAKER - single or double sharp cutaway mahogany body, black pickguard with model name stamp, mahogany neck, 22-fret rosewood fingerboard with pearl dot inlay, wrapover stop tailpiece, 3-per-side tuners with plastic buttons, nickel hardware, covered single coil pickup, volume/tone control, available in Sparkling Burgundy, Walnut, or Sunburst finish, mfg. 1959-1970.

1959-1960	N/A	$1,350	$1,150	$950	$750	$600	$450
1961-1965	N/A	$1,000	$850	$725	$600	$500	$400
1966-1970	N/A	$800	$675	$575	$500	$400	$300

Add 20% for Walnut, Sparkle Burgundy, Red or Blue finishes.

The single cutaway is the most desirable configuration of this model. In 1960, redesigned narrower pickup replaced original part/design. In 1961, double round cutaway body replaced original part/design. In 1962, Maestro vibrato became an option. In 1963, Cherry finish became available. In 1966, double sharp cutaway body, white pickguard, vibrato tailpiece, Fire Engine Red and Pelham Blue finishes replaced previous part/design. In 1967, Sparkling Burgundy finish became an option. In 1970, only Walnut finish was available.

Melody Maker 3/4 - similar to Melody Maker, except has 3/4 size body, available in Golden Sunburst finish, mfg. 1959-1970.

1959-1960	N/A	$800	$675	$575	$500	$400	$300
1961-1970	N/A	$700	$600	$500	$400	$300	$200

Melody Maker-D - similar to Melody Maker, except has 2 single coil pickups, available in Golden Sunburst finish, mfg. 1960-1970.

1960	N/A	$1,200	$1,050	$900	$750	$600	$450
1961-1965	N/A	$1,000	$875	$750	$625	$500	$375
1966-1970	N/A	$800	$675	$575	$500	$400	$300

Melody Maker III - similar to Melody Maker, except has 3 pickups, available in Pelham Blue or Sparkling Burgundy finishes, approx. 350 mfg. 1967-1970.

	N/A	$1,000	$875	$750	$625	$500	$375

Melody Maker-12 - similar to original Melody Maker, except has twelve strings, 6-per-side tuners, 2 mini humbuckers, approx. 210 mfg. 1967-1970.

	N/A	$800	$675	$575	$500	$400	$300

Add 35% for Pelham Blue and Sparkling Burgundy finishes.

In 1970, Pelham Blue and Sparkling Burgundy finishes were optional.

Melody Maker Double - similar to Melody Maker D, except has newer appointments, available in Cherry or Sunburst finshes, mfg. 1977-1983.

	N/A	$700	$575	$475	$400	$325	$250

MELODY MAKER REISSUE - single cutaway mahogany body, black pickguard, mahogany neck, 22-fret rosewood fingerboard with pearl dot inlay, narrow peghead, Tune-O-Matic bridge/stop tailpiece, 24 3/4 in. scale, 3-per-side tuners with pearloid buttons, chrome hardware, covered high-output humbucker pickup at bridge position, volume/tone control, available in Alpine White, Ferrari Red, Ebony, or Frost Blue finishes. Mfg. 1986-2000.

1986-1994	N/A	$650	$500	$400	$325	$250	$200
1995-2000	$375	$325	$275	$250	$225	$200	$185

Last MSR was $750.

GRADING	100% MINT	98% NEAR MINT	95% EXC+	90% EXC	80% VG+	70% VG	60% G

LES PAUL MELODY MAKER (LPMM) - single cutaway Santa Maria (or equivilant) body, Spanish cedar neck with rosewood fingerboard with dot inlays, single vintage P-90 pickup, Tune-O-Matic bridge with stopbar tailpiece, includes gig bag, three aged finishes, including Satin Cherry, Satin Ebony, or Satin Yellow finish, mfg. 2003-present.

MSR	$708	$525	$375	$325	$285	$250	$225	$200

ELECTRIC: MODERNE SERIES

MODERNE - originally designed as one of three Gibson modernistic concept guitars (with the Explorer and Flying V), this instrument was blue-printed in 1958. A debate still rages over whether or not they were actually built, as a 1958 Moderne has not yet been seen. There is some vague mention on a shipping list (that could also apply to the Explorer model). Tom Wheeler, in his book *American Guitars*, suggests that some were built - and when the music retailers responded in a negative way, Gibson sold some at a cut rate price to employees and destroyed others. Ted McCarty, who was president of Gibson at the time (and part designer of the three models), has guessed that a handful were built as prototypes.

It's hard to hang a price tag on something that hasn't been seen. Until one actually shows up, and can be authenticated by experts (materials, construction techniques, parts), there can't be an intelligent conversation about value.

MODERNE HERITAGE - single cutaway sharkfin style korina body, black pickguard, korina neck, 22-fret rosewood fingerboard with pearl dot inlay, Tune-O-Matic bridge/stop tailpiece, tulip blackface peghead with pearl logo inlay, inked serial number on peghead, 3-per-side tuners with plastic single ring buttons, gold hardware, 2 humbucker pickups, 2 volume/1 tone controls, 3-position switch, available in Natural, Red, White, or Ebony finishes, mfg. 1982-83.

	N/A	$2,700	$2,300	$1,800	$1,500	$1,200	$900

Initially, there were 500 guitars to be produced, but only 143 were actually manufactured. This is a reissue of the 1958 Moderne, with specifications from the blueprint.

ELECTRIC: NIGHTHAWK, BLUESHAWK, & HAWK SERIES

BLUESHAWK (DSBH, DSNB) - single cutaway poplar body, 2 f-holes, bound solid maple top, 25.5 in. scale, mahogany neck, 22-fret rosewood fingerboard with pearl diamond inlay, fixed bridge with strings through-body ferrules, blackface peghead with pearl double diamond/logo inlay, 3-per-side tuners with plastic buttons, gold hardware, 2 creme-colored P-90-style Blues 90 pickups with hum-cancelling dummy coil, volume/push/pull tone controls, 3-way selector, 6-position Varitone switch, includes gig bag, available in Chicago Blue (CB, new 1997), Ebony (EB), or Heritage Cherry (HC) finishes, current mfg.

MSR	$1,248	$850	$650	$550	$495	$450	$400	$350

BluesHawk w/Maestro (DSBH) - similar to BluesHawk (DSBH), except features a gold-plated Tune-O-Matic bridge/Maestro tremolo, available in Chicago Blue (CB), Ebony (EB) and Heritage Cherry (HC) finishes, mfg. 1997-2000.

$1,025	$850	$750	$650	$550	$450	$350

Last MSR was $1,486.

LITTLE LUCILLE (DSLL) - similar to Blueshawk, except has Tune-O-Matic bridge, and TP-6 tailpiece, 3-way selector switch with 6-position Varitone selector switch, gold hardware, Ebony, Blues Burst, or Wine Red finish, mfg. 1999-present.

MSR	$1,700	$1,250	$900	$800	$725	$675	$600	$550

THE HAWK - single cutaway mahogany body, mahogany neck, 25.5 in. scale, 22-fret rosewood fingerboard with dot inlay, wraparound bridge, blackface peghead with silkscreened logo, engraved "The Hawk" truss rod cover, 3-per-side tuners, chrome hardware, 2 exposed pole piece humbucker (490R) pickups, 1 volume/2 tone controls, 3-way selector, available in Ebony (EB) and Wine Red (WR) finishes, disc. 1998.

$525	$450	$400	$350	$300	$260	$220

NIGHTHAWK CUSTOM (DSNC) - single cutaway mahogany body, bound figured maple top, mahogany neck, 22-fret bound ebony fingerboard with pearl crown inlay, strings through bridge, bound blackface peghead with pearl plant/logo inlay, 3-per-side tuners with pearl buttons, gold hardware, 2 humbucker pickups, volume/push-pull tone controls, 5-position switch, available in Antique Natural (AN), Dark Wineburst, Fireburst (FI), Trans. Red, or Vintage Sunburst finishes, disc. 1999.

$1,025	$850	$750	$650	$550	$450	$350

Last MSR was $2,299.

In 1994, Translucent Amber (TA) finish was introduced, Dark Wineburst, Translucent Red and Vintage Sunburst finishes were discontinued.

Nighthawk Custom 3 Pickup (DSC3) - similar to Nighthawk Custom, except has three pickups (humbucker/single coil/humbucker pickups), available in Antique Natural (AN), Fireburst (FI), or Translucent Amber (TA) finishes, disc. 1999.

$1,025	$850	$750	$650	$550	$450	$350

Last MSR was $2,399.

Nighthawk Custom 3 Pickup/Floyd Rose (DSC3-FG) - similar to Nighthawk Custom 3 Pickup, except has double locking Floyd Rose vibrato and gold hardware, available in Antique Natural (AN), Fireburst (FI), or Translucent Amber (TA) finishes, mfg. 1994-99.

$825	$725	$650	$550	$450	$350	$275

Last MSR was $2,499.

**Gibson Melody Maker
courtesy George McGuire**

G

**Gibson Blueshawk
courtesy John Beeson
The Music Shoppe**

GRADING	100% MINT	98% NEAR MINT	95% EXC+	90% EXC	80% VG+	70% VG	60% G

NIGHTHAWK LANDMARK (DSLS) - single cutaway mahogany body, bound maple top, mahogany neck, 22-fret rosewood fingerboard with pearl dot inlay, fixed bridge, 3-per-side tuners with pearl buttons, gold hardware, 2 mini humbucker pickups, volume/push-pull tone controls, 5-position switch, Landmark Series decal noting the location of the National Park or Monument specific to each color, available in Everglades Green (EG), Glacier Blue (GB), Mojave Burst (MB), Navajo Turquoise (NT), or Sequoia Red (SR) finishes, mfg. 1995-99.

	$700	$600	$525	$450	$400	$350	$300

Last MSR was $1,339.

NIGHTHAWK SPECIAL (DSN-) - single cutaway mahogany body, bound maple top, mahogany neck, 22-fret rosewood fingerboard with pearl dot inlay, strings through bridge, blackface peghead with pearl logo inlay, 3-per-side tuners, gold hardware, 2 humbucker pickups, volume/push-pull tone controls, 5-position switch, available in Ebony (EB), Heritage Cherry (HC), or Vintage Sunburst (VS) finishes, disc. 1999.

	$650	$575	$500	$425	$350	$275	$250

Last MSR was $1,099.

Nighthawk Special 3 Pickup (DSN3) - similar to Nighthawk Special, except has humbucker/single coil/humbucker pickups, disc. 1999.

	$750	$650	$575	$500	$450	$425	$395

Last MSR was $1,199.

NIGHTHAWK STANDARD (DSNS) - single cutaway mahogany body, bound figured maple top, mahogany neck, 22-fret bound rosewood fingerboard with pearl parallelogram inlay, strings through bridge, bound blackface peghead with pearl plant/logo inlay, 3-per-side tuners with pearl buttons, gold hardware, 2 humbucker pickups, volume/push-pull tone controls, 5-position switch, available in Fireburst (FI), Trans. Amber (TA), Trans. Red, or Vintage Sunburst (VS) finishes, disc. 1999.

	$800	$725	$650	$550	$475	$400	$350

Last MSR was $1,599.

In 1994, Trans. Red finish was discontinued.

Nighthawk Standard 3 Pickup (DSS3) - similar to Nighthawk Standard, except has humbucker/single coil/humbucker pickups, available in Fireburst (FI), Trans. Amber (TA), and Vintage Sunburst (VS) finishes, disc. 1999.

	$895	$750	$650	$550	$450	$350	$275

Last MSR was $1,739.

Nighthawk Standard 3 Pickup/Floyd Rose (DSS3-FG) - similar to Nighthawk Standard 3 Pickup, except has double locking Floyd Rose vibrato and gold hardware, available in Fireburst (FI), Trans. Amber (TA), or Vintage Sunburst (VS) finishes, mfg. 1994-99.

	$700	$625	$550	$500	$450	$425	$395

Last MSR was $1,839.

ELECTRIC: RD SERIES

RD STANDARD - single cutaway asymmetrical hourglass style maple body, black pickguard, maple neck, 22-fret rosewood fingerboard with pearl dot inlay, Tune-O-Matic bridge/stop tailpiece, blackface peghead with logo decal, 3-per-side tuners, nickel hardware, 2 covered humbucker pickups, 2 volume/2 tone controls, 3-position switch, available in Cherry Sunburst, Ebony, Natural, or Tobacco Sunburst finishes, approx. 1,265 mfg. 1977-79.

	N/A	$650	$550	$450	$375	$325	$300

RD Artist - similar to RD Standard, except has an ebony fingerboard with block inlay, multi-bound peghead with pearl stylized f-hole/logo inlay, gold hardware, mini switch, active electronics. Approx. 2,350 mfg. 1977-79.

	N/A	$900	$800	$725	$650	$575	$500

In 1978, tunable stop tailpiece replaced original part/design.

RD-Custom/RD Custom 77 - similar to RD Standard, active solid state electronics, 4 knobs, 3-way pickup selector switch, one selector switch, two-way mini switch for model selection, large backplate, maple fingerboard, circuit board designed by the Moog synthesizer division of Norlin, available in Natural or Walnut finish, approx. 1,375 mfg. 1977-1979 only.

	N/A	$1,100	$950	$825	$725	$625	$525

ELECTRIC: SG SERIES

In 1961, the new SG (solid guitar) body shape with double pointed cutaway was originally intended to bring a new style to the Les Paul line. But without Les Paul´s approval they were renamed the SG during 1963. The first two years of SG production (1961-end of 1963) in this series have Les Paul logos on their pegheads or the area below the fingerboard (see Les Paul section).

SG STANDARD (MFG. 1963-1970) - double sharp cutaway mahogany body, layered black pickguard, one piece mahogany neck, 22-fret bound rosewood fingerboard with pearl trapezoid inlay, Tune-O-Matic bridge/side-pull vibrato, blackface peghead with pearl logo inlay, 3-per-side tuners, nickel hardware, 2 covered humbucker pickups, 2 volume/2 tone controls, 3-position switch, available in Cherry finish, mfg. 1963-1970.

1963-1965	N/A	$5,000	$4,500	$3,950	$3,500	$3,000	$2,600
1966-1970	N/A	$2,850	$2,500	$2,150	$1,800	$1,600	$1,400

In 1963, some instruments were produced with an ebony tailblock and pearl inlay.

SG Deluxe - double cutaway mahogany body, raised layered Les Paul style black pickguard, mahogany neck, 22-fret bound rosewood fingerboard with pearl dot inlay, Tune-O-Matic bridge/Bigsby-style vibrato tailpiece, blackface peghead with pearl logo inlay, 3-per-side tuners, chrome hardware, 2 covered humbucker pickups, 2 volume/2 tone controls mounted on layered black plate, 3-position switch, available in Cherry (most common), Ebony (rare, only 6 mfg.), Natural, or Walnut (common) finishes, mfg. 1971-74, and 1976.

	N/A	$795	$725	$550	$450	$400	$325

SG STANDARD (1972-1990 MFG.) - similar to SG Standard, except has pearl block fingerboard inlay, stop tailpiece, pearl crown peghead inlay, chrome hardware, available in Cherry (most common), Ebony (rare), Natural, Satin Walnut, Tobacco Sunburst, Walnut, or White finish, mfg. 1972-1981.

	N/A	$795	$725	$550	$450	$400	$325

Approx. 260 SG Standards were mfg. with Bigsby vibratos. In 1976 Cherry, Tobacco Sunburst and White finishes became available. A left-hand model in Walnut finish was available from 1973-79.

GRADING	100% MINT	98% NEAR MINT	95% EXC+	90% EXC	80% VG+	70% VG	60% G

SG Standard (1983-87 Mfg.) - same as SG Standard Reissue I, available in Cherry or Sunburst finishes, mfg. 1983-87.

| | N/A | $750 | $650 | $575 | $500 | $450 | $425 |

SG Standard (1989-1990 Mfg.) - similar to SG Standard Reissue I, except has trapezoid fingerboard inlay, available in Ebony or Wine Red finishes, mfg. 1989-1990.

| | N/A | $750 | $650 | $575 | $500 | $450 | $425 |

SG STANDARD (SGS-) - double cutaway mahogany body, mahogany neck, 22-fret bound rosewood fingerboard with pearl trapezoid inlay, Tune-O-Matic bridge/stop tailpiece, blackface peghead with pearl crown/logo inlay, 3-per-side tuners with plastic buttons, chrome hardware, layered black pickguard, 2 covered humbucker pickups, 2 volume/2 tone controls, 3-position switch, available in Candy Apple Blue (disc. 1994), Candy Apple Red (disc. 1994), Ebony (EB), Heritage Cherry (HC), Natural Burst (new 1999, limited edition), or TV Yellow (disc. 1994) finishes, current mfg.

| MSR | $1,658 | $1,100 | $825 | $750 | $650 | $575 | $500 | $450 |

Add $100 for Heritage Cherry and Natural Burst finish. Add approx. $200 for left-handed configuration.

SG Standard With Maestro (SGS-) - similar to SG Standard, except features a Maestro vibrato tailpiece, available Ebony (EB) finish, mfg. 1996-2000.

| | $1,350 | $1,050 | $950 | $850 | $725 | $600 | $475 |

Last MSR was $2,043.

SG '61 REISSUE (SG61) - double cutaway mahogany body, mahogany neck, 22-fret bound rosewood fingerboard with pearl trapezoid inlay, Tune-O-Matic bridge/stop or trapeze (new 2001, includes vibrola) tailpiece, blackface peghead with pearl plant/logo inlay, 3-per-side tuner with pearl buttons, nickel hardware, layered black pickguard, 2 covered humbucker pickups, 2 volume/2 tone controls, 3-position switch, Gibson deluxe lyre vibrola became optional in 2001-2002, available in Heritage Cherry (HC) finish, mfg. 1986-present.

| MSR | $2,278 | $1,600 | $1,400 | $1,200 | $995 | $850 | $700 | $600 |

Add $231 for Gibson deluxe lyre vibrola with trapeze tailpiece (disc. 2002).

Gibson SG '61 Reissue courtesy Gibson

SG VOODOO (SGSV) - features JuJu (JJ) finish and bright chrome hardware, mfg. 2002-04.

| | $975 | $750 | $675 | $600 | $550 | $500 | $450 |

Last MSR was $1,398.

THE SG (FIREBRAND SG) - double cutaway walnut body, walnut neck, 22-fret ebony fingerboard with pearl dot inlay, Tune-O-Matic bridge/stop tailpiece, blackface peghead with pearl crown/logo inlay, 3-per-side tuners, chrome hardware, layered black pickguard, 2 covered humbucker pickups, 2 volume/2 tone controls, 3-position switch, available in Natural satin nitrocellulose finish, limited mfg. 1979-1981.

| | N/A | $500 | $450 | $400 | $325 | $250 | $225 |

This model was renamed Firebrand SG in 1980, with the new name burned into top.

The SG Deluxe (Firebrand SG Deluxe) - similar to The SG (Standard), except has mahogany body/neck, available in Antique Mahogany, Ebony, Natural, or Wine Red finishes, mfg. 1979-1985.

| | N/A | $500 | $450 | $400 | $325 | $250 | $225 |

In 1980, renamed Firebrand SG Deluxe with new name burned into top.

SG EXCLUSIVE - similar to the the SG (Standard), except has mahogany body, black finish, cream binding on neck, cream pickguard, cream pickup covers, gold knobs, quail tap switch, TP-6 stop tailpiece, and truss rod cover that reads "Exclusive," approx. 475 mfg. 1979 only.

| | N/A | $995 | $900 | $800 | $725 | $650 | $575 |

SG ANGUS YOUNG SIGNATURE (SGAY) - similar to SG Classic, except has two pickups ('57 classic and Angus Young humbuckers), devil decal on headstock, engraved tailpiece with vibrator, nickel hardware, includes Angus Young signature on hardshell case, available in Aged Cherry (AC) finish only, mfg. 2000-present.

| MSR | $3,628 | $2,350 | $1,775 | $1,525 | $1,250 | $1,100 | $1,000 | $900 |

SG PETE TOWNSHEND SIGNATURE - features dual P-90 pickups, wraparound bridge/tailpiece, chrome hardware, back of headstock features Pete Townshend signature decal, available in Satin Mahogany Red finish, mfg. summer 2001-mid-2003.

| | $1,295 | $925 | $850 | $750 | $650 | $550 | $475 |

Last MSR was $1,845.

SG TONY IOMMI SIGNATURE - features two Tony Iommi humbuckers and silver crosses for fret inlays, signature decal on truss rod cover, chrome hardware, available in Ebony finish, mfg. 2001-2003.

| | $1,575 | $1,200 | $995 | $875 | $750 | $625 | $550 |

Last MSR was $2,298.

SG CLASSIC - double sharp cutaway mahogany body, patterned after the late 1960s SG Special, 2 P-90 pickups, 22-fret bound rosewood fingerboard with pearloid dot inlays, Tune-O-Matic bridge with ABR tailpiece, chrome hardware, includes gig bag, available in Ebony Stain or Heritage Cherry finish, mfg. 1999-2001.

| | $1,200 | $1,075 | $900 | $800 | $700 | $600 | $525 |

Last MSR was $1,537.

Gibson SG Classic courtesy Gibson

GRADING	100% MINT	98% NEAR MINT	95% EXC+	90% EXC	80% VG+	70% VG	60% G

SG CUSTOM - double sharp cutaway mahogany body, mahogany neck, 22-fret bound ebony fingerboard with pearl block inlay, Tune-O-Matic bridge, side-pull or Maestro vibrato, stop tailpiece became standard in 1972, multi-bound peghead with pearl split diamond inlay, 3-per-side tuners, gold hardware, white layered pickguard, 3 covered humbucker pickups, 2 volume/2 tone controls, 3-position switch, available in Ebony (rare, only 7 mfg. 1975), Cherry (approx. 200 mfg. 1972-79), Tobacco Sunburst (12 mfg. 1979 only), Walnut (most common), White (approx. 525 mfg. 1974-79), or Wine Red finishes, mfg. 1963-1980.

1963-1966	N/A	$5,750	$5,000	$4,500	$4,000	$3,500	$3,000
1967-1970	N/A	$2,850	$2,500	$2,200	$1,850	$1,650	$1,450
1970-1980	N/A	$1,750	$1,500	$1,200	$900	$800	$700

During 1963, Maestro vibrato replaced the original part/design. In 1972, stop tailpiece replaced previous part/design. The Bigsby vibrato became available in 1974 - approx. 60 were mfg. between 1974-79.

SG '62 Custom/SG Les Paul Custom - similar to SG Custom, except has three TAF humbucker pickups, Tune-O-Matic bridge, available in Antique Ivory finish, mfg. 1986-1991.

	N/A	$1,000	$850	$725	$600	$500	$400

In 1987, model was renamed SG Les Paul Custom. In 1990, Classic White finish was introduced.

SG DELUXE (SGD+) - double cutaway mahogany body, slim tapered mahogany neck, 22-fret rosewood fingerboard with pearl dot inlay, Tune-O-Matic bridge/Bigsby-style Maestro tremolo, blackface peghead with pearl logo inlay, 3-per-side tuners, chrome hardware, pearloid pickguard, 3 chrome-covered mini-humbucker pickups, volume/tone controls, 6-way rotary chickenhead switch, available in Blue Ice (BI), Ebony (new 1999), or Hellfire Red (HR) finishes, mfg. 1998-99.

	$1,200	$1,000	$900	$800	$700	$600	$525

SG LES PAUL (SG BODY STYLE) W/DELUXE MAESTRO (SG61) - features traditional SG style with Maestro deluxe vibrola, two '57 Classic humbucker pickups, black pickguard, Hertiage Cherry finish, mfg. 1999-2000.

	$1,895	$1,450	$1,275	$1,075	$995	$875	$795

Last MSR was $2,899.

SG JR. - double cutaway mahogany body, mahogany neck, 22-fret rosewood fingerboard with pearl dot inlay, Tune-O-Matic bridge/stop tailpiece, 3-per-side tuners with plastic buttons, nickel hardware, black pickguard, single coil pickup, volume/tone control, available in Cherry finish, mfg. 1963-1970.

1963-1965	N/A	$1,250	$1,075	$950	$850	$750	$650
1966-1970	N/A	$1,000	$900	$800	$700	$625	$550

Add 25% for TV finish (approx. 3,050 mfg. 1961-1968).

This model had an optional vibrato beginning in 1962. In 1961, The Les Paul Jr. adopted the SG body style, and featured a single P-90 pickup, laminated pickguard, and Les Paul Jr. peghead logo. In 1963, the Les Paul Jr. was renamed the SG Jr. In 1965, vibrato became standard.

SG Jr. (Recent Mfg. SGJ-) - double cutaway mahogany body, chrome hardware, current production model in Ebony or Wine Red finishes. Mfg. 1999-2002.

	$775	$525	$450	$400	$350	$295	$250

Last MSR was $1,075.

SG SPECIAL - double cutaway mahogany body, mahogany neck, 22-fret rosewood fingerboard with pearl dot inlay, stop tailpiece, blackface peghead with pearl logo inlay, 3-per-side tuners with plastic buttons, nickel hardware, layered black pickguard, 2 single coil pickups, 2 volume/2 tone control, 3-position switch, available in Ebony (25 mfg. 1971-73), Natural (approx. 450 mfg. 1971-77), Cherry (most common), Walnut (new 1971) or White (approx. 455 mfg. 1962-68, reintroduced 1972-78) finishes, mfg. 1963-1977.

1963-1965	N/A	$2,850	$2,500	$2,250	$1,950	$1,725	$1,500
1966-1970	N/A	$1,500	$1,300	$1,100	$925	$800	$700
1971-1977	N/A	$875	$775	$675	$600	$525	$450

Add 15% for White finish (1962-68 mfg.).

Approx. 750 SG Specials in Cherry finish were produced with Bigsby vibrato (mfg. 1972-77). Approx. 75 left-hand models in Cherry and Walnut finishes were mfg. between 1971-77. In 1965, vibrato became standard.

SG Special 3/4 - similar to SG Special, except has 3/4 size body, 19-fret fingerboard, available in Cherry Red finish, mfg. 1959-1961.

	N/A	$1,250	$1,050	$900	$800	$700	$600

SG Professional - similar to SG Special, except has a pearl logo, 2 black soapbar P-90 pickups, available in Cherry (common), Natural (approx. 315 mfg.) and Walnut (common) finishes, mfg. 1971-74.

	N/A	$650	$575	$500	$450	$400	$350

SG Studio - similar to SG Special, except has no pickguard, 2 humbucker pickups, 2 volume/1 tone controls, available in Natural finish, approx. 930 mfg. 1978 only.

	N/A	$550	$475	$400	$350	$300	$250

SG SPECIAL (SGSP) - double sharp cutaway mahogany body, maple neck, 22-fret rosewood fingerboard with pearl dot inlay, Tune-O-Matic bridge/stop tailpiece, blackface peghead with silkscreened logo inlay, 3-per-side tuners, chrome hardware, black pickguard, 2 humbucker pickups, volume/tone controls, 3-position switch. Available in Alpine White (disc. 1998), Ebony (EB), Ferrari Red (FR, disc.), Ebony Stain (Mfg. 1999-2000, limited edition), Plum (mfg. 1999-2000, limited edition), Creme (mfg. 1999-2000, limited edition), Wine Red (new 2001), Blue Teal Flip-Flop (new 2001), Platinum (new 2003), Pewter (mfg. 2002), or TV Yellow (disc. 1994) finishes, includes gig bag, current mfg.

MSR	$1,298	$900	$675	$550	$500	$450	$400	$375

Add $100 for Blue Teal Flip-Flop. Add $50 for Platinum finish.

SG Special Faded (SGSC) - similar to SG Special, except has one coat finish, available in Worn Cherry (WC) or Worn Brown (WB) finishes, includes gig bag, mfg. 2002-present.

MSR	$1,018	$675	$475	$425	$375	$330	$300	$275

GRADING	100% MINT	98% NEAR MINT	95% EXC+	90% EXC	80% VG+	70% VG	60% G

SG GOTHIC (SGG-) - similar to SG Special, except has Gothic finish, includes gig bag, new 2000-2002.

	$825	$725	$625	$525	$475	$425	$375

Last MSR was $1,383.

SG SUPREME (SGSU) - double sharp cutaway mahogany body with AA flame maple top, mahogany slim tapered (1959 style) neck with ebony fingerboard featuring split diamond inlays, bound neck and headstock, 2 P-90A black pickups (disc. 2001), two '57 Classic humbucker pickups, Tune-O-Matic bridge and stop tailpiece, gold hardware, available in Lavaburst (mfg. 2001-2003), Translucent Black (BL, new 2004), Fireburst (FI), Midnight Burst (MD, new 2001), or Emerald Burst (ED, new 2001) finish, mfg. 1999-present.

MSR	$2,878	$1,925	$1,425	$1,225	$1,050	$850	$725	$650

Gibson SG Les Paul w/Deluxe Maestro courtesy Gibson

SG TV - double rounded or SG style cutaway mahogany body, mahogany neck, 22-fret rosewood fingerboard with pearl dot inlay, wraparound stop tailpiece, 3-per-side tuners with plastic buttons, nickel hardware, small (mfg. 1966-68) or large black pickguard, single coil pickup, volume/tone control, available in Limed Mahogany and White finishes, mfg. 1959-1968.

1959-1961	N/A	$7,250	$6,000	$5,500	$5,000	$4,500	$4,000
1961-1965	N/A	$3,250	$2,750	$2,400	$2,100	$1,800	$1,550
1966-1968	N/A	$2,000	$1,750	$1,500	$1,300	$1,100	$925

In 1961, the SG-style body replaced the double rounded cutaway horns. This configuration was available in White finish. The Double Cutaway is fairly rare, and does not trade too often in the vintage guitar market.

SG-X LIMTED EDITION (SGX-) - double cutaway mahogany body, mahogany neck, 24.75 in. scale, 24-fret rosewood fingerboard with pearl dot inlay, Tune-O-Matic bridge/stop tailpiece, blackface peghead with logo, 3-per-side tuners, chrome hardware, white pickguard, 500T exposed polepiece humbucker pickups, volume/tone controls, coil-tap mini-switch, available in Carribean Blue (SB), Corona Yellow (SY), or Coral (SC) finishes, mfg. 1998 only.

	$575	$495	$450	$400	$350	$300	$275

Last MSR was $740.

SG-X (SGX-) - similar to the SG-X. Available in Ebony (EB) or Dark Wineburst (DW) finishes, mfg. 1998-2000.

	$550	$425	$375	$325	$275	$250	$225

Last MSR was $856.

SG-Z (SGZ-) - double cutaway mahogany body, slim tapered mahogany neck, 24-fret bound rosewood fingerboard with pearl split diamond inlay, Tune-O-Matic bridge/Z-shaped stop tailpiece with strings through-body, blackface peghead with pearl Z/Gibson logo inlay, 3-per-side tuners, black chrome hardware, pearloid pickguard, 500T single coil/490R humbucker exposed polepiece pickups, volume/tone controls, 3-way selector toggle, available in Platinum (PL), or Verdigris (VG) finishes, limited mfg. 1998 only.

	$850	$775	$700	$625	$550	$500	$450

Last MSR was $1,365.

SG '90 SINGLE - double sharp cutaway mahogany body, pearloid pickguard, maple neck, 24-fret bound ebony fingerboard with pearl split diamond inlay, strings through anchoring, blackface peghead with pearl crown/logo inlay, 3-per-side tuners, black chrome hardware, humbucker pickup, volume/tone control, 3-position switch, available in Alpine White, Heritage Cherry, or Metallic Turquoise finishes, mfg. 1989-1990.

	N/A	$525	$450	$395	$350	$325	$295

This model had an optional Steinberger KB double locking vibrato.

SG '90 Double - similar to SG '90 Single, except has single coil/humbucker pickups, mfg. 1989-1992.

	N/A	$550	$425	$400	$350	$325	$300

SG-100 - double cutaway mahogany body, black pickguard, mahogany neck, 22-fret rosewood fingerboard with dot inlay, tunable stop tailpiece, 3-per-side tuners, nickel hardware, single coil pickup, volume/tone control. Available in Cherry Sunburst (25 mfg. 1971 only) or Walnut (common) finishes, approx. 1,225 mfg. 1971-72.

	N/A	$400	$350	$300	$250	$225	$200

SG-200 - similar to SG-100, except has 2 single coil pickups, slide switch, available in Walnut (common) or Cherry Sunburst finish, mfg. 1971-72.

	N/A	$500	$425	$350	$300	$260	$230

SG-250 - similar to SG-100, except has 2 single coil pickups, 2 slide switches, available in Walnut (rare, approx. 30 mfg. only) or Cherry Sunburst finish.

	N/A	$500	$425	$350	$300	$260	$230

SG I - double cutaway mahogany body, black pickguard, mahogany neck, 22-fret rosewood fingerboard with dot inlay, tunable stop tailpiece, 3-per-side tuners, nickel hardware, single coil pickup, volume/tone control, available in Cherry (most common) or Walnut finishes, mfg. 1972-78.

	N/A	$450	$400	$350	$300	$260	$230

Add 40% for Junior pickup (approx. 60 mfg. 1972-73 only).

SG II - similar to SG I, except has 2 single coil pickups, slide switch, available in Walnut or Cherry finish, mfg. 1972-76.

	N/A	$450	$400	$350	$300	$260	$230

Add 20% for humbucker pickups (approx. 60 mfg. 1975 only).

SG III - similar to SG I, except has 2 single coil pickups, 2 slide switches, available in Cherry Sunburst finish. Approx. 950 were mfg. 1972-77.

	N/A	$450	$400	$350	$300	$260	$230

Gibson SG Supreme courtesy Gibson

GRADING	100% MINT	98% NEAR MINT	95% EXC+	90% EXC	80% VG+	70% VG	60% G

ELECTRIC: SONEX SERIES

SONEX-180 CUSTOM - single cutaway composite body, black pickguard, bolt-on maple neck, 22-fret ebony fingerboard with dot inlay, Tune-O-Matic bridge/stop tailpiece, blackface peghead with decal logo, 3-per-side tuners, chrome hardware, 2 exposed humbucker pickups, 2 volume/2 tone controls, 3-position switch, available in Ebony or White finishes, mfg. 1981-82.

	N/A	$375	$325	$300	$240	$210	$180

Sonex-180 Deluxe - similar to Sonex-180 Custom, except has 2-ply pickguard, rosewood fingerboard, available in Ebony finish, mfg. 1981-84.

	N/A	$375	$325	$300	$240	$210	$180

A left-handed variation was introduced during 1982.

Sonex Artist - similar to Sonex-180 Custom, except has rosewood fingerboard, tunable stop tailpiece, 3 mini switches, active electronics, available in Candy Apple Red or Ivory finishes, mfg. 1981-84.

	N/A	$450	$400	$350	$310	$270	$240

ELECTRIC: SPIRIT SERIES

SPIRIT I - double cutaway mahogany body, bound plain or figured maple top, tortoiseshell pickguard, mahogany neck, 2-fret rosewood fingerboard with pearl dot inlay, tunable wrapover bridge, blackface peghead with logo decal, 3- or 6-(new 1983)-per-side tuners with plastic buttons, chrome hardware, 1 exposed humbucker pickup, volume/tone control, available in Natural, Red, or Sunburst finishes, mfg. 1982-88.

	N/A	$500	$450	$400	$350	$300	$250

In 1983, 6-per-side tuner peghead replaced 3-per-side tuner, and figured maple top was disc.

Spirit II - similar to Spirit I, except has no pickguard, 2 exposed humbucker pickups, 2 volume/1 tone controls, mfg. 1982-88.

	N/A	$500	$450	$400	$350	$300	$250

Spirit II XPL - similar to Spirit I, except has bound fingerboard, Kahler vibrato, 6-on-a-side tuners, 2 exposed humbuckers pickups, 2 volume/1 tone controls, mfg. 1985-87.

	N/A	$350	$300	$250	$225	$200	$180

ELECTRIC: SUPER 400 CES SERIES

SUPER 400 CES - single round cutaway grand auditorium style body, arched spruce top, bound f-holes, raised multi-bound mottled plastic pickguard, figured maple back/sides, multiple bound body, 3-piece figured maple/mahogany neck, model name engraved into heel cap, 14/20-fret bound ebony fingerboard with point on bottom, pearl split block fingerboard inlay, adjustable rosewood bridge with pearl triangle wings inlay, gold trapeze tailpiece with engraved model name, multi-bound blackface peghead with pearl split diamond/logo inlay, pearl split diamond inlay on back of peghead, 3-per-side tuners, gold hardware, two single coil (P-90 or Alnico) or humbucker pickups, 2 volume/2 tone controls, 3-position switch, available in Ebony, Natural (introduced 1952), Sunburst (introduced 1951), or Wine Red finishes, 18 in. wide body, 21.75 in. long by 3.375 in. deep, 25.5 in. scale, limited mfg. (approx. 20-50 each year) 1951-1994.

1951-1954	N/A	$20,000	$18,000	$15,000	$9,300	$7,450	$6,700
1955-1959	N/A	$18,000	$15,000	$10,000	$7,200	$6,500	$5,900
1960-1969	N/A	$11,000	$9,600	$8,100	$7,500	$7,000	$6,450
1970-1974	N/A	$6,850	$6,300	$5,750	$5,200	$4,750	$4,250
1975-1985	N/A	$6,000	$5,300	$4,575	$3,850	$3,500	$3,350
1986-1994	N/A	$5,500	$5,000	$4,500	$4,000	$3,800	$3,650

Last MSR was $5,000.

Between 1951-53, P90 pickups were standard, during 1953-57, Alnico pickups were standard. In 1957, PAF humbucker pickups replaced Alnico pickups. In 1960, sharp cutaway replaced original part/design. In 1962, Pat. No. humbucker pickups replaced previous part/design. In 1969, round cutaway replaced previous part/design. In 1974, neck volute was introduced. In 1981, neck volute was discontinued. Super 400 CES models with PAF pickups (1957-1962) have sold for as high as $25,000. Instruments should be determined on a piece-by-piece basis as opposed to the usual market. The Super 400 CES model has been a platform for experimentation - ser. nos. of "one-offs" were custom ordered with special features. Models produced between 1955 and 1962 in Blonde finish will add apprx. 100% to the value. Current production instruments are part of the Historic Collection Series, found at the end of this section.

ELECTRIC: TAL FARLOW SERIES

TAL FARLOW - single round cutaway bound hollow body, arched figured maple top, bound f-holes, scroll style inlay on cutaway, raised black bound pickguard, maple back/sides/neck, 20 bound rosewood fingerboard with pearl reverse crown inlay, Tune-O-Matic bridge/trapeze tailpiece, rosewood tailpiece insert with pearl engraved block inlay, bound peghead with pearl crown/logo inlay, 3-per-side tuners, chrome hardware, 2 covered humbucker pickups, 2 volume/2 tone controls, 3-position switch, available in Brown Sunburst finish, approx. 215 mfg. 1962-1967.

	N/A	$10,000	$9,000	$8,000	$7,000	$6,000	$5,000

Current production instruments (Tal Farlow Reissue) are part of the Historic Collection Series, found at the end of this section.

ELECTRIC: TRINI LOPEZ SERIES

TRINI LOPEZ STANDARD - double round cutaway semi-hollow bound body, arched maple top, bound diamond holes, raised layered black pickguard, maple back/sides, mahogany neck, 22-fret bound rosewood fingerboard with pearl split diamond inlay, Tune-O-Matic bridge/trapeze tailpiece, ebony tailpiece insert with pearl model name inlay, 6-on-a-side tuners, chrome hardware, 2 covered humbucker pickups, 2 volume/2 tone controls, 3-position switch, available in Cherry finish, approx. 1,975 mfg. 1964-1971.

	N/A	$2,000	$1,800	$1,550	$1,375	$1,100	$995

Trini Lopez Deluxe - dimilar to Trini Lopez Standard, except has sharp cutaway, tortoise pickguard, 20-fret ebony fingerboard, available in Cherry Sunburst finish, approx. 315 mfg. 1964-1971.

	N/A	$2,500	$2,250	$1,925	$1,750	$1,500	$1,300

CUSTOM SHOP: GENERAL INFORMATION

The Gibson Guitar Corp. operates two Custom Shops - one in Nashville, TN (mostly electric mfg.), and one in Bozeman, MT (only acoustic mfg.). The Nashville Custom Shop was established in Gibson´s main production facility beginning in 1983. During 1993, they moved into a separate facility. During 2003, Gibson celebrated its 10th anniversary as a separate operation. The Custom Shops manufacture instruments for the Gibson Custom, Art, and Historic Divisions. The Historic Collection specializes in handcrafting exact reproductions of historically significant Gibson instruments, i.e., Les Pauls, SGs, Firebirds, and large body jazz guitars. The Custom Collection focuses on Custom Shop artist signature models and newer variations of some of Gibson´s older classics. The Art Guitars are mostly limited edition and one-of-a-kind guitars – most of these involve elaborate painted/inlaid scenes.

The Custom Shop listings are broken down into the following categories: Carved Top Series, ES Series, Designer Series, and the SG Series. The Custom Shop Les Pauls are separated into Historic Collection: Les Paul Series, and Custom Collection: Les Paul Series. Finally, Art guitars, one-of-a-kind and very limited editions can be found under Limited Editions - Various Models, and Misc.

The models listed below are either reproductions of Gibson classics (Historic Collection) or other Custom Shop models manufactured in a wide variety of models and configurations. In recent years, the Nashville Custom Shop has produced many limited edition instruments, and these are all grouped under: Custom Shop - Limited Editions - Various Models. Whenever possible, original MSRs and quantities produced are listed. Artist Signature models are listed separately within the individual categories. Whenever possible, Gibson factory model nomenclature (in some cases, only prefixes are listed) has been provided at the end of the model name, and appear in parenthesis. In some instances, you may see [ ] brackets, which indicates the color/finish abbreviation would appear in that spot.

Gibson Custom Shop/Historic Collection instruments are produced in limited quantities. Historic instruments are manufactured to the exact original specifications and in several cases, use the same tooling when available. Since most of these instruments see little or no use (the great majority remain NIC), most are in excellent+ condition, values below will only be listed down to the 95% condition factor, except on the limited editions, where typically only the MSR and quantity manufactured appear.

Custom Shop and Historic Collection instruments listed below can be differentiated by the Gibson Custom Shop or Historic Collection code reference in parenthesis at the end of each model listing. The finish and hardware can also be determined from this code using the last four letters.

Also refer to the *Blue Book of Acoustic Guitars* for more information on the acoustic Custom Shop models available from the Bozeman, MT Custom Shop.

Gibson Sonex-180 Custom courtesy Freedom Guitars Inc.

G

CUSTOM SHOP: CUSTOM COLLECTION ABBREVIATIONS

AG	Antique Gold	DW	Dark Wineburst or Diamond White	SB	Sienna Burst or Antique Sunburst (Lee Ritenour model only)
AN	Antique Natural	EB	Ebony or Black Sparkle (Lenny Kravitz model only)	SBM	Satin Blue Metallic (new 2003)
AW	Alpine White				
BB	Blueburst (new 2003)			SCM	Satin Copper Metallic (new 2003)
BCM	Blue Chameleon (new 2003)	EG	Emberglow		
		FC	Faded Cherry	SGMET	Sage Green Metallic (new 2003)
BG	Bigsby	FM	Firemist		
BLK	Black	GB	Gingerburst	SGM	Satin Green Metallic (new 2003)
BP	Black/White Bullseye	GH	Gold		
BS	Butterscotch	GML	Gold Maestro	SKB	Skynyrd Burst (new 2003)
BTG	Black to Gold (new 2003)	GT	Green Tiger (new 2003) or Gold Trapeze		
BTN	Black to Natural (new 2004)			SL	Silver
		HB	Honeyburst	SOR	Sunset Orange Metallic
BTW	Black to White (new 2004)	HC	Heritage Cherry	SSG	Sunset Glow
		HS	Heritage Cherry Sunburst	SSM	Satin Silver Metallic (new 2003)
BZ	Blues Burst	IG	Iguana Burst (new 2003)		
CAM	Camouflage (new 2004)	NA	Natural or Walnut	TA	Trans Amber
CB	Caramel Brown	NH	Nickel	TBK	Trans Black
CCM	Copper Chameleon (new 2004)	NM	Nickel Maestro	TB	Trans Blue
		NML	Nickel Maestro Long	TGB	Tangerine Burst
CH	Chrome	NT	Nickel Trapeze	TR	Trans Red
CHA	Cherry Aged (new 2003)	OTR	Orange to Red (new 2003)	3B	Triburst
CHM	Chameleon			TS	Tobacco Burst
CRB	Cranberry	PB	Pthalo Blue or Page Burst	TVW	TV White (new 2003)
CR	Cardinal Red	PC or PK	Peacock	VS	Vintage Sunburst
CS	Chablis	PCM	Purple Chameleon	WC	Washed Cherry (new 2003)
CS	Heritage Cherry Sunburst (Elegant Model)	PTMET	Pewter Metallic (new 2003)		
				WH	White (new 2003)
CW	Classic White	RB	Rockabilly Brown (new 2004)	WR	Wine Red
DR	Dicky Betts Red			YL	Yellow
DTB	Dark Tobacco Burst	RDMET	Red Metallic (new 2003)		

Gibson Tal Farlow courtesy Dave Rogers Dave's Guitar Shop

GRADING	100% MINT	98% NEAR MINT	95% EXC+	90% EXC	80% VG+	70% VG	60% G

CUSTOM SHOP: HISTORIC COLLECTION ABBREVIATIONS

AG	Antique Gold	GH	Gold	NML	Nickel Maestro Long
AN	Antique Natural	GM	Golden Mist Poly	NT	Nickel Trapeze
BG	Gold Bigsby	GML	Gold Maestro	PB	Pelham Blue
BR	Cremona Brown Sunburst	HB	Honeyburst	PW	Polaris White
BS	Butterscotch	HD	Heritage Darkburst	SM	Silver Mist Poly
CH	Chrome	HP	Heather Poly	TV	TV Yellow
CR	Cardinal Red	IG	Inverness Green	TVW	TV White
CW	Classic White	IT	Ice Tea	TS	Tobacco Sunburst
EB	Ebony	JB or OB	Oxblood	VB	Viceroy Brown Sunburst
ER	Ember Red	KG	Kerry Green	VS	Vintage Sunburst
FB	Frost Blue	NA	Natural	WC	Washed Cherry
FC	Faded Cherry	NH	Nickel	WR	Wine Red
FT	Faded Tobacco	NM	Nickel Maestro		

CUSTOM SHOP: CARVED TOP SERIES

BYRDLAND (HSBYWRGH) - single rounded cutaway multi-ply bound hollow body, solid spruce top, bound f-holes, maple back/sides/neck, 23.5 in. scale, 22-fret multi-ply bound ebony pointed fingerboard with pearl block inlay, ABR-1 bridge with rosewood base/trapeze tailpiece, multi-ply bound blackface peghead with pearl flowerpot/logo inlay, 3-per-side tuners, gold hardware, raised bound tortoise pickguard, 2 covered humbucker ('57 Classic PAF Reissue) pickups, 2 volume/2 tone controls, 3-way selector switch (on treble bout). Available in Wine Red, Natural, or Vintage Sunburst finish, Body Width 17 in., Body Depth 2.25 in., this model is part of the Historic Collection, mfg. 1998-present.

MSR	$7,930	$5,200	$3,150	$2,500	N/A	N/A	N/A	N/A

Byrdland (HSBYVSGH) - with Vintage Sunburst finish.

MSR	$9,705	$6,400	$4,250	$3,150	N/A	N/A	N/A	N/A

Byrdland (HSBYNAGH) - with Natural finish.

MSR	$11,717	$7,700	$5,000	$3,750	N/A	N/A	N/A	N/A

BYRDLAND FLORENTINE (HSBYFWRGH) - similar to the Byrdland, except features a single Florentine cutaway body, available in Wine Red, Natural, or Vintage Sunburst finish, Body Width 17 in., Body Depth 2.25 in., this model is part of the Historic Collection, new 1998.

MSR	$8,167	$5,375	$3,550	$2,650	N/A	N/A	N/A	N/A

Byrdland (HSBYFVSGH) - with Vintage Sunburst finish.

MSR	$9,942	$6,500	$4,250	$3,250	N/A	N/A	N/A	N/A

Byrdland (HSBYFNAGH) - with Natural finish.

MSR	$11,954	$7,800	$5,100	$3,800	N/A	N/A	N/A	N/A

WES MONTGOMERY (HSWMWRGH) - single round cutaway hollow body, carved spruce top, bound f-holes, raised bound tortoise pickguard, multibound body, carved flame maple back/sides, 5-piece maple neck, 20-fret multibound ebony fingerboard with pearl block inlay, Tune-O-Matic bridge on ebony base with pearl leaf inlay, engraved trapeze tailpiece with silver engraved insert, multibound blackface peghead with pearl torch/logo inlay, 3-per-side tuners, gold hardware, humbucker pickup, volume/tone control, available in Vintage Sunburst, Wine Red, Ebony (disc., reintroduced 2004), or Natural finish, this model is part of the Historic Collection, mfg. 1993-present.

MSR	$8,300	$5,800	$3,550	$2,450	N/A	N/A	N/A	N/A

Last MSR was $7,259.

Wes Montgomery (HSWMVSGH) - with Vintage Sunburst finish, current mfg.

MSR	$10,065	$6,800	$4,500	$3,300	N/A	N/A	N/A	N/A

Wes Montgomery (HSWMNAGH) - with Natural finish.

MSR	$12,136	$7,900	$5,500	$4,350	N/A	N/A	N/A	N/A

Wes Montgomery (HSWMEBGH) - with Ebony finish, reintroduced 2004-present.

MSR	$8,349	$5,500	$3,650	$3,100	N/A	N/A	N/A	N/A

L-4 CES MAHOGANY (HSL4M[ ]/WRGH) - single sharp cutaway bound body, carved spruce top, layered black pickguard, f-holes, mahogany back/sides/neck, 20-fret bound ebony fingerboard with pearl parallelogram inlay, Tune-O-Matic bridge on ebony base with pearl inlay on wings, trapeze tailpiece, blackface peghead with pearl crown/logo inlay, 3-per-side tuners with plastic buttons, gold hardware, 2 covered humbucker pickups, 2 volume/2 tone controls, 3-position switch, available in Wine Red, Ebony, Vintage Sunburst, and Natural finish, this model is from the Custom Collection, mfg. 1987-present.

MSR	$5,312	$3,425	$2,400	$1,800	N/A	N/A	N/A	N/A

This model was redesignated with the HSL4M (mahogany) family code during 2004.

L-4 CES (HSL4VSGH) - with Vintage Sunburst (VS) finish.

MSR	$5,900	$3,950	$2,650	$1,950	N/A	N/A	N/A	N/A

L-4 CES (HSL4NAGH) - with Natural (NA) finish.

MSR	$7,665	$5,100	$3,250	$2,525	N/A	N/A	N/A	N/A

Some earlier reissue models were available in Natural (NA) finish. Natural finish was briefly discontinued in 1996, then reintroduced in 1998.

GRADING	100% MINT	98% NEAR MINT	95% EXC+	90% EXC	80% VG+	70% VG	60% G

L-5 CES (HSLC{ }/GH) - single round cutaway bound body, carved spruce top, layered tortoise pickguard, bound f-holes, maple back/sides/neck, 20-fret bound pointed ebony fingerboard with pearl block inlay, ebony bridge with pearl inlay on wings, model name engraved trapeze tailpiece with chrome insert, multi-bound blackface peghead with pearl flame/logo inlay, 3-per-side tuners, gold hardware, 2 covered humbucker pickups, 2 volume/2 tone controls, 3-position switch, available in Natural, Wine Red, Ebony, or Vintage Sunburst finish, this model is part of the Historic Collection, current mfg.

MSR $9,914	$6,500	$4,350	$3,350	N/A	N/A	N/A	N/A

L-5 CES (HSLCVSGH) - with Vintage Sunburst finish, current mfg.

MSR $11,620	$8,250	$5,400	$4,150	N/A	N/A	N/A	N/A

L-5 CES (HSLCNAGH) - with Natural finish, current mfg.

MSR $13,620	$9,650	$6,500	$4,100	N/A	N/A	N/A	N/A

L-5 SIGNATURE (CSL5SGH) - scaled down body variation of the original L-5, spruce top, AAA maple back/rims, two '57 Classic humbucker pickups, ABR-1 bridge, with L-5 style tailpiece, 7-ply top binding, 3-ply back binding, available in Vintage Sunburst or Tangerine Burst, this model is part of the Custom Collection, mfg. 2001-04.

	$7,250	$5,150	$4,100	N/A	N/A	N/A	N/A

Last MSR was $10,913.

LEE RITENOUR L-5 SIGNATURE (CSL5SLRSBGH) - L-5 styling and body, step trapeze tailpiece, adjustable pole floating pickup mounted on pickguard, Antique Sunburst finish, limited mfg. beginning 2003.

MSR $11,642	$7,800	$5,500	$4,250	N/A	N/A	N/A	N/A

L-5 STUDIO (CSL5[ ]NH) - single rounded cutaway semi-hollow body, carved spruce top, black body binding, 2 f-holes, 20-fret ebony fingerboard with mother-of-pearl dot inlay, ABR-1 bridge with pearl inlay on wings/metal Bail raised tailpiece, blackface peghead with pearl logo inlay, 3-per-side Schaller tuners, "Ice Cube Marble" pickguard, nickel hardware, 2 covered humbucker ('57 Classic) pickups, 2 volume/2 tone controls, 3-position switch, available in Autumnburst (AB), Trans. Blue (BU), Trans. Red (TR), or Alpine White (new 1999) finish, this model was part of the Custom Collection, mfg. 1997-2000.

	$3,150	$2,600	$2,200	N/A	N/A	N/A	N/A

Last MSR was $5,226.

Add $546 for Alpine White finish (new 1999).

Early versions of this model were identified as being available in a Classic White finish.

Gibson L-4 CES Mahogany courtesy Gibson

SUPER 400 CES (HSS4[ ]GH/WRGH) - single sharp cutaway grand auditorium style body, arched spruce top, bound f-holes, raised multi-bound mottled plastic pickguard, figured maple back/sides, multiple bound body, 3-piece figured maple/mahogany neck, model name engraved into heel cap, 14/20-fret bound ebony fingerboard with point on bottom, pearl split block fingerboard inlay, adjustable rosewood bridge with pearl triangle wings inlay, gold trapeze tailpiece with engraved model name, multi-bound blackface peghead with pearl 5-piece split diamond/logo inlay, pearl 3-piece split diamond inlay on back of peghead, 3-per-side tuners, gold hardware, 2 pickups, 2 volume/2 tone controls, 3-position switch, available in Natural, Wine Red, Ebony, or Vintage Sunburst finish, this model is part of the Historic Collection, current mfg.

MSR $14,589	$9,500	$6,000	$4,500	N/A	N/A	N/A	N/A

Super 400 CES (HSS4VSGH) - with Vintage Sunburst finish, current mfg.

MSR $16,267	$11,500	$7,450	$5,400	N/A	N/A	N/A	N/A

Super 400 CES (HSS4NAGH) - with Natural finish, current mfg.

MSR $18,267	$13,000	$8,800	$6,500	N/A	N/A	N/A	N/A

CUSTOM SHOP: ES SERIES

In addition to the following CS/ES Models being listed in numerical sequence, the Tal Farlow, Paul Jackson, Jr., Le Grande, and Pat Martino Models are listed at the end of this section, since these models utilize the ES body style.

CS-336 - scaled down version of the ES-335, double rounded cutaway, semi-hollow, bound body, arched figured (Model CS-336F) or plain maple bookmatched top with center block being an integral part of the top and back, one piece hollow mahogany back and rim, single-ply creme binding on top, back, and fingerboard, 24.75 in. scale, two '57 classic humbucker pickups, rosewood fingerboard with pearloid dot fret markers, available in Faded Cherry (FC), Vintage Sunburst (VS), Tangerine Burst (TB), Trans. Amber (TA), or Ebony (EB) finishes, includes hardshell case, this model is part of the Custom Collection, mfg. 2002-present.

MSR $4,095	$2,700	$2,350	$1,750	N/A	N/A	N/A	N/A

LEE ROY PARNELL CS-336 CUSTOM AUTHENTIC SIGNATURE - 336 style body/appointments, custom authentic aged finish, super fat neck profile, ebony fingerboard, aged hardware, serialization includes LPR prefix, available in Ebony finish only, mfg. 2003-04.

	$2,725	$2,100	$1,725	N/A	N/A	N/A	N/A

Last MSR was $4,024.

CS-355 - similar in design as original ES-355 mfg. 1958-1982, figured maple top, back and sides, one-piece mahogany neck with 22-fret ebony fingerboard, 24.75 in. scale, two '57 Classic humbuckers, Tune-O-Matic bridge and stop tailpiece, available in Faded Cherry, Vintage Sunburst or Natural, this model is part of the Custom Collection, mfg. 2004-present.

MSR $7,705	$5,075	$3,600	$2,750	N/A	N/A	N/A	N/A

Add $995 for Natural finish.

Gibson L-5 CES courtesy LaVonne Wagner Music

G

GRADING	100% MINT	98% NEAR MINT	95% EXC+	90% EXC	80% VG+	70% VG	60% G

CS-356 FIGURED - scaled down ES-335 body style, includes two '57 Classic humbuckers, AAA figured bookmatched maple top, ABR-1/stop-bar or Bigsby tailpiece, gold hardware, Faded Cherry finish, mfg. 2001-present.

	MSR	$5,070	$3,325	$2,650	$1,975	N/A	N/A	N/A	N/A

Add $355 for Bigsby tailpiece.

ES-5 SWITCHMASTER (HS5S☐GH) - single rounded cutaway body, arched figured maple top, bound f-holes, 3-ply bound body, figured maple back/sides/neck, 20-fret multi-bound pointed fingerboard with pearl block inlay, ABR-1 adjustable bridge/ornate trapeze tailpiece, bound blackface peghead with pearl crown/logo inlay, 3-per-side tuners, gold hardware, raised layered black pickguard, 3 '57 Classic PAF covered pickups, 4-position selector switch on treble cutaway bout, 3 volume/3 tone controls, available in Vintage Sunburst finish, This model is part of the Historic Collection, disc. 2000, reintroduced 2002 and is currently produced.

	MSR	$6,083	$4,000	$3,150	$2,450	N/A	N/A	N/A	N/A

ES-5 Switchmaster (HS5SNAGH) - with Natural finish.

	MSR	$7,810	$5,125	$3,800	$3,200	N/A	N/A	N/A	N/A

ES-5 Switchmaster (HS5SWRGH) - with Wine Red finish, new 2005.

	MSR	$7,810	$5,125	$3,800	$3,200	N/A	N/A	N/A	N/A

ES-5 P (HS5SP☐GH) - similar to the ES-5 Switchmaster, except features P-90 pickups, available in Vintage Sunburst (VS) or Wine Red (WR) finishes, disc. 2000, reintroduced 2002 and is currently produced.

	MSR	$5,804	$3,800	$2,850	$2,300	N/A	N/A	N/A	N/A

ES-5 P (HS5SPNAGH) - with Natural finish, current mfg.

	MSR	$7,533	$4,950	$3,725	$3,150	N/A	N/A	N/A	N/A

ES-5 ALNICO (HS5A☐GH) - similar to ES Switchmaster, except features Alnico pickups, available Vintage Sunburst or Wine Red finishes, disc. 2000, reintroduced 2002 and is currently produced.

	MSR	$6,390	$4,200	$3,350	$2,750	N/A	N/A	N/A	N/A

ES-5 Alnico (HS5ANAGH) - with Natural finish.

	MSR	$8,119	$5,350	$4,050	$3,150	N/A	N/A	N/A	N/A

ES-5 P WITH 3 P-90 PICKUPS (HS5P[ ]GH) - similar to the ES-5 Switchmaster, except has 3 black P-90 pickups, 3 volume controls, 1 master tone control on treble bout, raised tailpiece, available in Vintage Sunburst (VS) or Wine Red (WR) finishes, this model was part of the Historic Collection, disc. 2000.

	$3,200	$2,650	$2,150	N/A	N/A	N/A	N/A

Last MSR was $5,357.

ES-5 P With 3 P-90 Pickups (HS5PNAGH) - with Natural finish.

	$4,175	$3,500	$3,000	N/A	N/A	N/A	N/A

Last MSR was $6,953.

ES-135 SWINGMASTER - features all maple construction (top, rims, back and neck), slim 22-fret ebony fingerboard, 2 P90 single coil pickups, nickel hardware, including Bigsby tailpiece with extended arm, multi-ply pickguard, custom pinup decal on upper bout, 4 different finishes, this model was part of the Custom Collection, mfg. 1999-2000.

	$2,200	$1,825	$1,500	N/A	N/A	N/A	N/A

Last MSR was $3,670.

ES-150 CHARLIE CHRISTIAN - styled after the original 1935 ES-150 used by Charlie Christian, features single "bar-style" high output pickup and Golden Sunburst finish, AAA spruce on top, back, and sides, one-piece mahogany neck with rosewood fingerboard and pearl block inlays, nickel hardware, single volume and single tone control, this model was part of the Custom Collection, limited mfg. 2000.

	$4,850	$3,250	$2,350	N/A	N/A	N/A	N/A

Last MSR was $6,470.

ES-175 SWINGMASTER - features maple top, back, rims, and mahogany neck with 20-fret ebony fingerboard, two '57 Classic humbucker pickups, nickel hardware, including ABR-1 bridge and Bigsby tailpiece with extended arm, multi-ply pickguard, custom pinup decal on upper bout, 4 different finishes, this model was part of the Custom Collection, mfg. 1999-2000.

	$2,850	$2,375	$1,975	N/A	N/A	N/A	N/A

Last MSR was $4,750.

ES-295 (ES95 PREFIX) - single sharp cutaway bound maple body, f-holes, raised white pickguard with etched flowers, maple neck, 20-fret bound rosewood fingerboard with pearl parallelogram inlay, Tune-O-Matic metal/rosewood bridge/trapeze tailpiece, blackface peghead with pearl plant/logo inlay, 3-per-side tuners with pearl buttons, nickel hardware, 2 covered stacked humbucker pickups, 2 volume/2 tone controls, 3-position switch, available in Antique Gold (AG) finish, this model was part of the Historic Collection, disc. 2000.

	$3,500	$2,925	$2,400	N/A	N/A	N/A	N/A

Last MSR was $5,838.

In 1997, the ES-295 was offered in Bullion Gold finish (ES95AGBN) with a Bigsby tremolo.

ES-295 With Bigsby (ES95A prefix) - similar to the ES-295, except features a Bigsby tremolo bridge, available in Antique Gold finish, mfg. 1998-2000.

	$3,700	$3,075	$2,500	N/A	N/A	N/A	N/A

Last MSR was $6,154.

ES-330 (HS30[ ]NH) - dual rounded cutaway semi-hollow bound body, arched maple top, f-holes, maple back/sides, mahogany neck, 22-fret bound rosewood fingerboard with pearloid dot inlay, ABR-1 bridge/raised trapeze tailpiece, blackface peghead with pearl logo inlay, 3-per-side tuners, nickel hardware, raised bound black pickguard, 2 'dog-eared' P-90 single coil pickups, 2 volume/2 tone controls, 3-way selector switch, available in Faded Cherry (FC), Viceroy Brown Sunburst (VB), or Vintage Sunburst (VS) finishes, this model was part of the Historic Collection, mfg. 1998-2000.

	$2,550	$2,125	$1,650	N/A	N/A	N/A	N/A

Last MSR was $4,250.

GRADING	100% MINT	98% NEAR MINT	95% EXC+	90% EXC	80% VG+	70% VG	60% G

ES-330 (HS30ANNH) - with Antique Natural finish.

		$3,050	$2,525	$2,000	N/A	N/A	N/A	N/A

Last MSR was $5,075.

1959 ES-335 DOT REISSUE (HS35P9[ ]NH) - double rounded cutaway semi-hollow bound body, arched maple top, f-holes, arched maple back, maple sides, set-in one-piece mahogany neck, 24.75 in. scale, 22-fret rosewood fingerboard with pearloid dot inlay, Tune-O-Matic bridge/stop tailpiece, blackface peghead with pearl crown/logo inlay, 3-per-side tuners, nickel hardware, raised layered black pickguard, 2 covered humbucker ('57 Classic PAF Reissue) pickups, 2 volume/2 tone controls, 3-position switch. Available in Faded Cherry (FC), Ebony (EB), Vintage Sunburst (VS) finishes, body width 16 in., body depth 1.75 in., this model is part of the Historic Collection, mfg. 1998-2000, reintroduced 2002 and is currently produced.

MSR	$5,963		$3,925	$2,850	$2,250	N/A	N/A	N/A	N/A

ES-335 Dot Reissue (HS35P9ANNH) - with Antique Natural finish.

MSR	$6,673		$4,450	$3,325	$2,600	N/A	N/A	N/A	N/A

Add $908 for extra figured wood (Model HS35F9ANNH, Mfg. 1999-2000).

1963 ES-335 BLOCK REISSUE (HS35P0[ ]NH) - similar to the 1959 ES-335 Dot Reissue, except has a 1963-style thin tapered neck, pearloid block fingerboard inlay, available in Faded Cherry (FC) or Vintage Sunburst (VS) finishes, this model is part of the Historic Collection, mfg. 1998-2000, reintroduced 2002 and is currently produced.

MSR	$5,963		$3,925	$2,850	$2,250	N/A	N/A	N/A	N/A

ES-335 Block Reissue (HS35P0ANNH) - with Antique Natural finish.

MSR	$6,673		$4,450	$3,325	$2,600	N/A	N/A	N/A	N/A

Add $908 for extra figured wood (Model HS35F0ANNH, Mfg. 1999-2000).

ES-336 (ES36NH) - dual rounded cutaway semi-hollow bound body, carved maple top, 2 f-holes, mahogany back/sides, set-in mahogany neck, 22-fret rosewood fingerboard with pearl dot inlay, Tune-O-Matic bridge/stop tailpiece, slimmed down blackface peghead with pearl Gibson logo inlay, 3-per-side tuners, nickel hardware, raised layered black pickguard, 2 covered humbucker pickups, 2 volume/2 tone controls, 3-way toggle switch, available in Emberglow (EG) or Wine Red (WR) finishes, this model was part of the Custom Collection, mfg. 1997-2000.

		$2,400	$1,950	$1,500	N/A	N/A	N/A	N/A

Last MSR was $3,989.

ES-345 (HS45[ ]GH) - double rounded cutaway semi-hollow bound body, arched maple top, f-holes, maple back/sides, mahogany neck, 22-fret bound rosewood fingerboard with pearl parallelogram inlay, ABR-1 bridge/stop tailpiece, blackface peghead with pearl crown/logo inlay, 3-per-side tuners, gold hardware, raised layered black pickguard, 2 covered humbucker ('57 Classic PAF Reissue) pickups, 2 volume/2 tone controls, 3-position selector switch, 6-way Vari-tone rotary switch, available in Faded Cherry (FC), Viceroy Brown Sunburst (VB), or Vintage Sunburst (VS) finishes, Body Width 16 in., Body Depth 1.75 in., this model was part of the Historic Collection, mfg. 1998-2000.

		$3,300	$2,750	$2,275	N/A	N/A	N/A	N/A

Last MSR was $5,501.

ES-345 (HS45ANGH) - with Antique Natural or Vintage Burst (new 1999) finish.

		$3,700	$3,100	$2,575	N/A	N/A	N/A	N/A

Last MSR was $6,176.

ES-345 WITH BIGSBY (HS45[ ]BG) - similar to the ES-345, except features a Bigsby tremolo bridge, available in Faded Cherry (FC), Viceroy Brown Sunburst (VB), or Vintage Sunburst (VS) finishes, this model was part of the Historic Collection, mfg. 1998-2000.

		$3,475	$2,900	$2,400	N/A	N/A	N/A	N/A

Last MSR was $5,775.

ES-345 With Bigsby (HS45ANBG) - with Antique Natural or Vintage Burst (new 1999) finish.

		$3,875	$3,225	$2,575	N/A	N/A	N/A	N/A

Last MSR was $6,450.

ES-345 WITH MAESTRO (HS45[ ]GML) - similar to the ES-345, except features a Maestro tailpiece. Available in Faded Cherry (FC), Viceroy Brown Sunburst (VB), or Vintage Sunburst (VS) finishes, this model was part of the Historic Collection, mfg. 1998-2000.

		$3,625	$3,025	$2,425	N/A	N/A	N/A	N/A

Last MSR was $6,049.

This model was part of the Custom Collection.

ES-345 With Maestro (HS45ANGML) - with Antique Natural or Vintage Burst (new 1999) finish.

		$4,050	$3,375	$2,650	N/A	N/A	N/A	N/A

Last MSR was $6,724.

ES-346 (ES346GH) - semi-hollow bound body, carved maple top, mahogany back/sides, set-in mahogany neck, Tune-O-Matic bridge/stop tailpiece, blackface peghead with pearl Gibson logo inlay, 3-per-side tuners, gold hardware, 2 covered humbucker pickups, volume/tone controls, 3-way toggle switch. Available in Emberglow (EG) or Gingerburst (new 1999) finish, mfg. 1997-2000.

		$2,750	$2,300	$1,950	N/A	N/A	N/A	N/A

Last MSR was $4,589.

Gibson ES-175 Swingmaster courtesy Gibson

G

GRADING	100% MINT	98% NEAR MINT	95% EXC+	90% EXC	80% VG+	70% VG	60% G

ES-350 T (HS50[ ]GH) - single rounded cutaway hollow bound body, arched figured curly maple top, multi-ply body binding, 2 bound f-holes, curly maple back/sides/neck, 24.75 in. scale, 22-fret bound rosewood fingerboard with pearl parallelogram inlay, adjustable rosewood bridge/ornate trapeze tailpiece, bound blackface peghead with pearl crown/logo inlay, 3-per-side tuners with plastic buttons, gold hardware, raised layered black pickguard, 2 covered humbucker ('57 Classic PAF) pickups, 2 volume/2 tone controls, 3-way selector toggle. Available in Viceroy Brown Sunburst (VB) and Vintage Sunburst (VS) finishes, body width 17 in., body depth 2.25 in., this model was part of the Historic Collection, mfg. 1998-2000.

	$3,575	$3,000	$2,475	N/A	N/A	N/A	N/A

Last MSR was $5,978.

ES-350 T (HS50ANGH) - with Antique Natural or Vintage Burst (new 1999) finish.

	$3,825	$3,250	$2,600	N/A	N/A	N/A	N/A

Last MSR was $6,370.

ES-446S - carved spruce top with braces carved into top, one-piece mahogany carved out body, rosewood fingerboard with pearl dot inlays, two '57 Classic humbuckers, nickel hardware, Tune-O-Matic bridge with bail tailpiece, under 7.5 lbs., available in Emberglow (EG), Faded Cherry (FC), Honeyburst (HB), Natural (NA), and Vintage Sunburst (VS), this model is part of the Custom Collection, mfg.1999-2003.

	$2,400	$1,850	$1,500	N/A	N/A	N/A	N/A

Last MSR was $3,550

TAL FARLOW (HSTFWRNH) - single round cutaway bound hollow body, arched figured maple top, bound f-holes, scroll style inlay on cutaway, raised black bound pickguard, maple back/sides/neck, 20-fret bound rosewood fingerboard with pearl reverse crown inlay, Tune-O-Matic bridge/trapeze tailpiece, rosewood tailpiece insert with pearl engraved block inlay, bound peghead with pearl crown/logo inlay, 3-per-side tuners, nickel hardware, 2 covered humbucker pickups, 2 volume/2 tone controls, 3-position switch, available in Wine Red (WR) finish, this model is part of the Historic Collection, current mfg.

MSR	$4,799	$3,200	$2,300	$1,800	N/A	N/A	N/A

Tal Farlow (HSTFVSNH) - with Vintage Sunburst finish (with nickel hardware), current mfg.

MSR	$4,973	$3,275	$2,425	$1,925	N/A	N/A	N/A

Tal Farlow (HSTF prefix) - with Viceroy Brown Sunburst (disc. 2003) or Natural finish (with nickel hardware), mfg. 1998-present.

MSR	$5,919	$3,925	$2,700	$2,100	N/A	N/A	N/A

PAUL JACKSON, JR. SIGNATURE - similar to ES-346, except made to the artist's specifications, with AAA figured maple top, available in Gingerburst or Wine Red finishes, this model is part of the Custom Collection, mfg. 1999-present.

MSR	$4,379	$3,000	$2,200	$1,700	N/A	N/A	N/A

LE GRANDE (HSLGGH) - custom shop edition of the Le Grand, with gold hardware. Available in Dark Wineburst (DW, new 2000), Vintage Sunburst, Chablis, Natural, or Trans. Amber finish, this model is part of the Custom Collection, mfg. 1998-present.

MSR	$11,632	$7,625	$5,400	$3,850	N/A	N/A	N/A

Add $2,012 for Chablis, Natural, or Trans Amber finishes (new 1999).

PAT MARTINO SIGNATURE - carved out mahogany thin body, AAA figured maple top on Custom Model, plain maple top on Standard Model, f-holes, two '57 Classic humbuckers, straight pull peghead, ebony fingerboard w/o inlays, nickel (Standard Model) or gold (Custom Model) hardware, Tune-O-Matic bridge with stop tailpiece, available in Caramel Brown (CB) or Heritage Cherry Sunburst (HS), this model is part of the Custom Collection, new 1999, Standard Model disc. 2000.

MSR	$4,675	$3,250	$2,475	$1,850	N/A	N/A	N/A

Subtract 10% for Standard Model.

LARRY CARLTON ES-335 - ES-335 style, plain maple body, mahogany neck, single cream binding, 22-fret rosewood fingerboard with small block inlays, three-per-side tuners, Tune-O-Matic bridge, stopbar tailpiece, two Classic '57 humbucker pickups, four knobs, three-way switch, chrome hardware, available in Carlton Sunburst finish, mfg. summer 2004-present.

MSR	$6,438	$4,650	$3,250	$2,500	N/A	N/A	N/A

A pilot run of 50 instruments was scheduled.

CUSTOM SHOP: DESIGNER SERIES

YAHOO! EXPLORER - limited edition model featuring Yahoo! graphics, purple swirl nitrocellulose finish, part of the Limited Edition Custom Collection.

	N/A	N/A	N/A	N/A	N/A	N/A	N/A

Lack of secondary marketplace activity on this model precludes accurate pricing.

1958 KORINA EXPLORER (DSKX PREFIX) - korina body, white pickguard, korina neck, 22-fret rosewood fingerboard with pearl dot inlay, Tune-O-Matic bridge/trapeze tailpiece, 6-on-a-side tuners, gold hardware, 2 humbucker pickups, 2 volume/1 tone controls, 3-position switch, available in Antique Natural finish, this model is part of the Historic Collection, current mfg.

MSR	$12,676	$8,275	$6,150	$4,300	N/A	N/A	N/A

ALLEN COLLINS SIGNATURE KORINA EXPLORER - one-piece korina body, aged by Tom Murphy, rosewood fingerboard with dot inlay, 2 Classic '57 humbuckers, A. Collins prefix in serialization, aged gold hardware, aged Antique Natural finish. limited edition of 100 mfg. 2003-04.

	$7,650	$6,250	$4,750	N/A	N/A	N/A	N/A

Last MSR was $11,716.

1957 KORINA FUTURA (CSMF PREFIX) - similar to the Explorer, except has a split 3-per-side headstock, available in Antique Natural (with gold hardware) finish, mfg. 1998-2003.

	$8,000	$5,950	$4,250	N/A	N/A	N/A	N/A

Last MSR was $12,071.

1958-59 KORINA FLYING V (DSKV PREFIX) - korina V-shaped body, white pickguard, korina neck, 22-fret rosewood fingerboard with pearl dot inlay, Tune-O-Matic bridge/stop tailpiece, 3-per-side tuners with plastic buttons, gold hardware, 2 humbucker pickups, 2 volume/1 tone controls, 3-position switch, available in Natural finish, this model is part of the Historic Collection, current mfg.

MSR	$12,072	$8,000	$5,950	$4,250	N/A	N/A	N/A

GRADING	100% MINT	98% NEAR MINT	95% EXC+	90% EXC	80% VG+	70% VG	60% G

1967 FLYING V REISSUE - mahogany V-shaped body, available in Antique Natural, Classic White, Ebony, Faded Cherry, or Tobaccoburst, this model is part of the Historic Collection, mfg. 2001-04.

	$2,400	$1,850	$1,450	N/A	N/A	N/A	N/A

Last MSR was $3,550.

LENNY KRAVITZ SIGNATURE 1967 FLYING V - patterned after Lenny Kravitz' '67 Flying V, features Black Sparkle finish, gold mirrored pickguard and gold hardware, includes Maestro vibrola, with "Lenny" engraved on the bass and custom shaped neck, white lined guitar case, this model is a Limited Edition, only 125 mfg. 2002-present.

MSR	$5,918	$3,900	$3,250	$2,450	N/A	N/A	N/A	N/A

FLYING V CUSTOM - features solid mahogany body and neck, two '57 Classic humbuckers, Les Paul appointments, available in Classic White or Faded Cherry, mfg. 2004-present.

MSR	$4,971	$3,300	$2,500	$2,000	$1,750	$1,500	$1,300	$1,100

Add $621 for Classic White finish.

FLYING V STANDARD FIGURED TOP - flame maple top, two-piece mahogany back, vintage trapezoid inlays on neck, two Burstbucker pickups, nickel hardware, Washed Cherry finish only, mfg. 2003-present.

MSR	$4,847	$3,200	$2,250	$1,950	$1,650	$1,350	$1,150	$975

1963 REVERSE FIREBIRD I (HSF1 PREFIX) - asymmetrical hourglass style mahogany body, through-body 9-ply laminated mahogany neck, 22-fret rosewood fingerboard with pearl dot inlay, wraparound tailpiece, wood/partial blackface reverse peghead with pearl logo inlay, 6 in a line banjo tuners, nickel hardware, multi-ply white pickguard, covered mini-humbucker pickup, volume/tone control, available in Vintage Sunburst (VS) finish, mfg. 1998-present.

MSR	$3,692	$2,450	$1,700	$1,250	N/A	N/A	N/A	N/A

The entire Firebird Series (I, III, V, VII) is available in Custom Colors (limited quantities): Cardinal Red, Ebony, Ember Red, Frost Blue, Inverness Green, Kerry Green, Pelham Blue, Polaris White, Golden Mist Poly, Heather Poly, and Silver Mist Poly (polyurethane). Firebird I, III, V, and VII are part of the Historic Collection Series, and are an Award level dealer exclusive models.

1964 REVERSE FIREBIRD III (HSF3 PREFIX) - similar to the 1963 Firebird I, except features a bound rosewood fingerboard, Tune-O-Matic bridge/Maestro vibrola tailpiece, 2 covered mini-humbucker pickups, 2 volume/2 tone controls, 3-way selector (mounted on pickguard on treble bout), available in Vintage Sunburst (VS) finish, mfg. 1998-present.

MSR	$4,524	$3,000	$2,200	$1,600	N/A	N/A	N/A	N/A

1965 REVERSE FIREBIRD V (HSF5 PREFIX) - similar to the 1963 Firebird I, except features a bound rosewood fingerboard with pearl trapezoid inlay, ABR-1 bridge/Maestro deluxe vibrola tailpiece, plastic handle on vibrola arm, 2 covered mini-humbucker pickups, 2 volume/2 tone controls, 3-way selector (mounted on pickguard on treble bout), available in Vintage Sunburst (VS) finish, mfg. 1998-present.

MSR	$5,343	$3,525	$2,650	$1,950	N/A	N/A	N/A	N/A

1965 REVERSE FIREBIRD VII (HSF7 PREFIX) - similar to the 1963 Firebird I, except features a bound ebony fingerboard with pearl block inlay, ABR-1 bridge/Maestro deluxe vibrola tailpiece, plastic handle on vibrola arm, gold hardware, 3 covered mini-humbucker pickups, 2 volume/2 tone controls, 3-way selector (mounted on pickguard on treble bout). Available in Vintage Sunburst (VS) finish, part of the Historic Collection, mfg. 1998-present.

MSR	$6,989	$4,625	$3,300	$2,500	N/A	N/A	N/A	N/A

NON REVERSE FIREBIRD (CS-NRFRBRD{ }GH) - non-reverse Firebird body style, choice of two humbuckers (available in CR, NA, or PB finishes, disc.), three mini-humbuckers (Ebony or TV White only) or three P-90 (Ebony or TV White only) pickups, mfg. 2003-present.

MSR	$2,582	$1,725	$1,275	$1,000	N/A	N/A	N/A	N/A

CUSTOM SHOP: SG SERIES

LES PAUL SG STANDARD REISSUE (SGSR PREFIX) - reissue of the Les Paul SG Standard, includes historically accurate heel shape, holly peg veneer, tapered peg head, vintage body shape and scarfing, two '57 Classic pickups, pearloid trapezoid inlays on fingerboard, ABR-1 bridge with stop bar or ABR-1 bridge with short Maestro vibrato, available in Faded Cherry, Classic White, or TV Yellow finish, this model is part of the Historic Collection, mfg. 2000-present.

MSR	$3,977	$2,625	$1,950	$1,500	N/A	N/A	N/A	N/A

Add $186 for Maestro vibrato. Add $310 for aged hardware (SGSRA prefix). Add $248 for Classic White or TV Yellow finish. Add approx. $200 for left-hand model.

LES PAUL SG SPECIAL REISSUE (SGSPR PREFIX) - reissue of the Les Paul SG Special, includes historically accurate heel shape, holly peg veneer, tapered peg head, vintage body shape and scarfing, two P-90 pickups, wraparound bridge or vibrato with short Maestro tailpiece, pearl dot inlays, available in Faded Cherry, Classic White, or TV Yellow finish, this model is part of the Historic Collection, mfg. 2000-present.

MSR	$3,418	$2,275	$1,700	$1,325	N/A	N/A	N/A	N/A

Add $296 for Maestro vibrato (disc.). Add $248 for Classic White or TV Yellow finish. Add approx. $200 for left-hand model.

LES PAUL SG CUSTOM REISSUE (SGC PREFIX) - double sharp cutaway mahogany body, white layered pickguard, mahogany neck, 22-fret bound ebony fingerboard with pearl block inlay, model Tune-O-Matic bridge/stop tailpiece, multi-bound peghead with pearl split diamond inlay, 3-per-side tuners, gold hardware, 3 covered humbucker pickups, 2 volume/2 tone controls, 3-position switch, available in Classic White or Faded Cherry (new 2000) finish, this model is part of the Historic Collection, current mfg.

MSR	$5,070	$3,350	$2,500	$1,825	N/A	N/A	N/A	N/A

Add approx. $200 for left-hand model.

Gibson ES-446S courtesy Gibson

Gibson Le Grande courtesy Gibson

GRADING	100% MINT	98% NEAR MINT	95% EXC+	90% EXC	80% VG+	70% VG	60% G

Les Paul SG Custom With Maestro (SGC Prefix) - similar to the Les Paul SG Custom, except features a Bigsby-style Maestro tremolo bridge, available in Classic White finish (with gold hardware), current mfg.

| MSR | $5,248 | $3,450 | $2,600 | $1,925 | N/A | N/A | N/A |

´63 CORVETTE STINGRAY SG LIMITED EDITION - double cutaway (SG-style) mahogany body carved to simulate the split rear window of a ´63 Stingray Corvette (with simulated chrome windows), set-in mahogany neck, 22-fret bound ebony fingerboard with mother-of-pearl "StingRay" inlay, wraparound bridge, blackface peghead with pearl checkered flag/logo inlay, 3-per-side tuners, chrome hardware, Corvette-style valve cover engraving chrome plated pickup, volume/tone controls, engraved serial number plate, available in Tuxedo Black, Sebring Silver, or Riverside Red finishes, mfg. 1996 only.

		$2,500	$2,250	$1,975	$1,750	$1,500	$1,350	$1,200

This model comes with a leather case, Certificate of Authenticity, and framed print of the original concept drawing of the Gibson 1963 Corvette Guitar. The 1963 Corvette Guitar was a Gibson Custom Shop model, and was produced in a limited edition of 150 instruments.

PETE TOWNSHEND SIGNATURE - replica of the SG Pete Townshend used during The Who's "Live at Leeds" concert in 1970, features Townshend's signature on back of headstock, includes handsigned certificate, exclusive flight case and protective cloth guitar cover, mfg. 2000 only.

		N/A	$3,000	$2,250	N/A	N/A	N/A	N/A

Last MSR was $4,588.

This model is part of the Custom Collection. Only 250 were manufactured.

TONY IOMMI SIGNATURE (SCST) - one-piece solid mahogany SG body, with original style 1961 neck joint, slim taper mahogany neck, 2 Tony Iommi signature humbucker pickups, ebony fingerboard with sterling silver cross inlays, nickel hardware, ABR-1 bridge with stop tailpiece, right- or left-handed, Ebony or Wine Red finish, this model is part of the Custom Collection, mfg. 1999-2004.

		$3,925	$2,950	$2,200	N/A	N/A	N/A	N/A

Last MSR was $5,905.

SG ELEGANT (SGELEGQ) - features quilt top, choice of Blueburst, Firemist, or Iguana Burst finishes, new 2005.

| MSR | $4,847 | $3,225 | $2,450 | $1,875 | N/A | N/A | N/A |

CUSTOM SHOP: HISTORIC COLLECTION LES PAUL SERIES

One of the more recent considerations on currently manufactured Les Paul Reissues is weight - in this case, less is better! Many dealers are now listing the weights of individual guitars, as they can vary from between 8.5 and 9.5 lbs.

Add approx. $200 for left-hand model, available on most currently manufactured Reissues below.

LES PAUL 1952 GOLD TOP REISSUE (LP52AGNT/LPR2AGNT) - single sharp cutaway solid mahogany body, bound carved maple top, mahogany neck, 22-fret bound rosewood fingerboard with pearl trapezoid inlays, raised trapeze tailpiece, blackface peghead with pearl logo inlay, 3-per-side tuners with plastic buttons, nickel hardware, raised cream pickguard, 2 creme P-90 single coil pickups, 2 volume/2 tone controls, 3-position switch, available in Antique Gold finish, this model is part of the Historic Collection, mfg. 1998-2004, LP52AGNT mfg. 2003-04.

		$2,400	$1,850	$1,450	N/A	N/A	N/A	N/A

Last MSR was $3,588.

Add $3,275 for aged finish by Tom Murphy (mfg. 2002, LPR2AAGNT).

LES PAUL 1954 GOLD TOP REISSUE (LP54AGNH/LPR4AGNH) - similar to the Les Paul 1952 Gold Top Reissue, except features wraparound bridge, and hardware similar to the original 1954 model, available in Antique Gold finish, LPR4AGNH introduced in 2003, current mfg.

| MSR | $4,055 | $2,700 | $1,900 | $1,500 | N/A | N/A | N/A |

Les Paul 1954 "Oxblood" Reissue (LP54JBNH/LPR4JBNH) - similar to the Les Paul '54 Gold Top Reissue, except features two '57 Classic PAF Reissue humbucker pickups, available in Oxblood finish (with nickel hardware), new 1998, LPR4JBNH introduced in 2003.

| MSR | $4,143 | $2,775 | $2,050 | $1,600 | N/A | N/A | N/A |

LES PAUL CUSTOM BLACK BEAUTY 1954 REISSUE (LPB4EBGH) - single sharp cutaway multi-bound mahogany body with carved top, raised bound black pickguard, mahogany neck, 22-fret bound ebony fingerboard with pearl block inlay, Tune-O-Matic bridge/stop tailpiece, multi-bound peghead with pearl split diamond/logo inlay, 3-per-side tuners with plastic buttons, gold hardware, 2 single coil pickups, 2 volume/2 tone controls, 3-position switch, available in Ebony finish, this model is part of the Historic Collection, current mfg.

| MSR | $5,674 | $3,725 | $2,650 | $1,875 | N/A | N/A | N/A |

Add $296 for Gold Bigsby tremolo (Model LPB4EBBG).

LES PAUL 1956 GOLD TOP REISSUE (LP56AGNH/LPR6AGNH) - single sharp cutaway solid mahogany body, bound carved maple top, mahogany neck, 22-fret bound rosewood fingerboard with pearl trapezoid inlays, Tune-O-Matic bridge/stop bar tailpiece, blackface peghead with pearl logo inlay, 3-per-side tuners with plastic buttons, nickel hardware, raised cream pickguard, 2 single coil pickups, 2 volume/2 tone controls, 3-position switch, available in Antique Gold Top finish, this model is part of the Historic Collection, mfg. 1990-current, LPR6AGNH mfg. 2003-present.

| MSR | $4,030 | $2,750 | $2,150 | $1,700 | N/A | N/A | N/A |

Add $3,163 (last retail value) for aged finish by Tom Murphy (LPR6AAGNH) - disc 2001.

LES PAUL CUSTOM BLACK BEAUTY 1957 REISSUE 2 PICKUP - single sharp cutaway multi-bound mahogany body with carved top, raised bound black pickguard, mahogany neck, 22-fret bound ebony fingerboard with pearl block inlay, Tune-O-Matic bridge/stop tailpiece, multi-bound peghead with pearl split diamond/logo inlay, 3-per-side tuners with plastic buttons, gold hardware, 2 humbucker pickups, 2 volume/2 tone controls, 3-position switch, available in Ebony or Faded Cherry (new 2001) finish, this model is part of the Historic Collection, current mfg.

| MSR | $5,970 | $3,925 | $2,650 | $1,875 | N/A | N/A | N/A |

Add $296 for Gold Bigsby tremolo (Model LPB7EBBG, new 2001). Add $2,131 for aged finish by Tom Murphy (mfg. 2003-04).

Les Paul Custom Black Beauty '57 Reissue 3 Pickups (LPB3 prefix) - similar to Les Paul Custom Black Beauty '57 Reissue, except has 3 pickups, available with Bigsby tremolo or master tone control, disc. 2004.

		$3,150	$2,350	$1,725	N/A	N/A	N/A	N/A

Last MSR was $4,679.

Add $291 for Gold Bigsby tremolo (Model LPB3EBBG). Add $829 for master tone (new 1999, Model LPB3MBGH).

GRADING	100% MINT	98% NEAR MINT	95% EXC+	90% EXC	80% VG+	70% VG	60% G

LES PAUL 1957 CUSTOM REISSUE (LPB7FCGH) - reissue of the 1957 Les Paul Custom, gold hardware, available in Faded Cherry (FC) finish only, This model was part of the Historic Collection, mfg. 2001, reintroduced 2004 and is currently produced.

MSR	$5,674		$3,725	$2,650	$1,875	N/A	N/A	N/A	N/A

LES PAUL 1957 GOLDTOP REISSUE (LP57AGNH/LPR7AGNH) - single sharp cutaway solid mahogany body, bound carved maple top, raised cream pickguard, mahogany neck, 22-fret bound rosewood fingerboard with pearl trapezoid inlays, Tune-O-Matic bridge/stop tailpiece, blackface peghead with pearl logo inlay, 3-per-side tuners with plastic buttons, nickel hardware, 2 humbucker pickups, 2 volume/2 tone controls, 3-position switch, available in Antique Goldtop finish or in darkback configuration (new 2001), this model is part of the Historic Collection, LPR7AGNH introduced in 2003, current mfg.

MSR	$4,030		$2,750	$2,150	$1,700	N/A	N/A	N/A	N/A

Add $3,124 (last retail price) for aged finish by Tom Murphy (LPR7AAGNH, mfg. 2001 only).

Also available with dark finished back and sides.

Les Paul '57 Goldtop Reissue with Aging & Amp - includes Tom Murphy aging, Reissue case and Gibson Amp, disc. 2001.

			$5,500	$4,000	$3,250	N/A	N/A	N/A	N/A

Last MSR was $9,663.

Les Paul 1957 Goldtop Custom Authentic (LPR7CAAGNH) - similar to the 1957 Les Paul Goldtop Reissue, except features aged finish and hardware, available in Goldtop finish, mfg. 2001-present.

MSR	$4,528		$3,000	$2,350	$1,875	N/A	N/A	N/A	N/A

LES PAUL 1958 PLAINTOP REISSUE (LPR8 PREFIX) - similar to the Les Paul '59 Flametop Reissue, except features a much less figured carved maple top, available in Washed Cherry (WC, new 2004), Faded Tobacco (FT, new 2004), Ice Tea (IT, new 2004), Heritage Cherry Sunburst (HS) or Vintage Red (VR) finishes, disc. 1999, reintroduced 2003 and is currently produced.

MSR	$4,030		$2,750	$2,150	$1,700	N/A	N/A	N/A	N/A

Last MSR was $4,970.

Les Paul '58 Figured Top Reissue (LPR8F/LPR8NH) - similar to the Les Paul '58 PlainTop Reissue, except features a slightly more figured carved maple top, available in Butterscotch (BS), Heritage Darkburst (HD, new 2002), Faded Tobacco (FT, new 2002), Ice Tea (IT, new 2002), Washed Cherry (WC, new 2002), or Vintage Red (VR, disc.) finishes (with nickel hardware), mfg. 1998-99, reintroduced 2001-2002.

			$4,450	$2,750	$2,150	N/A	N/A	N/A	N/A

Last MSR was $5,700.

Add $722 for Custom Authentic Series (aged finish and hardware, new 2001, CS-A58FG-NH). Add $913 for left-hand model.

Les Paul 1958 Plaintop Custom Auhtentic (LPR8CA) - similar to the 1958 Les Paul Plaintop Reissue, except features aged finish and hardware, available in Faded Tobacco (FT), Iced Tea (IT), or Worn Cherry (WT) finishes, mfg. 2003-present.

MSR	$4,528		$3,000	$2,350	$1,875	N/A	N/A	N/A	N/A

LES PAUL 1959 FLAMETOP REISSUE (LP59/LPR9 PREFIX) - single sharp cutaway solid mahogany body, bound carved curly maple top, raised cream pickguard, mahogany neck, 22-fret bound rosewood fingerboard with pearl trapezoid inlays, Tune-O-Matic bridge/stop tailpiece, blackface peghead with pearl logo inlay, 3-per-side tuners with plastic buttons, nickel hardware, 2 humbucker pickups, 2 volume/2 tone controls, 3-position switch, available in Heritage Darkburst (HD, disc. 2000, reintroduced 2002-2003), Washed Cherry (new 2003), Faded Tobacco (new 2003), Ice Tea (new 2004) or Heritage Cherry Sunburst (HS, disc. 2002) finishes, current mfg.

MSR	$7,467		$4,975	$3,850	$3,000	N/A	N/A	N/A	N/A

Add $470 for Custom Authentic Series (aged finish and hardware, new 2002, CS-A59-NH). Add $2,973 for aged finish by Tom Murphy (mfg. 2002, LPR9FA).

Les Paul '59 Figured Top Reissue (LPR9F) - similar to the Les Paul '59 Flametop Reissue, except features a less figured carved maple top, available in Heritage Cherry Sunburst (HS) or Vintage Red (VR) finishes, mfg. 1999-2000.

			$4,950	$4,100	$3,350	N/A	N/A	N/A	N/A

Last MSR was $8,162.

Les Paul '59 Plaintop Reissue (LPR9P) - similar to the Les Paul '59 Flametop Reissue, except features a much less figured carved maple top, available in Heritage Cherry Sunburst (HS) or Vintage Red (VR) finishes, mfg. 1999-2000.

			$3,775	$3,100	$2,500	N/A	N/A	N/A	N/A

Last MSR was $6,291.

LES PAUL 1960 FLAMETOP REISSUE (LPR0 PREFIX) - single sharp cutaway mahogany body, bound carved flame maple top, raised cream pickguard, mahogany neck, 22-fret rosewood fingerboard with pearl trapezoid inlay, Tune-O-Matic bridge/stop tailpiece, blackface peghead with pearl logo inlay, 3-per-side tuners with plastic buttons, nickel hardware, 2 covered humbucker pickups, 2 volume/2 tone controls, 3-position switch, available in Heritage Darkburst (HD, disc. 2002), Washed Cherry (new 2003), Faded Tobacco (new 2003), Ice Tea (IT, new 2004), or Heritage Cherry Sunburst (HS, disc. 2002) finishes, disc. 2001, reintroduced 2002.

MSR	$7,467		$4,925	$3,850	$3,000	N/A	N/A	N/A	N/A

Add $517 for Custom Authentic (mfg. 2004 only). Add approx. $600 for left-handed configuration.

This model is part of the Historic Collection, and is an Award level dealer exclusive model.

Gibson Tony Iommi
courtesy Gibson

Gibson Les Paul '58 Reissue
courtesy Gibson

G

GRADING	100% MINT	98% NEAR MINT	95% EXC+	90% EXC	80% VG+	70% VG	60% G

1957 LP JUNIOR SINGLE CUTAWAY (LPJRSC PREFIX) - single cutaway mahogany body, set-in mahogany neck, 22-fret rosewood fingerboard with pearl dot inlay, wraparound tailpiece, 3-per-side tuners with plastic buttons, nickel hardware, black pickguard, black 'dog-eared' P-90 single coil pickup, volume/tone controls, available in Faded Cherry (FC), Vintage Sunburst (VS), TV White (TVW, new 2003), or TV Yellow (TV) finishes, mfg. 1998-present.

	MSR	$2,895		$1,925	$1,400	$1,050	N/A	N/A	N/A	N/A

1958 LP JUNIOR DOUBLE CUTAWAY (LPJRDC PREFIX) - similar to the 1960 LP Special Single Cutaway, except features an offset double cutaway body, available in Faded Cherry (FC), TV White (TVW, new 2004), or TV Yellow (TV) finishes, mfg. 1998-present.

	MSR	$2,895		$1,925	$1,400	$1,050	N/A	N/A	N/A	N/A

1960 LP SPECIAL SINGLE CUTAWAY (LPSPSCNH) - single cutaway mahogany body, set-in mahogany neck, 22-fret rosewood fingerboard with pearl dot inlay, wraparound tailpiece, 3-per-side tuners with plastic buttons, nickel hardware, black pickguard, 2 black P-90 single coil pickups, 2 volume/2 tone controls, 3-way selector toggle switch. Available in Faded Cherry (FC), TV White (TVW, new 2004) or TV Yellow (TV) finishes, mfg. 1998-present.

	MSR	$2,895		$1,925	$1,400	$1,050	N/A	N/A	N/A	N/A

1960 LP Special Double Cutaway (LPSPDCNH) - similar to the 1960 LP Special Single Cutaway, except features an offset double cutaway body, available in Faded Cherry (FC), TV White (TVW, new 2004), or TV Yellow (TV) finishes, mfg. 1998-present.

	MSR	$2,895		$1,925	$1,400	$1,050	N/A	N/A	N/A	N/A

CUSTOM SHOP: CUSTOM COLLECTION LES PAUL SERIES

The upscale Les Paul Custom Collection models are produced in limited quantities in the Gibson Custom Shop, and will have the Custom Shop logo on the back of the headstock. One of the more recent considerations on currently manufactured Les Paul Reissues is weight. Many dealers are now listing the weights of individual guitars, as they can vary from between 8.5 and 9.5 lbs. Most Custom Shop models that show up in the vintage/used market as a rule are usually in 95% or better condition, since they are rarely played.

Add approx. $200 for left-hand models available on most currently manufactured LPs listed below.

LES PAUL 1968 CUSTOM FIGURED TOP (CS68LPCF PREFIX) - 1968 Les Paul Custom configuration with carved figured maple top, two '57 Classic humbucker pickups, gold hardware, ABR-1 bridge with stop tailpiece, choice of Antique Natural, Butterscotch, Heritage Cherry Sunburst, or Triburst finish, mfg. 2000-present.

	$3,300	$2,475	$1,975	N/A	N/A	N/A	N/A

Last MSR was $4,852.

Subtract $237 for Custom Authentic Series (aged Ebony finish and hardware, new 2001, CS-A68EBNH).

LES PAUL CATALINA (CSCAT[ ]NH) - single cutaway mahogany body, internal sound chambers, set-in mahogany neck, white bound carved maple top, 22-fret bound ebony fingerboard with pearl trapezoid inlay, Tune-O-Matic bridge/stop tailpiece, blackface peghead with pearl Custom Shop/Gibson logo inlays, white pearloid truss rod cover, 3-per-side tuners, nickel hardware, white pearloid pickguard, 2 covered humbucker ('57 Classic) pickups, 2 volume/2 tone controls, 3-way toggle switch, available in Canary Yellow (CY), Cascade Green (CG), or Riverside Red (RR) finishes, mfg. 1997-99.

	$2,225	$1,850	$1,450	N/A	N/A	N/A	N/A

Last MSR was $3,695.

The Riverside Red (RR) finish was a limited run finish.

LES PAUL CLASS 5 FIGURED/QUILT (CSC5/CSC5Q PREFIX) - features bound figured maple top, '60s profile neck with long tenon, 2 Burstbucker pickups, nickel hardware, single-ply cream binding on top/neck, available in Cranberry (CRB), Sienna Burst (SB), Trans. Amber (TA), Trans. Blue (TB), Trans. Black (TBK), or Tangerine Burst (TGB), mfg. 2001-04, Quilt Top mfg. 2003-04.

	$3,625	$2,750	$2,150	N/A	N/A	N/A	N/A

Last MSR was $5,385.

Add $601 for Quilt Top (new 2003).

LES PAUL CLASSIC MAHOGANY (CSMC[ ]NH) - features solid mahogany construction with carved figured mahogany top, and one-piece mahogany neck with long tenon, two '57 Classic zebra humbucker pickups, nickel hardware, available in Antique Natural (AN), Heritage Sunburst (HS), Trans. Red (TR), or Vintage Sunburst (VS), mfg. 2000 only, reintroduced 2002 only.

	$2,995	$2,200	$1,750	N/A	N/A	N/A	N/A

Last MSR was $4,379.

LES PAUL CUSTOM (LPC PREFIX) - similar features to Les Paul Custom mfg. 1957-1960 (more info under listing Les Paul: Custom Series subheading), multi-layered bindings, gold plated hardware, pearl block inlays, "Les Paul Custom" marked on truss rod cover, two Alnico humbucker pickups, available in Ebony (EB), Wine Red (WR), Alpine White (AW), or Heritage Cherry Sunburst (HS), mfg. 2004-present.

	MSR	$4,559		$3,075	$2,450	$2,000	$1,750	$1,500	$1,300	$1,100

LES PAUL ELEGANT FLAME (FIGURED, CSELNH) OR QUILT (CSELQNH) - single cutaway mahogany body, internal sound chambers, set-in mahogany neck, cream bound carved AAA grade maple top (disc. 2000) or quilt top (new 2001, subject to availability), 22-fret bound ebony fingerboard with abalone trapezoid inlay, Tune-O-Matic bridge/stop tailpiece, blackface peghead with pearl Custom Shop/Gibson logo inlays, black truss rod cover, 3-per-side tuners, nickel hardware, clear pickguard, 2 covered humbucker ('57 Classic) pickups, 2 volume/2 tone controls, 3-way toggle switch, available in Heritage Cherry Sunburst (HS, new 2001), Peacock (PK, new 2001), Antique Natural (AN), Butterscotch (BS), Cherry Sunburst (Mfg. 1999-2000), Tobacco Sunburst (Mfg. 1999-2000), or Firemist (FM, disc. 2000, reintroduced 2004) finishes, mfg. 1997-2004, Flametop disc. 2002.

	$3,400	$2,750	$2,000	N/A	N/A	N/A	N/A

Last MSR was $5,101.

Add $589 for Quilt Top.

GRADING	100% MINT	98% NEAR MINT	95% EXC+	90% EXC	80% VG+	70% VG	60% G

LES PAUL FLORENTINE (CSF-GH) - single cutaway semi-hollow mahogany body with center block, set-in mahogany neck, bound carved maple top, 2 f-holes (or diamond-shaped f-holes), white body binding (front and back), 22-fret bound ebony fingerboard with pearl block inlay, Tune-O-Matic bridge/stop tailpiece, bound blackface peghead with pearl split diamond/Gibson logo inlays, engraved "Les Paul Florentine" black truss rod cover, 3-per-side tuners, gold hardware, 2 covered humbucker ('57 Classic) pickups, 2 volume/2 tone controls, 3-way toggle switch, available in Ebony (EB), Emberglow (EG), Heritage Cherry Sunburst (new 1999), or Wine Red (WR) finishes, mfg. 1997-2000.

	$2,625	$2,150	$1,650	N/A	N/A	N/A	N/A

Last MSR was $4,359.

Les Paul Florentine Plus (CSFPGH) - similar to the Les Paul Florentine, except features a figured maple top, available in Antique Natural (AN), Emberglow (EG), Translucent Black (new 1999), or Heritage Cherry Sunburst (HS) finishes, mfg. 1997-2000.

	$2,995	$2,450	$1,950	N/A	N/A	N/A	N/A

Last MSR was $4,926.

LES PAUL ULTIMA (CSUL PREFIX, ET/GT SUFFIX) - single cutaway mahogany body, set-in mahogany neck, abalone/white bound carved AAA grade maple top, 22-fret bound ebony fingerboard with custom abalone inlay, Tune-O-Matic bridge/stop (ET suffix) or trapeze (GT suffix) tailpiece, blackface peghead with pearl Custom Shop/Gibson logo inlays, choice of butterfly (CSULBHSGH, disc. 2001), flame (CSULFHSGH), harp lady (CSULHHSGH), or tree of life (CSULTHSGH) fretboard inlay, gold truss rod cover, 3-per-side Grover Imperial tuners with metal or pearl buttons, gold hardware, 2 covered humbucker ('57 Classic) pickups, 2 volume/2 tone controls, 3-way toggle switch, available in Heritage Cherry Sunburst (HS) finish, mfg. 1997-present.

MSR	$10,545	$6,950	$5,050	$3,750	N/A	N/A	N/A	N/A

Add $269 for gold Ultima trapeze tailpiece (GT suffix).

ACE FREHLEY SIGNATURE LES PAUL (LPAF, LPFR) - single cutaway bound mahogany body, flame maple top, 22-fret bound ebony fingerboard with lightning bolt inlay/Frehley's signature in pearl script at 12th fret, bound black peghead with Ace peghead image, chrome hardware, Tune-O-Matic bridge/stop tail piece, no pickguard, 3 DiMarzio humbucker pickups, 2 volume/2 tone controls, 3-way toggle, available in Sunburst finish, mfg. 1997-2001.

	$4,000	$3,100	$2,500	$2,100	$1,850	$1,650	$1,425

Gibson Les Paul Class 5
courtesy Gibson

JIMMY PAGE SIGNATURE LES PAUL (LPPG) - single cutaway bound mahogany body, AA grade figured maple top, 22-fret bound rosewood fingerboard with trapezoid inlay, bound black peghead, gold hardware, Tune-O-Matic bridge/stop tail piece, cream pickguard with engraved "Jimmy Page" signature, 2 exposed polepiece humbucker pickups, 2 volume/2 tone controls (all push-pull for custom wiring and coil taps), 3-way selector toggle, available in Light Honey Burst (LB) finish, mfg. 1995-99.

	$4,000	$3,100	$2,500	$2,100	$1,850	$1,650	$1,425

Last MSR was $6,300.

JIMMY PAGE SIGNATURE LES PAUL (CURRENT) - carved figured maple top, solid mahogany back and one-piece neck, duplicates Jimmy Page's original 'Burst, including eliptical neck profile and single push/pull pot, available in three releases, mfg. 2004-present.

Jimmy Page First Release - pilot run of only 25, signed by Jimmy Page and aged by Tom Murphy, available through Gibson Super dealers only, limited mfg. 2004 only.

	$18,500	$14,000	$10,000	$8,000	$6,000	$5,000	$4,000

Last MSR was $23,669.

Jimmy Page Second Release - aged by Tom Murphy, available through Gibson Super dealers only, 150 mfg. 2004 only.

	$11,000	$8,500	$7,000	$6,250	$5,500	$4,750	$4,000

Last MSR was $16,556.

Jimmy Page Third Model/Custom Authentic - standard run with no limit or exclusivity, Custom Authentic version, mfg. 2004-present.

MSR	$9,401	$6,150	$4,350	$3,500	$2,750	$2,250	$1,850	$1,500

JOE PERRY SIGNATURE LES PAUL (LPJP, LPPR) - single cutaway mahogany body, bookmatched figured maple top, 22-fret rosewood fingerboard with trapezoid inlay, black peghead with white shell truss rod cover, Joe Perry's signature in white on body behind the bridge, black chrome hardware, Tune-O-Matic bridge/stop tail piece, white shell pickguard, 2 humbucker pickups, 2 volume/2 tone controls (treble tone control is push/pull), active mid-boost circuit, 3-way toggle, available in hand-stained Translucent Blackburst finish, mfg. 1997-99.

	$2,250	$1,600	$1,350	$1,100	$995	$875	$750

Last MSR was $3,296.

JOE PERRY SIGNATURE LES PAUL (CS-LPJPGT) - similar to previous Signature Model except has Aged Tiger Green Finish, and Burstbucker two and three pickups, limited mfg. 2003-present.

MSR	$5,958	$3,950	$2,850	$2,350	$1,850	$1,675	$1,375	$1,250

Add $313 for Bigsby tailpiece.

Gibson Les Paul Elegant Flame
courtesy Gibson

GRADING	100% MINT	98% NEAR MINT	95% EXC+	90% EXC	80% VG+	70% VG	60% G

ZAKK WYLDE SIGNATURE LES PAUL - features unmistakable B&W bullseye graphics or camo bullseye (new 2004, initial pilot run of 25 units, followed by standard run second release), or Natural Rough (disc.) top, 2 EMG black pickups, gold hardware, oiled, raw maple back, mfg. 1999-present.

MSR	$5,881		$3,900	$2,875	$2,400	$2,000	$1,675	$1,375	$1,250

Add $800 for Natural Rough top (disc. 2002).

DICKEY BETTS RED TOP SIGNATURE LES PAUL - features Dickey Betts Red Top finish, limited edition mfg. 2002-04.

			$3,550	$2,700	$2,200	$1,900	$1,625	$1,350	$1,225

Last MSR was $5,325.

PETER FRAMPTON SIGNATURE LES PAUL - features specially wired 3 pickup configuration with chambered back allowing for lightweight construction, Peter Frampton signature inlaid on 12th fret, custom style pearloid spilt diamond headstock inlay, available in Ebony finish only, mfg. 2000-present.

MSR	$5,800		$3,800	$2,775	$2,500	$2,150	$1,800	$1,550	$1,275

SLASH SIGNATURE LES PAUL - features plain maple top, two Seymour Duncan Alnico Pro 2 humbuckers and Fishman powerbridge, aged nickel hardware, truss rod cover marked "Slash", Custom Authentic Dark Tobacco Sunburst finish, initial pilot run of 25 units, followed by standard run second release, mfg. 2004-present.

MSR	$6,120		$4,000	$2,950	$2,350	$2,000	$1,800	$1,600	$1,400

GARY ROSSINGTON SIGNATURE LES PAUL - figured maple top, solid mahogany back, one-piece mahogany neck, 22-fret rosewood fingerboard, 24.75 in. scale, Burstbucker 2 and Burstbucker 3 pickups, two volume and controls knobs, 3-way switch, available in Skynyrd Burst, aged by Tom Murphy, limited edition of 250 mfg. 2002-04.

			$5,250	$3,850	$3,000	$2,600	$2,200	$1,800	$1,400

Last MSR was $7,691.

CARVED DIAMOND LES PAUL - custom carved maple top, solid mahogany back, one-piece mahogany neck, 22-fret rosewood fingerboard, two '57 Classic humbuckers, gold hardware, kidney bean tuners, three dimensional finish, available in Blue Chameleon multi-colors or Black to Gold finish, mfg. 2003-present.

MSR	$5,841		$3,875	$2,950	$2,500	$2,150	$1,750	$1,500	$1,250

Add $373 for Black to Natural or Black to White finishes.

CARVED FLAME LES PAUL - custom carved maple top featuring carved flames, solid mahogany back, one-piece mahogany neck, 22-fret rosewood fingerboard, two '57 Classic humbuckers, gold hardware, three dimensional finish, available in Chameleon multi-colors or Orange to Red, mfg. 2003-present.

MSR	$5,841		$3,875	$2,950	$2,500	$2,150	$1,750	$1,500	$1,250

Add $373 for Black to Natural or OTR finishes.

CRAZY HORSE LES PAUL - carved maple top, solid mahogany back, one-piece mahogany neck, 22-fret rosewood fingerboard, two '57 Classic humbuckers, nickel hardware, vintage tulip tuners, created in collaboration with Stacy David, limited edition of 25 beginning 2004.

Retail pricing is not currently available on this model.

LES PAUL 10TH ANNIVERSARY - carved maple top, solid mahogany back, one-piece mahogany neck with long neck tenon, 22-fret ebony fingerboard, 10th anniversary inlayed on 12th fret, gold engraved pickguard, pickup coves, and truss rod cover, Diamond White finish, limited edition of 50 mfg. 2003-04.

		$4,950	$4,250	$3,500	$2,750	$2,000	$1,500	$1,000

Last MSR was $6,894.

LES PAUL 1968 CUSTOM "THE DARKNESS" - single cutaway solid mahogany body with maple top, Les Paul Custom binding, mahogany neck, 22-fret ebony fingerboard with Ultima flame inlays, three-per-side tuners, Tune-O-Matic bridge, stop tailpiece, two Classic '57 humbucker pickups, four knobs, three-way switch, nickel hardware, available in Silver-Blue Sparkle, Silver-Red Sparkle, or Silver-Red sparkle finishes, 24.75 in. scale, mfg. summer 2004-present.

MSR	$8,000		$5,775	$3,950	$2,650	N/A	N/A	N/A	N/A

CUSTOM SHOP: LIMITED EDITIONS - VARIOUS MODELS

The Nashville Custom Shop has produced a number of limited editions over the years. These instruments are typically produced in limited quantities from 10 to approx. 300, depending on the configuration and original order. Total production and original MSRs have been provided if known. In some cases, a limited edition may be double listed within another category, and many recently manufactured custom shop limited edition LPs are separately listed and described under Custom Shop: Custom Collection Les Paul Series. On currently manufactured limited editions from the Custom Shop, standard 10% - 35% discounts apply for most instruments. On discontinued limited editions, the secondary marketplace values can be difficult to determine, since these instruments are very specialized, and appeal only to a small number of collectors and nitch enthusiasts.

Limited Edition LPs have included a '60 Corvette (total unknown, features distinctive two-tone aqua body and Corvette motifs), a Hard Rock Café, '60 Corvette LP (B&W, Corvette logo inlaid in neck), Dale Earnhardt (333 Mfg. 1999, black body with #3 on front), Dale Earnhardt Intimidator (No MSRP, 333 Mfg. 2000-2002, anniversary silver with "The Intimidator" inlaid on fretboard), Dale Earnhardt Jr. (No MSRP, Mfg. 2000-2002, Budweiser logo with #8 on body), X-Men Wolverine (50 Mfg. 2000, features X-Men motifs), Web-Slinger One (150 Mfg., features Spider-Man pattern), Dickey Betts '57 Les Paul Goldtop (no MSR), Old Hickory (200 Mfg. 1999), Playboy ($7,000 last MSR, 10 Mfg., features black body with white Playboy bunny logo and Playboy inlaid in fretboard), Playboy Rabbit Head (50 Mfg., body is shaped like a black rabbit head), and Playmate of the Year (50 Mfg. beginning 2001, features pink burst glitter finish).

During 2002, the Custom Shop released the following limited edition models: Indian Chief Les Paul (100 mfg. - MSR was $9,450), Bob Marley Les Paul Special (200 mfg. - MSR is $4,734), 1952 Les Paul Gold Top Aged (50 mfg. - MSR was $7,288), Non-Reverse Firebird Plus (60 mfg. in blue, red, and green swirl finishes - MSR was $3,309), Mahogany Explorer (15 mfg. in satin green, copper, blue and silver metallic finishes - MSR was $3,134), Mahogany Flying V (15 mfg. in satin green, copper, blue, and silver metallic finishes - MSR is $3,134), Mahogany Futura (MSR is $3,134), and the Flying V Custom (40 mfg. in Ebony - MSR was $4,734).

During 2003, the Custom Shop released the following limited edition models: Duane Allman 1959 Les Paul Aged (55 mfg. - MSR is $13,630), Gary Rossington Signature SG (250 mfg. - MSR is $4,614), L-4 CES Thin Body 10th Anniversary (30 mfg. - MSR is $7,337), Lee Roy Parnell CS-336 Custom Authentic Signature (MSR

GRADING	100% MINT	98% NEAR MINT	95% EXC+	90% EXC	80% VG+	70% VG	60% G

is $4,024), 10th Anniversary CS-356 (30 mfg. - MSR was $6,982), 10th Anniversary Les Paul Custom (40 mfg. - MSR is $6,894), 50th Anniversary Corvette (50 mfg. - MSR is $9,822), Flying V Standard Figured Top (MSR is $4,615), HUMMER Les Paul (100 mfg. - MSR was $9,467), SG Elegant Quilt (MSR is $4,615), SG Custom 10th Anniversary (40 mfg., MSR was $6,154), Mahogany Explorer w/Split Headstock (MSR is $3,134), Playboy Hottie SG (MSR was $4,497), and the Playboy CS-356 (MSR was $6,154).

During 2004, the Custom Shop released the following limited edition models: Jimmy Page Les Paul (3 releases - first release is 25 aged and signed units, MSR is $23,669, second release is 150 aged and signed units, MSR is $16,556, third release MSR is $9,456), Slash Les Paul (MSR is $6,036), Zakk Wylde camo bullseye Les Paul (MSR is $5,799), Duane Eddy Signature Model (MSR is $6,154), and the Copperhead SG (25 mfg., MSR is N/A).

CUSTOM SHOP: MISC.

L-4 S - single cutaway one-piece mahogany body, mahogany neck, multi-ply body binding, single-ply neck binding, 22-fret rosewood fingerboard with parallelogram inlays, three-per-side tuners, Tune-O-Matic bridge, stop tailpiece, two custom Burstbucker 2's with exposed coils, two knobs, three-way switch, nickel hardware, available in Cherry or Vintage Sunburst finishes, 24.75 in. scale, mfg. summer 2004-present.

	MSR	$4,024		$2,995	$2,000	$1,400	N/A	N/A	N/A	N/A

L-5 S - single cutaway solid mahogany body with maple top, three-piece mahogany neck, Les Paul Custom binding, 22-fret ebony fingerboard with pearl block inlays, three-per-side tuners, ABR-1 bridge, stop tailpiece, one custom Burstbucker 2 pickup, two knobs, three-way switch, gold hardware, available in Ebony finish, 24.75 in. scale, mfg. summer 2004-present.

	MSR	$5,444		$3,950	$2,600	$1,900	N/A	N/A	N/A	N/A

JOHNNY A. SIGNATURE MODEL - double cutaway design, features completely hollow body, AAA figured maple top, mahogany back and rims are carved from a single block of mahogany, resonates more like a flat-top than an archtop, 18/22-fret ebony fingerboard, with Bigsby or stop tailpiece, unbound f-holes, two '57 Classic humbucker pickups, nickel (stop) or gold hardware, serialization has JA prefix, only available in Sunset Glow finish, mfg. 2003-present.

	MSR	$5,281		$3,475	$2,600	$2,200	$1,800	$1,500	$1,300	$1,100

Add $359 for Bigsby.

DUANE EDDY SIGNATURE MODEL - single rounded cutaway body, highly figured maple top, back, and sides, 16 in. (w) x 20 1/4 x 3 in., custom wound single coil pickups and a custom LR Baggs bridge transducer which can be blended, Bigsby tremolo tailpiece, nickel hardware, Duane Eddy signature on scalloped pickguard, Rockabilly Brown finish, mfg. 2004-present.

	MSR	$6,241		$4,250	$3,350	$2,725	$2,300	$2,000	$1,750	$1,500

Gibson Zakk Wylde Les Paul
courtesy Gibson

ELECTRIC BASS: EB SERIES

EB - double sharp cutaway maple body, tortoise pickguard, maple neck, 20-fret maple fingerboard with pearl dot inlay, bar bridge, 30.5 in. scale, blackface peghead with logo decal, 2-per-side tuners, chrome hardware, covered humbucker pickup, volume/tone control, available in Natural finish, mfg. 1970 only.

	N/A	$900	$800	$700	$600	$500	$450

EB-O - SG shaped, double round cutaway mahogany body, black pickguard, mahogany neck, 20-fret rosewood fingerboard with pearl dot inlay, bar bridge, blackface peghead with pearl crown/logo inlay, 2-per-side Kluson banjo tuners, nickel hardware, covered humbucker pickup, volume/tone control, available in Cherry Red, Walnut (mfg. 1971-79), Ebony (approx. 10 mfg. 1971-75), or Natural (only 5 mfg. 1973 only) finish, mfg. 1959-1979.

1959-1960	N/A	$1,500	$1,325	$1,150	$975	$895	$850
1961-1979	N/A	$1,000	$825	$775	$595	$525	$450

In 1961, double sharp cutaway body, laminated pickguard, standard tuners replaced original part/design. In 1963, metal handrest was added, metal covered pickup replaced original part/design.

EB-OF - similar to EB-O, except has laminated pickguard, metal handrest, built-in fuzztone electronics with volume/attack controls and on/off switch, mfg. 1962-65.

	N/A	$1,200	$1,125	$1,050	$950	$895	$795

EB-OL - similar to EB-O, except has long scale length, mfg. 1970-77.

	N/A	$600	$525	$450	$395	$325	$250

EB-1 (GIBSON ELECTRIC BASS) - violin-shaped mahogany body, arched top with painted f-hole/purfling, raised black pickguard, mahogany neck, 20-fret rosewood fingerboard with pearl dot inlay, bar bridge, blackface peghead with pearl logo inlay, 2-per-side Kluson banjo tuners, nickel hardware, covered alnico pickup, volume/tone control, available in Dark Brown finish, approx. 550 mfg. 1953-58.

	N/A	$3,100	$2,850	$2,500	$2,200	$1,950	$1,750

This model was originally designated the Gibson Electric Bass. In 1958, after the introduction of the EB-2 model, the Gibson Electric Bass was commonly called the EB-1.

EB-1 (1970-1973 Mfg.) - similar to EB-1, except has standard tuners, one covered humbucker pickup, approx. 475 mfg. 1970-73.

	N/A	$1,500	$1,275	$1,050	$850	$775	$700

Gibson EB-O
courtesy Dave Rogers
Dave's Guitar Shop

GRADING	100% MINT	98% NEAR MINT	95% EXC+	90% EXC	80% VG+	70% VG	60% G

EB-2 - 335-style double round cutaway semi-hollow body, arched maple top, raised laminated pickguard, f-holes, bound body, maple back/sides, mahogany neck, 20-fret rosewood fingerboard with pearl dot inlay, bar bridge, blackface peghead with pearl crown/logo inlay, 2-per-side Kluson banjo tuners, nickel hardware, covered humbucker pickup, volume/tone control, available in Cherry, Natural or Sunburst finishes, mfg. 1958-1961.

	N/A	$2,500	$2,000	$1,695	$1,500	$1,250	$1,000

EB-2 models in Natural finish (Model EB-2 N) command a premium.

In 1959, baritone pushbutton control added; Black finish was introduced. In 1960, string mute added, standard tuners, redesigned pickup replaced original part/design; Cherry finish was introduced.

EB-2 (1964-1972 Mfg.) - similar to EB-2, except has standard tuners, metal covered humbucker pickup, available in Walnut or Sunburst finish, mfg. 1964-1970.

	N/A	$1,000	$900	$800	$700	$600	$500

In 1965, Cherry finish became an option.

EB-2D - similar to EB-2, except has standard tuners, 2 metal covered humbucker pickups, available in Cherry or Sunburst finishes, mfg. 1966-1970.

	N/A	$1,250	$1,125	$1,000	$900	$800	$700

In 1969, Burgundy and Walnut finishes were introduced.

EB-3 - SG style double sharp cutaway mahogany body, laminated black pickguard with finger rest, metal hand rest, mahogany neck, 30.5 in. scale, 20-fret rosewood fingerboard with pearl dot inlay, bar bridge, blackface peghead with pearl crown/logo inlay, 2-per-side Kluson tuners, nickel hardware, 2 covered humbucker pickups, 2 volume/tone controls, rotary switch, available in Cherry (most common), Ebony (rare, only 10 mfg. 1973), Natural (rare), Walnut (common), or White (rare, approx. 70 mfg. 1976-79) finish, mfg. 1961-1979.

1961-1969	N/A	$1,500	$1,200	$995	$875	$750	$650
1970-1979	N/A	$1,000	$875	$750	$650	$525	$495

In 1963, metal pickup covers were added. In 1969, metal bridge cover added, slotted peghead replaced original part/design, handrest, crown peghead inlay were removed. In 1971, Natural finish became available, Walnut finish became an option. In 1972, crown peghead inlay added, solid peghead replaced previous part/design. In 1976, White finish became available.

EB-3L - similar to EB-3, except has a longer 34.5 in. scale length, available in Cherry or Walnut finish, mfg. 1971-79.

	N/A	$675	$595	$495	$395	$350	$325

EB-4L - SG style double sharp cutaway mahogany body/neck, black laminated pickguard, 20-fret rosewood fingerboard with pearl dot inlay, bar bridge with metal cover, covered humbucker pickup, volume/tone control, 3-position switch, available in Cherry or Walnut finishes, mfg. 1972-79.

	N/A	$550	$450	$385	$275	$235	$200

EB-6 THINLINE - 335-style double round cutaway semi-hollow (EB-2 shaped) body, arched maple top, raised laminated pickguard, f-holes, bound body, maple back/sides, mahogany neck, 20-fret rosewood fingerboard with pearl dot inlay, bar bridge, blackface peghead with pearl crown/logo inlay, 3-per-side Kluson tuners with plastic buttons, nickel hardware, covered humbucker pickup, volume/tone control, pushbutton switch, available in Sunburst finish, mfg. 1960-61.

	N/A	$2,600	$2,200	$1,900	$1,600	$1,250	$1,050

EB-6 Solid Body - similar to EB-6 Thinline, except has double sharp cutaway solid mahogany (SG shaped) body, all metal tuners, approx. 135 shipped, mfg. 1961-67.

	N/A	$2,500	$2,100	$1,750	$1,500	$1,300	$1,200

In 1962, hand rest and string mute were added, 2 covered humbucker pickups, 2 volume/tone controls, 3-position switch replaced original part/design, pushbutton switch removed.

EB 650 - single sharp cutaway semi-hollow bound maple body, arched top, diamond soundholes, maple neck, 21-fret rosewood fingerboard with pearl dot inlay, adjustable rosewood bridge/trapeze tailpiece, blackface peghead with pearl vase/logo inlay, 2-per-side tuners, chrome hardware, 2 covered humbucker pickups, 2 volume/2 tone controls, available in Trans. Amber, Trans. Black, Trans. Blue, Trans. Purple, or Trans. Red finishes, disc. 1996.

	$1,375	$1,150	$1,000	$850	$750	$695	$625

Last MSR was $2,100.

EB 750 - similar to EB 650, except has deeper body, f-holes, figured maple back/sides, abalone inlay, gold hardware, 2 Bartolini pickups, volume/treble/bass/pan controls, active electronics, available in Ebony finish, disc. 1996.

	$1,425	$1,200	$1,050	$895	$795	$725	$650

Last MSR was $2,200.

Add $400 for Antique Natural and Vintage Sunburst finishes.

ELECTRIC BASS: MISC. MODELS

The instruments included in this subcategory are typically models that are not part of a series, and have not had a lot of production or standardized nomenclature. They will appear in alphabetical order.

CONTINENTAL BASS (BAC5) - five-string configuration, offset double cutaway body with long horns, smartwood body, neck-thru body maple neck, rosewood fingerboard, 3/2-per-side tuners, two Bassline pickups, four knobs, gold hardware, available in Natural Oil finish, new 2005.

MSR	$3,488	$2,325	$2,050	$1,725	$1,500	$1,325	$1,100	$975

EXPLORER BASS - radical offset hourglass alder body, maple neck, 21-fret rosewood fingerboard with pearl dot inlay, fixed bridge, blackface peghead with logo decal, 4-on-a-side tuners, chrome hardware, 2 humbucker pickups, 2 volume/1 tone controls, available in Ebony or Ivory finishes, mfg. 1984-87.

	N/A	$650	$575	$500	$450	$400	$350

In 1985 only, a Custom Graphics finish was available.

GRADING	100% MINT	98% NEAR MINT	95% EXC+	90% EXC	80% VG+	70% VG	60% G

FLYING V BASS - alder V-shaped body, maple neck, 21-fret rosewood fingerboard with pearl dot inlay, fixed bridge, blackface arrowhead-shaped headstock with logo decal, 2+2 tuners, chrome hardware, 2 humbucker pickups, volume/tone controls, available in Ebony, Ivory, or Natural finishes, mfg. 1978-1982.

	N/A	$795	$675	$595	$525	$495	$350

It is estimated that only 300 to 400 of these models were built.

G-3 - similar to Grabber, except has black pickguard, rosewood fingerboard, fixed bridge with cover, blackface peghead with logo decal, 3 single coil pickups, 3-position switch, available in Ebony (common), Wine Red (rare, less than 10 mfg. 1976-79), Natural, Walnut (rare, approx. 40 mfg. 1977-78 only), Natural Satin (most common), or Sunburst finishes, mfg. 1975-1982.

	N/A	$350	$300	$260	$230	$200	$175

In 1976, Ebony and Wine Red finishes became available. In 1977, Walnut finish became available.

GIBSON IV BASS - offset double cutaway alder body, maple neck, 22-fret ebony fingerboard with offset pearl dot inlay, fixed bridge, blackface peghead with logo decal, 2-per-side tuners, black hardware, 2 humbucker pickups, 2 volume/1 tone controls, available in Black, Red, or White finishes, mfg. 1987-89.

	N/A	$700	$600	$500	$400	$350	$325

GIBSON V BASS - similar to Gibson IV, except has 5 strings, 3/2-per-side tuners, mfg. 1987-89.

	N/A	$800	$695	$575	$450	$400	$375

GRABBER G-1 - offset double cutaway alder body, tortoise or black pickguard, bolt-on maple neck, 20-fret maple fingerboard with pearl dot inlay, Tune-O-Matic bridge with metal cover, string through-body tailpiece, logo peghead decal, 2-per-side tuners, chrome hardware, 1 movable pickup, volume/tone control, available in Ebony, Wine Red (common), Natural Satin (most common), Natural Maple Gloss, Black, White (rare, less than 60 mfg. 1976-77), Walnut (rare, approx. 75 mfg. 1977-78) or Natural finish, mfg. 1973-1982.

	N/A	$450	$400	$350	$300	$260	$230

In 1975, Ebony and Wine Red finishes became available. In 1976, Black and White finishes became available. In 1977, Walnut finish became available.

LELAND SKLAR SIGNATURE BASS (CSLS[ ]SN) - offset double cutaway maple body, bolt-on maple neck, 34 in. scale, 21-fret rosewood fingerboard with pearl dot inlay, fixed bridge, 4-on-a-side tuners, chrome hardware, 2 P-style EMG split-coil pickups, volume/blend/tone controls, available in Ebony (EB) or TriBurst (TBI) finishes, mfg. 1997-98.

$995	$900	$800	$725	$650	$575	$500

Last MSR was $2,219.

The Leland Sklar Signature Bass was a Gibson Custom Shop model. This model was developed in conjunction with bassist Leland Sklar (Phil Collens, Barefoot Servants).

Q-80 (Q-90) - offset double cutaway asymmetrical alder body, bolt-on maple neck, 22-fret rosewood fingerboard with pearl dot inlay, fixed bridge, blackface peghead with screened logo, 4-on-a-side tuners, chrome hardware, 2 humbucker pickups, 2 volume/1 tone controls, available in Ebony, Red, or Black finishes, mfg. 1987-1992.

	N/A	$650	$550	$475	$375	$325	$300

In 1988, this model was renamed Q-90. In 1989, fretless fingerboard became available.

RD STANDARD BASS - offset hourglass maple body, layered black pickguard, maple neck, 20-fret fingerboard with pearl dot inlay, Tune-O-Matic bridge/strings through anchoring, blackface peghead with pearl logo inlay, 2-per-side tuners, nickel hardware, 2 pickups, 2 volume/2 tone controls, available in Ebony or Natural finishes, mfg. 1977-1980.

	N/A	$750	$700	$625	$550	$500	$450

This model had an ebony fingerboard with Ebony finish only. Extreme rarity precludes accurate pricing on this model.

RD Artist Bass - similar to RD Standard Bass, except has winged "f" peghead inlay, two mini switches, active electronics, available in Ebony, Fireburst, Natural, or Sunburst finishes, mfg. 1977-1982.

	N/A	$800	$700	$625	$550	$500	$450

RD-77 - similar styling to the RD Artist Bass, only 6 mfg. 1977 only.

RIPPER L9-S - offset double cutaway alder body, black pickguard, bolt-on maple neck, 20-fret maple fingerboard with pearl dot inlay, Tune-O-Matic bridge with metal cover, string through-body tailpiece, blackface peghead with logo decal, 2-per-side tuners, chrome hardware, 2 humbucker pickups, volume/treble/bass controls, rotary switch, available in Tobacco Sunburst (rare), Ebony or Natural, Natural Maple Gloss (most common) Natural Satin finishes, mfg. 1973-1982.

	N/A	$600	$525	$450	$400	$350	$300

Add $75 for fretless ebony fingerboard with Sunburst finish (Ripper L9-FS).

In 1974, this model was renamed the Ripper. In 1975, fretless ebony fingerboard with Sunburst finish became available. In 1976, Tobacco Sunburst became available.

SB 300 - double sharp cutaway mahogany body/neck, 20-fret rosewood fingerboard with pearl dot inlay, fixed bridge with metal cover, blackface peghead with screened logo, 2-per-side tuners, chrome hardware, 2 single coil pickups with metal rings, volume/tone control, 3-position switch, control plate, available in Walnut finish, approx. 900 mfg. 1971-73.

	N/A	$350	$300	$260	$230	$200	$175

SB 350 - double sharp cutaway mahogany body/neck, thumbrest, 20-fret rosewood fingerboard with pearl dot inlay, bar bridge with metal cover, blackface peghead with pearl logo inlay, 2 covered humbucker pickups, volume/tone control, 2 on/off switches, available in Cherry, Natural, or Walnut finishes, mfg. 1972-75.

	N/A	$325	$275	$225	$195	$175	$150

Gibson EB-3
courtesy Dave Rogers
Dave's Guitars Shop

G

Gibson SB-350
courtesy Dave Rogers
Dave's Guitars Shop

GRADING	100% MINT	98% NEAR MINT	95% EXC+	90% EXC	80% VG+	70% VG	60% G

SB 400 - similar to SB 300, except has a long scale length, available in Cherry finish. Approx. 940 mfg. 1971-73.

| | N/A | $350 | $300 | $250 | $200 | $175 | $150 |

SB 450 - similar to SB 350, except has a long scale length, available in Cherry, Natural, or Walnut finish, mfg. 1972-76.

| | N/A | $375 | $325 | $275 | $225 | $195 | $175 |

SG-Z (BAZ-) - double sharp cutaway, SG style mahogany body and neck with rosewood fingerboard with split diamond inlays, dual Z-bass pickups, black pearloid pickguard, black chrome hardware, available in Heritage Cherry (HC) or Ebony (EB) finishes, mfg. 1998-2001.

| | $1,100 | $950 | $800 | $700 | $600 | $500 | $425 |

Last MSR was $2,152.

SG REISSUE BASS (BASG) - SG body style with one mini-humbucker bridge and one bass humbucker pickup, black pickguard, three knobs, gold hardware, available in Cherry (CH) or Ebony (EB) finishes, new 2005.

| MSR | $1,408 | $1,025 | $875 | $750 | $625 | $550 | $475 | $400 |

Add $120 for Heritage Cherry Sunburst finish.

VICTORY ARTIST - offset double cutaway asymmetrical alder body, black pickguard, bolt-on maple neck, 24-fret extended rosewood fingerboard with offset pearl dot inlay, fixed bridge, blackface peghead with screened logo, 4-on-a-side tuners, chrome hardware, 2 humbucker pickups, volume/treble/bass controls, electronics/phase switches, active electronics, available in Antique Fireburst or Candy Apple Red finishes, mfg. 1981-86.

| | N/A | $600 | $525 | $450 | $375 | $350 | $325 |

Victory Custom - similar to Victory Artist, except has no active electronics, mfg. 1982-84.

| | N/A | $525 | $450 | $375 | $300 | $275 | $250 |

Victory Standard - similar to Victory Artist, except has 1 humbucker pickup, volume/tone control, phase switch, no active electronics, available in Candy Apple Red or Silver finishes, mfg. 1981-87.

| | N/A | $425 | $375 | $300 | $250 | $225 | $200 |

ELECTRIC BASS: LES PAUL BASS SERIES

List Prices included a hardshell case.

LES PAUL BASS - single sharp cutaway solid mahogany body, bound body, control plate, mahogany neck, 24-fret bound rosewood fingerboard with pearl block inlay, fixed bridge with metal cover, bound peghead with pearl split diamond/logo inlay, 2-per-side tuners, chrome hardware, 2 humbucker pickups with metal rings, volume/treble/bass controls, 3-position pickup/tone switches, impedance/phase switches, available in Walnut finish, approx. 2,575 mfg. 1971-1976.

| | N/A | $1,000 | $900 | $800 | $700 | $600 | $525 |

LES PAUL SIGNATURE BASS - hollow offset double cutaway, arched maple top, raised cream pickguard, f-holes, maple back/sides, mahogany neck, 22-fret rosewood fingerboard with pearl trapezoid inlay, fixed bridge with cover, 2-per-side tuners, chrome hardware, humbucker pickup, plastic pickup cover with stamped logo, volume/tone controls, level switch, available in Gold Top or Sunburst finishes, approx. 625 mfg. 1973-79.

| | N/A | $1,250 | $1,100 | $950 | $800 | $700 | $600 |

This model had walnut back/sides with Gold Top finish.

LES PAUL TRIUMPH BASS - single sharp cutaway mahogany body, bound body, control plate, mahogany neck, 24-fret bound rosewood fingerboard with pearl block inlay, fixed bridge with metal cover, bound peghead with pearl split diamond/logo inlay, 2-per-side tuners, chrome hardware, 2 humbucker pickups with metal rings, volume/treble/bass controls, 3-position pickup/tone switches, impedance/phase switches, available in Walnut or White finishes, mfg. 1975-79.

| | N/A | $950 | $875 | $800 | $725 | $650 | $550 |

LES PAUL SMARTWOOD BASS - single cutaway semi-hollow mahogany body, flat maple top, set-in neck, 34 in. scale, 20-fret chechen fingerboard with mother-of-pearl trapezoid inlay, fixed bridge, 2-per-side tuners, gold hardware, 2 Gibson TB+ humbucker pickups, 2 volume/2 tone controls, 3-position pickup selector switch, Bartolini TCT active preamp, available in Antique Natural, Heritage Cherry Sunburst, Earthburst, Ebony, or Emerald handrubbed finishes (available in polyurethane option).

While advertised in 1998, this model was never produced. SmartWood is a program of the Rainforest Alliances, an international non-profit conservation organization that certifies that certain woods are harvested in a sustainable manner.

LES PAUL SPECIAL 4-STRING BASS - single cutaway mahogany body, set-in mahogany neck, 34 in. scale, 24-fret ebony fingerboard with pearl dot inlay, fixed bridge, 2-per-side tuners, black chrome hardware, 2 TB+ humbucker pickups, volume/blend/bass/treble controls, Bartolini TCT active preamp, available in Classic White, Ebony, Heritage Cherry Sunburst, or Trans. Amber polyurethane finishes, includes hardshell case, mfg. 1997-98.

| | $1,200 | $1,050 | $925 | $800 | $700 | $600 | $500 |

Last MSR was $2,100.

Les Paul Special 5-String - similar to the Deluxe except has five strings, 3/2-per-side tuners.

| | $1,300 | $1,125 | $950 | $825 | $700 | $600 | $500 |

Last MSR was $2,200.

Add $60 for lined fretless fingerboard, $60 for fretless fingerboard (unlined), $100 for chrome hardware, $100 for gold hardware, or $300 for LP Premium Plus flame maple top.

LES PAUL DELUXE 4-STRING BASS - similar to the Les Paul Special, except has pearl trapezoid fingerboard inlays, 2 Bartolini bass humbucker pickups, available in Clear, Heritage Cherry Sunburst, Honey Burst, Trans. Amber, Trans. Black, Trans. Blue, Trans. Green, Trans. Red, Vintage Sunburst polyurethane or Handrubbed Oil finishes, mfg. 1997-98.

| | $1,400 | $1,200 | $1,000 | $900 | $800 | $700 | $600 |

Last MSR was $2,300.

GRADING	100% MINT	98% NEAR MINT	95% EXC+	90% EXC	80% VG+	70% VG	60% G

Les Paul Deluxe 5-String - similar to the Deluxe except has five strings, 3/2-per-side tuners.

	$1,450	$1,250	$1,050	$925	$800	$700	$600

Last MSR was $2,400.

LES PAUL STANDARD BASS 4-STRING (BAL3) - similar to the Les Paul Special, except has
bound maple top, pearl trapezoid fingerboard inlay, chrome hardware, 2 piece bridge, two-per-side tuners, available in Clear (disc. 1998), Ebony (disc. 1998), Heritage Cherry Sunburst (HS), Honey Burst (HB), Trans. Amber (disc. 1998), Vintage Sunburst (VB) polyurethane or Handrubbed Oil (disc. 1998) finishes, mfg. 1997-present.

MSR	$2,708	$1,825	$1,325	$1,075	$925	$800	$700	$600

Les Paul Standard Bass 5-String - similar to the Standard except in 5-String configuration, 3/2-per-side tuners, disc. 1998.

	$1,750	$1,250	$1,075	$925	$825	$725	$625

Last MSR was $2,630.

Add $100 for chrome hardware.

LES PAUL DOUBLE CUTAWAY BASS (BLD4) - asymetrical double cutaway Les Paul body style,
22-fret fingerboard with dot inlay, two bass humbucker pickups, three knobs, chrome hardware, available in Black Cherry (BC) or Root Beer finishes, new 2005.

MSR	$1,888	$1,375	$1,175	$950	$825	$700	$600	$500

ELECTRIC BASS: LPB (LES PAUL BASS) SERIES

LPB-1 - single cutaway mahogany body/neck, 20-fret ebony fingerboard with pearl dot inlay, fixed bridge, blackface peghead with pearl logo inlay, 2-per-side tuners, black hardware, 2 covered humbucker pickups, volume/treble/bass/pan controls, active electronics, available in Ebony, Classic White, Heritage Cherry, or Translucent Amber finishes, mfg. 1992-96.

	$750	$625	$525	$425	$375	$350	$325

Last MSR was $1,050.

**Gibson SG Reissue Bass
courtesy Gibson**

In 1994, Translucent Amber finish was discontinued.

LPB-1/5 - similar to LPB-1, except has 5 strings, 2/3-per-side tuners, disc. 1996.

	$750	$625	$525	$425	$375	$350	$325

Last MSR was $1,050.

LPB-2 - similar to LPB-1, except has figured maple top, trapezoid fingerboard inlay, Bartolini pickups, available in Heritage Cherry Sunburst, Trans. Amber, Trans. Black, Trans. Blue and Trans. Red finishes, disc. 1996.

	$900	$800	$700	$625	$550	$475	$400

Last MSR was $1,475.

In 1994, Translucent Amber, Translucent Black, Translucent Blue and Translucent Red finishes were discontinued.

LPB-2/5 - similar to LPB-2, except has 5 strings, 2/3-per-side tuners, available in Heritage Cherry Sunburst or Translucent Amber finishes, disc. 1996.

	$925	$825	$725	$625	$550	$475	$400

Last MSR was $1,560.

LPB-2 Premium - similar to LPB-1, except has figured maple top, trapezoid fingerboard inlay, Bartolini pickups, available in Heritage Cherry Sunburst, Honey Burst, Trans. Amber, or Vintage Sunburst finishes, disc. 1996.

	$925	$825	$725	$625	$550	$475	$400

Last MSR was $1,560.

In 1994, Honey Burst and Vintage Sunburst finishes were discontinued.

LPB-3 - similar to LPB-1, except has bound maple top, abalone trapezoid fingerboard inlay, chrome hardware, available in Ebony finish, disc. 1996.

	$995	$875	$775	$675	$575	$475	$400

Last MSR was $1,650.

Add $200 for Heritage Cherry Sunburst, Honey Burst, and Vintage Sunburst finishes.

LPB-3 Plus - similar to LPB-1, except has bound figured maple top, abalone trapezoid fingerboard inlay, chrome hardware, available in Heritage Cherry Sunburst, Honey Burst, Trans. Amber, or Vintage Sunburst finishes, disc. 1994.

	$1,200	$1,050	$900	$800	$700	$600	$500

Last MSR was $2,150.

LPB-3 Premium Plus - similar to LPB-1, except has bound highest quality figured maple top, abalone trapezoid fingerboard inlay, chrome hardware, available in Heritage Cherry Sunburst, Honey Burst, Trans. Amber, or Vintage Sunburst finishes, disc. 1996.

	$1,475	$1,250	$1,000	$875	$775	$675	$575

Last MSR was $2,400.

**Gibson Les Paul
Standard Bass
courtesy Gibson**

In 1994, Translucent Amber finish was discontinued.

LPB-3/5 Premium Plus - similar to LPB-1, except has 5 strings, bound highest quality figured maple top, abalone trapezoid fingerboard inlay, 2/3-per-side tuners, chrome hardware, available in Heritage Cherry Sunburst, Honey Burst, or Vintage Sunburst finishes, mfg. 1994-96.

	$1,475	$1,250	$1,000	$875	$775	$675	$575

Last MSR was $2,400.

GRADING	100% MINT	98% NEAR MINT	95% EXC+	90% EXC	80% VG+	70% VG	60% G

ELECTRIC BASS: THUNDERBIRD SERIES

THUNDERBIRD - reverse body, two pickups, available in Ebony, Natural, Mahogany, or Tobacco Sunburst (most common), 500 mfg. 1979.

	N/A	$1,450	$1,250	$1,075	$925	$800	$700

THUNDERBIRD II - asymmetrical hourglass style mahogany body, layered white pickguard with engraved Thunderbird logo, thumb rest, through-body mahogany neck, 20-fret rosewood fingerboard with pearl dot inlay, Tune-O-Matic bridge/stop tailpiece, 6-on-a-side tuners, chrome hardware, single coil pickups with cover, volume/tone controls, available in Custom Color and Sunburst finishes, approx. 1,150 mfg. 1963-69.

1963-1965 (REVERSE)	N/A	$3,500	$3,100	$2,750	$2,300	$1,975	$1,600
1966-1969 (NON-REVERSE)	N/A	$2,150	$1,850	$1,650	$1,400	$1,300	$1,200

In 1965, body/neck were redesigned and replaced original part/design.

THUNDERBIRD IV - similar to Thunderbird II, except has 2 pickups. Approx. 600 mfg. 1964-69.

1963-1965 (REVERSE)	N/A	$4,500	$4,000	$3,600	$3,200	$2,800	$2,300
1966-1969 (NON-REVERSE)	N/A	$2,000	$1,775	$1,600	$1,400	$1,275	$1,150

In 1965, body/neck were redesigned and replaced original part/design.

THUNDERBIRD 1976 BICENTENNIAL - similar to Thunderbird, except has red and blue Centennial Thunderbird figure (with stars) on white pickguard, three point adjustable tailpiece, 34.5 in. scale, rosewood fingerboard with dot inlay, available in Ebony, Natural Mahogany, White (rare), or Sunburst finishes, mfg. 1976 only.

	N/A	$1,500	$1,295	$1,100	$875	$750	$700

THUNDERBIRD IV (BAT4) - asymmetrical hourglass style mahogany body, white pickguard with engraved Thunderbird symbol, through-body 9-piece mahogany/walnut neck, 20-fret ebony fingerboard with pearl dot inlay, fixed bridge, partial blackface peghead with pearl logo inlay, 4-on-a-side tuners, black chrome hardware, 2 covered pickups, 2 volume/1 tone controls, available in Cardinal Red (disc.), Classic White (CW), Ebony (EB), and Vintage Sunburst (VS), Natural (NA, 1999-2004), Natural Burst (NB, 1999-2004), or Ebony Stain (ES 1999-2004) finishes, mfg. 1987-present.

MSR	$2,418		$1,700	$1,250	$1,075	$775	$725	$675

In 1994, Cardinal Red and Vintage Sunburst finishes were discontinued; Tobacco Sunburst (TS) finish was introduced. In 1999, Vintage Sunburst was reintroduced. In 1998, Tobacco Sunburst (TS) finish was discontinued.

THUNDERBIRD NIKKI SIXX SIGNATURE BLACKBIRD - similar to Thunderbird IV, except has Flat Black finish and black chrome hardware, Thunderbird bridge with Opti-Grab handle, iron cross inlays in ebony fingerboard, on/off toggle switch, dual Thunderbird pickups with "Blackbird" pickguard, includes Nikki Sixx signature hardshell case, mfg. 2000-2002.

	$1,850	$1,350	$1,150	$900	$800	$725	$675

Last MSR was $2,691.

THUNDERBIRD STUDIO (BTS) - four- of five-string configuration Thunderbird body style with two black pickups, available in Cherry (CH) or Ebony (EB) finishes only, new 2005.

MSR	$1,408		$1,025	$875	$750	$625	$550	$475	$400

Add $80 for five-string configuration.

GIFFIN GUITARS

Instruments currently produced in Portland, OR, since 2004. Previously produced in San Fernando Valley, CA from 1988-2004, and in England from the late 1960s-1988.

Luthier Roger Giffin has been building custom guitars and basses since the late 1960s. He ran a guitar shop that built and repaired guitars in London, England. In the late 1970s, he designed a guitar that would later become the Steinberger M Series. Gibson took interest in the guitar and Giffin was offered a job at the West Coast Gibson Custom Shop. He moved to Los Angeles, CA in 1988, and worked there until all custom shop material was moved to Nashville in 1993. In 1994, Brett Allen and Giffin started the R & B Instrument Service in L.A., where they mainly did repairs. In 1997, Giffin decided to branch out on his own again and started building guitars. He produced guitars in L.A. until June, 2004, when he relocated to Portland, OR. Giffin builds guitars under the philosophy that a hands-on approach to guitar building allows himself to build unique and individual instruments. The very highest standard of hand building instruments is used. For more information or for ordering, contact Giffin directly (see Trademark Index).

ELECTRIC

Giffin produces a variety of instruments in 6- and 12-string configurations. His most popular model is possibly the Standard, which is a cross between the Stratocaster and Les Paul that he developed back in the 1970s. Other models include the Model-T, Macro, Micro, and Drop-Tuned (baritone style). Prices typically start around $2,500 - 3,000 depending on model and options. Giffin will also build instruments on a custom-order basis.

GILCHRIST, STEPHEN

Instruments currently built in Australia. Distributed by the Carmel Music Company of Carmel, CA.

Australian luthier Stephen Gilchrist is known for his high quality mandolins, mandolas and mandocellos. Gilchrist began building instruments in 1976, and spent 1980 in the U.S. working in Nashville, Tennessee at Gruhn Guitars. After 1980, Gilchrist returned to Australia and continues to produce guitars and mandolins. For further information regarding current model specifications and pricing, contact the Carmel Music Company directly (see Trademark Index). Gilchrist has built a number of acoustic and electric guitars; most of the electric guitars were built between 1987 to 1988. To make identification of these guitars a bit difficult, some models do not have the Gilchrist name anywhere on the instrument and none of them have a serial number.

GILES

Instruments previously produced in Bellingham, MA. Distributed by Giles USA/AD & G Enterprises of Bellingham, MA.

Designer/luthier Allen Giles offered a retro-styled/advanced composition guitar model that was reasonably priced. Giles' KL-200 model featured a bolt-on maple neck combined with a resin cast body. The resin cast body was designed to recreate the tonal and sustain qualities of more expensive tone woods. Both the body and the necks were produced in the USA. The composite guitar was offered in part due to other big-name manufacturers (Gibson, Martin) producing guitars out of more environmental-friendly products.

GRADING	100% MINT	98% NEAR MINT	95% EXC+	90% EXC	80% VG+	70% VG	60% G

ELECTRIC

The **KL-200** had an offset double cutaway resin cast body with a cutaway in the lower bout. The bolt-on maple neck had a hand-rubbed oil finish, and featured a 22-fret fingerboard of either maple or rosewood. The chrome (or black) hardware included a vintage-style 6-screw tremolo, and Sperzel locking tuners. The Bill Lawrence pickups were available in either a 3 single coil or 2 single/humbucker configuration; and had volume and tone controls, and a 5-way pickup selector. All electronic elements were mounted to a pearloid pickguard, available in Black, Candy Apple Red, Pearl White, Sea Foam Green, Viper Blue, Gold, Woodland Green, Teal, and Viper Red high gloss finishes. The last retail list price was $850, and Giles offered such custom shop upgrades as painted body color and pickguards, Floyd Rose or Point Technology tremolos, or different pickups. Even though these were built in the USA, prices do not command a premium and used models can be found for less than $400.

**Gibson Thunderbird IV
courtesy Gibson**

GITTLER

Instruments previously handbuilt by Allan Gittler in New York from mid-1970s to mid-1980s. Between 1986 and 1987 the Astron company of Israel produced commercial versions based on the original unique design.

Designer Allan Gittler introduced an electric guitar that expressed its design through function. This guitar is a unique design in that there is only a metal frame with frets welded on it – no wood exists in the guitar. Gittler produced the first 60 instruments himself in the U.S., and an additional 500 were produced by Astron in Israel under an agreement. A few Gittler basses were produced as well. In 1982, Gittler moved to Israel and took the Hebrew name of Avraham Bar Rashi. Bar Rashi offered a new, innovative, wood constructed design that further explores his guitar concepts for a few years. Gittler passed away in 2002 (information courtesy of Brian Gidyk, Vancouver, Canada).

ELECTRIC

GITTLER - metal frame guitar, no headstock, 31-frets, mfg. mid-1970s-mid-1980s.

	100%	98%	95%	90%	80%	70%	60%
1970S-1982	N/A	$3,500	$3,000	$2,500	$2,200	$1,900	$1,600
1984-1986	N/A	$1,500	$1,200	$1,000	$850	$700	$600

GLOBE

See Goodman. See chapter on House Brands.

This trademark has been identified as a House Brand of the Goodman Community Discount Center, circa 1958-1960 (source: Willie G. Moseley, *Stellas & Stratocasters*).

GLORY

Instruments currently produced in China.

Glory produces electric guitars and basses that are based mainly off traditional American designs including the Stratocaster, Telecaster, Les Paul, ES-335, Jazz Bass, and the Precision bass among others. For more information regarding the Glory brand, refer to the website (see Trademark Index).

GODIN

Instruments currently built in La Patrie and Princeville, Quebec, in Canada; and Berlin, New Hampshire since 1987. Distributed by La Si Do, Inc. of St. Laurent, Canada.

Although the trademark and instruments bearing his name are relatively new, Robert Godin has been a mainstay in the guitar building industry since 1972. Godin got his first guitar at age seven and never looked back. By the time he was 15, he was working at La Tosca Musique in Montreal selling guitars and learning about minor repairs and set up work. Before long, Robert´s passion for guitar playing was eclipsed by his fascination with the construction of the instruments themselves. In 1968 Godin set up a custom guitar shop in Montreal called Harmonilab. Harmonilab quickly became known for its excellent work and musicians were coming from as far away as Quebec City to have their guitars adjusted. Harmonilab was the first guitar shop in Quebec to use professional strobe tuners for intonating guitars.

Although Harmonilab´s business was flourishing, Robert was full of ideas for the design and construction of acoustic guitars. So in 1972, the Norman Guitar Company was born. From the beginning the Norman guitars showed signs of the innovations that Godin would eventually bring to the guitar market. Perhaps the most significant item about the Norman history is that it represented the beginning of guitar building in the village of La Patrie, Quebec. La Patrie has since become an entire town of guitar builders - more on that later.

By 1978, Norman guitars had become quite successful in Canada and France, while at the same time the people in La Patrie were crafting replacement necks and bodies for the electric guitar market. Before long there was a lineup at the door of American guitar companies that wanted Godin´s crew to supply all their necks and bodies.

In 1980 Godin introduced the Seagull guitar. With many innovations like a bolt-on neck (for consistent neck pitch), pointed headstock (straight string pull) and a handmade solid top, the Seagull was designed for an ease of play for the entry level to intermediate guitar player. Most striking was the satin lacquer finish. Godin borrowed the finishing idea that was used on fine violins, and applied it to the acoustic guitar. When the final version of the Seagull guitar went into production, Godin went about the business of finding a sales force to help introduce the Seagull into the U.S. market. Several independent U.S. sales agents jumped at the chance to get involved with this new guitar, and armed with samples off they went into the market. A couple of months passed, and not one guitar was sold. Rather than retreat back to Harmonilab, Godin decided that he would have to get out there himself and explain the Seagull guitar concept. So he bought himself an old Ford Econoline van and stuffed it full of about 85 guitars, and started driving through New England visiting guitar shops and introducing the Seagull guitar. Acceptance of this new guitar spread, and by 1985 La Si Do was incorporated and the factory in La Patrie expanded to meet the growing demand.

**Gibson Thunderbird Studio
courtesy Gibson**

GRADING	100% MINT	98% NEAR MINT	95% EXC+	90% EXC	80% VG+	70% VG	60% G

Godin introduced the La Patrie brand of classical acoustic guitars in 1982. The La Patrie trademark was used to honor the town's tradition of luthiery that had developed during the first ten years since the inception of the Norman guitars trademark. In 1985, Godin also introduced the Simon & Patrick line (named after his two sons) for people interested in a more traditional instrument. Simon & Patrick guitars still maintained a number of Seagull innovations.

Since Godin's factory had been producing necks and bodies for various American guitar companies since 1978, he combined that knowledge with his background in acoustic guitar design for an entirely new product. The Acousticaster was debuted in 1987, and represented the first design under the Godin name. The Acousticaster was designed to produce an acoustic sound from an instrument that was as easy to play as the player's favorite electric guitar. This was achieved through the help of a patented mechanical harp system inside the guitar. Over the past few years, the Godin name has become known for very high quality and innovative designs. Robert Godin is showing no signs of slowing down, having recently introduced the innovative models Multiac, LGX, and LGX-SA.

Today, La Si Do Inc. employs close to 500 people in four factories located in La Patrie and Princeville, Quebec (Canada), and Berlin, New Hampshire. Models of the La Si Do guitar family are in demand all over the world, and Godin is still on the road teaching people about guitars. In a final related note, the Ford Econoline van "died" with about 300,000 miles on it about 14 years ago, (Company History courtesy Robert Godin and Katherine Calder [Artist Relations], La Si Do, Inc., June 5, 1996).

PRODUCTION MODEL CODES

Godin is currently using a system similar to the original Gretsch system, in that the company is assigning both a model name and a four-digit number that indicates the color finish specific to that guitar model. Thus, the four digit code will indicate which model and color from just one number. References in this text will list the four digit variances for color finish within the model designations.

ELECTRIC: ARTISAN SERIES

ARTISAN ST I (MODEL 3990) - offset double cutaway light maple body, carved bird's-eye maple top, bolt-on rock maple neck, 22-fret rosewood or maple fingerboard with offset dot inlay, 21st fret pearl block inlay, Schaller 2000 tremolo, 6-on-a-side locking Schaller tuners, gold hardware, 3 Godin twin blade pickups, volume/tone controls, 5-position switch, available in Antique Violin Brown, Cognacburst, and Trans. Blue finishes, disc. 1998.

$875	$725	$625	$550	$450	$375	$275

Last MSR was $1,095.

Early models may have 22-fret ebony fingerboard with offset dot inlay/pearl block inlay at 21st fret, and a Wilkinson vibrato. Models were available in Trans. Black and Trans. Purple finishes.

Artisan ST Signature (Model 11675) - similar to Artisan ST-I, except has carved figured maple top, rock maple neck, maple or rosewood fingerboard, 3 Seymour Duncan Lil '59 pickups, disc.

$1,050	$850	$750	$650	$525	$425	$325

Last MSR was $1,295.

Add $350 for AAA Grade top.

Maple fingerboard: Available in Antique Violin Brown (Model 11667), Cognacburst (Model 11681), and Trans. Blue (Model 11675) finishes. Rosewood fingerboard: Available in Antique Violin Brown (Model 11698), Cognacburst (Model 11711), and Trans. Blue (Model 11704) finishes. Early models may feature a quilted maple top, and ebony fingerboards.

Artisan ST II - similar to Artisan ST I, except has carved arched top, vintage-style vibrato, 6-on-a-side non-locking tuners, 3 Godin twin blade passive pickups, volume/push/pull tone (Michael Braun EQ system) controls, 5-way selector switch, available in Blue and Black finishes, disc. 1995.

Research continues on the Artisan ST II model and pricing.

Artisan ST II Ultimate - similar to Artisan ST II, except has Wilkinson vibrato, 6-on-a-side staggered locking tuners, available in Blue and Black finishes, disc. 1995.

Research continues on the Artisan ST II Ultimate model and pricing.

Artisan ST IV - similar to Artisan ST I, except has vintage-style Schaller 4000 vibrato, 2 Tetrad (twin) blade/Tetrad Combo humbucker Godin pickups, available in Cognacburst high gloss and Violin Brown satin finishes, disc. 1997.

$675	$550	$475	$400	$350	$300	$250

Last MSR was $960.

This model has an optional maple fingerboard with black inlay.

Artisan ST V - similar to Artisan ST I, except has longer bass/shorter treble horns offset cutaway body, Canadian maple top, rosewood fingerboard with offset dot inlay, double locking vibrato, 6-on-a-side non-locking tuners, black hardware, Godin twin blade/Tetrad Combo humbucker pickups, volume/push/pull tone (Michael Braun EQ system) controls, 3-way selector switch, available in Trans. Amber, Trans. Blue, or Trans. Green finishes, disc. 1996.

Research continues on the Artisan ST V model and pricing.

Artisan ST VI - similar to Artisan ST V, except has Schaller Floyd Rose II double locking vibrato, non-locking tuners, black hardware, Tetrad Combo humbucker/Tetrad blade/Tetrad Combo humbucker Godin pickups, available in Black or Trans. Green finishes, disc. 1997.

$700	$575	$500	$425	$375	$325	$275

Last MSR was $990.

The Transparent Green finish was available with a figured maple top.

ARTISAN TC SIGNATURE (MODEL 4515, ARTISAN TC I) - single cutaway light maple body, carved figured maple top, bolt-on rock maple neck, 22-fret maple or rosewood fingerboard with offset dot inlay, "dish style" fixed bridge, 6-on-a-side tuners, gold hardware, 2 Godin Tetrad twin blade pickups, volume/tone controls, 3-position switch, disc. 1998.

$950	$800	$675	$575	$400	$425	$350

Last MSR was $1,195.

Maple fingerboard: Available in Antique Violin Brown (Model 4508), Cognacburst (Model 4522), and Trans. Blue (Model 4515) finishes. Rosewood fingerboard: Available in Antique Violin Brown (Model 4591), Cognacburst (Model 4614), and Trans. Blue (Model 4607) finishes. Early TC I models may have ebony fingerboards, bird's-eye maple necks, and the (push/pull) Michael Braun EQ system controls.

GRADING	100% MINT	98% NEAR MINT	95% EXC+	90% EXC	80% VG+	70% VG	60% G

Artisan TC II - similar to Artisan TC I, except has carved arched top, 2 Godin twin blade passive pickups, volume/push/pull tone (Michael Braun EQ system) controls, 3-way selector switch, available in White finish, disc. 1995.

Research continues on the Artisan TC II model and pricing.

ELECTRIC: G SERIES

The G Series body shape was derived from the Artisan ST V model.

G-1000 - longer bass/shorter treble horns offset cutaway light maple body, rock maple neck, 24.75 in. scale, 24-fret maple or rosewood fingerboard with dot inlay, vintage-style tremolo, 6-on-a-side tuners, gold hardware, pickguard, 2 Godin exposed polepiece single coil/humbucker pickups, volume/tone controls, 5-way selector switch, available in Black, Cognacburst, and Trans. Blue high gloss finishes; Trans. Amber, or Antique Violin (Burst) satin lacquer finishes, disc. 1996.

	N/A	$500	$450	$400	$350	$300	$250

G-4000 - similar to G-1000, except has deluxe Schaller vintage-style tremolo, Schaller locking tuners, available in Black, Cognacburst, Trans. Blue Burst, or Trans. Violet high gloss finishes; Antique Violin (Burst) satin lacquer finish, disc. 1996.

	N/A	$500	$450	$400	$350	$300	$250

G-5000 - similar to G-1000, except has 25.5" scale, rosewood fingerboard, no pickguard, Tetrad twin blade/Tetrad Combo humbucker pickups, Schaller Floyd Rose II locking tremolo, Schaller locking tuners, MFB mid filter EQ control, available in Black or Red high gloss finishes, disc. 1996.

	N/A	$550	$475	$425	$375	$325	$275

Godin LG SP90
courtesy Godin

ELECTRIC: LG SERIES

LG Series models were originally equipped with Godin Tetrad (hum cancelling single coil) pickups. The S designation indicates Seymour Duncan pickups.

LG S (MODEL 7882) - single cutaway Honduran mahogany body, mahogany neck, 24.75 in. scale, 24-fret Indian rosewood fingerboard with dot inlay, fixed tuneomatic-style bridge, 3-per-side Schaller 'Klouson' Pro Series tuners, matching finish headstock, black hardware, 2 Seymour Duncan custom humbucker pickups, volume/tone controls, 3-position switch, available in Natural (Model 7882) or Transparent Red (Model 7868) semi-gloss finishes, mfg. 1997-98.

	$600	$525	$450	$375	$300	$250	$200

Last MSR was $725.

Add $20 for Black Pearl (Model 10615) and CognacBurst (Model 7875) high gloss finishes.

LG Humbucker - similar to the LG S, except features 2 Godin Tetrad Combo pickups, volume/push/pull tone (MFB mid filter) controls, 5-way switch, available in Natural satin lacquer finish, disc. 1997.

MSR	$625	$500	$425	$375	$325	$275	$235	$195

Add $50 for Black Pearl, CognacBurst, Dark Gold, and Trans. Red high gloss finishes.

LG SP90 - single cutaway mahogany body, mahogany neck with rosewood fingerboard, 24.75 in. scale, 24-frets, 3-per-side tuners, strings through-body, 1 Volume/1 Tone, 2 Seymour Duncan SP90 single coil pickups, 3-way switch, fixed" tun-o-matic" style bridge, available in natural, Cognac, Dark Gold, Trans. Red, or Black Pearl finishes, current mfg.

MSR	$625	$500	$425	$375	$325	$275	$235	$195

Add $50 for Cognac Burst, Trans. Red, Black Pearl, or Dark Gold finishes.

LGT S (MODEL 11612) - similar to the LG S, except features a light maple body, Schaller Trem 2000 tremolo, 3-per-side Schaller locking tuners, pickguard, 2 Tetrad blade single coil/Seymour Duncan humbucker pickups, 5-way selector switch, available in Aqua (11612), Black Pearl (11643), Cream (11636), Trans. Blue (11629), or Trans. Red (11650) high gloss finishes, mfg. 1997-98.

	$650	$575	$500	$425	$350	$275	$200

Last MSR was $795.

LGT (Model 7493) - similar to the LGT S, except features 2 Godin single coil/Tetrad Combo pickups, volume/push/pull tone (MFB mid filter) controls, 5-way switch, available in Aqua (8742), Black (8780), Cream (8759), Trans. Blue (7493), or Trans. Red (7509) high gloss finishes, disc. 1997.

	$650	$575	$500	$425	$350	$275	$200

Last MSR was $795.

LG SIGNATURE - single cutaway mahogany body, carved flamed maple top, mahogany neck, rosewood fingerboard with offset dot inlays, 2 Seymour Duncan humbucker pickups, Schaller bridge, 2 knobs, 5-way switch, black hardware, available in Trans. Blue, Trans. Black, or Cognacburst finishes, current mfg.

MSR	$1,095	$900	$750	$650	$575	$500	$425	$350

Add $320 for AAA top.

ELECTRIC: LGX SERIES

The original **LGX** model featured both magnetic pickups and L.R. Baggs transducer saddles, and offered guitar players both the "electric voice" and the "acoustic voice" in the same instrument. A year later, the **LGX-SA** with Roland-Ready Synth Acess was introduced. The **LGXT** subsitutes a tremolo bridge for a Tune-O-Matic bridge/strings into-body; and the **LGX3** features 3 single coils instead of the two humbuckers on the LGX-SA.

GRADING	100% MINT	98% NEAR MINT	95% EXC+	90% EXC	80% VG+	70% VG	60% G

LGX (MODEL 7561) - rounded single cutaway mahogany body, carved figured maple top, 25.5 in. scale, mahogany neck, 22-fret rosewood fingerboard with dot inlay, "Godin style" tuneomatic bridge/strings into-body "fingers," 3-per-side tuners, gold hardware, 2 Godin Tetrad (twin blade) pickups, microtransducer bridge pickup, volume/tone/blend controls, 5-way magnetic pickup selector switch, magnetic/mix/transducer mini-switch, volume/treble/mid/bass transducer controls (4 sliders in bass bout), available in Black Pearl (10509), CognacBurst (10486), Mahogany (7578), Trans. Amber (7585), or Trans. Blue (7561) high gloss finishes, mfg. 1996-2002.

			$1,200	$1,000	$875	$750	$650	$550	$450

Last MSR was $1,475.

Add $50 for 2 Seymour Duncan custom humbucker pickups, available in Black Pearl (10516), CognacBurst (10493), Mahogany (7813), Trans. Amber (Model 7820), or Trans. Blue (7806) high gloss finishes. Add $350 for AAA Grade top.

LGX Left-Handed (Model 9718) - similar to the LGX-SA, except features a left-handed configuration, available in Mahogany (9718) high gloss finish, mfg. 1997-98.

			$1,350	$1,100	$950	$800	$650	$550	$450

Last MSR was $1,725.

LGX 3 (MODEL 11568) - rounded single cutaway maple body, 25.5 in. scale, mahogany neck, 22-fret rosewood fingerboard with dot inlay, "Godin style" tuneomatic bridge/strings into-body "fingers," 3-per-side tuners, gold hardware, 3 Seymour Duncan pickups (Lil '59s/Duckbucker), L.R. Baggs X-Bridge bridge pickup with custom preamp/EQ, volume/blend/tone controls, 5-way magnetic pickup selector switch, magnetic/mix/transducer mini-switch, volume/treble/mid/bass transducer controls (4 sliders in bass bout), available in Black Pearl (10568), Cream (11599), Trans. Blue (11582), or Trans. Red (11575) high gloss finishes, mfg. 1998-2002.

			$950	$825	$725	$650	$575	$500	$425

Last MSR was $1,250.

Add $170 for transparent colors.

LGX-SA WITH SYNTH ACCESS - rounded single cutaway mahogany body, carved figured maple top, 25.5 in. scale, mahogany neck, 22-fret ebony fingerboard with dot inlay, "Godin style" Tune-O-Matic bridge/strings into-body "fingers," 3-per-side tuners, gold hardware, 2 Godin Tetrad (twin blade) pickups, microtransducer bridge pickup, volume/synth volume/tone controls, 5-way magnetic pickup selector switch, magnetic/mix/transducer mini-switch, Program Up/Down synth control toggle mini-switch, volume/treble/mid/bass transducer controls (4 sliders in bass bout), 13 pin connector for Roland GR series guitar synths, 3 outputs (magnetics, bridge/mix, 13 pin connector), available in Black Pearl (10547), CognacBurst (10523), Mahogany (4911), Trans. Amber (4928), or Trans. Blue (4904) high gloss finishes, current mfg.

MSR	$1,795		$1,500	$1,300	$1,150	$1,000	$850	$725	$600

Add $320 for AAA top. Subtract $50 for no Seymour Duncan pickups.

LGX-SA With Synth Access Left-Handed (Model 9817) - similar to the LGX-SA, except features a left-handed configuration, available in Mahogany (9817) or Trans. Amber (Model 9824) high gloss finishes, mfg. 1997-2002.

			$1,700	$1,500	$1,300	$1,150	$1,000	$850	$700

Last MSR was $2,125.

Add $350 for AAA Grade top.

Earlier models may be designated Model 9770.

LGX T (MODEL 9688) - similar to the LGX-SA, except features maple body (no carved figured maple top), tremolo bridge, L.R. Baggs X-Bridge bridge pickup with custom preamp/EQ, 2 Seymour Duncan custom humbucker pickups, available in Black Pearl (10622), Cream (9701), Trans. Blue (9688), or Trans. Red (9695) high gloss finishes, mfg. 1997-present.

MSR	$1,595		$1,300	$1,150	$1,000	$850	$750	$650	$550

Add $320 for AAA Grade.

ELECTRIC: MISC. MODELS

EXIT 22 - single cutaway mahogany body, 24.75 in. scale, 12 in. radius rock maple neck, 22-fret maple or rosewood fingerboard, 3 Godin designed pickups in HSS configuration, fixed bridge, 6-on-one-side tuners, 5-way switch, 2 knobs, black hardware, available in Natural finish, mfg. 2004-present.

MSR	$495		$400	$350	$300	$250	$210	$170	$135

FLAT FIVE X - single cutaway body, carved maple top, silver maple leaf center with poplar wings, f-holes, 24.75 in. scale, mahogany neck, rosewood fingerboard, 2 Godin Flat Five humbucker pickups, Schaller acoustic transducer bridge, 3 knobs, 5-way switch, 1 mini switch, black hardware, available in Light Burst or Trans. Blue finishes, current mfg.

MSR	$1,995		$1,650	$1,450	$1,250	$1,100	$950	$800	$650

FREEWAY CLASSIC - offset double cutaway Strat style silver leaf maple body with poplar wings, 25.5 in. scale, 12 in. radius rock maple neck, 22-fret maple or rosewood fingerboard, 3 Godin designed pickups in HSH configuration, vintage tremolo bridge, 6-on-one-side tuners, 5-way switch, 2 knobs, chrome hardware, available in Black Pearl or Burgundy finishes, mfg. 2004-present.

MSR	$475		$395	$350	$300	$250	$200	$165	$130

Freeway Classic Leaftop - similar to the Freeway Classic, except has a premium grade highly figured maple top, available in Lightburst or Trans. Blue finishes, mfg. 2004-present.

MSR	$595		$495	$425	$375	$325	$275	$225	$175

MONTREAL - single cutaway chambered mahogany body, f-holes, 24.75 in. scale, mahogany neck, rosewood fingerboard, 2 Godin humbucker pickups, LR Baggs transducer bridge, custom pre-amp and 3 band EQ, 3 knobs, 5-way switch, black hardware, available in Natural finish, mfg. 2004-present.

MSR	$1,795		$1,500	$1,300	$1,150	$1,000	$850	$700	$550

GRADING	100% MINT	98% NEAR MINT	95% EXC+	90% EXC	80% VG+	70% VG	60% G

RADIATOR - single cutaway chambered Silver Leaf Maple body, Rock Maple neck, maple or rosewood fingerboard, dot position markers, 24.75 in. scale, 3-per-side tuners, 24 frets, 2 Godin-designed Low Noise single coil pickups, 2 Volume/1 Tone, full face white or black pearloid pickguard, available in Cream, Black Pearl, Black Chrome, Pace Car Blue, or Black Onyx finishes, current mfg.

MSR	$395	$325	$275	$245	$215	$185	$155	$125

Add $20 for Black Chrome finish.

SOLIDAC LEAFTOP - single cutaway Silver Leaf Maple body, mahogany neck with rosewood fingerboard, 22-frets, 25 ½" scale, 3-per-side tuners, tremolo bridge, 2 Volumes/1 Tone, two voice guitar with acoustic sound produced by a transducer equipped bridge and electric sounds by Godin design pickups in a humbucker-single-humbucker confuguration, 5-way switch, 2 outputs, available in high gloss Black Pearl, HG Trans. Red and HG Trans. Purple, current mfg.

MSR	$835	$675	$600	$525	$475	$425	$375	$325

XTSA LEAFTOP SYNTH ACCESS - single cutaway silver leaf maple body with poplar wings, 25.5 in. scale, 16 in. radius rock maple neck, ebony fingerboard, 3 Godin designed pickups in HSH configuration, tremolo bridge with RMC transducers, custom pre-amp and 3 band EQ, mulitple outputs for 13-pin Roland synth, 3 knobs, 5-way switch, 2 mini switches, chrome hardware, available in Dark Trans. Red or Trans. Black finishes, mfg. 2004-present.

MSR	$1,095	$900	$750	$650	$550	$475	$400	$325

MULTIAC JAZZ SYNTH ACCESS - Multiac style, silver leaf maple body with carved flame maple top, f-holes, 25.5 in. scale, silver leaf maple neck, ebony fingerboard, 1 mini-humbucker pickup, transducer bridge, custom RMC electronics, 13 pin output for synth, 2 knobs, gold hardware, available in Spruce or Lightburst flame finishes, current mfg.

MSR	$2,295	$1,900	$1,700	$1,500	$1,300	$1,150	$1,000	$850

ELECTRIC: SD SERIES

SD - single cutaway light maple body, bolt-on rock maple neck, 24.75 in. scale, 24-fret maple or rosewood fingerboard with dot inlay, vintage-style tremolo bridge, 6-on-a-side tuners, natural headstock finish, chrome hardware, pickguard, 2 Godin single coil/humbucker pickups, volume/tone controls, 5-position switch, current mfg.

MSR	$395	$325	$275	$245	$215	$185	$155	$125

Add $20 for Transparent colors. Maple fingerboard: Extreme Aqua (11117), Extreme Purple (11070), Trans. Blue (8896), Trans. Purple (10431), and Trans. Red (8902) high gloss finishes. Rosewood fingerboard: Extreme Aqua (11124), Extreme Purple (11087), Trans. Blue (Model 8827), Trans. Purple (10424), and Trans. Red (8834) high gloss finishes.

Maple Fingerboard: Available in Aqua (8872), Banana Cream (10752), Black Pearl (10455), Canary Yellow (10479), Cream (8865), Midnight Blue Pearl (10417), and Powder Blue (11032) high gloss finishes. Rosewood Fingerboard: Available in Aqua (8803), Banana Cream (10769), Black Pearl (10448), Canary Yellow (10462), Cream (8797), Midnight Blue Pearl (10400), and Powder Blue (11049) high gloss finishes.

SD With Schaller Floyd Rose (Model 9855) - similar to the SD, except features a Schaller licensed Floyd Rose tremolo, rosewood fingerboard (only), available in Aqua (Model 9831), Black Pearl (Model 10639), and Cream (Model 9879) high gloss finishes, disc 1999.

			$475	$425	$375	$325	$275	$225	$175

Last MSR was $625.

Add $20 for Trans. Blue (9855) and Trans. Red (9862) high gloss finishes.

SD Leaftop - similar to the SD, except has a premium grade of highly figured maple, available in Light Burst Quilted or Trans. Blue Flame finishes, current mfg.

MSR	$495	$400	$350	$300	$250	$200	$165	$130

SDXT - single cutaway silver leaf maple body with poplar wings, 25.5 in. scale, 12 in. radius rock maple neck, maple or rosewood fingerboard, 3 Godin designed pickups in HSH configuration, floating tremolo bridge, black pickguard, 2 knobs, 5-way switch, chrome hardware, available in Black Pearl, Red, or Midnight Blue finishes, current mfg.

MSR	$475	$395	$350	$300	$250	$210	$170	$130

SDXT Leaftop - similar to the SDXT, except has a premium grade of highly figured maple, available in Lightburst Quilted or Trans. Blue Flame finishes, current mfg.

MSR	$595	$495	$425	$375	$325	$275	$225	$175

ELECTRIC BASS

Add $350 for AAA Grade top.

BG 4 4-STRING - offset double cutaway 3-piece body, rock maple centre/light maple wings, 3-piece maple neck, 34 in. scale, 22-fret rosewood fingerboard with offset dot inlay, 2-per-side Schaller tuners, Schaller fixed bridge, EMG 40P5/EMG 40 soapbar pickups, volume/balance/dual EQ controls, available in Black (8766), Cream (9572), Trans. Blue (7424), or Trans. Red (9565) high-gloss finishes, current mfg.

MSR	$875	$700	$625	$550	$475	$425	$375	$325

BG 5 5-STRING - similar to the BG IV, except features a 5-string configuration, 3/2-per-side tuners, available in Black (8773), Cream (9596), Trans. Blue (7455), or Trans. Red (9589) high-gloss finishes, current mfg.

MSR	$975	$800	$725	$650	$575	$500	$425	$350

FREEWAY 4-STRING BASS - offset double cutaway silver leaf maple body, rock maple neck, 22-fret rosewood fingerboard with dot inlay, 2 Godin designed pickups, 3 knobs, chrome hardware, available in Black Pearl, Midnight Blue, or Burgundy finishes, current mfg.

MSR	$555	$450	$375	$325	$275	$235	$195	$155

Add $50 for Natural Flame SG finish.

Godin Exit 22
courtesy Godin

G

Godin SDXT Leaftop
courtesy Godin

GRADING	100% MINT	98% NEAR MINT	95% EXC+	90% EXC	80% VG+	70% VG	60% G

FREEWAY 5-STRING BASS - similar to the Freeway 4 Bass, except in 5-String configuration, 4/1-per-side tuners, current mfg.

MSR	$625		$500	$425	$350	$300	$250	$210	$170

Add $50 for Natural Flame SG finish.

SD BASS (MODEL 11735) - offset double cutaway maple body, maple neck, 34 in. scale, 22-fret rosewood fingerboard with offset dot inlay, 2-per-side tuners, fixed bridge, P/J-style Godin passive pickups, volume/tone controls, available in Black Pearl (11728), Cream (11742), Trans. Blue (11735), or Trans. Purple (11759) high-gloss finishes, mfg. 1998-2002.

			$450	$375	$325	$275	$235	$195	$165

Last MSR was $595 .

Add $100 for 5-string model.

SD PRO BASS (MODEL 11773) - similar to the SD Bass, except features Seymour Duncan Bassline pickups, available in Black Pearl (11766), Cream (11780), Trans. Blue (11773), or Trans. Purple (11797) high-gloss finishes, mfg. 1998-99.

			$675	$600	$525	$450	$400	$350	$300

Last MSR was $899.

GODWIN
Instruments previously built in Italy in the mid-1970s.

In 1967, Bob Murrell produced the first commercially available guitar that made organ sounds, named the GuitOrgan. The GuitOrgan featured Japanese-built hollowbody guitars and Baldwin-style circuitry. Following Murrell, the Vox company fused a Phantom model guitar with a Continental model organ around 1970, and named it the Guitar Organ. The Godwin company apparently thought that the third time was the charm when they introduced the Godwin Organ model guitar in the mid 1970s. Still a bargain if bought by the pound (not by the sound!), the Godwins were only produced for about a year. The instrument featured a double cutaway wood body, 2 independent single coil pickups, and 13 knobs - plus 19 switches! Even with a large amount of wood removed for the organ circuitry, the fairly deep-bodied guitar is still heavy (source: Tony Bacon, *The Ultimate Guitar Book*).

GOLDENTONE
Instruments previously produced in Japan during the 1960s.

The Goldentone trademark was used by U.S. importers Elger and its partner Hoshino Gakki Ten as one of the brandnames used in their joint guitar producing venture. Hoshino in Japan was shipping Fuji Gen Gakki-built guitars marketed in the U.S. as Goldentone, Elger, and eventually Ibanez. These solid body guitars featured original body designs in the early to mid 1960s (source: Michael Wright, *Guitar Stories*, Volume One).

GOLDEN WOOD
Instruments currently built in Gualala, CA.

The Golden Wood company is currently offering handcrafted guitars. For further information regarding specifications and pricing, please contact the Golden Wood company directly (see Trademark Index).

GOODFELLOW
See Lowden Guitars. Instruments currently built in Northern Ireland. Distributed in the US market by Quality First Products of Forest City, NC.

Goodfellow basses were introduced in the 1980s, and caught the eye of Lowden Guitars' Andy Kidd during an exhibit in Manchester. Kidd, originally offering to further spread the word and help subcontract some of the building, eventually acquired the company. These high quality basses feature select figured and exotic wood construction, as well as active tone circuitry and humbucking pickups designed by Kent Armstrong, available in 4-, 5-, or 6-string models, the ebony fingerboard spans a two octave neck. For further information, contact Lowden guitars directly (see Trademark Index).

GOODMAN
See chapter on House Brands.

This trademark has been identified as a House Brand of the Goodman Community Discount Center, circa 1961-1964. Previously, the company used the trademark of Globe (source: Willie G. Moseley, *Stellas & Stratocasters*).

GORDON SMITH GUITARS
Instruments currently produced in Partington, England since 1979.

This company builds both original designs and Fender/Gibson-style solid and semi-hollow body guitars. The name comes from the names of the two partners Gordon Whitham and John Smith. John Smith is the only one left in the partnership. All guitars are hand-crafted. Models feature company's own pickups and hardware, but hardware options changed through the years. There is a wide variety of models including the GS, GS Explorer, Gypsy, Graf Deluxe, Graduate, Griffin, Galaxy, Gemini (starting to see a pattern?), Classic S, Classic T, and Flying V Series.(Source: Tony Bacon and Paul Day, *The Guru's Guitar Guide*). For more information refer to their website (see Trademark Index).

GORDY
Instruments previously built in England from the mid 1980s-early 1990s.

Luthier Gordon Whitham founded Gordy guitars after he parted ways with the Gordon Smith Guitar company. Gordon produced original design solid body guitars such as the Red Shift, 1810, and Xcaster. Gordon also produced a headless Gordy bass. It is reported that Gordon stopped producing guitars in the early 1990s sometime and went into the electronic effect business. It is reported that a trainee of Gordon's still gives advice and does set-ups on Gordy guitars in the Manchester area.

GOSPEL
Instruments previously built in Bakersfield, California in the late 1960s. A second series was produced in Jonah's Ridge, North Carolina in the early 1980s.

In 1969, luthier Semie Moseley trademarked the Gospel brandname separate from his Mosrite company. Only a handful of late '60s Gospels were produced and featured a design based on Mosrite's Celebrity model guitar. Moseley also produced a Gospel model briefly under his own Mosrite label as well – the rare Gospel (trademark only) does not have the Mosrite name mentioned on the headstock. In the early '80s, Moseley again attempted to offer guitars to the gospel music industry. The Gospel guitars represent Semie Moseley's love of gospel music and his attempt to furnish gospel musicians with quality instruments, (Information courtesy of Andy Moseley and Hal Hammer, 1996).

GOYA

Instruments previously produced in Sweden circa 1900s to mid-1960s. Distributed by Hershman Musical Instrument Company of New York. Later Goya instruments were built in Korea from the early 1970s to 1996, and were distributed by The Martin Guitar Company, located in Nazareth, Pennsylvania.

The Goya trademark was originally used by the Hershman Musical Instrument Company of New York City, New York in the 1950s on models built by Sweden's Levin company (similar models were sold in Europe under the company's Levin trademark). Levin built high quality acoustic flattop, classical, and archtop guitars as well as mandolins. A large number of rebranded Goya instruments were imported to the U.S. market.

In the late 1950s, solidbody electric guitars and basses built by Hagstrom (also a Swedish company) were rebranded Goya and distributed in the U.S. as well. In 1963 the company changed its name to the Goya Musical Instrument Corporation. Goya was purchased by Avnet (see Guild) in 1966, and continued to import instruments such as the Rangemaster in 1967. By the late 1960s, electric solidbody guitars and basses were then being built in Italy by the EKO company. Avnet then sold the Goya trademark to Kustom Electronics. It has been estimated that the later Goya instruments of the 1970s were built in Japan.

The C. F. Martin company later acquired the Levin company, and bought the rights to the Goya trademark from a company named Dude, Inc. in 1976. Martin imported a number of guitar, mandolin, and banjo string instruments from the 1970s through to 1996. While this trademark is currently discontinued, the rights to the name are still held by the Martin Guitar company.

The Goya company featured a number of innovations that most people are not aware of. Goya was the first classic guitar line to put the trademark name on the headstock, and also created the ball end classic guitar string. Levin-Era Goya models feature interior paper label with the Goya trademark in a cursive style, and designated "Made by A.B. Herman Carlson Levin - Gothenburg, Sweden." Model and serial number appear on the label, as well as on the neck block.

ELECTRIC

While Goya mainly offered acoustic guitars, the first electrics debuted in the late 1950s. The first series of electrics were built by Hagstrom, and feature a sparkly plastic covering. A later series of electrics such as the Range Masters, were produced from 1967-1969 (by EKO of Italy) and featured pushbutton controls. Other Eko/Goya creations include the Panther, P-26, and P-46. Goya also offered a number of electric guitar amplifiers in the 1950s and 1960s.

GRAFFITI

Instruments previously built in England from the early to late 1980s.

While the instruments were indeed constructed in the UK, the parts themselves were from Italy or Japan. The guitars were medium-to-good quality Fender-styled solid body instruments (Source: Tony Bacon and Paul Day, *The Guru's Guitar Guide*).

GRAND

Instruments currently produced in China.

Grand produces entry level electric guitars and basses. There are various models and options offered.

GRANT

Instruments previously produced in Japan from the 1970s through the 1980s.

The Grant trademark was the brandname of a UK importer, and the guitars were medium quality copies of American designs (source: Tony Bacon and Paul Day, *The Guru's Guitar Guide*).

GRANTSON

Instruments previously produced in Japan during the mid-1970s.

These entry level guitars featured designs based on popular American models (Source: Tony Bacon and Paul Day, *The Guru's Guitar Guide*).

GRAY, KEVIN

Instruments previously built in Dallas, TX.

Luthier Kevin Gray built custom guitars, as well as performed repairs and restorations on instruments for a number of years.

ELECTRIC

Gray blended state of the art technology with handcrafted exotic wood tops. Standard features included a solid mahogany body and neck, 24-fret rosewood or ebony fingerboard, choice of 24 3/4 in. or 25 1/2 in. scale, and mother-of-pearl or abalone inlays. Gray also featured gold-plated hardware, Sperzel locking tuners, Seymour Duncan or Lindy Fralin pickups, and hand-rubbed lacquer finishes.

Gray offered four different variations of his custom guitars. The **Carved Top** (last retail was $2,995) featured an exotic wood top over the mahogany body, and had a set-neck. A **Marquetry Flat Top** (last retail was $2,995) had designs or scenes formed from exotic hardwoods, body binding, and a set-neck. An unsculpted exotic hardwood top and body binding was offered on the Flat Top (last retail was $2,795). Gray also built a **Contoured Top/Bolt-on** design (last retail was $2,495) with a carved maple top, maple neck, and either a maple, alder, or basswood body.

GRAZIOSO

See Futurama.

Godin BG 4 4-String
courtesy Godin

Godin Freeway 5-String Bass
courtesy Godin

GRADING	100% MINT	98% NEAR MINT	95% EXC+	90% EXC	80% VG+	70% VG	60% G

GRECO
Instruments previously produced in Japan during the 1960s.

Greco instruments were imported to the U.S. through Goya Guitars/Avnet. Avnet was the same major company that also acquired Guild in 1966 (source: Michael Wright, *Guitar Stories*, Volume One).

GREENE & CAMPBELL GUITARS
Instruments currently produced in New England, since 2002.

Greene and Campbell guitars produces high quality, professional grade instruments in America. In 2004, the company hired several former craftsmen from the defunct Guild Guitar Factory in Westerly Rhode Island. For more information contact Greene and Campbell directly (see Trademark Index).

ELECTRIC

Greene and Campbell's guitars come with great standard features, but they also offer several great options. List price on guitars starts at $1,500 with selling price around $1,000. Contact Greene and Campbell for more information on pricing and models.

GREMLIN
Instruments currently built in Asia. Distributed in the U.S. market by Midco International of Effingham, IL.

Gremlin guitars are entry level guitars at entry level prices designed for entry level students.

GRENDEL
Instruments currently built in Czechoslovakia. Distributed by Matthews & Ryan Musical Products, Inc., of New York City, NY.

Grendel basses are licensed by Michael Tobias Design (MTD Basses) and are built in the Czech Republic. Grendel basses are also available in the English music market under the Stadium trademark, and are offered through Bass Centre. Grendel basses are named after the monster character in the literary work **Beowulf**.

ELECTRIC BASS

GR4 4-STRING - offset double cutaway poplar body, bolt-on maple neck, 34 in. scale, 24-fret (plus 'Zero' fret) wenge fingerboard, 4-on-a-side headstock with wenge overlay, Schaller tuners, 2 single coil Bartolini pickups, volume/tone controls, toggle switch, Bartolini electronics, available in Pilsner Oil or Burgundy Sunburst, Coral Blue, Red, or Red Sunburst See-Through lacquer finishes, current mfg.

	MSR	$1,450		$1,150	$1,075	$995	$925	$750	$600	$450

GR4 FL - similar to the GR4, except has a flame maple top, current mfg.

	MSR	$1,510		$1,200	$1,100	$1,025	$950	$800	$650	$500

GR5 5-STRING - similar to the GR4 4-String, except in a 5-string configuration, 4/1 headstock, current mfg.

	MSR	$1,580		$1,250	$1,150	$1,050	$975	$800	$650	$500

GR5 FL - similar to the GR5, except has a flame maple top, current mfg.

	MSR	$1,650		$1,300	$1,175	$1,075	$995	$825	$675	$550

GRENN
Instruments previously built in Japan during the late 1960s.

Grenn guitars were a series of entry level semi-hollow body designs (source: Tony Bacon and Paul Day, *The Guru's Guitar Guide*).

GRETSCH
Instruments currently produced in the U.S. and Japan by the Fender Musical Instrument Corporation. Previously produced and distributed by the Fred Gretsch Company of Savannah, Georgia. Instruments originally produced in New York City, NY from the early 1900s to 1970. Production was moved to Booneville, AR from 1970 to 1979. Gretsch (as owned by D. H. Baldwin Piano Company) ceased production (of guitars) in 1981.

Friedrich Gretsch was born in 1856, and emigrated to America when he was 16. In 1883 he founded a musical instrument shop in Brooklyn which prospered. The Fred Gretsch Company began manufacturing instruments in 1883 (while Friedrich maintained his proper name, he "Americanized" it for the company). Gretsch passed away unexpectedly (at age 39) during a trip to Germany in April 1895, and his son Fred (often referred to as Fred Gretsch, Sr. in company histories) took over the family business (at 15!). Gretsch Sr. expanded the business considerably by 1916. Beginning with percussion, ukeleles, and banjos, Gretsch introduced guitars in the early 1930s, developing a well respected line of archtop orchestra models. In 1926 the company acquired the rights to K. Zildjian Cymbals, and debuted the Gretsch tenor guitar. During the Christmas season of 1929, the production capacity was reported to be 100,000 instruments (stringed instruments and drums); and a new midwestern branch was opened in Chicago, Illinois. In March of 1940 Gretsch acquired the B & D trademark from the Bacon Banjo Corporation. Fred Gretsch, Sr. retired in 1942.

William Walter Gretsch assumed the presidency of the company until 1948, and then Fred Gretsch, Jr. took over the position. Gretsch, Jr. was the primary president during the great Gretsch heyday, and was ably assisted by such notables as Jimmy Webster and Charles "Duke" Kramer (Kramer was involved with the Gretsch company from 1935 to his retirement in 1980, and was even involved after his retirement!). During the 1950s, the majority of Gretsch's guitar line was focused on electric six string Spanish instruments. With the endorsement of Chet Atkins and George Harrison, Gretsch electrics became very popular with both country and rock 'n roll musicians through the 1960s.

Outbid in their attempt to buy Fender in 1965, the D. H. Baldwin company bought Gretsch in 1967, and Gretsch, Jr. was made a director of Baldwin. Baldwin had previously acquired the manufacturing facilities of England's James Ormstron Burns (Burns Guitars) in September 1965, and Baldwin was assembling the imported Burns parts in Booneville, Arkansas. In a business consolidation, The New York Gretsch operation was moved down to the Arkansas facility in 1970. Production focused on Gretsch, and Burns guitars were basically discontinued.

In January of 1973 the Booneville plant suffered a serious fire. Baldwin made the decision to discontinue guitar building operations. Three months later, long-time manager Bill Hagner formed the Hagner Musical Instruments company and formed an agreement with Baldwin to build and sell Gretsch guitars to Baldwin from the Booneville facility. Baldwin would still retain the rights to the trademark. Another fire broke out in December of the same year, but the

GRADING	100% MINT	98% NEAR MINT	95% EXC+	90% EXC	80% VG+	70% VG	60% G

operation recovered. Baldwin stepped in and regained control of the operation in December of 1978, the same year that they bought the Kustom Amplifier company in Chanute, Kansas. Gretsch production was briefly moved to the Kansas facility, and by 1982 they moved again to Gallatin, Tennessee. 1981 was probably the last date of guitar production, but Gretsch drum products were continued at Tennessee. In 1983 the production had again returned to Arkansas.

Baldwin had experimented briefly with guitar production at their Mexican organ facilities, producing perhaps 100 Southern Belle guitars (basically renamed Country Gentlemans) between 1978 and 1979. When Gretsch production returned to Arkansas in 1983, the Baldwin company asked Charles Kramer to come out of retirement and help bring the business back (which he did). In 1984, Baldwin also sold off their rights to Kustom amps. In 1985 Kramer brokered a deal between Baldwin and Fred Gretsch III that returned the trademark back to the family.

Kramer and Gretsch III developed the specifications for the reissue models that are currently being built by the Terada company in Japan. The majority of Japanese-produced Gretsch models are brokered in the US market; however, there has been some "grey market" Japan-only models that have been brought into the US One such model, the White Penguin Reissue, was briefly offered through Gretsch to the US market - it is estimated that perhaps a dozen or so were sold through dealers.

In 1995, three models were introduced built in the U.S: **Country Club 1955** (model G6196-1955), **Nashville 1955** (model G6120-1955), and the **White Falcon I - 1955** (model G6136-1955), (Later company history courtesy Michael Wright, *Guitar Stories*, Volume One).

On January 1, 2003, Gretsch guitars was sold to Fender (FMIC) as the exclusive distributor, producer, developer, and marketer of Gretsch. Look for Fred Gretsch and Gretsch guitars in the Fender booth now at the NAMM shows! Fred is still consulting for Gretsch guitars.

Charles Duke Kramer first joined the Gretsch company at their Chicago office in 1935. When Kramer first retired in 1980, he formed D & F Products. In late 1981, when Baldwin lost a lease on one of their small production plants, Kramer went out and bought any existing guitar parts (about three 42-foot semi-trailers worth!). While some were sold back to the revitalized Gretsch company in 1985, Kramer still makes the parts available through his D & F Products company. D & F Products can be reached at: 6735 Hidden Hills Drive, Cincinnati, OH 45230 (513.232.4972).

PREVIOUS PRODUCTION MODEL CODES

The Gretsch company assigned a name and a four digit number to each guitar model. However, they would also assign a different, yet associated number to the same model in a different color or component assembly. This system helped expedite the ordering system, says Charles Duke Kramer, "you could look at an invoice and know exactly which model and color from one number." References in this text, while still incomplete, will list variances in the model designations.

CURRENT PRODUCTION MODEL CODES

Current Gretsch models may have a G preface to the four digit code, and also letters at the end that designate different bridge configuration (like a Bigsby tremolo), or a cutaway body style. Many of the reissue models also have a hyphen and four digit year following the primary model number designation that indicate a certain vintage-style year.

ELECTRIC: ANNIVERSARY SERIES

ANNIVERSARY MODEL 6124/6125 - single round cutaway semi-hollow maple body, arched top, bound body, f-holes, raised white pickguard with logo, mahogany neck, 21-fret ebony fingerboard with pearloid thumbnail inlay, roller bridge/G logo trapeze tailpiece, blackface peghead with logo inlay, peghead mounted nameplate with engraved diamond, 3-per-side tuners, chrome hardware, covered pickup, volume control on cutaway bout, 3-position tone switch, available in Sunburst (Model 6124), Two-Tone Green (Model 6125), or Two-Tone Tan finishes, mfg. 1958-1972.

1958-1960	N/A	$1,550	$1,350	$1,150	$950	$825	$700
1961-1964	N/A	$1,300	$1,100	$950	$850	$750	$650
1965-1972	N/A	$1,150	$1,000	$850	$700	$600	$500

Add $100 for Two-Tone Green finish.

In 1960, rosewood fingerboard replaced ebony fingerboard. In 1963, the Two Tone Tan was also designated as Model 6125.

DOUBLE ANNIVERSARY MODEL 6117/6118 - similar to Anniversary, except has 2 covered pickups, 2 volume controls, 3-position selector switch, available in Sunburst (Model 6117) or Two-Tone Green (Model 6118) finishes, mfg. 1958-1975.

1958-1961	N/A	$2,300	$2,000	$1,750	$1,550	$1,350	$1,150
1962-1965	N/A	$2,000	$1,750	$1,500	$1,300	$1,100	$900
1966-1975	N/A	$1,500	$1,300	$1,150	$1,000	$850	$700

Add $100 for Two-Tone Green finish.

In 1961, stereo output was optional. The Anniversary Stereo model was offered in Sunburst (Model 6111) and Two Tone Green (Model 6112) until 1963. In 1963, bound fingerboard was added, palm vibrato optional, stereo output was discontinued. In 1963, Two Tone Brown was also designated at Model 6118. In 1972, f-holes were made smaller, adjustable bridge replaced roller bridge, peghead nameplate was removed. In 1974, block fingerboard inlay replaced thumbnail inlay, and the sunburst finish designation became Model 7560.

ANNIVERSARY REISSUE MODEL G6124 - similar to Anniversary, except has rosewood fingerboard, available in Sunburst (Model G6124) or 2-Tone Green (Model G6125) finishes, mfg. 1993-99.

$1,200	$900	$750	$600	$550	$495	$450

Last MSR was $1,500.

Gretsch Anniversary
Model 6125
Blue Book Publications

Gretsch Double Anniversary
Model 6117
Blue Book Publications

GRADING	100% MINT	98% NEAR MINT	95% EXC+	90% EXC	80% VG+	70% VG	60% G

DOUBLE ANNIVERSARY REISSUE MODEL G6117/6118 (NO. 241-1001) - similar to Anniversary, except has rosewood fingerboard, 2 pickups, 2 volume controls, 3-position switch, available in Sunburst (Model G6117) or 2-Tone Green (Model G6118) finishes, mfg. 1993-99, reintroduced 2002 and is currently produced.

MSR	$2,325		$1,900	$1,600	$1,350	$1,100	$900	$750	$600

Add $100 for Model G6118 with Hilo ´Tron pickups and Sunburst finish. Add $120 for Bigsby tailpiece.

Double Anniversary Reissue Left-Hand Model G6118TLH (No. 240-1021) - similar to the Double Anniversary Reissue, except in a left-handed configuration, with a Bigsby taipiece, mfg. 1997-99, reintroduced 2004 and is currently produced.

MSR	$2,825		$2,300	$2,000	$1,750	$1,500	$1,300	$1,100	$900

Double Anniversary Reissue Junior Model G6118JR (No. 241-1002) - similar to the Double Anniversary except has a smaller body, available in Smoke Green finish, current mfg.

MSR	$2,275		$1,850	$1,600	$1,350	$1,150	$1,000	$850	$700

Add $120 for Bigsby tailpiece.

120th ANNIVERSARY G6118T (NO. 241-1003) - 120 year Anniversary Gretsch model, 2 TV Jones Classic Filter'Tron pickups, Bigsby vibrato tailpiece, chrome hardware, available in Bamboo Yellow/Copper Mist finish, mfg. 2004-present.

MSR	$2,925		$2,350	$2,050	$1,800	$1,550	$1,300	$1,050	$800

ELECTRIC: ASTRO-JET SERIES

ASTRO-JET MODEL 6126 - Offset double cutaway asymmetrical hardwood body, black pickguard, metal rectangle plate with model name/serial number on bass side cutaway, maple neck, 21-fret bound ebony fingerboard with thumbnail inlay, adjustamatic bridge/Burns vibrato, asymmetrical blackface peghead with silkscreen logo, 4/2-per-side tuners, chrome hardware, 2 exposed pickups, 3 controls, 3 switches, available in Red top/Black back/side finish, mfg. 1965-68.

	N/A	$1,400	$1,200	$1,050	$900	$750	$600

ELECTRIC: ATKINS AXE SERIES

ATKINS AXE MODEL 7685/7686 - single sharp cutaway bound hardwood body, white pickguard with logo, maple neck, 22-fret bound ebony fingerboard with white block inlay, Tune-O-Matic stop bridge, bound black face peghead with logo, 3-per-side tuners, chrome hardware, 2 covered humbucker pickups, 2 volume/2 tone controls, 3-position switch, available in Dark Grey (Model 7685) or Rosewood Stain (Model 7686) finishes, mfg. 1976-1981.

	N/A	$1,200	$1,050	$900	$775	$650	$550

Atkins Super Axe Model 7680/7681/7682 - similar to Atkins Axe, except has black plate with mounted controls, volume/3 effects controls, 2 effects switches, active electronics, available in Red (Model 7680), Dark Grey (Model 7681), and Sunburst (Model 7682), mfg. 1976-1981.

	N/A	$1,500	$1,300	$1,150	$1,000	$850	$700

AXE REISSUE MODEL G7685 (NO. 241-0507) - similar to the Atkins Axe, available in Dark Cherry Red or Walnut Satin (Model G7686), mfg. 1997-99, reintroduced 2002-03.

	$1,900	$1,650	$1,400	$1,150	$950	$750	$600

Last MSR was $2,325.

ELECTRIC: BST (BEAST) SERIES

Baldwin-owned Gretsch introduced the BST series from 1979 to 1981, and the series featured lower line models with a solid body construction and bolt-on necks, as well as higher priced models with neck-through designs.

BST-1000 SINGLE HUMBUCKER MODEL 8210/8216 - single cutaway solid body, bolt-on neck, 24-fret fingerboard, Tune-O-Matic stop bridge, 3-per-side tuners, chrome hardware, humbucker pickup, volume/tone controls, available in Brown (Model 8210) or Red (Model 8216), mfg. 1979-1981.

	N/A	$450	$375	$325	$275	$225	$175

Last MSR was $299.

BST-1000 Double Humbucker Model 8211/8215 - similar to the BST-1000, except has two humbucker pickups, 3-way selector switch, available in Brown (Model 8215) or Red (Model 8211), mfg. 1979-1981.

	N/A	$500	$425	$350	$300	$250	$200

The same model designation (BST-1000) was used on the two pickup version as well as the single pickup model. The four digit model/digit code would be the proper designator.

BST-1500 MODEL 8217 - similar to the BST-1000, and featured only one humbucker, available in Brown (Model 8217), mfg. 1981 only.

	N/A	$400	$350	$300	$250	$200	$150

BST-2000 MODEL 8220 - offset double cutaway solid body, bolt-on neck, 22-fret fingerboard, available in Brown (Model 8220) and Red (Model 8221), mfg. 1979-1980.

	N/A	$525	$450	$400	$350	$300	$250

BST-5000 MODEL 8250 - offset double cutaway solid body, laminated neck-through design, 24-fret fingerboard, carved edges around top, available in Red (Model 8250), mfg. 1979-1980.

	N/A	$550	$475	$425	$375	$325	$275

Last MSR was $695.

GRADING	100% MINT	98% NEAR MINT	95% EXC+	90% EXC	80% VG+	70% VG	60% G

ELECTRIC: BIKINI SERIES

BIKINI MODEL 6023 - double cutaway slide-and-lock poplar body with detachable poplar center block, raised white pickguard with logo, bolt-on maple neck, 22-fret maple fingerboard with black dot inlay, adjustable ebony bridge/trapeze tailpiece, black face peghead with logo, 3-per-side tuners, chrome hardware, exposed pickup, volume/tone control, available in Black finish, mfg. 1961-63.

	N/A	$1,850	$1,600	$1,350	$1,150	$950	$750

It is estimated that only 35 instruments were produced. The slide-and-lock body is named a "Butterfly" back and is interchangeable with 6-string or bass neck shafts. There is also a "Double Butterfly," able to accommodate both necks (Model 6025). Controls for this instrument are located on top of detachable center block. Double neck Bikini models are priced around $2,000 to $2,500.

ELECTRIC: BLACKHAWK SERIES

BLACKHAWK MODEL 6100/6101 - double round cutaway bound maple body, f-holes, raised silver pickguard with logo, maple neck, 22-fret bound fingerboard with thumbnail inlay, dot inlay above the 12th fret, tuning fork bridge, roller bridge/G logo Bigsby vibrato tailpiece, black face peghead with logo inlay, peghead mounted nameplate, 3-per-side tuners, chrome hardware, 2 covered pickups, volume control on upper bout, 2 volume controls, two 3-position switches, available in Black (Model 6101) or Sunburst (Model 6100) finishes, mfg. 1967-1972.

	N/A	$1,800	$1,550	$1,350	$1,150	$950	$750

ELECTRIC: BO DIDDLEY SERIES

Gretsch Bikini
courtesy Rob Lurvey

BO DIDDLEY MODEL 6138 (NO. 241-0102) - faithful reproduction of the famous Bo Diddley rectangular guitar, 17.75 in. X 9.25 in. X 2 in. rectangular alder body (semi-hollow body), 5-ply maple top, bound top and back, 3-piece rock maple set neck, 1957 style headstock, 3-per-side tuners, ebonized rosewood fingerboard with pearl dot position markers, 22-frets, 25.5 in. scale, bone nut, 2 FilterTron pickups with gold covers, 2 Volume/1 Tone control plus master volume, 3-way switch, gold Tune-O-Matic bridge, Gold "G" tailpiece, available in Solid Red finish, mfg. 2000-present.

MSR	$2,825		$2,300	$1,950	$1,700	$1,450	$1,200	$1,000	$800

Add $300 for left-hand model (Model G6138LH).

ELECTRIC ARCHTOP: BRIAN SETZER SERIES

BRIAN SETZER SIGNATURE MODEL G6120-SSL (NO. 240-0108) - single rounded cutaway bound body, arched 5-ply laminated flamed maple top, bound f-holes, 5-ply flame maple back, 7-ply laminated flame maple sides, maple neck, 24.5 in. scale, 22-fret bound ebony fingerboard with pearl thumbnail inlay, adjustamatic metal bridge with ebony base/Bigsby vibrato tailpiece, bound flame maple veneered peghead with pearl horseshoe/logo inlay, 3-per-side Sperzel locking tuners, gold hardware, raised gold pickguard with artist signature/model name/logo, 2 Gretsch Filtertron humbucker pickups, master volume/2 volume controls, 3-position/tone switches, available in Orange Stain Lacquer finish, mfg. 1994-present.

MSR	$4,175		$3,400	$3,000	$2,700	$2,400	$2,100	$1,800	$1,500

Add $150 for Orange Tiger Flame finish.

This model has optional dice volume control knobs (included). In 2004, TV Jones pickups were introduced.

Brian Setzer Signature Model G6120-SSU (No. 240-0107) - similar to Brian Setzer Model SSL, except available in Orange Stain or Green Stain non-laquer finishes, mfg. 1994-present.

MSR	$3,850		$3,100	$2,700	$2,400	$2,100	$1,800	$1,500	$1,200

In 2004, TV Jones pickups were introduced.

Brian Setzer Signature Model Left-Hand G6120-SSULH (No. 240-0120) - similar to Brian Setzer Model SSL, except in left-handed configuration, available in Orange Tiger Flame finish, current mfg.

MSR	$4,425		$3,600	$3,200	$2,800	$2,500	$2,200	$1,900	$1,600

BRIAN SETZER HOT ROD MODEL (NO. 240-0106/0111) - similar to Brian Setzer Signature model, except has 2 Specially-Wound Filter-Tron pickups with Alnico Magnets, pickups mounted closer to strings than usual, pickup selector switch, master volume control, 3-piece Rock Maple neck, Ebonized Rosewood fingerboard, silver pickguard with Gretsch logo, oversized f-holes, polished aluminum Bigsby tailpiece, chrome-plated nameplate on headstock, chrome-plated hardware, available in Flat Black (G6120SHBK), Regal Blue (G6120SHB), Tangerine (G6120SHT), Candy Apple Red (G6120SHA), or Purple (G6120SHP) finishes, mfg. 1999-present.

MSR	$3,125		$2,500	$2,200	$1,900	$1,650	$1,400	$1,200	$1,000

Add $200 for TV Jones pickups (Model G6120SHXTV, No. 240-0112).

ELECTRIC ARCHTOP: BROADKASTER SERIES

BROADKASTER HOLLOW BODY MODEL 7607/7608 - double round cutaway semi-hollow bound maple body, f-holes, raised black pickguard with logo, maple neck, 22-fret rosewood fingerboard with white dot inlay, adjustable bridge/G logo trapeze tailpiece, blackface peghead with logo, 3-per-side tuners, chrome hardware, 2 covered pickups, master volume/2 volume/2 tone controls, 3-position switch, available in Natural (Model 7607) or Sunburst (Model 7608) finishes, mfg. 1975-1980.

	N/A	$1,100	$950	$825	$700	$600	$500

This model was also available with Bigsby vibrato tailpiece in Natural (Model 7603) and Sunburst (Model 7604) finishes. In 1976, Tune-O-Matic stop tailpiece, 2 covered humbucker DiMarzio pickups replaced original parts/designs. Between 1977 and 1979, a Red finish was offered as Model 7609.

Gretsch Bo Diddley
courtesy Gretsch Guitars

GRADING	100% MINT	98% NEAR MINT	95% EXC+	90% EXC	80% VG+	70% VG	60% G

BROADKASTER SOLID BODY MODEL 7600/7601 - offset double cutaway maple body, white pickguard, bolt-on maple neck, 22-fret maple fingerboard with black dot inlay, fixed bridge, 3-per-side tuners, chrome hardware, 2 exposed pickups, 2 volume controls, pickup selector/tone switch, available in Natural (Model 7600) or Sunburst (Model 7601) finishes, mfg. 1975-1980.

	N/A	$600	$525	$450	$400	$350	$300

ELECTRIC/ELECTRIC ARCHTOP: CHET ATKINS SERIES

CHET ATKINS SOLID BODY MODEL 6121 - single cutaway routed solid mahogany body, bound maple top, raised gold pickguard with signature/logo, G brand on lower bout, tooled leather side trim, maple neck, 22-fret bound rosewood fingerboard with pearl block inlay with engraved western motif, adjustable bridge/Bigsby vibrato tailpiece, bound peghead with maple veneer and pearl steer's head/logo inlay, 3-per-side tuners, gold hardware, 2 exposed DeArmond pickups, control on cutaway bout, 2 volume/tone controls, 3-position switch, available in Red Orange finish, mfg. 1954-1963.

1954-1956	N/A	$5,500	$4,700	$4,200	$3,700	$3,200	$2,700
1957-1960	N/A	$5,200	$4,500	$4,000	$3,500	$3,000	$2,500
1961-1963	N/A	$5,000	$4,400	$3,900	$3,400	$2,1900	$2,400

The Bigsby vibrato was available with or without gold-plating. This model was originally issued with a jeweled Western styled strap. In 1957, an ebony fingerboard with humptop block inlay was introduced, Filter-tron pickups replaced original parts/design, G brand and tooled leather side trim were discontinued. In 1958, thumbnail fingerboard inlays replaced block inlays, steer's head peghead inlay replaced horseshoe inlay, tone control replaced by 3-position switch and placed by the pickup selector switch. In 1961, the body was changed to double cutaway style. In 1962, a standby switch was added.

CHET ATKINS COUNTRY GENTLEMAN MODEL 6122 - single round cutaway hollow bound maple body, simulated f-holes, gold pickguard with logo, maple neck, 22-fret bound ebony fingerboard with pearl thumbnail inlay, adjustable bridge/Bigsby vibrato tailpiece, bound blackface peghead with logo inlay, peghead mounted nameplate, 3-per-side tuners, gold hardware, 2 covered humbucker pickups, master volume/2 volume controls, two 3-position switches, available in Mahogany or Walnut finishes, mfg. 1957-1981.

1957-1961	N/A	$6,200	$5,300	$4,400	$3,700	$3,000	$2,300
1962-1965	N/A	$3,500	$3,100	$2,700	$2,300	$2,000	$1,700
1966-1969	N/A	$3,000	$2,500	$2,100	$1,800	$1,500	$1,200
1970-1981	N/A	$2,500	$2,100	$1,800	$1,500	$1,200	$1,000

A few of the early models had the Chet Atkins signpost signature on the pickguard, but this was not a standard feature. The f-holes on this model were inlaid in early production years, then they were painted on, sometimes being painted as if they were bound. A few models produced during 1960-1961 did have actual f-holes in them, probably special order items. The Bigsby vibrato tailpiece was not gold-plated originally. In 1961, double round cutaway body, bridge mute, standby switch and padded back became available. By 1962, gold-plated vibrato was standard. In 1972, this model became available with open f-holes. Between 1972 to 1980, a Brown finish was offered as Model 7670. In 1975, a tubular arm was added to the Bigsby vibrato. In 1979, vibrato arm was returned to a flat bar.

CHET ATKINS HOLLOW BODY/NASHVILLE MODEL 6120/7660 - single round cutaway bound maple body, arched top with stylized G brand, bound f-holes, raised gold pickguard with Chet Atkins' sign post signature/logo, maple neck, 22-fret bound rosewood fingerboard with pearl Western motif engraved block inlay, adjustable bridge/Bigsby vibrato tailpiece, bound blackface peghead with steerhead/logo inlay, 3-per-side tuners, gold hardware, 2 exposed DeArmond pickups, volume control on cutaway bout, 2 volume/tone controls, 3-position switch, available in Red, Red Amber, or Western Orange finishes, mfg. 1954-1980.

1954-1955	N/A	$7,800	$7,000	$6,400	$5,800	$5,200	$4,500
1956	N/A	$7,200	$6,400	$5,600	$4,800	$4,000	$3,200
1957	N/A	$6,700	$5,800	$5,100	$4,300	$3,500	$2,700
1958-1961	N/A	$5,500	$4,700	$4,000	$3,200	$2,700	$2,200
1962-1967	N/A	$2,800	$2,400	$2,000	$1,700	$1,400	$1,100
1968-1980	N/A	$2,000	$1,700	$1,400	$1,200	$1,000	$800

Some models were available with body matching pegheads. In 1956, engraved fingerboard inlay was discontinued, horseshoe peghead inlay replaced steer's head, vibrato unit was nickel plated. In 1957, humptop fingerboard inlay, Filter-tron pickups replaced original parts/designs, G brand on top discontinued. In 1958, ebony fingerboard with thumbnail inlay and adjustable bar bridge replaced original parts/designs. The tone control changed to a 3-position switch and was placed next to the pickup selector switch. In 1961, body was changed to a double round cutaway semi-hollow style with painted f-holes, pickguard had no signpost around Chet Atkins' signature, string mute, mute/standby switches (a few models were produced with a mute control) and back pad were added. In 1967, this model was renamed the Nashville, with Chet Atkins Nashville on pickguard and peghead mounted nameplate. In 1972, Tune-O-Matic bridge and elongated peghead were added, string mute and switch, nameplate were removed. Between 1972 to 1979, a Red finish was offered as Model 7660. In 1973, real f-holes were added. In 1975, tubular arm added to vibrato, hardware became chrome plated and the standby switch was removed. In 1979, flat vibrato arm replaced tubular arm.

CHET ATKINS TENNESSEAN MODEL 6119/7655 - single round cutaway hollow bound maple body, arched top, f-holes, raised black pickguard with Chet Atkins' signpost signature/logo, maple neck, 22-fret ebony fingerboard with pearl thumbnail inlay, adjustable bar bridge/Bigsby vibrato tailpiece, 3-per-side tuners, chrome hardware, exposed pickup, volume control, 3-position switch, available in Cherry, Dark Cherry Stain, Mahogany, or Walnut finishes, mfg. 1958-1980.

1958-1961	N/A	$2,900	$2,400	$2,000	$1,700	$1,400	$1,100
1962-1967	N/A	$2,500	$2,100	$1,800	$1,500	$1,200	$900
1968-1980	N/A	$2,000	$1,700	$1,400	$1,200	$1,000	$800

In 1961, solid maple top with painted f-holes, grey pickguard with logo, bound rosewood fingerboard, tuners with plastic buttons replaced original parts/designs; exposed pickup, 2 volume controls, tone switch were added. In 1962, Chet Atkins signature on pickguard, standby switch were added. In 1963, painted bound f-holes, padded back were added. In 1964, peghead nameplate became available. In 1970, real f-holes were added. In 1972, adjustamatic bridge replaced bar bridge, peghead nameplate was removed. Between 1972 to 1979, a Dark Red finish was offered as Model 7655.

GRADING	100% MINT	98% NEAR MINT	95% EXC+	90% EXC	80% VG+	70% VG	60% G

ELECTRIC ARCHTOP: CLIPPER SERIES

CLIPPER MODEL 6186/6187/6188 - single round cutaway bound maple body, arched top, f-holes, raised pickguard with logo, maple neck, 21-fret ebony fingerboard with white dot inlay, adjustable ebony bridge/trapeze tailpiece, blackface peghead with logo, 3-per-side tuners with plastic buttons, chrome hardware, exposed DeArmond pickup, volume/tone control, available in Natural (Model 6188), Beige/Grey (Model 6187), or Sunburst (Model 6186) finishes, mfg. 1958-1975.

1958-1969	N/A	$1,200	$1,050	$900	$750	$650	$550
1970-1975	N/A	$900	$750	$650	$550	$450	$350

The original release of this model had a deep, full body. By 1958, the body had a thinner, 335 style thickness to it. In 1963, a palm vibrato was offered as standard, though few models are found with one. In 1968, vibrato was no longer offered. In 1972, 2 pickup models became available. Between 1972 to 1975, a Sunburst/Black finish was offered as Model 7555.

ELECTRIC: COMMITTEE SERIES

COMMITTEE MODEL 7628 - double cutaway walnut body, clear pickguard, through-body maple/walnut neck, 22-fret rosewood fingerboard with pearl dot inlay, fixed bridge, bound peghead with burl walnut veneer and pearl logo inlay, 3-per-side tuners, chrome hardware, 2 covered humbucker pickups, 2 volume/2 tone controls, 3-position switch, available in Natural finish, mfg. 1975-1981.

	N/A	$550	$475	$400	$350	$300	$250

There are two versions of the Committee model: the dual cutaway body, with a pickguard between the two pickups; and the model with the slightly offset cutaway body (the bass bout is slightly larger than the treble bout).

ELECTRIC: CONVERTIBLE/SAL SALVADOR SERIES

CONVERTIBLE MODEL 6199/SAL SALVADOR MODEL - single round cutaway hollow maple body, spruce top, gold pickguard with logo, bound body/f-holes, maple neck, 21-fret bound rosewood fingerboard with pearl humptop block inlay, adjustable rosewood bridge/G logo trapeze tailpiece, bound blackface peghead with logo inlay, 3-per-side Grover Imperial tuners, gold hardware, exposed DeArmond pickup, volume/tone control, available in Bamboo Yellow and Ivory top with Copper Mist and Sunburst body/neck finishes, mfg. 1955-1968.

1955-1958	N/A	$2,750	$2,350	$2,000	$1,700	$1,400	$1,100
1959-1964	N/A	$2,300	$2,000	$1,700	$1,400	$1,200	$1,000
1965-1968	N/A	$1,800	$1,550	$1,300	$1,100	$900	$700

1The pickup and controls were pickguard mounted on this instrument. In 1957, ebony fingerboard with thumbnail inlay replaced original fingerboard/inlay. In 1958, this model was renamed the Sal Salvador. In 1965, block fingerboard inlay replaced thumbnail fingerboard inlay, controls were mounted into the instrument´s top.

Gretsch Chet Atkins Country Gentleman Model 6122 courtesy Dave Rogers Dave's Guitar Shop

ELECTRIC: CORVETTE SERIES

CORVETTE HOLLOW BODY MODEL 6183 - non-cutaway semi-hollow mahogany body, tortoise shell pickguard, mahogany neck, 20-fret rosewood fingerboard with pearl dot inlay, 2 f-holes, adjustable rosewood bridge/trapeze tailpiece, black face peghead with logo, 3-per-side tuners with plastic buttons, chrome hardware, single coil pickup, volume/tone control, available in Natural (Model 6183), Sunburst (Model 6182), or Gold (Model 6184) finishes, mfg. 1954-56.

	N/A	$1,350	$1,150	$1,000	$850	$750	$650

The semi-hollow Corvette was originally issued as the Electromatic Spanish model. Some models have necks with 21 frets instead of 20.

CORVETTE SOLID BODY MODEL 6132 - offset double cutaway mahogany body, 2 piece pickguard, mahogany neck, 21-fret rosewood fingerboard with pearl dot inlay, adjustable rosewood bridge/trapeze tailpiece, black face peghead with logo, 3-per-side tuners with plastic buttons, chrome hardware, exposed pickup, volume/tone control, available in Natural (Model 6132), or Platinum Grey (Model 6133) finishes, mfg. 1961-1978.

1961-1962	N/A	$900	$800	$700	$600	$500	$400
1963-1964	N/A	$800	$700	$600	$500	$425	$350
1965-1969	N/A	$700	$600	$500	$425	$375	$325
1970-1978	N/A	$550	$475	$425	$375	$325	$275

In 1963, cutaways were sharpened and changed, pickguard styling changed, metal bridge replaced ebony bridge, 1 pickup with vibrato (Model 6134) or 2 pickups (extra tone control and 3-position switch) with vibrato (Model 6135) became optional, Cherry finish was added, and Platinum Grey finish was discontinued. In 1964, peghead shape became rounded with 2/4 tuners per side. In 1966, the Silver Duke with Silver Glitter finish and the Gold Duke with Gold Glitter finish were produced. These guitars were stock 1966 Corvettes (Model 6135) with special finishes that were built specifically for the Sherman Clay Music store chain of the western U.S. Company brochures of the time did not identify the above Duke models. These models have been mis-identified as being named after Charles Duke Kramer, a long time Gretsch employee - but that was not the case. A small amount of these models exist.

Gretsch Clipper Model 6186 courtesy Glen Perkins Hand Picked Guitars

GRADING	100% MINT	98% NEAR MINT	95% EXC+	90% EXC	80% VG+	70% VG	60% G

ELECTRIC: COUNTRY CLASSIC SERIES

COUNTRY CLASSIC SINGLE CUTAWAY MODEL G6122 S (NO. 240-1105) - single rounded cutaway semi-hollow bound maple body, bound f-holes, 3-piece maple neck, 22-fret bound ebony fingerboard with pearl thumbnail inlay, ebony/metal Tune-O-Matic bridge/Bigsby vibrato tailpiece, bound blackface peghead with pearl logo inlay, peghead mounted metal nameplate, 3-per-side tuners, gold hardware, raised gold pickguard with model name/logo, 2 humbucker pickups, master volume/2 volume/1 tone controls, selector switch, available in Walnut Stain finish, body width 17 in., disc. 2003.

	$2,350	$2,050	$1,750	$1,500	$1,225	$975	$750

Last MSR was $2,925.

COUNTRY CLASSIC DOUBLE CUTAWAY MODEL G6122 (NO. 240-1101) - similar to the Country Classic I, except has double rounded cutaway body, current mfg.

MSR	$3,025	$2,450	$2,150	$1,850	$1,550	$1,300	$1,050	$850

Country Classic 12 String (Model G6122-12) - similar to the Country Classic, except features 12-string configuration, 6-per-side tuners, mfg. 1997-disc.

	$2,550	$2,200	$1,900	$1,600	$1,350	$1,050	$775

Last MSR was $3,100.

Country Classic TV Jones Pickups G6122SP (No. 240-1107) - similar to the Country Classic, except has TV Jones pickups, available in Walnut Stain finish, new 2004.

MSR	$3,875	$3,200	$2,700	$2,400	$2,100	$1,850	$1,600	$1,350

COUNTRY CLASSIC 1958 MODEL G6122-1958 (NO. 240-1102) - similar to the Country Classic, except features specifications based on the 1958 version, mfg. 1997-present.

MSR	$3,175	$2,550	$2,200	$1,900	$1,600	$1,300	$1,100	$900

COUNTRY CLASSIC 1959 MODEL G6122-1959 (NO. 240-1106) - similar to the Country Classic, except features specifications based on the 1959 version, mfg. 2003-present.

MSR	$3,575	$2,900	$2,500	$2,200	$1,900	$1,600	$1,300	$1,000

COUNTRY CLASSIC 1962 MODEL G6122-1962 (NO. 240-1103) - similar to the Country Classic, except features specifications based on the 1962 version, current mfg.

MSR	$3,175	$2,550	$2,200	$1,900	$1,600	$1,350	$1,100	$900

Country Classic 1962 Left-Handed Model G6122-1962 LH) - similar to the Country Classic 1962 Reissue, except in left-handed configuration, mfg. late 1994-99.

	$2,625	$2,325	$1,975	$1,750	$1,425	$1,150	$825

Last MSR was $3,300.

COUNTRY CLASSIC JUNIOR MODEL G6122 JR (NO. 240-1104) - double rounded cutaway semi-hollow bound body, laminated press-arched maple top and back, 3-ply laminated maple sides (mahogany linings), bound f-holes, set-in 2 piece rock maple neck, 24.6" scale, 22-fret bound ebonized rosewood fingerboard with Neo Classical style pearl (thumbnail) inlay, ebony/metal Tune-O-Matic bridge/Bigsby vibrato tailpiece, bound peghead with pearl logo inlay, peghead mounted metal nameplate, 3-per-side enclosed tuners, gold hardware, raised gold pickguard with model name/logo, 2 Filtertron pickups, master volume/2 volume/master tone controls, pickup selector switch, available in Walnut or Orange Stain finishes, body width 14 in., body depth 2.25 in., mfg. 1998-present.

MSR	$2,500	$2,000	$1,750	$1,550	$1,350	$1,150	$950	$750

Orange finish was introduced in 2001.

ELECTRIC: COUNTRY CLUB SERIES

COUNTRY CLUB MODEL 6192/6193/6196 - single round cutaway hollow body, arched laminated maple top, bound body, bound f-holes, raised bound tortoise pickguard, laminated figured maple back/sides, maple neck, 21-fret bound rosewood fingerboard with ivoroid block inlay, Melita bridge/"G" trapeze tailpiece, bound black face peghead with logo, 3-per-side Grover Statite tuners, gold hardware, 2 DeArmond single coil pickups, master volume/2 volume/1 tone controls, 3-position switch, available in Cadillac Green (Model 6196), Natural (Model 6193), and Sunburst (Model 6192) finishes, body width 17 in., mfg. 1954-1981.

1954-1956	N/A	$3,400	$3,000	$2,600	$2,200	$1,900	$1,600
1957-1959	N/A	$3,800	$3,400	$3,000	$2,600	$2,300	$2,000
1960-1963	N/A	$3,200	$2,800	$2,500	$2,200	$1,900	$1,600
1964-1969	N/A	$2,700	$2,400	$2,100	$1,800	$1,500	$1,200
1970-1974	N/A	$2,200	$1,900	$1,600	$1,400	$1,200	$1,000
1975-1979	N/A	$2,000	$1,700	$1,500	$1,300	$1,100	$900
1980-1981	N/A	$1,700	$1,400	$1,200	$1,000	$850	$700

Add 20% for Cadillac Green or Natural finishes.

In 1955, raised gold pickguard with logo replaced original parts/design. Raised black pickguards may also be found. In 1956, peghead truss rod cover was introduced. In 1958, PAF Filter' Tron humbucker pickups, master/2 volume controls, pickup/tone 3-position switches. In 1959, Grover Imperial tuners replaced original parts/design. By 1960, zero fret was introduced, Pat. Num. Filter'Tron pickups replaced original parts/design. In 1961, thinline body replaced original parts/design. In 1962, padded back, string mute with dial knob, standby switch was introduced. In 1964, Grover "kidney button" tuners replaced original parts/design, padded back, string mute/dial was discontinued. In 1965, deep body replaced original parts/design. In 1968, Cadillac Green finish was discontinued. By 1972, raised grey pickguard with engraved logo, block fingerboard inlay, adjustamatic/rosewood bridge, trapeze tailpiece with logo engraved black plastic insert replaced original parts/design. Between 1972 to 1974, the sunburst designation was changed to Model 7575, and Natural was changed to Model 7576. In 1974, master volume/2 volume/2 tone controls, 3-position switch replaced original parts/designs. In 1975, Antique Stain (Model 7577) finish was introduced, and the Sunburst finish was discontinued. In 1979 only, Walnut finish was available.

GRADING	100% MINT	98% NEAR MINT	95% EXC+	90% EXC	80% VG+	70% VG	60% G

Country Club Project-O-Sonic Model 6101 - similar to Country Club, except has bound ebony fingerboard with pearl thumbnail inlay, Grover Imperial tuners, PAF P.O.S. (Project-O-Sonic) Filter-Tron "stereo" pickups, treble/bass volume controls, 3-position treble/bass/closing switches, available in Cadillac Green (Model 6103), Natural (Model 6102), and Sunburst (Model 6101) finishes, mfg. 1958-1967.

	N/A	$3,200	$2,900	$2,600	$2,300	$2,000	$1,700

In 1959, zero nut, standard Pat. Num. Filter'Tron pickups begin to replace original parts/designs, 3 tone/ 1 pickup select, 3-position switches replaced original parts/designs.

COUNTRY CLUB MODEL G6196CG (NO. 241-1000) - single cutaway, 2 DynaSonic pickups, long "G" tailpiece, adjustable bridge, ebony fingerboard with pearl block position markers, 3-per-side tuners, 2 f-holes, detailed binding, gold hardware, available in Cadillac green, Sunburst, or Amber Natural finishes, 17 in. hollow body design, 2.75 in. depth, mfg. 2001-present.

MSR	$3,425		$2,750	$2,400	$2,100	$1,800	$1,500	$1,300	$1,100

    Add $160 for Bigsby tailpiece and FilterTron pickups.

1955 COUNTRY CLUB CUSTOM REISSUE MODEL G6196-1955) - similar to the Country Club, circa 1955. Carve solid spruce top, ebony fingerboard and bridge base, 24kt. gold plating on hardware, 2 Gretsch Dynasonic pickups, available with hand rubbed lacquer finish, available in Blue Sunburst OR Cadillac Green finishes, body width 17 in., mfg. 1995-99.

	$6,350	$5,500	$4,800	$4,100	$3,400	$2,700	$2,000

    Last MSR was $7,900.

ELECTRIC: COUNTRY ROC & DELUXE CHET SERIES

COUNTRY ROC MODEL 7620 - single cutaway routed mahogany body, bound arched maple top, raised pickguard with logo, G brand on lower bout, tooled leather side trim, maple neck, 22-fret bound ebony fingerboard with pearl block inlay with engraved western motif, adjustamatic bridge/"G" trapeze tailpiece with western motif belt buckle, bound peghead with figured maple veneer and pearl horseshoe logo/inlay, 3-per-side tuners, gold hardware, 2 exposed pickups, master volume/2 volume/2 tone controls, 3-position switch, available in Red Stain finish, mfg. 1974-79.

	N/A	$2,250	$1,950	$1,700	$1,450	$1,200	$950

DELUXE CHET MODEL 7680/7681 - single round cutaway semi-hollow bound maple body, bound f-holes, raised black pickguard with model name/logo, 3-piece maple neck, 22-fret bound ebony fingerboard with pearl thumbnail inlay, Tune-O-Matic bridge/Bigsby vibrato tailpiece, bound black face peghead with pearl logo inlay, 3-per-side tuners, chrome hardware, 2 exposed pickups, master volume/2 volume/2 tone controls, 3-position switch, available in Dark Red (Model 7680) or Walnut (Model 7681) finishes, mfg. 1973-75.

	N/A	$2,000	$1,700	$1,400	$1,200	$1,000	$800

In 1976, this model was renamed the Super Axe. See the Atkins Axe series.

ELECTRIC: DUANE EDDY SERIES

DUANE EDDY MODEL G6120DE - single round cutaway bound body, arched laminated maple top, 7-ply laminated maple back/sides, bound f-holes, raised pickguard with Duane Eddy's signature/logo, rock maple neck, 24.5 in. scale, 22-fret bound ebony fingerboard with pearl hump block inlay, adjustable Spacer Control bridge/chrome Bigsby vibrato tailpiece, bound blackface peghead, 3-per-side Gotoh tuners, gold hardware, 2 Dynasonic single coil pickups, volume control on cutaway bout, 2 volume/tone controls, 3-position switch, available in Ebony Burst (Model G6120 DE) and Orange (Model G6120 DEO) urethane finishes, body width 16.62 in., body depth 2.8 in., mfg. 1997-2002.

	$3,000	$2,600	$2,300	$2,000	$1,700	$1,400	$1,100

    Last MSR was $3,700.

ELECTRIC: DUO-JET & JET FIREBIRD SERIES

These guitars have a single cutaway body, unless otherwise noted. The body construction consists of a top cap over a highly routed body made of pine, maple, mahogany, or spruce. The top was then covered with a plastic material, similar to the covering used by Gretsch on their drums. Duo-Jets also featured a rosewood fingerboard, mahogany neck and 2 DeArmond Dynasonic pickups (again, unless noted otherwise).

DUO-JET MODEL 6128 - single cutaway routed mahogany body, bound maple top, raised white pickguard with logo, mahogany neck, 22-fret bound rosewood fingerboard with pearloid block inlay, adjustable bridge/G logo trapeze tailpiece, bound black face peghead with logo, 3-per-side tuners, chrome hardware, 2 exposed DeArmond pickups, master volume/2 volume/1 tone control, 3-position switch, available in Black or Sparkle finishes, mfg. 1953-1971.

1953-1957	N/A	$5,000	$4,300	$3,700	$3,100	$2,500	$1,900
1958-1960	N/A	$4,000	$3,400	$2,800	$2,200	$1,700	$1,300
1961-1962	N/A	$3,500	$3,100	$2,700	$2,200	$1,700	$1,200
1963-1967	N/A	$2,500	$2,100	$1,800	$1,500	$1,200	$900
1968-1971	N/A	$2,000	$1,700	$1,400	$1,200	$1,000	$800

    Add 25% for Cadillac Green finish.

This model was available as a custom order instrument with Green finish and gold hardware. In 1956, humptop fingerboard inlay replaced block inlay. In 1957, Filter-tron pickups replaced original parts/ design. In 1958, thumbnail fingerboard inlay and roller bridge replaced the original parts/designs, 3-position switch replaced tone control and placed by the other switch. In 1961, double cutaway body became available. In 1962, gold pickguard, Burns vibrato, gold hardware and standby switch replaced, or were added, items. From 1963-1966, Sparkle finishes were offered. In 1968, Bigsby vibrato replaced existing vibrato/tailpiece, treble boost switch added.

Gretsch Country Club Model 6192 courtesy: Dave Rogers Dave's Guitar Shop

Gretsch Country Classic TV Jones Pickups Model G6122SP courtesy Gretsch Guitars

GRADING	100% MINT	98% NEAR MINT	95% EXC+	90% EXC	80% VG+	70% VG	60% G

DUO JET REISSUE MODEL G6128 (NO. 241-0400) - single round cutaway mahogany body, bound arched maple top, raised white pickguard with logo, mahogany neck, 22-fret bound rosewood fingerboard with pearl humpblock inlay, adjustamatic bridge/G logo trapeze tailpiece, bound blackface peghead with pearl horseshoe/logo inlay, 3-per-side tuners, chrome hardware, 2 humbucker pickups, master/2 volume/1 tone controls, selector switch, available in Jet Black top finish, mfg. 1990-present.

MSR	$2,425		$1,950	$1,700	$1,450	$1,250	$1,050	$900	$750

Add $120 for optional chrome Bigsby tremolo (Model G6128T, No. 240-0400). Add $50 for Pumpkin finish (Model G6128 PT).

Duo-Jet Doubleneck Model G6128T-6/12 (No. 240-0409) - Similar to the Duo Jet (G6128), except features two necks (doubleneck configuration), mfg. 1998-present.

MSR	$4,850		$3,900	$3,400	$2,900	$2,500	$2,100	$1,800	$1,500

Duo Jet Custom Edition G6128TSP (No. 241-0403) - similar to the Duo Jet Reissue, except has DynaSonic pickups with a Bigsby tailpiece, available in Black finish, mfg. 2004-present.

MSR	$3,075		$2,500	$2,200	$1,950	$1,700	$1,450	$1,250	$1,050

DUO JET 1957 REISSUE MODEL G6128-1957 (NO. 241-0401) - single round cutaway mahogany body, bound arched maple top, raised white pickguard with logo, mahogany neck, 22-fret bound rosewood fingerboard with pearl humpblock inlay, adjustamatic metal bridge with rosewood base/tailpiece, bound blackface peghead with pearl logo inlay, 3-per-side tuners, chrome hardware, 2 humbucker pickups, master volume/2 volume/1 tone controls, 3-position switch, available in Black finish, mfg. 1994-present.

MSR	$2,775		$2,250	$2,000	$1,750	$1,550	$1,350	$1,150	$950

This model has an optional G logo trapeze tailpiece.

Duo Jet 1957 Reissue Left-Handed Model G6128-1957LH - similar to the Duo Jet 1957 Reissue, except in left-handed configuration, mfg. late 1994-disc.

			$2,400	$2,100	$1,850	$1,600	$1,350	$1,100	$850

Last MSR was $2,950.

Duo Jet 1962 Reissue with Bigsby Model G6128T-1957 (No. 240-0401) - similar to the Duo Jet 1957 Reissue, except with a Bigsby tailpiece, current mfg.

MSR	$2,925		$2,350	$2,000	$1,750	$1,500	$1,300	$1,100	$950

Duo Jet 1962 Reissue with Bigsby Model G6128T-1962 (No. 240-0402) - similar to the Duo Jet 1957 Reissue, except features specifications based on the 1962 version, mfg. 1996-present.

MSR	$2,575		$2,100	$1,850	$1,650	$1,450	$1,250	$1,100	$950

DUO JET CADILLAC GREEN G6128TCG (NO. 240-0408) - similar to the Duo Jet Reissue, except has a Bigsby tailpiece, Dynasonic pickups, Cadillac Green or Black finishes, and gold hardware, new 2005.

MSR	$3,325		$2,700	$2,350	$2,050	$1,800	$1,550	$1,200	$1,000

Add $35 for black finish with a fixed arm tailpiece (G6128T-DSV, No. 240-0411).

JET FIREBIRD MODEL 6131 - similar to Duo Jet, except has black pickguard with logo, 22-fret bound rosewood fingerboard with pearloid block inlay, adjustable bridge/G logo trapeze tailpiece, bound black face peghead with logo, 3-per-side tuners, chrome hardware, 2 exposed pickups, master/2 volume/1 tone control, 3-position switch, available in Red top/Black back/sides/neck finish, mfg. 1955-1971.

1955-1959	N/A	$4,500	$3,900	$3,300	$2,600	$2,000	$1,400
1960-1964	N/A	$3,500	$2,900	$2,400	$2,100	$1,700	$1,300
1965-1971	N/A	$2,000	$1,700	$1,400	$1,200	$1,000	$800

A few models were produced without the logo on the pickguard.

Jet Firebird Reissue Model G6131 (No. 241-0502) - similar to Duo Jet, gold pickguard, gold hardware, available in Cherry Red top finish, current mfg.

MSR	$2,425		$1,950	$1,700	$1,450	$1,250	$1,050	$900	$750

Add $120 for Bigsby tailpiece (Mmodel G6131T, No. 240-0502).

Jet Firebird Reissue Model G6131TDS (No. 240-0506) - similar to Duo Jet Reissue, except has Dynasonic pickups and a Bigsby tailpiece, new 2005.

MSR	$3,175		$2,550	$2,250	$1,950	$1,700	$1,500	$1,300	$1,100

Add $120 for Bigsby tailpiece (Mmodel G6131T, No. 240-0502).

ELECTRIC: ELLIOT EASTON SERIES

ELLIOT EASTON MODEL G6128 (NO. 240-0100) - A Duo-Jet guitar converted to Elliot Easton's specs, narrowed headstock, Sperzel locking tuners, two piece maple neck, Bigsby Tailpiece, available in Cadillac Green, Red, or Black finishes, current mfg.

MSR	$3,075		$2,500	$2,200	$1,900	$1,650	$1,400	$1,150	$900

Elliot Easton Left-Handed Model G6128LH (No. 240-0120) - similar to the Elliot Easton except in left-handed configuration, available in Cadillac Green or Red finishes, current mfg.

MSR	$3,325		$2,700	$2,350	$2,050	$1,800	$1,550	$1,300	$1,050

Add $40 for Bigsby tailpiece (G6128T, No. 240-0120).

ELECTRIC: ELECTROMATIC (SPANISH) SERIES

ELECTROMATIC SPANISH MODEL 6182 - hollow bound maple body, arched spruce top, f-holes, raised tortoise pickguard, maple neck, 14/20-fret rosewood fingerboard with white dot inlay, adjustable rosewood bridge/trapeze tailpiece, blackface peghead with engraved logo, Electromatic vertically engraved onto peghead, 3-per-side tuners with plastic buttons, chrome hardware, exposed DeArmond pickup, volume/tone control, available in Natural (Model 6185N) or Sunburst (Model 6185) finishes, mfg. 1940-1954.

1940-1949	N/A	$1,200	$1,050	$900	$750	$650	$550
1950-1954	N/A	$900	$750	$650	$550	$450	$350

GRADING	100% MINT	98% NEAR MINT	95% EXC+	90% EXC	80% VG+	70% VG	60% G

The original (1940) version of this model had a larger body style. By 1949, the body style was 16 inches across the bottom bouts. In 1952, the Sunburst finish was redesignated Model 6182, and the Natural finish was redesignated Model 6183. In 1955, this model was renamed Corvette, with a new peghead design. In 1957, a single round cutaway body became available.

ELECTRO II MODEL 6187/6188 - similar to Electromatic, except has 2 DeArmond pickups, available in Natural (Model 6188) and Sunburst (Model 6187) finishes, mfg. 1951-55.

	N/A	$2,000	$1,700	$1,400	$1,200	$1,000	$800

Electro IIC Model 6193 - similar to Electromatic, except has single round cutaway, gold hardware, 2 DeArmond pickups, available in Natural (Model 6193) or Sunburst (Model 6192) finishes, body width 17", mfg. 1951-53.

	N/A	$2,500	$2,100	$1,800	$1,500	$1,300	$1,100

In 1953, a truss rod was introduced, Melita bridge repaced original parts/design. In 1954, this model was renamed Country Club.

ELECTRIC: MALCOLM YOUNG SERIES

These models were developed by Gretsch and Malcolm Young (AC/DC), with assistance by Young´s guitar technician Alan Rogan. This model is based on Young´s early 1960s Jet Firebird that has been modified through the years.

MALCOLM YOUNG I MODEL G6131SMY (NO. 241-0103) - double rounded cutaway bound top, maple top, mahogany back/sides, no f-holes, laminated mahogany neck, 24.5" scale, 22-fret (plus Zero Fret) ebony fingerboard with Neo-Classical (thumbnail) inlays, bound blackface peghead with pearl logo inlay, 3-per-side deluxe enclosed tuners, chrome hardware, BadAss adjustable bridge, Filtertron pickup with Alnico magnets, volume control on cutaway bout, tone control on lower bout, available in Flamed Maple (Model G6131 SMYF), Natural Maple with Satin finish (Model G6131 SMY), or Red (Model G6131 SMYR), mfg. mid 1996-present.

MSR	$1,975		$1,600	$1,400	$1,200	$1,050	$900	$750	$600

Add $75 for Flamed Maple top (Model G6131 SMYF).

Malcolm Young II Model G6131MY (No. 241-0104) - similar to the Malcolm Young Signature model, except has two Filtertron pickups, 2 volume/1 tone controls, and pickup selector switch, available in Flamed Maple (Model G6131 MYF), Natural Maple with matte finish (Model G6131 MY), and Red (Model G6131 MYR), mfg. mid 1996-present.

MSR	$2,175		$1,750	$1,500	$1,300	$1,100	$950	$800	$650

Add $75 for Flamed Maple top (Model G6131 MYF).

ELECTRIC: MONKEES SERIES

MONKEES´ ROCK-N-ROLL MODEL MODEL 6123 - double round cutaway bound maple body, arched top, bound f-holes, raised white pickguard with Monkees/logo, maple neck, 22-fret bound rosewood fingerboard with pearl double thumbnail inlay, adjustable bridge/Bigsby vibrato tailpiece, blackface peghead with pearl logo inlay, peghead mounted nameplate, 3-per-side tuners, chrome hardware, 2 covered pickups, volume control on cutaway bout, 2 volume controls, pickup selector/2 tone switches, available in Red finish, mfg. 1966-68.

	N/A	$1,900	$1,650	$1,450	$1,250	$1,050	$900

The Monkees´ logo appears on the truss rod cover and pickguard.

ELECTRIC: NASHVILLE SERIES

NASHVILLE MODEL G6120 - single round cutaway semi-hollow bound maple body, raised gold pickguard with logo, bound f-holes, 3-piece maple neck, 22-fret bound ebony fingerboard with pearl block inlay, adjustamatic metal bridge with ebony base/Bigsby vibrato tailpiece, bound blackface peghead with pearl horseshoe/logo inlay, 3-per-side tuners, gold hardware, 2 humbucker pickups, master/2 volume/1 tone controls, selector switch, available in Black (Model G6120BK), Trans. Orange (Model G6120) or Blue Sunburst (Model G6120 BS) finishes, mfg. 1991-present.

MSR	$2,925		$2,350	$2,050	$1,800	$1,550	$1,300	$1,050	$800

Nashville Left-Handed Model G6120LH (No. 240-1221) - similar to the Nashville, except in left-handed configuration, mfg. late 1994-present.

MSR	$3,225		$2,600	$2,300	$2,000	$1,750	$1,500	$1,250	$1,000

Nashville Tiger Maple Model G6120TM (No. 240-1201) - similar to Nashville, except has figured maple body/neck, available in Amber Flame or Western finishes, current mfg.

MSR	$3,225		$2,600	$2,300	$2,000	$1,750	$1,500	$1,250	$1,000

Nashville Western Model G6120W (No. 240-1209) - similar to Nashville, except has stylized G brand on lower bass bout, model name in fence post on pickguard, engraved western motif fingerboard inlay, disc 2003.

			$2,350	$2,050	$1,800	$1,500	$1,225	$975	$750

Last MSR was $2,925.

Nashville Dynasonic Model G6120DS/DSV (No. 240-1210/1213) - similar to Nashville, except has Dynasonic pickups, mfg. 2003-present.

MSR	$2,925		$2,350	$2,050	$1,800	$1,550	$1,300	$1,050	$800

In 2005, this model was revised with Dynasonic pickups.

Nashville Dynasonic Western Model G6120DSW (No. 240-1301) - similar to Nashville Dyansonic, except has Western motif, mfg. 2003-present.

MSR	$3,025		$2,450	$2,150	$1,850	$1,550	$1,300	$1,050	$850

Gretsch Duo Jet Doubleneck
Blue Book Publications

Gretsch Monkees' Rock-N-Roll
Model 6123
courtesy Dave Rogers
Dave's Guitar Shop

GRADING	100% MINT	98% NEAR MINT	95% EXC+	90% EXC	80% VG+	70% VG	60% G

NASHVILLE DOUBLE NECK MODEL G6120-6/12 (NO. 240-1309) - similar to the Nashville, except has a 6-string and 12-string neck configurations, available in Orange Stain finish, mfg. 1997-present.

MSR	$5,375	$4,350	$3,800	$3,450	$3,100	$2,700	$2,300	$1,900

NASHVILLE DOUBLE CUTAWAY G6120DC (NO. 240-1204) - similar to the Nashville model except is in double cutaway configuration, TV Jones Pickups (new 2004), available in Orange Stain finish, mfg. 2003-present.

MSR	$3,900	$3,200	$2,800	$2,450	$2,150	$1,850	$1,550	$1,250

NASHVILLE JUNIOR MODEL G6120JR - similar to Nashville, except features full scale neck/half scale body, available in Brilliant Orange finish, disc. 1999.

	$1,600	$1,350	$1,150	$1,000	$850	$700	$550

Last MSR was $2,000.

Nashville Junior 2 Model G6120-JR2 (No. 240-1208) - similar to Nashville, except features full scale neck/smaller sized body, 2 Filtertron pickups, available in Orange Stain finish, mfg. 1998-present.

MSR	$2,475	$2,000	$1,700	$1,400	$1,200	$1,000	$850	$700

NEW NASHVILLE G6120N (NO. 240-1301) - similar to the Nashville model except has a deep single sharp cutaway, available in Orange Stain finish, mfg. 2003 only.

	$2,380	$2,050	$1,800	$1,550	$1,250	$1,050	$850

Last MSR was $2,975.

NASHVILLE WESTERN 1957 REISSUE MODEL G6120W-1957 (NO. 240-1205) - similar to Nashville Western, except is based on the 1957 model, available in Western Maple Stain finish, current mfg.

MSR	$3,325	$2,700	$2,350	$2,050	$1,800	$1,550	$1,200	$950

NASHVILLE 1960 REISSUE MODEL G6120-1960 (NO. 240-1206) - similar to Nashville, except is based on the 1960 model, available in Western Maple Stain finish, current mfg.

MSR	$3,125	$2,500	$2,150	$1,850	$1,550	$1,300	$1,050	$800

Nashville 1960 Reissue Left-Handed Model G6120-1960LH (No. 240-1226) - similar to the Nashville 1960 Reissue, except in left-handed configuration, mfg. late 1994-present.

MSR	$3,425	$2,750	$2,350	$2,050	$1,750	$1,450	$1,200	$975

1955 NASHVILLE CUSTOM REISSUE MODEL G6120-1955 - single round cutaway semi-hollow bound maple body, raised gold pickguard with logo, bound f-holes, 3-piece maple neck, 22-fret bound ebony fingerboard with pearl block inlay, adjustamatic metal bridge with ebony base/Bigsby vibrato tailpiece, bound blackface peghead with pearl horseshoe/logo inlay, 3-per-side tuners, gold hardware, 2 humbucker pickups, master/2 volume/1 tone controls, selector switch, available in Ebony or Trans. Orange finishes, mfg. 1995-99.

	$6,000	$5,250	$4,575	$3,900	$3,225	$2,550	$1,875

Last MSR was $7,500.

1955 Western Nashville Custom Reissue Model G6120W-1955 - similar to the 1955 Custom Reissue, except features an authentic G branded top and western motifs, mfg. 1997-99.

	$6,375	$5,575	$4,850	$4,150	$3,400	$2,725	$2,000

Last MSR was $7,960.

NASHVILLE WESTERN U.S. CUSTOM SHOP G6120WCST (NO. 240-1216) - Nashville style, DynaSonic pickups, Bigsby tailpiece, mfg. in the U.S. Gretsch Custom Shop, available in Western Maple Stain finish, mfg. 2004-present.

MSR	$9,000	$7,500	$6,000	$5,000	N/A	N/A	N/A	N/A

NASHVILLE SOLIDBODY G6121 (NO. 240-0505) - Duo Jet style body, Nashville appointments, select chambered mahogany body, one piece mahogany neck, two TV Jones Classic pickups, Bigsby tailpiece, available in Mahogany Stain with a Vintage Orange top, new 2005.

MSR	$3,250	$2,600	$2,250	$2,000	$1,750	$1,550	$1,350	$1,150

KEITH SCOTT NASHVILLE MODEL 6120KS (NO. 240-0200) - similar to the Nashville, except has brilliant gold top, dark mahogany sides and back, ebony fingerboard with neoclassical position markers, 16 in. wide multiple bound body, oversized f-holes, master and individual pickup volume controls, tone control, Gretsch Space Control bridge, Gretsch single coil Dyna-Sonic pickups, 24kt gold-plated hardware, available in Gold Top finish, mfg. 1999-present.

MSR	$4,025	$3,250	$2,850	$2,500	$2,200	$1,900	$1,650	$1,400

ELECTRIC: NEW JET SERIES

NEW JET MODEL G6114 (NO. 241-0501) - single cutaway mahogany body, carved flamed maple top, mahogany neck, rosewood fingerboard with Gretsch humped inlays, 3-per-side tuners, Dual TV Jones Filter-Tron pickups, Tune-O-Matic bridge, G-Stop tailpiece, 3-way switch, four knobs, available in Antique Maple, Trans. Red, or Trans. Black, mfg. 2002-03.

	$1,800	$1,550	$1,300	$1,100	$950	$800	$650

Last MSR was $2,225.

ELECTRIC: PRINCESS, RALLY, & RAMBLER SERIES

PRINCESS MODEL 6106 - offset double cutaway mahogany body, pickguard with "Princess" logo, mahogany neck, 21-fret rosewood fingerboard with pearl dot inlay, adjustable bridge/trapeze tailpiece, Tone Twister vibrato, body matching peghead with logo, 3-per-side tuners with plastic buttons, gold hardware, exposed pickup, volume/tone control, available in Blue, Pink, or White finishes, mfg. 1962-64.

	N/A	$2,300	$2,000	$1,700	$1,400	$1,200	$1,000

Pickguard color on this model was dependent on body color.

GRADING	100% MINT	98% NEAR MINT	95% EXC+	90% EXC	80% VG+	70% VG	60% G

RALLY MODEL 6104 - double round cutaway bound maple body, arched top, f-holes, raised pickguard with sportstripes/logo, maple neck, 22-fret bound rosewood fingerboard with pearl thumbnail inlay, dot inlay above 12th fret, adjustable bar bridge/Bigsby vibrato tailpiece, blackface peghead with logo inlay, 3-per-side tuners, chrome hardware, 2 exposed pickups, volume control on cutaway bout, 2 volume/tone controls, pickup selector/treble boost/standby switches, available in Bamboo Yellow top/Copper Mist back/side (Model 6105), or Rally Green (Model 6104) finishes, mfg. 1967-1970.

	N/A	$1,500	$1,300	$1,100	$950	$800	$650

RAMBLER MODEL 6115 - single sharp cutaway 3/4 size hollow bound maple body, f-holes, raised black pickguard with logo, maple neck, 20-fret rosewood fingerboard with white dot inlay, adjustable rosewood bridge/G logo trapeze tailpiece, bound blackface peghead with logo inlay, 3-per-side tuners with plastic buttons, chrome hardware, exposed DeArmond pickup, volume/tone control, available in Ivory top/Black body/neck finish, mfg. 1957-1961.

	N/A	$1,500	$1,300	$1,100	$950	$800	$650

In 1960, a round cutaway replaced original style cutaway.

ELECTRIC: REVEREND HORTON HEAT SERIES

REVEREND HORTON HEAT SIGNATURE G6120RHH (NO. 240-1217) - patterned after the Nashville model, features aged fingerboard, headstock binding, wide block Pearloid inlays, and other western motifs, bound oversized f-holes, two TV Jones Classic pickups, three knobs, two switches, clear pickguard, Bigsby tailpiece, available in Orange finish, new 2005.

MSR	$4,125	$3,400	$3,000	$2,700	$2,400	$2,100	$1,800	$1,500

ELECTRIC: ROC JET SERIES

ROC JET MODEL 6127 - single cutaway mahogany body, arched bound top, raised silver pickguard with logo, mahogany neck, 22-fret bound ebony fingerboard with pearloid halfmoon inlay and zero fret, adjustable bridge/G logo trapeze tailpiece, bound black face peghead with "Roc Jet" logo, 3-per-side tuners, chrome hardware, model nameplate on peghead, 2 humbucker pickups, 2 volume/2 tone controls, 3-position switch, available in Black (Model 6130) or Orange (Model 6127) finishes, mfg. 1969-1972.

	N/A	$1,200	$1,050	$900	$800	$700	$600

ROC JET MODEL 7610 - single cutaway mahogany body, arched bound top, raised silver pickguard with logo, mahogany neck, 22-fret bound rosewood fingerboard with pearloid thumbnail inlay, adjustable bridge/G logo trapeze tailpiece, bound black face peghead with logo, nameplate with serial number attached to peghead, 3-per-side tuners, chrome hardware, 2 exposed pickups, master volume on cutaway bout, 2 volume/2 tone controls, 3-position switch, available in Black (Model 7610), Porsche Pumpkin (Model 7611), Red (Model 7612), or Walnut Stain (Model 7613) finishes, mfg. 1970-1980.

	N/A	$950	$800	$700	$600	$500	$400

In 1972, the pickguard was redesigned, peghead nameplate was removed. In 1978, Tune-O-Matic stop tailpiece and covered humbucker DiMarzio pickups replaced original parts/designs.

ELECTRIC: ROUNDUP SERIES

ROUNDUP MODEL 6130 - single cutaway routed mahogany body, bound knotty pine top, raised tortoise pickguard with engraved steer's head, G brand on lower bout, tooled leather side trim, maple neck, 22-fret bound rosewood fingerboard with pearl block inlay with engraved western motif, adjustable bridge/G logo trapeze tailpiece with western motif belt buckle, bound peghead with pine veneer and pearl steer's head/logo inlay, 3-per-side tuners, gold hardware, 2 exposed DeArmond pickups, control on cutaway bout, 2 volume/tone controls, 3-position switch, available in Orange Stain finish, mfg. 1954-1960.

	N/A	$7,500	$6,500	$5,700	$5,000	$4,300	$3,500

This model was also available with mahogany and maple tops. This model was originally issued with a jeweled Western styled strap.

ROUNDUP REISSUE MODEL G6121W (NO. 240-0503/0504) - single round cutaway mahogany body, bound arched maple top, raised gold pickguard with logo, stylized G brand on lower bass bout, mahogany neck, 22-fret bound rosewood fingerboard with pearl engraved western motif block inlay, adjustamatic metal bridge with ebony base/Bigsby vibrato tailpiece, bound peghead with pearl horseshoe/logo inlay, 3-per-side tuners, gold hardware, 2 humbucker pickups, master/2 volume/1 tone controls, selector switch, available in Trans. Orange finish, current mfg.

MSR	$2,925	$2,350	$2,050	$1,800	$1,550	$1,300	$1,050	$800

ELECTRIC: SILVER JET & SPARKLE JET SERIES

SILVER JET MODEL 6129 - single cutaway routed mahogany body, bound Nitron plastic top, raised white pickguard with logo, mahogany neck, 22-fret bound rosewood fingerboard with pearloid block inlay, adjustable bridge/G logo trapeze tailpiece, bound black face peghead with logo, 3-per-side tuners, chrome hardware, 2 exposed pickups, master/2 volume/1 tone control, 3-position switch, available in Silver Sparkle finish, mfg. 1955-1963.

1955-1959	N/A	$5,500	$4,700	$4,000	$3,400	$2,800	$2,200
1960-1963	N/A	$4,500	$3,700	$3,100	$2,700	$2,300	$1,900

Any models with Silver Sparkle finish found after 1963 are Duo Jets with Sparkle finish (see Duo Jet models earlier in this section).

Gretsch Princess
Model 6106
Blue Book Publications

Gretsch Silver Jet Reissue
Model 6129
Blue Book Publications

GRADING		100% MINT	98% NEAR MINT	95% EXC+	90% EXC	80% VG+	70% VG	60% G

SILVER JET MODEL G6129 (NO. 241-0405) - single round cutaway mahogany body, bound arched maple top, raised white pickguard with logo, mahogany neck, 22-fret bound rosewood fingerboard with pearl humpblock inlay, adjustamatic bridge/G logo trapeze tailpiece, bound blackface peghead with pearl horseshoe/logo inlay, 3-per-side tuners, chrome hardware, 2 humbucker pickups, master/2 volume/1 tone controls, selector switch, available in Silver Sparkle top finish, current mfg.

MSR	$2,525	$2,050	$1,750	$1,450	$1,250	$1,050	$900	$750

Add $120 for optional Bigsby vibrato tailpiece (Model G6129T, No. 240-0405).

Silver Jet Left-Handed G6129T-1957LH - similar to the Silver Jet, except features a left-handed configuration, mfg. 1998-2002.

		$2,575	$2,225	$1,975	$1,650	$1,350	$1,100	$775

Last MSR was $3,200.

SILVER JET 1957 REISSUE MODEL G6129-1957 (NO. 241-0406) - single round cutaway mahogany body, bound arched maple top, raised white pickguard with logo, mahogany neck, 22-fret bound rosewood fingerboard with pearl humpblock inlay, adjustamatic metal bridge with rosewood base/G logo trapeze tailpiece, bound blackface peghead with pearl logo inlay, 3-per-side tuners, chrome hardware, 2 humbucker pickups, master volume/2 volume/1 tone controls, 3-position switch, available in Silver Sparkle finish, mfg. 1994-present.

MSR	$2,925	$2,350	$2,050	$1,800	$1,550	$1,300	$1,050	$800

Silver Jet 1957 Reissue with Bigsby Model G6129T-1957 (No. 240-0406) - similar to the Silver Jet 1957 Reissue, except has Bigsby tremolo, mfg. 1994-present.

MSR	$3,075	$2,500	$2,150	$1,900	$1,650	$1,400	$1,150	$900

SILVER JET 1962 REISSUE MODEL G6129T-1962 (NO. 240-0407) - similar to the Silver Jet, except features specifications based on the 1962 version and a Bigsby Tremolo, mfg. 1996-present.

MSR	$2,675	$2,150	$1,800	$1,500	$1,300	$1,100	$900	$700

SPARKLE JET MODEL G6129TX (NO. 240-0405) - single round cutaway mahogany body, bound arched maple top, raised white pickguard with logo, mahogany neck, 22-fret bound rosewood fingerboard with pearl humpblock inlay, Bigsby tremolo, bound blackface peghead with pearl horseshoe/logo inlay, 3-per-side tuners, chrome hardware, 2 humbucker pickups, master/2 volume/1 tone controls, selector switch, available in Black Sparkle (G6129TB), Champagne Sparkle (G6129TC), Green Sparkle (G6129TG), Gold Sparkle (G6129TAU), Light Blue Pearl Sparkle (G6129TL), or Red Sparkle (G6129TR) top finish, current mfg.

MSR	$2,675	$2,150	$1,800	$1,550	$1,300	$1,100	$900	$700

This model is also available as a 1962 Reissue with Champagne finish and a Bigsby Tremolo (Model G6129TC-1962, No. 240-0407). Black Sparkle finish was discontinued in 2002.

Sparkle Jet 1957 Reissue Model G6129G-1957 - similar to the Sparkle Jet, except features specifications based on the 1957 Reissue, available in Green Sparkle (G6129G-1957) or Gold Sparkle (G6129AU-1957) top finishes, disc.

		$2,100	$1,800	$1,600	$1,350	$1,150	$950	$750

Last MSR was $2,600.

ELECTRIC: SPECTRA SONIC SERIES

SPECTRA SONIC MODEL G6143 (NO. 240-1500) - single cutaway semi-hollow body, laminated spruce top, alder body, 3-piece mahogany neck, 22 fret African Padauk fingerboard with dot inlay, two humbucking pickups (T.V. Jones Classic & Plus), Bigsby Vibrato tailpiece, 3-per-side tuners, 3-way switch, two knobs (v, tone), chrome hardware, available in Black finish, mfg. 2002-present.

MSR	$2,500	$2,000	$1,750	$1,500	$1,300	$1,100	$900	$700

Spectra Sonic C-Melody Baritone Model G6144 (No. 240-1501) - similar to the Spectra Sonic except has a longer scale (29.25"), tuned differently, and has T.V. Jones Classic & MagnaTron pickups, available in Black finish, mfg. 2002-present.

MSR	$2,500	$2,000	$1,750	$1,500	$1,300	$1,100	$900	$700

ELECTRIC: STREAMLINER SERIES

STREAMLINER MODEL 6190 - single cutaway hollow bound body, arched top, f-holes, maple neck, 21-fret bound rosewood fingerboard with pearl hump-back inlay, roller bridge/G logo trapeze tailpiece, blackface peghead with nameplate, 3-per-side tuners with plastic buttons, chrome hardware, plastic pickguard, 1 single coil pickup, volume/tone controls, available in Natural (Model 6191), Yellow/Brown (Model 6189), Gold (Model 6189), or Sunburst (Model 6190) finishes, mfg. 1954-59.

	N/A	$2,000	$1,700	$1,450	$1,250	$1,050	$900

In 1958, a humbucker replaced the single coil pickup.

STREAMLINER MODEL 6102 - double round cutaway bound maple body, arched top, f-holes, maple neck, 22-fret bound rosewood fingerboard with pearl thumbnail inlay, dot inlay above 12th fret, roller bridge/G logo trapeze tailpiece, blackface peghead with nameplate, 3-per-side tuners with plastic buttons, chrome hardware, 2 covered pickups, master volume/2 volume controls, pickup selector/treble boost/standby switches, available in Cherry Red (Model 6103) or Sunburst (Model 6102) finishes, mfg. 1969-1975.

	N/A	$1,350	$1,150	$1,000	$850	$750	$650

In 1972, dot fingerboard inlay and nameplate were removed, Tune-O-Matic bridge replaced roller bridge. Between 1972 and 1975, the Red finish was redesignated Model 7566, and the Sunburst finish was redesignated Model 7565.

STREAMLINER MODEL G3150 (NO. 251-0201) - 16" single cutaway hollowbody design, Laminated maple top, back and sides, 24.5" scale, maple neck with rosewood fingerboard, neoclassical position markers, 2 Dynasonic single coil pickups, G tailpiece or Bigsby vibrato tailpiece, available in Cherry Red or Black (Model G3151) finishes, disc. 2003.

		$1,250	$1,050	$925	$850	$700	$575	$450

Last MSR was $1,560.

Add $95 for Cherry Red or White finish with Bigsby tailpiece (Models G3155 and G3156 respectively). Add $290 for left hand model in White or Black finish (Models GG3156LH and G 3156BKLH respectively).

GRADING	100% MINT	98% NEAR MINT	95% EXC+	90% EXC	80% VG+	70% VG	60% G

ELECTRIC: SUPER SERIES

SUPER AXE MODEL 7680 - refer to the Deluxe Chet Model.

SUPER CHET MODEL 7690 - single round cutaway hollow bound maple body, bound f-holes, raised black pickguard with engraved model name/logo, maple neck, 22-fret bound ebony fingerboard with abalone floral inlay, adjustamatic bridge/trapeze tailpiece with ebony insert with abalone floral inlay, bound blackface peghead with abalone floral/logo inlay, 3-per-side tuners, gold hardware, 2 exposed humbucker pickups, master volume/2 volume/2 tone controls all mounted on the pickguard, available in Red (Model 7690) or Walnut (Model 7691) finishes, mfg. 1972-1980.

1972-1975	N/A	$2,700	$2,300	$2,000	$1,700	$1,400	$1,100
1976-1980	N/A	$2,200	$1,900	$1,600	$1,400	$1,200	$1,000

This model was also available with Bigsby vibrato tailpiece.

SUPER GRETSCH MODEL G7690 - rounded double cutaway hollow bound body, laminated press-arched maple top and back, 7-ply laminated maple sides, bound f-holes, set-in 2 piece rock maple neck, 25.5 in. scale, 22-fret bound ebony fingerboard with abalone floral inlay, adjustable roller bridge on ebony base/Bigsby tremolo tailpiece, bound peghead with abalone floral/logo inlay, 3-per-side enclosed tuners, gold hardware, raised pickguard with logo, 2 Filtertron pickups, master volume/2 volume/master tone controls (body mounted), pickup selector switch, available in Shaded Golden Sunburst urethane finish, body width 17 in., body fepth 2.5 in., mfg. 1998-disc.

$2,400	$2,100	$1,700	$1,400	$1,200	$1,000	$800

Last MSR was $3,000.

This reissue model is based (in part) on the Super Chet model of the 1970s. Many modern refinements have modified the design.

Gretsch Silver Jet Model G6129T courtesy John Beeson The Music Shoppe

ELECTRIC: SYNCHROMATIC SERIES

SYNCHROMATIC MODEL G6040MCSS - single round cutaway jumbo style, arched maple top, bound fang soundholes, 3-stripe bound body, arched maple back, maple sides/neck, 14/20-fret bound rosewood fingerboard with pearl split humpblock inlay, adjustamatic metal bridge with ebony base/Bigsby vibrato tailpiece, bound blackface peghead with pearl model name/logo inlay, 3-per-side tuners, gold hardware, raised bound tortoise pickguard, humbucker pickup, volume/tone control, pickguard mounted pickup/controls, available in Natural finish, mfg. 1991-disc.

$2,000	$1,700	$1,400	$1,200	$1,000	$800	$600

Last MSR was $2,500.

SYNCHROMATIC JAZZ MODEL G410 - single round cutaway multi-bound auditorium style, carved spruce top, f-holes, flame maple back/sides/neck, 20-fret multi-bound ebony fingerboard with pearl split hump block inlay, adjustable ebony stairstep bridge/trapeze tailpiece, multi-bound blackface peghead with pearl logo inlay, 3-per-side Imperial tuners, gold hardware, raised bound flame maple pickguard, humbucker pickup, volume control, pickguard mounted pickup/control, available in Shaded finish, mfg. 1993-disc.

$4,600	$4,100	$3,700	$3,300	$2,900	$2,500	$2,100

Last MSR was $5,700.

Add $300 for Natural finish. (G410M) 2001.

SYNCHROMATIC ARCHTOP MODEL G3110 (NO. 251-0101) - 16.25 in. single cutaway hollow body design, laminated spruce top, Laminated Maple back and sides, maple set neck with rosewood fingerboard, neoclassical position markers, 2 cat´s-eye soundholes, synchronized bridge, 2 single coil Dynasonic pickups, available in Tobacco Sunburst finish, disc. 2003.

$1,300	$1,100	$950	$875	$725	$600	$475

Last MSR was $1,600.

Synchromatic Archtop Thinline Model G3140 (No. 251-0102) - similar to the Synchromatic except has a thinline body, available in Orange Stain or Black finishes, disc. 2003.

$1,200	$1,050	$900	$775	$650	$550	$425

Last MSR was $1,500.

ELECTRIC: TENNESSEE ROSE SERIES

TENNESSEE ROSE MODEL G6119 (NO. 240-1301) - single round cutaway semi-hollow bound maple body, raised silver pickguard with model name/logo, bound f-holes, maple neck, 22-fret bound rosewood fingerboard with pearl thumbnail inlay, ebony/metal Tune-O-Matic bridge/Bigsby vibrato tailpiece, black face peghead with pearl logo inlay, 3-per-side tuners, chrome hardware, 2 humbucker pickups, master volume/2 volume/1 tone controls, selector switch, available in Dark Cherry Red Stain finish, current mfg.

MSR	$2,625	$2,100	$1,800	$1,550	$1,300	$1,100	$900	$700

Tennessee Rose Left-Handed G6119 LH - similar to the Tennessee Rose, except in left-handed configuration, mfg. late 1994-present.

MSR	$2,925	$2,350	$2,050	$1,800	$1,550	$1,300	$1,050	$800

TENNESSEE ROSE 1962 MODEL G6119-1962 (NO. 240-1302) - similar to the Tennessee Rose, except is based on a 1962 configuration, available in Walnut finish, mfg. 1994-present.

MSR	$2,725	$2,200	$1,900	$1,650	$1,400	$1,150	$950	$750

This model is also available with Hilo 'Tron pickups and Burgandy finish (Model G6119-1962HT, No. 240-1303).

Gretsch Streamliner Model 6102 courtesy George McGuire

GRADING	100% MINT	98% NEAR MINT	95% EXC+	90% EXC	80% VG+	70% VG	60% G

Tennessee Rose 1962 Left-Handed G6119-1962HTLH (No. 240-1323) - similar to the Tennessee Rose HT, except in left-handed configuration, mfg. 1994-present.

	MSR	$3,075		$2,500	$2,150	$1,850	$1,600	$1,350	$1,100	$850

TENNESSEE ROSE SPECIAL G6119SP (NO. 240-1305) - similar to the Tennessee Rose, except is based on the late '50s models with a 2.5 in. deep body, 2 High Sensitive Filter'Tron pickups, Bigsby tailpiece, neo-classical dot markers, and a Gretsch rocking bar bridge, available in Deep Cherry Stain finish, mfg. 2004-present.

	MSR	$2,725		$2,200	$1,900	$1,650	$1,400	$1,150	$950	$750

ELECTRIC: TK, VAN EPS & VIKING SERIES

TK-300 MODEL 7625 - offset double cutaway solid body, white pickguard, bolt-on maple neck, 22-fret rosewood fingerboard with dot inlay, stop bridge, elongated "hockey stick" peghead, 6-on-a-side tuners, chrome hardware, 2 humbucker pickups, volume/tone controls, 3-way pickup selector switch, available in Red (Model 7624) or Natural (Model 7625) finishes, mfg. 1977-1981.

	N/A	$700	$625	$550	$475	$400	$325

VAN EPS MODEL 6079 - 7-string configuration, single round cutaway hollow bound maple body, bound f-holes, maple neck, 21-fret bound ebony fingerboard with pearl thumbnail inlay, tuning fork bridge, roller bridge/G logo trapeze tailpiece, bound blackface asymmetrical peghead with pearl logo inlay, peghead mounted nameplate, 4/3-per-side tuners, gold hardware, raised white pickguard with logo, 2 covered humbucker pickups, master volume/2 volume controls, pickup selector/tone/standby switches, available in Sunburst (Model 6079) or Walnut (Model 6080) finishes, mfg. 1968-1979.

1968-1971	N/A	$3,100	$2,600	$2,200	$1,800	$1,400	$1,000
1971-1979	N/A	$2,500	$2,100	$1,800	$1,500	$1,200	$900

Add 20% for Walnut finish.

The above model was a 7-string version. A 6-string version was also offered with 3-per-side tuners in Sunburst (Model 6081) and Brown (Model 6082), though it was discontinued in 1972. In 1972, peghead nameplate, tuning fork bridge and standby switch were removed, ebony bridge and chrome hardware replaced original parts/designs. Between 1972 to 1979, the Brown finish was redesignated Model 7581, and the Sunburst finish was redesignated Model 7580.

VIKING MODEL 6187 - double round cutaway hollow bound maple body, f-holes, 21-fret bound ebony fingerboard with pearl thumbnail inlay, offset dot inlay above 12th fret, string mute, roller bridge/Bigsby vibrato tailpiece with telescoping arm, bound blackface peghead with pearl logo inlay, peghead mounted nameplate, 3-per-side tuners, gold hardware, raised pickguard with Viking/logo, 2 covered humbucker rail pickups, master volume/2 volume controls, pickup selector/tone/mute/standby switches, leatherette back pad, available in Cadillac Green (Model 6189), Natural (Model 6188), or Sunburst (Model 6187) finishes, mfg. 1964-1974.

1964-1969	N/A	$2,000	$1,700	$1,400	$1,200	$1,000	$800
1970-1974	N/A	$1,500	$1,300	$1,100	$950	$800	$650

Early models had a Viking ship on the pickguard as well as the logos. In 1966, tuning fork bridge was added. In 1968, flat arm vibrato unit replaced original parts/design. In 1972, string mute, tuning fork and back pad were removed. Between 1972 and 1974, the Natural finish was redesignated Model 7586, and the Sunburst finish was redesignated Model 7585.

ELECTRIC: WHITE FALCOLN SERIES & VARIATIONS

WHITE FALCON MODEL 6136 - single round cutaway hollow bound maple body, arched spruce top, bound f-holes, maple neck, 21-fret bound ebony fingerboard with pearl "feather engraved" humptop block inlay, adjustable bridge/G logo tubular trapeze tailpiece, bound V styled white-face peghead with vertical Gold Sparkle wings/logo, 3-per-side Grover Imperial tuners, gold hardware, raised gold pickguard with falcon/logo, 2 exposed DeArmond pickups, master volume on cutaway bout, 2 volume/1 tone control, 3-position switch, available in White finish, mfg. 1955-1981.

1955	N/A	$25,000	$21,000	$18,000	$15,000	$12,000	$10,000
1956	N/A	$23,000	$19,000	$16,000	$13,000	$11,000	$9,000
1957	N/A	$21,000	$17,000	$14,000	$12,000	$10,000	$8,000
1958-1961	N/A	$18,000	$15,000	$13,000	$11,000	$9,000	$7,000
1962-1963	N/A	$8,000	$7,000	$6,200	$5,500	$4,700	$4,000
1964-1966	N/A	$7,000	$6,100	$5,300	$4,500	$3,700	$2,900
1967-1969	N/A	$5,000	$4,300	$3,600	$2,900	$2,300	$1,700
1970-1975	N/A	$4,500	$3,800	$3,200	$2,600	$2,200	$1,500
1976-1981	N/A	$4,000	$3,400	$2,800	$2,200	$1,700	$1,200

This instrument had Gold Sparkle binding and jeweled control knobs. The Gold Sparkle binding was not on all bound edges on the earliest models and it was sometimes omitted during this instruments' production run. In 1957, Filter-tron pickups replaced original parts/design. In 1958, arched maple top, thumbnail fingerboard inlay, horizontal peghead logo, roller bridge and tone switch (placed by pickup selector control) replaced original parts/designs, peghead mounted nameplate was added, though it was not placed on all instruments produced. Stereo output became optional (as Model 6137). In 1959, second version of stereo output offered with 3 tone switches placed by pickup selector switch.

In 1960, double mute with 2 controls and back pad were added. In 1962, double round cutaway body and Bigsby vibrato tailpiece became standard, it was offered as an option up to this time. Some models had a G logo tubular trapeze tailpiece. Stereo models had master volume control removed and pickup selector switch put in its place. In 1963, mute controls were changed to switches. In 1964, Gretsch G logo vibrato trapeze tailpiece and oval button tuners replaced original parts/designs. In 1965, offset dot fingerboard inlay above 12th fret was added, stereo tone switches were moved to lower bout and controls/switches were reconfigured. In 1966, tuning fork bridge was added. In 1972, Bigsby vibrato unit replaced Gretsch vibrato unit. Between 1972 to 1981, the model was redesignated Model 7594. In 1980, the non-stereo models were discontinued, and the double round cutaway stereo model (Model 7595) was available as a special order item.

White Falcon Reissue - reissue of original White Falcon design, available in White finish, mfg. 1972-1981.

	N/A	$4,500	$3,800	$3,300	$2,800	$2,300	$1,800

GRADING	100% MINT	98% NEAR MINT	95% EXC+	90% EXC	80% VG+	70% VG	60% G

WHITE FALCON CURRENT MFG. MODEL G6136 (NO. 241-1401) - single round cut-away semi-hollow bound maple body, bound f-holes, maple neck, 22-fret bound rosewood fingerboard with pearl block inlay, ebony/metal Tune-O-Matic bridge/Cadillac tailpiece, bound peghead with pearl gold sparkle logo inlay, 3-per-side tuners, gold hardware, raised gold pickguard with flying falcon, 2 humbucker pickups, master volume/2 volume/1 tone controls, selector switch, available in White finish, mfg. 1991-present.

	MSR	$4,175	$3,400	$3,000	$2,600	$2,200	$1,850	$1,500	$1,250

Also available with a Bigsby tailpiece at no additional cost.

White Falcon I Model G7593 (No. 240-1406) - similar to White Falcon 1955 Single Cutaway, except has Bigsby vibrato tailpiece, imported from Japan, mfg. 1991-present.

	MSR	$4,025	$3,250	$2,850	$2,450	$2,100	$1,750	$1,400	$1,150

White Falcon II Model G7594 (No. 240-1407) - similar to White Falcon I, except has double round cutaway body and Bigsby tremolo, imported from Japan, mfg. 1991-present.

	MSR	$4,025	$3,250	$2,850	$2,450	$2,100	$1,750	$1,400	$1,150

WHITE FALCON LEFT-HANDED MODEL G6136-1959LH (NO. 241-1423) - similar to the White Falcon 1959 model except in left-handed configuration, current mfg.

	MSR	$4,625	$3,800	$3,300	$2,900	$2,500	$2,100	$1,700	$1,400

BLACK FALCON 1955 SINGLE CUTAWAY MODEL G6136BK - single round cutaway semi hollow bound maple body, raised gold pickguard with flying falcon, bound f-holes, maple neck, 22-fret bound rosewood fingerboard with pearl block inlay, ebony/metal Tune-O-Matic bridge/Cadillac tailpiece, bound peghead with pearl gold sparkle logo inlay, 3-per-side tuners, gold hardware, 2 humbucker pickups, master volume/2 volume/1 tone controls, selector switch, available in Black finish, disc. 1999, reintroduced 2003 and is currently produced.

	MSR	$4,175	$3,400	$3,000	$2,600	$2,200	$1,850	$1,500	$1,250

Also available with a Bigsby tailpiece at no additional cost.

Black Falcon I Model G7593BK - similar to Black Falcon, except has a Bigsby vibrato tailpiece, disc. 1996, reintroduced current mfg.

	MSR	$4,025	$3,250	$2,850	$2,450	$2,100	$1,750	$1,400	$1,150

Gretsch Tennessee Rose Special G6119SP courtesy Gretsch

Black Falcon II Model G7594BK - similar to Black Falcon, except has a double round cutaway body instead of the single cutaway body, disc.

		$2,900	$2,500	$2,200	$1,875	$1,550	$1,225	$900

Last MSR was $3,600.

SILVER FALCOLN MODEL G 6136SL (G7594SL) - similar to White Falcon I, available in Silver finish, imported from Japan, mfg. 1997-99, reintroduced 2003-present.

	MSR	$4,175	$3,400	$3,000	$2,600	$2,200	$1,850	$1,500	$1,250

Also available with a Bigsby tailpiece at no additional cost.

WHITE FALCON JR. MODEL G7594JR (NO. 240-1408) - similar to White Falcon, except with a smaller, sleeker body, laminated maple top and back, gold fleck binding and white/black purfling, 7-ply laminated maple sides, f-holes, two-piece rock maple set neck, ebony fingerboard, 22-frets, white headstock with gold binding, gold truss rod cover, bone nut, two gold-plated Filtertron pickups, master volume, two pickup volume, master tone, selector switch, gold-plated hardware, available in White finish, mfg. 1999-2003.

		$2,580	$2,250	$2,000	$1,750	$1,550	$1,300	$1,050

Last MSR was $3,225.

STEPHEN STILLS WHITE FALCOLN MODEL G6136-1958 (NO. 240-0105) - similar to the White Falcon except to Stephen Stills specifications, has enlarged f-holes, his signature between the 18th and 21st fret inlaid, FilterTron pickups, available in Aged White finish, current mfg.

	MSR	$4,825	$3,900	$3,400	$3,000	$2,600	$2,300	$2,000	$1,700

1955 WHITE FALCON CUSTOM REISSUE MODEL G6136-1955 - similar to White Falcon 1955 Single Cutaway, except has a carved solid spruce top, ebony fingerboard and bridge base, 24kt. gold plating on hardware, 2 Gretsch Dynasonic pickups, available with hand rubbed lacquer finish, body width 17 in., mfg. 1995-99.

		$7,200	$6,300	$5,500	$4,700	$4,000	$3,300	$2,500

Last MSR was $8,900.

WHITE FALCON U.S. CUSTOM SHOP G6136CST (NO. 240-1404) - U.S. Custom Shop version based on the earliest White Falcons from the 1950s, includes DynaSonic pickups, and all signature Falcon trim, available in White finish, mfg. 2004-present.

	MSR	$11,000	$9,000	$8,000	$7,000	N/A	N/A	N/A	N/A

ELECTRIC: WHITE PENGUIN SERIES

This model debuted at the 1956 Music Industry trade show, and was produced in very small amounts while it was "available" until 1963. The only mention of this model from Gretsch was the appearance on the 1958 and 1959 price lists – it never appeared in any of the Gretsch catalogs.

This guitar is ultra rare; and of the 50 manufactured, only 19 are publicly accounted for. The *Blue Book of Electric Guitars* is aware of a small numbers of others not publicly accounted for that are in the hands of private collectors.

Gretsch White Falcon Model 6136 courtesy Dave Rogers Dave's Guitar Shop

GRADING	100% MINT	98% NEAR MINT	95% EXC+	90% EXC	80% VG+	70% VG	60% G

WHITE PENGUIN MODEL 6134 - single cutaway mahogany body, bound arched top, mahogany neck, 22-fret bound ebony fingerboard with pearl feather engraved humptop block inlay, adjustable bridge/G logo tubular trapeze tailpiece, bound V styled white face peghead with vertical Gold Sparkle wings/logo, 3-per-side Grover Imperial tuners, gold hardware, raised gold pickguard with penguin/logo, 2 exposed DeArmond pick-ups, master/2 volume/1 tone control, 3-position switch, available in White finish, mfg. 1955-1963.

	N/A	$80,000	$70,000	$60,000	$50,000	$40,000	$30,000

Originally released with banjo armrest attached to bass lower bout. This instrument had gold sparkle binding and jeweled control knobs. In 1957, Filter-tron pickups replaced original parts/design. In 1958, thumbnail fingerboard inlay, roller bridge replaced the original parts/designs, 3-position switch replaced tone control and was placed by the other switch. In 1959, horizontal logo/metal nameplate was applied to peghead. In 1961, double cutaway body became available.

WHITE PENGUIN (BLACK PENGUIN) MODEL G6134 (NO. 241-0509) - a reissue of the original White Penguin, available in White or Black finishes, mfg. 1996-present.

MSR	$3,975	$3,250	$2,850	$2,550	$2,200	$1,850	$1,500	$1,250

ELECTRIC: ELECTROMATIC/SYNCHROMATIC COLLECTION SERIES

Value line of guitars launched in 2000. Headstocks bear the Synchromatic logo and NOT Gretsch. The Gretsch logo is on the truss rod covers.

BO DIDDLEY G1810/5810 (NO. 270-2903/251-5405) - 17.75 in. X 9.75 in. rectangular body, bolt-on maple neck, rosewood fingerboard with dot position markers, 2 Gretsch humbucker pickups, adjustable bridge, 1 volume and 1 tone control plus master volume and master tone controls, 3-way switch, 3-per-side die-cast tuners, available in Red finish, mfg. 2000-present.

MSR	$500	$400	$350	$300	$250	$210	$170	$130

MINI-DIDDLEY G1850/5850 (NO. 251-2905/5406) - compact version of the Bo Diddley model, 8 in. X 15.5 in. body, 20 frets, 1 Gretsch humbucker pickup, bolt-on maple neck with rosewood fingerboard, dot position markers, wraparound tailpiece, 1 volume and 1 tone control, 2-way pickup enhancement switch, die-cast tuners, available in Red finish, mfg. 2000-present.

MSR	$420	$350	$300	$260	$230	$200	$160	$120

ELLIOT EASTON G1570/5570 (NO. 250-2901/5400) - single cutaway mahogany body with carved top, mahogany neck, rosewood fingerboard, Bigsby tailpiece, Dual Gretsch Humbucking pickups, available in Cadillac Green finish, current mfg.

MSR	$1,000	$750	$675	$600	$525	$450	$375	$300

DOUBLE JET G1910/5425T (NO. 251-3005/250-5040) - double cutaway body, bolt-on maple neck, rosewood fingerboard with dot position markers, 2 Gretsch humbucker pickups, black and white binding, adjustable bridge, pickup selector switch, master volume, 3-per-side die-cast tuners, available in Satin Amber, Black, Red, Gold Sparkle, or Silver Sparkle finishes, mfg. 2000-present.

MSR	$700	$525	$450	$400	$350	$300	$250	$200

ELECTROMATIC HOLLOW BODY G512X (NO. 250-5801) - single cutaway, laminated top/back/sides, maple neck, 22-fret rosewood fingerboard, black pickguard, 2 DeArmond single coil pickups, Adjusto-Matic bridge, Bigsby tailpiece, four knobs, 3-way switch, chrome hardware, available in Silver Sparkle, Light Blue, Gold Sparkle, Firebird Red, or Black finishes, mfg. 2004-present.

MSR	$1,200	$960	$850	$750	$675	$600	$525	$450

JET CLUB G1413 (NO. 251-3002) - single cutaway solid body, bolt-on maple neck with rosewood fingerboard, block position markers, 2 gretsch humbucker pickups, chrome Tune-O-Matic bridge, frosted pickguard, 2 volume and 2 tone controls, 3-way switch, 3-per-side die-cast tuners, available in Tobacco Sunburst finish, mfg. 2000-03.

			$350	$295	$250	$225	$195	$175	$150

Last MSR was $500.

JET PRO G1514/5235 (NO. 251-3003/5010) - similar to the other models in the Jet series, except has carved arched top, 2 Gretsch humbucker pickups, set maple neck with rosewood fingerboard, crown position markers, chrome plated Tune-O-Matic bridge, 2 volume and 2 tone controls, 3-way switch, 3-per-side die-cast tuners, available in Black, Silver Sparkle, Gold Sparkle, or Cherry Sunburst finishes, mfg. 2000-present.

MSR	$550	$425	$350	$300	$250	$220	$190	$160

Add $120 for Bigsby tailpiece.

In 2001, Black and Silver Sparkle finishes were introduced.

JET II G1315 (NO. 251-3001) - single cutaway solid body, bolt-on maple neck with rosewood fingerboard, dot position markers, 2 Gretsch humbucker pickups, chrome plated wraparound bridge, frosted pickguard, 1 volume and 1 tone control, 3-way switch, 3-per-side die-cast tuners, available in Sunburst finish, mfg. 2000-03.

			$295	$250	$225	$195	$175	$150	$125

Last MSR was $420.

JUNIOR JET G1121/5210 (NO. 251-3000/5030) - single cutaway solid body, bolt-on maple neck, rosewood fingerboard with dot position markers, chrome plated wraparound bride, 1 Gretsch single coil pickup, frosted pickguard, 1 volume and 1 tone control, 3-per-side die-cast tuners, available in Tobacco Sunburst, Black, Candy Apple Red, Regal Blue, Tangerine, or Purple finishes, mfg. 2000-present.

MSR	$350	$275	$235	$195	$165	$135	$105	$75

In 2001, Black, Candy Apple Red, Regal Blue, Tangerine and Purple finishes were introduced.

Junior Jet II G5220 (No. 251-5020) - similar to the Junior Jet, except has 2 mini-humbucker pickups, available in Tobacco Sunburst or Black finishes, mfg. 2004-present.

MSR	$400	$300	$260	$230	$200	$170	$140	$110

SPARKLE JET G1615 (NO. 251-3006) - single cutaway semi-hollow body design, bolt-on maple neck with rosewood fingerboard. Dot position markers, chrome wraparound bridge, 2 volume controls and 1 tone control, master volume, 3-way switch, 3-per-side die-cast tuners, available in Black, Silver, Blue, Gold, or Red finishes, mfg. 2000-04.

			$350	$300	$250	$220	$190	$160	$130

Last MSR was $450.

Add $100 for Bigsby tailpiece, new 2001.

A matching headstock with 1 f-hole is also available.

GRADING		100% MINT	98% NEAR MINT	95% EXC+	90% EXC	80% VG+	70% VG	60% G

Double Neck Sparkle Jet G1566 (No. 251-3901) - similar to the Sparkle Jet except has two necks, one bass and one guitar, available in Silver finish, mfg. 2002-present.

| MSR | $1,350 | $1,025 | $900 | $825 | $750 | $675 | $600 | $500 |

SPECIAL JET G525X (NO. 251-5000) - single cutaway mahogany body, mahogany neck, 22-fret rosewood fingerboard, black pickguard, 2 DeArmond single coil pickups, wrap around bridge and tailpiece, two knobs, 3-way switch, chrome hardware, available in Tobacco Sunburst, Cherry, or Black finishes, new 2004.

| MSR | $700 | $525 | $450 | $400 | $350 | $300 | $250 | $200 |

ELECTRIC BASS

BIKINI BASS MODEL 6024 - double cutaway slide-and-lock poplar body with detachable poplar center block, bolt-on maple neck, 17-fret maple fingerboard with black dot inlay, adjustable ebony bridge/stop tailpiece, black face peghead with logo, 2-per-side tuners, chrome hardware, humbucker pickup, volume/tone control, available in Black finish, mfg. 1961-63.

| | N/A | $1,600 | $1,400 | $1,200 | $1,050 | $900 | $750 |

The slide-and-lock body is called a Butterfly back and is interchangeable with 6-string or bass shafts. There was also a Double Butterfly, able to accommodate both necks. Controls for this instrument are located on top of detachable center block.

BROADKASTER MODEL 7605 - offset double cutaway maple body, white pickguard, bolt-on maple neck, 30.5 in. scale, 20-fret maple fingerboard with black dot inlay, fixed bridge with cover, 2-per-side tuners, chrome hardware, exposed pickup, volume/tone control, available in Natural (Model 7605) and Sunburst (Model 7606) finishes, mfg. 1975-79.

| | N/A | $700 | $625 | $550 | $475 | $400 | $325 |

BROADKASTER HOLLOW BODY BASS MODEL G6119B (NO. 241-6000) - single round cutaway semi-hollow bound maple body, bound f-holes, maple neck, 30.5 in. scale, 20-fret bound rosewood fingerboard with pearl thumbnail inlay, adjustamatic metal bridge with ebony base/trapeze tailpiece, blackface peghead with pearl logo inlay, 2-per-side tuners, chrome hardware, 2 humbucker pickups, 2 volume/1 tone controls, selector switch, available in Natural (Model G6119-B) or Trans. Orange (Model 6119-B/O) finishes, current mfg.

| MSR | $2,300 | $1,850 | $1,600 | $1,350 | $1,150 | $950 | $800 | $650 |

The Broadkaster Hollow Body Electric Bass is also known as the Tennessee Rose/Broadcaster.

Broadkaster Left-Handed (G6119-BLH) - similar to the Broadkaster bass, except in a left-handed configuration, mfg. late 1994-disc.

| | $2,200 | $1,900 | $1,600 | $1,300 | $1,000 | $850 | $700 |

Last MSR was $2,700.

Gretsch White Penguin
Model G6134
courtesy Gretsch

COMMITTEE BASS MODEL 7629 - double cutaway walnut body, clear pickguard, through-body maple/walnut neck, 22-fret rosewood fingerboard with pearl dot inlay, fixed bridge, bound peghead with burl walnut veneer and pearl logo inlay, 2-per-side tuners, chrome hardware, exposed pickup, volume/tone control, available in Natural (Model 7629) finish, mfg. 1977-1981.

| | N/A | $600 | $525 | $450 | $375 | $300 | $250 |

ELECTROTONE BASS G6073 (NO. 241-6002) - single smooth cutaway hollow body, two f-holes, body/neck binding, 22-fret rosewood fingerboard with side inlays, two-per-side tuners, Gretsch tailpiece, adjustable bridge, two ThunderTron pickups, three knobs, two switches, available in Burgundy Stain finish, new 2005.

| MSR | $2,675 | $2,200 | $1,900 | $1,650 | $1,400 | $1,200 | $1,000 | $800 |

JET BARITONE G1255/5265 (NO. 250-3903/251-5900) - similar to Jet Bass except is tuned differently, has a Bigsby tailpiece, available in Black Sparkle finish, mfg. 2002-present.

| MSR | $640 | $500 | $425 | $375 | $325 | $275 | $225 | $175 |

JET BASS LONG SCALE G1232 (NO. 251-3602) - similar to Junior Jet Bass except is in a long scale, available in Black Burst finish, mfg. 2002-03.

| | $475 | $425 | $350 | $300 | $250 | $200 | $150 |

Last MSR was $680.

JUNIOR JET BASS G1212 (NO. 251-3600) - single cutaway solid body, bolt-on maple neck, rosewood fingerboard with dot position markers, 2-per-side die-cast tuners, 1 mini-humbucker pickup, adjustable bridge, 1 volume and 1 tone control, available in Black Sunburst finish, mfg. 2000-03.

| | $270 | $225 | $175 | $150 | $125 | $95 | $65 |

Last MSR was $380.

JUNIOR JET II BASS G1222 (NO. 251-3601) - similar to Junior Jet Bass except has 2 humbucking pickups, available in Black Sunburst finish, mfg. 2000-03.

| | $350 | $295 | $250 | $195 | $150 | $125 | $95 |

Last MSR was $500.

LONG SCALE HOLLOW BODY BASS MODEL G6072 (NO. 241-6001) - double rounded cutaway hollow bound body, laminated maple top and back, 7-ply laminated maple sides, 2 bound f-holes, set-in 3-piece rock maple neck, 34 in. scale, 20-fret rosewood fingerboard with white dot inlay, adjustable bridge on ebony bass/G logo trapeze tailpiece, 2-per-side tuners, gold hardware, 2 covered pickups, Master volume/2 volume controls, tone/standby/pickup selector switches, round pad on back, available in Shaded Golden Sunburst finishes, body width 17 in., body depth 2 in., mfg. 1998-present.

| MSR | $2,300 | $1,850 | $1,600 | $1,350 | $1,150 | $950 | $800 | $650 |

Gretsch Electromatic Hollow
Body G5125
courtesy Gretsch

GRADING	100% MINT	98% NEAR MINT	95% EXC+	90% EXC	80% VG+	70% VG	60% G

MODEL 6070 (COUNTRY GENTLEMAN BASS) - double round cutaway hollow bound maple body, arched top with painted bound f-holes, finger rests, maple neck, 34 in. scale, 20-fret rosewood fingerboard with white dot inlay, string mute with switch, roller bridge/G logo trapeze tailpiece, bound blackface peghead with metal nameplate, 2-per-side tuners, gold hardware, covered pickup, volume control, tone/standby switches, round pad on back, available in Amber Red and Sunburst finishes, Body Width 17 in., mfg. 1962-1972.

	N/A	$1,050	$900	$800	$700	$600	$500

After 1972, this model was available only by special order.

MODEL 6071 - single round cutaway hollow bound maple body, 29 in. scale, painted bound f-holes, finger rests, maple neck, 21-fret rosewood fingerboard with white dot inlay, zero fret, string mute with switch, roller bridge/G logo trapeze tailpiece, blackface peghead with logo, 4-on-a-side tuners, gold hardware, covered pickup, volume control, tone/standby switches, available in Red Mahogany finish, body width 16 in., mfg. 1964-1972.

	N/A	$900	$750	$650	$550	$450	$350

In 1967, chrome hardware replaced gold hardware. After 1972, this model was available only by special order.

MODEL 6072 - similar to the Model 6070, except has 2 covered pickups, master/2 volume controls, pickup selector/tone/standby switches, available in Sunburst finish, mfg. 1968-1972.

	N/A	$1,250	$1,100	$950	$850	$750	$650

MODEL 6073 - similar to the Model 6071, except has 2 covered pickups, master/2 volume controls, pickup selector/tone/standby switches, available in Mahogany finish, mfg. 1968-1972.

	N/A	$1,100	$950	$800	$700	$600	$500

In 1967, chrome hardware replaced gold hardware.

MODEL 7615 - offset double cutaway asymmetrical mahogany body treble bout cutout, rosewood pickguard with finger rests, mahogany neck, 22-fret bound rosewood fingerboard with white dot inlay, fixed bridge, bound peghead with logo, 2-per-side tuners, chrome hardware, 2 exposed pickups, 2 controls, 3-position switch, available in Mahogany finish, mfg. 1972-75.

	N/A	$600	$525	$450	$375	$325	$275

SPECTRA SONIC BASS MODEL G6145 (NO. 241-6009) - TV Jones designed bass similar to the Spectra Sonic guitar, available in Black finish, current mfg.

MSR	$2,500	$2,000	$1,750	$1,500	$1,300	$1,100	$900	$700

TK 300 MODEL 7627 - offset double cutaway maple body with divot in bottom, white pickguard, bolt-on maple neck, 20-fret rosewood fingerboard, fixed bridge with cover, chrome hardware, 4-on-a-side tuners, exposed pickup, volume/tone control, available in Autumn Red Stain (Model 7626) or Natural (Model 7627) finishes, mfg. 1977-1981.

	N/A	$650	$575	$500	$425	$350	$275

In 1980, Natural finish was discontinued.

GRIMSHAW
Instruments previously produced in England from the 1950s through the late 1970s.

While this company is best known for its high quality archtop guitars, they also produced a notable semi-hollowbody design in the mid 1950s called the Short-Scale. In the early 1960s, Emile Grimshaw introduced the Meteor solid body guitar. The company then focused on both original and copies of American designs from the late 1960s on (Source: Tony Bacon and Paul Day, *The Guru's Guitar Guide*).

GRIS GRIS GUITARS
Instruments currently built in New Orleans, LA since 1998.

Gris Gris Guitars and Instruments was founded by Ted Graham in 1998. Graham, a rock and rhythm & blues guitar player since the late 1960s/early 1970s, was looking for a guitar with the "perfect look and sound" – so he created one. Using guitar bodies from different sources, Graham commissioned New Orleans Artist Perry Morgan to paint the bodies in one-of-a-kind Voodoo-style designs. Graham also customizes the electronics, to make the guitars "irresistible to the guitar player." All hand-painted instruments are completed in New Orleans. For further information regarding Gris Gris Guitars, contact Ted Graham directly (see Trademark Index).

Perry Morgan is a Magazine Street artist known to Jazzfest fans and others for his ornately painted silks, furniture, and other mediums with a sometime Caribbean tilt. Morgan and Graham attended and studied the 1998 exhibit "The Sacred Arts of Haitian VoDou" at the New Orleans Museum of Art to absorb the themes of the voodoo alters and other art forms from the island. New Orleans still retains its strong Haitian influence, evident today in its food and flavors, architecture, mood, and music.

GROOVE TOOLS
Groove Tools By Conklin. Instruments currently built in Korea. Distributed by Westheimer Corporation of Chicago, IL.

The Groove Tools line of bass guitars is based on designs from luthier Bill Conklin (see CONKLIN). The instruments are produced in Korea, and re-checked in the U.S. prior to shipping to the dealer thus maintaining a high level of quality.

ELECTRIC BASS

GT-4 - offset double cutaway swamp ash body with extended bass bout, figured maple top, bolt-on 5-ply wenge/purpleheart laminated neck with tilt-back headstock, 2-per-side tuners, 24-fret purpleheart fingerboard with dot inlays, fixed bridge, black hardware, 2 Conklin active soapbar pickups, volume/blend/bass/treble controls, available in Clear Hard or Cellophane Magenta finishes, 34 in. scale, current mfg.

MSR	$995		$695	$600	$525	$450	$400	$350	$300

This model is also available in fretless configuration.

GT-5 - similar to the GT-4, except has 5-string configuration, 3/2 headstock, current mfg.

MSR	$1,095		$770	$675	$600	$525	$450	$400	$350

This model is also available in fretless configuration.

GT-7 - similar to the GT-4, except has 7-string configuration, 4/3-per-side headstock, 7 piece laminated wenge/purpleheart neck, 2 Bartolini active soapbar pickups, current mfg.

MSR	$1,695		$1,195	$1,050	$925	$800	$700	$600	$500

This model is also available in fretless configuration.

GRADING	100% MINT	98% NEAR MINT	95% EXC+	90% EXC	80% VG+	70% VG	60% G

GT-BD7 BILL DICKENS SIGNATURE - similar to the GT-4, except has 7-string configuration, 4/3 headstock, 7-piece laminated Maple/Purpleheart neck, through-body design, swamp ash wings/curly maple top, gold hardware, 2 Bartolini "Bill Dickens" model pickups, custom Bartolini parametric frequency selector, brilliance/volume/blend/EQ controls, available in Clear Hard or Purple Burst finishes, current mfg.

	MSR	$2,395		$1,650	$1,450	$1,300	$1,150	$1,000	$850	$700

This 7-string model was developed in conjunction with bassist Bill Dickens.

GROSH, DON CUSTOM GUITARS

Instruments currently built in Canyon Country, CA since 1992.

Luthier/designer Don Grosh has been repairing and building guitars since the 1980s. In the 1980s, Grosh worked for a prominent Southern California guitar producer, and has worked with notable guitarists such as Steve Lukather. For the past five years, Grosh has been offering his fine handcrafted models out of his workshop. Grosh combines state of the art building techniques with quality tone woods and real lacquer finishes for a good looking/good sounding professional instrument.

GENERAL INFORMATION

All models are available with the following standard finishes, unless otherwise listed:

Bursts: Cherry Burst, Honey Burst, Tobacco Burst, Two-Color Burst, and Three-Color Burst.
Metallic Colors: Black, Blue, Burgundy, Deep Jewel Green, Gold, Purple, Red, and Teal Blue.
Solid Colors: Baby Blue, Black, Vintage Peach, Vintage Red, and Vintage White.
Transparent Colors: Amber, Black, Blonde, Blue, Butterscotch, Cherry, Green, Magenta, Orange, Purple, and Turquoise. All models have a 25.5 in. scale. There are other options as well as the following options; check website for more information: Grosh featured an **ElectraTone** series that have a retro Danelectro feel to them - and that´s a good thing! **ElectraTone** models feature a semi-hollow poplar body with a laminated vintage colored top, bolt-on neck, 22-fret rosewood fingerboard, vintage flat-mount bridge. Models are available with a choice of 2 P-90 single coils (**Model GE P-90**), 2 humbuckers (**Model GE H-H**), 2 lipstick tube single coils (**Model GE LIPSTICK**), or three single coil pickups (**Model GE SSS**); pickups are mounted to a pickguard. Retail list was $1,195 (the GE SSS 3 retail list was $1,250). A 12-string configuration model (**GE 12**) and a Baritone model (**GE BARATONE**) were announced for future consideration, but it is unknown if they were ever produced.

Add $200 for bird's-eye maple neck. Add $40 for ebony fingerboard. Add $30 for Jumbo (6100) or Tall Narrow (6105) frets. Add $30 for blend pot (allows pickup combinations not available on standard select switches). Add $30 for locking, standard, or Kluson tuners. Add $50 for white pearl, green pearl, mint, or tortoise shell pickguard. Add $50 for chrome or gold humbucker covers. Add $70 for mahogany or swamp ash body. Add $60 for Wilkinson bridge. Add $240 for Floyd Rose bridge. Add $120 for black hardware. Add $120 for gold hardware. Add $200 for 3 Lindy Fralin single coil pickups. Add $300 for Tie Dye finish. Add $250 for 2 single coil/1 humbucker Lindy Fralin pickups. Add $250 for highly figured (flame or quilt) maple top. Add $600 for RMC MIDI synth electronics. Add $200 for White Limba/Black Limba body. Add $300 for full hollow body routing with F-Holes. Add $300 for Solid Rosewood Neck.

ELECTRIC GUITARS

The Set Neck model was introduced in the early 2000s. This guitar represents Grosh's top of the line model. Features include a AAAAA quilt or flamed maple top, a full-access 22-fret neck, an a reinforced neck/headstock volute. Prices retail at $3,980 and $4,900 for the limited model. Options are available on this model as well.

BARITONE (MODEL BT) - S or T body shape, long scale, disc.

			$1,800	$1,550	$1,250	$1,050	$900	$750	$600

Last MSR was $2,250.

BENT TOP CUSTOM (MODEL BTC) - offset double cutaway basswood or mahogany body, contoured (bent) figured maple top, bolt-on maple neck, 22-fret maple or rosewood fingerboard with dot position markers, Grosh vintage tremolo or flat mount/string through-body bridge, 6-on-a-side headstock, chrome hardware, white or black pickguard, 3 single coil Seymour Duncan or DiMarzio pickups, volume/tone controls, 5-way selector switch, current mfg.

MSR	$2,880		$2,350	$2,150	$1,950	$1,650	$1,350	$1,100	$950

Bent Top Custom T (Model BTT) - similar to the Bent Top Custom, except has a single cutaway body design, current mfg.

MSR	$2,880		$2,350	$2,150	$1,950	$1,650	$1,350	$1,100	$950

CUSTOM CARVE TOP (MODEL CCT) - single cutaway mahogany body, arched (carved) figured maple top, bolt-on maple or mahogany neck, 22-fret maple or rosewood fingerboard with dot position markers, stop tail bridge, 6-on-a-side headstock, chrome hardware, 2 humbucker Seymour Duncan or DiMarzio pickups, volume/tone controls, 3-way selector, current mfg.

MSR	$3,180		$2,750	$2,500	$2,300	$2,050	$1,800	$1,550	$1,300

Hollow Carve Top (Model HCT) - similar to the Custom Carve Top, except has hollowed basswood or mahogany body (internal tone chamber).

MSR	$3,280		$2,800	$2,550	$2,350	$2,100	$1,850	$1,600	$1,325

ELECTRIC ACOUSTIC (MODEL EA) - single cutaway alder body, bolt-on maple or mahogany neck, 22-fret maple or rosewood fingerboard with dot position markers, stop tail bridge, 6-on-a-side headstock, chrome hardware, custom piezo transducer mounted in bridge, volume/tone controls, current mfg.

MSR	$2,880		$2,350	$2,150	$1,950	$1,650	$1,350	$1,100	$950

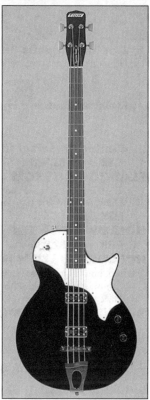

Gretsch Spectra Sonic Bass
Model G6145
courtesy Gretsch

G

Don Grosh Bent Top Custom
courtesy Don Grosh

GRADING	100% MINT	98% NEAR MINT	95% EXC+	90% EXC	80% VG+	70% VG	60% G

Electric Acoustic Trilogy (Model ET) - similar to the Electric Acoustic, except has rosewood bridge and Hipshot Trilogy tuning machine, current mfg.

		$2,400	$2,175	$1,950	$1,650	$1,350	$1,100	$950

Last MSR was $2,900.

Electric Acoustic Hybred (Model ET-H) - similar to the Electric Acoustic, except has magnetic pickups, selector switch, current mfg.

		$2,400	$2,175	$1,950	$1,650	$1,350	$1,100	$950

Last MSR was $2,900.

Electric Classical (Model EC) - similar to the Electric Acoustic, except has classical nylon strings and a rosewood bridge, current mfg.

MSR	$2,880	$2,350	$2,150	$1,950	$1,650	$1,350	$1,100	$950

FLAT TOP CUSTOM (MODEL FTC) - single cutaway basswood or mahogany body, figured maple top, bolt-on maple or mahogany neck, 22-fret maple or rosewood fingerboard with dot position markers, stop tail bridge, 6-on-a-side headstock, chrome hardware, 2 humbucker Seymour Duncan or DiMarzio pickups, volume/tone controls, 3-way selector, current mfg.

MSR	$2,880	$2,350	$2,150	$1,950	$1,650	$1,350	$1,100	$950

HOLLOW BENT TOP CUSTOM (MODEL HBTC) - similar to the Bent top except has a hollowed out body, current mfg.

MSR	$2,980	$2,400	$2,200	$1,975	$1,675	$1,400	$1,150	$950

HOLLOW CUSTOM (MODEL HC) - single cutaway basswood or mahogany hollowed-out body (internal tone chamber), figured maple top, bolt-on maple or mahogany neck, 22-fret maple or rosewood fingerboard with dot position markers, flat mount bridge, 6-on-a-side headstock, chrome hardware, 2 humbucker Seymour Duncan or DiMarzio pickups, volume/tone controls, 3-way selector, current mfg.

MSR	$2,980	$2,400	$2,200	$2,000	$1,700	$1,400	$1,150	$975

RETRO CLASSIC (MODEL RC) - offset double cutaway alder body, bolt-on maple neck, 22-fret maple or rosewood fingerboard with dot position markers, Grosh vintage tremolo or flat mount/string through-body bridge, 6-on-a-side headstock, chrome hardware, white or black pickguard, 3 single coil Seymour Duncan or DiMarzio pickups, volume/tone controls, 5-way selector switch. Current Mfg.

MSR	$2,500	$2,000	$1,800	$1,650	$1,500	$1,250	$1,050	$900

Retro Classic Pink Sparkle (Model RCPS) - similar to Retro Classic, except has a special Pink Sparkle finish, cream binding on top, disc.

		$1,750	$1,500	$1,300	$1,100	$950	$800	$650

Last MSR was $2,200.

RETRO CLASSIC VINTAGE T (MODEL RCVT) - single cutaway alder body, bolt-on maple neck, 22-fret maple or rosewood fingerboard with dot position markers, flat mount/string through-body bridge, 6-on-a-side headstock, chrome hardware, white or black pickguard, 2 single coil Seymour Duncan or DiMarzio pickups, volume/tone controls, 3-way selector switch, current mfg.

MSR	$2,500	$2,000	$1,800	$1,650	$1,500	$1,250	$1,050	$900

RETRO CLASSIC HOLLOW T (MODEL RCHT) - similar to the Retro Classic Vintage T, except has hollowed out body (internal acoustic tone chamber), current mfg.

MSR	$2,780	$2,250	$2,050	$1,850	$1,600	$1,300	$1,100	$950

ELECTRIC BASS

J4/P4 - Retro J or P body style, 4-string, Bad Ass II bridge, Hipshot Ultralight tuners, current mfg.

MSR	$2,600	$2,200	$1,900	$1,700	$1,500	$1,300	$1,100	$900

J5 - similar to J4, except in a 5-string configuration. 21 or 24 frets, Hipshot 5-string bridge, Hipshot Ultralight tuners, current mfg.

MSR	$2,800	$2,400	$2,100	$1,800	$1,600	$1,400	$1,200	$1,000

Add $400 for Quilt or Flame bent "arched" maple top.

GROSSMAN
See chapter on House Brands.

Before World War II, the majority of guitars were sold through mail-order distributors. The Grossman company distributed a number of guitars built for them with their trademark on the headstock (source: Tom Wheeler, *American Guitars*).

GROVES CUSTOM GUITARS
Instruments currently built in Tucson, AZ.

Luthier Gordon S. Groves is currently offering hand crafted guitar models. For further information regarding specifications and pricing, please contact luthier Groves directly (see Trademark Index).

GROWLER
See Palmer.

GRUGGETT GUITARS
Instruments currently built since 1961 by Gruggett Guitars located in Bakersfield, CA. Distributed by Stark-Marquadt of Bakersfield, CA or Jacobson's Service in Denver, CO.

Luthier Bill Gruggett originally worked at the Mosrite plant for Semie Moseley beginning in 1962. Gruggett worked his way up to a management position at Mosrite, but when he returned from a vacation in 1966, he found that he had been replaced. Gruggett then went to work for another ex-Mosrite employee named Joe Hall, who produced a limited amount of Hallmark "Sweptwing" guitars.

In 1967, Gruggett started his own Gruggett Guitars. He built the first forty models of the "Stradette" guitar in his garage, and then moved to a factory in downtown Bakersfield and hired four employees. Between 1967 and 1968, the company started around 300 guitars but only finished 120 of them. During that same year, Gruggett built thirty-five ES-335-style guitars for Ed Pregor of Hollywood (which carried Pregor's Epcore label). From 1969 to 1974, Gruggett ran the family's pipe and cable business. Two years later, when Semie Moseley returned to Bakersfield to reopen Mosrite, he called on

Gruggett to manage the plant. Unfortunately, Semie's venture ran out of operating capital four months later - and Gruggett was back to building his own models again.

Gruggett Guitars is still in full operation, and luthier Bill Gruggett is building a variety of designs from traditional solid body to handcarved custom guitars (source: Peter Jacobson, Jacobson's Service, and Hal Hammer).

GUDELSKY MUSICAL INSTRUMENTS
Instruments previously built in Vista, CA from 1985 to 1996.

Luthier Harris Paul Gudelsky (1964-1996) had apprenticed to James D'Aquisto before starting Gudelsky Musical Instruments. Gudelsky's personal goal was to try to build a more modern version of the archtop guitar. Gudelsky offered a small line of instruments exclusively on a customer order basis that included hollow body archtops (acoustic and electric/acoustic) ranged between $4,290 and $5,500; semi hollow bodies ranged from $4,235 to $4,400; and set-neck solid bodies ranged from $2,450 to $3,500. Paul Gudelsky was found fatally shot at his Vista, California home in May, 1996.

GUGINO
Instruments previously built in Buffalo, NY between the 1930s and 1940s.

Luthier Carmino Gugino built instruments that featured high quality conventional building (the frets, finish, carving, etc.) combined with very unconventional design ideas. As detailed by Jay Scott, certain models feature necks that screw on to the body, or have asymmetrical bodies, or an archtop that has a detachable neck/body joint/bridge piece that is removable from the body (source: Teisco Del Rey, *Guitar Player* magazine).

GUILD
Instruments currently produced in Westerly, RI since 1969. Distributed by the Fender Musical Instrument Corporation (FMIC) of Scottsdale, AZ. Guild was originally located in New York City between 1952 and 1956; production was moved to Hoboken, NJ, from late 1956 to 1968. In 1997, Guild (Fender FMIC) opened up a new Custom Shop in Nashville, TN.

Contrary to stories of a guild of old world-style craftsmen gathering to build these exceptional guitars, Guild was founded in 1952 by Alfred Dronge. Dronge, a Jewish emigrant from Europe, grew up in New York City and took jobs working for various music stores on Park Row. Dronge became an accomplished musician who played both banjo and guitar, and loved jazz music. His experience in teaching music and performing in small orchestras led to the formation of the Sagman and Dronge music store.

After World War II, Dronge gave up the music store in favor of importing and distributing Italian accordions. The Sonola Accordion Company was successful enough to make Dronge a small fortune. It is with this reputation and finances that Dronge formed Guild Guitars, Inc. with ex-Ephiphone sales manager George Mann. Incidentally, the Guild name came from a third party who was involved with a guitar amplifier company that was going out of business. As the plant was closing down Dronge and Gene Detgen decided to keep the name. The Guild company was registered in 1952.

As the original New York-based Epiphone company was having problems with the local unions, they decided to move production down to Philadelphia. Dronge took advantage of this decision and attracted several of their ex-luthiers to his company. Some of the workers were of Italian ancestry, and felt more comfortable remaining in the Little Italy neighborhood rather than moving to Pennsylvania.

The company was originally located in a New York loft from 1952 through 1956. They expanded into a larger workshop in Hoboken, New Jersey, in late 1956. Finally, upon completion of new facilities, Guild moved to Westerly, Rhode Island, in 1969.

As pop music in the 1960s spurred on a demand for guitars, musical instrument companies expanded to meet the business growth. At the same time, large corporations began to diversify their holdings. Most people are aware of the CBS decision to buy Fender in 1965, or Baldwin Piano's purchase of the Burns trademark and manufacturing equipment in 1967. In 1966 electronic parts producer Avnet Inc. bought Guild Musical Instruments, and Alfred Dronge stayed on as president. Dronge also hired Jim Deurloo (of Gibson and later Heritage fame) as plant manager in December 1969. Deurloo's commitment to quality control resulted in better consistency of Guild products.

Tragedy occurred in 1972 as Alfred Dronge was killed in an aircraft crash. The relationships he built with the members of the company dissipated, and the driving force of twenty years since the inception was gone. However, Leon Tell (Guild's vice president from 1963 to 1973) became the company president in 1973 and maintained that position until 1983.

In mid August of 1986, Avnet sold Guild to a management/investment group from New England and Tennessee. Officers of the newly formed Guild Music Corporation included company President Jerre R. Haskew (previously Chief Executive Officer and President of the Commerce Union Bank of Chattanooga Tennessee), Executive Vice President of Plant and Operations George A. Hammerstrom, and Executive Vice President of Product Development and Artist Relations George Gruhn (Gruhn later left the company in early 1988).

Unfortunately, the remaining members of the investment group defaulted on bank obligations in November of 1988, leading to a court supervised financial restructuring. The Faas Corporation of New Berlin, Wisconsin (now U.S. Musical Corporation) bought Guild in January 1989. Solid body guitar production was discontinued in favor of acoustic and acoustic-electric production (a company strength) although some electric models were reissued in the mid 1990s.

Most recently, the Guild company was purchased by Fender Musical Instrument Corporation in 1995. A recent 1996 catalog shows an arrangement of acoustic and acoustic-electric models, as well as some semi-hollowbody guitars and one solid body electric. Guild has introduced more solid body electrics lately; all current models are based on memorable Guild models from earlier years (such as the Starfire models). In 1997, Guild opened a new Custom Shop in Nashville, Tennessee. In 2001 production was moved to Corona, California.

Robert Benedetto signed a formal agreement with the Fender Musical Instrument Corporation (FMIC) on March 5th, 1999 to redesign both the Artist Award and X700 Stuart Models, which will continue to be made at the Guild factory in Westerly, Rhode Island. These newly redesigned models are scheduled for production by 2000. Changes include recarving the tops and backs, changing the bracing, and refining the f-hole and pickguard designs for both models. While the trademark Guild harp-style tailpiece remains, a mother-of-pearl "Benedetto" logo will be inlaid in the 19th fret on both models,(Reference source for early Guild history: Hans Moust, *The Guild Guitar Book*; contemporary history courtesy Jay Pilzer; Guild model information courtesy Bill Acton, Guild Guitars, Benedetto information courtesy of Cindy Benedetto).

**Don Grosh Hollow Custom
courtesy Don Grosh**

**Don Grosh Bass J5
courtesy Don Grosh**

GRADING	100% MINT	98% NEAR MINT	95% EXC+	90% EXC	80% VG+	70% VG	60% G

GUILD IDENTIFYING FEATURES

According to noted authority and Guild enthusiast Jay Pilzer, there are identifying features on Guild instruments that can assist in determining their year of production:

Knobs on Electrics: 1953-58 transparent barrel knobs; 1959-63 transparent yellowish top hat knobs with Guild logo in either chrome or gold; 1964-72 black top hat knobs, Guild logo, tone or vol; circa 1990-present black top hat with Guild logo, no numbers or tone/vol.

Electric Pickguards: Except for the Johnny Smith/Artist Award (which used the stairstep pickguard), Guild pickguards were rounded, following the shape of the guitar until 1963 when the stairstep became standard on archtop electrics.

Headstock Inlays: The earliest were simple Guild inverted V with triangular insert, with G logo below, later the triangular insert disappears, Chesterfield introduced on some models by 1957. In general the more elaborate the headstock, the higher price the instrument.

ELECTRIC ARCHTOP: MISC.

CE-100 CAPRI - single sharp cutaway hollow style, arched bound spruce top, raised bound black pickguard, 2 f-holes, maple back/sides/neck, 20-fret bound rosewood fingerboard with pearl block inlay, adjustable rosewood bridge/trapeze tailpiece, blackface peghead with pearl shield/logo inlay, 3-per-side tuners, chrome hardware, single coil pickup, volume/tone control, available in Black, Blonde and Sunburst finishes, mfg. 1953-1984.

N/A	$1,500	$1,400	$1,300	$1,250	$1,200	$1,100

This model had an optional Bigsby vibrato. In 1954, harp tailpiece replaced original parts/design. In 1962, humbucker pickup replaced original parts/design.

CE-100 D - similar to CE-100, except has 2 single coil pickups, 2 volume/2 tone controls, 3-position switch, mfg. 1952-1975.

N/A	$1,700	$1,600	$1,500	$1,400	$1,300	$1,200

Add $200 for factory-installed DeArmond pickups (a small number were produced with DeArmond pickups at Guild).

In 1962, 2 humbucker pickups replaced original parts/design.

DUANE EDDY 400 - single round cutaway semi-hollow body, arched bound spruce top, f-holes, raised black pickguard with Duane Eddy's signature, maple back/sides, mahogany neck, 20-fret bound rosewood fingerboard with pearl block inlay, adjustable bridge/Bigsby vibrato, bound peghead with pearl Chesterfield/logo inlay, 3-per-side tuners, chrome hardware, 2 covered humbuckers, 2 volume/2 tone controls, 3-position switch, mix control, available in Natural finish, mfg. 1963-69.

N/A	$3,300	$2,800	$2,400	$2,000	$1,700	$1,400

Duane Eddy 500 - similar to Duane Eddy 400, except has figured maple back/sides/neck, ebony fingerboard, gold hardware, mfg. 1962-1974.

N/A	$5,700	$5,000	$4,300	$3,700	$3,000	$2,400

BERT WHEEDON - similar to the Duane Eddy 400, except has a double cutaway and pickguard reads Bert Wheedon, mfg. 1963-65.

Rarity and lack of activity in the secondary marketplace precludes accurate pricing on this model. This model was produced for U.K. distribution.

GEORGE BARNES ACOUSTI-LECTRIC - single round cutaway hollow style, arched bound spruce top, bound pickup holes, raised black pickguard with logo, figured maple back/sides/neck, 20-fret bound rosewood fingerboard with pearl block inlay, adjustable rosewood bridge/harp style tailpiece, bound peghead with pearl shield/logo inlay, 3-per-side tuners with pearl buttons, chrome hardware, 2 covered humbucker pickups, 2 volume/2 tone controls, 3-way switch, pickguard mounted controls, available in Natural finish, mfg. 1964-67.

N/A	$7,000	$6,000	$5,000	$4,000	$3,200	$2,500

Bound slots were placed into the top of this instrument so that the pickups would not touch the top.

GEORGE BARNES GUITAR IN F - single round cutaway hollow small body, spruce top, bound pickup holes, raised black pickguard with logo, mahogany back/sides/neck, 20-fret bound rosewood fingerboard with pearl block inlay, adjustable rosewood bridge/harp tailpiece, bound blackface peghead with pearl f/logo inlay, 3-per-side tuners, chrome hardware, 2 humbucker pickups, 2 volume/2 tone pickguard mounted controls, 3-position switch, mfg. 1963-65.

The pickups in this instrument were held in place by a lengthwise support and did not touch the top of the guitar. Rarity and lack of activity in the secondary marketplace precludes accurate pricing on this model.

M-65 - single round cutaway hollowed mahogany body, bound spruce top, 2 f-holes, raised black laminated pickguard, mahogany neck, 22-fret bound rosewood fingerboard with pearl block inlay, adjustable metal bridge/harp tailpiece, blackface peghead with pearl logo inlay, 3-per-side tuners, nickel hardware, single coil pickup, volume/tone controls, available in Sunburst finish, mfg. 1962-68.

N/A	$1,350	$1,200	$1,050	$900	$750	$600

M-65 3/4 - similar to M-65, except has smaller body/scale length, mfg. 1962-1970.

N/A	$1,100	$950	$800	$700	$600	$500

PALOMA (NO. 360-6200) - chambered special design solid mahogany body and solid spruce top, ebony fingerboard, Chesterfield logo, side dots, classical style neck and headstock, high volume nylon electric with custom design pickup Fishman system, available in Black, or Amber, current mfg.

MSR	$2,500		$1,900	$1,600	$1,400	$1,200	$1,000	$850	$700

PEREGRINE (NO. 360-6000) - chambered special design solid mahogany body and top, rosewood fingerboard, Chesterfield logo, pearl dot inlay, high volume acoustic electric with custom design pickup Fishman system, available in Lake Placid Blue, black, or Red Trans., mfg. 2003-present.

MSR	$1,800		$1,400	$1,200	$1,050	$900	$775	$650	$550

STUDIO ST 301 - double cutaway archtop laminated maple body (similar to the T-100 with a double cutaway), one single coil or humbucker pickup, available in Cherry or Sunburst finishes, body width 16.675 in., body depth 1.875 in., mfg. 1968-1970.

N/A	$1,300	$1,100	$950	$800	$700	$600

Studio ST 302 - similar to the ST 301, except has 2 pickups, mfg. 1968-1970.

N/A	$1,350	$1,150	$1,000	$850	$750	$650

Studio ST 303 - similar to the ST 301, except has 2 pickups and a Bigsby tremolo, mfg. 1968-1970.

N/A	$1,700	$1,450	$1,250	$1,100	$950	$800

GRADING	100% MINT	98% NEAR MINT	95% EXC+	90% EXC	80% VG+	70% VG	60% G

Studio ST 304 - similar to the ST 301, except has 2 pickups and a thicker body, body depth 2.875 in., mfg. 1968-1970.

| | N/A | $1,900 | $1,650 | $1,400 | $1,200 | $1,050 | $900 |

T-50 - similar to X-50, except had thinline body, mfg. 1962-1982.

| | N/A | $800 | $700 | $625 | $550 | $500 | $450 |

T-100 - single sharp cutaway semi-hollow body, arched bound spruce top, 2 f-holes, mahogany back/sides/neck, 20-fret bound rosewood fingerboard with pearl dot inlay (later production models do not have bound necks), adjustable rosewood bridge/harp tailpiece, blackface peghead with pearl shield/logo inlay (shield does not appear on later models), 3-per-side Grover tuners, chrome hardware, raised black pickguard with 'Guild' in gold lettering, single coil pickup, volume/tone control, serial numbers appear on both back of headstock and on a paper label visible through the upper f-hole, available in Blonde or Sunburst finishes, mfg. 1960-1972.

| | N/A | $1,300 | $1,150 | $1,000 | $900 | $800 | $700 |

T-100 D - similar to T-100, except had 2 single coil pickups, 2 volume/2 tone controls, 3-position switch on upper horn.

| | N/A | $1,400 | $1,200 | $1,050 | $950 | $850 | $750 |

ELECTRIC ARCHTOP: ROBERT BENEDETTO SERIES

JOHNNY SMITH AWARD (BENEDETTO, NO. 360-9800) - single smooth cutaway hollow body, carved hand-graduated spruce top, solid carved figured maple back and sides, two bound f-holes, fully bound mutli-ply binding, five-piece curly maple neck, 20-fret ebony fingerboard with MOP block inlays and 19th fret Benedetto inlay, inlaid Johnny Smith headstock, three-per-side Grover gold plated hardware with imperial buttons, rosewood bridge, engraved harp tailpiece, black stairstep pickguard, single Benedetto S-6 mini humbucker pickup, single volume knob, gold hardware, available in Antique Burst, Honey Blonde, or Opulent Brown finishes, 17 in. width, 3 in. depth, 25 9/16 in. scale, mfg. summer 2002-present.

| MSR | $11,000 | $8,750 | $7,500 | $6,500 | $5,500 | N/A | N/A | N/A |

STUART (BENEDETTO, NO. 360-9500/9501) - single smooth cutaway hollow body, carved hand-graduated spruce top, solid carved figured maple back and sides, two bound f-holes, body and neck binding, five-piece curly maple neck, 20-fret ebony fingerboard with MOP block inlays and 19th fret Benedetto inlay, three-per-side Grover gold plated hardware, rosewood bridge, black stairstep pickguard, two Benedetto A-6 humbucker pickups, four knobs, gold hardware, available in Antique Burst, Honey Blonde, or Opulent Brown finishes, 25 9/16 in. scale, mfg. 2002-present.

| MSR | $10,000 | $8,000 | $7,000 | $6,000 | $5,000 | N/A | N/A | N/A |

In late 1999, this model was redesigned by Robert Benedetto, with limited production beginning at the Westerly, RI plant. New features include recarved top and back, refined f-hole and pickguard design, changed bracing, and mother-of-pearl "Benedetto" logo inlay on the 19th fret. A single pickup model is also available.

ELECTRIC ARCHTOP: M-75 ARISTOCRAT & BLUESBIRD SERIES

M-75 ARISTOCRAT - single rounded cutaway hollow mahogany body, bound spruce top, raised black laminated pickguard, mahogany neck, 22-fret bound rosewood fingerboard with pearl block inlay, adjustable metal bridge/harp tailpiece, blackface peghead with pearl logo inlay, 3-per-side tuners, gold hardware, 2 single coil pickups, 2 volume/2 tone controls, 3-position switch, available in Natural or Sunburst finishes, mfg. 1952-1963.

| | N/A | $2,700 | $2,300 | $2,000 | $1,800 | $1,600 | $1,450 |

The Aristocrat model was often called the Bluesbird.

M-75 BLUESBIRD STANDARD - similar to M-75 Aristocrat, except has semi-hollow body construction, pearl Chesterfield/logo inlay, chrome hardware, 2 humbucker pickups, mfg. 1968-1974.

| | N/A | $1,300 | $1,150 | $1,000 | $900 | $800 | $700 |

Last MSR was $425.

M-75 BLUESBIRD DELUXE (M-75 G BLUESBIRD) - similar to M-75 Aristocrat, except has pearl Chesterfield/logo inlay, 2 humbucker pickups, gold-plated hardware.

| | N/A | $1,200 | $1,050 | $900 | $800 | $700 | $600 |

Last MSR was $495.

The G designation in the production name indicated Gold-plated hardware.

M-75 S BLUESBIRD STANDARD (M-75 CS BLUESBIRD) - single round cutaway bound mahogany solid body, raised black laminated pickguard, mahogany neck, 22-fret bound rosewood fingerboard with pearl block inlay, Tune-O-Matic bridge/fixed tailpiece, blackface peghead with pearl Chesterfield/logo inlay, 3-per-side tuners, chrome hardware, 2 humbucker pickups, master volume/2 volume/2 tone controls, 3-position switch, available in Sunburst finish, mfg. 1970-1984.

| | N/A | $1,200 | $1,050 | $900 | $750 | $650 | $550 |

Last MSR was $425.

The S designation in the production name indicated solid body (instead of semi-hollow); the C designation indicated Chrome hardware.

M-75 S BLUESBIRD DELUXE (M-75 GS BLUESBIRD) - similar to M-75 S Bluesbird Standard (CS Bluesbird), except has gold hardware.

| | N/A | $1,000 | $850 | $750 | $650 | $550 | $450 |

Last MSR was $495.

The S designation in the production name indicated Solid body (instead of semi-hollow); the G designation indicated gold-plated hardware.

**Guild Peregrine Custom
courtesy Dave Rogers
Dave's Guitar Shop**

**Guild Stuart
courtesy Guild**

GRADING	100% MINT	98% NEAR MINT	95% EXC+	90% EXC	80% VG+	70% VG	60% G

BLUESBIRD REINTRODUCTION - similar to the M-75 S Bluesbird (CS Bluesbird), except had 3 single coils (or 2 single coils/humbucker with coil tap switch), mfg. 1985-88.

	N/A	$950	$825	$700	$600	$525	$450

BLUESBIRD STD (NO. 360-6400) - single round cutaway bound solid mahogany body, internal sound chambers, carved maple top, raised black pickguard, mahogany neck, 22-fret bound rosewood fingerboard with pearl block inlay, Tune-O-Matic bridge/stop tailpiece, blackface peghead with pearl Chesterfield/logo inlay, 3-per-side tuners, chrome hardware, 2 Seymour Duncan SH-1 humbucker pickups, 2 volume/2 tone controls, 3-position switch, available in Black, Gold Metallic, or Trans. Red finishes, mfg. 1995-2003.

	$1,700	$1,450	$1,250	$1,050	$900	$750	$600

Last MSR was $2,200.

Early models may also feature Natural and White finishes.

Bluesbird P90 (No. 360-6409) - similar to the Bluesbird, except has P-90 pickups, disc. 2003.

	$1,750	$1,500	$1,300	$1,100	$950	$800	$650

Last MSR was $2,300.

Bluesbird AAA Top (No. 360-6400) - similar to the Bluesbird, except features a carved AAA grade figured maple top, available in Amber, Cherry Sunburst, or Tobacco Sunburst finishes, mfg. 1998-2003.

	$1,800	$1,550	$1,350	$1,150	$1,000	$850	$700

Last MSR was $2,400.

Bluesbird AAA P90 (No. 360-6409) - similar to the Bluesbird, except has P-90 pickups, disc. 2003.

	$1,900	$1,650	$1,400	$1,200	$1,000	$850	$700

Last MSR was $2,500.

ELECTRIC ARCHTOP: STARFIRE SERIES

STARFIRE I - single sharp cutaway thin hollow bound maple body, arched top, f-holes, raised black pickguard with star/logo, maple neck, 20-fret bound rosewood fingerboard with pearl dot inlay, adjustable rosewood bridge/harp trapeze tailpiece, bound blackface peghead with pearl Chesterfield/logo inlay, 3-per-side tuners, chrome hardware, single coil pickup, volume/tone controls, available in Cherry Red, Ebony, Emerald Green, or Honey Amber finishes, mfg. 1961-66.

	N/A	$1,200	$1,050	$950	$850	$750	$650

This model had an optional mahogany body. In 1962, humbucker pickup replaced original parts/design.

STARFIRE II - similar to Starfire I, except has 2 single coil pickups, 2 volume/2 tone controls, mfg. 1961-1972.

	N/A	$1,350	$1,200	$1,050	$900	$800	$700

Between 1961 to 1962, some models were built with factory-installed DeArmond pickups. In 1962, 2 humbucker pickups replaced original parts/design.

Starfire II Recent Mfg. (No. 360-7200) - single Florentine cutaway thinline hollow body, raised black pickguard, 2 Guild SD-1 humbuckers, adjustable rosewood bridge/harp tailpiece, chrome hardware, 2 volume/2 tone controls, 3-way toggle, available in Antique Burst, Black, Blonde, or Trans. Red finishes, mfg. 1995-disc.

	$1,500	$1,300	$1,100	$950	$800	$650	$500

Last MSR was $1,999.

Left-handed model (Model 350-7220) available at no additional cost.

STARFIRE III - similar to Starfire I, except has Guild Bigsby vibrato, 2 single coil pickups, 2 volume/2 tone controls, mfg. 1961-1970.

1961-1966	N/A	$1,400	$1,250	$1,100	$1,000	$900	$800
1967-1970	N/A	$1,200	$1,050	$900	$800	$700	$600

Between 1961 to 1962, some models were built with factory-installed DeArmond pickups.

Starfire III Current Mfg. (No. 360-7300) - single Florentine cutaway thinline hollow body, raised black pickguard, 2 Guild SD-1 humbuckers, Bigsby bridge/tailpiece, chrome hardware, 2 volume/2 tone controls, 3-way toggle, available in Antique Burst, Black, Blonde, and Trans. Red finishes, mfg. 1995-present.

MSR	$2,200	$1,700	$1,500	$1,300	$1,100	$950	$800	$650

Left-handed model (Model 350-7320) available for an additional $72.

Starfire III P-90 Current Mfg. (No. 360-7309) - similar to the Starfire III except has P-90 pickups, disc. 2004.

	$1,750	$1,550	$1,350	$1,150	$1,000	$850	$700

Last MSR was $2,300.

STARFIRE IV - double round cutaway semi-hollow bound maple body, raised black pickguard, 2 f-holes, 3-piece maple neck, 22-fret bound rosewood fingerboard with pearl dot inlay, Tune-O-Matic bridge/harp trapeze tailpiece, pearl Chesterfield/logo peghead inlay, 3-per-side tuners, gold hardware, 2 humbucker pickups, 2 volume/2 tone controls, 3-position switch, available in Black, Blonde, Blue, Green, Red or Walnut finishes, mfg. 1963-1994.

1963-1971	N/A	$2,200	$1,900	$1,700	$1,500	$1,300	$1,100
1972-1980	N/A	$1,700	$1,500	$1,300	$1,150	$1,000	$850
1981-1990	N/A	$1,450	$1,250	$1,100	$950	$800	$650
1991-1994	N/A	$1,300	$1,100	$950	$825	$700	$600

Last MSR was $1,900.

In 1972, master volume control was introduced. In 1980, ebony fingerboard, stop tailpiece replaced original parts/design, master volume control was discontinued.

Starfire IV Current Mfg. (No. 360-7400) - double cutaway thinline hollow body, raised black pickguard, 2 Guild SD-1 humbuckers, bridge/stop tailpiece, chrome hardware, 2 volume/2 tone controls, 3-way toggle, available in Antique Burst, Black, Blonde, or Trans. Red finishes, mfg. 1995-present.

MSR	$2,500	$1,950	$1,650	$1,450	$1,250	$1,050	$900	$750

Left-handed model (Model 350-7420) available at no additional cost.

GRADING	100% MINT	98% NEAR MINT	95% EXC+	90% EXC	80% VG+	70% VG	60% G

STARFIRE V - similar to Starfire IV, except has pearl block fingerboard inlay, Guild Bigsby vibrato, master volume control, available in Cherry Red, Ebony, Emerald Green, or Honey Amber finishes, mfg. 1963-1972.

1963-1967	N/A	$2,400	$2,100	$1,850	$1,600	$1,400	$1,200
1968-1972	N/A	$1,900	$1,650	$1,400	$1,200	$1,050	$900

Add $100 for Amber or Green finish.

Starfire V Recent Mfg. (No. 350-7600) - similar to Starfire IV, except Curly Maple top and body, rosewood fingerboard with Pearloid block inlays, two SD-1 humbucker pickups, Guild Bigsby Model 7 Vibrato, chrome hardware, master volume control, available in Blonde (801), Antique Burst (837), or Emerald Green Trans. finishes, mfg. 1999-2002.

$1,800	$1,550	$1,250	$1,050	$900	$750	$600

Last MSR was $2,399.

Left-handed model (Model 350-7620) available for an additional $65.

STARFIRE VI - similar to Starfire IV, except has bound f-holes, ebony fingerboard with pearl block/abalone wedge inlay, Guild Bigsby vibrato, bound peghead with pearl shield/logo inlay, gold hardware, master volume control, available in Cherry Red, Ebony, Emerald Green, or Honey Amber finishes, mfg. 1963-1979.

N/A	$3,200	$2,800	$2,500	$2,200	$1,900	$1,600

STARFIRE XII - similar to Starfire IV, except has 12 strings, 6-per-side tuners, available in Cherry Red, Ebony, Emerald Green, or Honey Amber finishes, mfg. 1966-1975.

N/A	$1,700	$1,500	$1,300	$1,150	$1,000	$850

ELECTRIC ARCHTOP: X SERIES

X-50 GRANADA - hollow style body, arch spruce top, f-holes, raised black pickguard, bound body, mahogany back/sides/neck, 14/20-fret rosewood fingerboard with pearl dot inlay, adjustable rosewood bridge/trapeze tailpiece, blackface peghead with screened logo, 3-per-side tuners, humbucker pickup, volume/tone controls, available in Sunburst finish, mfg. 1952-1970.

N/A	$975	$900	$800	$725	$650	$575

X-60 - similar to the X-150, except has gold finish.

N/A	$1,600	$1,450	$1,350	$1,250	$1,175	$1,000

Guild Starfire
courtesy George McGuire

X-150 SAVOY (NO. 360-8400) - single rounded cutaway hollow body, bound laminated flame maple top, 2 f-holes, raised black pickguard, laminated flame maple back/sides, mahogany neck, 20-fret bound rosewood fingerboard with pearl block inlay, adjustable rosewood bridge/engraved harp tailpiece, pearl Chesterfield/logo peghead inlay, 3-per-side tuners, chrome hardware, Guild SD-1 humbucker pickup, volume/tone controls, available in Antique Burst or Blonde finishes, body depth 3.375 in., mfg. 1954-1965, reintroduced 1998-present.

1954-1962	N/A	$2,000	$1,700	$1,500	$1,300	$1,100	$950
1963-1965	N/A	$1,700	$1,500	$1,300	$1,100	$950	$800
MSR	$2,300	$1,750	$1,500	$1,250	$1,050	$900	$750	$600

Left-handed model (Model 350-8420) available at no additional cost.

X-150 D Savoy (No. 360-8500) - similar to the X-150 Savoy, except features 2 Guild SD-1 humbucking pickups, available in Antique Burst or Blonde finishes, body depth 3.375 in., mfg. 1998-2003.

$1,800	$1,550	$1,300	$1,100	$950	$800	$650

Last MSR was $2,400.

Left-handed model (Model 350-8520) available at no additional cost.

Rockabilly (X-160, No. 360-8600) - similar to the X-150 except has 2 DeArmond Model 2000 single coil pickups, single volume and tone control, Bigsby Vibrato tailpiece, available in Black, Tennessee Orange, or Metallic Blue finishes, disc. 2003.

$1,950	$1,650	$1,400	$1,150	$1,000	$850	$700

Last MSR was $2,600.

X-160 SAVOY - single round cutaway hollow body, bound curly maple archtop, 2 f-holes, bound black pickguard, curly maple back/sides/neck, 20-fret rosewood fingerboard with pearl dot inlay, adjustable rosewood bridge/Bigsby vibrato tailpiece, pearl Chesterfield/logo peghead inlay, 3-per-side tuners, chrome hardware, 2 humbucker pickups, 2 volume/2 tone controls, 3-position switch, available in Black, Blonde, or Sunburst finishes, mfg. 1991-95.

N/A	$1,200	$1,050	$900	$750	$650	$550

Last MSR was $1,600.

X-170 MANHATTAN (NO. 350-8000) - single round cutaway hollow body, bound curly maple archtop, 2 f-holes, black pickguard, curly maple back/sides/neck, 20-fret bound rosewood fingerboard with pearl block inlay, adjustable rosewood bridge/harp tailpiece, pearl Chesterfield/logo peghead inlay, 3-per-side tuners, chrome hardware, 2 Guild SD-1 humbucker pickups, 2 volume/2 tone controls, 3-position switch, available in Antique Burst or Blonde finishes, body width 16.625 in., body depth 2.5 in., mfg. 1988-2002.

$1,900	$1,600	$1,350	$1,150	$950	$800	$650

Last MSR was $2,499.

Left-handed model (Model 350-8020) available at no additional cost.

Earlier models may have a bound black pickguard and gold hardware.

Guild X-160
courtesy Guild

GRADING	100% MINT	98% NEAR MINT	95% EXC+	90% EXC	80% VG+	70% VG	60% G

X-170B Manhattan with Bigsby (No. 350-8100) - similar to the X-170 Manhattan, except has Bigsby bridge/tailpiece, body width 16.625 in., body depth 2.5 in., mfg. 1995-98.

| | $1,600 | $1,400 | $1,200 | $1,000 | $850 | $700 | $550 |

Last MSR was $2,099.

X-175 MANHATTAN - single round cutaway hollow body, bound spruce archtop, 2 f-holes, black laminated pickguard, maple back/sides, mahogany neck, 20-fret bound rosewood fingerboard with pearl block inlay, adjustable rosewood bridge/harp tailpiece, blackface peghead with pearl logo inlay, 3-per-side tuners, chrome hardware, 2 single coil soapbar pickups, volume/tone controls, 3-position switch, available in Blonde or Sunburst finishes, mfg. 1954-1984.

1954-1962	N/A	$2,100	$1,850	$1,650	$1,500	$1,350	$1,200
1963-1984	N/A	$1,700	$1,550	$1,400	$1,250	$1,100	$950

Until 1958, models had 1 volume and 1 tone controls. In 1962, 2 humbucker pickups replaced original parts/design.

X-180 PARK AVENUE (NO. 360-8000) - similar to the X-170, except has select curly maple body, gold hardware, bound headstock, Chesterfield logo, 2 Guild humbucker pickups, available in Blonde or Antique Burst finishes, disc. 2003.

| | $2,200 | $1,900 | $1,600 | $1,400 | $1,200 | $1,000 | $850 |

Last MSR was $2,900.

X-350 STRATFORD - single round cutaway hollow style, arched spruce top, raised black laminated pickguard, 2 bound f-holes, multibound body, maple back/sides/neck, 20-fret bound rosewood fingerboard with pearl block inlay, adjustable rosewood bridge/harp tailpiece, blackface peghead with pearl shield/logo inlay, 3-per-side tuners, gold hardware, 3 single coil pickups, volume/tone controls, 6 pickup pushbutton switches, available in Sunburst finish, mfg. 1952-1973.

| | N/A | $3,100 | $2,700 | $2,400 | $2,100 | $1,800 | $1,600 |

In 1962, 2 single coil pickups, 3-position switch replaced original parts/designs.

X-375 STRATFORD - similar to the X-350 except in Natural finish, mfg. 1952-1973.

| | N/A | $3,100 | $2,700 | $2,400 | $2,100 | $1,800 | $1,600 |

X-400 - similar to the X-175, except had 2 volume/2 tone controls and an early sunburst finish.

| | N/A | $2,200 | $1,900 | $1,650 | $1,450 | $1,250 | $1,100 |

X-440 - similar to the X-400, except had Blonde finish.

| | N/A | $2,200 | $1,900 | $1,650 | $1,450 | $1,250 | $1,100 |

X-500 - single round cutaway hollow style, bound arched laminated spruce top, 2 bound f-holes, bound tortoise pickguard, maple back/sides/neck, 20-fret bound ebony fingerboard with pearl block/abalone wedge inlay, adjustable ebony bridge, stylized trapeze tailpiece, bound peghead with pearl shield/logo inlay, 3-per-side Imperial tuners, gold hardware, 2 humbucker pickups, 2 volume/2 tone controls, 3-position switch, available in Blonde or Sunburst finishes, mfg. 1953-1995.

1953-1962	N/A	$3,100	$2,700	$2,400	$2,100	$1,800	$1,500
1963-1979	N/A	$2,800	$2,500	$2,200	$1,900	$1,650	$1,450
1980-1995	N/A	$2,500	$2,100	$1,850	$1,600	$1,350	$1,150

Last MSR was $3,800

X-550P (NO. 395-8800) - single Venetian cutaway semi-hollow body, 2 f-holes, laminated spruce top, laminated curly maple back & sides, five piece mahogany/maple neck, 20-fret ebony fingerboard with abalone and pearl block inlays, entire body binding, 2 Seymour Duncan single coil pickups, black pickguard, Bigsby tailpiece, four knobs, 3-way switch, gold hardware, available in Antique Burst, Black, or Blonde finishes, mfg. 2004-present.

| MSR | $5,500 | $4,250 | $3,750 | $3,400 | $3,100 | $2,800 | $2,500 | $2,200 |

X-700 STUART (NO. 350-8200) - single round cutaway hollow style, bound arched solid spruce top, 2 bound f-holes, bound tortoise pickguard, German maple back/sides, 5-piece maple neck, 20-fret bound ebony fingerboard with pearl block/abalone wedge inlay, adjustable ebony bridge/stylized trapeze tailpiece, bound peghead with pearl shield/logo inlay, 3-per-side Imperial tuners, gold hardware, 2 Guild SD-1 humbucker pickups, 2 volume/2 tone controls, 3-position switch, available in Antique Burst and Blonde finishes, body width 16 5/8 in., body depth 3 1/2 in., mfg. 1988-1999.

| | $3,100 | $2,700 | $2,400 | $2,100 | $1,800 | $1,600 | $1,400 |

Last MSR was $3,856.

X-700 STUART BENEDETTO - refer to individual listing within the Robert Benedetto Series.

X-770 STUART (NO. 395-8201) - this model was advertised by Guild during 1998 with the following specifications: single cutaway hollow style, solid spruce top, 2 f-holes raised pickguard, maple back/sides/neck, 25.5 in. scale, 20-fret bound ebony fingerboard with pearl and abalone inlay, adjustable ebony bridge, engraved harp tailpiece, bound peghead with pearl shield/logo inlay, 3-per-side tuners, gold hardware, Guild SD-1 humbucker pickup, volume/tone controls. Available in Antique Burst or Blonde high gloss finishes, body width 3 1/2", while advertised, this model has yet to be manufactured

ELECTRIC: BRIAN MAY SERIES

BRIAN MAY - offset double cutaway bound mahogany body, black laminated pickguard, 24-fret ebony fingerboard with pearl dot inlay, Tune-O-Matic bridge/Brian May vibrato, blackface peghead with pearl logo inlay, 3-per-side tuners, chrome hardware, 3 single coil Seymour Duncan pickups, volume/tone controls, 6 slide switches, available in Black, Trans. Green, Trans. Red, or White finishes, mfg. 1984-88.

| | N/A | $2,700 | $2,400 | $2,100 | $1,800 | $1,500 | $1,300 |

BRIAN MAY SIGNATURE - offset double cutaway bound mahogany body, black laminated pickguard, 24-fret ebony fingerboard with pearl dot inlay, Tune-O-Matic bridge/Brian May vibrato, blackface peghead with pearl logo inlay, 3-per-side tuners, chrome hardware, 3 single coil pickups, volume/tone controls, 6 slide switches, available in Trans. Red finish, mfg. 1994 only.

| | N/A | $2,700 | $2,300 | $2,000 | $1,700 | $1,500 | $1,300 |

In 1994, this model was offered in a limited edition of only 1,000 guitars.

GRADING	100% MINT	98% NEAR MINT	95% EXC+	90% EXC	80% VG+	70% VG	60% G

BRIAN MAY PRO - offset double cutaway mahogany body, bound mahogany top, black multilaminated pickguard, 24-fret ebony fingerboard with pearl dot inlay, Tune-O-Matic bridge/Brian May vibrato, mahogany peghead with pearl logo inlay, 3-per-side Schaller tuners, chrome hardware, 3 single coil Seymour Duncan pickups, volume/tone controls, 6 slide switches, available in Black, Trans. Green, Trans. Red, or White finishes, mfg. 1994-95.

	N/A	$1,650	$1,450	$1,250	$1,100	$950	$800

Last MSR was $1,800.

BRIAN MAY SPECIAL - similar to Brian May Pro, except has rosewood fingerboard, Tune-O-Matic bridge/stop tailpiece, available in Natural finish, mfg. 1994-95.

	N/A	$1,350	$1,200	$1,050	$900	$750	$600

Last MSR was $1,500.

BRIAN MAY STANDARD - offset double cutaway mahogany body, black multilaminated pickguard, 24-fret rosewood fingerboard with pearl dot inlay, Tune-O-Matic bridge/stop tailpiece, mahogany peghead with pearl logo inlay, 3-per-side Schaller tuners, chrome hardware, 3 single coil pickups, volume/tone controls, 6 slide switches, available in Black, Green, Red, or White finishes, mfg. 1994-95.

	N/A	$850	$750	$650	$575	$500	$425

Last MSR was $1,000.

This model has either 1 single coil/1 humbucker pickups or 2 humbucker pickups (both with coil tap). These pickup configurations were optional.

ELECTRIC: BURNSIDE SERIES

In the late 1980s Guild imported a number of solid body electrics as entry level instruments that had "Burnside by Guild" on the headstock. Further information on these models can be found under the Burnside listing in the *Blue Book of Electric Guitars*.

ELECTRIC: CROSSROAD SERIES

CROSSROADS (CR 1) - single cutaway semi-hollow mahogany body, bound figured maple top, figured maple neck, 22-fret bound rosewood fingerboard with pearl dot inlay, rosewood bridge with white black dot pins, blackface peghead with pearl shield/logo inlay, 3-per-side tuners, chrome hardware, humbucker/piezo bridge pickups, 2 volume/1 tone controls, 3-position switch, available in Amber, Black, or Natural finishes, mfg. 1994-95.

	N/A	$1,150	$1,000	$850	$725	$600	$500

Last MSR was $1,300.

CROSSROADS DOUBLE E - double neck configuration, mahogany body with acoustic side routed out, bound spruce top, mahogany neck, bound blackface peghead with pearl Chesterfield/logo inlay, 3-per-side tuners, chrome hardware; acoustic side features: round soundhole, 22-fret rosewood fingerboard with pearl dot inlay, rosewood bridge with white black dot pins, piezo bridge pickups; electric side features: 22-fret bound ebony fingerboard with abalone/pearl wedge/block inlay, Tune-O-Matic bridge/stop tailpiece, 2 exposed Seymour Duncan humbucker pickups, 2 volume/2 tone controls, two 3-position switches, available in Black or Natural finishes, mfg. 1993-95.

	N/A	$2,000	$1,700	$1,500	$1,300	$1,100	$900

Last MSR was $2,995.

CROSSROADS DOUBLENECK SLASH SIGNATURE MODEL (NO. 395-6120) - oversized (shared) single cutaway mahogany body, bound figured maple top, set-in necks, rosewood fingerboards. 12-string configuration (acoustic): round soundhole, spruce braced soundboard, 6-per-side tuners, custom pinless rosewood bridge, Fishman piezo bridge pickup, Fishman preamp. 6-string configuration (electric): 3-per-side tuners, Tune-O-Matic bridge/stop tailpiece, 2 humbucker pickups, volume/tone controls, 3-way selector switch, available in Black or Crimson Red Trans. high gloss finishes, mfg. 1997-disc.

$3,700	$3,350	$2,900	$2,400	N/A	N/A	N/A

Last MSR was $4,899.

This model was designed in conjunction with Doug Blair (See Blair Guitars LTD.) and guitarist Slash (Guns 'N Roses).

Crossroads Doubleneck AAA (No. 395-6130) - similar to Crossroads Doubleneck (Model 395-6120), except has AAA Maple solid top. Custom colors upon request, mfg. 1999 only.

$3,750	$3,250	$2,750	N/A	N/A	N/A	N/A

Last MSR was $4,999.

ELECTRIC: DETONATOR SERIES

DETONATOR (1ST SERIES) - offset double cutaway poplar body, bolt-on maple neck, 22-fret rosewood fingerboard with dot inlays, black hardware, 6-on-a-side headstock, 2 single coils/1 humbucker EMG active pickups, Floyd Rose locking vibrato, mfg. 1987-88.

	N/A	$650	$575	$500	$425	$350	$300

In 1988, this model changed designation to the Detonator II.

Detonator (2nd Series) - offset double cutaway poplar body, bolt on maple neck, 22-fret rosewood fingerboard with dot inlays, black hardware, 6-on-a-side headstock, 2 single coils/1 humbucker DiMarzio pickups, Guild/Mueller locking vibrato, mfg. 1988 only.

	N/A	$575	$500	$425	$350	$300	$250

**Guild X-350
courtesy John Beeson
The Music Shoppe**

**Guild Brian May
courtesy Phil Winfield**

GRADING	100% MINT	98% NEAR MINT	95% EXC+	90% EXC	80% VG+	70% VG	60% G

ELECTRIC: LIBERATOR SERIES

LIBERATOR - offset double cutaway poplar body, bolt on maple neck, 22-fret rosewood fingerboard with dot inlays, black hardware, 6-on-a-side headstock, 2 single coils/1 humbucker DiMarzio pickups, Guild/Mueller locking vibrato, mfg. 1988 only.

	N/A	$650	$550	$475	$400	$350	$300

LIBERATOR II - offset double cutaway poplar body, bolt on maple neck, 22-fret rosewood fingerboard with dot inlays, black hardware, 6-on-a-side headstock, 2 single coils/1 humbucker EMG active pickups, Floyd Rose locking vibrato, mfg. 1987-88.

	N/A	$700	$600	$525	$450	$400	$350

LIBERATOR ELITE - similar to the Liberator II, except had a flamed maple top, bound ebony fingerboard with rising sun inlays, gold hardware, active Bartolini pickups, mfg. 1988 only.

	N/A	$950	$825	$700	$600	$525	$450

ELECTRIC: M-80 & M-85 SERIES

M-80 - dual cutaway bound mahogany body, raised black laminated pickguard, mahogany neck, 22-fret bound rosewood fingerboard with pearl block inlay, Tune-O-Matic bridge/fixed tailpiece, blackface peghead with pearl Chesterfield/logo inlay, 3-per-side tuners, chrome hardware, 2 Guild Xr-7 humbucker pickups, master volume/2 volume/2 tone controls, 3-position switch, available in Black, Natural, Red, or White finishes, mfg. 1975-1983.

	N/A	$850	$750	$675	$600	$525	$450

In 1981, this model was offered with a maple top/mahogany back, 24-fret fingerboard, 2 volume/2 tone controls, and a 3-way pickup selector.

M-85 CS - similar to the M-80, mfg. 1975-1980.

	N/A	$900	$800	$700	$625	$550	$475

ELECTRIC: NIGHTBIRD SERIES

NIGHTBIRD - single cutaway bound chambered mahogany body and carved Sitka spruce or maple top, mahogany neck, 22-fret bound ebony fingerboard with diamond shaped inlays, finetune bridge/stop tailpiece, mfg. 1985-87.

	N/A	$1,800	$1,500	$1,300	$1,100	$950	$800

Designed in conjunction with George Gruhn.

NIGHTBIRD I - similar to the original Nightbird design, except has spruce top, unbound rosewood fingerboard, and unbound headstock, 2 DiMarzio pickups, separate coil tap and phase switches, and chrome hardware, mfg. 1987-88.

	N/A	$1,400	$1,200	$1,050	$900	$750	$600

NIGHTBIRD II - similar to the original Nightbird design with carved Sitka spruce top and ebony fingerboard, except has gold hardware, mfg. 1987-88.

	N/A	$1,400	$1,200	$1,050	$900	$750	$600

ELECTRIC: S SERIES

While the following models such as the S-250 through the S-284 **Aviator** have no accurate pricing information, there is some increased interest in these Guild solid bodies in the vintage and secondary market.

Most of these 1980s S Series models sell in the range between $350 and $600.

S-25 - offset double cutaway mahogany body, set neck, unbound top, 2 humbuckers, 1 volume and 1 tone control, mfg. 1981-83.

Rarity and lack of activity in the secondary marketplace precludes accurate pricing on this model.

S-26 - similar to the S-25, except very low production, mfg. 1983 only.

Rarity and lack of activity in the secondary marketplace precludes accurate pricing on this model.

S-50 JET STAR - offset double cutaway mahogany body with concave bottom bout, black pickguard, built-in stand, mahogany neck, 22-fret rosewood fingerboard with pearl dot inlay, adjustable metal bridge/vibrato tailpiece, 3-per-side tuners, chrome hardware, single coil pickup, volume/tone controls, available in Amber, Black, Cherry Red, Green, or Sunburst finishes, mfg. 1963-67.

	N/A	$750	$650	$575	$500	$425	$375

The S-50 Jet Star was the first model of Guild's solid body guitars.

S-56 D - similar to the S-60, except has DiMarzio pickups, mfg. 1979-1982.

Rarity and lack of activity in the secondary marketplace precludes accurate pricing on this model.

S-60 - offset double cutaway mahogany body, black pickguard, mahogany neck, 24-fret rosewood fingerboard with pearl dot inlay, Tune-O-Matic bridge/fixed tailpiece, 3-per-side tuners, chrome hardware, single pickup, volume/tone controls, available in Black, Red, or White finishes, mfg. 1977-1989.

	N/A	$550	$475	$400	$350	$300	$250

S-60 D - similar to S-60, except has 2 single coil DiMarzio pickups, 2 volume/2 tone controls, 3-position switch, mfg. 1977-1989.

	N/A	$600	$525	$450	$375	$325	$275

S-70 - similar to S-60, except has 3 single coil pickups, 3-position/2 mini switches, mfg. 1978-1982.

	N/A	$575	$500	$425	$375	$325	$275

S-70 AD - similar to S-70, except has an ash body and DiMarzio pickups, mfg. 1978-1982.

	N/A	$650	$550	$475	$400	$350	$300

S-90 - similar to the S-50, except featured a humbucker and a covered bridge/tailpiece assembly, mfg. 1970-76.

	N/A	$700	$625	$550	$475	$400	$350

GRADING	100% MINT	98% NEAR MINT	95% EXC+	90% EXC	80% VG+	70% VG	60% G

S-100 POLARA - offset double cutaway mahogany body with concave bottom bout, black laminated pickguard, built-in stand, mahogany neck, 22-fret rosewood fingerboard with pearl dot inlay, adjustable metal bridge/vibrato tailpiece, 3-per-side tuners, chrome hardware, 2 single coil pickups, 2 volume/2 tone controls, 3-position switch, available in Amber, Black, Cherry Red, Green, or Sunburst finishes, mfg. 1963-68.

| | N/A | $1,400 | $1,200 | $1,050 | $900 | $800 | $700 |

S-100 Polara Recent Mfg. (No. 350-6300) - offset double cutaway mahogany body, set-in mahogany neck, 22-fret bound rosewood fingerboard with pearl block inlay, adjustable metal bridge/stop tailpiece, 3-per-side tuners, chrome hardware, 2 Seymour Duncan humbucker pickups, 2 volume/2 tone controls, 3-way selector switch, available in Black, Natural, Trans. Red, or White finishes, mfg. 1995-2000.

| | $1,400 | $1,200 | $1,050 | $900 | $900 | $700 | $600 |

Last MSR was $1,569.

S-100 - offset double cutaway mahogany body, black pickguard with logo, mahogany neck, 22-fret bound rosewood fingerboard with pearl block inlay, adjustable metal bridge/vibrato tailpiece, blackface peghead with pearl Chesterfield/logo inlay, 3-per-side tuners, chrome hardware, 2 humbucker pickups, 2 volume/2 tone controls, 3-position switch, available in Amber, Black, Cherry Red, Green, or White finishes, mfg. 1970-74.

| | N/A | $1,100 | $950 | $825 | $700 | $600 | $500 |

In 1973, phase switch was introduced.

S-100 C - similar to S-100, except has carved acorn/leaves top, clear pickguard with logo, Tune-O-Matic bridge/fixed tailpiece, phase switch, stereo output, available in Natural finish, mfg. 1973-76.

| | N/A | $1,350 | $1,150 | $1,000 | $875 | $750 | $650 |

S-100 Deluxe - similar to S-100, except has Bigsby vibrato tailpiece, mfg. 1973-75.

| | N/A | $1,200 | $1,050 | $900 | $775 | $650 | $575 |

S-100 REISSUE - double cutaway mahogany body, black pickguard, mahogany neck, 22-fret bound rosewood fingerboard with pearl block inlay, Tune-O-Matic bridge/fixed tailpiece, blackface peghead with pearl Chesterfield/logo inlay, 3-per-side tuners, chrome hardware, 2 humbucker Guild pickups, 2 volume/2 tone controls, 3-position/coil tap switches, available in Black, Green Stain, Natural, Red Stain, Vintage White, or White finishes, mfg. 1994-95.

| | N/A | $850 | $725 | $600 | $500 | $425 | $350 |

Last MSR was $1,000.

S-100 Reissue G - similar to S-100 Reissue, except has gold hardware, mfg. 1994-95.

| | N/A | $850 | $750 | $650 | $550 | $475 | $400 |

Last MSR was $1,200.

S-200 THUNDERBIRD - offset double cutaway asymmetrical mahogany body with concave bottom bout, black pickguard, built-in stand, mahogany neck, 22-fret bound rosewood fingerboard with pearl block inlay, adjustable metal bridge/vibrato tailpiece, bound blackface peghead with pearl eagle/logo inlay, 3-per-side tuners, chrome hardware, 2 single coil pickups (some with humbuckers), 2 volume/2 tone controls, 3 pickup/1 tone slide switches, available in Amber, Black, Cherry Red, Green, or Sunburst finishes, mfg. 1963-1970.

| | N/A | $3,000 | $2,600 | $2,300 | $2,000 | $1,800 | $1,600 |

The Thunderbird model featured a folding stand built into the back of the body. While a unique feature, the stand was less than steady and prone to instability. Be sure to inspect the headstock/neck joint for any indications of previous problems due to the guitar falling over.

In 1987, pickup configuration changed to 2 single coils/1 humbucker.

S-250 - offset double cutaway mahogany body, set neck, bound top, chrome hardware, 2 humbuckers, 2 volume/2 tone controls, mfg. 1981-1983.

Rarity and lack of activity in the secondary marketplace precludes accurate pricing on this model.

S-260 - similar to the S-250, except produced in low numbers, mfg. 1983.

Rarity and lack of activity in the secondary marketplace precludes accurate pricing on this model.

S-270 FLYER (RUNAWAY OR SPRINT) - offset double cutaway body, bolt-on neck, 6-on-a-side "Blade" headstock, one EMG pickup, locking tremolo, mfg. 1983-85.

Rarity and lack of activity in the secondary marketplace precludes accurate pricing on this model.

S-271 Sprint (Flyer) - similar to S-270, except different pickup configuration, mfg. 1983-85.

Rarity and lack of activity in the secondary marketplace precludes accurate pricing on this model.

S-275 - offset double cutaway body, set neck, bound top, gold hardware, 2 humbuckers, 2 volume/1 tone control, 1 phase (or coil tap) switch, mfg. 1983-87.

Rarity and lack of activity in the secondary marketplace precludes accurate pricing on this model.

S-280 FLYER - offset double cutaway body, bolt-on neck, 22-fret fingerboard, 6-on-a-side headstock, 2 humbuckers, 2 volume/2 tone controls, mfg. 1983-86.

| | N/A | $400 | $350 | $300 | $250 | $200 | $150 |

S-281 FLYER - similar to S-280 Flyer, except has a locking tremolo and 1 volume/1 tone controls, mfg. 1983-86.

| | N/A | $425 | $350 | $300 | $250 | $200 | $150 |

S-282 - similar to S-280 Flyer, except has a set-in neck, 1 volume/1 tone controls, mfg. 1983-86.

| | N/A | $450 | $375 | $325 | $275 | $225 | $175 |

S-284 AVIATOR - symmetrical double cutaway body, set neck, 6-on-a-side "pointed" headstock, locking tremolo, 2 single/humbucker EMG pickups, volume/tone controls, mfg. 1984-88.

Rarity and lack of activity in the secondary marketplace precludes accurate pricing on this model.

Guild Nightbird II
courtesy Guild

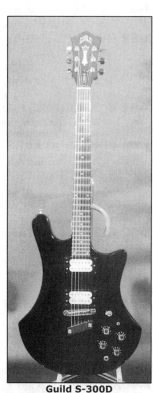

Guild S-300D
courtesy Sam J. Maggio

GRADING	100% MINT	98% NEAR MINT	95% EXC+	90% EXC	80% VG+	70% VG	60% G

S-285 AVIATOR - similar to S-284 Aviator, except has bound fingerboard and headstock, fancy fingerboard inlays, mfg. 1986-87.

Rarity and lack of activity in the secondary marketplace precludes accurate pricing on this model.

S-300 - offset double cutaway mahogany body, distinctly rounded tail end, black pickguard, mahogany neck, 24-fret ebony fingerboard with pearl dot inlay, Tune-O-Matic bridge/fixed tailpiece, blackface peghead with pearl Chesterfield/logo inlay, 3-per-side tuners, chrome hardware, 2 single coil pickups, 2 volume/2 tone controls, 3-position/phase switches, available in Black, Red, or White finishes, mfg. 1976-1989.

	N/A	$800	$700	$600	$525	$450	$375

S-300 A - similar to S-300, except has an ash body and maple neck, mfg. 1977-1982.

	N/A	$850	$750	$650	$575	$500	$425

S-300 D - similar to S-300, except has 2 DiMarzio humbucker pickups, mfg. 1977-1982.

	N/A	$850	$750	$650	$575	$500	$425

S-400 - similar to the S-300, except has set neck and active electronics, mfg. 1979-1982.

	N/A	$875	$750	$650	$575	$500	$450

S-400 A - similar to S-400, except ash body and maple neck, mfg. 1979-1982.

	N/A	$900	$750	$650	$575	$525	$475

ELECTRIC: T SERIES

T-250 - single cutaway ash body, black pickguard, controls mounted on metal plate, bolt-on maple neck, 22-fret maple fingerboard with black dot inlay, fixed bridge, 6-on-a-side tuners, gold hardware, 2 single coil EMG pickups, volume/tone controls, 3-position switch, available in Black, Blue, Red, or White finishes, mfg. 1986-circa 1990.

	N/A	$750	$675	$625	$575	$525	$475

The T-250 is sometimes referred to as the Roy Buchanan model.

T-200 - similar to the T-250.

	N/A	$825	$750	$700	$650	$600	$550

The T-200 is also sometimes called the Roy Buchanan model.

ELECTRIC: X SERIES

X-79 SKYHAWK - offset double cutaway asymmetrical mahogany body with fin like bottom bout, black pickguard, mahogany neck, 24-fret rosewood fingerboard with pearl dot inlay, Tune-O-Matic bridge/stop tailpiece, blackface peghead with pearl logo inlay, 3-per-side tuners, chrome tuners, 2 single coil pickups, 2 volume/1 tone controls, 3-position switch, available in Black, Green, Red, Sparkle, or White finishes, mfg. 1981-85.

	N/A	$800	$700	$600	$500	$425	$350

Rarity and lack of activity in the secondary marketplace precludes accurate pricing on this model. Guild records show only 172 models produced.

X-79-3 - similar to the X-79, except features 3 single coil pickups, volume/tone controls, 3 mini switches, mfg. 1981-85.

	N/A	$900	$800	$700	$600	$500	$400

X-80 SWAN - possibly related to either the X-79 or X-82, mfg. 1983-85.

Rarity and lack of activity in the secondary marketplace precludes accurate pricing on this model.

X-82 NOVA - asymmetrical angular body, 3 point headstock, chrome hardware, stop tailpiece, 2 humbuckers, 2 volume/2 tone controls, phase (or coil tap) switch, mfg. 1981-84.

	N/A	$900	$800	$700	$600	$500	$400

In 1983, a locking tremolo system was added.

Rarity and lack of activity in the secondary marketplace precludes accurate pricing on this model.

X-84 V - bolt neck, Guild or Kahler tremolo, mfg. 1983 only.

In 1983, Guild announced a new line of bolt neck, solid body electrics. To date, research has not indicated further specifications. Future updates will appear in subsequent editions of the Blue Book of Electric Guitars.

X-88 FLYING STAR - "Flying Star" asymmetrical angular body with sharp points, bolt-on neck, locking tremolo, 2 octave fingerboard with star inlays, 1 EMG pickup, mfg. 1984-85.

	N/A	$650	$575	$525	$475	$425	$350

Guitar design was inspired by members of the rock band Motley Crue. Some literature may refer to this model as the Crue Flying Star.

X-88 D Flying Star - similar to X-88 Flying Star, except has DiMarzio pickups, mfg. 1984-85.

	N/A	$675	$600	$525	$475	$425	$350

X-92 CITRON BREAKAWAY - offset solid body (bass side removable for travel), 3 single coil pickups, tremolo, 1 volume/1 tone control, 5-way selector switch, mfg. 1984-86.

	N/A	$750	$650	$550	$475	$425	$375

Designed by luthier Harvey Citron, originally of Veillette-Citron; now currently Citron Enterprises (see CITRON, HARVEY). The X-92 came with a travel/gig bag.

X-97 V - bolt neck, Guild or Kahler tremolo, mfg. 1983 only.

Rarity and lack of activity in the secondary marketplace precludes accurate pricing on this model.

X-100 BLADERUNNER - asymmetrical angular body that featured triangular sections removed, bolt-on neck, 6-on-a-side pointed headstock, locking tremolo, humbucking pickup, volume/tone controls, mfg. 1984-85.

	N/A	$1,800	$1,550	$1,350	$1,150	$1,000	$850

Designed by California based design team of David Newell and Andrew Desrosiers (See David Andrew Design Research).

X-108 V - bolt neck, Guild or Kahler tremolo, mfg. 1983 only.

Rarity and lack of activity in the secondary marketplace precludes accurate pricing on this model.

GRADING	100% MINT	98% NEAR MINT	95% EXC+	90% EXC	80% VG+	70% VG	60% G

X-2000 NIGHTBIRD - single cutaway routed out mahogany body, bound figured maple top, bound tortoise pickguard, mahogany neck, 22-fret bound ebony fingerboard with pearl block/abalone wedge inlay, Tune-O-Matic bridge/stop tailpiece, bound peghead with pearl shield/logo inlay, 3-per-side tuners, gold hardware, 2 humbucker pickups, volume/tone control, 3-position/single coil switches, available in Amberburst, Black, Cherry Sunburst, or Natural finishes, disc. 1994.

	N/A	$1,700	$1,500	$1,500	$1,100	$950	$800

Last MSR was $1,995.

X-3000 NIGHTINGALE - similar to X-2000, except has 2 f-holes, disc. 1994.

	N/A	$1,800	$1,550	$1,350	$1,150	$1,000	$850

Last MSR was $1,995.

ELECTRIC BASS: MISC.

Early Guild basses have a specially designed Guild single coil pickup made by Hagstrom in Sweden that is often mistaken for a humbucker. Some of these basses have an extra switch that activated a passive circuit and eliminated the hum associated with single coil pickups. This feature makes the basses more desirable and collectible.

ASHBORY - small curved teardrop body, neck-through design, 4-on-a-side tuners, chrome hardware, piezo pickup under bridge, volume/tone controls, mfg. 1986-88.

	N/A	$575	$500	$425	$375	$325	$275

It is estimated that only 2,000 instruments were produced. This compact bass had solid silicon tubing for strings, and, oddly enough, can approximate the sound of an upright bass. The Ashbory Bass has been reissued by Fender. It is Korean made with English electronics and retails for $400.

B-301 - offset double cutaway mahogany body, black laminated pickguard, mahogany neck, 20-fret rosewood fingerboard with pearl dot inlay, fixed bridge, blackface peghead with pearl Chesterfield/logo inlay, 2-per-side tuners, chrome hardware, single coil pickup, volume/tone controls, available in Black, Natural, White, or Red finishes, mfg. 1977-1981.

	N/A	$650	$575	$525	$475	$425	$375

In 1980, mahogany body/neck instruments were discontinued.

B-301A - similar to B-301, except instrument featured an ash body and maple neck, mfg. circa 1979-1981.

	N/A	$650	$575	$525	$475	$425	$375

B-302 - similar to B-301, except has 2 single coil pickups, 2 volume/2 tone controls, 3-position switch, mfg. 1977-1981.

	N/A	$800	$700	$625	$550	$475	$425

In 1980, mahogany body/neck instruments were discontinued.

B-302A - similar to B-302, except instrument featured an ash body and maple neck, mfg. circa 1979-1981.

	N/A	$800	$700	$625	$550	$475	$425

B-401 - rounded double cutaway body, set neck, 1 pickup, mfg. 1980-81.

	N/A	$725	$625	$550	$475	$400	$350

Total production for both the B-401 and B-402 was 335 instruments.

B-402 - similar to the B-401, except has 2 pickups, mfg. 1980-81.

	N/A	$750	$650	$575	$500	$450	$400

Total production for both the B-401 and B-402 was 335 instruments.

JET STAR BASS - offset double cutaway companion bass to the S-200 Thunderbird, S-100 Polara, and S-50 Jet Star guitars. It came with a Thunderbird style headstock with 2-per-side tuners until 1966 when it changed to 4 0n 1 side tuners. From 1964-1965 it had a Hagstrom style single col pickup, from 1966 to 1970 it came with Guild Mickey Mouse bass pickups, mfg. 1964-1970

1964-1965	N/A	$1,600	$1,400	$1,200	$1,000	$850	$700
1966-1970	N/A	$1,200	$1,000	$800	$700	$600	$500

JS BASS I - offset double cutaway mahogany body/neck, 21-fret rosewood fingerboard with pearl dot inlay, fixed bridge, blackface peghead with pearl Chesterfield/logo inlay, 2-per-side tuners, chrome hardware, humbucker pickup, volume/tone controls, available in Black, Natural and Sunburst finishes, mfg. 1970-78.

	N/A	$800	$700	$625	$550	$500	$450

This model had an optional fretless fingerboard. In 1972, tone switch was introduced, redesigned humbucker pickup replaced original parts/design.

JS Bass I LS - similar to JS Bass I, except has long scale length, mfg. 1976-78.

	N/A	$800	$700	$625	$550	$500	$450

JS BASS II - similar to JS Bass I, except has 2 humbucker pickups, 2 volume/2 tone controls, 3-position switch, mfg. 1970-78.

	N/A	$900	$800	$725	$650	$575	$525

In 1972, tone switch was introduced, redesigned humbucker pickups replaced original parts/design. In 1974 through 1976, a hand carved acorn/leaves body was offered.

JS Bass II LS - similar to JS Bass I, except has long scale length, 2 humbucker pickups, 2 volume/2 tone controls, 3-position switch, mfg. 1976-78.

	N/A	$900	$800	$700	$625	$575	$525

M-85 I - similar to the JS Bass I, except has a carved top, single cutaway semi-solid design, rosewood fingerboard with dot inlays, 30.75 in. scale, 1 Hagstrom single coil pickup, mfg. 1970-1980.

	N/A	$2,250	$1,950	$1,700	$1,450	$1,250	$1,050

Guild X-2000 Nightbird courtesy Guild

G

Guild JS Bass II courtesy

GRADING	100% MINT	98% NEAR MINT	95% EXC+	90% EXC	80% VG+	70% VG	60% G

M-85 II - similar to the M-85 I, except has 2 pickups, 2 volume/2 tone controls, mfg. 1970-1980.

	N/A	$2,700	$2,300	$2,000	$1,700	$1,500	$1,300

ST 4 - offset double cutaway asymmetrical poplar body, bolt-on maple neck, 22-fret rosewood fingerboard with pearl dot inlay, fixed bridge, 4-on-a-side tuners, black hardware, P/J-style pickups, 2 volume/tone controls, available in Black, Natural, or White finishes, disc. 1994.

	N/A	$550	$475	$425	$375	$325	$275

Last MSR was $795.

This model was also offered with a mahogany body.

ST 5 - similar to ST 4, except has 5 strings, 4/1 per side tuners, disc. 1994.

	N/A	$600	$525	$450	$400	$350	$300

Last MSR was $895.

X-701 - X shaped body with four offset corners, 2-per-side tuners, 21-fret fingerboard with dot inlay, single pickup, black pickguard, various metallic colors, mfg. 1982-84

	N/A	$850	$750	$650	$575	$500	$425

X-702 - similar to the X-701 except has two pickups, mfg. 1982-84.

	N/A	$950	$850	$750	$675	$600	$525

ELECTRIC BASS: PILOT SERIES

All models in the Pro Pilot series were available fretless at no extra cost.

PRO 4 - offset double cutaway asymmetrical maple body, bolt-on maple neck, 22-fret rosewood fingerboard with pearl dot inlay, fixed bridge, 4-on-a-side tuners, black hardware, 2 J-style active EMG pickups, 2 volume/tone controls, active preamp, available in Amber, Black, Natural, or White finishes, mfg. 1994-95.

	N/A	$750	$650	$575	$500	$425	$350

Last MSR was $1,100.

PRO 5 - similar to Pro 4, except has 5 strings, 4/1 per side tuners, disc. 1995.

	N/A	$800	$700	$625	$550	$475	$400

Last MSR was $1,200.

SB-600 PILOT - similar to the Pro 4, except has a poplar body and 2 DiMarzio pickups, mfg. 1983-88.

	N/A	$600	$525	$450	$375	$325	$275

SB-601 PILOT - similar to SB-600 Pilot, except has 1 pickup, mfg. 1983-88.

	N/A	$500	$425	$350	$300	$250	$200

SB-602 PILOT - similar to SB-600 Pilot, except has 2 EMG pickups and a bass vibrato, mfg. 1983-88.

	N/A	$625	$550	$500	$425	$375	$325

SB-603 PILOT - similar to SB-600 Pilot, except has 3 pickups, mfg. 1983-88.

	N/A	$550	$475	$425	$375	$325	$275

SB-604 PILOT - similar to SB-600 Pilot, except has different headstock design and EMG pickups, mfg. 1983-88.

	N/A	$550	$475	$425	$375	$325	$275

SB-605 PILOT - similar to SB-600 Pilot, except has 5 strings and EMG pickups, mfg. 1986-88.

	N/A	$650	$575	$525	$475	$425	$375

SB-902 ADVANCED PILOT - similar to the SB-600 Pilot, except has a flamed maple body, ebony fingerboard, and Bartolini pickups and preamp, mfg. 1987-88.

	N/A	$1,000	$850	$700	$600	$500	$400

SB-905 ADVANCED PILOT - similar to SB-902 Advanced Pilot, except has 5 strings, mfg. 1987-88.

	N/A	$1,100	$900	$750	$650	$550	$450

ELECTRIC BASS: SB SERIES

Prior to the introduction of the Pilot Bass and subsequent models in 1983, the four models in the SB series sported a vaguely Fenderish body design.

SB-201 - offset double cutaway ash body, set-in maple neck, 2-per-side headstock, 20-fret rosewood fingerboard, Chesterfield logo, split coil pickup, volume/tone controls, mfg. 1982-83.

	N/A	$675	$575	$500	$425	$375	$325

Some models have been spotted with a soapbar (large rectangular) pickup.

SB-202 - similar to SB-201, except features 2 pickups, 2 volume/2 tone controls, phase switch, mfg. 1982-83.

	N/A	$800	$700	$625	$550	$475	$400

SB-203 - similar to SB-201, except has 1 split coil pickup and 2 single coils, volume/tone controls, 3 mini-switches for pickup selection, mfg. 1982-83.

	N/A	$650	$575	$525	$475	$425	$375

SB-502 E - similar to SB-201, except has active electronics, mfg. 1982-83.

	N/A	$750	$675	$600	$525	$450	$375

SB-666 BLADERUNNER BASS - a companion piece to the X-100 Bladerunner guitar, the SB-666 bass shares similar body design features, but only 1 pickup, mfg. 1984-85.

	N/A	$1,500	$1,300	$1,100	$950	$800	$650

SB-608 FLYING STAR BASS - a companion piece to the X-88 Flying Star guitar, the SB-608 bass shares similar body design features, but only 1 pickup, mfg. 1984-85.

	N/A	$850	$750	$650	$550	$475	$400

GRADING	100% MINT	98% NEAR MINT	95% EXC+	90% EXC	80% VG+	70% VG	60% G

SB-608 E - similar to the SB-608 Flying Star, except has active EMG pickups, mfg. 1984-85.

	N/A	$850	$750	$650	$550	$475	$400

ELECTRIC BASS: STARFIRE SERIES

STARFIRE BASS I - double round cutaway semi-hollow bound maple body, thumb/finger rests, 2 f-holes, 3-piece maple neck, 20-fret rosewood fingerboard with pearl dot inlay, fixed bridge, pearl Chesterfield/logo peghead inlay, 2-per-side tuners, chrome hardware, humbucker pickup, volume/tone controls, available in Cherry Red, Ebony, Emerald Green, or Honey Amber finishes, mfg. 1964-1975.

	N/A	$1,300	$1,100	$950	$825	$700	$600

In 1970, Hagstrom-made single coil pickups were featured. This model also offered a mahogany body.

STARFIRE BASS II - similar to Starfire Bass I, except has 2 humbucker pickups, master volume control, bass boost switch, mfg. 1964-1977.

1964-1969	N/A	$1,500	$1,300	$1,100	$950	$850	$750
1970-1977	N/A	$1,350	$1,150	$1,000	$875	$750	$650

Starfire Bass II Current Mfg. (No. 350-7500) - double cutaway thinline semi-hollow body, laminated mahogany top/back/sides, body binding, 2 f-holes, maple neck, 21-fret rosewood fingerboard with dot inlay, fixed bridge, pearl logo peghead inlay, 2-per-side tuners, chrome hardware, 2 Guild humbucker pickups, 2 volume/2 tone controls, 3-way selector switch, additional switch, available in Antique Burst, Black, Blonde, or Trans. Red finishes, mfg. 1998-2002.

	$1,850	$1,550	$1,350	$1,150	$950	$800	$650

Last MSR was $2,299.

Left-handed model (Model 350-7520) available at no additional cost.

Guild X-702
courtesy

G

GUITAR COLLECTION
See also Bass Collection. Instruments previously manufactured in Japan from 1985 to 1992. Distributed by Meisel Music, Inc. of Springfield, NJ.

Guitar Collection (and Bass Collection) instruments are medium grade instruments with good hardware, and a modern, rounded body design. Their current appeal may fall in the range of the novice to intermediate player looking for a solid-feeling instrument. Guitar Collection instruments were originally distributed by Meisel Music, Inc. for a number of years between 1985 to 1992. Their on-hand stock was purchased by the Sam Ash music store chain of New York in 1994 and sold through the Sam Ash stores.

ELECTRIC

The **G 3 S** model (circa 1992) features a sleek, offset double cutaway alder body, bolt-on maple neck, 24-fret rosewood fingerboard (no inlay), fixed bridge, 3-per-side tuners, black hardware, single coil/humbucker pickups, volume and tone controls, and a 3-way toggle selector switch. The G 3 S model was available in Black, Magenta, and Pearl White finishes (original retail list unknown).

GUITAR FACTORY
Instruments currently built in Orlando, FL.

The Guitar Factory has been building and repairing guitars since 1972. They have offered an Electric/Acoustic E/A 12 Mono model that features a white limba hollow body, through-body white limba neck, 2 octave red locust fingerboard, red locust bridge, Sperzel tuners, 3 Bartolini single coil pickups/Fishman Matrix acoustic pickup, volume and tone controls. The suggested retail price is $3,600. Various options include pickup configuration, mono or dual outputs, choice of different woods, and hardware. For further information regarding specifications, other models and pricing, contact The Guitar Factory directly (see Trademark Index).

GUITAR FARM
Instruments currently built in Sperryville, VA.

The Guitar Farm is currently offering hand crafted guitar models. For further information regarding specifications and pricing, contact The Guitar Farm directly (see Trademark Index).

GUITORGAN
Instruments previously assembled in Waco, TX between 1969 to 1988 (the guitars were produced in Japan, and the electronics were built and installed in the U.S.). Distributed by Musiconics (MCI) of Waco, TX.

Inventor Bob Murrell introduced the GuitOrgan prototype at the 1967 Chicago NAMM show, along with partner Bill Mostyn and demonstrator Bob Wiley. Early home-built production began in 1967; a production factory was opened in 1968. Murrell's company started out as Murrell Electronics, which evolved into Musiconics International (MCI). Murrell combined his electronics and musical backgrounds in his vision of a guitar that could also offer Hammond organ-type sounds.

While developing his prototype, Murrell worked with Baldwin for his own organ circuitry (Baldwin was just beginning to import the Burns models to the U.S., and was interested in the various aspects of the guitar market). The finished product featured a fingerboard with segmented frets (six segments, one per string) wired to the internal controls. As a result, when a note or notes are fretted, the organ is triggered - and the note will sustain as long as the note stays fretted. The GuitOrgan allows players the option of either or both sounds of a guitar and the on-board

Guild SB-602 Pilot
courtesy Guild

GRADING	100% MINT	98% NEAR MINT	95% EXC+	90% EXC	80% VG+	70% VG	60% G

organ. Peavey later approximated this same segmented fret/wired-to-circuitry approach in their own MidiBass (later CyberBass) MIDI controller. GuitOrgans feature Murrell's own design of organ circuitry, with voices derived from Baldwin products (by permission). Early models were built in various guitars that could house the circuitry. Production models featured the wide hollowbody models from Ventura and Univox, built in Japan. Some models may also be Ibanez or Yamaha.

GuitOrgans have three jacks on the side of the body: Two standard 1/4 in. phono jacks, and a 3-point electrical jack for the wall plug (power supply). That's right, this guitar plugs into the wall! Using the two jacks, the player can run two amps (or two channels of the same amp). In the late 1980s, Murrell also began wiring the GuitOrgan with MIDI controls; the additional MIDI cost was $480. Murrell would also wire a customer-supplied guitar for $1,200. (Source: Teisco Del Rey, *Guitar Player* magazine).

ELECTRIC

The GuitOrgan had a list price of $995 in 1969, and the price rose up to $2,495 retail new by 1984. It is estimated that 3,000 instruments were produced between 1967 to 1984, but the final number is larger due to Murrell offering to build custom orders after 1984.

M-300 - offset double cutaway laminated hollow body, black raised pickguard, 21 (segmented) fret rosewood fingerboard with block inlay, Tune-O-Matic bridge/raised tailpiece, 3-per-side tuners, chrome hardware, 2 covered humbucker pickups, 2 volume/2 tone controls, 3-position switch, sustain knob/vibrato/8 voice switches, staccato switch, available in Sunburst finish, mfg. 1969-circa mid -1970s.

	N/A	$1,500	$1,250	$1,050	$900	$750	$600

The first production run of GuitOrgans were placed in the body of Ventura's Barney Kessel model. Later models were built into Univox's copy of a Gibson 335.

M-340 - similar to the M-300, except features miniturized electronics, mfg. mid to late 1970s (estimated).

	N/A	$1,400	$1,200	$1,050	$900	$750	$600

B-300 - similar to the M-340, except features Hammond organ-type sounds, mfg. late 1970s-early 1980s (estimated).

	N/A	$1,600	$1,350	$1,100	$950	$800	$650

B-35 - similar to the B-300, except features updated engineering, angled cuts on fret segments, mfg. mid to late 1980s (estimated).

	N/A	$1,600	$1,350	$1,100	$950	$800	$650

GUS GUITARS
Instruments currently produced in England since 1983.

Gus guitars have been produced since 1983. They produce guitars with the philosophy of: making instruments that look, feel, and sound special. Gus guitars indeed have a special look with a chrome metal border around the guitar. The looks of the guitar have also been compared to classic cars and bikes. Their flagship model is the G-1 for guitar and G-3 for bass. There are several variations of these models as well. For more information contact Gus Guitars directly (see Trademark Index).

GUYA
Instruments previously produced in Japan during the 1960s.

These instruments were generally entry level to good quality guitars based on Rickenbacker designs. Guya was the forerunner to Guyatone labeled guitars, and was built by the same company (see Guyatone). (Source: Michael Wright, *Guitar Stories*, Volume One).

GUYATONE
Instruments previously built in Japan from late 1950s to the mid-1970s.

The original company was founded by Mitsou Matsuki, an apprentice cabinet maker in the early 1930s. Matsuki, who studied electronics in night classes, was influenced by listening to Hawaiian music. A friend and renowned guitar player, Atsuo Kaneko, requested that Matsuki build a Hawaiian electric guitar. The two entered into business as a company called Matsuki Seisakujo, and produced guitars under the Guya trademark.

In 1948, a little after World War II, Matsuki founded his new company, Matsuki Denki Onkyo Kenkyujo. This company produced electric Hawaiian guitars, amplifiers, and record player cartridges. In 1951, this company began using the Guyatone trademark for its guitars. By the next year the corporate name evolved into Tokyo Sound Company. They produced their first solid body electric in the late 1950s. Original designs dominated the early production, albeit entry level quality. Later quality improved, but at the sacrifice of originality as Guyatone began building medium quality designs based on Fender influences. Some Guyatone guitars also were imported under such brandnames as Star or Antoria. (Source: Michael Wright, *Guitar Stories*, Volume One).

While traditional stringed instruments have been part of the Japanese culture, the guitar was first introduced to Japan in 1890. Japan did not even begin to open trade or diplomatic relations with the West until U.S. President Millard Fillmore sent Commodore Matthew C. Perry in 1850. In 1929 Maestro Andres Segovia made his first concert tour in Japan, sparking an interest in the guitar that has been part of the subculture since then. Japanese fascination with the instrumental rock group the Ventures also indicates that not all American design influences would be strictly Fender or Gibson; Mosrite guitars by Semie Moseley also were a large influence, among others.

Classic American guitar designs may have been an influence on the early Japanese models, but the influence was incorporated into original designs. The era of copying designs and details began in the early 1970s, but was not the basis for Japanese guitar production. As the entry level models began to get better in quality and meticulous attention to detail, then the American market began to take notice.

ELECTRIC

SOLIDBODY/HOLLOWBODY MODELS - models include various configurations, and complete specifications are unknown, mfg. 1950s-mid-1970s.

		N/A						
1950S		N/A	$450	$400	$350	$300	$250	$200
1960S		N/A	$400	$350	$300	$250	$200	$150
1970S		N/A	$350	$300	$250	$210	$170	$130

Section H

H.M.L. GUITARS

Instruments currently built in Seattle, WA since 1994.

H.M.L. Guitars was founded in 1994 by Howard Leese (guitarist, and 25 year veteran with the rock group Heart). Leese participates in all aspects of construction as the overall quality control inspector. He also allows every customer to help co-design their instruments for a more personal touch. H.M.L. guitars are totally hand built in Seattle by luthier Jack Pimentel.

The customer list for H.M.L. guitars includes such notables as Bruce Hastell, Mike Soldano, Val Kolbeck, Billy Gibbons, Jim Fiske, and (of course) Howard Leese himself, (company information courtesy Howard Leese, 1996).

ELECTRIC

Designed by Leese, the standard features of the H.M.L. model include a unique set of five hollow chambers placed throughout the body, in areas of acoustical sensitivity to better project "true" sound dissipation. For the fretboards, Leese prefers to use figured cocabola wood on the entire HML line due to its beauty, sound and feel. Other features include a carved tiger flame maple top with matched flame maple neck. Customers can even select their own choice of tops from Howard´s personal stock of aged, exotic woods, and can choose specific color finishes, pickups, and electronics.

**Hagstrom Corvette Condor
courtesy Richard Blake**

H.S. ANDERSON

Instruments previously produced in either Canada or CA, circa 1970s.

H.S. Anderson guitars were hand-made instruments built circa 1970s. Very little information is known about this trademark. A few examples include a Telecaster copy, a symmetrical double cutaway, and a mini-body called "The Apple." Most of these guitars appear to be mid- to high quality with various features. Any information on this trademark or the guitars would be welcome and can be submitted to the *Blue Book of Electric Guitars*. Any further updates will be included in upcoming editions.

HAGSTROM

Instruments currently produced since 2004. Currently distributed by American Music & Sound (AM&S) of Agoura Hills, CA. Previously produced in Sweden from circa 1957 through the early 1980s. Early distributors included the Hershman Musical Instrument Company of New York (under Goya logo) and Selmer, U.K. (under Futurama logo). In the mid-1970s, Ampeg became the U.S. distributor.

Hagstrom first began building guitars and basses in 1957, although many models appeared under the Futurama trademark in England (distributed by Selmer, U.K.) and either Hagstrom or Goya (distributed by Hershman Musical Instrument Company).

Hagstrom produced roughly 130,000 electric guitars and basses from 1958 to 1981 in Alvdalen, Sweden. During the early ´80s until 1983, a few instruments were manufactured under the Hagstrom name in Japan. Due to quality concerns and ever-increasing competition, the doors were eventually closed in 1983.

Distributors included the Hershman Musical Instrument Company of New York, the Merson Musical Supply Company of Westbury, New York, Selmer, U.K. and eventually Ampeg. The evolution of the Hagstrom line was rapid, and approximately 65 different models of guitars and basses were produced. (featured here are the more popular and well-known models). Early in its history, guitars were marketed in the U.K. as Futurama and in the US as Goya, Kent (a name that rarely appeared on the guitar and should not be confused with Kent trademark guitars) or Hagstrom. By 1965, all guitars were identified as Hagstrom.

Hagstrom produced both solid body and semi-hollowbody electrics, as well as an archtop model designed by luthier James L D'Aquisto. Also introduced was the first 8-string bass (four pairs of strings) and the "fastest neck in the world" which was accomplished by using an H-shape "expander stretcher" truss, a design that has allowed the necks to remain true even to this day.

In 2004, Hagstrom announced that they were building guitars again. This line was officially introduced at the 2005 NAMM show. The new line of Hagstrom guitars includes models for the vintage years such as the Swede and Hagstrom as well as some new designs. For more information contact Hagstrom directly (see Trademark Index).

ELECTRIC: 1950S-1980S MFG

Some Hagstrom models encountered at guitar shops and shows include the 1959 Les Paul-styled **ESP 24** hollowbody and 4 pickup **EDP 46 De Luxe**. These have all wood hollowbody interior construction with plastic exterior and were available in sparkle, pearloid or plain with a white pearloid "mother of toilet seat" fingerboard.

Some of the more frequently seen models are the **Kent I** and **H I**, equipped with two single coil pickups and 4 control slide switches. These had a complete Lucite molded top and vinyl back. The **H II** and **H III** models are easy to identify because the name is on the headstock, and the number of pickups corresponds with the model number (it is important to note that original parts for these guitars, especially the switches, are very difficult to find). Later came the **H II N**, which had two humbucker pickups.

The **Viking I** is equipped with two single coil pickups, one selector switch, individual tone and volume controls for each pickup and six-in-line tuners. As the Viking line is a semi-hollowbody, these have more of a 335 vibe to them. The **Viking II** is similar to the **V I**, except it has gold hardware and accents. (this is sometimes called the "Elvis guitar" as Elvis briefly played one in his ´68 comeback) The **Viking I N** (or **Scandia**) was equipped with two humbucker pickups, D´Aquisto-

**Hagstrom HII N OT
courtesy Kwinn E Kastrosky**

GRADING	100% MINT	98% NEAR MINT	95% EXC+	90% EXC	80% VG+	70% VG	60% G

designed 3-on-a-side tuners, separate volume and tone controls, pickup selector and a tone selector. It has a plain badge on the headstock. The **Viking** looks identical to the **V I N** except it has a floral headstock badge and a wood center block in the thinline hollowbody.

1963 brought out one of Hagstrom´s more unusual desings with the introduction of the **Impala** and **Corvette**. Shaped much like the Fender **Jaguar**, the necks were contoured and filled so they blended and flowed directly into the body. When the guitars began being imported into the U.S., the **Corvette** name had to be changed to **Condor**, as Gretsch already had the **Corvette** name registered.

Hagstrom´s **Swede**, a Les Paul-derived solidbody electric, was introduced in 1970. The suggested list price for the **Swede** (Model 803) in 1975 was $640. In 1977, the **Super Swede** made its debut. 1977 brought about the **Scandi**, a three single coil Strat-ish style. Most Hagstrom models had a corresponding bass available.

In 1969, Hagstrom debuted an f-hole archtop model designed by James D´Aquisto. The body was made of nine-ply laminate birch and these guitars were actually produced by Bjarton of Bjarnum, Sweden for Hagstrom. In 1976, Hagstrom manufactured and reintroduced the **Jimmy** model and in 1977 added the oval hole model. D´Aquisto did not make these guitars for Hagstrom. However he did purchase bodies from Hagstrom and used them in his own line of hollowbody electrics.

Hagstrom and Ampeg teamed up and introduced the **Patch 2000** guitar and synthesizer system in 1976. This system of a modified Swede model plus a footpedal had a list price of $2,000 in 1977. Due to the wiring design, it is advisable that you purchase both at the same time if the intention is to use it with a synthesizer. However the instrument plays as any other without the pedal.

It should be noted that the values decrease significantly when the conditions are 80% or less, as replacement parts for Hagstrom guitars and basses are very difficult to find. The publisher would like to thank Mr. Kwinn Kastrosky for his significant contributions to the Hagstrom section.

CORVETTE CONDOR - 3 single coil pickups, otherwise identical to the Impala.

	N/A	$1,200	$900	$800	$725	$425	$250

F12-S - 12-string version of the H II.

	N/A	$800	$650	$475	$325	$200	$150

H II (F-200) - similar to the H I but with all wood body, standand style pickguard and top mount angled jack plate, 2 single coil pickups, 4 control switches/1 standby switch.

	N/A	$600	$550	$400	$300	$175	$125

H III (F-300) - same as H II except has 3 single coils, 6 control/1 standby switch.

	N/A	$800	$650	$475	$325	$200	$150

H II N (HG 801) - birch body and neck, 2 humbuckers, 3-way pickups switch, 2 volume/2 tone control, adjustable bridge, Hagstrom "tremar" tremolo.

	N/A	$950	$800	$650	$550	$400	$250

Add 10% for mahogany.

H II N OT (HG 800) - same as the H II N except without tremolo.

	N/A	$1,200	$1,100	$850	$600	$400	$250

HAGSTROM "JIMMY" D´AQUISTO - single cutaway w/ f-holes, laminate birch ached top and back, adjustable ebony saddle and bridge base, 2 humbucker pickups, 2 volume/2 tone contols, 3-position pickup selector, 20-fret birch neck with ebony fretboard, block inlay, 24.75 in. scale, body length 20 in., width 15.75 in., depth 2.75 in.

	N/A	$1,300	$900	$750	$475	$300	$200

"Jimmy" Oval-hole - same body dimensions as the f-hole but with single oval hole, 1 humbucker pickup mounted in the soundhole, 1 volume/1 tone control mounted on the floating pickguard, nickel plated tailpiece.

	N/A	$1,800	$1,675	$1,400	$1,000	$750	$500

IMPALA - double cutaway, neck-through design, 2 single coils, 6 inline tuners, 8 control rocker switch bank w/ separate volume for rhythm and lead.

	N/A	$1,000	$825	$750	$650	$400	$250

KENT I/H I (F-11) - double cutaway plastic top vinyl covered back Strat-ish style design, 4 control switches, 1 volume control, two single coil, 6 inline tuners.

	N/A	$650	$600	$450	$375	$200	$150

SCANDI - very Strat-ish body style, ash body and neck, solid maple fretboard with black dot inlay, 3 covered single coils, 1 volume/3 tone controls, 3 individual pickups selector switches, 6 in-line Schaller machines, 2 tail strap buttons.

	N/A	$1,250	$1,000	$800	$725	$400	$250

SUPER SWEDE - single cutaway Les Paul-ish, maple body and neck, zero fret, jumbo silver nickel frets, set neck w/ ebony board and block inlay, 2 humbuckers, coil tapping switch, 3-way pickup selector, indiviual string tailpieces, fully adjustable roller bearing bridge, 2 tail strap buttons.

	N/A	$2,750	$2,500	$1,950	$1,650	$1,100	$750

SWEDE - Les Paul-ish in design, mahogany body and neck, 3-position tone/3-position pickup selector, ebony fretboard w/ block inlay, 2 humbucker pickups, 2 volume/2 tone controls, 3 on a side D´Aquisto Van Ghent machine heads, floral design on headstock, bolt on neck.

	N/A	$1,000	$900	$750	$475	$300	$200

Add 20% for Patch 2000.

VIKING I - thinline laminate f-hole hollowbody, 3-way toggle, 2 volume/2 tone control, 6 in line tuners, chrome fittings, dot inlays on rosewood fingerboard.

	N/A	$650	$600	$500	$400	$275	$150

Add $50 if with original Hagstrom Bigsby.

VIKING II - same look as the V I except with gold plated fittings and accessories. Block inlays on ebony fretboard, mfg. 1967-68.

	N/A	$1,000	$850	$700	$525	$400	$250

Add $75 if with original Hagstrom Bigsby.

VIKING I N (HG 802) - 2 humbucker pickups, 2 volume/2 tone controls, 3-position tone/3-position pickup switch, 3 on a side D´Aquisto designed Van Ghent tuners, plain badge on headstock, rosewood bridge base.

	N/A	$1,000	$850	$700	$600	$450	$300

GRADING	100% MINT	98% NEAR MINT	95% EXC+	90% EXC	80% VG+	70% VG	60% G

VIKING - similar to the Viking I N, but the body contains a solid wood center block, floral design on the headstock instead of the plain badge.

	N/A	$850	$750	$650	$550	$350	$250

ELECTRIC: 2004-CURRENT MFG.

In 2004, Hagstrom started producing guitars again. The **Swede** retails for $750 (left-handed version also available) and the **Super Swede** for $850. The **Viking** retails for $625 and the **Viking Deluxe** for $750. The Jazz Series comes in the **HJ-500 Jimmy** model for $850, the **HJ-600** for $895, and the **HL-500** for $895. The F Series has two sharp cutaways like an SG but in a Strat-style body. The **F-20** retails for $425, the **F-200** for $550, and the **F-200P** with tremolo for $629 (also available in left-handed configuration). The **F-300** has a basswood body and retails for $425 (also available in left-handed configuration) or $475 for sparkle finish. The Deluxe series is shaped like the Swede series, but is a solid-body. The **D2H** retails for $695 or $750 for a flamed finish. The **D2F** has a chambered body with a single f-hole and retails for $750 or $795 for a flamed finish.

ELECTRIC BASS: 1950S-1980S MFG.

Many of the Hagstrom six-string guitars had a bass model available as well. Most bass models are similar to their guitar counterparts. The exception to this is the **Super Swede Bass** and 8-String Bass. Prices for the bass models are approximately 10% higher than for the six-string models.

8 STRING - modeled after the H II, 4 sets of 2 strings, 2 single coil pickups.

	N/A	$1,200	$1,000	$900	$750	$500	$300

ELECTRIC BASS: 2004-CURRENT MFG.

Two bass guitars are scheduled to be released in addition to the new line of guitars. The **HB200** is a four-string that retails for $550 (also available in left-handed configuration). The **HB-280** is a eight-string like that of models in the past and retails for $695.

HALLMARK

Instruments previously built in Arvin, CA during the 1960s. The Hallmark trademark and design was reintroduced in January 1995 on a custom order basis. These custom order Hallmark guitars were built in Bakersfield, CA. Previously distributed by Front Porch Music of Bakersfield, CA. Hallmark was reintroduced again in the early 2000s by Bob Shade in Greenbelt, MD.

The Hallmark company was founded by Joe Hall, an ex-Mosrite employee, around 1967. The Sweptwing design, in its original dual cutaway glory, is strikingly reminiscent of a Flying V built backwards. According to ads run in *Guitar Player* magazine back in 1967, the model was available in a six-string, 12 string, bass, semi-hollowbody six-string, and doubleneck configurations. The suggested list price of the semi-hollowbody six-string was $265 in the same ad. According to luthier Bill Gruggett, Hallmark produced perhaps 40 guitars before the company ran out of money.
Models generally featured a 3-tuners-per-side headstock, two humbuckers, a triangular pickguard with the pickup selector mounted in the horn corner, a volume and tone knobs, and a stop tailpiece. The doubleneck version has to be more rare than the standard six string, although vintage Hallmarks don't turn up every day.
If you're still smitten by the original design, the good news is that they're available again! Custom order Hallmarks are being produced by Bob Shade in MD. The SweptWing is also available as an imported model for a reasonable price. Interested players are urged to contact the company directly (see Trademark Index).

ELECTRIC

The recent mfg. Sweptwing is available in several different configurations. The Vintage Series has a mahogany body with a bolt-on maple neck and a large white pickguard. The guitar retails for $795 and the bass for $725. The Custom series has a mahogany body with a flamed maple top and set mahogany neck and no pickguard. The guitar retails for $899 and the bass for $795.

SWEPTWING - backwards Flying V-style, 3-per-side tuners, 2 humbucker pickups, triangular pickguard, various other features, mfg. circa 1967.

	N/A	$600	$500	$450	$400	$350	$300

HAMATAR

Instruments previously built in Spicewood, TX circa early 1990s - 2000.

Luthier/designer Curt Meyers worked on an innovative design that featured primary and secondary guitar bodies that shared a similar neck. A central fret replaced the conventional nut, and there was a separate scale length for the left-hand and the right-hand. Dubbed the Model X-15, this guitar can produce two notes on a single string. Last known retail prices on the X-15 ran from $499 up to $4,000.
Meyers also produced a guitar called the **J.H. model** that was designed for players that favor the Jeff Healy fretting technique. The guitar consisted of a central body and a pair of necks that shared the same set of strings. Last known retail prices ranged from $1,400 to $4,000.

Hagstrom Super Swede
courtesy Kwinn E Kastrosky

Hagstrom Viking I
courtesy Kwinn E Kastrosky

GRADING	100% MINT	98% NEAR MINT	95% EXC+	90% EXC	80% VG+	70% VG	60% G

HAMBURGUITAR

Instruments currently built in Las Vegas, NV. Previously built in Westland, MI.

Hamburguitar guitar models are custom built by Bernie Hamburger. The instruments are available in 6-, 9-, and 12-string configurations, and feature a large number of configurations and options.

Several personalities have played Hamburguitars including the late George Harrision. A Hamburguitar was used for the recording and the video for *Real Love* on the Beatles Anthology II.

Options include a semi-hollow body choice of pickups, body binding, tremolo (where applicable), and a lacquer finish. For further information regarding pricing and specifications, please contact Bernie Hamburger at Hamburguitar directly (see Trademark Index).

ELECTRIC

Hamburger is currently offers models that base price at $1,950, and all feature Seymour Duncan pickups and a hand-rubbed tung oil finish. The **Innovator 9 String** has a bookmatched maple top, figured maple neck, and an ebony fingerboard. The lower 3 strings (E, A, D) are paired with strings tuned one octave above the pitch. Both the New Vintage and the **Model T** feature single cutaway body designs. The Model T has a stained bookmatched burl top with binding, mahogany body, maple neck and ebony fingerboard. The **Vintage Style** has a slab mahogany body, mahogany neck, rosewood fingerboard, P-90-style pickups, and starts at $1,450.

HAMER

Instruments originally produced in Arlington Heights, IL. Current production facilities were moved to New Hartford, CT in 1997. Hamer instruments are distributed by the Kaman Music Corporation of Bloomfield, CT. Hamer Guitars also has an entry level series of USA-designed guitars and basses that are built in Asia.

Hamer Guitars was co-founded by Paul Hamer and Jol Dantzig in 1976. In the early 1970s, the two were partners in Northern Prairie Music, a Chicago-based store that specialized in stringed instrument repair and used guitars. The repair section had been ordering so many supplies and parts from the Gibson facilities that the two were invited to a tour of the Kalamazoo plant. Later, Northern Prairie was made the first American Gibson authorized warranty repair shop.

Hamer, a regular gigging musician at the time, built a Les Paul-shaped short scale bass with Gibson parts that attracted enough attention for custom orders. By 1973, the shop was taking orders from some professional musicians as well. Hamer and Dantzig were both Gibson enthusiasts. Their early custom guitars were Flying V-based in design, and then later they branched out in Explorer-styled guitars. These early models were basically prototypes for the later production guitars, and featured Gibson hardware, Larry DiMarzio-wound pickups, figured tops, and lacquer finishes.

In the mid 1970s, the prices of used (beginning to be vintage) Fenders and Gibsons began to rise. The instruments offered by those same companies was perceived as being of lesser quality (and at higher prices). Hamer and Dantzig saw a market that was ignored by the major companies, so they incorporated Hamer USA. The first shop was set up in Palatine, Illinois. The first Hamer catalog from Fall 1975 shows only an Explorer-shaped guitar dubbed **The Hamer Guitar** (later, it became the Standard model) for the retail list price of $799. Hamer USA built perhaps 50 Standards between 1975 and 1978, an amount estimated to be ten to fifteen a year. In contrast, Gibson reissued the Explorer from 1976 to 1978 and shipped 3,300 of them! In 1978, Hamer debuted their second model, the Les Paul-ish Sunburst. While the Standard had jumped up to a retail price of $1,199, the Sunburst's lower price created new demands. In 1980, the company expanded into larger facilities in Arlington Heights, Illinois.

Paul Hamer left Hamer USA in 1987. A year later, Hamer was acquired by the Kaman Music Corporation. In March of 1997, Hamer production was shifted to new facilities in New Hartford, Connecticut. The Hamer company was given their own workspace, re-installed their same machinery (moved in from Illinois), and they operate their own finishing booth.

The Hamer company was first to offer black chrome hardware and double locking tremolos (right from Floyd Rose's basement!) on production guitars. During the 1980s, customized Hamer guitars sported LED position markers, built-in wireless transmitters, custom colors, custom graphics (like snake or 'dragon' skin).

SERIALIZATION, MODEL IDENTIFICATION, & PRICING OPTIONS

Jol Dantzig estimates that Hamer USA has built 48,000 guitars between 1975 and 1995. Serialization is easy to decipher, as the first digit in the serial number is the year the guitar was built. However, since the cycle repeats itself (0 to 9), knowing when the model was produced becomes the key.

Hamer USA (1975 to 1997): All instruments made in Illinois (1975-1996) and currently Connecticut (1997 to date) display either Hamer, or Hamer USA logo on the headstock.

1998 to Date: Models after 1997 specifically have the Hamer USA logo on the headstock.

Hamer Slammer Series: All instruments in the Slammer series are designed in the U.S., then manufactured overseas and distributed by Hamer. The design specifics on these models are similar to the USA models and have corresponding names, but the materials and components are not of similar quality.

Before 1998: Slammer series instruments up to 1997 have the Hamer Slammer Series logo on the headstock.

1998 to Date: CUIDADO! In a touching show of Solidarity in 1998, all Slammer series instruments now have a simple Hamer logo on the headstock (the serial number is on the back of the headstock). Be especially alert to the Hamer versus Hamer USA designated headstock logos.

Hamer USA Guitars are offered with a variety of options. A Natural finish or Black hardware options are available at no extra charge.

Add $35 for pickguard upgrade (tortoiseshell, pearloid, and mint green). Add $50 for Seymour Duncan pickup upgrade (per pickup). Add $75 for EMG pickup upgrade (per pickup). Add $75 for ebony fingerboard. Add $100 for color upcharge (color finish not listed by model). Add $105 for Gold hardware. Add $135 for crown fingerboard inlays. Add $425 for left-handed configuration. Add $500 for Ultimate Grade figured maple body.

ELECTRIC: ANNIVERSARY & MISC. SERIES

25TH ANNIVERSRY LIMITED EDITION (MODEL AN25L) - artist body style and neck made of Honduras Mahogany, Ivoroid bound body, neck, and headstock, sterling silver purfling inside binding, bookmatched flamed maple top with f-hole, ebony fingerboard, crown inlays starting at the first fret, sterling silver truss rod cover with 25th Anniversary engraving, bone nut, pearl inlaid Hamer logo, chrome Grover tuners, Seymour Duncan and Pearly gates pickups, sterling silver back plate with 25th Anniversary engraving, available in Cherry Trans. finish, silver GC-25 hardshell case included, mfg. 1999.

N/A	N/A	N/A	N/A	N/A	N/A	N/A

GRADING	100% MINT	98% NEAR MINT	95% EXC+	90% EXC	80% VG+	70% VG	60% G

25TH ANNIVERSARY EDITION (MODEL AN25E)

- similar to AN25L except does not have sterling silver purfling, truss rod cover, or back plate. bookmatched "Chevron" mahogany top, covered Seymour Duncan '59 and JB pickups, Grover tuners, tune-o-matic, stop tailpiece, available in Cherry Trans. finish, mfg. 1999 only.

	$1,000	$900	$800	$700	$60	$500	$400

Last MSR was $1,299.

30TH ANNIVERSARY LIMITED (MODEL 30ANLTD-NBN)

- Artist body style, one-piece Honduras mahogany chambered body, bookmatched AAAA flame maple top, 3-piece mahogany neck, 22-fret Brazilian rosewood fingerboard with MOP Victory inlays, fully bound body, 2 Seymour Duncan Antiquity pickups, three knobs, 3-way switch, nickel hardware, available in Natural Burst finish, new 2004.

MSR	$3,999	$3,300	$2,900	$2,600	$2,300	N/A	N/A	N/A

**Hamer 30th Anniversary
Limited
courtesy Hamer**

ELECTRIC: ARTIST SERIES

ARTIST (MODEL GATASO)

- offset double cutaway mahogany body, arched flamed maple top, mahogany set neck with rosewood fingerboard, dot inlays, 2 Seymour Duncan Seth Lover pickups, 2 volume/1 tone control, 3-way toggle, tune-o-matic bridge, 1 f-hole, tuned sound chamber, Schaller 3-on-a-side tuners, available in Honey (HY) or 59 Burst (59B) finishes, current mfg.

MSR	$2,810	$2,250	$1,950	$1,700	$1,450	$1,250	$1,100	$950

Red Transparent and Emerald Green finishes were introduced in 2001 and discontinued in 2002.

ARTIST CUSTOM (MODEL GATA)

- offset double cutaway mahogany body with sound chamber, arched bound bookmatched flamed maple top, mahogany neck, single f-hole, 22-fret bound rosewood fingerboard with mother-of-pearl crown inlay, tune-o-matic bridge/stop tailpiece, 3-per-side Schaller tuners, chrome hardware, 2 covered Seymour Duncan Seth Lover humbuckers, 1 volume/2 tone controls, 3-position switch, available in '59 Burst (59), Honey (HY), or Natural (NT) lacquer finishes, current mfg.

MSR	$3,185	$2,600	$2,300	$2,000	$1,800	$1,600	$1,400	$1,200

Natural finish discontinued in 1998. Honey finish discontinued in 1999. In 2001, Honey and Vintage Natural finishes were reintroduced along with Red Trans. or Emerald Green finishes.

ARTIST KORINA (MODEL ARTK)

- similar to Artist Mahogany except korina body and top, korina neck, 2 Seymour Duncan P-90 pickups, available in Vintage Korina or Jazzburst finishes, mfg. 2001-present.

MSR	$2,310	$1,850	$1,600	$1,350	$1,150	$1,000	$850	$700

Artist Korina HB (Model ARTKHB) - similar to Artist Korina except is equipped with two Seymour Duncan humbucker pickups, available in Vintage Korina finish, mfg. 2001-present.

MSR	$2,310	$1,850	$1,600	$1,350	$1,150	$1,000	$850	$700

ARTIST MAHOGANY (MODEL ARTM)

- offset double cutaway finest Honduran mahogany body and neck, book-matched arched top, single f-hole, rosewood fingerboard with mother-of-pearl dot position markers, 2 Seymour Duncan P-90 pickups, 3-per-side Grover tuners, stop tailpiece, tune-o-matic bridge, chrome hardware, 2 volume, 1 tone control, available in Silver Sparkle, Cherry Trans., Black, or Jazzburst finishes, mfg. 2001-present.

MSR	$2,310	$1,850	$1,600	$1,350	$1,150	$1,000	$850	$700

Artist Mahogany HB (Model ARTHB) - similar to Artist Mahogany except is equipped with two Seymour Duncan humbucker pickups, available in Silver Sparkle, Cherry Trans., Black, or Jazzburst finishes, mfg. 2001-present.

MSR	$2,310	$1,850	$1,600	$1,350	$1,150	$1,000	$850	$700

ARTIST STUDIO (MODEL GATASO)

- similar to the Artist, except has unbound carved bookmatched maple top, unbound fingerboard with pearl dot inlay, Wilkinson Hard Tail wraparound bridge, available in '59 Burst (59), Honey (HY), or Natural (NT) lacquer finishes, disc. 1998.

	$1,650	$1,450	$1,250	$1,100	$950	$800	$650

Last MSR was $2,199.

ARTIST ULTIMATE (MODEL ARTULT)

- offset double cutaway Honduran mahogany body with sound chamber, arched bookmatched Ultimate Grade figured maple top, mother-of-pearl body binding, set-in 3-piece mahogany neck, one bound f-hole, 24.75 in. scale, 22-fret mother-of-pearl bound ebony fingerboard with mother-of-pearl crown inlays, tune-o-matic bridge/stop tailpiece, 3-per-side Grover Super Rotomatic tuners, gold hardware, 2 covered Seymour Duncan Ultimate humbuckers, volume/2 tone controls, 3-position selector switch, available in Cognac (CN) Lacquer finish, mfg. 1998-present.

MSR	$6,000	$5,000	$4,200	$3,700	$3,200	$2,700	$2,300	$2,000

The Duncan Ultimate hand-wound pickups have covers handsigned by Seymour Duncan.

ELECTRIC: BLITZ SERIES

BLITZ

- radical offset hourglass body, set-in neck, 22-fret rosewood fingerboard with pearl dot inlay, double locking tremolo, 'drooping' peghead with screened logo, 3-per-side tuners, black hardware, 2 humbucker pickups, 2 volume/tone controls, 3-position switch, available in Black, Candy Red, Ice Pearl, or Metal Gray finishes, mfg. 1982-84.

	N/A	$700	$675	$600	$525	$450	$400

Blitz 6-Per-Side Tuners - similar to the Blitz except has 6-on-one-side-tuners, mfg. 1984-89.

	N/A	$850	$750	$650	$575	$500	$425

Last MSR was $1,125.

The Blitz model was the "updated" version of the Standard.

**Hamer Artist
courtesy George McGuire**

GRADING	100% MINT	98% NEAR MINT	95% EXC+	90% EXC	80% VG+	70% VG	60% G

ELECTRIC: CALIFORNIAN SERIES

CALIFORNIAN (MODEL GCAS) - offset double cutaway mahogany body, bolt-on rock maple neck, 25.5 in. scale, 27-fret rosewood fingerboard with pearl dot inlays, Floyd Rose tremolo, 6-on-a-side Schaller tuners, black hardware, slanted single coil/humbucker Slammer (or OBL) pickups, volume/tone controls, 3-way selector, mfg. 1988-1991.

	N/A	$950	$850	$750	$675	$600	$525

Last MSR was $1,500.

CALIFORNIAN CUSTOM (MODEL GCAC) - similar to the Californian, except features a set-in maple neck, ebony fingerboard with pearl boomerang inlay, Trem-single/trembucker Seymour Duncan pickups, mfg. 1988-1993.

	N/A	$1,100	$975	$850	$750	$650	$550

Last MSR was $2,000.

CALIFORNIAN DELUXE (MODEL CALDLX) - similar to the Californian, except features a mahogany body, bolt-on ivoroid bound maple neck, 27-fret rosewood fingerboard with boomerang inlays, locking tremolo and nut, 6-on-a-side black tuners 1 humbucker and 1 single coil Duncan Designed pickups, 1 volume control, 3-way toggle, available in Aztec Gold, disc 2002.

	$600	$525	$450	$375	$300	$250	$200

Last MSR was $790.

CALIFORNIAN ELITE (MODEL GCAE) - similar to the Californian, except has mahogany body, maple neck, 27-fret ebony fingerboard with pearl boomerang inlays, Floyd Rose tremolo, Tremstack (stacked single coil)/TrembuckerSeymour Duncan pickups, available in Aztec Gold, Black, Emerald Green, Natural, and Transparent Cherry finishes, mfg. 1987-1996.

	N/A	$800	$700	$625	$550	$475	$400

Last MSRwas $1,400.

Californian 12-String (Model G12S) - similar to the California Elite, except has 12-string configuration, figured maple top, 6-per-side tuners, disc. 1992.

	N/A	$1,000	$900	$800	$700	$600	$500

Last MSR was $1,700.

CALIFORNIAN DOUBLENECK (MODEL GDBS) - similar to the Californian Elite, except has doubleneck construction with a variety of configurations (12/6 strings are the most popular), both necks set-in (not bolt-ons), disc. 1996.

	N/A	$1,750	$1,500	$1,300	$1,100	$900	$700

Last MSR was $2,700.

CALIFORNIAN (MODEL CAL) - double offset cutaway mahogany body, bolt-on maple neck, slanted 27-fret rosewood fingerboard with dot inlay double locking tremolo, 6-on-a-side tuners, chrome hardware, single coil/humbucker pickups, 3-position switch, volume control, available in Aztec Gold, Black, or Cherry Trans. finishes, disc. 1999.

	$525	$450	$400	$350	$300	$250	$200

Last MSR was $749.

CALIFORNIAN (MODEL CX2) - double offset cutaway basswood body, maple neck, maple fingerboard with black dot inlays, 6-on-one-side tuners, two black humbucker pickups, two knobs (v, tone), 3-way switch, tune-o-matic bridge, STB, black hardware, available in Black, White, or Red finishes, mfg. 2003-present.

MSR	$330		$230	$200	$170	$150	$130	$110	$90

CALIFORNIAN (MODEL CX3) - similar to the CX2 Californian, except has H/S/H pickup configuration and rosewood fingerboard, available in Black or Gun Metal Blue finishes, mfg. 2003-present.

MSR	$420		$300	$250	$220	$190	$160	$130	$100

CALIFORNIAN QUILT (MODEL CX4Q) - similar to the CX2 Californian, except has 3 single coil pickups, quilted maple top, rosewood fingerboard, and a tremolo unit, available in Trans. Red, Trans. Violet, or Trans. Blue finishes, mfg. 2003-present.

MSR	$520		$360	$315	$275	$240	$210	$180	$150

CALIFORNIAN QUILT TOP (MODEL CALQ) - similar to the Californian except has maple body with quilted maple veneer top, maple neck with abalone binding, and single boomerang inlay on 12th fret, available in Trans. Red, mfg. 2003-present.

MSR	$600		$420	$350	$300	$260	$220	$180	$150

ELECTRIC: CENTAURA SERIES

CENTAURA (MODEL GCTS) - offset double cutaway alder body, bolt-on maple neck, 24-fret rosewood fingerboard with pearl offset inlay, Floyd Rose tremolo, reverse headstock, 6-on-a-side Schaller tuners, black hardware, 2 single coil/humbucker Seymour Duncan pickups, volume/tone control, 5-position switch, upper mids boost switch, available in Aztec Gold, Black, Emerald Green, or Trans. Cherry finishes, mfg. 1988-1993.

	N/A	$800	$700	$625	$550	$500	$450

Last MSR was $1,350.

CENTAURA DELUXE - similar to Centaura, except has ebony fingerboard, pearl boomerang inlay at 3rd/12th fret, chrome hardware, EMG pickups, disc. 1993.

	N/A	$1,100	$950	$850	$750	$650	$550

Last MSR was $1,800.

SLAMMER CENTAURA (MODEL CTM) - similar to the Centaura, except has maple fingerboard, standard vibrato, reverse headstock, available in Black, Blood Red, Candy Apple Red, 3-Tone Sunburst, or Vintage White finishes, disc. 1996.

	N/A	$325	$275	$235	$195	$165	$135

Last MSR was $500.

In 1994, Candy Apple Red and Vintage White finishes were introduced, Blood Red finish was discontinued.

GRADING	100% MINT	98% NEAR MINT	95% EXC+	90% EXC	80% VG+	70% VG	60% G

Slammer Centaura C (Model CTR) - similar to the Slammer Centaura, except has locking vibrato, reverse headstock, available in Amber Burst, Black Metalflake, Black Pearl, Candy Red, Cherry Metalflake, Trans. Cherry, Vintage White, or 3-Tone Sunburst finishes, disc. 1994.

	N/A	$375	$325	$275	$240	$210	$180

Last MSR was $600.

Slammer Centaura Deluxe - similar to the Slammer Centaura, except has curly sycamore body, locking vibrato, regular headstock, available in Trans. Purple and Trans. Walnut finishes, mfg. 1994-96.

	N/A	$350	$300	$250	$210	$180	$150

Last MSR was $540.

Slammer Centaura RC - similar to the Slammer Centaura, except has locking vibrato, regular headstock, available in Black or Trans. Cherry finishes, disc. 1996.

	N/A	$400	$350	$300	$270	$230	$200

Last MSR was $650.

ELECTRIC: CHAPPARRAL SERIES

CHAPPARRAL (MODEL GCHS) - offset double cutaway mahogany body, bolt-on maple neck, 25.5 in. scale, 24-fret ebony fingerboard with pearl boomerang inlay, double locking tremolo, 6-on-a-side tuners, black hardware, 2 single coil/humbucker Slammer pickups, volume/tone control, 5-position switch, mfg. 1988-1991.

	N/A	$750	$675	$600	$525	$450	$400

Last MSR was $1,500.

Chaparral with Sustainiac (Model GCSS) - similar to the Chaparral, except has Sustainiac device in neck pickup position, battery compartment on back, mfg. 1988-1991.

	N/A	$750	$675	$600	$525	$450	$400

Last MSR was $1,600.

CHAPPARRAL CUSTOM (MODEL GCHC) - Similar to the Chaparral, except has set-in maple neck, black hardware, 2 OBL stacked 'blade' single coil/1 Slammer humbucker pickups, volume/tone control, three 3-way mini-switches, mfg. 1986-88.

	N/A	$800	$700	$625	$550	$450	$350

Last MSR was $1,750.

The three mini-switches control pickup selection, bridge coil tapping, and single coil phase reversal.

CHAPPARRAL ELITE (MODEL GCHE) - similar to the Chaparral, except has alder body, chrome hardware, humbucker/single coil/humbucker pickups, volume/tone control, 5-position/2 mini-switches, active electronics, available in Aztec Gold, Black, Emerald Green, Natural, or Trans. Cherry finishes, mfg. 1988-1990.

	N/A	$700	$625	$550	$475	$425	$375

Last MSR was $1,400.

Chaparral Elite with Sustainiac (Model GCSE) - similar to the Chaparral Elite, except has Sustainiac device in neck pickup position, battery compartment on back, mfg. 1989-1990.

	N/A	$800	$700	$600	$525	$450	$375

Last MSR was $1,900.

**Hamer Centura
courtesy George McGuire**

ELECTRIC: DAYTONA SERIES

DAYTONA (MODEL GDAS) - offset double cutaway alder body, white pickguard, bolt-on maple neck, 25.5 in. scale, 22-fret maple fingerboard with black dot inlay, Wilkinson VS tremolo, 6-on-a-side locking Sperzel tuners, chrome hardware, 3 single coil Seymour Duncan pickups, 1 volume/2 tone controls, 5-position switch, available in 2-Tone Sunburst, Blue Trans., Emerald Green, Jade Trans., Kool Blue, Red Trans., Seafoam Green, Natural, or White Trans. finishes, mfg. 1994-98.

$775	$700	$625	$550	$475	$400	$325

Last MSR was $1,149.

Add $50 for optional rosewood fingerboard (Model GDAR).

Daytona SV - similar to Daytona, except features 3 active EMG single coil pickups, mfg. 1994-96.

$800	$700	$625	$550	$475	$400	$325

Last MSR was $1,200.

SLAMMER DAYTONA (MODEL DAM) - similar to the Daytona, except has maple body, Accutune II tremolo, 3 Slammer single coil pickups, available in Black, Candy Blue, Emerald Green, or Two Tone Burst finishes, mfg. 1994-98.

$350	$300	$260	$230	$200	$170	$140

Last MSR was $500.

Slammer Daytona (Model DAR) - similar to the Slammer Daytona, except has a rosewood fingerboard, available in Aztec Gold, Black (BK), Candy Blue (CB), Candy Red (CR), or Three-Tone Burst (3T) finishes, mfg. 1994-2001.

$350	$300	$260	$230	$200	$170	$140

Last MSR was $500.

In 1998, Two-Tone Sunburst (2T) finish was introduced; Aztec Gold finish was discontinued.

**Hamer Diablo
courtesy Hamer Guitars**

GRADING	100% MINT	98% NEAR MINT	95% EXC+	90% EXC	80% VG+	70% VG	60% G

ELECTRIC: DIABLO SERIES

DIABLO (MODEL GDBS) - offset double cutaway alder body, bolt-on maple neck, 24-fret rosewood fingerboard with pearl dot inlay, double locking Floyd Rose tremolo, blackface peghead with screened logo, 6-on-a-side tuners, chrome hardware, 2 exposed humbucker DiMarzio pickups, volume/tone controls, 5-position switch, available in Aztec Gold, Black, Cherry Trans., Emerald Green, Natural, or Red Trans. finishes, mfg. 1993-96.

	N/A	$700	$625	$550	$475	$400	$325

Last MSR was $950.

Diablo II (Model GDBS-II) - similar to the Diablo, except has DiMarzio humbucker/single coil/humbucker pickups, available in Aztec Gold, Black, Cherry Trans., Emerald Green, and Natural finishes, disc. 1998.

	$800	$725	$650	$575	$500	$425	$350

Last MSR was $1,274.

DIABLO DELUXE (MODEL DABDLX) - double offset cutaway maple body, ivoroid bound maple bolt-on neck, rosewood fingerboard with boomerang inlays, 2 Duncan Designed humbucker pickups, 2 volume/1 tone control, 3-way toggle, locking nut, Floyd Rose type tremolo bridge, chrome hardware, available in Emerald Green finish, disc. 2002.

	$550	$475	$425	$375	$325	$275	$200

Last MSR was $730.

SLAMMER DIABLO (MODEL DAB) - offset double cutaway maple body, bolt-on maple neck, 24.75 in. scale, 24-fret rosewood fingerboard with dot inlay, double locking tremolo, 6-on-a-side tuners, chrome hardware, 2 Duncan Designed exposed humbuckers, volume/tone controls, 5-position switch, available in Amberburst, Black (BK), or Emerald Green (EG) finishes, disc. 1999.

	$475	$425	$375	$325	$275	$225	$175

Last MSR was $689.

In 1995, Amberburst finish was discontinued. Amberburst and Black finishes discontinued in 1998.

Slammer Diablo II (Model DB2) - similar to the Slammer Diablo, except has humbucker/single coil/humbucker pickups, available in Aztec Gold, Black, or Candy Apple Red finishes, mfg. 1994-96.

	$475	$425	$375	$325	$275	$225	$175

Last MSR was $650.

Slammer Diablo SV (Model DB3) - similar to the Slammer Diablo, except has a standard vibrato, 3 single coil pickups, available in Amberburst, Black, or Candy Apple Red finishes, mfg. 1994-96.

	N/A	$350	$300	$250	$210	$180	$150

Last MSR was $550.

ELECTRIC: DUOTONE SERIES

DUOTONE (MODEL GDOS) - double cutaway semi-hollow mahogany body, bound spruce top, 3 round soundholes, mahogany neck, 22-fret bound rosewood fingerboard with pearl dot inlay, strings through rosewood bridge, blackface peghead with screened logo, 3-per-side tuners, chrome hardware, 2 exposed Seymour Duncan humbuckers, piezo bridge pickup, volume/2 tone controls, 3-way magnetic pickup selector, 3-position magnetic/piezo selector switch, on-board 3-band EQ, active electronics, available in '59 Burst, Black, or Natural finishes, mfg. 1994-98.

	$1,400	$1,250	$1,100	$975	$850	$700	$550

Last MSR was $2,199.

The on-board 3-band EQ is accessed through a panel on the rear of the body.

DuoTone P-90 (Model GDOS-90) - similar to the DuoTone, except has 2 single coil P-90-style soapbar pickups, available in '59 Burst, Black, Cherry Transparent, or Natural finishes, mfg. 1996 only.

	$1,400	$1,200	$1,100	$1,000	$850	$695	$550

Last MSR was $2,099.

DUOTONE (MODEL DUO) - modeled after the Duotone Custom, provides electric or acoustic sounds, separately or together, mahogany body with carved spruce top with one f-hole, two Duncan designed humbucker pickups, acoustic bridge mounted Piezo pickup with adjustable 3-band EQ, 3-way mini toggle switch, available in Jazz Burst or Cherry Sunburst finish, mfg. 1999-2003.

	$700	$575	$500	$425	$350	$300	$250

Last MSR was $950.

Jazz Burst finish discontinued 1999. Cherry Sunburst finished introduced 2000.

DUOTONE CUSTOM (MODEL DOUC) - double cutaway semi-hollow mahogany body, Ivoroid bound arched spruce top, one f-hole, set-in 3-piece mahogany neck, 24.75 in. scale, 22-fret bound East Indian rosewood fingerboard with pearl crown inlay, strings through rosewood bridge, blackface peghead with screened logo, 3-per-side tuners, chrome hardware, 2 covered Seymour Duncan humbucker ('59/JB) pickups, piezo bridge pickup, volume/2 tone controls, 3-way magnetic pickup selector, 3-position magnetic/piezo selector switch, on-board 3-band EQ, active electronics, available in Jazz Burst (JZ) or Natural (NT) lacquer finishes, mfg. 1998-present.

MSR	$3,000	$2,500	$2,200	$1,950	$1,700	$1,500	$1,300	$1,100

The on-board 3-band EQ is accessed through a panel on the rear of the body. Red Trans. finish introduced in 2001. Natural finish discontinued in 1999.

ELECTRIC: ECHOTONE SERIES

ECHOTONE (MODEL ECO) - classically styled, double cutaway design with solid maple bound back and top with bound f-hole, rosewood fingerboard with MOP dot inlays, 3-per-side tuners, two Duncan designed humbucker pickups with chrome covers, black pickguard, 3-way toggle switch, Keystone tuners, tune-o-matic, Stop tailpiece, available in Cherry Trans. or Two-Tone Sunburst finishes, mfg. 1999-present.

MSR	$520		$360	$310	$275	$240	$210	$180	$150

GRADING	100% MINT	98% NEAR MINT	95% EXC+	90% EXC	80% VG+	70% VG	60% G

Echotone Left-Handed (Model LECO) - similar to the Echotone, except in left-handed configuration, available in Cherry Trans. finish, new 2005.

MSR	$600	$420	$350	$300	$260	$220	$180	$150

ECHOTONE CUSTOM (MODEL ECC) - similar to Echotone except has pearl trapezoid fingerboard inlays, gold plated hardware, lyre tailpiece, available in Trans. Cherry finish, disc. 2002.

	$625	$550	$475	$425	$350	$300	$225

Last MSR was $849.

ELECTRIC: ECLIPSE SERIES

ECLIPSE (MODEL GECS) - offset double cutaway mahogany body, short body horns/rounded lower bout, set-in mahogany neck, 22-fret rosewood fingerboard with pearl dot inlay, Wilkinson Hardtail wraparound bridge, Lubritrak nut, blackface peghead with screened logo, 3-per-side tuners, chrome hardware, 2 Seymour Duncan mini-humbucker pickups, volume/tone controls, 3-way selector, available in Black, Cherry Trans. (CT), Candy Green (CG), Ferrari Red, or Vintage Orange (VO) finishes, mfg. 1995-99.

	$1,050	$900	$800	$700	$600	$500	$400

Last MSR was $1,399.

In 1998, Black and Ferrari Red finishes were discontinued.

Eclipse 12-String (Model GEC-12) - similar to the Eclipse, except has 12-string configuration, Hamer adjustable bridge, available in Cherry Tran. (CT), Candy Green (CG), or Vintage Orange (VO) finishes, disc. 1999.

	$1,200	$1,050	$900	$800	$700	$600	$500

Last MSR was $1,599.

SLAMMER ECLIPSE (MODEL ECS) - offset double cutaway mahogany body, short body horns/rounded lower bout, set-in mahogany neck, 22-fret rosewood fingerboard with dot inlay, trapeze bridge/stop tailpiece, 3-per-side tuners, chrome hardware, 2 mini-humbucker pickups, volume/tone controls, 3-way selector, available in Aztec Gold (AG), Black (BK), Cherry Trans. (CT), or Vintage Orange (VO) finishes, disc. 1999.

	$550	$475	$425	$375	$325	$275	$225

Last MSR was $725.

ELECTRIC: FIREBIRD SERIES

FB I - asymmetrical hourglass style mahogany body with raised center section, set-in maple neck, 22-fret ebony fingerboard with pearl boomerang inlay, double locking tremolo, reverse peghead, 6-on-a-side tuners, black hardware, Slammer humbucker pickup, volume/tone control, mfg. 1986-89.

	N/A	$700	$625	$575	$525	$475	$425

Last MSR was $1,200.

Hamer Duotone courtesy George McGuire

FB II - similar to the FB I, except has 2 humbuckers, 3-way selector, mfg. 1987-89.

	N/A	$750	$675	$600	$550	$500	$450

Last MSR was $1,400.

ELECTRIC: MAESTRO SERIES

MAESTRO 7-STRING - offset double cutaway body, set-in neck, reverse headstock, 7-on-the-other side tuners, mfg. 1990-91.

	N/A	$1,300	$1,100	$950	$850	$750	$650

Last MSR was $2,600.

The Maestro was a specialty model with a seven-string configuration. The Maestro originally debuted at the 1987 NAMM industry show. More research is being conducted into the specifications.

ELECTRIC: MIRAGE SERIES

MIRAGE (MODEL GMIR) - offset double cutaway mahogany body, carved figured koa top, mahogany neck, 25.5 in. scale, 22-fret rosewood fingerboard with pearl dot inlay, standard Wilkinson vibrato, 3-per-side Sperzel locking tuners, chrome hardware, 3 Seymour Duncan single coil rail pickups, volume/tone controls, 5-position selector, lead bypass switch, available in Cherry Trans. or Natural finishes, mfg. 1994-98.

	$1,300	$1,150	$1,000	$875	$750	$600	$475

Last MSR was $1,899.

MIRAGE II (MODEL GMIR-II) - similar to the Mirage, except has a carved maple top, 2 covered Seymour Duncan humbuckers, 3-way selector, no lead bypass switch, available in '59 Burst, Honey, Kool Blue, Red Trans., or Tobacco Sunburst finishes, disc. 1998.

	$1,350	$1,200	$1,000	$875	$750	$600	$475

Last MSR was $1,899.

MIRAGE MAPLE TOP (MODEL GMIM-II) - similar to the Mirage, except has a carved flame maple top, Wilkinson VS100 tremolo, 3-per-side Schaller locking tuners, 2 covered Seymour Duncan humbucker ('59/JB) pickups, 3-way selector (no lead bypass switch), available in Honey (HY), Kool Blue (KB), or Red Trans. (RT) lacquer finishes, mfg. 1998-99.

	$1,550	$1,350	$1,150	$1,000	$850	$700	$550

Last MSR was $2,099.

Hamer Eclipse courtesy George McGuire

GRADING	100% MINT	98% NEAR MINT	95% EXC+	90% EXC	80% VG+	70% VG	60% G

ELECTRIC: MONACO SERIES

MONACO (MODEL MON) - single cutaway hollow mahogany body, spruce arched top with f-holes, mahogany neck, 22-fret rosewood fingerboard with victory inlays, 3-per-side-tuners, dovetail neck joint, 2 Seymour Duncan humbucking pickups, three knobs (2 volume, 1 tone), 3-way switch, tune-o-matic bridge, Bigsby Vibrato, Schaller tuners, chrome hardware, available in Red Trans. finish, mfg. 2003-present.

	MSR	$3,060	$2,500	$2,200	$1,950	$1,700	$1,500	$1,300	$1,100

Monaco III (Model MON3) - similar to the Monaco, except has three Seymour Duncan P-90 pickups, two knobs, and five-way rotary switch, available in Red Trans. finish, new 2005.

	MSR	$3,560	$2,900	$2,600	$2,350	$2,100	$1,850	$1,600	$1,400

MONACO ELITE (MODEL MONEL) - similar to the Monaco Superpro except has a solid body, 24.75 in. scale, available in Indigo Blue, Black, Tobacco Sunburst, '59 Burst, or Aztec Gold finishes, mfg. 2003-present.

	MSR	$3,185	$2,600	$2,300	$2,000	$1,750	$1,550	$1,350	$1,150

Monaco Elite Mahogany (Model MONELM) - similar to the Monaco Elite, except has a mahogany body, available in Cherry Trans., Vintage Orange, 2-Tone Sunburst, or TV Blonde finishes, mfg. 2003-present.

	MSR	$2,310	$1,850	$1,600	$1,350	$1,150	$950	$800	$650

Monaco Elite P-90 (Model MONELP) - similar to the Monaco Elite, except has P-90 pickups, available in Goldtop finish, mfg. 2004-present.

	MSR	$2,935	$2,350	$2,050	$1,800	$1,550	$1,350	$1,200	$1,050

MONACO SUPERPRO (MODEL MONS) - similar to the Monaco except has a chambered body with no f-holes, book-matched flamed maple top, ivoroid binding, and no tremolo arm, available in Amberburst, '59 Burst, or Aztec Gold finishes, mfg. 2003-present.

	MSR	$3,185	$2,600	$2,300	$2,000	$1,750	$1,550	$1,350	$1,150

MONACO SUBTONE (MODEL MONST) - similar to the Monaco except is tuned to Baritone B-B, has dot inlays, has no binding, 26.5 in. scale, available in Black finish, mfg. 2003-present.

	MSR	$2,935	$2,350	$2,050	$1,800	$1,550	$1,350	$1,200	$1,050

ELECTRIC: NEWPORT SERIES

NEWPORT (MODEL NEW) - double cutaway body style, Ivoroid bound Honduras mahogany neck and body, neck has white dot inlays, hand carved, arched spruce top with two f-holes, two Hamer "Phat Cat" single coil pickups had built in Seymour Duncan's Custom Shop, these are designed so that they can be replaced with humbuckers without altering the pickup cavities, Tune-O-Matic bridge and Bigsby vibrato tailpiece, Grover Super Rotomatic tuners, Trans. Orange Sparkle finish, mfg. 1999-present.

	MSR	$2,810	$2,250	$1,950	$1,700	$1,450	$1,250	$1,050	$900

Black Cherry Burst and Jazzburst finishes introduced in 2000. Vintage Natural finish introduced in 2001.

NEWPORT KORINA (MODEL NEWK) - similar to Newport except has Korina top, tortoiseshell bound korina body, available in Vintage Korina finish, current mfg.

	MSR	$2,935	$2,350	$2,050	$1,800	$1,550	$1,350	$1,200	$1,050

NEWPORT PRO (MODEL NEWPRO) - same features as the Newport except has two Seymour Duncan Seth Lover pickups and a tune-o-matic bridge with a stop tailpiece, available in Trans. Orange Sparkle finish, mfg. 1999-present.

	MSR	$2,810	$2,250	$1,950	$1,700	$1,450	$1,250	$1,050	$900

Black Cherry Burst and Jazzburst finishes introduced in 2000. Vintage Natural finish introduced in 2001.

NEWPORT PRO CUSTOM (MODEL NEWPROC) - similar to Newport Pro except has ebony fingerboard, trapezoid position markers, trapeze tailpiece, gold hardware, available in Ruby Red finish, mfg. 2001-present.

	MSR	$3,310	$2,700	$2,400	$2,100	$1,850	$1,600	$1,400	$1,200

NEWPORT 12 STRING (MODEL NEW12) - similar to Newport Pro except in a 12-string configuration, maple body with bird's-eye Maple top, maple-set neck, rosewood fingerboard with dot position markers, two Seymour Duncan "Phat Cat" single coil pickups, 1 volume/1 tone control, 3-way toggle, tune-o-matic bridge, stop tailpiece, Grover Super Rotomatic tuners, 6-per-side tuners, available in Natural finish, mfg. 2001-present.

	MSR	$3,185	$2,600	$2,300	$2,000	$1,750	$1,550	$1,350	$1,150

ELECTRIC: PHANTOM SERIES

PHANTOM (PHAN) - offset double cutaway Honduran mahogany body, set-in 3-piece mahogany neck, 24.75 in. scale, 22-fret East Indian rosewood fingerboard with pearl dot inlays, tune-o-matic bridge/stop tailpiece, 3-per-side headstock, chrome hardware, black pickguard, Seymour Duncan 'triple coil' (combination single coil and humbucker) pickups, volume/tone controls, 3-way pickup selector, available in 2-Tone Sunburst (2T), Black (BK), or TV Blonde (TV) finishes, mfg. 1998 only.

			$1,150	$1,000	$900	$800	$700	$600	$500

Last MSR was $1,599.

PHANTOM CUSTOM (PHANC) - similar to the Phantom, except features a flamed maple top, Seymour Duncan HS-1 single coil/Seymour Duncan 'triple coil' pickups, 5 way rotary switch, available in Amberburst (AM) or Vintage Orange (VO) finishes, mfg. 1998-99.

			$1,400	$1,250	$1,100	$950	$850	$750	$650

Last MSR was $1,899.

PHANTOM A5 - sleek offset double cutaway mahogany body, set-in mahogany neck, 24.75 in. scale, 22-fret rosewood fingerboard with pearl dot inlays, double locking tremolo, 3-per-side headstock, black hardware, black pickguard, single coil/combination single coil and humbucker, volume/tone controls, 3-way pickup selector, 2-way single coil/humbucker mode switch, available in Black, Ice Pearl, Laser Pearl, Midnight Pearl, Red, or White finishes, mfg. 1982-84.

			N/A	$700	$625	$550	$475	$400	$325

GRADING	100% MINT	98% NEAR MINT	95% EXC+	90% EXC	80% VG+	70% VG	60% G

Phantom A5 6-On-One-Side Tuners - similar to the Phantom A5 except has six-on-one-side tuners, mfg. 1984-89.

	N/A	$600	$550	$500	$450	$400	$325

Last MSR was $850.

The Phantom A5 was developed in conjunction with guitarist Andy Summers (Police, solo artist).

PHANTOM 12-STRING - similar to the Phantom A5, except has 12-string configuration, fixed bridge, 6-per-side tuners, mfg. 1984-89.

	N/A	$600	$500	$425	$350	$275	$225

Last MSR was $1,100.

PHANTOM A7 - similar to the Phantom A5, except has both 1/4 in. phono and 24 pin synth interface, hex bridge pickup, 5-position switch, 3 synth control knobs, mfg. 1984-89.

	N/A	$550	$475	$400	$350	$300	$250

Last MSR was $1,700.

The Phantom A7 was equipped to interface with both the Roland G-300 Guitar Synth and the Synclavier system.

PHANTOM GT - similar to the Phantom A5, except has a single humbucker pickup, mfg. 1986-89.

	N/A	$550	$475	$400	$350	$300	$250

Last MSR was $1,450.

This model was developed in conjunction with guitarist Glenn Tipton (Judas Priest).

**Hamer Mirage
courtesy George McGuire**

ELECTRIC: PROTOTYPE SERIES

PROTOTYPE - dual cutaway mahogany body, set-in neck, 22-fret rosewood fingerboard with pearl dot inlays, fixed bridge, 3-per-side headstock, chrome hardware, black pickguard, combination single coil and humbucker ('tri-coil'), volume/tone controls, 3-way selector, available in Black, Blue, Red, or White finishes, mfg. 1981-89.

	N/A	$750	$675	$600	$525	$450	$375

Last MSR was $850.

This model was available with a locking tremolo system.

PROTOTYPE 12-STRING - similar to the Prototype, except in 12-string configuration, 6-per-side headstock, mfg. 1982-89.

	N/A	$800	$700	$625	$550	$475	$400

Last MSR was $1,100.

PROTOTYPE II - similar to the Prototype, except has additional single coil pickup (neck position), and additional toggle switch, mfg. 1984-89.

	N/A	$750	$675	$600	$525	$450	$375

Last MSR was $850.

PROTOTYPE SS - similar to the Prototype, except features rosewood or ebony fingerboard with crown (or dot) inlay, 6-per-side tuners, Floyd Rose or Kahler locking tremolo, 2 single coil/humbucker pickups, 2 selector toggle switches, mfg. 1985-89.

	N/A	$700	$625	$550	$475	$400	$325

Last MSR was $1,150.

ELECTRIC: SCARAB & SCEPTOR SERIES

SCARAB I - offset single cutaway body with J-hook bottom bout, set-in neck, 22-fret rosewood or ebony fingerboard with pearl dot (or pearl crown) inlay, 6-on-a-side tuners, double locking vibrato, chrome hardware, humbucker pickup, volume/tone control, available in various custom Candy, Day-Glo, Pearl, or Phosphorescent finishes, mfg. 1984-89.

	N/A	$550	$475	$400	$350	$300	$250

Last MSR was $1,000.

Scarab II - similar to the Scarab I, except has 2 humbucker pickups, 3-way selector, mfg. 1985-89.

	N/A	$650	$575	$500	$425	$350	$275

Last MSR was $1,450.

SCARAB (MODEL SCA, XT SERIES) - offset single cutaway with J-hook bottom bout alder body, set maple neck, 22-fret rosewood fingerboard with dot inlay, six-on-one-side tuners, two humbucker pickups, two knobs, three-way switch, black hardware, available in Black or Fire Engine Red finishes, new 2005.

MSR	$420	$300	$250	$220	$190	$160	$130	$100

SCEPTER (MODEL GSRC) - sharply beveled angular mahogany body, set-in rock maple neck, 24.75 in. scale, 24-fret ebony fingerboard with pearl boomerang inlays, Floyd Rose tremolo, 6-on-a-side tuners, black hardware, 2 humbuckers, 3-way selector, mfg. 1985-88.

	N/A	$650	$550	$450	$375	$300	$250

Last MSR was $1,650.

In 1985 Candy Apple Red was only available and early models only had 22 frets. Later models have 24 frets and black and red bodies.

**Hamer Newport
courtesy Hamer**

GRADING	100% MINT	98% NEAR MINT	95% EXC+	90% EXC	80% VG+	70% VG	60% G

ELECTRIC: SPECIAL SERIES

SPECIAL (MODEL GSPS) - double cutaway mahogany body, mahogany neck, 22-fret rosewood fingerboard with pearl dot inlay, tune-o-matic bridge/stop tailpiece, blackface peghead with screened logo, 3-per-side tuners, chrome hardware, 2 single coil Seymour Duncan soapbar pickups, 1 volume/2 tone controls, 3-position switch, available in 2-Tone Sunburst, Black, Cherry Trans. (CT), TV Blonde (TV), or Vintage White finishes, mfg. 1979-1998.

1979-1985	N/A	$900	$800	$725	$650	$575	$500
1986-1995	N/A	$800	$725	$650	$575	$500	$425
1996-1998	$950	$850	$750	$650	$550	$450	$350

Last MSR was $1,399.

In 1995, Vintage White finish was discontinued. In 1998, 2-Tone Sunburst and Black finishes were discontinued.

Special FM (Model GSPS-FM) - similar to Special, except has figured maple top, 2 Seymour Duncan humbucker ('59/JB) pickups, available in '59 Burst (59), Aztec Gold (AG), Blue Trans., Cherry Trans., Emerald Green, Natural, Salmon Blush, or Vintage Orange finishes, mfg. 1994-98.

$1,050	$925	$800	$675	$575	$475	$400

Last MSR was $1,599.

In 1996, Emerald Green, Salmon Blush, Cherry Trans., and Vintage Orange finishes were discontinued. In 1998, Blue Transparent and Natural finishes were discontinued.

SPECIAL KORINA JR. (MODEL GSPKJR) - double cutaway Korina body similar to the Les Paul Junior, set Korina neck, 22-fret rosewood fingerboard with dot inlay, three-per-side tuners, wraparound tailpiece, tortoiseshell pickguard, single dog-eared Seymour Duncan P-90 pickup, three knobs, Vintage Korina finish, new 2005.

MSR	$2,750	$2,200	$1,950	$1,750	$1,550	$1,350	$1,200	$1,050

SLAMMER SPECIAL (MODEL SPH) - similar to the Special, except has 2 humbucker pickups, available in 3-Tone Sunburst, Black, or Trans. Cherry finishes, mfg. 1994-95.

N/A	$400	$350	$300	$250	$200	$150

Last MSR was $650.

ELECTRIC: STANDARD SERIES

STANDARD (THE HAMER GUITAR) - explorer-style mahogany body, bound bookmatched curly maple top, mahogany set neck, 24.75 in. scale, 22-fret bound rosewood or ebony fingerboard with pearl dot (or crown) inlay, tune-o-matic bridge/stop tailpiece, chrome hardware, 6-on-a-side hockey stick headstock, 2 humbucker pickups, 2 volume/tone controls, 3-way selector on treble bout, available in Cherry Sunburst, Natural, Opaque Black, Opaque White, or Tobacco Sunburst finishes, mfg. 1974-1989.

1974-1978	N/A	$1,750	$1,500	$1,300	$1,100	$900	$700
1979-1984	N/A	$1,500	$1,300	$1,100	$950	$800	$650
1985-1989	N/A	$1,250	$1,050	$900	$750	$600	$450

Last MSR was $1,600.

It is estimated that Hamer USA built 50 Standards between 1975 and 1978 (roughly 10 to 15 a year).

STANDARD CUSTOM (MODEL GSTC) - Explorer-style mahogany body, bound bookmatched figured maple top, mahogany set 3-piece mahogany neck, 22-fret bound rosewood fingerboard with pearl crown inlay, tune-o-matic bridge/stop tailpiece, chrome hardware, 6-on-a-side hockey stick headstock, 2 Seymour Duncan exposed pole piece humbucker ('59/JB) pickups, 2 volume/tone controls, 3-way selector on treble bout, available in '59 Burst (59), Black, or Natural finishes, mfg. 1996-present.

MSR	$3,185	$2,600	$2,300	$2,000	$1,750	$1,550	$1,350	$1,150

In 1998, Black and Natural finishes were discontinued.

Standard Dot Inlay (Model GSTS) - similar to the Standard Custom (Model GSTC), except has unbound fingerboard and dot inlays, mfg. 1996 only.

$1,400	$1,200	$1,050	$900	$750	$625	$500

Last MSR was $1,899.

Standard Korina - similar to the Standard Custom, except features a solid korina (African limba wood) body, mfg. 1996 only.

N/A	N/A	N/A	N/A	N/A	N/A	N/A

Model has not traded sufficiently to quote pricing. This 1996 Limited Edition was held to 100 pieces.

STANDARD MAHOGANY (MODEL GSTM) - similar to the Standard Custom, except has solid one-piece mahogany body (no figured maple top), white pickguard, mother-of-pearl fingerboard inlay dots, 2 covered Seymour Duncan humbuckers, available in Black (BK) or Yellow Transparent (YT) finishes, disc. 1999.

$1,400	$1,200	$1,050	$900	$750	$625	$500

Last MSR was $1,899.

RICK NIELSEN SIGNATURE (MODEL RNS) - Standard body style with solid maple neck and body, rosewood fingerboard with mother-of-pearl dot inlays, two Duncan-designed humbucker pickups, white pickguard with Rick's caricature and facsimile signature, Keystone tuners, three-position toggle switch, chrome hardware, available in Aztec Gold (AG) finish, mfg. 1999-2000.

$700	$600	$525	$450	$375	$300	$250

Last MSR was $949.

STANDARD (MODEL STD, XT SERIES) - similar to the Standard (Model GSTM), except has alder body, white dot fingerboard inlay dots, 2 exposed pole piece Duncan Designed humbuckers, available in Aztec Gold or Black finish, mfg. 1998-present.

MSR	$520	$360	$310	$275	$240	$210	$180	$150

Black finish introduced in 2001.

GRADING	100% MINT	98% NEAR MINT	95% EXC+	90% EXC	80% VG+	70% VG	60% G

STANDARD FLAMETOP (MODEL STDF, XT SERIES) - similar to standard except has ivoroid bound body and neck, flat top, trapezoid position markers, available in Cherry Sunburst finish, mfg. 2001-present.

MSR	$600		$420	$350	$300	$260	$180	$150

JAZZ 5 (MODEL JZ5) - single cutaway design, finest flamed maple back and sides, arched spruce top, f-holes, bound top, back, and neck, two Duncan designed humbuckers, 3-per-side tuners, maple set neck, rosewood fingerboard with trapezoid position markers, trapeze tailpiece, chrome hardware, black pickguard, available in Natural finish, mfg. 2001-02.

	$900	$800	$725	$650	$550	$475	$400

Last MSR was $1,200.

ELECTRIC: STELLAR SERIES

STELLAR 1 (MODEL ST1) - double cutaway body design that allows access to all frets, solid maple neck and body, rosewood fingerboard with MOP dot inlays, two Duncan designed humbucker pickups, silky oak arched top, 3-way toggle switch, chrome deluxe tuners and hardware, tune-o-matic, stop tailpiece, available in Cherry Sunburst or Purpleburst, mfg. 1999-2000.

	$475	$400	$350	$300	$250	$200	$150

Last MSR was $629.

STELLAR 3 (MODEL ST3) - similar to Stellar 1 except has Duncan designed humbucker and 2 single coil pickups, 5-way switch, mini-toggle coil tap, Wilkinson Tremolo bridge, 1 volume/1 tone control, chrome hardware, available in Cherry Sunburst or black finishes, mfg. 2001-02.

	$525	$475	$425	$375	$325	$275	$225

Last MSR was $699.

ELECTRIC: STEVE STEVENS SERIES

These models were designed in conjunction with guitarist Steve Stevens (Billy Idol band). A third model, the Steve Stevens Custom (Model GSSC), was issued in 1989 with a retail list price of $1,700.

STEVE STEVENS I - dual cutaway body, set-in neck, 24-fret rosewood or ebony fingerboard with pearl dot (or crown) inlay, 6-on-a-side tuners, double locking tremolo, black hardware, 2 single coil/1 humbucker Slammer pickups, volume/tone controls, 3-way selector, 2-way switch, available in various custom finishes, mfg. 1984-1991.

	N/A	$700	$625	$550	$475	$400	$350

Last MSR was $1,400.

STEVE STEVENS II - offset double cutaway mahogany body, set-in rock maple neck, 25.5 in. scale, 22-fret rosewood fingerboard with pearl dot inlays, Floyd Rose tremolo, 6-on-a-side tuners, black hardware, slanted single coil/slanted humbucker pickups, volume/tone control, 3-way selector, mfg. 1986-1991.

	N/A	$750	$675	$600	$525	$450	$375

Last MSR was $1,500.

This model was also available with an ebony fingerboard with pearl crown inlays.

Hamer Special FM courtesy Hamer Guitars

ELECTRIC: STUDIO SERIES

Studio Series models, like the Archtop models, feature an arched, figured maple top. In 1998, two Archtop Custom models (the Archtop Custom and the Archtop GT Custom) have been renamed as Studio models.

STUDIO (MODEL GATS-SO) - slightly offset double cutaway mahogany body, arched flamed maple top, set-in 3-piece mahogany neck, 24.75 in. scale, 22-fret rosewood fingerboard with pearl dot inlay, Wilkinson Hardtail wraparound bridge, 3-per-side tuners, chrome hardware, 2 Seymour Duncan humbucker pickups, volume/2 tone controls, 3-position switch, available in '59 Burst (59), Aztec Gold (AG), Blue Trans., Cherry Trans., or Natural finishes, current mfg.

MSR	$2,685		$2,150	$1,850	$1,600	$1,400	$1,200	$1,000	$800

In 1996, tune-o-matic bridge/stop tailpiece replaced the Wilkinson hardtail wraparound. In 1998, Blue Trans., Cherry Trans., and Natural finishes were disc.

STUDIO MAHOGANY (MODEL STUM) - similar to Studio except has book-matched top, Grover tuners, available in Black or Cherry Trans. finishes, mfg. 2001-present.

MSR	$2,310		$1,850	$1,600	$1,350	$1,150	$1,000	$850	$700

STUDIO CUSTOM (MODEL GATC, ARCHTOP CUSTOM) - slightly offset double cutaway mahogany body, arched bound figured maple top, set-in 3-piece mahogany neck, 22-fret bound rosewood fingerboard with mother-of-pearl crown inlay, tune-o-matic bridge/stop tailpiece, 3-per-side tuners, chrome hardware, 2 exposed Seymour Duncan humbuckers, volume/2 tone controls, 3-position switch, available in '59 Burst (59), Aztec Gold, Blue Transparent, Cherry Transparent, or Natural lacquer finishes, mfg. 1992-97 (as Archtop Custom), 1998-current (as Studio Custom).

1992-1997		$1,600	$1,350	$1,150	$1,000	$850	$700	$550
1998-MSR $2,935		$2,350	$2,050	$1,800	$1,550	$1,350	$1,200	$1,050

In 1998, Aztec Gold, Blue Trans., Cherry Trans., and Natural lacquer finishes were discontinued.

Archtop Standard - similar to Archtop Custom (Model GATC), except has unbound fingerboard with pearl dot inlay, available in '59 Burst, Aztec Gold, Blue Trans., Cherry Trans., or Natural lacquer finishes, disc. 1996.

	N/A	$1,000	$850	$750	$650	$550	$450

Last MSR was $1,300.

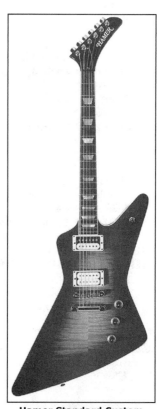

Hamer Standard Custom courtesy Hamer Guitars

GRADING	100% MINT	98% NEAR MINT	95% EXC+	90% EXC	80% VG+	70% VG	60% G

STUDIO P-90 (MODEL GAPC, ARCHTOP GT CUSTOM) - similar to Studio Custom, except has 2 creme Seymour Duncan P-90 soapbar single coil pickups, available in Gold Top (GT) finishes, current mfg.

	MSR	$2,685	$2,150	$1,850	$1,600	$1,400	$1,200	$1,000	$800

Archtop GT Custom (GAPC) - similar to the Studio P-90, available in Black or Gold Top finishes, disc. 1998.

		$1,350	$1,150	$1,000	$875	$750	$600	$475

Last MSR was $1,899.

Archtop GT Standard (Model GAPS) - similar to Archtop GT Custom (Model GAPC), except has unbound fingerboard with pearl dot inlay, available in Black or Gold Top finishes, disc. 1996.

		N/A	$1,000	$850	$725	$600	$500	$400

Last MSR was $1,299.

ELECTRIC: SUNBURST SERIES

SUNBURST - double cutaway mahogany body, arched bound figured maple top, set-in mahogany neck, 22-fret bound rosewood fingerboard with pearl dot (or crown) inlay, tune-o-matic bridge/stop tailpiece, 3-per-side tuners, chrome hardware, 2 humbucker pickups, 2 volume/1 tone controls, 3-position switch, available in Sunburst finish, mfg. 1977-1989.

1977-1982		N/A	$1,200	$1,050	$900	$800	$700	$600
1983-1989		N/A	$1,000	$850	$750	$650	$550	$450

Last MSR was $900.

SUNBURST ARCHTOP CUSTOM (MODEL SBCS) - double cutaway mahogany body, arched bound figured maple top, mahogany neck, 22-fret bound rosewood fingerboard with abalone crown inlay, tune-o-matic bridge/stop tailpiece, 3-per-side tuners, gold hardware, 2 Seymour Duncan humbucker pickups, 2 volume/1 tone controls, 3-position switch, available in '59 Burst, Aztec Gold, Blue Burst, Emerald Green, Natural, Salmon Blush, Trans. Blue, Trans. Cherry, or Vintage Orange finishes, mfg. 1991-95.

		N/A	$1,200	$1,050	$900	$800	$700	$600

Last MSR was $1,800.

SUNBURST ARCHTOP STANDARD (MODEL SBSS) - similar to Sunburst Archtop Custom, except has unbound fingerboard with pearl dot inlay, chrome hardware, disc. 1995.

		N/A	$1,100	$950	$800	$700	$600	$500

Last MSR was $1,600.

SUNBURST ARCHTOP STUDIO - similar to Sunburst Archtop Custom, except has unbound figured maple top, unbound rosewood fingerboard with pearl dot inlay, chrome hardware, mfg. 1994-95.

		N/A	$1,000	$850	$700	$600	$500	$400

Last MSR was $1,400.

SUNBURST ARCHTOP (MODEL SAT) - slightly offset double cutaway mahogany body, bound carved maple top, mahogany neck, 22-fret rosewood fingerboard with dot inlay, tune-o-matic bridge/stop tailpiece, 3-per-side tuners, chrome hardware, 2 Duncan Designed exposed pole piece humbucker pickups, volume/2 tone controls, 3-position switch, available in Black (BK), Gold Top (GT), and Vintage White finishes, disc. 1999.

		$475	$400	$350	$300	$250	$200	$150

Last MSR was $699.

In 1995, Vintage White finish was discontinued.

Slammer Archtop Flame Maple (Model SAT-F) - similar to the Slammer (Sunburst) Archtop, except features a carved flame maple top, available in Cherry Sunburst (CS) or Tobacco Sunburst (TS) finishes, current mfg.

	MSR	$520	$375	$325	$275	$240	$210	$180	$150

Tobacco Sunburst finish discontinued in 2000. Purpleburst and Blueburst finishes introduced in 2001.

Slammer Sunburst Flat Top (Model SFT) - similar to the Sunburst Archtop, except has a flat top (as opposed to contoured or carved), bound flamed top, available in Aztec Gold (AG), Black (BK), Cherry Sunburst (CS), Cherry Trans. (CT), or Vintage Orange (VO) finishes, disc. 1999.

		$575	$500	$425	$375	$325	$275	$225

Last MSR was $769.

SUNBURST ARCHTOP 2 (MODEL SAT2, XT SERIES) - similar to the Sunburst Archtop 1, except has more basic features, available in Black finish, current mfg.

	MSR	$420	$300	$260	$220	$190	$160	$130	$100

Sunburst Archtop P-90 (Model SATP90, XT Series) - similar to the Sunburst Archtop, except features two P-90 pickups, available in Goldtop finish, new 2005.

	MSR	$420	$300	$260	$220	$190	$160	$130	$100

SUNBURST ARCHTOP FLAMETOP (MODEL SATF, XT SERIES) - similar to the Sunburst Archtop 2, except has a flame maple top, available in Blue Burst, Cherry Sunburst, Honeyburst, or Purpleburst finishes, new 2005.

	MSR	$520	$360	$290	$250	$210	$180	$150	$130

Sunburst Archtop Flametop Left-Hand (Model LSATF, XT Series) - similar to the Sunburst Archtop Flametop, except in left-hand configuration, available in Honeyburst or Purpleburst finishes, new 2005.

	MSR	$600	$420	$350	$300	$250	$210	$180	$150

SUNBURST ARCHTOP QUILT (MODEL SATQ, XT SERIES) - similar to the Sunburst Archtop 2, except has a quilted maple veneer top and crown inlays, available in Trans. Black or Honeyburst finishes, current mfg.

	MSR	$600	$420	$350	$300	$260	$220	$180	$150

GRADING	100% MINT	98% NEAR MINT	95% EXC+	90% EXC	80% VG+	70% VG	60% G

SUNBURST FLATOP (MODEL SFX-2, XT SERIES) - similar to the Sunburst except has a flat top, basswood body, maple neck, black hardware, and rosewood fingerboard, available in Black Cherry, Pearl Blue, or White finishes, current mfg.

MSR	$330		$230	$200	$175	$150	$130	$110	$90

SUNBURST FLATOP (MODEL SFX-3, XT SERIES) - similar to the Sunburst Flat top except has a tortise pickguard, and white pickup covers, available in Gun Metal Blue or Gun Metal Black finishes, current mfg.

MSR	$420		$300	$260	$220	$190	$160	$130	$100

ELECTRIC: T-51 SERIES

T-51 (MODEL T51S) - single cutaway alder body, bolt-on hard rock maple neck, 22-fret maple fingerboard with black dot inlay, Wilkinson HT-100 bridge, 6-on-a-side Sperzel tuners, chrome hardware, black bakelite pickguard, 2 Seymour Duncan single coil pickups, volume/tone control, 3-position switch, controls mounted metal plate, available in Black, Butterscotch, Natural, Vintage Orange, or White Trans. finishes, mfg. 1994-98.

	$775	$700	$625	$550	$475	$400	$325

Last MSR was $1,149.

Add $50 for optional rosewood fingerboard (Model T51R).

T-51 Fishman Power Bridge (Model T51F) - similar to the T-51, except has a bridge-mounted Fishman transducer system, disc. 1998.

	$925	$850	$750	$650	$550	$450	$350

Last MSR was $1,399.

SLAMMER T-51 (MODEL T5M) - similar to the T-51, except has swamp ash body, fixed bridge, 2 Slammer single coil pickups, available in 2-Tone Sunburst (2T), Amberburst (AB), or Black (BK) finishes, mfg. 1994-99.

	$375	$325	$275	$235	$195	$160	$125

Last MSR was $499.

ELECTRIC: TLE & TRAD SERIES

TLE - single cutaway mahogany body, figured maple top, set-in rock maple neck, 24-fret rosewood fingerboard with pearl dot inlay, fixed bridge, black hardware, 6-on-a-side tuners, 3 single coil pickups, volume/tone controls, 5-way selector, mfg. 1986-89.

	N/A	$675	$600	$525	$450	$375	$300

Last MSR was $900.

TLE CUSTOM - single cutaway bound mahogany body, figured maple top, set-in rock maple neck, 24-fret ebony fingerboard with pearl boomerang inlay, Floyd Rose tremolo, black hardware, 6-on-a-side tuners, 2 OBL single coil/Slammer humbucker pickups, volume/tone controls, 5-way selector, mfg. 1987-89.

	N/A	$900	$800	$700	$600	$500	$400

Last MSR was $1,750.

TRAD '62 (T-62) - double offset cutaway alder body, white pickguard, bolt-on bird's-eye maple neck, 22-fret pau ferro fingerboard with pearl dot inlay, standard vibrato, Lubritrak nut, 6-on-a-side locking Sperzel tuners, 3 single coil Alnico pickups, volume control, 5-position switch, 3-band EQ with bypass switch, available in Daphne Blue, Emerald Green, Seafoam Green, 2-Tone Sunburst, 3-Tone Sunburst, Trans. Blue, Trans. White, or Vintage White finishes, mfg. 1992-95.

	N/A	$950	$850	$750	$675	$600	$525

Last MSR was $1,450.

In 1994, 3-Tone Sunburst was discontinued, Daphne Blue, Emerald Green, 2-Tone Sunburst, Transparent Blue and Transparent White finishes were introduced.

ELECTRIC: VANGUARD SERIES

VANGUARD (MODEL VAN) - trademark double cutaway body style, Honduras Mahogany neck with rosewood fingerboard, semi-hollow body with one f-hole, two Seymour Duncan P-90 pickups with black covers. Unique Silver Sparkle finish covers the entire body, back of neck and headstock, mfg. 1999-2000.

	$925	$825	$725	$650	$575	$500	$425

Last MSR was $1,299.

Trans. Cherry finish introduced 2000.

VANGUARD HB (MODEL VANHB) - similar to Vanguard except has Seymour Duncan '59 pickup in the neck position and Seymour Duncan JB pickup in the bridge position, mfg. 1999-2000.

	$1,050	$925	$850	$750	$675	$600	$525

Last MSR was $1,499.

ELECTRIC: VECTOR SERIES

The Vector model was originally available as a custom order only, and then later put into production. Models were built with and without a curly maple top, and with fixed bridge or Kahler tremolo.

Hamer Sunburst courtesy George McGuire

Hamer T-51 courtesy Hamer Guitars

GRADING	100% MINT	98% NEAR MINT	95% EXC+	90% EXC	80% VG+	70% VG	60% G

VECTOR (MAHOGANY) - Flying V-style mahogany body, set-in mahogany neck, 24.75 in. scale, 22-fret rosewood fingerboard with mother-of-pearl inlay, Schaller tuners, string through-body bridge, 2 humbuckers, 2 volume/tone controls, 3-way selector switch, available in Black and White Graphic, Cherry, Sunburst, Opaque Red, Trans. Blue, Trans. Green, and Trans. Yellow finishes, mfg. 1979-1989.

	N/A	$425	$350	$300	$250	$200	$150

Last MSR was $800.

Vector (Maple Top) - similar to the Vector, except has a curly maple top, mfg. 1979-1989.

	N/A	$475	$400	$350	$300	$250	$200

Last MSR was $900.

Vector KK (Mahogany) - similar to the Vector, except has a single humbucker pickup, mfg. 1985 to 1989.

	N/A	$450	$375	$300	$250	$200	$150

Last MSR was $1,450.

This model was designed in conjunction with guitarist K.K. Downing (Judas Priest).

Vector KK (Maple Top) - similar to the Vector KK, except has a curly maple top, mahogany body, mfg. 1985-89.

	N/A	$500	$425	$350	$300	$250	$200

Last MSR was $1,450.

VECTOR FLAMETOP (MODEL VECF) - Flying V-style alder body, flat flamed maple veneer, maple neck with ivoroid binding, rosewood fingerboard with boomerang inlays, two humbucking pickups, 3 knobs (2 volumes, tone), 3-way switch, tune-o-matic bridge, available in Cherry Sunburst finish, current mfg.

MSR	$520	$360	$310	$275	$240	$210	$180	$150

Add $50 for Cherry Sunburst finish.

VECTOR KORINA (MODEL GVKS) - FlyingV-style Korina body, set Korina neck, 22-fret rosewood fingerboard with dot inlay, three-per-side tuners, STB, white pickguard, two Seymour Duncan '59 humbucker pickups, three knobs, three-way switch, gold hardware, Vintage Korina finish, new 2005.

MSR	$3,750	$3,000	$2,650	$2,350	$2,100	$1,850	$1,650	$1,450

ELECTRIC: VINATGE & VIRTUOSO SERIES

VINTAGE S (MODEL GVSS) - offset double cutaway figured maple body, bolt-on bird's-eye maple neck, 22-fret pau ferro fingerboard with pearl dot inlay, standard ABM vibrato, Lubritrak nut, 6-on-a-side locking Sperzel tuners, 3 Seymour Duncan APS-1 single coil pickups, volume/tone controls, 5-position switch, 3-band EQ with bypass switch, available in '59 Burst, 3-Tone Sunburst, Amberburst, Aztec Gold, Cherry Sunburst, Natural, or Salmon Burst finishes, disc. 1996.

	$1,200	$1,050	$950	$825	$700	$575	$450

Last MSR was $1,800.

In 1994, Aztec Gold, Natural and Salmon Burst finishes were introduced, Cherry Sunburst finish was discontinued.

VIRTUOSO (MODEL GVTC) - offset double cutaway mahogany body, set-in maple neck, 26.25 in. scale, 36-fret rosewood fingerboard with pearl dot inlay, Floyd Rose tremolo, reverse headstock, 6-on-a-side tuners, humbucker 'rail' single coil pickup, volume controls, mfg. 1987-1991.

	N/A	$1,250	$1,100	$950	$850	$750	$650

Last MSR was $2,300.

ACOUSTIC ELECTRIC BASS

This model is included in the Electric Book because it is the only acoustic model that Hamer has made.

ACOUSTIC 12-STRING BASS (MODEL B12A) - single cutaway mahogany body, bound bookmatched figured maple top, maple set neck, 34 in. scale, round soundhole, 21-fret rosewood fingerboard with pearl dot inlay, fixed bridge, 6-per-side tuners, chrome hardware, 2 EMG pickups (EMG P mounted in soundhole/EMG HB mounted near bridge), 2 volume/tone controls, active electronics. In reality, this is a solid body instrument with an acoustic look, available in '59 Burst (59), Black, or White finishes, mfg. 1991-96, 1998-present.

MSR	$3,375	$2,800	$2,450	$2,100	$1,800	$1,600	$1,400	$1,200

In 1998, Black and White finishes were discontinued.

ELECTRIC BASS: PRICING OPTIONS

Hamer USA Basses are offered with a variety of options. A Natural finish or black hardware options are available at no extra charge.

Add $70 for EMG upgrade (per pickup). Add $105 for gold hardware.

ELECTRIC BASS: BLITZ SERIES

BLITZ (MODEL BBLS) - radical hourglass-shaped mahogany body, set-in maple neck, 34 in. scale, 21-fret rosewood fingerboard with pearl dot inlay, fixed bridge, 4-on-a-side tuners, chrome hardware, P/J-style pickups, 2 volume/tone control, available in various Hamer custom finishes, mfg. 1982-1991.

	N/A	$650	$575	$500	$425	$350	$275

Last MSR was $1,050.

BLITZ 5 STRING - similar to the Blitz Bass, except has 5-string configuration, mfg. 1985-89.

	N/A	$700	$625	$550	$475	$400	$325

Last MSR was $1,100.

This model was optional with a Kahler tremolo system.

GRADING	100% MINT	98% NEAR MINT	95% EXC+	90% EXC	80% VG+	70% VG	60% G

ELECTRIC BASS: CENTAURA SERIES

SLAMMER CENTAURA BASS (MODEL CB4) - offset double cutaway alder body, bolt-on maple neck, 34 in. scale, 21-fret maple or rosewood fingerboard with offset dot inlay, fixed bridge, 4-on-a-side tuners, chrome hardware, P/J-style pickups, 2 volume/tone controls, available in 3-Tone Sunburst, Black, Blood Red, Candy Apple Red, or Vintage White finishes, mfg. 1993-95.

	N/A	$325	$275	$225	$195	$150	$125

Last MSR was $500.

In 1994, Candy Apple Red and Vintage White finishes were introduced, and Blood Red finish was discontinued.

SLAMMER CENTAURA BASS 5 (MODEL CB5) - similar to the Slammer Centaura Bass, except in a 5-string configuration, reverse headstock, 2 J-style pickups, black hardware, available in 3-Tone Sunburst, Black, Black Metalflake, Black Pearl, Blue Metalflake, Candy Apple Red, Candy Red, or Vintage White finishes, mfg. 1993-95.

	N/A	$350	$300	$275	$225	$195	$150

Last MSR was $580.

In 1994, Black and 3-Tone Sunburst finishes were introduced, Black Metalflake, Black Pearl, Blue Metalflake and Candy Red finishes were discontinued.

ELECTRIC BASS: CHAPARRAL SERIES

CHAPARRAL BASS (MODEL BCHS) - offset double cutaway mahogany body, set-in rock maple neck, 20-fret rosewood fingerboard with pearl dot inlay, fixed bridge, 4-on-a-side tuners, chrome hardware, EMG P/J-style pickups, 2 volume/1 tone controls, active electronics, mfg. 1987-1995.

	N/A	$850	$750	$675	$600	$525	$450

Last MSR was $1,350.

CHAPARRAL BASS 5 STRING (MODEL B05S) - similar to Chaparral Bass, except has a 5-string configuration, mfg. 1987-1995.

	N/A	$950	$850	$750	$650	$550	$450

Last MSR was $1,500.

CHAPARRAL BASS MAX (MODEL BCMC) - similar to the Chaparral Bass, except has mahogany or figured maple body, 20-fret ebony fingerboard with pearl boomerang inlays, mfg. 1987-1991.

	N/A	$900	$800	$700	$625	$550	$450

Last MSR was $1,400.

Hamer Acoustic 12-String Bass courtesy Hamer Guitars

CHAPARRAL BASS 12-STRING (MODEL B12L) - similar to Chaparral Bass, except has 12-string configuration, mahogany body, Hamer brass fixed bridge, split-V headstock, 6-per-side Schaller tuners, 2 EMG DC-35 pickups, volume/pan/bass/treble controls, EMG BTS active electronics, stereo output jacks, available in Black (BK) or Cherry Trans. finishes, current mfg.

MSR	$3,000	$2,500	$2,200	$1,950	$1,700	$1,500	$1,300	$1,100

This model was designed in conjunction with bassist Tom Petersson (Cheap Trick). In 1998, Cherry Transparent finish was discontinued.

CHAPARRAL BASS 9 BOLT NECK, (MODEL B04S) - offset double cutaway alder body, bolt-on maple neck, 21-fret rosewood fingerboard with pearl dot inlay, fixed bridge, 4-on-a-side tuners, chrome hardware, P/J-style EMG pickups, 2 volume/1 tone controls, active electronics, available in Aztec Gold, Black, Candy Red, Natural, 3-Tone Sunburst, Trans. Cherry, Vintage White, or White finishes, mfg. 1989-1995.

	N/A	$850	$750	$650	$575	$500	$425

Last MSR was $1,400.

Chaparral 5-String Bass - similar to Chaparral Bass, except has a 5-string configuration, reverse headstock, additional mix control, mfg. 1989-1995.

	N/A	$950	$850	$750	$650	$550	$450

Last MSR was $1,550.

CHAPARRAL BASS 12 (MODEL CH12, XT SERIES) - similar to Chaparral 12 Bass except has mahogany body, maple neck with two truss rods, rosewood fingerboard with dot inlays, 2 Duncan Designed humbucker pickups, 1 volume/1 tone, 1 pan with active bass and treble, custom bridge, chrome hardware, available in Black or White Pearl finishes, mfg. 2001-present.

MSR	$900	$625	$550	$500	$450	$400	$350	$300

SLAMMER CHAPARRAL BASS (MODEL CHB) - similar to the Chaparral Bass, except has a maple body, chrome hardware, P/J-style pickups, available in 3-Tone Sunburst, Black, Candy Red, or Vintage White finishes, disc. 1996.

	N/A	$400	$350	$300	$250	$200	$150

Last MSR was $600.

In 1994, Black, Candy Red and Vintage White finishes were introduced.

SLAMMER CHAPARRAL BASS 5 (MODEL CH5) - similar to the Slammer Chaparral Bass, except in a 5-string configuration, reverse headstock, available in 3-Tone Sunburst, Black, or Candy Red finishes, disc. 1996.

	N/A	$450	$400	$350	$300	$250	$200

Last MSR was $700.

Hamer Chaparral Bass courtesy Hamer Guitars

GRADING	100% MINT	98% NEAR MINT	95% EXC+	90% EXC	80% VG+	70% VG	60% G

ELECTRIC BASS: CRUISEBASS SERIES

CRUISEBASS (MODEL BCRS) - sleek offset double cutaway alder body, bolt-on maple neck, 34 in. scale, 22-fret rosewood fingerboard with white dot inlay, 4-on-a-side headstock, Gotoh fixed bridge, chrome hardware, black pickguard, 2 Seymour Duncan J-style pickups, 2 volume/tone controls, available in 2-Tone Sunburst, Black, Black Cherry Burst, Candy Blue, Candy Green, Candy Red, Emerald Green, or White Trans. finishes, mfg. 1982-89.

	N/A	$850	$750	$650	$550	$475	$400

Last MSR was $1,150.

Cruise Bass (Model BCRT, Cruisebass 2-Tek) - similar to the Cruisebass, except features a 2-Tek bridge, 4-on-a-side Schaller closed housing tuners, available in 2-Tone Sunburst (with tortoise pickguard), Black (with pearloid pickguard), Candy Blue (with pearloid pickguard), or White (with tortoise pickguard) finishes, disc. 1999.

$1,125	$975	$850	$750	$625	$495	$375

Last MSR was $1,499.

Add $100 for an ebony fretless neck with inlaid maple fretlines (Model BCRT-F).

Cruise Custom (Model BCRT-A, Cruisebass Active) - similar to the Cruise Bass (BCRT), except features 2 J-Style EMG active pickups, active EMG electronics, available in 2-Tone Sunburst (with tortoise pickguard), Black (with pearloid pickguard), Candy Blue (with pearloid pickguard), or White (with tortoise pickguard) finishes, disc.

$1,300	$1,150	$1,000	$875	$725	$600	$475

Last MSR was $1,749.

Add $100 for an ebony fretless neck with inlaid maple fretlines (Model BCRT-A-F).

CRUISEBASS 5 - similar to the Cruisebass, except in a 5-string configuration, 5-on-a-side tuners, available in 2-Tone Sunburst, Black, Black Cherry Burst, Candy Blue, Candy Green, Candy Red, Emerald Green, or White Trans. finishes, mfg. 1982-89.

	N/A	$900	$800	$700	$600	$525	$450

Last MSR was $1,150.

Cruise 5 (Model BC5T, Cruisebass 5 2-Tek) - similar to the Cruisebass, except features a hand carved asymmetrical maple neck, 2-Tek bridge, 5-on-a-side Schaller closed housing tuners, available in 2-Tone Sunburst (with tortoise pickguard), Black (with pearloid pickguard), Candy Blue (with pearloid pickguard), or White (with tortoise pickguard) finishes, disc. 1999.

$1,200	$1,050	$925	$795	$650	$525	$400

Last MSR was $1,599.

Add $100 for an ebony fretless neck with inlaid maple fretlines (Model BC5T-F).

Cruise 5 Custom (Model BC5T-A, Cruisebass 5 Active) - similar to the Cruise 5 (BC5T), except features 2 J-Style EMG active pickups, active EMG electronics, available in 2-Tone Sunburst (with tortoise pickguard), Black (with pearloid pickguard), Candy Blue (with pearloid pickguard), or White (with tortoise pickguard) finishes, disc. 1999.

$1,500	$1,300	$1,150	$975	$825	$650	$500

Last MSR was $1,999.

Add $100 for an ebony fretless neck with inlaid maple fretlines (Model BC5T-A-F).

SLAMMER CRUISE 4 (MODEL CRS, SLAMMER CRUISE BASS) - sleek offset double cutaway maple body, bolt-on maple neck, 34 in. scale, 22-fret rosewood fingerboard with white dot inlay, 4-on-a-side tuners, Natural finish headstock, fixed bridge, chrome hardware, white (or tortoiseshell or black) pickguard, 2 J-style pickups, 2 volume/tone controls, available in Black (BK), Candy Blue (CB), or Two-Tone Sunburst (2T) finishes, disc. 2002.

$400	$350	$300	$250	$200	$160	$130

Last MSR was $580.

Slammer Cruise 5 (Model CRV, Slammer Cruisebass 5) - similar to the Cruisebass 5, except features a five-string configuration, 4/1-per-side headstock, available in Black (BK), Candy Blue (CB), or Two-Tone Sunburst (2T) finishes, disc 2002.

$465	$400	$350	$300	$250	$200	$150

Last MSR was $680.

ELECTRIC BASS: MISC. MODELS

FB IV - asymmetrical hourglass style mahogany body with raised center section, set-in maple neck, 34 in. scale, 21-fret rosewood fingerboard with pearl dot inlay, fixed bridge, reverse peghead, 4-on-a-side tuners, black hardware, P/J-style pickups, 2 volume/tone control, mfg. 1986-89.

	N/A	$800	$700	$625	$550	$500	$450

Last MSR was $1,200.

IMPACT BASS - Offset double cutaway mahogany body, set-in hard rock maple neck, 24-fret ebony fingerboard with pearl boomerang inlay, fixed bridge, 2-per-side tuners, gold hardware, 2 EMG pickups, 2 volume/treble/bass controls, active electronics, mfg. 1991-93.

	N/A	$1,500	$1,300	$1,100	$1,000	$900	$800

Last MSR was $2,500.

Specialty models were contructed with a neck-through design, pau ferro fingerboard, and used sapelle, purpleheart, and rosewood in their construction.

MONACO BASS (MODEL MONB) - single cutaway chambered mahogany body with a figured maple top, maple neck, 21-fret rosewood fingerboard with dot inlay, two-per-side tuners, two Seymour Duncan Phat Cat bass pickups, three knobs, chrome hardware, available in '59 Burst or Tobacco Sunburst finishes, new 2005.

MSR	$3,000		$2,500	$2,200	$1,950	$1,700	$1,500	$1,300	$1,100

GRADING	100% MINT	98% NEAR MINT	95% EXC+	90% EXC	80% VG+	70% VG	60% G

SCARAB BASS (MODEL BSCS) - offset single cutaway body with J-hook bottom bout, set-in neck, 34 in. scale, 21-fret rosewood fingerboard with pearl dot inlay, 4-on-a-side tuners, fixed bridge, chrome hardware, P/J-style pickups, 2 volume/tone control, available in various custom Candy, Day-Glo, Pearl, or Phosphorescent finishes, mfg. 1985-89.

	N/A	$650	$575	$500	$425	$350	$275

Last MSR was $1,000.

Scarab Bass 5 String - similar to the Scarab Bass, except has 5-string configuration, mfg. 1985-89.

	N/A	$700	$625	$550	$475	$400	$325

Last MSR was $1,100.

This model was also offered with a Kahler tremolo bridge.

STANDARD BASS - Explorer-style mahogany body, bound bookmatched curly maple top, mahogany set neck, 34 in. scale, 20-fret bound rosewood or ebony fingerboard with pearl dot inlay, Tune-O-Matic bridge/stop tailpiece, chrome hardware, 4-on-a-side hockey stick headstock, 2 humbucker pickups, 2 volume/tone controls, available in Cherry Sunburst, Natural, Opaque Black, Opaque White, or Tobacco Sunburst finishes, mfg. 1975-1983.

	N/A	$1,200	$1,050	$900	$800	$700	$600

Last MSR was $1,600.

STANDARD BASS (MODEL STB) - Explorer-style alder body, flat top, alder set neck with rosewood fingerboard, dot position markers, 2 Duncan Designed humbucker pickups, 2 volume/1 tone control, Gotoh-style tuners, chrome hardware, available in Black finish, mfg. 2001-02.

	$675	$600	$525	$475	$425	$375	$325

Last MSR was $900.

SUNBURST FLAT TOP (MODEL SFB, XT SERIES) - double cutaway basswood body with beveled edge, maple set neck, 24-fret rosewood fingerboard with crown inlay, two humbucker pickups, 3 knobs (2 volumes, 1 tone), Gotoh style bridge, 2-per-side tuners, black hardware, available in Black Cherry or Gun Metal Grey finish, mfg. 2003-present.

MSR	$600		$420	$350	$300	$260	$220	$180	$150

TWELVE STRING BASS (SHORT SCALE, MODEL B12S) - double cutaway figured maple body, maple set neck, 30.5 in. scale, 21-fret rosewood fingerboard with pearl dot inlay, fixed bridge, 6-per-side tuners, chrome hardware, 2 EMG pickups, 2 volume/1 tone controls, active electronics, available in '59 Burst, Aztec Gold, Black, Candy Red, Natural, Trans. Cherry, or White finishes, mfg. 1991-96.

	N/A	$1,400	$1,200	$1,050	$900	$750	$600

Last MSR was $2,000.

Twelve String Bass (Long Scale) - similar to Twelve String Bass (Short Scale) except has long scale fingerboard.

	N/A	$1,500	$1,300	$1,100	$950	$800	$650

Last MSR was $2,200.

This model was the forerunner to the Chaparral 12-String model.

Hamer 12-String Bass (Short Scale) courtesy Hamer Guitars

ELECTRIC BASS: VELOCITY SERIES

VELOCITY (MODEL VEL) - double offset cutaway bubinga body, 5-piece maple/bubinga neck, 24-fret rosewood fingerboard with dot inlays, single humbucker pickup, active electronics, 3 knobs (v, b, t), Gotoh style bridge, 2-per-side-tuners, chrome hardware, available in Natural Oil finish, mfg. 2003-04.

	$600	$525	$450	$375	$300	$250	$200

Last MSR was $800.

Velocity 2 (Model VEL2) - similar to the Velocity except has two Jazz-style pickups, mfg. 2003-04.

	$600	$525	$450	$375	$300	$250	$200

Last MSR was $800.

Velocity 5 (Model VEL5) - similar to the Velocity except has five-string configuration, mfg. 2003-04.

	$675	$600	$525	$450	$375	$325	$250

Last MSR was $900.

Velocity 2 5-String (Model VEL25) - similar to the Velocity except has five-string configuration, mfg. 2003-04.

	$675	$600	$525	$450	$375	$325	$250

Last MSR was $900.

This model is also available in fretless configuration.

VELOCITY 2 ASH (MODEL VEL2A) - similar to the Veolcity bass except has an ash body and matching color headstock, available in Honeyburst, Trans. Black, or Trans. Red finishes, mfg. 2003-present.

MSR	$600		$420	$350	$300	$260	$220	$180	$150

HAMILTONE

Instruments currently built in Fort Wayne, IN.

Luthier James M. Hamilton is currently offering a Limited Edition SRV custom guitar similar to the one that the late Stevie Ray Vaughn played on a number of occasions. This guitar is commissioned by Billy Gibbons of ZZ Top. He also produces pearl inlay necks that can be fitted in Stratocasters. For further information and specifications, please contact luthier Hamilton directly (see Trademark Index).

Hamer Monaco Bass courtesy Hamer Guitars

GRADING	100% MINT	98% NEAR MINT	95% EXC+	90% EXC	80% VG+	70% VG	60% G

HAMMERTONE GUITARS

Instruments currently built in Hamilton, Ontario.

Hammertone Guitars builds a 12-string Mando´tar that is tuned an octave higher than normal tuning. Hammertone is part of the F Bass company. For more information regarding this model, please contact the company directly (see Trademark Index).

HANEWINCKEL GUITARS

Instruments currently built in Artesia, CA.

Pete Hanewinckel and Hanewinckel Guitars is currently offering four different models of custom built bass guitars. All four models are all available in 4-, 5-, 6-, 7-, and 8-string configurations. Basses are constructed with a variety of tonewoods, as well as exotic woods, and feature Bartolini or Lane Poor pickups. Bolt-on models feature 6-bolt neck joints, and neck-through construction is optionally offered.

Retail prices in the Vintage series range between $1,600 up to $3,200; the Classic series prices fall between $1,900 and $3,500; Artist series models are between $2,300 and $4,000; the top-of-the-line Pro series ranges from $2,600 to $4,300. The newer Signature Series are between $2,900 and $4,500. There are also options available at added prices. For further information regarding body styles and specifications, please contact Hanewinckel Guitars directly (see Trademark Index).

HANG-DON

Instruments previously built in Vietnam during the 1970s.

These entry level guitars displayed a Fender-ish lean in design, although the composition and materials are basic (source: Tony Bacon, *The Ultimate Guitar Book*).

HARDBODY COMPOSITE GUITARS

Instruments previously built in Escondido, CA. Previously distributed by Bi-Mar International of Escondido, CA.

Designer George M. Clayton is an expert in composite (graphite) materials, and has a background in the aerospace field as well as yacht (Catamaran) building. Clayton was a former vice president and head designer for the Rainsong Guitar Company and previously offered the STS-1 solid body, graphite electric guitar.

The STS-1 (last MSR $1,750) features a neck-through molded design, ebony fingerboard, abalone inlays, active EMG 89 humbucker pickups, and three custom colors (red, white, or black).

HARMONIC DESIGN

Instruments previously built in Bakersfield, CA until 2003. Pickups currently produced.

Harmonic Design USA primarily builds custom pickups for many popular American models, such as the Stratocaster, Telecaster, and Les Paul. They have also built two retro-styled guitars for today´s players. The **Elektro** (last MSR $1,200) is a semi-hollow body 335 type guitar with a textured multi-flek finish. The **Tweedcaster** (last MSR $1,990) is a Fender-style guitar with aged tweed cloth covering the body and headstock. Harmonic Design mainly specializes in making custom pickups for many of the popular American design guitars. For more information on guitars or pickups refer to their website (see Trademark Index).

HARMONY

Instruments previously produced in the Chicago, IL area between the 1890s and 1975. Also previously produced in Korea from the mid-1970s through the late 1980s. See Chapter on House Brands.

The Harmony Company of Chicago, Illinois was one of the largest American musical instrument manufacturers. Harmony has the historical distinction of being the largest "jobber" house in the nation, producing stringed instruments for a number of different wholesalers. Individual dealers or distributors could get stringed instruments with their own brandname on it (as long as they ordered a minimum of 100 pieces). At one time the amount of instruments being produced by Harmony made up the largest percentage of stringed instruments being manufactured in the U.S. market (archtops, flattops, electric Spanish, Hawaiian bodies, ukuleles, banjos, mandolins, violins, and more).

Harmony was founded by Wilhelm J.F. Schultz in 1892. Schultz, a German immigrant and former foreman of Lyon & Healy´s drum division, started his new company with four employees. By 1884, the number of employees had grown to forty, and Shultz continued to expand into larger and larger factories through 1904. Shultz built Harmony up to a 125 employee workforce (and a quarter of a million dollars in annual sales) by 1915.

In 1916, the Sears, Roebuck Company purchased Harmony, and seven years later the company had annual sales of 250,000 units. Max Adler, a Sears executive, appointed Jay Kraus as vice-president of Harmony in 1925. The following year Jay succeeded founder Wilhelm Schultz as president, and continued expanding production. In 1930, annual sales were reported to be 500,000 units, with 35 to 40 percent being sold to Sears (catalog sales). Harmony had no branch offices, territorial restrictions, or dealer reps - wholesalers purchased the musical instruments and aggressively sold to music stores.

Harmony bought several trademarks from the bankrupt Oscar Schmidt Company in 1939, and their Sovereign and Stella lines were Harmony´s more popular guitars. In 1940, Krause bought Harmony by acquiring the controlling stock, and continued to expand the company´s production to meet the market boom during the 1950s and 1960s. Mr. Kraus remained president until 1968, when he died of a heart attack. Charles Rubovits (who had been with Harmony since 1935) took over as president, and remained in that position for two years. Kraus´ trust still maintained control over Harmony, and trust members attempted to form a conglomerate by purchasing Chicago-based distributor Targ & Dinner and a few other companies. Company (or more properly the conglomerate´s) indebtedness led to a liquidation auction to satisfy creditors - although Harmony continued to turn in impressive annual sales figures right up until the company was dissolved in 1974 (or early 1975). The loss of Harmony in the mid 1970s, combined with the decline of Kay/Valco, Inc. in 1969 (or 1970) definitely left the door wide open for Asian products to gain a larger percentage of the entry or student level guitar market (for example, W.M.I. began using the Kay trademark on Teisco-built guitars as early as 1973; these guitars were sold through department store chains through the 1970s), (Harmony company history courtesy Tom Wheeler, *American Guitars*, Harmony model information courtesy John Kinnemeyer of JK Lutherie, Ryland Fitchett of Rockohaulix, Ronald Rothman of Rothman´s Guitars).

GRADING	100% MINT	98% NEAR MINT	95% EXC+	90% EXC	80% VG+	70% VG	60% G

IDENTIFYING RE-BRANDED HARMONY TRADEMARKS

Harmony reportedly made 57 "different" brands throughout their productive years. Early models featured the Harmony trademark, or remained unlabeled for the numerous wholesalers. In 1928 Harmony introduced the Roy Smeck Vita series, and two years later the **Grand Concert** and **Hawaiian** models debuted. The **Vagabond** line was introduced in 1931, the **Cremona** series in 1934, and **Patrician** guitars later in 1938.

As Harmony was purchased by Sears, Roebuck in 1916, Harmony built a number of **Silvertone** models. Harmony continued to sell to Sears even after Kraus bought the company. Harmony bought a number of trademarks from the bankrupt Oscar Schmidt Company in 1939 (such as **La Scala**, **Stella**, **Sovereign**), as well as expanding their own brandnames with **Valencia**, **Monterey**, **Harmony Deluxe**, **Johnny Marvin**, **Vogue**, and many (like **Carelli** from the mid 1930s) that are being researched today! Although the Kay company built most of the **Airline** guitars for the Montgomery Ward stores, Harmony would sometimes be subcontracted to build Airlines to meet the seasonal shopping rush. National (Valco) supplied resonator cones for some Harmony resonator models, and probably bought guitar parts from Harmony in return.

HARMONY PRODUCTION & PRICING

The Harmony company of 4600 South Kolin Avenue in Chicago, Illinois built a great deal of guitars. Harmony catalogs in the early 1960s proudly proclaimed, "we´ve produced millions of instruments but we make them one at a time." Harmony guitars can be found practically anywhere: the guitar shop, the antique shop, the flea market, the Sunday garage sale right around the corner. Due to the vast numbers of Harmony guitars, and because the majority of them were entry level models, the vintage guitar market´s response is a collective shrug of the shoulders as it moves on to the higher dollar American built Fenders and Gibsons, etc. As a result, the secondary Harmony guitar market is rather hard to pin down. Outside of a few hardy souls like Willie Moseley, Ronald Rothman, Paul Day, and Tony Bacon, very little has been written about Harmony guitar models as a means to identify them. As a result, rather than use the exact model designations, most dealers tend to offer a "Harmony Acoustic," or a "'60s Harmony Archtop" through their ads or at guitar shows. It becomes difficult to track the asking prices of various models if the information regarding that model is not available.

The majority of Harmony guitars encountered today are generally part of the millions produced during the 1960s through the company´s closing in 1975. As most of them were entry level models, condition (especially physical condition) becomes a bit more critical in pricing. A dead mint Harmony Rocket is worth the money because it´s clean – a beat up, player´s grade Rocket might not be worth a second look to the interested party. However, the market interest is the deciding factor in pricing – the intrinsic value of (for example) a laminated body Harmony archtop will be the deciding factor in the asking price to the public.

The *Blue Book of Electric Guitars* continues to seek out additional input on Harmony models, specifications, dates of production, and any serialization information. This year´s section is the starting point for defining Harmony products. Additional information gathered on Harmony will be updated in future editions of the *Blue Book of Electric Guitars*.

Most Harmony guitars have been played and are in the average condition range. Most of these guitars are valued under $300. However, there are some models that may bring more money, especially if they are in excellent condition. We have listed some of the most popular models from the 1960s and 1970s. Keep in mind that Harmony produced hundreds of different models over the years. It is unrealistic to provide every single model ever produced because we simply do not have adequate information to make model descriptions. The information listed is from catalogs. Nine out of ten Harmony guitars are going to be in average condition and valued under $300.

Harmony models also carried the series designation on the headstock (i.e. Broadway, Monterey, Patrician, Soverign, etc.) in addition to the Harmony trademark.

For further information regarding Harmony acoustic guitars, please refer to the *Blue Book of Acoustic Guitars*.

Harmony H 66 Vibra Jet
courtesy Harmony

ELECTRIC: SINGLE CUTAWAY ELECTRIC MODELS

H 62 BLONDE (GRAND AUDITORIUM SIZE) - single cutaway body, laminated curly maple top/ laminated spruce back/sides, 2 segmented f-holes, heavy shell edge binding, 14/20-fret rosewood fingerboard with white block inlay, 3-per-side tuners, chrome hardware, adjustable bridge/metal tailpiece, raised black pickguard, 2 Harmony exposed pole piece pickups, 2 volume/2 tone controls, pickup selector switch (mounted on diamond-shaped plate on lower treble bout), available in Natural Blonde finish, length 41.25 in., body width 16.25 in., body depth 2.75 in., disc. 1966.

N/A	$850	$700	$550	$425	$350	$250

Last MSR was $199.50.

H 63 ESPANADA - similar to H 62 Blonde, except features a 14/20-fret ebonised hard maple fingerboard with pearlette inlay, white body binding, raised white binding, available in Black finish, length 41.25 in., body width 16.25 in., body depth 2.75 in., disc. 1966.

N/A	$850	$700	$550	$425	$350	$250

Last MSR was $199.50.

H 66 VIBRA JET - bound modified single cutaway body, laminated maple top/back/sides, 2 segmented f-holes, 20-fret rosewood fingerboard with white dot inlay, 3-per-side tuners, chrome hardware, adjustable bridge/raised tailpiece, raised bound black pickguard, 2 GoldenTone Index pickups, 2 volume/2 tone controls ("all in a single row" along lower bout), pickup selector switch (mounted on diamond-shaped plate on lower treble bout), built-in Transistorized Tremolo, Tremolo on/off switch/Tremolo speed/modulation controls mounted on a wedge-shaped controls plate, available in Sunburst Mahogany finish, length 40.5 in., body width 15.75 in., body depth 2 in., mfg. 1961-66.

N/A	$750	$600	$475	$375	$300	$200

Last MSR was $189.50.

The wedge-shaped (arrowhead) controls plate in mounted to the top of the guitar, and features an on/off switch, speed and depth control knobs.

GRADING	100% MINT	98% NEAR MINT	95% EXC+	90% EXC	80% VG+	70% VG	60% G

H 68 DEEP BODY CUTAWAY ARTISTS - single cutaway hollow body, bound arched spruce top, 2 bound segmented f-holes, 20-fret rosewood fingerboard with pearlette block inlay, 3-per-side tuners, chrome hardware, adjustable bridge/metal tailpiece, raised black pickguard, 2 DeArmond Golden Tone pickups, 2 volume/2 tone controls, 3-way pickup selector switch (mounted on diamond plate on treble bout), available in Brown Mahogany Shaded Sunburst finish, length 41 in., body width 16.25 in., body thickness 3.375 in., mfg. circa 1968-circa 1971.

	N/A	$900	$750	$600	$475	$350	$250

Last MSR was $219.50.

H 74 NEO-CUTAWAY (WITH BIGSBY VIBRATO) - modified single cutaway body, laminated maple top/back/sides, 2 segmented f-holes, celluloid edge binding, 20-fret rosewood fingerboard with white dot inlay, 3-per-side tuners, chrome hardware, adjustable bridge/Bigsby tailpiece, raised bound black pickguard, 2 GoldenTone Indox pickups, 2 volume/2 tone controls, pickup selector switch (mounted on diamond-shaped plate on lower treble bout), available in Sunburst finish, length 40.5 in., body width 15.75 in., body depth 2 in., disc. 1967.

	N/A	$900	$750	$600	$475	$350	$250

Last MSR was $219.50.

ELECTRIC: DOUBLE CUTAWAY ELECTRIC MODELS

H 60 METEOR (ULTRA THIN DOUBLE CUTAWAY) - dual cutaway hollow bound body, laminated maple top, laminated maple back/sides, 2 bound f-holes, 20-fret ebonized maple fingerboard with white block inlay, 3-per-side tuners, adjustable bridge/metal tailpiece, raised black pickguard, 2 pickups, 2 volume/2 tone controls, 3-way pickup selector switch (on treble bout), white truss rod cover, available in Shaded Sunburst finish, length 40.5 in., body width 15.75 in., body depth 2 in., mfg. circa 1968-1970.

	N/A	$650	$525	$425	$325	$250	$150

Last MSR was $219.50.

H 60 LH Meteor - similar to the H 60, except features a left-handed configuration, available in Shaded Sunburst finish, length 40.5 in., body width 15.75 in., body depth 2 in., mfg. circa 1968-circa 1970.

	N/A	$650	$550	$425	$350	$250	$150

Last MSR was $239.50.

H 61 METEOR (ULTRA THIN DOUBLE CUTAWAY) - similar to the H 60 Meteor, except features white dot fingerboard inlay, 2 GoldenTone pickups, black truss rod cover, available in Shaded Sunburst finish, length 40.5 in., body width 15.75 in., body depth 2 in., mfg. 1971-73.

	N/A	$650	$525	$425	$325	$250	$150

Last MSR was $219.50.

H 61 LH Meteor - similar to the H 61, except features a left-handed configuration, available in Shaded Sunburst finish, length 40.5 in., body width 15.75 in., body depth 2 in., mfg. 1971-73.

	N/A	$650	$550	$425	$350	$250	$150

Last MSR was $239.50.

H 64 DOUBLE CUTAWAY ELECTRIC (H 661) - dual cutaway hollow body, bound arched laminated maple top, laminated back/sides, 2 bound segmented f-holes, celluloid binding, 20-fret rosewood fingerboard with white dot inlay, 3-per-side tuners, chrome hardware, adjustable bridge/Bigsby True vibrato tailpiece, raised black pickguard, 2 DeArmond pickups, 2 volume/2 tone controls, 3-way pickup selector switch (mounted on diamond plate on treble bout), available in Shaded Sunburst finish, length 40.5 in., body width 15.75 in., body depth 2 in., mfg. 1967-1970.

	N/A	$850	$725	$600	$450	$350	$250

Last MSR was $249.50.

In 1973, the H 64 was redesignated the H6 61.

H 71 - double cutaway body, laminated maple top/back/sides, 24.25 in. scale, 20-fret rosewood fingerboard, 3-per-side Waverly tuners, Bigsby tremolo/adjustable bridge, 2 Harmony pickups, volume/tone controls, pickup selector switch, available in Sunburst finish, length 40.5 in., body width 15.75 in., mfg. circa 1971.

	N/A	$850	$725	$600	$450	$350	$250

Last MSR was $289.50.

This model was available in with a Bigsby tremolo bridge.

H 72 DOUBLE CUTAWAY ARCHED HOLLOW BODY ELECTRIC - dual cutaway hollow bound body, arched laminated maple top, laminated maple back/sides, 2 bound S-shaped f-holes (S-holes?), 24.25 in. scale, 20-fret bound ebonized maple fingerboard with white block inlay, 6-on-a-side Waverly tuners, adjustable bridge/raised art deco metal tailpiece, raised black pickguard, 2 DeArmond Golden Tone pickups, 2 volume/2 tone controls, 3-way pickup selector switch, available in Shaded Burgundy finish, length 40.5 in., body width 15.75 in., mfg. 1966-circa 1971.

	N/A	$525	$400	$325	$250	$175	$125

Last MSR was $239.50.

H 72 V - similar to the H 72, except features a Bigsby True vibrato bridge, available in Shaded Burgundy finish, length 40.5 in., body width 15.75 in., mfg. 1966-circa 1971.

	N/A	$600	$500	$400	$325	$250	$150

Last MSR was $289.50.

H 75 - double cutaway body, bound laminated curly maple arched top, laminated maple back/sides, 2 segmented f-holes, 20-fret rosewood fingerboard with white block inlay, 3-per-side tuners, chrome hardware, adjustable bridge/ornamental tailpiece, raised bound black pickguard, 3 DeArmond pickups with exposed pole pieces, 3 volume/3 tone controls, 3 pickup selector switches (mounted on oval plate on lower treble bout), available in Shaded Brown finish, length 40.5 in., body width 15.75 in., body depth 2 in., mfg. 1961-1971.

	N/A	$750	$600	$475	$375	$300	$200

Last MSR was $300.

The H 75's finish was also described as "Violin Brown Mahogany Shading with Sunburst Effect."

H 76 - similar to the H 75, except features a Bigsby True vibrato tailpiece, available in Shaded Brown finish, length 40.5 in., body width 15.75 in., mfg. 1966-1970.

	N/A	$800	$650	$525	$400	$325	$225

Last MSR was $350.

GRADING	100% MINT	98% NEAR MINT	95% EXC+	90% EXC	80% VG+	70% VG	60% G

H 77 - similar to the H 75, available in Shaded Warm Cherry Red finish, length 40.5 in., body width 15.75 in., body depth 2 in., mfg. 1963-1970.

| | N/A | $750 | $600 | $475 | $375 | $300 | $200 |

Last MSR was $300.

H 78 - similar to the H 77, except features a Bigsby True vibrato tailpiece, available in Shaded Warm Cherry Red finish, length 40.5 in., body width 15.75 in., mfg. 1966-1970.

| | N/A | $800 | $650 | $525 | $400 | $325 | $225 |

Last MSR was $350.

H 79 ULTRA THIN DOUBLE CUTAWAY 12-STRING - double cutaway body, bound laminated maple arched top, laminated maple back/sides, 2 segmented f-holes, 24.25 in. scale, 20-fret bound rosewood fingerboard with white block inlay, 6-per-side tuners, slotted headstock, chrome hardware, adjustable bridge/ornamental tailpiece, raised bound black pickguard, 2 DeArmond pickups, 2 volume/2 tone controls, 3-way pickup selector, available in Burgundy Red finish, length 41 in., body width 15.75 in., body depth 2 in., mfg. 1966-1970.

| | N/A | $900 | $750 | $600 | $450 | $350 | $250 |

Last MSR was $239.50.

ELECTRIC: BOB KAT & COLOR KAT (SILHOUETTE) SERIES

In 1963, Harmony debuted the Silhouette Series, which featured three solid body electric models. This Series was renamed the Bob Kat Series in 1969; the models with solid color finishes were renamed the Color Kat Series.

H 14 BOB KAT SINGLE PICKUP (H 14 SILHOUETTE) - similar to the H 15 Silhouette, except features one DeArmond Golden Tone pickup, volume/tone controls, rhythm/lead boost slide switch, available in Shaded Walnut Wood finish, length 36.75 in., body width 12.75 in., body thickness 1.5 in., mfg. 1963-circa 1971.

| | N/A | $250 | $200 | $170 | $140 | $110 | $80 |

Last MSR was $64.50.

Harmony H 74 Neo-Cutaway courtesy Harmony

H 14 V Bob Kat (H 14 Silhouette) - similar to the H 14 Silhouette, except features an adjustable bridge/No. 1750 (Type G) vibrato tailpiece, available in Shaded Walnut Wood finish, length 36.75 in., body width 12.75 in.", body thickness 1.5 in., mfg. 1966-circa 1971.

| | N/A | $275 | $225 | $195 | $160 | $130 | $100 |

Last MSR was $74.50.

H 15 BOB KAT (H 15 SILHOUETTE) - slightly offset double cutaway maple body, bolt-on hardwood neck, 24.25 in. scale, 20-fret ebonized maple fingerboard with white dot inlay, 6-on-a-side Waverly tuners, adjustable bridge/tailpiece with chrome cover, white pickguard, 2 DeArmond Golden Tone pickups, 2 volume/2 tone controls, 3-way pickup selector toggle, available in Shaded Walnut Wood finish, length 36.75 in., body width 12.75 in., body thickness 1.5 in., mfg. 1963-circa 1971.

| | N/A | $300 | $250 | $200 | $160 | $130 | $100 |

Last MSR was $87.50.

H 15 V Bob Kat (H 15 Silhouette) - similar to the H 15 Silhouette, except features an adjustable bridge/No. 1750 (Type G/Type W) vibrato tailpiece, available in Shaded Walnut Wood finish, length 36.75 in., body width 12.75 in., body thickness 1.5 in., mfg. 1966-circa 1971.

| | N/A | $325 | $275 | $225 | $195 | $165 | $135 |

Last MSR was $97.50.

H 16 COLOR KAT (B, R, W, H 16 SILHOUETTE, H 616) - slightly offset double cutaway maple body, bolt-on hardwood neck, 24.25 in. scale, 20-fret ebonized maple fingerboard with white dot inlay, 6-on-a-side Waverly tuners, adjustable ebonized maple bridge/Type W vibrato tailpiece, white pickguard, 2 DeArmond Golden Tone pickups, 2 volume/2 tone controls, 3-way pickup selector toggle, available in Candy Apple Red (Model H 16 R), Metallic Blue (Model H 16 B), or Gleaming White (Model H 16 W) finishes, length 36.75 in., body width 12.75 in., body thickness 1.5 in., mfg. 1967-circa 1973.

| | N/A | $325 | $275 | $225 | $195 | $165 | $135 |

Last MSR was $117.50.

The H 16's control knobs are larger than the H 15's 'top hat'-style knobs. The H 16 was redesignated the H 616 in 1973.

H 17 SILHOUETTE - similar to the H 15 Silhouette, except features an adjustable bridge/Type G vibrato with flat metal vibrato arm, available in Shaded Cherry Red finish, length 36.75 in., body width 12.75 in., body thickness 1.5 in., mfg. 1963-66.

| | N/A | $350 | $300 | $250 | $220 | $190 | $160 |

Last MSR was $127.50.

H 19 DE LUXE SILHOUETTE - similar to the H 15 Silhouette, except features larger body dimensions, 20-fret bound rosewood fingerboard with pearlette block inlay, black pickguard, adjustable bridge/Type H (No. 1749B) vibrato, available in Cherry Red finish, length 39.25 in., body width 13.25 in., body thickness 1.5 in., mfg. 1963-68.

| | N/A | $375 | $325 | $275 | $240 | $210 | $170 |

Last MSR was $177.50.

ELECTRIC: HOLLYWOOD SERIES

Hollywood arched (top) models have pickups, laminated hardwood bodies, and "Harmony Hollywood" stencilled on the peghead.

GRADING	100% MINT	98% NEAR MINT	95% EXC+	90% EXC	80% VG+	70% VG	60% G

H 37 - arched top hardwood body, 2 f-holes, 20-fret fingerboard with gold block inlay, 3-per-side tuners, chrome hardware, adjustable bridge/raised tailpiece, raised black pickguard, DeArmond pickup, volume/tone controls, available in Metallic Gold finish with Black center panel, length 40", body width 15.75 in., disc. circa 1965.

	N/A	$275	$225	$195	$165	$135	$105

Last MSR was $60.

H 39 - arched top hardwood body, 2 f-holes, 20-fret fingerboard with white block inlay, 3-per-side tuners, chrome hardware, adjustable bridge/raised tailpiece, raised black pickguard, DeArmond pickup, volume/tone controls, available in Shaded Brown Mahogany finish, length 40 in., body width 15.75 in., disc. circa 1965.

	N/A	$300	$250	$200	$170	$140	$110

Last MSR was $69.50.

H 41 - similar to the H 39, except has 2 DeArmond pickups, raised white pickguard, pointer control (pickup blend), disc. circa 1968.

	N/A	$325	$275	$225	$180	$150	$120

Last MSR was $87.50.

ELECTRIC: METEOR SERIES

H 70 METEOR - single cutaway body, bound laminated maple top/spruce back/sides, 2 segmented f-holes, 20-fret rosewood fingerboard with white block inlay, 3-per-side tuners, chrome hardware, adjustable bridge/raised tailpiece, raised black pickguard, 2 GoldenTone Index pickups, 2 volume/2 tone controls, pickup selector switch (mounted on diamond-shaped plate on lower treble bout), available in Sunburst finish, length 40.5 in., body width 15.75 in., body depth 2 in., disc. 1967.

	N/A	$650	$525	$425	$325	$250	$150

Last MSR was $179.50.

H 70 Meteor LH - similar to the H 70 Meteor, except in left-handed configuration, available in Sunburst finish, disc. 1967.

	N/A	$650	$525	$425	$350	$250	$150

Last MSR was $199.50.

H 71 METEOR - similar to the H 70 Meteor, available in Natural Blonde finish, disc. 1966.

	N/A	$650	$525	$425	$350	$250	$150

Last MSR was $199.50.

H 71 Meteor (H6 71) - similar to the H 71 Meteor, except features different Harmony pickups, control knobs, available in Natural Blonde finish, mfg. circa 1970-1972.

	100% MINT	98%	95%	90%	80%	70%	60%
1970-1972	N/A	$700	$575	$450	$375	$300	$200
1973-1975	N/A	$650	$525	$425	$350	$250	$150

Last MSR was $329.95.

This model was re-designated H6 71 in 1973.

ELECTRIC: REBEL SERIES

Harmony´s Rebel Series models featured volume/tone slider controls (per pickup) dubbed the Stick-Shift Controls. "You´ll know your settings - visually," claimed the 1971 catalog. Never mind appealing to the player´s aural sense, eh?

H 81 REBEL - offset dual cutaway hollow body, laminated maple top/back/sides, celluloid body binding, hardwood neck, 24.25 in. scale, 20-fret ebonized maple fingerboard with white dot inlay, 6-on-a-side Waverly tuners, adjustable metal bridge/tailpiece with chrome cover, chrome hardware, 2-piece white pickguard, DeArmond pickup, tone change on/off switch, volume/tone slider controls, available in Sunburst finish, length 38 in., body width 14 in., body thickness 1.75 in., mfg. 1969-circa 1972.

	N/A	$275	$225	$195	$165	$135	$105

Last MSR was $99.50.

H 82 REBEL (H 682) - offset dual cutaway hollow body, laminated maple top/back/sides, celluloid body binding, hardwood neck, 24.25 in. scale, 20-fret ebonized maple fingerboard with white dot inlay, 6-on-a-side Waverly tuners, adjustable metal bridge/tailpiece with chrome cover, chrome hardware, 2-piece white pickguard, 2 DeArmond pickups, 2 pickup selector on/off switches, 2 volume/2 tone slider controls, available in Sunburst finish, length 38 in., body width 14 in., body thickness 1.75 in., mfg. 1969-circa 1972 (as H 82), 1973-75 (as H 682).

	N/A	$300	$250	$210	$180	$150	$120

Last MSR was $119.50.

H 82 G - similar to the H 82, available in Shaded Avocado finish, length 38 in., body width 14 in., body thickness 1.75 in., mfg. 1969-circa 1972.

	N/A	$225	$185	$150	$120	$90	$60

Last MSR was $119.50.

ELECTRIC: ROCKET SERIES

The original Rocket series was discontinued in 1968; however, the "Slash One" series continued on from 1969 to 1972. Two Rocket models (H6 54 and H6 56) were offered between 1973 and 1975. The original Rockets had covered pickups and white control knobs; Slash One models have exposed pole piece pickups and white/gold Top Hat-style knobs. Body sizes and designs basically remained the same.

H 53 ROCKET I - single cutaway hollow hardwood bodies, celluloid body binding, 2 f-holes, 24.25 in. scale, 20-fret ebonized maple fingerboard with white dot markers, raised white pickguard (marked 'Harmony'), 3-per-side Waverly tuners, adjustable bridge/tailpiece, chrome hardware, Goldentone Index covered pickup, volume/tone controls, available in Red and Sunburst finishes, length 40.5 in., body width 15.75 in., body thickness 2 in., disc. 1968.

	N/A	$400	$325	$250	$200	$150	$95

Last MSR was $87.50.

GRADING	100% MINT	98% NEAR MINT	95% EXC+	90% EXC	80% VG+	70% VG	60% G

H 53/1 Rocket I - similar to H 53 Rocket I, except features a GoldenTone exposed pole piece pickup, available in Red and Sunburst finishes, length 40.5 in., body width 15.75 in., body thickness 2 in., mfg. 1969-1972 (as H 53/1), 1973-75 (as H 654).

	N/A	$350	$275	$225	$175	$125	$80

Last MSR was $99.50.

In 1973, the H 53/1 model was redesignated the H 654.

H 54 ROCKET II - similar to the H 53 Rocket I, except features 2 covered pickups, 2 volume/2 tone controls, pickup selector switch (mounted on diamond-shaped plate on lower treble bout), disc. 1968.

	N/A	$500	$425	$350	$275	$200	$125

Last MSR was $119.50.

H 54/1 Rocket II - similar to the H 53/1 Rocket I, except features 2 Goldentone pickups, 2 volume/2 tone controls, 3-way pickup selector switch (mounted on diamond-shaped plate on lower treble bout), length 40.5 in., body width 15.75 in., body thickness 2 in., mfg. 1969-1972 (as H 54/1), 1973-75 (as H 654).

	N/A	$450	$375	$300	$225	$175	$125

Last MSR was $134.50.

H 56 ROCKET VII - similar to the H 54 Rocket II, except features a vibrato tailpiece, mfg. 1966-68.

	N/A	$600	$525	$450	$375	$300	$200

Last MSR was $137.50.

H 56/1 Rocket VII - similar to the H 54/1 Rocket II, except features a vibrato tailpiece, length 40.5 in., body width 15.75 in., body thickness 2 in., mfg. 1969-1972 (as H 56/1), 1973-75 (as H 656).

	N/A	$500	$450	$400	$325	$250	$175

Last MSR was $149.50.

In 1973, the H 56/1 model was redesignated H 656.

H 59 ROCKET III - similar to the H 53 Rocket I, except features 3 covered pickups, 3 volume/3 tone controls ("in a single row" along lower bout), 4 way selector switch (on lower treble bout), disc. 1968.

	N/A	$700	$600	$500	$400	$275	$225

Last MSR was $147.50.

H 59/1 Rocket III - Similar to the H 53/1 Rocket I, except features 3 Goldentone pickups, 3 volume/3 tone controls, 4 way pickup selector switch (mounted on lower treble bout), length 40.5 in., body width 15.75 in., body thickness 2 in., mfg. 1969-1970.

	N/A	$650	$550	$450	$350	$275	$200

Last MSR was $159.50.

Harmony H-39
courtesy Harmony

ELECTRIC: ROY SMECK SERIES

Both models were endorsed by guitarist Roy Smeck (the "Wizard of the Strings").

H 57 ROY SMECK (SINGLE PICKUP) - arched auditorium-sized body, celluloid binding, laminated spruce top, 2 segmented f-holes, 20-fret bound rosewood fingerboard with white dot inlay, black peghead marked 'Roy Smeck', 3-per-side tuners, chrome hardware, adjustable bridge/raised tailpiece, raised black pickguard marked 'Harmony', exposed pole piece pickup, volume/tone controls, available in Shaded Brown Mahogany finish, length 40.5 in., body width 15.75 in., body depth 2 in., disc. circa 1965.

Last MSR was $105.

The secondary market is still undefined.

H 58 ROY SMECK (DOUBLE PICKUP) - similar to the H 57 Roy Smeck, except has 2 pickups, 2 volume/2 tone controls, 3-way switch (mounted on diamond-shaped pickguard on lower treble bout), raised white pickguard marked 'Harmony,' available in Natural top/Black back and sides finish, disc. circa 1965.

Last MSR was $135.

The secondary market is still undefined.

H 73 ROY SMECK ELECTRIC - arched semi-hollow single cutaway body, celluloid binding, laminated maple top, 2 f-holes, 20-fret rosewood fingerboard with white dot inlay, blackface peghead, 'Roy Smeck' logo on upper bass bout, 3-per-side tuners, chrome hardware, adjustable bridge/Type GA vibrato tailpiece, raised white pickguard, 2 DeArmond pickups, 2 volume/2 tone controls, 3-way toggle switch, available in opaque Mandarin Red finish, length 40.5 in., body width 15.75 in., body depth 2 in., mfg. 1963-circa 1968.

Last MSR was $175.

The secondary market is still undefined.

ELECTRIC: STRATOTONE SERIES

Harmony's slab cut solid body Stratotone was available circa mid to late 1950s (discontinued by 1961). While the Stratotone's name was (probably) derived from Fender's Stratocaster model, the slim single cutaway design hearkened back to the Telecaster. Solid body Stratotone models featured Harmony/DeArmond pickups and a 3 on a side headstock.
Harmony also produced 3 hollow body (tone chamber) Stratotone models that were discontinued circa 1965. These models featured DeArmond-designed GoldenTone Indox pickups and unique pickup selection/voicing controls.

Harmony H 59 Rocket II
courtesy Harmony

GRADING	100% MINT	98% NEAR MINT	95% EXC+	90% EXC	80% VG+	70% VG	60% G

H 45 STRATOTONE MARS (SINGLE PICKUP) - single cutaway hollow laminated body, white celluloid body binding, hardwood neck, 20-fret ebonised maple fingerboard with white dot inlay, 3-per-side tuners, chrome hardware, adjustable bridge/raised tailpiece, white pickguard, GoldenTone Indox pickup, volume/tone controls, 2 way treble/bass emphasis switch, available in Sunburst finish, length 17.75 in., body width 13.125 in., body thickness 2 in., disc. circa 1965.

	N/A	$350	$275	$225	$175	$125	$80

Last MSR was $72.50.

H 46 STRATOTONE MARS (DOUBLE PICKUP) - similar to the H 45 Mars, except has 2 GoldenTone pickups, 3-way switch, 2 stacked control knobs (volume/tone per pickup), disc. circa 1965.

	N/A	$375	$300	$250	$190	$150	$90

Last MSR was $98.50.

H 47 STRATOTONE MERCURY - single cutaway hollow body, laminated curly maple top/back, white celluloid body binding, hardwood neck, 20-fret rosewood fingerboard with white pearlette block inlay, 3-per-side tuners, chrome hardware, adjustable bridge/raised tailpiece, white pickguard, GoldenTone Indox pickup, volume/tone controls, 3-way rhythm/treble/bass emphasis switch, available in Sunburst finish, length 17.75 in., body width 13.125 in., body thickness 2 in., disc. circa 1965.

	N/A	$400	$325	$250	$200	$150	$95

Last MSR was $99.50.

The Mercury model's multi-purpose Switch has three settings: Rhythm (tone preset), Treble (preset with treble emphasis), and Bass (activates the tone control).

H 47 LH Stratotone Mercury - similar to the H 46 Mercury, except in left-handed configuration, disc. circa 1965.

	N/A	$425	$350	$275	$225	$160	$105

Last MSR was $117.50.

H 48 STRATOTONE MERCURY - similar to the H 47 Mercury, except has black pickguard, available in Natural Blonde finish, disc. circa 1965.

	N/A	$400	$325	$250	$200	$150	$95

Last MSR was $104.50.

H 49 DELUXE STRATOTONE JUPITER - single cutaway hollow body, laminated spruce top/curly maple back, white celluloid body binding, hardwood neck, 20-fret rosewood fingerboard with white block inlay, 3-per-side tuners, chrome hardware, adjustable bridge/raised tailpiece, black pickguard, 2 GoldenTone Indox pickup, 2 volume/2-tone/blender controls, 3-way selector, available in Gold Sunburst finish, length 17.75 in., body width 13.125 in., body thickness 2 in., disc. circa 1965.

	N/A	$450	$375	$295	$225	$175	$125

Last MSR was $147.50.

ELECTRIC BASS

H 22 HI-VALUE - single cutaway semi-hollow body, laminated maple top/back/sides, 2 segmented f-holes, 30 in. scale, celluloid body binding, 20-fret ebonised maple fingerboard with white dot inlay, 2-per-side Waverly tuners, adjustable rosewood bridge/covered metal endpiece, white "Stealth Fighter Jet"-shaped pickguard, GoldenTone (DeArmond) pickup, volume/tone controls, voicing switch, available in Sunburst Walnut finish, length 44.25 in., body width 15.75 in., body thickness 2 in., mfg. 1961-68.

	N/A	$500	$425	$350	$300	$250	$200

Last MSR was $109.50.

The voicing switch allows the option of the "full bass" or "lighter baritone" registers (possibly a low end filter capacitor control).

H 22/1 Hi-Value - similar to the H 22 Hi-Value, except features dual cutaway semi-hollow body, available in Sunburst finish, length 44.5 in., body width 15.75 in., body thickness 2 in., mfg. 1969-1972.

	N/A	$450	$375	$325	$275	$225	$175

Last MSR was $109.50.

H 25 SILHOUETTE DELUXE BASS - offset double cutaway hardwood body, bolt-on hardwood neck, 30 in. scale, 20-fret rosewood fingerboard with white dot inlay, 4-on-a-side Waverly tuners, adjustable metal bridge/string damper/tailpiece with chrome cover, Golden Tone pickup, volume/tone controls, 2 pushbutton volume/tone preset controls, available in Cherry Red finish, length 44.75 in., body width 13 in., body thickness 1.5 in., mfg. 1966-circa 1972.

	N/A	$350	$275	$225	$175	$125	$80

Last MSR was $139.50.

H 27 THIN HOLLOW DOUBLE CUTAWAY BASS - dual cutaway hollow body, bound laminated curly maple top, laminated maple back/sides, 2 segmented f-holes, 30" scale, 20-fret bound rosewood fingerboard with white dot inlay, 4-on-a-side Waverly tuners, adjustable metal bridge with nickel-plated cover, 2 GoldenTone pickups, 2 volume/2 tone controls, pickup selector switch, available in Sunburst finish, length 45 in., body width 15.75 in., body thickness 2 in., mfg. 1966-circa 1972.

	N/A	$500	$425	$350	$275	$200	$125

Last MSR was $199.50.

HARPERS

Instruments previously built in Apple Valley, CA.

Harper's Guitars is a family owned and operated business that designs and builds high quality, solid body electric guitars. According to Jon Harper, Harper's Guitars builds instruments in the traditional manner, by hand - which gives the models a quality, personality, and playability that cannot be obtained in a mass-produced instrument. Harper has stopped producing guitars because of increasing family concerns as well as other reasons. The Harper guitar website is still up and running and any current orders will be completed and shipped. For further information, contact Harper's Guitars directly (see Trademark Index).

A pair of custom-built models from Harper's include the Marin (last MSR was $1,695) that features a figured maple top over a mahogany body, and the Eric Bloom Signature Model (last MSR was $1,795), which was developed in part with guitarist Eric Bloom (Blue Oyster Cult).

GRADING	100% MINT	98% NEAR MINT	95% EXC+	90% EXC	80% VG+	70% VG	60% G

ELECTRIC

Both the **Monterey** and **Sierra** models feature basswood, poplar, or alder bodies, satin tung oil finished maple necks, a 25.5 in. scale, 22-fret maple fingerboards with black dot inlay, Sperzel locking tuners, Schaller non-tremolo bridges, and 2 DiMarzio humbuckers (volume control and 3-way toggle switch). Both models are available in a solid color finish with a last MSR of $1,595.

The **Mojave** model is similar to the above models, except features either an ash or mahogany body, 2TEK bridge, hand rubbed oil finish or choice of a translucent finish (last MSR was $1,895). Harper´s Guitars offers a wide range of options such as bookmatched tops, different body and neck woods, hardware, and inlays all available at additional costs.

HARPTONE

Instruments previously built in Newark, NJ 1966 to mid-1970s.

The Harptone company was a commercial successor to the Felsberg Company (circa 1893). During the 1930s, Harptone was more known for musical instrument accessories, although a few guitars were built between 1924 and 1942.

The Harptone Manufacturing Corporation was located at 127 South 15th Street in Newark, New Jersey (07107) during the early to mid 1960s. Harptone´s main guitar designer was Stan Koontz (who also designed Standel and his own signature guitars). Harptone´s guitar product line consisted of mainly acoustic guitar models, including acoustic archtop models.

When Micro-Frets closed operations in Maryland in either 1974 or 1975, the company assets were purchased by David Sturgill. Sturgill, who served as the company president of Grammer Guitars for three years, let his sons John and Danny gain access to leftover Micro-Frets parts. In addition to those parts, they had also purchased the remains of New Jersey´s Harptone guitar company. The two assembled a number of solid body guitars which were then sold under the Diamond-S trademark. Unfortunately, that business venture did not catch on, and dissolved sometime in 1976, (Company history courtesy Tom Wheeler, *American Guitars*).

Harptone instruments were built between 1966 to the mid -1970s. Research continues on the production dates per model, and as such none of the following models below will have an indicated date(s) of manufacture. Instruments can be dated by examining the components (pickups, hardware, tuners) and especially the potentiometers (where applicable). For further information regarding Harptone acoustic models, please refer to the *Blue Book of Acoustic Guitars*.

ELECTRIC BASS

400 BASS - semi-acoustic maple body, 19-fret rosewood fingerboard, adjustable metal bridge, Grover tuners, DeArmond pickup, volume/tone controls, body width 16 in., body thickness 1.75 in., 30.5 in. scale, mfg. late 1960s-early 1970s.

N/A	$500	$425	$350	$300	$250	$200

Last MSR was $299.95.

HARRISON CUSTOM GUITARS

Instruments currently built in West Yorkshire, England.

Harrison Custom Guitars build guitars with the belief that their small team of craftsmen can provide a genuine custom service. Guy Harrison is the guy (no pun intended), who is in charge of the operation.They build guitars only to order and by doing this they also introduce fresh ideas into the guitar market. For more information on Harrison guitars refer to their website (see Trademark Index).

HARTKE

Instruments previously built in Ashbury Park, NJ and overseas from 2000-03. Distributed by Samson Technologies, Corporation of Syosset, NY.

The Hartke company was co-founded in 1984 by Larry Hartke and they mainly produce bass amplifiers and speaker cabinets. With the success of the bass amplifiers Hartke decided to match up a guitar to go with it. The Hartke bass guitar has features that make it different than some entry level guitar. For more information on Hartke amplifiers, refer to the *Blue Book of Guitar Amplifiers*. For more information on Hartke basses refer to Hartke directly (see Trademark Index).

ELECTRIC BASS

Hartke produces both models that are affordable to anyone as well as higher end models with all the features that make it well worth its money. The **XL Series** are the top end models that have the following features: a select poplar sharp double cutawaybody, an aluminum neck, triple chrome plated headstock, Ebonol fingerboard with Nickel silver jumbo frets and a zero fret, 2 EMJ pickups (J & P), a Schaller 2000 chrome bridge, and a brushed aluminum pickguard. These guitars are available in Black, Medium Blue, Bright Yellow, Light Silver, Royal Purple, and Bright White, and come in either a four string (MSR $2,400) or a five string (MSR TBA) and an extra $100 for Custom colors (anything besides black). The **XK Series** is like the XL but toned down more and does not have many of the features that the XL does and is not produced in New Jersey. These guitars are only available in Black and a four string configuration (MSR $1,000) and five string (MSR $1,130).

The **NT Series** was offered for a short while in 2002, but no longer appears on the price list. The NT stood for "Neck Through Body" design with a smoother cutaway. It also has a maple body, 3-piece maple neck, rosewood fingerboard with 24 frets, two soap bar pickups and was available in Black or Trans. Red finishes. MSR was $680 for the four string black, $730 for the four string Trans. Red and five string Black, and $770 for the five string Trans. Red.

GRADING	100% MINT	98% NEAR MINT	95% EXC+	90% EXC	80% VG+	70% VG	60% G

The **WK Series** has the same smooth cutaways with a basswood body and no active electronics. MSR is $550 for the WK-4 in Silver, $600 for the WK-4 in Black Quilt Maple and the WK-5 Silver, and $650 for the WK-5 with Black Quilt Maple finish. The **AK Series** was the same as the WK except with chrome hardware and is only available in black. This guitar appears to be discontinued now. The AK-4 MSR was $500 and the AK-5 was $570. The **CK Series** are produced with the same high standard of the WK except with less features. The CK-4 is only available as a four string for $370 available in Black or Cherry Red finishes. The **HP Series** is new and is very affordable. Here, a basic bass is available as a four string in black or red finish for an MSR of $220.

Possibly one of the best inventions for the beginning guitar player is also offered, which would be the **Bass Gig Pack**. A SB-15 Bass is teamed up with a B-15 Combo bass amp in one package. The bass guitar is avilable in black or red. The amp has 15W, 1-6.5 in. speaker, 3 band EQ, effects loop, line out, and headphone jack. The package includes a guitar strap, gig bag, and instrument cable, all for an MSR of $430.

HAWK

See Framus and Klira. Instruments previously built in West Germany during the early 1960s.

The Hawk trademark was a brandname used by a UK importer. Instruments imported into England were built by either Framus or Klira in Germany, and are identical to their respective builder's models (source: Tony Bacon and Paul Day, *The Guru's Guitar Guide*).

HAYMAN

Instruments previously built in England during the mid-1970s.

In 1969, luthier Jim Burns (ex-Burns, Burns-Weill) was invited into the Dallas-Arbiter organization to develop a new line of guitars under the Hayman trademark. His working collaboration with Bob Pearson (ex-Vox) ultimately developed designs for three guitars and one bass. Woodworking and truss rod work were done by Jack Golder and Norman Holder, who had been with Jim Burns previously.

Instruments were produced from 1970 through 1973. Jim Burns moved on from Dallas-Arbiter in 1971, leaving Pearson to continue developing new ideas. When Dallas-Arbiter folded in the mid 1970s, Pearson joined with Golder and Holder to form the Shergold company. Hayman instruments, while not as flashy as their Burns predecessors, were still solid instruments, and also a link to formation of the later Shergold models.

According to authors Tony Bacon and Paul Day, the last two digits of a Hayman serial number indicate the year of manufacture. This practice began in 1974 (source: Paul Day, *The Burns Book*).

HAYNIE, LES

Instruments currently built in Eureka Springs, AR.

Les Haynie handcrafts custom guitars in his shop in Eureka Springs.

HEART/HEARTWOOD

Instruments previously built in England during the mid- to late 1980s. Renamed Heartwood in 1988.

Early models of these high quality original and Fender-style guitars had heart-shaped fretboard and headstock inlays (source: Tony Bacon and Paul Day, *The Guru's Guitar Guide*).

HEARTFIELD

Instruments previously produced in Japan from 1989 through 1994. Distributed by the Fender Musical Instruments Corporation located in Scottsdale, AZ.

As part of a reciprocal agreement, the Japanese Fuji Gen Gakki company that produced various Fender models received distribution assistance from FMIC for the Heartfield line. During the mid to late 1980s, various companies such as Jackson/Charvel popularized the superstrat concept: different pickup combinations and locking tremolos that updated the original Fender Stratocaster design. As Fender never had much success straying from the original Stratocaster design (like the Katana or Performer models), the Heartfield models filled a niche in promotion of designs "too radical" for the Fender trademark. Heartfield models were designed both at Fender USA and Fender Japan.

Some Heartfield models featured active electronics or other 'non-Fender' associated designs. Later production models may also have "Heartfield by Fender" on the headstock instead of the standard Heartfield logo.

ELECTRIC: ELAN SERIES

ELAN I - double offset cutaway mahogany body, bookmatched figured maple top, mahogany neck, 22-fret ebony fingerboard with pearl dot inlay, fixed bridge, 3-per-side tuners with pearl buttons, gold hardware, 2 humbucker pickups, volume/tone control, 5-position switch, available in Amber, Antique Burst, Crimson Trans., or Sapphire Blue Trans. finishes, mfg. 1991-93.

N/A	$700	$600	$525	$450	$400	$350

Last MSR was $1,120.

From 1991 to 1992, these models featured ivoroid bound figured maple top, bound fingerboard with triangle inlay, and humbucker/single coil/humbucker pickups.

ELAN II - similar to Elan I, except has locking Floyd Rose vibrato, locking tuners, chrome hardware.

N/A	$700	$600	$525	$450	$400	$350

Last MSR was $1,190.

ELAN III - similar to Elan I, except has double locking Floyd Rose vibrato, black hardware, humbucker/single coil/humbucker pickups.

N/A	$800	$700	$600	$500	$425	$350

Last MSR was $1,400.

GRADING	100% MINT	98% NEAR MINT	95% EXC+	90% EXC	80% VG+	70% VG	60% G

ELECTRIC: EX SERIES

EX I - double offset cutaway basswood body, mahogany neck, 22-fret rosewood fingerboard with pearl dot inlay, double locking Floyd Rose vibrato, 3-per-side tuners, black hardware, 3 single coil pickups, 2 in a humbucker configuration in bridge position, volume/tone/boost control, 5-position switch, series/parallel mini switch, active electronics, available in Black, Chrome Red, Frost Red, Midnight Blue, Montego Black or Mystic White finishes, mfg. 1992 only.

	N/A	$525	$400	$350	$275	$225	$175

EX II - similar to EX I, except has figured maple top, available in Amber, Antique Burst, Crimson Trans., or Sapphire Blue Trans. finishes, mfg. 1992 only.

	N/A	$550	$425	$350	$300	$250	$200

ELECTRIC: RR SERIES

RR 8 - offset double shorthorn cutaway alder body, white pickguard, mahogany neck, 22-fret rosewood fingerboard with pearl dot inlay, fixed bridge, 3-per-side tuners, chrome hardware, humbucker pickup, volume/tone control, 3 mini switches with LED's, active electronics, available in Blue Sparkle, Brite White, Frost Red and Yellow Sparkle finishes, mfg. 1991-93.

	N/A	$425	$375	$300	$250	$175	$150

RR 9 - similar to RR 8, except has standard vibrato, mfg. 1991-93.

	N/A	$475	$395	$325	$275	$225	$150

RR 58 - offset double short horn cutaway mahogany body, black pickguard, mahogany neck, 22-fret rosewood fingerboard with abalone dot inlay, fixed bridge, 3-per-side tuners, chrome hardware, 2 humbucker pickups, volume/tone control, 5-position switch, available in Blonde, Crimson Trans. or Emerald Green Trans. finishes, mfg. 1991-93.

	N/A	$550	$475	$425	$350	$275	$225

RR 59 - similar to RR 58, except has standard vibrato, locking tuners, 2 humbucker pickups, mfg. 1991-93.

	N/A	$600	$525	$450	$375	$300	$250

ELECTRIC: TALON SERIES

TALON - double offset cutaway basswood body, black pickguard, bolt-on maple neck, 22-fret rosewood fingerboard with pearl dot inlay, double locking Floyd Rose vibrato, 6-on-a-side tuners, black hardware, 2 single coil/1 humbucker pickups, volume/tone control, 5-position switch, available in Black, Chrome Red, Frost Red, Midnight Blue, Montego Black, or Mystic White finishes, mfg. 1991-93.

	N/A	$375	$325	$295	$250	$175	$150

Talon I - similar to Talon, except has humbucker/single coil/humbucker pickups, mfg. 1991-93.

	N/A	$450	$400	$350	$300	$250	$200

Talon II - similar to Talon, except has 24-fret fingerboard, 2 DiMarzio humbucker pickups, mfg. 1991-93.

	N/A	$525	$450	$395	$350	$275	$225

Talon III - similar to Talon, except has humbucker/single coil/humbucker pickups, mfg. 1991-93.

	N/A	$625	$525	$475	$400	$325	$250

Talon III R - similar to Talon III, except has a reverse headstock and no pickguard (rear loaded controls), mfg. 1991-93.

	N/A	$650	$550	$475	$400	$325	$275

TALON IV - double offset cutaway basswood body, black pickguard, bolt-on maple neck, 24-fret rosewood fingerboard with triangle inlay, 12th and 24th frets have additional red triangle inlay, double locking Floyd Rose vibrato, 6-on-a-side tuners, black hardware, humbucker/single coil/humbucker pickups, volume/tone control, 5-position switch, available in Black, Chrome Red, Frost Red, Midnight Blue, Montego Black, or Mystic White finishes, mfg. 1991-93.

	N/A	$675	$600	$525	$450	$375	$300

Talon V - similar to Talon IV, except has a reverse headstock, mfg. 1991-93.

	N/A	$650	$600	$525	$450	$375	$300

ELECTRIC BASS: DR SERIES

This series had an offset double cutaway alder body, bolt-on 3-piece maple/graphite neck, rosewood fingerboard with offset pearl dot inlay, fixed bridge, 2 J-style pickups, volume/tone/balance controls, 2 position switch, active electronics.

DR 4 - 22-fret fingerboard, 2-per-side tuners, chrome hardware, available in Black Pearl Burst, Blue Pearl Burst, Mystic White, or Red Pearl Burst finishes, mfg. 1991-93.

	N/A	$700	$750	$600	$500	$400	$325

DR 5 - 5 strings, 24-fret fingerboard, 2/3-per-side tuners, chrome hardware, mfg. 1991-93.

	N/A	$750	$700	$650	$550	$450	$350

DR 6 - 6 strings, 24-fret fingerboard, 3-per-side tuners, gold hardware, 2 humbucker pickups, available in Black, Chrome Red, Frost Red, Midnight Blue, or Mystic White finishes, mfg. 1991-93.

	N/A	$775	$725	$675	$625	$550	$450

GRADING	100% MINT	98% NEAR MINT	95% EXC+	90% EXC	80% VG+	70% VG	60% G

ELECTRIC BASS: DR C SERIES

This series had an offset double cutaway figured hardwood body, through-body 3-piece maple/graphite neck, 24-fret rosewood fingerboard with offset pearl dot inlay, fixed bridge, gold hardware, 2 J-style pickups, volume/tone/balance controls, 2-position switch, active electronics. This series is custom made, available in Antique Burst, Crimson Stain, Ebony Stain and Natural finishes.

DR 4 C - 2-per-side tuners, mfg. 1991-93.

	N/A	$1,150	$1,000	$950	$850	$675	$575

DR 5 C - 5-string configuration, 2/3-per-side tuners, mfg. 1991-93.

	N/A	$1,250	$1,100	$1,000	$900	$725	$625

DR 6 C - 6-string configuration, 3-per-side tuners, mfg. 1991-93.

	N/A	$1,300	$1,150	$1,100	$975	$850	$725

ELECTRIC BASS: PROPHECY SERIES

PR I - double cutaway basswood body, bolt-on maple neck, 22-fret rosewood fingerboard with pearl dot inlay, fixed bridge, graphite nut, 4-on-a-side tuners, chrome hardware, P-style/J-style pickups, volume/balance control, available in Black, Chrome Red, Frost Red, Midnight Blue, or Mystic White finishes, mfg. 1991-93.

	N/A	$500	$450	$395	$325	$250	$200

PR II - similar to PR I, except has ash body, gold hardware, volume/treble/bass controls, active electronics, available in Antique Burst, Crimson Trans., Natural, or Sapphire Blue Trans. finishes, mfg. 1991-93.

	N/A	$550	$495	$425	$375	$300	$250

PR III - similar to PR I, except has laminated ash body, through-body laminated maple neck, gold hardware, volume/treble/bass controls, active electronics, available in Antique Burst, Crimson Trans., Natural, or Sapphire Blue Trans. finishes, mfg. 1991-93.

	N/A	$750	$675	$625	$575	$450	$375

HEINS GUITARS

Instruments currently built in Sneek, The Netherlands.

Luthier Wim Heins has been building guitars since the late 1960s – and was motivated to build his first one at an early age because he was too young to actually buy a guitar! After his first experiment, Hein kept building and customizing guitars as a hobby. After one of his guitars Heins built for a friend began to receive some notice, Heins decided to go into business – so what started out as a hobby became a business.

Heins' specialized guitar building and repair shop in The Netherlands offers these handcrafted electric guitar and bass models direct to the player, with no middle man. His current brochure offers an overview of models with the reminder that it can "never be complete or represent the variety in guitars, because all of them are made to the exact specifications of the client." Today there are several models offered.

Personality and originality seem to be big parts of the Heins guitar models, as most of them feature premium figured woods, a sleek offset double cutaway body design, and quality pickups and hardware. Guitar models include the Dick and Zingana, as well as the 7-string Danny model. Basses include the 4-string Noest, 5-string TMF, and 6-string Pookie (which, oddly enough, is this author's nickname for his dog). For further information regarding prices and specifications, please contact Wim Heins at Heins Guitars directly (see Trademark Index).

HEIT DELUXE

Instruments previously produced in Japan circa late 1960s to early 1970s.

The Heit Deluxe trademark is a brand name applied to guitars imported into the U.S. market by an unidentified New York importer. Updated information from noted researcher Michael Wright has confirmed that certain Heit Deluxe models share similarities with Teisco Del Rey guitars, leading to the conclusion that Teisco/Kawai built many of the models for the Heit Deluxe brand name (source: Michael Wright, *Guitar Stories*, Volume One).

ELECTRIC

ELECTRIC SOLIDBODIES - various configurations often similar to Teisco Del Ray, mfg. late 1960s-early 1970s.

LOW-END MODELS	N/A	$150	$120	$100	$80	$60	$40
MID-END MODELS	N/A	$200	$160	$130	$100	$80	$60
HIGH-END MODELS	N/A	$250	$200	$160	$130	$100	$80

The more features the guitar has (pickups, electronics, woods, etc.), the higher end the guitar is.

HEMBROOK

Instruments currently built in TX. Distributed by Hembrook Custom Basses and Guitars of Texas.

Ranger Bob, a self-taught luthier, left the U.S. Army in 1992 and returned to the University of Texas. While playing a 5-string bass for a surf-rock band in Austin, Ranger Bob noticed some deficiencies in his instrument - which lead to his discovery that most 5-string basses he encountered were either just retreaded "vintage" designs with an additional string or trendy boutique models that didn't feature very practical designs.

After several years of research and discussion, Ranger Bob began building prototype instruments. During this prototype building, he encountered Texas Mesquite wood (normally considered a pesky shrub in Northern Texas). Mesquite is rare among woods in that it expands and contracts to changes in moisture equally in all directions. Most woods expand 2 or 3 times more across the grain than along the grain - which is why moisture changes can warp necks or bodies. Mesquite is an isometric wood, and thus Ranger Bob argues that it is the ideal neck wood. Through innovation, Ranger Bob and his company search out new components and durable material for their instruments, then integrate the components into the balanced structure. For more information regarding Hembrook contact them directly (see Trademark Index).

GRADING		100% MINT	98% NEAR MINT	95% EXC+	90% EXC	80% VG+	70% VG	60% G

**Heritage H-575
courtesy Heritage**

ELECTRIC BASS

Hembrook electric basses are priced at $1,700, $1,800, and $1,900, in 4, 5, and 6, string configurations (as well as an 8-string (disc. 2003), 30 in. scale baritone model, and two guitar models). U[right electric basses are available in 4-string ($2,000) and 5-string ($2,200). Hembrook bass necks feature straight grain Mesquite laminated to figured maple; the bodies are Honduran mahogany with a 1/4 in. burled Mesquite top. Ranger Bob sourced out parts and electronics from all over the world, and features Seymour Duncan pickups and preamps. Piezo-electric sensors are built in-house.

HERITAGE

Instruments currently built in Kalamazoo, MI since 1984. The company was incorporated on April 1, 1985. The Lasar Music Corporation is the exclusive sales and marketing company for Heritage Guitars, Inc.

The Gibson guitar company was founded in Kalamazoo in 1902. The young company continued to expand, and built production facilities at 225 Parsons Street (the first of a total of five buildings at that location) in 1917. In 1974, Gibson was acquired by the Norlin corporation, which also opened facilities the same year in Nashville, Tennessee. However, financial troubles led Norlin to consider shutting down either the Kalamazoo or Nashville facilities in the early 1980s. Even though the Kalamazoo plant was Gibson's home since 1917, the decision was made in July of 1983 by Norlin to close the plant. The doors at 225 Parsons Street closed in the fall of 1984.

Heritage Guitar, Inc. opened in 1985 in the original Gibson building. Rather than uproot and move to Tennessee, Jim Deurloo, Marvin Lamb, and J.P. Moats elected to leave the Gibson company, and stay in Kalamazoo to start a new guitar company. Members of the original trio were later joined by Bill Paige and Mike Korpak (other long time Gibson workers). Korpack left the Heritage company in 1985.

Jim Deurloo began working at Gibson in 1958, and through his career was promoted from neck sander to pattern maker up to general foreman of the pattern shop, machine shop, and maintenance. Deurloo was the plant manager at Guild between 1969 to 1974, and had been involved with the opening and tooling up of the newer Nashville facility in 1974. During this time period, Deurloo was also the head of engineering, and was later promoted to assistant plant manager. In 1978 Deurloo was named plant manager at the Kalamazoo facility.

Marv Lamb was hired by Gibson in 1956 to do hand sanding and other jobs in the wood shop (Lamb was one of the workers on the '58 Korina Flying Vs and Explorers). He was promoted through a series of positions to general foreman of finishing and final assembly, and finally to plant superintendent in 1974 (a position he held until Gibson closed the plant in 1984).

J.P. Moats was hired by Gibson in 1957 for sanding and final cleaning. Through promotions, Moats became head of quality control as well as the supervisor of inspectors, and later the wood inspector. While inspecting wood for Gibson, Moats was also in charge of repairs and custom orders.

Bill Paige, a graduate of the business school at Western Michigan University joined Gibson in 1975 as a cost accountant and other capacities in the accounting department. Paige is currently the Heritage controller, and handles all non-guitar manufacturing functions.

All current owners of Heritage continue to design models, and produce various instruments in the production facilities. Heritage continues to develop new models along with their wide range of acoustic, hollow body, semi-hollow, and electric guitar models. Heritage is also one of the few new guitar companies with models that are stocked in vintage and collectible guitar stores worldwide.

GENERAL INFORMATION & SERIALIZATION

Serialization started with the letter A in 1984.

Heritage offers a wide range of custom features. EMG, HRW, or Seymour Duncan pickups, special colors, special inlays, and choice woods may be ordered (call for custom quote). Unless specified, a hardshell case is optional with the guitar. Cases for the acoustics, jazz guitars, and basses run $170 while the cases for electric guitars are $160; cases for the Super Eagle model are $190.

Var-I-Phase is a Heritage innovation that provides coil tap capabilities as well as the ability to roll in the exact amount of in-phase/out-of-phase balance in the player's sound. It is a $300 option on numerous Heritage models. Here are some other pricing options:

Add $50 for engraved truss rod cover. Add $50 for installed chrome-covered pickups. Add $100 for an ebony fingerboard. Add $100 for a pickguard-mounted tone control on jazz models. Add $150 for MOP engraved truss rod cover. Add $150 for gold or black hardware. Add $150 for single bound extra pickguard. Add $150 for Heritage HRW pickup. Add $250 for mulitple bound extra pickguard. Add $300 for Var-I-Phase (see explanation). Add $300 for left-handed configuration. Add $500 for Custom-carved left-handed models. Add $400 for tap tuning of top and back (each).

ELECTRIC: CUSTOM CARVED HOLLOW BODY GUITARS

**Heritage SAE Custom
courtesy Heritage**

AMERICAN EAGLE - single round cutaway hollow style, tap tuned solid spruce carved top, 25.5 in. scale, bound body and f-holes, bound flame maple pickguard with pearl inlay, solid curly or bubbled maple back/sides, 5-piece figured maple neck, 20-fret bound ebony fingerboard with pearl/abalone American heritage inlays, ebony/rosewood bridge with pearl star inlay, Liberty Bell shaped trapeze tailpiece, red/white/blue-bound peghead with pearl eagle, stars, American Flag and Heritage logo inlay, pearl truss rod cover engraved with owner's name, 3-per-side Kluson tuners, gold hardware, pickguard-mounted Heritage jazz pickup with 3 star inlay on cover, volume control on pickguard, available in Natural finish, mfg. 1986-present.

MSR	$13,440	$10,500	$9,500	$8,500	$7,500	N/A	N/A	N/A

Price includes hardshell case.

GRADING		100% MINT	98% NEAR MINT	95% EXC+	90% EXC	80% VG+	70% VG	60% G

CONCERT MASTER - single sharp cutaway semi-hollow body, solid spruce carved top, multiple bound body, bound f-holes, bound curly maple pickguard, solid curly maple back/sides/neck, 20-fret ebony fingerboard with Heritage MOP block inlay, ebony bridge, finger tailpiece, bound peghead with pearl logo and name on truss rod, 3-per-side tuners, gold hardware, single premium Heritage humbucker pickup, LR Baggs bridge piezo, two knobs, available in various finishes, 25.5 in. scale, 18 in. body width, 3 in. body thickness, new 2005.

	MSR	$7,980		$6,200	$5,500	$4,800	$4,000	N/A	N/A	N/A

Add $400 for Translucent Custom finishes.

EAGLE - single round cutaway hollow style, solid mahogany top/pickguard, 25.5 in. scale, f-holes, cream-bound body, mahogany back/sides/neck, 20-fret rosewood fingerboard with pearl dot inlay, rosewood bridge/trapeze tailpiece, 3-per-side tuners, chrome hardware, pickguard-mounted Heritage jazz pickup, volume control on pickguard, available in standard finish, body width 17 in., body thickness 3 in., mfg. 1986-present.

	MSR	$3,190		$2,500	$2,150	$1,850	$1,600	$1,400	$1,200	$1,000

Add $200 for Translucent custom finishes. Add $250 for solid spruce top.

Eagle Classic - single round cutaway hollow style, solid carved spruce top, 25.5 in. scale, f-holes, bound maple pickguard, bound body, solid curly maple back/sides, 5-piece curly maple neck, 20-fret bound ebony fingerboard, ebony bridge/trapeze tailpiece, bound peghead, 3-per-side tuners, gold hardware, 1 floating (or 2 humbucker) pickups, 2 volume/tone controls, 3-position switch, available in Almond Sunburst and Antique Sunburst finishes, body width 17 in., body thickness 3 in., mfg. 1992-present.

	MSR	$4,225		$3,300	$2,850	$2,500	$2,200	$1,900	$1,700	$1,500

Add $400 for Translucent custom finishes.

Eagle TDC - similar to Eagle, except has thinner body style, tune-o-matic bridge, dual top routed pickups, available in Antique Sunburst finish, body width 17 in., body thickness 2.25 in., current mfg.

	MSR	$3,440		$2,700	$2,400	$2,050	$1,750	$1,500	$1,300	$1,100

Add $200 for Translucent custom finishes.

GOLDEN EAGLE - single round cutaway hollow style, solid spruce carved top, 25.5 in. scale, 7-ply bound body, bound f-holes, bound maple pickguard, curly maple back/sides/neck, 20-fret bound ebony fingerboard with pearl cloud inlay, ebony bridge with pearl V inlay, trapeze tailpiece, bound peghead with pearl eagle on tree and logo inlay, eagle inlay on back of headstock (with reg. no.), pearl truss rod cover with owner's name, 3-per-side Kluson tuners, gold hardware, pickguard-mounted Heritage jazz humbucker pickup, pickguard-mounted volume control, available in Antique Sunburst, Sunsetburst, Almond Sunburst, Antique Natural, or Natural finishes, body width 17 in., body thickness 3 in., mfg. 1985-present.

	MSR	$5,330		$4,150	$3,700	$3,250	$2,800	$2,500	$2,200	$1,900

Add $400 for Translucent custom finishes.

This model is available with a single floating pickup, dual humbucker, or single humbucker pickup configurations.

HENRY JOHNSON - single sharp cutaway semi-hollow body, solid spruce carved top, multiple bound body, bound f-holes, bound curly maple pickguard, solid curly maple back/sides/neck, 20-fret ebony fingerboard with MOP block inlay, ebony bridge, Heritage bail tailpiece, bound peghead with pearl logo and name on truss rod, 3-per-side tuners, gold hardware, two premium Heritage humbucker pickups, four knobs, available in various finishes, 25 in. scale, 17 in. body width, 3.25 in. body thickness, new 2005.

	MSR	$6,100		$4,700	$4,200	$3,800	$3,400	$3,000	$2,600	$2,200

Add $400 for Translucent Custom finishes.

JOHNNY SMITH (THE ROSE) - single round cutaway hollow style, solid spruce carved top, 25 in. scale, bound body, bound f-holes, bound curly maple pickguard, curly maple back/sides/neck, 20-fret ebony fingerboard with abalone block inlay, ebony bridge, individual finger-style trapeze tailpiece, bound peghead with abalone/pearl rose inlay, 3-per-side tuners, black hardware, pickguard-mounted Heritage jazz humbucker pickup, pickguard-mounted volume control, available in Antique Sunburst finish, body width 17 in., body thickness 3 in., mfg. 1989-2002.

				$4,500	$3,800	$3,500	$3,200	$2,900	$2,600	$2,300

Last MSR was $5,710.

Add $400 for Translucent Custom finishes.

This model is personally signed by Johnny Smith on the label.

SUPER EAGLE - single round cutaway hollow style, solid spruce carved top, 25.5 in. scale, bound body and f-holes, bound maple pickguard, curly maple back/sides/neck, 20-fret bound ebony fingerboard with pearl split block inlay, ebony bridge with pearl V inlay, trapeze tailpiece, bound peghead with pearl eagle on tree and logo inlay, pearl truss rod cover with owner's name, 3-per-side Grover Imperial tuners, gold hardware, single floating (or 2 humbucker) pickup(s), volume/tone controls and 3-position switch, available in Antique Sunburst finish, body width 18 in., body thickness 3 in., mfg. 1988-present.

	MSR	$5,985		$4,650	$4,100	$3,550	$3,100	$2,700	$2,300	$2,000

Add $400 for Translucent custom finishes.

SUPER KB - single sharp cutaway semi-hollow body, solid spruce carved top, multiple bound body, bound f-holes, bound curly maple pickguard, solid curly maple back/sides/neck, 20-fret ebony fingerboard with Heritage MOP block inlay, ebony bridge, finger tailpiece, bound peghead with pearl logo and name on truss rod, 3-per-side tuners, gold hardware, two premium Heritage humbucker pickups, four knobs, available in various finishes, 25.5 in. scale, 18 in. body width, 3 in. body thickness, new 2005.

	MSR	$7,135		$5,500	$4,800	$4,200	$3,500	N/A	N/A	N/A

Add $400 for Translucent Custom finishes.

SWEET 16 - single sharp cutaway hollow style, solid spruce carved top, multiple bound body, bound f-holes, bound curly maple pickguard, curly maple back/sides/neck, 20-fret ebony fingerboard with pearl split block inlay, ebony bridge with pearl 16 inlay, trapeze tailpiece, bound peghead with pearl "Sweet 16" and logo inlay, 3-per-side tuners, gold hardware, pickguard-mounted Heritage jazz humbucker, pickguard-mounted volume control, available in Almond Sunburst and Antique Sunburst finishes, body width 16 in., body thickness 2.75 in., mfg. 1987-present.

	MSR	$4,780		$3,700	$3,200	$2,800	$2,400	$2,100	$1,800	$1,500

Add $400 for Translucent Custom finishes.

This model can be found with either single top routed humbucker or dual top routed humbucker pickup configurations.

GRADING	100% MINT	98% NEAR MINT	95% EXC+	90% EXC	80% VG+	70% VG	60% G

ELECTRIC: PARSONS STREET PROJECT

PARSONS STREET - offset double cutaway solid mahogany body, curly maple top, 25.5 in. scale, mahogany neck, 22-fret bound rosewood fingerboard with pearl block inlay, tune-o-matic bridge/stop tailpiece, 3-per-side tuners, chrome hardware, 2 single coil/1 humbucker pickups, volume/tone control, 5-position and Var-I-Phase switch, available in Antique Sunburst, Antique Cherry Sunburst, or Natural finishes, mfg. 1989-1992.

	N/A	$900	$800	$700	$600	$500	$400

Last MSR was $1,345.

PARSONS STREET III - similar to the Parsons Street, except has hardwood body, maple neck, unbound rosewood fingerboard with pearl dot inlay, black chrome hardware, Kahler tremolo bridge, no Var-I-Phase switch, 2 mini switches, available in Black, Red, or White finishes, disc. 1991.

	N/A	$650	$550	$475	$400	$325	$275

Last MSR was $1,165.

This model was available with either a Shadow Piezo tremolo pickup or Shadow active humbucker pickup.

PARSONS STREET V - similar to the Parsons Street, except has bound body, Kahler tremolo bridge, volume/2 tone controls, no Var-I-Phase switch, 2 mini switches, available in Antique Sunburst and Antique Cherry Burst finishes, disc. 1991.

	N/A	$850	$750	$650	$550	$450	$350

Last MSR was $1,300.

This model was available with either a Shadow Piezo tremolo pickup or Shadow active humbucker pickup, and also available in Amber Trans., Black Trans., Blue Trans., Cherry Trans., Emerald Green Trans., Almond, Blue, Red, or Vintage Sunburst Trans. finishes.

ELECTRIC: MILENNIUM SERIES

Add $100 for Translucent Custom finishes for all Millennium models.

STANDARD ULTRA - single cutaway semi-hollow body, solid carved multiple white bound ultra curly maple top, single white bound, solid flat mahogany back and solid mahogany sides, f-holes, no pickguard, 1 piece mahogany neck, white bound ebony fingerboard, mother-of-pearl block position markers, 2 gold plated HRW pickups, 2 Volume/2-Tone controls, 3-way switch, 3-per-side tuners, available in Vintage Sunburst and other finishes, 24.75 in. scale, current mfg.

MSR	$3,040		$2,400	$2,050	$1,750	$1,500	$1,250	$1,050	$850

LIMITED EDITION 2001 ULTRA - single cutaway semi-hollow body, multiple white bound solid carved ultra curly maple top, single white bound flat ultra curly maple back, solid sides, f-holes, no pickguard, 1-piece mahogany neck, 24.75 in. scale, white bound ebony fingerboard, trapezoid outline markers, the words "Millennium," "2001," and "Kalamazoo" engraved in the last three position markers, 2 gold plated HRW pickups, 2 Volume/2-Tone controls, 3-way switch, individual gold plated tuners, gold plated stop tailpiece, adjustable bridge, 3-per-side tuners, available in Chestnut Sunburst and other finishes, disc. 2002.

	$2,400	$2,100	$1,800	$1,500	$1,200	$1,000	$800

Last MSR was $3,200.

BLACK BEAUTY DC (MILENNIUM DC) - double cutaway semi-hollow body, multiple white bound solid carved maple top, single white bound flat maple back and solid maple sides, f-holes, no pickguard, 1-piece mahogany neck, white bound ebony fingerboard with mother-of-pearl block position markers, 2 gold plated HRW pickups, 2 Volume/2-Tone controls, 3-way switch, individual gold plated tuners, gold plated stop tailpiece, adjustable bridge, available in Black finish, current mfg.

MSR	$2,565		$2,000	$1,750	$1,500	$1,300	$1,100	$950	$800

EAGLE CUSTOM - single cutaway semi-hollow body, solid carved multiple white bound ultra curly maple top, multiple white bound solid carved ultra curly maple back and solid sides, f-holes, no pickguard, 3-piece curly maple neck, multiple white bound ebony fingerboard, 22-frets, mother-of-pearl split block position markers, 2 gold plated HRW pickups, 2 Volume/2-Tone controls, 3-way switch, individual gold plated Imperial tuners, gold plated Heritage finger tailpiece, adjustable bridge, available in Burnt Amber and other finishes, 24.75 in. scale, disc. 2002.

	$3,600	$3,200	$2,900	$2,600	$2,300	$2,000	$1,700

Last MSR was $4,650.

EAGLE 2000 - single cutaway semi-hollow body, solid carved multiple white bound curly maple top, single white bound solid carved curly maple back and solid sides, no pickguard, 3-piece curly maple neck, 24 ¾" scale white bound ebony fingerboard with 22-frets, abalone block position markers, 2 gold plated Seth Lover pickups, 2 volume/2 tone controls, 3-way switch, individual gold plated Grover Imperial tuners, gold plated Heritage bail tailpiece, adjustable bridge, available in Old Style Sunburst and other finishes, current mfg.

MSR	$3,645		$2,850	$2,500	$2,200	$1,900	$1,650	$1,400	$1,150

H-155 - single cutaway semi-hollow body, solid carved multiple white bound curly maple top, single white bound flat curly maple back, solid sides, one-piece mahogany neck, single white bound mother-of-pearl headstock inlay, single white bound ebony fingerboard with mother-of-pearl block position markers, 2 gold plated Seth Lover pickups, 3-way switch, 2 volume/2 tone controls, individual gold plated tuners, 3-per-side tuners, gold plated stop tailpiece, adjustable bridge, available in Almond Sunburst and other finishes, 24.75 in. scale, current mfg.

MSR	$2,500		$1,950	$1,700	$1,450	$1,250	$1,050	$900	$750

H-158 - single cutaway semi-hollow body with laminated arched top and arched back, single cream bound top and back, no pickguard, 2 f-holes, rosewood cream bound fingerboard with 22 frets, mother-of-pearl dot inlays, 2

Heritage Eagle courtesy Buffalo Bros. Guitars

Heritage Super Eagle courtesy LaVonne Wagner Music

GRADING	100% MINT	98% NEAR MINT	95% EXC+	90% EXC	80% VG+	70% VG	60% G

humbucker pickups, selector switch in horn, 2 volume/2 tone control knobs, chrome plated machine heads, stop bar tailpiece and adj. bridge, mfg. 2001-present.

MSR	$2,215	$1,750	$1,500	$1,300	$1,100	$950	$800	$650

SAE CUSTOM - single cutaway mahogany body with carved maple top, 24.75 in. scale, f-holes, bound body, mahogany neck, 22-fret bound rosewood with pearl dot inlay, tune-o-matic bridge/stop tailpiece, 3-per-side tuners, chrome hardware, 2 humbucker pickups, Mike Christian transducer bridge-mounted pickup, 2 volume/1 tone controls, 3 mini toggle switches, available in Antique, Translucent Almond, Translucent Amber, Trans. Blue, Trans. Cherry, or Trans. Emerald Green finishes, mfg. 1992-present.

MSR	$2,600	$2,000	$1,700	$1,500	$1,300	$1,100	$950	$800

SAE Cutaway - similar to SAE Custom, except only has a mounted Mike Christian transducer bridge pickup and volume/tone control, disc. 1994.

N/A	$1,500	$1,300	$1,100	$950	$800	$650

Last MSR was $965.

ELECTRIC: MISC. MODELS

ALVIN LEE MODEL - 335 style, bound curly maple top/back/sides, f-holes, black pickguard, mahogany neck, 22-fret bound ebony fingerboard with pearl dot inlay, tune-o-matic bridge/stop tailpiece, 3-per-side tuners, chrome hardware, humbucker/single coil/humbucker pickup, 3 volume/2 tone controls, 3-position switch, available in Trans. Cherry finish, mfg. 1993-96.

	$1,500	$1,200	$1,000	$850	$700	$550	$400

Last MSR was $1,885.

GARY MOORE MODEL - single cutaway mahogany body, bound carved curly maple top, 24.75 in. scale, bound curly maple pickguard, mahogany neck, 22-fret bound rosewood fingerboard with pearl crown inlay, tune-o-matic bridge/stop tailpiece, black peghead with Gary Moore signature imprint, 3-per-side tuners, chrome hardware, 2 EMG humbucker pickups, 2 volume/2 tone controls, 3-position switch, available in Trans. Amber finish, disc. 1992.

N/A	$3,200	$2,800	$2,400	$2,000	$1,600	$1,200

Last MSR was $1,415.

This model has a certificate signed by the owners. This model featured a limited production of only 150 instruments: the first group included 75 models in Amber, the second group had 75 models in Almond Sunburst. The series number is stamped on the headstock, beneath ser. no.

LITTLE-ONE CM - small size asymmetrical double cutaway curly maple body/neck, 22-fret bound rosewood fingerboard with pearl dot inlay, tune-o-matic bridge/stop tailpiece, 3-per-side tuners, chrome hardware, humbucker pickup, volume control, available in Trans. Amber, Trans. Black, or Trans. Cherry finishes, mfg. 1992-94, reintroduced 2000-present.

MSR	$1,465	$1,150	$1,000	$850	$750	$650	$550	$450

List price includes gig bag. Also available as a poplar body, MSR $1,365.

MARK SLAUGHTER ROCK - radical single cutaway mahogany body/neck, 22-fret rosewood fingerboard with pearl dot inlay, tune-o-matic bridge/stop tailpiece, reverse headstock, 6-on-a-side tuners, chrome hardware, 2 single coil/1 humbucker pickups, volume/tone control, 5-position switch, available in Black, Red, or White finishes, mfg. 1992-95.

N/A	$850	$700	$600	$500	$400	$300

Last MSR was $1,135.

Add $200 for Kahler Spyder tremolo bridge.

STAT - offset double cutaway bound curly maple/mahogany body, mahogany neck, 22-fret rosewood fingerboard with pearl dot inlay, tune-o-matic bridge/stop tailpiece, 6-on-a-side tuners, chrome hardware, 2 single coil/1 humbucker pickups, volume/tone controls, 3 mini toggle pickup selector/1 mini toggle coil tap switches, available in Antique Sunburst, Antique Cherry Sunburst, or Cherry finishes, mfg. 1989-1991.

N/A	$800	$700	$625	$550	$475	$400

Last MSR was $785.

V.I.P. (V.I.P.-1) - offset double cutaway curly maple body, bolt-on mahogany neck, 25.5 in. scale, 22-fret rosewood fingerboard with pearl dot inlay, tune-o-matic bridge/stop tailpiece, 6-on-a-side tuners, blackface peghead with "The Heritage" logo, chrome hardware, humbucker pickup, volume/tone controls, coil tap mini toggle switch, phase or standby mini toggle switch, available in Trans. color finishes, mfg. 1986-1990.

N/A	$750	$650	$575	$500	$425	$350

Last MSR was $465.

Add $30 for fine tune tailpiece and locking nut. Add $30 for Kahler Flyer tremolo bridge.

In 1989, Fine Tune tailpiece, and Kahler Flyer tremolo bridge were discontinued. When both mini-switches are in the Up position, one is a coil tap switch and the other is a standby (signal on/off) switch. When both mini- switches are in the down position, the tone control becomes a Variable Phase control between the two pickup coils (0=out of phase, 10=in phase). A wide variety of tonal capabilities are thus offered to the guitarist.

V.I.P.-2 - similar to the V.I.P., except features 2 humbucker pickups, available in Trans. color finishes, mfg. 1986-1990.

N/A	$800	$700	$600	$525	$450	$375

Last MSR was $565.

Add $30 for fine tune tailpiece and locking nut. Add $30 for Kahler Flyer tremolo bridge.

In 1989, Fine Tune tailpiece, and Kahler Flyer tremolo bridge were discontinued.

ELECTRIC: H (SOLID BODIES) SERIES

Add $100 for Translucent Custom finishes.

GRADING	100% MINT	98% NEAR MINT	95% EXC+	90% EXC	80% VG+	70% VG	60% G

H-127 CUSTOM - single cutaway mahogany body, bound arch maple top, maple neck, 22-fret maple fingerboard with pearl dot inlay, tune-o-matic bridge/stop tailpiece, 6-on-a-side tuners, chrome hardware, 2 single coil pickups, volume/tone control, 3-position switch, available in Antique Sunburst or Sunsetburst finishes, mfg. 1992-96.

	N/A	$900	$800	$700	$600	$500	$400

Last MSR was $1,250.

H-127 Standard - similar to H-127 Custom, except has solid mahogany body, disc. 1992.

	N/A	$750	$625	$500	$450	$400	$325

Last MSR was $1,010.

H-140CM - single sharp cutaway mahogany body, bound curly maple top, white pickguard, mahogany neck, 22-fret rosewood fingerboard with pearl dot inlay, tune-o-matic bridge/stop tailpiece, 3-per-side tuners, chrome hardware, 2 exposed humbucker pickups, 2 volume/2 tone controls, 3-position switch, available in Standard or Translucent finishes, 24.75 in. scale, mfg. 1985-present.

MSR	$1,695	$1,325	$1,150	$1,000	$850	$750	$650	$550

This model with the gold top finish has a carved plain maple top, mfg. 1994-present.

H-140CMV - similar to the H-140CM, except has installed Heritage Var-I-Phase electronics, available in Standard or Translucent finishes, mfg. 1994-present.

MSR	$1,995	$1,550	$1,350	$1,200	$1,050	$900	$750	$650

H-147 - similar to H-140CM, except has plain maple top, bound ebony fingerboard with pearl block inlay, bound peghead and gold hardware, mfg. 1989-1992.

	N/A	$1,000	$850	$700	$600	$500	$400

Last MSR was $1,215.

H-150CM - single sharp cutaway mahogany body, bound carved curly maple top, white pickguard, mahogany neck, 22-fret bound rosewood fingerboard with pearl crown inlay, tune-o-matic bridge/stop tailpiece, 3-per-side tuners, chrome hardware, 2 covered humbucker pickups, 2 volume/2 tone controls, 3-position switch, available in various finishes, 24.75 in. scale, mfg. 1988-present.

MSR	$2,140	$1,650	$1,450	$1,300	$1,150	$1,000	$850	$700

H-150CM Classic - similar to H-150CM, except has 2 humbucker HRW or Seymour Duncan pickups, available in Standard or Translucent finishes, current mfg.

MSR	$2,290	$1,800	$1,550	$1,350	$1,200	$1,050	$900	$750

H-150CM Deluxe - similar to H-150CM, except has multiple-bound body, bound matching curly maple peghead, bound curly maple pickguard, gold hardware, 2 Seymour Duncan pickups, available in Standard or Translucent finishes, mfg. 1992-present.

MSR	$2,830	$2,200	$1,900	$1,650	$1,450	$1,250	$1,100	$950

This model is available on a limited basis. Price includes hardshell case.

H-150CM Ultra - similar to H-150CM Deluxe, except has ultra top, gold hardware, and 2 HRW pickups, available in Standard or Translucent finishes, mfg. 1992-present.

MSR	$3,040	$2,350	$2,050	$1,800	$1,600	$1,400	$1,200	$1,000

H-150CM 20th Anniversary - 20th Anniversary verison of the H-150CM, new 2005.

MSR	$3,925	$3,050	$2,700	$2,400	$2,150	N/A	N/A	N/A

H-150 SPECIAL - single sharp cutaway poplar body, bound carved plain maple top, mahogany neck, 22-fret bound rosewood fingerboard with pearl dot inlay, tune-o-matic bridge/stop tailpiece, 3-per-side tuners, chrome hardware, 2 humbucker pickups, 2 volume/2 tone controls, 3-position switch, available in Black and Old Style Sunburst finishes, 24.75 in. scale, mfg. 1994-2004.

MSR	$1,665	$1,300	$1,100	$950	$800	$700	$600	$500

H-150P - similar to H-150 Special, except has cream-bound solid poplar body, pearl dot fingerboard inlay, available in Blue, Red, or White finishes, mfg. 1992-98.

	$850	$725	$650	$550	$450	$375	$275

Last MSR was $1,050.

Add $100 for solid Gold finish.

H-157 - single sharp cutaway mahogany body, multiple white-bound carved solid maple top, 24.75 in. scale, mahogany neck, 22-fret bound ebony fingerboard with mother-of-pearl block inlay, tune-o-matic bridge/stop tailpiece, bound blackface peghead with pearl diamond/logo inlay, black pickguard, 3-per-side tuners, gold hardware, 2 volume/2 tone controls, 3-position switch, available in Standard or Translucent finishes, mfg. 1989-present.

MSR	$2,515	$1,950	$1,700	$1,500	$1,300	$1,150	$1,000	$850

H-170CM - double cutaway mahogany body, cream-bound carved solid curly maple top, mahogany neck, 22-fret rosewood fingerboard with pearl dot inlay, tune-o-matic bridge/stop tailpiece, 3-per-side tuners, chrome hardware, 2 humbucker pickups, 2 volume/2 tone controls, 3-position switch, available in Standard or Translucent finishes, 24.75 in. scale, mfg. 1996-present.

	$1,200	$1,050	$900	$800	$700	$600	$500

Last MSR was $1,550.

Heritage V.I.P.
courtesy Steve Cherne

H

Heritage H-150 CM Deluxe
courtesy Heritage

GRADING	100% MINT	98% NEAR MINT	95% EXC+	90% EXC	80% VG+	70% VG	60% G

H-170CM SM - similar to the H-170CM, except features 2 Seymour Duncan Stag Mag humbucker pickups, 2 push/pull (coil tap) volume controls, master tone control, mfg. 1998-2004.

	$1,325	$1,150	$1,000	$850	$700	$650	$550

Last MSR was $1,700.

H-357 - single round cutaway asymmetrical hourglass style mahogany body, white pickguard, through-body mahogany neck, 22-fret rosewood fingerboard with pearl dot inlay, tune-o-matic bridge/stop tailpiece, 6-on-a-side tuners, chrome hardware, 2 humbucker pickups, 2 volume/2 tone controls, 3-position switch, available in Antique Sunburst, Black, Blue, Red, or White finishes, mfg. 1989-1996.

	N/A	$1,700	$1,500	$1,300	$1,100	$950	$800

Last MSR was $1,350.

This model was also available with black pickguard and reverse headstock. Later models have a standard Heritage headstock. It is estimated that only 50 to 75 instruments were produced.

ELECTRIC: 500 SEMI-HOLLOW SERIES

Models in the 500 Series feature a semi-hollow body design.

ACADEMY CUSTOM - single rounded cutaway style, cream-bound curly maple top, f-holes, bound maple pickguard, curly maple back/sides, one piece mahogany neck, 22-fret bound rosewood fingerboard with pearl crown inlay, tune-o-matic bridge/stop tailpiece, bound peghead, 3-per-side tuners, gold hardware, 2 humbuckers, 2 volume/tone controls, 3-position switch, available in Almond Sunburst and Antique Sunburst finishes, 24.75 in. scale, 15 in. body width, 1.5 in. body thickness, mfg. 1992-present.

MSR	$2,600	$2,000	$1,700	$1,500	$1,300	$1,150	$1,000	$850

Add $100 for Natural or Translucent Color finishes: Amber Translucent, Black Translucent, Blue Translucent, Cherry Translucent, Emerald Green Translucent, or Vintage Sunburst Translucent.

PROSPECT STANDARD - dual cutaway smaller 335-style, cream-bound curly maple laminate top/back f-holes, solid curly maple sides, white pickguard, mahogany neck, 20-fret bound rosewood fingerboard with pearl dot inlay, rollermatic bridge/stop tailpiece, 3-per-side tuners, nickel/chrome hardware, 2 humbucker pickups, 2 volume/tone controls, 3-position switch, available in Almond Sunburst or Antique Sunburst finishes, 24.75 in. scale, 15 in. body width, 1.5 in. body thickness, mfg. 1991-present.

MSR	$2,235	$1,725	$1,500	$1,300	$1,150	$1,000	$850	$750

Add $100 for Translucent Custom finishes.

ROY CLARK MODEL - single round cutaway, bound curly maple top/back/sides, bound f-holes, bound maple pickguard, mahogany neck, 22-fret bound rosewood fingerboard with mother-of-pearl split block inlay, tune-o-matic roller bridge/stop tailpiece, bound peghead, 3-per-side tuners, gold hardware, 2 humbuckers, 2 volume/tone controls, 3-position switch, available in various finishes, 24.75 in. scale, 16 in. body width, 1.5 in. body thickness, mfg. 1992-present.

MSR	$2,985	$2,300	$2,000	$1,750	$1,500	$1,300	$1,100	$950

Add $100 for Translucent Custom finishes.

H-535 - double round cutaway semi-hollow body, cream-bound curly maple laminate top and back, solid curly maple sides, f-holes, curly maple pickguard, mahogany neck, 22-fret bound rosewood fingerboard with pearl dot inlay, tune-o-matic bridge/stop tailpiece, 3-per-side tuners, chrome hardware, 2 humbucker pickups, 2 volume/tone controls, 3-position switch, available in Antique Sunburst finish, 24.75 in. scale, 16 in. body width, 1.5 in. body thickness, mfg. 1987-present.

MSR	$2,235	$1,725	$1,500	$1,300	$1,150	$1,000	$850	$750

Add $100 for Translucent Custom finishes. Add $170 for HRW pickups.

H-535 Classic - similar to H-535, except has 2 Seymour Duncan humbuckers, mfg. 1996-present.

MSR	$2,385	$1,850	$1,600	$1,400	$1,200	$1,050	$925	$800

H-535 Custom - similar to H-535, except has pearl diagonal inlay and bound peghead with pearl logo inlay, available in Antique Sunburst or Transparent Black finishes, mfg. 1991-92.

	N/A	$1,100	$950	$825	$700	$600	$500

Last MSR was $1,490.

H-535 20th Anniversary - 20th Anniversary version of the H-535, new 2005.

MSR	$3,665	$2,850	$2,500	$2,200	$1,950	N/A	N/A	N/A

H-555 - similar to H-535, except has bound f-holes, curly maple neck, ebony fingerboard with abalone/pearl diamond/arrow inlay with block after 17th fret, bound peghead with abalone/pearl diamond/arrow and logo inlay, gold hardware, available in Standard or Translucent finishes, 16 in. body width, 1.5 in. body thickness, mfg. 1989-present.

MSR	$2,985	$2,300	$2,000	$1,750	$1,500	$1,300	$1,100	$950

Add $100 for Translucent Custom finishes. Add $170 for HRW pickups.

H-574 - single round cutaway hollow style, bound curly maple top/back/sides, f-holes, white pickguard, mahogany neck, 20-fret rosewood fingerboard with pearl dot inlay, tune-o-matic bridge/stop tailpiece, 3-per-side tuners, chrome hardware, 2 humbuckers, 2 volume/tone controls, 3-position switch, available in Antique Sunburst finish, mfg. 1989-1991.

	N/A	$1,000	$850	$725	$600	$500	$400

Last MSR was $1,250.

Add $50 for Natural finish.

GRADING	100% MINT	98% NEAR MINT	95% EXC+	90% EXC	80% VG+	70% VG	60% G

ELECTRIC: 500 HOLLOW BODY SERIES

H-516 - single round cutaway semi-hollow body, laminated arched curly maple top and back, solid curly maple sides, f-holes, one-piece mahogany neck, rosewood fingerboard, mother-of-pearl position markers, 20-frets, individual nickel plated tuners, nickel plated Heritage bail tailpiece, adjustable bridge, 2 chrome plated humbucking pickups, 2 volume/2 tone controls, 3-way switch, available in various finishes, 24.75 in. scale, disc. 2004.

| | $1,800 | $1,550 | $1,350 | $1,150 | $1,000 | $875 | $750 |

Last MSR was $2,320.

H-550 - single round cutaway hollow style, multiple white-bound curly maple laminate braced top, bound curly maple laminate back, solid curly maple sides, bound f-holes, bound curly maple pickguard, curly maple neck, 20-fret bound ebony fingerboard with pearl split-block inlay, tune-o-matic bridge/trapeze tailpiece, bound peghead with pearl split-block and logo inlay, 3-per-side tuners, chrome hardware, 2 humbucker pickups, 2 volume/tone controls, 3-position switch, available in various finishes, 25.5 in. scale, 17 in. body width, 3 in. body thickness, mfg. 1990-present.

| MSR | $3,370 | $2,600 | $2,300 | $2,000 | $1,750 | $1,500 | $1,300 | $1,100 |

Add $100 for Translucent Custom finishes.

H-575 - single sharp cutaway hollow style, cream-bound solid carved curly maple braced top, cream-bound curly maple back, curly maple sides, f-holes, curly maple pickguard, mahogany neck, 20-fret rosewood fingerboard with pearl dot inlay, rosewood bridge/trapeze tailpiece, 3-per-side tuners, chrome hardware, 2 humbuckers, 2 volume/2 tone controls, 3-position switch, available in Antique Sunburst finish, 24.75 in. scale, 16 in. body width, 2.75 in. body thickness, mfg. 1987-present.

| MSR | $2,720 | $2,100 | $1,800 | $1,550 | $1,350 | $1,200 | $1,050 | $900 |

Add $200 for Translucent Custom finishes.

H-575 Classic - similar to the H-575, except has 2 HRW or Seymour Duncan humbuckers, mfg. 1996-present.

| MSR | $2,870 | $2,250 | $1,950 | $1,700 | $1,500 | $1,300 | $1,100 | $950 |

H-575 Custom - similar to the H-575, except has white body binding, bound fingerboard with mother-of-pearl "hash mark" or block inlays, bound peghead with pearl logo inlay and gold hardware, available in Sunset Burst finish, mfg. 1989-present.

| MSR | $3,420 | $2,650 | $2,350 | $2,050 | $1,800 | $1,600 | $1,400 | $1,200 |

Add $200 for Translucent Custom finishes.

In 1998, block fingerboard inlays replaced the "hash mark" fingerboard inlays, and the headstock inlays were disc.

H-575 Gold Top - similar to the H-575, except has Gold Top, mfg. 2001-04.

| | $2,150 | $1,900 | $1,650 | $1,400 | $1,200 | $1,000 | $850 |

Last MSR was $2,800.

H-575MH - similar to the H-575 except has a solid carved spruce top, solid carved mahogany back, mahogany rim and neck, cream-bound rosewood fingerboard, bound pickguard and peghead, one four point floating HRW pickup in top, gold hardware, amber knobs, mfg. 2002-present.

| MSR | $3,200 | $2,500 | $2,200 | $1,900 | $1,650 | $1,400 | $1,200 | $1,050 |

H-576 - single rounded cutaway semi-hollow style with floating center block, cream-bound curly maple laminate top and back, solid curly maple sides, f-holes, bound curly maple pickguard/peghead, mahogany neck, 20-fret rosewood fingerboard with mother-of-pearl block inlay, bridge/stop tailpiece, 3-per-side tuners, chrome hardware, 2 humbuckers, 2 volume/2 tone controls, 3-position switch, available in Antique Sunburst finish, 24.75 in. scale, 16 in. body width, 2.75 in. body thickness, mfg. 1990-2004.

| | $1,995 | $1,750 | $1,500 | $1,300 | $1,100 | $950 | $800 |

Last MSR was $2,570.

Add $100 for Translucent Custom finishes.

**Heritage H-535
courtesy Wolfe Guitars**

ELECTRIC BASS

Heritage Electric Bass models were discontinued in 1999.

CHUCK JACOBS MODEL - offset double cutaway maple body, 5-piece laminated maple through-body neck, 34 in. scale, 24-fret bound rosewood fingerboard with pearl dot inlay, 5-string configuration, fixed bridge, bound peghead, 3/2-per-side tuners, black hardware, 2 EMG J-style active pickups, 2 volume/2 tone controls, available in Black, Red, or White finishes, disc.

| | $2,100 | $1,850 | $1,600 | $1,350 | $1,125 | $875 | $650 |

Last MSR was $2,600.

Chuck Jacobs CM - similar to the Chuck Jacobs model, except has curly maple body, available in Trans. Black, Trans. Cherry, or Sunsetburst finishes, disc.

| | $2,150 | $1,900 | $1,650 | $1,400 | $1,175 | $925 | $675 |

Last MSR was $2,700.

**Heritage H-575 Custom
courtesy Heritage**

GRADING	100% MINT	98% NEAR MINT	95% EXC+	90% EXC	80% VG+	70% VG	60% G

HB 2 - offset double cutaway hardwood body, bolt-on maple neck, 34 in. scale, 21-fret rosewood fingerboard with white circle inlays, 4-on-a-side tuners, chrome hardware, fixed bridge, P/J-style pickups, 2 volume/1 tone controls, available in Antique Sun Burst, Antique Cherry Burst, or Black finishes, disc. 1992.

	N/A	$650	$575	$525	$475	$425	$350

Last MSR was $755.

HB 1 - similar to the HB 2, except has one split P-style pickup, volume/tone control, series/parallel mini switch, disc. 1992.

	N/A	$525	$450	$400	$350	$325	$225

Last MSR was $655.

HB-IV - offset double cutaway maple body, through-body maple neck, 34 in. scale, 24-fret rosewood fingerboard with pearl dot inlay, fixed bridge, 2-per-side tuners, black hardware, 2 active EMG soapbar pickups, 2 volume/2 tone controls, available in Black, Red, or White finishes, disc.

	N/A	$1,600	$1,400	$1,200	$1,050	$850	$650

Last MSR was $2,000.

Add $100 for curly maple top and Translucent Color finishes: Black Translucent, Cherry Translucent, Antique Sunburst finishes.

HB-V - similar to HB-IV, except has 5-string configuration, 3/2-per-side tuners, available in Black, Red, or White finishes, disc.

	N/A	$1,700	$1,450	$1,300	$1,100	$900	$700

Last MSR was $2,125.

Add $100 for curly maple top and Translucent Color finishes: Black Translucent, Cherry Translucent, Antique Sunburst finishes.

HILL CUSTOM GUITARS

Instruments currently produced in Cleveland, OH since 2000.

John Hill reorganized Hill Guitars as Hill Custom Guitars in 2000. They focus on very high end custom guitars and basses while still offering a standard line of professional instruments. For more information contact John Hill directly (see Trademark Index).

ELECTRIC

Hill produced several different models and configurations. The HB Series are bolt-on neck designs. The **HB-GS** is a Strat-style Swamp Ash or Alder body and retails for $1,499. The **HB-GT** is a Tele-style Swamp Ash or Alder body and retails for $1,499. The HN Series are neck-thru-body designs. The **HN-GS** Standard is a double cutaway with mahogany body and retails for $1,859. The **HN-GS Elite** has an exotic top, ebony fingerboard, and retails for $2,459. The HS Series are set-neck designs. The **HS-GL Standard Arch Top** has a single cutaway with a mahogany body and retails for $2,299. The **HS-GL Elite Arch Top** has a multi-laminate neck with maple, purple heart, and padauk with an ebony fingerboard, mahogany body with figured top and retails for $3,259. The **HS-GP Standard Arch Top** has a double cutaway mahogany body and retails for $2,499. The **HS-GP Elite Arch Top** has a multi-laminate neck with maple, purple heart, and padauk with an ebony fingerboard, mahogany body with figured top and retails for $3,559. The **HS-GJ Jazz Arch Top** has a single cutaway mahogany body and retails for $3,699.

The **Hillster** is a double cutaway alder body with a maple neck and Seymour Duncan pickups. This model was introduced in 2005 and retails for $1,899.

ELECTRIC BASS

Hill produced several different models and configurations in electric bass. The HB Series are bolt-on models. The **HB-B4 Standard** is a four-string configuration alder or swamp ash body and retails for $2,199. The **HB-B4 Elite** has a multi-laminate neck and a figured top with walnut back and retails for $2,799. The **HB-B5 Standard** is a five-string configuration alder or swamp ash body and retails for $2,599. The **HB-B5 Elite** has a multi-laminate neck and a figured top with walnut back and retails for $3,299.

The HN Series feature neck-through-body designs. The **HN-B4 Standard** has a mahogany body and retails for $2,499. The **HN-B4 Elite** has a multi-laminate neck with padauk and purple heart stripes, a walnut core body, figured top and back, ebony fingerboard and retails for $3,299. The **HN-B5 Standard** has a mahogany body and retails for $2,999. The **HN-B5 Elite** has a multi-laminate neck with padauk and purple heart stripes, a walnut core body, figured top and back, ebony fingerboard and retails for $3,899. The **HN-B6 Standard** has a mahogany body and retails for $3,799. The **HN-B6 Elite** has a multi-laminate neck with padauk and purple heart stripes, a walnut core body, figured top and back, ebony fingerboard and retails for $4,699. The **HN-B7 Elite** is the same as the HN-B6 Elite except in seven-string configuration and retails for $5,499.

The **Motto** is a double cutaway alder body with a maple neck and Barolini pickups. This model was introduced in 2005 and retails for $1,899.

HILL GUITARS

Instruments previously built in Cleveland, OH from 1989 to 1994.

The Hill guitar company was founded by luthier Jon Hill in 1989. Hill Guitars produced many guitars and basses mostly custom shop, one of a kind type pieces. There were over 300 instruments built by 1994.

In 1994 Hill's extensive background in guitar building and design became an asset when he joined the re-formed Dean Guitars and moved its shop to Plant City, Florida in fall of 1995. As Vice President of Dean he was responsible for production which went on until early 1997, when the company disbanded. Hill moved back to Cleveland and started building guitars again as Hill Custom Guitars in 2000 (see Hill Custom Guitars).

ELECTRIC

Hill Guitars originally offered eight models of U.S. built guitars that ranged in price from $799 to $2,999; and four models of basses (each available in 4, 5, and 6-string configurations) that ranged from $1,197 to $2,120.

HOFNER

Instruments produced beginning 1887-1949 in Schonbach, and 1950-date in Bubenreuth, and Hagenau, Germany. Distributed in the U.S. by The Music Group in Sun Valley, CA. Previously distributed by Boosey & Hawkes Musical Instruments, Inc. of Libertyville, IL.

The Hofner instrument making company was originally founded by Karl Hofner in 1887. Originally located in Schonbach (in the area now called Czechoslovakia), Hofner produced fine stringed instruments such as violins, cellos, and double basses. Karl's two sons, Josef and Walter, joined the company in 1919 and 1921 (respectively), and expanded Hofner's market to North American and the Far East. Production of guitars began in 1925, in the area that was to become East Germany during the "Cold War" era. Following World War II, the Hofner family moved to West Germany and established a new factory in Bubenreuth in 1948. By 1950, new production facilities in Bubenreuth and Hanenau were staffed by over 300 Hofner employees.

The first Hofner electric archtop debuted in the 1950s. While various guitar models were available in Germany since 1949 (and earlier, if you take in the over 100 years of company history), Hofners were not officially exported to England until Selmer of London took over distributorship in 1958. Furthermore, Selmer's British models were specified for the U.K. only - and differ from those available in the German market.

The concept of a violin-shaped bass was developed by Walter Hofner (Karl's son) in 1956. Walter's idea to electrically amplify a bass was new for the company, but the hollow body model itself was based on family design traditions. The **500/1** model made its debut at the Frankfurt Music Fair the same year. While most people may recognize that model as the Beatle Bass popularized by Paul McCartney, the Hofner company also produced a wide range of solid, semi-hollow, and archtop designs that were good quality instruments.

Until 1997, Hofner products were distributed by EMMC (Entertainment Music Marketing Corporation, which focused on distributing the 500/1 Reissue violin electric bass. In 1998, distribution for Hofner products in the U.S. market was changed to Boosey & Hawkes Musical Instruments, Inc. of Libertyville, Illinois. Boosey & Hawkes wasted no time in introducing three jazz-style semi-hollow guitar models, which includes a **New President** (Model HP-55) model guitar. Boosey & Hawkes is also distributing Thomastik guitar and bass strings along with the Hofner accessories, (Hofner history source: Gordon Giltrap and Neville Marten, The Hofner Guitar - A History; and Tony Bacon, The Ultimate Guitar Book, Current Hofner product information courtesy Rob Olsen, Boosey & Hawkes Musical Instruments, Inc.).

**Hill HBGT
courtesy Hill Custom Guitars**

MODEL DATING INFORMATION

Hofner began installing adjustable truss-rods in their guitar necks beginning in 1960. Any model prior to that year will not have a truss-rod cover.

Between the late 1950s and early 1970s, Hofner produced a number of semi-hollow or hollowbody electric guitars and basses that were in demand in England. English distribution was handled by **Selmer** of London, and specified models that were imported. In some cases, English models are certainly different from the domestic models offered in Germany. There will always be interest in Hofners; either Paul McCartney's earlier association with the **Beatle Bass** or the thrill of a **Committee** or **Golden Hofner**.

From the late 1960s to the early 1980s, the company produced a number of guitar models based on popular American designs. In addition, Hofner also built a number of better quality original models such as **Alpha**, **Compact**, and **Razorwood** from the late 1970s to the mid 1980s. However, you have to know ´em before you tag ´em. The *Blue Book of Electric Guitars* recommends discussions with your favorite vintage dealers (it´s easier to figure them out when they´re in front of you). Other inquiries can be addressed either to Boosey & Hawkes as to models nomenclature and market value.

Some models listed have not been individually priced. In general, acoustic electric archtop models will range from $800-$1,100, semi-acoustic electric archtops from $900-$1,500, Hollow body basses from $1,000-$1,700 and solid body basses from $500-$750.

Demand is highest in the category of "Violin" basses and weakest in the category of solid body basses. The archtop models are also quite desirable with jazz artists who appreciate quality vintage instruments.

Hofner (and Boosey & Hawkes) is currently offering a wider range of models outside of the U.S. market. In fact, Hofner has 4 different series of acoustic guitars that are not represented below: the child-sized Jugend-/Schulergitarren (HS Series), classical-style **Konzertgitarren** (HF Series), environment-friendly **Green Line** (HGL Series), and the upscale **Meistergitarren** (HM Series). Electric models include the **Jazzica Standard** and **Jazzica Special**, **Vice President**, and **New President** , as well as the **Nightingale Standard** and the **Nightingale Special**. Electric bass models are the same.

ELECTRIC ARCHTOP: HOLLOW BODY MODELS

MODEL 450E - archtop hollowbody, laminated maple top, back and sides, rosewood fingerboard, white celluloid band position markers, bound top, celluloid pickguard, 3-per-side tuners, f-holes, lyre tailpiece, 1 pickup mounted at the fingerboard, no controls, available in sunburst finish and wine red finish on late production models, mfg. 1954-1984.

MODEL 455/S/E1 - archtop hollow body, laminated maple top and back, black and white celluloid bindings on top, back and f-holes, red-white celluloid inlays on the headstock, 3-per-side tuners, white pickguard, lyre tailpiece, celluloid band position markers. 1 adjustable pickup, volume, 3 sliding tone switches, available in Cherry Red and Blonde (Model 455/S/b/E1) finishes, mfg. early to late 1960s.

MODEL 456/S/B/E2 - archtop hollow body, single cutaway design, flame maple back and sides, bound top, back, fingerboard and f-holes, black pickguard, 3-per-side tuners, red, black, or white headstock, lyre tailpiece, celluloid band position markers, 2 adjustable pickups, 2 volume controls and 3 sliding tone switches or 2 volume and 2 tone controls, available in Blonde finish, mfg. circa 1961-62.

MODEL 457/S/E1 - archtop hollowbody, single cutaway design, spruce top, flame maple back and sides, bound top, back, fingerboard and f-holes, headstock decorated with gold plated clef and staff, 3-per-side tuners, celluloid band position markers, white pickguard, 1 adjustable pickup, 1 volume control and 3 sliding tone controls, lyre tailpiece, available in Brown Sunburst finish, mfg. circa 1961-1970.

MODEL 457/S/E2 - same as Model 457/S/E1 except has 2 adjustable pickups andand either 2 volume controls and 3 sliding tone switches or 2 volume and 2 tone controls, available in Brown Sunburst and Blonde (Model 457/S/b/E2) finishes, mfg. circa 1961-1970.

**Hofner 500/2 Bass
Blue Book Publications Archive**

GRADING	100% MINT	98% NEAR MINT	95% EXC+	90% EXC	80% VG+	70% VG	60% G

MODEL 462/S/E1 - archtop hollow body, selected spruce top, flame maple back and sides, 2-piece tailpiece, eliptical sound holes, bound top, back, fingerboard and f-holes, 3-per-side tuners, headstock has gold plated clef and staff, celluloid band fingerboard inlays (1 wide and 2 narrow), 1 adjustable pickup, 1 volume and 3 sliding tone switches, available in light brown varnish finish, mfg. circa 1954-1970.

MODEL 462/S/E3 - archtop hollow body, same as Model 462/S/E3 except has 3 adjustable pickups and 1 volume and 3 tone controls, pickup selector switch, available in Light Brown Varnish finish, mfg. circa 1954-1970.

MODEL 463/S/E2 - archtop hollow body, single cutaway design, sapeli mahogany back and sides, selected spruce top, bound mahogany fingerboard, wooden inlays and celluloid bindings on top and back, harp tailpiece, 3-per-side tuners, dark pickguard. 2 adjustable pickups, 2 volume and 2 tone controls, available in Shaded Brown finish, mfg. circa 1961-1970.

MODEL 465/S/E2 - archtop hollow body, single cutaway design, well selected fine spruce top, rosewood back and sides, wood and celluloid bindings on top, back, fingerboard and f-holes, mother-of-pearl headstock inlays (bell-fowers) and fingerboard position markers (1 narrow rectangle flanked by 2 pentagons that resemble arrowheads), ebony fingerboard, 3-per-side tuners, lucite pickguard, 2 pickups, early 1960s models had 2 volume controls and 3 sliding tone controls while late '60s models had 2 volume and 2 tone controls, lyre tailpiece, available in Light Brown finish, mfg. circa 1961-1970.

MODEL 470/S/E2 - archtop hollow body, single cutaway design, selected spruce top, best quality flame maple back and sides, wooden flower inlays on back, ebony fingerboard and headstock, gold plated hardware, bound top, back, fingerboard and f-holes, 3-per-side tuners, mother-of-pearl headstock inlays (Lillies) and position markers (1 narrow rectangle flanked by 2 pentagons that resemble arrowheads), lucite pickguard, 2 pickups, late 1950s models had 2 volume and 3 sliding tone controls. Mid '60s models had 3 sliding pickup selector switches and 2 volume and 1 tone control, available in High Polish Blonde finish, mfg. circa 1959-1994.

	N/A	$1,200	$1,050	$925	$800	$700	$600

MODEL 471/E2 - large archtop hollow body, selected spruce top, flame maple back and sides, florentine cutaway, celluloid binding on top and back, ebony fingerboard with mother-of-pearl inlays, 3-per-side tuners, black pickguard, lyre tailpiece, 2 pickups, 2 volume and 2 tone controls, pickup selector switch, available in Blonde finish, mfg. circa 1969-1977.

	N/A	$1,100	$950	$825	$700	$600	$500

MODEL AL2 - archtop hollow body, single cutaway design, spruce top, flame maple back and sides, wooden inlays on back, bound top and back, mother-of-pearl position markers, 1 pickup in the neck position, 1 volume, 1 tone control, 3-per-side tuners, lyre tailpiece, could be ordered with a piezo pickup under the bridge or with stereo output, available in Blonde and Shaded Brown finishes, mfg. 1978-1986.

MODEL AZ - archtop hollow body, single cutaway design, solid spruce top, flame maple back and sides, mother-of-pearl split block position markers, bound top and back, chrome hardware, lyre tailpiece, wooden pickguard, f-holes, 3-per-side tuners, available in Black and Antique Brown finishes, mfg. 1982-1991.

MODEL AZ AWARD - archtop hollow body, same as Model AZ except has V-style tailpiece, ebony fingerboard, gold plated hardware, available in Blonde and Bordeaux Red Sunburst finishes, mfg. 1982-1991.

VERYTHIN CLASSIC (MODEL HVC) - double cutaway semi-hollow bound body, German spruce top, highly flamed African maple back and sides, asymmetrically profiled European maple neck, 22-fret ebony fingerboard with genuine mother-of-pearl inlays, gold plated hardware, solid spruce tone block, individually carved and fitted by hand for a precise match to the top and back, uses no tone bars, specially designed Hofner/Kent Armstrong pickups, contemporary f-hole design, 2 volume and 2 tone controls, toggle switch, lyre tailpiece, gold hardware, available in Natural, Black, and Sunburst finishes, current mfg.

MSR   **$2,698**

JAZZICA CUSTOM (MODEL HJCL/HJ5-I) - single rounded cutaway semi-hollow bound body, solid carved German spruce top, laminated African Anigree back/sides, 2 bound cat's-eye f-holes, European hard rock maple neck, 25.75 in. scale, 24-fret bound ebony fingerboard with mother-of-pearl block inlay, 3-per-side Schaller tuners, matching finish peghead, adjustable ebony bridge/raised metal tailpiece, gold hardware, Hofner/Kent Armstrong floating pickup, volume/tone controls, available in Natural finish, current mfg.

MSR   **$3,190**

NEW PRESIDENT (MODEL HNP/HP55-I) - single rounded cutaway semi-hollow bound body, solid carved German spruce top, laminated flamed African Anigree back/sides, 2 f-holes, European hard rock maple neck, 25.75 in. scale, 24-fret bound ebony fingerboard with mother-of-pearl block inlay, 3-per-side Schaller tuners, bound blackface peghead with mother-of-pearl design inlay, adjustable ebony bridge/raised metal tailpiece, gold hardware, raised ebony pickguard, Hofner/Kent Armstrong 'floating' pickup, volume control, available in Natural finish, current mfg.

MSR   **$3,096**

VICE PRESIDENT (MODEL HVP) - single rounded cutaway semi-hollow bound body, solid handcarved German AAA spruce top, f-holes, highly flamed African maple back and sides, asymmetrically profiled European maple neck, 24-fret ebony fingerboard with genuine mother-of-pearl imlays, nickel plated hardware, mother-of-pearl "lily" inlay on headstock, fully adjustable Hofner/Kent Armstrong floating pickup with individually adjustable pole pieces, non-routed bridge and neck pickups, 3-way pickup selector switch, 2 tone and 2 volume controls, a single bass tonebar braces the top, available in Sunburst and Black finishes, disc.

Last MSR was $2,695.

NIGHTINGALE (MODEL HN35-I) - dual rounded cutaway semi-hollow bound body, laminated bird's-eye maple top/back/sides, 2 bound f-holes, solid German spruce sustain block, European hard rock maple neck, 25.75 in. scale, 24-fret bound ebony fingerboard with mother-of-pearl block inlay, 3-per-side Schaller tuners, bound blackface peghead with mother-of-pearl design inlay, tune-o-matic bridge/stop tailpiece with fine tuners, gold hardware, 2 Classic '57 humbucker pickups, 2 volume/2 tone controls, master volume control, 3-way pickup selector, stereo outputs, available in Antique Gold Sunburst finish, disc.

Last MSR was $3,350.

ELECTRIC ARCHTOP: SEMI-HOLLOW BODY MODELS

MODEL 125 - single cutaway, arched top and back, celluloid bound top and back, 3-per-side tuners, lyre tailpiece, dot position markers, 1 adjustable pickup, 1 volume and 1 tone control, black pickguard, available in Shaded Brown finish and Blonde (Model 125/b/E1), mfg. 1954-1970.

	N/A	$500	$400	$325	$250	$200	$150

MODEL 126/E2 - same as Model 125 except has 2 pickups, 2 volume and 2 tone controls, available in shaded brown finish, mfg. 1954-1970, also available in Blonde finish (Model 126/b/E2), mfg. 1956-1967.

	N/A	$600	$500	$400	$325	$250	$175

GRADING	100% MINT	98% NEAR MINT	95% EXC+	90% EXC	80% VG+	70% VG	60% G

MODEL 128/E2 - same basic design as Model 125 except has flame maple back and sides, bound fingerboard, mother-of-pearl headstock inlays and fingerboard position markers, available in Gold/Red Shaded finish with black sides and Blonde finish (Model 128/b/E2), mfg. 1961-1970.

	N/A	$700	$600	$500	$400	$300	$200

MODEL 459 (II) - violin-shaped body, 3-per-side tuners, celluloid band position markers, lyre tailpiece, 2 pickups, white pickguard, bound top, available in Brown Burst finish, mfg. 1967-1970.

	N/A	$1,500	$1,300	$1,150	$1,000	$900	$800

MODEL 4572 (II) - arched top, double cutaway design, 2 in. thick body, 3-per-side tuners, white celluloid binding on top and f-holes, 2 pickups, 2 volume and 2 tone controls with toggle switch or 1 volume and 2 tone controls, f-holes, black pickguard, available in sunburst finish, mfg. 1969-1988.

	N/A	$750	$650	$550	$475	$400	$325

MODEL 4574 - arched top, double cutaway design, flame maple back and sides, spruce top, 1.75 in. body, bound top, back and f-holes, 3-per-side tuners, celluloid band position markers, mother-of-pearl headstock inlays (bell flowers), 2 pickups, a variety of electronics available, available in Wine Red Shaded finish or Brown with Black sides, mfg. 1961-1976.

	N/A	$850	$750	$650	$550	$475	$400

MODEL 4577 - arched top, single florentine cutaway, 3-per-side tuners, 3 dot position markers, f-holes, 2 pickups, 1 volume and 1 tone control and a toggle switch, lyre tailpiece with vibrato bar, black pickguard, available in Brown Burst finish, mfg. 1967-1992.

	N/A	$900	$800	$700	$600	$500	$400

T2S - arched top, double cutaway design, flamed maple body with sustain block, bound top, back and f-holes, mother-of-pearl position markers, two 052 pickups, stop tailpiece, 3-per-side tuners, black pickguard, available in Walnut Brown and Sahara Yellow, mfg. 1978-1980.

**Hofner 459
courtesy Debbie Nix**

ELECTRIC BASS: HOLLOW BODY MODELS

MODEL 500/1 - violin-shaped body, spruce top, maple back and sides, 2 pickups, 2 volume and 2 tone controls on early models, 2 volume and 3 sliding tone controls on production since circa 1959, lyre tailpiece, dot position markers, 2-per-side tuners, available in Shaded Brown finish, mfg. 1956-present.

1956-1961	N/A	$3,500	$3,100	$2,700	$2,300	$2,200	$1,700
1962	N/A	$3,000	$2,600	$2,300	$2,000	$1,700	$1,500
1963	N/A	$2,800	$2,400	$2,100	$1,800	$1,600	$1,400
1964	N/A	$2,600	$2,200	$1,900	$1,700	$1,500	$1,300
1965	N/A	$2,400	$2,100	$1,800	$1,600	$1,400	$1,200
1966-1969	N/A	$2,000	$1,700	$1,500	$1,300	$1,100	$900
1970-1979	N/A	$1,500	$1,300	$1,100	$950	$800	$700
1980-1989	N/A	$1,200	$1,050	$900	$800	$700	$600
1990-1994	N/A	$1,000	$850	$725	$600	$500	$400

MODEL 500/2 - single cutaway design similar to Model 125, spruce top, maple back and sides, lyre tailpiece, 2-per-side tuners, dot position markers, 2 pickups, 2 volume controls and 3 sliding tone switches, white pickguard, available in Shaded Brown finish, mfg. 1965-1970.

1965-1966	N/A	$1,800	$1,500	$1,300	$1,100	$950	$800
1967-1970	N/A	$1,500	$1,250	$1,050	$900	$750	$600

MODEL 500/4 - arched top, double cutaway, f-holes, lyre tailpiece, 2-per-side tuners, dot position markers, 2 pickups, 3 rotary controls and a toggle switch, black pickguard, available in Brown Burst finish, mfg. 1969-1988.

1969-1979	N/A	$1,500	$1,300	$1,150	$900	$750	$600
1980-1989	N/A	$1,000	$850	$725	$600	$500	$400

MODEL 500/5 - arched top, single cutaway design, f-holes, 2-per-side tuners, lyre tailpiece, bound top, 2 pickups, 2 volume/2 tone controls, dot position markers, white pickguard, mother-of-pearl headstock inlay (lillies), available in Shaded Brown finish, mfg. 1961-1979.

1961-1965	N/A	$2,000	$1,700	$1,500	$1,300	$1,100	$900
1966-1969	N/A	$1,500	$1,300	$1,150	$900	$750	$600
1970-1979	N/A	$1,200	$1,050	$900	$800	$700	$600

MODEL 500/8 - arched top, double cutaway with florentine style horns, f-holes, celluloid band position markers, 2-per-side tuners, mother-of-pearl headstock inlays (lillies), 2 pickups, 2 volume/2 tone controls, toggle switch, black pickguard, available in Brown Burst finish, mfg. 1969-1977.

VINTAGE 63 VIOLIN BASS (MODEL 500/1-63, BEATLE BASS) - violin-style bound hollow body, arched solid German spruce top, laminated flame maple back/sides, 3-piece laminated maple/beech neck, 22-fret bound rosewood fingerboard with pearl dot inlay, adjustable rosewood bridge/trapeze tailpiece, bound blackface peghead, 2-per-side tuners, nickel hardware, raised pearloid pickguard with engraved logo, 2 "Staple Top" humbucker pickups, 2 volume controls, Rhythm/Solo tone selector switch, Bass On/Treble On pickup selector switches, controls mounted on a pearloid plate, available in Antique Brown Sunburst, Trans. Red, or Trans. Blue, current mfg.

	MSR	$2,570		$1,950	$1,750	$1,600	$1,450	$1,300	$1,150	$1,000

This model is available in a left-handed configuration with the same specifications.

**Hofner Vintage 63 Violin Bass
courtesy Dave Rogers
Dave's Guitar Shop**

GRADING	100% MINT	98% NEAR MINT	95% EXC+	90% EXC	80% VG+	70% VG	60% G

VINTAGE ´62 REISSUE BASS (MODEL 500/1-62) - violin style bound hollow body, arched solid German spruce top, laminated flame maple back and sides, 2 piece neck, rosewood fingerboard, 22-fret neck, pearl dot position markers, trapeze tailpiece, pearloid pickguard, bound top and back, 2-per-side strip tuners, nickel hardware, 2 "Staple Top" humbucker pickups, 2 volume controls, Rhythm/Solo tone selector switch, Bass On/Treble On pickup selector switches, available in Antique Brown Sunburst finish, based on Paul McCartney´s 1962 Violin Bass, current mfg.

	MSR	$2,774		$2,100	$1,900	$1,700	$1,550	$1,400	$1,250	$1,100

DELUXE VIOLIN BASS (MODEL 5000/1) - violin-style bound hollow body, arched German spruce top, tortoise body binding, laminated flame maple back/sides, solid European hard rock maple neck, 22-fret bound ebony fingerboard with pearl double dot inlay, adjustable ebony bridge/raised trapeze tailpiece, bound blackface peghead with mother-of-pearl diamond inlay, 2-per-side tuners, gold hardware, raised black pickguard with engraved logo, 2 "Staple Top" humbucker pickups, 2 volume controls, Rhythm/Solo tone selector switch, Bass On/Treble On pickup selector switches, controls mounted on a black plate, available in Natural finish, current mfg.

	MSR	$2,994		$2,250	$2,000	$1,800	$1,600	$1,450	$1,300	$1,150

ELECTRIC BASS: SOLID BODY MODELS

MODEL 182 - double cutaway, 1 piece maple neck with rosewood fingerboard, 4-on-a-side tuners, dot position markers, 2 pickups, 2 volume controls and 3 sliding tone controls, black pickguard, available in Red, Ivory, Ice Blue, or Shaded Brown finish, mfg. 1962-1985.

MODEL 183 - shaped similar to Stratocaster, 4-on-a-side tuners, dot position markers, 2 pickups, 2 volume controls and 1 tone switch, white pickgurad, mfg. 1975-1983.

MODEL 185 - offset double cutaway design, 4-on-a-side tuners, celluloid band position markers, 2 pickups, 2 volume/2 tone controls, pickup control switches, black pickguard, mfg. 1962-1983.

MODEL 186 - single cutaway body similar to Telecaster, 4-on-a-side tuners, dot position markers, 2 pickups, 1 volume and 1 tone control, pickup selector switch, covered bridge, available in ivory finish, mfg. 1971-73.

MODEL 187 (I) - double sutaway design similar to SG, solid mahogany body, 2-per-side tuners, mother-of-pearl block position markers and headstock inlays, 2 pickups, 2 volume and 2 tone controls, toggle switch, white pickguard, covered bridge, mfg. 1971-72.

MODEL 188 (I) - 6-string bass, offset double cutaway design, 4/2 tuner configuration, celluloid band position markers, 3 pickups, tremolo bridge. Mfg. 1963 only. Also available as Model 188 (II), similar to Model 188 (I) except 6 tuners on one side, mfg. 1964-1970.

HOHNER

Instruments currently produced in Korea, although earlier models from the 1970s were built in Japan. Currently distributed in the U.S. by HSS (a Division of Hohner, Inc.), located in Richmond, VA.

The Hohner company was founded in 1857, and is currently the world´s largest manufacturer and distributor of harmonicas. Hohner offers a wide range of solidly constructed musical instruments. The company has stayed contemporary with the current market by licensing designs and parts from Ned Steinberger, Claim Guitars (Germany), and Wilkinson hardware.

In addition to their guitar models, Hohner also distributes Sonor drums, Sabian cymbals, and Hohner educational percussion instruments. For Revelation or Rockford brand guitars see their respective series in this book.

ELECTRIC: MISC

CARIBBEAN PEARL - single rounded cutaway maple body, bolt-on maple neck, 22-fret rosewood fingerboard with pearloid dot inlay, tune-o-matic bridge/stop tailpiece, 3-per-side die-cast tuners, gold hardware, 2 covered humbucker pickups, volume/tone controls, 3-way selector switch, available in Pearl Berry Red (PBR), Pearl Island Blue (PIB), or Pearl Oyster Black (POB) Ivoroid Top (and matching headstock) finishes with matching stained (Blue, Red, Black) backs, mfg. 1998-2002.

			$450	$375	$325	$275	$225	$175	$125

Last MSR was $599.

G3T - Steinberger-style headless maple body, through-body maple neck, 24-fret rosewood fingerboard with white dot inlay, Steinberger vibrato, black hardware, 2 single coil/humbucker EMG pickups, volume/tone control, 3 mini switches, passive filter in tone control, available in Black, Grey Nickel Satin, or White finishes, mfg. 1990-present.

MSR	$799		$575	$495	$425	$375	$325	$250	$195

Add $60 for left-handed version (G3TLH).

In 1994, White finish was discontinued.

The Jack Guitar - similar to G3T, except has asymmetrical double cutaway body, available in Black or Metallic Red finishes, disc. 1994.

	N/A		$500	$425	$375	$325	$275	$225

Last MSR was $765.

HT CST - single cutaway alder body, white pickguard, bolt-on maple neck, 22-fret maple fingerboard with black dot inlay, fixed bridge, 6-on-a-side tuners, chrome hardware, 2 single coil pickups, volume/tone controls, 3-way switch, available in Sunburst or Trans. Violet finishes, disc.

		$395	$350	$300	$275	$225	$175	$125

Last MSR was $525.

Add $50 for ATN active electronics and pearloid pickguard with Black finish (Model HT CST AP).

JT60 - offset double cutaway maple body, tortoise pickguard, bolt-on maple neck, 22-fret rosewood fingerboard with pearl dot inlay, standard vibrato, 6-on-a-side tuners, chrome hardware, 3 single coil pickups, 2 volume/tone controls, 5-position switch, advance tone passive electronics, available in Ivory or Sea Foam Green finishes, mfg. 1992-96.

	N/A		$325	$275	$235	$195	$165	$135

Last MSR was $480.

GRADING	100% MINT	98% NEAR MINT	95% EXC+	90% EXC	80% VG+	70% VG	60% G

OSC - single cutaway solid ash lightweight body, bolt-on maple neck, 22-fret maple fingerboard with dot inlay, three-per-side Grover tuners, fixed bridge, three single coil pickups, three knobs, five-way switch, brushed chrome hardware, available in Trans. Amber, Trans. Black, or Trans. Red finishes, new 2005.

MSR	$649	$490	$425	$375	$325	$275	$225	$175

OSC Archtop - similar to the OSC, except has an arched flame maple top, and Tesla Plasma pickups in H/S/H configuration, available in Cherry Sunburst, Natural Satin, or Trans. Black finishes, new 2005.

MSR	$679	$510	$450	$400	$350	$300	$250	$200

TABU - double cutaway solid mahogany body with arched quilted maple top, set mahogany neck, 24-fret rosewood fingerboard with dot inlay, matching headstock with three-per-side Grover tuners, fixed bridge, STB, two Tesla Plasma II humbucker pickups, four knobs, three-way switch, chrome hardware, available in Cherry Sunburst, Trans. Blue, or Trans. Green finishes, new 2005.

MSR	$749	$575	$500	$425	$375	$325	$275	$225

Tabu DC - similar to the Tabu, except has no quilted top or binding, 22-fret fingerboard with Batman inlay, stop tailpiece, and exposed pickups, available in Natural, Trans. Black, or Yellow finishes, new 2005.

MSR	$699	$525	$450	$400	$350	$300	$250	$200

ELECTRIC: CLASSIC CITY SERIES

THE BATON ROUGE - single cutaway alder body with contoured top, bolt-on maple neck, 22-fret rosewood fingerboard with pearloid dot inlay, wraparound bridge, blackface peghead, 3-per-side die-cast tuners, chrome hardware, 2 exposed pole piece humbucker pickups, volume/tone controls, 3-way toggle selector, available in Butterscotch or Cherry Sunburst finishes, mfg. 1998-2002.

	$250	$225	$190	$150	$120	$95	$75

Last MSR was $359.

THE SPRINGFIELD - similar to the Baton Rouge, except features 3 single coil pickups, classic-style tremolo bridge, white pickguard, available in Black and Uptown Blue finishes, mfg. 1998-2002.

	$225	$195	$170	$130	$105	$85	$60

Last MSR was $309.

THE BIRMINGHAM - slightly offset double cutaway alder body with contoured top, bolt-on maple neck, 22-fret rosewood fingerboard with pearloid dot inlay, wraparound bridge, natural finish peghead, 6-on-a-side die-cast tuners, chrome hardware, 2 exposed pole piece humbucker pickups, volume/tone controls, 3-way toggle selector, available in Black or Candy Apple Red finishes, mfg. 1998-2002.

	$240	$215	$185	$145	$115	$90	$70

Last MSR was $339.

THE RENO - similar to the Birmingham, except features single coil/humbucker pickups, tele-style fixed bridge, black pickguard, available in Vintage Sunburst finish, mfg. 1998-2002.

	$225	$195	$170	$130	$105	$85	$60

Last MSR was $309.

ELECTRIC: HL & HS SERIES

HL59 - single sharp cutaway solid maple body, bound figured maple top, black pickguard, mahogany neck, 22-fret bound rosewood fingerboard with pearl crown inlay, tune-o-matic bridge/stop tailpiece, bound peghead with pearl pineapple/logo inlay, 3-per-side tuners, chrome or gold hardware, 2 humbucker pickups, 2 volume/tone controls, 3-way switch, available in Black, Cherry Sunburst, Gold Top, Ivory, or Violin finishes, mfg. 1990-96.

	N/A	$400	$325	$275	$225	$180	$140

Last MSR was $625.

Add $35 for left-handed version (Model HL59LH).

HL60 - single sharp cutaway maple body, black pickguard, mahogany neck, 22-fret bound rosewood fingerboard with pearl dot inlay, tune-o-matic bridge/stop tailpiece, blackface peghead with pearl coconut/logo inlay, 3-per-side tuners, chrome hardware, 2 single coil pickups, 2 volume/2 tone controls, 3-position switch, available in Cherry Red finish, mfg. 1994-96.

	N/A	$350	$300	$250	$210	$170	$130

Last MSR was $575.

HL90 - similar to the HL59, except features a bound maple/mahogany body, white pickguard, bound peghead with pearl diamond/logo inlay, 3-per-side tuners, chrome hardware, 2 PAF pickups, available in Gold Top finish, mfg. 1992-96.

	N/A	$450	$400	$350	$300	$250	$200

Last MSR was $690.

HLP75 - similar to HL59, except has white pickguard, bolt-on neck, diamond peghead inlay, available in Antique Sunburst and Black finishes, mfg. 1990-91.

	N/A	$275	$225	$175	$150	$125	$100

Last MSR was $375.

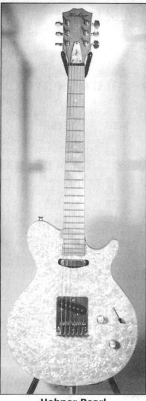

**Hohner Pearl
courtesy Mark Rice**

**Hohner HL59
courtesy Hohner**

GRADING	100% MINT	98% NEAR MINT	95% EXC+	90% EXC	80% VG+	70% VG	60% G

ELECTRIC: REVOLUTION SERIES

REVOLUTION STANDARD (HRGSTDII) - double offset cutaway basswood body, maple bolt on neck, 24-fret rosewood fingerboard with dot inlay, 6-on-one-side tuners, black pickguard, 2 Humucking pickups, three knobs (v, 2 tones), 3-way switch, tremolo unit, chrome hardware, available in Black Metallic or Blue Metallic Satin, mfg. 2002-present.

	MSR	$299	$225	$190	$175	$150	$125	$95	$75

This model is also available with 2 single coil and 1 humbucker pickups, available in Gray Metallic Satin or Red Metallic Satin finishes (Model HRGSTDIII).

REVOLUTION DELUXE (HRGDLXII) - double offset cutaway basswood body, maple bolt on neck, 24-fret rosewood fingerboard with dot inlay, 6-on-one-side tuners, 2 Mighty Mite Humbucker pickups, three knobs (v, 2 tones), 3-way switch, coil tap, Wilkinson tremolo unit, platinum nickel or cosmo black hardware, available in Blue Burst or Black Hammered, mfg. 2002-present.

	MSR	$499	$350	$310	$275	$240	$205	$175	$150

This model is also available with 2 single coil and 1 humbucker pickups, available in Antique Violin Dark or Cherry Sunburst finishes (Model HRGDLXIII).

ELECTRIC: STANDARD SERIES

HS35 (SE35) - semi-hollow body, maple bound top/back/sides, black pickguard, mahogany neck, 22-fret rosewood fingerboard with pearl dot inlay, tune-o-matic bridge/stop tailpiece, pearl pineapple/logo peghead inlay, chrome hardware, 2 humbucker pickups, 2 volume/tone controls, 3-position switch, available in Natural, Cherry Red, or Tobacco Sunburst finishes, mfg. 1990-present.

	MSR	$499	$375	$325	$275	$235	$195	$160	$130

Early versions of this model may feature gold hardware, and Black, Sunburst, or White finishes. In 2005, block inlays were introduced.

HS40 (SE400) - single round cutaway hollow body, maple bound top/back/sides, f-holes, black pickguard, mahogany neck, 22-fret bound rosewood fingerboard with pearl block inlay, tune-o-matic bridge/trapeze tailpiece, bound peghead with pearl pineapple/logo inlay, 2 humbucker pickups, 2 volume/tone controls, 3-position switch, available in Natural, Tobacco Sunburst, Trans. Red, or Vintage Sunburst finishes, mfg. 1992-present.

	MSR	$599	$450	$375	$325	$275	$235	$190	$160

HS45 - single round cutaway hollow body, maple bound top/back/sides, f-holes, black pickguard, mahogany neck, 22-fret bound rosewood fingerboard with pearl block inlay, tune-o-matic bridge/trapeze tailpiece, bound peghead with pearl pineapple/logo inlay, 2 humbucker pickups, four knobs, three-position switch, available in Natural, Trans. Red, or Vintage Sunburst finishes, new 2005.

	MSR	$649	$490	$400	$350	$300	$250	$210	$180

HS59 (ST59) - double offset cutaway alder body, white pickguard, bolt-on maple neck, 22-fret maple fingerboard with black dot inlay, standard vibrato, 6-on-a-side tuners, chrome hardware, 3 single coil pickups, volume/2 tone controls, 5-way switch, available in Black and Sunburst finishes, mfg. 1990-98.

			$375	$325	$275	$225	$175	$150	$125

Last MSR was $479.

Add $20 for left-handed configuration with Sunburst finish (Model HS59LH). Add $20 for pearloid pickguard with Black or Sunburst finish (Model HS59P). Add $35 for ATN active electronics with Trans. Blue or Trans. Red finishes (Model HS59A). Add $55 for ATN active electronics and pearloid pickguard with Trans. Blue or Trans. Red finishes (Model HS59AP).

HS65 - rounded single cutaway maple body, flamed maple top, bolt-on maple neck, 22-fret rosewood fingerboard with dot inlay, tremolo, 3-per-side tuners, gold hardware, 2 single coil/humbucker pickups, volume/tone controls, 5-way switch, available in Cherry Sunburst finish, mfg. 1997-98.

		$375	$325	$275	$225	$175	$150	$125

Last MSR was $479.

HS75 - similar to HS65, except features bird's-eye maple top, set-in neck, chrome hardware, 2 humbuckers, 3-way switch, available in Blonde finish, mfg. 1997-98.

		$400	$350	$300	$250	$200	$175	$150

Last MSR was $499.

HS85 - similar to HS65, except features pearloid top, 2 single coil pickups, 3-way switch, available in White Pearloid finish, mfg. 1997-98.

		$450	$400	$350	$300	$250	$200	$150

Last MSR was $599.

HS90 - double offset cutaway maple body, bolt-on maple neck, 24-fret rosewood fingerboard with dot inlay, tremolo, 6-on-a-side tuners, gold hardware, 2 single coil/humbucker pickups, volume/tone controls, 5-way switch, available in Natural Satin finish, mfg. 1997-2000.

		$425	$375	$325	$275	$225	$200	$150

Last MSR was $549.

HJ3 - single cutaway semi-hollow mahogany body with figured maple top, 2 f-holes, B/N/H binding, set mahogany neck, 22-fret rosewood fingerboard with trapezoid inlays, black headstock with three-per-side tuners, tune-o-matic bridge, stop tailpiece, cream pickguard, two Tesla humbucker pickups, four knobs, three-way switch, chrome hardware, available in Trans. Amber finish, new 2005.

	MSR	$799	$600	$525	$450	$400	$350	$300	$250

HJ4 - single cutaway semi-hollow mahogany body with arched mahogany top, 2 f-holes, B/N/H binding, set mahogany neck, 22-fret rosewood fingerboard with trapezoid inlays, black headstock with three-per-side tuners, tune-o-matic bridge, stop tailpiece, black pickguard, two Tesla humbucker pickups, four knobs, three-way switch, gold hardware, available in Trans. Blue finish, new 2005.

	MSR	$799	$600	$525	$450	$400	$350	$300	$250

HJ5 - single cutaway semi-hollow mahogany body with arched spruce top, 2 f-holes, B/N/H binding, set mahogany neck, 22-fret rosewood fingerboard with split parallelogram inlays, black headstock with three-per-side tuners, rosewood bridge, trapeze tailpiece, black pickguard, two Tesla humbucker pickups, four knobs, three-way switch, gold hardware, available in Vintage Sunburst finish, new 2005.

	MSR	$799	$600	$525	$450	$400	$350	$300	$250

GRADING	100% MINT	98% NEAR MINT	95% EXC+	90% EXC	80% VG+	70% VG	60% G

**Hohner HS75
courtesy Billy Ray Bush**

ELECTRIC: ST SERIES

ST CUSTOM - double offset cutaway flame maple body, bolt-on maple neck, 22-fret rosewood fingerboard with abalone dot inlay, double locking vibrato, 6-on-a-side tuners, black hardware, 2 single coil/humbucker EMG pickups, volume/tone control, 3 mini switches, available in Cherry Sunburst finish, mfg. 1990-1991.

| | N/A | $675 | $625 | $525 | $425 | $375 | $325 |

Last MSR was $1,050.

ST LYNX - similar to ST Custom, except features maple body, 24-fret rosewood fingerboard with white dot inlay, single coil/humbucker EMG pickups, 3-position switch, available in Metallic Blue or Metallic Red finishes, mfg. 1990-94.

| | N/A | $475 | $375 | $350 | $275 | $250 | $200 |

Last MSR was $740.

ST METAL S - similar to the ST Lynx, except features 22-fret rosewood fingerboard with white shark tooth inlay, 2 single coil/1 humbucker EMG pickups, volume/tone control, 3 mini switches, available in Black, Black Crackle, or Pearl White finishes, mfg. 1990-91.

| | N/A | $425 | $375 | $325 | $250 | $225 | $175 |

Last MSR was $630.

ST SCORPION - similar to ST Lynx, except features a 22-fret rosewood fingerboard with Whitesnake tooth inlays, three mini switches, two knobs with coil tap, optional Steinberger KB double locking vibrato unit, mfg. 1990-94.

| | N/A | $475 | $375 | $350 | $275 | $250 | $200 |

ST VICTORY - similar to the ST Lynx, except features black pickguard, 22-fret rosewood fingerboard with white dot inlay, reverse headstock, humbucker pickup, available in Metallic Dark Purple or Metallic Red finishes, mfg. 1990-91.

| | N/A | $400 | $350 | $275 | $250 | $225 | $175 |

Last MSR was $575.

ELECTRIC: TE SERIES

TE CUSTOM - single cutaway bound maple body, white pickguard, bolt-on maple neck, 21-fret rosewood fingerboard with white dot inlay, fixed bridge, 6-on-a-side tuners, chrome hardware, 2 single coil pickups, volume/tone control, 3-position switch, available in 3-Tone Sunburst finish, mfg. 1992-96.

| | N/A | $350 | $300 | $250 | $200 | $160 | $120 |

Last MSR was $500.

TE Custom XII - similar to TE Custom, except has 12-string configuration, black pickguard, 2 humbucker pickups, available in Black finish, mfg. 1990-93.

| | N/A | $350 | $300 | $250 | $200 | $160 | $120 |

Last MSR was $550.

TE Prinz - similar to TE Custom, except features bound flamed maple body, tortoise pickguard, 21-fret maple fingerboard with black dot inlay, available in Natural finish, mfg. 1990-96.

| | N/A | $375 | $325 | $275 | $225 | $175 | $125 |

Last MSR was $565.

ELECTRIC BASS: MISC. MODELS

B BASS IV - Offset double cutaway maple body, through-body maple neck, 24-fret rosewood fingerboard with white dot inlay, Steinberger DB bridge, 2-per-side tuners, black hardware, 2 J-style Designed by EMG pickups, 2 volume/tone controls, active tone electronics with switch and LED, available in Black, Natural Satin, Trans. Black, Trans. Blue, or Trans. Red finishes, mfg. 1990-present.

| MSR | $825 | $625 | $550 | $475 | $425 | $350 | $295 | $225 |

B Bass B - similar to B Bass, except has bolt-on maple neck, available in Lake Placid Blue, Trans. Black, or Trans. Red finishes, mfg. 1994-96.

| | N/A | $375 | $325 | $275 | $235 | $195 | $150 |

Last MSR was $600.

B Bass V - similar to B Bass, except in 5-string configuration, available in Black, Natural Satin, Trans. Black, Trans. Blue, or Walnut Stain finishes, current mfg.

| MSR | $875 | $650 | $575 | $500 | $425 | $350 | $275 | $225 |

B Bass VI - similar to B Bass, except in 6-string configuration, available in Natural finish, current mfg.

| MSR | $1,050 | $750 | $650 | $575 | $500 | $425 | $350 | $275 |

B BASS IV QUILT (BBASSIVQ) - similar to the B Bass except has a quilted maple top, available in Antique Violin Dark finish, current mfg.

| MSR | $875 | $650 | $575 | $500 | $425 | $350 | $275 | $225 |

B Bass Quilt V (BBASSVQ) - similar to the B Bass Quilt except in 5-string configuration, current mfg.

| MSR | $945 | $725 | $650 | $550 | $450 | $375 | $300 | $250 |

B Bass Quilt VI (BBASSVIQ) - similar to the B Bass Quilt except in 6-string configuration, current mfg.

| MSR | $1,125 | $800 | $725 | $650 | $575 | $475 | $350 | $275 |

GRADING	100% MINT	98% NEAR MINT	95% EXC+	90% EXC	80% VG+	70% VG	60% G

B 500 - sleek offset double cutaway maple body, bolt-on maple neck, 24-fret rosewood fingerboard with white dot inlay, fixed bridge, 2-per-side tuners, chrome hardware, P/J-style pickups, 2 volume/2 tone controls, available in Metallic Red finish, mfg. 1997-2002.

		$425	$350	$325	$275	$225	$175	$125

Last MSR was $549.

HPB - offset double cutaway hardwood body, white pickguard, bolt-on maple neck, 20-fret maple fingerboard with black dot inlay, fixed bridge, 4-on-a-side tuners, chrome hardware, P/J-style pickup, volume/tone control, available in Black finish, disc. 2000.

		$375	$325	$275	$250	$200	$175	$125

Last MSR was $489.

Add $10 for left-handed configuration (HPB LH).

HZB - similar to HPB, except features 2 J-style single coil pickups, tortoiseshell pickguard, 2 volume/tone controls, controls mounted on a metal plate, available in Ivory finish, disc.

		$375	$325	$275	$250	$200	$175	$125

Last MSR was $495.

This model is available with a fretless fingerboard (Model HZB FL).

HZAB - similar to HZB, except has 2 J-style Designed by EMG active pickups, available in Vintage Sunburst and Walnut Satin finishes, disc.

		$495	$425	$375	$325	$275	$225	$175

Last MSR was $649.

PHOENIX STANDARD - offset double cutaway agathis body, bolt-on maple neck, 24-fret rosewood fingerboard with offset pearloid dot inlay, fixed bridge, natural finish peghead, 2-per-side die-cast tuners, chrome hardware, 2 HPC-4 Deluxe soapbar pickups, 2 volume/tone controls, available in Black and Candy Apple Red finishes, mfg. 1998-2002.

		$285	$225	$180	$140	$110	$95	$75

Last MSR was $399.

Add $10 for left-handed configuration (PHO-LH).

Phoenix Deluxe - similar to the Phoenix Standard, except features Louisiana swamp ash body, 2 HPC-4 Custom active/passive pickups, gold hardware, abalone fingerboard dot inlay, active electronics LED indicator, available in Desert Walnut Stain finish, mfg. 1998-2002.

		$425	$375	$325	$275	$225	$175	$125

Last MSR was $599.

ELECTRIC BASS: HEADLESS SERIES

B2 - Steinberger-style maple body, through-body maple neck, 24-fret rosewood fingerboard with white dot inlay, Steinberger bridge, black hardware, 2 humbucker pickups, 2 volume/1 tone controls, available in Black and Red finishes, mfg. 1990-92.

		N/A	$350	$300	$275	$225	$200	$150

Last MSR was $550.

B2A - similar to B2, except features mini switch, active electronics, LED lights, available in Black and Red finishes, mfg. 1990-92.

		N/A	$450	$375	$300	$250	$225	$175

Last MSR was $625.

Add $35 for left-handed version.

B2ADB - similar to B2A, except has Steinberger DB bridge, available in Black or Metallic Red finishes, mfg. 1992-present.

MSR	$850	$575	$495	$425	$375	$325	$275	$225

B2AFL - similar to B2A, except is fretless with an ebonol fingerboard, mfg. 1990-92.

		N/A	$450	$400	$350	$300	$250	$200

Last MSR was $695.

B2AV - similar to B2A, except features 5-string configuration, available in Walnut Stain finish, current mfg.

MSR	$850	$575	$500	$425	$375	$325	$275	$225

B2B - Steinberger style maple body, bolt-on maple neck, 24-fret rosewood fingerboard with white dot inlay, Steinberger bridge, black hardware, P/J-style pickups, 2 volume/tone controls, available in Black finish, mfg. 1992-present.

MSR	$565	$425	$375	$325	$275	$225	$180	$150

B2V - similar to B2B, except in a 5-string configuration, available in Black finish, mfg. 1990-92.

		N/A	$450	$400	$350	$300	$250	$200

Last MSR was $675.

THE JACK BASS CUSTOM - offset double cutaway maple body, through-body headless maple neck, 24-fret rosewood fingerboard with white dot inlay, Steinberger bridge, black hardware, 2 J-style pickups, 2 volume/tone controls, active tone electronics with switch and LED, available in Black, Metallic Red, or Natural finishes, mfg. 1990-2000.

		$650	$575	$450	$375	$300	$275	$225

Last MSR was $875.

Add $75 for 5-string configuration (The Jack Bass Custom 5).

GRADING	100% MINT	98% NEAR MINT	95% EXC+	90% EXC	80% VG+	70% VG	60% G

ELECTRIC BASS: REVOLUTION SERIES

REVOLUTION STANDARD (HRBSTD) - double offset cutaway agathis body, bolt-on maple neck, 24-fret rosewood fingerboard with dot inlay, matching color headstock, 2-per-side tuners, black pickguard, 2 select EMG Humbucker pickups, three knobs (2 v, tone), chrome hardware available in Black, Candy Apple Red, or Lake Placid Blue finishes, mfg. 2002-present.

MSR	$379	$275	$225	$195	$175	$150	$125	$95

Add $20 for left-handed configuration, available in Black finish (HRBSTDLH).

REVOLUTION DELUXE (HRBDLX) - double offset cutaway ashwood/mahogany body, bolt-on maple neck, 24-fret rosewood fingerboard with dot inlay, matching color headstock, 2-per-side tuners, black pickguard, 2 select EMG Humbucking pickups, active tone controls with switch, three knobs (2 v, tone), chrome hardware available in Natural Oil finish, mfg. 2002-present.

MSR	$599	$425	$365	$325	$275	$225	$175	$125

Revolution Deluxe 5 (HRB5DLX) - similar to the Revolution Deluxe except in five-string configuration, mfg. 2002-present.

MSR	$699	$495	$425	$375	$325	$250	$200	$150

HOLIDAY

See chapter on House Brands.

This trademark has been identified as a House Brand distributed by Montgomery Wards and Alden's department stores. Author/researcher Willie G. Moseley also reports seeing a catalog reprint showing Holiday instruments made by Harmony, Kay, and Danelectro. Additional information in regards to instruments with this trademark will be welcome, especially any Danelectro with a Holiday logo on the headstock (source: Willie G. Moseley, *Stellas & Stratocasters*).

HOLLISTER GUITARS

Instruments previously built in Dedham, MA.

Luthier Kent Hollister offers high quality, custom built guitars such as the **Archtop** ($3,000), **Semi-hollow** ($1,900), **Carved Top Solid Body** ($1,500), and **The Plank** ($1,200). The Plank is an electric solid body with neck-through design. Hollister also created the **Archtop Bass** ($2,800), which features a central soundhole (as opposed to f-holes). Just the thing to swing with the archtop guitarists!

HOLMAN

Instruments previously built in Neodesha, KS during the late 1960s. Distributed by Holman-Woodell, Inc. of Neodesha, KS.

The Holman-Woodell company built guitars during the late 1960s in Neodesha, Kansas (around 60 miles due south from Topeka). While they were producing guitars for Wurlitzer, they also built their own Holman brand as well as instruments trademarked Alray and 21st Century. The Holman-Woodell company is also famous for building the La Baye "2 x 4" guitars for Wisconsin-based inventor Dan Helland. The Holman-Woodell company also released a number of faux "2 x 4s" built from leftover parts with the "Holman" logo after the La Baye company went under (source: Michael Wright, *Guitar Stories*, Volume One).

HOLMES, TOM

Instruments previously built in TN circa 1970s to 1980s.

Luthier Tom Holmes custom built numerous high quality, solid body guitars for a number of years for artists such as Billy Gibbons (ZZ Top), Bo Diddley, and others. In the mid 1970s, Holmes came up with a design for a "triple coil" (i.e., a pickup that could be split into a single coil and a humbucker instead of just splitting a dual coil), and custom built guitars to bring the idea to the marketplace. The T.H.C. guitars were completely handcrafted (save for the tuners and the bridge) by Holmes, and a majority of the guitars were sold through Larry Henrikson's Ax-in-Hand Guitar Shop in Dekalb, Illinois. Other T.H.C. models include a limited run of Holmes/Gibbons "Cadillac" guitars (based on the Gretsch Cadillac model played by Bo Diddley).

In the mid 1980s, Holmes became involved with the Gibson Guitar company. Holmes designed the tooling for some of the company production, and was a part of Gibson's '57 Classic pickup reissue. During his work on the reissue pickup, Holmes worked on a P.A.F. design similar to the original vintage pickups. With the success of his design, Holmes went into business with his own company, hand winding his P.A.F. reproductions and stamping out the proper pickup cover to go with it.

Holmes' pickups have appeared in certain limited production models from the large guitar manufacturing companies, and are very popular in Japan and Germany as aftermarket reissues. For further information on his P.A.F. reproductions, contact Tom Holmes directly (see Trademark Index), (Collector's tip courtesy David Larson at Audio Restoration, and Larry Henrikson at Ax-in-Hand).

HOLST, STEPHEN

Instruments currently built in Eugene, OR since 1984.

Luthier Stephen Holst began building guitars in 1984, and through inspiration and refinement developed the models currently offered. Holst draws on his familiarity of Pacific Northwest tonewoods in developing tonal qualities in his handcrafted instruments. Holst specifically works with the customer commissioning the instrument, tailoring the requests to the specific guitar. In addition, Holst has experimented in other designs such as nylon string, 7- and 12-string, and baritone archtops.

ELECTRIC SEMI HOLLOW & THINLINE SERIES

At the request of several jazz performers, Holst designed the **K 250** thinline semi-hollow guitars. The K 250 draws on the inspiration and design of the K 200 arch-top, combined with a highly figured black walnut top and peghead overlay. The body width is 15 in. and the electronics are the Tom Doyle D1 pickup system. List price is $4,000. There are other models including the K100, K200, and Classical Guitar that are listed in the *Blue Book of Acoustic Guitars*.

HONDO

Instruments currently produced in Korea. Distributed by MBT International of Charleston, South Carolina. Between 1974 to early 1980s some models were produced in Japan.

The Hondo guitar company was originally formed in 1969 when Jerry Freed and Tommy Moore of the International Music Corporation (IMC) of Fort Worth, Texas, combined with the recently formed Samick company. IMC's intent was to introduce modern manufacturing techniques and American quality standards to the Korean guitar manufacturing industry.

The Hondo concept was to offer an organized product line and solid entry level market instruments at a fair market price. The original Korean products were classical and steel-string acoustic guitars. In 1972, the first crudely built Hondo electrics were built. However, two years later the product line took a big leap forward in quality under the new Hondo II logo. Hondo also began limited production of guitars in Japan in 1974.

By 1975, Hondo had distributors in 70 countries worldwide, and had expanded to producing stringed instruments at the time. In 1976, over 22,000 of the Bi-Centennial banjos were sold. The company also made improvements to the finish quality on their products, introduced scalloped bracing on acoustics, and began using a higher quality brand of tuning machines.

Hondo was one of the first overseas guitar builders to feature American-built DiMarzio pickups on the import instruments beginning in 1978. By this year, a number of Hondo II models featured designs based on classic American favorites. In 1979, over 790,000 Hondo instruments were sold worldwide. All guitar production returned to Korea in 1983. At that point, the product line consisted of 485 different models!

In 1985, IMC acquired major interest in the Charvel/Jackson company, and began dedicating more time and interest in the higher end guitar market. The Hondo trademark went into mothballs around 1987. However, Jerry Freed started the Jerry Freed International company in 1989, and acquired the rights to the Hondo trademark in 1991 (the "Est. 1969" tagline was added to the Hondo logo at this time). Freed began distribution of a new line of Hondo guitars. In 1993, the revamped company was relocated to Stuart, Florida; additional models added to the line were produced in China and Taiwan.

The Hondo Guitar Company was purchased by the MBT International in 1995. MBT also owns and distributes J.B. Player instruments. The Hondo product line was revamped for improved quality while maintaining student-friendly prices. Hondo celebrated their 25th year of manufacturing electric guitars in 1997 (source: Tom Malm, MBT International; and Michael Wright, *Guitar Stories*, Volume One).

ELECTRIC

Hondo guitars generally carried a new retail price range between $179 and $349 (up to $449). While their more unusual-designed model may command a slightly higher price, the average used price may range between $125 (good condition) up to $250 for basic models, and can range from $200-$400 for higher end models. Models such as the Machine Gun model can bring up to $500, the Longhorn up to $450 and the Longhorn double neck up to $750.

Current Hondo electric solid body models include the **H720M** (list $299), a traditional style double cutaway model with bolt-on maple neck, 21-fret rosewood fingerboard, vintage-style tremolo, white pickguard, 3 single coil pickups, volume/2 tone controls, and a 5-way selector switch. The **H715** (list $199) has a plywood body, nato neck, kuku wood fingerboard, black pickguard, humbucker, and volume/tone controls.

The **All Star series** debuted in the fall of 1983, and featured Fender-based models with a slimmed down Telecaster-ish headstock.

Paul Dean (Loverboy) endorsed and had a hand in designing two solid body models in 1983. The Hondo version could even be seen as a dry run for Dean's later association with the Kramer company. The **Dean II** had a stop tailpiece and two humbuckers, and the **Dean III** featured three single coils and a standard tremolo.

The **Deluxe Series** was first offered in 1982, and featured 11 classical and 22 steel string acoustic models. The electric line featured 9 variations on the Les Paul theme, including the **H-752** double cutaway LP. A 'strat' of sorts carried the designation **H-760**, a B.C. Rich inspired model with humbuckers and three mini-switches was the **H-930**, and a 335 repro was designated the **H-935**. Many carried a new list price between $229 and $299.

Texas luthier/designer Mark Erlewine licensed a pair of designs to Hondo for the **Erlewine Series** in 1982 and 1983. His **Chiquita** travel guitar had a scale of 19" and an overall 27.5 in. length; and the headless **Lazer** was a full scale (25.5 in.) guitar with an overall length of 31 in.. A third model, named the **Automatic** was offered as well. List prices ranged from $199 to $349.

Unveiled in late 1984, the **Fame Series** featured Fender-based reproductions with the Fame logo in a spaghetti-looking lettering. However, the spelling and outline would be a give-away from a distance (if their intention was so bold...).

In 1985, noted luthier/designer **Harry Fleishman** licensed the Flash bass, a headless, bodiless, 2 octave neck, Schaller Bridge equipped, magnetic and piezo-driven electric bass that was based on one of his high quality original designs. Fleishman also designed a Tele-ish acoustic/electric similar to the Kramer Ferrington models that were available.

The **Longhorn series** featured a guitar (model **HP 1081**) and bass (model **H 1181**) constructed of solid wood bodies and bolt-on necks. The guitar had a 32-fret neck, single humbucker, fixed bridge, brass nut, volume/tone controls, as well as a coil tap and phase mini switches. The bass model had a 2 octave neck, P-style split pickup, volume/tone controls, and a mini switch. Both were available in Cream Sunburst, Metallic Bronze, and Natural Walnut finishes during the early 1980s.

The **MasterCaster Series** were mid 1980s models advertised as having solid ash bodies, Kahler Flyer locking tremolos, and Grover tuners.

The **Professional Series** was introduced in 1982, and had a number of classical and steel string models. More importantly, there was a number of electric Strat-style guitars that were presumably built by Tokai in Japan. Tokai was one of the reproduction companies of the mid-to-late 1970s that built pretty good Strats – much to Fender's displeasure.

Standard Series guitars were also introduced in the early 1980s, and were Hondo's single or double pickup entry level guitars. The acoustic models were beginner's guitars as well. The Standard line did offer 11 banjo models of different add-ons and four distinct mandolins.

**Hopf Spcial
courtesy Mark Stodghill**

ELECTRIC BASS

New Hondo electric solid body basses feature the **H820M** (list $335), a traditonal style double cutaway model with bolt-on maple neck, 20-fret rosewood fingerboard, black pickguard, P-style pickup, volume and tone controls. The similarly designed H815 (list $249) has a 29.75 in. scale, nato neck, and kuku wood fingerboard.

HOOTENANNY

See chapter on House Brands.

This trademark has been identified as a "sub-brand" from the budget line of Chris guitars by the Jackson-Guldan company. However, another source suggests that the trademark was marketed by the Monroe Catalog House (source: Willie G. Moseley, *Stellas & Stratocasters*).

HOPF

Instruments previously made in Germany from the late 1950s through the mid-1980s.

The Hopf name was established back in 1669, and lasted through the mid 1980s. The company produced a wide range of good quality solid body, semi-hollow, and archtop guitars from the late 1950s on. While some of the designs do bear an American design influence, the liberal use of local woods (such as beech, sycamore, or European pine) and certain departures from conventional styling give them an individual identity (source: Tony Bacon, *The Ultimate Guitar Book*).

ELECTRIC GUITAR

SATURN 63 ARCHTOP - semi-hollow body, 6-on-one-side tuners, two pickups, clear raised pickguard inscribed with "Hopf", tremolo, one pickup selector switch, one tone switch, and volume knob, mfg. circa 1950s-1960s.

	N/A	$850	$750	$650	$550	$450	$350

Guitar is equipped with a 3 pin DIN plug instead of a 1/4" jack on control panel. Make sure the original cable is with the guitar when it is purchased!

HOSONO GUITAR WORKS

Instruments previously produced in Glendale, CA.

Hosono Guitar Works produced fine quality instruments for a number of years.

HOT LICKS

Instruments currently built in Florida. Distributed by Hot Licks Musical Instruments of Pound Ridge, NY. Previously produced in PA.

The Hot Licks guitar models are the signature series from Arlen Roth (if you have seen any of his videos, then you know the caliber of his playing). These models feature single cutaway bodies and 2 single coil pickups in a decidely Tele-style guitar. Hot Licks mainly focuses on instructional videos.

Hot Licks guitars feature lightweight ash bodies, bird's-eye maple necks, and bird's-eye or rosewood fingerboards. Models are available in Classic Sunburst, Safari Green, Roadmaster Red, Vintage Cream, and that well-known Del Fuego Black with Flames custom paint finishes. Retail price is $1,695 (the custom Flame job is an additional $300).

HOWARD (JAPAN MFG.)

Instruments previously produced in Japan, circa 1960s.

Instruments under the Japanese-produced Howard trademark thus encountered have been bolt-on neck Fender Strat copies of decent quality. Retail prices in the late 1960s ranged between $79 to $119 (source: Roland Lozier, Lozier Piano & Music).

HOYER

Current production instruments are distributed internationally by Mario Pellarin Musikwaren of Cologne, Germany. Instruments built in West Germany from the late 1950s through the late 1980s.

The Hoyer company produced a wide range of good to high quality solid body, semi-hollow body, and archtop guitars, with some emphasis on the later during the 1960s. During the early 1970s, there was some production of solid bodied guitars with an emphasis on classic American designs.

The Hoyer trademark was re-introduced in the 1990s with the cheerful "A Legend is Back!" motto. Hoyer is currently offering a wide range of acoustic and electric guitars in Europe; a U.S. distributor has not yet been named. Further information on Hoyer instruments is available through the company; contact them directly (see Trademark Index) (source: Tony Bacon and Paul Day, *The Guru's Guitar Guide*).

ELECTRIC

Hoyer currently is offering a handful of Guild- and Gibson-esque electric guitar models. The semi-hollow single Florentine cutaway Jazz '57 model has a 16" wide body, 2 covered humbuckers, a 3 tuners per side headstock, a 20-fret rosewood fingerboard with white block inlays, and an adjustable rosewood bridge/raised chrome tailpiece. The Jazz '57 is also available with gold hardware, and in Metallic Gold or Tobacco Sunburst finishes. The single rounded cutaway **Cat** model has a 17 in. body width, and is available in Black, Foam Green, and Wine Red finishes. On the Gibson front, the single cutaway **Junior 90** model has a solid mahogany body, 2 P-90 soapbars or 2 chrome covered humbucker pickups, and Blonde, Wine Red, Black, and Metallic Gold finishes; the **3-35** model is pretty self-explanatory once you remove the dash, and is available in Cherry Red and Tobacco Sunburst finishes. Hands down ´50s cool goes to the Hoyer **Bo** model, a double humbucker, solid alder rectangular, set-in mahogany neck, maraca shakin´, Willie and the Hand Jive, Bo Diddley-style guitar!

HUBER, NIK

Instruments currently built in Rodgau, Germany since 1993. Distributed by Nik Huber Guitars of Rodgau, Germany.

Luthier Nik Huber has been building guitars for over three years. In addition to his PRS-inspired models, he maintains a repair shop and guitar sales room. Huber's woodworking skills and finishes have attracted notice from many local players as well as notables such as Paul Reed Smith (PRS Guitars). Huber models are available with numerous custom options, such as gold hardware, Tom Holmes pickups, Mann Made tremolos, L.R. Baggs bridges, custom inlays, quilted maple tops, and others. For further information regarding Nik Huber models, please contact luthier Huber directly (see Trademark Index).

ELECTRIC

Huber offers three distinctive models, all with highly figured wood tops and translucent finishes (a tip of the lutherie cap to PRS). Huber´s original design with a slightly offset single cutaway **Dolphin** model has a mahogany body, quilted maple top, mahogany or bird´s-eye maple neck, bird´s-eye maple or maple-bound rosewood fingerboard, and a dolphin headstock inlay. This model has a 25.5 in. scale length, Wilkinson or Schaller tremolo, and Seymour Duncan (humbucker) pickups. The decidedly single cutaway **Orca** model has a curly maple top, 24.75 in. scale, tune-o-matic bridge/stop tailpiece, 3-per-side Schaller M6 tuners, and Seymour Duncan Antiquity humbuckers.

The offset double cutaway **Steve Lauer** model has a mahogany body, quilted maple top, bird´s-eye maple neck/fingerboard, and a bat headstock inlay. This model also has a 25.5 in. scale length, MannMade tremolo, and Joe Barden deluxe pickups. There is also a **Custom** guitar where anything goes. The owner of the guitar has it built to his/her exact specifications and is made to look and sound just how they want it.

HUMAN BASE

Instruments currently built in Waldems, Germany. Distributed in the U.S. market by Salwender International of Orange, California.

Human Base produces four models of high quality bolt neck and neck-through bass guitars. Currently, Salwender International is distributing the Base X bolt-on neck model in the U.S. market. Additional specifications and information are available through either Human Base or Salwender International directly (see Trademark Index).

ELECTRIC BASS

The following Human Base models are available in the U.S. market: The Bass X, The Max, The Jonas, The Class X, and The X-Over. The Bass X Series features an offset double cutaway ash body, bird´s-eye maple top, rear-mounted bolt-on neck (neck extends well into the back of the body and bolts in), 22-fret rosewood fingerboard, fixed bridge, 2 Bartolini pickups, volume/tone controls, active electronics, and is available in various Translucent matte finishes. Retail is $2,380 for the 4-string, $2,550 for the 5-string, and $2,805 for the 6-string.

The Max series has a larger body and several options. Retail is $3,911 for the 4-string, $3,959 for the 5-string, and $5,305 for the 6-string. The Jonas series retails for the same prices as the Max series. The Class X series has a very large treble bout and is the priciest model in the lineup. The retail prices are $5,101 for the 4-string, $5,781 for the 5-string, and $6,461 for the 6-string. The X-Over retails for $2,584 for the 4-string, $2,805 for the 5-string, and $3,060 for the six string. Refer to the Salwender website for all the options and specifications.

HUNTINGTON

Instruments currently distributed by Actodyne General Incorporated.

In 1997, Actodyne General Incorporated debuted a new line of sleek, electric guitar and bass models. Actodyne is the maker of the popular Lace Helix guitar pickups. For further information, contact Actodyne General Incorporated directly (see Trademark Index).

HURRICANE

Instruments previously produced in Japan during the late 1980s.

The Hurricane trademark shows up on medium quality superstrat and solid body guitars based on popular American designs (source: Tony Bacon and Paul Day, *The Guru's Guitar Guide*).

HUSKEY

Instruments previously built in MO.

Huskey Guitar Works guitar building started in 1979 with one goal - to create a line of instruments that were both innovative and eye catching. Rick and Jackie Huskey found that instruments of the late 1970s did not have the amount of natural sustain that they were looking for.

To increase the amount of sustain, the Huskeys incorporated the same materials used by luthiers for generations in the first of their designs. The Stormtrooper design brought about the development of the SustainArm, an innovation that increases the sustain of the Huskey guitars by reducing the tension along the neck. The SustainArm is an integral extension of the body, attaching on the low E side of the neck. The SustainArm also enabled them to extend the lower treble side cutaway, and allowed unrestricted access to the fretboard (some fretboards are equipped with as many as 36 frets), (Company history courtesy Rick and Jackie Huskey).

ELECTRIC

Huskey Guitar Works offered several models of high quality, custom built guitars that featured original designs and neck-through construction. Models include the Axeminister, Keeper, Usurper, Yarnspinner. Last retail prices ranged from $2,599 to $2,699. Guitar models were available in 6-, 9-, and 12-string configurations;

left-handed configurations are available at no extra charge. These guitars have not shown up in the second-hand market to determine a price.

FREEDOMFIGHTER - wedge-shaped body with sustain arm, through-body neck, 6-on-a-side tuners, Kahler tremolo bridge, EMG 89 humbucker pickup, volume/tone controls.

Last MSR was $2,599.

HARBINGER - dual cutaway maple/mahogany body with sustain arm, 5-piece through-body neck, 6-on-a-side Sperzel locking tuners, Kahler Pro tremolo bridge, 2 EMG (85/89) humbucker pickups, volume/tone controls, 3-way toggle selector.

Last MSR was $2,699.

STORMTROOPER - maple/alder body with sustain arm, 5-piece neck, 29-fret ebony fingerboard, 6-per-side Sperzel locking tuners, Kahler Pro tremolo, leg rest, EMG 89 humbucker, volume/tone controls.

Last MSR was $2,699.

ELDER - similar to the Stormtrooper, except features ash and mahogany body.

Last MSR was $2,699.

PEACEMAKER - similar to the Stormtrooper, except features an alder body.

Last MSR was $2,699.

HUTTL

Instruments previously built in Germany from the 1950s to the 1970s.

The Huttl trademark may not be as well-known as other German guitar builders such as Framus, Hopf, or Klira. While their designs may be as original as the others, the quality of workmanship is still fairly rough in comparison.

HY-LO

Instruments previously produced in Japan during the mid to late 1960s.

These entry level solid body guitars feature designs based on classic American favorites. One such model (designation unknown) featured an offset double cutaway body and six on a side tuners like a strat, but two single coil pickups and volume and tone controls.

HYUNDAI

Instruments currently built in Korea. Distributed in the U.S. through Hyundai Guitars of West Nyack, NY.

Hyndai offers a range of medium quality guitars designed for beginning students that have designs based on popular American classics.

Human Bass Bass-X
courtesy Salwender

Human Bass JBX
courtesy Salwender

NOTES

Section I

IBANEZ

Instruments currently produced in Japan since the early 1960s, and some models produced in Korea since the 1980s. Ibanez guitars are distributed in the U.S. by Ibanez USA (Hoshino) in Bensalem, PA. Other distribution offices include Quebec (for Canada), Sydney (for Australia), and Auckland (for New Zealand).

The Ibanez trademark originated from the Fuji plant in Matsumoto, Japan. In 1932, the Hoshino Gakki Ten, Inc. factory began producing instruments under the Ibanez trademark. The factory and offices were burned down during World War II, and were revived in 1950. By the mid 1960s, Hoshino was producing instruments under various trademarks such as Ibanez, Star, King's Stone, Jamboree, and Goldentone.

In the mid 1950s, Harry Rosenbloom opened the Medley Music store outside Philadelphia. As the Folk Music boom began in 1959, Rosenbloom decided to begin producing acoustic guitars and formed the Elger company (named after Rosenbloom's children, Ellen and Gerson). Elger acoustics were produced in Ardmore, Pennsylvania between 1959 and 1965.

In the 1960s, Rosenbloom travelled to Japan and found a number of companies that he contracted to produce the Elger acoustics. Later, he was contacted by Hoshino to form a closer business relationship. The first entry level solid body guitars featuring original designs first surfaced in the mid 1960s, some bearing the Elger trademark, and some bearing the Ibanez logo. One of the major keys to the perceived early Ibanez quality is due to Hoshino shipping the guitars to the Elger factory in Ardmore. The arriving guitars would be re-checked, and set up prior to shipping to the retailer. Many distributors at the time would just simply ship product to the retailer, and let surprises occur at the unboxing. By reviewing the guitars in a separate facility, Hoshino/Ibanez could catch any problems before the retailer - so the number of perceived flawed guitars was reduced at the retail/sales end. In England, Ibanez was imported by the Summerfield Brothers, and sometimes had either the CSL trademark or no trademark at all on the headstock. Other U.K. distributors used the Antoria brand name, and in Australia they were rebranded with a Jason logo.

In the early 1970s, the level of quality rose as well as the level of indebtedness to classic American designs. It has been argued that Ibanez' reproductions of Stratocasters and Les Pauls may be equal to or better than the quality of Norlin era Gibsons or CBS era Fenders. While the *Blue Book of Electric Guitars* would rather stay neutral on this debate (we just list them, not rate them), it has been suggested by outside sources that next time close your eyes and let your hands and ears be the judge. In any event, the unauthorized reproductions eventually led to Fender's objections to Tokai's imports (the infamous headstock sawing rumour), and Norlin/Gibson taking Hoshino/Ibanez/Elger into court for patent infringement.

When Ibanez began having success basically reproducing Gibson guitars and selling them at a lower price on the market, Norlin (Gibson's owner at the time) sent off a cease-and-desist warning. Norlin's lawyers decided that the best way to proceed was to defend the decorative (the headstock) versus the functional (body design), and on June 28th, 1977 the case of Gibson vs. Elger Co. opened in Philadelphia Federal District Court. In early 1978, a resolution was agreed upon: Ibanez would stop reproducing Gibsons if Norlin would stop suing Ibanez. The case was officially closed on February 2, 1978.

The infringement lawsuit ironically might have been the kick in the pants that propelled Ibanez and other Japanese builders to get back into original designs. Ibanez stopped building Gibson exact reproductions, and moved on to other designs. By the early 1980s, certain guitar styles began appealing to other areas of the guitar market (notably the Hard Rock/Heavy Metal genre), and Ibanez's use of famous endorsers probably fueled the appeal. Ibanez's continuing program of original designs and artist involvement continued to work in the mid to late 1980s, and continues to support their position in the market today, (Source: Michael Wright, *Guitar Stories*, Volume One).

**Ibanez UV7
courtesy Ibanez**

MODEL DATING & IDENTIFICATION

It may be easier to date an Ibanez guitar knowing when key hardware developments were introduced.

1977: Ibanez' Super 80 "Flying Finger" humbuckers with chrome covers.

1980: Ornate (or just large) brass bridges/tailpieces, and brass hardware.

1984: 'Pro Rocker' locking tremolo system.

1985: 'Edge' double locking tremolo system.

1987: Debut of the DiMarzio-made IBZ USA pickups.

1990: 'Lo-Pro' Edge tremolo system. In addition to the Ibanez company's model history, a serialization chart is provided in the back of the Blue Book of Guitars to further aid the dating of older Ibanez guitars (not all potentiometer builders use the EIA source code, so overseas-built potentiometer codes on Japanese guitars may not help in the way of clues).

1959-1967: Elger Acoustics are built in Ardmore, Pennsylvania; and are distributed by Medley Music, Grossman Music (Cleveland), Targ and Dinner (Chicago), and the Roger Balmer Company on the west coast. Elger imported from Japan the Tama acoustics, Ibanez acoustics, and some Elger electrics.

1962-1965: Introduction of entry level bolt-neck solid body electrics, and some set-neck archtop electrics by 1965.

1971-1977: The copy era begins for Ibanez (Faithful Reproductions) as solid body electrics based on Gibson, Fender, and Rickenbacker models (both bolt-ons and set-necks) arrive. These are followed by copies of Martin, Guild, Gibson, and Fender acoustics. Ibanez opens an office and warehouse outside of Philadelphia, Pennsylvania to maintain quality control on imported guitars in 1972.

1973: Ibanez's Artist series acoustics and electrics are debuted. In 1974, the Artist-style neck joint; later in 1976 an Artist 'Les Paul' arrives. This sets the stage for the LP variant double cutaway Artist model in 1978.

1975: Ibanez began to use a meaningful numbering system as part of their warranty program. In general, the letter stands for the month (January = A, February = B, etc.) and the following two digits are the year.

**Ibanez 92UCGR1
courtesy Ibanez**

GRADING	100% MINT	98% NEAR MINT	95% EXC+	90% EXC	80% VG+	70% VG	60% G

1977: Ibanez´s first original design, the Iceman, arrives with a rather excited lower bout and goosebeak headstock. A bass with the neck-through design (similar to a Rickenbacker 4001) is available, and a full series of neck-through designs are available in the Musician models. The George Benson GB-10 model and more original design series like the Performer, Professional, Musician, and Concert also appear.

1979-1980: Musician Series basses, Studio Series guitars, and an 8-string bass (MC-980) debut in 1979. The semi-hollowbody AS Series are introduced a year later.

1981-1987: Ibanez switches to the bolt-neck Strat design and other variants in the Roadster series, followed by the Blazer in 1981, and the Roadstar II models by 1982. The Pro Line and RS Series solid bodies appears in 1984. The early 1980s are the time for pointy body designs such as the Destroyer II (Explorer- based model), X Series Destroyers, ´headless´ Axstar models, and the original extreme pointy-ness of the XV-500. Jazz boxes like the AM Series semi-hollowbody guitars are introduced in 1982, followed by the FG Series a year later. In 1984, the Lonestar acoustics are introduced, and Ibanez responds to the MIDI challenge of Roland by unveiling the IMG-2010 MIDI guitar system.

1987: Ibanez hits the Hard Rock/Heavy Metal route full bore with popular artist endorsements and the Power, Radius, and Saber (now ´S´) series. These models have more in common with the ´superstrat´ design than traditional design. The early to mid 1980s is when Ibanez really begins making inroads to the American guitar consumer.

1988: Steve Vai's JEM appears on the U.S. market. Ibanez covers the entry level approach with the EX Series, built in Korea. The experimental Maxxas solid-looking hollowbody electric is unleashed.

1990: In 1990, the Steve Vai JEM 7-string Universe model (it's like six, plus one more!) proceeds to pop young guitarists' corks nationwide. The Ibanez American Master series, a product of the new American Custom Shop, is introduced.

1991: Reb Beach's Voyager model (Ladies and Gentlemen, nothing up my sleeve, and nothing behind the tremolo bridge!)intrigues players who want to bend up several semitones.

1992-1993: The ATL acoustic/electric design in unveiled and RT Series guitars debut in 1993.

(This overview, while brief, will hopefully identify years, trends, and series. For further information and deeper clarification, please refer to Michael Wright's *Guitar Stories*, Volume One.)

ELECTRIC: JUMP START PACKAGE

This Jump Start Package includes the electric guitar, GT10 amplifier with built in Over Drive circuit, PL5 PowerLead Distortion foot pedal, gig bag, instructional video, digital auto tuner, strap, cable, picks, chord chart, and a free subscription to *Plugged In* (the official Ibanez newsletter).

JUMP START PACKAGE (IJS40) - offset double cutaway agathis body, bolt-on maple neck, 21-fret maple fingerboard with black dot inlay, standard tremolo, 6-on-a-side tuners, chrome hardware, white pickguard, 2 single coil/humbucker pickups, volume/tone controls, 5-way selector, available in Black, Jewel Blue, or Candy Apple Red finishes, current mfg.

MSR	$360	$275	$225	$200	$175	$150	$125	$100

Jump Start Package (IJS70M) - similar to the (IJS40) guitar model, except features humbucker/single coil/humbucker pickups, available in Black or Metallic Green finishes, mfg. 1998-99.

	$400	$350	$300	$275	$250	$225	$195

Last MSR was $499.

Jump Start Package (IJS720) - similar to the (IJS40) guitar model, except features a GRX 7-String guitar, 7-string book and video, available in Black finish, mfg. 2001-03.

	$350	$300	$275	$240	$225	$190	$145

Last MSR was $500.

ELECTRIC: ARTCORE SERIES

The Artcore Series replaced the Artstar Series. All models in this series are hollowbody archtops that are mainly based on some of Gibson's popular designs such as the ES-5, ES-175, and ES-335.

AF75 - single cutaway jumbo hollow body archtop ES-5 style, maple back/top/sides, two f-holes, body binding, mahogany neck, 22-fret rosewood fingerboard with block inlay, three-per-side tuners, fixed bridge, trapeze tailpiece, pickguard, two humbucker pickups, four knobs, three-way switch, chrome hardware, available in Brown Sunburst, Trans. Blue Sunburst, or Trans. Orange finishes, mfg. 2003-present.

MSR	$430	$325	$275	$235	$195	$160	$130	$100

In 2005, Orange Trans. finish was introduced with cream colored knobs and pickguard (Model AF75D).

AFS75T - similar to the AF75, except has a Vintage Vibrato tailpiece, available in Trans. Blue, Trans. Red, or Turquoise finishes, mfg. 2003-present.

MSR	$500	$375	$325	$275	$235	$195	$160	$130

In 2004, Turquoise finish was introduced with cream colored knobs and pickguard (Model AFS75TD).

AFS77T - single cutaway jumbo hollow body archtop ES-5 style, maple back/top/sides, two f-holes, body binding, three-piece maple/mahogany neck, 22-fret rosewood fingerboard with block inlay, three-per-side tuners, Vintage Vibrato tailpiece, pickguard, two exposed humbucker pickups, four knobs, three-way switch, black hardware, available in Metallic Gray finish, mfg. 2004-present.

MSR	$530	$400	$350	$300	$250	$210	$180	$150

AF85 - single cutaway jumbo hollow body archtop ES-5 style, flame maple top/back/sides, two f-holes, body binding, three-piece maple/mahogany neck, 22-fret rosewood fingerboard with block inlay, three-per-side tuners, fixed bridge, trapeze tailpiece, pickguard, two humbucker pickups, four knobs, three-way switch, chrome hardware, available in Violin Sunburst finish, mfg. 2003-present.

MSR	$570	$430	$375	$325	$275	$225	$190	$160

AF105 CUSTOM - single cutaway jumbo hollow body archtop ES-5 style, flame maple top/back/sides, two f-holes, body binding, five-piece maple/bubinga neck, 22-fret rosewood fingerboard with block inlay, three-per-side tuners, wood tailpiece, pickguard with knobs mounted on it, single humbucker pickup, two knobs, gold hardware, available in Natural finish, new 2005.

MSR	$930	$700	$625	$550	$450	$400	$350	$300

Also available as the AF105F, except has two humbucker pickups and knobs mounted on body with a three-way switch.

GRADING	100% MINT	98% NEAR MINT	95% EXC+	90% EXC	80% VG+	70% VG	60% G

AG75 - single cutaway jumbo hollow body archtop, maple back/top/sides, two f-holes, body binding, mahogany neck, 22-fret rosewood fingerboard with block inlay, three-per-side tuners, fixed bridge, trapeze tailpiece, pickguard, two humbucker pickups, four knobs, three-way switch, chrome hardware, available in Brown Sunburst finish, mfg. 2003-present.

MSR	$430	$325	$275	$235	$195	$160	$130	$100

In 2005, Orange Trans. finish was introduced with cream colored knobs and pickguard (Model AF75D).

AG85 - single cutaway jumbo hollow body archtop ES-5 style, figured bubinga top/back/sides, two f-holes, body binding, three-piece maple/mahogany neck, 22-fret rosewood fingerboard with block inlay, three-per-side tuners, fixed bridge, trapeze tailpiece, pickguard, two humbucker pickups, four knobs, three-way switch, chrome hardware, available in Trans. Red finish, mfg. 2003-present.

MSR	$570	$430	$375	$325	$275	$225	$190	$160

AK85 - single sharp cutaway jumbo hollow body archtop ES-175 style, spruce top flame maple back and sides, two f-holes, body binding, three-piece maple/mahogany neck, 22-fret rosewood fingerboard with block inlay, three-per-side tuners, rosewood bridge, trapeze tailpiece, matching pickguard, two humbucker pickups, four knobs, three-way switch, chrome hardware, available in Dark Violin Sunburst finish, mfg. 2004-present.

MSR	$570	$430	$375	$325	$275	$225	$190	$160

AM73 - double cutaway thin hollow body archtop ES-335 style, maple back/top/sides, two f-holes, body binding, mahogany neck, 22-fret rosewood fingerboard with dot inlay, three-per-side tuners, fixed bridge, pickguard, two humbucker pickups, four knobs, three-way switch, chrome hardware, available in Trans. Brown finish, mfg. 2003-present.

MSR	$400	$300	$250	$220	$180	$150	$120	$90

In 2005, Orange Trans. finish was introduced with cream colored knobs and pickguard (Model AF75D).

AM73T - similar to the AM73, except has a Vintage Vibrato bridge/tailpiece, Trans. Red finish, mfg. 2003-04.

	$375	$325	$275	$235	$195	$160	$130

Last MSR was $500.

AM77 - double cutaway thin hollow body archtop ES-335 style, maple back/top/sides, two f-holes, body binding, three-piece maple/mahogany neck, 22-fret rosewood fingerboard with block inlay, three-per-side tuners, Vintage Vibrato tailpiece, pickguard, two exposed humbucker pickups, four knobs, three-way switch, black hardware, available in Nebula Black finish, mfg. 2004 only.

	$360	$310	$260	$220	$180	$150	$120

Last MSR was $480.

AM77T - similar to the AM77, except has a Vintage Vibrato bridge/tailpiece, new 2005.

MSR	$530	$400	$350	$300	$250	$210	$180	$150

AS73 - double cutaway thin hollow body archtop ES-335 style, maple back/top/sides, two f-holes, body binding, mahogany neck, 22-fret rosewood fingerboard with dot inlay, three-per-side tuners, fixed bridge, pickguard, two humbucker pickups, four knobs, three-way switch, chrome hardware, available in Brown Sunburst or Trans. Cherry finishes, mfg. 2003-present.

MSR	$400	$300	$250	$220	$180	$150	$120	$90

In 2005, Orange Trans. finish was introduced with cream colored knobs and pickguard (Model AF75D).

AS83 - double cutaway thin hollow body archtop ES-335 style, flame maple top/back/sides, two f-holes, body binding, three-piece maple/mahogany neck, 22-fret rosewood fingerboard with block inlay, three-per-side tuners, fixed bridge, pickguard, two humbucker pickups, four knobs, three-way switch, chrome hardware, available in Violin Sunburst finish, mfg. 2004-present.

MSR	$570	$430	$375	$325	$275	$225	$190	$160

AWD82 - offset double cutaway thin hollow body archtop RG style, bubinga top, maple top and sides, two f-holes, body binding, three-piece maple/mahogany neck, 22-fret rosewood fingerboard with AWL block inlay, three-per-side tuners, fixed bridge, two humbucker pickups, two knobs, three-way switch, chrome hardware, available in Trans. Blue finish, new 2005.

MSR	$480	$360	$310	$270	$230	$190	$160	$130

AWD82L - similar to the AWD82, except has a maple top/back/sides with abalone binding and inlays, Black finish, new 2005.

MSR	$570	$430	$375	$325	$275	$235	$195	$160

AWD82T - similar to the AW82, except has a tremolo bridge, Trans. Red finish, new 2005.

MSR	$530	$400	$350	$300	$250	$210	$180	$150

AXD71 - single cutaway ES-125 style body, maple top/back/sides, single f-hole, body binding, mahogany neck, 22-fret rosewood fingerboard with dot inlay, three-per-side tuners, fixed bridge, two humbucker pickups, two knobs, three-way switch, chrome hardware, Black finish, mfg. 2004 only.

	$300	$250	$210	$180	$150	$120	$90

Last MSR was $400.

AXD81 - single cutaway ES-125 style body, maple top/back/sides, single f-hole, body binding, three-piece maple/mahogany neck, 22-fret rosewood fingerboard with Artcore dot inlay, three-per-side tuners, fixed bridge, two humbucker pickups, two knobs, three-way switch, chrome hardware, Violin Sunburst finish, mfg. 2004 only.

	$360	$310	$270	$230	$190	$160	$130

Last MSR was $480.

Ibanez AF75
courtesy Ibanez

Ibanez AG75
courtesy Ibanez

GRADING		**100%** MINT	**98%** NEAR MINT	**95%** EXC+	**90%** EXC	**80%** VG+	**70%** VG	**60%** G

AXD82 - single cutaway ES-125 style body, spruce top, maple back and sides, two f-holes, body binding, three-piece maple/mahogany neck, 22-fret rosewood fingerboard with Artcore dot inlay, three-per-side tuners, fixed bridge, trapeze tailpiece, two humbucker pickups, two knobs, three-way switch, chrome hardware, Dark Violin Sunburst finish, new 2005.

	MSR	$500		$375	$325	$275	$235	$195	$160	$130

Last MSR was $480.

AXF74 - ES-125 style body, maple top/back/sides, two f-holes, body binding, mahogany neck, 22-fret rosewood fingerboard with dot inlay, three-per-side tuners, fixed bridge, trapeze tailpiece, cream pickguard, two humbucker pickups, two knobs, three-way switch, chrome hardware, Pale Blue finish, mfg. 2004 only.

		$300	$250	$210	$180	$150	$120	$90

Last MSR was $400.

FTM60 - offset single cutaway semi-acoustic Talman style body, maple top/back/sides, single f-hole, body binding, mahogany neck, 22-fret rosewood fingerboard with dot inlay, three-per-side tuners, fixed bridge, sparkle pickguard, two humbucker pickups, two knobs, three-way switch, chrome hardware, Turquoise finish, mfg. 2004 only.

		$250	$200	$170	$140	$110	$90	$70

Last MSR was $330.

FWD60 - offset double cutaway thin hollow body archtop RG style, maple top/back/sides, two f-holes, body binding, three-piece maple/mahogany neck, 22-fret rosewood fingerboard with dot inlay, three-per-side tuners, fixed bridge, two humbucker pickups, two knobs, three-way switch, chrome hardware, available in Trans. Orange finish, new 2005.

	MSR	$400		$300	$250	$210	$180	$150	$120	$90

TXD71 - offset single cutaway semi-acoustic Talman style body, maple top/back/sides, single f-hole, body binding, mahogany neck, 22-fret rosewood fingerboard with dot inlay, three-per-side tuners, fixed bridge, two humbucker pickups, two knobs, three-way switch, chrome hardware, Black finish, mfg. 2004 only.

		$300	$250	$210	$180	$150	$120	$90

Last MSR was $400.

ELECTRIC: ARTIST SERIES

Artist Series models debuted in 1973. By 1977/1978, there were at least three variations being offered: The **Artist** (Model 2618), which had a dual cutaway body engraved tailpiece, gold hardware, 2 humbuckers with engraved pickup covers, and dot fingerboard inlays. The **Artist EQ** (Model 2623), a favorite of guitarist Steve Miller during this time period, had an onboard 3-band EQ (three extra knobs).

In 1981, the **Artist Model AR-300** featured a tiger maple (flamed) top and Super 58 humbuckers with coil taps.

Many of the late 1970s Les Paul-styled Artist models are seeing a pricing resurgence of $700 to $900 in the vintage market. The 1980s models are less collectible at this point and are asking between $500-$650.

Between July 1972 and July 1973, luthier Rex Bogue constructed the heavily inlaid doubleneck "Double Rainbow" guitar for jazz guitarist Mahavishnu John McLaughlin (the inlay work alone was over 80 hours!). McLaughlin´s doubleneck attracted the attention of Jeff Hasselberger at Ibanez, who received Bogue´s permission to duplicate the "look" of the guitar. Ibanez´ vaguely SG-shaped doubleneck re-creation debuted in the 1975 Ibanez catalog as the **Model 2670**, under the **Professional** or **Artist Autograph** series. While the **Model 2670** was available from 1975 through 1980, it is estimated that only a dozen were actually produced. The 1975 retail list for the **Model 2670** was $1,500. The Artist Series was reintroduced by Ibanez in 1997.

AR200 ARTIST - dual cutaway mahogany body, bound maple top, set-in maple neck, 22-fret rosewood fingerboard with pearl dot inlay, 3-per-side tuners, chrome hardware, Full Tune II bridge/stop tailpiece, 2 humbucker pickups, 2 volume/2 tone controls, 3-way pickup selector, available in Black or Trans. Red finishes, mfg. 1997-99, reintroduced 2004-and is currently produced.

	MSR	$660		$495	$425	$375	$325	$275	$225	$175

Add $75 for flamed maple top, only on models produced between 1997-99.

AR250 ARTIST - double cutaway select mahogany body, Flamed maple top, 1-piece maple set neck, rosewood fingerboard with pearl dot inlays, 22 large frets, 3-per-side tuners, Full Tune II bridge, 1 ea. IBZ AH-1 and IBZ AH-2 humbucker pickups, chrome hardware, available in Vintage Burst finish, disc. 2003.

		$600	$525	$450	$400	$350	$300	$250

Last MSR was $800.

AR300 ARTIST - double cutaway select mahogany body, flamed maple top, 3-piece maple set neck, rosewood fingerboard with pearl block inlays, 22 large frets, 3-per-side tuners, br-eg bridge, 2 Super HB-58 humbucker pickups, chrome hardware, available in Honey Sunburst finish, mfg. 2004-present.

	MSR	$800		$600	$525	$450	$400	$350	$300	$250

AR700 ARTIST - similar to the AR200, except features 3-piece maple neck, abalone dot fingerboard inlay, Gibralter II bridge/stop tailpiece, gold hardware, 2 Super 58 humbuckers, available in Stained Brown Sunburst finish, mfg. 1997-99.

		$1,050	$850	$750	$650	$595	$525	$450

Last MSR was $1,299.

AR2000 ARTIST PRESTIGE - similar to the AR200, except features a flamed maple top, 3-piece maple neck, abalone dot fingerboard inlay, Gibralter II bridge/stop tailpiece, gold hardware, 2 Super 58 humbuckers, available in Vintage Violin finish, mfg. 1997-2003.

		$1,500	$1,250	$1,200	$1,100	$995	$895	$750

Last MSR was $2,000.

AR3000 ARTIST - double cutaway select mahogany body, AAA flamed maple top, 3-piece maple set neck, rosewood fingerboard with pearl block inlays, 22 medium frets, 3-per-side tuners, Gibralter II bridge, 2 Super HB-58 humbucker pickups, gold hardware, available in Vintage Violin finish, mfg. 2004 only.

		$1,650	$1,400	$1,200	$1,050	$900	$775	$650

Last MSR was $2,130.

GRADING	100% MINT	98% NEAR MINT	95% EXC+	90% EXC	80% VG+	70% VG	60% G

ELECTRIC: ARTSTAR SERIES

AF80 - single rounded cutaway semi-hollow style, bound maple top, bound f-holes, raised black pickguard, maple back/sides, set-in maple neck, 22-fret bound rosewood fingerboard with pearl dot inlay, adjustable rosewood bridge/trapeze tailpiece, bound blackface peghead with screened flower/logo, 3-per-side tuners, chrome hardware, 2 covered humbucker pickups, 2 volume/2 tone controls, 3-position switch, available in Vintage Sunburst finish, mfg. 1994-96.

	N/A	$450	$375	$325	$275	$225	$175

Last MSR was $650.

AF120 - similar to AF80, except features bound spruce top, 20-fret fingerboard with pearl/abalone block inlay, gold hardware, 2 Ibanez Super 58 humbucker pickups, available in Brown Sunburst finish, disc.2003.

	$750	$650	$575	$495	$425	$325	$250

Last MSR was $1,000.

AF200 - similar to the AF80, except features bound spruce top, bound f-holes, raised pickguard, 3-piece mahogany/maple set-in neck, 20-fret bound ebony fingerboard with pearl/abalone rectangle inlays, ebony bridge with trapeze tailpiece, gold hardware, 2 Super 58 humbuckers, available in Antique Violin finish, mfg. 1991-98.

	$1,500	$1,425	$1,200	$1,000	$900	$725	$550

Last MSR was $2,199.

AF207 7-String - similar to AF200, except features 7-string configuration, 4/3-per-side tuners, one DiMarzio humbucker pickup, available in Antique Violin finish, mfg. 1997-2001.

	$2,250	$1,950	$1,700	$1,500	$1,300	$1,100	$850

Last MSR was $3,000.

AF220 - similar to the AF200, except features maple top/back/sides, 20-fret bound rosewood fingerboard with pearl block inlay, adjustable rosewood bridge/GE 103B metal tailpiece, available in Butterscotch Trans. finish, mfg. 1998-99.

	$1,525	$1,225	$1,025	$925	$825	$725	$600

Last MSR was $1,899.

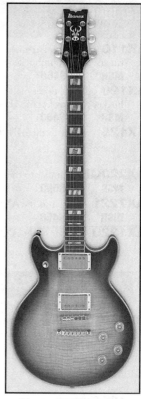

Ibanez AR300 Artist courtesy Ibanez

AM200 - double cutaway semi-hollow style, burl mahogany top with bound body/f-holes, raised pickguard, burl mahogany back/sides, 3-piece mahogany/maple set-in neck, 20-fret bound rosewood fingerboard with pearl abalone rectangle inlay, tune-o-matic bridge stop tailpiece, bound peghead, 3-per-side nylon head tuners, gold hardware, 2 Super 58 humbuckers, volume/tone control, 3-position selector switch, available in Antique Violin finish, mfg. 1991-96.

	N/A	$950	$800	$675	$550	$475	$400

Last MSR was $1,500.

AS50 - double cutaway semi-hollow style, maple top/back/sides, f-holes, raised black pickguard, bolt-on maple neck, 22-fret bound rosewood fingerboard with pearl dot inlay, Full Tune II bridge/stop tailpiece, 3-per-side tuners, chrome hardware, 2 humbucker pickups, 2 volume/2 tone controls, 3-position switch, available in Butterscotch Trans. or Brown Sunburst finishes, mfg. 1998-99.

	$350	$295	$260	$225	$195	$165	$125

Last MSR was $499.

AS80 - double cutaway semi-hollow style, bound maple top, bound f-holes, raised black pickguard, maple back/sides/neck, set-in neck, 22-fret bound rosewood fingerboard with abalone dot inlay, tune-o-matic bridge/stop tailpiece, bound blackface peghead with screened flower/logo, 3-per-side tuners, chrome hardware, 2 covered Super 58 humbucker pickups, 2 volume/2 tone controls, 3-position switch, available in Butterscotch Trans. or Vintage Sunburst finishes, mfg. 1994-2001.

	N/A	$550	$475	$425	$375	$325	$275

Last MSR was $800.

AS120 - similar to AS80, except features pearl/abalone block fingerboard inlay, gold hardware, available in Trans. Red finish, disc. 2003.

	$675	$575	$525	$450	$375	$300	$225

Last MSR was $900.

AS180 - similar to AS80, except features 3-piece maple/mahogany set-in neck, cream dot fingerboard inlay, Gibralter II tune-o-matic bridge/wrap-around tailpiece, available in Stained Sunburst finish, disc. 1999.

	$1,100	$950	$800	$695	$575	$475	$350

Last MSR was $1,399.

AS200 - similar to AS80, except features bound flame maple top, flame maple back/sides, 3-piece mahogany/maple neck, pearl/abalone block fingerboard inlay, Gibralter II tune-o-matic bridge/wrap-around tailpiece, gold hardware, available in Antique Violin finish, mfg. 1991-2001.

	$1,575	$1,350	$1,200	$1,000	$850	$700	$525

Last MSR was $2,100.

ELECTRIC: AX SERIES

AXS32 - double offset mahogany body, 3-piece mahogany neck, 22-fret bound rosewood fingerboard with 12th fret inlay, STB bridge, 3-per-side tuners, two humbucker pickups (AH3, AH4), four knobs, 3-way switch, chrome hardware, available in Dark Red Stained Flat or Trans. Flat Black finishes, current mfg.

MSR	$530		$399	$350	$300	$250	$200	$160	$130

Ibanez AF200 courtesy Ibanez

GRADING	100% MINT	98% NEAR MINT	95% EXC+	90% EXC	80% VG+	70% VG	60% G

AX110 - double offset mahogany body, three-piece AX maple neck, 22-fret bound rosewood fingerboard with dot inlay, fixed bridge, three-per-side tuners, single humbucker pickup, two knobs, black hardware, Weathered Brown finish, new 2005.

MSR	$460		$350	$290	$250	$220	$190	$160	$130

AX120 - double offset mahogany body, AX maple neck, 22-fret bound rosewood fingerboard with dot inlay, fixed bridge, 3-per-side tuners, two humbucker pickups (AH3, AH4), four knobs, 3-way switch, chrome hardware, available in Antique Bronze or Gray Nickel finishes, current mfg.

MSR	$400		$300	$250	$210	$175	$150	$125	$95

AX125 - similar to the AX120 except has a Downshifter D-tuner on the bridge, available in Black finish, mfg. 2001-04.

	$340	$275	$225	$200	$175	$145	$115

Last MSR was $450.

AX220QM - similar to the AX120 except has a quilted maple top, available in Biker Black finish, mfg. 2001-present.

MSR	$500		$375	$325	$275	$225	$200	$160	$130

AX7221 - similar to the AX120 except is in 7-string configuration, available in Gray Pewter finish, mfg. 2001-present.

MSR	$450		$350	$300	$250	$210	$180	$150	$120

AX1220 - similar to the AX120 except has different pickups, available in Biker Black finish, mfg. 2003 only.

	$750	$675	$600	$525	$475	$425	$375

Last MSR was $1,000.

ELECTRIC: BLAZER SERIES

Earlier Blazer models (1980s) featured 2 mini-switches for coil tap and phase functions, and metallic finishes with matching color headstocks.

BL850 - offset double cutaway alder body, bolt-on maple neck, 22-fret rosewood fingerboard with pearl dot inlay, 6-on-a-side tuners, chrome hardware, pearloid pickguard, Gotoh 510AT tremolo, humbucker/single coil/humbucker pickups, volume/tone controls, 5-way selector, available in Black or Vintage Burst finishes, disc. 1999.

1980-1989	N/A	$400	$325	$275	$225	$175	$125
1990-1999	N/A	$500	$425	$350	$300	$250	$200

Last MSR was $679.

BL1025 - similar to the BL850, except features Wilkinson VSV tremolo, available in Cayman Green and Vintage Burst finishes, disc. 1999.

	$750	$650	$575	$495	$425	$325	$250

Last MSR was $999.

ELECTRIC: DOUBLE AXE SERIES

The Ibanez **Double Axe** model was available from (circa) 1974-76. The Double Axe was Ibanez´ take on the Gibson EDS-1275; Gibson first produced the EDS-1275 between 1963 and 1968, then discontinued the model. Ibanez began issuing their Double Axe in 1974, probably in limited production amounts. Then, in 1977, Gibson again began producing the EDS-1275 (Model DSED currently) and has done so since then. Coincidence? Or to coincide with the Led Zeppelin tours and the frequent use by guitarist Jimmy Page?

The **Double Axe** (Model 2402) was available in a 6-string/12-string doubleneck configuration, a 4-string bass/6-string guitar doubleneck configuration, and an odd dual 6-string doubleneck configuration. All models were available in Cherry or Walnut finishes, with the same list price of $425. All three were also available in a custom Ivory finish for $450.

ELECTRIC: EX SERIES

EX Series models were available from 1988 to 1994.

EX160 - offset double cutaway maple body, bolt-on maple neck, 22-fret rosewood fingerboard with pearl dot inlay, standard vibrato, 6-on-a-side tuners, chrome hardware, 2 single coil/1 humbucker pickups, volume/tone control, 5-position switch, available in Black or Matte Stain finishes, mfg. 1988-1994.

	N/A	$250	$210	$180	$150	$125	$100

Last MSR was $330.

EX170 - similar to the EX160, except features 22-fret maple fingerboard with black dot inlay, humbucker/single coil/humbucker pickups, available in Black, Blue Night, or Matte Violin finishes, mfg. 1988-1994.

	N/A	$250	$210	$180	$150	$130	$100

Last MSR was $350.

EX270 - similar to EX170, except has locking vibrato, black hardware, available in Black, Blue Night, or Candy Apple finishes, mfg. 1988-1994.

	N/A	$300	$250	$210	$180	$140	$110

Last MSR was $470.

EX350 - offset double cutaway basswood body, bolt-on maple neck, 22-fret bound rosewood fingerboard with triangle inlay, double locking vibrato, 6-on-a-side tuners, chrome hardware, humbucker/single coil/humbucker Ibanez pickups, volume/tone control, 5-position switch, available in Black, Burgundy Red, Desert Yellow, or Laser Blue finishes, mfg. 1988-1994.

	N/A	$350	$300	$250	$210	$170	$130

Last MSR was $570.

EX360 - similar to EX350, except features 2 single coil/humbucker Ibanez pickups, available in Black, Dark Grey, Jewel Blue, or Purple Pearl finishes, mfg. 1988-1992.

	N/A	$350	$300	$250	$210	$170	$130

Last MSR was $500.

EX365 - similar to EX350, except features reverse headstock, single coil/humbucker Ibanez pickups, available in Black, Laser Blue, or Ultra Violet finishes, mfg. 1988-1992.

	N/A	$350	$300	$250	$210	$170	$130

Last MSR was $480.

GRADING	100% MINT	98% NEAR MINT	95% EXC+	90% EXC	80% VG+	70% VG	60% G

EX370 - offset double cutaway basswood body, bolt-on maple neck, 22-fret bound rosewood fingerboard with triangle inlay, double locking vibrato, 6-on-a-side tuners, chrome hardware, humbucker/single coil/humbucker Ibanez pickups, volume/tone control, 5-position switch, available in Black, Burgundy Red, Jewel Blue, or Ultra Violet finishes, mfg. 1988-1994.

	N/A	$350	$300	$250	$210	$170	$130

Last MSR was $570.

EX370 FM - similar to EX370, except has flame maple top, gold hardware, available in Antique Violin, Cherry Sunburst, or Wine Burst finishes, disc. 1994.

	N/A	$375	$325	$275	$225	$190	$155

Last MSR was $650.

EX1500 - offset double cutaway maple body, bolt-on maple neck, 22-fret maple fingerboard with black dot inlay, standard vibrato, 6-on-a-side tuners, gold hardware, tortoise pickguard, humbucker/single coil/humbucker pickups, volume/tone control, 5-position switch, available in Antique Violin or Black finishes, mfg. 1993-94.

	N/A	$300	$250	$210	$170	$140	$110

Last MSR was $430.

EX1700 - similar to EX1500, except has bound body, no pickguard, chrome hardware, available in Cherry Sunburst or Trans. Turquoise finishes, mfg. 1993-94.

	N/A	$350	$300	$250	$210	$170	$130

Last MSR was $430.

EX3700 - offset double cutaway basswood body, bound flame maple top, bolt-on maple neck, 24-fret maple fingerboard with black dot inlay, double locking vibrato, 6-on-a-side tuners, gold hardware, humbucker/single coil/humbucker Ibanez pickups, volume/tone control, 5-position switch, available in Trans. Purple, Trans. Red, or Trans. Turquoise finishes, mfg. 1993-94.

	N/A	$400	$350	$300	$250	$200	$150

Last MSR was $650.

ELECTRIC: FRANK GAMBALE SIGNATURE (FGM) SERIES

The FGM Series was co-designed by guitarist Frank Gambale, and debuted in 1991.

FGM100 - sculpted thin offset double cutaway mahogany body, one-piece maple neck, 22-fret bound rosewood fingerboard with body matching color sharktooth inlay, double locking vibrato, 6-on-a-side tuners, black hardware, DiMarzio humbucker/DiMarzio single coil/Ibanez humbucker pickups, volume/tone control, 5-position selector switch, available in Black, Desert Sun Yellow, Pink Salmon, or Sky Blue finishes, mfg. 1991-94.

	N/A	$800	$700	$600	$500	$400	$300

Last MSR was $1,300.

FGM200 - similar to the FGM100, except features unbound 22-fret rosewood fingerboard with clay dot inlay, strings through Gotoh fixed bridge, DiMarzio humbucker/single coil/humbucker pickups, available in Black or White finishes, mfg. 1994-96.

	N/A	$900	$775	$650	$550	$450	$350

Last MSR was $1,500.

FGM300 - similar to the FGM100, except features 22-fret bound rosewood fingerboard with pearl sharktooth inlay, DiMarzio humbucker/single coil/humbucker pickups, available in Desert Yellow Sun or Metallic Green finishes, mfg. 1994-96.

	N/A	$1,000	$850	$700	$600	$500	$400

Last MSR was $1,700.

FGM400 - similar to the FGM100, except features a quilted maple top, 22-fret bound rosewood fingerboard with pearl block/Frank Gambale signature inlay at 12th fret, 2 single coil/humbucker Ibanez pickups, available in Blazer Blue finish, mfg. 1997-99.

	$1,650	$1,450	$1,275	$1,100	$900	$725	$550

Last MSR was $2,199.

In 1998, Quilted Maple translucent finish was introduced; Blazer Blue finish was discontinued. When the FGM400 was first introduced, the quilted maple top was a $200 option. This optional model was known as the FGM400 QM, which was available in Quilted Maple finish. A year later, the FGM400 QM model was discontinued; the quilted maple top which was optional before became a production model.

ELECTRIC: GAX SERIES

GAX30 - dual cutaway basswood body, maple neck, 22-fret rosewood fingerboard with pearl dot inlay, fixed bridge, 3-per-side tuners, chrome hardware, 2 AX humbucker pickups, 2 volume/2 tone control, 3-position switch, available in Black, Jewel Blue, or Trans. Red finishes, mfg. 2004-present.

MSR	$220	$165	$140	$120	$100	$80	$65	$50

GAX70 - dual cutaway agathis body, maple neck, 22-fret rosewood fingerboard with pearl dot inlay, Full Tune II bridge/stop tailpiece, 3-per-side tuners, chrome hardware, 2 exposed pole piece humbucker pickups, 2 volume/2 tone control, 3-position switch, available in Black, Butterscotch Transparent, Jewel Blue, or Trans. Red finishes, mfg. 1997-present.

MSR	$280	$210	$175	$155	$135	$115	$95	$75

Add $40 for left-handed configuration.

Ibanez EX370 FM
courtesy Ibanez

Ibanez FGM100
courtesy Ibanez

GRADING	100% MINT	98% NEAR MINT	95% EXC+	90% EXC	80% VG+	70% VG	60% G

GAX75 - similar to the GAX70 except has a Short Stop II bridge with downshifter, available in Gray Pewter finish, mfg. 2001-present.

	MSR	$330	$250	$215	$175	$150	$125	$105	$80

ELECTRIC: GEORGE BENSON (GB) SERIES

The GB Series was co-designed by George Benson. The first model, the **GB10**, was introduced in 1978. Along with the GB10 was the **GB20**, which featured a 16 in. body width and a single floating humbucker. The **GB30** was introduced in 1985, and the special **GB12** (celebrating the 12th Anniversary of the GB10) was introduced in 1990.

GB5 - single round cutaway hollow style, arched spruce top, bound f-holes, raised bound maple pickguard, bound body, maple back/sides, maple/mahogany 3-piece neck, 20-fret bound ebony fingerboard with pearl split block inlay, ebony bridge with pearl curlicue inlay, ebony tailpiece, bound blackface peghead with pearl flower/logo, 3-per-side tuners with pearloid buttons, gold hardware, 2 humbucker Ibanez pickups, 2 volume/2 tone controls, 3-position switch, available in Brown Sunburst finish, mfg. 1994-96.

			$1,600	$1,450	$1,300	$1,150	$1,000	$875	$725

Last MSR was $2,900.

GB10 - single round cutaway hollow style, arched spruce top, bound f-holes, raised bound black pickguard, bound body, flamed maple back/sides, 3-piece maple/mahogany neck, 22-fret bound ebony fingerboard with pearl/abalone split block inlay/George Benson signature block inlay at 21st fret, ebony bridge with pearl arrow inlays, ebony/metal tailpiece, bound peghead with abalone torch/logo inlay, 3-per-side tuners with pearloid buttons, gold hardware, 2 Ibanez humbucker pickups, 2 volume/2 tone controls, 3-position switch, available in Brown Sunburst or Natural finishes, mfg. 1978-present.

1978-1995		N/A	$2,300	$2,000	$1,700	$1,450	$1,250	$1,050
1996-MSR	$3,330	$2,500	$2,200	$1,900	$1,600	$1,400	$1,200	$1,000

GB10JS - similar to the GB10, except features maple back/sides, bound rosewood fingerboard, rosewood bridge, available in Brown Sunburst finish, disc. 1999.

		$1,199	$975	$850	$725	$625	$500	$375

Last MSR was $1,499.

GB12 LIMITED EDITION GEORGE BENSON 12TH ANNIVERSARY MODEL - single round cutaway hollow style, arched flame maple top/back/sides, abalone and plastic bound body and f-holes, raised matched pickguard, 22-fret ebony fingerboard with special GB-12 inlay/George Benson signature scroll inlay at 21st fret, ebony bridge with flower inlay, gold and ebony tailpiece with vine inlay, bound peghead with abalone logo and George Benson 12th Anniversary Ibanez inlays, 3-per-side nylon head tuners, gold hardware, 2 humbucker Ibanez pickups, 2 volume/tone controls, 3-position switch, available in Brown Sunburst finish, mfg. 1990-92.

		$1,300	$1,100	$1,000	$850	$750	$625	$500

Last MSR was $2,000.

GB30 - single round cutaway hollow style, arched maple top/back/sides, bound body and f-holes, raised black pickguard, mahogany neck, 22-fret bound ebony fingerboard with offset pearl dot inlay/George Benson signature block inlay at 21st fret, tune-o-matic bridge/stop tailpiece, bound peghead with abalone logo and George Benson standard Ibanez inlay, 3-per-side nylon head tuners, black hardware, 2 humbucker pickups, 2 volume/tone controls, 3-position switch, available in Black or Trans. Red finishes, mfg. 1985-1992.

		N/A	$900	$775	$650	$550	$450	$350

Last MSR was $1,300.

GB100 - single round cutaway hollow style, arched flame maple top/back/sides, bound f-holes, abalone bound body, raised maple pickguard, 22-fret bound ebony fingerboard with special pearl GB12 inlay, ebony bridge with flower inlay, metal/ebony tailpiece with pearl vine inlay, bound blackface peghead with abalone torch/logo inlay, 3-per-side tuners with pearloid buttons, gold hardware, 2 humbucker Ibanez pickups, 2 volume/2 tone controls, 3-position switch, available in Brown Sunburst finish, mfg. 1993-96.

		N/A	$1,900	$1,650	$1,400	$1,200	$1,000	$800

Last MSR was $2,500.

GB200 - Venetian cutaway hollowbody, spruce top, maple back and sides, 3-piece maple/mahogany set neck, bound ebony fingerboard with GB 200 Pearl position markers, 20 medium frets, ebony bridge, 2 IBZ Super 58 humbucker pickups, gold hardware, available in Brown Sunburst finish, current mfg.

	MSR	$3,730	$2,800	$2,400	$2,100	$1,800	$1,550	$1,350	$1,150

ELECTRIC: GOLDEN OLDIES SERIES

Proof that Ibanez was willing to take on the established American companies was established in 1974 when Ibanez introduced the **Golden Oldies Series**. The four instruments were modeled after Gibson´s stalwart designs, with a little tongue in cheek renaming. The **Rocket Roll** was Ibanez´ version of a Flying V, the **Firebrand** was a Firebird copy, the **Deluxe ´59er** was a flametop LP with sunburst finish steal (even to the right year in the name!), and the **FM Jr.** was the Ibanez version of the Les Paul TV Junior (FM ´radio´ derived from TV - Get it?). This series was produced from 1974-75.

Both the Rocket Roll and the Firebrand had the Ibanez logo on their respective truss rod covers; the Deluxe ´59er and FM Jr. had the Ibanez logo across their headstocks. Golden Oldies models featured solid or sunburst finishes, similar to their namesakes.

The **Rocket Roll** model was designated **Model 2387**. Ibanez also had a **Rocket Roll** Bass 4-string model designated **Model 2387-B**, but few have turned up on the secondary market.

ELECTRIC: GHOSTRIDER SERIES

The Ghostrider Series was introduced in 1994.

GR320 - double cutaway bound alder body, mahogany neck, 22-fret bound rosewood fingerboard with pearl dot inlay, strings through fixed bridge, 3-per-side tuners, black hardware, 2 Ibanez humbucker pickups, volume/tone control, 3-position switch, available in Black or Cherry finishes, mfg. 1994-96.

		N/A	$450	$375	$325	$275	$225	$175

Last MSR was $700.

GRADING	100% MINT	98% NEAR MINT	95% EXC+	90% EXC	80% VG+	70% VG	60% G

GR520 - similar to the GR320, except features bound carved maple top, 22-fret bound rosewood fingerboard with abalone/pearl split block inlay, tune-o-matic bridge/stop tailpiece, bound blackface peghead with screened logo, 3-per-side tuners with pearloid buttons, gold hardware, available in Orange Sunburst or Vintage Sunburst finishes, mfg. 1994-96.

	N/A	$500	$425	$350	$300	$250	$200

Last MSR was $800.

Ibanez GB10
courtesy Ibanez

ELECTRIC: GSA/GSZ SERIES

GSA20 - double offset cutaway agathis body, GSA maple neck, 22-fret rosewood fingerboard with dot inlay, standard tremolo, 6-on-one-side tuners, two humbucker pickups (PSND1 & PSND2), available in Black finish, disc. 2004.

	$220	$185	$150	$125	$100	$80	$60

Last MSR was $290.

GSA60 - similar to the GSA60 except has two single coil pickups and a humbucker, available in Black or Jewel Blue finishes, current mfg.

MSR	$300	$225	$190	$155	$130	$110	$90	$70

GSZ120 - offset double cutaway poplar body, maple neck, 22-fret rosewood fingerboard with dot inlay, three-per-side tuners, standard bridge, two humbucker pickups, three knobs, three-way switch, black hardware, available in Black Night or Silver finishes, new 2005.

MSR	$286	$215	$180	$155	$130	$105	$80	$60

ELECTRIC: GX/GRG/GRX SERIES

Models RX20, RX20 L, and RX40 were part of the RX Series from 1994 until 1997. In 1998, these models were redesignated with a ´G´ prefix and added to the GRX Series.

GRG170 DX - offset double cutaway basswood body, maple neck, 24-fret rosewood fingerboard with sharktooth inlays, black headstock with six-per-side tuners, FAT 10 tremolo bridge, two humbucker and one single coil pickups, two knobs, five-way switch, chrome hardware, Black Night or Jewel Blue finishes, new 2005.

MSR	$330	$230	$190	$160	$140	$120	$100	$80

GRX20 (RX20) - offset double cutaway agathis body, bolt-on maple neck, 22-fret maple fingerboard with black dot inlay, standard tremolo, 6-on-a-side tuners, chrome hardware, white pickguard, 2 humbucker pickups, volume/tone control, 3-position switch, available in Black, Blue Night, or Deep Green finishes, mfg. 1994-present.

MSR	$220	$175	$155	$140	$115	$100	$80	$60

In 1998, rosewood fingerboard replaced the maple fingerboard; Jewel Blue finish was introduced; Blue Night and Deep Green finishes were discontinued.

GRX20 L (RX20 L) - similar to the RX20, except in left-handed configuration, available in Black finish, current mfg.

MSR	$330	$260	$230	$210	$180	$150	$120	$90

GRX40 (RX40) - similar to the RX20, except features rosewood fingerboard with pearl dot inlay, 2 single coil/humbucker pickups, 5-way selector, available in Black, Blue Night, or Deep Green finishes, disc. 1999.

	$180	$165	$150	$135	$115	$90	$70

Last MSR was $269.

In 1998, Candy Apple Red and Jewel Blue finishes were introduced; Blue Night and Deep Green finishes were discontinued. In 1999, alder body replaced agathis and Metallic Red and Metallic Grape finishes were introduced while Blue Night and Deep Green were discontinued.

GRX70 - similar to the RX20, except features rosewood fingerboard with pearl dot inlay, humbucker/single coil/humbucker pickups, 5-way selector, available in Black or Metallic Green finishes, mfg. 1998-99.

	$215	$175	$150	$135	$115	$95	$75

Last MSR was $299.

GRX720 - similar to the GRX40 except is in 7-string configuration, available in black finish, mfg. 2001-03.

	$300	$250	$210	$180	$150	$125	$95

Last MSR was $400.

ELECTRIC: ICEMAN SERIES

The original Iceman model (PS10) was introduced in 1978.

IC200 - single horn cutaway asymmetrical bound mahogany body with pointed bottom bout, ic maple neck, 22-fret bound rosewood fingerboard with pearl dot inlay, tune-o-matic bridge/stop tailpiece, 3-per-side tuners, chrome hardware, 2 humbucker pickups, volume/tone controls, 3-position switch, available in Black or Brown Sunburst finishes, mfg. 2004-present.

MSR	$530	$375	$325	$275	$235	$195	$165	$135

In 2005, Black finish was disc.

IC300 - single horn cutaway asymmetrical bound basswood body with pointed bottom bout, bolt-on maple neck, 22-fret bound rosewood fingerboard with pearl dot inlay, tune-o-matic bridge/stop tailpiece, 3-per-side tuners, chrome hardware, 2 Ibanez humbucker pickups, volume/tone controls, 3-position switch, available in Black or Blue finishes, mfg. 1994-2003.

	$495	$425	$375	$325	$275	$225	$175

Last MSR was $650.

Ibanez GB12
courtesy Ibanez

GRADING	100% MINT	98% NEAR MINT	95% EXC+	90% EXC	80% VG+	70% VG	60% G

IC400 - single horn cutaway asymmetrical bound mahogany body with pointed bottom bout, ic set maple neck, 22-fret bound rosewood fingerboard with Iceman parallelogram inlay, tune-o-matic bridge/stop tailpiece, 3-per-side tuners, chrome hardware, 2 Ibanez humbucker pickups, 2 volume, 2 tone controls, 3-position switch, available in Black finish, mfg. 2004-present.

	MSR	$700	$525	$450	$400	$350	$300	$250	$200

IC500 - similar to the IC300, except features pearloid bound body, raised pearloid pickguard, abalone dot fingerboard inlay, bound blackface peghead with pearl logo inlay, 3-per-side tuners with pearloid buttons, cosmo black hardware, available in Black finish, mfg. 1994-96.

	$800	$650	$595	$525	$450	$400	$325

Last MSR was $1,300.

ICJ100 WZ - single horn cutaway asymmetrical mahogany body with pointed bottom bout, abalone bound maple top/back, set-in maple neck, 22-fret bound rosewood fingerboard with pearl/abalone block inlay, Lo Pro II locking tremolo, 3-per-side tuners, chrome hardware, 2 Ibanez humbucker pickups, volume/tone (push/pull coil tap) controls, 3-position switch, available in Green Galaxy finishes, disc. 1999.

	$1,525	$1,300	$1,150	$995	$825	$650	$500

Last MSR was $1,999.

This model was designed in conjunction with J. (White Zombie).

ICX220 - single horn cutaway asymmetrical basswood body with pointed bottom, three-piece X maple neck, 24-fret bound rosewood fingerboard with pearl dot inlay, tune-o-matic bridge/stop tailpiece, three-per-side tuners, two humbucker pickups, volume/tone controls, three-way switch, chrome hardware, Black finish, new 2005.

	MSR	$400	$300	$250	$210	$180	$150	$120	$90

ELECTRIC: JEM SERIES

The JEM Series was co-designed by Steve Vai, and introduced in 1987. All models in the series have a Monkey Grip hand slot routed in the bodies.

JEM555 - offset double cutaway American basswood body, bolt-on maple neck, 24-fret rosewood fingerboard with pearl dot/vine inlay with Steve Vai signature block inlay at 24th fret, Lo TRS II tremolo, 6-on-a-side tuners, charcoal hardware, humbucker/single coil/humbucker DiMarzio pickups, volume/tone control, 5-position switch, available in Black or White finishes, mfg. 1994-2002.

	$875	$725	$650	$550	$475	$395	$300

Last MSR was $1,200.

Add $100 for left-handed configuration (Model JEM555L). Available in Black finish only. The left-handed configuration was discontinued in 1998.

JEM7 V - offset double cutaway alder body, pearloid pickguard, bolt-on maple neck, 24-fret ebony fingerboard with pearl/abalone vine inlay, Lo Pro Edge tremolo, 6-on-a-side tuners, gold hardware, humbucker/single coil/humbucker DiMarzio pickups, volume/tone control, 5-position switch, available in White finish, mfg. 1994-present.

	MSR	$2,800	$2,100	$1,800	$1,550	$1,300	$1,100	$950	$800

Add $75 for Sparkle Blue finish.

JEM7 D - similar to JEM7 V, except has American Basswood body, rosewood fingerboard, screw-head position markers, 2 DiMarzio Breed humbucker pickups and 1 Dimarzio Special single coil in the center position, chrome hardware, available in Black finish, disc. 2004.

	$1,350	$1,150	$1,000	$875	$750	$650	$550

Last MSR was $1,730.

JEM7 - similar to the JEM7 V, except features an American basswood body, brushed aluminum pickguard, 24-fret rosewood fingerboard with screw inlay, brushed chrome hardware, available in Burnt Stain Blue finish, disc. 1999.

	$1,400	$1,200	$1,050	$925	$795	$650	$500

Last MSR was $1,999.

JEM77 GMC (GREEN MULTI-COLOR) - offset double cutaway basswood body, transparent pickguard, bolt-on maple neck, 24-fret rosewood fingerboard with fluorescent vine inlay, double locking vibrato, 6-on-a-side tuners, charcoal hardware, humbucker/single coil/humbucker DiMarzio pickups, volume/tone control, 5-position switch, available in Green Multi Color finish, mfg. 1992-94.

	N/A	$1,400	$1,200	$1,050	$900	$775	$650

Last MSR was $2,100.

JEM77 BFP (Blue Floral Pattern) - similar to JEM77 GMC, except has maple fingerboard with Blue vine inlay, body matching peghead, available in Blue Floral Pattern finish, mfg. 1991-96.

	N/A	$1,300	$1,100	$950	$825	$700	$600

Last MSR was $2,000.

JEM77 FP (Floral Pattern) - similar to JEM77 GMC, except has green/red vine fingerboard inlay, body matching peghead, available in Floral Pattern finish, mfg. 1988-1999.

	N/A	$1,350	$1,150	$1,000	$875	$750	$625

JEM77 PMC (Purple Multi-Color) - similar to JEM77 GMC, except has a maple fingerboard with 3 color pyramid inlay, available in Purple Multi Color finish, mfg. 1991-92.

	N/A	$1,400	$1,200	$1,050	$900	$775	$650

Last MSR was $2,100.

JEM777 - offset double cutaway basswood body, black pickguard, bolt-on maple neck, 24-fret maple fingerboard with 3 color vanishing pyramid inlay, double locking vibrato, 6-on-a-side tuners, charcoal hardware, humbucker/single coil/humbucker DiMarzio pickups, volume/tone control, 5-position switch, available in Desert Sun Yellow finish, mfg. 1992-96.

	N/A	$1,200	$1,050	$925	$800	$700	$600

Last MSR was $1,800.

JEM777 V - similar to JEM777, except features alder body, available in Black finish, disc. 1994.

	N/A	$1,100	$950	$825	$700	$600	$500

Last MSR was $1,700.

GRADING		100% MINT	98% NEAR MINT	95% EXC+	90% EXC	80% VG+	70% VG	60% G

JEM777B - similar to the JEM777, except has a basswood body, five-piece Prestige maple/walnut neck, and Rock Mirror finish, new 2005.

MSR	$3,100	$2,350	$2,000	$1,750	$1,500	$1,300	$1,100	$900

Ibanez JEM777
courtesy Ibanez

ELECTRIC: JPM SERIES

The JPM Series was co-designed with guitarist John Petrucci (Dream Theatre).

JPM100 - offset double cutaway basswood body, bolt-on 1-piece maple neck, 24-fret bound rosewood fingerboard with offset pearl dot inlay, Lo Pro Edge double locking tremolo, 6-on-a-side tuners, black hardware, 2 DiMarzio humbucker pickups, volume/tone control, 3-position switch, available in P4 (Part 4) Black/Green/Blue graphic matte finish, mfg. 1998-99.

			$1,100	$950	$825	$725	$600	$495	$375

Last MSR was $1,499.

JPM P3 - similar to the JPM except available in P3 (Part 3) Black/White graphic finish, disc. 1997.

			$1,200	$1,050	$925	$795	$650	$525	$400

Last MSR was $1,599.

ELECTRIC: JET KING SERIES

JTK1 - offset double cutaway, basswood body, three-piece maple neck, 22-fret rosewood neck with narrow side inlays, three-per-side tuners with plastic knobs, standard bridge, STB with plate, chrome pickguard, two humbucker pickups, two knobs, three-way switch, two retro switches, chrome hardware, available in Brown Sunburst, Butterscotch Trans., or Metallic Light Blue finishes, mfg. 2002-present.

MSR	$400	$300	$250	$210	$180	$150	$120	$90

JTK2 - offset double cutaway Talman style, basswood body, three-piece maple neck, 22-fret rosewood neck with offset triangle inlays, six-on-one-side tuners, standard bridge, STB with plate, two pickguards, two humbucker pickups, two knobs, three-way switch, two retro switches, chrome hardware, available in Brown Sunburst, or Coral Pink finishes, mfg. 2004-present.

MSR	$400	$300	$250	$210	$180	$150	$120	$90

ELECTRIC: JOE SATRIANI (JS) SERIES

The JS Series was co-designed by Joe Satriani, and debuted in 1990.

JS1 - offset double cutaway contoured basswood body, bolt-on maple neck, 22-fret rosewood fingerboard with pearl dot inlay, double locking vibrato, 6-on-a-side tuners, chrome hardware, humbucker/single coil/humbucker DiMarzio pickups, volume/tone control, 5-position switch, available in Black, Inferno Red, or White finishes, mfg. 1991-94.

		N/A	$900	$775	$650	$550	$450	$350

Last MSR was $1,200.

JS3 - similar to JS1, except has 2 humbucker DiMarzio pickups, 3-position switch, available in Custom Graphic finish, mfg. 1990 only.

		N/A	$1,500	$1,250	$1,050	$925	$800	$700

Last MSR was $2,300.

JS4 - similar to JS1, except has 2 humbucker DiMarzio pickups, 3-position switch, available in Electric Rainbow finish, mfg. 1993 only.

		N/A	$1,600	$1,300	$1,100	$950	$800	$700

Last MSR was $2,300.

JS5 - similar to JS1, except has 2 humbucker DiMarzio pickups, 3-position switch, available in Rainforest finish, mfg. 1992 only.

		N/A	$1,600	$1,300	$1,100	$950	$800	$700

Last MSR was $2,300.

JS6 - similar to JS1, except has mahogany body, fixed bridge, 2 humbucker DiMarzio pickups, 3-position switch, available in oil finish, mfg. 1993 only.

		N/A	$1,600	$1,300	$1,100	$950	$800	$700

Last MSR was $2,300.

JS 10TH ANNIVERSARY CHROME LIMITED EDITION - offset double cutaway contoured luthite body, bolt-on one-piece maple neck, 22-fret rosewood fingerboard with pearl dot inlay, Edge double locking tremolo, 6-on-a-side tuners, chrome hardware, 2 DiMarzio JS10TH humbucker pickups, volume/tone control, 3-position switch, available in Chrome finish, mfg. 1998-99.

		$2,400	$2,000	$1,750	N/A	N/A	N/A	N/A

Last MSR was $3,000.

JS100 - offset double cutaway contoured basswood body, bolt-on one-piece maple neck, 22-fret rosewood fingerboard with pearl dot inlay/Joe Satriani block inlay at 21st fret, Lo TRS II double locking tremolo, 6-on-a-side tuners, chrome hardware, 2 Ibanez humbucker pickups, volume/tone control, 3-position switch, available in Black and Trans. Red finishes, mfg. 1994-present.

MSR	$900	$675	$600	$525	$450	$375	$300	$225

Ibanez JS-4
courtesy Ibanez

GRADING	100% MINT	98% NEAR MINT	95% EXC+	90% EXC	80% VG+	70% VG	60% G

JS600 - similar to JS100, except has STB, available in Black or White finishes, mfg. 1994-96.

	N/A	$600	$525	$450	$375	$300	$225

Last MSR was $700.

JS700 - similar to JS100, except features mahogany body, one-piece mahogany neck, wraparound bridge, 2 P-90 style single coil pickups, available in Trans. Red finish, disc. 1999.

	$725	$625	$525	$450	$375	$300	$225

Last MSR was $899.

JS1000 - offset double cutaway contoured mahogany body, bolt-on maple neck, 22-fret rosewood fingerboard with abalone dot inlay/Joe Satriani block inlay at 21st fret, double locking tremolo, 6-on-a-side tuners, charcoal hardware, 2 DiMarzio humbucker (PAF Pro/Fred) pickups, volume/tone control, 3-position switch, hi-pass filter push/pull switch in volume control, coil tap push/pull switch in tone control, available in Black Pearl and Trans. Blue finishes, mfg. 1994-96, 1998-present.

MSR	$1,770	$1,325	$1,150	$1,000	$850	$750	$650	$550

In 1998, White finish was introduced; Transparent Blue finish was discontinued.

JS1200 - similar to the JS1000, except has an edge-pro tremolo bridge, available in Candy Apple finish, mfg. 2004-present.

MSR	$1,830	$1,375	$1,150	$1,000	$900	$800	$700	$600

JS2000 - similar to the JS1000, except available in Champagne Gold finish, mfg. 2003-04.

	$1,250	$1,100	$950	$825	$700	$600	$500

Last MSR was $1,660.

JS6000 - similar to the JS1000, except features strings through fixed bridge, available in Oil or Trans. Red finishes, mfg. 1994-96.

	N/A	$1,000	$875	$750	$650	$550	$450

Last MSR was $1,400.

ELECTRIC: JOHN SCOFIELD (JSM) SERIES

JSM100 - double cutaway thin hollow flamed maple body, f-holes, mahogany neck, 22-fret bound ebony fingerboard with pearl/abalone block inlays, 2 IBZ Super 58 Humbucker pickpus, Gibralter II bridge, 3-per-side tuners, four knobs, switch, gold hardware, available in Vintage Sunburst finish, mfg. 2001-present.

MSR	$2,800	$2,100	$1,850	$1,600	$1,400	$1,200	$1,000	$850

ELECTRIC: KORINA SERIES

Introduced a year after the **Golden Oldies** Series, the **Korina** Series models is another example of Ibanez really sticking it to Gibson. If the series name was the battle cry, then the actual models are the equivalent of the Marines landing. Ibanez introduced three models based on Gibson´s futuristic designs of 1958: The **Rocket Roll Sr.** was a copy of the Flying V, the **Futura** was the Moderne copy, and **Destroyer** was their take on the Explorer model. All models had an original retail list price of $395, and featured an Ibanez script logo on the headstock similar (from a distance...hmmm). While one reliable vintage source estimates that the ´Korina´ is in fact tinted Japanese ash, interest in these three models has seen a resurgence in the past couple of years. This series lasted from 1975-77.

One note of moderate interest (it´ll win you a drink in a bar bet), the **Korina Series** Ibanez Flying V copy was named the **Rocket Roll Sr.** Why Sr.? The first Ibanez **Rocket Roll** model was the solid finish **Golden Oldies Series** model!

The Korina series is again seeing a lot of attention from players and dealers, now in the Vintage Guitar market. The three models all can be found with price tags ranging from $800 to $1,000 at guitar shows; market research has indicated that they actually sell in the area between $550/$600 up to $800.

ELECTRIC: KORN SIGNATURE SERIES

K7 - double offset cutaway mahogany body 7-string tuned to A, 5 piece maple/bubinga neck, 24-jumbo fret bound rosewood figerboard with K-7 inlay around 12th fret, 7-on-one-side tuners, matching color headstock, two DiMarzio pickups, Lo Pro Edge 7 bridge with U bar, one knob, switch, polished chrome hardware, available in Blade Gray or Firespeak Blue finishes, mfg. 2001-present.

MSR	$2,000	$1,500	$1,300	$1,100	$950	$825	$700	$600

ELECTRIC: MIKE MUSHOCK SIGNATURE SERIES

MMM1 - offset double cutaway mahogany body, three-piece mahogany/purple wood neck-thru body, 22-fret rosewood fingerboard, three-per-side tuners, MM bridge, STB, two humbucker pickups, two knobs, five-way switch, chrome hardware, Mahogany Oil finish, 28 in. scale, mfg. 2002-present.

MSR	$1,000	$750	$650	$575	$500	$450	$400	$350

ELECTRIC: MISC. MODELS

DT200 - single cutaway Explorer style mahogany body, three-piece maple neck, 22-fret rosewood fingerboard with dot inlay, six-on-one-side tuners, standard bridge, two humbucker pickups, three knobs, three-way switch, chrome hardware, available in Candy Apple or Vintage Amber finishes, mfg. 2004-present.

MSR	$530	$400	$350	$300	$250	$210	$180	$150

RVX220 - Flying V-style with longer bass bout basswood body, three-piece maple neck, 24-fret rosewood fingerboard with dot inlay, six-on-one-side tuners, standard bridge, two humbucker pickups, two knobs, three-way switch, chrome hardware, available in Candy Apple or Vintage Amber finishes, new 2005.

MSR	$400	$300	$250	$210	$180	$150	$120	$90

GRADING	100% MINT	98% NEAR MINT	95% EXC+	90% EXC	80% VG+	70% VG	60% G

ELECTRIC: NOODLES SIGNATURE SERIES

NDM1 - Talman style basswood body, three-piece maple neck, 22-fret rosewood fingerboard with pearl dot inlay, matching headstock with three-per-side tuners, fixed bridge, two humbucker and one single coil pickups, two knobs, five-way switch, black hardware, hand-wrapped in duct tape with a poly gray finish, mfg. 2003-present.

MSR	$660	$495	$425	$375	$325	$275	$225	$175

ELECTRIC: PAT METHENY SIGNATURE (PM) SERIES

The PM Series was designed in conjunction with Pat Metheny. The PM100 model debuted in 1996.

PM20 - similar to the PM100, except features 22-fret bound rosewood fingerboard, rosewood bridge piece, ivoroid body binding, available in Natural or Trans. Black finishes, mfg. 1997-99.

	$1,125	$925	$800	$695	$575	$475	$350

Last MSR was $1,399.

PM100 - slightly offset semi-hollow body, abalone bound maple top/back/sides, 2 bound f-holes, set-in mahogany neck, 22-fret bound ebony fingerboard with pearl/abalone block inlay/Pat Metheny signature block at 21st fret, raised ebony bridge/metal tailpiece, gold hardware, 3-per-side tuners, black peghead with Ibanez logo/slash diamond inlay, Ibanez Super 58 covered humbucker, volume/tone control, available in Black or Natural finishes, mfg. 1996-present.

MSR	$3,330	$2,500	$2,150	$1,900	$1,700	$1,500	$1,300	$1,100

PM120 - similar to Model PM100, except has Abalone/Pearl Block position markers, 2 IBZ Silent 58 humbucking pickups, available in Black or Natural finishes, current mfg.

MSR	$3,460	$2,600	$2,300	$2,000	$1,750	$1,550	$1,350	$1,150

Ibanez K7
courtesy Ibanez

ELECTRIC: PAUL GILBERT SERIES

PGM Series was designed in conjunction with Paul Gilbert (Racer X, Mister Big).

PGM30 - offset double cutaway basswood body, painted f-holes, bolt-on one-piece maple neck, 24-fret rosewood fingerboard with pearl dot inlay, Lo TRS II double locking tremolo, reverse peghead with screened logo, 6-on-the-other-side tuners, chrome hardware, Ibanez humbucker/single coil/humbucker pickups, volume control, 5-position switch, available in White finish, disc. 1998, reintroduced 2000-03.

	$600	$525	$450	$375	$300	$225	$175

Last MSR was $800.

PGM301 - offset double cutaway basswood body, painted f-holes, bolt-on one-piece maple neck, 24-fret maple fingerboard with pearl dot inlay, fixed bridge, reverse peghead with matching color, 6-on-a-side tuners, chrome hardware, DiMarzio humbucker/single coil/humbucker pickups, volume control, 5-position switch, available in White finish, mfg. 2004-present.

MSR	$1,570	$1,200	$1,050	$925	$800	$700	$600	$500

PGM500 - similar to the PGM30, except features strings through fixed bridge, gold hardware, DiMarzio humbucker/single coil/humbucker pickups, available in Candy Apple finish, mfg. 1994-96.

	N/A	$900	$775	$650	$550	$450	$350

Last MSR was $1,300.

PGM900 PMTC - single rounded cutaway mahogany body, 2 painted f-holes, bolt-on one-piece maple neck, 22-fret rosewood fingerboard with pearl dot inlay, fixed bridge, 3-per-side tuners, gold hardware, 2 Ibanez Super 58 humbucker pickups, volume control, 3-position switch, available in Trans. Red finish, mfg. 1998-99.

	$1,050	$825	$725	$625	$525	$475	$425

Last MSR was $1,299.

ELECTRIC: R SERIES

R442 - offset double cutaway alder body, bolt-on maple neck, 22-fret maple fingerboard with black dot inlay, locking vibrato, 6-on-a-side locking tuners, black hardware, 2 single coil/1 humbucker Ibanez pickups, volume/tone control, 5-position switch, available in Trans. Blue, Trans. Cherry, or Trans. Sunburst finishes, mfg. 1992 only.

	N/A	$425	$350	$325	$275	$225	$175

Last MSR was $700.

R540 LTD - offset double cutaway basswood body, bolt-on maple neck, 22-fret bound rosewood fingerboard with sharktooth inlay, double locking tremolo, 6-on-a-side tuners, black hardware, humbucker/single coil/humbucker Ibanez pickups, volume/tone control, 5-position switch, available in Black, Candy Apple, or Jewel Blue finishes, mfg. 1992-96.

	N/A	$600	$525	$450	$400	$350	$300

Last MSR was $1,000.

R540 - similar to R540 LTD, except has pearl dot inlay, 2 single coil/humbucker Ibanez pickups, available in Blue Burst finish, mfg. 1992 only.

	N/A	$600	$525	$450	$400	$350	$300

Last MSR was $950.

R540 HH - similar to R540, except has 2 Ibanez humbucker pickups, available in White finish.

	N/A	$600	$525	$450	$400	$350	$300

Last MSR was $930.

Ibanez R540 LTD
courtesy Ibanez

GRADING	100% MINT	98% NEAR MINT	95% EXC+	90% EXC	80% VG+	70% VG	60% G

R542 - similar to the R540 LTD, except featured alder body, 22-fret rosewood fingerboard with abalone oval inlay, 3 Ibanez single coil pickups, available in Blue, Candy Apple, or White finishes, mfg. 1992 only.

	N/A	$550	$475	$400	$350	$300	$250

Last MSR was $800.

ELECTRIC: RT/RV SERIES

RT150 - offset double cutaway alder body, white pickguard, bolt-on maple neck, 24-fret rosewood fingerboard with pearl dot inlay, standard vibrato, 6-on-a-side tuners, chrome hardware, humbucker/single coil/humbucker pickups, volume/tone control, 5-position switch, available in Black or Deep Red finishes, mfg. 1993 only.

	N/A	$300	$250	$200	$170	$140	$110

Last MSR was $400.

RT450 - similar to RT150, except has tortoise pickguard, locking tuners, Ibanez pickups, available in Amber, Black, or Tobacco Sunburst finishes, mfg. 1993 only.

	N/A	$350	$300	$250	$210	$170	$130

Last MSR was $550.

RT452 - similar to RT450, except has 12 strings, fixed bridge, 6-per-side tuners, available in Amber finish, mfg. 1993 only.

	N/A	$400	$350	$300	$250	$200	$150

Last MSR was $650.

RT650 - offset double cutaway alder body, bound gravure top, pearloid pickguard, bolt-on maple neck, 24-fret bound rosewood fingerboard with pearl dot inlay, standard vibrato, 6-on-a-side locking tuners, chrome hardware, humbucker/single coil/humbucker Ibanez pickups, volume/tone control, 5-position switch, available in Trans. Blue or Trans. Red finishes, mfg. 1993 only.

	N/A	$450	$375	$325	$275	$225	$175

Last MSR was $750.

RV470 - similar to the RT650, except features unbound gravure top, transparent pickguard, 22-fret rosewood fingerboard with pearl dot inlay, gold hardware, available in Purpleburst or Tobaccoburst finishes, mfg. 1993 only.

	N/A	$500	$425	$350	$300	$250	$200

Last MSR was $850.

ELECTRIC: RG SERIES

The RG Series debuted in 1985.

RG170 - similar to the RG220, except features an agathis body, maple fingerboard with black dot inlay, standard tremolo bridge, humbucker/single coil/humbucker pickups, 5-position switch, available in Black, Jewel Blue, or Metallic Green finishes, mfg. 1997-2004.

	$250	$220	$195	$170	$150	$125	$95

Last MSR was $310.

In 1998, Metallic Green was discontinued.

RG220 - offset double cutaway basswood body, bolt-on one-piece maple neck, 24-fret rosewood fingerboard with dot inlay, single locking tremolo, 6-on-a-side tuners, chrome hardware, 2 humbucker pickups, volume/tone control, 3-position switch, available in Black or Metallic Green finishes, mfg. 1994-99.

	$325	$275	$235	$195	$160	$130	$100

Last MSR was $479.

RG270 - offset double cutaway basswood body, bolt-on maple neck, 24-fret maple fingerboard with black dot inlay, double locking tremolo, 6-on-a-side tuners, chrome hardware, humbucker/single coil/humbucker pickups, volume/tone control, 5-position switch, available in Black, Jewel Blue, or Metallic Green finishes, mfg. 1994-2001.

	$375	$325	$285	$245	$205	$165	$125

Last MSR was $500.

Add $50 for 24-fret bound rosewood fingerboard with white sharktooth inlay, black hardware (Model RG270 DX).

Early model may feature Crimson Metallic or Emerald Green finishes.

RG320 - offset double cutaway basswood body, bolt-on maple neck, 24-fret rosewood fingerboard with pearl dot inlay, double Lo TRS II tremolo, 6-on-a-side tuners, chrome hardware, 2 humbucker pickups, volume/tone control, 3-position switch, available in Grey Pewter matte finishes, mfg. 1997-2003.

	$450	$375	$325	$295	$250	$195	$150

Last MSR was $600.

RG320FM - similar to the RG320 except has a flamed maple top, available in Trans. Lavender or Amber finishes, mfg. 2004-present.

MSR	$600	$450	$375	$325	$275	$235	$195	$160

Last MSR was $700.

RG320QS - similar to the RG320 except has a mahogany body with a quilted Sapele top, available in Trans. Red finish, mfg. 2001-03.

	$525	$450	$375	$325	$275	$225	$175

Last MSR was $700.

RG321 - offset double cutaway basswood body, maple neck, 24-fret bound rosewood fingerboard, two humbucker pickups, fixed bridge, 6-on-one-side, two knobs, five-way switch, chrome hardware, available in Royal Blue finish, mfg. 2004 only.

	$250	$210	$180	$150	$120	$100	$80

Last MSR was $330.

RG321MH - similar to the RG321, except has a mahogany body, available in Mahogany Oil finish, mfg. 2004-present.

MSR	$370	$260	$220	$190	$170	$150	$120	$90

GRADING	100% MINT	98% NEAR MINT	95% EXC+	90% EXC	80% VG+	70% VG	60% G

RG350 DX/EX - similar to the RG320, except features a bound rosewood fingerboard with pearl sharktooth inlay, black hardware, mirror (or white pearloid) pickguard, H/S/H pickups, available in Black or White finishes, mfg. 1997-present.

MSR	$530		$375	$325	$280	$240	$210	$180	$150

RG370 - offset double cutaway basswood body, maple neck, 24-fret bound rosewood fingerboard, two humbucker pickups, Edge-Pro tremolo bridge, 6-on-one-side, two knobs, five-way switch, black hardware, available in Moon Shadow finish, mfg. 2004 only.

	$300	$250	$210	$180	$150	$120	$90

Last MSR was $400.

RG370DX - similar to the RG370, except has a bound fingerboard with Sharktooth inlays, available in Electric Blue or Black finishes, mfg. 2004-present.

MSR	$480		$340	$290	$250	$220	$190	$160	$130

RG420 - similar to the RG320, except features black hardware, Lo TRS tremolo, 2 humbucker (V7/V8) IBZ pickups, available in Black or Royal Blue finishe, mfg. 1997-99.

	$495	$425	$375	$325	$275	$225	$175

Last MSR was $679.

RG450 - offset double cutaway basswood body, transparent pickguard, bolt-on maple neck, 24-fret maple fingerboard with black dot inlay, double locking vibrato, 6-on-a-side tuners, black hardware, humbucker/single coil/humbucker Ibanez pickups, volume/tone control, 5-position switch, available in Black, Emerald Green, or Purple Neon finishes, mfg. 1994-98.

	$350	$300	$275	$250	$200	$175	$150

Last MSR was $585.

RG450 DX - similar to RG450, except has bound rosewood fingerboard with white sharktooth inlay, black hardware, available in Black or White finishes, mfg. 1994-98.

	$600	$500	$425	$375	$300	$250	$195

Last MSR was $749.

RG470 - similar to the RG450, except features 24-fret rosewood fingerboard with pearl dot inlay, available in Black, Jewel Blue, or Mediterranean Green finishes, mfg. 1993-2002.

	$525	$450	$375	$325	$275	$225	$175

Last MSR was $700.

Add $100 for left-handed configuration (Model RG470 L). Available in Jewel Blue finish only.

Early RG470 models may feature Crimson Metallic and Emerald Green finishes. In 1998, the RG470 L was discontinued in Jewel Blue, and offered in Black finish only.

RG470 FM - similar to RG470, except has bound figured maple top, maple fingerboard with black dot inlay, available in Trans. Black or Trans. Purple finishes, mfg. 1994-96.

	N/A	$450	$375	$325	$275	$225	$175

Last MSR was $700.

RG470 FX - similar to RG470, except has strings-through fixed bridge, available in Black or Laser Blue finishes, mfg. 1994-96.

	N/A	$325	$275	$235	$195	$165	$135

Last MSR was $480.

RG470 XL - similar to RG470, except has a 27" neck, available in Black Pearl finish, mfg. 2001-02.

	$600	$525	$450	$400	$350	$300	$250

Last MSR was $800.

RG520 - offset double cutaway basswood body, bolt-on one-piece maple neck with bubinga reinforcement, 24-fret maple fingerboard with dot inlay, Edge double locking vibrato, 6-on-a-side tuners, chrome hardware, 2 humbucker (V7/V8) IBZ pickups, volume/tone control, 5-position switch, available in Grey Pewter matte finish, mfg. 1997-99.

	$550	$475	$425	$375	$300	$250	$200

Last MSR was $799.

RG520 QS - similar to the RG520, except features a mahogany body, quilted sapele top, available in Trans. Black or Trans. Blue finishes, mfg. 1997-2002.

	$699	$600	$525	$450	$375	$325	$250

Last MSR was $930.

RG550 - offset double cutaway basswood body, black pickguard, bolt-on maple neck, 24-fret maple fingerboard with black dot inlay, double locking vibrato, 6-on-a-side tuners, black hardware, humbucker/single coil/humbucker Ibanez pickups, volume/tone control, 5-position switch, available in Black finish, mfg. 1991-2002.

	$650	$575	$500	$425	$350	$275	$200

Last MSR was $820.

Early models may feature Electric Blue, Candy Apple, and Desert Sun Yellow finishes.

RG550 DX - similar to RG550, except has body-color-matched mirror pickguard, available in Laser Blue or Purple Neon finishes, disc. 1994.

	N/A	$600	$525	$450	$400	$350	$300

Last MSR was $850.

**Ibanez RG370DX
courtesy Ibanez**

**Ibanez RG550 DX
courtesy Ibanez**

GRADING	100% MINT	98% NEAR MINT	95% EXC+	90% EXC	80% VG+	70% VG	60% G

RG550 LTD - similar to RG550, except has body-color-matched mirror pickguard, bound rosewood fingerboard with pearl sharktooth inlay, black hardware, available in Black or Purple Neon finishes, mfg. 1994-96.

	N/A	$650	$575	$500	$425	$375	$325

Last MSR was $1,000.

RG560 - similar to RG550, except has rosewood fingerboard with pearl dot inlay, 2 single coil/humbucker Ibanez pickups, available in Black, Candy Apple, or Jewel Blue finishes, mfg. 1992 only.

	N/A	$525	$425	$350	$300	$250	$200

Last MSR was $750.

RG565 - similar to RG550, except has body-color matched fingerboard inlay, reverse headstock, single coil/humbucker Ibanez pickups, available in Candy Apple, Emerald Green, or Laser Blue finishes, mfg. 1992 only.

	N/A	$550	$450	$375	$350	$300	$250

Last MSR was $800.

RG570 - similar to the RG550, except features 24-fret rosewood fingerboard with pearl dot inlay, available in Black Pearl or Purple Pearl finishes, mfg. 1992-2002.

	$625	$550	$475	$400	$350	$275	$225

Last MSR was $820.

Add $80 for Flaked Blue and Flaked Green Metal Flake finishes. Add $150 for left-handed configuration (Model RG570L). Available in Jewel Blue finish only. The left-handed configuration was discontinued in 1996.

Early models may have Candy Apple, Emerald Green, Jewel Blue, and Purple Neon finishes.

RG570 FM - similar to RG570, except has flame maple top, available in Amber, Trans. Blue or Trans. Cherry finishes, mfg. 1992 only.

	N/A	$600	$525	$450	$375	$300	$250

Last MSR was $850.

RG750 - offset double cutaway basswood body, bolt-on maple neck, 24-fret bound maple fingerboard with sharktooth inlay, double locking vibrato, bound peghead, 6-on-a-side tuners, black hardware, humbucker/single coil/humbucker Ibanez pickups, volume/tone control, 5-position switch, available in Black or Candy Apple finishes, mfg. 1992 only.

	N/A	$675	$600	$525	$450	$375	$300

Last MSR was $1,000.

RG760 - similar to RG750, except features rosewood fingerboard, 2 single coil/humbucker Ibanez pickups, available in Black, Jewel Blue, or Emerald Green finishes, mfg. 1992 only.

	N/A	$675	$600	$525	$450	$375	$300

Last MSR was $1,000.

RG770 - similar to the RG750, except features 24-fret bound rosewood fingerboard with pearl sharktooth inlay, available in Black or Emerald Green finishes, mfg. 1991-94.

	N/A	$700	$625	$550	$475	$400	$325

Last MSR was $1,000.

This Model was available with transparent pickguard, maple fingerboard with body-color-matched sharktooth inlay (Model RG770DX). Available in Laser Blue and Violet Metallic finishes.

RG1077XL - double offset cutaway basswood body, Wizard maple neck with bubinga reinforcement, 24 fret bound rosewood fingerboard with dot inlay, Lo Pro Edge 7 bridge, 2 Dimarzio humbuckers & 1 single coil, chrome hardware, available in Royal Blue finish, mfg. 2001-02.

	$1,150	$1,000	$925	$825	$725	$625	$475

Last MSR was $1,500.

RG1200 - similar to the RG750, except features flame maple top, pearloid pickguard, 24-fret bound rosewood fingerboard with abalone oval inlay, humbucker/Ibanez single coil/DiMarzio humbucker pickups, available in Trans. Red or Trans. Blue finishes, mfg. 1992 only.

	N/A	$950	$825	$700	$625	$525	$425

Last MSR was $1,350.

RG1550 - similar to the RG550 except has a Prestige neck and a Edge-Pro tremolo system, mfg. 2003-present.

	$575	$500	$425	$375	$325	$275	$200

Last MSR was $750.

The RG1550 replaced the RG550 with the new neck and new tremolo system.

RG2120X - offset double cutaway mahogany solid body, 3-piece maple neck, rosewood fingerboard, 24 jumbo frets, Wizard neck type, Double Locking Tremelo, L.R. Baggs piezo pickups, Double Edge bridge, 6 on 1 side tuners, 1 ea. V7 and V8 humbucker pickups, available in Trans. Blue finish, disc. 2004.

	$1,2500	$1,100	$950	$825	$700	$600	$500

Last MSR was $1,660.

RG2027X 7-STRING - offset double cutaway mahogany body, 3-piece maple neck, rosewood fingerboard, abalone offset position marker at the 12th fret, 24 large frets, Wizard 7 neck type, Double Edge 7 bridge, 1 ea IBZ V7-7 & IBZ V8-7 humbucker pickups, available in Vintage Violin finish, disc.

	$1,275	$1,175	$1,075	$975	$875	$750	$625

Last MSR was $1,699.

RG3120 PRESTIGE - offset double cutaway mahogany body, figured maple top, bolt-on 3-piece maple neck, 24-fret rosewood fingerboard with pearl dot inlay, Lo Pro Edge tremolo, 6-on-a-side tuners, chrome hardware, 2 DiMarzio humbucker (PAF PRfo/Tone Zone) pickups, volume/tone control, 3-position switch, available in Twilight Blue finish, mfg. 1997-2003.

	$1,125	$975	$825	$700	$595	$475	$375

Last MSR was $1,500.

GRADING	100% MINT	98% NEAR MINT	95% EXC+	90% EXC	80% VG+	70% VG	60% G

RG3220 PRESTIGE - similar to the RG3120, except features a quilted maple top, available in Twilight Blue or Vintage Red finishes, mfg. 1998-99.

	$1,200	$1,050	$900	$750	$625	$500	$395

Last MSR was $1,599.

RG7321 - offset double cutaway basswood body, 7-string, 5-piece Wizard maple/walnut neck, 24-fret rosewood fingerboard with dot inlay, standard bridge, two humbucker pickups (AH1-7, AH2-7), two knobs, switch, 7-on-one-side tuners, black hardware, available in Black finish, mfg. 2001-present.

MSR	$500	$350	$300	$260	$230	$190	$160	$130

RG7420 7-STRING - offset double cutaway basswood body, 7-string, one-piece maple neck with Bubinga reinforcement, Wizard-7 All Access neck, rosewood fingerboard, dot position markers, 24 jumbo frets, Lo TRS-7 bridge, 1 ea. IBZ V7-7 & 1 IBZ V8-7 humbucker pickup, available in Black Pearl or Magenta Crush finishes, disc. 2003.

	$600	$525	$450	$400	$350	$300	$250

Last MSR was $800.

Also available with a 27 in. neck and fixed bridge (Model RG7421XL).

RG7421 - similar to the RG7420 except has a fixed bridge, available in Black finish, disc. 2001.

	$575	$500	$425	$375	$325	$275	$225

Last MSR was $750.

RG7620 7-STRING - 7-string configuration, offset double cutaway basswood body, bolt-on one-piece maple neck, 24-fret bound maple fingerboard with pearl dot inlay, Lo Pro Edge 7 tremolo, 7-on-a-side tuners, black hardware, 2 DiMarzio Blaze II humbuckers, volume/tone control, 5-position switch, available in Black or Royal Blue finishes, disc. 2001.

	$975	$850	$745	$640	$535	$430	$325

Last MSR was $1,300.

In 1998, DiMarzio Blaze II humbuckers replaced the DiMarzio RG7 Special humbuckers.

RG7621 7-String - similar to the RG7620, except features a fixed bridge, available in Black or White finishes, mfg. 1997-99.

	$725	$625	$525	$450	$395	$325	$250

Last MSR was $1,000.

Ibanez RG565 courtesy Ibanez

RGT42 DX FX - offset double cutaway mahogany body, Wizard II neck-thru maple/walnut neck, 24-fret rosewood fingerboard with deluxe sharktooth inlays, black headstock with six-per-side tuners, fixed bridge, two humbucker pickups, two knobs, five-way switch, Black Flat finish, new 2005.

MSR	$700	$490	$425	$375	$325	$275	$225	$175

RGT42 DX - similar to the RGT42, except has an Edge Pro II tremolo bridge, Black Pearl finish, new 2005.

MSR	$800	$575	$500	$425	$350	$300	$250	$200

RGT42 DX FM - similar to the RGT42 DX, except has a flame maple top, Trans. Lavender Flat finish, new 2005.

MSR	$900	$630	$550	$475	$425	$375	$325	$275

ELECTRIC: RG PRESTIGE SERIES

RGA121 - offset double cutaway mahogany body maple arched top, five-piece Wizard Prestige maple/walnut neck, 24-fret rosewood fingerboard with dot inlays, black headstock with six-on-one-side tuners, Gibraltar Plus bridge, pickguard, two humbucker pickups, two knobs, five-way switch, available in Natural Flat or Violin Flat finishes, new 2005.

MSR	$1,200	$850	$750	$675	$600	$525	$450	$400

RGT220H - offset double cutaway mahogany body, five-piece thru-body Wizard Prestige maple/wenge neck, 24-fret rosewood fingerboard with dot inlay, six-on-one-side tuners, Edge Pro bridge, two DiMarzio humbucker pickups, two knobs, five-way switch, Natural finish, new 2005.

MSR	$1,930	$1,350	$1,150	$1,000	$900	$800	$700	$600

RGT220A - similar to the RGT220H, except has an ash body, new 2005.

MSR	$2,000	$1,400	$1,200	$1,050	$900	$775	$650	$550

RGT320Q - offset double cutaway mahogany body with a AAA flame maple top, five-piece thru-body Wizard Prestige maple/wenge neck, 24-fret rosewood fingerboard with dot inlay, matching headstock with six-on-one-side tuners, Edge Pro bridge, two DiMarzio humbucker pickups, two knobs, five-way switch, Royal Brown Burst finish, new 2005.

MSR	$2,660	$1,900	$1,700	$1,500	$1,350	$1,200	$1,050	$900

RGA321F - offset double cutaway mahogany body with AAA flame maple arched top, five-piece Wizard Prestige maple/walnut neck, 24-fret rosewood fingerboard with dot inlays, black headstock with six-on-one-side tuners, Gibraltar Plus bridge, pickguard, two DiMarzio humbucker pickups, two knobs, five-way switch, Sapphire Blue finish, new 2005.

MSR	$1,930	$1,350	$1,150	$1,000	$900	$800	$700	$600

RG1520G - offset double cutaway basswood body, five-piece Wizard Prestige maple/walnut neck, 24-fret rosewood fingerboard with dot inlay, black headstock with six-on-one-side tuners, Edge Pro bridge with piezo for Roland GK output, two humbucker pickups, three knobs, five-way switch, two mini switches, Black Pearl finish, new 2005.

MSR	$1,400	$995	$900	$800	$725	$650	$575	$500

RG1527 - similar to the RG1570, except in seven-string configuration, and has two humbucker pickups, Royal Blue finish, new 2005.

MSR	$1,100	$775	$700	$625	$550	$475	$400	$350

Ibanez RG770 DX courtesy Ibanez

GRADING	100% MINT	98% NEAR MINT	95% EXC+	90% EXC	80% VG+	70% VG	60% G

RG1570 - offset double cutaway basswood body, five-piece Wizard Prestige maple/walnut neck, 24-fret rosewood fingerboard with dot inlay, black headstock with six-on-one-side tuners, Edge Pro bridge, two humbucker and one single coil pickups in H/S/H configuration, two knobs, five-way switch, available in Mirage Blue or Mirage Red finishes, mfg. 2003-present.

	MSR	$1,000	$700	$625	$550	$475	$425	$375	$325

The RG1570 replaced the RG570 with the new neck and new tremolo system.

RG1570 Left-Hand - similar to the RG-1570, except in left-handed configuration, Black finish, new 2005.

	MSR	$1,100	$775	$675	$600	$525	$450	$400	$350

RG1820X - offset double cutaway basswood body, five-piece Wizard Prestige maple/walnut neck, 24-fret rosewood fingerboard with dot inlay, black headstock with six-on-one-side tuners, double Edge Pro bridge with piezos for Roland GK output, two humbucker pickups, four knobs, five-way switch, one mini switch, Galaxy Black finish, new 2005.

	MSR	$1,330	$950	$850	$775	$700	$625	$550	$425

RG2550E - offset double cutaway basswood body, five-piece Wizard Prestige maple/walnut neck, 24-fret rosewood fingerboard with dot inlay, black headstock with six-on-one-side tuners, Edge Pro bridge, pickguard, two humbucker and one single coil DiMarzio pickups in H/S/H configuration, two knobs, five-way switch, Galaxy Black finish, new 2005.

	MSR	$1,170	$825	$725	$650	$575	$500	$425	$375

RG2570E - offset double cutaway basswood body, five-piece Wizard Prestige maple/walnut neck, 24-fret rosewood fingerboard with brown mirror sharktooth inlays, black headstock with six-on-one-side tuners, Edge Pro bridge, pickguard, two humbucker and one single coil DiMarzio pickups in H/S/H configuration, two knobs, five-way switch, Vital Silver finish, new 2005.

	MSR	$1,170	$825	$725	$650	$575	$500	$425	$375

RG2620 - offset double cutaway basswood body, five-piece Wizard Prestige maple/walnut neck, 24-fret rosewood fingerboard with dot inlays, black headstock with six-on-one-side tuners, Edge Pro bridge, pickguard, two DiMarzio humbucker pickups, two knobs, five-way switch, Cubed Blue finish, new 2005.

	MSR	$1,500	$1,050	$900	$825	$750	$675	$600	$525

RG3120F - offset double cutaway mahogany body with AAA flame maple top, five-piece Wizard Prestige maple/walnut neck, 24-fret rosewood fingerboard with dot inlays, black headstock with six-on-one-side tuners, Edge Pro bridge, pickguard, two DiMarzio humbucker pickups, two knobs, five-way switch, Aged Natural or Dark Amber finishes, new 2005.

	MSR	$1,930	$1,350	$1,150	$1,000	$900	$800	$700	$600

ELECTRIC: RX SERIES

RX160 - offset double cutaway maple body, bolt-on maple neck, 22-fret rosewood fingerboard with pearl dot inlay, standard vibrato, 6-on-a-side tuners, chrome hardware, humbucker/single coil/humbucker pickups, volume/tone control, 5-position switch, available in Black, Blue Night, or Red finishes, mfg. 1994-96.

	N/A	$225	$195	$170	$150	$120	$90

Last MSR was $340.

RX170 - similar to RX160, except has maple fingerboard with black dot inlay, available in Emerald Green, Trans. Blue, or Trans. Red finishes, mfg. 1994-96.

	N/A	$250	$210	$180	$155	$125	$95

Last MSR was $360.

RX270 - similar to RX160, except has bound body, maple fingerboard with black dot inlay, available in Black, Cherry Sunburst, or Trans. Green finishes, mfg. 1994-96.

	N/A	$300	$250	$210	$170	$140	$110

Last MSR was $430.

RX240 - offset double cutaway agathis body, bolt-on maple neck, 22-fret rosewood fingerboard with pearl dot inlay, TZ30 modern tremolo, 6-on-a-side tuners, chrome hardware, white pickguard, 2 single coil/humbucker pickups, volume/tone control, 5-way selector, available in Candy Apple, Metallic Green, or Sunburst finishes, disc. 1998.

	$295	$250	$225	$195	$165	$135	$100

Last MSR was $399.

RX350 - similar to the RX160, except features pearloid pickguard, 22-fret maple fingerboard with black dot inlay, cosmo black hardware, humbucker/single coil/humbucker Ibanez pickups, available in Black, Emerald Green, Trans. Red, or Trans. Turquoise finishes, mfg. 1994-96.

	N/A	$325	$275	$235	$195	$155	$115

Last MSR was $480.

RX352 - similar to RX350, except has 12 strings, fixed bridge, 6-on-a-side tuners, available in Black finish, mfg. 1994 only.

	N/A	$400	$350	$300	$250	$200	$150

Last MSR was $580.

RX650 - similar to the RX350, except features bound figured maple top, 22-fret bound rosewood fingerboard with pearl dot inlay, available in Trans. Green, Trans. Purple, or Trans. Red finishes, mfg. 1994-96.

	N/A	$400	$350	$300	$250	$200	$150

Last MSR was $570.

RX750 - similar to the RX350, except features padauk/mahogany/padauk body, 22-fret rosewood fingerboard with pearl dot inlay, gold hardware, available in Natural finish, mfg. 1994 only.

	N/A	$650	$575	$500	$425	$350	$300

Last MSR was $1,000.

ELECTRIC: S, SA, SC, SCA, SV, & SZ SERIES

The S Series was originally introduced as the **Saber** Series in 1987.

GRADING	100% MINT	98% NEAR MINT	95% EXC+	90% EXC	80% VG+	70% VG	60% G

SCA220 - offset double cutaway mahogany body, 1-piece maple neck, rosewood fingerboard with pearl dot position markers, 22 large frets, Short Stop II bridge, 2 IBZ V6 humbucker pickups, chrome hardware, available in Black Pearl finish, disc. 2003.

	$490	$425	$375	$325	$275	$225	$175

Last MSR was $650.

S CLASSIC SC420 - thin contoured offset double cutaway mahogany body, one-piece bolt-on maple neck, 22-fret rosewood fingerboard with pearl dot inlay, Short Stop II wraparound bridge, 3-per-side tuners, chrome hardware, 2 Ibanez humbucker pickups, top-mounted volume/tone controls, 3-position switch, available in Black or Black Cherry finishes, mfg. 1997-2004.

	$750	$650	$575	$500	$400	$325	$250

Last MSR was $1,000.

S CLASSIC SC500 N (NYLON STRING) - similar to the S Classic SC420, except features a nylon string configuration, spruce top, one-piece mahogany neck, 22-fret bound ebony fingerboard with abalone dot inlay, slotted headstock, gold hardware, piezo bridge pickup, volume/tone controls, available in Natural finish, mfg. 1998-99.

	$950	$800	$700	$600	$500	$425	$325

Last MSR was $1,299.

Ibanez RG1570
courtesy Ibanez

S CLASSIC SC620 - similar to the S Classic SC420, except features bound flame maple top, 22-fret bound ebony fingerboard with abalone/pearl oval inlay, gold hardware, available in Amber Pearl finish, mfg. 1997-99.

	$1,050	$925	$800	$695	$575	$475	$350

Last MSR was $1,399.

S470 - sculpted thin offset double cutaway mahogany body, bolt-on maple neck, 22-fret rosewood fingerboard with pearl dot inlay, Lo TRS II double locking tremolo, 6-on-a-side tuners, chrome hardware, humbucker/single coil/humbucker IBZ pickups, volume/tone control, 5-position switch, available in Black, Jewel Blue, or Mediterranean Green finishes, mfg. 1991-present.

MSR	$640	$450	$375	$325	$275	$225	$200	$175

Add $80 for left-handed configuration (Model S470 L), available in Black finish only.

Early models may feature Natural Oil, Transparent Blue, and Transparent Red finishes.

S470 FM - similar to S470, except has a flame maple top, available in British Racing Green finish, mfg. 1998-99.

	$750	$600	$550	$500	$450	$400	$325

Last MSR was $950.

S470QS - similar to Model S470 except, has quilted sapele/mahogany body, available in Trans. Red finish, disc. 2004.

	$715	$625	$550	$450	$350	$295	$250

Last MSR was $950.

SF470 - similar to S470, except has tune-o-matic bridge/stop tailpiece, available in Black or Trans. Red finishes, mfg. 1991-96.

	N/A	$600	$525	$450	$375	$300	$225

Last MSR was $850.

S470 DX QM - similar to the S470, except has a quilted maple top and deluxe inlays, Charcoal Brown, Natrual Fade, or Trans. Lavender finishes, new 2005.

MSR	$800	$575	$500	$425	$375	$325	$275	$225

S520EX - double offset mahogany body, three-piece Wizard II maple neck, 22-fret bound rosewood fingerboard with 12th fret inlay, black headstock with six-on-one-side tuners, ZR tremolo bridge, two humbucker pickups, two knobs, five-way switch, black hardware, Black finish, new 2005.

MSR	$730	$515	$450	$375	$325	$275	$225	$175

S540 - offset double cutaway mahogany body, bolt-on maple neck, 22-fret maple fingerboard with abalone oval inlay, pearl Custom Made inlay at 21st fret, double locking vibrato, 6-on-a-side tuners, cosmo black hardware, humbucker/single coil/humbucker Ibanez pickups, volume/tone control, 5-position switch, available in Cayman Green, Jade Metallic, or Oil finishes, mfg. 1987-1996.

	N/A	$800	$675	$550	$475	$400	$325

Last MSR was $1,200.

In 1994, Cayman Green finish was introduced, Jade Metallic was discontinued.

S540 LTD - similar to S540, except has bound rosewood fingerboard with sharktooth inlay, bound peghead, chrome hardware, available in Trans. Blue finish, mfg. 1991-99.

	$1,075	$925	$800	$695	$575	$475	$350

Last MSR was $1,399.

Early models may feature Black, Emerald Green, Jewel Blue, Lipstick Red, and Purple Neon finishes.

S540 BM - similar to S540, except has burl mahogany top, bound rosewood fingerboard, gold hardware, available in Antique Violin finish, disc. 1996.

	N/A	$900	$775	$650	$550	$475	$400

Last MSR was $1,300.

Ibanez S-540
courtesy Ibanez

S540 FM - similar to S540, except has flame maple top, bound rosewood fingerboard with abalone oval inlay, chrome hardware, available in Trans. Purple or Trans. Turquoise finishes, disc. 1997.

	N/A	$1,000	$850	$725	$600	$500	$425

Last MSR was $1,450.

GRADING	100% MINT	98% NEAR MINT	95% EXC+	90% EXC	80% VG+	70% VG	60% G

S540 QM - similar to S540, except has quilted maple top, bound rosewood fingerboard with pearl dot inlay, chrome hardware, available in Trans. Blue finish, disc. 1999.

	$1,050	$900	$750	$650	$550	$450	$350

Last MSR was $1,399.

S1520 (S1620) - offset double cutaway mahogany body, 1-piece maple neck with Bubinga reinforcement, bound rosewood fingerboard, 22 jumbo frets, Wizard All Access neck, "S" Special on 12th fret, Lo Pro Edge bridge, 1 ea. IBZ QM-1 and IBZ QM-2 humbucker pickups, available in Black Pearl finish, disc. 2003.

	$1,050	$900	$750	$650	$599	$550	$499

Last MSR was $1,400.

Add $200 for figured bubinga top (Model S1520FB).

S2020X - offset double cutaway mahogany body, 3-piece maple neck, rosewood fingerboard, 22 jumbo frets, Wizard neck style, Double Edge bridge, 1 ea. MQ-1 and QM-2 humbucker pickups, L.R. Baggs piezo pickup system, available in Antique Violin finish, disc. 2003.

	$1,200	$1,075	$999	$899	$799	$699	$550

Last MSR was $1,600.

S2075FW - double offset mahogany body with poplar burl top, five-piece Wizard II Prestige maple/bubinga neck, 22-fret bound rosewood fingerboard with 12th fret Prestige inlay, black headstock with six-on-one-side tuners, ZR with D-Tuner tremolo bridge, two humbucker and one single coil DiMarzio pickups in H/S/H configuration, two knobs, five-way switch, Hoeny Sunburst finish, new 2005.

MSR	$1,460	$1,025	$900	$800	$725	$650	$575	$500

S2540 NT S PRESTIGE - sculpted thin offset double cutaway figured sapelle mahogany body, bolt-on 3-piece maple neck, 22-fret bound rosewood fingerboard with pearl ´S´ special inlay, Lo Pro Edge double locking tremolo, 6-on-a-side tuners, gold hardware, humbucker/single coil/humbucker IBZ pickups, volume/tone control, 5-position switch, available in Natural finish, mfg. 1997-99.

	$1,600	$1,400	$1,200	$1,000	$850	$700	$600

Last MSR was $1,999.

S7420 7-STRING - offset double cutaway mahogany body, 1-piece maple neck with bubinga reinforcement, Wizard 7 All Access neck, rosewood fingerboard, 22 jumbo frets, Lo TRS7 bridge, 1 ea. IBZ V7-7 and IBZ V8-7 humbucker pickups, available in Black Pearl finish, disc. 2000.

	$975	$875	$775	$675	$550	$450	$350

Last MSR was $1,300.

S5407 7-STRING - sculpted thin offset double cutaway mahogany body, bolt-on maple neck, 7-string configuration, 22-fret rosewood fingerboard with pearl dot inlay, double locking tremolo, 7 on one side tuners, black hardware, 2 single coil/humbucker DiMarzio pickups, volume/tone control, 5-position switch, available in Black finish, mfg. 1991-92.

	$950	$800	$700	$600	$525	$425	$350

Last MSR was $1,300.

SA160 - offset double cutaway mahogany body, 1-piece maple neck, rosewood fingerboard with pearl dot position markers, 22 jumbo frets, TZ30 bridge, 2 single coil pickups and 1 humbucker pickup, chrome hardware, available in Black, Metallic Grape, Royal Blue, Vampire Kiss, or Weathered Brown finishes, current mfg.

MSR	$450	$350	$300	$250	$225	$200	$175	$150

In 2005, an SAT bridge was introduced.

SA160AH - similar to the SA160 except has an ash body, available in Trifade Burst finish, mfg. 2004-present.

MSR	$530	$400	$325	$275	$235	$195	$165	$135

SA160QM - similar to the SA160 except has a quilted maple top, mfg. 2001-present.

MSR	$550	$425	$350	$300	$250	$225	$195	$175

SA220FM - offset double cutaway mahogany body with flame maple arched top, three-piece maple neck, 22-fret rosewood fingerboard with dot inlay, matching headstock with six-on-one-side tuners, SAT30S tremolo bridge, two humbucker pickups, two knobs, five-way switch, chrome hardware, Trans. Lavender finish, new 2005.

MSR	$600	$420	$350	$300	$250	$210	$180	$150

SA320X - offset double cutaway mahogany body with arched top, three-piece maple neck, 22-fret rosewood fingerboard with dot inlay, matching headstock with six-on-one-side tuners, double SAT tremolo bridge with piezos, two humbucker pickups, two knobs, five-way switch, two outputs, chrome hardware, Metallic Black finish, new 2005.

MSR	$870	$625	$550	$475	$425	$375	$325	$275

SA1260 - offset double cutaway mahogany body with arched top, three-piece Prestige maple neck, 22-fret rosewood fingerboard with dot inlay, black headstock with six-on-one-side tuners, SAT Pro tremolo bridge, one humbucker and two single coil pickups, two knobs, five-way switch, chrome hardware, Antique Violin finish, mfg. 2004-present.

MSR	$860	$600	$525	$450	$400	$350	$300	$250

SA2020FM - offset double cutaway mahogany body with flame maple arched top, five-piece Prestige maple/walnut neck, 22-fret rosewood fingerboard with 12th fret Prestige inlay, matching headstock with six-on-one-side tuners, double SAT tremolo bridge with piezos, two DiMarzio humbucker pickups, two knobs, five-way switch, chrome hardware, Vintage Violin finish, new 2005.

MSR	$1,000	$700	$625	$550	$475	$425	$375	$325

SV420 - similar to S470, except has flamed maple top, 2 Ibanez humbucker pickups, gold hardware, TZ100 modern tremolo, available in Butterscotch Trans. finish, disc. 1997.

	$650	$575	$500	$425	$375	$295	$225

Last MSR was $900.

SV470 - similar to S470, except has standard vibrato, locking tuners, gold hardware, available in Black, Oil, or Trans. Red finishes, mfg. 1993-96.

	$650	$575	$500	$425	$375	$300	$225

Last MSR was $900.

GRADING	100% MINT	98% NEAR MINT	95% EXC+	90% EXC	80% VG+	70% VG	60% G

SZ320 - offset double cutaway thick mahogany body with arched maple top, three-piece mahogany neck, 22-fret rosewood fingerboard with dot inlay, black headstock with six-on-one-side tuners, Gibraltar III bridge, two humbucker pickups, three knobs, three-way switch, chrome hardware, available in Black or Weathered Brown finishes, mfg. 2002-present.

	MSR	$573		$430	$375	$325	$275	$235	$195	$160

Model SZ320MH is the same as the SZ320 except has a full mahogany body.

SZ520QM - offset double cutaway thick mahogany body with arched quilted maple top, three-piece mahogany neck, 22-fret rosewood fingerboard with 12th fret special inlay, black headstock with three-per-side tuners, Gibraltar III bridge, STB, two humbucker pickups, three knobs, three-way switch, chrome hardware, available in Blackberry, Bright Blue, or Gold Amber Burst finishes, mfg. 2002-present.

	MSR	$666		$500	$425	$375	$325	$275	$235	$190

SZ720FM - offset double cutaway thick mahogany body with arched flame maple top, three-piece mahogany neck, 22-fret rosewood fingerboard with special flame inlays, bound black headstock with three-per-side tuners, Gibraltar III bridge, STB, two humbucker pickups, three knobs, three-way switch, chrome hardware, available in Trans. Gray finish, mfg. 2004-present.

	MSR	$840		$630	$550	$475	$400	$350	$300	$250

SZ2020FM - offset double cutaway thick mahogany body with arched flame maple top, five-piece maple/walnut neck, 22-fret rosewood fingerboard with 12th-fret Prestige inlay, matching headstock with three-per-side tuners, MM bridge, two Seymour Duncan humbucker pickups, three knobs, three-way switch, chrome hardware, available in Trans. Black Flat finish, new 2005.

	MSR	$1,330		$1,000	$875	$750	$675	$600	$525	$450

Ibanez SA160 courtesy Ibanez

ELECTRIC: SERIES II SERIES

Ibanez had a number of upscale models in the mid 1970s, but it is estimated that only a small number of these models were produced. The **Artwood Nouveau**, perhaps inspired by Ibanez' Rex Bogue-derived **Model 2670**, was a Strat copy with a carved mahogany body and carved headstock. The intriguing **Custom Agent (Model 2405)** featured a bound, ornate Les Paul body and notched headstock. **Custom Agent** models had a retail list price of $448 in 1976. The **Black Eagle Bass** was a Jazz Bass model with maple fingerboard and pearl inlaid pickguard with eagle inlay design. These models were produced between 1975 and 1977.

ELECTRIC: TALMAN SERIES

When this series first debuted in 1994, the bodies were made out of Resoncast, a composite wood material. Later models have wood construction. This series is not to be confused with the acoustic models; see the *Blue Book of Acoustic Guitars*.

TC220 - similar to the TC420, except features an agathis body, standard tremolo, 2 exposed pole piece humbucker pickups, available in Black or Deep Green finishes, mfg. 1998-99.

		$300	$250	$225	$195	$150	$125	$100

Last MSR was $399.

TC420 - offset slight double cutaway basswood body, bolt-on maple neck, 22-fret rosewood fingerboard with pearl dot inlay, Full Action II modern tremolo, 3-per-side tuners, natural wood headstock with screened logo, white pickguard, chrome hardware, 2 chrome cover humbucker pickups, volume/tone control, 3-position switch, available in Black, Flaked Silver Metal Flake, or Mediterranean Green finishes, disc. 1999.

		$450	$375	$300	$250	$200	$175	$125

Last MSR was $499.

Add $50 for Flaked Silver Metal Flake finish.

TC420 L - similar to the TC420, except features a left-handed configuration, available in Mediterranean Green finish, mfg. 1998-99.

		$475	$395	$325	$275	$225	$195	$150

Last MSR was $599.

TC630 - offset slight double cutaway light ash body, bolt-on maple neck, 22-fret rosewood fingerboard with pearl dot inlay, TT50 vintage-style tremolo, 3-per-side tuners, natural wood headstock with screened logo, white pearloid pickguard, chrome hardware, 3 single coil lipstick tube pickups, volume/tone controls, 5-position switch, available in Black or Ivory (w/red tortoiseshell pickguard) finishes, disc. 1998.

		$525	$450	$395	$325	$275	$225	$175

Last MSR was $669.

TC740 - similar to the TC630, except features alder body, Gotoh 510AT tremolo, 2 single coil lipstick tube chrome cover humbucker pickups, available in Black or Mint Green finishes, disc. 1999.

		$650	$525	$450	$395	$325	$275	$200

Last MSR was $799.

TC825 - similar to the TC630, except features Bigsby tremolo, 2 chrome cover humbucker pickups, 3-position selector, available in Flaked Blue or Flaked Silver Metal Flake finishes, disc. 1999.

		$750	$625	$550	$475	$395	$325	$250

Last MSR was $949.

Ibanez SZ720FM courtesy Ibanez

GRADING	100% MINT	98% NEAR MINT	95% EXC+	90% EXC	80% VG+	70% VG	60% G

TC5300 - offset double cutaway body, cream pickguard, bolt-on figured maple neck, 22-fret rosewood fingerboard with pearl dot inlay, standard vibrato, 3-per-side tuners, chrome hardware, 3 single coil lipstick tube pickups, volume/tone control, 5-position switch, available in Azure Blue Burst, Royal Orangeburst, Black, Pale Blue, or Bravure Flame Amber finishes, mfg. 1994-96.

	N/A	$375	$325	$275	$235	$195	$165

Last MSR was $550.

Add $25 for Azure Blue Burst or Royal Orangeburst finishes. Add $50 for Gravure Flame Amber finish.

TV650 - single cutaway bound body, 3-layer white pickguard, bolt-on figured maple neck, 22-fret rosewood fingerboard with pearl dot inlay, standard vibrato, 3-per-side tuners, gold hardware, humbucker/single coil/humbucker pickups, volume/tone control, 5-position switch, available in White finish, mfg. 1994-96.

	N/A	$450	$375	$325	$275	$225	$175

Last MSR was $700.

TV750 - Similar to TV650, except has unbound body, available in Gravure Quilted Brown Sunburst finish, mfg. 1994-96.

	N/A	$425	$375	$325	$275	$225	$175

Last MSR was $700.

ELECTRIC: UNIVERSE SERIES

This series of 7-string guitar models was co-designed by Steve Vai, and debuted in 1990.

UV7 - offset double cutaway basswood body, bolt-on maple neck, 24-fret rosewood fingerboard with pearl dot inlay, Lo Pro Edge 7 double locking tremolo, 7-on-a-side tuners, black pickguard, chrome hardware, humbucker/single coil/humbucker DiMarzio pickups, volume/tone control, 5-position switch, available in Black finish, mfg. 1990-98.

	$1,450	$1,250	$1,050	$950	$825	$650	$500

Last MSR was $1,999.

UV7 P - similar to UV7, except has white pickguard, pearl abalone pyramid inlay, available in White finish, disc. 1994.

	N/A	$1,200	$1,050	$925	$800	$700	$600

Last MSR was $1,700.

UV77 - similar to UV7, except has 3 color pyramid inlay, available in Multi-Colored finish, disc. 1994.

	N/A	$1,400	$1,200	$1,050	$900	$750	$600

Last MSR was $2,200.

UV777 - similar to UV7, except features disappearing pyramid fingerboard inlay, available in Black finish, current mfg.

MSR	$2,440	$1,850	$1,600	$1,400	$1,200	$1,000	$850	$700

ELECTRIC: USA EXOTIC WOOD & CUSTOM GRAPHIC SERIES

The Ibanez Custom Shop was moved to North Hollywood, California in 1990. Ibanez Made in USA and American Master models are produced at this location.

UCEWFM (FLAME MAPLE) & UCEWQM (QUILTED MAPLE) - offset double cutaway mahogany body, highly figured maple top, bolt-on bird's-eye maple neck, 24-fret rosewood fingerboard with pearl dot inlay, double locking tremolo, 6-on-a-side tuners, black hardware, humbucker/Ibanez single coil/DiMarzio humbucker pickups, volume/tone control, 5-position switch, available in Natural, Trans. Blue, Trans. Ebony, or Trans. Purple finishes, mfg. 1992 only.

	N/A	$1,200	$1,050	$900	$775	$650	$525

Last MSR was $1,700.

92 UCGR1 - offset double cutaway basswood body, bolt-on maple neck, 24-fret bound rosewood fingerboard with sharktooth inlay, double locking tremolo, 6-on-a-side tuners, bound peghead, black hardware, DiMarzio single coil/Ibanez humbucker pickups, volume/tone control, available in "Ice World" finish, mfg. 1992 only.

	N/A	$1,000	$875	$750	$650	$550	$450

Last MSR was $1,550.

92 UCGR2 - similar to 92UCGR1, except has reverse headstock, DiMarzio humbucker/Ibanez single coil/DiMarzio humbucker pickups, available in "No Bones About It" finish.

	N/A	$1,000	$875	$750	$650	$550	$450

Last MSR was $1,600.

92 UCGR3 - similar to 92UCGR1, except has reverse headstock, 2 Ibanez humbucker pickups, available in "Grim Reaper" finish.

	N/A	$1,000	$875	$750	$650	$550	$450

Last MSR was $1,550.

92 UCGR4 - similar to 92UCGR1, except has unbound fingerboard with pearl dot inlay, DiMarzio humbucker/Ibanez single coil/DiMarzio humbucker pickups, available in "Angel Depart" finish.

	N/A	$1,000	$875	$750	$650	$550	$450

Last MSR was $1,550.

92 UCGR5 - similar to 92UCGR1, except has unbound maple fingerboard with black dot inlay, DiMarzio single coil/humbucker pickups, available in "Unzipped" finish.

	N/A	$1,000	$875	$750	$650	$550	$450

Last MSR was $1,500.

92 UCGR6 - similar to 92UCGR1, except has unbound rosewood fingerboard with pearl dot inlay, DiMarzio humbucker/Ibanez single coil/DiMarzio humbucker pickups, available in "Sea Monster" finish.

	N/A	$1,000	$875	$750	$650	$550	$450

Last MSR was $1,550.

GRADING	100% MINT	98% NEAR MINT	95% EXC+	90% EXC	80% VG+	70% VG	60% G

92 UCGR7 - similar to 92UCGR1, except has reverse headstock, DiMarzio humbucker/Ibanez single coil/ DiMarzio humbucker pickups, available in "Alien's Revenge" finish.

	N/A	$1,000	$875	$750	$650	$550	$450

Last MSR was $1,600.

92 UCGR8 - similar to 92UCGR1, except has unbound maple fingerboard with black dot inlay, 2 DiMarzio humbucker pickups, available in Cosmic Swirl II finish.

	N/A	$1,000	$875	$750	$650	$550	$450

Last MSR was $1,500.

ELECTRIC: VOYAGER SERIES

The Voyager Series was co-designed by Reb Beach, and was introduced in 1991.

RBM1 - offset double cutaway mahogany body with vibrato wedge cutaway, metal pickguard, bolt-on maple neck, 22-fret rosewood fingerboard with pearl dot inlay, double locking tremolo, 6-on-a-side tuners, gold hardware, 2 single coil/humbucker pickups, volume control, 5-position switch, available in Black, Blue, or Candy Apple finishes, mfg. 1991-94.

	N/A	$800	$700	$625	$550	$475	$400

Last MSR was $1,200.

RBM2 - similar to RBM1, except has koa top, Bolivian rosewood neck/fingerboard, available in Natural finish, disc. 1994.

	N/A	$1,500	$1,300	$1,100	$950	$800	$650

Last MSR was $2,100.

RBM10 - offset double cutaway mahogany body with lower wedge cutaway, metal control plate, bolt-on maple neck, 22-fret rosewood fingerboard with pearl dot inlay, double locking tremolo, 6-on-a-side tuners, gold hardware, 2 single coil/humbucker pickups, volume control, 5-position switch, available in Black or Emerald Green finishes, mfg. 1994-96.

	N/A	$600	$525	$450	$375	$300	$250

Last MSR was $800.

RBM400 - similar to RBM10, except has Bolivian rosewood neck/fingerboard, clay dot fingerboard inlay, Ibanez pickups, available in Oil finish, mfg. 1994-96.

	N/A	$1,200	$1,050	$900	$800	$700	$600

Last MSR was $1,500.

Ibanez UV777 courtesy Ibanez

ELECTRIC BASS

Ibanez' Jump Start Packages include an electric bass guitar, bass amplifier, gig bag, instructional video, digital auto tuner, strap, cable, picks, and a free subscription to *Plugged In* (the official Ibanez newsletter).

TR50BK (IJSTR50 JUMP START PACKAGE) - offset double cutaway agathis body, bolt-on maple neck, 22-fret maple fingerboard with black dot inlay, fixed bridge, 4-on-a-side tuners, chrome hardware, black pickguard, P-style pickup, volume/tone controls, available in Black and Blue Night finishes, mfg. 1997 only.

$400	$325	$275	$225	$175	$135	$95

Last MSR was $499.

JUMP START PACKAGE (IJSB70) - offset double cutaway agathis body, bolt-on maple neck, 22-fret rosewood fingerboard with pearl dot inlay, fixed bridge, 4-on-a-side tuners, chrome hardware, P-style pickup, volume/tone controls, available in Black and Jewel Blue finishes, mfg. 1998-99.

$385	$325	$295	$250	$225	$195	$150

Last MSR was $479.

ELECTRIC BASS: AFFIRMA SERIES

This series was designed by Swiss luthier, Rolf Spuler. His design incorporates a neck that extends half-way through the body with individual bridges for each string. There is a thumb slot, a pearl/abalone AFR insignia, and a pearl block with Ibanez and the serial number inscriptions inlaid into the body, located between the single coil pickup and the bridge system. All models are available in a fretless configuration at no additional charge.

A104 - offset double cutaway asymmetrical saman (or kralo walnut or flame maple) body, maple neck, 24-fret ebony fingerboard with offset pearl inlay at 12th fret, 4 Mono Rail bridges, tuning lever on low string bridge, body matching peghead veneer, 2-per-side tuners, black hardware, single coil/4 bridge piezo pickups, volume/concentric treble/bass/mix controls, active electronics, available in Natural finish, mfg. 1991-93.

	N/A	$1,250	$1,050	$900	$800	$700	$600

Last MSR was $1,900.

A105 - similar to A104, except has 5 strings, 5 Mono Rail bridges, 3/2-per-side tuners, mfg. 1991-93.

	N/A	$1,500	$1,300	$1,150	$1,000	$850	$750

Last MSR was $2,000.

ELECTRIC BASS: ARTCORE SERIES

AGB140 - single smooth cutaway Les Paul Bass style hollow body, maple top/back/sides, 2 f-holes, body binding, three-piece maple/mahogany neck, 22-fret rosewood fingerboard with dot inlay, two-per-side tuners, Gibraltar III bridge, single pickup, two knobs, chrome hardware, available in Trans. Brown finish, 34 in. scale, mfg. 2004-present.

MSR	$530		$400	$350	$300	$250	$210	$180	$150

Ibanez RBM2 courtesy Ibanez

GRADING	100% MINT	98% NEAR MINT	95% EXC+	90% EXC	80% VG+	70% VG	60% G

ASB140 - double cutaway hollow body, maple top/back/sides, 2 f-holes, body binding, three-piece maple/mahogany neck, 22-fret rosewood fingerboard with dot inlay, two-per-side tuners, Gibraltar III bridge, single pickup, two knobs, chrome hardware, available in Brown Sunburst finish, 34 in. scale, mfg. 2004-present.

MSR	$530	$400	$350	$300	$250	$210	$180	$150

ELECTRIC BASS: ATK SERIES

ATK Series basses were introduced in 1995.

ATK300 - offset double cutaway light ash body, bolt-on 3-piece maple neck, 22-fret maple fingerboard with black dot inlay, ATK Custom surround fixed bridge, 2-per-side tuners, chrome hardware, triple coil pickup, volume/3-band EQ tone controls, pickup character mini switch, available in Black or Vintage Burst finishes, disc. 1999.

		$525	$450	$400	$350	$275	$225	$195

Last MSR was $749.

ATK305 - similar to the ATK300, except in a 5-string configuration, 2/3-per-side tuners, disc. 1999.

		$600	$525	$450	$400	$325	$275	$225

Last MSR was $849.

ELECTRIC BASS: BTB SERIES

BTB300 BG - offset double cutaway mahogany body with bubinga top, 5-piece maple and walnut neck, 34 in. scale, 23-fret rosewood fingerboard with dot inlay, 2 Ibanez SPJ-4B pickups, Mono-Rail II, 3 knobs, 2-per-side tuners, available in Walnut Flat finish, mfg. 2004-present.

MSR	$650	$495	$425	$375	$325	$275	$225	$175

BTB305 BG - similar to the BTB300 BG, except in 5-string configuration, 3/2-per-side tuners, new 2004.

MSR	$750	$575	$500	$425	$375	$325	$275	$225

BTB400QM - offset double cutaway basswood body, quilted maple top, 5 piece maple/walnut neck, 24-fret rosewood fingerboard with pearl dot inlay, two IBZ DFR-4 pickups, 2-per-side tuners, mono-rail II bridge, active EQ, five knobs, chrome hardware, available in Trans. Red, mfg. 2001-present.

MSR	$700	$525	$450	$400	$350	$275	$225	$175

BTB405QM - similar to the BTB400QM except is in five-string configuration, available in Trans. Black or Blue Burst finishes, mfg. 2001-present.

MSR	$800	$600	$525	$450	$375	$300	$250	$195

BTB406QM - similar to the BTB400QM except is in six-string configuration, available in Trans. Black finish, mfg. 2001-present.

MSR	$900	$675	$600	$525	$450	$375	$300	$250

BTB500 (BTB510) - offset double cutaway ash body, 4-string, 35" scale, 3-piece maple neck, rosewood fingerboard with Pearl Dot position markers, 24 medium frets, Mono-Rail II bridge, 1 ea. IBZ DFR-N and IBZ DFR-B pickups, available in Walnut Flat finish, disc. 2003.

		$750	$650	$575	$500	$450	$399	$350

Last MSR was $1,000.

In 2001, the BTB500 was replaced by the BTB510, which features a mahogany body.

BTB505 (BTB 515) - similar to Model BTB500, except in a 5-string configuration, available in Walnut Flat or Trans. Flat Black finishes, disc. 2003.

		$925	$800	$675	$625	$575	$525	$475

Last MSR was $1,300.

In 2001, the BTB505 was replaced by the BTB515, which features a mahogany body.

BTB1000 - Double offset cutaway mahogany body, maple back, flamed maple top, 5-piece maple/bubinga BTB4 Prestige neck, 24-large fret rosewood fingerboard with abalone dot inlay, two IBZ DFR pickups, Mono-Rail II bridge, 2-per-side tuners, active EQ, silver nickle hardware, available in oil finish, mfg. 2001-04.

		$1,350	$1,150	$1,000	$875	$750	$650	$550

Last MSR was $1,730.

BTB1005 - similar to the BTB1000 except is in five string configuration, mfg. 2001-04.

		$1,450	$1,250	$1,100	$950	$825	$700	$600

Last MSR was $1,860.

BTB1006 - similar to the BTB1000 except is in six string configuration, mfg. 2001-04.

		$1,500	$1,300	$1,150	$1,000	$875	$750	$650

Last MSR was $1,930.

BTB 1205E PRESTIGE - five-string configuration, offset double cutaway mahogany body with flame maple top and maple back, Prestige neck-thru five-piece maple/walnut neck, 24-fret rosewood fingerboard with offset abalone dot inlays, 3/2-per-side tuners, Monorail bridge, two Bartolini custom pickups, five knobs, Bartolini 3-Band active electronics, chrome/black hardware, Natural finish, new 2005.

MSR	$1,330	$1,000	$875	$750	$675	$600	$525	$450

BTB 1206E PRESTIGE - similar to the BTB1205E, except in six-string configuration, and three-per-side tuners, new 2005.

MSR	$1,440	$1,100	$950	$825	$725	$650	$575	$500

ELECTRIC BASS: CT SERIES

CTB1 - offset double cutaway maple body, bolt-on 3-piece maple neck, 22-fret rosewood fingerboard with pearl dot inlay, die-cast fixed bridge, 2-per-side tuners, chrome hardware, P/J-style Ibanez pickups, 2 volume/tone controls, available in Black, Blue Night, Red, or White finishes, mfg. 1992 only.

		N/A	$300	$250	$200	$175	$150	$125

Last MSR was $450.

Add $50 for left-handed configuration (Model CTB1L).

GRADING	100% MINT	98% NEAR MINT	95% EXC+	90% EXC	80% VG+	70% VG	60% G

CTB3 - similar to CTB1, except has CT Custom fingerboard inlay, black hardware, 2 volume/tone controls, available in Black, Blue Night, Natural, or Trans. Red finishes, disc. 1992.

	N/A	$375	$325	$275	$250	$225	$150

Last MSR was $600.

CTB5 - similar to CTB1 except features CT Custom fingerboard inlay, 5-string configuration, 3/2-per-side tuners, black hardware, 2 J-style EMG pickups, 2 volume/tone controls, available in Black, Natural, or Trans. Red finishes, mfg. 1992 only.

	N/A	$450	$375	$325	$275	$250	$200

Last MSR was $700.

ELECTRIC BASS: DOUG WIMBISH SIGNATURE (DWB) SERIES

DWB-1 - offset double cutaway maple body, 4-string, 5-piece maple/bubinga neck-thru body, rosewood fingerboard with abalone/pearl position markers, Accu-Cast B20 bridge, 1 ea. IBZ AFR-P and IBZ AFR-J pickups, gold hardware, available in Trans. Blue finish, disc. 2002.

	$2,250	$2,050	$1,850	$1,650	$1,450	$1,250	$1,050

Last MSR was $3,000.

DWB-2 - similar to Model DWB-1, except has bolt-on 3-piece maple neck, available in Royal Wine Sunburst finish, disc. 2002.

	$1,275	$1,075	$875	$750	$695	$650	$595

Last MSR was $1,700.

DWB-3 - similar to the DWB-1 except has a custom 2 band EQ and EMG 35P4 and 35J pickups, available in Trans. Orange finish, mfg. 2003-present.

MSR	$1,300		$975	$850	$750	$675	$600	$525	$450

DWB35 - similar to the DWB3, except in 5-string configuration, available in Bright Blue finish, new 2004.

MSR	$1,400		$1,050	$900	$800	$700	$625	$550	$475

ELECTRIC BASS: ERGODYNE (EDA, EDB, & EDC) SERIES

Ergodyne Series basses feature Luthite, a light weight synthetic body material. The Ergodyne Contemporary Series (EDC) models have sleeker bodies than the regular Ergodyne series models, with two contoured areas on the top, extended bass horn, and indented areas under the controls.

EDA900 - offset double cutaway Luthite body, 3-piece maple EDA4 neck, 24-medium fret rosewood fingerboard with dot inlay on 12th fret, 2-per-side tuners, single IBZ-DFR pickup, active electronics, four knobs, Mono-Rail II bridge, chrome hardware, available in Silver Flat finish, mfg. 2001-04.

	$600	$525	$475	$425	$350	$300	$250

Last MSR was $800.

EDA905 - similar to the EDA900 except is in five-string configuration, available in Silver Flat or Flare Orange Flat finishes, mfg. 2001-04.

	$675	$595	$525	$450	$375	$325	$275

Last MSR was $900.

EDB300 - offset double cutaway rounded Luthite body, bolt-on one-piece maple neck, 24-fret rosewood fingerboard with pearl dot inlay, standard fixed bridge, 2-per-side tuners, chrome hardware, 2 Ibanez DX 'soapbar' pickups, 2 volume/tone controls, available in Black or Jewel Blue finishes, disc. 1998.

	$450	$375	$325	$275	$225	$175	$150

Last MSR was $549.

EDB350 - similar to the EDB300, except features 1 Ibanez DX pickup, Accu-Cast B20 bridge, black hardware, Phat bass boost circuitry, disc. 1998.

	$500	$425	$375	$325	$275	$225	$175

Last MSR was $629.

EDB400 - similar to the EDB300, except features Accu-Cast B20 bridge, black hardware, 2 volume/3-band EQ controls, available in Black or Jewel Blue finishes, disc. 1998.

	$525	$450	$395	$325	$275	$225	$175

Last MSR was $679.

EDB405 - similar to the EDB400, except features a 5-string configuration, 3/2-per-side headstock, disc. 1998.

	$575	$525	$450	$395	$325	$250	$200

Last MSR was $799.

EDB500 - offset double cutaway rounded Luthite body with "slap contour area," bolt-on one-piece maple neck, 24-fret rosewood fingerboard with pearl dot inlay, standard fixed bridge, 2-per-side tuners, black hardware, 2 IBZ DXH soapbar pickups, 2 volume/bass/treble controls, Phat Bass boost active EQ, available in Gray Pewter matte finish, mfg. 1998-2002.

	$425	$350	$300	$250	$225	$195	$150

Last MSR was $580.

EDB600 - similar to the EDB300, except features Accu-Cast B20 bridge, chrome hardware, 2 volume/3-band EQ controls, available in Gray Pewter, White Pearl or Mystique Purple matte finishes, mfg. 1998-present.

MSR	$680		$525	$450	$400	$350	$300	$250	$200

Ibanez BTB405Q
courtesy Ibanez

Ibanez CTB5
courtesy Ibanez

GRADING	100% MINT	98% NEAR MINT	95% EXC+	90% EXC	80% VG+	70% VG	60% G

EDB605 - similar to the EDB300, except features 5-string configuration, 3/2-per-side tuners, Accu-Cast B25 bridge, 2 volume/3-band EQ controls, available in Gray Pewter or Mocca matte finishes, mfg. 1998-present.

MSR	$750	$575	$500	$425	$350	$300	$250	$200

Note: MSR $750 with $575 $500 $425 $350 $300 $250 $200.

EDB690 - offset double cutaway Luthite body, 5-piece maple and bubinga neck, rosewood fingerboard with Pearl dot position markers, 24 medium frets, 2-per-side tuners, Accu-Cast B20 bridge, 2 IBZ DXH hign output humbuckers, 3-band active EQ, available in Burled Art Grain finish, disc. 2001.

	$600	$525	$450	$375	$325	$275	$225

Last MSR was $800.

EDC700 - sleek offset double cutaway rounded Luthite body with "slap contour areas," bolt-on one-piece maple neck, 24-fret rosewood fingerboard with pearl dot inlay, Accu-Cast B20 bridge, 2-per-side tuners, chrome hardware, 2 IBZ SFR soapbar pickups, 2 volume/bass/treble/Vari-mid controls, available in Black Pearl or Night Navy finishes, mfg. 1998-2002.

	$625	$550	$475	$400	$350	$295	$225

Last MSR was $850.

EDC710 - similar to the EDC700 except has a new triple coil pickup with three settings, available in Copper Brush Flat finish, mfg. 2003 only.

	$510	$450	$375	$325	$275	$225	$175

Last MSR was $680.

EDC705 - similar to the EDC700, except features 5-string configuration, 3/2-per-side tuners, Accu-Cast B25 bridge, black hardware, 2 volume/3-band EQ controls, available in Black Pearl finishes, mfg. 1998-2002.

	$725	$625	$550	$475	$400	$325	$250

Last MSR was $950.

EDC715 - similar to the EDC705 except has a new triple coil pickup with three settings, available in Copper Brush Flat finish, mfg. 2003 only.

	$575	$500	$425	$350	$300	$250	$200

Last MSR was $750.

ELECTRIC BASS: EX SERIES

EXB404 - offset double cutaway maple body, bolt-on 3-piece maple neck, 22-fret rosewood fingerboard with pearl dot inlay, die-cast fixed bridge, 4-on-a-side tuners, chrome hardware, P/J-style pickups, 2 volume/tone controls, available in Black, Burgundy Red, Crimson Metallic, or Jewel Blue finishes, disc. 1996.

	N/A	$300	$250	$210	$180	$150	$120

Last MSR was $450.

Add $40 for left-handed configuration (Model EXB404L), available in Black finish.

EXB445 - similar to the EXB404, except features 5-string configuration, 4/1-per-side tuners, black hardware, 2 J-style EMG pickups, available in Black, Burgundy Red, or Jewel Blue finishes, disc. 1996.

	N/A	$350	$300	$250	$200	$160	$130

Last MSR was $550.

ELECTRIC BASS: GAX SERIES

GAXB150 - double cutaway alder body with contoured top, maple neck, 20-fret rosewood fingerboard with dot inlay, two-per-side tuners, B-10 bridge, dual coil soap bar pickup, single knob, three-way switch, chrome hardware, available in Black, Metallic Blue, or Metallic Red finishes, 32 in. scale, mfg. 2003-present.

MSR	$240	$180	$150	$130	$110	$90	$70	$50

ELECTRIC BASS: GSR SERIES

GSR100 - similar to Model GSR200, except has 1 PSND-P pickup, available in Black, Silver, or Metallic Blue finishes, current mfg.

MSR	$243	$185	$160	$140	$120	$100	$80	$60

Add $100 for left-hand configuration (Model GSR 100L).

In 2005, Silver finish was introduced.

GSR200 - offset double cutaway Agatis body, 4-string, 1-piece maple neck, roswood fingerboard with pearl dot position markers, 22 medium frets, 2-per-side tuners, Standard 4-string bridge, 1 ea. PSND-P and PSND-J pickups, chrome hardware, available in Black, Jewel Blue, or Trans. Red finishes, current mfg.

MSR	$286	$200	$170	$145	$125	$105	$85	$70

Add $50 for left-handed configuration.

GSR200FM - similar to the GSR200, except has a flame maple top, available in Trans. Fireburst Blue or Trans. Brown Sunburst finishes, new 2005.

MSR	$343	$260	$220	$190	$160	$140	$120	$100

GSR205 - similar to Model GSR200, except in a 5-string configuarion, standard 5-string bridge, 2 IBZ J5 pickups, available in Black finish, current mfg.

MSR	$400	$300	$250	$225	$200	$175	$150	$125

Add $75 for left-handed configuration.

ELECTRIC BASS: GTR (TR) SERIES

The TR50, TR70, and TR75 models were originally part of the TR Series from 1994-97. In 1998, these models were redesignated the GTR Bass Series models. In 1998, Jewel Blue and Metallic Green finishes were introduced; Blue Night and Deep Green finishes were discontinued.

GRADING	100% MINT	98% NEAR MINT	95% EXC+	90% EXC	80% VG+	70% VG	60% G

GTR50 (TR50) - offset double cutaway agathis body, bolt-on maple neck, 22-fret maple fingerboard with pearl dot inlay, standard fixed bridge, 4-on-a-side tuners, chrome hardware, black pickguard, split P-style pickup, volume/tone controls, available in Black, Blue Night, or Deep Green finishes, mfg. 1994-99.

	$200	$175	$150	$135	$115	$95	$65

Last MSR was $259.

Add $140 for left-handed configuration (Model GTR50 L). Available in Black finish only.

GTR70 (TR70) - similar to TR50, except features P/J-style pickups, available in Black, Blue Night, or Deep Green finishes, disc. 1999.

	$235	$195	$175	$150	$125	$100	$75

Last MSR was $299.

GTR75 (TR75) - similar to TR50, except features 5-string configuration, 4/1-per-side headstock, 2 IBZ J-style pickups, available in Black or Blue Night finishes, disc. 1999.

	$375	$300	$265	$225	$190	$155	$115

Last MSR was $459.

Ibanez EXB445
courtesy Ibanez

ELECTRIC BASS: GARY WILLIS SIGNATURE (GWB) SERIES

GWB1 - offset double cutaway Swamp Ash body, 3-piece maple neck, ebony fretless fingerboard, pearl dot position markers, STD-5 bridge, 1 ea. Bartolini GW and Bartolini NTBT pickups, black hardware, available in Natural Flat finish, disc. 2004.

	$1,550	$1,350	$1,150	$1,000	$850	$700	$550

Last MSR was $2,000.

GWB2 - similar to Model GWB1, except has 24 medium frets, available in Trans. Black Flat finish, disc. 2002.

	$1,350	$1,150	$1,050	$950	$850	$750	$650

Last MSR was $1,800.

GWB35 - 5-string configuration, offset double cutaway basswood body, 3-piece maple neck, ebony fretless fingerboard, pearl dot position markers, B-105 bridge, SFR-GWB Custom pickup, active electronics, black hardware, available in Black Flat finish, mfg. 2004-present.

MSR	$800	$600	$525	$450	$400	$350	$300	$250

GWB105 - five-string configuration, offset double cutaway light ash body, three-piece maple neck, ebonol fretless fingerboard with offset pearl dot inlays, B-105 bridge, two Bartolini pickups, two knobs, black hardware, available in Natural Flat finish, new 2005.

MSR	$1,300	$975	$850	$750	$675	$600	$525	$450

Last MSR was $2,000.

ELECTRIC BASS: ICEMAN SERIES

ICB200 - single horn cutaway asymmetrical mahogany body with pointed bottom bout, bolt-on maple neck, 22-fret rosewood fingerboard with pearl dot inlay, B-10 bridge, 2-per-side tuners, 2 MHC4 pickups, 3 knobs, chrome hardware, available in Brown Sunburst finish, mfg. 2004-present.

MSR	$530	$400	$325	$275	$235	$195	$165	$135

Last MSR was $580.

ICB300 - single horn cutaway asymmetrical mahogany body with pointed bottom bout, raised cream pickguard, bolt-on maple neck, 22-fret bound rosewood fingerboard with pearl dot inlay, fixed die-cast bridge, 2-per-side tuners, chrome hardware, 2 Ibanez pickups, 2 volume/tone controls, 3-position switch, available in Black or Blue finishes, mfg. 1994-96.

	N/A	$400	$350	$300	$250	$200	$150

Last MSR was $580.

ICB500 - similar to the ICB300, except features pearloid bound mahogany body, raised pearloid pickguard, 22-fret bound rosewood fingerboard with abalone dot inlay, bound blackface peghead with pearl logo inlay, cosmo black hardware, available in Black finish, mfg. 1994-96.

	N/A	$900	$800	$700	$600	$500	$400

Last MSR was $1,300.

ELECTRIC BASS: KORN SIGNATURE SERIES

FIELDY K5 - five-string configuration, offset double cutaway mahogany body with padauk top and back, five-piece wenge/walnut neck, 24-fret rosewood fingerboard with K5 12th fret inlay, Fieldy signature on headstock with 2/3-per-side tuners, die-cast bridge, two ADX pickups, four knobs, gold hardware, Oil finish, mfg. 2002-present.

MSR	$1,000	$750	$650	$575	$500	$425	$375	$325

ELECTRIC BASS: ROADGEAR (RD) SERIES

RD300 - offset double cutaway with extended bass horn, agathis body, maple neck, 24-fret rosewood fingerboard with dot inlay, four-on-one-side tuners, B-100 bridge, two pickups, three knobs, chrome hardware, available in Black or Navy Metallic finishes, mfg. 2004-present.

MSR	$300	$225	$185	$150	$125	$105	$85	$65

In 2005, Navy Metallic finish was introduced.

Ibanez GWB35
courtesy Ibanez

GRADING		100% MINT	98% NEAR MINT	95% EXC+	90% EXC	80% VG+	70% VG	60% G

RD500 - offset double cutaway with extended bass horn, basswood body with quilted maple top, maple neck, 24-fret rosewood fingerboard with dot inlay, four-on-one-side tuners, Accu-Cast B-205 bridge, two Duncan/Ibanez pickups, four knobs, chrome hardware, available in Sunburst finish, mfg. 2004-current.

	MSR	$550	$425	$350	$300	$250	$210	$180	$150

RD505 - similar to the RD500, except in five-string configuration, 4/1-per-side tuners, available in Sunburst finish, new 2005.

	MSR	$600	$450	$375	$325	$275	$235	$195	$165

RD900FM - offset double cutaway with extended bass horn, mahogany body with flame maple top, maple neck, 24-fret rosewood fingerboard with abalone dot inlay, matching headstock with four-on-one-side tuners, Accu-Cast B-400 bridge, two Bassline pickups, four knobs, chrome hardware, available in Natural finish, new 2005.

	MSR	$900	$675	$600	$525	$450	$400	$350	$300

ELECTRIC BASS: SB SERIES

SB1200 - similar to the SB1500, except features a mahogany body, available in Black, Blue, or White finishes, mfg. 1992 only.

		N/A	$700	$600	$525	$450	$375	$300

Last MSR was $1,200.

SB1500 - offset double cutaway bubinga (or padauk or wenge) body, bolt-on 5-piece bubinga/wenge neck, 22-fret ebony fingerboard with abalone oval inlays, AccuCast-B bridge, 4-on-a-side tuners, chrome hardware, P/J-style EMG pickups, 2 volume/tone controls, active electronics, available in Natural finish, mfg. 1992 only.

		N/A	$900	$800	$700	$600	$500	$400

Last MSR was $1,500.

ELECTRIC BASS: SOUNDGEAR (SR) SERIES

Soundgear Series basses were introduced in 1987, and feature the SD GR by Ibanez logo on their headstocks. In 1998, Natural and Jewel Blue finishes were introduced; Blue Night and Metallic Green finishes were discontinued.

SR300 - sleek offset double cutaway agathis body, bolt-on 3-piece maple neck, 24-fret rosewood fingerboard with pearl dot inlay, standard fixed bridge, 2-per-side tuners, chrome hardware, P/J-style Ibanez DX pickups, 2 volume/tone controls, available in Black, Blue Night, or Metallic Green finishes, disc. 1999.

		$325	$250	$225	$200	$175	$125	$100

Last MSR was $399.

Add $100 for left-handed configuration (Model SR300 L), available in Black finish. Also available in fretless configuration.

SR300 DX - similar to the SR300, except features Phat bass boost circuitry, available in Black or Metallic Green finishes, current mfg.

	MSR	$380	$285	$250	$225	$200	$175	$150	$125

Add $75 for left-handed configuration (Model SR300DXL), available in Black finish.

This model is also available with a fretless fingerboard.

SR305 - similar to the SR300, except features a 5-string configuration, 3/2-per-side tuners, 2 Ibanez DX soapbar pickups, available in Black or Blue Night finishes, mfg. 1997-99.

		$375	$325	$295	$250	$225	$195	$165

Last MSR was $499.

SR305 DX - similar to the SR305, except features Phat bass boost circuitry, available in Black or Metallic Green finishes, current mfg.

	MSR	$450	$350	$300	$260	$230	$195	$160	$130

SR390 - offset double cutaway ash body, bolt-on 3-piece maple neck, 24-fret rosewood fingerboard with pearl dot inlay, standard fixed bridge, 2-per-side tuners, black hardware, 2 IBZ DX soapbar pickups, 2 volume/tone controls, Phat bass boost circuitry, available in Butterscotch or Trans. Red finishes, mfg. 1998-99.

		$400	$350	$300	$275	$225	$200	$150

Last MSR was $529.

SR400 - offset double cutaway soft maple body, bolt-on 3-piece maple neck, 24-fret rosewood fingerboard with pearl dot inlay, die-cast fixed bridge, 2-per-side tuners, black hardware, P/J-style Ibanez DX pickups, 2 volume/3-band EQ tone controls, available in Black, Jewel Blue, Mediterranean Green, or Natural finishes, mfg. 1993-present.

	MSR	$540	$400	$350	$300	$250	$210	$170	$130

Add $50 for left-handed configuration (Model SR400 L) or fretless fingerboard (Model SR400 FL). Both models were only available in a Black finish.

Early models may feature Candy Apple and Crimson Metallic finishes. In 1997, the left-handed configuration and fretless fingerboard option were both discontinued.

SR405 - similar to SR400, except has 5-string configuration, 3/2-per-side tuners, 2 Ibanez DX soapbar pickups, available in Black, Jewel Blue, or Natural finishes, mfg. 1994-present.

	MSR	$650	$500	$450	$400	$350	$295	$225	$185

SR406 - similar to SR400, except has 6-string configuration, 3-per-side tuners, 2 Ibanez DX soapbar pickups, available in Black finish, disc. 2003.

		$600	$525	$450	$395	$325	$275	$225

Last MSR was $800.

SR480 - offset double cutaway mahogany body, 4-string, 5-piece maple/Wenga neck, rosewood fingerboard with pearl dot position markers, 24 medium frets, Die Cast 4-String bridge, 1 IBZ DXP pickup and 1 IBZ DXJ pickup, EQBIII 3-band active EQ, black hardware, available in Stained Oil finish, disc. 2003.

		$525	$450	$400	$350	$300	$225	$185

Last MSR was $700.

GRADING	100% MINT	98% NEAR MINT	95% EXC+	90% EXC	80% VG+	70% VG	60% G

SR485 - similar to Model SR480, except in a 5-string configuration, Die Cast 5-String bridge, available in Stained Oil finish, disc. 2003.

	$600	$525	$450	$395	$325	$275	$225

Last MSR was $800.

SR500 - offset double cutaway maple body, bolt-on 3-piece maple neck, 24-fret rosewood fingerboard with pearl dot inlay, fixed bridge, 2-per-side tuners, black hardware, P/J-style active Ibanez pickups, volume/treble/bass/mix controls, active electronics, available in Black, Emerald Green, Jewel Blue, Natural, or Trans. Turquoise finishes, mfg. 1993-96.

	N/A	$475	$400	$350	$300	$250	$200

Last MSR was $700.

Add $50 for left-handed configuration (Model SR500 L), available in Black finish.

SR500 (Current Mfg.) - similar to the SR-500, except has a mahogany body with a five-piece wenge/bubinga neck, abalone oval inlays, Bartolini pickups, and Bartolini active electronics, available in Brown Mahogany finish, mfg. 2004-present.

MSR	$700	$525	$450	$400	$350	$300	$250	$200

SR505 - similar to SR500, except has 5-string configuration, 3/2-per-side tuners, 2 J-style EMG pickups, available in Black, Natural, Trans. Red, or Trans. Turquoise finishes, mfg. 1993.

	N/A	$550	$475	$400	$350	$300	$250

Last MSR was $800.

SR505 (Current Mfg.) - similar to the current mfg. of the SR500, except in five-string configuration, 3/2-per-side tuners, mfg. 2004-present.

MSR	$750	$575	$500	$425	$375	$325	$275	$225

SR506 - similar to SR500, except has 6-string configuration, 3-per-side tuners, 2 Ibanez ADX active humbucker pickups, Vari-Mid 3-band EQ, available in Black or Natural finishes, mfg. 1994-98.

	N/A	$650	$575	$500	$425	$375	$325

Last MSR was $999.

SR506 (Current Mfg.) - similar to the current mfg. SR500, except in six-string configuration, three-per-side tuners, mfg. 2004-present.

MSR	$800	$600	$525	$450	$400	$350	$300	$250

SR590 - similar to SR500, except has gold hardware, available in Natural or Trans. Turquoise finishes, mfg. 1994-96.

	N/A	$500	$425	$375	$300	$250	$200

Last MSR was $750.

SR800 - offset double cutaway basswood body, bolt-on 3-piece maple neck, 24-fret rosewood fingerboard with pearl dot inlay, AccuCast B20 (formerly B IV) bridge, 2-per-side tuners, black hardware, P/J-style Ibanez AFR pickups, volume/blend/Vari-mid 3-band EQ controls, available in Black, Dark Metallic Green, or Metallic Blue finishes, disc. 2003.

	$600	$525	$460	$395	$330	$265	$200

Last MSR was $800.

Add $100 for fretless fingerboard version (Model SR800 F), mfg. 1992 only. Add $150 for left-handed version (Model SR800 L), disc. 1994.

Early models may feature Candy Apple, Cayman Green, Jewel Blue, and Royal Blue finishes. In 1998, Arctic Blue and Cherry Fudge finishes were introduced.

SR800 A - similar to SR800, except has ash body, available in Amber or Trans. Black finishes, mfg. 1997-99.

	$625	$550	$495	$425	$350	$295	$225

Last MSR was $849.

SR885 - similar to SR800, except has 5-string configuration, 3/2-per-side tuners, AccuCast B25 bridge, 2 Ibanez ADX active pickups, available in Black or Metallic Blue finishes, mfg. 1991-2003.

	$700	$625	$550	$475	$395	$325	$240

Last MSR was $900.

Early models may feature Candy Apple, Laser Blue, and Royal Blue finishes. In 1998, Arctic Blue finish was introduced.

SR886 - similar to SR885, except has 6-string configuration, 3-per-side tuners, available in Black or Candy Apple finishes, mfg. 1992 only.

	N/A	$900	$800	$700	$600	$500	$400

Last MSR was $1,400.

SR890 - offset double cutaway ash body, bolt-on 3-piece maple neck, 24-fret rosewood fingerboard with pearl dot inlay, fixed bridge, 2-per-side tuners, gold hardware, P/J-style Ibanez active pickups, volume/treble/2 mid/bass/mix controls, available in Trans. Cherry or Trans. Turquoise finishes, mfg. 1993 only.

	N/A	$650	$550	$475	$400	$350	$300

Last MSR was $1,000.

SR895 - similar to SR890, except has 5-string configuration, 3/2-per-side tuners, mfg. 1993 only.

	N/A	$800	$700	$600	$500	$425	$350

Last MSR was $1,200.

**Ibanez SB1500
courtesy Ibanez**

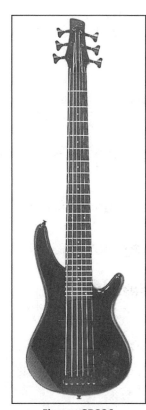

**Ibanez SR886
courtesy Ibanez**

GRADING	100% MINT	98% NEAR MINT	95% EXC+	90% EXC	80% VG+	70% VG	60% G

SR 900 (1992 MFG.) - similar to the SR890, except features an AccuCast-B bridge, P/J-style Ibanez pickups, 2 volume/tone controls, available in Emerald Green or Purple Neon finishes, mfg. 1992 only.

	N/A	$600	$500	$425	$350	$300	$250

Last MSR was $900.

SR900 (CURRENT MFG.) - offset double cutaway figured maple body, five-piece maple/bubinga neck-thru body, 24-fret rosewood fingerboard with abalone oval inlays, two-per-side tuners, Accu-Cast B20 bridge, two Bartolini pickups, five knobs, Bartolini active electronics, black chrome hardware, available in Antique Violin Flat, Trans. Black, or Trans. Flat Black finishes, new 2005.

MSR	$1,040	$780	$700	$625	$550	$475	$400	$325

SR905 - similar to the SR900, except in five-string configuration, 3/2-per-side tuners, available in Charcoal Brown Flat finish, new 2005.

MSR	$1,100	$825	$725	$650	$575	$500	$425	$350

SR950 - similar to SR900, except has ebony fingerboard with abalone oval inlay, gold hardware, available in Trans. Cherry or Trans. Turquoise finishes, disc.

	N/A	$650	$550	$475	$400	$350	$300

Last MSR was $1,000.

SR990 QS - offset double cutaway mahogany body, quilted sapele top, bolt-on 5-piece bubinga/wenge neck, 24-fret wenge fingerboard with abalone oval inlay, AccuCast B20 bridge, 2-per-side tuners, chrome hardware, Ibanez P/J-style AFR pickups, volume/blend/Vari-mid 3-band EQ controls, available in Stained Oil finish, mfg. 1998-99.

	$700	$600	$525	$450	$375	$325	$250

Last MSR was $949.

SR1010 - offset double cutaway mahogany body, bolt-on 5-piece bubinga/wenge neck, 24-fret wenge fingerboard with abalone oval inlay, AccuCast B20 (previously B IV) bridge, 2-per-side tuners, chrome hardware, Ibanez P/J-style AFR pickups, volume/blend/Vari-mid 3-band EQ controls, available in Stained Oil finish, disc. 1999.

	$850	$725	$625	$550	$450	$375	$275

Last MSR was $1,099.

In 1998, SFR pickups replaced AFR pickups.

SR1015 - similar to SR1010, except has 5-string configuration, 3/2-per-side tuners, AccuCast B25 bridge, 2 Ibanez ADX humbucker pickups, available in Stained Oil finish, disc. 1999.

	$1,000	$895	$750	$650	$525	$425	$325

Last MSR was $1,249.

In 1998, SFR pickups replaced ADX pickups.

SR1016 - similar to SR1300, except has 6-string configuration, 3-per-side tuners, die-cast bridge, black hardware, 2 Ibanez ADX humbucker pickups, available in Stained Oil finish, disc. 1999.

	$1,100	$950	$795	$675	$575	$450	$350

Last MSR was $1,349.

In 1998, DXP pickups replaced ADX pickups.

SR1200 - offset double cutaway mahogany body, figured maple top, through body 5-piece bubinga/wenge neck, 24-fret rosewood fingerboard with abalone oval inlay, die-cast bridge, 2-per-side tuners, black hardware, Ibanez P/J-style AFR pickups, volume/blend/Vari-mid 3-band EQ controls, available in Butterscotch Trans, or Natural finishes, mfg. 1994-98.

	$925	$750	$675	$595	$495	$400	$300

Last MSR was $1,199.

SR1205 - similar to SR1200, except has 5-string configuration, 3/2-per-side tuners, 2 Ibanez ADX humbucker pickups, available in Butterscotch Trans. or Natural finishes, mfg. 1994-98.

	$1,000	$900	$795	$675	$575	$450	$350

Last MSR was $1,349.

SR1300 - offset double cutaway padauk body, bolt-on 5-piece bubinga/wenge neck, 24-fret wenge fingerboard with pearl dot inlay, fixed bridge, 2-per-side tuners, cosmo black hardware, P/J-style Ibanez pickups, volume/treble/2 mid/bass/mix controls, available in Oil finish, disc. 1996.

	$900	$750	$675	$595	$525	$425	$350

Last MSR was $1,400.

SR1305 - similar to SR1300, except has 5-string configuration, 3/2-per-side tuners, 2 Ibanez active humbucker pickups, disc. 1996.

	$1,000	$800	$725	$650	$550	$475	$400

Last MSR was $1,600.

SR1306 - similar to SR1300, except has 6-string configuration, 3-per-side tuners, 2 Ibanez active humbucker pickups, disc. 1996.

	$1,100	$900	$825	$725	$625	$550	$450

Last MSR was $1,800.

SR1500 - offset double cutaway bubinga or padauk body, bubinga/wenge 5-piece neck, 22-fret ebony fingerboard with pearl dot inlay, fixed bridge, 2-per-side tuners, black hardware, P/J-style EMG pickups, 2 volume/tone controls, available in Natural finish, mfg. 1991-92.

	N/A	$850	$750	$650	$575	$500	$425

Last MSR was $1,400.

SR2000 - offset double cutaway maple body, through body 5-piece maple/walnut neck, 24-fret wenge fingerboard with abalone oval inlay, fixed bridge, 2-per-side tuners, gold hardware, P/J-style Ibanez pickups, volume/treble/2 mid/bass/mix controls, available in Oil or Trans. Purple finishes, mfg. 1993 only.

	N/A	$1,000	$875	$750	$650	$550	$450

Last MSR was $1,600.

GRADING	100% MINT	98% NEAR MINT	95% EXC+	90% EXC	80% VG+	70% VG	60% G

SR2005 - similar to SR2000, except has 5-string configuration, 3/2-per-side tuners, 2 J-style Ibanez pickups, mfg. 1993 only.

	N/A	$1,200	$1,050	$900	$800	$700	$600

Last MSR was $1,900.

SR3000 - offset double cutaway mahogany body, 5-piece wenge/bubinga neck, 24-fret wenge fingerboard with abalone oval inlay, 2 IBZ SFR pickups, Mono-Rail II bridge with D-tuner, active EQ, black hardware, available in Stained Oil finish, mfg. 2001-04.

	$1,050	$900	$825	$750	$650	$550	$450

Last MSR was $1,400.

SR3005 - similar to the SR3000 except is in five string configuration, mfg. 2001-04.

	$1,125	$975	$875	$800	$700	$600	$500

Last MSR was $1,500.

SR3006 - similar to the SR3000 except is in six string configuration, mfg. 2001-04.

	$1,200	$1,050	$900	$800	$700	$600	$525

Last MSR was $1,600.

SR5000 SR PRESTIGE - offset double cutaway mahogany/walnut/mahogany body, bolt-on 5-piece bubinga/wenge neck, 24-fret wenge fingerboard with abalone oval inlay, Monorail bridge pieces with D-Tuner, 2-per-side tuners, gold hardware, Ibanez P/J-style AFR pickups, volume/blend/Vari-mid 3-band EQ controls, available in Mahogany finish, disc. 1999.

	$1,500	$1,250	$1,100	$995	$775	$650	$475

Last MSR was $1,899.

In 1998, 2 IBZ SFR soapbar pickups replaced the P/J-style AFR pickups.

SR5005 SR PRESTIGE - similar to SR5000, except has 5-string configuration, 3/2-per-side tuners, 5 Monorail bridge pieces, 2 Ibanez ADX humbucker pickups, disc. 1999.

	$1,600	$1,300	$1,150	$1,000	$800	$675	$500

Last MSR was $1,999.

In 1998, 2 IBZ SFR soapbar pickups replaced the 2 ADX humbucker pickups.

Ibanez SR950
courtesy Ibanez

ELECTRIC BASS: SOUNDGEAR PRESTIGE SERIES

SR1000EFM - offset double cutaway maple body with flame maple top, five-piece maple/bubinga neck-thru body design, 24-fret rosewood fingerboard with offset abalone oval inlays, two-per-side tuners, Monorail bridge, two Bartolini pickups, four knobs, black chrome hardware, Natural finish, new 2005.

MSR	$1,330		$1,000	$875	$750	$650	$575	$500	$425

SR1000EWN - offset double cutaway mahogany body with walnut top, five-piece maple/bubinga neck-thru body design, 24-fret rosewood fingerboard with offset abalone oval inlays, two-per-side tuners, Monorail bridge, two Bartolini pickups, four knobs, black chrome hardware, Natural finish, new 2005.

MSR	$1,330		$1,000	$875	$750	$650	$575	$500	$425

SR1005EFM - similar to the SR1000EFM, execpt in five-string configuration, 2/3-per-side tuners, new 2005.

MSR	$1,460		$1,100	$950	$825	$700	$625	$550	$475

SR1005EWN - similar to the SR1000EWN, execpt in five-string configuration, 2/3-per-side tuners, new 2005.

MSR	$1,460		$1,100	$950	$825	$700	$625	$550	$475

SR1006EFM - similar to the SR1000EFM, execpt in six-string configuration, three-per-side tuners, new 2005.

MSR	$1,570		$1,175	$1,025	$900	$775	$675	$600	$525

ELECTRIC BASS: SOUNDGEAR 'X'TREME SERIES

The 'X'Treme Soundgear Series feature the traditional feel of the SR series with powerful pickups for a no-frills model with lots of volume.

SRX300 - offset double cutaway SR style basswood body, maple neck, 24-fret rosewood fingerboard with pearl dot inlays, two-per-side tuners, Accu-Cast B-100 bridge, two PFR pickups, four knobs, chrome hardware, available in Iron Pewter or Moon Shadow finishes, mfg. 2004-present.

MSR	$430		$325	$275	$235	$195	$160	$130	$100

SRX400 - offset double cutaway SR style soft maple body, three-piece maple neck, 24-fret rosewood fingerboard with pearl dot inlays, two-per-side tuners, Accu-Cast B-100 bridge, white pickguard, single PFR pickup, two knobs, chrome hardware, available in Indigo Blue Burst, Dark Stain Flat, or Martini Olive finishes, mfg. 2003-present.

MSR	$530		$400	$350	$300	$250	$210	$180	$150

In 2005, Martini Olive finish was disc.

SRX500 - offset double cutaway SR style basswood body with flame maple top, three-piece maple neck, 24-fret rosewood fingerboard with pearl dot inlays, two-per-side tuners, Accu-Cast B-200 bridge, two PFR pickup, four knobs, chrome hardware, available in Honey Sunburst, Stained Blue Burst, or Trifade Burst finishes, mfg. 2003-present.

MSR	$630		$475	$400	$350	$300	$250	$210	$170

In 2004, Trifade Burst finish was introduced.

SRX505 - similar to the SRX500, except in five-string configuration, 2/3-per-side tuners, available in Trans Black finish, mfg. 2003-present.

MSR	$680		$510	$450	$375	$325	$275	$225	$180

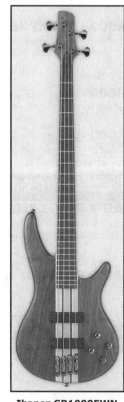

Ibanez SR1000EWN
courtesy Ibanez

GRADING	100% MINT	98% NEAR MINT	95% EXC+	90% EXC	80% VG+	70% VG	60% G

SRX700 - offset double cutaway SR style light ash body, five-piece maple/walnut neck-thru-body, 24-fret rosewood fingerboard with pearl dot inlays, two-per-side tuners, Accu-Cast B-200 bridge, two PFR pickup, four knobs, chrome hardware, available in Honey Sunburst finish, mfg. 2003-present.

	MSR	$900		$675	$600	$525	$450	$400	$350	$300

SRX705 - similar to the SRX700, except in five-string configuration, 2/3-per-side tuners, available in Natural finish, mfg. 2003-present.

	MSR	$930		$700	$625	$550	$475	$425	$375	$325

ELECTRIC BASS: TRB (TR) SERIES

TR Series basses were introduced in 1992, and were originally designated TRB (B for Bass) in the model names.

TRB1 - offset double cutaway alder body, bolt-on maple neck, 22-fret rosewood fingerboard with pearl dot inlay, die cast fixed bridge, 4-on-a-side tuners, black hardware, P/J-style pickups, 2 volume/tone controls, available in Black, Candy Apple, Jewel Blue, or Trans. Blue finishes, mfg. 1991-93.

		N/A	$325	$275	$235	$195	$165	$135

Last MSR was $430.

Add $50 for left-handed version (Model TRB1L), available in Black finish only.

TRB2 - similar to TRB1, except has ash body, gold hardware, available in Lavender Stain and Walnut Stain finishes, mfg. 1993 only.

		N/A	$375	$325	$275	$235	$195	$165

Last MSR was $530.

TRB3 - similar to TRB1, except has basswood body, P/J-style Ibanez pickups, 2 volume/tone controls, available in Black, Blue, or Lipstick Red finishes, mfg. 1992 only.

		N/A	$425	$350	$300	$250	$210	$175

Last MSR was $650.

TRB15 - similar to TRB1, except has 5-string configuration, 4/1 per side tuners, 2 J-style pickups, available in Black or Trans. Red finishes, mfg. 1993 only.

		N/A	$375	$325	$275	$235	$195	$165

Last MSR was $530.

TRB100 - offset double cutaway alder body, bolt-on maple neck, 22-fret rosewood fingerboard with pearl dot inlay, fixed bridge, 4-on-a-side tuners, black hardware, P/J-style pickups, volume/tone/mix control, available in Black, Candy Apple, Jewel Blue, or Trans. Blue finishes, mfg. 1994-96.

		N/A	$325	$275	$235	$195	$165	$135

Last MSR was $450.

TRB105 - similar to TRB100, except has 5-string configuration, 4/1 per side tuners, 2 J-style pickups, available in Black or Trans. Red finishes, mfg. 1994-96.

		N/A	$375	$325	$275	$235	$195	$165

Last MSR was $550.

TRB200 - similar to the TRB100, except features an ash body, gold hardware, available in Lavender Stain or Walnut Stain finishes, mfg. 1994-96.

		N/A	$375	$325	$275	$235	$195	$165

Last MSR was $550.

TR500 (TR EXPRESSIONIST) - offset double cutaway alder body, bolt-on maple neck, 22-fret rosewood fingerboard with pearl dot inlay, EB70 Dual Mount bridge, 4-on-a-side tuners, chrome hardware, pickguard, 2 Ibanez PT single coil pickups, volume/tone/3-band EQ controls, available in Black, Mint Green, or Vintage Burst finishes, disc. 1998.

		$550	$450	$395	$325	$275	$225	$175

Last MSR was $679.

TR505 - similar to the TR500, except features 5-string configuration, 4/1 per side tuners, tortoiseshell pickguard, available in Vintage Burst finish, disc. 1998.

		$650	$525	$450	$395	$325	$275	$200

Last MSR was $799.

TR600 - similar to the TR500, except features AccuCast B20 bridge, pearloid pickguard, available in Cayman Green or Royal Blue finishes, disc. 1998.

		$650	$525	$450	$395	$325	$275	$200

Last MSR was $799.

ELECTRIC BASS: USA CUSTOM AMERICAN MASTER SERIES

MAB 4 FM (FLAME MAPLE) - offset double cutaway mahogany body, figured maple top, maple/purple heart 3-piece through body neck, 24-fret rosewood fingerboard with pearl dot inlay, Wilkinson fixed bridge, 2-per-side tuners, black hardware, P-style/J-style EMG pickups, 2 volume/tone controls, available in Natural finish, disc. 1992.

		N/A	$1,500	$1,300	$1,175	$1,050	$925	$700

Last MSR was $2,600.

MAB 5 BE (BIRD'S-EYE MAPLE) - similar to MAB4FM, except has bird's-eye maple top, 5-string configuration, 3/2-per-side tuners, disc. 1992.

		N/A	$1,700	$1,400	$1,275	$1,150	$1,000	$850

Last MSR was $2,800.

ELECTRIC BASS: VERDINE WHITE SIGNATURE SERIES

VWB1 - offset double cutaway alder body, 3-piece maple neck, ebony fingerboard with Abalone dot position markers, 24 jumbo frets, Accu-Cast B20 bridge, 1 ea. IBZ AFR-P and IBZ AFR-J pickups, chrome hardware, available in Cream finish, disc. 2002.

		$975	$875	$775	$725	$650	$550	$450

Last MSR was $1,300.

IMAGE

Instruments previously built in Taiwan in the mid-1980s.

The Image line consisted of entry level to mid-quality designs based on classic American models, (source: Tony Bacon and Paul Day, *The Guru's Guitar Guide*).

IMPERIAL

Instruments previously produced in Italy circa 1963-1966 (later models were produced in Japan until circa 1968).

The Imperial trademark is a brand name used by U.S. importer Imperial Accordion Company of Chicago, Illinois. Imperial instruments consisted of solid body electric guitars and basses (source: Michael Wright, *Vintage Guitar Magazine*).

ITALIA

Instruments currently produced in Korea. Distributed by LPD Music International in Madison Heights, MI.

Italia guitars are built with inspiration from the 1960s Italian guitars using 21st century technologies. Their models feature unique designs, often with a sparkle finish. Retail prices start at $549 and range up to $699 for most models. There are some models that are pricier such as the Double Neck. For more information refer to their web site (see Trademark Index).

**Ibanez SRX700
courtesy Ibanez**

**Italia Modena
courtesy International Vintage**

NOTES

Section J

J.B. PLAYER

Instruments currently produced in Asia. Distributed by MBT International of Charleston, SC. MBT International, owner of J.B. Player, is the parent company to the Hondo Guitar Company, Musicorp, Engl USA, and MBT Lighting and Sound.

J.B. Player offers a wide range of entry to student level instruments in acoustic or electric solid body guitars and basses. Most models are based off of popular American designs. Many higher quality models may appeal to working musicians, and feature such parts as Schaller hardware, Wilkinson bridges, and APC pickups. All models are listed on their website; refer to it for more information (see Trademark Index).

GRADING	100% MINT	98% NEAR MINT	95% EXC+	90% EXC	80% VG+	70% VG	60% G

ELECTRIC: ARTIST SERIES

J.B. Player JBA-460
courtesy J.B. Player

JB-400-AM - single cutaway semi-hollowbody, bound flame maple top, bound 'fang' style soundhole, mahogany back/sides/neck, 22-fret bound ebonized rosewood fingerboard with pearl dot inlay, Tune-O-Matic bridge/stop tailpiece, bound peghead, 3-per-side tuners, gold hardware, 2 humbucker pickups, volume/tone control, 3-position switch, available in Natural finish, disc. 1996.

	N/A	$1,200	$1,050	$900	$750	$600	$450

Last MSR was $1,900.

JB-400-AL - similar to the JB-400-AM, except features a black bound maple top, basswood back/sides, bolt-on maple neck, 24-fret rosewood fingerboard with pearl dot inlay, single coil/humbucker pickups, available in White finish, disc. 1996.

	N/A	$900	$800	$700	$600	$500	$400

Last MSR was $1,475.

JBA-440 - dual cutaway semi-hollow alder body, body binding, one f-hole, alder back/sides, maple neck, 22-fret bound rosewood fingerboard with pearl block inlay, Tune-O-Matic bridge/stop tailpiece, blackface peghead, 3-per-side tuners, gold hardware, 2 humbucker pickups, volume/tone control, 3-position switch, available in Black gloss finish, mfg. 1998-2003.

	$500	$425	$375	$325	$275	$225	$175

Last MSR was $699.

JBA-460 - similar to JBA-440, except features raised white pickguard, 2 volume/2 tone controls, available in Brown Sunburst finish, mfg. 1998-2003.

	$525	$450	$395	$350	$295	$250	$195

Last MSR was $735.

JBA-500 - offset double cutaway alder body, carved ash top, maple neck, 22-fret rosewood fingerboard with pearl wedge inlay, standard vibrato, 6-on-a-side tuners, black hardware, humbucker/single coil/humbucker covered APC pickups, volume/tone control, 5-position switch, available in Amber or Walnut finishes, mfg. 1994-98.

	$575	$500	$450	$400	$325	$275	$200

Last MSR was $795.

JBA-600 - offset double cutaway hardwood body, mahogany neck, 24-fret rosewood fingerboard with pearl dot inlay, standard vibrato, 3-per-side tuners, gold hardware, 2 humbucker covered APC pickups, volume/tone control, 3-position switch, available in Black or Cherryburst finishes, mfg. 1994-98.

	$650	$575	$500	$450	$375	$295	$225

Last MSR was $895.

JBA-700 - slightly offset double cutaway alder body, bolt-on maple neck, 22-fret rosewood fingerboard with pearl dot inlay, standard vibrato, 3-per-side tuners, gold hardware, white pearloid pickguard, 3 lipstick-style single coil pickups, volume/tone control, 5-position switch, available in Candy Red or Ivory finishes, mfg. 1998-2003.

	$295	$250	$205	$165	$130	$110	$85

Last MSR was $415.

JBA-750 - similar to JBS-700, except features Wilkinson tremolo, pearloid pickguard, available in Candy Red or Dark Metallic Blue finishes, mfg. 1998-2003.

	$325	$295	$265	$230	$205	$175	$150

Last MSR was $519.

JBA-L3 - single cutaway ash body, bolt-on maple neck, 24-fret rosewood fingerboard with dot inlay, Wilkinson tremolo, 6-on-a-side tuners, gold hardware, 3 single coil pickups, volume/tone control, 5-position switch, available in Vintage Sunburst finish, disc. 2003.

	$595	$525	$450	$425	$375	$295	$225

Last MSR was $825.

JBA-L4 - similar to the JBA-L3, except features Tune-O-Matic bridge/stop tailpiece, 2 humbuckers, 3-way switch, available in Vintage Sunburst or Tobacco Sunburst finishes, current mfg.

	$450	$375	$300	$250	$225	$200	$150

Last MSR was $629.

J.B. Player JBA-L3
courtesy J.B. Player

GRADING	100% MINT	98% NEAR MINT	95% EXC+	90% EXC	80% VG+	70% VG	60% G

JBA-LTD - similar to the JBA-L4, except features an alder body, 22-fret rosewood fingerboard, standard vibrato, chrome hardware, 2 covered APC humbucker pickups, volume/tone control, 3-position switch, available in Natural finish, mfg. 1994-96.

	N/A	$375	$325	$275	$235	$195	$165

Last MSR was $600.

ELECTRIC: JBG SERIES

JBG150 - single cutaway Les Paul style, bolt-on neck, no pickguard, two humbucker pickups, two knobs, three-way switch, chrome hardware, available in Black or Wine Red finishes, current mfg.

MSR	$199		$140	$110	$90	$75	$60	$45	$30

JBG155 - single cutaway Telecaster style, bolt-on neck, 21-fret maple fingerboard, two single coil pickups, two knobs, three-way switch, six-on-one-side tuners, chrome hardware, available in Cherry Sunburst or Natural finishes, current mfg.

MSR	$199		$140	$110	$90	$75	$60	$45	$30

JBG165 - double cutaway Stratocaster style, bolt-on maple neck, 21-fret rosewood fingerboard, three single coil pickups, three knobs, five-way switch, six-on-one-side tuners, chrome hardware, available in Aqua, Black, Blue, Pearl White, Red, or Sunburst finishes, current mfg.

MSR	$199		$140	$110	$90	$75	$60	$45	$30

Add $10 for left-handed configuration (available in Black, Pearl White, or Suburst finishes).

JBG175 - similar to the JBG165, except has a quilted finish, available in Trans. Blue, Trans. Green, or Trans. Red finishes, current mfg.

MSR	$199		$140	$110	$90	$75	$60	$45	$30

JBG250 - double cutaway ES-335 style, maple top/back/sides, 2 f-holes, b/n binding, rosewood fingerboard with dot inlay, 3-per-side tuners, stop tailpiece, black pickguard, two humbucker pickups, four knobs, three-way switch, chrome hardware, available in Cherry or Vintage Sunburst finishes, current mfg.

MSR	$599		$420	$350	$300	$260	$230	$200	$170

ELECTRIC: PG/PGP SERIES

In 1998, the Professional Series PGP-111 models featured advanced "quilted" or "flamed" photo tops, a system that resembles figured maple tops.

PG-111-B3 - offset double cutaway hardwood body, black pickguard, bolt-on maple neck, 22-fret rosewood fingerboard with pearl dot inlay, double locking vibrato, 6-on-a-side tuners, black hardware, 3 single coil pickups, volume/2 tone controls, 5-position switch. Available in Black Pearl, Red Pearl, or White Pearl finishes, mfg. 1994-96.

	N/A	$300	$250	$210	$170	$130	$90

Last MSR was $485.

PG-111-HS - similar to PG-111-B3, except has 2 single coil/1 humbucker pickups, disc. 1996.

	N/A	$325	$275	$235	$195	$165	$135

Last MSR was $500.

PG-121 - similar to PG-111-B3, except has no pickguard, volume/tone control, 3 mini switches in place of 5-position switch, coil split in tone control, available in Black Pearl, Black/White Crackle, Fl. Pink, Fl. Yellow, Red/White Crackle, or White Pearl finishes, disc. 1996.

	N/A	$350	$300	$250	$210	$180	$150

Last MSR was $600.

PGP-111-PQ - offset double cutaway alder body, bolt-on maple neck, 22-fret rosewood fingerboard with pearl dot inlay, standard vibrato, 6-on-a-side tuners, gold hardware, pearloid pickguard, 3 single coil pickups, volume/2 tone controls, 5-position switch, available in Amber (quilted) or Cherry (flamed) photo top Sunburst finishes, mfg. 1998-2003.

	$325	$275	$250	$225	$175	$150	$115

Last MSR was $450.

PGP-111-DPQ - similar to PGP-111-P, except has 3 Duncan Designed single coil pickups, available in Amber (quilted) or Cherry (flamed) photo top Sunburst finishes, mfg. 1998-2003.

	$375	$325	$275	$250	$200	$175	$125

Last MSR was $540.

PGP-111-HDP - similar to PGP-111-P, except has 2 Duncan Designed single coil/Duncan Designed humbucker pickups, available in Amber (quilted) or Cherry (flamed) photo top Sunburst finishes, mfg. 1998-2001.

	$395	$350	$295	$275	$250	$195	$125

Last MSR was $560.

PGP-111 - similar to PGP-111-P, except has maple body/neck, neck-through construction, EMG pickups, available in Black, Black/White Crackle, Fluorescent Yellow, Red, Red/White Crackle, Red/Yellow Crackle, White, or White Pearl finishes, disc. 1994.

	$350	$325	$275	$225	$200	$175	$150

Last MSR was $550.

PGP-112 - single cutaway maple body, ash top and back, bolt-on maple neck, 22-fret maple fingerboard with dot inlay, fixed vibrato, 6-on-a-side tuners, gold hardware, tortoiseshell pickguard, 2 single coil pickups, volume/tone controls, 3-position switch, metal controls plate, available in Natural, Cherry Sunburst, Antique Burst, Cherry Gloss, or Trans. Black finishes, mfg. 1998-2003.

	$305	$260	$230	$195	$165	$135	$100

Last MSR was $435.

PGP-120 - shark fin style maple body, maple neck, 22-fret rosewood fingerboard with pearl triangle inlay, double locking vibrato, 6-on-a-side tuners, black hardware, 2 single coil/1 humbucker EMG pickups, volume/tone control, 5-position switch, available in Black, Black Pearl, or Black/White Crackle finishes, disc. 1994.

	N/A	$500	$450	$400	$350	$300	$250

Last MSR was $800.

GRADING	100% MINT	98% NEAR MINT	95% EXC+	90% EXC	80% VG+	70% VG	60% G

PGP-121 - similar to PG121, except has maple body/neck, neck-through construction, EMG pickups, available in Black, Black Pearl, Fluorescent Pink, Fluorescent Pink/Blue Crackle, Fluorescent Yellow Crackle, Ultra Violet, or White Pearl finishes, disc. 1994.

	N/A	$400	$350	$300	$250	$200	$150

Last MSR was $650.

PGP-150A - offset double cutaway hardwood body, bolt-on maple neck, 24-fret rosewood fingerboard with offset pearl dot inlay, standard vibrato, 6-on-a-side tuners, black hardware, 2 single coil/humbucker pickups, volume/tone controls, 5-position switch, available in Amber or Cherryburst finishes, mfg. 1994-96.

	N/A	$350	$300	$250	$210	$170	$140

Last MSR was $595.

ELECTRIC: SHG SERIES

SHG-111 - offset double cutaway hardwood body, bolt-on maple neck, 22-fret maple fingerboard with black dot inlay, standard vibrato, 6-on-a-side tuners, chrome hardware, white pickguard, 3 single coil pickups, volume/2 tone controls, 5-position switch, available in Black, Gun Metal Grey, Pink, Phantom Blue, Red, Red/White Crackle, Terminator Red, Ultra Violet, White, 2-Tone Sunburst, or 3-Tone Sunburst finishes, disc. 2003.

	$250	$215	$175	$150	$125	$105	$85

Last MSR was $339.

This model also available with rosewood fingerboard with pearl dot inlay. In 1994, Gun Metal Grey, Pink, Phantom Blue, Red/White Crackle, Terminator Red, Ultra Violet, and White finishes were discontinued. In 1996, Metallic red, Metallic Blue, and Ivory finishes were introduced; 2-Tone Sunburst finish was discontinued.

SHGL-111 - similar to SHG-111, except features a left-handed configuration, available in 3-Tone Sunburst, Black, Ivory, Metallic Blue, or Metallic Red finishes, disc.

	N/A	$250	$220	$190	$160	$130	$100

Last MSR was $360.

SHG-112 - single cutaway hardwood body, black pickguard, bolt-on maple neck, 22-fret maple fingerboard with black dot inlay, fixed bridge, 6-on-a-side tuners, chrome hardware, 2 single coil pickups, volume/tone controls, 3-position switch, available in Aged Blonde, Black, Cherry Sunburst, or Natural finishes, disc. 2003.

	$250	$215	$175	$150	$125	$100	$75

Last MSR was $339.

In 1996, 3-Tone Sunburst, Ivory, Metallic Blue, and Metallic Red finishes were introduced; Aged Blonde, Cherry Sunburst, and Natural finishes were discontinued.

SHG-112-HSS - similar to SHG-112 (2S), except has 2 single coil/humbucker pickups, available in Aged Blonde, Black, Cherry Sunburst, or Natural finishes, disc. 1994.

	N/A	$250	$200	$170	$140	$110	$80

Last MSR was $430.

SHG-121 - soloist body style offset double cutaway hardwood body, ash top, cream binding, bolt-on maple neck, 22-fret rosewood fingerboard with pearl dot inlay, Tune-O-Matic bridge/stop tailpiece, 6-on-a-side tuners, chrome hardware, 2 humbucker pickups, volume/tone controls, 3-way position switch, available in Antique Violin, Trans. Black, or Trans. Red finishes, mfg. 1998-2001.

	$275	$225	$175	$150	$125	$100	$75

Last MSR was $349.

SHG-122 - similar to SHG-121, except has 2 single coil/humbucker pickups, volume/2 tone controls, standard tremolo, available in Antique Violin or Trans. Red finishes, mfg. 1998-2001.

	$295	$250	$195	$175	$150	$125	$100

Last MSR was $369.

SHG-150 - single rounded cutaway nato body, 22-fret rosewood fingerboard with white dot inlay, fixed bridge, 3-per-side die-cast tuners, chrome hardware, 2 humbucker pickups, volume/tone controls, 3-position switch, available in Black Gloss, Trans. Amber, or Wine Red finishes, mfg. 1998-2003.

	$195	$175	$155	$135	$115	$95	$75

Last MSR was $279.

SHG-160 - offset double cutaway nato body, bolt-on maple neck, 22-fret rosewood fingerboard with black dot inlay, standard vibrato, 6-on-a-side tuners, chrome hardware, 2 single coil/humbucker pickups, volume/tone controls, 5-position switch, available in Metallic Black, Metallic Gold, Cherry Sunburst finishes, mfg. 1998-2003.

	$205	$180	$160	$140	$120	$95	$75

Last MSR was $289.

ELECTRIC BASS: ARTIST SERIES

JBA-B1 N - offset double cutaway hardwood body, maple neck, 24-fret rosewood fingerboard with pearl offset dot inlay, fixed bridge, 3/2-per-side tuners, chrome tuners, 2 J-style pickups, 2 volume/2 tone controls, available in Black or Natural finishes, mfg. 1994-98.

	$625	$550	$475	$425	$350	$275	$225

Last MSR was $850.

J.B. Player PGP-112
courtesy J.B. Player

J

J.B. Player SHG-111
courtesy J.B. Player

GRADING	100% MINT	98% NEAR MINT	95% EXC+	90% EXC	80% VG+	70% VG	60% G

JBA-B2 - single cutaway alder body, maple neck, 20-fret rosewood fingerboard with dot inlay, fixed bridge, 2-per-side tuners, gold tuners, 2 J-style pickups, 2 volume/2 tone controls, available in Black finish, disc. 1998.

	$475	$425	$375	$325	$275	$225	$175

Last MSR was $650.

Add $75 for 5-string configuration (Model JBA-B2V).

JBA-B3 4-STRING - offset double cutaway solid ash body with extended bass horn, 5-piece maple through-body neck, 24-fret rosewood fingerboard with dot inlay, fixed bridge, 2-per-side tuners, chrome tuners, P/J-style pickups, volume/blend/2 tone controls, active electronics, available in Natural Gloss (N) or Cherry Matte (CH) finishes, disc.

	$850	$725	$625	$550	$450	$375	$275

Last MSR was $1,115.

JBA-B3 B (Bolt-On) - similar to the JBA-B3, except features bolt-on maple neck, volume/2 tone controls, 3-way switch, active/passive switching, available in Natural Gloss (N) or Vintage Sunburst (VS) finishes, disc. 2003.

	$450	$400	$350	$325	$275	$225	$175

Last MSR was $625.

Add $20 for Transparent Black gloss finish (Model JBA-B3 B T).

JBA-B5 5-STRING - similar to the JBA-B3, except has 5-string configuration, 3/2-per-side tuners, available in Natural Gloss (N) or Cherry Matte (CH) finishes, disc. 2003.

	$850	$775	$675	$575	$495	$395	$300

Last MSR was $1,209.

JBA-B5 B (Bolt-On) - similar to the JBA-B5, except features bolt-on maple neck, volume/2 tone controls, 3-way switch, active/passive switching, available in Natural Gloss (N) or Vintage Sunburst (VS) finishes, disc. 2003.

	$505	$450	$395	$350	$300	$250	$195

Last MSR was $719.

JBA-B6 6-STRING - similar to the JBA-B3, except has 6-string configuration, 3-per-side tuners, 7-piece maple through-body neck, 2 humbucker pickups, 2 volume/2 tone controls, available in Cherry Matte (CH) finishes, disc. 2003.

	$950	$850	$750	$650	$525	$425	$325

Last MSR was $1,329.

ELECTRIC BASS: JBB SERIES

JBB113 - double cutaway P-Bass style, bolt-on maple neck, rosewood fingerboard with dot inlay, four-on-one-side tuners, white pickguard, single split pickup, two knobs, chrome hardware, available in Black, Sunburst, or White finishes, 34 in. scale, current mfg.

MSR	$249	$175	$140	$115	$95	$75	$60	$45

JBB115 - five-string configuration, double cutaway Ernie Ball Sterling style, bolt-on maple neck, rosewood fingerboard with dot inlay, 3/2-per-side tuners, white pickguard, single humbucker pickup, two knobs, chrome hardware, available in Black, Metallic Blue, or Metallic Red finishes, 34 in. scale, current mfg.

MSR	$289	$200	$160	$130	$105	$85	$65	$50

JBB117 - double cutaway J-Bass style, bolt-on maple neck, rosewood fingerboard with dot inlay, four-on-one-side tuners, white pickguard, two jazz-style pickups, three knobs, chrome hardware, available in Black, Pearl White, or Sunburst finishes, 34 in. scale, current mfg.

MSR	$249	$175	$140	$115	$95	$75	$60	$45

ELECTRIC BASS: PROFESSIONAL SERIES

PGP-113 - offset double cutaway maple body, black pickguard, bolt-on maple neck, 20-fret rosewood fingerboard with pearl dot inlay, 4-on-a-side tuners, black hardware, P/J-style EMG pickups, volume/tone control, 3-position switch, available in Black, Black Pearl, Red, Red Pearl, or White Pearl finishes, disc. 1994.

	N/A	$250	$200	$170	$140	$110	$80

Last MSR was $425.

PGP-114 - similar to the PGP-113, except features hardwood body, 24-fret rosewood fingerboard with pearl dot inlay, 2-per-side tuners, chrome hardware, volume/2 tone controls, available in Black Pearl finish, mfg. 1994-96.

	N/A	$300	$250	$210	$170	$130	$90

Last MSR was $495.

PGPB-4B - double offset cutaway body, quilted photo top, bolt-on maple neck, 24-fret rosewood fingerboard with dot inlay, P- and J-style pickups, three knobs, 2-per-side tuners, available in Ivory, Metallic Red, or Metallic Blue finishes, disc. 2003.

	$330	$275	$225	$190	$150	$125	$90

Last MSR was $469.

Add $15 for Metallic Red or Metallic Blue finishes. Add $15 for left-handed configuration (PGPLB-4B).

PGPB-4BQT - double offset cutaway body, quilted photo top, bolt-on maple neck, 24-fret rosewood fingerboard with dot inlay, P- and J-style pickups, three knobs, 2-per-side tuners, available in Trans. Purple, Trans. Blue, or Trans. Green finishes, disc. 2003.

	$375	$300	$250	$200	$160	$130	$95

Last MSR was $519.

GRADING	100% MINT	98% NEAR MINT	95% EXC+	90% EXC	80% VG+	70% VG	60% G

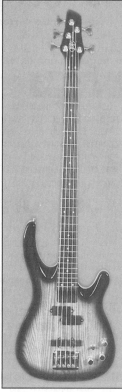

ELECTRIC BASS: SLEDGEHAMMER SERIES

SHB-113 - offset double cutaway hardwood body, black pickguard, bolt-on maple neck, 20-fret rosewood fingerboard with pearl dot inlay, fixed bridge, black hardware, P-style pickup, volume/tone control, available in Black, Red, or White finishes, disc.

	$295	$250	$225	$195	$150	$125	$95

Last MSR was $379.

J. REYNOLDS

Instruments currently produced in Asia. Distributed by Midco Music, which is part of MBT International of Charleston, SC.

J. Reynolds offers entry level guitars based on popular American designs at a competitive price. For more information refer to their website (see Trademark Index).

ELECTRIC

JR3 - single cutaway Les Paul Junior style, poplar body, bolt-on neck, 22-fret rosewood fingerboard with dot inlay, single humbucker pickup, two knobs, chrome hardware, black finish, current mfg.

MSR	$160		$120	$100	$85	$70	$55	$40	$25

JR4 - single cutaway Telecaster style, poplar body, bolt-on neck, 21-fret rosewood fingerboard with dot inlay, two single coil pickups, two knobs, chrome hardware, Black or Natural Honey finish, current mfg.

MSR	$200		$140	$115	$95	$80	$65	$50	$35

JR6 - double cutaway Stratocaster style, poplar body, bolt-on neck, 21-fret rosewood fingerboard with dot inlay, three single coil pickups, three knobs, chrome hardware, available in Antique Sunburst, Black, Natural Honey, Trans. Blue, Trans. Purple, Trans. Blue, or Vintage White finishes, current mfg.

MSR	$160		$120	$100	$85	$70	$55	$40	$25

Add $5 for S/S/H pickup configuration (Model JR66).

JR8 - single cutaway Les Paul style, poplar body, bolt-on neck, 22-fret rosewood fingerboard with dot inlay, two humbucker pickups, four knobs, pickguard, chrome hardware, available in Cherry Sunburst finish, current mfg.

MSR	$260		$185	$155	$130	$110	$90	$70	$50

Add $20 for set-neck version, available in Black finish.

ELECTRIC BASS

JR7 - double cutaway P-style poplar body, 20-fret rosewood fingerboard with dot inlay, single P-style pickup, two knobs, white pickguard, chrome hardware, available in Antique Sunburst, Black, Natural Honey, Trans. Blue, or Trans. Red finishes, current mfg.

MSR	$200		$140	$115	$95	$80	$65	$50	$35

This model is also available in mini-versions and left-hand configuration.

J.B. Player JBA-B5 B
courtesy J.B. Player

JD

See Jay Dee. Instruments previously built in England.

JDS

Instruments currently built in Asia. Exclusively distributed by Wolf Imports of St. Louis, MO.

JDS Limited Edition instruments are medium quality acoustic and solid body electric guitars that feature designs based on popular American classics.

JG

Instruments previously produced in Italy during the late 1960s.

The SA series featured four models of medium quality but original designs. Readers are encouraged to write and share whether or not they also share similarities to other Italian-produced guitars of this era! Results will be published in future editions of the *Blue Book of Electric Guitars* (source: Tony Bacon and Paul Day, *The Guru's Guitar Guide*).

JHS

Instruments previously built in Japan during the late 1970s.

The JHS trademark was the initials of the UK importer John Hornby Skewes, who founded his import company in 1965 (See Encore). The generally good quality instruments featured both original designs and those based on classic American designs. The line focused primarily on solid body guitars, much like the Encore line today (source: Tony Bacon and Paul Day, *The Guru's Guitar Guide*).

Jackson Dinky Reverse
courtesy Jackson

JJ GUITARS

Instruments currently built in Shipton on Stour, England.

JJ (Hucke) Guitars were designed over a period of eighteen months where they took over 1,000 years of playing experience and put that into their guitars. JJ Guitars' models are handcrafted with figured maple tops and translucent finishes. Retail prices are listed on their website in British pounds. For further information regarding model specification and pricing, contact JJ Guitars directly (see Trademark Index).

ELECTRIC

These following models were previoulsy produced. The sleek double cutaway Antarctica model has a mahogany body, bolt-on maple neck with shaped heel, 24-fret rosewood fingerboard, reverse headstock, 2 humbuckers 5-way ´mega-switch,´ Schaller Pro licensed Floyd Rose tremolo. A carved maple top is optional on this model. The Arctic III has similar construction techniques as the Antarctica, except has a rounder lower bout and regular 6-on-a-side tuner headstock. This model is complete with the carved maple top. The Sahara model has a single rounded cutaway mahogany solid body with a through-body mahogany neck, carved maple top, 24-fret rosewood fingerboard, Tune-O-Matic bridge/stop tailpiece, 2 Seymour Duncan humbuckers, gold hardware, and 3-per-side Schaller tuners. The Jewel was produced between 2000-04 and featured a mahogany body and neck. The JJ Special was produced between 2000-04 and was available in Blue and Gold. Models introduced in 2003/2004 include the JJ Retro Lux, Electra, Electra V, Retro, Retro HB, and left-handed model. Retail prices start at £949.

JP GUITARS

Formerly Pimentel Guitars. Instruments currently produced in Pullyallup, WA.

Luthier Jack Pimentel is currently offering the JP and JP II models of stand-up, compact body electric basses. Pimentel´s basses share the same dimensions as an original upright bass (same fingerboard radius, neck contour, string spacing, and scale length); however, his models feature a detachable neck for ease in traveling and shipping. For more information refer to their website (see Trademark Index).

ELECTRIC GUITAR & BASS

There are four different guitar models currently offered. The CT series features mahogany bodies, figured maple tops, and mahogany necks. The fingerboard is made of either rosewood, ebony, or cocobola and the pickup configuration consists of humbuckers and one single coil. The **CT Standard** retails for $2,750. The **CT Custom** has a carved top and retails for $3,150. The **CT Deluxe** has custom inlay work. The **FT Standard** is like the CT series except has an alder body, maple neck, and retails for $2,250.

All bass models are constructed of seasoned hardwoods which feature internal tone chambers, and EMG active EQ circuitry and piezo electric pickups. The **JP I** Upright Bass has a retail list price of $2,200; the **JP II** features a hand carved wood top (list $2,950); and the **JP II Deluxe** has a hand carved flame or quilted maple top and gold hardware (list $3,450). A custom flight case is available for $475, and the upright´s stand is $100.

JTG OF NASHVILLE

Instruments currently built in Japan and Mexico. Previously distributed by JTG of Nashville located in Nashville, TN.

JTG of Nashville, used to import quality Japanese and Mexican acoustic guitars. JTG is no longer importing guitars and they focus mainly on children's toys and books. They offered a solid body electric during the mid 1980s.

ELECTRIC

The **Infinity** solid body electric guitar was designed by Dave Petschulat, and had a body profile similar to a sharpened Explorer. The **Infinity** had a highly angular ash body, curly maple neck, six-on-a-side headstock, one humbucking pickup, a custom tremolo, and was offered with either charcoal gray or white with red accents, and red with a light gray accent. The last suggested retail price (circa mid 1980s) was $595.

JACKSON

Instruments currently built in Ontario, CA & Japan. Jackson USA and Jackson Custom Shop series guitars are built in Ontario, CA. Jackson Professional Series guitars are built in Japan. Previously distributed in the U.S. by International Music Corporation of Fort Worth, TX. Currently distributed by Fender Musical Instrument Coporation of Scottsdale, AZ.

The Charvel/Jackson Guitar company was founded in 1978 after Grover Jackson bought out Wayne Charvel´s Guitar Repair shop in Azusa, California. As the bolt-neck custom-built Charvel guitars gained popularity with the up-and- coming West Coast rock musicians, it became a necessity that standardized models were established. By 1983, neck- through designs were introduced with the Jackson logo on the headstock. Jackson/Charvel was first licensed (in 1985) and later acquired (in 1986) by the International Music Company (IMC) of Fort Worth, Texas.

In about 1992, upper end Charvels began to be incorporated into the Jackson line (essentially becoming the Jackson Professional Series). American-built models have "Made in U.S.A." logo on the headstock; the Japanese-built Professional series models do not.

In 2002, Fender Musical Instruments Corporation (FMIC) purchased the rights to the Jackson/Charvel trademark. Jackson is now part of Fender´s increasing empire.

MODEL DESIGNATIONS & COLOR CODES

In 1996, the models in the product line were renamed from their usual name plus designation (ex.: a Rhoads Standard) to a simpler 3 or 4 digit abbreviation (Rhoads Standard = RR2). Older models discontinued prior to 1996 will retain their original designation, while new models and continuing production models will follow the new designation.

In 2002, Fender purchased the company and the product code began to be listed. Wherever there is a current model there is the typical Fender SKU code where any guitar can be identified.

On the USA Select and the Artist Series there are several color options available at an addtional price as follows:

> Add $35 for Black Cherry, Black Forest, Candy Apple Green, Candy Blue, Cobalt Blue, Cream, Deep Candy Red, Gold, Ivory, Red Blue Pearl, Silver Sparkle, Snow White, Ultra Violet Burst, and Yellow Gold Pearl. Add $70 for Amber Sunburst, Burnt Cherry Sunburst, Cherry Sunburst, Natural, Tobacco Sunburst, Trans. Black, Trans. Blue, Trans. Green, Trans. Red, and Violin Brown. Add $175 for Black Ghost Flames, Blue Bengal, Blue Ghost Flames, Eerie Dess Swirl, Green Ghost Flames, Hot Rod Flames, Lightning Sky, Pile O' Skulls, Shattered Glass, Snakeskin, Tan and Blue Flames, USA Flag, and Yellow Bengal.

GRADING	100% MINT	98% NEAR MINT	95% EXC+	90% EXC	80% VG+	70% VG	60% G

ELECTRIC: AX/S SERIES

The AX/S Series was introduced in 1999 and offers many outstanding features at very affordable prices.

D10 - dinky style body constructed of alder with 24-fret maple neck, rosewood fingerboard with dot inlays, JT-480s bridge and two JE10 pickups, chrome hardware, available in Black, Metallic Blue, or Metallic Red finishes, disc. 1999.

	$300	$250	$225	$200	$175	$150	$100

Last MSR was $425.

D10 PRO - similar to D10 except has shark fin neck inlays, one JA-10N pickup and one JA-10B pickup. JB-480 bridge, chrome hardware, available in Black, Metallic Red, or Metalic Blue finishes, disc. 1999.

	$340	$275	$250	$225	$200	$175	$150

Last MSR was $485.

K10 - Kelly body style, alder body, maple neck with rosewood fingerboard, dot inlays, JT-480s bridge, two JE10 pickups, chrome hardware, available in Black, Metallic Blue, or Metallic Red, disc. 1999.

	$350	$285	$260	$240	$210	$185	$160

Last MSR was $495.

K10 PRO - similar to K10 except has shark fin neck inlays, one JA-10N and one JA-10B pickup, JB-480 bridge, chrome hardware, available in Black, Metallic Red, or Metallic Blue finishes, disc. 1999.

	$390	$325	$275	$250	$225	$200	$175

Last MSR was $555.

R10 - Rhoads body style, alder body, maple neck with rosewood fingerboard, dot inlays, JT-480s bridge and two JE10 pickups, chrome hardware, available in Black, Metallic Red, or Metallic Blue, disc. 1999.

	$350	$285	$260	$240	$210	$185	$160

Last MSR was $495.

R10 PRO - similar to R10 except has shark fin neck inlays, one JA-10 pickup and one JA-10B pickup, JB-480 bridge, chrome hardware, available in Black, Metallic Red, or Metallic Blue, disc. 1999.

	$390	$325	$275	$250	$225	$200	$175

Last MSR was $555.

Jackson Original Rhoads
courtesy Jackson

J

ELECTRIC: CONCEPT SERIES

The Concept series was available briefly from 1993 through late 1994. Continuing popularity led to introduction of the Performer Series in 1995, which combined the best design aspects of the Concept series models with new innovations.

JDR-94 - offset double cutaway poplar body, bolt-on maple neck, 24-fret rosewood fingerboard with pearl offset dot inlay, double locking vibrato, reverse blackface peghead with screened logo, 6-on-a-side tuners, black hardware, humbucker/single coil/humbucker pickups, volume/tone control, 5-position switch, available in Black, Bright Red, or Dark Metallic Blue finishes, mfg. 1993-94.

	N/A	$400	$325	$275	$235	$195	$165

Last MSR was $595.

JDX-94 - similar to JDR-94, except has standard fingerboard dot inlay, fixed bridge, standard peghead design, 2 single coil/1 humbucker pickups configuration, available in Black, Bright Red, or Dark Metallic Blue finishes, mfg. 1993-94.

	N/A	$375	$325	$275	$235	$195	$165

Last MSR was $550.

JRR-94 - shark fin poplar body, black pickguard, bolt-on maple neck, 24-fret rosewood fingerboard with pearl dot inlay, Tune-O-Matic bridge/strings through-body tailpiece, blackface peghead with screened logo, 6-on-a-side tuners, black hardware, 2 humbucker pickups, 2 volume/1 tone controls, 3-position switch, available in Black, Bright Red, or Dark Metallic Blue finishes, mfg. 1993-94.

	N/A	$400	$325	$275	$235	$195	$165

Last MSR was $595.

JSX-94 - offset double cutaway poplar body, bolt-on maple neck, 24-fret rosewood fingerboard with pearl offset dot inlay, double locking vibrato, blackface peghead with screened logo, 6-on-a-side tuners, black hardware, 2 single coil/1 humbucker pickups, volume/tone control, 5-position switch, available in Black, Bright Red, or Dark Metallic Blue finishes, mfg. 1993-94.

	N/A	$400	$325	$275	$235	$195	$165

Last MSR was $595.

ELECTRIC: DINKY (DK, DX, & DR) SERIES

The Jackson Dinky model is a scaled down 7/8th size SuperStrat model (an updated, modern version of the industry standard Strat - of course, the Dinky body shape is now an industry standard as well), featuring 2 single coils and a humbucker in the bridge condition.

Add $35 for Amber Sunburst, Trans. Blue, Trans. Black, or Trans. Red finishes.

Jackson King V
courtesy Jackson

GRADING	100% MINT	98% NEAR MINT	95% EXC+	90% EXC	80% VG+	70% VG	60% G

DINKY STANDARD - offset double cutaway basswood body, transparent pickguard, bolt-on maple neck, 24-fret rosewood fingerboard with colored dot inlay, double locking vibrato, 6-on-a-side tuners, black hardware, 2 stacked coil/humbucker Jackson pickups, volume/tone control, 5-position switch, available in Black, Candy Blue, Dark Metallic Red, or Snow White finishes, mfg. 1991-93.

	N/A	$550	$475	$400	$350	$300	$250

Last MSR was $895.

DX1 (DINKY XL) - offset double cutaway basswood body, bolt-on maple neck, 24-fret bound rosewood fingerboard with pearl sharkfin inlay, double locking vibrato, 6-on-a-side tuners, black hardware, 2 stacked coil/1 humbucker Jackson pickups, volume/tone control, 5-position switch, available in Deep Metallic Blue, Metallic Black and Pearl White finishes, mfg. 1992-98.

	$700	$600	$500	$400	$350	$300	$250

Last MSR was $995.

Dinky XL (Trans) - similar to Dinky XL, except has flame maple top, available in Cherry Sunburst, Trans. Blue, Trans. Red, or Trans. Violet finishes, mfg. 1993-95.

	$750	$650	$550	$450	$400	$350	$300

Last MSR was $1,095.

DX2 (DINKY EX) - offset double cutaway basswood body, black pickguard, bolt-on maple neck, 24-fret rosewood fingerboard with pearl dot inlay, double locking vibrato, 6-on-a-side tuners, black hardware, humbucker/single coil/humbucker Jackson pickups, volume/tone control, 5-position switch, available in Black, Deep Metallic Blue, Deep Metallic Red, or Snow White finishes, mfg. 1993-98.

	$500	$450	$395	$325	$275	$250	$225

Last MSR was $745.

DR3 (DINKY REVERSE TRANS) - similar to Dinky Reverse, except has poplar body, flame maple top, available in Black, Natural Green Sunburst, Natural Purple Sunburst, Natural Red Sunburst, or Trans. Blue finishes, mfg. 1994-2001.

	$595	$525	$450	$400	$350	$300	$250

Last MSR was $845.

In 1998, Transparent Green and Tobacco Sunburst (with mahogany body) finishes were introduced; Natural Green Sunburst, Natural Purple Sunburst, and Natural Red Sunburst finishes were discontinued.

DR5 (DINKY REVERSE) - offset double cutaway basswood body, bolt-on maple neck, 24-fret maple (or rosewood) fingerboard with offset dot inlay, reverse headstock, double locking vibrato, 6-on-a-side tuners, black hardware, 2 humbucker Jackson pickups, volume/tone control, 3-position switch, available in Black, Candy Blue, Dark Metallic Violet, or Stone finishes, mfg. 1992-98.

	$525	$450	$375	$325	$275	$225	$175

Last MSR was $745.

In 1994, the Stone finish was discontinued.

DR6 - similar to DR3 except string through-body, Tune-O-Matic type bridge, available in Black, Deep Candy Blue or Dark Metallic Red finishes, mfg. 2000-01.

	$450	$375	$325	$275	$235	$195	$165

Last MSR was $695.

Add $50 for Tobacco Sunburst and Burnt Cherry Sunburst finishes.

DR7 7 STRING - similar to DR6 except in a 7-string configuration, available in Black or Deep Candy Blue finishes, disc. 2001.

	$630	$500	$425	$350	$275	$200	$125

Last MSR was $895.

DK2 (DINKY, NO. 290-1000) - offset double cutaway poplar body, bolt-on maple neck, 22-fret rosewood fingerboard with pearl sharkfin inlay, double locking vibrato, 6-on-a-side tuners, chrome hardware, 2 single coil/humbucker pickups, volume/tone control, 5-position switch, available in Black, Dark Metallic Red, Satin Black, Midnight Blue Sparkle or Deep Metallic Violet finishes, mfg. 1998-present.

MSR	$675		$475	$400	$350	$300	$260	$230	$190

Add $35 for Trans. finishes (Amber Sunburst, Black, Blue, or Red). Add $70 for Crimson Swirl, Eerie Dess Swirl, or Hot Rod Flames finishes. Add $250 for Blue & Orange Flames or Skulls finishes.

DK2L (No. 290-1001) - similar to the DK2, except in left-hand configuration, available in Black or Dark Metallic Red finishes, mfg. 1998-present.

MSR	$725		$520	$450	$400	$350	$300	$250	$200

Add $35 for Trans. finishes (Blue or Red).

DK2FS (No. 290-1002) - similar to the DK2 except has Firestorm electronics, mfg. 1998-present.

MSR	$750		$525	$450	$400	$350	$300	$250	$200

Add $35 for Trans. finishes (Blue or Red).

DK2FF (No. 290-1004) - similar to the DK2 except has a Flame Fingerboard, available in Black finish, mfg. 2003-present.

MSR	$1,100		$800	$700	$600	$525	$450	$375	$325

DK2S (No. 290-1003) - similar to the DK2 except has a Sustainer Driver/Pickup for effects, available in Black finish, mfg. 2003-present.

MSR	$900		$650	$575	$500	$425	$375	$325	$275

Add $35 for Trans. finishes (Amber Sunburst, Black, Blue, or Red).

SDK2 - smaller (Super Dinky) style, offset double cutaway poplar or ash body, bolt-on maple neck, 24-fret bound rosewood (or maple) fingerboard with pearl sharkfin inlay, double locking vibrato, 6-on-a-side tuners, black hardware, humbucker/single coil/humbucking Jackson pickups, volume/tone control, 5-position switch, available in Black, Cobalt Blue, Red Pearl Satin, Cobalt Blue Satin, or Graphite finishes, mfg. 1996-98.

	$450	$375	$325	$295	$250	$225	$175

Last MSR was $625.

GRADING	100% MINT	98% NEAR MINT	95% EXC+	90% EXC	80% VG+	70% VG	60% G

DKMG (NO. 290-0100) - similar to the DK2 except has a basswood body, 2 EMGHZ pickups, and a JT580LP bridge, available in Black, Black Forest, Cobalt Blue, or Satin Black finishes, mfg. 2002-present.

MSR	$900	$650	$575	$500	$425	$375	$325	$275

DKMGFF (No. 290-0107) - similar to the DKMG, excpt has a flame fingerboard, available in Black finish, mfg. 2003-present.

MSR	$1,100	$800	$700	$600	$525	$450	$375	$325

DKMGT (No. 290-0101) - similar to the DKMG, excpt has a JT390 Tunamatic STB bridge, available in Black, Black Forest, Candy Blue, or Satin Black finishes, mfg. 2002-present.

MSR	$850	$600	$525	$450	$400	$350	$300	$250

Add $70 for Cobalt Blue Swirl finish.

DKMGFFT (No. 290-0106) - similar to the DKMGT, excpt has a flame fingerboard, available in Black finish, mfg. 2003-present.

MSR	$1,050	$750	$650	$575	$500	$425	$375	$325

DK27 (No. 290-0102) - similar to the DKMG except has no flame veneer on top, available in Black, Black Forest, or Cobalt Blue finishes, mfg. 2002-present.

MSR	$850	$600	$525	$450	$400	$350	$300	$250

ELECTRIC: FB SERIES

FB2 - offset asymmetrical hourglass shaped poplar body, bolt-on maple neck, 24-fret rosewood fingerboard with dot inlays, chrome hardware, JT580 locking tremolo, 2 exposed humbuckers, 1 volume knob, 3-way selector switch, available in Black, Mint Green, or Vintage White finishes, mfg. 1996-97.

		$525	$475	$450	$425	$375	$325	$275

Last MSR was $795.

FB2 T - similar to the FB2, except has JT390 Tune-O-Matic/stop tailpiece, mfg. 1996-97.

		$575	$500	$450	$375	$325	$275	$250

Last MSR was $725.

Jackson DX 1 (Dinky XL)
courtesy Jackson

ELECTRIC: FUSION SERIES

FUSION EX - offset double cutaway basswood body, black pickguard, bolt-on maple neck, 24-fret rosewood fingerboard with offset white dot inlay, double locking vibrato, 6-on-a-side tuners, black hardware, 2 single coil/1 humbucker Jackson pickups, volume/tone control, 5-position switch, available in Black, Deep Metallic Blue, Dark Metallic Red, or Snow White finishes, mfg. 1992-95.

	N/A	$450	$375	$325	$275	$235	$195

Last MSR was $695.

FUSION HH - offset double cutaway mahogany body, bolt-on maple neck, 24-fret bound rosewood fingerboard with offset pearl dot inlay, double locking vibrato, 6-on-a-side tuners, black hardware, 2 humbucker Jackson pickups, 3-position switch, available in Black or Trans. Red finishes, mfg. 1992-95.

	N/A	$600	$525	$450	$375	$300	$250

Last MSR was $895.

In 1992, basswood body with Black finish was optional. In 1994, basswood body was discontinued.

FUSION PRO - offset double cutaway basswood body, bolt-on maple neck, 24-fret bound ebony fingerboard with pearl sharkfin inlay, double locking vibrato, bound peghead with pearl Jackson logo inlay, 6-on-a-side tuners, black hardware, 2 stacked coil/humbucker Jackson pickups, volume/tone control, 5-position and bypass switches, active electronics, available in Bright Red, Candy Blue, Metallic Black, or Pearl White finishes, mfg. 1992-94.

	N/A	$800	$700	$625	$550	$475	$400

Last MSR was $1,295.

Fusion Pro (Trans) - similar to Fusion Pro, except has flame maple top, available in Cherry Sunburst, Trans. Amber, Trans. Blue, or Trans. Red finishes, disc. 1994.

	N/A	$850	$750	$650	$575	$500	$425

Last MSR was $1,395.

FUSION XL - offset double cutaway basswood body, bolt-on maple neck, 24-fret bound ebony fingerboard with pearl sharkfin inlay, double locking vibrato, bound peghead with pearl Jackson logo inlay, 6-on-a-side tuners, black hardware, 2 stacked coil/1 humbucker Jackson pickups, volume/tone control, 5-position switch, available in Deep Metallic Blue, Dark Metallic Red, Metallic Black, or Snow White finishes, mfg. 1992-94.

	N/A	$650	$550	$475	$400	$350	$300

Last MSR was $995.

Fusion XL (Trans) - similar to Fusion XL, except has flame maple top, available in Cherry Sunburst, Trans. Blue, Trans. Red, or Trans. Violet finishes, mfg. 1992-94.

	N/A	$675	$575	$500	$425	$375	$325

Last MSR was $1,095.

FX1 (FUSION STANDARD) - offset double cutaway basswood body, bolt-on maple neck, 24-fret rosewood fingerboard with pearl offset dot inlay, double locking vibrato, bound peghead with screened Jackson logo

Jackson Fusion HH
courtesy Jackson

GRADING	100% MINT	98% NEAR MINT	95% EXC+	90% EXC	80% VG+	70% VG	60% G

inlay, 6-on-a-side tuners, black hardware, 2 stacked coil/1 humbucker Jackson pickups, volume/tone control, 5-position switch, available in Black, Candy Blue, Dark Metallic Red, or Snow White finishes, mfg. 1992-96.

	N/A	$600	$525	$450	$375	$300	$250

Last MSR was $895.

ELECTRIC: INFINITY, JTX, & JRS SERIES

INFINITY PRO - double cutaway asymmetrical mahogany body, bound figured maple top, set in mahogany neck, 22-fret bound rosewood fingerboard with pearl diamond/abalone dot inlay, double locking vibrato, bound peghead with pearl Jackson logo inlay, 6-on-a-side tuners, chrome hardware, 2 humbucker Jackson pickups, volume/tone control, 3-position switch, available in Cherry Sunburst, Star Glo, Trans. Blue, Trans. Red, or Trans. Violet finishes, mfg. 1992-94.

	N/A	$950	$850	$750	$650	$550	$450

Last MSR was $1,495.

Infinity XL - double cutaway asymmetrical bound basswood body, bolt-on maple neck, 22-fret rosewood fingerboard with abalone dot inlay, double locking vibrato, 6-on-a-side tuners, black hardware, 2 humbucker Jackson pickups, volume/tone control, 3-position switch, available in Black, Deep Metallic Blue, Dark Metallic Red, or Magenta finishes, mfg. 1992-94.

	N/A	$650	$575	$500	$425	$350	$300

Last MSR was $995.

JTX STD - single cutaway basswood body, pearloid pickguard, bolt-on maple neck, 24-fret maple fingerboard with black dot inlay, double locking Floyd Rose vibrato, 6-on-a-side tuners, chrome hardware, single coil/humbucker Jackson pickup, volume control, 3-position/mini switches, available in Black, Deep Metallic Blue, Deep Metallic Red, Magenta, Trans. Pearl Purple, or Snow White finishes, mfg. 1993-95.

	N/A	$450	$375	$325	$275	$225	$175

Last MSR was $695.

In 1994, Transparent Pearl Purple and Snow White finishes were introduced, Deep Metallic Blue and Magenta were discontinued.

JTX (Trans) - similar to JTX, except has ash body, available in Trans. Black, Trans. Blue, Trans. Pearl Purple, or Trans. Red finishes, mfg. 1993 only.

	N/A	$400	$325	$275	$235	$195	$165

Last MSR was $645.

JRS-2 - offset double cutaway ash body, bolt-on maple neck, 25.5 in. scale, 22-fret rosewood or maple fingerboard, Wilkinson VS-50 vibrato, reverse natural finish headstock, 6-on-the-other side tuners, chrome hardware, Kent Armstrong humbucker, volume control, available in Black, Bright Red, Electric Blue, Trans. Black, or Trans. White finishes, mfg. 1997-98.

	$525	$450	$350	$275	$225	$175	$125

Last MSR was $745.

Add $50 for Transparent finish.

ELECTRIC: KELLY SERIES

KE3 (NO. 290-2000) - similar to Kelly STD, except has pearl sharkfin fingerboard inlay, available in Black, Dark Metallic Blue, or Dark Metallic Violet finishes, mfg. 1994-present.

MSR	$750		$525	$450	$400	$350	$300	$250	$200

Add $35 for Transparent finish (Trans. Blue and Trans. Red). Add $70 for Crimson Swirl or Eerie Dress Swirl finishes. Add $250 for Skulls finish.

In 1998, Midnight Blue Sparkle, Trans. Blue, and Trans. Red finishes were introduced; Dark Metallic Blue and Dark Metallic Violet finishes were discontinued.

KE4 (KELLY STD) - single sharp cutaway radical hourglass style poplar body, bolt-on maple neck, 24-fret rosewood fingerboard with pearl dot inlay, double locking Floyd Rose vibrato, 6-on-a-side tuners, chrome hardware, 2 humbucker Jackson pickups, volume control, 3-position switch, available in Black, Deep Metallic Blue, Deep Metallic Red, or Deep Metallic Violet finishes, mfg. 1993-98.

	$550	$475	$400	$325	$275	$225	$175

Last MSR was $795.

KV3 - V-style poplar body, bolt-on maple neck, 22-fret rosewood fingerboard with pearl sharkfin inlay, double locking vibrato, 6-on-a-side tuners, chrome hardware, 2 Duncan Design humbucker pickups, volume/tone controls, 3-position switch, available in Black or Midnight Blue Sparkle finishes, mfg. 1998-2001.

	$600	$525	$475	$425	$375	$325	$250

Last MSR was $875.

Add $50 for Transparent finishes with maple tops (Cherry Sunburst, Trans. Blue, and Trans Red).

ELECTRIC: PERFORMER (PS) SERIES

Continuing popularity of the Concept series led to introduction of the Performer Series in 1995, which combined the best design aspects of the Concept series models with new innovations.

Add $50 for alder body/flamed maple top in Trans. finish (Trans. Blue, Trans. Green, Trans. Purple, or Trans. Red), available on all models.

PS-1 - offset double cutaway alder body, bolt-on maple neck, 24-fret rosewood fingerboard with dot inlay, JT490 fulcrum vibrato, blackface peghead with screened logo, 6-on-a-side tuners, black hardware, black pickguard, 2 single coils/1 humbucker pickups, volume/tone control, 5-position switch, available in Black, Red Violet Metallic, Blue Green Metallic, Black Cherry, or Deep Metallic Blue finishes, mfg. 1995-99.

	$385	$335	$285	$250	$215	$185	$145

Last MSR was $545.

GRADING	100% MINT	98% NEAR MINT	95% EXC+	90% EXC	80% VG+	70% VG	60% G

PS-2 - similar to PS-1, except has double locking JT500 tremolo and no pickguard, available in Black, Red Violet Metallic, Blue Green Metallic, Black Cherry, or Deep Metallic Blue finishes, mfg. 1995-2003.

	$425	$350	$315	$265	$240	$210	$170

Last MSR was $595.

PS-3 - Sharkfin style alder body, black pickguard, bolt-on maple neck, 24-fret rosewood fingerboard with dot inlay, Tune-O-Matic bridge/strings through-body tailpiece, blackface peghead with screened logo, 6-on-a-side tuners, black hardware, 2 humbucker pickups, 2 volume/1 tone controls, 3-position switch, available in Black, Red Violet Metallic, Blue Green Metallic, Black Cherry, or Deep Metallic Blue finishes, mfg. 1995-99.

	$425	$350	$315	$265	$240	$210	$165

Last MSR was $595.

PS-3T - similar to PS-3, except has double locking JT500 tremolo, available in Black, Red Violet Metallic, Blue Green Metallic, Black Cherry, or Deep Metallic Blue finishes, mfg. 1995-2001.

	$475	$400	$350	$325	$275	$240	$200

Last MSR was $675.

PS-4 - offset double cutaway alder body, bolt-on maple neck, 24-fret rosewood fingerboard with offset dot inlay, double locking vibrato, reverse blackface peghead with screened logo, six-on-the-other side tuners, black hardware, humbucker/single coil/humbucker pickups, volume/tone control, 5-position switch, available in Black, Red Violet Metallic, Blue Green Metallic, Black Cherry, or Deep Metallic Blue finishes, mfg. 1995-2001.

	$450	$400	$350	$325	$275	$225	$175

Last MSR was $645.

PS-6 - asymmetrical "Kelly"-style alder body, bolt-on maple neck, 24-fret rosewood fingerboard with dot inlay, Tune-O-Matic bridge/stop tailpiece, blackface peghead with screened logo, 6-on-a-side tuners, chrome hardware, 2 humbucker pickups, 2 volume/1 tone controls, 3-position switch, available in Black, Red Violet Metallic, Blue Green Metallic, Black Cherry, or Deep Metallic Blue finishes, mfg. 1997-98.

	$450	$375	$325	$300	$250	$225	$175

Last MSR was $625.

PS-6T - similar to the PS-6, except features JT-500 double locking tremolo, black hardware, mfg. 1997-2001.

	$475	$400	$350	$300	$275	$225	$175

Last MSR was $675.

PS-7 - offset double cutaway alder body, bolt-on maple neck, 22-fret rosewood fingerboard with dot inlay, Wilkinson VS-50 vibrato, 6-on-a-side tuners, chrome hardware, black pickguard, 2 single coils/humbucker pickups, volume/tone control, 5-position switch, available in Black, Red Violet Metallic, Blue Green Metallic, Black Cherry, or Deep Metallic Blue finishes, mfg. 1995-2001.

	$400	$350	$300	$275	$240	$195	$165

Last MSR was $575.

Jackson KE3
courtesy Jackson

J

ELECTRIC: PHIL COLLEN SERIES

PHIL COLLEN MODEL - unbalanced double cutaway poplar body, through-body maple neck, 24-fret bound ebony fingerboard with pearl sharkfin inlay, double locking vibrato, bound peghead with pearl Jackson logo inlay, 6-on-a-side Gotoh tuners, black hardware, single coil/humbucker Jackson pickups, volume control, 3-position switch, available in Metallic Black, Pearl White, or Radiant Red Pearl finishes, mfg. 1991 only.

	N/A	$1,100	$950	$825	$700	$600	$500

Last MSR was $1,695.

PC1 PHIL COLLEN (NO. 280-3050) - offset double cutaway koa body, quilted maple top, bolt-on maple neck, 24-fret quilted maple fingerboard, Original Floyd Rose locking tremolo, gold hardware, Floyd Rose Sustainer pickup/DiMarzio HS-2 single coil/DiMarzio Super 3 humbucker, volume/tone control, five-way position switch, available in Au Naturel, Chlorine, Euphoria, Mocha, Root Beer, or Solar Trans. finishes, mfg. 1996-present.

MSR	$3,000		$2,200	$1,900	$1,700	$1,500	$1,300	$1,100	$900

Add $150 for left-handed configuration (No. 280-3120).

Designed in conjunction with Phil Collen (Def Leppard).

PC3 PHIL COLLEN - offset double cutaway mahogany body, quilted maple top, bolt-on maple neck, 24-fret quilted maple fingerboard, Wilkinson VS50 tremolo, chrome hardware, 2 single coil/humbucker Duncan Design pickups, volume/tone control, 5-way position switch, available in Trans. Amber, Trans. Green, or Trans. Red finishes, mfg. 1998-2001.

	$750	$675	$600	$550	$500	$425	$300

Last MSR was $995.

Designed in conjunction with Phil Collen (Def Leppard).

ELECTRIC: PLAYERS CHOICE SERIES

The Player´s Choice series was released from 1993 to 1995 and incorporated many of the most requested options from the Jackson Custom Shop. Standardization of designs yielded lower retail list prices.

Jackson PC1 Phil Collen
courtesy Jackson

GRADING	100% MINT	98% NEAR MINT	95% EXC+	90% EXC	80% VG+	70% VG	60% G

EXOTIC DINKY - offset double cutaway koa body, bound quilted maple top, bolt-on maple neck, 24-fret bound pau ferro fingerboard with offset pearl dot inlay, double locking vibrato, bound peghead with pearl logo inlay, 6-on-a-side tuners, gold hardware, 2 stacked coil/humbucker Seymour Duncan pickups, volume/tone control, 5-position switch, available in Tobacco Sunburst, Trans. Blue, Trans. Purple or Trans. Red finishes, mfg. 1993-95.

	N/A	$1,700	$1,450	$1,200	$1,000	$800	$600

Last MSR was $2,400.

FLAMED DINKY - similar to Exotic Dinky, except has flame maple body, bound ebony fingerboard with pearl sharkfin inlay, black hardware, Jackson pickups, available in Trans. Black, Trans. Blue, or Trans. Purple finishes, mfg. 1993-95.

	N/A	$1,500	$1,300	$1,100	$900	$700	$550

Last MSR was $2,200.

KING V - V-style poplar body, through-body maple neck, 22-fret bound ebony fingerboard with pearl sharkfin inlay, fixed locking bridge, bound peghead with pearl logo inlay, 6-on-a-side tuners, black hardware, 2 volume/1 tone controls, 5-position switch with opposite switching, available in Black finish, mfg. 1993-95.

	N/A	$1,500	$1,300	$1,100	$900	$700	$550

Last MSR was $2,200.

ORIGINAL RHOADS - Sharkfin style poplar body, gold pickguard, through-body maple neck, 22-fret bound ebony fingerboard with pearl sharkfin inlay, Tune-O-Matic bridge, strings through tailpiece with V plate, 6-on-a-side tuners, gold hardware, 2 humbucker Seymour Duncan pickups, 2 volume/1 tone controls, 3-position switch, available in Black finish, mfg. 1993-95.

	N/A	$1,500	$1,300	$1,100	$900	$700	$550

Last MSR was $2,200.

PHIL COLLEN - offset double cutaway maple body, through-body maple neck, 24-fret bound ebony fingerboard with pearl sharkfin inlay, double locking vibrato, bound peghead with pearl Jackson logo inlay, 6-on-a-side Gotoh tuners, black hardware, single coil/humbucker Jackson pickups, volume control, 3-position switch, available in Metallic Black or Pearl White finishes, mfg. 1993-95.

	N/A	$1,600	$1,400	$1,200	$1,000	$800	$600

Last MSR was $2,300.

RHOADS 10 STRING - Sharkfin style quilted maple body, through-body maple neck, 22-fret bound ebony fingerboard with pearl sharkfin inlay, double locking vibrato, bound peghead with pearl Jackson inlay, double R truss rod cover, 6-on-a-side tuners, 4 tuners located on bridge end of instrument, gold hardware, volume control, 3-position switch, available in Trans. Black finish, mfg. 1993-95.

	N/A	$1,600	$1,400	$1,200	$1,000	$800	$600

Last MSR was $2,500.

This model was designed in conjunction with guitarist Dan Spitz (Anthrax).

AT2 T - offset double cutaway basswood body, bolt-on maple neck, 22-fret rosewood fingerboard with white dot inlay, chrome hardware, wraparound stop tailpiece, 2 chrome covered humbuckers, volume/tone controls, 3-way selector switch, available in Black, Deep Metallic Red, Cherry Sunburst, or Trans. Purple finishes, mfg. 1996-98.

	$675	$550	$475	$425	$350	$295	$225

Last MSR was $895.

Add $50 for Transparent finish and gravure top.

ELECTRIC: RANDY RHOADS SERIES

RR1 USA RHOADS (NO. 280-3060) - similar to Rhoads EX except has black pickguard, bound ebony fingerboard with pearl sharkfin inlay, bound peghead with pearl logo inlay, volume/2 tone controls, 3-way switch, available in Black, Black Pearl, Blue Green Pearl, Electric Blue, Ferrari Red, Gun Metal Grey, Metallic Black, Pavo Purple, or Sea Foam Green finishes, mfg. 1987-present.

1987-1995	N/A	$1,500	$1,250	$1,050	$900	$800	$700
1996-MSR $2,600	$1,850	$1,600	$1,400	$1,200	$1,050	$900	$750

Add $150 for left-handed configuration (No. 280-3160).

In 1998, Metallic Black finish was introduced; Gun Metal Gray and Blue Green Metallic finishes were discontinued.

RR1T (No. 280-3061) - similar to RR1 except has a Tune-O-Matic string through-body, SH4B bridge pickup, available in Blue Green Pearl, black, Black Pearl, Cobalt Blue, Electric Blue Metallic, Ferrari Red, Gun Metal Gray, Metallic Black, or Pavo Purple finishes, current mfg.

MSR	$2,600	$1,850	$1,600	$1,400	$1,200	$1,050	$900	$750

Add $150 for left-handed configuration (No. 280-3161).

RR2 - similar to RR1, except has maple gravure top, bolt-on neck, 22-fret ebony fingerboard, available in Black, Deep Metallic Blue, Dark Metallic Red, or Snow White finishes, mfg. 1996-98.

	$1,000	$850	$700	$600	$550	$425	$350

Last MSR was $1,295.

RR3 (NO. 280-3000) - similar to RR1 except has alder body with flamed maple top, bolt-on rock maple neck with rosewood fingerboard, sharkfin position markers, Duncan Designed 103B and 103N humbucker pickups, JT580LP bridge, available in Black or Deep Candy Blue finishes, mfg. 1995-present.

MSR	$750	$525	$450	$400	$350	$300	$250	$200

Add $35 for Trans. finishes (Black, Blue, or Red). Add $70 for Crimson Swirl or Eerie Dess Swirl finishes.

RR4 (RHOADS EX) - Sharkfin style poplar body, bolt-on maple neck, 22-fret rosewood fingerboard with pearl dot inlay, double locking vibrato, 6-on-a-side tuners, black hardware, 2 humbucker Jackson pickups, volume control, 3-position switch, available in Black, Bright Red, Candy Blue, Snow White, or Stone finishes, mfg. 1992-98.

	$550	$475	$400	$350	$300	$250	$200

Last MSR was $745.

Add $50 for Transparent finishes.

GRADING	100% MINT	98% NEAR MINT	95% EXC+	90% EXC	80% VG+	70% VG	60% G

RR5 (NO. 290-3002) - similar to the RR1 except has a neck-thru body, and a JT390 bridge STB, available in Black finish, mfg. 2001-present.

MSR	$1,500		$1,075	$925	$800	$725	$650	$575	$500

Add $35 for Trans. finishes (Natural, Blue, Red, or Violin Brown). Add $70 for Ivory with Black pinstripes finish.

RR7 - similar to RR1T except in a 7-string configuration, available in Black or Deep Candy Blue finishes, disc. 2001.

	$650	$550	$475	$425	$400	$325	$250

Last MSR was $895.

RWR ROSWELL RHOADS - futuristic rounded sharkfin style poplar body, bolt-on maple neck, 25.5 in. scale, 22-fret rosewood fingerboard with crop circle inlay, Tune-O-Matic bridge/strings through-body ferrules, 3-per-side tuners, black hardware, Duncan Design humbucker pickups, volume control, available in Black or Midnight Blue Sparkle finishes, disc. 2001.

	$700	$600	$525	$450	$400	$325	$275

Last MSR was $975.

RANDY RHOADS LIMITED EDITION - Sharkfin style maple body, through-body maple neck, 22-fret bound ebony fingerboard with pearl block inlay, standard vibrato, bound peghead, truss rod cover with overlapping RR stamped into it, 6-on-a-side tuners, gold hardware, 2 humbucker Jackson pickups, 2 volume/tone controls, 3-position switch located on top side of body, available in White finish with Black pinstriping around body edge, mfg. 1992 only.

N/A	$1,600	$1,400	$1,200	$1,050	$900	$750

Last MSR was $2,495.

This was a reproduction of the original series that was co-designed by Randy Rhoads and luthier Grover Jackson. Only 200 reproductions were built.

ELECTRIC: SURFCASTER (SC) SERIES

SC1 SURFCASTER - slightly offset single rounded cutaway semi-hollow mahogany body, bound ash top, bound wedge soundhole, bolt-on maple neck, 25.5 in. scale, 24-fret bound rosewood (or maple) fingerboard with pearl sharkfin inlay, GTB100 wraparound bridge, bound peghead with screened logo, 3-per-side tuners, squared off headstock, chrome hardware, pearloid pickguard, lipstick-style single coil/chrome covered humbucker pickups, volume/tone control, 3-position switch, available in Trans. Black, Trans. Green, Trans. Ivory, or Trans. Red finishes, mfg. 1998-2001.

	$735	$625	$575	$500	$450	$350	$275

Last MSR was $1,045.

In 1999, Trans. Green and Trans. Ivory finishes were disc.

SC3 - similar to SC1 except has two single coil pickups and one humbucking pickup, STB, available in Black or Sea Foam Green finishes, disc. 2001.

	$725	$600	$550	$500	$450	$400	$325

Last MSR was $995.

SC4 (NO. 290-1500) - Surfcaster style alder body with flame maple veneer, bolt-on rock maple neck, 22-fret rosewood fingerboard with dot inlay, white tortise pickguard, 3-per-side tuners, 3 Duncan Design single coil pickups, JT390 Tune-O-Matic bridge STB, chrome hardware, available in Black, Dark Metallic Blue, Dark Metallic Red, or Sea Foam Green finishes, mfg. 2002-03.

	$425	$360	$310	$275	$250	$200	$175

Last MSR was $607.

Add $35 for Trans. Red or Trans. Blue finishes.

SC12 12-STRING - similar to SC3 except in a 12-string configuration, ash body, J370 bridge, 2 Duncan Designed LS101 pickups, available in Black or Sea Foam green finishes, disc. 2001.

	$925	$750	$675	$575	$500	$425	$350

Last MSR was $1,245.

OC1 - similar to the Surfcaster, except has solid basswood body, 1 Chandler LST lipstick-style single coil/exposed pole piece humbucker, available in Gun Metal Gray, Metallic Violet, or Vintage White finishes, mfg. 1996-97.

	$575	$500	$440	$380	$325	$290	$250

Last MSR was $725.

ELECTRIC: SOLOIST SERIES

SOLOIST ARCHTOP - offset double cutaway mahogany body, arched flame maple top, through-body maple neck, 24-fret bound ebony fingerboard with pearl sharkfin inlay, Tune-O-Matic bridge with through-body string holders, bound peghead with pearl Jackson logo inlay, 6-on-a-side Gotoh tuners, black hardware, 2 humbucker Jackson pickups, volume/tone control, 3-position switch, available in Cherry Sunburst, Trans. Amber, Trans. Blue, or Trans. Red finishes, mfg. 1989-1991.

N/A	$950	$850	$750	$650	$550	$450

Last MSR was $1,495.

Add $200 for double locking vibrato.

Jackson RR4 (Rhoads EX) courtesy Jackson

Jackson Surfcaster courtesy Willie's American Guitar

GRADING	100% MINT	98% NEAR MINT	95% EXC+	90% EXC	80% VG+	70% VG	60% G

SOLOIST STANDARD - offset double cutaway poplar body, bolt-on maple neck, 24-fret rosewood fingerboard with dot inlay, double locking vibrato, 6-on-a-side tuners, black hardware, 2 stacked coil/humbucker Jackson pickups, 1 volume/1 tone control, 5-position switch, available in Bright Red, Deep Metallic Blue, Metallic Blue, or Pearl White finishes, mfg. 1991-95.

	N/A	$700	$625	$550	$475	$400	$325

Last MSR was $995.

SOLOIST USA - offset double cutaway poplar body, through-body maple neck, 24-fret bound ebony fingerboard with pearl sharkfin inlay, double locking vibrato, bound peghead with pearl Jackson logo inlay, 6-on-a-side tuners, black hardware, 2 stacked coil/1 humbucker Jackson pickups, volume/tone/mid boost controls, 5-position switch, active electronics, available in Bright Red, Deep Metallic Blue, Metallic Blue, or Pearl White finishes, mfg. 1991-95.

	N/A	$1,400	$1,200	$1,050	$900	$750	$600

Last MSR was $2,295.

SL1 USA SOLOIST (NO. 280-3070) - offset double cutaway poplar body, through-body maple neck, 24-fret bound ebony fingerboard with pearl sharkfin inlay, Original Floyd Rose tremolo, bound peghead with pearl Jackson logo inlay, 6-on-a-side tuners, black hardware, 2 Duncan stacked humbuckers/Duncan TB4 humbucker pickups, volume/tone/mid boost controls, 5 way switch, active electronics, available in Blue Green Pearl, Deep Candy Red, Gun Metal Gray, or Metallic Black finishes, mfg. 1991-present.

MSR	$2,450	$1,750	$1,500	$1,300	$1,100	$950	$800	$650

Also available as the SL1T with tremolo, at no additional cost. Add $150 for left-handed configuration (No. 280-3170)

This model is available with optional custom graphics, and is also available in left-handed configuration. See finish list for additional colors.

SL2 (SOLOIST XL) - similar to SL1, except has ebony fingerboard with no inlays, 2 exposed humbuckers, chrome hardware, screened logo, and no active electronics, available in Deep Metallic Blue, Dark Metallic Red, Metallic Black, or Pearl White finishes, mfg. 1996-98.

	$1,000	$875	$750	$625	$575	$425	$350

Last MSR was $1,395.

Add $100 for mother-of-pearl sharkfin neck inlay (Model SL2 S).

SL2H USA SOLOIST (NO. 280-3071) - similar to the SL1 Soloist, except has two humbucker pickups, available in Black, Black Pearl, Blue Green Pearl, Electric Blue, Ferrari Red, Gun Metal Grey, Metallic Black, Pavo Purple, or Sea Foam Green, current mfg.

MSR	$2,450	$1,750	$1,500	$1,300	$1,100	$950	$800	$650

Also available as the SL2HT with tremolo for no additional cost. Add $150 for left-handed configuration (No. 280-3171).

Also available in left-handed configuration (No. 280-3171), and is available with other color options, see list.

SL2H MAH USA Soloist (No. 280-3072) - similar to the SL2H Soloist, except has a mahogany body with a flamed maple top and mahogany thru neck, available in Amber Sunburst, Burnt Cherry Sunburst, Cherry Sunburst, Mahogany, Natural, Tobacco Sunburst, Trans. Black, Trans. Blue, Trans. Green, Trans. Red, or Violin Brown finishes, current mfg.

MSR	$3,000	$2,200	$1,900	$1,700	$1,500	$1,300	$1,100	$900

Add $150 for left-handed configuration (No. 280-3172).

SLATQH (No. 280-3073) - similar to the SL2H MAH Soloist, except has a mahogany body with a .75 in. quilted maple top and mahogany thru neck, available in Amber Sunburst, Burnt Cherry Sunburst, Cherry Sunburst, Mahogany, Natural, Tobacco Sunburst, Trans. Black, Trans. Blue, Trans. Green, Trans. Red, or Violin Brown finishes, current mfg.

MSR	$3,200	$2,400	$2,100	$1,850	$1,600	$1,400	$1,200	$1,000

Add $150 for left-handed configuration (No. 280-3173).

SL3 (NO. 290-4000) - similar to the SL1 Soloist, except has a rock maple neck, rosewood fingerboard, JT580LP bridge, and 3 Seymour Duncan pickups (Distortion, Hot Rail, and Cool Rail single coils), available in Black or Satin Black finishes, mfg. 2002-present.

MSR	$1,500	$1,075	$925	$850	$725	$650	$575	$500

Add $35 for Trans. finishes (Amber Sunburst, Natural, Blue, Red, and Violin Brown).

SLS SOLOIST SUPERLIGHT (NO. 280-3073) - offset double cutaway mahogany body, contoured flame maple top, through-body mahogany neck, 24-fret bound rosewood fingerboard, 3-per-side pointed headstock, Tune-O-Matic bridge/stop tailpiece, chrome hardware, 2 humbuckers, volume/tone controls, available in Black, Tobacco Sunburst, or Trans. Orange burst finishes, mfg. 1997-98, reintroduced 2003-04.

	$2,300	$2,000	$1,750	$1,550	$1,350	$1,150	$950

Last MSR was $3,100.

Add $20 for optional flame maple top (this option was discontinued in 1998). Add $150 for left-handed configuration (No. 280-3172).

In 1998, Burst Cherry Sunburst and Trans. Black finishes were introduced; Black, Tobacco Sunburst, and Trans. Orange Burst finishes were discontinued.

SLSMG SOLOIST (NO. 290-0104) - Soloist shape, mahogany body, mahogany neck-thru, bound ebony fingerboard, 2 EMGHZ pickups, JT390 bridge STB, black hardware, available in Satin Black finish, mfg. 2001-present.

MSR	$1,350	$950	$850	$775	$700	$625	$550	$475

Add $35 for Violin Brown finish.

SHS1 SHANNON SOLOIST - offset double cutaway poplar body, through-body maple neck, 25.5 in. scale, 24-fret bound ebony fingerboard with pearl sharkfin inlay, 6-on-a-side pointed headstock, Original Floyd Rose tremolo, chrome hardware, 2 single coil/humbucker Seymour Duncan pickups, volume/tone controls, 5 way selector, available in Black, Blue Ghost Flames, or Slime Green finishes, mfg. 1998.

	$1,350	$1,150	$1,000	$895	$750	$600	$475

Last MSR was $1,895.

GRADING	100% MINT	98% NEAR MINT	95% EXC+	90% EXC	80% VG+	70% VG	60% G

ELECTRIC: SS SERIES

Jackson offered the Short Scale series guitars with a scale length of 24.75 in. instead of the usual 25.5 in. scale normally employed. This shorter scale length was an option on the Fusion series for a number of years.

SS1 - offset shallow double cutaway arched basswood or ash body, bolt-on maple neck, 22-fret rosewood fingerboard with dot inlay, 3-per-side headstock, chrome hardware, 2 humbuckers, Wilkinson VS-100 tremolo, volume/tone controls, 3-way switch, available in Black, Cobalt Blue, Blue Green Pearl, or Red Pearl Satin finishes, mfg. 1996-97.

	$525	$475	$400	$375	$275	$200	$175

Last MSR was $795.

SS2 - similar to the SS1, except has polar body, no arched top, and Tune-O-Matic stop tailpiece, mfg. 1996-97.

	$450	$375	$325	$275	$175	$150	$125

Last MSR was $695.

ELECTRIC: STEALTH & TH SERIES

STEALTH HX - similar to Stealth EX, except has Tune-O-Matic bridge, strings through-body tailpiece, 3 humbucker Jackson pickups, available in Black, Deep Metallic Blue, Deep Metallic Red, or Deep Metallic Violet finishes, mfg. 1991-95.

	N/A	$375	$325	$275	$235	$195	$165

Last MSR was $595.

STEALTH PRO - offset double cutaway basswood body, bolt-on maple neck, 22-fret ebony fingerboard with offset pearl dot inlay, double locking vibrato, blackface peghead with pearl logo inlay, 6-on-a-side tuners, black hardware, 2 single coil/humbucker Jackson pickups, volume/tone control, 5-position switch, available in Metallic Blue finish, mfg. 1991-93.

	N/A	$750	$650	$575	$500	$425	$350

Last MSR was $1,195.

STEALTH PRO TRANS - similar to Stealth Pro, except has ash body, body matching peghead without pearl inlay, available in Trans. Amber finish, mfg. 1991-93.

	N/A	$800	$700	$625	$550	$475	$400

Last MSR was $1,295.

This model was available with figured maple top in Trans. Blue and Trans. Violet finishes.

STEALTH XL - similar to Stealth Pro, except has ash body, rosewood fingerboard, available in Trans. Amber, Trans. Blue, Trans. Red, or Trans. Violet finishes, mfg. 1991-93.

	N/A	$550	$475	$400	$325	$300	$225

Last MSR was $895.

TH1 (STEALTH EX) - offset double cutaway basswood or ash body, bolt-on maple neck, 22-fret rosewood fingerboard with offset pearl dot inlay, double locking vibrato, 6-on-a-side tuners, black hardware, 2 single coil/humbucker Jackson pickups, volume/tone control, 5-position switch, available in Black, Metallic Violet, Graphite, Cobalt Blue Satin, or Red Pearl Satin finishes, mfg. 1991-97.

	$550	$450	$350	$275	$250	$225	$200

Last MSR was $795.

Add $100 for left-handed configuration of this model.

TH2 - similar to the TH1, except has Jackson Custom Fulcrum non-locking tremolo and pointy profile straight pull 3-per-side headstock, mfg. 1996-97.

	$525	$425	$325	$275	$225	$200	$175

Last MSR was $725.

ELECTRIC: STUDENT JS SERIES

JS 1 DINKY (NO. 290-0010) - similar to the JS 20 except has two humbucker pickups, available in Black, Dark Metallic Blue, or Dark Metallic Red finishes, mfg. 2003-present.

MSR	$285		$210	$175	$145	$125	$105	$85	$65

JS 20 DINKY (NO. 290-0011) - offset double cutaway alder body, bolt-on maple neck, 22-fret rosewood fingerboard with dot inlay, SG 23 non-locking vibrato, blackface peghead with logo, 6-on-a-side tuners, chrome hardware, 2 single coil/1 humbucker pickups, volume/tone control, 5-position switch, available in Black, Metallic Blue, or Metallic Red finishes, mfg. 1996-present.

MSR	$300		$220	$185	$150	$125	$105	$85	$65

Add $35 for Trans. finishes (Amber Sunburst, Tobacco Sunburst, Blue, or Red).

JS 30 (NO. 290-0012) - similar to JS 20, except features 2 humbuckers, available in Black, Dark Metallic Blue, Dark Metallic Red, or Gun Metal Grey finishes, mfg. 1997-98, 2000-present.

MSR	$450		$325	$275	$225	$190	$160	$130	$100

Add $35 for Trans. finishes (Black or Blue).

JS 30 KE/KV/RR/WR (NO. 290-0013/4/5/6) - Kelly, King V, Rhoads, or Warrior body style, available in Dark Metallic Red, Dark Metallic Blue, or Black finishes, new 2004.

MSR	$428		$300	$250	$210	$170	$135	$115	$100

Jackson Soloist Standard
courtesy Jackson

J

Jackson SL2 Soloist XL
courtesy Jackson

GRADING	100% MINT	98% NEAR MINT	95% EXC+	90% EXC	80% VG+	70% VG	60% G

ELECTRIC: SWEE-TONE SERIES

The Swee-Tone series was introduced in 2002. These guitars are produced in the Jackson/Charvel USA Custom Shop. These models include the ATSC, AT2H, AT90, AT3, BTSC, BT2H, BT90, and Jazz guitars.

ARCHTOP ATSC - double cutaway arched body, Sitka or Englemann Spruce body wings, hard rock maple top, Honduran mahogany neck-thru-body, 22-fret ebony fingerboard with dot inlay, 2 Seymour Duncan single coil pickups, 3 knobs, 5-way switch, STB bridge, chrome hardware, available in Amber Lager Burst, Blonde, Cabernet, Caramel, or Faded Cherry Sunburst finishes, mfg. 2002-present.

	MSR	$3,000		$2,200	$1,900	$1,700	$1,500	$1,300	$1,100	$900

Also available with 2 Seymour Duncan humbucker pickups (AT2H). Add $150 for 2 Seymour Duncan stacked P-90 pickups (AT90). Add $225 for 3 Seymour Duncan P-90 pickups (AT3). Add $150 for left-handed configuration.

BENT TOP BTSC - double cutaway bent body, Sitka or Englemann Spruce body wings, hard rock maple top, Honduran mahogany neck-thru-body, 22-fret ebony fingerboard with dot inlay, 2 Seymour Duncan single coil pickups, 3 knobs, 5-way switch, STB bridge, chrome hardware, available in Amber Lager Burst, Blonde, Cabernet, Caramel, or Faded Cherry Sunburst finishes, mfg. 2002-present.

	MSR	$2,950		$2,150	$1,850	$1,650	$1,450	$1,250	$1,050	$850

Also available with 2 Seymour Duncan humbucker pickups (BT2H). Add $25 for 2 Seymour Duncan stacked P-90 pickups (BT90). Add $100 for 3 Seymour Duncan P-90 pickups (BT3). Add $150 for left-handed configuration.

JAZZ'R SC - single cutaway body, Sitka or Englemann Spruce body wings, hard rock maple top, Honduran mahogany neck-thru-body, 22-fret ebony fingerboard with dot inlay, 2 Seymour Duncan single coil pickups, 3 knobs, 3-way switch, STB bridge, chrome hardware, available in Amber Lager Burst, Blonde, Cabernet, Caramel, or Faded Cherry Sunburst finishes, mfg. 2002-present.

	MSR	$3,000		$2,200	$1,900	$1,700	$1,500	$1,300	$1,100	$900

Add $75 for 2 Seymour Duncan humbucker pickups (AT2H). Add $150 for left-handed configuration.

ELECTRIC: USA SERIES

Jackson USA models are built in Ontario, California in the same facility as the Jackson Custom Shop.

AT1 - offset double cutaway mahogany (with quilt maple top) or poplar body, bolt-on maple neck, 22-fret ebony fingerboard, chrome hardware, Wilkinson VS-100 tremolo, 2 chrome covered humbuckers, volume/tone controls, 3-way selector switch, available in Black, Deep Candy Red, Blue Green Pearl, Trans. Blue, Trans. Green, Cherry Sunburst, or Trans. Black finishes, mfg. 1996-98.

	$1,200	$1,050	$950	$850	$750	$675	$550
				Last MSR was $1,495.			

Add $150 for Transparent finish.

AT1 T - similar to the AT1, except features a Wilkinson GB-100 stop tailpiece and chrome humbucker covers, disc. 1998.

	$1,100	$975	$850	$750	$675	$575	$500
				Last MSR was $1,445.			

Add $150 for Transparent finish.

DK1 USA DINKY (NO. 280-3010) - offset double cutaway poplar body, bound quilted maple top, bolt-on maple neck, 22-fret bound ebony fingerboard with offset pearl dot inlay, Original Floyd Rose vibrato, bound peghead with pearl logo inlay, 6-on-a-side tuners, gold hardware, 2 stacked coil/humbucker Seymour Duncan pickups, volume/tone control, 5-position switch, available in Black, Black Pearl, Blue Green Pearl, Electric Blue, Ferrari Red, Gun Metal Grey, Metallic Black, Pavo Purple, or Sea Foam Green finishes, mfg. 1993-98, 2000-present.

	MSR	$2,200		$1,600	$1,400	$1,250	$1,100	$950	$800	$650

Add $150 for left-handed configuration (No. 280-3110).

In 1998, bound quilted maple top was only available on transparent finish models. See list for additional colors.

SDK1 - similar to the DK1, except has smaller (Super Dinky) and lighter poplar or ash body, rosewood or maple fingerboard, and humbucker/single coil/humbucking pickups, available in Black, Cobalt Blue, Orange/Gold Pearl, Gun Metal Grey, Deep Candy Red, or Graphite finishes, mfg. 1996-97.

	$1,000	$875	$750	$675	$595	$500	$475
				Last MSR was $1,295.			

DR2 - similar to the Dinky Reverse (DR5), except has a poplar (or ash) body, JT580 locking tremolo, 2 Duncan humbuckers, and ebony fingerboard. Available in Black, Ultra Violet Burst, Deep Candy Red, Graphite, and Cobalt Blue Satin finishes, mfg. 1996-1998.

	$1,100	$950	$825	$725	$600	$495	$375
				Last MSR was $1,445.			

FUSION USA - offset double cutaway basswood body, bolt-on maple neck, 24-fret bound ebony fingerboard with pearl sharkfin inlay, double locking vibrato, bound peghead with pearl Jackson logo inlay, 6-on-a-side tuners, black hardware, 2 stacked coil/1 humbucker Jackson pickups, volume/tone control, 5-position and bypass switches, active electronics, available in Bright Red, Candy Blue, Metallic Black, or Pearl White finishes, mfg. 1992-94.

	N/A	$1,500	$1,300	$1,150	$1,000	$850	$700

JJ1 - offset dual cutaway poplar or korina body (bass horn slightly extended), bolt-on maple neck, 25.5 in. scale, 22-fret rosewood fingerboard with dice inlay 12th fret markers, 3-per-side headstock, chrome hardware, Wilkinson GTB 100 stop tailpiece, 2 exposed humbuckers, volume/tone control, 3 way selector, available in Black, Silver Sparkle, or Natural finishes, mfg. 1996-2001.

	$1,000	$895	$775	$675	$575	$495	$400
				Last MSR was $1,295.			

Add $100 for transparent finish (Transparent Red).

This model was designed in conjunction with Scott Ian (Anthrax). This model is also available with a Wilkinson VS-100 tremolo as Model JJ1 W (this option was discontinued in 1998).

GRADING	100% MINT	98% NEAR MINT	95% EXC+	90% EXC	80% VG+	70% VG	60% G

JJ2 USA SCOTT IAN (NO. 280-3020) - similar to the JJ1 except has an alder body, maple or mahogany thru-neck, ebony fingerboard, and Seymour Duncan/Scott Ian humbucker pickups, available in Black, Black Pearl, Blue Green Pearl, Electric Blue, Ferrari Red, Gun Metal Grey, Metallic Black, Pavo Purple, or Sea Foam Green finishes, disc. 2004.

	$1,750	$1,500	$1,300	$1,100	$950	$800	$650

Last MSR was $2,450.

Add $150 for left-handed configuration (No. 280-3120).

See list for additional colors.

JJ4 - similar to JJ1 except has string through-body, Tune-O-Matic style bridge, dot position markers, available in black or Deep Candy Blue, disc. 2001.

	$560	$450	$375	$300	$250	$175	$125

Last MSR was $745.

Add $50 for Tobacco Sunburst finish.

JJ4 Tattoo - similar to JJ4 except available in Tattoo finish which is black with intricate white pin-striping job on guitar's top, disc. 2001.

	$635	$510	$425	$350	$275	$200	$150

Last MSR was $845.

JJP - single cutaway mahogany body, bolt-on mahogany neck, 24.75 in. scale, 22-fret rosewood fingerboard with dot inlay, 3-per-side tuners, squared off headstock, chrome hardware, DiMarzio humbucker, Tune-O-Matic bridge/stop tailpiece, volume control, available in Black, Purple, or Tobacco Sunburst finishes, mfg. 1997-98.

	$900	$750	$650	$550	$475	$395	$300

Last MSR was $1,195.

JRS-1 - offset double cutaway ash body, bolt-on maple neck, 25.5 in. scale, 22-fret maple fingerboard, Wilkinson VS-100 vibrato, reverse natural finish headstock, 6-on-the-other side tuners, chrome hardware, Seymour Duncan humbucker, volume control, available in Black, Electric Blue, Trans. Black, Trans. Red, or Trans. White finishes, mfg. 1997-98.

	$975	$800	$700	$600	$525	$450	$350

Last MSR was $1,245.

Jackson JJ2 USA Scott Ian
courtesy Jackson

J

1997 PETER MAX LIMITED EDITION JRS-1 - similar to the JRS-1, available in a hand painted finish by artist Peter Max, mfg. 1997 only.

Too few of these exist for accurate statistical representation. In 1997, Jackson offered a very limited series of guitars hand painted by artist Peter Marx. Series I models were to be painted all over, and limited to a total of 12 pieces. Series II models were to be painted on the face of the body only, and limited to 24 pieces. However, a total of only 4 pieces were actually completed out of the entire project. There has not been a price determined because of no activitiy on the market and the rarity.

KE1 (KELLY PRO) - single sharp cutaway radical hourglass style poplar body, through-body maple neck, 24-fret bound ebony fingerboard with pearl sharkfin inlay, Kahler APM 3310 non-locking fixed bridge, 6-on-a-side tuners, black hardware, Duncan TB4 humbucker pickup, volume control, available in (Metallic) Black, Trans. Black, or Snow White Pearl finishes, mfg. 1994-2001.

	$1,200	$1,000	$895	$775	$650	$550	$425

Last MSR was $1,695.

Add $100 for transparent finish with maple top (Transparent Black). Add $150 for Original Floyd Rose tremolo (Model KE1 F-this option was discontinued in 1998).

This model was designed in conjunction with Marty Freidman (Megadeth).

KE2 USA KELLY (NO. 280-3030) - similar to the KE1, except features a Floyd Rose tremolo, 2 Seymour Duncan humbucker pickups, available in Black, Black Pearl, Blue Green Pearl, Electric Blue, Ferrari Red, Gun Metal Grey, Metallic Black, Pavo Purple, or Sea Foam Green finishes, mfg. 1998-present.

MSR	$2,600	$1,850	$1,600	$1,400	$1,200	$1,050	$900	$750

KV1 (KING V PRO-MUSTAINE) - V-style poplar body, through-body maple neck, 24-fret bound ebony fingerboard with pearl sharkfin inlay, fixed locking Kahler APM 3310 bridge, bound peghead, 6-on-a-side tuners, black hardware, 2 Seymour Duncan humbucker pickups, 2 volume/1 tone controls, 3-position switch, available in Black, Cherry Sunburst, or Sparkle Silver Metallic finishes, mfg. 1993-2001.

	$1,450	$1,200	$1,050	$900	$750	$600	$450

Last MSR was $1,795.

Add $100 for Transparent Black finish.

In 1994, Cherry Sunburst finish was introduced. In 1998, Natural finish with Korina body was introduced; Cherry Sunburst and Sparkle Silver Metallic finishes were discontinued.

KV2 (KING V STD. MFG. 1993-97) - V-style poplar body, bolt-on maple neck, 22-fret rosewood fingerboard with pearl dot inlay, double locking Floyd Rose vibrato, 6-on-a-side tuners, black hardware, 2 Jackson humbucker pickups, volume control, 3-position switch, available in Black, Bright Red, Candy Blue, or Snow White finishes, mfg. 1993-97.

	N/A	$500	$425	$375	$325	$275	$225

Last MSR was $795.

Jackson KE2 USA Kelly
courtesy Jackson

GRADING	100% MINT	98% NEAR MINT	95% EXC+	90% EXC	80% VG+	70% VG	60% G

KV2 (USA KING V MFG. 1998-CURRENT NO. 280-3040) - similar to the KV2 (Formerly King V Std.), except features maple through-body neck, 22-fret ebony fingerboard with sharkfin inlay, 2 Seymour Duncan humbucker pickups, available in Black, Black Pearl, Blue Green Pearl, Electric Blue, Ferrari Red, Gun Metal Grey, Metallic Black, Pavo Purple, or Sea Foam Green finishes, mfg. 1998-present.

MSR	$2,600	$1,850	$1,600	$1,400	$1,200	$1,050	$900	$750

Add $150 for left-handed configuration (No. 280-3140).

KV2T (NO. 280-3041) - similar to the KV2, new 2003-present.

MSR	$3,000	$2,200	$1,900	$1,700	$1,500	$1,300	$1,100	$900

Add $150 for left-handed configuration (No. 280-3141).

ELECTRIC: WARRIOR SERIES

WARRIOR PRO - radically offset X-shaped poplar body, through-body maple neck, 24-fret bound ebony fingerboard with pearl sharkfin inlay, double locking vibrato, bound peghead with pearl Jackson logo inlay, 6-on-a-side Gotoh tuners, black hardware, 3 single coil Jackson pickups, volume/tone control, 5-position and mid range sweep switches, available in Candy Blue, Ferrari Red, Midnight Black, Pearl Yellow, or Snow White Pearl finishes, mfg. 1991 only.

	N/A	$1,300	$1,100	$950	$800	$700	$600

Last MSR was $1,695.

WR1 USA WARRIOR (NO. 280-3080) - offset X-shaped alder body, maple thru-neck, 24-fret ebony fingerboard with triangle inlays, 6-on-a-side tuners, 2 Seymour Duncan humbucking pickups, Floyd Rose tremolo, volume/tone control, 3-way switch, available in Standard colors, current mfg.

MSR	$2,600	$1,850	$1,600	$1,400	$1,200	$1,050	$900	$750

Add $150 for left-handed configuration (No. 280-3180).

WRMG WARRIOR (NO. 290-0105) - similar to the Warrior except has a poplar body, maple neck with rosewood fingerboard, 2 EMGHZ pickups, JT580LP bridge, and a TurboCharger, available in Black, Black Forest, or Cobalt Blue finishes, current mfg.

MSR	$900	$650	$575	$500	$425	$375	$325	$275

Add $35 for Trans. finishes (Black, Blue, or Green).

WARRIOR USA - radically offset X-shaped poplar body, through-body maple neck, 24-fret bound ebony fingerboard with pearl sharkfin inlay, double locking vibrato, bound peghead with pearl Jackson logo inlay, 6-on-a-side Gotoh tuners, black hardware, 3 single coil Jackson pickups, volume/tone control, 5-position and midrange sweep switches, available in Candy Blue, Ferrari Red, Midnight Black, Pearl Yellow, or Snow White Pearl finishes, mfg. circa mid- to late 1980s.

	N/A	$1,800	$1,500	$1,200	$1,000	$800	$600

Last MSR was $2,950.

This model was available as a custom order only.

SDTL1 - single cutaway ash body, bolt-on maple neck, 22-fret maple fingerboard, screened logo, 6-on-a-side tuners, 2 Armstrong single coil pickups/Wilkinson power bridge, 2 volume controls, push/pull pot fader, 3-way selector, stereo output jack, mfg. 1996 only.

	$1,000	$850	$725	$600	$525	$450	$375

Last MSR was $1,395.

ELECTRIC: X SERIES

DX6 (NO. 290-1101) - offset double cutaway poplar body with flame veneer, bolt-on maple neck, 22-fret rosewood fingerboard with dot inlay, 3-per-side tuners, 2 Duncan design HB-103 pickups, Tunamatic STB bridge, 2 knobs (v, tone), 3-way switch, chrome hardware, available in Black, Dark Metallic Blue, or Dark Metallic Red, mfg. 2001-03.

	$350	$295	$250	$215	$185	$150	$120

Last MSR was $500.

Add $35 for Amber Sunburst finish (No. 290-1102).

DX7 - offset double cutaway solid body, 7-string configuration, alder body, bolt-on maple neck, rosewood fingerboard with sharkfin position markers, JT790 Tunamatic bridge, string through-body, reverse headstock, 7-on-a-side tuners, 1 volume/1 tone, 3-way switch, 2 Duncan Designed HB7 humbucker pickups, available in Black, Dark Metallic Blue, or Dark Metallic Red finishes, disc. 2001.

	$350	$300	$250	$200	$175	$150	$100

Last MSR was $499.

DX10 - similar to DX6 except in a 6-string configuration, JT500 single locking bridge, Armstrong 213 and Armstrong 214 humbucker pickups, dot position markers, available in Black, Dark Metallic Red or Dark Metallic Blue finishes, disc. 2001.

	$325	$275	$235	$195	$165	$135	$105

Last MSR was $425.

DX10-D (No. 290-1103) - similar to DX10 except has sharkfin position markers, available in black, Dark Metallic Red, or Dark Metallic Blue finishes, current mfg.

MSR	$525	$370	$325	$275	$235	$195	$165	$135

Add $35 for Trans. finishes (Amber Sunburst, Tobacco Sunburst, Blue, Red).

DX10-DFS (No. 290-1104) - similar to the DX10D except has Duncan Design Firestorm electronics, mfg. 2001-present.

MSR	$630	$450	$375	$325	$275	$235	$195	$165

Add $35 for Trans. finishes (Amber Sunburst, Tobacco Sunburst, Blue, Red).

GRADING	100% MINT	98% NEAR MINT	95% EXC+	90% EXC	80% VG+	70% VG	60% G

DXMG (No. 290-0103) - similar to the DX10 except has a poplar body, bound neck, 2 EMGHZ pickups, available in Black or Gun Metal Grey finishes, mfg. 2001-present.

MSR	$675	$475	$400	$350	$300	$250	$210	$170

JX10 (NO. 290-1200) - similar to the DX10 except has three single coil Duncan Designed pickups, available in Black, Dark Metallic Blue, or Dark Metallic Red finishes, mfg. 2002-03.

	$250	$215	$180	$150	$125	$95	$65

Last MSR was $357.

Add $35 for Trans. finishes (Amber Sunburst, Tobacco Sunburst, Blue, Red).

KX10 - single cutaway design with sweeping lower bout, solid alder body, bolt-on maple neck, rosewood fingerboard with dot position markers, JT500 single locking bridge, 1 Volume/1 Tone, 3-way slotted switch, 1 Armstrong 213 and 1 Armstrong 214 humbucker pickups, available in Black, Dark Metallic Red, or Dark Metallic Blue finishes, disc. 2001.

	$375	$300	$250	$225	$200	$175	$125

Last MSR was $495.

KX10-D - similar to KX10 except has sharkfin position markers, JT500 double locking bridge, available in Black, Dark Metallic Red, or Dark Metallic Blue, disc. 2001.

	$425	$350	$300	$250	$225	$200	$150

Last MSR was $555.

KVX10 (NO. 290-1300) - Flying V poplar body with flamed maple veneer, bolt-on maple neck, 24-fret rosewood fingerboard with triangle inlays, 6-on-one-side tuners, 2 Duncan Design HB-103 pickups, JT390 Tune-O-Matic STB bridge, two knobs (v, tone), 3-way switch, chrome hardware, available in black, Dark Metallic Blue, or Dark Metallic Red finishes, mfg. 2002-present.

MSR	$675	$475	$400	$350	$300	$250	$210	$170

Add $35 for Trans. finishes (Amber Sunburst, Trans. Blue, or Trans. Red). Add $70 for Cobalt Blue Swirl finish.

RX10 - Rhoads style alder body, bolt-on maple neck, rosewood fingerboard with dot position markers, JT500 single locking bridge, 1 volume/1 tone, 3-way toggle, 1 Armstrong 213 and 1 Armstrong 214 humbucker pickups, available in Black, Dark Metallic Red, or Dark Metallic Blue finishes, disc. 2001.

	$375	$300	$250	$225	$200	$175	$125

Last MSR was $495.

RX10-D (No. 290-1400) - similar to RX10 except has sharkfin position markers and JT500 double locking bridge, available in black, Satin Black, Dark Metallic Red, or Dark Metallic Blue finishes, current mfg.

MSR	$675	$475	$400	$350	$300	$250	$210	$170

Add $70 for Trans. finishes (Amber Sunburst, Trans. Blue, Trans. Red, or Cobalt Blue Swirl).

WRXT WARRIOR (NO. 290-1600) - X shaped poplar body, bolt-on maple neck, 24-fret rosewood fingerboard with triangle inlays, 6-on-side tuners, 2 Duncan Design Detonator humbucking pickups, JT580LP bridge, two knobs (v, tone), 3-way switch, chrome hardware, available in Black, Dark Metallic Blue, or Dark Metallic Red, mfg. 2002-present.

MSR	$675	$475	$400	$350	$300	$250	$210	$170

Add $35 for Trans. Blue or Trans. Red finishes.

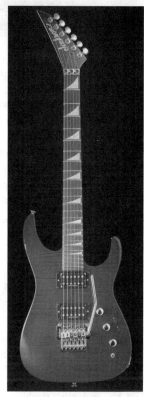

Jackson DX10-DFS courtesy Jackson

ELECTRIC: CUSTOM SHOP GUITARS

Current literature indicates that the Jackson Custom Shop has been creating custom guitars longer than any production facility in the U.S. A current example of their custom artistry would be the **Roswell Rhoads**, an advanced sharkfin design machined out of 6061-TS aircraft grade aluminum that features LSR tuners, "crop circle" neck inlays, and a Tom Holmes humbucker pickup. The Jackson Custom Shop briefly featured custom pyrography finishes, a wood burning technique by artist Dino Muradian that offers a high degree of drawing and shading on the guitar´s wood body.

Currently, the Jackson Custom Shop is offering a wide range of body and neck woods, pickup selection, custom wiring, custom or airbrushed finishes, and innovative body designs. Custom guitars take 4 to 12 months for delivery. Contact Jackson Guitars or a local Jackson dealer for a full price quote.

CUSTOM SHOP GUITAR MODEL (BASE PRICE) - alder (or basswood or poplar) body, quartersawn maple neck, 25.5 in. scale, 22 (or 24) fret maple (or rosewood or ebony) fingerboard with sharkfin or dot inlay, Gotoh tuners, chrome or black hardware, choice of pickups and configuration, available in Solid, Candy Colors, Metallic, or Pearl finishes, current (specialty) mfg.

The Custom Shop prices retailed at the following: Bolt-On Neck $2,880, Through-Body Neck $3,420, Bolt-On Double Neck $4,320. Neck Through Double Neck $5,220. Seven-string configuration $120. Mahogany, Korina, or Lacewood $60. Koa $250. Solid Figured Maple $950. Flame or Quilted Maple Veneer $120. Pricing needs to be determined individually as each model is different. List prices include an SKB case.

ELECTRIC BASS: ANTI-GRAVITY SERIES

The Jackson Anti-Gravity series was released in 2003 and features a new, radical design. Retail prices start at $2,800 and go up from there. Look for more information in further edtions.

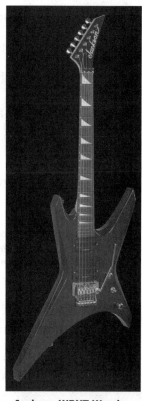

Jackson WRXT Warrior courtesy Jackson

GRADING	100% MINT	98% NEAR MINT	95% EXC+	90% EXC	80% VG+	70% VG	60% G

AG4 (NO. 280-9000) - double offset unique shaped body, solid spruce body, 24-fret Madagascar rosewood fingerboard with dot inlays, 2-per-side tuners, 2 Basslines STK J2 pickups, 5 rosewood knobs, 3-way switch, Hipshot bridge, black hardware, available in Black Pearl, Blue Green Pearl, Electric Blue, Ferrari Red, Gun Metal Grey, Metallic Black, Sea Foam Green, or Black finishes, mfg. 2003-present.

MSR	$3,200		$2,400	$2,100	$1,850	$1,600	$1,400	$1,200	$1,000

Add $75 for highly-figured maple top (Model AG4Q, No. 280-9001). Add $150 for left-handed configuration (No. 280-9100).

AG5 (NO. 280-9002) - similar to the AG4, except in 5-string configuration, 3/2-per-side tuners, mfg. 2003-present.

MSR	$3,300		$2,500	$2,200	$1,900	$1,650	$1,450	$1,250	$1,050

Add $75 for highly-figured maple top (Model AG4Q, No. 280-9002). Add $150 for left-handed configuration (No. 280-9102).

ELECTRIC BASS: CONCERT SERIES

Add $35 for Trans. finishes including Amber Sunburst, Tobacco Sunburst, Blue , Red, Green, Ivory, and Burnt Cherry Sunburst.

C4 P - sleek offset double cutaway poplar body, bolt-on maple neck, 34 in. scale, 24-fret rosewood fingerboard with pearl dot inlay, chrome hardware, JB340 fixed bridge, 2-per-side tuners, 2 Duncan Design J-style pickups, volume/blend/tone controls, available in Black, Deep Candy Blue, or Dark Metallic Red finishes, mfg. 1998-2001.

			$450	$400	$350	$325	$275	$225	$175

Last MSR was $645.

C4 A - similar to the C 4 P, except features 2 Duncan Design SB101 soapbar pickups, Armstrong PAB-20 preamp. Available in Black and Deep Candy Blue finishes, mfg. 1998-2001.

			$550	$475	$425	$375	$325	$275	$225

Last MSR was $795.

C4 J - similar to the C 4 P, except features 2 Duncan Design JB104 Alnico J-style pickups, available in Black, Deep Candy Blue, or Dark Metallic Red finishes, mfg. 1998 only.

			$500	$425	$350	$300	$250	$200	$175

Last MSR was $725.

C5 P - sleek offset double cutaway poplar body, bolt-on maple neck, 34 in. scale, 24-fret rosewood fingerboard with pearl dot inlay, chrome hardware, JB350 fixed bridge, 3/2-per-side tuners, 2 Duncan Design SB101 pickups, volume/blend/tone controls, available in Black, Deep Candy Blue, or Dark Metallic Red finishes, mfg. 1998-2001.

			$525	$450	$400	$350	$300	$250	$200

Last MSR was $745.

C5 A (No. 290-9001) - similar to the C5 P, except features 2 Duncan Design SB101 pickups, Armstrong PAB-20 preamp, available in Black, Dark Metallic Red, or Deep Candy Blue finishes, mfg. 1998-2002.

			$450	$375	$325	$275	$225	$175	$150

Last MSR was $642.

C5MJ (No. 290-9002) - similar to the C5A except has Duncan Design pickups: SB101, JB102N, mfg. 1998-present.

			$450	$375	$325	$275	$225	$175	$150

Last MSR was $642.

C20 (NO. 290-9000) - sleek offset double cutaway poplar body, bolt-on maple neck, 21-fret rosewood fingerboard with pearl dot inlay, chrome hardware, RBB10 fixed bridge, Jackson P/J-style pickups, volume/blend/tone controls, available in Black, Metallic Blue, or Metallic Red finishes, mfg. 1998-present.

MSR	$450		$325	$275	$235	$195	$165	$135	$105

CMG (NO. 290-9003) - Precision style alder body, bolt-on maple neck, 22-fret rosewood fingerboard with triangle inlay, 4-on-one-side tuners, 2 EMGHZ35 pickups, JB340 Convertible bridge, active electronics, five knobs, black hardware, available in Black, Black Forest, or Cobalt Blue finishes, mfg. 2001-present.

MSR	$900		$650	$575	$500	$425	$375	$325	$275

CONCERT EX - offset double cutaway poplar body, bolt-on maple neck, 22-fret rosewood fingerboard with white dot inlay, fixed bridge, 4-on-a-side tuners, black hardware, Jackson P/J-style pickups, volume/tone/mix control, available in Black, Bright Red, Candy Blue, Snow White, or Stone finishes, mfg. 1992-95.

		N/A	$425	$350	$300	$250	$200	$150

Last MSR was $595.

In 1994, Bright Red and Snow White finishes were discontinued.

CONCERT XL - similar to Concert EX, except has bound fingerboard with pearl sharkfin inlay, available in Black Cherry, Deep Metallic Blue, Dark Metallic Red, Metallic Black, or Pearl White finishes, mfg. 1992-95.

		N/A	$550	$475	$425	$375	$325	$275

Last MSR was $895.

In 1994, Pearl White finish was discontinued.

CONCERT V - similar to Concert EX, except has 5 strings, bound fingerboard with sharkfin inlay, Kahler fixed bridge, volume/treble/bass/mix controls, active electronics, available in Black Cherry, Dark Metallic Blue, or Metallic Black finishes, mfg. 1992-95.

		N/A	$600	$525	$450	$400	$350	$300

Last MSR was $995.

GRADING	100% MINT	98% NEAR MINT	95% EXC+	90% EXC	80% VG+	70% VG	60% G

ELECTRIC BASS: FUTURA SERIES

FUTURA EX (WINGER BASS) - double cutaway asymmetrical offset poplar body, bolt-on maple neck, 22-fret rosewood fingerboard with pearl dot inlay, fixed bridge, 4-on-a-side tuners, black hardware, P/J-style Jackson pickups, volume/tone/mix control, available in Black, Deep Metallic Blue, Magenta, or Snow White finishes, mfg. 1992-95.

	N/A	$500	$425	$350	$300	$250	$200

Last MSR was $795.

Add $100 for left-handed version.

The Winger Bass was co-designed in conjunction with Kip Winger.

FUTURA PRO (WINGER BASS) - double cutaway asymmetrical offset maple body, through-body maple neck, 21-fret ebony fingerboard with pearl dot inlay, Kahler fixed bridge, 4-on-a-side tuners, black hardware, 2 EMG pickups, volume/treble/bass/mix control, active electronics, available in Candy Red, Metallic Black, or Pearl White finishes, mfg. 1992-93.

	N/A	$1,300	$1,100	$950	$800	$650	$500

Last MSR was $1,795.

Futura Pro (Trans) - similar to Futura Pro, except has lacewood body/neck and has body color matching bound peghead, available in Carmel Lace, Cinnabar, or Natural finishes, disc. 1993.

	N/A	$1,350	$1,150	$1,000	$850	$700	$550

Last MSR was $1,895.

FUTURA XL - similar to Futura Pro, except has Jackson fixed bridge and P/J-style pickups, available in Dark Metallic Red, Metallic Black, or Pearl White finishes, disc. 1993.

	N/A	$900	$800	$700	$600	$525	$450

Last MSR was $1,295.

Futura XL Trans - similar to Futura Pro (Trans), except has Jackson fixed bridge and P/J-style pickups, available in Trans. finishes, disc. 1993.

$975	$825	$700	$550	$500	$450	$400

Last MSR was $1,395.

Jackson Concert EX
courtesy Jackson

ELECTRIC BASS: MISC. MODELS

EL1 - sleek offset double cutaway basswood body, maple neck, 21-fret rosewood fingerboard, black hardware, fixed bridge, P/J Jackson pickups, volume/blend/tone controls, available in Black, Cobalt Blue, or Red Pearl finishes, mfg. 1996-98.

$625	$550	$475	$425	$375	$325	$295

Last MSR was $745.

Add $50 for transparent finish.

JJ BASS (U.S. MFG.) - dual cutaway poplar body, bolt-on maple neck, 30 in. scale, 19-fret rosewood fingerboard with pearl dot inlay, Hipshot fixed bridge, 2-per-side tuners, chrome hardware, Seymour Duncan Basslines humbucker pickup, volume/3 tone controls, available in Black or Interference Flame finishes, mfg. 1998-2001.

$1,200	$1,050	$900	$775	$650	$550	$425

Last MSR was $1,695.

Add $200 for Interference Flame finish.

JM6 - offset double cutaway poplar body, bolt-on maple neck, 34 in. scale, 21-fret rosewood fingerboard with pearl dot inlay, JB340 fixed bridge, 4-on-a-side tuners, natural finish headstock, chrome hardware, Armstrong MM-1 humbucker pickup, volume/tone controls, available in Black, Retro Green, or Retro Red finishes, mfg. 1998 only.

$425	$375	$325	$295	$250	$195	$150

Last MSR was $595.

JM6 PJ - similar to the JM6, except features Duncan Design P/J-style pickups, available in Black, Retro Green, or Retro Red finishes, mfg. 1998.

$425	$375	$325	$295	$250	$195	$150

Last MSR was $595.

JS-40 - offset double cutaway alder body, bolt-on maple neck, 22-fret rosewood fingerboard with white dot inlay, fixed bridge, 4-on-a-side tuners, black hardware, P/J-style pickups, volume/tone/mix control, available in Black, Metallic Blue, or Metallic Red finishes, mfg. 1997-2001.

$295	$240	$215	$185	$155	$130	$100

Last MSR was $395.

JZB-1 - sleek offset double cutaway alder body, quilted maple top, bolt-on maple neck, 21-fret pau ferro fingerboard, black hardware, fixed bridge, 2 EMG soapbar pickups, volume/blend/tone controls, available in Amber Sunburst, Trans. Black, or Trans. Purple finishes, mfg. 1997-98.

$1,200	$1,000	$900	$795	$675	$550	$425

Last MSR was $1,695.

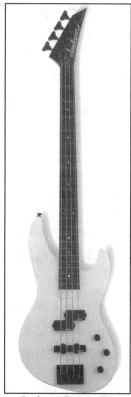

Jackson Futura EX
courtesy Jackson

GRADING	100% MINT	98% NEAR MINT	95% EXC+	90% EXC	80% VG+	70% VG	60% G

JZB-2 - similar to the JZB-1, except features an alder (or ash) body, rosewood fingerboard, cream pickguard, 2 Jackson J-style pickups. Available in Black, Electric Blue, Cherry Sunburst, or Tobacco Sunburst finishes, mfg. 1997-98.

	$975	$825	$725	$625	$525	$425	$325

Last MSR was $1,295.

KB1 KELLY BASS - single sharp cutaway radical hourglass style poplar body, through-body maple neck, 22-fret bound rosewood fingerboard with pearl dot inlay, fixed bridge, 4-on-a-side tuners, black hardware, Jackson P/J pickups, volume/blend/tone controls, available in Black or Cobalt Blue finishes, mfg. 1994-2001.

	$525	$450	$400	$350	$300	$250	$200

Last MSR was $745.

KBX KELLY BASS (NO. 290-9100) - similar to the KB1 Kelly Bass except has alder body, and Duncan Design pickups, available in Black or Deep Candy Blue finishes, mfg. 2002-03.

	$500	$425	$375	$325	$275	$225	$175

Last MSR was $714.

Add $35 for Trans. Red, Trans. Blue, or Wine Red finishes. Add $70 for Eerie Dess Swirl finish.

PS-5 - offset double cutaway alder body, bolt-on maple neck, 22-fret rosewood fingerboard with white dot inlay, fixed bridge, 4-on-a-side tuners, black hardware, Jackson P/J-style pickups, volume/tone/mix control, available in Black, Deep Metallic Blue, Red Violet Metallic, Blue Green Metallic, or Black Cherry finishes, mfg. 1997-99.

	$425	$350	$300	$250	$210	$180	$150

Last MSR was $595.

Add $50 for alder body/flamed maple top in Trans. finish (Trans. Blue, Trans. Green, Trans. Purple, and Trans. Red).

TBX - single cutaway asymmetrical hourglass poplar body, through-body maple neck, 21-fret bound rosewood fingerboard with pearl sharkfin inlay, fixed bridge, bound blackface peghead with screened logo, 4-on-a-side tuners, black hardware, 2 humbucker EMG pickups, 2 volume/tone controls, available in Black, Dark Metallic Violet, or Scarlet Green Metallic finishes, mfg. 1994-95.

	N/A	$1,100	$950	$800	$650	$550	$450

Last MSR was $1,695.

ELECTRIC BASS: CUSTOM SHOP BASSES

The Jackson Custom Shop is currently offering a wide range of body and neck woods, pickup selection, custom wiring, custom or airbrushed finishes, and innovative body designs. Custom guitars take 4 to 12 months for delivery. Contact Jackson Guitars or a local Jackson dealer for a full price quote.

CUSTOM SHOP BASS MODEL (BASE PRICE) - alder (or basswood or poplar) body, quartersawn maple neck, 25.5 in. scale, 22- (or 24) fret maple (or rosewood or ebony) fingerboard with sharkfin or dot inlay, Gotoh tuners, chrome or black hardware, choice of pickups and configuration, available in Solid, Candy color, Metallic, or Pearl finishes, current (specialty) mfg.

The Retail prices on basses are as follows: Bolt-on Bass $2,760, Neck-Thru Bass $3,120. List prices include an SKB case.

JACKSON, DOUGLAS R.

Instruments currently built in Destin, FL. Distributed through the Douglas R. Jackson Guitar Shop of Destin, FL.

Luthier Douglas R. Jackson handcrafts his own acoustic and electric guitars, which are built on commission. On occasion, Jackson may build a model on speculation, but that is not the norm. All models are marketed through his guitar shop.

Jackson attended a guitar building school in the Spring of 1977. While enrolled, he was hired by the school to teach and perform repairs. Jackson taught two classes in the 1977 school year, and helped build over 150 instruments (plus his own personal guitars and repairs). Jackson then went to work for a vintage guitar dealer on and off for three years, while he studied just about anything he could get his hands on. During this research phase, Jackson continued to build three or four guitars a year (in addition to his shop repairs).

In 1986, Jackson moved from Arizona to his present location in Destin, Florida (the Pensacola/Fort Walton Beach area). Jackson currently owns and operates a 1,500 square foot building that houses his guitar shop and manufacturing equipment, (Biography courtesy Douglas R. Jackson).

Jackson estimates that he has built close to 150 instruments consisting of acoustic and electric 6- and 12-string guitars, electric basses and mandolins, resonator guitars, ukuleles, and dulcimers.

ELECTRIC

Jackson´s electric models start at $1,000 for a set neck or neck-through style, and go up depending on choice of woods, electronics, and the hardware selected. Jackson estimates that the prices of his used electrics range from $600 and up. Jackson supplies a hard shell case for all of his handcrafted instruments. Further information regarding specifications and pricing, please contact Douglas R. Jackson directly (see Trademark Index).

JAGARD

Instruments currently built in Japan, Taiwan, and China by the Eikosha Musical Instrument Co., Inc. Previously distributed in the U.S. by V. J. Rendano, located in Boardman, OH.

Jagard electric guitars feature solid ash and solid maple bodies.

JAGGER

Instruments currently produced in Korea. Distributed by Sangjin Industrial Co. Ltd.

Jagger has released a series of guitars that look like Stratocasters and are described as "...the birth of dirty metal," whatever that is supposed to mean. They are available with metal pickguards in copper, silver, or gold colors, hard tail or tremolo bridges, and single coil or humbucking pickups. These guitars were designed by Q-Parts for Sangjin Industrial Co. Ltd.

GRADING	100% MINT	98% NEAR MINT	95% EXC+	90% EXC	80% VG+	70% VG	60% G

JAMBOREE

Instruments previously produced in Japan.

The Jamboree trademark was a brand name used by U.S. importers Elger/Hoshino of Ardmore, Pennsylvania. Jamboree, along with others like Goldentone, King's Stone, and Elger were all used on Japanese guitars imported to the U.S. Elger/Hoshino evolved into Hoshino USA, the distributor of Ibanez guitars (source: Michael Wright, *Guitar Stories*, Volume One).

JAMMER

Instruments currently produced in Asia. Distributed by VMI Industries (Vega Musical Instruments) of Brea, CA.

Jammer instruments are designed with the entry level and student guitarist in mind.

JANSEN

Instruments previously produced in Auckland, New Zealand from the 1960s through the 1970s.

Jansen guitars and amplifiers were manufactured by Beverly Bruce and Goldy Ltd., who continued to produce amplifiers and P.A. gear through the late 1980s. During the 1960s and 1970s, Jansen guitars were the most popular brand in New Zealand. One notable U.S. example of Jansen guitars was the Jazzman model that was used by the Surfaris.

Jansen guitars were basically Fender-style copies. The Invader model was based on the Stratocaster, while the Beatmaster and Jazzman were based on the Telecaster and Jaguar, respectively. Jansen basses also played "follow the leader," with the Rock Bass and Beat Bass models emulating the Precision and Telecaster basses. Further market surveys will review playability and production quality. Rarity and lack of activity in the secondary marketplace precludes accurate pricing on this model.

JAROCK

Instruments previously built in Japan during the early 1980s.

These guitars are medium quality Stratocaster-styled solid body guitars (source: Tony Bacon and Paul Day, *The Guru's Guitar Guide*).

JAROS CUSTOM GUITARS

Instruments currently built in Rochester, Pennsylvania since 1995. Distribution is handled directly at Jaros Custom Guitars, Guitar Land in San Clemente, and Doc's Vintage Guitars in West Los Angeles, CA.

Combining years of cabinetmaking and guitar playing, Harry Jaros and his son James decided to build a couple of guitars as a father-and-son project. When the beautifully crafted original models turned out to have great tone and playability, the family hobby quickly became a business venture as they decided to produce more of these handcrafted instruments and make them available for everyone to enjoy!

From coast to coast, Jaros has a pair of guitar players currently endorsing his custom guitars: Jon Butcher, and Bruce Gatewood.

DR Jackson Curly Purple Heart courtesy Douglas R. Jackson

ELECTRIC

Jaros handcrafted guitars feature a 12" neck radius. Both models are available in a semi-hollow (internal tone chambers) and solid body configurations. Other options include a 24-fret fingerboard; choice of tiger, quilt or bird's-eye maple; translucent lacquer colors; and distinct custom abalone and mother-of-pearl inlay. There are no price up charges for left-handed models.

CUSTOM 22 CARVED TOP - slightly offset double cutaway mahogany body, bookmatched AAA figured maple carved top, figured maple back, through-body eastern hard rock maple or mahogany neck, 25" scale, 22-fret rosewood (or ebony or paduak) fretboard with original design inlays, chrome or gold hardware, 3-per-side Schaller tuners, two Seymour Duncan humbucker pickups, volume/tone controls (push/pull pots wired for coil tapping), 3-way selector switch, available in Clear or Sunburst nitrocellulose finishes, mfg. 1996-present.

    MSR $2,799

    List price includes hardshell case.

CUSTOM 22 FLATTOP - similar to the Custom 22 Carve Top, except has flat bookmatched AAA figured maple top, mfg. 1995-present.

    MSR $2,799

ACOUSTIC/ELECTRIC HYBRID GUITAR - sound chambered carved inside, stereo or mono operation, bookmatched AAA flamed maple top and back, mahogany neck-through body, custom made LR Baggs saddles, Seymour Duncan pickups, available in Natural finish, current mfg.

JAX

Instruments previously produced in Taiwan during the early 1980s.

These solid body guitars consist of entry level designs based on classic American models (source: Tony Bacon and Paul Day, *The Guru's Guitar Guide*).

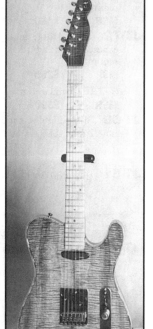

DR Jackson Custom Electric courtesy Douglas R. Jackson

GRADING	100% MINT	98% NEAR MINT	95% EXC+	90% EXC	80% VG+	70% VG	60% G

JAY DEE

Instruments currently built in Birmingham, England since 1977.

The Jay Dee trademark sometimes appears as JD on the headstock of these high quality original design guitars. Luthier John Diggins has been quite successful in building a quality instrument through the years, and has produced some models based on classic American designs as well.

Jay Dee **Supernatural** basses were distributed in the U.S. for a length of time by Aspen & Associates starting in 1985. Aspen & Associates are the non-tube side of Aspen Pittman´s Groove Tubes company (source: Tony Bacon and Paul Day, *The Guru's Guitar Guide*).

Jay Dee has also had endorsees such as Geezer Butler and Tony Iommi from Black Sabbath and Angus Young. Jay Dee features both electric guitars and basses. For more information and availability, refer to their website (see Trademark Index).

JAY G

See chapter on House Brands.

This trademark has been identified as a sub-brand from the budget line of Chris guitars by the Jackson-Guldan company of Columbus, Ohio (source: Willie G. Moseley, *Stellas & Stratocasters*).

JAY TURSER

Instruments currently produced in Asia. Distributed by Music Industries Corporation of Floral Park, NY.

Music Industries is currently offering a wide range of Jay Turser solid body electric instruments. These instruments are student and entry level instruments with fairly good quality necks and electronics, and are offered in a good number of finishes.

Jay Turser models are offered in the following colors: Antique (ANS), Black (BK), Blue Sparkle (BLSP), Cherry Sunburst (CS), Matt Green (MG), Natural Honey (NH), Purple Sunburst (PS), Red Sunburst (RS), Red Sparkle (RSP), Silver Sparkle (SSP), Transparent Black (TB), Transparent Blue (TBL), Transparent Moss Green (TMG), Transparent Red (TR), Tobacco Sunburst (TS), and Violin Shade (VS) finishes.

ELECTRIC: MODELS JT 10 - JT-81

JT-10L - 1/2 size LP-style solid body, mahogany neck, rosewood fingerboard, 3-per-side tuners, 2 humbucker pickups, 2 volume/2 tone controls, available in Black, Purple Sunburst, Trans. Blue, Trans. Red, or Tobacco Sunburst finishes, disc.

		$135	$110	$95	$85	$65	$50	$35

Last MSR was $179.

JT-30 - 1/2 size Strat-style solid body, maple neck, rosewood fingerboard, 6-on-a-side tuners, 3 single coil pickups, volume/tone controls, 5-way switch, available in Natural Honey, Trans. Black, Trans. Blue, or Trans. Red finishes, current mfg.

MSR	$180	$135	$110	$95	$85	$65	$50	$35

JT-50 - double cutaway solid body similar to SG design, maple set neck, rosewood fingerboard, dot position markers, 3-per-side tuners, 2 humbucker pickups, 2 Volume/2-Tone controls, black pickguard, chrome hardware, stop tailpiece, available in Black, Walnut, or Trans. Red finish, current mfg.

MSR	$340	$260	$190	$170	$150	$130	$110	$90

JT-50 Custom - similar to JT-50 except has gold plated tuners and gold hardware, available in Black, Ivory, Trans. Red, or Purple Sunburst, current mfg.

MSR	$400	$300	$225	$200	$175	$150	$125	$100

JT-72 - offset double cutaway ash body, flame maple top, 22-fret maple neck, rosewood fingerboard with dot position markers, 3-per-side tuners, 2 exposed coil humbucker pickups, 3-way switch, tremolo tailpiece, available in Trans. Red, Trans. Blue, Trans. Black, or American Flag finishes, current mfg.

MSR	$360	$275	$210	$180	$150	$130	$110	$90

JT-72F - similar to the JT-72, except has a flamed maple top, available in Natural or Trans. Red finishes, new 2004.

MSR	$390	$295	$250	$210	$180	$150	$120	$90

JT-80 - offset double cutaway Rick-style solid body, maple set neck, rosewood fingerboard, 3-per-side die-cast tuners, 3 chrome covered pickups, 2 volume/2 tone controls, mid pickup control, available in Black or Red Sunburst finishes, disc. 1999.

		$330	$225	$200	$175	$150	$100	$75

Last MSR was $439.

JT-81 - similar to the JT-80, except features double cutaway hollowbody, available in Black or Red Sunburst finishes, disc. 1999.

		$340	$230	$200	$175	$150	$100	$75

Last MSR was $459.

ELECTRIC: MODELS JT 134 - JT-142

JT-134 - single cutaway semi-hollow body, contoured top, 22-fret mahogany neck with rosewood fingerboard, dot position markers, 3-per-side tuners, 2 humbucking pickups, Tune-O-Matic bridge, 2 Volume/2-Tone controls, 3-way switch, die-cast tuners, trapeze tailpiece, f-holes, black pickguard, available in Antique Sunburst, Natural, or Black finishes, current mfg.

MSR	$430	$335	$275	$225	$190	$160	$130	$100

Left-handed version available in Tobacco Sunburst finish.

JT-134 Vine - similar to the JT-134 except has an abalone & MOP vine inlay and gold hardware, mfg 2002-present.

MSR	$600	$430	$375	$325	$295	$250	$195	$150

JT-134DC - similar to JT-134 except, in a double cutaway version, flame maple top, available in Antique Sunburst, Cherry Sunburst, or Blue finishes, mfg. 2001-present.

MSR	$480	$350	$300	$250	$195	$175	$150	$125

Left-handed version available in Tobacco Sunburst finish.

GRADING	100% MINT	98% NEAR MINT	95% EXC+	90% EXC	80% VG+	70% VG	60% G

JT-134DC Vine - similar to the JT-134DC except, has abalone and mother-of-pearl vine inlay the full length of the fingerboard, available in Antique Sunburst, Black, Trans. Blue, or Cherry Sunburst finishes, mfg. 2001-present.

MSR	$600	$430	$375	$325	$295	$250	$195	$150

JT-135 - dual cutaway semi-hollowbody, arched top, maple set neck, rosewood fingerboard, 3-per-side die-cast tuners, Tune-O-Matic bridge/stop tailpiece, 2 covered humbucker pickups, raised black pickguard, 2 volume/2 tone controls, 3-way toggle switch, available in Cherry Sunburst, Natural Honey, Trans. Red, or Tobacco Sunburst finishes, current mfg.

MSR	$410		$305	$210	$185	$165	$140	$105	$80

Left-handed version available in Tobacco Sunburst finish.

JT-135D - similar to the JT-135, except features an arched flame maple top, available in Natural Honey or Antique Sunburst finishes, current mfg.

MSR	$440		$330	$225	$200	$180	$150	$100	$75

JT-136 - (3" body depth) single cutaway semi-hollowbody, arched top, maple set neck, rosewood fingerboard, 3-per-side Kluson tuners, Tune-O-Matic bridge/stop tailpiece, raised black pickguard, 2 covered humbucker pickups, 2 volume/2 tone controls, 3-way toggle switch, available in Antique Sunburst, Black, Natural Honey, Tobacco Sunburst, Cherry Sunburst, Trans. Red, or Violin Shade finishes, current mfg.

MSR	$450		$350	$275	$225	$185	$155	$125	$100

Left-handed version available in Tobacco Sunburst finish.

JT-136 Vine - similar to the JT-136 except has vine fingerboard inlay, available in Black, Cherry Sunburst or Tobacco Sunburst finishes, mfg. 2001-present.

MSR	$650		$470	$410	$350	$300	$250	$200	$150

JT-137 - semi-acoustic, thin line body with flame maple top, hard maple neck, rosewood fingerboard, 2 covered pickups, 2 volume/1 tone control, adjustable bridge, gold die-cast tuners, available in Black, Tobacco Sunburst, or Natural finishes, current mfg.

MSR	$530		$385	$325	$275	$225	$175	$150	$105

JT-140 COLONEL - single cutaway hollowbody, arched ash top, maple set neck, rosewood fingerboard with pearl block/abalone inlays, 3-per-side tuners, classic jazz-style tremolo, f-holes, 2 humbucker pickups, 2 volume/2 tone controls, 3-way switch, gold hardware, black pickguard, available in White or Black finishes, current mfg.

MSR	$730		$565	$475	$400	$325	$300	$275	$225

JT-141 MONTERREY - single cutaway hollowbody, arched top, maple set neck, rosewood fingerboard with pearl block/abalone inlays, 3-per-side tuners, f-holes, 1 humbucker pickup, 1 volume/1 tone control, trapeze tailpiece, gold hardware, black pickguard, available in Trans. Red, Cherry Sunburst, or Tobacco Sunburst finishes, current mfg.

MSR	$630		$490	$400	$325	$275	$250	$225	$175

JT-142 - double cutaway hollow body, arched top, set maple neck, rosewood fingerboard with block and triangle inlay, 2 humbucking pickups, gold hardware, trapeze tailpiece, raised pickguard, four knobs, 3-way switch, gold hardware, available in Trans. Blue, Trans. Black, Trans. Red, or Tobacco Sunburst finishes, mfg. 2002-present.

MSR	$80		$450	$375	$300	$250	$225	$200	$150

Jay Turser JT-30 courtesy Jay Turser

ELECTRIC: MODELS JT 200 - JT-270

JT-200C - single cutaway solid body, contoured top, mahogany set neck, rosewood fingerboard, 3-per-side covered tuners, Tune-O-Matic bridge/stop tailpiece, raised black pickguard, 2 covered humbucker pickups, 2 volume/2 tone controls, 3-way toggle switch, available in Black, Purple Sunburst, Red Sunburst or Gold Metallic (JT-200GT) finishes, current mfg.

MSR	$350		$270	$210	$175	$150	$125	$100	$75

Left-handed version available in Black finish.

JT-200D - similar to the JT-200, except has a flame maple top, available in Red Sunburst, Trans. Red, or Tobacco Sunburst finishes, current mfg.

MSR	$480		$375	$300	$225	$185	$160	$135	$110

JT-200DLX - similar to the JT-200, except has block fingerboard inlays, gold hardware, and available in Natural finish, new 2004.

MSR	$525		$385	$325	$275	$225	$175	$140	$105

JT-200 PRO - double cutaway lightweight solid body, contoured flame maple top, 22-fret hard maple set neck, rosewood fingerboard with dot position markers, 3-per-side tuners, 2 humbucker pickups, adjustable bridge, 2 volume/2 tone controls, 3-way switch, gold die-cast tuners, stop tailpiece, white pickguard, available in Red Sunburst, Purple Sunburst, Trans. Red, or Trans. Black finishes, current mfg.

MSR	$390		$300	$235	$200	$175	$150	$125	$100

JT-200 DRAGON - single cutaway solid body with contoured flame maple top, 22-fret mahogany set neck, rosewood fingerboard, 3-per-side tuners, abalone and mother-of-pearl Dragon inlay full length of fingerboard, 2 humbucker pickups, adjustable bridge, 2 volume/2 tone controls, 3-way switch, die-cast tuners, gold hardware, black pickguard, available in Antique Sunburst or Red Sunburst finishes, disc. 2000.

		$525	$475	$450	$400	$375	$350	$300

Last MSR was $699.

Jay Turser JT-200 D courtesy Jay Turser

GRADING		100% MINT	98% NEAR MINT	95% EXC+	90% EXC	80% VG+	70% VG	60% G

JT-200 SERPENT - similar to JT-200 Dragon, solid body with flame maple top, 22-fret mahogany set neck, rosewood fingerboard, 2 humbucker pickups, adjustable bridge, 2 volume/2 tone controls, 3-way switch, die-cast tuners, gold hardware, abalone and mother-of-pearl serpent inlay full length of fingerboard, available in Trans. Red, Trans. Black, Tobacco Sunburst, Trans. Moss Green, Purple Sunburst, Red Sunburst and Antique Sunburst finishes, mfg. 2001-present.

MSR	$700	$540	$475	$400	$325	$275	$225	$175

JT-200 VINEQMT - similar to the JT-200 except has a quilted maple top and abalone & MOP vine inlay, available in Black, Purple Sunburst, or Tobacco Sunburst finishes, mfg. 2002-present.

MSR	$700	$540	$475	$400	$325	$275	$225	$175

JT-230 - offset double cutaway body, set neck, maple fingerboard with offset black inlays, 2 exposed humbucker pickups, STB, Tune-O-Matic bridge, 3-per-side tuners, 2 knobs, 5-way switch, available in Metallic finishes, new 2004.

MSR	$325	$245	$205	$170	$145	$125	$95	$75

JT-250 - offset double cutaway solid ash body, contoured top, maple set neck, rosewood fingerboard, 3-per-side die-cast tuners, 2 point tremolo, 2 humbucker pickups, volume/tone controls, 3-way toggle switch, available in Purple Sunburst, Red Sunburst, Trans. Blue, or Trans. Red finishes, disc. 1999.

		$365	$275	$250	$225	$200	$175	$125

Last MSR was $489.

JT-250G - similar to Model JT-250 except has gold plated tuners and gold plated hardware, available in Black or Trans. White finishes, disc. 2000.

		$390	$290	$265	$245	$215	$190	$150

Last MSR was $519.

JT-270 - double cutaway thinline, solid body with f-holes, set maple neck, 24-fret rosewood fingerboard with dot inlays, 2 humbucker pickups, all-in-one bridge, chrome hardware, two knobs, 3-way switch, available in Black or Natural finishes, mfg. 2002-present.

MSR	$430	$330	$275	$240	$205	$175	$150	$125

JT-270F - similar to the JT-270 except has a flame maple top, available in Black, Natural Honey, Trans. Blue, or Trans. Red, mfg. 2002-present.

MSR	$450	$345	$295	$250	$215	$180	$155	$125

JT-280 - offset double cutaway Mosrite style body, set-neck, 2 P-90 style pickups, vibrato tailpiece, available in Triple Tobacco Sunburst or Vintage Creamy White finishe, new 2004.

MSR	$500	$375	$325	$275	$235	$195	$165	$135

ELECTRIC: MODELS JT 300 - JT-1000

JT-300 - offset double cutaway solid body, maple set neck, rosewood fingerboard, 6-on-a-side covered tuners, standard tremolo, white pickguard, 3 single coil pickups, volume/2 tone controls, 5-way toggle switch, available in Black, Natural Honey, Purple Sunburst, Trans. Black, Trans. Blue, Trans. Moss Green, Trans. Red, or Tobacco Sunburst finishes, current mfg.

MSR	$250	$190	$150	$125	$100	$75	$65	$50

JT-300M - similar to the JT-300 except has a one piece maple neck, available in Black, Natural Honey, Vintage Creamy White, or Two-Tone Sunburst, mfg. 2002-present.

MSR	$270	$205	$165	$135	$110	$85	$70	$55

JT-300PAK - similar to the JT-300 except has a built in 6 Watt practice amp, available in Black, Trans. Blue, Trans. Red, or Tobacco Sunburst, mfg. 2002-present.

MSR	$325	$245	$205	$170	$145	$125	$95	$75

JT-300QMT - similar to JT-300 except, has quilted maple top, pearloid pickguard, gold hardware, available in Trans. Black, Purple Sunburst, Trans. Blue, Trans. Moss Green, Trans. Red, Natural Honey, or Tocbacco Sunburst finishes, mfg. 2001-03.

		$225	$175	$150	$125	$105	$75	$60

Last MSR was $300.

JT-300Vine - similar to the JT-300 except has an abalone & MOP vine inlay, available in Purple Sunburst, Trans. Black, Trans. Blue, Trans. Red, or Tobacco Sunburst, mfg. 2002-present.

MSR	$330	$250	$210	$180	$150	$125	$100	$75

JT-301 - similar to the JT-300, except features a solid light ash body, white pearloid pickguard, available in Black finish, disc. 1999.

		$210	$160	$135	$110	$85	$75	$60

Last MSR was $279.

JT-301QMT - similar to the JT-301 except has a flamed maple top and gold hardware, available in Trans. Black, Trans. Blue, Trans. Red, or Tobacco Sunburst finishes, mfg. 2002-03.

		$225	$190	$150	$125	$100	$75	$60

Last MSR was $300.

JT-301MQMT - similar to the JT-301QMT except has a one piece maple neck, available in Natural, Trans. Blue, or Trans. Red, finishes, mfg. 2002-03.

		$255	$215	$175	$150	$125	$95	$75

Last MSR was $340.

JT-302 - similar to the JT-300, except features a solid ash body, maple fingerboard, white pearloid pickguard, available in Natural Honey, Trans. Blue, or Trans. Red finishes, disc. 2000.

		$250	$190	$165	$150	$125	$100	$75

Last MSR was $329.

JT-700 7-STRING - 7-string, offset double cutaway solid body, maple neck, rosewood fingerboard with dot position markers, 7-on-a-side tuners, two exposed coil humbucking pickups, 1 Volume/1 Tone control, 3-way switch, fixed tailpiece, disc. 2003.

		$225	$190	$175	$150	$125	$95	$65

Last MSR was $300.

GRADING	100% MINT	98% NEAR MINT	95% EXC+	90% EXC	80% VG+	70% VG	60% G

JT-1000 - double cutaway ash body, maple neck-thru body, rosewood fingerboard, 2 humbuckers, Floyd Rose tremolo, two knobs, available in Natural or Burgandy finishes, mfg. 2002-present.

MSR	$560	$435	$360	$300	$260	$225	$195	$150

ELECTRIC: MODELS JT MISC.

JT-BLUES - sculpted double cutaway solid body, 22-fret bolt-on maple neck, rosewood fingerboard with dot position markers, adjustable nut, 2 humbucking pickups, 1 volume/1 tone control, 3-way switch, chrome hardware, die-cast 6-on-a-side tuners, reverse headstock, white pearloid pickguard, available in Natural, Trans. Red, or Trans. Black finishes, disc. 2002.

		$235	$175	$150	$125	$100	$75	$50

Last MSR was $309.

JT-BRANSON - same body style as JT-Blues, has two single coil Phantom pickups, available in Natural, Trans. Red or Trans. Black finishes, disc. 2002.

		$225	$160	$140	$115	$90	$60	$40

Last MSR was $299.

JT-CALIFORNIA - same body style as JT-Branson and JT-Blues, has 3 single coil Phantom pickups, available in Natural, Trans. Red, or Trans. Black finishes, disc. 2002.

		$240	$180	$160	$135	$110	$95	$60

Last MSR was $319.

JT-HAWK - offset double cutaway solid body, maple neck, rosewood fingerboard, 3-per-side die-cast tuners, fixed bridge, white pearloid pickguard, 2 humbucker pickups, volume/tone controls, 3-way toggle switch, available in Blue Sparkle, Red Sparkle, Silver Sparkle, or Trans. Blue finishes, disc. 2000.

		$210	$160	$145	$130	$115	$90	$65

Last MSR was $279.

JT-Hawk BB - similar to JT-Hawk except has 3 humbucker pickups, 1 volume/1 tone, 3-way switch, pearloid pickguard, classic jazz-style tailpiece with tremolo, disc. 2000.

		$279	$200	$175	$150	$125	$100	$75

Last MSR was $399.

Jay Turser JT-200 Serpent courtesy Jay Turser

JT-Hawk/12 - similar to the JT-Hawk except in 12-string configuration, available in Trans. Red or Black finishes, mfg. 2002-present.

MSR	$410	$320	$250	$210	$180	$150	$125	$95

JT-RES - single cutaway acoustic/electric solid poplar body, resonator, hard maple neck, rosewood fingerboard with dot position markers, 1 piezo and 1 covered pickup, 1 volume/2 tone controls, chrome die-cast tuners, 3-per-side tuners, available in See-Thru Red or Antique Natural Sunburst finishes, current mfg.

MSR	$400	$305	$225	$175	$150	$125	$100	$75

JT-900RES - acoustic resonated guitar, 1 lipstick pickup, die-cast tuners, 1 volume/1 tone control and mixing control, available in Cherry Sunburst, See-Thru Black, or Tobacco Sunburst finishes, mfg. 2001-2003.

		$280	$215	$185	$165	$140	$105	$75

Last MSR was $370.

JT-SHARK - solid body instrument with body shaped like a shark, tailfin headstock, 3-per-side tuners, 1 humbucker pickup and 2 single coil pickups, tremolo bridge, 5-way switch, two knobs, chrome hardware, current mfg.

MSR	$500	$375	$325	$285	$250	$225	$195	$150

JT-LT - classic single cutaway lightweight solid body design, rosewood fingerboard with dot position markers, 6-on-a-side die-cast tuners, 2 pickups, 3-way switch, white pickguard, available in Black or Ivory finishes, mfg. 2001-present.

MSR	$200	$150	$125	$110	$95	$75	$60	$40

JT-LT Custom - similar to Model JT-LT except, has maple fingerboard, gold hardware, pearloid pickguard, available in Antique Sunburst or See-Thru Red finishes, mfg. 2001-present.

MSR	$250	$190	$150	$125	$105	$85	$65	$45

JT-SOLOSLIM - offset double cutaway thinline ash body, 24-fret maple neck with rosewood fingerboard, dot position markers, 2 humbucker and 1 single coil pickup, floating tremolo, 1 volume/1 tone control, 5-way switch, die-cast tuners, 6-on-a-side tuners, chrome hardware, available in Natural finish, disc. 2000.

		$325	$240	$210	$180	$155	$125	$95

Last MSR was $429.

JT-HORN - offset double cutaway solid body, 24-fret maple neck, rosewood fingerboard with dot position markers, 1 humbucker and 1 single coil pickup, tremolo, 1 volume/1 tone control, 3-way switch, 6-on-a-side die-cast tuners, chrome hardware, available in Metallic Red or Metallic Blue finishes, disc. 2002.

		$230	$195	$175	$150	$125	$95	$65

Last MSR was $329.

JT-SLIMMER - offset double cutaway solid ash body, thin-line design, 22-fret maple neck with rosewood fingerboard, oval position markers, 2 humbuckers and 1 single coil pickup, floating tremolo, 1 volume/1 tone control, 5-way switch, die-cast tuners, available in Trans. Red, Purple Sunburst, or Trans. Moss Green finishes, disc. 2002.

		$250	$225	$195	$175	$150	$125	$95

Last MSR was $359.

Jay Turser JT-Hawk/12 courtesy Jay Turser

GRADING	100% MINT	98% NEAR MINT	95% EXC+	90% EXC	80% VG+	70% VG	60% G

JT-SG - dual cutaway solid body, maple set neck, rosewood fingerboard, 3-per-side die-cast tuners, Tune-O-Matic bridge/stop tailpiece, black pickguard, 2 covered humbucker pickups, 2 volume/2 tone controls, 3-way toggle switch, available in Trans. Red finish, disc. 1999.

		$250	$200	$175	$150	$125	$100	$75

Last MSR was $339.

JT-SPECTRE - radical offset sweeping solid body design, reverse headstock, 6-on-a-side tuners, 25.5 in. scale, rosewood fingerboard with scallop position markers, 1 humbucker pickup and 2 single coil pickups, 1 volume/1 tone control, 5-way switch, precision vibrato bridge, adjustable nut, available in Metallic Red, Metallic Black, or Metallic Silver finishes, disc. 2002.

		$349	$299	$275	$250	$225	$195	$150

Last MSR was $500.

JT-SPIRITE - radical teardrop shaped solid body, reverse headstock, 6-on-a-side tuners, 25.5 in. scale, rosewood fingerboard with dot position markers, 1 humbucker pickup and 2 single coil pickups, 1 volume/1 tone control, 5-way switch, precision vibrato, adjustable nut, available in Fl. Yellow, Fl, Red, or Fl. Blue finishes, disc. 2002.

		$335	$295	$250	$225	$195	$175	$135

Last MSR was $480.

JT-STILETTE - double cutaway sheet aluminum body, reverse headstock, 6-on-a-side tuners, 25.5 in. scale, rosewood fingerboard with scallop position markers, 1 humbucker pickup and 2 single coil pickups, 1 volume/1 tone control, 5-way switch, precision vibrato, adjustable nut, available in Aluminum/Black finish, disc. 2002.

		$419	$350	$295	$250	$225	$195	$150

Last MSR was $600.

ELECTRIC BASS

JTB-2B - violin-shaped semi-hollow body, maple set neck, rosewood fingerboard, 2-per-side die-cast tuners, chrome hardware, white pearloid pickguard, 2 chrome covered humbucker pickup, 2 volume controls, 3 tone slide switches, available in Violin Shade finish, current mfg.

MSR	$410		$310	$230	$200	$175	$150	$125	$100

Add $50 for Natural finish (Model JTB-2B/N).

Also available in left-handed configuration.

JTB-2B/GBK - similar to the JTB-2B except has gold hardware, available in Black finish, mfg. 2002-present.

MSR	$430		$335	$260	$220	$190	$160	$135	$105

JTB-40 - 1/2 size P-style solid body, maple neck, rosewood fingerboard, 4-on-a-side tuners, P-style split pickup, volume/tone controls, available in Trans. Black, Trans. Blue, or Trans. Red finishes, current mfg.

MSR	$240		$180	$135	$120	$105	$90	$75	$60

JTB-134 - double offset hollow body, f-holes, 2 humbucker pickups, 4 knobs, chrome hardware, available in Tobacco Sunburst finish, new 2004.

MSR	$450		$345	$295	$250	$215	$180	$155	$125

Add $35 for active electronics (Model JTB-600A).

JTB-400C - offset double cutaway solid body, maple neck, rosewood fingerboard, 4-on-a-side tuners, chrome hardware, P-style split pickup, volume/tone controls, available in Antique, Black, Trans. Moss Green, Natural Honey, Trans. Black, Trans. Red, Trans. Blue, or Tobacco Sunburst finishes, disc. 2003.

		$225	$170	$150	$130	$110	$90	$70

Last MSR was $300.

JTB-400QMT - similar to Model JTB-400 except, has quilted maple top, pearloid pickguard and gold hardware, available in Natural Honey, Tobacco Sunburst, Trans. Black, Trans. Red, or Trans. Blue finishes, mfg. 2001-present.

MSR	$350		$245	$195	$175	$150	$125	$95	$65

JTB-401 - P-style bass, pickguard like the early 50s P-basses, maple fingerboard, single humbucker, two knobs, chrome hardware, available in Vintage Creamy White, Vintage Sunburst, or Black finishes, new 2004.

MSR	$260		$195	$150	$125	$105	$85	$65	$45

JTB-402 - J-style bass, rosewood fingerboard, 2 J-style pickups, three knobs, chrome hardware, available in Tobacco Sunburst or Black finishes, new 2004.

MSR	$275		$205	$160	$135	$110	$90	$70	$50

JTB-440 - similar to the JTB-400, except has a exposed pole piece humbucking pickup, round white pickguard, volume/2 tone controls, chrome 1/2-moon controls plate, available in Purple Sunburst, Trans. Black, Trans. Blue, or Trans. Red finishes, disc. 2003.

		$235	$195	$160	$140	$120	$100	$80

Last MSR was $320.

JTB-440D - similar to the JTB-440 except has a mirror like pickguard, available in Cherry Sunburst, Natural, or Purple Sunburst finishes, mfg. 2002-03.

		$310	$245	$195	$175	$150	$125	$100

Last MSR was $410.

JTB-445 - similar to the JTB-440, except in a 5-string configuration, maple neck, rosewood fingerboard, open back tuners, humbucker pickup, 1 volume/2 tone controls, available in Purple Sunburst, Trans. Blue, Trans. Red, Natural Honey, or Black finishes, current mfg.

MSR	$400		$310	$245	$200	$175	$150	$125	$100

JTB-500 - offset double cutaway solid body, maple neck, rosewood fingerboard, 2-per-side tuners, black hardware, P/J-style pickup, 2 volume/tone controls, available in Trans. Black, Trans. Blue, or Trans. Red finishes, current mfg.

MSR	$310		$245	$190	$160	$140	$120	$100	$80

JTB-500QMT - similar to the JTB-500, except has a quilted maple top, available in Natural Honey, Trans. Blue, or Trans. Red finishes, mfg. 2002-03.

		$265	$215	$180	$155	$130	$110	$85

Last MSR was $350.

GRADING	100% MINT	98% NEAR MINT	95% EXC+	90% EXC	80% VG+	70% VG	60% G

JTB-550 - similar to the JTB-500, except has a 5-string configuration, 3/2-per-side tuners, available in Natural, Trans. Black, Trans. Blue, or Trans. Red finishes, current mfg.

MSR	$330	$260	$205	$170	$150	$130	$110	$90

JTB-500QMT - similar to the JTB-550, except has a quilted maple top, available in Natural Honey, Trans. Black, Trans. Blue, or Trans. Red finishes, mfg. 2002-03.

		$295	$235	$185	$155	$130	$110	$85

Last MSR was $390.

JTB-600 - double offset curved body, flame maple top, basswood body, 24-fret fingerboard with dot inlay, 2 pickups, 4 knobs, gold hardware, available in Cherry Sunburst, Green Sunburst, Purple Sunburst, or Natural finishes, new 2004.

MSR	$450	$345	$295	$250	$215	$180	$155	$125

Add $35 for active electronics (Model JTB-600A).

JTB-900 - offset double cutaway solid ash body, maple neck, rosewood fingerboard, 2-per-side tuners, matte chrome hardware, P/J-style pickup, 2 volume/tone controls, available in Natural Honey, Trans. Blue, or Trans. Red finishes, disc. 2000.

		$300	$225	$200	$175	$150	$125	$100

Last MSR was $399.

JTB-1004 - offset double sharp cutaway ash body, maple neck-thru body, 24-fret rosewood fingerboard with dot inlay, 2 pickups, active electronics, five knobs, available in Mahogany, Natural, or Trans. Red finishes, mfg. 2002-03.

		$495	$425	$375	$325	$275	$225	$175

Last MSR was $660.

JTB-HAWK - double cutaway, maple neck, 21-fret rosewood fingerboard with oval inlays, white pickguard, 2-per-side tuners, single humbucker pickup, two knobs, chrome hardware, available in Purple Sunburst, Trans. Blue, Black, or Trans. Red, mfg. 2002-present.

MSR	$340	$255	$215	$180	$155	$130	$110	$85

JTB-WB - Warwick-style offset double cutaway solid ash body, maple neck, rosewood fingerboard, 2-per-side tuners, matte chrome hardware, 2 J-style pickup, 2 volume/tone controls, available in Natural Honey or Matte Green finishes, disc. 1999.

		$260	$200	$175	$150	$125	$110	$90

Last MSR was $349.

JT-SCARABE - radical sweeping offset body design similar to the Spectre guitar, reverse headstock, 4 on 1 side tuners, rosewood fingerboard with scallop position markers, 34 in. scale, 1-twin coil pickup, 1 volume/1 tone control, available in Metallic Black, Metallic Red, or Metallic Silver finishes, disc. 2002.

		$375	$325	$275	$250	$225	$195	$150

Last MSR was $529.

**Jay Turser JTB-500
courtesy Jay Turser**

JAYXZ

Instruments currently built in Lakeland, FL.

Jeffrey David Patterson was born January 9, 1956 in Lakeland, Florida, where he still manages to survive to this day with the help and understanding of his wife, Mary, and sons, Colin and Kyle (as well as Mom, Dad, brothers, friends, and so on, and so on). Patterson's life was typical of a young boy growing up in central Florida: hanging around orange groves, the Cuban Missile Crisis - and that one fateful Sunday night when the Beatles played on the Ed Sullivan show. Like so many other kids that night, Patterson turned to his parents and said, "I wanna guitar for Christmas!" It took a great deal of convincing, but he did get a guitar for Christmas. The first guitar made the most beautiful necklace that any boy could want, but it was not much of a guitar. This began the quest of one little boy that only wanted to get more out of this thing we call guitar.

It was in fact Patterson's second guitar (an unplayable Teisco from W.T. Grant Co.) that inspired him to experiment with the 'action' of a guitar. Matchbook covers, toothpicks, and even small bits of gravel made for good shim stock to improve the playability of the neighbors' cheap "axes-du-joir." At 14, Patterson picked up bass when it was discovered that the Credence Clearwater Revival cover band he was in sucked so bad because there were three rhythm guitars and a drummer. This is what set the stage for the "Component Multineck System" of today.

Patterson began building guitars and other stringed instruments from scratch in 1984 when he became frustrated with the concept of permanent double-neck instruments. 6-string and 12-string necks were an easy choice, but with bass it was a different question altogether. Should the configuration be an 8-string and a 4-string, or fretted and fretless, or what? After thirteen years of hit and miss research, Patterson came up with a new development.

Patterson's Jayxz (pronounced "Jakes") Musical Implements company is currently offering guitars that feature a "Component Multineck System." The CMS concept allows the player to combine various string configuration bodies together to form a doubleneck instrument. Furthermore, Patterson's instruments are also convertible: the tuners and bridge are all mounted on the same easy to remove piece of the instrument called the "Tailstock." After loosening the strings a bit, the tailstock is unbolted and the anchoring hardware is slid off the other end. Patterson estimates that a changeover can be done in less than fifteen minutes, (Biography courtesy Jeff Patterson, September 1998).

Jayxz CMS models are available in 10 different models (string configurations). Prices per each standard model start at $750.

**Jay Turser JTB-Hawk
courtesy Jay Turser**

GRADING	100% MINT	98% NEAR MINT	95% EXC+	90% EXC	80% VG+	70% VG	60% G

JEANNIE

Instruments previously built in Pittsburg, CA. Guitar accessories currently produced.

Jeannie specializes in making custom pickguards. However, they have produced a guitar in the past. The Jeannie Talon VIII 8-string features a jazz-style solid body guitar (different wood choices are available) with a eagle's claw-shaped headstock. This model has an ebony fingerboard, pearl-covered headstock/pickguard/strat-style single coil pickups (with eight pole pieces) and a hand-built custom bridge. The suggested retail price began at $2,000. In addition, Jeannie also offers other guitar parts. Jeannie's pickguards are available with custom engraving, holographic designs, exotic wood pickguards, or custom designs. For more information on Jeannie visit their website (see Trademark Index).

JEDSON

Instruments previously produced in Japan from the late 1960s through the late 1970s.

The Jedson trademark appears on entry to student level solid body and semi-hollowbody guitars; some models with original design and some models based on classic American designs (source: Tony Bacon and Paul Day, *The Guru's Guitar Guide*).

JEM

Instruments previously built in Carle Place, NY during the mid- to late 1980s.

Before Ibanez's Steve Vai Jem model, Jem Custom Guitars was offering custom body designs, paint jobs, and electronic packages. Jem President Joe Despagni's ads used to run "As seen on MTV and on stage with Steve Vai."

Pre-Ibanez Jem guitars are definitely eye-catching, quality built electrics. Prices in the secondary market will reflect quality of workmanship, wood types in construction, and custom work. While the more custom body designs may currently be out of fashion with the retro fascination, these are not guitars to sell cheap.

JENNINGS

Instruments previously built in Japan, others were assembled in England during the early 1970s.

Jennings produced instruments at different quality levels. On one hand, there's the entry level solid body guitars based on classic American designs. On the other hand, there are some higher quality "tiny-bodied" solid body guitars. Some guitars were also assembled in England using Japanese and English parts. Instruments should be examined on an individual basis, and then priced accordingly (source: Tony Bacon and Paul Day, *The Guru's Guitar Guide*).

JENNINGS, DAVE

Instruments previously built in England during the late 1980s.

Luthier David Jennings produced some very respectable original design solid body guitars. Jennings primarily worked as a custom builder, so the overall number of instruments available might perhaps be rather limited (source: Tony Bacon and Paul Day, *The Guru's Guitar Guide*).

JENNINGS-THOMPSON

Instruments previously built in Austin, Texas.

Jennings-Thompson was a high quality, limited production company located in Austin. Ross Jennings, a former employee of Wayne Charvel (and also a production manager at B.C. Rich), personally built all his instruments along with another luthier. They limited production to about 30 basses and guitars a year, and worked with the customer to ensure that the commissioned instrument would be exactly tailored to their individual playing style. Pendulum and Spectrum basses had a retail price beginning at $3,699 (4-string) up to $4,099 (6-string). Their guitars carried a list price of $2,599.

JERRY BIX

Instruments previously built in England during the early 1980s.

While the Musician and Exotic series had some vestiges of Fender-ish styling to them, the Ptera guitars featured original designs. This company also produced some high quality custom models as well.

JERRY JONES

Instruments currently built in Nashville, TN since 1981. Distributed by Jerry Jones Guitars of Nashville, TN.

Luthier Jerry Jones began repair and guitar building at Nashville's Old Time Pickin' Parlour in 1978. By 1980, he had opened his own shop and was building custom guitars as well as designing his own original models. Jones' company has been specializing in reproducing Danelectro models and parts; however, the designs have been updated to improve upon original design flaws and to provide a more stable playing instrument (source: Tony Bacon and Paul Day, *The Guru's Guitar Guide*).

ELECTRIC

All instruments in this series are available in: Bahama Green, Black, Blood Red/Caramel vinyl, Copper, Gold, Mustard, New Copper/Maroon vinyl, Red, and Turquoise finishes. The Almond finish is currently discontinued. Jerry Jones also offers these optional 'Burst finishes: Bloodburst (Blood/Cream), Copperburst, Seaburst (Black/Turquoise), and Turquoise/White.

> **Add $50 for a Neptune bridge (fixed bridge with metal saddles) on below listed models. Add $75 for Sunburst or optional Burst finishes ($150 on the Doubleneck model).**

DELUXO - single cutaway semi-hollowbody, select maple top, carved heel neck joint, 23-fret rosewood fingerboard with pearl dot inlay, fixed metal bridge, 3-per-side tuners, Natural finish headstock, chrome hardware, transparent (or matching finish) pickguard with silk-screened Deluxo logo, 2 single coil lipstick pickups, dual concentric volume/tone controls, 3-position selector switch, mfg. 1998-2001.

$720	$650	$575	$500	$425	$350	$250

Last MSR was $895.

GRADING	100% MINT	98% NEAR MINT	95% EXC+	90% EXC	80% VG+	70% VG	60% G

Deluxo 12-String - similar to the Deluxo, except in 12-string configuration, mfg. 1998-2001.

	$800	$725	$625	$550	$450	$375	$275

Last MSR was $995.

Deluxo Baritone guitar - similar to the Deluxo except has a longer neck and is tuned to B, mfg. 1998-2001.

	$720	$650	$575	$500	$425	$350	$250

Last MSR was $895.

GUITARLIN - deep double cutaway poplar body with hollow sound channels, masonite top/back, transparent pickguard, bolt-on poplar neck, 31-fret rosewood fingerboard with white dot inlay, fixed bridge with rosewood saddle, 3-per-side tuners, chrome hardware, 2 lipstick pickups, volume/tone control, 3-position switch, disc.

	$625	$550	$475	$400	$350	$275	$200

Last MSR was $795.

LONGHORN DOUBLENECK - similar to Guitarlin, except has 2 necks: 6-string guitar configuration and 6-string bass configuration, 3 lipstick tube pickups per guitar neck, 2 lipstick tube pickups per bass neck, disc.

	$1,350	$1,175	$1,000	$885	$750	$595	$450

Last MSR was $1,665.

MASTER ELECTRIC SITAR - single cutaway poplar body, transparent pickguard, 13 sympathetic strings with own nut/bridge/lipstick pickup, bolt-on poplar neck, 21-fret rosewood fingerboard with white dot inlay, fixed buzz bridge/through-body tailpiece, 6-on-a-side tuners, chrome hardware, 2 lipstick pickups, 3 volume/tone controls, available in Black Gator, Original Gator, Turquoise Gator, White Gator, or other listed finishes, mfg. 1990-present.

MSR	$900		$725	$625	$550	$475	$400	$325	$275

Supreme Electric Sitar - similar to the Master Electric Sitar, except has 2 independent necks, one is regular length and the other is short with a fretless fingerboard, available in Gatorburst finish, mfg. 2004-present.

MSR	$1,200		$950	$850	$750	$650	$575	$500	$425

Baby Electric Sitar - miniature sitar with a single six-string neck, small body with a single pickup, available in Black Gator, Cream Gator, Red Gator, or Turq Gator finishes, mfg. 2004-present.

MSR	$650		$525	$450	$400	$350	$300	$250	$200

SHORTHORN - double cutaway poplar body, white pickguard, bolt-on poplar neck, 21-fret rosewood fingerboard with pearl dot inlay, fixed bridge with rosewood saddle, 3-per-side tuners, chrome hardware, 3 lipstick pickups, volume/tone control, 5-position switch, current mfg.

MSR	$950		$760	$650	$575	$500	$400	$325	$275

Shorthorn 2 Pickup - similar to Shorthorn, except has 2 lipstick tube single coil pickups, mfg. 1997-2001, 2004-present.

MSR	$900		$725	$625	$550	$475	$400	$325	$250

Jerry Jones Shorthorn courtesy Jerry Jones

SHORTHORN BARITONE - single cutaway poplar body, transparent pickguard, bolt-on poplar neck, 23-fret rosewood fingerboard with pearl dot inlay, tuned to B, fixed bridge with rosewood saddle, 3-per-side tuners, chrome hardware, 2 lipstick pickups, volume/tone controls, 3-position switch, current mfg.

MSR	$950		$760	$650	$575	$500	$400	$325	$275

Shorthorn Baritone 2 Pickup - similar to the Shorthorn Baritone, except has 2 lipstick pickups, current mfg.

MSR	$900		$725	$625	$550	$475	$400	$325	$250

SINGLE CUTAWAY - similar to Shorthorn, except has single round cutaway style body, current mfg.

MSR	$950		$760	$650	$575	$500	$400	$325	$275

Single Cutaway 2 Pickup - similar to Single Cutaway, except has 2 lipstick tube single coil pickups, mfg. 1997-2001, 2004-present.

MSR	$900		$725	$625	$550	$475	$400	$325	$250

SINGLE CUTAWAY BARITONE - similar to Shorthorn Baritone, except has single round cutaway style body, current mfg.

MSR	$950		$760	$650	$575	$500	$400	$325	$275

Single Cutaway Baritone 2 Pickup - similar to the Single Cutaway, except has two lipstick single coil pickups, current mfg.

MSR	$900		$725	$625	$550	$475	$400	$325	$250

TWELVE STRING - similar to Single Cutaway, except has 12-string configuration, 6-per-side tuners, fixed bridge with metal saddles, 3 pickups, current mfg.

MSR	$1,000		$800	$700	$625	$550	$475	$400	$325

Twelve String 2 Pickup - similar to the Twelve String, except has two lipstick single coil pickups, current mfg.

MSR	$950		$760	$650	$575	$500	$425	$350	$275

Shorty Octave 12-String - similar to the Twelve String, except is in a Longhorn body with an octave neck, mfg. 2003-present.

MSR	$900		$725	$625	$550	$475	$400	$325	$250

Jerry Jones Single Cutaway courtesy Jerry Jones

GRADING	100% MINT	98% NEAR MINT	95% EXC+	90% EXC	80% VG+	70% VG	60% G

ELECTRIC BASS

LONGHORN 4 (SHORT SCALE) - double deep cutaway bound poplar body with hollow sound chambers, transparent pickguard, bolt on poplar neck, 30 in. scale, 24-fret rosewood fingerboard with white dot inlay, fixed bridge with rosewood saddle, 2-per-side tuners, chrome hardware, 2 lipstick pickups, volume/tone control, 3-position switch, current mfg.

	MSR	$900		$725	$625	$550	$475	$400	$325	$250

LONGHORN 6 - similar to Longhorn 4, except has 6-string configuration, 3-per-side tuners, current mfg.

	MSR	$900		$725	$625	$550	$475	$400	$325	$250

SHORTHORN 4 - double cutaway, Indian rosewood fingerboard, current mfg.

	MSR	$900		$725	$625	$550	$475	$400	$325	$250

SINGLE CUTAWAY 4 - similar to Longhorn 4, except has single cutaway style body, disc. 1992.

	N/A	$400	$325	$275	$225	$195	$175

Last MSR was $595.

SINGLE CUTAWAY 6 - similar to Longhorn 4, except has single cutaway style body, 6-string configuration, disc. 1992.

	N/A	$400	$325	$275	$225	$195	$175

Last MSR was $595.

JERZY DROZD

Instruments currently built in Barcelona, Spain.

Jerzy Drozd offers several bass guitars. They use the philosophy of three parts when building guitars: science, artisan work, and art. Bass guitars can be as simple as a Basic 4-String, and can be as elaborate as a 10-String Custom Model. The **Obsession** Series basses features several models that have unlimited options. There are also Limited Editions and Special Basses. For additional information regarding model specification and pricing, contact Jerzy Drozd directly (see Trademark Index).

JOE'S GUITARS

Instruments previously built in Salt Lake City, UT.

Joe's Guitars offered a number of handcrafted guitar models and one bass model. All guitar models featured a recessed Tune-O-Matic bridge, Seymour Duncan pickups, and a hardshell case. Models included the Cobra (last retail was $1,349) and Cobra SX (last retail was $1,699), the hollowbody Cobra XT (last retail was $1,995), bolt-on neck model Viper (last retail was $1,349) and the Viper XS (last retail was $1,699).

JOHN BIRCH GUITARS

Instruments currently built in England since 1970.

John Birch Guitars was founded in Birmingham, England in 1970 by luthier John Birch. Birch offered custom repair and guitar building service; the custom guitars were based on popular models (i.e., Fender/Gibson designs) of the day, but featured new construction methods like through-body necks, improved truss rod design, and pickups such as the hyperflux, biflux, and multiflux. In the 1980s he teamed up with Barry Kirby to build the Cobra models, including the highly imaginative Cobra "Rook" for Rook Music (Birch is more renowned for his custom guitar building).

In 1993, John Birch Guitars relocated to Nottingham, England. The company began offering an original series of guitar models as well as MIDI implementation, (Some historical background courtesy Tony Bacon, *The Ultimate Guitar Book*).

ELECTRIC

Birch's handcrafted **Classic Guitars** range for 1998 all share the main features of John Birch Guitars. The standard features include through-body neck, sculptured neck-to-body joint, 24-fret fingerboard, full back scratch plate (pickguard), Birch Full Range humbuckers (or single coil), or multimode for MIDI version. Choice of custom color finishes.

Current model designs include the **J1** and **J2** a double cutaway with two humbuckers; the **SG** (traditional SG shape) with 2 humbuckers; the 2 humbucker **LP** (traditional LP shape); and the **ST**, a traditional Strat-style guitar with single coils or humbuckers. Prices for the models with John Birch Pickups and a stop tailpiece begin at $2,278. The Special Series base prices at $3,038.

ELECTRIC BASS

John Birch basses are offered in 4- 5- and 6-string configurations. Models feature a 22-fret fingerboard, and are available in the **J1**, **J2**, **SG**, **LP**, and 4001 body styles. Prices for a 4-string with JB Hyperflux (or 2 J-style) pickups starts at $2,278. There is an up charge for MIDI access and EMG pickups. For further information regarding model specifications and pricing, contact John Birch Guitars directly (see Trademark Index).

JOHNNY REB

Instruments currently produced in Asia. Distributed by Johnny Reb Guitars (L.A. Guitar Works) of Reseda, CA.

Those "Rock 'n Rebels" **Johnny Reb** models sport single cutaway 'Tele'-style bodies that combine a wood top to a fiberglass back and sides. The total weight of this traditional design (yet un-traditional production technique) is only 5 pounds - a welcome relief to those "chicken-pickers" playing 4 and 5 hour bar gigs.

The hollow Johnny Reb models are available with ash, figured maple, or mahogany tops with an f-hole, molded fiberglass backs, bolt-on maple necks with rosewood or maple fingerboards, 6-on-a-side chrome tuners, 2 single coil pickups, volume and tone controls, and a 3 way toggle selector. Retail list price is only $399. For further information regarding the Johnny Reb guitars, contact the company directly (see Trademark Index).

GRADING	100% MINT	98% NEAR MINT	95% EXC+	90% EXC	80% VG+	70% VG	60% G

JOHNSON

Instruments currently produced in Asia. Distributed by the Music Link of Brisbane, CA.

The Music Link's Johnson guitars offers a wide range of acoustic and electric guitars, with prices aimed at the entry level and student guitarists. All models are listed on their website, and for individual model specs, please contact Music Link directly (see Trademark Index). There are also various practice amps in the Johnson line, as well as numerous accessories like cases, Quartz tuners, and tuning machines.

ELECTRIC

Johnson did offer two higher end models. The **JE-500-R Tiger Stripe** is a double cutaway arched top, much like a PRS. It has two humbucker pickups along with a tremolo unit, and last MSR was $579. The **JE-550-Y Hawk Eye** is like the Tiger Stripe except has a bird's-eye maple top and black hardware for $599. There are also hollowbody electric guitars available including the **Tone Master**, **Dragon Fly**, and **Las Vegas**.

DEL MAR (JS-800) - double cutaway Stratocaster style body, various pickup configurations, various finishes, current mfg.

MSR	$159	$110	$90	$75	$60	$45	$30	$15

Add $15 for left-handed configuration. Add $5 for Special configuration.

DEL SOL (JT-800) - single cutaway Telecaster style body, two single coil pickups, various finishes, current mfg.

MSR	$159	$110	$90	$75	$60	$45	$30	$15

SOLARA (JS-900) - single cutaway Les Paul style, arched top, two humbucker pickups, four knobs, available in various finishes, current mfg.

MSR	$280	$195	$165	$140	$120	$100	$80	$60

Add $25 for the Solara Elite.

ELECTRIC BASS

Johnson electric guitars and basses have a pointed headstock, with all tuners on one side. Johnson basses have solid alder bodies and maple necks. The **JJ-140** is the higher end of the bass market. It features an Amberburst finish and retails for $399. There is also a five string available (**JJ-150**) for $499. The **Catalyst** series are available in four, five, and six string configurations and start at $349.

JJ-800 - double cutaway J-Bass style, two J-style pickups, three knobs, various finishes, current mfg.

MSR	$199	$140	$115	$95	$75	$60	$45	$30

JP-800 - double cutaway P-Bass style, single split P-style pickups, two knobs, various finishes, current mfg.

MSR	$199	$140	$115	$95	$75	$60	$45	$30

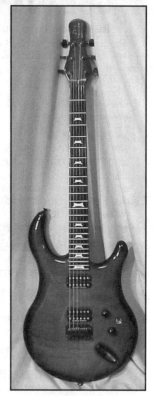

Jon Kammerer Blue Electric
courtesy Jon Kammerer

JOHNSON'S EXTREMELY STRANGE MUSICAL INSTRUMENT COMPANY

Instruments currently built in Burbank, CA.

Luthier Bruce Johnson specializes in Scroll Basses, which are distinctive horizontal electric basses with scroll-style headstocks and a warm tone like an upright bass. This bass design was originally manufactured by Ampeg from '66 to '69, and the most common model is known as the AEB-1. Johnson's website has extensive historical and technical information about the Ampeg Scroll Bassses, and he also does restorations and supplies parts for them.

In 1997, Johnson developed and introduced new generations versions of the Scroll Bass design, known as the AEB-2 (fretted) and the AUB-2 (fretless). These basses retain the style and character of the original Ampegs, but have been completely re-engineered to improve the quality, function and tone. These basses are specifically designed to bring out the tone of flatwound strings, and have a rich, cello-like sound. Each of these basses is hand built to order in Johnson's shop in Burbank, CA.

From '97 through '99, Johnson worked in cooperation with St. Louis Music, Inc., and some of those instruments were sold under the Ampeg name. The partnership has been mutually dissolved, and Johnson now sells his instruments directly to musicians worldwide through his website.

In 2000, Johnson introduced the SSB, a unique short scale bass patterned after a rare model that Ampeg manufactured in 1967. In the fall of 2001, Johnson introduced a new-generation version of the Ampeg ASB-1 "Devil Bass." For more information refer to the website (see Trademark Index).

ELECTRIC BASS

The AEB-2 Scroll Bass retails for $2,100. The AUB-2 Fretless Scroll Bass retails for $1,900. The SSB Short Scale Bass retails for $1,350. There is a slight discount if payment is made all in advance.

JOKER

See C & R Guitars.

Jon Kammerer Metal Electric
courtesy Jon Kammerer

JOLANA

Instruments previously produced in Czechoslovakia, circa 1960s.

While researching a number of guitar trademarks, associate editor Walter Murray of Frankenstein Fretworks came across two b&w photographs of Jolana instruments in the book *Musical Instruments: An Illustrated History* [Crown Publishers, New York], by Alexander Buchner. The photos illustrate at least four different models of Jolana guitars, ranging from electric models to semi-hollow (or hollow) models. Author Tony Bacon, in *The Ultimate Guitar Book*, calls the two examples he has viewed "Entry level production solid bodies, (but) have original designs with headstocks that seem to echo the Fender Swinger." Now that's rocking out behind the Iron Curtain! (source: Walter Murray, Frankenstein Fretworks; Alexander Buchner, *Musical Instruments: An Illustrated History* [Crown Publishers, New York]; and Tony Bacon, *The Ultimate Guitar Book*).

ELECTRIC

The Jolana solid body electric has an asymmetrical double cutaway body, laminated fingerboard with dot fretmarkers, chrome hardware, adjustable floating bridge/tremolo tailpiece, 3 humbucker pickups, volume and tone controls, four (possibly a fifth) white rocker switches on pickguard.

Jolana hollow or semi-hollow models (**Tornado** model?) feature a Gibson ES-style body, 6-per-side tuners/Strat-style string guides, 21-fret laminated fretboard with dot markers, 2 f-holes, trapeze tailpiece/Bigsby-like tremolo combination, 3 single coil pickups, volume and tone controls, 4 rocker switches on raised pickguard, additional rocker switch/2 finger wheels on upper horn. The "Jolana" logo is located on the lower bout with either a music staff design or in script typeface (without music staff design).

ELECTRIC BASS

The Jolana electric bass model has a maple neck with laminated (darker) wood fingerboard, white or pearloid dot fretmarkers, four on a side tuners with pearloid buttons. No further information ascertained.

JONES, TED NEWMAN

Instruments currently built in Austin, TX.

Luthier Ted Newman Jones is offering handcrafted custom instruments in his Austin workshop.

JON KAMMERER GUITARS

Instruments currently manufactured by Jon Kammerer Guitars located in Keokuk, IA, since 2000.

Luthier Jon Kammerer originally started manufacturing his unique acoustic instruments because of a 1995 thesis project for industrial design school. After much research, it was determined that up to 2/3 of the sound waves in an acoustic guitar bounce into a corner and directly back onto themselves, canceling each other. Also, the standard boxy appearance of an acoustic guitar had not been changed for a long time. This led to his experimentation with both ceramic and fiberglass guitar bodies. Utilizing state-of-the-art CAD/CAM software and computer controlled milling machines, every wood part in a Kammerer guitar is machine made to high tolerances. The unique contoured body is cut out of two blanks, then precisely glued at the center. All Kammerer instruments include a dual action truss rod, 4-screw neck, Gotoh tuning machines, cast acrylic saddle and nut, strap mounting buttons, and a hard shell case. In 2002, Jon started producing solid body and cored body electric guitars as well.

Jon Kammerer electric guitars are available as a double cutaway solid body ($895 MSR), double cutaway cored body ($950), large hollow body electric ($1,075), large deep body jazz guitar with cat's-eye soundholes ($1,175). Options are as follows: exotic wood fretboard ($50), abalone or MOP inlay ($50), Trans. finish ($200), Sunburst finish ($200), standard pickups (any combination $100 MSR), Seymour Duncan pickups (3 S.C. $220, 2 S.C., 1 Hum $240, 2 Hum $175, 1 S.C., 1 Hum $150), and an extra tone control ($25). A new "Flag" guitar is available, which features the flag of the USA and retails for $3,000, and $2,000 for the Wave solid body. Please contact Jon Kammerer directly for more information (see Trademark Index).

JOODEE

See Daion. Instruments previously produced in Japan from the late 1970s through the 1980s.

Joodee instruments were produced by luthier Shiro Tsuji and the T & Joodee Guitar company. Due to the demand in Japan for the Gem B series and others, very few instruments were exported to the U.S. market.

JORDAN GUITARS

Formerly JVE Guitars. Instruments currently built in Rankin, IL.

Luthier Patrick Jordan custom builds guitars and sitars. Unlike the Coral/Danelectro design, Jordan places the 12 sympathetic strings to the rear of the instrument. Jordan features the usual North American hardwoods such as Ash, Alder, Basswood, Cherry, Maple, and Walnut, but others such as Birch, Poplar, and Sycamore are optional. Jordan's favorite tone wood is Osage Orange. Jordan's custom template/order sheet gives the player making the commission some control over aspects of the construction, while Jordan maintains control over pickup placement and hardware placement. Jordan also offers custom bodies as replacement parts. Prices on guitars start at $1,500, bodies range from $150 to $880, and sitars range from $3,835 to $4,400. For further information, contact Patrick Jordan directly (see Trademark Index).

JUBAL GUITARS

Instruments currently built in Olean, NY.

Jubal's Merlin Deluxe is designed and built by Gregory Swier. This dual cutaway model features a hand-carved mahogany body, mahogany neck-through design, 24-fret ebony fingerboard/ebony headstock overlay, 3-per-side Schaller tuners, Gotoh bridge/stop tailpiece, lipstick tube-style single coil/nickel covered Gibson Classic '57+ humbucker pickups, volume/tone controls, and a 3-way selector. Available in custom colors, clear lacquer, or oil finishes. The list price of $2,250 includes an ultralite case.

JUDD GUITARS

Instruments currently built in Cranbrook (British Columbia), Canada.

Judd custom instruments are produced in Cranbrook, British Columbia. For information regarding model specifications and pricing, please contact Judd Guitars directly (see Trademark Index).

Section K

K.B. PRO

See Knowbudge.

KICS (USA)

See RAJ Guitar Crafts.

KALAMAZOO

See chapter on House Brands.

In the late 1930s, the Gibson guitar company decided to offer their own entry level guitars. While similar to models built for other distributors (Cromwell, Fascinator, or Capital) in construction, the Kalamazoo line was originally only offered for about five years. Models included flattop and archtop acoustics, lap steels (and amps), and mandolins.

Pre-war Kalamazoo instruments, like other Gibson budget instruments, do not have an adjustable truss rod (a key difference), have different construction techniques, and have no identifying Gibson logo.

In the mid-1960s, Gibson again released an entry level series of guitars under the Kalamazoo trademark, except all models were electric solid body guitars (except a flattop acoustic) that had a double offset cutaway body, bolt-on necks, 6-on-a-side headstock, and one or two pickups. The body profile of late 1960s models then switched to even dual cutaways. The second run of Kalamazoo models came to an end in the early 1970s. These post-war models do feature an adjustable truss rod.

Kalamazoo serial numbers are impressed into the back of the headstock, and feature six digits like the regular Gibson line. However, the Kalamazoo numbers do not match or correspond with the Gibson serialization (in the back of this book). Further information regarding Kalamazoo serialization will appear in future editions of the *Blue Book of Electric Guitars* (source: Walter Carter, *Gibson Guitars: 100 Years of an American Icon*).

GRADING	100% MINT	98% NEAR MINT	95% EXC+	90% EXC	80% VG+	70% VG	60% G

ELECTRIC

KG-1 - offset double cutaway body, bolt-on neck, rosewood fingerboard with dot inlay, Melody Maker pickup with white cover, 6-on-a-side tuners, available in Red, White, or Blue finishes, mfg. 1965-1970.

N/A	$225	$195	$165	$135	$105	$75

Add $50 for vibrato (Model KG-1A).

In 1968, the body shape changed to one that is similar to an SG, but has no beveled edges in the cutaways like Gibson SG's.

KG-2 - offset double cutaway body, bolt-on neck, rosewood fingerboard with dot inlay, 2 Melody Maker pickups with white covers, 6-on-a-side tuners, available in Red, White, or Blue finishes, mfg. 1965-1970.

N/A	$275	$235	$190	$150	$120	$100

Add $50 for vibrato (Model KG-2A).

In 1968, the body shape changed to one that is similar to an SG, but has no beveled edges in the cutaways like Gibson SG's.

KALIL

Instruments currently built in McComb, MS.

Luthier Edward E. Kalil builds instruments to custom order. Kalil currently offers acoustic steel and nylon models, as well as solid body electrics. Costs will vary due to complexity of the design and appointments.

Kalil began building guitars after attending a class at Guitar Research and Design (GRD) run by Charles Fox in South Strafford, Vermont. Kalil's class instructor was George Morris. Kalil has been a member of the Guild of American Luthiers (G.A.L.) since 1981, and a member of A.S.I.A. (Association of Stringed Instrument Artisans) since 1988.

Kalil instruments can be easily identified by the Kalil headstock logo. Kalil also offers the Lick En Stik travel guitar, a full scale instrument with a compact body and built-in amp (with variable distortion). For further information, contact luthier Edward E. Kalil directly (see Trademark Index).

KAMICO

See chapter on House Brands.

This trademark has been identified as the House Brand of the Kay Guitar company. As one of the leading suppliers of House Brand guitars, Kay also supplied an entry level budget line of guitars to various musical instrument distributors (source: Willie G. Moseley, *Stellas & Stratocasters*).

KAPA

Instruments previously built in Hyattsville, MD between 1962 and 1970.

Kapa guitars were designed and built by Kope Veneman and Company during a successful eight-year production. Veneman, a Dutch immigrant, was running a music store during the early 1960s that imported German and Italian guitars. In 1962, Veneman founded his own production facility, and named the company based on initials from his

GRADING	100% MINT	98% NEAR MINT	95% EXC+	90% EXC	80% VG+	70% VG	60% G

family member's first names: Kope, his son Albert, his daughter Patricia, and his wife Adeline. During the eight-year run, the Kapa company produced nearly 120,000 decent quality, fair-priced instruments.

ELECTRIC

Kapa guitars were available in four basic body styles, and in three variants thereof (six-string, twelve-string, and bass guitar). These models include a mini-Strat (**Challenger**), a mini-Jazzmaster (**Continental**), a teardrop shape (**Minstrel**), and a thinline hollowbody (also a **Challenger**, with different model designations). However, the names are not always consistent with the body styles, and can lead to some confusion. Kapa also produced an unofficial model named the **Cobra**, which is a single pickup model assembled with leftovers from regular production runs.

Kapa guitars were offered with bolt-on necks, 6-on-a-side headstocks (or four, if a bass), and many sported a Jazzmaster-ish tremolo system. Early Challenger solid bodies had 2 pickups and a 3-way toggle switch (original retail price $229); Deluxe or Wildcat models had three pickups (original retail price $275). The Continental
model debuted around 1966 with a slightly slimmer body and differently cut horns, and sliding on/off pickup switches (original retail price $199). The teardrop-shaped Minstrel model (original retail price $269) had three single coil pickups, on/off sliders, master volume, and three tone knobs. Kapa also produced most of their models in 6-string, 12-string, and bass configurations. Keep in mind, however, that the preceding was a rough approximation - it is possible to find models that have different parts than the standard designs (source: Michael Wright, *Guitar Stories*, Volume One).

ARCHTOP ES-335 STYLE - double cutaway ES-335 style archtop, 2 f-holes, body binding, rosewood fingerboard, 6-on-one side tuners, 2 humbucker pickups, four knobs, black raised pickguard, available in various finishes, mfg. 1969-1970.

	N/A	$300	$250	$210	$170	$130	$90

CHALLENGER - double cutaway mini-Stratocaster style body, bolt-on neck, various neck configurations, Jazzmaster style tremolo, 2 humbucker or 3 single coil pickups, 3 knobs, switch, available in various finishes, mfg. 1962-1970.

	N/A	$350	$300	$250	$200	$150	$100

Circa 1966, the single pickup switch was changed from a three-way to two on/off switches.

COBRA - similar to the Continental, except had a small pickguard and single pickup, mfg. mid- to late 1960s.

	N/A	$250	$200	$170	$140	$110	$80

CONTINENTAL - double cutaway mini-Jazzmaster style body, bolt-on neck, various neck configurations, Jazzmaster-style tremolo, 2 humbucker or 3 single coil pickups, 3 knobs, one or two switches, available in various finishes, mfg. 1966-1970.

	N/A	$350	$300	$250	$200	$150	$100

MINSTREL - teardrop-shaped body, three single coil pickups, on/off slider switches, four knobs (MV, 3 tone), available in various finishes, mfg. 1968-1970.

	N/A	$350	$300	$250	$200	$150	$100

KARERA

Instruments previously produced in Korea. Distributed by the V.J. Rendano Music Company, Inc. of Youngstown, OH.

Karera offered a wide range of electric guitars and basses that featured classic American designs from the 1990s. These good quality instruments may appeal to entry level up to student guitarists. Suggested new retail prices ranged from $175 up to $375 on guitar models, and $300 to $500 on electric basses. Victor J. Redando of the distributing company passed away in 2002.

KASUGA

Instruments previously produced in Japan from the late 1960s through the early 1980s.

Kasuga produced guitars of both original designs and designs based on classic American models. While the quality is medium to good on both solid body or semi-hollowbody guitars, it is generally the "reproduction" models that are found in the music stores. One reader wrote in to report that his Tele-style model plays "pretty good, and has a good feeling neck." Readers with additional photos or information concerning original design Kasuga guitars are invited to write the *Blue Book of Electric Guitars*.

KAWAI

Instruments previously built in Japan circa 1956 to mid-1970s; imported models since the late 1970s. No current importation. Previously distributed in the U.S. market by Kawai America Corporation of Compton, CA.

While Kawai continues to be a dominant company in keyboards (notably their high quality pianos and synthesizers) they have been and continue producing good quality guitars and basses. Although their entire product line is not available in the U.S. market, Kawai does feature a number of startling original designs in addition to a number of models based on classic American designs.

The Kawai company began producing their own guitars back in 1956, and had participated in exporting to the American market. In 1967, the Kawai corporation purchased the Teisco company (of Teisco Del Rey guitar fame). Kawai continued distributing the Teisco line in the U.S. through 1973, but then concentrated on domestic distribution of Kawai products thereafter.

Kawai returned to the American marketplace in the mid-1980s with a line of quality bass guitar models, and reissued the Teisco Spectrum Five model in the early 1990s. Recent electric bass models included the ash body/bolt-on maple neck **RB 65A** (list $899), the 5-string **RB 865A** (list $1,095), and the koa/maple body, maple/mahogany through-body neck **FIIB 110 KS** (list $1,395).

ELECTRIC

MISC. ARCHTOPS - various configurations, mfg. 1950s-late 1970s.

	N/A	$350	$300	$250	$200	$150	$100

MISC. SOLIDBODIES - various configurations, mfg. 1950s-late 1970s.

	N/A	$400	$350	$300	$250	$200	$150

GRADING	100% MINT	98% NEAR MINT	95% EXC+	90% EXC	80% VG+	70% VG	60% G

KAY

See chapter on House Brands. Instruments previously built between the 1930s and the late 1960s. Kay stringed instruments were manufactured and distributed by the Kay Musical Instrument Company of Chicago, IL. Kay, along with Harmony, were the two larger suppliers of House Brand instruments for distributors and retailers. The Kay trademark returned in the 1970s. Currently, the instruments are produced in Asia, and are distributed by A.R. Musical Enterprises, Inc. of Fishers, IN.

The roots of the Kay Musical Instruments company began back in 1890, when the Groeschel Company of Chicago, Illinois first began building bowl-back (or potato bug) mandolins. In 1918 Groeschel was changed to the Stromberg-Voisenet Company, and incorporated in 1921. Vice-president C.G. Stromberg directed production of guitars and banjos under the Mayflower trademark (see Mayflower). This Stromberg is not to be confused with luthier Charles Stromberg (and son Elmer) of Boston, Massachusetts. Stromberg-Voisenet introduced the process of laminating wood tops and backs in 1924, and also began arching instrument tops and backs. Henry Kay Kuhrmeyer, who later became company president, offered use of his middle name on the more popular Kay-Kraft series of Stromberg-Voisenet's guitars, mandolins, and banjos.

The Kay era began when Henry Kay Kuhrmeyer bought the Stromberg-Voisenet company in 1928. Kuhrmeyer renamed the company Kay Musical Instruments in 1931, and began mass-producing stringed instruments. Kay, like Washburn at the turn of the century, claimed production of almost 100,000 instruments a year by the mid 1930s. Kay instruments were both marketed by the company itself, and produced for jobbers (distributors) and retail houses under various names. Rather than produce a list here, the *Blue Book of Electric Guitars* has attempted to identify Kay-produced House Brands throughout the alphabetical listing in this text. Many of these instruments were entry level or student instruments then, and should be considered entry level even now. But as Jay Scott (author of *'50s Cool: Kay Guitars*) points out, "True, the vast majority of Kay's student-grade and intermediate guitars were awful. But the top of each line - banjo, guitar and mandolin (especially the acoustic and electric jazz guitars and flattop acoustics) - were meritorious pieces of postwar musical art."

Kay introduced upright basses in 1937, and marketed them under both the Kay trademark and K. Meyer (a clever abbreviation of Kuhrmeyer?). After Leo Fender debuted his Precision electric bass at the 1951 NAMM trade show, Kay was the first company to join Fender in the electric bass market as they introduced their K-162 model in 1952. Kay also went on to produce some of the coolest mixtures of classic archtop design and '50s modern acrylic headstocks on the "Gold K" line that debuted in 1957.

Kay 400 Series Professional courtesy George McGuire

The Kay Musical Instrument company was sold to an investment group headed by Sydney Katz in 1955. Katz, a former manager of Harmony's service department, was more aggressive and competitive in the guitar market. Kay's production facilities expanded to try to meet the demand of the guitar market in the late 1950s and early 1960s. A large number of guitars were produced for Sears under the Silvertone trademark. At the peak of the guitar boom in 1964, Kay moved into a new million dollar facility located near Chicago's O'Hare Airport.

Unfortunately, by 1965 the guitar market was oversaturated as retail demand fell off. While Kay was still financially sound, Katz sold the company to Seeburg. Seeburg, a large jukebox manufacturer based in Chicago, owned Kay for a period of two years. At this time, the whole guitar industry was feeling the pinch of economics. Seeburg wanted to maintain its niche in the industry by acquiring Valco Guitars, Inc. (see National or Dobro) and producing their own amplifiers to go with the electric Kay guitars. Bob Keyworth, the executive vice-president in charge of Kay, suggested the opposite: Seeburg should sell Kay to Valco.

Robert Engelhardt, who succeeded Louis Dopyera in Valco's ownership in 1962, bought Kay from Seeburg in June 1967. Valco moved into the Kay facilities, but Engelhardt's company was under-financed from the beginning. Engelhardt did make some deal with an investment group or financial company, but after two years the bills couldn't be paid. The investment group just showed up one day and changed the plant locks. By 1969 or 1970, both Valco Guitars Inc., and the Kay trademark were out of business.

The rights to the Kay name were acquired by Sol Weindling and Barry Hornstein, who were importing Teisco Del Rey (Kawai) guitars to the U.S. market with their W.M.I. importing company. W.M.I. began putting the Kay name on the Teisco products beginning in 1973, and continued on through the 1970s.

In 1980, Tony Blair of A.R. Enterprises purchased the Kay trademark. The Kay trademark is now on entry level/beginner guitars built in Asia (1950s/1960s company history courtesy Jay Scott, *'50s Cool: Kay Guitars*; contemporary history courtesy Michael Wright, *Vintage Guitar Magazine*).

ELECTRIC: BARNEY KESSEL MODELS

When guitarist Barney Kessel began endorsing Kay guitars, his signature appeared on the pickguards of the various Barney Kessel guitar models. By 1960, the signature was removed as Kessel had moved on to endorsing Gibson products.

BARNEY KESSEL JAZZ SPECIAL (MODEL 8700 S) - semi-hollowbody, 24.75 in. scale, 3-per-side tuners, 2 pickups, mfg. 1957-1960.

	N/A	$1,700	$1,350	$1,050	$800	$600	$400

This was the premier model of the Gold "K" Line of Barney Kessel guitar models. This model was also available with a Blonde finish (Model 8700 B).

Barney Kessel Jazz Special (Model 8701 S) - similar to the Kessel Jazz Special (Model 8700 S), except features one pickup, mfg. 1957-1960.

	N/A	$1,500	$1,200	$900	$700	$500	$300

This model was also available with a Blonde finish (Model 8701 B).

Kay 450 Professional courtesy George McGuire

GRADING	100% MINT	98% NEAR MINT	95% EXC+	90% EXC	80% VG+	70% VG	60% G

BARNEY KESSEL ARTIST (MODEL 6700 S) - semi-hollowbody, 24.75 in. scale, 3-per-side tuners, 2 pickups, mfg. 1957-1960.

	N/A	$2,000	$1,700	$1,400	$1,100	$900	$700

The Artist model was the intermediate-sized model of the Gold "K" Line of Barney Kessel guitar models. This model was also available with a Blonde finish (Model 6700 B).

Barney Kessel Artist (Model 6701 S) - similar to the Kessel Artist (Model 6700 S), except features one pickup, mfg. 1957-1960.

	N/A	$1,900	$1,600	$1,300	$1,000	$800	$600

This model was also available with a Blonde finish (Model 6701 B).

BARNEY KESSEL PRO (MODEL 1700 S) - single cutaway LP-style body, 2 pickups, mfg. 1957-1960.

	N/A	$1,900	$1,600	$1,300	$1,000	$800	$600

Introduced as a Les Paul-styled guitar in 1954, the Pro became the entry level model in the Gold "K" Line of Barney Kessel guitar models in 1957. This model was also available with a Blonde finish (Model 1700 B).

Barney Kessel Pro (Model 1701 S, Mfg. 1957 - 1960) - similar to the Kessel Pro (Model 1700 S), except features one pickup, mfg. 1957-1960.

	N/A	$1,800	$1,500	$1,200	$900	$700	$500

This model was also available with a Blonde finish (Model 1701 B).

PRO (MODEL K172-S) - 24.75 in. scale, 3-per-side tuners, one pickup, mfg. 1954-57.

The secondary market is still undefined. This model was also available with a Blonde finish (Model K172-B) and Grey Transparent finish called "Harewood" (Model K172-H).

ELECTRIC: UPBEAT SERIES

Upbeat models also echo some of that '50s coolness, and were available between 1957 and 1960.

UPBEAT (MODEL K 8980 S) - semi-hollowbody, one pickup, 3-per-side tuners on headstock, mfg. 1957-1960.

	N/A	$1,000	$800	$600	$450	$300	$200

This model was also available in a Blonde finish (Model K 8980 B), and Jet Black finish (Model K 8980 J).

Upbeat (Model K 8990 S) - similar to the Upbeat (Model K8980S) except has 2 pickups, mfg. 1957-1961.

	N/A	$1,200	$950	$750	$550	$400	$275

This model was also available in a Blonde finish (Model K 8990 B), and Jet Black finish (Model K 8990 J).

Upbeat (Model K 8995 S) - similar to the Upbeat (Model K8980S) except has 3 pickups, mfg. 1957- 1961.

	N/A	$1,300	$1,000	$800	$600	$450	$300

This model was also available in a Blonde finish (Model K 8995 B), and Jet Black finish (Model K 8995 J).

KAY KRAFT

Sometimes hyphenated as Kay-Kraft. See Kay. Instruments previously produced in Chicago, IL from the mid-1920s to the mid-1950s.

Henry Kay Kuhrmeyer, who worked his way up from company secretary, treasurer, and later to president of Stromberg-Voisenet, lent his middle name to a popular selling line of guitars, mandolins, and banjos. When Kuhrmeyer gained control of Stromberg-Voisenet and changed the name to Kay Musical Instruments, he continued to use the Kay Kraft trademark. Instruments using this trademark could thus be either Stromberg-Voisenet or Kay (depending on the label) but was still produced by the same company in the same facilities.

KELLER CUSTOM GUITARS

Instruments currently built in Mandan, ND, since 1993.

Randall Keller handcrafts custom guitars out of high quality wood and parts as opposed to mass production versions. The **Keller Custom Pro** is offered with a large variety of different woods, hardware choices, and finishes to the customer commissioning the guitar. Prices are around $2,000 new, but contact Keller for a price quote.

KELLETT ALUMINUM GUITARS

Instruments currently manufactured in Santa Clara, CA.

Peter Kellett is an established California artist acknowledged for his pioneering work with dye colors on anodized aluminum. Currently, he is making an aluminum instrument patterned after the Stratocaster, with choice of maple or rosewood neck. He also sells the bodies separately, and finishes are multi-colored anodized and/or aluminum nickel. For more information, please contact the company directly (see Trademark Index).

KELLISON, T. R.

Instruments currently built in Billings, Montana since 1978.

Luthier T.R. Kellison has been handcrafting custom instruments since 1978.

KELLY GUITARS

See Carmine Street Guitars.

GRADING	100% MINT	98% NEAR MINT	95% EXC+	90% EXC	80% VG+	70% VG	60% G

KEN BEBENSEE GUITARS AND BASSES

Instruments currently built in North San Juan, CA. Previously built in Nevada City and San Luis Obispo, CA.

Luthier Ken Bebensee began building basses and guitars in high school as a musician trying to develop his own style. While studying engineering and industrial technology at Cal Poly State University (San Luis Obispo), Bebensee continued to refine and improve on his designs.

In 1983, Bebensee began offering custom-built instruments. Bebensee works out of an old wooden shop in San Luis Obispo, and custom creates a handful of instruments per year. Bebensee's instruments are custom built from the highest grade of sustained yield, exotic woods. For further information (the full-color brochure is breathtaking!), please contact luthier Bebensee directly (see Trademark Index).

Bebensee estimates that he has created over eighty instruments since 1983. Bebensee has finished twenty basses and guitars since his color brochure of 1997, most of them custom orders from professional musicians for recording and live performance. The headstock reads "KB." In 2001/02, Ken Bebensee Guitars and Basses was relocated to Nevada City, California. In 2004, they relocated again to North San Juan, CA.

ELECTRIC

Bebensee offers the following as standard features on all his handcrafted instruments: a 24-fret fingerboard, laminated neck-through body design, graphite nut, 100% copper foil shielding in the electronics cavity, Tung Oil/urethane finish, Sperzel locking or Gotoh or Hipshot tuners, Bartolini (or Lane Poor or DiMarzio or Seymour Duncan) pickups, and his own KB bridge. Bebensee also features a list of additional cost options on any of his models.

Bebensee's **Big Fatty Guitar** features neck-through body design combined with a semi-hollow body and 2 f-holes. The **Bear-o-Tone** guitar is a 28 in. scale baritone with a semi-hollow body, while the similarly shaped **Jazz '96 Guitar** features an ebony tailpiece, 2 active pickups and bridge mounted piezo system. The **Blue Funk Guitar** is a carved solid body model with scrolled horn, Bigsby tremolo, and Blue Metallic polyester finish. A testimony to his craft, the **Gothic Angel** has an elaborately carved body with abalone and mother-of-pearl fingerboard inlays. The **San Luis Archtop** is an acoustic model with a carved spruce top, koa back, cherry sides, and matching set of cat's-eye f-holes.

The base list prices for an electric 6-string guitar starts at $2,920, 7-string or Baritone is $3,250, and an 8-String or baritone is $3,450.

Kay 405 Professional
courtesy George McGuire

ELECTRIC BASS

In addition to his fine guitar models, Bebensee offers a number of high quality electric bass guitars. The **Zeus** combines a sleek, offset double cutaway hollowbody with a Bartolini MM magnetic pickup and bridge mounted piezo system, while the **Space Bass** has a carved spruce top and Lane Poor MM pickup. The **Pisces** is a semi-hollow design with Bartolini triple coil pickup, active preamp, 5-position rotary switch, and piezo pickup mounted in the bridge. Other models like the **Deuce**, **Falcon**, **Solar**, and **Baroque** are all solid body guitars featuring exotic woods and offset cutaway rounded bodies.

The list price for a 4-string bass starts at $2,980. Bebensee also offers 5-, 6-, and 7-string bass configurations (priced respectively at $3,260, $3,480, and $3,600). In 2004, and 8- and 10-string versions became available for $3,720 and $3,960, respectively.

KEN SMITH BASSES, LTD.

Instruments currently built in Perkasie, PA and Japan. Distributed by Ken Smith Basses, Ltd. of Perkasie, PA.

Luthier Ken Smith's original career was as a professional studio musician. Inspired by his need for a better quality bass guitar, he built one! His efforts introduced the concept of a high quality custom bass designed to meet the needs of a professional player. Smith spent a number of years in the early 1970s researching luthier information and building designs. By 1978, he opened his business, and in 1980, the first Smith basses were introduced.

ELECTRIC BASS: ANNIVERSARY SERIES

Add $100 for fretless fingerboard models. Add $200 for left-handed versions.

20TH ANNIVERSARY - offset double cutaway tiger maple body core/black walnut or mahogany laminate, figured (flamed, birds-eye, and charcoal flamed) California redwood top and back, hard rock maple/bubinga laminate neck, 24-fret Macassar ebony fingerboard with mother-of-pearl top and side dot position markers, fixed bridge, figured California redwood peghead with pearl logo inlay, 2-per-side tuners, gold hardware, 2 humbucker pickups, volume/treble/bass/mix controls, series/parallel switches, active electronics, available in Natural finish, mfg. 1998-99.

N/A	N/A	N/A	N/A	N/A	N/A	N/A

Last MSR was $6,170.

20th Anniversary 5-string - similar to the 20th Anniversary except in 5-string configuration, 3/2-per-side tuners.

N/A	N/A	N/A	N/A	N/A	N/A	N/A

Last MSR was $6,170.

20th Anniversary 6-string - similar to the 20th Anniversary except in 6-string configuration, 3-per-side tuners.

N/A	N/A	N/A	N/A	N/A	N/A	N/A

Last MSR was $6,170.

A total of 40 Anniversary basses are scheduled. Serial numbers will designate the order in which the basses were produced, and what string configuration.

Kay Professional Bass
courtesy George McGuire

K

GRADING	100% MINT	98% NEAR MINT	95% EXC+	90% EXC	80% VG+	70% VG	60% G

25TH ANNIVERSARY - Fusion body style, five- or seven-piece laminated wings of tiger maple, quilted maple, or figured walnut, core of western quilted maple, tiger maple, mahogany, or walnut, five-or seven-piece laminated maple and morado neck-thru body with graphite inlaid bars, two-per-side tuners, two humbucker soapbar pickups, five knobs, Classic finish, mfg. 2004-present.

MSR	N/A	$5,850	$5,200	$4,600	$4,000	N/A	N/A	N/A

25th Anniversary 5-String - similar to the 25th Anniversary, except in five-string configuration and 3/2-per-side tuners, mfg. 2004-present.

MSR	N/A	$6,000	$5,300	$4,700	$4,100	N/A	N/A	N/A

25th Anniversary 6-String - similar to the 25th Anniversary, except in six-string configuration and 3-per-side tuners, mfg. 2004-present.

MSR	N/A	$6,300	$5,600	$5,000	$4,500	N/A	N/A	N/A

25th Anniversary 7-String - similar to the 25th Anniversary, except in seven-string configuration and 4/3-per-side tuners, mfg. 2004-present.

MSR	N/A	$7,500	$6,500	$5,800	$5,200	N/A	N/A	N/A

ELECTRIC BASS: BSR/BT SERIES

BSR4J - offset double cutaway body with pointed bottom, solid figured maple or walnut body wings, bolt-on three-piece maple neck, 24-fret bubinga fingerboard with offset dot inlays, matching headstock with two-per-side tuners, standard bridge, two J-Style pickups, five knobs, chrome hardware, Stradivari Gold Oil finish, mfg. 1997-present.

MSR	N/A	$2,325	$2,000	$1,750	$1,550	$1,350	$1,150	$1,000

Add $80 for gold or black hardware.

Later models feature a morado/pau ferro fingerboard. In 2004, an 18-volt electronics system was introduced.

BSR5J - similar to the BSR4J, except in five-string configuration with 3/2-per-side tuners, mfg. 1997-present.

MSR	N/A	$2,400	$2,100	$1,850	$1,600	$1,400	$1,200	$1,050

BSR4J-MW - similar to the BSR 4J, except has a bookmatched walnut top over figure maple body, mfg. 1997-present.

MSR	N/A	$2,550	$2,200	$1,900	$1,650	$1,450	$1,250	$1,100

Later models feature a morado/pau ferro fingerboard. In 2004, an 18-volt electronics system was introduced.

BSR5J-MW - similar to the BSR4J-MW, except in five-string configuration with 3/2-per-side tuners, mfg. 1997-present.

MSR	N/A	$2,625	$2,300	$2,000	$1,750	$1,500	$1,300	$1,100

BSR4M/CR4M - offset double cutaway body with pointed bottom, tiger maple, walnut, avodire, quilted maple, lacewood, or swamp ash body wings, bolt-on three-piece maple neck, 24-fret morado/pau ferro fingerboard with offset dot inlays, matching headstock with two-per-side tuners, standard bridge, two humbucker soap bar pickups, five knobs, chrome hardware, Stradivari Gold Oil finish, mfg. 1997-present.

MSR	N/A	$2,475	$2,150	$1,875	$1,625	$1,425	$1,225	$1,025

Add $80 for gold or black hardware. Add $80 for ebony fingerboard

In 2004, an 18-volt electronics system was introduced.

BSR5M/CR5M - similar to the BSR4M, except in five-string configuration with 3/2-per-side tuners, mfg. 1997-present.

MSR	N/A	$2,550	$2,200	$1,900	$1,650	$1,450	$1,250	$1,050

BSR6M/CR6M - similar to the BSR4M, except in six-string configuration with 3-per-side tuners, mfg. 1997-present.

MSR	N/A	$2,700	$2,300	$2,000	$1,750	$1,500	$1,300	$1,100

BSR4MW/CR4MW - similar to the MSR4M/CR4M, except has three-piece laminated wings with either bookmatched tiger maple top/back with a walnut core or a bookmatched walnut top/back with a tiger maple core, mfg. 1997-present.

MSR	N/A	$2,775	$2,400	$2,100	$1,800	$1,550	$1,350	$1,150

Add $80 for ebony fingerboard.

In 2004, an 18-volt electronics system was introduced.

BSR5MW/CR5MW - similar to the BSR4MW/CR4MW, except in five-string configuration with 3/2-per-side tuners, mfg. 1997-present.

MSR	N/A	$2,850	$2,450	$2,150	$1,850	$1,600	$1,400	$1,200

BSR6MW/CR6MW - similar to the BSR4MW/CR4MW, except in six-string configuration with 3-per-side tuners, mfg. 1997-present.

MSR	N/A	$3,000	$2,600	$2,250	$1,950	$1,700	$1,450	$1,250

BSR4P/CR4V - similar to the MSR4M/CR4M, except has three-piece laminated wings with a bookmatched top/back of tiger maple, quilted maple, walnut, bubinga, shedua, avodire, imbuia, lacewood, or koa, a core of western quilted maple, tiger maple, mahogany, or walnut, and a five-piece laminated maple and morado neck with graphite inlaid bars, current mfg.

MSR	N/A	$3,150	$2,700	$2,350	$2,050	$1,800	$1,600	$1,400

Add $80 for ebony fingerboard.

In 2004, an 18-volt electronics system was introduced.

BSR5P/CR5V - similar to the BSR4P/CR4V, except in five-string configuration, 3/2-per-side tuners, current mfg.

MSR	N/A	$3,225	$2,750	$2,400	$2,150	$1,850	$1,650	$1,450

BSR6P/CR6V - similar to the BSR4P/CR4V, except in six-string configuration, 3-per-side tuners, current mfg.

MSR	N/A	$3,375	$2,900	$2,500	$2,200	$1,950	$1,700	$1,500

BSR4MS/BT4MSV - offset double cutaway body with pointed bottom, tiger maple, black walnut, or quilted maple body wings, neck-thru-body three-piece maple neck with graphite inlaide bars, 24-fret morado/pau ferro fingerboard with offset dot inlays, matching headstock with two-per-side tuners, standard bridge, two humbucker soap bar pickups, five knobs, chrome hardware, Stradivari Gold Oil finish, current mfg.

MSR	N/A	$3,075	$2,600	$2,250	$1,950	$1,700	$1,500	$1,300

Add $80 for ebony fingerboard.

In 2004, an 18-volt electronics system was introduced.

GRADING		100% MINT	98% NEAR MINT	95% EXC+	90% EXC	80% VG+	70% VG	60% G

BSR5MS/BT5MSV - similar to the BSR4MS/BT4MSV, except in five-string configuration with 3/2-per-side tuners, current mfg.

MSR	N/A	$3,150	$2,700	$2,350	$2,050	$1,800	$1,600	$1,400

BSR6MS/BT6MSV - similar to the BSR4MS/BT4MSV, except in five-string configuration with 3/2-per-side tuners, current mfg.

MSR	N/A	$3,300	$2,800	$2,400	$2,100	$1,850	$1,650	$1,450

BSR4GN/BT4G - offset double cutaway body with pointed bottom, tiger maple, walnut, quilted maple, bubinga, shedua, avodire, imbuia, lacewood, or koa three-piece laminated body wings, neck-thru-body five-piece maple and bubinga neck with graphite inlaide bars, 24-fret ebony fingerboard with offset dot inlays, matching headstock with two-per-side tuners, standard bridge, two humbucker soap bar pickups, five knobs, gold hardware, Stradivari Gold Oil finish, mfg. 1997-present.

MSR	N/A	$3,750	$3,200	$2,800	$2,450	$2,100	$1,800	$1,550

In 2004, an 18-volt electronics system was introduced.

BSR5GN/BT5G - similar to the BSR4GN/BT4G, except in five-string configuration with 3/2-per-side tuners, mfg. 1997-present.

MSR	N/A	$3,825	$3,275	$2,850	$2,500	$2,150	$1,850	$1,600

BSR6GN/BT6G - similar to the BSR4GN/BT4G, except in six-string configuration with 3-per-side tuners, mfg. 1997-present.

MSR	N/A	$3,975	$3,350	$2,900	$2,550	$2,200	$1,900	$1,650

BSR4EG/BT4EG - offset double cutaway body with pointed bottom, five-piece laminated tiger maple, figured walnut, quilted maple, morado, zebrawood, cocobola, or ebony with a walnut back body wings, western quilted maple, tiger maple, mahogany, or walnut core, five-piece maple and morado neck-thru-body, 24-fret ebony ferro fingerboard with offset dot inlays, matching headstock with two-per-side tuners, standard bridge, two humbucker soap bar pickups, five knobs, Stradivari Gold Oil finish, mfg. 1997-present.

MSR	N/A	$4,500	$3,950	$3,500	$3,100	$2,700	$2,350	$2,000

In 2004, an 18-volt electronics system was introduced.

BSR5EG/BT5EG - similar to the BSR4EG/BT4EG, except in five-string configuration with 3/2-per-side tuners, mfg. 1997-present.

MSR	N/A	$4,500	$3,950	$3,500	$3,100	$2,700	$2,350	$2,000

BSR6EG/BT6EG - similar to the BSR4EG/BT4EG, except in six-string configuration with 3-per-side tuners, mfg. 1997-present.

MSR	N/A	$4,650	$4,100	$3,600	$3,200	$2,800	$2,400	$2,050

BSR7EG - similar to the BSR4EG/BT4EG, except in seven-string configuration with 4/3-per-side tuners, mfg. 1997-present.

MSR	N/A	$6,300	$5,600	$5,000	$4,500	$4,000	$3,600	$3,200

Ken Smith BSR4MS courtesy Ken Smith

ELECTRIC BASS: BLACK TIGER SERIES

BLACK TIGER BSR4TN/BT4TNV - offset double cutaway BSR style body, three-piece laminated rare figured black walnut body wings, walnut back, five-piece laminated maple and bubinga neck-thru-body with graphite inlaid bars, two-per-side tuners, standard bridge, two humbucker soapbar pickups, five knobs, gold hardware, Classic finish, mfg. 2002-present.

MSR	N/A	$4,050	$3,500	$3,100	$2,750	$2,400	$2,100	$1,800

Black Tiger BSR5TN/BT5TNV - similar to the Black Tiger BSR4TN/BSR4TNV, except in five-string configuration with 3/2-per-side tuners, mfg. 2002-present.

MSR	N/A	$4,050	$3,500	$3,100	$2,750	$2,400	$2,100	$1,800

Black Tiger BSR6TN/BT6TNV - similar to the Black Tiger BSR4TN/BSR4TNV, except in six-string configuration with 3-per-side tuners, mfg. 2002-present.

MSR	N/A	$4,200	$3,600	$3,200	$2,800	$2,450	$2,150	$1,850

BLACK TIGER ELITE BSR4TNE/BT4TNVE - similar to the Black Tiger, except has exhibition grade black walnut wood with contrasting laminates, mfg. 2002-present.

MSR	N/A	$4,950	$4,400	$3,900	$3,500	$3,100	$2,700	$2,400

Black Tiger Elite BSR5TNE/BT5TNVE - similar to the Black Tiger Elite BSR4TNE/BT4NVE, except in five-string configuration with 3/2-per-side tuners, mfg. 2002-present.

MSR	N/A	$4,950	$4,400	$3,900	$3,500	$3,100	$2,700	$2,400

Black Tiger Elite BSR6TNE/BT6TNVE - similar to the Black Tiger Elite BSR4TNE/BT4NVE, except in six-string configuration with 3-per-side tuners, mfg. 2002-present.

MSR	N/A	$5,100	$4,500	$4,000	$3,550	$3,150	$2,750	$2,450

ELECTRIC BASS: BURNER SERIES

ARTIST - double cutaway mahogany body with exotic wood top/back, bolt-on maple/walnut 5-piece neck, 24-fret rosewood fingerboard with pearl dot inlay, fixed bridge, 2-per-side tuners, black hardware, 2 humbucker pickups, volume/treble/bass and mix controls, active electronics, available in Antique Natural finish, disc. 1998.

		$1,925	$1,550	$1,000	$800	$720	$660	$600

Last MSR was $2,399.

Ken Smith BSR5NT courtesy Ken Smith

GRADING	100% MINT	98% NEAR MINT	95% EXC+	90% EXC	80% VG+	70% VG	60% G

Artist V - similar to Artist, except has 5 strings, 3/2-per-side tuners, disc. 1998.

	$2,000	$1,625	$1,050	$840	$755	$690	$630

Last MSR was $2,499.

Artist VI - similar to Artist, except has 6 strings, 3-per-side tuners, disc. 1998.

	$2,150	$1,750	$1,150	$920	$830	$760	$690

Last MSR was $2,699.

CUSTOM - double cutaway figured maple body, bolt-on maple/walnut 5-piece neck, 24-fret rosewood fingerboard with pearl dot inlay, fixed bridge, 2-per-side tuners, black hardware, 2 J-style pickups, volume/treble/bass and mix controls, active electronics, available in Trans. Antique Natural, Trans. Candy Red, or Trans. Cobalt Blue finishes, disc. 1998.

	$1,600	$1,300	$980	$840	$775	$630	$480

Last MSR was $1,999.

Custom V - similar to Custom, except has 5 strings, 3/2-per-side tuners, disc. 1998.

	$1,675	$1,365	$1,080	$945	$830	$725	$565

Last MSR was $2,099.

Custom VI - similar to Custom, except has 6 strings, 3-per-side tuners, disc. 1998.

	$1,850	$1,495	$1,150	$980	$850	$760	$670

Last MSR was $2,299.

DELUXE - double cutaway swamp ash body, bolt-on maple neck, 24-fret pau ferro fingerboard with pearl dot inlay, fixed brass bridge, 2-per-side tuners, black hardware, 2 J-style pickups, 2 volume/1 treble/1 bass controls, active electronics, available in Antique Natural, Trans. Candy Apple Red, Trans. Cobalt Blue finishes, disc. 1998.

	$1,525	$1,235	$1,000	$880	$775	$640	$480

Last MSR was $1,899.

Deluxe V - similar to Deluxe, except has 5 strings, 3/2-per-side tuners, disc. 1998.

	$1,600	$1,300	$1,050	$920	$800	$680	$530

Last MSR was $1,999.

Deluxe VI - similar to Deluxe, except has 6 strings, 3-per-side tuners, disc. 1998.

	$1,750	$1,425	$1,140	$1,065	$985	$825	$770

Last MSR was $2,199.

STANDARD - double cutaway alder body, bolt-on maple neck, 24-fret pau ferro fingerboard with pearl dot inlay, fixed brass bridge, 2-per-side tuners, black hardware, 2 J-style pickups, 2 volume/1 treble/1 bass controls, active electronics, available in Electric Blue, Ivory White, Onyx Black and Scarlet Red finishes, disc. 1998.

	$1,350	$1,100	$930	$860	$720	$630	$520

Last MSR was $1,699.

Standard V - similar to Standard, except has 5 strings, 3/2-per-side tuners, disc. 1998.

	$1,450	$1,150	$975	$880	$750	$665	$550

Last MSR was $1,799.

Standard VI - similar to Standard, except has 6 strings, 3-per-side tuners, disc. 1998.

	$1,600	$1,300	$1,050	$920	$800	$680	$525

Last MSR was $1,999.

ELECTRIC BASS: C.R. CUSTOM SERIES

C.R. CUSTOM IV BOLT-ON - double cutaway maple body, figured maple wings, bolt-on 3-piece maple neck, 24-fret pau ferro fingerboard, fixed brass bridge, blackface peghead with pearl logo inlay, 2-per-side tuners, chrome hardware, 2 humbucker pickups, volume/treble/bass/mix controls, active electronics, available in Natural finish, mfg. 1993-96.

	$1,925	$1,550	$1,375	$1,200	$935	$760	$675

Last MSR was $2,400.

This model has swamp ash wings as an option.

C.R. Custom V Bolt-On - similar to C.R. Custom IV, except has 5 strings, 3/2-per-side tuners, mfg. 1993-96.

	$2,000	$1,625	$1,200	$960	$860	$790	$720

Last MSR was $2,500.

C.R. Custom VI Bolt-On - similar to C.R. Custom IV, except has 6 strings, 3-per-side tuners, mfg. 1993-96.

	$2,075	$1,695	$1,250	$1,000	$900	$825	$750

Last MSR was $2,600.

C.R. CUSTOM IV - double cutaway mahogany body, figured maple top/back, through-body 3-piece maple neck, 24-fret pau ferro fingerboard with pearl dot inlay, fixed brass bridge, 2-per-side tuners, chrome hardware, 2 humbucker pickups, volume/treble/bass/mix controls, active electronics, available in Natural finish, mfg. 1993-96.

	$2,250	$1,825	$1,600	$1,395	$1,175	$965	$750

Last MSR was $2,800.

This group of instruments was formerly the Chuck Rainey Series. This model has koa, oak and walnut bodies, and black and gold hardware as options.

C.R. Custom V - similar to C.R. Custom IV, except has 5 strings, 3/2-per-side tuners, mfg. 1992-96.

	$2,325	$1,885	$1,650	$1,425	$1,185	$950	$725

Last MSR was $2,900.

GRADING	100% MINT	98% NEAR MINT	95% EXC+	90% EXC	80% VG+	70% VG	60% G

C.R. Custom VI - similar to the C.R. Custom V, except has 6 strings, 3/2-per-side tuners, mfg. 1992-96.

		$2,400	$1,950	$1,700	$1,475	$1,225	$995	$750

Last MSR was $3,000.

ELECTRIC BASS: FUSION SERIES

FUSION F4MS - offset double cutaway body, exotic top over tiger maple or tiger maple over black walnut body wings, three-piece neck-thru body maple neck with graphite inlaid bars, two per-side tuners, standard bridge, two humbucker soapbar pickups, five knobs, mfg. 2004-present.

MSR	N/A	$3,300	$2,800	$2,400	$2,100	$1,850	$1,650	$1,450

Fusion F5MS - similar to the Fusion F4MS, except in five-string configuration and 3/2-per-side tuners, mfg. 2004-present.

MSR	N/A	$3,375	$2,850	$2,450	$2,150	$1,900	$1,700	$1,500

Fusion F6MS - similar to the Fusion F4MS, except in six-string configuration and 3-per-side tuners, mfg. 2004-present.

MSR	N/A	$3,525	$3,000	$2,600	$2,250	$2,000	$1,750	$1,550

ELECTRIC BASS: G SERIES

This series has graphite rods adjacent to the truss rod for added strength and durability.

B.M.T. ELITE IV - offset double cutaway mahogany body with walnut/maple veneer, figured maple top/back, through-body 7-piece bubinga/maple/ovankol neck, 24-fret pau ferro fingerboard with pearl dot inlay, fixed brass bridge, blackface peghead with pearl logo inlay, 2-per-side tuners, gold hardware, 2 humbucker pickups, volume/treble/mid/bass/mix controls, active electronics, available in Natural finish, mfg. 1993-96.

		$3,525	$2,850	$2,500	$2,175	$1,825	$1,495	$1,150

Last MSR was $4,400.

This model has bubinga, koa, lacewood, pau ferro top/walnut back, ovankol, walnut and zebrawood bodies, ebony fingerboard, black and chrome hardware as an option.

B.M.T. Elite V - similar to B.M.T. Elite IV, except has 5 strings, 3/2-per-side tuners, mfg. 1993-96.

		$3,600	$2,925	$2,575	$2,225	$1,875	$1,525	$1,175

Last MSR was $4,500.

B.M.T. Elite VI - similar to B.M.T. Elite IV, except has 6 strings, 3-per-side tuners, mfg. 1993-96.

		$3,675	$2,975	$2,625	$2,265	$1,900	$1,550	$1,200

Last MSR was $4,600.

B.T. CUSTOM IV - double cutaway mahogany body, figured maple top/back, through-body 5-piece maple/mahogany neck, 24-fret ebony fingerboard with pearl dot inlay, fixed brass bridge, blackface peghead with pearl logo inlay, 2-per-side tuners, black hardware, 2 humbucker Smith pickups, volume/concentric treble-bass/mix controls, active electronics, available in Charcoal Gray, Electric Blue, Natural, or Scarlet Red finishes, disc. 1996.

		$3,125	$2,535	$2,225	$1,900	$1,600	$1,285	$975

Last MSR was $3,900.

This model has bubinga, koa, lacewood, pau ferro, ovankol and zebrawood bodies with Natural finish, pau ferro fingerboard, chrome and gold hardware as options.

B.T. Custom V - similar to B.T. Custom IV, except has 5 strings, 3/2-per-side tuners, disc. 1996.

		$3,250	$2,600	$2,275	$1,950	$1,640	$1,325	$1,000

Last MSR was $4,000.

B.T. Custom VI - similar to B.T. Custom IV, except has 6 strings, 3-per-side tuners, disc. 1996.

		$3,275	$2,650	$2,335	$2,000	$1,695	$1,375	$1,050

Last MSR was $4,100.

**Smith B.T. Custom V
G Series
courtesy Ken Smith**

K

KENDRICK

Instruments currently built in Pflugerville, TX since 1994.

In 1989, Gerald Weber started Kendrick Amplifiers in Pflugerville, Texas. Originally dedicated to reproducing the classic Fender tweeds in exact detail, Kendrick has grown to include their own unique designs. Weber was the first designer to build a vintage-style amp complete with hand-wiring. Weber also joined a network of hand-built amplifier designers that shared an interest in helping musicians gain a knowledge of the workings of their favorite guitar amps.

Weber has been writing his monthly column for *Vintage Guitar Magazine* for a number of years now, and this was the first technical article that the magazine had ever printed. Weber is also the author of *A Desktop Reference of Hip Vintage Guitar Amps and Tube Talk for the Guitarist and Tech*, both of which gather together numerous technical tips for tube amplifiers.

ELECTRIC

Beginning in 1994, Weber offered two guitar models in addition to his amplifier line. Kendrick´s Continental model was designed as a tribute to Stevie Ray Vaughan and the Austin blues scene; the Town House model was named after the club in Texas where ZZ Top started their career. Both models are available in other custom colors.

**Smith C.R. Custom VI
O Series
courtesy Ken Smith**

GRADING	100% MINT	98% NEAR MINT	95% EXC+	90% EXC	80% VG+	70% VG	60% G

CANARY - single cutaway Les Paul style Honduran mahogany body, Brazilian canarywood neck, Madagascar rosewood fingerboard, 2 custom wound humbucker pickups, tune-o-matic bridge, four knobs, available in Sunburst Nitrocellulose finish, current mfg.

MSR	$3,295	$3,295	N/A	N/A	N/A	N/A	N/A

CONTINENTAL - offset angular swamp ash body, maple neck, 22-fret Brazilian rosewood fingerboard with pearl Texas-shaped inlay, 6-on-a-side tuners, chrome hardware, vintage-style tremolo, pickguard, 3 Lindy Fralin single coil vintage repro pickups, volume/2 tone controls, 5-way switch, available in Sunburst nitrocellulose lacquer finish, mfg. 1994-present.

MSR	$2,995	$2,995	N/A	N/A	N/A	N/A	N/A

SIRIUS - single cutaway Les Paul-style Honduran mahogany body, ivoroid binding, rosewood fingerboard, 3-per-side tuners, 2 P-90 pickups, four knobs, 3-way switch, current mfg.

MSR	$2,295	$2,295	N/A	N/A	N/A	N/A	N/A

TOWN HOUSE - single cutaway mahogany body, arched maple top, set-in mahogany neck, 22-fret Brazilian rosewood fingerboard with pearl Texas-shaped inlay, 3-per-side tuners, chrome hardware, tune-o-matic bridge, bridge/stop tailpiece, raised pickguard, 2 Lindy Fralin humbucker pickups, 2 volume/2 tone controls, 3-way selector, available in Sunburst nitrocellulose lacquer finish, mfg. 1994, 1996-present.

MSR	$3,295	$3,295	N/A	N/A	N/A	N/A	N/A

Town House Limited Edition - similar to the Town House, except has a solid Brazilian rosewood neck, tailpiece, and bridge, chambered Hoduran mahogany body, and an Adirondack spruce top, current mfg.

MSR	$5,995	$5,995	N/A	N/A	N/A	N/A	N/A

Currently, Kendrick has enough Brazilian rosewood to build four, and only four, of these guitars.

KENT

Instruments previously produced in Korea and Japan circa 1960s. Distributed in the U.S. by Buegeleisen & Jacobson of New York, NY; Maxwell Meyers in TX; Southland Musical Merchandise Corporation in NC; and Harris Fandel Corporation in MA.

The Kent trademark was used on a full line of acoustic and solid body electric guitars, banjos, and mandolins imported into the U.S. market during the 1960s. Some of the earlier Kent guitars were built in Japan by either the Teisco company or Guyatone, but the quality level at this time is down at the entry or student level. The majority of the models were built in Korea (source: Walter Murray, Frankenstein Fretworks; and Michael Wright, *Guitar Stories*, Volume One). The address for Kent Guitars (as distributed by Buegeleisen & Jacobson) during the 1960s was 5 Union Square, New York (New York 10003).

ELECTRIC

690 - offset double cutaway solid body, 17-fret bolt-on neck with black plastic binding, vertical rectangular position markers, 6-on-a-side tuners, 4 single coil pickups, chrome pickguard, 6 rocker switches for pickup control, 2 roller dials for volume and tone, tremolo tailpiece, adjustable bridge, available in Black/Yellow Sunburst finish.

	N/A	$200	$160	$130	$100	$75	$50

830 - maple top/back/sides, 24.75 in. scale, 23-fret rosewood fingerboard, 3-per-side tuners, roller bridge, 2 Kent pickups, volume/tone controls, pickup selector switch, available in Sunburst finish, length 42.5 in., body width 15.625 in., body depth 1.625 in., mfg. circa late 1960s-early 1970s.

	N/A	$300	$260	$230	$200	$170	$140

Last MSR was $99.

831 12-STRING - maple top/back/sides, round soundhole, 24.75 in. scale, 23-fret rosewood fingerboard, roller bridge, 6-per-side tuners, 2 pickups, volume/tone controls, pickup selector switch, length 42.5 in., body width 15.625 in., body thickness 1.625 in., mfg. circa late 1960s-early 1970s.

	N/A	$350	$300	$250	$210	$175	$150

Last MSR was $110.

ELECTRIC BASS

832 BASS - semi-acoustic maple body, 30.5 in. scale, 23-fret rosewood fingerboard, 2-per-side tuners, roller bridge, 2 Kent pickups, volume/tone controls, pickup selector switch, length 45.75 in., body width 19 in., body depth 1.625 in., mfg. circa late 1960s-early 1970s.

	N/A	$275	$235	$205	$175	$145	$115

Last MSR was $110.

KERCORIAN

Instruments previously built in Royal Oak, Michigan 1997-2000.

Jeff Kercorian founded Kercorian Bass Guitars in January of 1997. Kercorian, an electric bassist for many years, handled the bass model designs and electronics; and Jim Sebree, an instrument builder for the past twenty-five years, constructed the models.

ELECTRIC BASS

There was no charge for the fretless neck option. Exotic wood tops and backs were also offered.

Add $40 for fretless neck with inlaid lines. Add $50 for gold hardware. Add $75 for Hipshot D tuner. Add $80 for EMG 2-band EQ. Add $120 for EMG 3-band EQ.

SURREALIST - offset double cutaway body with exaggerated bass horn, eastern hard rock maple neck-through design, 34 in. scale, mahogany body wings, padauk (or purpleheart) top/back, 24-fret ebony fingerboard with mother-of-pearl dot inlay, chrome hardware, 2-per-side headstock, Gotoh tuners, Schaller fixed bridge, active EMG (or passive Bartolini) humbucking pickup, volume/tone controls, Neutrik locking output jack.

	N/A	N/A	N/A	N/A	N/A	N/A	N/A

Last MSR was $1,299.

This model was also available with bird's-eye maple/walnut top/back, walnut top/maple veneer, lacewood top/back, or walnut top/padauk and maple veneer.

KIMAXE

Instruments currently produced in Korea and China. Distributed by Kenny & Michael's Co., Inc. of Los Angeles, CA.

Kimaxe guitars are manufactured by Sang Jin Industrial Company, Ltd., which has a head office in Seoul, Korea and manufacturing facilities in four different places (Inchon, Bupyong, and Kongju, Korea; Tien Jin, China). Sang Jin Industrial Company, Ltd. is better known as a main supplier of guitars to world famous companies such as Fender, Hohner, and other buyers' own brand names for the past ten years. Sang Jin builds almost 10,000 guitars for these accounts each month. In 1994, Sang Jin established its own subsidiary (Kenny and Michael's Company) in Los Angeles in order to distribute their own lines of Kimaxe electric guitars and Corina acoustic guitars.

The Kimaxe line mainly offers quality solid body electric guitars and basses with designs based on classic American models at very affordable prices. For further information contact Kenny & Michael's Co., Inc. directly (see Trademark Index).

KIMBARA

Instruments previously produced in Japan from the late 1960s to 1990. Current trademark reintroduced to British marketplace in 1995. Instruments currently produced in China. Distributed in the U.K. by FCN Music.

The Kimbara trademark was a brand name used by a UK importer on these Japanese-produced budget level instruments. Kimbara acoustics were first introduced in England in the late 1960s. During the 1970s, the Kimbara trademark was also applied to a number of solid body guitars based on classic American designs as well. Kimbara instruments are generally mid- to good quality budget models, and a mainstay in the British market through 1990. In 1995, FCN Music began importing Chinese-built classical and dreadnought acoustic guitars into England. Retail price-wise, the reborn line is back in its traditional niche (source: Jerry Uwins, *Guitar the Magazine* [UK]).

KIMBERLY

Instruments currently produced in Seoul, Korea. Distributed by the Kimex Trading Co., Ltd. of Seoul, Korea. Instruments produced in Japan, circa 1960s to early 1970s. Previously distributed by Lafayette Company catalog sales.

Kimberly guitars were originally manufactured by Kawai Guitars (and pianos), located in Hamamatsu, Japan, and imported by Limmco, Inc., owned by Bob Seidman. The company tried to fill the void left by the discontinuance of the Kay & Harmony trademarks. Photographic evidence of a Kimberly-branded May Queen (yes, that infamous Teisco model!) arrived at the offices of the *Blue Book of Electric Guitars* in the 1990s. Fellow guitar enthusiasts are invited to send in photographs and information regarding Kimberly guitars (source: Mr. Bob Seidman, Seidman Sales, Ft. Lauderdale, FL.).

ELECTRIC

Current production of guitars under the Kimberly trademark is the Kimex Trading Co., Ltd. of Seoul, Korea. Kimex produces a number of guitar and bass models that favor classic American designs, and are designed with the entry level guitarist and student in mind.

While some of the currently produced Kimberly models feature solid alder, the majority of bodies are ply-constructed. Retail prices for the **KS-100** strat-styled model begin at $219, while a **KT-200** Tele-ish model lists for $329. For further information on models and pricing of current Kimberly instruments, contact the Kimex Trading Co., Ltd. directly (see Trademark Index).

KINAL

Instruments currently produced in Vancouver, British Columbia (Canada), since 1972.

Luthier Mike Kinal has been custom building and designing handcrafted guitars since the late 1960s. Kinal began building six-string solid body electrics, and produced the **Kinal Standard** in October, 1972. In 1974, Kinal designed the solid body carved top **Kinal Custom**, which became the trademark design throughout the 1970s and 1980s. In 1976, Kinal started to concentrate on bass guitar designs and produced a number of basses. Kinal turned his attention to the creation of the **Voyager Archtop** jazz guitar in 1988.

Mike Kinal now offers a line of guitars and basses with special emphasis on tonality, balance, and comfort. Kinal basses are available with a wide variety of custom finishes including figured and exotic tonewoods tops, headstock laminates, black, gold and two-tone hardware, thumb platforms, neck inlays, and active electronics. Contact Kinal to discuss your custom instrument needs (see Trademark Index, company history courtesy Mike Kinal, April 1977).

ELECTRIC

The **Voyager Archtop**'s body wood is all aged figured maple, and matched for color, tone, and grain pattern. Tops are made from Sitka or Englemann spruce. All tops and backs are hand graduated and tuned. The Voyager archtop is available in single cutaway or non-cutaway versions, and is available in a 25 in. or 25.5 in. scale. The fingerboard, bridge, pickguard, and tailpiece are all made from ebony, and the floating-type pickup is a Benedetto or Bartolini. The Voyager archtop is offered in Natural, Violin, or Sunburst finishes with clear coats of nitrocellulose lacquer. In current production, the retail list price is $5,000 for a non-cutaway, $6,500 for a single cutaway, and $8,000 for a Deluxe model. Other options are available at addtional costs.

CUSTOM - single cutaway Honduran mahogany body, arched bookmatched figured maple top, set-in Honduran mahogany neck, 22 nickel fret rosewood fingerboard with crown inlays, Schaller tuners and bridge, 2 humbucking pickups, 2 volume/2 tone controls, 3-way selector switch, available in Sunburst, Trans. Black, or Trans. Red finishes, current mfg.

MSR   **$3,200**

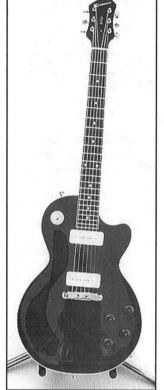

**Ken Smith BSR4MS
courtesy Ken Smith**

K

**Kinal MK4-B
courtesy Kinal**

STANDARD - offset double cutaway alder, korina, maple, or swamp ash body, set-in neck, 22 nickel fret rosewood fingerboard, chrome hardware, 3 single coil pickups, volume/tone/blend controls, 5-way selector switch, available in Black, Cherry Red, Cobalt Blue, or Sunburst finishes, current mfg.

    MSR   **$1,800**

      This model is available in a 24 2/3 in. scale, 25 in. scale, 25.5 in. scale lengths.

ELECTRIC BASS

DK 4-B - symmetrical double cutaway, contoured hollow body of alder, ash, maple or mahogany with a spruce top with soundholes. 34 in., 34.5 in., and 35 in. scales, 21- or 24-fret ebony, rosewood or maple fingerboard, chrome hardware, 1 single coil/piezo pickups, available in Natural, Burst, or Trans. finishes, disc.

                                                Last MSR was $2,250.

   DK 5-B 5-String - similar to DK 4-B, except in a 5-string configuration, current mfg.

    MSR   **$2,800**

MK 4 - offset double cutaway mahogany, alder, or swamp ash body core with bookmatched exotic hardwood top and backs, through-body laminated purpleheart/eastern maple or wenge neck, 34 in. or 35 in. scale, ebony fingerboard, 2 pickups, volume/blend/treble/mid/bass controls, active electronics, available in a highly polished clear polyester finish, disc.

                                                Last MSR was $2,400.

   MK 5 5-String - similar to the MK 4, except in a 5-string configuration, disc.

                                                Last MSR was $2,700.

MK 4-B - offset double cutaway alder, ash, korina or maple body, bolt-on graphite-reinforced hard maple neck, 34 in. or 35 in. scale, 24-fret ebony fingerboard, fixed bridge (front or rear loading of strings), 2 single coil Bartolini (or Fralin or Lane Poor) pickups, volume/blend/tone controls, available in Natural, Sunburst, Trans. Black, Trans. Blue, or Trans. Red finishes, current mfg.

    MSR   **$1,650**

   MK 5-B 5-String - similar to the MK 4-B, except in a 5-string configuration, current mfg.

    MSR   **$1,850**

   MK 6-B 6-String - similar to the MK 4-B, except in a 6-string configuration, current mfg.

    MSR   **$2,050**

   MK21-B - similar to the MK 4-B, except in five-string configuration and has 21 frets, disc. 2003.

                                                Last MSR was $2,100.

MK 21 - 5-string configuration, offset double cutaway alder, swamp ash, or korina body, maple neck with graphite reinforcement, 21-fret rosewood fingerboard, 3/2-per-side tuners, two pickups (Jazz/Soap, 2 Soap, 2 Jazz, or Jazz/MM), active electronics, four knobs, three-way switch, available in Trans. Black, Trans. Blue, Trans. Green, Trans. Red, Cherry, Nicotine, or Tobacco finishes, mfg. 2004-present.

    MSR   **$2,100**

SK 4-B - symmetrical double cutaway contour alder, ash, korina or maple body, bolt-on graphite reinforced hard maple neck, 34 in., 34.5 in., or 35 in. scale, 21 or 24-fret ebony, rosewood or maple fingerboard, fixed bridge (front or back loading strings), chrome hardware, 1 single coil and 1 humbucker pickup with coil tap (Bartolini or Basslines), available in Natural, Burst, or Trans. finishes, current mfg.

    MSR   **$1,650**

   SK 5-B 5-String - similar to SK 4-B, except in a 5-string configuration, current mfg.

    MSR   **$1,850**

   SK 6-B 6-String - similar to SK 4-B, except in a 6-string configuration, current mfg.

    MSR   **$2,100**

KING, DAVID

Instruments currently built in Portland, OR, since early 1990s.

Luthier Dave King hand-builds a number of custom basses ranging from minimalist body travel basses to ornately carved and inlaid instruments featuring on-board electronic tuners, active electronics, and headphone amplifiers. Most of King's instruments are custom orders and few of them come up for resale. King estimates he builds five or six guitars a year. For more information or a custom quote, contact King directly (see Trademark Index).

ELECTRIC BASS

David King´s philosophy is to build basses that are as comfortable and easy to play as possible. To this end, all specifications such as body dimension, materials, electronics, and finishes are customer specified. King custom machines all of his own headless hardware from solid brass and aluminum. King´s designs combine the latest advances in materials and electronics, with non-endangered and certified tonewoods.

The headless **DK** travel bass (last MSR $1,700) weighs in at 5 pounds. The **Ultralight** headless model (last MSR $1,900) features a khaya, swamp ash, or butternut body, while the **D Bass 4** headless model features exotic wood bodies (last MSR $2,100). The **Kappa** traditional model has a 2-per-side headstock, and a bolt-on or neck-through design (last MSR $2,200).

In the 2000s, King changed the way basses were named. There are two simple series, the Standard and the Basic. A Basic model starts with just a guitar and options are added to that. A four-string starts at $2,200, a five-string starts at $2,500, and a six-string starts at $2,800. The Standard model has more features than the Basic features and there are few options. A four-string starts at $3,200, a five-string starts at $3,600, a six-string starts at $4,000, a seven-string starts at $4,400, and an eight-string starts at $4,000.

KING´S STONE

Instruments previously produced in Japan.

The King's Stone trademark was a brand name used by U.S. importers Elger/Hoshino of Ardmore, Pennsylvania. King's Stone, along with others like Goldentone, Jamboree, and Elger were all used on Japanese guitars imported to the U.S. Elger/Hoshino evolved into Hoshino USA, distributor of Ibanez guitars (source: Michael Wright, *Guitar Stories*, Volume One).

GRADING		100% MINT	98% NEAR MINT	95% EXC+	90% EXC	80% VG+	70% VG	60% G

KINGSTON

Instruments previously produced in Japan from 1958 to 1967, and distributed in the U.S. by Westheimer Importing Corporation of Chicago, IL.

The Kingston brand name was used by U.S. importer Westheimer Importing Corporation of Chicago, Illinois. Jack Westheimer, who was one of the original guitar importers and distributors, is currently president of Cort Musical Instruments of Northbrook, Illinois. The Kingston trademark was used on a product line of acoustic and solid body electric guitars, electric bass guitars, banjos, and mandolins imported into the U.S. market during the 1960s. It has been estimated that 150,000 guitars were sold in the U.S. during the 1960s. Some of the earlier Kingston guitars were built in Japan by either the Teisco company or Guyatone (source: Michael Wright, *Guitar Stories*, Volume One).

ELECTRIC

MISC. SOLIDBODIES - various configurations, mfg. 1960s.

		100%	98%	95%	90%	80%	70%	60%
LOW END		N/A	$150	$120	$100	$80	$60	$40
HIGH END		N/A	$200	$160	$130	$100	$80	$60

**Kinal MK5-B
courtesy Kinal**

K

KLEIN, STEVE

Instruments currently produced in Sonoma, CA since 1976.

Steve Klein first began building electric guitars in Berkeley, California in 1967. A year later, Klein's grandmother introduced him to Dr. Michael Kasha at the University of California in Berkeley. Klein built his first acoustic after that meeting. He briefly attended the California College of Arts and Crafts in 1969, but left to continue building guitars.

In 1970, Klein built his second acoustic guitar. He moved to Colorado in the winter of 1970-1971, but later that summer accepted a job at The American Dream guitar shop back in San Diego (this shop was later bought by Bob Taylor and Kurt Listug, and grew into Taylor Guitars).

The third guitar Steve Klein built also had Kasha-inspired designs. Klein travelled to Detroit via Colorado, and met Richard Schneider. Schneider was building Kasha-style classical guitars at the time, and Klein thought that he was going to stay and apprentice with Schneider. Schneider looked at Klein's current guitar and said "Congratulations, you're a guitar builder," and sent Klein back home.

In the fall of 1972, Klein received his business license. He designed the current acoustic body shape and flying brace, and started work on the Electric Bird guitar. Later the next summer, Klein had finished the first L-457 acoustic, and by 1974 had finished three more acoustics; his first 12-string guitar and his first small (39.6 in.) body. Klein made a deal with Clayton Johnson (staff member of 'Bill Gramm Presents') to be able to get into concerts to show guitars to professional musicians. Klein got to meet such notables as Stills, Crosby, Young, David Lindly, Doc Watson, Roy Buchanan, John Sebastion (Loving Spoonful), and others. In the summer of 1975, Klein went to Los Angeles with guitars to meet J.D. Souther; he received a commission from Joni Mitchell, and set up shop in Oakland.

In 1976, Klein finally settled into his current shop space in Sonoma. He continued building and designing guitars while doing some repair work. Two years later, he finished Joni Mitchell's guitar, and the Electric Bird as well. In 1979, Klein met Steve Kauffman at a G.A.L. convention in Boston. That same year, Klein and Carl Margolis began developing a small electric model that was nicknamed Lumpy by David Lindly. Klein also did a side project of antique repair, furniture, and chairs for George Lucas at the Skywalker Ranch. On a more personal note, Klein married Lin Marie DeVincent in the spring of 1985, and Michael Hedges played at their wedding.

The MK Electric model was designed in conjunction with Ronnie Montrose in 1986. By 1988, the small Klein electric design was finished, and was debuted at a trade show in 1989. Klein Electric Division was started later that same year, and Steve Klein began designing an acoustic Harp guitar for Michael Hedges. A year later the acoustic Harp project was dropped in favor of an electrical Harp design instead (Hedges and guitar appeared on the cover of the October 1990 issue of *Guitar Player* magazine).

In the early 1990s, Klein began designing an acoustic bass guitar for and with Bob Taylor of Taylor Guitars. The first prototypes were assembled by Steve Kauffman in 1993. A large acoustic guitar order came in from Japan a year later, and the shipment was sent in 1995. In order to concentrate on the acoustic guitar production, Klein sold his Electric Division to Lorenzo German that same year, and the Electric Division still operates out of the original Klein Sonoma facilities. The Taylor/Klein acoustic bass went into production in 1996, and currently there is a waiting period on acoustic models.

In 1997, Klein went into business with Ed Dufault and opened Klein's Sonoma Music. Located on Broadway in Sonoma, California, the music shop services the local community as well as offering acoustic guitars built by Klein and other high grade builders like Michael Lewis.

ELECTRIC

Steve Klein began producing electric guitars in 1989, and production continued at the Klein facility through 1997. In 1995, Lorenzo German bought the Electric Division, and he continues to produce high quality electrics. (See Klein Electric Guitars).

KLEIN ELECTRIC GUITARS

Instruments currently produced in Linden, CA since 2000. Previously produced in Discovery Bay, CA from 1998-2000. Previously produced in Sonoma, CA from 1976-1997.

In 1988, Steve Klein finished designing a smaller electric guitar that featured a more ergonomic body style. This model debuted at the 1989 NAMM show, and the Klein Electric Division was started later that same year. In order to concentrate on his acoustic guitar production, Steve Klein sold his Electric Division to Lorenzo German in 1995, and the Electric Division operated out of the original Klein Sonoma facilities through 1997. In 1998, production moved to Discovery Bay, California. Lorenzo German continues to work and promote the high quality electric models. In 2000, the address changed one again to Linden, California.

**Klein E.G. Electric K-Bass
courtesy Loranzo German**

Current notable guitarists using the Klein electric include David Torn, Bill Frisell, Mick Goodrick, Lou Reed, Henry Kaiser, and Ken Hatfield.

ELECTRIC

The Klein Electric guitar model has an overall length of 31.5 in. Klein electric models are optional with a number of custom features.

Add $145 for a custom finish. Add $220 for a Novax fingerboard. Add $385 for a Steinberger Trans-Trem bridge. Add $169 for a chambered body (internal tone chambers). Add $353 for Joe Barden pickups. Add $88 for additional Seymour Duncan Alnico Pro II pickup (middle position). Add $88 for H.D. Z90 pickups. Add $575 for RMC Piezo pickups.

BF-96 - offset ergonomic swamp ash body, bolt-on one-piece headless rosewood neck, 25.5 in. scale, 24-fret rosewood fingerboard, Steinberger S-Trem bridge, pickguard, Seymour Duncan Jazz/Alnico II Pro/'59 humbucker pickups, volume/tone controls, 5-way selector switch, available in Black or Gloss White finishes, weight 6.5 lbs., current mfg.
MSR $3,250

DT-96 - offset ergonomic alder or basswood body, bolt-on one-piece headless rosewood neck, 25.5 in. scale, 24-fret rosewood fingerboard, Steinberger S-Trem bridge, Seymour Duncan Jazz/'59 humbucker pickups, volume/tone controls, 5-way selector switch, available in Black or Pearl White finishes, weight 7.5 lbs., current mfg.
MSR $2,675

ELECTRIC BASS

K BASS 4-STRING - offset ergonomic swamp ash or alder body with extended bass horn, bolt-on Moses Graphite neck, fretless rosewood fingerboard, 2 EMG (35P4/35J) pickups, 2 volume/tone stacked BTC controls, available in Black and Copper or Metallic Blue Zolatone finishes, current mfg.
MSR $2,525

Add $665 for a maple neck with rosewood or ebony fingerboard. Add $800 for a rosewood neck. Add $100 for a neck with a DB tuner. Add $185 for a Moses Graphite five-string neck. Add $285 for gloss finish.

KLIRA

Instruments currently produced in Germany since the late 1950s.

The Klira trademark originated in 1887 by builder Johannes Klier (another text gives "Otto" as his first name). The first company electrics appeared in 1958, and solid body guitars followed in 1960. Throughout the 1960s, Klira produced Fender-ish original designs; but as the 1970s started, the emphasis was put on versions of Fender and Gibson designs. Instruments are generally good quality functional guitars, and many have multi-laminate necks (akin to a wood butcher block, source: Tony Bacon, *The Ultimate Guitar Book*).

KNIGHT

Instruments previously made in England during the 1970s and 1980s. Instruments are currently built in Surrey, England.

Luthier Dick Knight (1907-1996) was a well-respected British guitar maker, and examples of his work were collected world-wide. Knight (born Stanley Charles Knight) specialized in archtop guitar construction, notably the Imperial model. While Knight began building his first guitars in the 1930s, he became more prominent in the 1970s (and 1980s), and featured such clients as Dave Gilmour, Paul McCartney, Pete Townshend, and Mike Rutherford (among others).

During Knight's formative years in the 1930s he worked for Lagonda, the motor vehicle manufacturer. After work, Knight would construct wood items at home, and lost the tips of his fingers in an accident. As this accident prevented him from playing guitar, he turned to making instruments as a hobby. At the outbreak of World War II, Knight met Ben and Lew Davis (the owners of Selmers music shop in London), as well as Joe Van Straten (Selmers' shop manager). In addition to instrument repair, Van Straten suggested the two work on producing a quality English archtop. When finances would not permit the business to carry on, Selmers asked Knight to produce some guitars.

Later, when Knight's wife became ill, he left his work at Selmers and professional guitar making for seventeen years. During this time period, he did produce a number of instruments under the Knight logo. Some of his earliest models do not have a name on the headstock. In addition to his archtop models, Knight produced flattop acoustic, solid body and 335-style guitars. All Knight's instruments were produced with the same high degree of quality. Recently, Knight's son-in-law Gordon Wells has been continuing to produce guitars and keep the Knight name alive in the guitar-building world (source: Keith Smart, *The Zemaitis Guitar Owners Club*).

KNOWBUDGE

Instruments previously built in Santa Barbara, CA, during the late 1990s.

KnowBudge Productions (a.k.a. K.B. Pro) built each guitar over a time period of nine months up to one year.

ELECTRIC

The 1996 Pinaka **T.C. 1-441** had a retail price of $18,369.27. The six-string hollowbody guitar also featured a sculptured Brunzchelle design, 22-fret ebony neck and graphite nut, fixed bridge, and passive electronics (volume control, on/off switch, volume bypass switch).

The 1998 6-string electric **Pinaka 411** (retail list $45,936.72) features a sleek Brunzchelle hollowbody with ebony fingerboard, 6-on-a-side reverse headstock, fully adjustable non-tremolo bridge, passive electronics (designed for use solely with tube amps), volume control, on/off switch, and a volume bypass switch. The output jack is located towards the rear main fin.

The final installment of the Pinaka series is the 1998 **Star** model. 108 guitars were built and 20 sold to the public. This guitar features a water resistant rubber finish and a Nightglow Waterproof pickup. The pickups are designed to be used with a tube amplifier. The fingerboard is ebony and special strings from K.B. Pro need to be used because regular strings will scratch the finish. This guitar retailed for $72,032.27.

Information courtesy KnowBudge Productions, 5-15-97.

KNUTSON LUTHIERY

Instruments currently built in Forrestville, CA, since 1978.

Luthier John Knutson has been building and repairing stringed instruments in and around the San Francisco Bay area since 1978. As a custom builder of acoustic, archtop, and electric instruments, Knutson has produced hundreds of guitars, mandolins, dulcimers, and basses (including custom double- and triple-neck combinations). For further information, contact luthier John Knutson directly (see Trademark Index).

Knutson is currently producing the **Messenger Upright Electric Bass** (retail list $2,450, $2,650 for passive electronics, $2,850 for passive/active electronics, and $3,050 for the Messenger/Barbera active electonics), the **Songbird Electric Mandolin** (list $2,250), and the **Messenger Electric Guitar** (retail list $1,450). John Knutson holds the exclusive rights to the Songbird, Ecotone, and Messenger trademarks.

KOLL GUITAR COMPANY

Instruments currently built in Portland, OR since 1993. Previously produced in Long Beach, CA from 1990-93.

Luthier Saul Koll combines his background in art (sculpture) and his ten-year experience with instrument repair to design and construct his quality guitars. Most Koll instruments are custom ordered, although he does offer four basic models based on, but not replicas of, vintage style instruments. Koll's guitars are constructed with fine quality tone woods and a glued neck joint design. For further information, contact luthier Koll directly (see Trademark Index).

**Knight Electric Model
courtesy Keith Smart**

The solidbody models have a unique double cutaway. The **Jr. Glide** features a single P-90 pickup and retails for $1,699. The **Superior** was introduced in 1997, has a deeper cutaway, two pickups, and retails for $1,850. The **Duo Glide** has a chambered body and retails for $2,399. The **Spectro Glide 12-String** has a chambered body and retails for $2,499. The **Super Glide Almighty** has a chambered mahogany body with a handcarved figured maple top and retails for $3,499.

Archtop models were first built in 1992, feature a single round cutaway, and many options are available. The **Rose City** has an Alaska sitka top with Pacific Northwest Big Leaf maple back and sides and retails for $3,599. The **Rose City 7** is the same as the Rose City, except in seven-string configuration and retails for $3,799. The **New Rose** was introduced in 2004, features an upgraded Rose City, and retails for $5,000. Koll bought the Bridgetown series in 2000. The **Bridgetown** is a 17 in. body with elaborate decoration and detail, and retails for $6,500. The **Bridgetown 7** is the same as the Bridgetown, except in seven-string configuration and retails for $6,900.

The **Thunder Glide Ali** bass has a shape similar to the solidbody guitars and is made of solid alder, a maple neck, and retails for $1,995. The **Thunderglide Eli Corbet Bass** was developed with Todd Corbett and retails for $2,849. The **Thunderglide Ali Eric Wilson Bass** was developed for Eric Wilson and retails for $3,499.

KONA

Instruments currently produced in Asia. Distributed by M&M Merchandisers of Ft. Worth, TX.

M&M Merchandisers has owned pawn shops since 1976 and done a lot of buying and selling of instruments as well as other products. In July, 2001, they introduced a line of guitars built overseas. There are acoustics, electrics, and guitar amplifiers. Kona guitars are quality instruments at affordable prices. Most retail prices are between $200 and $400. For more information contact M&M Merchandisers (see Trademark Index).

KOONTZ

See also Standel and Harptone. Instruments previously built in Linden, NJ.

Luthier Stan Koontz designed several different models of acoustic and electric guitars and basses for Bob Crooks' Standel company. The instruments were built in Harptone's New Jersey facilities, and have the Standel logo on the peghead. Koontz also built his own custom guitars that featured striking innovations as side-mounted electronics and a hinged internal f-hole cover. Stan passed away in the late 1980s (source: Tom Wheeler, *American Guitars*).

KRAMER

Instruments previously produced in Neptune, NJ. Kramer (the original BKL company) was located in Neptune, NJ, since its inception in 1975 to the late 1980s. Production of Kramer (KMI) instruments was at facilities in Eatontown, NJ. Kramer Guitars is currently a division of Gibson Musical Instruments, located in Nashville, TN. Distributed worldwide by MusicYo.com.

Gary Kramer and Dennis Berardi founded the firm in October of 1975 to produce guitars. Kramer, one of the ex-partners of Travis Bean, brought in his guitar-building know-how to Berardi's previous retail experience. In the following April, Peter J. LaPlaca joined the two. LaPlaca had worked his way up through Norlin to vice presidency before joining Kramer and Berardi. The original company is named after their three initials: B, K, and L. Kramer (BKL) opened the Neptune factory on July 1, 1976. The first Kramer guitar was co-designed by luthier Phil Petillo, Berardi, and Kramer. Once the prototypes were completed and the factory tooled up, the first production run was completed on November 15, 1976. The first solid body guitars featured an original body design, and a bolt-on aluminum neck with rear wood inlays.

One month after the first production run was finished, Gary Kramer left the BKL company. Guitar production under the Kramer trademark continued. By the early 1980s, the company line consisted of fourteen different guitar and bass designs with a price range of $649 to $1,418. Kramer's high profile continued to rise, thanks to an exclusive

**1998 Knowbudge Pinaka 441
courtesy Knowbudge**

GRADING	100% MINT	98% NEAR MINT	95% EXC+	90% EXC	80% VG+	70% VG	60% G

endorsement deal with Edward Van Halen. In the mid-1980s, the company flourished as they had the sole license to market the Floyd Rose tremolo system.

In 1985, Berardi bought the Spector company; production and distribution of Spector basses then originated from Kramer's facilities in New Jersey. Throughout the late 1980s, Kramer was one of the guitar companies favored by the hard rock/heavy metal bands (along with Charvel/Jackson). However, the company went into bankruptcy in 1989, attempted refinancing several times, and was purchased at auction by a group that incorporated the holdings under the company name of Kramer Musical Instruments in 1995. The newly-reformed Kramer (KMI) company had also acquired the rights to the Spector trademark and Spector instruments designs. Kramer (KMI) was located in Eatontown, New Jersey.

Kramer (KMI) reintroduced several new models at industry trade shows in 1995, again sporting an aluminum neck design. However, the company never did directly bring any large amount of products to the musical instrument market.

In 1997, the Gibson corporation acquired the Kramer trademark. By 1998, Gibson was displaying Kramer-trademarked models at the Summer NAMM industry show, and ads in the print media followed a month later. It has been indicated by some Gibson company officials that the Kramer SuperStrat style models will be produced in Korea (like current Epiphone models).

MODEL INFORMATION & FINISHES

Aluminum Neck Models: The first solid body guitars offered in 1975 featured aluminum necks with the open or prong V-shape. This is the first identifying clue in comparing a Travis Bean versus a Kramer, as all Travis Bean models have a closed top (which forms a enclosed ´T´). The first Kramer models featured original body designs and two Kramer pickups (they have Kramer on the pickup covers). In 1978 the DMZ Custom series offered DiMarzio pickups.

Wood Neck Models: By 1982, the aluminum neck construction was phased out for a more conventional wood neck/wood body guitars. All high end Kramer USA and Custom models were produced in America. The Focus series of guitars (1985-1989) were built in Japan. Striker series and AeroStar series (also 1985-1989) were built in Korea.

When Kramer switched over to the more conventional wood neck/wood body guitars, the Natural finishes that they were using were phased out in favor of new solid finishes (these colors may also be found on the later aluminum neck models as well): Arctic White, Aztec Rust, Electric Yellow, Flame Red, Midnight Black, Pacific Blue, Slate Blue, and Sundance Orange finishes.

ELECTRIC: AEROSTAR SERIES

The AeroStar series was produced in Korea during the mid-1980s as an entry level to the more expensive U.S. produced Kramers, and have the EMG Select pickups in them.

ZX 10 - offset double cutaway body, single humbucker pickup, six-on-a-side tuners, mfg. mid-1980s.

	N/A	$150	$120	$100	$80	$60	$40

ZX 20 - offset double cutaway body, two humbucker pickups, six-on-a-side tuners, mfg. mid-1980s.

	N/A	$175	$145	$125	$105	$85	$65

ZX 30/ZX 30H - offset double cutaway body, 3 single coil (ZX 30) or H/S/S (ZX 30H) pickups, six-on-a-side tuners, mfg. mid-1980s.

	N/A	$200	$170	$145	$120	$95	$75

ELECTRIC: ALUMINUM NECK SERIES

Earlier aluminum neck models from 1976 like the 450 feature a laminated "cutting board" style wood body, stop tailpiece, an aluminum plate over the area where the neck bolts to the body, and the 3-per-side "prong" aluminum headstock. The 450 model featured 2 humbuckers, 2 volume and 2 tone controls, and a 3-way pickup selector switch. Other models featured 3 single coil pickups. Research continues on models 250, 350, 450 G, and 650 to designate the differences. Aluminum neck models are generally priced from $250 to $500 in good condition. While most dealers are happy to sell them, some dealers are holding on to them and cranking up the asking price in the theory that these models may someday be collectible. However, the early models are still "as heavy as a bear" (as we say up north, don´t you know) - and when the neck warms up, the tuning goes out. You be the judge!

250/350/450G/650 - offset double cutaway body, aluminum neck, prong style headstock, various controls and pickups, mfg. late 1970s.

	N/A	$500	$425	$350	$300	$250	$200

ELECTRIC: BARETTA SERIES

BARETTA - offset double cutaway Stratocaster style, bolt-on maple neck, 22-fret rosewood fingerboard, six-on-one-side pointed headstock, Floyd Rose tremolo, single diagonally mounted pickup, single knob, black hardware, available in various finishes, mfg. 1984-86.

	N/A	$500	$425	$375	$325	$275	$225

ELECTRIC: DMZ CUSTOM SERIES

DMZ CUSTOM 1000 - offset double cutaway maple body, bolt-on aluminum neck with wood inserts, 21-fret ebanol fingerboard with white dot inlay, prong 3-per-side headstock, Schaller tuners, bridge/stop tailpiece, aluminum or stainless steel hardware, 2 DiMarzio Super Distortion humbuckers, volume/tone controls, 3-way selector switch, available in Natural finish, mfg. 1978-1982.

	N/A	$550	$475	$400	$325	$250	$200

Last MSR was $629.

DMZ CUSTOM 2000 - similar to the DMZ Custom 1000, except has 2 DiMarzio Dual Sound humbuckers, 2 mini switches (coil taps), disc.

	N/A	$600	$525	$450	$375	$300	$225

Last MSR was $649.

DMZ CUSTOM 3000 - similar to the DMZ Custom 1000, except has 3 DiMarzio SDS-1 single coil pickups, 5-way selector switch, disc.

	N/A	$600	$525	$450	$375	$300	$225

Last MSR was $559.

DMZ CUSTOM 6000G - similar to the DMZ Custom 1000, except has a bird´s-eye maple top, aluminum neck, two humbucker pickups and active electronics, mfg. 1978-1982.

	N/A	$575	$500	$425	$350	$275	$225

GRADING	100% MINT	98% NEAR MINT	95% EXC+	90% EXC	80% VG+	70% VG	60% G

ELECTRIC: DUKE (HEADLESS) SERIES

Kramer's headless guitars and basses debuted between 1981 and 1982. Steinberger's new designs certainly were reviewed throughout the market, apparently.

DUKE STANDARD - headless design, aluminum neck, 22-fret neck, single pickup, mfg. 1981-82.

	N/A	$500	$425	$350	$300	$250	$200

This model was also available with a Floyd Rose Tremolo and two pickups.

DUKE SPECIAL - headless design, aluminum neck, 22-fret neck, two pickups, mfg. 1981-82.

	N/A	$550	$475	$400	$325	$250	$200

This model was also available with a Floyd Rose Tremolo and two pickups.

ELECTRIC: FOCUS SERIES

Focus series guitars were the Japanese-produced entry level models in 1984. A bit better than the AeroStars, but cheaper price-wise than the U.S. Pacer models. Another model named after a Ford vehicle, maybe this is where Ford gets their ideas!

FOCUS 1000 - offset double cutaway, single pickup, 6-on-one-side pickups, tremolo, mfg. 1984-88.

	N/A	$350	$300	$250	$210	$175	$125

FOCUS 2000 - similar to the Focus 1000, except has two pickups, mfg. 1984-88.

	N/A	$400	$350	$300	$250	$200	$150

FOCUS 3000 - similar to the Focus 1000, except has three pickups, mfg. 1984-88.

	N/A	$450	$375	$325	$275	$225	$175

ELECTRIC: PACER SERIES

The Pacer series was introduced in 1983, and were generally pretty good quality guitars now unfairly associated with the 1980s "hair band" heavy metal groups (although some would argue that the "hair bands" were to real metal what dryer lint is to an angora sweater). These guitars were around $1,200 when they were new.

PACER - offset double cutaway, pointy headstock, maple neck, rosewood fingerboard, 2 single coil and a humbucker Seymour Duncan pickups, three knobs (v, 2 tones), Floyd Rose Tremolo, mfg. 1983-84.

	N/A	$550	$475	$400	$325	$250	$200

Pacer Custom - similar to the Pacer except has dual humbucker pickups and gold hardware, mfg. 1983-84.

	N/A	$600	$525	$450	$375	$300	$225

Pacer Deluxe - similar to the Pacer, except has optional "Flicker," mfg. 1983-84.

	N/A	$650	$575	$475	$400	$325	$250

Pacer Imperial - similar to the Pacer Custom, mfg. mid-1980s.

	N/A	$600	$525	$450	$375	$300	$225

ELECTRIC: SIGNATURE SERIES

GENE SIMMONS AXE - "Olde English Executioner Axe"-style maple (or ash) body, bolt-on aluminum neck with rear wood inserts, 22-fret ebanol fingerboard, chrome hardware, 3-per-side "prong" headstock, 2 DiMarzio humbuckers, volume/tone controls, 3-way switch, available in Black and Silver custom polyester finish, mfg. 1980-81.

	N/A	$2,200	$1,900	$1,600	$1,300	$1,000	$800

Last MSR was $799.

Kramer produced a matching bass model. Both had limited runs of 1000 instruments, numbered and signed by Gene Simmons (KISS).

GORKY PARK - Ballalaika-shaped guitar, bolt-on maple neck, mfg. 1986-87.

	N/A	$650	$575	$475	$400	$325	$250

This model was designed in conjunction with the Russian heavy metal band Gorky Park in 1989.

KRAMER-RIPLEY STEREO GUITAR RSG-1 - offset double cutaway body, 6-on-a-side headstock, Floyd Rose locking tremolo, volume/tone controls, mfg. 1985-87.

	N/A	$800	$700	$600	$500	$425	$350

Last MSR was $1,349.

Designed by luthier Steve Ripley. Guitar features a six-channel stereo mix, with a panning pot for each string.

PAUL DEAN SIGNATURE - offset double cutaway body, ebony fingerboard, 6-on-a-side pointy headstock, Floyd Rose locking tremolo system, 2 Seymour Duncan Vintage Staggered single coils/Seymour Duncan JB humbucker pickups, volume/tone controls, 3 on/off pickup switches, mfg. 1986-88.

	N/A	$600	$525	$450	$375	$300	$225

Last MSR was $1,400.

RICHIE SAMBORA SIGNATURE - offset double cutaway body, maple fingerboard with black star inlays, 6-on-a-side pointy headstock, gold hardware, Floyd Rose locking tremolo system, 2 Seymour Duncan humbucker pickups, volume/tone controls, 5-way selector switch, mfg. 1988-1991.

	N/A	$600	$525	$450	$375	$300	$225

Last MSR was $1,380.

**Kramer Custom Shop
Bon Jovi Model
Courtesy Eric Ernest**

K

**Kramer Baretta
courtesy Brian Goff**

GRADING		100% MINT	98% NEAR MINT	95% EXC+	90% EXC	80% VG+	70% VG	60% G

ELECTRIC: STRIKER SERIES

The Striker series, like the AeroStar series, was produced in Korea in the mid-1980s. Similar intent, slightly different features.

STRIKER - double offset cutaway, similar to the Aerostar series, two single coil and one humbucker pickups, mfg. mid-1980s.

	N/A	$300	$250	$200	$160	$130	$95

DOUBLENECK STRIKER - similar to the Striker, except in doubleneck electric and acoustic configuration, current mfg.

MSR	N/A	$600	$525	$450	$400	$350	$300	$250

ELECTRIC BASS: DMZ CUSTOM SERIES

DMZ CUSTOM 4000 - offset double cutaway maple body, bolt-on aluminum neck with wood inserts, 21-fret ebanol fingerboard with white dot inlay, prong 2-per-side headstock, Schaller tuners, bridge/stop tailpiece, aluminum or stainless steel hardware, 2 DiMarzio dual coil humbuckers, volume/tone controls, 3-way selector switch, active EQ, available in Natural finish, mfg. 1978-1982.

	N/A	$650	$550	$450	$375	$300	$225

Last MSR was $679.

ELECTRIC BASS: MIDI SERIES

In the mid-1980s, Kramer retailed a MIDI interface unit designed by IVL Technologies called the Pitchrider 7000. Ideally, any guitar could be hooked up to the Pitchrider 7000 using a hexaphonic pickup, have guitar information converted to a MIDI signal, and send that signal to any MIDI compatible synthesizer. Although not a guitar per se, this tool can add an extra dimension to an existing guitar (providing it tracks the note information properly). In 1988, the Pitchrider (Mark II) had a list price of $649; an additional MFS-40 foot switch was optional for an additional $150.

KRUNDAAL

Instruments previously built in Italy circa early to mid-1960s.

Krundaal instruments designed by Italian motorcycle and guitar appreciator, Wandré Pelotti (1916-1981). Wandré instruments may bear a number of different brand names (such as **Davoli**, **Framez**, **Avalon**, or **Avanti**), but the Wandré logo will appear somewhere. Wandré guitars were personally produced by Pelotti from 1956 or 1957 to 1960; between 1960 to 1963, by Framez in Milan, Italy; and from 1963 to 1965 by Davoli. Under the Krundaal logo a stamped "A. Davoli, Made in Italy" designation can be found (source: Tony Bacon, *The Ultimate Guitar Book*).

ELECTRIC

BIKINI - rounded body design, stylized W bridge, two single coil Davoli pickups, mfg. circa 1963-65.

	N/A	$850	$725	$625	$550	$450	$350

This model features an attached portable amplifier.

KUSTOM

Instruments previously built in Chanute, KS during the late 1960s.

The Kustom Amplifier company, builders of the famous tuck-and-roll covered amps, produced four different guitar models in their Kansas factory from 1967 to late 1969. Bud Ross, the founder/designer of Kustom, was a bassist-turned-second-guitarist in the late 1950s who had a knack for electronics and wiring. Ross teamed up with Fred Berry, and Kustom amps debuted at the summer 1965 NAMM show. Eventually the line ranged from small combos to huge P.A.s and bass cabinets (imagine the amp backline at a Creedence Clearwater Revival show, and you'll get an idea about the range of the Kustom product line).

In 1967, Doyle Reeding approached Ross about building guitars. Along with Wesley Valorie, the three began designing electric guitars. Guitar wizard Roy Clark, who later became a Kustom amp endorser, also had input on the Kustom design. These semi-hollowbody guitars featured two-piece carved-out top glued to a two-piece carved-out back (similar to the Microfrets design). Ross estimates that between 2,000 and 3,000 were produced during the two years, all in the Kansas facility (source: Michael Wright, *Guitar Stories*, Volume One).

ELECTRIC

All models featured a common body design, and differed in the hardware and pickups that were installed.

K200 A - dual cutaway semi-hollow body, bolt-on maple neck, 22-fret bound rosewood fingerboard with dice dot inlays, cat's-eye f-hole, zero fret, chrome-plated nut, 3+3 winged headstock, black pickguard, Bigsby tremolo system, 2 DeArmond humbuckers, 2 volume/2 tone controls, 3-way pickup selector switch, available in Black, Black Ash, Blue, Natural, Red, Sunburst, White Ash, Wineburst, or Zebra finishes, mfg. 1967-late 1969.

	N/A	$800	$700	$600	$500	$400	$300

The burgundy to green Wineburst finish is also called Watermelon Burst by collectors.

K200 B - similar to the K200 A, except has double dot inlay on fingerboard, trapeze tailpiece, and 2 DeArmond single coils, mfg. 1967-late 1969.

	N/A	$750	$625	$550	$450	$375	$300

K200 C - similar to the K200 A, except has smaller unwinged headstock design, white pickguard, and less fancy tuning machines, mfg. 1967-late 1969.

	N/A	$700	$575	$500	$400	$325	$250

GRADING	100% MINT	98% NEAR MINT	95% EXC+	90% EXC	80% VG+	70% VG	60% G

ELECTRIC BASS

K200 D - dual cutaway semi-hollow body, bolt-on maple neck, 21-fret rosewood fingerboard with single dot inlays, cat's-eye f-hole, zero fret, chrome-plated nut, 2-per-side winged headstock, black pickguard, bass bridge/stop tail-piece, 2 DeArmond 4-pole single coil pickups, 2 volume/2 tone controls, 3-way pickup selector switch, available in Black, Black Ash, Blue, Natural, Red, Sunburst, White Ash, Wineburst, or Zebra finishes, mfg. 1967-late 1969.

	N/A	$800	$700	$600	$500	$400	$300

KYDD

Instruments currently built in Upper Darby, PA. Distributed by Modulus Guitars of Novato, CA.

Luthier/inventor Bruce Kaminsky, a freelance bassist, designed the Kydd Carry-On bass electric bass to replicate the sounds of an upright acoustic bass in a six pound, 35.5 in. overall length instrument. This smaller instrument is set up on a tripod stand, and has a 30 in. scale (as compared to a 41 in. plus scale on the old doghouse acoustics). Over the past couple of years, Kaminsky estimates that he has sold at least 100 instruments. Recently, the Modulus Guitars company set up a distribution deal with Kaminsky to further distribute his basses. For further information, please contact luthier Kaminsky directly (see Trademark Index).

ELECTRIC BASS

K BASS - solid hard maple minimalist body/neck, granadillo fingerboard with pearl side position markers, maple adjustable bridge, chrome string clamp and tuning system, Fishman transducers, volume/tone controls, available in a hand rubbed, ultra-thin finish, 35.5 in. overall length, 30 in. scale, current mfg.

MSR **$1,795**

Add $200 for curly maple body/neck.

List price includes a tripod stand and padded gig bag.

K 5 5-String - similar to the K 4 4-String, except in five-string configuration, current mfg.
MSR **$1,995**

K 6 6-String - similar to the K 4 4-String, except in six-string configuration, current mfg.
MSR **$2,195**

KYLE, DOUG

Instruments currently built in Hampstead (Devon), England.

Doug Kyle is currently offering handcrafted guitars.

K

NOTES

Section L

LTD

Instruments currently built in Korea. Distributed by the ESP Guitar Company, of North Hollywood, CA, since 1994.

LTD instruments are designed and distributed by the ESP Guitar Company. All of the designs are based on current ESP models, and offer a cost effective way to own the same ESP style instruments. LTD also have Starter packs that inlcude a guitar or bass, amp, tuner, gig bag, strap, cable, and a lesson CD-ROM.

GRADING	100% MINT	98% NEAR MINT	95% EXC+	90% EXC	80% VG+	70% VG	60% G

ELECTRIC: 50 SERIES

AX-50 - offset four-point sharp-edged agathis body, maple neck, rosewood fingerboard with dot inlay, 3-per-side tuners, STB, two humbucker pickups, two knobs, three-way switch, black hardware, available in Black Satin or Silver Satin finishes, 25.5 in. scale, new 2005.

	MSR	$349		$250	$210	$180	$150	$130	$110	$90

EC-50 - single cutaway agathis body, maple neck, rosewood fingerboard, two humbucker pickups, 3-per-side tuners, black hardware, available in Titanium or Black finishes, mfg. 2003-present.

	MSR	$299		$225	$190	$160	$140	$120	$95	$70

EX-50 - Explorer-style agathis body, maple neck, rosewood fingerboard, two humbucker pickups, 6-on-one-side tuners, black hardware, available in Titanium or Black finishes, mfg. 2003-present.

	MSR	$319		$240	$200	$170	$150	$125	$100	$75

F-50 - offset sharp-edged agathis body, maple neck, rosewood fingerboard, two humbucker pickups, 3-per-side tuners, black hardware, available in Titanium, Black Cherry or Black finishes, mfg. 2003-present.

	MSR	$319		$240	$200	$170	$150	$125	$100	$75

H-50 - offset double cutaway agathis body, maple neck, rosewood fingerboard, two humbucker pickups, 3-per-side tuners, black hardware, available in Electric Blue or Black finishes, mfg. 2003-present.

	MSR	$299		$225	$190	$160	$140	$120	$95	$70

M-50 - offset double cutaway agathis body, maple neck, rosewood fingerboard, two humbucker pickups, 6-on-one-side tuners, black hardware, tremolo, available in Blue Satin, Black Satin or Grey Satin finishes, mfg. 2003-present.

	MSR	$249		$190	$160	$140	$120	$100	$80	$60

MH-50 - offset double cutaway agathis body, maple neck, rosewood fingerboard, two humbucker pickups, 6-on-one-side tuners, black hardware, tremolo, available in Black Cherry or Black finishes, mfg. 2003-present.

	MSR	$299		$225	$190	$160	$140	$120	$95	$70

Add $30 for Tremolo.

VIPER-50 - sharp SG-ish double cutaway agathis body, maple neck, rosewood fingerboard, two humbucker pickups, 3-per-side tuners, black hardware, available in Grey Satin or Black finishes, mfg. 2003-present.

	MSR	$299		$210	$180	$160	$140	$120	$95	$70

LTD AX-50
courtesy LTD

ELECTRIC: 100 SERIES

E-100 - single cutaway alder body, bolt-on maple neck, 22-fret rosewood fingerboard with white dot inlay, tune-o-matic bridge/stop tailpiece, 3-per-side headstock, chrome hardware, 2 LTD exposed pole piece humbucker pickups, volume/tone controls, 3-position selector, available in Black, Candy Apple Red, or Pearl White finishes, mfg. 1998-99.

				$350	$300	$250	$225	$175	$150	$100

Last MSR was $429.

EC-100QM - single cutaway agathis body with quilted maple top, maple neck, 24-fret rosewood fingerboard, two humbucker pickups, 3-per-side tuners, black hardware, available in See-Thru Black Cherry finish, mfg. 2002-present.

	MSR	$399		$280	$240	$210	$180	$150	$120	$95

H-100 - offset double cutaway arched top alder body, bolt-on maple neck, 22-fret rosewood fingerboard with white dot inlay/block inlay on 12th fret, tune-o-matic bridge/stop tailpiece, 'curved point' peghead, 3-per-side tuners, chrome hardware, 2 LTD humbucker pickups, volume/tone controls, 3-way selector toggle, available in Black, Candy Apple Red, and Pearl White finishes, mfg. 1998-2002.

				$285	$225	$200	$175	$150	$125	$100

Last MSR was $399.

H-100FM - similar to the H-100, except has an agathis body with a flamed maple top, available in See-Thru Aqua, mfg. 2003-present.

	MSR	$399			$280	$225	$200	$175	$150	$125	$100

LTD EC-50
courtesy LTD

GRADING	100% MINT	98% NEAR MINT	95% EXC+	90% EXC	80% VG+	70% VG	60% G

M-100 - offset double cutaway alder body, bolt-on maple neck, 22-fret rosewood fingerboard with white dot inlay (logo block inlay at 12th fret), LTD licensed Floyd Rose tremolo, reverse peghead, 6 on-the-other-side tuners, black hardware, 2 LTD humbucker pickups, volume/tone control, 3-position switch, available in Black, Candy Apple Red, or Pearl White finishes, mfg. 1998-2001.

		$275	$225	$190	$175	$150	$100	$75

Last MSR was $399.

M-100FM - similar to the M-100, except has an agathis body with a flamed maple top, available in See-Thru Black, mfg. 2003-present.

MSR	$399	$280	$225	$200	$175	$150	$125	$100

MH-100 - similar to H-100, except has Floyd Rose Licensed bridge, 24 XJ frets, and two EMG-HZ humbucker pickups, available in See-Through Black, See-Through Black Cherry, or See-Through Aqua finishes, mfg. 1999-2002.

		$389	$315	$250	$225	$200	$170	$150

Last MSR was $499.

MH-100QM - similar to the MH-100, except has an agathis body with a quilted maple top, available in See-Thru Aqua, mfg. 2003-present.

MSR	$399	$280	$230	$200	$175	$150	$125	$100

Add $30 for tremolo.

MV-100 - offset double cutaway basswood body, bolt-on maple neck, rosewood fingerboard with offset dot position markers, model name inlaid at 12th fret, black hardware, tune-o-matic bridge with string through body, 24 XJ frets, LTD LB-100 and LR-100 pickups, 1 volume/1 tone, 3-way toggle, available in Black, Metallic Gold, Ice Blue, or Teal finishes, mfg. 2001-02.

		$320	$275	$250	$225	$200	$175	$150

Last MSR was $399.

VIPER-100FM - sharp SG-ish double cutaway agathis body with flamed maple top, maple neck, rosewood fingerboard, two humbucker pickups, 3-per-side tuners, black hardware, available in See-Thru Black finish, mfg. 2002-present.

MSR	$399	$280	$225	$200	$175	$150	$125	$100

ELECTRIC: 200 SERIES

E-200 (LTD ECLIPSE) - single cutaway alder or mahogany body, bolt-on maple neck, 22-fret bound rosewood fingerboard with white dot inlay (logo block inlay at 12th fret), tune-o-matic bridge/stop tailpiece, 3-per-side headstock, chrome hardware, 2 Duncan-designed exposed pole piece humbucker pickups, volume/tone controls, 3-position selector, available in Black, Honey Sunburst, See-Through Blue, See-Through Purple, or See-Through Red finishes, mfg. 1996-99.

		$475	$400	$350	$295	$250	$200	$150

Last MSR was $549.

EC-200QM - single cutaway agathis body with quilted maple top, 3-piece mahogany neck, 24-fret rosewood fingerboard with dot inlay and 12th fret model name inlay, 2 EMG-HZ humbucker pickups, Tune-O-Matic bridge, 3 knobs, black hardware, available in See-Thru Black finish, mfg. 2004-present.

MSR	$599	$420	$350	$300	$250	$210	$180	$150

EXP-200 (LTD E.X.P.) - radical offset hourglass alder body, bolt-on maple neck, 22-fret rosewood fingerboard with white dot inlay, tune-o-matic bridge/stop tailpiece, black 'drooping' peghead with screened logo, 6-on-a-side tuners, black hardware, 2 Duncan-designed humbuckers, volume/tone controls, 3-position switch, available in Black or Olympic White finishes, mfg. 1996-99.

		$575	$500	$425	$375	$300	$250	$175

Last MSR was $719.

F-200 - offset double cutaway body with a gothis flavor, basswood body, bolt-on maple neck, rosewood fingerboard with arrowhead position markers, black hardware, Floyd Rose Licensed bridge, 24 XJ frets, 2 humbucker EMG HZ pickups, 3-per-side tuners, locking nut, available in Black, Black Cherry, Midnight Purple, or Gunmetal Blue finishes, mfg. 2000-03.

		$450	$375	$325	$275	$225	$175	$135

Last MSR was $649.

FB-200 - 27 in. baritone scale, offset double cutaway basswood body with gothic styling, bolt-on maple neck, rosewood fingerboard with arrowhead position markers, 3-per-side tuners, black hardware, tune-o-matic bridge, 24 XJ frets, 2 humbucker EMG HZ pickups, EMG Afterburner Active Gain Boost, 1 volume/1 tone control, toggle, available in Black finish, mfg. 2001 only.

		$575	$525	$475	$450	$400	$375	$325

Last MSR was $749.

H-200 (LTD HORIZON) - offset double cutaway alder or mahogany arched top body with natural binding, bolt-on maple neck, 24-fret bound rosewood fingerboard with white dot inlay/block inlay on 12th fret, tune-o-matic bridge/stop tailpiece, bound 'curved point' peghead, 3-per-side tuners, chrome hardware, 2 Duncan-designed humbucker pickups, volume/tone controls, 3-way selector toggle, available in Black, Honey Sunburst, See-Through Blue, See-Through Purple, or See-Through Red finishes, mfg. 1995-2000.

		$409	$3755	$325	$275	$225	$175	$125

Last MSR was $549.

H-201 - similar to Model H-200 except has mahogany body with flamed maple top, block position markers and model name inlaid at 12th fret, black hardware, natural top and body binding, Duncan-designed HB-102 pickup set, 1 volume/1 tone control, 5-way Megaswitch, available in See-Through Green, See-Through Red, See-Through Orange, or See-Through Blue, mfg. 2001 only.

		$480	$450	$425	$400	$350	$325	$300

Last MSR was $599.

H-202 - similar to the H-201, available in See-Thru Red, See-Thru Green, or See-Thru Blue, mfg. 2002-03.

		$350	$290	$250	$220	$180	$150	$120

Last MSR was $499.

GRADING	100% MINT	98% NEAR MINT	95% EXC+	90% EXC	80% VG+	70% VG	60% G

M-2 - offset double cutaway hardwood body, bolt-on neck, 24-fret rosewood fingerboard with white dot inlay (logo block inlay at 12th fret), double locking vibrato, reverse 'pointy' blackface peghead with screened logo, 6-on-the-other-side tuners, black hardware, single coil/humbucker ESP pickups, volume control, 3-position switch, available in Black finish, mfg. 1995-98.

	$750	$700	$625	$550	$450	$350	$275

Last MSR was $1,095.

Add $100 for See-Through Blue, See-Through Purple, or See-Through Red finishes.

M-200 - offset double cutaway alder body, bolt-on maple neck, 22-fret rosewood fingerboard with arrowhead inlays (logo block inlay at 12th fret), recessed Floyd Rose Standard tremolo, reverse peghead, 6-on-the-other-side tuners, black hardware, 2 Duncan-designed humbucker pickups, volume/tone control, 3-position switch, available in Black, Pearl White, See-Through Blue, or See-Through Red finishes, mfg. 1998-2000.

	$429	$375	$300	$250	$200	$175	$125

Last MSR was $599.

M-200 FM - similar to the M-200, except has a flame maple top, available in See-Thru Black or See-Thru Black Cherry finishes, current mfg.

MSR	$599	$420	$350	$300	$250	$210	$180	$150

M-201 - similar to Model M-200 except basswood body, white neck binding, EMG HZ H-1 pickup set, 1 volume/1 tone control, 3-way toggle and EMG After Burner, available in Black, Black Gold, Gunmetal Blue, or Titanium finishes, mfg. 2001 only.

	$490	$450	$400	$350	$300	$250	$200

Last MSR was $649.

M-250 (LTD MIRAGE) - similar to the LTD M-200, except features 2 rail humbuckers/exposed pole piece humbucker Duncan-designed pickups, 5-way selector switch, available in Black, Pearl White, See-Through Blue, or See-Through Red finishes, mfg. 1996-2000.

	$495	$425	$375	$300	$250	$175	$125

Last MSR was $629.

Early versions of this model may have a Wilkinson tremolo, and (2 single coil/humbucker) ESP pickups.

M-251 - similar to Model M201 except has EMG-HZ H-1B, S-1, H-1N pickups, 5-way toggle, available in Black, Black Gold, Gunmetal Blue, or Titanium finishes, mfg. 2001 only.

	$510	$450	$400	$350	$300	$250	$200

Last MSR was $679.

LTD Viper-100FM courtesy LTD

MH-200 - similar to H-200, except has Floyd Rose Licensed bridge, available in See-Through Black, See-Through Black Cherry, or See-Through Aqua finishes, mfg. 1999-2000.

	$499	$450	$400	$350	$300	$250	$200

Last MSR was $649.

MHB-200 - similar to the MH-200, except in baritone configuraiton, available in Titanium or Black finishes, mfg. 2004-present.

MSR	$599	$420	$350	$300	$250	$210	$180	$150

L

MH-201 - similar to the MH200, except has a quilted maple top and HB102 Duncan-designed pickups, available in See-Thru Purple, See-Thru Red, or See-Thru Blue finishes, mfg. 2001-03.

	$420	$350	$300	$260	$230	$195	$150

Last MSR was $599.

MV-200 - similar to Model MV-100 except has mahogany body with flamed maple top, natural top and body binding, white binding on neck, Duncan-designed HB-102B and HR-101 pickups, available in See-Through Red, See-Through Blue, See-Through Purple, or See-Through Orange finishes, mfg. 2001-02.

	$440	$400	$350	$300	$250	$200	$175

Last MSR was $549.

RS-200 - modified star-shaped mahogany body, maple bolt-on neck with rosewood fingerboard, arrowhead neck inlays, white neck binding, 24 XJ frets, Floyd Rose licensed bridge, two EMG-HZ humbucker pickups, black hardware, available in Black, Grey Satin, Midnight Purple, or Gun Metal Blue finishes, mfg. 1999 only.

	$575	$525	$450	$399	$350	$299	$250

Last MSR was $749.

ULTRA TONE - offset double cutaway hardwood body, 22-fret bound rosewood fingerboard with white dot inlay, tune-o-matic bridge/stop tailpiece, chrome hardware, black/white marbleized pickguard, 3-per-side vintage-style tuners, screened logo/graphic on headstock, 2 covered ESP humbuckers, 2 volume/tone controls, 3-way selector, available in Black finish, mfg. 1996-98.

	$625	$575	$500	$450	$375	$300	$225

Last MSR was $895.

ULTRA-200 - similar to the LTD Ultra Tone, except features an alder body, white pearloid pickguard, blackface peghead with silk-screened LTD logo, 2 Duncan-designed humbuckers, available in Black, Pearl White, or Three-Tone Sunburst finishes, mfg. 1998-99.

	$670	$580	$510	$440	$370	$300	$225

Last MSR was $895.

LTD M-200FM courtesy LTD

GRADING	100% MINT	98% NEAR MINT	95% EXC+	90% EXC	80% VG+	70% VG	60% G

V-200 - Flying V-shaped alder body, bolt-on maple neck, 22-fret rosewood fingerboard with white dot inlay, tune-o-matic bridge/stop tailpiece, black pointed peghead with screened logo, 3-per-side tuners, chrome hardware, 2 Duncan-designed humbuckers, volume/tone controls, 3-position switch, available in Black or Olympic White finishes, mfg. 1998-99.

	$575	$500	$425	$375	$300	$250	$175

Last MSR was $719.

V-250 - similar to V-200, except has mahogany body, arrowhead neck inlays, white neck binding, two EMG-HZ humbucker pickups, Floyd Rose licensed bridge, and black hardware, available in Black, Grey Satin, Midnight Purple, or Gun metal Blue finishes, mfg. 1999-2000.

	$595	$500	$450	$399	$350	$299	$250

Last MSR was $749.

VB-200 - offset sharp double cutaway mahogany body, 3-piece maple neck, 24-fret rosewood fingerboard with dot and 12th fret model name inlays, 2 EMG-HZ humbucker pickups, Tune-O-Matic bridge, 2 knobs, 3-way switch, black hardware, available in See-Thru Black Cherry or Black finishes, mfg. 2004-present.

MSR	$599	$420	$350	$300	$250	$210	$180	$150

VIPER-200FM - offset sharp double cutaway agathis body, flamed maple top, 3-piece maple neck, 24-fret rosewood fingerboard with dot and 12th fret model name inlays, 2 EMG-HZ humbucker pickups, Tune-O-Matic bridge, 2 knobs, 3-way switch, 3-per-side tuners, black hardware, available in See-Thru Black Cherry finish, mfg. 2004-present.

MSR	$599	$420	$350	$300	$250	$210	$180	$150

ELECTRIC: 250/260/350 SERIES

AX-250 - offset four-point sharp-edged basswood body, bolt-on maple neck, rosewood fingerboard with custom tribal inlay, 3-per-side tuners, STB, two EMG humbucker pickups, two knobs, three-way switch, black hardware, available in Black finish, 25.5 in. scale, new 2005.

MSR	$799	$575	$500	$425	$375	$325	$275	$225

AX-350 - 4-point cutaway mahogany body, 3-piece mahogany neck, 24-fret rosewood fingerboard with custom tribal graphic inlay, 2 EMG 81 humbucker pickups, Tune-O-Matic bridge, STB, 2 knobs, 3-way switch, black hardware, available in Black finish, mfg. 2004 only.

	$600	$525	$450	$375	$325	$275	$225

Last MSR was $849.

Add $35 for Floyd Rose tremolo, available in See-Thru Blue finish.

EX-250 - radically shaped mahogany body, maple bolt-on neck, rosewood fingerboard with dot position markers, EX-250 inlaid at the 12th fret, black hardware, tune-o-matic bridge, 22 XJ frets, 2 Duncan-designed humbucker pickups, 6-on-a-side tuners, 1 volume/1 tone control, toggle, available in Black, Black Cherry, Midnight Purple, or Gunmetal Blue finishes, mfg. 2000 only.

	$450	$425	$400	$375	$350	$325	$300

Last MSR was $599.

EX-260 - Explorer-styled agathis body, 3-piece maple neck, 22-fret rosewood fingerboard with dot and 12th fret model name inlays, 2 EMG-HZ humbucker pickups, Tune-O-Matic bridge, 3 knobs, 6-on-a-side tuners, black hardware, available in Titanium or Black finishes, mfg. 2004-present.

MSR	$599	$420	$350	$300	$250	$210	$180	$150

EX-350 - similar to Model EX-250 except has mahogany set neck, Floyd Rose Licensed bridge, 2 humbucker EMG HZ pickups, available in Black, Black Cherry, Midnight Purple, or Gunmetal Blue, mfg. 2000 only.

	$600	$550	$500	$450	$400	$375	$350

Last MSR was $799.

EX-351 - similar to the EX-250, except has 2 EMG-HZ pickups, available in Titanium or Black finishes, mfg. 2002-03.

	$420	$350	$300	$250	$210	$170	$130

Last MSR was $599.

Add $150 for Diamond Plate finish (Model EX-351D).

F-250 - offset double cutaway agathis body with contoured sides, 3-piece maple neck, 24-fret rosewood fingerboard with arrowhead and 12th fret model name inlays, 2 EMG-HZ pickups, 2 knobs, 3-way switch, Floyd Rose tremolo, black hardware, available in Titanium or Black finishes, mfg. 2004-present.

MSR	$649	$460	$375	$325	$275	$235	$190	$160

H-250 - offset double cutaway Strat-style agathis body, flamed maple top, 3-piece maple neck, 24-fret rosewood fingerboard with dot and 12th fret model name inlays, 2 EMG-HZ humbucker pickups, Tune-O-Matic bridge, 2 knobs, 3-way switch, 3-per-side tuners, chrome hardware, available in See-Thru Blue or See-Thru Red finishes, mfg. 2004-present.

MSR	$599	$420	$350	$300	$250	$210	$180	$150

MH-250NT - offset double cutaway Strat-style agathis body, flame maple top, 3-piece maple neck, 24-fret rosewood fingerboard with offset block and 12th fret model name inlays, 2 EMG-HZ humbucker pickups, Tune-O-Matic bridge, 2 knobs, 3-way switch, 3-per-side tuners, black hardware, available in Deep Brown Sunburst finish, mfg. 2004-present.

MSR	$599	$420	$350	$300	$250	$210	$180	$150

Add $30 for Floyd Rose tremolo, available in See-Thru Black finish.

ELECTRIC: 300 SERIES

EC-300 - single cutaway mahogany body, 3-piece maple neck, 24-fret rosewood fingerboard, two EMG-HZ humbucker pickups, binding, 3-per-side tuners, black hardware, available in See-Thru Black Cherry, Vintage Sunburst, or Black finishes, mfg. 2002-03.

	$450	$400	$350	$300	$250	$200	$150

Last MSR was $649.

GRADING	100% MINT	98% NEAR MINT	95% EXC+	90% EXC	80% VG+	70% VG	60% G

EC-300P - similar to the EC-300, except has two Duncan-designed P-90 pickups, available in Black or Metallic Gold finishes, mfg. 2002-03.

	$399	$340	$290	$250	$210	$180	$140

Last MSR was $569.

EC-300ATS - similar to the EC-300, except has two Duncan-designed HB-102 pickups, creme full body binding, and 22 frets, available in Black or Metallic Gold finishes, mfg. 2002-03.

	$495	$425	$375	$325	$275	$225	$175

Last MSR was $699.

F-300FM - offset double cutaway body with a gothis flavor, mahogany body, bolt-on maple neck, rosewood fingerboard with arrowhead position markers, black hardware, tune-o-matic bridge, STB, 24 XJ frets, 2 humbucker EMG HZ pickups, 3-per-side tuners, available in See-Thru Black finishes, mfg. 2003 only.

	$595	$525	$475	$425	$375	$325	$250

Last MSR was $849.

H-300 - similar to H-200, except has mahogany neck-through body with figured maple top, mahogany neck with rosewood fingerboard, two EMG-HZ humbucker pickups, available in See-Through Black, See-Through Black Cherry, or See-Through Aqua finishes, mfg. 1999-2000.

	$600	$500	$450	$400	$350	$325	$300

Last MSR was $749.

H-301 - similar to Model H-300 except has flamed maple top, maple neck, tune-o-matic bridge with stop tailpiece, EMG HZ H-1 pickup set, available in See-Through Green, See-Through Red, See-Through Blue, or See-Through Orange finishes, mfg. 2001 only.

	$575	$500	$450	$400	$350	$325	$300

Last MSR was $749.

H-302 - similar to the H-301, available in Amber Sunburst, See-Thru Black Cherry, or See Thru Black, mfg. 2002-03.

	$495	$425	$375	$325	$275	$225	$175

Last MSR was $699.

HB-300 - 27 in. baritone scale double offset cutaway maple body, 3-piece maple body, 24-fret rosewood fingerboard with offset blocks and model name at 12th fret inlays, 3-per-side tuners, two Duncan-designed HB-102 pickups, tune-o-matic bridge, STB, two knobs, toggle switch, black hardware, available in Titanium or Black finishes, mfg. 2002-03.

	$450	$400	$350	$300	$250	$200	$150

Last MSR was $649.

LTD EX-260
courtesy LTD

M-300 - similar to M-200, except has mahogany neck-through body with figured maple top, mahogany neck with rosewood fingerboard, white neck binding, 2 EMG-HZ humbucker pickups, available in See-Through Black, See-Through Black Cherry, or See-Through Aqua finishes, mfg. 1999-2000.

	$625	$525	$475	$425	$375	$325	$275

Last MSR was $799.

Also available with two EMG-HZ humbucker pickups and one single coil pickup for an additional $30 (LTD M-350). Disc. 2000. Last MSR was $829.

M-302 - similar to the M-300, except has arrowhead inlays and a Floyd Rose tremolo, available in Natural Gloss, See-Thru Black Cherry, or See-Thru Black finishes, mfg. 2003 only.

	$525	$450	$400	$350	$300	$250	$195

Last MSR was $749.

MH-300 - similar to MH-200, except has mahogany neck-through body with figured maple top, mahogany neck with rosewood fingerboard, and two EMG-HZ pickups, available in See-Through Black, See-Through Black Cherry, or See-Through Aqua finishes, mfg. 1999-2000.

	$675	$575	$525	$475	$425	$375	$325

Last MSR was $849.

MH-301 - similar to Model MH-300 except has quilted maple top, maple neck-through body, EMG-HZ H-1 pickup set, available in See-Through Purple, See-Through Red, See-Through Green, or See-Through Blue finishes, mfg. 2001-03.

	$560	$495	$450	$400	$350	$275	$225

Last MSR was $799.

MV-300 - similar to Model MV-200 except has neck-through body, EMG-HZ H-1B, S-1 pickups, available in See-Through Red, See-Through Blue, See-Through Purple, or See-Through Orange finishes, mfg. 2001-02.

	$565	$525	$475	$450	$400	$350	$300

Last MSR was $749.

VB-300 - 27 in. baritone scale, offset double cutaway mahogany body, maple set neck, rosewood fingerboard with dot inlays and model name inlaid at the 12th fret, black hardware, 3-per-side tuners, tune-o-matic bridge, white neck binding, 24 XJ frets, 2 humbucker EMG HZ pickups and EMG Afterburner Active Gain Boost, available in Black finish, mfg. 2001-03.

	$490	$425	$375	$325	$290	$275	$250

Last MSR was $699.

LTD H-250
courtesy LTD

GRADING	100% MINT	98% NEAR MINT	95% EXC+	90% EXC	80% VG+	70% VG	60% G

VIPER-300 - offset double cutaway design, mahogany body, maple set neck, rosewood fingerboard with dot position markers, Viper 300 inlaid at the 12th fret, black hardware, 3-per-side tuners, tune-o-matic bridge, white neck binding, 24 XJ frets, 2 humbucker EMG HZ pickups, available in Black or See-Through Cherry finishes, mfg. 2000 only.

	$490	$465	$425	$400	$375	$350	$325

Last MSR was $649.

VIPER-301 - similar to Viper 300 except has rosewood fingerboard with flag inlays and model name at the 12th fret, tune-o-matic bridge with stop tailpiece, EMG HZ H-1 pickup set, 1 volume/1 tone control, toggle, available in black or See-Through Black Cherry finishes, mfg. 2001-03.

	$475	$425	$375	$325	$275	$225	$175

Last MSR was $649.

ELECTRIC: 400 SERIES

AX-400 - offset four-point sharp-edged mahogany body, three-piece set mahogany neck, 24-fret bound rosewood fingerboard with custom tribal inlay, 3-per-side tuners, tune-o-matic bridge, STB, two EMG humbucker pickups, two knobs, three-way switch, black hardware, available in Black finish, 25.5 in. scale, new 2005.

MSR	$999	$700	$625	$550	$475	$425	$375	$325

EC-400 - single cutaway mahogany body, 3-piece mahogany neck, 24-fret rosewood fingerboard with flag inlays and 12th fret model name inlay, 2 EMG-81 humbucker pickups, Tune-O-Matic bridge, 3 knobs, black hardware, available in Vintage Sunburst, See-Thru Black Cherry, or Black finishes, mfg. 2004-present.

MSR	$849	$600	$525	$450	$400	$350	$300	$250

EC-400AT - similar to the EC-400, except has 2 Seymour Duncan JB/59 humbucker pickups, 22-fret fingerboard, full body binding, and chrome hardware, available in Metallic Gold or Black finishes, mfg. 2004-present.

MSR	$799	$575	$500	$425	$375	$325	$275	$225

EX-400 - Explorer-style mahogany body, 3-piece mahogany neck, 22-fret rosewood fingerboard with flag inlays and 12th fret model name inlay, 2 EMG-81 humbucker pickups, Tune-O-Matic bridge, 2 knobs, black hardware, available in Black finish, mfg. 2004-present.

MSR	$849	$600	$525	$450	$400	$350	$300	$250

EX-400BD - similar to the EX-400, except has a black diamond plate on the top, mfg. 2004-present.

MSR	$999	$700	$625	$550	$475	$400	$350	$300

F-400FM - offset double cutaway mahogany body with contoured sides, flamed maple top, 3-piece maple neck, 22-fret rosewood fingerboard with custom tribal graphic inlay, 2 EMG-81 humbucker pickups, Tune-O-Matic bridge, 2 knobs, 3-way switch, black hardware, available in See-Thru Black finish, mfg. 2004-present.

MSR	$999	$700	$600	$525	$450	$375	$325	$275

H-400 - offset double cutaway Strat-style mahogany body, flame maple top, 3-piece mahogany neck, 24-fret rosewood fingerboard with dot and 12th fret model name inlay, 2 Seymour Duncan JB/59 humbucker pickups, Tune-O-Matic bridge, 2 knobs, 5-way switch, black hardware, available in Amber Sunburst or Amber Cherry Sunburst finishes, mfg. 2004-present.

MSR	$799	$575	$500	$425	$375	$325	$275	$225

HYBRID-400 - double cutaway mahogany body, 3-piece mahogany neck, 22-fret rosewood fingerboard with dot and 12th fret model name inlay, Seymour Duncan JB humbucker and Duncan-designed TE-101R pickups, flat-mount bridge with STB, 2 knobs, 3-way switch, black hardware, available in Vintage Sunburst, See-Thru Black Cherry, or Black finishes, mfg. 2004-present.

MSR	$699	$490	$425	$350	$300	$250	$210	$180

MH-400NT - offset double cutaway Strat-style mahogany body, flame maple top, 3-piece mahogany neck, 24-fret rosewood fingerboard with offset block and 12th fret model name inlay, 2 EMG 81 humbucker pickups, Tune-O-Matic bridge, STB, 2 knobs, 5-way switch, black hardware, available in See-Thru Black finish, mfg. 2004-present.

MSR	$849	$600	$525	$450	$375	$325	$275	$225

Add $35 for Floyd Rose tremolo, available in See-Thru Blue finish. Also available in baritone configuration (Model MHB-400).

MHB-400 - similar to the MH-400, except in baritone configuraiton, available in Black Satin finish, mfg. 2004-present.

MSR	$849	$600	$525	$450	$400	$350	$300	$250

VB-400 - offset sharp double cutaway mahogany body, 3-piece maple neck, 24-fret rosewood fingerboard with dot and 12th fret model name inlays, 2 EMG-81 humbucker pickups, Tune-O-Matic bridge, 2 knobs, 3-way switch, black hardware, available in Black finish, mfg. 2004-present.

MSR	$849	$600	$525	$450	$400	$350	$300	$250

VIPER-400 - offset sharp double cutaway mahogany body, 3-piece mahogany neck, 24-fret rosewood fingerboard with flag and 12th fret model name inlay, 2 EMG 81 humbucker pickups, Tune-O-Matic bridge, 2 knobs, 3-way switch, black hardware, available in Vintage Sunburst, See-Thru Black Cherry, Olympic White, or Black finishes, mfg. 2004-present.

MSR	$849	$600	$525	$450	$400	$350	$300	$250

Viper-407 - similar to the Viper 400, except in seven-string configuration, 3/4-per-side tuners, available in Black Satin finish, new 2005.

MSR	$899	$630	$550	$475	$425	$375	$325	$275

ELECTRIC: DELUXE (1000) SERIES

EC-1000 - single sharp cutaway mahogany body with flamed maple top, 3-piece mahogany neck, 24-fret rosewood fingerboard with abalone flags and model name at 12th fret inlays, full guitar abalone binding, matching color headstock, 3-per-side tuners, two EMG-81 humbucker pickups, TonePros System II locking bridge, chrome hardware, available in Amber Sunburst, Black, or See-Thru Black Cherry finishes, mfg. 2002-present.

MSR	$1,049	$750	$650	$575	$500	$425	$375	$325

Add $70 for Black finish with no flamed maple top and gold hardware. Add $105 for Black Cherry Sunburst finish with quilted maple top.

GRADING	100% MINT	98% NEAR MINT	95% EXC+	90% EXC	80% VG+	70% VG	60% G

H-1000 - double offset cutaway mahogany body with flamed maple top, 3-piece maple neck, 24-fret rosewood fingerboard with abalone offset block and model name at 12th fret inlays, full white with abalone body binding, two JB/59 Seymour Duncan pickups, TonePros locking bridge, two black knobs, five-way switch, black hardware, available in Black, Amber Sunburst, or See-Thru Aqua, mfg. 2002-present.

MSR	$1,049	$750	$650	$550	$475	$425	$375	$325

    Add $70 for Black finish with EMG-81 pickups.

M-1000FM - double offset cutaway maple body with flamed maple top, 3-piece maple neck, 24-fret rosewood fingerboard with abalone arrowheads and model name at 12th fret inlays, neck and headstock white with abalone purfling binding, 6-on-the-other-side tuners, two EMG-81 humbucker pickups, original Floyd Rose tremolo unit, two knobs, five-way switch, available in See-Thru Black finish, mfg. 2002-present.

MSR	$1,369	$975	$875	$800	$725	$650	$550	$450

MH-1000 - offset double cutaway Strat-style mahogany body, 3-piece maple neck, 24-fret rosewood fingerboard with offset block and 12th fret model name inlay, 2 EMG 81 humbucker pickups, Tone Pros locking bridge with STB, 2 knobs, 5-way switch, black hardware, available in See-Thru Black Cherry or Black finishes, mfg. 2004-present.

MSR	$1,049	$750	$650	$550	$475	$425	$375	$325

    Add $75 for See-Thru Black Cherry finish with Seymour Duncan pickups and quilt maple top.

VIPER 1000FM - double sharp cutaway mahogany body with flamed maple top, 3-piece mahogany neck, 24-fret rosewood fingerboard with abalone flags and model name at 12th fret inlays, neck and headstock white with abalone binding, 3-per-side tuners, 2 EMG-81 pickups, TonePros locking bridge, two knobs, three-way switch, black hardware, available in See-Thru Black finish, mfg. 2003-present.

MSR	$1,199	$850	$750	$675	$625	$575	$500	$400

ELECTRIC: SIGNATURE SERIES

AL-600 - offset sharp double cutaway mahogany body, set mahogany three-piece neck, 24-fret bound rosewood fingerboard with spade inlays, bound headstock, three-per-side tuners, TonePros locking bridge, STB, black pickguard, two EMG humbucker pickups, two knobs, three-way switch, chrome hardware, avaialble in Three-Tone Sunburst finish, new 2005.

MSR	$1,099	$775	$675	$600	$525	$475	$400	$325

AXXION DAVE MUSTAINE - double cutaway X-shaped body with slightly extended lower bass bout, mahogany body, set three-piece mahogany neck, 24-fret ebony fingerboard with XX inlays, three-per-side tuners, TonePros locking bridge, STB, two Seymour Duncan humbucker pickups, three knobs, three-way switch, black hardware, available in Black finish, 25.5 in. scale, new 2005.

MSR	$1,149	$800	$700	$625	$550	$500	$450	$375

DEVIL GIRL - composite body shaped like a "devil girl" and devil wings, maple neck, 22-fret rosewood fingerboard with devil's tail and flames inlays, EMG-HZ H-4 humbucker pickup, tune-o-matic STB bridge, 6-on-one side tuners, black hardware, available in Fire Red Satin finish, mfg. 2003 only.

		$650	$575	$525	$475	$425	$375	$325

                   Last MSR was $899.

DV8-R (DAVE MUSTAINE) - sharp Flying V mahogany body, neck-thru mahogany neck, 24-fret rosewood bound fingerboard with first fret eight ball inlay, bound headstock with six-on-one-side tuners, TonePros locking bridge, STB, black pickguard, two Seymour Duncan humbucker pickups, three knobs, three-way switch, black hardware, available in Black, Metallic Silver, or Snow White finishes, 25.5 in. scale, mfg. 2003-present.

MSR	$1,149	$800	$700	$625	$550	$500	$450	$375

DV-200 DAVE MUSTAINE - sharp Flying V basswood body, bolt-on maple neck, 24-fret rosewood bound fingerboard with first fret eight ball inlay, bound headstock with six-on-one-side tuners, tune-o-matic bridge, STB, black pickguard, two Duncan-designed humbucker pickups, three knobs, three-way switch, black hardware, available in Black finish, 25.5 in. scale, mfg. 2004-present.

MSR	$699	$490	$425	$375	$325	$275	$235	$190

GL-500K (GEORGE LYNCH) - offset double cutaway alder body, bolt-on maple neck, rosewood fingerboard with dot position markers, model name at 12th fret, black hardware, Floyd Rose Licensed bridge, 22 XJ frets, Duncan-designed HB-103, SC-101 pickups, 1 volume with push/pull pickup selector, custom graphics, mfg. 2001-02.

		$750	$700	$650	$600	$550	$500	$450

                   Last MSR was $999.

GL-500T (George Lynch) - similar to Model GL-500K except has different graphic (tiger stripes), mfg. 2001-02.

		$750	$700	$650	$600	$550	$500	$450

                   Last MSR was $999.

GL-600MT (GEORGE LYNCH) - similar to the GL-500T, except has a maple body, maple fingerboard, single Seymour Duncan TB-12 pickup, available in custom Yellow and Black graphics, mfg. 2003-04.

		$850	$775	$700	$625	$575	$525	$450

                   Last MSR was $1,199.

GL-600FB - similar to the GL-600MT, except is in baritone configuration and has a flamed body, mfg. 2003-04.

		$850	$775	$700	$625	$575	$525	$450

                   Last MSR was $1,199.

LTD F-400FM
courtesy LTD

LTD MH-400NT
courtesy LTD

L

GRADING	100% MINT	98% NEAR MINT	95% EXC+	90% EXC	80% VG+	70% VG	60% G

GL-600SS - similar to the GL-600MT, except has Screamin' Demon finish, new 2005.

MSR	$1,249	$875	$775	$700	$625	$575	$525	$450

GRYNCH (JAMES HETFIELD) - baritone offset double cutaway mahogany body, maple set neck, 24-fret rosewood fingerboard with dot inlay and 12th fret Grynch, matching color headstock, 3-per-side tuners, two EMG humbucker pickups, TonePros system II locking bridge, two knobs, toggle switch, EMG Afterburner electronics, black hardware, available in Black with green and red flames, mfg. 2003 only.

		$850	$775	$700	$625	$575	$525	$450

Last MSR was $1,199.

JH-600 (JEFF HANNEMAN) - double cutaway maple neck-through-body, maple neck, rosewood fingerboard with "S" and key inlays, 24 XJ frets, two EMG-81 humbucker pickups, white N/H binding, Floyd Rose bridge, 2 knobs, 3-way switch, black hardware, available in Black finish, mfg. 2004-present.

MSR	$1,349	$950	$850	$775	$700	$625	$525	$425

JP-600 (JARDEL PAISANTE) - offset double cutaway mahogany body, 3-piece maple neck, large tortoise pickguard, 22-fret rosewood fingerboard with flag and 12th fret model name inlays, 2 EMG 81 humbucker pickups, Tone Pros locking bridge, 2 knobs, 5-way switch, 3-per-side tuners, chrome hardware, available in Black finish, mfg. 2004-present.

MSR	$1,099	$775	$675	$600	$525	$450	$400	$350

JAMES HETFIELD "TRUCKSTER" - single cutaway Les Paul-style mahogany body, set three-piece mahogany neck, 22-fret rosewood fingerboard with flag and 12th fret ESP inlays, matching headstock with JH initial and three-per-side tuners, Tone Pros Locking bridge, stop tailpiece, two EMG active pickups, three knobs, three-way switch, chrome hardware, finished in Aged Primer Grey with custom black, white, and red wear marks, 24.75 in. scale, new 2005.

MSR	$1,349	$950	$850	$775	$700	$625	$525	$425

K-500 (KELLY HAYES) - single cutaway EC style mahogany body, maple neck, 24-fret rosewood fingerboard with cold spider inlays, two EMG-HZ pickups, TonePros bridge, STB, two knobs, three-way switch, black hardware, available in Black Satin finish, mfg. 2002-04.

		$600	$550	$500	$450	$400	$350	$275

Last MSR was $849.

KH-202 (KIRK HAMMETT) - similar to the KH-502, except has a basswood body, Black finish, mfg. 2003-present.

MSR	$699	$490	$425	$350	$300	$250	$210	$180

KH-203 (KIRK HAMMETT) - similar to the KH-503, except has a basswood body, Black finish, mfg. 2003-present.

MSR	$699	$490	$425	$350	$300	$250	$210	$180

KH-502 (KIRK HAMMETT) - offset double cutaway alder body, maple neck-through body, rosewood fingerboard with dot position markers, skull and crossbones at 12th fet, black hardware, Floyd Rose Licensed bridge, 24 XJ frets, EMG-HZ H-1 pickup set, 2 volume/1 tone control, 3-way slotted switch, available in Black, mfg. 2001-02.

		$750	$700	$650	$600	$550	$500	$450

Last MSR was $999.

KH-503 (KIRK HAMMETT) - single cutaway alder body, maple neck-through body, rosewood fingerboard with dot position markers and spiders at the 12th fret, black hardware, Floyd Rose Licensed bridge, 24 XJ frets, EMG-HZ H-1 pickup set, 2 volume/1 tone control, 3-way toggle, available in Black, mfg. 2001-02.

		$750	$700	$650	$600	$550	$500	$450

Last MSR was $999.

KH-602 (KIRK HAMMETT) - similar to the KH-502, except has a maple body, two EMG-81 humbucker pickups, and an original Floyd Rose tremolo, available in Black finish, mfg. 2003-present.

MSR	$1,349	$950	$850	$775	$700	$625	$550	$475

KH-603 (KIRK HAMMETT) - similar to the KH-503, except has a maple body, two EMG-81 humbucker pickups, and an original Floyd Rose tremolo, available in Black finish, mfg. 2003-present.

MSR	$1,349	$950	$850	$775	$700	$625	$550	$475

MC-200 (MAX CAVALERA) - similar to the MC-500, except has a basswood body, Brazil Green finish, mfg. 2003-present.

MSR	$649	$450	$375	$325	$275	$225	$180	$140

MC-500 (MAX CAVALERA) - offset double cutaway alder body, maple neck-through body, rosewood fingerboard with dot position markers and XXX at 12th fret, black hardware, tune-o-matic bridge with string-through body, white neck binding, 24 XJ frets, 1 Duncan-designed HB-103B pickup, 1 volume control, available in Brazil Green finish, mfg. 2001-02.

		$750	$700	$650	$600	$550	$500	$450

Last MSR was $999.

MC-600 (MAX CAVALERA) - similar to the MC-500, except has a maple body, and a Seymour Duncan SH-6 pickup, Brazil Green finish with graphics, mfg. 2003-present.

MSR	$1,049	$750	$675	$600	$525	$475	$400	$325

SC-200 (STEVEN CARPENTER) - similar to the SC-200, except has a basswood body, available in Black or See-Thru Green finishes, mfg. 2003-present.

MSR	$649	$450	$375	$325	$275	$225	$180	$140

SC-500 (STEVEN CARPENTER) - offset double cutaway alder body, maple neck-through body, rosewood fingerboard with model name inlaid at 12th fret, chrome hardware, tune-o-matic bridge with string-through body, white neck binding, 24 XJ frets, Duncan-designed HB-102 Set and SC-101 single coil pickup, 1 volume/1 tone control, 3-way slotted switch, available in Black and See-Through Green finishes, mfg. 2001-02.

		$750	$700	$650	$600	$550	$500	$450

Last MSR was $999.

GRADING	100% MINT	98% NEAR MINT	95% EXC+	90% EXC	80% VG+	70% VG	60% G

SC-600 (STEVEN CARPENTER) - similar to the SC-600, except has a maple body, Seymour Ducan SH-4 and HB-102N pickups, Tone Pros locking bridge, available in Natural Gloss or Three-Tone Burst finishes, mfg. 2003-present.

| MSR | $1,049 | $750 | $675 | $600 | $525 | $450 | $375 | $325 |

SC-607 - similar to the SC-600, except in seven-string configuration, available in Black or Natural gloss finish, mfg. 2003-present.

| MSR | $1,299 | $925 | $850 | $775 | $700 | $600 | $525 | $450 |

SC-607B - similar to the SC-600, except in 7-string and baritone configuration, available in Natural Gloss or Black finishes, mfg. 2004-present.

| MSR | $1,349 | $950 | $850 | $775 | $700 | $625 | $525 | $425 |

TA-500 (TOM ARAYA) - 4-string bass, offset double cutaway alder body, maple neck-through body, rosewood fingerboard with dot inlays and pentagrams at the 12th fret, black hardware, LTD BB-04 bridge, 24 XJ frets, EMG 35-HZ pickup set, volume, pan, B-30 Active EQ, available in Black, mfg. 2001-02.

| | | $750 | $700 | $650 | $600 | $550 | $500 | $450 |

Last MSR was $999.

ELECTRIC: 30TH ANNIVERSARY SERIES

These guitars represent ESP's 30 years in the guitar industry (1975-2005).

EC-2005 - EC-style mahogany body, set three-piece mahogany neck, 24-fret ebony fingerboard with 12th fret 30 inlay, skull headstock with three-per-side tuners, tune-o-matic bridge, STB, two EMG humbucker pickups, two knobs, three-way switch, black hardware, Black Satin finish, new 2005.

| MSR | $899 | $630 | $550 | $475 | $425 | $375 | $325 | $275 |

F-2005 - F-style mahogany body, set three-piece mahogany neck, 24-fret ebony fingerboard with 12th fret 30 inlay, skull headstock with three-per-side tuners, tune-o-matic bridge, STB, two EMG humbucker pickups, two knobs, three-way switch, black hardware, Black Satin finish, 25.5 in. scale, new 2005.

| MSR | $999 | $700 | $625 | $550 | $475 | $425 | $375 | $325 |

VIPER-2005 - Viper-style mahogany body, set three-piece mahogany neck, 24-fret ebony fingerboard with 12th fret 30 inlay, skull headstock with three-per-side tuners, tune-o-matic bridge, STB, two EMG humbucker pickups, two knobs, three-way switch, black hardware, Black Satin finish, 24.75 in. scale, new 2005.

| MSR | $899 | $630 | $550 | $475 | $425 | $375 | $325 | $275 |

LTD JH-600 Jeff Hanneman
courtesy LTD

ELECTRIC: 7-STRING SERIES

M-107 - offset double cutaway basswood body, bolt-on 7-string maple neck, rosewood fingerboard with dot inlays and M-107 at the 12th fret, string through body bridge, 22 XJ frets, 2 humbucker LTD 7 pickups, black hardware, reverse headstock, 7-on-one-side tuners, 1 volume/1 tone control, toggle, available in Black Satin, Blue Satin and Purple Satin finishes, mfg. 2000 only.

| | | $375 | $350 | $325 | $300 | $275 | $250 | $225 |

Last MSR was $499.

M-207 - similar to Model M-107, except has arrowhead position markers, M-207 inlaid at the 12th fret, Floyd Rose Licensed 7 Bridge, 2 humbucker Duncan-designed 7 pickups, available in black, Black Cherry, Midnight Purple, or Gunmetal Blue finishes, mfg. 2000 only.

| | | $600 | $550 | $500 | $450 | $400 | $350 | $300 |

Last MSR was $799.

M-307 - similar to Model M-207, except has neck-through body, mahogany body, mahogany neck with rosewood fingerboard, white neck binding, M-307 inlaid at the 12th fret, 2 humbucker EMG HZ-707 pickups, available in Black, Black Cherry, Midnight Purple, or Gunmetal Blue, mfg. 2000-01.

| | | $650 | $600 | $550 | $500 | $450 | $400 | $375 |

Last MSR was $849.

MH-307 - similar to Model M-307, except has mahogany body with figured maple top, block position markers, M-307 inlaid at the 12th fret, available in See-Through Black, See-Through Black Cherry, or See-Through Aqua, mfg. 2000-01.

| | | $675 | $625 | $575 | $525 | $475 | $425 | $375 |

Last MSR was $899.

F-207 - offset double cutaway body design with a gothis look, basswood body, bolt-on 7-string maple neck, rosewood fingerboard with arrowhead position markers, black hardware, Floyd Rose Licensed 7 bridge, 24 XJ frets, 2 humbucker EMG HZ-707 pickups, 3 and 4 headstock tuner configuration, available in Black, Black Cherry, Midnight Purple, or Gunmetal Blue, mfg. 2000 only.

| | | $600 | $550 | $500 | $450 | $400 | $350 | $300 |

Last MSR was $799.

H-207 - offset double cutaway ash body, bolt-on 7-string maple neck, rosewood fingerboard with block inlays, black hardware, tune-o-matic 7 bridge, white neck binding, natural body binding, 24 XJ frets, 2 humbucker Duncan Design 7 pickups, 1 volume/1 tone control, toggle, 3 and 4 headstock tuner configuration, available in See-Through Black, See-Through Black Cherry, or See-Through Aqua, mfg. 2000 only.

| | | $525 | $475 | $450 | $400 | $350 | $300 | $250 |

Last MSR was $699.

LTD MC-600 Max Cavalera
courtesy LTD

GRADING		100% MINT	98% NEAR MINT	95% EXC+	90% EXC	80% VG+	70% VG	60% G

H-307 - similar to Model H-207, except has neck-thru body, mahogany body with figured maple top, mahogany neck, 2 humbucker EMG HZ-707 pickups, available in See-Through Black, See-Through Black Cherry, or See-Through Aqua, mfg. 2000-01.

			$600	$550	$500	$450	$400	$350	$300

Last MSR was $799.

ELECTRIC BASS: 50 & H-4 SERIES

B-50 - double offset agathis body, maple neck, rosewood fingerboard, two pickups, three knobs, 2-per-side tuners, black hardware, available in Black, Titanium, or Black Cherry finishes, mfg. 2002-present.

MSR	$249		$175	$150	$130	$110	$95	$75	$55

B-55 - similar to the B-50, except in five-string configuration, 3/2-per-side tuners, mfg. 2003-present.

MSR	$299		$210	$175	$150	$130	$110	$95	$75

H-4 BASS - sleek offset double cutaway hardwood body, maple neck, 24-fret rosewood fingerboard with offset white dot inlay, 2-per-side curved point headstock with screened logo, fixed bridge, black hardware, P/J-style ESP pickups, volume/blend/tone controls, available in Black, Candy Apple Red, Metallic Purple, or Metallic Blue finishes, mfg. 1995-98.

			$625	$575	$500	$450	$375	$300	$225

Last MSR was $895.

ELECTRIC BASS: 100 SERIES

B-100 SPECIAL - slightly offset double cutaway alder body, bolt-on maple neck, 21-fret rosewood fingerboard with white dot inlay, 2-per-side headstock with screened logo, fixed bridge, chrome hardware, LTD exposed pole piece humbucker pickup, volume/tone controls, available in Black, Candy Apple Red, or Pearl White finishes, mfg. 1998-99.

			$399	$350	$300	$250	$225	$175	$125

Last MSR was $499.

B-104 - double cutaway basswood body with offset waist, maple bolt-on neck with rosewood fingerboard, dot inlays, 24 XJ frets, 4 String Deluxe Bass bridge, 2 LTD soapbar pickups with mid control, chrome hardware, available in Black, Grey Satin, Metallic Red, or Electric Blue finishes, mfg. 1999-2003.

			$255	$215	$180	$150	$130	$100	$75

Last MSR was $359.

B-105 - similar to B-104 Bass, except in a 5-string configuration, available in Black, Grey Satin, Metallic Red, or Electric Blue finishes, mfg. 1999-2003.

			$280	$250	$210	$170	$140	$110	$80

Last MSR was $399.

B-154 - offset double cutaway agathis body, flame maple top, maple neck, 24-fret rosewood fingerboard with dot and 12th fret model name inlays, 2 ESP SB pickups, ESP DB bridge, four knobs, black hardware, available in See-Thru Red or See-Thru Blue finishes, mfg. 2004-present.

MSR	$399		$280	$235	$205	$175	$145	$115	$90

B-155 - similar to the B-154, except in five-string configuration, available in Amber Sunburst or See-Thru Black finishes, mfg. 2004-present.

MSR	$449		$315	$260	$230	$200	$170	$140	$110

F-104 - offset double cutaway sculpted agathis body, bolt-on maple neck with rosewood fingerboard, white dot inlays, 24 XJ frets, 4 String Deluxe Bass bridge, two pickups with 2-band active EQ, black hardware, available in Black, Titanium or Grey Satin finishes, mfg. 2003-present.

MSR	$429		$300	$250	$210	$170	$140	$110	$80

VIPER-104 - sharp double cutaway agathis body, maple neck, rosewood fingerboard, two pickups, 2 band active EQ, 2-per-side tuners, black hardware, available in Black or Grey Satin finishes, mfg. 2003-present.

MSR	$429		$300	$250	$210	$170	$140	$110	$80

ELECTRIC BASS: 200 SERIES

In 2003 the B-200 Series recieved flamed maple tops and colors See-Thru Black Cherry and See-Thru Black were introduced.

B-204(FM) - offset double cutaway basswood body, bolt-on maple neck, 24-fret rosewood fingerboard with white dot inlay, 2-per-side headstock with screened logo, fixed bridge, chrome hardware, 2 EMG HZ soapbar pickups, volume/blend/bass/treble controls, EMG active EQ, available in Red or Natural finishes, mfg. 1998-2003.

			$425	$375	$335	$290	$250	$210	$175

Last MSR was $579.

B-205(FM) - similar to the B-204, except in 5-string configuration, 3/2-per-side tuners, available in Red or Natural finishes, mfg. 1998-2003.

			$450	$400	$350	$300	$250	$225	$185

Last MSR was $629.

B-206FM - similar to the B-204, except in 6-string configuration, 3-per-side tuners, available in Natural Gloss finish, mfg. 2003-present.

MSR	$749		$525	$450	$375	$325	$275	$240	$200

B-208FM - similar to the B-204, except in 8-string configuration, 4-per-side tuners, available in See-Thru Black finish, mfg. 2002-present.

MSR	$799		$575	$500	$425	$375	$325	$275	$225

This bass has two four-strings that are tuned an octive apart, which is similar to a 12-string guitar.

B-254 - offset double cutaway agathis body, flame maple top, 5-piece maple neck, 24-fret rosewood fingerboard with dot and 12th fret model name inlays, 2 EMG 35-HZ pickups, ESP BB bridge with STB, five knobs, Cosmo black hardware, available in Amber Sunburst or See-Thru Black finishes, mfg. 2004-present.

MSR	$649		$460	$400	$350	$300	$250	$210	$170

GRADING	100% MINT	98% NEAR MINT	95% EXC+	90% EXC	80% VG+	70% VG	60% G

B-255 - similar to the B-254, except in five-string configuration, available in Natural Gloss or See-Thru Black finishes, mfg. 2004-present.

| MSR | $699 | $490 | $425 | $375 | $325 | $275 | $235 | $190 |

EC-254 - single cutaway mahogany body, creme binding (B/N/H), 5-piece maple/walnut neck, 22-fret rosewood fingerboard with dot and 12th fret model name inlays, 2 EMG HZ pickups, Tune-O-Matic bridge, three knobs, chrome hardware, available in See-Thru Black Cherry or Black finishes, mfg. 2004-present.

| MSR | $649 | $450 | $400 | $350 | $300 | $260 | $230 | $190 |

Add $35 for See-Thru Black Cherry finish.

F-204 - offset double cutaway sculpted mahogany body, bolt-on maple neck with rosewood fingerboard, white dot inlays, 24 XJ frets, 4 String Deluxe Bass bridge, two EMG-HZ pickups with 3-band active EQ, black hardware, available in Black, Titanium, Grey Satin, Midnight Purple, or Gun metal Blue finishes, mfg. 1999-2003.

| | | $500 | $425 | $375 | $325 | $275 | $225 | $175 |

Last MSR was $699.

F-205 - similar to F-204 Bass, except in a 5-string configuration, available in Black, Grey Satin, Midnight Purple, or Gun Metal Blue finishes, mfg. 1999-2003.

| | | $525 | $475 | $425 | $375 | $325 | $275 | $225 |

Last MSR was $749.

F-254 - offset double cutaway with many points and contours, agathis body, 5-piece maple/walnut fingerboard with dot and 12th fret model name inlays, 2 EMG-HZ pickups, ESP-BB bridge, five knobs, Cosmo black hardware, available in Titanium or Black finishes, mfg. 2004-present.

| MSR | $699 | $495 | $425 | $375 | $325 | $275 | $235 | $195 |

F-255 - similar to the F-254, except in five-string configuration, available in Gun Metal Blue finish, mfg. 2004-present.

| MSR | $749 | $525 | $450 | $400 | $350 | $300 | $250 | $200 |

VIPER-254 - offset sharp double cutaway mahogany body, 5-piece maple/walnut neck, 21-fret rosewood fingerboard with dot and 12th fret model name inlays, 2 EMG HZ pickups, ESP-BB bridge with STB, five knobs, black hardware, available in See-Thru Black Cherry, Olympic White, or Black finishes, mfg. 2004-present.

| MSR | $649 | $450 | $400 | $350 | $300 | $260 | $230 | $190 |

ELECTRIC BASS: 300 SERIES

In 2003 The B-200 Series recieved flamed maple tops and colors See-Thru Black Cherry and See-Thru Black were introduced.

B-304(FM) - similar to B-204 Bass, except has Neck-Through mahogany body, maple neck with rosewood fingerboard, available in See-Through Black, See-Through Black Cherry, or 2-Tone Sunburst finishes, mfg. 1999-2003.

| | | $550 | $500 | $450 | $400 | $350 | $300 | $250 |

Last MSR was $759.

B-305(FM) - similar to B-304 Bass, except in a 5-string configuration, available in See-Through Black, See-Through Black Cherry, or 2-Tone Sunburst finishes, mfg. 1999-2003.

| | | $575 | $525 | $475 | $425 | $350 | $300 | $250 |

Last MSR was $799.

C-304 - unique offset double cutaway maple body with quilted maple or bubinga top, 5-piece maple/walnut thru body neck, 24-fret rosewood fingerboard with dot inlay, matching headstock, 2-per-side tuners, two EMG 35-HZ pickups, active EQ, five knobs, gold hardware, available in Honey Satin Natural, See-Thru Blue, or See-Thru Red finishes, mfg. 2002-03.

| | | $550 | $500 | $450 | $400 | $350 | $300 | $250 |

Last MSR was $779.

C-305 - similar to the C-304, except in five-string configuration, 3/2-per-side tuners, mfg. 2002-03.

| | | $585 | $535 | $485 | $425 | $375 | $320 | $270 |

Last MSR was $829.

EC-304ATS - single sharp cutaway mahogany body, five-piece maple neck, rosewood fingerboard with flag inlays, two EMG 35-HZ pickups, 2-per-side tuners, tune-o-matic bridge, cream body binding, three knobs, available in Black or See-Thru Red finishes, mfg. 2002-03.

| | | $525 | $475 | $425 | $375 | $325 | $275 | $225 |

Last MSR was $749.

Add $35 for See-Thru Red finish, which has a flamed maple top (Model EC-304ATSFM).

VIPER-304 - sharp double cutaway mahogany body, 5-piece maple neck, rosewood fingerboard, two EMG pickups, active EQ, 2-per-side tuners, STB, five knobs, black hardware, available in Black or See-Thru Black Cherry finishes, mfg. 2002-03.

| | | $525 | $475 | $425 | $375 | $325 | $275 | $225 |

Last MSR was $749.

VIPER-305 - similar to the Viper-304, except in five-string configuration, mfg. 2003 only.

| | | $575 | $525 | $475 | $425 | $350 | $300 | $250 |

Last MSR was $799.

LTD B-155 courtesy LTD

LTD F-255 courtesy LTD

GRADING	100% MINT	98% NEAR MINT	95% EXC+	90% EXC	80% VG+	70% VG	60% G

ELECTRIC BASS: 400 SERIES

B-404 - offset double cutaway mahogany body, quilt maple top, 5-piece maple/walnut neck, 24-fret rosewood fingerboard with dot and 12th fret model name inlays, 2 EMG 35-DC/P5 pickups, ESP BB bridge with STB, five knobs, Cosmo black hardware, available in Dark Brown Sunburst or See-Thru Black Cherry finishes, mfg. 2004-present.

MSR	$999		$700	$625	$550	$475	$400	$350	$300

B-405 - similar to the B-404, except in five-string configuration, available in Amber Sunburst or See-Thru Black finishes, mfg. 2004-present.

MSR	$1,049		$750	$650	$575	$500	$425	$375	$325

EC-404 - single cutaway mahogany body, flame maple top, 5-piece maple/walnut neck, 22-fret rosewood fingerboard with flag and 12th fret model name inlays, 2 EMG active pickups, ESP BB bridge, three knobs, Cosmo black hardware, available in See-Thru Black finish, mfg. 2004-present.

MSR	$999		$700	$625	$550	$475	$400	$350	$300

DF-404 - offset double cutaway mahogany body with contours, 5-piece maple neck, 24-fret rosewood fingerboard with tribal graphic inlay, 2 EMG active pickups, ESP BB bridge, five knobs, Cosmo black hardware, available in Black finish, new 2004.

MSR	$999		$700	$625	$550	$475	$400	$350	$300

VIPER-404 - offset sharp double cutaway mahogany body, flame maple top, 5-piece maple/walnut neck, 21-fret rosewood fingerboard with flag and 12th fret model name inlays, 2 EMG active pickups, ESP BB bridge, five knobs, black hardware, available in See-Thru Black Cherry finish, mfg. 2004-present.

MSR	$999		$700	$625	$550	$475	$400	$350	$300

ELECTRIC BASS: DELUXE (1000) & SIGNATURE SERIES

B-2005 30TH ANNIVERSARY - B-style mahogany body, set five-piece maple/walnut neck, 24-fret ebony fingerboard with 12th fret 30 inlay, skull headstock with two-per-side tuners, ESP BB-604 bridge, two EMG humbucker pickups, five knobs, black hardware, Black Satin finish, 35 in. scale, new 2005.

MSR	$999		$700	$625	$550	$475	$425	$375	$325

J-1004 - double offset ash body with quilted maple top, maple neck, rosewood fingerboard with dot inlay, matching headstock, 4-on-one-side tuners, two EMG humbucker pickups, four knobs, gold hardware, available in Natural Gloss or See-Thru Red finishes, mfg. 2003-present.

MSR	$1,189		$840	$750	$675	$600	$525	$450	$375

J-1005 - similar to the J-1004, except in five-string configuration, mfg. 2003-present.

MSR	$1,239		$875	$775	$700	$625	$550	$475	$400

JM-500 (JEREMY MARSHALL) - double offset cutaway ash body, five-piece maple/walnut neck, 24-fret ebony fingerboard with cold spider inlays, two EMG 40-DC pickups, active EQ, five knobs, black chrome hardware, available in Black Satin finish, mfg. 2002-03.

			$700	$625	$550	$500	$425	$375	$325

Last MSR was $999.

MD-500 (MARCELO DIAS) - double smooth cutaway maple body, maple neck, 22-fret ebony fingerboard with symbol inlays, two Duncan-designed MM pickups, active EQ, five knobs, black chrome hardware, available in Grey Satin finish, mfg. 2002-03.

			$700	$625	$550	$500	$425	$375	$325

Last MSR was $999.

TA-200 (TOM ARAYA) - double sharp edged cutaway basswood body, maple neck, 24-fret rosewood fingerboard with pentagram inlays, two EMG 35-HZ pickups, three knobs, black hardware, available in Black finish, mfg. 2003-present.

MSR	$799		$575	$500	$425	$350	$300	$250	$200

TA-600 (TOM ARAYA) - similar to the TA-200, except has a maple body and active electronics, availalbe in Black finish, mfg. 2003-present.

MSR	$1,199		$850	$750	$675	$625	$550	$450	$375

LUK

See Launhardt & Kobs.

LA BAYE

Instruments previously built in Neodesha, KS in 1967. Designed and distributed by The La Baye Company in Green Bay, WI. Current information can be obtained through Henri's Music of Green Bay (and Appleton), WI.

Inventor Dan Helland conceived the notion of a minimal-bodied guitar while working at Henri's Music Shop in Green Bay, Wisconsin during the mid-1960s. After receiving some support from owner Henri Czachor and others, Helland had the Holman-Woodell company of Neodesha, Kansas build the first (and only) run of forty-five instruments. La Baye guitars share similar stock hardware pieces and pickups installed on Wurlitzer guitars of the same era, as Holman-Woodell were building a number of different trademarked instruments during the mid- to late 1960s.

After receiving the first shipment, Helland attended the 1967 Chicago NAMM show (the same show where Ovation first debuted). Unfortunately, the minimal body concept was so far advanced that the market didn't catch up until Steinberger released his first bass in the 1980s! La Baye instruments were produced in 1967, and a total of forty-five were shipped to Helland.

Identification is pretty straightforward, given that the 3+3 headstock will say La Baye and sometimes 2 x 4. The 22-fret neck bolts to the rectangular body, and controls are mounted on top and bottom of the body. There were four models: the six-string and twelve-string guitars, and the short-scale (single pickup) bass as well as the long-scale (2 pickup) bass. However, keep in mind that there are only forty-five official La Baye instruments (others were later offered by Holman and 21st Century, from the same factory that built the initial models- source: Michael Wright, *Guitar Stories*, Volume One).

GRADING	100% MINT	98% NEAR MINT	95% EXC+	90% EXC	80% VG+	70% VG	60% G

LA GUITAR FACTORY

Instruments currently produced in Charlotte, NC since 1997.

LA Guitar Factory consists of luthiers Ari Lehtela and Luke Luther. They use a wide variety of materials to produce acoustic and electric guitars, primarily hollow body archtop jazz electrics. They also produce bass guitars along with a variety of other products. There are also several options available on each guitar. For more information contact LA Guitar Factory directly (see Trademark Index).

ELECTRIC

Most of LA Guitar Factory's guitars are electric. The **Jazz Wonder** is the flagship of the line and features a spruce top with flamed maple back and sides. Other models include the **Jazz Tango**, **The Blue Model**, **Jazz 'Tela**, and the **8-A**. The semi-hollowbody and solid guitars include the **'Tela** and the **Lukacaster**.

LACE GUITARS

Also Lace Helix. Instruments currently built in Huntington Beach, CA since 1979. Distributed by AGI (Actodyne General Inc.) of Huntington Beach, CA.

AGI's Lace Guitars feature a revolutionary neck design: the ergonomically correct Lace Helix Twisted Neck. The Twisted Neck has a 20 degree twist that follows the natural twist of the player's hand as it travels up and down the fingerboard. While the prototypes were introduced during 1997, production finally began in late 1999, after CNC production problems had been solved. Lace also manufactures a Helix 10.8 degree neck that bolts on to a Fender Stratocaster neck pocket (with clear gloss finish and Jim Dunlop frets). The retail price is $400.

ELECTRIC

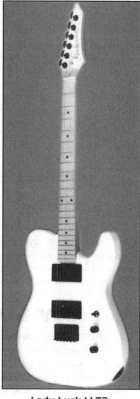

**Lady Luck LLT3
courtesy Lady Luck**

ACELA - Lace style hollow basswood/poplar body, bolt-on maple neck, 21-fret maple fingerboard, 3-per-side tuners, Lace Sensor Acoustic Bronze pickups, two black knobs, chrome hardware, available in Black, Coral, Vintage Burst, or White finishes, disc. 2003.

	$450	$400	$350	$300	$250	$200	$150

Last MSR was $599.

CALIFORNIA CLASSIC - offset double cutaway mahogany body, mahogany neck, rosewood fingerboard with dot position markers, 3 Lace PS-900 Ultra Vintage pickups, fulcrum full-contact tremolo or wraparound bridge may be specified, 2-pickup variation may be special ordered, choice of a variety of traditional nitrocellulose finishes, disc. 2003.

	$1,275	$1,050	$950	$850	$725	$600	$500

Last MSR was $1,699.

CALIFORNIA GOLD RUSH - offset double cutaway ash body, bolt-on maple neck with maple fingerboard, 3 Lace Ultra Vintage PS-900 pickups or 3 single coil size Lace Ultra Vintage pickups, full contact tremolo or wraparound bridge, available in Black, Red and Three-Tone Vintage Sunburst grain enhanced nitrocellulose translucent finishes, disc. 2003.

	$1,350	$1,100	$975	$850	$725	$600	$500

Last MSR was $1,799.

CALIFORNIA TWISTER 10.8 NECK - Strat-style body, bolt-on maple neck, maple or rosewood fingerboard, tortiseshell pickguard, choice of 2 Hot Gold Dually's, 3 Holy Grail Single coils, or 2 Lace Hot Gold's and a Dually for pickups, two knobs, switch, tremolo, available in Black finishes, current mfg.

MSR	$1,299	$1,000	$900	$825	$700	$550	$475	$400

Add $75 for Hot Golds (SSH) or Chrome Dome (SSS) pickup configurations.

CYBERCASTER 10.8 NECK - Lace-style swamp ash body, 10.8 degree maple neck, maple fingerboard, 3-per-side tuners, USA Lace Hemi Humbucker pickups, black carbon pickguard, chrome wrap-around bridge, two knobs, 3-way switch, chrome hardware, available in Butterscotch or Black finishes, current mfg.

MSR	$1,599	$1,250	$1,100	$950	$800	$650	$550	$450

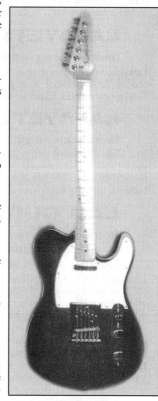

HUNTINGTON - Strat-style poplar body, maple bolt-on neck, 21-fret rosewood neck with dot inlay, 3-per-side tuners, two powered by Lace humbucker pickups, white pickguard, three black knobs, tremolo, five-way switch, available in Red or Black finishes, current mfg.

MSR	$250	$190	$175	$150	$130	$110	$95	$75

Huntington Limited Edition Drop & Gain Model - similar to the Huntington except has Lace Drop and Gain pickups, tortoise pickguard, available in Metallic Blue finish, current mfg.

MSR	$499	$350	$300	$260	$230	$200	$170	$140

Huntington PT - similar to the Huntington, excep it has 3 Gold Lace Sensor Made in U.S.A. pickups, available in Black or Red finishes, new 2004.

MSR	$469	$330	$280	$250	$220	$190	$160	$130

Add $20 for Lace Holy Grail, Chrome Dome, AlumiTone, or SSD configuraiton of Lace Gold Sensor pickups.

LACE HELIX GLASS - sleek offset double cutaway Avanti lightweight fiberglass body, maple neck, 25.5 in. scale, rosewood fingerboard with offset mother-of-pearl dot inlay, 6-on-a-side Sperzel tuners, fixed bridge, chrome or gold hardware, 2 Lace humbucker pickups, black mini data volume/tone controls, pickup selector switch, available in Black, Acto-Blue, Red, Yellow, or White finishes, disc. 2003.

	$1,500	$1,200	$1,000	$825	$700	$600	$550

Last MSR was $1,995.

**Lady Luck LLT1
courtesy Lady Luck**

GRADING	100% MINT	98% NEAR MINT	95% EXC+	90% EXC	80% VG+	70% VG	60% G

LACE HELIX WOOD - sleek offset double cutaway mahogany body, maple neck, 25.5 in. scale, rosewood fingerboard with offset mother-of-pearl dot inlay, 6-on-a-side Sperzel tuners, fixed bridge or stop tailpiece, chrome or gold hardware, 3 single coil (or 2 humbucker) Lace pickups, black mini data volume/tone controls, pickup selector switch, available in Black, Acto-Blue, Red, Yellow, or White finishes, disc. 2003.

$1,500	$1,200	$1,000	$825	$700	$600	$550

Last MSR was $1,995.

LG-1 - offset double cutaway alder body, maple neck, 25.5 in. scale, slab rosewood fingerboard with offset mother-of-pearl dot inlay, 6-on-a-side locking Sperzel tuners, ABM bridge, features ActoTone virtual acoustic pickup system, chrome or gold hardware, 3 Lace California convertible pickups, 2 volume/1 tone controls, pickup selector switch, disc. 2003.

$925	$800	$700	$600	$500	$400	$350

Last MSR was $1,300.

Add $300 for LG-1 California/Custom (includes carved ash top, and Super Vintage Lace Holy Grail pickups).

LADO

Instruments currently built in Pickering, Ontario. Instruments were previously built in Scarborough, Ontario (Canada) since the early 1970s.

Lado founder and company president Joe Kovacic initially learned the guitar-building craft in Zagreb, Croatia. Kovacic gained luthier experience in Austria and Germany before leaving Europe to move to North America in 1971. Every handcrafted bass and guitar is backed by over thirty years experience, and current suggested retail prices fall between $799 and $999. Lado also offers a Lutherie school with four different courses. For further information, please contact Lado directly (see Trademark Index).

LADY LUCK

Instruments currently produced in Korea since 1986. Distributed in the U.S., Europe, and South America by Lady Luck Industries, Inc. of Cary, IL.

President Terresa Miller has been offering a wide range of imported, affordable guitars that are designed for beginning students up to working professionals. Lady Luck guitar models are designed in the U.S. (specifications and colors). Lady Luck also offers several models of electric bass guitars along with the line of acoustic and electric guitars.

In addition to the Lady Luck and Nouveau brands, Lady Luck Industries also distributes Adder Plus pickups and EV Star Cables.

ELECTRIC

Lady Luck's **La Femme** model guitars (list $995) feature a female-figure sculpted, styrene body and Bill Lawrence Keystone pickups. Available in White or Black finishes.

The **Nouveau** series models like the **LLS-2N** featured an offset double cutaway solid ash body, 2 single coils/humbucker pickups, standard tremolo, and 6-on-a-side tuners. The **LLS-2NFR** model featured a licensed Floyd Rose bridge. Retail list prices begin at $375.

LLS-models feature an offset double cutaway body, while the **LLP**- and **LLT**-models feature single cutaway bodies. The **Retrospect** line features designs based on classic American favorites, with prices that begin at $210 (**LLS1**) to $250 (LLS2), and up through $280 (**LLT1**).

LAFAYETTE (JAPAN MFG.)

Instruments previously produced in Japan during the 1960s, and distributed by LaFayette Electronics.

Lafayette instruments were shorter-scaled beginner instruments imported to the U.S. and sold through LaFayette Electronics' catalogs. The LaFayette product line consisted of amplifiers, thinline acoustic/electric archtops, and solid body electric guitars and basses. Many models built by Japan's Guyatone company, although some may also be Teisco models (source: Michael Wright, *Vintage Guitar Magazine*).

LAFAYETTE (KOREA MFG.)

Instruments currently built in Korea. Distributed by the More Company of Pooler, GA.

The More Company, distributors of Synsonic instruments, is also offering a wide range of acoustic and acoustic/electric guitars; and solid body electric guitars and basses. Acoustic models like the **SW 690** have a retail list price of $460; acoustic/electrics start at $500. Solid body electric models range from $350 up to $625, and basses run from $575 to $650. For additional information regarding models, specifications, and pricing, please contact Lafayette (a More Company) directly (see Trademark Index).

LAG GUITARS

Instruments currently built in Bedarieux, France. Hotline by LAG series is currently produced in Korea (Hotline models are designed in France and built to specifications in Korea). Currently imported and distributed by the Sandell Trading Company, located in Clearwater Beach, FL.

LAG has been building guitars in France since 1980. LAG began building the high quality **Beast** superstrat designed solid bodies, and later introduced the **Roxanne Prestige** and **Roxanne Classic** double cutaway LP-ish model. One of the more original designs developed by the LAG company was to offer a Floyd Rose locking tremolo on the **Roxanne Prestige**, a move un-duplicated by any of the American companies like Gibson, Hamer, Dean (or others with Gibson-esque guitar designs).

Led by Michael Chavarria, the Bedarieux facility currently has eleven workers. LAG has currently cut back on custom models in favor of offering more options on the four series in the new line. LAG specifically uses flamed maple tops on all of their models, and features electronics by DiMarzio, Fishman, and Seymour Duncan; and Schaller, Sperzel, and Wilkinson hardware.

LAG also produces the "Le Key" portable MIDI keyboard controller, a sleek 37-key model worn on a strap just like a guitar. LAG guitars is also offering a Jumbo-style acoustic model with either mahogany or rosewood back and sides. This model is also available in an acoustic/electric configuration.

GRADING	100% MINT	98% NEAR MINT	95% EXC+	90% EXC	80% VG+	70% VG	60% G

ELECTRIC

The superstrat **Beast** models feature offset double cutaway basswood bodies, bolt-on maple necks, tremolo bridges, and 6 tuners on a side headstocks. Models include the **Standard**, flamed maple topped **Supreme**, humbucker/single coil/humbucker **Custom**, and the semi-hollow **Thinline**.

The traditional style **Blues** models all feature double cutaway bodies, with distinctive white pearloid pickguards that cover the pickup area forward to the treble and bass horns. Both the **Standard** and **Louisiane** models feature a humbucker/single coil SuperTele configuration (the Louisiane has gold hardware), while the **Nashville** has 2 single coils and a humbucker in the bridge position.

The **Rockline** series is LAG´s modern superstrat models, with a humbucker/single coil/humbucker pickup configuration and sleek double cutaway body shape. Models include the **Standard** and **Avenue**; the **Metalmaster** model has been in production for over ten years.

As mentioned above, **Roxanne** models feature a dual cutaway mahogany body and glued-in neck, and feature two humbuckers and a 3-tuners-per-side headstock. Both the **Standard** and **Classic** models are straight ahead classic LP-style guitars (the Classic has a flamed maple top and Sunburst finish); the **Prestige** features a tune-o-matic bridge and raised metal tailpiece; and the eye-catching **Floyd** model features a recessed Floyd Rose tremolo.

In 1994, Lag introduced the new **Hotline** Series. Hotline guitar designs are conceived in France and built to LAG specifications in Korea. Both the **TB1** and the **RK1** models come equipped with the new Duncan-designed pickups, and are available in one of three colors: Black See-Through, Green See-Through, or Red See-Through. Interested guitarists are invited to contact the LAG company directly (see Trademark Index).

**LAG Blues Deluxe
courtesy LAG Guitars**

LAKEFRONT

Instruments previously built in Mossville, IL circa early 1980s

Lakefront Musical Instruments offered a number of high quality solid body electric guitars. Instruments featured a neck-through construction, 21-fret fingerboard, 3-per-side gold plated Grover tuner, and laminated body construction that featured oak, zebrawood, rosewood, walnut, curly maple, and bird´s-eye maple. Hardware and pickups were specified by the buyer. Suggested list prices are still unknown at this date. Last given address for Lakefront was Lakefront Musical Instruments, Box 48, Mossville, IL 61552.

LAKLAND

Instruments currently built in Chicago, IL since 1994. The Skyline Series is produced overseas.

Luthier Dan Lakin has been playing and buying/selling bass guitars for a number of years. In 1994, he began offering a high quality, custom-built electric bass with a design based on Leo Fender´s later models.

ELECTRIC BASS: 4 & 5 STRING MODELS

Lakland models are differentiated by the pickup configuration. All models (except the Joe Osborn Signature model) are available in a 4- and 5-string configuration, and in three different appointment levels. 4-String models are optional with a Hipshot Bass Xtender (D-Tuner) for $100.

4-94 - slightly offset double cutaway body, bolt-on quatersawn maple neck with 2 graphite reinforcement bars, 34 in. scale, 22-fret maple (or rosewood) fingerboard with dot inlay, 4-on-a-side tuners, fixed bridge with round metal plate, chrome hardware, single coil/humbucker Bartolini (or Seymour Duncan Bassline) pickups, volume/pan/bass/mid/treble controls, coil tap switch, mfg. 1994-present.

4-94 Standard - swamp ash body with Translucent or Sunburst finish.

MSR	$3,300	$2,475	$2,150	$1,850	$1,650	$1,350	$1,050	$900

4-94 Classic - alder body with Metallic finish (with optional white pickguard).

MSR	$3,300	$2,475	$2,150	$1,850	$1,650	$1,350	$1,050	$900

4-94 Deluxe - swamp ash body with quilted or flamed maple top, Translucent or Sunburst finish.

MSR	$3,700	$2,775	$2,400	$2,100	$1,750	$1,450	$1,250	$975

55-94 - similar to the 4-94, except features a 35 in. scale, 5-string configuration, 3/2-per-side tuners, mfg. 1994-present.

55-94 Standard - swamp ash body with Translucent or Sunburst finish.

MSR	$3,600	$2,700	$2,300	$2,000	$1,725	$1,425	$1,150	$950

55-94 Classic - alder body with Metallic finish (with optional white pickguard).

MSR	$3,600	$2,700	$2,300	$2,000	$1,725	$1,425	$1,150	$950

55-94 Deluxe - swamp ash body with quilted or flamed maple top, Translucent or Sunburst finish.

MSR	$4,100	$3,075	$2,650	$2,350	$2,050	$1,750	$1,450	$1,100

4-63 - similar to the 4-94, except features 2 J-style single coil Bartolini (or Basslines or Lindy Fralin) pickups, disc. 2002.

4-63 Standard - swamp ash body with Translucent or Sunburst finish.

	$2,250	$1,950	$1,650	$1,450	$1,250	$1,050	$850

Last MSR was $3,000.

4-63 Classic - alder body with Metallic finish (with optional white pickguard).

	$2,250	$1,950	$1,650	$1,450	$1,250	$1,050	$850

Last MSR was $3,000.

**LAG Roxanne
courtesy LAG Guitars**

GRADING	100% MINT	98% NEAR MINT	95% EXC+	90% EXC	80% VG+	70% VG	60% G

4-63 Deluxe - swamp ash body with quilted or flamed maple top, Translucent or Sunburst finish.

	$2,550	$2,250	$1,950	$1,650	$1,350	$1,150	$950

Last MSR was $3,400.

55-63 - similar to the 4-63, except features a 35 in. scale, 5-string configuration, 3/2-per-side tuners, Bartolini and Bassline pickups, disc 2002.

55-63 Standard - swamp ash body with Translucent or Sunburst finish.

	$2,475	$2,175	$1,875	$1,675	$1,375	$1,075	$875

Last MSR was $3,300.

55-63 Classic - alder body with Metallic finish (with optional white pickguard).

	$2,475	$2,175	$1,875	$1,675	$1,375	$1,075	$875

Last MSR was $3,300.

55-63 Deluxe - swamp ash body with quilted or flamed maple top, Translucent or Sunburst finish.

	$2,850	$2,550	$2,250	$1,950	$1,650	$1,350	$995

Last MSR was $3,800.

4-76 - similar to the 4-94, except features one MM (humbucker) Bartolini (or Basslines) pickup, volume/bass/mid/treble controls, disc. 2000, reintroduced 2005 and is currently produced.

4-76 Standard - swamp ash body with Translucent or Sunburst finish, disc. 2000, reintroduced 2005 and is currently produced.

MSR	$3,200	$2,400	$2,100	$1,850	$1,600	$1,400	$1,200	$1,000

4-76 Classic - alder body with Metallic finish (with optional white pickguard), disc. 2000, reintroduced 2005 and is currently produced.

MSR	$3,200	$2,400	$2,100	$1,850	$1,600	$1,400	$1,200	$1,000

4-76 Deluxe - swamp ash body with quilted or flamed maple top, Translucent or Sunburst finish, disc. 2000, reintroduced 2005- and is currently produced.

MSR	$3,600	$2,700	$2,400	$2,100	$1,800	$1,550	$1,300	$1,100

4-DUAL J - similar to 4-76 except features two Lindy Fralin "J" style pickups, mfg. 2001-02.

4-Dual J Standard - swamp ash body, available in Translucent White, Translucent Blonde, Amber, Burgundy, Natural, Blue, Three-Tone Sunburst, Tobacco Sunburst, Cherry Sunburst, or Teal Sunburst finishes.

	$2,150	$1,850	$1,550	$1,250	$1,050	$850	$725

Last MSR was $2,880.

4-Dual J Classic - alder body, available in Shoreline Gold, Inca Silver, Teal Green, Sea Foam Green, Lake Placid Blue, Sherwood Green, Burgundy Mist, Candy Apple Red, Fiesta Red, Sonic Blue, Olympic White, or Black finishes.

	$2,150	$1,850	$1,550	$1,250	$1,050	$850	$725

Last MSR was $2,800.

4-Dual J Deluxe - swamp ash body with flame or quilt maple top, available in Amber, Burgundy, Natural, Blue, Three-Tone Sunburst, Tobacco Sunburst, Teal Sunburst, or Cherry Sunburst finishes.

	$2,850	$2,550	$2,250	$1,950	$1,650	$1,350	$995

Last MSR was $3,300.

55-76 - similar to the 4-76, except features a 35 in. scale, 5-string configuration, 3/2-per-side tuners, disc. 2000, reintroduced and is currently produced.

55-76 Standard - swamp ash body with Translucent or Sunburst finish, disc. 2000, reintroduced 2005 and is currently produced.

MSR	$3,500	$2,650	$2,300	$2,000	$1,700	$1,450	$1,250	$1,050

55-76 Classic - alder body with Metallic finish (with optional white pickguard), disc. 2000, reintroduced 2005 and is currently produced.

MSR	$3,500	$2,650	$2,300	$2,000	$1,700	$1,450	$1,250	$1,050

55-76 Deluxe - swamp ash body with quilted or flamed maple top, Translucent or Sunburst finish, disc. 2000, reintroduced 2005 and is currently produced.

MSR	$4,000	$3,000	$2,600	$2,300	$2,000	$1,750	$1,550	$1,350

55-DUAL J - similar to 55-76, except features two Lindy Fralin "J" style pickups, mfg. 2001-02.

55-Dual J Standard - swamp ash body, available in Amber, Burgundy, Natural, Blue, Three-Tone Sunburst, Tobacco Sunburst, Cherry Sunburst, Teal Sunburst, Translucent White, or Translucent Blonde finishes.

	$2,400	$2,100	$1,800	$1,500	$1,200	$995	$850

Last MSR was $3,200.

55-Dual J Classic - alder body, available in Shoreline Gold, Inca Silver, Teal Green, Lake Placid Blue, Sherwood Green, Burgundy Mist, Candy Apple Red, Sonic Blue, Seafoam Green, Fiesta Red, Olympic White, or Black finishes.

	$2,400	$2,100	$1,800	$1,500	$1,200	$995	$850

Last MSR was $3,200.

55-Dual J Deluxe - swamp ash body, flame or quilt maple top, available in Amber, Burgundy, Natural, Blue, Three-Tone Sunburst, Tobacco Sunburst, Cherry Sunburst, or Teal Sunburst finishes.

	$2,775	$2,475	$2,175	$1,875	$1,575	$1,375	$1,050

Last MSR was $3,700.

HOLLOWBODY - built in collaboration with Michael Tobias, two Bartolini humbucker pickups, 2-per-side Hipshot Ultra-light tuners, East Indian rosewood fingerboard with bird's-eye maple position markers, quartersawn rock maple neck with graphite reinforcement bars, 1 f-hole, mfg. 2000-present.

Hollowbody Standard - carved mahogany back and sides, carved maple top, available in Shoreline Gold, Inca Silver, Teal Green, Lake Placid Blue, Sherwood Green, Burgundy Mist, Candy Apple Red, Sonic Blue, Seafoam Green, Fiesta Red, or Olympic White finishes.

MSR	$3,600	$2,700	$2,400	$2,100	$1,800	$1,500	$1,200	$950

Hollowbody Deluxe - carved mahogany back and sides, carved Maple Top AAA-Flame, available in Three-Tone Sunburst or Tobacco Sunburst finishes.

MSR	$4,200	$3,150	$2,750	$2,450	$2,150	$1,850	$1,550	$1,250

GRADING	100% MINT	98% NEAR MINT	95% EXC+	90% EXC	80% VG+	70% VG	60% G

Hollowbody Deluxe Limited Edition - carved mahogany back and sides, carved maple top AAAAA-Flame, available in Three-Tone Sunburst and Tobacco Sunburst finishes, disc 2002.

	100%	98%	95%	90%	80%	70%	60%
	$3,600	$3,200	$2,800	$2,500	$2,200	$1,900	$1,550

Last MSR was $4,800.

ELECTRIC BASS: SIGNATURE SERIES

JERRY SCHEFF SIGNATURE - offset double cutaway body, 22-frets, quartersawn rock maple neck, bird's-eye maple with ebony dots or East Indian rosewood with bird's-eye maple dots fingerboard, two Kent Armstrong Split-Tube low-output pickups, onboard Bartolini 3-band preamp, white pickguard.

Standard 4 - 34 in. scale, swamp ash body, Hipshot tapered shaft tuners, available in Amber, Burgundy, Natural, Blue, Three-Tone Sunburst, Tobacco Sunburst, Cherry Sunburst, or Teal Sunburst, Translucent White, or Translucent Blonde finishes.

MSR	$3,200	$2,400	$2,050	$1,800	$1,500	$1,200	$975	$750

Classic 4 - 34 in. scale, alder body, Hipshot tapered shaft tuners, available in Shoreline Gold, Inca Silver, Teal Green, Lake Placid Blue, Seafoam Green, Sherwood Green, Fiesta Red, Burgundy Mist, Candy Apple Red, Sonic Blue, Olympic White, or Black finishes.

MSR	$3,200	$2,400	$2,050	$1,800	$1,500	$1,200	$975	$750

Deluxe 4 - 34 in. scale, swamp ash body, Hipshot tapered shaft tuners, available in the same finishes as the Standard Model minus Translucent White, or Translucent Blonde, current mfg.

MSR	$3,700	$2,775	$2,400	$2,100	$1,750	$1,400	$1,100	$850

Standard 5 - 35 in. scale, swamp ash body, Hipshot Ultralight tuners, available in the same finishes as its 4-string counterpart.

MSR	$3,600	$2,700	$2,350	$2,050	$1,650	$1,350	$1,050	$800

Classic 5 - 35 in. scale, alder body, Hipshot Ultralight tuners, available in the same finishes as its 4-string counterpart.

MSR	$3,600	$2,700	$2,350	$2,050	$1,650	$1,350	$1,050	$800

Deluxe 5 - 35 in. scale, swamp ash body, quilt/flame maple top, Hipshot Ultralight tuners, available in the same finishes as its 4-string counterpart.

MSR	$4,100	$3,075	$2,700	$2,350	$2,050	$1,750	$1,400	$1,050

Lakland Model 494
courtesy LTD

BOB GLAUB SIGNATURE - offset double cutaway alder or ash body, 34 in. scale, quartersawn maple neck w/ graphite reinforcement, 20-fret East Indian rosewood fingerboard or maple fingerboard, Lindy Fralin pickups, 1 volume/1 tone passive, Hipshot tapered shaft tuners, Lakland design dual access strings-through body or bridge, available in 3-Tone Sunburst, black, Olympic White, Candy Apple Red Metallic, Teal Green Metallic, Lake Placid Blue Metallic, Sherwood Green Metallic, Shoreline Gold Metallic, Inca Silver, Burgundy Mist, Translucent White, or Natural finishes, current mfg.

MSR	$3,100	$2,325	$2,000	$1,650	$1,350	$1,100	$900	$750

Add $375 for "P & J" configuration with Fralin linear hum-canceling "J" pickup.

JOE OSBORN SIGNATURE - offset double cutaway alder body, bolt-on quatersawn maple neck with 2 graphite reinforcement bars, 34 in. scale, 20-fret Indian rosewood fingerboard with pearl dot inlay, 4-on-a-side Hipshot tuners, fixed bridge, chrome hardware, tortoiseshell (or vintage white) pickguard, 2 J-style single coil Bartolini (or Lindy Fralin) pickups, 2 stack knob volume/tone controls, metal controls plate, available in Three-Tone Sunburst, Black, Olympic White or Metallic finishes, current mfg.

MSR	$3,600	$2,700	$2,350	$2,050	$1,650	$1,350	$1,050	$800

Add $225 for active system with Bartolini pickups and custom-made 3-band EQ preamp.

Joe Osborn 5-String Signature - similar to the Joe Osborn signature, except in 5-string configuration, current mfg.

MSR	$3,900	$2,925	$2,500	$2,200	$1,750	$1,425	$1,100	$850

Add $225 for active system with Bartolini pickups and custom-made 3-band EQ preamp.

ELECTRIC BASS: SKYLINE SERIES

In 2002, Lakland introduced the Skyline series. These are guitars that are designed off of the popular U.S. Lakland models and are assembled overseas. They are then delivered to their shop in Chicago, where the final manufacturing process takes place including the electronics and pickups on most instruments. This gives anyone who wants to play guitar, an entry level model at price that just about anyone can afford.

SKYLINE 44-01 STANDARD FOUR-STRING - offset double cutaway ash body, bolt-on maple neck, 22-fret maple, rosewood, or fretless rosewood fingerboard, four-on-one-side tuners, two Bartolini spilt coil soapbar pickups, five knobs, chrome hardware, available in 3-Tone Sunburst, Black, Candy Apple Red, Cherry Sunburst, Inca Silver, Lake Placid Blue, or Natural finishes, mfg. 2002-present.

MSR	$950	$675	$575	$500	$450	$400	$350	$300

Skyline 44-02 Standard Four-String - similar to the Skyline 44-01, except has active electronics, mfg. 2002-present.

MSR	$1,599	$1,125	$975	$850	$750	$625	$550	$475

Skyline 44-02 Deluxe Four-String - similar to the Skyline 44-01, except has active electronics and a quilted maple top veneer, available in 3-Tone Sunburst, Cherry Sunburst, or Natural finishes, mfg. 2002-present.

MSR	$1,799	$1,275	$1,100	$950	$850	$775	$700	$625

Lakland Joe Osborn
5-String Signature
courtesy LTD

L

GRADING		100% MINT	98% NEAR MINT	95% EXC+	90% EXC	80% VG+	70% VG	60% G

SKYLINE 55-01 STANDARD FIVE-STRING - offset double cutaway ash body, bolt-on maple neck, 22-fret maple, rosewood, or fretless rosewood fingerboard, 3/2-per-side tuners, two Bartolini spilt coil soapbar pickups, five knobs, chrome hardware, available in 3-Tone Sunburst, Black, Candy Apple Red, Cherry Sunburst, Inca Silver, Lake Placid Blue, or Natural finishes, mfg. 2002-present.

MSR	$999		$700	$600	$525	$475	$425	$375	$325

Skyline 55-02 Standard Five-String - similar to the Skyline 55-01, except has active electronics, mfg. 2002-current

MSR	$1,699		$1,200	$1,050	$925	$800	$700	$625	$550

Skyline 55-02 Deluxe Five-String - similar to the Skyline 55-01, except has active electronics and a quilted maple top veneer, available in 3-Tone Sunburst, Cherry Sunburst, or Natural finishes, mfg. 2002-present.

MSR	$1,899		$1,350	$1,200	$1,050	$925	$800	$725	$650

LAUNAY KING

Instruments previously built in England during the mid-1970s.

These high quality solid body guitars featured original design stylings and "ultra-comprehensive" active circuitry. The entire line consisted of two different series of guitars, the **Swayback** series and the **Prototype** series (source: Tony Bacon and Paul Day, *The Guru's Guitar Guide*).

LAUNHARDT & KOBS

Instruments currently produced in Wetslar, Germany.

Launhardt & Kobs specialize in high quality acoustic guitar models. Their classical series feature models like the **Prelude**, **Sarabande**, **Bourree**, and **Romantika** with slotted headstocks and traditional Spanish-style bodies. The jumbo-style models include the 6-string **Jack D.** and the 12-string **William D.** guitars.

Launhardt & Kobs also produces five Jazz Guitar (archtop) models, all with a 650 mm scale and choice of Attila Zoller or EMG pickups. In addition to the archtop models, Launhardt & Kobs also offers a Strat-style solid body **Model 1** and Tele-ish **Model 2** models under the LUK trademark.

The **Averell D.** akustik (acoustic bass) model has a single rounded cutaway body, and a 865 mm scale length. Both the **Model 3** and **Model 4** solid body electric basses have Jazz bass-stylings.

LAWRENCE, KENNETH

Instruments currently built in Arcata, CA since 1986.

Luthier Kenneth Lawrence had a six-year background in European style furniture and cabinet building before he began working at Moonstone Guitars. Lawrence worked with owner/luthier Steve Helgeson for five years constructing guitars and basses at Moonstone before starting his own Lawerence Instruments in 1986. Lawerence also draws upon his twenty-eight year bass playing background in his designs. For additional information, contact luthier Kenneth Lawrence directly (see Trademark Index).

ELECTRIC BASS

Lawrence crafts high quality instruments from responsibly harvested rainforest hardwoods from southern Mexico and Central America. This forestry project is monitored and endorsed by the Rainforest Alliance. The exotic woods featured in Lawrence´s instruments like Grenadillo, Katalox, and Chechen share similar sonic characteristics to traditional hardwood choices. In the past two years, Lawrence increased the scale length on his 5- and 6-string basses to 35 in. for improving the articulation of the entire instrument (most notably the lower frequencies). Other custom options are available per model (call for pricing and availability).

The **Associate** has an offset double cutaway 2-piece alder or ash body, bolt-on hard maple neck, 34 in. (35 in. on 5- and 6-string models) scale, 24-fret grenadillo or rosewood fingerboard, Gotoh tuners, Gotoh fixed bridge, black hardware, custom Basslines pickups, volume/tone controls, 2-band EQ active electronics, and is available in an Oil finished neck/satin finished body. Retail pricing is: $2,370 for the 4-string, $2,570 for the 5-string, and $2,770 for the 6-string. Options:

The **Sonority** is similar to the Associate, except features through-body neck construction, and is available in an Oil finished neck/satin finished body. This model is now discontinued. Last retail prices were: $2,550 for a 4-string, $2,750 for a 5-string, and $2,950 for the 6-string. The Sonority has the same custom options as the Associate.

The **Brase** has an offset double cutaway 2-piece alder or ash body with upper horn in contact with the neck between the 11th and 15th fret ("braced"), set-in 3-piece hard maple neck with graphite spars, 35 in. scale, 24-fret grenadillo fingerboard, Gotoh tuners, Gotoh fixed bridge, custom Basslines or Lane Poor pickups, volume/tone controls, 3-band EQ active electronics with bypass, and is available in an Oil finished neck/satin finished body. Retail pricing is: $3,880 for the 5-string and $4,080 for the 6-string. Options:

The **Chamberbass** has a sculpted, semi-acoustic offset double cutaway ash or mahogany body, spruce or redwood soundboard (top), set-in hard maple neck, 35 in. scale, black ebony or katalox fretless fingerboard, Gotoh tuners, Gotoh fixed bridge, black hardware, custom Basslines or Lane Poor pickups/piezo bridge pickup, volume/tone controls, and is available in an Oil finished neck/satin finished body. Retail pricing is $5,050 for the 5-string and $5,250 for the 6-string. Options:

Add $50 for gold hardware. Add $60 for Katalox fretless (lined or unlined) fingerboard. Add $75 for a 21-fret neck "Scallop." Add $100 for a maple fretboard. Add $140 for a bird's-eye or flamed maple fingerboard. Add $170 for contrasting wood binding on fretboards and rear cover plate. Add $175 for hand rubbed Oil and Wax finish. Add $175 for a Maccassar or Indian black ebony fretless fingerboard. Add $200 to $250 for Clear or Transparent color high gloss polyester finishes. Add $240 to $320 for highly figured wood top.

Add $160 to $200 for Blue, Red, Purple, and Tobacco Burst satin finish. Add $175 for a hand-rubbed tung oil and wax finish on body. Add $250 for a stained color with oil and wax finish (Red, Blue, Purple, Yellow, and Clear). Add $260 for Transparent clear high gloss polyester finish. Add $320 for Transparent color high gloss finish. Add $260 to $340 for highly figured wood top.

Add $100 for a select Spruce top. Add $120 for fretted fingerboard. Add $260 for Transparent clear high gloss polyester finish. Add $320 for Transparent color high gloss finish. Add $260 to $340 for highly figured wood top.

LEA ELECTRIC GUITARS

Instruments currently built in East Islip, NY.

Solid body and semi-hollow construction guitars are custom-made to order. Lea Guitars are handcrafted of exotic and colorful tone woods and feature "through-body" neck construction, bookmatched top, single or double cutaway body designs, choice of body and fingerboard woods, 22- or 24-fret fingerboard, hand-rubbed laquer or oil finish, choice of hardware and pickup configurations. The "Century" model is a unique single cutaway design that blends beauty and function. The Century model now features a slightly larger body for improved tone and balance. Base price for the Century model is $1,795. Note: Base price includes a large selection of wood options.

LEDUC

Instruments currently built in France, and distributed by Leduc Instruments of Sun Valley, CA. They are also available through World Arts of East Northport, NY.

Luthier/designer Christophe Leduc's high quality electric guitars and basses are built with distinctive tone woods and exacting handcrafting. Leduc's **U-Guitar** features a free-floating soundboard and semi-hollow construction, with pickups and hardware mounted through the soundboard to the body. The U models range in price from $3,295 to $4,195; the semi-acoustic U (**Utopia**) Bass models range in retail price from $2,995 to $3,895.

PAD series basses feature Padauk wood construction in the neck, fingerboard, body, and even the knobs for a unity of resonances. PAD basses are offered in 4-, 5-, or 6-string variations. Prices start at $2,150, and on up to $2,895.

Masterpiece models feature a maple and bubinga neck-through-body design. Thier current price list is listed in Euros. For further information, contact Leduc Instruments directly (see Trademark Index).

LEGEND CUSTOM GUITARS

Instruments currently built in Dartmouth (Nova Scotia), Canada.

Zane O'Brien, luthier and musician behind Legend guitars, has been doing fine woodworking since 1970 and converted over to building electric guitars in 1988. The three-man shop turns out high quality electric guitars and basses for the discriminating musician who knows what they want in a finely crafted instrument.

Considerable time and effort is made in selecting only the best grades of woods for the bodies and necks. The book matched tops are usually figured maple or some exotic wood. The rear mounted pickup design bodies (pickups are installed through the back cavity - a patent is pending) really does a lot to keep the weight down as well as enhances the overall look of the instrument because you only see the top of the pickup when looking at the front of the guitar. This look is similar to how a pickup would look in a pickguard - but without the pickguard. Legend guitar models range in price from $900 to $2,000 (Canadian dollars). For further information regarding pricing and model specifications, please contact Zane O'Brien at Legend Custom Guitars directly (see Trademark Index).

Earlier Legend guitars had Fender-style headstocks, but this was changed in 1996. The current "sickle"-style headstock is more unique, simple, and pleasing to the eye.

Hardware and electronics vary depending on customer preferences, price, and availability. Other shape bodies are also available and custom designs are invited. All Legend guitars have a one-year limited warranty on material and workmanship. Legend guitars are played and endorsed by such well-known artists as George Hebert (Anne Murray Band) and Al McCumber (Lenny Gallant Band), to name a few (company information courtesy Zane O'Brien).

Legend Electric Model courtesy Legend Custom Guitars

ELECTRIC: GENERAL INFORMATION

The Legend necks are either 25.5 in. or 24.75 in. scale, have a standard 12 in. radius fingerboard, are either 21 or 22-fret, come with a bi-flex two way adjustable truss rod (no skunk stripe on back), six tuners in a line headstock design, and are available in Natural Maple finish or vintage amber. Necks are available in other exotic fingerboard woods besides rosewood, ebony, maple, etc.

All Legend guitars are produced in a variety of translucent finishes, solid color finishes, metallic finishes, and glitter finishes (all of which are clear coated with a high quality catalyzed urethane lacquer and polished to a glass like deep finish). Many of the guitars have headstocks finished to match the body.

ELECTRIC: CARVED TOP SERIES

The Legend Carved Top/Arch-top is a double cutaway shape like a Strat, but narrower through the waist, has more pronounced horns, and is deeper and more rounded. The rear body contour is also deeper and more rounded. The following are examples of current Legend Carved Top models: The Legend **Purpleheart Carved Top** features a poplar body, purpleheart carved top, rear-routed control and pickup cavities, creme body binding, bolt-on tiger maple neck, 22-fret purpleheart fingerboard with pearl dot inlay, 6-on-a-side Schaller tuners, chrome hardware, strings-through the body fixed bridge, 2 single coil/humbucker pickups, volume/tone controls, 5-way selector switch. This model has a Cherry Burst polyester base/Polyurethane lacquer clear coat (topcoat). The current list price is $875 (Canadian).

The Legend **Bird's-eye Maple** model is similar to the Purpleheart, except features a book matched birds-eye maple top, mahogany body, ebony fingerboard, and 3 active SA EMG single coil pickups. This model has a similar Cherry Burst polyester base/Polyurethane lacquer clear coat (topcoat), and the current list price is $1,375 (Canadian).

The Legend **Tiger Maple** (flamed maple) model is similar to the Purpleheart, except features a book matched tiger maple top over the poplar body, ebony fingerboard, 2 single coil/Jeff Beck humbucker Seymour Duncan pickups, and mini-toggle (series/parallel/split humbucker) switch. This model has a Teal Green Burst polyester base/Polyurethan lacquer clear coat (topcoat), and the current list price is $1,495 (Canadian).

Legend Custom Electric courtesy Legend Custom Guitars

GRADING	100% MINT	98% NEAR MINT	95% EXC+	90% EXC	80% VG+	70% VG	60% G

ELECTRIC: TELE SERIES

The Tele-style Legend bodies are like the vintage Fenders, but with book matched tops, binding, and exotic woods. Here are current Legend Tele models for example purposes:

The Legend **Silver Sparkle** Tele features a poplar body, conventional pickup cavities, custom silver sparkle pickguard, black body binding, bolt-on maple neck, 22-fret bound bocote fingerboard with pearl dot inlay, 6-on-a-side Gotoh tuners, black hardware, strings-through the body fixed bridge, 2 single coil pickups, volume/tone controls, 5-way selector switch. This model has a Silver Sparkle polyester base/Polyurethane lacquer clear coat (topcoat). The current list price is $1,295 (Canadian). A similar model with a Dusty Rose Sparkle/Silver Sparkle Back finish and Bill Lawrence pickups lists at $1,375 (Canadian).

The Legend **Pau Amarello** Tele model is similar to the Silver Sparkle Tele, except features a book matched Pau Amarello top, white pickguard, white body binding, rosewood fingerboard with gold pearl dot inlay, and chrome hardware. This model has a Natural finish polyester base with an airbrushed brown edging/Polyurethane lacquer clearcoat (topcoat). The current list price is $950 (Canadian).

The Legend **Pearloid-Bound** Tele model is similar to the Silver Sparkle Tele, except features a rosewood fingerboard, pearloid body binding/pearloid pickguard, gold-plated hardware/neck pickup cover, and Schaller tuners. This model has a White polyester base/Polyurethane lacquer clearcoat (topcoat), and the current list price is $975 (Canadian).

LEW CHASE

Instruments previously built in Japan during the late 1970s.

Guitars for the Lew Chase trademark were built by Azumi prior to introduction of their own trademark in the early 1980s. Azumi instruments were generally medium quality solid bodies; expect the same of Lew Chase branded guitars (source: Tony Bacon and Paul Day, *The Guru's Guitar Guide*).

LIBERTY, GENE

Instruments currently built in Sheridan, IL, since the 1970s.

Gene Liberty, at the Ultimate Guitar Repair Shop, has been building high-end custom guitars and basses and doing major repair work full-time since the 1970s. Facilities include complete metal and wood-working shops, with custom-built computer controlled machinery for engineering and building prototypes and experimental designs. The shop also designs and builds tools, fixtures, and machines specific to guitar construction and repair. For more information contact Liberty directly (see Trademark Index).

ELECTRIC

Guitars and basses made here are mainly exotic wood, neck-through-body construction, and the buyer can be the designer, with control of all parameters. Some special options can include through-body dovetail neck construction, interchangeable plug-in pickups, custom designed pearl and abalone shell, and gold or silver wire inlay and engraving, non-standard fingerboard radii and fret scale lengths and any type of special wiring. The shop also makes a limited number of acoustic and archtop jazz guitars to order.

The solid body guitar and bass models have a retail price that starts at $1,800; the acoustic guitar models start at $2,200; and the archtop guitar models have a retail price that begins at $3,500.

LIGHTWAVE SYSTEMS

Formerly Audio Optics. Instruments previously manufactured in Japan by Tune Guitar Technology Co., Ltd. Lightwave pickups currently built in Carpinteria, CA. Previously built in Santa Barbara, CA. Distributed by Lightwave Systems, Inc. of Carpinteria, CA.

The Lightwave pickup system uses a patented new technology of optical scanning in their innovative pickup designs in place of the older magnetic field system. The design team at Lightwave Systems spent ten years creating and perfecting the system, which is composed of optical/piezo sensing elements for each string. The company plans to release their own bass, electroacoustic and electric guitar models, retrofit kits for popular instruments, or as an OEM system for bass and guitar.

According to the company, here's how it works: a string of any composition is illuminated by an infrared light source, so that the string casts a shadow on a pair of high speed photo detectors. When the string is vibrated, the size and shape of the shadow changes in direct proportion to the frequency. This modulates a current passing through the photo sensors - and the current is then amplified. The Lightwave pickup works with any string composition, is totally immune to hum and buzz, and has no self-dampening of string sustains.

ELECTRIC BASS

LIGHTWAVE CUSTOM MANIAC - exotic hardwood body, 25-fret rosewood fingerboard, bolt-on neck. Pickup system utilizes Lightwave infrared pickups, with piezo sensors; cable and power supply included, controls include Ice Tone (for glassy brilliant highs), disc.

$2,000 $1,700 $1,500 $1,300 $1,100 $900 $750

Last MSR was $1,999.

Add $1,000 for 5-string configuration.

LINC LUTHIER

Instruments currently built in Upland, CA since 1991.

Designer Linc Luthier offers handcrafted instruments that feature exotic hardwoods. All bodies are semi-acoustic, and are designed to create an instrument that is lighter in weight as well as possessing greater audio character. Linc also eliminates any plastic, paint, or screws in their quest for functional simplicity - thus, all pickup systems are passive, not active (which requires a battery). Tone is a combination of the overall design coupled with the wood combinations required to produce a certain sound (bright, dark, woody, heavy on the mid-range, etc.). No two instruments have been exactly alike, which means that custom options are used often. The body-to-neck joint is the strongest in the world (patented). For more information contact Linc Luthier directly (see Trademark Index).

GRADING	100% MINT	98% NEAR MINT	95% EXC+	90% EXC	80% VG+	70% VG	60% G

ELECTRIC

Guitar models generally feature a stacked humbucker/dual coil humbucker combination (other custom variations available), with volume and pan controls. Linc features a 24-fret fingerboard, Kahler tremolo or Schaller stop tailpiece, gold hardware, and a clear hand rubbed finish. Retail list prices start at $2,310 for the **Guitar** model, and $2,750 for a **Baritone** configuration.

ELECTRIC BASS

Electric Basses are crafted the same way as the Guitar models, and feature Bartolini pickups and volume/pan controls. **Bass** models are available in 4-string (retail $2,300), 5-string ($2,970), 6-string ($3,410), and 8-string configurations ($3,520); **Double Neck** instruments start at $6,400.

LINCOLN

Instruments previously produced in Japan between the late 1970s and the early 1980s.

Lincoln instruments featured both original designs and designs based on classic American favorites; most guitars considered good quality (source: Tony Bacon and Paul Day, *The Guru's Guitar Guide*).

LINDELL

Instruments previously produced in Japan during the mid-1960s.

Research continues into the Lindell trademark, as the producing company in Japan and the American distributor have yet to be identified. Further information will be reported in future editions of the *Blue Book of Electric Guitars*.

LINDERT

Instruments currently built in Chelan, WA since 1986.

Charles Lindert has been building guitars since 1986, in the state of Washington. The current Loco-Motive Series gets its name in part from the old railway stop near the Chelan Falls facility, near Lake Chelan and the Columbia River. Now president of his own company, Lindert is ably assisted by Larry Krupla (Production Manager) and Jennifer Sheda (Public Relations). All Lindert instruments are easily recognizable by Lindert's eye-catching Thumbs Up patented headstock.

Lindert has produced a range of guitar models that run from vintage-inspired to advanced, forward-thinking styles. Several of Lindert's models feature the Missing Link switch, which allows pickup combinations of neck/bridge, or all three single coils on together (combinations that are not available on traditional 3 single coil pickup systems).

ELECTRIC: BEACHMASTER, CONDUCTOR, & DIESEL SERIES

BEACHMASTER - offset double cutaway/offset waist alder body, bolt-on maple neck, 22-fret rosewood fingerboard, 6-on-a-side tuners, fulcrum tremolo bridge, beveled top, chrome hardware, 3 single coil pickups, 1 volume/2 tone controls, 5-way selector/phase/Missing Link switch, available in Black, Blue, Red, Sunburst, or White finishes, disc. 1995.

	N/A	$700	$625	$550	$475	$350	$275

Last MSR was $1,099.

Beachmaster II - similar to the Beachmaster, except no phase/Missing Link switches, disc. 1996.

	N/A	$500	$425	$350	$275	$225	$175

Last MSR was $649.

CONDUCTOR - similar to the Locomotive T, except treble horn has more pronounced point, 2 humbucker pickups, spiderweb-style 5 large/5 small fabric "grille" inserts behind bridge, mfg. 1998-present.

MSR	$858	$650	$575	$500	$425	$350	$300	$250

Add $140 for extended 30" scale and 24-fret fingerboard (Model Conductor Bass VI).

DIESEL S - offset double cutaway body, bolt-on maple neck, 22-fret rosewood fingerboard, six-on-one-side tuners, chrome hardware, cream colored pickguard, 6 fabric "grille" inserts on top (behind bridge), fixed bridge, 3 single coil pickups, volume/tone controls with chickenhead knobs, 5-way selector switch, available in textured Beechwood brown finish, mfg. 1998-present.

MSR	$798	$600	$525	$450	$375	$325	$275	$225

Add $134 for extended 30" scale and 24-fret fingerboard (Model Diesel S Bass VI).

Diesel T - similar to the Diesel S, except has a single cutaway body, 2 single coil pickups, and 3-way selector, mfg. 1998-present.

MSR	$738	$550	$475	$400	$350	$300	$250	$200

Add $194 for extended 30" scale and 24-fret fingerboard (Model Diesel T Bass VI).

ELECTRIC: LEVITATOR SERIES

The Levitator series offset double cutaway body shape featured louvered soundholes and an integral hand grip on the upper bout. Levitators were optional with a 24-fret fingerboard, a Floyd Rose style tremolo, and Starr pickup selector switches.

GRADING	100% MINT	98% NEAR MINT	95% EXC+	90% EXC	80% VG+	70% VG	60% G

LEVITATOR ESCAPE ARTIST - semi-hollow offset double cutaway body, bolt-on maple neck, 22-fret rosewood fingerboard, 6-on-a-side tuners, fixed bridge, louvered soundholes and built-in hand grip on the upper bout, chrome hardware, 2 single coil pickups, volume/tone controls, 3-way selector/phase switches, available in Black, Blue, Red, Sunburst, or White finishes, disc. 1995.

	N/A	$700	$625	$550	$475	$350	$275

Last MSR was $1,099.

LEVITATOR ILLUSIONIST - similar to the Levitator Escape Artist, except has 3 single coil pickups, 5-way selector/phase/single-dual switches, disc. 1995.

	N/A	$700	$625	$550	$475	$350	$275

Last MSR was $1,099.

LEVITATOR MERLIN - similar to the Levitator Escape Artist, except has 2 humbucker pickups, 2 volume/2 tone knobs, 3-way selector/phase/single-dual switches, disc. 1995.

	N/A	$750	$675	$600	$525	$425	$325

Last MSR was $1,199.

LEVITATOR PRO-MAGICIAN - similar to the Levitator Escape Artist, except has 2 single coil/humbucker pickups, 5-way selector/phase/single-dual switches, disc. 1995.

	N/A	$750	$675	$600	$525	$425	$325

Last MSR was $1,299.

ELECTRIC: LOCOMOTIVE SERIES

The Locomotive series was originally produced as the Victor series. The series/models were introduced in late 1995, and renamed in 1996. Locomotive models feature a three-piece body construction design similar to '50s Danelectro guitars, and have a 25.5 in. scale. The Baritone-style Bass VI configurations have a 30 in. scale length, and a 24-fret fingerboard.

LOCOMOTIVE S - offset double cutaway body, bolt-on maple neck, 22-fret rosewood fingerboard, six-on-one-side tuners, chrome hardware, cream colored pickguard, 9 fabric "grille" inserts on top (behind bridge), fixed bridge, 3 single coil pickups, volume/tone controls with chickenhead knobs, 5-way selector switch, available in textured Beechwood brown finish, mfg. 1995-present.

MSR	$798	$600	$525	$475	$395	$325	$275	$200

Add $184 for extended 30 in. scale and 24-fret fingerboard (Model LocoMotive S Bass VI).

LocoMotive T - similar to the Locomotive S, except has a single cutaway body, 2 single coil pickups, and 3-way selector, mfg. 1995-present.

MSR	$738	$550	$475	$425	$375	$295	$250	$195

Add $200 for extended 30 in. scale and 24-fret fingerboard (Model LocoMotive T Bass VI).

FRANKLIN - similar to the Locomotive T, except treble horn has more pronounced point, 2 humbucker pickups, 2 fabric "grille" inserts behind bridge, mfg. 1996-present.

MSR	$858	$650	$550	$495	$425	$350	$295	$225

Add $140 for extended 30 in. scale and 24-fret fingerboard (Model Franklin Bass VI).

2 THUMBS UP DOUBLENECK - similar to the Locomotive S, except has double neck configuration, 30 in. scale upper bass neck/25.5 in. scale lower guitar neck, 3 single coil pickups (per neck), neck electronics selector, tortoiseshell pickguard, mfg. 1997-present.

MSR	$1,998	$1,500	$1,300	$1,150	$1,000	$850	$700	$550

ELECTRIC: GREENBACK, SKYLINER, & TWISTER SERIES

GREENBACK T - similar to the Locomotive T, except treble horn has more pronounced point, tonyte dollar green semi-hollowbody model, 3 single coil pickups, halfmoon fabric grille inserts behind bridge. Available in Greenback Green/Cream finish, mfg. 1997-present.

MSR	$990	$750	$650	$575	$500	$425	$350	$275

This model is inspired by the modern art of Diego Rivera.

SKYLINER - offset double cutaway body, bolt-on maple neck, 25.5 in. scale, 22-fret rosewood fingerboard, six per side tuners, chrome hardware, rocket ship pickguard/grille panel, fixed bridge, 2 single coil/humbucker pickups, volume/tone controls with chickenhead knobs, 5-way selector switch, available in textured Beechwood Brown finish, mfg. 1997-present.

MSR	$858	$650	$575	$500	$425	$350	$295	$225

Add $140 for extended 30 in. scale and 24-fret fingerboard (Model Skyliner Bass VI).

Americana Skyliner - similar to Skyliner, except features Red Body finish, blue fabric panel inserts, and white pickguard, mfg. 1997-98.

	$600	$525	$475	$400	$325	$275	$225

Last MSR was $859.

TWISTER S - offset double cutaway body, bolt-on maple neck, 22-fret rosewood fingerboard, six on one side tuners, chrome hardware, cream colored pickguard, 6 fabric "grille" inserts on top (behind bridge) in a fan-shaped pattern, fixed bridge, 3 single coil pickups, volume/tone controls with chickenhead knobs, 5-way selector switch, available in textured Beechwood Brown finish, mfg. 1998-present.

MSR	$798	$600	$525	$450	$375	$325	$275	$225

Add $184 for extended 30 in. scale and 24-fret fingerboard (Model Twister S Bass VI).

Twister T - similar to the Twister S, except has a single cutaway body, 2 single coil pickups, and 3-way selector, mfg. 1998-present.

MSR	$738	$550	$475	$400	$350	$300	$250	$200

Add $194 for extended 30 in. scale and 24-fret fingerboard (Model Twister T Bass VI).

GRADING	100% MINT	98% NEAR MINT	95% EXC+	90% EXC	80% VG+	70% VG	60% G

ELECTRIC: SHOOTING STAR & TELEPORTER SERIES

SHOOTING STAR 2HB - assault rifle-style alder body, bolt-on maple neck, 22-fret rosewood fingerboard, 6-on-a-side tuners, fixed bridge, built-in hand grip on the upper bout, chrome hardware, 2 humbucker pickups, 1 volume/2 tone controls, 3-way selector/coil tap switches, available in Black, Blue, Red, Sunburst, or White finishes, disc. 1995.

	N/A	$650	$575	$500	$425	$350	$275

Last MSR was $849.

Shooting Star HSS - similar to the Shooting Star 2HB, except has 2 single coil/humbucker pickups, disc. 1995.

	N/A	$675	$600	$525	$450	$375	$300

Last MSR was $899.

TELEPORTER - semi-hollow single cutaway body, bolt-on maple neck, 22-fret rosewood fingerboard, 2 f-holes, beveled edges, 6-on-a-side tuners, fixed bridge, chrome hardware, 2 humbucker pickups, 2 volume/2 tone controls, 3-way selector toggle, 2 coil tap mini switches, available in Black, Blue, Red, Sunburst, or White finishes, disc. 1995.

	N/A	$700	$625	$550	$475	$350	$275

Last MSR was $1,099.

Teleporter II - similar to the Teleporter, except has fulcrum tremolo, and no coil tap switches, disc. 1995.

	N/A	$500	$425	$375	$325	$275	$225

Last MSR was $599.

ELECTRIC: TRIBUTE & VENTRILOQUIST SERIES

TRIBUTE - offset double cutaway alder body, bolt-on maple neck, 22-fret rosewood fingerboard, 6-on-a-side tuners, fulcrum tremolo bridge, chrome hardware, 3 single coil pickups, 1 volume/2 tone controls, 5-way selector switch, available in Black, Blue, Red, Sunburst, or White finishes, disc. 1995.

	N/A	$600	$525	$450	$375	$325	$275

Last MSR was $949.

This model was also available with a pearloid pickguard as the Tribute Ultra II (retail list was $649).

VENTRILOQUIST 2HB - Flying V-style alder body, bolt-on maple neck, 22-fret rosewood fingerboard, 6-on-a-side tuners, fixed bridge, built-in hand grip on the upper bout, chrome hardware, 2 humbucker pickups, 1 volume/2 tone controls, 3-way selector/coil tap switches, available in Black, Blue, Red, Sunburst, or White finishes, disc. 1995.

	N/A	$700	$625	$550	$475	$350	$275

Last MSR was $1,099.

Ventriloquist HSS - similar to the Ventriloquist 2HB, except has 2 single coil/humbucker pickups, disc. 1995.

	N/A	$725	$650	$550	$475	$350	$275

Last MSR was $1,149.

ELECTRIC BASS

LEVITATOR WAND - semi-hollow offset double cutaway body, bolt-on maple neck, 30 in. scale, 24-fret rosewood fingerboard, 4-on-a-side tuners, fixed bridge, louvered soundholes and built-in hand grip on the upper bout, chrome hardware, 3 single coil pickups, volume/tone controls, 5-way selector/phase/Missing Link switches, available in Black, Blue, Red, Sunburst, or White finishes, disc. 1995.

	N/A	$800	$700	$600	$500	$400	$300

Last MSR was $1,399.

LOCOMOTIVE P BASS - offset double cutaway body, bolt-on maple neck, 34 in. scale, 22-fret rosewood fingerboard, four-on-one-side tuners, chrome hardware, cream colored pickguard, 9 fabric-type grille inserts on top (reversed/before bridge), fixed bridge, split-coil pickup, volume/tone controls with chickenhead knobs, available in textured Beechwood Brown finish, current mfg.

MSR	$729	$525	$450	$395	$350	$275	$225	$175

LINE 6

Instruments currently produced since 2002. Amplifiers and other modeling devices currently produced in Agoura Hills, CA since 1996.

Line 6 was established in 1996. Even though they are a relatively new company, they have been very successful. Line 6 products can be described as taking musical products, such as amplifiers, and combining with up-to-date technology. Line 6's first patent was a digital modeling amp, which almost all amplifier companies have given a try at now. This was a result of realizing the need to get a number of amplifier tones out of one amplifier. Not only was this Line 6's idea, but this is the theory behind all modeling amps. The AxSys 212 was the first product to hit the shelves in 1996, and many amplifiers followed. Shortly thereafter, another idea was tackled by the staff at Line 6; to make an amplifier that would sound great in the recording studio. The POD was the answer to this, as it could plug into a tape recorder, or even a computer. This is a kidney shaped device that has all the effects with a line out jack for recording purposes. Line 6 is currently still producing state-of-the-art amps and leading the industry as far as technology. They have also released the Variaxe guitar, which is a modeling type of guitar. For more information refer to their website (see Trademark Index).

GRADING	100% MINT	98% NEAR MINT	95% EXC+	90% EXC	80% VG+	70% VG	60% G

ELECTRIC

VARIAX MODELER - offset double cutaway contoured body, maple neck, 22-fret rosewood neck with dot inlay, no exposed pickups, pickguard, 3-per-side tuners, three knobs (v, tone, effect selector), 1/4 in. guitar jack, available in Candy Apple Red, Sunburst, or Black finishes, mfg. 2002-present.

MSR	$1,400		$900	$800	$725	$650	$575	$500	$425

There are around two dozen effects that the guitar can reproduce, such as a 12-string, banjo, acoustic, etc.

VARIAX 700 MODELER - offset double cutaway contoured body, maple neck, 22-fret rosewood neck with rounded block inlay, no exposed pickups, pickguard, 3-per-side tuners, three knobs (v, tone, effect selector), Custom Baggs tremolo bridge, XLR and 1/4 in. guitar jack, available in Trans. Red, Trans. Blue, Trans. Amber, or Black finishes, mfg. 2003-present.

MSR	$1,900		$1,450	$1,250	$1,100	$950	$800	$700	$600

Add $100 for Trans. Red, Trans. Blue, or Trans. Amber finishes.

There are around two dozen effects that the guitar can reproduce, such as a 12-string, banjo, acoustic, etc.

LINN SAHLI

Instruments currently built in Palm Desert, CA.

Linn Sahli guitars feature two dual coil humbuckers that electronically recreate fourteen sound configurations by connecting the individual coils of the pickups in either series or parallel. Thus, the guitar can move from the sound of a Strat to a Les Paul with the change of a pickup selector. Any of these fourteen configurations can be programmed into the six pickup selectors, and an onboard voice will indicate which pickup selection has been chosen during the programming stage.

Linn Sahli guitars also feature six individual bridge pieces/string retaining tailpieces, which separate the string "crosstalk" found in one-piece bridges. Current models include the double cutaway Model A (list $3,099) and single cutaway Model T (list $3,099). Both models feature AAA grade flamed maple tops, mahogany bodies, one-piece mahogany necks, and Translucent or Solid Color finishes. Linn Sahli basses are offered in 4- and 5-string configurations. The LSJ model (list $1,999) has a swamp ash or curly maple body, rock maple neck with rosewood fingerboard, and is finished in Translucent colors. The 5-string LSJ-5 Artist (list $2,499) features a through-body neck construction.

LION

See Egmond. Instruments previously built in Holland during the late 1960s.

Guitars carrying the Lion trademark were built by the Egmond guitar company during the late 1960s. These low quality to entry level instruments featured both original and American designs based on classic favorites in both solid and semi-hollowbody configurations (source: Tony Bacon and Paul Day, *The Guru's Guitar Guide*).

LOGABASS

Instruments currently built in Japan, and distributed by Leduc Instruments of Sun Valley, CA. Instruments are also available through World Arts of East Northport, NY.

Logabass instruments are high quality basses that feature a headless design and patented bridge/tuning gear. All models have Bartolini electronics, and are available in 4-, 5-, and 6-string configurations (with fretted or fretless fingerboards).

LOPER

Instruments previously built in Hawthorne, FL 1995-2000. Distributed by Guitar Works of Hawthorne, FL.

Luthier Joe Loper built high quality custom bass guitars that feature a neck-through design. His original designs contained a number of stylish innovations that indicate fine attention to detail.

LORD

Instruments previously built in Japan, in the 1960s.

Guitars with the Lord trademark originated in Japan, and were distributed in the U.S. by the Halifax company (source: Michael Wright, *Guitar Stories*, Volume One). Used Lord electric guitars can generally be found priced between $75 and $150, depending upon condition.

LOTUS

Instruments currently produced in Korea, China, and India. Distributed by Midco International of Effingham, IL.

Lotus guitars are designed for the student or entry level guitarist. Lotus offers a wide range of acoustic and electric guitar models (a little something for everyone!). In addition to the Electric guitar models, Lotus also offers 4 dreadnought acoustics, 2 banjo models, and 4 mandolins. Lotus Electric Basses are offered in a Precision-style L760, as well as a Jazz-style model L750JSB and two modern design basses (L770 4-string and L780 5-string).

ELECTRIC

The **L660** Strat-styled guitar (list $235) features a solid ash body, rosewood fingerboard, 3 single coils, and a standard tremolo bridge (available in Black, Red, White, and Tobacco Burst), as well as a left-handed configuration. The upscale **L680** model (list $269) features a pearloid pickguard, and is available in Black Pearl Burst, Blue Pearl Burst, Crimson Burst, Metallic Green, and Silver Red Burst; the **L685** (list $289) has gold hardware and a Transparent Teak woodgrain finish. The **L690** model is similar to the L660, except features 2 single coil and one humbucker pickups. SuperStrat models include the **L1110** and **L1190**, which have 3 tuners per side headstocks, black pickguards, and different pickup configurations.

Lotus offers two different single cutaway body models: the Tele-ish **L590** and the LP-style **L520** models. Lotus also offers a dual cutaway laminated wood semi-hollow **L800TBU** model, as well as 4 "mini" downsized models (list $259 to $289).

LOWRY GUITARS

Instruments previously built in Concord, CA from 1975 to early 1990s.

Lowry guitars offered custom built, reverse stringing, headless guitar models. The **Modaire** model was offered in several design variations and was priced from $1,250 up to $3,000. Last address for the Lowry company was given as 2565 Cloverdale Avenue, Unit J, Concord, California 94518 (510.827.4803).

LUCENA

Instruments previously distributed by Music Imports of San Diego, CA.

Music Imports offered a number of quality Lucena guitar models.

LYLE

Instruments previously built in Japan from 1969 to 1980. Distributed by the L.D. Heater company of Beaverton, OR.

The Lyle product line consisted of acoustic and acoustic/electric archtop guitars, as well as solid body electric guitars and basses. These entry level to intermediate quality guitars featured designs based on popular American models. These instruments were manufactured by the Matsumoku company, who supplied models for both the Arai (Aria, Aria Pro II) company and the early 1970s Epiphone models (source: Michael Wright, *Vintage Guitar Magazine*). Lyle also produced a cheaper guitar called the Heater.

ELECTRIC

MISC. ELECTRIC MODELS - various configurations, solidbody and hollowbody, mfg. 1969-1980.

	N/A	$175	$150	$125	$100	$75	$50

**Lyric Mars
courtesy Lyric Guitars**

LYNX

Instruments previously produced in Japan during the mid-1970s.

The Lynx trademark is the brand name used by a UK importer, and can be found on very low budget/low quality solid body guitars (source: Tony Bacon and Paul Day, *The Guru's Guitar Guide*).

LYON, G.W.

Trademark of instruments built in Korea since the early 1990s. Previously distributed in the U.S. by Washburn International of Vernon Hills, IL.

G.W. Lyon offered a range of instruments designed for the student or beginner guitarist at affordable prices and decent entry level quality.

LYRIC

Instruments currently built in Tulsa, OK.

Designer John Southern drew upon his personal playing experience in designing the Lyric custom guitar. The primary interest was versatility, so that the guitar would have numerous tonal options available through the pickups and switching system. Southern spent two years developing the prototypes (built in Tulsa by hand), and is now offering six different guitars and one bass model. All guitars come with custom-made hardshell cases.

ELECTRIC

The following listed prices may vary depending on options (call for price quote). Prices include a hardshell tweed case.

The **Jupiter** model (retail list $6,900) is the design that Southern started with. The three-inch deep AAA-grade Curly maple body is 13 in. wide across the lower bout, and features a 4/2 (per side tuners) headstock design, 20-fret ebony fingerboard with special **Quasar** position marker inlay, 3 coil-tapped Seymour Duncan humbuckers, and a bridge mounted piezo pickup. The center humbucker is a custom converted Woody acoustic guitar pickup. Controls include two 3-way toggles, two push/pull knobs, and a Pinky-Knob master volume control. This ingenious design is complemented by a gold plated Lyric tailpiece and banjo-style custom tuning pegs with abalone buttons.

The **Mars** model is similar in construction, except features a Barcus Berry bridge transducer and a single coil-tapped mini-humbucker. Controls include a blend, push/pull tone, and Pinky Swell knobs. The Curly maple body is 1.75 in. deep, and the ebony fingerboard has the Mars Dot inlay pattern. Current list price is $3,300.

The **Venus** model (retail list $4,500) is an acoustic/electric version of the Jupiter that features a split coil Johnny Smith pickup and an L.R. Baggs bridge transducer and preamp, and a 1 11/16 in. deep body. It is available in a 3 in. depth to accommodate an additional graphic EQ, or with an extra magnetic pickup and blend controls.

The Lyric **Lady** (retail list $4,675) is a thicker body version made from hard maple, with a hollower construction and exquisite female figure pearl position markers on ebony. Humbucker pickup placement is conventional neck and bridge, with two coil top option and a blend with a Barcus Berry under saddle thin line pickup. It has no pinky knob and features chrome hardware and Steinberger tuners.

**Lyric Venus
courtesy Lyric Guitars**

The **Saturn** is a thin 1.75 in. Honduras mahogany body with multiple spiderweb-shaped chambers, under an exquisite book matched curly maple cap. The Saturn has a one piece mahogany neck and Quazar fingerboard inlay on finest ebony. The double Johnny Smith custom "Duncan" pickups are coil tapped and floating. The Saturn is priced retail at $3,500. For a moderately priced custom guitar, the Saturn will play rings around its competitors.

The Lyric **Mercury** solid body is offered in a swamp ash, poplar, alder, walnut, or cherry, with a maple or mahogany neck. The pickups are 6 pole piece coil-tapped humbuckers and a stop tail piece. The tuners are conventional Gotohs, and the specialty colors of clear or copper tone sparkle are offered ($1,800 retail price).

ELECTRIC BASS

The **Zeus** Bass (retail list $N/A) features a laminated walnut and maple neck-through design, hollowed curly maple body, 22-fret ebony fingerboard, burled walnut veneer on headstock/rear access panel, EMG active pickups, and an 18-volt onboard preamp.

L

Section M

MCI INTERTEK

Instruments previously produced in Japan from 1983-85. Distributed by MCI of Arlington, TX.

John Burkhead started MCI Intertek and produced various models of electric guitars. A designer/consultant to the company was possibly Gene Fields of Fender fame. In 1985, Fred Gretsch Guitars purchased the company. Saxon brand pickups were used in these guitars. Information courtesy: Walter Murray, *Frankenstein Fretworks*.

GRADING	100% MINT	98% NEAR MINT	95% EXC+	90% EXC	80% VG+	70% VG	60% G

ELECTRIC

EX 3000 - asymmetrical hourglass-shaped body Gibson Explorer-style, maple neck, 22-fret rosewood fingerboard, pointed headstock with 6-on-a-side tuners, locking nut and locking bridge with tremolo, 3 black covered humbucker pickups, two knobs (v, tone), 3 individual switches, available in black finish, mfg. 1983-85.

	N/A	$125	$100	$80	$65	$50	$35

RR 3000 - sharkfin offset V Jackson Original Rhodes style, maple neck, 22-fret rosewood fingerboard, pointed headstock with 6-on-a-side tuners, locking nut and locking bridge with tremolo, no pickguard, 2 black covered humbucker pickups, two knobs (v, tone), 3-way switch, available in Pearl finish, mfg. 1983-85.

	N/A	$125	$100	$80	$65	$50	$35

RT 2000 - single cutaway Telecaster-style mahogany body with flamed maple top, body binding, maple neck, 22-fret rosewood fingerboard, pointed headstock with 6-on-a-side tuners, locking nut and locking bridge with tremolo, no pickguard, 3 single coil pickups, two knobs (v, tone) on Telecaster-style plate, 5-way switch, gold hardware, available in Sunburst finish, mfg. 1983-85.

	N/A	$150	$125	$105	$90	$75	$60

This model was also available with a humbucker pickup in the bridge position (Model RT 2200).

SS 1000 - double cutaway Stratocaster-style body, maple neck, 22-fret rosewood fingerboard, pointed headstock with 6-on-a-side tuners, locking nut and locking bridge with tremolo, baby blue pickguard, 3 single coil pickups, three knobs (v, 2 tone), 5-way switch, gold hardware, available in White finish, mfg. 1983-85.

	N/A	$125	$100	$80	$65	$50	$35

Add $25 for two humbucker or three humbucker configurations.

This model was also available with a humbucker pickup in the bridge position (Model SS 3000), two humbuckers (Model SX 2000, pearl finish), and three humbuckers (Model SX 3000, black finish).

MD

See Metal Driver (Sumer Musical Instruments, Co. Ltd.) & Music Drive (Sumer Musical Instruments, Co. Ltd.).

MDX

Instruments currently built in West Point, MA. Distributed by MDX Sound Lab of West Point, MA.

Dann Maddox and partners have combined custom guitar and bass building and a computer website to introduce the concept of a "virtual custom shop." After nine years of custom building instruments at the regional level, MDX chose to use the Internet to go international with their handcrafted guitars.

Orders can be received at their website and guitars can be designed wholly through the Internet. This allows the customer to interactively design the guitar, and MDX the capabilities to construct it. Contact MDX through their website for more information (see Trademark Index).

MJ GUITAR ENGINEERING

Instruments currently built in Rohnert Park, CA, since the 1970s.

MJ Guitars is a small, family owned and operated manufacturing company and has been in business for more than 25 years. They specialize in high quality handmade production guitars. For more information, refer to the Trademark Index.

ELECTRIC

Mirage guitars feature a graphite-reinforced U-shaped open headstock with a logo that reads **M J MIRAGE**, a semi-hollow-body, and sleek double cutaway profile. In addition to the listed finishes, Mirage offers Custom Color finishes as well.

CATALINA - double offset smooth cutaway hollow poplar body, maple top, maple neck, bound rosewood fingerboard, 3-per-side tuners, two Seymour Duncan Custom '59 pickups, three knobs, single switch, chrome hardware, current mfg.

MSR	$5,500		$5,500	$4,500	$3,700	$2,900	$2,400	$2,000	$1,600

Catalina LX - similar to the Catalina, except has a bird's-eye maple neck and exotic maple top, current mfg.

MSR	$7,500		$7,500	$6,000	$5,000	$4,200	$3,400	$2,800	$2,200

**MJ Guitar Catalina
courtesy MJ Guitar**

M

GRADING	100% MINT	98% NEAR MINT	95% EXC+	90% EXC	80% VG+	70% VG	60% G

MIRAGE STANDARD - sleek offset double cutaway poplar body, carved maple top, set-in maple neck, 24.625 in. scale, 22-fret rosewood fingerboard with cream bar position markers, 3-per-side open headstock, Gotoh tuners, chrome hardware, tune-o-matic bridge/stop tailpiece, 2 Seymour Duncan humbuckers, 2 volume/1 tone controls, 3-way selector switch, current mfg.

MSR	$2,495	$2,300	$2,000	$1,750	$1,500	$1,250	$1,050	$850

Mirage Classic - similar to the Mirage Standard, except features mahogany body, carved maple or mahogany top, maple or mahogany set-in neck, nickel hardware, 2 Seymour Duncan P-90 pickups, disc.

	$2,300	$2,000	$1,750	$1,500	$1,250	$1,050	$850

Last MSR was $2,695.

Mirage Custom - similar to the Mirage Standard, except has mahogany body, carved exotic wood top, flame or bird's-eye maple neck, ebony fingerboard, gold hardware, current mfg.

MSR	$3,695	$2,960	$2,500	$2,200	$1,900	$1,650	$1,300	$1,100

MIRAGE GT - similar to the Mirage Standard, except features a 25.5 in. scale, internal tone chambers, tele-style bridge, 2 Seymour Duncan Alnico Pro II single coil pickups, available in Cream, Lake Placid Blue, or Sea Foam Green finishes, current mfg.

MSR	$2,495	$2,300	$1,850	$1,600	$1,400	$1,200	$950	$800

Mirage Rally - similar to the Mirage GT, except has Wilkinson VS100 tremolo, 3 Seymour Duncan single coil pickups, 5-way selector switch, available in Black, Red, and Silver finishes, current mfg.

MSR	$2,895	$2,700	$2,400	$2,100	$1,800	$1,550	$1,200	$1,000

ROADSTER - poplar body, bolt-on maple neck, 25.5 in. scale, 2 Seymour Duncan Alnico II Pro pickups, VS100 Tremolo or fixed bridge, hand made in the U.S.A., current mfg.

MSR	$1,595	$1,400	$1,200	$1,050	$900	$750	$625	$500

SPEEDSTER - radical offset single cutaway solid poplar body, maple neck, rosewood fingerboard, wrap around bridge, 6-on-one-side tuners, pickguard, two EMG pickups, chrome hardware, current mfg.

MSR	$1,595	$1,395	$1,150	$1,025	$900	$750	$600	$500

ELECTRIC BASS

M4 ROCKCRUSHER - sharp double offset cutaway poplar body, maple top, 3-piece maple/mahogany neck, rosewood fingerboard, two EMG pickups, four knobs, EMG BTS system, chrome hardware, disc. 2003.

Last MSR was $2,795.

M5 ROCKCRUSHER - similar to the M4, except in five-string configuration, disc. 2003.

Last MSR was $2,895.

MTD

Instruments currently built in Kingston, NY since 1994.

Luthier Michael Tobias has been handcrafting guitars and basses since 1977. The forerunner of MTD, Tobias Guitars was started in Orlando, Florida in April 1977. Tobias' first shop name was the Guitar Shop, and he sold that business in 1980 and moved to San Francisco to be partners in a short-lived manufacturing business called Sierra Guitars. The business made about fifty instruments and then Tobias left San Francisco in May of 1981 to start a repair shop in Costa Mesa, California.

Several months later, Tobias left Costa Mesa and moved to Hollywood. Tobias Guitars continued to repair instruments and build custom basses for the next several years with the help of Bob Lee and Kevin Almieda (Kevin went on to work for Music Man). The company moved into 1623 Cahuenga Boulevard in Hollywood, and after a year quit the repair business. Tobias Guitars added Bob McDonald, lost Kevin to Music Man, and then got Makoto Onishi. Then the business grew in leaps and bounds. In June of 1988 the company had so many back orders, it did not accept any new orders until the January NAMM show in 1990.

After several attempts to move the business to larger, better-equipped facilities, Michael Tobias sold Tobias Guitars to Gibson on January 1, 1990. Late in 1992, it was decided that in the best corporate interests, Tobias Guitars would move to Nashville. Michael Tobias left the company in December 1992, and was a consultant for Gibson as they set up operations in Nashville.

By contractual agreement, after Tobias' consulting agreement with Gibson was up, he had a one-year non-competition term. That ended in December 1993. During that time, Tobias moved to The Catskills in upstate New York and set up a small custom shop. Tobias started designing new instruments and building prototypes in preparation for his new venture. The first instruments were named Eclipse. There are 50 of them and most all of them are 35 in. bolt-ons. There are three neck-throughs. Tobias finally settled on MTD as the company name and trademark. As of October 1,1997, he had delivered 250 MTD instruments, including bolt-on basses, guitars, neck-through basses, and acoustic bass guitars.

Michael Tobias is currently building nearly 100 instruments per year, with the help of Chris Hofschneider (who works two days per week). Chris has at least 15 years experience, having worked for Sam Koontz, Spector Guitars, Kramer, and being on the road with bands like Bon Jovi and other New Jersey-based bands. Michael Tobias is also doing design and development work for other companies, such as Alvarez, Brian Moore Guitars, Modulus Guitars, Lakeland, American Showster (with Chris Hofschneider) and the new Czech-built Grendel basses (source: Michael Tobias, MTD fine handmade guitars and basses).

ELECTRIC BASS

All MTD instruments are delivered with a wenge neck/wenge fingerboard, or maple neck/wenge fingerboard; 21 frets plus a "zero" fret, 35 in. scale length. Prices include plush hardshell cases.

The standard finish for body and neck is a tung oil base with a urethane top coat. Wood choices for bodies: swamp ash, poplar, and alder. Other woods, upon request, may require upcharges. Exotic tops are subject to availability. Beginning 2000, all MTD Basses come equipped with the Buzz Feiten Tuning System. MTD basses feature custom Bartolini active pickups and electronics, volume/pan/treble/mid/bass controls, and internal trim pot to adjust the gain. Options:

Add $100 for a lined fretless neck. Add $100 for an ebony fingerboard. Add $100 for a matching peghead. Add $50-$100 for a matching truss rod. Add $150 for a hand-rubbed oil stain. Add $200 for satin epoxy coating on lined or unlined fretless fingerboard. Add $200 for epoxy/oil urethane finished maple fingerboard. Add $200 for a 24-fret fingerboard. Add $200 for a walnut body. Add $300 for a korina, African satinwood (Avadore), or lacewood body. Add $300 for a wenge neck. Add $350 for a left-handed model. Add $400 for lacquer finish: Sunburst (amber or brown), See-Throughs (transparency) of Red, Coral Blue, or Honey Gold. Add $500 for a 10 Top of burl, flamed, or quilted maple, myrtle, or mahogany.

GRADING	100% MINT	98% NEAR MINT	95% EXC+	90% EXC	80% VG+	70% VG	60% G

435 - 4-string configuration, 2-per-side headstock, mfg. 1994-present.
  MSR $3,400

535 - 5-string configuration, 2/3-per-side headstock, mfg. 1994-present.
  MSR $3,600

635 - 6-string configuration, 3-per-side headstock, mfg. 1994-present.
  MSR $3,800

MTD 735-24 - 7-string configuration, 4/3-per-side tuners, 24-fret fingerboard, current mfg.
  MSR $4,600

HEIR - similar to the Kingston, except has an additional Jazz pickup in the neck position, available in Tobacco Sunburst or Trans. Dark Cherry Sunburst finishes, mfg. 2003-present.

MSR	$829	$650	$575	$500	$450	$400	$350	$300

  Add $40 for fretless configuration.

Heir 5 - similar to the Heir, except in five-string configuration, mfg. 2003-present.

MSR	$879	$700	$625	$550	$475	$425	$375	$325

  Add $40 for fretless configuration.

KINGSTON - 4-string bass, 24-fret, basswood body, maple neck, rosewood fingerboard, passive MM style humbucker pickup, mfg. 2001-present.

MSR	$649	$500	$440	$390	$350	$300	$250	$200

  Add $20 for colors. Add $20 for fretless configuration. Add $20 for left-handed configuration.

Kingston 5 - similar to the Kingston, except in 5-string configuration, mfg 2001-present.

MSR	$699	$550	$475	$425	$375	$325	$275	$225

  Add $20 for colors. Add $20 for fretless configuration. Add $20 for left-handed configuration.

SARATOGA - double offset cutaway basswood body, figured maple top, matching headstock, 4-on-one-side tuners, bolt-on maple neck, rosewood or maple fingerboard, 2 Bartolini pickups, 2-band EQ, three knobs, switch, Style B Bridge, available in Amber, Dark Cherry, or Tobacco Sunburst finishes, mfg. 2001-present.

MSR	$1,499	$1,150	$1,050	$950	$850	$725	$600	$475

  Add $80 for fretless configuration.

Saratoga 5 - similar to the Saratoga, except in five-string configuration, 4/1-per-side tuners, mfg. 2001-present.

MSR	$1,599	$1,200	$1,050	$925	$800	$700	$600	$500

  Add $80 for fretless configuration.

MTD 535
courtesy MTD

McCURDY, RIC

Instruments currently built in New York City, NY.

Luthier Ric McCurdy has been producing custom guitars since 1983. Originally based in Santa Barbara, California, he moved to New York City in 1991 where he studied archtop guitar building with Bob Benedetto. Since then, he has been concentrating on building archtops and one-off custom guitars.

Currently using McCurdy guitars are ECM recording artist John Abercrombie and studio ace Joe Beck. All archtops feature the Kent Armstrong adjustable pole piece pickup which can be used with steel or bronze strings. For further information contact McCurdy directly (see Trademark Index).

ELECTRIC

The **Moderna** is a single cutaway archtop guitar, 16 in. wide at lower bout. This model features flame maple back and sides with a Sitka spruce top, multi-fine line binding on body head and pickguard, graphite-reinforced maple neck with 25.5 in. scale, and abalone or pearl block inlays on a 22-fret ebony fingerboard. The finish is Nitrocellulose Lacquer.

The vintage styled **Kenmare** archtop is 17 in. across the lower bout, and has AAAA flame maple back and sides, and a Sitka spruce top. Other aspects of this model include bound f-holes, multi-ply fine line binding, 25.5 in. scale, graphite-reinforced maple neck, split block inlay on 22-fret ebony fingerboard, vintage peghead inlay, and Cremona Amber Nitrocellulose finish.

McCurdy's **Perfecta** is a single cutaway model that is 16 in. across the lower bout, and has bound Faux Holes, a single humbucking pickup, maple top/back/sides and neck, 25.5 in. scale, graphite-reinforced neck, ebony fingerboard, and a nitrocellulose lacquer finish.

The **Monaco** features pickups mounted to the body for added versatility in live performances. The spruce top and flame maple back and sides are augmented by Kent Armstrong or Seymour Duncan humbucker pickups.

McINTURFF, TERRY C.

Instruments currently built in Holly Springs, NC since 1977. Distributed by Terry C. McInturff Guitars, Inc. of Holly Springs, NC.

McInturff has been building and servicing guitars since 1977. McInturff's varied luthiery and musical experiences have resulted in the rare opportunities to experiment with guitar designs and to test those designs on stage and in the studio.

McCurdy Archtop
courtesy Ric McCurdy

ELECTRIC

All McInturff guitars are standard with full RF shielding and shock protection circuitry. List price includes a deluxe hardshell case. Some options available include upgrading maple tops, adding binding and purfling, optional pickup configurations, neck carves, custom electronics, solo switch and a rainbow of gorgeous nitrocellulose finishes. 2003 is marking the 25th Anniversary of McInturff guitars, so he is releasing a number of limited production guitars in celebration.

TCM POLARIS - offset double cutaway slab Honduran mahogany body, and Honduran mahogany graphite-reinforced neck, abalone dot inlay, chrome hardware, fixed bridge, TCM Zodiac humbuckers with 5-way switch, available in 4 transparent colors, disc.

Last MSR was $1,995.

Polaris Pro - similar to the TCM Polaris, except features a 1/4 in. 3A Grade maple top, available in 22 finishes, mfg. 1998-disc.

Last MSR was $2,295.

TCM MONARCH - offset double cutaway design, solid mahogany body with deep dish carve. Paua shell "rope" inlay, chrome hardware, fixed or vibrato bridge, six pickup configurations available at no extra cost, available in 4 transparent finishes, current mfg.

MSR $2,695

TCM EMPRESS - offset double cutaway design with deep dish carved 3A Grade maple top, Paua shell "rope" inlay, chrome hardware, fixed or vibrato bridge, 2 TCM single coil pickups and 1 TCM Zodiac Humbucker in the bridge position, available in 22 finishes with many options, current mfg.

MSR $2,995

TCM ROYAL - offset double cutaway design with deep dish carved mahogany top, features tuned chamber and acoustic port, paua shell "rope" inlay, chrome hardware, fixed bridge, TCM T90 soapbar pickups stock, available in 4 transparent finishes, current mfg.

MSR $2,695

TCM GLORY STANDARD - offset double cutaway design with deep dish carved 4A Grade maple top and matching headstock, features semi-hollow chamber, paua shell "slash" inlay, chrome hardware, fixed or vibrato bridge, 2 TCM Zodiac humbucker pickups, available in 22 finishes with options, current mfg.

MSR $2,995

TCM Glory Custom - offset double cutaway design with deep dish carved 5A Grade maple top and matching headstock, features semi-hollow chamber, Paua shell "slash" inlay, gold hardware, fixed or vibrato bridge, locking tuners, bound neck and headstock, any pickup configuration, available in 22 finishes, current mfg.

MSR $4,200

TCM TAURUS STANDARD - single cutaway design with traditional carved 4A Grade maple top and matching headstock, features "fan-style" tone chambers, 17-degree headstock pitch, paua shell "crest" inlay, chrome hardware, fixed bridge, locking tuners, TCM Zodiac neck and bridge humbuckers, 2 vol/1 tone and blade switch, available in 22 finishes, current mfg.

MSR $3,400

TCM Taurus Sportster - similar to the TCM Taurus Standard, except has a full mahogany body, basically a toned-down version of the Standard, current mfg.

MSR $2,995

TCM Taurus Standard "T" - similar to Taurus Standard, except features a fully functional vibrato bridge that does not rob the tone, 9-degree pitch headstock, chrome hardware, locking tuners, available in 22 finishes, current mfg.

MSR $3,400

TCM Taurus Custom - similar to Taurus Standard, except has Master Grade maple top and matching headstock, bound body, neck, and headstock, paua shell "slash" inlay, gold hardware, available in any finish currently offered, current mfg.

MSR $6,000

TCM Taurus Tree of Life - similar to taurus Custom, except features reserve stock maple top and matching headstock, exquisite tree of life inlay features red and green abalone, MOP, and paua shell on an ebony fingerboard framed with paua shell purfling, extends to the peghead for a dramatic but tasteful touch, current mfg.

MSR $10,000

TCM ZODIAC - body design and liberal design approach similar to the Glory Custom, features best materials and finest grades of woods, 100 piece paua shell, MOP, and silver zodiac inlay depicts accurate constellations, mountains, planets, and 12th fret sun, custom birthday inlay available to match the sky on the day you were born, available in 22 finishes, current mfg.

MSR $5,200

TCM Zodiac Custom - same as the TCM Glory, except features solid African Limba wood neck and body, disc.

Last MSR was $5,150.

McLAREN

Instruments currently built in San Diego, CA.

Bruce McLaren worked many years as a design engineer in the defense industry and played bass guitar in several amateur bands. When the design of new defense products came to a halt, he started a company (McLaren Products) which manufactures electric bass guitars.

McLaren Products of San Diego, California produces distinctive, highly figured 4- and 5-string basses. Because of a tracer mill-type cutting tool developed by Bruce McLaren, a fully carved and beveled body (both front and back) can be produced economically. The body has a unique outline sometimes described as a cross between "an SG and a Strat," and features strips of solid figured hardwoods rather than figured veneer glued onto a lightweight body core (which is done on most figured wood basses being offered today). Due to the extensive carving, the basses weigh in at a light 8.5 pounds.

ELECTRIC BASS

The necks are made of hard maple with a carefully designed truss rod arrangement which pulls the fingerboard to the optimum curvature for a very low action. The truss rod is also positioned in the neck so that it will offset the tendency that all basses have for the tuner head to twist (this tendency is caused by the fact that the tension in D strings is about 15 pounds greater than that for E strings). Pickups used are active EMG in a P/J arrangement which makes it possible to individually adjust the volume of each string and gives a wide range of tones. The pickups are fully shielded and produce no hum or buzz either with the hands on or off the strings.

Three body styles are produced, and each are offered with 4- or 5-string configurations - fretted or fretless. The price ranges from $1,530 (**QC4** 4-string) up to $1,850 (**BB5** 5-string).

McNAUGHT GUITARS

Instruments currently built in Charlotte, NC since 1989.

While he has been building guitars part time for the past eight years, David Thomas McNaught began building full time in 1997. McNaught's guitar playing background started in his childhood, performing to his favorite band's songs with a tennis racket! While learning to play an actual guitar, McNaught sometimes became dissatisfied with the construction. Many of his first guitars became customized (changing parts and pickups). This customizing combined his family's woodworking background and gave him the idea to begin building his own designs. Many of the ideas used in his guitar designs are based on a player's point of view. For more information contact McNaught directly (see Trademark Index).

ELECTRIC

The signature series is available in any shape there is and many features and options are usually added. Other models include the Vintage Double Cut, Phoenix Rising, G-4, and G-5. Four- and five-string basses are in the workings.

McSWAIN GUITARS

Instruments currently built in Los Angeles, CA.

Luthier Stephen McSwain produces elaborate hand carved guitar bodies that he later builds into full guitars. McSwain's high degree of relief turns the bodies into playable works of art. Contact luthier McSwain for pricing quote and commission date availability directly (see Trademark Index).

MACDONALD, S.B. CUSTOM INSTRUMENTS

Instruments currently built in Huntington (Long Island), NY, since the 1980s.

Luthier S.B. MacDonald has been building and restoring stringed instruments for 20 years. His instruments are built by special order and designed around the needs of each customer. MacDonald offers acoustic, electric, and resophonic instruments. He is also a columnist for *20th Century Guitar* and *Acoustic Musician* magazines.

One of MacDonald's custom instruments is the Resonator Electric, a vintage-style semi-hollow body guitar with a resonator cone. The Resonator Electric features a maple neck, 21-fret ebony fingerboard, 6-on-a-side Grover tuners, Tele-style neck pickup/Fishman transducer in resonator cone, volume and tone controls, and cool retro colors. For further information on this model and others, contact luthier S.B. MacDonald directly (see Trademark Index).

McInturff TCM Empress
courtesy Terry McInturff

MADEIRA

See Guild. Instruments previously built in Japan during the early 1970s to late 1980s.

The Madeira line was imported to augment Guild sales in the U.S. between 1973 and 1974. The first run of solid body electrics consisted of entry level reproductions of classic Fender, Gibson, and even Guild designs (such as the S-100). The electric models were phased out in a year (1973 to 1974), but the acoustics were continued.

The solid body electrics were reintroduced briefly in the early 1980s, and then again in 1990. The line consisted of three guitar models (ME-200, ME-300, ME-500) and one bass model (MBE-100). All shared similar design accoutrements such as bolt-on necks and various pickup configurations (source: Michael Wright, *Vintage Guitar Magazine*).

ELECTRIC

EARLY MODELS - various configurations and appointments, mfg. early 1970s

N/A	$200	$170	$140	$120	$100	$80

1980/1990 MODELS - various configurations and appointments, models may consist of ME-200, ME-300, and ME-500, the main difference is the pickup configuration, mfg. early 1980s and early 1990s.

N/A	$150	$130	$110	$90	$70	$50

MAGNATONE

Instruments previously built in CA circa mid-1950s through late 1960s.

Magnatone is more recognized for their series of brown and gold amplifiers produced during the early 1960s than the company's guitars. Magnatone was originally founded as the Dickerson Brothers in Los Angeles, California circa 1937. The company began building phonographs, lap steels, and amplifiers. In 1947, the company was known as Magna Electronics. By the mid-1950s, they were offering electric Spanish hollowbody guitars designed by Paul Bigsby. Like Standel (and the early years at Fender), Magnatone wanted a guitar line to offer retailers.

In 1959, Magna Electronics merged with Estey Electronics (which was run by Roy and Ken Chilton). The guitar line was redesigned by Paul Barth in 1961, and four different models were offered. Magnatone also offered **Estey** thinline electric guitars in the late 1960s that were imported in from Italy. Magnatone maintained showrooms on both coasts, with one in West Hempstead, New York, and the other in Torrance, California (source: Tom Wheeler, American Guitars; and Michael Wright, *Vintage Guitar Magazine*).

ELECTRIC: MARK SERIES

Magnatone debuted the **Mark** series in 1956, which consisted of single cutaway/one pickup **Mark III Standard**; the single cutaway/two pickup **Mark III Deluxe**; the double cutaway **Mark IV**; and the double cutaway model that was equipped with a Bigsby tremolo called the **Mark V**. Both the Mark IV and the Mark V models were designed by Paul Bigsby.

McInturff Zodiac
courtesy Terry McInturff

M

GRADING		100% MINT	98% NEAR MINT	95% EXC+	90% EXC	80% VG+	70% VG	60% G

ELECTRIC: STARSTREAM SERIES

In 1962, Paul Barth (of National/Rickenbacker/Bartell fame) designed four models that consisted of a 1- or 2-pickup solid body model, a 3/4 scale beginner´s electric guitar, and an electric/acoustic (retail prices ranged from $99 to $299). The guitar line was renamed the **Starstream** series in 1965, and all models were redesigned with a double cutaway body. There were three electric/acoustics models (that ranged from $350 to $420), and three solid body electrics (one a 3/4 size) and a bass guitar (ranging from $170 to $290).

MAGNUM GUITARS

Instruments currently built in Ione, WA.

Magnum guitars are produced by Arndt Anderson and built out of magnesium and aluminum. The magnesium guitar started out in 1983 by Shark Byte Engineering. Between then and now, Anderson worked on machining for the aerospace and defense industry. After the military was downsized and Arndt was looking for work, he continued to build equipment for sensors and other technology. He also started to produced the guitars on a more regular basis. The magnesium guitar looks heavy but is really light and has an amazing sound. The designs are very unique and the options are almost endless. For more information refer to their website (see Trademark Index).

MAGNUS KREMPEL CUSTOM INSTRUMENTS

Instruments currently built in Weinback, Germany.

Luthier Magnus Krempel is currently offering a number of 4-, 5-, and 6-string electric basses and custom instruments.

MALDEN

Instruments currently produced overseas. Distributed by Malden Guitars in Los Angeles, CA.

Malden produces quality instruments at competitive prices. Some designs are based on Paul Reed Smith and others have a Gibson Les Paul and Fender Stratocaster. Models start at $549 and the most expensive model is listed at $899. For more information contact Malden directly (see Trademark Index).

MANNE GUITARS

Instruments currently built in Schio, Italy, since 1986. Distributed in the U.S. by Atlanta Custom Guitars in Gainesville, GA.

Andrea Ballarin and Manne Guitars have been producing handcrafted instruments in Italy since 1986. Manne creates finely crafted instruments that are based on original designs. His philosophy is to hand-craft the finest instrument and make it available worldwide at a reasonable price. For more information contact the distributor or Manne directly (see Trademark Index).

ELECTRIC: SEMIACUSTICA SERIES

The **SemiAcustica** model is addressed to both folk acoustic and semi-hollow body guitar players. The neck is the same used on the **Taos** models. The offset double cutaway body is constructed with light poplar, and features a spruce top. The body is closed to prevent feedback at loud performances. A special element is placed under the bridge to "dump" top vibrations and simulate the minor sustain, which is a characteristic of acoustic guitars.

SEMIACUSTICA GUITAR - offset double cutaway hollow basswood body, spruce or Italian burled poplar top, six-on-one-side tuners, blendable magnetic and piezo pickups, black hardware, current mfg.

MSR	$4,304		$3,400	$3,000	$2,700	$2,400	$2,100	$1,800	$1,500

This model has a piezo pickup under the bridge and a magnetic pickup near the neck which allows for a mix to get all the different tones (from the full-bodied sound of the humbucker to the crisp and clean sound of the piezo). The bridge has a special design for fast string changing and compensation adjustment.

ELECTRIC: TAOS SERIES

TAOS STANDARD - offset double cutaway alder body, bolt-on multi-laminated asymmetrical shaped neck, 640 mm scale, 24-fret phenolic fingerboard, 6-on-a-side tuners, Fishman Powerbridge with piezo pickups, 2 single coils/splittable (coil tap) humbucker, 5-way selector switch, available in a Satin finish, current mfg.

			$1,050	$900	$800	$700	$600	$500	$400

Last MSR was $1,350.

Add $100 for Antique Sunburst finish.

This model is factory built in Europe.

Taos PB Flame - similar to the Taos '98, except features a mahogany body, flame maple top, available in a High Gloss finish, current mfg.

			$1,400	$1,200	$1,050	$900	$800	$700	$600

Last MSR was $1,790.

TAOS - double cutaway mahogany body with a high-quality flame maple or Italian Burl carved top, set neck, 6-on-a-side tuners, HH or SSH pickup configuration, two knobs, 5-way switch, Wikinson tremolo bridge, available in High Gloss finish, current mfg.

MSR	$5,148		$4,000	$3,500	$3,100	$2,700	$2,400	$2,100	$1,800

ELECTRIC BASS

The semi-hollow **AcoustiBass** instrument features an acoustic chamber under the bridge. The strings pass through the body and then over a saddle which has a piezo element. Manne also added a magnetic pickup in the bridge position that adds an additional mellow tone. The AcoustiBass model features the simplified volume, balance, and tone controls, which gives a broad spectrum of sounds (going from a dark, woody double bass sound, to a crisp biting sound). The 4-string version of the AcoustiBass has a retail list price of $4,042, the 5-string version lists at $4,244, and the 6-string at $4,548.

GRADING	100% MINT	98% NEAR MINT	95% EXC+	90% EXC	80% VG+	70% VG	60% G

BASIC XLR - offset double cutaway heavy ash body (45mm thickness), multi-laminated asymmetrical shaped neck, 864 mm scale, 24-fret phenolic fingerboard, 4-on-a-side tuners, 2 epoxy sealed splittable (coil tapped) Manne Soapbar pickups (with double shielding), volume/push/pull tone pot, pick-up selector, passive circuitry, current mfg.

MSR	$4,510	$3,500	$3,100	$2,800	$2,500	$2,200	$1,900	$1,600

Basic XLR 5-String - similar to the Basic XLR, except in five-string configuration, five-on-one-side tuners, current mfg.

MSR	$4,572	$3,550	$3,150	$2,800	$2,500	$2,200	$1,900	$1,600

SPECIAL BASS - offset double cutaway with long bass horn, heavy ash body with Italian burl poplar top, 24-fret fingerboard, 5-on-one-side tuners, humbucker and single coil pickups, two knobs, gold hardware, High Gloss finish, disc. 2004.

$4,300	$3,800	$3,400	$3,100	$2,800	$2,500	$2,200

Last MSR was $5,528.

Manne Semiacustica Guitar
courtesy Manne Guitars

MANSON

A.B. Manson & Company. Instruments currently built in Devon, England since the late 1970s. Distributed in the U.S. by S.A. Music of Santa Barbara, CA.

Stringed instruments bearing the Manson name come from two separate operations. Acoustic guitars, mandolins, bouzoukis (and even triplenecks!) are built by Andrew Manson at A.B. Manson & Company. Electric guitars and electric basses are built by Hugh Manson at Manson Handmade Instruments. Andrew and Hugh Manson have been aplying their luthier skills for over twenty-five years. Both Mansons draw on a wealth of luthier knowledge as they tailor the instrument directly to the player commissioning the work.

Hand sizing (for neck dimensions), custom wiring, or custom choice of wood - it's all done in-house. Both facilities are located in Devon, and both Mansons build high quality instruments respective of their particular genre. U.S. retail prices are around $3,275 for various models like the **Dove**, **Heron**, and **Sandpiper**. For further information regarding model specifications, pricing, and availability, please contact either Andrew or Hugh Manson directly (see Trademark Index).

According to authors Tony Bacon and Paul Day (*The Guru's Guitar Guide*), Manson instruments can be dated by the first two digits of the respective instrument's serial number.

MANTRA

Instruments currently produced in Italy.

The Mantra **MG** series is constructed of lightweight magnesium alloy, with a bolt-on wood neck. Casting of the innovative body is handled in Italy, while the necks are built in the U.S. by Warmoth Guitars.

MAPSON, JAMES L.

Instruments currently built in Santa Ana, CA, since 1995.

Luthier James L. Mapson individually tailors both acoustic and electro-coustic archtop guitars by commission, balancing both design and construction to achieve performance goals for the professional musician. Beginning his career in 1995, James is largely self-taught. After considerable study of construction theory, he settled upon pursuing the D'Angelico approach, passed down and further developed by James L. D'Aquisto and subsequently by John Monteleone. Today Jim continues this approach to acoustic design, as well as his own designs to improve the electric archtop for performance and recording-minded clientele. Noted players using Mapson's instruments include Mundell Lowe, Ron Eschete, Frank Potenza and John Abercrombie. For more information contact Mapson directly (see Trademark Index).

M

ELECTRIC ARCHTOP

Acoustic models do not have exposed pickups. The Solo is a 16 or 17 in. body Neo-classic acoustic archtop and lists for $7,500. The Lusso is a 16 or 17 in. body traditional acoustic archtop and lists for $12,500. The Avante is a 17 or 18 in. body advanced acoustic archtop and lists for $7,500. There is only one of these built per year and in the past two were built per year.

Electric models have exposed pickups. The Bopcity is a 16 in. electric archtop and lists for $5,550. The Jazz Standard is a 15 in. tinline body available in a flat back with arch top for $4,500 or arched back and top for $5,500. The Jazz Bandit is a 13.5 in. thinline body available in a flat back with arch top for $4,500 or arched back and top for $5,500.

MARATHON

See chapter on House Brands.

This trademark had been identified as a House Brand previously used by Abercrombie & Fitch during the 1960s by author/researcher Willie G. Moseley. However, a number of newer guitars sporting the same trademark have been recently spotted. These guitars are built in Korea by the Samick company, and serve as an entry level instrument for the novice guitarist.

James Mapson Jazz Standard
courtesy James Mapson

GRADING	100% MINT	98% NEAR MINT	95% EXC+	90% EXC	80% VG+	70% VG	60% G

MARCHIONE

Instruments currently handcrafted in Houston, TX. Previously produced in New York (Manhattan), NY, since 1993.

Stephen Marchione builds recording quality archtop and special commission guitars. Marchione's clientele primarily consists of New York's top studio and stage players, and he has received commissions from the likes of Mark Whitfield, John Abercrombie, Vernon Reed, and Mark Knopfler. Other notables playing Marchione's guitars are George Wadenius (Steely Dan's *Alive in America* CD), Mark Stewart (Bang on a Can's *Music for Airports* CD), and Kenny Brescia and Ira Seigel (sound track for the Broadway smash *Rent*).

Marchione approaches his craft from many different angles. He understands players' sound and comfort needs as a guitar player himself. Marchione also seriously studies the great guitar and violin instruments in order to build archtop guitars that function as pinnacle pieces. When a player brings in a D'Aquisto or D'Angelico to Marchione's Manhattan shop, Marchione scrutinizes the instrument's construction, draws blueprints, and then quizzes the player about the instrument's best qualities. These important elements are then incorporated into his own designs.

The violin tradition has also figured prominently in Marchione's building. A hands-on understanding of cello arching is crucial to Marchione's ability to recreate the arching subtleties that imbue his archtop guitars with full acoustic volume and tambour. Marchione's friendship with violin maker Guy Rabut has impressed upon Marchione the importance of incorporating centuries of stringed instrument knowledge. Their friendship has also given Marchione the opportunity to measure and draw plans from Guarnieri cellows as well as Rabut's renowned instruments.

Personal musicianship, an exacting approach to guitar making, and the experience of hand building almost three hundred acoustic archtops, neck-throughs, and electric guitars are the groundwork for each and every Marchione guitar, (Company information courtesy Stephanie Green).

ELECTRIC ARCHTOP

MARCHIONE ARCHTOP - 16, 17, or 18 in. body width, hollow body archtop, AAAAA Englemann Spruce top, highly figured maple back and sides, 2 f-holes, all wood binding, African ebony fingerboard, MOP headstock inlay, 3-per-side tuners, narrow pickguard, fancy tailpiece, hand wound floating pickup, available in various finishes, current mfg.

16 IN. MSR $16,500	$16,500	$15,500	$15,000	$14,000	$12,000	N/A	N/A
17 IN. MSR $20,000	$20,000	$19,000	$17,500	$15,000	$13,000	N/A	N/A
18 IN. MSR $22,000	$22,000	$21,000	$19,000	$17,000	$15,000	N/A	N/A

WHITFIELD ARCHTOP - 16 in. body width, hollow body archtop, AAAAA Englemann Spruce top, highly figured maple back and sides, 2 f-holes, single ply all wood binding, sugar maple neck, African ebony fingerboard, African ebony MOP and zulu headstock inlay, 3-per-side tuners, narrow African ebony pickguard, fancy tailpiece with zulu wood, hand wound floating pickup, available in red finish, current mfg.

MSR $18,500	$18,500	$17,500	$16,000	$14,500	$13,000	N/A	N/A

ELECTRIC: BOLT-ON NECK MODELS

The **Bolt-On** model is the workhorse of New York's studio and stage players. Marchione builds his Bolt-On neck guitars to deliver incomparable sustain even with a tremolo, clear ringing sound, and easy playing low action. The sustain and sound quality are products of Marchione's full contact press fitting of the neck, machine heads, and bridge posts. When a string is attacked, the tone is transmitted through the instruments instantaneously with nothing lost to sloppy fitting. Marchione levels the fingerboard under string tension to ensure a stable, easy playing, buzz free neck. All electronic components are military grade, and Marchione uses custom audio tapered potentiometers. He also maximizes the signal path by employing a custom wiring configuration.

ELECTRIC: NECK-THROUGH BODY MODELS

Marchione's Neck-Through the body construction technique gives the player a wide palette: everything from a fat neck sound to full throttle bridge sound and all the mixes in-between. The comfort and playability of the neck are as integral to Marchione's guitars as great tone, so he cuts the neck to fit the player's hand. The neck is constructed from a three piece Sugar maple laminate, and the 24-fret fingerboard is available with a choice of ebony or rosewood. This three piece neck laminate is ultra stable and delivers clear highs, a responsive midrange, and a deep resonant bass register. The body is constructed of light weight Quilted maple. Aside from the beauty of the quilt figuring, a solid maple body gives the guitar an acoustic quality that is unobtainable with standard electric guitar woods. Spruce wood is used for the body of the Nylon string versions.

CARVED TOP MODEL - double cutaway Stratocaster style highly flamed maple top and mahogany or spruce back, bolt-on sugar maple neck, 22-fret ebony fingerboard, matching color headstock with 6-on-a-side tuners, vibrato bridge, two humbucker pickups, two knobs, switch, gold hardware, available in various finishes, current mfg.

MSR $6,500	$5,500	$5,000	$4,500	$4,000	$3,500	N/A	N/A

NECK-THROUGH MODEL - double cutaway Stratocaster style AAAAA highly flamed maple body, neck-thru-body hard rock maple neck, 22-fret ebony fingerboard, matching color headstock with 6-on-a-side tuners, two humbucker pickups, two knobs, switch, gold hardware, available in various finishes, current mfg.

MSR $6,500	$5,500	$5,000	$4,500	$4,000	$3,500	N/A	N/A

MARCO POLO

Instruments previously built in Japan circa early 1960s. Distributed by the Marco Polo Company of Santa Ana, CA.

The Marco Polo product line offered acoustic flattops, thinline hollowbody acoustic/electric guitars, and solid body electric guitars and basses. These inexpensive Japanese-built instruments were the first to be advertised by its U.S. distributors, Harry Stewart and the Marco Polo company. While the manufacturers are currently unknown, it is estimated that some of the acoustics were built by Suzuki, and some electric models were produced by Guyatone (source: Michael Wright, *Vintage Guitar Magazine*).

MARI BY REDIVIVUS

Instruments currently built in Torino, Italy, since 1985.

Mari by Redivivus was established by the Mari Brothers in 1985, which was just a shop for repairing and customizing instruments. In the later part of the 1980s they started to put together something for their own instrument. In 1990 the first Mari bass was born and up until 1994 it was a custom order only. In 1995 production increased up to five models, and today their price list is four pages long! There are several models available and currently they are only available in Europe. For more information refer to their website (see Trademark Index).

MARINA

Instruments currently produced in Korea since the late 1980s.

These medium quality solid body guitars sported both original and designs based on classic Fender styles (source: Tony Bacon and Paul Day, *The Guru's Guitar Guide*).

MARLEAUX

Instruments currently built in Clausthal-Zellerfeld, Germany. Distributed in the U.S. market by Joey G.'s Music.

One of Europe's finest custom houses, Marleaux custom basses are now available in the U.S., as distributed by Dan Lenard of Luthiers Access Group. There are several different models being offered including: The **Consat** and the headless **Betra**. Options are the norm - neck-through or bolt-on construction, one piece bodies, or exotic tops and backs (over 40 varieties of tonewoods are available). For additional information regarding model specifications, wood options, and pricing, contact Marleaux directly (see Trademark Index).

MARLIN

Instruments currently produced in Korea. Instruments were previously produced in East Germany. Since 1989, the trademark "Marlin by Hohner" has been produced in Korea.

The Marlin trademark originally was the brand name of a UK importer. The first **Sidewinder** and **Slammer** series were medium quality strat-styled solid body guitars from East Germany. When production moved to Korea, the models changed to **Blue Fin**, **Master Class**, **State of the Art**, **Loner**, and **Nastie** designations.

In 1989, a variation of the trademark appeared. Headstocks now bore a **Marlin by Hohner** description. Still Korean produced, but whether this is a new entry level series for the Hohner company or a Marlin variant is still being researched. Any further information can be submitted directly to the *Blue Book of Electric Guitars*, (source: Tony Bacon and Paul Day, *The Guru's Guitar Guide*).

MARLING

Instruments previously produced in Japan during the mid-1970s.

As the Italian-based EKO guitar company was winding down, they were marketing an EKO guitar copies built in Japan (although they may have been built by EKO). EKO offered a number of Marling acoustic models, as well as electric guitars. These guitar models were poor quality compared to the 1960s Italian EKOs (source: Michael Wright, *Guitar Stories*, Volume One).

**Marchione Archtop
courtesy Steven Marchione**

MARTIN

Instruments previously produced in Nazareth, Pennsylvania until 1982. C.F. Martin & Company was originally founded in New York in 1833. Acoustic instruments currently built since 1839.

Even though Martin has produced mostly acoustic instruments over the decades, the company information and history have been provided below for the benefit of the reader. Martin made their last pure electric instruments during 1982.

The Martin Guitar company has the unique position of being the only company that has always been helmed by a Martin family member. Christian Frederick Martin, Sr. (1796-1873) came from a woodworking (cabinet making) family background. He learned guitar building as an employee for Johann Stauffer, and worked his way up to Stauffer's foreman in Vienna (Austria). Martin left Stauffer in 1825, and returned to his birthplace in Markneukirchen (Germany). Martin got caught up in an on-going dispute between the violin makers guild and the cabinet makers guild. Martin and his family emigrated to America in the fall of 1833, and by the end of the year set up a full line music store. The Martin store dealt in all types of musical instruments, sheet music, and repairs - as well as Martin's Stauffer-style guitars.

After six years, the Martin family moved to Nazareth, Pennsylvania. C.A. Zoebich & Sons, their New York sales agency, continued to hold "exclusive" rights to sell Martin guitars; so the Martin guitars retained their New York labels until a business falling-out occurred in 1898. The Martin family settled outside of town, and continued producing guitars that began to reflect less of a European design in favor of a more straightforward design. Christian Martin favored a deeper lower bout, Brazilian rosewood for the back and sides, cedar for necks, and a squared-off slotted peghead (with 3 tuners per side). Martin's scalloped X-bracing was developed and used beginning in 1850 instead of the traditional "fan" bracing favored by Spanish luthiers (fan bracing is favored on classical guitars today).

In 1852, Martin standardized his body sizes, with "1" the largest and "3" the smallest (size 2 and 2 1/2 were also included). Two years later, a larger "0" and smaller "5" sizes were added as well. Martin also standardized his style (or design) distinctions in the mid 1850s, with the introduction of Style 17 in 1856 and Styles 18 and 27 a year later. Thus, every Martin guitar has a two-part name: size number and style number. Martin moved into town in 1857 (a few blocks north of town square), and built his guitar building factory right next door within two years.

C.F. Martin & Company was announced in 1867, and in three years a wide range of Styles were available. A larger body size, the 00 debuted in 1877. Under the direction of C.F. Martin, Jr. (1825-1888), the company decided to begin producing mandolins - which caused the business split with their New York sales agency. Martin bowl-back mandolins were offered beginning in 1895, three years before the snowflake inlay Style 42 became available. Also as important, Martin began serializing their guitars in 1898. The company estimated that 8,000 guitars had been built between 1833 to 1898; and so started the serialization with number 8,000. This serialization line is still intact today (!), and functions as a useful tool in dating the vintage models. The 15" wide body Size 000, as well as more pearl inlay on Martin guitars were introduced in 1902, which led to the fancier Style 45 two years later.

A major materials change occurred in 1916, as mahogany replaced cedar as the chosen wood for neck building. White celluloid (ivoroid) became the new binding material in 1918. The Martin company also took a big technological leap in 1922, as they adapted the Model 2 - 17 for steel strings instead of gut strings (all models would switch to steel string configuration by 1929). To help stabilize the new amount of stress in the necks, an ebony bar

**Marchione Custom Electric
courtesy Marchione**

M

GRADING	100% MINT	98% NEAR MINT	95% EXC+	90% EXC	80% VG+	70% VG	60% G

was embedded in the neck (the ebony bar was replaced by a steel T-Bar in 1934). Martin briefly built banjos in the early to mid 1920s, and also built a fair share of good quality ukuleles and tiples.

In 1929, Martin was contacted by Perry Bechtel who was looking for a flattop guitar with 14 frets clear of the body (Martin's models all joined at the 12th fret). The company responded by building a 000 model with a slimmed down 14/20-fret neck - announced in the 1930 catalog as the OM (Orchestra Model) (the 14/20-fret neck was adopted by almost all models in the production line by 1934). Martin also began stamping the model name into the neck block of every guitar in 1931.

While the Jazz Age was raising a hubaloo, Martin was building archtop guitars. The three C models were introduced in 1931, and the R-18 two years later. Martin arch top production lasted until 1942. The arch tops of 1931 have since been overshadowed by another model that debuted that year - Martin's 16" wide Dreadnought size. Guitar players were asking for more volume, but instead of making a bigger "0000" body, Martin chose to design a new type of acoustic guitar. Martin was already building a similar type of guitar originally as a model for the Oliver Ditson company in 1916; they just waited for the market to catch up to them!

The dreadnought acoustic (so named after large World War I battleships) with X-bracing is probably the most widely copied acoustic guitar design in the world today. A look at today's music market could confirm a large number of companies building a similar design, and the name "dreadnought" has become an industry standard. Back in the 1930s, a singing cowboy of some repute decided to order a dreadnought size guitar in the Style 45. Gene Autry became the first owner of Martin's D-45.

Due to the use of heavy gauge steel strings, the Martin company stopped the practice of "scalloping" (shaving a concave surface) the braces on their guitar tops. 1947 saw the end of herringbone trim on the guitar tops, due to a lack of consistent sources (either German or American). The first two dozen (or so) 1947 D-28 models did have herringbone trim. Some thirty years later, Martin's HD-28 model debuted with the "restored" scalloped bracing and herringbone trim (this model is still in production today).

The folk boom of the late 1950s increased the demand for Martin guitars. The original factory produced around 6,000 guitars a year, but that wasn't enough. Martin began construction on a new facility in 1964, and when the new plant opened a year later, production began to go over 10,000 guitars a year. While expansion of the market is generally a good thing, the limited supply of raw materials is detrimental (to say the least!). In 1969, Brazil put an embargo on rosewood logs exported from their country. To solve this problem, Martin switched over to Indian rosewood in 1969. Brazilian rosewood from legal sources does show up on certain limited edition models from time to time.

The 1970s was a period of fluctuation for the Martin company. Many aggressive foreign companies began importing products into the U.S. market, and were rarely challenged by complacent U.S. manufacturers. To combat the loss of sales in the entry level market, Martin started the Sigma line of overseas-produced guitars for dealers. Martin also bought Levin, the Swedish guitar company in 1973. The Size M, developed in part by Mark Silber, Matt Umanov, and Dave Bromberg, debuted in 1977. E Series electric guitars were briefly offered beginning in 1979 (up until 1983). A failed attempt at union organization at the Martin plant also occurred in the late 1970s. Martin's Custom Shop was formally opened in 1979, and set the tone for other manufacturers' custom shop concepts.

The late C.F. Martin III, who had steered the company through the Great Depression, said that 1982 was the most devastating year in the company's history. The balance of the 1980s produced some innovations and radical changes at the Martin company. It was 1985 when current CEO and Chairman of the Board Chris F. Martin IV assumed his duties at the youthful age of 28. The Martin Guitar of the Month program, a limited production/custom guitar offering was introduced in 1984 (and continued through 1994, prior to the adoption of the Limited Edition series) as well as the new Jumbo J Series. The most mind-boggling event occurred the next year: The Martin Company adopted the adjustable truss rod in 1985! Martin always maintained the point of view that a properly built guitar wouldn't need one. The Korean-built Stinger line of solid body electrics was offered the same year as the Shenandoah line of Japanese-produced parts/U.S. assembly.

The Martin company continues producing guitars only in Pennsylvania. The recent Road Series models, with their CNC-carved necks and laminated back and sides are being built in the same facilities producing the solid wood bodies and custom shop models. The X Series was introduced in 1998, and features HPL (high pressure laminate) constructed components, decal rosette, screened headstock logo, and patented neck mortise. Martin has brought all model production (figuratively and literally) under one roof. During 1999, Martin proudly opened up its new 85,000 square foot addition, making this facility one of the most state of the art guitar plants on the planet. Production has risen to 225 guitars per day. This new efficient technology also has enabled Martin to keep consistent high quality production within the U.S., while actually lowering consumer costs.

At the recent NAMM show, Martin introduced their new DXM model, a unique instrument with a composite body and top. Martin continues to do product research with other tone woods, and is vitally concerned with dwindling supplies of traditional woods. Martin also adheres to the guidelines and conservation efforts set by such organizations as the Forest Stewardship Council, Rainforest Foundation International, and SmartWood Certified Forestry (Certified Wood products) (source: Mike Longworth, *Martin Guitars: A History*; Walter Carter, *The Martin Book: A Complete History of Martin Guitars*; Tom Wheeler, *American Guitars*, and Martin factory brochures/catalogs.).

ELECTRIC: E SERIES

These models have offset round double cutaway bodies, mahogany necks, round wave cresting style peghead, and 3-per-side tuners.

E-18 - 9-piece maple/rosewood/walnut body, 22-fret rosewood fingerboard with pearl dot inlay, Leo Quan wrapped bridge, brass nut, rosewood peghead veneer with CFM logo decal, Sperzel tuners, chrome hardware, 2 humbucker covered DiMarzio pickups, 2 volume/2 tone controls, 3-position/phase switches, available in Natural finish, mfg. 1979-1982.

	N/A	$750	$650	$575	$500	$400	$300

Brass control knobs found on earlier models, replaced by black plastic on later models.

EM-18 - 9-piece maple/rosewood/walnut body, 22-fret rosewood fingerboard with pearl dot inlay, Leo Quan wrapped bridge, brass nut, rosewood peghead veneer with CFM logo decal, Sperzel tuners, chrome hardware, 2 humbucker exposed DiMarzio pickups, 2 volume/2 tone controls, 3-position/phase/coil tap switches, available in Natural finish, mfg. 1979-1982.

	N/A	$750	$650	$575	$500	$400	$300

A few models found with Mighty Mite pickups, brass control knobs found on earlier models, replaced by black plastic on later models.

E-28 - mahogany body, through-body neck, 24-fret ebony fingerboard with pearl dot inlay, Schaller tune-o-matic tailpiece, ebony peghead veneer with CFM logo decal, Schaller tuners, chrome hardware, 2 humbucker exposed Seymour Duncan pickups, 2 volume/treble/bass controls, 3-position/phase/bypass switches, active electronics, available in Sunburst finish, mfg. 1981-82.

	N/A	$850	$750	$650	$550	$450	$350

GRADING	100% MINT	98% NEAR MINT	95% EXC+	90% EXC	80% VG+	70% VG	60% G

ELECTRIC: F SERIES

These guitars have a 3 on a side traditional squared Martin headstock.

F-50 - single round cutaway semi-hollow bound plywood body, f-holes, raised black pickguard, mahogany neck, 20-fret rosewood fingerboard with white dot inlay, adjustable plexiglass bridge/trapeze tailpiece, 3-per-side tuners, chrome hardware, adjustable exposed pickup, volume/tone control, available in Sunburst finish, mfg. 1961-65.

	N/A	$1,100	$950	$800	$675	$550	$450

Approximately 519 of these instruments were made.

F-55 - similar to F-50, except has 2 pickups, 2 volume/2 tone controls, 3-position switch, mfg. 1961-65.

	N/A	$1,300	$1,150	$1,000	$875	$750	$650

Approximately 665 of these instruments were made.

F-65 - similar to F-50, except has double cutaway, Bigsby style vibrato, 2 pickups, 2 volume/2 tone controls, 3-position switch.

	N/A	$1,500	$1,300	$1,150	$1,000	$850	$700

Approximately 566 of these instruments were made.

ELECTRIC: GT SERIES

These guitars have a non-traditional large headstock, with 2 sharp upper corners scooping down to the center, and a Lower Bout Width of 16 in.

GT-70 - single round cutaway semi hollow bound plywood body, arch top, f-holes, raised white pickguard, mahogany neck, 22-fret bound rosewood fingerboard with white dot inlay, adjustable bridge/Bigsby style vibrato, bound peghead with logo decal, 3-per-side tuners, chrome hardware, 2 exposed pickups, 2 volume/2 tone controls, 3-position switch, available in Black or Burgundy finishes, mfg. 1965-68.

	N/A	$1,300	$1,150	$1,000	$875	$750	$650

Approximately 453 of these instruments were made.

GT-75 - similar to GT-70, except has double round cutaways, mfg. 1965-68.

	N/A	$1,500	$1,300	$1,150	$1,000	$850	$700

Approximately 751 instruments (total) were made.

GT-75-12 - similar to GT-70, except has twelve strings, double round cutaways, mfg. 1965-68.

	N/A	$1,400	$1,200	$1,050	$900	$775	$650

This model had a traditional style headstock.

ELECTRIC BASS

These models have offset round double cutaway body, mahogany neck, round wave cresting style peghead, and 2-per-side tuners.

EB-18 - 9-piece maple/rosewood/walnut body, 22-fret rosewood fingerboard with pearl dot inlay, Leo Quan fixed bridge, brass nut, rosewood peghead veneer with CFM logo decal, Grover tuners, chrome hardware, exposed DiMarzio pickup, volume/tone control, 2-position switch, available in Natural finish, mfg. 1979-1982.

	N/A	$700	$625	$575	$500	$425	$350

EB-28 - mahogany body, through-body mahogany neck, 22-fret ebony fingerboard with pearl dot inlay, Schaller tune-o-matic bridge/stop tailpiece, rosewood peghead veneer with CFM logo decal, Schaller tuners, chrome hardware, P/J-style exposed DiMarzio pickups, 2 volume/treble/bass controls, 3-position/phase/bypass switches, active electronics, available in Sunburst finish, mfg. 1981-82.

	N/A	$800	$700	$600	$500	$400	$300

Last MSR was $1,254.

This model was also offered with a fretless fingerboard. Approximately 217 of these instruments were made.

MARVEL

See also Premier. Instruments previously built in Japan circa 1950s to mid-1960s.

The Peter Sorkin Music Company of New York, New York was an importer/distributor of Premier guitars and amplifiers. Many Premier guitars were built in New York using Italian or other foreign parts, and sometimes the instruments would be rebranded (**Marvel, Royce, Bell-Tone,** or **Strad-O-Lin**). Marvel guitars have been identified as the budget line distributed by Sorkin. Marvel guitars may be completely imported or have parts that are imported (which would make the guitar partially U.S. built: a helpful tip for all you American xenophobes) (source: Michael Wright, *Guitar Stories*, Volume One).

MASTER

Instruments currently built in Los Angeles, CA.

Luthier George Gorodnitski has been building fine handcrafted acoustic and semi-hollowbody electric guitars for a number of years. For further information, please contact luthier Gorodnitski directly (see Trademark Index).

Martin E-18
courtesy Dave Rogers
Dave's Guitar Shop

Martin F-55
courtesy Michale Patton

M

MASTER'S BASS

Instruments currently built in Waco, TX.

For 12 years, the Master's Bass Company has specialized in building handcrafted electric basses. Each Master's bass is a combination of ergonomic design, choice exotic and domestic hardwoods, custom electronics, and the finest bass hardware available.

The **Reality** bass has a 3-piece maple neck and soft maple body wings (retail price $1,995 to $2,250); the **Dream** Bass features a 5-piece neck and bookmatched tops and backs ($3,899 and $4,299); and the top-of-the-line **Fantasy** bass has a 7-piece neck and bookmatched exotic wood tops and backs ($4,599 to $4,999). All basses are offered in 4-, 5-, and 6-string configuration, although 7-string models are an option.

MASTERTONE

Instruments previously produced by Gibson from the 1920s to the 1940s. See chapter on House Brands.

While the Mastertone designation was applied to high end Gibson banjos in the 1920s, the Mastertone trademark was used on a Gibson-produced budget line of electric guitars beginning in 1941. Some acoustic "Hawaiian" guitars from the 1930s by Gibson also carried the Mastertone label. While built to the same standards as other Gibson guitars, they lack the one "true" Gibson touch: an adjustable truss rod. House Brand Gibsons were available to musical instrument distributors in the late 1930s and early 1940s (source: Walter Carter, *Gibson Guitars: 100 Years of an American Icon*).

MATON

Instruments currently produced in Bayswater North, Australia since 1946.

Maton is Australia's longest established guitar manufacturer. The Maton trademark was established in 1946 by British emigre Bill May, a former woodworking teacher. His trademark name was a combination of his last name and tone, which is what every luthier seeks.

In the 1940s, it was a commonly held belief among Australian guitarists and musical instrument retailers that American guitars were the best in the world. Bill May may have subscribed to that general idea, it didn't stop him from questioning why Australians shouldn't build their own guitars. As May related in a 1985 interview, "I wanted to make better guitars, beyond what people thought you had the ability to do. People asked 'How do you think you can do it, you've never been to see how it's done and what do you know about it? And it's Australia. You don't know anything here. If you want good instruments, you have to wait and get them from America.' But I didn't believe that."

May was raised with craftsman skills and a positive attitude, both for his own self esteem and for his country. Bill May originally completed his apprenticeship in cabinet making, and later an honors course in art and graphic design before he spent ten years as a woodwork teacher. When May couldn't find a decent sounding guitar in a reasonable price range, he began building guitars in the garage of his Thornbury home. While there was no wealth of guitar building information back in the 1940s, May learned from the various guitars that passed through his hands. Production tools for the time period were the same sort used by furniture craftsmen, like chisels, planes, or the occasional belt-sander or bench saw. Rather than knock out copies of American models, May produced designs that were distinctive in appearance and sound - and featured Australian woods and distinctly Australian names. After the humble beginnings in his garage, a factory was established outside of Melbourne in 1951. Maton guitars began to be offered through local stores; by the mid 1960s Maton instruments had established a solid reputation throughout Australia.

May passed away on his 75th birthday in 1993, but the company continues to produce quality acoustic guitars. The modern factory located in Bayswater is certainly different from Maton's original site in Canterbury, but the traditional use of hand craftsmanship still co-exists with the new CNC router at the plant. While the focus of current production has been on acoustic guitars, the company also promises that there will be a return of production electrics later on. Maton estimates that 80,000 guitars were sold in the past forty years. The current company builds over 400 acoustics per month. For more information refer to their website (see Trademark Index).

Sources: Company history courtesy John Stephenson, *The Maton Book* (1997). Additional model descriptions courtesy Linda Kitchen (Bill May's daughter) and Haidin Demaj, Maton Guitars).

ELECTRIC

A brief listing of their previous quality electric solid body guitars include such models as the **Wedgtail**, **Flamingo**, **Fyr Byrd**, and **Ibis**.

Semi-hollowbodies include the **Slender Line, Starline**, and **Supreme** models. Maton has a variety of electric guitars for sale, retail price starting at $1,299. The MS Series is there current line of guitars.

MAXINE

Instruments currently produced in China. Distributed by Bejing Eternal Musical Instrument Corp. Ltd.

Maxine is a company that makes an endless amount of guitars. Pretty much any color, design, and configuration is available. They are mainly entry level guitars and don't sell for much. It is unknown if a U.S. distributor has been established yet. For more information refer to their website and good luck reading it (see Trademark Index).

MAXTONE

Instruments currently produced in Taiwan, and distributed by the Ta Feng Long Enterprises Company, Ltd. of Tai Chung, Taiwan.

Maxtone instruments are designed with the entry level to student quality guitars. For further information, contact Maxtone directly (see Trademark Index).

MAYA

See also El Maya. Instruments previously produced in Japan from the mid-1970s through the mid-1980s.

Maya guitars span the range of entry level to medium quality solid body, semi-hollowbody, and archtops that feature both original designs and other designs based on classic American favorites. The Maya company also produced a secondary trademark called "El Maya" that featured good quality Fender-based designs as well as some originals (source: Tony Bacon and Paul Day, *The Guru's Guitar Guide*).

MAYFAIR

Instruments previously produced in Japan, circa 1960s.

Research continues on the Mayfair trademark.

MEAN GENE GUITARS

Instruments previously built in CA between 1989 to 1991.

Gene Baker was a partner in a short lived business arrangement that specialized in guitar building, repair, rehearsal hall rental, and retail sales of guitar-related products. In 1990, Baker also released an instructional video and manual titled *Mean Gene's Insane Lead Guitar Manual* (source: Gene Baker, Baker Guitars USA).

Baker estimates that about 50 instruments were produced (many with custom colors and graphics), and usually built from ground up on customer's specifications. Baker still services them at his current shop.

MEAZZI

Instruments previously produced in Italy from 1963 to 1969.

The Meazzi company has been a seller, distributor, and even a producer of musical instruments in Italy for over the past 50 years. Between 1963 and 1969, Meazzi offered a wide range of electric guitars and basses. These instruments exude a lot of character (similar to other 1960s production guitars) but offer the vintage guitar collector some real eye-catching models. Best of all, the guitars are pretty good quality for playing, too!
(source: Marino Meazzi, Meazzi S.P.A. of Paderno, Italy; model text derived from the book celebrating Meazzi's 50th Anniversary, *Meazzi's All Stars* by Marco Cogliati (Paderno, Italy); model dating estimations courtesy Carlos Juan, Collectables & Vintage '95, Stuttgart, Germany)

ELECTRIC

Most Meazzi models featured an "in-line" tuner headstock and bolt-on neck, similar to Fender style production. Keeping in line with the 1960s designs, many popular Meazzi models had a vague Burns and Fender Jaguar/Jazzmaster design feel. However, pickguard design and appointments are 100% original Meazzi. All hardware is chrome. Meazzi instruments are more plentiful in Europe than in the U.S. Until the secondary market is defined in the U.S., accurate used market prices are not available.

Meazzi offered a number of archtop guitar models between 1964 to 1969. The **Cerri** archtop had a single pickup, and was the top of the line. The two pickup **Zuccheri** was produced in very limited amounts, making it a fairly rare model. Some of the hollow body guitar models offered between 1964 to 1969 include the **Continental**, which featured 2 pickups and a tremolo bridge; and the 2 pickup model **Sheptre**.

The **Corsair** solid body had an offset double cutaway design, black pickguard, 22-fret fingerboard, 6-on-a-side headstock, metal bridge/mute/tremolo tailpiece, 2 pickups, volume and tone controls. The **Mustang** has a similar body design, but features 3 single coil pickups and a different tremolo bridge configuration. Both models available between 1964 to 1969.

The **Diamond** solid body electric guitar model was briefly produced between 1963 to 1964. The Diamond had one pickup, a sparkle finish top, and a celluloid back overlay.

The **Jupiter** solid body guitar model has an offset double cutaway body (no forward horns), bolt-on neck, 22-fret fingerboard, 6-on-a-side tuners, 2 single coil pickups, half plastic pickguard/half chrome plated pickguard, chrome plate on upper bass bout with a curved slider (fader) volume control, raised metal bridge/tremolo, 2 tone controls, and a curved slider (fader) volume control on lower half of the chrome plated pickguard. This model was also available with 2 DeArmond pickups, or as a hollowbody with additional preamp and blend controls. The **Baby Jupiter** guitar model is similar in design, except features a full length white plastic pickguard, one tone control, and a smaller chrome controls plate with a white curved slider (fader) volume control. Both models were produced between 1964 to 1969, and were available in Black, Blue, Green, Red, Red Sunburst, and Yellow Sunburst finishes.

The dual cutaway **Lovely** has a 22-fret fingerboard, 2 single coil pickups, metal bridge/tremolo tailpiece all mounted on an oversized white pickguard/top overlay; the similarly designed **Zephir**

features different pickups, and a different metal bridge/mute/tremolo bridge set up. However, the tremolo bridge is mounted on the body.

The **Zodiac** forgoes the sleek body designs of the other models in favor of a single cutaway "artist's palette" shape similar to a **Teisco May Queen**. This solid body model has a 22-fret fingerboard, 2 pickups, metal bridge/mute/tremolo, volume and tone controls. Available between 1964 to 1969.

ELECTRIC BASS

The **Diamond** solid body electric bass model, similar to the electric guitar model, was briefly produced between 1963 to 1964. The Diamond Bass had one pickup, a sparkle finish top, and a celluloid back overlay. Another model, the **Double** featured similar construction, but is the rarer of the two, and was also produced between 1963 and 1964.

Most Meazzi electric solid body basses featured a rosewood fingerboard with dot position markers and 4-on-a-side tuners. Meazzi basses were available in Black, Green, Red, and Sunburst finishes with matching or natural finished headstock.

The **Jupiter Bass** solid body has an offset double cutaway body (no forward horns), 20-fret fingerboard, 2 pickups, half plastic pickguard/half chrome plated pickguard, chrome plate on upper bass bout with a curved slider (fader) volume control, fixed bridge, chrome bridge cover, 2 tone controls, and a curved slider (fader) volume control on lower half of the chrome plated pickguard. The **Baby Jupiter** is similar in design, except features a full length white plastic pickguard, one tone control, and a smaller chrome controls plate with a white curved slider (fader) volume control. Both models were produced between 1964 and 1969.

The **Kadett Extra** bass has a dual cutaway solid body, 20-fret fingerboard, large white pickguard, chrome bridge/metal tailpiece, chrome bridge color, 2 gold/chrome colored pickups, volume and tone controls, and a three way selector switch. The Kadett Extra was produced between 1964 and 1969.

The **Meteor** bass was offered in two versions: one pickup (**Meteor Bass I**) or with two pickups as the **Meteor Bass Extra**. Both versions featured an offset double cutaway body (no forward horns), 20-fret fingerboard, oversized white pickguard, fixed bridge, chrome bridge cover, volume and tone controls (the Extra has an additional 3-way toggle switch). Both versions were available between 1964 and 1969.

**Martin EB-18
courtesy John Beeson
The Music Shoppe**

**Maton BB1200 Hollowbody
courtesy Maton**

M

The offset double cutaway **Tiger** bass has a 21-fret fingerboard and an oversized white pickguard/top overlay – the 2 pickups, volume and tone controls, and metal bridge/tailpiece are all mounted to it. The tailpiece has a chrome cover. While the Tiger was available between 1964 and 1969, it has been noted that very few were actually made.

Other Meazzi bass models issued between 1964 and 1969 include the violin-shaped **Effe** hollowbody; and the **Prinz** and **Spezial** hollow body models. All the hollow body basses have two pickups.

MEGAS GUITARS

Instruments currently built in San Francisco, CA since 1989.

Luthier Ted Megas has been building guitars since 1975, and in 1989 began building archtop guitars, which represented the best combination of his musical interests and his knowledge and skills as a woodworker. Megas builds about twelve of his quality instruments each year. For more information, please contact luthier Megas directly (see Trademark Index).

ELECTRIC

The **Athena** is classically styled with multi-lined plastic bindings throughout; split block MOP inlays on fingerboard; abalone dot side position markers; X-bracing; MOP nut; precision machined brass tailpiece construction with ebony overlay; and Schaller tuning machines with ebony buttons. List prices range from the 16 in. body width ($6,800), 17 in. width ($7,150), and the 18 in. width ($7,700).

The **Apollo** features wood bindings, abalone, dot side position makers, X-bracing; cello style f-holes, MOP nut, precision machined brass tailpiece construction with ebony overlay, and Schaller tuning machines with ebony buttons. List prices range from the 16 in. body width ($5,950), 17 in. width ($6,275), and the 18 in. width ($6,800).

The **Spartan** has a single bound body, neck, and peg head, parallel bracing, bone nut, ebony tailpiece with brass anchor, and gold Gotoh tuning machines. List prices range from the 16 in. body width ($5,000), 17 in. width ($5,300), and the 18 in. width ($5,700).

The **Athena** solid-body model is available with a choice of a solid, chambered, or hollow body, carved AAA flamed maple top, back, and sides, multi-lined bindings, graphite reinforced neck, ebony fingerboard, bridge, and front and back peg head overlay, brass tailpiece, gold hardware, Kent Armstrong pickup, volume and tone control, and retail is $4,450. There are options such as a seven string and left-handed versions.

The **Spartan** solid-body model is available with a choice of a solid or chambered body, carved spruce top, mahogany back and neck, single bound binding, graphite reinforced neck, ebony fingerboard and peg head overlay, tune-o-matic bridge and stop tailpiece, gold hardware, Kent Armstrong humbucker pickup, volume and tone control, and retail is $3,450. There are options such as a seven-string and left-handed versions.

Add $275 for custom shading or sunburst. Add $400 for left-handed configuration. Add $550 for 7-string configuration.

MELANCON GUITARS

Instruments currently built in Thibodaux, LA.

Luthier Gerard Melancon´s Artist models offer an upscale "version" of Strat- and Tele-style models, with heavily figured (flame and quilt) maple tops over ash (or alder or mahogany) body woods. Melancon also features high grade hardware and pickups in his construction. Models differ in their appointments, and Melancon offers a range of custom options to personalize each instrument built.

ELECTRIC

Melancon offers a variety different versions of the Artist, like the **Pro Artist** model (list $2,000), The **P90 Pro Artist** model ($2,200), **Vintage Artist** model (list $2,300), the **Classic Artist** ($2,500), the **P90 Artist** ($2,600), the **Custom Artist** ($2,700), and the **Cajun Gentleman** ($2,800). There are also bass guitars available in four-string ($2,400) and five-string ($2,700) configurations.

MELOBAR

Instruments currently built in Sweet, ID since1967.

Melobar was founded by designer Walt Smith to provide steel guitarists the opportunity to stand up and also be able to play chord voicings without the traditional pedals or knee levers. Smith, a teacher/performer (and cattle rancher), passed away at age 70 in 1990. His son, Ted Smith, continues to operate the family-run business, providing these high quality instruments to steel guitarists.

Walt Smith continued to make improvements on his initial design through the years, and the refinement produced the Powerslide "88 model in the late 1980s. The model can be operated with 10 strings or six, and features a Bill Lawrence pickup. Other model variations featured body designs based on Strat, Explorer, or Flying V shapes; the same designs were offered in a comfortable foam body as well.

Some of the original metal acoustic Melobars were built by Dobro, while the first electric solid body models were produced by Semie Moseley (of Mosrite fame) (source: Teisco Del Rey, *Guitar Player magazine*).

Jim Frost is now the president of Melobar as of 2004. Melobar is bringing back all the lines of guitars after a pause in production over a few years. Ted Smith still serves on the board of directors for Melobar, and helps teach the guitar building process. Black Canyon Guitars are showing Melobar guitars at shows around the country. For more information contact Melobar directly (see Trademark Index).

MELODY

Instruments previously produced in Italy from the late 1970s through to the mid-1980s.

Melody produced guitars that were based on American designs, but were of good quality. Typically guitars like this were modeled after popular designs with poor quality. Melody original design guitars were built much better as well. The Blue Sage series was introduced in 1982, and included a model called the **Nomad** that featured a built-in amp and speaker (source: Tony Bacon, *The Ultimate Guitar Book*).

MEMPHIS

Instruments currently produced in Korea (recent circa). Distributed by C. Bruno of Bloomfield, Connecticut.

Memphis electric guitars and basses are entry level to medium quality instruments designed for the student guitarist. Models encountered so far are the bolt-on neck Fender copies (Strats, Teles, P-basses). Headstocks have a silk-screened "Memphis" logo; guitars usually have a thick polyurethane solid finish, so let´s not ask how ply the body wood is. One higher end model with a locking tremolo system and two exposed coil humbuckers was encountered by contributing editor Walter Murray (source: Walter Murray, *Frankenstein Fretworks*).

GRADING		100% MINT	98% NEAR MINT	95% EXC+	90% EXC	80% VG+	70% VG	60% G

ELECTRIC/BASS

MISC. ELECTRICS - various configurations and appointments, mfg. 1990s.

ELECTRIC		N/A	$150	$125	$105	$90	$75	$60
BASS		N/A	$125	$105	$90	$75	$60	$45

MENKEVICH GUITARS

Instruments currently built in Philadelphia, PA.

Luthier Michael Menkevich has been handcrafting quality guitars for a number of years. He builds classical guitars from original designs to reproductions of popular models.

MERCHANT BASS

Instruments currently built in New York, NY.

Luthier/designer Steve Merchant has been offering quality, electric, upright basses for a number of years. Merchant starts with a core bass and builds it to order. 50% is due when ordering a model. The four string bass retails at $2,400 and the five string at $2,750. For further information contact luthier/designer Steve Merchant directly (see Trademark Index).

MERCURIO

Instruments currently produced in Chanhassen, MN since 2004.

Mercurio produces guitars that feature interchangeable pickup modules. Pickups can be changed in a matter of seconds through FireWireT technology. Mercurio's PickupPaksT plug into a guitar from the back. Any pickup configuration and pickups from most major manufacturers can be used. Their guitars are built with a mix of materials including aluminum, exotic plastics, carbon composites, and tone woods. For more information contact Mercurio directly (see Trademark Index).

**Megas Guitars Athena
courtesy Megas Guitars**

ELECTRIC

Mercurio offers guitars built in the traditional Stratocaster and Telecaster style. The Strat style comes in three different variations. The Classic S is the traditional double cutaway with a pickguard. The Modern S is a double cutaway with a maple top and no pickguard. The CarveTop S is a double cutaway with a 5/8 in. sculpted maple top. The Telecaster comes in two models. The Classic T is a traditional single cutaway "slab" style. The Modern T is a single cutaway with a forearm and tummy cuts. Several finish options are available as well as different woods in the guitar for an upcharge. These guitars work with just about any pickup configuration: humbuckers, P-90s, single coils, active, and passive. Prices start at $2,999.

MERCURY GUITARS

Instruments previously built in Berkeley, CA 1994-2000.

Mercury Guitars consisted of three people: Linda Delgado, partner Doug Pelton, and employee Norm Devalier. Mercury Guitars focused on the design of the **Artemis**, **El Grande**, and **Vintage** guitar models. Mercury Guitars wanted to provide the player with a point of reference from which to begin (hence the reference to the vintage instrument).

The staff at Mercury Guitars hand selected all woods, seeking to use renewable sources while insuring good resonant qualities. Their finish choice also affirmed their commitment to the environment as they utilized a water based product which was specifically engineered for the guitar industry.

ELECTRIC

The Artemis model had a single cutaway alder body, 2 single coil pickups, maple neck with rosewood fingerboard, and one piece bridge (last price $730). The upscale **El Grande** model has an alder body with figured maple top, ebony fingerboard with 26.1 in. scale length, 2 humbucker pickups, and a tune-o-matic bridge/stop tailpiece. Last list price was $1,550. Mercury also produced a 4-string bass, dubbed the **Casper**, which featured a humbucker pickup.

MERLIN

Instruments previously produced in Korea during the late 1970s.

The Merlin trademark was a brand name of a UK importer. The Merlin guitar was an extremely entry level, single pickup solid body guitar. As we like to say up north in the winter time, I prefer to buy my wood by the truckload, not piece by piece (source: Tony Bacon and Paul Day, *The Guru's Guitar Guide*; Firewood advice courtesy the good ol' boys down at the Manistique General Store 'n Liquor Emporium).

MERMER GUITARS

Instruments currently built in Sebastian, FL, since 1983.

Luthier Richard Mermer, Jr. is producing concert quality, handcrafted instruments designed and built for the individual. Steel string, nylon string, electric-acoustic instruments, and acoustic Hawaiian steel guitars are offered.

All Mermer guitars feature: solid wood construction, choice of select tone woods, decorative wood binding, custom wood and stone inlay, custom scale lengths, fully compensated saddles and precision intonation, adjustable truss rod, choice of hardware and accessories, and optional pickup and microphone installation. Mermer produces about 12 instruments a year. For a list of options and additional information refer to their website (see Trademark Index).

GRADING	100% MINT	98% NEAR MINT	95% EXC+	90% EXC	80% VG+	70% VG	60% G

MESROBIAN

Instruments currently built in Salem, MA, since 1995.

Luthier Carl Mesorbian began woodworking at the age of seven, and recieved his first guitar at the age of fourteen. Like many luthiers, Carl worked on making furniture cabinet after completing the a program in this industry in Boston. After this he began repairing guitars, and eventually made two of his own. Carl then attended Dick Boak´s guitar making class in New Jersey, and has been producing guitars ever since. For further information contact Carl directly (see Trademark Index).

ELECTRIC ARCHTOP

Mesrobian guitars are similar to the D´Angelico style with the big archtops and fancy headstocks. The **Standard**, which is actually the highest end model, retails for $4,250. The **Special** with less features is $3,750, and the **Session** is very basic for $2,750. Custom one-off models are also available.

MESSENGER

Instruments previously built in San Francisco, CA between 1968 and 1971. Distributed by Musicraft of San Francisco, CA.

Messenger guitars and basses featured a single piece metal alloy neck in a design that pre-dated Travis Bean and Kramer instruments. Messenger instruments also feature distinctive f-holes, a thin body, and mono or stereo output. Available in a six or twelve string configuration. Colors included Morning Sunburst, Midnight Sunburst, and Rojo Red (source: Michael Wright, *Vintage Guitar Magazine*).

ELECTRIC

ELECTRIC ARCHTOP - double cutaway thin hollowbody archtop, distinct f-holes, alloy-metal neck, rosewood fingerboard, mono or stereo output, available in Morning Sunburst, Midnight Sunburst, or Rojo Red, mfg. 1968-1971.

	N/A	$2,000	$1,700	$1,500	$1,300	$1,100	$900

MESSENGER BASS

See Knutson Luthiery. Instruments currently built in Forestville, CA since 1992.

The **Messenger Upright Electric Bass** is a limited edition, handcrafted, numbered, and signed instrument built by luthier John Knutson. It is designed to make the transition between acoustic and electric playing as natural and rewarding as possible. For more information, please contact the company directly (see Trademark Index).

METAL DRIVER

Also MD. See Music Drive. Instruments previously built in Korea. Previously distributed by Sumer Musical Instruments Co., Ltd. of Japan.

The Sumer Musical Instruments company briefly offered an aluminum body (with bolt-on wood neck) model which featured the Abel Axe aluminum body, also similar to the model offered under the **Rogue** trademark. Other **MD** and **Metal Driver** models during this time period feature wood bodies similar to designs offered by Ibanez and Jackson. All electric guitars and basses were good quality instruments that appealed to the working or semi-professional musician (see Music Drive).

METROPOLITAN

Instruments currently built in Houston, TX since 1995. Distributed by Alamo Music Products of Houston, TX.

Metropolitan Guitars was originally conceived by David Wintz (of Robin Guitars fame), based on the idea that others would find the retro styling of the old National **Glenwood** as appealing as he did. While the original National Glenwood models had a formed plastic body and a bolt-on metal neck, Wintz´ current **Tanglewood** model features a "map-shaped" wood body, and a mahogany set-in neck. Wintz debuted the Tanglewood series in March, 1996. Two more series, the Glendale and the Westport, followed a year later. The **Glendale** model has a single cutaway body, more rounded than the Tanglewood, but similar large body dimensions. The **Westport** model has a scaled down, rounded body. For more information contact Metropolitan directly (see Trademark Index).

ELECTRIC

GLENDALE CUSTOM - single cutaway African Fakimba body, scooped edges on body creating a raised top, one-piece set mahogany neck, rosewood fingerboard with MOP butterfly inlays, 3-per-side tuners, Art Deco tailpiece, truss rod cover, and pickguard, two humbucker pickups, four knobs, three-way switch, chrome hardware, available in Tobacco Sunburst, Pearl Aqua Blue, Jet Black, or custom colors, mfg. 1997-present.

MSR	$2,750		$2,200	$2,000	$1,850	$1,700	$1,550	$1,400	$1,250

Glendale Custom Acoustic - similar to the Glendale Custom, except has a L.R. Baggs Piezo bridge pickup, 6 knobs, and push/pull for pickups, mfg. 1997-present.

MSR	$3,295		$2,650	$2,450	$2,250	$2,100	$1,950	$1,800	$1,650

GLENDALE DELUXE - single cutaway African Fakimba body, scooped edges on body creating a raised top, one-piece set mahogany neck, rosewood fingerboard with MOP dot inlays, 3-per-side tuners, Art Deco tailpiece, truss rod cover, and pickguard, two humbucker pickups, four knobs, three-way switch, nickle plated hardware, available in Tobacco Sunburst, Pearl Aqua Blue, Jet Black, or custom colors, mfg. 1997-present.

MSR	$1,870		$1,500	$1,350	$1,200	$1,050	$950	$850	$750

GLENDALE SUPER ACOUSTIC - single cutaway African Fakimba body with flame maple top, scooped edges on body creating a raised top, laminated flame maple neck, ebony fingerboard with MOP butterfly inlays, 3-per-side tuners, Art Deco tailpiece, truss rod cover, and pickguard, two humbucker pickups, L.R. Baggs piezo bridge pickup, six knobs, three-way switch, gold hardware, available in Tobacco Sunburst, Pearl Aqua Blue, Jet Black, or custom colors, mfg. 1997-present.

MSR	$4,950		$4,000	$3,600	$3,300	$3,100	$2,900	$2,700	$2,500

GRADING	100% MINT	98% NEAR MINT	95% EXC+	90% EXC	80% VG+	70% VG	60% G

TANGLEWOOD CUSTOM - double cutaway with pointed bass bout and cutout lower treble bout basswood body, scooped edges on body creating a raised top, one-piece set mahogany neck, rosewood fingerboard with MOP butterfly inlays, 3-per-side tuners, Art Deco tailpiece, truss rod cover, and pickguard, two humbucker pick-ups, four knobs, three-way switch, chrome hardware, available in Tobacco Sunburst, Pearl Aqua Blue, Jet Black, or custom colors, mfg. 1996-present.

	MSR	$2,750		$2,200	$2,000	$1,850	$1,700	$1,550	$1,400	$1,250

Tanglewood Custom Acoustic - similar to the Tanglewood Custom, except has a L.R. Baggs Piezo bridge pickup, 6 knobs, and push/pull for pickups, mfg. 1996-present.

MSR	$3,295		$2,650	$2,450	$2,250	$2,100	$1,950	$1,800	$1,650

TANGLEWOOD DELUXE - double cutaway with pointed bass bout and cutout lower treble bout basswood body, scooped edges on body creating a raised top, one-piece set mahogany neck, rosewood fingerboard with MOP dot inlays, 3-per-side tuners, Art Deco tailpiece, truss rod cover, and pickguard, two humbucker pickups, four knobs, three-way switch, nickle plated hardware, available in Tobacco Sunburst, Pearl Aqua Blue, Jet Black, or custom colors, mfg. 1996-present.

MSR	$1,870		$1,500	$1,350	$1,200	$1,050	$950	$850	$750

WESTPORT CUSTOM - single cutaway Les Paul size African Fakimba body, scooped edges on body creating a raised top, one-piece set mahogany neck, rosewood fingerboard with MOP butterfly inlays, 3-per-side tuners, Art Deco tailpiece, truss rod cover, and pickguard, two humbucker pickups, four knobs, three-way switch, chrome hardware, available in Tobacco Sunburst, Pearl Aqua Blue, Jet Black, or custom colors, mfg. 1997-present.

MSR	$2,750		$2,200	$2,000	$1,850	$1,700	$1,550	$1,400	$1,250

Westport Custom Acoustic - similar to the Westport Custom, except has a L.R. Baggs Piezo bridge pickup, 6 knobs, and push/pull for pickups, mfg. 1997-present.

MSR	$3,295		$2,650	$2,450	$2,250	$2,100	$1,950	$1,800	$1,650

WESTPORT DELUXE - single cutaway Les Paul size African Fakimba body, scooped edges on body creating a raised top, one-piece set mahogany neck, rosewood fingerboard with MOP dot inlays, 3-per-side tuners, Art Deco tailpiece, truss rod cover, and pickguard, two humbucker pickups, four knobs, three-way switch, nickle plated hardware, available in Tobacco Sunburst, Pearl Aqua Blue, Jet Black, or custom colors, mfg. 1997-present.

MSR	$1,870		$1,500	$1,350	$1,200	$1,050	$950	$850	$750

WESTPORT SUPER ACOUSTIC - single cutaway Les Paul size African Fakimba body with flame maple top, scooped edges on body creating a raised top, laminated flame maple neck, ebony fingerboard with MOP butterfly inlays, 3-per-side tuners, Art Deco tailpiece, truss rod cover, and pickguard, two humbucker pickups, L.R. Baggs piezo bridge pickup, six knobs, three-way switch, gold hardware, available in Tobacco Sunburst, Pearl Aqua Blue, Jet Black, or custom colors, mfg. 1997-present.

MSR	$4,950		$4,000	$3,600	$3,300	$3,100	$2,900	$2,700	$2,500

Metropolitan Glendale Custom
courtesy Metropolitan

MIAMI

Instruments previously produced in Japan during the mid-1970s.

The Miami trademark is the brand name used by a British importer. Instruments tended to be entry level solid body guitars (source: Tony Bacon and Paul Day, *The Guru's Guitar Guide*).

MICHAEL

Instruments previously built in Japan during the mid-1980s.

The Michael trademark was a brand name used by a UK importer. The "Metro" model was a medium quality strat design solid body (source: Tony Bacon and Paul Day, *The Guru's Guitar Guide*).

MICHAEL DOLAN CUSTOM GUITARS

Instruments currently built in Santa Rosa, Sonoma County, CA since 1977.

Luthier Michael Dolan has been handcrafting quality guitars for over twenty years. After Dolan graduated from Sonoma State University with a Bachelor of Arts degree in Fine Arts, he went to work for a prestigious bass and guitar manufacturer. Dolan's full service shop offers custom built guitars and basses (solid body, archtop, acoustic, neck-through, bolt-on, set-neck, and headless) as well as repairs and custom painting. He and his staff work in domestic and exotic woods, and use hardware and electronics from all well-known manufacturers. Finishes include their standard acrylic top coat/polyester base, nitrocellulose, and hand rubbed oil.

As luthier Dolan likes to point out, a "Custom Guitar is a unique expression of the vision of a particular individual. Because there are so many options and variables, offering a price list has proven to be impractical." However, Dolan's prices generally start at $1,250 and the average cost may run between $1,500 to $2,500. Prices are determined by the nature of the project, and the costs of components and building materials.

Working with their custom guitar order form, Michael Dolan can provide a firm up-front price quote. All custom guitars are guaranteed for tone, playability, and overall quality.

MICHIGAN

Instruments previously produced in East Germany from the late 1950s through the early 1960s.

The Michigan trademark was a brand name utilized by a British importer. Quality ranged from entry level to intermediate on models that were either solid body, semi-hollow, or archtop (source: Tony Bacon and Paul Day, *The Guru's Guitar Guide*).

Metropolitan Glendale Custom
courtesy Metropolitan

GRADING	100% MINT	98% NEAR MINT	95% EXC+	90% EXC	80% VG+	70% VG	60% G

MICK, BOB

Instruments currently built in Tucson, AZ. Distributed directly by Bob Mick Guitars of Tucson, AZ.

Luthier Bob Mick has a JM-1 ($1,299) short scale bass "built like our top-of-the-line basses, only smaller!" Mick also features the M-4 ($3,150) neck-through design that features maple and exotic woods in its construction. There are also five and six string versions as well. Furthermore, luthier Mick can custom build any basses from simple designs to the exotic in bolt-on or neck-through.

MICRO-FRETS

Instruments currently built in Frederick MD since 2004. Previously built in Frederick, MD between 1967 and 1974.

During the expansion of the pop music market in the 1960s, many smaller guitar producers entered the electric instrument market to supply the growing public demand for guitars. One such visionary was Ralph J. Jones, who founded the Micro-Frets organization in 1967. Jones, who primarily handled design concepts, electronics, and hardware innovations, received financial backing from his former employer (a successful Maryland real estate magnate). It is estimated that Jones began building his prototypes in 1965, at his Wheaten, Maryland workshop. By 1967 production began at the company factory located at 100 Grove Road in Frederick, Maryland. Ralph J. Jones was the company president and treasurer, and was assisted by F.M. Huggins (vice-president and general manager) and A.R. Hubbard (company secretary) as well as the working staff.

Micro-Frets guitars were shown at the 1968 NAMM show. The company did the greatest amount of production between 1969 and 1971, when 1,700 of the less than 3,000 total guitars were made. Jones passed away sometime in 1973, and was succeeded by Huggins as president.

When Micro-Frets closed operations in Maryland in either 1974 or 1975, the company assets were purchased by David Sturgill. Sturgill, who served as the company president of Grammer Guitars for three years, let his sons John and Danny gain access to leftover Micro-Frets parts. In addition to those parts, they had also purchased the remains of New Jersey's Harptone guitar company. The two assembled a number of solid body guitars which were then sold under the "Diamond-S" trademark. Unfortunately, that business venture did not catch on, and dissipated sometime in 1976, (Micro-Frets enthusiast Jim Danz, began detailing a listing of Micro-Frets serial numbers. His results appeared in a company history by Michael Wright in *Vintage Guitar* magazine).

Micro-Frets is back in business and run by Will Meadors and Paul Rose. After the trademark spent many years in mothballs, these two men revived it and are selling guitars again. The new models are based on the vintage models of the past. Parts are also available. For more information contact Micro-Frets directly (see Trademark Index).

SERIALIZATION

The entire production of the Micro-Frets company is less than 3,000 guitars and basses produced. As in the case of production guitars, neck plates with stamped serial numbers were pre-purchased in lots, and then bolted to the guitars during the neck attachment. The serial numbers were utilized by Micro-Frets for warranty work, and the four digit numbers do fall roughly in a usable list.

This list should be used for rough approximations only:

Between the company start-up in 1967 and 1969, serial numbers were 1000 to 1300 (around 300 instruments produced). During the transition period, a couple of dozen instruments were produced. From 1969 to 1971, serial numbers 1323 to 3000 (around 1,700 instruments were produced). Finally, in the company's home stretch between 1971 to 1974, serial numbers 3000 to 3670 (roughly 700 instruments were produced).

BODY CONSTRUCTION STYLES

Furthermore, a survey of company production indicates three predominant styles or construction similarities shared by various production models through the years. Again, this information is a rough approximation based on viewed models, and any errors in it are the fault of this author (so don't blame Jim Danz!): Style I (1967 to 1969): Most of the Micro-Fret guitars are actually hollow bodied guitars built by joining two separate top and bottom slabs of routed-out solid wood. As a result, earlier models will feature a side gasket on the two body halves. The early vibrato design looks similar to a Bigsby. The pickguard will have two levels, and the thumb wheel controls are set into a scalloped edge on the top half. Pickups will be DeArmond, Micro-Frets **Hi-Fis**, or German-made Schallers or possibly Hofners. Tuning pegs will be Grovers (some with pearl grips) or Schallers (on the high end models).

Style II (1969 to 1971): The side gaskets are gone, but side seams should be noticeable. The bi-level pickguard is white, the top half is shorter than the lower, and now conventional knobs are utilized. Guitars now sport only Micro-Fret pickups, but there are a number of different designs. According to Bill Lawrence (Bill Lawrence Guitar Company/Keystone Pickups), Micro-Frets approached him at the 1968 NAMM show and contracted him to design both the pickups and the manufacturing process. Micro-Frets pickups were then produced in-house by the company.

Style III (1971 or 1972 until 1974): No side seams are visible, but by then a number of solid body guitars were being introduced as well. The bi-level pickguard now has a clear plastic short top half. Micro-Fret pickups are again used, although some were built with extra booster coils and three switches for tonal options. There are still some unsubstantiated reports of possible 12-string versions, or even a resonator model!

ELECTRIC

CALIBRA I - 22-fret rosewood fingerboard, adjustable metal nut, 6-on-a-side tuners, adjustable bridge, chrome hardware, 2 Micro-Frets pickups, volume/tone controls, pickup selector switch, mfg. 1969-circa 1972.

	N/A	$750	$700	$650	$575	$500	$425

Last MSR was $299.

The Calibra I model was similar to an earlier model, the Golden Comet.

Calibra - similar to the Calibra I, except features a fixed bridge/tailpiece, mfg. 1971-circa 1972.

	N/A	$700	$650	$600	$550	$475	$400

Last MSR was $269.

HUNTINGTON - maple top/back/sides, 22-fret rosewood fingerboard, adjustable metal nut, 6-on-a-side tuners, adjustable bridge, chrome hardware, 2 Micro-Frets pickups, volume/tone controls, pickup selector switch, mfg. 1967-circa 1973.

	N/A	$900	$825	$750	$675	$600	$525

Last MSR was $599.

ORBITER - triple cutaway body, controls on the bottom edge of the pickguard, features a built-in wireless transmitter, mfg. 1968-69.

	N/A	$950	$875	$825	$750	$650	$550

This model should come equipped with a receiver unit.

GRADING	100% MINT	98% NEAR MINT	95% EXC+	90% EXC	80% VG+	70% VG	60% G

SIGNATURE - thin dual cutaway hardwood body with pointed horns, maple neck, 22-fret rosewood fingerboard, adjustable metal Micro-nut, 6-on-a-side tuners, Calibrato bridge, chrome hardware, 2 Micro-Frets MF pickups, volume/tone controls, pickup selector switch, available in Black, Maraschino Cherry, Standard Sunburst, or Walnut finishes, mfg. 1969-circa 1972.

	N/A	$650	$600	$550	$500	$425	$350

Last MSR was $349.

The Signature Model was also offered in a Baritone model (30 in. scale), mfg. 1971-74.

SPACETONE - dual rounded cutaway thin body, maple top/back/sides, white celluloid body binding, maple neck, 22-fret rosewood fingerboard, adjustable metal Micro-nut, 6-on-a-side tuners, Calibrato tremolo, chrome hardware, split level white pickguard, 2 Micro-Frets Hi Fi pickups, volume/tone controls, pickup selector switch, available in Black, Martian Sunburst, or Standard Sunburst finishes, mfg. 1967-circa 1973.

	N/A	$800	$750	$675	$600	$525	$450

Last MSR was $449.

STAGE II - maple top/back/sides, 22-fret rosewood fingerboard, adjustable metal nut, 6-on-a-side tuners, adjustable bridge, chrome hardware, 2 Micro-Frets pickups, volume/tone controls, pickup selector switch, mfg. 1969-circa 1971.

	N/A	$675	$600	$550	$500	$425	$350

Last MSR was $359.

The Stage II Model was also offered in a Baritone model (30 in. scale), mfg. 1972-74.

ELECTRIC BASS

RENDEVOUS - similar to the Thundermaster, except features one pickup, mfg. 1967-69.

	N/A	$600	$550	$500	$425	$350	$300

Last MSR was $295.

SIGNATURE BASS - solid body, 30 in. (or 34 in.) scale, 20-fret rosewood fingerboard, adjustable metal nut, 4-on-a-side tuners, adjustable bridge, chrome hardware, 2 Micro-Frets pickups, volume/tone controls, pickup selector switch, mfg. 1969-circa 1972.

	N/A	$650	$600	$550	$475	$400	$325

Last MSR was $299.

This model was available with a fretless fingerboard.

STAGE II BASS - slightly offset double cutaway body, maple body, 30 in. (or 34 in.) scale, maple neck, 20-fret rosewood fingerboard, adjustable metal Micro-nut, 2-per-side tuners, adjustable bridge, chrome hardware, Micro-Frets Hi Fi pickup, volume/tone controls, available in Black, Maraschino Cherry, Standard Sunburst, or Walnut finishes, mfg. 1969-circa 1972.

	N/A	$650	$575	$525	$450	$375	$300

Last MSR was $299.

This model was available with a fretless fingerboard.

THUNDERMASTER BASS - thin dual rounded cutaway maple body, white celluloid body binding, 30 in. (or 34 in.) scale, 20-fret rosewood fingerboard, adjustable metal Micro-nut, 2-per-side tuners, adjustable bridge, chrome hardware, 2 Micro-Frets Hi Fi pickups, volume/tone controls, pickup selector switch, available in Martian Sunburst or Standard Sunburst finishes, mfg. 1967-1973.

	N/A	$700	$650	$600	$550	$475	$400

Last MSR was $425.

This model was available with a fretless fingerboard.

MIDI AXE

Instruments currently produced in Everett, WA. Distributed by the Virtual DSP Corporation of Everett, WA.

The Virtual DSP Corporation has unveiled a custom electric guitar which incorporates a state of the art pitch-to-MIDI tracking system. The MIDI Axe features 6 separate RMC piezo electric pickups (built into the tremolo bridge), which combines their signal into a direct output signal. MIDI Axe is the first MIDI system to allow full software upgradability; software updates are available by download at the company's website, which is no longer up.

MIGHTY MITE

Replacement parts and instruments were previously built in the U.S. during the 1970s and early 1980s. Replacement parts are currently distributed by Westheimer Corporation of Northbrook, IL.

The Mighty Mite company was probably better known for its high quality replacement parts it produced rather than the guitars they made available. Mighty Mite parts are still currently offered (source: Tony Bacon and Paul Day, *The Guru's Guitar Guide*).

M

MIKE LULL CUSTOM GUITARS

Instruments currently built in Bellevue, WA.

Luthier Mike Lull has been building guitars for several bands in the Seattle area for years. Lull and two partners opened their own repair shop based on Lull's customizing and repair talents in 1978. Lull has been the sole owner of the Guitar Works since 1983 and still offers repair and restoration services in addition to his custom-built instruments.

ELECTRIC

Mike Lull Custom Guitars now offers a number of different guitar models. Currently the only guitar available is the SX Guitar Model, which is a traditional strat design and retails for $2,699. Last Retail Prices on the **Classic** models range from $1,695 up to $2,195; the **Modern Soloist** is $2,595, and the **Custom Carved Top** is $2,895. The **Vintage** model definitely brings back the feel of an older Strat. Models feature alder, mahogany, or swamp ash bodies, rock maple necks, maple or rosewood (or ebony) fingerboards, and Seymour Duncan or Van Zandt pickups.

ELECTRIC BASS

The 4-string bass models like the **Modern Jazz** and **Vintage P/J** prices start at $2,199 up to $2,499, and the 5-string **Modern 5** and the 35 in. scale **Modern 535** models are priced at $2,499 to $2,999. For further information, contact Mike Lull Custom Guitars directly (see Trademark Index).

MILLENNIUM GUITARS

Instruments currently produced in Pasadena, CA.

Millennium Guitars have a new Model ML-2000 ($2,880 MSR) that features a body made from polished, clear coated aluminum. The ML-2001 ($2,430 MSR) has traditional construction, and utilizes purple sparkle chip resistant enameled bodies in either gloss or wrinkle finish.

MILLER

Instruments currently built in Rossbach, Germany.

Miller custom instruments are constructed from carbon graphite fibers or hemp, leading to the company's motto "Don't Smoke it, Play it!" Hempline models are semi-hollow in construction, including the neck and headstock. These advanced design aspects place the Miller company on the cutting edge of guitar technology and construction. For additional information concerning models and pricing, contact the Miller company directly (see Trademark Index).

MINARIK GUITARS

Instruments currently produced in Van Nuys, CA since 2002.

Luthier M.E. Minarik builds custom solidbody and chambered guitars with radical body designs. Minarik worked under Bernie Rico Sr. from B.C. Rich and is responsible for the Goddess Warlock, India Twin Double Neck, Poseidon Exclusive, and Twilight Serenade Acoustic. For more information contact Minarik directly (see Trademark Index).

ELECTRIC

The Studio X-Treme series are priced at $1,349 for Midnight Black finish and $1,399 for Sunburst finish. The Super Custom series starts at $3,000. The Professional Series starts at $4,995. There are several options available, especially on the higher end guitars. Models are available in most series. The Diablo features a double cutaway body with eight points along the edge. The Inferno is a double cutaway with wood cut to look like flames on the bottom. The Goddess is a more conserved body shape with an offset double cutaway and a small notch on the bottom.

MIRAGE

Instruments previously produced in Taiwan during the late 1980s.

Entry level to intermediate quality guitars based on classic American designs (source: Tony Bacon and Paul Day, *The Guru's Guitar Guide*).

MIRAGE GUITAR WORKS

Instruments currently produced in Manchester, MD since the 1980s. Previously built in Etters, PA from 1978-early 1980s.

Luthier Paul Gabot is the founder of Mirage Guitar Works (MGW). MGW opened in 1978, and the first guitars were primarily built from acrylic sheet or cast polyester. In 1985, Gabot started building guitars out of wood but continues to produce guitars mainly out of alternative materials. Guitars are built in very limited productions and many are built as full custom instruments. In 1998, MGW started an import series from Korea. These guitars are solidbodies with high-quality appointments. Only 50 guitars are built at a time, and a total of 500 built in a series. Gabot tries to introduce one new model a year and discontinue one after 500 are built. In 2004, a series of acoustic guitars was introduced as a limited production of around 50 guitars a year. For more information contact MGW directly (see Trademark Index).

ELECTRIC

Mirage Guitars offers original design electric guitars with see through bodies constructed of acrylic or polyester. The **Mindbender I** had a bolt-on maple neck, 6-on-a-side tuners, and 2 MightyMite humbuckers or 3 single coils. Available in clear, tinted, and opaque. Retail list price began at $795.

MODULUS GUITARS

Instruments currently built in Novato, CA since 1997. Previously built in San Francisco, CA 1978-1997.

Geoff Gould, an aerospace engineer and bass player, was intrigued by an Alembic-customized bass he saw at a Grateful Dead concert. Assuming that the all wood construction was a heavy proposition, he fashioned some samples of carbon graphite and presented them to Alembic. An experimental model with a graphite neck was displayed in 1977, and a patent issued in 1978. Gould formed the Modulus Graphite company with other ex-aerospace partners to provide necks for Alembic, and also build necks for Music Man's Cutlass bass model as well as their own Modulus Graphite guitars. Modulus Graphite's first products were Fender-style replacement necks, but in the early 1980s five- and six-string bass models were introduced. Since then, the Modulus neck patent has been licensed to several companies, and Modulus has supplied finished necks to Alvarez Yairi, Aria, Cort, Ibanez, Moonstone, Peavey, Status, Steinberger, Tokai, and Zon as well. For more information contact Modulus directly (see Trademark Index).

GRADING	100% MINT	98% NEAR MINT	95% EXC+	90% EXC	80% VG+	70% VG	60% G

ELECTRIC: BLACKKNIFE SERIES

Blackknife series guitars feature bolt-on graphite/epoxy composite necks with phenolic/ebonol fingerboards (unless otherwise listed). All models are available with the following standard finishes, unless otherwise listed: Amber, Clear Blue, Clear Green, Clear Red, Deep Black, Monza Red, Pure White, Sea Foam Green, Surf Green, and Vintage Pink. The following options were available on the Blackknife models:

> Add $50 for black or gold hardware. Add $100 for body matching colored neck. Add $100 for Wilkinson tremolo bridge. Add $100 for 3-Tone Sunburst or Translucent Cream finish. Add $100 for Custom Color finishes: Black Cherry, Blue/Greenburst, Blue/Purpleburst, Blue Velvet, Charcoal Metalflake, Cherryburst, Clear Black, Green Velvet, Honeyburst and Purple Metalflake. Add $150 for Candy Apple Blue, Candy Apple Green, or Candy Apple Red finish. Add $175 for 2TEK bridge. Add $200 for double locking tremolo.

CLASSIC (MODEL BC6) - offset double cutaway alder body, bolt-on graphite neck, 25.5 in. scale, 22-fret phenolic fingerboard with white dot inlay, ABM fixed bridge, 6-on-a-side tuners, chrome hardware, humbucker/single coil/humbucker EMG pickups, volume/tone controls, 5-way selector, available in Black, Cream, Green, Red, or White finishes, disc. 1996.

	N/A	$1,200	$1,050	$900	$775	$650	$525

Last MSR was $1,999.

Classic (Model GIMCL) - similar to the Classic (Model BC6), except has flamed maple top, gold hardware, Wilkinson VS-100 tremolo, 3 mini-switches, disc. 1994.

	N/A	$1,500	$1,250	$1,050	$875	$725	$600

Last MSR was $2,495.

MODEL T (MODEL MT6/GITNT) - single cutaway alder body, bolt-on graphite neck, 25.5 in. scale, 22-fret phenolic fingerboard with white dot inlay, strings through-body bridge, 6-on-a-side tuners, chrome hardware, 2 Seymour Duncan single coil pickups, volume/tone controls, 3-way selector, available in Black, Cream, Green, Red, or White finishes, disc. 1996.

	N/A	$1,000	$850	$700	$600	$500	$400

Last MSR was $1,699.

Modulus Special 3H courtesy Modulus

Model T Custom (Model GI1NT-C) - similar to Model T, except has figured maple top, black hardware, 1 Seymour Duncan/1 Van Zandt single coil pickups, disc. 1994.

	N/A	$1,250	$1,050	$900	$775	$650	$525

Last MSR was $2,095.

SPECIAL (MODEL BS6) - offset double cutaway alder body, bolt-on graphite neck, 22-fret phenolic fingerboard with white dot inlay, ABM fixed bridge, 6-on-a-side tuners, chrome hardware, 2 HS-2 single coil/1 humbucker DiMarzio pickups, volume/tone controls, 5-way selector, available in Black, Cream, Green, Red, or White finishes, mfg. 1994-96.

	N/A	$1,200	$1,050	$900	$775	$650	$525

Last MSR was $1,999.

Special 3H (Model GIS3HT) - similar to the Special (Model BS6), except has double locking Floyd Rose tremolo, 2 EMG-SA single coil/1 EMG 85 humbucker pickups, 3 mini-switches, disc. 1994.

	N/A	$1,200	$1,050	$900	$775	$650	$525

Last MSR was $1,995.

Special 3H Custom (Model GIS3HT-C) - similar to Special 3H (Model GIS3HT), except has figured maple top, and black hardware, disc. 1994.

	N/A	$1,450	$1,250	$1,100	$950	$800	$650

Last MSR was $2,395.

VINTAGE (MODEL BV6/GIS3VT) - offset double cutaway alder body, bolt-on graphite neck, 25.5" scale, 22-fret fingerboard with white dot inlay, vintage-style 2-point tremolo, 3-layer white pickguard, chrome hardware, 3 Van Zandt single coil pickups, volume/2 tone controls, 5-way selector, available in Black, Cream, Green, Red, or White finishes, disc. 1996.

	N/A	$1,100	$950	$825	$700	$600	$500

Last MSR was $1,899.

Vintage Custom (Model GIS3VT-C) - similar to Vintage, except has figured maple top, black hardware, disc. 1994.

	N/A	$1,350	$1,150	$1,000	$850	$700	$550

Last MSR was $2,295.

ELECTRIC: BLACKKNIFE CUSTOM SERIES

The following models have a through-body graphite neck. Options are similar to the bolt-on neck Blackknife models.

BOB WEIR SIGNATURE (MODEL BW6/GIBW) - offset double cutaway alder body, cocabola top, through-body graphite neck, 24-fret phenolic fingerboard with white dot inlay, double locking Floyd Rose tremolo, 6-on-a-side tuners, black hardware, 2 single coil/1 humbucker EMG pickups, volume/tone/active electronics control, 3 mini-switches, disc. 1996.

	N/A	$2,200	$1,800	$1,500	$1,300	$1,100	$900

Last MSR was $3,499.

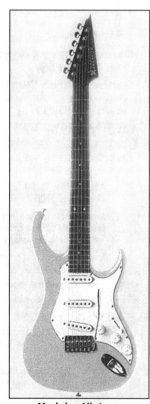

Modulus Vintage courtesy Modulus

M

GRADING	100% MINT	98% NEAR MINT	95% EXC+	90% EXC	80% VG+	70% VG	60% G

CUSTOM (MODEL GIMCT) - offset double cutaway alder body, figured maple top, through-body neck, 24-fret phenolic fingerboard with white dot inlay, double locking Floyd Rose vibrato, 6-on-a-side tuners, gold hardware, humbucker/single coil/humbucker EMG pickups, volume/tone/active electronics control, 3 mini-switches, disc. 1994.

	N/A	$1,800	$1,550	$1,300	$1,100	$950	$800

Last MSR was $2,995.

Custom 12-String (Model GIMF-12) - similar to the Custom, except in a 12-string configuration, 6-per-side tuners, mfg. 1991-92.

	N/A	$1,700	$1,450	$1,250	$1,050	$900	$750

Last MSR was $2,695.

ELECTRIC: GENESIS SERIES

Genesis series guitars have a graphite composite central core in the neck surrounded by spruce, cedar, alder, or figured maple; the fingerboard is granadillo.

Add $50 for 2 single coil/1 humbucker DiMarzio pickups (there is no additional charge for substituting 2 DiMarzio humbuckers for the 3 single coils). Add $100 for ABM tremolo bridge. Add $200 (and up) for highly figured maple/graphite neck. Add $225 for 2TEK bridge.

GENESIS ONE (MODEL G1/GO6) - offset double cutaway alder body, bolt-on graphite/spruce (or graphite/soma, graphite/alder, or graphite/red cedar) neck, 22-fret granadillo fingerboard with white dot inlay, white (or black) pickguard, ABM fixed bridge, 6-on-a-side Schaller tuners, chrome hardware, 3 DiMarzio dual-blade single coil-sized humbucker pickups, volume/tone controls, 5-way selector, available in Black, Green, Red, or White finishes, mfg. 1996-present.

MSR	$2,199	$1,600	$1,400	$1,200	$1,050	$900	$750	$600

Add $50 for tortoiseshell, white or black pearl pickguard. Add $100 for 2-Tone or 3-Tone Sunburst finish. Add $150 for Candy Apple Blue, Candy Apple Green, or Candy Apple Red finish.

Genesis One with Tremolo (Model G1T) - similar to the Genesis One, except has an ABM tremolo bridge, mfg. 1997-present.

MSR	$2,299	$1,700	$1,450	$1,250	$1,100	$950	$800	$650

GENESIS TWO (MODEL G2/GT6) - similar to the Genesis One, except has figured maple top, no pickguard (rear-routed body), available in BlueStone, GreenStone, GrayStone, or RedStone finishes, mfg. 1996-present.

MSR	$2,499	$1,850	$1,600	$1,350	$1,150	$1,000	$850	$700

Add $100 for BlueStoneBurst, GreenStoneBurst, and RedStoneBurst finishes. Add $200 for highly figured quilt or flamed maple top.

Genesis Two with Tremolo (Model G2T) - similar to the Genesis Two, except has an ABM tremolo bridge, mfg. 1997-present.

MSR	$2,699	$2,000	$1,700	$1,450	$1,250	$1,050	$900	$750

GENESIS THREE (MODEL G3) - offset double cutaway alder or soma body, set-in graphite/soma (or graphite/red cedar) neck, 25 in. scale, 22-fret granadillo fingerboard with white dot inlay, black pickguard, fixed bridge, 3-per-side tuners, chrome hardware, 2 custom soapbar-style humbuckers (or 2 full size humbuckers) pickups, 2 volume/1 tone controls, 5-way selector, available in Black, Blue, Creme, Green, and Red solid finishes; Blue, Green, Honey, or Rose Transparent colors, mfg. 1998-2003.

	$1,600	$1,400	$1,200	$1,000	$825	$675	$525

Last MSR was $1,999.

Add $100 for Cherryburst and Honeyburst finishes. Add $200 for quilt or flame maple top.

Genesis Three Carved Top (Model G3CT) - similar to the Genesis Three, except has a carved top, mfg. 2002-present.

MSR	$2,899	$2,150	$1,850	$1,600	$1,350	$1,150	$950	$800

Genesis Three Semi-Hollow (Model G3SH) - similar to the Genesis Three, except has a semi-hollow wider 15 in. body and a stylized soundhole, mfg. 2001-02, reintroduced 2004.

MSR	$3,099	$2,250	$1,950	$1,700	$1,450	$1,250	$1,050	$850

ELECTRIC BASS: PRICING OPTIONS

The following options were available on earlier models from Modulus: The following options are available on current models: There has always been a premium on exotic wood tops throughout the history of Modulus. Here are the current options:

Add $100 for Kahler bridge upgrade. Add $100 for black or gold hardware. Add $100 for body matching colored neck. Add $600 for piezo bridge pickup (4-string). Add $700 for piezo bridge pickup (5-string). Add $800 for piezo bridge pickup (6-string).

Add $100 for fretless fingerboard (with or without lines). Add $100 for BlueStoneBurst, GreenStoneBurst, and RedStoneBurst finishes. Add $225 for 2TEK bridge. Add $50 for EMG-DC pickup(s) with active treble/mid/bass controls (BQC). Add $75 for Bartolini pickups with treble/bass controls (NTBT). Add $125 for Bartolini pickups with treble/mid/bass controls (NTMB)

Add $100 for bubinga or purpleheart top (clear finish only). Add $200 for chakte kok top (clear finish only). Add $200 (and up) for highly figured quilt or flame maple. Add $300 for burl or spalted maple (clear finish only).

ELECTRIC BASS: FLEA SERIES

FLEA BASS (MODEL FB4) - offset double cutaway alder body, bolt-on graphite neck, 34 in. scale, 22-fret phenolic fingerboard with white dot inlay, white (or black) multi-layer pickguard, Gotoh bridge, 4-on-a-side tuners, chrome hardware, Lane Poor MM4 pickup, volume/treble/bass controls, Bartolini NTBT active EQ, available in Black, Gray, Red, or White Semi-Gloss finishes, mfg. 1997-present.

MSR	$2,799	$2,050	$1,800	$1,550	$1,300	$1,100	$900	$750

Add $50 for Lane Poor MM4 pickup and Bartolini NTMB active EQ (treble/mid/bass controls). Add $50 for Bartolini MM pickup and Bartolini NTMB active EQ (treble/mid/bass controls). Add $75 for J style pickups. Add $100 for ABM bridge. Add $250 for Blue, Gold, Purple, or Silver Metalflake finish with matching headstock.

This model is also available with Basslines by Seymour Duncan MM pickup and electronics or Bartolini MM pickup/NTBT active EQ at no extra up charge.

GRADING	100% MINT	98% NEAR MINT	95% EXC+	90% EXC	80% VG+	70% VG	60% G

Flea Bass 5-String (Model FB5) - similar to the Flea Bass, except has a 5-string configuration, mfg. 1997-present.

MSR	$2,999		$2,200	$1,900	$1,650	$1,400	$1,150	$950	$800

Add $75 for J style pickups.

ELECTRIC BASS: J SERIES

VINTAGE J BASS (MODEL VJ4/GVJ4/BSJV) - sleek offset double cutaway swamp ash body, bolt-on graphite neck, 34 in. scale, 21-fret phenolic fingerboard with white dot inlay, Gotoh bridge, 4-on-a-side tuners, tortoiseshell pickguard, chrome hardware, 2 Bartolini J pickups, 2 volume/treble/bass controls, available in Black, Cream, Green, Red, or White finishes, mfg. 1994-present.

MSR	$2,199		$1,600	$1,350	$1,150	$1,000	$850	$700	$550

Add $225 for VJ-4 with flamed maple top.

In 1996, Green, Red, and White finishes were discontinued. Earlier models may feature 2 EMG-JV pickups and EMG-BTS active electronics. In 1997, the option of no pickguard/rear-routed controls was offered at no extra premium.

DELUXE J (MODEL DJ4/BSJV-C) - similar to Vintage J, except has figured maple top, no pickguard (rear-routed body), available in Amber, Blue, Green, Purple, Red Transparent finishes; Black Cherry, Blue, Blue over Red, Green, Orange Crush, Pink over Blue, Royal Velvet, and Red over Blue Velvet finishes, mfg. 1994-96.

	N/A	$1,350	$1,150	$1,000	$850	$700	$600

Last MSR was $2,199.

ELECTRIC BASS: M-92 SERIES

M92-4 (MODEL BSM4) - offset double cutaway alder or poplar body, bolt-on graphite neck, 35 in. scale, 24-fret phenolic fingerboard with white dot inlay, fixed bridge, 2-per-side tuners, black (or pearloid) pickguard, chrome hardware, EMG-35 DC humbucker pickup, volume/treble/bass controls, active electronics, mfg. 1994-96.

	N/A	$1,100	$950	$825	$700	$600	$500

Last MSR was $1,899.

M92-5 (Model BSM5) - similar to M92-4, except has 5 strings, Schaller bridge, 3/2-per-side tuners, EMG-40 DC humbucker pickup, mfg. 1994-96.

	N/A	$1,250	$1,050	$900	$775	$650	$525

Last MSR was $2,099.

Modulus M92-4
courtesy Modulus

ELECTRIC BASS: GENESIS SERIES

The Genesis MTD series was the result of the combined efforts of Modulus Guitars and designer Michael Tobias.

Add $75 for 2-Tone Sunburst, 3-Tone Sunburst, Blue/Green Sunburst, Blue/Purple Sunburst, CherryBurst, or HoneyBurst finish. Add $75 for Metallic finishes in Blue, Green, Light Plum, or Red.

GENESIS MT4 (MODEL BG4) - offset double cutaway alder or light ash body, bolt-on graphite/alder (or graphite/cedar or graphite/spruce) neck, 34 in. scale, 24-fret granadillo fingerboard with white dot inlay, ABM bridge, 4-on-a-side tuners, black hardware, 2 J-style Bartolini pickups, volume/treble/bass controls, available in Amber, Blue, Clear Gloss, Clear Satin, Gloss Black, Green, Orange Crush, Purple, or Red finishes, mfg. 1997-98, reintroduced 2003-present.

MSR	$3,199		$2,350	$2,050	$1,800	$1,550	$1,300	$1,100	$900

Genesis MT5 (Model BG5) - similar to the Genesis MT4, except has a 5-string configuration, 35 in. scale, 22-fret fingerboard, 5-on-a-side tuners, mfg. 1997-98, reintroduced 2003-present.

MSR	$3,399		$2,500	$2,200	$1,900	$1,650	$1,400	$1,150	$950

ELECTRIC BASS: OTEIL SERIES

OTEIL BASS LIMITED EDITION (MODEL OB6) - offset double cutaway semi-hollow mahogany body, cedar or spruce top, slash-style f-hole, bolt-on graphite neck, 35 in. scale, 24-fret phenolic or granadillo fingerboard with white inlay, ABM fixed bridge, 3-per-side tuners, black hardware, 2 Lane Poor soapbar pickups, 2 volume/treble/mid/bass controls, available in Purpleburst or Deep Transparent Purple finishes, mfg. 1998-2001.

	N/A	$3,000	$2,500	$2,200	$1,900	$1,600	$1,300

Last MSR was $3,999.

ELECTRIC BASS: PRIME SERIES

Add $50 for Amber, Blue, Green or Red Clear Color finish. Add $100 for 2-Tone or Cherry Sunburst finish.

MODULUS PRIME-4 (MODEL BSP4) - offset double cutaway ash body, bolt-on neck, 24-fret cocobola fingerboard, fixed bridge, 2-per-side tuners, chrome hardware, humbucker pickup, volume/treble/bass controls, active electronics, available in Natural finish, mfg. 1994 only.

	N/A	$1,200	$1,050	$900	$775	$650	$525

Last MSR was $1,995.

Modulus Quantum
5 SPi Custom
courtesy Modulus

M

GRADING	100% MINT	98% NEAR MINT	95% EXC+	90% EXC	80% VG+	70% VG	60% G

MODULUS PRIME-5 (MODEL BSP5) - similar to Modulus Prime-4, except has 5 strings, Schaller bridge, 3/2-per-side tuners, mfg. 1994 only.

	N/A	$1,350	$1,150	$1,000	$850	$700	$600

Last MSR was $2,195.

MODULUS PRIME-6 (MODEL BSP6) - similar to Modulus Prime-4, except has 6 strings, APM bridge, 3-per-side tuners, mfg. 1994 only.

	N/A	$1,500	$1,250	$1,050	$875	$725	$600

Last MSR was $2,495.

ELECTRIC BASS: SONICHAMMER SERIES

The SonicHammer series was originally announced as the **SledgeHammer** series. In 1997, aspects of the SonicHammer design became the foundation for the **Flea Bass** .

SONICHAMMER (SLEDGEHAMMER MODEL SH4) - offset double cutaway alder or swamp ash body, bolt-on graphite neck, 34 in. scale, 21-fret phenolic fingerboard with white dot inlay, tortoiseshell pickguard, Gotoh bridge, 4-on-a-side tuners, chrome hardware, 3-coil Bartolini pickup, volume/treble/bass controls, available in Black, Cream, Green, Red, or White finishes, mfg. 1996 only.

	N/A	$1,200	$1,050	$900	$775	$650	$525

Last MSR was $2,199.

DELUXE SONICHAMMER (DELUXE SLEDGEHAMMER MODEL DSH4) - similar to the Sledgehammer, except has a figured maple top, swamp ash body, available in Amber, Blue, Green, Purple, Red Transparent finishes; Black Cherry, Blue, Blue over Red, Green, Orange Crush, Pink over Blue, Royal Velvet, or Red over Blue Velvet finishes, mfg. 1996 only.

	N/A	$1,400	$1,200	$1,050	$900	$750	$600

Last MSR was $2,399.

ELECTRIC BASS: QUANTUM STANDARD SERIES

QUANTUM 4 SPi STANDARD (MODEL BSQ4XL) - offset double cutaway alder/poplar body, bolt-on graphite neck, 35 in. scale, 24-fret fingerboard with white inlay, Modulus/Gotoh fixed bridge, 2-per-side tuners, chrome hardware, 2 active EMG-soapbar pickups, 2 volume/treble/bass controls, mfg. 1995-96.

	N/A	$1,200	$1,050	$900	$775	$650	$525

Last MSR was $2,199.

The treble/bass controls are concentric in some models.

QUANTUM 5 SPi STANDARD (MODEL BSQ5XL) - similar to Quantum 4 SPi Standard, except has 5 strings, Schaller bridge, 3/2-per-side tuners, mfg. 1995-96.

	N/A	$1,400	$1,200	$1,050	$900	$750	$600

Last MSR was $2,399.

QUANTUM 6 SPi STANDARD (MODEL BSQ6XL) - similar to Quantum 4 SPi Standard, except has 6 strings, APM bridge, 3-per-side tuners, mfg. 1995-96.

	N/A	$1,600	$1,400	$1,200	$1,000	$850	$700

Last MSR was $2,699.

ELECTRIC BASS: QUANTUM CUSTOM SERIES

QUANTUM 4 (MODEL Q4) - offset double cutaway alder body, figured maple top, bolt-on graphite neck with relief-adjustment system, 35 in. scale, 24-fret phenolic or granadillo fingerboard with white inlay, ABM fixed bridge, 2-per-side tuners, chrome (or gold or black) hardware, 2 EMG-DC pickups, volume/balance/treble/bass controls, available in Amber, Blue, Clear Gloss, Clear Satin, Green, Orange Crush, Purple, and Red Transparent finishes; BlueStone, GrayStone, GreenStone, and RedStone finishes; Black Cherry, Blue, Blue over Red, Green, Pink over Blue, Royal Blue, or Red over Blue Velvet finishes, mfg. 1996-present.

MSR	$3,699	$2,700	$2,400	$2,100	$1,800	$1,500	$1,300	$1,100

QUANTUM 5 (MODEL Q5) - similar to the Quantum 4, except has 5-string configuration, 3/2-per-side headstock, mfg. 1996-present.

MSR	$3,899	$2,850	$2,500	$2,200	$1,900	$1,600	$1,350	$1,150

Quantum Wide 5 (Model QW5) - similar to the Quantum 4, except has 5-string configuration on a 6-string-sized fingerboard/neck, 3/2-per-side headstock, mfg. 1996-present.

MSR	$4,099	$3,000	$2,650	$2,300	$2,000	$1,700	$1,450	$1,200

QUANTUM 6 (MODEL Q6) - similar to the Quantum 4, except has 6-string configuration, 3-per-side headstock, mfg. 1996-present.

MSR	$4,099	$3,000	$2,650	$2,300	$2,000	$1,700	$1,450	$1,200

QUANTUM 4 SPi CUSTOM (MODEL BSQ4XL-C) - similar to the Quantum 4, except has fixed Modulus/Gotoh bridge, black hardware, 2 active EMG pickups, 2 volume/treble/bass controls, disc. 1996.

	N/A	$1,700	$1,400	$1,150	$950	$800	$650

Last MSR was $2,499.

QUANTUM 5 SPi CUSTOM (MODEL BSQ5XL-C) - similar to Quantum 4 SPi Custom, except has 5 strings, Schaller bridge, 3/2-per-side tuners, disc. 1996.

	N/A	$1,800	$1,500	$1,200	$1,000	$850	$700

Last MSR was $2,699.

QUANTUM 6 SPi CUSTOM (MODEL BSQ6XL-C) - similar to Quantum 4 SPi Custom, except has 6 strings, APM bridge, 3-per-side tuners, disc. 1996.

	N/A	$2,000	$1,700	$1,400	$1,100	$950	$800

Last MSR was $2,999.

GRADING	100% MINT	98% NEAR MINT	95% EXC+	90% EXC	80% VG+	70% VG	60% G

ELECTRIC BASS: SWEETSPOT SERIES

QUANTUM 4 SWEETSPOT (MODEL Q4SS) - offset double cutaway alder body, figured maple top, bolt-on graphite neck with relief-adjustment system, 35 in. scale, 24-fret composite or granadillo fingerboard with white inlay, ABM fixed bridge, 2-per-side tuners, chrome (or black or gold) hardware, EMG-DC pickup, volume/treble/bass controls, active electronics. Available in Amber, Blue, Clear Gloss, Clear Satin, Green, Orange Crush, Purple, and Red Transparent finishes; BlueStone, GrayStone, GreenStone, and RedStone finishes; Black Cherry, Blue, Blue over Red, Green, Pink over Blue, Royal Blue, or Red over Blue Velvet finishes, mfg. 1996-2003.

	$2,150	$1,850	$1,600	$1,350	$1,100	$875	$650

Last MSR was $2,699.

QUANTUM 5 SWEETSPOT (MODEL Q5SS) - similar to the Quantum 4 SweetSpot, except has 5-string configuration, 3/2-per-side headstock, mfg. 1996-2003.

	$2,250	$1,950	$1,750	$1,450	$1,200	$950	$750

Last MSR was $2,899.

Quantum Wide 5 SweetSpot (Model QW5SS) - similar to the Quantum 4 SweetSpot, except has 5-string configuration on a 6-string-sized fingerboard/neck, 3/2-per-side headstock, mfg. 1996-2003.

	$2,400	$2,050	$1,850	$1,525	$1,250	$1,000	$800

Last MSR was $3,099.

QUANTUM 6 SWEETSPOT (MODEL Q6SS) - similar to the Quantum 4 SweetSpot, except has 6-string configuration, 3-per-side headstock, mfg. 1996-2003.

	$2,450	$2,100	$1,900	$1,550	$1,250	$1,000	$800

Last MSR was $3,099.

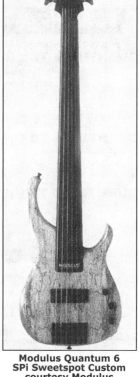

QUANTUM 4 SWEETSPOT TURBO (MODEL Q4SST) - similar to the Quantum 4 SweetSpot, except has extra EMG-DC pickup, master volume/balance/treble/bass controls, available in Amber, Blue, Green, Orange Crush, Purple, Red, and Turquoise Transparent finishes; Black Cherry, Blue, Blue over Red, Green, Pink over Blue, Royal Blue, or Red over Blue Velvet finishes, mfg. 1996 only.

N/A	$1,750	$1,450	$1,175	$975	$825	$675

Last MSR was $2,599.

QUANTUM 5 SWEETSPOT TURBO (MODEL Q5SST) - similar to the Quantum 4 SweetSpot Turbo, except has 5-string configuration, 3/2-per-side headstock, mfg. 1996 only.

N/A	$1,850	$1,550	$1,300	$1,100	$900	$700

Last MSR was $2,799.

Quantum Wide 5 SweetSpot Turbo (Model QW5SST) - similar to the Quantum 4 SweetSpot Turbo, except has 5-string configuration on a 6-string-sized fingerboard/neck, 3/2-per-side headstock, mfg. 1996 only.

N/A	$2,000	$1,700	$1,400	$1,150	$950	$800

Last MSR was $2,999.

Modulus Quantum 6 SPi Sweetspot Custom courtesy Modulus

QUANTUM 6 SWEETSPOT TURBO (MODEL Q5SST) - similar to the Quantum 4 SweetSpot Turbo, except has 6-string configuration, 3-per-side headstock, mfg. 1996 only.

N/A	$2,000	$1,700	$1,400	$1,150	$950	$750

Last MSR was $2,999.

QUANTUM 4 SPi SWEETSPOT CUSTOM (MODEL BSQ4XL-SS-C) - similar to the Quantum 4 SweetSpot, except has phenolic fingerboard, Modulus/Gotoh fixed bridge, gold or black hardware, volume/treble/bass controls, active electronic, mfg. 1994-96.

N/A	$1,250	$1,050	$900	$775	$650	$525

Last MSR was $2,095.

QUANTUM 5 SPi SWEETSPOT CUSTOM (MODEL BSQ5XL-SS-C) - similar to Quantum 4 SPi Sweet Spot Custom, except has 5-string configuration, Schaller bridge, 3/2-per-side tuners, mfg. 1994-96.

N/A	$1,350	$1,150	$1,000	$850	$700	$550

Last MSR was $2,299.

QUANTUM 6 SPi SWEETSPOT CUSTOM (MODEL BSQ6XL-SS-C) - similar to Quantum 4 SPi Sweet Spot Custom, except has 6-string configuration, APM bridge, 3-per-side tuners, mfg. 1994-96.

N/A	$1,750	$1,450	$1,175	$975	$825	$675

Last MSR was $2,599.

QUANTUM 4 SPi SWEETSPOT STANDARD (MODEL BSQ4XL-SS) - similar to the Quantum 4 SPi Sweet Spot Custom, except has alder/poplar body (no figured maple top), chrome hardware, mfg. 1994-95.

N/A	$1,050	$900	$775	$650	$550	$450

Last MSR was $1,799.

QUANTUM 5 SPi SWEETSPOT STANDARD (MODEL BSQ5XL-SS) - similar to Quantum 4 SPi Sweet Spot Standard, except has 5-string configuration, Schaller bridge, 3/2-per-side tuners, mfg. 1994-95.

N/A	$1,200	$1,050	$900	$775	$650	$525

Last MSR was $1,999.

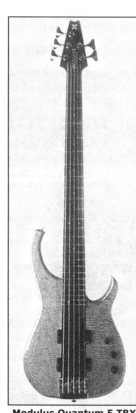

QUANTUM 6 SPi SWEETSPOT STANDARD (MODEL BSQ6XL-SS) - similar to Quantum 4 SPi Sweet Spot Standard, except has 6-string configuration, APM bridge, 3-per-side tuners, mfg. 1994-96.

N/A	$1,350	$1,150	$900	$775	$650	$525

Last MSR was $2,299.

Modulus Quantum 5 TBX courtesy Modulus

GRADING	100% MINT	98% NEAR MINT	95% EXC+	90% EXC	80% VG+	70% VG	60% G

ELECTRIC BASS: QUANTUM THRU-BODY SERIES

Beginning in 1996, neck-through bass and guitar models were available on a custom order basis only.

QUANTUM 4 TBX (MODEL BIQ4XL) - offset double cutaway alder body, figured maple top, through-body graphite neck, 35 in. scale, 24-fret phenolic fingerboard with white dot inlay, fixed Modulus/Gotoh bridge, graphite/epoxy nut, 2-per-side Modulus/Gotoh tuners, gold hardware, 2 EMG soapbar humbuckers, 2 volume/treble/bass controls, active EMG-BQCS EQ, disc. 1996.

N/A	$2,700	$2,400	$2,100	$1,800	$1,500	$1,200

Last MSR was $3,699.

Some models may have concentric ("stacked") treble/bass controls.

QUANTUM 5 TBX (MODEL BIQ5XL) - similar to 4 TBX, except has 5-string configuration, ABM or Schaller bridge, 3/2-per-side tuners, disc. 1996.

N/A	$3,000	$2,650	$2,300	$2,000	$1,700	$1,400

Last MSR was $4,099.

QUANTUM 6 TBX (MODEL BIQ6XL) - similar to 4 TBX, except has 6-string configuration, ABM or Kahler bridge, 3-per-side tuners, mfg. 1992-96.

N/A	$3,400	$3,000	$2,600	$2,300	$2,000	$1,700

Last MSR was $4,499.

MOLL CUSTOM INSTRUMENTS

Instruments currently built in Springfield, MO, since 1996.

Luthier Bill Moll offers premium custom crafted archtop guitars, carved archtop bass guitars, and solid body electric bass models, as well as repair and restoration services for stringed instruments. Much of Moll's training since 1975 has been in the specific application of acoustical physics, so instruments are built to perform acoustically before electronics are considered. Denise Moll has also been studying lutherie with her husband since 1997, and contributes greatly to the output of the shop. They are one of the few married couples building as a team. Moll still builds custom solid body basses in limited numbers. Moll also offers a custom shop where just about anything can be made. All you have to do is ask. For more information refer to their website (see Trademark Index).

ELECTRIC ARCHTOP

Moll Custom Instruments offer four archtop models in either a 16 in., 17 in., or 18 in. body width (a 19 in. body width is an option for an additional $500). The **Classic** (list $3,500) has a solid carved X-braced spruce top, solid carved maple back/sides/neck, ebony fingerboard, solid brass tailpiece, and Gotoh tuners. The **Classic Custom** is based off of D'Aquisto's model and lists for $6,500. The **Express** (list $6,000) is a modern design archtop with teardrop-shaped soundholes. The D´Angelico-derived **New Yorker** has the fancy inlays and stairstep bridge and pickguard that most jazz players lust after (list $7,500). A **John Pizzarelli** model is available for $4,000. The **Working Man's Hero** is built on a CNC machine and lists for $2,750.

Moll custom basses feature laminated figured maple and American walnut in their through-body neck designs, and use active Seymour Duncan Basslines soapbar pickups. Prices run from $2,800 (4-string), to $3,000 (5-string), and up to $3,250 (6-string) base list prices.

MONROE

Instruments previously built near El Paso, TX circa late 1980s-1999.

Luthier Robert Monroe Turner was a former apprentice to *Guitar Player* columnist and repairer Dan Erlewine. Turner founded Monroe Guitars in 1988 and debuted his line of high quality, solid body electrics at the 1989 NAMM Show (source: Tom Wheeler, *American Guitars*).

MONTCLAIR

See chapter on House brands.

This trademark has been identified as a House Brand of Montgomery Wards (source: Willie G. Moseley, *Stellas & Stratocasters*).

MONTELEONE, JOHN

Instruments currently built in Islip, NY, since 1976.

Luthier John Monteleone has been building guitars and mandolins since the 1970s. A contemporary of James D´Aquisto, Monteleone performed repair and restoration work for a number of years while formulating his own archtop designs. Monteleone's archtop guitars feature such unique ideas as a flush-set truss rod cover, recessed tuning machine retainers, and a convex radius headstock. For further information, please contact luthier John Monteleone directly (see Trademark Index).

ELECTRIC ARCHTOP

Models include archtop designs. The **Radio City** features a single rounded cutaway. The **Radio Flyer** is a single rounded cutaway with cat's-eye soundholes. The **Eclipse** is a single rounded cutaway with an oval soundhole. The **Grand Artist** features a scroll type bass bout with f-holes. All guitars are available in 16 in., 17 in., or 18 in. body widths. Many other options are also available. Prices start at $10,000. Used prices for instruments in excellent condition can range from $15,000 - $20,000 and above.

MONZA

Instruments previously built in Holland, unknown production date.

While Monza guitars sports a Made in Holland sticker on the back of the headstock, the electronics and tailpiece/bridge on one identified model are clearly Italian (possibly 1960s?). The instrument features 20-fret neck, six on a side headstock and tuners, two pickups, a tremolo/bridge unit, 3 switches, 3 volume/tone knobs, and a offset double cutaway with a scroll on the bass horn reminiscent of the 1960s Premier guitars (source: Teisco Del Rey, *Guitar Player*, February 1984).

M

GRADING	100% MINT	98% NEAR MINT	95% EXC+	90% EXC	80% VG+	70% VG	60% G

MOON GUITARS

Instruments currently built in Japan since 1979. Previously distributed in the U.S. market by the Luthiers Access Group of Chicago, IL.

The Moon corporation is known primarily for their modern take on the traditional jazz-style bass originated by Leo Fender. The last few years has seen Moon develop new modern design basses to compliment these jazz basses. The Climb series, and GLB line offer new choices from Japan's premier bass builder. For more information contact Moon directly (see Trademark Index).

MOON GUITARS LTD.

Instruments currently built in Glascow, Scotland, since 1979.

Moon Guitars was established by Jimmy Moon in 1979, and the Moon Guitars name has become synonymous with custom built instruments of very high quality as they are producing modern instruments with strong traditional roots. Originally, Moon Guitars produced acoustic guitars, mandolins, mandolas, and dulcimers. Moon moved into the electric market during the eighties, producing for an impressive client list of famous names. A shift in the market pre-emptied a return to building acoustics and mandolins (while continuing with custom built electrics, basses, and electric mandolins).

Moon Guitars' latest successful development is the Moon electro acoustic mandolin, which comes in various body shapes with a piezo-based pickup system. For further information, please contact Moon Guitars Ltd. directly (see Trademark Index).

MOONSTONE

Instruments currently built in Eureka, CA (guitar production has been in different locations in CA since 1972). Distributed directly by Moonstone Guitars of Eureka, CA.

Moll 4-String Bass courtesy Moll

In 1972, self-taught luthier Steve Helgeson began building acoustic instruments in an old shingle mill located in Moonstone Heights, California. By 1974, Helgeson moved to Arcata, California, and began producing electric Earth Axe guitars. By 1976, Helgeson had moved to a larger shop and increased his model line and production. Helgeson hit boom sales in the early 1980s, but tapered off production after the market shifted in 1985. Rather than shift with the trends, Helgeson preferred to maintain his own designs. In 1988, a major disaster in the form of a deliberately set fire damaged some of his machinery. Steve's highly figured wood supply survived only a minor scorching. Helgeson moved and reopened his workshop in 1990 at the current location in Eureka, California, where he now offers a wide range of acoustic and electric guitars and basses. In addition to the standard models,

All Moonstone instruments are constructed from highly figured woods. Where burl wood was not used in the construction, the wood used is highly figured. Almost all necks are reinforced with veneers, or stringers. Bass necks are reinforced with through-body graphite stringers. Moonstone has always utilized exotic woods such as African purpleheart, paduak, wenge, koa, mahogany, Sitka and Engelmann spruce, myrtlewood, and black burl walnut.

Some older models can also be found with necks entirely made of graphite composite with phenolic fingerboards. Helgeson commissioned Modulus Graphite to produce these necks, and used them on models like the Eclipse Standard, Deluxe Basses, Vulcan Standard and Deluxe guitars, the M-80, D-81 Eagle 6- and 12-string models, as well as the D-81 Standard and the Moondolin (mandolin). In 1981, most wood necks were reinforced with a Graphite Aluminum Honeycomb Composite (G.A.H.C.) beam with stainless steel adjustment rod. Moonstone also offers custom guitars designed in accordance with the customer's request. All current prices include a hardshell case. For further information regarding current acoustic guitar models, please refer to the *Blue Book of Acoustic Guitars*.

ELECTRIC: EAGLE SERIES

EAGLE - double cutaway hand carved burl maple body, 5-piece maple/paduak neck, 24-fret paduak bound ebony fingerboard with pearl bird inlay, LQBA bridge/tailpiece, walnut burl peghead veneer with pearl halfmoon/logo inlay, 3-per-side tuners, gold hardware, 2 humbucker Bartolini pickups, 2 volume/1 tone controls, 3-position switch, push/pull preamp switch in volume control, active electronics, available in Natural finish, mfg. 1980-84.

N/A	$3,500	$2,800	$2,300	$1,900	$1,500	$1,100

Last MSR was $2,780.

A licensed falconer, Helgeson's inspiration for this model came from the training and hunting with his raptors. Only 11 of these guitars were built in this series.

EAGLE LIMITED EDITION - double cutaway hand carved burl maple body, (127 individual hand carved feathers) 5-piece maple/paduak neck, 24-fret bound ebony fingerboard with Moonstone original pearl bird inlay, bridge/tailpiece, walnut burl peghead veneer with pearl halfmoon/logo inlay, 3-per-side tuners, gold hardware, 2 humbucker Bartolini pickups, 2 volume/2 tone controls, 3-position switch, active electronics, available in Natural finish, disc.

N/A	N/A	N/A	N/A	N/A	N/A	N/A

Last MSR was $7,480.

ELECTRIC: ECLIPSE SERIES

ECLIPSE DELUXE - offset double cutaway paduak core body, bookmatch burl top/back, through-body 2-piece maple neck, 24-fret bound ebony fingerboard with pearl diamond/star inlay, LQBA bridge/tailpiece, burl walnut peghead veneer with pearl halfmoon/logo inlay, 3-per-side tuners, gold hardware, 2 humbucker covered Bartolini pickups, 2 volume/2 tone controls, 3-position/phase switches, available in Natural finish, mfg. 1979-1983.

N/A	$1,800	$1,500	$1,200	$1,000	$850	$700

Last MSR was $1,435.

Moonstone Eagle courtesy Steve Helgeson

GRADING	100% MINT	98% NEAR MINT	95% EXC+	90% EXC	80% VG+	70% VG	60% G

ECLIPSE STANDARD - offset double cutaway mahogany core body, bookmatch burl top/back, through-body 2-piece maple neck, 24-fret rosewood fingerboard with pearl dot inlay, LQBA bridge/tailpiece, burl wood peghead veneer with screened logo, 3-per-side tuners, gold hardware, 2 humbucker covered Bartolini pickups, 2 volume/tone controls, 3-position/phase switches, available in Natural finish, mfg. 1979-1983.

| | N/A | $1,600 | $1,350 | $1,100 | $900 | $750 | $600 |

Last MSR was $1,215.

Eclipse Standard 12 - similar to Standard except has 12 strings, Leo Quan tunable bridge, 6-per-side tuners, mfg. 1979-1983.

| | N/A | $1,650 | $1,400 | $1,150 | $950 | $800 | $650 |

Last MSR was $1,325.

Eclipse Standard Doubleneck - similar to the Standard and the Standard 12 (two necks sharing the same body) with each neck having separate electronics and a 3-position neck selector, mfg. 1979-1983.

| | N/A | $2,500 | $2,000 | $1,750 | $1,500 | $1,250 | $950 |

Last MSR was $2,055.

ELECTRIC: EXPLODER & FLAMING V SERIES

EXPLODER - radical offset hourglass burl wood body, through-body 2-piece maple neck, 24-fret rosewood fingerboard with pearl dot inlay, LQBA bridge/tailpiece, figured wood peghead veneer with screened logo, 3-per-side tuners, gold hardware, 2 humbucker covered Bartolini pickups, 2 volume/1 tone controls, 3-position/phase switches, available in Natural finish, mfg. 1980-83.

| | N/A | $1,600 | $1,350 | $1,100 | $900 | $750 | $600 |

Last MSR was $965.

This model had DiMarzio pickups as an option.

FLAMING V - V-style burl wood body, through-body 2-piece maple neck, 24-fret rosewood fingerboard with pearl dot inlay, LQBA bridge/tailpiece, figured wood peghead veneer with screened logo, 3-per-side tuners, gold hardware, 2 humbucker covered Bartolini pickups, 2 volume/1 tone controls, 3-position/phase switches, available in Natural finish, mfg. 1980-84.

| | N/A | $1,600 | $1,350 | $1,100 | $900 | $750 | $600 |

Last MSR was $965.

DiMarzio pickups were an option.

ELECTRIC: M80 & PULSAR SERIES

M-80 - double cutaway semi-hollowbody, carved figured maple top/back/sides, f-holes, raised multi layer black pickguard, bound body, 2-piece figured maple neck, 24-fret bound ebony fingerboard with abalone snowflake inlay, LQBA bridge/tailpiece, figured wood peghead veneer with abalone half-moon/logo inlay, 3-per-side tuners, gold hardware, 2 covered Bartolini humbucker pickups, 2 volume/tone controls, 3-position/phase switches, available in Natural finish, mfg. 1980-84.

| | N/A | $1,800 | $1,600 | $1,400 | $1,200 | $950 | $750 |

Last MSR was $1,690.

Burl walnut pickguard, tunable bridge/tailpiece, PAF pickups, Orange-Honey finish and Tobacco Burst finish were an option.

M-80 REISSUE - double cutaway semi-hollow (with sustain block through-body) or hollow-body (bracing carved in) body, carved figured maple top/back/sides, 25.5 in. scale, f-holes, 2-piece quarterswan hard maple neck, 22-fret bound ebony fingerboard with abalone starflake inlay, tailpiece, ebony peghead veneer with abalone halfmoon/mother-of-pearl logo inlay, 3-per-side Schaller tuners, gold hardware, 2 Seymour Duncan pickups, 2 volume/2 tone controls, 3-position/phase switches, available in Natural finish, current mfg.

MSR   **$4,200**

Add $500 for Sunburst finish.

This model is optional with cat's-eye f-holes, pickguard, tune-o-matic bridge/stop tailpiece, pickup selection, and Sunburst or Color toner finishes.

PULSAR - mini radical offset hourglass alder body, black pickguard, maple neck, 24-fret rosewood fingerboard with pearl dot inlay, LQBA bridge/tailpiece, blackface peghead with screened logo, 3-per-side tuners, gold hardware, DiMarzio (or Lawrence) pickup, volume/tone control, available in Black finish, mfg. 1980-83.

| | N/A | $1,450 | $1,250 | $1,100 | $950 | $800 | $650 |

Last MSR was $810.

PULSAR STANDARD REISSUE - similar to Pulsar, available in Natural or Sunburst finish, mfg 2000 only.

Last MSR was $2,530.

Add $275 for Sunburst finish.

ELECTRIC: VULCAN & Z-80 SERIES

VULCAN DELUXE - double cutaway carved burl maple body, 5-piece maple/padauk neck, 24-fret bound ebony fingerboard with pearl diamond/star inlay, LQBA bridge/tailpiece, burl walnut peghead veneer with pearl halfmoon/logo inlay, 3-per-side tuners, gold hardware, 2 humbucker covered Bartolini pickups, master volume/2 volume/2 tone controls, 5 position tone control, 3-position/boost switches, active electronics, available in Natural finish, mfg. 1977-1984.

| | N/A | $2,000 | $1,700 | $1,400 | $1,200 | $1,000 | $800 |

Last MSR was $1,680.

VULCAN STANDARD - double cutaway mahogany body, bound carved bookmatch burl maple top, 2-piece maple neck, 24-fret rosewood fingerboard with pearl dot inlay, LQBA bridge/tailpiece, burl maple peghead veneer with screened logo, 3-per-side tuners, gold hardware, 2 humbucker covered Bartolini pickups, 2 volume/tone controls, 3-position/phase switches, available in Natural finish, mfg. 1977-1984.

| | N/A | $1,800 | $1,500 | $1,250 | $1,050 | $850 | $700 |

Last MSR was $1,215.

GRADING	100% MINT	98% NEAR MINT	95% EXC+	90% EXC	80% VG+	70% VG	60% G

VULCAN STANDARD REISSUE - dual cutaway mahogany body, carved flamed or quilted maple top, set-in mahogany neck, 22-fret bound fingerboard with pearl dot inlay, stop-ABR tailpiece, 3-per-side Grover tuners, gold hardware, 2 Seymour Duncan humbucker pickups, 2 volume/2 tone controls, 3-position switch, available in Natural finish, current mfg.

MSR   **$3,000**

    Add $400 for Sunburst finish.

This model is optional with a Madagascar rosewood fretboard, PAF pickups, nickel hardware, and Cherry Mahogany or Honey Sunburst finishes.

Z-80 REISSUE - dual cutaway semi-hollow (parabolic baffles under bridge) body, Englemann spruce floating top, 2 7/8 in. thick rims with Grill soundholes in the cutaways, 25.5 in. scale, 2-piece quarterswan figured hard maple neck, 22-fret bound ebony fingerboard with abalone starflake inlay, trapeze tailpiece/ABR1 tune-o-matic bridge, ebony peghead veneer with abalone halfmoon/mother-of-pearl logo inlay, 3-per-side Schaller tuners, gold hardware, 2 Seymour Duncan humbucker pickups, volume/tone controls, 3-position switch, available in Natural finish, current mfg. (special order only).

MSR   **$6,000**

This reissue is based on the model Helgeson designed in the mid 1980s (only two of the original series were built).

**Moonstome Vulcan Deluxe
courtesy Fly by Night**

ELECTRIC BASS

Moonstone offers special order custom designed models whose price must be quoted individually upon request.

M-80 BASS - offset double cutaway semi-hollow body, four-string configuration, carved flame maple top, mahogany body wings, 35 in. scale, 2 f-holes, through-body 5-piece maple/purpleheart neck, 22-fret bound ebony fingerboard with abalone large diamond inlay, Alembic tailpiece, 3/2-per-side Schaller tuners, gold hardware, 2 Alembic pickups, 2 volume/2 tone controls, 3-position switch, Alembic electronics, available in Natural finish, disc. 2003.

	N/A	N/A	N/A	N/A	N/A	N/A	N/A
					Last MSR was $3,520.		

    Add $275 for 5-string model.

ECLIPSE DELUXE - offset double cutaway padauk core body, bookmatch burl top/back, through-body 2-piece maple neck, 24-fret bound ebony fingerboard 24-fret bound ebony fingerboard with pearl diamond/star inlay, fixed bridge, burl walnut peghead veneer with pearl halfmoon/logo inlay, 2-per-side tuners, gold hardware, 2 J-style Bartolini pickups, 2 volume/tone controls, 3-position/phase switches, available in Natural finish, mfg. 1980-84.

	N/A	$1,500	$1,250	$1,050	$900	$750	$600
					Last MSR was $1,495.		

ECLIPSE STANDARD - offset double cutaway mahogany core body, bookmatch burl top/back, through-body 3-piece maple/padauk neck with graphite stringers, 24-fret rosewood fingerboard with pearl dot inlay, fixed bridge, burl maple peghead veneer with screened logo, 2-per-side tuners, gold hardware, 2 J-style Bartolini pickups, 2 volume/tone controls, phase switch, available in Natural finish, mfg. 1980-84.

	N/A	$1,350	$1,150	$950	$750	$650	$550
					Last MSR was $1,295.		

EXPLODER - radical offset hour glass burl wood body, through-body 3-piece maple/padauk neck with graphite stringers, 24-fret rosewood fingerboard with pearl dot inlay, fixed bridge, burl maple peghead veneer with screened logo, 2-per-side tuners, gold hardware, 2 J-style Bartolini pickups, 2 volume/1 tone controls, 3-position/phase switches, available in Natural finish, mfg. 1980-83.

	N/A	$1,300	$1,100	$950	$800	$650	$550
					Last MSR was $1,265.		

FLAMING V - V-style burl wood body, through-body 3-piece maple/padauk neck with graphite stringers, 24-fret rosewood fingerboard with pearl dot inlay, fixed bridge, maple burl peghead veneer with screened logo, 2-per-side tuners, gold hardware, 2 J-style Bartolini pickups, 2 volume/1 tone controls, 3-position/phase switches, available in Natural finish, mfg. 1981.

	N/A	$1,400	$1,200	$1,000	$850	$700	$550
					Last MSR was $1,265.		

NEPTUNE - carved figured maple top, swamp ash wings, 5-piece hard rock maple, purple heart stringers, boundy ebony fretboard, graphite reinforced adj. truss rod, ebony head veneer inlaid with mother-of-pearl and abalone crescent, Schaller tuners, Bartollini active pickups and tone circuit, gold ABM bridge, mfg. 2000-present.

MSR   **$3,700**

    Add $675 for Burst and Thunderbird inlays.

Neptune 5-String - similar to the Neptune, except in five-string configuration, mfg. 2000-present.

MSR   **$4,000**

    Add $675 for Burst and Thunderbird inlays.

**Moonstone Vulcan Reissue
courtesy Steve Helgeson**

M

VULCAN - double cutaway burl maple body, 3-piece maple/padauk neck, 24-fret bound ebony fingerboard with pearl diamond/star inlay, fixed bridge, burl walnut peghead veneer with pearl halfmoon/logo inlay, 2-per-side tuners, gold hardware, humbucker covered Bartolini "P" pickup, 2 volume/tone controls, active tone circuit, available in Natural finish, mfg. 1982-84.

	N/A	$1,250	$1,100	$950	$800	$675	$550

Last MSR was $1,055.

Vulcan II - similar to Vulcan, except has carved top, mfg. 1982-84.

	N/A	$1,300	$1,150	$1,000	$850	$700	$550

Last MSR was $1,155.

MORALES

Instruments previously produced in Japan by Zen-On circa late 1960s.

The Morales product line offered thinline hollowbody acoustic/electric and hollowbody electric guitars, as well as solid body electric guitars, basses, and mandolins. This brand may not have been imported into the U.S. market (source: Michael Wright, *Vintage Guitar Magazine*).

MORCH GUITARS

Instruments currently built in Orsted, Denmark since 1970.

In 1970 Johnny Morch started to manufacture electric guitars in cooperation with his father, Arne Morch. The first standard models were made in great numbers in a sort of handmade "batch" production: a carpenter made the body, a painter did the lacquer-work, an engraver cut out the pickguard, and the rest was made by Morch himself (assembling, adjustment, and final delivery to the music shops for retail).

In the middle of 1970 Morch started to cooperate with the guitarist Thomas Puggard-Muller, who designed Morch´s "curl"-models which were later published in the Danish Design Index and thus shown all over the world. For years Thomas was involved with the firm, and his close contact with the professional world of music has sold Morch instruments to a great many well-known musicians at home as well as abroad.

Since then the firm has expanded in the opposite way of most other companies. Now the entire production takes place exclusively in Morch´s workshop, and there is a close contact between the musician and the craftsman. All instruments are literally handmade and adjusted exactly to the needs of the individual musician, (Company history courtesy Johnny Morch, Morch Guitars).

Importation of Morch instruments to Britain began in 1976. These models may be found in greater abundance in Europe than in the U.S. Currently, the company is offering 2 guitar models, and 4-, 5-, and 6-string bass models. Prices range from □2,800 up to □4,800.

MORELLI, C.M.

Instruments previously built in Port Chester, NY.

C. M. Morelli offered custom models that featured various body and neck materials, hardware, pickup, and finish options. Retail prices started at $1,899, and Morelli built custom body and headstock shapes, 4-, 6-, 8-, 10-, 12-string and double-neck models. C.M. Morelli also offered custom imprinted picks and accessories.

MORGAINE

Instruments currently built in Boppard, Germany, since 1994. Previously distributed in the U.S.A. by Salwender International.

Morgaine guitars are entirely handmade by experienced Master Luthier Jorg Tandler. Necks are carved the traditional way with a draw knife, body contours carefully shaped, and the arched tops are chiseled similar to the way violin makers carve violin tops. Morgaine guitars feature hand selected woods, Lindy Fralin pickups, Wilkinson VSV tremolos, Schaller or Gotoh tuners, and nitrocellulose lacquer finishes.

ELECTRIC

Morgaine standard finishes include 2-Tone, Cherry, or Tobacco Sunburst finishes. Custom colors include Fiesta Red, Surf Green, and Vintage White.

AUSTIN - Honduran mahogany body/neck, 22-fret Indian rosewood fingerboard with pearl dot inlay, vintage bone nut, tune-o-matic bridge, custom wound Lindy Fralin bridge pickup, volume/tone controls, mfg. 1997-present.

MSR $2,599

BEAUTY - Honduran mahogany body/neck, American soft maple top, bound Brazilian rosewood fingerboard, 2 custom wound Lindy Fralin humbucker pickups, volume/tone controls, available in Faded Cherry Sunburst and Tobacco Sunburst finishes, mfg. 1995-present.

MSR $5,059

STRAT ´54 - swamp ash body, hard rock maple neck, 22-fret maple fingerboard, vintage bone nut, Wilkinson VSV tremolo, 3 custom wound Lindy Fralin pickups, volume/tone controls, available in Sunburst and all custom finishes, mfg. 1994-present.

MSR $3,195

STRAT ´57 - similar to Strat ´54, except features alder body, available in Sunburst and all custom finishes, mfg. 1994-present.

MSR $3,195

STRAT ´61 - similar to Strat ´54, except features alder body, 22-fret Brazilian rosewood fingerboard, available in Sunburst and all custom finishes, mfg. 1994-present.

MSR $3,195

MORIDAIRA

See also Morris. Instruments previously produced in Japan.

The Moridaira company is an OEM manufacturer of guitars for other companies, under different trademark names. The company has produced a wide range of entry level to very good quality guitars through the years, depending on the outside company´s specifications. Circa 2003, they were no longer an OEM manufacturer.

MORRIS

Instruments currently produced in Korea. Distributed by the Moridaira company of Tokyo, Japan.

The Moridaira company offers a wide range of acoustic and solidbody electric guitars designed for the beginning student up to the intermediate player under the Morris trademark. They no longer produce solidbody electric guitars. Moridaira has also built guitars (OEM) under other trademarks for a number of other guitar companies.

MORTORO, GARY

Instruments currently built in Miami, FL since 1991.

Luthier Gary Mortoro has been building handcrafted instruments since 1991, under the guidance and direction of Master Luthier and Archtop Builder Robert Benedetto. Gary´s dedication to the crafting of his guitars combined with his playing ability has resulted in an instrument not only of fine detail and craftsmanship, but of exquisite sound and beauty. Some of the players who own a Mortoro are George Benson, Tony Mottola, Jimmy Vivino, Rodney Jones, Gene Bertoncini, Joe Cinderella, and Jimmy Buffet.

Mortoro currently offers six different models that are available in carved or laminate versions. For further information, please contact Gary Mortoro directly (see Trademark Index).

ELECTRIC

Carved models have select tops and backs with matching sides and neck. **Laminate** models feature laminated tops and backs, with necks and sides of flamed maple. All models feature a single cutaway and come in 14 in., 16 in., or 17 in. bodies. Body thickness is up to the player´s choice. Motoro guitars feature ebony for the fingerboard, pickguard, bridge, and tailpiece, Pearl inlay, Schaller tuners, and a floating Mortoro pickup by Kent Armstrong. Models come with a hard shell case and warranty. A number of options; custom colors, custom inlays, 7 string models, etc. are also available.

The **Free Flight** (Volo Libero) has no body (or neck) binding, narrow or traditional pickguard. The Carved Solid Top/Back version retails for $6,500 and the laminated body version retails for $4,500.

The **Songbird** (L´uccello Cantante) black/white body binding, narrow or traditional pickguard with inlay, inlaid tailpiece. The Carved solid top and back version retails for $8,900 and the laminated version retails for $5,500.

The **Starling** (Il Storno) has multiple "bird" soundholes in upper and lower bout, "bird" cutout on side of upper bout, no body/neck binding, 12th fret pearl inlay, narrow pickguard. The Carved solid top and back version retails for $7,800 and the laminated version is $5,300. Mortoro´s non-traditional "bird" soundholes in place of f-holes sets the Starling (Il Storno) into a new area where form and function cross into a nicely voiced, pleasant to the eye archtop design.

The **Free Bird** (Uccello Libero) has 2 "bird" soundholes (instead of 2 f-holes), "bird" cutout on side of upper bout, no body/neck binding, 12th fret pearl inlay, narrow pickguard. The Carved solid top and back version retails for $6,500 and the laminated version is $4,500.

The **Parrot** was designed for Jimmy Buffett. The F-holes are in parrot shape, parrot inlays are used, and the color is Parrot green. Retail price is $6,000 for the laminate and $8,600 for the carved.

The **Song of Verona** is a carved model with the finest master grade European spruce and maple and retails for $12,500.

The **Riva of Garda** is the top of the line model in a 14 in. body with the finest woods and retails for $18,000.

**Morgaine Beauty
courtesy Salwender
International**

MOSCATO

Instruments currently built in Uchaux, France.

Jean-Luc Moscato´s namesake company offers a number of high quality, unique design electric guitars and basses. Moscato, ably assisted by Paul Lairat, Antoine Drescher, and Jean-Philippe Hubin, produces ornate laminated curved body guitars like the Flame, the **Legend**, and the **Devil In You**; and basses like the **Funk Bass** and the Legend Bass. For further information regarding specifications and pricing, please contact Moscato directly (see Trademark Index).

MOSES GRAPHITE MUSICAL INSTRUMENTS

Instruments currently produced in Eugene, OR.

Stephen Mosher has been offering high quality replacement graphite necks for several years. Moses, Inc. lists a large number of graphite necks available for 4-, 5-, and 6-string bass, baritone guitars, and 6-string guitars. For further information regarding pricing, models, and availability, please contact Moses, Inc. directly (see Trademark Index).

ELECTRIC BASS

Moses Graphite is a full service custom shop, and offers additional luthier supplies. The **Starhwak** series and the **Vertical Jump** series are also available.

M

**Mortoro Parrot
courtesy Mortoro**

MOSRITE

Instruments previously produced in Bakersfield, CA during the 1960s; earlier models built in Los Angeles, CA during the mid- to late 1950s. Distribution in the 1990s was handled by Unified Sound Association, Inc. Production of Mosrite guitars ceased in 1994. There were other factory sites around the U.S. during the 1970s and 1980s: other notable locations include Carson City, NV; Jonas Ridge, NC; and Booneville, AR (previous home of Baldwin-operated Gretsch production during the 1970s).

Luthier/designer Semie Moseley (1935-1992) was born in Durant, Oklahoma. The family moved to Bakersfield, California when Moseley was 9 years old, and Semie left school in the seventh grade to travel with an evangelistic group playing guitar.

Moseley, 18, was hired by Paul Barth to work at Rickenbacker in 1953. While at Rickenbacker, Moseley worked with Roger Rossmeisl. Rossmeisl's "German carve" technique was later featured on Moseley's guitar models as well. Moseley was later fired from Rickenbacker in 1955 for building his own guitar at their facilities. In the later years, Moseley always credited Barth and Rossmeisl (and the Rickenbacker company) for his beginning knowledge in guitar building.

With the help of Reverend Ray Boatright, who cosigned for guitar building tools at Sears, Moseley began building his original designs. The Mosrite trademark is named after Moseley and Boatright ("-rite"). After leaving Rickenbacker, Moseley built custom instruments for various people around southern California, most notably Joe Maphis (of "Town Hall Party" fame). Moseley freelanced some work with Paul Barth's "Barth" guitars, as well as some neck work for Paul Bigsby.

After traveling for several months with another gospel group, Moseley returned to Bakersfield and again set up shop. Moseley built around 20 guitars for Bob Crooks (Standel). When Crooks asked for a Fender-styled guitar model, Moseley flipped a Stratocaster over, traced the rough outline, and built the forerunner to the Ventures model!

After Nokie Edwards (Ventures) borrowed a guitar for a recording session, Stan Wagner (Ventures Manager) called Moseley to propose a business collaboration. Mosrite would produce the instruments, and use the Venture's organization as the main distributor. The heyday of the Mosrite company was the years between 1963 and 1969. When the demand set in, the company went from producing 35 guitars a month to 50 and later 300. The Mosrite facility had 105 employees at one point, and offered several different models in addition to the Ventures model (such as the semi-hollowbody Celebrity series, the Combo, and the Joe Maphis series).

In 1963, investors sold the Dobro trademark to Moseley, who built the first 100 or 150 out of parts left over from the Dobro plant in Gardenia. Later Bakersfield Dobros can be identified by the serial number imprinted on the end of the fingerboard. The Mosrite company did not build the amplifiers which bear the Mosrite trademark; another facility built the Mosrite amplifiers and fuzz pedals, and paid for the rights to use the Mosrite name.

The amplifier line proved to be the undoing of Mosrite. While some of the larger amplifiers are fine, one entry level model featured a poor design and a high failure rate. While covering for returns, the Ventures organization used up their line of credit at their bank, and the bank shut down the organization. In doing so, the Mosrite distribution was shut down as well. Moseley tried a deal with Vox (Thomas Organ) but the company was shut down in 1969. Moseley returned to the Gospel music circuit, and transferred the Dobro name to OMI in a series of negotiations.

Between the mid 1970s and the late 1980s, Moseley continued to find backers and sporadically build guitars. In 1972, Guitar Player magazine reported that "Semie Moseley is now working with Reinhold Plastics, Inc. to produce Mosrite of California guitars." Later that year, Moseley set up a tentative deal with Bud Ross at Kustom (Kustom Amplifiers) in Chanute, Kansas. Moseley was going to build a projected 200 guitars a month at his 1424 P Street location, and Ross' Kustom Electronics was going to be the distributor. This deal fell through, leaving Moseley free to strike up another deal in April of 1974 with Pacific Music Supply Company of Los Angeles, California. Pacific Music Supply Company had recently lost their Guild account, and was looking for another guitar line to distribute. One primary model in 1974 was the solid body Model 350 Stereo. The **Brass Rail** model was developed around 1976/1977. While shopping around his new model with "massive sustain," Moseley met a dealer in Hollywood Music in Los Angeles. This dealer had connections in Japan, and requested that Moseley begin recreating the original-style Ventures models. Moseley set out to build 35 to 50 of these reproductions per month for a number of months. Several years after Moseley recovered from an illness in 1983, he began rebuilding his dealer network with a number of models like the **V-88**, **M-88**, and **Ventures 1960s Reissues** . These models were built at his Jonas Ridge location.

Moseley's final guitar production was located in Booneville, Arkansas. The Unified Sound Association was located in a converted Walmart building, and an estimated 90% to 95% of production was earmarked for the Japanese market.

Moseley passed away in 1992. His two biggest loves were Gospel music, and building quality guitars. Throughout his nearly forty year career, he continued to persevere in his guitar building. Unified Sound Association stayed open through 1994 under the direction of Loretta Moseley, and then later closed its doors as well.

Information courtesy of Andy Moseley and Hal Hammer [1996]; additional information courtesy Willie G. Moseley, *Stellas and Stratocasters*, and Tom Wheeler, *American Guitars*; Mosrite catalogs and file information courtesy John Kinnemeyer, JK Lutherie; model dating estimations courtesy Carlos Juan, Collectables & Vintage '95, Stuttgart, Germany.

MODEL IDENTIFICATION

Mosrite guitars are easily identifiable by the "M" notch in the top of the headstock. Mosrite models produced in the 1960s have a "M" initial in a edged circle, and "Mosrite" (in block letters) "of California" (in smaller script) logo.

Contrary to vintage guitar show information in the current "Age of Fendermania," Mosrite instruments were not available in those (rare) Fender finishes like Candy Apple Red and Lake Placid Blue. Catalog colors were identified as Blue or Red.

Mosrite did offer option colored finishes like Metallic Blue and Metallic Red. Semie's designs offered numerous innovations, most notable being the Vibra-Mute vibrato. This item was designed for the Ventures models and can be used to help identify early Mosrite instruments. The early vibratos (pre-1966) have Vibra-Mute and Mosrite on them, while later vibratos have Mosrite alone on them. More distinction can be made among the earliest instruments with Vibra-Mutes by observing the casting technique used. While the early vibratos were sandcast, later units were die-cast (once funding was available). In 1973 all guitar & basses models used the new humbucker pickups. No official Ventures models of any type, except a few Mark 1's that were exported to Japan, were produced with the Ventures logo after 1967.

During the heyday of Mosrite production in Bakersfield, model designations in the catalog would list a **Mark I** to designate a 6-string model, **Mark XII** to indicate the 12-string version, and **Mark X** to designate the bass model within a series. These Mark designations are a forerunner to – but not the same usage as – the later **1967-1969 Mark** "No Logo" series.

PRODUCTION DATES

Mosrite models in this edition of the *Blue Book of Electric Guitars* feature estimated dates of production for each model. Just as it is easy to take for granted a sunny day in the Summer until it rains, most dealers and collectors take a Mosrite model as "Just a Mosrite" without really double checking the true nature of which model it really is. Of course, the corollary of this way of thinking is to assume that the Mosrite in question is going to end up in the Far East with the rest of them! Is Johnny Ramone the only current American guitar player to use these guitars? Are there no mega-Mosrite collectors? Ventures fans unite!

GRADING	100% MINT	98% NEAR MINT	95% EXC+	90% EXC	80% VG+	70% VG	60% G

The *Blue Book of Electric Guitars* is actively seeking additional input on Mosrite models, specifications, date of production, and any serialization information. This year´s section is the official "Line Drawn in the Sand" for Mosrite fans – assume that this is the bottom, or the foundation to build upon. Any extra information gathered on Mosrite will be updated in future editions of the *Blue Book of Electric Guitars*. For the time being, assume that all Production Dates are either CIRCA and/or ESTIMATED.

For further information regarding Mosrite acoustic and resonator guitar models, please refer to the *Blue Book of Acoustic Guitars*

ELECTRIC: 300 & BRASS RAIL SERIES

300 - single cutaway solid body, maple neck, rosewood fingerboard with double dot inlay, 3-per-side tuners, chrome hardware, one exposed pole piece humbucker pickup, volume/tone controls, available in Natural finish, mfg. 1973-75.

	N/A	$650	$550	$475	$425	$350	$275

350 STEREO - similar to the 300, except features white pickguard, 2 exposed pole piece humbucker pickups, 2 volume/2 tone controls, pickup selector toggle switch, on/off switch, 2 side-mounted jacks, available in Natural Wood finish, mfg. 1973-75.

	N/A	$700	$625	$550	$450	$375	$300

All controls are mounted on the pickguard.

BRASS RAIL STANDARD - offset double cutaway hardwood body, maple neck, 22 brass frets mounted into a brass rail running the length of the rosewood fingerboard, 3-per-side tuners, brass hardware, 2 pickups, volume/tone controls, 3-way toggle selector, available in Natural finish, mfg. 1976-77.

	N/A	$1,400	$1,200	$1,000	$850	$700	$600

BRASS RAIL DELUXE - similar to the Brass Rail, except has active circuitry, available in Natural finish, mfg. 1976-77.

	NA/	$1,700	$1,350	$1,000	$875	$750	$650

It is estimated that only 75 Brass Rail Deluxe models were built.

**Mosrite Celebrity
courtesy The Music Shoppe**

ELECTRIC: CELEBRITY SERIES

Celebrity Series instruments feature a semi-hollow body, and 2 f-holes. The Celebrity Series featured the CE I, CE II deluxe version and the CE III economical version. Vibrato bridges were offered on each model for an additional $30 (retail list).

CELEBRITY I (MARK I, CE I, # 202) - arched top and back, 2.75 in. body depth, semi-hollow double cutaway body, spruce top, maple back/sides, double body binding, 2 bound f-holes, maple neck, 24.5 in. scale, zero fret, 22-fret bound rosewood fingerboard, roller bridge/vibrato tailpiece, 3-per-side deluxe chrome tuners, chrome hardware, 2 black single coil pickups with exposed pole pieces, volume/tone controls, white "apostrophe" plastic controls plate on lower bout, available in Transparent Cherry Red, or Transparent Sunburst finishes, mfg. 1966-69.

	N/A	$900	$800	$700	$600	$500	$400

Last MSR was $448.

In 1968, Cherryburst, Deep Black, Metallic Blue, Metallic Red, and Pearl White finishes were introduced.

Celebrity I 12-String (CE I Mark XII, Model 204) - similar to the Celebrity 1, except has 12-string configuration, 6-per-side tuners, mfg. 1966-69.

	N/A	$900	$800	$700	$600	$500	$400

Last MSR was $485.

This model had the Moseley vibrato as an option.

Celebrity I (1972-1973) - similar to the Celebrity 1 (Model # 202), except features raised black pickguard, volume/tone controls mounted on a rounded "half-moon" plastic controls plate (with 3-way toggle and 1/4 in. jack, available in Red or Sunburst finishes, mfg. 1972-73.

	N/A	$700	$600	$500	$425	$350	$275

Last MSR was $498.

CELEBRITY (MARK I, CE II, # 211) - bound arched top, 1 13/16 in. body width, semi-hollow body, spruce top, maple back/sides, maple neck, 2 bound f-holes, 24.5 in. scale, 22-fret bound rosewood fingerboard, roller bridge, vibrato tailpiece, 3-per-side deluxe chrome tuners, raised white pickguard, chrome hardware, 2 adjustable pickups, volume/tone controls, 3-way selector switch, white "apostrophe" plastic controls plate on lower bout, available in Trans. Cherry Red or Trans. Sunburst finishes, mfg. 1965-69.

	N/A	$1,000	$900	$800	$700	$600	$500

Last MSR was $369.

In 1968, Cherryburst, Deep Black, Metallic Blue, Metallic Red and Pearl White finishes were introduced.

Celebrity 12-String (Mark XII, CE II, # 213) - similar to the Combo, except has 12-string configuration, 6-per-side tuners, adjustable bridge, mfg. 1965-69.

	N/A	$1,000	$900	$800	$700	$600	$500

Last MSR was $419.

This model had the Moseley vibrato as an option.

M

GRADING	100% MINT	98% NEAR MINT	95% EXC+	90% EXC	80% VG+	70% VG	60% G

CELEBRITY (MARK I, CE III, # 220) - similar to the Combo (Mark I) (Model CE II), except features 1.875 in. body depth, maple top, curly maple back/sides, white body purfling, Indian rosewood fretboard, 2 black pickups, adjustable bridge, and 3-per-side enclosed tuners with white buttons, available in Trans. Cherry Red or Trans. Sunburst finishes, mfg. 1965-69.

	N/A	$850	$750	$650	$550	$450	$350

Last MSR was $279.

In 1968, Cherryburst, Deep Black, Metallic Blue, Metallic Red, and Pearl White finishes were introduced. This model had the Moseley vibrato as an option.

Celebrity (Mark XII, CE III, # 222) - similar to the Combo, except has 12-string configuration, 6-per-side tuners, adjustable bridge, available in Trans. Cherry Red or Trans. Sunburst finishes, mfg. 1965-69.

	N/A	$850	$750	$650	$550	$450	$350

Last MSR was $329.

This model had the Moseley vibrato as an option.

Celebrity III (1972-1973) - similar to the Celebrity III (Model # 220), except features adjustable roller bridge/raised tailpiece, raised white pickguard, volume/tone controls mounted on a rounded "half-moon" plastic controls plate (with 3-way toggle and 1/4 in. jack), available in Red and Sunburst finishes, mfg. 1972-73.

	N/A	$700	$600	$500	$425	$350	$275

Last MSR was $298.

ELECTRIC: COMBO SEMI-ACOUSTIC SERIES

Combo Series models have a semi-acoustic hollow body that is slightly larger than the Mark I solid body.

COMBO I (MARK I, MODEL 300) - hollow body, 1.5 in. body depth, spruce top, maple back/sides, double body binding, hard rock maple neck, one bound f-hole, zero fret, 24.5 in. scale, 22-fret bound Indian rosewood fingerboard with dot inlay, roller bridge/Mosrite vibrato tailpiece, 3-per-side Kluson deluxe chrome tuners, white pickguard, chrome hardware, 2 adjustable pickups, volume/tone controls, 3-way selector switch, available in Trans. Cherry Red or Trans. Sunburst finishes, mfg. 1966-69.

	N/A	$1,400	$1,200	$1,000	$850	$700	$550

Last MSR was $398.

In 1968, Cherryburst, Deep Black, Metallic Blue, Metallic Red, and Pearl White finishes were introduced.

Combo 1 12-String (Mark XII, Model 302) - similar to the Combo, except has 12-string configuration, 6-per-side tuners, adjustable bridge, available in Trans. Cherry Red or Trans. Sunburst finishes, mfg. 1965-69.

	N/A	$1,250	$1,050	$900	$750	$600	$450

Last MSR was $448.

This model had the Moseley vibrato as an option.

ELECTRIC: GOSPEL SERIES

In the early 1990s, Moseley offered three models in the **Gospel Victory** series. The **Gospel Victory I** and **Gospel Victory II** had semi-hollowbodies, similar to the original Gospel model. The **Gospel Victory III** model was a solid body version. All three models were briefly built between 1990 to 1992.

GOSPEL (MARK I, MODEL 600) - bound arched top, arched back, 2.75 in. body width, semi-hollowbody, select maple top, maple back/sides, maple neck, 2 bound f-holes, 24.5 in. scale, 22-fret bound rosewood fingerboard, "Mosrite of California/Gospel Guitar" headstock logos, roller bridge/vibrato tailpiece, 3-per-side tuners, raised black pickguard, chrome hardware, 2 black single coil pickups with exposed pole pieces, 2 volume/2 tone controls, 3-way selector switch, black "apostrophe" plastic controls plate on lower bout, available in Natural finish with tinted Golden Brown headstock, mfg. 1967-69.

	N/A	$1,100	$950	$800	$700	$600	$500

Last MSR was $498.

Gospel 12-String (Mark XII, Model 602) - similar to the Gospel, except has 12-string configuration, 6-per-side tuners adjustable bridge, available in Natural finish, mfg. 1967-69.

	N/A	$1,050	$900	$775	$650	$550	$450

Last MSR was $529.

This model had the Moseley vibrato as an option.

ELECTRIC: JOE MAPHIS SERIES

Joe Maphis Model instruments were designed in conjunction with guitarist Joe Maphis. These semi-hollow models (the walnut back is carved out, and then glued to a spruce top) have controls mounted on the pickguard.

JOE MAPHIS (MODEL MARK I, # 501) - slightly offset double semi-hollow body, 1.5 in. body depth, bound spruce top, walnut back, hard rock maple neck, 24.5 in. scale, 22-fret celluloid bound rosewood fingerboard, laminated black (or white) shell pickguard, deluxe adjustable roller bridge/vibrato tailpiece, 3-per-side tuners, chrome hardware, 2 adjustable pickups, volume/tone controls, available in Natural and Transparent Sunburst finishes, mfg. 1965-69.

	N/A	$1,400	$1,200	$1,000	$850	$700	$550

Last MSR was $498.

Joe Maphis 12-String (Model Mark XII, # 503) - similar to the Joe Maphis, except has 12-string configuration, 6-per-side tuners, available in Natural finish, mfg. 1965-69.

	N/A	$1,500	$1,300	$1,000	$850	$725	$600

Last MSR was $589.

In 1967, Blue and Sunburst finishes were introduced.

GRADING	100% MINT	98% NEAR MINT	95% EXC+	90% EXC	80% VG+	70% VG	60% G

JOE MAPHIS DOUBLENECK (MODEL MARK XVIII) - similar to the Joe Maphis, except has 2 necks in a 12-string/6-string configuration, 6-per-side tuners/adjustable bridge (12-string neck), 3-per-side tuners/ Moseley vibrato (6-string neck) 1.25 in. body depth, available in Natural or Trans. Sunburst finishes, mfg. 1965-69.

	N/A	$2,800	$2,500	$2,200	$1,900	$1,600	$1,300

Last MSR was $689.

This model was optional with a 4-string Bass neck. This model was optional with Metallic Blue and Metallic Pearl White finishes (1960s retail list was an additional $30).

Joe Maphis Doubleneck (Model VII) Reissue - similar to the Joe Maphis Doubleneck (Model Mark XVIII), available in Black, Sunburst, or White finishes, mfg. 1990, 1992-94.

	N/A	N/A	N/A	N/A	N/A	N/A	N/A

Last MSR was $3,000.

Model has not traded sufficiently to quote pricing.

Joe Maphis JM 65 (1966-1967) - similar to the Joe Maphis, except has 2 necks in a mandolin/6-string configuration, 2-per-side tuners (mandolin neck), 3-per-side tuners (6-string neck), available in Black or Sunburst finishes, mfg. 1966-67.

	N/A	$1,500	$1,200	$1,000	$800	$650	$500

ELECTRIC: 1988 & RAMONES SERIES

MOSRITE 1988 GUITAR (M-88) - offset double cutaway basswood body, no German carve body ridge, 3-piece laminated maple neck, zero fret, 22-fret laminated curly maple/rosewood fingerboard, "Mosrite 1988" logo on headstock, vibrato or fixed bridge, 3-per-side tuners, chrome hardware, fixed bridge, 2 creme-colored Alnico single coil pickups, volume/tone controls, 3-position switch, side-mounted 1/4 in. jack, available in Banana, Diamondized Ebony Black, Diamondized Money Green, Diamondized Ruby Red, or Sunburst finishes, mfg. circa 1988.

	N/A	$1,200	$1,000	$850	$700	$550	$400

Last MSR was $1,100.

Mosrite 1988 Guitar with Vibrato bridge - similar to the Mosrite 1988, except has a vibrato bridge.

	N/A	$1,400	$1,200	$1,000	$850	$700	$550

Last MSR was $1,260.

The headstock logo on M-88 models reads "Mosrite 1988, Made In U.S.A."

RAMONES MODEL - offset double cutaway basswood or alder body, maple neck, 22-fret rosewood fingerboard with double dot inlay, 3-per-side tuners, natural wood headstock with Mosrite/Ramones logo, tune-o-matic bridge/stop tailpiece, black pickguard, chrome hardware, black covered Mosrite pickup, volume control, topmounted jack, available in Gold finish, mfg. circa 1992.

	N/A	$2,500	$2,200	$1,900	$1,600	$1,300	$1,000

This model was designed in conjunction with long time Mosrite player Johnny Ramone (The Ramones).

ELECTRIC: VENTURES SERIES

In the early 1960s, Semie Moseley entered into an agreement with the Ventures organization to build the Ventures model guitar. Ventures model guitars built between 1959 and 1964 have a **Mosrite of California** logo and "The Ventures Model" on the headstock. After the business agreement with the Ventures faltered, Mosrite produced a **MARK** model (and variants) that were Ventures-style models without the "Ventures" logo or affiliation mentioned.

VENTURES MODEL (1959-1962) - offset double cutaway hardwood body, set-in maple neck, 22-fret bound rosewood fingerboard (sand casted) Vibramute vibrato bridge, chrome hardware, white pickguard, 2 black single coil pickups, volume/tone controls, 3-position switch, available in Sunburst finish, mfg. 1959-1962.

	N/A	N/A	N/A	N/A	N/A	N/A	N/A

Model has not traded sufficiently to quote pricing. It is estimated that only 40 of these guitars were built.

Ventures Model (1963) - similar to the Ventures Model (1959-1963), except features a bound body, side-mounted jack, available in Sunburst or White Pearl finishes, mfg. 1963 only.

1963	N/A	$6,700	$5,900	$5,200	$4,400	$3,600	$2,700

Ventures Model (1964-1965) - similar to the Ventures Model (1959-1963), except features side-mounted jack, (no body binding), available in Red, Sunburst, or White Pearl finishes, mfg. 1964-65.

1964	N/A	$5,000	$4,300	$3,700	$3,200	$2,500	$1,900
1965	N/A	$3,500	$3,200	$2,750	$2,400	$2,000	$1,600

VENTURES (MODEL MARK I, # 102) - offset double cutaway hardwood body, bolt-on maple neck, 24.5 in. scale, 22-fret bound rosewood fingerboard, deluxe bridge/vibrato tailpiece, "Mosrite of California/The Ventures Model" headstock logo, chrome hardware, white pickguard, 2 black single coil pickups, volume/tone controls, 3-position switch, Vibramute bridge, available in Metallic Blue, Metallic Red, or Sunburst finishes, mfg. 1965-67.

	N/A	$3,200	$2,700	$2,200	$1,700	$1,400	$1,100

Last MSR was $438.

Ventures with Moseley tailpiece - similar to the Ventures Mark 1, except has a Moseley tailpiece, mfg. 1965-68.

	N/A	$2,500	$2,100	$1,700	$1,300	$1,100	$900

Last MSR was $398.

Ventures Mark Series models do not have a bound body.

Mosrite Joe Maphis Doubleneck courtesy Willie's American Guitar

M

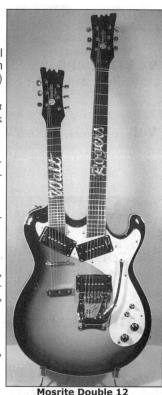

Mosrite Double 12 Electric Hollow courtesy Abalone Vintage

GRADING	100% MINT	98% NEAR MINT	95% EXC+	90% EXC	80% VG+	70% VG	60% G

Ventures (Model Mark V, # 101) - similar to the Ventures (Mark I), except features a short scale fingerboard, smaller body, 24.5 in. scale, adjustable bridge, available in Blue, Red, Sunburst, or White finishes, mfg. 1963-67.

	N/A	$2,000	$1,700	$1,400	$1,100	$900	$700

Last MSR was $299.95.

VENTURES 12-STRING (MODEL MARK XII, # 104) - similar to the Ventures (Mark I), except features 12-string configuration, 6-per-side tuners, Vibramute bridge, available in Metallic Blue, Metallic Red, or Sunburst finishes, mfg. 1965-67.

	N/A	$1,750	$1,500	$1,250	$1,050	$850	$650

Last MSR was $489.

Ventures 12-String with fixed tailpiece - similar to the Ventures 12-string, except has a fixed tailpiece, mfg. 1965-67.

	N/A	$1,250	$1,100	$900	$750	$600	$500

Last MSR was $449.

VENTURES DOUBLENECK (MODEL MARK XVIII, # 105) - similar to the Ventures (Mark I), except has 2 necks in a 12-string/6-string configuration, 6-per-side tuners (12-string neck), 3-per-side tuners (6-string neck), available in Metallic Blue, Metallic Red, or Sunburst finishes, mfg. 1964-67.

	N/A	$2,500	$2,100	$1,700	$1,400	$1,150	$950

Last MSR was $689.

VENTURES II - offset double cutaway hardwood body, bolt-on maple neck, 22-fret rosewood fingerboard, roller bridge/vibrato or Moseley tailpiece, chrome hardware, white pickguard, 2 pickups, volume/tone controls, 3-position switch, available in Red and Sunburst finishes, mfg. 1965-67.

	N/A	$1,300	$1,100	$950	$800	$650	$500

ELECTRIC: VENTURES "NO LOGO" MARK SERIES (MFG. 1967-69)

Between 1967 and 1969, Mosrite continued to produce a Ventures model guitar. However, as the company had no affiliation with the group, the Mark series models have no "The Ventures Model" logo on them.

MARK I - offset double cutaway solid body, bolt-on maple neck, 24.5 in. scale, 22-fret bound Indian rosewood fingerboard, roller bridge/vibrato bridge, chrome hardware, white pickguard, 2 black single coil pickups, volume/tone controls, 3-position switch, available in Cherryburst, Deep Black, Metallic Blue, Metallic Red, Pearl White, Trans. Cherry Red, or Trans. Sunburst finishes, mfg. 1967-69.

	N/A	$1,100	$950	$800	$650	$500	$450

MARK III (1984-1986) - similar to the Mark I, except features 3 single coil pickups, available in Sunburst finish, mfg. 1984-86.

	N/A	$850	$750	$650	$550	$450	$350

MARK V - similar to the Mark I, except features a smaller body, 1.125 in. body depth, roller bridge/vibrato tailpiece, 3-per-side tuners with white buttons, mfg. 1967-69.

	N/A	$1,000	$850	$700	$575	$450	$375

MARK XII 12-STRING - similar to the Mark I, except has 12-string configuration, 6-per-side tuners, adjustable bridge, mfg. 1967-69.

	N/A	$1,050	$950	$800	$650	$500	$450

ELECTRIC: VENTURES "NO LOGO" V SERIES (MFG. 1973-75)

The Mark Series was given humbuckers in place of their usual single coil pickups during production between 1973 to 1975 as the **V-II**. The **V-I Standard**, with two single coil pickups, was offered beginning in 1972.

V-I STANDARD - offset double cutaway solid body, bolt-on maple neck, 22-fret bound rosewood fingerboard with dot inlay, roller bridge/vibrato bridge, 3-per-side tuners, natural finish headstock, white pickguard, chrome hardware, 2 black single coil pickups with exposed pole pieces, 2 volume/1 tone controls, 3-position switch, available in Red and Sunburst finishes, mfg. circa 1972-75.

	N/A	$600	$525	$450	$350	$300	$225

Last MSR was $398.

V-II - offset double cutaway solid body, bolt-on maple neck, 22-fret bound rosewood fingerboard, roller bridge/vibrato bridge, 2-per-side tuners, natural finish headstock, white pickguard, chrome hardware, white pickguard, 2 black humbucker pickups with exposed pole pieces, 2 volume/2 tone controls, 3-position switch, 2 bypass switches, available in Red or Sunburst finishes, mfg. 1973-75.

	N/A	$550	$475	$400	$350	$250	$175

Last MSR was $398.

ELECTRIC: VENTURES REISSUE MODELS

Semie Moseley produced a limited amount of Ventures reissue models in the late 1980s through the early 1990s. It is estimated that a large percentage of these guitars were shipped to, and remain in Japan.

VENTURES EARLY 1960S REISSUE (BOLT-ON) - offset double cutaway basswood or alder body, bolt-on maple neck, 22-fret rosewood fingerboard, vibrato bridge or tailpiece, 3-per-side tuners, chrome hardware, white pickguard, 2 black Alnico single coil pickups, volume/tone controls, 3-position switch, available in Black, Sunburst, or White finishes, mfg. circa 1987-1990.

	N/A	$2,200	$1,900	$1,600	$1,300	$1,000	$800

Last MSR was $2,200.

VENTURES EARLY 1960S REISSUE (VENTURES REISSUE '63) - bound offset double cutaway alder body, glued-in maple neck, bound rosewood fingerboard, (original-style sand cast) Vibramute vibrato bridge, 3-per-side tuners, chrome hardware, white pickguard, 2 black Alnico single coil pickups, volume/tone controls, 3-position switch, side-mounted jack, available in Black, Sunburst, or White finishes, mfg. circa 1987-1990.

	N/A	$2,500	$2,200	$1,900	$1,600	$1,300	$1,000

Last MSR was $2,598.

The announced reserved serial numbers were # 87001 through # 87150. It is unknown at this date how many models were produced.

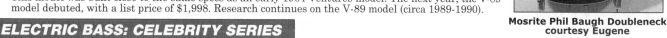

GRADING	100% MINT	98% NEAR MINT	95% EXC+	90% EXC	80% VG+	70% VG	60% G

VENTURES 40TH ANNIVERSARY - similar to the Ventures Reissue '63, except features gold-plated hardware, available in Black, Sunburst, or White finishes, mfg. circa 1992.

	N/A	N/A	N/A	N/A	N/A	N/A	N/A

Lack of secondary marketplace activity precludes accurate pricing on this model. The 40th Anniversary model celebrated the first Semie Moseley guitar built in 1952 (1952-1992). Research continues on the Ventures 40th Anniversary.

NOKIE EDWARDS MODEL - bound offset double cutaway alder body, glued-in maple neck, bound rosewood fingerboard, (original-style sand cast) Vibramute vibrato bridge, "Nokie" logo, 3-per-side tuners, chrome hardware, white pickguard, 2 black Alnico single coil pickups, volume/tone controls, 3-position switch, side-mounted jack, available in Black, Sunburst, or White finishes, mfg. circa 1989-1990.

	N/A	N/A	N/A	N/A	N/A	N/A	N/A

Last MSR was $2,000.

Lack of secondary marketplace activity precludes accurate pricing on this model.

NOKIE EDWARDS 30TH ANNIVERSAY MODEL - similar to the Nokie Edwards Model, with alder or basswood body, "Nokie Anniversary" logo, mfg. circa 1992.

	N/A	N/A	N/A	N/A	N/A	N/A	N/A

Lack of secondary marketplace activity precludes accurate pricing on this model.

VENTURES 1988 (V-88) - offset double cutaway basswood body, 3-piece laminated maple neck, zero fret, 22-fret bound rosewood fingerboard, "Mosrite/The Ventures Model/1988" logo on headstock, vibrato bridge, chrome hardware, white pickguard, 2 black covered Alnico single coil pickups, volume/tone controls, 3-position switch, available in Banana, Diamondized Ebony Black, Diamondized Money Green, Diamondized Ruby Red, and Sunburst finishes, mfg. circa 1988.

	N/A	$2,200	$1,900	$1,600	$1,300	$1,000	$800

Last MSR was $1,460.

This model was built close to the same specs as an early 1964 Ventures model. The next year, the V-89 model debuted, with a list price of $1,998. Research continues on the V-89 model (circa 1989-1990).

**Mosrite Phil Baugh Doubleneck
courtesy Eugene**

ELECTRIC BASS: CELEBRITY SERIES

In 1968, Cherryburst, Deep Black, Metallic Blue, Metallic Red, and Pearl White finishes were introduced.

CELEBRITY I BASS (MARK X, MODEL CE I, # 203) - arched top and back, 2.75 in. body depth, semi-hollow double cutaway body, spruce top, maple back/sides, bound top and back, 2 bound f-holes, maple neck, 30.25 in. scale, 20-fret bound rosewood fingerboard, fixed bridge, chrome bridge cover, 2-per-side tuners, chrome hardware, 2 black pickups with exposed pole pieces, volume/tone controls, 3-way selector switch, white "apostrophe" plastic controls plate on lower bout, available in Trans. Cherry Red or Trans. Sunburst finishes, mfg. 1966-69.

	N/A	$800	$700	$600	$500	$400	$300

Last MSR was $398.

CELEBRITY BASS (MARK X, MODEL CE II, # 212) - semi-hollowbody, spruce top, maple back/sides, double body binding, maple neck, one bound f-hole, bound rosewood fingerboard, 2-per-side tuners, adjustable bridge/metal tailpiece, chrome bridge cover, chrome hardware, 2 adjustable pickups, volume/tone controls, 3-way selector switch, available in Trans. Cherry Red or Trans. Sunburst finishes, mfg. 1965-69.

	N/A	$1,000	$875	$750	$650	$550	$450

Last MSR was $349.

CELEBRITY BASS (MARK X, MODEL CE III, # 221) - similar to the Combo (Mark I) (Model CE II), except features maple top, curly maple back/sides, white body purfling, Indian rosewood fretboard, 2 black pickups, and 2-per-side enclosed tuners with white buttons, available in Trans. Cherry Red or Trans. Sunburst finishes, mfg. 1965-69.

	$850	$750	$650	$550	$450	$350

Last MSR was $279.

ELECTRIC BASS: COMBO, GOSPEL, & JOE MAPHIS SERIES

COMBO 1 BASS (MARK X, 301) - hollow body, spruce top, maple back/sides, double body binding, hard rock maple neck, one bound f-hole, 30.25 in. scale, 20-fret bound rosewood fingerboard, 2-per-side Kluson deluxe chrome tuners, adjustable bridge, chrome bridge cover, chrome hardware, 2 adjustable pickups, volume/tone controls, 3-way selector switch, available in Trans. Cherry Red or Trans. Sunburst finishes, mfg. 1966-69.

	N/A	$1,000	$850	$700	$600	$500	$375

Last MSR was $369.

GOSPEL BASS (MARK X, 601) - bound arched top, arched back, 2.75 in. body width, semi-hollow body, select maple top, maple back/sides, maple neck, 2 bound f-holes, 30.25 in. scale, 20-fret bound rosewood fingerboard, "Mosrite of California/Gospel Guitar" headstock logos, adjustable bridge, 2-per-side tuners, raised black pickguard, chrome hardware, 2 black pickups with exposed pole pieces, 2 volume/2 tone controls, 3-way selector switch, black "apostrophe" plastic controls plate on lower bout, available in Natural finish with tinted Golden Brown headstock, mfg. 1967-69.

	N/A	$1,100	$950	$850	$750	$650	$500

Last MSR was $469.

**Mosrite Celebrity Bass CE III
courtesy Atomic Guitars**

M

GRADING	100% MINT	98% NEAR MINT	95% EXC+	90% EXC	80% VG+	70% VG	60% G

JOE MAPHIS BASS (MODEL MARK X, 502) - semi-hollowbody, bound spruce top, 1.5 in. body depth, walnut back, maple neck, 30.25 in. scale, 20-fret rosewood fingerboard, fixed bridge, laminated black (or white) shell pickguard, chrome bridge cover, 2-per-side tuners, chrome hardware, 2 adjustable pickups, volume/tone controls, 3-way selector switch, available in Natural or Trans. Sunburst finishes, mfg. 1965-69.

	N/A	$1,150	$975	$850	$750	$650	$525

Last MSR was $449.

ELECTRIC BASS: VENTURES SERIES

VENTURES MODEL BASS (1963-1965) - bound offset double cutaway hardwood body, set-in maple neck, 20-fret bound fingerboard, adjustable bridge, chrome hardware, 2-per-side tuners, white pickguard, 2 black pickups, volume/tone controls, 3-position switch, side-mounted jack, available in Sunburst or White Pearl finishes, mfg. 1963-65.

	N/A	$4,000	$3,500	$3,000	$2,500	$2,000	$1,500

VENTURES BASS (MODEL MARK X, # 103) - offset double cutaway hardwood body, bolt-on maple neck, 30.25 in. scale, 20-fret bound rosewood fingerboard with dot inlay, "Mosrite of California/The Ventures" headstock logo, fixed bridge, chrome hardware, white pickguard, 2 black single coil pickups, volume/tone controls, 3-position switch, available in Metallic Blue, Metallic Red, or Sunburst finishes, mfg. 1963-66.

	N/A	$2,000	$1,700	$1,400	$1,200	$1,000	$800

Last MSR was $330.

Ventures Mark Series models do not have a bound body.

MARK X BASS - offset double cutaway solid body, bolt-on maple neck, 30.25 in. scale, 20-fret bound Indian rosewood fingerboard, adjustable bridge, chrome hardware, white pickguard, 2 black pickups, volume/tone controls, 3-position switch, available in Cherryburst, Deep Black, Metallic Blue, Metallic Red, Pearl White, Transparent Cherry Red, or Transparent Sunburst finishes, mfg. 1967-69.

	N/A	$1,400	$1,200	$1,050	$900	$750	$600

While similar to the 1963-1969 Ventures Bass model, the Mark X Bass does not have a "The Ventures Model" logo on the headstock.

ELECTRIC BASS: V SERIES

V-I BASS (V I STANDARD BASS) - offset double cutaway solid body, bolt-on maple neck, 20-fret bound rosewood fingerboard with double dot inlay, adjustable bridge/stop tailpiece, chrome bridge cover, 2-per-side tuners, Natural finish headstock, white pickguard, chrome hardware, white pickguard, 2 black pickups with exposed pole pieces, volume/tone controls, 3-position switch, available in Red or Sunburst finishes, mfg. circa 1972-75.

	N/A	$700	$600	$500	$400	$325	$250

Last MSR was $398.

V-II BASS - similar to the V-I Bass, except features 2 black humbucker pickups with exposed pole pieces, 2 pickup bypass switches, available in Red or Sunburst finishes, mfg. 1973-75.

	N/A	$750	$650	$550	$450	$375	$300

Last MSR was $398.

ELECTRIC BASS: REISSUE MODELS

MOSRITE 1988 BASS (M-88 BASS) - offset double cutaway basswood body, no German carve body ridge, 3-piece laminated maple neck, zero fret, 20-fret laminated curly maple/rosewood fingerboard, "Mosrite 1988" logo on headstock, vibrato or fixed bridge, 2-per-side tuners, chrome hardware, 2 creme colored Alnico pickups, volume/tone controls, 3-position switch, side-mounted 1/4 in. jack, available in Banana, Diamondized Ebony Black, Diamondized Money Green, Diamondized Ruby Red, or Sunburst finishes, mfg. 1988-89.

	N/A	$1,500	$1,200	$1,000	$800	$650	$500

The headstock logo on M-88 models reads "Mosrite 1988, Made In U.S.A."

VENTURES VINTAGE BASS (SET-NECK) - bound offset double cutaway alder body, glued-in maple neck, 20-fret bound rosewood fingerboard, fixed bridge, 2-per-side tuners, chrome hardware, white pickguard, 2 black Alnico single coil pickups, volume/tone controls, 3-position switch, side-mounted jack, available in Black, Sunburst, or White finishes, mfg. circa 1990.

	N/A	$2,700	$2,400	$2,100	$1,800	$1,500	$1,200

Last MSR was $2,748.

Ventures Vintage Bass (Bolt-On) - similar to the Ventures Vintage Bass (Set-Neck), except has a bolt-on neck, mfg. circa 1990.

	N/A	$2,400	$2,100	$1,800	$1,500	$1,200	$900

Last MSR was $2,350.

VENTURES 1988 BASS (V-88 BASS) - offset double cutaway basswood body, 3-piece laminated maple neck, 20-fret bound rosewood fingerboard, "Mosrite/The Ventures Model/1988" logo on headstock, 2-per-side tuners, fixed tailpiece, chrome hardware, 2 black pickups, volume/tone controls, 3-position switch, available in Banana, Diamondized Ebony Black, Diamondized Money Green, Diamondized Ruby Red, or Sunburst finishes, mfg. circa 1988.

	N/A	$2,000	$1,700	$1,400	$1,100	$900	$700

Last MSR was $1,460.

The next year, the V-89 Bass model debuted, with a list price of $2,148. Research continues on the V-89 Bass model (circa 1989-1990).

GRADING	100% MINT	98% NEAR MINT	95% EXC+	90% EXC	80% VG+	70% VG	60% G

MOURADIAN

Instruments currently built in Cambridge, MA since 1989. Instruments were previously built in Winchester, Massachusetts between 1980, 1982 and 1988.

Mouradian custom basses are high quality instruments generally associated with bassist Chris Squire (Yes) due to his continued use of his CS-74 model. Other noted Mouradian bass players include Pat Badger (Extreme).

Jim Mouradian first built Squire's custom bass in 1980, and formed a production company in 1982. Mouradian Guitars was initially based in Winchester, Massachusetts for the first 6 years, and then moved to Cambridge, Massachusetts in 1989. Jim and his son, Jon, continued to produce custom-built electric basses while offering repair services.

The Mouradian company expanded their production capabilities in 1997/1998 when Jim and John teamed up with Martin Flanders (see Flanders Archtop Guitars) and Pat Badger. Badger, a former employee before his band Extreme hit nationally, has returned to the company that originally hired him, (Preliminary research courtesy Jeff Meyer; company information courtesy Jon Mouradian).

ELECTRIC BASS

Mouradian **CS-74** "**Chris Squire**" basses have an unusual curved body design. The **CS-74** (retail list starting at $3,795) features a neck-through design, graphite-reinforced rock maple neck, 22-fret ebony fingerboard, 3 custom made humcancelling pickups, 3 on/off pickup selector switches, and an active EQ. This model is available with numerous options, including a 5-String configuration (**CS-75**).

Mouradian's newest model is the **Reality Bass**, available in 4-String (retail list $1,895) and 5-String (retail list $1,895) configurations. This model has either a swamp ash or alder body, 21-fret rosewood or bird's-eye maple fingerboard, strings through-body bridge, Hipshot Ultralite tuners, EMG 35 P4/35 J pickups, and stacked volume/tone controls. The **Reality Bass** is optional with different electronic packages, exotic woods, custom finishes, or in a fretless configuration. All Mouradian basses are built in the U.S., and are available direct from the company in Massachusetts.

MUDGE BASSES

Instruments currently built in Oakland, CA.

Mudge basses are individually handcrafted "one at a time" in the Mudge shop, and feature hand carved bodies and necks. All woods are also hand selected by Mudge. Basses have a mahogany body with exotic or domestic bookmatched top. Necks are handcarved maple with contrasting wood stripes of Walnut or Purpleheart. For further information, contact Mudge Basses directly (see Trademark Index).

ELECTRIC BASS

Mudge bass models are available in the **DN4** 4-string (list $1,800) and 5-string **DN5** (list $2,000) configurations. The offset double cutaway body is carved from Honduran mahogany and topped with Wenge, Zebrawood, Cocabolo, or Pau Ferro; bird's-eye maple necks feature a Pau Ferro fingerboard and mother-of-pearl side dots. Mudge basses have chrome hardware, Hipshot or Leo Quan BadAss II bridges, 2 EMG J-style pickups, and have hand rubbed oil finishes. The CK Models have the same general specs as the DN's, except the boby material is Ash (list $1,600 4-string) and ($1,800 5-string).

MULTI-STAR

See Musima. Instruments previously produced in East Germany during the 1970s and 1980s.

The Multi-Star trademark was a brand name used by the Musima company on a series of solid body guitars featuring designs based on popular American classics (source: Tony Bacon and Paul Day, *The Guru's Guitar Guide*).

MULTIVOX

Instruments previously produced in New York City, NY during the 1950s and 1960s. Later models had imported hardware but were still "built" in New York.

Multivox was the manufacturing subsidiary of the Peter Sorkin Music Company, which built products under the Premier trademark. Sorkin began the Multivox company in the mid 1940s. Multivox eventually established a separate corporate identity, and continued in existence for fourteen or so years after the Sorkin company closed down in the 1970s (source: Michael Wright, *Guitar Stories*, Volume One). The Multivox trademark is now used on a line of effect pedals.

ELECTRIC

SCROLL-BODY ELECTRIC - double cutaway with scroll on bass bout, solid mahogany body, rosewood fingerboard with dot inlay, 3-per-side tuners, trapeze tailpiece, sparkle pickguard, single P-90 pickup, two knobs, gold hardware, available in Natural finish, mfg. late 1950s-mid 1960s.

N/A	$750	$650	$575	$500	$425	$350

MUNCY

Instruments are currently built in Kingston, TN.

Luthier Gary Muncy designed the solid body "Bout Time" model that features a new innovative neck design. Constructed from CNC machined aluminum, the neck's fretboard is made from bloodwood which is then shaped between the sunken frets similar to scalloping. Fingering notes occurs in the in-between areas so the string makes contact at the raised area.

**Mosrite Ventures Bass
courtesy Jerry Yensan**

**Multi-Vox Premier
courtesy Waco Vintage**

M

MURPH

Instruments previously built in San Fernando, CA between 1965 and 1966.

Designer/inventor Pat Murphy was responding to his children's musical interests when he began manufacturing Murph guitars in the mid 1960s. Murphy put the family-run shop together with equipment picked up at auctions, and contracted a violin maker named Rick Geiger to help with production. After a falling out with Geiger, Murphy began manufacturing guitars in the midsummer of 1965.

The company originally was to be called York, but a brass instrument manufacturer of the same name caused them to use the Murph trademark. Pat Murphy estimated that perhaps 1,200 to 1,500 guitars were built in the one year production span. Models were built in lots of 50, and a total of nearly 100 guitars were built a week. Bridges and tremolos were from the Gotz company in Germany, and the tuning machines were Klusons. Pickups were hand wound in the guitar production facility. Pat Murphy was also contracted to make a small number of guitars for Sears under the Silvertone label (source: Teisco Del Rey, *Guitar Player* magazine).

ELECTRIC

Models included the semi-hollow **Gemini**, and the solid body **Squire**. Some of the Squire seconds were finished with vinyl upholstery and snap buttons and were designated the **Westerner** model. The Gemini had a retail price of $279, the Squire I (one pickup) at $159.50, and the Squire II (two pickups) listed at $189.50. One model called the **Continental IV** was a single pickup semi-hollowbody design that was priced around $239.

Murphy also produced a full-size kit guitar called the **Tempo**, corresponding bass guitar models for the line, and heart-shaped bodied guitars in six or twelve string configurations.

MUSIC DRIVE

Also M D. Instruments currently produced in Korea by Sumer Korea. Previously distributed in the U.S. by Sumer USA, located in Huntington Beach, CA.

The Sumer Musical Instruments Co., Ltd. is currently offering a wide range of electric guitar and bass models under the **Music Drive** (or **MD**) trademark. Most models are good quality designs intended for the intermediate to working professional guitarist. There are a wide range of electric and bass models. Standard Series instruments feature heel-less bolt-on hard maple necks, rosewood fingerboards, chrome hardware, and numerous solid/transparent/metallic finishes.

MUSIC MAN

See Ernie Ball/Music Man for models produced 1984-present. Instruments previously produced in Fullerton, CA between 1976 and 1982.

The original Music Man company was put together in March of 1972 by two ex-Fender executives. Tom Walker (a chief salesman) and Forrest White (ex- vice president and general manager of Fender) made their mark early, with a successful line of guitar amplifiers. In 1976, Music Man introduced new solid body guitar models designed and built by Leo Fender. After abiding by a ten year "no compete" clause in the sale of Fender Electrical Instrument Company (1965-1975), Fender's CLF Research factory provided Music Man with numerous guitar and bass models through an exclusive agreement.

Leo Fender and George Fullerton (another ex-Fender employee) began building facilities for CLF Research in December of 1974. Fullerton was made vice president of CLF in March 1976, and the first shipment of instruments from CLF to Music Man was in June of the same year. Some of the notable designs in early Music Man history are the Sabre and Stingray series of guitars and basses.

In 1978, the controlling interest at Music Man expressed a desire to buy the CLF factory and produce instruments directly. Fender and Fullerton turned down repeated offers, and Music Man began cutting production orders. The controversy settled as CLF Research stopped manufacturing instruments for Music Man in late 1979. Fender then began working on new designs for his final company, G & L.

Music Man's trademark and designs were purchased in 1984 by Ernie Ball. The Ernie Ball company, known for its string sets and Earthwood basses, set up production in its San Luis Obispo factory. Ernie Ball/Music Man has retained the high level of quality from original Fender/CLF designs, and has introduced some innovative designs to their current line (See Ernie Ball/Music Man).

The three year span of the original Music Man company saw the release of such models as the Sabre I and Sabre II, as well as the Sting Ray I and Sting Ray II guitars. Perhaps even better known are the Sabre Bass, Sting Ray Bass, and Cutlass Bass. The Sting Ray was available with either strings through the body or strings through the bridge. It is estimated that less than 300 Cutlass basses were built.

ELECTRIC

SABRE I - offset double cutaway, maple neck, flat fingerboard, two pickups, available in various colors, mfg. 1978-1982.

	N/A	$750	$650	$575	$500	$425	$350

SABRE II - offset double cutaway, maple neck, 7.5 in radius fingerboard, two pickups, otherwise similar to the Sabre I, available in various colors, mfg. 1978-1982.

	N/A	$750	$650	$575	$500	$425	$350

STINGRAY I - offset double cutaway, maple neck, flat fingerboard, two pickups, available in various colors, mfg. 1978-1982.

	N/A	$750	$650	$575	$500	$425	$350

STINGRAY II - offset double cutaway, maple neck, 7.5 in radius fingerboard, two pickups, otherwise similar to the Stingray I, available in various colors, mfg. 1978-1982.

	N/A	$750	$650	$575	$500	$425	$350

ELECTRIC BASS

CUTLASS I - mfg. 1982-87.

	N/A	$1,800	$1,500	$1,200	$1,000	$800	$600

CUTLASS II - mfg. 1982-87.

	N/A	$1,800	$1,500	$1,200	$1,000	$800	$600

GRADING	100% MINT	98% NEAR MINT	95% EXC+	90% EXC	80% VG+	70% VG	60% G

SABRE BASS - offset double cutaway P-bass style body, maple neck, maple fingerboard, two pickups, 3/1-per-side tuners, 3 knobs, available in various finishes, mfg. 1978-1987.

	N/A	$1,000	$850	$725	$600	$500	$400

This model is continued in the Ernie Ball section from 1988 to 1991.

STINGRAY BASS - offset double cutaway, single pickup, 3/1-per-side tuners, available in various finishes, mfg. 1976-1984.

		N/A					
1976-1979	N/A	$2,000	$1,700	$1,400	$1,200	$1,000	$800
1980-1984	N/A	$1,500	$1,250	$1,050	$850	$700	$550

**Murph Squire Bass
courtesy Seph Gilchrest**

MUSICIAN SOUND DESIGN

Instruments previously built in Koln (Cologne), Germany. Other products currently built.

Musician Sound Design offered a sleek (yet pointy) custom guitar model. They currently focus on guitar and bass effects as well as some other products. For further information, contact Musician Sound Design directly (see Trademark Index).

MUSICVOX

Instruments currently produced in Korea since 1996. Distributed by Musicvox of Cherry Hill, NJ.

Owner Matt Eichen's new Musicvox Spaceranger guitar features a unique new design that will certainly gather attention any time a player takes it out of the case! Eichen combined the oversized headstock with an equally-oversized treble-side horn for resonance purposes, which gives the Spaceranger design increased sustain.

After two years of expanding into a retail/distributor base, Eichen decided to take the guitars right to the players worldwide with direct sales. As as result, the factory pricing for direct sales has radically reduced the retail list price. In Austin Power's *Goldmember*, MusicVox's guitars are used in the band Ming Tea in the movie, Yeah Baby!

Early versions (1996-1997 Mfg.) of the Spaceranger guitar model featured either an alder or an ultralight ash body. Finishes included solid color urethane colors like Red Alert, All Systems Green, Black Hole, Ignition Yellow, and White Hot. Nitrocellulose Sunburst and Transparent finishes were also available.

ELECTRIC

The current version **Spaceranger** guitar model features a single cutaway/enlarged lower bout light mahogany body, 24.75 in. scale, bolt-on Canadian maple neck, 21-fret rosewood (or maple) fingerboard with dot (or block) inlays, fixed bridge, 2/4 per side vintage-style keystone tuners on a curved/enlarged headstock, pickguard, 3-way selector switch, and volume/tone controls. Spacerangers fire up the frequencies via a pair of either black P-90 style single coils, PAF- or mini-style covered humbuckers (chrome or gold covers), or Toaster-style pickups with chrome/black covers. Trapeze and tremolo tailpieces are available by special order. Current retail is $750 for the Spaceranger. The **Space Cadet** has somewhat of a less radical body and retails for $799.99.

Finishes include solid colors like Black (with white body binding), Candy Apple Red, Seafoam Green, Taxicab Yellow, and White (with triple black body binding). Transparent finishes include Bookmatched Flame Maple Top with Cherry Sunburst, Fireglow Sunburst, Korina, and Three Tone Sunburst. Sparkle Top finishes include Gold Stardust and Silver Stardust.

ELECTRIC BASS

The **Spaceranger Bass** features a similar construction as the guitar model, except has a 30 in. scale, 20-fret fingerboard, rosewood bridge/trapeze tailpiece, 1/3-per-side vintage-style keystone tuners, and a pair of either mini-style or large special design covered humbuckers (chrome or gold covers). Retail price on this model is $750. The **Space Cadet** has somewhat of a less radical body and retails for $799.99. A 12-string bass is also available for $899.99.

Finishes include solid colors like Black (with white body binding), Candy Apple Red, and White (with triple black body binding). Transparent finishes include Bookmatched Flame Maple Top with Cherry Sunburst, Korina, and Three-Tone Sunburst. Sparkle Top finishes include Gold Stardust and Silver Stardust.

MUSIMA

Instruments currently produced in Germany since the late 1950s.

The Musima company has been producing a number of solid body and semi-hollowbody guitars with original designs since the late 1950s. It has been reported by other sources that a number of guitars were exported to Britian under the *Otwin & Rellog* trademark. These guitars were available through the early 1960s, then the company issued their own medium quality solid body guitars such as the **707** and **708** during the mid-1960s. The company continues to produce good quality guitars for the international guitar market. Any additional information on this trademark is welcome and can be submitted directly to the *Blue Book of Electric Guitars* (source: Tony Bacon, *The Ultimate Guitar Book*).

NOTES

Section N

9STEIN

Instruments currently built in the U.S. Distributed by Michael Reizenstein in Yonkers, NY.

Designer Michael Reizenstein's nine-string combination bass and guitar has an offset, ergonomic body design that features a fully adjustable armrest (which also gives control of the instrument positioning). The guitar features a tune-o-matic bridge/stop tailpiece, humbucker pickup, 5/4-per-side headstock, and built-in Boss TU-12 tuner. The 9Stein combination bass and guitar is built by luthier Tommy Doyle. For further information, please contact Michael Reizenstein directly (see Trademark Index).

N.I.C.E. GUITARS

Instruments currently built in Basel, Switzerland.

N.I.C.E., or Nature Is Continuously Evolving, produces several high quality guitars. Guitars can be ordered directly from their website. For further information regarding model specifications and pricing, please contact N.I.C.E. directly (see Trademark Index).

NS DESIGN

Instruments currently produced in Nobleboro, ME, and previously produced in Walpole, ME.

Designer Ned Steinberger founded NS Design in 1993 as a means to independently develop new and innovative stringed instrument designs. While not really a production center in the factory sense, some of the ideas that are explored here may have an impact on the musical instrument industry again! Prices start at $2,800 for the four-string, $3,200 for the five-string, and $5,200 for the six-string. They have expanded with more models including cellos, violins, and violas. For more information, refer to their website (see Trademark Index).

NYC MUSIC PRODUCTS

Instruments currently built in Brooklyn, NY. Distributed by Matthews & Ryan Musical Products of Brooklyn, NY.

NYC bass guitars are built by the luthiers at Fodera with a more traditional design, and are designed for the bass player who is looking for the quality of a Fodera bass at a more affordable price.

ELECTRIC BASS

Before 1998, the **Empire** bass was offered in 2 variations: the **Model 1** (list $2,000), which featured an alder body and a northern rock maple bolt-on neck; and the **Model 2** (list $2,000) which had a swamp ash body, northern rock maple bolt-on neck, and a maple fingerboard. The addition of an optional high grade curly maple or quilted maple top was an extra $500, a Brazilian rosewood fingerboard was an extra $250, and Seymour Duncan Antiquity pickups ran an additional $150.

The current model **Empire Bass** is offered in a 4-string or 5-string configuration. Both models have either an alder or swamp ash body, bolt-on northern rock maple neck, 21-fret rosewood fingerboard with mother-of-pearl inlay dots (or maple with ebony dots), Seymour Duncan, EMG or Bartolini pickups, black or gold hardware, and a Clear Natural Satin finish. Models are optionally offered with a Moses Graphite neck (add $270 for a wooden fingerboard). The **Empire** 4-string model (list $2,400) has a scale length of 34 in.; the **Empire** 5-string model has a 35 in. scale (list $3,200).

The addition of an optional high grade curly maple or quilted maple top is an extra $250. Optional urethane lacquer finishes in custom colors are $250, while a high gloss clear finish is $150.

NYS

Instruments currently built in upstate NY by luthier Chirstopher Hofschneider by the company name of Black Creek Musical Instrument Co., which is located in Middleburgh, NY.

NYS Guitars are handmade in upstate, NY by Chris, under the name of NYS. As a company they build handcrafted six-string guitars and four- and five-string electric basses. NYS has built some amazing guitars for amazing players. For more information, contact NYS directly (see Trademark Index).

NADINE

Instruments previously produced in Japan during the late 1980s.

The Nadine trademark is a brand name used by a British importer. Nadine guitars are good quality Fender-derived and Superstrat models (source: Tony Bacon and Paul Day, *The Guru's Guitar Guide*).

NADY

Instruments previously built in Asia by Fernandes and Cort. Distributed circa mid-1980s by Nady Systems, Inc. of Emeryville, CA.

The Nady company is best known for its wireless guitar and microphone systems that were introduced in 1977. In 1985, Nady introduced a guitar model (**Lightning**) and a bass model (**Thunder**) that featured a built-in wireless unit in a production guitar. Nady also offered a 300-watt Mosfet bass amp that was rack mountable, as well as a 100 watt Mosfet rack mountable guitar head.

Nady instrument design featured a maple through-neck design, offset double cutaway alder bodies (or wings), 6-on-a-side (four for the bass) tuning machines, 24-fret ebony fingerboard with mother-of-pearl lightning bolt inlays,

National Resoelectric courtesy Dave Rogers Dave's Guitar Shop

National Town & Country courtesy George McGuire

black hardware, and a black finish. The Lightning had two humbucker pickups and a locking tremolo system, while the Thunder had a P/J pickup combination. The guitars are equipped with 1/4 in. jacks so they can still be used conventionally. However, the proper complete package would be the instrument and the 501 VHF receiver. Although Nady instruments came with the 501 VHF receiver, they could be upgraded to the 601 or 701 receiver as well.

Pricing for these instruments depends on condition, playability, working electronics, and receiver (the 501 system was okay for the earlier time period; Nady builds a much better wireless system now). Instrument prices can range between $250 and $600.

NAPOLITANO, ARTHUR

Instruments currently built in Allentown, NJ, since 1993.

Luthier Arthur Napolitano began building electric guitars in 1967, and offered repair services on instruments in 1978 in Watchung, New Jersey. Napolitano moved to Allentown in 1992, and began building archtop guitars in 1993. Napolitano currently offers several different archtop models like the **Primavera**, **Acoustic**, **Philadelphian**, **Jazz Box**, and a **Seven-String** model. Prices range from $4,900 to $9,800. For more information, contact Napolitano directly (see Trademark Index).

NATIONAL

Instruments previously produced in Los Angeles, CA from the mid-1920s to the mid-1930s. Instruments produced in Chicago, IL from mid-1930s to 1969. After National moved production to Chicago in the mid-1930s, they formally changed the company name to Valco (but still produced National brand guitars). Instruments produced in Japan circa 1970s. Distributed by Strum'N Drum of Chicago, IL. When Valco went out of business in 1969, the National trademark was acquired by Strum'N Drum, who then used the trademark on a series of Japanese-built guitars.

The Dopyera family emigrated from the Austro-Hungary area to Southern California in 1908. In the early 1920s, John and Rudy Dopyera began producing banjos in Southern California. They were approached by guitarist George Beauchamp to help solve his volume (or lack thereof) problem with other instruments in the vaudeville orchestra. In the course of their conversation, the idea of placing aluminum resonators in a guitar body for amplification purposes was developed. John Dopyera and his four brothers (plus some associates like George Beauchamp) formed National in 1925.

The initial partnership between Dopyera and Beauchamp lasted for about two years, and then John Dopyera left National to form the Dobro company. National's corporate officers in 1929 consisted of Ted E. Kleinmeyer (pres.), George Beauchamp (sec./gen. mngr.), Adolph Rickenbacker (engineer), and Paul Barth (vice pres.). In late 1929, Beauchamp left National, and joined up with Adolph Rickenbacker to form Ro-Pat-In (later Electro String/Rickenbacker).

At the onset of the American Depression, National was having financial difficulties. Louis Dopyera bought out the National company, and, as he owned more than 50% of the stock in Dobro, "merged" the two companies back together (as National Dobro). In 1936, the decision was made to move the company to Chicago, Illinois. Chicago was a veritable hotbed of mass-produced musical instruments during the early to pre-World War II 1900s. Manufacturers like Washburn and Regal had facilities there, and major wholesalers and retailers like the Tonk Bros. and Lyon & Healy were based there. Victor Smith, Al Frost, and Louis Dopyera moved their operation to Chicago, and in 1943 formally announced the change to Valco (the initials of their three first names: Victor-Al-Louis Company). Valco worked on war materials during World War II, and returned to instrument production afterwards. Valco produced the National/Supro/Airline fiberglass body guitars in the 1950s and 1960s, as well as wood-bodied models.

In 1969 or 1970, Valco Guitars, Inc. went out of business. The assets of Valco/Kay were auctioned off, and the rights to the National trademark were bought by the Chicago, Illinois-based importers Strum'N Drum. Strum'N Drum, which had been importing Japanese guitars under the **Norma** trademark, were quick to introduce National on a line of Japanese-produced guitars that were distributed in the U.S. market. Author/researcher Michael Wright points out that the National "Big Daddy" bolt-neck black LP copy was one of the first models that launched the Japanese "Copy Era" of the 1970s. Early company history courtesy Bob Brozman, The History and Artistry of National Resonator Instruments; model descriptions compiled by Dave Hull. "Copy Era" National information courtesy Michael Wright.

For information regarding the National resonator models, please refer to the *Blue Book of Acoustic Guitars*.

N

ELECTRIC

AVALON (MODEL 1134) - single smooth cutaway, bound fingerboard with block inlay, black pickguard, 2 metal covered pickups, adjustable rosewood bridge, trapeze tailpiece, rounded headstock with 3-per-side plastic butterfly tuners, 2 knobs on treble bout, 1 switch on upper treble bout, 12 in. wide, available in Blonde finish with black back and sides, mfg. 1956-57.

N/A	$850	$750	$650	$575	$500	$425

BOLERO (MODEL 1132) - single smooth cutaway, unbound fingerboard with dot inlay, single metal covered pickup, pickguard, adjustable rosewood bridge, trapeze tailpiece, symmetrical peghead with 3-per-side plastic butterfly tuners, 12 in. wide, available in Sunburst finish with black back and sides, mfg. 1956-57.

N/A	$700	$600	$525	$450	$375	$300

GLENWOOD/GLENWOOD DELUXE (MODEL 1105) - single rounded cutaway, fully bound body, white plastic backplate, 2 metal covered pickups, black pickguard, bound fingerboard with diamond enclosed in block inlays, 6 knobs on bass side, single switch on treble side, 3-per-side tuners, gold hardware, 12.25 in. wide body, available in Natural finish with black back and sides, mfg. 1954-1961.

N/A	$1,250	$1,100	$950	$800	$700	$600

In 1957, a small script peghead logo was placed above the National shield and plastic butterfly tuners replaced the metal ones. In 1958, this model was renamed the Glenwood Deluxe and the body size was increased to 13.625 in., another knob was added to the treble side, metal tuners were reintroduced, and a Bigsby vibrato tailpiece was introduced.

GLENWOOD 98 - "map-shaped" Res-o-glass body, rounded treble bout cutaway, pointy bass bout, diamond enclosed by block fingerboard inlays, 2 standard and 1 bridge pickups, 3 knobs on treble side, 3-way switch, Bigsby vibrato, beveled edges on peghead to show lines, chrome plated hardware, available in Pearl White finish, black neck-back finish, mfg. 1962-65.

N/A	$2,500	$2,200	$1,900	$1,600	$1,400	$1,200

In 1964, a master volume knob near the jack was added.

GRADING	100% MINT	98% NEAR MINT	95% EXC+	90% EXC	80% VG+	70% VG	60% G

GLENWOOD 99 - "map-shaped" Res-o-glass body, rounded treble bout cutaway, pointy bass bout, diamond enclosed by block fingerboard inlays, 2 standard and 1 bridge pickups, plate tailpiece, beveled edges on peghead to show lines, 3 knobs on treble side, 3 knobs on bass side, 3-way switch, chrome plated hardware, available in Snow White finish, mfg. 1962-65.

	N/A	$2,800	$2,400	$2,100	$1,800	$1,500	$1,300

In 1963, a Bigsby Vibrato was introduced with gold hardware and Sea-Foam Green finish. In 1964, a master volume knob near the jack was added.

VAL-PRO 82/NEWPORT 82 - "map-shaped" Res-o-glass body, rounded treble bout cutaway, pointy bass bout, quarter circle inlays, single pickup, 3 knobs on treble side, 3-way switch, chrome plated hardware, available in Scarlet finish, mfg. 1962-65.

	N/A	$1,500	$1,300	$1,100	$950	$800	$650

In 1963, the Val-Pro 82 was renamed the Newport 82 with a pointed treble horn, the switches and knobs were moved to bass side, vibrato was added, and the finish was changed to Pepper Red. A few models were produced in the late 1960s from leftover parts.

VAL-PRO 84/NEWPORT 84 - "map-shaped" Res-o-glass body, rounded treble bout cutaway, pointy bass bout, quarter circle inlays, 1 standard and 1 bridge pickup, 3 knobs on treble side, 3-way switch, chrome plated hardware, available in Arctic White finish, mfg. 1962-65.

	N/A	$1,700	$1,500	$1,300	$1,100	$900	$750

In 1963, the Val-Pro 84 was renamed the Newport 84 with a pointed treble horn, vibrato added, and the finish was changed to Sea Foam Green. A few models were produced in the late 1960s from leftover parts.

VAL-PRO 88/NEWPORT 88 - "map-shaped" Res-o-glass body, rounded treble bout cutaway, pointy bass bout, quarter circle inlays, 2 standard and 1 bridge pickup, 6 knobs on treble side, 3-way switch, chrome plated hardware, available in Raven Black finish, mfg. 1962-65.

	N/A	$2,000	$1,750	$1,500	$1,300	$1,100	$900

In 1963, the Val-Pro 88 was renamed the Newport 88 with a pointed treble horn, vibrato added and the knobs were moved to the bass side and put in groups of 2. A few models were produced in the late 1960s from leftover parts.

National Avalon
courtesy George McGuire

NEAL MOSER GUITARS

Instruments currently built in Glendora, CA. Distributed by GMW Guitar Works of Glendora, CA.

Neal Moser began his career in guitars in 1964 and worked with industry leaders such as Vox, B.C. Rich, and Wayne Charvel. Neal Moser Guitars built both electric and archtop guitar models, as well as bass models in the **Empire** series. Neal retired in 1998 and only consults with Lee Garver of GMW. He also does specialized work for others by appointment only. For further information, please contact Neal Moser Guitars directly (see Trademark Index).

NED CALLAN

See also CMI, Shaftesbury, PC, and Simms-Watts. Instruments previously built in England from the early to late 1970s.

The Ned Callan trademark is a pseudonym for custom luthier Peter Cook. Cook successfully mass-produced enough decent quality solid body guitars to warrant other trademarks: Shaftesbury and Simms-Watts were the brand names of British importers; PC (Cook's initials) and CMI (guessing Cook Musical Instruments?) and perhaps other marketing devices. Outside of the headstock moniker, the guitars themselves seemed the same (source: Tony Bacon and Paul Day, *The Guru's Guitar Guide*).

ELECTRIC: FIRST SERIES

The two models in the First Series were produced between 1970 and 1975. Both had 2 single coil pickups, 4 controls, and a selector switch. The **Custom** model featured offset dual cutaways, while the **Salisbury** only had a single cutaway body design.

ELECTRIC: SECOND SERIES

The two models in the Second Series were even more similar: both shared the same rounded body design with two forward horns that earned them the nicknames of "Nobbly Neds," two pickups, and two control switches plus a selector switch. The **Hombre** had chrome pickups, while the **Cody** had black pickups. Both models were produced from 1973 to 1975.

NEO

Instruments currently produced in Buckingham, PA since 1991. Distributed by NEO Products, Inc. of Buckingham, PA.

Neo custom guitars and basses feature a body of tough, clear acrylic and a Neon tube (plus power supply) that lights up as the instrument is played. The **Neo** guitars were developed to provide extra visual effects that neon lighting can provide to a musician in the course of a performance. The **Basic** model has a retail price of $1,995, and features a 22-fret ebony fingerboard and 2 EMG humbuckers with active preamp. Additionally, the company has expanded its line to include the **Spitfire** electric violin.

National Val-Pro 88
courtesy George McGuire

N

NERVE

Instruments previously built in England during the mid-1980s.

There were three different high quality models produced by Nerve. The original design solid body guitars were "headless," meaning no headstocks at the end of the neck. Model designations were the Energy, the Reaction, and the System. Any additional information would be appreciated and can be submitted directly to the *Blue Book of Electric Guitars* (source: Tony Bacon and Paul Day, *The Guru's Guitar Guide*).

NEUSER

Instruments currently built in Modra, Slovakia. Distributed by the Neuser Co., Ltd. of Finland.

Neuser handcrafts high quality custom basses that are available in 4-, 5-, and 6-string configurations. Robert Neuser began building bass guitars by himself in 1977. The Neuser Company was originated in 1989. Within a few years, the company brought together a fine team of professional craftsmen. Neuser basses feature a number of body and neck wood combinations as well as finish options (contact the company for a price quote).

The **Crusade** model features a two-piece alder body, flame maple top, glued-in five-piece neck, 22-fret ebony fingerboard, Neuser soapbar pickups and EBS active electronics. Basses are finished in high gloss nitrocellulose.

The neck-through-body design of the **Courage** has a 2-piece body of ash (or alder, bubinga, mahogany, or maple) in different combinations, a five-piece maple/mahogany neck or bubinga neck, 24-fret ebony fingerboard, and custom Bartolini pickups, EBS or Bartolini active electronics.

The **Cloudburst** has a nine-piece maple/mahogany or bubinga neck-through-body construction, five-piece ash (or alder or bubinga, or mahogany, or maple) body in different combinations, 24-fret ebony fingerboard, Bartolini custom pickups, and EBS or Bartolini active electronics. The Cloudburst is available in high gloss nitrocellulose or wax-oil finish. There is also a **Chase** bass available.

Neuser has another design that features a combination of a traditional electric bass guitar and a hammer system where the player can control the hammers that hit the strings with a piano-like key mechanism. The **Claudia Claw-Hammer** bass is available in bubinga with a maple plate, Bartolini pickups, active electronics, and a wax-oil finish. For further information, refer to their website (see Trademark Index).

NICKERSON

Instruments currently built in Northampton, MA since the early 1980s.

Luthier Brad Nickerson, born and raised in Cape Cod, Massachusetts, has been building archtop guitars since 1982. Nickerson attended the Berklee College of Music, and worked in the graphic arts field for a number of years. While continuing his interest in music, Nickerson received valuable advice from New York luthier Carlo Greco, as well as Cape Cod violin builder Donald MacKenzie. Nickerson also gained experience doing repair work for Bay State Vintage Guitars (Boston), and The Fretted Instrument Workshop (Amherst, Massachusetts).

With his partner Lyn Hardy, Nickerson builds archtop, flattop, and electric guitars on a custom order basis. Nickerson is also available for restorations and repair work. For further information regarding specifications and availability, please contact Nickerson Guitars directly (see Trademark Index).

NIEMINEN, KARI

See Versoul.

Prior to the introduction of the Versoul trademark, luthier Kari Nieminen of Finland used his name on his hand-built guitars. Nieminen, an industrial designer, teaches at the University of Art and Design in Helsinki.

NIGHTINGALE

Instruments currently built in England since the late 1980s.

Luthier Bernie Goodfellow features original designs on his high quality solid body guitars (source: Tony Bacon and Paul Day, *The Guru's Guitar Guide*).

NINETEEN NINETYSEVEN

Previous trademark of instruments (both electric and bass) previously marketed by Akai during 1998.

Previous models included the **SB410 Bass, SB511 Bass, SB411 Bass, CG112 Electric, CG112LE Electric,** and the **SG112 Electric**. Limited mfg. and importation to date. Very little information is known about these instruments.

NINJA

Instruments currently produced in Korea since the late 1980s.

The Ninja trademark is a brand name used by a British importer on these entry level to intermediate quality guitars. The instrument designs are based on classic American favorites (source: Tony Bacon and Paul Day, *The Guru's Guitar Guide*).

NOBLE

Instruments previously produced in Italy circa 1950s to 1964. Production then shifted to Japan circa 1965 to 1969. Distributed by Don Noble and Company of Chicago, IL.

Don E. Noble, accordionist and owner of Don Noble and Company (importers), began business importing Italian accordions. By 1950, Noble was also importing and distributing guitars (manufacturer unknown). In 1962, the company began distributing EKO and Oliviero Pigini guitars, and added Wandre instruments the following year.

In the mid-1960s, the Noble trademark was owned by importer/distributor Strum´N Drum of Chicago. The Noble brand was then used on Japanese-built solid body electrics (made by Tombo) through the late 1960s.

When the Valco/Kay holdings were auctioned off in 1969, Strum´N Drum bought the rights to the National trademark. Strum´N Drum began importing Japanese-built versions of popular American designs under the National logo, and discontinued the Noble trademark during the same time period (source: Michael Wright, *Vintage Guitar Magazine*).

NOBLES, TONY

Instruments currently built in Waverly, TX.

Shellacious! Luthier Tony Noble builds high quality guitars and also writes a column in *Vintage Guitar Magazine*. For further information, contact Precision Guitarworks directly (see Trademark Index).

GRADING	100% MINT	98% NEAR MINT	95% EXC+	90% EXC	80% VG+	70% VG	60% G

NORMA

Instruments previously built in Japan between 1965 and 1970 by the Tombo company. Distributed by Strum'N Drum, Inc., of Chicago, IL.

These Japanese-built guitars were distributed in the U.S. market by Strum'N Drum, Inc. of Chicago, IL. Strum'N Drum also distributed the Japanese-built Noble guitars of the mid- to late 1960s, and National solid body guitars in the early 1970s (source: Michael Wright, *Guitar Stories*, Volume One).

ELECTRIC

MISC. ELECTRIC MODELS - various configurations, six- or twelve-string configuration, double cutaway bodies, white pickguard in various pieces, 2-4 pickups, knobs, switches, available in Sunburst or sparkle finishes, mfg. late 1960s.

	100%	98%	95%	90%	80%	70%	60%
2 PICKUPS	N/A	$400	$325	$275	$225	$175	$125
3 PICKUPS	N/A	$450	$375	$300	$250	$200	$150
4 PICKUPS	N/A	$500	$425	$350	$275	$225	$175

MISC. BASS MODELS - various configurations and appointments, may include solidbody and hollowbody, mfg. late 1960s.

	100%	98%	95%	90%	80%	70%	60%
	N/A	$250	$200	$170	$140	$110	$80

NORTH AMERICAN GUITARS

Instruments currently built in Largo, FL, since 1961.

The North American Instrument Company has been building fine, hand-made guitars since 1962. They produce guitar models such as the Texas Special, Florida Bluesmaster, American Artist, and the American Legend guitars. They have guitars based on the traditional Stratocaster design as well as their own original designs. Pricing starts at $2,085 and can range up to $6,000 and above depending on the options. For more information refer to their website (see Trademark Index).

NORTON

Instruments currently manufactured in Belgrade, MT.

Norton instruments are modular in design allowing for switching of pickups and body modules. This is done through a system of metal rails that even allow for changing placement of a pickup. For more information refer to their website (see Trademark Index).

Nickerson Archtop courtesy Nickerson

ELECTRIC: MODULAR MODELS

PYTHON - serpentine modular body with snake's head being the upper bout, quartersawn maple neck, rosewood fingerboard with dot position markers, 25.5 in. scale, 6-on-a-side tuners, standard with 2 humbucker pickups, modular system allows for switching of pickups, coil tap, gold hardware, 1 volume/1 tone, 3-way switch, available in Red or Black finishes, current mfg.
MSR $1,795

AEM - modular body, quartersawn maple neck, rosewood fingerboard with dot position markers, 25.5 in. scale, other scales on request, 3-per-side tuners, two exposed coil humbucker pickups, other pickup mudules available, coil tap or phase available, tremolo bridge, 1 volume/1 tone control, available in Black, Blue, Red, Copper, or Green finishes, current mfg.
MSR $1,795

ADM - modular body, quartersawn maple neck, rosewood fingerboard with dot position markers, 3-per-side tuners, 25.5 in. scale, other scales available, two exposed coil humbucker pickups, other pickup modules available, coil tap or phase available, 1 volume/1 tone control, 3-way switch, available in Red, Black, or Blue finishes, current mfg.
MSR $1,695

DR. BILL - modular body, quartersawn maple neck, rosewood fingerboard with dot position markers, 3-per-side tuners, 25.5 in. scale, other scales available, 2 humbucking pickups, other pickup modules available, phase and coil tap available, 1 volume/1 tone control, 3-way switch, available in Blue finish, disc. 2000.
Last MSR was $1,450.

ELECTRIC: PERFORMER SERIES

NBG-6 - offset double cutaway body with the look of the modular models, body features a large oval cutout in lower bout, rosewood fingerboard with dot position markers, 6-on-a-side tuners, three humbucker pickups, 1 volume/1 tone, 3-way switch, stop tailpiece, available in Red or Sunburst finishes, current mfg.
MSR $899

MARK 1 - offset double cutaway body, maple neck and fingerboard, black dot position markers, 6-on-a-side tuners, 2 exposed coil humbucker pickups, tremolo bridge, 1 volume/1 tone control, 3-way switch, available in Cherryburst finish, current mfg.
MSR $399

MARK II - similar to Mark 1 except has Floyd Rose Licensed tremolo, available in Sunburst finish, current mfg.
MSR $499

Norma 12-String courtesy John Oldag

N

MARK III - similar to Mark II except has gold hardware and higher grade top, available in Redburst finish.
    MSR   **$599**

ELECTRIC BASS: MODULAR MODELS

MERLIN - modular body, quartersawn mapleneck, rosewood fingerboard with dot position markers, 4-on-a-side tuners, two pickups, different pickup modules available, 1 volume/1 tone control, 3-way switch, available in Black finish, current mfg.
    MSR   **$1,795**

NOUVEAU GUITARS

See Lady Luck.

NOVA GUITARS

See Buscarino, John. Instruments previously built in FL starting in 1981.

Luthier John Buscarino founded the Nova Guitar Company in 1981, and produced a number of high quality solid body electric guitars under that logo before changing to his current trademark of Buscarino. Buscarinio currently focuses on acoustic and acoustic archtop models.

NOVAX

Instruments currently built in San Leandro, CA since 1985. Novak has built custom guitars since 1970, in locations from NY to CA.

Luthier Ralph Novak began playing guitar at age fourteen in 1965, and also began experimenting with guitar design, modifying guitars, and making (crude) custom parts.

By age sixteen, Novak was repairing and customizing guitars for friends and doing some freelance repair for local music stores. Novak continued part-time repairwork through high school at Stuyvesant in New York, and through college at Brooklyn College, where he studied music. By age nineteen, Novak was working with Charles LoBue at GuitarLab in Greenwich Village in New York. Later, he quit college to work full-time at GuitarLab, where he worked with some of New York City's finest guitarists and built custom guitars. In his spare time Novak began working on innovative designs with LoBue.

Around 1975, LoBue and GuitarLab moved uptown to Alex's Music on West 48th Street. Novak stayed at Alex's for about a year, and then began freelance repair work for several stores on West 48th as well as seeing private clients in his repair shop in a downtown loft.

In 1978, Novak and LoBue moved to the San Francisco Bay area, and worked together until LoBue moved back to New York City. Novak stayed in the Bay area and worked at Subway Guitars in Berkeley, later becoming a partner and helping to build it into the viable repair shop it is today. In 1985, Novak left the partnership to open his own repair shop in Oakland, where he also built several custom instruments per year. In 1989, Novak received a U.S. patent for his "Fanned Fret" system, and began working on prototypes to find the optimum scale length combination for guitar and bass. In 1992 the Novax fretboard was mentioned in *Business Week* magazine's "1992 Idea Winners," and received the Industrial Design Society Award for Excellence in 1993 (the last music-related award was Ned Steinberger's headless bass in 1982).

The first official Novax guitar was completed in 1993, as the result of several years of researching and developing and gathering opinions and suggestions from players of all styles of music. Novak eventually obtained custom hardware for his system, and since then has concentrated on building Expression series and Tribute model guitars and basses. Due to the labor-intensive nature of the work, Novak has "retired" from the daily repair business to focus directly on his guitars, (biography courtesy Ralph Novak, March 18, 1996)

The patented Novax Fanned Fretboard has been licensed out to such notables as Dingwall Designer Guitars, Klein Custom Guitars, and Acacia Instruments, and, in late 1995, Moses Graphite announced retrofit epoxy-graphite Novax-style necks for Precision and Jazz basses.

ELECTRIC: EXPRESSION SERIES

The Expression Guitars are set-neck models with ergonomic body shapes that are highly carved for comfort and beauty. The new **Expression 8 String** was designed in conjunction with Charlie Hunter, and incorporates 3 bass strings and 5 guitar strings for a wide spectrum of sound. Current retail on this model is $4,500.

Novak's 6- or 7-string hollow body model named the **A-X** which is constructed "under tension" so the finished guitar is bright and responsive. Models range in price from $2,950 up to $3,250.

The **Expression Classic** has an offset double cutaway body features choices of walnut, maple, lacewood, zebrano, swamp ash, or birch; vertical-grain Eastern rock maple neck, patented 22-fret "fanned fret" design, choice of fingerboard materials such as wenge, purpleheart, paduak, rosewood, ebony, or bird's-eye maple; choice of three nut widths, Bartolini pickups, volume knob, rotary switching tone knob, pickup blend knob, 3-per-side headstock design and chrome tuners, available in Natural finish, mfg. 1993-current and MSR is $2,650 including the case. Options include:

The **Expression Custom** has an offset double cutaway body features a laminate design of highly figured bookmatched maple over a body core of paduak, lacewood, or purpleheart; vertical-grain Eastern rock maple neck, patented 22-fret "fanned fret" design, choice of wood-bound fingerboard materials such as wenge, purpleheart, paduak, rosewood, ebony, or bird's-eye maple; choice of three nut widths, Bartolini pickups, active circuitry (4 different choices), volume knob, rotary switching tone knob, pickup blend knob, gold or black chrome hardware, 3-per-side headstock design, available in Natural finish, current mfg. and retail is $3,150, including the case. Add $200 for vertical-grain Paduak neck.

The **Expression Baritone** has an offset double cutaway body features choice of walnut, birch, or lacewood; vertical-grain Eastern rock maple neck, patented 22-fret "Fanned Fret" design, choice of fingerboard materials such as wenge, purpleheart, paduak, rosewood, or ebony; Bartolini Soapbar pickups, extra bass-cut circuitry, volume knob, rotary switching tone knob, pickup blend knob, gold or black chrome hardware, 3-per-side headstock design, available in Natural finish, current mfg. retail is $2,850, including a gig bag. The Baritone model is a specially designed long-scale guitar in "B" tuning.

    Add $120 for Active circuitry with gain boost and active/passive switching. Add $175 for Active circuitry with treble and bass boost (16 Db cut/boost).

ELECTRIC: TRIBUTE SERIES

The Tribute models are built in tribute to the pioneering work of Leo Fender, and feature bolt-on necks as well as body designs that recall the classic lines of Fender's work. The Tribute Guitar has a Tribute body designs are either single cutaway ("Tele") or double cutaway ("Strat") based solids available in alder, ash, or swamp ash (body styles are also available in non-traditional laminated exotic woods), patended "Fanned Fret" fingerboard, Bartolini pickups mounted to the pickguard, Bartolini circuitry, traditional hardware and styling, current mfg. and retail is $1,950.

    Add $500 for laminated body and rear routed electronics (eliminates pickguard).

ELECTRIC BASS

Novak´s 5-string electric bass, named the **Mo´ B**, is constructed with birch, lacewood, maple, or walnut. Models can be ordered as a Custom, with laminated body and bound fretboard (with wood choices similar to the Expression Custom guitar model).

The **Expression Bass 4-String** has an offset double cutaway body features choice of walnut, birch, maple, or lacewood; vertical-grain eastern rock maple neck, patented "fanned fret" design, choice of fingerboard materials such as wenge, purpleheart, paduak, rosewood, or ebony; Bartolini Soapbar pickups, Bartolini circuitry, volume knob, tone knob, pickup blend knob, 2-per-side headstock design, available in Natural finish, current mfg. and retail is $2,650. The Expression Bass 5-string retails for $2,750, and the 6-string is $2,850.

The **Expression Custom Bass** offset double cutaway body features a laminate design of highly figured bookmatched maple over a body core of paduak, lacewood, or purpleheart; vertical-grain eastern rock maple neck, patented "fanned fret" design, choice of wood-bound fingerboard materials such as wenge, purpleheart, paduak, rosewood, ebony, or bird´s-eye maple; Bartolini pickups, Bartolini circuitry, volume knob, tone knob, pickup blend knob, gold or black chrome hardware, 2-per-side headstock design, available in Natural finish, current mfg. and retail is $3,150 including the case. The 5-String is $3,250, and the 6-string is $3,350.

The **Tribute Bass** has a Tribute body designs are a double cutaway ("Precision") or ("Jazz") based solids available in alder, ash, or swamp ash (body styles are also available in non-traditional laminated exotic woods), patented "Fanned Fret" fingerboard, Bartolini pickups mounted to the pickguard, Bartolini circuitry, traditional hardware and styling, current mfg. and retail is $2,400.

Add $500 for laminated body and rear routed electronics (eliminates pickguard). Add $175 for active tone shaping electronics.

**Novax Charlie Hunter
courtesy Novax**

N

NOTES

Section O

OFB GUITARS

See Pat Wilkins. Instruments previously built in Virginia Beach, VA during the early 1990s.

OLP

Officially Licensed Product. Instruments currently produced in China since the early 2000s. Distributed in the U.S. by HHI in Cincinnati, OH.

OLP (Officially Licensed Product) offers guitars based on many designs including the Ernie Ball-style Eddie Van Halen model. OLP also offers other designs with the patented 4/2-per-side tuners. For more information, contact OLP directly (see Trademark Index).

OLP MM1
courtesy OLP

GRADING	100% MINT	98% NEAR MINT	95% EXC+	90% EXC	80% VG+	70% VG	60% G

ELECTRIC

MM1 - single cutaway Eddie Van Halen-style basswood body, North American maple neck and 22-fret fingerboard with dot inlay, 4/2-per-side tuners, non-locking tremolo bridge, two dirty finger humbucker pickups, single knob, 3-way switch, chrome hardware, available in Black Sparkle, Candy Red, Desert Gold, Mint Green, Lava Pearl, or Red Hot finishes, mfg. 2002-present.

MSR	$300		$200	$170	$150	$130	$110	$90	$70

Also available in left-handed configuration.

MM4 - double cutaway basswood body, North American maple neck, 22-fret rosewood fingerboard with dot inlay, 4/2-per-side tuners, non-locking tremolo bridge, S/S/H pickups, two knobs, 5-way switch, chrome hardware, available in Candy Red or Stratus Blue Sparkle finishes, current mfg.

MSR	$300		$220	$180	$150	$130	$110	$90	$70

O´HAGAN

Instruments previously built in St. Louis Park (a suburb of Minneapolis), MN from 1979 to 1983. Distributed by the Jemar Corporation of St. Louis Park, MN.

O´Hagan guitars were developed by Jerry O´Hagan. O´Hagan, a former clarinetist and music teacher, began importing the Grande brand acoustic guitars from Japan in 1975. In 1979, the O´Hagan guitar company was formed to build quality, affordable solid body guitars. Two years later, the company incorporated as the Jemar Corporation (this designation can be found on the back of post-1981 models).

In 1983, both a nationwide recession and a resurgence in traditional guitar design (the beginning of "Strat-mania") took a toll on the four-year-old company. When a bank note became due, the company was unable to pay. The I.R.S. had an outstanding bill due as well, and seized company holdings to auction off. The O´Hagan company, which tried to provide quality guitars at an affordable price, closed its door for good. It is estimated that only 3,000 instruments were produced during the company´s four-year production, with the majority being the NightWatch models.

Serialization ran one of two ways during the company´s production: The first serial number code was **YYMXXX**, with the first two digits indicating the year, the third (and sometimes fourth) digit the month, and the final digits provided the sequential numbering. The second code was probably instituted in the 1980s, as only one digit indicated the year. The second serial code was **MYMXXX**, with the first and third digits indicating the month, the second digit the year, and the last three digits sequential numbering (source: Michael Wright, *Guitar Stories*, Volume One).

VISUAL IDENTIFICATION FEATURES

Headstock Identification: O´Hagan instruments can be identified by the O´Hagan decal, or a glued-on stylized "O H" logo which also featured a cloverleaf (or sometimes just the cloverleaf). Instruments may also sport a "Jemar Corporation" decal back by the serial number.

Pickup Identification: One dating method to use is based on the instrument´s pickup (if the original pickups are still installed). Instruments built between 1979 and 1980 had pickups by Mighty Mite; in 1981, they were switched to DiMarzio; and finally O´Hagan settled on Schaller pickups in 1982 and 1983.

ELECTRIC

The most eye-catching model was the **Shark** (basic retail list $529), which was introduced in 1979. The body design recalls a rounded-off Explorer, and features maple and walnut in a neck-through design. The vaguely offset headstock features 3+3 tuning machine alignment, and the guitar has two humbuckers, a 3-way pickup selector switch, two volume knobs, and a master tone knob. Other models may feature push/pull coil tap potentiometers (this option cost an extra $90), and a phase switch. O´Hagan also developed the **NightWatch** model, initially a single cutaway LP-style guitar (original retail list $479), and then joined by a dual cutaway model (same retail list price) of the same name.

In 1980, O´Hagan introduced his most popular model, the **Twenty Two** (retail list $529). This model, again built of maple and walnut, is based on the popular Flying V design. The **Laser** model, a sort of Strat-based design, featured a six-on-a-side headstock and either three single coils or a humbucker. As O´Hagans were basically hand-built custom instruments, various options can be found on existing models, and models were available in a left-handed configuration.

O

GRADING	100% MINT	98% NEAR MINT	95% EXC+	90% EXC	80% VG+	70% VG	60% G

LASER - offset double cutaway Strat-style body with different pointed ends, maple body with maple/walnut neck-thru design, 22-fret fingerboard, either 3 single coil or a single humbucker pickup, 6-on-one-side tuners, two knobs, single switch, available in various colors, mfg. 1981-83.

	N/A	$500	$425	$350	$300	$250	$200

NIGHTWATCH - single (Les Paul) or double (Les Paul Junior) cutaway body, 2 humbucker pickups, 3-per-side tuners, 3 knobs, 2 switches, available in various finishes, mfg. 1981-83.

	N/A	$450	$375	$325	$275	$225	$175

SHARK - offset Explorer style body with not-quite-as-sharp points, maple body with maple and walnut neck-thru design, 22-fret fingerboard with dot inlay, 3-per-side tuners, 2 humbucker pickups, 3 knobs, 2 switches, available in various finishes, mfg. 1979-1983.

	N/A	$600	$500	$425	$350	$300	$250

TWENTY-TWO - Flying V-style body, maple body, maple/walnut neck-thru design, 22-fret fingerboard with dot inlay, 2 humbucker pickups, 3-per-side tuners, 3 knobs, 2 switches, available in various finishes, mfg. 1980-83.

	N/A	$550	$475	$400	$325	$275	$225

ELECTRIC BASS

All guitar models had a bass counterpart (original retail prices ran an additional $10 to $50 extra, depending on the model). Bass models were available as a Regular, which had one pickup; or a Special, which had two pickups.

OAHU

Instruments previously built by Kay, from the 1930s to the 1960s, however the Oahu trademark was used all the way up into the 1980s. Previously distributed by the Oahu Publishing Company of Cleveland, OH.

The Oahu Publishing Company offered Hawaiian- and Spanish-style acoustic guitars, lap steels, sheet music, and a wide range of accessories during the Hawaiian music craze of pre-war America. Catalogs stress the fact that the company is a major music distributor, but the instruments were really built by the Kay Musical company. They produced a number of Hawaiian style guitars in the 1930s and 1940s, primarily. In the late 1930s, Oahu developed a line of lap steel guitars and amplifiers. Information courtesy: Michael Wright, *Guitar Stories*, Volume Two.

OAKLAND

Instruments previously produced in Japan from the late 1970s through the early 1980s.

These good quality solid body guitars featured both original designs and designs based on classic American favorites (source: Tony Bacon and Paul Day, *The Guru's Guitar Guide*).

ODELL

Instruments previously produced by the Vega Guitar Company of Boston, MA, and distributed through the Vega Guitar catalog circa early 1930s to the early 1950s.

Odell acoustic guitars with slotted headstocks were offered through early Vega Guitar catalogs in the early 1930s. In the 1932 catalog, the four Odell models were priced above Harmony guitars, but were not as pricey as the Vega models.

Other Odell mystery guitars appear at guitar shows from time to time. David Pavlick is the current owner of an interesting arch top model. The three-tuners-per-side headstock features a decal which reads "Odell - Vega Co., - Boston," and features a 16.5 in. archtop body, one Duo-Tron pickup, 20-fret neck, volume/tone controls mounted on the trapeze tailpiece. Inside one f-hole there is "828H1325" stamped into the back wood. Any additional information would be appreciated and can be submitted directly to the *Blue Book of Electric Guitars* (source: David J. Pavlick, Woodbury, CT).

ODYSSEY

Instruments previously built in North Vancouver, British Columbia (Canada), from 1976 to 1981.

Odyssey Guitars, Ltd. was founded in 1976 by partners Attila Balogh (luthier/production manager) and Joe Salley (sales manager). The preliminary guitar model was featured both as a carved top model with body binding and diamond-shaped fingerboard inlays, as well as a non-bound version in mahogany or ash body. In 1981, Balogh and Salley parted ways and dissolved the company.

Salley still retains the rights to the Odyssey name, and sells Odyssey Accessories at the Wes-Can company in Surrey, British Columbia. In March 1983, Balogh was commissioned by Paul Dean (Loverboy) to produce a limited run of fifty Paul Dean models. While these models were similar to the custom handcrafted guitar that Paul Dean himself built, they had nothing to do with Odyssey guitars. Balogh then worked with Ray Ayotte to set up the Ayotte Drum Company. Attila Balogh was killed in an accident in November of 1987. Balogh is remembered as being a true craftsman in every sense of the word, (company history and model information courtesy Mike Kinal, April 1997).

MODEL DATING IDENTIFICATION

1976-1977: The 3-per-side headstock has a slight dip in the center, bass and treble horns are relatively short.

1978-1979: Redesigned body has lengthened bass and treble horns, center of headstock has a rounded up area.

1980-1981: Introduction of the bolt-neck **Attila** models, headstock has an **AA** logo.

ELECTRIC

The first series of Odyssey guitars featured an ornate carved top/bound body model called the **Carved Guitar**, which had a retail price of $1,195. The non-bound body version was available in a mahogany or ash body. All models featured a 3-per-side headstock, set-neck design, 2 DiMarzio humbuckers, Schaller tuners, brass nut/hardware, and a high gloss, hand-rubbed finish. The **Mahogany Guitar** model listed for $895, and the **Ash Guitar** was $995. Both non-bound guitar models were offered with a corresponding Bartolini Hi-A pickup equipped 4-string bass model with similar listed prices.

The **Attila (AA) Series** were offered between 1980 and 1981, and featured the Odyssey guitar and bass design with a bolt-on (instead of set-in) neck. Pricing is estimated to be around the Hawk series level.

In late 1978, the body design was retooled, and the headstock profile was redesigned. The previous Carved Guitar model became the **Carved Top Series 100**. The G100 has a carved bookmatched figured maple top, set-in neck, 24.75 in. scale, 3-per-side headstock, herringbone body binding, maple headstock veneer, 24-fret bound ebony fingerboard with mother-of-pearl dot inlays, tune-o-matic bridge/stop tailpiece, brass hardware, Schaller or Grover tuners, 2 DiMarzio Dual Sound humbucker pickups, 2 volume/2 tone controls, 2 coil tap switches, 3-way pickup selector switch, available in Tobacco Shaded (TS) or Wine Shaded (WS) finishes, mfg. 1978-1981. Last MSR was $1,195.

In 1978, the previous Ash Guitar model became the **Carved Top Series 200**. The G200 has a double cutaway carved ash body, set-in neck, 24.75 in. scale, 3-per-side headstock, 24-fret bound ebony fingerboard with abalone inlays, tune-o-matic bridge/stop tailpiece, brass hardware, Schaller or Grover tuners, 2 DiMarzio Dual Sound humbucker pickups, 2 volume/2 tone controls, 2 coil tap switches, 1 phase switch, 3-way pickup selector switch, available in Tobacco Shaded (TS) or Wine Shaded (WS) finishes, mfg. 1978-1981. Last MSR was $995.

In 1978, the previous Mahogany Guitar model became the **Mahogany Series 300**. The G300 has a double cutaway mahogany body, set-in neck, 24.75 in. scale, 3-per-side headstock, 24-fret bound ebony fingerboard with abalone inlays, tune-o-matic bridge/stop tailpiece, brass hardware, Schaller or Grover tuners, 2 DiMarzio Dual Sound humbucker pickups, 2 volume/2 tone controls, 1 phase switch, 3-way pickup selector switch, available in Tobacco Shaded (TS) or Wine Shaded (WS) finishes, mfg. 1978-1981. Last MSR was $895.

Based on Odyssey guitar designs, the Hawk model was designated the economy series with a maple body, Natural finish, and different hardware choices.

G400 has a double cutaway maple body, set-in neck, 24.75 in. scale, 3-per-side headstock, 24-fret bound ebony fingerboard with dot inlays, tune-o-matic bridge/stop tailpiece, brass hardware, Schaller or Grover tuners, 2 DiMarzio humbuckers, volume/tone controls, 3-way pickup selector switch, available in Natural finish, mfg. 1978-1981. Last MSR was $595 and add $50 for Tobacco Shaded (TS) or Wine Shaded (WS) finishes.

The G500 featured a neck-through body design, a free-floating spruce top, double cutaway semi-hollow body, spruce top, neck-through body, 24.75 in. scale, 3-per-side headstock, 24-fret bound ebony fingerboard with mother-of-pearl inlays, hand carved ebony bridge/stop tailpiece, brass hardware, Schaller or Grover tuners, 2 DiMarzio humbucker pickups, 2 volume/ 2 tone controls, 2 coil tap switches, 1 phase switch, 3-way pickup selector switch, available in Tobacco Shaded (TS) or Wine Shaded (WS) finishes, mfg. 1978-1981. Last MSR was $1,995. Add $200 for optional 6-band on board EQ.

Odyssey´s **Custom Series 600** offered the customer the choice of any Odyssey guitar style, exotic or noble hardwoods, DiMarzio Dual Sound, PAF, Super II pickups, or Bartolini Hi-A pickups, 2 volume/2 tone controls, 2 coil tap switches, 1 phase switch, 6-band onboard graphic EQ, 3-way pickup selector switch, available in Tobacco Shaded (TS) or Wine Shaded (WS) finishes, mfg. 1978-1981. Last MSR was $1,995. Add $200 for optional 6-band onboard EQ.

Odyssey's **Custom Series 600** offered the customer the choice of any Odyssey guitar style, exotic or noble hardwoods. DiMarzio Dual Sound, PAF, Super II pick-ups, or Bartolini Hi-A pickups, 2 volume/2 tone controls, 2 coil tap switches, 1 phase switch, 6-band onboard graphic EQ, 3-way pickup selector switch. The **G600** guitar or the **B600** bass was available in Tobacco Shaded (TS) or Wine Shaded (WS) finishes, and either model had a list price of $1,495. Odyssey offered a **Custom V** and **Custom X-plorer** models that featured neck-through body construction, rosewood fingerboards, a bone nut, 2 DiMarzio pickups, Gotoh Gut machine heads, a Leo Quan Badass bridge, volume/tone controls, phase switch, 3-way selector switch. The V had a 3+3 "Flying V" headstock, while the X-plorer had a six-on-a-side headstock. Both models were offered at $999 with a hardshell case.

O'Hagan Model Twenty-Two courtesy George McGuire

ELECTRIC BASS

The **B100 Carved Top Bass** has a carved bookmatched figured maple top, set-in neck, 34 in. scale, 2-per-side headstock, herringbone body binding, maple headstock veneer, 24-fret bound ebony fingerboard with mother-of-pearl dot inlays, tune-o-matic/stop tailpiece, brass hardware, Schaller or Grover tuners, 2 Bartolini Hi-A pickups, 2 volume/2 tone controls, 3-way pickup selector switch, available in Tobacco Shaded (TS) or Wine Shaded (WS) finishes, mfg. 1978-1981. Last MSR was $1,195.

The **B200 Carved Ash Bass** has a double cutaway ash body, set-in neck, 34 in. scale, 2-per-side headstock, 24-fret bound ebony fingerboard with abalone inlays, tune-o-matic/stop tailpiece, brass hardware, Schaller or Grover tuners, 2 Bartolini Hi-A pickups, 2 volume/2 tone controls, 3-way pickup selector switch, and is available in Tobacco Shaded (TS) or Wine Shaded (WS) finishes, mfg. 1978-1981. Last MSR was $995.

The **B300 Mahogany Bass** has a double cutaway mahogany body, set-in neck, 34 in. scale, 2-per-side headstock, 24-fret bound ebony fingerboard with abalone inlays, tune-o-matic/stop tailpiece, brass hardware, Schaller or Grover tuners, 2 Bartolini Hi-A pickups, 2 volume/2 tone controls, 3-way pickup selector switch, and is available in Tobacco Shaded (TS) or Wine Shaded (WS) finishes, mfg. 1978-1981. Last MSR was $895.

The **B400 Hawk Bass** has a double cutaway maple body, set-in neck, 34 in. scale, 2-per-side headstock, 24-fret bound ebony fingerboard with dot inlays, Leo Quan Badass bridge, brass hardware, Schaller or Grover tuners, DiMarzio P-bass-style split pickup, volume/tone controls, pickup selector switch, and is available in Natural finish, mfg. 1978-1981. Last MSR was $595. Add $50 for Tobacco Shaded (TS) or Wine Shaded (WS) finishes.

The **B500 Semi-Acoustic Bass** has a double cutaway semi-hollowbody, spruce top, neck-through body, 34 in. scale, 2-per-side headstock, 24-fret bound ebony fingerboard with mother-of-pearl inlays, hand carved ebony bridge/stop tailpiece, brass hardware, Schaller or Grover tuners, 2 Bartolini pickups, 2 volume/2 tone controls, 3-way pickup selector switch, and is available in Tobacco Shaded (TS) or Wine Shaded (WS) finishes, mfg. 1978-1981. This model was available with a fretted or unfretted fingerboard. Last MSR was $1,995. Add $200 for optional 6-band onboard EQ.

OLD KRAFTSMAN

Instruments previously produced by Gibson and Kay circa 1930s-1960s. See chapter on House Brands.

This trademark has been identified as a House Brand of Speigel, and was sold through the Speigel catalogs. The Old Kraftsman brand was used on a full line of acoustic, thinline acoustic/electric, and solid body guitars from circa 1930s to the 1960s. Old Kraftsman instruments were probably built by various companies in Chicago, including Kay and some models by Gibson (source: Michael Wright, *Vintage Guitar Magazine*).

ONYX

Instruments previously built in Korea during the 1980s.

The Onyx trademark was the brand name of an Australian importer. These solid body guitars were generally entry level to intermediate quality. However, the late '80s model **1030** bears a passing resemblance to a Mosrite Mark I with modern hardware (source: Tony Bacon, *The Ultimate Guitar Book*).

OPTEK

See Smartlight.

OPUS

Instruments previously produced in Japan in the mid-1970s

The Opus trademark is a brand name of U.S. importers Ampeg/Selmer (source: Michael Wright, *Guitar Stories*, Volume One).

ORANGE

Instruments previously produced in Korea during the mid-1970s.

While this solid body guitar did feature an original body design and two humbucking pickups, the finish was painted black! (source: Tony Bacon and Paul Day, *The Guru's Guitar Guide*).

ORBIT

See Teisco Del Rey. Instruments previously built in Japan during the mid- to late 1960s.

The Orbit trademark is the brand name of a UK importer. Orbit guitars were produced by the same folks who built Teisco guitars in Japan, so while there is the relative coolness of the original Teisco design, the entry level quality is the drawback (source: Tony Bacon and Paul Day, *The Guru's Guitar Guide*).

ORPHEUM

See also Lange. Instruments currently produced in Asia since 2001 and distributed by Tacoma Guitars. Instruments previously manufactured in Chicago, IL circa 1930s to 1940s. Distributed by William L. Lange Company of New York, NY, and by C. Bruno & Son. Instruments later manufactured in Japan circa 1960s. Distributed by Maurice Lipsky Music Company, Inc., of New York, NY.

The Orpheum trademark goes back to 1901. Orpheum guitars were first introduced by distributor William L. Lange Company of New York in the mid-1930s. The Orpheum brand instruments were also distributed by C. Bruno & Son during this early period. It is estimated that some of the Orpheum models were built in Chicago, Illinois by the Kay company.

Lange's company went out of business in the early 1940s, but New York distributor Maurice Lipsky resumed distribution of Orpheum guitars circa 1944. The Maurice Lipsky Music Company continued distributing Orpheum guitars through to the 1960s (see also Domino, source: Tom Wheeler, *American Guitars*; Orpheum Manufacturing Company catalog courtesy John Kinnemeyer, JK Lutherie).

Until more research is done in the Orpheum area, prices will continue to fluctuate. Be very cautious in the distinction between the American models and the later overseas models produced in Japan. "What the market will bear" remains the watchword for Orpheums.

Orpheums are available once again. They are distributed by Tacoma guitars and offered at a competitive price.

OSCAR SCHMIDT

Instruments currently produced in Korea. Distributed by U.S. Music Corp. in Mundelein, IL.

The original Oscar Schmidt company was based in Jersey City, New Jersey, and was established in the late 1800s by Oscar Schmidt and his son, Walter. The Oscar Schmidt company produced a wide range of stringed instruments and some of the trade names utilized were Stella, Sovereign, and LaScala, among others. The company later changed its name to Oscar Schmidt International, and, in 1935 or 1936, followed with the Fretted Instrument Manufacturers. After the company went bankrupt, the Harmony Company of Chicago, Illinois purchased rights to use Oscar Schmidt's trademarks in 1939.

In the late 1900s, the Oscar Schmidt trademark was revived by the Washburn International Company of Illinois. Oscar Schmidt currently offers both acoustic guitars and other stringed instruments for the beginning student up to the intermediate player (source: Tom Wheeler, *American Guitars*).

In 1999, Oscar Schmidt released a semi-hollow body electric model, the OE30. Please contact Music Corp. directly for more information (see Trademark Index).

ELECTRIC

OE30 - double cutaway hollow body, maple top/back/sides, 2 f-holes, rosewood fingerboard, 3-per-side tuners, black pickguard, two humbucker pickups, four knobs, chrome hardware, available in Black or Cherry finishes, mfg. 1999-present.

	MSR	$350		$225	$175	$145	$120	$100	$80	$60

OE30DL - similar to the OE30, except has a flamed maple top and gold hardware, available in Blue Burst or Tobacco Sunburst finishes, mfg. 2003-present.

	MSR	$400		$250	$200	$170	$140	$120	$100	$80

OE40 - single cutaway full-bodied jazz hollow body, maple top/back/sides, 2 f-holes, rosewood fingerboard with split block inlays, 3-per-side tuners, black pickguard, fancy tailpiece, two humbucker pickups, four knobs, gold hardware, available in Tobacco Sunburst finish, mfg. 2003-present.

	MSR	$500		$300	$250	$220	$190	$160	$130	$100

OX10 - offset double cutaway Strat-style hardwood body, maple neck, rosewood fingerboard, six-on-one-side tuners, Fulcrum tremolo bridge, SSH pickups, two knobs, five-way switch, chrome hardware, available in Black, Blue, or Red finishes, mfg. 2004-present.

	MSR	$220		$140	$110	$90	$70	$55	$40	$25

GRADING	100% MINT	98% NEAR MINT	95% EXC+	90% EXC	80% VG+	70% VG	60% G

ELECTRIC BASS

OB20 - double cutaway semi-hollow maple body, two f-holes, mahogany neck, rosewood fingerboard, standard bridge and stop tailpiece, two passive soapbar pickups, four knobs, three-way switch, chrome hardware, available in Black or Blue Burst finishes, current mfg.

	MSR	$450		$270	$230	$200	$170	$150	$130	$110

OB30 - offset double cutaway hardwood body, maple neck, 24-fret rosewood fingerboard, matching headstock, fixed bridge, single split pickup, two knobs, chrome hardware, available in Black, Metallic Blue, Natural Satin, or Trans. Red finishes, current mfg.

	MSR	$280		$170	$140	$120	$100	$80	$60	$45

OTHON

Instruments currently built in Orangevale, CA.

Luthier Robert Othon currently offers a range of high quality, solid body guitars that feature a lightweight top of solid rock. Othon's patented process produces a layer of stone so thin that it adds only six to eight ounces to the total weight. Both the Classic and the **Highlander** feature offset double cutaway alder bodies, while the **Viking** has a Honduran mahogany body and a slight flare to the forward horns. The **Traditional** features a single cutaway swamp ash body, 2 single coils, and a fixed bridge. All models feature bolt-on hard rock maple necks and 25 1/2" scale lengths. For further information, contact luthier Robert Othon directly (see Trademark Index).

OTWIN

See Musima. Instruments previously built in East Germany in the late 1950s to early 1960s.

Instruments with the Otwin brand name were built by the Musima company in Germany beginning in the late 1950s. Earlier models were available in original designs of both solid body and semi-hollowbody configurations through the early 1960s (source: Tony Bacon and Paul Day, *The Guru's Guitar Guide*).

OVATION

Instruments currently built in New Hartford, CT since 1967. Distribution is handled by the Kaman Music Corporation of Bloomfield, CT. Solidbody electrics and semi-hollow electrics are no longer produced.

The Ovation guitar company, and the nature of the Ovation guitar's synthetic back are directly attributed to founder Charles H. Kaman's experiments in helicopter aviation. Kaman, who began playing guitar back in high school, trained in the field of aeronautics and graduated from the Catholic University in Washington, D.C. His first job in 1940 was with a division of United Aircraft, home of aircraft inventor Igor Sikorsky. In 1945, Kaman formed the Kaman Aircraft Corporation to pursue his helicopter-related inventions.

As the company began to grow, the decision was made around 1957 to diversify into manufacturing products in different fields. Kaman initially made overtures to the Martin company, as well as exploring both Harmony and Ludwig drums. Finally, the decision was made to start fresh. Due to research in vibrations and resonances in the materials used to build helicopter blades, guitar development began in 1964 with employees John Ringso and Jim Rickard. In fact, it was Rickard's pre-war Martin D-45 that was used as the "test standard." In 1967, the Ovation company name was chosen, incorporated, and settled into its new facilities in New Hartford, Connecticut. The first model named that year was the Balladeer.

Ovation guitars were debuted at the 1967 NAMM show. Early players and endorsers included Josh White, Charlie Byrd, and Glen Campbell. Piezo pickup-equipped models were introduced in 1972, along with other models. During the early 1970s, Kaman Music (Ovation's parent company) acquired the well-known music distributor Coast and also part of the Takamine guitar company. By 1975, Ovation decided to release an entry level instrument, and the original Applause/Medallion/Matrix designs were first built in the U.S. before production moved into Korea.

In 1986, Kaman's oldest son became president of Kaman Music. Charles William "Bill" Kaman II had begun working in the Ovation factory at age fourteen. After graduating college in 1974, Bill was made Director of Development at the Moosup, Connecticut plant. A noted Travis Bean guitar collector (see Kaman's Travis Bean history later in this book), Bill Kaman remained active in the research and development aspect of model design. Kaman helped design the Viper III and the UK II solid bodies.

Bill Kaman gathered all branches of the company under one roof as the Kaman Music Corporation (KMC) in 1986. As the Ovation branch was now concentrating on acoustic and acoustic/electric models, the corporation bought the independent Hamer company in 1988 as the means to re-enter the solid body guitar market. Furthermore, KMC began distributing Trace-Elliot amplifiers the same year, and bought the company in 1992. The Kaman Music Corporation acts as the parent company, and has expanded to cover just about all areas of the music business. As a result, the Ovation branch now concentrates specifically on producing the best acoustic guitars, with the same attention to detail that the company was founded on (source: Walter Carter, *The History of the Ovation Guitar*).

FOUR DIGIT MODEL CODES

Ovation instruments are identified by a four-digit model code. The individual numbers within the code will indicate production information about that model. The first digit is generally 1.

The second digit describes the type of guitar. The third digit indicates the depth of the guitar's bowl. The fourth digit indicates the model (for the first 8 acoustics). The color code follows the hyphen after the four-digit model number. Colors available on Ovation guitars are Sunburst (1), Red (2), Natural (4), Black (5), White (6), LTD Nutmeg/Anniversary Brown/Beige/Tan (7), Blue (8), Brown (9), Barnwood [a grey to black sunburst] (B), and Honeyburst (H). Other specialty colors may have

Oscar Schmidt OE40
courtesy Oscar Schmidt

O

Oscar Schmidt OB 20 Bass
courtesy Oscar Schmidt

GRADING	100% MINT	98% NEAR MINT	95% EXC+	90% EXC	80% VG+	70% VG	60% G

a 2- or 3-letter abbreviation, (information collected in Mr. Carter´s Ovation Appendices was researched and compiled by Paul Bechtoldt). For further information regarding Ovation acoustic models, please refer to the *Blue Book of Acoustic Guitars*.

ELECTRIC

Although Ovation´s solid body guitars are generally overshadowed by the fine acoustic models, they still are good playable instruments that offer a change of pace from the traditional market favorites. Ovation introduced the **Electric Storm** semi-hollowbody guitars in 1968, and they were available through 1973. The Electric Storm models featured bodies built in Germany, and hardware by Schaller. American-built solid bodies were presented beginning 1972, and various models survived through to 1983. Early models featured an on-board FET preamp, and are probably the first production guitars with "active electronics."

In 1984, Ovation produced the **Hard Body** series, which featured Korean-built necks and bodies, DiMarzio pickups and Schaller hardware. The Hard Body series was only briefly offered for a year, and can be identified by the natural wood strip bearing the Ovation name on the lower section of the four- or six-on-a-side headstocks. The 3+3 headstock looks similar to other Ovation headstocks. Model names range from **GP** (Guitar Paul) which had a retail price of $399, to the **GS** (Guitar Strat) models which ranged in price from $315 to $425. Those names seem pretty self-explanatory in regards to the models they resembled. Both solid body guitars and basses were offered. In 1988, Kaman bought the independent **Hamer** company, a move which brought the company back into the solid body guitar field in a competitive way.

BREADWINNER (MODEL 1251) - "kidney"-shaped mahogany body, mahogany neck, 3-per-side headstock, dot fingerboard inlay, two large single coil pickups, master volume knob, master tone knob, midrange filter switch, three-way pickup selector switch, available in a textured Black, White, Tan, or Blue finish, mfg. 1972-79.

	N/A	$625	$550	$450	$375	$300	$225

Last MSR was $349.

In 1975, single coil pickups were replaced by humbuckers. In 1976, Blue finish was discontinued.

DEACON (MODEL 1252) - single cutaway body, diamond shaped position markers, master volume knob, master tone knob, midrange filter switch, three-way pickup selector switch, available in Sunburst finish, mfg. 1973-1982.

	N/A	$600	$525	$450	$375	$300	$225

Last MSR was $449.

In 1975, single coil pickups were replaced by humbuckers. In 1976, colors were expanded to Red, Black, and Natural finishes.

Deacon Deluxe - similar to the Deacon, except featured different hardware and pickups, mfg. 1972-1980.

	N/A	$650	$575	$500	$400	$325	$250

Deacon Twelve String (Model 1253) - similar to the Deacon, except in 12-string configuration, mfg. 1976-1980.

	N/A	$550	$475	$400	$325	$250	$175

ECLIPSE (MODEL K-1235) - economy model of the Electric Storm series, semi-hollow, available in Black finish only, mfg. 1971-73.

	N/A	$500	$425	$350	$300	$250	$200

HURRICANE (MODEL K-1120) - 12-string configuration, double cutaway semi-hollow body, gold-plated hardware, two DeArmond humbucker pickups, master volume knob, two separate tone control knobs, phase switch on bass bout, pickup balance/blend switch on treble bout, available in Natural, Nutmeg, or Walnut Green finishes, mfg. late 1968-69.

	N/A	$500	$425	$350	$275	$225	$175

This is the same as the Thunderhead in 12-string configuration.

PREACHER (MODEL 1281) - double cutaway mahogany body, two humbucker pickups, 24.5 in. scale, mfg. 1975-1982.

	N/A	$450	$375	$300	$250	$200	$150

Preacher Deluxe (Model 1282) - similar to the Preacher, except features a series/parallel pickup switch and a midrange control, mfg. late 1975-78.

	N/A	$500	$425	$350	$275	$225	$175

Preacher Deluxe Twelve String (Model 1283) - similar to the Preacher Deluxe, except in twelve-string configuration, mfg. late 1975-78.

	N/A	$450	$375	$300	$250	$200	$150

THUNDERHEAD (MODEL K-1360/K-1213/K-1233) - double cutaway semi-hollow body, gold-plated hardware, two DeArmond humbucker pickups, master volume knob, two separate tone control knobs, phase switch on bass bout, pickup balance/blend switch on treble bout, available in Natural, Nutmeg, or Walnut Green finishes, mfg. 1968-1972.

	N/A	$425	$350	$300	$250	$200	$150

Thunderhead (Model K-1460) with vibrato was introduced in 1968. In 1970, the Thunderhead changed designation to K-1213; the Thunderhead with vibrato was designated K-1212. In 1971, Electric Storm models were offered in Red, Nutmeg, and Black. In the Spring of 1971, the Thunderhead changed its designation to K-1233; the Thunderhead with vibrato was designated K-1234.

Thunderhead With Vibrato (Model K-1460/K-1212/K-1234) - similar to the Thunderhead except with vibrato, mfg. 1968-1972.

	N/A	$450	$375	$325	$275	$225	$175

TORNADO (MODEL K-1160/K-1211/K-1231) - similar to the Thunderhead model, except features separate volume knobs for each pickup, chrome hardware, and no phase switch, available in Red or Sunburst finishes, mfg. late 1968-1973.

	N/A	$475	$400	$325	$275	$225	$150

Tornado (Model K-1260) with vibrato was introduced in 1968. In 1970, the Tornado changed designation to K-1211; the Tornado with vibrato was designated K-1212. In the Spring of 1971, the Tornado changed designation to K-1231; the Tornado with vibrato was designated K-1232.

Tornado With Vibrato (Model K-1260/K-1212/K-1232) - similar to the Tornado, except has vibrato, mfg. 1968-1973.

	N/A	$500	$425	$350	$275	$225	$175

GRADING	100% MINT	98% NEAR MINT	95% EXC+	90% EXC	80% VG+	70% VG	60% G

UK II (MODEL 1291) - double cutaway Urelite (Urethane) material on an aluminum frame, set-neck design, two humbucker pickups, two volume knobs, two tone knobs, series/parallel pickup switching, three-way pickup selector switch on upper bass bout, mfg. 1980-82.

	N/A	$725	$625	$525	$450	$350	$250

Last MSR was $550.

The UK II designation was short for Ultra Kaman II.

ULTRA GP/GS - single cutaway (GP) or double cutaway (GS) solidbody in a variety of configurations, one, two, or three pickups, available in various finishes, mfg. 1985-late 1980s.

	N/A	$250	$200	$170	$140	$110	$80

VIPER (MODEL 1271) - single cutaway ash body, bolt-on one-piece maple neck, maple or ebony fingerboard, two single coil pickups, 25 in. scale, master volume knob, master tone knob, three-way pickup selector switch, mfg. 1975-1983.

	N/A	$425	$350	$300	$250	$200	$150

Last MSR was $395.

While most bodies were built of ash, some were built using maple or mahogany.

VIPER III (MODEL 1273) - similar to the Viper, except has three single coil pickups with different individual windings, and three on/off pickup selector switches, mfg. 1975-1983.

	N/A	$475	$400	$325	$275	$225	$175

ELECTRIC BASS

MAGNUM I (MODEL 1261) - double offset cutaway mahogany body, graphite reinforced neck, humbucker pickup (neck position) and double coil pickup (bridge position), stereo output, string mute, mfg. 1974-1982.

	N/A	$625	$550	$475	$400	$350	$300

Last MSR was $570.

MAGNUM II (MODEL 1262) - similar to the Magnum I, except featured a 3-band active EQ, mfg. 1974-1982.

	N/A	$675	$600	$525	$450	$375	$325

Last MSR was $685.

MAGNUM III (MODEL 1263) - similar to the Magnum I, except features less radical body styling (deeper bass bout cutaway), two split-coil humbuckers, mfg. 1978-1983.

	N/A	$625	$550	$475	$400	$350	$300

Last MSR was $570.

MAGNUM IV (MODEL 1264) - similar to the Magnum II, except features less radical body styling (deeper bass bout cutaway), two split-coil humbuckers, mfg. 1978-1983.

	N/A	$675	$600	$525	$450	$375	$325

Last MSR was $685.

TYPHOON I (MODEL K-1140) - similar to the Thunderhead guitar model, except in four-string bass version, mfg. late 1968-69.

	N/A	$575	$500	$450	$375	$325	$250

TYPHOON II (MODEL K-1240/K-1222) - similar to the Typhoon I model, except initial models have a smaller body and shorter cutaway horns, mfg. late 1968-1972.

	N/A	$600	$525	$450	$375	$325	$250

Originally catalogued as the Williwaw, which means Mountain Wind (in keeping with the Electric Storm motif). In mid-1969, the body design was changed to resemble other Electric Storm models. In 1970, the Typhoon II changed designation to K-1222.

TYPHOON III (MODEL K-1340) - similar to the Typhoon I, except fretless, mfg. 1969-1970.

	N/A	$575	$500	$450	$375	$325	$250

TYPHOON IV (MODEL K-1216) - similar to the Typhoon III, mfg. 1970-72.

	N/A	$575	$500	$450	$375	$325	$250

TYPHOON V (MODEL K-1217) - mfg. 1971-72.

	N/A	$600	$525	$450	$375	$325	$250

ULTRA HARD UB - double cutaway P-Bass style, 4-on-one-side tuners, available in various finishes, mfg. 1985-late 1980s.

	N/A	$200	$160	$130	$100	$80	$60

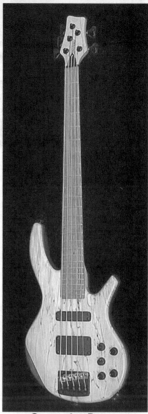

Overwater Basses
Evolution
courtesy Overwater Basses

OVERWATER BASSES

Instruments currently built in the United Kingdom since the late 1970s.

Luthier Chris May has been building high quality guitars and basses since 1978. May has built a number of custom basses with innovative designs, such as the **C Bass** (1985) which features a lower-than-standard tuning of C-F-Bb-Eb. This 36 in. scale bass was tuned two full steps below conventional four-string tuning.

In 1995, The Overwater Guitar Company moved to their new headquarters in Carlisle, Cumbria (the last town on A69 before Scotland). The new Overwater Jam Factory, Ltd. features two rehearsal studios, a 24-track recording facility, and a retail outlet for musical equipment sales in addition to May's workshops. May also helped develop the Delta line of bass amplification for Carlsboro. For more information on Overwater, refer to their website (see Trademark Index).

ELECTRIC

May offers the **Advance** custom guitar and the "**S**" and "**T**" **Traditional** series models in one of three configurations: The **Standard** has a one-piece neck-through design, and solid wings. The **Deluxe** features a one- or two-piece neck-through design, and an overlaid flat top. The **Pro** configuration is a one- or two-piece neck-through with a carved top. Bolt-on necks are also offered.

Advance necks can be walnut, mahogany, or maple, and the bodies constructed of solid mahogany or walnut (with the option of a flat or carved maple top). Traditional series guitars are generally built with maple necks and either sycamore, light ash, or alder bodies. Fingerboards can be rosewood, ebony, or maple. Customers can specify pickup and electronics, and choice of finish.

ELECTRIC BASS

Chris May is featuring three bass models: the original styles of the **Progress** and **Fusion**, as well as the traditional styled "J" model. Basses are offered in 4-, 5-, 6-, 7-, and 8-string configurations (only 4- and 5-string on the "J" series). Again, there are three different variants in the bass model offering: the **Classic** has a two- or three-piece neck-through design and solid wings. The **Deluxe** features a three-piece neck-through design with laminated wings, and the **Pro** has similar construction with multi-laminated wings. While the "J" series features a bolt-on neck, the body can still be upgraded to a Deluxe or a Pro. Bass necks can be laminated of maple/walnut or maple/sycamore, and the bodies constructed of sycamore, maple or walnut. The traditional "J" basses are generally built with maple necks and either sycamore, light ash, walnut, or alder bodies. Fingerboards can be rosewood, ebony, or maple. Customers can specify pickup and electronics, and choice of finish. There are the **Elite**, **Evolution**, and **Anniversary** Series that are available as well.

Section P

PBC

See Bunker Guitars. Instruments previously built in Coopersburg, PA from 1989 to 1996.

The PBC Guitar Technology company is the collaboration between John Pearse, Dave Bunker, and Paul Chernay. Pearse and Bunker met at the 1988 NAMM show in California. Pearse was promoting his strings and high tech pickups, while Bunker was demonstrating his Touch guitar. The two were later joined by Chernay, a long-time friend of Pearse. Luthier Bunker's previous guitar designs, while radical for their time, were designed in a way to solve certain inherent solid body design flaws. PBC Guitar Technology introduced both the Tension-Free neck design and the Wishbone hollowbody series.

After the PBC Guitar Technology company went out of business in 1996, Dave Bunker began building guitars under his old Bunker Guitars trademark in 1998 (see Bunker Guitars). Bunker's new company planned on offering PBC-style models in late 1998/early 1999.

The Tension-Free design involves a solid 3/8 in. steel bar that runs inside the length of the neck, and transfers all the string pull directly to the body of the instrument. This leaves the outer wood neck and fretboard free from the loading that would normally lead to neck warpage, and the solid steel core carries all neck vibration to the body. Tension-Free necks have appeared on other manufacturer's models (such as Ibanez' USA Prestige Series models).

ELECTRIC: GTS, GTX, & TOUCH SERIES

PBC offered a number of custom options in regards to woods, finishes, electronics, and other player-oriented concerns. In the early 1990s, PBC offered the GTS electric solid body series. Models featured PBC pickups, 25 in. scale, 24-fret fingerboards, Tension-Free necks, and six-on-a-side tuners. The **GTS 200** (list $1,095 to $1,595) featured a offset double cutaway body, Floyd Rose tremolo system, 2 PBC Banshee single coils and 1 PBC Spectrutone humbucker pickup.

The **GTS 350** (list $1,195 to $1,695) was a single cutaway model with 2 PBC Spectrutone humbucking pickups, coil taps, Tension-Free neck, and a through-the-body bridge. A semi-hollowbody version, the **GTS 350 SH** (list $1,595 to $1,895) featured similar hardware.

The GTX series of the early 1990s was a marriage of conventional guitar shapes and the Touch series electronics. GTX guitars had a unique angular body design, 25 in. scale, and 2 humbuckers (actually pre-amped Hex pickups similar to the Touch guitar system). The **GTX 200 H** (list $1,895) had the tuning keys on the headstock, while the **GTX Hammer** (list $1,995) featured reverse tuning (tuning keys on the bridge). A fairly advanced system that offered great sustain and keyboard-like note attack - the guitar is actually off until you hammer or pick a note!

The Dave Bunker Signature Series Touch Guitar models offered an instrument that can be played by touching the strings. This innovative instrument combines a 6-string guitar neck, 4-string bass guitar neck, and the PBC Hexaphonic pickups/electronics package. The **GTT 1000** was a high quality, basic model listed at $1,695, and had a solid color finish. The **GTT 2000** (list $2,195) doubled the number of hexaphonic pickups per neck, and thus tripled the tonal options. The top of the line GTT 3000 added a series of adjustable bandpass filters to the 20 hexaphonic pickups, as well as the option of a clear lacquer finish on the natural wood models. The new list price on the **GTT 3000** models ranged from $2,995 to $3,295.

GRADING	100% MINT	98% NEAR MINT	95% EXC+	90% EXC	80% VG+	70% VG	60% G

ELECTRIC: WISHBONE SERIES

Wishbone Hollowbody guitars have an innovative design. Rather than mount the bridge to the solid, carved top like other conventional designs, Bunker's bridge floats on a wishbone/multi laminate wood beam that extends from the heel block to the underneath of the bridge. A brass bar couples the block to the bridge, leaving the top of the guitar free to resonate like an acoustic guitar top.

The Wishbone series consists of three hollowbody archtop models, and an Arlen Roth Signature model. All four models include the Tension-Free neck and Wishbone bridge support beam. Tops are carved from solid bookmatched figured maple, and the bodies are carved from blocks of tone woods.

Add $100 for ebony fingerboard. Add $100 for AAA grade maple top. Add $100 for neck binding. Add $250 for left-handed configuration. Add $250 for EMG piezo bridge transducer.

AC 200 - 2 in. deep single cutaway maple (or alder, or walnut) body, carved arched solid figured maple top, 2 f-holes, eastern hard rock maple neck, 25.5 in. scale, 22-fret rosewood (or maple or morado) fingerboard with dot inlay, carved ebony (or rosewood or morado) Wishbone bridge, brass saddles, 3+3 tuners, chrome hardware, Bill Lawrence Keystone pickups, volume/blend/tone controls, available in Natural, Amberburst, Rubyburst, or Vintageburst finishes, disc. 1996.

N/A	$1,000	$850	$700	$600	$500	$400

Last MSR was $1,795.

In 1996, Jewel Top finishes were introduced. Finishes include Trans. Amber, Trans. Emerald, and Trans. Ruby tops with natural back and sides.

ARLEN ROTH SIGNATURE AC 200 - similar to the AC 200, except has a 6-on-a-side headstock with screened signature, available in Rubyburst or satin finish Amberburst, disc. 1996.

N/A	$1,100	$950	$800	$700	$600	$500

Last MSR was $1,795.

GRADING	100% MINT	98% NEAR MINT	95% EXC+	90% EXC	80% VG+	70% VG	60% G

AC 300 - similar to the AC-200, except has 3.5 in. body depth, disc. 1996.

| | N/A | $1,200 | $1,050 | $900 | $750 | $650 | $550 |

Last MSR was $1,995.

AC 312 - similar to the AC 300, except has 12-string configuration, disc. 1996.

| | N/A | $1,300 | $1,150 | $1,000 | $850 | $700 | $600 |

Last MSR was $2,495.

ELECTRIC BASS: GTB SERIES

Companion basses to the GTS series guitars of the early 1990s can be viewed as forerunners to today´s current models. Both the 200 series and the 350 series offered Tension-Free necks and through-the-body bridges, 34 in. scale, 24-fret fingerboards, and PBC pickups. The **GTB 200** (list $995) featured a offset double cutaway body, four-on-a-side headstock, and chrome hardware. A five-string version, the **GTB 205** (list $1,295) featured similar hardware.

Both the four-string **GTB 350** and five-string **GTB 355** headless models have the same features as the current models. However, the newer designs have a more pronounced inverse body curve by the bridge. Earlier models had prices that ranged from $1,195 to $1,895.

Later GTB models featured Tension-Free necks and through-the-body bridges.

Add $100 for fretted or fretless ebony fingerboards. Add $100 for AAA grade maple top. Add $200 for EMG BTC active tone circuit. Add $350 for left-handed configuration. Add $900 for patented Hex Mute electronics.

GTB 354 - double cutaway alder body, figured maple top, 5-piece laminated maple and walnut neck, 34 in. scale, 24-fret rosewood (or maple or morado) fingerboard with dot inlay, PBC through-the-body bridge, 2+2 tuners, gold or chrome hardware, two EMG DC pickups, volume/tone controls, pickup selector switch, available in Natural, Amberburst, Vintageburst, or Trans. Emerald, Ruby, Sapphire, Amethyst (Purple), or Onyx finishes, disc. 1996.

| | N/A | $900 | $800 | $700 | $600 | $500 | $400 |

Last MSR was $1,495.

This model is available in a headless configuration (tuners on bridge) at no extra charge.

GTB 355 - similar to the GTB 354, except has a 5-string configuration, 3/2 headstock, disc. 1996.

| | N/A | $1,000 | $850 | $750 | $650 | $550 | $450 |

Last MSR was $1,795.

This model is available in a headless configuration (tuners on bridge) at no extra charge.

GTB 356 - similar to the GTB 354, except has a 6-string configuration, 3-per-side headstock, disc. 1996.

| | N/A | $1,100 | $950 | $800 | $700 | $600 | $500 |

Last MSR was $2,095.

The GTB 356 is available only in the headless configuration.

ELECTRIC BASS: WISHBONE SERIES

Both models include the Tension-Free neck and Wishbone bridge support beam. Tops are carved from solid bookmatched figured maple, and the bodies are carved from blocks of tone woods.

Add $100 for headless neck. Add $100 for fretted or fretless ebony fingerboards. Add $100 for AAA grade maple top. Add $200 for EMG BTC active tone circuit. Add $350 for left-handed configuration. Add $900 for patented Hex Mute electronics.

AB 400 - 2 in. deep double cutaway maple (or alder, or walnut) body, carved arched solid figured maple top, 2 f-holes, 5-piece laminated maple and walnut neck, 34 in. scale, 22-fret rosewood (or maple or morado) fingerboard with dot inlay, carved ebony (or rosewood or morado) Wishbone bridge, brass saddles, 2+2 tuners, chrome hardware, two EMG DC pickups, volume/tone controls, pickup selector switch, available in Natural, Amberburst, Vintageburst, or Trans. Emerald finishes, disc. 1996.

| | N/A | $1,300 | $1,150 | $1,000 | $850 | $700 | $600 |

Last MSR was $2,495.

AB 500 - similar to the AB 400, except has a 5-string configuration, 3/2 headstock, disc. 1996.

| | N/A | $1,450 | $1,250 | $1,100 | $950 | $800 | $650 |

Last MSR was $2,795.

PC

See also Ned Callan. Instruments previously built in England from the early 1970s through the mid-1980s.

The PC brand is the trademark of custom luthier Peter Cook, who produced the original design Axis solid body guitar for a number of years (source: Tony Bacon and Paul Day, *The Guru's Guitar Guide*).

PACK LEADER

Instruments previously built in England during the late 1970s.

This high quality solid body guitar was built by luthier Roger Bucknall (Fylde Guitars), and its original design was available in either a rosewood or walnut version. For further information on Roger Bucknall, see Fylde (source: Tony Bacon and Paul Day, *The Guru's Guitar Guide*).

PALM BAY

Instruments currently built in England.

Palm Bay is currently offering a number of high quality electric guitars. Models like the Cyclone have an offset double cutaway mahogany body and maple top, maple neck, ebony fingerboard, licensed Floyd Rose bridge, DiMarzio humbuckers, and a Palm Tree inlay at the first fret. Other models include the Cyclone SE-X and Tidal Wave EXP.

PALM GUITAR

Instruments currently built in Southbury, CT.

The Palm Guitar is advertised as the World's smallest electric guitar. This guitar is truly portable as it is only 26 in. long and weighs in at three pounds. The body is made out of a carbon fiber graphite composite so it won't warp in excessive heat or cold. For more information refer to their website (see Trademark Index).

ELECTRIC

The Palm guitar is available in three different models. The **Basic**, is just what it sounds like, designed for economy and retails for $1,100. The **Standard** includes a Seymour Duncan pickup and other options. This retails for $1,500. A **Custom** model is also available, which put's you in the designer's chair and this guitar starts at $1,500. There is also a bass model available.

PALMER

Instruments currently produced in Asia since the late 1980s. Distributed by Chesbro Music Company of Idaho Falls, ID, and Tropical Music Corporation of Miami, FL.

Both the Chesbro Music Company and Tropical Music Corporation are distributing Palmer brand acoustic and classical models. These models are geared towards the entry level or student guitarist.

During the late 1980s, Palmer offered instruments that were entry level solid body guitars that feature designs based on traditional American designs. Solid body models were marketed under the trademark (or model designation) of Biscayne, Growler, Baby, and Six. The **Biscayne** trademark is still distributed by Tropical Music Corporation. Palmer electric guitars are usually priced in the used market between $75 and $300.

PANGBORN

Instruments previously built in England from the late 1970s to the late 1980s.

Luthier Ashley Pangborn has specialized in high quality custom order solid body guitars, as well as standard models such as the Warrior and the Warlord (source: Tony Bacon and Paul Day, *The Guru's Guitar Guide*).

PAO CHIA

Instruments currently produced in China. Distributed by the Guangzhou Bourgade Musical Instruments Factory Co. Ltd.

Pao Chia instruments have been produced since 1988. They produce an entire line of acoustic guitars, as well as classical guitars, and electric guitars and basses. These instruments are mainly entry level models at entry level prices. For more information in Chinese, refer to their website (see Trademark Index).

PARADIS

Instruments currently built in Switzerland.

Luthier Rolf Spuler, designer of the Ibanez AFR Affirma series in the early 1990s, continues to offer advanced design high quality instruments.

PARKER

Instruments currently produced in Wilmington, MA, since 2003. Distributed by U.S. Music Corp. in Mundelein, IL. Previously produced in New York from 1992-2003. Previously distributed by Korg USA of New York, NY.

Designer Ken Parker began building unconventional archtop guitars in the 1970s. He then took a job with (now defunct) Stuyvesant Music in New York City, working both in the repair shop as well as building Guitar Man instruments. Parker's background in repairing and customizing guitars became the groundwork for the innovative design of the Fly guitar.

In 1982, Parker met Larry Fishman (Fishman Transducers) while reviewing a prototype bass. Parker and Fishman joined forces, and attended the 1985 NAMM music industry show to gain financial backing for the new Fly model. The new guitar design attracted some interest in the market, but Parker and Fishman were interested in protecting the design, rather than let unauthorized versions show up in the marketplace. Around 1990, Korg USA (distributor of Marshall amplifiers and Korg keyboards in the U.S. market) took interest in the design and production applications. The Fly guitar debuted at the 1992 NAMM show.

Parker guitars are carved from solid wood, and then have a thin layer of carbon/glass/epoxy composite material applied as a strengthening measure. The fingerboard and peghead veneer on these instruments are made from the same synthetic composite material. While the futuristic design and composite material tends to mystify vintage-minded guitar owners, the Fly is still 95% wood.

In 2003, Parker introduced the Parker Custom Shop. Customers can now have guitars built to their specifications, where just about anything goes. Contact Parker for information on the Custom Shop (see Trademark Index). In 2003, they became a part of U.S. Music Corp., which also owns Washburn, Randall Amplifiers, and Oscar Schmidt.

ELECTRIC: FLY SERIES

All instruments in this series have the following specs: offset double cutaway carved poplar one piece body/neck, 24-fret carbon/fiber epoxy fingerboard, blackface peghead with screened logo, 6-on-a-side locking Sperzel tuners, and black hardware. Instruments are finished in a gloss urethane paint.

Palm Guitar Electric Standard courtesy Palm Guitar

P

GRADING	100% MINT	98% NEAR MINT	95% EXC+	90% EXC	80% VG+	70% VG	60% G

F - fixed Parker bridge, 2 exposed humbucker pickups, master volume/volume/tone controls, 3-position switch, mfg. 1994 only.

	N/A	$1,150	$1,000	$875	$750	$650	$550

Last MSR was $1,625.

FV - standard Parker vibrato, vibrato tension wheel, 2 exposed humbucker pickups, master volume/volume/tone controls, 3-position switch, mfg. 1994 only.

	N/A	$1,300	$1,150	$1,000	$850	$725	$600

Last MSR was $1,910.

FD - fixed Parker bridge, 2 exposed humbucker/6 piezo bridge pickups, master volume/humbucker volume/tone controls, stacked volume/tone piezo control, two 3-position switches, mfg. 1994 only.

	N/A	$1,350	$1,200	$1,050	$900	$750	$600

Last MSR was $1,960.

FLY ARTIST (FAV) - similar to the Fly Deluxe, except features a solid Sitka spruce body, vibrato bridge, piezo bridge mounted pickup, magnetic pickups, available in Trans. Cherry or Rootbeer Metallic finishes, mfg. 1996-2002.

	$2,950	$2,400	$2,000	$1,750	$1,500	$1,200	$895

Last MSR was $4,167.

In 1997, Transparent Butterscotch (BS) finish was introduced; Transparent Cherry and Rootbeer Metallic finishes were disc.

FLY CONCERT (FCT) - similar to the Fly Deluxe, except features a solid Sitka spruce body, piezo bridge pickups, and no magnetic pickup system, available in Trans. Cherry or Rootbeer Metallic finishes, mfg. 1996-2002.

	$2,000	$1,650	$1,400	$1,225	$1,000	$850	$650

Last MSR was $3,444.

In 1997, Transparent Butterscotch (BS) finish was introduced; Transparent Cherry and Rootbeer Metallic finishes were disc. In 1998, Ebony (E) - a solid Ebony Pearl finish was introduced. In 2000, Ebony (E) finish was disc.

FLY CLASSIC (FCV) - similar to the Fly Deluxe, except features a solid mahogany body, and finished top, available in Dusty Black (DB), Trans. Cherry (TC) or Metallic Rootbeer (RB) finishes, mfg. 1996-present.

MSR	$3,198	$2,350	$1,950	$1,600	$1,300	$1,050	$850	$625

In 1997, Natural Mahogany (NM), Teal (T), Transparent Blue (TB), and Transparent Emerald (TE) finishes were introduced. In 2000, Transparent Blue, Transparent Emerald, Teal, and Metallic Rootbeer finishes were disc.

Fly Classic Standard (FCVST) - non-piezo model, mahogany body with basswood neck, custom wound DiMarzio humbucker pickups, 24 hardened stainless steel frets, Parker vibrato system, locking Sperzel tuners, push-pull tone control coil-tap enables six pickup settings, available in Trans. Cherry or Natural Mahogany finishes, mfg. 2001-02.

	$1,900	$1,500	$1,350	$1,150	$950	$825	$600

Last MSR was $2,675.

FLY DELUXE (FDV) - standard Parker vibrato, vibrato tension wheel, 2 exposed humbucker/6 piezo bridge pickups, master volume/humbucker volume/tone controls, stacked volume/tone piezo control, two 3-position switches, available in Dusty Black (DB), Majik Blue (MB), Galaxie Gray, Euro Red, Pearl White (PW), Ruby Red (RR), Ice Blue Burst (IBSB), Italian Plum (IP), Emerald Green (EG), or Antique Gold (AG) finishes, mfg. 1994-present.

MSR	$2,998	$2,275	$1,800	$1,500	$1,200	$1,000	$800	$600

In 1998, Heather Grey (HG) finish was introduced; Galaxie Gray and Euro Red finishes were disc. In 2000, Pearl White (PW) finish was disc.

Fly Deluxe Standard (FDVST) - non-piezo model, poplar body and basswood neck, custom wound DiMarzio humbucker pickups, 24 hardened stainless steel frets, Parker vibrato system, locking Sperzel tuners, push/pull tone control coil-tap enables 6 pickup settings, available in Ruby Red (RR), Dusty Black (DB), or Majik Blue (MB), mfg. 2001-02.

	$1,725	$1,400	$1,200	$995	$875	$775	$675

Last MSR was $2,425.

FLY MAPLE CLASSIC (FCVM) - Fly Classic with maple body, Transparent Hazelnut Brown finish, mfg. 1999-2001.

	$2,425	$1,850	$1,550	$1,250	$1,050	$850	$625

Last MSR was $3,325.

In 2000, Trans. Cherry (TC) finish was introduced.

FLY MAPLE CUSTOM (FMCV) - select maple body, basswood neck, 2 custom wound DiMarzio humbucker magnetic pickups, Fishmad piezo active preamp/mixer system, parker high performance vibrato, available in Trans. Cherry finish, mfg. 2001-02.

	$2,425	$1,950	$1,725	$1,550	$1,375	$1,200	$1,050

Last MSR was $3,325.

FLY MOJO - Fly style carved mahogany body, mahogany neck, 24-fret carbon glass epoxy fingerboard, 2 Seymour Duncan humbucker pickups, aluminum vibrato bridge, 3 knobs, 2 switches, black hardware, available in Dusty Black, Natural Mahogany, or Trans. Cherry, mfg. 2004-present.

MSR	$3,398	$2,500	$2,050	$1,750	$1,500	$1,250	$1,000	$750

Add $75 for Natural Mahogany or Trans. Cherry finishes.

Fly Mojo Singlecut - similar to the Fly Mojo, except has a single cutaway body with no tremolo, available in Dusty Black, Natural Mahogany, or Trans. Cherry finishes, new 2005.

MSR	$2,698	$2,050	$1,750	$1,500	$1,250	$1,000	$800	$600

Fly Mojo Flame - similar to the Fly Mojo, except has a AAA Flame maple top, available in Trans. Green, Trans. Blue, or Black Cherry Burst finishes, mfg. 2004-present.

		$2,850	$2,500	$2,100	$1,700	$1,450	$1,200	$950

MSR $3,798

Fly Mojo Flame Singlecut - similar to the Fly Mojo Flame, except has a single cutaway body with no tremolo, available in Black Cherry Burst, Trans. Blue Burst, or Trans. Green Burst finishes, new 2005.

MSR	$2,998	$2,275	$1,800	$1,550	$1,300	$1,050	$850	$650

P

GRADING	100% MINT	98% NEAR MINT	95% EXC+	90% EXC	80% VG+	70% VG	60% G

FLY SUPREME (FSV) - similar to the Fly Deluxe, except features a solid maple body, and finished top, available in Trans. Honey (TH) or Sunburst (SB) finishes, mfg. 1996-2002.

| | $3,500 | $3,200 | $2,900 | $2,500 | $2,200 | $1,900 | $1,500 |

Last MSR was $5,111.

In 2000, Sunburst finish was disc.

SPANISH FLY - electric/classical nylon string guitar with solid Sitka spruce body, basswood neck, and ebony bridge with tie block, Butterscotch finish, mfg. 1999-2002.

| | $3,000 | $2,700 | $2,400 | $2,100 | $1,800 | $1,500 | $1,200 |

Last MSR was $4,139.

MIDIFLY (MIDFV) - features MidiAxe DSP-MIDI guitar system with vibrato, stereo output, Fishman piezo system, and DiMarzio magnetic pickups, MIDI in-out, Sunburst, Natural Mahogany or Heather Gray finish, mfg. 1999-2002.

| | $2,500 | $2,200 | $1,800 | $1,500 | $1,200 | $950 | $725 |

Last MSR was $3,611.

In 2000, Sunburst and Natural Mahogany finishes were disc.

FLY DELUXE SINGLE II (FDV2) - solid poplar body with basswood neck, custom wound Dimarzio humbucker and 2 single coil pickups plus 6-element Fishman piezo pickups, Custom Fishman Active Filtering Preamp, 5-way pickup selector, exclusive parker neck with carbon and glass fingerboard, stainless steel frets, presicion aluminum bridge with stainless steel saddles, Sperzel locking tuners, 3.5-5 lbs, available in Heather Gray (HG), Dusty Black (DB), or Ruby Red (RR) finishes, mfg. 2000-02.

| | $2,200 | $1,800 | $1,575 | $1,350 | $1,125 | $975 | $825 |

Last MSR was $3,050.

Parker Fly Classic
courtesy Parker

FLY HARDTAIL (FHT) - basswood body & basswood neck, custom Sperzel Drop-D tuner, carbon & glass fingerboard, jumbo stainless steel frets, 2 custom wound DiMarzio humbuckers plus Fishman 6-element piezo pickups, Custom Fishman Active Filtering Preamp, non-vibrato bridge with stainless steel saddles, available in Stealth Gray (SG) finish, mfg. 2000-02.

| | $2,125 | $1,750 | $1,500 | $1,300 | $1,100 | $950 | $800 |

Last MSR was $2,972.

FLY HARDTAIL STANDARD (FHTST) - non-piezo model, basswood body and neck, custom wound DiMarzio humbucker pickups, 24 jumbo, hardened stainless steel frets, non-vibrato bridge, locking Sperzel tuners with custom Drop-D, push/pull tone control coil-tap enables 6 pickup settings, available in Stealth Gray finish, mfg. 2001-02.

| | $1,825 | $1,600 | $1,400 | $1,200 | $1,000 | $850 | $725 |

Last MSR was $2,550.

FLY JAZZ (FJZ) - mahogany body and basswood neck, 2 custom wound DiMarzio humbuckers with a specially voiced neck pickup plus Fishman 6-element piezo pickups, Custom Fishman Filtering Preamp, exclusive Parker neck with stainless steel frets, Sperzel locking tuners, carbon & glass fingerboard, precision aluminum bridge with stainless steel saddles, available in Trans. Cherry (TC) finish, mfg. 2000-02.

| | $2,675 | $2,300 | $1,850 | $1,550 | $1,250 | $975 | $750 |

Last MSR was $3,750.

ELECTRIC: NIGHTFLY SERIES

The 1997/1998 NiteFly models now have the ability to mix electric and acoustic sound through one amp as well as two in stereo. Parker´s **NiteMix** (Model PNM1) magnetic mixer/preamp box is designed specifically for NFV1 and NFV2 Nitefly models to allow the individual outputs to be combined through a single guitar amplifier (list $160).

NITEFLY (NFV1) - offset double cutaway solid maple body, bolt-on neck (composed of modulus carbon/glass fiber), 22-fret fingerboard, 6-on-a-side locking Sperzel tuners, pickguard, free-floating vibrato, 3 single coil Dimarzio pickups/Fishman passive piezo-transducer bridge pickup, volume/tone controls, 5-way selector switch (magnetic pickups), piezo volume knob, piezo/magnetic selector switch, available in Black Pearl, White Pearl, Sunburst, Trans. Red, or Trans. Blue finishes, mfg. 1996-98.

| | $950 | $800 | $675 | $595 | $495 | $395 | $300 |

Last MSR was $1,199.

NITEFLY (NFV2) - similar to the NiteFly, except features 2 single coil DiMarzio pickups/DiMarzio humbucker, mfg. 1996-98.

| | $1,000 | $825 | $725 | $650 | $525 | $425 | $325 |

Last MSR was $1,249.

NITEFLY (NFV3) - offset double cutaway solid maple body, bolt-on basswood (reinforced by a back layer of carbon/glass/epoxy composite), 22-fret composite fingerboard, 6-on-a-side locking Sperzel tuners, black pickguard, Parker vibrato, 3 DiMarzio single coil pickups/Fishman piezo transducer bridge pickup, volume/tone controls, 5-way selector switch (magnetic pickups), piezo volume knob, piezo/magnetic selector switch, available in Black Pearl (B), White Pearl (W), Sunburst (SB), Trans. Red (TR), or Trans. Blue (TB) finishes, mfg. 1998-2000.

| | $975 | $850 | $750 | $650 | $525 | $425 | $325 |

Last MSR was $1,299.

NITEFLY (NFV4) - similar to the NiteFly, except features 2 single coil DiMarzio pickups/DiMarzio humbucker, available in Black Pearl (B), White Pearl (W), Sunburst (SB), Trans. Red (TR), or Trans. Blue (TB) finishes, mfg. 1998-2000.

| | $1,000 | $875 | $775 | $675 | $550 | $450 | $350 |

Last MSR was $1,349.

Parker Fly Mojo Flame
courtesy Parker

P

GRADING	100% MINT	98% NEAR MINT	95% EXC+	90% EXC	80% VG+	70% VG	60% G

NITEFLY-SA (NFVSA) - Nitefly configuration, carved swamp ash body and mahogany bolt-on neck, carbon & glass fingerboard, stainless steel frets, Nitefly vibrato system with stainless steel saddles, precision aluminum bridge, 2 DiMarzio single coil pickups and 1 DiMarzio humbucker pickup, 6-element Fishman piezo pickup, Sperzel locking tuners, available in Black, Sunburst, Trans. Red, or Trans. Blue, mfg. 1999-present.

	MSR	$1,848	$1,400	$1,100	$925	$800	$400	$600	$525

NITEFLY-SA STANDARD (NFVSAST) - non-piezo model, swamp ash body, mahogany bolt-on neck, custom wound DiMarzio pickups, 22 hardened stainless steel frets, locking Sperzel tuners, 5-way pickup selector switch, available in Black, Sunburst, Trans. Red, or Trans. Blue, mfg. 2001-02.

	$1,025	$800	$725	$675	$600	$650	$495

Last MSR was $1,444.

NITEFLY-M (NFVM) - similar to Nitefly-SA except mahogany body and neck, 2 DiMarzio humbucker pickups, available in Black, Sunburst, Natural, Trans. Red, or Trans. Blue, mfg. 1999-present.

	MSR	$1,748	$1,300	$1,050	$875	$750	$675	$575	$500

NITEFLY MOJO - Fly-style carved mahogany body, bolt-on mahogany neck, 22-fret carbon glass epoxy fingerboard, 2 Seymour Duncan humbucker pickups, aluminum vibrato bridge, 3 knobs, 2 switches, black hardware, available in Dusty Black, Natural Mahogany, or Trans. Cherry, mfg. 2004-present.

	MSR	$2,098	$1,550	$1,300	$1,050	$900	$775	$650	$550

Add $75 for Natural Mahogany or Trans. Cherry finishes.

Nitefly Mojo Flame - similar to the NiteFly Mojo, except has a AAA Flame maple top, available in Trans. Blue or Cherry Sunburst finishes, mfg. 2004-present.

	MSR	$2,498	$1,850	$1,550	$1,250	$1,050	$850	$700	$550

Nitefly Mojo Southern - similar to the Nitefly Mojo, except has two single coil Duncan pickups, a black pickguard, and controls mounted on a metal plate vertically, available in Blonde and Butterscotch finishes, new 2005.

	MSR	$1,848	$1,400	$1,100	$950	$800	$700	$600	$500

ELECTRIC: P SERIES

P-36 - Fly design, carved ash body, bolt-on maple neck, pickguard, single coil bridge and soap bar neck pickups, Fishman Piezo, available in Natural or Blonde finishes, mfg. 2004-present.

	MSR	$999	$650	$550	$475	$400	$350	$300	$250

P-38 (P38VA) - similar to Nitefly, select ash body and bolt-on maple neck with rosewood fingerboard, 22 jumbo nickel frets, custom Parker alnico humbucker and 2 single coil pickups, pearloid pickguard, Wilkinson licensed vibrato bridge system featuring Fishman piezo pickups, custom Fishman active preamp with "Smart Switching" output jack for mixing magnetic and piezo signals, available in Black, Sunburst, Trans. Blue, or Trans. Red, mfg. 2000-2003.

	$600	$500	$425	$375	$350	$325	$250

Last MSR was $849.

P-38 STANDARD (P38VAST) - non-piezo model, ash body, bolt-on maple neck with rosewood fingerboard, custom wound DiMarzio pickups, 22 jumbo nickel-silver frets, Wilkinson licensed vibrato, 5-way pickup selector switch, available in Black, Sunburst, or Trans. Red finishes, mfg. 2001-02.

	$525	$425	$350	$300	$260	$230	$200

Last MSR was $749.

P-40 (P40VA) - ash body, bolt-on maple neck with rosewood fingerboard, 1 humbucker pickup and 2 single coil custom wound Parker alnico magnetic pickups, Wilkinson licensed vibrato with Fishman piezo active preamp/mixer system, available in Steel Gray, Trans. Red, or Trans. Black finishes, mfg. 2001-03.

	$725	$650	$575	$500	$425	$350	$275

Last MSR was $999.

P-42 - Fly design, carved mahogany body, bolt-on mahogany neck, 2 humbucker pickups, Fishman Piezo, stop-tail bridge, available in Metallic Gray or Metallic Black finishes, mfg. 2004-present.

	MSR	$799	$525	$450	$400	$350	$300	$250	$200

P-44 (P44VM) - solid mahogany body, flamed maple top, maple bolt-on neck, rosewood fingerboard, 2 custom wound Parker Alnico humbucking pickups, Wilkinson-licensed Vibrato, Fishman active piezo pickup preamp/mixer, Grover locking tuners, three knobs, switch, chrome hardware, available in Tobacco Sunburst, Cherry Sunburst, or Trans. Charcoal, mfg. 2001-03.

	$850	$700	$625	$550	$475	$400	$325

Last MSR was $1,149.

PM-10 - single cutaway mahogany arched top body, set mahogany neck, stop bridge and tailpiece, no pickguard, two Parker Stinger humbucker pickups, two knobs, three-way switch, available in Black or Natural finishes, new 2005.

	MSR	$799	$525	$450	$400	$350	$300	$250	$200

PM-20 - single cutaway mahogany body, carved quilted bubinga or flame maple top, set mahogany neck, stop bridge and tailpiece, no pickguard, two Parker Stinger humbucker pickups, two knobs, three-way switch, available in Quilted Bubinga or Flame Maple Traditional Sunburst finishes, new 2005.

	MSR	$899	$600	$525	$450	$375	$325	$275	$225

ELECTRIC: FLY SELECT SERIES

BRONZE FLY - Fly design, carved Sitka spruce body, basswood neck, 24-fret carbon-glass epoxy fingerboard, 6 Element Fishman piezo pickup, 2 knobs, black hardware, available in Trans. Butterscotch finish, mfg. 2004-present.

	MSR	$3,398	$2,500	$2,100	$1,800	$1,500	$1,250	$1,000	$750

GRADING	100% MINT	98% NEAR MINT	95% EXC+	90% EXC	80% VG+	70% VG	60% G

FLY ARTIST - Fly design, carved Sitka spruce body, basswood neck, 24-fret carbon-glass epoxy fingerboard, 2 DiMarzio Humbucker pickups, 6 Element Fishman piezo pickup, 3 knobs, 2 switches, aluminum vibrato bridge, black hardware, available in Trans. Butterscotch finish, mfg. 2004-present.

| | MSR | $4,198 | | $3,600 | $3,100 | $2,600 | $2,100 | $1,800 | $1,500 | $1,200 |

FLY SUPREME - Fly design, carved Big Lake maple body, basswood neck, 24-fret carbon-glass epoxy fingerboard, 2 DiMarzio Humbucker pickups, 6 Element Fishman piezo pickup, 3 knobs, 2 switches, aluminum vibrato bridge, black hardware, available in Trans. Honey finish, mfg. 2004-present.

| | MSR | $5,198 | | $4,400 | $3,600 | $3,000 | $2,500 | $2,100 | $1,800 | $1,500 |

NYLON FLY - Fly nylon-string design, carved Sitka spruce body, wide basswood neck, 24-fret carbon-glass epoxy fingerboard, 6 Element Fishman piezo pickup, 2 knobs, gold hardware, available in Trans. Butterscotch finish, mfg. 2004-present.

| | MSR | $4,398 | | $3,800 | $3,200 | $2,700 | $2,100 | $1,800 | $1,500 | $1,200 |

ELECTRIC BASS: FLY BASS SERIES

FLY BASS (FB4) - double offset parker type spruce top body with quilted maple top and back, mahogany neck, 24 stainless-steel fret glass/carbon fingerboard, 2 custom-wound DiMarzio Ultra-Jazz pickups, Fisman piezo active pickup preamp/mixer system, four-on-one-side tuners, five black knobs, switch, available in Natural or Trans. Red finishes, mfg. 2002-present.

| | MSR | $3,198 | | $2,400 | $1,950 | $1,700 | $1,450 | $1,250 | $1,050 | $850 |

FLY BASS FIVE-STRING (FB5) - similar to the Fly Bass, except in five-string configuration, available in Natural or Trans. Red finishes, mfg. 2002-present.

| | MSR | $3,298 | | $2,500 | $2,050 | $1,750 | $1,500 | $1,275 | $1,075 | $875 |

FLY MOJO BASS - Fly Bass 4-string configuration, Sitka Spruce body with quilted maple top and back, carbon reinforced neck, 24-fret carbon-glass fingerboard, 2 humbucker pickups, 3 knobs, black hardware, available in Dusty Black or 3-Tone Sunburst finishes, new 2004.

| | MSR | $2,898 | | $2,200 | $1,750 | $1,450 | $1,150 | $950 | $750 | $600 |

Parker Nitefly SA
courtesy Parker

PARKSONS

Instruments currently produced in Korea. Distributed by Paxphil in Korea.

Parksons produces an entire line of acoustic guitars as well as electrics, basses, banjos, mandolins, and resonators. These guitars are mainly entry level instruments that retail for under $200. Refer to their website for more information and a full listing of every guitar that they produce (see Trademark Index).

PATRICK EGGLE GUITARS

Instruments currently produced in Coventry, England since 1991.

Eggle started building guitars in the late 1970s. He spent much of the 1980s building and repairing guitars. In the early 1990s he started building solidbody guitars under the name Patrick Eggle Guitars. In 1995, he left the company in pursuit to work alone. He spent the next few years doing repairs and building various instruments. In 2001, he started to build guitars again, but this time they were acoustic configurations. He worked in Bedforshire, England for a while until he moved to the U.S. Flattop and archtop guitars are currently produced in Hendersonville, NC. For more information refer to Patrick James Eggle Guitars in the *Blue Book of Acoustic Guitars* as he only produces acoustic flattops and archtops currently.

The company continued production of instruments. In January 1997, Patrick Eggle Guitars was purchased by music retailers Musical Exchanges, which has stores in Coventry and Birmingham (England). Between 1993 and 1994, two models (New York-USA and Los Angeles-USA) were assembled with Patrick Eggle components in Santa Barbara, California. However, full production is again completely centered in England. Patrick Eggle has several models available currently, however they are all in England and appear only in pounds versus dollars on the price sheet. Not many guitars find their way over to the U.S. and because of this, it's hard to determine prices on these guitars. There was also a series of archtop guitars released for the U.S. that retail between $6,500 and $8,500. For more information contact Patrick Eggle Guitars directly (see Trademark Index).

ELECTRIC: BERLIN SERIES

The Berlin model was voted the Making Music British Guitar of the Year award in 1995.

DELUXE - offset double cutaway maple body, carved figured maple top, mahogany neck, 24-fret ebony fingerboard with abalone dot inlay, abalone maple leaf inlay on 12th fret, locking Wilkinson vibrato, 3-per-side locking Sperzel tuners, gold hardware, 2 humbucker Eggle pickups, volume/coil tap control, 3-position switch, available in Antique Gold, Bahamian Blue, Burny Amber, Burgundy Burst, Chardonnay Rouge, Chardonnay Rouge Burst, Cherry, Cherry Burst, Citrus Green, Citrus Green Burst, Deep Sea Blue, Emerald Isle Blue, Pink Glow, Pink Glow Burst, Purple Haze, Shamu Blue, Shamu Blue Burst, Tobacco Burst, Vintage Gold Burst, or Walnut finishes, disc. 1994.

| | | N/A | $1,000 | $850 | $725 | $600 | $500 | $400 |

Last MSR was $1,400.

Parker Fly Bass
courtesy Parker

P

GRADING	100% MINT	98% NEAR MINT	95% EXC+	90% EXC	80% VG+	70% VG	60% G

PLUS - offset double cutaway mahogany body, carved figured maple top, mahogany neck, 24-fret ebony fingerboard with abalone dot inlay, tune-o-matic bridge/stop tailpiece, body matching peghead, 3-per-side locking Sperzel tuners, chrome hardware, 2 humbucker Eggle pickups, volume/tone control, 3-position switch, coil tap in tone control, available in Antique Gold, Bahamian Blue, Chardonnay Rouge, Cherry, Pink Glow, or Walnut finishes, disc. 1994.

	N/A	$550	$475	$400	$350	$300	$250

Last MSR was $800.

Add 10% for gold hardware.

PRO - offset double cutaway mahogany body, carved figured maple top, mahogany neck, 22-fret ebony fingerboard with abalone dot inlay, tune-o-matic bridge/stop tailpiece, body matching tailpiece, 3-per-side locking Sperzel tuners, chrome hardware, 2 humbucker Eggle pickups, volume/tone control, 3-position switch, available in Antique Gold, Bahamian Blue, Burgundy Burst, Chardonnay Rouge, Chardonnay Rouge Burst, Cherry, Cherry Burst, Deep Sea Blue, Emerald Isle Blue, Pink Glow, Pink Glow Burst, Purple Haze, Tobacco Burst, Vintage Gold Burst, or Walnut finishes, disc.

	N/A	$2,000	$1,700	$1,400	$1,200	$1,000	$800

Last MSR was $2,400.

The Berlin Pro is also offered with a 24-fret fingerboard, gold hardware, or Wilkinson VS 100 tremolo.

STAGE - offset double cutaway mahogany body, carved figured maple top, mahogany neck, 24-fret ebony fingerboard with abalone dot inlay, tune-o-matic bridge/stop tailpiece, body matching tailpiece, 3-per-side locking Sperzel tuners, chrome hardware, 2 humbucker Eggle pickups, volume/tone control, 3-position switch, available in Antique Gold, Bahamian Blue, Burgundy Burst, Chardonnay Rouge, Chardonnay Rouge Burst, Cherry, Cherry Burst, Deep Sea Blue, Emerald Isle Blue, Pink Glow, Pink Glow Burst, Purple Haze, Tobacco Burst, Vintage Gold Burst, or Walnut finishes, disc.

	N/A	$1,000	$850	$725	$600	$500	$400

Last MSR was $1,400.

STANDARD - offset double cutaway mahogany body, carved figured maple top, mahogany neck, 24-fret ebony fingerboard with abalone dot inlay, tune-o-matic bridge/stop tailpiece, body matching tailpiece, 3-per-side locking Sperzel tuners, chrome hardware, 2 humbucker Eggle pickups, volume/tone control, 3-position switch, available in Black, Natural, or White finishes, disc. 1994.

	N/A	$425	$350	$300	$250	$200	$150

Last MSR was $600.

Add 10% for gold hardware.

UK DLX-4HT - offset double cutaway mahogany body, highest quality (AAAA) carved figured maple top, mahogany neck, 22-fret ebony fingerboard with abalone maple leaf inlay, tune-o-matic bridge/stop tailpiece, 3-per-side Sperzel tuners, chrome hardware, 2 humbucker Eggle pickups, volume/tone control, 3-position switch, available in Natural finish, disc. 1994.

	N/A	$2,200	$1,800	$1,500	$1,200	$1,000	$800

Last MSR was $2,850.

UK DLS-4A - similar to UK DLX-4HT, except has Wilkinson vibrato, locking Sperzel tuners, disc. 1994.

	N/A	$2,300	$1,900	$1,600	$1,300	$1,000	$800

Last MSR was $3,100.

UK PLUS ULTRA - offset double cutaway mahogany body, carved figured maple top, mahogany neck, 22-fret ebony fingerboard with abalone dot inlay, tune-o-matic bridge/stop tailpiece, 3-per-side Sperzel tuners, chrome hardware, 2 humbucker Eggle pickups, volume/tone control, 3-position switch, available in Antique Gold, Cherry, Cherry Burst, or Tobacco Burst finishes, disc. 1994.

	N/A	$1,300	$1,100	$950	$800	$700	$600

Last MSR was $1,900.

UK Plus-1A - offset double cutaway mahogany body, carved figured maple top, mahogany neck, 22-fret ebony fingerboard with abalone dot inlay, tune-o-matic bridge/stop tailpiece, 3-per-side Sperzel tuners, chrome hardware, 2 humbucker Eggle pickups, volume/tone control, 3-position switch, available in Natural finish, disc. 1994.

	N/A	$950	$825	$700	$600	$500	$400

Last MSR was $1,300.

UK Plus-2A - similar to Plus-1A, except has higher quality (AA) carved maple top, disc. 1994.

	N/A	$1,050	$900	$775	$650	$550	$450

Last MSR was $1,500.

UK Plus-3A - similar to Plus-1A, except has higher quality (AAA) carved maple top, abalone maple leaf fingerboard inlay, disc. 1994.

	N/A	$1,300	$1,100	$950	$825	$700	$600

Last MSR was $1,940.

UK PRO ULTRA - offset double cutaway mahogany body, carved figured AAA maple top, mahogany neck, 24-fret ebony fingerboard with abalone dot inlay, locking Wilkinson vibrato, 3-per-side locking Sperzel tuners, chrome hardware, 2 humbucker Eggle pickups, volume/tone control, 3-position switch, available in Antique Gold, Cherry, Cherry Burst, or Tobacco Burst finishes, disc. 1994.

	N/A	$1,700	$1,400	$1,200	$1,000	$800	$600

Last MSR was $2,450.

UK Pro-3A - offset double cutaway mahogany body, carved figured AAA maple top, mahogany neck, 24-fret ebony fingerboard with abalone dot inlay, locking Wilkinson vibrato, 3-per-side locking Sperzel tuners, chrome hardware, 2 humbucker Eggle pickups, volume/tone control, 3-position switch, available in Natural finish, disc. 1994.

	N/A	$1,500	$1,300	$1,100	$950	$800	$600

Last MSR was $2,200.

ELECTRIC: LEGEND SERIES

JS - offset double cutaway, maple body, carved figured maple top, figured maple neck, 24-fret ebony fingerboard with pearl maple leaf inlay, locking Wilkinson vibrato, ebony veneer on peghead, 3-per-side locking Sperzel tuners, 2 active humbucker Reflex pickups, volume/tone control, 3-position switch, coil tap in volume control, active electronics, available in Antique Gold, Bahamian Blue, Burny Amber, Burgundy Burst, Chardonnay Rouge, Chardonnay Rouge Burst, Cherry, Cherry Burst, Citrus Green, Citrus Green Burst, Deep Sea Blue, Emerald Isle Blue, Natural, Pink Glow, Pink

GRADING	100% MINT	98% NEAR MINT	95% EXC+	90% EXC	80% VG+	70% VG	60% G

Glow Burst, Purple Haze, Shamu Blue, Shamu Blue Burst, Tobacco Burst, Vintage Gold Burst, or Walnut finishes, disc. 1994.

	N/A	$1,250	$1,100	$950	$800	$675	$550

Last MSR was $1,750.

This instrument was designed for Big Jim Sullivan. This model had black hardware as an option.

ELECTRIC: LOS ANGELES SERIES

PLUS - offset double cutaway maple body, bolt-on maple neck, 24-fret maple fingerboard with black pearl dot inlay, locking Wilkinson vibrato, 3-per-side locking Sperzel tuners, chrome hardware, 3 dual rail pickups, volume/tone control, 5-position rotary switch, mini switch, active electronics, available in Antique Gold, Cherry, Cherry Burst, Citrus Green, Pink Glow, Purple Haze, Shamu Blue, or Shamu Blue Burst finishes, disc. 1994.

	N/A	$575	$500	$425	$350	$300	$250

Last MSR was $850.

PRO - offset double cutaway maple body, bolt-on maple neck, 24-fret maple fingerboard with black pearl dot inlay, locking Wilkinson vibrato, ebony peghead veneer, 3-per-side locking Sperzel tuners, gold hardware, 3 stacked coil Reflex pickups, volume/tone control, 5-position rotary switch, active electronics, available in Antique Gold, Burgundy Burst, Chardonnay Rouge, Chardonnay Rouge Burst, Cherry, Cherry Burst, Citrus Green, Citrus Green Burst, Pink Glow, Pink Glow Burst, Purple Haze, Shamu Blue, Shamu Blue Burst, or Vintage Gold Burst finishes, disc. 1994.

	N/A	$750	$650	$575	$500	$425	$350

Last MSR was $1,100.

STANDARD - offset double cutaway maple body, bolt-on maple neck, 24-fret maple fingerboard with black pearl dot inlay, locking Wilkinson vibrato, 3-per-side locking Sperzel tuners, chrome hardware, 3 dual rail pickups, volume/tone control, 5-position rotary switch, mini switch, active electronics, available in Black, Natural, USA Blue, USA Pink, USA Red, or USA Yellow finishes, disc. 1994.

	N/A	$450	$375	$325	$275	$225	$175

Last MSR was $650.

USA-HT - offset double cutaway alder body, pearloid pickguard, bolt-on maple neck, 22-fret rosewood fingerboard with pearl dot inlay, fixed Wilkinson bridge, 3-per-side Sperzel tuners, 2 single coil/humbucker Seymour Duncan pickups, volume/tone control, 5-position rotary switch, mini switch, active electronics, available in Calypso Green, Creme, Iris Red, Mauve, or Silver Metallic finishes, disc. 1994.

	N/A	$750	$650	$575	$500	$425	$350

Last MSR was $1,100.

**Patrick Eggle Berlin Pro
courtesy Patrick Eggle Guitars**

Creme finish available with tortoise pickguard only.

USA-T - similar to USA-HT, except has locking Sperzel tuners, Wilkinson vibrato, disc. 1994.

	N/A	$800	$700	$600	$525	$450	$375

Last MSR was $1,200.

ELECTRIC: NEW YORK SERIES

DELUXE - offset double cutaway semi-hollow mahogany body, carved bound figured maple top, maple/rosewood neck, 22-fret ebony fingerboard with pearl NY inlay at 12th fret, tune-o-matic bridge, string-through body tailpiece, 3-per-side Sperzel tuners, gold hardware, 2 humbucker pickups, volume/tone control, 3-position switch, coil tap in tone control, available in Antique Gold, Bahamian Blue, Burny Amber, Burgundy Burst, Chardonnay Rouge, Chardonnay Rouge Burst, Cherry, Cherry Burst, Citrus Green, Citrus Green Burst, Deep Sea Blue, Emerald Isle Blue, Pink Glow, Pink Glow Burst, Purple Haze, Shamu Blue, Shamu Blue Burst, Tobacco Burst, Vintage Gold Burst, or Walnut finishes, disc. 1994.

	N/A	$425	$350	$300	$250	$200	$150

Last MSR was $600.

PLUS - offset double cutaway mahogany body, pearloid pickguard, bolt-on maple neck, 22-fret rosewood fingerboard with offset pearl dot inlay, tune-o-matic bridge, string-through body tailpiece, 3-per-side Sperzel tuners, chrome hardware, single coil/humbucker pickups, volume/tone control, mini switch, coil tap in tone control, available in Antique Gold, Burny Amber, Cherry, Citrus Green, or Deep Sea Blue, disc. 1994.

	N/A	$475	$400	$350	$300	$250	$200

Last MSR was $675.

Add 10% for gold hardware.

STANDARD - offset double cutaway mahogany body, pearloid pickguard, bolt-on maple neck, 22-fret rosewood fingerboard with offset pearl dot inlay, tune-o-matic bridge, string-through body tailpiece, 3-per-side Sperzel tuners, chrome hardware, single coil/humbucker pickups, volume/tone control, mini switch, coil tap in tone control, available in Black, Natural, USA Blue, USA Pink, USA Red, or USA Yellow finishes, disc. 1994.

	N/A	$350	$300	$250	$200	$160	$130

Last MSR was $500.

**Patrick Eggle Berlin Pro
courtesy Patrick Eggle Guitars**

P

GRADING	100% MINT	98% NEAR MINT	95% EXC+	90% EXC	80% VG+	70% VG	60% G

UK PLUS - offset double cutaway mahogany body, AA figured maple top, bolt-on maple neck, 22-fret rosewood fingerboard with offset pearl dot inlay, tune-o-matic Wilkinson bridge, string-through body tailpiece, 3-per-side Sperzel tuners, chrome hardware, 2 humbucker Seymour Duncan pickups, volume/tone control, 3-position switch, available in Cherry Burst, Deep Sea Blue, or Vintage Gold finishes, disc. 1994.

	N/A	$1,000	$875	$750	$650	$550	$450

Last MSR was $1,500.

USA MODEL R - offset double cutaway mahogany body, bolt-on maple neck, 22-fret rosewood fingerboard with offset pearl dot inlay, tune-o-matic Wilkinson bridge/stop tailpiece, 3-per-side Sperzel tuners, chrome hardware, 2 single coil Seymour Duncan pickups, volume/tone control, 3-position switch, available in Amber, Natural Oil, Red, or Red Oil finishes, disc. 1994.

	N/A	$700	$600	$500	$400	$325	$250

Last MSR was $1,000.

Add $100 for strings-through body tailpiece.

USA MODEL T - similar to USA Model R, except has single coil/humbucker Seymour Duncan pickups, disc. 1994.

	N/A	$700	$600	$500	$400	$325	$250

Last MSR was $1,000.

Add $100 for strings-through body tailpiece.

PATTERSON GUITARS

Instruments currently built in Falcon Heights, MN.

Patterson Guitars is currently offering high quality electric guitars, basses, and archtop models. Options include left-handed configuration, custom inlays, neck scale, and clear or colored lacquer finishes. For further information, please contact Patterson Guitars directly (see Trademark Index).

ELECTRIC

The Patterson **At Series Archtop Jazz Guitars** feature hand-carved German spruce tops, German curly maple back, multi-lined binding throughout, traditionally shaped f-holes, 3- to 5-piece curly maple neck, 22-fret ebony fingerboard, ebony tailpiece, pickguard and bridge, 1 custom-made, dual-coil pickup, gold tuners, and hard shell case. List price is $8,000.

The Patterson **Pt Series Guitars** feature a neck-through, multi-laminated body and graphite reinforced neck with your choice of numerous exotic woods, 24-fret ebony, wenge, or maple fingerboard, custom oil finish, 2 custom-made, humingbucker pickups with Patterson active or passive electronics, light-weight aluminum alloy tuners and precision adjustable bridge. List price is $2,400.

ELECTRIC BASS

The Patterson **Pb Series Basses** feature a bolt-on neck 4-, 5-, and 6-string models, high-gloss base coat/clear urethane finished body, 5-piece graphite reinforced neck, 24-fret ebony, wenge, maple, or phenolic fingerboard front and back peghead veneer, 3-ply laminated pickguard, cast aluminum alloy tuning gears, precision adjustable bridge, fine multi-lined binding, inlaid fret markers, Petterson passive or active high-definition electronics packages, 2 made for Patterson dual coil soapbar pickups. List price is $2,200 to $2,600.

The Patterson **Pt Series Basses**

feature a neck-through 4-, 5-, and 6-string models, multi-laminated body and graphite reinforced neck with your choice of numerous exotic woods, 26-fret ebony, wenge, maple or phenolic fingerboard, custom oil finish, 2 custom-made soapbar, dual-coil pickups with Patterson active 4-band EQ or passive electronics, light-weight aluminum alloy tuners and precision adjustable bridge. List price is $2,800 to $3,200.

PAUL, BRIAN

Instruments currently built in Plano, TX.

Luthier Brian Paul Prokop is currently handcrafting two electric guitar solid body models that feature original designs. Paul originally introduced the **Pro-22**, and this year also unveiled the new Artist Series model.

ELECTRIC

Both models feature a carved curly maple top, Honduran mahogany body, mahogany or figured maple neck, 22-fret ebony (or rosewood or maple) fingerboard, abalone and mother-of-pearl fingerboard inlays, Sperzel locking tuners, Seymour Duncan pickups, volume/tone controls, and a Wilkinson bridge (hard tail or floating tremolo system). Guitars are finished in aniline dyes and nitrocellulose lacquer (the current retail price includes a hardshell case). The **Pro-22** model has 2 humbuckers: Seymour Duncan Pearly Gates and Jeff Beck models. The **Artist Series** model has 3 Seymour Duncan Hot Stack single coils, or the option of humbuckers (like the Pro-22).

PAUL REED SMITH GUITARS (PRS)

Current manufacturer located in Stevensville, MD, 1996-present. Previously manufactured in Annapolis, MD 1985-1996.

Combining the best aspects of vintage design traditions in modern instruments, luthier Paul Reed Smith designed a guitar that became very influential during the late 1980s. With meticulous attention to detail, design, and production combined with the concept of graded figured wood tops, PRS guitars have become touchstone in today's guitar marketplace. The concept of a 10 top (denoting clearly defined figure across the entire maple top with no dead spots) was introduced by PRS Guitars, and the phrase, "It's a 10 top with birds," has become magic for both PRS players and collectors.

Paul Reed Smith built his first guitar for a college music class. Drawing on his high school shop classes and his musical experiences, his first attempt gained him an *A*.

Working out of his home attic in Annapolis, MD during the mid 1970s, Smith began designing and revising his guitar models while involved with the guitar repair trade. He continued to work out of a small repair shop for the better part of eight years, and was selling a number of handcrafted guitars between 1976 through 1984 without any major advertising. By 1982, he had finished designing and building a guitar that combined traditional design with his original ideas.

In 1985, Smith received some major financial backing and was able to start limited handmade production of the PRS Custom model. This limited partnership business arrangement guaranteed his high quality products would finally be marketed and advertised within the guitar industry. One major difference between PRS and other guitar companies of the 1980s is Smith made, or had exclusively made, all of his own components for his own guitars. Of course, choosing highly figured woods for construction also helped to ensure his instruments maintained a high level of quality and eye appeal. Through the years, Smith has continued to experiment with pickup design, body and neck variations, and even amplification and speaker systems.

In 1990, a PRS amplifier was introduced. The HG-70 Harmonic Generator amplifier head and 4 x 12 in. cabinet had a retail price of $2,208; the 212 combo version had a list price of $1,795, and less than 400 total were manufactured (please refer to the *Blue Book of Guitar Amplifiers* for more information on this model).

In addition to the various Limited Edition models, PRS continues to offer the Private Stock models which are very limited in production and individually handcrafted.

In 1994, PRS introduced the McCarty Model as a tribute to Ted McCarty, Gibson's President from 1950-1966.

Entering the new millenium, PRS continued to expand its model lineup with a new Singlecut Series. During 2001, the company introduced an entry-level, fine quality Santana SE Model, manufactured in Korea per PRS specs. During 2002, PRS introduced its new Dragon 2002, the first new Dragon since the Dragon 2000 in 1999. Additionally, PRS improved the Santana SE Model with new cosmetics, features, colors, and pickups, in addition to providing its extensive lineup of instruments manufactured in Stevensville, MD. During late May of 2003, the company launched the Brazilian Series, with only 1,500 instruments being made in the Custom 22, Custom 24, and McCarty models. This new series features Brazilian rosewood fretboards, headstock veneer, and truss rod cover. The Santana Brazilian was also released at the same time, with Brazilian rosewood neck and fretboard. During winter NAMM of 2004, PRS introduced new models, including the Modern Eagle, Custom 22/12, 513 Rosewood, SE EG, and SE Soapbar.

As in the past, tone and player performance have become the key elements on all PRS instruments. Additionally, collectibility on older PRS instruments, especially those guitars manufactured in the 1980s/early 1990s with killer wood and/or 10 tops, has continued to be strong, with prices having risen dramatically over the past decade.

Paul Reed Smith Santana III courtesy Dave Rogers Dave's Guitar Shop

CURRENT PRS FINISHES

PRS offers a wide variety of stains and colors referred to as finish groups. Because the choice of colors within these groups change regularly, it is recommended to go to the PRS website: http://www.prsguitars.com, and check out the current availability on both colors and finishes. Also, since each PRS guitar is unique in terms of wood, colors and stains can vary from one instrument to the next, and it is always recommended to look at the colors per instrument at a PRS dealer.

Current finish groups are as follows: A (translucent finish on maple with natural maple edge) - includes Amber, Black Cherry, Black Sunburst, Blue Matteo, Cherry Sunburst, Dark Cherry Sunburst, Emerald Green, Gray Black, Natural, Orange, Purple, Teal Black, Tobacco Sunburst, Tortoise Shell, Turquoise, Vintage Sunburst, Vintage Yellow, Whale Blue, Ruby, and Tri-Color Sunburst. B (translucent finish on maple with matching maple edge) - includes Royal Blue, Scarlet Ed, Tobacco Wrap Around Burst, Violin Amber, Violin Amber 'Burst, and Dark Cherry Wrap Around 'Burst. C (translucent finish on maple with natural maple edge) - includes Amber, Black Cherry, Black Sunburst, Blue Matteo, Dark Cherry Sunburst, Gray Black, McCarty Sunburst, McCarty Tobacco 'Burst, Orange, Natural, Teal Black, Tortoise Shell, Turquoise, Vintage Yellow, Whale Blue, Ruby, Tri-Color Sunburst. D (translucent finish on maple with matching maple edge) - includes Violin Amber, Violin Amber 'Burst, Tobacco Wrap Around 'Burst, Dark Cherry Wrap Arouns 'Burst. E (translucent toner on solid mahogany) - includes Black Sunburst, Natural Mahogany, Translucent Blue, Translucent Orange, Translucent Purple, Translucent Turquoise, Translucent Vintage Cherry, Translucent Walnut. F (opaque colors) - includes Black, Platinum Metallic, and Old Gold Metallic. G (opaque colors with natural maple edge) - includes Black, Old Gold Metallic (gold top), and Platinum Metallic. J (translucent toner on solid ash) - includes Black Sunburst, Natural Ash, Translucent Emerald Green, Translucent Vintage Cherry, Tri-Color Sunburst, and Translucent Turquoise. K (translucent finish on maple with natural maple edge) - includes Amber, Black Cherry, Black Sunburst, Blue Matteo, Cherry Sunburst, Emerald Green, Gray Black, Natural, Orange, Purple, Tobacco Sunburst, Tortoise Shell, Turquoise, Vintage Sunburst, Vintage Yellow, Whale Blue, Ruby, and Tri-Color Sunburst. M (translucent finish on maple with matching maple edge) - includes Royal Blue, Scarlet Red, Tobacco Wrap Around 'Burst, and Dark Cherry Wrap Arouns 'Burst. P (opaque colors on swamp ash) - includes Black. R (translucent finish on spruce) - includes Black Sunburst, Tobacco Sunburst, Tri-Color Sunburst, and Vintage Natural. S (opaque colors with natural spruce edge) - includes Black and Old Gold Metallic (gold top). T (translucent finish on maple for inset Bass top) - includes Amber, Black Cherry, Black Sunburst, Cherry Sunburst, Dark Cherry Sunburst, Emerald Green, Gray Black, Natural, Orange, Purple, Royal Blue, Scarlet Red, Teal Black, Tobacco Sunburst, Tortoise Shell, Turquoise, Vintage Sunburst, Vintage Yellow, Violin Amber, Violin Amber 'Burst, Whale Blue, and Tri-Color Sunburst. W (translucent toner on solid alder) - includes Black Sunburst, Translucent Emerald Green, Translucent Vintage Cherry, Tri-Color Sunburst, and Translucent Turquoise. X (satin unltra thin nitro, Modern Eagle only) - includes Faded Blue Jean, Abalone, Slate, Charcoal, Red Tiger, McCarty Amber, Emerald, and Old Natural.

TREBLE POSITION PICKUPS

The following pickups represent current pickup listings with descriptions.

HFS: Stock on Custom 24s, CE 24s and Standard 24s. Originally meaning Hot, Fat and Screams, the HFS features a powerful ceramic magnet and hot coils for an aggressive tone when cranked, clear highs, searing midrange and thumping bass. This pickup is compatible with the 5 position rotary pickup selector.

Dragon II Treble: Stock on Custom 22s, CE 22s and Standard 22s. The nickel silver cover and months of tweaking have resulted in an alnico pickup with McCarty like tones and a little more output. This pickup is compatible with the 5 position rotary pickup selector.

McCarty Treble: Stock on the McCarty Model and McCarty Standard. Using a unique manufacturing process inspired by Ted McCarty, combined with a vintage alnico magnet and special nickel silver cover, give the McCarty its silvery vintage tone. This pickup contains a few more turns on the coils to balance it with the bass position pickup.

Archtop Treble: Stock on the archtop and hollowbodies. This is a clearer, less powerful version of our McCarty bass pickup. This pickup was specifically designed to match well with the PRS Piezo system and is good for many styles of music.

1989 Paul Reed Smith Custom w/bird inlays courtesy Dave Rogers Dave's Guitar Shop

P

GRADING	100% MINT	98% NEAR MINT	95% EXC+	90% EXC	80% VG+	70% VG	60% G

PRS #6 Treble: Stock on the Singlecut Trem. This is similar in sound to our PRS #7 but without the cover and is again a result of our tweaking. Clear and well balanced across the entire tonal spectrum, this pickup is very alive and sounds excellent distorted. (disc. 2004).

PRS #7 Treble: Stock on the Singlecut. This may be one of the best treble pickups from PRS. It´s powerful and clear with vintage alive characteristics. It is also used on stage by many touring bands.

Dragon Treble: Not currently stock on any model. This pickup is fat with lots of clarity and sounds great clean or at high gain. A powerful ceramic magnet combined with a high number of turns produces a huge sound; good for driving high gain type amps. This pickup is compatible with the 5 position rotary pickup selector.

Santana Treble: Stock on the Santana II. On many occasions, Carlos Santana has taken guitars out of our shipping room and used them in concert that evening. This is the pickup he originally came to rely upon.

Santana III Treble: Stock on the Santana III. This is the pickup Carlos is currently using - Similar to Dragon II´s but tweaked for Carlos. This pickup will give you smooth tones for all styles of music.

Tremonti Treble: Stock on the Mark Tremonti Signature model. The Tremonti Treble pickup is specifically wound to Mark´s specifications with powerful custom magnets. This is the hottest, most aggressive pickup currently offered.

Artist Treble: Sounds clear and full with tons of tone. This bridge pickup is built similar to the Artist Bass with extra turns for warmth. For blues, rock and jazz.

BASS POSITION PICKUPS

Vintage Bass: Stock on Custom 24s, CE 24s and Standard 24s. This alnico pickup provides round, clear tone to complement the HFS and also works well when coil tapped. This pickup is compatible with the 5 position rotary pickup selector.

Dragon II Bass: Stock on Custom 22s, CE 22s and Standard 22s. The nickel silver cover and our tweaking have resulted in a rich bass position humbucker with enough output and clarity for any style of playing. This pickup is compatible with the 5 position rotary pickup selector.

McCarty Bass: Stock on the McCarty Model and McCarty Standard. Using a unique manufacturing process inspired by Ted McCarty, combined with a vintage alnico magnet and special nickel silver cover, give this McCarty a nice vintage tone.

Archtop Bass: Stock on the archtop and hollowbodies. This is also a clearer, less powerful version of our McCarty bass pickup. The pickup was specifically designed to match well with the PRS Piezo system and is good for many styles of music including jazz and rhythm guitar.

PRS #6 Bass: Stock on the Singlecut Trem. Clear, warm and extremely well balanced across the entire tonal spectrum. (Disc. 2004).

PRS #7 Bass: Stock on the Singlecut. It is a full range pickup with vintage alive characteristics. It is also highly recommended and used on stage by many touring bands.

Dragon Bass: Not currently stock on any model. This pickup has a great combination of rich, warm bass with sweet in.angelic in. high end. The vintage alnico magnet and winding process result in a pickup that is beautiful for solos and rhythm. This pickup is compatible with the 5 position rotary pickup selector.

Santana Bass: Stock on the Santana II. On many occasions, Carlos Santana has taken guitars out of our shipping room and used them in concert that evening. This is the pickup he originally came to rely upon and continues to be one of his favorite bass pickups.

Santana III Bass: Stock on the Santana III. Again Carlos´ pickup of choice - this pickup is essentially a Santana bass pickup with a cover. It has less output than the Santana III treble pickup resulting in the perfect combination.

Tremonti Bass: Stock on the Mark Tremonti Signature model. The Tremonti Bass pickup features an alnico magnet and is the perfect compliment to the Tremonti Treble pickup. This is the same pickup Mark uses in concert and in the studio for is rhythm sounds.

A wide variety of PRS Pickups are available as aftermarket replacement parts, both in nickel and gold finishes. Prices range from $120 to $130.

Artist Bass: Driven by vintage alnico, this neck pickup has a unique and beautiful tone. The winding is a little hotter than the Vintage Bass.

HARDWARE, WOOD, & DATING INFORMATION

In addition to a fairly straight forward serialization method (see PRS Serialization in the back of this text), there are a number of ways to supplement guitar dating by inspecting various features on the instrument. During late 1991, the sweet switch was discontinued. In 1991, PRS stopped offering Brazilian rosewood fingerboards, and began offering very good quality Indian rosewood. Brazilian rosewood fingerboards are still available through limited edition models or custom-built models. PRS began using mother-or-pearl inlay in place of abalone shell inlay. In 1993, PRS introduced the one piece stop tailpiece. In 1995, the large, long neck heel was introduced. The two-piece tremolo bridge replaced the one-piece tremolo bridge. Standard post-1985 Custom/Standard Model electronics/hardware included two PRS Hybrid pickups, 5-position rotary switch, volume control and sweet toggle switch, PRS tremolo system, Schaller/PRS locking tuners and low friction nut. A master tone pot (3 knobs total) replaced the sweet switch in November of 1991. Pickups were originally standard treble and standard bass. End slugs on E and B were changed in 1987 to reduce high end, these were changed on the CE, Custom and Standard to HFS Treble and Vintage Bass by November 1991.

1985-CURRENT MFG. SET NECK FEATURES

PRS instruments manufactured during 1985-87 evolved from the pre-´85 all mahogany guitar. By 1985, standard set neck features included back angled 3 on-a-side non-veneered headstock, one piece mahogany glued in neck, regular shape, 25 in. scale length, 24-fret, single action truss road (double action truss rod fitted from late 1991), 10 in. radiused Indian rosewood fingerboard (Brazilian rosewood was standard until it was phased out by early 1990-91 on all but top-line limited edition models such as the Dragon), mother-of-pearl abalone moon inlays (birds were optional), and one piece mahogany body or back.

Electronics included: PRS ´Hybrid´ pickup system, 5-position rotary switch, volume control and Sweet switch. A master tone replaced Sweet switch in November 1991. Pickups were originally Standard Treble and Standard Bass. End slugs on E and B changed in 1987 to reduce high end. Changed on CE, Custom and Standard to HFS Treble and Vintage Bass by November 1991. PRS Tremolo System, Schaller/PRS locking tuners, low friction nut.

ELECTRIC: ARTIST SERIES

Please also check under the McCarty Series for the McCarty Archtop Artist.

ARTIST SERIES I - replaced Signature Series, offset double cutaway mahogany body, carved flame maple top, mahogany wide-fat neck, 24-fret rosewood fingerboard with abalone bird inlay, standard PRS vibrato, abalone signature peghead inlay, inlayed abalone headstock logo on rosewood headstock overlay, 3-per-side locking PRS tuners, chrome hardware, 2 PRS Artist Series humbucker pickups, volume/tone/5-position control, Certificate of Authenticity, special thin finish, available in Amber, Dark Cherry Sunburst, Indigo and Teal Black finishes, mfg. 1991-93.

$3,000	$2,650	$2,275	$1,895	$1,500	$1,375	$1,250

Last MSR was $3,780.

In 1993, a 22-fret maple bound fingerboard replaced original parts/design, semi hollowbody, stop tailpiece, and gold hardware became options.

GRADING	100% MINT	98% NEAR MINT	95% EXC+	90% EXC	80% VG+	70% VG	60% G

ARTIST SERIES II - similar to the Artist, except has carved figured maple top, 25 in. scale, maple bound 22-fret rosewood fingerboard with abalone bird inlay, PRS wrap over bridge/tailpiece, maple bound peghead with abalone signature inlay, gold hardware, 2 PRS Artist Series humbucker pickups, available in Amber, Dark Cherry Sunburst, Indigo, or Teal Black finishes, mfg. 1993-96.

	$3,950	$3,400	$3,000	$2,650	$2,200	$1,750	$1,575

Last MSR was $4,400.

This model comes complete with a Certificate of Authenticity from PRS. Options included a leather or hardshell case, semi-hollowbody, quilted maple top, PRS tremolo system or humbucker/single/humbucker pickup configuration.

ARTIST SERIES LIMITED EDITION - similar to Artist II, except with abalone purfling on neck, headstock and truss rod cover, 14 kt. gold bird inlays, mother-of-pearl and abalone eagle inlayed on the headstock, leather/hardshell case. 200 mfg. 1994-96.

	$6,750	$5,800	$4,850	$3,750	$3,000	$2,600	$2,200

Last MSR was $7,000.

ARTIST SERIES III - similar to the Artist II, except has mahogany back with exceptional artist grade maple top, paua bound 22-fret wide-fat or wide-thin mahogany neck with rosewood fingerboard with paua shell bird inlay, paua bound peghead with paua signature inlay, paua purfling on the neck, headstock, and truss rod cover, Artist Series pickups, 5-way rotary switch, volume/tone, gold PRS stoptail and locking tuners, available in Amber, Dark Cherry Sunburst, Indigo and Teal Black finishes, mfg. 1996-97.

	$4,300	$3,800	$3,350	$2,875	$2,450	$2,150	$1,850

Last MSR was $4,800.

Add $700 for quilted maple top.

This model comes complete with hardshell leather case and a Certificate of Authenticity from PRS. This model has the standard PRS tremolo system, or a semi-hollowbody optional at no extra charge.

ARTIST SERIES IV - similar to the Artist III, except has mahogany back with exceptional artist grade maple top, bound 22-fret wide-fat or wide-thin mahogany neck, rosewood fingerboard with etched solid 14kt. gold bird inlays, gold purfling on neck, headstock and truss rod cover, original PRS etched gold bird inlay on headstock, 2 PRS McCarty pickups with goldplated nickel silver covers, gold hardware, gold PRS stop tailpiece and locking tuners, available in Amber, Dark Cherry Sunburst, Indigo, or Teal Black finishes, mfg. 1996-97.

	$6,000	$5,300	$4,400	$3,750	$3,000	$2,600	$2,200

Last MSR was $7,600.

Add $700 for quilted maple top.

This model comes complete with hardshell leather case and a Certificate of Authenticity from PRS. This model has the standard PRS tremolo system, or a semi-hollowbody optional at no extra charge.

SANTANA MODELS - please refer to the Santana Series in this section for more information and pricing on this series.

Paul Reed Smith 2004 CE 22 Maple Top courtesy John Beeson The Music Shoppe

ELECTRIC: CE (CLASSIC ELECTRIC) BOLT-ON SERIES

In 1995, Alder body wood on CE models was changed to Mahogany.

CE 22 (CE 22 BOLT-ON) - offset double cutaway carved alder or mahogany (mfg. 1995-2000) body, bolt-on maple neck, 22-fret rosewood fingerboard with abalone dot inlay, 25 in. scale, satin black headstock finish, PRS stoptail (new 1995) or PRS tremolo system, 3-per-side PRS locking tuners, chrome hardware, 2 covered PRS Dragon II humbucker pickups, volume/tone control, 5-position rotary switch, available in Black Sunburst, Natural, Trans. Green, Trans. Orange, Trans. Purple, Trans. Turquoise, Trans. Blue, Trans. Walnut, or Trans. Vintage Cherry finishes, mfg. 1994-2000.

	$1,150	$1,000	$900	$825	$695	$575	$425

Last MSR was $1,720.

Add $70 for 3-way toggle selector switch and push/pull tone control (coil tap capabilities). Add $280 for gold hardware.

This model was available in the following 1998 custom opaque colors: Antique White, Black, Seafoam Green, Ocean Turquoise, Cabernet Metallic, Deep Purple Metallic, Forest Green Metallic, Old Gold Metallic, Orange Mica Pearl Metallic, Platinum Metallic, Royal Blue Metallic, and Strawberry Pearl Metallic finishes. List price includes case.

CE 22 Maple Top (CE 22 Bolt-On Maple Top) - similar to the CE 22 Bolt-on, except has carved figured maple top, wide fat neck, stop tailpiece and wide-thin neck profile disc. 2001, a wide variety of colors have been available on this model, and currently, it is available in K, M, or G colors/finishes, mfg. 1994-present.

MSR	$2,650	$2,000	$1,550	$1,325	$1,075	$900	$725	$575

Add $500 for flame maple 10 top (disc.). Add $750 for quilt maple 10 top (disc.). Add $390 for gold hardware. Add $70 for 3-way toggle selector switch and push/pull tone control (coil tap capabilities).

Subtract $200 for finish group G.

Currently, this model is only available with wide-fat neck and tremolo beginning 2001. In 1998, Turquoise and Whale Blue finishes were introduced; Dark Blue, Natural, and Scarlet Sunburst finishes were disc. This model is also available in the 1998 custom opaque finishes with natural maple edge.

P

GRADING	100% MINT	98% NEAR MINT	95% EXC+	90% EXC	80% VG+	70% VG	60% G

CE 22 MAHOGANY - offset double cutaway carved mahogany body, bolt-on mahogany neck, 22-fret rosewood fingerboard with dot inlay, three-per-side tuners, PRS tremolo, two Dragon II covered humbucker pickups, two knobs, five-way switch, chrome hardware, available in various finishes, new 2005.

MSR	$2,400	$1,800	$1,550	$1,350	$1,150	$1,000	$850	$750

Add $390 for gold hardware.

This model is also available with a volume and push/pull tone control with a three-way pickup switch.

CE 24 (CE BOLT-ON) - offset double cutaway carved alder or mahogany (mfg. 1995-2000) body, bolt-on maple neck, (wide-thin became optional in 1999), 24-fret rosewood fingerboard with abalone dot inlay, 25 in. scale, unfaced satin black headstock finish, PRS stoptail (mfg. 1995-2001) or PRS tremolo system, 3-per-side PRS locking tuners, chrome hardware, 2 humbucker PRS pickups (one HFS and one Vintage Bass, new 1991), volume/tone control, 5-position rotary switch (1st year issue had 3-way switch with large bat), available in Black, Black Sunburst, Classic Red, Natural, Pearl Black, or Vintage Cherry finishes, mfg. 1988-1999.

		$1,300	$1,100	$975	$825	$695	$575	$425

Last MSR was $1,720.

Add $70 for 3-way toggle selector switch and push/pull tone control (coil tap capabilities). Add $320 for gold hardware. Add $80 for 1996-1997 custom colors (Electric Blue, Electric Red, Pearl White, Black Holoflake, Blue Holoflake, Burgundy Holoflake, Green Holoflake, Gold Holoflake, Red Holoflake, and Silver Holoflake).

In 1998, Translucent Green, Translucent Orange, Translucent Purple, Translucent Turquoise, Translucent Walnut, and (Translucent) Vintage Cherry finishes were introduced; Black, Classic Red, and Pearl Black finishes were disc. This model is available in the following 1998 custom opaque colors: Antique White, Black, Seafoam Green, Ocean Turquoise, Cabernet Metallic, Deep Purple Metallic, Forest Green Metallic, Old Gold Metallic, Orange Mica Pearl Metallic, Platinum Metallic, Royal Blue Metallic, and Strawberry Pearl Metallic finishes.

CE 24 Maple Top (CE Bolt-On Maple Top) - similar to CE Bolt-On, except has HFS bridge and Vintage Bass neck pickups, thin neck, stop tailpiece and regular neck profile disc. 2001, wide thin neck with tremolo beginning 2001, available in K, M or G colors/finishes, mfg. 1989-present.

MSR	$2,650	$2,000	$1,550	$1,325	$1,075	$900	$725	$575

Add $260 for mother-of-pearl bird inlays on neck (this option disc. in 1998). Add $360 for gold hardware. Add $70 for 3-way toggle selector switch and push/pull tone control (coil tap capabilities). Add $500 for flame maple 10 top. (Option disc. 1999). Add $700 for quilt maple 10 top. (Option disc. 1999).

Subtract $200 for finish group G.

In 1998, Turquoise and Whale Blue finishes were introduced; Dark Blue, Natural, and Scarlet Sunburst finishes were disc. This model is also available in the 1998 custom opaque finishes with natural maple edge. List price includes case.

CE 24 MAHOGANY - offset double cutaway carved mahogany body, bolt-on mahogany neck, 24-fret rosewood fingerboard with dot inlay, three-per-side tuners, PRS tremolo, one HFS and one Vintage humbucker pickups, two knobs, five-way switch, chrome hardware, available in various finishes, new 2005.

MSR	$2,400	$1,800	$1,550	$1,350	$1,150	$1,000	$850	$750

Add $390 for gold hardware.

This model is also available with a volume and push/pull tone control with a three-way pickup switch.

ELECTRIC: CUSTOM SERIES

CUSTOM 22 - based on Dragon Series I, but w/o the inlay, tremolo, or stoptail options, wide thin or wide fat neck profiles available, features a 22-fret fingerboard and 2 covered PRS Dragon II humbucker pickups, non-locking tuners on stop tailpiece became standard from March 6, 2001 - Jan. 2002, then changed to Phase II locking PRS tuners, left-handed version new 1999, includes case, available in A, B, or G colors/finishes, mfg. 1993-present.

MSR	$3,000	$2,200	$1,750	$1,450	$1,250	$1,000	$750	$650

Add $370 for 20th Anniversary model (Mfg. 2005). Add $590 for flame maple 10 top. Add $790 for quilt maple 10 top. Add $320 for abalone bird inlay. Add $70 for 3-way toggle selector switch and push/pull tone control (coil tap capabilities). Add $390 for gold hardware. Add $240 for semi-hollowbody option (disc. 2002). Add $1,380 for Artist Package Flame and $1,580 for Artist Package Quilt: Artist Grade flame or quilted maple top, translucent toned back, rosewood headstock veneer, Paua bird inlay in neck, and gold hardware. Add approx. 15% for left-hand model (not available in 24-fret or with Artist Package option).

Subtract $200 for finish group G.

The 10-top and Artist Package options were introduced in 1998. During 2005, a 20th Anniversary model was released, which has "20th" on the truss-rod cover and special "Birds in Flight" fingerboard inlays.

Brazilian Series Custom 22 - similar to Custom 22, Brazilian fretboard and headstock overlay, pink heart abalone birds and signature, the word "Brazilian" is inlayed on the face of the headstock in green abalone ripple, gold/nickel hybrid hardware configuration (similar to the Dragon 2002), 10 top only. Limited run of 500 guitars all signed and numbered on backplate 2003-2004.

		$3,350	$2,750	$1,975	$1,500	$1,250	$995	$800

Last MSR was $4,150.

Add $200 for quilt maple.

CUSTOM 22 SOAPBAR - similar to Custom 22 except has 3 Seymour Duncan soapbar single coil pickups, 5-way blade pickup selector, 1 volume/1 tone control, rock maple neck and fretboard (rosewood fretboard optional), regular D neck carve, PRS tremolo bridge, mfg. 1998-2001.

		$2,100	$1,675	$1,450	$1,300	$1,100	$850	$750

Last MSR was $2,800.

Add $200 for quilt top. Add $550 for 10 top flame. Add $750 for 10 top quilt. Add $200 for rock maple fingerboard with antique maple tint. Add $280 for abalone bird inlays. Add $360 for gold hardware.

GRADING	100% MINT	98% NEAR MINT	95% EXC+	90% EXC	80% VG+	70% VG	60% G

CUSTOM 24 - offset double cutaway mahogany body, carved figured maple top, mahogany neck, 24-fret rosewood fingerboard with abalone/pearl moon inlay, 25 in. scale, PRS tremolo system or PRS stoptail (mfg. circa 1993-2001), 3-per-side low mass cam style locking tuners, chrome hardware, Phase II tuners became standard 2002, 2 humbucker PRS pickups (one HFS and one Vintage Bass), volume/tone control, 5-position rotary switch, 10-top became an option in 1987, available in many colors, including current finish groups A, B, and G. Vintage Yellow is most desirable in early mfg., black headstock, includes leather case, mfg. 1985-present.

1985-1991 W/ 10-TOP & BIRDS	$4,500	$4,150	$3,550	$3,100	$2,650	$2,350	$2,000
1985-1991 W/O 10-TOP & BIRDS	$2,750	$2,350	$2,000	$1,750	$1,500	$1,250	$995
MSR	$3,000	$2,200	$1,750	$1,450	$1,250	$1,000	$750	$650

Add $370 for 20th Anniversary model (Mfg. 2005). On current mfg., add $590 for flame maple 10 top. Add $790 for quilt maple 10 top. Add $320 for abalone bird inlay. Add $70 for 3-way toggle selector switch and push/pull tone control (coil tap capabilities). Add $390 for gold hardware. Add $240 for semi-hollowbody option (disc. 2002). Add $1,380 for Artist Package Flame and $1,580 for Artist Package Quilt: Artist Grade flame or quilted maple top, translucent toned back, rosewood headstock veneer, Paua bird inlay in neck, and gold hardware. Add approx. 15% for left-hand model (not available in 24-fret or with Artist Package option). Early mfg. with low serial numbers in 90%+ original condition will bring a 10%-30% premium.

Subtract $200 for finish group G.

Prices for pre-1992 Custom 24 models (with sweet switch) can vary significantly depending on the quality of the top wood, condition, and finish.

In 1998, Teal Black, Turqoise, Violin Amber, and Violin Amber Sunburst finishes were introduced; Scarlet Sunburst finish was disc. This model has a Wide-Thin neck optional. Sweet switch and Brazilian rosewood fretboard was disc. Nov. 1991. During 2005, a 20th Anniversary model was released, which has "20th" on the truss-rod cover and special "Birds in Flight" fingerboard inlays.

Brazilian Series Custom 24 - similar to Custom 24, Brazilian fretboard and headstock overlay, pink heart abalone birds and signature, the word "Brazilian" is inlayed on the face of the headstock in green abalone ripple, gold/nickel hybrid hardware configuration (similar to Dragon 2002), 10 top only. Limited run of 500 guitars all signed and numbered on backplate beginning 2003.

MSR	$4,150	$3,250	$2,650	$1,925	$1,500	$1,250	$995	$800

Add $200 for quilt maple.

Custom 24 Metal - heavy metal version of the Custom 24 with custom striped finish, mfg. 1985-87.

$1,995	$1,750	$1,500	$1,300	$1,075	$900	$725

This model appeared on the cover of the first PRS color catalog.

CUSTOM 22/12 - similar to Custom 22, except is 12-string, electronics include two PRS 12-string pickups with covers and a Lindy Fralin single coil center pickup, 3-way toggle pickup selector, volume and tone control, available in A, B, or G colors/finishes, mfg. 2004-present.

MSR	$3,400	$2,600	$2,250	$1,950	$1,650	$1,350	$1,000	$800

Add $590 for flame maple 10 top. Add $790 for quilt maple 10 top. Add $320 for abalone bird inlay. Add $390 for gold hardware. Subtract $200 for finish group G.

ELECTRIC: DRAGON SERIES

DRAGON - offset double cutaway mahogany body on Dragons I-III and Dragon 2000, arched bound flame maple top, mahogany neck, 22-fret ebony fingerboard with intricate dragon inlay, PRS wrap over bridge/tailpiece, abalone signature inlay on peghead, 3-per-side locking PRS tuners, gold hardware, 2 uncovered humbucker PRS pickups, volume/tone control, 5-position rotary control, available in Amber, Dark Cherry Sunburst, Indigo and Teal Black finishes, mfg. on a yearly basis, in limited numbers. Each year the dragon inlays became more elaborate. Dragon I-IIIs have virtually dried up in the used marketplace.

Dragon I (Mfg. 1991-92) - first 22-fret PRS instrument, featured new PRS stop tail (wrap over bridge), increased headstock angle, Dragon pickups, wide-fat neck and gold hardware, features elaborate dragon inlayed in fretboard (201 pieces, abalone, turquoise, and mother-of-pearl, 50 mfg.

$29,500	$25,000	$20,000	N/A	N/A	N/A	N/A

Last MSR was $8,000.

Dragon II (Mfg. 1993) - similar to Dragon I, except has 218-piece dragon fingerboard inlay utilizing abalone, gold, coral, malachite, onyx, and mother-of-pearl, 100 mfg.

$25,000	$21,500	$15,750	N/A	N/A	N/A	N/A

Last MSR was $11,000.

Dragon III (Mfg. 1994) - similar to Dragon II, except has 238-piece fingerboard inlay, utilizing gold, red, and green abalone, mother-of-pearl, mammoth ivory and stone, 100 mfg.

$25,000	$21,500	$15,750	N/A	N/A	N/A	N/A

Last MSR was $16,000.

Dragon 2000 (Mfg. 2000) - similar specs as the McCarty model, Brazilian rosewood neck and fretboard with no fretboard inlay, Dragon inlay on body made of 242 pieces of mastadon ivory, rhodonite, agoya, coral, onyx, sugilite, chrysocola, red, green, and pink abalone and paua, includes leather presentation case and certificate of authenticity, 50 mfg. 1999-2000.

$25,000	$21,500	$15,750	N/A	N/A	N/A	N/A

Last MSR was $20,000.

Paul Reed Smith
2004 Custom 22
courtesy John Beeson
The Music Shoppe

P

Paul Reed Smith
Dragon 1
courtesy John A. Sazy, M.D.

GRADING	100% MINT	98% NEAR MINT	95% EXC+	90% EXC	80% VG+	70% VG	60% G

Dragon 2002 Singlecut (Mfg. 2002) - single cut body and lower fretboard elaborately inlayed over 85% of the body with 272 pieces Mammoth Ivory, Green Ripple Abalone, Abalone Sparkle, Paua Select, Paua Heart, Green Heart Abalone, Brown Lip MOP, Black Lip MOP, Orange Red Spiney, Gold MOP, Black Onyx, Blue Chrysacola, Brazilian rosewood neck, 2 covered nickel humbucker PRS pickups, gold tailpiece, available in Black Cherry, Whale Blue, or Gray Black, 100 mfg. 2002 only.

	$25,000	$16,750	$12,000	N/A	N/A	N/A	N/A

Last MSR was $30,000.

ELECTRIC: EG BOLT-ON SERIES

The EG Bolt-on models had two slightly different body designs, the Series I was a square shape, and the Series II was a rounder shaped body.

EG BOLT-ON SERIES I - square shape, offset double cutaway alder body, white pickguard, bolt-on maple neck, 22-fret rosewood fingerboard with pearl dot inlay, standard PRS tremolo system, Schaller non-locking tuners, chrome hardware, humbucker/single coil/humbucker pickups, volume control, push/pull tone control, 5-position switch, coil tap in tone control, available in Black, Black Sunburst, Classic Red, or Seafoam Green finishes, mfg. 1990-91.

	$800	$650	$575	$475	$395	$350	$300

Last MSR was $1,280.

This model also available with 2 single coil/1 humbucker pickups with coil tap in tone control (EG 3), and 3 single coil pickups with dual tone- in-tone control (EG 4).

EG Bolt-On LH - similar to EG Bolt-On, except in left-handed configuration, mfg. 1993 only.

	$750	$700	$625	$500	$450	$400	$350

Last MSR was $1,285.

EG BOLT-ON SERIES II MAPLE TOP - similar to EG Bolt-On, except has round shaped, Alder body, wide thin maple neck, 22-fret rosewood fretboard, scratchplate mounted pickups in three formats, h/s/h, s/s/h, s/s/s, volume, tone, 5-way selector, coil taps, PRS tremolo, locking machines, EG bolt-on maple top adds three piece maple, '10' option, available in Black Cherry Burst, Black Sunburst, Emerald Green Burst, Grey Black Burst, Purple Burst, Royal Blue Burst, Scarlet Burst, Tri-Color Sunburst, or Whale Blue Burst finishes, mfg. 1992-95.

	$950	$795	$725	$595	$475	$425	$375

Last MSR was $1,580.

Add 15% for 10-top in 95%+ original condition.

In 1994, Black Cherry Burst, Emerald Green Burst, Purple Burst, Royal Blue Burst, Scarlet Burst, Tri-Color Sunburst and Whale Blue Burst finish were introduced.

EG Bolt-On LH Maple Top - similar to EG Bolt-On Maple top, except in left-handed configuration, available in Black Sunburst or Grey Black Sunburst finishes, mfg. 1993 only.

	$950	$795	$725	$595	$475	$425	$375

Last MSR was $1,585.

ELECTRIC: LIMITED EDITION/ANNIVERSARY MODELS

AWARD SERIES - mahogany body, regular maple neck with Brazilian rosewood fretboard with moon inlays, gold hardware, 5-way switch and stop tailpiece with tune-o-matic, 24-fret, "Award Series 10/20" hand marked in gold on back of headstock, 20 mfg. for top PRS dealers circa 1990.

	$3,750	$3,250	$2,900	$2,650	$2,325	$2,000	$1,800

1990/91 LIMITED EDITION MODEL - semi-hollowbody with cedar, redwood or maple top, signature grade wood, gold hardware, tune-o-matic bridge and stopbar tailpiece (a few tremolo eqipped guitars were made), signed and numbered, 300 mfg. 1990-91.

	$4,950	$4,450	$3,850	$3,250	$2,650	$2,175	$1,725

10TH ANNIVERSARY MODEL - offset double cutaway mahogany body, carved figured maple top, Artist Limited Edition style with wide-fat or wide-thin mahogany neck, 25 in. scale, abalone bound 22-fret ebony fingerboard with engraved gold abalone bird inlays, Gold PRS wrap over bridge/tailpiece, abalone bound peghead with engraved PRS Eagle and mother-of-pearl 10th Anniversary ribbon inlay, abalone bound truss rod cover, 3-per-side Gold PRS locking tuners, gold hardware, 2 Gold McCarty humbucker pickups, volume and push/pull tone control, 3-position switch, available in Amber, Dark Cherry Sunburst, Indigo, Purple, or Teal Black finishes, 200 mfg. 1995 only.

	$7,500	$5,800	$4,900	$4,100	$3,200	$2,750	$2,250

Last MSR was $6,600.

Add $750 for a quilted maple top.

This model comes complete with hardshell leather case and a Certificate of Authenticity from PRS. This model was also available with semi-hollowbody, or a PRS tremolo system.

GOLDEN EAGLE LIMITED EDITION - basswood body, Brazilian rosewood fingerboard, 22-fret curly maple neck, original carving by Floyd L. Scholz of golden eagle or bald eagle on body, engraved solid gold bird inlays, McCarty electronics, gold hardware and PRS stoptail bridge, very limited edition mfg. 1997 only.

	$17,500	$15,000	$12,500	$10,000	N/A	N/A	N/A

Last MSR was $24,000.

ELECTRIC: MCCARTY SERIES

Introduced in 1994, the McCarty Model instrument was built as a tribute to Ted McCarty, the company president who was responsible for many model and part innovations during his tenure with the Gibson company during the 1950s. In 1998, 3 archtop and 2 hollowbody models were added to the McCarty Series.

GRADING	100% MINT	98% NEAR MINT	95% EXC+	90% EXC	80% VG+	70% VG	60% G

McCARTY MODEL - offset double cutaway mahogany thick body, East Coast maple top, 1/8 in. thicker mahogany back, mahogany Wide-Fat neck, (East Indian rosewood neck became optional in 1998), 22-fret rosewood fingerboard with pearl and abalone moon inlays, PRS stop tailpiece, blackface peghead with screened logo, 3-per-side vintage-style tuners with plastic buttons, covered Dragon Bass PRS humbuckers (changed to McCarty Series type in 1995, and includes a push/pull coil-tap on the tone control, 3-way toggle pickup selector, includes case, many colors and finishes have been available, current finish groups are C, D, and G, mfg. 1994-present.

MSR	$3,150		$2,350	$1,950	$1,575	$1,350	$1,050	$950	$725

> Add $590 for flame 10 Top. Add $320 for abalone bird inlays. Add $600 for East Indian rosewood neck (only available with stoptail bridge). Add $200 for PRS tremolo and low mass locking tuners (disc.). Add $390 for gold hardware. Add approx. 15% for left-hand model.
>
> Subtract $200 for finish group G.

The first 100 instruments were signed and numbered.

In 1998, Amber, Black Sunburst, Tortoiseshell, Vintage Yellow, Violin Amber, and Violin Amber Burst finishes were introduced.

Brazilian Series McCarty - similar to McCarty Model, Brazilian fretboard and headstock overlay, pink heart abalone birds and signature, the word "Brazilian" is inlayed on the face of the headstock in green abalone ripple, gold/nickel hybrid hardware configuration, 10 top only. Limited run of 500 guitars all signed and numbered on backplate beginning 2003.

MSR	$4,150		$3,250	$2,650	$1925	$1,500	$1,250	$995	$800

> Add $600 for East Indian rosewood neck.

McCARTY STANDARD - similar to McCarty Model, except has carved solid mahogany body (no maple top), only offered with stoptail bridge option, includes case, many color and finishes have been available, current finish groups are E and F, mfg. 1995-present.

MSR	$2,800		$2,000	$1,675	$1,350	$1,175	$1,000	$850	$725

> Add $550 for flame 10 Top (disc. 2004). Add $320 for abalone bird inlays. Add $600 for East Indian rosewood neck. Add $390 for gold hardware. Add $200 for PRS tremolo and low mass locking tuners (disc.).

Current finish groups include E and F. In 1998, Black Sunburst, Trans. Green, Trans. Orange, Trans. Purple, Trans. Turquoise, and Trans. Walnut finishes were introduced; Black, Custom Black, and Gold Top finishes were disc. In 2000, Trans. Green, Deep Purple Metallic, Ocean Turquoise, Forest Green Metallic, Orange Mica Pearl, Royal Blue Metallic, and Strawberry Pearl Metallic finishes were disc. and Trans. Vintage Cherry, and Natural Mahogany finishes were introduced.

Brazilian McCarty Model - similar to McCarty Standard Model, except has Brazilian rosewood fingerboard and neck, limited edition - each headstock individually signed and numbered, 250 mfg. 1999 only.

			$3,350	$2,975	$2,600	$2,300	$1,975	$1,700	$1,500

McCARTY SOAPBAR - similar to McCarty Model, except has mahogany body/carved east coast maple top or carved solid mahogany body, 2 Seymour Duncan Soapbar single coil pickups, volume/tone controls, 3-way toggle switch, many colors and finishes have been available, current finish groups are C, D, and G, mahogany body/carved maple top, includes case, mfg. 1998-present.

MSR	$3,150		$2,350	$1,925	$1,550	$1,350	$1,075	$950	$725

> Add $200 for PRS tremolo and low mass locking tuners (disc.). Add $590 for flame 10 Top. Add $320 for abalone bird inlays. Add $600 for East Indian rosewood neck. Add $390 for gold hardware.
>
> Subtract $200 for Group G finish.

McCARTY SOAPBAR STANDARD - similar to McCarty Soapbar except has carved solid mahogany body (no maple top), many colors/finish has been available, current finish groups include E and F, current mfg.

MSR	$2,800		$2,000	$1,700	$1,375	$1,200	$1,000	$875	$725

> Add $320 for abalone bird inlays. Add $600 for East Indian rosewood neck. Add $390 for gold hardware.

ARCHTOP - offset double cutaway hollow body, carved spruce top, Artist grade flame maple back, carved mahogany sides, Wide-Fat mahogany neck with paua bird inlays, 22-fret Brazilian rosewood fingerboard with pearl and abalone moon inlays, Brazilian rosewood veneer headstock with paua signature, adjustable gold PRS stoptail bridge, gold hardware, 3-per-side low mass tuners with ebony buttons, 2 McCarty Archtop pickups, L.R. Baggs/PRS Piezo bridge system with individual string voicing, volume/tone controls, 3-position toggle switch, includes case, body depth (rim) 2.75 in., body depth (bridge) 4 in., available ini finish group R, mfg. 2002-2004.

			$4,750	$4,150	$3,650	$3,150	$2,600	$2,200	$1,850

Last MSR was $6,000.

McCARTY ARCHTOP SPRUCE - offset double cutaway hollow body, carved spruce top, carved mahogany back/sides, Wide-Fat mahogany neck, 22-fret rosewood fingerboard with pearl and abalone moon inlays, headstock (matches back/neck), adjustable PRS stoptail bridge, 3-per-side low mass tuners with ebony buttons, 2 McCarty Archtop pickups, volume/tone controls, 3-position toggle switch, includes case, available in Satin Vintage Natural finish, body depth (rim) 2.75 in., body depth (bridge) 4 in., mfg. 1998-2001.

			$2,600	$2,100	$1,800	$1,600	$1,400	$1,250	$1,000

Last MSR was $3,300.

> Add $280 for abalone bird inlays. Add $320 for gold hardware. Add $650 for LR Baggs/PRS Piezo bridge system, patent applied for, individual string voicing, real acoustic guitar modeling.

A Piezo bridge pickup option was available beginning 1999.

**Paul Reed Smith
2002 Dragon Singlecut
courtesy John A. Sazy, M.D.**

**Paul Reed Smith
2004 McCarty Model
courtesy John Beeson
The Music Shoppe**

GRADING	100% MINT	98% NEAR MINT	95% EXC+	90% EXC	80% VG+	70% VG	60% G

McCARTY ARCHTOP I - similar to McCarty Archtop Spruce except has carved figured maple top, carved mahogany back and sides, 22-fret wide-fat mahogany neck, rosewood fingerboard, pearl and abalone moon inlays, wide fat neck, rosewood veneer headstock, adjustable PRS stop tailpiece, two McCarty Archtop pickups, 1 volume/1 tone control, 3-way toggle pickup selector, available in Amber, Black Cherry, Black Sunburst, Dark Cherry Sunburst, Gray Black, McCarty Sunburst, natural, McCarty Tobacco Burst, Teal Black, Tortoise Shell, Turquoise, Vintage Yellow, Whale Blue, Cherry Sunburst, Violin Amber, or Violin Amber Burst, mfg. 1998-2001.

	$2,775	$2,575	$2,300	$2,100	$1,900	$1,700	$1,500

Last MSR was $3,700.

Add $200 for quilt top. Add $550 for 10 top flame. Add $750 for 10 top quilt. Add $280 for Abalone bird inlays. Add $320 for gold hardware. Add $650 for LR Baggs/PRS piezo bridge system, patent-pending, individual string voicing, real acoustic guitar modeling.

McCARTY ARCHTOP II - similar to the McCarty Archtop, except features carved Custom Grade figured maple top and back, with mahogany sides and rosewood headstock veneer, includes case, available in Amber, Black Cherry, Black Sunburst, Dark Cherry Sunburst, McCarty Tobacco Sunburst, McCarty Sunburst, Natural, Tobacco Sunburst, Vintage Sunburst, Violin Amber, or Violin Amber Burst finishes, mfg. 1998-2001.

	$2,600	$2,300	$2,000	$1,800	$1,600	$1,400	$1,200

Last MSR was $3,900.

Add $280 for abalone bird inlays. Add $1,100 for flame 10 top and back. Add $1,500 for quilt 10 top and back. Add $320 for gold hardware. Add $650 for LR Baggs/PRS piezo bridge system, patent-pending, individual string voicing, real acoustic guitar modeling.

McCARTY ARCHTOP ARTIST - similar to the McCarty Archtop II, except features carved Artist Grade figured maple top and back, 22-fret Brazilian rosewood fingerboard with 14kt gold-outlined abalone bird inlay, rosewood headstock veneer, gold hardware, includes case, available in Amber, Black Cherry, Black Sunburst, Dark Cherry Sunburst, Gray Black, McCarty Tobacco Sunburst, McCarty Sunburst, Natural, or Tobacco Sunburst finishes, mfg. 1998-2002.

	$7,500	$6,250	$5,500	$5,000	$4,500	$4,000	$3,000

Last MSR was $10,000.

Add $650 for LR Baggs/PRS Piezo bridge system, patent-pending, individual string voicing, real acoustic guitar modeling.

This model was available by special order only. "McCarty Archtop Artist" and the instrument´s number in this series is printed on the back of the headstock in gold. This model was also available with either flame or quilt top and back (no extra charge). Optional finishes iuncluded Amber, Black Cherry, Gray Black, McCarty Sunburst, Tiger´s Eye, Turquoise, Violin Amber, and Violin Amber Burst double-stained finishes (no extra charge). The double-stained finishes were only available on the McCarty Archtop Artist model and Private Stock models.

McCARTY HOLLOWBODY - offset double cutaway hollowbody, carved spruce top, carved mahogany back/sides, Wide-Fat mahogany neck, 22-fret rosewood fingerboard with pearl and abalone moon inlays, headstock (matches back/neck), PRS stoptail bridge, 3-per-side low mass tuners with ebony buttons, 2 McCarty Archtop pickups, volume/tone controls, 3-position toggle switch, available in Satin Vintage Natural finish (spruce top); Amber, Black Cherry, Black Sunburst, Dark Cherry Sunburst, McCarty Tobacco Sunburst, McCarty Sunburst, Natural, Tobacco Sunburst, Vintage Sunburst, Violin Amber, or Violin Amber Burst high gloss finishes (maple top), includes case, body depth (rim) 1.75 in., body depth (Bridge) 3 in. Mfg.1998-2003.

	$2,650	$2,250	$1,950	$1,750	$1,550	$1,350	$1,150

Last MSR was $3,600.

Add $160 for adjustable PRS stoptail bridge. Add $280 for abalone bird inlay. Add $360 for gold hardware. Add $650 for LR Baggs/PRS Piezo bridge system, patent applied for, individual string voicing, real acoustic guitar modeling. Add $200 for quilt top. Add $550 for flame 10 Top. Add $750 for quilt 10 Top (disc.).

A Piezo bridge pickup option was added in 1999.

McCarty Hollowbody I - similar to the McCarty Hollowbody, except features carved Custom Grade figured maple top and carved mahogany back and sides, includes case, currently available in C, D, and G finish groups, mfg. 1998-present.

MSR	$3,800		$2,800	$2,350	$2,000	$1,775	$1,550	$1,350	$1,150

Add $590 for flame 10 Top. Add $550 for quilt top (disc. 2002). Add $320 for abalone bird inlay. Add $160 for adjustable PRS stoptail bridge. Add $390 for gold hardware. Add $650 for LR Baggs/PRS Piezo bridge system, patent applied for, individual string voicing, real acoustic guitar modeling. Add $750 for quilt 10 Top (disc.). Add $1,380 for Artist Package with flame maple and paua bird inlays.

Subtract $200 for finish group G.

McCarty Hollowbody II - similar to the McCarty Hollowbody I, except features carved maple top and back with carved mahogany sides, includes case, this model has been available in Amber, Black Cherry, Black Sunburst, Dark Cherry Sunburst, McCarty Tobacco Sunburst, McCarty Sunburst, Natural, Tobacco Sunburst, Vintage Sunburst, Violin Amber, or Violin Amber Burst finishes, current finish groups include C, D, and G, mfg. 1998-present.

MSR	$4,000		$2,950	$2,450	$2,175	$1,950	$1,625	$1,400	$1,200

Add $160 for adjustable PRS stoptail bridge. Add $320 for abalone bird inlay. Add $390 for gold hardware. Add $650 for LR Baggs/PRS Piezo bridge system (new 1999), patent applied for, individual string voicing, real acoustic guitar modeling. Add $1,100 for quilt top and back (disc. 2002). Add $1,180 for flame 10 top and back. Add $1,500 for quilt 10 top and back (disc.). Add $1,380 for Artist's Package with flame maple and paua bird inlays.

Subtract $200 for finish group G.

McCarty Hollowbody Spruce - similar to McCarty Hollowbody I and II except has carved spruce top, current finish groups are R and S, mfg. 1998-present.

MSR	$3,400		$2,650	$2,000	$1,850	$1,600	$1,450	$1,250	$1,000

Add $320 for abalone bird inlays. Add $160 for adjustable PRS stop tailpiece. Add $390 for gold hardware. Add $650 for LR Baggs/PRS piezo bridge system, patent applied for, individual string voicing, real acoustic guitar modeling.

Subtract $200 for finish group S.

GRADING	100% MINT	98% NEAR MINT	95% EXC+	90% EXC	80% VG+	70% VG	60% G

ROSEWOOD LIMITED - offset double cutaway mahogany McCarty style body, carved curly maple top, mahogany back, wide-fat East Indian rosewood neck, 22-fret Brazilian rosewood fingerboard with elaborate PRS etched tree of life (consisting of abalone, Brown Lip mother-of-pearl, coral, gold, and mammoth ivory materials) inlay, PRS wraparound bridge, tree of life and signature peghead inlay, gold vintage tuners or gold PRS tremolo with gold PRS locking machines, gold hardware, 2 PRS McCarty humbuckers with gold plated nickel silver covers, gold anodized PRS stoptail, volume/tone controls, 3-position toggle switch, available in Black Cherry, Grey Black, Purple, Violin Amber, or Violin Amber Sunburst finishes, 100 mfg. 1996 only.

	100%	98%	95%	90%	80%	70%	60%
	$10,500	$9,500	$8,500	N/A	N/A	N/A	N/A

Last MSR was $13,000.

This model comes complete with hardshell leather case and a Certificate of Authenticity from PRS.

ELECTRIC: MISC.

SE EG - mahogany body with arm carve and pickguard, mahogany neck with 22-fret rosewood fingerboard, 25 in. scale, moon inlays, wide fat neck carve, PRS tremolo or stop tailpiece, PRS non-locking tuners, S/S/S or S/S/H pickup configuration, five-way blade pickup selector, volume and tone controls, available in Metallic Red with white pickguard, Metallic Blue with white pickguard, Antique White with tortoiseshell pickguard, mfg. 2004-present.

MSR	$658	$500	$425	$325	$275	$250	$225	$200

SE BILLY MARTIN - offset double cutaway design, solid mahogany body with set-in mahogany neck, two black soapbar pickups, 25 in. scale, 22-fret fingerboard with green Billy Martin designed inlays, wide fat neck carve, PRS tremolo or stop tailpiece, PRS non-locking tuners, two soapbar pickups, 3-way toggle pickup selector, volume and tone controls, black hardware, available in Flat Black finishes, mfg. in Korea, includes Cordura gig bag, new 2005.

MSR	$638	$500	$425	$375	$325	$285	$250	$225

SE SOAPBAR - single cutaway design, solid mahogany body with set-in mahogany neck, two black soapbar pickups, 25 in. scale, 22-fret fingerboard with moon inlays, wide fat neck carve, PRS trememlo or stop tailpiece, PRS non-locking tuners, two soapbar pickups, 3-way toggle pickup selector, volume and tone controls, available in Vintage Cherry or Black Burst, mfg. in Korea, includes Cordura gig bag. Limited mfg. 2004 only - disc. due to litigation.

$475	$425	$375	$325	$285	$250	$225

Last MSR was $598.

**Paul Reed Smith SE GE
courtesy John Beeson
The Music Shoppe**

SE SOAPBAR II - offset double cutaway design, solid mahogany body with set-in mahogany neck, two black soapbar pickups, 25 in. scale, 22-fret fingerboard with moon inlays, wide fat neck carve, PRS trememlo or stop tailpiece, PRS non-locking tuners, two soapbar pickups, 3-way toggle pickup selector, volume and tone controls, available in Antique White, Black, Tobacco Sunburst, or Tobacco Sunburst finishes, mfg. in Korea, includes Cordura gig bag, new 2005.

MSR	$598	$475	$425	$375	$325	$285	$250	$225

DAVE NAVARRO SIGNATURE - offset double cutaway carved maple top with mahogany back, set mahogany neck, 24-fret rosewood fingerboard with bird MOP inlays, matching headstock with Dave Navarro truss-rod cover and three-per-side tuners, PRS tremolo, one HFS and one Vintage humbucker pickups, two knobs, three-way switch, gold hardware, available in Jet White finish without natural maple edge, new 2005.

MSR	$3,400	$2,600	$2,250	$1,900	$1,650	$1,450	$1,250	$1,050

MODERN EAGLE - offset double cutaway, carved figured maple top and mahogany body, Brazilian rosewood neck and fretboard, RP pickups with satin covers, 3-way toggle selector, volume and tone control, 22-fret fingerboard, wide fat neck profile, rippled abalone bird inlays with Modern Eagle headstock inlay, features ultra thin nitrocellulose finish, includes leather case, stoptail or tremolo tailpiece, current finish group is X, mfg. 2004-present.

MSR	$8,000	$5,950	$5,000	$4,400	$3,600	$3,000	$2,650	$2,300

513 ROSEWOOD - offset double cutaway with carved 10-top maple front, mahogany body with Brazilian rosewood neck and fretboard, 25.25 in. scale, 22-fret fingerboard with new 513 style bird inlays, thin profile body, five proprietary PRS single coil pickups allowing thirteen modern and vintage sounds, compensated scalloped nut, redesigned neck joint, volume and tone controls with two blade switches, PRS tremolo bridge, current finish groups are A and B, mfg. 2004-present.

MSR	$6,400	$5,000	$4,300	$3,750	$3,250	$2,650	$2,250	$1,900

ELECTRIC: PRIVATE STOCK MODELS

PRS Private Stock models are very limited, non-production instruments, and are available in most models. To date, over 750 Private Stock instruments have been manufactured since April, 1996. These guitars are built from very special pieces of tone wood(s), and each instrument is individually made to custom order by a small team of senior craftsmen led by luthier Joseph Knaggs. Production is very limited, and each one is personally checked and play tested by the team and Paul Reed Smith, in addition to being personally signed, dated, and numbered by Paul Reed Smith. A unique certificate signed by Paul Reed Smith, describing the materials and construction also accompanies every Private Stock guitar.

Since each Private Stock guitar is custom built to order, prices for new instruments can vary significantly, depending on the instrument´s configuration, woods, finishes, and inlays. Prices typically vary from $6,500 - $20,000, and it is recommended that the company verify the original configuration of each Private Stock instrument (see Trademark Index for contact information).

**Paul Reed Smith Santana II
courtesy Dave Rogers
Dave's Guitar Shop**

GRADING	100% MINT	98% NEAR MINT	95% EXC+	90% EXC	80% VG+	70% VG	60% G

ELECTRIC: SANTANA SERIES

SANTANA MODEL - this model reproduces Santana's original model, offset double cutaway mahogany pre-1985 body shape with Paua shell purfling, carved Artist Grade maple top, mahogany neck, 24.5 in. scale, 24-fret (11.5 in. radius) rosewood fingerboard with rippled abalone bird inlays, PRS tremolo system, PRS Eagle inlay on natural wood headstock, abalone OM symbol inlaid on truss rod cover, 3-per-side PRS locking tuners, chrome hardware, 2 Santana Zebra Coil humbucker pickups, volume/tone control, 2 mini switch pickup selectors, available in Santana Yellow finish (with Natural Mahogany back), includes leather case, first 100 signed and numbered, mfg. 1995-98.

	$5,750	$5,000	$4,500	$4,000	$3,500	$3,000	$2,500

Last MSR was $6,000.

In 1998, Brazilian rosewood fingerboard replaced rosewood fingerboard; rosewood headstock overlay replaced natural wood headstock finish; 3-way toggle replaced 2 mini switch pickup selectors. In 1998, the PRS stoptail bridge and gold hardware were optional. This model was also available in Amber, Black Cherry, Black Sunburst, Cherry Sunburst, Dark Cherry Sunburst, Emerald Green, Grey Black, Orange, Purple, Royal Blue, Scarlet Red, Teal Black, Tobacco Sunburst, Tortoise Shell, Turquoise, Vintage Sunburst, Violin Amber, Violin Amber Sunburst, and Whale Blue finishes.

SANTANA II MODEL - almost identical to the Santana Model, except has artist grade wood, Brazilian rosewood fretboard and headstock veneer, eagle inlayed on headstock, one 3-way McCarty style selector switch rather than two mini-toggle switches, master volume control, master tone control, rippled abalone bird inlays, many finishes available (groups A and B), including Santana Yellow finish, includes leather case, mfg. 1999-present.

MSR	$8,000	$6,000	$5,000	$4,500	$4,000	$3,500	$3,000	$2,500

This model is also available in Amber, Black Sunburst, Black Cherry, Dark Cherry Sunburst, Emerald Green, McCarty Sunburst, McCarty Tobacco Sunburst, Teal Black, Tobacco Sunburst, Vintage Sunburst, Violin Amber Sunburst, and Whale Blue finishes. In 2000, Cherry Sunburst, Gray Black, Natural, Orange, Purple, Tortoise Shell, Turquoise, Vintage Yellow, Royal Blue, Scarlet Red finishes introduced.

SANTANA III MODEL - similar to the Santana II model, but less ornate, 1 piece South American mahogany body, two-piece curly carved maple top, Santana wide-fat mahogany 24-fret neck, 24.5 in. scale, 11.5 in. radius, East Indian rosewood fingerboard with abalone bird inlays, two Santana III pickups with covers, 1 volume/1 tone control, 3-way selector, headstock color matches back/neck, PRS tremolo 14-1, low mass locking tuners, electronics and tremolo cavity cover, many finishes available (groups A and B), including Santana Yellow, mfg. 2000-present.

MSR	$3,800	$2,850	$2,600	$2,375	$2,175	$1,975	$1,750	$1,550

Add $590 for 10 top flame. Add $390 for gold hardware.

SANTANA BRAZILIAN - features Brazilian rosewood neck and fretboard, 11.5 in. radius, 24.5 in. scale, eagle on H.S. Santana fret wire, Green Ripple Abalone birds, 10 top (choice of quilt or flame), Santana II purfling, Santana III pickups, gold/nickel hardware (similar to Dragon 2002), includes leather case, finish groups include A, B, and Santana Yellow. Limited run of 200 guitars with engraved and numbered backplate, mfg. 2003.

	$6,500	$5,500	$4,750	$4,250	$3,750	$3,250	$2,750

Last MSR was $9,000.

SANTANA SE - entry level Santana model, mahogany body and mahogany 22-fret set neck, rosewood fingerboard with SE shell (disc. mid 2002) or white pearloid (new mid-2002) inlays, gloss black headstock with Santana SE logo, unbound (disc.) or bound fingerboard and headstock (new mid 2002), PRS designed tremolo or stop tailpiece, PRS designed non-locking tuners, 2 covered humbucker (disc. 2002) or 2 uncovered open coil pickups (new mid 2002), 1 volume/1 tone control, 3-way selector switch, with (new mid 2002) or w/o (disc. mid 2002) small contoured 3-layer pickguard, current production has contoured lower about for player comfort. Available in Royal Blue (disc. 2003), Tobacco Sunburst (new 2002), Pearl White (mfg. 2002-2003), Silver (mfg. 2002-2003), Grey Black (disc.), Teal (disc.), Aqua Metallic (mfg. 2002-2003), Black (new 2004), or Vintage Cherry finishes, includes Cordura gig bag, mfg. in Korea, mfg. 2001-present.

MSR	$738	$495	$400	$365	$335	$300	$285	$260

ELECTRIC: SIGNATURE SERIES

SIGNATURE MODEL - based on the Custom 24, the first ultimate quality wood grade PRS model, extremely figured maple top (artist grade) with bird fret inlays, hand signed in back of headstock by Paul Reed Smith, 1,000 mfg. 1986-1990.

	$6,750	$5,700	$5,000	$4,250	$3,800	$3,375	$3,000

Prices for Signature models (with sweet switch) can vary significantly depending on the quality of the top wood, condition, and finish.

ELECTRIC: SINGLECUT/MARK TREMONTI SERIES

SINGLECUT - single cutaway body design, thick mahogany back, carved maple top, 22-fret mahogany neck, rosewood fingerboard with abalone dot inlays, wide, fat neck, headstock color matches back/neck, PRS stop tailpiece, Vintage tuners, two covered PRS #7 pickups, 3-way toggle switch on upper bout, 2 volume/2 tone controls, most recent finish groups include A, B, C, and G, mfg. 2000-disc. 2004 due to litigation.

	$2,650	$2,350	$2,150	$1,825	$1,675	$1,550	$1,375

Last MSR was $3,300.

Add $200 for quilt top. Add $590 for 10 top flame. Add $790 for 10 top quilt. Add $320 for abalone bird inlays. Add $390 for gold hardware. Add $1,380 for Artist package Flame and $1,580 for Artist package Quilt: Paua bird inlays in neck, rosewood headstock veneer with paua signature, Artist grade top and translucent toned back, gold hardware, leather case.

Subtract $200 for finish group G.

Brazilian Rosewood Singlecut - similar to Singlecut Model, except has solid Brazilian rosewood neck and fretboard, gold vintage style tuners, gold strap buttons, gold jack plate and screws, gold toggle ring, gold anodized stop tailpiece, nickel studs, PRS #7 pickups with brushed nickel covers and gold fillister screws, 180 pf cap on volume controls, limited production, 250 mfg. 2001 only.

	$3,650	$3,250	$2,875	$2,300	$2,000	$1,700	$1,475

Last MSR was $4,400.

P

GRADING	100% MINT	98% NEAR MINT	95% EXC+	90% EXC	80% VG+	70% VG	60% G

Singlecut Tremolo - similar to Singlecut, except has McCarty Style switching, thinner body, maple top, available in 9 colors, PRS Tremolo and Phase II locking tuners, PRS #6 zebra bobbin pickups, available in Vintage Sunburst, Dark Cherry Sunburst, Black Cherry, Whale Blue, Emerald Green, Grey Black, Dark Cherry Wrap Around Burst, Custom Black (optional), or Platinum (optional) finishes, gig bag included, mfg. 2002-present.

	$2,075	$1,850	$1,525	$1,325	$1,050	$925	$825

Last MSR was $2,840.

Add $590 for 10 top flame. Add $790 for 10 top quilt. Add $320 for abalone bird inlays. Add $390 for gold hardware. Add $1,380 for Artist package Flame and $1,580 for Artist package Quilt: paua bird inlays in neck, rosewood headstock veneer with paua signature, artist grade top and translucent toned back, gold hardware, leather case.

Subtract $200 for Custom Black or Platinum finish.

MARK TREMONTI MODEL - single cutaway design, thick mahogany back with carved maple top, 22-fret mahogany neck, rosewood fingerboard with mother-of-pearl bird inlays, Mark Tremonti 12th fret inlay, headstock color matches back/neck, truss rod cover with mother-of-pearl purfling, PRS adjustable stop tailpiece, PRS locking tuners, two Tremonti pickups, 3-way toggle pickup selector, 2 volume/2 tone controls, includes case, available in Black or Platinum finish, mfg. 2001-04 due to litigation.

	$2,650	$2,400	$2,150	$1,950	$1,750	$1,550	$1,350

Last MSR was $3,500.

TREMONTI SE MODEL - single cutaway design, solid mahogany body, 22-fret one piece mahogany neck with dot inlays, bound body and fingerboard, PRS adjustable stop tailpiece, two Tremonti pickups without covers, 3-way toggle pickup selector, 2 volume/2 tone controls, includes Cordura gig bag, available in Black or Platinum finish only, mfg. 2002-04 due to litigation.

	$460	$400	$350	$300	$250	$225	$200

Last MSR was $638.

Paul Reed Smith Singlecut courtesy Dave Rogers Dave's Guitar Shop

ELECTRIC: SPECIAL & STUDIO SERIES

SPECIAL - developed for the 'hard rock/metal player,' wide-thin neck, trem-up routing for a full tone up, volume and tone controls with 5 way rotary, HFS Treble pickup, PRS single coil in middle, HFS Bass pickup (changed to Vintage Bass humbucker by 1989), mfg. 1988-1991.

	$1,450	$1,275	$1,075	$900	$725	$575	$475

STUDIO - similar to Special, except has standard neck profile, Hot Vintage treble pickup and two PRS single coil pickups, mfg. 1988-1991.

	$1,450	$1,275	$1,075	$900	$725	$575	$475

While this model was discontinued in 1991, the humbucker/single coil/single coil (h/s/s) pickup configuration was offered as an option until 1997.

ELECTRIC: STANDARD SERIES

STANDARD 22 - offset double cutaway carved mahogany body, set-in mahogany neck, 22-fret rosewood fingerboard with pearl and abalone moon inlay, 25 in scale, color-matching headstock, PRS tremolo system or PRS stoptail bridge, 3-per-side locking PRS tuners, chrome hardware, 2 PRS Dragon II humbucker pickups, volume/tone control, 5-position rotary switch, current finish groups include E and F, includes case, mfg. 1994-present.

MSR	$2,730	$1,995	$1,675	$1,350	$1,050	$950	$825	$600

Add $320 for abalone bird inlays. Add $390 for gold hardware.

This model has wide thin or wide fat neck profiles available. In 1998, Black Sunburst, Natural, Translucent Green, Translucent Orange, Translucent Purple, Translucent Turquoise, and Translucent Walnut finishes were introduced; Black and Pearl Black finishes were disc. In 2004, the 3-way toggle selector pickup became an option available at no charge - previously, it was a $70 option.

Standard 22 Maple Top - similar to the Standard 22, except features mahogany body, carved maple top, includes case. Available in Antique White, Black, Seafoam Green, Ocean Turquoise, Cabernet Metallic, Deep Purple Metallic, Forest Green Metallic, Old Gold Metallic, Orange Mica Pearl Metallic, Platinum Metallic, Royal Blue Metallic, and Strawberry Pearl Metallic finishes with natural maple edge (some models may have a natural gloss finish on the back), mfg. 1998-99.

	$1,650	$1,250	$1,150	$950	$850	$750	$600

Last MSR was $2,300.

Add $70 for 3-way toggle selector switch and push/pull tone control (coil tap capabilities). Add $260 for abalone bird inlays. Add $280 for gold hardware.

STANDARD 24 (STANDARD) - offset double cutaway carved mahogany body/neck, 24-fret rosewood fingerboard with pearl and abalone moon inlay, 25 in. scale, standard PRS tremolo system or PRS stoptail bridge, 3-per-side locking PRS tuners, chrome hardware, 2 humbucker PRS pickups (one HFS and one Vintage Bass), volume/tone control, 5-position rotary switch, includes case, available in Black, Natural, Pearl Black, or Vintage Cherry finishes, mfg. 1987-present.

1985-1991 W/ BIRDS		$2,450	$2,100	$1,750	$1,500	$1,250	$1,000	$875
1985-1991 W/O BIRDS		$1,950	$1,750	$1,500	$1,250	$995	$875	$675
MSR	$2,730	$1,995	$1,675	$1,350	$1,050	$950	$825	$600

Add $80 for 1996/1997 Custom colors (Custom Black, Electric Blue, Electric Red, Gold Top, Pearl White, Black Holoflake, Blue Holoflake, Burgundy Holoflake, Green Holoflake, Gold Holoflake, Red Holoflake, and Silver Holoflake - disc.). Add $240 for a semi-hollowbody (this option disc. in 1998). Add $320 for abalone bird inlays on neck. Add $390 for gold hardware. Early mfg. with low serial numbers in 90%+ original condition will bring a 10%-30%+ premium.

Paul Reed Smith Standard 24 courtesy John Beeson The Music Shoppe

P

GRADING	100% MINT	98% NEAR MINT	95% EXC+	90% EXC	80% VG+	70% VG	60% G

Sweet switch and Brazilian rosewood fretboard were disc. Nov., 1991. The Standard Model nomenclature was introduced in 1987, after two years of regular production. Current finish groups include E and F. In 1998, Black Sunburst, Natural, Trans. Green, Trans. Orange, Trans. Purple, Trans. Turquoise, and Trans. Walnut finishes were introduced; Black and Pearl Black finishes were disc. During 2004, an optional 3-way toggle selector switch and push/pull tone control (coil tap capabilities) became available at no charge - previously it was a $70 option. During 2005, a 20th Anniversary model was released, which has "20th" on the truss-rod cover and special "Birds in Flight" fingerboard inlays.

Standard 24 Maple Top - similar to the Standard 24, except features mahogany body, carved maple top, available in Antique White, Black, Seafoam Green, Ocean Turquoise, Cabernet Metallic, Deep Purple Metallic, Forest Green Metallic, Old Gold Metallic, Orange Mica Pearl Metallic, Platinum Metallic, Royal Blue Metallic, and Strawberry Pearl Metallic finishes with natural maple edge (some models may have a Natural gloss finish on the back), list price includes case, mfg. 1998-99.

			$1,650	$1,250	$1,150	$950	$850	$750	$600

Last MSR was $2,300.

Add $70 for 3-way toggle selector switch and push/pull tone control (coil tap capabilities). Add $260 for abalone bird inlays. Add $280 for gold hardware.

SWAMP ASH SPECIAL - offset double cutaway carved swamp ash (or black ash) body, bolt-on maple neck, 22-fret maple fingerboard with abalone dot inlay, toned clear headstock finish, PRS stoptail bridge (disc. 2001) or PRS tremolo, 3-per-side locking PRS tuners, chrome hardware, PRS McCarty humbucker/Seymour Duncan Vintage Rail single coil/PRS McCarty humbucker pickups, volume/push-pull tone (coil tap) controls, 3-position toggle switch, includes case, current finish groups include J and P, mfg. 1996-present.

MSR	$2,730		$1,995	$1,675	$1,350	$1,050	$950	$825	$600

Add $320 for abalone bird inlays. Add $300 for figured maple neck/figured maple fingerboard. Add $390 for gold hardware.

Subtract $200 for finish group P.

In 1998, Natural and Tri-Color Sunburst finishes were introduced; Grey Black finish was disc. (previously 1997 Custom colors).

ELECTRIC BASS

The PRS basic electric bass models were available with bolt-on or set-in neck joint configurations. Basic features included a PRS preamp, 5 position rotary switch, deep and clear tone controls, and PRS hardware. The bolt-on neck models had alder bodies, or alder bodies with figured maple tops; the set-in neck models had solid mahogany, or mahogany bodies with maple tops. Approx. 600 PRS basses were manufactured 1986-1992. Desirable options on the PRS bass models include the bird inlays, and a figured maple 10 Top.

BASS 4/BASS 5 - solid alder body, bolt-on rock maple neck, rosewood or maple fretboard with dot inlays, 3 single coil pickups, 1 hum canceling, mfg. 1990-91.

4-STRING	$1,500	$1,300	$1,100	$950	$825	$700	$600
5-STRING	$1,700	$1,500	$1,300	$1,100	$950	$825	$700

CE BASS-4/BASS-5 (MAPLE TOP) - maple top, alder back, bolt-on rock maple neck, rosewood or maple fretboard, dot inlay, 3 single coil pickups, 1 hum canceling, mfg. 1990-91.

	$1,100	$975	$850	$725	$600	$525	$450

CURLY BASS-4/CURLY BASS-5 - maple top, mahogany back, rock maple neck, Brazilian rosewood fretboard, moon inlay, 3 single coil pickups, 1 hum canceling, mfg. 1987-1991.

4-STRING	$1,950	$1,750	$1,550	$1,375	$1,100	$975	$850
5-STRING	$3,200	$2,875	$2,500	$2,200	$2,000	$1,800	$1,600

Add 20%-30% for 10-top (flame or quilt), gold hardware and bird inlays.

These models were available with an optional 10-top, gold hardware, bird inlays or a quilted top.

ELECTRIC BASS - offset double cutaway alder body, (optional swamp ash body available), bolt-on rock maple neck, rosewood or rock maple 21-fret ingerboard, 34 in. scale, abalone dot inlays, PRS machined brass bridge, 20-1 low mass tuners, 2-per-side tuners, 2 PRS high inductance passive magnetic pickups, (v/v/t with high end switchable audio preamp), 2 volume/1 master tone control, optional gold hardware, optional LR Baggs Piezo bridge system with 3 band active EQ, and selector switch for piezo (piezo option discontinued in 2001), current finish groups are F, J, and W, mfg. 2000-04.

		$1,800	$1,600	$1,300	$1,050	$925	$800	$700

Last MSR was $2,400.

Add $400 for swamp ash body. Add $1,000 for figured maple neck with rosewood or figured maple fingerboard. Add $320 for abalone bird inlays. Add $390 for gold hardware. Add $750 for LR Baggs/PRS piezo bridge system, patent applied for, individual string voicing, 3 band active EQ, selector switch for piezo, magnetic, or both (disc.). Add $200 for Black Sunburst, Translucent Emerald Green, Translucent Vintage Cherry, Tri-Color Sunburst, and Translucent Turquoise finishes (alder body only). Add $200 for finish groups F and W with alder body.

Subtract $200 for finish groups F and J with swamp ash body.

ELECTRIC BASS MAPLE TOP - similar to Electric Bass except, alder back, curly maple inset top, current finish groups are T and F, mfg. 2000-04.

	$2,100	$1,950	$1,775	$1,550	$1,275	$1,000	$895

Last MSR was $2,800.

Add $590 for 10 top flame. Add $1,000 for figured maple neck with rosewood or figured maple fingerboard. Add $320 for abalone bird inlays. Add $390 for gold hardware. Add $750 for LR Baggs/PRS piezo bridge system, patent applied for, individual string voicing, 3-band active EQ, selector switch for piezo, magnetic, or both (disc.).

Subtract $200 for finish group F.

GRADING	100% MINT	98% NEAR MINT	95% EXC+	90% EXC	80% VG+	70% VG	60% G

BASS FOUR - offset double cutaway solid mahogany body and rock maple neck, Brazilian rosewood fretboard with moon inlays (birds were optional), 34 in. scale, 2-per-side headstock, 3 single coil pickups, 1 hum canceling, volume/tone/pickup selector controls, gold hardware optional, available in Translucent finishes, mfg. 1987-1991.

		$1,800	$1,600	$1,400	$1,200	$1,000	$800	$600

Last MSR was $1,500.

Add 15% for Curly Bass Model with maple top. Add $700 for 10-Top w/birds in 95%+ condition.

Subtract $200 for alder body/bolt-on neck.

Bass Five - similar to the Bass Four, except has 5-string configuration, 3/2 headstock, mfg. 1987-1991.

		$1,300	$1,200	$1,100	$1,000	$800	$600	$400

Last MSR was $1,600.

Subtract $200 for alder body/bolt-on neck.

SIGNATURE SERIES 4 OR 5 STRING - signature (artist grade) maple top, mahogany back, rock maple neck, Brazilian rosewood fretboard, abalone bird inlay, 3 single coil pickups, 1 hum canceling, optional gold hardware and quilted top, mfg. 1987-1991.

		$2,150	$1,850	$1,750	$1,500	$1,250	$1,000	$895

PAWAR GUITARS

Instruments currently built in Willoughby Hills, OH.

The idea for Pawar guitars was discussed in 1995 between Jay Pawar and Jeff Johnston, and the first guitar came in 1999. Pawar Guitars are handcrafted in the U.S., and currently available in 3 models. All models come standard with the Pawar positive tone system (P.T.S.), and feature carved maple tops, lightweight swamp ash backs, maple necks, and rosewood fretboards. Please contact the company directly for more information (see Trademark Index).

Paul Reed Smith Electric Bass courtesy Dave Rogers Dave's Guitar Shop

ELECTRIC

Dot Neck Inlay Option $100, all 3 models. Bigsby B5 Vibrato Tailpiece with Roller Bridge Option $200, all 3 models. Quilt Maple Top Option $100, Prestige Model Only. bird's-eye maple top Option $200, Prestige Model Only.

TURN OF THE CENTURY PLAYER - offset cutaway solid body, unique scroll upper bout, carved maple top, light weight swamp ash back, maple neck, rosewood fingerboard, 25 1/2" scale, jumbo frets, set neck, tunematic bridge, string-through body retainer, Sperzel non-locking tuners, recessed Dunlop strap locks, Pawar Positive Tone System with 20 pre-set classic tones, 2 Seymour Duncan pickups, Gun Metal Gray back, available in Sterling Silver, Drama Gold, or Midnight Black finishes, current mfg.

MSR	N/A	$1,999	$1,650	$1,400	$1,200	$1,050	$900	$750

TURN OF THE CENTURY STAGE - similar to Turn Of The Century Player except comes standard with premium hand selected woods and Translucent Ivory finished back, available in Copper Tan, Cobalt Blue, or Emerald Green finishes, current mfg.

MSR	N/A	$2,325	$1,950	$1,700	$1,450	$1,300	$1,150	$975

TURN OF THE CENTURY PRESTIGE - similar to Turn Of The Century Stage except has highly figured maple top, matching figured maple headstock veneers, premium light weight swamp ash back, ivoroid bound bird's-eye maple neck, select rosewood fingerboards, available in Antiqueburst, Natural, Cherryburst, or Tobaccoburst translucent finishes, current mfg.

MSR	N/A	$2,625	$2,200	$1,950	$1,700	$1,500	$1,300	$1,100

PEAL

Instruments currently produced in Korea. Distributed by the Ye-Il International Company.

Peal produces a line of acoustic, electric, bass, and round back guitars that are mainly entry level instruments. For more information refer to their website (see Trademark Index).

PEAR CUSTOM

Instruments currently built in Pleasanton, CA.

Luthier Tom Palecki offers custom electric guitar design and construction and custom painting in a wide variety of traditional and high tech colors. Our instruments are exclusively electric and consultations are by appointment only. Prices begin at $2,000 and up for design and construction depending on complexity of design and color. Pear Custom are also the inventors of the Turbotune guitar and bass string winder and Turbotune Drum Key currently licensed to Dean Markley Strings for world wide sales. For further information, please contact Pear Custom Guitars directly (see Trademark Index).

PEARL

Instruments previously produced in Italy starting in the late 1970s (production then moved to Japan). Production ended sometime in the early 1980s.

The Pearl trademark appeared on a number of instruments manufactured (at first) by the Gherson company of Italy. These medium quality guitars featured both original designs on some models, and copies of classic American designs on others. Production of Pearl guitars moved to Japan (circa 1978-1979) and continued on for another couple of years. Although Italy had a tradition of guitar manufacture throughout the years, the cheaper labor costs that Japan was featuring at the time eventually won out in production considerations (source: Tony Bacon and Paul Day, *The Guru's Guitar Guide*).

Pawar Turn of the Century Prestige courtesy Pawar

P

GRADING	100% MINT	98% NEAR MINT	95% EXC+	90% EXC	80% VG+	70% VG	60% G

PEARL RIVER

Instruments currently produced in China.

Pearl River produces an entire line of acoustic guitars, as well as electric guitars. Pearl River guitars is a derivative of the Pearl River Guitar Company. They are mainly entry level instruments at an entry level prices. For more information refer to their website (see Trademark Index).

PEAVEY

Instruments currently built in Meridian and Leaksville, MS. Distributed by Peavey Electronics Corporation of Meridian, MS since 1965. Peavey also has a factory and distribution center in Corby, England to help serve and service the overseas market.

Peavey Electronics is one of the very few major American musical instrument manufacturers still run by the original founding member and owner. Hartley Peavey grew up in Meridian, Mississippi and spent some time working in his father's music store repairing record players. He gained some recognition locally for the guitar amplifiers he built by hand while he was still in school, and decided months prior to college graduation to go into business for himself. In 1965 Peavey Electronics was started out of the basement of Peavey's parents' home. Due to the saturated guitar amp market of the late 1960s, Peavey switched to building P.A. systems and components. By 1968 the product demand was great enough to warrant building a small cement block factory on rented land and hire another staff member.

The demand for Peavey products continued to grow, and by the early 1970s the company's roster had expanded to 150 employees. Emphasis was still placed on P.A. construction, although both guitar and bass amps were doing well. The Peavey company continued to diversify and produce all the components needed to build the finished product. After twelve years of manufacturing, the first series of Peavey guitars was begun in 1977, and introduced at the 1978 NAMM show. An advertising circular show compared the price of an American built T-60 (plus case) for $350 versus the Fender Stratocaster's list price of $790 or a Gibson Les Paul for $998.50 (list). In light of those list prices, it's also easy to see where the Japanese guitar makers had plenty of maneuvering room during their copy era.

The T-Series guitars were introduced in 1978, and the line expanded from three models up to a total of seven in five years. In 1983, the product line changed, and introduced both the mildly wacky Mystic and Razer original designs (the Mantis was added in 1984) and the more conservative Patriot, Horizon, and Milestone guitars. The Fury and Foundation basses were also added at this time. After five years of stop tailpieces, the first Peavey Octave Plus vibratos were offered (later superseded by the Power bend model). Pickup designs also shifted from the humbuckers to single or double blade pickups.

Models that debuted in 1985 included the vaguely stratish Predator, and the first doubleneck (!), the Hydra. In response to the guitar industry shifting to superstrat models, the Impact was introduced in 1986. Guitars also had the option of a Kahler locking tremolo, and two offsprings of the '84 Mantis were released: The Vortex I or Vortex II. The Nitro series of guitars were available in 1987, as well as the Falcon, Unity, and Dyna-Bass. Finally, to answer companies like Kramer or Charvel, the Tracer series and the Vandenberg model(s) debuted in 1988.

As the U.S. guitar market grew more conservative, models like the Generation S-1 and Destiny guitars showed up in guitar shops. Peavey basses continued to evolve into sleeker and more solid instruments like the Palaedium, TL series or B Ninety. 1994 saw the release of the MIDIBASE (later the Cyberbass) that combined magnetic pickups with a MIDI-controller section.

One of Peavey's biggest breakthroughs in recent years was the development of the Peavey EVH amplifier, developed in conjunction with Edward Van Halen. Due to the success and acceptance of the EVH 5150 amplifier, Van Halen withdrew his connection with his signature Ernie Ball model (which is still in production as the Axis model), and designed a new **Wolfgang** model with Peavey. This new model had a one year waiting period from when it was announced at the NAMM industry trade show to actual production. Many Peavey dealers who did receive early models generally sold them at new retail (no discount) for a number of months due to slow supply.

Rather than stay stuck in a design holding pattern, Peavey continues to change and revise guitar and bass designs, and they continue the almost twenty year tradition of American built electric guitars and basses.

Model History, nomenclature, and description courtesy Grant Brown, Peavey Repair section. Information on virtually any Peavey product, or a product's schematic is available through Peavey Repair. Grant Brown, the head of the Repair section, has been with Peavey Electronics for over eighteen years.

ELECTRIC: AXCELERATOR SERIES

AXCELERATOR - offset double cutaway poplar (or swamp ash) body, pearloid pickguard, bolt-on maple neck, 22-fret rosewood fingerboard with pearl dot inlay, Peavey Power Bend III non-locking tremolo, 6-on-a-side locking tuners, chrome hardware, 3 Db2 dual blade humbucker pickups, volume/tone control, 5-position switch, available in Black, Candy Apple Red, Metallic Gold, Trans. Blue, or Trans. Red finishes, mfg. 1994-98.

$600	$525	$450	$375	$325	$275	$200

Last MSR was $799.

AXCELERATOR AX - similar to Axcelerator, except has swamp ash body, Floyd Rose double locking vibrato, non-locking tuners, gold hardware 2 Db2 dual blade/1 Db4 quad blade humbucker pickups, 3-way turbo (allows bridge pickup to be tapped as single coil, dual coil, and full humbucker modes) switch, available in Blonde, Trans. Blue, Trans. Green, or Trans. Red finishes, mfg. 1995-98.

$600	$525	$450	$375	$325	$275	$200

Last MSR was $799.

This model had maple fingerboard with black dot inlay as an option.

AXCELERATOR F - similar to Axcelerator, except has swamp ash body, Floyd Rose double locking vibrato, non locking tuners, gold hardware 2 dual blade/1 quad blade humbucker pickups, available in Blonde, Trans. Blue, Trans. Green, or Trans. Red finishes, mfg. 1994 only.

$475	$400	$350	$325	$275	$250	$200

Last MSR was $799.

Options such as swamp ash body and AX pickup assembly (2 Db2 dual blade and 1 Db4 quad blade humbuckers) were offered on the regular Axcelerator. The Axcelerator F model evolved into the Axcelerator AX model.

ELECTRIC: STEVE CROPPER SERIES

CROPPER CLASSIC - single cutaway mahogany body with figured maple top, bolt-on hard rock maple neck, 22-fret rosewood fingerboard, Db2 dual blade humbucker, Db4 quad blade humbucker, gold hardware, master volume and tone controls, 3-way pickup selector switch, two position coil-tap switch, available in Black, Onion Green, Memphis Sun, Tiger Eye, Harlequin Violet, or Rhythm Blue finishes, case included, current mfg.

MSR	$1,200		$975	$850	$775	$700	$625	$550	$425

This model was designed in conjunction with guitarist Steve Cropper.

GRADING	100% MINT	98% NEAR MINT	95% EXC+	90% EXC	80% VG+	70% VG	60% G

ELECTRIC: DEFENDER & DESTINY SERIES

DEFENDER - offset double cutaway poplar body, white laminated pickguard, bolt-on maple neck, 24-fret rosewood fingerboard with pearl dot inlay, double locking Floyd Rose vibrato, 6-on-a-side tuners, chrome hardware, exposed humbucker/single coil/humbucker pickups, volume/tone control, 5-position switch, available in Black, Candy Apple Red, Cobalt Blue, or White finishes, mfg. 1994-95.

N/A	$300	$250	$210	$170	$130	$90

Last MSR was $590.

Defender F - similar to Defender, except has alder body, black pearloid laminated pickguard, humbucker/single coil rail/humbucker pickups, available in Metallic Purple, Metallic Silver, Pearl Black, or Pearl White finishes, mfg. 1994-95.

N/A	$500	$425	$350	$300	$250	$200

Last MSR was $799.

DESTINY - offset double cutaway poplar body, through body rock maple neck, 24-fret bound rosewood fingerboard, pearl dot inlays, Kahler double locking vibrato, 6-on-a-side tuners, black hardware, 2 high output single coil/1 Alnico humbucker pickups, volume/tone control, 5-position pickup selector and coil tap switch, available in Black, Blue, White, or Red finishes, mfg. 1989-1994.

N/A	$400	$350	$300	$250	$200	$150

Last MSR was 699.95.

Destiny Custom - offset double cutaway mahogany body, quilted maple top, through body flamed maple neck, 24-fret bound rosewood fingerboard, pearl oval inlay at 12th fret, double locking vibrato, 6-on-a-side tuners, gold hardware, 2 high output single coil/1 Alnico humbucker pickups, volume/tone control, 5-position pickup selector and a coil tap switch, available in Honey Burst, Trans. Black, Trans. Blue, Trans. Honey Burst, or Trans. Red finishes, mfg. 1989-1994.

N/A	$550	$450	$375	$325	$275	$225

Last MSR was $1,000.

ELECTRIC: DETONATOR SERIES

DETONATOR - offset double cutaway poplar body, bolt-on hard rock maple neck, 24-fret rosewood fingerboard with pearl dot inlay, Peavey Floyd Rose double locking tremolo, 6-on-a-side tuners, chrome hardware, ceramic humbucker/single coil/humbucker configuration, volume/tone control, 5-position switch, white laminated pickguard, available in Candy Apple Red, Cobalt Blue, Gloss Black, or, Gloss White finishes, disc. 1998.

$450	$375	$325	$275	$225	$175	$150

Last MSR was $589.

DETONATOR AX - similar to the Detonator, except has alder body, Alnico humbucker/Db2 dual blade single coil/Alnico humbucker configuration, Power Bend III tremolo system, locking tuning machines, pearloid pickguard, available in Metallic Purple, Metallic Silver, Pearl Black, or Pearl White finishes, disc. 1998.

$550	$500	$450	$375	$325	$250	$175

Last MSR was $779.

DETONATOR JX - similar to the Detonator, except has poplar body, 2 single coil/humbucker ceramic pickups, Power Bend II tremolo system, non-locking tuning machines, white laminated pickguard, available in Gloss Black, Gloss Dark Blue, Gloss White, or Gloss Red finishes, disc. 1998.

| | | $300 | $260 | $230 | $200 | $175 | $150 | $100 |

$300	$260	$230	$200	$175	$150	$100

Last MSR was $419.

ELECTRIC: EVH WOLFGANG SERIES

The EVH Wolfgang series was designed in conjunction with Edward Van Halen. Van Halen, who had great success with the Peavey 5150 amplifiers he also helped develop, named the guitar model after his son.

EVH WOLFGANG (STOP TAILPIECE/SOLID COLORS) - offset double cutaway bound basswood body, arched top, bolt-on graphite-reinforced bird's-eye maple neck, 22-fret bird's-eye maple fingerboard with black dot inlays, 25.5 in. scale, adjustable bridge/stop tailpiece, 3-per-side headstock, chrome tuners, chrome hardware, 2 ceramic humbuckers, volume/tone controls, 3-position pickup selector, available in Gloss Black or Gloss Ivory finishes, mfg. 1996-2004.

EVH Wolfgang (Floyd Rose/Solid Colors) - similar to the EVH Wolfgang, except has a Peavey Floyd Rose double locking tremolo system with a D-Tuner dropped D tuning knob, mfg. 1996-2004.

$1,350	$1,175	$950	$800	$675	$550	$425

Last MSR was $1,800.

EVH Wolfgang (Stop Tailpiece/Transparent Colors) - similar to the EVH Wolfgang, except features a arched quilted maple top, stop tailpiece/non-tremolo bridge, available in Trans. Amber, Trans. Purple, Trans. Red, Trans. Blue, Trans. Green, Trans. Dark Cherry Sunburst, Sea Foam, Vintage Gold, Cherry Sunburst, or Sunburst finishes, mfg. 1996-2004.

$1,425	$1,200	$1,025	$875	$750	$600	$450

Last MSR was $1,880.

P

GRADING	100% MINT	98% NEAR MINT	95% EXC+	90% EXC	80% VG+	70% VG	60% G

EVH Wolfgang (Floyd Rose/Transparent Colors) - similar to the EVH Wolfgang, except has a arched quilted maple top, Peavey Floyd Rose double locking tremolo system with a **D-Tuna** dropped D tuning knob, available in Trans. Amber, Trans. Purple, Trans. Red, Trans. Blue, Trans. Green, Trans. Dark Cherry Sunburst, Sea Foam, Vintage Gold, Cherry Sunburst, or Sunburst finishes, mfg. 1996-2004.

	$1,650	$1,400	$1,150	$975	$825	$675	$550

Last MSR was $2,200.

EVH WOLFGANG SPECIAL - offset double cutaway basswood body, bolt-on maple neck, 22-fret maple fingerboard with black dot inlays, 25.5 in. scale, adjustable bridge/stop tailpiece, 3-per-side headstock, chrome tuners, chrome hardware, 2 humbuckers, volume/tone controls, 3-position pickup selector, available in Gloss Black, Gloss Ivory, Vintage Gold, Gloss Purple, or Sunburst finishes, mfg. 1997-2004.

	$900	$750	$625	$525	$450	$375	$300

Last MSR was $1,200.

Also available with rosewood fingerboard.

EVH Wolfgang Special Flametop - similar to EVH Wolfgang Special except, has High Grade Flame Maple Top, hand detailed flame body binding, Case included, available in Gloss Black, Trans. Red, Trans. Purple, Trans. Amber, Trans. Sunburst, or Trans. Dark Cherry Sunburst finishes, disc. 2004.

	$1,250	$1,050	$900	$800	$725	$650	$575

Last MSR was $1,650.

Also available with rosewood fingerboard.

EVH Wolfgang Special ST - similar to EVH Wolfgang Special except, has recessed tune-o-matic bridge and stop tailpiece, case included, available in Gloss Black, Gloss Ivory, Gloss Purple, Vintage Gold, Tobacco Sunburst finishes, disc. 2004.

	$700	$600	$525	$475	$425	$375	$325

Last MSR was $1,000.

Also available with rosewood fingerboard.

EVH Special EXP Quilt Top - similar to the EVH Special, except has a quilted maple top over a basswood body, available in Trans. Blue, Trans. Maroon, Amber, or Sunburst finishes, mfg. 2004 only.

	$725	$625	$550	$475	$400	$350	$300

Last MSR was $900.

ELECTRIC: FALCON SERIES

FALCON - double offset cutaway poplar body, bolt-on bi-laminated maple neck, 22-fret maple fingerboard, 25.5 in. scale, 6-on-a-side tuners, three single coil pickups, Kahler locking tremolo system, volume/tone controls, five way pickup selector, white pickguard, mfg. 1986-88.

	N/A	$250	$200	$175	$150	$125	$100

Last MSR was $399.50.

FALCON ACTIVE - similar to the Falcon, except body was restyled to sleeker design lines, flame maple bi-laminated neck with rosewood or flame maple fingerboard, and active Bi-FET pickups replaced the original passive system, active electronics powered by an onboard 9-volt battery, mfg. 1988-89.

	N/A	$325	$275	$250	$225	$175	$150

Last MSR was $549.

FALCON CLASSIC - similar to the Falcon Active, except has Flame Maple bi-laminated neck and Flame Maple fingerboard, 3 passive single coil pickups, Power Bend non-locking tremolo system, mfg. 1988-89.

	N/A	$225	$175	$150	$135	$105	$75

Last MSR was $349.50.

FALCON CUSTOM - similar to the Falcon, except featured a rosewood fingerboard and different fingerboard radius, mfg. 1986-1990.

	N/A	$300	$250	$200	$175	$150	$125

Last MSR was $449.50.

In 1988, the Falcon Custom´s body design was restyled into a sleeker profile similar to the Falcon Classic and Falcon Active that were offered that same year. In 1988, flame maple neck with rosewood or maple fingerboards replaced the standard rock maple neck. In 1989, changes involved a figured maple neck with a rosewood fingerboard, pickups were upgraded to the HRS (Hum Reducing System) models, carved maple top over poplar body, gold hardware, Power Bend II tremolo and locking tuning machines, and a graphite nut.

FALCON STANDARD - similar to the Falcon Classic, except has a Figured Maple bi-laminated neck and rosewood fingerboard, 3 HRS (Hum Reducing System) passive single coil pickups, Power Bend II non-locking tremolo and graphite saddles, locking tuning machines, mfg. 1989-1990.

	N/A	$225	$175	$150	$135	$105	$75

Last MSR was $349.50.

ELECTRIC: FIRENZA SERIES

FIRENZA (IMPACT FIRENZA) - offset double cutaway mahogany body, bolt-on maple neck, 22-fret rosewood fingerboard with pearl dot inlay, 25 in. scale, recessed tune-o-matic bridge/stop tailpiece, 3-per-side tuners, chrome hardware, 2 soapbar single coil pickups, volume/tone control, 3-position selector switch, available in Ivory, Gloss Black, Sunburst, Trans. Cherry, or Trans. Walnut finishes, disc. 2000.

	$525	$450	$395	$350	$295	$225	$175

Last MSR was $699.

An early Impact Firenza model may have 2 single coil/humbucker pickups, poplar body, or tremolo bridge. Also available in Powder Blue, Red, Seafoam Green, and White finishes.

FIRENZA AX (IMPACT FIRENZA AX) - similar to the Impact Firenza, except features a swamp ash body, Power Bend III standard tremolo, locking tuners, 2 covered humbucker pickups, 5-way pickup selector, available in Antique Blonde, Pearl Black, Sunburst, or Trans. Red finishes, disc. 2000.

	$650	$575	$500	$425	$350	$275	$200

Last MSR was $899.

This model was an option with an alder body, and available in Metallic Silver, Pearl Black, or Trans. Grape with pearloid pickguard, or Sunburst with tortoiseshell pickguard finishes.

P

GRADING	100% MINT	98% NEAR MINT	95% EXC+	90% EXC	80% VG+	70% VG	60% G

FIRENZA JX (IMPACT FIRENZA JX) - similar to the Impact Firenza, except features basswood body, fixed bridge, 2 single coil/humbucker pickups, 5-way pickup selector, available in Gloss Black, Gloss Ivory, or Gloss Red finishes, mfg. 1997-2000.

		$480	$390	$345	$295	$250	$200	$150

Last MSR was $599.

ELECTRIC: G-90 SERIES

G-90 - offset double cutaway poplar body, bolt-on rock maple neck, 24-fret bound rosewood fingerboard with pearl dot inlay, Floyd Rose double locking tremolo, reverse headstock, 6-on-a-side tuners, black hardware, 2 HRS single coil/1 Alnico tapped humbucker pickups, volume/tone control, 5-position pickup selector, coil tap switch, available in Black, Blue, Eerie Dess Black, Eerie Dess Blue, Eerie Dess Multi, Eerie Dess Red, Pearl White, Raspberry Pearl, or Sunfire Red finishes, disc. 1994.

	N/A	$350	$300	$275	$250	$200	$150

Last MSR was $600.

**Peavey Generation
EXP ACMQT
courtesy Peavey**

ELECTRIC: GENERATION SERIES

GENERATION S-1 - single cutaway mahogany body, flame maple top, bolt-on laminated maple neck, 22-fret rosewood fingerboard with pearl dot inlay, fixed brass bridge, graphlon nut, 6-on-a-side tuners, gold hardware, active single coil/humbucker pickup, volume/tone control, 3-position pickup selector, coil tap switch, available in Trans. Amber, Trans. Black, Trans. Blue, or Trans. Red finishes, mfg. 1988-1994.

	N/A	$450	$400	$350	$300	$250	$200

Last MSR was $800.

GENERATION S-2 - similar to Generation S-1, except has Kahler double locking tremolo system, mfg. 1990-94.

	N/A	$450	$400	$350	$300	$250	$200

Last MSR was $800.

GENERATION S-3 - similar to Generation S-1, except has hollow sound chambers, maple fingerboard with black dot inlay, 3 stacked coil pickups, coil tap in tone control, available in Trans. Black, Trans. Blue, Trans. Honey Sunburst, or Trans. Red finishes, mfg. 1991-94.

	N/A	$275	$250	$225	$200	$175	$150

Last MSR was $500.

GENERATION CUSTOM - similar to Generation S-1, except has solid poplar body, flame maple neck, ebony fingerboard, black hardware, black chrome Kahler double locking tremolo, active electronics, Peavey single coil/humbucker pickups, volume/tone controls, 3-way pickup selector, coil tap switch, mfg. 1989-1994.

	N/A	$450	$400	$350	$300	$250	$200

Last MSR was $799.

GENERATION STANDARD - similar to Generation S-1, except has solid poplar body, flame maple bi-laminated neck, 22-fret flame maple fingerboard, chrome hardware, 6-on-a-side headstock, 2 single coil pickups, master volume/master tone controls, and 3-way pickup selector, mfg. 1989-1994.

	N/A	$250	$210	$180	$150	$130	$100

Last MSR was $429.

GENERATION EXP - single cutaway basswood body, 21-fret rosewood fingerboard with dot inlays, white pickguard, HSS pickup configuration, two knobs and switch on metal plate, chrome hardware, available in Candy Apple Red, Trans. Blue, Gold, Sunburst, or Black finishes, mfg. 2003-present.

MSR	$250		$195	$165	$140	$120	$100	$80	$60

Add $175 for the ACM Peavey circuit, with 3 knobs and stereo output.

GENERATION EXP ACM QT - single cutaway basswood body with quilted maple top, 22-fret rosewood fingerboard with dot inlays, white pickguard, HSH pickup configuration, 3 knobs and switch, Peavey ACM circuit, chrome hardware, available in Brown Sugar, Sunburst, Wine Red, Purple, or Orange finishes, mfg. 2003-present.

MSR	$700		$525	$450	$400	$350	$300	$250	$200

GENERATION CUSTOM USA ACM - single cutaway alder body with laminated pearliod top, 22-fret maple fingerboard with dot inlays, 3 Vintage P-90 pickups, 3 knobs, 5-way switch, Peavey ACM circuit, steel plate bridge, chrome hardware, available in Red, White, Blue, or Custom Color finishes, mfg. 2004 only.

	$1,250	$1,050	$900	$750	$650	$550	$450

Last MSR was $1,600.

ELECTRIC: HP SERIES

The HP Signature Series is named after Hartley Peavey, the founder of Peavey.

HP SIGNATURE EX - offset double cutaway agathis body with flame maple veneer top, set maple neck, 22-fret rosewood fingerboard with block inlays, 2 humbucker pickups, Tune-o-matic bridge and tailpiece, 3-per-side tuners, 3 knobs, 3-way switch, gold-plated hardware, available in Metallic Gold, Sunburst, or Black finishes, 24.75 in. scale, mfg. 2004-present.

MSR	$400		$300	$250	$210	$180	$150	$120	$90

**Peavey HP Signature EX
courtesy Peavey**

GRADING	100% MINT	98% NEAR MINT	95% EXC+	90% EXC	80% VG+	70% VG	60% G

HP SIGNATURE EXP - offset double cutaway three-piece mahogany body with quilted maple veneer top, full body binding, set mahogany neck, 24-fret rosewood fingerboard, 2 humbucker pickups, Tune-o-matic bridge and tailpiece, 3-per-side tuners, 3 knobs, 3-way switch, gold-plated hardware, available in Metallic Gold, Sunburst, or Black finishes, 24.75 in. scale, mfg. 2004-present.

MSR	$700	$525	$450	$400	$350	$300	$250	$200

HP SIGNATURE USA CUSTOM - offset double cutaway one-piece mahogany body with AAAAA quilted maple veneer top, set mahogany neck, 24-fret ebony fingerboard, 2 humbucker pickups, Tune-o-matic bridge and tailpiece, 3-per-side tuners, 3 knobs, 3-way switch, gold-plated hardware, available in Tiger Eye, Vintage Burst, or Custom Color finishes, 24.75 in. scale, mfg. 2004-present.

MSR	$2,400	$1,800	$1,550	$1,350	$1,150	$950	$800	$700

ELECTRIC: HORIZON SERIES

HORIZON - offset double cutaway hardwood body, bi-laminated hard rock maple neck, 23-fret rosewood neck, 24.75 in. scale, chrome hardware, 6-on-a-side tuners, 2 dual blade humbucker pickups, stop tailpiece, master volume control, two tone controls (one per pickup), 3-way pickup selector, available in Natural, White, Black, or Sunburst finishes, mfg. 1983-86.

N/A	$250	$210	$180	$150	$130	$100

Last MSR was $379.

The tone control for the humbucking pickups allows the capability of single or dual coil mode. Turning counterclockwise to 7 brings the second coil into operation. Tone circuitry is standard in function between 7 and 0.

HORIZON II - similar to the Horizon, except features an extra in. single blade single coil pickup in the middle position (extra 3-way switch controls the middle pickup only: off/phase with the other pickups/out-of-phase with the other pickups), mfg. 1983-86.

N/A	$300	$250	$225	$200	$175	$125

Last MSR $349-$499.

This model had the option of a Peavey Octave Plus tremolo system.

Horizon II Custom - similar to the Horizon II, except features a black phenolic fingerboard and pearl or metallic finishes, mfg. 1984-85.

N/A	$325	$275	$250	$225	$175	$135

Last MSR $475-$525.

ELECTRIC: HYDRA SERIES

HYDRA DOUBLENECK - offset double cutaway hardwood body, bi-laminated hard rock maple necks in a 12/6 configuration, 24-fret maple fingerboards, both necks in 24.75 in. scale, 2 dual blade humbuckers per neck, master volume knob, two tone knobs (one per pickup), 3-way pickup selector (6 string), 3-way pickup selector (12-string), 3-way neck selector switch, mfg. 1984-86.

N/A	$550	$475	$425	$375	$325	$275

Last MSR was $1,099.

The tone control for the humbucking pickups allows the capability of single or dual coil output. Fully opening the pot to 10 achieves single coil mode. Turning counterclockwise to 7 brings the second coil into operation. Tone circuitry is standard in function between 7 and 0.

JEFF COOK HYDRA DOUBLENECK - similar to Hydra, except has Kahler double locking tremolo system on six-string neck, as well as Jeff Cook on headstock, mfg. 1985-86.

N/A	$750	$650	$575	$500	$425	$350

Last MSR was $1,299.50.

This model had design input from Jeff Cook (Alabama).

ELECTRIC: IMPACT SERIES

The Impact Series, introduced in 1985, featured superstrat styling and a sleek body profile. The later Impact series (Firenza, Milano, and Torino) further explored the Impact body design with other pickup configurations such as dual humbuckers. The Impact Firenza series later evolved into its own Firenza series (see Firenza Series).

IMPACT 1 - offset double cutaway Poplar body, hard rock neck, 22-fret Polyglide polymer fingerboard with pearl dot inlay, Kahler locking tremolo system, 6-on-a-side tuners, Black chrome or gold-on-brass hardware, 2 P-6 single coils/1 P-12 humbucker pickups, master volume control, master tone control, three pickup selector mini-switches, available in Pearl Black or Pearl White finishes, mfg. 1985-87.

N/A	$425	$375	$325	$275	$240	$200

Last MSR was $749.50.

Impact 1 Unity - similar to Impact 1, except has an ebony fingerboard, neck-through design, black chrome hardware, 2 single coil/Alnico humbucker pickups, available in Pearl Black or Pearl White finishes, mfg. 1987-89.

N/A	$450	$400	$350	$325	$275	$225

Last MSR was $799.

IMPACT 2 - similar to Impact 1, except has a rosewood fingerboard (instead of synthetic fingerboard), available in Pearl Black or Pearl White finishes, mfg. 1985-87.

N/A	$300	$250	$225	$190	$150	$125

Last MSR was $519.

IMPACT MILANO - offset double cutaway maple body, figured maple top, 25 in. scale, bolt-on rock maple neck, 24-fret rosewood fingerboard with pearl dot inlay, Power Bend III standard vibrato, 6-on-a-side locking tuners, chrome hardware, 2 Alnico exposed humbucker pickups, volume/tone control, 5-position switch, available in Antique Amber, Metallic Green, Trans. Blue or Trans. Red finishes, mfg. 1994-95.

N/A	$400	$350	$300	$250	$200	$150

Last MSR was $799.

P

GRADING	100% MINT	98% NEAR MINT	95% EXC+	90% EXC	80% VG+	70% VG	60% G

IMPACT TORINO I - offset double cutaway mahogany body, figured maple top, 25 in. scale, set-in mahogany neck, 24-fret rosewood fingerboard with pearl/abalone 3-D block inlay, tune-o-matic bridge/stop tailpiece, 6-on-a-side tuners, chrome hardware, 2 Alnico exposed humbucker pickups, volume/tone control, 5-position switch, available in Cherry Sunburst, Honey Sunburst, Metallic Gold, or Trans. Red finishes, mfg. 1994-95.

	N/A	$500	$450	$400	$350	$300	$250

Last MSR was $999.

IMPACT TORINO II - similar to Impact Torino I, except had a Power Bend III standard vibrato and locking tuners, mfg. 1994-95.

	N/A	$500	$450	$400	$350	$300	$250

Last MSR was $999.

ELECTRIC: JACK DANIEL'S SERIES

JACK DANIEL'S EX - single cutaway mahogany body, arched and contoured top, mahogany set-neck, 22-fret rosewood fingerboard with block inlay, Jack Daniel's on headstock with three-per-side tuners, standard stop tailpiece, two high output Peavey humbucker pickups, three knobs with Old No. 7, three-way switch, chrome hardware, available in Black finish with Jack Daniel's graphic, new 2005.

MSR	$500		$375	$325	$275	$240	$210	$180	$150

JACK DANIEL'S EXP - single cutaway mahogany body, AAAAA quilted maple top, contoured back, mahogany set-neck, 22-fret ebony fingerboard with 11-13 Old No. inlay, Jack Daniel's on headstock with three-per-side tuners, standard stop tailpiece, STB, two high output Peavey humbucker pickups, three knobs with Old No. 7, three-way switch, chrome hardware, available in Trans. Whiskey or Trans. Charcoal finishes, 24.75 in. scale, new 2005.

MSR	$900		$600	$525	$450	$400	$350	$300	$250

JACK DANIEL'S USA - single cutaway mahogany body, AAAAA arched quilted maple top, contoured back, mahogany set-neck, 22-fret ebony fingerboard with 11-13th fret Old No. 7 inlay, custom control, switch, and truss-rod covers made of aged Jack Daniel's wooden whiskey barrels, Jack Daniel's on headstock with three-per-side tuners, Dual-Compression tailpiece, STB, two high output Peavey humbucker pickups, three knobs with Old No. 7, three-way switch, chrome hardware, available in Trans. Whiskey, Trans. Charcoal, or custom color finishes, 24.75 in. scale, new 2005.

MSR	$2,600		$1,950	$1,700	$1,500	$1,300	$1,100	$950	$800

ELECTRIC: JAZZ FUSION SERIES

JF-1 EXP - double cutaway hollow body archtop, maple plywood body with quilt veneer, two f-holes, cream body and neck binding, set mahogany neck, 22-fret rosewood fingerboard with block inlays, three-per-side tuners, black pickguard, Tune-O-Matic bridge and stop tailpiece, two humbuckers, four knobs, three-way switch, gold hardware, available in Black, Sunburst, or Trans. Red finishes, new 2005.

MSR	$400		$300	$250	$210	$180	$150	$120	$90

Peavey Limited EXP courtesy Peavey

ELECTRIC: LIMITED SERIES

LIMITED EXP - double offset cutaway alder body, quilted maple top, bolt-on neck, 22-fret rosewood fingerboard, two humbucking pickups (HH) or 2 single coils and a humbucker (SSH), two knobs, switch, 6-on-one-side tuners, Hipshot Ultra Glide tremolo bridge, chrome hardware, available in Midnight Blue, Green, Red, or Sunburst finishes, mfg. 2001-04.

	$450	$375	$325	$275	$225	$185	$145

Last MSR was $520.

LIMITED VT/HB/ST - double offset cutaway ash body, flamed maple top, bolt-on neck, 22-fret rosewood fingerboard, two humbucking pickups (HB), 2 single coils and a humbucker (ST), or 3 single coils (VT), two knobs, switch, 6-on-one-side tuners, Hipshot Ultra Glide tremolo bridge, chrome hardware, available in Black, Violet, Midnight Blue, Margarita, or Tiger Eye finishes, mfg. 2001-04.

	$825	$750	$700	$650	$575	$500	$425

Last MSR was $1,100.

Add $150 for custom colors.

Limited VT/HB/ST Quilted Top - similar to the Limited, except has a quilted maple top, available in Black, Violet, Midnight Blue, Margarita, or Tiger Eye finishes, mfg. 2001-04.

	$975	$900	$825	$750	$650	$550	$450

Last MSR was $1,300.

Add $150 for custom colors.

ELECTRIC: MANTIS SERIES

MANTIS - single cutaway Flying V (pointy V?) hardwood body, bi-laminated hard rock maple neck, 23-fret rosewood neck, 24.75 in. scale, chrome hardware, 6-on-a-side tuners, 1 dual blade humbucker pickup, fixed bridge, master volume and master tone control, mfg. 1984-86.

	N/A	$325	$275	$225	$190	$150	$100

Last MSR was $269.50.

This model had the Octave Plus tremolo system as an option.

Peavey Jazz Fusion JF-1 courtesy Peavey

GRADING	100% MINT	98% NEAR MINT	95% EXC+	90% EXC	80% VG+	70% VG	60% G

MANTIS LT - similar to the Mantis, except features a Kahler Flyer locking tremolo, black pickguard, mfg. 1985-86.

| | N/A | $375 | $325 | $275 | $225 | $200 | $150 |

ELECTRIC: MILESTONE SERIES

MILESTONE - offset double cutaway hardwood body, bi-laminated hard rock maple neck, 24-fret rosewood neck, 24.75 in. scale, chrome hardware, 6-on-a-side tuners, 2 dual blade humbucking pickups, fixed bridge, master volume control, two tone controls (one per pickup), 3-way pickup selector, pickup phase switch (either in or out-of-phase), mfg. 1983-86.

| | N/A | $250 | $225 | $200 | $175 | $150 | $125 |

Last MSR was $449.

This model had the Octave Plus tremolo system as an option. The tone control for the humbucking pickups allows the capability of single or dual coil output. Fully opening the pot to 10 achieves single coil mode. Turning counterclockwise to 7 brings the second coil into operation. Tone circuitry is standard in function between 7 and 0.

MILESTONE CUSTOM - similar to the Milestone, except features a phenolic fingerboard, available in Pearl or Metallic finishes, mfg. 1985-86.

| | N/A | $300 | $250 | $225 | $200 | $175 | $150 |

Last MSR was $499.

MILESTONE 12 - similar to the Milestone, except in 12-string configuration, mfg. 1985-86.

| | N/A | $350 | $300 | $250 | $225 | $200 | $150 |

Last MSR was $519.50.

ELECTRIC: MYSTIC SERIES

MYSTIC - offset double cutaway-dual rounded wings hardwood body, bi-laminated hard rock maple neck, 23-fret rosewood neck, 24.75 in. scale, chrome hardware, 6-on-a-side tuners, 2 dual blade humbucker pickups, fixed bridge, master volume control, two tone controls (one per pickup), 3-way switch, available in Blood Red, White, Frost Blue, Inca Gold, Silver, Sunfire Red, or Black finishes, mfg. 1983-86.

| | N/A | $300 | $250 | $225 | $200 | $175 | $150 |

Last MSR was $399.

This model had the Octave Plus tremolo system as an option. The tone control for the humbucking pickups allows the capability of single or dual coil output. Fully opening the pot to 10 achieves single coil mode. Turning counterclockwise to 7 brings the second coil into operation. Tone circuitry is standard in function between 7 and 0.

ELECTRIC: NITRO SERIES

The Nitro Series debuted in 1986, and featured a number of models designed towards Hard Rock players.

NITRO I - dual offset cutaway hardwood body, bi-laminated maple neck, 22-fret rosewood fingerboard, 25.5 in. scale, 6-on-a-side pointy headstock, black hardware, Peavey Precision tuners, Kahler locking tremolo system, exposed pole piece humbucker, master volume knob, mfg. 1986-89.

| | N/A | $300 | $275 | $225 | $175 | $150 | $125 |

Last MSR was $399.50.

Nitro I Active - similar to the Nitro I, except features active circuitry and an extra tone control knob, system requires a 9-volt battery, mfg. 1988-1990.

| | N/A | $375 | $325 | $275 | $250 | $225 | $175 |

Last MSR was $549.

Nitro I Custom - similar to the Nitro I, except features recessed Floyd Rose/Kahler locking tremolo, mfg. 1987-89.

| | N/A | $350 | $300 | $275 | $200 | $150 | $125 |

Last MSR was $499.50.

NITRO II - dual offset cutaway hardwood body, bi-laminated maple neck, 22-fret rosewood fingerboard, 25.5 in. scale, 6-on-a-side headstock, black hardware, Peavey Precision tuners, Kahler locking tremolo system, two exposed pole piece humbuckers, master volume knob, master tone knob, 3-way pickup selector switch, mfg. 1987-89.

| | N/A | $325 | $275 | $225 | $200 | $150 | $125 |

Last MSR was $449.50.

NITRO III - dual offset cutaway hardwood body, bi-laminated maple neck, 22-fret rosewood fingerboard, 25.5 in. scale, 6-on-a-side headstock, black hardware, Peavey Precision tuners, Kahler locking tremolo system, 2 exposed pole piece single coil pickups, 1 exposed pole piece humbuckers, master volume knob, master tone knob, 3 individual pickup selector mini switches, mfg. 1987-89.

| | N/A | $350 | $300 | $275 | $200 | $150 | $125 |

Last MSR was $499.50.

Nitro III Custom - similar to the Nitro III, except features Alnico pickups and recessed Floyd Rose/Kahler locking tremolo system, mfg. 1987-89.

| | N/A | $400 | $350 | $300 | $250 | $200 | $150 |

Last MSR was $599.50.

NITRO LIMITED - similar to the Nitro III, except features 22-fret ebony fingerboard, gold hardware, neck-through body design, Alnico pickups and recessed Floyd Rose/Kahler locking tremolo system, mfg. 1987-89.

| | N/A | $575 | $525 | $475 | $400 | $325 | $250 |

Last MSR was $1,000.

NITRO C-2 - dual offset cutaway hardwood body, bi-laminated maple neck, 22-fret rosewood fingerboard, 25.5 in. scale, 6-on-a-side headstock, black hardware, Peavey Precision tuners, Floyd Rose locking tremolo system, 1 HRS single coil pickup (middle position), 2 Alnico humbuckers, master volume knob, master tone knob, 3 individual pickup selector mini switches, mfg. 1990-92.

| | N/A | $400 | $350 | $300 | $250 | $200 | $150 |

Last MSR was $599.

P

GRADING	100% MINT	98% NEAR MINT	95% EXC+	90% EXC	80% VG+	70% VG	60% G

NITRO C-3 - similar to the Nitro C-2, except features 2 Alnico single coil/Alnico humbucker pickups, mfg. 1990-92.

	N/A	$425	$350	$300	$250	$200	$150

Last MSR was $599.

ELECTRIC: ODYSSEY SERIES

ODYSSEY - single cutaway mahogany body, carved flame maple top, set mahogany neck, 24-fret bound ebony fingerboard with white arrow inlay, 24.75 in. scale, tune-o-matic bridge/stop tailpiece, graphlon nut, bound peghead, 3-per-side tuners, gold hardware, 2 humbucker Alnico pickups, 2 volume/2 tone controls, 3-position and coil split switches, straplocks, available in '59 Vintage Sunburst, Tobacco Sunburst, Trans. Black, Trans. Blue, or Trans. Red finishes, mfg. 1990-94.

	N/A	$650	$575	$475	$400	$325	$250

Last MSR was $1,000.

ODYSSEY 25TH ANNIVERSARY - similar to Odyssey, except has bound quilted maple top, 2 color pearl 3D block fingerboard inlay, black hardware, black pearl tuning machines, straplocks, available in Trans. Black finish, disc.

	$900	$750	$650	$575	$500	$425	$350

Last MSR was $1,300.

ELECTRIC: PATRIOT SERIES

PATRIOT - double cutaway hardwood body, bi-laminated hard rock maple neck, 23-fret fingerboard, 23.75 in. scale, chrome hardware, 6-on-a-side headstock, graphlon top nut, black laminated pickguard, 2 single coil blade pickups, volume/tone controls, 3-way pickup selector switch, mfg. 1983-86.

	N/A	$200	$175	$150	$125	$100	$75

Last MSR ranged $229-$299.

PATRIOT PLUS - similar to the Patriot model, except features dual blade humbucker in the bridge position instead of a single coil, and a 24.75 in. scale, mfg. 1983-86.

	N/A	$225	$195	$175	$150	$110	$75

Last MSR was $249.

The tone control for the humbucking pickups allows the capability of single or dual coil output. Fully opening the pot to 10 achieves single coil mode. Turning counterclockwise to 7 brings the second coil into operation. Tone circuitry is standard in function between 7 and 0.

PATRIOT WITH TREMOLO - similar to the Patriot model, except features a 24.75 in. scale, a Power Bend standard tremolo, 1 humbucker in the bridge position, and a volume control, mfg. 1986-1990.

	N/A	$225	$195	$175	$150	$110	$75

Last MSR was $259.50.

ELECTRIC: PREDATOR SERIES

The Predator models were introduced in the mid-1980s, and the first model featured a dual humbucker, locking tremolo design. After several years, the design was modified to three single coils pickups instead, and later to the popular single/single/humbucker variant.

PREDATOR (1985-88 MFG.) - double cutaway hardwood body, bi-laminated hard rock maple neck, 23-fret fingerboard, 24.75 in. scale, chrome hardware, 6-on-a-side headstock, black laminated pickguard, Kahler Flyer locking tremolo system, 2 exposed pole piece humbucker pickups, volume control, tone controls, 3-way pickup selector switch, mfg. 1985-88.

	N/A	$275	$225	$200	$175	$150	$125

Last MSR was $399.50.

PREDATOR (1990-2000 MFG.) - offset double cutaway poplar body, white pickguard, bolt-on maple neck, 22-fret maple fingerboard with black dot inlay, 25.5 in. scale, Power Bend standard vibrato, 6-on-a-side tuners, chrome hardware, 3 single coil pickups, volume/2 tone controls, 5-position switch, available in Gloss Black, Metallic Red, or Metallic Dark Blue finishes, mfg. 1990-2000.

	$240	$200	$175	$150	$125	$100	$75

Last MSR was $299.

In 1996, when the Predator AX was disc., the Predator model was upgraded with the rosewood fingerboard, 2 single coil/1 humbucker pickups, and Power Bend III tremolo system. Early versions of the Predator model were offered in Black, Red, and White finishes. In 1999, Gloss Red finish was added and Metallic Red and Metallic Dark Blue were disc.

Predator Sunburst - similar to the Predator, available in a Sunburst finish, disc. 1999.

	$240	$200	$175	$150	$125	$100	$75

Last MSR was $299.

Predator AX - similar to Predator, except has rosewood fingerboard with pearl dot inlay, 2 single coil/1 humbucker pickups, volume/tone control, 3-position mini switch, available in Black, Powder Blue, Red, or White finishes, mfg. 1994-95.

	N/A	$200	$160	$130	$110	$90	$70

Last MSR was $349.

P

GRADING	100% MINT	98% NEAR MINT	95% EXC+	90% EXC	80% VG+	70% VG	60% G

Predator DX - similar to Predator AX, except has maple fingerboard, mfg. 1994-95.

	N/A	$200	$160	$130	$110	$90	$70

Last MSR was $349.

PREDATOR PLUS - similar to Predator, except has solid poplar body, 3-on-a-side headstock with straight string pull and ergonomic tuner placement, master tone and volume control, chrome hardware, available in Black, Sunburst, Metallic Dark Blue, or Metallic Titanium finishes, mfg. 1999-2002.

	$300	$250	$200	$150	$100	$75	$50

Last MSR was $390.

Predator Plus Transparent - similar to the Predator, except available in Trans. Red, or Trans. Green finishes, mfg. 1999-2002.

	$325	$275	$225	$175	$125	$100	$75

Last MSR was $400.

Predator Plus Maple Fingerboard - similar to the Predator, except has a maple fingerboard, available in Black, Metallic Dark Blue, Metallic Titanium, or Sunburst finishes, mfg. 1999-2002.

	$325	$275	$225	$175	$125	$95	$65

Last MSR was $400.

Add $10 for Transparent Colors.

Predator Plus Left-Hand - similar to the Predator Plus, except in left-handed configuration, mfg. 1999-2002.

	$325	$275	$225	$185	$135	$100	$75

Last MSR was $420.

Add $10 for Transparent Colors.

Predator Plus HB - similar to Predator Plus except, has 2 high ourput humbucker pickups with black pickup rings, 3-way pickup selector, Master Volume, Master Tone, available in Gloss Black, Cobalt Blue, Metallic Gold, Metallic Garnet Red, or Metallic Titanium finishes, disc 2002.

	$209	$150	$130	$110	$90	$70	$50

Last MSR was $300.

PREDATOR PLUS ST7 - similar to the Predator Plus, except in 7-string configuration, available in Black, Cashmere, Charcoal Metallic Violet, and Metallic Titanium, mfg. 2001-2002.

	$350	$300	$250	$200	$160	$130	$100

Last MSR was $460.

Add $30 for Floyd Rose Tremolo (Model Predator Plus TR7).

PREDATOR PLUS EXP - offset double cutaway body, 22-fret rosewood fingerboard with dot inlay, 2 humbucker pickups, Floyd Rose licensed tremolo, black hardware, available in Candy Apple Red, Metallic Topaz Blue, or Black finishes, mfg. 2003-present.

MSR	$290	$225	$190	$165	$145	$125	$105	$85

Add $20 for left-handed configuration, new 2004.

ELECTRIC: RAPTOR SERIES

RAPTOR I - offset double cutaway body, white pickguard, bolt-on maple neck, 21-fret rosewood fingerboard with white dot inlay, 25.5 in. scale, Power Bend standard vibrato, 6-on-a-side tuners, chrome hardware, 3 single coil pickups, volume/2 tone controls, 5-position switch, available in Gloss Black, Gloss Red, or Gloss White finishes, disc. 2000.

	$175	$150	$125	$115	$100	$85	$65

Last MSR was $219.

Raptor I Sunburst - similar to the Raptor I. Available in Sunburst finish, disc. 2000.

	$190	$175	$150	$125	$100	$85	$75

Last MSR was $229.

RAPTOR PLUS EXP - similar to Raptor I, except has multi-lam body, 3-on-a-side headstock with straight string pull and ergonomic tuner placement, master tone control, hum-canceling in positions 2 and 4, master volume control, available in Sunburst or White finishes, mfg. 1999-present.

MSR	$200	$160	$140	$125	$115	$100	$85	$65

Add $10 for Metallic Garnet red finish (Raptor Plus Metallic). Add $20 for left-hand model (Raptor Plus LH).

Raptor Plus TK - similar to Raptor Plus except, has covered single coil pickup in the neck position and high output single coil pickup in the bridge position, available in Glass Black, Cobalt Blue, Metallic Gold, Metallic Garnet Red, or Metallic Titanium finishes, disc 2002.

	$215	$195	$175	$150	$130	$110	$95

Last MSR was $310.

ELECTRIC: RAZER & REACTOR SERIES

RAZER - offset double cutaway-angular hardwood body, bi-laminated hard rock maple neck, 23-fret maple neck with black dot inlays, 24.75 in. scale, chrome hardware, 6-on-a-side tuners, 2 dual blade humbucking pickups, fixed bridge, master volume control, two tone controls (one per pickup), 3-way pickup selector, available in Blood Red, White, Frost Blue, Silver, Inca Gold, Sunfire Red, or Black finishes, mfg. 1983-86.

	N/A	$325	$275	$225	$175	$150	$100

Last MSR was $399.50.

This model had the Octave Plus tremolo system as an option. The tone control for the humbucking pickups allows the capability of single or dual coil output. Fully opening the pot to 10 achieves single coil mode. Turning counterclockwise to 7 brings the second coil into operation. Tone circuitry is standard in function between 7 and 0.

GRADING	100% MINT	98% NEAR MINT	95% EXC+	90% EXC	80% VG+	70% VG	60% G

REACTOR - single cutaway poplar body, white pickguard, metal controls mounted plate, bolt-on maple neck, 22-fret maple fingerboard with black dot inlay, 25.5 in. scale, strings-through fixed bridge, 6-on-a-side tuners, chrome hardware, 2 single coil pickups, volume/tone control, 3-position switch, available in Gloss Black, Gloss Red, or Gloss White finishes, disc. 1999.

	$325	$275	$250	$225	$200	$150	$125

Last MSR was $409.

Reactor AX - similar to Reactor, except has alder or swamp ash body, and 2 Db2-T dual blade humbucker pickups, available in Gloss Black, Powder Blue, Sea Green (Alder body: pearloid pickguard), Blonde or Sunburst (swamp ash: tortoiseshell pickguard), disc. 1999.

	$450	$375	$325	$275	$225	$175	$150

Last MSR was $559.

ELECTRIC: ROTOR SERIES

ROTOR EX - Explorer style body with notched body sides, mahogany body, 24-fret rosewood fingerboard with block inlay, white body binding, 2 humbucker pickups, Floyd Rose licensed tremolo, 3 knobs, 3-way switch, black hardware, available in Candy Apple Red or Black finishes, 24.75 in. scale, mfg. 2004-present.

MSR	$400	$300	$250	$210	$180	$150	$120	$90

ROTOR EXP - Explorer style body with notched body sides, mahogany neck-thru body, 24-fret rosewood fingerboard with block inlay, shell and white B/N/H binding, 2 humbucker pickups, Tune-o-matic bridge, 3 knobs, 3-way switch, black hardware, available in Cherry, Pearl White, or Black finishes, 24.75 in. scale, mfg. 2004-present.

MSR	$1,000	$750	$650	$575	$500	$425	$375	$325

ROTOR MARK SILVESTRI/PROXIMITY EFFECT - Rotor body style, abalone fingerboard and headstock binding, features Proximity Effect graphics, mfg. 2004-present.

MSR	$700	$525	$450	$400	$350	$300	$250	$200

ELECTRIC: T SERIES

The T series guitars and basses were originally designed by Chip Todd in 1977, and debuted at the 1978 NAMM show. The three prototypes shown were T-60 and T-30 guitars, and a T-40 bass. Chip Todd was primarily an engineer who repaired guitars on the side. Todd was hired out of his Houston guitar repair shop, and initially handled the drafting and design by himself. Hartley Peavey had a great deal of input on the initial designs, and the tone circuit was invented by noted steel guitarist Orville Red Rhodes. Todd was eventually assisted by Gerald Pew, Bobby Low, and Charley Gressett. According to researcher Michael Wright, Chip Todd left Peavey in 1981 and currently works in the TV satellite electronics – although he does have a new patent on guitar design that he is considering applying for. Peavey´s initial concept was to use machinery to control efficiency and quality control. Borrowing an idea from gun manufacturing, Peavey bought a controlled carving machine to maintain strict tolerances in design. In a seeming parallel to the Fender debut of **plank guitars** and other derisive comments in 1951 leading to the other manufacturers then building solid body electrics in 1952, the guitar industry first insisted that *you can´t build guitars on a computer*! A year later, everybody was investigating numerical controllers (and later the CAD/CAM devices - now CNC machines). If Leo Fender is the father of the mass produced solid body guitar (among other honors), then Hartley Peavey is the father of the modern solid body production technique, (source material courtesy Michael Wright, *Guitar Stories*, Volume One).

T-15 - double offset cutaway body, bolt-on bi-laminated rock maple neck, 20-fret fingerboard, 23.5 in. scale, chrome hardware, 6-on-a-side tuners, cream and black laminated pickguard, two oversized in.blade in. style single coil pickups, master volume knob, master tone knob, 3-way pickup selector switch, available in Natural finish, mfg. 1981-83.

	N/A	$250	$225	$200	$160	$130	$95

Last MSR was $199.50.

The T-15 was offered with the optional Electric Case. The molded plastic case´s center area contained a 10 watt amp and 5 in. speaker, and had a pre- and post-gain controls, and an EQ control. The Electric Case can be viewed as Peavey´s solid state version of Danelectro´s tube Amp-in-Case concept. The T-15 Guitar with Electric Case retailed as a package for $259.50.

T-25 - double offset cutaway body, bolt-on bi-laminated rock maple neck, 23-fret fingerboard, 24.75 in. scale, chrome hardware, 6-on-a-side tuners, two double blade style humbucking pickups, master volume control, two tone controls (first for the neck pickup and the other for the bridge pickup), 3-way pickup selector switch, available in Natural, Sunburst, Sunfire Red, or Frost Blue finishes, mfg. 1982-83.

	N/A	$225	$195	$175	$150	$115	$75

Last MSR $299.50-$374.50.

The tone control for the humbucking pickup allows the capability of single or dual coil output. Fully opening the pot to 10 achieves single coil mode. Turning counterclockwise to 7 brings the second coil into operation. Bridge pickup is full humbucking at the 0 setting.

T-25 Special - similar to the T-25, except features a black phenolic fingerboard and black laminated pickguard, available in Gloss Black finish, mfg. 1982-83.

	N/A	$250	$200	$175	$150	$135	$95

Last MSR was $399.50.

Peavey Raptor Plus EXP
courtesy Peavey

Peavey Rotor EXP
courtesy Peavey

GRADING	100% MINT	98% NEAR MINT	95% EXC+	90% EXC	80% VG+	70% VG	60% G

T-26 - double offset cutaway body, bolt-on bi-laminated rock maple neck, 23-fret fingerboard, 24.75 in. scale, chrome hardware, 6-on-a-side tuners, three blade style single coil pickups, master volume control, two tone controls (first for the neck pickup and the other for the bridge pickup), five way pickup selector switch, available in Natural, Sunburst, Sunfire Red, or Frost Blue finishes, mfg. 1982-83.

	N/A	$250	$225	$195	$175	$150	$125

Last MSR ranged $324-$419.

Both the neck and the bridge single coil pickup have their own tone control. The center pickup does not have a tone control, but functions through either of the two tone controls when employed in the humbucker modes.

T-27 - double offset cutaway body, bolt-on bi-laminated rock maple neck, 23-fret fingerboard, 24.75 in. scale, chrome hardware, 6-on-a-side tuners, two in.blade in.style single coil pickups and one double blade style humbucker, master volume control, two tone controls (first for neck and middle pickups and the other for the bridge pickup), five way pickup selector switch, available in Natural, Sunburst, Sunfire Red, or Frost Blue finishes, mfg. 1982-83.

	N/A	$275	$225	$195	$175	$150	$125

Last MSR ranged $344-$419.

The tone control for the humbucker pickup allows the capability of single or dual coil output. Fully opening the pot to 10 achieves single coil mode. Turning counterclockwise to 7 brings the second coil into operation. Bridge pickup is full humbucking at the 0 setting.

T-27 Limited - similar to the T-27, except features upgraded electronics and a rosewood neck, mfg. 1982-83.

	N/A	$275	$225	$195	$175	$150	$125

Last MSR was $374.50.

T-30 - double offset cutaway body, bolt-on bi-laminated rock maple neck, 20-fret fingerboard, 23.5 in. scale, 6-on-a-side tuners, three blade style single coil pickups, master volume knob, master tone knob, five way pickup selector switch, available in Natural finish, mfg. 1981-83.

	N/A	$175	$150	$125	$100	$75	$50

Last MSR was $259.50.

The T-30 Guitar/Electric Case package retailed at $319.50.

T-60 - double offset cutaway body, bolt-on bi-laminated rock maple neck, 23-fret maple fingerboard, 25.5 in. scale, chrome hardware, 6-on-a-side tuners, two in.double blade in. style humbucking pickups, two volume controls, two tone controls (one per pickup), pickup phase switch, 3-way pickup selector switch, available in Natural, Black, White, or Sunburst finish, mfg. 1978-1988.

	N/A	$300	$250	$200	$175	$150	$100

Last MSR $399.50-$459.50.

Finishes other than Natural command a higher premium. Original case adds a small premium.

The T-60 was the first Peavey production guitar, and had a rosewood fingerboard as an option. In 1982, Blood Red and Burgundy finishes were available. The original Red Rhodes-designed pickups allows the capability of single or dual coil output. Fully opening the pot to 10 achieves single coil mode. Turning counterclockwise to 7 brings the second coil into operation, and achieving full range humbucker tone. Rotation of the control from 7 to 0 further contours the tone circuit. The Phase switch is a two position switch which reverses the coil relationship in the bridge pickup when the pickup switch is in the middle position: up is in phase, and down is out-of-phase.

T-1000 LT - double offset Western Poplar body, rock maple neck, 24-fret rosewood fingerboard, Recessed Floyd Rose licensed Double locking tremolo system, 2 single coil and 1 coil-tapped humbucker pickups, master volume control, master tone control, 5-way pickup selector switch, mfg. 1992-94.

	N/A	$400	$350	$325	$275	$250	$200

Last MSR was $699.

T-JR (JUNIOR) - similar to the T-60 guitar, except featured an octave neck and smaller body dimensions (like a mandolin), mfg. 1982-83.

	N/A	$175	$150	$125	$100	$85	$70

Last MSR was $199.95.

ELECTRIC: TRACER SERIES

The original Tracer model was introduced in 1988. Subsequent models were styled to compete with Charvel/Jackson, Ibanez, and Kramer instruments in the Hard Rock music genre.

TRACER I - offset double cutaway poplar body, bolt-on bi-laminated maple neck, 22-fret maple fingerboard with black dot inlay, 25.5 in. scale, Power Bend standard tremolo, graphlon nut, 6-on-a-side tuners, chrome hardware, 1 humbucker pickup, volume/tone control, available in Black, Red, or White finishes, mfg. 1988-1994.

	N/A	$250	$220	$190	$150	$125	$100

Last MSR was $299.

Tracer (Second Version): In 1991, after numerous Tracer models had been offered, the original Tracer was turbo charged from its basic model design with the addition of 2 single coil pickups, 24-fret maple fingerboard, a new 24.75 in. scale, and a five way pickup selector switch (The Second Version of the Tracer was similar to the Tracer Custom without the Kahler locking tremolo).

TRACER II - similar to the Tracer 1, except features single coil/humbucker pickups, 3-way pickup selector switch, available in Black, Metallic Blue, Metallic Red, or White finishes, mfg. 1989-1990.

	N/A	$300	$250	$225	$175	$130	$95

Last MSR was $359.

Tracer II '89 - similar to the Tracer II, with the 24.75 in. scale, yet shares all the same hardware and configuration of the previous Tracer II, mfg. 1989-1991.

	N/A	$300	$250	$225	$175	$130	$95

Last MSR was $359.

The only verifiable difference is the scale length. Whip out the measuring stick. Whip it out!

TRACER LT - similar to the Tracer II, except has rosewood fingerboard with white dot inlay, Floyd Rose double locking vibrato, black hardware, available in Black, Metallic Blue, Metallic Red, or White finishes, mfg. 1991-94.

	N/A	$300	$250	$225	$195	$160	$115

Last MSR was $424.

GRADING	100% MINT	98% NEAR MINT	95% EXC+	90% EXC	80% VG+	70% VG	60% G

TRACER CUSTOM - similar to the Tracer II with the 2 single coil/humbucker pickups, but maintains the original 25.5 in. scale. Other additions include a 5-way pickup selector switch, coil tap, black hardware, Kahler/Floyd Rose double locking tremolo, mfg. 1989-1990.

	N/A	$375	$325	$275	$225	$175	$125

Last MSR was $529.

Tracer Custom '89 - similar to the Tracer Custom, except has shorter 24.75 in. scale length, also similar to the revised Tracer II, except the Custom '89 has a locking Kahler tremolo and the Tracer doesn't, mfg. 1989-1991.

	N/A	$350	$300	$250	$200	$175	$125

Last MSR was $459.

TRACER DELUXE - similar to the Tracer II, except has a Kahler/Floyd Rose locking tremolo and black hardware; the Deluxe model maintains the original 25.5 in. scale and 22-fret fingerboard, mfg. 1988-1990.

	N/A	$300	$260	$230	$190	$150	$110

Last MSR was $429.

Tracer Deluxe '89 - similar to the Tracer Deluxe, except has shorter 24.75 in. scale, 24-fret maple fingerboard, mfg. 1989-1991.

	N/A	$325	$295	$240	$200	$160	$125

Last MSR was $459.

This model has a reverse headstock as an option.

ELECTRIC: V-TYPE SERIES

V-TYPE NTB - offset double cutaway body with notched body sides, neck-thru body, 24-fret rosewood fingerboard with 12th fret inlay, abalone binding and inlays, 2 ceramic humbucker pickups, reverse 6-on-a-side tuners, two knobs, 3-way switch, available in Trans. Purple, Pearl White, or Black finishes, new 2004.

MSR	$800	$600	$525	$450	$400	$350	$300	$250

Add $75 for Floyd Rose licensed tremolo.

ELECTRIC: VANDENBURG SERIES

The Vandenburg series of the late 1980s was designed in conjunction with guitarist Adrian Vandenburg.

VANDENBURG SIGNATURE - offset double cutaway poplar body with side slot cuts, bolt-on bi-laminated maple neck, 24-fret ebony fingerboard with pearl dot inlay, 24.75 in. scale, Kahler/Floyd Rose double locking vibrato, reverse headstock, 6-on-the-other-side tuners, black hardware, single coil/Alnico humbucker pickups, volume/tone control, 3-position switch, available in '62 Blue, Black, Pearl White, Raspberry Pearl, Rock-It Pink, or Sunfire Red finishes, mfg. 1988-1994.

	N/A	$600	$500	$425	$350	$300	$250

Last MSR was $850.

This model came new with a certificate signed by Adrian Vandenberg.

VANDENBURG CUSTOM - offset double cutaway mahogany body with side slot cuts, set maple neck, 24-fret rosewood fingerboard with white stripes and arrows inlay, 24.75 in. scale, Kahler/Floyd Rose double locking vibrato, reverse headstock, 6-on-the-other-side tuners, black hardware, 1 HCS single coil/1 Alnico humbucker pickups, 2 master volume controls, 3-position pickup selector knob, available in Trans. Honey Sunburst, Trans. Pink, or Trans. Violet finishes, mfg. 1989-1994.

	N/A	$800	$700	$600	$525	$450	$375

Last MSR was $1,299.

The neck pickup volume control has a push-pull coil-tap built in. The coil tap directly affects the bridge humbucker, and converts it from single coil to humbucker mode.

VANDENBURG QUILT TOP - offset double cutaway mahogany body with side slot cuts, carved Quilted Maple top, set mahogany neck, 24-fret bound rosewood fingerboard with white stripes and arrows inlay, Floyd Rose double locking vibrato, reverse headstock, 6-on-the-other-side tuners, gold hardware, 2 humbucker pickups, volume/tone control, 3-position pickup selector switch, coil tap mini switch, available in Trans. Honey Sunburst, Trans. Pink, or Trans. Violet finishes, mfg. 1990-94.

	N/A	$900	$800	$700	$600	$525	$450

Last MSR was $1,399.

VANDENBURG PUZZLE - similar to the Vandenberg Quilt Top, except features a one piece mahogany body with carved top, and Black finish with white puzzle graphics, mfg. 1989-1992.

	N/A	$900	$800	$700	$600	$525	$450

Last MSR was $1,599.

ELECTRIC: VORTEX SERIES

VORTEX 1 - single cutaway flared hardwood body, bi-laminated maple neck, 22-fret Polyglide polymer fingerboard, 25.5 in. scale, black hardware, 6-on-a-side tuners, Kahler locking tremolo system, two P-12 adjustable pole piece humbucking pickups, master volume knob, master tone knob, 3-way selector switch, available in Jet Black, Fluorescent Red, Fluorescent Pink, or Pearl White finishes, mfg. 1985-86.

	N/A	$400	$350	$300	$250	$210	$175

Last MSR was $699.50.

Peavey T-60
courtesy David Vareberg

Peavey V-Type NTB
courtesy Peavey

P

GRADING	100% MINT	98% NEAR MINT	95% EXC+	90% EXC	80% VG+	70% VG	60% G

VORTEX 2 - similar specifications as the Vortex 1, except features a tapered sharkfin/Flying V body design. All other pickup and hardware descriptions as previously described, available in Jet Black, Fluorescent Red, Fluorescent Pink, or Pearl White finishes, mfg. 1985-86.

	N/A	$425	$375	$325	$275	$225	$175

Last MSR was $699.50.

ELECTRIC BASS: AXCELERATOR SERIES

AXCELERATOR - offset double cutaway poplar body, pearloid pickguard, bolt-on maple neck, 21 rosewood fingerboard with pearl dot inlay, fixed bridge, 4-on-a-side tuners, chrome hardware, 2 VFL active covered humbucker pickups, volume/stacked tone/mix controls, available in Candy Apple Red, Cobalt Blue, Metallic Gold, Metallic Green, or Pearl Black finishes, system requires a 9-volt battery, mfg. 1994-98.

$475	$400	$350	$300	$250	$200	$150

Last MSR was $600.

Axcelerator Fretless - similar to Axcelerator, except has fretless pau ferro fingerboard, available in Candy Apple Red, Cobalt Blue, Metallic Gold, or Pearl Black finishes, mfg. 1994-95.

$500	$425	$350	$300	$250	$200	$150

Last MSR was $650.

AXCELERATOR 5 - similar to Axcelerator, except has 5 strings, 4/1-per-side tuners, 35 in. scale, Wilkinson WBB5 bridge, available in Candy Apple Red, Metallic Purple, Metallic Silver, or Pearl Black finishes, disc. 1999.

$575	$500	$425	$375	$325	$275	$225

Last MSR was $769.

The revised design Axcelerator is optional with a fretless neck.

AXCELERATOR 6 - similar to Axcelerator 5, except has 6 strings, 3-per-side tuners, 35 in. scale, 21-fret pau ferro fingerboard with white dot inlays, Wilkinson WBB6 bridge, 2 VFL-6 humbucker pickups, available in Candy Apple Red, Metallic Purple, Metallic Gold, or Pearl Black finishes, mfg. 1997-99.

	$850	$725	$625	$525	$450	$375	$275

Last MSR was $1,118.

AXCELERATOR PLUS - similar to Axcelerator, except has swamp ash body and pau ferro fingerboard, available in Blonde or Sunburst finish with a tortoiseshell pickguard, or Trans. Grape or Trans. Red finish with pearloid pickguard, disc. 1999.

	$600	$525	$450	$375	$325	$275	$200

Last MSR was $799.

AXCELERATOR 2-T - offset double cutaway poplar body, pearloid pickguard, bolt-on maple neck, 21 rosewood fingerboard with pearl dot inlay, 2-Tek bridge, 4-on-a-side tuners, chrome hardware, 2 VFL active covered humbucker pickups, volume/stacked tone/mix controls, available in Candy Apple Red, Cobalt Blue, Metallic Gold, Metallic Green, or Pearl Black finishes, system requires a 9-volt battery, mfg. 1996-99.

	$725	$625	$525	$450	$375	$300	$225

Last MSR was $899.

In 1996, the standard Axcelerator model was offered with a 2-Tek bridge. While physically the same specifications as the original, the addition of the 2-Tek technology opens up the sonic qualities by a perceptible amount.

ELECTRIC BASS: B SERIES

B-NINETY - offset double cutaway poplar body with access scoops, bolt-on bi-laminated maple neck, 21-fret rosewood fingerboard with white dot inlay, 34 in. scale, fixed bridge, graphlon nut, 4-on-a-side mini bass tuners, black hardware, P/J-style pickups, 2 volume/master tone controls, available in '62 Blue, Black, Charcoal Gray, Pearl White, Raspberry Pearl, or Sunfire Red finishes, mfg. 1990-94.

	N/A	$300	$250	$225	$200	$160	$110

Last MSR was $499.

This model was optional in a left-handed configuration.

B-Ninety Active - similar to B-Ninety, except has active electronics, mfg. 1990-94.

	N/A	$325	$275	$250	$225	$190	$125

Last MSR was $549.

B-QUAD-4 - deep offset double cutaway flame maple body, bolt-on Modulus Graphite neck, 24-fret phenolic fingerboard with pearl B inlay at 12th fret, fixed bridge, 4-on-a-side tuners, gold hardware, 2 covered active humbucker/4 piezo bridge pickups, master volume, 2 stacked volume/tone controls, piezo volume/tone controls, stereo/mono switch, Dual mono/stereo 1/4 in. outputs, available in Trans. Teal or Trans. Violet finishes, mfg. 1994-98.

$1,600	$1,375	$1,200	$1,050	$875	$700	$525

Last MSR was $2,118.

The B-Quad-4 was designed in conjunction with bassist Brian Bromberg. This model has black hardware with Natural and White finishes as an option. Instrument contains on-board 4 x 2 stereo mixing controls for the piezo pickup system. There are four pairs of volume/stereo panning controls on the back plate for adjustment of the stereo field from the dual output jacks.

B-Quad-5 - similar to the B-Quad-4, except has 5-string configuration, 5-on-a-side tuners, mfg. 1995-98.

$1,850	$1,575	$1,375	$1,195	$995	$795	$600

Last MSR was $2,418.

ELECTRIC BASS: CIRRUS SERIES

The Cirrus models were introduced in 1997. All models feature a 35 in. scale, through-body laminated neck (walnut/maple or maple/purpleheart), graphite reinforced neck and peghead, 24-fret pau ferro fingerboard, ABM bridge, 2 VFL humbuckers, volume/balance knobs, treble/mid/bass EQ controls. Each model is available fretless.

GRADING	100% MINT	98% NEAR MINT	95% EXC+	90% EXC	80% VG+	70% VG	60% G

CIRRUS 4 - walnut body with select bookmatched exotic wood tops, 4-string configuration, 2-per-side tuners, available in hand-rubbed satin and oil finishes, mfg. 1997-present.

	MSR	$1,700		$1,375	$1,200	$1,050	$900	$750	$650	$550

> **Add $75 for highly figured redwood top (Cirrus 4 Redwood) or Peacock Blue option with a maple top (Cirrus 5 Peacock Blue). Add $150 for Claro walnut body (Cirrus 4 Claro Walnut). Add $600 for Quilt Top Tiger Eye option.**

Cirrus 4 BXP - similar to the Cirrus 4, except has an agathis back with a maple veneer top, available in Bubinga Top Natural, Darkwood Top Natural, or Quilt Top Tiger Eye, mfg. 2004-present.

MSR	$720		$550	$475	$400	$350	$300	$250	$200

Cirrus 4 Bolt-On - similar to the Cirrus 4, except has a solid mahogany body and bolt-on neck, available in Natural finish, 34 in. scale, new 2005.

MSR	$1,300		$1,050	$900	$775	$650	$550	$475	$400

CIRRUS 5 - walnut body with select bookmatched exotic wood tops, 5-string configuration, 3/2-per-side tuners, available in hand-rubbed satin and oil finishes, mfg. 1997-present.

MSR	$1,900		$1,550	$1,300	$1,100	$950	$800	$700	$600

> **Add $75 for highly figured redwood top (Cirrus 5 Redwood) or Peacock Blue option with a maple top (Cirrus 5 Peacock Blue). Add $150 for Claro Walnut body (Cirrus 5 Claro Walnut). Add $600 for Quilt Top Tiger Eye option.**

Cirrus 5 BXP - similar to the Cirrus 5, except has an agathis back with a maple veneer top, available in Bubinga Top Natural, Darkwood Top Natural, or Quilt Top Tiger Eye, mfg. 2004-present.

MSR	$800		$600	$525	$450	$400	$350	$300	$250

Cirrus 5 Bolt-On - similar to the Cirrus 5, except has a solid mahogany body and bolt-on neck, available in Natural finish, 34 in. scale, new 2005.

MSR	$1,500		$1,200	$1,050	$900	$800	$700	$600	$500

CIRRUS 6 - alder body with figured redwood wood top, 6-string configuration, 3-per-side tuners, available in high gloss finish, mfg. 1997-present.

MSR	$2,100		$1,700	$1,500	$1,300	$1,150	$1,000	$850	$700

> **Add $75 for Peacock Blue option with a maple top (Cirrus 6 Peacock Blue). Add $150 for Claro Walnut body (Cirrus 6 Claro Walnut). Add $600 for Quilt Top Tiger Eye option.**

Peavey Cirrus 4 BXP Bass
courtesy Peavey

ELECTRIC BASS: CYBERBASS SERIES

MIDIBASE - offset double cutaway alder body, maple neck, 21-fret rosewood fingerboard with white dot inlay, fixed bridge, graphlon nut, 4-on-a-side tuners, black hardware, 2 humbucker pickups, 2 volume/tone/mix controls, bypass switch, available in Pearl White finish, mfg. 1992-93.

		N/A	$1,200	$1,050	$900	$750	$625	$500

Last MSR was $1,800.

Basic concept and MIDI controller design by Australian bassist and electrical engineering student Steve Chick. Chick began working on a bass synthesizer in his spare time in 1982, put out his own MB4 retrofit system during the mid 1980s, and began working with the Peavey corporation in 1991. In early 1994, the MidiBass name was changed to Cyberbass (See Cyberbass).

CYBERBASS (MIDIBASS) - offset double cutaway poplar body, black pearloid laminated pickguard, bolt-on maple neck, 22-fret rosewood fingerboard with pearl dot inlay, fixed bridge, 4-on-a-side tuners, chrome hardware, 2 covered active humbucker pickups, 2 stacked controls, mini switch, available in Candy Apple Red, Montana Green, or Pearl Black finishes, mfg. 1994-98.

	$1,400	$1,175	$1,000	$895	$750	$600	$450

Last MSR was $1,799.

This model has volume/volume/MIDI volume/master tone controls and can be used to trigger a synthesized sound module, sound bass notes through the conventional magnetic pickups, or combine the two.

CYBERBASS 5 - similar to the Cyberbass, except has 5-string configuration, 5-on-a-side tuners, mfg. 1995-98.

	$1,500	$1,200	$1,100	$995	$825	$650	$500

Last MSR was $1,999.

ELECTRIC BASS: DYNA-BASS SERIES

DYNA-BASS - offset double cutaway poplar body, bolt-on bi-laminated maple neck, 21-fret rosewood fingerboard with white dot inlay, 34 in. scale, Schaller fixed bridge, graphlon nut, 4-on-a-side mini tuners, gold hardware, 2 active humbucker pickups, volume control, 2 stacked tone controls, pickup blend control, active/passive bypass mini switch. System requires a 9-volt battery, available in '62 Blue, Black, Charcoal Gray, Pearl White, or Sunfire Red finishes, mfg. 1985-1994.

		N/A	$450	$375	$325	$275	$225	$175

Last MSR was $729.

In 1991, the original Super Ferrite pickups were changed to newer humbucker style. In 1986, the Dyna-Bass was offered with an optional Kahler Bass Tremolo (retail list $929).

DYNA-BASS 5 - similar to Dyna-Bass, except has 5 strings, 4/1-per-side tuners, 5 string Schaller bridge, and 34 in. scale, mfg. 1987-1994.

		N/A	$475	$400	$350	$300	$250	$200

Last MSR was $799.50.

Peavey Cirrus 5 Bolt-On Bass
courtesy Peavey

GRADING	100% MINT	98% NEAR MINT	95% EXC+	90% EXC	80% VG+	70% VG	60% G

DYNA-BASS UNITY - similar to Dyna-Bass, except has active P/J pickups, neck-through construction, black chrome hardware, and 21-fret ebony fingerboard, mfg. 1987-1990.

	N/A	$475	$400	$350	$300	$250	$200

Last MSR was $799.

Dyna-Bass Unity Ltd. - similar to Dyna-Bass Unity, except has figured maple top, gold hardware, available in Honey Sunburst finish, mfg. 1988-1990.

	N/A	$600	$550	$500	$450	$375	$300

Last MSR was $1,100.

ELECTRIC BASS: FORUM SERIES

FORUM (FIRST VERSION) - offset double cutaway poplar body, white laminated pickguard, bolt-on bi-laminated Eastern maple neck, 21-fret rosewood fingerboard with pearl dot inlay, 34 in. scale fixed bridge, graphlon nut, 4-on-a-side tuners, chrome hardware, P-style/J-style ceramic humbucker pickups, 2 volume/tone control, available in Black, Red, or White finishes, mfg. 1993-98.

$375	$325	$275	$250	$200	$175	$125

Last MSR was $499.

Forum (Second Version): In 1995, the P/J pickup combination was replaced with an active humbucker in the P-style position. The three controls switched to volume/treble/bass. This second configuration is the current model.

FORUM 5 - similar to Forum (Second Version), except features 5-String configuration, 35 in. scale, alder or swamp ash body, Peavey fixed bridge, 2 active VFL-Plus humbuckers, volume/pickup blend/tone controls, available in Pearl White, Pearl Black (alder bodies); Trans. Grape, Sunburst (swamp ash bodies) finishes, disc. 1998.

$600	$525	$450	$395	$325	$275	$200

Last MSR was $789.

FORUM AX - similar to Forum (Second Edition), except features alder or swamp ash bodies, ABM fixed bridge, 2 active VFL humbuckers, volume/pickup blend/tone controls, available in Candy Apple Red, Pearl Black (alder bodies); Blonde, or Sunburst (swamp ash bodies) finishes, disc. 1998.

$550	$475	$425	$350	$300	$250	$175

Last MSR was $729.

FORUM PLUS - similar to Forum (First Version), except has P/J-style active pickups, available in Candy Apple Red, Cobalt Blue, Metallic Green, or Pearl Black finishes, mfg. 1993-95.

	N/A	$450	$375	$325	$275	$225	$175

Last MSR was $520.

ELECTRIC BASS: FOUNDATION SERIES

FOUNDATION - offset double cutaway poplar body, bolt-on maple neck, 21-fret maple fingerboard with black dot inlay, fixed bridge, 34 in. scale, graphlon nut, 4-on-a-side tuners, chrome hardware, 2 single coil pickups, 2 volume/tone control, available in Gloss Black, Gloss Red, Sunburst, or Gloss White finishes, mfg. 1983-2002.

$425	$350	$300	$250	$225	$175	$150

Last MSR was $600.

Add $30 for Foundation model with rosewood fingerboard.

In 1994, Sunburst finish was disc.

Foundation Fretless - similar to Foundation, except has fretless rosewood fingerboard with fret lines, disc. 1999.

$350	$275	$250	$225	$175	$150	$125

Last MSR was $429.

FOUNDATION 5 - similar to Foundation, except has 5 strings, 4/1-per-side tuners, disc.

$475	$400	$350	$275	$250	$200	$160

Last MSR was $650.

FOUNDATION CUSTOM - similar to the Foundation, except features a black phenolic fingerboard and pearly or metallic finishes, mfg. 1984-85.

	N/A	$325	$250	$225	$195	$175	$140

Last MSR $394.50-$474.50.

FOUNDATION S - similar to Foundation, except has P/J-style humbucker pickups, hardwood body, 2 volume/tone control, mfg. 1986-1990.

	N/A	$350	$300	$250	$225	$175	$125

Last MSR was $419.50.

Foundation S Active - similar to Foundation S, except has active Bi-Fet P/J-style humbucker pickups (system requires a 9-volt battery), mfg. 1988-1990.

	N/A	$400	$350	$300	$250	$200	$150

Last MSR was $449.50.

ELECTRIC BASS: FURY SERIES

FURY - offset double cutaway poplar body, white pickguard, bolt-on maple neck, 21-fret maple fingerboard with black dot inlay, 34 in. scale, fixed bridge, graphlon nut, 4-on-a-side tuners, chrome hardware, P-style pickup, volume/tone control, available in Gloss Black, Gloss Red, Sunburst, or Gloss White finishes, mfg. 1983-1998.

$300	$250	$195	$175	$150	$125	$100

Last MSR was $399.

The original 1983 Fury model was similar in design to the earlier T-20. In 1994, the Sunburst finish was disc.

GRADING	100% MINT	98% NEAR MINT	95% EXC+	90% EXC	80% VG+	70% VG	60% G

FURY II - solid Agathis body with sculpted front and back contours, 34 in. scale, maple neck, dual expanding truss rod with adjustable wheel, rosewood fingerboard, 21-frets, die-cast bridge with machined steel saddles, mini tuners, 9V powered active pickup and electronics, 8 dB boost/cut for bass, mid, treble, thumb rest, satin chrome plated hardware, available in Black, Sunburst, Metallic Garnet Red, Metallic Dark Blue, or Metallic Titanium finishes, mfg. 1999-2003.

	$300	$250	$225	$200	$175	$150	$100

Last MSR was $400.

Add $20 for left-hand model (Fury II LH).

FURY 4 QUILT TOP - offset double cutaway solid body, 4-string, 34 in. scale, 21-frets, Quilted Maple top, solid maple neck with rosewood fingerboard, 2 VFL internally-active pickups, 3-band active EQ, single master volume, mid, bass, and treble controls, satin chrome hardware, available in Trans. Red, Trans. Blue, Trans. green, or Sunburst finishes, disc. 2003.

	$350	$275	$225	$200	$175	$150	$125

Last MSR was $500.

FURY V QUILT TOP - similar to Fury V Quilt Top except, in a 6-string configuration, available in Trans. Red, Trans. Blue, Trans. Green, or Sunburst finishes, disc. 2003.

	$425	$350	$325	$275	$250	$225	$175

Last MSR was $600.

FURY VI QUILT TOP - similar to Fury V Quilt Top except, in a 6-string configuration, available in Trans. Red, Trans. Blue, Trans. Green, or Sunburst finishes, disc. 2003.

	$495	$425	$375	$350	$325	$275	$225

Last MSR was $700.

ELECTRIC BASS: G SERIES

G BASS - offset double cutaway solid alder body, bolt-on composite graphite neck, 35 in. scale, 21-fret pau ferro fingerboard with white dot inlay, fixed bridge, graphlon nut, 4-on-a-side tuners, chrome hardware, VLF Plus humbucker pickup, volume/3 band EQ controls, available in Holoflack Black, Holoflake Red, or Holoflake Green finishes, mfg. 1997-2002.

	$700	$595	$525	$450	$395	$325	$250

Last MSR was $919.

G 5 BASS - similar to the G Bass, except features 5-string configuration, 5-on-a-side tuners, 2 VFL pickups, ABM bridge, volume/blend/3 band EQ, available in Holoflack Black, Holoflake Red, Charcoal Grey, Metallic Dark Blue, or Vintage Sunburst finishes, mfg. 1998-2002.

	$1,050	$895	$750	$640	$545	$450	$350

Last MSR was $1,400.

**Peavey Fury VI Quilt Top
courtesy Dave Rogers
Dave's Guitar Shop**

ELECTRIC BASS: GRIND SERIES

GRIND 4 - offset double cutaway alder body, hard rock maple neck, 24-fret Pau Ferro rosewood fingerboard with dot inlays, j and p style pickups, on-board active 3-band EQ, active electronics, four knobs, 2-per-side tuners, black hardware, available in Black, Silver Pearl, Metallic Orange, or Charocal Metallic Violet finish, mfg. 2001-03.

	$900	$775	$700	$625	$550	$475	$400

Last MSR was $1,200.

GRIND 5 - similar to the Grind 4, except in five-string configuration, mfg. 2001-03.

	$1,050	$900	$800	$700	$625	$550	$450

Last MSR was $1,400.

GRIND 4 BXP - similar to the Grind 4, except not made in the U.S.A., has an agathis body, and 9-volt system, available in Topaz Blue, mfg. 2002-present.

MSR	$500	$400	$325	$275	$225	$200	$150	$100

GRIND 5 BXP - similar to the Grind 4, except in five-string configuration, mfg. 2001-present.

MSR	$550	$450	$375	$325	$275	$250	$225	$175

GRIND 6 BXP - similar to the Grind 4, except in six-string configuration, mfg. 2003-present.

MSR	$600	$495	$425	$375	$325	$275	$235	$195

ELECTRIC BASS: MILESTONE SERIES

MILESTONE II - offset double cutaway body, single piece maple neck, 20-fret rosewood fingerboard, 34 in. scale, fixed bridge, one split-coil pickup, 4-on-a-side tuners, chrome hardware, white laminated pickguard, volume/tone controls, available in Gloss Black, Gloss Red, Gloss White, or Powder Blue Sunburst finishes, disc. 1999.

	$215	$175	$155	$135	$115	$95	$75

Last MSR was $269.

Add $10 for Milestone II in Sunburst finish.

**Peavey Grind 5 BXP
courtesy Peavey**

P

GRADING	100% MINT	98% NEAR MINT	95% EXC+	90% EXC	80% VG+	70% VG	60% G

MILESTONE III - balanced, comfortable body styling with front and back contours, 34 in. scale, maple neck, rosewood fingerboard, dual expanding truss rod with adjustable wheel, 2 single coil J-style pickups (hum-cancelling when used together), stamped steel bridge, two volume controls, master tone control, chrome hardware, available in Black, White, Sunburst, Metallic Garnet Red, or Metallic Dark Blue finishes, mfg. 1999-present.

MSR	$210	$170	$140	$120	$100	$80	$65	$50

Add $20 for left-hand configuration.

MILESTONE IV - similar to Milestone III, except has 1 split coil P-style pickup, available in Black, White, Sunburst, Metallic Garnet Red or Metallic Dark Blue finishes, mfg. 1999-2003.

		$225	$180	$160	$140	$120	$100	$85

Last MSR was $300.

Add $20 for left-hand configuration. Add $125 for Bass Stage Pack.

MILESTONE V - similar to Milestone III, except 5-String configuration, available in Black, Burgundy Red, Sunburst, or Metallic Topaz Blue finishes, mfg. 2001-03.

		$300	$250	$200	$175	$150	$125	$100

Last MSR was $400.

ELECTRIC BASS: MILLENIUM SERIES

MILLENNIUM 4BN - offset double cutaway solid alder body, graphite reinforced hard rock maple neck, 35" scale, Bird's-eye Maple fingerboard, Active VFL pickups, active 3-band EQ, Hipshot bridge, available in Neon Blue, Gold Sparkle, Charcoal Metallic Violet, Trans. Blonde, Candy Apple Red, Tobacco Sunburst, Peacock Blue Metallic, or Pearl Black finishes, disc. 2003.

		$900	$800	$700	$650	$600	$550	$500

Last MSR was $1,300.

Millenium J4 - similar to the Millenium 4 basses, except has J-style pickups, available in Sunburst, Candy Apple Red, Blonde, or Seafoam Green, mfg. 2001-04.

		$775	$675	$550	$500	$450	$395	$325

Last MSR was $1,100.

Millennium 4 Pau Ferro or Maple - similar to Millennium 4 BN except, has a maple Pau Ferro fingerboard, same finish options, disc. 2002.

		$775	$675	$550	$500	$450	$395	$325

Last MSR was $1,100.

Millennium 4 Plus BN - similar to Millenium 4BN except, has bird's-eye maple neck, Hipshot D-Tuner. Available in Transparent Black Teal, Royal Blue, Tiger Eye, Black Violet, Peacock Blue, Tobacco Sunburst, Vintage Sunburst, Ruby Red, Cashmere Metallic, Harlequin Violet/Gold, disc. 2003.

		$1,125	$1,025	$950	$895	$850	$795	$750

Last MSR was $1,600.

Millenium J4 Plus - similar to the Millenium 4 Plusbasses, except has J-style pickups, available in Tiger Eye, Royal Blue, Margarita, or Trans. Green finishes, mfg. 2001-04.

		$975	$875	$775	$695	$650	$595	$550

Last MSR was $1,400.

Millennium 4 Plus Pau Ferro or Maple - similar to Millenium 4 Plus BN except, has Pau Ferro fingerboard, solid alder body with flame maple top. Same finish options, disc. 2003.

		$975	$875	$775	$695	$650	$595	$550

Last MSR was $1,400.

MILLENNIUM 5 BN - similar to Millennium 4BN except, in a 5-string model, available in Neon Blue, Gold Sparkle, Charcoal Metallic Violet, Transparent Blonde, Candy Apple Red, Tobacco Sunburst, Peacock Blue Metallic, or Pearl Black finishes, disc. 2002.

		$1,125	$1,025	$925	$825	$725	$625	$525

Last MSR was $1,600.

Millennium 5 Pau Ferro or Maple - similar to Millennium 5 BN except, has Pau Ferro or Maple fingerboard, same finish options, disc. 2004.

		$975	$875	$775	$695	$650	$595	$550

Last MSR was $1,400.

Millennium 5 Plus BN - similar to Millennium 5 BN except, has solid alder body with flame maple top. bird's-eye maple fingerboard. Same finish options, disc. 2004.

		$1,350	$1,225	$1,125	$1,025	$925	$825	$725

Last MSR was $1,900.

Millennium 5 Plus Pau Ferro or Maple - similar to Millennium 5 Plus BN except, with Pau Ferro or Maple fingerboard, same finish options, disc. 2003.

		$1,200	$1,100	$995	$895	$795	$695	$595

Last MSR was $1,700.

MILLENNIUM 4 BXP - offset double cutaway basswood body with quilted maple top, 2 J-Style pickups, STB, 3 knobs, black hardware, available in Trans. Black, Trans. Blue, Tiger Eye, or Sunburst finishes, mfg. 2003-present.

MSR	$290	$225	$190	$165	$145	$125	$105	$85

Add $20 for left-handed configuration. Add $85 for Peavey VFL active pickups (Model AC BXP).

MILLENNIUM 5 BXP - similar to the Millenium 4 BXP, except in 5-string configuration, available in Trans. Black, Trans. Blue, Tiger Eye, or Sunburst finishes, mfg. 2003-present.

MSR	$320	$250	$225	$200	$175	$150	$125	$100

Add $85 for Peavey VFL active pickups (Model AC BXP).

P

GRADING	100% MINT	98% NEAR MINT	95% EXC+	90% EXC	80% VG+	70% VG	60% G

ELECTRIC BASS: PALAEDIUM & PATRIOT SERIES

PALAEDIUM - offset double cutaway three piece alder body, bolt-on maple neck, 21-fret ebony fingerboard with pearl dot inlay, 34 in. scale, Leo Quan Bad Ass II fixed bridge, graphlon nut, 4-on-a-side tuners, gold hardware, 2 humbucker pickups, volume/tone/mix control, available in Trans. Amber, Trans. Red, or Trans. Violet finishes, mfg. 1991-94.

	N/A	$475	$400	$350	$325	$275	$225

Last MSR was $800.

The Palaedium model was developed in conjunction with bassist Jeff Berlin.

PATRIOT - offset double cutaway maple or southern ash body, bi-laminated maple neck, 21-fret fingerboard, 34 in. scale, fixed bridge, four on a side tuners, chrome hardware, graphlon nut, one single coil pickup, black laminated pickguard, volume/tone controls, available in Gloss or Satin finishes, mfg. 1984-88.

	N/A	$225	$185	$150	$125	$110	$85

Last MSR ranged $225-$332.

Patriot Custom - similar to the Patriot, except features a rosewood fingerboard and color matched peghead, mfg. 1986-88.

	N/A	$325	$275	$225	$175	$135	$95

Last MSR was $310.

ELECTRIC BASS: RJ, RSB, & RUDY SARZO SERIES

RJ-IV - offset double cutaway maple body, neck-through body bi-laminated maple neck, 21-fret Mahassar ebony fingerboard with pearl arrow inlay, fixed bridge, graphlon nut, 4-on-a-side mini tuners, Hipshot Bass Extender Key, black hardware, P/J-style active pickups, volume control, 3 band EQ controls, pickup selector toggle switch, available in Black Pearl Burst, Blue Pearl Burst, Purple Pearl Burst, or Red Pearl Burst finishes, mfg. 1990-94.

	N/A	$575	$525	$475	$425	$375	$300

Last MSR was $1,049.

Peavey Milestone V Bass courtesy Peavey

Model designed in conjunction with bassist Randy Jackson. This model was optional with a koa body/neck, rosewood fingerboard, and Hipshot D-Tuner.

RSB - offset double cutaway poplar body, bolt-on rock maple neck, 24-fret maple fingerboard with black dot inlay, 34 in. scale, fixed brass bridge, 4-on-a-side mini tuners, gold hardware, graphlon nut, 2 VFL active humbucker pickups, volume/tone/mix controls, available in Black finish, mfg. 1993-95.

	N/A	$425	$350	$300	$250	$200	$150

Last MSR was $700.

RSB Koa - similar to RSB, except has koa body, pau ferro fingerboard with pearl dot inlay, available in Oil finish, mfg. 1993-95.

	N/A	$500	$425	$375	$325	$275	$225

Last MSR was $800.

RUDY SARZO SIGNATURE - offset double cutaway ash body, through body maple/purpleheart 5-piece neck, 24-fret ebony fingerboard with pearl oval inlay, fixed Schaller brass bridge, brass nut, 4-on-a-side tuners, gold hardware, 2 ceramic humbucker pickups, volume/tone/3 band EQ controls, bypass switch, active electronics, available in Trans. Black, Trans. Red, or Trans. Violet finishes, mfg. 1989-1994.

	N/A	$650	$600	$525	$475	$400	$325

Last MSR was $1,100.

ELECTRIC BASS: T SERIES

The T series guitars and basses were originally designed by Chip Todd in 1977, and three models debuted in 1978 (T-60 and T-30 guitars, and a T-40 bass).

T-20 - double offset cutaway maple or southern ash body, bi-laminated hard rock maple neck, 21-fret maple fingerboard, 34 in. scale, chrome hardware, fixed bridge, four on a side headstock, single blade single coil pickup, volume knob, tone knob, brown laminated pickguard, available in Natural, Sunfire Red, or Frost Blue finishes, mfg. 1982-85.

	N/A	$350	$300	$250	$200	$150	$120

Last MSR ranged $299-$374.

This model was also available with a fretless neck.

T-40 - double offset cutaway body, bolt-on bi-laminated rock maple neck, 23-fret fingerboard, 34 in. scale, chrome hardware, fixed bridge, four on a side tuners, two in.double blade in. style humbucking pickups, two volume controls, two tone controls (one per pickup), pickup phase switch, 3-way pickup selector switch, brown laminated pickguard, available in Natural, White, Black, or Sunburst finishes, mfg. 1978-1988.

	N/A	$400	$350	$300	$250	$200	$150

Last MSR ranged $399-$484.

Peavey Millenium J-4 Bass courtesy Peavey

The T-40 was the first Peavey production bass. This model was also offered with a fretless neck. In 1982, Blood Red and Burgundy finished were offered. The original Red Rhodes-designed pickups allows the capability of single or dual coil output. Fully opening the tone potentiometer to 10 achieves single coil mode. Turning counterclockwise to 7brings the second coil into operation, and achieving full range humbucking tone. Rotation of the control from 7 to 0 further contours the tone circuit. The Phase switch is a two position switch which reverses the coil relationship in the bridge pickup when the pickup switch is in the middle position (up is in phase, and down is out-of-phase).

P

GRADING	100% MINT	98% NEAR MINT	95% EXC+	90% EXC	80% VG+	70% VG	60% G

T-45 - double offset cutaway hardwood body, bi-laminated hard rock maple neck, 21-fret maple fingerboard, 34 in. scale, chrome hardware, fixed bridge, four on a side tuners, dual blade humbucker, master volume knob, two tone knobs, available in Black, White, Sunburst, Blood Red, or Burgundy finishes, mfg. 1982-86.

	N/A	$450	$375	$325	$275	$225	$175

Last MSR $434.50-$459.50.

The humbucking pickup can be used in either single coil or dual coil mode. Fully opening the tone potentiometer to 10 achieves single coil mode. Turning counterclockwise to 7 brings the second coil into operation, and achieving full range humbucking tone. Rotation of the control from 7 to 0 further contours the tone circuit.

ELECTRIC BASS: TL SERIES

TL-FIVE - offset double cutaway eastern flame maple body, neck-through body maple/purpleheart 5-piece neck, 24-fret ebony fingerboard with pearl oval inlay, Schaller fixed brass bridge, graphlon nut, 3/2-per-side tuners, gold hardware, 2 Super Ferrite humbucker pickups, volume/blend controls, treble/mid/bass controls, bypass mini-toggle, 3-band active electronics, available in Honey Sunburst, Trans. Black, Trans. Blue, Trans. Emerald, Trans. Red, or Trans. Violet finishes, mfg. 1988-1998.

	$1,150	$1,000	$875	$750	$650	$550	$450

Last MSR was $1,699.

In 1991, the VFL humbuckers were introduced. In 1994, the Transparent Violet finish was disc.

TL-SIX - similar to TL-Five, except features 6 strings, pearl arrow fingerboard inlay, 4/2-per-side tuners, Kahler 6-string bridge, gold hardware, 2 P-style pickups, mfg. 1989-1998.

	$1,300	$1,110	$950	$800	$700	$625	$475

Last MSR was $1,899.

ELECTRIC BASS: UNITY SERIES

UNITY - offset double cutaway poplar body with scoop access styling, neck-through body bi-laminated maple neck, 21-fret rosewood fingerboard with pearl dot inlay, fixed bridge, graphlon nut, 4-on-a-side tuners, black hardware, P/J-style pickups, 2 volume/tone control, available in '62 Blue, Black, Charcoal Gray, Pearl White, or Sunfire Red finishes, mfg. 1987-1994.

	N/A	$425	$350	$325	$275	$250	$175

Last MSR was $700.

Unity Koa - similar to Unity, except has koa body, solid koa neck-through design, gold hardware, available in Natural finish, mfg. 1988-1994.

	N/A	$450	$375	$350	$300	$250	$200

Last MSR was $750.

PEDULLA-ORSINI

Instruments previously built in MA circa 1974 to 1975.

The Pedulla-Orsini trademark was used by Mike Pedulla and Sam Orsini, who collaborated on custom basses, guitars, and banjo construction. Pedulla was a violinist and had a college music degree, teamed up with Orsini. The majority of work that they concentrated on was mostly instrument repair. Pedulla then went on to form M.V. Pedulla Guitars, and became very well-known for his high quality bass models.

PEDULLA, M.V.

Instruments currently built in MA since 1975.

The M.V. Pedulla company was founded back in 1975 by Michael Vincent Pedulla. They originally produced some acoustic guitars, as well as electrics (one model was outfitted with MIDI system compatible with the Roland GR-700 series). Once he created the unique design that led to the MVP and Buzz bass models, they began to specialize directly in high quality handcrafted basses.

Stock equipment found on M.V. Pedulla basses include Bartolini pickups and on-board preamps, ABM bridges, and Pedulla/Gotoh tuning machines. All models are available in fretted or fretless configuration.

GENERAL INFORMATION/FINISHES

Available colors include: Amber, Amber Sunburst, Arctic Night, Charcoal, Cherry, Cherry Sunburst, Emerald Green, Gold, Green/Blue Sunburst, Light Gold, Natural, Peacock Blue, Rose, Tobacco Sunburst, Vintage Cherry, Vintage Cherry Sunburst, or Violet.
The following Candy Colors are also available: Black, Blue, Green, Purple, Red, or Teal.
All models are available in either fretted or fretless configurations.

Add $400 for customer's signature on headstock. Add $500 for polyester finish on ET Thunderbass and ETB Thunderbolt models.

ELECTRIC BASS: BUZZ SERIES

This series consists of 2 models, the **MVP** and the **BUZZ**. The **MVP** has a fretted fingerboard, while the **BUZZ** is fretless – all other aspects are identical. Bassists Mark Egan and Tim Landers helped design and perfect the Buzz Bass.
Earlier specifications and nomenclature differ slightly from Pedulla´s current model offerings. When the MVP/Buzz **Standard** featured a flame maple body and chrome tuners, the upgrade to black or gold hardware was called the **Deluxe**; a higher grade (AA) flamed maple with black or gold hardware was designated the **Custom**; and the next higher grade (AAA) flame maple with black or gold hardware was labeled a **Signature**. Black, chrome, or gold hardware is now standard, and MVP/Buzz basses are offered in the AA or AAA grade flame maple bodies.

Add $800 above the AAA price for AAAAA grade or quilted maple body (the quilted maple body known as the Limited Edition version).

P

GRADING	100% MINT	98% NEAR MINT	95% EXC+	90% EXC	80% VG+	70% VG	60% G

BUZZ STANDARD - offset double cutaway flame maple body, through body maple laminate neck, fretless ebony fingerboard, fixed bridge, brass nut, 2-per-side tuners, chrome hardware, P/J-style Bartolini pickups, volume/tone/mix control, active electronics, available in Champagne, Black, Lime Green, Metallic Midnight Blue, Red, or White finishes, disc. 1994.

	N/A	$1,400	$1,200	$1,050	$900	$800	$700

Last MSR was $1,775.

This model was optional with 2 J-style or 2 Bartolini humbucker pickups.

PENTABUZZ STANDARD - similar to the Buzz Standard, except features 5-string configuration, 3/2-per-side tuners, disc. 1994.

	N/A	$1,600	$1,400	$1,200	$1,050	$900	$750

Last MSR was $2,075.

HEXABUZZ STANDARD - similar to the Buzz Standard, except features 6-string configuration, 3-per-side tuners, 2 J-style Bartolini pickups, disc. 1994.

	N/A	$1,800	$1,600	$1,400	$1,200	$1,050	$900

Last MSR was $2,275.

This model had 2 Bartolini humbucker pickups as an option.

OCTABUZZ STANDARD - similar to the Buzz Standard, except features 8-string configuration (4 pairs/tuned an octave apart), 4-per-side tuners, disc. 1994.

	N/A	$1,700	$1,500	$1,300	$1,100	$950	$800

Last MSR was $2,075.

BUZZ AA - offset double cutaway figured Eastern maple body, AA figured, through body quartersawn maple neck, fretless ebony fingerboard, fixed bridge, brass nut, 2-per-side tuners, black or gold hardware, choice of in.soapbar in. (or P/J-style or J/J-style) Bartolini pickups, volume/tone/blend control, active electronics, available in various finishes (see list), current mfg.

MSR	$3,495	$2,800	$2,350	$2,000	$1,700	$1,400	$1,150	$900

Buzz AAA - similar to the Buzz AA except has a AAA figured maple body.

MSR	$3,795	$3,050	$2,500	$2,150	$1,800	$1,500	$1,200	$950

PENTABUZZ AA - similar to the Buzz AA, except in 5-string configuration, 3/2-per-side tuners, current mfg.

MSR	$3,795	$3,050	$2,500	$2,150	$1,800	$1,500	$1,200	$950

Pentabuzz AAA - similar to the Pentabuzz, except has a AAA grade figured maple body.

MSR	$4,095	$3,300	$2,800	$2,350	$1,950	$1,600	$1,300	$1,000

Add $400 for optional wide spacing (19 mm) fingerboard.

HEXABUZZ AA - similar to the Buzz, except in 6-string configuration, 3-per-side tuners, current mfg.

MSR	$3,995	$3,200	$2,700	$2,250	$1,850	$1,550	$1,250	$975

Hexabuzz AAA - similar to the Hexabuzz AA except has a AAA figured maple body.

MSR	$4,295	$3,450	$2,950	$2,500	$2,050	$1,700	$1,400	$1,100

OCTABUZZ AA - similar to the Buzz, except in 8-string configuration (4 pairs/tuned an octave apart), 4-per-side tuners, current mfg.

MSR	$4,095	$3,300	$2,800	$2,350	$1,950	$1,600	$1,300	$1,000

Octabuzz AAA - similar to the Octabuzz, except has a AAA figured maple body.

MSR	$4,395	$3,550	$3,000	$2,550	$2,100	$1,750	$1,450	$1,150

ELECTRIC BASS: MVP SERIES

MVP4 STANDARD - offset double cutaway flame maple body, through body maple laminate neck, 24-fret ebony fingerboard with pearl dot inlay, fixed bridge, brass nut, 2-per-side tuners, chrome hardware, P/J-style Bartolini pickups, volume/tone/mix control, active electronics, available in Champagne, Black, Lime Green, Metallic Midnight Blue, Red, or White finishes, disc. 1994.

	N/A	$1,400	$1,200	$1,050	$900	$800	$700

Last MSR was $1,775.

This model was optional with 2 J-style or 2 Bartolini humbucker pickups.

MVP5 STANDARD - similar to the MVP4 Standard, except features 5-string configuration, 3/2-per-side tuners, disc. 1994.

	N/A	$1,600	$1,400	$1,200	$1,050	$900	$750

Last MSR was $2,075.

MVP6 STANDARD - similar to the MVP4 Standard, except features 6-string configuration, 3-per-side tuners, 2 J-style Bartolini pickups, disc. 1994.

	N/A	$1,800	$1,600	$1,400	$1,200	$1,050	$900

Last MSR was $2,275.

This model had 2 Bartolini humbucker pickups optional.

MVP8 STANDARD - similar to the MVP Standard, except features 8-string configuration (4 pairs/tuned an octave apart), 4-per-side tuners, disc. 1994.

	N/A	$1,700	$1,500	$1,300	$1,100	$950	$800

Last MSR was $2,075.

**Pedulla Pentabuzz Standard
courtesy M.V. Pedulla**

**Pedulla Rapture R135
courtesy M.V. Pedulla**

P

GRADING	100% MINT	98% NEAR MINT	95% EXC+	90% EXC	80% VG+	70% VG	60% G

MVP4 AA - offset double cutaway hard Eastern figured maple body, through body quartersawn maple neck, 24-fret ebony fingerboard with pearl dot inlay, fixed bridge, brass nut, 2-per-side tuners, black, chrome, or gold hardware, choice of soapbar (or P/J-style or J/J-style) Bartolini pickups, volume/tone/blend control, active electronics, available in various finishes (see list), current mfg.

MSR	$3,495		$2,800	$2,350	$2,000	$1,700	$1,400	$1,150	$900

MVP4 AAA - similar to the MVP4 AA, except has a AAA figured maple body.

MSR	$3,795		$3,050	$2,650	$2,150	$1,800	$1,500	$1,200	$950

MVP5 AA - similar to the MVP4, except in 5-string configuration, 3/2-per-side tuners, current mfg.

MSR	$3,795		$3,050	$2,650	$2,150	$1,800	$1,500	$1,200	$950

MVP5 AAA - similar to the MVP5, except has a AAA figured maple body.

MSR	$4,095		$3,300	$2,800	$2,350	$1,950	$1,600	$1,300	$1,000

Add $400 for optional wide spacing (19 mm) fingerboard.

MVP6 AA - similar to the MVP4, except in 6-string configuration, 3-per-side tuners, current mfg.

MSR	$3,995		$3,200	$2,700	$2,250	$1,850	$1,550	$1,250	$975

MVP6 AAA - similar to the MVP6 except has a AAA figured maple body.

MSR	$4,295		$3,450	$2,950	$2,500	$2,050	$1,700	$1,400	$1,100

MVP8 AA - similar to the MVP4, except features 8-string configuration (4 pairs/tuned an octave apart), 4-per-side tuners, current mfg.

MSR	$4,095		$3,300	$2,800	$2,350	$1,950	$1,600	$1,300	$1,000

MVP8 AAA - similar to the MVP8, except has a AAA figured maple body.

MSR	$4,395		$3,550	$3,000	$2,550	$2,100	$1,750	$1,450	$1,150

ELECTRIC BASS: MARK EGAN SIGNATURE SERIES

This series is co-designed by bassist Mark Egan. Every model except the doubleneck is available in fretless configuration.

Add $800 for AAAAA grade or quilted maple body (the quilted maple body was formerly known as the Limited Edition version).

ME 4 - sleek offset double cutaway AAA Grade flame maple body, through body maple neck, 24-fret ebony fingerboard with pearl dot inlay, ebony thumb rest, fixed bridge, brass nut, 2-per-side Gotoh tuners, gold hardware, 2 J-style pickups, volume/tone/mix controls, active electronics, available in Amber, Amber Sunburst, Cherry, Cherry Sunburst, Light Gold, Natural, or Peacock Blue gloss polyester finishes, disc. 2002.

			$3,200	$2,700	$2,250	$1,850	$1,550	$1,250	$975

Last MSR was $3,995.

ME 5 - similar to ME 4, except in 5-string configuration, 3/2-per-side tuners, disc. 2002.

			$3,450	$2,950	$2,500	$2,050	$1,700	$1,400	$1,100

Last MSR was $4,295.

Add $400 for optional wide spacing (19 mm) fingerboard.

ME 6 - similar to ME 4, except in 6-string configuration, 3-per-side tuners, disc. 2002.

			$3,600	$3,000	$2,600	$2,200	$1,800	$1,500	$1,200

Last MSR was $4,495.

ME 4-F+8 DOUBLENECK - offset double cutaway AAA Grade maple body, doubleneck configuration: fretless 4-string/fretted 8-string, disc. 2002.

			N/A	N/A	N/A	N/A	N/A	N/A	N/A

Last MSR was $9,999.

ELECTRIC BASS: RAPTURE SERIES

Rapture Series pickguard/finish combinations run: Pearl pickguards on solid finishes, tortoiseshell on Light Gold and Tobacco Sunburst finishes. Fretless configurations are available on all models.

RAPTURE RBSB-4 - sleek offset double cutaway soft Eastern curly maple body, bolt-on satin-finished maple neck, 22-fret rosewood or maple fingerboard with pearl dot inlay, fixed bridge, 2-per-side tuners, chrome hardware, pickguard, one Bartolini soapbar pickup, volume/treble/bass controls, mid-cut mini switch, TBT electronics, available in various finishes (see list), mfg. 1995-present.

MSR	$2,195		$1,800	$1,500	$1,250	$1,000	$800	$650	$500

Rapture RBSB-5 - similar to Rapture RB4, except in 5-string configuration, 3/2-per-side tuners, mfg. 1995-present.

MSR	$2,395		$1,950	$1,650	$1,400	$1,150	$900	$700	$550

RAPTURE RBJ2-4/RBPJ-4 - similar to the RB4, except features 2 J-style or P-style and J-style Bartolini pickups, volume/blend/treble/bass controls, mfg. 1996-present.

MSR	$2,495		$2,000	$1,700	$1,400	$1,150	$900	$750	$600

Rapture RBJ2-5/RBPJ-5 - similar to Rapture RBJ2-4, except in 5-string configuration, 3/2-per-side tuners, current mfg.

MSR	$2,695		$2,200	$1,850	$1,500	$1,200	$950	$825	$650

RAPTURE 2000 RBJ2-4/RBPJ-4 - similar to the Rapture series, except has a AA-flamed maple body and headstock, a 5A bird's-eye maple neck, and PJ or JJ pickups, mfg. 2001-present.

MSR	$2,995		$2,450	$2,050	$1,700	$1,450	$1,200	$950	$700

Rapture 2000 AAA RBJ2-4/RBPJ-4 - similar to the Rapture 2000, except has a AAA flamed maple top and headstock, mfg. 2001-present.

MSR	$3,295		$2,700	$2,300	$1,900	$1,550	$1,250	$1,000	$800

RAPTURE 2000 RBJ2-5/RBPJ-5 - similar to the Rapture 2000, except in five-string configuration, mfg. 2001-present.

MSR	$2,895		$2,300	$1,850	$1,550	$1,300	$1,100	$900	$700

GRADING	100% MINT	98% NEAR MINT	95% EXC+	90% EXC	80% VG+	70% VG	60% G

Rapture 2000 AAA RBJ2-5/RBPJ-5 - similar to the Rapture 2000, except has a AAA flamed maple top and headstock, mfg. 2001-present.

| | MSR | $3,195 | | $2,550 | $2,050 | $1,750 | $1,500 | $1,250 | $1,050 | $800 |

ELECTRIC BASS: SERIES II SERIES

All of these models were available with a fretless fingerboard.

Add $200 for soapbar or P/J-style active pickups. Add $200 for A Grade flame maple. Add $400 for AA Grade flame maple.

S-II 4 - offset double cutaway poplar body, bolt-on maple neck, 22-fret rosewood fingerboard with pearl dot inlay, fixed bridge, brass nut, 2-per-side Gotoh tuners, black hardware, P/J-style Bartolini pickups, volume/tone/mix controls, available in Black, Champagne, Lime Green, Midnight Blue, Red, Yellow, or White finishes, disc. 1992.

| | N/A | $900 | $800 | $700 | $625 | $550 | $475 |

Last MSR was $1,295.

S-II 5 - similar to S-II 4, except has 5-string configuration, 3/2-per-side tuners, disc. 1992.

| | N/A | $1,100 | $950 | $800 | $700 | $600 | $500 |

Last MSR was $1,695.

S-II 6 - similar to S-II 4, except has 6-string configuration, 3-per-side tuners, disc. 1992.

| | N/A | $1,300 | $1,100 | $950 | $800 | $675 | $550 |

Last MSR was $1,895.

ELECTRIC BASS: THUNDERBASS SERIES

This series has 2 variations: the ThunderBass, which features a fretted fingerboard, and the ThunderBuzz, which is fretless.

THUNDERBASS T4 AA - sleek offset double cutaway figured maple body, through body maple/bubinga 5-piece neck, 24-fret ebony fingerboard with pearl dot inlay, fixed bridge, 2-per-side MVP/Gotoh tuners, black, chrome, or gold hardware, 2 Bartolini soapbar pickups, volume/tone/pan controls, available in various finishes (see list), mfg. 1993-present.

| MSR | $3,495 | | $2,800 | $2,400 | $2,000 | $1,700 | $1,400 | $1,150 | $900 |

Thunderbass T4 AAA Grade - similar to the Thunderbass except has a AAA figured maple body, current mfg.

| MSR | $3,795 | | $3,050 | $2,500 | $2,150 | $1,800 | $1,500 | $1,200 | $950 |

Pedulla Thunderbolt 4 courtesy M.V. Pedulla

THUNDERBASS T5 AA - similar to Thunderbass T4, except in 5-string configuration, 3/2-per-side tuners, current mfg.

| MSR | $3,795 | | $3,050 | $2,500 | $2,150 | $1,800 | $1,500 | $1,200 | $950 |

Thunderbass T5 AAA Grade - similar to the Thunderbass T5, except has a AAA figured maple body, current mfg.

| MSR | $4,095 | | $3,300 | $2,800 | $2,350 | $1,950 | $1,600 | $1,300 | $1,000 |

THUNDERBASS T6 AA - similar to Thunderbass T4, except in 6-string configuration, 3-per-side tuners, current mfg.

| MSR | $3,995 | | $3,200 | $2,700 | $2,250 | $1,850 | $1,550 | $1,250 | $975 |

Thunderbass T6 AAA Grade - similar to the Thunderbass T8, except has a AAA figured maple body, current mfg.

| MSR | $4,295 | | $3,450 | $2,950 | $2,500 | $2,050 | $1,700 | $1,400 | $1,100 |

THUNDERBASS T8 AA - similar to Thunderbass T4, except has 8-string configuration (4 pairs of strings/tuned an octave apart), 2-per-side tuners, 4 tuners on bottom bout, mfg. 1994-present.

| MSR | $4,095 | | $3,300 | $2,800 | $2,350 | $1,950 | $1,600 | $1,300 | $1,000 |

Thunderbass T8 AAA Grade - similar to the Thunderbass T8, except has a AAA figured maple body, current mfg.

| MSR | $4,395 | | $3,550 | $3,000 | $2,550 | $2,100 | $1,750 | $1,450 | $1,150 |

ELECTRIC BASS: THUNDERBUZZ SERIES

THUNDERBUZZ T4-F AA - sleek offset double cutaway figured maple body, through body maple/bubinga 5-piece neck, fretless ebony fingerboard, fixed bridge, 2-per-side MVP/Gotoh tuners, black, chrome, or gold hardware, 2 Bartolini soapbar pickups, volume/tone/pan controls, available in various finishes (see list), mfg. 1993-2003.

| | $2,500 | $2,050 | $1,750 | $1,500 | $1,250 | $1,050 | $800 |

Last MSR was $3,195.

Thunderbuzz T4-FAAA Grade - similar to the Thunderbuzz except has a AAA figured maple body, disc. 2003.

| | $2,725 | $2,250 | $1,900 | $1,600 | $1,350 | $1,100 | $850 |

Last MSR was $3,495.

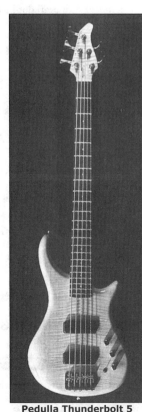

Pedulla Thunderbolt 5 courtesy M.V. Pedulla

THUNDERBUZZ T5-F AA - similar to Thunderbuzz T4-F, except has 5-string configuration, 3/2-per-side tuners, disc. 2003.

| | $2,725 | $2,250 | $1,900 | $1,600 | $1,350 | $1,100 | $850 |

Last MSR was $3,495.

Thunderbuzz T5-F AAA Grade - similar to the Thunderbuzz except has a AAA figured maple body, disc. 2003.

| | $3,000 | $2,500 | $2,100 | $1,750 | $1,450 | $1,150 | $875 |

Last MSR was $3,795.

P

GRADING	100% MINT	98% NEAR MINT	95% EXC+	90% EXC	80% VG+	70% VG	60% G

THUNDERBUZZ T6-F AA - similar to Thunderbuzz T4-F, except has 6-string configuration, 3-per-side tuners, disc. 2003.

	$2,900	$2,400	$2,000	$1,700	$1,400	$1,100	$900

Last MSR was $3,695.

Thunderbuzz T6-F AAA Grade - similar to the Thunderbuzz except has a AAA figured maple body, disc. 2003.

	$3,150	$2,550	$2,150	$1,800	$1,500	$1,200	$950

Last MSR was $3,995.

THUNDERBUZZ T8-F AA - similar to Thunderbuzz T4-F, except has 8-string configuration (4 pairs of strings/tuned an octave apart), 2-per-side tuners, 4 tuners on bottom bout, mfg. 1994-2003.

	$3,050	$2,500	$2,100	$1,750	$1,450	$1,150	$875

Last MSR was $3,795.

Thunderbuzz T8-F AAA Grade - similar to the Thunderbuzz except has a AAA figured maple body, disc. 2003.

	$3,275	$2,850	$2,400	$1,900	$1,600	$1,300	$1,050

Last MSR was $4,095.

ELECTRIC BASS: THUNDERBASS EXOTIC TOP (ET) SERIES

This series has 2 variations: the ET ThunderBass, which features a fretted fingerboard, and the ET ThunderBuzz, which is fretless.

Add $300 for AAAAA quilted maple top. Add $500 for polyester finish (with or without color).

ET4 - sleek offset double cutaway flame maple body, bubinga (or cocobola, AAAAA flame maple, quilted maple, or zebra) top, through body neck, 24-fret ebony fingerboard with pearl dot inlay, fixed bridge, brass nut, 2-per-side Gotoh tuners, black, chrome, or gold hardware, 2 Bartolini humbucker pickups, volume/tone/mix controls, active electronics, available in Natural oil/urethane finish, current mfg.

MSR	$3,495	$2,800	$2,400	$2,000	$1,700	$1,400	$1,150	$900

ET5 - similar to ET4, except has 5-string configuration, 3/2-per-side tuners, current mfg.

MSR	$3,795	$3,050	$2,500	$2,150	$1,800	$1,500	$1,200	$950

ET6 - similar to ET4, except has 6-string configuration, 3-per-side tuners, current mfg.

MSR	$3,995	$3,200	$2,700	$2,250	$1,850	$1,550	$1,250	$975

ET8 - similar to ET4 except has 8-string configuration (4 pairs of strings/tuned an octave apart), 2-per-side tuners on peghead, 4 tuners on bottom bout, mfg. 1994-present.

MSR	$4,095	$3,300	$2,800	$2,350	$1,950	$1,600	$1,300	$1,000

ELECTRIC BASS: THUNDERBOLT SERIES

The Thunderbolt Series is the bolt-on neck version of the Thunderbass design. All of these models are available with a fretless fingerboard.

THUNDERBOLT TB4 AA - sleek offset double cutaway figured maple body, through body satin-finished neck, 22-fret rosewood or maple fingerboard with pearl dot inlay, fixed bridge, 2-per-side tuners, black, chrome, or gold hardware, 2 Bartolini soapbar pickups, volume/tone/pan controls, mini switch, active electronics, available in various finishes (see list), mfg. 1994-present.

MSR	$2,895	$2,350	$1,850	$1,500	$1,200	$950	$800	$650

Thunderbolt TB4 AAA Grade - similar to the Thunderbolt TB4 except has a AAA figured maple body.

MSR	$3,195	$2,600	$2,200	$1,800	$1,500	$1,200	$950	$750

THUNDERBOLT TB5 AA - similar to Thunderbolt TB4, except has 5-string configuration, 3/2-per-side tuners, current mfg.

MSR	$2,995	$2,450	$2,050	$1,700	$1,450	$1,200	$950	$700

Thunderbolt TB AAA Grade - similar to the Thunderbolt TB5 except has a AAA figured maple body.

MSR	$3,295	$2,700	$2,300	$1,900	$1,550	$1,250	$1,000	$800

THUNDERBOLT TB6 AA - similar to Thunderbolt TB4, except has 6-string configuration, 3-per-side tuners, current mfg.

MSR	$3,095	$2,500	$2,050	$1,700	$1,400	$1,150	$900	$700

Thunderbolt TB6 AAA Grade - similar to the Thunderbolt TB6 except has a AAA figured maple body.

MSR	$3,395	$2,750	$2,300	$1,900	$1,550	$1,200	$950	$725

ELECTRIC BASS: THUNDERBOLT EXOTIC TOP (ET) SERIES

THUNDERBOLT ETB4 - sleek offset double cutaway figured maple body, AAAAA flame maple (or bubinga or cocobola or quilt or zebra) top, bolt-on 5-piece maple/bubinga neck, 22-fret rosewood or maple fingerboard with pearl dot inlay, fixed bridge, 2-per-side tuners, black, chrome, or gold hardware, 2 Bartolini soapbar pickups, volume/tone/pan controls, mini switch, active electronics, available in Oil/urethane finish, mfg. 1998-present.

MSR	$2,995	$2,450	$2,050	$1,700	$1,450	$1,200	$950	$700

THUNDERBOLT ETB5 - similar to Thunderbolt ETB4, except in 5-string configuration, 3/2-per-side tuners, mfg. 1998-present.

MSR	$3,095	$2,500	$2,050	$1,700	$1,400	$1,150	$900	$700

THUNDERBOLT ETB6 - similar to Thunderbolt ETB4, except in 6-string configuration, 3-per-side tuners, mfg. 1998-present.

MSR	$3,295	$2,700	$2,300	$1,900	$1,550	$1,250	$1,000	$800

PEERLESS

Instruments currently produced in Korea.

Peerless is another Korean guitar manufacture that produces entry level instruments. Several archtop electrics are available, mostly in traditional Gibson ES or D'Angelico designs. Contact the company for more information (see Trademark Index).

PENCO

Instruments previously produced in Japan circa 1970s. Distributed by the Philadelphia Music Company of Philadelphia, PA.

This trademark has been identified as a House Brand of the Philadelphia Music Company of Philadelphia, Pennsylvania, the U.S. distributor of these Japanese-built instruments. The Pennco (sometimes misspelled Penco) brand name was applied to a full range of acoustic and solid body electric guitars, many entry level to intermediate quality versions of popular American designs (source: Michael Wright, *Vintage Guitar Magazine*).

PENNCREST

See chapter on House Brands.

This trademark has been identified as a House Brand of J.C. Penney's (source: Willie G. Moseley, *Stellas & Stratocasters*).

PENSA CLASSIC

Instruments currently built in New York, NY since 1995. Distributed by Rudy's Music Shop of New York City, NY.

Rudy Pensa continues the tradition of producing high quality custom guitars first started in 1985 with his collaboration with John Suhr under the Pensa-Suhr trademark. Early Pensa-Suhrs were cast in the superstrat sort of design, with Floyd Rose tremolos and EMG electronics. When Suhr left in 1990, other builders like Larry Fitzgerald, Mas Hino, and Paul Blomstrom joined the workshop. Today, the Pensa Classic guitar models are beginning to grow more Gibson-esque with dual humbuckers and tune-o-matic bridge/stop tailpiece combinations like the Deluxe and Pensa Custom. However, the classic MK model is still being offered.

PENSA-SUHR

Instruments previously produced in New York, NY between the mid-1980s and early 1990s.

Rudy Pensa founded Rudy's Music Shop on West 48th street in New York back in 1978. Rudy's Music Shop features both retail instruments, amps, and effects as well as vintage classics. In 1983 John Suhr added a repair section to the shop, and within two years the pair collaborated on custom guitars and basses. Pensa-Suhr instruments feature exotic woods, pickup and wiring options, and other upgrades that the player could order. Pensa-Suhr instruments were high quality, and built along the lines of classic American designs.

In 1989, John Suhr moved to California and teamed up with Bob Bradshaw to open up a custom pedalboard/custom guitar shop. In 1994, Suhr joined the Fender custom shop as a Master Builder, and has been active in helping modernize the Fender Precision designs as well as his Custom Shop duties. Rudy Pensa maintained Rudy's Music Shop in New York City, and continues producing guitars and basses under the Pensa Classic trademark.

PERFORMANCE

Instruments currently built in Hollywood, CA.

The Performance guitar shop has been building custom guitars, doing custom work on guitars, and performing quality repair work for a good number of years.

The **Corsair 22** model features a double cutaway ash body, 22-fret Maple neck, 2 humbuckers, Schaller Floyd Rose locking tremolo, volume and tone knobs, pickup selector switch and Performance tuners. The guitar comes complete with an oil finish, and has a retail price beginning at $1,850. Performance also offers the **Corsair 24**, a similar model guitar that features a 24-fret fingerboard (two octaves). Retail price begins at $1,950.

PERRON

Instruments currently built in Elkhart, IN.

Michael Perron is an independent guitar manufacturer that produces five per month, as well as custom guitars and basses. All Perron guitars are high quality instruments that have a solid feel to them. For further information, please contact Michael Perron directly (see Trademark Index).

PETE BACK GUITARS

Instruments currently built in Richmond (North Yorkshire), England since 1975.

Luthier Pete Back is noted for his custom handcrafted guitars of the highest quality. His electric, folk and classical guitar construction uses the finest woods available. Pete has his own original designs, but will make whatever the guitarist requires. He also offers repairs (refretting, set-ups, and resprays). Back's prices start at 650 (English pounds), depending on parts and materials.

PETILLO GUITARS

Instruments currently manufactured in Ocean, NJ, since 1966.

Luthier Phillip J. Petillo has been creating, repairing, and restoring guitars and other instruments since the 1960s. Petillo was one of the original co-designers of the Kramer aluminum neck guitar in 1976, and built the four prototypes for Kramer (BKL). Later, he severed his connections with the company.

Currently, Petillo makes custom handcrafted acoustic carved top and back guitars, flattop acoustics, semi-hollowbody guitars, and solid body guitars and basses. Petillo also makes and repairs the bowed instruments. Petillo, a holder of a BS, MS, and PhD in Engineering, also offers his talents in Engineering for product development, research and development, engineering, and prototype building for the musical instruments industry.

Phillip and Lucille Petillo are the founders and officers of a research corporation that develops devices and technology for the medical industry. While seeming unrelated to the music industry, the Phil-Lu Incorporated company illustrates Petillo's problem-solving skills applied in different fields of study.

**Pedulla ET5
courtesy M.V. Pedulla**

**Pedulla Thunderbolt 5
courtesy M.V. Pedulla**

P

Petillo estimates that he hand builds between 8 to 20 guitars a year on his current schedule. Prices begin at $1,200 and are priced by nature of design and materials utilized. Custom Marquetry Inlay and other ornamental work is priced by the square inch. Petillo offers 170 different choices of lumbers, veneers, and mother-of-pearl.

Restoration, alteration and repair work are price quoted upon inspection of the instrument. In addition, he markets his patented products such as Petillo Frets, the Acoustic Tonal Sensor, Petillo Strings and Polish, and a fret micro-polishing system.

Some of his clients include: Tal Farlow, Chuck Wayne, Jim Croce, Elvis Presley, James Taylor, Tom Petty, Howie Epstein, Dave Mason, The Blues Brothers, Bruce Springsteen, Gary Talent, Steve Van Zant, Southside Johnny, and many others.

PHANTOM GUITAR WORKS

Instruments currently built in Clatskanie, OR since 1992.

Phantom Guitar Works produces a number of modern versions of Vox classic designs, keeping true to the spirit of the original model while updating some of the hardware to produce a stabile player's guitar. Phantom was founded by Jack Charles in 1992. All guitars built today are constructed in the U.S.A. For a period of time, some models were produced overseas. Phantom warns customers to beware of cheap Chinese copies that are in violation of their trademark. For more information contact Phantom directly (see Trademark Index).

ELECTRIC

Models in the Phantom product line include the **Mandoguitar**, the five sided **Phantom** and **Phantom Bass**, the **Teardrop**, **Teardrop B.J.**, and the **Teardrop Bass**. Most models list at $599 and may be additional for certain finishes.

PHIL

Instruments currently produced in Korea.

The Myung Sung Music Ind. Co., Ltd. is currently offering a wide range of well constructed electric guitar models. There is a large variety of styles, configurations, colors, and affordable price points. Construction utilizes top quality laminates, rosewood, spruce, mahogany, and build quality is top shelf. The **Phil Pro** Series offers models with offset double cutaway bodies, bolt-on necks, and double locking tremolo systems. For more information on the current model lineup, availability, and pricing, please contact The Myung Sung Music Ind. Co., Ltd.

ELECTRIC: REVIVAL SERIES

The **MSG 625** has an offset double cutaway solid body with flamed archtop, maple set neck, rosewood fingerboard, 22-frets, pearl block inlays, 3-per-side tuners, 2 humbucker pickups, 2 volume, 1 tone, 3-way switch, gold hardware, available in Purple Burst finish only, current mfg.

The **MSG 635** has an offset double cutaway solid body with oak archtop, maple set neck, rosewood fingerboard with dot inlays, 24-frets, 3-per-side tuners, 2 humbucker pickups, 1 volume, 1 tone, 3-way switch, chrome hardware, available in Cherry Sunburst finish only, current mfg.

The **MSG 640** has an offset double cutaway solid body with burled archtop, maple set neck, rosewood fingerboard with dot inlays, 24-frets, 3-per-side tuners, 2 humbucker pickups with exposed coils and 1 single coil pickup, 1 volume, 1 tone, five way switch, vibrato tailpiece, chrome hardware, available in Transparent Black finish only, current mfg.

The **MSG 650L** has an offset double cutaway solid body with flame top, maple set neck, rosewood fingerboard with dot inlays, 22-frets, 3-per-side tuners, 1 volume, 1 tone, 3-way switch, pearloid pickguard, 2 humbucker pickups, gold hardware, available in Blue Burst finish only, current mfg.

The **MSG 65 5** has an offset double cutaway semi-hollowbody design, maple set neck, rosewood fingerboard with dot inlays, 22-frets, 3-per-side tuners, pearloid body binding, single elliptical soundhole, 2 humbucker pickups with exposed zebra coils, gold hardware, available in Yellow Burst finish only, mfg. 2001-present.

The **MSG 678** has an offset double cutaway semi-hollowbody design, quilted arch top, maple set neck, rosewood fingerboard with pearloid steer head inlays, 22-frets, 3-per-side tuners, 1 volume, 1 tone, 3-way switch, 2 humbucker pickups with exposed zebra coils, 2 elliptical soundholes, gold hardware, available in Green Burst finish only, mfg. 2001-present. The **MSG 678A** is the same as the MSG 678 but with Black Pearl hardware and Amber Burst finish, mfg. 2001-present.

The **MSG 688** has an offset double cutaway solid body with flame top, maple set neck, rosewood fingerboard with pearl block inlays, 22-frets, 3-per-side tuners, string though body, 2 volume, 1 tone, 3-way switch, 2 Seymour Duncan humbucker pickups, pearl body binding, large pearl eagle inlay on guitar top, available in Trans. Red or Trans. Blue finish, current mfg.

The **PSM 700T** has an offset double cutaway solid body design, body constructed in laminated bands of maple, walnut and bubinga, arch top, neck-through body, neck constructed of maple, walnut and bubinga, rosewood fingerboard with pearl dot inlays, 24-frets, 6-on-a-side tuners, Wilkinson bridge with vibrato bar, 1 volume, 1 tone, five way switch, 2 Bill Lawrence humbucker pickups and 1 single coli alnico pickup, chrome hardware, available in Natural finish only, mfg. 2001-present.

ELECTRIC: ARDENT SERIES

The **MSF 201** has an offset double cutaway solid body, flame top, bolt-on maple neck, rosewood fingerboard with dot inlays, 24-frets, locking nut, 6-on-a-side tuners, Floyd Rose 200 bridge, 1 volume, 1 tone, five way switch, 2 exposed coil humbucker pickups and 1 single coil pickup, gold hardware, available in Transparent Purple finish only, current mfg.

The **MSF 231** has an offset double cutaway solid body, bolt-on maple neck, rosewood fingerboard with offset dot inlays, locking nut, 24-frets, 6-on-a-side tuners, Floyd Rose 200 bridge, 1 volume, 1 tone, five way switch, 2 single coil pickups and 1 exposed coil humbucker pickup, chrome hardware, available in Dark Metallic Blue finish only, current mfg.

The **MSF 237** has an offset double cutaway solid body, bolt-on maple neck, rosewood fingerboard with offset dot inlays, 24-frets, locking nut, 6-on-a-side tuners, Floyd Rose 200 bridge, 1 volume, 1 tone, five way switch, 2 exposed coil humbucker pickups and 1 single coil pickup, black hardware, available in Black finish only, current mfg.

The **MSF 275** is a 7-string, offset double cutaway solid body, oak top, bolt-on maple neck, rosewood fingerboard with dot inlays, 22-frets, 7-on-a-side tuners, locking nut, Floyd Rose 700 bridge, 1 volume, 1 tone, 3-way switch, 2 exposed coil humbucker pickups and 1 single coil pickup, chrome hardware, available in Yellow Burst finish only, mfg. 2001-present.

The **MSF 276** is a 7-string, offset double cutaway solid body, bolt-on maple neck with rosewood fingerboard, dot inlays, 24-frets, 7-on-a-side tuners, locking nut, Floyd Rose 700 bridge, 2 exposed coil humbucker pickups, 1 volume, 1 tone, 3-way switch, chrome hardware, available in Rainbow Pearl finish only, mfg. 2001-present.

The **MSF 277** is a 7-string, offset double cutaway solid body, bolt-on maple neck with rosewood fingerboard, dot inlays, 24-frets, locking nut, 7-on-a-side tuners, Floyd Rose 700 bridge, 2 humbucker pickups, 1 volume, 1 tone, 3-way switch, black hardware, available in black finish only, current mfg.

The **MSF 301** has an offset double cutaway solid body, flamed archtop, bolt-on maple neck with rosewood fingerboard, chevron inlays, 24-frets, locking nut, 6-on-a-side tuners, Floyd Rose 500 bridge, 2 Bill Lawrence humbucker pickups and 1 single coil pickup, 1 volume, 1 tone, five way switch, Black Pearl hardware, available in Transparent Blue finish only, current mfg.

The **MSF 302** has an offset double cutaway solid body with oak archtop, bolt-on maple neck, rosewood fingerboard with dot inlays, 24-frets, locking nut, 6-on-a-side tuners, Floyd Rose bridge, 2 single coil pickups and 1 humbucker pickup, 1 volume, 1 tone, five way switch, chrome hardware, available in Transparent Amber finish only, current mfg. The **MSF 303** is similar to **MSF 302** except has black hardware and is available in Metallic Green finish, current mfg.

The **MSF 531** has an offset double cutaway solid body, flame double archtop, bolt-on maple neck, rosewood fingerboard with shark fin inlays, 24-frets, locking nut, 6-on-a-side tuners, Floyd Rose 500 bridge, 2 Bill Lawrence humbucking pickups and 1 single coil pickup, 1 volume, 1 tone, five way switch, gold hardware, available in Transparent Red finish only, current mfg.

The **MSL 988** has an Explorer style solid body with flame top, set or bolt-on necks available, rosewood fingerboard with dot inlays, 22-frets, 2 Alnico ZB humbucker pickups with exposed coils, 2 volume, 1 tone, 3-way switch, Black Pearl hardware, available in Purple Burst finish only, mfg. 2001-present. The **MSS 235** has an offset double cutaway solid body, oak top, bolt-on maple neck, rosewood fingerboard with dot inlays, 22-frets, locking nut, 6-on-a-side tuners, 2 single coil pickups and 1 exposed coil humbucker pickup, 1 volume, 1 tone, five way switch, chrome hardware, available in Trans. Green finish only, current mfg.

The **MSV 983** has a V shaped solid body with flame top, available with set or bolt-on maple neck, rosewood fingerboard with dot inlays, 22-frets, 6-on-a-side tuners, 2 exposed coil humbucker pickups, 2 volume, 1 tone, 3-way switch, chrome hardware, available in Green Burst finish only, current mfg.

The **MSW 202** has an offset double cutaway solid body, burl top, bolt-on maple neck, rosewood fingerboard with pearl block inlays, 22-frets, locking nut, 6-on-a-side tuners, Wilkinson bridge, 2 exposed coil humbucker pickups, 1 volume, 1 tone, 3-way switch, gold hardware, available in Trans. Black finish, current mfg.

The **MSW 206** has an offset double cutaway solid body, flame top, bolt-on maple neck, rosewood fingerboard with offset dot inlays, locking nut, 24-frets, 6-on-a-side tuners, 2 exposed coil humbucker pickups and 1 single coil pickup, 1 volume, 1 tone, five way switch, chrome hardware, available in Trans. Blue finish only, current mfg.

The **MSW 255** has an offset single cutaway body, quilted top, maple through neck, rosewood fingerboard, 22-frets, 6-on-a-side tuners, Wilkinson bridge, 1 Bill Lawrence humbucker and 2 single coil pickups, 1 volume, 1 tone, five way switch, satin chrome hardware, available in Natural finish only, mfg. 2001-present.

The **MSW 577** has an offset double cutaway solid body with flame round top, bolt-on 5-piece maple neck, rosewood fingerboard with dot inlays, 22-frets, 6-on-a-side tuners, 2 single coil and 1 humbucker pickup, 1 volume, 1 tone, five way switch, black hardware, available in Cherry Sunburst finish only, current mfg.

ELECTRIC HOLLOWBODY

The **FM 800** has a double cutaway semi-hollowbody, bird´s-eye maple top, back and sides, maple set neck, rosewood fingerboard with pearl block inlays, 22-frets 3-per-side tuners, 2 humbucker pickups, lyre tailpiece, 2 volume, 2 tone, 3-way switch, gold hardware, available in Cherry finish only, disc. 2000.

The **FM 805** has a double cutaway semi-hollowbody, maple top, back, and sides, maple set neck, rosewood fingerboard with pearl block inlays, 22-frets, 3-per-side tuners, 2 humbucker pickups, stop tailpiece, 2 volume, 2 tone, 3-way switch, chrome hardware, available in Black finish only, disc. 2000.

The **FM 810** has a double cutaway semi-hollowbody, flame maple top, maple back and sides, maple set neck, rosewood fingerboard with pearl block inlays, 22-frets, 3-per-side tuners, 2 humbucker pickups, 2 volume, 2 tone, 3-way switch, gold hardware, available in Trans. Amber finish only, mfg. 2001-present. The **FM 815** is the same as FM 805 except has lyre tailpiece and is available in Yellow Burst finish only. Disc. 2000.

The **FM 820** has a double cutaway semi-hollowbody, bird´s-eye maple top, back and sides, maple set neck, rosewood fingerboard with pearl block inlays, 22-frets, 3-per-side tuners, 2 humbucker pickups, stop tailpiece, 2 volume, 2 tone, 3-way switch, gold hardware, available in Cherry Sunburst finish, disc. 2000.

The **FM 827** has a double cutaway semi-hollowbody, maple top, back and sides, maple set neck, rosewood fingerboard with dot inlays, 22-frets, 3-per-side tuners, 2 humbucking pickups, 2 volume, 2 tone, 3-way switch, chrome hardware, available in 2-Tone Sunburst finish only, current mfg.

The **FMA 830** has a single cutaway semi-hollowbody, maple top, maple back and sides, maple set neck, rosewood fingerboard with pearl block inlays, 22-frets, 3-per-side tuners, 2 humbucker pickups, 2 volume, 2 tone, 3-way switch, chrome hardware, available in 2-Tone Sunburst finish only, current mfg.

The **FMA 850** has a single cutaway semi-hollowbody, Florentine cutaway, maple top, back, and sides, maple set neck, rosewood fingerboard with pearl block inlays, 3-per-side tuners, 22-frets, vibrato bridge, 2 humbucker pickups, 2 volume, 2 tone, 3-way switch, chrome hardware, available in Trans. red finish, disc. 2000.

The **FMA 870** has a single cutaway semi-hollowbody, spruce top, sycamore back and sides, maple set neck, rosewood fingerboard with pearl block inlays, 22-frets, 3-per-side tuners, 2 humbucker pickups, 2 volume, 2 tone, 3-way switch, gold hardware, available in Trans. Amber finish only, current mfg. The **FMA 88** has a single cutaway semi-hollowbody, spruce top, sycamore back and sides, maple set neck, rosewood fingerboard with pearl block inlays, 22-frets, 3-per-side tuners, 1 humbucker pickup, black pickguard, 1 volume, 1 tone, gold hardware, available in Yellow Burst finish only, disc. 2000.

ELECTRIC BASS: COMMAND BASS SERIES

The **PBM 43T** has a offset double cutaway solid body, round top, maple set neck, rosewood fingerboard with dot inlays, 24-frets, 2-per-side tuners, 2 pickups, 1 volume, 2 tone, 1 balance, chrome hardware, available in Rainbow Pearl finish only, mfg. 2001-present.

The **PBM 46E** has an offset double cutaway solid body, mahogany round top, 5-piece set neck, rosewood fingerboard with dot inlays, 24-frets, 2-per-side tuners, 2 pickups, volume, middle, bass, and balance controls, gold hardware, available in Natural finish only, mfg. 2001-present.

The **PBM 47T** has an offset double cutaway soft maple solid body, maple/walnut/bubinga neck-through body, rosewood fingerboard with dot inlays, 24-frets, 2-per-side tuners, 2 Music Man 4 pickups, 1 volume, 2 tone, 1 balance, gold hardware, available in Natural finish only, current mfg.

The **PBM 48** has an offset double cutaway solid body, ash round top, maple bolt-on neck, rosewood fingerboard with dot inlays, 24-frets, 4 on 1 side tuners, 2 pickups, volume, bass, mid, and balance controls, chrome hardware, available in Natural finish only, mfg. 2001-present.

**Petillo Guitar
courtesy Petillo Guitars**

The **PBM 56E** has a 5-string, offset double cutaway solid body, burl round top, maple set neck, rosewood fingerboard with dot inlays, 24-frets, 3/2 tuners, 2 pickups, volume, middle, bass and balance controls, gold hardware, available in Brown Burst finish only, mfg. 2001-present.

The **PBM 58-8** has a 8-string, offset double cutaway solid body, available with bolt-on or set maple neck, rosewood fingerboard with dot inlays, 24-frets, 4-per-side tuners, 2 GB-4 pickups, controls for volume, treble, mid, bass and balance, chrome hardware, available in Pearl White finish only, mfg. 2001-present.

The **PBM-58-12** has a 12-string, offset double cutaway solid body, quilted round top, set or bolt-on maple neck, rosewood fingerboard with dot inlays, 24-frets, 6-per-side tuners, 2 GB-4 pickups, volume, mid, bass and balance controls, chrome hardware, available in Trans. Black finish only, mfg. 2001-present.

The **PBM-59T** has a 5-string, offset double cutaway solid body, oak round top, maple/walnut/bubinga neck-through body, 24-frets, 3/2 tuners, 2 Music Man 5 pickups, 1 volume, 2 tone, 1 balance, gold hardware, available in Trans. Amber finish only, current mfg.

PHILIP KUBICKI TECHNOLOGY

Instruments currently built and distributed by Philip Kubicki Technology of Santa Barbara, CA. Factory direct sales. Instruments previously built in Clifton, NJ.

Luthier Phil Kubicki began building acoustic guitars at age 15. Kubicki was one of the first employees hired by Roger Rossmeisel at Fender, and was part of Rossmeisl's staff during production of the LTD model. After leaving Fender, Kubicki gained a reputation for his custom guitar building. He formed his own company, Philip Kubicki Technology (PKT) to produce acoustic guitars, components (especially high quality necks), and short scale travel electric guitars.

In 1983, Kubicki formalized design plans for the Ex Factor 4 bass. This revolutionary headless-designed bass debuted in 1985. In 1988, Kubicki entered into a trademark and licensing deal with Fender Musical Instruments Corporation which allowed him time for research while Fender built, distributed, and marketed the concept of the Factor bass. By 1992, the deal was dissolved, and Kubicki regained control of his bass designs.

Currently, Kubicki continues to oversee distribution of his namesake basses. In addition, Kubicki is available for guitar repair and refretting of vintage, acoustic, and jazz guitars in Santa Barbara, California.

ELECTRIC

Many people are not aware of the custom guitars that luthier Kubicki has built. There are two models of short scale travel guitars, built in quantities of less than 300: The Arrow (a Flying V) and another based roughly on a Les Paul. Both instruments have high quality pickups and hardware, and are generally signed and numbered by Kubicki. Kubicki has also built a number of quality acoustic guitars, again in limited amounts.

ELECTRIC BASS

All instruments are available in Bahama Green, Black, Charcoal Pearl, Midnight Blue Pearl, Red, Tobacco Sunburst, Transparent Blue Burst, Transparent Burgundy, Red, White and Yellow finishes. Kubicki also makes custom basses that feature exotic woods and the like. For more information on these refer to the website to see what is in stock.

EX FACTOR 4 - offset double cutaway wave style maple body with screened logo, laminated maple neck, 32 in. to 36 in. scale, 24-fret ebony fingerboard, fixed aluminum bridge with fine tuners (reverse tuning design), 4 string anchors on peghead with low E string clasp (D Tuner), black hardware, 2 Kubicki humbucker pickups, stacked volume/mix control, stacked treble/bass control, 5-position rotary switch, active electronics, mfg. 1985-present.

MSR	$2,795		$2,250	$1,750	$1,500	$1,300	$1,050	$850	$650

This model has fretless fingerboard or ⅝-string configuration optional. The E string clasp allows the player access to the two fret extension (i.e., down to D without retuning) on the headstock.

Factor 4 - similar to Ex Factor 4, except has no low E string clasp (D Tuner), 34 in. scale, current mfg.

MSR	$2,595		$2,075	$1,675	$1,470	$1,265	$1,050	$855	$650

There was also a Factor 5-string produced in the late 1980s.

KEY FACTOR 4 - offset double cutaway wave style maple body with screened logo, bolt-on laminated maple neck, 24-fret rosewood fingerboard, fixed aluminum bridge, 2-per-side tuners, black hardware, 2 Kubicki humbucker pickups, stacked volume/mix control, stacked treble/bass control, 5-position rotary switch, active electronics, mfg. 1994-present.

MSR	$1,795		$1,450	$1,200	$1,000	$850	$700	$550	$425

Add $130 for maple fingerboard. Add $130 for fretless fingerboard.

Key Factor 5 - similar to Key Factor 4, except has 5 strings, 3/2-per-side tuners, mfg. 1994-present.

MSR	$1,995		$1,550	$1,300	$1,100	$900	$750	$600	$475

PHOENIX GUITAR COMPANY

Instruments previously produced in Phoenix, AZ, from 1994-96.

Througout the late 1980s and into the early 1990s, Intel chip designer George Leach pursued the construction of guitars as a hobby during his vacation time from work. He attended guitar construction seminars around the country including one given by Frank Finochio. By 1993, he came to the conclusion that the only way to fully indulge in guitar building was to open his own company. In early 1994, he purchased a two-building property in downtown Phoenix, Arizona. Matt Minton was hired as the production manager. Later in 1994, two other luthiers were hired. The property was divided into a retail shop in the front building and production in the back. The retail shop sold Heritage, Santa Cruz, and Breedlove for new instruments and also dealt with used instruments. They also performed repairs.

George focused on a model called the Nylon OM, which he considered to be the ultimate fingerstlye acoustic. Most other instruments were custom order guitars based on pre-war style-28 Martins. There were less than 50 instruments built by the company. In late 1995, George's entire original staff was hired away by Gibson, and he closed the shop. He finished up production on the few outstanding orders from a shop in his garage. In 1996, he was still building a few guitars with the name Phoenix, but has since ceased. Information courtesy: David Costner, May, 2001.

ELECTRIC

Serial numbers were attached to guitars and the following scheme can be used. Seven numbers were utilized MMYYXXX with MM being the month, YY being the year, and XXX being the production number starting with 001.

The **Chuck Hill** electric featured an alder body with a figured maple top, Fender vintage style tremolo, and three single coil pickups. The price was $1,400 and two were produced. Various Fender electric guitars were built with prices ranging from $800 to $1,200. About 6 of these were produced.

PICKARD

Instruments previously built in England from the late 1970s through the mid-1980s.

These good quality solid body guitars feature original designs, pickups and hardware by custom builder Steve Pickard (source: Tony Bacon and Paul Day, *The Guru's Guitar Guide*).

PIGNOSE

Instruments currently produced overseas. Distributed by Pignose in Las Vegas, NV.

Pignose amplifiers have been around since 1972. A kid went to a distributor in Oakland with this prototype amp that was built in a wooden box. The idea of a portable, battery operated amp wasn't taken by storm from the distributor in Oakland. He later gave a prototype to Terry Kath of Chicago who took interest in the idea. The volume knob kept coming loose and he brought it his tech. The rubber knob was melted and when it was fixed, Terry said that it looked like a pig's nose. Some of the first models were produced with these pignose knobs, and there only two of them known in existence. It's funny how names sometimes come about.

This amp was one of the first that was completely portable amplifier. Now Pignose offers amps that are run strictly on DC battery power along with a rechargeable model. Not only are these amps novel ideas, they are also fairly cheap. They currently offer a wide range of products, including some tube models. They also have some electric guitar models available now. A full size electric model PEG is available for $169. For more information contact Pignose directly (see Trademark Index).

PLAYER

Instruments previously built in Scarsdale, NY during the mid-1980s.

The Player model MDS-1B attempted to give the musician control over his sound by providing pop-in modules that held different pickups. The MDS-1B model was routed for two modules (other models were either routed for one or three). The plastic modules that housed the DiMarzio pickups were inserted from the back of the guitar into mounting rings that had four phospor-bronze self-cleaning contacts. Empty modules were also available if the musician wanted to install his own choice of pickups to the guitar.

The offset double cutaway body was one piece Honduran mahogany, and featured a bolt-on neck with either rosewood or ebony or maple fingerboards. The headstock had six on one side Gotoh mini tuners, and the bridge was a Kahler locking tremolo. The scale length was 25 1/2 in. and had 22-frets. Controls consisted of a master volume and master tone, individual volume knobs for each pickup, and a 3-way pickup selector switch. The price of $1,100 included a hardshell case, but the pickups were optional!

PLAYMATE

Instruments currently produced in China, Korea, or Japan. Distributed by Dean Musical Instruments and Aramadillo Enterprises in Clearwater, FL.

Playmate is a trademark used by the Dean Musical Instrument company. These guitars represent beginner guitars that are priced very affordable. The models are based off of some of Dean's popular models like the Avalanche and Evo. Most guitars retail for less than $200 and most guitars are available for sale around $100. Player packs are also available. For more information contact Dean directly (see Trademark Index).

PLEASANT

Instruments previously produced in Japan circa late 1940s through the mid 1960s.

These Japanese-built solid body guitars were built between 1947 to 1966. The manufacturer is still unknown. There is no evidence of the brand being imported to the American market (source: Michael Wright, *Vintage Guitar Magazine*).

POOLE CUSTOM GUITARS

Instruments previously built in Kent, England.

Luthier Sid Poole built handcrafted custom made electric guitars. Poole bypassed the world of CNC or CAD/CAM and did all the body and neck shaping by hand, as well as spraying the nitrocellulose finishes himself. These handcrafted instruments are heavily favored by many of the United Kingdom's guitar players such as Bernie Marsden (Whitesnake) and Geoff Whitehorn (Paul Rodgers Band).

The majority of Poole's instruments were built as custom order only, and many feature a wide variety of options. The *Blue Book of Electric Guitars* advises that these instruments be appraised individually by a competent dealer/collector with a lot of experience.

PREMIER

Instruments currently produced in Korea, since the early 1990s. Distributed in the U.S. market by Entertainment Music Marketing Corporation (EMMC) of Deer Park, NY. Instruments previously produced in New York from the 1930s to the 1970s. Later models were manufactured in Japan.

Premier was the brand name of the Peter Sorkin Music Company. Premier-branded solid body guitars were built at the Multivox company of New York, and distribution of those and the later Japanese built Premiers was handled by the Sorkin company of New York City, New York. Other guitars built and distributed (possibly as rebrands) were Royce, Strad-o-lin, Belltone, and Marvel.

Premier E-Model
courtesy Ablone Vintage

Philip Kubicki
Ex Factor 4
courtesy Philip Kubicki

P

GRADING	100% MINT	98% NEAR MINT	95% EXC+	90% EXC	80% VG+	70% VG	60% G

Premier solid body guitars featured a double offset cutaway body, and the upper bout had a "carved scroll" design, bolt-on necks, a bound rosewood fingerboard, 3+3 headstocks (initially; later models featured 6-on-a-side), and single coil pickups. Later models of the mid to late 1960s featured wood bodies covered in sparkly plastic.

Towards the end of the U.S. production in the mid 1960s, the **Custom** line of guitars featured numerous body/neck/electronics/hardware parts from overseas manufacturers like Italy and Japan. The guitars were then assembled in the U.S, and available through the early 1970s.

Some models, like the acoustic line, were completely made in Japan during the early 1970s. Some Japanese-built versions of popular American designs were introduced in 1974, but were discontinued two years later. By the mid 1970s, both the Sorkin company and Premier guitars had ceased. Multivox continued importing and distributing Hofner instruments as well as Multivox amplifiers through the early 1980s. Hofners are currently distributed by the Entertainment Music Marketing Corporation of New York, as well as the current line of Premier solid body electric guitars and basses (source: Michael Wright, *Guitar Stories*, Volume One).

Current Premier models are built in Korea, and feature a slimmed (or sleek) strat-style guitar body and P-style bass body. New list prices range are around $200-$300.

ELECTRIC

SCROLLBODY E-721/E-725/E-729/E-733 - double cutaway with scroll bass bout, bolt-on neck, rosewood fingerboard with dot inlay, 3-per-side or 6-on-a-side (older) tuners, long pickguard, single pickup, various knobs, nickle hardware, available in Ruby (E-721), Natural (E-725), Ebony (E-729), or Sunburst (E-733) finishes, mfg. 1958-1970.

1958-1962	N/A	$500	$425	$350	$300	$250	$200
1962-1965	N/A	$400	$325	$275	$225	$175	$125
1965-1970S	N/A	$300	$250	$200	$170	$140	$100

In 1963, the style was changed to a plastic covered body

PROFILE

Instruments previously produced in Japan during the mid- to late 1980s.

Profile guitars are generally good quality models based on Fender designs (source: Tony Bacon and Paul Day, *The Guru's Guitar Guide*).

PULSE

Instruments previously built in Korea during the mid- to late 1980s.

These entry level to intermediate quality solid body guitars feature designs based on classic American favorites (source: Tony Bacon and Paul Day, *The Guru's Guitar Guide*).

PURE-TONE

See chapter on House Brands.

This trademark has been identified as a House Brand of Selmer (UK) (source: Willie G. Moseley, *Stellas & Stratocasters*).

PUNISHER

By Gene Simmons. Instruments previously produced in CA during the mid-1990s.

The Gene Simmons Punisher is a bass guitar built to the exact specifications of Kiss bassist, Gen Simmons. Each bass was individually numbered and signed. It is unknown how many of these were produced. An unknown guitar maker produced this guitar and distributed by GHS.

ELECTRIC BASS

GENE SIMMONS PUNISHER - double pointed cutaway body with point at bottom, 24-fret rosewood fingerboard with diamond inlays, 2-per-side tuners, two EMG pickups (1 J-style, 1 P-style), 2 knobs, 3-way switch, Schaller bridge and hardware, chrome hardware, available in Black, Tobacco Sunburst, or Two-Tone Natural Wood finishes, mfg. circa mid 1990s.

N/A	$1,200	$1,000	$850	$700	$600	$500

Last MSR was $1,500

P

Section Q

QUEST

Instruments previously built in Japan during the mid-1980s. Distribution in the U.S. market was handled by Primo, Inc. of Marlboro, MA.

Quest solid body guitars featured some original designs as well as designs based on classic American favorites. Overall, the quality of the instruments were medium to good, a solid playable rock club guitar.

ELECTRIC

Some of the instruments featured in the Quest line while they were briefly imported to the U.S. were an Explorer copy with turned-down point on the treble horn (**ATAK-6X**), and a Bass model similar to a P-Bass with squared off horns and P/J pickup combination (**Manhatten M3-BZ**). Quest instruments are generally priced between $175 and $350.

QUEST MINI GUITARS

Instruments currently distributed by Music Industries Corporation, located in Floral Park, NY.

These mini instruments come in 2 basic configurations: the AP-5 Traveler guitar, and the AP-7 Baby Shark. Both are 3/4 scale, the AP-5 Traveler features a solid wood body and neck, and both have a built-in amplifier/speaker.

Q

NOTES

Q

Section R

R. HAYES INSTRUMENTS

Please refer to the H (Hayes) section in this text.

Following three-and-a-half years of designing, prototyping, and licensing negotiations, Rick Hayes and R. Hayes Instruments of Cincinnati, Ohio, unveiled the first in a series of unique licensed sculpted guitars at the 1998 Summer Session NAMM show in Nashville. Leading the product line is a **Bugs Bunny** model with a worldwide limited edition of only one hundred pieces. It is not simply a guitar with characters sculpted into it, it is a character "sculpted" into a guitar - with the integrity of value with a Warner Bros. stamp of approval. This guitar marries artistic form with outstanding musical attributes. Each instrument is part of the complete set of one hundred, yet the nature of the handwork involved ensures that each is unique in its own right.

As part of the baby boomer generation, Hayes grew up with the Looney Tunes characters - and now he can share them with his teenage sons who find them as captivating as ever. Following a stint with Kenner Products working as a designer on the original Star Wars toy line, Hayes has since managed to keep a hand in music- and art-related projects at all times. Hayes admits that this has been his most exciting project to date.

Following the Bugs Bunny model will be a **Sylvester** with Tweety Bird model, then **Yosemite Sam** and on to several other Warner Bros. character guitars. Negotiations are currently underway with other unrelated licensing entities, as well as other Warner Bros. movie properties. Regardless of the model, only top-of-the-line materials and parts are chosen for their musical and aesthetic qualities. The retail price is $12,000 per instrument, and they will be sold through the R. Hayes website, Warner Bros. Studio stores, and through select retail outlets (company information courtesy Lyn Ebbing, R. Hayes Instruments).

ELECTRIC

The Bugs Bunny guitar is constructed of top grade AAA maple that is individually carved and painstakingly sanded, then airbrushed, clearcoated, and buffed to a high gloss shine. The Canadian hard rock maple neck is reinforced with a unique two-way double action adjustable truss rod, and topped with a natural ebony fingerboard detailed with intricate mother-of-pearl inlay. The neck is then secured with a custom engraved and numbered solid brass neckplate. Added features include a custom-wound humbucker pickup, LP JR. bridge, Gotoh locking tuners, and a graphite nut. Retail price is $12,000, and the edition is limited to only one hundred pieces. Each instrument travels in a custom fit Anvil ATA (Air Travel Association) approved flight case with combination lock, and is accompanied by a color Certificate of Authenticity placed in a gold embossed leather portfolio hand signed by Hayes. Additional measures have been taken to provide authenticity protection.

R & L

See Roman & Lipman.

RAJ GUITAR CRAFTS

Instruments currently built in Asia. Distributed by L.A. Guitar Works of Reseda, CA.

All RAJ models are constructed from Southsea hardwoods, and feature meticulously inlaid shells that highlight the body designs. The current models include the **Warbird** ($1,295), which possesses a body design that follows "superstrat" lines. The **Panther** ($1,395) body design is reminiscent of the Fender Jaguar model, albeit with more flowing body curves. The **Shark's** ($1,195) original design suggests a cross between a Flying V and Bo Diddley's rectangular guitar of the 1950s (prettier than the description suggests). All models feature a one-piece maple neck, or maple with rosewood fingerboard with the S.A.T. (Side Adjustment Truss rod) which allows for neck adjustments while the guitar is still fully strung.

RKS GUITARS

Instruments currently produced in Thousand Oaks, CA since circa 2000.

RKS Guitars was co-founded by Ravi Sawhney and Dave Mason. These guitars are hand-built in the U.S. and represent thousands of hours in designing and testing. The Open Architecture design on the guitar allows the guitar to be taylored to many different players. The front of the guitar is split into three parts. The body is a molded polymer and two open chambers are held together by aluminum or wood rods. For more information, contact RKS directly (see Trademark Index).

ELECTRIC

RKS guitars come in a variety of styles, yet they all have the same basic design. The **Original** is the first model to be released and is a double cutaway solidbody. The Original is also available as a hollow body. The **Boomerang** is a Flying V type of style. The **Wave** is another double cutaway with flared sides at the bottom. A five-string bass is also available.

RWK GUITARS

Instruments currently built in Highland Park, IL since 1991. Distributed by RWK Guitars of Highland Park, IL.

After achieving some success repairing guitars both for himself and friends in the music business, Bob Karger started hand-making guitars in 1991. He wanted to build something that was not only contemporary, but would also stand the test of time. That is why the company slogan is "Classic Guitars Built Today." The initial design, which, to date, is the only design built, is named "SET." This is an acronym for Solid Electric Through-neck.

RKS Boomerang
courtesy RKS Guitars

RKS Wave
courtesy RKS Guitars

R

GRADING	100% MINT	98% NEAR MINT	95% EXC+	90% EXC	80% VG+	70% VG	60% G

His goal is to build a guitar which takes advantage of what has been developed so far in the solid electric guitar world and go that extra step. The body is highly contoured, highlighted by the noticeable lack of an upper bout, to provide comfort and ease of play. Its through-neck design, along with having the strings anchored through the back of the body, is directly aimed at generating maximum sustain. Because they are handmade, this provides the flexibility of being able to substitute parts and variation in construction aspects, such as neck feel and radius, to easily suit the musician's preference, (biography courtesy Bob Karger, RWK Guitars, July 18, 1996).

ELECTRIC

S.E.T. (SOLID ELECTRIC THROUGH-NECK) - single cutaway ergonomically shaped maple body, solid maple through-neck design, cream top binding, 24-fret bound ebony fingerboard with dot inlay, string through-body bridge, 3-per-side Schaller tuners, gold-plated hardware, 2 humbucker pickups, 2 volume and 2 tone controls, 3-position switch, Translucent Natural finish, current mfg.

MSR	$800		$800	$725	$650	$575	$500	$400	$300

PHOENIX - Gibson Reverse Firebird body design, solid mahogany, neck-thru body construction, rosewood fingerboard, two mini-humbucking pick-ups, volume and tone bell knobs, banjo style tuners, tune-o-matic style bridge, chrome or gold hardware, current mfg.

MSR	N/A

RAINSONG

All-graphite acoustic guitars currently produced in Woodinville, WA since 2001. Projection Series and Parlor Series instruments produced in Korea with soundboards built in Woodinville, WA. Distributed by RainSong Graphite Guitars. All-graphite instruments were previously produced in Maui, HI from 1994-2001. No Rainsong full-electric guitars are currently produced.

RainSong Graphite Guitars was founded by Dr. John A Decker Jr. in Maui, Hawaii. Decker, a physicist with degrees in engineering, began researching and developing composite acoustic guitars in 1985. The goal was to produce a fine-sounding, high-quality composite acoustic guitar that would be impervious to changes in humidity and temperature. Members of the design team included Dr. Decker, noted luthier Lorenzo Pimentel and composites expert George Clayton. In December, 1994, after a prolonged research and development period, full production facilities were opened in Maui, Hawaii. The first generation of RainSongs were built using traditional bracing patterns. By 1997, the company offered a complete range of acoustic guitars, acoustic basses, and jazz archtops.

In 1998, Ashvin Coomar took over as the President/CEO of the company. With an engineering and business background, Coomar hit the road running. With the help of Dr. Decker, Coomar developed a new soundboard technology, called Projection Tuned Layering™, that dramatically improved the volume and bass response of the instruments. In 1999, RainSong decided to narrow its line to one offering, the WS1000, that used the new Projection Tuned Layering™ technology. By late 2000, the company began leveraging the success of the WS1000 by introducing other models that used the same technology.

In 2001, RainSong relocated its entire operations to Woodinville, Washington. This move was based on economics – better access to materials and skilled craftsmen and lower shipping costs. The company currently employs seven people. Decker is now the chairman and continues to reside in Maui, Hawaii.

ELECTRIC

JZ1000 - slim body cutaway jazz guitar design, equipped with EMG dual active humbucker pickups, trapeze tailpiece, all-graphite construction, mfg. 1999-2001.

	$1,900	$1,750	$1,500	$1,250	$1,100	$995	$775

Last MSR was $2,295.

RALEIGH

Instruments currently built in Chicago, IL. Distributed by the Aloha Publishing and Musical Instrument Company of Chicago, IL.

The Aloha company was founded in 1935 by J.M. Raleigh. True to the nature of a House Brand distributor, Raleigh's company distributed both Aloha instruments and amplifiers and Raleigh brand instruments through his Chicago office. Acoustic guitars were supplied by Harmony, and initial amplifiers and guitars for the Aloha trademark were supplied by the Alamo company of San Antonio, Texas. By the mid-1950s, Aloha was producing their own amps, but continued using Alamo products (source: Michael Wright, *Vintage Guitar Magazine*).

RALSTON

Instruments currently built in Grant Town, WV.

Ralston currently offers three models with regular or figured maple tops, two humbuckers, volume/tone controls, switching for series/parallel or single coil, and rosewood fingerboards. The **R/B** is a double cutaway body style for rock or blues players, while the **V** is a single cutaway for all styles of music. Ralston's **Original** model is all that (and a bag of picks) - a novel eye-catching design with two forward body cutaways as well as two cutaways on the rear bout as well! Contact Ralston for pricing and availability.

RAMTRACK

Instruments currently built in Redford, MI. Distributed by World Class Engineered Products, Inc. of Redford, MI.

The innovative people at Ramtrack have attempted to answer the age-old dilemma of the working musician: how many guitars do you need to bring to a show to convincingly recreate famous guitar sounds? Obviously, a single coil pickup does not sound like a humbucker, and different configurations of pickups exist on a multitude of solid body guitar designs. The Ramtrack guitar design consists of a solid body guitar with cassettes containing different pickup combinations that are removable from the body.

Inventor James Randolph came up with the concept for the Ramtrak when he was faced with compromising his playing style to accommodate the type of guitar loaded with the proper pickups needed to record the tracks for any given song, i.e.: Strats play and sound different than a Les Paul. Though the concept of removable pickups is not a new one, Ramtrack excels in the execution of how the cassettes are installed and removed from the guitar. Ramtrak requires no tools for changing the pickup cassette.

GRADING	100% MINT	98% NEAR MINT	95% EXC+	90% EXC	80% VG+	70% VG	60% G

Ramtrak guitars (**Model RG-ST**) feature a pacific maple body, bolt-on hardrock maple neck, 22-fret rosewood fingerboard, standard tremolo, and an aluminum extrusion cassette plate. Pickup cassettes are loaded with the most popular pickups on the market. The guitars are presently manufactured by CNC in Korea, and parts are shipped to Michigan (where final assembly and inspection takes place).

RANGE RIDER

See chapter on House Brands.

This trademark has been identified as a House Brand of the Monroe Catalog House (source: Willie G. Moseley, *Stellas & Stratocasters*).

RANSOM

Instruments currently built in San Francisco, CA.

Ransom custom builds high quality bass guitars in a 4-, 5-, and 6-string configuration. Basses are constructed of alder bodies with quilted or flame maple tops, 24-fret maple, rosewood, or ebony fingerboards, and feature Bartolini, EMG, or Seymour Duncan pickups. Retail prices range from $1,500 to $2,200. For further information, contact Ransom directly (see Trademark Index).

RAREBIRD

Instruments currently built in Denver, CO since 1978. Distributed by the Rarebird Guitar Laboratory of Denver, CO.

Luthier Philip Bruce Clay apprenticed in a small Denver repair shop from 1974 to 1976, where he learned the basics of guitar repair. Later, he attended the Guitar Research and Design Center in Vermont (under the direction of Charles Fox), and graduated in February of 1978.

The **Rarebird** objective has been to build a durable, high quality instrument since the opening of its shop. Custom options are virtually limitless with over fifty species of hardwood on hand, and Clay´s twenty-plus years of experience can help guide the customer to the tones so desired. Clay´s approach is to simply talk the customer through the different options, systematically explaining the combinations. Having built over 1,200 instruments since 1978, Clay celebrated his 25th Anniversary in 2003.

Noted **Rarebird** features are multi-laminate necks and graphite reinforcements for stability, heelless bodies - either neck-through or set-in (glued in) for sustain and complete access, and semi-hollow guitar designs to achieve a rich and full balanced tone. For more information, refer to Rarebird´s website (see Trademark Index).

Ramtrak Guitar w/Pickup Modules courtesy Ramtrak

ELECTRIC

Rarebird produces several different electric guitar and bass models. Prices start at $1,200 for standard production models and $2,250 for custom made instruments. Most of the custom models are available in a variety of options. Bass guitars come in five- and six-string configurations. Mini guitars are available and start at $500.

RAT FINK

Instruments currently produced since 2002. Currently distributed by Lace Music of Huntington Beach, CA.

Rat Fink is a series of amplifiers and guitars that are based on characters that were created by "Big Daddy" Ed Roth. These products were released at the Winter NAMM show in 2002. There was an animated video of these characters playing in the Lace booth featuring the new amplifiers and guitars. Rat Fink has appeared more on show cars and other related memorabilia. Ken Mitchroney has painted designs on Rat Fink guitars as well.

ELECTRIC

GUITAR - double cutaway original design body, 21-fret rosewood fingerboard with dot inlay, reverse six-per-side tuners, two humbucker pickups, two knobs, three-way switch, chrome hardware, available in Flat Black, Flat Gray, Red, or Flat Pearl White with Ed Roth graphics, mfg. 2002-present.

MSR	$369		$250	$200	$170	$140	$120	$100	$80

The Rat Pack is available with a guitar in Red finish and a 10W amplifier. Retail is $499.

RAVER

Instruments previously produced in Japan during the mid-1970s.

These very entry level solid body guitars featured 2 pickups, which leads one to ask why two when costs are being cut everywhere else in the overall design (source: Tony Bacon and Paul Day, *The Guru´s Guitar Guide*).

RAY RAMIREZ BASSES

Instruments currently built in Humacao, Puerto Rico.

Ray Ramirez is currently producing the Caribbean Series Electric Upright Bass in wood and also in fiberglass. The instrument is a modern version of the Ampeg Baby Bass. The electronics include a diaphragm pickup for a deep punch and clear sound suitable for Jazz, as well as Latin music. For more information refer to their website (see Trademark Index).

Rarebird Dynohawk courtesy Rarebird

R

REBETH

Instruments previously built in England during the early 1980s.

Luthier Barry Collier built a number of custom guitars during the early 1980s, and has a strong eye for original designs (source: Tony Bacon, *The Ultimate Guitar Book*).

REDONDO

See chapter on House Brands.

This trademark has been identified as a House Brand of the Tosca Company (source: Willie G. Moseley, *Stellas & Stratocasters*).

REDWING GUITARS

Instruments currently produced in St. Albans, United Kingdom.

Luthier Patrick Eggle (of Patrick Eggle Guitars fame) left his namesake company in 1994 to start Redwing Guitars. He continues to focus on high quality solid body electric guitars that feature his original designs.

Current models, like the **Tornado Signature** and **Ventura Signature**, feature alder bodies with figured maple tops, bird's-eye maple necks, Jim Cairnes pickups, Schaller tuners, and Wilkinson bridges. For further information regarding pricing and specifications, please contact luthier Patrick Eggle directly (see Trademark Index).

REEDMAN

Instruments currently built in Korea. Distributed by Reedman America of Whittier, CA.

The Reedman Musical Instrument company is currently offering a wide range of good quality acoustic, acoustic/electric, and solid body electric guitars. For further information, please contact Reedman America directly (see Trademark Index).

REITH GUITARS

Instruments currently produced in Castle Rock, CO.

Luthier Todd Reith produces entirely hand-built guitars made in the U.S. He trained as a luthier in Boston, MA under master builders Thomas Knatt and Adam Zois. Reith is a computer engineer and uses his guitars with some of this technology. Reith offers his slogan, "Uncompromising detail and commitment to total quality!" He builds one-of-a-kind guitars with no compromises in parts or workmanship. For more information, contact Reith directly (see Trademark Index).

RELLOG

See Musima. Instruments previously built in East Germany in the late 1950s to early 1960s.

Instruments with the Rellog brand name were built by the Musima company in Germany during the late 1950s on. Earlier models were available in original designs of both solid body and semi-hollowbody configurations through the early 1960s (source: Tony Bacon and Paul Day, *The Guru's Guitar Guide*).

RENAISSANCE

Instruments previously produced in Malvern, PA from 1977 to 1980.

Renaissance guitars was founded by John Marshall, Phil Goldberg, and Dan Lamb in the late 1970s. Marshall, who played guitars in a number of local bands in the 1960s, was friends with local luthier Eric Schulte. Schulte, a former apprentice of Sam Koontz (Harptone and Standel guitars) taught Marshall guitar-building skills. In 1977, Marshall began gathering information and building jigs, and received some advice from Augustino LoPrinzi on a visit to New Jersey. Goldberg was then a current owner of a northern Delaware music store, and Lamb was a studio guitarist with prior experience from Musitronics (the effects company that built Mu-tron and Dan Armstrong modules). A number of wooden guitar and bass prototypes were built after the decision to use plexiglass was agreed upon.

In 1979, the then-fledgling company was experiencing financial troubles. Marshall left the company, and a new investor named John Dragonetti became a shareholder. Unfortunately, the company's financial position, combined with the high cost of production, did not provide any stability. Renaissance guitars closed down during the fall of 1980.

In a related sidenote, one of the Renaissance employees was guitarist/designer Dana Sutcliffe. Sutcliffe went on to form his Dana Guitar Design company, and was involved in guitar designs for St. Louis Music's Alvarez line in 1990. One awarding-winning model was the Dana Scoop guitar, which won the Music Retailer's Most Innovative award in 1992 (source: Michael Wright, *Guitar Stories*, Volume One).

Production is estimated to be around 300 to 330 instruments within three years. Serialization for Renaissance instruments has one (or two) digits for the month, two following digits for the year, and the remainder of the digits indicating consecutive production (thus, M[M]YYXXXX).

ELECTRIC/ELECTRIC BASS

Renaissance instruments were constructed from either greyish Bronze, Clear, or See Through Black Plexiglass. Necks were built of laminated maple, with ebony fingerboards and brass position markers. The 3-per-side (2-per-side for bass) headstocks had Schaller tuning machines; the instruments featured DiMarzio pickups, a brass nut and bridge, and an active circuit designed by Dan Lamb and Hank Zajac. The plexiglass models are bringing around $500.

The original 1979 product line consisted of the **Model SPG** single cutaway guitar (list $725), the **Model SPB** single cutaway bass with 2 P-Bass DiMarzios (list $750), and the **Model DPB** double cutaway bass with 1 P-Bass DiMarzio (list $625). A smaller number of pointy horn double cutaway basses and guitars were later developed (**S-100G** or **B, S-200B, T-100B,** and **T-200G**).

SPG - single cutaway guitar, plexiglass body, laminated maple neck, ebony fingerboard, 3-per-side tuners, DiMarzio pickups, mfg. late 1970s.

N/A	$650	$550	$475	$400	$325	$250

SPB - single cutaway bass, plexiglass body, laminated maple neck, ebony fingerboard, 2-per-side tuners, 2 P-Bass DiMarzio pickups, mfg. late 1970s.

N/A	$700	$600	$500	$425	$350	$275

DPB - double cutaway bass, plexiglass body, laminated maple neck, ebony fingerboard, 2-per-side tuners, 1 P-Bass DiMarzio pickup, mfg. late 1970s.

N/A	$750	$650	$550	$450	$350	$275

GRADING		100% MINT	98% NEAR MINT	95% EXC+	90% EXC	80% VG+	70% VG	60% G

T-200G - double cutaway B.C. Rich Bich style body, plexiglass body, laminated maple neck, 24-fret ebony fingerboard, 3-per-side tuners, two DiMarzio pickups, mfg. late 1970s.

		N/A	$650	$550	$475	$400	$325	$250

RENAISSANCE GUITAR COMPANY

Instruments currently built in Santa Cruz, CA. Sales and marketing are done by John Connolly & Co. in Northport, NY.

Renaissance Guitars are built by luthier Rick Turner, one of the original three partners that formed Alembic in 1970. In 1978, he left Alembic to form Turner Guitars, and opened a workshop in 1979 in Novato, California. Although artists such as Lindsey Buckingham favored Turner's guitars, the company was closed in 1981. Turner's records show that approximately 130 instruments were built during that time period (1979-1981).

Rick Turner is well-known and respected for his innovative designs that oftentimes utilize a retro style with state-of-the-art construction, materials, and most importantly, his proprietary electronics, which give amazing results. As well as building instruments, Rick Turner has written countless columns on guitar building, repairs, and products profiles in guitar magazines. Turner reopened his guitar shop in 1989, and now offers a range of instruments under both the Renaissance and Ricker Turner trademarks.

AMPLI-COUSTIC & ELECTRIC: RENAISSANCE SERIES

The Renaissance series is completed in a semi-hollowbody fashion: the solid cedar top is glued to a neck extension that runs the length of the rosewood of mahogany body. This design also features the Turner "Reference Piezo" 18-volt system.

Add $450 for New Zealand paua abalone purfling with contrasting top stripes. Add $250 for New Zealand paua abalone purfling on non-slotted pegheads. Add $350 for High Reniassance option with gloss finish with purfling and special woods (suffix H).

RENAISSANCE "AMPLI-COUSTIC" STEEL STRING RS-6 - cedar top with clear poly finish, bolt-on maple neck, walnut or cherry sides/back, Turner designed piezo bridge pickup with 18-volt Highlander preamp, low noise, volume and tone controls, current mfg.

MSR	$1,950		$1,600	$1,400	$1,250	$1,100	$950	$825	$700

RS-6-B - similar to the RS-6, except is baritone, current mfg.

MSR	$2,000		$1,600	$1,400	$1,250	$1,100	$950	$825	$700

RS-12 - similar to the RS-6, except is 12-string, current mfg.

MSR	$2,175		$1,750	$1,550	$1,400	$1,250	$1,100	$950	$800

RS-12-B - similar to the RS-12, except is baritone, current mfg.

MSR	$2,225		$1,800	$1,600	$1,400	$1,250	$1,100	$950	$800

RENAISSANCE "AMPLI-COUSTIC" STEEL STRING RN-6 - similar to RS-6, except is nylon string with bolt-on mahogany neck, current mfg.

MSR	$2,010		$1,650	$1,450	$1,250	$1,100	$950	$825	$700

RN-6-H - similar to the RN-6, except has hybrid steel/nylon with slim 14-fret mahogany neck, slot head, and Thomastik/Infeld ropecore strings, current mfg.

MSR	$2,060		$1,700	$1,500	$1,300	$1,150	$1,000	$875	$750

RENAISSANCE STEEL STRING (RSS-1) - cedar top, mahogany laminate back and sides, bound in black, mahogany neck with adjustable truss rod, 24-fret rosewood fingerboard (joins body at 14th fret), 25 21/32 in. scale, paua shell dot inlays and side dots, Turner "Reference Piezo" system, 18-volt Highlander Audio buffer electronics, one volume knob, Natural finish, disc. 1998.

Last MSR was $1,675.

RSS-2 - similar to the RSS-1, except features a Rosewood laminate back and sides, ebony fingerboard, tortoise celluloid binding with half-herringbone purfling around top, multiple veneer overlays on peghead, disc. 1998.

Last MSR was $2,050.

RENAISSANCE NYLON STRING (RNS-1) - similar to the RSS-1, except rosewood neck width at nut is 2 in. or 1.875 in., and paua shell side dots only, disc. 1998.

Last MSR was $1,650.

RNS-2 - similar to the RNS-1, except features a rosewood laminate back and sides, ebony fingerboard, tortoise celluloid binding with half-herringbone purfling around top, multiple veneer overlays on peghead, disc. 1998.

Last MSR was $2,100.

AMPLI-COUSTIC & ELECTRIC: T SERIES

MODEL T - a new series designed in 1996, with the blues or bottleneck player in mind, the Model T is a modern recreation of the early 1930s George Beauchamp/Paul Barth "double horseshoe" magnetic "Rick" pickup featuring Alnico magnets, affixed to a solid Honduran mahogany or American swamp ash (disc.) body that has a colorful front and back laminate of Formica Color-Core. The hard rock maple bolt-on neck features an adjustable truss rod and double graphite reinforcing, and is designed for heavier strings. Though the design screams retro, the hardware is quite modern, including a Wilkinson stop bridge/tailpiece, and Schaller nickel roller bridge. Options include the Wilkinson GTB 100 combination bridge; or Bigsby and Schaller "tune-o-matic" roller bridge combined with either a Turner Bar tailpiece, Bigsby vibrato, or the Hipshot Trilogy (multiple tunings) tailpiece, Standard colors include Rosetta Boomerang, Arctic White, Black, Ferrari Red, and Hawaiian Blue, current mfg.

MSR	$1,900		$1,550	$1,350	$1,200	$1,050	$900	$775	$650

Add $200 for Bigsby and Schaller roller bridge. Add $300 with Hipshot Trilogy multi-tuning tailpiece.

Renaissance Electric Bass
courtesy Bass Palace

Renaissance G.C. Ampli-Coustic
courtesy Renaissance G.C.

R

GRADING	100% MINT	98% NEAR MINT	95% EXC+	90% EXC	80% VG+	70% VG	60% G

ELECTRIC BASS: ELECTROLINE SERIES

Electroline basses feature exotic wood, bolt-on necks, reinforcing graphite bars, and Turner-designed pickups and electronics.

ELECTROLINE 1 EL-434-P - swamp ash or Honduran mahogany body, bolt-on bird's-eye maple neck, fretted or fretless ebony or pakka wood fingerboard, 34 in. scale, Wilkinson bridge with Turner Reference Piezo pickups, Schaller or Hipshot Ultra-lite tuning machines, on-board Highlander Audio electronics, multiple veneer overlays on peghead, available in Vintage Clear, Translucent Maroon, Indigo, or Forest Green, current mfg.

MSR	$2,800	$2,300	$2,050	$1,850	$1,650	$1,500	$1,350	$1,100

Add $250 for piezo and single Turner "Diamond" magnetic pickup. Add $500 for two Diamond pickups. Add $100 for Custom colors.

Electroline Special ELS-434-P - similar to the EL-434-P, except has a solid swamp ash body, plain maple neck, and a piezo pickup only, disc. 2004.

	$1,700	$1,500	$1,350	$1,200	$1,050	$925	$800

Last MSR was $2,090.

Add $250 for piezo and single Turner "Diamond" magnetic pickup. Add $375 for two Diamond pickups.

ELECTROLINE 1 EL-535-P - similar to the EL-434-P Electroline except is in 5-string configuration with a 35 in. scale neck, current mfg.

MSR	$3,100	$2,500	$2,200	$1,950	$1,750	$1,550	$1,400	$1,250

Add $300 for piezo and two Turner "Diamond" magnetic pickups. Add $100 for Custom colors.

Electroline Special ELS-535-P - similar to the EL-535-P, except has a solid swamp ash body, plain maple neck, and a piezo pickup only, disc. 2004.

MSR	$2,230	$1,800	$1,600	$1,400	$1,250	$1,100	$975	$850

Add $375 for piezo and two Turner "Diamond" magnetic pickups.

ELECTROLINE 2 - similar to the Electroline 1, except features a 21-fret fretted neck, Turner "Diamond T" magnetic pickup system, and blending electronics, disc. 2001.

Last MSR was $2,430.

Add $240 for 5-string configuration (Model EL-25). Add $90 for Gold, Silver Flake, or 3-Tone Sunburst custom color.

ELECTRIC BASS: RENAISSANCE BASS AMPLI-COUSTIC SERIES

Add $450 for New Zealand Paua abalone purfling with contrasting top stripes. Add $250 for New Zealand paua abalone purfling on non-slotted pegheads.

RENAISSANCE RB-4-FRETTED/FRETLESS BASS - cedar top, maple neck with graphite reinforcement, walnut or cherry sides/back, current mfg.

MSR	$2,075	$1,700	$1,500	$1,300	$1,150	$1,000	$875	$750

RB-4 Special - similar to the RB-4, except has a maple neck with graphite and oiled body, current mfg.

MSR	$1,935	$1,550	$1,350	$1,200	$1,050	$900	$775	$650

RENAISSANCE RB-5 FRETTED/FRETLESS BASS - similar to RB-4, except is 5-string, fretless version is $2,305, current mfg.

MSR	$2,260	$1,850	$1,650	$1,500	$1,350	$1,200	$1,050	$900

RB-5 Special - similar to the RB-5, except has a maple neck with graphite and oiled body, current mfg.

MSR	$2,115	$1,700	$1,500	$1,350	$1,200	$1,050	$925	$800

RENO, G.H.

Instruments previously built in Tulsa, OK since 1984.

In 1984, G.H. "Jerry" Reno already a working guitarist in Tulsa, Oklahoma, set out to produce his own line of custom built guitars. His idea was a better feeling, playing, and sounding guitar "geared to the experienced player." The modest guitar shop grew into a 4,000 square foot factory, just off the famed Route 66 in Tulsa, Oklahoma. Specimans can be found dating back to the 1980s. For more information, contact G.H. Reno directly (see Trademark Index)..

ELECTRIC

No two Reno solidbody electric guitars are exactly alike. Jerry Reno, the master craftsman and chief designer at G.H. Reno, creates a tour de force in his quality, innovative designs exemplified by, but not limited to three different styles: **Hideaway**, **Honkey Tonk**, and **Rebel**. From its 4,000 square foot facility, highly customized one-of-a-kind classics are made to order. Reno bolt-on guitar necks are constructed from hard rock maple and feature select maple or pau ferro fingerboards. Guitar bodies are made from a variety of woods including swamp ash, maple, and Honduran mahogany. Special inlays and custom paint adorn many of Reno's creations. Vinyl graphics, "glow-dot" side markers, and "Single/Double Barrel" custom wound pickups are the newest additions to the ever increasing list of available options. With a current starting price of $1,495, an original "Reno" guitar can still be built to suit. Available colors include Burnt Orange, Light Blue, Light Green, Medium Blue, Metallic Gold, as well as trans. finishes and custom colors.

RESURRECTION GUITARS

Instruments currently built in Jensen Beach, FL since 1994.

In addition to building custom instruments of every conceivable type, Luthiers Pat O'Donnell and Tim O'Donnell also offer their own line of standard guitars that are true workhorses. The Standard line of guitars starts with The Barebones at $1,500, the Standard at $1,850, the Stereo Thin Line at $2,500, and the Tulip Hollow Body at $3,200. Their custom instruments all feature a laminated neck and a plethora of woods to choose from...achieving an amazing sounding instrument and a work of art. Resurrection Guitars has gained a notable reputation for the quality repair work thay have been doing for fifteen years.

R

GRADING	100% MINT	98% NEAR MINT	95% EXC+	90% EXC	80% VG+	70% VG	60% G

Resurrection Guitars is authorized by Pete Cripe to build exact replicas of the Jerry Garcia "Lightning Bolt" guitar (which was built for Jerry by Pete's son, the late Steve Cripe). These guitars are available by custom order, and only a very limited number will be obtainable. For more information, refer to the Resurrection website (see Trademark Index).

REVELATION

Also HSS Revelation. Instruments previously built in Czechoslovakia from 1993 to 1996. Distributed by Hohner/HSS, Inc., of Richmond, VA.

Revelation series guitars featured designs formulated by the Hohner Guitar Research Team, an international group consisting of English, French, German, and U.S. luthiers. Continuing that international flavor, the guitar model itself features European and Indian woods, English pickups, German tuners, American tremolo system/roller nut, and was produced in Czechoslokavia!

ELECTRIC: REVELATION SERIES

Both Revelation models feature an on-board ATN (Advanced Tonal Network) passive electronic system that is engaged at the push/pull tone switch. In bypass, the signal travels from the pickups to the volume control then directly to the output jack. In active, the signal travels from the pickups to volume to 2 tone controls (then on to the output jack). Tone control 1 is a treble roll-off, while Tone control 2's center detent offers treble cut or pickup resonance.

RTS - sleek offset double cutaway poplar body, bolt-on maple neck, 25.5 in. scale, 24-fret rosewood fingerboard with offset pearl dot inlay, Wilkinson VS100 tremolo, Wilkinson roller nut, 6-on-a-side Schaller M6 tuners, 3 Entwistle-White single coil pickups, black pickguard, volume/2 tone controls (1 is push/pull), 5-way selector, ATN passive electronic system, available in Black, Marble Red, Marble White, Red, Sunburst, Trans. Blue, Trans. Honey, or Trans. Red polyurethane finishes, mfg. 1993-96.

N/A	$500	$425	$375	$325	$275	$225

Last MSR was $899.

RTX - similar to the RTS, except has middle and bridge pickups in humbucker configuration, 3-way switch, active tone electronics, mfg. 1993-96.

N/A	$500	$425	$375	$325	$275	$225

Last MSR was $899.

**G.H. Reno Hideaway
courtesy G.H. Reno**

REVEREND

Instruments currently built in Warren, MI. Distributed by Reverend Musical Instruments of Warren, MI. Previously in Eastpointe, MI.

Joe Naylor, cofounder of J.F. Naylor Engineering (Naylor Amps) formed Reverend Musical Instruments in March, 1997 to produce American-made, vintage-style guitars. Naylor, a graduate of the Roberto-Venn School of Luthiery in 1987, has been designing and custom building guitars for the past ten years. Reverend is currently a factory-direct order company, which eliminates the middle man. Visit their website for all the information on ordering and pricing (see Trademark Index).

ELECTRIC

Reverend briefly offered the Black Cat model, which was similar to the Avenger model. The Black Cat differed in that it had no arm rest, but did have a solid white pickguard, single coil/humbucker pickup combination, volume control (no tone control), and 3-way selector switch. The Black Cat was available in Jet Black finish only (hence the name), and had a retail list price of $598. This model is only available with a rosewood fingerboard.

The **Reverend** guitar line features a wood-based phenolic top and back mated to a six-inch-wide white mahogany center block (total weight is only 6.5 pounds). Reverend models are finished with whitewall sides and **Reflecto-Hyde** tops and backs; this super tough finish is available in '57 Turquoise (disc.), '69 Orange, Aged Burgundy, Aged Yellow, Aged White (disc.), Deep Sea Teal, Fire Engine Red (disc.), Jet Black, Hunter Green (disc.), Indigo Blue (disc.), and Sky Blue finishes.

Reverend guitars are available in two different levels. The Premium line of guitars are the full-fledged version that has been produced since the start of Reverend. The Workhorse guitars are cheaper in price as they feature a single-ply pickguard, non-locking tuners, and various other limited options to keep the cost down.

Add $10 for maple fingerboard. Add $25 for phase or studio switch wiring. Add $30 for Graph Tech Guitar Bridge Saddles. Add $35 for Flame Maple or Red Mahogany wood look finishes. Add $35 for Lake Superior Blue, Moroccan Gold or Lava Swirl brushed aluminum finishes. Add $50 for Sperzel locking tuners. Add $75 for Fulcrum tremolo. Add $75 for Ultimate Bigsby tremolo. Add $150 for Hawaiian brushed aluminum finish. Add $150 for Hot Rod Flames brushed aluminum finish. Add $180 for Hawaiian smoked chrome finish. Add $180 for Hot Rod Flames smoked chrome finish.

AVENGER TL - slightly offset double cutaway semi-hollowbody, Reflecto-Hyde phenolic top and back, bolt-on satin finished maple neck, 25.5 in. scale, 22-fret rosewood fingerboard with white dot inlay, fixed bridge, chrome hardware, whitewall sides, white pearloid pickguard, chrome plated arm rest, six-on-a-side sealed die-cast tuners, 3 Kent Armstrong single coil pickups, volume/tone controls, 5-way selector, available in '57 Turquoise, Aged White (with tortoiseshell pickguard), Fire Engine Red, Hunter Green, Indigo Blue, or Jet Black, mfg. 1997-present.

MSR	$1,199		$700	$625	$550	$500	$450	$400	$350

The Jet Black finish is optional with a tortoiseshell pickguard.

**Reverend Commando
courtesy George McGuire**

R

GRADING	100% MINT	98% NEAR MINT	95% EXC+	90% EXC	80% VG+	70% VG	60% G

Avenger GT - similar to the Avenger TL, except has a humbucker in the bridge position, coil tap, mfg. 1997-1999, 2001-04.

	$699	$650	$600	$550	$500	$450	$390

Last MSR was $1,249.

Avenger TL Workhorse - similar to the Avenger Premium, except has a single-ply pickguard, non-locking tuners, various other limited options, available in '69 Orange, Aged Burgundy, Aged Yellow, Deep Sea Teal, Jet Black, or Sky Blue finishes, mfg. 2003-present.

MSR	$949	$550	$475	$425	$375	$325	$275	$225

COMMANDO GT - offset double cutaway body, Reflecto-Hyde phenolic top and back, bolt-on maple neck, 22-fret rosewood or maple neck with dot inlay, 6-on-one-side tuners, two single coil and one humbucker pickup, two knobs, five-way switch, coil tap switch, chrome hardware, available in '69 Orange, Aged Burgundy, Aged Yellow, Deep Sea Teal, Jet Black, or Sky Blue finishes, mfg. 1998-2001, 2004-present.

MSR	$1,249	$725	$650	$575	$525	$475	$425	$375

Commando GT Workhorse - similar to the Commando GT, except has a single-ply pickguard, non-locking tuners, various other limited options, mfg. 2003-present.

MSR	$979	$575	$500	$450	$400	$350	$300	$250

HITMAN - Reverend tele-style bridge pickup, zebra neck humbucker with coil tap, 3-way pickup selector, available in standard colors, disc.

	$725	$650	$595	$550	$495	$450	$375

Last MSR was $899.

ROCCO - offset double cutaway body, Reflecto-Hyde phenolic top and back, bolt-on maple neck, 22-fret rosewood or maple neck with dot inlay, 6-on-one-side tuners, two humbucker pickups, two knobs, five-way switch, two coil tap switches, chrome hardware, available in '69 Orange, Aged Burgundy, Aged Yellow, Deep Sea Teal, Jet Black, or Sky Blue finishes, mfg. 1997-present.

MSR	$1,249	$725	$650	$600	$550	$500	$450	$390

Rocco Workhorse - similar to the Rocco, except has a single-ply pickguard, non-locking tuners, various other limited options, mfg. 2003-present.

MSR	$979	$575	$500	$450	$400	$350	$300	$250

SLINGSHOT - offset double cutaway body, Reflecto-Hyde phenolic top and back, bolt-on maple neck, 22-fret rosewood or maple neck with dot inlay, 6-on-one-side tuners, two P-90 pickups, two knobs, three-way switch, two coil tap switches, chrome hardware, available in '69 Orange, Aged Burgundy, Aged Yellow, Deep Sea Teal, Jet Black, or Sky Blue finishes, mfg. 1998-present.

MSR	$1,199	$700	$625	$575	$525	$475	$425	$375

Slingshot Workhorse - similar to the Slingshot, except has a single-ply pickguard, non-locking tuners, various other limited options, mfg. 2003-present.

MSR	$949	$550	$475	$425	$375	$325	$275	$225

Slingshot Custom - similar to the Slingshot, except has 3 P-90 pickups, current mfg.

MSR	$1,249	$725	$650	$600	$550	$500	$450	$390

Slingshot Custom Workhorse - similar to the Slingshot Custom, except has a single-ply pickguard, non-locking tuners, various other limited options, mfg. 2003-present.

MSR	$979	$575	$500	$450	$400	$350	$300	$250

SPY - similar to the Avenger, except has 3 chrome lipstick tube pickups, solid white pickguard, mfg. 1997-2001.

	$725	$650	$595	$550	$495	$450	$375

Last MSR was $899.

WOLFMAN - offset double cutaway body, Reflecto-Hyde phenolic top and back, bolt-on maple neck, 22-fret rosewood or maple neck with dot inlay, 6-on-one-side tuners, two Rev-Tron humbucker pickups, two knobs, three-way switch, chrome hardware, available in '69 Orange, Aged Burgundy, Aged Yellow, Deep Sea Teal, Jet Black, or Sky Blue finishes, mfg. 2004-present.

MSR	$1,199	$700	$625	$575	$525	$475	$425	$375

Wolfman Workhorse - similar to the Wolfman, except has a single-ply pickguard, non-locking tuners, various other limited options, mfg. 2004-present.

MSR	$949	$550	$475	$425	$375	$325	$275	$225

ELECTRIC BASS

All Reverend basses were disc. in 2004. The last day to order was September 30, 2004.

BRADHOUSER 5 BASS - similar to the Rumblefish, except has two double J-Style pickups, disc. 2004.

	$875	$775	$725	$675	$625	$550	$475

Last MSR was $1,499.

RUMBLEFISH/RUMBLEFISH PJ BASS - slightly offset double cutaway semi-hollowbody, Reflecto-Hyde phenolic top and back, bolt-on satin finished maple neck, 34 in. scale, 21-fret rosewood fingerboard with white dot inlay, fixed bridge, chrome hardware, whitewall sides, white pearloid pickguard, chrome plated arm rest, four-on-a-side sealed die-cast tuners, 2 Kent Armstrong J-style pickups, 2 volume/1 tone controls, available in '57 Turquoise, Aged White (with tortoiseshell pickguard), Fire Engine Red, Hunter Green, Indigo Blue, or Jet Black, mfg. 1998-2004.

	$725	$650	$600	$550	$500	$450	$390

Last MSR was $1,249.

The Jet Black finish is optional with a tortoiseshell pickguard.

RUMBLEFISH XL BASS - similar to Rumblefish except has 1 volume/1 tone control, 3-position voicing switch (parallel, single coil, series), disc. 2001.

	$725	$625	$550	$495	$450	$395	$350

Last MSR was $929.

RUMBLEFISH 5L BASS - 5-string, long scale version of the Rumblefish, with 2 Reverend J-style pickups, 21-fret 35 in. scale aluminum reinforced neck with rosewood fingerboard, lightweight construction, mfg. 1999-2004.

	$750	$675	$625	$575	$525	$475	$400

Last MSR was $1,299.

REYNOLDS

Instruments currently built in Austin, TX.

Luthier Ed Reynolds began repairing instruments in 1974 and then building in 1976. While based in Chicago, Illinois, Reynolds gained a reputation for being a quality repairman. In 1991, Reynolds relocated to Austin, Texas and has continued to build electric guitars and basses.

RIBBECKE, TOM

Instruments currently built in Healdsburg, California. Previously built in the Santa Rosa and the San Francisco bay area in California.

Luthier Tom Ribbecke has been building and repairing guitars and basses for over twenty-three years in the San Francisco bay area. Ribbecke's first lutherie business opened in 1975 in San Francisco's Mission District, and remained open and busy for ten years. In 1985, Ribbecke closed down the storefront in order to focus directly on client commissions.

Ribbecke guitars are entirely hand built by the luthier himself, while working directly with the customer. Beyond his signature and serial number of the piece, Ribbecke also offers a history of the origin of all materials involved in construction.

All prices quoted are the base price new, and does not reflect additions to the commissioned piece. For further information, please contact luthier Tom Ribbecke directly (see Trademark Index). The *Blue Book of Acoustic Guitars* also has information on acoustic models.

ELECTRIC

THINLINE STYLE STANDARD (TESTADURA) - instrument constructed of first grade domestic maple or rosewood back and sides, solid carved top and back, ebony pickguard, carbon fiber braced, master volume and tone controls, dot inlays, and chrome hardware, available in Natural finish, current mfg.

MSR   **$8,000**

Add $400 for Sunburst finish. Add $450 for wood body binding.

RICH, B.C.

Please refer to the B section of this text.

RICHELIEU

Instruments previously built in Bridgeport, CT from 1982 to 1984.

The Richelieu company was founded by a pair of musicians to produce good quality guitars in their regional area. For a period of about three years, the Richelieu company produced customized neck-through-body **Spectre** guitars. Customers could specify various pickups and finishes. It has been confirmed that the company produced seventy-five guitars and a few bass models. A second model, the **Black Rock**, had name badges but the model itself was never produced. Unfortunately, the company ran out of funds before the model design really took off. Serial numbers are impressed into the back of the headstock (source: David J. Pavlick, Woodbury, CT).

ELECTRIC

Spectre guitars feature a neck-through design, and a Honduran mahogany body shaped roughly like a cross between an SG (dual pointy cutaways) and a Strat (rounded lower bout). Spectres feature a Gibson-esque 3-per-side headstock, chrome hardware, Leo Quan wraparound tailpiece, white pickguard, 2 humbuckers, volume and tone controls, 3-way toggle for pickup selection, and a coil tap mini-switch. Due to production problems with grain-matching the wood, most Spectre models had solid finishes (such as Blue/Gray, White, Purple, and various sparkle finishes) as opposed to a Natural wood finish. Earlier models have a screened Richelieu logo on a black peghead, block print Spectre badge, one large toggle/one mini-toggle switch, Grover tuning pegs, and DiMarzio pickups. Later models have a headstock decal that reads "Richelieu USA," an arrowhead-shaped Spectre truss rod cover, one large toggle/two mini-toggle switches, and Schaller tuners. The top cutaway was also opened up for easier playing access.

RICKENBACKER

Instruments currently produced in Santa Ana, CA. Distributed by Rickenbacker International Corporation of Santa Ana, CA. Rickenbacker instruments have been produced in CA since 1931.

In 1925, John Dopyera (and brothers) joined up with George Beauchamp and Adolph Rickenbacker and formed National to build resonator guitars. Beauchamp's attitudes over spending money caused John Dopyera to leave National and start the Dobro company. While at National, Beauchamp, Rickenbacker and Dopyera's nephew, Paul Barth, designed the Frying Pan electric lap steel. In 1929 or 1930, Beauchamp was either forced out or fired from National - and so allied himself with Adolph Rickenbacker (National's tool and die man) and Barth to form Ro-Pat-In. In the summer of 1931, Ro-Pat-In started building aluminum versions of the Frying Pan prototype. Early models have "Electro" on the headstock. Two years later, "Rickenbacker" (or sometimes "Rickenbacher") was added to the headstock, and Ro-Pat-In was formally changed to the Electro String Instrument Corporation. Beauchamp left Electro sometime in 1940, and Barth left in 1956 to form his own company.

In December of 1953, F.C. Hall bought out the interests of Rickenbacker and his two partners. The agreement stated that the purchase was complete, and Electro could "continue indefinitely to use the trade name Rickenbacker." Hall, founder of Radio-Tel and the exclusive Fender distributor, had his Fender distributorship bought out by Leo Fender and Don Randall. The Rickenbacker company was formed in 1965 as an organizational change (Electro is still the manufacturer, and Rickenbacker is the sales company). Rickenbacker instruments gained popularity as the Beatles

**Reverend Wolfman
courtesy
reverendguitars.com**

**Rickenbacker 325
courtesy Rickenbacker**

R

GRADING	100% MINT	98% NEAR MINT	95% EXC+	90% EXC	80% VG+	70% VG	60% G

relied on a number of their guitars in the 1960s. One slight area of confusion: the model names and numbers differ from the U.S. market to models imported to the U.K. market during the short period in the 1960s when Rose Morris represented Rickenbacker in the U.K (at all other times, the model numbers worldwide have been identical to the U.S. market).

In 1984, John Hall (F.C. Hall's son) officially took control by purchasing his father's interests in both the Rickenbacker, Inc. and Electro String companies. Hall formed the Rickenbacker International Corporation (RIC) to combine both interests (source: John C. Hall, Chief Executive Officer, Rickenbacker International Corporation; and Tom Wheeler, *American Guitars*).

EXPORT MODEL DESIGNATIONS

During the five years in the mid- to late 1960s (1964-1969), Rickenbacker exported a handful of models to the Rose, Morris & Company, Ltd. in England for European sales. Many of the export models have a corresponding U.S. model, although the export hollowbody models have f-holes rather than the slash hole (or none at all). Rickenbacker designated the export models with an "S" after the model number; Rose, Morris gave them a completely different number! For further information regarding Rickenbacker acoustic models, please refer to the *Blue Book of Acoustic Guitars*.

ELECTRIC: ELECTRO-SPANISH & MANDOLINS

Rickenbacker pegheads are generally of the same pattern and design. They have 3-per-side tuners and plastic, or metal, logo imprinted plates. Twelve-string pegheads, while roughly similar to the six-string pegheads, are not the same size and have 6 tuners (3-per-side) running parallel to the peghead face and 6 tuners running perpendicular with routed slots in the peghead face to accommodate string winding.

Rickenbacker currently offers the 5002V58 Mandolin, a vintage-style solid body electric mandolin based on a similar model issued in 1958. The current reproduction has a maple and walnut laminated body, 8-string configuration, and single coil pickups. Available in Fireglo or Mapleglo finishes (retail list is $1,489). Most Rickenbacker instrument necks are maple (however, some are maple/shedua laminates). Pickguards and peghead plates are usually color matched, and controls are usually pickguard mounted (any differences will be listed where appropriate). Rickenbacker color finishes include Fireglo, Jetglo, Mapleglo, Midnight Blue, Red, Turquoise, and White. Midnight Blue, Red, and White finishes come standard with black hardware, binding, nameplate, and pickguard. Fireglo, Jetglo, Mapleglo, and Turquoise finishes come standard with chrome hardware, white binding, nameplate, and pickguard. The Vintage Reissue Series models are only available with chrome parts. In 1964, Rickenbacker's "R" style trapeze tailpieces replaced all other trapeze tailpieces.

ELECTRO SPANISH - folk style, maple top, f-holes, bound body, maple back/sides/neck, 14/19-fret rosewood fingerboard with pearl dot inlay, rosewood bridge/trapeze tailpiece, pearl veneer on classic style peghead with metal logo plate, horseshoe pickup, available in Stained finish, mfg. 1932-35.

	N/A	$2,500	$2,200	$1,900	$1,600	$1,300	$1,000

In 1934, body binding and volume control were added. This model was superseded by the Ken Roberts model.

KEN ROBERTS ELECTRO-SPANISH - concert style, laminated bound mahogany top, f-holes, laminated mahogany back/sides, mahogany neck, 17/22-fret bound rosewood fingerboard with white dot inlay, compensating bridge/Kauffman vibrato tailpiece, pearloid peghead veneer with brass logo plate, 3-per-side tuners, nickel hardware, horseshoe pickup, volume control, available in Two-Tone Brown finish, mfg. 1935-1940.

	N/A	$1,200	$1,000	$850	$700	$575	$450

From 1935-1937, the volume control was octagon shaped. In 1938, round volume control with ridges replaced original parts/design.

ELECTRIC: 200 SERIES

220 HAMBURG - double cutaway maple body, through-body maple neck, 24-fret rosewood fingerboard with pearloid dot inlay, fixed bridge, 3-per-side tuners, 2 humbucker pickups, 2 volume/2 tone controls, 3-position switch, available in Fireglo, Jetglo, Mapleglo, Midnight Blue, Red, or White finishes, mfg. 1987-1995.

	N/A	$575	$450	$325	$300	$275	$250

Last MSR was $900.

260 EL DORADO - similar to 220, except has bound body/fingerboard, gold hardware, disc. 1995.

	N/A	$700	$525	$375	$350	$325	$275

Last MSR was $1,050.

ELECTRIC: 300 SERIES

This series utilizes a hollowbody, white binding, inlaid fingerboard and Rick-o-Sound jacks. These are available in Fireglo or Natural Grain finish (unless otherwise indicated). The 300 Series has also been called the Capri Series.

310 - offset pointed double cutaway semi hollow 3/4 size maple body, 21-fret rosewood fingerboard with white dot inlay, tune-o-matic bridge/trapeze tailpiece, chrome hardware, 2 covered pickups, volume/tone control, 3-position switch, available in Autumnglo, Fireglo, Mapleglo, Natural, or Two-Tone Brown finishes, mfg. 1958-1971, reintroduced 1981-88.

1958-1964	N/A	$3,500	$2,750	$2,300	$1,950	$1,700	$1,450
1965-1971	N/A	$2,500	$1,850	$1,500	$1,350	$1,150	$950
1981-1988	N/A	$500	$450	$400	$350	$300	$250

In 1963, a mixer control was added. Instruments were inconsistently produced with and without f-holes.

315 - similar to 310, except has Kauffman vibrato, mfg. 1958-1975.

1958-1964	N/A	$3,500	$2,750	$2,300	$1,950	$1,700	$1,450
1965-1969	N/A	$2,500	$1,850	$1,500	$1,350	$1,150	$950
1970-1975	N/A	$1,500	$1,100	$850	$700	$550	$400

320 - offset pointed double cutaway semi-hollow 3/4 size maple body, bi-level pickguard, through-body maple neck, 21-fret rosewood fingerboard with pearloid dot inlay, tune-o-matic bridge/R-style trapeze tailpiece, 3-per-side tuners, chrome hardware, 3 chrome bar pickups, 2 volume/2 tone/mix controls, 3-position switch, available in Fireglo, Jetglo, Mapleglo, Midnight Blue, Red, or White finishes, mfg. 1958-1994.

1958-1964	N/A	$5,000	$4,500	$4,000	$3,500	$3,000	$2,500
1965-1971	N/A	$3,500	$3,100	$2,650	$2,250	$1,950	$1,700
1972-1994	N/A	$1,000	$850	$700	$600	$500	$400

Last MSR was $1,000.

GRADING	100% MINT	98% NEAR MINT	95% EXC+	90% EXC	80% VG+	70% VG	60% G

325 - similar to 320, except has Kauffman vibrato, available in Fireglo, Mapleglo, Natural, or Two-Tone Brown finishes, mfg. 1958-1975.

1958-1964	N/A	$6,000	$5,300	$4,600	$3,900	$3,500	$3,000
1965-1971	N/A	$4,500	$3,800	$3,100	$2,350	$1,950	$1,500
1972-1975	N/A	$1,000	$850	$700	$600	$500	$400

330 - offset double cutaway semi-hollow maple body, wedge-shaped soundhole, bi-level pickguard, through-body maple neck, 24-fret rosewood fingerboard with pearl dot inlay, tune-o-matic bridge/R-style trapeze tailpiece, 3-per-side tuners, 2 single coil pickups, 2 volume/2 tone/mix controls, 3-position switch, available in Fireglo, Jetglo, Mapleglo, Midnight Blue, Red, or White finishes, mfg. 1958-present.

1958-1964	N/A	$2,500	$2,000	$1,700	$1,400	$1,100	$850
1965-1971	N/A	$2,000	$1,600	$1,300	$1,050	$900	$700
1972-1993	N/A	$1,000	$850	$700	$600	$500	$400
1994-MSR $1,419	$1,100	$900	$775	$650	$595	$450	$350

In 1963, a mixer control was added.

330/12 - similar to 330, except has 12 strings, 6-per-side tuners, mfg. 1965-present.

1965-1971	N/A	$2,200	$1,800	$1,500	$1,300	$1,100	$850
1972-1993	N/A	$1,300	$1,100	$900	$750	$625	$550
1994-MSR $1,529	$1,250	$1,000	$800	$675	$575	$475	$375

331 LIGHT SHOW - similar to 330, except has Plexiglass top with frequency controlled flashing lights, mfg. 1970-75.

	N/A	$7,500	$6,500	$5,500	$4,500	$3,800	$3,000

Originally, this model was released with an external power supply box. This model is nicknamed the Light Show.

340 - offset double cutaway semi-hollow maple body, wedge soundhole, bi-level pickguard, through-body maple neck, 24-fret rosewood fingerboard with pearl dot inlay, tune-o-matic bridge/R-style trapeze tailpiece, 3-per-side tuners, 3 single coil pickups, 2 volume/2 tone/mix controls, 3-position switch, available in Fireglo, Jetglo, Mapleglo, Midnight Blue, Red, or White finishes, mfg. 1958-present.

1958-1994	N/A	$1,200	$1,050	$900	$750	$600	$450
1995-MSR $1,549	$1,200	$1,000	$850	$700	$600	$500	$400

340/12 - similar to 340, except has 12 strings, 6-per-side tuners, mfg. 1994-present.

MSR $1,749	$1,300	$1,100	$950	$800	$675	$550	$450

350 LIVERPOOL - offset pointed double cutaway semi-hollow maple body, bi-level pickguard, through-body maple neck, 24-fret rosewood fingerboard with pearloid dot inlay, tune-o-matic bridge/R-style trapeze tailpiece, 3 chrome bar pickups, 2 volume/2 tone/mix controls, 3-position switch, stereo output, available in Fireglo, Jetglo, Mapleglo, Midnight Blue, Red, or White finishes, mfg. 1985-1995.

	N/A	$900	$750	$600	$475	$350	$275

Last MSR was $1,270.

360 - offset double cutaway semi-hollow maple body, wedge-shaped soundhole, pickguard, through-body maple neck, 21-fret bound rosewood fingerboard with pearl triangle inlay, tune-o-matic bridge/R-style trapeze tailpiece, 2 single coil pickups, 2 volume/2 tone diamond controls, 3-position switch, wired for stereo, available in Autumnglo, Black, Fireglo, Natural, or Two Tone Brown finishes, mfg. 1958-present.

1958-1964	N/A	$3,000	$2,500	$2,000	$1,500	$1,300	$1,100
1965-1974	N/A	$2,000	$1,700	$1,400	$1,150	$1,000	$850
1975-1993	N/A	$1,300	$1,100	$900	$750	$600	$450
1994-MSR $1,549	$1,250	$1,000	$875	$725	$625	$500	$400

The above description is referred to as the Old Style which ran from 1958 to 1964. In 1964, the 360 New Style was released and featured an unbound rounded top, bound soundhole and checkered body binding which ran from 1964 to 1990. In the early 1960s, round control knobs and bi-level pickguards began replacing original parts/designs. In 1960, stereo output became optional. In 1963, a mixer control was added. When the model 360 was reissued, the current model has no body binding or slash f-hole binding.

360 6/12 Convertible - 12-string, unique string damping device allows convertible operation from 12 to 6 string.

	N/A	$2,700	$2,300	$1,900	$1,600	$1,300	$1,000

360/12 - similar to 360, except has 12 strings, 6-per-side tuners, mfg. 1964-present.

1966-1969	N/A	$2,500	$2,100	$1,850	$1,500	$1,250	$1,050
1970-1993	N/A	$1,500	$1,200	$1,000	$800	$650	$500
1994-MSR $1,669	$1,350	$1,150	$975	$800	$675	$550	$450
1964-1965	N/A	$3,500	$3,000	$2,600	$2,100	$1,700	$1,400

When the model 360/12 was reissued, it featured no body binding or slash f-hole binding.

Rickenbacker 330 courtesy Dave Rogers Dave's Guitar Shop

Rickenbacker 331 Light Show courtesy Dave Rogers Dave's Guitar Shop

R

GRADING	100% MINT	98% NEAR MINT	95% EXC+	90% EXC	80% VG+	70% VG	60% G

360 WB (365 OR 360 VB) - offset double cutaway semi-hollow maple body, wedge-shaped soundhole, pickguard, through-body maple neck, 21-fret bound rosewood fingerboard with pearl triangle inlay, tune-o-matic bridge/trapeze tailpiece, 2 single coil pickups, 2 volume/2 tone diamond controls, 3-position switch, available in Autumnglo, Black, Fireglo, Natural, or Two-Tone Brown finishes, mfg. 1958-1995.

1958-1964	N/A	$3,500	$3,000	$2,500	$2,100	$1,700	$1,300
1965-1987	N/A	$1,500	$1,200	$1,050	$900	$750	$550
1988-1995	N/A	$1,200	$1,050	$900	$750	$600	$450

Last MSR was $1,320.

In 1985, this model was reintroduced as 360 VB featuring Old Style body, high gain pickups and R-style tailpiece. In 1991, this model was renamed the 360 WB. In 1997, this model was renamed the 365.

360/12 WB - similar to 360WB, except has 12 strings, 6-per-side tuners, disc. 1995.

1958-1964	N/A	$5,000	$4,300	$3,600	$2,950	$2,500	$1,950
1965-1967	N/A	$6,500	$5,800	$5,000	$4,350	$3,600	$2,900
1968	N/A	$5,000	$4,300	$3,600	$2,950	$2,500	$1,950
1969-1995	N/A	$1,250	$1,050	$900	$750	$600	$450

Last MSR was $1,530.

370 - offset double cutaway semi-hollow maple body, wedge-shaped soundhole, pickguard, through-body maple neck, 21-fret bound rosewood fingerboard with pearl triangle inlay, tune-o-matic bridge/R-style trapeze tailpiece, 3 single coil pickups, 2 volume/2 tone diamond controls, 3-position switch, available in Autumnglo, Black, Fireglo, Natural, or Two-Tone Brown finishes, mfg. 1958-present.

1961-1964	N/A	$3,000	$2,500	$2,000	$1,500	$1,300	$1,100
1965-1971	N/A	$2,200	$1,800	$1,500	$1,200	$900	$700
1972-1993	N/A	$1,500	$1,200	$1,000	$800	$650	$500
1994-MSR $1,699	$1,300	$1,100	$925	$775	$650	$525	$400
1958-1960	N/A	$5,000	$4,000	$3,200	$2,600	$2,000	$1,500

370/12 - similar to 370, except 12 strings, 6-per-side tuners, mfg. 1965-present.

1965-1971	N/A	$1,500	$1,200	$1,000	$850	$700	$550
1972-MSR $1,829	$1,450	$1,150	$995	$875	$695	$575	$500

370 WB - similar to 370, except has tune-o-matic bridge/vibrato tailpiece, mfg. 1994-95.

	N/A	$1,250	$1,050	$900	$750	$600	$450

Last MSR was $1,555.

370/12 WB - similar to 370, except has 12 strings, tune-o-matic bridge/vibrato tailpiece, 6-per-side tuners, mfg. 1958-1995.

1958-1968	N/A	$5,200	$4,500	$3,700	$2,900	$2,500	$2,000
1969-1994	N/A	$1,300	$1,100	$900	$750	$600	$450

Last MSR was $1,655.

380L LAGUNA - offset double cutaway semi-hollow walnut body, slash (wedge-shaped) soundhole, set-in maple neck, 24-fret maple fingerboard with black dot inlay, Rickenbacker fixed bridge, 3-per-side tuners, gold hardware, walnut/maple laminate headstock veneer, 2 humbucker pickups, 2 volume/2 tone controls, 3-position switch, available in Oil finish, current mfg.

MSR	$1,699	$1,300	$1,100	$950	$800	$675	$550	$425

380L PZ Laguna - similar to the 380L Laguna, except has bridge-mounted piezo pickups, active electronics, current mfg.

MSR	$1,999	$1,550	$1,250	$1,100	$950	$775	$650	$525

381 - offset sharp double cutaway semi-hollow maple body, carved top, white bi-level pickguard, checkered bound body, bound wedge-shaped soundhole, through-body maple neck, 21-fret bound rosewood fingerboard with pearl triangle inlay, tune-o-matic bridge/trapeze tailpiece, chrome hardware, 2 chrome bar pickups, 2 volume/2 tone/mix controls, 3-position switch, available in Brownburst or Natural finishes, mfg. 1958-1963, reintroduced 1968-1974.

1958-1963	N/A	$5,000	$4,300	$3,600	$2,950	$2,500	$2,100
1969-1974	N/A	$2,500	$2,000	$1,500	$1,300	$1,100	$850

The original run of this series, 1958-early 1960s, had single pickguards, 2 controls. Fingerboard inlay was both dot and triangle. There were also a number of variations that Rickenbacker produced, some with f-shaped soundholes and some with vibratos.

ELECTRIC: 400 SERIES

The tulip style body shape acquired its nickname from the cutaways radiating out at a 45 degree angle, curving outwards to rounded point, then curving back.

400 COMBO - tulip style maple body, gold pickguard, through-body maple neck, 21-fret rosewood fingerboard with white dot inlay, covered pickup, volume/tone control, 2-position switch, available in Blue Green, Golden, or Jet Black finishes, mfg. 1956-58.

	N/A	$1,500	$1,250	$1,000	$800	$650	$500

This was the first through-body neck construction that Rickenbacker manufactured. In 1957, an extra switch was added.

420 - cresting wave style maple body, white pickguard, through-body maple neck, 21-fret rosewood fingerboard with white dot inlay, fixed bridge, chrome hardware, chrome bar pickup, volume/tone control, 2-position switch, available in Sunburst finish, mfg. 1965-1984.

1965-1969	N/A	$1,200	$1,050	$900	$750	$600	$500
1970-1984	N/A	$1,000	$850	$725	$600	$500	$400

425 - similar to 420, except has vibrato, mfg. 1958-1973.

1958-1964	N/A	$1,250	$1,100	$900	$750	$600	$500
1965-1973	N/A	$1,000	$850	$725	$600	$500	$400

This model replaced the 400 Combo. In 1965, the vibrato was added, at which time the 420 was introduced as the non-vibrato instrument in this style.

GRADING	100% MINT	98% NEAR MINT	95% EXC+	90% EXC	80% VG+	70% VG	60% G

450 COMBO - cresting wave style maple body, white pickguard, through-body maple neck, 21-fret rosewood fingerboard with pearl dot inlay, fixed bridge, chrome hardware, 2 chrome bar pickups, 2 volume/2 tone controls, 3-position switch, available in Black, Fireglo, Natural, or Sunburst finishes, mfg. 1957-1984.

1957-1968	N/A	$1,500	$1,250	$1,000	$850	$725	$600
1969-1984	N/A	$1,200	$1,050	$900	$750	$600	$500

This model was introduced with a tulip style body, metal pickguard, 2 controls and a rotary switch located on the upper treble bout. It was manufactured this way for one year. In 1958, the cresting wave body style was introduced. In 1966, the 4 controls were introduced. From 1962 to 1977, 3 pickups were optional.

450/12 - similar to 450, except has 12 strings, 6-per-side tuners, mfg. 1964-1985.

1965-1968	N/A	$1,500	$1,250	$1,000	$850	$725	$600
1969-1984	N/A	$1,200	$1,050	$900	$750	$600	$500

460 - similar to 450, except has bound body, bound fingerboard with pearl triangle inlay, mixer control, mono output jack on pickguard, available in Black, Fireglo, or Natural finishes, mfg. 1961-1985.

1961-1968	N/A	$1,700	$1,450	$1,150	$950	$800	$650
1969-1985	N/A	$1,300	$1,100	$950	$800	$675	$550

This model is similar to the model 620 (which has stereo outputs), which may lead to some confusion and/or mis-identification of the proper model designation.

480 - cresting wave style maple body, white pickguard, bolt-on maple neck, 24-fret bound rosewood fingerboard with white dot inlay, covered tune-o-matic bridge/R style trapeze tailpiece, cresting wave style peghead, chrome hardware, 2 single coil exposed pickups, 2 volume/2 tone controls, 3-position switch, mfg. 1973-1984.

	N/A	$800	$675	$550	$500	$450	$400

481 - similar to 480, except has bound body, slanted frets, pearl triangle fingerboard inlay, 2 humbucker exposed pickups, phase switch, mfg. 1973-1984.

	N/A	$850	$725	$600	$525	$450	$400

483 - similar to the 481, except has three pickups, mfg. 1973-1984.

	N/A	$900	$750	$650	$550	$475	$425

**Rickenbacker 360
courtesy Dave Rogers
Dave's Guitar Shop**

ELECTRIC: 600 SERIES

600 COMBO - offset double cutaway maple body, carved top, black pickguard, maple neck, 21-fret rosewood fingerboard with white dot inlay, fixed bridge, chrome hardware, single coil horseshoe pickup, volume/tone control, 2-position switch, available in Blonde finish, mfg. 1954-59.

	N/A	$1,700	$1,400	$1,150	$950	$800	$650

These instruments had both set and bolt-on necks. According to Rickenbacker's own records, there were apparently quite a few variations of this model. These models were on the price lists as having cresting wave style bodies until 1969, though none were ever produced.

610 - cresting wave style maple body, bi-level pickguard, through-body maple neck, 21-fret rosewood fingerboard with pearl dot inlay, tune-o-matic bridge/R-style trapeze tailpiece, 3-per-side tuners, 2 single coil pickups, 2 volume/2 tone/mix controls, 3-position switch, available in Fireglo, Jetglo, Mapleglo, Midnight Blue, Red, or White finishes, mfg. 1987-1998.

	$750	$600	$475	$350	$300	$250	$200

Last MSR was $1,000.

610/12 - similar to 610, except has 12 strings, 6-per-side tuners, disc. 1998.

	$825	$550	$425	$375	$325	$275	$225

Last MSR was $1,100.

615 (610 VB) - similar to 610, except has roller bridge/vibrato tailpiece, chrome hardware, 2 chrome bar pickups, 2 volume/2 tone controls, available in Black, Fireglo, or Natural finishes, mfg. 1962-1977, reintroduced as the 610VB from 1985 to 1990.

1962-1965	N/A	$1,500	$1,300	$1,100	$950	$800	$650
1966-1969	N/A	$1,300	$1,100	$950	$800	$650	$500
1970-1977	N/A	$1,000	$850	$725	$600	$500	$400

620 - similar to 610, except has bound body, bound fingerboard with pearl triangle inlay, 2 single coil exposed pickups, wired for stereo, available in Fireglo, Jetglo, Mapleglo, Midnight Blue, Red, or White finishes, mfg. 1977-present.

1977-1990	N/A	$1,100	$950	$800	$650	$525	$400
1991-MSR $1,299	$995	$850	$700	$575	$475	$400	$325

620/12 - similar to 620, except has 12 strings, 6-per-side tuners, mfg. 1981-present.

1981-1990	N/A	$1,300	$1,100	$950	$800	$650	$500
1991-MSR $1,419	$1,100	$875	$750	$650	$550	$450	$350

In 1989, the deluxe trim was replaced by standard trim.

**Rickenbacker 615
courtesy Dave Rogers
Dave's Guitar Shop**

GRADING	100% MINT	98% NEAR MINT	95% EXC+	90% EXC	80% VG+	70% VG	60% G

625 (620 VB) - similar to 610, except has bound body, bound fingerboard with pearl triangle inlay, roller bridge/vibrato tailpiece, 2 chrome bar pickups, available in Fireglo, Jetglo, Mapleglo, Midnight Blue, Red, or White finishes, mfg. 1977-1994.

1977-1985	N/A	$1,500	$1,300	$1,100	$950	$800	$650
1986-1994	N/A	$1,150	$950	$800	$675	$550	$400

Last MSR was $1,450.

In 1985, this model was reintroduced as the 620 VB (mfg. 1985 to 1990).

650 COMBO - offset double sharp cutaway maple body, carved top, pickguard, maple neck, 21-fret rosewood fingerboard with white dot inlay, fixed bridge, single coil horseshoe pickup, volume control, available in Natural or Turquoise Blue finishes, mfg. 1957-1960.

	N/A	$1,700	$1,400	$1,150	$950	$800	$650

In late 1957, a chrome bar pickup replaced the horseshoe pickup.

660 - cresting wave style figured 'charactered' maple body, checkered body binding, through-body maple neck, 21-fret bound rosewood fingerboard with pearl triangle inlay, tune-o-matic bridge/trapeze tailpiece, gold bi-level pickguard, gold peghead logoplate, 3-per-side tuners, chrome hardware, 2 vintage-style pickups, 2 volume/2 tone/mix controls, 3-position switch, available in Fireglo or Jetglo finish, mfg. 1998-present.

MSR	$1,879	$1,450	$1,250	$1,100	$1,000	$850	$750	$600

660/12 - similar to the 660, except features 12-string configuration, 6-per-side tuners, 12 saddle bridge, mfg. 1998-present.

MSR	$1,999	$1,550	$1,350	$1,200	$1,100	$950	$850	$700

ELECTRIC: 650 SERIES (CURRENT MFG.)

All models in this series have a cresting wave style body, pickguard, maple through-body neck, 24-fret maple fingerboard with black dot inlay, fixed bridge, 3-per-side tuners, 2 humbucker pickups, 2 volume/2 tone/mix controls, 3-position switch. Available in Natural finish (unless otherwise listed). Mfg. 1991 to date.

650A ATLANTIS - maple body, 24 frets, chrome hardware and pickplate. Two humbucker pickups, available in Vintage Turquoise finish only, disc. 2003.

	$1,000	$800	$700	$575	$495	$400	$325

Last MSR was $1,299.

650C COLORADO - walnut body, 24 frets, two humbucker pickups, chrome hardware and pickplate, available in Jetglo Black finish only, mfg. 1994-present.

MSR	$1,299	$1,000	$800	$700	$575	$495	$400	$325

650D DAKOTA - walnut body, 24 frets, two humbucker pickups, walnut peghead laminate, chrome hardware and pickplate, available in Natural Oil finish, current mfg.

MSR	$999	$800	$675	$575	$500	$400	$325	$250

650F FRISCO (650E EXCALIBER) - 24 frets, two humbucker pickups, African vermilion body, African vermilion peghead laminate, gold hardware, available in Clear High Gloss finish, disc. 2003.

	$1,100	$900	$775	$650	$525	$425	$350

Last MSR was $1,419.

650S SIERRA - 24 frets, two humbucker pickups, solid walnut body, walnut peghead laminate, gold hardware, available in Natural Oil finish, current mfg.

MSR	$1,099	$900	$750	$625	$550	$450	$375	$275

ELECTRIC: 800 SERIES

800 (COMBO) - offset double cutaway maple body, carved top, black pickguard, maple neck, 21-fret rosewood fingerboard with white dot inlay, fixed bridge, chrome hardware, double coil horseshoe pickup, 2 volume controls, 2 selector switches, available in Blonde or Turquoise Blue finishes, mfg. 1954-59.

	N/A	$1,500	$1,200	$1,000	$850	$700	$550

In 1957, the pickguard was enlarged and the controls were mounted on it, a chrome bar pickup replaced one of the "horseshoe" pickups, and Turquoise Blue finish became optional. This model was on the price list through 1969, though it was no longer available.

850 COMBO - offset double sharp cutaway maple body, carved top, pickguard, maple neck, 21-fret rosewood fingerboard with white dot inlay, fixed bridge, double coil horseshoe pickup, volume/tone controls, 2 switches, available in Natural or Turquoise Blue finishes, mfg. 1957-1960.

	N/A	$1,800	$1,500	$1,200	$950	$700	$600

In late 1957, the horseshoe pickup was replaced by a single coil horseshoe and chrome bar pickups. This model was on the price lists through 1967. There were several variations of this model that were made with 3 pickup designs or through-body neck constructions.

ELECTRIC: 900 & 1000 SERIES

900 - tulip style 3/4 size maple body, white pickguard, through-body maple neck, 21-fret rosewood fingerboard with white dot inlay, fixed bridge, chrome hardware, single coil pickup, volume/tone control, 2-position switch, available in Black, Brown, Fireglo, Gray, or Natural finishes, mfg. 1957-1980.

	N/A	$800	$700	$600	$525	$450	$400

In 1958, a chrome bar pickup replaced the original pickup. In 1961, Fireglo finish became optional. By 1974, cresting wave body style became standard.

950 - similar to 900, except has 2 pickups, mfg. 1957-1980.

	N/A	$850	$750	$625	$550	$475	$425

In 1958, a chrome bar pickup replaced the original pickup. In 1961, Fireglo finish became optional. By 1974, cresting wave body style became standard.

GRADING	100% MINT	98% NEAR MINT	95% EXC+	90% EXC	80% VG+	70% VG	60% G

1000 - similar to 900, except has 18-fret fingerboard, mfg. 1957-1971.

	N/A	$800	$700	$600	$525	$475	$425

In 1958, a chrome bar pickup replaced the original pickup. In 1961, Fireglo finish became optional.

ELECTRIC: EXPORT SERIES

Between 1964 and 1969, Rickenbacker exported a number of models to the Rose, Morris & Company, Ltd. in England for exclusive distribution in the U.K. and European sales. The export models have a corresponding U.S. model, although the export hollow body models have f-holes rather than the slash hole (or none at all).

1997 - offset double cutaway semi-hollow maple body, f-style soundhole, white bi-level pickguard, through-body maple neck, 21-fret rosewood fingerboard with pearl dot inlay, tune-o-matic bridge/trapeze tailpiece, 3-per-side tuners, chrome hardware, 2 pickups, 2 volume/2 tone/mix controls, 3-position switch, available in Fireglo finish, mfg. 1964-69.

	N/A	$2,000	$1,700	$1,400	$1,100	$850	$650

In 1966, Autumnglo finish was introduced. The 1997 export model corresponded to the U.S. 335 model.

ELECTRIC: LIMITED EDITION SERIES

Production totals and original list prices courtesy Rickenbacker.

230GF GLENN FREY LIMITED EDITION - (Series 200/2000 style) double cutaway maple body, chrome pickguard with Glenn Frey signature, through-body maple neck, 24-fret maple fingerboard (finished in Gloss Jet Black) with pearl dot inlay, fixed bridge, chrome peghead logo plate, 3-per-side tuners, black hardware, 2 humbucker pickups, chrome volume/tone control, 3-position mini switch, available in Gloss Jet Black finish, disc. 2000.

	$950	$800	$650	$550	$475	$425	$375

Last MSR was $1,199.

Only 1,000 instruments were scheduled. Each instrument includes a Certificate of Authenticity signed by Glenn Frey. Price includes a deluxe hardshell case.

**Rickenbacker 620
courtesy John Beeson
The Music Shoppe**

325JL JOHN LENNON LIMITED EDITION - offset double cutaway semi-hollow 3/4 size Eastern rock maple body, white bi-level pickguard with John Lennon signature and graphic, through-body maple neck, 21-fret rosewood fingerboard with pearl dot inlay, tune-o-matic bridge/vintage vibrato, white peghead logoplate, 3-per-side tuners, chrome hardware, 3 vintage-style pickups, 2 volume/2 tone/mix controls, 3-position switch, available in Jetglo finish, mfg. 1990-94.

	N/A	$1,500	$1,300	$1,100	$950	$800	$650

Last MSR was $1,700.

Only 974 instruments were produced (953 Model 325JL, 21 Model 325JL LH left-handed configuration). Each instrument includes an individually numbered Certificate of Authenticity. This model was optional with vintage-style hardshell case with silver covering and crushed velvet lining. A total of 2,000 instruments from the John Lennon Series (models 325, 355, 355/12) were produced.

350SH SUSANNA HOFFS LIMITED EDITION - offset sharp double cutaway semi-hollow maple body, bi-level pickguard with Susanna Hoffs signature, checkered body binding, through-body maple neck, 24-fret bound rosewood fingerboard with pearl triangle inlay, tune-o-matic bridge/R-style trapeze tailpiece, 2 'chrome bar'/1 HB-1 humbucker pickups, 2 volume/2 tone/mix controls, 3-position switch, stereo output, available in Jetglo finish, mfg. 1988-1991.

	N/A	$2,000	$1,700	$1,400	$1,200	$1,000	$800

Last MSR was $1,279.

Only 250 instruments were produced. Each instrument includes an individually numbered Certificate of Authenticity.

355JL JOHN LENNON LIMITED EDITION - offset double cutaway semi-hollow Eastern rock maple body, white bi-level pickguard with John Lennon signature and graphic, through-body maple neck, 21-fret rosewood fingerboard with pearl dot inlay, tune-o-matic bridge/trapeze tailpiece, white peghead logoplate, 3-per-side tuners, chrome hardware, 3 vintage-style pickups, 2 volume/2 tone/mix controls, 3-position switch, available in Jetglo finish, mfg. 1990-94.

	N/A	$1,600	$1,350	$1,150	$1,000	$850	$700

Last MSR was $1,730.

Only 691 instruments were produced (660 Model 355JL, 8 Model 355JL LH left-handed configuration, 23 Model 355JL VB). Each instrument includes an individually numbered Certificate of Authenticity. This model was optional with vintage-style hardshell case with silver covering and crushed velvet lining.

355/12JL John Lennon Limited Edition - similar to 355JL John Lennon, except has 12-string configuration, 6-per-side tuners, mfg. 1990-94.

	N/A	$1,600	$1,350	$1,150	$1,000	$850	$700

Last MSR was $1,830.

Only 334 instruments were produced (329 Model 355/12JL, 5 Model 355/12JL LH left-handed configuration). Each instrument includes an individually numbered Certificate of Authenticity. This model was optional with vintage-style hardshell case with silver covering and crushed velvet lining.

360CW CARL WILSON LIMITED EDITION - circa 1965 styling, 21-fret, checked binding, vintage pickups, vintage case, disc.

	$1,500	$1,250	$1,000	$900	$800	$700	$600

Last MSR was $1,999.

**Rickenbacker 650S Sierra
courtesy John Beeson
The Music Shoppe**

R

GRADING	100% MINT	98% NEAR MINT	95% EXC+	90% EXC	80% VG+	70% VG	60% G

360/12CW CARL WILSON LIMITED EDITION 12-STRINGS - similar to 360CW except in a 12-string configuration, disc.

	$1,650	$1,350	$1,050	$950	$850	$750	$650

Last MSR was $2,149.

370/12RM ROGER McGUINN LIMITED EDITION - offset double cutaway semi-hollow maple body, bound wedge-shaped soundhole, bi-level pickguard with Roger McGuinn signature, checkered body binding, through-body maple neck, 21-fret bound rosewood fingerboard with pearl triangle inlay, tune-o-matic bridge/R-style trapeze tailpiece, 6-per-side tuners, chrome hardware, 3 vintage-style pickups, 2 volume/2 tone/mix controls, 3-position switch, customized circuitry, available in Fireglo, Jetglo, or Mapleglo finishes, mfg. 1988 only.

	N/A	$4,000	$3,400	$2,800	$2,200	$1,600	$1,000

Last MSR was $1,399.

Only 1,000 instruments were produced. Each instrument includes an individually numbered Certificate of Authenticity. The first 250 certificates were signed by Roger McGuinn. This model was optional without the enhanced, customized electronics (retail list price $1,299). This model has become very collectible and has sold on ebay for as high as $4,500.

381JK JOHN KAY LIMITED EDITION - double cutaway semi-hollow maple body, carved top/back, checkered body binding, bound wedge style soundhole, silver pickguard with John Kay signature and wolf head logo, through-body maple neck, 21-fret bound rosewood fingerboard with pearl triangle inlay, tune-o-matic bridge/R-style trapeze tailpiece, silver peghead logoplate, 3-per-side tuners, chrome hardware, 2 HB-1 humbucker pickups, 2 volume/2 tone/mix controls, 4-position/phase switches, active electronics, mono or stereo outputs, available in Jetglo finish, mfg. 1988-1997.

	N/A	$1,600	$1,350	$1,100	$900	$750	$600

Last MSR was $1,699.

Scheduled production amount unknown. Each instrument includes an individually numbered Certificate of Authenticity. Price included a hardshell luggage case.

660/12TP TOM PETTY LIMITED EDITION - cresting wave style figured Eastern rock maple body, checkered body binding, gold bi-level pickguard with Tom Petty signature, checkered body binding, through-body maple neck, 21-fret bound rosewood fingerboard with pearl triangle inlay, tune-o-matic bridge/trapeze tailpiece, gold pickguard, gold peghead logoplate, 6-per-side tuners, chrome hardware, 2 pickups, 2 volume, 2 tone/mix controls, 3-way switch, available in Fireglo or Jetglo finish, mfg. 1991-97.

	N/A	$1,700	$1,400	$1,150	$950	$800	$650

Last MSR was $1,849.

Only 1,000 instruments were produced (807 Model 660/12TP FG, 6 Model 660/12TP LH FG, 186 Model 660/12TP JG, 1 Model 660/12TP LH). Each instrument includes an individually numbered Certificate of Authenticity. Price included a Rickenbacker vintage case.

1997PT PETE TOWNSHEND LIMITED EDITION - offset double cutaway semi-hollow maple body, (violin) f-hole, white bi-level pickguard with Pete Townshend signature, through-body maple neck, 21-fret rosewood fingerboard with pearl dot inlay, tune-o-matic bridge/'R' trapeze tailpiece, 3-per-side tuners, chrome hardware, 3 vintage-style pickups, 2 volume/2 tone/mix controls, 3-position switch, available in Fireglo finish, mfg. 1987 only.

	N/A	$2,000	$1,700	$1,400	$1,150	$950	$750

Last MSR was $1,225.

Only 250 instruments produced. 1997PT models were individually numbered and came with a Certificate of Authenticity signed by John Hall (CEO, Rickenbacker).

ELECTRIC: VINTAGE REISSUE SERIES

The instruments in this series are reproductions from the 1960s, using vintage-style pickups, hardware, and knobs. Rickenbacker typically produces more than 10,000 instruments per year since their debut in 1984. The Vintage Series models are produced in small production lots of 25 to 50 instruments.

1997 - offset double cutaway semi-hollow maple body, (violin) f-hole, white bi-level pickguard, through-body maple neck, 21-fret rosewood fingerboard with pearl dot inlay, tune-o-matic bridge/trapeze tailpiece, 3-per-side tuners, chrome hardware, 2 pickups, 2 volume/2 tone/mix controls, 3-position switch, available in Fireglo, Jetglo, or Mapleglo finishes, disc. 2000.

	$1,350	$1,150	$900	$775	$650	$525	$475

Last MSR was $1,799.

1997 SPC - similar to 1997, except has 3 pickups, mfg. 1993-2000.

	$1,500	$1,250	$975	$850	$695	$550	$500

Last MSR was $1,949.

1997 VB - similar to 1997, except has vibrato tailpiece, mfg. 1988-1995.

	$950	$800	$700	$575	$500	$425	$350

Last MSR was $1,500.

325V59 HAMBURG - offset double cutaway semi hollow 3/4 size maple body, gold bi-level pickguard, through-body maple neck, 21-fret rosewood fingerboard with pearl dot inlay, tune-o-matic bridge/Bigsby vibrato tailpiece, 3-per-side tuners, chrome hardware, 3 pickups, 2 volume/2 tone controls, 3-position switch, available in Jetglo or Mapleglo finishes, mfg. 1991-2000.

	$1,750	$1,300	$1,000	$895	$750	$600	$500

Last MSR was $2,069.

This model, a reproduction based on a similar model most popular in 1959, is actually derived from an earlier design.

325V63 MIAMI - similar to 325V59, except has white pickguard, vintage vibrato, 2 volume/2 tone/mix controls, available in Jetglo finish, disc. 2000.

	$1,700	$1,275	$1,050	$875	$750	$600	$500

Last MSR was $2,069.

This model is derived from the 1959 revision of the Model 325.

GRADING	100% MINT	98% NEAR MINT	95% EXC+	90% EXC	80% VG+	70% VG	60% G

350V63 LIVERPOOL - offset sharp double cutaway semi-hollow maple body, bi-level pickguard, through-body maple neck, 21-fret rosewood fingerboard with pearloid dot inlay, tune-o-matic bridge/trapeze tailpiece, 3 chrome bar pickups, 2 volume/2 tone/mix controls, 3-position switch, stereo output, available in Jetglo finish, mfg. 1994-present.

MSR	$2,129	$1,750	$1,400	$1,150	$1,000	$875	$750	$525

This model is styled after the classic 325 series guitars.

350/12V63 *Liverpool 12* - similar to 350V63, except has 12 strings, 6-per-side tuners, mfg. 1994-present.

MSR	$2,249	$1,800	$1,500	$1,200	$1,000	$895	$775	$550

360V64 - offset double cutaway semi-hollow bound maple body, wedge soundhole, white bi-level pickguard, through-body maple neck, 21-fret rosewood fingerboard with pearl triangle inlay, tune-o-matic bridge/trapeze tailpiece, 3-per-side tuners, chrome hardware, 2 pickups, 2 volume/2 tone/mix controls, 3-position switch, available in Fireglo finish, disc. 2000.

		$1,450	$1,200	$995	$850	$695	$600	$500

Last MSR was $1,949.

This reproduction is based on the 1964 Deluxe 360 model.

360/12V64 - similar to 360V64, except has 12 strings, 6-per-side tuners, available in Fireglo finish, mfg. 1985-2000.

		$1,500	$1,250	$1,050	$900	$750	$650	$550

Last MSR was $2,069.

381V69 - offset double cutaway semi-hollow bound maple body, figured maple top/back, bound wedge soundhole, white bi-level pickguard, checkered bound body, through-body maple neck, 21-fret bound rosewood fingerboard with pearl triangle inlay, tune-o-matic bridge/R-style trapeze tailpiece, 3-per-side tuners, chrome hardware, 2 pickups, 2 volume/2 tone/mix controls, 3-position switch, available in Fireglo, Jetglo, or Mapleglo finishes, mfg. 1987-present.

MSR	$2,859	$2,200	$1,850	$1,450	$1,250	$1,000	$875	$750

This model is derived from a design released in 1957.

381/12V69 - similar to 381V69, except has 12 strings, 6-per-side tuners, mfg. 1989-present.

MSR	$2,999	$2,300	$1,900	$1,500	$1,300	$1,100	$900	$800

ELECTRIC: C SERIES

325C58 HAMBURG - semi-hollowbody, 21-fret, short scale, 3 pickups, gold pickguard, Kauffman Vib-rola. Vintage reissue case included, available in Mapleglo or Jetglo finishes, mfg. 2001-present.

MSR	$3,199	$2,400	$2,000	$1,600	$1,400	$1,100	$900	$750

325C64 MIAMI - semi-hollowbody, 21-fret, short scale, 3 pickups, RIC vibrato, white pickguard, vintage reissue case included, available in Jetglo finish only, mfg. 2001-present.

MSR	$2,999	$2,250	$1,850	$1,450	$1,250	$1,000	$800	$650

360/12C64 - semi-acoustic, 21 frets, full scale, 2 pickups, trapeze tailpiece, double bound, vintage reissue case included, available in Fireglo finish, mfg. 2001-present.

MSR	$3,199	$2,400	$2,000	$1,600	$1,400	$1,100	$900	$750

ELECTRIC: DOUBLENECK SERIES

362/12 - offset double cutaway semi hollow checkered bound maple body, bound wedge-shaped soundhole, white pickguard, through-body maple/walnut laminate necks, 24-fret bound rosewood fingerboards with pearl triangle inlay, tune-o-matic bridges/R style tailpieces, 6-per-side/3-per-side tuners, chrome hardware, 2 single coil exposed pickups per neck, 2 volume/2 tone/mix controls, two 3-position switches, stereo output, available in Natural finish, mfg. 1975-1985.

	N/A	$2,500	$2,100	$1,800	$1,500	$1,200	$900

This was a special order instrument.

4080 - cresting wave style bound maple body, 2-piece black pickguard, maple necks, bound rosewood fingerboards with pearl triangle inlay, fixed bridge for bass neck, tune-o-matic/R style trapeze tailpiece for guitar neck, cresting wave style pegheads, 2-per-side tuners for bass neck, 3-per-side tuners for guitar neck, chrome hardware, 2 single coil exposed pickups per neck, 2 volume/2 tone/1 mix controls, two 3-position switches, stereo output, available in Natural finish, mfg. 1975-1985.

	N/A	$2,500	$2,100	$1,800	$1,500	$1,200	$900

Bass neck may be maple/walnut laminate and had 20 frets. The guitar neck had 24 frets.

4080/12 - similar to 4080, except has 12 strings, 6-per-side tuners on the guitar neck, mfg. 1978-1985.

	N/A	$2,400	$2,100	$1,800	$1,500	$1,200	$900

ELECTRIC BASS: 2000 SERIES

2020 HAMBURG - double cutaway maple body, through-body maple neck, 20-fret rosewood fingerboard with pearl dot inlay, fixed bridge, 2-per-side tuners, 2 single coil pickups, 2 volume/2 tone controls, toggle switch, active electronics, available in Fireglo, Jetglo, Mapleglo, Midnight Blue, Red, or White finishes, mfg. 1984-1995.

	N/A	$700	$600	$500	$425	$350	$275

Last MSR was $1,000.

**Rickenbacker
325C58 Hamburg
courtesy Rickenbacker**

**Rickenbacker 4000
courtesy Rickenbacker**

R

GRADING	100% MINT	98% NEAR MINT	95% EXC+	90% EXC	80% VG+	70% VG	60% G

2060 EL DORADO - similar to 2020, except has double bound body, bound fingerboard, gold hardware, disc. 1995.

	N/A	$750	$650	$550	$450	$375	$300

Last MSR was $1,200.

ELECTRIC BASS: 3000 SERIES

3000 - offset double cutaway Strat style body, 30 in. scale, 1 humbucker pickup, standard headstock, 2 knobs, available in various finishes, mfg. 1975-1984.

	N/A	$750	$650	$575	$500	$425	$350

3001 - offset double cutaway Strat style body, 33.5 in. scale, 1 humbucker pickup, standard headstock, 3 knobs, available in various finishes, mfg. 1975-1984.

	N/A	$750	$650	$575	$500	$425	$350

ELECTRIC BASS: 4000 SERIES

All models in this series have the following, unless otherwise listed: cresting wave style maple body, pickguard, through-body maple neck, 20-fret rosewood fingerboard, fixed bridge, 2-per-side tuners, single coil/horseshoe pickups, 2 volume/2 tone controls, 3-position switch.

4000 - cresting wave style maple body, white pickguard, through-body mahogany neck, 20-fret rosewood fingerboard with white dot inlay, fixed bridge, cresting wave peghead with maple laminate wings, 2-per-side tuners, chrome hardware, horseshoe pickup, volume/tone control, available in Autumnglo, Brownburst, Black, Fireglo, or Natural finishes, mfg. 1955-1987.

1957-1960	N/A	$5,000	$4,500	$3,900	$3,300	$2,800	$2,200
1961-1964	N/A	$4,000	$3,400	$2,800	$2,300	$1,800	$1,300
1965-1969	N/A	$2,500	$2,100	$1,800	$1,500	$1,250	$950
1970-1987	N/A	$1,250	$1,050	$900	$750	$600	$500

This was the first production Rickenbacker Bass guitar. In 1955, only a handful of instruments were produced. In 1958, a walnut neck replaced the mahogany neck. In 1960, a maple/walnut laminated neck replaced the walnut neck. Fireglo finish became optional. In 1963, a bridge string mute was added and Autumnglo and Black finishes became optional. In 1964, the horseshoe pickup was replaced by a single coil pickup with a metal cover.

4001 - cresting wave style checkered bound maple body, white pickguard, through-body maple/walnut neck, 20-fret bound rosewood fingerboard with pearl triangle inlay, fixed bridge, cresting wave peghead, 2-per-side tuners, chrome hardware, bar/horseshoe pickups, 2 volume/2 tone controls, 3-position switch, available in Fireglo or Natural finishes, mfg. 1961-1986.

1961-1964	N/A	$5,000	$4,300	$3,600	$3,100	$2,600	$2,000
1965-1969	N/A	$3,500	$3,000	$2,600	$2,200	$1,750	$1,400
1970-1972	N/A	$2,500	$2,100	$1,800	$1,500	$1,300	$1,000
1973-1977	N/A	$1,500	$1,250	$1,050	$900	$775	$650
1978-1986	N/A	$1,000	$850	$750	$625	$500	$400

In the early 1960s, a few models had ebony fingerboards. In 1964, the horseshoe pickup was replaced by a single coil pickup with a metal cover. In 1965, Natural finish became optional. Stereo output was originally a special order item on the 4001 until 1971 when it became optional.

4001C64 - similar to 4001 except has horseshoe pickup, Kluson style tuners, neck-through body, available in Mapleglo or Fireglo finishes, mfg. 2001-present.

MSR	$2,999	$2,300	$2,050	$1,850	$1,750	$1550	$1,350	$1,050

4001C64S - similar to 4001C64 except has rehaped body and reversed head, available in Mapleglo finish, mfg. 2001-present.

MSR	$3,199	$2,450	$2,200	$2,000	$1,850	$1,650	$1,450	$1,150

4001 FL - similar to 4001, except has a fretless fingerboard, disc.

	N/A	$4,500	$3,800	$3,100	$2,500	$2,100	$1,800

This model was available only by special order.

4001 S - similar to 4001, except has unbound body, dot fingerboard inlay, mfg. 1964-67, reintroduced 1980-86.

1964-1967	N/A	$5,000	$4,300	$3,600	$3,100	$2,600	$2,000
1980-1986	N/A	$1,250	$1,050	$900	$750	$650	$500

This was also known as the export Model 1999. Original release instruments were manufactured in low quantities and are rare finds. This was the model made famous by Paul McCartney and Chris Squire.

4002 - similar to 4000, except has checkered bound figured maple body, figured maple/walnut 5-piece neck, bound ebony fingerboard with pearl triangle inlay, 2 humbucker exposed pickups, 2 volume/2 tone controls, 3-position switch, stereo and direct outputs, available in Mapleglo or Walnut finishes, mfg. 1981 only.

	N/A	$1,200	$1,050	$900	$775	$650	$550

This was a Limited Edition instrument.

4003 - cresting wave style bound maple body, 2-piece white pickguard, through-body maple neck, 20-fret bound rosewood fingerboard with pearl triangle inlay, fixed bridge, cresting wave style peghead, 2-per-side tuners, chrome hardware, 2 single coil exposed pickups (metal cover over bridge pickup), 2 volume/2 tone controls, 3-position switch, stereo output, available in Natural finish, mfg. 1973-present.

1973-1994	N/A	$1,250	$1,050	$900	$750	$625	$500
1995-MSR	$1,529	$1,200	$950	$795	$695	$575	$475	$400

In 1985, pickguard was replaced with one piece unit.

4003 FL - similar to 4003, except has a fretless fingerboard with pearl dot inlay, current mfg.

MSR	$1,529	$1,200	$950	$795	$695	$575	$475	$400

GRADING	100% MINT	98% NEAR MINT	95% EXC+	90% EXC	80% VG+	70% VG	60% G

4003 S - similar to 4003, except has no binding, dot fingerboard inlay, mono output, available in Red finish, mfg. 1980-1995.

	N/A	$1,200	$1,000	$850	$725	$600	$500

Last MSR was $1,200.

4003/S5 - similar to 4003, except in 5-string configuration, 3/2-per-side tuners, no binding, dot fingerboard inlay, mono output, mfg. 1987-2003.

	$1,250	$995	$850	$750	$625	$475	$395

Last MSR was $1,649.

4003/S8 - similar to 4003, except has 8 strings, no binding, dot fingerboard inlay, 4-per-side tuners, mono output, mfg. 1987-2003.

	$1,500	$1,275	$1,100	$895	$750	$595	$475

Last MSR was $1,919.

4004C CHEYENNE - cresting wave style walnut body, through-body maple neck, 20-fret maple fingerboard with black dot inlay, fixed bridge, cresting wave style peghead with walnut laminates, 2-per-side tuners, gold hardware, 2 humbucker exposed pickups, volume/tone control, 3-position mini switch, available in Natural finish, mfg. 1993-2000.

	$1,200	$975	$850	$750	$625	$495	$395

Last MSR was $1,569.

4004CII CHEYENNE II - similar to 4004C Cheyenne except has super contoured maple and walnut body, bubinga fingerboard, gold parts, available in translucent colors, mfg. 2001-present.

MSR	$1,949	$1,475	$1,250	$1,150	$1,000	$900	$800	$650

4004L LAREDO - similar to 4004C, except has hardwood body, chrome hardware, available in Jetglo finish, mfg. 1994-present.

MSR	$1,749	$1,350	$1,100	$925	$795	$675	$550	$425

The 4004L Laredo has been available in all standard colors since 1995.

4005 - offset double cutaway semi-hollow maple body, rounded top, bound wedge-shaped soundhole, white pickguard, through-body maple/walnut laminate neck, 21-fret bound rosewood fingerboard with pearl triangle inlay, tune-o-matic bridge/R style trapeze tailpiece, cresting wave style peghead, 2-per-side tuners, chrome hardware, 2 single coil exposed pickups, 2 volume/2 tone/mix controls, 3-position switch, available in Fireglo or Natural finishes, mfg. 1965-1984.

1965-1969	N/A	$4,000	$3,400	$2,900	$2,400	$1,900	$1,400
1970-1974	N/A	$2,500	$2,100	$1,800	$1,500	$1,200	$950
1975-1984	N/A	$1,500	$1,250	$1,050	$900	$750	$600

4005 WB - similar to 4005, except has bound body, mfg. 1966-1984.

	N/A	$5,000	$4,300	$3,500	$3,000	$2,400	$1,600

4005/6 - similar to 4005, except has 6 strings, 3-per-side tuners, mfg. 1965-1978.

	N/A	$4,500	$3,800	$3,200	$2,500	$2,100	$1,700

4005/8 - similar to 4005, except has 8 strings, 4-per-side tuners, mfg. 1967-1984.

	N/A	$3,500	$2,800	$2,300	$1,850	$1,450	$1,150

4008 - cresting wave style bound maple body, white pickguard, through-body maple neck, 21-fret bound rosewood fingerboard with pearl triangle inlay, fixed bridge, cresting wave style peghead, 4-per-side tuners, chrome hardware, 2 single coil exposed pickups (metal cover over bridge pickup), 2 volume/2 tone controls, 3-position switch, available in Fireglo or Natural finishes, mfg. 1972-1984.

	N/A	$1,000	$850	$775	$700	$625	$550

This model was available on special order only.

ELECTRIC BASS: LIMITED EDITION SERIES

2030GF GLENN FREY LIMITED EDITION - double cutaway maple body, chrome pickguard with Glenn Frey signature, through-body maple neck, 20-fret ebony fingerboard with pearl dot inlay, fixed bridge, chrome peghead logoplate, 2-per-side tuners, black hardware, 2 humbucker pickups, chrome volume/tone control, 3-position mini switch, available in Jetglo finish, disc. 1995.

	N/A	$850	$750	$675	$600	$525	$450

Last MSR was $1,050.

4001CS CHRIS SQUIRE LIMITED EDITION - cresting wave Eastern rock maple body, white pickguard with Chris Squire signature, through-body maple neck, 20-fret vermilion fingerboard with pearl dot inlay, fixed bridge, white peghead logoplate, 2-per-side tuners, chrome hardware, single coil/horseshoe pickups, 2 volume/2 tone controls, 3-position switch, available in Cream Lacquer finish, disc. 2000.

	$1,600	$1,400	$1,200	$1,000	$800	$700	$600

Last MSR was $1,899.

Only 1,000 instruments are scheduled. The fingerboard and peghead on this model are carved from one piece of African vermilion. Price includes a Rickenbacker vintage case.

Rickenbacker 4003 courtesy Dave Rogers Dave's Guitar Shop

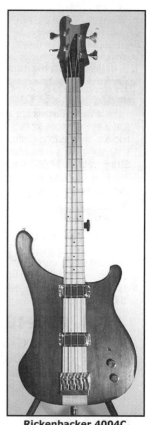

Rickenbacker 4004C Cheyenne Blue Book Publications

R

GRADING	100% MINT	98% NEAR MINT	95% EXC+	90% EXC	80% VG+	70% VG	60% G

4004LK LEMMY KILMISTER LIMITED EDITION - cresting wave style highly carved walnut body, through-body maple neck, 20-fret rosewood fingerboard with pearl dot inlay, fixed bridge, black/white checked body binding, cresting wave style peghead, 2-per-side tuners, gold hardware, 3 humbucker pickups, volume/tone control, 5-position switch, available in Oil finish, mfg. 1998-2003.

	$2,200	$1,950	$1,800	$1,600	$1,400	$1,200	$900

Last MSR was $2,799.

Price includes a standard Rickenbacker case.

4001V63 - cresting wave style maple body, white pickguard, through-body maple neck, 20-fret rosewood fingerboard with pearl dot inlay, fixed bridge, 2-per-side tuners, chrome hardware, single coil/horseshoe pickups, 2 volume/2 tone controls, 3-position switch, available in Fireglo and Mapleglo finishes, mfg. 1984-2000.

	$1,600	$1,300	$1,100	$950	$775	$650	$500

Last MSR was $2,069.

This model was derived from the 4001 bass that was popular in 1963.

RICKMANN

Instruments previously built in Japan during the late 1970s.

The Rickmann trademark is a brand name used by a UK importer. Instruments are generally intermediate quality copies of classic American designs (source: Tony Bacon and Paul Day, *The Guru's Guitar Guide*).

RICO

See B.C. Rich.

RIPLEY, STEVE

Instruments currently built in Tulsa, OK since 1983.

Luthier Steve Ripley had established a reputation as both a guitarist and recording engineer prior to debuting his Stereo Guitar models at the 1983 NAMM show. Ripley's designs were later licensed by Kramer (BKL). In 1986, Ripley moved to Tulsa, Oklahoma and two years later severed his relationship with Kramer. Any further information would be appreciated and can be submitted directly to the *Blue Book of Electric Guitars* (source: Tom Wheeler, *American Guitars*).

RITTER BASS GUITARS

Instruments currently built in Bad Durkheim, Germany since 1991. Distributed worldwide by Ritter Bass Guitars of Bad Durkheim, Germany.

Luthier/designer Jens Ritter originally apprenticed as an traditional woodworker. During his apprenticeship, Ritter was also an accomplished electric bassist who played in German Jazz and Fusion bands.

At the age of eighteen, Ritter began building custom basses for local bass players. After a few years the name Jens Ritter was a synonym for high end custom basses in Europe. In 1999, Ritter invented a new Tremolo System for bass guitars (4-string, 5-string and 6-string). It works with miniature ball bearings. In 2001, he developed a special body sound material called Galpera. This material has an similar sound characteristic to hard maple and it can be covered with chrome or gold. All instruments are completely hand-made and unique. For further information regarding specifications, pricing, and U.S. dealers contact the Ritter Bass Guitars website (see Trademark Index).

ELECTRIC BASS

Ritter's **Basic-Basses** are a more standardized model from his custom basses. The Basic Bass model has an offset cutaway figured maple (flamed, quilted, bird's-eye, etc.) one (or two) piece hand shaped body, bolt-on graphite neck, 34 in. scale, fretted phenolic or fretless wood fingerboards, 2 Bartolini soapbar humbuckers, volume/tone controls, 3-band EQ controls with active/passive switch, and a custom built Ritter bridge. Basic Basses are finished in a Balm finish, consisting of an oil and wax application (a high gloss polyester lacquer finish is optional for an additional $200). The 1998 announced prices run from $3,870 (**4-String fretless**; $4,050 **4-string fretted**) to $4,500 (**5-string fretless**; $4,770 **5-string fretted**) up to $5,200 (**6-string fretless**; $5,490 **6-string fretted**).

There are now several models being offered, including the **Classic**, the **Roya**, the **Okon**, the **Raptor**, the **Jupiter**, and the **Seal**. They have parametric electronics and 2 triplebuckers (3-coil pickups) and are available in Gold and high gloss Piano Lacquer finishes.

RITZ

See WRC Guitars. Instruments previously built in Calimesa, CA from 1989 to 1990.

Ritz guitars are high quality solid body designs by Wayne R. Charvel (of Charvel/Jackson fame). After a year of production, the Ritz trademark was then superseded by the current **WRC** or **WRC Guitars** (Wayne R. Charvel) trademark. During the year of production under the Ritz name, only a handful of guitars were produced, (Information courtesy Eric J. Galletta, WRC Guitars).

Refer to WRC models for descriptions and pricing information. Due to the limited supply, these models may not appear in the secondary market unless sold by the original owner.

RIVERHEAD

Also Riverhead Guitars. Instruments currently built in Japan since the mid-1980s. Distributed in the U.S. by American Riverhead of Bolingbrook, IL. Distributed in Japan by Headway Co., Ltd. of Japan.

The Headway Company's RiverHead guitar models currently feature a number of different designs. Good quality construction and materials are featured on these instruments (source: Tony Bacon and Paul Day, *The Guru's Guitar Guide*).

GRADING	100% MINT	98% NEAR MINT	95% EXC+	90% EXC	80% VG+	70% VG	60% G

ELECTRIC

An earlier River Head model was the Unicorn, which featured 2 pickups, a smaller original shaped body, and a "headless" neck (no headstock; reverse stringing). Authors Bacon and Day mention a guitar model RUG2090 (Riverhead Unicorn Guitar 2090 perhaps?).

The **Diva** series offers a stylistically different take on the conventional strat-style design, while the **Gracia** series of guitars is more "Ernie Ball/Music Man" influenced. Retail list prices begin at $1,099.

ELECTRIC BASS

Gracia basses are based on the offset double cutaway Jazz body design, and are available in 4- and 5-string configuration. Gracia models have alder or quilted maple top/alder bodies, one-piece maple necks, ebony or rosewood or maple fingerboards, Gotoh hardware (black or gold), 2 Alnico J-style pickups, 2 volume/1 tone controls, and translucent colors. Retail list prices begin at $1,049.

**Ritter "Smor"
Custom 5-String
courtesy Steve Cherne**

ROBELLI, CARLO

Instruments previously produced in Japan circa 1970s. Distributed by Sam Ash of New York, NY.

Carlo Robelli instruments were good quality instruments based on popular American models. They may look like they were produced in Kalamazoo, but the instruments are definitely Asian in construction. Most instruments are in 80% to 90% condition; and generally priced between $175 to $299.

ROBERTS

Instruments previously built in Brea, CA during the early 1990s.

Inventor Curt Roberts and his artist wife, Elizabeth, invented a four-sided guitar neck as a means to supply guitarists with a number of alternative tunings on a single instrument. The **Roto-Caster** was available in 2-, 3-, or 4-neck configurations.

The last given address for Roberts Roto-Neck was 471 West Lambert Rd., Suite 104, Brea, California 92621 (714.256.7276), (FAX) 714.256.7288.

ROBIN GUITARS

Instruments currently built in Houston, TX since 1982. Distributed by Alamo Music Products of Houston, TX.

In 1972, David Wintz teamed up with a friend to open a guitar shop in Houston, Texas. After ten years of dealing, repairing, and restoring vintage guitars, Wintz began building quality instruments and offering them for sale. In addition to building guitars, Wintz began offering Rio Grande pickups in 1993. Originated by veteran pickup winder Bart Wittrock, the Rio Grande pickups are offered in a variety of sounds/applications and colors - including sparkle finishes!

As a further supplement to the standard models listed below, Robin's Custom Shop can assemble virtually anything on a special order basis. Custom graphics and a variety of finishes are also available. Robin guitars feature Rio Grande pickups as standard equipment.

ELECTRIC: AVALON SERIES

Add $325 for Bigsby Tailpiece. Add $350 for abalone dolphin inlay on neck.

AVALON CLASSIC - single cutaway mahogany body, figured maple top, mahogany neck, 22-fret rosewood fingerboard with abalone dot inlay, tune-o-matic bridge/stop tailpiece, blackface peghead with pearl logo inlay, 3-per-side tuners with plastic buttons, nickel hardware, 2 exposed humbucker Seymour Duncan pickups, volume/tone control, 3-position switch, available in Antique Violinburst, Antique Amber, or Antique Tobaccoburst finishes, mfg. 1994-present.

MSR	$2,995	$2,400	$1,950	$1,675	$1,400	$1,150	$925	$750

AVALON DELUXE - single cutaway ash body, figured maple top, mahogany neck, 22-fret rosewood fingerboard with pearl dot inlay, tune-o-matic bridge/stop tailpiece, blackface peghead with pearl logo inlay, 3-per-side tuners with plastic buttons, nickel hardware, 2 exposed humbucker Seymour Duncan pickups, volume/tone control, 3-way switch, available in Metallic Gold or Cherry finishes, mfg. 1994-present.

MSR	$1,995	$1,600	$1,300	$1,100	$950	$800	$650	$500

AVALON FLATTOP - single cutaway ash body, tortoise multilam pickguard, mahogany neck, 22-fret rosewood fingerboard with pearl dot inlay, tune-o-matic bridge/stop tailpiece, blackface peghead with screened logo, 3-per-side tuners with plastic buttons, nickel hardware, 2 exposed humbucker Seymour Duncan pickups, volume/tone control, 3-position switch, available in Old Blonde or Metallic Gold finishes, mfg. 1994-present.

MSR	$1,750	$1,400	$1,150	$975	$825	$675	$550	$450

AVALON GRAND CLASSIC - single cutaway mahogany body with a carved figured maple top, one piece mahogany set neck, 22-fret ebony fingerboard with abalone dot inlays, 2 Rio Grande humbucking pickups, tune-o-matic tailpiece, MOP headstock inlay, 3-per-side tuners, fully bound, two knobs (v, tone), gold hardware, mfg. 2001-present.

MSR	$4,295	$3,450	$2,950	$2,600	N/A	N/A	N/A	N/A

**Robin Avalon
courtesy Sam Baker**

R

GRADING	100% MINT	98% NEAR MINT	95% EXC+	90% EXC	80% VG+	70% VG	60% G

AVALON PRO - single cutaway mahogany body with a carved arched maple top, one piece mahogany set neck, 22-fret rosewood fingerboard with MOP dot inlays, 2 Rio Grande humbucking pickups, tune-o-matic tailpiece, 3-per-side tuners, fully bound, two knobs (v, tone), nickel hardware, available in Vintage Yellow or Cherry finishes, mfg. 2000-present.

	MSR	$1,795		$1,450	$1,200	$1,000	$850	$700	$575	$475

ELECTRIC: MACHETE SERIES

All models in this series have reverse single cutaway asymmetrical bodies with terraced cuts on front and back. Pegheads are asymmetrically V-shaped.

MACHETE CUSTOM - figured maple body, through-body maple neck, 24-fret ebony fingerboard with pearl dot inlay, double locking vibrato, blackface peghead with screened logo, 4/2-per-side Sperzel tuners, black hardware, 2 Seymour Duncan blade humbucker pickups, volume/tone control, 3-position switch, available in Antique Amber or Ruby Red finishes, mfg. 1991-95.

	N/A	$1,600	$1,400	$1,200	$1,050	$900	$750

Last MSR was $2,195.

In 1994, mahogany body, figured maple top, set mahogany neck, rosewood fingerboard, tune-o-matic bridge/stop tailpiece, chrome hardware, pole piece humbucker pickups replaced original parts/designs.

Machete Custom Classic - figured maple body, through-body maple neck, 24-fret ebony fingerboard with pearl dot inlay, double locking vibrato, blackface peghead with screened logo, 4/2-per-side tuners, black hardware, 2 Seymour Duncan blade humbucker pickups, volume/tone control, 3-position switch, available in Antique Amber or Ruby Red finishes, mfg. 1991-95.

	N/A	$1,700	$1,500	$1,300	$1,100	$950	$800

Last MSR was $2,395.

In 1994, mahogany body, excellent grade figured maple top, set mahogany neck, tune-o-matic bridge/stop tailpiece, chrome hardware, pole piece humbucker pickups replaced original parts/designs.

MACHETE DELUXE - mahogany body, through-body mahogany neck, 24-fret rosewood fingerboard with pearl dot inlay, double locking vibrato, body matching peghead with screened logo, 4/2-per-side tuners, black hardware, 2 Seymour Duncan blade humbucker pickups, volume/tone control, 3-position switch, available in Cherry finish, mfg. 1991-95.

	N/A	$1,500	$1,300	$1,100	$950	$800	$650

Last MSR was $1,995.

In 1994, poplar body, set maple neck, pole piece humbucker pickups replaced original parts/designs.

MACHETE SPECIAL - ash body, bolt-on maple neck, 24-fret rosewood fingerboard with pearl dot inlay, double locking vibrato, blackface peghead with screened logo, 4/2-per-side tuners, black hardware, 2 humbucker PJ Marx pickups, volume/tone control, 3-position switch, available in Natural Oil finish, mfg. 1991-94.

	N/A	$700	$600	$500	$425	$350	$275

Last MSR was $995.

MACHETE STANDARD - ash body, bolt-on maple neck, 24-fret rosewood fingerboard with pearl dot inlay, double locking vibrato, body matching peghead with screened logo, 4/2-per-side tuners, black hardware, 2 Seymour Duncan blade humbucker pickups, volume/tone control, 3-position switch, available in Blue or Cherry finishes, current mfg.

	MSR	$2,195		$1,800	$1,500	$1,250	$1,000	$800	$650	$500

Add $225 for double locking tremolo. Add $380 for abalone dolphin inlays on neck.

ELECTRIC: MEDLEY SERIES

All models in this series have V-shaped peghead as an option.

MEDLEY SPECIAL - offset double cutaway ash body, bolt-on maple neck, 24-fret rosewood fingerboard with pearl dot inlay, double locking Floyd Rose vibrato, reverse blade peghead, 6-on-a-side Sperzel tuners, black hardware, single coil/humbucker exposed pickups, volume control, 3-position switch, available in Oil finish, mfg. 1991-95.

	N/A	$700	$600	$500	$425	$350	$275

Last MSR was $995.

MEDLEY STANDARD - offset double cutaway swamp ash or basswood body, bolt-on maple neck, 24-fret rosewood fingerboard with pearl dot inlay, double locking Floyd Rose vibrato, reverse blade peghead, 6-on-a-side Sperzel tuners, black hardware, single 2 exposed Seymour Duncan humbucker pickups, volume/tone control, 3-position switch, available in Blue, Cherry, Natural, Pearl Black, or Purple finishes, mfg. 1991-present.

	MSR	$1,995		$1,600	$1,300	$1,100	$925	$750	$600	$450

Add $225 for double locking tremolo. Add $380 for abalone dolphin inlays on neck.

Medley Standard II-Texas Curly Slabtop - similar to Medley Standard II, except has mahogany body, curly maple top, available in Natural finish, disc. 1995.

	N/A	$1,250	$1,050	$900	$750	$625	$500

Last MSR was $1,820.

Medley Standard II-Texas Quilted Slabtop - similar to Medley Standard II, except has mahogany body, quilted maple top, available in Natural finish, disc. 1995.

	N/A	$1,300	$1,100	$900	$750	$625	$500

Last MSR was $1,870.

MEDLEY STANDARD IV - offset double cutaway hardwood body, bolt-on maple neck, 24-fret rosewood fingerboard with pearl dot inlay, double locking Floyd Rose vibrato, reverse blade peghead, 6-on-a-side Sperzel tuners, black hardware, 2 stacked coil rail/1 pole piece Seymour Duncan humbucker exposed pickups, volume/tone control, 5-position switch, available in Blue, Cherry, Green, Pearl White, or Purple finishes, mfg. 1991-95.

	N/A	$1,000	$850	$725	$600	$500	$400

Last MSR was $1,580.

GRADING	100% MINT	98% NEAR MINT	95% EXC+	90% EXC	80% VG+	70% VG	60% G

Medley Standard IV-Curly - similar to Medley Standard IV, except has curly maple body, mfg. 1991-94.

	N/A	$1,200	$1,050	$900	$750	$625	$500

Last MSR was $1,920.

MEDLEY VI EXOTIC TOP - offset double cutaway hardwood body, bound figured maple top, bolt-on maple neck, 24-fret rosewood fingerboard with pearl dot inlay, double locking Floyd Rose vibrato, reverse blade peghead, 6-on-a-side Sperzel tuners, black hardware, single coil rail/exposed pole piece Seymour Duncan humbucker pickups, volume/tone control, 5-position switch, mfg. 1991-95.

	N/A	$1,200	$1,050	$900	$750	$625	$500

Last MSR was $1,790.

MEDLEY STUDIO IV - offset double cutaway ash body, bolt-on maple neck, 24-fret maple fingerboard with black dot inlay, standard Wilkinson vibrato, reverse blade peghead, 6-on-a-side locking Sperzel tuners, chrome hardware, 2 single coil rail/1 exposed pole piece humbucker Seymour Duncan pickups, volume/tone control, 5-position switch, disc. 1995.

	N/A	$1,100	$950	$800	$700	$600	$500

Last MSR was $1,595.

ELECTRIC: RANGER SERIES

RANGER - offset double cutaway poplar body, pearloid pickguard, controls mounted on a metal plate, bolt-on maple neck, 22-fret rosewood fingerboard with pearl dot inlay, fixed strings through bridge, reverse peghead, 6-on-a-side tuners, chrome hardware, humbucker/2 single coil pickups, volume/tone control, 5-position switch, available in Pearl Black, Pearl Red, or Pearl White finishes, mfg. 1991-2000.

$1,275	$1,050	$925	$795	$650	$525	$395

Last MSR was $1,595.

Add $100 for ash body.

In 1994, standard peghead replaced original parts/design.

**Robin Machette Standard
courtesy Robin Guitars**

RANGER CUSTOM - offset double cutaway bound ash body, white pickguard, metal controls mounted plate, bolt-on figured maple neck, 22-fret rosewood fingerboard with pearl dot inlay, fixed strings through bridge, reverse peghead, 6-on-a-side tuners, chrome hardware, humbucker/2 single coil pickups, volume/tone control, 5-position switch, available in Cherry, Orange, or Three-Tone Sunburst finishes, mfg. 1991-present.

MSR	$1,895		$1,500	$1,250	$1,025	$850	$700	$550	$425

In 1994, standard peghead replaced original parts/design.

Ranger Custom Exotic Top - similar to Ranger Custom, except has bound figured maple top, pearloid pickguard, standard peghead, disc. 1995.

	N/A	$1,100	$950	$800	$700	$600	$500

Last MSR was $1,620.

RANGER REVIVAL - offset double cutaway hardwood body, pearloid pickguard, bolt-on maple neck, 22-fret rosewood fingerboard with pearl dot inlay, standard vibrato, 6-on-a-side Sperzel tuners, 3 single coil pickups, 1 volume/2 tone controls, 5-position switch, disc. 2000.

$1,200	$800	$600	$475	$425	$395	$350

Last MSR was $1,595.

Add $100 for ash body.

RANGER SPECIAL - offset double cutaway ash body, controls mounted on a metal plate, bolt-on maple neck, 22-fret rosewood fingerboard with pearl dot inlay, fixed strings through bridge, reverse peghead, 6-on-a-side tuners, chrome hardware, humbucker/2 single coil pickups, volume/tone control, 5-position switch, available in Natural Oil finish, mfg. 1991-95.

	N/A	$700	$600	$500	$425	$350	$275

Last MSR was $995.

In 1994, standard peghead replaced original parts/design.

RANGER STUDIO - offset double cutaway ash body, white pickguard, controls mounted on a metal plate, bolt-on maple neck, 22-fret rosewood fingerboard with pearl dot inlay, fixed strings through bridge, reverse peghead, 6-on-a-side locking Sperzel tuners, chrome hardware, 3 single coil pickups, volume/tone control, 5-position switch. Available in Cherry Sunburst, Three-Tone Sunburst, Tobacco Sunburst, Two-Tone Sunburst, Unburst, Violin Sunburst and the following Transparent finishes: Blue, Bone White, Charcoal Black, Cherry, Green, Honey, Lavender, Natural, Old Blonde, Orange, Purple, Rootbeer, Violet, or Yellow, mfg. 1991-95.

	N/A	$1,000	$850	$725	$600	$500	$400

Last MSR was $1,540.

In 1994, standard peghead replaced original parts/design.

WRANGLER - similar to Ranger Standard, except has vintage-style fixed bridge, available in 3-Tone Sunburst, Old Blonde, or Black finishes, disc.

$1,275	$1,050	$925	$795	$650	$525	$395

Last MSR was $1,595.

Add $750 for optional Parson White B-Bender.

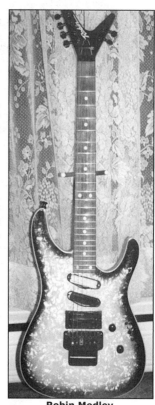

**Robin Medley
courtesy Bob Smith**

R

GRADING	100% MINT	98% NEAR MINT	95% EXC+	90% EXC	80% VG+	70% VG	60% G

ELECTRIC: RAIDER & TEDLEY SERIES

RAIDER STANDARD II - asymmetrical double cutaway reverse hardwood body, bolt-on maple neck, 24-fret rosewood fingerboard with pearl dot inlay, double locking vibrato, reverse headstock, 6-on-a-side tuners, black hardware, 2 humbucker Seymour Duncan pickups, volume/tone control, 3-position switch, available in Blue, Cherry, Natural, Pearl Black, or Purple finishes, disc. 1992.

	N/A	$950	$875	$725	$600	$525	$450

Last MSR was $1,450.

Raider Standard IV - similar to Ranger Standard II, except has 2 stacked coil/1 humbucker Seymour Duncan pickups, tone control, 5-position/coil tap switch, Available in Blue, Cherry, Green, Pearl White, OR Purple finishes, disc. 1992.

	N/A	$1,000	$875	$750	$650	$550	$475

Last MSR was $1,520.

TEDLEY STANDARD VI - single cutaway hardwood body, bolt-on maple neck, 24-fret rosewood fingerboard with pearl dot inlay, double locking vibrato, reverse headstock, 6-on-a-side tuners, black hardware, stacked coil/humbucker Seymour Duncan pickups, volume/tone control, 3-position switch, available in Cherry, Orange, Pearl Black, or Purple finishes, mfg. 1991-94.

	N/A	$1,025	$875	$725	$575	$525	$450

Last MSR was $1,450.

ELECTRIC: SAVOY SERIES

SAVOY CLASSIC - single cutaway mahogany semi-hollow body, carved curly maple top, mahogany neck, 22-fret rosewood fingerboard with abalone dot inlay, 24.75" scale, tune-o-matic bridge/stop tailpiece, 2 f-holes, blackface peghead with pearl logo inlay, 3-per-side tuners with plastic buttons, nickel hardware, 2 Rio Grande humbuckers, volume/tone control, 3-position switch on upper bass bout, available in Antique Violinburst, Antique Amber, or Wine Red, disc. 2000.

	$2,400	$1,975	$1,725	$1,495	$1,250	$1,000	$750

Last MSR was $2,995.

Add $325 for Bigsby Tailpiece.

Savoy Dolphin Classic - similar to the Savoy Classic, except has dolphin inlays, current mfg.

MSR	$3,795	$3,050	$2,600	$2,200	$1,850	$1,450	$1,150	$850

SAVOY STANDARD (DELUXE) - single cutaway swamp ash solid or poplar semi-hollow body, carved arched top, mahogany neck, 22-fret rosewood fingerboard with pearl dot inlay, 2 f-holes, tune-o-matic bridge/stop tailpiece, blackface peghead with pearl logo inlay, 3-per-side tuners with plastic buttons, nickel hardware, 2 Rio Grande humbucker pickups, volume/tone control, 3-position switch on upper bass bout, available in Metallic Gold, Cherry, Orange, or Old Blonde finishes, current mfg.

MSR	$2,195	$1,750	$1,450	$1,250	$1,050	$900	$750	$600

Add $325 for Bigsby Tailpiece. Add $380 for abalone dolphin inlay on neck.

Cherry finish can be supplemented with an optional Bigsby and gold-plated hardware. This model was renamed the Savoy Standard sometime in the early 2000s.

SAVOY PRO - single cutaway mahogany body, carved arched maple top, mahogany set neck, 22-fret rosewood fingerboard with MOP dot inlay, 2 f-holes, tune-o-matic bridge/stop tailpiece, blackface peghead with pearl logo inlay, 3-per-side tuners with plastic buttons, nickel hardware, 2 Rio Grande humbucker pickups, volume/tone control, 3-position switch on upper bass bout, available in Antique Tobacco Sunburst or Cherry finishes, current mfg.

MSR	$1,795	$1,450	$1,200	$1,000	$850	$700	$575	$475

ELECTRIC BASS

In 1998, Robin Guitars introduced the **Freedom Bass**, a model with classic body styling and Rio Grande ´Powerbucker´ passive pickups. The Freedom Bass was offered in a 4-string (list $1,595) and 5-string ($1,695) configurations. The **Freedom Bass Active** was offered with humbucker pickups and active electronics in 4-string (list $1,795) and 5-string (list $1,895) configurations.

JAYBIRD (RANGER JAYBIRD) - offset double cutaway asymmetrical ash body, pearloid pickguard, controls mounted on a metal plate, bolt-on maple neck, 20-fret rosewood fingerboard with pearl dot inlay, fixed bridge, reverse peghead, 4-on-a-side tuners, chrome hardware, 2 J-style pickups, volume/tone control, 3-position switch, mfg. 1991-1996, 1998-2000.

	$1,200	$1,050	$925	$795	$650	$525	$395

Last MSR was $1,595.

This model is similar to the Ranger Bass, but with the Jaybird body style. In 1994, standard peghead replaced original parts/design.

JAYWALKER (RANGER JAYWALKER) - offset double cutaway asymmetrical ash body, figured maple top, bolt-on maple neck, 20-fret ebony fingerboard with pearl dot inlay, fixed bridge, 4-on-a-side tuners, black hardware, 2 J-style Bartolini pickups, volume/treble/bass/mix controls, mfg. 1991-96.

	N/A	$1,100	$950	$825	$700	$600	$500

Last MSR was $1,865.

Jaywalker Active - similar to the Jaywalker, except features ´Double J´ pickups, active electronics, available in 3-Tone Sunburst or Tobacco Sunburst finishes, disc.

	N/A	$1,200	$1,000	$875	$750	$650	$550

Last MSR was $1,995.

R

GRADING	100% MINT	98% NEAR MINT	95% EXC+	90% EXC	80% VG+	70% VG	60% G

MACHETE V 5 STRING - reverse single cutaway asymmetrical body with 'terraced' ash body, bolt-on maple neck, 24-fret rosewood fingerboard with pearl dot inlay, fixed Schaller bridge, V-shaped peghead, 3/2-per-side tuners, black hardware, 2 Bartolini pickups, volume/treble/bass/mix controls, active electronics, available in Trans. Cherry, Trans. Green, or Pearl Black finishes, mfg. 1991-96, 1998-2000.

	$1,600	$1,400	$1,175	$995	$875	$675	$550

Last MSR was $2,195.

In 1994, ebony fingerboard replaced original parts/design.

MEDLEY - offset double cutaway ash body, bolt-on maple neck, 24-fret rosewood fingerboard with pearl dot inlay, fixed bridge, V-shaped peghead, 2-per-side tuners, black hardware, P/J-style pickups, volume/tone control, 3-position switch, available in Pearl Black, Pearl White, Trans. Blue, or Trans. Cherry finishes, mfg. 1991-96, 1998-2000.

	$1,200	$1,050	$925	$795	$650	$525	$395

Last MSR was $1,595.

In 1994, reverse blade peghead replaced original parts/design.

RANGER - offset double cutaway ash body, black pickguard, controls mounted on a metal plate, bolt-on maple neck, 20-fret maple fingerboard with black dot inlay, fixed bridge, reverse peghead, 4-on-a-side Sperzel tuners, chrome hardware, P/J-style pickups, volume/tone control, 3-position switch, available in Pearl Black, Pearl Red, or Trans. Old Blonde finishes, mfg. 1991-96.

	N/A	$950	$825	$700	$600	$500	$400

Last MSR was $1,265.

In 1994, standard peghead replaced original parts/design.

Ranger Bass VI - similar to Ranger, except has 24-fret rosewood fingerboard with pearl dot inlay, fixed strings through bridge, 6-on-a-side Sperzel tuners, 3 single coil pickups, disc. 1994.

	N/A	$1,000	$850	$725	$600	$500	$400

Last MSR was $1,365.

Ranger Special - similar to Ranger, except has no pickguard, rosewood fingerboard, disc. 1994.

	N/A	$700	$600	$500	$425	$350	$300

Last MSR was $995.

Robin Savoy
courtesy David Wertz

ROBINSON

Instruments currently built in Newburyport, MA.

Robinson Custom Guitars currently offers two models (SC-1 and SC-2) as well as custom design solid body electrics. Options include choice of woods, figured or exotic tops, hardware, and pickups.

ROCKINGER

Instruments and parts currently produced in Germany since 1978.

Rockinger has been producing numerous high quality replacement parts for a number of years; it seems only natural for them to produce quality original design guitars as well (source: Tony Bacon, *The Ultimate Guitar Book*). For more information refer to their website (see Trademark Index).

ROCKOON

Instruments previously produced in Japan by Kawai.

Good quality solid body guitars and basses featuring superstrat and original designs. Basses are the sleeker body design prevalent since the mid 1980s (RB series). Superstrats such as the RG, RF, or RGT series feature variations on single/humbucker pickup combinations. Rockoon guitars are equipped with Rockoon/Kawai or Shadow pickups, and Schaller hardware.

ROCKSON

Instruments previously built in Taiwan during the late 1980s.

Rockson solid body guitars featured designs based on the then-popular "superstrat" design, and other Fender-derived designs (source: Tony Bacon and Paul Day, *The Guru's Guitar Guide*).

ROCKWOOD

See Hohner. Instruments previously produced in Korea. Previously distributed in the U.S. by HSS (a Division of Hohner, Inc.), located in Richmond, VA.

The Hohner company was founded in 1857, and is currently the world's largest manufacturer and distributor of harmonicas. Hohner offers a wide range of solidly constructed musical instruments. The Rockwood (or Rockwood Pro) models are good student level Strat-style electrics. The Rockwood name is currently used on starter drumsets offered by Hohner.

ELECTRIC

LX 100G - double offset cutaway maple body, black pickguard, bolt-on maple neck, 22-fret rosewood fingerboard with pearl dot inlay, standard vibrato, 6-on-a-side tuners, chrome hardware, 3 single coil pickups, 2 volume/tone controls, 5-position switch, available in Black and Red finishes, mfg. 1992-96.

	N/A	$150	$125	$100	$90	$80	$75

Last MSR was $260.

R

GRADING	100% MINT	98% NEAR MINT	95% EXC+	90% EXC	80% VG+	70% VG	60% G

LX 200G - similar to LX100G, except has white pickguard, 2 single coil/humbucker pickups, volume/tone control, coil split switch, available in Black and White finishes, mfg. 1992-96.

	N/A	$200	$175	$150	$125	$110	$100

Last MSR was $330.

LX 250G - single sharp cutaway bound maple body, white pickguard, mahogany neck, 22-fret bound rosewood fingerboard with pearl crown inlay, tune-o-matic bridge/stop tailpiece, 3-per-side tuners, chrome hardware, 2 humbucker pickups, 2 volume/2 tone controls, 3-position switch, available in Antique Sunburst or Black finishes, mfg. 1992-96.

	N/A	$220	$190	$160	$125	$115	$100

Last MSR was $375.

RP-150G - double offset cutaway maple body, bolt-on maple neck, 22-fret rosewood fingerboard with dot inlay, vintage-style tremolo bridge, 6-on-a-side tuners, chrome hardware, white pickguard, 3 exposed pole piece single coil pickups, 2 volume/1 tone controls, 5-position switch, available in Black, Candy Apple Red, Ivory, Metallic Blue, Turquoise, or Two-Tone Sunburst finishes, disc.

$200	$175	$150	$125	$100	$85	$75

Last MSR was $275.

Add $25 for maple fingerboard (Model RP-180G). This model was discontinued in 1997.

ELECTRIC BASS

LX100B - offset double cutaway hardwood body, bolt-on maple neck, 21-fret rosewood fingerboard with white dot inlay, fixed bridge, 4-on-a-side tuners, chrome hardware, P-style pickup, volume/tone control, available in Black or Red finishes, mfg. 1992-96.

	N/A	$200	$170	$140	$120	$100	$80

Last MSR was $300.

LX200B - similar to LX100B, except has short scale neck, disc. 1996.

	N/A	$170	$140	$120	$100	$90	$80

Last MSR was $270.

LX300B - similar to LX100B, except has white pickguard, P/J-style pickups, 2 volume/tone control, disc. 1994.

	N/A	$220	$190	$160	$140	$120	$100

RP150B LONG SCALE BASS - offset double cutaway hardwood body, bolt-on maple neck, 21-fret rosewood fingerboard with white dot inlay, fixed bridge, 4 on a side tuners, chrome hardware, P-style pickup, volume/tone controls, available in Black, Red, or Sunburst finishes, disc.

$250	$215	$190	$165	$140	$115	$85

Last MSR was $325.

RP120B SHORT SCALE BASS - similar to the RP150B, except features 20-fret fingerboard, shorter scale, downsized body, available in Black finish, disc.

$215	$185	$165	$140	$120	$95	$75

Last MSR was $289.

ROGER

Instruments previously built in West Germany from the late 1950s to mid-1960s.

Luthier Wenzel Rossmeisl built very good to high quality archtop guitars as well as a semi-solid body guitar called "Model 54." Rossmeisl derived the trademark name in honor of his son, Roger Rossmeisl.

Roger Rossmeisl (1927-1979) was raised in Germany and learned luthier skills from his father, Wenzel. One particular feature was the "German Carve," a feature used by Wenzel to carve an indented plane around the body outline on the guitar's top. Roger Rossmeisl then travelled to America, where he briefly worked for Gibson in Kalamazoo, Michigan (in a climate not unlike his native Germany). Shortly thereafter he moved to California, and was employed at the Rickenbacker company. During his tenure at Rickenbacker, Rossmeisl was responsible for the design of the Capri and Combo guitars, and custom designs. His apprentice was a young Semie Moseley, who later introduced the "German Carve" on his own Mosrite brand guitars. Rossmeisl left Rickenbacker in 1962 to help Fender develop their own line of acoustic guitars (Fender had been licensing Harmony-made Regals up till then), and later introduced the Montego and LTD archtop electrics.

ROGERS

See chapter on House Brands.

This trademark has been identified as a House Brand of Selmer (UK) (source: Willie G. Moseley, *Stellas & Stratocasters*).

ROGUE

Instruments currently produced in Korea. Distributed by Musician's Friend of Medford, OR.

Musician's Friend distributes a line of good quality student and entry level instruments through their mail order catalog. Musician's Friend now offers a wide range of good quality guitars at an affordable price. For further information, contact Musician's Friend directly (see Trademark Index).

ROK AXE

Instruments currently produced in Korea. Distributed by Muse of Inchon, Korea.

The Muse company is currently offering a wide range of electric guitar and bass models, as well as a number of acoustic guitar models. Rok Axe models are generally fine entry level to student quality instruments. Rok Axe instruments are distributed by several companies. Prices generally start around $100.

R

ROKKOR

Instruments currently produced in Asia. Distributed by the L.A. Guitar Works of Reseda, CA.

Rokkor electric guitars are currently offered as part of a guitar & amp package designed for the beginning guitarist. The strat-styled models is available in Candy Red or 3-Tone Sunburst finishes, maple or rosewood fingerboards, and chrome hardware. List price for the guitar/amp package is $338.

ROLAND

Instruments previously built in Japan by Fuji Gen Gakki during the late 1970s through mid-1980s (these instruments feature both a 1/4 in. phono plug and a 24-pin cable attachment). Distributed in the U.S. by Roland Musical Instruments of Los Angeles, CA.

The Roland company was founded in Japan, and has been one of the premier synthesizer builders since its inception in 1974. By 1977, the company began experimenting with guitar synthesis. Traditionally, synthesizers have been linked with keyboards as their key mechanism is easier to adapt to trigger the synthesized voice. Early keys on keyboards were as simple as the lightswitch in your house: press down for "on," release for "off!" As synthesizers continued to evolve (today's model uses microprocessors similar to a home PC computer), the keys provided more information like "velocity"(how hard the key was struck, held, or released - just like a piano).

In 1977, Roland reasoned that the keyboard provided the controlling information to the synthesizer, or was the "controller." In a similar parallel, then, Roland introduced a guitar "controller" and a separate synthesizer. The first system (1977-1980) featured the **GS-500** guitar and the **GR-500** synth, a vaguely Gibsonish single cutaway model with 10 plus switches. The GR-500 featured sounds from the then-current Roland keyboard synths, and the unit was fairly large and full of switches.

Roland's second series (1980-1984) was a direct improvement on their initial design. The **GR-100** (yellow box) and the **GR-300** (blue box) units are much more compact and designed to be placed on the floor - like "synth stompboxes." Roland introduced four guitar models: two models (**202** and **505**) were based on Fender-ish body styles, and the other two (**303** and **808**) were more Gibson-esque in their designs. The first bass-driven synth was also introduced with the **G-33** "controller" and the **GR-33B** synth in a floor package. These specific instruments were built for Roland by Fuji Gen Gakki (builders for Ibanez, Greco, and Fender's Squire series).

The tracking, or reproduction of note(s) struck and when, by these early 1980s systems was better than the GS-500/GR-500 system. The tracking (response time) has always been the biggest hurdle to overcome in guitar systhesis, with many units being rejected by guitarists because they don't respond quick enough, or with the same dynamics as the original part. Fair enough, but when you consider the amount of information provided by striking one note on a guitar string (pitch, note length, bend, vibrato, etc) you can see the innate difficulty Roland struggled with.

The third series (1984-1986) is the most eye-catching system from Roland. The effects pedal look of the blue and yellow boxes was replaced by the sleek looking **GR-700** and **GR-700B** (bass unit). Standard Fender and Gibson guitar designs were replaced by the **G-707** guitar and **G-77** bass "controllers" which featured an offset design (that made lap placement damn near impossible!), and a "stabilizer bar" that ran from the body to the headstock. The futuristic designs looked exciting, and certainly were high quality, but the unusual appearance led to a quick exit from the market.

One of the key downfalls to the whole Roland system of synthesis was the fact that a guitar player had to buy the full package from Roland. No matter what your favorite guitar was, you could only approach synthesizing sounds through a Roland model guitar. Alternate keyboard controllers had been available to keyboardists for a number of years, and the "controller" just had to be a collection of keys that could trigger a synth. Thanks to the advent of MIDI and formalized MIDI codes beginning in 1982, company A's controller could run Company B and Company C's synthesizers. In 1988 (possibly 1987), Roland made an important breakthrough when they introduced the **GK-1 Synthesizer Driver**. The GK-1 was a small black rectangular decoder unit that was held in place by the strap button on the lower bout of the guitar. Guitar signals were picked up with a hex-designed string pickup that mounted near the bridge of your favorite guitar, as well as a 1/4" phone plug to pick up additional information from the magnetic pickups. The signal ran back to the **GM-70 GR-MIDI Converter** rack unit, and signal information was then split into MIDI and regular guitar signal for additional sound reinforcement. The GK-1 had onboard controls for master volume and balance, as well as continuous controller #1 and #2. Just like the previous GR series synths (GR-100, GR-300, GR-700), the GK-1/GM-70 connected with a 24-pin cable. Therefore (and mentioned in the Roland advertising), a "G" Series guitar can also work with the GM-70. While the GS Series forerunner only works with itself, any "G Series guitar can work with any "G" Series synth (just check for the 24-pin connector). At this point, Roland got out of the guitar business, and completely into the guitar synthesis business because they finally supplied a "box" that you could slip on your favorite guitar.

In 1989, modernization stepped in when Roland revamped the GK-1 with the **GK-2**. Gone was the 24-pin bulky block connector in favor of a slim, rounded 13-pin cable. The GK-2 slimmed into a smaller triangular unit that took up less space on the lower bout of the player's guitar, and the GM-70 evolved into the **GR-50** single space rack unit. Currently, Roland markets an upgraded synth driver (**GK-2A**), which some companies such as Fender and Godin build directly into production models. The rack mounted GR-50 has been redesigned into the **GR-1** floor unit (shades of the GR-100!), and the GR-1's 200 "voices" can be expanded into 400 total with in the unit - as well as driving an external synthesizer. Roland also offers a **GR-09** floor unit, and a single half-rack unit called the **GI-10** (which converts Roland GK-2A information into standard MIDI information). Furthermore, Roland has recently introduced a new unit called the **VG-8** (for virtual guitar) which processes the information sent by a GK-2A driver into different (non-synth) pathways to create a whole new category of "guitar processing."

One of the first things to check for when encountering a Roland synth-guitar is that 24-pin cable. The 24-pin design was proprietary for this system, and does not a similar design available at the local computer store - and they are currently "out of stock" on this crucial item at Roland. So even if you aren't going to use the synthesizer, just having the cable brings the value up!

Original list price of the GR-100 was $595; the GR-300 was $995 (!). There was a splitter box called the US-2 that could be used to patch the two units together.

R

GRADING	100% MINT	98% NEAR MINT	95% EXC+	90% EXC	80% VG+	70% VG	60% G

ELECTRIC/SYNTHESIZER CONTROLLER

Roland's dedication to the guitar synth made them the de facto industry standard. During Roland's second series of guitar synths (1980 to 1984) a number of other guitar builders also produced instruments that could "drive" the Roland **GR-100** and **GR-300** synthesizers (and later the **GR-70**0). The following prices listed after each model reflect the 1986 retail price: Gibson Les Paul ($1,299) and Explorer ($1,049); Hamer A 7 Phantom ($1,500); Modulus Graphite Blacknife Special Synth Controller ($1,500); M.V. Pedulla MVP-S guitar ($1,745) Steinberger GL2T-GR ($2,250); Zion Turbo Synth ($1,395). If you do find the following instruments, now you know why they have the funny plug and extra knobs on them! In the mid to late 1980s, Aria built a number of guitar controllers with magnetic pickups, piezo pickups, and a Roland GR- MIDI system all onboard. These models may have "Aria Custom Shop" on the headstock. Aria offered the MIDI system in the PE DLX MID model, FL MID model, and AVB MID 4 bass model. All have extra synth controlling knobs and both a 1/4 in. phono and a 13-pin DIN jacks mounted on the sides.

G-202 - offset double cutaway body, 6-on-a-side tuners, 2 humbuckers, pickup selector switch on pickguard's treble bout, 2 volume and 2 tone knobs, three synth dedicated switches, mfg. 1980-84.

	N/A	$600	$500	$425	$350	$300	$250

The G-202 guitar controller was designed to be used in conjunction with the GR-100 and GR-300 model synthesizers.

G-303 - slightly offset double cutaway body, 3+3 headstock, 2 humbuckers, pickup selector switch on upper bass bout, 2 volume and 2 tone knobs, chrome hardware, 3 dedicated synth switches, bridge, and stop tailpiece, mfg. 1980-84.

	N/A	$600	$500	$425	$350	$275	$225

The G-303 guitar controller was designed to be used in conjunction with the GR-100 and GR-300 model synthesizers.

G-505 - offset double cutaway body, six-on-a-side tuners, 3 single coils, 5-way pickup selector switch on pickguard's treble bout, 2 volume and 2 tone knobs, tremolo bridge, three synth dedicated switches, mfg. 1980-84.

	N/A	$650	$550	$475	$400	$325	$275

The G-505 guitar controller was designed to be used in conjunction with the GR-100 and GR-300 model synthesizers.

G-707 - asymmetrical "sharkfin" body with extra "stabilizing" graphite arm that connects to headstock, reverse six on a side headstock, 2 covered humbuckers, selector switch, mfg. 1983-86.

	N/A	$1,000	$850	$750	$650	$550	$450

The G-707 guitar controller was designed to be used in conjunction with the GR-700 model synthesizer. The whole package, when introduced in 1983, had a retail price of $2,995 (Guitar controller, $995; GR-700 floor unit, $1,995).

G-808 - slightly offset double cutaway body, laminated central strip with body "wings," 3+3 headstock, 2 humbuckers, pickup selector switch on upper bass bout, 2 volume and 2 tone knobs, gold hardware, 3 dedicated synth switches, bridge, and stop tailpiece, mfg. 1980-84.

	N/A	$900	$750	$650	$550	$450	$350

The G-808 guitar controller was designed to be used in conjunction with the GR-100 and GR-300 model synthesizers.

GS-500 - single cutaway hardwood body, 2 humbuckers, 3+3 headstock, pickup selector switch, 2 volume and 2 tone knobs, extra synth-dedicated knobs and switches, mfg. 1977-1980.

	N/A	$850	$750	$650	$550	$475	$400

The GS-500 guitar controller was designed to be used in conjunction with the GR-500 model synthesizer.

ELECTRIC BASS/SYNTH CONTROLLER

G-33 - offset double cutaway body, four on a side tuners, 1 magnetic pickup/1 hex MIDI pickup, fixed bridge, 1 volume and 2 tone knobs, assorted synth-dedicated controls, mfg. 1980-84.

	N/A	$600	$500	$425	$375	$325	$250

The G-33 guitar controller was designed to be used in conjunction with the GR-33B model synthesizer.

B-88 - Similar to the G-33, except featured a center laminated strip and 2 body "wings," and same pickup/synth configuration, available in Natural finish, mfg. 1980-84.

	N/A	$700	$600	$500	$425	$350	$275

The G-88 guitar controller was designed to be used in conjunction with the GR-33B model synthesizer.

G-77 - asymmetrical "sharkfin" body with extra "stabilizing" graphite arm that connects to headstock, reverse four on a side headstock, 2 pickups, selector switches, mfg. 1984-85.

	N/A	$500	$425	$350	$300	$250	$175

The G-77 guitar controller was designed to be used in conjunction with the G-700B model synthesizer.

ROMAN, ED

Guitar manufacturer and dealer located in Las Vegas, NV since 2002. Previously located in Danbury, CT until circa 2002.

In 1998, luthier/designer Ed Roman opened his own custom guitar company (see Roman & Lipman).

Roman is definitely a guitar-oriented individual. His website on the internet is possibly the largest site dedicated to guitars, and features information, articles, opinions, and various services available for custom built guitars. Roman is also a large buyer and seller in the secondary guitar market, and favors good quality, well built guitars.

Ed Roman also maintains another company called Exotic Tonewoods that makes pieces of exotic woods available to custom luthiers and guitar builders. Due to the variances in wood, hardware, and pickups, the following models show no listed "base" price. However, these high quality instruments are still fairly reasonable for the options available to the player. Please contact Ed Roman Guitars directly (see Trademark Index) for a current listing of the various trademarks and manufacturers they are representing currently.

ELECTRIC

Roman´s previous custom-built model is the **Edberger** which can best be described as a cross between a Steinberger double cutaway model and an Ernie Ball ´Van Halen´ model. The **Edberger** has the headless, reverse stringing design of a Steinberger combined with an Original Steinberger TransTrem or S Trem tremolo bridge; but also maintains the offset shallow cutaway feel of the Ernie Ball. Edberger models were available with Korina, basswood, alder, mahogany, or swamp ash bodies; quilted, burled, flame, or spalted maple tops; birds-eye maple or ebony fingerboards; choice of pickups (Tom Holmes, Duncan, EMG, Dimarzio); choice of Original Steinberger TransTrem or S Trem tremolo; solid wood or Strandular Graphite neck; and literally 100 different color finishes. Edberger models were available in left-handed and 12-string configurations, or with custom inlays. Roman also offered other custom-built models like the **Fly-berger**, **X-berger**, and current Leslie West signature models. Roman´s **Mystery Guitar** model has a solid Honduran mahogany body, neck-through design, archtop quilted or flamed maple tops, 24-fret bound ebony fingerboard, abalone purfling, and choice of hardware and pickups (Tom Holmes, Duncan, DiMarzio, PRS, or EMG). For further information regarding custom options and pricing, please contact Ed Roman at Ed Roman Guitars directly (see Trademark Index).

ROMAN & LIPMAN

Instruments previously built in Danbury, CT from 1991 to 1997. Distributed by Roman & Lipman Guitars of Danbury, CT. See Ed Roman.

Luthier Ed Roman and his partner Barry Lipman founded R & L in the early 1990s to offer custom-built instruments to players who were not satisfied with the usual production guitars. R & L, a successful division of the East Coast Music Mall, began offering custom instruments that featured the "most spectacular" wood available. After seven years, Ed Roman left to form his own custom guitar company.

All Roman & Lipman instruments were hand built in the U.S. with American components, with the exception of certain imported exotic woods. Roman & Lipman also offered numerous hardware, pickup, and electronic options. As a result, any Roman & Lipman bass encountered in the secondary market (which is a fairly rare event), must be viewed and priced as a custom-built instrument; in other words, priced for what the market will bear.

ELECTRIC

Due to the variances in wood, hardware, and pickups, the following models show no listed "base" price. However, these high quality instruments are still fairly reasonable for the options available to the player. Certain models have been listed for $1,995 up to $2,995 in past publications.

The following model descriptions are the general parameters for the listing as each instrument was basically a custom order. In other words, there is no "standard" base model — guidelines, body designs, and customer satisfaction were the rules of thumb.

The **Penetrator** guitar was first introduced in 1991, and was Roman & Lipman´s neck-through solid body guitar. This model boasts a straight string pull with a 3-per-side headstock design; choices of over 15 different body woods, 10 different fingerboard woods, pickups, bridges and electronics. The neck-through design also sports Roman & Lipman´s trademarked "No heel neck joint."

The **Sceptre** guitar was introduced in 1992, and was Roman & Lipman´s bolt-on neck model. This traditional style guitar boasts high quality tone-wood bodies such as koa, quilted maple and mahogany combinations, myrtlewood, spalted maple, burl maple, and over 10 more choices. Numerous fingerboard materials include pau ferro, brazilian rosewood, snakewood, koa, macassar ebony, flame maple, figured wenge, and others. R & L also offered numerous hardware, pickup, and electronic options.

ELECTRIC BASS

The Intruder bass was offered beginning in 1994 as a four, five, or six string hand constructed instrument. Featuring such tone woods as quilted maple, koa, korina, congalo alves, and bubinga, these basses have a five piece neck-through-body construction. Different scale lengths, a variety of electronics, pickups combine with R & L´s exclusive "Posi-Phase" bridge systems which helps detract the Low B phase cancellation problems on 5 and 6 string models. The Invader bass was introduced in 1996. A slightly different body design differentiates the Invader from its older brother, the Intruder, but both basses share similar woods, construction, and options.

ROSCOE GUITARS

Instruments currently built in Greensboro, NC since 1971.

Luthier Keith Roscoe opened a shop in Greensboro, North Carolina in 1971 called The Guitar Shop. From its early origins of four or five guitars a year, the workshop turned into a production facility capable of 20 to 30 guitars a month. Roscoe had produced over 900 custom guitars by 1990, and three quarters of them featured custom airbrush or color finishes (source: Tom Wheeler, *American Guitars*).

Keith Roscoe now focuses on bass guitars. His models feature neck and body woods selected from his collection, and special attention is given to matching the woods for both sound and beauty. For further information, please contact Roscoe Guitars directly (see Trademark Index).

ELECTRIC BASS GUITARS

Other options available on all models include ebony, bird´s-eye maple, diamondwood, fretless, and fretless with lines fingerboards, custom inlays, choice of quilted or bird´s-eye maple, cocobola, burl maple, burl myrtle, burl redwood bodies, exhibition grade tops of quilted maple, flame maple, figured maple and other exotic woods. Left-handed models are available for an additional $135. There is also a Century Bass available in five string configuration ($3,250), and a six-string ($3,450).

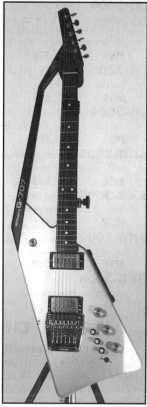

**Rolan G-707
courtesy Rob's Island Guitars**

R

LG-3000 - offset solid body, choice of Spanish cedar, mahogany or swamp ash, 4 strings, 24 frets, choice of rosewood, maple, diamond wood, or spalted purple heart, 34 in. scale, small body, figured or flamed maple top, 2 Bartolini pickups plus standard 2-way EQ & Bartolini preamp, Gotoh or Hipshot tuners, black Hipshot bridge, available in Antique Yellow, Bright Yellow, Emerald Green, Bright Red, Roscoe Red, Cordovan, Purple, Aqua, Cobalt Blue, Faded Blue Jean, Orange, Tobacco Sunburst, Amber, or Black, current mfg.

    MSR   **$2,495**

LG-3005 - similar to Model LG-300 except in a 5-string configuration, 35 in. scale, otherwise same features and choice of colors as its 4 string brother, current mfg.

    MSR   **$2,950**

LG-3006 - offset double cutaway LG solid body, similar to LG-3000 and LG-3005 except in a 6-string configuration, same features and colors options as those models, designed in conjunction with Jimmy Haslip, current mfg.

    MSR   **$3,175**

SKB-3005 - offset double cutaway body, standard 5-string design, body slightly larger than LG series basses, 35 in. scale, 24 frets, same color choices and options as previously listed, current mfg.

    MSR   **$2,950**

SKB-3006 - offset double cutaway body, standard 6-string design, body slightly larger than LG series basses, 35 in. scale, 24 frets, same color choices and options as previously listed, current mfg.

    MSR   **$3,175**

SKB-3007 - similar to Model SKB-3006 except in a 7-string configuration, can be strung with a low F# or high F, same color options and features as other models, current mfg.

    MSR   **$3,550**

SKB-3008 - similar to Model SKB-3007 except in an 8-string configuration, tuned from low F# to High F (.20 wound), same choice of colors and options as other models, disc.

Last MSR was $3,695.

ROSE GUITARS

Instruments previously built in Nashville, TN 1981-1998.

These high quality handcrafted guitars feature American made hardware and pickups, as well as highly figured tops. Rose´s custom guitars have been played by a number of Nashville's better-known guitar players and session players. Rose, originally an Oregon native, moved to Nashville in the late 1970s. In 1981, he launched both the Rose Guitar Center in Henderson (right outside Nashville) and Jonathan Rose custom guitars. The Rose Guitar Center was been in the same location for the past fifteen years, and featured both new and used instrument sales as well as repair and custom work. Jonathan was ably assisted by his wife Angela, and both could be found either at the shop, or at vintage shows displaying their guitars, (Biography courtesy Jonathan and Angela Rose, June 1996).

Since 1981, Rose built over 200 custom guitars. Of the 200, 25 were basses. The serialization began in 1981 with #1, and Rose maintained a list of the original specifications, colors, woods, and original owners for each and every one.

ELECTRIC

The following models were all available in Translucent, Emerald Green, Amber, Burgundy, Deep Water Blue, Two-tone Heritage Cherry Burst, and Two-tone Tobacco Burst finishes. Additional custom options include:

    Add $595 for a Parsons-White String Bender. Add $200 for a marbleized finish. Add $700 for a tree of life neck inlay. Add $375 for a mini tree of life inlay. Add $400 for a horse and horse shoe inlay. Add $100 for top binding. Add $250 for top binding with Abalone. Add $250 for a Floyd Rose Tremolo. Add $200 for a Wilkerson Convertible Bridge.

CUSTOM - single cutaway hollow swamp ash body, flamed maple top, two Van Zantz humbucker pickups, one single coil pickup, bird´s-eye maple neck with bird´s-eye fingerboard, and gold hardware, disc.

Last MSR was $1,695.

ELITE - double cutaway alder or mahogany body, quilted or flamed maple top, two Seymour Duncan pickups, and chrome or gold hardware, disc.

Last MSR was $2,495.

F-HOLE HOLLOWBODY - hollow swamp ash body, two Van Zantz single coil pickups, bird´s-eye maple neck with Brazilian rosewood fingerboard, and chrome hardware, disc.

Last MSR was $1,295.

STANDARD - single cutaway alder body, flame or quilted maple top, contoured back, three Seymour Duncan Alnico pro II single coil pickups, bird´s-eye maple neck with ebony fingerboard, and gold hardware, disc.

Last MSR was $1,595.

7/8 STRAT STYLE - offset double cutaway swamp ash body, bird´s-eye maple neck, ebony fingerboard, three Seymour Duncan single coil pickups, and chrome hardware, disc.

Last MSR was $1,295.

ROSETTI

See Egmond and Shergold. Instruments previously produced in Holland during the early 1960s through the mid-1970s; one solid body model built in England by another company in 1969.

The Rosetti trademark was a brand name used by a UK importer. The Rosetti name turned up on Dutch-built Egmond solid and semi-hollowbody guitars during the 1960s. The same British importer also stocked a Shergold-made solid body model "Triumph" in 1969 (source: Tony Bacon and Paul Day, *The Guru's Guitar Guide*).

ROTOSOUND

Instruments previously built in England in the mid-1970s.

English custom luthier John Birch both designed and built the Rotosound instruments. This high quality solid body did not have any cut-aways in the overall design, and a modular pickup configuration offered the variety of 10 different plug-ins (source: Tony Bacon and Paul Day, *The Guru's Guitar Guide*).

R

ROWAN CUSTOM GUITARS

Instruments currently built in Garland, TX, since 1997.

Rowan Custom Guitars is a small company in Garland, Texas. Headed by Mike Rowan, this company handcrafts their solid and semi-solid guitars "one at a time" to focus attention to the details and construction techniques. Rowan stives to provide the best instrument possible without pricing guitars out of most people's reach. For further information regarding specifications and options, contact Rowan Custom Guitars directly (see Trademark Index).

ELECTRIC

Rowan offers several guitar models: the RSN (Journeyman) Set Neck (list $2,500, and $2,750 for a quilted maple top), the RC (list $1,700), the RCT-1 (disc., last MSR $2,495), RCT-2 (disc., last MSR $2,495), the RCT-3 (disc., last MSR $2,495), the Cimarron ($3,000), the Sierra ($3,300) the hollowbody Montara I (list $3,500), and Montara II (list $2,750) models.

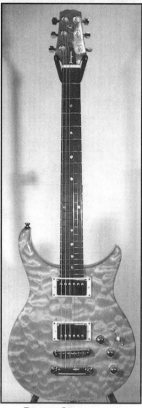

Rowan Journeyman courtesy Rowan Custom Guitars

ROY CUSTOM GUITARS

Instruments currently built in Chelmsford (Ontario), Canada. Previously produced in Sudbury.

Roy Custom Guitars offers a completely handcrafted instrument that is available in either left- or right-handed configurations. The **RR Custom Electric Guitar** features a curly maple or cherry wood carved top over a Honduran mahogany or alder back. The five piece maple and wenge set-neck has an ebony or rosewood fingerboard, and either gold plated or chromed Gotoh hardware.

ROYAL

Instruments currently built in England since 1980.

Some of these high quality solid body guitars feature designs based on previous Fender and Gibson favorites. Other original designs include the Medusa and Electra models (source: Tony Bacon and Paul Day, *The Guru's Guitar Guide*).

ROYALIST

See chapter on House Brands.

This trademark has been identified as a House Brand of the RCA Victor Records Store (source: Willie G. Moseley, *Stellas & Stratocasters*).

RUSTLER

Instruments previously produced in Mason City, IA, during the mid-1990s.

Rustler Guitars combined the classic look found in desirable, vintage, single cutaway guitars with the sound, playability, and quality of a custom builder. Instruments were constructed of a curly maple top over alder back and side bodies, and feature gold hardware, 6-on-a-side tuners, and rosewood, maple, or ebony fingerboards.

RYBSKI

Instruments currently built in Wartrace, Tennessee. Previously distributed by Luthiers Access Group of Chicago, Illinois.

Luthier Slawomir Rybski Waclawik brings close to twenty years of research to the development and custom building of each bass. Waclawik, a bassist himself, combines exotic woods with modern designs.

ELECTRIC BASS

Instruments all feature 34 in. scale, and a 24-fret (two octave) neck design. Rybski pickups were designed by the luthier and Poland´s sound wiz Jan Radwanski. Rybski makes his own pickups and preamp, and the pickups feature a wood cover that match the top of the instrument.

BASIC - cherry (or mahogany or ash) body, padauk neck, 2 Rybski "single coil" pickups, active electronics, master volume/blend/treble/bass controls, current mfg.

    MSR   **$2,750**

        Add $200 for 5-string configuration. Add $350 for 6-string configuration.

PRO - ash (or padauk, or zebrawood, or bubinga) body, padauk (or zebrawood, or purpleheart, or rosewood) top, padauk (or purpleheart or Satinwood) neck, 2 Rybski "double coil" pickups, master volume/blend/treble/bass controls, pickup coil switches, parallel/series switch, active electronics, current mfg.

    MSR   **$3,250**

        Add $250 for 5-string configuration. Add $500 for 6-string configuration.

SPECIAL - zebrawood (or purpleheart, or wenge, or satinwood, or ash) body, zebrawood (or purpleheart, or rosewood, or bubinga, or wenge) top, purpleheart (or satinwood, or pau ferro, or jatoba) neck, 2 Rybski "double coil" pickups, master volume/blend/treble/mid/bass controls, pickup coil switches, parallel/series switch, active electronics (9 or 18-volt system), current mfg.

    MSR   **$3,650**

        Add $250 for 5-string configuration. Add $500 for 6-string configuration.

R

NOTES

Section S

S-101

Instruments currently produced in China. Distributed by American Sejung Corporation in Walnut, CA.

The Sejung Musical Instrument Corporation produces the S-101 line of guitars and was introduced in 2002. They have a 600,000 square foot manufacturing facility and produce a wide variety of fretted instruments, guitar amplifiers, and pianos. Currently they have over fifty different electric models being produced. For more information, visit their website (see Trademark Index).

S.D. CURLEE USA

Instruments previously built in Matteson, IL from 1975 to 1982.

In the early 1970s, Randy Curlee was the owner of a Chicago based music store. Curlee recognized a need for an inexpensive, hand built quality guitar; and in the late 1970s the instruments he offered ranged in price from $350 (guitar models) to $399 (basses). Curlee thought that the S.D. moniker was better than using his first name. Curlee was also the first to plan on overseas reproductions occurring, and devised a plan to circumvent that from happening (See S.D. Curlee Internatonal). After the company closed in 1982, Curlee was involved in Yamaha's guitar production. Curlee also marketed the Zoom sound processors before leaving the music industry.

It is estimated that 15,000 instruments were built during the seven years of production. The majority were basses, and about 3,000 were guitars. Instruments with three digit serial numbers up to around 1000 are the first production models, and serial numbers under 4000 are from the mid- to late 1970s. After number 4000, the numbering scheme changed (source: Michael Wright, *Guitar Stories*, Volume One).

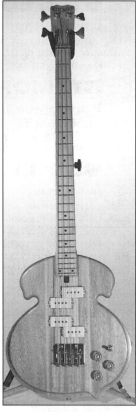

S.D. Curlee Bass courtesy Guy Bruno

GRADING	100% MINT	98% NEAR MINT	95% EXC+	90% EXC	80% VG+	70% VG	60% G

ELECTRIC

Typical of the times when everybody thought that brass parts helped with sustaining properties, S.D. Curlee instruments featured a squared brass nut, brass bridge, brass neck plate and electronics cover. Necks consisted of hard rock maple, and bodies consisted of exotic woods like butcher block maple, brazilian or honduran mahogany, black walnut, purpleheart, koa, and (later models) poplar. Hardware included Schaller tuners, DiMarzio pickups, and BadAss bridges. Headstocks were 3+3 (2+2 on basses), and featured a master volume knob and a tone knob per pickup, as well as a pickup selector toggle. The neck sat halfway into the body in a channel, and had four bolts in a large rear plate (sort of a bolt-on/set-neck hybrid).

Individual models are hard to determine, as there were some variations during production. At least 8 different models were named, although the first three (Standards I, II, and III) are the original models that the following five were variants of. Finally, as the company was closing down in 1982, Curlee built some Destroyer, Flying V, and other original shapes.

MISC. ELECTRIC MODELS - various designs, mfg. 1975-1982.

	N/A	$550	$475	$425	$375	$325	$275

MISC. BASS MODELS - various designs, mfg. 1975-1982.

	N/A	$500	$425	$375	$325	$275	$225

S.D. CURLEE INTERNATIONAL

See Hondo. Instruments previously built in Japan from the late 1970s to the mid-1980s, as well as in Korea during the same time period.

In the mid 1970s, Randy Curlee proposed a deal with Jerry Freed of Hondo Guitars to build licensed designs of his guitars. Curlee planned to beat other unlicensed copies to the market, and make money on the reproductions as well. Guitars had similar designs as the S.D. Curlee USA models, except had S.D. Curlee Design Series across the peghead, and Aspen model designation as well.

Curlee also licensed the design to the Matsumoku company in Japan, who produced similar looking models under the S.D. Curlee International logo. The Japanese-produced models were marketed and sold mainly in the Oriental market, while the Hondo versions were distributed in the U.S. as well as the U.K. Some models were distributed by J.C. Penney and Global dealers, and some of the Global dealers even rebranded them under the Global trademark (source: Michael Wright, *Guitar Stories*, Volume One).

ST. BLUES

Instruments previously built in Memphis, TN circa mid- to late 1980s. Distributed by S & T Workshop of Memphis, TN.

St. Blues instruments were distributed by the S & T Workshop in Memphis, Tennessee. These high quality electric solid body guitars were favored by such guitarists as Joe Walsh and Jeff Carlisi (.38 Special). Models include the dual cutaway Bluescaster and the single Florentine cutaway Bluesmaster. If you're thinking we're gonna "Tele" ya which Fender-style model they are based on, you're wrong! But consider this: Both models featured maple or rosewood fingerboards, 6-on-a-side tuners, 2 single coil pickups, a fixed bridge, and volume/tone controls plus a three way selector switch mounted on a metal controls plate.you be the judge! Retail list prices are still unavailable. The last given address for St. Blues/S & T Workshop was 1492 Union, Memphis, Tennessee 38104.

S

ST. GEORGE

Instruments previously produced in Japan during the mid- to late 1960s.

The St. George trademark was a brand name used by U.S. importer Buegeleisen & Jacobson of New York, New York. It has also been reported that instruments bearing the St. George label were imported by the WMI Corporation of Los Angeles, California. These entry level solid body guitars featured some original body designs, but low production quality (source: Michael Wright, *Guitar Stories*, Volume One).

ST. MORITZ

Instruments previously produced in Japan circa 1960s.

While the St. Moritz trademark was a brand name used on Japanese-built guitars, neither the U.S. distributor nor the Japanese manufacturer has been identified. Some models appear to be Teisco/Kawai. Most are the shorter scale beginner´s guitar, and are available in a thinline hollowbody or solid body design (source: Michael Wright, *Vintage Guitar Magazine*).

SGD LUTHERIE

Instruments previously built in Hoboken, NJ and Orange NJ.

Luthier David Schwab first began repairing and modifying basses and guitars back in 1972. Schwab, who began playing bass in 1969, built his first hand-made guitar in 1976, a prototype solid body nylon stringed classical. Another original design was the **MantaRay** 8-string bass, which first debuted in 1980. In the mid 1980s, Schwab was working at American Showster Guitars, making the '57 **Chevy Tailfin** model for such players as Billy Gibbons, Robin Crosby (Ratt), and Terence Trent D´Arby. The first of these guitars he built appeared in an edition of *Playboy* , in a section on unique holiday gifts.

For the past two years, SGD Lutherie has been located in a 150 year old building (once the home of Guild Guitars) in Hoboken, New Jersey. After having problems with the building´s owners, Schwab has returned to his former location in Orange, New Jersey. Schwab is currently not producing any guitars.

SMD

Instruments currently built in New York.

Luthier Chris Stambaugh began building high quality string instruments for his friends and himself out of necessity: they needed the quality but couldn´t afford the retail prices. Stambaugh, born and raised in North Berwick, Maine, started building guitars during his tenure at a furniture building company. In 1995, his band won the Maine Musician´s Award for Originality.

Stambaugh is currently attending the Wentworth Institute of Technology and is majoring in Industrial Design. Stambaugh was chosen for the Arioch Scholar program, and is one of three students attending on the program´s full scholarship. His stated goal is to craft the highest quality instruments for a fair market price, using environmentally friendly techniques and form and function designs drawn from his educational background.

ELECTRIC

The **SMD Custom** 6-string features a neck-through-body design, and oil finish, Stambaugh´s standard peghead and body pattern. Everything else about the guitar is left to the customer´s choice: tonewoods, pickups, electronics, hardware, neck inlays, and wiring style is based on the preference of the player commissioning the guitar, and is covered in the base price starting at $1,200. Further options of a gloss finish (add $150) or a tremolo bridge (add $150) are priced extra.

ELECTRIC BASS

Stambaugh´s **SMD Custom Bass** is available in 4-, 5-, or 6-string configurations. Similar to the SMD Custom guitar, luthier Stambaugh only specifies an oil finish, peghead and body pattern (the look of the instrument). All other options are left to the customer´s choice. While there is no option for a bass tremolo, the gloss finish option is an extra $150. Retail prices start at $1,300 (4-string), $1,450 (5-string), up to $1,600 (6-string model). Luthier Stambaugh is also building custom designed banjos (including a Banjo Bass).

SMT GUITARS

Instruments currently built in Great Falls, VA since 1992.

Scientifico Musico Technographique (SMT Guitars) is a full custom guitar manufacturing company that produces 30 instruments a year in limited production. Their instruments are inspired by the work of Paul Bigsby and Nat Daniels (Danelectro) with a touch of Zemaitis thrown in. These instruments are known for their wacky designs, pearl inlay, and excellent playability. Elements of fine art, '40s industrial design, and American hot rod culture are seen in these instruments. SMT has created guitars for Andy Gill (Gang of Four), Chris Isaak, and Billy F. Gibbons (ZZ Top). Due to the customer´s involvement in the design process, SMT guitars are not sold in stores and are available directly from the manufacturer, (Company information courtesy Steven Metz, SMT Guitars).

SSD

See Spector. Instruments previously built in Korea from 1991-98. Previously distributed exclusively in North America by Armadillo Enterprises of Clearwater, FL.

Stuart Spector co-founded Spector Guitars in 1976, and became well-known for the sleek, neck-through-body design that proved popular with bass players. In 1985, Kramer (BKL) bought the company while Stuart Spector maintained a consulting position for three years.

In 1989, Spector left Kramer and founded Stuart Spector Designs, Ltd. He introduced the SD bass in 1992, and along with Joe Veillette began handcrafting instruments, using custom-made hardware and fine hardwoods. Veillette left SSD in the spring of 1996 to work on his own designs as well as do outside consulting for other firms. Stuart Spector reacquired the rights to his Spector trademark in 1997. Both the U.S. and European produced models became the Spector line, while the current Korean produced models retained the SSD trademark.

The U.S. built NS and SD series models were previously built in Woodstock, New York from 1992 to 1996; and the Europe series models in Czechoslovakia from 1995 to 1996.

S

GRADING	100% MINT	98% NEAR MINT	95% EXC+	90% EXC	80% VG+	70% VG	60% G

ELECTRIC BASS: KOREA SERIES

NS94 (NS-K-4) - offset double cutaway soft maple body, through-body maple neck, rosewood fingerboard with dot inlays, 34 in. scale, black die-cast fixed bridge, blackface peghead with pearl logo inlay, 2-per-side tuners, black hardware, 2 EMG HZ humbucker pickups, two volume/treble/bass EQ controls, active electronics, available in Gloss Black finish, disc. 1998.

	$750	$675	$595	$500	$425	$325	$250

Last MSR was $950.

NS94S - similar to the NS94, available in Amber Stain, Black Stain, Blue Stain, Honeyburst, Matte Natural, Natural, Padauk Stain, and Red Stain finishes, disc. 1998.

	$775	$695	$625	$525	$450	$350	$275

Last MSR was $995.

NS95 (NS-K-5) - similar to NS94, except has 5-string configuration, 3/2-per-side tuners, available in Gloss Black finish, disc. 1998.

	$800	$725	$650	$550	$475	$375	$295

Last MSR was $1,050.

NS95S - similar to NS95, available in Amber Stain, Black Stain, Blue Stain, Honeyburst, Matte Natural, Natural, Padauk Stain, or Red Stain finishes, disc. 1998.

	$825	$725	$675	$575	$500	$395	$300

Last MSR was $1,095.

Sadowsky Vintage Tele Style courtesy Sadowsky Guitars

SADOWSKY

Instruments currently produced in Brooklyn, NY since 1979. Distributed by Sadowsky Guitars Ltd. of Manhattan, NY.

Roger Sadowsky, a noted East Coast repairman and luthier, has been providing quality customizing and repairs in his shop since 1979. Sadowsky originally apprenticed with Master Luthier Augustino LoPrinzi in New Jersey between 1972 to 1974. He then spent five years as the head of the service department for Medley Music Corporation located outside of Philadelphia, Pennsylvania. Upon opening his own shop, Sadowsky initially concentrated on proper instrument set-ups and repair for studio musicians and touring personnel. This background of repair work on top- notch personal instruments became the basis for Sadowsky's later designs.

Sadowsky's instruments are based on time-tested Fender designs, with a primary difference being the attention paid to the choice of woods. The better a guitar sounds acoustically translates into a better sound when used electronically. The nature of custom work versus production line assembly insures that a player will get the features specified, and Sadowsky has also introduced his own custom active preamps and circuitry. Current staff members include Norio Imai and Ken Fallon.

Sadowsky builds an outboard version of his bass preamp for players unable (or unwilling, in the case of a vintage instrument) to have a preamp installed in their instruments. This preamp simply consists of a volume, bass, and treble knobs, but the simplicity of the controls belies the sophisticated nature of the circuitry.

ELECTRIC

THE SADOWSKY GUITAR - offset double cutaway, undersized Strat style alder body, 22-fret maple neck, Morado fingerboard, dot position markers, 6-on-a-side tuners, 3 single coil Sadowsky pickups, vintage style tremolo bridge, by-passable preamp with midrange boost and boost gain, available in Lake Placid Blue finish, current mfg.

MSR   **$2,500**

Add $75 for swamp ash body. Add $200 for bent (arched) maple top. Add $50 for Black hardware. Add $75 for Gold Hardware. Add $200 for Vintage Color Matching Headstock.

VINTAGE TELE - Tele style swamp ash body, 22-fret maple neck with maple fingerboard, dot position markers, 6-on-a-side tuners, six-saddle vintage style bridge, 2 Joe Barden pickups, Sadowsky preamp, available in Trans. White finish, current mfg.

MSR   **$3,150**

Add $50 for Black Hardware. Add $75 for Gold Hardware. Add $200 for Vintage Color Matching Headstock.

ELECTRIC NYLON STRING GUITAR - Tele-style body, Quilted Maple top on alder, 22-fret maple neck, Morado fingerboard with dot position markers, 6-on-a-side tuners, Piezo crystal transducer with Sadowsky preamp, available in Cherry Sunburst finish, curent mfg.

MSR   **$3,250**

Add $500 for MIDI option.

ELECTRIC BASS

THE SADOWSKY BASS - offset double cutaway slightly undersized Jazz Bass style body, available in Standard, Vintage, or Modern features, 21-fret maple neck, alder body, Sadowsky J style pickups, active tone circuit, preamp, 4-string, available in Candy Apple Red finish, current mfg.

MSR   **$2,425**

Add $75 for swamp ash body. Add $275 for bent (arched) maple top. Add $150 for Vintage Style Basses. Add $200 for Vintage Color Matching Headstock. Add $50 for Black Hardware. Add $75 for Gold Hardware. Add $100 for Hipshot Bass D-Tuner. Add $100-250 for Fretless Basses. Add $100 for Passive Tone/Stacked Preamp.

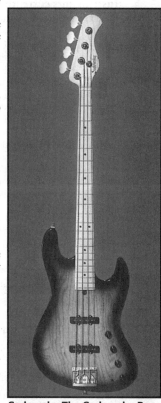

Sadowsky The Sadowsky Bass courtesy Sadowsky Guitars

S

SAKAI

Instruments previously produced in Japan during the early 1970s.

The Sakai trademark is a brand name of a United Kingdom importer on these entry level to intermediate instruments. The solid and semi-hollowbody guitars have some original designs and designs based on classic American favorites (source: Tony Bacon and Paul Day, *The Guru's Guitar Guide*).

T. SAKASHTA GUITARS

Instruments currently built in Van Nuys, CA. Distribution is directly handled by T. Sakashta Guitars of Van Nuys, CA.

Luthier Taku Sakashta builds high quality acoustic Archtop and steel string guitars. All are offered with custom options per model.

ELECTRIC: JAM MASTER SERIES

The Jam Master model is a double cutaway archtop semi-hollowbody electric guitar, and features differing wood and finish options for the three models. However, the three models do share some similar construction points, such as a Gaboon ebony (or cocobola) pickguard, Gotoh or Schaller tuning machines, and a Sakashta original design aluminum tailpiece (or Gotoh or Schaller tailpiece). The Jam Master features a Tom Holmes H-450 humbucker in the neck position, and a Tom Holmes H-453 humbucker in the Bridge position. Electronics includes 2 volume knobs, 2 tone knobs with series/parallel switching, and a three way pickup selector toggle switch.

Other options include a maple neck on models two or three, a solid brass tailpiece that replaces stock Gotoh or Schaller, gold hardware, a Two-tone sunburst, or a Three-tone sunburst.

The **Jam Master Model One** features a book matched Calelo walnut top, back and matching sides; the bound American black walnut neck has a Gaboon ebony fingerboard and pearl inlays. The Model One is available in high gloss nitrocellulose Natural or Transparent Black finish.

The **Jam Master Model Two**

is constructed of book matched bigleaf maple top, back and matching sides; the bound neck is of Honduran mahogany and has a Brazilian rosewood fingerboard with pearl inlays. The Model Two is finished in a high gloss nitrocellulose Blonde, Cherry Red, or Transparent Black finish.

The final **Jam Master, Model Three** sports a book matched Sitka spruce top and bigleaf maple back and matching sides. The bound eastern rock maple neck has a Gaboon ebony fingerboard and pearl inlays, and is offered in a high gloss nitrocellulose Blonde, Cherry Red, or Transparent Black finish.

SAKURA

Instruments previously produced in Japan during the mid-1970s. Production moved to Korea during the 1980s.

The Sakura trademark is a brand name of a U.K. importer. Entry level to intermediate quality instruments with some original design and others favoring classic American designs (source: Tony Bacon and Paul Day, *The Guru's Guitar Guide*).

SAMICK

Instruments currently produced in Korea since 1965. Current production of instruments is in Korea and City of Industry, CA. Distributed in the U.S. market by Samick Music Corporation of City of Industry, CA.

For a number of years, the Samick corporation was the phantom builder of instruments for a number of other trademarks. When the Samick trademark was finally introduced to the U.S. guitar market, a number of consumers thought that the company was brand new. However, Samick has been producing both upright and grand pianos, as well as stringed instruments for nearly forty years.

The Samick Piano Co. was established in Korea in 1958. By January of 1960, they had started to produce upright pianos, and within four years became the first Korean piano exporter. One year later in 1965, the company began manufacturing guitars, and by the early 1970s expanded to produce grand pianos and harmonicas as well. In 1973 the company incorporated as the Samick Musical Instruments Mfg. Co., Ltd. to reflect the diversity it encompassed. Samick continued to expand into guitar production. They opened a branch office in Los Angeles in 1978, a brand new guitar factory in 1979, and a branch office in West Germany one month before 1981.

Throughout the 1980s Samick continued to grow, prosper, and win awards for quality products and company productivity. The Samick Products Co. was established in 1986 as an affiliate producer of other products, and the company was listed on the Korean Stock Exchange in September of 1988. With their size of production facilities (the company claims to be cranking out over a million guitars a year, according to a recent brochure), Samick could be referred to as modern day producer of House Brand guitars as well as their own brand. In the past couple of years Samick acquired Valley Arts, a guitar company known for its one-of-a-kind instruments and custom guitars. This merger stabilized Valley Arts as the custom shop wing of Samick, as well as supplying Samick with quality American designed guitars.

Samick continues to expand their line of guitar models through the use of innovative designs, partnerships with high exposure endorsees (like Blues Saraceno and Ray Benson), and new projects such as the Robert Johnson Commemorative and the D'Leco Charlie Christian Commemorative guitars. Samick Company History courtesy Rick Clapper; Model Specifications courtesy Dee Hoyt.

In addition to their acoustic and electric guitars and basses, Samick offers a wide range of other stringed instruments such as autoharps, banjos, mandolins, and violins.

ELECTRIC ARCHTOP: AMERICAN CLASSIC CHARLIE CHRISTIAN ESTATE SERIES

All Charlie Christian Estate Series models have a 16 in. lower body width and 2.5 in. body depth (a portion of Estate Series sales proceeds go directly to respective surviving family members).

CCTS 650 BK - single cutaway hollowbody, bound top, solid top/back, set-in neck, 22-fret fingerboard with white split block inlay, 2 f-holes, 3-per-side tuners, tune-o-matic bridge/stop tailpiece, gold hardware, raised matching pickguard, 2 covered humbuckers, 2 volume/2 tone controls (with coil tap), 3-way pickup selector, available in Black finish, mfg. 1996-98.

	$900	$775	$690	$600	$520	$435	$350

Last MSR was $1,190.

CCFT 650 GS - similar to the CCTS 650 BK, except has rosewood bridge/gold plated trapeze tailpiece, available in Golden Sunburst finish, mfg. 1996-98.

	$900	$775	$690	$600	$520	$435	$350

Last MSR was $1,190.

GRADING	100% MINT	98% NEAR MINT	95% EXC+	90% EXC	80% VG+	70% VG	60% G

CCTT 650 WH - similar to the CCTS 650 BK, except has tune-o-matic bridge/trapeze tailpiece, available in White finish, mfg. 1996-98.

	$900	$775	$690	$600	$520	$435	$350

Last MSR was $1,190.

ELECTRIC ARCHTOP: LASALLE SERIES

JZ 1 - single cutaway hollowbody, select spruce top, quilt maple sides and back, 22-fret rosewood fingerboard with block inlay, two humbucker pickups, jazz style bridge, 3-per-side Grover tuners, four knobs (2v, 2 tone), available in Antique Natural or Vintage Sunburst finishes, case included, current mfg.

MSR	$1,196	$750	$650	$575	$500	$450	$400	$350

JZ 2 - single cutaway hollowbody, select spruce top, quilt maple sides and back, 22-fret rosewood fingerboard with block inlay, two Duncan design humbucker pickups, jazz style bridge, 3-per-side Grover tuners, four knobs (2v, 2 tone), available in Antique Natural, Vintage Sunburst, or Wine Red finishes, case included, current mfg.

MSR	$1,916	$1,200	$1,050	$925	$800	$700	$600	$500

JZ 2 LTD Limited Edition - similar to the JZ 2, except has a Bigsby tremolo bridge/tailpiece and special inlays, available in Pearl White finish, mfg. 2004-present.

MSR	$2,116	$1,350	$1,200	$1,050	$925	$800	$700	$600

JZ 3 - similar to the JZ 2, except has a single sharp cutaway, available in Antique Natural, Vintage Sunburst, or Wine Red finishes, case included, current mfg.

MSR	$1,916	$1,200	$1,050	$925	$800	$700	$600	$500

JZ 4 - similar to the JZ 2, except has a single pickup and no knobs or switches, available in Antique Natural or Brown Sunburst finishes, case included, current mfg.

MSR	$1,796	$1,125	$975	$850	$725	$625	$550	$475

ELECTRIC ARCHTOP: ROYALE SERIES

RL 1 - single cutaway hollowbody, nato arched top, nato back and sides, bolt-on neck, 22-fret rosewood fingerboard with dot inlay, two humbucker pickups, 3-per-side Grover tuners, black pickguard, 4 knobs (2v, 2 tone), 3-way switch, available in Trans. Red, Trans. Blue, or Black finishes, mfg. 2001-present.

MSR	$556	$350	$290	$250	$210	$180	$150	$120

RL 2 - similar to the RL 1, except has a set neck, available in Brown Sunburst or Trans. Red finishes, mfg. 2001-present.

MSR	$776	$490	$425	$375	$325	$275	$225	$175

Add $20 for left-handed configuration, available in Trans. Red finish only.

RL 3 - single cutaway hollowbody, quilted maple arched top, striped mahogany back and sides, set neck, 22-fret rosewood fingerboard with trapezoid inlay, two Duncan Designed humbucker pickups, 3-per-side Grover tuners, black pickguard, 4 knobs (2v, 2 tone), 3-way switch, available in Amber or Original Sunburst finishes, mfg. 2001-present.

MSR	$1,316	$850	$750	$675	$600	$525	$450	$400

RL 4 - similar to the RL 3, except has mahogany top, back, and sides, 8-ply binding, and block inlays, available in Black, Pearl White, or Wine Red finishes, mfg. 2001-present.

MSR	$1,356	$875	$775	$700	$625	$550	$475	$425

RL 4 LTD Limited Edition - similar to the RL 4, except has a Bigsby tremolo/bridge and special inlays, available in Pearl White finish, mfg. 2004-present.

MSR	$1,996	$1,250	$1,100	$950	$850	$750	$650	$550

RL 5 - similar to the RL 3, except has select spruce top, mahogany back, and sides, jazz tailpiece, and parallelogram inlays, available in Vintage Sunburst finish, mfg. 2001-present.

MSR	$1,356	$875	$775	$700	$625	$550	$475	$425

ELECTRIC: ALTERNATIVE SERIES

All American Classics by Valley Arts models are optional with Seymour Duncan pickups as an upgrade.

Add $160 for 2 Seymour Duncan single coil pickups (upgrade). Add $180 for 3 Seymour Duncan single coil pickups (upgrade). Add $200 for Seymour Duncan single/single/humbucker pickups (upgrade).

KJ-540 (AURORA) - offset double cutaway alder body, bolt-on maple neck, 24-fret bound rosewood fingerboard with pearl dot inlay, double locking vibrato, 6-on-a-side tuners, black hardware, single coil/humbucker pickup, volume/tone control, 3-position switch, available in Aurora finish, disc. 1994.

	N/A	$300	$250	$210	$180	$150	$120

Last MSR was $490.

KR-564 GPE (HAWK) - offset double cutaway alder body, bolt-on maple neck, 24-fret bound rosewood fingerboard with pearl triangle inlay, double locking vibrato, 6-on-a-side tuners, black hardware, 2 single coil rail/1 humbucker pickups, volume/2 tone controls, 5-position switch, available in Hawk Graphic finish, disc. 1994.

	N/A	$350	$300	$250	$210	$180	$150

Last MSR was $580.

**Samick LaSalle JZ 3
courtesy Samick**

**Samick Royale RL 1
courtesy Samick**

S

GRADING	100% MINT	98% NEAR MINT	95% EXC+	90% EXC	80% VG+	70% VG	60% G

KR-564 GPSK (Viper) - similar to the Hawk, except features a Viper Graphic finish, disc. 1994.

	N/A	$400	$350	$300	$260	$220	$180

Last MSR was $650.

KR-654 GPS (NIGHTBREED) - similar to the Hawk, except features a Nightbreed Graphic finish, disc. 1994.

	N/A	$400	$350	$300	$260	$220	$180

Last MSR was $650.

ELECTRIC: AMERICAN CLASSIC RAY BENSON SERIES

Earlier versions of the Ray Benson Signature Series (model DTR-100) featured similar designs like a contoured alder body, but did not include a maple top. Other differing features include 2 single coil pickups and a 3-way selector switch. These models were available in Black (BK) and Tobacco Sunburst (TS) finishes.

STR-100 TS - contoured single cutaway alder body, figured maple top, bolt-on maple neck, 25.5 in. scale, 21-fret maple fingerboard with black dot inlay, fixed bridge, 6-on-a-side die-cast tuners, chrome hardware, violin-shaped white pearloid pickguard, humbucker/Hot Rail/single coil Duncan-Designed pickups, volume/tone (push/pull coil tap) control, 5-position switch, controls mounted on metal plate, available in Tobacco Sunburst finish, disc. 1999.

	$350	$300	$270	$230	$195	$160	$120

Last MSR was $470.

STR-100 AM - similar to the STR-100 TS, except features flame maple top, humbucker/2 single coil pickups, available in Amber Flame finish, disc. 2001.

	$575	$475	$425	$375	$325	$275	$195

Last MSR was $750.

STR-200 TBK - similar to the STR-100 TS, except features flame maple top, gold hardware, Texas-shaped white pearloid pickguard, humbucker/2 single coil pickups, available in Trans. Black finish, disc. 2001.

	$625	$525	$475	$425	$375	$325	$250

Last MSR was $825.

STR-200KF N - similar to STR-200 TBK, except in Kus finish, this is the NAMM 100th Anniversary Model, mfg. 2001 only.

	$675	$600	$525	$475	$425	$375	$325

Last MSR was $897.

ELECTRIC: AMERICAN CLASSIC BLUES SARACENO SERIES

Blues Saraceno TV Twenty models may feature a "-cicle" finish, a *Burst*-style finish in non-traditional ´Burst colors.

BS ASH - offset rounded cutaway solid alder body, bolt-on maple neck, 25.5 in. scale, 22-fret maple fingerboard with offset black dot inlay, strings through-body fixed bridge, 3-per-side die-cast tuners, black hardware, 2 single coil/humbucker Duncan-Designed pickups, volume/tone (push/pull coil tap) controls, 5-way selector switch, available in Black (BK), Raid Red (RA), or White (WH) finishes, disc. 1999.

	$450	$390	$345	$295	$250	$200	$150

Last MSR was $600.

Add $50 for Black/Red/Grey (BRGR) or Red/Yellow/Black (RYB) Plaid finishes (Model BS ASH PP).

BS AVH - similar to the BS ASH, except features vintage-style tremolo, available in Black (BK), Raid Red (RA), and White (WH) solid finishes; Berry-cicle (BEC), Cherry-cicle (CHC), Cream-cicle (CRC), Fudge-cicle (FUC), Grape-cicle (GRC), Lemon-cicle (LEC), and Lime-cicle (LIC) "burst" finishes, disc. 1999.

	$450	$390	$345	$295	$250	$200	$150

Last MSR was $600.

Add $50 for Black (MBKF), Blue (MBLF), Gold (MGF), Green (MGRF), and Silver (MSF) Metal Flake finish (Model BS AVH). Add $50 for Blue/Burgundy/Black (BLBUBC) or Orange/Green/Gold (OGNGDC) Plaid finishes (Model BS AVH PP).

BS ALG - similar to the BS ASH, except features licensed Floyd Rose locking tremolo, 2 Duncan-Designed humbuckers, volume control, 3-way selector switch, available in Black (BK), Raid Red (RA), or White (WH) finishes, disc. 1999.

	$525	$455	$400	$345	$290	$235	$175

Last MSR was $700.

Add $50 for Black/Yellow/Blue (BYBL) or White/Blue/Red (WBLR) Plaid finishes (Model BS ALG PP).

ELECTRIC: AMERICAN CLASSIC JAZZ SERIES

HF-650 (BLUENOTE) - single rounded cutaway bound hollowbody, arched maple top, raised black pickguard, 2 f-holes, maple back/sides/neck, 22-fret bound rosewood fingerboard with abalone/pearl block inlay, adjustable rosewood bridge/trapeze tailpiece, bound blackface peghead with pearl vines/logo inlay, 3-per-side tuners, gold hardware, 2 covered humbucker pickups, 2 volume/2 tone controls, 3-position switch, available in Natural (N) or Sunburst (SB) finishes, disc. 2001.

	$850	$750	$700	$650	$595	$550	$495

Last MSR was $1,125.

HJ-650 - L-5 style maple body, single rounded cutaway, maple set neck, rosewood fingerboard, 20-frets, 25.5 in. scale, block position markers, 3-per-side tuners, 2 f-holes, die-cast tuners, gold hardware, 2 humbucker pickups, 2 volume/2 tone controls, adjustable bridge, trapeze tailpiece, available in Natural or Tobacco Sunburst finishes, disc. 2001.

	$875	$800	$725	$650	$600	$550	$495

Last MSR was $1,155.

HJ-650/CN - similar to Model HJ-650, except has single Florentine cutaway, available in Natural finish, disc. 2001.

	$900	$800	$725	$650	$600	$550	$495

Last MSR was $1,200.

S

GRADING	100% MINT	98% NEAR MINT	95% EXC+	90% EXC	80% VG+	70% VG	60% G

HJ-650 TSB LH - similar to Model HJ-650, except in left-hand configuration, available in Tobacco Sunburst finish, disc. 2001.

	$875	$800	$725	$650	$600	$550	$495

Last MSR was $1,155.

HJ-650 TSB (WABASH) - single round cutaway arched hollowbody, maple top, bound holes, raised black pickguard, bound body, 17 in. lower body bout, maple back/sides/neck, 20-fret bound rosewood fingerboard with pearl block inlay, adjustable rosewood bridge/trapeze tailpiece, bound peghead with pearl flower/logo inlay, 3-per-side tuners, gold hardware, 2 humbucker pickups, 2 volume/2 tone controls, 3-position switch, available in Natural or Sunburst finishes, disc. 1999.

	$575	$500	$440	$380	$320	$260	$195

Last MSR was $770.

Add $10 for Natural finish (Model HJ-650 N).

HJS-650 TR VS - similar to the HJ-650 TSB, except features abalone bound top/bound raised pickguard, solid spruce top, 17.5 in. lower body bout, bigsby tremolo bridge, available in Abalone Sunburst finish, disc 2001.

	$1,275	$1,100	$965	$830	$695	$560	$425

Last MSR was $1,700.

HJ-660N - similar to HJ-650, except has Tiger top, 3 P-90 pickups and Vintage style tailpiece. Available in Natural finish, mfg. 2001 only.

	$950	$815	$700	$625	$550	$450	$350

Last MSR was $1,275.

Samick HJ-650 N
courtesy Samick

HJ-850 OR - L-5 style body, arched spruce top, arched maple back and sides, set maple neck, rosewood fingerboard, 20 frets, 25.5 in. scale, 2 humbucker pickups, 2 volume/2 tone controls, chrome hardware, Grover tuners, tune-o-matic bridge with vibrato, available in Orange finish, mfg. 2001 only.

	$850	$725	$625	$550	$475	$400	$325

Last MSR was $1,137.

SAT-450 (KINGSTON) - double rounded cutaway semi-hollowbody, arched flame maple top, bound body, bound f-holes, raised black pickguard, maple back/sides, mahogany neck, 22-fret bound rosewood fingerboard with pearl dot inlay, tune-o-matic bridge/stop tailpiece, bound peghead with pearl leaf/logo inlay, 3-per-side tuners, chrome hardware, 2 humbucker pickups, 2 volume/2 tone controls, 3-position switch, available in Black, Cherry Sunburst, Golden Sunburst, or Natural finishes, disc. 1995.

	N/A	$350	$300	$250	$210	$180	$150

Last MSR was $530.

SAT-650 CSTT (KINGSTON CLASSIC) - double cutaway semi-hollowbody, arched tigertail flame maple top, bound f-holes, raised black pickguard, maple back/sides, mahogany neck, 22-fret bound rosewood fingerboard with pearl diamond inlay, tune-o-matic bridge/stop tailpiece, bound peghead with pearl leaf/logo inlay, 3-per-side tuners, gold hardware, 2 humbucker pickups, 2 volume/2 tone controls, 3-position switch, available in Cherry Sunburst or Natural finishes, disc. 2001.

	$850	$750	$695	$650	$595	$550	$475

Last MSR was $1,140.

Add $60 for Natural finish (Model SAT-650 TT N).

SAT-650 PBE - similar to SAT-650 CSTT except features pink bird's-eye top, back and sides, disc. 2001.

	$875	$775	$695	$650	$595	$550	$495

Last MSR was $1,185.

SAB-650 BGS - similar to the SAT-650 CSTT, except features bird's-eye maple top/back/sides, available in Burgundy finish, disc. 2000.

	$600	$525	$450	$375	$300	$250	$200

Last MSR was $790.

ELECTRIC: AMERICAN CLASSIC LP SERIES

LP-750 - single cutaway mahogany body, bound mother-of-pearl covered top, set-in mahogany neck, 24.75 in. scale, 24-fret ebony fingerboard with pearl block inlay, bound mother-of-pearl covered headstock, 3-per-side tuners, chrome hardware, tune-o-matic bridge/stop tailpiece, 2 humbucker pickups with chrome covers, 2 volume/2 tone controls, 3-way selector, disc. 2001.

	$1,050	$900	$790	$680	$570	$460	$350

Last MSR was $1,400.

ELECTRIC: AMERICAN CLASSIC TRAD-S SERIES

Instruments in this series have an offset double cutaway body, bolt-on maple neck, 21-fret fingerboard, 6-on-a-side tuners, chrome hardware, 3 single coil pickups, 1 volume/2 tone controls, 5-position switch as following features (unless otherwise listed).

DCL-9500 SDQ AN - carved quilt maple top, abalone body binding, set-in neck, ebony fingerboard, tune-o-matic bridge/stop tailpiece, 2 Duncan humbucker pickups, volume/tone controls, 3-way selector, disc. 2000.

	$600	$520	$460	$395	$330	$265	$200

Last MSR was $800.

S

GRADING	100% MINT	98% NEAR MINT	95% EXC+	90% EXC	80% VG+	70% VG	60% G

JAD-120 BGS - offset body design, solid maple neck, 25.5 in. scale, 22-fret fingerboard, die-cast tuners, Schaller tremolo, 2 S-90 pickups, volume/tone controls, 3-way selector, aAvailable in Burgundy Sunburst, mfg. 1997-98.

	$340	$300	$265	$230	$190	$155	$115

Last MSR was $450.

MFN-130 BLS - solid maple neck, 25.5 in. scale, 22-fret fingerboard, die-cast tuners, Wilkinson tremolo, 3 S-90 pickups, volume/tone controls, available in Blue Burst finish, mfg. 1997-98.

	$375	$325	$285	$245	$205	$165	$125

Last MSR was $500.

RL-660 A TR - plank body, bird's-eye maple neck, 25.5 in. scale, 24-fret ebony fingerboard with white dot inlay, gold hardware, tune-o-matic bridge/stop tailpiece, 2 single coil/humbucker pickups, volume/tone controls, available in Trans. Red finish, disc. 1999.

	$375	$325	$285	$245	$205	$165	$125

Last MSR was $500.

SCM-1 G FAM - arched mahogany body, flame maple top, bird's-eye maple neck, 25.5 in. scale, 24-fret ebony fingerboard with white dot inlay, gold hardware, licensed Floyd Rose tremolo, 2 single coil/humbucker Duncan pickups, volume/tone controls, available in Natural Flame finish, disc. 1999.

	$450	$390	$345	$295	$250	$200	$150

Last MSR was $600.

SSM-1 - alder body, 22-fret maple fingerboard with black dot inlay, 3 single coil pickups, vintage-style tremolo, white pickguard, 6-on-a-side die-cast tuners, available in Black, Lake Placid Blue, Metallic Red, Natural Satin, Sea Foam Green, Tobacco Sunburst, or White finishes, mfg. 1994-2001.

	$395	$350	$295	$250	$195	$150	$95

Last MSR was $525.

In 1999, Florescent Green, Cherry Sunburst, Burgundy Mist finishes were introduced.

SSM-1 LH - similar to the SSM-1, except in a left-handed configuration, available in Black or Metallic Red finishes, disc. 2001.

	$425	$375	$325	$275	$225	$175	$125

Last MSR was $570.

SSM-2 - similar to the SSM-1, except features 22-fret rosewood fingerboard with white dot inlay, licensed Floyd Rose tremolo, 2 single coil/humbucker pickups, volume/tone controls, available in Lake Placid Blue, Metallic Red, or Trans. Black finishes, mfg. 1994-98.

	$330	$290	$255	$220	$185	$150	$110

Last MSR was $440.

SSM-3 - similar to the SSM-1, except features 22-fret rosewood fingerboard with white dot inlay, licensed Floyd Rose tremolo, gold hardware, 2 single coil/humbucker pickups, volume/tone controls, available in Black or Tobacco Sunburst finishes, mfg. 1994-98.

	$375	$325	$285	$245	$205	$165	$125

Last MSR was $500.

SMX-3 - bound carved mahogany body, bird's-eye maple neck, 25.5 in. scale, 22-fret bound ebony fingerboard with pearl dot inlay, bound headstock, licensed Floyd Rose tremolo, gold hardware, 2 single coil/humbucker pickups, volume/tone controls, available in Cherry Sunburst finish, mfg. 1994-96.

	$390	$325	$295	$260	$225	$195	$165

Last MSR was $650.

SMX-4 - similar to the SMX-3, except features tune-o-matic bridge/stop tailpiece, available in Trans. Blue or Trans. Red finishes, mfg. 1994- 2000.

	$450	$390	$345	$295	$250	$200	$150

Last MSR was $600.

ELECTRIC: AMERICAN CLASSIC TRAD-T SERIES

Instruments in this series have a single cutaway body design, bolt-on maple neck, 21-fret fingerboard, "Tele"-style fixed bridge, 6-on-a-side tuners, chrome hardware, 2 single coil pickups, volume/tone control, 3-position switch as following features (unless otherwise listed).

TA-630 DLX TR - contoured alder body, flame maple top, rosewood fingerboard with white dot inlay, TM2 tremolo, gold hardware, pearloid pickguard, 3 single coil lipstick tube pickups, available in Trans. Red finish, disc. 2000.

	$340	$295	$260	$225	$190	$150	$115

Last MSR was $450.

Earlier versions may feature a Purple Burst finish (model TA-630 DLX PS).

TL-650 K N - quilted kusu body, 22-fret rosewood fingerboard with white dot inlay, tune-o-matic bridge/stop tailpiece, die-cast tuners, gold hardware, 2 humbucker pickups, available in Oyster finish, mfg. 1994-98.

	$450	$365	$320	$275	$230	$185	$140

Last MSR was $560.

SMX-1 - bound carved ash body, 24-fret bound ebony fingerboard with pearl dot inlay, double locking Floyd Rose vibrato, gold hardware, 2 single coil/humbucker pickups, 5-position switch, available in Cherry Sunburst or Vintage Sunburst finishes, mfg. 1994-96.

	N/A	$375	$325	$275	$235	$195	$150

Last MSR was $650.

SMX-2 VS - bound carved ash body, 24-fret maple fingerboard with pearl dot inlay, tune-o-matic bridge/stop tailpiece, die-cast tuners, gold hardware, available in Vintage Sunburst finish, mfg. 1994-2000.

	$425	$370	$325	$280	$235	$190	$145

Last MSR was $570.

This model is available with a 24-fret rosewood fingerboard and Tobacco Sunburst finish (model SMX-2 R TS).

S

GRADING	100% MINT	98% NEAR MINT	95% EXC+	90% EXC	80% VG+	70% VG	60% G

STM-1 - ash body, 22-fret maple fingerboard with black dot inlay, Gotoh locking tuners, available in Natural finish, mfg. 1994-96.

	N/A	$200	$160	$130	$110	$90	$70

Last MSR was $350.

ELECTRIC: ARTIST ELECTRIC SOLID BODY SERIES

DS-100 - offset double cutaway hardwood body, bolt-on maple neck, 25.5 in. scale, 21-fret maple fingerboard with black dot inlay, standard tremolo, 6-on-a-side tuners, chrome hardware, white pickguard, 3 single coil pickups, volume/2 tone controls, 5-position switch, available in Black, Metallic Red, Sunburst, or White finishes, mfg. 1994-98.

	$190	$165	$145	$125	$100	$85	$65

Last MSR was $250.

DS-410 - similar to the DS-100, except features 21-fret rosewood fingerboard, 2 single coil/humbucker pickups, available in Black, Metallic Red, Sunburst, or White finishes, disc. 1999.

	$195	$170	$150	$130	$110	$90	$65

Last MSR was $260.

FV-450 - flying V-style nato body, set-in neck, 24.75 in. scale, 22-fret rosewood fingerboard with white dot inlay, 3-per-side Gotoh tuners, tune-o-matic bridge/stop tailpiece, 2 humbucker pickups, volume/2 tone controls, 3-way selector switch, available in Black or Metallic Red finishes, disc. 2001.

	$435	$375	$325	$275	$225	$175	$125

Last MSR was $585.

Samick SSM-2 PW
courtesy Samick

KR-660 AC (ICE CUBE) - offset double cutaway acrylic body, bolt-on maple neck, 24-fret bound rosewood fingerboard with pearl V inlay, licensed Floyd Rose tremolo, 6-on-a-side die-cast tuners, gold hardware, 2 single coil/humbucker pickups, volume/tone controls, 5-position switch, available in Clear finish, disc. 1999.

	$525	$455	$400	$345	$290	$230	$175

Last MSR was $700.

KK-660 BB - similar to the KR-660 AC, except features a bamboo body, available in Natural Bamboo finish, disc. 1999.

	$520	$450	$395	$340	$285	$230	$175

Last MSR was $690.

LC-650 - single cutaway body, bound arched top, set-in nato neck, 24.75 in. scale, 22-fret rosewood fingerboard with white block inlay, 3-per-side Gotoh tuners, diamond/logo headstock inlay, gold hardware, tune-o-matic bridge/stop tailpiece, 2 humbucker pickups, 2 volume/2 tone controls, 3-way selector, available in Black or Cherry Sunburst finishes, mfg. 1997-2001.

	$650	$550	$495	$450	$395	$350	$275

Last MSR was $855.

LS-450 - single cutaway body, bound arched flame top, set-in nato neck, 24.75 in. scale, 22-fret rosewood fingerboard with white block inlay, 3-per-side Gotoh tuners, chrome hardware, tune-o-matic bridge/stop tailpiece, 2 humbucker pickups, 2 volume/2 tone controls, 3-way selector, available in Cherry Sunburst or Wine Red finishes, mfg. 1997-2001.

	$600	$500	$450	$395	$350	$295	$250

Last MSR was $825.

In 1999, Transparent Burgundy finish was introduced.

LS-450 (Metal Flake) - similar to LS-450, except features bound arched top, available in Granite Gold, Metallic Green Flake, Metallic Gold, Metallic Gold Flake, or Metallic Red Flake finishes, mfg. 1997-2001.

	$675	$575	$475	$425	$375	$325	$275

Last MSR was $900.

In 1999, Metallic Blue Flake, Bubinga, and Pink Bird's-eye Maple finishes were introduced.

LS-450-12 CS - similar to LS-450, except in a 12-string configuration, 6-per-side tuners, available in Cherry Sunburst finish, mfg. 1997-2001.

	$675	$575	$475	$425	$375	$325	$275

Last MSR was $900.

LSE-450 HS - similar to LS-450, except features an arched top, bolt-on nato neck, available in Honey Sunburst finish, mfg. 1997-2001.

	$425	$375	$325	$275	$225	$175	$125

Last MSR was $570.

In 1999, Wine Red finish was introduced.

MFV BK - "mini" flying V-style guitar, 19 in. scale, stop tailpiece, humbucker pickup, volume/tone control, available in Black finish, disc. 2000.

	$200	$175	$155	$135	$115	$190	$70

Last MSR was $270.

MLP BK - "mini" LP-style guitar, 19 in. scale, stop tailpiece, humbucker pickup, volume/tone control, available in Black finish, disc. 2000.

	$200	$175	$155	$135	$115	$190	$70

Last MSR was $270.

Samick SMX-2VS
courtesy Samick

S

GRADING	100% MINT	98% NEAR MINT	95% EXC+	90% EXC	80% VG+	70% VG	60% G

MST R - "mini" strat-style guitar, 19 in. scale, 2 single coil pickups, volume/tone control, 3-way switch, available in Metallic Red finish, disc. 2000.

| | $200 | $175 | $155 | $135 | $115 | $190 | $70 |

Last MSR was $270.

SG-450 - dual cutaway SG-style nato body, set-in neck, 24.75 in. scale, 22-fret rosewood fingerboard with white dot inlay, 3-per-side Gotoh tuners, tune-o-matic bridge/stop tailpiece, black pickguard, 2 humbucker pickups, volume/2 tone controls, 3-way selector switch, available in Black, White, or Wine Red finishes, mfg. 1997-2001.

| | $475 | $425 | $375 | $325 | $275 | $225 | $175 |

Last MSR was $630.

Earlier versions of an SG-style model had white block fingerboard inlay, and were only available in Wine Red finish (model SG 450 WR).

SVE-130 (SOUTHSIDE) - offset double cutaway alder body, bolt-on maple neck, 25.5 in. scale, 21-fret maple fingerboard with black dot inlay, vintage-style tremolo, 6-on-a-side standard tuners, chrome hardware, white pickguard, 3 single coil pickups, volume/2 tone controls, 5-position switch, available in Black, Metallic Red, Sunburst, or White finishes, disc. 1999.

| | $220 | $190 | $170 | $145 | $120 | $100 | $75 |

Last MSR was $290.

SVE-130 LH - similar to the SVE-130, except in a left-handed configuration, available in Black or Metallic Red finishes, disc 2001.

| | $325 | $275 | $250 | $225 | $175 | $125 | $95 |

Last MSR was $450.

In 2000, Black finish was disc.

SVE-130 SD TS - similar to the SVE-130, except features 3 Duncan single coil pickups, available in Sunburst finish, disc. 1999.

| | $255 | $220 | $195 | $170 | $140 | $115 | $85 |

Last MSR was $340.

SV-430 (SOUTHSIDE SPECIAL) - similar to SVE-130, except has 22-fret rosewood fingerboard with pearl dot inlay, disc. 1996.

| | N/A | $200 | $160 | $130 | $110 | $90 | $70 |

Last MSR was $270.

SS-430 (Southside Classic) - similar to the SVE-130, except features 22-fret rosewood fingerboard with pearl dot inlay, standard vibrato, available in Antique Orange, Candy Apple Red, Pacific Blue, SeaMist Green, or Tobacco Sunburst finishes, disc. 1994.

| | N/A | $225 | $195 | $165 | $140 | $120 | $100 |

Last MSR was $340.

SS-430 (Southside Legend) - similar to the SVE-130, except features an ash body, 22-fret rosewood fingerboard with pearl dot inlay, standard vibrato, available in Natural or Trans. Ivory finishes, disc. 1994.

| | N/A | $225 | $195 | $165 | $140 | $120 | $100 |

Last MSR was $340.

SV-460 (SOUTHSIDE HEAVY) - similar to SVE-130, except has black pickguard, 22-fret rosewood fingerboard with pearl dot inlay, 2 single coil/1 humbucker pickups, disc. 1996.

| | N/A | $200 | $160 | $130 | $110 | $90 | $70 |

Last MSR was $280.

TO-120 (UPTOWN) - single cutaway ash body, bolt-on maple neck, 25.5 in. scale, 21-fret maple fingerboard with black dot inlay, fixed bridge, 6-on-a-side tuners, chrome hardware, white pickguard, 2 single coil pickups, volume/tone control, 3-position switch, controls mounted on metal plate, available in Butterscotch or Trans. Ivory finishes, disc. 1996.

| | N/A | $210 | $170 | $140 | $120 | $100 | $80 |

Last MSR was $290.

TO-120 A N (Uptown Legend) - similar to Uptown, except has alder body, black pickguard, die-cast tuners, available in Natural finish, disc 2001.

| | $400 | $350 | $300 | $250 | $195 | $150 | $95 |

Last MSR was $540.

TO-320 BK (UPTOWN CLASSIC) - similar to TO-120 A N, except has gold hardware, available in Black finish, disc 2001.

| | $415 | $375 | $325 | $275 | $225 | $175 | $125 |

Last MSR was $555.

ELECTRIC: AVION SERIES

AV 1 - single cutaway Les-Paul stlye nato body, bolt-on neck, 22-fret rosewood fingerboard with dot inlay, 2 humbucker pickups, 3-per-side Grover tuners, two knobs (v, tone), 3-way switch, chrome hardware, available in Black, Vintage Sunburst, or Wine Red finishes, current mfg.

| MSR | $388 | $250 | $200 | $160 | $130 | $100 | $80 | $60 |

AV 2 - similar to the AV 1, except has a set neck, available in Trans. Red, Trans. Blue, or Cherry Sunburst finishes, disc. 2003.

| | $310 | $250 | $210 | $180 | $150 | $120 | $90 |

Last MSR was $496.

AV 3 - similar to the AV 2, except has a flamed arched maple top and crown inlays, available in Trans. Red, Trans. Blue, Vintage Sunburst, or Cherry Sunburst finishes, current mfg.

| MSR | $616 | $390 | $325 | $275 | $235 | $195 | $165 | $135 |

AV 3 LH - similar to the AV 3, except in left-handed configuration, Cherry Sunburst finish, current mfg.

| MSR | $656 | $415 | $350 | $300 | $250 | $210 | $180 | $150 |

AV 4 - similar to the AV 2, except has a quilted maple top, available in Trans. Red, Trans. Blue, or Amber finishes, current mfg.

| MSR | $916 | $600 | $525 | $450 | $400 | $350 | $300 | $250 |

S

GRADING	100% MINT	98% NEAR MINT	95% EXC+	90% EXC	80% VG+	70% VG	60% G

AV 5 - similar to the AV 2, except has a mahogany top and 2 P-90 pickups, available in Wine Red finish, disc. 2003.

	$360	$300	$250	$210	$180	$150	$120

Last MSR was $576.

AV 6 - similar to the AV 3, except has a quilted maple arched top, available in Original Sunburst, Trans. Red, Trans. Emerald Green, or Vintage Sunburst finishes, current mfg.

MSR	$1,116	$700	$600	$525	$450	$400	$350	$300

AV 7 - similar to the AV 3, except has a mahogany arched top and 8-ply binding, available in Black finish, current mfg.

MSR	$1,116	$700	$600	$525	$450	$400	$350	$300

ELECTRIC: BLUES SARACENO RADIO TEN ARTIST SERIES

BS VG - offset rounded cutaway alder body, bolt-on maple neck, 25.5 in. scale, 22-fret maple fingerboard with off-set black dot inlay, vintage-style tremolo, 3-per-side die-cast tuners, black hardware, 2 humbucker pickups, volume control, 3-way selector switch, available in Black (BK), Raid Red (RA), or White (WH) finishes, disc. 1999.

	$265	$230	$205	$175	$150	$120	$90

Last MSR was $350.

Add $50 for Pink (MPF) or Purple (MPUF) Metal Flake finishes (Model BS VG). Add $50 for White/Blue/Black (WBLB) or White/Red/Black (WRB) Plaid finishes (Model BS VG PP).

BS SH - similar to the BS VG, except features tune-o-matic bridge/stop tailpiece, 2 single coil/humbucker pickups, volume/tone (push/pull coil tap) controls, 5-way selector switch, available in Black (BK), Raid Red (RA), or White (WH) finishes, disc. 1999.

	$300	$260	$230	$200	$165	$135	$100

Last MSR was $400.

Add $50 for Red (MRF) Metal Flake finish (Model BS SH). Add $50 for White/Green/Black (WGNB) or White/Orange/Black (WOB) Plaid finishes (Model BS SH PP

Samick TO-120 AN
(Uptown Legend)
courtesy Samick

ELECTRIC: COBRA SERIES

CA 2 - double sharp cutaway heavy metal style sculpted mahogany body, set neck, 22-fret rosewood fingerboard with dot inlays, 2 Duncan Designed Humbucker pickups, 3-per-side Grover tuners, four knobs (2v, 2 tone), 3-way switch, available in Black or Metallic Silver finishes, current mfg.

MSR	$480	$360	$310	$275	$240	$200	$160	$130

ELECTRIC: CONCORD SERIES

CD 2 - offset double cutaway sculpted body with an arched top, multi-ply black binding, set mahogany neck, 24-fret rosewood fingerboard with offset dot inlays, three-per-side tuners, adjustable bridge, stop tailpiece, two Duncan design humbucker pickups, two knobs, three-way switch, chrome hardware, available in Metallic Black finish, 25.5 in. scale, mfg. 2004-present.

MSR	$1,116	$700	$600	$525	$450	$400	$350	$300

CD 3 - similar to the CD 2, except has a High Tech quilt top, available in Trans. Black Cherry finish, 25.5 in. scale, mfg. 2004-present.

MSR	$1,196	$750	$650	$575	$500	$425	$375	$325

ELECTRIC: FASTBACK SERIES

FB 1 - offset single cutaway sixties style bound agathis body, high tech Quilt top, bolt-on neck, 22-fret rosewood fingerboard with dot inlays, 3-per-side Grover tuners, standard tremolo, two Duncan Designed direct mount humbucker pickups, three knobs (2v, tone), 3-way switch, chrome hardware, available in Trans. Red, Trans. Blue, or Trans. Black finishes, current mfg.

MSR	$416	$260	$220	$190	$160	$140	$120	$100

FB 2 - similar to the FB 1, except a quilted maple top and a Floyd style locking tremolo and nut, available in Trans. Red, Trans. Blue, or Trans. Black finishes, disc. 2003.

	$550	$475	$425	$375	$325	$275	$225

Last MSR was $880.

FB 3 - similar to the FB 1, except a quilted maple arched top, mahogany body, set neck, rosewood fingerboard with crown inlay, no tremolo, and has four knobs, available in Trans. Red, Amber, or Vintage Sunburst finishes, disc. 2003.

	$625	$550	$475	$425	$375	$325	$275

Last MSR was $1,000.

ELECTRIC: FORMULA SERIES

FA 1 - single cutaway Tele-style agathis body, bolt-on neck, 22-fret rosewood fingerboard, two single coil pickups, 3-per-side tuners, two knobs (v, tone), 3-way switch, white pickguard, chrome hardware, available in Black or Metallic Red finishes, current mfg.

MSR	$356	$225	$185	$160	$140	$120	$100	$80

Samick Avion AV 6
courtesy Samick

S

GRADING		100% MINT	98% NEAR MINT	95% EXC+	90% EXC	80% VG+	70% VG	60% G

FA 2 - single cutaway Tele-style bound alder body, quilted maple top, bolt-on neck, 22-fret maple fingerboard, two single coil & one humbucker Duncan Designed pickups, 3-per-side Grover tuners, two knobs (v, tone), 5-way switch, white pickguard, chrome hardware, available in Trans. Blue or Trans. Red finishes, current mfg.

	MSR	$636	$400	$325	$275	$235	$195	$165	$135

ELECTRIC: GT SERIES

GT 1 - Flying-V style agathis body, set neck, 22-fret rosewood fingerboard with dot inlay, two humbucker pickups, 3-per-side tuners, three knobs (2v, tone), 3-way switch, chrome hardware, available in Black or Metallic Red finishes, disc. 2003.

				$310	$260	$220	$190	$160	$130	$100

Last MSR was $496.

GT 2 - Flying-V style bound mahogany body, quilted maple top, set neck, 22-fret rosewood fingerboard with crown inlay, two Duncan Designed humbucker pickups, 3-per-side tuners, three knobs (2v, tone), 3-way switch, chrome hardware, available in Trans. Red or Trans. Blue finishes, disc. 2003.

				$430	$360	$320	$280	$240	$200	$160

Last MSR was $688.

ELECTRIC: INTERCEPTOR SERIES

The Interceptor Series includes models IC 1, IC 2, IC 3, and IC 4. This series was discontinued in 2003 and replaced by the Incerceptor II series, which are models IC 10, IC 20, and IC 30.

IC 1 - offset double cutaway agathis body, bolt-on neck, 24-fret rosewood fingerboard, one humbucker and two single coil pickups, 3-per-side chrome tuners, three knobs (v, 2 tone), 5-way switch, available in Black or Wine Red finishes, disc. 2003.

				$215	$175	$145	$125	$105	$85	$65

Last MSR was $344.

IC 2 - similar to the IC 1, except has an oak overlay top, available in Trans. Red, Trans. Black, Trans. Blue, or Trans. Emerald Green finishes, disc. 2003.

				$240	$195	$160	$130	$110	$90	$70

Last MSR was $384.

IC 3 - similar to the IC 2, except two Duncan Designed humbucker pickups, vintage pickguard, and a locking tremolo, available in Metallic Midnight Blue or Metallic Wine Red finishes, disc. 2003.

				$480	$400	$350	$300	$250	$210	$180

Last MSR was $768.

IC 4 - similar to the IC 3, except has a high tech quilt top, alder body, two Duncan Designed humbucker and one single coil pickups, vintage pickguard, and a locking tremolo, available in Trans. Red or Trans. Violet finishes, disc. 2003.

				$550	$475	$425	$375	$325	$275	$225

Last MSR was $880.

IC 10 - offset double cutaway sculpted body, bolt-on maple neck, 24-fret rosewood fingerboard with offset dot inlays, three-per-side tuners, hard tail bridge, two humbucker pickups, three knobs, five-way switch, chrome hardware, available in Corvette Yellow, Metallic Black, Metallic Silver, or Metallic Red finishes, 25.5 in. scale, mfg. 2004-present.

	MSR	$372	$235	$195	$165	$140	$120	$100	$80

IC 20 - similar to the IC 10, except has a vintage style tremolo, available in Cobalt Blue, Metallic Black, Metallic Silver, or Metallic Red finishes, 25.5 in. scale, mfg. 2004-present.

	MSR	$412	$260	$220	$190	$160	$130	$110	$90

IC 30 - similar to the IC 10, except has a High Tech quilt top and vintage style tremolo, available in Trans. Blue or Trans. Red finishes, 25.5 in. scale, mfg. 2004-present.

	MSR	$796	$500	$425	$375	$325	$275	$225	$175

ELECTRIC: MALIBU SERIES

MB 1 - offset double cutaway Strat style nato body, bolt-on neck, 22-fret rosewood fingerboard with dot inlays, 3-single coil pickups, 3 knobs (v, 2 tone), 5-way switch, white pickguard, 3-per-side Grover tuners, standard tremolo, available in Black, Cobalt Blue, Tobacco Sunburst, Red, Pearl White, Corvette Yellow, Metallic Red, Metallic Gold, Metallic Silver, or Metallic Midnight Blue finishes, current mfg.

	MSR	$316	$200	$160	$130	$110	$90	$70	$50

Add $20 for left-handed configuration, available in Black finish only.

MB 1 M - similar to the MB 1, except has a maple fingerboard, available in Black, Cobalt Blue, or Metallic Red finishes, current mfg.

	MSR	$336	$210	$170	$140	$120	$100	$80	$60

MB 2 - similar to the MB 1, except has a single humbucker with two single coil pickups in HSS configuration, available in Black, Metallic Red, Metallic Gold, Metallic Midnight Blue, Tobacco Sunburst, or Vintage Sunburst finishes, mfg. 2004-present.

	MSR	$356	$225	$185	$150	$130	$110	$90	$70

MB 3 - similar to the MB 1, except has a Wilkinson tremolo, maple fingerboard, Duncan Designed pickups, and a vintage pickguard, available in Metallic Wine Red, Metallic Red, Pearl White, or Metallic Dark Blue finishes, disc. 2003.

				$390	$325	$275	$235	$195	$165	$135

Last MSR was $616.

MB 4 - similar to the MB 3, except has a High Tech Quilt top, and one humbucker and two single coil Duncan Design pickups, available in Trans. Red, Trans. Violet, or Vintage Sunburst finishes, disc. 2003.

				$430	$360	$320	$280	$240	$200	$170

Last MSR was $688.

GRADING	100% MINT	98% NEAR MINT	95% EXC+	90% EXC	80% VG+	70% VG	60% G

MB 30 - similar to the MB 1, except has three single coil Duncan design pickups, available in Metallic Wine Red or Metallic Midnight Blue finishes, mfg. 2004-present.

	MSR	$556		$350	$275	$235	$195	$165	$135	$110

MB 50 - similar to the MB 30, except has one humbucker and two single coil Duncan design pickups in HSS configuration, available in Metallic Wine Red or Metallic Midnight Blue finishes, mfg. 2004-present.

	MSR	$596		$375	$300	$250	$210	$180	$150	$120

ELECTRIC: METALHEAD SERIES

MH 2 - offset double highly sculpted body with numerous points, set mahogany neck, 24-fret rosewood fingerboard with dot inlay, three-per-side tuners, adjustable bridge, stop tailpiece, two Duncan design humbucker pickups, four knobs, three-way switch, black hardware, available in Black, Metallic Silver, or Metallic Red finishes, mfg. 2004-present.

	MSR	$1,036		$650	$575	$500	$450	$400	$350	$300

ELECTRIC: PERFORMANCE SERIES

KR-664 NM (LEGACY) - offset double cutaway alder body, bolt-on maple neck, 24-fret bound rosewood fingerboard with pearl boomerang inlay, double locking vibrato, 6-on-a-side tuners, gold hardware, 2 single coil rail/1 humbucker pickups, volume/tone control, 5-position/coil tap switches, available in Natural finish, disc. 1994.

N/A	$350	$300	$250	$210	$170	$130

Last MSR was $560.

KRT-664 (PROPHET) - similar to KR-664, except has ash body, through-body neck, available in Trans. Black or Trans. Red finishes, disc. 1994.

N/A	$375	$325	$275	$225	$175	$135

Last MSR was $600.

KR-665 ARS (STINGER) - similar to the KR-664, except has bound alder body, available in Antique Red, Sunburst, or Black finishes, disc. 1994.

N/A	$350	$300	$250	$210	$170	$130

Last MSR was $540.

Samick Interceptor IC 10 courtesy Samick

KV-130 (RENEGADE) - offset double cutaway alder body, bolt-on maple neck, 24-fret maple fingerboard with black dot inlay, standard vibrato, 6-on-a-side tuners, chrome hardware, 3 single coil pickups, volume/tone control, 5-position switch, available in Cobalt Blue or Metallic Red finishes, disc. 1994.

N/A	$225	$195	$165	$135	$115	$95

Last MSR was $380.

KV-450 (SCANDAL) - similar to Renegade, except has bound rosewood fingerboard, 2 humbucker pickups, 2 volume/1 tone control, 3-position switch, available in Fluorescent Green or Metallic Black finishes, disc. 1994.

N/A	$175	$145	$125	$105	$85	$65

Last MSR was $300.

SR-660 (SCORPION) - offset double cutaway alder body, bolt-on maple neck, 24-fret bound rosewood fingerboard with pearl boomerang inlay, double locking vibrato, 6-on-a-side tuners, gold hardware, 2 single coil/1 humbucker pickups, volume/tone control, 5-position switch, push/pull coil tap in tone control, available in Black, Metallic Red, or Pearl White finishes, disc. 1994.

N/A	$300	$250	$210	$180	$150	$120

Last MSR was $520.

YR-660 (SCORPION PLUS) - similar to Scorpion, except has sharktooth fingerboard inlay, direct switch, available in Black, Blue, Metallic Red, or Pearl White finishes, disc. 1994.

N/A	$250	$200	$160	$130	$100	$70

Last MSR was $450.

ELECTRIC: ROCKWELL SERIES

RW 1 - Explorer-style agathis body, set neck, 22-fret rosewood fingerboard with dot inlay, two humbucker pickups, 3-per-side tuners, three knobs (2v, tone), 3-way switch, chrome hardware, available in Black or Metallic Red finishes, disc. 2003.

$310	$260	$220	$190	$160	$130	$100

Last MSR was $496.

RW 2 - Explorer-style bound mahogany body, quilted maple top, set neck, 22-fret rosewood fingerboard with crown inlay, two Duncan Designed humbucer pickups, 3-per-side tuners, three knobs (2v, tone), 3-way switch, chrome hardware, available in Trans. Violet or Trans. Red finishes, disc. 2003.

$430	$360	$320	$280	$240	$200	$160

Last MSR was $688.

Samick Malibu MB 1 courtesy Samick

S

GRADING	100% MINT	98% NEAR MINT	95% EXC+	90% EXC	80% VG+	70% VG	60% G

ELECTRIC: STANDARD SOLID BODY SERIES

LS-10 - offset double cutaway hardwood body, bolt-on nato neck, 21-fret rosewood fingerboard with white dot inlay, vintage-style tremolo, chrome hardware, 6-on-a-side standard tuners, white pickguard, 3 single coil pickups, volume/tone control, 3-way selector, available in Black, Metallic Red, Sunburst, or Trans. Cherry finishes, disc 2001.

	$195	$175	$150	$125	$95	$80	$60

Last MSR was $277.

Add $18 for Metallic Red, Transparent Cherry and Blue finishes.

In 1999, Blue finish was introduced.

LS-11 - offset double cutaway hardwood body, bolt-on maple neck, 25.5 in. scale, 21-fret rosewood fingerboard with white dot inlay, vintage-style tremolo, chrome hardware, 6-on-a-side standard tuners, white pickguard, 3 single coil pickups, volume/2 tone controls, 5-way selector switch, available in Black, Burgundy Sunburst, Metallic Red, Red Marble, Red Sunburst, Sunburst, or Trans. Cherry finishes, disc 2001.

	$225	$195	$175	$150	$120	$90	$65

Last MSR was $295.

Add $12 for Red Marble, Metallic Red and Trans Cherry finishes.

In 1999, Red Sunburst finish was disc.

LS-11 D BK LH - similar to the LS-11, except in left-handed configuration, die-cast tuners, available in Black finish, disc 2001.

	$265	$225	$175	$150	$125	$95	$75

Last MSR was $355.

LS11M - similar to LS-11, except has maple fingerboard, availvble in Metallic Red, Black, or Metallic Dark Blue finishes, mfg. 2001 only.

	$199	$175	$150	$125	$95	$75	$50

Last MSR was $277.

LS-110 - similar to the LS-11, except features 3 Duncan single coil pickups, available in Black, Red, and Sunburst finishes, disc. 1999.

	$215	$190	$170	$145	$120	$100	$75

Last MSR was $287.

LS-35 BDS (LS-310 DB) - offset double cutaway hardwood body, bolt-on maple neck, 25.5 in. scale, 21-fret rosewood fingerboard with white dot inlay, vintage-style tremolo, black hardware, 6-on-a-side die-cast tuners, pickguard, 2 single coil/humbucker pickups, volume/tone controls, 5-way selector switch, available in Black, Natural, Orange Sunburst, Trans. Red, or Vintage Sunburst finishes, mfg. 1997-98.

	$180	$155	$140	$120	$100	$80	$60

Last MSR was $237.

LS-36 D - offset double cutaway hardwood body, oak veneer top, bolt-on maple neck, 25.5 in. scale, 21-fret rosewood fingerboard with white dot inlay, vintage-style tremolo, chrome hardware, 6-on-a-side die-cast tuners, pickguard, 2 single coil/humbucker pickups, volume/tone controls, 5-way selector switch, available in Brown Sunburst, Orange Sunburst, Trans. Black, Trans. Blue, or Trans. Cherry finishes, mfg. 1997-98.

	$165	$140	$125	$110	$90	$75	$55

Last MSR was $217.

A similar model, LS-36 SD was announced in 1997, but this model has yet to be manufactured.

LS-40 D - similar to the LS-36 D, except features 2 humbucker pickups, standard tremolo, 3-way selector, available in Natural, Orange Sunburst, Trans. Blue, or Trans. Cherry finishes, mfg. 1997-98.

	$165	$140	$125	$110	$90	$75	$55

Last MSR was $217.

LS-45 D - similar to the LS-36 D, except features single body binding, 2 humbucker pickups, standard tremolo, available in Trans. Blue, Trans. Cherry, or Vintage Sunburst finishes, mfg. 1997-98.

	$170	$145	$130	$110	$95	$80	$60

Last MSR was $224.

LS-41 DS OS - offset double cutaway hardwood body, bolt-on maple neck, 25.5 in. scale, 21-fret rosewood fingerboard with white dot inlay, vintage-style tremolo, chrome hardware, 6-on-a-side die-cast tuners, pickguard, humbucker/single coil/humbucker pickups, volume/tone controls, 5-way selector switch, available in Orange Sunburst finish, mfg. 1997-2000.

	$170	$150	$135	$115	$100	$80	$60

Last MSR was $226.

LSM-80 T - student 7/8 size offset double cutaway hardwood body, bolt-on nato neck, rosewood fingerboard with white dot inlay, vintage-style tremolo, chrome hardware, 6-on-a-side enclosed gear tuners, white pickguard, single coil/humbucker pickups, volume/tone control, 3-way selector, available in Black or Red finishes, mfg. 1997-2001.

	$175	$150	$125	$95	$75	$65	$50

Last MSR was $235.

LT-11 BK (P-757 BK) - single cutaway hardwood body, bolt-on maple neck, 25.5 in. scale, 21-fret rosewood fingerboard with white dot inlay, fixed bridge, chrome hardware, 6-on-a-side enclosed gear tuners, white pickguard, 2 single coil pickups, volume/tone control, 3-way selector, controls mounted on a metal plate, available in Black finish, disc 2001.

	$255	$225	$195	$150	$125	$95	$75

Last MSR was $340.

LT-11 SS - similar to the LT-11 BK, available in Silver Sunburst finish, mfg. 1997-98.

	$190	$165	$145	$125	$105	$85	$65

Last MSR was $250.

GRADING	100% MINT	98% NEAR MINT	95% EXC+	90% EXC	80% VG+	70% VG	60% G

SL-21 (SL-22) - single cutaway hardwood body (flat, not arched top), nato neck, 24.75 in. scale, 21-fret rosewood fingerboard with white dot inlay, tune-o-matic bridge/stop tailpiece, chrome hardware, 3-per-side standard tuners, 2 humbucker pickups, 2 volume/2 tone control, 3-way selector, available in Black, Golden Sunburst, Silver Sunburst, or Vintage Sunburst finishes, disc 2001.

	$250	$195	$175	$150	$125	$95	$70

Last MSR was $340.

SL-21 S TC (SL-22 S TC) - similar to the SL-21, available in Trans. Cherry finish, disc 2001.

	$265	$225	$195	$150	$125	$95	$75

Last MSR was $355.

ELECTRIC: T SERIES

RANGER 3 - single cutaway contoured alder body, bolt-on maple neck, 21-fret rosewood fingerboard with pearl dot inlay, strings through fixed bridge, 6-on-a-side tuners, gold hardware, pearloid pickguard, 3 single coil pickups, volume/tone control, 5-position switch, available in Black or Blue finishes, mfg. 1994-96.

	N/A	$275	$225	$195	$165	$135	$105

Last MSR was $500.

ELECTRIC: TORINO SERIES

TR 1 - double sharp SG-ish cutaway body style, nato body, set neck, 22-fret rosewood fingerboard with dot inlay, pickguard, two humbucker pickups, 3-per-side die-cast tuners, four knobs (2v, 2 tone), 3-way switch, available in Wine Red or Black finishes, current mfg.

MSR	$496	$310	$250	$210	$180	$150	$120	$90

TR 2 - similar to the TR 1, except has a High Tech Quilt top, mahogany body, Duncan Designed pickups, and crown inlays, available in Vintage Sunburst or Trans. Red finishes, current mfg.

MSR	$696	$435	$375	$325	$275	$235	$195	$165

TR 3 - similar to the TR 1, except has a bound alder body, High Tech Quilt top, no pickguard, and only two knobs, available in Trans. Emerald Green, Original Sunburst, or Vintage Sunburst finishes, current mfg.

MSR	$1,116	$700	$600	$525	$450	$400	$350	$300

Samick Torino TR 3
courtesy Samick

TR 4 - similar to the TR 1, except has a bound alder body with a carved top, no pickguard, only two knobs, gold hardware, available in Metallic Black, Metallic Cherry Burst, or Pearl White finishes, mfg. 2004-present.

MSR	$1,116	$700	$600	$525	$450	$400	$350	$300

ELECTRIC: ULTRAMATIC SERIES

UM 1 - offset double cutaway bound flat nato body, set neck, 22-fret rosewood fingerboard with dot inlays, two humbucker pickups, 3-per-side grover tuners, two knobs (v, tone), 3-way switch, chrome hardware, available in Black, Purple, or Wine Red finishes, current mfg.

MSR	$496	$310	$250	$210	$180	$150	$120	$90

UM 2 - similar to the UM 1, except has a High Tech Quilt top, available in Trans. Red or Trans. Blue finishes, disc. 2003.

	$340	$275	$235	$195	$165	$135	$110

Last MSR was $536.

UM 3 - similar to the UM 1, except has a High Tech Quilt arched top and Duncan Designed pickups, available in Trans. Red, Original Sunburst, Vintage Sunburst, or Trans. Emerald Green finishes, current mfg.

MSR	$1,116	$700	$600	$525	$450	$400	$350	$300

UM 4 - similar to the UM 31, except has a Wilkinson vibrato bridge, available in Trans. Red, Trans. Blue, Original Sunburst, Vintage Sunburst, or Trans. Emerald Green finishes, disc. 2003.

	$650	$575	$475	$425	$375	$325	$275

Last MSR was $1,040.

ELECTRIC BASS: AMERICAN CLASSIC SOLID BODY

All American Classics by Valley Arts bass models are optional with Bartolini pickups as an upgrade.

Add $225 for Bartolini P/J pickups for 4-string configuration (upgrade). Add $235 for Bartolini P/J pickups for 5-string configuration (upgrade).

BTB-460 TS - violin-shaped body, 2 humbucker pickups, 2 volume/2 tone controls, available in Tobacco Sunburst finish, mfg. 1997-2000.

	$590	$515	$455	$390	$325	$265	$200

Last MSR was $790.

CB-630 RSBU N (THUNDER) - sleek offset scooped double cutaway alder body, bubinga top, bolt-on maple neck, 34 in. scale, 24-fret rosewood fingerboard with pearl dot inlay, fixed bridge, 4-on-a-side die-cast tuners, gold hardware, P/J-style pickups, volume/tone control, 3-position switch, available in Natural finish, disc 2001.

	$565	$475	$425	$375	$325	$275	$225

Last MSR was $750.

Some early models may also have Black Finishing Net, Granite White Sunburst, or Pearl White finishes.

Samick Ultramatic UM 1
courtesy Samick

S

GRADING	100% MINT	98% NEAR MINT	95% EXC+	90% EXC	80% VG+	70% VG	60% G

CB-630 RSQT US - similar to the CB-630 RSBU N, except features a quilted maple top, available in Light Vapor Green finish, disc 2001.

	$615	$525	$450	$395	$355	$295	$250

Last MSR was $825.

FB-430 SQ PS - 7/8 scale sleek offset double cutaway body, quilt top, bolt-on maple neck, 34 in. scale, 20-fret rosewood fingerboard with pearl dot inlay, fixed bridge, 4-on-a-side die-cast tuners, chrome hardware, P/J-style pickups, 2 volume/tone control, available in Purple Burst finish, disc. 2000.

	$340	$295	$260	$225	$190	$150	$115

Last MSR was $450.

In 1999, Transparent Red finish was introduced and Purple Burst finish was disc.

SCBM-1 B TBL - offset double cutaway carved ash body, bolt-on maple neck, 20-fret rosewood fingerboard with pearl dot inlay, fixed bridge, 4-on-a-side tuners, black hardware, P/J-style pickups, 2 volume/1 tone controls, active electronics, available in Trans. Blue, Trans. Black, or Trans. Red finishes, mfg. 1994-2000.

	$415	$360	$315	$275	$230	$185	$140

Last MSR was $550.

Add $80 for gold hardware with Transparent Black finish (model SCBM-1 G TB).

In 1996, Trans. Black and Trans. Red finishes were disc.

SCBM-2 B TBL - similar to SCBM-1 B, except has 5-string configuration, 4/1-per-side tuners, available in Trans. Blue finish, mfg. 1994-2000.

	$450	$390	$345	$295	$250	$200	$150

Last MSR was $600.

SCBM-2 G - similar to SCBM-1 B, except has 5-string configuration, 4/1-per-side tuners, gold hardware, available in Trans. Blue or Trans.Red finishes, mfg. 1994-2000.

	$450	$390	$345	$295	$250	$200	$150

Last MSR was $600.

Earlier models may also feature Cherry Sunburst and Trans. Black finishes. In 1999, Trans. Black finish was reintroduced.

SJM-1 - J-style offset double cutaway alder body, bolt-on maple neck, 20-fret rosewood fingerboard with white dot inlay, fixed bridge, pickguard, 4-on-a-side tuners, chrome hardware, 2 J-style pickups, volume/tone controls, available in Black or 3 Color Sunburst finishes, disc. 1999.

	$300	$260	$230	$200	$165	$135	$100

Last MSR was $400.

SMBX-1 FCS - offset double cutaway mahogany body, bound carved flame maple top, bolt-on maple neck, 34 in. scale, 20-fret bound ebony fingerboard with pearl dot inlay, fixed bridge, bound peghead, 4-on-a-side tuners, gold hardware, P/J-style pickups, 2 volume/tone controls, active electronics, available in Flame Cherry Sunburst finish, mfg. 1994-2000.

	$480	$435	$380	$325	$270	$215	$160

Last MSR was $640.

SMBX - similar to SMBX-1 FCS, except has 5-string configuration, 4/1-per-side tuners, available in Flame Cherry Sunburst or Flame Trans. Black finishes, mfg. 1994-2000.

	$525	$455	$400	$345	$290	$230	$175

Last MSR was $700.

SPM-1 - contoured offset double cutaway alder body, bolt-on maple neck, 20-fret maple fingerboard with black dot inlay, fixed bridge, pickguard, 4-on-a-side tuners, white pickguard, chrome hardware, P-style split pickup, volume/tone controls, available in Black or 3 Color Sunburst finishes, disc. 1999.

	$285	$250	$220	$190	$160	$125	$95

Last MSR was $380.

Some early models may also feature Pearl White finish.

YBT-6629 - sleek offset double cutaway ash body, 6-string configuration, through-body maple/walnut neck, 34 in. scale, 24-fret ebony fingerboard with pearl dot inlay, fixed bridge, 4/2-per-side die-cast tuners, gold hardware, 2 J-style pickups, 2 volume/2 tone controls, 3-way selector, active electronics, available in Trans. Black or Walnut finishes, mfg. 1994-2001.

	$1,250	$1,050	$950	$850	$750	$650	$550

Last MSR was $1,650.

Some early models may also feature a Transparent Red finish. In 1999, Transparent Black finish was disc.

ELECTRIC BASS: ARTIST SOLID BODY SERIES

DB-100 - P-style offset double cutaway hardwood body, bolt-on maple neck, 20-fret maple fingerboard with black dot inlay, fixed bridge, pickguard, 4-on-a-side Schaller tuners, white pickguard, chrome hardware, P-style split pickup, volume/tone controls, available in Black or Metallic Red finishes, disc. 2000.

	$210	$185	$165	$140	$115	$95	$70

Last MSR was $280.

JB-420 (JAVELIN) - offset double cutaway contoured alder body, bolt-on maple neck, 34 in. scale, 21-fret rosewood fingerboard with white dot inlay, vintage-style fixed bridge, 4-on-a-side tuners, chrome hardware, white pickguard/thumb rest, 2 J-style pickups, 2 volume/tone controls, controls mounted on a metal plate, available in Black, Pearl White, or Sunburst finishes, disc. 2000.

	$265	$230	$205	$175	$150	$120	$90

Last MSR was $350.

In 1996, Pearl White finish was disc.

LB-539 (AURORA) - offset double cutaway alder body, maple neck, 24-fret rosewood fingerboard, fixed bridge, 4-on-a-side tuners, black hardware, P/J-style pickup, volume/mid/bass/balance controls, available in Aurora Multi Palette finish, disc. 1994.

	N/A	$300	$250	$210	$180	$150	$120

Last MSR was $520.

S

GRADING	100% MINT	98% NEAR MINT	95% EXC+	90% EXC	80% VG+	70% VG	60% G

MPB MR - "mini" P-style bass, 26 in. scale, chrome hardware, black pickguard, split P-style pickup, volume/tone controls, available in Metallic Red finish, disc. 2000.

	$250	$215	$190	$165	$140	$110	$85

Last MSR was $330.

PB-110 (PRESTIGE) - P-style offset double cutaway solid alder body, bolt-on maple neck, 34 in. scale, 20-fret maple fingerboard with black dot inlay, vintage-style fixed bridge, 4-on-a-side Schaller tuners, chrome hardware, black pickguard/thumb rest, split P-style pickup, volume/tone controls, available in Black, Metallic Red, or White finishes, disc. 2000.

	$240	$210	$185	$160	$135	$110	$80

Last MSR was $320.

PB-110 LH - similar to the PB-110, except in a left-handed configuration, available in Black and Metallic Red finishes, disc. 2001.

	$375	$325	$275	$225	$175	$125	$95

Last MSR was $495.

XBT-637 (PROPHET) - offset double cutaway alder body, through-body 3-piece maple neck, 24-fret rosewood fingerboard with pearl dot inlay, fixed bridge, 4-on-a-side tuners, gold hardware, P/J-style pickups, volume/tone control, 3-position switch, available in Trans. Black, Trans. Blue, or Trans. Red finishes, disc. 1994.

	N/A	$350	$300	$250	$210	$180	$150

Last MSR was $600.

YB-410 (PRESTIGE GT) - sleek contoured offset double cutaway solid alder body, bolt-on maple neck, 34 in. scale, 24-fret rosewood fingerboard with pearl dot inlay, fixed bridge, 4-on-a-side die-cast tuners, chrome hardware, split P-style pickup, volume/tone controls, available in Black, Trans. Blue, or Tobacco Sunburst finishes, disc. 2000.

	$270	$235	$210	$180	$150	$120	$90

Last MSR was $360.

In 1999, White finish was introduced.

YB-410 BK LH - similar to the YB-410, except in a left-handed configuration, available in Black finish, mfg. 1997-2001.

	$395	$350	$295	$250	$195	$150	$95

Last MSR was $540.

YB-430 - similar to the YB-410, except features P/J-style pickups, 3-way selector switch, available in Tobacco Sunburst or Trans. Blue finishes, disc 2001.

	$425	$375	$325	$275	$225	$175	$125

Last MSR was $570.

In 2000, Tobacco Sunburst finish was disc.

YB-430 BB - similar to the YB-430, except features bamboo body, available in Natural finish, mfg. 1997-98.

	$355	$305	$270	$230	$195	$160	$120

Last MSR was $470.

YB 530 FL - similar to the YB-410, except features P/J-style pickups, fretless rosewood fingerboard, black hardware, available in Black or Red finishes, mfg. 1994-2001.

	$435	$375	$325	$275	$225	$175	$125

Last MSR was $585.

YB-639 (THUNDERBOLT) - sleek offset double cutaway alder body, bolt-on maple neck, 24-fret rosewood fingerboard with pearl lightning bolt inlay, fixed bridge, 4-per-side tuners, gold hardware, P/J-style active pickups, volume/treble/bass/balance controls, available in Black, Grayburst, Metallic Red, or Pearl White finishes, disc. 1994.

	N/A	$275	$225	$185	$155	$125	$95

Last MSR was $450.

YB5-639 (THUNDER-5) - sleek contoured offset scooped double cutaway solid alder body, 5-string configuration, bolt-on maple neck, 34 in. scale, 24-fret rosewood fingerboard with pearl dot inlay, fixed bridge, 4/1 on a side die-cast tuners, gold hardware, P/J-style pickups, 2 volume/tone controls, 3-way selector switch, active/passive circuitry, available in Black, Granite Gold, Metallic Red, or White finishes, disc. 2001.

	$585	$495	$395	$350	$295	$250	$195

Last MSR was $780.

YB5-639 BK LH - similar to YB5-639, except in a left-handed configuration, available in Black finish, mfg. 1997-2001.

	$595	$495	$395	$350	$295	$250	$195

Last MSR was $810.

YB6-629 WA - similar to YB5-639, except features 6-string configuration, 4/2-per-side tuners, 2 J-style pickups, active circuitry, available in Walnut finish, mfg. 1997-2001.

	$1,000	$900	$800	$700	$600	$475	$350

Last MSR was $1,350.

A similar model (model YBT6-629) featured maple/walnut through-body neck design, 24-fret ebony fingerboard with pearl dot inlay, and Trans. Black, Trans. Red, or Walnut finishes.

Samick SJM-1
courtesy Samick

Samick SMBX-1
courtesy Samick

S

GRADING	100% MINT	98% NEAR MINT	95% EXC+	90% EXC	80% VG+	70% VG	60% G

ELECTRIC BASS: CORSAIR SERIES

CR 1 - double cutaway agathis body, bolt-on neck, 22-fret rosewood fingerboard with offset dot inlay, J-J pickups, white pickguard, 2-per-side tuners, two knobs, chrome hardware, available in Black, Antique Ivory, Red, Tobacco Sunburst, Covette Yellow, Natural, or Cobalt Blue finishes, current mfg.

MSR	$376	$235	$190	$160	$130	$110	$90	$70

CR 1 3 - similar to the CR 1, except in 30 in. scale, available in Black finish, new 2005.

MSR	$356	$225	$185	$150	$125	$105	$85	$65

CR 1 5 - similar to the CR 1, except in five-string configuration, 3/2-per-side tuners, available in Cobalt Blue or Metallic Red finishes, new 2005.

MSR	$436	$275	$225	$190	$160	$130	$110	$90

CR 2 - double cutaway agathis body, oak overlay, bolt-on neck, 22-fret rosewood fingerboard with offset dot inlay, split P pickup, 2-per-side tuners, two knobs, chrome hardware, available in Brown Sunburst, Trans. Blue, Trans. Black, or Trans. Red finishes, disc. 2003.

		$225	$185	$150	$130	$110	$90	$70

Last MSR was $360.

CR 3 5 - double cutaway alder body, 5-string, bolt-on neck, 22-fret rosewood fingerboard with offset dot inlay, P/J pickups, 3/2-per-side tuners, three knobs, chrome hardware, available in Red, Cobalt Blue, or Black finishes, disc. 2003.

		$310	$250	$210	$180	$150	$120	$100

Last MSR was $496.

CR 4(M) - double cutaway alder body, high tech Quilted top, bolt-on neck, 22-fret rosewood or maple fingerboard with offset dot inlay, JJ pickups, 2-per-side tuners, vintage pickguard, three knobs, chrome hardware, available in Trans. Red, Trans. Blue, Trans. Emerald Green, Vintage Sunburst, Black, Metallic Midnight Blue, or Metallic Wine Red finishes, disc. 2003.

		$360	$300	$250	$210	$180	$150	$120

Last MSR was $576.

CR 4 5 - similar to the CR 4, except in five-string configuration, 3/2-per-side tuners, available Trans. Emerald Green or Trans. Blue finishes, disc. 2003.

		$460	$400	$350	$300	$250	$210	$170

Last MSR was $728.

ELECTRIC BASS: FAIRLANE SERIES

FN 1 - offset double cutaway agathis body, bolt-on neck, 22-fret maple fingerboard with offset dot inlay, split P pickup, white pickguard, 2-per-side tuners, three knobs, chrome hardware, available in Tobacco Sunburst, Black, Metallic Red, or Cobalt Blue finishes, current mfg.

MSR	$356	$225	$185	$155	$135	$115	$95	$75

Add $20 for left-handed configuration, available in Tobacco Sunburst finish only.

FN 1 5 - similar to the FN 1, except in five-string configuration, 3/2-per-side tuners, available in Black finish, new 2005.

MSR	$396	$250	$210	$180	$150	$120	$100	$80

FN 2 - offset double cutaway agathis body, oak overlay, bolt-on neck, 22-fret rosewood fingerboard with offset dot inlay, split P pickup, 2-per-side tuners, two knobs, chrome hardware, available in Natural, Trans. Black or Trans. Red finishes, disc. 2003.

		$225	$185	$155	$135	$115	$95	$75

Last MSR was $360.

Add $10 for left-handed configuration, available in Trans. Black finish.

FN 3 5 - offset double cutaway alder body, 5-string, bolt-on neck, 22-fret rosewood fingerboard with offset dot inlay, P/J pickups, 3/2-per-side tuners, three knobs, chrome hardware, available in Metallic Red or Black finishes, disc. 2003.

		$335	$275	$235	$195	$165	$135	$105

Last MSR was $536.

FN 4(M) - offset double cutaway alder body, high tech Quilted top, bolt-on neck, 22-fret rosewood or maple fingerboard with offset dot inlay, JJ pickups, 2-per-side tuners, vintage pickguard, three knobs, chrome hardware, available in Trans. Violet, Trans. Blue, Original Sunburst, Vintage Sunburst, Black, Metallic Midnight Blue, or Metallic Wine Red finishes, current mfg.

MSR	$596	$375	$325	$275	$235	$195	$165	$135

FN 5 4 - offset double cutaway alder body, high tech Quilted top, bolt-on neck, 22-fret rosewood fingerboard with offset dot inlay, Deluxe active pickups, 2-per-side tuners, four knobs, chrome hardware, active electronics, available in Vintage Sunburst finish, new 2005.

MSR	$1,116	$700	$600	$525	$450	$400	$350	$300

FN 5 5 - offset double cutaway alder body, high tech Quilted top, 5-string, bolt-on neck, 22-fret rosewood fingerboard with offset dot inlay, Deluxe active pickups, 3/2-per-side tuners, four knobs, chrome hardware, active electronics, available in Trans. Emerald Green or Trans. Red finishes, current mfg.

MSR	$1,156	$725	$625	$550	$475	$425	$375	$325

FN 5 6 - similar to the FN 5 5, except in 6-string configuration, 3-per-side tuners, available in Trans. Red finish, current mfg.

MSR	$1,316	$850	$750	$675	$600	$525	$450	$375

ELECTRIC BASS: MISC. MODELS

COBRA BASS CAB 2 - offset double sharp cutaway heavy metal sculpted ash body, neck thru body, 22-fret rosewood fingerboard with dot inlay, two active pickups, active electronics, 2-per-side tuners, four knobs, black hardware, available in Black or Mirror Tips finishes, current mfg.

MSR	$1,396	$875	$775	$675	$600	$525	$450	$400

GRADING	100% MINT	98% NEAR MINT	95% EXC+	90% EXC	80% VG+	70% VG	60% G

TABU BASS TBB 2 - offset radical double cutaway bound alder body, neck thru body, laminated maple neck, 24-fret rosewood fingerboard with offset dot inlays, 2-per-side tuners, 2 active pickups, active electronics, four knobs, chrome hardware, available in Trans. Black finish, current mfg.

		$875	$775	$675	$600	$525	$450	$375

Last MSR was $1,396.

ULTRAMATIC BASS UMB 2 - offset double cutaway alder body, high-tech quilted maple top, set-neck, 22-fret rosewood fingerboard with offset dot inlays, 2 active pickups, active electronics, 2-per-side tuners, 4 knobs, chrome hardware, available in Original Sunburst finish, disc. 2003.

$850	$750	$650	$575	$500	$425	$350

Last MSR was $1,344.

ELECTRIC BASS: ROYALE SERIES

ROYALE BASS RLB 2 - single cutaway hollowbody, arched quilted maple top, mahogany sides and back, set neck, 22-fret rosewood fingerboard with crown inlays, two active pickups, active electronics, four knobs, chrome hardware, available in Vintage Sunburst finish, disc. 2004.

$790	$700	$625	$550	$475	$400	$350

Last MSR was $1,264.

ROYALE BASS RLB 3/RLB 4 - single cutaway hollowbody, arched quilted maple top, mahogany sides and back, set neck, 22-fret rosewood fingerboard with crown inlays, two active pickups, active electronics, four knobs, chrome hardware, available in Black (RLB 4) or Vintage Sunburst (RLB 3) finishes, mfg. 2004-present.

MSR	$1,436	$900	$800	$700	$625	$550	$475	$400

ELECTRIC BASS: STANDARD SOLID BODY SERIES

LB-11 - P-style offset double cutaway hardwood body, bolt-on maple neck, 34 in. scale, 20-fret rosewood fingerboard with white dot inlay, vintage-style fixed bridge, 4-on-a-side Schaller tuners, chrome hardware, black pickguard, split P-style pickup, volume/tone controls, available in Black, Red, or Sunburst finishes, disc 2001.

$250	$195	$170	$155	$125	$95	$70

Last MSR was $328.

Samick Corsair CR 1 Bass courtesy Samick

FB-15 S (LB-11 NP) - similar to the LB-11, except features solid maple neck, scooped contoured body, die-cast tuners, no pickguard, available in Trans. Black, Natural, Trans. Red, or Vintage Sunburst finish, mfg. 1997-2001.

$265	$225	$195	$175	$150	$125	$95

Last MSR was $355.

LBJ-21 TS - J-style offset double cutaway hardwood body, bolt-on maple neck, 34 in. scale, 20-fret rosewood fingerboard with white dot inlay, vintage-style fixed bridge, 4-on-a-side die-cast tuners, chrome hardware, pickguard, 2 J-style pickups, volume/tone controls, available in Tobacco Sunburst finish, mfg. 1997-2001.

$250	$225	$195	$175	$150	$125	$95

Last MSR was $337.

LBM-10 SB (MPB-11 SB) - short scale P-Style bass, 30 in. scale, black pickguard, split P-style pickup, volume/tone controls, available in Sunburst finish, disc. 2001.

$210	$175	$150	$125	$110	$95	$65

Last MSR was $280.

SANDNER

Instruments previously produced between 1948 and 1959.

The Sandner trademark can be found on a series of acoustic archtops. These models may have Alosa or Standard on the headstock (or tailpiece). Research continues into the Sandner (or Alosa) trademark.

SANO

Instruments previously produced in Italy circa late 1960s.

Sano electric models resemble the Fender Jaguar. The Sano 3-way pickup selector toggle switch's positions are labeled as routed inscriptions in the pickguard; the positions are labeled T, ALL, and B. Apparently they stand for "Top," "ALL" (both pickups combined), and "Bottom" - something gets lost in translation from Italian.

The Sano electric has an offset double cutaway asymmetrical solid body (wood unknown), bolt-on maple neck, 22-fret rosewood fingerboard with white dot inlay, 6-on-a-side chrome tuners, floating bridge/vibrato tailpiece, w/b/w laminated plastic pickguard, 2 single coil pickups, volume and tone controls, 3-way selector. Available in solid finishes. The neckplate is inscribed "N. 1000," perhaps the model designation. Sano electric guitars in average condition are worth around $150 (source: Walter Murray, *Frankenstein Fretworks*).

SANOX

Instruments previously produced in Japan from the late 1970s through the mid-1980s.

Intermediate to good quality guitars featuring some original designs and some designs based on American classics (source: Tony Bacon and Paul Day, *The Guru's Guitar Guide*).

Samick Fairlane FN 5 6 Bass courtesy Samick

S

SANTUCCI

Instruments currently produced in Rome, Italy. Distributed in the U.S. market by the Santucci Corporation of New York City, NY.

The ten-string Santucci TrebleBass was developed by Sergio Santucci, a professional musician who has played guitar all over the world. Santucci began to develop the idea of combining the guitar and bass onto a one necked instrument as he was very fond of both. The desire to reproduce the original sound of the 4-string bass together with the guitar was "so strong that I had destroyed five instruments to achieve this project," notes Santucci. The **Treblebas** combines the 6-strings of a guitar with the 4-strings of a bass all on one neck, and is especially designed to expand the two-handed tapping style of play. The active circuitry of the individual guitar/bass pickups are wired to separate outputs (thus processing the two individual outputs to their respective amplification needs), and can be switched on and off independently. The two octave fretboard and custom made Gotoh tremolo/bass tailpiece give any guitarist ample room for exploration across the sonic range. For further information, contact designer Santucci directly (see Trademark Index).

ELECTRIC

The **Treblebass** has an offset double cutaway alder body, through-body 5-piece maple neck, 24-fret ebony fingerboard with pearl dot inlay, custom-made Gotoh bridge consisting of: fixed bridge, bass; standard vibrato, guitar; 4/6-per-side tuners, chrome Gotoh hardware, split-bass/single coil/humbucker-guitar EMG pickups, 2 concentric volume/tone controls, 2 mini switches, available in White, Black, Red, Green, Yellow, and Blue finishes with silk screened logo, mfg. 1990-current, and MSR is $1,980.

SARDONYX

Instruments previously built in New York City, NY circa early 1970s.

Sardonyx custom built guitars and basses were constructed in Greenwich Village in New York City. One source indicates that they were available in Matt Uminov Guitars in the West Village. Further research continues on the Sardonyx trademark, (preliminary research courtesy Jeff Meyer).

SARRICOLA

Instruments previously built in Lake Thunderbird, IL.

Luthier Bill Sarricola, an ex-Hamer employee, offered four different custom-built guitar models. Sarricola models feature three different equipment packages on each guitar, as well as other custom options.

SATELLITE

Instruments previously produced in Japan during the late 1970s. Current production moved to Korea through the early to late 1980s.

The Satellite trademark is the brand name of a United Kingdom importer. These entry level to intermediate quality solid body and semi-hollowbody guitars featured both original and designs based on popular American classics (source: Tony Bacon and Paul Day, *The Guru's Guitar Guide*).

SAXON

Instruments previously built in Japan during the mid-1970s.

The Saxon trademark is a brand name utilized by a United Kingdom importer. These medium quality solid body guitars featured Gibson-based designs (source: Tony Bacon and Paul Day, *The Guru's Guitar Guide*).

SCHACK BASSES

Instruments currently produced in Hammerbach, Germany.

Luthier Andy Schack has been building bass guitars since the 1970s. Schack offers handcrafted basses in a 4-, 5-, or 6-string configuration and exotic wood tops. He is also known for having many firsts in the bass guitar industry. For further information, contact Schack Guitars directly (see Trademark Index).

ELECTRIC

The **SG 665 BASIC** has an offset double cutaway asymmetrical figured maple body, maple neck, 24-fret ebony fingerboard, fixed bridge, 3-per-side Sperzel tuners, Schack ETS 2D bridge, chrome hardware, 2 humbucker Seymour Duncan pickups, volume/tone control, 3-position switch, available in Transparent Stain finish, and last MSR was $1,800.

The **SG 665 CUSTOM** is similar to Basic, except has Flamed Maple body and gold hardware. The last MSR was $2,030.

The **SG 665 CLASSIC** is similar to Custom, except model features further appointments. The last MSR was $2,650

Add $250 for tremolo system.

ELECTRIC BASS

The Unique Series features the basic Unique body design that is offered in both bolt-on and neck-through models. The Unique IV Neck-Through Basic is also available in a Custom, Artwood, and Rootwood configurations (exotic tops). Contact Schack for exotic wood availability, or for a price quote on a bookmatched top/back.

The **Unique IV Bolt-On Basic** has an offset double cutaway asymmetrical bubinga body, bolt-on maple neck, 24-fret ebony fingerboard, fixed Schack ETS-3D bridge, 2-per-side tuners, black hardware, 2 Basstec JB-4 single coil pickups, 2 volume controls, 3 knob treble/mid/bass EQ control with active electronics, available in Natural finish, and MSR is $2,800. **Unique V Bolt-On Basic** is similar to the Unique IV, except has 5-string configuration, and MSR is $2,990. **Unique VI Bolt-On Basic** is similar to the Unique IV, except has 6-string configuration, and MSR is $3,475.

The **Unique IV Bolt-On Custom** is similar to the Unique IV Bolt-On Basic, except features exotic wood construction and gold hardware and MSR is $3,460. The **Unique V Bolt-On Custom** is similar to the Unique IV Custom, except has 5-string configuration, and MSR is $3,676. The **Unique VI Bolt-On Custom** is similar to the Unique IV Custom, except has 6-string configuration, and MSR is $4,130.

The **Unique IV Neck-Through Basic** has an offset double cutaway asymmetrical maple body, goncalo alves top, through-body 9 piece maple/bubinga neck, 24-fret ebony fingerboard, fixed bridge, 2-per-side tuners, black hardware, 2 Basstec single coil pickups, 2 volume controls, and a 3 knob treble/mid/bass EQ controls with active electronics, available in Natural finish, and MSR is $3,590. The **Unique V Neck-Through Basic** is similar to the Unique IV Neck-Through, except has a 36 in. scale and 5-strings, and MSR is $3,930. The **Unique VI Neck-Through Basic** is similar to the Unique IV Neck through, except has a 36" scale and 6-strings, and MSR is $4,270.

Add $140 for fretless neck with fret inlay stripes. Add $336 for two piece bookmatched top.

SCHAEFER GUITARS

Instruments currently built in Duluth, MN. Previously built in Hillsboro, TX and Fort Worth, TX until 2003.

Luthier Ed Schaefer studied classical guitar in college while working as a guitar tech at R.B.I. The Rhythm Band Instrument Company was a sister company of I.M.C. (International Music Corporation - See Hondo or Charvel/Jackson). Schaefer's main job was fret re-surfacing and set-ups on imported guitars that sat out on ships for too long! Schaefer's first lutherie attempt was building a classical guitar (with the guidance of Irving Sloan's guitar construction book). In 2003, Schaefer relocated to the Land of 10,000 Lakes.

Schaefer Freddy
courtesy Ed Scheafer

ELECTRIC ARCHTOP

Schaefer's archtop models feature AAA Sitka or Englemann spruce tops, American sycamore backs and sides, and 3-piece sycamore necks. Schaefer's professional painting background has led him to the opinion that "Nitrocellulose lacquer - the only way" to finish guitars. Schaefer is currently constructing his archtop guitars on a custom order, commission basis. For further information regarding specifications and pricing, please contact Ed Schaefer directly (see Trademark Index).

CASANOVA - thinline double cutaway body, quilted or flamed maple top, sides, and back, three-piece maple neck, split-block MOP inlay on fingerboard, gold Grover Deluxe tuners, Art Deco headstock inlay, bound entire guitar, f-holes, pickguard and tailpiece, 2 Kent Armstrong gold covered humbucker pickups, available in high gloss nitrocellulose lacquer finish, tweed hardshell case included, current mfg.

    MSR   **$4,500**

JAZZ SINGER - 16 in. or 17 in. archtop bodies, Venetian cutaway, Flamed Maple back and sides, Sitka Spruce top, Three-piece Flamed Maple neck, unbound headstock, single-ply bound top and back, single-ply bound Ebony fingerboard, single-ply bound f-holes, single-ply bound Ebony pickguard, gold Grover tuners, adjustable Ebony bridge, 25 in. fret scale, double action truss rod, double carbon-fiber reinforced neck, headstock inlay, available in Light Vintage Amber nitrocellulose lacquer finish, tweed hardshell case included.

    MSR   **$6,000**

ELEGANTE - 16 in. or 17 in. archtop bodies, Venetian cutaway, Flamed Maple sides and back, Sitka Spruce top, three-pieced Flamed Maple neck, five-ply bound headstock, three-ply bound Ebony fingerboard, nine-ply bound top and back, three-ply bound f-holes, three-ply bound Ebony pickguard, gold Schaller tuners, adjustable Ebony bridge, 25 in. fret scale, double action truss rod, double carbon-fiber reinforced neck, headstock inlay, available in Light Vintage Amber nitrocellulose lacquer finish, tweed hardshell case included, disc. 2000.

    Last MSR was $6,500.

RHYTHMASTER - 17.75 in. archtop body, select flamed maple sides and back, hand carved top, 3 1/4" sides, three-piece flamed maple neck, split-block inlay on fingerboard, double-action truss rod, gold Grover Deluxe tuners, Art Deco headstock inlay, five-ply bound entire guitar, f-holes, pickup, pickguard and tailpiece, available in high gloss nitrocellulose lacquer finish, tweed hardshell case included, current mfg.

    MSR   **$8,500**

SWINGMASTER - 17 in. archtop body, select Sitka Spruce top, select aged maple sides and back, hand carved top, 3.25 in. sides, three-piece hard rock maple neck, solid ebony fingerboard, block inlay on fingerboard, double-action truss rod, gold Grover Deluxe tuners, custom headstock inlay, custom .030 five-ply bound body, custom .030 three-ply bound headstock, neck, f-holes, pickguard and tailpiece, available in high gloss nitrocellulose lacquer finish. Tweed hardshell case included, current mfg.

    MSR   **$8,000**

MIKE OVERLY CUSTOM - 16 in. or 17 in. archtop bodies, Venetian cutaway, Flamed Maple back and sides, Sitka Spruce top, three-piece Flamed Maple neck, five-ply bound headstock, three-ply bound Ebony fingerboard, nine-ply bound top and back, three-ply bound f-holes, three-ply bound Ebony pickguard, custom fretboard end, custom bound tailpiece, custom bound truss-rod cover, gold Schaller tuners, adjustable Ebony bridge, 25 in. fret scale, double action truss rod, double carbon-fiber reinforced neck, headstock inlay, available in Light Vintage Amber nitrocellulose lacquer finish, tweed hardshell case included.

    MSR   **$7,000**

SCHECTER

Instruments currently produced in Los Angeles, CA. Production of high quality replacement parts and guitars began in Van Nuys, CA in 1976.

The Schecter company, named after David Schecter, began as a repair/modification shop that also did some customizing. Schecter began making high quality replacement parts (such as Solid Brass Hardware, Bridges, Tuners, and the MonsterTone and SuperRock II pickups) and build-your-own instrument kits. This led to the company offering of quality replacement necks and bodies, and eventually to their own line of finished instruments. Schecter is recognized as one of the first companies to market tapped pickup assemblies (coil tapping can offer a wider range of sound from an existing pickup configuration). Other designers associated with Schecter were Dan Armstrong and Tom Anderson.

In 1994, Michael Ciravolo took over as the new director for Schecter Guitar Research. Ciravolo introduced new guitar designs the same year, and continues to expand the Schecter line with new innovations and designs.

In 1998, Schecter and Maestro Alex Gregory teamed up to offer the 7-String Limited Edition Signature model based on the patented specifications and neck profile of Gregory's original 1989 model. This signature model will be individually numbered, and comes with a signed Certificate of Authenticity (list $2,595) (source: Tom Wheeler, *American Guitars*).

By the mid 1980s, Schecter was offering designs based on early Fender-style guitars in models such as the Mercury, Saturn, Hendrix, and Dream Machine. In the late 1980s Schecter also had the U.S. built Californian series as well as the Japan-made Schecter East models. Currently, the entire Schecter guitar line is built in America.

S

GRADING	100% MINT	98% NEAR MINT	95% EXC+	90% EXC	80% VG+	70% VG	60% G

GENERAL INFORMATION

Schecter offers a number of options on their guitar models. Seymour Duncan, EMG, Van Zandt, Lindy Fralin, and Mike Christian piezo pickups are available (call for price quote).

Add $50 for left-handed configuration. Add $100 for Sperzel Locking Tuners. Add $50 for black or gold hardware (Disc. Option). Add $75 for matching headstock. Add $175 for Wilkinson VS-100 tremolo (Disc. Option). Add $250 for Original Floyd Rose tremolo. Add $300 for flame koa or lacewood top (Disc. Option).

ELECTRIC: AVENGER SERIES

AVENGER - sleek offset double cutaway arched mahogany body, maple neck, 25.5 in. scale, 22-fret rosewood fingerboard with block inlay, 6-on-a-side Sperzel tuners, black headstock with screened logo, tune-o-matic bridge/stop tailpiece, chrome hardware, 2 Seymour Duncan exposed humbuckers, volume/tone controls, 3-way toggle switch, available in Black, Candy Apple Red, See-Through Red, or Antique Yellow finishes, mfg. 1997-present.

MSR	$2,095		$1,750	$1,500	$1,300	$1,100	$900	$700	$500

Add $400 for EMG pickups and reverse headstock (Model Avenger Mach 2).

Avenger 7 - similar to the Avenger, except in 7-string configuration, disc. 2003.

		$1,995	$1,750	$1,500	$1,300	$1,100	$800	$600

Last MSR was $2,495.

ELECTRIC: CONTOURED EXOTIC TOP (CET) SERIES

C.E.T. - offset double cutaway mahogany or swamp ash body, flame or quilted maple tops, bolt-on bird's-eye maple neck, 22-fret maple or rosewood fingerboard with dot inlay, fixed bridge (or vintage-style tremolo), 6-on-a-side Sperzel locking tuners, chrome hardware, 3 single coil pickups, volume/tone controls with coil tapping capabilities, 5-position switch, available in Sunburst or Custom See-Through color finishes, current mfg.

MSR	$2,695		$2,025	$1,750	$1,500	$1,300	$1,050	$850	$650

This model is also available with 2 single coil/1 humbucker pickups configuration. C.E.T. models are also optional with hollow internal "tone" chambers (technically a C.E.T.-H). In 1996, a version called the C.E.T. Deluxe was offered that specifically featured 3 single coil pickups and a vintage-style tremolo (retail list was also $2,295). This version is inherent in the current listing for the C.E.T. model. Early versions of this model are available in Black Cherry, Brown Sunburst, Honeyburst, Transparent Aqua, Transparent Purple, Transparent Turquoise, Vintage Cherry Sunburst, and Oil/Wax finishes.

C.E.T.-7 -offset double cutaway 7-string model, semi-hollowbody, rosewood fingerboard with dot position markers, 7-on-1-side tuners, 2 humbucker pickups and 1 single coil pickup in the middle position, 1 Volume/1 Tone control, 5-way switch,choice of finishes, disc. 2003.

		$2,300	$2,050	$1,850	$1,600	$1,350	$1,100	$850

Last MSR was $2,895.

C.E.T. PT - similar to the C.E.T., except has single cutaway body, 2 humbucker pickups, 3-way toggle switch, mfg. 1996-98.

		$1,850	$1,600	$1,395	$1,195	$975	$750	$575

Last MSR was $2,295.

ELECTRIC: DIAMOND SERIES

006 - offset double cutaway mahogany body, bolt-on maple neck with rosewood fingerboard, diamond position markers. 3-per-side tuners, 25.5 in. scale, Grover tuners, black hardware, non-tremolo bridge, 22 jumbo frets, 2 Duncan Design pickups, 1 single coil and 1 humbucker, available in Black Satin, Gray Satin, or Walnut Stain finishes, mfg. 2001-03.

		$460	$400	$350	$300	$250	$200	$150

Last MSR was $649.

006 BlackJack - similar to the 006, except has 2 Duncan Designed humbucker pickups, black hardware, available in Gloss Black finishes, new 2004.

MSR	$799		$560	$475	$425	$375	$325	$275	$225

006 Deluxe - similar to 006 model except, has a basswood body, bolt-on neck, diamond high-output pickups, and no body binding, available in Satin Black or Vampire Red Satin finishes, new 2003.

MSR	$449		$300	$250	$220	$190	$160	$130	$105

006 Elite - similar to 006 model except, has mahogany body with flame maple top, maple set neck, diamond position markers at the 12th fret, tune-o-matic bridge, bound neck, 24 jumbo frets, 2 Duncan Design pickups, 1 humbucker and 1 single coil, available in Black Cherry or See-Through Black finishes, mfg. 2001-present.

MSR	$799		$560	$495	$450	$375	$325	$275	$225

007 - offset double cutaway mahogany body, 7-string, bolt-on maple neck with rosewood fingerboard, diamond position markers, 25.5 in. scale, Grover tuners, black hardware, non-tremolo bridge, 24 jumbo frets, 1 Duncan Designed humbucker pickup and 1 Duncan Designed single coil pickup, available in Black, Walnut Gloss, or Black satin finishes, disc. 2001.

		$485	$425	$375	$325	$275	$225	$175

Last MSR was $649.

007 Elite - similar to 007 model except, has mahogany body with flame maple top, maple set neck, diamond position markers at the 12th fret, available in See thru Black or Black Cherry finishes, current mfg.

MSR	$849		$595	$525	$450	$375	$325	$275	$225

A-1 -offset double cutaway mahogany body, upswept horns, bolt-on maple neck with rosewood fingerboard, diamond position markers, 6-on-a-side tuners, 25.5 in. scale, tune-o-matic bridge, Grover tuners, black hardware, 24 jumbo frets, 2 Duncan Designed humbucker pickups, available in Black, Dark Metallic Blue , Metallic Red, Gun Metal Gray, or Silver Satin finishes, disc. 2000.

		$485	$450	$395	$350	$295	$250	$175

Last MSR was $649.

GRADING	100% MINT	98% NEAR MINT	95% EXC+	90% EXC	80% VG+	70% VG	60% G

A-1 Elite - similar to A-1 model except, has neck-through-body, available in Black, Ultra Voilet, or Silver Satin finishes, disc 2001.

	$599	$550	$495	$450	$395	$350	$295

Last MSR was $799.

A-7 - similar to A-1 model except, in a 7-string configuration, Non-Trem 7 bridge, available in Black, Dark Metallic Blue, Silver Satin, Metallic Red, or Gun Metal Gray finishes, disc. 2000.

	$560	$495	$450	$395	$350	$295	$225

Last MSR was $749.

A-7 Elite - similar to A-1 Elite model except, in a 7-string configuration, available in Black, Ultra Violet, or Silver Satin finishes, disc 2001.

	$675	$625	$575	$525	$475	$425	$375

Last MSR was $899.

AVENGER - similar body design to A-1 and A-7 models except, has basswood body, dot position markers, Crème body biding, 2 Duncan Design pickups, available in Black Satin, Gray Satin, or Walnut Stain finishes, mfg. 2001-03.

	$595	$525	$450	$375	$325	$275	$225

Last MSR was $849.

AVIATION: BOMBER GIRL/FLYING TIGER - PT body style, mahogany body, mahogany neck, 22-fret rosewood fingerboard with Stars and Bars inlays, Duncan Designed H/S pickup configuration, two knobs, 3-way switch, PT-H bridge, 6-on-a-side tuners, available in either Bomber Girl or Flying Tiger finishes, new 2004.

MSR	$699	$495	$425	$375	$325	$275	$225	$175

C-1 - offset double cutaway mahogany body, bolt-on maple neck with rosewood fingerboard, diamond position markers, 3-per-side tuners, 24 jumbo frets, 24.75 in. scale, bound body, tune-o-matic bridge, black hardware, 2 Duncan Designed humbucker pickups, string through-body, 1 Volume/1 Tone control, 3-watt switch, available in Silver Top, Electric Blue, Gray Satin, or Black finishes, disc. 2003.

	$475	$400	$350	$300	$250	$200	$150

Last MSR was $649.

**Schecter C.E.T.
courtesy Schecter**

Add $100 for left-hand model. Add $35 for Extended scale model (C-1 EX).

C-1 BlackJack - similar to C-1 model except has 2 Seymour Duncan pickups, black hardware, available in Gloss Black finish, new 2004.

MSR	$799	$560	$495	$450	$375	$325	$275	$225

Also available in an extended version at no additional cost.

C-1 Plus - similar to C-1 model except, has flame maple top and maple set neck, rosewood fingerboard with Vector position markers, chrome hardware, available in Charcoal Gray Burst, Vintage Sunburst, Cherry Sunburst, or Black Cherry finishes, current mfg.

MSR	$799	$560	$495	$450	$375	$325	$275	$225

C-1 FR - similar to the C-1 Plus, except has a Floyd Rose locking tremolo, available in Gloss Black finish, mfg. 2002-present.

MSR	$849	$595	$525	$450	$375	$325	$275	$225

C-1 Elite - similar to the C-1 Plus, except has abalone binding, flame maple top (Amber), and single 12th fret inlay, available in Black (chrome hw) or Amber (gold hw) finishes, mfg. 2002-present.

MSR	$899	$630	$550	$475	$400	$350	$300	$250

C-1 Classic - similar to the C-1, except has a quilted maple top, and vine of life inlay, available in Antique (gold hw), Vintage 3-Tone Sunburst (gold hw) or Trans. Blue (chrome hw) finishes, mfg. 2002-present.

MSR	$999	$700	$625	$550	$475	$375	$325	$275

C-1 E/A - similar to the C-1, except has a hollowbody with a quilted maple top, chrome hardware, piezo pickup, and split block inlay, available in Trans. Black or Dark Vintage Sunburst finishes, mfg. 2002-present.

MSR	$999	$700	$625	$550	$475	$375	$325	$275

C/SH-1 - similar to the C-1 Plus, except has a semi-hollow body with a flame maple top and f-holes, available in Tobacco Sunburst or Vintage Trans. Red finishes, new 2004.

MSR	$849	$595	$525	$450	$375	$325	$275	$225

C-7 - similar to C-1 model except, in a 7-string configuration, ash body, 25.5 in. scale, Non-Trem 7 bridge, available in Black, Gray Satin, See-Through Blue, See-Through Red, or Walnut Gloss finishes, disc. 2000.

	$560	$495	$450	$395	$350	$295	$225

Last MSR was $749.

C-7 BlackJack - similar to the C-7, except has 2 Seymour Duncan humbucker pickups, black hardware, available in Black Gloss finish, new 2004.

MSR	$849	$595	$525	$450	$400	$350	$300	$250

C-7 Plus - similar to C-1 Plus Model except, in a 7-string configuration, 25.5 in. scale, Non-Trem 7 bridge, available in Charcoal Gray Burst, Vintage Sunburst, Cherry Sunburst, or Black Cherry finishes, disc 2001.

	$599	$550	$499	$450	$399	$350	$299

Last MSR was $799.

**Schecter S Series Model
courtesy Schecter**

S

GRADING	100% MINT	98% NEAR MINT	95% EXC+	90% EXC	80% VG+	70% VG	60% G

HELLCAT - offset double cutaway basswood body, bolt-on maple neck, 22-fret rosewood fingerboard with dot inlay, 3 Duncan Designed MH-101 pickups, pickguard, VS-50 tremolo, two knobs, 3-way switch, chrome hardware, available in Ice Blue or 3-Tone Sunburst finishes, current mfg.

	MSR	$649	$475	$425	$375	$325	$275	$225	$175

Hellcat VI - similar to the Hellcat, except in 6-string bass configuraiton that similar to the Fender VI electric, available in 3-Tone Sunburst or Gloss Black finishes, new 2004.

	MSR	$749	$560	$495	$425	$375	$325	$275	$225

JAZZ ELITE - single cutaway hollow body, maple body with quilted maple top, set 3-piece mahogany neck, 22-fret rosewood fingerboard with abalone block inlays, raised black pickguard, 2 Duncan Designed HB-101 humbucker pickups, four knobs, 3-way switch, trapeze tailpiece, gold hardware, available in Black Cherry or Vintage Natural Gloss finishes, new 2004.

	MSR	$899	$630	$550	$475	$425	$375	$325	$275

OMEN-6 - offset double cutaway basswood body, bolt-on maple neck, rosewood fingerboard with dot position markers, 3-per-side tuners, 25.5 in. scale, Diamond tuners, Chrome hardware, tune-o-matic bridge, 24 jumbo frets, 2 Diamond humbucker pickups, available in Gloss Black, Electric Blue, Black Satin, or Walnut Stain finishes, mfg. 2001-present.

	MSR	$449	$300	$250	$220	$190	$160	$130	$105

Omen-7 - similar to Omen-6 model except, in 7-string cinfiguration, black hardware, 2 Duncan Design humbucker pickups, available in Gloss Black, Walnut Stain, Electric Blue, or Black Satin finishes, current mfg.

	MSR	$499	$350	$300	$250	$210	$175	$150	$125

PT -single cutaway Tele-style alder body, bolt-on maple neck, 22-fret maple fingerboard with black dot inlays, 6-on-one side tuners, creme body binding, 2 Duncan Design H-103 pickups, two knobs, 3-way switch, black hardware, available in Gloss Black finish, current mfg.

	MSR	$599	$425	$350	$300	$250	$200	$160	$130

PT Vintage - similar to the PT, except has a rosewood fingerboard, traditional single coil Duncan Designed pickups, and pickguard, available in 2-Tone Sunburst or Trans. Red finishes, new 2004.

	MSR	$599	$425	$350	$300	$250	$200	$160	$130

PT BlackJack - similar to the PT, except has 2 Duncan Designed humbucker pickups, black hardware, available in Gloss Black finishes, new 2004.

	MSR	$799	$560	$475	$425	$375	$325	$275	$225

PT CUSTOM -single cutaway Tele-style mahogany body, quilted maple top, set 3-piece maple neck, 22-fret rosewood fingerboard with 3-ply crown inlays, 3-per-side tuners, abalone body binding, 2 Duncan Design HB-102 pickups, two knobs, 3-way switch, gold hardware, available in Trans. Honey or Antique Amber finishes, mfg. 2003-present.

	MSR	$799	$560	$495	$450	$375	$325	$275	$225

S-1 - double cutaway mahogany body, bolt-on maple neck with rosewood fingerboard, diamond position markers, 3-per-side tuners, 24.75 in. scale, Grover tuners, chrome hardware, 22 jumbo frets, 2 Duncan Designed humbucker pickups, available in Black, See-Through Cherry, Violet Burst, Crimson Burst, or Army Green Burst finishes, disc 2001, reintroduced 2003-present.

	MSR	$699		$495	$425	$375	$325	$275	$225	$175

S-1 BlackJack - similar to the S-1, except has 2 Duncan Designed humbucker pickups, black hardware, available in Gloss Black finishes, new 2004.

	MSR	$799	$560	$475	$425	$375	$325	$275	$225

S-1 Elite - similar to S-1 model except, has a flamed maple top, abalone body binding, and gothic cross inlays, available in Black Cherry or Antique Amber finishes, mfg. 2002-present.

	MSR	$899	$600	$550	$475	$400	$350	$300	$250

S-1 Flame - similar to S-1 model except, has a green or purple flamed finish, mfg. 2002-present.

	MSR	$799	$560	$495	$450	$395	$350	$295	$250

S-1 Flame Deluxe - similar to the S-1 Flame, except has a basswood body and Ghost Flame graphics, new 2004.

	MSR	$499	$350	$300	$260	$220	$190	$160	$130

S-1 Plus - similar to S-1 model except, has mahogany body with flame maple top, maple set neck, Cream neck binding, available in See-Through Black, Black Chery, or Trans Green Burst finishes, disc 2002.

	$560	$495	$450	$395	$350	$295	$250

Last MSR was $749.

SCORPION - double cutaway mahogany body, tuned B-B, maple set neck with rosewood fingerboard, diamond position marker at the 12th fret, 25.5 in. scale, 24 jumbo frets, 3-per-side tuners, black hardware, 2 Duncan Designed humbucker pickups, available in Black Satin finish, current mfg.

	MSR	$699	$495	$450	$400	$375	$325	$275	$225

Scorpion Tribal - similar to the Scorpion, except has a full tribal fingerboard inlay, available in Gloss Black finish, mfg. 2002-03.

	$595	$550	$475	$400	$350	$300	$250

Last MSR was $899.

T-1 - offset double cutaway mahogany body, bolt-on maple neck with rosewood fingerboard, diamond position markers, 22 jumbo frets, 25.5 in. scale, Grover Tuners, tune-o-matic bridge, 1 Duncan Designed humbucker pickup and 1 Duncan Designed single coil pickup, available in Black, See-Thru Cherry, Walnut Gloss, or Dark Metallic Purple finishes, disc. 2000.

	$450	$400	$350	$300	$250	$200	$150

Last MSR was $599.

T-7 - similar to T-I model except, in a 7-string configuration, 24 jumbo frets, available in Black, See-Through Cherry, Walnut Gloss, or Dark Metallic Purple finishes, disc. 2000.

	$525	$475	$425	$375	$325	$275	$225

Last MSR was $699.

S

GRADING	100% MINT	98% NEAR MINT	95% EXC+	90% EXC	80% VG+	70% VG	60% G

TSH-1 - offset double cutaway semi-hollow mahogany body, flame maple top, bolt-on maple neck with rosewood fingerboard, diamond position markers, 22 jumbo frets, 25.5 in. scale, tune-o-matic bridge/trapeze, Grover tuners, chrome hardware, 3-per-side tuners, 1 Duncan Designed humbucker pickup and 1 Duncan Designed single coil pickup, white pearloid pickguard, available in Trans. Honey, See thru Black, Black Cherry, or Vintage Trans-Orange finishes, current mfg.

MSR	$649	$475	$425	$375	$325	$275	$225	$175

TSH-12 - similar to TSH-1 except, in a 12-string configuration, 6-per-side tuners, available in Vintage Trans Orange, Black Cherry, See-Through Black, or Trans. Honey finishes, current mfg.

MSR	$699	$495	$450	$400	$350	$300	$250	$200

TEMPEST (SPECIAL) - similar to TSH-1 model except, has a solid mahogany body, dot position markers, Crème body binding, 2 Duncan Design humbucker pickups, available in Gloss Black and Gold Top finishes, mfg. 2001-present.

MSR	$699	$495	$425	$350	$300	$250	$210	$170

TEMPEST CUSTOM - similar to the Tempest, except has a maple top and split crown inlays, available in Gloss Black (gold hw), Vintage White (chrome hw), or Antique Sunburst (chrome hw), mfg. 2002-present.

MSR	$799	$560	$495	$450	$375	$325	$275	$225

ULTRA - offset single cutaway mahogany body with raised center, set 3-piece mahogany neck with ultra access, 22-fret rosewood fingerboard with dot inlay, black pickguard, 2 Duncan Designed HB-102 humbucker pickups, TonePros system bridge, 2 knobs, 3-way switch, 4/2-per-side tuners, chrome hardware, available in Vintage Cherry or Vintage Sunburst finishes, new 2004.

MSR	$699	$495	$425	$350	$300	$250	$210	$170

V-1 PLUS - offset double cutaway mahogany body with flame maple top, bolt-on maple neck with rosewood fingerboard, diamond position markers, 24 jumbo frets, 25.5 in. scale, 6-on-a-side tuners, Floyd Rose bridge with vibrato, 2 Duncan Designed humbucker pickups plus 1 Duncan Designed single coil pickup in the middle position, 1 Volume/1 Tone control, 5-way switch, available in See-Through Black, Trans. Amber, Trans. Purple Burst, or Trans. Blue Burst finishes, disc. 2001.

	$525	$475	$425	$375	$325	$275	$225

Last MSR was $699.

ELECTRIC: DIAMOND ARTIST SERIES

Schecter Diamond Series S-1
courtesy Schecter

JERRY HORTON SIGNATURE MODEL - offset double cutaway mahogany body, bolt-on maple neck, rosewood fingerboard with "roach" position marker at the 12th fret, 25.5 in. scale, tune-o-matic bridge, Grover tuners, black hardware, body and headstock binding, 24 jumbo fets, 2 Seymour Duncan humbucker pickups, available in Gloss black, Gloss Red, Gloss White, or Gloss Grey finishes, mfg. 2001-03.

	$700	$625	$575	$525	$475	$425	$350

Last MSR was $999.

M-33 MIKE TEMPESTA SIGNATURE MODEL - slightly offset double cutaway mahogany body with maple top, maple set neck, rosewood fingerboard with "Skulls" position marker at the 12th fret, 24.75 in. scale, tune-o-matic bridge, Grover tuners, black hardware, bound body and neck, 22 jumbo frets, 2 Duncan Design humbucker pickups, available in Black Satin, Gray Satin, or Silver Satin finishes, disc. 2003.

	$700	$625	$575	$525	$475	$425	$350

Last MSR was $999.

TOMMY LEE SIGNATURE - double offset cutaway Explorer-ish style mahogany body, set maple neck, 22-fret rosewood fingerboard with stripper girls inlays, single Seymour Duncan humbucker pickup, 6-on-other side tuners, one volume knob, chrome hardware, available in Satin Black or Pearl White finishes, mfg. 2003 only.

	$700	$625	$575	$525	$475	$425	$350

Last MSR was $999.

TERRY CORSO SIGNATURE - double offset 006-ish style mahogany body, figured maple top, set maple neck, 24-fret rosewood fingerboard with 12th fret AAF inlay, two Seymour Duncan humbucker pickups, 3-per-side tuners, two knobs, 3-way switch, black hardware, available in Vintage Natural Gloss finish, disc. 2003.

	$700	$625	$575	$525	$475	$425	$350

Last MSR was $999.

TROUBLE VALLI SIGNATURE - double Scropion-ish style mahogany body, set maple neck, 22-fret rosewood fingerboard with stars and tattoos inlays, Seymour Duncan humbucker and single coil pickups, 3-per-side tuners, two knobs, 3-way switch, chrome hardware, available in Electric Blue or Metallic Green finishes, disc. 2003.

	$700	$625	$575	$525	$475	$425	$350

Last MSR was $999.

ELECTRIC: H SERIES

The "H" Series were offered between 1994 and 1996, and featured 2 hollow internal "tone" chambers, choice of pickup confiurations, and transparent finishes. Other options included Wilkinson or Floyd Rose tremolos.

Schecter Diamond Series
Tempest
courtesy Schecter

S

GRADING	100% MINT	98% NEAR MINT	95% EXC+	90% EXC	80% VG+	70% VG	60% G

E.T.-H - offset double cutaway mahogany body with 2 internal routed sound chambers, figured maple top, stylized f-hole, bolt-on bird's-eye maple neck, 22-fret maple or rosewood fingerboard with dot inlay, fixed strings through bridge, 6-on-a-side tuners, black hardware, 2 humbucker pickups, volume/tone controls with coil tap capability, 3-position switch, available in Black Cherry, See-Through Aqua, See-Through Purple, See-Through Turquoise, or Vintage Cherry Sunburst finishes, mfg. 1994-96.

	N/A	$1,500	$1,250	$1,050	$900	$750	$600

Last MSR was $2,195.

C.E.T.-H - similar to E.T.-H, except does not have stylized f-hole, mfg. 1994-96.

	N/A	$1,700	$1,400	$1,150	$950	$800	$650

Last MSR was $2,495.

This model is also similar to the solid body version C.E.T.

PT C.E.T.-H (PT Hollow) - similar to the C.E.T.-H, except has single cutaway body, mfg. 1995-96.

	N/A	$1,700	$1,400	$1,150	$950	$800	$650

Last MSR was $2,495.

ELECTRIC: HELLCAT SERIES

HELLCAT (SPITFIRE) - slightly offset alder body, maple neck, 22-fret rosewood fingerboard with dot inlay, 6-on-a-side locking Sperzel tuners, pearloid pickguard, chrome hardware, Wilkinson VS-100 tremolo, 3 Seymour Duncan covered mini-humbuckers, volume/tone controls, pickup selector switch, available in Black Sparkle, Blue Sparkle, Burgundy Mist, Candy Apple Red, and White Pearl finishes with matching headstock, mfg. 1996-present.

MSR	$2,095	$1,675	$1,450	$1,250	$1,050	$850	$700	$500

Subtract $100 for 2 tapped humbuckers or 2 mini humbuckers (Model Hellcat NT).

HELLCAT 10 STRING - similar to Hellcat, except in 10-string configuration, tune-o-matic bridge/string through-body ferrules, 7/3 headstock, mfg. 1996-99.

	$1,550	$1,350	$1,195	$1,000	$850	$675	$495

Last MSR was $1,895.

ELECTRIC: HOLLYWOOD SERIES

The Hollywood Series was introduced in 1996. These models are also optional with hollow internal "tone" chambers.

HOLLYWOOD CUSTOM - offset double cutaway mahogany or swamp ash body, highly figured maple tops, bird's-eye maple neck, 22-fret maple or rosewood fingerboard with dot inlay, Wilkinson VS-100 tremolo, 6-on-a-side Sperzel locking tuners, chrome hardware, 2 single coil/1 humbucker pickups, volume/tone controls with coil tapping capabilities, 5-position switch, available in Vintage Sunburst or Hand Tinted Custom color finishes, mfg. 1996-present.

MSR	$2,895	$2,325	$2,025	$1,750	$1,450	$1,200	$950	$700

HOLLYWOOD CLASSIC - similar to the Hollywood Custom, except has arched flame or quilted maple top, 24.75 in. scale, 24-fret fingerboard, 3-per-side tuners, tune-o-matic bridge/strings through-body ferrules, 2 covered humbuckers, mfg. 1996-present.

MSR	$2,995	$2,395	$2,100	$1,800	$1,500	$1,250	$975	$725

This model is also available in a 25.5 in. scale with a 22-fret fingerboard.

HOLLYWOOD LTD. - offset double cutaway mahogany or swamp ash body, exotic wood tops, bird's-eye maple neck, 22-fret maple or rosewood fingerboard with dot inlay, Wilkinson VS-100 tremolo, 6-on-a-side Sperzel locking tuners, chrome hardware, 2 single coil/1 humbucker pickups, volume/tone controls with coil tapping capabilities, 5-position switch, available in Custom color finishes, mfg. 1996-99.

	$2,350	$2,050	$1,775	$1,500	$1,300	$1,050	$900

Last MSR was $2,895.

ELECTRIC: LIMITED EDITION SERIES

CALIFORNIA CUSTOM (CUSTOM) - offset double cutaway figured maple body, bolt-on bird's-eye maple neck, 22-fret rosewood fingerboard with dot inlay, double locking Schaller vibrato, 6-on-a-side tuners, gold hardware, 2 single coil/1 humbucker pickups, volume/tone control, 5-position switch, available in Black Aqua, Black Cherry, Black Purple, Black Turquoise, Brown Sunburst, Honeyburst, Trans. Turquoise, or Vintage Cherry Sunburst finishes, disc. 1998.

	$2,100	$1,800	$1,595	$1,375	$1,100	$900	$800

Last MSR was $2,995.

In 1994, Black Aqua and Black Purple finishes were introduced; Black Turquoise, Brown Sunburst and Honeyburst finishes were disc.

CS-1 - offset double cutaway arched exotic wood body (bird's-eye maple, flamed "Tiger" maple, Hawaiian flamed koa, or flame walnut), set-in neck, 24.75 in. scale, 24-fret rosewood fingerboard with dot inlay, tune-o-matic bridge/string through-body ferrules, 3-per-side Sperzel tuners, gold hardware, 2 Seymour Duncan Seth Lover humbuckers, volume/tone controls, 3-position switch, available in a hand-rubbed Natural Oil finish, mfg. 1995-2003.

	$3,025	$2,500	$2,150	$1,850	$1,500	$1,200	$1,000

Last MSR was $4,295.

Each instrument is hand numbered and comes with a Certificate of Authenticity.

KORINA CLASSIC - offset double cutaway arched korina body, set-in korina neck, 24.75 in. scale, 22-fret rosewood fingerboard with dot inlay, tune-o-matic bridge/string through-body ferrules, 3-per-side Sperzel tuners, gold hardware, 2 Seymour Duncan Seth Lover humbuckers, 2 volume/1 tone controls, 3-position switch, available in Antique Yellow finish, mfg. 1997 only.

	$2,750	$2,300	$1,950	$1,600	$1,350	$1,100	$900

Last MSR was $3,895.

1997 production limited to 12 guitars. Each instrument is hand stamped and comes with a Certificate of Authenticity.

GRADING	100% MINT	98% NEAR MINT	95% EXC+	90% EXC	80% VG+	70% VG	60% G

ELECTRIC: PT SERIES

PT (USA) - single cutaway bound alder body, bolt-on maple neck, 22-fret maple or rosewood fingerboard with dot inlay, Tele-style strings-through fixed bridge, 6-on-a-side Sperzel locking tuners, black hardware, 2 humbucker pickups, volume/tone controls with coil tap access, 3-position switch, available in Gloss Black, Gold, Metallic Blue, Metallic Red, or Snow White finishes, current mfg.

	MSR	$1,995		$1,595	$1,350	$1,150	$950	$800	$650	$500

This model debuted on The WHO's 1982 farewell tour.

PT CET - similar to PT Model except has contoured exotic top (CET), choice of fingerboard woods, choice of hardware color, choice of pickups, choice of tremolo or hardtail, other options, available in Trans., Sunburst or Natural oil finishes, current mfg.

	MSR	$2,695		$2,150	$1,800	$1,550	$1,350	$1,150	$950	$700

PT S/S (PT/2 S) - similar to PT, except has white pickguard, 2 single coil pickups, available in 3-Tone Sunburst, Fire Engine Red, Gloss Black, Gold, or Snow White finishes, mfg. 1994-99.

$1,350	$1,195	$1,050	$895	$725	$575	$425

Last MSR was $1,595.

PT-X - similar to the PT, except has bound mahogany body, available in Gloss Black, Gold, See-Through Red, Snow White, or Tobacco 'Burst, mfg. 1995-99.

$1,500	$1,325	$1,150	$1,000	$825	$650	$475

Last MSR was $1,795.

PT CUSTOM - single cutaway mahogany body, carved bound figured maple top, bolt-on birdseye maple neck, 22-fret maple or rosewood fingerboard with dot inlay, tune-o-matic bridge/string through-body ferrules, 6-on-a-side tuners, gold hardware, 2 Seymour Duncan covered humbuckers, volume/tone controls with coil tap capabilities, 3-position switch, available in Orange Violin, See-Through Black, or Vintage Cherry Sunburst finishes, mfg. 1992-98.

$1,750	$1,500	$1,325	$1,150	$950	$800	$650

Last MSR was $2,495.

PT-X DELUXE - similar to the PT-X, except has no body binding, available in Gloss Black, See-Through Blue, See-Through Emerald, See-Through Red, or Tobacco 'Burst finishes, mfg. 1996-99.

$1,350	$1,195	$1,050	$895	$725	$575	$425

Last MSR was $1,595.

ELECTRIC: S (STANDARD) SERIES

S STANDARD - offset double cutaway swamp ash body, bolt-on maple neck, 22-fret maple or rosewood fingerboard with dot inlay, fixed bridge (or vintage-style tremolo), 6-on-a-side tuners, chrome hardware, black pickguard, 3 single coil pickups, volume/tone with coil tap control, 5-position switch, available in Natural Oil finish, mfg. 1994-present.

	MSR	$1,595		$1,275	$1,050	$850	$750	$650	$550	$400

This model has 2 single coil/1 humbucker pickups configuration optional. Early versions of this model have bird's-eye maple necks, and Natural Oil/Wax or Vintage Oil/Wax finishes.

S CLASSIC - similar to the "S" Standard, except has arched swamp ash body, 24.75 in. scale, 24-fret maple or rosewood fingerboard, 3-per-side headstock, tune-o-matic bridge/stop tailpiece, 2 exposed humbuckers, 2 volume/1 tone controls, 3-way toggle switch, mfg. 1996-present.

	MSR	$1,595		$1,275	$1,050	$850	$750	$650	$550	$400

S-7 7 STRING - offset double cutaway Superstrat body made from southern swamp ash, 25.5 in. rock maple neck, maple or rosewood fingerboard, several variations of pickups available, nom-tremolo through-body bridge, Sperzel tuners, available in Natural or Tinted oil finishes, disc. 2003.

$1,595	$1,350	$1,150	$950	$800	$650	$500

Last MSR was $1,995.

S PT - similar to the "S" Standard, except has single cutaway swamp ash body, black (or white) pickguard/metal controls plate, Tele-style fixed bridge, 2 single coil pickups, mfg. 1995-present.

	MSR	$1,595		$1,275	$1,050	$850	$750	$650	$550	$400

This model has single coil/humbucker, or humbucker/single coil pickups configuration as an option.

ELECTRIC: SCORPION SERIES

The Scorpion Series models feature slightly offset dual cutaway bodies with rounded lower bouts.

SCORPION ELITE - similar to Scorpion except, has body handbuilt from 1 piece of Honduran Mahogany, highly figured flame maple top, composite center laminate, 24.75 in. medium scale bolt-on quartersawn rock maple neck, Ebony fingerboard, 2 Seymour Duncan Seth Lover humbucker pickups, hard-tail bridge, available in Transparent finishes, disc. 2000.

$1,725	$1,525	$1,325	$1,125	$925	$725	$595

Last MSR was $2,295.

**Schecter C.E.T.-H
courtesy Bob Smith**

**Schecter California Custom
courtesy George McGuire**

S

GRADING	100% MINT	98% NEAR MINT	95% EXC+	90% EXC	80% VG+	70% VG	60% G

ELECTRIC: SUNSET SERIES

SUNSET CUSTOM - offset double cutaway ash body, rock maple neck, 22-fret maple or rosewood fingerboard with dot inlay, vintage-style tremolo, 6-on-a-side Sperzel locking tuners, chrome hardware, 2 single coil/1 humbucker pickups, volume/tone controls with coil tapping capabilities, 5-position switch, available in See-Through Black, See-Through Blue, See-Through Green, See-Through Honey Sunburst, See-Through Purple, or See-Through Red finishes with natural binding, mfg. 1996-99.

	$1,350	$1,195	$1,050	$895	$725	$575	$425

Last MSR was $1,695.

Add $200 for single coil/humbucker pickup configuration (Model Sunset Custom H/S).

SUNSET 7 - body similar to Sunset Classic, hand carved swamp ash body, 25.5 in. scale maple neck, rosewood fingerboard, dot position markers, 2 Schecter "tapped" Superock-7 humbucker pickups, non-trem through body bridge, Sperzel tuners, 5/2 tuner configuration, natural body binding, scouped headstock, available in soild or transparent finishes, disc. 2003.

	$1,925	$1,600	$1,350	$1,150	$950	$800	$650

Last MSR was $2,395.

SUNSET CLASSIC - similar to the Sunset Custom, except has arched ash body, 24.75 in. scale, 24-fret fingerboard, black headstock with screened logo, 3-per-side tuners, tune-o-matic bridge/strings through-body ferrules, 2 exposed humbuckers, mfg. 1996-present.

MSR	$1,995		$1,595	$1,350	$1,150	$950	$800	$650	$500

ELECTRIC: TEMPEST SERIES

TEMPEST (USA) - slightly offset mahogany body, maple neck, 25.5 in. scale, 22-fret rosewood fingerboard with dot inlay, 3-per-side Sperzel tuners, black headstock with screened logo, 5-ply black pickguard, tune-o-matic bridge/trapeze tailpiece, chrome hardware, 2 Seymour Duncan P-90 pickups, 2 volume/1 tone controls, 3-way toggle switch, available in Black, See-Through Red, T.V. Yellow, or Vintage Sunburst finishes, mfg. 1997-present.

MSR	$1,995		$1,595	$1,350	$1,150	$950	$800	$650	$500

TEMPEST CUSTOM - similar to the Tempest, except has bound maple top, tune-o-matic bridge/stop tailpiece, 2 Seymour Duncan exposed Alnico Pro humbuckers, available in Black, Burgundy, or Vintage Gold-Top finishes, mfg. 1997-present.

MSR	$2,095		$1,675	$1,450	$1,250	$1,050	$850	$700	$550

ELECTRIC: TRADITIONAL SERIES

Traditional Series models have been the cornerstone of the Schecter company for the past twenty years.

TRADITIONAL - offset double cutaway alder or swamp ash body, bolt-on rock maple neck, 22-fret maple or rosewood fingerboard with dot inlay, vintage-style tremolo, 6-on-a-side Sperzel locking tuners, chrome hardware, white pickguard, 3 single coil pickups, volume/tone controls with coil tapping capabilities, 5-position switch, available in 2-Tone Sunburst, 3-Tone Sunburst, Burgundy Mist, Candy Red, Gloss Black, Lake Placid Blue, Sea Foam Green, See-Through Aqua, See-Through White, Sonic Blue, Vintage Blonde, or Vintage Red finishes, current mfg.

MSR	$1,995		$1,595	$1,350	$1,150	$950	$800	$650	$500

This model has 2 single coil/1 humbucker pickups configuration as an option. Early versions of this model have bird's-eye maple necks, and were available in Cherry Sunburst, Metallic Gold, Brownburst, Vintage Black, and Vintage White finishes.

TRADITIONAL PT - similar to the Traditional, except has single cutaway body, black (or white) pickguard/metal controls plate, Tele-style fixed bridge, 2 single coil pickups, available in 3-Tone Sunburst, Gloss Black, Natural Gloss, See-Through White, or Vintage Blonde finishes, mfg. 1996-present.

MSR	$1,995		$1,595	$1,350	$1,150	$950	$800	$650	$500

This model has single coil/humbucker, or humbucker/single coil pickups configuration as an option.

ELECTRIC BASS: USA SERIES

Schecter also offers options on their bass models. Seymour Duncan and EMG pickups, active EQ circuitry, and custom 4-, 5-, 6-string basses are available (call for price quote). The Contoured Exotic Top model was formerly an option on the Bass/4 model between 1992 to 1994; the C.E.T. model officially debuted in 1995.

Add $100% for left-handed configuration. Add $50 for Black or Gold Hardware. Add $75 for matching headstock. Add $100 for Hipshot D-Tuner. Add $300 for 2-TEK bridge. Add $300 for flame koa or lacewood top.

B/4 (BASS/4) - similar to the Tradition, except has no pickguard/control plate (rear-routed body), P/J-style or 2 J-Style pickups, available in Gloss Black, Honeyburst, See-Through Blue, See-Through Green, See-Through Purple, or Vintage White finishes, mfg. 1992-98.

	$1,400	$1,200	$1,000	$875	$725	$575	$425

Last MSR was $1,695.

Early versions of this model have bird's-eye maple necks and ash bodies. In 1996, Burgundy Mist, See-Through Red, and See-Through White finishes were introduced; Honeyburst, See-Through Green, and See-Through Purple finishes were disc.

BASS/5 - similar to the Bass/4, except in 5-string configuration, 5-on-a-side headstock, mfg. 1992-94.

	$1,550	$1,250	$1,100	$975	$825	$675	$525

Last MSR was $2,095.

BARON 4 (BARON IV) - single cutaway bound mahogany body, bolt-on maple neck, 21-fret maple or rosewood fingerboard with dot inlay, fixed bridge, chrome hardware, 4-on-a-side tuners, Seymour Duncan Basslines humbucker pickup, volume/tone controls, 6 position rotary switch, available in Antique Yellow, Black, See-Through Red, or Vintage Gold-top finishes, mfg. 1996-2000.

	N/A	$1,400	$1,225	$1,050	$875	$675	$500

Last MSR was $1,895.

BARON 5 (BARON V) - similar to Baron IV, except in 5-string configuration, 5-on-a-side headstock, mfg. 1996-2000.

	N/A	$1,500	$1,275	$1,100	$900	$700	$525

Last MSR was $1,995.

S

GRADING	100% MINT	98% NEAR MINT	95% EXC+	90% EXC	80% VG+	70% VG	60% G

C.E.T. 4 - offset double cutaway ash body, flame or quilted maple top, bolt-on bird's-eye maple neck, 21-fret maple or rosewood fingerboard with dot inlay, fixed bridge, 4-on-a-side tuners, chrome hardware, 2 J-style MonsterTone pickups, 2 volume/1 tone controls, available in Sunburst and Custom See-Through color finishes, mfg. 1995-98.

	N/A	$1,750	$1,525	$1,300	$1,075	$850	$625

Last MSR was $2,495.

This model is available with P/J-style pickup configuration.

C.E.T. B/4 H - similar to the C.E.T. 4, except has hollow internal "tone" chambers, available in See-Through Aqua, See-Through Black, See-Through Black Cherry, See-Through Honey, See-Through Honeyburst, See-Through Purple, or See-Through Turquoise finishes, disc. 1996.

	N/A	$1,800	$1,550	$1,300	$1,075	$900	$650

Last MSR was $2,695.

C.E.T. 5 - similar to C.E.T. 4, except in 5-string configuration, 5-on-a-side headstock, mfg. 1995-98.

	N/A	$1,900	$1,600	$1,350	$1,100	$950	$700

Last MSR was $2,695.

HELLCAT (SPITFIRE) - slightly offset double cutaway alder body, bolt-on rock maple neck, 21-fret maple or rosewood fingerboard with dot inlay, fixed bridge, 4-on-a-side tuners, chrome hardware, pearloid pickguard, 3 Kent Armstrong lipstick pickups, volume/tone controls, 6 position rotary pickup selector, available in Black Sparkle, Blue Sparkle, Burgundy Mist, Candy Apple Red, or White Pearl finishes with matching headstock, mfg. 1996-2000.

	$1,525	$1,325	$1,150	$1,000	$825	$650	$475

Last MSR was $1,895.

MODEL T (USA) - offset double cutaway heavy ash body, bolt-on rock maple neck, 21-fret rosewood or maple fingerboard with dot inlay, fixed bridge, 4-on-a-side tuners, chrome hardware, black pickguard, P/J-style Monstertone pickups, volume/tone controls mounted on metal control plate, available in 2-Tone Sunburst, Black, Natural Gloss, See-Through White, or Vintage Blonde finishes, mfg. 1995-present.

MSR	$1,995	$1,595	$1,350	$1,150	$950	$800	$650	$500

This model is also available with 2 volume (no tone) controls configuration. This model was designed in conjunction with Rob DeLeo (Stone Temple Pilots).

Schecter Traditional PT
courtesy Schecter

S STANDARD-J - sleek offset double cutaway swamp ash body, bolt-on rock maple neck, 21-fret rosewood or maple fingerboard with dot inlay, fixed bridge, 4-on-a-side tuners, chrome hardware, black pickguard, P/J-style Monstertone pickups, 2 volume/1 tone controls, available in Natural Oil finish, mfg. 1995-present.

MSR	$1,595	$1,275	$1,050	$900	$750	$650	$525	$400

S STANDARD -P (S VINTAGE) - similar to the "S" Standard, except has P-style split pickup, volume/tone controls, mfg. 1995-present.

MSR	$1,595	$1,275	$1,050	$900	$750	$650	$525	$400

S '51 - similar to the "S" Standard, except has Seymour Duncan vintage single coil pickup, volume/tone controls mounted on chrome control plate, mfg. 1997-99.

	$1,050	$900	$775	$675	$550	$450	$325

Last MSR was $1,295.

S STANDARD-J5 ("S" 5-STRING) - similar to the "S" Standard, except in 5-string configuration, 5-on-a-side tuners, 2 J-Style pickups, mfg. 1997-present.

MSR	$1,695	$1,350	$1,150	$975	$825	$700	$550	$450

SUNSET BASS - offset double cutaway ash body, bolt-on bird's-eye maple neck, 21-fret maple or rosewood fingerboard with dot inlay, fixed bridge, 4-on-a-side tuners, chrome hardware, P/J-style pickups, 2 volume/1 tone controls, available in Black, Honeyburst, See-Through Blue, See-Through Green, See-Through Purple, or See-Through Red finishes with natural wood binding, mfg. 1996 only.

	N/A	$1,200	$1,050	$900	$750	$600	$450

Last MSR was $1,695.

TEMPEST - slightly offset double cutaway mahogany body, rock maple neck, 21-fret rosewood fingerboard with pearl dot inlay, fixed bridge, 2-per-side tuners, black headstock with screened logo, chrome hardware, 5-ply black pickguard, covered humbucker/mini-humbucker pickups, 2 volume/tone controls, available in Antique Yellow, Gloss Black, See-Through Cherry, T.V. Yellow, or Vintage Gold-top finishes, mfg. 1997-99.

			$1,550	$1,350	$1,150	$1,000	$825	$650	$475

Last MSR was $1,895.

Add $200 for maple top and creme body binding (Model Tempest Custom).

TRADITIONAL J - offset double cutaway alder or swamp ash body, bolt-on rock maple neck, 21-fret rosewood or maple fingerboard with dot inlay, fixed bridge, 4-on-a-side tuners, chrome hardware, black pickguard, 2 J-style Monstertone pickups, 2 volume/1 tone controls mounted on metal control plate, available in 2-Tone Sunburst, 3-Tone Sunburst, Gloss Black, Natural Gloss, See-Through White, or Vintage White finishes, mfg. 1994-present.

MSR	$1,995	$1,595	$1,350	$1,150	$950	$800	$650	$500

TRADITIONAL "P" - similar to the Traditional, except has one-piece white pickguard, P-style Monstertone pickup, available in 2-Tone Sunburst, 3-Tone Sunburst, Gloss Black, Natural Gloss, See-Through White, or Vintage Blonde finishes, mfg. 1997-present.

MSR	$1,995	$1,595	$1,350	$1,150	$950	$800	$650	$500

TRADITIONAL 5-STRING - similar to the Traditional, except in 5-string configuration, 5-on-a-side headstock, mfg. 1995-98.

		$1,500	$1,300	$1,100	$975	$800	$650	$475

Last MSR was $1,895.

Schecter Hellcat
courtesy George McGuire

S

GRADING	100% MINT	98% NEAR MINT	95% EXC+	90% EXC	80% VG+	70% VG	60% G

ELECTRIC BASS: DIAMOND/STILETTO SERIES

Scheter has introduced a series like what the Diamond Series is to guitars for basses.

BARON - single cutaway Telecaster style mahogany body, bolt-on maple neck, 22-fret rosewood fingerboard with dot inlay, single Duncan Designed MM pickup, Hipshot bridge, 4-on-one side tuners, 4 knobs, chrome hardware, available in Gloss Black finish, mfg. 2003-present.

	MSR	$799		$575	$500	$425	$375	$325	$275	$225

Also available as the Baron H Hollowbody for no additional cost.

C-4 - offset double cutaway mahogany body with figured maple top, bolt-on multi-laminate maple/walnut neck, 24-fret rosewood fingerboard with vector inlay, 2 EMG HZ pickups, S-Tek bridge, 2-per-side tuners, 4 knobs, chrome or gold hardware, available in Black Cherry or Antique Amber finishes, mfg. 2003-present.

	MSR	$699		$495	$425	$350	$300	$250	$210	$170

C-5 - similar to the C-4, except in 5-string configuration, 2/3-per-side tuners, mfg. 2003-present.

	MSR	$749		$560	$475	$400	$350	$300	$250	$200

CV-4 - offset double cutaway alder body, 6 bolt-on maple neck, 24-fret rosewood fingerboard with vector inlay, 2 Duncan Designed pickups, Hipshot bridge, 4-on-one-side tuners, 5 knobs, chrome hardware, available in Gloss Black or Dark Vintage Sunburst finishes, mfg. 2003-present.

	MSR	$699		$495	$425	$350	$300	$250	$210	$170

CV-5 - similar to the CV-4, except in 5-string configuration, 2/3-per-side tuners, mfg. 2003-present.

	MSR	$749		$560	$475	$400	$350	$300	$250	$200

CALIFORNIA CUSTOM 4 - offset double cutaway J-style alder body with figured maple top, bolt-on maple neck, 21-fret rosewood fingerboard with dot inlay, 2 EMG J-style pickups, 4-on-one-side tuners, 4 knobs, Hipshot bridge, chrome hardware, available in Black Cherry or Dark Vintage Sunburst finishes, mfg. 2003-present.

	MSR	$899		$630	$550	$475	$425	$375	$325	$275

California Custom 5 - similar to the California Custom 4, except in 5-string configuration, 2/3-per-side tuners, mfg. 2003-present.

	MSR	$949		$675	$600	$525	$450	$400	$350	$300

MODEL T - offset double cutaway P-Bass style alder body, bolt-on maple neck, 21-fret rosewood fingerboard with dot inlay, Seymour Duncan Bassline P/J configuration, P-style pickguard, 4-on-one side tuners, vintage style bridge, 3 knobs on metal plate, chrome hardware, available in 3-Tone Sunburst or Black finishes, mfg. 2003-present.

	MSR	$849		$600	$525	$450	$400	$350	$300	$250

OMEN 4 - offset double cutaway basswood body, bolt-on maple neck, 24-fret rosewood fingerboard with dot inlay, 2 Diamond Active pickups, standard bridge, 2-per-side tuners, 4 knobs, chrome or black hardware, available in Gloss Black or Walnut Satin finishes, mfg. 2003-present.

	MSR	$499		$350	$300	$250	$210	$180	$150	$120

Omen 5 - similar to the Omen 4, except in 5-string configuration, 2/3-per-side tuners, mfg. 2003-present.

	MSR	$549		$390	$325	$275	$225	$195	$165	$135

Omen 8 - similar to the Omen 4, except in 8-string configuration (4 strings in octave), available in Gloss Black finish only, mfg. 2003-present.

	MSR	$549		$390	$325	$275	$225	$195	$165	$135

SB-1 FLAME - double cutaway mahogany body, set maple neck, 22-fret rosewood fingerboard with black pearl flame inlay, 2 EMG HZ pickups, deluxe body binding, 2-per-side tuners, 4 knobs, Custom bridge, black chrome or chrome hardware, available in Ghost Flame or Hot Rod Flame finishes, mfg. 2003-present.

	MSR	$799		$575	$500	$425	$375	$325	$275	$225

SB-1 Flame Deluxe - similar to the SB-1 Flame, except has a basswood body, pearl dot inlays, and Diamond Active pickups, mfg. 2003-present.

	MSR	$499		$350	$300	$250	$220	$190	$160	$130

SCORPION BASS - double cutaway Scorpion style mahogany body, set maple neck with graphite rods, 24-fret rosewood fingerboard with 12th fret diamond inlay, 2 EMG HZ pickups, Hipshot bridge, 4 knobs, 2-per-side tuners, black hardware, available in Satin Black finish, mfg. 2003-present.

	MSR	$799		$575	$500	$425	$375	$325	$275	$225

STILETTO CUSTOM 4 - offset double cutaway mahogany body with figured maple top, bolt-on multi-laminate maple/walnut neck, 24-fret rosewood fingerboard with offset dot inlay, 2 EMG HZ pickups, S-Tek bridge, 2-per-side tuners, 4 knobs, black or gold hardware, available in Natural Satin or Black Cherry finishes, mfg. 2003-present.

	MSR	$699		$495	$425	$350	$300	$250	$210	$170

Stiletto Custom 5 - similar to the Stiletto Custom 5, except in 5-string configuration, 2/3-per-side tuners, mfg. 2003-present.

	MSR	$749		$560	$475	$400	$350	$300	$250	$200

STILETTO DELUXE 4 - offset double cutaway basswood body, bolt-on maple neck, 24-fret rosewood fingerboard with offset dot inlay, 2 Diamond Active pickups, Diamond bridge, 2-per-side tuners, 4 knobs, chrome hardware, available in Vintage White or Gloss Black finishes, mfg. 2003-present.

	MSR	$499		$350	$300	$250	$210	$180	$150	$120

Stiletto Deluxe 5 - similar to the Stiletto Deluxe 4, except in 5-string configuration, 2/3-per-side tuners, mfg. 2003-present.

	MSR	$549		$390	$325	$275	$225	$195	$165	$135

STILETTO ELITE 4 - offset double cutaway mahogany body with figured maple top, multi-laminate maple/walnut neck-thru design, 24-fret rosewood fingerboard with 12th fret diamond inlay, 2 EMG HZ pickups, S-Tek bridge, 2-per-side tuners, 4 knobs, gold hardware, available in Honey Sunburst or Black Cherry finishes, mfg. 2003-present.

	MSR	$849		$600	$525	$450	$400	$350	$300	$250

Stiletto Elite 5 - similar to the Stiletto Elite 4, except in 5-string configuration, 2/3-per-side tuners, mfg. 2003-present.

	MSR	$899		$630	$550	$475	$425	$375	$325	$275

GRADING	100% MINT	98% NEAR MINT	95% EXC+	90% EXC	80% VG+	70% VG	60% G

STILETTO STUDIO 4 - offset double cutaway mahogany body with bubinga top, multi-laminate maple/walnut neck-thru design, 24-fret rosewood fingerboard with offset dot inlays, 2 EMG HZ pickups, Diamond Custom bridge, 2-per-side tuners, 5 knobs, gold hardware, Honey Satin finish, mfg. 2003-present.

MSR	$899	$630	$550	$475	$425	$375	$325	$275

Stiletto Studio 5 - similar to the Stiletto Studio 4, except in 5-string configuration, 2/3-per-side tuners, mfg. 2003-present.

MSR	$949	$675	$600	$525	$450	$400	$350	$300

Stiletto Studio 6 - similar to the Stiletto Studio 4, except in 6-string configuration, 3-per-side tuners, mfg. 2003-present.

MSR	$999	$700	$625	$550	$475	$425	$375	$325

Stiletto Studio 8 - similar to the Stiletto Studio 4, except in 8-string configuration (4-string octaves), 4-per-side tuners, mfg. 2003-present.

MSR	$999	$700	$625	$550	$475	$425	$375	$325

SCHON

Instruments previously built in CA (later Canada) circa 1987-1990.

Schon guitars are so named for their namesake, guitarist Neal Schon (of Journey fame). Rather than just sign off on a production guitar, Schon actually put up his own money and design contributions to get the Schon guitar into production.

Schon guitar models were originally built by Charvel/Jackson´s west coast production facilities; production later shifted to Larrivee Guitars in Canada during their brief flirtation with electric solid body models (circa 1987-1988).

ELECTRIC

Schon guitar models are generally well crafted instruments; models occasionally turn up at guitar shows and over the Internet.

NS-STD - single cutaway alder body wings, through-body solid maple neck, 25.5 in. scale, 24-fret bound ebony fingerboard with pearl dot inlay, 6-on-a-side Schaller tuners, sloped pointed headstock, chrome hardware, 2 Schon custom humbuckers, tune-o-matic bridge/individual stop finger tailpiece, volume/tone controls, five way selector switch, available in a lacquer finish, mfg. 1987-1990.

	N/A	$800	$725	$650	$525	$450	$350

Last MSR was $1,199.

NS-STD W/TREMOLO - same as the NS-STD, except has a Kahler tremolo instead of the stylish stop tailpiece, mfg. 1987-1990.

	N/A	$950	$850	$750	$650	$550	$450

Last MSR was $1,399.

NS-SC - same as the NS-STD, except has 2 single coils and 1 humbucker, Kahler tremolo, mfg. 1987-1990.

	N/A	$975	$875	$775	$675	$575	$450

Last MSR was $1,499.

SCHULTE, C. ERIC

Instruments currently built in Frazerview (Malvern), PA since the early 1950s.

Luthier Eric Shulte began repairing instruments in the early 1950s, mostly his own and for his close friends. Soon afterward, Schulte began building semi- hollowbody guitars of his own design that featured a distinct six-on-a-side headstock, two humbuckers, dual cutaway body with florentine-style horns, and a raised pickguard (a much cooler version of a Gibson Trini Lopez model, if you will). Schulte currently builds a number of different style models now. Schulte is mostly self-taught, although he did learn a good bit in the 1960s while working at the Philadelphia Music Company of Limerick, Pennsylvania. Sam Koontz, the late builder of Koontz guitars also worked there and the two shared trade secrets. During the Bluegrass and Folk music heydays Schulte made more than 130 fancy five-string banjo necks.

Schulte´s Music Company of Malvern, Pennsylvania offers both new and used musical instruments, amplifiers, instrument repair and customizing, and his own custom electric guitars and basses. Schulte has been repairing and building guitars for forty-seven years and is still at it as he enjoys the work, challenges, and the opportunity to meet some wonderful musicians.

Some of Schulte´s more notable customers were the late Jim Croce, Paul Stanley (Kiss), Randy Bachmann and Blair Thornton (B.T.O.), Joe Federico, Sergio Franchi, Bill Fisher, Chuck Anderson, Banjo Joe Dougherty, Dennis Sandole, and Roger Sprung, (Biographical information courtesy C. Eric Shulte, July 1997).

SEBRING

Instruments previously built in Korea. Distributed by V.M.I. Industries of Brea, CA.

Sebring instruments are designed towards the intermediate level guitar student.

SEDONA

Instruments previously built in Asia. Distributed by V.M.I. Industries of Brea, CA.

Sedona offers a range of instruments that appeal to the beginning guitarist and entry level player. For further information, contact V.M.I Industries directly (see Trademark Index).

Schecter Bass/5
courtesy Schecter

Schon NS-STD
Blue Book Publications

S

SEIWA

Instruments previously built in Japan during the mid-1980s.

These medium quality solid body guitars featured Fender-based designs, often with two or three single coil pickups (source: Tony Bacon and Paul Day, *The Guru's Guitar Guide*).

SEKOVA

Instruments previously produced in Japan.

Sekova brand instruments were distributed in the U.S. market by the U.S. Musical Merchandise Corporation of New York, New York (source: Michael Wright, *Guitar Stories*, Volume One).

SELMER LONDON

See also Hofner. Instruments previously built in West Germany from the late 1950s to the early 1970s.

Selmer London was the distribution branch of the Selmer company in the United Kingdom. Selmer London distributed the French-built Selmers, as well as imported the Hofner-built semi-hollowbody models. While a number retained the Hofner trademark, some Hofners were rebranded "Selmer." Hofner also produced a number of UK-only export models which were distributed by Selmer London; such as the President and Golden Hofner (top of the hollowbody electric range).

Selmer semi-hollowbody models to watch for include the **Triumph** (single cutaway and a single pickup), **Diplomat** (single cutaway but two pickups), the **Emperor** and the **Astra** (two cutaways and two pickups). In the early 1970s, Selmer also marketed a solid body guitar called the **Studio** (source: Tony Bacon and Paul Day, *The Guru's Guitar Guide*).

SERIES 10

Instruments previously produced in Korea, and distributed by St. Louis Music of St. Louis, MO.

Series 10 instruments are designed for the entry level to intermediate guitar player, and feature designs based on classic American favorites.

SEVER

Instruments currently built in Izola, Slovenia. Distributed by Sever Musical Instruments and Equipment, Ltd. of Izola, Slovenia.

Sever is offering solid body electric guitar models that feature several innovative hardware and design ideas. Sever instruments are hand crafted out of select tone woods, and feature top electronics and hardware. For further information, contact Sever Musical Instruments and Equipment, Ltd. directly (see Trademark Index).

SHADOW

Instruments previously built in West Germany from 1988 through 1994. Disturbed through Shadow Electronics of America, Inc. of Stuart, FL.

Shadow produced high quality solid body guitars for six years. The company still continues to produce their high quality pickups and transducers, as well as their SH-075 Quick Mount MIDI guitar system. The SH-075 Quick Mount MIDI system combines a hex pickup and the output of a guitar's magnetic pickups to generate a MIDI signal. The SH-075 also has an onboard alphanumeric keypad for sending program changes, assigning MIDI channels, tuning, and other functions. The splitter box at the other end of the MIDI cable decodes the signal into MIDI information and an analog sound from the pickups. Shadow pickups can be ordered as aftermarket replacements, and also can be found in other guitar manufacturers' products.

MISC. MODELS

In addition to the numerous high quality guitar models listed below, Shadow also produced a solid body classical guitar. The Shadow **Solid Body Classical** had a retail list price around $1,250.

ELECTRIC: G SERIES

All G Series models were available in Blue Stain, Cognac Stain and Red Stain finishes unless otherwise noted.

G 202 - offset double cutaway ash body, bolt-on maple neck, 24-fret rosewood fingerboard with pearl dot inlay, double locking vibrato, 6-on-a-side tuners, chrome hardware, 2 stacked coil/1 active humbucker Shadow pickups, volume/tone control, coil split switch in volume control, on/off switch in tone control, 5-position switch, available in the three listed finishes, as well as a Black Stain finish, disc. 1994.

	N/A	$975	$800	$650	$580	$535	$485

Last MSR was $1,625.

This model was also available with black or gold hardware.

G 213 - offset double cutaway Brazilian Cedro body, flame maple top/bolt-on neck, 24-fret rosewood fingerboard with pearl dot inlay, double locking vibrato, 6-on-a-side tuners, gold hardware, 2 stacked coil/1 active humbucker pickups, volume/tone control, coil split switch in volume control, on/off switch in tone control, 5-position switch, disc. 1994.

	N/A	$1,050	$900	$800	$725	$650	$575

Last MSR was $1,995.

G 214 - similar to G 213, except has quilted maple top and bird's-eye maple neck, disc 1994.

	N/A	$1,200	$1,025	$875	$800	$725	$650

Last MSR was $2,200.

G 233 - similar to G 213, except has no magnetic pickups, standard bridge, piezo bridge pickup, volume control, 3-band EQ, active electronics.

	N/A	$950	$800	$625	$550	$500	$450

Last MSR was $1,575.

GRADING	100% MINT	98% NEAR MINT	95% EXC+	90% EXC	80% VG+	70% VG	60% G

G 234 - similar to the G 233, except has a quilted maple top and bird's-eye maple neck.

	N/A	$950	$800	$625	$550	$500	$450

Last MSR was $1,575.

G 235 - similar to the G 233, except has a bird's-eye maple top and neck.

	N/A	$950	$800	$625	$550	$500	$450

Last MSR was $1,575.

G 243 - similar to G 233, except has standard bridge, Shadow humbucker with 5-band EQ/piezo bridge pickup with 3-band EQ, 2 volume controls, active electronics, disc. 1994.

	N/A	$1,000	$875	$725	$625	$575	$525

Last MSR was $1,770.

G 244 - similar to the G 243, except has a quilted maple top and bird's-eye maple neck.

	N/A	$1,000	$875	$725	$625	$575	$525

Last MSR was $1,770.

G 245 - similar to the G 233, except has a bird's-eye maple top and neck.

	N/A	$1,000	$875	$725	$625	$575	$525

Last MSR was $1,770.

**Shadow S-100
courtesy Shadow**

ELECTRIC: S SERIES

All S Series models were available in Black, Blue Stain, Blue Thunder, Cognac Stain, Gold, Red Stain, Red Thunder, Tobacco Stain, Violet Stain, White and White Thunder finishes.
All S Series models were available with black, chrome, or gold hardware.

S 100 - offset double cutaway basswood body, bolt-on maple neck, 22-fret rosewood fingerboard with pearl dot inlay, double locking vibrato, 6-on-a-side tuners, 2 single coil/1 humbucker Shadow pickups, volume/tone control, 5-position switch, disc. 1994.

	N/A	$600	$500	$425	$350	$325	$300

Last MSR was $995.

S 110 - similar to S 100, except has active humbucker pickup, on/off switch, tone control, active electronics.

	N/A	$750	$625	$500	$450	$400	$350

Last MSR was $1,225.

S 120 - similar to S 100, except has 2 active humbucker pickups, 2 volume controls and 3-position switch.

	N/A	$800	$650	$525	$475	$425	$375

Last MSR was $1,315.

S 121 - similar to the S 120, except has an alder body.

	N/A	$800	$650	$525	$475	$425	$375

Last MSR was $1,315.

S 130 (SHP-1) - similar to S 100, except has no magnetic pickups, standard bridge, piezo bridge pickup, volume control, 3-band EQ, active electronics, mfg. 1990-94.

	N/A	$675	$550	$450	$400	$350	$325

Last MSR was $1,125.

S 131 - similar to the S 130, except has an alder body.

	N/A	$675	$550	$450	$400	$350	$325

Last MSR was $1,125.

S 140 - similar to S 130, except has standard bridge, Shadow humbucker with 5-band EQ/piezo bridge pickup with 3-band EQ, 2 volume controls, active electronics.

	N/A	$800	$650	$525	$475	$425	$375

Last MSR was $1,315.

This model is also available with an alder body (S 141).

S 141 - similar to the S 140, except has an alder body.

	N/A	$800	$650	$525	$475	$425	$375

Last MSR was $1,315.

SHAFTESBURY

See also Ned Callan. **Instruments previously manufactured in Italy and Japan from the late 1960s to the early 1980s. One English-built model was produced during the overall time period.**

The Shaftesbury trademark is the brand name of a UK importer. Shaftesbury instruments were generally medium to good quality versions of American designs. The Shaftesbury line featured both solid and semi-hollowbody guitars and basses. To hazard a guess, I would assume that the Italian production was featured early on in the late 1960s; as costs rose the importer chose to bring in Japanese-built guitars sometime around the mid-to-late 1970s. As luthier Peter Cook was busy during the 1970s mass-producing decent quality guitars under the Ned Callan, Simms-Watts, and CMI brand names the 1970s would be a good "guess-timate" for the introduction of Ned Callan/Shaftesbury model instruments (source: Tony Bacon and Paul Day, *The Guru's Guitar Guide*).

**Shadow S-130
courtesy Shadow**

S

SHANE

Instruments currently built in Fairfax, VA.

Shane has been offering quality custom built guitars for a number of years. Both the **S100 SC** and the **S350 Targa** offer traditional style bodies, while the **SJ Series** features a more modern style. Shane's **SB-1000** bass (retail list $399) has 24-fret fingerboard, 34 in. scale, P/J-style pickups, and a 2-per-side headstock.

SHELTONE

Instruments previously produced in Japan during the 1960s.

The Sheltone trademark is a brand name used by a UK importer. Sheltone instruments are entry level solid body or semi-hollowbody guitars (source: Tony Bacon and Paul Day, *The Guru's Guitar Guide*).

SHERGOLD

Instruments currently built in England since 1968 (the company is currently concentrating on custom orders).

Luthier Jack Golder was one of the mainstays of the Burns London company during the early 1960s, and stayed with the company when it was purchased in 1965 by the American Baldwin Organ company. Baldwin also acquired Gretsch in 1967. Baldwin was assembling imported Burns parts in Booneville, Arkansas. In 1970 moved the New York Gretsch operation to this facility as it phased out Burns guitar production.

Norman Holder, the ex-Burns mill foreman, rejoined Jack Golder during production of Hayman guitars (and once again affiliated with Jim Burns, who handled some of the Hayman designs). When Dallas-Arbiter, the distributor of Hayman guitars, went under in 1975 both Golder and Holder decided to continue working together on their own line of guitars. Some of the Hayman refinements carried over into the Shergold line (like the Hayman 4040 bass transforming into the Shergold Marathon bass), but the original design concept can be attributed to this team.

The Shergold company has also supplied a number of UK builders with necks and bodies under contract. These companies include BM, Jim Burn's Burns UK, Hayman (under Dallas-Arbiter), Peter Cook's Ned Callan, Pangborn, and Rosetti's "Triumph" model. Author Tony Bacon, in *The Ultimate Guitar Book*, notes that Shergold was the last company to make guitars (and parts) in quantity in the United Kingdom.

Possibly one of the easier trademarks to figure out model designations as the pickguard carries both the "Shergold" and model name on it! Shergold models generally feature a double cutaway solid body, and two humbucker pickups. Models include the Activator, Cavalier, Marathon (bass), Masquerador, Meteor, Modulator, and custom-built doublenecks (source: Paul Day, *The Burns Book*).

SHERWOOD

See chapter on House Brands.

This trademark has been identified as a House Brand of Montgomery Wards (source: Willie G. Moseley, *Stellas & Stratocasters*).

SHINE

Instruments currently produced in China and Korea. Distributed by the Saein Musical Instrument Co. LTD.

Shine produces a wide variety of electric solidbody and archtop guitars as well as basses. Most of their designs are based on popular American models, however they do have some original models. It is unknown if there is an American distributor. For more information refer to their website (see Trademark Index).

SIEGMUND

Instruments currently built in Tujunga, CA.

Siegmund Guitars currently produces classic handcrafted archtop, resophonic, and solid body electric guitars, as well as amplifier cabinets and cases. Siegmund features unique and fine quality, original design guitars. They were previously produced in Austin, Texas. For more information contact Siegmund (see Trademark Index).

SIERRA (U.S. MFG.)

Sierra (Excaliber Series). Instruments previously built in San Francisco, CA in 1981.

Sierra Guitars was a well-conceived but short-lived company that handcrafted the Excaliber line of guitars and basses. Founded in 1981 by Michael Tobias and Ron Armstrong, the San Francisco-based company lasted only one year and produced 50 instruments, (Model specifications and company history source: Hal Hammer).

ELECTRIC

All Excaliber instruments feature a three piece laminated neck-through design, stainless steel truss rod, chrome plated brass hardware, and select hardwoods. There was a $100 charge for left-handed instruments, and a $100 up charge for a vibrato bridge. Given the relatively small number of total instruments produced, accurate pricing on the following models is not available. Secondary market prices may have some relationship to the original list prices as offered in 1981.

MODEL 6.1 - offset double cutaway body, 24.75 in. scale neck, 3-per-side headstock, stop tailpiece, humbucker pickup, volume/tone controls, available in Natural finish, mfg. 1981 only.

Last MSR was $1,299.

Model 6.1 A - similar to the 6.1, except had active electronics and mini toggle switch.

Last MSR was $1,429.

MODEL 6.2 - offset double cutaway body, 24.75 in. scale neck, 3-per-side headstock, stop tailpiece, 2 humbucker pickups, 2 volume/1 tone controls, selector toggle switch, available in Natural finish, mfg. 1981 only.

Last MSR was $1,449.

Model 6.2 A - similar to the 6.2, except had active electronics and mini toggle switch.

Last MSR was $1,582.

ELECTRIC BASS

There was no charge for the fretless neck option.

MODEL 4.1 - offset double cutaway body with slightly elongated bass bout, 2-per-side headstock, 2 octave fretted neck, one pickup, volume/tone controls, available in Natural finish, mfg. 1981 only.

Last MSR was $1,429.

Model 4.1 A - similar to the 4.1, except had active electronics and mini toggle switch.

Last MSR was $1,559.

MODEL 4.2 - offset double cutaway body with slightly elongated bass bout, 2-per-side headstock, 2 octave fretted neck, two pickup, 2 volume/1 tone controls, available in Natural finish, mfg. 1981 only.

Last MSR was $1,579.

Model 4.2 A - similar to the 4.2, except had active electronics and mini toggle switch.

Last MSR was $1,712.

SIERRA (UK MFG.)

Instruments previously built in England during the early to mid-1960s.

The Jetstar model was a medium quality solid body guitar that featured a design based on Fender; the Jetstar even featured three single coil pickups (source: Tony Bacon and Paul Day, *The Guru's Guitar Guide*).

SIERRA DESIGNS

Instruments previously built in Portland, OR during the early 1980s.

Sierra Designs was founded in 1983 by Gene Fields. Fields, who worked at Fender from 1961 to 1983, eventually joined the Fender R & D section in 1966. Fields was the designer of the Starcaster, Fender's bolt neck answer to the ES-335 in the mid 1970s (source: Teisco Del Rey, *Guitar Player Magazine*, March 1991).

SIGGI GUITARS

Instruments currently built in Hattenhofen, Germany, since 1994.

Luthier Siegfried Braun is currently offering a handcrafted electric guitars that feature a direct pull (for strings) headstock, CNS neck system, and flamed or quilted maple tops. For further information regarding model specifications and pricing, contact Siggi Guitars directly (see Trademark Index).

SIGMA

Instruments previously assembled in Asia, with final finishing/inspection in Nazareth, PA. Distributed by the C. F. Martin Guitar Company of Nazareth, PA.

In 1970, the Martin Guitar Company expanded its product line by introducing the Sigma line. The instruments begin their assembly in Japan, and then are shipped in to Pennsylvania where the Martin company can oversee the final finishing and setup. Sigma guitars are great introductory models to the classic Martin design (source: Michael Wright, *Guitar Stories*, Volume One).

ELECTRIC

While the focus of the Sigma line has been primarily acoustic guitars (after all, Sigma is a division of the Martin Guitar Company), there were a handful of solid body guitars and basses distributed during the early 1970s. Two models, the SBG2-6 and SBE2-9 resemble Gibson SGs. The **SBE2-9** is similar to the **SBG2-6**, except has a Bigsby-style vibrato. The Sigma **SBF2-6** features a telecaster-style body mated to a 3 tuners on a side headstock. The **SBB2-8** electric bass has a vaguely Fender Precision-style body (in the earlier Telecaster bass body style) with a 2 tuners on a side headstock.

These guitars don't show up to much on the market. When they do they are worth what Martin Electrics are worth to the Martin's but on a Sigma level.

SIGNATURE

Instruments previously produced in Aurora, Ontario, Canada from 1987 to 1990.

The Signature Guitar Company was founded by Russ Heinl. Heinl collaborated with Alex Lifeson of Rush to design most models. Guitars were produced from 1987 to 1990. Information courtesy: Scott Citrigno, July, 2003.

ELECTRIC

Signature produced six different guitar models over its lifespan. The Crusader, the Pegasus, the Oracle, the Odyssey, the Aurora, and the Excaliber Bass. The Oracle features and alder contoured body with a highly flamed maple top, rock maple neck, ebony fingerboard with offset and 21st MOP Oracle inlay, Floyd Rose licensed tremolo, two humbuckers, one single coil pickup in H/S/H configuration, two knobs, coil tap, three mini-switches, and gold hardware.

SIGNET

Instruments previously produced in Japan circa early 1970s.

The Signet trademark was a brand name used by U.S. importers Ampeg/Selmer (source: Michael Wright, *Guitar Stories*, Volume One).

SILVER CADET

Instruments previously produced in Korea. Previously distributed in the U.S. market by Ibanez (Hoshino USA) of Bensalem, PA.

The Silver Cadet guitar line provides an entry level step into the wonderful world of electric guitars (buy a guitar, plug it into a loud amp, and then tell your parents! They'll either cut your allowance or cut off your electricity). The current quality of these instruments, like other contemporary entry level guitars, is a lot better today than it was twenty or thirty years ago for a beginning student.

Silvertone Electric Model courtesy Dale Hanson

Silvertone Electric Model courtesy George McGuire

S

ELECTRIC

ZR140 - offset double cutaway hardwood body, black pickguard, bolt-on maple neck, 21-fret rosewood fingerboard with pearl dot inlay, standard vibrato, 6-on-a-side tuners, chrome hardware, 2 single coil/1 humbucker pickups, volume/tone control, 5-position switch, available in Black, Red and White finishes, mfg. 1994-96.

	N/A	$180	$150	$120	$100	$80	$60

Last MSR was $250.

ZR350 - similar to ZR140, except has double locking vibrato, humbucker/single coil/humbucker pickups, available in Black, Red, or White finishes, mfg. 1994-96.

	N/A	$300	$250	$200	$160	$130	$100

Last MSR was $430.

ELECTRIC BASS

ZTB100 - offset double cutaway hardwood body, black pickguard, bolt-on maple neck, 22-fret rosewood fingerboard with pearl dot inlay, fixed bridge, 4-on-a-side tuners, chrome hardware, P-style pickup, volume/tone control, available in Black or Red finishes, mfg. 1994-96.

	N/A	$225	$190	$160	$130	$110	$90

Last MSR was $300.

SILVER STAR

Instruments currently produced in Korea. Distributed by Un Sung Musical Instruments Co. LTD.

Silver Star is a trademark of guitars produced by Un Sung music. Un Sung produces over fifty thousand guitars a year. They offer many popular American designs as well as some of their original models. On the cover of their brochure they feature a triple neck guitar. It is unknown if there is an American distributor. For more information visit their website (see Trademark Index).

SILVERTONE

See chapter on House Brands. Instruments currently built in Korea. Distributed by the Samick Corporation.

This trademark has been identified as a House Brand owned and used by Sears and Roebuck between 1941 to 1970. There was no company or factory; Sears owned the name and applied it to various products from such manufacturers as Harmony, Valco, Danelectro, and Kay. Sears and Roebuck acquired Harmony in 1916 to control its respectable ukulele production. Harmony generally sold around 40 percent of its guitar production to Sears. The following is a word of caution: Just because it says Silvertone, do not automatically assume it is a Danelectro! In fact, study the guitar to determine possible origin (Harmony, Valco and Kay were originally built in Illinois, Danelectro in New Jersey; so all were U.S. However, mid 1960s models were built in Japan by Teisco, as well!). Best of all, play it! If it looks good, and sounds okay - it was meant to be played. As most Silvertones were sold either through the catalog or in a store, they will generally be entry level quality instruments.

Certain Silvertone models have garnered some notoriety, such as the Danelectro-produced combination of guitar and amp-in-case. Sears also marketed the Teisco company's TRG-1 (or TRE-100) electric guitar with amp built in! This guitar has a six-on-a-side "Silvertone" headstock, and a single cutaway *pregnant Telecaster* body design (the small built-in speaker is in the *tummy*). Harmony produced a number of electric hollowbody guitars (like the Sovereign) for the Silvertone label; Kay also offered a version of their **Thin Twin** model as well as arch top models.

The publisher would like to thank Scott Sanders for his contributions to the Silvertone section.

Samick has revived the Silvertone line and is now producing a full assortment of models. A big part of Silvertone now is Paul Stanly of Kiss, who has an entire line of guitars. Look for more information on Silvertone guitars in upcoming editions of *The Blue Book of Electric Guitars*.

ELECTRIC

1300 - single cutaway, U-series body with 13.25 in. lower bout width, Masonite semi-solid construction, clear or white pickguard, bolt-on neck, 21-fret rosewood fingerboard with dot inlay, metal trapezoidal bridge with rosewood stick saddle, Coke-bottle shaped peghead, 3-per-side tuners with plastic buttons, single coil lipstick tube pickup, volume/tone control with selector switch, available in Copper (Model 1300) and Black (Model 1302) finishes, mfg. 1958-59.

	N/A	$375	$325	$260	$220	$175	$150

1301 - similar to Model 1300 except has 2 single coil lipstick tube pickups, 2 stacked volume/tone controls with 3-position selector switch, available in Copper (Model 1301) or Black (Model 1303) finishes, mfg. 1958-59.

	N/A	$400	$325	$275	$225	$180	$150

1305 - similar to Model 1300 except has 3 single coil lipstick tube pickups, 3 stacked volume/tone controls, available in White/Black Sunburst finish, mfg, 1958-59.

	N/A	$425	$350	$300	$250	$200	$150

These models are often referred to as U models by collectors because they are almost identical to the U series of guitars that Danelectro manufactured with the Danelectro logo.

1317 - single cutaway with 11.75 in. lower bout width, Masonite semi-solid construction, clear pickguard, bolt-on neck, 21-fret rosewood fingerboard with dot inlay, metal trapezoidal bridge with rosewood stick saddle, Coke-bottle shaped peghead, 3-per-side tuners with plastic buttons, single coil lipstick tube pickup, volume/tone control with selector switch, available in Black (Model 1317) or Bronze (Model 1321) finishes, mfg. 1957-58.

	N/A	$375	$325	$260	$220	$175	$150

1319 - similar to Model 1317 except has 2 single coil lipstick tube pickups, 2 stacked volume/tone controls. Available in Black (Model 1319) and Bronze (Model 1323) finishes, mfg. 1957-58.

	N/A	$400	$325	$275	$225	$180	$150

These models are similar to the U models except for a shorter lower bout width of 11.75 in. and shorter overall length. Collectors call them "peanut body" models.

GRADING	100% MINT	98% NEAR MINT	95% EXC+	90% EXC	80% VG+	70% VG	60% G

1357 - single cutaway, solid poplar body covered in vinyl, 11.75 in. lower bout width, clear or dark brown pickguard, bolt-on neck, 20-fret rosewood fingerboard with dot inlay, metal trapezoidal bridge with rosewood stick saddle, Coke-bottle shaped peghead wider at the bottom, 3-per-side tuners with plastic buttons, single coil lipstick tube pickup, volume/tone control with selector switch, available in Tan with Ginger sides finish and the following Custom Colors: Flame Red with Black sides, Yellow with black sides, Bronze with Mint Green sides, Coral with White sides (All custom colors Model 1358), mfg. 1955-57.

| | N/A | $350 | $300 | $250 | $215 | $175 | $150 |

1359 - similar to Model 1357 except has 2 single coil lipstick tube pickups, 2 stacked knob volume/tone controls, 3-position selector switch. Available in Tan with Ginger sides finish and the following Custom Colors: Flame Red with Black sides, Yellow with black sides, Bronze with Mint Green sides, Coral with White sides (All custom colors Model 1360), mfg. 1955-57.

| | N/A | $375 | $325 | $260 | $220 | $180 | $150 |

1375 - single cutaway, solid poplar body covered in vinyl, 11.75 in. lower bout width, white pickguard, bolt-on neck, 20-fret rosewood fingerboard with dot inlay, metal trapezoidal bridge with rosewood stick saddle, Coke-bottle shaped peghead covered with white, plastic overlay, lightning bolt under logo and wider at the bottom, 3-per-side tuners with plastic buttons, single coil pickup mounted under pickguard, volume/tone control, available in Maroon, mfg 1954-55.

| | N/A | $425 | $375 | $300 | $250 | $200 | $150 |

1377 - similar to Model 1375 except has 2 covered pickups, 2 volume/tone controls, 3-position selector switch, available in Maroon, mfg. 1954-55.

| | N/A | $425 | $375 | $300 | $250 | $200 | $150 |

1415 - identical to Model 1417 except pickguard is cut in a half circle around the lipstick tube pickup instead of flush up against it, available in Bronze (Model 1415) or Black (Model 1416) finishes, mfg. 1960 only.

| | N/A | $375 | $325 | $260 | $220 | $180 | $150 |

1417 - single cutaway, U-series body with 13.25 in. lower bout width, Masonite semi-solid construction, clear or white pickguard, bolt-on neck, 21-fret rosewood fingerboard with dot inlay, metal trapezoidal bridge with rosewood stick saddle, "dolphin-nose" shaped peghead, 6-on-a-side tuners with plastic buttons, single coil lipstick tube pickup, volume/tone control with selector switch, available in Bronze (Model 1417) or Black (Model 1419) finishes, mfg. 1959-1960, 1961-62.

| | N/A | $400 | $325 | $275 | $225 | $185 | $150 |

Silvertone Electric Model courtesy George McGuire

1448 - offset double cutaway asymmetrical body, Masonite semi-solid construction, white pickguard, bolt-on neck, 18-fret rosewood fingerboard with dot inlay, metal trapezoidal bridge with rosewood stick saddle, 6-on-a-side tuners with plastic buttons, single coil lipstick tube pickup, volume/tone control, available in Black with metallic accents finish, mfg. 1962-67.

| | N/A | $375 | $325 | $260 | $220 | $180 | $150 |

This model is known as an amp-in-case model because the case came fitted with a 3-watt amplifier and a 5-inch speaker. In 1964, a 6-inch speaker replaced the 5-inch speaker. In 1964, metal "skate-key" tuners replaced the tuners with plastic buttons.

1449 - similar to Model 1448 except has 21-fret rosewood fingerboard, two single coil lipstick tube pickups, 2 stacked volume/tone controls with 3-position selector switch, available in Black with metallic accents finish, mfg. 1963-64.

| | N/A | $425 | $350 | $300 | $250 | $200 | $150 |

This model is known as an amp-in-case model because the case came fitted with a 5-watt amplifier, tremolo and an 8-inch speaker.

1450 - offset double cutaway asymmetrical body, solid wood covered with veneer, tortoise-shell pickguard, bolt-on neck, 21-fret rosewood fingerboard with dot inlay, metal trapezoidal vibrato bridge with rosewood stick saddle, 6-on-a-side metal "skate-key" tuners, 2 single coil lipstick tube pickups with 4 volume/tone controls, 3-position selector switch, available in Red Sunburst finish, mfg. 1965-66.

| | N/A | $450 | $375 | $325 | $275 | $225 | $175 |

This model was only listed in the 1965 Sears Christmas catalog. However, since 1966 models do exist, it is probable that they were produced and sold in stores to use up available stock.

1451 - offset double cutaway asymmetrical body, solid wood covered with veneer, white pickguard, bolt-on neck, 18-fret rosewood fingerboard with dot inlay, metal trapezoidal bridge with rosewood stick saddle, 6-on-a-side metal "skate-key" tuners, single coil lipstick tube pickup with volume/tone control, available in Black finish, mfg. 1967-68.

| | N/A | $375 | $325 | $260 | $220 | $180 | $150 |

This model is known as an amp-in-case model because the case came fitted with a 3-watt amplifier and a 6-inch speaker.

1452 - similar to 1451 except 21-fret fingerboard, vibrato bridge, Fender-like peghead shape, 2 single coil lipstick tube pickups with 4 volume/tone controls, available in Red Sunburst finish, mfg. 1967-68.

| | N/A | $400 | $325 | $275 | $220 | $180 | $150 |

This model is known as an amp-in-case model because the case was fitted with a 5-watt amplifier, tremolo and an 8-inch speaker.

1457 - offset double cutaway asymmetrical body, Masonite semi-solid construction, white pickguard, bolt-on neck, 21-fret rosewood fingerboard with dot inlay, metal trapezoidal bridge with rosewood stick saddle, 6-on-a-side tuners with metal "skate-key" tuners, 2 single coil lipstick tube pickups with stacked volume/tone controls, 3-position selector switch, available in Red Sunburst with metallic accents finish, mfg. 1964-67.

| | N/A | $350 | $300 | $250 | $210 | $180 | $150 |

This model is known as an amp-in-case model because the case was fitted with a 5-watt amplifier, tremolo and an 8-inch speaker. Price includes amp as well.

S

Silvertone Solid-Body Electric courtesy George McGuire

GRADING	100% MINT	98% NEAR MINT	95% EXC+	90% EXC	80% VG+	70% VG	60% G

1480 - single cutaway, U-series body with 13.25 in. lower bout width, Masonite semi-solid construction, clear or white pickguard, bolt-on neck, 18-fret rosewood fingerboard with dot inlay, metal trapezoidal bridge with rosewood stick saddle, dark brown or natural Coke-bottle shaped peghead, 3-per-side tuners with plastic buttons, single coil lipstick tube pickup mounted centrally between neck joint and bridge, volume/tone control, available in Brown with metallic accents finish, mfg. 1958 only.

	N/A	$375	$325	$260	$220	$180	$150

These models were only available through the Sears Christmas catalog. Although they were no longer listed in the Christmas Catalog after 1960, the existence of post-1960 models indicates that they were still being manufactured and sold at Sears stores through at least 1961, probably to use up existing stock.

1450 - identical to Model 1480 (Not to be confused with the Model 1450 solidbody above), mfg. 1959.

1456 - identical to Model 1450 except pickguard is cut in a half circle around the lipstick tube pickup instead of flush up against it, mfg. 1960-61.

ELECTRIC BASS

1373 - single cutaway, U-series body with 13.25 in. lower bout, Masonite semi-solid construction, clear or white pickguard, bolt-on neck, 24-fret rosewood fingerboard with dot inlay, trapezoidal bridge with rosewood stick saddle, Coke-bottle shaped peghead, 3-per-side tuners with plastic buttons, 2 single coil lipstick tube pickups, stacked volume/tone controls with 3-position selector switch, available in Black finish, mfg. 1957-59.

	N/A	$375	$325	$260	$220	$180	$150

This model was a 6-string bass that was tuned like a guitar, but an octave lower.

1442 - offset double cutaway asymmetrical body, solid wood covered with veneer, white pickguard, bolt-on neck, 30-inch scale, 22-fret rosewood fingerboard with dot inlay, metal trapezoidal bridge with rosewood stick saddle, 4-on-a-side metal tuners, single coil lipstick tube pickup with volume/tone control, selector switch, available in Brown sunburst finish, mfg. 1966-68.

	N/A	$425	$350	$300	$250	$200	$150

1443 - similar to Model 1442 except tortoiseshell pickguard, 34-inch scale, 2 single coil lipstick tube pickups, 4 volume/tone controls with 3-position selector switch, available in Red Sunburst finish, mfgd. 1966-68.

	N/A	$425	$350	$300	$250	$200	$150

1444 - single cutaway, U-series body with 13.25 in. lower bout, Masonite semi-solid construction, clear or white pickguard, bolt-on neck, 24-fret rosewood fingerboard with dot inlay, trapezoidal bridge with rosewood stick saddle, "dolphin-nose" shaped peghead, 4-on-a-side tuners with plastic or metal buttons, single coil lipstick tube pickup, volume/tone control, available in Black finish, mfg. 1959-1966.

	N/A	$375	$325	$260	$220	$180	$150

SIMMONS GUITARS

Instruments currently produced Hendersonvill, NC.

Simmons guitars produces high-quality, hand made, limited production four and five-string electric bass guitars. Guitars are built out of quality hardwoods and electronics. The body features neck-through design with a double action truss-rod. Barolini active pickups and electronics are installed. Four-string models start at $1,730 and five-string models start at $1,830. For more information contact Simmons directly (see Trademark Index).

(GENE) SIMMON'S PUNISHER BASS

See Punisher Bass.

SIMMS-WATTS

See also Ned Callan. Instruments previously produced in England during the mid-1970s.

The Simms-Watts trademark is the brand name used on England's own Ned Callan guitars. In fact, without the difference of the headstock label, the instruments are the same as, and produced by, Ned Callan (Peter Cook) (source: Tony Bacon and Paul Day, *The Guru's Guitar Book*).

SIMPSON

Instruments previously produced in New Zealand during the 1960s.

Luthier Ray Simpson built his first electric guitar in 1941. Production continued throughout the 1960s. A representational model called the **Pan-O-Sonic** combines both strat-designated overtones with original bridge and wiring designs (the three single coil pickups each have their own on/off switch.) If wired differently from a standard 3 or 5-way selector, this switching could offer some pickup combinations not offered traditionally! Anyone with further information on Simpson guitars is invited to write to the *Blue Book of Electric Guitars* (source: Tony Bacon, *The Ultimate Guitar Book*).

SIMPSON HOT ROD GUITARS

Instruments previously built in Clearwater, FL.

Sam Simpson offeried some well-built and hand crafted electric guitar models. Most models featured a highly figured maple top and quality pickups and hardware.

SIMPSON-JAMES

Instruments currently built in Westfield, MA since 1993.

Simpson-James basses are hand built in Westfield, Massachusetts by luthiers Christopher Mowatt and Robert Clarke. The company was established in 1993 with the vision of providing custom electric basses to local professional musicians. The basses produced have been unique in that no two instruments were alike, each being a prototype in design and function. Simpson-James currently offers four different neck-through **SJ-4** 4-string models (list prices range from $1,100 to $1,600), and two **SJ-5** 5-string models (list $2,100). The **Performer Series**, introduced in 1996, is a rebirth of the Great American Workhorse of basses. Offering the same quality in a bolt-neck design, Performer series 4- and 5-strings range from $1,250 to $2,000. According to product director Christopher Mowatt, Simpson-James is currently hand-building between 2 to 5 instruments per month in their efforts to maintain strict quality control.

S

SINGER

Instruments currently produced in China.

Singer produces a large amount of acoustic, electric, and bass guitars that are mainly based on popular American designs. They have some original designs as well. It is unknown who the American distributor is. For more information contact their website (see Trademark Index).

SLAMMER

By Hamer. Instruments currently produced in Asia since 1990. Distributed by the Kaman Music Corp. in Bloomfield, CT.

Slammer is Hamer's entry level line of guitars that is produced in Asia. Some models are based on Hamer's regular production designs, while some are based on other popular American models. All prices retail for less than $400 and most guitars can be purchased for around $200. For more information contact the Kaman Music Corp. (see Trademark Index).

SMARTLIGHT

Instruments currently produced in Korea. Distributed in the U.S. by Optek Music Systems, Inc. of Windham, NH. Previously of Raleigh, NC. Earlier instruments may have the Optek or Smartlight trademark on the headstock. Current models have an "SL" logo on the headstock.

Optek Music Systems was formed by Rusty Shaffer in 1989 as a means to help educate new and existing guitarists through the use of the SmartLIGHT Interactive System(TM) for guitar. The SmartLIGHT guitar has LED lights in the neck that light up guitar fingerings to show guitarists precisely where to place their fingers. The SmartLIGHT connects to a personal computer. Players can learn to play specific songs which have been recorded on MIDI albums by using the company's MIDI driver in conjunction with a general sequencer program. They can also learn chord fingerings of their choice by using software that allows them to choose chords, scales, or notes in any of twelve musical keys and illuminate those fingerings on the guitar, (Company information courtesy Michelle Gouldsberry). It looks like the new name may be Fretlight (check their website).

Three SmartLIGHT electric guitars and one SmartLIGHT bass guitar are offered for all playing levels. The entry level 30-A electric (factory direct $379.95) has a solid black body with one piezo pickup. The intermediate 30-B electric ($479.95) in Natural or Translucent Blue has one piezo pickup and two single coil pickups. The advanced 30-C electric ($679.95) in Orange Sunburst has a bird's-eye maple top and back, Seymour Duncan pickups, and gold hardware. The advanced 40-C electric bass ($699.95) is made of the same materials as the 30-C, and includes the Seymour Duncan Lightnin' Rod bassline active/passive pickup system. The Smartlight guitars are produced in the same Korean factory that makes guitars for companies like Fender, Gibson's Epiphone brand, and Washburn. The U.S. Optek facility checks quality control, assembly, and set-ups prior to shipping.

SMITH, KEN

See Ken Smith Basses, LTD.

SOLA-SOUND

Instruments previously produced in Japan during the early 1970s.

The Sola-Sound trademark was a brand name used by a UK importer. These medium quality solid body guitars featured designs based on classic American favorites (source: Tony Bacon and Paul Day, *The Guru's Guitar Book*).

SONGBIRD GUITARS

Instruments currently made in Asia, and distributed by Songbird Guitars, in Cranberry, PA.

Songbird Guitars imports both acoustic and electric instruments.

SONNET

Instruments previously produced in Japan.

Sonnet guitars were distributed in the U.S. by the Daimaru New York Corporation of New York, New York (source: Michael Wright, *Guitar Stories*, Volume One).

SPALT BASSES

Instruments currently produced in Los Angeles, CA.

Spalt produces high quality basses that feature odd designs. The Matrix and Terminator aren't your everyday bass. Spalt also has the Wiper pickup. This is a pickup that can be "swept" back and forth on the body to get an infinite number of sounds by having the pickup situated differently. Prices start around $2,500. For more information refer to their website (see Trademark Index).

SPECTOR

Current trademark owned by Stuart Spector Design, Ltd., located in Saugerties, NY. Instruments are built in Woodstock, NY (USA Handmade Series), THE Czech Republic (Europe Series) Korea (Professional Series) and China (Performance Series). Instruments originally built in Brooklyn, NY from 1976 through 1985. After Kramer (BKL) bought the company, production moved to Neptune, NJ between 1985 and 1989. Some late 1980s Kramer/Spector models were produced in Japan.

**Silvertone Jupiter
courtesy George McGuire**

S

GRADING	100% MINT	98% NEAR MINT	95% EXC+	90% EXC	80% VG+	70% VG	60% G

Two members of the Brooklyn Woodworkers Co-operative, Stuart Spector and Alan Charney, established Spector Guitars in 1976. The initial SB-1 bass and G-1 guitar both featured neck-through-body design. Another member of the co-op was Ned Steinberger, who was designing and building furniture. Stuart began searching for a new bass design and Ned offered to assist. Ned built a prototype bass that would influence bass guitar design forever. He designed the NS-1 bass. "The idea of attaching the body parts at an angle and then curving the top was intended to give the instrument a more attractive appearance, and the compound curve on the back is for comfort," states Ned. It was this prototype instrument more than any other that set the stage for my work in musical instrument design. The cusved body Spector NS was an instant classic. The NS-1 was updated to the two pickup NS-2, and bolt-on neck versions(NS-1B and NS-2JA) were added to the line in 1982.

Spector sold the company to Kramer Music Products in 1985. Kramer continued to produce the NS-2 bass, and introduced the first imported Spector basses, including the NS-2A, In June, 1987, Stuart debuted the NS-5 5-string bass for Kramer production. All production ceased when Kramer went into bankruptcy in 1989.

Stuart Spector´s current company, Stuart Spectpr Designs, Ldt, introduced the new SD bass series in 1991 under the "SSD" name. In December 1992 SSD relaunched the NS bass series.

The Gibson Guitar Corp. purchased the Kramer trademark in 1997, and Stuart Spector Designs purchased the rights to the Spector trademark. All instruments since 1997 sport the original "SS" logo (company information courtesy Stuart Spector).

MODEL PRODUCTION LOCATION BY DATE

1976-1985: Brooklyn, New York.

1985-1990: Neptune, New Jersey under Kramer.

1991-1996: Woodstock, New York as **S S D**.

1993-1996: Czech Republic as **S S D**.

1997-date: USA Handmade, Czech Republic, Korea and China production with original Spector trademark.

ELECTRIC: BLACKHAWK SERIES

The Blackhawk guitar design and development by Chris Hofschneider features a mahogany body with a flame maple top, bolt-on maple neck, rosewood fingerboard, 25.5" scale, black hardware, and Schaller tuners.

European production models like the **Blackhawk CR** with a Wilkinson stop tailpiece lists at $995, while the Blackhawk with Schaller/Floyd Rose tremolo lists at $1,295 (Model BH-FR). Choice of finishes included Black, Blue, and Red Stain finishes, and Cherry Sunburst.

Spector also offers a **Blackhawk Custom USA** (Model BHK-FB) which is built in the U.S. and features Tom Holmes, EMG, or Seymour Duncan P-90 pickups, chrome hardware, and a fixed bridge (list $1,799). The Blackhawk with Original Floyd Rose tremolo (Model BHK-FR) has a list price of $2,029. The optional Gold plated hardware is an additional $80. The U.S.-built Blackhawk guitars are available in Amber Stain, Black & Blue, Black & Teal, Black Cherry, Black Oil, Black Stain, Blueburst, Blue Stain, Cherry Sunburst, Clear Gloss, Forest Green, Golden Stain, Green/Blueburst, Ivory, Magenta Stain, Orange Stain, Red Stain, Teal Stain, Tobacco Sunburst, Teal Stain, and Violet Stain.

ELECTRIC BASS: PERFORMANCE SERIES

Ned Steinberger Spector designs from the late 1970s featured models like the **NS-1**, which had a single humbucker pickup, neck-through design, 2-per-side headstock. This model opened the door for others such as the **NS-1 B**, a bolt-on neck model; the **NS-2** (2 humbuckers); and the **NS-2 J** which featured 2 EMG pickups. Early Spector basses still command good money on the vintage market.

PERFORMER 4 (NS-2000 B) - similar to the NS-2000, except features a bolt-on neck, mfg. 1998-present.

	MSR	$549		$390	$340	$290	$250	$200	$165	$135

This model is produced in China. In 2003, the NS-2000-B was renamed the Performer 4.

PERFORMER 5 - similar to the Performer 4, except in 5-string configuration, mfg. 2004 only.

	$425	$375	$325	$275	$235	$195	$160

Last MSR was $579.

ELECTRIC BASS: PROFESSIONAL SERIES

NS-2000/4 - offset double cutaway body, through-body neck, 34 in. scale, 24-fret rosewood fingerboard with pearl dot inlays, fixed bridge, blackface peghead with pearl logo inlay, 2-per-side tuners, chrome hardware, two humbucker pickups, volume/tone controls, available in Natural finish, mfg. 1998-2002.

	$650	$575	$500	$450	$400	$350	$300

Last MSR was $995

Add $100 for 5-string configuration (Model NS2000-5).

This model was produced in Korea.

LEGEND 4 - offset double cutaway basswood body, bolt-on maple neck, 24-fret rosewood fingerboard, 2 EMG-HZ pickups, 2-per-side tuners, 4 knobs, gold hardware, available in Amberburst, Slate Grey, or Black Cherry finishes, mfg. 2004-present.

	MSR	$849		$600	$525	$450	$400	$350	$300	$250

Legend 5 - similar to the Legend 4, except in 5-string configuration, 3/2-per-side tuners, mfg. 2004-present.

	MSR	$899		$625	$550	$475	$425	$375	$325	$275

Legend 6 - similar to the Legend 4, except in 6-string configuration, 3-per-side tuners, mfg. 2004-present.

	MSR	$949		$675	$600	$525	$450	$400	$350	$300

Q4 (NS2000) - offset double cutaway basswood body, quilted maple top, bolt-on neck, 24-fret rosewood fingerboard with dot inlay, two active EMG pickups, four knobs, 2-per-side tuners, black hardware, available in Amberburst, Black Stain, Blue Stain, or Black Cherry finishes, disc. 2004.

	$550	$475	$400	$350	$300	$250	$200

Last MSR was $749.

GRADING	100% MINT	98% NEAR MINT	95% EXC+	90% EXC	80% VG+	70% VG	60% G

Q5 (NS2000) - similar to the Q4, except in five-string configuration, 3/2-per-side tuners, disc. 2004.

	$575	$500	$425	$375	$325	$275	$225

Last MSR was $799.

Q6 (NS2000) - similar to the Q4, except in six-string configuration, 3-per-side tuners, disc. 2004.

	$600	$525	$450	$400	$350	$300	$250

Last MSR was $849.

REX 4 - offset single cutaway maple body, rock maple neck-thru body, 24-fret rosewood fingerboard with dot inlay, two EMG pickups, four knobs, 2-per-side-tuners, black hardware, Rex Brown of Pantera Signature model, available in Black Stain or Holoflash Black, current mfg.

MSR	$1,199	$850	$750	$675	$600	$525	$450	$375

Rex 5 - similar to the Rex 4, except in five-string configuration, 3/2-per-side tuners, current mfg.

MSR	$1,299	$925	$825	$725	$650	$575	$500	$425

SPECTORCORE 4 - similar to the Q4, except has semi-hollow tone chambers and a Fishman power bridge pickup, available in Black, Teal, Amberburst, or Black Stain finishes, mfg. 2002-present.

MSR	$899	$650	$575	$500	$425	$375	$325	$275

Spectorcore 5 - similar to the Spectorcore 4, except in five-string configuration, 3/2-per-side tuners, current mfg.

MSR	$949	$675	$600	$525	$450	$400	$350	$300

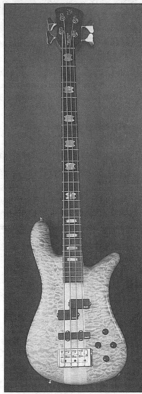

**Spector NS Bass
courtesy Spector**

ELECTRIC BASS: BOB SERIES

Stuart Spector designed the BOB models in 1996. These models feature a bolt-on neck design, and are built in the USA.

Add $175 for a high gloss finish (HG). Add $200 for a figured maple top (FIG-MPL).

BOB 4 - offset double cutaway swamp ash body, 6 bolt, bolt-on maple neck, pau ferro fingerboard, fixed brass bridge, blackface peghead with pearl logo inlay, 2-per-side tuners, gold hardware, EMG DC pickup, volume/treble/bass controls, available in Matte Natural finish, mfg. 1996-99.

	$1,000	$900	$825	$750	$650	$550	$450

Last MSR was $1,295.

BOB 4 Deluxe - similar to the BOB 4, except features 2 EMG DC pickups, EMG 3-band EQ, mfg. 1996-99.

	$1,200	$1,050	$950	$850	$750	$650	$550

Last MSR was $1,565.

BOB 5 - similar to BOB 4, except has 5-string configuration, 3/2-per-side tuners, mfg. 1996-99.

	$1,050	$950	$850	$750	$650	$550	$450

Last MSR was $1,395.

BOB 5 Deluxe - similar to BOB 4, except has 5-string configuration, 3/2-per-side tuners, 2 EMG DC pickups, EMG 3-band EQ, mfg. 1996-99.

	$1,250	$1,100	$975	$875	$775	$675	$575

Last MSR was $1,665.

ELECTRIC BASS: EUROPE SERIES

The NS-CR basses are built in the Czech Republic, and were first offered in 1995.

4 NS 4 CR - offset double cutaway soft maple body, through-body graphite-reinforced maple neck, rosewood fingerboard with dot inlays, solid fixed brass bridge, blackface peghead with pearl logo inlay, 2-per-side tuners, gold hardware, EMG P/J-style pickups, 2 volume/treble/bass EQ controls, active electronics, available in Fire Engine Red, Gloss Black, or White finishes, 34 in. scale, mfg. 1995-99.

	$1,300	$1,100	$950	$825	$700	$600	$500

Last MSR was $1,795.

Euro (NS 4 CRFM) - similar to the NS 4 CR, except features a figured maple body, gold Schaller tuners, available in Amber, Blackburst, Black Cherry, Black Stain, Clear Gloss, Natural Oil, Plum Stain, and Red Stain finishes, disc. 2004.

	$1,650	$1,400	$1,200	$1,000	$850	$700	$550

Last MSR was $2,299.

Euro 4 LX - similar to the Euro 4, except has an alder body with a figured top, mfg. 2003-present.

MSR	$2,199	$1,550	$1,350	$1,200	$1,050	$900	$800	$700

NS 5 CR - similar to NS 4 CR, except has 5-string configuration, 3/2-per-side tuners, EMG 40 DC pickups, disc. 1999.

	$1,450	$1,250	$1,050	$900	$775	$650	$525

Last MSR was $1,995.

Euro 5 (NS 5 CRFM) - similar to NS 4 CRFM, except has 5-string configuration, 3/2-per-side gold Schaller tuners, EMG 40 DC pickups, available in Amber, Blackburst, Black Cherry, Black Stain, Clear Gloss, Natural Oil, Plum Stain, or Red Stain finishes, disc. 2004.

	$1,800	$1,550	$1,350	$1,150	$1,000	$850	$700

Last MSR was $2,499.

Euro 5 LX - similar to the Euro 5, except has an alder body with a figured maple top, mfg. 2003-present.

MSR	$2,399	$1,700	$1,500	$1,300	$1,150	$1,000	$900	$800

S

GRADING	100% MINT	98% NEAR MINT	95% EXC+	90% EXC	80% VG+	70% VG	60% G

EURO 6 LX - similar to the Euro 4 LX, except in six-string configuration, new 2005.

MSR	$2,899	$2,100	$1,800	$1,600	$1,400	$1,200	$1,050	$900

REBOP 4 - offset double cutaway European alder body, bolt-on 3-piece rock maple neck, 24-fret rosewood fingerboard with dot inlay, two EMG pickups, Spector active electronics, 2-per-side-tuners, gold hardware, available in Tobacco Sunburst, Black Stain, Amber, or Black Cherry Burst finishes, mfg. 2002-present.

MSR	$1,499	$1,050	$900	$800	$700	$625	$550	$475

Rebop 5 - similar to the Rebop 4, except in five-string configuration, 3/2-per-side tuners, mfg. 2002-present.

MSR	$1,599	$1,125	$975	$850	$750	$675	$600	$525

ELECTRIC BASS: JN SERIES

In 1995, Spector offered a custom bass series based on a model built for Jason Newsted (formerly of Metallica, now part of Voivod). These neck-through models featured EMG pickups, piezo bridges and electronics, a black oil finish, and fiber optic illuminated side markers. List prices were $4,900 (**JN-4P**), $5,075 (**JN-5P**), and $5,350 (**JN-6P**) respectively.

ELECTRIC BASS: USA SERIES

In the USA Series, the NS models were designed by Ned Steinberger (based on his original curved back model from 1976). The SD models were designed by Stuart Spector in 1992. Current U.S. models are optional with bridge-mounted piezo pickup systems.

NS 2 - offset double cutaway figured maple body, through-body 3-piece maple neck, 24-fret pau ferro fingerboard with pearl crown inlays, 34 in. scale, solid fixed brass bridge, blackface peghead with pearl logo inlay, 2-per-side tuners, gold hardware, P/J-style EMG pickups, volume/mix/stacked 2-band EQ controls, 9-volt active electronics, available in Natural Oil finish, current mfg.

MSR	$4,999	$3,800	$3,200	$2,700	$2,300	$1,900	$1,600	$1,300

> **Add $750 for high gloss finish (Model NS 2 HG). Available in Amber Stain, Black & Blue, Black & Teal, Black Cherry, Black Oil, Black Stain, Blueburst, Blue Stain, Cherry Sunburst, Clear Gloss, Forest Green, Golden Stain, Green/Blueburst, Ivory, Magenta Stain, Orange Stain, Red Stain, Teal Stain, Tobacco Sunburst, Teal Stain, and Violet Stain.**

NS 2 J - similar to the NS 2, except features a bolt-on 3-piece neck, swamp ash body, black hardware, 24-fret pau ferro fingerboard, 2 J-style EMG pickups, EMG active electronics, available in Natural Oil finish, current mfg.

MSR	$2,699	$1,950	$1,700	$1,500	$1,300	$1,150	$1,000	$850

> **Subtract $200 for swamp ash body. Add $175 for high gloss finish (Model NS 2 J HG). Add $175 for optional curly maple body. Add $200 for exotic top.**

NS-JH5 - similar to the NS 2 J, except in five-string configuration, and has EMG-40TW pickups, current mfg.

MSR	$2,899	$2,100	$1,800	$1,550	$1,350	$1,200	$1,050	$900

> **Subtract $200 for swamp ash body. Add $200 for exotic top.**

NS-JH6 - similar to the NS 2 J, except in six-string configuration, and has EMG-45TW pickups, current mfg.

MSR	$3,099	$2,250	$1,950	$1,700	$1,450	$1,250	$1,100	$950

> **Subtract $200 for swamp ash body. Add $200 for exotic top.**

NS-4 - similar to the NS-2, except has EMG-35DC pickups and an 18 volt active electronic system, current mfg.

MSR	$4,999	$3,800	$3,200	$2,700	$2,300	$1,900	$1,600	$1,300

NS 4-20 LIMITED EDITION 20TH ANNIVERSARY - similar to the NS 4, except features AAAAA Western quilted maple body, ebony fingerboard with hand cut swimming trout inlay of mother-of-pearl/abalone/copper/aluminum, mfg. 1996 only.

	N/A	N/A	N/A	N/A	N/A	N/A	N/A

Last MSR was $11,000.

This model comes with a Certificate of Authenticity signed by Stuart Spector, and a hardshell case.

NS 5 - similar to NS 4, except in 5-string configuration, 3/2-per-side tuners, EMG 40 DC pickup, disc. 1999.

	$3,000	$2,500	$2,100	$1,800	$1,500	$1,200	$950

Last MSR was $4,000.

> **Add $500 for high gloss finish (Model NS 5 HG).**

NS 5XL - similar to the NS 5, except has a 35 in. scale neck, and EMG-40-DC pickups, current mfg.

MSR	$5,299	$4,000	$3,400	$2,900	$2,500	$2,100	$1,700	$1,300

NS-6 - similar to NS 4, except in 6-string configuration, 3-per-side tuners, EMG 45 DC pickups, disc. 1999.

	$3,200	$2,700	$2,300	$1,900	$1,600	$1,300	$1,000

Last MSR was $4,200.

> **Add $500 for high gloss finish (Model NS 6 HG).**

NS 6XL - similar to the NS 6, except has a 35 in. scale neck, and EMG-40-DC pickups, current mfg.

MSR	$5,499	$4,250	$3,600	$3,100	$2,600	$2,200	$1,800	$1,400

NS 535 5-STRING - offset double cutaway figured maple body, through-body 3-piece maple neck, 24-fret pau ferro fingerboard with pearl crown inlays, 35 in. scale, solid fixed brass bridge, blackface peghead with pearl logo inlay, 3/2-per-side tuners, gold hardware, two EMG 40 DC soapbar pickups, volume/mix/stacked 2-band EQ controls, 18-volt active electronics, available in Natural Oil finish, mfg. 1998-99.

	N/A	N/A	N/A	N/A	N/A	N/A	N/A

REX 4USA - similar to the Rex 4, except made in USA and has a AAAA figured maple top, current mfg.

MSR	$4,999	$3,800	$3,200	$2,700	$2,300	$1,900	$1,600	$1,300

Rex 5USA - similar to the Rex 4USA, except in five-string configuration, current mfg.

MSR	$5,299	$4,000	$3,400	$2,900	$2,500	$2,100	$1,700	$1,300

GRADING	100% MINT	98% NEAR MINT	95% EXC+	90% EXC	80% VG+	70% VG	60% G

SPECIAL

Instruments previously built in Yugoslavia circa mid-1960s.

These entry level solid body guitars were built by the Muzicka Naklada company, which was based in Yugoslavia. The model 64 sports a vaguely Fender-ish body design and three single coils, as well as 5 knobs and 3 switches (source: Tony Bacon, *The Ultimate Guitar Book*).

SPIRAL

Instruments currently built in Van Nuys, CA. Distributed by Alfa Export Office, Inc. of Van Nuys, CA.

Spiral high quality electric guitars are crafted by the same people that build the Xotic custom basses and Trilogic pickups. Spiral's **SEG-Standard** features a two-piece ash or alder double cutaway body, bolt-on neck, 25.5" scale, maple or rosewood fingerboard, 4 Trilogic T/L pickups arranged as a 2 single coil/humbucker configuration, Wilkinson VS-100 G tremolo, master volume/high pass filter/low pass filter controls, coil tap mini-switch, and 5-way pickup selector (list $1,980). The **SEG-Pro** is similar to the SEG-Standard, except features a flame or quilted maple top over an ash body (list $2,480). Both models are available in Black, Seafoam Green, Red, and White solid finishes; or Black, Blue, Green, Red, White, Yellow, or Special Burst transparent colors.

SQUIER

Instruments currently produced in Mexico, Korea, and China. Distributed by the Fender Musical Instrument company of Scottsdale, AZ. Instruments first produced in Japan circa 1982; later production shifted to Korea in 1987 (to the Young Chang Akki factory).

In 1982, the Fender division of CBS established **Fender Japan** in conjunction with Kanda Shokai and Yamano music. Production of the Squier instruments, originally intended for European distribution, began in 1983 at the Fugi Gen Gakki facilities in Matsumoto, Japan. The Squier trademark was based on the V.C. Squier string-making company that produced strings for Fender in the 1950s, and was later acquired by Fender (under CBS) in 1965. What was intended as a European Commodity soon became a way for Fender to provide entry level instruments for students and beginning players.

The Squier trademark was introduced in 1983, and Squier II series was introduced circa 1986. In 1996, the Squier line was greatly expanded by Fender, with the introduction of various different series.

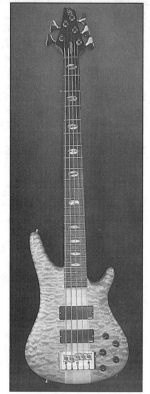

Spector SD Bass courtesy Spector

PRODUCTION MODEL CODES

Fender´s current Squier instruments are produced in Mexico, Korea and China. Fender products are identified by a part number that consists of a three digit location/facility code and a four digit model code (the two codes are separated by a hyphen). The second/third digit combination designates the production location: The first digit after the hyphen will indicate which country is the place of origin: For example, the model designated 033-0600 would be the Chinese-produced Affinity Series Strat. Squier instruments are directly based on Fender designs, and either carry a large Squier by Fender or Fender - Squier Series on the headstock.

ELECTRIC: MISC. MODELS

BULLET (NO. 031-0000) - beginner or student level Strat, maple neck, 21 frets, rosewood fingerboard with dot position markers, 3 single coil pickups, 6-on-a-side tuners, 25.5 in. scale, hard-tail bridge, available in Black, Baltic Blue, or Torino Red finishes, mfg. 2000-present.

MSR	$166		$100	$85	$70	$60	$50	$35	$25

Also available as the Bullet Special with a single humbucker pickup.

DUO-SONIC (NO. 033-0702) - hardwood body, maple neck, 22.7 in. scale, 20-fret fingerboard, fixed bridge, 2 single coil pickups, available in Black, Arctic White, or Torino Red, mfg. 1998-2000.

			$160	$140	$120	$100	$80	$60	$45

Last MSR was $229.

ESPRIT (NO. 034-3000) - similar double cutaway basswood body, body binding, set mahogany neck, 22-fret rosewood fingerboard with dot block inlay, 3-per-side tuners slightly offset, standard bridge, two Duncan Designed humbucker pickups, four knobs, three-way switch, chrome hardware, available in Antique Burst, Black, or Wine Satin finishes, new 2005.

MSR	$666		$400	$325	$275	$225	$175	$140	$110

JAGMASTER (NO. 027-1600) - offset double cutaway basswood body, bolt-on maple neck, 24 in. scale, 22-fret rosewood fingerboard with white dot inlay, 6-on-a-side tuners, vintage-style tremolo, chrome hardware, brown shell pickguard, 2 humbucker pickups, volume/tone controls, 3-way switch, available in 3-Tone Sunburst, Black, Candy Apple Red, Sonic Blue, or Vintage White finishes, disc. 2000.

			$350	$300	$275	$225	$175	$125	$75

Last MSR was $499.

M-80 BOLT-ON (NO. 034-4000) - offset double cutaway basswood body, bolt-on mahogany neck, 22-fret rosewood fingerboard with dot block inlay, 3-per-side tuners slightly offset, standard bridge, two Duncan Designed humbucker pickups, four knobs, three-way switch, chrome hardware, available in Black, Walnut Satin, or Wine Red Metallic finishes, new 2005.

MSR	$333		$200	$170	$145	$125	$100	$90	$75

Squier Bullet courtesy Fender

S

GRADING	100% MINT	98% NEAR MINT	95% EXC+	90% EXC	80% VG+	70% VG	60% G

M-80 SET-NECK (NO. 034-4100) - offset double cutaway basswood body, set mahogany neck, 22-fret rosewood fingerboard with dot block inlay, 3-per-side tuners slightly offset, standard bridge, two Duncan Designed humbucker pickups, four knobs, three-way switch, chrome hardware, available in Amber Satin, Black, or Crimson Red Trans. finishes, new 2005.

MSR	$666	$400	$325	$275	$225	$175	$140	$110

STANDARD CYCLONE (NO. 032-0500-5XX) - cyclone style smaller contoured body, single coil and humbucker pickups, vintage-style tremolo, bolt-on neck, 22-fret rosewood fingerboard with dot inlay, 6-on-one-side tuners, two knobs, 3-way switch, available in Black, Cobalt Blue Metallic, or Blue Metallic finishes, mfg. 2003-present.

MSR	$333	$200	$170	$145	$125	$100	$90	$75

STANDARD JAGMASTER (NO. 032-0700) - similar to Jagmaster, except has solid alder body, available in Candy Apple Red, Silver Sparkle, 3-Tone Sunburst, Black, or Montego Black finishes, mfg. 2000-present.

MSR	$416	$250	$215	$175	$150	$125	$100	$75

This model was redesigned for 2004.

SQUIER '51 (NO. 032-5100) - Stratocaster body crossed with Telecaster designs, early P-Bass style pickguard, Angled Strat and Humbucker pickup, 2 knobs on metal plate, Telecaster-style headstock, available in 2-Color Sunburst, Vintage Blonde, or Black finishes, new 2004.

MSR	$249	$150	$130	$110	$95	$75	$60	$40

SUPER-SONIC (NO. 027-1500) - rounded double cutaway alder body, bolt-on maple neck, 24 in. scale, reverse headstock, 22-fret rosewood fingerboard with white dot inlay, 6-on-the-other-side tuners, vintage-style tremolo, chrome hardware, 3-ply white/metal pickguard, 2 humbucker pickups, volume/tone controls, 3-way switch, available in Black or Olympic White finishes, disc. 2000.

	$350	$300	$275	$225	$175	$125	$75

Last MSR was $499.

Add $75 for Blue Sparkle or Silver Sparkle finishes.

VENUS (NO. 027-1700) - double cutaway basswood body with rounded lower bout, bolt-on maple neck, 25.5 in. scale, 22-fret bound rosewood fingerboard with white dot inlay, 6-on-a-side tuners, tune-o-matic bridge/strings through-body ferrules, chrome hardware, white shell pickguard, single coil/humbucker pickups, volume control, 3-way switch, available in 3-Tone Sunburst, Black, or Surf Green finishes with matching headstock, disc. 2000.

	$350	$300	$275	$225	$175	$125	$75

Last MSR was $499.

Venus XII (Model 027-1800) - similar to Venus, except features 12-string configuration, 6-per-side tuners, 2 Seymour Duncan split single coil pickups, volume/tone controls. Disc. 2000.

	$625	$575	$525	$475	$400	$325	$225

Last MSR was $799.

ELECTRIC: BULLET SERIES

Squier Bullet guitars and basses were produced in Japan between 1983 and 1988. Bullets have a telecaster-style headstock with a Squier by Fender - Bullet/star with a "1" in the center logo. Retail list prices in the early 1980s ranged between $279 and $419. The average used price today ranges from $125 up to $175.

ELECTRIC: SERIES 24 SERIES

The Series 24 guitars aren´t based on some of Gibson´s popular models, but they do have a similarity to them.

M-50 (NO. 034-5000) - single cutaway agathis body, bolt-on nato neck, 22-fret rosewood fingerboard with dot inlay, 3-per-side tuners, 2 humbucker pickups, pickguard, ABAT bridge, four knobs, 3-way switch, chrome hardware, available in Black or Crimson Red finishes, mfg. 2002-04.

	$185	$155	$130	$110	$90	$70	$50

Last MSR was $309.

M-70 (NO. 034-7000) - similar to the M-50, except has a set mahogany neck, and two Duncan Design humbucker pickups, available in Moon Blue or Black finishes, mfg. 2002-04.

	$415	$350	$310	$275	$225	$175	$125

Last MSR was $690.

M-77 (NO. 034-7700) - similar to the M-70, except has a carved maple top, available in Cherry Sunburst, Wine Red Metallic, or Black finishes, mfg. 2002-04.

	$495	$410	$350	$300	$250	$200	$150

Last MSR was $818.

S-65 (NO. 034-6500) - double sharp SG-ish cutaway agathis body, bolt-on nato neck, 22-fret rosewood fingerboard with dot inlay, 3-per-side tuners, two humbucker pickups, ABAT bridge, four knobs, 3-way switch, chrome hardware, available in Black or Crimson Red finishes, mfg. 2002-03.

	$185	$155	$130	$110	$90	$70	$50

Last MSR was $309.

S-73 (NO. 034-7300) - similar to the S-65, except has a set-mahogany neck, block inlays, and 2 Duncan Designed humbucker pickups, available in Black or Wine Red Metallic finishes, mfg. 2002-03.

	$440	$365	$325	$275	$225	$175	$125

Last MSR was $727.

STARFIRE (NO. 034-2000) - double cutaway semi-hollow 335-ish maple body, arched maple top, set maple neck, 22-fret rosewood fingerboard with dot inlay, 2 Duncan Designed humbucker pickups, four knobs, 3-way switch, chrome hardware, available in Natural or Crimson Red Trans. finishes, mfg. 2002-04.

	$599	$525	$450	$375	$325	$275	$225

Last MSR was $999.

GRADING	100% MINT	98% NEAR MINT	95% EXC+	90% EXC	80% VG+	70% VG	60% G

X-155 (NO. 034-2000) - single cutaway hollow 175-ish jazz maple body, arched maple top, set maple neck, 22-fret rosewood fingerboard with block inlay, 2 Duncan Designed humbucker pickups, pickguard, four knobs, 3-way switch, chrome hardware, available in White Heat (Cobalt Blue with white flames), Natural, or Tobacco Sunburst finishes, mfg. 2002-present.

MSR	$830	$500	$425	$350	$300	$250	$200	$150

ELECTRIC: SHOWMASTER SERIES

SHOWMASTER HH SKULL & CROSSBONES (NO. 132-3300) - offset sharp double cutaway basswood body, bolt-on maple neck, 24-fret rosewood fingerboard with dot inlays, reversed headstock, 1 single coil & 1 Duncan Design humbucker pickups, Floyd Rose tremolo, two knobs, 5-way switch, available in Black finish with skull and crossbone graphic, mfg. 2003-present.

MSR	$500	$300	$250	$210	$180	$150	$120	$95

SHOWMASTER JASON ELLIS SIGNATURE (NO. 132-3000) - offset sharp double cutaway basswood body, bolt-on maple neck, 24-fret rosewood fingerboard with skull and crossbone inlays, reversed headstock, 2 humbucker pickups, Floyd Rose tremolo, two knobs, 5-way switch, available in Black Metallic or Red Metallic finishes with graphic, mfg. 2002-present.

MSR	$449	$270	$225	$200	$170	$140	$110	$90

SHOWMASTER RALLY STRIPE (032-3600) - offset sharp double cutaway agathis body, bolt-on maple neck, 24-fret rosewood fingerboard with dot inlays, 3-per-side tuners, 2 humbucker pickups, hardtail bridge, two knobs, 3-way switch, available in Black with red stripe or Silver with black stripe, mfg. 2003-present.

MSR	$449	$270	$225	$200	$170	$140	$110	$90

ELECTRIC: STAGEMASTER SERIES

Squier Standard Jagmaster
courtesy Fender

STAGEMASTER SUB-SONIC DELUXE (NO. 032-4805) - offset double cutaway solid basswood body, maple neck-through-body with reverse "small" Strat headstock,6-on-a-side tuners, rosewood fingerboard, 27 in. scale, 24 frets, master volume and tone, 2 exposed coil humbucker pickups, available in Metallic Black, mfg. 2001-02.

	$420	$350	$300	$250	$200	$150	$100

Last MSR was $699.

STAGEMASTER DELUXE HH (NO. 132-4800) - offset double cutaway solid basswood body, maple neck-through-body with "small" reverse Strat headstock, rosewood fingerboard, 24 frets, 6-on-a-side tuners, Floyd Rose licensed double locking tremolo, master volume and tone, 2 humbucker pickups, available in Shoreline Gold Metallic, Atlantic Blue Metallic, or Wine Red Metallic finishes, disc. 2002.

	$360	$300	$250	$210	$180	$150	$130

Last MSR was $599.

Stagemaster Deluxe HSH (No. 132-4900) - similar to Stagemaster Deluxe HH, except has 2 humbucker pickups and 1 single coil pickup in the middle position, available in Pewter Gray Metallic, Black Metallic, or Emerald Green Metallic finishes, disc. 2002.

	$360	$300	$250	$210	$180	$150	$130

Last MSR was $599.

STAGEMASTER HSS (NO. 132-3700) - offset double cutaway solid alder body, maple neck with rosewood fingerboard, 24 medium-jumbo frets, 6-on-a-side tuners, 2 single coil pickups and 1 humbucker pickup in the bridge position, available in Black Metallic, Cobalt Blue Metallic, or Purple Metallic finishes, disc. 2002.

	$270	$225	$190	$160	$130	$105	$75

Last MSR was $449.

Stagemaster HSS NLT (No. 032-2700) - similar to Stagemaster HSS, except has Floyd Rose licensed non-locking twin pivot tremolo, available in Black Metallic, Cobalt Blue Metallic, or Purple Metallic finishes, mfg. 2001-02.

	$210	$175	$150	$130	$110	$90	$65

Last MSR was $349.

Stagemaster HH (No. 132-3800) - similar to Stagemaster HSS, except has 2 humbucker pickups. Available in Black Metallic, Cobalt Blue Metallic and Purple Metallic finishes, disc. 2002.

	$270	$225	$190	$160	$130	$105	$75

Last MSR was $449.

Stagemaster HSH (No. 132-3900) - similar to Stagemaster HH, except has 2 humbucker pickups and 1 single coil pickup in the middle position, available in Black Metallic, Cobalt Blue Metallic, or Purple Metallic finishes, disc. 2002.

	$270	$225	$190	$160	$130	$105	$75

Last MSR was $449.

STAGEMASTER 7 FR (NO. 132-3807) - similar to Stagemaster HH, except in a 7-string configuration, 2 high-output humbucker pickups, Floyd Rose licensed tremolo, available in Black Metallic, Cobalt Blue Metallic, or Purple Metallic finishes, disc. 2002.

	$330	$275	$250	$225	$195	$150	$105

Last MSR was $549.

Squier Showmaster
Jason Ellis Signature
courtesy Fender

S

GRADING	100% MINT	98% NEAR MINT	95% EXC+	90% EXC	80% VG+	70% VG	60% G

Stagemaster 7 HT (Model 032-3837) - similar to Stagemaster 7 FR, except has a "Hard-Tail" bridge, available in Black Metallic, Cobalt Blue Metallic, or Purple Metallic finishes, disc. 2002.

	$270	$225	$190	$160	$130	$105	$75

Last MSR was $449.

ELECTRIC: STRATOCASTER SERIES

The following models are based on Fender´s Stratocaster design, and all have an offset double cutaway body, bolt-on maple neck, 6-on-a-side tuners, chrome hardware, 3 single coil pickups, volume/2 tone controls, and 5-way selector (unless otherwise listed).

AFFINITY STRAT (NO. 033-0600/031-0600) - offset double cutaway hardwood body, 22-fret rosewood fingerboard with white dot inlay, tremolo, chrome hardware, white pickguard, 3 single coil pickups, volume/2 tone controls, 5-way selector, available in 2-Tone Sunburst, Metallic Red, Metallic Blue, Baltic Blue, Arctic White, Black, Aztec Gold, or Torino Red finishes, current mfg.

MSR	$249		$150	$130	$110	$95	$75	$60	$40

In 2001, British Racing Green, Baltic Blue and Galactic Purple finishes were introduced. In 2003, Aztec Gold was introduced. In 2004, 2-Tone Sunburst, Metallic Red, and Metallic Blue were introduced.

AFFINITY FAT STRAT (NO. 031-0700) - similar to Affinity Strat, except has a humbucker pickup in the bridge position, available in Metallic Red, Metallic Blue, Monego Black, Black, Arctic White, British Racing Green, Torino Red, or Baltic Blue finishes, mfg. 2001-present.

MSR	$249		$150	$130	$110	$95	$75	$55	$40

PRO TONE STRATOCASTER (NO. 033-2900) - ash body, 21-fret rosewood fingerboard with white dot inlay, gold hardware, white shell pickguard, vintage style tremolo, available in Crimson Red Trans. or Sapphire Blue Trans. finishes, disc. 1998.

	$375	$325	$275	$250	$200	$175	$125

Last MSR was $529.

This model is also available with a maple fingerboard with black dot inlay (Model 033-2902).

Pro Tone Stratocaster (Model 033-2600) - ash body, 21-fret rosewood fingerboard with white dot inlay, chrome hardware, red shell pickguard, available in Olympic White w/ matching headstock, disc. 1998.

	$350	$300	$275	$225	$195	$150	$125

Last MSR was $499.

Pro Tone Stratocaster (Model 033-2700) - ash body, 21-fret rosewood fingerboard with white dot inlay, chrome hardware, white shell pickguard, available in 3-Tone Sunburst finish, disc. 1998.

	$350	$300	$275	$225	$195	$150	$125

Last MSR was $499.

Pro Tone Stratocaster (Model 033-2802) - ash body, 21-fret maple fingerboard with black dot inlay, chrome hardware, aged pickup covers/control knobs, white pickguard, available in Vintage Blonde finish, disc. 1998.

	$350	$300	$275	$225	$195	$150	$125

Last MSR was $499.

This model is also available in left-handed configuration (Model 033-2822).

Pro Tone Fat Strat (Model 133-3102) - ash body, 22-fret maple fingerboard with black dot inlay, gold hardware, black shell pickguard, licensed Floyd Rose tremolo, 2 single coil/humbucker pickups, volume/tone controls, available in Black finish, disc. 1998.

	$450	$375	$350	$295	$250	$200	$150

Last MSR was $639.

STANDARD STRATOCASTER (NO. 033-1600) - alder body, 21-fret rosewood fingerboard with black dot inlay, chrome hardware, vintage-style tremolo, 3-ply white pickguard, available in Arctic White, Black, Brown Sunburst, Midnight Blue, or Midnight Wine finishes, disc. 1998.

	$200	$170	$145	$125	$100	$90	$75

Last MSR was $289.

This model is available with a maple fingerboard with white dot inlay (Model 033-1602). This model is available in a left-handed configuration (Model 033-1620) in Black and Brown Sunburst finishes.

Standard Fat Stratocaster (No. 033-1702) - similar to the Standard Stratocaster, except has 2 single coil/humbucker pickups. Available in Midnight Blue and Midnight Wine finishes, disc. 1998.

	$215	$175	$150	$135	$115	$100	$75

Last MSR was $299.

STANDARD STRATOCASTER 1998-2000 MFG. (NO. 013-2102) - poplar body, 21-fret maple fingerboard with black dot inlay, chrome hardware, vintage-style tremolo, 3-ply white pickguard, available in Arctic White, Black, Brown Sunburst, Lake Placid Blue, or Crimson Red Metallic finishes, mfg. 1998-2000.

	$225	$195	$165	$135	$115	$95	$75

Last MSR was $329.

Add $30 for a left-handed configuration (Model 013-2120) in Black, Arctic White, Brown Sunburst, Crimson Red Metallic, and Lake Placid Blue finishes.

This model is available with a rosewood fingerboard with white dot inlay (Model 013-2100).

Standard Fat Stratocaster (Model 013-2202) - similar to the Standard Stratocaster, except has 2 single coil/humbucker pickups, available in Arctic White, Black, Brown Sunburst, Lake Placid Blue, or Crimson Red Metallic finishes, mfg. 1998-2000.

	$235	$200	$175	$150	$125	$100	$85

Last MSR was $339.

Add $120 for Floyd Rose II tremolo (Model 113-2202) in Black, Arctic White, Brown Sunburst, Crimson Red Metallic, and Lake Placid Blue finishes. The Standard Fat Strat With Floyd Rose is available with a rosewood fingerboard (Model 113-2200).

S

GRADING	100% MINT	98% NEAR MINT	95% EXC+	90% EXC	80% VG+	70% VG	60% G

STANDARD STRATOCASTER 2001-CURRENT MFG. (NO. 032-1600)
- similar to Standard Stratocaster (Model 013-3102), except hassolid agathis body, maple neck, 22-fret rosewood fingerboard, large headstock, die-cast tuners, twin pivot bridge with satin-anodized saddles, 3 Alnico single coil pickups, available in Black & Chrome (Gloss Black with mirrored pickguard), 3-Color Sunburst, Sherwood Green Metallic, Candy Apple Red, Black Metallic, Shoreline Gold, Cherry Sunburst, Antique Burst, Satin Pewter Metallic, Walnut Satin, or Purple Metallic finishes, mfg. 2001-present.

	MSR	$333		$200	$170	$145	$125	$100	$90	$75

Add $20 for 3-Color Sunburst finish.

Also available with maple fingerboard (Model 032-1602). In 2004, Black & Chrome were introduced.

Standard Stratocaster Left-Hand (No. 032-1620)
- similar to the Standard Stratocaster, except in left-hand configuration, available in 3-Color Sunburst, Antique Burst, or Metallic Black finishes, current mfg.

MSR	$383		$230	$175	$150	$125	$100	$90	$75

STANDARD FAT STRATOCASTER (NO. 032-1700)
- similar to Standard Fat Stratocaster (Model 013-2202), except has solid agathis body, high-output humbucker in the bridge position, 22-frets, large headstock, black pickguard and knobs, black tremolo tip and pickup covers, available in 3-Color Sunburst, Shoreline Gold, Black Metallic, Candy Apple Red, Sherwood Green Metallic, Satin Pewter Metallic, Walnut Satin, or Purple Metallic finishes, mfg. 2001-present.

MSR	$333		$200	$170	$140	$120	$105	$90	$75

Standard Fat Strat 7 (No. 032-1807)
- similar to Standard Fat Stratocaster, except in a seven string configuration, available in 3-Color Sunburst, Black Metallic, Sherwood Green Metallic, Candy Apple Red, Purple Metallic and Shoreline Gold finishes, mfg. 2001-02.

		$270	$225	$190	$160	$130	$105	$75

Last MSR was $449.

Squier Affinity Fat Strat courtesy Squier/Fender

DOUBLE FAT STRATOCASTER (NO. 032-1800)
- similar to Standard Fat Stratocaster, except has 2 humbucker pickups, available in Sherwood Gold, Candy Apple Red, Sherwood Green Metallic, Purple Metallic, 3-Color Sunburst, Satin Pewter Metallic, Walnut Satin, or Black Metallic finishes, mfg. 2001-present.

MSR	$333		$200	$170	$130	$115	$100	$85	$75

Standard Double Fat Strat 7HT (Model 032-1837)
- similar to Double Fat Stratocaster, except has Hard-Tail bridge, available in 3-Color Sunburst, Black Metallic, or Purple Metallic finishes, mfg. 2001-present.

		$270	$225	$190	$160	$130	$105	$75

Last MSR was $449.

DELUXE STRATOCASTER (NO. 032-1660)
- similar to the Standard Stratocaster, except has a flame (3-Tone Sunburst) or quilt maple (Antique Burst) top, mfg. 2004-present.

MSR	$416		$250	$215	$175	$150	$125	$100	$75

TOM DELONGE STRAT
- Stratocaster alder body 21-fret rosewood fingerboard, single Duncan Design Detonator humbucker pickup, hardtail bridge, engraved neckplate with Tom Delonge's name, available in Surf Green, Black, or Polar White finishes, mfg. 2001-03.

		$180	$150	$130	$110	$90	$70	$50

Last MSR was $300.

ELECTRIC: TELECASTER SERIES

The following models are based on Fender's Telecaster, and all have an single cutaway body, bolt-on maple neck, 6-on-a-side tuners, 2 single coil pickups, tele-style bridge, volume/tone controls, contols mounted on a metal plate, and 3-way selector (unless otherwise listed).

AFFINITY TELE (NO. 031-0202)
- similar to Affinity Tele (Model 033-0200), except has solid alder body, new die-cast tuners, available in Butterscotch Blonde, Metallic Red, Metallic Blue, Black, Baltic Blue, Torino Red, or Arctic White finishes, mfg. 2000-present.

MSR	$283		$170	$150	$135	$115	$95	$75	$55

CHAMBERED TELE (NO. 034-0200)
- similar to the Telecaster, except has a chambered body with two Duncan Designed humbucker pickups and narrow block inlays, available in Black, Ebony Satin, Walnut Satin, or Wine Satin, new 2005.

MSR	$666		$400	$325	$275	$225	$175	$140	$110

PRO TONE FAT TELE (NO. 033-3700)
- ash body, 21-fret rosewood fingerboard with white dot inlay, chrome hardware, red shell pickguard, humbucker/single coil pickups, available in Natural finish, disc. 1998.

		$350	$300	$275	$225	$195	$150	$125

Last MSR was $499.

PRO TONE THINLINE TELE (NO. 033-3802)
- semi-hollow bound ash body, f-hole, 21-fret maple fingerboard with black dot inlay, gold hardware, white shell pickguard, available in Crimson Red Trans. finish, disc. 1998.

		$400	$350	$300	$275	$225	$195	$150

Last MSR was $579.

STANDARD TELECASTER (NO. 033-1202)
- alder body, 21-fret maple fingerboard with black dot inlay, chrome hardware, 3-ply white pickguard, 2 single coil pickups, available in Black, Blond, Brown Sunburst, or Midnight Wine finishes, disc. 1998.

		$200	$175	$150	$135	$115	$95	$75

Last MSR was $289.

Squier Double Fat Stratocaster courtesy Squier/Fender

S

GRADING	100% MINT	98% NEAR MINT	95% EXC+	90% EXC	80% VG+	70% VG	60% G

STANDARD TELECASTER 1998-2000 MFG. (NO. 013-2302) - poplar body, 21-fret maple fingerboard with black dot inlay, chrome hardware, 3-ply white pickguard, 2 single coil pickups, available in Black, Arctic White, Brown Sunburst, Lake Placid Blue, or Crimson Red Metallic finishes, mfg. 1998-2000.

	$235	$195	$175	$150	$125	$95	$75

Last MSR was $339.

STANDARD TELECASTER 2001-CURRENT MFG. (NO. 032-1200) - similar to Standard Telecaster (Model 032-2302), except has solid agathis body, 2 single coil Alnico pickups, available in Black & Chrome (Black body with mirrored pickguard), 3-Color Sunburst, Sherwood Green Metallic, Vintage Blonde, Black Metallic, Candy Apple Red, Antique Burst, Walnut Satin, or Purple Metallic finishes, mfg. 2001-current

MSR	$333	$200	$170	$145	$125	$105	$90	$75

Add $20 for 3-Color Sunburst and Vintage Blonde finishes.

Also available as a Special version with no pickguard (No. 032-1400).

STANDARD FAT TELECASTER (NO. 032-1300) - similar to Standard Telecaster (Model 013-2302), except has 1 humbucker pickup in the neck position and 1 single coil Alnico pickup, available in 3-Color Sunburst, Shoreline Gold, Sherwood Green Metallic, Vintage Blonde, Black Metallic, Antique Burst, or Candy Apple Red finishes, mfg. 2000-present.

MSR	$333	$200	$170	$140	$120	$100	$90	$75

Add $20 for 3-Color Sunburst and Vintage Blonde finishes.

Double Fat Tele Deluxe - similar to Standard Fat Telecaster, except has solid mahogany carved top body, mahogany set neck, 2 humbucker pickups, available in Black Metallic, Atlantic Blue Metallic and Frost Red Metallic finishes, disc 2001.

	$330	$275	$250	$225	$195	$150	$105

Last MSR was $549.

TELE (NO. 033-0200) - hardwood body, maple neck, 21-fret rosewood fingerboard, 2 single coil pickups, available in Black, Arctic White, or Torino Red, mfg. 1998-2000.

	$180	$160	$140	$120	$100	$80	$60

Last MSR was $259.

TELE CUSTOM (NO. 032-7502) - similar to the Telecaster Standard, except has a neck humbucker pickup, a hybrid of the '72 Tele Custom and Tele Deluxe, available in Black finish, mfg. 2004-present.

MSR	$333	$200	$170	$145	$125	$105	$90	$75

Add $25 for two humbucker pickups (Tele Custom II).

THINLINE TELE (NO. 034-0100) - alder bound semi-hollow body, set maple neck, two Duncan Designed humbucker pickups and narrow block inlays, available in Black, Crimson Trans., or Natural finishes, new 2005.

MSR	$600	$360	$290	$250	$210	$170	$140	$110

ELECTRIC BASS: MISC MODELS

BRONCO BASS (NO. 031-0902/033-0902) - hardwood body, maple neck, 30 in. scale, 19-fret maple fingerboard, single coil pickup, available in Black, Arctic White, or Torino Red, mfg. 1998-present.

MSR	$249	$150	$125	$110	$100	$90	$75	$50

In 2000, Arctic White finish was disc.

MB-4 MODERN BASS (NO. 032-8000) - offset double cutaway agathis modern style body, thin easy access neck, 22-fret rosewood fingerboard with dot inlay, PJ pickups, three knobs, 2-per-side tuners, available in Black Metallic, Black Cherry Burst, Cobalt Blue Metallic, or Pewter Grey Metallic, mfg. 2002-present.

MSR	$300	$180	$150	$135	$120	$100	$85	$65

In 2005, Black Cherry Burst was introduced.

MB-4 Skulls & Crossbones (No. 032-8001) - similar to the MB-4, except has Skull & Crossbone inlays and graphics, available in Black Metallic, mfg. 2003-present.

MSR	$333	$200	$170	$145	$125	$100	$90	$75

MB-5 MODERN BASS (NO. 032-8005) - similar to the MB-4, except in five-stirng configuration, 3/2-per-side tuners, and J-J pickups, mfg. 2002-present.

MSR	$383	$230	$180	$150	$130	$110	$90	$75

MUSICMASTER BASS (NO. 033-0300) - sleek double cutaway alder body, 30 in. scale, 18 fret rosewood fingerboard with white dot inlay, chrome hardware, fixed bridge, white pickguard, Vista-Tone single coil pickup, volume/tone controls, available in Arctic White, Black, Shell Pink, or Sonic Blue finish with matching headstock, disc. 2000.

	$280	$240	$215	$185	$160	$130	$100

Last MSR was $399.

ELECTRIC BASS: JAZZ BASS SERIES

STANDARD JAZZ BASS (NO. 033-1500) - sleek offset double cutaway alder body, bolt-on maple neck, 20-fret rosewood fingerboard with white dot inlay, fixed bridge, chrome hardware, white/metal pickguard, 2 single coil pickups, 2 volume/tone controls, available in Black, Brown Sunburst, or Midnight Wine finishes, disc. 1998.

	$225	$195	$175	$150	$125	$100	$75

Last MSR was $309.

S

GRADING	100% MINT	98% NEAR MINT	95% EXC+	90% EXC	80% VG+	70% VG	60% G

STANDARD JAZZ BASS (NO. 013-2500) - sleek offset double cutaway poplar body, bolt-on maple neck, 20-fret rosewood fingerboard with white dot inlay, fixed bridge, chrome hardware, white/metal pickguard, 2 single coil pickups, 2 volume/tone controls, available in Black, Brown Sunburst, Arctic White, Crimson Red Metallic, and Lake placid Blue finishes, disc. 2000.

		$250	$195	$175	$150	$125	$100	$75

Last MSR was $349.

STANDARD JAZZ BASS (NO. 032-6500) - similar to Standard Jazz Bass (old), except has solid agathis body, available in 3-Color Sunburst, Candy Apple Red, Shoreline Gold, Sherwood Green Metallic, Black Metallic, or Purple Metallic finishes, mfg. 2001-present.

MSR	$383	$230	$180	$150	$130	$110	$90	$75

AFFINITY J BASS (NO. 031-0760) - similar to the J Bass, except has 2 single coil pickups, available in Metallic Red, Metallic Blue, or Black finishes, mfg. 2004-present.

MSR	$300	$180	$150	$130	$110	$90	$70	$50

ELECTRIC BASS: PRECISION BASS SERIES

The following models are based on Fender´s Precision Bass, and all have an offset double cutaway body, bolt-on maple neck, 34 in. scale, 4-on-a-side tuners, split single coil pickup, volume/tone controls, unless otherwise listed.

AFFINITY P-BASS (NO. 031-0400/033-0400) - offset double cutaway hardwood body, 21-fret rosewood fingerboard with white dot inlay, fixed bridge, chrome hardware, white pickguard, 1 P-style split pickup, volume/tone controls, available in Arctic White, Black, or Torino Red finishes, current mfg.

MSR	$300	$180	$150	$130	$110	$90	$70	$50

In 2001, Baltic Blue finish was introduced.

P-BASS SPECIAL (NO. 033-0500) - similar to the P-Bass, except features P/J-style pickups, available in Black, Arctic White, and Torino Red, mfg. 1998-2000.

		$195	$175	$155	$135	$120	$100	$75

Last MSR was $279.

STANDARD P-BASS SPECIAL (NO. 032-1500) - similar to P-Bass Special, except has, solid Agathis body, Jazz Bass neck, 20-frets, standard hardware, available in 3-Color Sunburst, Sherwood Green Metallic, Candy Apple Red, Black Metallic, Shoreline Gold, or Purple Metallic finishes, current mfg.

MSR	$383	$230	$180	$150	$130	$110	$90	$75

Add $30 for left-hand model (Model 032-1520).

Standard P-Bass Special 5 (No. 032-1505) - similar to the Standard P-Bass Special, except in five-string configuration and 3/2-per-side tuners, current mfg.

MSR	$416	$250	$215	$185	$155	$130	$110	$90

PRO TONE P J BASS (NO. 033-5000) - ash body, 20-fret rosewood fingerboard with white dot inlay, chrome hardware, fixed bridge, red shell pickguard, P/J-style Alnico pickups, 2 volume/tone controls, available in Black finish with matching headstock, disc. 1998.

		$375	$350	$300	$275	$225	$175	$125

Last MSR was $539.

PRO TONE PRECISION BASS FIVE (NO. 033-3802) - ash body, 5-string configuration, 20-fret rosewood fingerboard with white dot inlay, 5-on-a-side tuners, gold hardware, fixed bridge, white shell pickguard, 2 "soapbar" pickups, 2 volume/tone controls, available in Crimson Red Trans. finish, disc. 1998.

		$475	$400	$375	$325	$275	$225	$175

Last MSR was $679.

STANDARD PRECISION BASS (NO. 033-1400) - alder body, 20-fret rosewood fingerboard with white dot inlay, fixed bridge, chrome hardware, white pickguard, P-style pickup, volume/tone controls, available in Black, Brown Sunburst, or Midnight Wine finishes, disc. 1998.

		$200	$175	$150	$135	$125	$100	$75

Last MSR was $299.

This model is available in a left-handed configuration (Model 033-1420) in Brown Sunburst finish.

STANDARD PRECISION BASS (NO. 013-2400) - poplar body, 20-fret rosewood fingerboard with white dot inlay, fixed bridge, chrome hardware, white pickguard, P-style pickup, volume/tone controls, available in Black, Arctic white, Brown Sunburst, Lake Placid Blue, or Crimson Red Metallic finishes, disc. 2000.

		$250	$195	$175	$150	$125	$100	$75

Last MSR was $339.

STACCATO

Instruments previously built in London, England from the early 1980s to around 1986.

In the late 1970s, painter/sculptor/guitarist Pat Townsend designed Staccato Drums, asymmetrical shaped drums that flared out from the heads. In 1982, he devised a modular guitar with a fiberglass/polyurethane foam body and magnesium alloy neck section. The necks are interchangeable on the body. Last given company address for Townsend was: Pat Townsend, 100 Kingsgate Road, London, England (NW6).

Squier Standard Fat Telecaster courtesy Squier/Fender

Squier P-Bass Special courtesy Squier/Fender

S

ELECTRIC

These high quality guitars featured neck platform of magnesium alloy, which has the pickups and hardware; while the wood or fiberglass solid body has the electronics and controls. Both the bridge (fixed or tremolo) and the nut are magnesium alloy. Neck choices for guitar were 6- or 12-string configuration; basses were available with 4- or 8-string configurations, fretted or fretless. In the early 1980s the Staccato list price was around $1,800 (models were still handmade). It is estimated that only 50 completed instruments were produced.

STADIUM

Also Bass Centre Stadium. See Grendel.

STAGG

Instruments previously built in Japan during the mid-1970s.

The Stagg trademark is a brand name of a UK importer. Stagg instruments were entry level to low quality solid body guitars that featured designs based on popular American classics (source: Tony Bacon and Paul Day, *The Guru's Guitar Guide*).

STAGG (CURRENT MFG.)

Instruments currently produced.

Stagg produces a wide variety of acoustic, electric, and bass guitars. They also produce guitar amplifiers and accessories for all of these. Refer to their website for more information (see Trademark Index).

STANDEL

Instruments previously produced in Newark, NJ during the late 1960s. Distributed by Standel of Temple City, CA.

The Standel company was founded by Bob Crooks (an electronics engineer) in the early 1960s, and rose to some prominence in the mid 1960s because of their solid-state amplifiers. The Standel name was derived from Crooks' previous radio repair business, Standard Electronics.

After learning electronics from correspondence courses, Crooks began working for Lockheed, and was promoted to engineer in charge of their Electronics Standards Lab. In his spare time, Crooks repaired radios in his garage. He was introduced to Paul Bigsby in the early 1950s, who was looking for someone to build amplifiers. Crooks began experimenting with semi-conductors in 1961, and two years later had developed a high power solid state amp. While the company did well during the 1960s, faulty parts and component failures in 1970 led to erosion of the Standel quality reputation. Crooks later sold the company to CMI in Chicago, and worked for them for two years (source: Willie Moseley, *Vintage Guitar Magazine*).

Crooks later worked at Barcus Berry, and furthered his investigations into tube and transistor amplifiers. Crooks devised a invention that compensated for speaker errors by modifying the signal going into the amplifier. Crooks named the unit the Sonic Maximizer, and it is still being produced by the BBE Sound Corporation of Long Beach, California. See the *Blue Book of Guitar Amplifiers* for more information on Standel Amps.

ELECTRIC

In the early 1960s, Bob Crooks asked Semie Moseley (Mosrite) to design a Fender-style solid body guitar for the Standel product line. Moseley's quick response was to flip over a Fender and trace the body outline! Moseley only built about 20 guitars for Crooks, but his *flipped over* original design became the foundation for the **Mosrite Ventures** model.

In 1966 or 1967, Crooks was contacted by the Harptone company of New Jersey with an offer to build guitars for Standel. Harptone hired luthier Stan Koontz to design a number of acoustic and electric guitars and basses for the Standel company. The instruments were built in Harptone's New Jersey facilities, and have the Standel logo on the peghead. Their production began gearing up right as Crooks began having problems with his amplifiers. According to interviews with Koontz, only a few hundred of Standel instruments were produced.

STAR

See Guyatone. Instruments previously produced in Japan during the early to mid-1960s.

While the Star trademark has been reported as a brand name used by an English importer, the trademark also appeared in the U.S. market distributed by Hoshino Gakki Ten (later Hoshino USA, distributor of Ibanez). No matter how you slice the bread, the loaf comes from the same oven. While the quality of these entry level solid body guitars was okay at best, they at least sported original designs. It is believed that Guyatone (Tokyo Sound Company) built the Star instruments.

Classic American guitar designs may have been an influence on the early Japanese models, but the influence was incorporated into original designs. The era of copying designs and details began in the early 1970s, but was not the basis for Japanese guitar production. As the entry level models began to get better in quality with meticulous attention to detail, then the American market began to take notice.

STARFIELD

Instruments previously produced in Japan and America. Distributed by Starfield America, located in North Hollywood, CA.

These higher end guitars were a side project of the Hoshino company, although no brochures directly linked Starfield to Hoshino/Ibanez. Starfield is no longer offered in the U.S. market (Hoshino continued to offer these quality instruments to other markets around the world).

ELECTRIC: AMERICAN SERIES

AMERICAN CLASSIC - offset double cutaway alder body, white pickguard, bolt on maple neck, 22-fret maple fingerboard with offset black dot inlay, standard Wilkinson vibrato, 3-per-side locking Magnum tuners, chrome hardware, 3 stacked coil Seymour Duncan pickups, volume/tone control, 5-position switch, available in Pearl White, Pewter, Popsicle, Sail Blue, or Tangerine finishes, disc. 1994.

N/A	$700	$600	$500	$400	$350	$300

Last MSR was $1,000.

Ebony fingerboard with offset pearl dot inlay was optional.

GRADING	100% MINT	98% NEAR MINT	95% EXC+	90% EXC	80% VG+	70% VG	60% G

AMERICAN CUSTOM - similar to American Classic, except has mahogany body, flame maple top, no pickguard, gold hardware, 2 humbucker Seymour Duncan pickups, available in Tobacco Sunburst, Trans. Cherry, Trans. Green, or Trans. Grey finishes, disc. 1994.

	N/A	$910	$780	$650	$525	$450	$375

Last MSR was $1,300.

AMERICAN SPECIAL - single sharp cutaway asymmetrical mahogany body, carved flame maple top, bolt-on maple neck, 22-fret maple fingerboard with offset black dot inlay, fixed Wilkinson bridge, 3-per-side tuners, chrome hardware, 2 humbucker Seymour Duncan pickups, volume/tone control, 5-position switch, available in Tobacco Sunburst, Trans. Cherry, Trans. Green, or Trans. Grey finishes, disc. 1994.

	N/A	$875	$750	$625	$500	$450	$375

Last MSR was $1,250.

Ebony fingerboard with offset pearl dot inlay was optional.

AMERICAN STANDARD - similar to American Special, except has alder body, standard Wilkinson vibrato, locking Magnum tuners, 3 stacked coil Seymour Duncan pickups, available in Pearl White, Pewter, Popsicle, Sail Blue, or Tangerine finishes, disc. 1994.

	N/A	$675	$575	$475	$375	$325	$275

Last MSR was $950.

AMERICAN TRAD - similar to American Classic, except has mahogany body, black pickguard, fixed bridge, 2 humbucker Seymour Duncan pickups, available in Trans. Cream, Trans. Green, Trans. Grey, Trans. Mustard, or Trans. Red finishes, disc. 1994.

	N/A	$700	$600	$500	$400	$350	$300

Last MSR was $1,000

ELECTRIC: SJ SERIES

SJ CLASSIC - offset double cutaway alder body, white pickguard, bolt-on maple neck, 22-fret rosewood fingerboard with offset pearl dot inlay, standard vibrato, 3-per-side tuners, chrome hardware, 3 single coil pickups, volume/tone control, 5-position switch, available in Black, Blue Mist, Cream, Destroyer Grey, Mint Green, or Peach finishes, disc. 1994.

	N/A	$275	$240	$200	$160	$140	$120

Last MSR was $400.

**Standel Model 5209
courtesy George McGuire**

SJ CUSTOM - similar to SJ Classic, except has arched swamp ash body, no pickguard, locking Magnum tuners, available in Trans. Blue, Trans. Cherry, Trans. Cream, Trans. Green, or Trans. Grey finishes, disc. 1994.

	N/A	$425	$350	$300	$250	$200	$175

Last MSR was $600.

SJ LIMITED - single sharp cutaway asymmetrical semi hollow-style, bound bird's-eye maple top, flower petal soundhole, mahogany back, bolt-on maple neck, 22-fret rosewood fingerboard with offset pearl dot inlay, fixed bridge, 3-per-side tuners, chrome hardware, 2 humbucker pickups, volume/tone control, 5-position switch, available in Tobacco Sunburst, Trans. Cherry, Trans. Green, or Trans. Grey finishes, disc. 1994.

	N/A	$450	$375	$325	$250	$225	$195

Last MSR was $650.

SJ TRAD - similar to SJ Classic, except has mahogany body, black pickguard, locking Magnum tuners, 2 single coil/1 humbucker pickups, available in Trans. Cream, Trans. Green, Trans. Grey, Trans. Mustard, or Trans. Red finishes, disc. 1994.

	N/A	$425	$350	$300	$250	$200	$175

Last MSR was $600.

STARFIRE

Instruments currently built in Japan, Taiwan, and China by the Eikosha Musical Instrument Co., Inc. Distributed in the U.S. by V. J. Rendano, located in Boardman, OH.

Starfire electric guitars feature solid ash bodies and maple necks. For more information about current model lineup, availability, and pricing, please contact the distributor directly (see Trademark Index).

STARFORCE

Instruments previously produced in Korea. Initially exported by Tropical Music of Miami, FL prior to their purchase of the Dean company.

The Starforce company was started in 1988. These medium quality solid body guitars feature designs based on the original Stratocaster, as well as the superstrat. With the introduction of models such as the 8007 with its more original body design, and several bass guitar models, Starforce sought to expand its market niche, but apparently isn't producing any guitars at this moment (source: Tony Bacon, *The Ultimate Guitar Book*).

STARK

Instruments currently produced in Bakersfield, CA.

Luthier David Stark offers custom built guitars, as well as guitar refinishing, repairs, and restorations. Stark has been buliding guitars one at a time since 1982. All guitars are custom built and prices start at $1,200. Stark studied under noted luthier Bill Gruggett for three years, and credits his design sense to Gruggett. For more information on Stark guitars refer to their website (see Trademark Index).

S

GRADING		100% MINT	98% NEAR MINT	95% EXC+	90% EXC	80% VG+	70% VG	60% G

STARWAY

Instruments previously manufactured in Japan during the mid-1960s.

The Starway trademark was a brand name used by a UK importer. Starway guitars tend to be entry level solid bodies that sport original designs (source: Tony Bacon and Paul Day, *The Guru's Guitar Guide*).

STATUS

Also Status Graphite. Formerly Strata. Instruments currently built in Essex, England since 1983.

Designer/luthier Rob Green has been building stringed instruments that feature carbon graphite neck-through-body designs since the early 1980s. According to author Tony Bacon, Status was the first British guitar that featured carbon graphite parts. For further information regarding current Status Graphite models, specifications, and pricing, contact Status Graphite directly (see Trademark Index).

Many of these high quality solid body instruments have no headstock (save for 1990s Matrix model) and either two humbuckers or three single coil pickups. The Series II model features wood wings on either side of the neck as it passes through the body. The Model 2000 is all graphite in its composition, the Model 4000 is a resin-composite body.

ELECTRIC BASS: ENERGY SERIES

Three new finishes are now available for the Stealth bass model; Amber, Blue, and Red.

ENERGY 4 - offset double cutaway ash body, bolt-on maple neck, 24-fret rosewood fingerboard, fixed bridge, 2-per-side tuners, black hardware, 2 Status pickups, volume/tone/mix controls, available in Amber, Black, Green, Natural, or Red finishes, current mfg.

MSR	$1,649	$1,116	$837	$700	$560	$505	$460	$420

This model also available with walnut body and fretless fingerboard.

ENERGY 5 - similar to Energy 4, except has 5-string configuration, 3/2-per-side tuners.

MSR	$1,899	$1,196	$797	$795	$635	$575	$525	$475

ENERGY 6 - similar to Energy 4, except has 6-string configuration, 3-per-side tuners.

MSR	$2,099	$1,196	$797	$795	$635	$575	$525	$475

ELECTRIC BASS: OTHER SERIES

Status introduced the new Groove Bass in 1998. The Groove Bass features an offset double cutaway alder or tulipwood body, and has a **Tri-Max** triple coil pickup (the two outer pickups generate the signal, the middle pickup is the hum-cancelling coil). The Groove Bass is available in 4- (list $1,599) and 5-string (list $1,799) configurations, and in 2-Tone Sunburst, Old English White, and Claret finishes.

Status Graphite has several other models currently available. For more information on them and pricing, refer to their website (see Trademark Index).

STAUFER

Instruments currently built in Durnau, Germany, 2003-present. Previously produced in Eschenbach, Germany until 2003.

Luthier Andre Waldenmaier is currently offering handcrafted guitars, as well as custom repair services. For additional information regarding the high quality guitars, or the repair services, contact Andre Waldenmaier directly (see Trademark Index).

ELECTRIC

Staufer offers his guitars in a few standard versions. However, just about any custom order is possible. The Vintage S-Caster features 3 single coil pickups and vintage tremolo. The Vintage T-Caster has a Tele shape with 2 single coil pickups. The S-Caster Dinky Deluxe is a modern Strat style with S/S/H pickup configuration with a Wikinson tremolo. The T-Caster Dinky Deluxe is a modern Tele style with S/S/H pickup configuration and a Wikinson tremolo.

STEINBERGER

Instruments currently produced in Nashville, TN. Distributed by Gibson Musical Instruments of Nashville, TN (Steinberger is a division of the Gibson Guitar Corporation). Instruments originally manufactured in NY, then NJ. Steinberger was purchased by the Gibson Guitar Corporation in 1987 (after a preliminary 1986 agreement).

Ned Steinberger, like Leo Fender and Nathan Daniels, was an instrument designer who didn't play any instruments. Steinberger revolutionized the bass guitar from the design point-of-view, and popularized the use of carbon graphite in musical instruments.

Ned Steinberger majored in sculpture at the Maryland Institute College of Art. Steinberger moved to New York in the 1970s after graduating, and started working as a cabinet maker and furniture designer. He soon moved into a space at the Brooklyn Woodworkers Co-operative and met a guitar builder named Stuart Spector. In 1976 Steinberger began suggesting ideas that later became the NS-1 bass ("NS" for Steinberger's entails, and "1" for the number of pickups). The NS-2, with two pickups, was introduced later. Steinberger's involvement with the NS design led him to originally consider mounting the tuning machines on the body instead of at the peghead. He produced his first "headless" bass in early 1978, built entirely out of wood. Displeased with the end result due to the conventional "dead spots" on the neck (sympathetic vibrations in the long neck cancel out some fundamentals, also called the "wolf" tone in acoustic guitars), Steinberger took the instrument and covered it in fiberglass. His previous usage of the stiff reinforcing fibers in furniture making and boat building did not prepare him for the improved tone and sustain the covered bass then generated.

In 1978, Steinberger continued to experiment with graphite. Actually, the material is a molded epoxy resin that is strengthened by carbon and glass fibers. This formed material, also popular in boat hulls, is said to have twice the density and ten times the "stiffness"of wood - and to be stronger and lighter than steel! Others who have utilized this material are Geoff Gould of Modulus Graphite, Status (UK), Ovation, and Moses Instruments. Steinberger publicly displayed the instrument at a 1979 U.S. Trade Show, hoping to sell the design to a guitar company. When no offers materialized, he formed the Steinberger Sound Corporation in 1980 with partners P. Robert Young (a plastics engineer) and Hap Kuffner and Stan Jay of Mandolin Brothers.

In 1980, the Steinberger bass was debuted at both the MusicMesse in Frankfurt and the NAMM show in Chicago. One of the hot design trends of the 1980s was the headless, reverse tuning instrument - although many were built of wood. Rather than fight "copycat" lawsuits, Steinberger found it easier to license the body and tuning design to other companies. In 1986 the Gibson Guitar corporation agreed to buy Steinberger Sound, and by 1990 had

S

GRADING	100% MINT	98% NEAR MINT	95% EXC+	90% EXC	80% VG+	70% VG	60% G

taken full control of the company. Steinberger continued to serve as a consultant and later developed the Transtrem and DB system detuner bridge

Steinberger is now distributed by online by musicyo.com, which handles several of Gibson's subsidiaries. Visit their website for current model information and pricing. Look for more current models to be in future editions of the *Blue Book of Electric Guitars*.

ELECTRIC: K SERIES

This series was co-designed by Steve Klein.

GK 4S - radical ergonomic style basswood body, black pickguard, bolt-on Steinberger Blend neck, 24-fret phenolic fingerboard with white dot inlay, Steinberger vibrato, black hardware, 2 single coil/1 humbucker EMG pickups, volume/tone control, 5-position switch, available in Black or White finishes, mfg. 1990-94.

	N/A	$1,050	$900	$725	$650	$600	$550

Last MSR was $1,800.

GK 4S-A - similar to GK 4S, except has active electronics, mfg. 1990-94.

	N/A	$1,250	$1,025	$820	$745	$675	$625

Last MSR was $2,050.

This model had Klein's autograph on the body.

GK 4T - similar to GK 4S, except has TransTrem vibrato, mfg. 1990-94.

	N/A	$1,400	$1,150	$900	$800	$725	$675

Last MSR was $2,250.

ELECTRIC: L SERIES

GL 2 (STANDARD) - one piece body/neck construction, rectangular body, 24-fret phenolic fingerboard with white dot inlay, Steinberger vibrato, black hardware, 2 humbucker EMG pickups, volume/tone control, 3-position switch, available in Black finish, mfg. 1989-2001.

	$1,725	$1,300	$1,075	$875	$775	$700	$650

Last MSR was $2,150.

Add $200 for White finish. Add $250 for active pickups. Add $400 for left-handed configuration. Add $450 for Transtrem bridge. Add $500 for 12-string version, no vibrato available.

GL 4 (PRO) - one piece body/neck construction, rectangular body, 24-fret phenolic fingerboard with white dot inlay, Transtrem vibrato, black hardware, 2 single coil/1 humbucker EMG pickups, volume/tone control, 5-position switch, available in Black finish, mfg. 1989-2001.

	$2,250	$1,450	$1,175	$975	$850	$775	$700

Last MSR was $2,850.

GL 7 (ELITE) - one piece body/neck construction, rectangular body, 24-fret phenolic fingerboard with white dot inlay, TransTrem vibrato, black hardware, humbucker/single coil/humbucker EMG pickups, volume/tone control, 5-position/coil split switches, active electronics, gold engraving, signed certificate, available in Black finish, mfg. 1989-2001.

	$2,350	$1,900	$1,600	$1,280	$1,150	$1,055	$960

Last MSR was $2,950.

ELECTRIC: M SERIES

GM 2S - double cutaway maple body, bolt-on Steinberger Blend neck, 24-fret phenolic fingerboard with white dot inlay, Steinberger vibrato, black hardware, 2 humbucker EMG pickups, volume/tone control, 3-position switch, available in Black, Candy Apple Red, Electric Blue, or White finishes, disc. 1995.

	N/A	$1,050	$900	$725	$650	$575	$525

Last MSR was $1,800.

Add $500 for 12-string version with no vibrato.

GM 2T - similar to GM 2S, except has TransTrem vibrato, disc. 1995.

	N/A	$1,400	$1,150	$900	$825	$750	$675

Last MSR was $2,250.

GM 4 (STANDARD) - double cutaway maple body, bolt-on Steinberger Blend neck, 24-fret phenolic fingerboard with white dot inlay, Steinberger vibrato, black hardware, 2 single coil/1 humbucker EMG pickups, volume/tone control, 5-position switch, available in Black, Candy Apple Red, Electric Blue, or White finishes, mfg. 1988-2001.

	$1,525	$1,150	$950	$800	$700	$625	$575

Last MSR was $1,900.

Add $250 for active pickups. Add $450 for Transtrem bridge. Add $600 for 12-string configuration.

GM 7S (PRO) - double cutaway maple body, bolt-on Steinberger Blend neck, 24-fret phenolic fingerboard with white dot inlay, Steinberger vibrato, black hardware, humbucker/single coil/humbucker EMG pickups, volume/tone control, 5-position/coil split switches, active electronics, available in Black, Candy Apple Red, Electric Blue, or White finishes, disc. 2001.

	$2,075	$1,550	$1,300	$1,050	$950	$875	$775

Last MSR was $2,350.

Steinberger SL2 Standard courtesy Steinberger

S

GRADING	100% MINT	98% NEAR MINT	95% EXC+	90% EXC	80% VG+	70% VG	60% G

GM 7T (Pro) - similar to GM 7S, except has TransTrem vibrato, active electronics, disc. 2001.

		$2,250	$1,825	$1,425	$1,175	$1,075	$900	$825

Last MSR was $2,800.

ELECTRIC: R SERIES

GR 4 - offset double cutaway maple body, bolt-on Steinberger Blend neck, 24-fret phenolic fingerboard with white dot inlay, R Trem vibrato, black hardware, 2 single coil rails/1 humbucker Seymour Duncan pickups, volume/tone control, 5-position switch, available in Black, Candy Apple Red, Electric Blue, or White finishes, disc. 1995.

	N/A	$900	$750	$600	$475	$425	$375

Last MSR was $1,390.

ELECTRIC: S SERIES

S STANDARD - offset double cutaway poplar body with bottom bout cutaway, bolt-on Steinberger Blend neck, 24-fret phenolic fingerboard with white dot inlay, standard vibrato, reverse peghead, 6-on-a-side gearless tuners, humbucker/single coil/humbucker exposed pickups, volume/tone control, 5-position/coil split switches, available in Black or White finishes, disc. 1995.

	N/A	$1,400	$1,150	$900	$800	$725	$675

Last MSR was $2,250.

S PRO - similar to S Standard, except has mahogany body, bound maple top, TransTrem vibrato, active electronics, available in Black, Cherry Sunburst, Fireburst, or White finishes, current mfg.

	N/A	$1,600	$1,300	$1,050	$925	$850	$775

Last MSR was $2,600.

GS 7ZA - offset double cutaway hardwood body, bolt-on Steinberger Blend neck, 24-fret phenolic fingerboard with white dot inlay, standard vibrato, reverse headstock, Knife Edge Knut, 6-on-a-side gearless tuners, black hardware, humbucker/single coil/humbucker pickups, volume/tone control, 5-way pickup selector/coil split switches, active electronics, available in Black, Candy Apple Red, Electric Blue, Purple, or White finishes, disc. 1992.

	N/A	$1,700	$1,400	$1,150	$950	$800	$725

Last MSR was $2,450.

GS 7TA - similar to GS 7ZA, except has TransTrem vibrato, disc.

	N/A	$1,800	$1,500	$1,200	$1,000	$850	$750

Last MSR was $2,800.

ELECTRIC BASS: L SERIES

XL 2 (STANDARD) - one piece molded body/neck construct, rectangle body, 24-fret phenolic fingerboard with white dot inlay, Steinberger bridge, black hardware, 2 humbucker EMG pickups, 2 volume/1 tone controls, available in Black finish, mfg. 1979-present.

MSR	$2,100	$1,675	$1,250	$1,050	$850	$750	$675	$625

Add $200 for White finish. Add $200 for fretless fingerboard (lined or unlined). Add $400 for left-handed configuration.

XL 2D (PRO) - similar to XL 2, except has Steinberger DB bridge, current mfg.

MSR	$2,400	$1,925	$1,450	$1,200	$950	$850	$775	$725

XLW 5 - similar to XL 2, except has 5-string configuration, current mfg.

MSR	$2,500	$2,000	$1,625	$1,250	$975	$850	$775	$725

ELECTRIC BASS: M SERIES

XM 2 - double cutaway maple body, bolt-on Steinberger Blend neck, 24-fret phenolic fingerboard with white dot inlay, Steinberger bridge, black hardware, 2 humbucker EMG pickups, 2 volume/1 tone control, available in Black, Candy Apple Red, Electric Blue, or White finishes, disc. 1995.

	N/A	$1,000	$850	$700	$600	$525	$475

Last MSR was $1,600.

Add $100 for fretless fingerboard. Add $250 for active electronics.

XM 2D - similar to XM 2, except has Steinberger DB bridge, disc. 1995.

	N/A	$1,050	$900	$750	$625	$550	$500

Last MSR was $1,700.

XM 2-5 - similar to XM 2, except has 5-string configuration, disc. 1995.

	N/A	$1,100	$950	$800	$650	$575	$525

Last MSR was $1,800.

ELECTRIC BASS: Q SERIES

XQ 2 (STANDARD) - offset double cutaway maple body, bolt-on Steinberger Blend neck, 24-fret phenolic fingerboard with white dot inlay, Steinberger bridge, black hardware, 2 humbucker EMG pickups, 2 volume/1 tone controls, available in Black, Candy Apple Red, Electric Blue, or White finishes, disc.

	N/A	$1,050	$900	$750	$625	$550	$500

Last MSR was $1,700.

Add $100 for fretless fingerboard.

GRADING	100% MINT	98% NEAR MINT	95% EXC+	90% EXC	80% VG+	70% VG	60% G

XQ 2D (PRO) - similar to XQ 2, except has Steinberger DB bridge, disc.

	N/A	$1,100	$950	$800	$650	$575	$500

Last MSR was $1,800.

XQ 2-5 - similar to XQ 2, except has 5-string configuration, disc.

	N/A	$1,250	$1,050	$825	$750	$675	$600

Last MSR was $2,050.

ELECTRIC BASS: DOUBLENECK SERIES

GM 4S/GM 4-12 - refer to model GM 4S, in 6 & 12-string versions, in this section for details, disc. 1995.

	N/A	$2,700	$2,300	$2,000	$1,700	$1,400	$1,200

Last MSR was $4,100.

GM 4T/GM4-12 - refer to model GM 4T, in 6 & 12-string versions, in this section for details, disc. 1995.

	N/A	$3,000	$2,500	$2,100	$1,800	$1,500	$1,300

Last MSR was $4,600.

GM 4S/XM 2 - refer to models GM 4S and XM 2, in 6-string guitar and 4-string bass models, in this section for details, disc. 1995.

	N/A	$2,600	$2,200	$1,900	$1,600	$1,300	$1,000

Last MSR was $4,000.

GM 4T/XM 2 - refer to models GM 4T and XM 2, in 6-string guitar and 4-string bass models, in this section for details, disc. 1995.

	N/A	$2,900	$2,500	$2,100	$1,800	$1,500	$1,300

Last MSR was $4,500.

Steinberger S Pro
courtesy Steinberger

STELLA

See Harmony. See Oscar Schmidt. Instruments previously produced by Oscar Schmidt in the early 1900s, produced by Harmony from the 1940s to the 1970s, and recently produced and distributed by MBT International from the late 1990s to the early 2000s.

Stella was a name used on guitars by Oscar Schmidt in the late 1800s and early 1900s. Harmony purcahsed the trademark circa 1940 and produced instruments until circa 1970s. MBT International reintroduced the name in the late 1990s with a line of acoustic guitars and accessories priced competitively.

STEPHEN´S

Instruments currently built in Seattle, WA. Distributed by Stephen´s Stringed Instruments, located in Seattle, WA.

Luthier/designer Stephen Davies created the Extended Cutaway (EC) that appears on his own instruments as well as licensed to certain Washburn models. Davies updated the 1950s four bolt rectangular neckplate with a curved "half moon" five bolt that helps lock the neck into the neck pocket. This innovative design eliminates the squared block of wood normally found at the end of a neck pocket, allowing proper thumb/hand placement as notes are fretted higher up on the neck and also avoids the old style side-to-side neck motion.

GENERAL INFORMATION

In 1996, the electric guitar models were offered at three different price levels. The **Basic** level offers a straight ahead model with solid hardware and Seymour Duncan pickups. At the next level, the **Standard** offers vintage and custom colors, and hand rubbed finishes in the choice of nitrocellulose lacquers or polyurethane for durability. At the **Prime** level, the instruments are offered with exotic wood necks and bodies. Furthermore, each of the three levels can be upgraded from stock quality parts to an enhanced or custom option depending on the customer´s order.

ELECTRIC: S SERIES

Some following models may be configured above the Basic level. Contact the company for further information. Pricing as of 2001, was the same on all three of the S models (S-2114, S-2122, and the S-2166). The Basic price is $1,395, the Standard price is $1,695, and the Prime version is $1,995.

S-2114 (SATIN MODEL S) - offset double cutaway alder body, bolt-on maple neck, 22-fret maple or rosewood fingerboard with dot inlay, through-body or stop tailpiece, 6-on-a-side tuners, nickel hardware, either 3 single coil or 2 humbucker Seymour Duncan pickups, 1 volume and 1 tone control, 3 or 5-position switch, available in Oil or Satin finish, mfg. 1995-present.

S-2122 (CLASSIC DREAM) - offset double cutaway alder body, bolt-on maple neck, 22-fret maple or rosewood fingerboard with dot inlay, vintage-style tremolo, 6-on-a-side tuners, nickel hardware, 3 single coil Seymour Duncan pickups, 1 volume and 1 tone control, 5-position switch, available in a Cream finish, mfg. 1995-present.

S-2166 (BLACK AND WHITE) - offset double cutaway alder body, bolt-on maple neck, 22-fret maple fingerboard with dot inlay, Schaller locking tremolo, 6-on-a-side tuners, black hardware, 3 single coil Seymour Duncan pickups, 1 volume and 1 tone control, 5-position switch, available in Black finish, mfg 1995-present.

Steinberger XL2T
courtesy Steinberger

S

GRADING	100% MINT	98% NEAR MINT	95% EXC+	90% EXC	80% VG+	70% VG	60% G

S-22EC - offset double cutaway alder body, bolt-on maple neck, 22-fret ebony fingerboard with pearl dot inlay, double locking vibrato, 6-on-a-side tuners, black hardware, 2 single coil/1 humbucker Seymour Duncan pickups, volume/tone control, 5-position switch, available in Raw finish, mfg. 1992-93.

	N/A	$1,000	$900	$800	$700	$625	$550

Last MSR was $1,575.

Add $20 for maple fingerboard. Add $170 for figured maple top. Subtract $20 for rosewood fingerboard. Add $70-$100 for Black, Cherry Sunburst, Natural and Tobacco Sunburst finishes.

ELECTRIC: T SERIES

Some following models may be configured above the Basic level. Contact the company for further information. Pricing as of 2001, was the same on all three of the T models (T-3111, T-3315, and the T-9111). The Basic price is $1,395, the Standard price is $1,695, and the Prime version is $1,995.

T-3111 (RAW MODEL T) - single cutaway ash or alder body, bolt-on maple neck, 22-fret maple or rosewood fingerboard with dot inlay, vintage-style bridge, 6-on-a-side tuners, nickel hardware, 2 single coil Seymour Duncan pickups, 1 volume and 1 tone control, 3-position switch, available in Tung Oil or Satin Lacquer finish, mfg. 1995-present.

T-3315 (BLUES MACHINE) - single cutaway ash body with three internal sound chambers, bolt-on maple neck, 22-fret maple or rosewood fingerboard with dot inlay, vintage-style bridge, 6-on-a-side tuners, nickel hardware, 2 single coil Seymour Duncan pickups, 1 volume and 1 tone control, 3-position switch, optional eight-note f-hole, mfg. 1995-present.

T-9111 (HONEY BURST) - single cutaway flamed maple top over alder body, bolt-on maple neck, 22-fret maple or rosewood fingerboard with dot inlay, vintage-style bridge, 6-on-a-side tuners, gold hardware, 2 single coil Seymour Duncan pickups, 1 volume and 1 tone control, 3-position switch, mfg. 1995-present.

T-22EC - single cutaway ash body, black pickguard, bolt-on maple neck, 22-fret rosewood fingerboard with pearl dot inlay, strings through-body bridge, 6-on-a-side tuners, chrome hardware, 2 single coil Seymour Duncan pickups, volume/tone control, 3-position switch, available in Black or Natural finishes, mfg. 1992-93.

	N/A	$1,050	$925	$800	$700	$625	$550

Last MSR was $1,595.

Add $20 for maple fingerboard. Add $30 for ebony fingerboard. Add $200 for figured maple top. Add $30 for Butterscotch, Cherry Sunburst and Tobacco Sunburst finishes.

STEVENS ELECTRICAL INSTRUMENTS

Instruments currently built in Alpine, TX.

For the past thirty years, luthier Michael Stevens has been performing his high quality guitar building and stringed instrument repairs in California and Texas. Stevens, along with John Page, was hired by Fender in 1986 to open their Custom Shop and construct individually-ordered, custom-built instruments.

In 1967, Stevens headed for Berkeley, California to study bronze casting with Peter Voucas, and also to "intercept a woman I was chasing," notes Stevens. Neither of the two happened at the time, but he did run into a great music scene and his life took a turn. While in Berkeley, Stevens met Larry Jameson through a mutual friend - it turned out that they were dating the same woman. Jameson was just starting a guitar repair shop in Oakland near Leo's Music (up above an amp shop called Magic Music Machines). In the long and short of it, Jameson got the girl, but Stevens got a job. Six months later the two moved to the corner of Rose and Grove in Berkeley and opened the Guitar Resurrection. Stevens credits Jameson for teaching him "what a guitar really was" and how to repair guitars by hand. Stevens and Jameson ran the Guitar Resurrection from 1969 to 1974. Stevens recalled a few notable memories during this time period, such as perhaps the first vintage guitar show circa 1970/1971 at Prune Music in Mill Valley, California; and getting vinyl plastic laminated from Hughs Plastic (a chore in itself) being the first to offer routed after market pickguards. After 1974, Stevens left to train Arabian horses for a number of years.

In 1978, Stevens moved to Austin, Texas. One of his early associates was Bill Collings. Stevens continued to make a name for himself performing repairs and building custom guitars for Christopher Cross (a double neck), Paul Glasse (a mandolin model), and Junior Brown's "Guit-Steel" hybrid. Stevens was hired by Fender in 1986 as Senior design engineer for their new Custom shop. While at Fender, Stevens designed the first set-neck Fender model, the LJ (named in honor of Larry Jameson). Perhaps only thirty-five to forty of these instruments were constructed. Stevens was the first Master builder at Fender to have his logo on his instruments, (Biograhy courtesy Michael Stevens).

Currently, Michael Stevens is back in Alpine, Texas. After a few years chasing cattle and "recharging his batteries," he is beginning production on a new line of Stevens guitars. For more information and pictures of his new shop, refer to his website (see Trademark Index).

ELECTRIC

LJ - single cutaway semi-hollow mahogany body, western curly carved maple top, ivoroid body binding, set mahogany neck, 22-fret Madagascar Kingwood fingerboard with dot inlay, Kingwood peghead veneer, 3-per-side tuners, Tune-O-Matic bridge, black pickguard, two humbucker pickups, three knobs, three-way switch, available in various finishes, current mfg.

MSR	$7,500	$7,500	N/A	N/A	N/A	N/A	N/A	N/A

CLASSIC - double cutaway semi-hollow mahogany body, western curly carved maple top, ivoroid body binding, set mahogany neck, 22-fret Madagascar Kingwood fingerboard with dot inlay, Kingwood peghead veneer, 3-per-side tuners, Tune-O-Matic bridge, black pickguard, two humbucker pickups, three knobs, three-way switch, chrome hardware, available in Natural or Sunburst finishes, 24.625 in. scale, current mfg.

MSR	$8,500	$8,500	N/A	N/A	N/A	N/A	N/A	N/A

This model is based on a shrunken ES-335.

FETISH - Flying V two-piece korina body, one-piece korina neck, 22-fret Brazilian rosewood fingerboard with dot inlay, Kingwood peghead veneer, 3-per-side tuners, Vintage style bridge with V tailpiece, white pickguard, two Tom Holmes humbucker pickups, three knobs, three-way switch, gold or nickle hardware, available in Natural finish, 24.625 in. scale, current mfg.

MSR	$15,000	$15,000	N/A	N/A	N/A	N/A	N/A	N/A

This model is based on the Gibson Flying V from 1957-59.

S

GRADING	100% MINT	98% NEAR MINT	95% EXC+	90% EXC	80% VG+	70% VG	60% G

ELECTRIC BASS

SLANT 4 - uniquely shaped double cutaway alder body, hard rock maple neck, 22-fret Madagascar Kingwood fingerboard, four-on-one-side tuners, STB, T6 Aluminum bridge plate, black or white pickguard, two Steven's pickups, two knobs, three-way switch, two hidden mini-switches, chrome hardware, available in various finishes, current mfg.

BOLT ON MSR $2,800	$2,800	N/A	N/A	N/A	N/A	N/A	N/A
SET NECK MSR $3,200	$3,200	N/A	N/A	N/A	N/A	N/A	N/A

SLANT 5 - similar to the Slant 4, except in five-string configuration with 4/1-per-side tuners, current mfg.

BOLT ON MSR $3,200	$3,200	N/A	N/A	N/A	N/A	N/A	N/A
SET NECK MSR $3,600	$3,600	N/A	N/A	N/A	N/A	N/A	N/A

SLANT 6 - similar to the Slant 4, except in six-string configuration with 4/2-per-side tuners, current mfg.

BOLT ON MSR $3,400	$3,400	N/A	N/A	N/A	N/A	N/A	N/A
SET NECK MSR $3,800	$3,800	N/A	N/A	N/A	N/A	N/A	N/A

**Stevens Electric Instruments
Model LJ
courtesy Jimmy Wallace**

STEWART GUITAR COMPANY

Instruments currently built in Swansboro, NC.

The Stewart Guitar Company specializes in their traveling guitars. The **Road Runner** guitar features a special tool-free neck connection system which allows the neck to be removed or re-assembled quickly without removing or detuning the strings. This system, dubbed the Clip Joint, allows for a full size guitar to be stored and carried in a briefcase-sized carrying case. A **Stow-Away** model is also available. For further information, contact the Stewart Guitar company directly (see Trademark Index).

STICK ENTERPRISES, INC.

Instruments currently produced in Woodland Hills, CA.

Although not a guitar or a bass, the Stick instrument is a member of the guitar family. Company literature refers to the Stick as a 'Touchboard' instrument, and that's the best definition and description for the various models. Designer/innovator Emmett Chapman designed the 8-string Stick Bass (2001, $1,700 MSR), 10-string Stick ($1,600 MSR, $1,800 for EMG pickup) or 12-string Grand Stick ($1,900 MSR, $2,100 for EMG pickup) as a "Touch" instrument to complement his two-handed guitar style. Stick instruments feature minimalist bodies.

The NS/Stick Model ($1,700 MSR) came about from a collaboration between Emmett Chapman and Ned Steinberger, utilizing a very low action and 2 pair of single coil pickups. Sticks incorporate a unique headstock configuration with a joint reverse-tuning bridge. Learning how to play this work of art may be quite a challenge, but the fruits of your labors would be more than rewarding! For further information, please contact Stick Enterprises (see Trademark Index).

STILES, GILBERT L.

Instruments previously built in Independence, WV and Hialeah, FL between 1960 and 1994.

Luthier/designer Gilbert L. Stiles (1914-1994) had a background of working with wood, be it mill work, logging or house building. In 1960, he set his mind to building a solid body guitar, and continued building instruments for over the next thirty years. In 1963, Stiles moved to Hialeah, Florida. Later on in his career, Stiles also taught for the Augusta Heritage Program at the Davis and Elkins College in Elkins, West Virginia.

Stiles built solid body electrics, arch tops, flattop guitars, mandolins, and other stringed instruments. It has been estimated that Stiles had produced over 1,000 solid body electric guitars and 500 acoustics during his career. His arch top and mandolins are still held in high esteem, as well as his banjos.

Stiles guitars generally have Stiles or G L Stiles on the headstock, or Lee Stiles engraved on a plate at the neck/body joint of a bolt-on designed solid body. Dating a Stiles instrument is difficult, given that only the electric solids were given serial numbers consecutively, and would only indicate which number guitar it was, not when built (source: Michael Wright, *Guitar Stories*, Volume One).

STONEHENGE II

Instruments previously built in Castelfidardo, Italy during the mid-1980s.

Luthier Alfredo Bugari designed his tubular metal-bodied guitar in a semi-solid, semi-hollowbody closed triangular design. A photo of this unique guitar was featured in author/researcher Tony Bacon's 1993 book, *The Ultimate Guitar Book*.

STRAD-O-LIN

Instruments previously produced in New York during the 1950s and 1960s. Later models manufactured in Japan.

Strad-O-Lin was a brand name of the Peter Sorkin Music Company. A number of solid body guitars were built at the Multivox company of New York, and distribution of those and the later Japanese built models were handled by the Sorkin company of New York City, New York. Other guitars built and distributed (possibly as rebrands) were Royce, Premier, Belltone, and Marvel.

**Stevens Electric Instruments
Model Fetish (Flying V)
courtesy Jimmy Wallace**

S

STRATA

See Status Graphite. Instruments previously made in England during the 1980s.

STRATOSPHERE

Instruments previously built in Springfield, MO between 1954 and 1958.

Inventor/designer Russ Deaver and his brother Claude formed the Stratosphere company in 1954, and introduced what is estimated to be the first doubleneck guitar that featured both six- and twelve-string necks. By comparison, Gibson did not release their model until 1958, while other designer contemporaries (Mosrite, Bigsby) had built doublenecks with a smaller octave neck.

In 1955, Stratosphere offered three models: a single neck six string (retail $134.50) called the Standard, the single neck twelve string version ($139.50) and the doubleneck 6/12 ($300). It was estimated that less than 200 instruments were built (source: Teisco Del Rey, *Guitar Player Magazine*).

STUART GUITAR DESIGNS

Instruments currently built in Cincinnati, OH.

Following a successful career as a musician in Europe and North America (including composing and performing music for European television and film), artist Stuart Christopher Wittrock returned to Cincinnati, Ohio. Between 1991 to 1997, he performed authorized warranty repairs for virtually every major guitar manufacturer. With 18 months and 2,000 hours design time invested, Wittrock and his team at Stuart Guitar Designs unveiled its first limited production model in 1997. Notable features include a proprietary wood bridge, tone chambers in the neck, "Broken-in" fingerboard, and aged wood, (Company information courtesy Stuart C. Wittrock, September 1997).

STUDIO KING

See chapter on House Brands.

While this trademark has been identified as a House Brand, the distributor is currently unknown at this time. Look for more information in future listings of the *Blue Book of Electric Guitars* (source: Willie G. Moseley, *Stellas & Stratocasters*).

STUMP PREACHER GUITARS

Instruments currently produced in Woodinville, WA.

John Devitry and staff at Stump Preacher Guitars continue to offer an innovative full scale "travel guitar" that is only 27" long! The **Stump Preacher** is currently available in 3 models, the Straight 6 (6 tuners on left or right side of body, $995 MSR), the Stumpy V6 (3 tuners on each side of body, $950 MSR), and the Teardrop V6 (3 tuners on each side of body, $799 MSR). These Stump Preacher models are constructed of high impact polyurethane and feature a neck core which can be adjusted for density, therefore producing different tones. The guitars are equipped with an EMG dual model (disc.) or Lace transducer pickup (various configurations), rosewood fingerboard, Schaller tuners, and a headless neck/reverse tuning system that is highly innovative! Currently, there are 8 different finishes to choose from. All Stump Preacher guitars have a built-in headphone amplifier. For further information, please contact Stump Preacher Guitars directly (see Trademark Index).

SUKOP

Instruments currently built in Angelfire, NM. Distributed by Sukop Electric Guitars of Clifton, NJ.

Luthier Stephen Sukop has been building basses since the 1980s. Sukop is currently offering a number of high quality, custom, handmade bass guitar models. Each Sukop bass is available in a 4-, 5-, or 6-string configuration (fretted or unfretted), and in 34 in. scale, 35 in. scale, and 36 in. scale length. Sukop basses feature a 7-piece laminated neck-through design, Bartolini pickups, Gotoh tuners, and a Kahler bridge. Contact Sukop For further information and ccurrent pricing (see Trademark Index).

SUMBRO

Instruments previously built in Japan during the mid- to late 1970s.

The Sumbro trademark is a brand name of UK importer Summerfield Brothers. These entry level to medium quality solid body guitars feature some original designs, as well as designs based on classic American favorites (source: Tony Bacon and Paul Day, *The Guru's Guitar Guide*).

SUNN

Instruments previously produced in India from 1989 to 1991. Distributed by the Fender Musical Instruments Corporation (FMIC) of Scottsdale, AZ.

The Sunn trademark, similar to the same used on the line of P.A. and amplifier equipment, was applied to a line of entry level strat replicas built in India. Oddly enough, the strat-styled guitar carries a "Mustang" designation in the headstock (source: Tony Bacon, *The Ultimate Guitar Book*). For more information on Sunn amplifiers, refer to the *Blue Book of Guitar Amplifiers*.

SUNTECH

Instruments previously produced in Japan circa late 1970s to early 1980s.

The only Suntech trademark instruments encountered so far have been bolt-on neck Fender-style Strat copies. These instruments are very nice reproductions of the Strat model. Research continues on the Suntech trademark (source: Roland Lozier, Lozier Piano & Music).

SUPER TWENTY

Instruments previously manufactured in Japan during the mid-1960s.

The Super Twenty trademark is a brand name used by a UK importer. This entry level solid body guitar featured an original design and three single coil pickups.

SUPERIOR

See chapter on House Brands.

While this trademark has been identified as a House Bran", the distributor is currently unknown. As information is uncovered, future editions of the *Blue Book of Electric Guitars* will be updated (source: Willie G. Moseley, *Stellas & Stratocasters*).

S

SUPERTONE

See chapter on House Brands.

This trademark has been identified as a House Brand of Sears, Roebuck and Company between 1914 to 1941. Instruments produced by various (probably) Chicago-based manufacturers, especially Harmony (then a Sears subsidiary). Sears used the Supertone trademark on a full range of guitars, lap steels, banjos, mandolins, ukuleles, and amplifiers.

In 1940, then-company president Jay Krause bought Harmony from Sears by acquiring the controlling stock, and continued to expand the company's production. By 1941, Sears had retired the Supertone trademark in favor of the new Silvertone name. Harmony, though a separate business entity, still sold guitars to Sears for sale under this new brand name (source: Michael Wright, *Vintage Guitar Magazine*).

SUPRO

See chapter on House Brands.

The Supro trademark was the budget brand of the National Dobro company (See National or Valco), who also supplied Montgomery Wards with Supro models under the **Airline** trademark. National offered budget versions of their designs under the Supro brand name beginning in 1935.

When National moved to Chicago in 1936, the Supro name was on wood-bodied lap steels, amplifiers, and electric Spanish arch top guitars. The first solid body Supro electrics were introduced in 1952, and the fiberglass models began in 1962 (there's almost thirty years of conventionally built guitars in the Supro history).

In 1962, Valco Manufacturing Company name was changed to Valco Guitars, Inc. (the same year that fiberglass models debuted). Kay purchased Valco in 1967, so there are some Kay-built guitars under the Supro brand name. Kay went bankrupt in 1968, and both the Supro and National trademarks were acquired by Chicago's own Strum 'N Drum company. The National name was used on a number of Japanese-built imports, but not the Supro name.

Archer's Music of Fresno, California bought the rights to the Supro name in the early 1980s. They marketed a number of Supro guitars constructed from new old stock (N.O.S.) parts for a limited period of time (source: Michael Wright, *Vintage Guitar Magazine*).

Some of these Valco-built models were constructed of molded fiberglass bodies and bolt-on wood/metal necks. While Supro pickups may sound somewhat funky to the modern ear, there is no denying the '50s cool appeal. Play 'em or display 'em. Either way, you can't go wrong.

Supros are on the higher end of desirability as far as House Brand Instruments and are generally priced between $350 and $750, depending on color and amount of knobs. Look for more individual model listing in upcoming editions of the *Blue Book of Electric Guitars* .

**Supro Valco
courtesy David Hill**

SURFRITE

Instruments previously built in Bakersfield, CA in 1967.

The Surfrite prototypes were created by Al Hartel for Mosrite in early 1967, and were built outside the plant. There are five identified prototypes: 2 basses, 2 guitars, and 1 twelve string. The rounded body design also features 2 outside arms that run parallel to the neck and join back behind/part of the headstock. Too labor intensive for production? Well, if they're called prototypes, there's a real good chance that they didn't go into full production (source: Teisco Del Rey, *Guitar Player Magazine*, December 1991).

SURINE

Instruments currently built in Denver, CO since 1992.

Scott M. Surine combined his twenty-five years bass playing experience with his graphic arts background in design to offer several models of high quality custom basses. Surine, who holds a Bachelor of Arts degree from Arizona State University, works with luthier Scott Lofquist (a noted Denver guitar builder). Surine basses have been offered since 1992, and a new model was introduced in 1996.

Surine basses are owned and played by musicians such as David Hyde (Delbert McClinton), Me'Shell NdegeOcello (Maverick Recording Artist), Tiran Porter (Doobie Brothers), and Reginald Veal (Branford Marsalis).

Surine basses are available with custom options such as customer-specified string spacing, neck profile contouring, lined or unlined fretless fingerboards, and left-handed versions at no charge. There is a minimal up charge for other variations such as transparent colors, different electronics packages, and some exotic hardwood caps. Hardshell cases and gig bags are available for $150 and $130 respectively.

All Surine basses share the same body construction as neck-through design, double cutaway body that reaches to the 24th fret, Bartolini pickups and TCT on- board pre-amp (9-volt), Gotoh tuners, Wilkinson bridge, and double truss rods for 5-, 6-, and 7-string models (a single truss rod is in the 4-string model).

Surine has also introduced the Quest, Regency, and Homage models. The Quest and Regency are variations of the Protocol, and the Homage is a Jazz bass type of guitar. Look for more information on these models in further editions of the *Blue Book of Electric Guitars*.

ELECTRIC BASS: AFFINITY SERIES

The Affinity models have symmetrical body horns, and Bartolini BC soapbar pickups.

The **Affinity Series I** features symmetrical double cutaway Honduras mahogany body core, choice of exotic woods top and bottom caps and matching headstock, 5-piece flamed maple neck-through construction, 24-fret ebony fingerboard and mother-of-pearl dot inlays, black or gold hardware, brass nut, volume/preamp on-off controls, concentric bass/treble boost/ cut controls, available in Clear Satin Acrylic finish, and the 4-string retails for $5,595, 5-String is $5,895, 6-String is $6,195, and the 7-String is $6,495.

The **Affinity Series II** features symmetrical double cutaway body wings of hard maple, mahogany, southern ash, alder, or walnut with matching headstock; 3-piece hard maple neck-through construction, 24-fret rosewood fingerboard and mother-of-pearl dot inlays, black hardware, brass nut, volume/preamp on-off controls, concentric bass/treble boost/cut controls, available in Clear Satin Acrylic finish, and the 4-string retails for $4,695, 5-String is $4,995, 6-String is $5,295, and the 7-String is $5,595.

**Surine Affinity Series I
Six-String Bass
courtesy Surine**

S

The **Affinity Series III** features symmetrical double cutaway body wings of hard maple, mahogany, or alder, 1-piece hard maple neck-through construction, 24-fret rosewood fingerboard and mother-of-pearl dot inlays, chrome hardware, bone nut, passive Bartolini pickups, volume/bass/treble controls, available in Hand-Oiled finish, and the 4-string retails for $4,095, 5-String is $4,395, and the 6-String is $4,695.

The **Affinity Series X** has all the features of the Series 1, except for body and headstock veneers and a seven-piece maple through-body neck. The 4-string retails for $6,495, the 5-string for $6,795, the 6-string for $7,095, and the 7-string for $7,395.

ELECTRIC BASS: ESPRIT SERIES

Introduced in 1996, the Esprit body design falls somewhere between the Affinity´s symmetrical horns and the Protocal´s exaggerated top horn. Esprit series basses feature Bartolini Jazz/Jazz pickups.

The **Esprit Series I** has an offset double cutaway Honduras mahogany body core, choice of exotic woods top and bottom caps and matching headstock, 5-piece flamed maple neck-through construction, 24-fret ebony fingerboard and mother-of-pearl dot inlays, black or gold hardware, brass nut, volume/preamp on-off controls, concentric bass/treble boost/cut controls, available in Clear Satin Acrylic finish, and the 4-string retails for $5,595, 5-String is $5,895, 6-String is $6,195, and the 7-String is $6,495.

The **Esprit Series II** has an offset double cutaway body wings of hard maple, mahogany, southern ash, alder, or walnut with matching headstock; 3-piece hard maple neck-through construction, 24-fret rosewood fingerboard and mother-of-pearl dot inlays, black hardware, brass nut, volume/preamp on-off controls, concentric bass/treble boost/cut controls, available in Clear Satin Acrylic finish, and the 4-string retails for $4,695, 5-String is $4,995, 6-String is $5,295, and the 7-String is $5,595.

The **Esprit Series III** has an offset double cutaway body wings of hard maple, mahogany, or alder; 1-piece hard maple neck-through construction, 24-fret rosewood fingerboard and mother-of-pearl dot inlays, chrome hardware, bone nut, passive Bartolini pickups, volume/bass/treble controls, available in Hand-Oiled finish, and the 4-string retails for $4,095, 5-String is $4,395, and the 6-String is $4,695.

The **Esprit Series X** has all the features of the Series 1, except for body and headstock veneers and a seven-piece maple through-body neck. The 4-string retails for $6,495, the 5-string for $6,795, the 6-string for $7,095, and the 7-string for $7,395.

ELECTRIC BASS: PROTOCOL SERIES

The Protocol model favors an exaggerated top horn, and Bartolini Precision/Jazz pickups.

The **Protocol Series I** has an offset double cutaway Honduras mahogany body core, choice of exotic woods top and bottom caps and matching headstock, 5-piece flamed maple neck-through construction, 24-fret ebony fingerboard and mother-of-pearl dot inlays, black or gold hardware, brass nut, volume/preamp on-off controls, concentric bass/treble boost/cut controls, available in Clear Satin Acrylic finish, and the 4-string retails for $5,595, 5-String is $5,895, 6-String is $6,195, and the 7-String is $6,495.

The **Protocol Series II** has an offset double cutaway body wings of hard maple, mahogany, southern ash, alder, or walnut with matching headstock; 3-piece hard maple neck-through construction, 24-fret rosewood fingerboard and mother-of-pearl dot inlays, black hardware, brass nut, volume/preamp on-off controls, concentric bass/treble boost/cut controls, available in Clear Satin Acrylic finish, and the 4-string retails for $4,695, 5-String is $4,995, 6-String is $5,295, and the 7-String is $5,595.

The **Protocol Series III** has an offset double cutaway body wings of hard maple, mahogany, or alder; 1-piece hard maple neck-through construction, 24-fret rosewood fingerboard and mother-of-pearl dot inlays, chrome hardware, bone nut, passive Bartolini pickups, volume/bass/treble controls, available in Hand-Oiled finish, and the 4-string retails for $4,095, 5-String is $4,395, and the 6-String is $4,695.

The **Protocol Series X** has all the features of the Series 1, except for body and headstock veneers and a seven-piece maple through-body neck. The 4-string retails for $6,495, the 5-string for $6,795, the 6-string for $7,095, and the 7-string for $7,395.

SUZUKI

Instruments currently built in Korea. Currently distributed in the U.S. market by Suzuki Guitars of San Diego, CA.

Suzuki, noted for their quality pianos, offered a range of acoustic and electric guitars designed for the beginning student to intermediate player. In 1996, the company discontinued the guitar line completely. Suzuki guitars are similar to other trademarked models from Korea at comparable prices. There are now guitars and amplifiers again available by Suzuki.

SWEAGLE

Instruments currently produced in Korea. Distributed by Sweagle of Sweden.

Sweagle used to be Eagle, but changed their name to Sweagle in 2001. They produce a wide variety of guitars and basses in Korean under Swedish design.

SWITCH

Instruments currently produced. Distributed by Switchmusic.com, Inc. in Ontario, CA.

Switch produces a wide variety of electric guitars, electric basses, and guitar amplifiers. Most guitars are based on original designs and have unique features. Prices list typically between $400 and $600 depending upon model. Switch also produces custom and signature guitars. For more information contact Switch directly (see Trademark Index).

SYLVAN

Instruments previously built in England during the late 1980s.

The Duke model was a high quality solid body guitar that had a through-body neck as part of its original design (source: Tony Bacon and Paul Day, *The Guru's Guitar Guide*).

SYNSONICS

Instruments currently built in Korea since 1989. Distributed by The More Company of Pooler, GA.

These entry level solid body guitars feature a built in amplifier and three inch speaker that can be defeated by an on/off switch. The overall design is Les Paul-derived with a thinner width body and a bolt-on neck, with the speaker mounted in the body area behind the stop tailpiece. Synsonics also builds a mini solid body guitar dubbed the Junior Pro.

S

Section T

21ST CENTURY GUITARS

Instruments previously built in Neodesha, KS during the late 1960s. Distributed by Holman-Woodell, Inc. of Neodesha, KS.

The Holman-Woodell company built guitars during the late 1960s in Neodesha, Kansas (around sixty miles due south from Topeka). While they were producing guitars for **Wurlitzer**, they also built their own Holman brand as well as instruments trademarked Alray. The Holman-Woodell company is also famous for building the **La Baye** 2 x 4 guitars. The La Baye 2 x 4 guitar model was introduced at the 1967 Chicago NAMM show by inventor Dan Helland. Unfortunately, the radical body-less design proved too far-ahead thinking for the guitar market, and the La Baye trademark officially ended that year. However, the Holman-Woodell company built a number of 2 x 4 guitars out of spare parts, and marketed them first under the Holman trademark. When new owners took over the production facilities, other instruments were released under the **21st Century** trademark. It has been estimated that perhaps up to one hundred faux "2 x 4"s were built, but reception of the later instruments was equal to the indifference generated by the first attempt (source: Michael Wright, *Guitar Stories*, Volume One).

TDL GUITAR WORKS

Instruments currently built in Atascadero, CA.

Luthier Tony DeLacugo handcrafts custom guitars and basses that feature an ergonomic body design. Models are available with various pickups, bridges, and hardware options. All guitars are produced under the name DeLacugo. For more information on these guitars, refer to their website (see Trademark Index).

ELECTRIC

The **DC Guitar** guitar model features a contoured mahogany body, maple neck, humbucker pickups (with coil taps), and metal-flake finishes, and is now discontinued, (last MSR was $3,200). The **Excelsior** guitar model has an ergonomic contoured mahogany body, and a bolt-on maple neck (list $3,500).

**TV Jones Model 6 7-String
courtesy TV Jones Guitars**

ELECTRIC BASS

DeLacugo´s Excelsior Bass model features a contoured ergonomic mahogany body, 3-piece bolt-on neck, 24-fret fingerboard, and a Candy Apple metal flake finish (list $3,500 for the 4-String, and $3,850 for the 5-String).

TV JONES GUITARS

Instruments currently built in Whittier, CA.

Luthier Thomas V. Jones has been building quality guitars for a number of years. Jones currently produces a wide variety of pickups as well. For more information refer to the website (see Trademark Index).

ELECTRIC

MODEL 5 BARITONE - single cutaway chambered (semi-hollow) mahogany body, figured maple top, f-hole, set-in maple neck, 29.28 in. scale, 24-fret ebony fingerboard, 3-per-side tuners, floating ebony bridge/ebony tailpiece, black hardware, EMG 91 pickups, volume/tone controls, available in Honey finish, mfg. 1996-2000.

Last MSR was $2,100.

Add $150 for fingerboard inlay. Add $150 for metal bridge/tailpiece. Add $175 for 2 pickups. Add $200 for Sunburst finish.

Model 5 Baritone 7-String - similar to the Model 5 Baritone, except features 7-string configuration, 4/3-per-side headstock, mfg. 1996-2000.

Last MSR was $2,400.

MODEL 6 JAZZ - single rounded cutaway semi-hollow laminated body, German spruce top, figured German maple back/sides, basswood body core, 2 f-holes, set-in mahogany neck, 25 in. scale, ebony fingerboard, 3-per-side tuners, raised ebony fingerboard, floating ebony bridge/ebony tailpiece, black hardware, EMG 91 pickups, volume/tone controls, available in Honey finish, body width: 16 inches, body depth: 2.25 inches, mfg. 1996-present.

MSR $6,000

Add $125 for fingerboard inlay. Add $200 for Sunburst finish. Add $400 for wood body binding.

Model 6 Jazz 7-String - similar to the Model 6 Jazz, except features 7-string configuration, 4/3-per-side headstock, mfg. 1996-present.

MSR $6,500

SPECTRA SONIC - single cutaway chambered semi-hollow body, spruce top, tortoiseshell body binding, set-in alder neck, 24.62 in. scale, 22-fret padauk fingerboard with white dot inlay, 3-per-side Kluson tuners, tortoiseshell headstock overlay, ABR-1 bridge/Bigsby tremolo, nickel hardware, tortoiseshell pickguard, 2 humbucker pickups, volume/tone controls, 3-way selector switch, available in Honey finish (disc.), Black and Pewter finishes, mfg. 1996-present.

MSR $3,500

Add $100 for "tub-tone" 5-way switch. Add $125 for bound f-hole. Add $150 for Sparkle finish. Add $200 for Filter-Tron pickups. Add $200 for Sunburst finish. Add $200 for Black lacquer finish.

**TV Jones Spectra Sonic
courtesy TV Jones Guitars**

T

GRADING	100% MINT	98% NEAR MINT	95% EXC+	90% EXC	80% VG+	70% VG	60% G

SPECTRA SONIC "C MELODY" BARITONE - similar to Spectra Sonic, except 29.3 in. scale and set maple neck, tune-o-matic stainless steel saddles, "C melody" pickups, available in Black and Pewter finishes, current mfg.

    MSR $3,700

SPECTRA SONIC BASS - similar to Spectra Sonic, except has 33 in. scale and set maple neck, 2 TV Jones Filter'Tron pickups with adjustable poles, available in Black and Pewter finishes, current mfg.

    MSR $3,600

TAKEHARU

Instruments previously produced in Japan during the early 1980s.

These good quality solid body and semi-hollowbody guitars featured original designs. Any information on this trademark would be appreciated and can be submitted directly to the *Blue Book of Electric Guitars* (source: Tony Bacon and Paul Day, *The Guru's Guitar Book*).

TALKOVICH, S. GUITARS

Instruments currently built in Woodstock, GA.

Luthier S. Talkovich is currently building guitars in the mold of the classic American designs, but with contemporary parts, hardware, and design features that are the 1990s - not the 1950s. Talkovich features one piece southern swamp ash bodies, rockwood necks, Lindy Fralin or Rio Grande pickups, Sperzel tuners, and Wilkinson hardware. Rockwood, a process used by Greg Curbow (Curbow String Instruments), is a hardwood composite that is bound by a thermo-setting phenolic resin. This process also eliminates any problems inherent in regular wood necks such as weather fluctuations, humidity, and warping. Talkovich modernized the bolt-on neck process by designing a shifted four bolt pattern, as well as a sculpted neck/heel joint. For more information contact Talkovich directly (see Trademark Index).

ELECTRIC

Talkovich currently offers two models of his guitars. The **TSS 3** features a one piece swamp ash body, black rockwood neck with either a black or ash rockwood 21-fret fingerboard, dot inlays, Sperzel tuners, three Lindy Fralin or Rio Grande single coils, Wilkinson bridge, full shielded control cavity, and Graph-tech nut. Finishes include Natural, or a $75 option of a Black top, Tinted finish, or 'Burst finish. Retail lists at $1,875, and includes a deluxe padded gig bag. The **TSFT 3** is similar to the TSS 3, except that it features a "Fancy Top" of bookmatched American Hard Rock Maple or American Black Walnut. Retail with the deluxe padded gig bag is $2,175.

TANARA

Instruments currently built in Korea and Indonesia. Distributed by the Chesbro Music Company of Idaho Falls, ID.

Tanara offers a range of acoustic and electric guitars designed for the entry level to student guitarist.

ELECTRIC

TC80 - single cutaway body, 6-on-a-side covered tuners, tele-style fixed bridge, chrome hardware, pickguard, 2 single coil pickups, volume/tone controls, 3-way selector, available in Black or Ivory finishes, current mfg.

MSR	$309	$230	$200	$175	$155	$130	$105	$80

TG100 - LP-style single cutaway body, carved solid maple top, East Indian rosewood fingerboard, compensating bridge, 3-per-side chrome tuners, 2 humbucker pickups, available in Black or Cherry Red Sunburst finishes, current mfg.

MSR	$389	$295	$250	$220	$190	$160	$130	$100

TS30 - offset double cutaway body, bolt-on mahogany neck, 25 1/2 in. scale, 21-fret rosewood fingerboard, standard tremolo, 6-on-a-side covered tuners, chrome hardware, pickguard, 3 single coil pickups, volume/2 tone controls, available in Black or Brown Sunburst finishes, current mfg.

MSR	$249	$190	$160	$140	$125	$100	$85	$65

TD33 - similar to the TS30, except features a maple neck, available in Black or Red finishes, current mfg.

MSR	$269	$200	$175	$155	$135	$115	$90	$70

TS40 - similar to the TS30, except features 2 single coil/humbucker pickups, available in Black and Brown Sunburst finishes, current mfg.

MSR	$269	$200	$175	$155	$135	$115	$90	$70

TD44 - similar to the TS40, except features a maple neck, available in Black or Red finishes, current mfg.

MSR	$289	$215	$190	$170	$145	$120	$100	$75

ELECTRIC BASS

TSP25 - offset double cutaway body, bolt-on mahogany neck, 34 in. scale, 20-fret rosewood fingerboard, fixed bridge, 4-on-a-side die-cast tuners, chrome hardware, pickguard, P-style split pickup, volume/tone controls, available in Black and Brown Sunburst finishes, current mfg.

MSR	$279	$210	$180	$160	$140	$115	$95	$70

TDP30 - similar to the TSP25, except features a maple neck, available in Black or Red finishes, current mfg.

MSR	$299	$225	$195	$170	$150	$125	$100	$75

TSPJ35 - similar to the TSP25, except features P/J-style pickups, 2 volume/1 tone controls, available in Black or Brown Sunburst finishes, current mfg.

MSR	$299	$225	$195	$170	$150	$125	$100	$75

TDPJ40 - similar to the TSPJ35, except has a maple neck, available in Black or Red finishes, current mfg.

MSR	$309	$230	$200	$175	$155	$130	$105	$80

T

TANGLEWOOD

Instruments currently produced in Korea and Indonesia. Distributed by the European Music Company, Ltd. of Kent, England.

The European Music Company, Ltd. is currently offering a wide range of acoustic and electric guitar models under the Tanglewood trademark. These solidly built instruments offer the beginning and intermediate player a quality guitar for the price. For more information and pricing, contact Tanglewood directly (see Trademark Index).

TAUSCH HANDMADE GUITARS

Instruments currently built in Buch, Germany.

Rainer Tausch is currently offering a number of semi-acoustic single cutaway electrics. The **Series 665** model has a maple body (in its basic version), and is available in different body thicknesses, with an additional piezo bridge pickup, and with a tremolo. The 665 is available in a black varnish or oil/wax finish. Prices are listed online, but are in Euros. For further information, contact Rainer Tausch directly (see Trademark Index).

TEIGEN GUITARS

Instruments currently built in Naples, FL.

Luthier Ross Teigen builds lightweight, distinctly designed custom guitars and basses. Teigen has been building guitars and basses since 1979, and attended the Technical College in Red Wing, Minnesota for stringed instrument construction and repair. Teigen worked in Minneapolis, Naples (Florida), and Miami before establishing Teigen Guitars in 1986 on the edge of the Florida Everglades, where he lives with his wife and three children. Teigen guitars feature original designs. For further information on models, prices, and custom options, please contact luthier Teigen directly (see Trademark Index).

TEISCO

See Teisco Del Rey. Instruments previously produced in Japan. Distributed in the U.S. by Westheimer Musical Instruments of Evanston, IL.

One of the original Teisco importers was George Rose of Los Angeles, California. Some instruments may bear the shortened "Teisco" logo, many others were shipped in unlabeled. Please: no jokes about Teisco "no-casters," (source: Michael Wright, *Guitar Stories*, Volume One).

Teisco Del Rey ET-460
Blue Book Publications

TEISCO DEL REY

Instruments previously produced in Japan from 1956 to 1973. Distributed in the U.S. by Westheimer Musical Instruments of Evanston, IL.

In 1946, Mr. Atswo Kaneko and Mr. Doryu Matsuda founded the Aoi Onpa Kenkyujo company, makers of the guitars bearing the Teisco and other trademarks (the company name roughly translates to the Hollyhock Soundwave or Electricity Laboratories). The Teisco name was chosen by Mr. Kaneko, and was used primarily in domestic markets. Early models include lap steel and electric-Spanish guitars. By the 1950s, the company was producing slab-bodied designs with bolt-on necks. In 1956, the company name was changed to the Nippon Onpa Kogyo Co., Ltd. - but the guitars still stayed Teisco!

As the demand for guitars in the U.S. market began to expand, Mr. Jack Westheimer of WMI Corporation of Evanston, Illinois started to import Japanese guitars in the late 1950s, perhaps circa 1958. WMI began importing the Teisco-built Kingston guitars in 1961, and also used the Teisco Del Rey trademark extensively beginning in 1964. Other Teisco-built guitars had different trademarks (a rebranding technique), and the different brand names will generally indicate the U.S. importer/distributor. The Japanese company again changed names, this time to the Teisco Co. Ltd. The Teisco line included all manners of solid body and semi-hollowbody guitars, and their niche in the American guitar market (as entry level or beginner's guitars) assured steady sales.

In 1967, the Kawai Corporation purchased the Teisco company. Not one to ruin a good thing, Kawai continued exporting the Teisco line to the U.S. (although they did change some designs through the years) until 1973. Due to the recent popularity in the Teisco name, Kawai actually produced some limited edition Teisco Spectrum Five models lately in Japan, although they were not made available to the U.S. market (source: Michael Wright, *Vintage Guitar Magazine*).

One dating method for identifying Teisco guitars (serial numbers are non-existent, and some electronic parts may not conform to the U.S. EIA code) is the change in pickguards that occurred in 1965. Pre-1965 pickguards are plastic construction, while 1965 and post-1965 pickguards are striped metal.

Pricing on Teisco Del Rey models and other Teiscos remains a bit strange. Most models that hang on walls are tagged at $99 (and sometimes lower), but clean cool shaped models sometimes command the $200 to $300 range. However, due to the association of the Spectrum Five model with Eddie Van Halen (he posed with a Spectrum Five on the cover of some German music magazine, if the story is true), some Spectrum Fives are now priced (used) at $1,000!

TELE-STAR

Instruments previously produced in Japan circa late 1960s to 1983.

The Tele-Star trademark was distributed in the U.S. by the Tele-Star Musical Instrument Corporation of New York, New York. Tele-Star offered a full range of acoustic, thinline acoustic/electric hollowbody, and solid body electric guitars and basses. Many built by Kawai of Japan, and some models feature sparkle finishes (source: Michael Wright, *Vintage Guitar Magazine*).

Tele-Star has reappeared again in recent years. John Thomas Riboloff worked for Gibson in the late 1980s and later on incorporated the CrossRoads Musical Instruments in Nashville, Tennessee. Recently, new Tele-Star models were produced. It is unknown at this point if these two trademarks are connected.

Teisco Del Rey
courtesy Nancy Patterson

T

GRADING	100% MINT	98% NEAR MINT	95% EXC+	90% EXC	80% VG+	70% VG	60% G

ELECTRIC

ELECTRIC SOLIDBODIES - various configurations, may include one, two, or three pickups, various knobs and switches, mfg. 1960s-1970s.

	N/A	$250	$200	$160	$130	$100	$80

TEMPEST

Instruments previously produced in Japan during the early 1980s.

These entry level to medium quality solid and semi-hollowbody guitars featured both original designs and designs based on popular American classics (source: Tony Bacon and Paul Day, *The Guru's Guitar Guide*).

TERRY ROGERS GUITARS

Instruments currently produced in TN.

Terry Rogers designed the Mallie electric guitar in 1999, and it is currently built by luthier John Suhr. For more information, including availability and pricing, please contact the company directly (see Trademark Index).

ELECTRIC

The **Mallie** has an offset double cutaway solid basswood body, patented body design, best quality bookmatched flame or quilted maple top, ivoroid bound body, straight grain hard maple neck with museum grade bird´s-eye maple fingerboard and matching quilt maple headstock, 22 medium frets, 3-per-side Sperzel tuners, DiMarzio custom patented design pickups, pickups are split by push/pull tone circuitry, 3-position LP style toggle switch, Floyd Rose design Gotoh locking bridge, available in Trans. Blue, Trans. Green, Trans. Purple, Trans. Ruby, Trans. Red, Trans. Violet, Trans. Gold, Trans. Lemon, Faded Burst, Cherry Burst, ´59 Burst, Tobacco, NAMM Flame, Honey Burst, Gloss Black, or Vintage Gold finishes, mfg. 2000-present.

There are also several other models available now. Visit Terry´s website for more information (see Trademark Index).

TEUFFEL

Instruments currently built in Germany. Distributed in Germany by S K C Graphite of Aschaffenburg, Germany.

Teuffel´s guitar models are unconventional new perspectives on the traditional design of the electric guitar. All models are custom-built in Germany, and feature top-rate construction details. Teuffel models feature moveable Alnico pickups, so the magnetic sources of tone generation can thus be varied for a wide range of tonal customizing.

ELECTRIC

The Teuffel **Birdfish** model has a minimalist metal frame, which reduces the design of an electric guitar to its essential components. The central elements consist of two aluminum sculptures of a bird and a fish, which provides the frame for components to be connected, vibrations transmitted, and interaction with the musician´s body. Resonator cylinders (up to two) can be attached across the top of the frame, and consist of both a maple core (Red) and swamp ash core (Blue). A wiring harness provides for interchanging the pickups, and are connected by a central rod for placement by twisting or sliding. Strings are run reverse from the headstock to a Steinberger-style bridge/tailpiece, and the bird´s-eye maple neck has 22-frets. The entire Birdfish guitar set consists of the Birdfish frame, 4 body resonators, five pickups, and a heavily padded and lined nubuk leather bag. The retail list price is quoted at $4,924.

The **Coco**, retains the moveable pickup concept. However, the Coco has an angular body with round pointed horns instead of a minimalist metal body. This body is constructed of a pearwood core, surrounded by a lightweight composite material and a polymer finish. The 22-fret bird´s-eye maple neck has a 6-on-a-side headstock and LSR tuners. The Coco has a Wilkinson tremolo bridge/LSR roller nut, 3 splitable Alnico pickups, volume/tone controls, and a five way selector switch. This model has been out of production since 2002.

The **Tesla** is a seven-string guitar with a low-B string. This is a more traditional design with a full body. The neck is made out of bird´s-eye maple and connects to the body at the 8th fret. There is no headstock and the strings are all tuned at the bridge. There are two hand-wound pickups, and control by three push button switches that all have different functions. The guitar is finished in a glow in the dark luminescent finish. When the lights are off it has a light green glow to it! This guitar is also available as a six-string version.

THOMAS, HARVEY

Also appears as Thomas Custom Guitars, or simply Thomas. Instruments previously built in Kent, WA during the early 1960s.

Flamboyant luthier Harvey Thomas built quality semi-hollowbody guitars whose designs bent the "laws of tradition" that conservative semi-hollowbody guitars normally adhere to. Thomas is also well-known for his explorations into the solid body design world as well. Models include the **Mandarin**, the **Mod**, **Riot King**, or the **Maltese Surf**er .

Most Thomas guitars feature 6-on-a-side headstock that looks like it could be hung up, a slim neck design, and 21-fret fingerboard that is clear of the body, and glitter or mirror pickguards. The Maltese Surfer looks like a Maltese Cross with a neck attached to one of the four sides. You´ll know one when you see one, but you won´t believe what you´re looking at! (source: Tony Bacon, *The Ultimate Guitar Book*).

THOMPSON, CARL

Instruments currently built in Brooklyn, NY since 1974.

Luthier Carl Thompson moved to New York in 1967, and began working as a repairman in Dan Armstrong´s guitar shop as a means to round out his income as a musician. In 1971 he formed a new shop with fellow guitarist Joel Frutkin, and by 1974 was working on his own bass guitar designs. Thompson has built basses for such luminaries as Anthony Jackson, Stanley Clarke, and Les Claypool.

Luthier Thompson generally produces five or six basses a year. Thompson maintains a small shop in Stahlstown, Pennsylvania to rough out body blanks or cut neck blanks, while his final shaping, finishing, and electronics are performed in his Brooklyn workshop (source: Tom Wheeler, *American Guitars*). Prices on basses start at $3,500 for a four-string with each additional string an extra $1,000. Several options are available, so the best way to get an accurate price on a guitar is to contact Thompson directly (see Trademark Index).

THORNTON, C. P.

Instruments currently built in Bryant Pond, ME since the mid-1980s.

Luthier Charles ("Chuck P.") Thornton began building custom guitars and basses in the mid 1980s that featured neck-through designs. While Thornton also worked for Dana Bourgeios in the early 1990s, his current focus is on handcrafted violins. Guitar and bass models are still available on a special order basis.

All Thornton guitar and bass models feature neck-through construction, and have the serial numbers stamped into the fretboard (Research courtesy Jim Shine, Oxford, Maine).

THUNDER BAY BASSES

Instruments currently built in Asia. Distributed by Sound Trek Distributors of Tampa, FL.

Thunder Bay instruments are good quality basses designed for the entry or student level up to the medium grade player. For further information on model specs and pricing, contact Sound Trek Distributors directly (see Trademark Index).

TIMTONE

Instruments currently built in Grand Forks (British Columbia), Canada, since 1992.

Timtone guitars are highly regarded handcrafted instruments designed for each client and built in small batches of four at a time. Luthier Tim Diebert is currently building about twenty instruments a year. He sells direct to the end user, ensuring a truly personalized, no compromise project. Using either the MK or the MK7 Series, the BT Series and the Rikiyabass body styles as a platform, Tim Diebert offers a large array of base features and options. For more information contact Timtone directly (see Trademark Index).

ELECTRIC

Tele-Star Mona
Blue Book Publications

Base Price includes many body shape and top wood choices, pickups and layout, switching choices, scale length, neck shape and size, fret gauge, tuners, colors and sunbursts, headstock styles, fingerboard wood choices, two styles of forearm rests and client designated control layout.

The **MK** Series guitar has a base price of $3,500, while the 7-string **MK7** guitar has a base price of $2,400. Options include different bridges, chambered bodies, fingerboard binding, MOP and sterling silver side markers, 2 styles of diamond face markers, fancy custom inlay work, special exotic wood tops, multi-laminated necks and bodies, 24kt. Gold-plated hardware, including the Steinberger gearless headstock tuners, black hardware, laser engraved cavity cover plate and custom-made cases, special requests and concept instruments.

Electronic options include Varitone controls, dual output piezo bridge saddles, custom Timtone pickups, 3rd or 4th pickup, 3 output MIDI equipped guitar with additional piezo and magnetic outputs or all three signals routing choices and a switchable and adjustable active output.

The **Rikiyabass** model has two main versions, one having the usual headstock and the other being headstockless. Multi-laminated body with fancy maple top over or with laminations showing, 4- or 5-string, fretted or fretless, ebony or Pau Ferro fingerboard, ABM hardware, Seymour Duncan 18V active 2 soapbar system with 3-band EQ and balance control and slap contour switch. There are several other models and configurations available.

TOBIAS

Instruments currently produced in Korea and Nashville, TN. Tobias Guitars are distributed by Gibson Guitar Corporation. Tobias Basses have been a division of the Gibson Guitar Corporation since January 1990. Production facilities were moved from Hollywood, California to Nashville, TN in 1992. Prior to purchase by Gibson, Tobias Basses were based in Hollywood, CA from 1981 to December 1989.

As related by luthier Michael Tobias, "Tobias Guitars was started in Orlando, Florida in April 1977. The first serial number I used was 0178 - January 1978. After 578, I went back to 179. My first shop name was the Guitar Shop. I sold that business in 1980 and moved to San Francisco to be partners in a short lived manufacturing business called Sierra Guitars. We made about 50 instruments. I left San Francisco in May of 1981 and started a repair shop in Costa Mesa, California.

I stayed in Costa Mesa for several months and then moved to Hollywood. The first California serial number was 240, and it was a solid mahogany 6-string guitar. The first South California number was 250. It was a mahogany LP junior style neck-through, one of four made.

Tobias Guitars continued to repair instruments and build custom basses for the next several years with the help of Bob Lee and Kevin Almieda (Kevin went on to work for Music Man). We moved into 1623 Cahuenga Boulevard in Hollywood and after a year quit the repair business. We added Bob McDonald, lost Kevin to Music Man, and then got Makoto Onishi. The business grew by leaps and bounds. In June of 1988, we had so many back orders that we did not accept any new orders until the January NAMM show in 1990.

After several attempts to move the business to larger, better equipped facilities, I sold Tobias Guitars to Gibson on 1/1/90. The first Tobias Gibson serial number was 1094. At that point, Gibson was instrumental in moving us to a bigger shop in Burbank and setting us up with a great spray booth and dust collection system. We finally met So. Cal safety codes. Basses built during the 1990-1992 era were built initially by the same crew that had helped establish Tobias Basses as one of the most sought after basses on the planet. We added several people during 1990, and ended up with a great ten-man shop.

Thomas Maltese Cross
courtesy Brian Goff

Business was still very good. We were not able to make anywhere near enough basses to fill the orders. Instead of trying to jack up production, we tried to get outside vendors to build for us. We had 110 **Model T** basses made for us by a very fine builder in New England, and then we got the Terada factory in Nagoya, Japan to make the **Standard** bass for us. This was and is a great bass, but the dollar-to-yen ratio killed the project. There were about 400 Standards. Late in 1992, it was decided that in best corporate interests Tobias Guitars would move to Nashville. After much deliberation, no one from the original Tobias Guitars crew went to Nashville. The final LA Tobias/Gibson serial number is 2044. Despite Gibson's ownership of Tobias, all of the basses made up to 2044 were built by my regular

GRADING	100% MINT	98% NEAR MINT	95% EXC+	90% EXC	80% VG+	70% VG	60% G

crew. We also built about 60 basses that were not numbered or finished by us. Those would be the first production from Tobias/Nashville.

I left the company in December of 1992, and was a consultant for Gibson as they set up operations in Nashville. They had some trouble at first, but have since done a fairly good job making Tobias basses.

By contractual agreement, after my consulting agreement with Gibson was up, I had a one year non competition term. That ended in December of 1993. During that time I moved to The Catskills in upstate New York and set up a small custom shop. I started designing new instruments and building prototypes in preparation for my new venture,"(Biography courtesy Michael Tobias, February 22, 1996).

ELECTRIC BASS: BASIC SERIES

B4 - offset double cutaway asymmetrical alder body, through body maple/bubinga neck, 24-fret wenge fingerboard, fixed bridge, 2-per-side tuners, black hardware, 2 Bartolini pickups, 2 volume/treble/midrange/bass controls, bypass switch, active electronics, available in Natural finish, current mfg.

MSR	$4,300	$2,900	$2,400	$2,000	$1,700	$1,400	$1,150	$900

Add $60 for fretless fingerboard. Add $200 for polyurethane finish. Add $250 for left-handed configuration.

This model has bubinga, figured maple, lacewood, walnut, or zebrawood body, maple/purpleheart neck as options.

B5 - similar to B4, except has 5 strings, current mfg.

MSR	$4,500	$3,000	$2,500	$2,100	$1,800	$1,500	$1,200	$950

B6 - similar to B4, except has 6 strings, current mfg.

MSR	$4,700	$3,150	$2,650	$2,200	$1,900	$1,600	$1,300	$1,000

ELECTRIC BASS: CLASSICAL SERIES

C4 - offset double cutaway asymmetrical laminated body, through body flame maple/purpleheart neck, 24-fret wenge fingerboard, fixed bridge, 2-per-side tuners, black hardware, 2 Bartolini pickups, 2 volume/treble/midrange/bass controls, bypass switch, active electronics, available in Natural finish, current mfg.

MSR	$5,100	$3,400	$2,900	$2,500	$2,100	$1,800	$1,500	$1,200

Add $60 for fretless fingerboard. Add $200 for polyurethane finish. Add $250 for left-handed configuration.

This model may have gold or chrome hardware. Neck may have walnut/purpleheart or walnut/bubinga laminate, maple may replace walnut in some configurations. This model also available in bird's-eye maple/wenge, bubinga/wenge/alder, flame maple/wenge/walnut, lacewood/wenge/alder, purpleheart/walnut, walnut/wenge/alder, walnut/wenge/walnut, or zebra/wenge/alder laminate body.

C5 - similar to C4, except has 5 strings, current mfg.

MSR	$5,200	$3,500	$3,000	$2,600	$2,150	$1,850	$1,550	$1,250

C6 - similar to C4, except has 6 strings, current mfg.

MSR	$5,300	$3,600	$3,100	$2,700	$2,250	$1,900	$1,600	$1,300

Last MSR was $4,700.

ELECTRIC BASS: GROWLER SERIES

GR4 - offset double cutaway body with symmetrical maple/purpleheart neck, 24-fret wenge fingerboard, fixed bridge, 2-per-side tuners, black hardware, 1 Bartolini quad-coil pickup with active 18-volt preamp and 2 contour switches, volume/tone controls, current mfg.

MSR	$2,200	$1,500	$1,250	$1,050	$900	$750	$650	$550

Add $60 for fretless fingerboard. Add $200 for polyurethane finish.

GR5 - similar to GR4, except features 5-string configuration, 3/2-per-side tuners, current mfg.

MSR	$2,400	$1,600	$1,300	$1,100	$950	$825	$700	$600

Last MSR was $2,100.

ELECTRIC BASS: KILLER B SERIES

KB4 - offset double cutaway asymmetrical swamp ash body, bolt-on maple/purpleheart 5-piece neck, 24-fret wenge fingerboard, fixed bridge, 2-per-side tuners, black hardware, 2 Bartolini pickups, 2 volume/treble/midrange/bass controls, bypass switch, active electronics, available in Oil finish, current mfg.

MSR	$2,900	$1,950	$1,650	$1,450	$1,250	$1,050	$900	$750

Add $200 for polyurethane finish. Add $60 for fretless fingerboard. Add $250 for left-handed configuration.

This model also available with alder, maple or lacewood body.

KB5 - similar to KB4, except has 5 strings, current mfg.

MSR	$3,000	$2,050	$1,750	$1,500	$1,300	$1,100	$950	$800

KB6 - similar to KB4, except has 6 strings, current mfg.

MSR	$3,100	$2,100	$1,800	$1,550	$1,350	$1,150	$1,000	$850

ELECTRIC BASS: PRO-STANDARD SERIES

PS4 - offset double cutaway asymmetrical figured maple body, through body maple/bubinga 5-piece neck, 24-fret rosewood fingerboard, fixed bridge, 2-per-side tuners, black hardware, 2 Bartolini pickups, volume/mix and 3-band EQ controls, active electronics, available in Black, Natural, Trans. Candy Amber, Trans. Candy Blue, Trans. Candy Red, or White finishes, mfg. 1994-96.

	N/A	$1,300	$1,050	$800	$700	$600	$500

Last MSR was $2,000.

This model has bubinga or zebra body with Natural finish as options.

T

GRADING	100% MINT	98% NEAR MINT	95% EXC+	90% EXC	80% VG+	70% VG	60% G

PS5 - similar to PS4, except has 5 strings, 3/2-per-side tuners, mfg. 1994-96.

	N/A	$1,400	$1,100	$900	$750	$650	$550

Last MSR was $2,100.

PS6 - similar to PS4, except has 6 strings, 3-per-side tuners, mfg. 1994-96.

	N/A	$1,500	$1,200	$950	$800	$700	$600

Last MSR was $2,300.

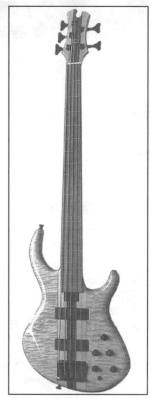

Tobias B5
courtesy Tobias

ELECTRIC BASS: RENEGADE SERIES

Renegade Series instruments were introduced in 1998.

RENEGADE 4 - offset double cutaway alder body, bolt-on maple neck, 24-fret fingerboard, fixed brass bridge, 2-per-side tuners, black hardware, single coil/humbucker Bartolini pickups, 2 volume/push/pull contour tone controls, active electronics, available in Amber, Black, Blue, Green, or Red finishes, mfg. 1998-2001.

	$1,000	$850	$725	$600	$500	$400	$300

Last MSR was $1,490.

Renegade 5 - similar to Renegade 4, except has 5-string configuration, 3/2-per-side tuners, mfg. 1998-2001.

	$1,100	$950	$800	$675	$550	$450	$350

Last MSR was $1,590.

ELECTRIC BASS: SIGNATURE SERIES

S4 - offset double cutaway asymmetrical laminated body, through body laminate neck, 24-fret wenge fingerboard, fixed bridge, 2-per-side tuners, black hardware, 2 Bartolini pickups, 2 volume/treble/midrange/bass controls, bypass switch, active electronics, available in Natural finish, current mfg.

MSR	$7,100		$5,000	$4,200	$3,600	$3,000	$2,500	$2,000	$1,500

This model may have gold or chrome hardware. This model also available in bubinga/wenge/bubinga, lacewood/wenge/lacewood, or zebra/wenge/zebra laminate body.

S5 - similar to S4, except has 5 strings, current mfg.

MSR	$7,200		$5,100	$4,300	$3,700	$3,100	$2,600	$2,100	$1,600

S6 - similar to S4, except has 6 strings, current mfg.

MSR	$7,300		$5,200	$4,400	$3,800	$3,200	$2,700	$2,200	$1,700

ELECTRIC BASS: STANDARD SERIES

ST4 - offset double cutaway asymmetrical ash body, through body maple/bubinga 5-piece neck, 24-fret rosewood fingerboard, fixed bridge, 2-per-side tuners, black hardware, 2 Bartolini pickups, volume/mix and 3-band EQ controls, active electronics, available in Black, Natural, Trans. Candy Amber, Trans. Candy Blue, Trans. Candy Red, or White finishes, disc. 1996.

	N/A	$1,300	$1,050	$900	$750	$650	$550

Last MSR was $1,850.

ST5 - similar to ST4, except has 5 strings, disc 1996.

	N/A	$1,400	$1,150	$950	$800	$700	$600

Last MSR was $1,950.

ST6 - similar to ST4, except has 6 strings, disc 1996.

	N/A	$1,500	$1,250	$1,000	$850	$725	$600

Last MSR was $2,300.

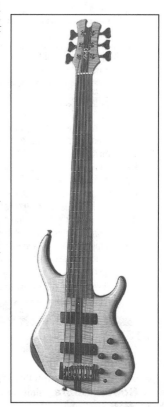

Tobias C6
courtesy Tobias

ELECTRIC BASS: TOBY DELUXE SERIES

The Toby Deluxe series is now available again on MusicYo´s website. Prices are considerably more affordable then the models that were produced in the 1990s. Retail prices are not given, and everything on the site is sold as wholesale.

TD4 - offset double cutaway asymmetrical maple body, bolt-on maple neck, 24-fret rosewood fingerboard, fixed bridge, 2-per-side tuners, chrome hardware, 2 J-style humbucker pickups, volume/mix/3-band EQ controls, active electronics, available in Black, Natural, Trans. Candy Amber, Trans. Candy Blue, Trans. Candy Red, or White finishes, mfg. 1994-96.

	N/A	$700	$600	$500	$425	$350	$275

Last MSR was $900.

TD5 - similar to TD4, except has 5 strings, 3/2-per-side tuners, mfg. 1994-96.

	N/A	$800	$700	$600	$500	$400	$300

Last MSR was $1,000.

ELECTRIC BASS: TOBY PRO SERIES

The Toby Pro series is now available again on MusicYo´s website. Prices are considerably more affordable then the models that were produced in the 1990s. Retail prices are not given, and everything on the site is sold as wholesale.

T

GRADING	100% MINT	98% NEAR MINT	95% EXC+	90% EXC	80% VG+	70% VG	60% G

TP4 - offset double cutaway asymmetrical maple body, through body maple/wenge 5-piece neck, 24-fret rosewood fingerboard, fixed bridge, 2-per-side tuners, chrome hardware, 2 humbucker pickups, volume/mix/3-band EQ controls, active electronics, available in Black, Natural, Trans. Candy Amber, Trans. Candy Blue, Trans. Candy Red, or White finishes, mfg. 1994-96.

	N/A	$900	$775	$650	$550	$450	$350

Last MSR was $1,200.

TP5 - similar to TP4, except has 5 strings, 3/2-per-side tuners, mfg. 1994-96.

	N/A	$1,000	$850	$725	$600	$500	$400

Last MSR was $1,300.

TP6 - similar to TP4, except has 6 strings, 3-per-side tuners, mfg. 1994-96.

	N/A	$1,100	$950	$800	$675	$550	$450

Last MSR was $1,400.

TOKAI

Instruments currently produced in Japan since the early 1960s.

Tokai instruments were very good Fender- and Gibson-based replicas produced during the mid- to late 1970s. After 1978 the company built instruments based on these classic American designs, then further branched out into some original designs and ´superstrat´ models. These models are becoming increasingly collectible and are starting to bring some higher dollars. There are a few websites out there dedicated to Tokai instruments. Lawsuits have been filed against Tokai because of their strikingly close copies of popular instruments. Tokai still builds guitars, but they are original designs only.

ELECTRIC

LS LES PAUL STYLE - single cutaway Les Paul body style, two humbuckers, four knobs, essentially a copy of the 1958-1960 Les Paul 'Burst, available in Cherry Sunburst or other finishes, mfg. mid-1970s.

	N/A	$550	$475	$400	$350	$300	$250

ST STRATOCASTER STYLE - offset double cutaway Stratocaster style, three single coil pickups, white pickguard, essentially a copy of the Stratocaster, available in various finishes, mfg. 1970s.

	N/A	$450	$375	$325	$275	$225	$175

TOM ANDERSON GUITARWORKS

Instruments currently produced in Newbury Park, CA since 1984.

Luthier/designer Tom Anderson founded Tom Anderson Guitarworks in 1984, following a stint at Schecter as vice president from 1977 to 1984. Anderson´s interest and exploration of tonewoods and the overall interaction of the guitar´s parts have led to a refined and defined tone in his instruments.

All specs and orders are maintained on the company database. For anyone interested in recreating his or her favorite Anderson instrument, each guitar has a file in the database. Furthermore, there´s a good chance the original builder is still on staff - and that someone will probably remember building the first instrument!

According to Roy Fought, nearly 6,000 instruments have been produced in the company´s eight year history. According to Fought, the company is structured towards building guitars for the individual player´s style, and that the tonewood and pickup combinations are combined to enhance what the player wants to get out of his instrument.

GENERAL INFORMATION

All models in this series are available in these finishes: 6120 Orange, Baby Blue, Black, Blonde, Bora Bora Blue, Cherry Burst, Honey Burst, Metallic Purple, Natural, Seafoam Green, Three-Color Burst, Tobacco Burst, Transparent Amber, Transparent Blonde, Transparent Blue, Transparent Green, Transparent Magenta, Transparent Purple, Transparent Red, Transparent White, Transparent Yellow, White and White Pearl. A special Cajun Red or Cajun Magenta is an option at an additional $90.

Metallic colors are offered as an additional $100 option. These finishes include Anthracite (Grey), Black Cherry, Burgundy Mist, Candy Apple Red, Electric Blue, Lake Placid Blue, Ruby, Sapphire, Sparkle Gold, Sparkle Plum, Sparkle Purple, and Shoreline Gold.

Anderson guitars are available with variations of the 5-way switching, or Anderson´s own Switcheroo system. The Switcheroo consists of a four switch passive system - the three mini-switches are used for selecting any combination of neck/middle/bridge pickups, while the fourth Blower mini-switch goes from any pickup selection directly to the bridge pickup at full output.

Chrome hardware is stock on the guitar models. In 1996, Anderson adopted the Buzz Feiten Tuning system as standard for all guitars produced. This system helps compensate for inaccuracies inherent in guitar design (other builders such as Washburn have also begun using this system). For other model options and wood choices, please contact the company.

> **Add $80 for the black hardware option. Add $150 for the gold hardware option. Add $450 for L.R. Baggs X-Bridge (an acoustic bridge transducer and preamp circuit). Add $70 for Swamp ash body. Add $70 for Mahogany back. Add $100 for bound koa top.**

ELECTRIC: COBRA SERIES

COBRA - single cutaway mahogany body, bound figured maple top, 24.75 in. scale, bolt-on mahogany neck, 22-fret rosewood fingerboard w/pearl dot inlay, fixed bridge, 6-on-a-side locking tuners, chrome hardware, 2 humbucker pickups, volume/tone control, 5-position switch, mfg. 1993-present.

MSR	$3,270	$2,500	$2,100	$1,800	$1,500	$1,200	$1,000	$800

This model is available with a vintage tremolo bridge.

Hollow Cobra - similar to Cobra, except has two hollow internal sound chambers, mfg. 1994-present.

MSR	$3,330	$2,550	$2,150	$1,800	$1,500	$1,200	$1,000	$800

COBRA S - similar to the Cobra, except features a double cutaway body, mfg. 1997-present.

MSR	$3,250	$2,500	$2,100	$1,800	$1,500	$1,200	$1,000	$800

GRADING	100% MINT	98% NEAR MINT	95% EXC+	90% EXC	80% VG+	70% VG	60% G

Hollow Cobra S - similar to Cobra S, except has two hollow internal sound chambers, mfg.1994-present.

MSR	$3,310		$2,500	$2,150	$1,800	$1,500	$1,200	$1,000	$800

COBRA SPECIAL - similar to the Cobra, except features all mahogany body, 2 P-90 style (Anderson P1 and P3) pickups, mfg. 1998-present.

MSR	$3,070		$2,350	$1,900	$1,600	$1,300	$1,100	$900	$700

ELECTRIC: DROP TOP SERIES

Tom Anderson introduced the Drop Top model in 1992. The Dropped or bent top feel is the contouring similar to other models, but features a thick top of bookmatched maple or koa.

DROP TOP - offset double cutaway basswood body, 25.5 in. scale, bound figured maple top, bolt-on maple neck, 22-fret maple fingerboard with black dot inlay, standard vibrato, 6-on-a-side locking tuners, chrome hardware, 2 single coil/1 humbucker pickups, volume/tone control, 4 mini switches, mfg. 1991-present.

MSR	$3,100		$2,400	$1,950	$1,650	$1,350	$1,150	$950	$750

This model is also available with the following options: alder or lacewood body; pau ferro, palisander or rosewood fingerboard; fixed bridge or double locking vibrato; and left-handed configuration.

Hollow Drop Top - similar to the Drop Top, except has hollowed internal tone chambers, mfg. 1996-present.

MSR	$3,160		$2,450	$2,000	$1,650	$1,350	$1,150	$950	$750

DROP TOP CLASSIC - similar to Drop Top, except has pearloid or black satin pickguard, mfg. 1993-present.

MSR	$3,100		$2,400	$1,950	$1,650	$1,350	$1,150	$950	$750

Add $100 for bound koa top.

Hollow Drop Top Classic - similar to the Drop Top, except has hollowed internal tone chambers, mfg. 1996-present.

MSR	$3,160		$2,450	$2,000	$1,650	$1,350	$1,150	$950	$750

DROP TOP T - similar to Drop Top, except has single cutaway body, mfg. 1993-present.

MSR	$3,100		$2,400	$1,950	$1,650	$1,350	$1,150	$950	$750

This model is also available with the following options: alder or lacewood body; pau ferro, palisander or rosewood fingerboard; fixed bridge or double locking vibrato; and left-handed configuration.

Tokai Les Paul "Reborn" courtesy Rick Wilkiewicz

ELECTRIC: HOLLOW T SERIES

The Hollow T series features a swamp ash or basswood body with hollowed out sides and a solid central section (slightly wider than the pickup´s width). These hollow internal tone chambers help produce a light weight guitar that still has the tonal characteristics of solid body models. This idea has been offered on other models in the Anderson line as well.

HOLLOW T - single cutaway swamp ash body with two internal hollow sound chambers, 25.5 in. scale, bolt-on maple neck, 22-fret maple fingerboard with black dot inlay, fixed bridge, 6-on-a-side locking tuners, chrome hardware, 2 hum-cancelling pickups, volume/tone control, 4 mini switches, current mfg.

MSR	$2,850		$2,200	$1,800	$1,500	$1,200	$1,000	$800	$650

Add $200 for maple top.

This model is available with these options: pau ferro, palisander or rosewood fingerboard with pearl dot inlay; standard or double locking vibrato, choice of pickups; and left-handed configuration.

Hollow T Contoured - similar to Hollow T, except has contoured top/back, redesigned sound chambers, mfg. 1995-present.

MSR	$2,910		$2,250	$1,850	$1,500	$1,200	$1,000	$800	$650

HOLLOW T CLASSIC - similar to Hollow T, except has white pickguard and metal plate containing volume/tone controls and 5-way selector switch, current mfg.

MSR	$2,850		$2,200	$1,800	$1,500	$1,200	$1,000	$800	$650

Add $200 for maple top.

Hollow T Classic Contoured - similar to Hollow T, except has contoured top/back, redesigned sound chambers, pearloid pickguard, 2 single coil pickups, 5-position switch, mfg. 1995-present.

MSR	$2,910		$2,250	$1,850	$1,500	$1,200	$1,000	$800	$650

ELECTRIC: GRAND AM, PRO AM, & CLASSIC SERIES

GRAND AM - offset double cutaway lacewood body, 25.5 in. scale, bolt-on maple neck, 22-fret maple fingerboard with black dot inlay, double locking vibrato, 6-on-a-side tuners, chrome hardware, 2 single coil/1 humbucker pickups, volume/tone control, 4 mini switches, disc. 1994.

			N/A	$1,700	$1,400	$1,150	$900	$700	$550

Last MSR was $2,400.

This model was available with all the Anderson options when it was offered. The exotic, upscale cousin to the Pro Am model.

Tokai Stratocaster Style courtesy Rick Wilkiewicz

GRADING	100% MINT	98% NEAR MINT	95% EXC+	90% EXC	80% VG+	70% VG	60% G

PRO AM - offset double cutaway swamp ash body, 25.5 in. scale, bolt-on maple neck, 22-fret pau ferro fingerboard with pearl dot inlay, double locking vibrato, 6-on-a-side tuners, chrome hardware, volume/tone control, 4 mini switches, mfg. circa mid 1980s-present.

MSR	$2,500	$1,900	$1,600	$1,350	$1,100	$950	$800	$650

Add $70 for mahogany body.

This model is also available with the following options: alder or basswood body; maple, palisander or rosewood fingerboard; fixed bridge or standard vibrato; locking tuners; left-handed configuration.

THE CLASSIC - offset double cutaway swamp ash body, 25.5 in. scale, white pickguard, bolt-on maple neck, 22-fret maple fingerboard with black dot inlay, standard vibrato, 6-on-a-side locking tuners, chrome hardware, 3 single coil pickups, volume/tone control, 4 mini switches, current mfg.

MSR	$2,500	$1,900	$1,600	$1,350	$1,100	$950	$800	$650

This model is also available with the following options: alder or basswood body; black satin pickguard; palisander, pau ferro or rosewood fingerboard with pearl dot inlay; fixed bridge or double locking vibrato; and left-handed configuration.

Baritom Classic - similar to the Classic, except in baritone configuration, current mfg.

MSR	$2,700	$2,100	$1,750	$1,400	$1,150	$950	$800	$650

Hollow Classic - similar to The Classic model, except has hollowed internal tone chambers, mfg. 1996-present.

MSR	$2,910	$2,250	$1,850	$1,500	$1,200	$1,000	$800	$650

TOMKINS

Instruments currently built in Harbord, Australia.

These high quality solid body guitars are custom built by luthier Allan Tomkins, and feature designs based on popular Fender classics. Tomkins' guitars are crafted from exotic Australian hardwoods and softwoods such as Tasmanian King Billy pine, black heart sassafrass, queensland silky oak, crab apple birch, or coachwood. Instruments feature Gotoh tuners and bridges, 21-fret necks, Seymour Duncan or Bill Lawrence pickups, and a nitro-cellulose lacquer finish. For more information refer to their website (see Trademark Index).

TOMMYHAWK

Instruments currently built in NJ. Distributed by Tom Barth's Music Box of Dover, NJ.

Designer Tom Barth offers a 24 in. travel-style guitar that is a one-piece carved mahogany body (back, sides, neck, and bracing). The solid spruce top, bridge, and top bracing are then glued on - forming a solid, tone projecting little guitar! In 1997, the soundhole was redesigned into a more elliptical shape. Barth's full size (25.5 in. scale) electric/acoustic has a double cutaway body, Tele-style neck with a 21-fret rosewood or maple fingerboard, and a Seymour Duncan Duckbucker pickup.

TOMMY'S SPECIAL GUITARS

Instruments currently built in Viersen, Germany. Previously distributed in the U.S. by Salwender International of Orange, CA. Distributed in Europe by Tommy's Special Guitars of Viersen, Germany.

Luthier Thomas Metz has been handcrafting high quality solid and semi-solid electric guitars for a number of years. The distinctive feature of the Tommy's Special Guitars model is the systematic respect for the wood and physical sound properties. Each instrument is the technical synthesis of these characteristics. Metz' basic model features an alder, ash or mahogany Strat- or Tele-style body, rock maple neck with rosewood fingerboard, chrome tuners, tunomatic bridge/stop tailpiece (or vintage-style Gotoh tremolo), and EMG pickups. Custom options include a semi-acoustic body with quilted maple top, carved quilted maple top, or bird's-eye maple neck.

TONEMASTER

See chapter on House Brands.

This trademark has been identified as a House Brand ascribed to several distributors such as Harris-Teller of Illinois, Schmidt of Minnesota, and Squire of Michigan. While one recognized source has claimed that instruments under this trademark were built by Harmony, author/researcher Willie G. Moseley has also seen this brand on a Valco-made lap steel (source: Willie G. Moseley, *Stellas & Stratocasters*).

TONESMITH

Instruments currently built in Rogers, MN, since 1984.

Luthier Kevin Smith opened his GLF Custom shop for guitar repairs and custom building in 1984. In 1996, he began building prototypes for a new guitar design, which in 1997 developed into a full line with different models. For more information, refer to their website (see Trademark Index).

ELECTRIC

The ToneSmith series has several different models: The model **316** (the 1997 new offset body shape), model 320, (double cutaway model), model **412** (1996 offset double cutaway body), and the model **510** (a 1996 single cutaway design). All models are available in Guitar, Baritone, and Bass configurations.

After the customer selects the body style and configuration, a decision is made to the level of features. The **Special** has an alder body and top, maple neck with black or ivoroid binding, rosewood fingerboard, pearl dot inlays, solid colors, and nickel or chrome hardware. The **Custom** has a bound mahogany (or alder, or ash) body, flame or bird's-eye maple (or mahogany, alder or ash) top, ivoroid (or pearl or tortoiseshell) bound maple neck, rosewood fingerboard, pearl diamond wing inlay, semi-transparent or burst finishes, and nickel or chrome hardware.

The **Deluxe** is similar to the Custom, except has ebony (or bubinga) fingerboards, sparkle finishes, and optional gold hardware. All ToneSmith models are optional with an acoustic bridge pickup, Bigsby tremolo, or custom ordered colors. The Ultra Lite Version substitutes a spruce body and spruce or maple top for the regular body and top.

T

TOP TWENTY

Instruments previously produced in Japan between 1965 and 1976.

The Top Twenty trademark is a brand name used by a UK importer. These entry level quality instruments featured a solid body construction and some original designs (source: Tony Bacon and Paul Day, *The Guru's Guitar Guide*).

TOTEM GUITARS

Instruments currently built in Three Rivers, CA.

Totem offers several high quality guitars with bolt-neck designs, ash bodies and maple or myrtle tops, and quality hardware. These guitars are by Spalt guitars. For more information on Totem guitars, refer to their website (see Trademark Index).

TOYOTA

Instruments previously produced in Japan circa early 1970s.

Toyota guitars were distributed in the U.S. by the Hershman company of New York, New York. The Toyota trademark was applied to a full range of acoustic, thinline acoustic/electric hollow body, and solid body electric guitars and basses (source: Michael Wright, *Guitar Stories*, Volume One).

TRACE ELLIOT

Instruments previously built in England by Status. Previously distributed in the U.S. market by Trace Elliot USA of Darien, IL.

If you're a bass player, you've probably tested or use Trace Elliot amplification. In the 1990s, Trace developed amplifiers for both acoustic and electric guitars. Trace Elliot is offered a line of bass guitars built by the Status company in England.

ELECTRIC BASS

T-Series basses feature bolt-on necks, a four on one side headstock, and 2 single coil J-style pickups with an additional hum-cancelling dummy coil, volume/blend/tone controls, and an active EQ. Last Retail prices range from $1,899 up to $2,599. The **T-Bass 1998 Special Edition** features a Candy Apple Red finish with matching headstock, an aged pickguard, and 2 exposed pole Alnico stacked humbucking pickups. Only 100 4-string and 100 5-string models were scheduled to be built.

**Tommy's Special Guitars
Moderne
courtesy Salwender**

TRADEMARK STRINGED INSTRUMENTS

Instruments currently built in Athens, OH, since 1990.

Luthier Tom Hirst has been in the guitar building business since 1990. He was a technical assitance rep for Stewart-McDonald. He also has a regular column called "The Drawing Board" in *Guitar Digest* Magazine. Hirst builds all sorts of guitars including electric guitars, acoustic guitars, basses, mandolins, violins, and dulcimers. He mainly specializes in the electric guitar and bass field. Prices are more than reasonable for a guitar of quality like this. For more information refer to their website (see Trademark Index).

TRADITION GUITARS

Instruments currently produced. Distributed by Tradition Guitars in Tullahoma, TN.

Tradition builds guitars that have very low retail prices compared to guitars of the same caliber in other brands. Tradition feels that many guitars have gone up in price but have gone the other way as far as value. Tradition is striving for a high-quality guitar that doesn't cost a lot. They have a full line of electric guitars and basses that are generally based on popular American designs. For more information refer to their website (see Trademark Index).

TRAVELER

Instruments currently built in Redlands, CA, since 1992. Distributed by OMG Music.

Designer J. Corey Oliver offers a full scale travel-style guitar that is only 28 inches in overall length (full size 24.75 in. fret board), and two inches thick. For more information refer to their website (see Trademark Index).

ELECTRIC

Constructed of either maple or mahogany, the Traveler (basic list $500) has a single coil pickup (an optional Fishman transducer is also offered), and a storable lower arm for playing in the sitting position, and a unique Stethophone headset that requires no power source. The Traveler Speedster features an armrest and retails for $500 in Gloss Black finish and $540 for Candy Apple Red Metallic finish. The Escape model is also available in steel or nylon string configuraiton and features an on-board EQ. Retail price is $500 for this. The Traveler Bass was introduced in November 2004, that features a full 35 in. scale body, 4.5 lbs, and retails for $499.

TRAVIS BEAN

Instruments previously built in Sun Valley, California from 1974 to 1979.

The following Travis Bean history is reprinted here courtesy of Bill Kaman, who has been a Travis Bean fan from the beginning. Additional information supplied by Richard Oblinger (Obe), a Travis Bean employee; and Travis Bean, the man behind it all.

Travis Bean: It's the name of a California motorcycle enthusiast who decided in the early '70s that aluminum would be a step forward in guitar design. He thought that it would be a much more stable material for the necks. Using a neck-through-to-the-bridge design also improved the sound and sustain of the guitars. While Travis played some

**Tonesmith 316 Custom
courtesy Dale Hanson**

T

guitar, he was a drummer and kept a drum kit set up at the factory to back up players when they were there to check out equipment.

The company was founded in 1974 and lasted five years, closing in August of 1979. They produced about 3,650 guitars and basses which are as viable an instrument today in the '90s as they were when they were built. Initial production began in 1974 and continued until December 1977 when the factory was closed for "reorganization." In June 1978, it reopened and continued until August 1979, when the plug was pulled by the investors who had "reorganized" the company. Sashi Pattell, an Indian guy, was the major investor and "drove" the company for the last twelve months. During the first six months of 1978, limited "unofficial" production continued with a partial production crew who often took guitars in lieu of wages.

In 1977, the guitars were sold through Rothschild Distribution but that ended with the reorganization. When the company closed in 1979, everything was sold off at auction. Mighty Mite bought about 200 bodies and most of the guitar parts but never really did anything with them. There were about thirty TB500 necks left over and it's not known who bought these. Mighty Mite itself was closed and auctioned off a few years later.

The first guitar Travis ever built was a 'Melody Maker' body shape with Gibson humbucker pickups. The aluminum neck had a welded-on peghead and bolted to the body. The neck attachment plate was inlaid in the body and extended back to under the bridge. After experimenting with this guitar a while the idea of a neck-through-to-the-bridge design began to take shape. A second prototype was built which was much closer to the production design in neck and body configuration. This guitar has a serial number of "1," and used Fender humbucker pickups. After these two guitars, limited production began. These first "limited production" guitars were TB1000 Artists and were produced in 1974. The serial numbers started with #11 and went to #20. These guitars were handmade by Travis and Mark McElwee, Travis' partner in the company, and are quite similar in construction to the second pre-production prototype. The bodies were Koa, Teak, Padauk, Zebra wood, and Alder (Guitar #11 and #18 are known to be Padauk). The necks on these were quite different from the later production models produced on a lathe. These were hand carved from a solid block of Reynolds T6061 aluminum and are solid under the fingerboard and solid through the body. The necks have a wide and flat profile which is noticeably thinner than the later production which are much fuller and more rounded. The pickups on these first guitars are humbuckers using Fender bobbins and Alnico magnets; and have "Travis Bean" engraved on the chrome pickup covers. The guitars are quite thin, about the same thickness as the 1979 final production Artists. Another interesting aspect of these guitars is the peghead. The angle is flatter than later production (about six degrees versus a production angle of twelve degrees). There is also about an extra inch between the nut and the beginning of the 'T' cutout. In this extra space there is bolted an aluminum block with 6 holes acting as a string tree to hold the tension over the nut. Later production guitars with the steeper angle didn't need this tie down.

In all, there are quite a few differences between these first 10 prototypes and the production models ranging from the body thickness and top contour, peghead dimensions and angle, neck profile and shape of the body insert piece, to the pickup engraving. These guitars are a bit crude compared to the later production; but after all, they are the first ones made.

Production of the 1000 series continued throughout 1974 with the 1000 Standard being introduced approximately six months after the startup. This guitar had all the same dimensions as the 1000 Artist, only differing in that the body was not carved and it had dot fingerboard inlays rather than the large pearl blocks of the Artist. It was a solid 1.75 in. all over. The run of serial numbers on Standards and Artists began with #21 and continued until #1000. At that point the lines were split and each continued with #1001, #1002, etc. While it is unclear if the production records of these first 1000 guitars still exist, it is estimated that there were approximately 1/3 Artists and 2/3 Standards. All the bodies were koa and most were finished Natural; however, the factory did offer Black, White, and Red. Both straight color and pearl color were offered. There were also several Dark Blue Pearl guitars made (there were two Silver guitars made: one for Joe Perry [of Aerosmith] a Standard #1738; and a Wedge Guitar [# 53] for Al Austin). The koa bodies continued until late 1978 when the painted models began to use magnolia and poplar. The Natural finishes continued to use mostly Koa although a natural magnolia is known to exist. All these guitars used black speed knobs which Travis bought directly from Gibson until for some reason Gibson shut them off. After that, clear speed knobs were used. In late 1978 and 1979, black metal knobs were used. Internally, these were referred to as "Sansui" knobs because they looked like they were off a home stereo set! The machine heads were Schaller and Grover and alternated without any pattern throughout the years of production. Towards the end of the company, Gotoh machine heads were used, particularly on the 500 model. The last Artist produced was serial number 1425 and the last Standard produced was serial number 1782. In all, there were about 755 Artists and 1,442 Standards produced.

The TB2000 Bass was introduced in late 1974. The first prototype had serial number "0" and is of similar construction to the first ten guitars. However, it is much more like a production guitar in that it doesn't have that "handmade" look of the first 10 guitars. This bass is pictured in the first catalog on the TB2000 models. This bass also had an aluminum nut (the only one made this way). All other production Travis Beans were made with brass nuts. The neck was hand carved by Travis and has a thick squarish feel. It was solid as was the section in the body. The body had a 1/4" edge radius and was koa. Production started with serial number 11 and the bodies were more rounded and contoured. They were all koa and made in Natural and the same colors as the guitars. A fretless version was available, as was a short scale model bass. In all about twelve short scale basses were made, two of which were for Bill Wyman in October 1978 (serial number 892 and 893). The last bass made was serial number 1033. In all there were 1,023 basses made.

The 500 model was meant to be a less expensive single coil version of the 1000 model. The first guitars were produced in late 1977, just before the reorganization shutdown. The first nine guitars were quite different from the balance of production. These had standard 1 3/4" thickness bodies but the aluminum body extension was set in from the top rather than sliding into the middle of the body and being exposed at the back. These guitars had uncoated necks, and the bodies were much more square than later production. Most of these first 500s went to performers like Jerry Garcia and Rory Gallager (who had three pickup guitars). Mark McElwee kept one made with a Koa body. In June of 1978 when production resumed with guitar #20 the bodies were more slimmer and had a slanted off center shape. The pickguards also were more stylized, and the majority of the necks were coated with the black Imron paint that was used to give the guitar necks a "warmer" feel. There were several made with three pickups (serial numbers 11, 12, 270). Up until around serial number 290, the pickups had black plastic covers with the pole piece exposed. After #290, the covers were solid black plastic with a molded-in stylized "Travis Bean" logo. The majority of the 500s had magnolia bodies although there were some made from poplar. Most were painted Black, White, or Red although there were some Naturals made. The last 500 was serial number 362 so there were a total of 351 TB500 guitars produced. There were plans for a 500 model Bass but it was never completed.

The Wedges are perhaps the most unique guitars and basses produced by Travis Bean. They were the "Stage" guitars, and the Travis Bean version of a 'Flying V'. They were introduced in 1976 and built for two years. In total, 45 TB3000 Wedge guitars and 36 TB4000 Wedge basses were produced. All the basses were produced in the 1.75 in. thickness. Most of the guitars were 1 3/4" thick, with the exception of the last few (for example, Wedge guitar #49 is 1.75 in., but the next to the last one produced [# 55] was 1.375 in. thick. Also, # 49 has a one piece fingerboard and # 55 is two-piece). The majority of the Wedges were produced in pearl colors: white, black, and red. An interesting point is that the bodies were the same overall size for both guitars and bass.

There were two doublenecks built. Both were double six strings and used Artist necks. One was a red Wedge and the other a natural Artist. There were also six 5-string guitars made that were Standards and are serial numbered 1732 to 1737. These went to Keith Richards, Travis Bean, Richard Oblinger, Mark McElwee, and Bill Lominic (the head machinist at the company). All these were coated necks and were 1.375 in. thick. Left-handed guitars and basses were also available and lefty 1000 Artists and Standards, as well as 2000 basses are known to exist. There were no lefty Wedges or 500s built. There were requests over the years for special custom bodies on guitars, but these requests were turned down. Travis felt that building the custom "one-offs" would dilute the impact of the market place of the standard production. There exist today several instruments with custom bodies (for example: a MAP guitar and a Flying V) but these were retrofitted to existing guitars and not done at the Bean factory.

Throughout the production there were several significant changes that took place. The first change was that the horns of the guitars and basses were widened. This was around mid-1977. This was a suggestion from Rothchild Distributing and it was felt that this would improve playability and sales. An estimate is that this took place on Artists around #1100, Standards #1250, and Basses #440. The second change is that the bodies were made thinner by .375 in. This is estimated to have taken place around #1200 on Artists, #1400 on Standards, and #580 on Basses and was probably phased in around the first part of 1978. The third change was that the fingerboards went to a two piece construction. This took place just about the same time as the thinner bodies. Initially, the fingerboard was rosewood (although some early guitars had ebony; they also experimented with phenolic) and was a standard thickness. The center portion of the neck under the fingerboard was machined away to make it lighter. There was a rib left down the middle to support the fingerboard. On the later version the fingerboard was again rosewood, but half the thickness it had been previously. A thin piece of aluminum was added under the fingerboard to bring the fingerboard assembly back to standard thickness. On these guitars the center rib was not left in the middle of the neck since the aluminum underlay would fully support the wood. Also in 1978, a slight radius was introduced to the fingerboard. Up until this they had all been flat like a classical guitar (except for the prototype bass [#0] which has a seven-degree radius). The fourth change that took place around mid-1977 was the coating of the necks. One of the constant complaints about Travis Beans was that the necks felt "cold" and some found them objectionable (it´s a good thing that these complainers didn´t play saxophones!). In response to this the company introduced the option of a black Imron coated neck. Imron is a heavy duty automobile enamel. It was felt that this heavy finish would make the necks feel slightly warmer, and since it was a spray-on finish it would be more like a standard guitar neck. This was an option on any guitar or bass (and as mentioned, pretty much a standard on the 500 series).

There was another small change in the machining of the aluminum piece in the body of the guitars. Approximately the first 300 TB1000 guitars made had the aluminum section in the body cavity machined from the side to take out the weight. The middle of the aluminum was cut completely away so there was a back section, visible at the back of the guitar; and a top section, which the pickups sat on. The rear most portion of the extension under the bridge was left solid. This was then glued into the body after it was finished. From around serial number 300, on the body section of the aluminum was machined from the top which created a "U" shaped channel under the guitar top and pickups. The rear end portion under the bridge was again solid. The improvement in this design was that it created a much more rigid structure in the body of the guitar, plus it allowed the body to be screwed to the neck extension by two wood screws through the walls of the "U" channel under the front pickup. Those two screws plus the three that fasten the bridge to the aluminum through the wood body are all that hold it together. This design made it much easier to remove the neck should it need work or work on the body. The pickups sat directly on either side of the "U" channel and were held in place by allen screws mounted from the rear.

The serial number of the guitar is stamped onto the face of the peghead just above the nut. It was also stamped into the aluminum under the neck pickup. On some it was also written on the bottom of the "U" channel. It was written on the body in two places: the interior of the control cavity, and in the space between the pickups on the inside. On the painted bodies the number in the control cavity was often painted over, and therefore not visible. It is interesting to note that bass #477 has body #478 so either bass #478 has #477 body or the #477 body had a problem and they just used the next body on the assembly line. This does prove that necks and bodies are interchangeable.

Where is Travis Bean today? By the time the company was sold at auction, Travis had his fill of production headaches, Music Industry BS, and demanding visits from the Taxmen. He took some time off. Being a tinkerer at heart, and someone who is happier using his hands and building things, he eventually began work building sets for the movie studios (which he continues to do today). His personal interest in music has stayed strong, and he has kept playing - focusing mostly on his drumming. Being true to his machinist/designer/tinker side, he has also developed a new style of rack setup for drums that allows for fast set-up and tear-down. So the answer is, Travis is alive and well and still playing in California (source: C. William Kaman, II, President [Kaman Music Corporation], May 6, 1994).

SERIALIZATION AND MODEL PRODUCTION

The following chart is a rough accounting of the production by year and serial number:

Model No.	1974 to Jan. 1976	Jan. 1976 to Dec. 1977	Jan. 1978 to June 1979	Total
TB500	-	-	11-362	351
TB1000A	11-400	400-1000,1000-1162	1163-1425	755
TB1000S	-	1056	1157-1782	1422
TB2000	11-200	201-763	764-1033	1023
TB3000	-	11-50	51-56	45
TB4000	-	11-47	-	36
Totals	600	1444	1611	3652

Travis Bean guitars are offered in the range between $1,000 and $1,250; the rarer Wedge models command a higher price (a total of 45 Wedge guitars and 36 Wedge basses were produced between 1976 and 1978). Prices today are typically found between $1,000 and $1,500.

TREKER

Instruments currently built in Draper, UT.

Treker offers a range of quality guitar and bass models that feature the exclusive Floating Neck technology. Handcrafted bodies are joined to a neck that has an internal tension bar which offers structural support and allows the fretboard to vibrate free of the traditional static load of the neck/truss rod/fingerboard design. For further information regarding individual models and specifications, or on the Floating Neck concept, please contact Treker directly (see Trademark Index).

T

TRIGGS GUITARS

Instruments currently hand built in Lawrence, KS. Previously manufactured in Kansas City, KS and Nashville, TN.

Luthier Jim Triggs has been building instruments since the mid -1970s. While at Gibson during 1986-1992, Jim wore many hats, including Artist Relations, Custom Shop Manager, Archtop Guitar Supervisor, Custom Mandolin Builder, and Art Guitar Designer. Jim left Gisbon in March of 1992, and has been custom building ever since, including many stars. His more famous clients have included: Alan Jackson, Steve Miller, Elliot Easton, Pat Martino, Mundell Lowe, Vince Gill, and Marty Stuart.

Jim´s son Ryan is currently working with him in the shop, and this "team," maybe the only father & son duo currently working on archtops together. The Triggs Boys keep busy with a constant back order of flattops, archtops, and F-5 style mandolins. Much of Jim´s time in the shop is spent on design work for other companies. Several models are in Cort Guitars line already, and 4 Triggs designed "Tradition Guitars" debuted at the Nashville Summer NAMM Show in July, 2001.

The sky´s the limit with a Triggs guitar. Flattop prices start at $2,000, archtops around $3,000, and F-5s for around $10,000. Please contact Triggs directly for more information and a personal price quotation (see Trademark Index), if the aliens haven´t abducted him (again!).

TRUETONE

See chapter on House Brands.

This trademark has been identified as a House Brand of Western Auto. Built by Kay in the 1960s, the six-on-a-side headstock shape shared with this trademark has been dubbed "duck´s bill" or "platypus" in reference to the rather bulbous nature of the design (source: Willie G. Moseley, *Stellas and Stratocasters*).

TRUSSART, JAMES

Instruments currently built in Los Angeles, CA. Previously built in Paris, France.

French luthier James Trussart was a custom electric guitar builder who began building in 1980, and rose to some notice during the 1980s in Paris (the "James Trusear Guitar Station" was the name of Trussart´s shop). Trussart has created instruments for both Eric Clapton and bassist Nathan East. While it was rumored that Trussart may have retired several years ago, Trussart is still custom crafting the steel bodied instruments that bear his namesake. For further information regarding model designations and pricing, contact James Trussart directly (see Trademark Index), (Preliminary information courtesy Jeff Meyer). Trussart created his version of Strat and Tele designs that featured exceptional craftsmanship, and were retail priced around $3,000. Trussart´s creations feature steel bodies, or engraved metal tops and headstocks over the instrument bodies. Many creations are one-of-a-kind designs. Research still continues on Trussart´s custom instruments and the models bearing the James Trusear trademark. For more information refer to Trussart´s website (see Trademark Index).

TUBULAR INSTRUMENT CO. INC.

Instruments previously built in Staten Island, NY.

Tubular Instrument Co. built a unique, light wooden string called the "Tube Bass."

TUNE GUITAR TECHNOLOGY CO., LTD.

Current trademark of instruments manufactured in Tokyo, Japan since 1983.

Tune Guitar Technology Co., Ltd. offers many different series of high quality basses and guitars. Tune Basses all possess innovative, original designs and quality hardware and electronics.

ELECTRIC BASS: BASS MANIAC CUSTOM SERIES

TBC-4 S - offset double cutaway walnut/padauk/bubinga body, bolt-on 3-piece maple neck, 25-fret rosewood fingerboard with white dot inlay, fixed Gotoh bridge, 2-per-side Gotoh tuners, black hardware, P/J-style humbucker Tune pickups, volume/treble/bass/mix controls, active electronics, available in Natural finish, current mfg.

MSR	$1,399		$1,050	$850	$750	$650	$550	$450	$350

TBC-5 S - similar to TBC-4 S, except has 5 string configuration, fixed Tune bridge, 3/2-per-side tuners, current mfg.

MSR	$1,699		$1,275	$1,025	$900	$775	$650	$525	$425

ELECTRIC BASS: KINGBASS SERIES

TWB-4 - offset double cutaway walnut/padauk/bubinga body with pointed bottom bout, bolt-on 3-piece maple neck, 24-fret ebony fingerboard with white dot inlay, fixed Gotoh bridge, body matching peghead with raised logo, 2-per-side Gotoh tuners, gold hardware, 2 humbucker Tune pickups, volume/treble/bass/mix/filter controls, active electronics, available in Natural finish, current mfg.

MSR	$2,249		$1,800	$1,350	$1,125	$900	$810	$740	$675

Add $100 for figured maple top.

TWB-5 - similar to TWB-4, except has 5 strings, 3/2-per-side tuners, current mfg.

MSR	$2,449		$1,825	$1,470	$1,225	$1,000	$875	$700	$615

TWB-6 - similar to TWB-4, except has 6 strings, 3-per-side tuners, current mfg.

MSR	$2,480		$1,860	$1,500	$1,325	$1,150	$975	$800	$620

ELECTRIC BASS: ZI NECK THROUGH SERIES

Zi3-4 - offset double cutaway walnut/padauk/bubinga body with pointed bottom bout, through body 3-piece maple neck, 24-fret ebony fingerboard with white dot inlay, fixed Tune bridge, body matching veneered peghead, 2-per-side Gotoh tuners, gold hardware, 2 humbucker Tune pickups, volume/treble/bass/mix/filter controls, active electronics, available in Natural finish, current mfg.

MSR	$2,599		$1,950	$1,600	$1,400	$1,225	$1,025	$850	$650

Zi3-5 - similar to Zi3-4, except has 5 strings, 3/2-per-side tuners, current mfg.

MSR	$2,799		$2,100	$1,680	$1,485	$1,290	$1,100	$900	$700

GRADING	100% MINT	98% NEAR MINT	95% EXC+	90% EXC	80% VG+	70% VG	60% G

Zi3-6 - similar to Zi3-4, except has 6 strings, 3-per-side tuners, current mfg.

	MSR	$2,999		$2,250	$1,800	$1,590	$1,380	$1,170	$960	$750

TURNER, RICK

Instruments currently built in Santa Cruz, CA. Distributed by Rick Turner Guitars of Topanga, CA. Previously built in Topanga, CA.

Luthier Rick Turner was one of the original three partners that formed Alembic in 1970. In 1978, he left Alembic to form Turner Guitars, and opened a workshop in 1979 in Novato, California. Although artists such as Lindsey Buckingham favored Turner's guitars, the company was closed in 1981. Turner's records show that approximately 130 instruments were built during that time period (1979-1981).

As well as building instruments, Rick Turner has written countless columns on guitar building, repairs, and products profiles in guitar magazines. Turner reopened his guitar shop in 1989, and now offers a range of instruments.

Please refer to the Renaissance section in this text for more information on these models manufactured by Rick Turner.

ELECTRIC: MODEL # SERIES

Tyler, James Mongoose courtesy James Tyler

Add $400 for AAA flamed or quilted top wood. Add $225 for Rick Turner Piezo bridge with proprietary blending electronics (BNC electronics only). Add $250 for matching bird´s eye maple peghead, fingerboard, pickup ring, tailpiece, and nickel pickup cover (disc.). Add $100 for custom colors such as Gold, Silver, Translucent Blue, Translucent Green, or others (disc.). Add $200 for optional Mike Christian Piezo bridge and Turner blending electronics (disc.).

MODEL ONE - also known as the Lindsey Buckingham guitar, features semi-hollow body and unique rotating single pickup design, trapeze tailpiece, 130 were manufactured before they became a custom shop model. Model One guitars and basses are now available through the custom shop only. Please allow 6-18 months for delivery, this custom shop model carries the Turner brand.

MODEL 1-A - single cutaway arched top mahogany top and back, bound in black, five piece laminated neck with multi layer veneer overlays on peghead, 24-fret black bound rosewood fingerboard (15 frets clear of the body), nickel plated hardware, single Turner Humbucking pickup, Schaller tuners and roller bridge, Turner "stop" tailpiece, one volume and one tone knob, available in a deep Red stain on the mahogany body and High Gloss Urethane finish, 24.75 in. scale, current mfg.

	MSR	$3,620		$3,100	$2,600	$2,250	$1,950	$1,750	$1,600	$1,450

Model 1-B - similar to the Model 1-A, except has an active buffer and line driver preamp, current mfg.

	MSR	$3,880		$3,300	$2,750	$2,375	$2,050	$1,825	$1,700	$1,500

Model 1-C - similar to the Model 1-A, except has a quasi-parametric EQ. This model is the duplicate to the original Model 1 (1979-1981), current mfg.

	MSR	$4,170		$3,600	$3,000	$2,550	$2,150	$1,900	$1,800	$1,550

MODEL 1-A CC - similar to the Model 1-A, except has a cedar core body with walnut, current mfg.

	MSR	$3,620		$3,100	$2,600	$2,250	$1,950	$1,750	$1,600	$1,450

Model 1-B-CC - similar to the Model 1-A, except has an active buffer and line driver preamp, current mfg.

	MSR	$3,880		$3,300	$2,750	$2,375	$2,050	$1,825	$1,700	$1,550

Model 1-C-CC similar to the Model 1-A, except has a quasi-parametric EQ, current mfg.

	MSR	$4,170		$3,600	$3,000	$2,550	$2,150	$1,900	$1,750	$1,600

MODEL 2 - similar to the Model 1-A, except that an added Turner humbucker pickup is added to the bridge position, disc. 2000.

Last MSR was $2,325.

MODEL 3-A - similar to the Model 1-A, except has an extended 27-fret ebony fingerboard (17 frets clear of the body), 24.75 in. scale, disc. 2000.

Last MSR was $2,335.

Model 3-B - similar to the Model 3-A, except has an active buffer and line driver preamp, disc. 2000.

Last MSR was $2,485.

Model 3-C - similar to the Model 3-A, except has a quasi-parametric EQ, disc. 2000.

Last MSR was $2,585.

ELECTRIC: JUNIOR SERIES

The Junior series was offered beginning in 1995. All models have an alder body, one piece maple neck, and no bindings or wood laminates. By saving on labor and some wood costs, the retail price of the Junior series is about $500 less than the Models 1,2, or 3; however, the same hardware and electronic options are offered on the Juniors as is on the regular models. The **Model 1-A, Jr.** features similar design to the Model 1-A, single pickup, painted alder body, rosewood fingerboard, and passive electronics at a list price of $2,360. The **Model 1-B, Jr.** is the same except has an active buffer and line driver preamp built in ($2,620), and the **Model 1-C, Jr.** features a quasi-parametric EQ ($2,910). All were available in Red, Maroon, Cobalt Blue, or Forest Green. Add $77.25 for a Three Color Sunburst. This series was discontinued.

T

TURTLETONE

Instruments previously built in Tempe, AZ.

Luthier/designer Walter G. Gura produced a number of solid body instruments that feature interesting and innovative designs. Though Turtletone was a relatively small company, they utilized a number of high tech devices like CAD/CAM (Computer Aided Design/Computer Aided Manufacturing) instruments. The CAD/CAM devices also assisted in customer-specified unusual body designs, as the design could be plotted prior to construction. Turtletone guitars featured maple bodies and necks, ebony fingerboards, DiMarzio pickups, and Kahler or Grover hardware. List price for the standard instrument was $1,600, and many special orders/options were available per customer order.

TUXEDO

Instruments previously made in England, West Germany, and Japan during the early to mid 1960s. Some guitars may also carry the trademark of Dallas.

The Tuxedo and Dallas trademarks are the brand names used by a UK importer/distributor. Some of the early solid body guitars were supplied by either **Fenton-Weill** or **Vox** in Britain, and other models were imported entry level German and Japanese guitars that featured some original design guitars (source: Tony Bacon and Paul Day, *The Guru's Guitar Guide*).

TYLER, JAMES

Instruments currently built in Van Nuys, CA.

Luthier James Tyler and his staff are currently building and offering a fairly wide range of custom solid body guitars and basses. Models are constructed of quality tonewoods, Wilkinson bridges, Schaller locking tuners, and "Tyler spec'd" Lindy Fralin or Seymour Duncan pickups.

ELECTRIC

Tyler guitars feature an offset, double cutaway body design and bolt-on bird´s-eye maple neck. In the **Studio Elite** series, bodies are constructed out of mamy-wood, and some models have a figured maple top "Bent Over Arm Contour." Prices range from $2,495 (**Studio Elite Psychedelic Vomit**) to $2,765 (**Studio Elite**) and up to $3,350 (**Studio Elite Deluxe**).

Tyler´s **Mongoose** series is the top of the line Tyler Guitar. Models feature Honduran mahogany bodies, and flame maple tops (except for the **Mongoose Special** and **Mongoose Acoustic Electric**). The maple cap under the **Mongoose Gold Top** is not flamed (nor is the gold finish translucent, if you think about it - so the flame wouldn´t be apparent). Prices run from $3,065 on the **Mongoose Gold Top** to $3,550 (**Mongoose Special**). For further information regarding these and other Tyler guitar models, contact Tyler Guitars directly (see Trademark Index).

TYM

Instruments currently built in Australia.

Tym guitars was founded in 1997. These are in the words of the luthier, Tim, basically copies of Mosrites. Production is approximately twenty-five instruments per year. All models are available in left-hand configuration also. For more information refer to their website (see Trademark Index).

ELECTRIC

All models are listed on their website, but they are in Australian dollars. Contact the compoany for what each model goes for in other countries.

The **Johnny Model** has an offset double cutaway body, copy of Johnny Ramone´s Mosrite Ventures MKII, solid body with two humbuckers or single coil pickups, Tune-O-Matic bridge, stop tailpiece, Kluson style tuners, 1 volume/1 tone control, 3-way selector switch, black or white 3-ply pickguard, available in any solid or metallic color and MSR in the U.S. was $750.

The **Johnny Deluxe Model** is similar to the Johnny Model, except has Moseley type vibrato and cast aluminum top hat knobs, choice of maple or ash neck with a zero fret, a more faithful reproduction of the Mosrite Ventures MK II, and MSR in the U.S. was $830.

The **Johnny Ramone Model** is similar to the Johnny deluxe model, except has 1 Seymour Duncan mini humbucker and 1 DiMarzio "Fat Strat" pickup, Mosrite style bridge and stop tailpiece, Grover style tuners, 1 volume/1 tone control, 3-way selector switch, black or white 3-ply pickguard, available in a selection of body timbers. Available in White, Blue or Metallic Gold finishes and MSR in the U.S. was $890.

The **Versatone Model** has an offset double cutaway Mosrite style body, same specs as Johnny Ramone Model, except has angled neck pickup, tune-o-matic bridge, Jazzmaster style vibrato and MSR in the U.S. was $800.

The **Versatone Deluxe Model** is similar to Versatone Model, except has Moseley type vibrato and Mosrite style cast aluminum top hat knobs, zero fret, painted neck binding, 2 P-90 pickups with surrounds, choice of ash or maple body and MSR in the U.S. was $890.

The **Versatone Deluxe VIII** is a copy of Mosrite VIII made in the mid -80s by Semie Moseley, carved top, no pickguard, basswood body, 1 volume control, 3 mini-toggles for pickup on/off, laminated rosewood and maple fingerboard and MSR in the U.S. was $950.

The **Mosrong Model 500** has a Mosrite-ish solid body design, available with 2 single coil pickups or 1 single coil and 1 humbucker in the bridge position, carved top, available with stop tailpiece or Jazzmaster style tremolo and MSR in the U.S. was $500.

There are several other configurations available on these three general models. Look for more information in further editions of the *Blue Book of Electric Guitars*.

Add $75 for aluminum neck. Add $35 for rock maple neck. Add $55 for each Seymour Duncan pickup. Add $70 for each Seymour Duncan mini-humbucker. Add $55 for each Kent Armstrong mini-humbucker. Add $40 for 3-color Sunburst finish. Add $20 for Moseley style left-hand tremolo.

Section U

U.S. MASTERS GUITAR WORKS

Instruments currently built in Middleton, WI.

The U.S. Masters Guitar Works drew on their retail and repair backgrounds while designing and producing the **Vector** and **Sportster** series of guitars, as well as the EP series four- and five-string bass models. There are select retail dealers, but they sell most of their product factory direct. Suggested list prices include a deluxe hardshell case. For more information on ordering and pricing (as it can change), visit their website (see Trademark Index).

GRADING	100% MINT	98% NEAR MINT	95% EXC+	90% EXC	80% VG+	70% VG	60% G

ELECTRIC: EP SERIES

EP GUITAR - offset double cutaway with an extended bass bout and shorter treble bout, Honduras mahogany body with a flame maple top, birdseye maple neck, six-on-one side tuners, fixed bridge, STB, various pickup configurations, available in deluxe high gloss finishes, 37.125 in. overall length, 25.5 in. scale, current mfg.

	MSR	$1,899		$1,300	$1,150	$1,000	$900	$800	$700	$600

> Add $100 for gold hardware. Add $100 for Point Classic tremolo bridge. Add $175 for Floyd Rose tremolo. Add $200 for grade 5 flame maple top. Add $200 for highly figured select birdseye maple neck.

ELECTRIC: LEGRAND SERIES

The LeGrand Series is the U.S. Masters re-engineering of the classic Strat design. This model features a locking neck joint to augment the standard bolt-on connection, a low profile heel, and additional pickup blend control. Standard LeGrand finishes include Black, Fine Metallic Candy, Red, Fine Metallic Blue; transparent finishes include Cherry, Purple, and Royal Blue. Deluxe LeGrand finishes are an additional $75, and include Sunburst, Amber, and Emerald Green.

LEGRAND - offset double cutaway Stratocaster style soft maple body, captive neck joint, rock maple neck, six-per-side tuners, six screw vintage style tremolo bridge, various pickup configurations, available in various finishes, current mfg.

	MSR	$1,599		$1,150	$1,000	$875	$750	$650	$550	$450

> Add $40 for pearl pickguard. Add $100 for gold hardware.

LEGRAND LEGEND - offset double cutaway Stratocaster style swamp ash body, captive neck joint, birdseye maple neck, six-per-side tuners, Point Classic tremolo bridge, various pickup configurations, available in various finishes, current mfg.

	MSR	$1,999		$1,400	$1,200	$1,050	$900	$800	$700	$600

> Add $40 for pearl pickguard. Add $100 for gold hardware.

LEGRAND CUSTOM LEGEND - offset double cutaway Stratocaster style swamp ash or mahogany body with a grade five flame maple top, captive neck joint, birdseye maple neck, six-per-side tuners, Point Classic tremolo bridge, various pickup configurations, available in various finishes, current mfg.

	MSR	$2,399		$1,700	$1,500	$1,300	$1,150	$1,000	$900	$800

> Add $40 for pearl pickguard. Add $100 for gold hardware.

ELECTRIC: SPORTSTER SERIES

The **Versatek** model (last MSR $999) has a fixed bridge and 2 HH Versatek pickups; the Classic (last MSR $1,074) has a floating tremolo bridge and 2 single coils/humbucker pickup configuration. The **Sportster F Classic** substitutes a Floyd Rose tremolo in place of the floating tremolo bridge, (last MSR $1,345). The **Hammer** model has a similar Floyd Rose tremolo, and features Hammer pickups (last MSR $1,320).

SPORTSTER - double cutaway body with rounded bass bout, soft maple body, six-per-side tuners, fixed bridge, black pickguard, HSS pickup configuration, available in deluxe High Gloss finishes, current mfg.

	MSR	$1,500		$1,150	$1,000	$875	$750	$650	$550	$450

> Add $70 for left-handed configuration. Add $100 for gold hardware. Add $100 for Point Classic tremolo. Add $100 for birdseye maple neck. Add $175 for Floyd Rose tremolo.

SPORTSTER SKINNY - double cutaway body with rounded bass bout, soft maple or mahogany body, black or cream body binding, six-per-side tuners, fixed bridge, two humbucker or two P-90 pickup configuration, available in deluxe High Gloss finishes, 1.3 in. thick body, current mfg.

	MSR	$1,799		$1,250	$1,100	$950	$850	$750	$650	$550

> Add $70 for left-handed configuration. Add $100 for gold hardware.

Sportster Skinny Flametop - similar to the Sportster Skinny, except has a grade 5 flame maple top and birdseye maple neck, current mfg.

	MSR	$2,199		$1,600	$1,400	$1,200	$1,050	$900	$800	$700

Sportster Skinny Quilttop - similar to the Sportster Skinny, except has a grade 5 quilted maple top and birdseye maple neck, current mfg.

	MSR	$2,499		$1,800	$1,550	$1,350	$1,150	$1,000	$900	$800

GRADING	100% MINT	98% NEAR MINT	95% EXC+	90% EXC	80% VG+	70% VG	60% G

ELECTRIC: SUPER T SERIES

SUPER T - single cutaway Telecaster style swamp ash body, rock maple neck, six-per-side tuners, fixed bridge, two humbucker pickups, various finishes, current mfg.

	MSR	$1,799	$1,250	$1,100	$975	$850	$750	$650	$550

SUPER T DELUXE - single cutaway Telecaster style lacewood body with a grade five flame maple top, body binding, birdseye maple neck, six-per-side tuners, fixed bridge, pearl pickguard, two humbucker pickups, various finishes, current mfg.

	MSR	$2,299	$1,650	$1,450	$1,250	$1,100	$975	$850	$750

SUPER T HOLLOW - single cutaway Telecaster style hollow mahogany body with a thin curly maple top, body birdseye maple neck, six-per-side tuners, fixed bridge, two humbucker pickups, various finishes, current mfg.

	MSR	$2,199	$1,600	$1,400	$1,200	$1,050	$925	$800	$700

ELECTRIC: VECTOR SERIES

Vector model guitars have an offset double cutaway Honduran mahogany bodies and contoured book-matched figured maple tops (AAA maple tops are available for an extra $300). Standard Vector opaque finishes include Black, Fine metallic Candy, Red, Fine Metallic Blue; transparent finishes include Amber, Cherry, Emerald Green, Sunburst, Purple, Royal Blue, Deep Blue, and Clear Gloss.

The **Vector Standard** has a list price of $1,899. The **Vector Versatek** model (list $1,449) has a fixed bridge and 2 HH Versatek pickups; the **Vector F Classic** (list $1,840) has a Floyd Rose bridge and 2 single coils/humbucker pickup configuration. The **Vector Artist** (list $1,497) has a fixed bridge and 2 single coil/humbucker pickups, while the **Vector Artist Special** substitutes a Point tremolo in place of the fixed bridge, and has a retail list price of $1,680. The **Vector Hammer** model has a similar Floyd Rose tremolo, and features 2 Hammer pickups (list $1,840).

These limited edition models are similar to the regular Vector models, but are constructed with solid Australian lacewood. Models include the **Lacewood Versatek** (list $1,160), **Lacewood F Classic** (list $1,490), **Lacewood Artist** (list $1,200), **Lacewood Artist Special** ($1,345), and the **Lacewood Hammer** (list $1,490). Lacewood Vector Transparent gloss finishes are an additional $250, and feature Amber, Cherry, Emerald Green, Royal Blue, and Purple.

VECTOR - offset double cutaway Honduras mahogany body with a contoured flame maple top, birdseye maple neck, six-on-one-side tuners, fixed bridge, STB, various pickup configurations, available in trans. high gloss finishes, 35 in. overall length, 25.5 in. scale, current mfg.

	MSR	$1,899	$1,300	$1,150	$1,000	$900	$800	$700	$600

Add $100 for gold hardware. Add $100 for Point Classic tremolo bridge. Add $175 for Floyd Rose tremolo. Add $200 for grade 5 flame maple top. Add $200 for highly figured select birdseye maple neck.

This model is also available with a lacewood body.

ELECTRIC BASS: EP SERIES

The **EP41 P** has a split P-style pickup (list $1,599), and the **EP41 S** has two soapbar pickups (list $1,245). **EP42** models feature figured wood bodies like curly maple and lacewood; prices range from $1,849 to $1,999. The **EP43** has Australian Lacewood or genuine mhogany with a bookmatched flame maple top, and lists for $1,999. The **EP53** is the five string version of the EP43 and lists for $2,149. The **EP44** has 3 pieces of Australian Lacewood with the sections seperated by different types of wood, and lists for $2,199. The **EP54** is the five string version of the EP44 and lists for $2,349.

The **EP45** has Australian Lacewood or genuine mahogany with the sections separated by different types of wood, and lists for $2,199. The **EP55** is the five string version of the EP45 and lists for $2,349. The EP50 5-String series have a similar construction to the EP40 models, and prices that range from $1,295 (**EP51P**) up to $2,199 (**EP55C**). There is a wide range of bass models and options to choose from. For additional information regarding model specifications and pricing, contact the U.S. Masters directly (see Trademark Index).

EP4 - offset double cutaway mahogany body, rock maple neck, 24-fret pao ferro fingerboard fingerboard with offset dot inlays, 3/1-per-side tuners, standard bridge, single split pickup, four knobs, chrome hardware, available in Natural finish, current mfg.

	MSR	$945	$675	$600	$525	$475	$425	$375	$325

EP5 - similar to the EP4, except in five-string configuration with 3/2-per-side tuners, current mfg.

	MSR	$999	$725	$625	$550	$500	$450	$400	$350

UNICORD

See UNIVOX. Instruments previously produced in Japan.

The Merson Musical Supply Company of Westbury, New York was the primary importer of Univox guitars. Merson evolved into Unicord, and also became a distributor for Westbury brand guitars (source: Michael Wright, *Guitar Stories*, Volume One).

UNITED

Instruments previously made in Elizabeth, NJ during the 1940s.

United guitars was owned by Frank Forcillo, ex-D'Angelico worker and long time friend. D'Angelico put his name on a series of plywood body guitars (Model G-7) that were built at either United or Code (also from New Jersey). The plywood instruments featured solid wood necks fashioned by D'Angelico, but the construction was handled out in the United plant. D'Angelico used to stock these guitars in his showroom/workshop in New York City. D'Angelicos by United were not numbered or recorded. The body design is perhaps more reminiscent of a Gibson ES-175, and used to carry the designation G 7 (source: Paul William Schmidt, *Acquired of the Angels*).

GRADING	100% MINT	98% NEAR MINT	95% EXC+	90% EXC	80% VG+	70% VG	60% G

UNIVOX

Instruments previously built in Japan circa 1969 to 1978. Distributed in the U.S. by the Merson Musical Supply Company of Westbury, NY.

Univox instruments were imported into the U.S. by the Merson Musical Supply Company of Westbury, New York. **Merson Musical Supply** later evolved into the **Unicord** company. The Univox trademark was offered on a full range of acoustic, thinline acoustic/electric hollowbody, and solid body electric guitars and basses. The majority of the Univox guitars produced were built by Arai of Japan (See Aria), and are entry level to intermediate quality for players (source: Michael Wright, *Guitar Stories*, Volume One).

ELECTRIC/ELECTRIC BASS

MISC. ELECTRIC - various configurations in hollowbody and solidbody configurations, mfg. 1960s-1970s.

	100%	98%	95%	90%	80%	70%	60%
	N/A	$500	$425	$350	$300	$250	$200

MISC. ELECTRIC BASSES - various configurations in hollowbody and solidbody configurations, mfg. 1960s-1970s.

	100%	98%	95%	90%	80%	70%	60%
	N/A	$450	$375	$325	$275	$225	$175

**Univox Custom Bass
courtesy The Music Shoppe**

NOTES

Section V

VF GUITARWORKS

Instruments currently built in Naples, Italy.

VF Guitarworks produces a line of electric guitars and basses. They have more than twenty different tonewoods to chose from on their guitars and basses. Prices on their guitars start at $1,150 and for the basses $1,250. For more information on VF Guitarworks visit their website (see Trademark Index).

VACCARO

Instruments currently built in Asbury Park, NJ. Distributed by the Vaccaro Guitar Company of Asbury Park, NJ.

The Vaccaro Guitar Company's debut in 1998 at the music industry NAMM show was one of the most colorful and stylish in years. This new company was formed in April of 1997 to begin producing its vibrant designs and innovative manufacturing techniques. Guitar manufacturing in the United States has been decreasing significantly, and today most of the world's production is done in Korea, Mexico, and Japan. The Vaccaro Guitar company seeks to bring quality guitar building back to America.

The Vaccaro Guitar company was founded by Henry Vaccaro, Sr. (chairman of the board) and Henry Vaccaro, Jr. (president). Henry Vaccaro, Sr. is not new to the guitar industry. Vaccaro, Sr. was one of the original founders of Kramer Music Products, Inc. (KMP), a premier American guitar manufacturing company. Vaccaro, Sr. served as a board member from 1976 to 1982, when he was elected Chairman of KMP's Board of Directors. He successfully guided the company into becoming one of America's largest guitar manufacturers, with sales in 1987 exceeding $15,000,000. Vacarro served as chairman from 1982 to 1988. Vacarro, Sr. was also the founder and president of the Henry V. Vaccarro Corporation, a statewide building construction firm that completed a number of high dollar construction projects. Vaccaro, Sr. dissolved this company when he began testing the prototypes of the new 'V' aluminum neck.

The entire Vaccaro guitar line was conceived by Vaccaro, Jr., stemming from a graphics and fashion background with extensive work in artist management. Vaccaro, Jr. drew from his experience to design a line of stylistic guitars. During the past 5 years, extensive research and testing had been conducted for the development of the Vaccaro 'V' neck that would be featured on all Vaccaro guitars and basses. The stability of the 'V' neck leads to the elimination of frequent adjustments and replacements.

In 1976, Kramer Music Products introduced the patented **Power Forged Aluminum T-Neck** guitar; from 1976 to 1980 total sales were in excess of $6,000,000. In 1981, the aluminum neck was discontinued, as it was too costly to produce compared to the conventional wooden neck. Vacarro, Sr. and luthier Dr. Phillip Petillo re-evaluated the original 1976 aluminum neck while researching the 'V' neck. Part of the problems encountered with the original T-Neck was the heavy weight (21 ounces), high manufacturing costs, and temperature conductibility (the neck would go out of tune under extreme heat or the chill of a cold neck was uncomfortable to guitarists). Vaccaro's new V neck features an aluminum core surrounded by wood (only 2 ounces heavier than a conventional wood neck, which is barely noticeable in a properly balanced body), an Ebanol synthetic fingerboard, and an adjustable truss rod for the desired bow or play in the neck.

GRADING	100% MINT	98% NEAR MINT	95% EXC+	90% EXC	80% VG+	70% VG	60% G

ELECTRIC

ASTROLITE (MODEL AST) - dual cutaway alder body, bolt-on aluminum/wood 'V' neck, 25.5 in. scale, 22-fret ebanol fingerboard with pearl diamond inlay, Schaller roller saddle bridge/stop tailpiece, 3-per-side tuners, chrome hardware, 2 Thruster Humbucker pickups, volume/tone control, 3-way position toggle switch, available in Black, Deja Blue, Pepto Pink, Triple Mint, or White finishes, current mfg.

MSR	$1,349		$1,100	$900	$775	$650	$550	$450	$350

COMET - offset dual cutaway basswood body, bolt-on figured wood 'V' neck, 25.5 in. scale, 22-fret ebanol fingerboard with pearl diamond inlay, Schaller roller saddle bridge/stop tailpiece, 3-per-side tuners, chrome hardware, 2 soapbar single coil pickups, volume/tone control, 3-way position toggle switch, available in Black, Red Glo, or White finishes, disc. 2003.

			$750	$675	$600	$550	$475	$400	$325

GENERATOR X (MODEL GX) - offset double cutaway alder body with pointed horns, bolt-on aluminum/wood 'V' neck, 25.5 in. scale, 22-fret ebanol fingerboard with pearl diamond inlay, Schaller roller saddle bridge/Bigsby tremolo, 3-per-side tuners, chrome hardware, 2 single coil/humbucker Rio Grande pickups, volume/tone control, 3-way position toggle switch, 5-way rotary selector. Available in Black, Deja Blue, Fire Burst, Pepto Pink, Orangeade, Retro Burst, or Triple Mint finishes, current mfg.

MSR	$1,499		$1,125	$925	$775	$650	$550	$450	$350

GROOVE JET (MODEL GJ) - offset double cutaway alder or mahogany body with pointed horns, bolt-on aluminum/wood 'V' neck, 25.5 in. scale, 22-fret ebanol fingerboard with pearl diamond inlay, Schaller roller saddle bridge/stop tailpiece, 3-per-side tuners, chrome hardware, 2 covered humbucker Seymour Duncan pickups, 2 volume/2 tone control, 3-way position toggle switch, available in Black, Corduroy, Emerald Stain, Orangeade, Red Glo, Retro Burst, Sapphire Stain, or White finishes, current mfg.

MSR	$1,349		$1,100	$900	$775	$650	$550	$450	$350

GRADING	100% MINT	98% NEAR MINT	95% EXC+	90% EXC	80% VG+	70% VG	60% G

X-RAY (MODEL XRG) - offset double cutaway alder body, bolt-on aluminum/wood 'V' neck, 25.5 in. scale, 22-fret ebanol fingerboard with pearl diamond inlay, Schaller roller saddle bridge/strings through-body ferrules, 3-per-side tuners, chrome hardware, white pearloid pickguard, single coil/humbucker Rio Grande pickups, volume/tone controls, 3-way position toggle switch, coil tap mini-switch, available in Black, Blue Sparkle, Green Sparkle, Orange Sparkle, Purple Sparkle, or Red Sparkle finishes, current mfg.

MSR $1,399	$1,125	$925	$775	$650	$550	$450	$350

ELECTRIC BASS

M-80 BASS (MODEL M-80) - offset double cutaway alder body with pointed horns, bolt-on aluminum/wood 'V' neck, 34 in. scale, 20-fret ebanol fingerboard w/pearl diamond inlay, fixed Schaller bridge, 2-per-side tuners, chrome hardware, P/J-style Basslines pickups, volume/pan/tone controls, available in Black, Fire Burst, Orangeade, Red Glo, Sapphire Stain, Amber, Emerald Stain, or White finishes, disc.

	$1,000	$850	$725	$600	$500	$400	$300

Last MSR was $1,549.

X-RAY BASS (MODEL XRB) - offset double cutaway alder body, bolt-on aluminum/wood 'V' neck, 34 in. scale, 20-fret ebanol fingerboard with pearl diamond inlay, fixed Schaller bridge, 2-per-side tuners, chrome hardware, white pearloid pickguard, P/J-style Basslines pickups, volume/pan/tone controls, available in Black, Blue Sparkle, Green Sparkle, Orange Sparkle, Purple Sparkle, or Red Sparkle finishes, current mfg.

MSR $1,499	$1,125	$925	$775	$650	$550	$450	$350

COMET BASS - similar to the Generator Bass, except has Comet shaped body, disc. 2003.

	$850	$775	$700	$625	$525	$425	$350

GENERATOR X BASS - offset double cutaway swamp ash body, bolt-on aluminum/wood 'V' neck, 34 in. scale, 20-fret ebanol fingerboard with pearl diamond inlay, Schaller 2000 bridge, 2-per-side tuners, chrome hardware, white pearloid pickguard, 2 J-style Basslines pickups, volume/pan/tone controls, available in Black, Blue Deja, White, Pepto Pink, Triple Mint, Amber, or Red Glo finishes, current mfg.

MSR N/A	$1,100	$900	$775	$650	$550	$450	$350

VALCO

See National.

Louis Dopyera bought out the National company, and as he owned more than 50% of the stock in Dobro, "merged" the two companies back together (as National Dobro). In 1936, the decision was made to move the company to Chicago, Illinois. Chicago was a veritable hotbed of mass produced musical instruments during the early to pre-World War II 1900s. Manufacturers like Washburn and Regal had facilities, and major wholesalers and retailers like the Tonk Bros. and Lyon & Healy were based there. Victor Smith, Al Frost, and Louis Dopyera moved their operation to Chicago, and in 1943 formally announced the change to VALCO (the initials of their three first names: V-A-L company). Valco worked on war materials during World War II, and returned to instrument production afterwards. Valco produced the National/Supro/Airline fiberglass body guitars in the 1950s and 1960s, as well as wood-bodied models. In the late 1960s, Valco was absorbed by the Kay company (See Kay). In 1968, Kay/Valco Guitars, Inc. went out of business. Both the National and the Supro trademarks were purchased at the 1969 liquidation auction by Chicago's Strum 'N Drum Music Company (source: Tom Wheeler, *American Guitars*).

VALLEY ARTS

Trademark currently owned and distributed by Gibson since late 2002. Instruments previously produced in City of Industry, CA since 1993. Previous production was based in North Hollywood, CA from 1979 to 1993. Previously distributed by the Samick Music Corporation of City of Industry, CA.

Valley Arts originally began as a North Hollywood teaching studio in 1963. The facilities relocated to Studio City, California and through the years became known as a respected retail store that specialized in professional quality music gear. Production moved back to North Hollywood and into larger facilities in 1989, and luthier/co-owner Michael McGuire directed a staff of 15 employees.

In 1992, the Samick corporation became involved in a joint venture with Valley Arts, and by June of 1993 had acquired full ownership of the company. Samick operated Valley Arts as the custom shop wing for the company, as well as utilizing Valley Arts designs for their Samick production guitars built overseas.

In 2002, Mike McGuire and Al Carness, who both founded Valley Arts in the beginning, became part of the company again when Gibson acquired the company. Al is now the manager of the Valley Arts retail Store and Mike is the operations manager for the Gibson Custom Shop. Valley Arts is current a custom order only guitar manufacturer. There are online order forms to select what you want. They are also a repair shop for guitars. Visit their website for more information (see Trademark Index).

All models were available with the following standard finishes, unless otherwise listed: Antique Burst, Antique Natural Burst, AquaMarine Burst, Blue Burst, Blue with Black Burst, Candy Red, Emerald Green, Fire Burst, Green Burst, Green with Black Burst, Green Teen, Kelly Green, Marteen Gold, Midnight Blue, Natural, Orange Teen, Oriental Blue, Purple Teen, Red with Black Burst, Sunset Gold, Trans. Black, Trans. Blue, Trans. Cream, Trans. Green, Trans. Purple, Violet Burst, Watermelon Burst, and White.

ELECTRIC: CALIFORNIA PRO SERIES

CALIFORNIA PRO (MODEL 7 RS) - 7/8 scale offset double cutaway alder body, bolt-on quartersawn maple neck, 24-fret rosewood fingerboard with abalone inlay, 6-on-a-side tuners, pickguard, gold hardware, stop tail bridge, 2 single coil/humbucker Duncan pickups, volume/tone controls, 5-way selector switch, vailable in Antique Burst, Fire Burst, Marteen Gold, Orange Teen, Purple Teen, Trans. Red, Trans. White, Transparent finishes: Black, Burgundy, Candy Blue, Candy Red, Hunter Green, or White solid finishes, disc 2002.

	$900	$780	$685	$590	$495	$390	$300

Last MSR was $1,199.

This model is available with a maple fingerboard (Model 7 MS), or with a Wilkinson vintage-style tremolo (Model 7 R; maple fingerboard option is Model 7 M).

GRADING	100% MINT	98% NEAR MINT	95% EXC+	90% EXC	80% VG+	70% VG	60% G

California Pro Deluxe (Model Deluxe 7 R) - similar to the California Pro, except has 7/8 scale ash body, Wilkinson vintage-style tremolo, pearloid pickguard, disc.

	$975	$850	$745	$640	$535	$430	$325

Last MSR was $1,299.

This model is available with a maple fingerboard (Model Deluxe 7 M).

California Pro Deluxe (Model Deluxe 8 R) - similar to the California Pro Deluxe (Model Deluxe 7 R), except has full-sized ash body, 22-fret rosewood neck, 3 Duncan single coil pickups, disc.

	$975	$850	$745	$640	$535	$430	$325

Last MSR was $1,299.

This model is available with a maple fingerboard (Model Deluxe 8 M).

California Pro Deluxe T (Model Deluxe 8 R T) - similar to the California Pro Deluxe (Model Deluxe 7 R), except has full-sized ash body, 22-fret rosewood neck, gold tele-style fixed bridge, 2 Duncan single coil pickups, mfg. 1997-2002.

	$975	$850	$745	$640	$535	$430	$325

Last MSR was $1,299.

This model is available with a maple fingerboard (Model Deluxe 8 M T).

ELECTRIC: CUSTOM PRO SERIES

Both Custom Pro Bent Top and quilted maple top models feature a wide variety of customer-specified options such as pickup configuration, choice of Duncan or EMG pickups, bridge configurations, and finishes.

CUSTOM PRO BENT TOP 'S' (MODEL C8BS) - offset double cutaway alder body, quilted maple top, bolt-on bird's-eye maple neck, 22-fret ebony fingerboard, 6-on-a-side tuners, gold hardware, volume/tone controls, 5-way selector switch, disc. 2002.

	$1,600	$1,350	$1,150	$1,000	$850	$700	$550

Last MSR was $2,200.

Custom Pro Bent Top 'T' (Model C8BT) - similar to the Custom Pro Bent Top 'S', except features a single cutaway body design, disc. 2002.

	$1,600	$1,350	$1,150	$1,000	$850	$700	$550

Last MSR was $2,200.

CUSTOM PRO BENT TOP 7/8 'S' (MODEL C7BS) - similar to the Custom Pro Bent Top 'S', except features a 7/8 scale offset double cutaway body design, disc. 2002.

MSR	$2,200	$1,600	$1,350	$1,150	$1,000	$850	$700	$550

Custom Pro Bent Top 7/8 'T' (Model C7BT) - similar to the Custom Pro Bent Top 'S', except features a 7/8 scale single cutaway body design, disc. 2002.

	$1,600	$1,350	$1,150	$1,000	$850	$700	$550

Last MSR was $2,200.

CUSTOM PRO QUILT 'S' (MODEL C8QS) - offset double cutaway quilted maple body, bolt-on bird's-eye maple neck, 22-fret ebony fingerboard, 6-on-a-side tuners, gold hardware, volume/tone controls, 5-way selector switch, disc. 2002.

	$2,200	$1,800	$1,500	$1,250	$1,050	$900	$750

Last MSR was $3,100.

Custom Pro Quilt 'T' (Model C8QT) - similar to the Custom Pro Quilt 'S', except features a single cutaway body design, disc. 2002.

	$2,200	$1,800	$1,500	$1,250	$1,050	$900	$750

Last MSR was $3,100.

CUSTOM PRO QUILT 7/8 'S' (MODEL C7QS) - similar to the Custom Pro Quilt 'S', except features a 7/8 scale offset double cutaway body design, disc. 2002.

	$2,200	$1,800	$1,500	$1,250	$1,050	$900	$750

Last MSR was $3,100.

Custom Pro Quilt 7/8 'T' (Model C7QT) - similar to the Custom Pro Quilt 'S', except features a 7/8 scale single cutaway body design, disc. 2002.

	$2,200	$1,800	$1,500	$1,250	$1,050	$900	$750

Last MSR was $3,100.

CUSTOM PRO - offset double cutaway ash body, bolt-on bird's-eye maple neck, 24-fret rosewood fingerboard with pearl dot inlay, double locking vibrato, 6-on-a-side tuners, gold hardware, white or black pickguard, 2 single coil/1 humbucker EMG pickups, volume/tone control, 5-position switch, available in Burnt Amber, Fireburst, Sunset Gold, Trans. Blue, Trans. Cream, Trans. Green, or Trans. Red finishes, disc. 1994.

	N/A	$1,400	$1,150	$900	$750	$600	$500

Last MSR was $1,995.

Add $300 for quilted maple body with ebony fingerboard.

STANDARD PRO - offset double cutaway maple body, black pickguard, bolt-on maple neck, 24-fret rosewood fingerboard with pearl dot inlay, double locking vibrato, 6-on-a-side tuners, black or chrome hardware, 2 single coil/1 humbucker EMG pickups, volume/tone control, 5-position switch, available in Black, Candy Red, Metallic Teal, or White finishes, disc. 1993.

	N/A	$1,400	$1,150	$900	$750	$600	$500

Last MSR was $1,995.

**Vaccaro X-Ray
courtesy Henry Vaccaro, Jr.**

GRADING	100% MINT	98% NEAR MINT	95% EXC+	90% EXC	80% VG+	70% VG	60% G

V

CUSTOM PRO CARVED TOP (MODEL VACTCP) - offset double cutaway mahogany body, bound flame maple carved top, set-in mahogany/bird's-eye maple neck, 24.75 in. scale, 22-fret bound ebony fingerboard with block inlays, tune-o-matic bridge/stop tailpiece, gold hardware, 2 Seymour Duncan PAF reissue humbuckers, 2 volume/master tone controls, 3-position switch, mfg. 1997-2002.

	$2,400	$2,080	$1,825	$1,580	$1,315	$1,060	$800

Last MSR was $3,200.

CUSTOM PRO DOUBLE NECK (MODEL VA12/6BS) - offset double cutaway alder body, quilted top, bolt-on 12-string and 6-string maple necks, 25.5 in. scale, 22-fret ebony fingerboards, chrome hardware; the 12- string neck has a fixed bridge, 3 EMG single coil pickups, volume control, 5-way selector; the 6-string neck has Wilkinson tremolo, 2 single coil/humbucker EMG pickups, volume control, 5-way selector, overall master tone control, 3-way neck selector switch, mfg. 1997-2002.

	$3,375	$3,000	$2,625	$2,250	$1,875	$1,500	$1,125

Last MSR was $4,500.

CUSTOM PRO EXOTIC WOOD (MODEL C7WS41D) - 7/8 scale offset double cutaway walnut body, bolt-on walnut neck with Spanish Luthiers joint, 24-fret ebony fingerboard, Original Floyd Rose tremolo, 6-on-a-side tuners, gold hardware, humbucker/Rail-F Duncan Custom pickups, volume/tone control, 3-position switch, available in Tung Oil finish, mfg. 1997-2002.

	$1,650	$1,430	$1,255	$1,080	$900	$725	$550

Last MSR was $2,200.

Different species of wood may vary in price.

CUSTOM PRO LITE (MODEL C7SS25D) - 7/8 scale offset double cutaway swamp ash body, bolt-on (Interlock technology) bird's-eye maple neck, 24-fret ebony fingerboard, Wilkinson vintage tremolo, 6-on-a-side tuners, gold hardware, 2 single coil/humbucker Seymour Duncan pickups, volume/tone control, 5-way switch, mfg. 1997-2002.

	$1,200	$1,040	$915	$785	$660	$530	$400

Last MSR was $1,600.

Custom Pro Lite (Model C7SS41D) - similar to the Custom Pro Lite (Model C7SS25D), except has bolt-on or Interlock neck joint, quartersawn maple or bird's-eye maple neck, rosewood fingerboard, black veneer headstock, Original Floyd Rose tremolo, gold or black hardware, humbucker/Rail-F Duncan Custom pickups, mfg. 1997-2002.

	$1,275	$1,100	$965	$830	$695	$560	$425

Last MSR was $1,700.

CUSTOM PRO S/L (MODEL SL8SS22E) - offset double cutaway swamp ash body, bolt-on bird's-eye maple neck, 22-fret ebony fingerboard, Original Floyd Rose vibrato, 6-on-a-side tuners, chrome hardware, black pickguard, 2 single coil/humbucker EMG pickups, volume/tone control, 5-position switch, available in Fireburst finish (body and neck), mfg. 1997-2002.

	$1,350	$1,170	$1,025	$880	$740	$595	$450

Last MSR was $1,800.

CUSTOM PRO L-1 (VACPL1) - offset double cutaway, alder, mahogany, or swamp ash body, two piece quilt maple, flame maple, or koa top, birdseye maple neck, 22-fret rosewood fingerboard with dot inlay, Duncan, EMG Active, or Valley Arts pickups in S/S/H, S/S/S, or H/H configuration, hard tail bridge, 3 knobs, 5-way switch, 6-on-one-side tuners, black or gold hardware, available in Custom Colors, mfg. 2003-present.

MSR	$3,000		$2,150	$1,850	$1,600	$1,350	$1,150	$1,000	$850

Add $225 for Floyd Rose or Wilkinson tremolo.

Custom Pro L-2 (VACPL2) - similar to the Custom Pro L-1, except in a 7/8 size body, 24.75 in. scale, 24-fret fingerboard, and 2 knobs, mfg. 2003-present.

MSR	$2,900		$2,050	$1,750	$1,500	$1,250	$1,050	$900	$750

Add $225 for Floyd Rose or Wilkinson tremolo.

CUSTOM PRO S-1 (VACPS1) - offset double cutaway, one piece quilt maple, swamp ash, mahogany, or alder top, bird's-eye maple neck, 22-fret rosewood fingerboard with dot inlay, Duncan, EMG Active, or Valley Arts pickups in S/S/H, S/S/S, or H/H configuration, hard tail bridge, 3 knobs, 5-way switch, 6-on-one-side tuners, black or gold hardware, available in Custom Colors, mfg. 2003-present.

MSR	$4,700		$3,400	$2,900	$2,500	$2,100	$1,800	$1,500	$1,200

Add $225 for Schaller Floyd Rose or Wilkinson tremolo.

Custom Pro S-2 (VACPS2) - similar to the Custom Pro S-1, except in a 7/8 size body, 24.75 in. scale, 24-fret fingerboard, and 2 knobs, mfg. 2003-present.

MSR	$4,700		$3,400	$2,900	$2,500	$2,100	$1,800	$1,500	$1,200

Add $225 for Schaller Floyd Rose or Wilkinson tremolo.

ELECTRIC: LUTHIER'S CHOICE SERIES

LUTHIER'S CHOICE (MODEL C7-LC) - single cutaway mahogany body, bound carved top, bird's-eye maple neck, 24-fret ebony fingerboard, bound painted headstock, tune-o-matic bridge/stop tailpiece, gold hardware, 2 Duncan P-90 pickups, recessed volume/tone controls, 3-way selector, available in Antique Burst or Tobacco Sunburst finishes, disc.

	$1,875	$1,625	$1,425	$1,220	$1,015	$825	$625

Last MSR was $2,500.

LUTHIER'S CHOICE 2 (MODEL C7-LC2) - similar to the Luthier's Choice, except has herringbone-bound top, 2 single coil/humbucker EMG pickups, 5-way selector, disc.

	$1,875	$1,625	$1,425	$1,220	$1,015	$825	$625

Last MSR was $2,500.

LUTHIER'S CHOICE JR. (MODEL C7-LC/JR) - similar to the Luthier's Choice, except without bound carved top; features mahogany neck, 24-fret rosewood fingerboard, chrome hardware, disc.

	$1,100	$945	$830	$715	$600	$480	$365

Last MSR was $2,450.

GRADING	100% MINT	98% NEAR MINT	95% EXC+	90% EXC	80% VG+	70% VG	60% G

V

ELECTRIC: MASTER SIGNATURE SERIES

RAY BENSON CUSTOM (MODEL VARB2) - single cutaway alder body, quilted maple top, maple neck, 25.5 in. scale, 22-fret maple (or rosewood or ebony) fingerboard, 6-on-a-side tuners, fixed bridge, chrome hardware, violin-shaped pearloid pickguard, humbucker/Hot Rail/single coil pickups, volume/tone controls, 5-way selector, disc.

	$1,600	$1,350	$1,150	$1,000	$850	$700	$550

Last MSR was $2,200.

Add $200 for flame maple top.

RAY BENSON CUSTOM TEXAS T (MODEL VARBTT) - oversized single cutaway alder body, quilted maple top, bird's-eye maple neck, 25.5 in. scale, 22-fret ebony fingerboard, 6-on-a-side tuners, fixed bridge, gold hardware, Texas 'T' or violin-shaped pearloid pickguard, humbucker/Hot Rail/single coil pickups, volume/tone (push/pull) controls, 5-way selector, disc.

	$2,025	$1,755	$1,540	$1,325	$1,100	$890	$675

Last MSR was $2,700.

Add $500 for body and headstock binding.

BLUES SARACENO CUSTOM (MODEL VABSC) - single rounded cutaway alder body, maple neck, 24.75 in. scale, 24-fret maple or rosewood fingerboard with offset colored position markers, 3-per-side tuners, Floyd Rose tremolo, black hardware, 2 Duncan Trembuckers, volume control, 3-way selector, disc.

	$1,425	$1,235	$1,080	$930	$780	$630	$475

Last MSR was $1,900.

Add $200 for glitter finish.

BLUES SARACENO CUSTOM BENT-TOP (MODEL VABSCB) - single rounded cutaway alder body, quilted maple top, bird's-eye maple neck, 24.75 in. scale, 24-fret ebony fingerboard with offset abalone position markers, 3-per-side tuners, Floyd Rose tremolo, black hardware, Duncan Trembucker/Duncan 59 humbucker pickups, volume control, 3-way selector, disc.

	$1,875	$1,625	$1,425	$1,225	$1,020	$825	$625

Last MSR was $2,495.

BLUES SARACENO CUSTOM FLATTOP (MODEL VASSH) - single rounded cutaway alder body, quartersawn maple neck, 25.5 in. scale, 22-fret rosewood or maple fingerboard w/offset colored position markers, 3-per-side tuners, through-body stringing fixed bridge, black or gold hardware, 2 single coil/1 humbucker pickups, volume control, 5-way selector, available in all Valley Arts Solid colors plus Berry-cicle, Cherry-cicle, Cream-cicle, Fudge-cicle, Grape-cicle, Lemon-cicle, and Lime-cicle finishes, disc.

	$1,200	$1,040	$915	$785	$660	$530	$400

Last MSR was $1,600.

BRENT MASON (VAMSS1MPHF1) - T-style design (Telecaster) swamp ash body, maple neck, 22-fret maple fingerboard with black dot inlay, black Tele-style pickguard, matching color headstock, S/S/H pickups with Gibson Mini-humbucker in neck, and Seymour Duncan Hot and Classic Stacks, 3 knobs and 3-way switch mounted on gold plate, 6-on-one-side tuners, gold hardware, available in Matte Pewter finish, new 2004.

MSR	$3,000	$2,150	$1,850	$1,600	$1,350	$1,150	$1,000	$850

STEVE LUKATHER SIGNATURE - offset double cutaway ash body, black pickguard, bolt-on bird's-eye maple neck, 24-fret ebony or rosewood fingerboard with pearl dot inlay, double locking vibrato, 6-on-a-side tuners, gold hardware, 2 single coil/1 humbucker EMG pickups, volume/tone control, 5-position switch, available in Fireburst finish, disc. 1993.

	N/A	$1,300	$1,100	$950	$800	$650	$500

Last MSR was $2,075.

This model was co-designed by Steve Lukather (Toto, Los Lobos) and has his signature on the back of the headstock.

ELECTRIC: STUDIO PRO SERIES

STUDIO PRO (MODEL SH7SR) - 7/8 scale offset double cutaway hardwood body, bolt-on quartersawn maple neck, 24-fret rosewood fingerboard, 6-on-a-side tuners, black or chrome hardware, vintage-style tremolo, slanted single coil/humbucker Duncan Design pickups, volume/tone controls, 5-way selector switch, available in Black (BK) or White (WH) finishes, mfg. 1997-2002.

	$750	$650	$575	$500	$425	$350	$275

Last MSR was $998.

STUDIO PRO (MODEL HH7TR) - similar to the Studio Pro, except has 7/8 scale single cutaway hardwood body, tune-o-matic bridge, 2 Duncan Design humbuckers, available in Black (BK) or White (WH) finishes, disc.

	$750	$650	$575	$500	$425	$350	$275

Last MSR was $998.

V

GRADING	100% MINT	98% NEAR MINT	95% EXC+	90% EXC	80% VG+	70% VG	60% G

ELECTRIC: T SERIES

T-SERIES (VATSS1) - single cutaway Telecaster style swamp ash body, maple neck, 22-fret maple or rosewood fingerboard with dot inlay, Tele-style pickguard, 2 Seymour Duncan vintage Stack pickups, 6-on-one-side tuners, 2 knobs and 3-way switch mounted on metal plate, gold hardware, available in Custom Colors, new 2004.

	MSR	$2,132		$1,500	$1,300	$1,150	$1,000	$850	$700	$550

T-SERIES BENT TOP (VABTH1) - single cutaway Telecaster hollow mahogany body, single f-hole on bass side, mahogany neck, 22-fret rosewood fingerboard with dot inlay, 3 Seymour Duncan pickups in S/S/H, 6-on-one-side tuners, 3 knobs and 5-way switch, gold hardware, available in Custom Colors, new 2004.

	MSR	$2,460		$1,750	$1,500	$1,300	$1,100	$950	$800	$650

ELECTRIC BASS: CAL PRO BASS SERIES

CAL PRO BASS IV (MODEL BASS IV) - offset double cutaway swamp ash body, bolt-on maple neck, 34 in. scale, 21-fret rosewood fingerboard, 4-on-a-side Valley Arts tuners, gold hardware, Wilkinson WBB-4 fixed bridge, P/J-style pickups, volume/tone controls, available in Antique Burst, Fire Burst, Marteen Gold, Orange Teen, Purple Teen, Trans. Red, or Trans. White finishes, disc.

$1,050	$900	$790	$680	$570	$460	$350

Last MSR was $1,399.

Add $275 for 2TEK bridge.

CAL PRO BASS V (MODEL BASS V) - similar to the Cal Pro Bass IV, except has 5-string configuration, Wilkinson WBB-5 bridge, disc.

$1,125	$975	$855	$735	$615	$495	$375

Last MSR was $1,499.

Add $275 for 2TEK bridge.

ELECTRIC BASS: CUSTOM PRO BASS SERIES

CUSTOM BASS (MODEL SKCB) - offset double cutaway mahogany body, bolt-on bird's-eye maple neck, 34 in. scale, 21-fret ebony fingerboard, fixed bridge, 4-on-a-side tuners, gold hardware, double P-style pickups, volume/tone controls, disc.

$1,125	$975	$855	$735	$615	$495	$375

Last MSR was $1,500.

CUSTOM BENT BASS (MODEL BBT) - offset double cutaway alder body, quilted maple top, bolt-on bird's-eye maple neck, 34 in. scale, 21-fret ebony fingerboard, fixed bridge, 4-on-a-side tuners, gold hardware, P/J-style EMG pickups, volume/tone controls, disc.

$1,500	$1,300	$1,140	$980	$820	$660	$500

Last MSR was $2,000.

Add $275 for 2TEK bridge.

This model is also available in a 5-string configuration.

CUSTOM QUILT BASS (MODEL BQB) - offset double cutaway carved herringbone bound quilted maple body, bolt-on bird's-eye maple neck, 34 in. scale, 21-fret ebony fingerboard with pearl dot inlay, fixed bridge, herringbone bound peghead, 4-on-a-side tuners, gold hardware, P/J-style EMG or Bartolini pickups, volume/tone controls, disc.

$2,625	$2,275	$2,000	$1,715	$1,435	$1,155	$875

Last MSR was $3,500.

Add $275 for 2TEK bridge.

This model is also available in a 5-string configuration. Earlier versions of this model had black hardware, pickup configurations (2 P-style or 2 J-style), rosewood fingerboards, and active electronics as options.

STUDIO PRO (MODEL SPB-IV) - offset double cutaway hardwood body, bolt-on quartersawn maple neck, 34 in. scale, 21-fret rosewood fingerboard, 4-on-a-side tuners, black or chrome hardware, Wilkinson bridge, P-style pickup, volume/tone controls, available in Black (BK) or White (WH) finishes, mfg. 1997-2002.

$750	$650	$570	$490	$410	$330	$250

Last MSR was $998.

CUSTOM PRO (VACBS1) - offset double cutaway alder body, quilt maple or flame maple top, birdseye maple neck, 24-fret birdseye maple or ebony fingerboard with dot inlay, 2 Seymour Duncan or EMG pickups in P/J configuration, 3 knobs, 4-on-one-side tuners, gold hardware, available in Custom Color finishes, new 2004.

	MSR	$3,000		$2,150	$1,850	$1,600	$1,350	$1,150	$1,000	$850

VANTAGE

Instruments currently produced in Korea. Original production was based in Japan from 1977 to 1990. Distributed by Music Industries Corporation of Floral Park, NY, since 1987.

This trademark was established in Matsumoku, Japan, around 1977. Instruments have been manufactured in Korea since 1990. Vantage offers a wide range of guitars designed for the beginning student to the intermediate player.

ELECTRIC: 100 SERIES

All models in this series have offset double cutaway laminated body, bolt-on maple neck, 24-fret maple fingerboard with offset black dot inlay, standard vibrato, and 6-on-a-side tuners, unless otherwise listed. Keep in mind there are hundreds of indiividual models in existence and not all of them will be listed here.

GRADING	100% MINT	98% NEAR MINT	95% EXC+	90% EXC	80% VG+	70% VG	60% G

111T - chrome hardware, single coil/humbucker pickup, volume/tone control, 3-position switch, available in Black, Cherry Sunburst, Red, or Tobacco Sunburst finishes, current mfg.

MSR	$359	$270	$235	$200	$175	$150	$120	$90

Add $10 for left-handed version of this model (Model 111T/LH).

118T - chrome hardware, 2 single coil/1 humbucker pickups, volume/2 tone controls, 5-position switch, available in Black, Cherry Sunburst and Tobacco Sunburst finishes, current mfg.

MSR	$330	$250	$215	$190	$165	$140	$115	$85

118DT - double locking vibrato, black hardware, 2 single coil/1 humbucker pickups, volume/2 tone controls, 5-position switch, available in Gold Granite, Marble Stone, Metallic Black, or Red Granite finishes, current mfg.

MSR	$459	$345	$300	$260	$225	$190	$150	$115

ELECTRIC: 200 SERIES

All models in this series have offset double cutaway alder body, bolt-on maple necks, 24-fret maple fingerboard with offset black dot inlay, standard vibrato, 6-on-a-side tuners, black hardware, volume/2 tone controls, 5-position switch.

213T - 3 single coil pickups, available in Tobacco Sunburst or Trans. Blue finishes, disc.

	$250	$215	$180	$145	$130	$120	$110

Last MSR was $360.

218T - 2 single coil/1 humbucker pickups, available in Trans. Black, Trans. Blue, or Trans. Red finishes, disc.

	$260	$225	$185	$150	$135	$120	$110

Last MSR was $370.

ELECTRIC: 300 SERIES

This series is the same as the 200 Series, except has rosewood fingerboards.

311T - single coil/humbucker pickup, available in Metallic Black Cherry or Metallic Blue finishes, disc.

	$275	$225	$190	$150	$135	$120	$110

Last MSR was $380.

320T - humbucker/single coil/humbucker pickups, available in Metallic Black, Metallic Black Cherry, or Pearl White finishes, disc.

	$300	$235	$195	$155	$140	$125	$115

Last MSR was $390.

ELECTRIC: 400 SERIES

This series is the same as the 300 Series, except has double locking vibrato.

418DT - 2 single coil/1 humbucker pickups, available in Black Fishnet, Black Sandstone, Metallic Black, or Red Sandstone finishes, disc.

	$375	$300	$250	$200	$170	$155	$145

Last MSR was $480.

ELECTRIC: 600 SERIES

635V - double cutaway semi-hollow style nato body, bound body/F-holes, raised black pickguard, nato neck, 22-fret rosewood fingerboard with offset pearl dot inlay, tunematic/stop tailpiece, 3-per-side tuners, chrome hardware, 2 humbucker pickups, 2 volume/2 tone controls, 3-position switch, available in Black, Cherry Sunburst, or Walnut finishes, current mfg.

MSR	$569	$425	$370	$250	$200	$160	$115	$70

Add $40 for gold hardware with Natural finish.

ELECTRIC: 700 SERIES

All models in this series have offset double cutaway alder body, bolt-on maple neck, 24-fret rosewood fingerboard with offset pearl dot inlay, double locking vibrato, 6-on-a-side tuners, black hardware, volume/2 tone controls, 5-position switch, unless otherwise noted.

718DT - 2 single coil/1 humbucker pickups, coil tap, available in Burgundy, Dark Marble Stone, Trans. Black or Trans. Red finishes, disc.

	$375	$300	$250	$200	$180	$165	$150

Last MSR was $500.

720DT - humbucker/single coil/humbucker pickups, coil tap, available in Dark Marble Stone, Multi-color, or Red Granite finishes, disc.

	$425	$350	$275	$220	$200	$180	$165

Last MSR was $550.

728GDT - figured maple top, bound fingerboard, gold hardware, 2 single coil/1 humbucker pickups, coil tap, available in Antique Violin finish, disc.

	$475	$400	$325	$250	$225	$205	$190

Last MSR was $630.

**Vantage 635 V
courtesy Vantage**

**Vantage 728 GDT
courtesy Vantage**

V

GRADING	100% MINT	98% NEAR MINT	95% EXC+	90% EXC	80% VG+	70% VG	60% G

ELECTRIC: 800 SERIES

All models in this series have offset double cutaway alder body, bound figured maple top, bolt-on maple neck, bound rosewood fingerboard with offset pearl dot inlay, double locking vibrato, body matching bound peghead, 6-on-a-side tuners, volume/2 tone controls, 5-position switch.

818DT - black hardware, 2 single coil/1 humbucker pickups, coil tap, available in Trans. Black, Trans. Blue, or Trans. Red finishes, disc.

	100%	98%	95%	90%	80%	70%	60%
	$375	$300	$250	$200	$180	$165	$150

Last MSR was $500.

Add $30 for gold hardware (Model 818GDT).

820GDT - gold hardware, humbucker/single coil/humbucker pickups, coil tap, available in Trans. Blue or Trans. Burgundy finishes, disc.

	100%	98%	95%	90%	80%	70%	60%
	$440	$330	$275	$220	$200	$180	$165

Last MSR was $550.

ELECTRIC: 900 SERIES

928GDT - offset double cutaway ash body, through body 7-piece maple rosewood neck, 24-fret rosewood fingerboard with offset pearl dot inlay, double locking vibrato, 6-on-a-side tuners, gold hardware, 2 single coil/1 humbucker pickups, volume/2 tone controls, 5-position/coil tap switches, available in Transparent Burgundy finish, disc.

	100%	98%	95%	90%	80%	70%	60%
	$675	$525	$425	$340	$305	$280	$255

Last MSR was $850.

ELECTRIC BASS

225B-1 - offset double cutaway alder body, bolt-on maple neck, 20-fret maple fingerboard with offset black dot inlay, fixed bridge, 2-per-side tuners, chrome hardware, P-style pickup, volume/tone control, available in Black, Dark Blue Sunburst, or Red finishes, current mfg.

MSR	$399	$295	$220	$165	$130	$120	$110	$100

330B - similar to 225B, except has rosewood fingerboard with offset pearl inlay, black hardware, P-style/J-style pickups, 2 volume/1 tone controls, available in Trans. Black, Trans. Blue, or Trans. Red finishes, current mfg.

MSR	$459	$350	$300	$265	$225	$190	$155	$115

This model is also available with fretless fingerboard.

525B - similar to 330B, except has higher quality bridge, available in Black Fishnet or Red Granite finishes, disc.

	100%	98%	95%	90%	80%	70%	60%
	$335	$250	$210	$170	$150	$135	$125

Last MSR was $420.

725B - offset double cutaway asymmetrical alder body, bolt-on maple neck, 24-fret rosewood fingerboard with offset pearl dot inlay, fixed bridge, 2-per-side tuners, black hardware, P-style/J-style pickups, 2 volume/2 tone controls, available in Black, Dark Marble Stone, Metallic Black, Pearl White, Red, or Trans. Red finishes, current mfg.

MSR	$499	$375	$325	$285	$245	$200	$150	$125

Add $20 for left-handed version (Model 725B-LH).

This model is also available with fretless fingerboard.

750B - similar to 725B, except has 5-strings, 3/2-per-side tuners, available in Blue Marble Stone or Pearl White finishes, current mfg.

MSR	$539	$400	$350	$300	$265	$225	$175	$135

Add $50 for active electronics.

930B - offset double cutaway asymmetrical ash body, through body 7-piece maple/rosewood neck, 24-fret rosewood fingerboard with offset pearl dot inlay, fixed bridge, 2-per-side tuners, gold hardware, P-style/J-style pickups, 2 volume/2 tone controls, available in Trans. Burgundy or Trans. Purple finishes, current mfg.

MSR	$849	$635	$550	$485	$415	$350	$285	$215

VANTEK

Instruments currently produced in Korea, and distributed by Music Industries Corporation of Floral Park, NY.

These instruments are built with the entry level player or beginning student in mind by Vantage in Korea.

VEGA

Instruments currently built in Korea, and distributed by Antares. Originally, Vega guitars were produced in Boston, MA.

The predessor company to Vega was founded in 1881 by Swedish immigrant Julius Nelson, C. F. Sunderberg, Mr. Swenson, and several other men. Nelson was the foreman of a 20-odd man workforce (which later rose to 130 employees during the 1920s banjo boom). Nelson, and his brother Carl, gradually bought out the other partners, and incorporated in 1903 as Vega (which means ′star′). In 1904, Vega acquired banjo maker A.C. Fairbanks & Company after Fairbanks suffered a fire, and Fairbank′s David L. Day became Vega′s general manager.

Vega built banjos under the Bacon trademark, named after popular banjo artist Frederick J. Bacon. Bacon set up his own production facility in Connecticut in 1921, and a year later wooed Day away from Vega to become the vice president in the newly reformed Bacon & Day company. While this company marketed several models of guitars, they had no facility for building them. It is speculated that the Bacon & Day guitars were built by the Regal company of Chicago, Illinois.

In the mid 1920s, Vega began marketing a guitar called the **Vegaphone**. By the early 1930s, Vega started concentrating more on guitar production, and less on banjo making. Vega debuted its Electrovox electric guitar and amplifier in 1936, and a electric volume control foot pedal in 1937. Vega is reported to have built over 40,000 guitars during the 1930s.

V

In the 1940s, Vega continued to introduce models such as the Duo-Tron and the Supertron; and by 1949 had become both a guitar producer and a guitar wholesaler as it bought bodies built by Harmony. In 1970, Vega was acquired by the C.F. Martin company for its banjo operations. Martin soon folded Vega's guitar production, and applied the trademark to a line of imported guitars. Ten years later, Martin sold the Vega trademark rights to a Korean guitar production company (source: Tom Wheeler, *American Guitars*).

VEILLETTE GUITARS

Instruments currently built in Woodstock, NY.

Joe Veillette has worked with both Harvey Citron and Stuart Spector as well as doing custom work under his own brand name. Veillette is co-designer with Michael Tobias of the Alvarez Avante series of acoustic guitars, baritones, and basses. Veillette currently is building his own namesake **Mark III Baritone 12-String**, **Mark VI Baritone 6-String**, and **Mark IV Bass**. Veillette's baritones are used by Steve Miller, Brad Whitford (Aerosmith), Neal Schon, and John Sebastian. For further information, please contact Veillette Guitars directly (see Trademark Index).

Even though Veillette Guitars appear to be acoustic electric instruments, the company refers to them as electric/acoustic, and because of this, these models are included in the *Blue Book of Electric Guitars*.

One of Veillette's new ideas is a Baritone-scale replacement neck that fits a Strat or Tele model's neck pocket. The Deep Six baritone conversion necks is marketed by WD Products.

Vantage 928GDT
courtesy Vantage

ELECTRIC

There is also a nylon string version of the 6- and 7-string for $1,975 and $2,000, respectively.

VEILLETTE MK III BARI-12 - 12-string configuration, semi-solid body design, single cutaway poplar body, figured maple top, bolt-on hard rock maple neck, 26 1/16 in. scale, 24-fret maple fingerboard, zero fret, rosewood bridge, 6-per-side mini Gotoh tuners, chrome hardware, piezo bridge pickup, volume/3-band active EQ controls, available in Black stain finish, mfg. 1997-98.

Last MSR was $1,950.

This model was available as a standard tuned 12-string (list price $1,600) with a 24 1/8" scale, and 22-fret fingerboard, in addition to a 6-string baritone (last MSR was $1,750). Other options included different colors and finishes, fingerboard materials, and a left-handed configuration.

VEILLETTE MK IV 6/12-STRING - 6/12-string configuration, standard tuned, the most recent design evolution, mfg. 1999-present.

    MSR   **$1,925**

        Add $150 for 12-string. Add $300 for additional Seymour Duncan pickup.

VEILLETTE MK IV BARITONE 6/12-STRING - similar to the Mk IV, except features a 6/12-string baritone configuration, 3-per-side tuners, available in Black stain finish, mfg. 1998-present.

    MSR   **$2,000**

        Add $200 for 12-string). Add $300 for additional Seymour Duncan pickup.

VEILLETTE MK IV 7-STRING - 7-string instrument with 26.1 in. scale length, features System 500 Alvarez piezo preamp combo, mfg. 1999-present.

    MSR   **$2,350**

        Add $350 for Kent Armstrong pickup.

ELECTRIC BASS

There is also a single-cutaway bass available for a retail of $3,050.

VEILLETTE MK IV BASS - semi-solid body design, single cutaway poplar body, figured maple top, bolt-on hard rock maple neck, 34 in. scale, 20-fret maple (or rosewood) fingerboard, zero fret, 2-per-side Gotoh tuners, rosewood bridge, chrome hardware, piezo bridge pickup, volume/3-band active EQ controls, available in Black, Amber, Stone, or Deep Red Stain finishes, mfg. 1997-present.

    MSR   **$2,050**

        Add $200 for 5-string. Add $500 for 6-string. Add $525 for 8-string.

VEILLETTE-CITRON

Instruments previously built in Brooklyn and Kingston, NY from 1976 to 1983.

The Veillette-Citron company was founded in 1975 by namesakes Joe Veillette and Harvey Citron. Rather than copy the current staus quo, both Veillette and Citron built high quality neck-through guitar and bass models that featured brass hardware and their own pickups. The Veillette-Citron company made their official debut at the 1976 NAMM show, and production followed soon after. Working by themselves, and sometimes joined by a workforce of up to five employees, Veillette-Citron instruments were entirely handcrafted.

After the company closed its doors in 1983, Citron went on to write straightforward, fact-filled columns for *Guitar Player* magazine (also *Bass Player* and *Guitar World*) and produced a 90 minute video tape entitled Basic Guitar Set-Up and Repair (Homespun Tapes). Citron also licensed the X-92 'Breakaway' to the Guild company in 1985. Citron debuted a new line of guitars and basses in 1994, which featured both bolt-on and neck-through designs and Citron- designed pickups.

Joe Veillette began performing with the musical group the Phantoms during the 1980s, and returned to guitar building in 1991 when he formed a partnership with Stuart Spector. Veillette reintroduced his Shark Baritone guitar, and later left to start his own shop. In addition to custom built guitars, Veillette has also done some consulting work for other instrument manufacturers (source: Baker Rorick, *Vintage Guitar Magazine*).

Ventura V-1400
courtesy Sam Maggio

VEKTOR ELECTRIC UPRIGHT

Instruments currently built in Viersen, Germany. Distributed by Vecktor directly. Previously distributed in the U.S. market by R2 Musical of Manhattan, NY, L.A. Bass Exchange of Tarzana, CA, and Stein on Vine of Hollywood, CA.

In 1969, Sven Henrik Gawron began studying the doublebass at the age of twelve. Ten years later he attended the Folkwang-Hochschule Conservatory in Essen, Germany, and participated in several modern jazz foundations. Gawron began seriously studying the repair and restoration of acoustic double basses in 1980, which lead to his opening of **Studio fur Kontrabasse** eight years later as a music shop specializing in doublebasses, pickups, and amplification. Gawron collaborated with M.B. Schulz Design in Dusseldorf in 1992 to develop the prototype of the **Vectorbass**, a slim, modern electric upright bass. The aim of Vektor is to combine modern design with traditional sound of the acoustic double bass. Vecktor Germany, is a registered trademark and Vektor Basses are played in bands including, Prince's New Power Generation (Rhonda Smith), Herbie Hancock (Matthew Garrison), and Oregon (Glen Moore).

ELECTRIC BASS

The **Vektor Electric Upright** is available as a four-string instrument in two different scales: the 36 in. scale Vektor Bassett and 41 in. scale Vektor Upright Bass (5-string is optional). The Upright comes in different traditional stains, three-piece maple body, ebony fingerboard and tailpiece, and custom made Schaller-mechanics. All instruments are delivered with body support attachment, telescopic endpin, and professional gig bag. Prices start around $5,000. For more information contact Sven-Henrik Gawron directly (see Trademark Index).

VELENO

Instruments currently built in St. Petersburg, FL.

Designer/guitar teacher John Veleno came up with the idea for an aluminum body guitar in 1967, and began producing them in 1970. It is estimated that only 185 instruments were built: 10 are a travel guitar (based on an idea by B.B. King), one is a bass guitar, and two were specially built for Todd Rungren in 1977 that were shaped like an ankh.

Veleno guitars were numbered sequentially in the serialization. Production ran from late 1970 through 1975 (maybe 1976) (source: Michael Wright, *Vintage Guitar Magazine*). For more information on Veleno guitars, refer to their website (see Trademark Index).

ELECTRIC

Veleno guitars have an equal horn dual cutaway profile body, and are constructed of two halves of routed aluminum blanks that are later combined together. Finished in gold or chrome plating (some have other anodized colors). The neck is an aluminum/magnesium composite, and the ´V´-shaped peghead was designed by Veleno´s wife (the red stone on the headstock is a replica of her birthstone, a ruby).

Veleno guitars now have a certificate of authenticity for each guitar which is the owner´s fingerprint. There are detailed records and history for each guitar that is fingerprinted.

VENTURA

Instruments previously produced in Japan circa 1970s.

Ventura guitars were distributed in the U.S. market by C. Bruno & Company of New York, New York. Ventura models were both full body and thinline hollowbody electric archtop guitars, and generally medium to good quality versions of popular American models (source: Michael Wright, *Guitar Stories*, Volume One; and Sam Maggio).

During the 1970s, a Barney Kessel Custom-style copy (the model is a V-1400, by the way) had a suggested retail price of $199.50.

ELECTRIC

LES PAUL COPY - single cutaway style, comes in a variety of configurations, two humbucker pickups, very similar to the Gibson Les Paul, mfg. 1970s.

	N/A	$300	$250	$200	$170	$140	$120

SEMI-HOLLOW ARCHTOPS - various configurations including an ES-175 style and Barney Kessel model, mfg. 1970s.

	N/A	$450	$375	$325	$275	$225	$175

VENTURES

See Wilson Brothers Guitar Company. For old Ventures models see Mosrite.

VERSOUL

Instruments currently built in Helsinki, Finland since 1994.

Versoul Ltd. was founded in 1994 by Kari Nieminen, who has over twenty years background in guitar making and design. Nieminen combines concern for the acoustic tone of his instruments with his innovative designs to produce a masterful instrument. Nieminen´s production is on a limited basis (he estimates about one guitar a week) in his humidity controlled workshop.

One of Nieminen´s newest model is the electric solid body **Raya**. This model is constructed out of Finnish alder, with a set-in mahogany neck, and 22-fret ebony fingerboard. The Raya features two Versoul single coil pickups, and a reverse headstock. Versoul has also recently released a Caspian electric twelve-string Sitar, and a Swan Model semi-acoustic guitar. There is also the **Henry** model, which is a Les-Paul looking guitar. There are other models available such as resonators electric guitars, bass guitars, sitars, and bariton guitars For further information, please contact luthier Nieminen directly (see Trademark Index).

VESTAX

Instruments currently built in Japan. Distributed by the Vestax Corporation of Fairfield, CA.

Vestax offers high quality guitars including one model that echos the classic designs of the 1940s and 1950s, as well as a semi-hollow electric model. The D´Angelico-Vestax **Phil Upchurch** model is a single cutaway New Yorker-style acoustic with bound body, two bound f-holes, bound headstock, three-

GRADING	100% MINT	98% NEAR MINT	95% EXC+	90% EXC	80% VG+	70% VG	60% G

per-side gold tuners, 22-fret bound ebony fingerboard with pearl block inlay, raised rosewood pickguard, adjustable rosewood bridge/´stair step´ rosewood tailpiece, floating humbucker pickup. Vestax´s **Superior Limited Series** semi-hollow **GV-98** looks like a double cutaway Strat or PRS design, but features hollowed out tone chambers under the flamed maple top. The GV-98 has a Wilkinson VSVG (GG) tremolo bridge, two single coil/humbucker pickups, and 22-fret fingerboard.

VESTER

Instruments previously built in Korea during the early 1990s. Distributed in the U.S. market by Midco International of Effingham, IL.

The Vester trademark was established in 1990 by Midco International, and widely distributed these solid body guitars that were designed for the entry level beginner to the intermediate guitarist. Midco discontinued the Vester trademark in 1994 in favor of their popular Lotus line of guitars.

**Vester FSR 330
courtesy Vester**

ELECTRIC

JAR 1370 - offset double cutaway carved alder body, bolt-on maple neck, 24-fret rosewood fingerboard with pearl shark tooth inlay, double locking vibrato, 6-on-a-side Gotoh tuners, black hardware, 2 single coil/1 humbucker alnico pickups, volume/tone/preamp controls, 5-position switch, available in Metallic Ice Blue, Metallic Red, or Pearl White finishes, disc. 1994.

	N/A	$450	$375	$300	$250	$200	$175

Last MSR was $600.

JAR 1380 - offset double cutaway mahogany body, carved bound figured maple top, bolt-on maple neck, 24-fret rosewood fingerboard with mixed shark tooth/dot inlay, block "Vester" inlay at 24th fret, double locking vibrato, 6-on-a-side tuners, black hardware, 2 active humbucker pickups, volume/tone control, 3-position switch, available in Cherry Burst, Trans. Black, or Trans. Green finishes, disc. 1994.

	N/A	$550	$475	$400	$325	$250	$200

Last MSR was $700.

JAR 1400 - offset double cutaway alder body, bolt-on maple neck, 22-fret rosewood fingerboard with mixed pearl shark tooth/dot inlay, double locking vibrato, 6-on-a-side Gotoh tuners, black hardware, 2 single coil/1 humbucker pickups, volume/tone control, 5-position and coil tap switches, available in Fluorescent Yellow, Metallic Dark Blue, Metallic Red, or Pearl White finishes, disc. 1994.

	N/A	$450	$375	$300	$250	$200	$175

Last MSR was $600.

JAR 1412 - offset double cutaway alder body, bolt-on maple neck, 24-fret rosewood fingerboard with pearl dot inlay, fixed bridge, 12-string headstock, 6-per-side Gotoh tuners, black hardware, 2 humbucker pickups, volume/tone control, 3-position switch, available in Metallic Dark Blue, Metallic Red, or Pearl White finishes, disc. 1994.

	N/A	$450	$375	$300	$250	$200	$175

Last MSR was $600.

JFA 500 - semi-hollow offset double cutaway alder body, bound spruce top, lightning bolt soundhole, maple neck, 22-fret rosewood fingerboard with pearl dot inlay, tunomatic bridge/stop tailpiece, 6-on-a-side tuners, chrome hardware, single coil/humbucker pickups, volume/tone control, 3-position switch, coil split in tone control, available in Red, Tobacco Sunburst, or White finishes, disc. 1994.

	N/A	$275	$225	$200	$175	$150	$125

Last MSR was $400.

JJM 1010 - offset double cutaway alder body, black pickguard, bolt-on maple neck, 22-fret maple fingerboard w/ black dot inlay, standard vibrato, 6-on-a-side tuners, chrome hardware, 2 single coil/1 humbucker pickups, volume/tone control, 5-position switch, available in Black, Red, or White finishes, disc. 1994.

	N/A	$225	$180	$150	$120	$100	$75

Last MSR was $300.

JJM 1020 - similar to JJM 1010, except has 24 frets, double locking vibrato, humbucker/single coil/humbucker pickups, available in Black, Fluorescent Yellow, Red, or White finishes, disc. 1994.

	N/A	$375	$300	$250	$200	$175	$150

Last MSR was $500.

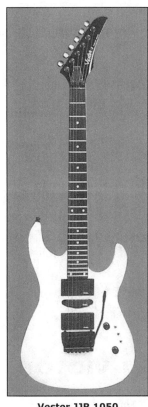

JJR 550 - offset double cutaway alder body, bolt-on maple neck, 22-fret rosewood fingerboard with pearl dot inlay, double locking vibrato, 6-on-a-side tuners, chrome hardware, single coil/humbucker pickups, volume control, 3-position switch, available in Blue Green, Metallic Gold, or Rubine Red finishes, disc. 1994.

	N/A	$250	$210	$175	$140	$120	$100

Last MSR was $340.

Add $30 for Graphic Designs finish.

JJR 1070 - offset double cutaway alder body, bolt-on maple neck, 24-fret rosewood bound fingerboard with pearl inverted V inlay, double locking vibrato, 6-on-a-side tuners, black hardware, humbucker/single coil/humbucker pickups, 3 mini switches, available in Pearl White finish, disc. 1994.

	N/A	$350	$275	$225	$190	$150	$125

Last MSR was $460.

Add $40 for Graphic Designs finish.

**Vester JJR 1050
courtesy Vester**

V

GRADING	100% MINT	98% NEAR MINT	95% EXC+	90% EXC	80% VG+	70% VG	60% G

JJR 1170 - offset double cutaway alder body, set maple neck, 24-fret rosewood fingerboard with pearl shark tooth inlay, double locking vibrato, 6-on-a-side tuners, black hardware, 2 single coil/1 humbucker alnico pickups, volume/tone and preamp controls, 3 mini switches, active electronics, available in Black finish, disc. 1994.

	N/A	$325	$275	$225	$200	$150	$110

Last MSR was $440.

JJR 1175 - similar to JJR 1170, except has 2 humbucker pickups, no preamp control or mini switches, 5-position switch, available in Metallic Charcoal Grey or Pearl White finishes, disc. 1994.

	N/A	$325	$275	$225	$200	$150	$110

Last MSR was $440

Subtract $40 for Crackle Blue/Green/Red/Yellow, Crackle Silver/Blue, or Crackle Yellow/Blue finishes.

JJR 1290 - offset double cutaway alder body, bound figured maple top, bolt-on maple neck, 24-fret bound rosewood fingerboard with pearl dot inlay, double locking vibrato, 6-on-a-side Gotoh tuners, black hardware, 2 single coil/1 humbucker pickups, volume/tone control, 5-position switch, available in Cherry Sunburst, Trans. Blue, Trans. Green, or Trans. Red finishes, disc. 1994.

	N/A	$350	$275	$225	$190	$150	$125

Last MSR was $470.

Models with the Transparent Red finish have reverse headstocks.

JJR 1462 - doubleneck construction. with one side being similar to JAR 1412 and the other being similar to JJR 1030. Both necks have 22-fret rosewood fingerboards with pearl dot inlay, 3-position neck selector switch included, available in White finish, disc. 1994.

	N/A	$900	$825	$750	$650	$550	$450

Last MSR was $1,200.

OAR 1500 - offset double cutaway asymmetrical mahogany body, carved maple top, set mahogany neck, 24-fret rosewood fingerboard with pearl dot inlay, standard vibrato, 3-per-side Gotoh locking tuners, chrome hardware, 2 humbucker pickups, volume tone control, 3-position and coil split mini switches, available in Metallic Red, Pearl Blue, or Pearl White finishes, disc. 1994.

	N/A	$450	$375	$300	$250	$200	$175

Last MSR was $600.

ELECTRIC BASS

OPR 436 - offset double cutaway asymmetrical maple body, bolt-on maple neck, 24-fret rosewood fingerboard with pearl dot inlay, fixed bridge, 2-per-side tuners, chrome hardware, P-style/J-style pickups, 2 volume/1 tone controls, available in Black or Metallic Red finishes, disc. 1994.

	N/A	$275	$250	$225	$190	$150	$120

Last MSR was $380.

OPR 935 - similar to OPR 436, except has alder body and black hardware, available in Black, Blue, or Metallic Red finishes, disc. 1994.

	N/A	$290	$260	$230	$195	$150	$125

Last MSR was $400.

OPR 935EQ - similar to OPR 935, except has volume/treble/bass and mix controls and active electronics, available in Black or Metallic Red finishes, disc 1994.

	N/A	$300	$275	$240	$200	$160	$125

Last MSR was $420.

OPR 1135 - offset double cutaway asymmetrical alder body, bolt-on maple neck, 24-fret rosewood fingerboard with pearl dot inlay, fixed bridge, 2-per-side tuners, black hardware, 2 humbucker pickups, 2 volume/1 tone controls, available in Black or White finishes, disc. 1994.

	N/A	$325	$275	$250	$200	$170	$135

Last MSR was $450.

OPR 1135EQ - similar to OPR 1135, except has volume/treble/bass and mix controls and active electronics, disc 1994.

	N/A	$375	$325	$275	$225	$175	$150

Last MSR was $500.

OPR 1235 - similar to OPR 1135, except has 5 strings, 3/2-per-side tuners, P-style/J-style pickups, 1 volume/2 tone controls, 3-position mini switch, available in Black or Metallic Red finishes, disc. 1994.

	N/A	$375	$325	$275	$225	$175	$150

Last MSR was $500.

OPR 1335EQ - similar to OPR 1235, except has 2 humbucker pickups, volume/treble/bass and mix controls and active electronics, available in Black or Pearl White finishes, disc. 1994.

	N/A	$400	$350	$300	$250	$200	$160

Last MSR was $550.

OPR 1435EQ - offset double cutaway carved alder body, bolt-on 5-piece maple/mahogany neck, 24-fret rosewood fingerboard with pearl dot inlay, fixed bridge, 2-per-side tuners, black hardware, P-style/J-style pickups, volume/treble/bass/mix controls, active electronics, available in Fl. Blue, Metallic Charcoal Grey, or Pearl White finishes, disc. 1994.

	N/A	$390	$340	$290	$240	$200	$160

Last MSR was $530.

VICTOR

See chapter on House Brands.

This trademark has been identified as a House Brand of the RCA Victor Record Stores (source: Willie G. Moseley, *Stellas & Stratocasters*).

GRADING	100% MINT	98% NEAR MINT	95% EXC+	90% EXC	80% VG+	70% VG	60% G

VIGIER

Instruments currently produced in Evry, France since 1980. Distributed in the U.S. by Salwender International of Orange, CA.

Luthier Patrice Vigier has been offering high quality solid body instruments since the early 1980s, and features advanced original designs. Vigier guitars and basses are known for the high technology used in their design process. For example, the **Nautilus** model bass that debuted in 1983 had an on board circuitry design that allowed instant access to nineteen pre-programmed control settings that were stored by the player. In 1997, Vigier celebrated ten years that they have been producing their **10/90 Neck**. This neck is composed of 10% carbon graphite, 90% wood; the graphite is used to stabilize and strengthen the wood neck. In just the past few years, a number of the guitar manufacturers in the guitar and bass building industry adopted graphite for the same reason. Vigier was previously distributed by Palyers International of San Dimas, California.

In 1980, Vigier introduced the Delta Metal fingerboard. This fingerboard was made from a unique alloy, produced sustain comparable to fretted instruments, was rich in harmonics, featured a uniform hard surface that stayed even (no dips or valleys), and was certainly visually exciting. Vigier has re-issued the Delta Metal fingerboard in 1998 as an option on models like the Passion and Arpege. Models like the Excalibur guitar and Excess bass with the Delta Metal fingerboard will be called the Surfreter.

ELECTRIC

ARPEGE III (MODEL V6ECVC) - offset double cutaway asymmetrical flame maple body, through body maple neck, 22-fret Phenowood fingerboard, double locking vibrato, 3-per-side tuners, black hardware, 2 humbucker pickups, volume/tone/mix controls, 3-position/memory switches, coil split in volume control, available in Antique Violin, Ash, Aquatic Blue, Burgundy, Emerald Green, French Kiss, Honey, Night Blue, or Red Trans. finishes, disc 2001.

$3,300	$2,700	$2,365	$2,000	$1,695	$1,350	$1,025

Last MSR was $4,144.

**Vigier Excalibur Ultra
courtesy Salwender
International**

EXCALIBUR ORIGINAL (MODEL VE6-CV3) - offset double cutaway ash body, mirrored pickguard, bolt-on maple neck, 24-fret maple fingerboard with black dot inlay, double locking vibrato, 6-on-a-side Gotoh tuners, chrome hardware, 3 single coil Seymour Duncan pickups, volume/tone control, 5-position switch, available in Antique Violin, Clear Red, Urban Blue, Urban Green, Urban Metal, Black, Honey, Natural Malt, Ocean Blue, or Wine Fire finishes, current mfg.

MSR	$2,400	$1,925	$1,600	$1,350	$1,150	$1,000	$850	$700

Excalibur Custom (Model VE6-CVC3) - similar to Excalibur, except has bound flame maple top, body color matching head stock, HSS or HSH DiMarzio pickups, current mfg.

MSR	$2,987	$2,400	$2,100	$1,850	$1,650	$1,450	$1,250	$1,100

Excalibur Special - similar to Excalibur, except has bound flame maple top, white pickguard, rosewood fingerboard, and HSH DiMarzio pickups, current mfg.

MSR	$2,597	$2,100	$1,850	$1,600	$1,400	$1,200	$1,050	$900

Also available as a hard-tail model.

Excalibur Ultra - similar to Excalibur, except has no pickguard and, and HSH EMG pickups, current mfg.

MSR	$2,980	$2,400	$2,100	$1,850	$1,650	$1,450	$1,250	$1,100

Excalibur Indus - similar to Excalibur, except has two humbucker Dimarzio pickups, available in textured Black finish, current mfg.

MSR	$1,921	$1,550	$1,350	$1,200	$1,050	$900	$775	$650

Excalibur Supra 7 - similar to Excalibur, except in 7-string configuration, available in Antique Violin, Black, Clear Red, Natural Alder, Urban Blue, or Urban Metal finishes, current mfg.

MSR	$2,475	$2,000	$1,750	$1,550	$1,350	$1,200	$1,050	$900

EXCALIBUR SUPRA SURFRETER - similar to Excalibur, except has a delta metal fretless fingerboard, available in High Gloss or Natural Matte finishes, current mfg.

MSR	$2,670	$2,150	$1,900	$1,700	$1,500	$1,300	$1,150	$1,000

EXPERT TEXAS BLUES (MODEL VEX6-CVT3) - offset double cutaway, alder body, bolt-on maple neck, 22-fret rosewood or maple fingerboard, choice of 3 single coil Dimarzio pickups (Retro 54, Standard 63, or Texas Blues), pickguard, two knobs, 5-way switch, Vigier 2010 tremolo unit, available in Antique Violin, Black, Natural Alder, Retro Blue, Retro Red, or Retro White finishes, current mfg.

MSR	$2,379	$1,950	$1,700	$1,500	$1,300	$1,150	$1,000	$850

MARILYN - radical offset double cutaway with sharp points, alder body, thru-neck maple, 24-fret rosewood fingerboard, 2 Dimarzio humbucker pickups, two knobs, 3-way switch, Fixed Shaller Bridge, available in Black finish current mfg.

MSR	$2,970	$2,400	$2,100	$1,850	$1,650	$1,450	$1,250	$1,100

PASSION III (MODEL VP6-CVC) - offset double cutaway asymmetrical alder body, half through body carbon fiber weave neck, 24-fret Phenowood fingerboard, double locking vibrato, pearl logo inlay on peghead, 3-per-side tuners with quick winders, chrome hardware, 2 single coil/1 humbucker Seymour Duncan pickups, push/pull volume control with active electronics switch, 6-position rotary tone control with parametric EQ, 3-position switch, available in Antique Violin, Black, Burnt Metal, Devil Burnt Metal, Ferrari Red, Flip-Flop Blue, Fuschia, Lemon, Natural, Night Blue, Pearl White, Peppermint, Silver Black, Sunburst Grey, or Trans. Red finishes, disc.

$2,600	$2,250	$1,975	$1,695	$1,425	$1,140	$865

Last MSR was 3,462.

**Vigier Expert Texas Blues
courtesy Salwender
International**

V

GRADING	100% MINT	98% NEAR MINT	95% EXC+	90% EXC	80% VG+	70% VG	60% G

ELECTRIC BASS

ARPEGE CUSTOM III (MODEL V4ECC) - offset double cutaway asymmetrical flame maple body, through body maple neck, 21-fret Phenowood fingerboard, fixed bridge, 2-per-side tuners, black hardware, 2 single coil pickups, volume/tone/mix/bypass controls, memory switch, available in Antique Violin, Ash, Aquatic Blue, Burgundy, Devil Burnt, Emerald Green, French Kiss, Honey, Night Blue, or Red Trans. finishes, current mfg.

MSR	$5,016	$4,000	$3,400	$2,900	$2,500	$2,200	$1,900	$1,600

Add $250 for fretless configuration.

Arpege Custom 5 (Model V5ECC) - similar to the Arpege Custom Bass, except in five-string configuration, current mfg.

MSR	$5,422	$4,400	$3,700	$3,200	$2,800	$2,400	$2,100	$1,800

Arpege Custom 6 (Model V6ECC) - similar to the Arpege Custom Bass, except in six-string configuration, current mfg.

MSR	$5,422	$4,400	$3,700	$3,200	$2,800	$2,400	$2,100	$1,800

Also available in fretless configuration.

EXCESS (MODEL VE4EC) - double offset cutaway alder body, bolt-on half-through carbon fiber weave/maple neck, 24-fret maple or rosewood fingerboard, fixed bridge, 4-on-a-side tuners, chrome hardware, black pickguard, 2 single coil pickups, volume/tone/mix controls, available in Antique Violin, Ash, Black, Clear Black, Clear Red, Natural Matte, or Ocean Blue finishes, current mfg.

MSR	$2,450	$1,999	$1,750	$1,550	$1,350	$1,200	$1,050	$900

Add $350 for metal fretless fingerboard.

During 1998, this model incorporated the Silencer hum canceling system. Also available with a fretless rosewood fingerboard.

PASSION STANDARD III (MODEL VP4ECS) - double offset cutaway asymmetrical alder body, half through carbon fiber weave neck, 21-fret Phenowood fingerboard, fixed bridge, 2-per-side tuners, black hardware, 2 single coil pickups, volume/tone/mix controls, parametric EQ/active electronic switches, available in Antique Violin, Black, Devil Burnt Metal, Ferrari Red, Flip-Flop Blue, Fuschia, Lemon, Natural, Night Blue, Pearl White, Peppermint, Silver Black, Sunburst Grey, or Trans. Red finishes, current mfg.

MSR	$3,416	$2,750	$2,300	$1,950	$1,650	$1,350	$1,075	$825

Add $700 for bass delta metal fingerboard.

During 1999, this model incorporated the Silencer hum canceling system.

Passion III Custom (Model VP4-ECC) - similar to Passion III, except has flame maple body, chrome hardware, available in Antique Violin, Aquatic Blue, Ash, Burgundy, Devil Burnt, Emerald Green, French Kiss, Honey, Night Blue, or Red finishes, current mfg.

MSR	$4,409	$3,600	$3,000	$2,500	$2,100	$1,800	$1,500	$1,250

Add $325 for 5-string version of this model (Model VP5-ECC). Add $625 for 6-string version of this model (Model VP6-ECC).

Also available with a fretless phenowood fingerboard.

VINTAGE

Instruments currently produced in Asia. Distributed by John Hornby Skewes & Co., Ltd. of Garforth (Leeds), England.

The Vintage trademark is the brand name of U.K. distributor John Hornby Skewes & Co., Ltd. These guitars are based on mostly popular American designs at entry-level prices. For more information and specific models and prices, contact JHS directly (see Trademark Index).

VINTIQUE

Instruments currently manufactured in Bergenfield, NJ.

Vintique manufactures world class handcrafted guitars by Jay Monterose. They manufacture the Vintique Model 5394 Custom guitar, and have made guitars for legendary guitar player Danny Gatton. They are currently not taking any orders due to their long backorder list. Vintique was previously produced in College Park, Maryland. For more information regarding this trademark, please visit their website (see Trademark Index).

VIRTUOSO

Instruments currently built in England since 1986.

Custom builder Jerry Flint produces a number of high quality solid body instruments based on classic Fender designs (source: Tony Bacon and Paul Day, *The Guru's Guitar Guide*).

VISION

Instruments previously produced in Japan during the late 1980s.

These medium to good quality solid body guitars featured a design based on the classic Stratocaster (source: Tony Bacon and Paul Day, *The Guru's Guitar Guide*).

VIVI-TONE

Instruments previously built in Kalamazoo, MI circa early 1930s.

After pioneering such high quality instruments for Gibson in the 1920s (such as the F-5 Mandolin), designer/engineer/builder Lloyd Loar founded the Vivi-Tone company to continue exploring designs too radical for Gibson. It is rumored that Loar designed a form of stand-up bass that was amplified while at Gibson, but this prototype was never developed into a production model.

Loar, along with partners Lewis A. Williams and Walter Moon started Vivi-Tone in 1933. Loar continued building his pioneering designs, such as an acoustic guitar with sound holes in the rear, but failed to find commercial success. However, it is because of his early successes at Gibson that researchers approach the Vivi-tone designs with some wonderment instead of discounting the radical ideas altogether (source: Tom Wheeler, *American Guitars*).

V

Lloyd Loar's electric Vivi-Tone guitars were some of the first to feature pickups. Because of his popularity with Gibson and the patents he has for this type of guitar, these instruments are quite collectible. Instruments could easily start at $1,000 for average guitars are go above $3,000 for the right model in excellent condition. The *Blue Book of Electric Guitars* recommends getting a couple opinions when dealing with a Vivi-Tone.

VLINE

Instruments previously built in France circa early 1980s.

Vline headless-style instruments feature an extremely unusual design, and featured all graphite construction. Vline instruments were offered for a limited time prior to problems concerning international copyrights on the tuning systems (See Steinberger). Vline instruments were offered in both guitar

and bass configurations. It is estimated that only 100 total instruments were produced. Further research continues for future editions of the *Blue Book of Electric Guitars*, (Preliminary research courtesy Jeff Meyer).

VOGEL GUITARS

Instruments currently produced in Vaca de Castro, Quito, Ecuador in South America since 1995. Distributed in the U.S. by Vogel Guitars in Walnut, CA.

Bob Vogel produces electric, electric bass, and acoustic guitars in Ecuador. He was born in Pasadena California, and lived near the famous Eddie and Alex Van Halen. In 1988, he went to Equador for missionary work and ended up marrying a woman he met there. After moving there in 1991, he looked into building guitars. By 1995, two others and himself started building guitars. For more information contact Bob Vogel directly (see Trademark Index).

VOGEL CUSTOM MADE GUITARS

Instruments currently built in Germany.

Vogel guitars is part of Custom Made Guitars and that consists of Vogel and Schmidt luthiers. Vogel currently bulid the Balance guitar, which is electric and acoustic. It has a chambered sound system in the body to make it sound acoustic but has all the features of an electric guitar. For more information contact the company directly (see Trademark Index).

**Vox Super Ace
courtesy Vox**

VOX

Instruments previously built in England from 1961 to 1964; production was then moved to Italy for the U.S. market from the mid-1960s until 1969 or 1970. After Italian production ceased, some solid body models were built in Japan during the 1980s.

The Vox company, perhaps better known for its amplifier design, also built fashionable and functional guitars and basses during the 1960s. While the early guitar models produced tended to be entry level instruments based on popular Fender designs, later models expressed an originality that fit in well with the 1960s British "Pop" music explosion.

Thomas Walter Jennings was born in London, England on February 28, 1917. During World War II he saw action with the English Royal Engineers, and received a medical discharge in 1941. By 1944 Jennings had a part-time business dealing in secondhand accordions and other musical instruments, and by 1946 had set up shop. Along with fellow musical acquaintance Derek Underdown, Jennings produced the Univox organ in 1951 and formed the Jennings Organ Company not long after. Based on the success of his organs for several years, Jennings teamed up with engineer Dick Denney to build amplifiers under the Vox trademark. In mid 1958, Jennings reincorporated the company as Jennings Musical Instruments (JMI). When rock ´n roll hit Britain, Vox amps were there.

The first Vox guitars were built in 1960 and introduced in 1961. Early models like the **Stroller** or **Clubman** were entry level instruments based on Fender designs. Quality improved a great deal when Vox brought in necks built by EKO in Recanati, Italy. Tom Jennings then assembled a three engineer design team of Bob Pearson (quality and materials control), Mike Bennett (prototypes), and Ken Wilson (styling design) to develop a more original-looking instrument. The resulting 5-sided Phantom in late 1962 featured a Strat-ish three single coil pickup selection and a Bigsby-derived tremolo. Further **Phantom** models were developed in 1963, as well as the **Mark** series ("teardrop" body shapes). When production moved to Italy in 1964, Vox guitars were built by EKO. Vox also offered a 12-string **Mandoguitar**, and a double cutaway 12-string called the **Bouzouki**. A number of hollowbody models such as the **Lynx**, **Bobcat**, and **Cougar** were made by Crucianelli in Italy during the mid 1960s.

In order to generate funds for the company, Jennings sold a substantial amount of shares to the Royston group in 1964, and later that same year the entire shareholding was acquired. JMI was officially renamed Vox Sound Ltd. Thomas Organ was already supplying JMI for organs in the British market, and was looking for a reciprocal agreement to import Vox amps to the U.S. market. However, Joe Benaron (president of Thomas Organ) was really into transistors, and began supplementing the British tube models with solid-state amps developed at Thomas laboratories at Sepulveda, California.

The Vox line began the slump that befell other corporate-run music instrument producers during the late 1960s and 1970s. Soon Japanese-built models appeared on the market with Voxton on their headstock, including a Les Paul-derived issued in 1970. Later, the Vox name appeared on a series of original design solid body guitars (24 series, 25 series, **White Shadows**) during the early to mid 1980s. These were produced by Aria Pro in Japan. Distribution in the U.S. during this time period was through the Pennino Music Company of Westminster, California; and Allstate Music Supply Corporation of Greensboro, North Carolina.

The Vox trademark was later purchased by the Korg company (Korg USA in the American Market). Korg USA distributes Korg synthesizers, Marshall Amplifiers, Parker guitars, and the new line of Vox amplifiers in the U.S. market. In 1998, Korg/Vox debuted 5 "new" electric guitar models which feature designs based on previous Vox models.

**Vox Bobcat
courtesy Vox**

V

GRADING	100% MINT	98% NEAR MINT	95% EXC+	90% EXC	80% VG+	70% VG	60% G

The Editor wishes to thank Mr. Jim Rhoads of Rhoads Music for his assistance in upgrading this section. For even more information regarding Vox instruments, visit his website at http://members.aol.com/rhoadsmusi/store.html and the associated site www.voxshowroom.com.

GENERAL INFORMATION & MODEL NAME IDENTIFICATION

Vox´s new models include the Mark III model VM3B with Bigsby tremolo (list $1,400), the Mark III model VM3F with fixed tailpiece (list $1,200), the Mark III model VM3CFWD with fixed tailpiece, chrome pickguard, and matching finish headstock (list $1,300), the Mark VI model VM6V with Bigsby tremolo (list $1,400), and the Mark XII model VMXII 12-string guitar (list $1,400).

Identification of Vox instruments is fairly easy, as the model names generally appear on the pickguards. However, there are models and configurations that do need to be doublechecked! Collectible Vox guitars seem to be the models built between 1962 and 1969.

ELECTRIC: ACE-MANDOGUITAR SERIES

ACE - offset double cutaway body, bolt-on neck, 6-on-a-side headstock, 2 single coil pickups, chrome hardware, volume/2 tone controls, 3-way selector switch, available in White, Red, and Sunburst finishes, mfg. 1961-66.

	N/A	$350	$275	$200	$150	$100	$75

Super Ace - similar to the Ace, except has three single coil pickups. Pickup selector switch mounted on lower treble bout, mfg. 1961-66.

	N/A	$400	$325	$250	$200	$150	$100

APACHE - asymmetrical rounded body, 6-on-a-side tuners, 3 single coil pickups, chrome hardware, vibrato bridge, volume/2 tone knobs, pickup selector switch, mfg. 1961-66.

	N/A	$600	$500	$425	$350	$275	$225

APOLLO - single florentine cutaway hollowbody, 6-on-a-side headstock, 1 single coil pickup with black cover, raised white pickguard, 2 f-holes, chrome hardware, trapeze bridge, volume/tone controls. Features an "E tuner" on/off switch, a Treble/Bass boost on/off switch and control, and Distortion on/off switch and control all mounted on a metal plate on lower body bout, available in Sunburst or Cherry finishes, mfg. 1967-68.

	N/A	$700	$600	$500	$400	$350	$300

BOBCAT - dual cutaway hollowbody, 3+3 headstock, 3 single coil pickups, raised white pickguard, 2 f-holes, chrome hardware, roller bridge/tremolo system, 2 volume/2 tone controls, pickup selector switch, mfg. 1965-67.

	N/A	$750	$650	$550	$450	$375	$325

BOSSMAN - single cutaway hollowbody, rounded treble bout, 6-on-a-side headstock, 1 single coil pickup with black cover, raised white pickguard, 2 f- holes, chrome hardware, trapeze bridge, volume/tone controls. Features an "E tuner" on/off switch, a Treble/Bass boost on/off switch and control, and Distortion on/off switch and control all mounted on a metal plate on lower body bout, available in Sunburst or Cherry finishes, mfg. 1967-68.

	N/A	$600	$500	$450	$400	$350	$275

BULLDOG - offset double cutaway body with beveled ridge along top edge, 3+3 headstock, 3 single coils, chrome hardware, vibrato bridge, volume/2 tone controls, pickup selector switch on lower treble bout, mfg. 1966 only.

	N/A	$800	$700	$600	$500	$400	$300

A two pickup variation of the Bulldog became the Invader model in 1967. U.K. catalogs also showed a picture of a 2 pickup Bulldog in 1969, which led some people to believe that this configuration was still available in the later time period. The Bulldog model is a relatively rare solid body electric.

CHEETAH - dual cutaway hollowbody, 6-on-a-side headstock, 2 single coil pickups with chrome covers, raised black pickguard, 2 f-holes, chrome hardware, roller bridge/tremolo system, volume/2 tone controls, pickup selector switch, "E tuner" on/off switch mounted on lower treble bout. "On-board" effects mounted on a metal plate features a Treble/Bass boost on/off switch and control, Distortion on/off switch and control, "Repeat Percussion" (a repeating echo-like function) on/off switch and control, available in Sunburst or Cherry finishes, mfg. 1967-68.

	N/A	$650	$575	$500	$425	$350	$275

CLUBMAN - offset double cutaway body, bolt-on neck, 19-fret neck with white dot position markers, 6-on-a-side tuners, chrome hardware, bridge/fixed tailpiece, 2 single coil pickups, 2 volume/1 tone knobs, white pickguard, available in White or Red finishes, mfg. 1961-66.

	N/A	$400	$325	$250	$200	$150	$100

CONSORT (FIRST SERIES) - similar to the Super Ace, except has smaller rounded off horns, a Bigsby-styled tremolo system, Sycamore neck and rosewood fingerboard, available in Red or Sunburst finishes, mfg. 1961-63.

	N/A	N/A	N/A	N/A	N/A	N/A	N/A

Consort (Second Series) - similar to the Consort (First Series), except has a different Vox vibrato, mfg. 1963-65.

	N/A	N/A	N/A	N/A	N/A	N/A	N/A

DELTA - similar to the Phantom model, except has knobs everywhere! Controls mounted on a black pickguard: built-in "E" tuner, distortion booster, treble/bass boost, and "Repeat Percussion" 2 single coil pickups, roller bridge/"Bigsby"-style tremolo, available in White finish, mfg. 1967-68.

	N/A	$1,500	$1,350	$1,250	$1,150	$950	$800

GRAND PRIX - single florentine cutaway hollowbody, 6-on-a-side headstock, 2 Ferro-Sonic single coil pickups with chrome covers, 21-fret neck with white block inlays, raised black pickguard, 2 f-holes, chrome hardware, roller bridge/tremolo system, hand operated wah-wah control, volume/2 tone controls, pickup selector switch, "E tuner" on/off switch mounted on a small metal plate. "On-board" effects mounted on a metal plate features a Treble/Bass boost on/off switch and control, Distortion on/off switch and control, "Wah Wah" control, and "Repeat Percussion" (a repeating echo-like function) on/off switch and control, available in Sunburst or Cherry finishes, mfg. 1967-68.

	N/A	$1,500	$1,350	$1,250	$1,150	$950	$800

HARLEM - offset double cutaway body, 6-on-a-side headstock, 2 single coils, chrome hardware, white pickguard, volume/2 tone controls, pickup selector switch located on upper bass bout, mfg. 1966 only.

	N/A	$550	$475	$350	$300	$250	$175

The fingerboard on the Harlem model is scalloped on the treble side, and straight on the bass side. Retail price of the Vox Harlem in 1965 was $189!

V

GRADING	100% MINT	98% NEAR MINT	95% EXC+	90% EXC	80% VG+	70% VG	60% G

HURRICANE - similar to the Spitfire, except only has 2 single coil pickups (no mid body pickup), mfg. 1965-67.

	N/A	$450	$400	$300	$250	$200	$150

Retail price of the Vox Hurricane in 1965 was $169.

INVADER - offset Mosrite-styled double cutaway solid body, 6-on-a-side tuners, 22-fret neck with white block inlays, ornate inlaid headstock design, 2 single coil pickups, chrome hardware, Bigsby-styled tremolo, hand operated wah-wah control, 1 volume/2 tone knobs, pickup selector switch, built-in "E" tuner. "On-board" effects mounted on the black pickguard includes a Treble/Bass boost on/off switch and control, Distortion on/off switch and control, "Wah Wah" control, and "Repeat Percussion" (a repeating echo-like function) on/off switch and control, available in Sunburst finish, mfg. 1967-68.

	N/A	$1,500	$1,350	$1,250	$1,150	$950	$800

LYNX - dual cutaway hollowbody, 3+3 headstock, 3 single coil pickups, raised white pickguard, 2 f-holes, chrome hardware, roller bridge/tremolo system, 2 volume/2 tone controls, pickup selector switch, mfg. 1964-67.

	N/A	$650	$575	$500	$425	$350	$275

Super Lynx Deluxe - similar to the Lynx, except has two single coil pickups and black control knobs, mfg. 1964-67.

	N/A	$750	$650	$550	$475	$400	$325

MANDOGUITAR - rounded single cutaway body, 6+6 headstock, octave-sized neck. 2 single coils, chrome hardware, white pickguard, volume/tone controls, pickup selector switch, mfg. 1964-66

ITALIAN	N/A	$2,500	$2,000	$1,800	$1,600	$1,300	$1,000
UK	N/A	$3,000	$2,700	$2,400	$2,200	$1,750	$1,250

ELECTRIC: MARK SERIES

MARK VI ACOUSTIC - teardrop shaped semi-hollowbody, 6-on-a-side tuners, chrome hardware, roller bridge/tremolo system, f-hole, 3 single coils, raised chrome pickguard, volume/2 tone controls and pickup selector all mounted on metal control plate on lower rear bout, mfg. 1965-67.

ITALIAN	N/A	$1,000	$800	$700	$600	$500	$350
UK	N/A	$1,500	$1,300	$1,100	$900	$700	$500

MARK VI (SOLID BODY) - this model was originally called the Phantom MK III, mfg. 1963-67.

ITALIAN	N/A	$1,200	$1,000	$800	$700	$575	$450
UK	N/A	$1,700	$1,400	$1,200	$950	$700	$500

MARK VI SPECIAL - similar to the Mark VI Acoustic, except has solid body, 6 push buttons mounted on pickguard, controls mounted to the body, and extra control knob near the pickup selector, mfg. only in the UK, 1964-67.

	N/A	$2,000	$1,700	$1,400	$1,100	$900	$700

MARK IX (9 STRING GUITAR) - similar to the Mark VI, except has a 3+6 headstock design, 9 strings (3 single bass, 3 pairs treble), white pickguard, volume/2 tone controls, pickup selector switch, mfg. 1964-67.

ITALIAN	N/A	$900	$750	$650	$550	$450	$350
UK	N/A	$1,250	$1,050	$900	$800	$700	$500

MARK XII - similar to the Mark IX, except has 6+6 headstock and 12 strings, mfg. 1964-67.

ITALIAN	N/A	$1,000	$800	$700	$600	$500	$350
UK	N/A	$1,500	$1,300	$1,100	$900	$700	$500

ELECTRIC: PHANTOM SERIES

The first Phantom series guitars are the first original designs from the Vox company. Some of the other early model solid body guitars introduced prior to 1962 were generally entry level models based on Fender designs.

PHANTOM I - original series solid body electric, mfg. only in the UK 1962-63.

	N/A	$2,200	$1,800	$1,500	$1,300	$1,050	$850

PHANTOM II - similar to the Phantom I, features some variations on the first model, mfg. only in the UK with Italian necks, mfg. 1962-63.

	N/A	$1,700	$1,400	$1,200	$1,050	$900	$750

PHANTOM VI - 5-sided body, 6-on-a-side "spearpoint" headstock, chrome hardware, roller bridge/tremolo system, 3 single coil pickups, white pickguard, volume/2 tone controls, pickup selector knob, mfg. 1962-67.

ITALIAN	N/A	$1,200	$950	$750	$600	$475	$350
UK	N/A	$2,000	$1,700	$1,400	$1,100	$900	$700

PHANTOM XII - similar to the Phantom VI, except has 12 strings, mfg. 1963-67.

ITALIAN	N/A	$1,200	$950	$750	$600	$475	$350
UK	N/A	$2,000	$1,700	$1,400	$1,100	$900	$700

PHANTOM XII STEREO - similar to the Phantom XII, except has a stop tailpiece, three split 3+3 single coil pickups, 3 volume/3 tone knobs for bass side pickups mounted on upper forward side of the body, 3 volume/3 tone knobs for treble side pickups mounted on lower rear side of the body, three on/off stereo pickup function selectors, one 5-way pickup selector switch, mfg. 1966-68.

ITALIAN	N/A	$1,500	$1,350	$1,200	$1,050	$900	$750
UK	N/A	$2,500	$2,100	$1,800	$1,500	$1,200	$1,000

Vox Hurricane courtesy Dale Hanson

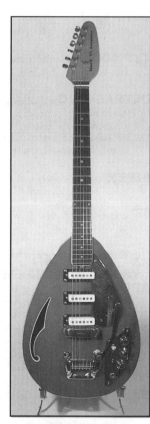

Vox Mark VI Acoustic courtesy Rockohaulix

GRADING	100% MINT	98% NEAR MINT	95% EXC+	90% EXC	80% VG+	70% VG	60% G

PHANTOM GUITAR ORGAN - similar to the Phantom VI, except has extra tone generating circuitry housed in body, 2 single coil pickups, organ on/off switch, 3-way pickup selector knob, guitar tone knob, guitar volume knob, organ volume knob, 6 push buttons, octave knob, organ tone knob, flute voice knob, 3 sustain/percussion controls, mfg. 1966 only.

	100%	98%	95%	90%	80%	70%	60%
UK	N/A	$2,200	$1,800	$1,600	$1,400	$1,200	$1,000

ELECTRIC: SHADOW-VIPER SERIES

SHADOW - offset double cutaway body, 6-on-a-side headstock, 3 single coil pickups, chrome hardware, white pickguard, tremolo, squarish tremolo cover has Vox logo on it, volume/2 tone controls, pickup selector knob on lower treble bout, mfg. 1960-65.

	N/A	$800	$700	$600	$525	$450	$375

SOUNDCASTER - similar to the Super Ace, except has a mute switch (for introducing "novel banjo effects") built near bridge, and contoured body, available in Red, White, Blue, or Black finishes, mfg. 1962-66.

	N/A	N/A	N/A	N/A	N/A	N/A	N/A

SPITFIRE - offset double cutaway body, 6-on-a-side tuners, chrome hardware, white pickguard, tremolo bridge, 3 single coils, volume/2 tone controls, pickup selector switch located on lower treble bout, mfg. 1965-67.

	N/A	$500	$400	$300	$250	$200	$150

STARSTREAM - teardrop hollowbody, 6-on-a-side headstock, 2 Ferro-Sonic single coil pickups with chrome covers, 21-fret neck with white block inlays, ornate headstock inlays around logo, raised black pickguard, 1 f-hole, chrome hardware, roller bridge/tremolo system, hand operated wah-wah control, volume/2 tone controls, pickup selector switch, "E tuner" on/off switch mounted on a small metal plate. onboard effects mounted on a metal plate features a Treble/Bass boost on/off switch and control, Distortion on/off switch and control, Wah-Wah control, and "Repeat Percussion" (a repeating echo-like function) on/off switch and control, available in Sunburst or Cherry finishes, mfg. 1967-68.

	N/A	$1,500	$1,350	$1,200	$1,050	$850	$650

Starstream XII - similar to the Starstream, except has a 6+6 headstock and 12-string configuration.

	N/A	$1,500	$1,350	$1,200	$1,050	$850	$650

STROLLER - similar to the Clubman model, except only has one single coil pickup, available in Red or White finishes, mfg. 1960-66.

	N/A	$350	$275	$225	$150	$100	$75

TEMPEST XII - offset double cutaway body, 6+6 headstock (12-string), 3 single coil pickups, chrome hardware, tremolo, white pickguard, volume/2 tone controls, pickup selector switch located in lower treble bout, mfg. 1965-67.

	N/A	$525	$450	$375	$300	$225	$150

THUNDERJET - double offset cutaway solid body, 22-fret neck with dot inlay, 6-on-a-side tuners, 1 black single coil pickup, chrome hardware, roller bridge/Bigsby-styled tremolo system, 1 volume/2 tone knobs, built-in "E" tuner, Treble/Bass boost on/off switch and control, and Distortion on/off switch and control. Controls all mounted on a white pickguard, available in Sunburst, White, or Cherry finishes, mfg. 1967-68.

	N/A	$350	$275	$200	$150	$100	$75

TORNADO - single cutaway semi-hollowbody design, 2 f-holes, raised white pickguard, roller bridge/trapeze tailpiece, 3-per-side asymmetrical headstock, 1 pickup (neck position), 1 volume knob and 1 tone knob, mfg. 1965-67.

	N/A	$350	$275	$200	$150	$100	$75

TYPHOON - similar to the Tornado model, except has a 3+3 headstock, 2 single coil pickups, and the pickup selector switch is located on the upper bass bout, mfg. 1965-67.

	N/A	$500	$400	$350	$300	$250	$150

ULTRASONIC - dual cutaway hollowbody, 6-on-a-side headstock, 2 single coil pickups with chrome covers, 21-fret neck with white block inlays, raised black pickguard, 2 f-holes, chrome hardware, roller bridge/tremolo system, hand operated wah-wah control, volume/2 tone controls, pickup selector switch, "E tuner" on/off switch mounted on lower treble bout. "On-board" effects mounted on a metal plate features a Treble/Bass boost on/off switch and control, Distortion on/off switch and control, Wah-Wah control, and "Repeat Percussion" (a repeating echo-like function) on/off switch and control, available in 6 and 12-string versions, available in Sunburst or Cherry finishes, mfg. 1967-68.

	N/A	$1,400	$1,200	$1,000	$850	$700	$550

VIPER - dual cutaway hollowbody, 6-on-a-side headstock, 2 Ferro-Sonic single coil pickups with chrome covers, 21-fret neck with white block inlays, raised black pickguard, 2 f-holes, chrome hardware, trapeze Vox tailpiece, volume/2 tone controls, pickup selector switch, "E tuner" on/off switch mounted on lower treble bout. "On-board" effects mounted on a metal plate features a Treble/Bass boost on/off switch and control, Distortion on/off switch and control, Wah-Wah control, and "Repeat Percussion" (a repeating echo-like function) on/off switch and control, available in Sunburst or Cherry finishes, mfg. 1968 only.

	N/A	$600	$500	$400	$300	$250	$175

ELECTRIC BASS

APOLLO IV - single cutaway hollowbody, four-on-a-side headstock, 1 single coil pickup, raised white pickguard, 2 f-holes, chrome hardware, roller bridge/trapeze tailpiece, volume/tone controls. "On-board" effects mounted on a metal plate features a "G tuner" on/off switch, Treble/Bass boost on/off switch and control, and Distortion on/off switch and control, mfg. 1967-68.

	N/A	$700	$600	$500	$400	$300	$200

ASTRO IV - violin-shaped semi-hollowbody, four-on-a-side tuners, 21-fret neck with white dot inlays, 2 single coil pickups, raised black pickguard, trapeze bridge, 1 volume/2 tone knobs, built-in "G" tuner mounted on a small metal plate, pickup selector switch. "On-board" effects mounted on a metal plate features a Treble/Bass boost on/off switch and control, and Distortion on/off switch and control, mfg. 1967-69.

	N/A	$800	$700	$600	$500	$400	$300

BASSMASTER - offset double cutaway body, four-on-a-side tuners, 2 single coil pickups, white pickguard, chrome hardware, volume/tone controls, mfg. 1961-64.

	N/A	$350	$275	$225	$175	$125	$75

GRADING	100% MINT	98% NEAR MINT	95% EXC+	90% EXC	80% VG+	70% VG	60% G

CONSTELLATION IV - teardrop shaped semi-hollowbody, four-on-a-side tuners, chrome hardware, fixed bridge, f-hole, 2 chrome covered single coils, raised black pickguard, volume/2 tone controls and pickup selector. "On-board" effects mounted on a metal plate features a "G tuner" on/off switch, Treble/Bass boost on/off switch and control, and Distortion on/off switch and control, mfg. 1967-68.

	N/A	$1,500	$1,300	$1,200	$1,050	$900	$750

MARK IV - teardrop solid body, four-on-a-side tuners, 2 single coil pickups, fixed bridge, volume/tone controls, pickup selector switch, mfg. 1965-68.

ITALIAN	N/A	$1,000	$800	$700	$600	$475	$350
UK	N/A	$1,500	$1,350	$1,200	$1,050	$900	$750

PHANTOM IV - 5-sided body, four-on-a-side tuners, fixed bridge, chrome hardware, white pickguard, 2 single coil pickups, volume/tone controls, pickup selector switch, mfg. 1965-68.

ITALIAN	N/A	$1,000	$800	$700	$600	$475	$350
UK	N/A	$1,500	$1,350	$1,200	$1,050	$900	$750

STINGER IV - teardrop shaped semi-hollowbody, four-on-a-side tuners, chrome hardware, fixed bridge, f-hole, 2 chrome covered single coils, raised black pickguard, volume/2 tone controls and pickup selector, mfg. 1968 only.

	N/A	$700	$600	$500	$400	$300	$200

WYMAN BASS - teardrop shaped semi-hollowbody, solitary slash f-hole, 2 pickups, 1 volume knob and 1 tone knob, four-on-a-side "spear" headstock, mfg. 1966-67.

	N/A	$2,000	$1,800	$1,600	$1,400	$1,200	$1,000

This model was endorsed by Bill Wyman (Rolling Stones). A protective snap-on pad was attached to the back of the Wyman bass.

VULCAN

Instruments previously produced in Korea during the mid-1980s.

Vulcan trademark instruments featured designs based on Fender and Gibson classics. However, these solid body guitars were low to entry level quality, and may appeal to the novice player only (source: Tony Bacon and Paul Day, *The Guru's Guitar Guide*).

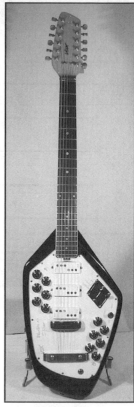

Vox Phantom XII Stereo courtesy Abalone Vintage

Vox Ultrasonic courtesy Fretware Guitars

NOTES

Section W

W. PAUL GUITARS, INC.

Instruments currently built in Waukesha, WI.

Designer William Paul Jarowsky's objective was to construct a guitar which enhanced the sound quality as well as the playability. Jarowsky developed the patented **Soundport System** electric guitars, which features a contoured semi-hollow body with top soundports hand-sculpted into the hollow chambers between the pickups.

All models feature a through-body neck, and contoured bodies. The **Natural** is the original version of Jarowsky's design, and features a high gloss, satin, or hand-rubbed finish that brings out the grain patterns of the wood. The **Plus** model features a variety of Translucent stains on an all maple or all ash body; the **Ultra** features high gloss solid finishes. Jarowsky's Limited and **Limited** Special models feature selected and exotic woods in their constructions. Currently, the Superior Classic (with elaborate, full length vine inlay) retails for $9,000, including Ameritage case. For additional information regarding wood availability (Timeless Timber wood is sawn from sawmill logs submerged underwater until 1991), and pricing, contact W. Paul Guitars directly (see Trademark Index).

WEM

See Watkins. Instruments previously built in England.

WEM (Watkins Electric Music) was the first of two name changes for the Watkins company (1960-1982).

WAL

Instruments currently built by Electric Wood in High Wycombe (Bucks), England since 1978.

In the mid 1970s, Pete Stevens joined London-based repairman Ian Waller to design the Wal Custom bass guitar. In 1978 the two incorporated into the company called Electric Wood, and produced numerous custom basses. Ian Waller later passed away; however, Stevens continues production to date.

WM GUITARS

Instruments currently built in Santa Fe, NM.

Will Miller and the craftsmen at WM Guitars in Santa Fe are custom building guitar and bass models in the foothills of the Sangre de Cristo mountains. Models are available with set-in or bolt-on necks. Instruments are created with maple, mahogany, wenge, and ebony woods, and feature an oil finish. For further information regarding models and pricing, contact Will Miller at WM Guitars directly (see Trademark Index).

As part of the company's philosophy of ecology, a tree is planted for every instrument the company builds.

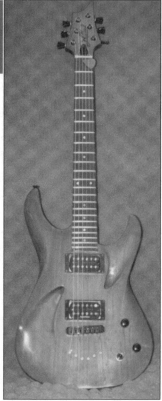

**W. Paul Ash-Plus
courtesy W. Paul**

WRC GUITARS

Instruments previously built in Calimesa, CA from 1989 to the mid-1990s. Distributed by WRC Music International, Inc. of Hemet, CA.

After designing guitar models that updated and surpassed their original inspirations, luthier/designer Wayne R. Charvel left his namesake company. Charvel did design one model for Gibson (the US-1) that quite frankly looks like a Charvel Model 6 with "Gibson" on the (Charvel-style) pointy headstock.

In 1989, Wayne Charvel formed a new company that produced guitars under the Ritz trademark. Only a handful were built before the logo was changed to WRC (Wayne R. Charvel) in 1990. WRC has been producing a number of "one- off" specialty guitars. The Neptune Series, which uses seashells as part of the top inlay, was designed in conjunction with current staff member Eric J. Galletta.

WRC Music International also operates the Park Hill Music Studio, a recording studio that has produced a number of recording dates.

GRADING	100% MINT	98% NEAR MINT	95% EXC+	90% EXC	80% VG+	70% VG	60% G

ELECTRIC: CLASSIC SERIES

The Classic series model has the following features optional: standard Wilkinson vibrato, double locking Floyd Rose vibrato, single cutaway body with 2 single coil pickups, volume/tone control, 3-position switch.

WRC CLASSIC - offset double cutaway alder body, bolt-on maple neck, 24-fret rosewood fingerboard with pearl dot inlay, strings through Wilkinson bridge, 3-per-side Grover tuners, chrome hardware, 2 single coil/1 humbucker Kent Armstrong exposed pickups, volume/tone controls, 3 mini switches, available in Black, Blond, Candy Apple Red, Electric Blue, Seafoam Green, Pearl White, Trans. Blue, Trans. Green, Trans. Tangerine, or White finishes, mfg. 1994-mid-1990s.

$750	$575	$500	$425	$350	$300	$250

Last MSR was $900.

**W. Paul Flame Maple Plus
courtesy W. Paul**

GRADING	100% MINT	98% NEAR MINT	95% EXC+	90% EXC	80% VG+	70% VG	60% G

ELECTRIC: EXOTIC SERIES

The Exotic series model has the following features optional: ebony or maple fingerboards, standard Wilkinson vibrato with locking Gotoh tuners, double locking Floyd Rose vibrato, chrome or gold hardware, single cutaway body with 2 single coil pickups, volume/tone control, 3-position switch.

WRC EXOTIC - offset double cutaway alder body, figured wood top, bolt-on maple neck, 24-fret rosewood fingerboard with pearl dot inlay, strings through Wilkinson bridge, 3-per-side Grover tuners, black hardware, 2 single coil/1 humbucker exposed pickups, volume/tone controls, 3 mini switches, available in Cherry Burst, Honey Burst, Natural, Tobacco Burst, Trans. Candy Blue, Trans. Candy Green, Trans. Candy Purple, Trans. Candy Red, or Trans. Candy Tangerine finishes, mfg. 1994-mid 1990s.

	N/A	$1,250	$1,100	$1,000	$900	$750	$500

Last MSR was $1,600.

ELECTRIC: NEPTUNE SERIES

This series, designed by Wayne R.Charvel and Eric J. Galletta, uses Pacific seashells for finish. It is estimated that only 80 Neptune Series models have been built to date. Only the Custom and Deluxe models have the following features optional: standard Wilkinson vibrato with locking Grover tuners or double locking Floyd Rose vibrato, multiple variations of pickup and control configurations.

CUSTOM - offset double cutaway basswood body, bolt-on figured maple neck, 22-fret ebony fingerboard, strings through Wilkinson bridge, 3-per-side Gotoh tuners, gold hardware, 2 Seymour Duncan humbucker pickups, volume/tone controls, 3-position switch. Available in Black Snake, Neptune Avalon, Neptune Gold, Neptune Violet Oyster, Paua, Tiger Cowrie, or White Nautilus shell finishes, disc.

$2,700	$2,400	$2,100	N/A	N/A	N/A	N/A

Last MSR was $3,000.

This model has the following features optional: 24-fret fingerboard, rosewood or maple fingerboard, abalone or pearl fingerboard inlay, black (or cloud, dolphin, or dot) fingerboard inlay design.

DELUXE - similar to the Custom, except features 24-fret rosewood fingerboard with abalone dot inlay, tune-o-matic bridge/stop tailpiece, black hardware, Seymour Duncan exposed humbucker pickup, volume control, available in Black Snake, Neptune Avalon, Neptune Violet Oyster, or Tiger Cowrie shell finishes, disc.

$2,100	$1,850	$1,500	N/A	N/A	N/A	N/A

Last MSR was $2,400.

This model has the following features optional: ebony or maple fingerboard, pearl dot fingerboard inlay, chrome or gold hardware.

STANDARD - similar to the Custom, except features an alder body, bolt-on maple neck, 24-fret rosewood fingerboard with pearl dot inlay, double locking Floyd Rose vibrato, 3-per-side Grover tuners, chrome hardware, available in Neptune Avalon Shell finish, disc.

$1,750	$1,500	$1,250	N/A	N/A	N/A	N/A

Last MSR was $2,000.

This model has standard Wilkinson vibrato with locking Grover tuners as an option.

WABASH

See chapter on House Brands.

This trademark has been identified as a House Brand of Wexler (source: Willie G. Moseley, *Stellas & Stratocasters*).

WANDRE´

See Davoli. Instruments previously produced in Italy during the mid-1950s through the late 1960s. Distributed in the U.S. by Don Noble and Company, and in the U.K. by Jennings Musical Industries, Ltd. (JMI).

Wandre guitars help define where art design and guitar production cross. Designed by Italian motorcycle and guitar appreciator, Wandre´ Pelotti (1916-1981) was an artist and sculptor from Milan. Wandre´ instruments are oddly shaped thinline hollowbody electric or solid body electric guitars with either Framez or Davoli pickups.

Wandre´ guitars were personally produced by Pelotti from 1956/1957 to 1960. Between 1960 and 1963, the designs were produced by Framez in Milan, Italy; then by Davoli from 1963 to 1965. Pelotti supervised construction from 1966 to 1969 in his own factory.

Wandre´s instruments may bear a number of different brand names, but the Wandre´ logo will appear somewhere. Other brand names include Davoli, Framez, JMI, Noble, Avalon, Avanti I, Krundaal, and possibly others (source: Tony Bacon and Paul Day, The Guru´s Guitar Guide; and Michael Wright, *Vintage Guitar Magazine*).

These solid body (and some hollowbody) guitars featured aluminum necks (called "Duraluminum") with wood fingerboards, and plastic coverings on the body. Finishes include multi-color or sparkle, as well as linoleum and fiberglass body parts. The **B.B.** model was named in honor of actress Brigitte Bardot. The futuristic body designs of the **Rock Oval**, **Spazial**, and **Swedenbass** may have some visual appeal, but the level of playing quality isn´t as high as the coolness factor may indicate.

WARR

Instruments currently built in Thousand Oaks, CA, since 1993.

Warr guitars was founded in 1993 in Long Beach, California. They later moved to Thousand Oaks, California. Luthier/designer Mark D.Warr is offering the Touch-style Guitar (Model TSG) instrument that features a conventional body, but can be played in a variety of styles.

Luthier Magnus Krempel is building the Warr Guitar for the European market with permission from Mark Warr. Krempel´s Warr models have an additional option of a Wilkinson tremolo system for the four or five high strings (see Magnus Krempel). For additional information, please contact Mark Warr directly (see Trademark Index).

GRADING	100% MINT	98% NEAR MINT	95% EXC+	90% EXC	80% VG+	70% VG	60% G

ELECTRIC

The Artist Series starts at $2,695 for the eight- and ten-string models, and $2,795 for the 12-string model. The Artisan Series are semi-hollow body models that start at $2,985 for eight-strings, $3,095 for a 10-string, and $3,185 for the 12-string. The Trey Gunn Signature series starts at $2,995 for eight and ten string and $3,095 for 12-string. The Phalanx Series starts at $3,200 for a 12-string and $3,400 for a 14-string. Several options are also available.

WARRIOR

Instruments currently built in Rossville, GA since 1995.

Warrior Annointed Hand Made Instruments is currently offers high quality custom-built bass models that feature bolt-on and neck-through designs, exotic woods, and an innovative "through-body stringing" that corrects the floppy feeling of the low B-string.

ELECTRIC GUITAR

Warrior has a full line of guitars that are as of high quality as their bass couterparts are. There are models such as the Guardian and Soldier which are more on the basic side, and then there are highly customized models avaialable. There are always different models for sale and being produced. Visit their website for information and full listings on each and every model (see Trademark Index).

ELECTRIC BASS

Warrior´s **Standard** model features bodies with a purpleheart center and mahogany or maple wings, a bolt-on neck, figured bookmatched tops, bird´s-eye maple or purpleheart fingerboards, Seymour Duncan humbucker pickup, and volume/tone controls.

The **Studio** model has a through-body 3-ply laminated neck with a purpleheart center and choice of mahogany or maple (or wenge or walnut) sides, figured bookmatched tops, wenge, bird´s-eye maple or purpleheart fingerboards, and 2 Bartolini or Seymour Duncan pickups.

Both the **Standard Plus** and **Studio Plus** neck-through models are also available in bolt-on neck configurations. These models feature a wide range of figured wood laminated tops and back, and multi-ply necks. The base retail price ranges from $2,900 up to $10,000, depending on the options and wood choices. There are also several customized models available.

**Warwick Bass
courtesy Warwick**

WARWICK

Instruments currently produced in Markneukirchen, Germany by Warwick GmbH & Co., Musicequipment KG since 1982. Distributed exclusively in the U.S. by Dana B. Goods of Santa Barbara, CA.

Hans Peter Wilfer, son of Framus´ Frederick Wilfer, established the Warwick trademark in 1982 in Erlangen (Bavaria). Wilfer literally grew up in the Framus factories of his father, and learned all aspects of construction and production right at the source. The high quality of Warwick basses quickly gained notice with bass players worldwide.

In 1995, Warwick moved to Markneukirchen (in the Saxon Vogtland) to take advantage of the centuries of instrument-making traditions. Construction of the new plant provided the opportunity to install new state-of-the-art machinery to go with the skilled craftsmen. The Warwick company continues to focus on producing high quality bass guitars; and since 1993, Warwick also offers a full range of bass amplification systems and speaker cabinets.

For information regarding the Warwick **Alien** acoustic bass model, please refer to the *Blue Book of Acoustic Guitars*.

GENERAL INFORMATION & OPTIONS

An ebony fretless fingerboard is available on all models at no additional charge. A few models are available in left-hand configuration and if not they are a special order but there is no additional cost. The following options are available on all models from Warwick:

Add 15% for left-handed version. Add $75 for black, chrome, or gold hardware. Add $125 for dot inlays. Add $125 for ebony fingerboard on fretted instruments. Add $100 for a D tuner. Add $150 for short or medium necks. Add $225 for Extra long scale neck. Add $250 for owner's name inlay. Add $250 for wide string spacing. Add $250 for high-polish colors on bolt-on bass models. Add $400 for high-polish colors on neck-through models. Add $500 for Bird's eye Maple body upgrade (maple body models only). Add $600 for LED fret markers.

ELECTRIC BASS: BUZZARD SERIES

BUZZARD - offset double cutaway zebrano body, wenge/zebrano neck, 24-fret wenge fingerboard, pearl model name peghead inlay, 4-on-a-side tuners, gold hardware, 2 P-style MEC pickups, volume/treble/mid/bass/mix controls, active electronics, available in Natural finish, disc. 1995.

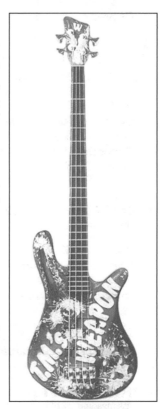

N/A	$2,400	$2,150	$1,850	$1,400	$1,250	$1,100

Last MSR was $3,900.

This model was designed by John Entwistle (The Who), and is not available with fretless fingerboard.

**Warwick Bass w/Graphics
courtesy Warwick**

GRADING	100% MINT	98% NEAR MINT	95% EXC+	90% EXC	80% VG+	70% VG	60% G

BUZZARD BOLT-ON - offset double cutaway zebrano body, bolt-on ovangkol neck, 24-fret wenge fingerboard, 2-per-side tuners, gold hardware, 2 P-style MEC pickups, 3 knobs, active electronics, available in Natural finish, mfg. 2003-present.

MSR	$2,399	$1,950	$1,700	$1,500	$1,300	$1,100	$950	$800

Buzzard Bolt-On 5-String - similar to the Buzzard Bolt-On, except in five-string configuration, 3/2-per-side tuners, mfg. 2003-present.

MSR	$2,599	$2,100	$1,800	$1,550	$1,350	$1,150	$1,000	$900

BUZZARD LTD 2003 - offset double cutaway zebrano body, ovangkol neck, 26-fret wenge fingerboard with numeric MOP fretboard inlays, 4-on-a-side tuners, gold hardware, 2 P-style MEC pickups, 3 knobs, active electronics, available in Red or Black Metallic Flip Flop finishes, mfg. 2003-present.

MSR	$5,499	$4,400	$3,900	$3,400	$2,900	$2,500	$2,100	$1,800

ELECTRIC BASS: CORVETTE SERIES

Ash bodies and colors are sometimes available on the Corvette Standard models.

CORVETTE PRO LINE - offset double cutaway contoured ash body, 3-piece wenge neck, 24-fret wenge fingerboard, 2-per-side tuners, gold hardware, 2 J-style active MEC pickups, 2 volume/1 tone controls, available in Blue Ocean, Burgundy Red, Honey Violin, or Nirvana Black oil finishes, mfg. 1994-95, reintroduced 2001-present.

MSR	$1,899	$1,525	$1,300	$1,100	$950	$800	$700	$600

When the Corvette Pro Line was reintroduced it featured a maple body.

Corvette Pro Line 5-String - similar to Corvette Pro, except has 5 strings, 3/2-per-side tuners, mfg. 1994-95, reintroduced 2001-present.

MSR	$2,099	$1,700	$1,450	$1,250	$1,050	$900	$750	$650

Corvette Pro Line 6-String - similar to Corvette Pro, except has 6-strings, 3-per-side tuners, mfg. 1994-95, reintroduced 2001-present.

MSR	$2,399	$1,950	$1,700	$1,450	$1,250	$1,100	$950	$800

CORVETTE LIMITED - similar to Corvette Pro Line, except features a semi-hollowbody design and f-holes. Production was limited to 100 instruments.

	N/A	N/A	N/A	N/A	N/A	N/A	N/A

There has not been sufficient trading of this model to quote prices.

CORVETTE ALTUS - offset double cutaway contoured ash body, flamed maple top, 3-piece wenge neck, 24-fret wenge fingerboard, 2-per-side tuners, gold hardware, MEC large pole soapbar active pickup, volume/3-band EQ controls, Seymour Duncan Basslines MM electronics, available in Natural oil finishes, disc 1999.

	$1,200	$1,050	$925	$775	$650	$500	$375

Last MSR was $1,499.

Add $125 for Basslines SMB-4A Alnico pickups.

The Altus model features an ash body with flamed maple top separated by a walnut veneer inlay. The fretless fingerboard is ebony.

Corvette Altus 5-String - similar to Corvette Altus, except has 4-piece wenge neck, 5 strings, 3/2-per-side tuners, disc 1999.

	$1,350	$1,195	$1,050	$895	$725	$575	$425

Last MSR was $1,699.

Add $125 for Basslines SMB-5A Alnico pickups.

CORVETTE STANDARD - offset double cutaway contoured 2- (or 3-) piece bubinga body, bolt-on wenge neck, 24-fret wenge fingerboard, 2-per-side tuners, chrome hardware, 2 J-style passive pickups, 2 volume/1 tone controls, available in Natural oil finishes, mfg. 1996-present.

MSR	$1,299	$1,050	$900	$775	$650	$550	$450	$350

Corvette Standard Active - similar to Corvette Standard, except has 2 active J-style pickups, mfg. 1996-present.

MSR	$1,499	$1,200	$1,050	$900	$750	$650	$550	$450

Corvette Standard 5-String - similar to Corvette Standard Active, except has 5 strings, 3/2-per-side tuners, mfg. 1996-present.

MSR	$1,699	$1,375	$1,200	$1,050	$900	$775	$650	$550

Corvette Standard 6-String - similar to Corvette Standard (Active), except has 6-strings, 3-per-side tuners, mfg. 1996-present.

MSR	$1,999	$1,600	$1,350	$1,150	$1,000	$875	$750	$650

CORVETTE FNA JAZZMAN - offset double cutaway contoured 2- (or 3-) piece swamp ash with maple cap body, bolt-on wenge neck, 24-fret wenge fingerboard, 2-per-side tuners, gold hardware, 2 MEC large pole & J SC passive/active pickups, 2 volume/1 tone controls, available in Natural and Trans. satin finishes, mfg. 1999-present.

MSR	$2,149	$1,725	$1,500	$1,300	$1,100	$950	$800	$750

Corvette FNA Jazzman 5-String - similar to Corvette FNA Jazzman, except has 5 strings, 3/2-per-side tuners, mfg. 1999-present.

MSR	$2,349	$1,900	$1,650	$1,450	$1,250	$1,050	$925	$800

Corvette FNA Jazzman Ltd 2002 - similar to Corvette FNA Jazzman, except hasa swirly bubinga cap, and is hand signed by Hans Peter Wilfer, 80 made for the U.S. market, mfg. 2002-03.

	$1,850	$1,600	$1,300	$1,000	N/A	N/A	N/A

Last MSR was $2,499.

Corvette FNA Jazzman Ltd 2004 - similar to Corvette FNA Jazzman, except has a flamed koa top on swamp ash and is hand signed by Hans Peter Wilfer, 60 made for the U.S. market, mfg. 2002-present.

MSR	$2,499	$2,000	$1,700	$1,500	$1,300	N/A	N/A	N/A

CORVETTE HOT ROD LTD. 2005 - offset double cutaway contoured two-piece swamp ash body with AAAA flame maple top, multi-layer Ekanga and maple veneer, four-piece flame maple neck, 24-fret flame maple fingerboard with planet inlays, 3/2-per-side tuners, two soapbar H/H pickups, three knobs, black hardware, available in Natural finish, new 2005.

MSR	$2,799	$2,250	$1,950	$1,700	$1,500	N/A	N/A	N/A

GRADING	100% MINT	98% NEAR MINT	95% EXC+	90% EXC	80% VG+	70% VG	60% G

Corvette Hot Rod LTD. 2005 5-String - offset double cutaway contoured two-piece swamp ash body with AAAA flame maple top, multi-layer Ekanga and maple veneer, three-piece flame maple neck, 24-fret flame maple fingerboard with planet inlays, two-per-side tuners, two P-style split pickups, three knobs, black hardware, available in Natural finish, new 2005.

MSR	$2,499	$2,000	$1,700	$1,500	$1,300	N/A	N/A	N/A

CORVETTE $$ (DOUBLE BUCK) - offset double cutaway contoured swamp ash body, three-piece ovangkol neck, 24-fret wenge fingerboard, two-per-side tuners, two MM pickups, four knobs, two mini-switches, black hardware, available in Natural and Trans. Oil finishes, new 2005.

MSR	$1,699	$1,375	$1,200	$1,050	$900	$775	$650	$550

Corvette $$ (Double Buck) 5-String - similar to the Corvette $$, except in five-string configuration, 3/2-per-side tuners, new 2005.

MSR	$1,999	$1,600	$1,400	$1,200	$1,050	$900	$775	$650

ELECTRIC BASS: CRUISER SERIES

CRUISER - Explorer-style pointed hollow mahogany body with quilted maple or Ziricote wood back and top, four-piece flame maple neck, 24-fret ebony fingerboard with spirit inlays, two-per-side tuners, two MEC active P-style split pickups, four knobs, gold hardware, available in various finishes, new 2005.

MSR	$5,599	$4,500	$3,800	$3,300	$2,800	N/A	N/A	N/A

ELECTRIC BASS: DOLPHIN SERIES

DOLPHIN PRO I - offset double cutaway asymmetrical boire/rosewood body, half through-body 7-piece wenge/zebrano neck, 24-fret wenge fingerboard with pearl dolphin inlay, 2-per-side tuners, chrome hardware, MEC J-style/humbucker pickups, concentric volume-balance/concentric treble-bass control, MEC active electronics, push/pull electronics switch in volume control, push/pull coil split switch in tone control, available in Natural oil finish, current mfg.

MSR	$4,249	$3,400	$2,900	$2,500	$2,150	$1,800	$1,500	$1,200

In 1996, gold hardware replaced chrome.

**Warwick Fortress One
courtesy Warwick**

Dolphin Pro I 5-String - similar to Dolphin Pro I, except has 5 strings, 3/2-per-side tuners, current mfg.

MSR	$4,549	$3,650	$3,150	$2,700	$2,300	$2,000	$1,700	$1,400

DOLPHIN PRO II - offset double cutaway asymmetrical ash body, bolt-on 3-piece maple neck, 24-fret wenge fingerboard, 2-per-side tuners, chrome hardware, 2 MEC J-style pickups, volume/concentric treble-bass/balance controls, active electronics, push/pull electronics switch in volume contro, available in Black, Black Stain, Blue, Blue Stain, Red Stain, or Wine Red finishes, disc. 1994.

	N/A	$1,200	$1,000	$875	$750	$675	$600

Last MSR was $2,050.

This model had Bartolini or EMG pickups as an option.

DOLPHIN SN - offset double cutaway asymmetrical Afzalea body with sound chambers, glued in ovangkol neck, 24-fret wenge fingerboard with pearl dolphin inlay, 2-per-side tuners, chrome hardware, MEC P-style/humbucker pickups, active electronics, gold hardware, available in Natural oil finish, current mfg.

MSR	$2,599	$2,100	$1,800	$1,550	$1,350	$1,150	$1,000	$850

Dolphin SN 5-String - similar to Dolphin SN, except has 5 strings, 3/2-per-side tuners and active JJ style pickups, current mfg.

MSR	$2,799	$2,250	$1,900	$1,650	$1,400	$1,200	$1,050	$900

ELECTRIC BASS: FORTRESS SERIES

FORTRESS (FORTRESS ONE) - offset double cutaway 3-piece maple body, bolt-on 3-piece wenge neck, 24-fret wenge fingerboard, 2-per-side tuners, chrome hardware, MEC Gold P/J-style active pickups, volume/treble/bass/balance control, active MEC electronics, available in Black, Blue, Green, Honey, Natural Maple, Red, or Violet satin finishes, disc 2000.

$1,350	$1,150	$950	$800	$700	$600	$500

Last MSR was $1,799.

Fortress R & B Standard 4-String - similar to Fortress, except has an ash body, and MEC P/J-style passive pickups, mfg. 1994-99.

$1,000	$925	$850	$750	$600	$550	$425

Last MSR was $1,199.

Fortress 5 String - similar to Fortress, except has 5 strings, 3/2-per-side tuners, 2 MEC J-style active pickups, active MEC electronics, mfg. 1994-2000.

$1,500	$1,300	$1,100	$950	$800	$700	$600

Last MSR was $1,999.

FORTRESS FLASHBACK - offset double cutaway 2- (or 3-) piece ash body, bolt-on wenge neck, 24-fret wenge fingerboard, 2-per-side tuners, chrome hardware, celluloid mother-of-pearl pickguard, 2 MEC lipstick tube pickups, passive volume/blend/tone controls, available in Honey, Natural, or Red finishes, mfg. 1996-99.

$1,200	$1,050	$825	$650	$600	$550	$500

Last MSR was $1,499.

Add $200 for 2-Tek bridge upgrade (factory installation).

**Warwick Streamer Bolt-On
courtesy Warwick**

W

GRADING	100% MINT	98% NEAR MINT	95% EXC+	90% EXC	80% VG+	70% VG	60% G

Fortress Flashback 5 String - similar to Fortress Flashback, except has 5 strings, 3/2-per-side tuners, mfg. 1996-99.

	$1,350	$1,050	$900	$850	$725	$650	$525

Last MSR was $1,699.

Add $200 for 2-Tek bridge upgrade (factory installation).

FORTRESS MASTERMAN - offset double cutaway 2-piece maple body, bolt-on wenge neck, 24-fret wenge fingerboard, 2-per-side tuners, side dot fret markers, chrome hardware, MEC dual J-style active pickup, volume/blend controls, 2 independent sets of bass/treble controls, 2 preamps, available in Honey, Natural, and Red finishes, mfg. 1996-2000.

	$1,500	$1,300	$1,100	$950	$800	$700	$600

Last MSR was $1,999.

Fortress Masterman 5 String - similar to Fortress Masterman, except has 5 strings, 3/2-per-side tuners, mfg. 1996-2000.

	$1,650	$1,450	$1,200	$1,050	$925	$775	$650

Last MSR was $2,199.

ELECTRIC BASS: INFINITY SERIES

INFINITY SN - double cutaway semi-hollow body, bird's-eye or flamed maple top, ovangkol back, glued in ovangkol neck with wenge fingerboard, active 2-way electronics, 2 MEC J-style pickups, black hardware, available in Natural finish, mfg. 2002-present.

MSR	$2,499	$2,000	$1,700	$1,450	$1,250	$1,100	$950	$800

Infinity SN 5-String - similar to the Infinity SN, except in five-string configuration, 3/2-per-side tuners, mfg. 2002-present.

MSR	$2,699	$2,175	$1,850	$1,600	$1,400	$1,200	$1,050	$900

INFINITY LTD 2000 - similar to the Infinity SN, except has a ovangkol body with birdseye or AAA flamed maple top, and passive/active MEC J & MEC large pole pickups, mfg. 2000-present.

MSR	$4,699	$3,800	$3,300	$2,800	$2,400	$2,100	$1,800	$1,500

Infinity SN 5-String - similar to the Infinity SN, except in five-string configuration, 3/2-per-side tuners, mfg. 2002-present.

MSR	$4,999	$4,000	$3,400	$2,900	$2,500	$2,200	$1,900	$1,600

ELECTRIC BASS: KATANA SERIES

KATANA - offset double cutaway swamp ash body with flame maple top, ovangkol neck, 24-fret ebony fingerboard with MOP fisheye inlay, 2 MEC active J/J pickups, MEC 3-band electronics, 2-per-side tuners, four knobs, gold hardware, available in various finishes, mfg. 2004-present.

MSR	$2,899	$2,350	$2,000	$1,750	$1,500	$1,300	$1,100	$950

Katana 5-String - similar to the Katana, except in 5-String configuration, 3/2-per-side tuners, mfg. 2004-present.

MSR	$3,199	$2,600	$2,200	$1,900	$1,650	$1,450	$1,250	$1,100

KATANA BOLT-ON - offset double cutaway swamp ash body with flame maple top, bolt-on ovangkol neck, 24-fret ebony fingerboard with MOP fisheye inlay, 2 MEC active J/J pickups, MEC 2-band electronics, 2-per-side tuners, four knobs, chrome hardware, available in various finishes, mfg. 2004-present.

MSR	$1,999	$1,600	$1,400	$1,200	$1,000	$850	$750	$650

Katana Bolt-On 5-String - similar to the Katana Bolt-On, except in 5-String configuration, 3/2-per-side tuners, mfg. 2004-present.

MSR	$2,199	$1,775	$1,500	$1,300	$1,100	$950	$800	$700

ELECTRIC BASS: STREAMER SERIES

The Streamer CT is also available in the LX version, which is a wide neck.

STREAMER BOLT-ON - offset double cutaway contoured cherry body, bolt-on maple/bubinga neck, 24-fret wenge fingerboard with pearl dot inlay, 2-per-side tuners, chrome hardware, P/J-style active MEC pickups, 2 volume/2 tone controls, available in Natural finish, disc. 1996.

	N/A	$1,400	$1,150	$900	$750	$695	$600

Last MSR was $2,100.

Streamer Bolt-On 5-String - similar to Streamer Bolt-On, except has 5 strings, 3/2-per-side tuners, 2 J-style active MEC pickups, disc. 1996.

	N/A	$1,600	$1,300	$1,050	$950	$850	$750

Last MSR was $2,500.

Streamer Bolt-On 6-String - similar to Streamer, except has 6-strings, 7-piece neck, 3-per-side tuners, 2 humbucker active MEC pickups, mfg. 1994-96.

	N/A	$1,800	$1,500	$1,150	$1,000	$925	$850

Last MSR was $2,800.

STREAMER JAZZMAN - offset double cutaway contoured 2- or 3-piece swamp ash body with maple top, ovangkol neck, 24-fret wenge fingerboard with pearl dot inlay, 2-per-side tuners, gold hardware, MEC large pole and J SC passive/active pickups, volume/treble/bass controls, active MEC electronics, available in Natural or Trans. satin finishes, mfg. 2001-present.

MSR	$2,499	$2,000	$1,700	$1,500	$1,300	$1,150	$950	$800

Streamer Jazzman 5-String - similar to the Streamer Jazzman, except in five-string configuration, 3/2-per-side tuners, mfg. 2001-present.

MSR	$2,699	$2,175	$1,850	$1,600	$1,400	$1,200	$1,050	$900

STREAMER CT - offset double cutaway contoured 2-piece flamed maple body, bolt-on wenge neck, 24-fret wenge fingerboard with pearl dot inlay, 2-per-side tuners, chrome hardware, MEC P/J-style active pickups, volume/treble/bass controls, active MEC electronics, chrome finish available in High Polish Black, Blue, Green, Honey, Natural Maple, Red, or Violet finishes, mfg. 1996-present.

MSR	$3,699	$3,000	$2,550	$2,200	$1,850	$1,600	$1,400	$1,200

GRADING	100% MINT	98% NEAR MINT	95% EXC+	90% EXC	80% VG+	70% VG	60% G

Streamer CT 5 String - similar to Streamer LX, except has 5 strings, 3/2-per-side tuners, 2 MEC J-style active pickups, mfg. 1996-present.

MSR	$3,999		$3,200	$2,700	$2,300	$2,000	$1,700	$1,450	$1,250

Streamer CT 6 String - similar to Streamer LX, except has 6 strings, 3-per-side tuners, 2 Bassline soapbar active pickups, mfg. 1997-present.

MSR	$4,299		$3,450	$2,950	$2,550	$2,150	$1,800	$1,500	$1,200

STREAMER PRO-M - offset double cutaway contoured 2-piece flamed maple body, bolt-on wenge neck, 24-fret wenge fingerboard, side pearl dot fret markers, 2-per-side Gotoh tuners, brass hardware, MEC dual J-style active pickup, volume/blend controls, separate treble/bass controls, 2 preamp electronics, available in Black, Blue, Green, Honey, Natural Maple, Red, or Violet satin finishes, mfg. 1996-2000.

		$1,650	$1,450	$1,200	$1,050	$900	$750	$650

Last MSR was $2,199.

Streamer Pro-M 5 String - similar to Streamer LX, except has 5 strings, 3/2-per-side tuners, mfg. 1996-2000.

		$1,800	$1,550	$1,300	$1,100	$950	$825	$750

Last MSR was $2,399.

STREAMER STAGE I - offset double cutaway contoured maple body, through-body 5-piece maple/bubinga neck, 24-fret wenge fingerboard with pearl dot inlay, 2-per-side tuners, gold hardware, P/J-style MEC pickups, volume/treble/bass/balance control, active MEC electronics, push/pull electronics switch in volume control, available in Natural finish, current mfg.

MSR	$3,499		$2,800	$2,400	$2,100	$1,800	$1,550	$1,300	$1,050

In 1996, Black, Blue, Green, Honey, Natural Maple, Red, and Violet satin finishes were introduced.

Streamer Stage I 5-String - similar to Streamer Stage I, except has 5 strings, 7-piece maple/wenge neck, 3/2-per-side tuners, 2 humbucker Bartolini pickups, current mfg.

MSR	$3,899		$3,150	$2,700	$2,300	$1,950	$1,700	$1,450	$1,250

In 1994, 7-piece maple/bubinga neck replaced original parts/design. In 1996, Basslines soapbar pickups replaced original parts/design.

Streamer Stage I 6-String - similar to Streamer Stage I, except has 6-strings, 7-piece maple/wenge neck, 3-per-side tuners, 2 humbucker Bartolini pickups, current mfg.

MSR	$4,199		$3,400	$2,900	$2,500	$2,100	$1,800	$1,550	$1,300

In 1994, 7-piece maple/bubinga neck replaced original parts/design. In 1996, basslines soapbar pickups replaced original parts/design.

STREAMER STAGE II - offset double cutaway contoured afzelia body, half through 7-piece wenge/afzelia neck, 24-fret ebony fingerboard with pearl/abalone Tao inlay, abalone W peghead inlay, 2-per-side tuners, gold hardware, 2 MEC J-style active pickups, volume/concentric treble-bass/mid/balance control, MEC active electronics, push/pull electronics switch in volume control, available in Natural finish, current mfg.

MSR	$3,799		$3,050	$2,650	$2,250	$1,900	$1,600	$1,350	$1,100

This model has Bartolini or EMG pickups as an option. In 1994, wenge fingerboard replaced original parts/design.

Streamer Stage II 5-String - similar to Streamer Stage II, except has 5 strings, 3/2-per-side tuners, current mfg.

MSR	$4,099		$3,300	$2,800	$2,400	$2,050	$1,750	$1,500	$1,250

STREAMER STAGE III - offset double cutaway asymmetrical boire body, half through-body 7-piece wenge/zebrano neck, 24-fret ebony fingerboard with pearl oval inlay, 2-per-side tuners, chrome hardware, 1 single coil/1 humbucker pickups, concentric volume-balance/concentric treble-bass control, active electronics, available in Natural finish, disc. 1990.

		N/A	$2,500	$2,000	$1,600	$1,300	$1,000	$800

Last MSR was $3,600.

ELECTRIC BASS: THUMB SERIES

THUMB BASS - offset double cutaway asymmetrical contoured 2-piece bubinga body, half through-body 7-piece wenge/bubinga neck, 24-fret wenge fingerboard, 2-per-side tuners, black hardware, 2 MEC Gold J-style pickups, volume/concentric treble-bass/concentric mid-balance control, active MEC electronics, available in Natural oil finish, current mfg.

MSR	$3,599		$2,900	$2,400	$2,100	$1,800	$1,550	$1,300	$1,100

Thumb Bass 5-String similar to Thumb Bass, except has 5 strings, 3/2-per-side tuners, current mfg.

MSR	$3,899		$3,150	$2,650	$2,300	$1,950	$1,650	$1,400	$1,200

Thumb Bass 6-String - similar to Thumb Bass, except has 6 strings, 3-per-side tuners, 2 humbucker Bartolini pickups, current mfg.

MSR	$4,199		$3,400	$2,900	$2,500	$2,100	$1,800	$1,550	$1,300

In 1996, Bassline soapbar pickups replaced the Bartolini humbuckers.

THUMB BOLT ON - offset double cutaway asymmetrical contoured walnut body, bolt-on 3-piece wenge neck, 24-fret wenge fingerboard, 2-per-side tuners, chrome hardware, 2 J-style MEC pickups, volume/concentric treble-bass/concentric mid-balance controls, active MEC electronics, available in Natural finish, mfg. 1994-present.

MSR	$1,999		$1,600	$1,400	$1,200	$1,050	$900	$750	$600

In 1998, black hardware replaced chrome hardware; ovankol body replaced the walnut body.

Warwick Thumb Bolt-On 5-String courtesy Dave Rogers Dave's Guitar Shop

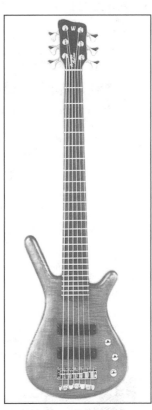

Warwick Thumb Bass courtesy Warwick

GRADING	100% MINT	98% NEAR MINT	95% EXC+	90% EXC	80% VG+	70% VG	60% G

Thumb Bolt On 5-String - similar to Thumb Bolt On, except has 5 strings, 4-piece wenge neck, 3/2-per-side tuners, mfg. 1994-present.

MSR	$2,199	$1,775	$1,500	$1,300	$1,100	$950	$800	$650

Add $175 for wide neck.

Thumb Bolt On 6-String - similar to Thumb Bolt On, except has 6 strings, 5-piece wenge neck, 3-per-side tuners, 2 humbucker MEC pickups, mfg. 1994-present.

MSR	$2,399	$1,925	$1,650	$1,400	$1,200	$1,000	$850	$700

Add $175 for wide neck.

In 1996, bassline soapbar pickups replaced the MEC humbuckers.

THUMB BLEACHED BLONDE LTD 2003 - similar to the Thumb, except has a AAAA flamed maple top, active MEC electronics, and chrome hardware, mfg. 2003-04.

		$2,000	$1,750	$1,500	$1,250	$1,100	$995	$900

Last MSR was $2,499.

ELECTRIC BASS: TRIUMPH SERIES

TRIUMPH ELECTRIC UPRIGHT - 3/4 scale (Electric Upright Bass) body, flamed maple body, arched select Bavarian spruce top, maple neck, rosewood fingerboard, Rubner satin engraved machine heads, scrolled headstock, Mec quad magnetic pickup/preamp system, mfg. 1996-present.

MSR	$4,399	$3,550	$3,100	$2,600	$2,200	$1,900	$1,600	$1,350

This model was designed by Hans Peter Wilfer, and was based on a Framus bass designed by his father. This model comes with a gig bag and stand.

Triumph Electric Upright 5-String - similar to the Triumph Electric Upright, except features 5 string configuration and a 3/2-per-side headstock, mfg. 1996-present.

MSR	$4,699	$3,800	$3,200	$2,800	$2,400	$2,100	$1,800	$1,500

ELECTRIC BASS: VAMPYRE SERIES

VAMPYRE SN - offset double cutaway body with sharp edges and crevices, flamed maple body, set-ovangkol neck, with Wenge fingerboard, active MEC J/TJ pickups, MEC 2-way electronics, four knobs, 2-per-side tuners, black hardware, available in oil finish, colored oil finish, or high polish, mfg. 2003-present.

MSR	$2,299	$1,850	$1,600	$1,350	$1,150	$1,000	$850	$750

Vampyre SN 5-String - similar to the Vampyre, except in five-string configuration, 3/2-per-side tuners, mfg. 2003-present.

MSR	$2,499	$2,000	$1,750	$1,500	$1,300	$1,100	$950	$800

VAMPYRE LTD 2003 - similar to the Vampyre SN, except has an ash body with quilted maple top, ebony fingerboard with f clef inlays, 3-way MEC electronics, and MEC J-pickups, mfg. 2003-present.

MSR	$5,299	$4,300	$3,600	$3,100	$2,700	N/A	N/A	N/A

Vampyre LTD 5-String - similar to the Vampyre LTD, except in five-string configuration, 3/2-per-side tuners, mfg. 2003-present.

MSR	$5,599	$4,500	$3,800	$3,300	$2,800	N/A	N/A	N/A

WASHBURN

Instruments currently produced both in Chicago, IL and Korea. Distributed by Washburn International, located in Vernon Hills, IL. Historically, Washburn instruments were produced in the Chicago, IL area from numerous sources from the late 1800s to 1940s. When the trademark was revived in the 1960s, instruments were produced first in Japan, and then later in Korea.

The Washburn trademark was originated by the Lyon & Healy company of Chicago, Illinois. George Washburn Lyon and Patrick Joseph Healy were chosen by Oliver Ditson, who had formed the Oliver Ditson Company, Inc. in 1835 as a musical publisher. Ditson was a primary force in music merchandising, distribution, and retail sales on the East Coast. In 1864 the Lyon & Healy music store opened for business. The late 1800s found the company ever expanding from retail, to producer, and finally distributor. The Washburn trademark was formally filed for in 1887, and the name applied to quality stringed instruments produced by a manufacturing department of Lyon & Healy.

Lyon & Healy were part of the Chicago musical instrument production conglomerate that produced musical instruments throughout the early and mid 1900s. As in business, if there is demand, a successful business will supply. Due to their early pioneering of mass production, the Washburn facility averaged up to one hundred instruments a day! Lyon & Healy/Washburn were eventually overtaken by the Tonk Bros. company, and the Washburn trademark was eventually discarded.

When the trademark was revived in 1964, the initial production of acoustic guitars came from Japan. Washburn electric guitars were re-introduced to the American market in 1979, and featured U.S. designs on Japanese-built instruments. Production of the entry level models was switched to Korea during the mid to late 1980s. As the company gained a larger foothold in the guitar market, American production was reintroduced in the late 1980s as well. Grover Jackson (ex-Jackson/Charvel) was instrumental in introducing new designs for Washburn for the Chicago series in 1993.

In 1998, Washburn adopted the Buzz Feiten Tuning System on the American-produced models. The Buzz Feiten Tuning System is a new tempered tuning system that produces a more "in-tune" guitar.

Early company history courtesy of John Teagle in his book *Washburn: Over One Hundred Years of Fine Stringed Instruments*. The actual history is a lot more involved and convoluted than the above outline suggests, and Teagle's book does a fine job of unravelling the narrative.

ELECTRIC: CARVED TOP (P/CENTURIAN) SERIES

All P Series models are equipped with the Buzz Feiten Tuning System.

GRADING	100% MINT	98% NEAR MINT	95% EXC+	90% EXC	80% VG+	70% VG	60% G

CT2K (P2) - slightly offset single cutaway mahogany body, mahogany neck, 22-fret rosewood fingerboard with pearl dot inlay, tune-o-matic bridge/stop tailpiece, blackface peghead, 3-per-side Grover tuners, chrome hardware, white pickguard, 2 exposed coil humbucker pickups, volume/tone controls, 3-position toggle switch, available in Black, Tiffany Blue, or Sapphire Blue finishes, mfg. 1997-99.

	$650	$500	$425	$375	$325	$275	$200

Last MSR was $879.

CT290K (P2 90) - similar to P2, except has 2 black P-90-style single coil pickups, available in Trans. Blue or Trans. Red finishes, mfg. 1997-99.

	$650	$500	$425	$375	$325	$275	$200

Last MSR was $879.

CT2QK (P2 Q) - similar to P2, except has a quilted maple top, available in Cherry Sunburst finish, mfg. 1997-2002.

	$700	$550	$450	$400	$350	$300	$250

Last MSR was $939.

CTP (PLUS/P3, U.S. MFG.) - slightly offset single cutaway bound sapele body, sapele neck, 22-fret rosewood fingerboard with pearl dot inlay, tune-o-matic bridge/Schaller fine tuner tailpiece, blackface peghead, 3-per-side Grover tuners, chrome hardware, 2 Seymour Duncan humbucker pickups, volume/tone controls, 3-position toggle switch, available in Antique Natural, Black, or Trans. Bordeaux Red finishes, mfg. 1997-99.

	$1,275	$1,025	$850	$750	$650	$500	$400

Last MSR was $1,699.

CTS (STUDIO) - similar to CTP. Available in Butterscotch Matte, Natural Matte, or Red Matte, mfg. 1999-2002.

	$975	$825	$725	$625	$525	$400	$300

Last MSR was $1,299.

CTSTD (STANDARD/P4, U.S. MFG.) - slightly offset single cutaway bound mahogany body, mahogany neck, 22-fret ebony fingerboard with pearl dot inlay, tune-o-matic bridge/Schaller fine tuner tailpiece, blackface peghead, 3-per-side Schaller locking tuners, chrome hardware, 2 Seymour Duncan humbucker pickups, volume/tone controls, 3-position toggle switch, available in Black or Cherry Sunburst finishes, mfg. 1997-99.

	$1,425	$1,150	$1,000	$850	$750	$600	$500

Last MSR was $1,899.

CTDLX (P4 DLX, U.S. MFG.) - similar to P4, except has a bound quilted maple top, bound fingerboard, 2 volume/2 tone controls, available in Cherry Sunburst, BlueBurst, or Tobacco Sunburst finishes, mfg. 1997-99.

	$1,650	$1,300	$1,150	$975	$800	$625	$550

Last MSR was $2,199.

**Washburn HB35
courtesy Washburn**

ELECTRIC: CLASSIC (HOLLOW BODY) SERIES

HB15 - hollow body ES-125 style mahogany body, 2 f-holes, 14/20-fret rosewood fingerboard with dot inlay, single Vintage pickup, raised pickguard with two knobs mounted on it, trapeze tailpiece, 3-per-side tuners, chrome hardware, available in Tobacco Sunburst finish, mfg. 2004-present.

MSR	$400	$300	$250	$220	$190	$160	$130	$100

HB15C Cutaway - similar to the HB15, except in cutaway configuration, new 2005.

MSR	$450	$315	$260	$230	$200	$170	$140	$110

HB30 - double cutaway semihollow style, arched flamed sycamore top, raised black pickguard, bound body/f-holes, flamed sycamore back/sides, maple neck, 20-fret bound rosewood fingerboard with pearl dot inlay, tune-o-matic bridge/stop tailpiece, bound blackface peghead with pearl diamond/W/logo inlay, 3-per-side Grover tuners, chrome hardware, 2 humbucker Washburn pickups, 2 volume/2 tone controls, 3-position switch, available in Cherry, Tobacco Sunburst, or Wine Red finishes, mfg. 1994-96, 1998-present.

MSR	$500	$350	$300	$260	$220	$190	$160	$130

Wine red finish discontinued 1999.

HB32 - double cutaway semihollow style, mahogany body, two f-holes, bound body and f-holes, 20-fret bound rosewood fingerboard with pearl dot inlay, tune-o-matic bridge/stop tailpiece, matching headstock with 3-per-side Grover tuners, two humbucker Washburn pickups, four knobs, three-way switch, distressed gold hardware, available in Distressed Mahogany finish, new 2005.

MSR	$500	$350	$300	$260	$220	$190	$160	$130

HB35 (S) - double cutaway semihollow style, arched flamed sycamore top, raised black pickguard, bound body/f-holes, flamed sycamore back/sides, maple neck, 20-fret bound rosewood fingerboard with pearl split rectangle inlay, tune-o-matic bridge/stop tailpiece, bound blackface peghead with pearl diamond/W/logo inlay, 3-per-side Grover tuners, gold hardware, 2 humbucker Washburn pickups, 2 volume/2 tone controls, 3-position switch, available in Natural, Tobacco Sunburst, or Wine Red finishes, current mfg.

MSR	$900	$630	$550	$500	$450	$350	$300

Tobacco Sunburst finish discontinued 1999. Later models have the Buzz Feiten Tunin System.

J3 - single sharp cutaway ES-175 style, spruce top, maple back and sides, two f-holes, bound body/neck/f-holes, mahogany neck, 14/20-fret rosewood fingerboard with block inlays, three-per-side tuners, adjustable rosewood bridge, W tailpiece, black pickguard, two humbucker pickups, four knobs, three-way switch, chrome hardware, available in Natural or Tobacco Sunburst finishes, new 2005.

MSR	$500	$315	$260	$230	$200	$170	$140	$110

**Washburn HB15
courtesy Washburn**

GRADING	100% MINT	98% NEAR MINT	95% EXC+	90% EXC	80% VG+	70% VG	60% G

J4 - single sharp cutaway ES-175 style, flame maple top/back/sides, oval soundhole, bound body and neck, mahogany neck, 14/20-fret rosewood fingerboard with dot inlays, three-per-side tuners, adjustable rosewood bridge, W tailpiece, black pickguard, single mini-humbucker pickups, two knobs mounted on pickguard, gold hardware, available in Honeyburst finish, new 2005.

	MSR	$600	$420	$350	$300	$250	$210	$170	$130

J5 - single sharp cutaway ES-175 style, spruce top, maple back and sides, two f-holes, bound body/neck/f-holes, mahogany neck, 14/20-fret rosewood fingerboard with abalone block inlays, three-per-side tuners, adjustable rosewood bridge, W tailpiece, black pickguard, two humbucker pickups, four knobs, three-way switch, gold hardware, available in Tobacco Sunburst finish, new 2005.

	MSR	$650	$475	$400	$350	$300	$250	$200	$150

J-6 MONTGOMERY (J-6 S) - single rounded cutaway hollow body, arched spruce top, raised black pickguard, bound body/2 f-holes, maple back/sides, maple neck, 20-fret bound rosewood fingerboard with split rectangle abalone inlay, adjustable tune-o-matic bridge/metal 'W' trapeze tailpiece, bound blackface peghead with abalone diamond/W/logo inlay, 3-per-side Grover tuners, gold hardware, 2 humbucker pickups, 2 volume/2 tone controls, 3-position switch, available in Natural or Tobacco Sunburst finishes, disc. 2004.

$850	$775	$700	$625	$525	$425	$325

Last MSR was $1,200.

In 1994, flamed sycamore back/sides replaced original parts/design.

J-8 MEMPHIS - similar to the J-6 Montgomery, except features maple top, 2 P-90-style single coil pickups, available in Black or Natural finishes, mfg. 1997-99.

$825	$725	$625	$525	$400	$300	$200

Last MSR was $1,099.

J-9 WASHINGTON - single rounded cutaway hollowbody, arched maple top, raised black pickguard, bound body/2 f-holes, maple back/sides, maple neck, 20-fret bound rosewood fingerboard with split rectangle abalone inlay, adjustable tune-o-matic bridge/metal 'W' trapeze tailpiece, bound blackface peghead with abalone diamond/W/logo inlay, 3-per-side Grover tuners, chrome hardware, 2 humbucker pickups, 2 volume/2 tone controls, 3-position switch, available in Wine Red finish, mfg. 1997-present.

$775	$700	$625	$575	$500	$400	$300

Last MSR was $1,100.

J-9 V G Washington - similar to the J-9 Washington, except features gold hardware, Bigsby tremolo, available in Black finish, mfg. 1997-2004.

$850	$775	$700	$625	$525	$425	$325

Last MSR was $1,200.

J-10 - single cutaway hollow style, arched solid spruce top, bound body and f-holes, raised bound tortoise pickguard, flame maple back/sides, multi layer maple neck, 20-fret bound ebony fingerboard with pearl/abalone split rectangle inlay, ebony bridge, trapeze tailpiece, bound peghead with abalone Washburn logo and stylized inlay, 3-per-side pearl button tuners, gold hardware, 2 humbucker pickups, 2 volume/tone controls, 3-position switch, available in Natural or Tobacco Sunburst finishes, disc. 1992.

$1,250	$1,100	$950	$800	$700	$600	$500

Last MSR was $1,800.

J-14 REGAL (U.S. MFG.) - single rounded cutaway hollowbody, arched maple top, raised black pickguard, bound body/2 f-holes, maple back/sides, maple neck, 20-fret bound ebony fingerboard with split rectangle abalone inlay, adjustable tune-o-matic bridge/Bigsby tremolo, bound blackface peghead with abalone diamond/W/logo inlay, 3-per-side Grover tuners, chrome hardware, 2 Seymour Duncan humbucker pickups, 2 volume/2 tone controls, 3-position switch & Washburn Reso-Tone Tailpiece, available in Natural or Trans. Wine Red finishes, mfg. 1998-99.

$1,725	$1,525	$1,425	$1,325	$1,200	$1,125	$1,000

Last MSR was $2,299.

This model features the Buzz Feiten Tuning System.

J-15 PARAMOUNT (U.S. MFG.) - similar to the J-9 Washington, except features adjustable tune-o-matic bridge/metal 'W' trapeze tailpiece, spruce top & sycamore back and sides. Lifetime Warranty, available in Natural or Tobacco Sunburst finishes, mfg. 1998-2000.

$2,250	$1,950	$1,850	$1,750	$1,600	$1,500	$1,300

Last MSR was $2,999.

This model features the Buzz Feiten Tuning System.

WP50 - single cutaway style, carved bound flame maple top, mahogany body/neck, raised white pickguard, 22-fret bound rosewood fingerboard with pearl trapezoid inlay, tune-o-matic bridge/stop tailpiece, 3-per-side pearl button tuners, chrome hardware, 2 humbucker Washburn pickups, 2 volume/tone controls, 3-position switch, available in Cherry Sunburst or Tobacco Sunburst finishes, disc. 1992.

N/A	$425	$350	$300	$250	$225	$175

Last MSR was $600.

WP80 - similar to WP50, except has carved maple top, black raised pickguard, ebonized fingerboard and gold hardware, available in Black or White finishes, disc. 1992.

N/A	$475	$400	$350	$275	$225	$200

Last MSR was $680.

WT522 - single cutaway alder body, figured ash top, white pickguard, controls mounted on a metal plate, bolt-on maple neck, 21-fret maple fingerboard with black dot inlay, strings through Wilkinson bridge, 6-on-a-side Grover tuners, chrome hardware, 2 single coil Washburn pickups, volume/tone control, available in Black, Blonde, or Tobacco Sunburst finishes, mfg. 1994-96.

N/A	$375	$300	$250	$200	$175	$150

Last MSR was $500.

ELECTRIC: CULPRIT (CP) SERIES

Culprit Series instruments were the second series of models designed in conjunction with guitarist Dimebag Darrell (Pantera), and were introduced in 1998. The **CP2003** is available in Transparent Bordeaux Red (list $1,099) and Black (list $1,149) finishes. These guitars were discontinued by 2000.

W

GRADING	100% MINT	98% NEAR MINT	95% EXC+	90% EXC	80% VG+	70% VG	60% G

ELECTRIC: DAN DONEGAN SERIES

Dan Donegan is the guitar player for Disturbed.

MAYA STANDARD DD70 (U.S. MFG.) - offset double pointed cutaway with lower end pointed on treble bout and rounded on bass bout, poplar body, maple neck, 22-fret rosewood fingerboard with pearl dot inlays, matching headstock with three-per-side tuners, TonePros bridge, STB, two Seymour Duncan humbucker pickups, two knobs, three-way switch, Buzz Feiten Tuning System, chrome hardware, available in Metallic Gray finish, 25.5 in. scale, new 2005.

MSR	$1,500		$1,125	$975	$850	$750	$675	$600	$525

MAYA PRO DD75 (U.S. MFG.) - offset double pointed cutaway with lower end pointed on treble bout and rounded on bass bout, mahogany body with maple cap, mahogany neck, 22-fret rosewood fingerboard with pearl dot inlays, matching headstock with three-per-side Sperzel locking tuners, TonePros bridge, STB, two Seymour Duncan humbucker pickups, two knobs, three-way switch, Buzz Feiten Tuning System, chrome hardware, available in Black finish, 25.5 in. scale, new 2005.

MSR	$2,700		$2,050	$1,800	$1,600	$1,400	$1,200	$1,050	$900

ELECTRIC: DIME SERIES

Dime Series instruments were designed in conjunction with guitarist Dimebag Darrell (Pantera).

DIME 3 (U.S. MFG.) - Flying V with forward treble horn mahogany body, black body binding, set-in mahogany neck, 22-fret rosewood fingerboard with pearl dot inlay, Floyd Rose double locking vibrato, 'V'-shaped peghead, 3-per-side Grover tuners, black hardware, 2 Seymour Duncan humbucker pickups, volume/tone controls, 3-position toggle switch, Buzz Feiten tuning system, available in Dime Slime (Greenish), Dime Bolt (Lightning graphic), or Red Bolt finishes, disc. 2003.

$1,900	$1,500	$1,325	$1,150	$975	$800	$650

Last MSR was $2,500.

DIME 3 ST (U.S. MFG.) - similar to the DIME 3, except available in Heavy Metal finish, disc. 2004.

$2,700	$2,300	$2,000	$1,700	$1,400	$1,100	$800

Last MSR was $3,600.

DIME 32 - four point X style body with shortened bass bout solid wood body, 22-fret rosewood fingerboard with dot inlay, 2 Washburn humbucker pickups, 3 knobs, 3-way switch, chrome hardware, available in Black finish, mfg. 2004 only.

$375	$325	$275	$235	$195	$165	$135

Last MSR was $500.

DIME 332 - Flying V with forward treble horn alder body, mahogany neck, 22-fret rosewood fingerboard with pearl dot inlay, tune-o-matic bridge/stop tailpiece, 'V'-shaped peghead, 3-per-side Grover tuners, chrome hardware, 2 Washburn humbucker pickups, volume/tone controls, 3-position toggle switch, available in Black or Red finishes, mfg. 1998-2003.

$400	$350	$325	$275	$200	$175	$125

Last MSR was $550.

DIME 333 - similar to the DIME332, except features a Floyd Rose locking tremolo bridge, available in BlackJack, DimeSlime Green, and DimeBolt (graphic) finishes, disc. 2003.

$795	$700	$600	$525	$450	$375	$325

Last MSR was $1,060.

DIME 2 ST - similar to the DIME333, except features a Floyd Rose locking tremolo bridge, mahogany body, and dual color gloss finish, available in Heavy Metal finish, disc. 2004.

$725	$650	$575	$500	$425	$375	$300

Last MSR was $950.

DIME ST PRO - four point X style body with shortened bass bout mahogany body, maple neck, set neck, 22-fret rosewood fingerboard with pearl lightning bolt inlay, Seymour Duncan '59 reissue and Dimebucker pickups, 3 knobs, 3-way switch, Floyd Rose style tremolo, black hardware, available in Blackburst or Cherryburst finishes, mfg. 2004 only.

$1,350	$1,150	$1,000	$850	$725	$600	$500

Last MSR was $1,750.

DIME V - Flying V style body, set neck, 24-fret rosewood fingerboard with dot and 12th fret skull inlays, 2 High-output humbucker pickups, STB, 3 knobs, 3-way switch, available in Jungle Camo or Black gloss finishes, mfg. 2004 only.

$425	$375	$325	$275	$235	$195	$165

Last MSR was $550.

Dime V Pro - similar to the Dime V, except has a mahogany body with maple top, V-shaped inlays, stop-tail bridge, and a Seymour Duncan '59 reissue and Dimebucker pickups, available in Carmelburst or Flame graphics, mfg. 2004 only.

$975	$875	$775	$700	$625	$550	$475

Last MSR was $1,300.

Washburn J-6 Montgomery
courtesy Washburn

Washburn Dan Donegan
Maya Pro DD75
courtesy Washburn

GRADING	100% MINT	98% NEAR MINT	95% EXC+	90% EXC	80% VG+	70% VG	60% G

ELECTRIC: FALCON SERIES

FALCON - double cutaway mahogany body, bound carved maple top, through-body mahogany neck, 22-fret bound rosewood fingerboard with brass circle inlay, strings through bridge, bound blackface peghead with screened logo, 3-per-side tuners, chrome hardware, 2 humbucker Washburn pickups, 2 volume/2 tone controls, 3-position switch, available in Sunburst finish, mfg. 1980-86.

	N/A	$250	$200	$175	$125	$100	$75

FALCON STANDARD - similar to Falcon, except has coil tap switch (in tone controls), available in Sunburst finish, mfg. 1980-86.

	N/A	$300	$225	$175	$150	$125	$100

FALCON DELUXE - similar to Falcon, except has abalone fingerboard inlay, coil tap switch (in tone controls), available in Sunburst finish, mfg. 1980-86.

	N/A	$350	$275	$225	$175	$150	$125

ELECTRIC: HARD ROCK SERIES

NX3 - offset double cutaway solid alder body, bolt-on Stephen's cutaway neck, rosewood fingerboard, 6-on-a-side tuners, two WB630 HH pickups, Floyd Rose tremolo, two knobs, 3-way switch, Buzz Feiten Tuning System, available in Black, Natural Matte, or Army Green finishes, mfg. 2002-03.

	$700	$625	$550	$475	$425	$375	$325

Last MSR was $1,000.

NX6 (U.S.A. MFG.) - offset double cutaway solid alder or Padauk body, bolt-on Stephen's cutaway neck, rosewood fingerboard, 6-on-a-side tuners, two EMG HH pickups, hard tail bridge, two knobs, 3-way switch, Buzz Feiten Tuning System, available in Industrial Black or Natural Matte finishes, mfg. 2002-03.

	$1,050	$975	$900	$825	$750	$650	$550

Last MSR was $1,400.

Add $300 for Seymour Duncan pickups.

NX6TM - similar to the NX6, except has a Timeless Timber body and Seymour Duncan pickups, available in Natural Matte finish, mfg. 2002-03.

	$1,875	$1,550	$1,300	$1,100	$950	$800	$650

Last MSR was $2,500.

WR150 - offset double cutaway solid body, maple neck, rosewood fingerboard with offset dot position markers, jumbo frets, 6-on-a-side tuners, 2 single coil pickups and 1 humbucking pickup, 1 volume/1 tone, slotted switch, Fulcrum bridge, vibrato tailpiece, chrome hardware, available in Metallic Blue, Metallic Purple, Metallic Red, or Caribbean Blue, mfg. 2000-02.

	$239	$200	$175	$150	$125	$100	$75

Last MSR was $320.

WR150Q - similar to Model WR150 except has quilted top, available in Tobacco Sunburst finish only, mfg. 2000 only.

	$275	$225	$200	$175	$150	$125	$100

Last MSR was $370.

WG580 - offset double cutaway solid body, maple neck, rosewood fingerboard with dot position markers, jumbo frets, 2 humbucking pickups and 1 single coil pickup, slotted switch, 1 volume/1 tone, 6-on-a-side tuners, black hardware, available in Black, Metallic Blue, or Metallic Purple, mfg. 2000-02.

	$560	$500	$450	$400	$350	$300	$250

Last MSR was $749.

CS780 - offset double cutaway solid body, maple neck, rosewood fingerboard with sharkfin position markers, faceted body, jumbo frets, 6-on-a-side tuners, locking nut, Floyd Rose bridge, 1 volume/1 tone, slotted switch, gold hardware, 2 humbucker pickups and 1 single coil pickup, available in Metallic Purple or Pearl White, mfg. 2000-02.

	$635	$575	$525	$475	$425	$375	$300

Last MSR was $849.

RS980 - offset double cutaway solid body, maple neck, rosewood fingerboard with sharkfin position markers, jumbo frets, reverse headstock, locking nut, Floyd Rose bridge, 2 humbucker pickups and 1 single coil pickup, black hardware, 1 volume/1 tone, slotted switch, available in Tobacco Sunburst or Metallic Gray, mfg. 2000-02.

	$650	$600	$550	$500	$450	$400	$350

Last MSR was $869.

ELECTRIC: IDOL SERIES

All models in this series have a sharp single cutaway body, four knobs, 3-way switch, and 3-per-side tuners.

P170 PILSEN (USA MFG.) - mahogany body with carved top, mahogany neck, 22-fret rosewood fingerboard with dot inlays, two Seymour Duncan humbucker pickups, TonePros bridge, stop tail piece, Buzz Feiten Tuning System, gold hardware, available in Black, Metallic Blue, Rootbeer, or Ruby Red finishes, mfg. 2004-present.

MSR	$2,000		$1,400	$1,200	$1,050	$900	$800	$700	$600

W114 - hard wood body, bolt-on maple neck, no pickguard, hard tail bridge, 2 humbucker pickups, chrome hardware, available in Metallic Gray, Metallic Blue, or Black finishes, mfg. 2004-present.

MSR	$250		$195	$160	$130	$110	$90	$70	$50

WI24 - maple body, STB, rosewood fingerboard with dot inlays, two humbucker pickups, chrome hardware, hard tail bridge, available in Metallic Blue, Metallic Grey, or Black finishes, mfg. 2002-03.

	$250	$200	$170	$140	$110	$85	$65

Last MSR was $330.

W

GRADING	100% MINT	98% NEAR MINT	95% EXC+	90% EXC	80% VG+	70% VG	60% G

WI64 - mahogany body, rosewood fingerboard with dot inlays, two humbucker pickups, chrome hardware, stop tail bridge, Buzz Feiten Tuning System, available in Trans. Red, Platinum Metallic, or Black finishes, mfg. 2002-present.

	MSR	$600	$450	$375	$325	$275	$235	$195	$165

WI64DL - similar to the WI64, except has a quilted maple top and gold hardware, available in Trans. Blue, Trans. Green, or Vintage Sunburst finishes, mfg. 2002-present.

	MSR	$700	$525	$450	$400	$350	$300	$250	$200

WI64DL Baritone - similar to the WI64, except is tuned to baritone, available in Black finish, mfg. 2002-03.

$650	$575	$500	$425	$375	$300	$250

Last MSR was $850.

WI65 - mahogany body, one-piece mahgoany set-neck, rosewood fingerboard with dot inlays, two Seymour Duncan humbucker pickups, chrome hardware, stop tail bridge, Buzz Feiten Tuning System, available in Coal (Matte Black) finish, mfg. 2002-03.

$700	$625	$550	$475	$425	$375	$325

Last MSR was $1,000.

WI66V - mahogany body with quilted arched maple top, one-piece mahgoany set-neck, rosewood fingerboard with block inlays, two WB630 high output humbucking pickups, chrome hardware, flush tremolo, Buzz Feiten Tuning System, available in Carmel Burst, Wine Burst, or Trans. Blue finishes, mfg. 2002-03.

$700	$625	$550	$475	$425	$375	$325

Last MSR was $1,000.

W166 PRO - mahogany body with quilted arched maple top, one-piece mahgoany set-neck, 22-fret rosewood fingerboard with pearl wing inlays, full body binding B/N/H, two Seymour Duncan humbucker pickups, chrome hardware, Tune-o-matic bridge, Buzz Feiten Tuning System, available in Quilted Trans. Black, Trans. Blue, or Trans. Wine Red finishes, mfg. 2004-present.

	MSR	$1,100	$825	$725	$650	$575	$500	$425	$350

W167 PRO - mahogany hollow body with AAA figured maple arched top, single f-hole, one-piece mahgoany set-neck, 22-fret rosewood fingerboard with pearl wing inlays, multi-layer binding B/N/H, two Seymour Duncan humbucker pickups, black chrome hardware, Tune-o-matic bridge, Buzz Feiten Tuning System, available in Quilted Trans. Tobacco Sunburst or Cherry Sunburst finishes, mfg. 2004-present.

	MSR	$1,100	$825	$725	$650	$575	$500	$425	$350

WI68 (USA MFG.) - mahogany body with AAA figured maple top, reveal binding, one-piece mahgoany set-neck, rosewood fingerboard with block inlays, two Seymour Duncan humbucking pickups, gold hardware, stop tail bridge, Buzz Feiten Tuning System, available in Carmel Burst, Cognac, Blueburst, Trans. Bordeaux Red, Blackburst, Amber, or Trans. Blue finishes, mfg. 2002-present.

	MSR	$2,600	$1,950	$1,700	$1,500	$1,300	$1,100	$950	$800

**Washburn Idol P170 Pilsen
courtesy Washburn**

ELECTRIC: JENNIFER BATTEN SERIES

JB80 - offset double alder body with flamed maple top, bolt-on maple neck, rosewood fingerboard with dot position markers, 3-per-side tuners, 3 WB630 pickups, Floyd Rose bridge, locking nut, Buzz Feiten Tuning System, 1 volume/1 tone, slotted switch, available in Caramel Burst finish, mfg. 2002-04.

$900	$825	$750	$675	$600	$500	$400

Last MSR was $1,200.

JB100 (U.S. MFG.) - offset double cutaway swamp ash and flamed maple body, maple neck, rosewood fingerboard with dot position markers, 3-per-side tuners, 1 Duncan JB Jr. and 2 Duckbucker pickups, Floyd Rose bridge. locking nut, Buzz Feiten Tuning System, 1 volume/1 tone, slotted switch, available in Caramel Burst, White, or Honey finishes, mfg. 2000-03.

$1,425	$1,250	$1,100	$975	$850	$750	$600

Last MSR was $1,900.

JB100 MIDI (U.S. MFG.) - similar to Model JB100 except includes a Roland GK-2 pickup, available in Caramel Burst, White, or Honey finishes, mfg. 2000-03.

$1,875	$1,550	$1,350	$1,150	$1,000	$900	$750

Last MSR was $2,500.

ELECTRIC: JON DONAIS SERIES

FACE ERASER X81 (U.S. MFG.) - offset double cutaway sepele body with flame maple top, set sepele neck, 22-fret ebony fingerboard, matching headstock with six-on-one-side Sperzel tuners, TonePros bridge, STB, two EMG pickups, two knobs, Buzz Feiten Tuning System, black hardware, available in Natural or Trans. Red finishes, new 2005.

	MSR	$2,900	$2,200	$1,900	$1,700	$1,500	$1,300	$1,150	$1,000

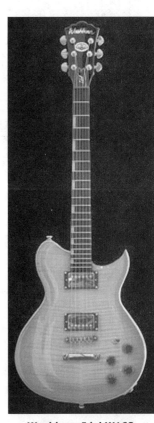

**Washburn Idol W168
courtesy Washburn**

GRADING	100% MINT	98% NEAR MINT	95% EXC+	90% EXC	80% VG+	70% VG	60% G

W

ELECTRIC: KC SERIES

KC20 - offset double cutaway hardwood body, arched top and back, scalloped cutaways, bolt-on maple neck, 22-fret rosewood fingerboard with pearl dot inlay, standard vibrato, 6-on-a-side tuners, chrome hardware, 2 single coil/1 humbucker Washburn pickups, volume/tone control, 5-position switch, available in Black or White finishes, disc. 1992.

	N/A	$250	$200	$175	$150	$125	$100

Last MSR was $350.

Add $50 for left-handed configuration (Model KC20 LH).

KC40 - offset double cutaway alder body, arched top and back, bolt-on maple neck, 22-fret rosewood fingerboard with pearl dot inlay, double locking vibrato, 6-on-a-side tuners, chrome hardware, 2 single coil/humbucker Washburn pickups, volume/tone control, 5-position switch, available in Black or White finishes, disc. 1992.

	N/A	$325	$275	$225	$175	$150	$125

Last MSR was $470.

Add $70 for left-handed configuration (Model KC40 LH).

KC42 - similar to KC40, except has reverse peghead, available in Black, Woodstone Fl. Red, or Woodstone Fl. Yellow finishes, disc. 1992.

	N/A	$350	$300	$250	$200	$175	$150

Last MSR was $500.

KC44 - similar to KC40, except has humbucker/single coil/humbucker Washburn pickups, available in Black Rain or White Rain finishes, disc. 1992.

	N/A	$350	$300	$250	$200	$175	$150

Last MSR was $500.

KC70 - similar to KC40, except has black hardware, 3 individual pickup selector and coil tap switches, available in Black, Metallic Black Cherry, White Rain, Woodstone Brown, Woodstone Red, or Woodstone Silver finishes, disc. 1992.

	N/A	$450	$400	$325	$250	$225	$175

Last MSR was $650.

Add $100 for left-handed configuration (Model KC70 LH).

KC90 - offset double cutaway alder body, arched top and back, scalloped cutaways, bolt-on maple neck, 24-fret rosewood fingerboard with pearl dot inlay, double locking vibrato, 6-on-a-side tuners, black hardware, 2 Seymour Duncan single coil/1 humbucker pickups, 5-position and coil tap switches, available in Black, Blond, Metallic Red, Natural Gold, Trans. Red, or White finishes, disc. 1992.

	N/A	$625	$575	$500	$425	$350	$300

Last MSR was $970.

ELECTRIC: LAREDO SERIES

All the instruments in this series were hand built in Chicago, and featured Seymour Duncan or Bill Lawrence pickups.

LT82 - single cutaway alder body, bolt-on maple neck, 22-fret maple fingerboard with black dot inlay, strings through Wilkinson bridge, 6-on-a-side Gotoh tuners, chrome hardware, white pickguard, 2 single coil pickups, volume/tone control, 3-position switch, controls mounted on a metal plate, available in Black, Natural, Trans. Blue, Trans. Red, Tobacco Sunburst, or Vintage Sunburst finishes, mfg. 1992-96.

	N/A	$575	$500	$425	$350	$300	$250

Last MSR was $800.

This model was optional with an ash body, pearloid pickguard, abalone dot fingerboard inlay, or a rosewood fingerboard with pearl dot inlay.

LT92 - similar to LT82, except features an ash body, pearloid pickguard, available in Natural or Tobacco Sunburst finishes, disc. 1996.

	N/A	$700	$600	$525	$450	$375	$300

Last MSR was $1,000.

This model has rosewood fingerboard with pearl dot inlay as an option.

ELECTRIC: MAGNUM SERIES

MR250 - single Florentine cutaway semi-hollow mahogany body, 2 small f-holes (near bridge), mahogany neck, 22-fret rosewood fingerboard with pearl dot inlay, tune-o-matic bridge/stop tailpiece, 3-per-side Grover tuners, chrome hardware, 2 exposed coil humbucker pickups, volume/tone controls, 3-position toggle switch, available in Antique Natural or Trans. Bordeaux Red finishes, mfg. 1997-99.

	$900	$725	$650	$550	$475	$395	$300

Last MSR was $1,199.

MR400 (U.S. MFG.) - similar to the MR250, except features 2 P-90-style single coil pickups. Bigsby/Roller Bridge is optional, Buzz Feiten tuning system, available in Honey or Trans. Red finishes, mfg. 1997-2000.

	$1,650	$1,450	$1,200	$1,000	$850	$700	$550

Last MSR was $2,199.

This model features the Buzz Feiten Tuning System.

MR450 (U.S. MFG.) - similar to the MR450, except features 2 Seymour Duncan humbucker pickups, available in Honey or Trans. Red finishes, mfg. 1997-2000.

	$1,500	$1,200	$1,050	$925	$795	$650	$500

Last MSR was $1,999.

GRADING	100% MINT	98% NEAR MINT	95% EXC+	90% EXC	80% VG+	70% VG	60% G

ELECTRIC: MAVERICK (BT & WM) SERIES

**Washburn BT10
courtesy Washburn**

BT2 - slightly offset double cutaway mahogany body, maple neck, 22-fret rosewood fingerboard with pearl dot inlay, tune-o-matic bridge/stop tailpiece, 3-per-side Grover tuners, chrome hardware, 2 exposed coil humbucker pick-ups, volume/tone controls, 3-position toggle switch, available in Black, Cherry Sunburst, Caribbean Blue, and Tiffany Blue finishes, mfg. 1998-2002.

	$240	$190	$150	$125	$110	$95	$75

Last MSR was $340.

Add $50 for Metal Flake Blue and Metal Flake Silver finishes. Caribbean Blue discontinued 1999.

BT2 Q - similar to BT2, except features a quilted maple top, available in Vintage Sunburst finish, mfg. 1998-2002.

	$260	$240	$220	$200	$140	$120	$100

Last MSR was $370.

BT3 - similar to BT2, except features tremolo bridge, white pickguard, 3 single coil pickups, volume/2 tone controls, 5-way selector switch, available in Black, Cherry Sunburst, Ivory, Tiffany Blue, or Red finishes, mfg. 1997-99.

	$250	$200	$175	$150	$135	$115	$95

Last MSR was $349.

BT4 - similar to BT2, except features tremolo bridge, 2 single coil/humbucker pickups, volume/tone controls, 5-way selector switch, available in Black, Dark Blue, or Tobacco Sunburst finishes, mfg. 1997-2002.

	$240	$190	$150	$125	$110	$95	$75

Last MSR was $340.

BT4 Q - similar to BT4, except features a quilted maple top, available in Cherry Sunburst finish, mfg. 1998-2002.

	$260	$240	$220	$200	$140	$120	$100

Last MSR was $370.

BT4 Q LH - similar to BT4, except features a quilted maple top, left-handed configuration, available in Cherry Sunburst finish, mfg. 1998-2002.

	$280	$240	$200	$175	$150	$125	$100

Last MSR was $400.

BT6 - similar to BT2, except features Floyd Rose tremolo bridge, humbucker/single coil/humbucker pickups, volume/tone controls, 5-way selector switch, available in Metal Flake Black, Galactic Blue, or Trans. Wine Red finishes, mfg. 1998-99.

	$450	$375	$325	$295	$250	$195	$150

Last MSR was $599.

BT8 - slightly offset double cutaway mahogany body, bound body, maple neck, 22-fret rosewood fingerboard with pearl dot inlay, tune-o-matic bridge/stop tailpiece, 3-per-side Grover tuners, chrome hardware, 2 exposed coil humbucker pickups, volume/tone controls, 3-position toggle switch, available in Honey Sunburst, Trans. Red, or Trans. Purple finishes, mfg. 1997-99.

	$550	$450	$395	$350	$295	$250	$195

Last MSR was $749.

BT9 - similar to BT8, except features maple fingerboard, black hardware, tremolo bridge, white pickguard, 2 single coil/humbucker pickups, volume/2 tone controls, 5-way selector switch, available in Trans. Blue or Trans. Red finishes, mfg. 1997-99.

	$525	$425	$375	$325	$275	$225	$175

Last MSR was $699.

BT10 - similar to BT8, except features Floyd Rose tremolo bridge, available in Trans. Dark Blue, or Trans. Red finishes, mfg. 1997-99.

	$525	$425	$375	$325	$275	$225	$175

Last MSR was $899.

BTM MINI - similar to BT2, except features smaller "mini" body, available in Metallic Dark Blue finish, mfg. 1998-disc.

	$175	$150	$130	$110	$95	$75	$60

Last MSR was $230.

WM100 (WMSTD, U.S. MFG.) - slightly offset double cutaway mahogany body, wood body binding, mahogany neck, 22-fret rosewood fingerboard with pearl dot inlay, tune-o-matic bridge/Schaller stop tailpiece, 3-per-side Grover tuners, chrome hardware, 2 Seymour Duncan humbucker pickups, volume/tone controls, 3-position toggle switch, Buzz Feiten Tuning System, available in Cobalt Blue, Trans. Bordeaux Red, or Honey finishes, mfg. 1997-99.

	$1,275	$1,000	$895	$775	$650	$550	$425

Last MSR was $1,699.

WM200 (WMP, U.S. MFG.) - similar to WM100, except features swamp ash body, maple neck, white pickguard, 2 single coil/humbucker Seymour Duncan pickups, volume/2 tone controls, 5-way selector switch, Buzz Feiten Tuning System, available in Black, Trans. Bordeaux Red, or Vintage Sunburst finishes, mfg. 1997-99.

	$1,125	$900	$795	$695	$595	$475	$375

Last MSR was $1,499.

GRADING	100% MINT	98% NEAR MINT	95% EXC+	90% EXC	80% VG+	70% VG	60% G

WMS (U.S. MFG.) - similar to WM200 (MWP), but available in Butterscotch Matte, Natural Matte, or Red Matte finishes, mfg. 1999-2000.

	$750	$600	$500	$400	$350	$300	$250

Last MSR was $999.

WM612 (U.S. MFG.) - similar to WM100, except features one (or two) Seymour Duncan pickups/piezo bridge pickups, 2 volume/2 tone controls, pickup selector switch(es), Buzz Feiten Tuning System, available in Vintage Sunburst finish, mfg. 1998-2000.

	$2,999	$2,699	$2,399	$2,100	$1,800	$1,500	$1,200

Last MSR was $3,999.

ELECTRIC: MERCURY SERIES

Mercury Series instruments were produced in Asia and U.S. All of the U.S.-built instruments in the Mercury series were produced in Chicago, and featured Seymour Duncan or Bill Lawrence pickups.

MG30 - offset double cutaway hardwood body, bolt-on maple neck, 24-fret rosewood fingerboard with offset pearl dot inlay, double locking vibrato, 6-on-a-side tuners, chrome hardware, 2 single coil/1 humbucker Washburn pickups, volume/tone control, 5-position switch with coil tap, available in Metallic Red, Pacific Blue Rain, or Tobacco Sunburst finishes, disc. 1994.

	N/A	$325	$275	$240	$200	$175	$125

Last MSR was $480.

MG34 - similar to MG30, except has maple fingerboard with black offset dot inlay, humbucker/single coil/humbucker pickups, available in Black, Metallic Dark Blue, or Purple Rain finishes, disc. 1994.

	N/A	$350	$300	$250	$200	$175	$150

Last MSR was $500.

MG40 - offset double cutaway alder body, white pickguard, bolt-on maple neck, 24-fret rosewood fingerboard with offset pearl dot inlay, double locking vibrato, 6-on-a-side tuners, black hardware, volume/tone control, 5-position switch with coil tap, available in Black, Ice Pearl, Metallic Red, or Pearl Blue finishes, disc. 1994.

	N/A	$400	$350	$275	$225	$200	$175

Last MSR was $570.

MG42 - similar to MG40, except has 2 humbucker pickups, available in Metallic Purple and Midnight Blue Metallic finishes, disc. 1994.

	N/A	$400	$350	$275	$225	$200	$175

Last MSR was $570.

MG43 - similar to MG40, except has maple fingerboard with offset black dot inlay, 3 single coil pickups, available in Black or Metallic Red finishes, disc. 1994.

	N/A	$350	$300	$250	$225	$200	$150

Last MSR was $550.

MG44 - similar to MG40, except has maple fingerboard with offset black dot inlay, humbucker/single coil/humbucker pickups, available in Black, Black Cherry Metallic, Metallic Red, or Midnight Blue Metallic finishes, disc. 1994.

	N/A	$425	$350	$275	$225	$200	$175

Last MSR was $590.

MG52 - offset double cutaway hardwood body, white pickguard, bolt-on maple neck, 24-fret rosewood fingerboard with offset pearl dot inlay, tune-o-matic bridge/stop tailpiece, 6-on-a-side tuners, chrome hardware, 2 humbucker Washburn pickups, volume/tone control, 5-way switch with coil tap, available in Metallic Dark Blue or Tobacco Sunburst finishes, disc. 1994.

	N/A	$300	$250	$225	$175	$150	$125

Last MSR was $430.

MG70 - offset double cutaway alder body, flamed maple top, transparent pickguard, bolt-on maple neck, 24-fret rosewood fingerboard with offset pearl dot inlay, double locking vibrato, 6-on-a-side tuners, gold hardware, volume/tone control, 5-position switch with coil tap, available in Trans. Blue or Vintage Sunburst finishes, disc. 1994.

	N/A	$475	$400	$350	$275	$225	$200

Last MSR was $700.

MG72 - similar to MG70, except has 2 humbucker pickups, available in Trans. Purple or Vintage Sunburst finishes, disc. 1994.

	N/A	$490	$425	$350	$275	$225	$200

Last MSR was $700.

MG74 - similar to MG70, except has maple fingerboard with offset black dot inlay, humbucker/single coil/humbucker pickups, available in Trans. Purple or Vintage Sunburst finishes, disc. 1994.

	N/A	$500	$425	$350	$275	$225	$200

Last MSR was $720.

MG90 (U.S. MFG.) - offset double cutaway mahogany body, bolt-on maple neck, 24-fret rosewood fingerboard with offset pearl dot inlay, standard Wilkinson vibrato, 6-on-a-side locking Gotoh tuners, chrome hardware, 2 single coil/humbucker exposed pole piece pickups, volume/tone control, 5-position switch, available in Natural finish, mfg. 1994-96.

	N/A	$650	$550	$475	$400	$325	$275

Last MSR was $900.

MG94 (U.S. MFG.) - similar to MG90, except features alder body, 24-fret maple fingerboard with offset black dot inlay, double locking vibrato, 6-on-a-side tuners, chrome hardware, humbucker/single coil/humbucker pickups, available in Green Iridescent, Iridescent, Midnight Blue Metallic, or 3-Tone Sunburst finishes, disc. 1994.

	N/A	$675	$600	$500	$400	$350	$300

Last MSR was $1,000.

This model has rosewood fingerboard with pearl dot inlay as an option.

GRADING	100% MINT	98% NEAR MINT	95% EXC+	90% EXC	80% VG+	70% VG	60% G

MG100 PRO (U.S. MFG.) - similar to the MG90, except features an ash body, available in Antique Natural, Trans. Blue, Trans. Red, or Vintage Sunburst finishes, mfg. 1994-96.

	N/A	$725	$650	$550	$450	$375	$325

Last MSR was $1,199.

MG102 (U.S. MFG.) - offset double cutaway ash body, bolt-on maple neck, 24-fret rosewood fingerboard with offset pearl dot inlay, standard Wilkinson vibrato, 6-on-a-side locking Gotoh tuners, chrome hardware, 2 humbucker exposed pickups, volume/tone control, 5-position switch, available in Antique Natural, Trans. Blue, or Trans. Red finishes, mfg. 1994-96.

	N/A	$700	$625	$525	$425	$350	$300

Last MSR was $1,100.

MG104 (U.S. MFG.) - offset double cutaway alder body, quilted maple top, bolt-on maple neck, 24-fret maple fingerboard with offset black dot inlay, double locking vibrato, 6-on-a-side tuners, chrome hardware, humbucker/single coil/humbucker pickups, volume/tone control, 5-position switch, available in Trans. Red, or Vintage Sunburst finishes, disc. 1994.

	N/A	$700	$625	$525	$425	$350	$300

Last MSR was $1,100.

MG112 (U.S. MFG.) - offset double cutaway alder body, bound quilted maple top, bolt-on maple neck, 24-fret rosewood fingerboard with offset pearl dot inlay, tune-o-matic bridge/stop tailpiece, 6-on-a-side Gotoh tuners, chrome hardware, 2 humbucker exposed pickups, volume/tone control, 5-way switch, available in Black, Trans. Blue, Trans. Purple, Trans. Red, or Vintage Sunburst finishes, mfg. 1992-96.

	N/A	$750	$650	$550	$450	$375	$325

Last MSR was $1,200.

In 1994, ash body, double locking Floyd Rose vibrato replaced original parts/designs, quilted maple top, Trans. Red finish were disc.

MG120 (U.S. MFG.) - offset double cutaway mahogany body, quilted maple top, bolt-on maple neck, 24-fret rosewood fingerboard with offset pearl dot inlay, standard Wilkinson vibrato, 6-on-a-side locking Gotoh tuners, chrome hardware, 2 single coil/humbucker exposed pickups, volume/tone control, 5-position switch, available in Trans. Blue, Trans. Red, or Vintage Sunburst finishes, mfg. 1994-96.

	N/A	$775	$675	$600	$500	$450	$350

Last MSR was $1,300.

MG122 ARTIST (U.S. MFG.) - similar to MG120, except features 2 exposed humbucker pickups, available in Trans. Purple, Trans. Red, or Vintage Sunburst finishe, mfg. 1994-96.

	N/A	$800	$725	$650	$550	$475	$375

Last MSR was $1,499.

MG142 (U.S. MFG.) - similar to MG120, except features 24-fret ebony fingerboard with offset pearl dot inlay, tune-o-matic bridge/stop tailpiece, graphite nut, 6-on-a-side tuners, 2 humbucker pickups, available in Trans. Red or Vintage Sunburst finishes, disc. 1994.

	N/A	$850	$750	$675	$600	$525	$450

Last MSR was $1,700.

MG154 (U.S. MFG.) - similar to MG142, except has double locking vibrato, humbucker/single coil/humbucker pickups, disc. 1994.

	N/A	$875	$800	$725	$650	$550	$475

Last MSR was $1,800.

MG300 - offset double cutaway hardwood body, bolt-on maple neck, 24-fret rosewood fingerboard with offset pearl dot inlay, double locking Floyd Rose vibrato, 6-on-a-side tuners, chrome hardware, 2 single coil/humbucker exposed Washburn pickups, volume/tone control, 5-position switch, available in Ice Pearl, Metallic Red, or Pacific Blue Rain finishes, mfg. 1994-96.

	N/A	$325	$275	$250	$200	$175	$150

Last MSR was $500.

MG340 - offset double cutaway hardwood body, bolt-on maple neck, 24-fret maple fingerboard with offset black dot inlay, double locking Floyd Rose vibrato, 6-on-a-side tuners, chrome hardware, humbucker/single coil/humbucker exposed Washburn pickups, volume/tone control, 5-position switch, available in Black, Pearl Blue, or Purple Rain finishes, mfg. 1994-96.

	N/A	$375	$300	$250	$225	$175	$150

Last MSR was $579.

MG401 - offset double cutaway alder body, figured ash top, bolt-on maple neck, 24-fret rosewood fingerboard with offset pearl dot inlay, standard Schaller vibrato, 6-on-a-side tuners, chrome hardware, 2 single coil/humbucker exposed Washburn pickups, volume/tone with coil tap control, 5-position switch, available in Antique Natural, Blonde, Natural, or Trans. Burgundy finishes, mfg. 1994-96.

	N/A	$450	$375	$325	$275	$225	$175

Last MSR was $699.

MG522 - offset double cutaway alder body, figured ash top, bolt-on maple neck, 24-fret rosewood fingerboard with offset pearl dot inlay, tune-o-matic bridge/stop tailpiece, 6-on-a-side tuners, chrome hardware, 2 humbucker exposed Washburn pickups, volume/tone with coil tap control, 3-position switch, available in Tobacco Sunburst or Trans. Black finishes, mfg. 1994-96.

	N/A	$350	$300	$275	$225	$175	$150

Last MSR was $530.

GRADING	100% MINT	98% NEAR MINT	95% EXC+	90% EXC	80% VG+	70% VG	60% G

MG700 - offset double cutaway alder body, figured sycamore top, bolt-on maple neck, 24-fret rosewood fingerboard with offset pearl dot inlay, double locking Floyd Rose vibrato, 6-on-a-side Grover tuners, gold hardware, 2 single coil/humbucker exposed Washburn pickups, volume/tone control, 5-position switch, available in Antique Natural or Vintage Sunburst finishes, mfg. 1994-96.

	N/A	$450	$400	$350	$275	$225	$200

Last MSR was $700.

MG701 - similar to MG700, except features a standard Wilkinson vibrato, 6-on-a-side locking Schaller tuners, chrome hardware, available in Antique Natural, Trans. Blue, or Vintage Sunburst finishes, mfg. 1994-96.

	N/A	$475	$425	$375	$325	$275	$225

Last MSR was $730.

MG821 - similar to the MG700, except features a bound figured sycamore top, standard Wilkinson vibrato, 6-on-a-side locking Schaller tuners, chrome hardware, 2 exposed humbucker Washburn pickups, volume/tone with coil tap control, 5-position switch, available in Tobacco Sunburst or Trans. Burgundy finishes, mfg. 1994-96.

	N/A	$500	$450	$375	$325	$275	$250

Last MSR was $780.

ELECTRIC: NUNO BETTENCOURT SERIES

This series was co-designed with Nuno Bettencourt and features the patented Extended Stephen´s Cutaway. All of the U.S.-built instruments in this series were produced in Chicago, and featured Seymour Duncan or Bill Lawrence pickups.

N1 - offset double cutaway alder body, bolt-on maple neck, 22-fret rosewood fingerboard with pearl dot inlay, standard tremolo, reverse headstock, 6-on-a-side Grover tuners, chrome hardware, 2 Washburn humbucker pickups, volume control, 3-way switch, available in Natural Matte or Padauk Stain finishes, mfg. 1997-99, 2005-present.

MSR	$300	$210	$180	$160	$140	$120	$100	$80

N2 - similar to the N1, except features a Floyd Rose double locking vibrato, 2 humbucker (Washburn/Bill Lawrence) pickups, available in Natural Matte or Padauk Stain finishes, disc. 1999, reintroduced 2005-present.

MSR	$600	$420	$350	$300	$250	$210	$170	$140

N4E A (U.S. MFG.) - offset double cutaway alder body, bolt-on maple neck, 22-fret ebony fingerboard with pearl dot inlay, Floyd Rose double locking vibrato, reverse peghead, 6-on-a-side Grover tuners, chrome hardware, 2 Seymour Duncan humbucker pickups, volume control, 3-position switch, Buzz Feiten Tuning System, available in Natural Matte finish, mfg. 1992-98, 2001.

	$1,125	$975	$850	$725	$625	$495	$375

Last MSR was $1,499.

N4E P (U.S. Mfg.) - similar to N4EA, except has padauk body, mfg. 1992-96, 2001.

	$1,000	$900	$800	$695	$575	$500	$400

Last MSR was $1,599.

N4E SA (U.S. Mfg.) - similar to N4EA, except has swamp ash body, Buzz Feiten Tuning System, available in Natural Matte, Paduak Stain Natural Matte, or Vintage Sunburst finishes, mfg. 1994-present.

MSR	$2,200	$1,650	$1,400	$1,200	$1,050	$900	$750	$600

N4E QM (U.S. Mfg.) - similar to N4EA, except has quilted maple top, Buzz Feiten Tuning System, available in Tobacco Sunburst or Wineburst finishes, mfg. 1997-99.

	$1,500	$1,200	$1,050	$900	$775	$625	$500

Last MSR was $1,999.

N4 Vintage (U.S. Mfg.) - similar to N4EA, except has an aged solid alder body, and aged hardware, Buzz Feiten Tuning System, and the N4 graphic on body, available in Natural Matte, finish, mfg. 2002-present.

MSR	$2,000	$1,500	$1,200	$1,050	$900	$775	$625	$500

N5 (U.S. MFG.) - double offset cutaway solid alder body with Stephen's cutaway, bird's-eye maple neck, 22-fret birdseye maple fingerboard with dot inlay, reverse six-on-one-side tuners, Floyd Rose tremolo, anaodized aluminum pickguard, three single coil Seymour Duncan pickups, two knobs, Buzz Feiten Tuning system, black hardware, available in Black, Cream, Military Green, or Tobacco Sunburst finishes, new 2005.

MSR	$2,700	$2,050	$1,800	$1,600	$1,400	$1,200	$1,050	$900

N6 (U.S. MFG.) - double offset cutaway solid alder body with Stephen's cutaway, bird's-eye maple neck, 22-fret birdseye maple fingerboard with dot inlay, reverse six-on-one-side tuners, Floyd Rose tremolo, anaodized aluminum pickguard, two single coil and one humbucker Seymour Duncan pickups, two knobs, Buzz Feiten Tuning system, chrome hardware, available in Black, Cream, Military Green, or Tobacco Sunburst finishes, new 2005.

MSR	$2,700	$2,050	$1,800	$1,600	$1,400	$1,200	$1,050	$900

ELECTRIC: PAUL STANLEY SERIES

Paul Stanley Series instruments were designed in conjunction with guitarist Paul Stanley (KISS), and were introduced in 1998. The entry level **PS100 B** features an alder body, 2 humbucker pickups and a tune-o-matic bridge (list $599); the **PS500 B** features a mahogany body and neck (list $1,249). The U.S.-built **PS2000 B** has Seymour Duncan pickups, and an ebony fingerboard tempered with the Buzz Feiten Tuning System (list $2,499). All models are available in a Black finish only.

PS2000 ROSE (PAUL STANLEY LIMITED EDITION OF 50) - similar to Model PS2000 except has a recreation of Paul´s Rose tattoo on the top just above the tailpiece. Each guitar is hand signed by Paul on the back along with its series number, comes with certificate of authenticity and a deluxe luggage quality hard case, limited mfg. during 2000.

	N/A	N/A	N/A	N/A	N/A	N/A	N/A

Last MSR was $3,999.

W

GRADING	100% MINT	98% NEAR MINT	95% EXC+	90% EXC	80% VG+	70% VG	60% G

ELECTRIC: SCOTT IAN SERIES

Scott Ian is the guitar player for Anthrax.

IAN STANDARD SI70 (U.S. MFG.) - double pointed cutaway body, poplar body, maple neck, 22-fret rosewood fingerboard with pearl dot inlays, matching headstock with three-per-side tuners, TonePros bridge, STB, two Seymour Duncan humbucker pickups, two knobs, three-way switch, Buzz Feiten Tuning System, chrome hardware, available in Black or Titanium finishes, 25.5 in. scale, new 2005.

	MSR	$1,500	$1,125	$975	$850	$750	$675	$600	$525

IAN PRO SI75 (U.S. MFG.) - double pointed cutaway body, mahogany body with carved top, deep-set V-mahogany neck, 22-fret ebony fingerboard with Scott Ian Anthragram inlays, matching headstock with three-per-side Sperzel locking tuners, TonePros bridge, STB, single Seymour Duncan humbucker pickup, single knob, Buzz Feiten Tuning System, chrome hardware, available in Black finish, 25.5 in. scale, new 2005.

	MSR	$2,700		$2,050	$1,800	$1,600	$1,400	$1,200	$1,050	$900

Washburn N2
courtesy Washburn

ELECTRIC: SHADOW SERIES

Washburn´s Shadow Series instruments are double cutaway body models. The **WS4** (list $349) features 3 single coil pickups and a fulcrum tremolo bridge; the **WS6** (list $349) has 2 single coils and a humbucker pickup configuration.

ELECTRIC: SILVERADO SERIES

This series incorporates the Stephen´s Extended Cutaway neck joint, and has rosewood or maple fingerboards. All the instruments in this series were hand built in Chicago, and featured Seymour Duncan or Bill Lawrence pickups.

LS93 - offset double cutaway ash body, pearloid pickguard, bolt-on maple neck, 22-fret fingerboard with pearl dot inlay, standard Wilkinson vibrato, 6-on-a-side locking Gotoh tuners, chrome hardware, 3 single coil pickups, volume/2 tone controls, 5-position switch, available in Black, Natural, Trans. Blue, Trans. Red, or Vintage Sunburst finishes, mfg. 1994-96.

		N/A	$600	$525	$450	$375	$325	$275

Last MSR was $1,000.

LT93 - similar to the LS93, except features an alder body, 22-fret maple fingerboard with black dot inlay, standard vibrato, 6-on-a-side locking tuners, available in Black or Tobacco Sunburst finishes, mfg. 1992-94.

		N/A	$675	$550	$525	$475	$400	$350

Last MSR was $1,300.

LT103 - similar to LT93, except has flame maple or swamp ash body, available in Natural or Tobacco Sunburst finishes, disc. 1994.

		N/A	$750	$625	$550	$475	$400	$350

Last MSR was $1,600.

ELECTRIC: STAGE SERIES

Stage Series models were available from Washburn between 1979 and 1986, and represent some of the first electric guitar models from the revamped Washburn company. These models featured U.S. designs, and were produced in Japan.

The **A-5** had an original retail price of $399; the **A-10** retail list was $599; and the **A-20** had a retail price of $699. Models with a tremolo (vibrato) bridge have a "V" designation in their model name (for example, A-10-V).

Stage Series models in player´s grade condition generally can be found priced between $75 and $175.

ELECTRIC: STEPHEN´S EXTENDED CUTAWAY SERIES

EC26 ATLANTIS - offset double cutaway basswood body, bolt-on maple neck, 26-fret rosewood fingerboard with pearl dot inlay, locking vibrato, 6-on-a-side locking tuners, chrome hardware, single coil/humbucker Seymour Duncan pickup, volume/tone control, 5-position switch, available in Black, Red, or White finishes, disc. 1991.

		N/A	$650	$575	$500	$425	$350	$325

Last MSR was $1,100.

This model featured the Stephen´s Extended Cutaway neck joint.

ELECTRIC: STEVE STEPHENS SIGNATURE SERIES

This series was co-designed with Steve Stevens (Billy Idol band). All of the U.S.-built instruments in this series were produced in Chicago, and featured Seymour Duncan or Bill Lawrence pickups.

SS40 - offset double cutaway poplar body, bolt-on maple neck, 22-fret maple fingerboard with abalone inlay, double locking Floyd Rose vibrato, 6-on-a-side Grover tuners, gold hardware, 2 angled humbucker exposed Washburn pickups, volume control, 5-position switch, available in Black finish, mfg. 1992-96.

		N/A	$500	$425	$350	$300	$250	$200

Last MSR was $800.

In 1994, black dot fingerboard inlay replaced the original abalone inlay.

Washburn Scott Ian
Ian Pro S175
courtesy Washburn

W

GRADING	100% MINT	98% NEAR MINT	95% EXC+	90% EXC	80% VG+	70% VG	60% G

SS80 (U.S. MFG.) - offset double cutaway poplar body, bolt-on maple neck, 22-fret maple fingerboard with abalone dot inlay, double locking vibrato, 6-on-a-side tuners, gold hardware, 2 humbucker pickups, volume control, 3-position switch, available in Black finish, mfg. 1992-96.

	N/A	$800	$700	$600	$525	$450	$400

Last MSR was $1,500.

SS100 (U.S. MFG.) - similar to SS80, except has black dot inlay, black hardware, available in Vintage Frankenstein Graphic finishes, mfg. 1992-94.

	N/A	$900	$800	$700	$625	$550	$475

Last MSR was $1,800.

ELECTRIC: USA CUSTOM SPECIALTIES SERIES

PT3 (U.S. MFG.) - heavy offset "V" mahogany body, 1/2 in. maple top, ebony fingerboard with dot position markers, 2 Seymour Duncan humbucking pickups and 1 single coil pickup, Grover 18-1 tuners, 3-per-side tuners, Buzz Feiten Tuning System, black hardware, available in Triple Black or Candy Apple Red finishes, mfg. 2000-02.

	$1,350	$1,150	$950	$850	$750	$650	$550

Last MSR was $1,800.

PTK (U.S. MFG.) - similar to Model PT3 except has korina body, ebony set neck, ebony fingerboard, EMG and Duncan pickups, Buzz Feiten Tuning System, available in Korina Gloss finish, mfg. 2000-02.

	$1,875	$1,500	$1,300	$1,150	$1,05 0	$900	$750

Last MSR was $2,500.

ELECTRIC: WINGS SERIES

All of the U.S.-built instruments in this series were produced in Chicago, and featured Seymour Duncan or Bill Lawrence pickups.

SB50 (U.S. MFG.) - double cutaway mahogany body, black pickguard, mahogany neck, 22-fret rosewood fingerboard with pearl dot inlay, tune-o-matic bridge/stop tailpiece, 3-per-side vintage Keystone tuners, chrome hardware, 2 single coil soapbar pickups, volume/2 tone controls, 3-position switch, available in Ivory, Tobacco Sunburst, or Wine Red finishes, mfg. 1992-94.

	N/A	$550	$475	$400	$325	$300	$275

Last MSR was $900.

SB80 - double cutaway mahogany body, arched bound flame maple top, raised white pickguard, mahogany neck, 22-fret bound rosewood fingerboard with pearl wings inlay, tune-o-matic bridge/stop tailpiece, 3-per-side tuners, chrome hardware, 2 humbucker Washburn pickups, 2 volume/2 tone controls, 3-position switch, available in Natural or Vintage Sunburst finishes, disc. 1996.

	N/A	$475	$400	$325	$295	$275	$250

Last MSR was $750.

SB100 (U.S. MFG.) - similar to SB50, except has bound arched figured maple top, no pickguard, bound fingerboard with pearl stylized V inlay, 2 humbucker pickups, available in Cherry Sunburst or Vintage Sunburst finishes, mfg. 1992-94.

	N/A	$1,250	$1,050	$900	$800	$725	$650

Last MSR was $2,500.

ELECTRIC: X SERIES

X-10/X-11/X-12 - offset double cutaway Strat style solid wood body, bolt-on maple neck, rosewood (X-10, X-12) or maple (X-11) fingerboard with offset dot inlay, 6-on-a-side tuners, 3 Washburn pickups in H/S/S configuration (X-10, X-11) or 2 Humbuckers (X-12), Flushtrem bridge, two knobs, 5-way switch, chrome hardware, available in Metallic Cherry, Metallic Blue, Metallic Gray, or Black finishes, mfg. 2004-present.

MSR	$250	$195	$160	$130	$110	$90	$70	$50

Add $30 for quilt maple top (Model X-12Q).

X-20 - offset double cutaway Strat-ish solid maple body, bolt-on maple neck, rosewood fingerboard with offset dot inlay, 6-on-a-side tuners, HSS WB630 pickups, Flushtrem bridge, two knobs, 5-way switch, chrome hardware, available in Metallic Cherry, Metallic Blue, or Metallic Gray finishes, mfg. 2002-03.

	$250	$200	$170	$140	$110	$85	$65

Last MSR was $330.

This model is available with a maple fingerboard with black finish (Model X-21).

X-22 - offset double cutaway Strat-ish solid maple body, bolt-on maple neck, rosewood fingerboard with offset dot inlay, 6-on-a-side tuners, HSS WB630 pickups, hard tail bridge, two knobs, 3-way switch, chrome hardware, available in Metallic Blue or Metallic Gray finishes, mfg. 2002-03.

	$250	$200	$170	$140	$110	$85	$65

Last MSR was $330.

X-22Q - similar to the X-22, except has a quilted maple top in Vintage Sunburst finish, mfg. 2002-03.

	$275	$225	$190	$160	$130	$100	$75

Last MSR was $360.

X-30 - offset double cutaway Strat style solid carved alder body, bolt-on maple neck, rosewood fingerboard with X inlay, 6-on-a-side tuners, 2 Washburn Headhunter humbucker pickups, STB, two knobs, 5-way switch, chrome hardware, available in Walnut or Black finishes, mfg. 2004-present.

MSR	$600	$450	$375	$325	$275	$235	$195	$165

X-33 - offset double cutaway Strat style solid carved alder body, bolt-on maple neck, maple or rosewood fingerboard with X inlay, 6-on-a-side tuners, 3 Washburn Shaman single coil pickups, Fulcrum tremolo, 3 knobs, 5-way switch, chrome hardware, available in Tobacco Sunburst or Black finishes, mfg. 2004-present.

MSR	$600	$450	$375	$325	$275	$235	$195	$165

W

GRADING	100% MINT	98% NEAR MINT	95% EXC+	90% EXC	80% VG+	70% VG	60% G

X-40 - offset double cutaway Strat-ish solid maple body, rosewood fingerboard with dot, 11-13 fret X inlay, 6-on-a-side tuners, HSH pickups, Floyd Rose tremolo, two knobs, 5-way switch, black hardware, Buzz Feiten Tuning System, available in Black, Metallic Polar Blue, or Platinum Metallic finishes, mfg. 2002-present.

MSR	$1,100	$800	$700	$625	$550	$475	$400	$325

X-50 - offset double cutaway Strat-ish solid mahogany body with arched quilted maple top, rosewood fingerboard with 11-13 fret X inlay, 6-on-a-side tuners, HH WB630 pickups, STB, two knobs, 3-way switch, chrome hardware, Buzz Feiten Tuning System, available in Wine Burst, Trans Blue, or Carmel Burst finishes, mfg. 2002-present.

MSR	$900		$675	$600	$525	$450	$375	$325	$275

ELECTRIC: 7-STRING SERIES

WG587 - offset double cutaway carved mahogany body, maple neck, rosewood fingerboard with dot position markers, tune-o-matic bridge, locking nut, vibrato tailpiece, 7-on-1-side tuners, 2 humbucker pickups and 1 single coil pickup, black hardware, available in Metallic Red or Metallic Gray finishes, mfg. 2000-02.

	$560	$500	$450	$400	$350	$300	$250

Last MSR was $749.

WG587V - similar to WG587 but is equipped with a Floyd Rose bridge, available in Metallic Red or Metallic Gray, mfg. 2000-02.

	$675	$600	$550	$500	$450	$400	$300

Last MSR was $899.

SONIC 7 (S7) (USA) - offset double cutaway solid mahogany body, maple neck, figured maple fingerboard with black dot position markers, 6 plus 1 headstock tuner configuration, Buzz Feiten Tuning System, hardtail bridge, string-through-body design, 2 humbucker pickups, 2 volume/1 tone, slotted switch, black hardware, available in Metallic Purple or Heavy Metal finishes, mfg. 2000-02.

	$1,200	$1,000	$900	$850	$800	$700	$550

Last MSR was $1,600.

SONIC 7V (S7V) (USA) - similar to Model S7 except has Floyd Rose bridge, available in Metallic Purple or Heavy Metal finishes, mfg. 2000-02.

	$1,275	$1,050	$950	$900	$800	$700	$600

Last MSR was $1,700.

Washburn X-12 courtesy Washburn

ELECTRIC BASS: AXXESS SERIES

XS2 - offset double cutaway hardwood body, maple neck, 24-fret rosewood fingerboard with pearl dot inlay, fixed bridge, 4-on-a-side tuners, chrome hardware, P-style Washburn pickup, push/pull volume/tone control, available in Black, Red, or White finishes, disc. 1992.

	N/A	$300	$250	$200	$175	$150	$125

Last MSR was $400.

XS4 - offset double cutaway alder body, maple neck, 24-fret rosewood fingerboard with pearl dot inlay, fixed bridge, 4-on-a-side tuners, chrome hardware, P-style/J-style Washburn pickups, volume/treble/bass controls, active electronics, available in Black or Red finishes, disc. 1992.

	N/A	$350	$300	$250	$200	$175	$150

Last MSR was $480.

XS5 - similar to XS4, except has 5 strings, 4/1 tuners and 2 J-style Washburn pickups, available in Black, Red, or White finishes, disc. 1992.

	N/A	$425	$350	$300	$250	$200	$175

XS6 - similar to XS4, except has 6 strings, available in Metallic Cherry Black, or Pearl White finishes, disc. 1992.

	N/A	$450	$375	$300	$250	$200	$175

Last MSR was $600.

XS8 - similar to XS4, except black hardware, 2 single coil Status pickups and active 2-band EQ fader control, available in Charcoal Rain, Black, or White finishes, disc. 1992.

	N/A	$550	$450	$375	$300	$250	$200

Last MSR was $800.

ELECTRIC BASS: BANTAM (XB) SERIES

XB100 - offset double cutaway asymmetrical mahogany body, bolt-on maple neck, 20-fret rosewood fingerboard with pearl dot inlay, fixed bridge, 2-per-side tuners, chrome hardware, P-style WB100 pickup, volume/tone controls, available in Black, Titanium Ice, Natural Matte, Metallic Blue, Metallic Cherry, Metallic Purple, and Black Metal Flake finishes, mfg. 1997-2004.

	$190	$160	$140	$120	$100	$80	$60

Last MSR was $265.

Add $30 for XB100 Flame Tobacco Sunburst finish (mfg. 1999-2000).

XB100Q - similar to the XB100, except has a quilted maple top with Tobacco Sunburst finish, disc. 2004.

	$235	$200	$175	$150	$125	$100	$75

Last MSR was $330.

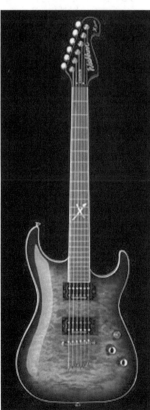

Washburn X-50 courtesy Washburn

GRADING	100% MINT	98% NEAR MINT	95% EXC+	90% EXC	80% VG+	70% VG	60% G

XB120 - offset double cutaway asymmetrical alder body, bolt-on maple neck, 20-fret rosewood fingerboard with pearl dot inlay, fixed bridge, 2-per-side tuners, black hardware, Soapbar pickups, volume/tone controls, available in Black, Trans. Blue, or Trans Red finishes, disc. 2004.

	$300	$260	$230	$200	$170	$140	$110

Last MSR was $430.

XB125 - similar to the XB120, except in five-string configuration, 3/2-per-side tuners, available in Black finish, disc. 2004.

	$375	$325	$275	$235	$195	$165	$135

Last MSR was $500.

XB125Q - similar to the XB125, except has a quilted maple top with Tobacco Sunburst finish, disc. 2004.

	$400	$350	$300	$260	$230	$190	$160

Last MSR was $530.

XB200 - offset double cutaway asymmetrical hardwood body, bolt-on maple neck, 20-fret rosewood fingerboard with offset pearl dot inlay, fixed bridge, 2-per-side tuners, chrome hardware, P/J-style Washburn WB500 pickups, 2 volume/2 tone controls, available in Black, Metallic Red, or Pearl Blue finishes, mfg. 1994-2000.

	$375	$295	$250	$225	$195	$150	$125

Last MSR was $499.

Add $50 for left-handed configuration (Model XB200 LH), available in Caribbean Blue finish only. Add $50 for XB200 Flame Tobacco Sunburst finish.

This model is available with a fretless fingerboard (Model XB200 FL). Available in Black finish only.

XB400 - offset double cutaway asymmetrical alder body, figured ash top, bolt-on maple neck, 20-fret rosewood fingerboard with offset pearl dot inlay, fixed bridge, 2-per-side tuners, chrome hardware, 2 Washburn humbucker pickups, 2 volume/2 tone controls, active electronics, available in Tobacco Sunburst, Trans. Burgundy, or Trans. Blue finishes, mfg. 1994-99.

	$625	$575	$525	$450	$375	$300	$225

Last MSR was $849.

In 1996, Natural Matte and Transparent Red finishes were introduced; Tobacco Sunburst and Trans. Burgundy finishes were disc.

XB500 - similar to XB400, except has 5-string configuration, 3/2-per-side tuners, available in Black and Natural finishes, mfg. 1994-99.

	$675	$550	$495	$425	$350	$295	$225

Last MSR was $899.

In 1996, Trans. Blue and Trans. Red finishes were introduced. Trans. Blue disc. 1998. Early models may have 2 P-style split coil pickups.

XB600 - similar to XB400, except has 6-string configuration, 3-per-side tuners, available in Black and Natural finishes, mfg. 1994-99.

	$850	$725	$650	$575	$475	$395	$300

Last MSR was $1,199.

In 1996, Trans. Blue and Trans. Red finishes were introduced. By 1999, offered only in Natural Matte finish. Early models may have 2 P-style split coil pickups.

XB800 - offset double cutaway asymmetrical alder body, figured sycamore top, bolt-on maple neck, 24-fret rosewood fingerboard with offset pearl dot inlay, fixed bridge, 2-per-side tuners, gold hardware, 2 humbucker Status pickups, volume/treble/bass/pan controls, active electronics, available in Antique Natural, Trans. Burgundy, Trans. Blue, or Vintage Sunburst finishes, mfg. 1994-96.

	N/A	$550	$475	$400	$325	$275	$225

Last MSR was $800.

XB900 (U.S. MFG.) - offset double cutaway asymmetrical swamp ash body, bolt-on maple neck, 24-fret rosewood fingerboard with offset pearl dot inlay, fixed bridge, 2-per-side tuners, black hardware, Seymour Duncan Bassline soapbar pickup, volume/3-band EQ controls, active electronics, Buzz Feiten Tuning System, available in StoneWash Blue, Antique Satin, or StoneWash Red finishes, mfg. 1997-2000.

	$1,125	$900	$795	$695	$595	$475	$375

Last MSR was $1,499.

XB900JJ (U.S. Mfg.) - similar to XB900, but has 2 Jazz pickups and is available in Butterscotch Matte and Natural Matte finishes, mfg. 1999-2000.

	$975	$850	$750	$650	$525	$425	$325

Last MSR was $1,299.

XB900PJ (U.S. Mfg.) - similar to XB900, but has 1 Jazz and 1 "P" pickup, available in Butterscotch Matte and Natural Matte finishes, mfg. 1999-2000.

	$975	$850	$750	$650	$525	$425	$325

Last MSR was $1,299.

XB920 (U.S. MFG.) - similar to XB900, except has Bartolini custom pickups, Buzz Feiten Tuning System available in bubinga, Natural Matte, or African Zebra finishes, current mfg.

MSR	$2,200	$1,650	$1,400	$1,200	$1,050	$900	$750	$600

XB925 (U.S. MFG.) - similar to XB920, except has 5-string configuration, 3/2-per-side tuners, Bartolini custom pickups, Buzz Feiten Tuning System available in Antique Stain, Bubinga, Cherry Sunburst, Vintage Sunburst, or African Zebra finishes, mfg. 1997-present.

MSR	$2,350	$1,775	$1,500	$1,300	$1,100	$950	$800	$650

XB926 (U.S. MFG.) - similar to the XB925, except in 6-string configuration, current mfg.

MSR	$2,450	$1,850	$1,550	$1,350	$1,150	$1,000	$850	$700

XB928 (U.S. MFG.) - similar to the XB925, except in 8-string configuration, current mfg.

MSR	$2,600	$1,950	$1,650	$1,400	$1,200	$1,050	$1,000	$850

XB1000 (U.S. MFG.) - offset double cutaway asymmetrical ash body, bolt-on maple neck, 24-fret rosewood fingerboard with pearl dot inlay, fixed Wilkinson bridge, blackface peghead with screened logo, 2-per-side Gotoh tuners, chrome hardware, humbucker Bartolini pickup, volume/mid/concentric treble/bass controls, available in Black, Trans. Blue, or Trans. Red finishes, mfg. 1994-96.

	N/A	$1,000	$850	$725	$600	$500	$400

Last MSR was $1,500.

GRADING	100% MINT	98% NEAR MINT	95% EXC+	90% EXC	80% VG+	70% VG	60% G

ELECTRIC BASS: FORCE & TAURUS SERIES

FORCE 4 - offset double cutaway bubinga body, neck-thru body, 24-fret rosewood fingerboard, 2 ABT pickups, monorail bridge, four knobs, 2-per-side tuners, active electornics, chrome hardware, available in Natural Matte finish, current mfg.

MSR	$800	$600	$525	$450	$375	$300	$250	$200

Force 5 - similar to the Force 4, except in five-string configuration, current mfg.

MSR	$900	$675	$600	$525	$450	$375	$300	$225

T12 - offset double cutaway basswood body, bolt-on maple neck, 24-fret rosewood fingerboard, single P-style pickups, two knobs, two-per-side tuners, chrome hardware, available in Black, Metallic Blue, Metallic Red, or Natural Satin finish, new 2005.

MSR	$300	$210	$180	$160	$140	$120	$100	$80

T14 - offset double cutaway basswood body, bolt-on maple neck, 24-fret rosewood fingerboard, one J-style and one P-style pickups, three knobs, two-per-side tuners, chrome hardware, available in Black, Cognac, or Natural Satin finish, new 2005.

MSR	$350	$250	$210	$180	$160	$140	$120	$100

T14Q - similar to the T14, except has a quilted maple top, available in Quilt Trans. Blue, or Quilt Tobacco Sunburst finishes, new 2005.

MSR	$400	$280	$240	$210	$180	$160	$140	$120

T24 - offset double cutaway stained mahogany body, neck-thru body, 24-fret rosewood fingerboard, 2 Jazz style pickups, four knobs, 2-per-side tuners, active electornics, chrome hardware, available in Natural Matte finish, current mfg.

MSR	$500	$350	$300	$260	$220	$190	$160	$130

T25 - similar to the T24, except in five-string configuration, current mfg.

MSR	$600	$420	$350	$300	$260	$220	$190	$160

Washburn XB400 courtesy Washburn

ELECTRIC BASS: M SERIES

M10 (U.S. MFG.) - offset double cutaway maple body, maple bolt-on neck, rosewood fingerboard with 12th fret skull and crossbones inlays, Seymour Duncan J-style pickups, two knobs, fixed bridge, 2-per-side tuners, chrome hardware, available in Natural Matte, Industrial Black, or Army Green finishes, disc. 2003.

	$1,200	$1,050	$925	$800	$700	$600	$500

Last MSR was $1,600.

This model is also available with P/J-style pickups (Model M12).

M13 (U.S. MFG.) - similar to the M10, except has LED's and Army Flag finish, disc. 2003.

	$1,500	$1,300	$1,100	$950	$800	$650	$550

Last MSR was $2,000.

ELECTRIC BASS: MERCURY (MB) SERIES

MB2 - offset double cutaway hardwood body, bolt-on maple neck, 24-fret rosewood fingerboard with offset pearl dot inlay, fixed bridge, 4-on-a-side tuners, chrome hardware, P-style pickup, volume/tone control, available in Black, Pacific Blue Rain, or White finishes, disc. 1994.

	N/A	$325	$275	$225	$200	$175	$125

Last MSR was $470.

MB4 - offset double cutaway alder body, bolt-on maple neck, 24-fret rosewood fingerboard with offset pearl dot inlay, fixed bridge, 4-on-a-side tuners, chrome hardware, P-style/J-style Washburn pickups, volume/treble/bass controls, 3-position switch, active electronics, available in Black, Black Cherry Metallic, Ice Pearl, Midnight Blue Metallic, or Natural finishes, disc. 1994.

	N/A	$375	$325	$275	$225	$200	$150

Last MSR was $550.

This model was also available with a maple fingerboard with black dot inlay.

MB5 - similar to MB4, except has 5-string configuration, 4/1 per side tuners, 2 J-style pickups, available in Black, Ice Pearl, or Natural finishes, disc. 1994.

	N/A	$475	$400	$325	$275	$225	$175

Last MSR was $670.

MB6 - similar to MB4, except has 6-string configuration, 4/2-per-side tuners, 2 J-style pickups, available in Natural finish, disc. 1994.

	N/A	$525	$450	$375	$300	$250	$225

Last MSR was $750.

Washburn Taurus T24 Bass courtesy Washburn

W

GRADING	100% MINT	98% NEAR MINT	95% EXC+	90% EXC	80% VG+	70% VG	60% G

MB8 - offset double cutaway alder body, flame maple top, bolt-on maple neck, 24-fret rosewood fingerboard with offset pearl dot inlay, fixed bridge, 4-on-a-side tuners, gold hardware, 2 humbucker active Status pickups, volume/treble/bass/mix controls, active electronics, available in Tobacco Sunburst, Trans. Blue, or Trans. Purple finishes, disc. 1994.

	N/A	$550	$475	$400	$350	$300	$250

Last MSR was $800.

This model was also available with a maple fingerboard with black dot inlay.

MB40 - offset double cutaway soft maple body, bolt-on maple neck, 24-fret rosewood fingerboard with dot inlays, 2 MPB500 pickups, five knobs, 2-per-side tuners, active electronics, chrome hardware, available in Metallic Gray finishes, current mfg.

MSR	$1,200	$900	$825	$750	$675	$600	$500	$400

ELECTRIC BASS: MISC. MODELS

AB 90 - single smooth cutaway hollow body, 2 f-holes, bolt-on maple neck, 21-fret rosewood fingerboard with split abalone block inlays, 2 soapbar pickups, four knobs, Washburn W tailpiece, chrome hardware, available in Walnut or Black finishes, mfg. 2004-present.

MSR	$1,200	$900	$825	$750	$675	$600	$500	$400

AB 95 - similar to the AB 90, except in 5-string configuration, 3/2-per-side tuners, mfg. 2004-present.

MSR	$1,300	$975	$875	$800	$725	$650	$550	$450

B200 - single cutaway alder body, bound carved maple top, 3-piece maple neck, 22-fret bound rosewood fingerboard with pearl dot inlay, fixed bridge, 2-per-side tuners, chrome hardware, 2 Washburn pickups, 2 volume/2 tone controls, available in Metallic Dark Blue finish, disc. 1994.

	N/A	$525	$450	$375	$325	$275	$225

Last MSR was $750.

BOOTSY (U.S. MFG.) - Bootsy Collins signature, star shaped body with pointed horns, mahogany body with maple top, maple neck, 24-fret birdseye maple fingerboard with pearl star inlays, 2 Seymour Duncan STKJ2 humbucker pickups, Bad Ass II bridge, 2-per-side tuners, gold hardware, available in Pearl White finish with Swarovski Austrian crystals, current mfg.

MSR	$4,500	$3,500	$3,000	$2,600	$2,200	N/A	N/A	N/A

ELECTRIC BASS: RB SERIES

RB2002 - double offset cutaway soft maple body, bolt-on maple neck, 24-fret rosewood fingerboard with dot inlay, Hammerhead system, humbucker and jazz pickups, active electronics, four knobs, pickguard, 2-per-side tuners, available in Black or Mahogany Satin oil finishes, disc. 2003.

	$675	$600	$525	$450	$400	$350	$300

Last MSR was $900.

RB2502 - similar to the RB2002, except in five-string configuration, available in Black or Caribbean Blue finishes, disc. 2003.

	$750	$675	$600	$525	$450	$375	$325

Last MSR was $1,000.

ELECTRIC BASS: SHADOW SERIES

Washburn´s Shadow Series bass instruments are double cutaway body models. The **WP4** (list $364) features a P-style split pickup and deluxe die-cast bridge; the **WJ4** (list $364) has 2 J-style pickups.

ELECTRIC BASS: STATUS 1000 SERIES

S60 - offset double cutaway one piece maple body/neck construction, walnut top/back laminates, 24-fret carbonite fingerboard, no headstock, tunable bridge, brass hardware, 2 single coil Status pickups, volume/tone control, active electronics with fader control, available in Black or White finishes, disc. 1992.

	N/A	$700	$600	$500	$400	$350	$300

Last MSR was $1,000.

S70 - similar to S60, Available in Natural, Trans. Blue, or Trans. Red finish, disc. 1994.

	N/A	$800	$725	$600	$500	$425	$350

Last MSR was $1,200.

This model was also available with fretless fingerboard (Model S70 FL).

WATERSTONE GUITARS

Instruments currently produced overseas and set up in Nashville, TN, since 2004.

Waterstone Guitars was created by a group of individuals who love guitars and music. Their goal is to bring quality built, exceptional sounding, and reasonably priced guitars to the market place. Guitars are designed and developed in the U.S., produced overseas, and then inspected at their shop in Nashville, TN. For more information contact Waterstone directly (see Trademark Index).

ELECTRIC

Waterstone produces a variety of instruments including, solidbody guitars, hollowbody archtops, acoustics, and bass guitars. Prices on the Signature hollowbody series retail for around $650, solidbodies are around $480, the bass guitars around $475, and the Tom Petersson Bass Collection starts at $1,730.

W

WATKINS

Instruments previously built in England from circa 1961 to 1982. Trademark was changed to W.E.M. (Watkins Electric Music) in the late 1960s, and then to Wilson in the 1970s.

Watkins (W.E.M.) were known primarily for their amplifiers; however, many players in Great Britain started out on a Watkins Rapier guitar. Borrowing heavily on Leo Fender's Stratocaster design, the guitars were available in 2-, 3-, or 4-pickup models. Guitars were designated by the model number: **Rapier 22** (2 pickups), **Rapier 33** (3 pickups), and **Rapier 44** (4 pickups). Models were available in a Bright Red or Black finish. A bass guitar counterpart was produced, and featured 2 pickups. These instruments started being produced around 1961.

Sid Watkins was responsible for the guitar making, as well as the cabinets for the various W.E.M. amps and W.E.M. CopiCats (an echo effect box distributed in the U.S. by Guild in the mid 1960s). The electronics were fitted to the amps by Sid's brother, Charlie. W.E.M. supplied many festivals in the 1960s with their P.A. systems. Watkins produced one of the first guitar synths. The **Fifth Man** featured a number of effects plus a primitive drum box. The guitar was demonstrated on the British television programe **Tomorrow's World**.

At the end of the 1960s, some of the Watkins guitars were branded W.E.M. The last change of name in the 1970s was Wilson (this was the maiden name of Sid's mother). Sid branched out into semi-acoustic guitars which became very popular. These models were favored by Roy Wood of Wizard (The Move). The guitar's popularity grew in Germany, and Sid would load up his V.W. camper to take them over himself.

As a footnote, Watkins made some guitars for Vox, when Vox apparently could not keep up with the demand for their instruments. As another matter of interest, G Plan (a British furniture company) also produced some guitars for the company.
Source: Keith Smart, Zemaitis Guitar Owners Club. Smart was an employee at Watkins/W.E.M. during the 1970s. Additional model information courtesy Tony Bacon and Paul Day, *The Guru's Guitar Guide.*

ELECTRIC

The Watkins trademark appears on entry level to medium quality solid body and semi-hollowbody models that primarily appealed to student players. Models include such designation as the **Rapier**, **Circuit 4**, **Mercury**, **Ranger**, and **Sapphire**. As indicated earlier, production was maintained until 1982 and the trademark name changed (or should we say evolved) twice during this company's history.

WAYNE

Instruments currently built in Paradise, CA since 1998.

Wayne guitars is currently operated by Wayne Chavel and his son Michael. Wayne has been producing guitars since 1962, and has produced guitars for many famous artists. Wayne has worked for Fender, Gibson, and B.C. Rich. Visit Wayne's website for more information (see Trademark Index).

ELECTRIC

There are several other models available. Visit the website for descriptions and pricing.
The **Hydra** has an outrageous body design, Premium grade Alder body, AAA bird's-eye maple neck, 22-fret neck, Original Floyd Rose tremolo bridge in chrome or non-tremolo brass bridge, available with the Eddie Van Halen D-tuna which allows the E string to be dropped to D without unclamping, ebony, rosewood, or maple fingerboards, Gotoh tuners, chrome or brass knobs, chrome or brass/gold hardware, one pickup variation available with volume control, two pickup variation has volume control and three-way switch, available in Jet Black, Bright Red, Candy Red, Corvette Yellow, Orange, Dark Purple, Metallic Lavender, Lime Green, Hand Rubbed Oil, Rock White, and Cherry Sunburst, custom graphics are also available, and MSR is $2,400. The **Rock Legend** has a double cutaway body design, technical specifications are the same as the Hydra Model, and MSR is $2,800. The **Star Guitar** has modified star shaped body design, technical specifications are the same as the Hydra Model. The **Wayne Special** has a double cutaway body, Flame or Quilted Maple top, Select Alder body, Cream Ivoroid binding and pickup bezels, compound radius fingerboard of ebony, rosewood, or maple. Other specifications are the same as the Hydra Model, available in Trans. Amber, Trans. Blue, Trans. Purple, Trans. Red, Natural, and Cherry Sunburst finishes.

WEEDON, BERT

Trademark of instruments previously built in West Germany in the mid-1960s.

While the Bert Weedon trademark was a brand name used by a UK importer, Bert Weedon was a famous British guitarist best known for his daily guitar lessons on British radio. Weedon was normally associated with Hofner guitars throughout his career. The **Zero One** model was a semi-hollowbody with a single cutaway and two pickups (source: Tony Bacon and Paul Day, *The Guru's Guitar Guide*).

WELSON

Instruments previously produced in Italy from the early 1970s to the early 1980s.

The Welson company produced medium quality guitars based on Gibson designs, as well as their own original designs and semi-hollowbody models. Welson also built guitars for the Vox company, and for Wurlitzer (U.S.) (source: Tony Bacon and Paul Day, *The Guru's Guitar Guide*).

WESTBURY

See Unicord. Instruments previously produced in Japan between 1978 and 1981.

The Merson Musical Supply Company of Westbury, New York was the primary importer of Univox guitars. Merson evolved into Unicord, and also became a distributor for Westbury brand guitars. Westbury instruments featured a set neck design on both the solid body electric guitars and basses, and generally had two humbuckers on the guitar models (some also had a vari-tone switch). Westbury guitars are generally medium to good quality original designs (source: Michael Wright, *Guitar Stories*, Volume One).

**Washburn AB95 Bass
courtesy Washburn**

**Washburn Bootsy Bass
courtesy Washburn**

GRADING	100% MINT	98% NEAR MINT	95% EXC+	90% EXC	80% VG+	70% VG	60% G

ELECTRIC

CUSTOM - offset dual cutaway body, arched top, set-in neck, 22-fret ebony fingerboard with white block inlay, 3 on a side headstock, bridge/stop tailpiece, chrome hardware, bound black peghead with Westbury logo and W design, 2 covered humbucker pickups, 2 volume/2 tone controls, 3-way switch, 5-position pickup tap/phase control, mfg. 1978-1981.

	N/A	$425	$350	$300	$250	$175	$125

CUSTOM S similar to the Custom, except has bound body, rosewood fingerboard, gold hardware, 2 DiMarzio humbuckers, mfg. 1980-81.

	N/A	$450	$375	$325	$275	$225	$150

ELECTRIC BASS

TRACK IV BASS - offset dual cutaway body, set-in neck, 20-fret ebony fingerboard with white dot inlay, 2-per-side headstock, fixed bridge, chrome hardware, black peghead with Westbury logo and W design, black pickguard, 2 P-style pickups, volume/blend/tone controls, mfg. 1978-1981.

	N/A	$400	$350	$300	$250	$200	$150

WESTONE

Instruments previously produced in Japan from circa late 1970s to mid 1980s. Subsequent instruments were built in Korea. Distributed in the U.S. by St. Louis Music of St. Louis, Missouri. Trademark re-introduced to British marketplace in 1996 by FCN Music. Instruments currently produced in Korea.

The Matsumoku company of Japan had been manufacturing guitars for other trademarks (such as Aria, Epiphone, and Vantage) since the 1960s. In 1981, Matsumoku decided to market their own original designs under their own trademark in addition to their current production for others. Westone guitars were originally marketed in the U.K. prior to the U.S. market. Matsumoku guitars are generally well-built, solid playing guitars that featured innovative design ideas.

In 1984, St. Louis Music announced that it would be merging Westone with their Electra brand (which was introduced back in 1971). Through the mid 1980s, models were sold under the Electra/Westone imprint, then Westone only as the Electra brand aspect was discontinued. In 1987, Matsumoku stopped producing instruments, so guitar production switched to Korea.

While the brand is not currently available in the U.S. market, FCN Music recently began importing Korean-built models into England. The current series consists of five models of medium to good quality.

ELECTRIC

Most guitars were designed as part of a certain series. The overall body design would then feature different pickup combinations, or the addition of a tremolo; popular series includes the Pantera (1986-1987), Thunder (1981-1987), Spectrum (1984-1987), Phoenix, Dynasty, Futura, Custom Pro, and the Clipper Six (1986-1988). The Clipper Six series was designed by Mark Ray of the United Kingdom. Many of the guitar series were produced in limited quantities. Matsumoku-produced Electra/Westone guitars should have serialization beginning with a **4** or **84**.

SPECTRUM ST - solid body, 22-fret bolt-on neck, dot position markers, chrome hardware, 6-on-a-side tuners, 1 volume/1 tone control, toggle switch, no pickguard, tremolo, 2 exposed coil humbuckers.

	N/A	$250	$225	$200	$175	$150	$125

WILDE USA

See Bill Lawrence Guitar Company LLC.

WILKES

Instruments currently built in England since the mid-1970s.

These high quality solid body guitars feature both original and designs based on popular American classics. Models include the Answer, Extrovert, Poet, Skitzo, and the Slut (?!). We know what you're thinking, and you are absolutely correct: Send photos and information for future updates of the Wilkes guitar models to the *Blue Book of Electric Guitars* (source: Tony Bacon and Paul Day, *The Guru's Guitar Book*).

WILKINS GUITAR FINISHES

Instruments currently built in Van Nuys, CA. Distributed by Wilkins Guitar Finishes of Van Nuys, CA. Instruments previously built in Portsmouth, VA.

Luthier Pat Wilkins has been acknowledged as a premier finisher of quality instruments for well over the past ten years. Some of his recent handiwork can be viewed on such models as the U.S. produced Pacifica models for Yamaha, as well as his namesake handcrafted models (other examples occasionally turn up as prototypes displayed at industry trade shows - but no further hints will be dropped).

Prior to moving to California, Wilkins joined former Schecter Research President Bill Ricketts and ex-Zion Guitars luthier Kenny Marshall in custombuilding limited production guitars and basses in the 1980s. The **OFB Guitars** custom models were built in Portsmouth, Virginia.

Wilkins' former models feature bolt-on neck, tilt-back headstocks, locking machine heads, numerous different pickup combinations, and spectacular finishes. For further information regarding custom finishes, please contact Wilkins Guitar Finishes directly (see Trademark Index).

WILSON

See Watkins. Instruments previously built in England.

The Wilson logo is the final one used by the Watkins company (1960-1982). They offered a wide variety of guitars that were handmade. Look for more information on models in further editions of the *Blue Book of Electric Guitars* (source: Tony Bacon, *The Ultimate Guitar Book*).

GRADING	100% MINT	98% NEAR MINT	95% EXC+	90% EXC	80% VG+	70% VG	60% G

WINSTON

Instruments previously produced in Japan circa early 1960s to late 1960s. Distributed in the U.S. by Buegeleisen & Jacobson of New York, NY.

The Winston trademark was a brand name used by U.S. importers Buegeleisen & Jacobson of New York, New York. The Winston brand appeared on a full range of acoustic guitars, thinline acoustic/electric archtops, and solid body electric guitars and basses. Winston instruments are generally the shorter scale beginner's guitar. Although the manufacturers are unknown, some models appear to be built by Guyatone (source: Michael Wright, *Vintage Guitar Magazine*).

ELECTRIC

MISC. ELECTRIC GUITARS - various configurations in solidbody and semi-hollow body electrics, mfg. 1960s.

	N/A	$225	$200	$175	$150	$125	$100

WITTMAN

Instruments currently built in Williamsport, PA since the early 1990s.

Wittman basses featured exotic woods and a sleek body profile, and different stringing configurations. The Aurora's sleek profile features an extended bass horn, and slimmed back treble bout cutaway.

ELECTRIC BASS

Models are designed with headstock as well as reverse tuned bridge (headless). The Aurora is available in 4-, 5-, and 6-string configurations. For those seeking a more traditional body shape, Wittman also offers a J/P shape design. Prices range from $1,900 to $2,300 for the different Aurora string configurations, and $1,500 to $1,900 for the traditional design. All models feature walnut, maple, polar, ash, or cherry bodies, a bolt-on neck (neck-through is optional), maple, ebony or rosewood fingerboard, EMG DC or Bartolini soapbar pickup, a Spinstrap, and on-board ProTuner. For further information regarding model specifications and pricing, contact Wittman Guitars directly (see Trademark Index).

WOLLERMAN GUITARS

Instruments currently built in Sheffield, IL. Wollerman Guitars also builds instruments for Supervolt, Stone Axe, Biggun, Brick, and Junk trademarks. Wollerman Guitars also markets Ledsled amplification and V-Max pickups.

Luthier/designer Mark Wollerman has been building handcrafted instruments since 1983. Wollerman, a guitarist himself, built his "new" guitar years ago when his finances were low. The Devastator, Wollerman's first handcrafted guitar, was used constantly as he participated with bands. Outside of a few model revisions, the same guitar is still currently produced. Wollerman founded his company in the early 1980s on the premise of building affordable guitars for musicians.

Wollerman offers over 170 guitar body designs, each which are available in eight different lines and five different sizes. Wollerman also offers electric mandolins and electric violins. Wollerman instruments are currently available both in the U.S., and in 21 countries worldwide. A large 112 page catalog of options and body styles is available for a nominal fee. For further information, please contact Wollerman guitars directly (see Trademark Index).

According to Mark Wollerman, some of the more popular body styles are the **Raider, Swept-Wing, Pro-57, J.P. 63, Blaster, Twister, Torqmaster,** and the **Junkmaster.**

ELECTRIC

All Standard Wollerman guitars feature a 25.5 in. scale, 21-fret rosewood fingerboard, graphite nut, Pro sealed tuning pegs, heavy duty hardtail bridge, chrome hardware, one standard humbucking pickup, and one volume control. Wollerman models have individual unique features that differentiate from model to model. Options can be added or subtracted to come up with custom versions of each model. The **Pearl Deluxe** features the full Power Tone bodies with highly figured tops available in White, Black, Gold, Red, Blue, or Green pearloid. Sides are finished in Black or White Naugahyde, and backs in a Gloss White. The **Super Pearl Deluxe** is an extra cost option of pearloid backs instead of Gloss White. There are many custom paint and solid body options, and the retail price lists at $429 and up. The **Biggun** series is a special variation of the **Wollerman, Supervolt, Brick,** and **Rawhide** lines. Models feature a 10% oversized body, 27 in. scale length, and 1.75 in. neck width (at nut). A true Baritone neck (28.5 in.) is also available. Retail prices list at $449 and up.

Supervolt models feature bodies similar to the full Power Tone bodies, except have Gloss White textured Fiberglass tops and backs and choice of pickguards/sidetrim in Black, Red, White, Blue, Yellow, and Green. Other options include color coordinated pickup covers, and swirl pickguards. Retail prices begin at $319 and up. The **Brick Series** is similar to the Supervolt, except feature tops, backs, and sides that resemble brick walls! Models feature gray "cement lines" and Red, White, Black, or Brown bricks. **Stone Axe** models feature the Full Power Tone bodies and pickguards, but the bodies have a finish like they were carved out of stone. Colors include Turquoise Dust, Red Quartz, Gray Stone, Sandstone, Pueblo Stone, Black Stone, Soap Stone, and Ironstone. Retail prices list at $339 and up.

Rawhide series guitars have the Wollerman Full Power Tone bodies with tops and backs constructed of "Leatherwood," and pickguards covered in black or white Naugahyde. Retail list begins at $299 and up. The **Junk Guitar** and bass series is the "enviromentally conscious" line from Wollerman. These instruments feature a neck-through-body design based on laminating the extra wood left over from other projects. These laminated bodies feature a natural look, durable all wood construction, and decent tone. A number of other guitar companies began building multi-laminated wood body guitars as far back as

Wright G.T. Soloette courtesy Skip Harrison

the 1970s, all with high end prices. However, this series is moderately priced, and begins at $259 and up. The Special Guitar Operations is the high end custom shop maintained by Wollerman.

S.G.O. guitars and basses (list $499 and up) feature the best parts, pickups, and woods available - as well as the flexibility for custom designs. Most bass guitar orders are processed through the S.G.O., and **Wollerman basses** (list $299 and up) feature a 34 in. scale, rosewood fingerboard, chrome hardware, a JB pickup, and one volume control. Most of the guitar designs are available in bass format. Wollerman also produces **4-string Tenor** guitars (list $239 and up), **Mini** guitars (similar to the full scale models, yet begin at $229 and up), electric Mandolins ($199 and up), and left-handed guitars (most models, and parts are available too - list $219 and up).

WOODY´S CUSTOM GUITARS

Instruments currently produced in New York City since mid-1970s.

Luthier/designer Woody Phiffer has been building and producing innovative high quality guitars for several years. Phiffer´s guitars always feature high quality construction and shaping, and immaculate translucent finishes.

Phiffer´s current custom model features a carved top and back, carved pickup covers, exotic woods, mutli-layer body binding, and quality hardware and pickups.

WORLD TEISCO

See Teisco Del Rey.

WRIGHT GUITAR TECHNOLOGY

Instruments currently built in Eugene, OR.

Luthier Wright was briefly involved with Stephen Mosher´s Moses Graphite necks, and then turned to producing a good quality travel guitar. The **Soloette** model has even traveled on the NASA´s space shuttle recently! The Soloette is factory order direct only. For more information regarding the Soloette and pricing, contact Wright Guitar Technology directly (see Trademark Index).

WURLITZER

Instruments previously built in America during the 1960s. Wurlitzer then began importing models from Italy during the 1970s.

During the 1960s, Wurlitzer distributed guitars built in the Holman-Woodell facility in Neodesha, Kansas (makers of other trademarks such as Holman, Alray, 21st Century, and La Baye). Instruments were medium quality solid or semi-hollowbody guitars. As U.S. production prices rose, Wurlitzer began importing semi-hollowbody guitars built by the Welson company in Italy in the early 1970s.

Section X

XOTIC GUITARS

Instruments currently built in Los Angeles, CA. Distributed by Prosound Communications, Inc. in San Fernando, CA.

Xotic builds high quality basses with exotic woods and premium hardware. Xotic is also building Trilogic pickups and preamps, as well as the Spiral guitar models (See SPIRAL). In 1999, Xotic started making effect pedals.

ELECTRIC GUITAR

Xotic produces two types of electric guitars and they are based on the popular Telecaster and Stratocaster. The **XSG** has a Strat shaped body. The **XTG** has a Telecaster shaped body. These guitars are built to feel like the original vintage models of the time.

ELECTRIC BASS

There is no additional charge for left-handed configurations. Xotic does offer a number of additional custom options per model.

The **XB-1** has an offset double cutaway 2-piece ash or alder body, bolt-on 3-piece maple neck, 34 in. scale, 24-fret maple fingerboard with black dot inlay, Gotoh bridge, Kent Armstrong pickup, volume/tone controls, Xotic P-1 preamp, available in Black, Red, White, or Burst finishes, available in 4-string with 2 per side Gotoh GB70E tuners, and 5-String with 3/2-per-side tuners.

The **XB-2 Standard** has an offset double cutaway ash or alder body, bolt-on 3-piece maple, 34 in. scale, 24-fret bird´s-eye maple fingerboard with abalone dot inlay, Hipshot Ultralite tuners, Kahler bridge, 2 Kent Armstrong pickups, master volume/blend/master tone controls, 3-band EQ controls, Xotic Super 125 preamp, available in Transparent color finishes, available in 4-string with 2 per side tuners, and 5-string with 3/2-per-side tuners.

The **XB-2 Custom** is similar to the XB-2 Standard, except features exotic wood top and back (bubinga, padauk, quilted maple, or zebrawood), ebony fingerboard with aluminum rings design inlay, available in Clear Semigloss finish, available in 4-string with 2 per side tuners, 5-string with 3/2-per-side tuners, and 6-string with 3-per-side tuners.

The **XB-2 Premier** is similar to the XB-2 Standard, except features maple, ash or alder body, special exotic wood top and back (figured maple, Macassar ebony, Madrone burl, maple burl, spalted maple, or ziricote), set-in maple neck, ebony fingerboard with aluminum rings design inlay, available in Clear Semigloss finish, available in 4-string with 2 per side tuners, 5-string with 3/2-per-side tuners, 6-string with 3-per-side tuners.

The **XB-3 Standard** 5-String has an offset double cutaway ash or alder body, bolt-on 3-piece maple, 34 in. scale, 21-fret bird´s-eye maple fingerboard with abalone dot inlay, 3/2-per-side Hipshot Ultralite tuners, Kahler bridge, 2 original single coil pickups, volume/blend/tone controls, available in Transparent color finishes, mfg. 1998-present.

The **XB-3 Custom** 5-String is similar to the XB-3 Standard 5-String, except features exotic wood top and back (bubinga, padauk, quilted maple, or zebrawood), ebony fingerboard with aluminum rings design inlay, available in Clear Semigloss finish.

The **XB-3 Premier** is similar to the XB-3 Standard 5-String, except features maple, ash or alder body, special exotic wood top and back (figured maple, Macassar ebony, Madrone burl, maple burl, spalted maple, or ziricote), set-in maple neck, ebony fingerboard with aluminum rings design inlay, available in Clear Semigloss finish.

The **XPB** has a body shape like a Precision bass. The body is hollow ash with STB, a maple neck, 21-fret rosewood fingerboard with dot inlay, Aero Type 3 pickup, 4-on-a-side hip-shot ultra light tuners, Hip Shot bridge, pickguard, available in natural oil finish.

Add $150 for cocobola, kingwood, or macassar ebony fingerboard. Add $200 for fretless fingerboard. Add $300 for custom model with set neck.

XTone PC-1
courtesy ESP/XTone

XTONE GUITARS

Instruments currently produced overseas, since 2003. Distributed by the ESP company.

XTone guitars were introduced in 2003 at the summer NAMM show. The XTone series is similar to the LTD series that ESP also has. The XTone line feature semi-hollow body models that have an original shape. Bigsby vibrato units are available on some models.

ELECTRIC SEMI-HOLLOW BODY

GRADING	100% MINT	98% NEAR MINT	95% EXC+	90% EXC	80% VG+	70% VG	60% G

PA-1 SEMI-ACOUSTIC - single cutaway semi-hollow mahogany body, three-piece maple neck, 22-fret rosewood fingerboard with pearl block inlays, body/neck/headstock binding, three-per-side tuners, rosewood bridge, B-Band Electret film transducer pickup system, three knobs, chrome hardware, available in Black or Brown Sunburst finish, new 2005.

MSR	$699		$495	$425	$375	$325	$275	$230	$190

Add $70 for flame maple top with Brown Sunburst finish.

XTone PS-2
courtesy ESP/XTone

GRADING	100% MINT	98% NEAR MINT	95% EXC+	90% EXC	80% VG+	70% VG	60% G

PC-1 - single cutaway semi-hollow mahogany body with flame maple top, single f-hole, three-piece maple neck, 22-fret rosewood fingerboard with pearl and abalone block inlays, body/neck/headstock binding, three-per-side tuners, tune-o-matic bridge with stop tailpiece, raised black pickguard, two Seymour Duncan humbucker pickups, four knobs, three-way switch, gold hardware, available in Blonde or Brown Sunburst finishes, mfg. 2004-present.

	MSR	$869		$625	$550	$475	$425	$375	$325	$275

PC-1V - similar to the PC-1, except has a Bigsby vibrato bridge/tailpiece, mfg. 2003-present.

	MSR	$899		$650	$575	$500	$450	$400	$350	$300

PC-2 - double cutaway semi-hollow mahogany body with flame maple top, single f-hole, three-piece maple neck, 22-fret rosewood fingerboard with pearl and abalone block inlays, body/neck/headstock binding, three-per-side tuners, tune-o-matic bridge with stop tailpiece, raised black pickguard, two Seymour Duncan humbucker pickups, four knobs, three-way switch, gold hardware, available in Black or See-Thru Red finishes, mfg. 2004-present.

	MSR	$819		$575	$500	$425	$375	$325	$275	$225

Add $35 for See-Thru Red finish.

PC-2V - similar to the PC-2, except has a Bigsby vibrato bridge/tailpiece, mfg. 2003-present.

	MSR	$849		$600	$525	$450	$400	$350	$300	$250

Add $35 for See-Thru Red finish.

PS-1 - single cutaway semi-hollow mahogany body with flame maple top, single f-hole, three-piece maple neck, 22-fret rosewood fingerboard with pearl block inlays, body/neck/headstock binding, three-per-side tuners, tune-o-matic bridge with stop tailpiece, raised black pickguard, two humbucker pickups, four knobs, three-way switch, chrome hardware, available in Black finish, mfg. 2004-present.

	MSR	$529		$375	$325	$275	$235	$190	$160	$130

PS-1V - similar to the PS-1, except has a licensed Bigsby vibrato bridge/tailpiece, mfg. 2003-present.

	MSR	$569		$400	$350	$300	$260	$220	$180	$140

PS-2 - double cutaway semi-hollow mahogany body with flame maple top, single f-hole, three-piece maple neck, 22-fret rosewood fingerboard with pearl block inlays, body/neck/headstock binding, three-per-side tuners, tune-o-matic bridge with stop tailpiece, raised black pickguard, two humbucker pickups, four knobs, three-way switch, chrome hardware, available in Candy Apple Red finish, mfg. 2004-present.

	MSR	$529		$375	$325	$275	$235	$190	$160	$130

PS-2V - similar to the PS-2, except has a licensed Bigsby vibrato bridge/tailpiece, mfg. 2003-present.

	MSR	$569		$400	$350	$300	$360	$220	$180	$140

Section Y

YAMAHA

Instruments currently produced in U.S., Taiwan, and Indonesia. Distributed in the U.S. by the Yamaha Corporation of America, located in Buena Park, CA. Instruments previously produced in Japan. Yamaha company headquarters is located in Hamamatsu, Japan.

Yamaha has a tradition of building musical instruments for over one hundred years. The first Yamaha solid body electric guitars were introduced to the American market in 1966. While the first series relied on designs based on classic American favorites, the second series developed more original designs. In the mid-1970s, Yamaha was recognized as the first Oriental brand to emerge as a prominent force equal to the big-name US builders.

Production shifted to Taiwan in the early 1980s as Yamaha built its own facility to maintain quality. In 1990, the Yamaha Corporation of America (located in Buena Park, California) opened the Yamaha Guitar Development (YGD) center in North Hollywood, California. The Yamaha Guitar Development center focuses on design, prototyping, and customizing both current and new models. The YGD also custom builds and maintains many of the Yamaha artist's instruments. The center's address on Weddington Street probably was the namesake of the Weddington series instruments of the early 1990s.

The Yamaha company is active in producing a full range of musical instruments, including band instruments, stringed instruments, amplifiers, and P.A. equipment.

ELECTRIC: AES SERIES

The two AES Series models debuted in 1998.

GRADING		100% MINT	98% NEAR MINT	95% EXC+	90% EXC	80% VG+	70% VG	60% G

AES 420 - single cutaway solid contoured mahogany body, set mahogany neck, 21-fret rosewood fingerboard with dot inlay, three-per-side tuners, wrap-around bridge, two humbucker pickups, three knobs, three-way switch, black or chrome hardware, available in Black or Metallic Red finishes, mfg. 2004-present.

	MSR	$650	$460	$400	$350	$300	$250	$200	$150

AES 500 - single rounded cutaway nato body, bolt-on maple neck, 25.5 in. scale, 22-fret rosewood fingerboard with pearl dot inlay, wraparound bridge, 3-per-side tuners, chrome hardware, pearloid stealth fighter-shaped pickguard, 2 chrome covered humbucker pickups, 2 volume/tone controls, 3-way selector switch, available in Black, Cream White, Gold, or Silver gloss finishes, mfg. 1998-2000.

		$450	$350	$300	$250	$200	$175	$150

Last MSR was $599.

AES 520 - single cutaway solid contoured mahogany body, set mahogany neck, 22-fret rosewood fingerboard with dot inlay, three-per-side tuners, original AES bridge, two humbucker pickups, three knobs, three-way switch, black or chrome hardware, available in Black/Gray Metallic or Satin Black finishes, 26.25 in. scale, new 2005.

	MSR	$800	$560	$475	$400	$350	$300	$250	$200

This model is a Drop-6, which means it has a longer scale length that is good for dropped tunings.

AES 620 - single cutaway solid contoured mahogany body with a flame maple top, set mahogany neck, 22-fret rosewood fingerboard with dot inlay, three-per-side tuners, original AES bridge, two Seymour Duncan humbucker pickups, three knobs, three-way switch, chrome hardware, available in Faded Burst, Royal Blue, or Trans. Dark Red finishes, 24.75 in. scale, mfg. 2004-present.

	MSR	$800	$560	$475	$400	$350	$300	$250	$200

Add $50 for left-handed configuration.

AES 620HB - similar to the AES 620, except has a semi-hollow mahogany body with a flame maple top, and single original design f-hole, available in Blonde or Old Violin Sunburst finishes, 24.75 in. scale, new 2005.

	MSR	$900	$630	$550	$475	$425	$375	$325	$275

AES 720 - single cutaway solid contoured mahogany body, set mahogany neck, 22-fret rosewood fingerboard with dot inlay, three-per-side tuners, original AES bridge, two DiMarzio humbucker pickups, three knobs, three-way switch, black or chrome hardware, available in Black/Blue Metallic or Black/Gray Metallic finishes, 24.75 in. scale, mfg. 2004-present.

	MSR	$1,000	$700	$625	$500	$450	$400	$350	$300

AES 800 - single rounded cutaway alder body, mahogany top, bolt-on maple neck, 25.5 in. scale, 22-fret rosewood fingerboard with pearl dot inlay, tune-o-matic bridge/individual fingers tailpiece, 3-per-side tuners, chrome hardware, tortoiseshell jimmy cap-shaped pickguard, 2 DiMarzio Q-100 hum-cancelling soapbar humbucker pickups, volume/tone/phase controls, 5-way selector switch, available in Brown Sunburst or Cherry Sunburst finishes, mfg. 1998-2000.

		$600	$500	$450	$400	$350	$300	$250

Last MSR was $799.

AES 800 B - similar to AES 800, except has alder body, Bigsby tailpiece, master volume, master tone, coil cut, 3-way selector switch, available in Blue finish, disc.

		$750	$650	$600	$550	$500	$450	$400

Last MSR was $999.

Yamaha AES 420 courtesy Yamaha

Yamaha AES 620 courtesy Yamaha

GRADING		100% MINT	98% NEAR MINT	95% EXC+	90% EXC	80% VG+	70% VG	60% G

AES 920 - single cutaway solid contoured African mahogany body with maple top, set African mahogany neck, 22-fret rosewood fingerboard with dot inlay, three-per-side tuners, original AES bridge, two Seymour Duncan humbucker pickups, three knobs, three-way switch, chrome hardware, available in Charcoal Gray or Honey Burst finishes, 24.75 in. scale, mfg. 2004-present.

	MSR	$2,500		$1,750	$1,500	$1,300	$1,100	$950	$800	$650

AES 1500 - single round cutaway semi-hollowbody, arched sycamore top, maple back/sides, set maple/mahogany neck with rosewood fingerboard, 22 frets, 2 DiMarzio Q-100 Humbuckers, gold hardware, 3-way selector switch, 2 volume/2 tone controls, coil splitting, 3-per-side tuners, tune-o-matic bridge, available in Orange or Pearl Snow White finishes, 24.75 in. scale, mfg. 1999-present.

	MSR	$2,400		$1,900	$1,650	$1,450	$1,250	$1,100	$950	$800

AES 1500 B (New) - similar to AES 1500, except has Bigsby B-6 tailpiece, available in Orange and Black finishes, mfg. 1999-present.

	MSR	$2,600		$2,100	$1,800	$1,550	$1,350	$1,150	$1,000	$850

AES FRANK GAMBALE SIGNATURE MODEL - designed in conjunction with guitarist Frank Gambale, features Fretwaves tuning system, carved top, double cutaway lightweight mahogany body, rear mounted bolt-on neck with ebony fingerboard, 25.5 in. scale, 3-per-side tuners, VS-100G bridge, 2 Seymour Duncan Hot Rails and 1 Seymour Duncan JB in the bridge position, master volume, master tone, push/pull coil tap, 5-position switch, available in Black or White finishes, mfg. 2001-present.

	MSR	$3,000		$2,250	$1,900	$1,600	$1,350	$1,150	$1,000	$850

AES AD6 AMIR DERAKH SIGNATURE - single cutaway AES style contoured alder body, bolt-on maple neck, 24-fret maple fingerboard with offset block inlays, three-per-side tuners, tune-o-matic bridge, black pickguard, single DiMarzio humbucker pickup, single knob, black hardware, available in Midnight Blue or Nimbus Gray finishes, mfg. 2003-present.

	MSR	$2,200		$1,550	$1,350	$1,200	$1,050	$900	$800	$700

This model is a Drop-6, which means it has a longer scale length that is good for dropped tunings.

AES RS7 RYAN SHUCK SIGNATURE - seven-string configuration, single cutaway AES style contoured alder body, bolt-on maple neck, 24-fret maple fingerboard with offset block inlays, three-per-side tuners, tune-o-matic bridge, black pickguard, single DiMarzio humbucker pickup, single knob, black hardware, available in Black or Rusty Red finishes, 26.25 in. scale, mfg. 2003-present.

	MSR	$2,300		$1,600	$1,350	$1,200	$1,050	$900	$800	$700

This model is a Drop-7, which means it has a longer scale length that is good for dropped tunings.

ELECTRIC: IMAGE SERIES

AE 500 - single cutaway archtop semi-hollow electric maple/mahogany laminate body, two custom f-holes, body and neck binding, set mahogany neck, 22-fret rosewood fingerboard with dot inlay, three-per-side tuners, original AES bridge, raised pickguard, two humbucker pickups, four knobs, three-way switch, chrome hardware, available in Black or Brown Sunburst finishes, new 2005.

	MSR	$650		$490	$425	$375	$325	$275	$225	$180

AE 1200 S - single round cutaway hollowbody, laminated spruce top, bound body and f-holes, raised bound tortoise pickguard, beech/birch back/sides, mahogany neck, 20-fret bound ebony fingerboard with abalone split block inlay, metal/grenadilla bridge with trapeze tailpiece, bound peghead, 3-per-side tuners, gold hardware, 2 humbucker pickups, 2 volume/tone controls, 3-position switch, coil split in tone controls, available in Antique Stain or Natural finishes, disc. 1996.

		N/A		$1,200	$1,000	$800	$650	$550	$450	

Last MSR was $1,800.

AES 1500 - single round cutaway hollowbody, curly maple top, bound body and f-holes, raised black pickguard, maple back/sides, 3-piece maple neck, 22-fret bound rosewood fingerboard with pearl dot inlay, bridge/stop tailpiece, abalone Yamaha symbol and scroll inlay on peghead, 3-per-side tuners, gold hardware, 2 DiMarzio humbucker pickups, 2 volume/tone controls, 3-position switch, coil split in tone controls, available in Orange Stain or Pearl Snow White finishes, disc. 1998.

				$1,900	$1,525	$1,150	$850	$750	$595	$525

Last MSR was $1,999.

AES 1500 B - similar to AES 1500, except has Bigsby vibrato, available in Antique Sunburst, Black, Natural and Orange Stain finishes, mfg. 1994-98.

				$1,395	$1,250	$1,100	$975	$775	$650	$600

Last MSR was $2,399.

AEX 500 - single rounded cutaway semi-hollowbody, laminated spruce top, bound body, 2 f-holes, laminated back/sides, bolt-on maple neck, 22-fret rosewood fingerboard with pearl dot inlay, adjustable rosewood bridge/metal trapeze tailpiece, blackface peghead with scroll/logo inlay, 3-per-side tuners, gold hardware, covered humbucker/piezo bridge pickups, master volume/pickup blend controls, 3 band EQ controls, available in Black or Brown Sunburst finishes, mfg. 1998-2000.

				$525	$450	$425	$400	$375	$350	$300

Last MSR was $699.

AEX 500 N(2) - nylon string, semi-hollow alder body, laminated spruce top, maple bolt-on neck, rosewood fingerboard, 22 frets, 1-way piezo pickup with 3-band EQ, rosewood bridge, master volume, gold hardware, available in Natural gloss and Solid Black finishes, 24.75 in. scale, disc. 2003.

				$525	$450	$425	$375	$350	$325	$275

Last MSR was $750.

AEX 502 - single cutaway, semi-hollow alder body with maple veneer, f-holes, maple bolt-on neck, rosewood fingerboard, 22-frets, 2 P-90 style pickups with "Dog Ear" covers, tune-o-matic bridge with stop tailpiece, 24.75 in. scale, master volume, master tone, 3-way selector switch, gold hardware, available in Brown Sunburst, Solid Black, or Orange stain finishes, disc. 2000.

				$485	$425	$400	$350	$325	$300	$250

Last MSR was $649.

GRADING	100% MINT	98% NEAR MINT	95% EXC+	90% EXC	80% VG+	70% VG	60% G

AEX 520 - similar to AEX 502, except has mini-humbucker pickups with covers, available in Brown Sunburst, Solid Black, or Orange stain finishes, disc. 2000.

		$525	$450	$425	$375	$350	$325	$275

Last MSR was $699.

AEX 1500 - single rounded cutaway hollow body, arched sycamore top, raised black pickguard, bound body and f-holes, figured maple back/sides/neck, 20-fret bound ebony fingerboard with pearl dot inlay, adjustable ebony bridge/trapeze tailpiece, bound blackface peghead with pearl scroll/logo inlay, 3-per-side tuners, gold hardware, humbucker/piezo bridge pickups, humbucker volume/tone controls, piezo volume/tone/3-band EQ controls, available in Antique Stain, Faded Burst, or Natural finishes, mfg. 1994-98.

		$1,250	$1,150	$975	$725	$650	$595	$500

Last MSR was $1,999.

AEX 1500 CURRENT MFG. - jazz archtop body, sycamore top, maple back and sides, ebony fingerboard, 20 frets, Floating Johnny Smith style humbuckers, bridge piezo, gold hardware, humbucker volume, tone, piezo pre-amp system with 3-band EQ, blend, volume, adjustable mid-range, ebony/bone bridge, 24.75 in. scale, co-designed with Martin Taylor, available in Natural or Antique Sunburst finishes, mfg. 1999-present.

MSR	$2,000	$1,500	$1,300	$1,150	$1,050	$895	$775	$675

Yamaha AES-1500B
courtesy Yamaha

ELECTRIC: PACIFICA SINGLE CUTAWAY SERIES

PAC 102 S - single cutaway alder body, bolt-on maple neck, 22-fret bubinga fingerboard with pearl dot inlay, fixed bridge, 6-on-a-side tuners, chrome hardware, white pickguard, 2 single coil pickups, volume/tone controls, 3-position switch. Available in Black, Brown Satin, and Natural satin finishes, mfg. 1994-2000.

		$275	$195	$150	$125	$115	$100	$85

Last MSR was $349.

PAC 120 S - single cutaway alder body, bolt-on maple neck, 22-fret bubinga fingerboard with pearl dot inlay, strings through fixed bridge, 6-on-a-side tuners, chrome hardware, 2 humbucker pickups, volume/tone controls, 3-position switch, available in Antique Sunburst, Black, or Yellow Natural finishes, mfg. 1994-2003.

		$250	$195	$175	$150	$125	$100	$90

Last MSR was $339.

In 1998, Natural Satin finish was introduced; Antique Sunburst and Yellow Natural finishes were disc. In 1999, Brown Satin was introduced.

PAC 302 S - single cutaway bound alder body, bolt-on maple neck, 22-fret rosewood fingerboard with pearl dot inlay, New Vintage fixed bridge, 6-on-a-side tuners, gold hardware, white pearloid pickguard, 2 single coil pickups, volume/tone controls, 3-position switch, available in Cherry Sunburst, Charcoal Grey, or Trans. Blue finishes, disc. 1999.

		$375	$295	$250	$225	$175	$150	$125

Last MSR was $479.

PAC 311 MS - Mike Stern body style, alder body with ash veneer, maple neck and fingerboard, 22-frets, 1 humbucker pickup, 1 "Hot Rail" style pickup, 3-position, selector, master volume, master tone, fixed bridge, black pickguard, chrome hardware, available in Natural, Vintage Blonde, or Orange Stain finishes, disc. 2003.

		$410	$325	$275	$250	$195	$165	$135

Last MSR was $549.

PAC 402 S - single cutaway bound alder body with 'high definition' top, bolt-on maple neck, 22-fret rosewood fingerboard with pearl dot inlay, New Vintage fixed bridge, 6-on-a-side tuners, gold hardware, white pearloid pickguard, 2 single coil pickups, volume/tone controls, 3-position switch, available in High Definition Amber Burst, High Definition Violin Sunburst, or High Definition Trans. Green finishes, disc.

		$425	$350	$300	$250	$200	$175	$150

Last MSR was $579.

812 S - single cutaway alder body, black pickguard, bolt-on maple neck, 24-fret rosewood fingerboard with pearl dot inlay, double locking vibrato, 6-on-a-side tuners, black hardware, 2 stacked coil/1 humbucker pickups, volume/tone control, 5-position switch with coil split, available in Black, Dark Red Metallic, or Lightning Blue finishes, disc. 1994.

		N/A	$500	$425	$350	$300	$250	$200

Last MSR was $730.

PAC 1511 MS MIKE STERN SIGNATURE MODEL - single cutaway bound 2-piece white ash body, bolt-on maple neck, 22-fret maple fingerboard with dot inlay, New Vintage fixed bridge, 6-on-a-side tuners, chrome hardware, black pickguard, 2 Seymour Duncan single coil pickups, volume/tone controls, 3-position switch, available in Natural gloss finish, mfg. 1996-present.

MSR	$1,500	$1,150	$900	$800	$700	$625	$475	$350

RGXTT TY TABOR SIGNATURE MODEL - designed in conjunction with Ty Tabor of King's X, off-set double cutaway body constructed of American Basswood wings and a stepped maple center, 2 Seymour Duncan Vintage Rails and 1 Seymour Duncan JB in the bridge position, 4-pole 5-way switch, master volume, master tone, coil capacitor cut push/pull switch, Wilkinson VS100G tremolo bridge, rosewood fingerboard, 22-frets, 3-per-side tuners, available in Trans. Red Sunburst, Trans. Green Sunburst, or Trans. Purple Sunburst finishes, disc. 2003.

		$1,125	$1,025	$925	$825	$725	$625	$499

Last MSR was $1,600.

Yamaha AEX 1500
courtesy Yamaha

GRADING	100% MINT	98% NEAR MINT	95% EXC+	90% EXC	80% VG+	70% VG	60% G

RGXTTD6 (Drop 6) Ty Tabor Signature Model - similar to Model RGXTT except, in a 26.25 in. scale, used together with heavier strings to provide deep-throated tones, available in Trans. Green Sunburst or Trans. Purple Sunburst, mfg. 2001-03.

| | $1,189 | $1,075 | $975 | $875 | $775 | $675 | $550 |

Last MSR was $1,700.

1221 M S - single cutaway basswood body, black pickguard, bolt-on maple neck, 24-fret maple fingerboard with black slash inlay, double locking vibrato, 6-on-a-side tuners, black hardware, humbucker/stacked coil/humbucker DiMarzio pickups, volume/tone control, 5-position switch with coil split, available in Black or Yellow Pearl finishes, disc. 1994.

| | N/A | $700 | $600 | $525 | $450 | $375 | $300 |

Last MSR was $1,060.

1230 S - single cutaway basswood body, black pickguard, bolt-on maple neck, 24-fret maple fingerboard with black slash inlay, double locking vibrato, 6-on-a-side tuners, black hardware, 3 DiMarzio humbucker pickups, volume/tone control, 5-position switch with coil split, available in Black or Dark Blue Metallic finishes, disc. 1994.

| | N/A | $700 | $600 | $525 | $450 | $375 | $300 |

Last MSR was $1,060.

PACIFICA USA 1 - single curved cutaway bound alder body, figured maple top, bolt-on maple neck, 22-fret rosewood fingerboard with pearl dot inlay, Wilkinson VSV vintage tremolo, 6-on-a-side Sperzel Tremlock tuners, gold hardware, white pearloid pickguard, 2 Seymour Duncan single coil/Seymour Duncan custom humbucker pickups, volume/tone controls, 5-position switch, metal controls plate, available in Natural, Trans. Blue, or Violin Sunburst finishes, mfg. 1996-2000.

| | $1,550 | $1,300 | $1,150 | $1,000 | $850 | $700 | $600 |

Last MSR was $1,899.

This model is constructed at the U.S. Yamaha Guitar Development center, featuring Warmoth bodies and necks, Seymour Duncan pickups, Wilkinson tremolo bridges, and Sperzel tuners.

ELECTRIC: PACIFICA DOUBLE CUTAWAY SERIES

PAC 012 - offset double cutaway agathis body, bolt-on maple neck, 22-fret sonokeling fingerboard with dot inlay, six-on-one-side tuners, vintage tremolo bridge, two single coil and one humbucker pickup in SSH configuration, white pickguard, two knobs, five-way switch, chrome hardware, available in Black, Metallic Dark Blue, or Metallic Dark Red finishes, mfg. 2004-present.

| MSR | $250 | | $175 | $150 | $130 | $110 | $90 | $70 | $50 |

PAC 112 - offset double cutaway alder body, bolt-on maple neck, 22-fret bubinga fingerboard with pearl dot inlay, standard vibrato, 6-on-a-side tuners, chrome hardware, white pickguard, 2 single coil/humbucker pickups, volume/tone controls, 5-position switch, Available in Antique Sunburst, Black, or Yellow Natural finishes, mfg. 1994-2003.

| | $290 | $215 | $165 | $140 | $155 | $110 | $95 |

Last MSR was $379.

Add $70 for left-handed configuration (Model PAC112 L). Add $20 for maple fingerboard (Model PAC112 M).

In 1999, Natural Satin, Brown Satin & Vintage White finishes were introduced; Antique Sunburst & Natural Yellow finishes were disc.

PAC 112J - similar to the PAC 112, except has a rosewood fingerboard, available in Black, Lake Blue, Metallic Red, Trans. Green, or Violin Sunburst finishes, mfg. 2004-present.

| MSR | $300 | | $225 | $185 | $150 | $130 | $110 | $90 | $70 |

PAC 303-12 12-STRING - offset double cutaway alder body, bolt-on maple neck, 22-fret rosewood fingerboard with pearl dot inlay, fixed bridge, 6-per-side tuners, gold hardware, white pearloid pickguard, 3 single coil pickups, volume/tone controls, 5-position switch, available in Trans. Blue or Trans. Cherry finishes, disc. 1999.

| | $525 | $425 | $375 | $325 | $275 | $225 | $175 |

Last MSR was $699.

PAC 303-12 II - double cutaway 12-string, alder body with ash veneer top, maple neck, rosewood fingerboard, 22-frets, 3-single coil pickups, 5-position selector switch, master volume, master tone, bridge with individual intonation adjustment, black pickguard, chrome hardware, available in Old Violin Sunburst, or Honey Burst, disc. 2003.

| | $485 | $410 | $340 | $295 | $250 | $215 | $150 |

Last MSR was $649.

PAC 312 - offset double cutaway alder body, bolt-on maple neck, 22-fret rosewood fingerboard with pearl dot inlay, vintage-style tremolo, 6-on-a-side tuners, gold hardware, white pearloid pickguard, 2 single coil/humbucker pickups, volume/tone controls, 5-position switch, available in Charcoal Grey, Cherry Sunburst, or Trans. Blue finishes, disc.

| | $375 | $300 | $275 | $225 | $195 | $150 | $125 |

Last MSR was $499.

PAC 312 II - double cutaway body, alder body with ash veneer top, maple neck with rosewood fingerboard, 22-frets, 2 single coil pickups and 1 humbucker pickup, 5-position switch, master volume, master tone, vintage tremolo, black pickguard, chrome hardware, available in Old Violin Sunburst, Trans. Red, or Trans. Dark Green finishes, disc. 2003.

| | $400 | $325 | $295 | $250 | $225 | $175 | $145 |

Last MSR was $539.

PAC 412 - offset double cutaway bound alder body with high definition top, bolt-on maple neck, 22-fret rosewood fingerboard with pearl dot inlay, vintage-style tremolo, 6-on-a-side tuners, gold hardware, white pearloid pickguard, 2 single coil pickups, volume/tone controls, 3-position switch, available in High Definition Amber Burst, High Definition Violin Sunburst, or High Definition Trans. Green finishes, disc.

| | $425 | $350 | $300 | $250 | $200 | $175 | $150 |

Last MSR was $579.

GRADING	100% MINT	98% NEAR MINT	95% EXC+	90% EXC	80% VG+	70% VG	60% G

PAC 412V - offset double cutaway alder body, bolt-on maple neck, 22-fret rosewood fingerboard with dot inlay, six-on-one-side tuners, Yamaha tremolo bridge, two single coil and one humbucker pickup in SSH configuration, black pickguard, two knobs, five-way switch, chrome hardware, available in Natural, Old Violin Sunburst, or Trans. Black finishes, mfg. 2004-present.

MSR	$600	$450	$375	$325	$275	$235	$190	$160

PAC 604 W - offset double cutaway select alder body, bolt-on maple neck, 22-fret rosewood fingerboard with pearl dot inlay, standard vibrato, 6-on-a-side tuners, chrome hardware, pearloid pickguard, 2 single coil/humbucker pickups, volume/tone control, 5-position switch, available in Antique Sunburst, Black, Cherry Sunburst, or Sea Foam Green finishes, mfg. 1994-2003.

		$695	$495	$425	$325	$295	$265	$235

Last MSR was $849.

In 1998, Trans. Blue finish was introduced; Sea Foam Green finish was disc. In 1999, Antique Sunburst finish was disc.

PAC 612V - offset double cutaway alder body with a flame maple top, bolt-on maple neck, 22-fret rosewood fingerboard with dot inlay, six-on-one-side tuners, Yamaha tremolo bridge, two single coil and one Seymour Duncan humbucker pickup in SSH configuration, black pickguard, two knobs, five-way switch, chrome hardware, available in Natural, Orange Stain, or Trans. Black finishes, 25.5 in. scale, mfg. 2004-present.

MSR	$900	$675	$600	$525	$450	$400	$350	$300

PAC 812 W - offset double cutaway select alder body, maple veneer top, bolt-on maple neck, 22-fret rosewood fingerboard with pearl dot inlay, Wilkinson VS100 tremolo, 6-on-a-side tuners, brushed aluminum hardware, white pearloid pickguard, 2 single coil/humbucker Seymour Duncan pickups, volume/tone control, 5-way selector switch, available in Natural, Trans. Blue, or Violin Sunburst finishes, mfg. 1998-present.

MSR	$1,149	$950	$800	$750	$650	$595	$550	$495

821 - offset double cutaway alder body, black pickguard, bolt-on maple neck, 24-fret rosewood fingerboard with pearl dot inlay, double locking vibrato, 6-on-a-side tuners, black hardware, humbucker/stacked coil/humbucker pickups, volume/tone control, 5-position switch with coil split, available in Black, Dark Red Metallic, or Lightning Blue finishes, disc. 1994.

	N/A	$500	$425	$350	$300	$250	$200

Last MSR was $730.

This model was also available with reverse peghead (Model 821R).

904 - offset double cutaway alder body, ash top, white pickguard, bolt-on maple Warmoth neck, 22-fret rosewood fingerboard with pearl dot inlay, 6-on-a-side tuners, nickel hardware, 2 single coil/humbucker pickups, volume/tone controls, 5-position switch, available in Faded Blue, Faded Burst, Old Violin Sunburst, or Trans. Black finishes, mfg. 1994-96.

	N/A	$800	$700	$600	$500	$400	$300

Last MSR was $1,250.

912 J - offset double cutaway swamp ash body, white pickguard, bolt-on maple neck, 22-fret fingerboard with pearl dot inlay, double locking vibrato, 6-on-a-side tuners, chrome hardware, 2 stacked coil/humbucker DiMarzio pickups, volume/tone control, 5-position switch, available in Black, Crimson Red, Faded Burst, or Trans. Blue finishes, disc. 1996.

	N/A	$800	$700	$600	$500	$400	$300

Last MSR was $1,250.

1212 - offset double cutaway basswood body, black pickguard, bolt-on maple neck, 24-fret rosewood fingerboard with pearl slash inlay, double locking vibrato, 6-on-a-side tuners, black hardware, 2 stacked coil/humbucker DiMarzio pickups, volume/tone control, 5-position switch with coil split, available in Black, Dark Blue Metallic, or Dark Red Metallic finishes, disc. 1994.

	N/A	$700	$600	$525	$450	$375	$300

Last MSR was $1,060.

1221 - similar to 1212, except has humbucker/stacked coil/humbucker DiMarzio pickups, available in Black and Dark Blue Metallic Flake finishes, disc. 1994.

	N/A	$700	$600	$525	$450	$375	$300

Last MSR was $1,060.

1221 M - similar to 1221, except has maple fingerboard with black slash inlay, disc. 1994.

	N/A	$700	$600	$525	$450	$375	$300

Last MSR was $1,060.

1230 - similar to 1221, except has 3 humbucker DiMarzio pickups, available in Black, Dark Red Metallic, or Lightning Blue finishes, disc. 1994.

	N/A	$700	$600	$525	$450	$375	$300

Last MSR was $1,060.

1412 - offset double cutaway mahogany body with 2 tone chambers, arched flame maple top, 7-piece maple/mahogany through body neck, 24-fret bound ebony fingerboard with abalone/pearl block inlay, double locking vibrato, 6-on-a-side tuners, chrome hardware, 2 stacked coil/humbucker DiMarzio pickups, volume/tone control, 5-position switch with coil split, available in Blonde, Cherry, Faded Burst, Rose Burst, or Trans. Black finishes, disc. 1994.

	N/A	$1,400	$1,150	$950	$800	$700	$600

Last MSR was $2,200.

Yamaha Pacifica USA 1
courtesy Dave Rogers
Dave's Guitar Shop

Yamaha Pacifica 112
courtesy Yamaha

GRADING	100% MINT	98% NEAR MINT	95% EXC+	90% EXC	80% VG+	70% VG	60% G

PACIFICA USA 2 - offset double cutaway bound basswood body, figured maple top, bolt-on maple neck, 22-fret rosewood fingerboard with pearl dot inlay, Wilkinson VS100 floating tremolo, 6-on-a-side Sperzel Tremlock tuners, gold hardware, white pearloid pickguard, 2 Seymour Duncan single coil/Seymour Duncan custom humbucker pickups, volume/tone controls 5-position switch, available in Natural, Trans. Blue, or Violin Sunburst finishes, mfg. 1996-2000.

	$1,550	$1,300	$1,150	$1,000	$850	$700	$600

Last MSR was $1,899.

This model is constructed at the U.S. Yamaha Guitar Development center, featuring Warmoth bodies and necks, Seymour Duncan pickups, Wilkinson tremolo bridges, and Sperzel tuners.

ELECTRIC: RGZ/RGX SERIES

RGZ 112 P - offset double cutaway alder body, black pickguard, bolt-on maple neck, 22-fret bubinga fingerboard with pearl dot inlay, standard vibrato, 6-on-a-side tuners, chrome hardware, 2 single coil/humbucker pickups, volume/tone control, 5-position switch, available in Black, Lightning Blue, or Vivid Red finishes, disc. 1994.

	N/A	$175	$150	$125	$115	$100	$85

Last MSR was $300.

RGX 120 D - offset double cutaway alder body, bolt-on maple neck, 22-fret bubinga fingerboard with pearl dot inlay, standard vibrato, 6-on-a-side tuners, chrome hardware, 2 humbucker pickups, volume/tone controls, 3-position switch, available in Black, Vintage Red, or White finishes, mfg. 1994-98.

	$250	$200	$175	$150	$125	$115	$100

Last MSR was $349.

RGX 121 D (RGZ 121 P) - similar to RGX 120 D, except has humbucker/single coil/humbucker pickups, 5-way switch, available in Black, Blue Metallic, Vintage Red, or Yellow Natural finishes, disc. 1998.

	$275	$225	$200	$175	$150	$125	$100

Last MSR was $379.

RZX 121 S - similar to RGX 120 D except, has one single coil pickup in the middle position in addition to two humbuckers, rosewood fingerboard, vintage tremolo, available in Mist Purple, Mist Raspberry, Satin Black, or Shelby Blue finishes, disc. 2003.

	$349	$299	$249	$199	$149	$99	$65

Last MSR was $499.

RGX 320FZ - offset double cutaway contoured mahogany body, set mahogany neck, 22-fret rosewood fingerboard with dot inlay, matching headstock with three-per-side tuners, original AES bridge, two humbucker pickups, two knobs, three-way switch, chrome hardware, available in Black or Pewter finishes, new 2005.

MSR	$570	$400	$325	$275	$235	$190	$160	$130

RGZ 321 P - similar to RGZ 120 D, except has double locking vibrato, humbucker/single coil/humbucker pickups, 5-position switch, available in Black, Lightning Blue, or 3D Blue, disc. 1994.

	N/A	$275	$225	$195	$175	$150	$125

Last MSR was $460.

RGX 420 S - offset double cutaway alder body, bolt-on neck, rosewood fingerboard with dot position markers, 25.5 in. scale, 24 frets, 6-on-a-side tuners, 2 humbucker pickups, 5-way switch, master volume, master tone, double locking tremolo, available in Grey Satin, Mist Green, or Satin Black finishes, disc. 2003.

	$419	$350	$295	$250	$195	$150	$95

Last MSR was $599.

RGX 420 SD6 (Drop 6) - similar to Model RGX 420 S except, has a 26.25 in. scale, the longer scale and heavier strings provide a deep-throated tone, mfg. 2001-03.

	$450	$395	$350	$295	$250	$195	$150

Last MSR was $649.

RGX 421 D - offset double cutaway alder body, bolt-on maple neck, 24-fret rosewood fingerboard with pearl dot inlay, double locking vibrato, 6-on-a-side tuners, chrome hardware, volume/tone controls, 5-position switch, available in Aqua, Black Pearl, Natural, or Red Metallic finishes, mfg. 1994-98.

	$425	$375	$295	$225	$200	$175	$150

Last MSR was $599.

This model was optional with a maple fingerboard (Model RGZ 421 D M).

RGX 520FZ - offset double cutaway contoured mahogany body with flame maple top, body and neck binding, set mahogany neck, 22-fret rosewood fingerboard with 12th fret custom inlay, matching 3-D headstock with three-per-side tuners, original AES bridge, two humbucker pickups, two knobs, three-way switch, black/chrome hardware, available in Trans. Black or Trans. Dark Red finishes, new 2005.

MSR	$710	$500	$425	$350	$300	$260	$220	$180

RGZ 612 P - offset double cutaway alder body, black pickguard, bolt-on maple neck, 24-fret rosewood fingerboard with pearl dot inlay, double locking vibrato, 6-on-a-side tuners, black hardware, 2 single coil/humbucker pickups, volume/tone control, 5-position switch with coil split, available in Black, Dark Red Metallic, or Lightning Blue finishes, disc. 1994.

	N/A	$500	$425	$350	$300	$250	$200

Last MSR was $720.

RGZ 612 PL - similar to RGZ 612 P, except has a left-handed configuration, disc. 1994.

	N/A	$550	$450	$375	$325	$275	$225

Last MSR was $830.

GRADING	100% MINT	98% NEAR MINT	95% EXC+	90% EXC	80% VG+	70% VG	60% G

RGX 621 D (RGZ 621 P) - offset double cutaway alder body, bolt-on maple neck, 24-fret rosewood fingerboard with pearl offset dot inlay, double locking vibrato, 6-on-a-side tuners, black hardware, humbucker/single coil/humbucker pickups, volume/tone controls, 5-position switch, available in Antique Sunburst, Black, Blue Metallic, or Red Metallic finishes, disc. 1995

	N/A	$525	$450	$375	$325	$275	$225

Last MSR was $800.

RGX 820 R - offset double cutaway basswood body, bolt-on maple neck, 22-fret rosewood fingerboard with green dot inlay, double locking vibrato, reverse peghead, 6-on-a-side tuners, black hardware, 2 humbucker pickups, volume control, 3-position switch, available in Black, Green Plaid, or Red Metallic finishes, mfg. 1993-95.

	N/A	$700	$600	$525	$450	$375	$300

Last MSR was $1,050.

RGX 821 - offset double cutaway alder body, bolt-on maple neck, 24-fret rosewood fingerboard with abalone oval inlay (fingerboard is scalloped from the 20th to the 24th fret), double locking vibrato, 6-on-a-side tuners, gold hardware, humbucker/single coil/humbucker pickups, volume/tone controls, 5-position switch, available in Antique Sunburst, Blackburst, Faded Blue, or Violetburst finishes, mfg. 1994-96.

	N/A	$650	$550	$475	$400	$325	$250

Last MSR was $1,000.

ELECTRIC: SA SERIES

SA 500 - double cutaway archtop semi-hollow electric maple body, two custom f-holes, body and neck binding, set mahogany neck, 22-fret rosewood fingerboard with dot inlay, three-per-side tuners, original AES bridge, raised pickguard, two humbucker pickups, four knobs, three-way switch, chrome hardware, available in Black or Brown Sunburst finishes, new 2005.

MSR	$600	$450	$390	$340	$300	$250	$200	$160

Yamaha RGX 421 D courtesy Yamaha

SA 800 - dual cutaway semi-hollowbody, laminated beech/birch top/back, alder center block, laminated mahogany/birch sides, bound body, 2 f-holes, mahogany neck, 22-fret bound rosewood fingerboard with pearl dot inlay, tunomatic bridge/stop tailpiece, 3-per-side tuners, chrome hardware, raised black pickguard, 2 covered humbucker pickups, 2 volume/2 tone controls, 3-position toggle switch, available in Black, Natural, or Wine Red finishes, mfg. 1983-89.

	N/A	$600	$525	$450	$375	$300	$225

Last MSR was $699.

SA 1100 - double cutaway semi-hollowbody, laminated maple top/back/sides, bound body, raised black pickguard, mahogany neck, 22-fret bound rosewood fingerboard with pearl dot inlay, bridge/stop tailpiece, 3-per-side tuners, chrome hardware, 2 humbucker pickups, 2 volume/tone controls, 3-position switch, coil split in tone controls, available in Black, Brown Sunburst, Natural, or Orange Sunburst finishes, disc. 1994.

	N/A	$800	$700	$600	$525	$450	$375

Last MSR was $1,050.

SA 2000 - similar to SA 1100, except has curly maple top, ebony fingerboard with abalone split block inlay, bound peghead with abalone Yamaha logo/stylized inlay, gold hardware, available in Brown Sunburst or Violin Sunburst finishes, mfg. 1981-89.

	N/A	$1,000	$850	$725	$600	$500	$400

Last MSR was $995.

Add $100 for left-handed configuration (Model SA 2000 L). Mfg. 1982 to 1989.

Early versions feature a laminated beech/birch top and back.

SA 2100 - similar to SA 1100, except has laminated beech/birch top and back, 2 covered Alnico humbucker pickups, ebony fingerboard with abalone split block inlay, bound peghead with abalone Yamaha logo/stylized inlay, gold hardware, available in Brown Sunburst or Violin Sunburst finishes, mfg. 1985-86.

	N/A	$1,000	$850	$725	$600	$500	$400

Last MSR was $1,299.

SA 2200 - similar to SA 1100, except has flame maple top, maple neck, ebony fingerboard with abalone split block inlay, bound peghead with abalone Yamaha logo/stylized inlay, gold hardware, available in Brown Sunburst or Violin Sunburst finishes, mfg. 1992-present.

MSR	$2,300	$1,800	$1,275	$1,075	$925	$775	$670	$575

ELECTRIC: SBG SERIES

In the 1980s, Yamaha introduced the SG (Solid Body Guitar) models. Guitar fans familiar with those specific initials will recognize that this situation wouldn´t last long! The SG Series later became the SBG (Solid Body Guitar) Series.

SBG 500 - dual pointed cutaway agathis body, bound carved maple top, maple neck, 24.75 in. scale, 22-fret bound rosewood fingerboard with pearl dot inlay, tune-o-matic bridge/stop tailpiece, 3-per-side tuners, chrome hardware, 2 exposed pole piece humbucker pickups, 2 volume/2 tone controls, 3-way toggle switch, available in Burgundy or Brown Sunburst finishes, mfg. 1981-83.

	N/A	$350	$300	$250	$210	$180	$150

Last MSR was $550.

Add $60 for left-handed configuration (Model SBG 550 L).

Yamaha RGX 621 D courtesy Yamaha

GRADING	100% MINT	98% NEAR MINT	95% EXC+	90% EXC	80% VG+	70% VG	60% G

SBG 500 B - dual pointed cutaway nato body, bound body, bolt-on nato neck, 24.75 in. scale, 22-fret rosewood fingerboard with pearl dot inlay, tunomatic bridge/stop tailpiece, 3-per-side tuners, chrome hardware, 2 exposed pole piece humbucker pickups, 2 volume/2 tone controls, 3-way toggle switch, available in Black, Cherry Sunburst, or Gold finishes, mfg. 1998-2003.

	$550	$495	$450	$400	$350	$300	$250

Last MSR was $739.

SBG 700 S - dual pointed cutaway mahogany body, bound body, set-in mahogany neck, 24.75 in. scale, 22-fret rosewood fingerboard with pearl dot inlay, tune-o-matic bridge/stop tailpiece, 3-per-side tuners, gold hardware, 2 exposed pole piece humbucker pickups, 2 volume/2 tone controls (with coil tap capabilities), 3-way toggle switch, available in Black, Brown Sunburst, Cherry Sunburst, or Trans. Green finishes, mfg. 1998-2003.

	$1,050	$925	$875	$795	$725	$675	$625

Last MSR was $1,399.

Brown Sunburst finish discontinued 2000.

SBG 1000 - dual pointed cutaway mahogany body, bound carved maple top, set-in mahogany neck, 24.75 in. scale, 22-fret bound rosewood fingerboard with pearl split triangle inlay, tune-o-matic bridge/stop tailpiece, 3-per-side tuners, bound headstock, chrome hardware, black pickguard, 2 humbucker pickups, 2 volume/2 tone controls (with coil tap capabilities), 3-way toggle switch, available in Black or Cherry Sunburst finishes, mfg. 1982-989.

	N/A	$600	$500	$425	$350	$275	$200

Last MSR was $795.

Add $105 for left-handed configuration (Model SBG 1000 L).

SBG 2000 - similar to SBG 1000, except features set-in laminated maple/mahogany neck, 22-fret bound ebony fingerboard with pearl split triangle inlay, available in Black, Brown Sunburst, Cherry Sunburst, or Deep Green finishes, mfg. 1981-89.

	N/A	$800	$700	$600	$525	$450	$375

Last MSR was $1,045.

Add $130 for left-handed configuration (Model SBG 2000 L).

SBG 3000 - similar to SBG 1000, except features Mexican abalone body binding, set-in laminated maple/mahogany neck, 22-fret bound ebony fingerboard with mother-of-pearl/Mexican abalone split triangle inlay, gold hardware, engraved stop tailpiece, available in Metallic Black, Metallic Gold, or Wine Red finishes, mfg. 1983-89.

	N/A	$1,000	$850	$725	$600	$500	$400

Last MSR was $1,295.

This model was equipped with an optional brass pickguard (to replace the factory installed black plastic pickguard).

ELECTRIC: SC SERIES

SC Series instruments have a body style reminiscent of a "flipped over" Strat, with the treble bout horn extending further out than the bass horn.

SC 400 - (reversed) offset double cutaway mahogany and ash body, through body mahogany neck, 25.5 in. scale, 22-fret rosewood fingerboard with pearl dot inlay, fixed bridge, 6-on-a-side tuners, chrome hardware, 3 Alnico 5 single coil pickups, volume/tone controls, 5-way selector switch, available in Persimmon Red or Oil Stain finishes, mfg. 1982-83.

	N/A	$300	$250	$210	$180	$150	$120

Last MSR was $475.

SC 600 - similar to SC 400, except features a maple/mahogany/ash/alder laminated body, maple/mahogany neck, available in Persimmon Red or Oil Stain finishes, mfg. 1982-83.

	N/A	$350	$300	$250	$210	$180	$150

Last MSR was $615.

ELECTRIC: SGV SERIES

Reintroduction of a mid-60´s design with updated features.

SGV 300 - offset double cutaway alder body, maple neck with rosewood fingerboard, dot position markers, 22 frets, 6-on-a-side tuners, Yamaha original ball bearing tremolo system, 3 Yamaha single coil pickups, volume, tone, balance controls, 3-way switch, available in Black, Red Metallic, Pearl Green, or Canary Yellow finishes, disc. 2003.

	$385	$325	$275	$225	$200	$150	$125

Last MSR was $549.

SGV 800 - similar to SGV 300 except, has 2 single coil Alnico-5 pickups, 2 volume/1 tone control, pearloid pickguard, available in Black Sparkle, Blue Sparkle, or Red Sparkle finishes, disc. 2003.

	$489	$425	$375	$325	$275	$225	$175

Last MSR was $699.

ELECTRIC: SHB & SSC SERIES

SHB 400 - offset double cutaway alder body, maple neck, 24.75 in. scale, 22-fret rosewood fingerboard with pearl dot inlay, fixed bridge, 3-per-side tuners, chrome hardware, 2 exposed pole piece humbucker pickups, volume/tone controls, 3-way toggle switch, available in Chestnut and Natural finishes, mfg. 1981-83.

	N/A	$350	$300	$250	$210	$180	$150

Last MSR was $450.

GRADING	100% MINT	98% NEAR MINT	95% EXC+	90% EXC	80% VG+	70% VG	60% G

SSC 500 - offset double cutaway alder body, maple neck, 25.5 in. scale, 21-fret rosewood fingerboard with pearl dot inlay, fixed bridge, 3-per-side tuners, chrome hardware, 3 bar-magnet single coil pickups, volume/tone controls, 3 mini-toggle pickup selector switches, available in Burgundy, Brown Sunburst, or Natural finishes, mfg. 1981-83.

| | N/A | $400 | $350 | $300 | $250 | $210 | $180 |

Last MSR was $550.

ELECTRIC: WEDDINGTON SERIES

SPECIAL - single cutaway mahogany body, set in mahogany neck, 22-fret rosewood fingerboard with pearl dot inlay, adjustable bar bridge/tailpiece, 3-per-side tuners, chrome hardware, 2 humbucker DiMarzio pickups, 2 volume/tone controls, 5-position switch with coil split, available in Black, Cherry, or Cream White finishes, disc. 1994.

| | N/A | $625 | $550 | $400 | $350 | $325 | $300 |

Last MSR was $1,000.

CLASSIC - similar to Special, except has arched bound maple top, bound fingerboard with pearl split block inlay, pearl Yamaha symbol and stylized oval inlay on peghead and tune-o-matic bridge/stop tailpiece, available in Cherry Sunburst, Metallic Black, or Metallic Red top/Natural sides finishes, disc. 1995.

| | N/A | $800 | $650 | $575 | $500 | $425 | $350 |

Last MSR was $1,600.

CUSTOM - similar to Classic, except has figured maple top, mahogany/maple neck, ebony fingerboard with pearl/abalone inlay, ebony veneer on peghead with pearl Yamaha symbol and stylized scroll inlay, available in Cherry, Faded Burst, or Roseburst finishes, disc. 1995.

| | N/A | $1,000 | $850 | $725 | $600 | $500 | $400 |

Last MSR was $2,200.

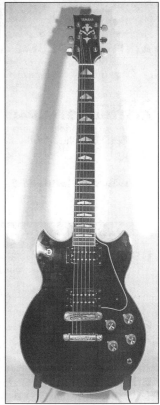

Yamaha SG-2000 courtesy San Diego Guitars

ELECTRIC BASS: ATTITUDE SERIES

ATTITUDE CUSTOM - offset double cutaway alder body, white pickguard, bolt-on maple neck, 21-fret maple fingerboard with offset black slot inlay, solid brass fixed bridge with 4 built-in piezo electric pickups, 4-on-a-side tuners, chrome hardware, woofer/P-style/piezo DiMarzio pickups, volume/tone control, mini toggle pickup selector switch, stereo outputs, available in Crimson Red, Dark Blue Metallic, or Light Violet Metallic finishes, disc. 1996.

| | N/A | $1,000 | $850 | $725 | $600 | $500 | $400 |

Last MSR was $1,500.

ATTITUDE DELUXE - offset double cutaway alder body, white pickguard, bolt-on maple neck, 21-fret rosewood fingerboard with pearl dot inlay, fixed bridge, 4-on-a-side tuners, chrome hardware, Yamaha "Six Pack" pickup, volume/tone control, 5-position switch, available in Metallic Black, Metallic Red, Pacific Blue, or White finishes, disc. 1994.

| | N/A | $550 | $475 | $400 | $350 | $300 | $250 |

Last MSR was $900.

ATTITUDE LIMITED - offset double cutaway alder body, white pickguard, bolt-on maple neck, 34 in. scale, 21-fret maple fingerboard with offset black slot inlay, solid brass fixed bridge, 4-on-a-side tuners, "Hipshot" XTender, chrome hardware, Dimarzio bass pickups, 2 volume/tone controls, mini-toggle pickup select switches, stereo outputs, available in Lightning Red or Thunder Blue finishes, disc. 1992.

| | N/A | $1,200 | $1,000 | $850 | $700 | $575 | $450 |

Last MSR was $1,800.

The Attitude Limited was designed in conjunction with bassist Billy Sheehan (Mr. Big).

ATTITUDE LIMITED II BILLY SHEEHAN SIGNATURE MODEL - similar to Limited, except has pearloid pickguard, scalloped fingerboard from 17th through 21st fret, black hardware, available in Black and Sea Foam Green finishes, mfg. 1994-present.

| MSR | $1,899 | $1,350 | $1,100 | $950 | $775 | $650 | $575 | $450 |

The Limited II was designed in conjunction with bassist Billy Sheehan (Mr. Big).

ATTITUDE X BILLY SHEEHAN 10TH ANNIVERSARY MODEL - similar to Limited Edition II except, features position markers that are Billy's fingerprints, pearloid pickguard, available in Purple Metallic or Black Metallic, commemorates the 10th anniversary of the Attitude line, mfg. 2001-03.

| $1,399 | $1,199 | $1,099 | $999 | $899 | $799 | $650 |

Last MSR was $1,999.

ATTITUDE PLUS - offset double cutaway alder body, white pickguard, bolt-on maple neck, 21-fret rosewood fingerboard with pearl dot inlay, fixed bridge, 4-on-a-side tuners, chrome hardware, P-style pickup, volume/tone control, available in Black, Sea Foam Green, or Red finishes, disc. 2003.

| $295 | $250 | $225 | $195 | $175 | $150 | $95 |

Last MSR was $399.

Yamaha Attitude Limited II courtesy Yamaha

GRADING	100% MINT	98% NEAR MINT	95% EXC+	90% EXC	80% VG+	70% VG	60% G

ATTITUDE SPECIAL - offset double cutaway alder body, white pickguard, bolt-on maple neck, 21-fret maple fingerboard with offset black slot inlay, fixed bridge, 4-on-a-side tuners, chrome hardware, DiMarzio Woofer/DiMarzio P-style pickups, 2 volume/1 tone controls, available in Black, Lightning Red, Sea Foam Green, or Thunder Blue finishes, mfg. 1994-96.

	N/A	$450	$375	$325	$275	$225	$175

Last MSR was $700.

ATTITUDE STANDARD - offset double cutaway alder body, white pickguard, bolt-on maple neck, 21-fret rosewood fingerboard with pearl dot inlay, fixed bridge, 4-on-a-side tuners, chrome hardware, P/J-style pickups, volume/tone control, 3-position switch, available in Black Pearl, Crimson Red, Dark Blue Metallic, or White finishes, disc. 1996.

	N/A	$550	$475	$400	$350	$300	$250

Last MSR was $800.

Attitude Standard 5 - similar to Standard, except in 5-string configuration, 4/1 per side tuners, disc. 1994.

	N/A	$600	$525	$450	$375	$325	$275

Last MSR was $930.

ELECTRIC BASS: BB SERIES

BB200 - offset double cutaway alder body, bolt-on maple neck, 21-fret rosewood fingerboard with pearl dot tuners, fixed bridge, 4-on-a-side tuners, chrome hardware, P-style pickup, volume/tone control, available in Black, Vivid Red, or White finishes, disc. 1994.

	N/A	$300	$250	$210	$180	$150	$120

Last MSR was $370.

This model was optional with a fretless fingerboard (Model BB200 F).

BB300 - similar to BB200, except has redesigned bridge, disc. 1994.

	N/A	$350	$300	$250	$210	$180	$150

Last MSR was $430.

This model was optional in a left-handed version (Model BB300 L).

BB350 - offset double cutaway alder body, bolt-on maple neck, 21-fret rosewood fingerboard with pearl dot inlay, fixed bridge, 4-on-a-side tuners, chrome hardware, 2 J-style pickups, 2 volume/tone controls, available in Black, Blue Metallic, Natural, or Vintage Red finishes, mfg. 1994-96.

	N/A	$350	$300	$50	$210	$180	$150

Last MSR was $500.

BB400 - offset double cutaway alder body, bolt-on maple neck, 33.875 in. scale, 21-fret rosewood fingerboard with pearl dot tuners, fixed bridge, 4-on-a-side tuners, chrome hardware, P-style pickup, volume/tone control, available in Chestnut or Natural finishes, mfg. 1981-83.

	N/A	$500	$425	$350	$300	$250	$200

Last MSR was $450.

Add $50 for a left-handed configuration (Model BB400 L).

BB 414 - offset double cutaway alder body, bolt-on maple neck, 21-fret rosewood fingerboard with wide oval inlays, four-on-one-side tuners, vintage style bridge, one single split and one soapbar pickups, two knobs, three-way switch, chrome hardware, available in Black Pearl, Metallic Orange, or Wine Red finishes, new 2005.

MSR	$600	$420	$350	$300	$260	$230	$190	$160

Add $25 for left-handed configuration.

BB 415 - similar to the BB 414, except in five-string configuration, 3/2-per-side tuners, new 2005.

MSR	$650	$450	$375	$325	$275	$235	$190	$160

BB 614 - offset double cutaway alder body, bolt-on maple neck, 21-fret rosewood fingerboard with wide oval inlays, four-on-one-side tuners, vintage style bridge, one single split and one soapbar pickups, five knobs, chrome hardware, available in Black Pearl, Pewter, or Yellow Natural finishes, 34 in. scale, new 2005.

MSR	$700	$500	$425	$375	$325	$275	$235	$190

Add $25 for left-handed configuration. Add $25 for fretless configuration.

BB1000 S - offset double cutaway alder, laminated maple/mahogany through-body neck, 33.875 in. scale, 21-fret rosewood fingerboard with pearl dot tuners, fixed bridge, 4-on-a-side tuners, chrome hardware, P/J-style pickups, volume/tone controls, 3-way selector toggle, available in Persimmon Red or Brown Stain finishes, mfg. 1982-89.

	N/A	$550	$475	$400	$350	$300	$250

Last MSR was $720.

This model may also have a maple or mahogany body.

BB 615 - similar to the BB 614, except in five-string configuration, 4/1-per-side tuners, new 2005.

MSR	$750	$525	$450	$400	$350	$300	$250	$200

BB1200 S - similar to the BB1000 S, except features an ebony fingerboard with pearl oval inlays, P-style pickup, 3-band EQ, on/off mini-switch, available in Burgundy or Deep Green finishes, mfg. 1982-89.

	N/A	$600	$525	$450	$375	$300	$250

Last MSR was $850.

This model was optional with a fretless fingerboard (Model BB1200 S F).

GRADING		100% MINT	98% NEAR MINT	95% EXC+	90% EXC	80% VG+	70% VG	60% G

BB1500 A - offset double cutaway alder body, black lam pickguard, bolt-on maple neck, 21-fret rosewood fingerboard with pearl dot inlay, brass fixed bridge, 4-on-a-side tuners, gold hardware, 2 stacked humbucker pickups, volume/treble/mid/bass/mix controls, active electronics, available in Black pearl, Natural, or Wine Red finishes, mfg. 1994-96.

		N/A	$650	$550	$475	$400	$325	$275

Last MSR was $1,000.

This model was optional with a fretless fingerboard (Model BB1500 A F).

BB2000 - offset double cutaway alder body, laminated maple/mahogany through-body neck, 33.875 in. scale, 21-fret ebony fingerboard with pearl oval tuners, fixed bridge, 4-on-a-side tuners, chrome hardware, P/bar-magnet J-style pickups, volume/tone controls, 3-way selector toggle, available in Natural or Brown Stain finishes, mfg. 1982-89.

		N/A	$600	$525	$450	$375	$300	$250

Last MSR was $989.

Add $100 for a left-handed configuration (Model BB2000 L). Mfg. 1983 to 1989.

This model was optional with a fretless fingerboard (Model BB2000 F).

BB 2004 - offset double cutaway Nathan East style alder and maple body, maple/premium grade mahogany neck-thru body, 24-fret rosewood fingerboard with block inlay, matching headstock with two-per-side tuners, individual string bridge, one split single-coil and one single coil pickups, five knobs, chrome hardware, available in Black, Natural Satin, or White finishes, mfg. 2004-present.

MSR	$1,800		$1,300	$1,100	$950	$825	$700	$600	$500

BB 2005 - similar to the five-string configuration, 3/2-per-side tuners, mfg. 2004-present.

MSR	$2,000		$1,400	$1,200	$1,050	$900	$800	$700	$600

BB3000MA MICHAEL ANTHONY SIGNATURE MODEL - offset double cutaway neck-through body design, 4-on-a-side tuners, nickel hardware, Hipshot D-Tuner, custom chile pepper position markers, available in Black or Green finishes, mfg. 2001-present.

MSR	$3,300		$2,300	$2,000	$1,700	$1,500	$1,300	$1,100	$900

BB5000 A - offset double cutaway alder body, mahogany/maple through body neck, 24-fret ebony fingerboard with pearl oval inlay, 5-string fixed bridge, 4/1-per-side tuners, brass hardware, P/J-style pickups, volume/tone/mix controls, active electronics, available in Cream White, Gun Metal Blue or Purple Pearl finishes, disc. 1994.

		N/A	$1,200	$1,000	$850	$700	$575	$450

Last MSR was $1,700.

Yamaha BB East courtesy Yamaha

BB EAST (NATHAN EAST SIGNATURE) - offset double cutaway alder body, figured maple top, bolt-on maple neck, 24-fret ebony fingerboard with pearl block inlay, brass fixed bridge, figured maple veneered peghead with screened artist's signature/logo, 3/2-per-side tuners, gold hardware, 2 humbucker pickups, volume/treble/mid/bass/mix controls, active electronics, available in Amberburst or Trans. Blue finishes, mfg. 1994-present.

MSR	$3,500		$2,500	$2,100	$1,800	$1,600	$1,400	$1,200	$1,000

This model was co-designed by bassist Nathan East.

BB G 4 - offset double cutaway alder body with high definition top, bolt-on maple neck, 24-fret rosewood fingerboard with pearl dot inlay, vintage-style fixed bridge, 2-per-side tuners, gold hardware, 2 single coil pickups, volume/tone/blend controls, available in High Definition Amber Burst, or High Definition Trans. Blue finishes, disc.

		$495	$395	$350	$300	$275	$225	$175

Last MSR was $649.

BB G 4 S - BBN4 upgraded with active electronics, 2 active humbuckers, gold hardware, volume, pan, bass, treble boost/cut, die-cast bridge, available in Sunburst, Blue, Pearl Snow White, or Black, disc. 2003.

		$450	$375	$295	$275	$225	$195	$165

Last MSR was $649.

BB G 5 - similar to the BB G 4, except features a 5-string configuration, 3/2-per-side tuners, available in High Definition Amber Burst or High Definition Trans. Blue finishes, disc.

		$525	$450	$375	$325	$295	$250	$195

Last MSR was $699.

BB G 5 S - BBN5 upgraded with active electronics, 2 active humbuckers, gold hardware, volume, pan, bass, treble boost/cut, die-cast bridge, available in Sunburst, Blue, Pearl Snow White, or Black finishes, disc. 2003.

		$525	$425	$375	$325	$295	$250	$195

Last MSR was $699.

BB N 4 - offset double cutaway alder body, bolt-on maple neck, 24-fret rosewood fingerboard with pearl dot inlay, vintage-style fixed bridge, 2-per-side tuners, chrome hardware, 2 single coil pickups, volume/tone/blend controls, available in Black, Brown Satin, or Natural Satin finishes, disc. 2003.

		$425	$325	$295	$250	$225	$175	$145

Last MSR was $549.

Add $80 for left-handed configuration (Model BB N 4 L). Fretless fingerboard available at no extra cost (Model BB N 4 F).

BB N 5 - similar to the BB N 4, except features a 5-string configuration, 3/2-per-side tuners, available in Black, Brown Satin, or Natural Satin finishes, disc. 2003.

		$425	$350	$275	$250	$200	$175	$150

Last MSR was $599.

Yamaha BBN5 Bass courtesy John Beeson The Music Shoppe

GRADING	100% MINT	98% NEAR MINT	95% EXC+	90% EXC	80% VG+	70% VG	60% G

BB N 5 A - similar to the BB N 4, except features figured maple top, 5-string configuration, 3/2-per-side tuners, 2 Alnico active single pickups with dummy coils, master volume, pan, bass cut/boost, treble cut/boost, 3 band EQ controls, active electronics, available in Amber Burst or Trans. Blue finishes, disc.

		$1,125	$950	$850	$750	$700	$600	$500

Last MSR was $1,499.

ELECTRIC BASS: BEX SERIES

BEX 4C - single cutaway hollow alder body, rosewood fingerboard with dot position markers, 21 frets, rosewood bridge, 1 humbucker pickup and 1 piezo pickup on the bridge, Master Volume, Balance, 3 band EQ, available in Dark Blue Burst, Orange Stain, or Brown Sunburst finish, mfg. 2001-present.

MSR	$1,050	$750	$650	$575	$500	$425	$375	$325

BEX-BS BILLY SHEEHAN - single sharp cutaway semi-hollow alder and birch body with a maple top, two custom f-holes, bolt-on maple neck, 21-fret rosewood fingerboard with mulitple dot inlays, two-per-side tuners, standard bridge, two humbucker pickups, four knobs, chrome hardware, available in Magenta finish, mfg. 2004-present.

MSR	$1,400	$1,000	$875	$775	$700	$625	$550	$475

ELECTRIC BASS: RBX SERIES

RBX 6 JM JOHN MYUNG SIGNATURE MODEL - double cutaway alder body with figured maple veneer, maple neck, ebony fingerboard with abalone "infinity" inlays, 24 frets, 2 active double coil pickups, volume, pan, bass, treble boost/cut, solid brass bridge, gold hardware, 35 in. scale, available in Turquoise Blue or Ruby Red finishes, current mfg.

MSR	$1,600	$1,125	$995	$900	$850	$795	$750	$650

RBX 170 - offset double cutaway agathis body, bolt-on maple neck, 24-fret rosewood fingerboard with dot inlay, two-per-side tuners, standard bridge, one split single coil and one regular single coil pickups, three knobs, black chrome hardware, available in Black, Metallc Dark Blue, or Metallic Red finishes, mfg. 2004-present.

MSR	$280	$200	$160	$130	$110	$90	$70	$50

RBX 250 - offset double cutaway alder body, bolt-on maple neck, 22-fret rosewood fingerboard with pearl dot inlay, fixed bridge, 4-on-a-side tuners, chrome hardware, P-style pickup, volume/tone controls, available in Black, Blue Indo, Crimson Red, Lightning Blue, Natural, or Pearl Snow White finishes, disc. 1996.

		N/A	$250	$210	$180	$150	$120	$90

Last MSR was $330.

RBX 350 - similar to RBX 250, except has P/J-style pickups, volume/tone/mix controls, available in Aqua, Black, Blue Indo, Brown Stain, Crimson Red, Lightning Blue, or Pearl Snow White finishes, disc. 1996.

		N/A	$300	$250	$210	$180	$150	$120

Last MSR was $400.

RBX 350 L - similar to RBX 350, except has left-handed configuration, disc. 1996.

		N/A	$325	$275	$225	$180	$150	$120

Last MSR was $520.

RBX 260 - offset double cutaway alder body, bolt-on maple neck, 24-fret rosewood fingerboard with pearl dot inlay, low mass fixed bridge, 2-per-side tuners, chrome hardware, P-style pickup, volume/tone controls, available in Black, Red, Blue Satin, or Natural Satin finishes, mfg. 1996-2000.

	$250	$200	$175	$150	$125	$100	$95

Last MSR was $349.

This model is optional with a fretless fingerboard (Model RBX 260 F) MSR $429. Available in left-handed configuration (Model RBX 260 L) MSR $449.

RBX 360 - similar to RBX 260, except has P/J-style pickups, volume/tone/pan controls, available in Black or Brown Satin finishes, mfg. 1996-2003.

	$380	$295	$275	$250	$195	$165	$125

Last MSR was $499.

Add $90 for left-handed configuration (Model RBX 360 L). Disc. 1999.

RBX 374 - offset double cutaway alder body, bolt-on maple neck, 24-fret rosewood fingerboard with dot inlay, matching 3-D headstock with two-per-side tuners, standard bridge, two humbucker pickups, four knobs, black hardware, available in Black, Flat Silver, or Metallic Red finishes, mfg. 2004-present.

MSR	$550	$390	$330	$280	$240	$200	$160	$130

RBX 375 - similar to the RBX 374, except in five-string configuration, 3/2-per-side tuners, mfg. 2004-present.

MSR	$600	$420	$350	$300	$250	$220	$180	$150

RBX 460 - offset double cutaway alder body with high definition top, bolt-on maple neck, 24-fret rosewood fingerboard with pearl dot inlay, low mass fixed bridge, 2-per-side tuners, gold hardware, P/J-style pickups, volume/tone/blend controls, available in Trans. Blue or Trans. Red finishes, disc.

	$450	$350	$300	$275	$225	$195	$150

Last MSR was $579.

RBX 650 - similar to RBX 350, except has black hardware, available in Black Pearl, Dark Blue Metallic, Faded Blue, Natural, or Red Metallic finishes, mfg. 1992-96.

		N/A	$450	$375	$325	$275	$235	$195

Last MSR was $700.

GRADING	100% MINT	98% NEAR MINT	95% EXC+	90% EXC	80% VG+	70% VG	60% G

RBX 760 A - offset double cutaway alder body, ash veneer top, bolt-on maple neck, 24-fret rosewood fingerboard with pearl dot inlay, low mass fixed bridge, 2-per-side tuners, gold hardware, 2 humbucker pickups, volume/blend/bass/treble controls, active electronics, available in Trans. Blue, Trans. Green, or Trans. Red finishes, disc. 2003.

| | $565 | $445 | $395 | $345 | $285 | $235 | $185 |

Last MSR was $749.

Add $100 for 5-string configuration, 3/2-per-side tuners (Model RBX 765 A).

RBX1000 - offset double cutaway sculpted ash body, bolt-on maple neck, 24-fret rosewood fingerboard with pearl dot inlay, fixed brass bridge, 4-on-a-side tuners, chrome hardware, P/J-style pickups, volume/treble/bass/mix controls, active electronics, available in Blue Stain, Brown Stain, Natural, Trans. Black, or Trans. Violet finishes, disc. 1996.

| | N/A | $700 | $600 | $525 | $450 | $375 | $300 |

Last MSR was $1,100.

ELECTRIC BASS: SBV SERIES

SBV 500 - reintroduction of a mid-60s design, offset radical double cutaway alder body, bolt-on neck, rosewood fingerboard, dot position markers, 20 frets, Vintage bridge, 2 Felight single coil pickups, 2 volume/1 tone control, available in Red Metallic, Shelby Blue, or Canary Yellow, 34 in. scale, disc. 2003.

| | $419 | $350 | $295 | $250 | $195 | $150 | $95 |

Last MSR was $599.

ELECTRIC BASS: TRB SERIES

TRB 4 - offset double cutaway carved ash body, bolt-on maple neck, 34 in. scale, 24-fret rosewood fingerboard with pearl dot inlay, brass fixed bridge, 2-per-side brass tuners, gold hardware, 2 stacked humbucker pickups, volume/treble/mid/bass/mix controls, active electronics, available in Blue Stain, Brown Stain, Cherry Sunburst, or Natural finishes, mfg. 1994-98.

| | $1,200 | $900 | $750 | $600 | $550 | $495 | $450 |

Last MSR was $1,599.

**Yamaha RBX 350 II
courtesy Yamaha**

TRB 4 P - similar to TRB 4, except features an offset double cutaway figured maple/rosewood/maple body, maple/mahogany neck-through body, 34 in. scale, 24-fret ebony fingerboard with pearl dot inlay, solid brass bridge, 2-per-side brass tuners, P/J-style/piezo bridge pickups, volume/treble/bass/2 mix controls, piezo pickup switch, available in Red Blonde, Trans. Blue, or Trans. Red Sunburst finishes, disc. 1994.

| | N/A | $1,200 | $1,000 | $800 | $720 | $660 | $600 |

Last MSR was $2,000.

TRB 4 II - offset double cutaway ash body, maple neck, 35 in. scale, 24-fret rosewood fingerboard with pearl dot inlay, fixed brass bridge, 2-per-side tuners, gold hardware, 2 humbucker pickups, volume/pan/treble cut and boost/mid/bass controls, available in Amber Burst, Trans. Blue Burst, or Magenta Burst finishes, mfg. 1998-present.

| MSR | $1,600 | $1,195 | $1,000 | $900 | $800 | $700 | $650 | $575 |

TRB 5 - offset double cutaway carved ash body, bolt-on maple neck, 34 in. scale, 24-fret rosewood fingerboard with pearl dot inlay, brass fixed bridge, 3/2-per-side brass tuners, gold hardware, 2 stacked humbucker pickups, volume/treble/mid/bass/mix controls, active electronics, available in Amber Stain, Blue Stain, Charcoal Gray, or Cherry Sunburst finishes, mfg. 1994-98.

| | $1,250 | $950 | $800 | $650 | $575 | $525 | $475 |

Last MSR was $1,699.

TRB5 P - similar to TRB5, except features an offset double cutaway figured maple/rosewood/maple body, maple/mahogany through body neck, 34 in. scale, 24-fret ebony fingerboard with pearl dot inlay, solid brass bridge, 3/2-per-side brass tuners, P/J-style/piezo bridge pickups, volume/treble/bass/2 mix controls, piezo pickup switch, available in Red Blonde, Trans. Blue, or Trans. Red Sunburst finishes, disc. 1996.

| | N/A | $1,250 | $1,150 | $925 | $825 | $750 | $695 |

Last MSR was $2,500.

TRB 5 II - offset double cutaway ash body, maple neck, 35 in. scale, 24-fret rosewood fingerboard with pearl dot inlay, fixed brass bridge, 3/2-per-side tuners, gold hardware, 2 humbucker pickups, volume/pan/treble cut and boost/mid/bass controls, available in Amber Burst, Trans. Blue Burst, or Magenta Burst finishes, mfg. 1998-present.

| MSR | $1,700 | $1,250 | $1,050 | $950 | $850 | $800 | $695 | $625 |

TRB 5 F II - similar to the TRB 5 II, except features a fretless fingerboard, available in Amber Burst, Trans. Blue, Burst, or Magenta finishes, mfg. 1998-present.

| MSR | $1,800 | $1,375 | $1,100 | $950 | $850 | $800 | $750 | $625 |

In 1999, Magenta finish was discontinued.

TRB 5 P II - similar to Model TRB 5 F II except, available with maple, bubinga or ovankol top, neck-through body, ebony fingerboard, Yamaha BPZ bridge, 2 double coil Alnico V pickups plus piezo pickup, 3-band EQ, pickup balance control, available in Natural finish, current mfg.

| MSR | $4,000 | $2,799 | $2,499 | $2,199 | $1,899 | $1,599 | $1,299 | $999 |

TRB 5 L II - similar to the TRB 5 II, except features a left-handed configuration, available in Amber Burst, Trans. Blue Burst, or Magenta finishes, mfg. 1998-present.

| MSR | $1,900 | $1,425 | $1,150 | $995 | $850 | $750 | $695 | $625 |

In 1999, Magenta finish was discontinued.

**Yamaha TRB 6
courtesy Yamaha**

GRADING	100% MINT	98% NEAR MINT	95% EXC+	90% EXC	80% VG+	70% VG	60% G

TRB 6 - offset double cutaway carved ash body, bolt-on maple neck, 34 in. scale, 24-fret rosewood fingerboard with pearl dot inlay, brass fixed bridge, 3-per-side brass tuners, gold hardware, 2 stacked humbucker pickups, volume/treble/mid/bass/mix controls, active electronics, available in Amber Stain or Charcoal Gray finishes, mfg. 1994-98.

		$1,300	$1,000	$900	$725	$650	$595	$550

Last MSR was $1,999.

TRB6 P - similar to TRB6, except features an offset double cutaway figured maple/rosewood/maple body, maple/mahogany through body neck, 34 in. scale, 24-fret ebony fingerboard with pearl dot inlay, solid brass bridge, 3-per-side brass tuners, 2 J-style/piezo bridge pickups, volume/treble/bass/2 mix controls, piezo pickup switch, available in Red Blonde, Trans. Blue, or Trans. Red Sunburst finishes, disc. 1996.

		N/A	$1,400	$1,200	$1,000	$925	$850	$750

Last MSR was $2,700.

TRB 6 II - offset double cutaway ash body, maple neck, 35 in. scale, 24-fret rosewood fingerboard with pearl dot inlay, fixed brass bridge, 3-per-side tuners, gold hardware, 2 humbucker pickups, volume/pan/treble cut and boost/mid/bass controls, available in Amber Burst, Trans. Blue Burst, or Magenta finishes, mfg. 1998-present.

MSR	$2,000	$1,495	$1,295	$1,150	$1,050	$925	$875	$675

TRB 6P II - similar to Model TRB 6 II except, has choice of maple, bubinga or ovankol top, neck-through body, ebony fingerboard, 2 Double Coil Alnico V pickups plue piezo pickup mounted on the bridge, volume, balance, piezo volume and 3-band EQ, available in natural finish, current mfg.

MSR	$4,400	$3,079	$2,775	$2,475	$2,175	$1,875	$1,575	$1,275

TRB 1005 - offset double cutaway maple and alder body, bolt-on maple neck, 24-fret rosewood fingerboard with dot pearl inlays, matching headstock with 3/2-per-side tuners, individual bridge, two Alnico hum-cancelling pickups, six knobs, gold and black hardware, available in Natural, Trans. Black, or Trans. Dark Red finishes, new 2005.

MSR	$1,300	$925	$800	$700	$625	$550	$475	$400

Add $75 for fretless configuration. Add $75 for left-handed configuration.

TRB 1006 - similar to the TRB 1005, except has six strings, three-per-side tuners, new 2005.

MSR	$1,450	$1,025	$900	$800	$700	$625	$550	$475

TRB JP (JOHN PATITUCCI SIGNATURE) - offset double cutaway alder body, carved figured maple top, bolt-on maple neck, 34 in.3 scale, 24-fret ebony fingerboard with pearl 3/4 oval inlay, brass fixed bridge, figured maple veneered peghead with screened artist's signature/logo, 3-per-side brass tuners, gold hardware, 2 stacked humbucker pickups, volume/treble/mid/bass/mix controls, active electronics, available in Amber Stain or Charcoal Gray finishes, mfg. 1994-present.

MSR	$4,000	$3,000	$2,500	$2,100	$1,800	$1,600	$1,400	$1,200

This model was co-designed by bassist John Patitucci.

YAMAKI

See Daion. Instruments previously produced in Japan during the late 1970s through the 1980s.

YAMATO

Instruments previously produced in Japan during the late 1970s to the early 1980s.

Yamato guitars are medium quality instruments that feature both original and designs based on classic American favorites (source: Tony Bacon and Paul Day, *The Guru's Guitar Guide*).

YUNKER, ERIC

Instruments previously built in San Francisco, CA during the early 1980s.

Luthier Eric Yunker (1953-1985) was described as "a man of many skills - poet, printer, inventor, graphic artist, musician, guitar sculptor." Yunker's instruments combined the sculpting aspect of a guitar body with playability, as well. One of the Yunker guitars is on display in the ZZ Top display area at the Rock and Roll Hall of Fame and Museum in Cleveland, Ohio (source: Jas Obrecht, *Guitar Player Magazine*).

YURIY

Instruments previously built in Wheeling, IL, from 1990 to 2002.

Luthier Yuriy Shishkov was born in 1964 in St. Petersburg. As with many other guitar makers, Shishkov began his career from discovering a big personal attraction to music. After spending ten years playing guitars that he found unsatisfactory, Yuriy attempted to build his own instrument in 1986. The results amazed everyone who played the instrument, including Yuriy himself! From this initial bit of success, Yuriy gained a reputation as a luthier as well as several orders for guitars.

In 1990, Yuriy moved to Chicago, Illinois. A year later, he secured a job at Washburn International, a major guitar company based in Chicago. His experience with personal guitar building lead him to a position of handling the difficult repairs, restorations, intricate inlay work, company prototypes, and the custom-built instruments for the artist endorsees.

Yuriy is no longer producing guitars as of 2002. He is currently the senior master builder at the Fender Custom Shop. You can still reach him, however (see Trademark Index).

ELECTRIC

Yuriy's electric **Angel** models range in price from $1,950 up to $3,500. Yuriy offers a number of options on his instruments, such as inlays, exotic woods, pickups, hardware, and bindings. He also works with the player commissioning the guitar to insure that the finished result is exactly what the player is specifying. Prices were the last advertised.

Section Z

ZAK

Instruments currently built in Gdansk, Poland. Distributed by Mayones Company of Gdansk, Poland.

The Mayones Company (Zenon Dziewulski) is currently offering a number of good quality solid body electric guitar and bass models. Production models feature the SuperStrat´styling, while the Custom Shop models are heavily into Tone Woods and Natural finishes. For further information regarding models and pricing, contact the Mayones Company directly (see Trademark Index).

ZEMAITIS

Instruments previously handcrafted in England 1957-2001.

Tony Zemaitis was born Antanus (Anthony) Casimere (Charles) Zemaitis in 1935. While his grandparents were Lithuanian, both Tony and his parents were born in the U.K. At age 16 he left college to be an apprentice at cabinet making. As part of a hobby, he refashioned an old damaged guitar found in the family attic. In 1955, the first turning point to luthiery. Zemaitis built his first "half decent" guitar, a classical, nylon string with peghead. In the mid to late 1950s, Zemaitis served for two years in Britian´s National Service.

Upon his return to civilian life, Zemaitis continued his guitar building hobby, only now a number of the guitars began turning up onto the folk scene. By 1960, he was selling guitars for the price of the materials, and a number of the originals that Zemaitis calls "Oldies" still exist. Early users include Spencer Davis, Long John Baldry, and Jimi Hendrix.

In 1965, Zemaitis´ hobby had acquired enough interest that he was able to become self employed. By the late 1960s, the orders were coming in from a number of top players such as Ron Wood, Eric Clapton, and George Harrison. The house and shop all moved lock, stock, and barrel to Kent in 1972. A **Student** model was introduced in 1980, but proved to be too popular and time-consuming to produce the number of orders, so it was discontinued.

In 1995, Zemaitis celebrated the 40th Anniversary of the first classical guitar he built in 1955. Guitar production was limited to ten guitars a year. Sadly in August of 2002, Tony Zemaitis passed away. His family and friends commented that despite retirement he couldn´t stay out of the workshop.

A few years ago, George Harrison lent three of his Zemaitis acoustic models to an exhibition in the U.K. organized by Viscount Linley (Princess Margaret´s son).

Source: Tony Zemaitis, March 1996 and Keith Smart, 2001. Information courtesy Keith Smart and Keith Rogers, *The Z Gazette:* magazine of the Zemaitis Guitar Owners Club based in England.

AUTHENTICITY

In the late 1980s, Zemaitis was surprised to see that his guitars were even more valuable in the secondhand market than originally priced. As his relative output was limited, an alarming trend of forgeries has emerged in England, Japan, and the U.S. Serial numbers identification and dating on guitars will continue to be unreported in this edition, due to the number of forgeries that keep turning up (and we´re not going to add tips to the "help-yourself merchants" as Tony likes to call them). To clarify matters simply: Tony Zemaitis has granted NO ONE permission to build reproductions and NO licensing deals have been made to any company.

POINTS TO CONSIDER WHEN BUYING A ZEMAITIS

Prior to spending a large amount of money on what may very well turn out to be a copy of a Zemaitis, it is always best to ask for advice.

There are German, Japanese, and English copies. At first glance they may look a little like a Zemaitis, but they will not sound like one due to the use of second-rate materials. Because of the mass produced nature of these fakes, the intonation and general finish will be inferior to the genuine article. Even more alarming, what starts out as a cheap copy changes hands once or twice and eventually ends up being advertised as the real thing without proper research.

The more difficult fakes to spot are the genuine Zemaitis guitars that started life as a cheaper version (Student or Test model), and has been unofficially upgraded. In other words, a plain front guitar suddenly becomes a Pearl Front guitar. While parts and pieces will be genuine, the newer finish and general appearance are nothing like the real thing.

Always ask for a receipt, even if you are not buying from a shop. Always check the spelling of "Zemaitis." Look at the engraving, and make sure that it is engraved by hand (not photo etching – it is too clean and has not been worked on by hand, reprinted courtesy Keith Smart, *The Z Gazette*).

The *Blue Book of Electric Guitars* strongly recommends two or three written estimates of any Zemaitis instrument from accredited sources. If possible, ask to see the original paperwork. Here are two more serious tips: Usually the person who commissioned the guitar has their initials on the truss rod cover. Also, review the printed label and logo (there´s only one correct spelling for Mr. Zemaitis´ name – and contrary to word of mouth, he did not intentionally misspell it on his guitars. Prices easily start at $10,000 and can go to and above $25,000.

MODEL DESCRIPTIONS

Here is a brief overview of model histories and designations. During the late 1950s, a few basic acoustic models were built to learn about sizes, shapes, wood response, and soundholes. From 1960 to 1964, guitar building was still a hobby, so there was no particular standard; also, the paper labels inside are hand labeled.

In 1965, Zemaitis turned pro and introduced the **Standard**, **Superior**, and **Custom** models of acoustic guitars. These terms are relative, not definitive as there is some overlapping from piece to piece. While some soundholes are round, there are a number of acoustic guitars built with the heart shaped soundhole.

The electric solidbody guitar was discussed and inspired by Eric Clapton on a visit to Zemaitis´ workshop in 1969. The handful of early models had aluminum plates on the faces, and later were followed by solid silver, then finally returned to aluminum as the British tax people proved difficult. Zemaitis´ good friend and engraver Danny O´Brien handles the ornate engraving on the M/F (**Metal Front**) models. The first test guitar was sold off cheaply at the time, but the second was purchased by Tony McPhee (Groundhogs); the third guitar built was purchased by Ron Wood. The M/F guitar model has since moved worldwide. There is a variation model called the **Disc Front** which has a round faced metal plate around the pickups as opposed to the entire front. An ultimate version called the Pearl Front is just that: a pearl topped solid body guitar – and the written description hardly does justice to the actual piece.

The **Student** model was introduced in 1980. Designed as a basic guitar that could be later upgraded, the model proved so popular that it was quickly discontinued for fear that the production would overtake other work altogether! In the late 1980s, clients began asking for either more decorations or copies of older models. At this point Zemaitis upgraded his system to the **Custom**, **Deluxe**, and **Custom Deluxe** which are still in use to date. Again, these three models are relative, not definitive as some crossing back and forth does go on.

ZENBU GUITARS

Instruments currently built in CA since 1978. Distributed by Zenbu Guitars of Sacramento, CA.

Luthier/designer Toshi Hiraoka has been producing custom-built guitars for specific clients for the past twenty years. Zenbu Guitars is available by appointment only.

ZEN-ON

Instruments previously produced in Japan circa 1946 to late 1960s.

The Zen-On brand appears on a full range of intermediate quality solid body electric guitars and basses, as well as thinline acoustic/electric hollowbody guitars and electric mandolins. By the late 1960s the company began using the Morales trademark (See Morales). The Japanese manufacturer is unknown, and Zen-On was not heavily imported into the U.S. market (source: Michael Wright, *Vintage Guitar Magazine*).

ELECTRIC

MISC. ELECTRIC GUITARS - various configurations in solidbody and semi-hollow body forms, mfg. 1950s and 1960s.

N/A	$150	$125	$100	$80	$60	$40

ZENTA

Instruments previously produced in Japan in the late 1960s to the late 1970s. During the 1970s, production moved to Korea.

These entry level solid body and semi-hollowbody guitars featured both original design and designs based on classic American favorites (source: Tony Bacon and Paul Day, *The Guru's Guitar Guide*).

ZENTECH

Instruments currently built in Girdwood, AK.

Dave Hill´s Zentech Instruments is a small custom shop that specializes in limited production, high quality custom-built electric guitars and basses. Zentech combines classic and free-thinking designs, select woods, high tech electronics, and precision bridges and tuners (Schaller, Smith, and Steinberger) in their instruments. In 1996, Zentech began offering archtop acoustics that featured twenty-year-old Sitka spruce.

All instruments have a ten-year guarantee, and prices include a hardshell case. Zentech also offers numerous custom options in hardware and exotic woods (call for pricing and availability).

ELECTRIC

The **Zentech SE** (base retail $1,000) has a cedar body and quilted maple top, rosewood fingerboard, inline headstock, chrome or black hardware, vintage-style hardtail bridge, 2 Chandler Zebra humbuckers, volume/tone controls, and a three way pickup selector.

The **Zentech ST** (base retail $1,200) has an offset double cutaway teak body, maple neck, Schaller tuners, and 2 Chandler Zebra humbuckers. It is wired in stereo, and has coil taps, phase switch, gold hardware, and tune-o-matic bridge/stop tailpiece. Slightly related is the **Tasmanian Micro**, a travel guitar with a full scale (25.5 in.) maple neck, smaller teak body, maple fingerboard, chrome hardware, single pickup, and single volume knob. Designed to fit in the overhead bin of a Boeing 727, this model is complete with a padded gigbag for $700.

Zentech´s Artist Series contains the **Shark**, which was designed in conjunction with Yupik Eskimo artist Jack Abraham. The Shark has the same appointments as the SE model, but a very original body shape (base retail $1,500).

ELECTRIC BASS

All Zentech basses can be ordered in 4-, 5-, 6-, and 7-string configurations, and with any combination of options. The following price quotes reflect the model discussed.

The **Darth Fretless 5** has a teak body with rather pointy forward horns, a through-body neck, fretless ebony fingerboard, locking tuners, graphite nut, 2 J-style pickups, active EQ, volume/blend/tone controls. This 5-string model has a base retail of $1,350.

A quilted walnut, dual cutaway rounded body signifies the **RB 5** bass. The RB 5 has a similar pickup/EQ/controls package as the Darth, and is priced at $1,300 in the 5-string configuration.

The **Zebra 6** 6-string has an offset cutaway body, through-body rock maple neck, ebony fingerboard, 2 Bartolini pickups, and volume/pan/tone controls. Zebra 6-strings have a base retail of $1,500.

GRADING	100% MINT	98% NEAR MINT	95% EXC+	90% EXC	80% VG+	70% VG	60% G

ZETA

Instruments currently built in Oakland, CA since 1982. Distributed by Zeta Music Systems, Inc. of Oakland, CA.

Zeta currently offers quality acoustic/electric violins, and a MIDI violin synthesizer in addition to the current Crossover models of electric bass. Zeta is now available as factory order direcet, which means you can order straight from the factory on their website. For more information refer to their website (see Trademark Index).

ELECTRIC

MIRROR 6 - rounded asymmetrical double cutaway ash body, bolt-on maple neck with aluminum and graphite headstock reinforcement, 24-fret ebony fingerboard with offset white block inlay, strings through body bridge, reverse headstock, 6 on the other side Gotoh tuners, black hardware, single coil/humbucker EMG pickups, hex MIDI pickup, volume/tone/blend/MIDI controls, 3 on/off switches (pickups or hex/synth), available in Black, Metallic Grey, Pearl White, Red, or Sea Foam Green finishes, mfg. 1989-1994.

**Zeta Crossover 5
Courtesy Zeta**

	N/A	$1,900	$1,500	$1,200	$1,000	$800	$600

Last MSR was $2,995.

Add $800 for modified Kahler double locking tremolo.

The Mirror 6 guitar functioned as a MIDI controller, and requires the Mirror 6 rack unit. Programming and parameter editing in the rack unit can be accessed through the guitar controls.

ELECTRIC BASS

Zeta currently offers the **Crossover** bass, which allows bassists the flexibility of two playing positions: either upright (the bass mounted on a specially designed stand) or on a shoulder strap. The 6-string configuration is available as the **Rob Wasserman** Signature model (list price is $3,895). Additionally, Zeta currently manufactures the E-Series Bass ($1,499 MSR), the Performer Bass ($1,999 MSR), Performer Upright ($2,500 MSR), and the Jazz Upright ($5,995).

Add $500 for flame or curly maple top (in Vintage Sunburst). Add $500 for exotic woods (koa, figured walnut, and zebrawood).

CROSSOVER 4 (MODEL XB-304) - sleek offset body design, set-in neck, fretless fingerboard, 2-per-side tuners, magnetic pickup, volume/tone controls, available in hand-oiled Natural, Black, or White finishes, current mfg.

MSR	N/A	$2,295	$1,950	$1,750	$1,500	$1,250	$1,050	$950

Crossover 5 (Model XB-305) - similar to the Crossover 4, except in a 5-string configuration. Current Mfg.

MSR	N/A	$2,295	$1,950	$1,750	$1,500	$1,250	$1,050	$950

PRISM - offset double cutaway ash body, bolt-on maple neck, 34 in. scale, 24-fret rosewood fingerboard with offset white block inlay, Zeta adjustable bridge, graphite laminated reverse headstock with aluminum stabilizing bar, 4 on the other side Gotoh tuners, black hardware, bridge mounted piezo pickups, volume/bass/presence controls, 3-way attentuation switch, available in Gloss Black, Anthracite Grey, Pearl White, Red, or Sea Foam Green finishes, mfg. 1988-1991.

	N/A	$900	$800	$700	$600	$500	$400

Last MSR was $1,495.

The 3-way attentuation switch was designed to allow switching between a P-Bass sound, a Steinberger-type sound, or the acoustic-like Zeta sound.

ZIM GAR

Instruments previously produced in Japan circa 1960s. Distributed in the U.S. by the Gar Zim Musical Instrument Corporation of Brooklyn, NY.

Zim Gar instruments were distributed by U.S. importer Gar Zim Musical Instrument Corporation of Brooklyn, New York. During the 1960s, Zim Gar offered the shorter scale beginner's solid body electric guitars and basses. The Japanese manufacturer is currently unknown.

Zim Gar budget electric guitars were available through Kmart stores during the 1960s. The two-pickup model had a list price of $29.95; the three-pickup model was $39.95 (source: Roland Lozier, Lozier Piano & Music; and Michael Wright, *Guitar Stories*, Volume One).

ELECTRIC

MISC. ELECTRIC GUITARS - various configurations including solidbodies, mfg. 1960s.

	N/A	$175	$150	$125	$105	$90	$75

ZIMMERLY, KEVIN

Instruments currently produced in Bay Shore, NY since 1993.

Luthier Kevin Zimmerly has been building high quality custom basses for the last three years. Zimmerly draws on his background of over twenty-two years in the music industry for design ideas and innovations, and has two current models: The **RKZ** (an offset double cutaway body) and the "**Silly Bass**" (an extreme treble side cutaway design).

GRADING	100% MINT	98% NEAR MINT	95% EXC+	90% EXC	80% VG+	70% VG	60% G

ELECTRIC BASS

The **RKZ** has an offset double cutaway body, ash, (or mahogany, maple, poplar, alder) body wings, through-body 3-piece maple neck, ebony fingerboard with dot inlays, Schaller or Wilkinson bridge, Gotoh tuners, chrome hardware, EMG pickups, volume/tone controls, available in 4-string with 3/1-per-side tuners, and a MSR $1,059, a 5-string with 3/2-per-side tuners, and an MSR $1,175, and a 6-string with 3-per-side tuners and an MSR $1,295.

The **SILLY BASS** is similar to the RKZ, except features an offset body with an extreme cutaway on the treble side, for range to the entire fretboard, available in 4-string with 2-per-side tuners, and MSR $959, a 5-string with 3/2-per-side tuners and an MSR $1,075, and a 6-string with 3-per-side tuners, and an MSR $1,195.

ZOID LIGHT GUITARS

Instruments currently built in Tampa, FL. Previous production was located in Melbourne, FL.

Zoid (Research and Development) **Light Guitars** offers a guitar model that features high density transparent bodies and internal lighting systems. The Light Guitar is available in three body shapes (and thirty-two colors).

ZION

Instruments currently built in Greensboro, NC since 1980. Distributed by Zion Guitar Technology of Greensboro, NC.

Luthier Ken Hoover founded Zion Guitar Technology in 1980, after six years of repairs, restorations, and custom building experience. In 1983, Zion was commissioned by *Guitar Player* magazine to build the **Silver Bird** model that was featured on the cover - and commissioned again in 1991 to build the **Burning Desire** model for cover art. Hoover has worked with such artists as Phil Keaggy and Ty Tabor (King's X), as well as custom builders such as Joe Barden and Pat Wilkins.

Zion guitars have been famous for their high quality and amazing custom finishes, and the Zion guitar staff maintains an output of forty to fifty guitars a month. From 1980 to 1993, the peghead logo had block lettering and triangular wings. In 1994, Zion redesigned their peghead logo to feature a bold signature look, with a large "Z".

ELECTRIC

Current price includes a hardshell case (unless otherwise noted).

Add $100 for gold hardware. Add $100 for glossy, tinted finish on neck.

ACTION SERIES - offset double cutaway basswood body, bolt-on maple neck, 25.5 in. scale, 22-fret rosewood (or ebony or bird's-eye maple) fingerboard, vintage style tremolo, bone nut, pearl pickguard/backplate, 6-on-a-side Sperzel Trim-lok tuners, chrome hardware, 3 Seymour Duncan vintage replica single coil pickups, volume/tone control, 5-way selector switch, available in Black, Natural, or White finishes, mfg. 1997-disc.

Last MSR was $1,150.

Price includes deluxe gig bag.

BURNING DESIRE - offset double cutaway basswood body, bolt-on maple neck, 22-fret ebony fingerboard with pearl dot inlay, standard Kahler vibrato, graphite nut, 6-on-a-side locking Sperzel tuners, chrome hardware, 2 stacked coil/1 humbucker Joe Barden pickups, volume/tone control, 3 pickup selector mini switches, 1 bypass-to-humbucker mini switch, available in Black with Neon Flames finish, disc. 1994.

	N/A	$2,100	$1,795	$1,395	$1,175	$995	$895

Last MSR was $2,995.

This model was one of Zion's Limited Edition Series. The pickup selector mini switch had three positions: series, off, and parallel.

CLASSIC MAPLE - offset double cutaway basswood body, carved arched bound figured maple top, bolt-on maple neck, 25.5 in. scale, 22-fret ebony (or bird's-eye maple) fingerboard with pearl dot inlay, Kahler Steeler locking vibrato, recessed bridge area, 6-on-a-side Sperzel Trim-lok tuners, black hardware, 2 single coil/1 humbucker Seymour Duncan (or Fralin or Barden Deluxe) pickups, volume/tone control, 5-position switch, available in Amber Top, Black, Trans. Blue Burst, Tobacco Burst, or Vintage Burst finishes, current mfg.

MSR	$2,895	$2,300	$1,950	$1,700	$1,450	$1,200	$950	$700

In 1995, Black, Transparent Blue Burst, and Vintage Burst finishes were discontinued. Honey Burst, Purple Burst, and Transparent Teal finishes were introduced. Past models were also available with Zion, EMG, Ultrasonic, or PJ Marx pickups.

Frosted Marble - similar to Classic Maple, except has basswood body, Zion Versa-Tone pickups, and custom Frosted Marble finish with matching headstock. Available in Deep Blue, Fire Orange, Intense Red, Jade Green, or Purple Frosted Marble finishes, mfg. 1994-96, reintroduced.

MSR	N/A	$1,900	$1,700	$1,450	$1,200	$1,000	$750	$550

Graphic Series - similar to Classic Maple, except has basswood body, choice of 5-way selector or 3 pickup selector mini switches, and a bypass-to-humbucker mini switch, and custom airbrushed design or specialty finish, available in Frosted Marble, Guilded Frost, Marble Rock, Metal Marble, Splatter Rock and Techno Frost finishes, disc. 1994, reintroduced 1998-present.

1990-1994	N/A	$1,300	$1,100	$900	$750	$600	$475
1998-MSR $2,640	$2,100	$1,850	$1,600	$1,375	$1,125	$895	$650

The current version of the Graphic Series has many custom options, "Features determine the exact price." The pickup selector mini switch had three positions: series, off, and parallel. Available in Burning Desire, Frosted Marble, Metal Marble, and Silverbird graphic finishes, 1998-present.

ELITE - offset double cutaway Strat-ish alder body, rosewood or maple fingerboard with dot inlays, custom electronics in SSS or SSH configurations, 6-on-a-side tuners, pickguard, chrome hardware, Wilkinson VSVG tremolo, available in Black Pearl, White Pearl, Red Pearl, Champaign, or Shoreline Gold, new 2003.

MSR	$1,499	$1,200	$1,050	$900	$800	$700	$600	$500

RT CLASSIC - similar to the Classic Maple, except has chrome hardware, bone nut, Mann resophonic tremolo, available in Amber Top, Honey Burst, Purple Burst, Tobacco Burst, or Trans. Teal finishes, disc.

	$2,100	$1,850	$1,600	$1,375	$1,125	$895	$650

Last MSR was $2,640.

GRADING	100% MINT	98% NEAR MINT	95% EXC+	90% EXC	80% VG+	70% VG	60% G

RT Classic Professional - similar to the RT Classic, except has swamp ash or mahogany body, Skyway tremolo, mfg. 1998-disc.

	$2,450	$2,150	$1,900	$1,650	$1,450	$1,250	$1,050

Last MSR was $3,060.

METRO - mahogany body, figured maple top, bolt-on maple neck, 25.5 in. scale, 22-fret rosewood (or bird's-eye maple or ebony) fingerboard, Mann resophonic tremolo, bone nut, 6-on-a-side Sperzel Trim-lok tuners, chrome hardware, 2 Barden Deluxe (or Seymour Duncan or Fralin) humbuckers, 2 volume/2 tone push/pull controls, 3-way selector switch, available in Amber Top, Honey Burst, Purple Burst, Tobacco Burst, or Trans. Teal finishes, mfg. 1997-disc.

	$1,900	$1,675	$1,450	$1,250	$1,050	$900	$750

Last MSR was $2,395.

PICKASSO - similar to Burning Desire, except has black hardware and Zion Versa-Tone pickups, available in Black, Blue/Purple/Pink and Pink/Orange/Yellow, and White finishes, disc. 1994.

	N/A	$1,800	$1,500	$1,200	$950	$825	$750

Last MSR was $2,495.

This model was one of Zion's Limited Edition Series.

PRIMERA - single cutaway mahogany body, AAA grade figured maple top, set-in mahogany neck, 24.75 in. scale, 22-fret rosewood fingerboard with mother-of-pearl royal crown inlays, tunomatic bridge/stop tailpiece (or Mann resophonic tremolo), 3-on-a-side Sperzel Trim-lok tuners, gold hardware, 2 Joe Barden Two-Tone (or Lindy Fralin) humbuckers, 2 volume/2 tone push/pull controls, 3-way selector switch, available in Amber Top or Honey Burst finishes, mfg. 1994-present.

MSR	$3,495	$2,800	$2,500	$2,200	$1,950	$1,750	$1,500	$1,250

Phil Keaggy Signature Model Primera - similar to the Primera, except has 2 custom Seymour Duncan humbuckers, and Phil Keaggy signature imprint on headstock, mfg. 1997-disc.

	$3,250	$2,800	$2,500	$2,200	$1,900	$1,700	$1,500

Last MSR was $3,995.

This is a Limited production model. Model includes a laminated Certificate of Authenticity. The push/pull controls throw the humbuckers into parallel for a brighter tone.

Zion Classic Maple Courtesy Zion

T MODEL - offset double cutaway basswood body, pearloid pickguard, bolt-on maple neck, 22-fret ebony (or maple) fingerboard with pearl dot inlay, standard Gotoh vibrato, graphite nut, 6-on-a-side locking Sperzel tuners, 3 stacked coil Zion pickups, volume/tone control, 5-position switch, available in Black, Cream and Tobacco Burst finishes, mfg. 1991-96.

	N/A	$1,100	$975	$825	$695	$550	$395

Last MSR was $1,595.

In 1995, Lindy Fralin pickups replaced original parts/designs.

Maple Top T - similar to T Model, except has figured maple top and Zion vibrato, available in Blue Burst, Purple Burst, Tobacco Burst, or Vintage Burst finishes, mfg. 1991-95.

	N/A	$1,250	$1,050	$900	$775	$625	$495

Last MSR was $1,995.

BENT TOP MAPLE T - offset double cutaway basswood body, Bent (contoured) figured maple top, bolt-on maple neck, 25.5 in. scale, 22-fret rosewood (or ebony or bird's-eye maple) fingerboard, Mann resophonic tremolo, 6-on-a-side Sperzel Trim-lok tuners, bone nut, chrome hardware, pearl pickguard and backplate, 3 Lindy Fralin single coil pickups with white 6-hole covers, volume/tone controls, 5-position switch, available in Blue Burst, Honey Burst, Purple Burst, or Tobacco Burst finishes, mfg. 1996-present.

MSR	$2,695	$2,150	$1,800	$1,550	$1,300	$1,100	$850	$600

Left Maple Top - similar to the Bent Top Maple T, except in left-handed configuration, mfg. 1991-present.

1991-1995		$1,400	$1,195	$1,050	$900	$775	$625	$495
MSR	$2,695	$2,150	$1,800	$1,550	$1,300	$1,100	$850	$600

From 1991 to 1995, the Left Maple Top model was similar to the Maple Top T (except as a left-hander). When the Bent or contoured top Maple T was introduced in 1996, the Left Maple Top model followed the new design configuration.

THE FIFTY - single cutaway swamp ash body, bolt-on maple neck, 25.5 in. scale, 22-fret bird's-eye maple (or ebony or rosewood) fingerboard, tele-style fixed bridge, 6-on-a-side Sperzel Trim-lok tuners, bone nut, chrome hardware, black bakelite pickguard, 2 Seymour Duncan vintage replica single coil pickups, chrome controls plate, volume/tone controls, 3-position switch, available in Butterscotch, Honey Burst, Mary Kaye, or Trans. Orange finishes, mfg. 1994-present.

MSR	$2,295	$1,850	$1,550	$1,350	$1,150	$950	$750	$550

In 1997, Zion redesigned their 6-saddle bridge, and replaced it with vintage-styled 3 shared-saddle bridge (angled for intonation correction).

THE NINETY - single cutaway swamp ash thin-line body, figured maple top, bolt-on maple neck, 25.5 in. scale, f-hole, 22-fret bird's-eye maple (or ebony or rosewood) fingerboard, tele-style fixed bridge, 6-on-a-side Sperzel Trim-lok tuners, bone nut, gold hardware, 2 Joe Barden Deluxe single coil pickups, gold controls plate, volume/tone controls, 3-position switch, available in Blue Burst, Honey Burst, Tobacco Burst or Trans. Orange finishes, mfg. 1994-present.

MSR	$2,695	$2,150	$1,800	$1,550	$1,300	$1,100	$850	$600

In 1997, Zion redesigned their 6-saddle bridge, and replaced it with vintage-styled 3 shared-saddle bridge (angled for intonation correction).

Zion The Fifty Courtesy Zion

GRADING	100% MINT	98% NEAR MINT	95% EXC+	90% EXC	80% VG+	70% VG	60% G

TY TABOR SIGNATURE MODEL - offset double cutaway basswood body, maple top, bolt-on maple neck, 25.5 in. scale, 22-fret rosewood fingerboard with pearl dot inlay, Mann resophonic tremolo, 6-on-a-side Sperzel Trim-lok tuners, gold hardware, black pickguard with Ty Tabor signature imprint, 3 Joe Barden Strat Deluxe single coil pickups, special taper tone control, 3 on/off push button pickup selectors with red button caps, available in Deep Opaque Red with special design position markers on back of neck, mfg. 1994-disc.

		$1,850	$1,600	$1,395	$1,195	$995	$775	$575

Last MSR was $2,295.

ULTRA GLIDE - single cutaway basswood body, carved maple top, 24.75 in. scale, 24-fret fingerboard, Kahler "Steeler" tremolo w/ auto latch, 2 humbuckers, mfg. 1991-92.

	N/A	$1,250	$1,050	$900	$775	$650	$500

Last MSR was $1,995.

This model was one of Zion's Limited Edition Series.

ELECTRIC BASS

RAD BASS - offset double cutaway basswood body, bolt-on maple neck, 20-fret ebony fingerboard, fixed bridge, 4-per-side Gotoh tuners, black hardware, P-style/J-style EMG pickups, 2 volume/1 tone controls, available in Amber Top, Classic Black, Purple Burst, Tobacco Burst, Transparent Blue Burst, and Vintage Burst finishes, disc. 1994.

	N/A	$1,250	$1,050	$900	$775	$625	$495

Last MSR was $1,995.

RAD BASS GRAPHIC MODEL - similar to the Rad Bass, except features specialty airbrush design or specialty finish, available in Frosted Marble Blue, Frosted Marble Purple, Frosted Marble Red, or Techno-Frost finishes, disc. 1992.

	N/A	$1,100	$950	$800	$650	$550	$450

Last MSR was $1,595.

Graphic finishes were available on the Rad Bass starting in 1993.

RAD BASS MAPLE TOP - similar to the Rad Bass, except had a figured maple top over basswood body, disc. 1992.

	N/A	$1,200	$1,000	$825	$750	$650	$575

Last MSR was $1,795.

ZOLLA

Instruments currently built in San Diego, CA, since 1979.

Zolla Guitars has been building high quality custom guitars, necks, and bodies in Southern California since 1979. Zolla also provides neck and body parts for various companies and individual luthiers.

Zolla's **BZ** series features three guitar models with a corresponding bass design. The BZ series overall features an offset, double cutaway body design. For further information regarding finished guitars or basses, or for guitar bodies and neck parts, call Zolla Guitars directly (see Trademark Index).

ZON

Instruments currently built in Redwood City, CA since 1987. Previous production was in Buffalo, NY from 1982 to 1987.

Luthier/musician Joseph M. Zon originally began building instruments in upstate New York back in 1982. Four years later Zon Guitars moved into larger facilities across country in California to meet the greater demand for his high quality basses.

ELECTRIC BASS: MICHAEL MANNING HYPERBASS SERIES

Prior to 1998, the Hyperbass model with detunable keys and bridge was labeled the Version II. Currently, the Version I is featured with detunable or non-detunable keys. A third version of the Hyperbass, **Version III** featured the detunable Zon/ATB bridge, detunable Zon/Gotoh/Hipshot tuners, and a piezo body pickup (last retail list was $7,995). The Version III was discontinued in 1998; the Zon piezo bridge option is still available for Zon basses. This instrument was co-designed by Michael Manring, and features a 3 octave fingerboard.

VERSION I - offset deep cutaway teardrop poplar body, curly maple top, composite neck, fretless phenolic fingerboard, blackface peghead with screened model name/logo, black hardware, humbucker Bartolini pickup, volume/treble/bass controls, ZP2-S active electronics, fixed Schaller bridge, available in Natural top/Black back finishes, current mfg.

MSR $5,395

Version I with Detunable Zon/ATB bridge - detunable Zon/Gotoh/Hipshot tuners.

Last MSR was $6,995.

ELECTRIC BASS: LEGACY ELITE SERIES

LEGACY ELITE - offset double cutaway poplar-core body, choice of bookmatched figured wood top, composite neck, 34 in. scale, 24-fret phenolic fingerboard with pearl dot inlay, fixed Zon bridge, blackface peghead with screened model name/logo, 2-per-side Schaller tuners, chrome hardware, 2 Bartolini dual coil pickups, volume/pan/bass/mid/treble boost/cut controls, ZP2-D active electronics. Available in Black, Emerald Green, Heather, Ice Blue, Lazer Blue, Midnight Blue, Mint Green, Mist Green, Natural, Pearl Blue, Porsche Red, Powder Blue, or Yellow finishes, current mfg.

MSR $4,395

This model is optional with the following tops: bird's-eye maple, California walnut, curly maple, goncalo alves, koa, mangowood, myrtlewood, quilted maple, or zebrawood.

Legacy Elite V - similar to Elite, except has 5 strings, 3/2-per-side tuners, mfg. 1986-present.

MSR $4,795

Legacy Elite VI - similar to Elite, except has 6 strings, 3-per-side tuners, mfg. 1988-present.

MSR $5,195

LEGACY ELITE SPECIAL - similar to the Legacy Elite, except features a bookmatched bubinga top, 2 Bartolini multi coil pickups, available in Natural top/Black back finishes, current mfg.
MSR $4,495

Legacy Elite V Special - similar to Elite Special, except has 5 strings, 3/2 tuners per side, current mfg.
MSR $4,995

Legacy Elite VI Special - similar to Elite Special, except has 6 strings, 3 tuners per side, current mfg.
MSR $5,395

STANDARD - offset double cutaway ash body, bolt-on composite neck, 24-fret phenolic fingerboard, fixed Zon bridge, blackface peghead with screened model name/logo, 2-per-side Zon/Gotoh tuners, chrome hardware, 2 Bartolini humbucker pickups, volume/pan/bass/mid/treble boost/cut controls, ZP2-D active electronics, available in Natural or Trans. finishes, disc.

Last MSR was $2,495.

This model has figured maple body optional.

Standard V - similar to Standard, except has 5 strings, 3/2-per-side tuners, disc.

Last MSR was $2,795.

Standard VI - similar to Standard, except has 6 strings, 3-per-side tuners, disc.

Last MSR was $3,095.

ELECTRIC BASS: SONUS SERIES

Both the Sonus 4/1 and 5/1 feature a single humbucker pickup, while the Sonus and Sonus Special models feature two pickups.

SONUS 4/1 - offset double cutaway alder body, bolt-on composite neck, 24-fret phenolic fingerboard, fixed Zon bridge, blackface peghead with screened model name/logo, 2-per-side Zon/Gotoh tuners, chrome hardware, humbucker pickup, 2 volume/treble/bass controls, active electronics, available in Dark Metallic Blue, Heather, High Gloss Black, or Metallic Red finishes, 34 in. scale, current mfg.
MSR $2,595

Sonus 4/2 - similar to the Sonus 4/1, except has 2 custom wound humbucker pickups, mfg. 2002-present.
MSR $2,995

SONUS 5/1 - similar to the Sonus 4/1, except in five string configuration, 3/2-per-side tuners, current mfg.
MSR $2,795

This model is optional with 22-fret fingerboard and a 35 in. scale.

Sonus 5/2 - similar to the Sonus 5/1, except has 2 custom wound humbucker pickups, mfg. 1999-present.
MSR $3,295

SONUS 4 - offset double cutaway ash body, bolt-on composite neck, 34 in. scale, 24-fret phenolic fingerboard, fixed Zon bridge, blackface peghead with screened model name/logo, 2-per-side Zon/Gotoh tuners, chrome hardware, 2 Bartolini single coil pickups, 2 concentric volume/treble/bass controls, active electronics, available in Natural or Trans. finishes, current mfg.
MSR $2,995

Sonus 5 - similar to Sonus, except has 5 strings, 3/2-per-side tuners, current mfg.
MSR $3,395

Sonus 6 - similar to Sonus, except has 6 strings, 3-per-side tuners, current mfg.
MSR $3,895

Sonus 8 - similar to the Sonus, except has 8 strings, 4-per-side tuners, 2 special multi-coil pickups, available in Natural finish, current mfg.
MSR $3,295

SONUS 4 SPECIAL - similar to the Sonus, except features a bookmatched bubinga top, 2 special multi-coil pickups, available in Natural polyester gloss finish, current mfg.
MSR $3,495

Sonus 5 Special - similar to Sonus Special, except has 5 strings, 3/2-per-side tuners, current mfg.
MSR $3,795

Sonus 6 Special - similar to Sonus Special, except has 6 strings, 3-per-side tuners, current mfg.
MSR $4,295

SONUS CUSTOM - similar to the Sonus, except features a 2-piece swamp ash body, bookmatched figured wood top, 2 special multi-coil pickups, available in Trans. or custom color finishes, current mfg.
MSR $3,195

Sonus Custom 5 - similar to Sonus Custom, except has 5 strings, 3/2-per-side tuners, current mfg.
MSR $3,495

Sonus Custom 6 - similar to Sonus Custom, except has 6 strings, 3-per-side tuners, mfg. 1998-present.
MSR $3,495

SONUS STUDIO 4 - 4 string model with 2 custom wound dual coil pickups and independent EQ per pickup, 22-fret, 35 in. scale, mahogany/figured maple body, mfg. 2002-present.
MSR $3,995

**Zon Standard 4
courtesy Zon**

**Zon Sonus 5 Special
courtesy Zon**

SONUS STUDIO 5 - 5-string model with 2 custom wound dual coil pickups and independent EQ per pickup, 22-fret, 35 in. scale, mahogany/figured maple body, mfg. 1999-present.

    MSR   **$4,195**

    Sonus Studio 519 - similar to the Sonus Studio, except has 19mm string spacing, mfg. 2002-present.

    MSR   **$3,495**

SONUS LIGHTWAVE 4 - 4 string model with infared optical pickup system and piezo bridge, black hardware, natural ash body, mfg. 2002-present.

    MSR   **$3,475**

    Extreme rarity precludes accurate pricing on this model. If and when one surfaces, the asking price could be in the $7,500 and up range. The pickups on this instrument were set under the pickguard, making the guitar appear to have no pickups. Due to unknown circumstances, this model never went into full production. There are few of these instruments to be found, and though they were featured in 1965 sales brochures, they would have to be considered prototypes. Most seasoned Fender dealers have never seen a Marauder. In the 1965-1966 catalog, the newly introduced Marauder carried a list price of $479. Compare this to the then-current list price of the Stratocaster's $281! This model had an optional standard vibrato. In 1966, the "second generation" Marauder featured 3 exposed pickups (which replaced original hidden pickups). According to Gene Fields, who was in the Fender R z1z1z1 D section at the time, 8 prototypes were built: 4 with regular frets and 4 with slanted frets.

    Sonus Lightwave 5 - similar to the Sonus Lightwave 5, except in five-string configuration, mfg. 2002-present.

    MSR   **$3,795**

    This model was renamed the RD Custom 77 in 1979.

ZORKO

Instruments previously built in Chicago, IL during the early to mid-1960s.

The Zorko trademark is the brand name of the Dopyera Brothers (See Dobro and Valco), and was used to market an electric pickup-equipped upright "mini-bass." In 1962, Everett Hull from Ampeg acquired the rights to the design. Hull improved the design, and Jess Oliver devised a new 'diaphragm-style' pickup. The Ampeg company then marketed the model as the "Baby Bass," (source: Tony Bacon and Barry Moorhouse, *The Bass Book*).

Some models in between 70% to 90% have been seen priced between $650 and $1,200. Pricing depends on condition of the body; also, compare pickups between the Zorko and an Ampeg. There may be retro fit kits from Azola, Clevinger, or some of the pickup companies (piezo bridge kits) that may fit a Zorko mini-bass.

ZWIER, JACK

Instruments currently produced in the Netherlands, since 1988.

Luthier Jack Zwier has been building and repairing guitars since 1988. In 1990, he attended the College for Musical Instrument Building in Belgium. He has produced over 150 hand crafted guitars and most of them are one-offs. Prices start at $800 for electric guitars. For more information contact luthier Zwier directly (see Trademark Index).

SERIALIZATION

POTENTIOMETER CODING: SOURCE DATE CODE

An Important Instrument Dating Breakthrough developed by Hans Moust (author, *The Guild Guitar Book*)

Stamped on every potentiometer (volume and tone *pots*) is a six- or seven-digit *source code* that tells who made the pot, as well as the week and the year. The *source dating* code is an element of standardization that is administered by the Electronics Industries Association (EIA), formed in 1924. The EIA assigns each manufacturer a three-digit code (there are some with one, two or four digits). Moust's research has indicatedthat there are no source date codes on any guitar pots before the late 1940s, and no single-digit year code after 1959 (six-digit source code).

It's fairly easy to crack the source code. The first three digits indicate the company that built the potentiometer. Sometimes these digits may be separated by a space, a hyphen, or a period. The most common company codes are:

137	CTS	304	Stackpole
140	Clarostat	134	Centralab
106	Allen Bradley	381	Bourns Networks

If the code is only six digits long, then the fourth digit is the year code (between 1947 and 1959). If the code is seven digits long, then the fourth and fifth digits indicate the year. The final two digits in either of the codes indicate the week of the year the potentiometer was built. Any final two digits with a code number over 52 possibly indicate a part number instead of a week of the year code.

When dating an instrument by the 'pot code,' keep two things in mind: The potentiometers must be original to the piece (new solder, or a date code that is off by ten or more years is a good giveaway to spot replacement pots); and the pot code only indicates when the potentiometer was built! If the pot is an original, it indicates a date before which the guitar could not have been built – so it's always a good idea to have extra reference material around.

Moust's research has indicated that virtually all Fenders from 1966 to 1969 have pots dated from 1966. Moust has speculated that when CBS bought Fender, they found a good deal on pots and bought a three-year supply. Guild apparently had the same good fortune in 1979, for when Moust visited the factory they still had a good supply of '79 pots - which explains why every Guild since then has had simillarly dated pots!

Finally, a word of caution: not all potentiometer manufacturers subscribed to the EIA source code date, and early Japanese components did not use the international coding like the American and European builders. If the code does not fit the above criteria, don't force it and skew your dating results.

(Source: George Gruhn and Walter Carter, **Guitar Player magazine,** *October 1990)*

ALEMBIC

Every instrument the company has produced has a corresponding instrument file which contains the original work order (specifications), returned warranty, and any other relevant paperwork.

In general, the first two numbers in the serial number are the year the instrument was completed and the letter code designates the model. The final two to five digits indicate the individual instrument and its place in the overall Alembic production. Alembic started with the number 1 in 1972, and has progressed sequentially ever since. An "A" or "B" after the serial number indicates the rare occasion when a serial number has been duplicated.

On new instruments, the serial number is stamped on the truss rod cover and also in the electronics cavity (Epic and Orion models have the number stamped on the back of the peghead and in the electronics cavity). On older instruments, the serial number is stamped directly on the ebony fingerboard below the 24th fret. The earliest Alembic models have serial numbers stamped on top of the headstock.

ARIA/ARIA PRO II

Aria started using serial numbers in the mid-1970s, and models before this have no serial number. Several different schemes have been used for serialization. Guitars built between 1979 and 1987 may use either one of these formats: YNNNNN or YYNNNNNN. The first one or two digits indicate the year. A 79XXXXX would be a 1979 and a 2XXXXXX would be a 1982. Some models built in Korea may use a year and week code for the first four digits.

Serial numbers after 1987 are unknown at this point. Keep in mind that several variations have been used and anything is quite possible.

(Source: Michael Wright/Aria)

B. C. RICH

Bernardo Chavez Rico learned his luthier skills from his father, Bernardo Mason Rico. When the B.C. Rich trademark was adopted, Rico built acoustic guitars for the first two years, and then switched to custom-built solid body electrics. When production formally commenced in 1972, the first 350 guitars were numbered sequentially.

In 1974, a serial number code was devised. The five-digit serial number was encoded YYZZZ, with the first two digits indicating the year and the last three indicating consecutive production. By the late 1970s, they ran out of numbers and had to begin using serial numbers meant for the following years production. In 1980, the year digits were two years ahead, and by 1981, they were off by four years!

Currently, the American-made B.C. Rich serialization does provide numbers which correspond to the year, as well as the quantity of guitars that were built in that year. For example:

953001995(	300th instrument produced)
960021996(	2nd instrument produced)

The serialization on the Import series models is for identification only, and does not depict the year of manufacture. B.C. Rich does maintain records that indicate the year of manufacture (and the manufacturer) if they are needed.

(Source: Bernie Rich, President/Founder of B.C. Rich International; and Michael Wright, **Vintage Guitar Magazine***)*

BENEDETTO

To date, Robert Benedetto has completed over 750 musical instruments. 466 are archtop guitars, with the remainder being compromised of 51 violins, five violas, one classical guitar, two mandolins, 11 semi-hollow electrics, 209 electric solidbody electric guitars and basses, and one cello. The 11 semi-hollow electrics include six unique, carved top, semi-hollow electrics made between 1982 and 1986. The other five include three prototypes for, and two finished examples of, his new "benny" semi-hollow electric line introduced in 1998. The 209 electric solid bodies include 157 electric guitars and 52 electric basses. Benedetto began making them in 1986 with John Buscarino. He stopped making them in the Spring of 1987. The 11 semi-hollow electrics and the one classical guitar are included in the archtop guitar serial numbering system. The two mandolins have no serial numbers. The violins, violas, and cello have their own serial number system (starting with #101) as do the electric solid body guitars and basses (starting with #1001).

Serial Numbers:

All Benedetto archtop guitars (except his first two) are numbered in one series, electric solidbodies and basses each have their own separate series, as do the violins, violas and cello. Archtop guitars have a four- or five- digit serial number with configuration ##(#)YY. two (or three) digits ##(#) indicate ranking, beginning with #1 in 1968.

The last two digits (YY) indicate the year.

Example: 43599 was made in 1999 and is the 435th archtop made since 1968.

From Robert Benedetto's *Archtop Guitar Serial Number Logbook*

Note: year listed on the right indicates date shipped, not made:

NUMBER	YEAR
0168 (#1)*	1968
0270 (#2)*	1970
0372	1972
0473	1973
0575-0676	1976
0777-1177	1977
1277-2778	1978
2879-4279	1979
4380-5580	1980
5681-7381	1981
7482-9582	1982
9682-10983	1983
11084-11984	1984
12085-12885	1985
12986-13586	1986
13686-13987-A	1987
14087-16488	1988
16588-19189	1989
19289-22490-A	1990
22591-25091	1991
25192-28092	1992
28193-30293	1993
30393-32994	1994
33095-36595	1995
36696-39496	1996
39597-40697	1997
40798-4349	1998
43599-45199	1999
45200-46200	2000
46301-46601	2001

* Actual number in log: Benedetto did not adopt his current serial number system until his third guitar, serial #0372.

Seven guitar serial numbers are follwed by the letter "A". Example: archtop guitar #23891 and #23891-A are two separate instruments even though both are numbered the "238th".

Further information and a full serial number list can be found in Robert Benedetto's book, Making an Archtop Guitar (Center stream Publishing/Hal Leonard, 1994).

BIGSBY, PAUL

Bigsby serial numbers can be found on the guitars stamped down by the lower strap button, and on pedal steels near the leg attachment. Serialization corresponds with the date produced (month/day/year).

CARVIN

Originally founded by Lowell C. Kiesel as the pickup-building L. C. Kiesel Company, Carvin has expanded through the years into a full line mail order company that offers guitars, basses, amplifiers, P.A. gear, and replacement parts. The company initially offered kit-built guitars, and, by 1964, completed models.

The 2,000 to 4,000 instruments built between 1964 and 1970 did not have serial numbers. The first serial number issued in 1970 was number 5000, and numbers since then have been sequential. Serial numbers up until the late 1990s were stamped on the jackplate. On models with rounded edges and no jackplates, the serial number was stamped into the end of the fingerboard unless it was maple. In that case, the number may be stamped inside the control cavity cover plate.

Carvin's serialization is sequential, but there appears to be no logical order in the way they are assigned. A TL60 built in 2002 has a serial number of 63663 while a Bolt built in 2000 has a serial number of 82398, and an LB70 bass built in 1998 has a serial number of 63094. The following chart of serial numbers contains several overlaps in numbers. The numbers recorded represent the lowest and highest numbers found for each year. More possibilities exist. Carvin suggests dating your guitar by certain features rather than the serial

number. Refer to the Carvin Museum website for more information: www.carvinmuseum.com.

YEAR	NUMBER
1970-1979	5000-10019
1980-1983	10768-15919
1984-1987	13666-25332
1988-1990	22731-25683
1991-1994	25359-42547
1995-1999	45879-81427
2000-PRESENT	56162-

(Source: Carvin Museum)

CHARVEL

Charvel began using four-digit serial numbers in November, 1981, beginning with 1001. Guitars built previous to this have no serialization. In order to correctly identify the year of your guitar, check the neckplate, body, and neck with the correct logo. The serial number is stamped onto the raised letter neckplate and runs to 5491. Plates with the number 5492 are considered non-authentic because several of these plates escaped the factory and were easy to forge. Five-digit serial numbers also appear occasionally. USA production ended in 1986. Current serial numbers are unknown at this time.

NUMBER	YEAR
1001-1095	1981
1096-1724	1982
1725-2938	1983
2939-4261	1984
4262-5303	1985
5304-5491	1986

(Source: Bret Dennis, www.sandimascharvel.com)

D'ANGELICO

Master Luthier John D'Angelico (1905-1964) opened his own shop at age 27, and every guitar was hand built - many to the specifications or nuances of the customer commissioning the instrument. In the course of his brief lifetime, he created 1,164 numbered guitars, as well as unnumbered mandolins, novelty instruments, and the necks for the plywood semi-hollowbody electrics. The objective of this list is to help identify the production of numbered guitars.

D'Angelico kept a pair of ledger books and some loose sheets of paper as a log of the guitars created, models, date of completion (or possibly the date of ship-meng), the person or business to whom the guitar was sold, and the date. The following list is a rough approximation of the ledgers and records.

First *Loose Sheets*	
1002-1073	1932-1934
Ledger Book One	
1169-1456	1936-1939
1457-1831	1940-1949
1832-1849	1950
Ledger Book Two	
1850-2098	1950-1959
2099-2122	1960
2123	1961
Second *Loose Sheets*	
2124-2164	Dates not recorded

Again, it must be stressed that the above system is a guide only. In 1991, author Paul William Schmidt published a book entitled *Acquired of the Angels: The Lives and Works of Master Guitar Makers John D'Angelico and James L. D'Aquisto* (The Scarecrow Press, Inc.; Metuchen, N.J. & London). In Appendix 1 the entire ledger information is reprinted save information on persons or businesses to whom the guitar was sold. This book is recommended to anyone seeking information on luthiers John D'Angelico and James L. D'Aquisto.

D'AQUISTO

Master luthier James L. D'Aquisto (1935-1995) met John D'Angelico around 1953. At the early age of 17, D'Aquisto became D'Angelico's apprentice, and by 1959 was handling the decorative procedures and other lutherie jobs.

D'Aquisto, like his mentor before him, kept ledger books as a log of the guitars created, models, date of completion (or possibly the date of shipmeng), the person or business to whom the guitar was sold, and the date. The following list is a rough approximation of the ledger. As the original pages contain some idiosyncrasies, the following list will by nature be inaccurate as well, and should only be used as a guide for dating individual instruments. The objective of this list is to help identify the production of numbered guitars.

The D'Aquisto Ledger

NUMBER	YEAR
1001-1035	1965-1969
1036-1084	1970-1974
1085-1133	1975-1979
1134-1175	1980-1984
1176-1228	1985-1990

Beginning in 1988, serialization started with 1230. 1257 was D'Aquisto's last serial number on non-futuristic models.

Other guitars that D'Aquisto built had their own serial numbers. For example, solid body and semi-hollow body guitars from 1976 to 1987 had an *E* before the three-digit number. D'Aquisto also built some classical models, some flat-top acoustics, and some hollowbody electric models (hollowbody guitars run from #1 to #30, 1976 to 1980; and #101 to #118, 1982 to 1988).

In 1991, author Paul William Schmidt published a book entitled *Acquired of the Angels: The Lives and Works of Master Guitar Makers John D'Angelico and James L. D'Aquisto* (The Scarecrow Press, Inc.; Metuchen, N.J. & London). In Appendix 2, the entire ledger information is reprinted up to the year 1988 except for information on persons or businesses to whom the guitar was sold. This book is recommended to anyone seeking information on luthiers John D'Angelico and James L. D'Aquisto.

DANELECTRO

Danelectro serial numbers are usually located in the neck pocket, although they do also turn up in other hidden areas of the body. Most Danelectros carry a four-digit code. The code pattern is XXYZ: XX is the week of the year (01-52), Y is still a mystery (batch code or designator?), and Z is the last digit of the production years. As the Z number is duplicated every ten years, model designation and features should also be used in determining the date. Some guitars built during the first nine weeks of each year (01 through 09, XX code) may not have the 0 as the first number.

There are two variations on this code. In late 1967, the **Coral** and **Dane** series were offered, and were numbered with a ZXX code. The other original models still maintain their four-digit code. However, the **Convertible** model (a Pre-'67 series) was cosmetically changed in 1968 to a Dane-style headstock, and changed to the new three-digit code.

(Serialization courtesy of Paul Bechtoldt and Doug Tulloch, Guitars from Neptune. *This book is the definitive listing for models, specifications, and company information - plus it carries many examples of the company's advertising as a reference tool)*

DEAN

Serialization for the *Made in the U.S.A.* instruments is fairly straightforward to decipher. The serial numbers were stamped onto the back of the headstock, and the first two digits of the serial number are the year of manufacture. The following five digits represent the instrument number. Examples of this would be:

NUMBER	YEAR
79 00619	1979
81 39102	1981
02 15268	2002

The imported Deans do not carry the stamped and year-coded serial numbers, and would have to be dated through configuration, headstock design, and other design factors. Contact Dean for more information on imported models.

(Source: Dean Guitars)

EPIPHONE

1935-1944: Acoustic guitars were introduced in 1930, and were built in New York City, New York through 1953. Electric models were introduced in 1935. Company manufacturing was moved to Philadelphia due to union harrass-ment in New York, and Epiphone continued on through 1957. Serial numbers on original Epiphones can be found on the label.

NUMBER	YEAR
000-249	1935
250-749	1936
750-1499	1937
1500-2499	1938
2500-3499	1939
3500-4999	1940
5000-6499	1941
6500-7499	1942
7500-8299	1943
8300-9000	1944

1945-1950: Between about 1945 and 1950, the number prefixes 15, 25, 26, 60, 75, and 85 were assigned to specific models. These were followed by three digits which were the actual "serial" number. Dating is unknown from the last numbers of the serial number.

NUMBER	MODEL
15	CENTURY HAWAIIAN
25	ZEPHYR SPANISH
26	ZEPHYR SPANISH
60	CENTURY SPANISH
75	ZEPHYR DELUXE
85	ZEPHYR DELUXE REGENT

1950-1957: In 1951, electric instruments were brought under the same numbering system as acoustics, and serial numbers were relocated to a paper label in the instrument's interior. Some transitional instruments bear both impressed numbers and a paper label with differing numbers. The latter are more accurate for use in dating.

NUMBER	YEAR
59000S	1950
60000S-63000S	1951
64000S	1952
64000S-66000S	1953
67000S	1954
68000S	1955
69000S	1957

1958-1961: In May of 1957, Epiphone was purchased by CMI and became a division of Gibson. Gibson built Epiphone guitars in Kalamazoo from 1958 to 1970. Hollow body guitars had the serial number on the inside label, and pre-fixed with "A-", plus four digits for the first three years (note: this is different than the similar Gibson serialization). Electric solid body guitars had the serial number inked on the back of the headstock (Y XXX or Y XXXX) and the first number indicates the year: "8" (1958), "9" (1959), and "0" (1960) (note: this is similar to the Gibson serialization).

NUMBER	YEAR
A 1000S	1959
A 2000S	1959-1960
A 3000S-A4312	1960-EARLY 1961

1961-1970: In 1961, the numbering scheme changed as all models had the serial number pressed into the back on the headstock. There were numerous examples of duplication of serial numbers, so when dating a Epiphone from this time period, consideration of parts/configuration and other details is equally important.

NUMBER	YEAR
100-42440	1961
42441-61180	1962
61450-64222	1963
64240-71040	1964
71041-96600	1962, 1963, 1964
96601-99999	1963

NUMBER	YEAR
000001-099999	1967
100000-106099	1963, 1967
106100-108999	1963
109000-109999	1963, 1967
110000-111549	1963
111550-115799	1963, 1967
115800-118299	1963
118300-120999	1963, 1967
121000-139999	1963
140000-140100	1963, 1967
140101-144304	1963
144305-144380	1963, 1964
144381-149864	1963
149865-149891	1964
149892-152989	1963
152990-174222	1964
174223-176643	1964, 1965
176644-250335	1964
250336-305983	1965
306000-310999	1965, 1967
311000-320149	1965
320150-320699	1967
320700-329179	1965
329180-330199	1965, 1967
330200-332240	1965, 1967, 1968
332241-348092	1965
348093-349100	1966
349121-368638	1965
368640-369890	1966
370000-370999	1967
380000-385309	1966
390000-390998	1967
400001-406666	1966
406667-409670	1966, 1967, 1968
409671-410900	1966
410901-419999	NO ENTRIES
420000-429193	1966
500000-500999	1965, 1966,1968, 1969
501009-501600	1965
501601-501702	1968
501703-502706	1965, 1968
503010-503109	1968
503405-520955	1965, 1968
520956-530056	1968
530061-530850	1966, 1968, 1969
530851-530993	1968, 1969
530994-539999	1969
540000-540795	1966, 1969
540796-545009	1969
555000-556909	1966
558012-567400	1969
570087-570643	1966
570645-570755	1966, 1967
570857-570964	1966
580000-580080	1969
580086-580999	1966, 1967, 1969
600000-600998	1966, 1967, 1968 (LOW END)
600000-606090	1969 (HIGH END)

NUMBER	YEAR
700000-700799	1966, 1967
750000-750999	1968, 1969
800000-800999	1966, 1967, 1968, 1969
801000-812838	1966, 1969
812900-819999	1969
820000-820087	1966, 1969
820088-823830	1966*
824000-824999	1969
828002-847488	1966, 1969
847499-858999	1966, 1969
859001-895038	1967
895039-896999	1968
897000-898999	1967, 1969
899000-899999	1968
900000-901999	1970
910000-999999	1968

1970-PRESENT (FOREIGN): In 1970, production of Epiphone instruments moved to Japan. Japanese Epiphones were manufactured between 1970 and 1983. According to author/researcher Walter Carter, the serial numbers on these are unreliable as a usable tool for dating models. Comparison to catalogs is one of the few means available for dating these instruments. Earlier Kalamazoo labels were generally orange with black printing and said "Made in Kalamazoo", while the Japanese instruments featured blue labels which read "Epiphone of Kalamazoo, Michigan" (note that it doesn't say "Made in Kalamazoo", nor does it say "Made in Japan"). Rules of thumb are, by nature, research of the model should be more thorough than just glancing at the label. Serial numbers from Japanese-made models are still unknown.

During the early 1980s, the Japanese production costs became pricey due to the changing ratio of the dollar to the yen. Production then moved to Korea where a different serialization system was used.

NUMBER	YEAR	TYPE
1000	1985	SOLIDBODIES
4000000S	1985	HOLLOWBODIES
4100000S	1985	HOLLOWBODIES
5060000S	1985	SOLIDBODIES
5080000S	1985	SOLIDBODIES
5090000S	1985	HOLLOWBODIES
5100000S	1985	SOLIDBODIES

Current Epiphones manufactured overseas typically utilize a seven- or eight-digit serial number, the first digit being the last one or two numbers of the year of manufacture, and the third and fourth digits being the week of manufacture. Many of these instruments have an alphabetical character designating the manufacturing facility (i.e., S3061789 refers to an instrument mfg. June, 1993 by Samick, R5068265 indicates an instrument mfg. during 1995 by Aria. S02104385 indicates a Samick model produced in October, 2002. Models produced in the late 1990s and early 2000s are more likely to have the eight-digit system.

1977-PRESENT (U.S.): Some top-of-the-line Epiphones were produced in the U.S. at Gibson's Kalamazoo, Nashville, and Montana facilities since the mid-70s. Like Gibson numbers, there are eight digits in the complete number, and this number follows the code of YDDDYNNN. The YY (first and fifth digits) indicate the year it was built. DDD indicates the day of the year (so DDD can't be above 365), and the NNN indicates the instrument's production ranking for that day (NNN = 021 = 21st guitar built). The Nashville facility begins each day at number 501, and the Montana workshop begins at number 001 (as did Kalamazoo). However, in 1994, the Nashville-produced Epiphones were configured as YYNNNNNN: YY = 94 (the year) and NNNNNN is the ranking for the entire year. Example: 82303025 was built on the 230th day of 1983 and was the 25th instrument built at Kalamazoo that day.

***Source: Walter Carter,* Epiphone: The Complete History, *Walter Carter and George Gruhn,* Gruhn's Guide to Vintage Guitars.**

FENDER

Serial numbers, in general, are found on the bridgeplate, the neckplate, the backplate, or the peghead. From 1950 to 1954, serial numbers are found on the bridgeplate or vibrato backplate. From 1954 to 1976, the serial numbers were found on the neckplate, either the top or the bottom of the plate. From 1976 to date, the serial number appears with the peghead decal. Vintage Reissues have their serial numbers on the neckplate and have been in use since 1982.

The Fender company also stamped (or handwrote) the production date on the heel of the neck, in the body routs, on the pickups, and near the wiring harness (the body, pickup, and wiring dating was only done sporadically, during certain time periods). However, the neck date (and body date) indicate when the neck (or body) part was completed! Fender produces necks and guitar bodies separately, and bolts the two together during final production. Therefore, the date on the neck will generally be weeks or months before the actual production date.

When trying to determine the manufacturing date of an instrument by serialization, it is best to keep in mind that there are no clear-cut boundaries between where the numbers began and when they ended. There was constant overlapping of serial numbers between years and models.

1950-1954: From 1950 to 1954, each guitar model had its own serialization group. Telecasters have different numbers than Stratocasters and P-Basses.

TELECASTER/ESQUIRE/BROADCASTER/NO-CASTER

NUMBER	YEAR
33-860	1950-1952
0005-0746	1950-1952
0748-1331	1951-1952
0161-0470	1951-1952
2911-5368	1951-1954

STRATOCASTER

NUMBER	YEAR
UNDER 6000	1954

PRECISION BASS

NUMBER	YEAR
161-357	1951
299-619	1952
0001-0160	1952
0161-0470	1951-1952
0475-0840	1952-1953
0848-1897	1953-1954

1954-1963: In late 1954, the serialization became standard for all models. The numbers are still a bit random, but most of them can be grouped into general categories. The following numbers represent where most numbers will fall into categories. However, the lowest and highest numbers represent serial numbers that have dated to a certain year. In 1955, 1957, and 1958, a "0" or a "-" may precede the number.

NUMBER	LOWEST	HIGHEST	YEAR
0001-6000S	0001	10146	1954
7000-8000S	3152	10798	1955
09000-16000S	7895	16957	1956
17000-24000S	10604	28522	1957
25000-33000S	022526	40644	1958
34000-43000S	022878	51593	1959
44000-58000S	39993	66626	1960
59000-70000S	55531	77754	1961
71000-93000S	69520	96203	1962
94000-99000S	81977	99924	1963

1962-1965: In 1962, as the serialization count neared 100000, they did not expand to six digits. Instead, an L preceded a five-digit sequence. It ran this way from 1962 to 1965. A few examples exist from 1962.

NUMBER	LOWEST	HIGHEST	YEAR
L00001-L19000S	L00001	L60330	1963
L20000-L59000S	L08825	L92560	1964
L60000-L99000S	L23537	L99944	1965

1965-1976: In 1965, when CBS bought Fender Musical Instruments, Inc., the serialization came to be known as the F Series, due to an "F" being stamped onto the neckplate. This series of numbers ran from 1965 to 1976. The approximate numbers and years are as follows:

NUMBER	LOWEST	HIGHEST	YEAR
100000-110000S	100173	158977	1965
120000-170000S	112172	261343	1966
180000-210000S	156657	263115	1967
220000-251000S	204352	262774	1968
252000-291000S	224160	290835	1969
292000-298000S	278916	304089	1970
290000-344000S	261863	331031	1971
345000-370000S	258495	654030	1972
380000-530000S	316987	602615	1973
540000-590000S	417024	677199	1974
600000-656000S	595121	717257	1975
657000-660000S			1976
670000-700000S			1971-1976

A way to cross-check the serialization from 1973 to 1976 is to check the production dates on the neck.

NUMBER	YEAR
400000S	EARLY 1973 TO LATE 1976
500000S	LATE 1973 TO LATE 1976
600000S	MID 1974 TO MID 1976
700000S	MID 1976 TO LATE 1976

1976-PRESENT (U.S.): In late 1976, Fender decided to move to a new numbering scheme for their serialization. The numbers appeared on the pegheads, and, for the remainder of 1976, they had a prefix of 76 in bold or S6 preceding a five-digit sequence. In 1977, the serialization went to a letter for the decade, followed by five or six digits with the first one indicating the last number of the year. For the most part, the number after the letter is the year, but it may bleed over into the following year. The letter code stands for the first letter of the decade: S for the '70s, E for the '80s, N for the '90s, and Z for the '00s. Some examples: E32575 is a guitar built in 1982, and N502587 is a guitar built in 1995 or 1996. Several exceptions exist in Fender's serialization - make sure to read the entire section for all models.

NUMBER	YEAR
760000S	1976, 1977
800000S	1979, 1980, 1981
1000000-8000000S	1976-1981
S100000-S600000S	1979-1982
S700000-S770000S	1977
S740000-S800000S	1978
S810000-S870000S	1979
S880000-S980000S	1980
S950000-S990000S	1981
E000000-E100000S	1979-1982
E110000-E120000S	1980-1983
E200000S	1982
E300000-E310000S	1983
E320000-E390000S	1984-1985
E400000S	1984, 1985, 1987
E800000S	1988, 1989
E900000S	1989, 1990
N900000S	1990
N000000S	1990
N100000S	1991, 1992
N200000S	1992, 1993
N300000S	1993, 1994
N400000S	1994, 1995
N500000S	1995, 1996

NUMBER	YEAR
N600000S	1996, 1997
N700000S	1997, 1998
N800000S	1998, 1999
N900000S	1999, 2000
Z000000S	2000, 2001
Z100000S	2001, 2002
Z200000S	2002, 2003
Z300000S	2003, 2004
Z400000S	2004, 2005
Z500000S	2005, 2006

While the idea was fine, the actuality was a different matter. Instrument production did not meet the levels for which decals had been produced, so there are several overlapping years. Sometimes several prefixes can be found within a single year's production. After 1991, the numbers became fairly standard and the letter and first digit prefix can be used accurately. Here is the revised table of letter/digit year codes:

CODE	DATE
S7	JAN. 1977-APR. 1978
S8	DEC. 1977-DEC. 1978
S9	NOV. 1978-AUG. 1981
E0	JUN. 1979-DEC. 1981
E1	DEC. 1980-JAN. 1982
E2	DEC. 1981-JAN. 1983
E3	DEC. 1982-JAN. 1985
E4	DEC. 1983-EARLY 1988
E8	1988-1989
E9	1989-1990
N9	1990
N0	1990-1991

25 Prefix: 25th Anniversary Stratocaster produced 1979 to 1980 25XXXXX.

AMXN Prefix: California Series electric guitars and basses, AMXN + six digits.

C Prefix: Collector's Series

CA Prefix: Stratocaster Gold, produced 1981 to 1983, CA + five digits.

CB Prefix: Precision Bass Special produced1981, Jazz Bass Gold produced 1982, CB + five digits.

CC Prefix: Stratocaster Walnut produced 1981 to 1983, CC + five digits.

CD Prefix: Precision Bass Special produced 1982, CD + five digits.

CE Prefix: Precision Bass Special produced 1981, Black & Gold Telecaster produced 1981 to 1983, CE + five digits.

CN Prefix: Fender and Squier guitars produced in Korea, production dates and numbers unknown.

CO Prefix: Precision Bass Special produced 1982, CO + five digits.

D Prefix: Jazz Bass produced from 1981 to 1982, D + six digits.

DN Prefix: American Deluxe electric guitars and basses, produced 1998 to 1999, DN+ six digits.

DZ Pefix: American Deluxe electric guitars and basses produced 2000-present, DZ + corresponding year (1 digit) + five or six digits.

FN Prefix: U.S.-built guitars and basses that are for export. Some examples may be found back into the U.S., FN + six digits.

G Prefix: The Strat produced 1980-1983, G + six digits.

GO Prefix: Precision Bass Special produced 1982, Stratocaster Gold produced 1982-1983, GO + five digits.

I Prefix: Limited number of guitars built for export only in 1989 and 1990. They feature Made in USA stamped on the heel of the neck, very few of these may be found in the U.S., one + six digits.

LE Prefix: Blonde Jaguars and Jazzmasters that were sold as a three-piece set with a Blonde Deluxe Reverb Amp, produced in 1994 only, LE + six digits.

MN Pefix: Mexican-made models produced in the 1990s.

NC Prefix: Squier Stratocaster Bullets, production and numbers unknown.

SE/SN/SZ Prefix: Signature Series guitars and basses, produced 1988-1989. These serial numbers follow the same numbering scheme as most standard guitars. Examples: SE900056 is a Signature 1989, N701025 is a Signature 1997.

T Prefix: Tribute Series instruments.

V Prefixes: (introduced circa 1982) designate Vintage Reissue Series. These guitars have a VXXXXXX designation with the numbers only representing production number.

VN Prefix: Fender and Squier guitars produced in Korea, production dates and numbers unknown.

XN Prefix: FSR and '52 Telecasters.

Several variations of serial numbers have been used by Fender. More schemes may exist, especially from the custom shop and/or limited editions, etc.

1982-PRESENT (JAPAN): Fender Japan was established in March, 1982, in a negotiation between CBS/Fender, Kanda Shokai, and Yamano Music. Instruments were built by Fuji Gen Gakki, initially for the European market. When the Vintage/Reissues models were offered in the early 1980s, a V in the serial number indicated U.S. production, while a JV stood for Fender Japan-built models. For the first two years of Japanese production, serial numbers consisted of a two-letter prefix to indicate the year, followed by five digits. In late 1984, this code was changed to a single-letter prefix and six digits. After 1997, some of the letters were regurgitated. These should not be confused with earlier models, and the later models should have "Crafted in Japan" on the headstock.

NUMBER	YEAR
A + 6 DIGITS	1985-1986, 1997-1998
B + 6 DIGITS	1985-1986
C + 6 DIGITS	1985-1986
E + 6 DIGITS	1984-1987
F + 6 DIGITS	1986-1987
G + 6 DIGITS	1987-1988
H + 6 DIGITS	1988-1989
I + 6 DIGITS	1989-1990
J + 6 DIGITS	1989-1990
JV + 5 DIGITS	1982-1984
K + 6 DIGITS	1990-1991
L + 6 DIGITS	1991-1992
M + 6 DIGITS	1992-1993
N + 5 DIGITS	1995-1996
N + 6 DIGITS	1993-1994
O + 5 DIGITS	1997-2000
O + 6 DIGITS	1994-1995
P + 5 DIGITS	1999-2002
P + 6 DIGITS	1995-1996
Q + 5 DIGITS	2002-2004
Q + 6 DIGITS	1993-1994
R + 5 DIGITS	2004-2005
S + 6 DIGITS	1994-1995
SQ + 5 DIGITS	1983-1984
T + 6 DIGITS	1994-1995
U + 6 DIGITS	1995-1996
V + 6 DIGITS	1996-1997

1990-PRESENT (MEXICO): Mexican instruments were first produced in 1990 with the Standard Series. Serialization is pretty straightforward, with a few models that overlap each year.

NUMBER	YEAR
MN0 + 5 DIGITS	1990-1991
MN1 + 5 DIGITS	1991-1992
MN2 + 5 DIGITS	1992-1993
MN3 + 5 DIGITS	1993-1994
MN4 + 5 DIGITS	1994-1995

NUMBER	YEAR
MN5 + 5 DIGITS	1995-1996
MN6 + 5 DIGITS	1996-1997
MN7 + 5 DIGITS	1997-1998
MN8 + 5 DIGITS	1998-1999
MN9 + 5 DIGITS	1999-2000
MZ0 + 5 DIGITS	2000-2001
MZ1 + 5 DIGITS	2001-2002
MZ2 + 5 DIGITS	2002-2003
MZ3 + 5 DIGITS	2003-2004
MZ4 + 5 DIGITS	2004-2005
MZ5 + 5 DIGITS	2005-2006

Dating a Fender instrument by serialization alone can get you within an approximate range of years, but this should not be used as a definitive means to determine the year of actual production. In order to date your guitar more accurately, it is necessary to date everything from the original parts.

Source: A.R. Duchossoir; Michael Wright, Vintage Guitar Magazine, Walter Carter and George Gruhn, Gruhn's Guide to Vintage Guitars, and FMIC.

FRAMUS

Framus serial numbers were generally placed on the back of the peghead or on a label inside the body. The main body of the serial number is followed by an additional pair of digits and a letter. This additional pair of numbers indicate the production year.

For example:

51334 63L	1963
65939 70L	1970

Source: Tony Bacon and Barry Moorehouse, The Bass Book, GPI Books, 1995.

G & L

According to G & L expert Paul Bechtoldt, all production serial numbers started at #500, as prior numbers were reserved for special instruments or presentations. All G & L models have a date in the neck pocket of the instrument for reliable dating. Most G & L instruments have both body and neck dating, leading to some confusion as to the actual building date. However, the final authority exists in the G & L log book - manually looking up the serial number of the instrument.

1980-1996: All G & L serial numbers are seven digits long, with the first digit being a letter prefix indicating a guitar ("G") system or bass ("B") system.

1997-Date: In 1997, all guitar models and L-1505 and L-2500 basses changed to a six-digit sequence beginning with **CL** (in honor of founder Clarence Leo Fender), followed by four numbers.

The two guitar models to have their own prefix digits and numbering system were the Broadcaster ("BC") and George Fullerton Signature model ("GF").

First Recorded Serial Number For Each Year

YEAR	GUITAR	BASS
1980	G000530	B000518
1981	G003122	B001917
1982	G009886	B008525
1983	G011654	B010382
1984	G013273	B014266
1985	G014690	B016108
1986	G017325	B017691
1987	G020241	B018063
1988	G023725	B019627
1989	G024983	B020106
1990	G026344	B021788
1991	G027163	B023013
1992	G029962	B024288

Information courtesy Paul Bechtoldt, G & L: Leo's Legacy, Woof Associates, 1994. This book is a must-have for anyone interested in G & L instruments, as the book documents models, variations, and the company history.

GIBSON

Identifying Gibson instruments by serial number is tricky at best, and downright impossible in some cases. The best method of identifying them is to use a combination of the serial number, the factory order number and any features that are particular to a specific time. (i.e. logo design change, headstock volutes, etc).

In addition to the above serial number information, Gibson also used Factory Order Numbers (F O N) to track batches of instruments being produced at the time. In the earlier years at Gibson, guitars were normally built in batches of forty instruments. Gibson's Factory Order Numbers were an internal coding that followed the group of instruments through the factory. Thus, the older Gibson guitars may have a serial number and a F O N. The F O N may indicate the year, batch number, and the ranking (order of production within the batch of forty).

This system is useful in helping to date and authenticate instruments. There are three separate groupings of numbers that have been identified and which are used for their accuracy. The numbers are usually stamped or written on the instrument's back and seen through the lower f-hole or round soundhole, or maybe impressed on the back of the headstock.

Code Letter F O Ns were discontinued after 1941, and any instruments made during or right after World War II do not bear an F O N codes. In 1949, a four digit F O N was used, but not in conjunction with any code letter indicating the year.

From 1952-1961, the F O N scheme followed the pattern of a letter, the batch number, and an instrument ranking number (when the guitar was built in the run of forty). The F O N is the only identification number on Gibson's lower grade models (like the ES-125, ES-140, J-160E, etc.) which do not feature a paper label. Higher grade models (such as the Super 400, L-5, J-200, etc.) feature both a serial number **and** a FON. When both numbers are present on a higher grade model, remember that the FON was assigned at the beginning of the production run, while the serial number was recorded later (before shipping). The serial number would properly indicate the actual date of the guitar.

1935-1947: The first production electric guitars appeared in 1935. These guitars picked up on the serialization, which was already established by the acoustic models. The serial numbers started with number 100 for acoustics and around 90000 for electrics. This system ran to 99999 for both acoustics and electrics. All numbers are approximate. In most cases, only the upper end instruments were assigned identification numbers. Serial numbers appear ink-stamped on a white paper label. FONs were first used in 1935. Other FONs may appear that aren't listed here that were produced during WWII. From 1935 to 1937, the letter appeared between the batch and instrument numbers (i.e. 722 A 23, 465 D 58, 863 E 02). The number is ink-stamped inside the guitar on the back. In 1938, the FON was changed to a two- or three-letter prefix before the batch and instrument numbers. The first letter indicates the year, the second indicates the brand (i.e. G for Gibson, K for Kalamazoo), and the third (if applicable) for electric. The FON is either ink-stamped on the label or on the back of the headstock.

SERIAL NUMBERS

APPROX. LAST NUMBER	YEAR
92800	1935
94100	1936
95200	1937
95750	1938
96050	1939
96600	1940
97400	1941
97700	1942
97850	1943
98250	1944
98650	1945
99300	1946
99999	1947

FACTORY ORDER NUMBERS (FON)

LETTER	YEAR
A	1935
B	1936
C	1937
D	1938
DA	1938
E(X, OR OTHER LETTERS)	1939
E	1941
F	1940
FA	1940
G	1941
H	1942

1947-1961 (HOLLOWBODIES): Gibson changed their serialization system once they reached 99999 and decided they did not want to go to a six-digit system. Instead, they added an A prefix followed by a three-, four-, or five-digit number. The new system started on April 28, 1947 with number A 100. The last number was used on February 21, 1961. From 1947 to early 1955, white oval labels were used. In early 1955, the label was changed to an orange oval. Serial numbers are on the label and FONs are ink-stamped on the inside back of the guitar. FONs consisted of a letter, four-digit batch number, and count number (i.e. Y 2230 21, V 4867 8, R 6785 15). FONs were discontinued after Gibson changed to the new serialization system in 1961.

SERIAL NUMBERS

APPROX. LAST NUMBER	YEAR
A 1304	1947
A 2665	1948
A 4413	1949
A 6597	1950
A 9419	1951
A 12462	1952
A 16101	1953
A 18667	1954
A 21909	1955
A 24755	1956
A 26819	1957
A 28880	1958
A 32284	1959
A 35645	1960
A 36147	1961

FACTORY ORDER NUMBERS (FON)

LETTER/NUMBER	YEAR
700-1000S	1947
1100-3700S	1948
3700-4500S	EARLY 1949

(FON)LETTER/NUMBER	YEAR
2000S	LATE 1949
3000-5000S	1950
6000-9000S	1951
Z	1952
Y	1953
X	1954
W	1955
V	1956
U	1957
T	1958
S	1959
R	1960
Q	1961

1952-1961 (SOLIDBODIES): When production of solidbody guitars began,

an entirely new serial number system was developed. Though not used on the earliest instruments produced (those done in 1952), a few of these instruments have three digits stamped on the headstock top. Sometime in 1953, instruments were ink stamped on the headstock back with 5- or 6-digit numbers, the first digit indicating the year, and the following digits indicating production numbers (Y NNNN or Y NNNNN). The production numbers run in a consecutive order and, aside from a few oddities in the change over years (1961-1962), it is fairly accurate to use them when identifying solid body instruments produced between 1953 and 1961. Later models typically feature six-digit numbers. Examples of this system:

    4 2205 = 1954
    6 14562 = 1956
    0 3865 = 1960

1961-1970: In 1961, Gibson started a new serial number system that covered all instrument lines. It consisted of numbers that were impressed into the wood. This is generally considered to be the most confusing out of all Gibson's serial number systems used between the years 1961 and 1970. There are several instances where batches of numbers are switched in order and duplicated, not just once, but up to four times, and seem to be randomly assigned throughout the decade.

Note: If "MADE IN USA" is stamped in the back of the headstock near the serial number, the guitar is not from the 1960s, but the 1970s. In this case, please refer to the next section on serializationf for 1970-1975 guitars.

NUMBER	YEAR
100-42440	1961
42441-61180	1962
61450-64222	1963
64240-71040	1964
71041-96600	1962, 1963, 1964
96601-99999	1963
000001-099999	1967
100000-106099	1963, 1967
106100-108999	1963
109000-109999	1963, 1967
110000-111549	1963
111550-115799	1963, 1967
115800-118299	1963
118300-120999	1963, 1967
121000-139999	1963
140000-140100	1963, 1967
140101-144304	1963
144305-144380	1963, 1964
144381-149864	1963
149865-149891	1964
149892-152989	1963
152990-174222	1964
174223-176643	1964, 1965
176644-250335	1964
250336-305983	1965
306000-310999	1965, 1967
311000-320149	1965
320150-320699	1967
320700-329179	1965
329180-330199	1965, 1967
330200-332240	1965, 1967, 1968
332241-348092	1965
348093-349100	1966
349121-368638	1965
368640-369890	1966
370000-370999	1967
380000-385309	1966

NUMBER	YEAR
390000-390998	1967
400001-406666	1966
406667-409670	1966, 1967, 1968
409671-410900	1966
410901-419999	NO ENTRIES
420000-429193	1966
500000-500999	1965, 1966,1968, 1969
501009-501600	1965
501601-501702	1968
501703-502706	1965, 1968
503010-503109	1968
503405-520955	1965, 1968
520956-530056	1968
530061-530850	1966, 1968, 1969
530851-530993	1968, 1969
530994-539999	1969
540000-540795	1966, 1969
540796-545009	1969
555000-556909	1966
558012-567400	1969
570087-570643	1966
570645-570755	1966, 1967
570857-570964	1966
580000-580080	1969
580086-580999	1966, 1967, 1969
600000-600998	1966, 1967, 1968 (LOW END)
600000-606090	1969 (HIGH END)
700000-700799	1966, 1967
750000-750999	1968, 1969
800000-800999	1966, 1967, 1968, 1969
801000-812838	1966, 1969
812900-819999	1969
820000-820087	1966, 1969
820088-823830	1966*
824000-824999	1969
828002-847488	1966, 1969
847499-858999	1966, 1969
859001-895038	1967
895039-896999	1968
897000-898999	1967, 1969
899000-899999	1968
900000-901999	1970
910000-999999	1968

1970-1975: From 1970 to 1975 the method of serializing instruments at Gibson became even more random. All numbers were impressed into the wood and a six-digit number was assigned, though no particular order was given and some instruments had a letter prefix. The orange labels inside hollow bodied instruments were discontinued in 1970 and were replaced by white and orange rectangular labels on the acoustics, and small black, purple, and white rectangular labels were placed on electric models.

In 1970, the words **MADE IN USA** were impressed into the back of instrument headstocks (though a few instruments from the 1950s also had this. The difference between a 1960s and a 1970s Gibson model is the "MADE IN USA" stamp on the back of the headstock.

NUMBER	YEAR
000000S	1973
100000S	1970-1975
200000S	1973-1975
300000S	1974-1975

NUMBER	YEAR
400000S	1974-1975
500000S	1974-1975
600000S	1970, 1971, 1972, 1974, 1975
700000S	1970, 1971, 1972
800000S	1973, 1974, 1975
900000S	1970, 1971, 1972
6 DIGITS + A	1970
A + 6 DIGITS	1973, 1974, 1975
B + 6 DIGITS	1974, 1975
C + 6 DIGITS	1974, 1975
D + 6 DIGITS	1974, 1975
E + 6 DIGITS	1974, 1975
F + 6 DIGITS	1974, 1975

When the Nashville Gibson plant was opened in 1974, it was decided that the bulk of the production of products would be run in the South; the Kalamazoo plant would produce the higher end (fancier) models in the North. Of course, many of the older guitar builders and craftsmen were still in Kalamazoo, and if they weren't ready to change how they built guitars, then they may not have been ready to change how they numbered them! Certain guitar models built in the late 1970s can be used to demonstrate the old-style, six-digit serial numbers. It is estimated that Gibson's Kalamazoo plant continued to use the six-digit serial numbers through 1978 and 1979. So double check the serial numbers on those 1970s L-5s, Super 400s, and Super 5 BJBs!

1975-1977: During the period from 1975 to 1977, Gibson used a transfer that had eight-digit numbers. The first two indicate the year (99=1975, 00=1976 and 06=1977), the following six digits are in the 100000 to 200000 range. *MADE IN USA* was also included on the transfer and some models had *LIMITED EDITION* also applied. A few bolt-on neck instruments had a date ink stamped on the heel area.

NUMBER	YEAR
99XXXXXX	1975
00XXXXXX	1976
06XXXXXX	1977

1977-PRESENT: In 1977, Gibson first introduced the serialization method that is in practice today. This updated system utilizes an impressed, eight-digit numbering scheme that covers both serializing and dating functions. The Custom/Historic/Art divisions do not use this system. Certain models in the Standard series do not follow this, either. Please refer to the end of the section for exceptions. The pattern is as follows:

YDDDYPPP

YY is the production year

DDD is the day of the year

PPP is the plant designation and/or instrument rank.

In 1994, for Gibson's Centennial, they used a special serialization. Every serial number started with 94 followed by six digits, which were the production dates and number (YYNNNNNN).

The three PPP numbers 001-499 indicate Kalamazoo production from 1977 to 1984. The Kalamazoo numbers were discontinued in 1984 when the factory closed. The three PPP numbers 500-999 indicate Nashville production from 1977 to 1989.

All currently manufactured Gibsons (non-custom shop) are stamped with a hand arbor, and start at 300 or 500, and continue until production is finished that day. This hand stamp used to be reset daily at #300 or #500 for all the LP style headstocks. The other shapes (Flying V, T-Bird, Explorer, etc.) were started at 700.

When acoustic production began at the plant in Bozeman, Montana (in 1989), the series' numbers were reorganized. Bozeman instruments began using 001-299 designations and, in 1990, Nashville instruments began using 300-999 designations. It should also be noted that the Nashville plant has not reached the 900s since 1977, so these numbers have been reserved for prototypes. Examples:

70108276 means the instrument was produced on Jan. 10, 1978, in Kalamazoo and was the 276th instrument stamped that day.

82765501 means the instrument was produced on Oct. 3, 1985, in Nashville and was the 1st instrument stamped that day.

03202652 means the instrument was produced on November 16, 2002 and was the 152nd instrument stamped that day (assuming they started at 500).

There are a few exceptions to this system.

Centennial Year/Models: 1994 is the most notable exception, with the first two numbers representing the year, so all models start with 94 and are followed by six digits. The Centennial models produced for the 1994 model year have an inked-on serial number that is six digits long. The serial number appears as YYYYMM. The first four represent the number produced. They all started on 1894, which represents instrument #1, and 1994 would be instrument #101. The last two digits indicate the month of the guitar released. A new model was released each month with a total of fourteen different models that includes two prototypes. The last two numbers will range from one to fourteen.

Special Runs/Limited Editions: Certain special editions in the 1970s and 1980s may feature serial numbers with six digits in the configuration of YY NNNN. The YY indicates the year and the NNNN is the instrument ranking.

Les Paul Classic: The 1960 Les Paul Classic features a six-digit number like the models had in the late 1950s and early 1960s. The serial number works just like it did back then with the first number indicating the last number in the year of production. For example, 2 15678 would be either a 1992 or 2002, and a 6 15890 would be a 1996. These models have been produced since 1990, so every ten years the numbers will recycle.

Reissues: Early Les Paul reissues produced between the late 1970s and 1993 should have an inked-on serial number on the back of the headstock. The first number should indicate the last year of the production. For example, 8 0358 would be a 1988. The Heritage Flying V, Moderne, and Chet Atkins CE produced between 1981 and 1983 will feature a serial number with a letter prefix followed by three digits. The letter may range from A through K, and the number started at 001. Most numbers finished at 099 and would move to the next letter. However, certain models do feature higher numbers than 100. The Heritage Series Explorer produced between 1982 and 1983 has a serial number that starts with 1 + 4 digits. These digits are strictly production numbers.

In 1992, the serialization of reissues became standard. The configuration of M YNNN is still in use by Gibson. The M indicates the model code, specifically the last digit of the year of the reissue. The Y indicates the last number of the year of the guitar, and the NNN are the production numbers. For example, 4 8256 indicates a 1954 Les Paul reissue built in 1998 and is the 256th instrument of the year. The following codes represent most of the reissues:

NUMBER	MODELS
2	1952 LES PAUL
4	1954 LES PAUL
6	1956 LES PAUL
7	1957 LES PAUL
8	1958 LES PAUL, EXPLORER
9	1959 LES PAUL, FLYING V
0	1960 LES PAUL

In 1997, Gibson reissued many of the 1960s models. A similar serialization system was used, but it is different than the 1950s reissues. The configuration consists of YYNNNM, where the YY is the last two years of the guitar's construction date, the NNN is the production number, and the M is the model code, specifically the last year of the reissue. For example, 021568 indicates a 1968 Les Paul Custom reissue built in 2002 and was the 156th instrument built that year. The following codes represent most of the reissues:

NUMBER	MODELS
1	SG/LES PAUL
3	1963 FIREBIRD I
4	1964 FIREBIRD III
5	1965 FIREBIRD V/FIREBIRD VII
8	1968 LES PAUL CUSTOM

CUSTOM SHOP: Most custom shop models use the configuration of Y9NNN or Y9NNNN (if the production run is higher than 1000 units in a year). The Y indicates the last digit of the year the guitar was built. 9 is assigned to every custom shop guitar, and the last three or four digits are production numbers.

Historic ES models use a slightly different system than the Custom Shop. The configuration consists of a letter prefix + MYNNN. The letter, which is usually an A or B, indicates that it is part of the Historic Collection, the M indicates the last year of reissue model, the Y indicates the last number of the year the guitar was built, and the final NNN digits are production numbers.

Custom Shop Signature Models use a serialization system with the artists initials and the instrument production number.

Other models such as the Gibson Les Paul Classic may use serialization that was used on the models during that time period. These would be six-digit serial numbers.

Source: A.R. Duchossoir, Gibson Electrics, The Classic Years *and* **Walter Carter and George Gruhn,** Gruhn's Guide to Vintage Guitars.

GRETSCH

The first Gretsch electric guitar appeared in 1940. Before World War II, By 1949, small labels bearing "Fred Gretsch Mfg. Co.," serial and model number replaced the penciled numbers inside the instruments. This label was replaced by a different style label, an orange and grey one, sometime in 1957. A few variations of this scheme occurred throughout the company's history, the most common being the use of impressed numbers in the headstock of instruments, beginning about 1949. Serial numbers were also stamped into the headstock nameplate of a few models. The numbers remain consecutive throughout and the following chart gives approximations of the years they occurred.

1940-1949: Serial numbers were penciled onto labels on the inside backs of Gretsch's higher-end instruments. The number can usually be viewed from the bass side f-hole. Numbers were assigned consecutively, but little is known about year-to-year specifics.

APPROX. NUMBERS	YEARS
001 - 1000	1939-1945
1001 - 2000	1946-1949

1949-1965: The label changed to read: The "Fred Gretsch Mfg. Co." with the company's address in New York. There are two spots where the model is printed and serial number is written in. The serial number should be in red and the model number written in blue or black. The label could be viewed from the f-hole on hollowbody models. On solidbody models, the number was placed inside the electronic compartment either on the wood or on the control plate. Some models produced in the 1960s may have the number impressed into the back of the headstock.

APPROX. NUMBERS	YEAR
2000 - 3000S	1950
3000 - 5000S	1951
5000 - 6000S	1952
6000 - 8000S	1953
8000 - 12000S	1954
12000 - 16000S	1955
16000 - 21000S	1956
21000- 26000S	1957
26000 - 30000S	1958
30000 - 34000S	1959
34000 - 39000S	1960
39000 - 45000S	1961
45000 - 52000S	1962
52000 - 63000S	1963
63000 - 77000S	1964
77000 - 85000S	1965

1965-1972: In the latter part of 1965, Gretsch decided to begin using a date coded system of serialization. It consists of the first digit (sometimes two) that identified the month; the second or third identifying the year, and the remaining digit (or digits) represented the number of the instrument in production for that month. Some examples of this system would be:

997	September, 1969 (7th instrument produced)
11255	November, 1972 (55th instrument produced)
70250	July, 1968 (250th instrument produced)

On solid body instruments, impressed headstock numbers were used. In 1967, *Made in USA* was added. Hollow body instruments still made use of a label placed on the inside back of the instrument.

1973-1981: In 1973, the label style changed once again, becoming a black and white rectangle with *Gretsch Guitars* and the date-coded serialization on it. A hyphen was also added between the month and the year to help avoid confusion.

Serialization Examples:

12-4387	December, 1974 (387th Instrument Produced)
3-745	March, 1977 (45th Instrument Produced)
10-056	October, 1980 (56th Instrument Produced)

1989-PRESENT: Contemporary Gretsch serialization beginning in 1989 utilizes nine digits in a YYMMmmm(m)xxx format. YY indicates the last two digits of the year (i.e., 01 = 2001). M or MM indicates the month of the year (1-12). mmm(m) references the model number with either three or four digits (i.e., a 6136 reads 136). x(xx) refers to a one-to-three digit production count. Examples: A currently manufactured Country Club Model (Model No. 6196) with ser. no. 01319652 indicates it was built in March of 2001, the last three numbers of the model number are next - 196. 52 indicates the production count. A Model No. 6121 Roundup with a ser. no. of 999121447 indicates it was built in Sept. of 1999, 121 represents the last three digits of the model number, and 447 is the production count.

GUILD

Guild Serialization went through three distinct phases, and can be both a helpful guide as well as confusing when trying to determine the manufacturing date of a guitar. The primary idea to realize is that most Guild models use a **separate serial numbering system for each guitar model** - there is no "overall system" to plug a number into! While serial numbers are sometimes a helpful tool, other dating devices like potentiomter codes or dating by hardware may be more exact.

1952-1965: Between the inception of the Guild company in 1952 and 1965, the serialization was sequential for all models.

APPROXIMATE LAST NUMBER	YEAR
350	1952
840	1953
1526	1954
2468	1955
3830	1956
5712	1957
8348	1958
12035	1959
14713	1960
18419	1961
22722	1962

APPROXIMATE LAST NUMBER	YEAR
28943	1963
38636	1964
46606	1965

1966-1969: While some models retained the serialization from the original series, many models were designated with a two-letter prefix and an independent numbering series for each individual model between 1966 and 1969.

Continued Original Serialization Series

APPROXIMATE LAST NUMBER	YEAR
46608	1966
46637	1967
46656	1968
46695	1969

The models that were numbered with the new two-letter prefix started each separate serial number series with 101.

1970-1979: The following chart details the serial numbers as produced through the 1970s. There are no corresponding model names or numbers for this time period.

APPROXIMATE LAST NUMBER	YEAR
50978	1970
61463	1971
75602	1972
95496	1973
112803	1974
130304	1975
149625	1976
169867	1977
190567	1978
211877	1979

1979-1989: In 1979, Guild returned to the separate prefix/serial number system. Serial numbers after the two-letter prefix in each separate system began with 100001 (thus, you would need a serialization table for each model/by year to date by serialization alone). In 1987, a third system was devised. In some cases, the **Model Designation** became the *prefix* for the serial number. For example:

D300041   D-30, #0041 (41st D-30 instrument produced)

With acoustic models, you can cross-reference the model name to the serial number to judge the rest of the serialization; the resulting serial number must still be checked in the serialization table.

1990-PRESENT: Guild continued with the separate prefix/serialization system. In 1994, only the model prefix and last serial numbers for each model were recorded; better records continued in 1995.

Guild Custom Shop: The three Guild Custom Shop models (**45th Anniversary**, **Deco**, and **Finesse**) all use a completely different serial numbering system. Each instrument has a serial number on the back of the headstock that indicates which number it is out of the complete series. Inside the guitar there is a seven-digit code: The first three numbers (starting with 500) indicate the production sequence, while the last four digits indicate the date of production (the fourth and seventh digit <u>in reverse</u> indicate the year, the fifth and sixth digits are the month).

Guild has a series of charts available on their website (www.guildguitars.com - Ask Mr. Gearhead) to help date a Guild model during its different manufacturing periods. It is recommended that you refer to this information, as there are many charts needed for the individual model serialization. Through the years (and different owners of the company), some of the historical documentation has been lost or destroyed. However, these tables are some of the most comprehensive available to the public. They are up to date through December 1997.

*(Serialization reference source: Hans Moust, **The Guild Guitar Book**; and Jay Pilzer, Guild Authority; additional company information courtesy Bill Acton, Guild Guitars)*

HAMER

Hamer serial numbers are fairly easy to understand, given that the first digit in the instrument's serial number is the last digit of the year the instrument was produced (1986 would be a **6**, for instance). The use of a single digit means that those numbers will cycle every ten years (0 to 9); instrument production dates now have more relevance.

From 1974 to 1981, Hamer USA employed two separate serial numbering systems, one for custom instruments, and one for production models:

Custom Instruments: These instruments are easily recognized by the use of a four-digit number stamped into the wood on the back of the peghead. The numbers ran from #0000 through #0680. All of the early Hamer USA Standards and 12-string basses, as well as a number of prototype instruments, were included in this serial numbering system.

Production Models: Production models are stamped (initially with ink, later in the wood, on the back of the peghead) with either a five or six-digit serial number. The first digit indicates the year that the instrument was built. The next four or five digits are sequentially stamped in order of production. For example, serial number 7 0001 was built in 1977, and was the first production model guitar built. Similarly, 0 1964 was built in 1980, and was the 1,964th production guitar built. The serial numbering sequence by decade is indicated below:

NUMBER	YEAR
7 0001-9 1450	1970S
0 1451-9 24192	1980S
0 24193- 9 50155	1990S
0 50156-	2000S

Hamer Serialization courtesy Jol Dantzig & Frank Rindone Hamer USA.

HOFNER

The sequence of Hofner serial numbers does not provide an exact method for dating Hofner guitars. Hofners were available in Germany since 1949 (and earlier, if you consider over 100 years of company history); but were not officially exported to England until Selmer of London took over distributorship in 1958. Furthermore, Selmer British models were specified for the U.K. only - and differ from those available in the German market.

However, research from author Paul Day indicated a dating scheme based on the pickups installed versus the time period. Keep in mind that there will be transitional models, and combinations do appear. Finally, a quick rule of thumb: Adjustable truss-rods were installed in necks beginning in 1960. Anything prior will not have a truss-rod cover.

DATE	PICKUP STYLE
1953-1959	Six *star-slot* pole piece (built by Fuma)
1957-1960	Black, White, or Brown plastic, with plain tops. Ends can be square or oval.
1960-1961	Rectangular metal case with four black slits in the top. Hofner *diamond* logo.
1961-1963	Rectangular metal case, six slot-screw **or** six rectangular pole pieces. The Hofner *diamond* logo appears on many of these.
1963-1967	Rectangular metal case, six slot-screw **and** six rectangular pole pieces.
1967-1978	Rectangular metal case, a single central bar magnet, plus six small slot-screw pole pieces.

Hofner then introduced a number of guitars based on Classic American favorites from the late 1960s on. These instruments used OEM pickups from Schaller, Shadow, and DiMarzio.

Information courtesy Paul Day, and was featured in Gordon Giltrap and Neville Marten's The Hofner Guitar - A History (International Music Publications Limited, 1993). The Giltrap and Marten book is an overview of Hofner models produced between the late 1950s and the early 1970s, and a recommended read for those interested in Hofner guitars or British pop and rock from the 1960s.

IBANEZ

Ibanez offers a wide selection of models with a corresponding wide range of features. This means there are a lot of models and, of course, a lot of different model numbers to try and keep track of. Ibanez serial numbers never indicated the model number, and still don't. Most solid body Ibanez guitars and basses didn't feature model numbers until recently, and even then, only on Korean-made instruments. On some semi-hollow models, some model numbers will appear on the label visible through the f-hole.

Here's how the Ibanez model numbers work (of course, there are always exceptions - but for the Ibanez models commonly encountered, this system applies pretty consistently).

SERIES: the first in the model number designate the series: RG550BK, RG Series; SR800BK is a Soundgear, etc. Also, in the Artstar lines, AS indicates (A)rtstar (S)emihollow, AF indicates (A)rtstar (F)ull hollow.

FINISH: the last two letters designate the finish: RG550BK, Black finish; RX240CA, Candy Apple. **Exceptions:** finishes such as Amber Pearl and Stained Oil Finish use three letters: AMP, SOL, etc. (having offered so many finishes, Ibanez is running out of traditional two letter cominations!)

The numbers following the Series letters indicate two items:

1. Point of Manufacture

On solid body guitars and basses, the numbers 500 and above indicate Japanese manufacture: RG550BK, SR800BK, BL850VB, the numbers 400 and below indicate Korean manufacture: SR400BK, RX240MG, etc.

This system doesn't apply to hollow bodies, and many signature guitars. J of White Zombie's signature model, the IJ100WZ is made in Japan, as is the JPM100.

2. Pickup Configuration

On solid body guitars only, the last 2 numbers indicate pickup configuration:

20= two humbucking pickups with or w/o pickguard (ex: TC420MD)

30 = three single coils with or w/o pickguard (no current models)

40 = sin/sin/hum with a pickguard (ex: TC740MN)

50 = hum/sin/hum with a pickguard (ex: RG550BK)

60 = sin/sin/hum with no pickguard (no current models)

70 = hum/sin/hum with no pickguard (ex: RG570FBL)

Exceptions: Of course! For example, TC825 (which has 2 humbuckers and a pickguard) and BL1025 (hum/sin/hum with a pickguard), etc.

IBANEZ SERIALIZATION

Author/researcher Michael Wright successfully discussed the Ibanez/Hoshino history in his book, *Guitar Stories Volume One* (Vintage Guitar Books, 1995). Early serial numbers and foreign-built potentiometer codes on Japanese guitars aren't much help in the way of clues, but Ibanez did institute a meaningful numbering system as part of their warranty program in 1975.

1975-1987: In general, Ibanez serial numbers between 1975 and 1987 had seven digits, arranged XYYZZZZ. The letter prefix "X" stands for the month (January = A, February = B, etc. on to L); the next following two digits (YY) are the year. The last four digits indicate the number of instruments built per month through a particular production date.

An outside source indicated that the month/letter code prefix was discontinued in 1988, and the previous dating code was discontinued in 1990. However, in 1987 the XYYZZZZ still appeared the same, but the new listing shifted to XYZZZZZ.

1987-1997: The opening alphabetical prefix "X" now indicates production **location** instead of month: F (Fuji, Japan), or C (Cort, Korea). The first digit "Y" indicates the year: As in 198Y and 199Y. Bright-eyed serialization students will have already noticed that while the year is obtainable, the decade isn't! Because of this, it is good to have a working knowledge of which models were available in approximately. which time periods. All following numbers again are the production ranking code (ZZZZZ).

1997-PRESENT: In mid-1997, Ibanez changed the format, and the second two digits after the alphabetical prefix indicate the last two digits of the actual year of production (i.e, F0003680 indicates a guitar built in Fuji during 2000).

CE Designation: In late 1996, in addition to the serial number on the back of the headstock, Ibanez electric guitars and basses added the "CE" designation. This indicated that the product met the electronic standards of the European Common Market, similar to our UL approval.

For more information on individual Ibanez guitar models, refer to *Ibanez - The Untold Story*, by Paul Specht, Michael Wright, Jim Donahue, and Pat Lefferts. This book features all of the history about Ibanez and features individual model listings. It may be easier to date the guitar from the production time that it was produced.

(Source: Michael Wright, Guitar Stories Volume One, Jim Donahue, Ibanez Guitars)

MARTIN

Martin electric guitars were only produced between 1961 and 1968, and again in 1979 until 1982. For a complete listing of serial numbers, please refer to the *Blue Book of Acoustic Guitars*.

NUMBER	YEAR
181297	1961
187384	1962
193327	1963
199626	1964
207030	1965
217215	1966

NUMBER	YEAR
230095	1967
241925	1968
419900	1979
430300	1980
436474	1981
439627	1982

(Source: Lon Werner, The Martin Guitar Company)

MATSUMOKU

(Includes various models from ARIA PRO II, VANTAGE, WASH-BURN, WESTONE)

Any Matsumoku-produced instrument will have the first number as the identifier for the year, or possibly a two-digit combination. Matsumoku stopped production in Japan in 1987, so an initial digit of "8" cannot be 1988 - the combination of the "8" plus the next digit will give the eighties designation.

The Matsumoku company built guitars for a number of trademarks. Although the Aria Company started their own "ARIA" guitar production in the 1960s, Matsumoku built guitars for them under contract from 1980 to 1987. Matsumoku also built guitars for **Vantage** between 1980 and 1986.

In 1979, the new series of **Washburn** electrics were designed in America, and produced in Japan by Matsumoku. After the success of supplying guitars for other companies' trademarks, Matsumoku marketed their own **Westone** instruments between 1981 and 1987. As Matsumoku stopped production in Japan in 1987, Westone production was moved to Korea.

(Dating information courtesy Tony Bacon and Paul Day, The Guru's Guitar Guide, Bold Strummer Ltd, 1990)

MICRO-FRETS

Micro-Frets produced less than 3,000 guitars and basses. As in the case of production guitars, neck plates with stamped serial numbers were pre-purchased in lots, and then bolted to the guitars during the neck attachment. The serial numbers were utilized by Micro-Frets for warranty work, and the four-digit numbers do fall roughly in a usable list. This list should be used for rough approximations only.

NUMBER	YEAR
1000-1300	1967-1969
1323-3000	1969-1971
3000-3670	1971-1974

MOONSTONE

The most important factor in determining the year of manufacture for Moonstone instruments is that each model had its own set of serial numbers. There is no grouping of models by year of manufacture.

NUMBER	YEAR
EAGLE (Electrics)	
52950-52952	1980
52953-52954	1981
52955-52959	1982
52960	1983
EARTHAXE	
(26 total instruments made)	
0001-0013	1975
0014-0026	1976
ECLIPSE Guitar models	
(81 total instruments made)	
79001-79003	1979
8004-8036	1980
8037-8040	1981
1041-1052	1981
1053-1075	1982
1076-1081	1983
ECLIPSE Bass models	
(124 total instruments made)	

NUMBER	YEAR
3801-3821	1980
3822-3828	1981
3029-3062	1981
3063-3109	1982
3110-3118	1983
3119-3123	1984
EXPLODER Guitar models	
(65 total instruments made)	
7801-7806	1980
7007-7020	1981
7021-7052	1982
7053-7065	1983
EXPLODER Bass models	
(35 total instruments made)	
6801-6803	1980
6004-6013	1981
6014-6031	1982
6032-6035	1983
FLYING V Guitar models	
(52 total instruments made)	
5801-5812	1980
5013-5028	1981
5029-5045	1982
5046-5048	1983
5049-5052	1984
FLYING V Bass models	
(6 total instruments made)	
9001-9006	1981
M-80	
(64 total instruments made)	
4801-4808	1980
4809-4816	1981
4017-4031	1981
4032-4052	1982
4053-4064	1983
MOONDOLINS	
T001-T002	1981
T003-T006	1983
T007	1984
VULCAN Guitar models	
(162 total instruments made)	
5027	1977
5028-5034	1978
107835-107838	1978
17939-179115	1979
179116-179120	1980
80121-80129	1980
80130-80134	1981
8135-8167	1981
8168-8185	1982
8186-8191	1983
7988-7991	1984
VULCAN Bass models	
(19 total instruments made)	
V001-V002	1982
V003-V016	1983
V017-V019	1984

MUSIC MAN

The serial numbers found on the original Music Man/Leo Fender's CLF produced instruments ("pre-Ernie Ball") are not encoded in a system that indicates the production date, but such information can be found on the end of the neck. As with the earlier Fenders, the neck would have to be removed from the body to view this information.

The Ernie Ball Music Man serialization utilizes a numbering system that indicates the year through the first two digits (for example: 93537 = 1993).

PAUL REED SMITH (PRS)

PRS regular production set neck five-digit serialization is fairly easy to decipher: The first digit of the instrument's serial number corresponds to the last digit of the year (i.e., 199"X") the guitar was built. The rest of the numbers correspond to that guitar's production number off the line.

Prefix Number	Years of Mfg.
0	1990, 2000
1	1991, 2001
2	1992, 2002
3	1993, 2003
4	1994, 2004
5	1985, 1995, 2005
6	1986, 1996, 2006
7	1987, 1997
8	1988, 1998
9	1989, 1999

Example: 7 2385 = 1987, 2,385th guitar built

However, just like the Hamer serialization, this number will cycle every ten years - so knowing when the model was available becomes critical. Keep in mind that the serial numbers from the 1980s will be relatively low numbers; serial numbers from the mid-1990s will be much higher.

Example: 7 25385 = 1997, 25,385th guitar built

Example: 050427 (McCarty Soapbar) = 2000, 50,427th guitar built

Example: 155765 (Custom Soapbar) = 2001, 55,765th instrument built

Before 1990, serial ranges were approximately 0001-0400 for 1985, 041-1700 for 1986, 1701-3500 for 1987, 3501-5400 for 1988, 5401-7600 for 1989, 7601-10100 for 1990 (start of five-digit numbers).

PRS CE (Classic Electric) models have one extra number inserted between the first digit (year designator) and before the number of the guitar. They are numbered in sequence (1988 began with 0001, and 1999 ended at approx. 20,000).

Example: 9 CE19759 = 1999, 19,759th guitar built

EG Models manufactured 1990-1995 have their own serial number range, approx. 0001-3300.

PRS bolt-on and set neck basses were manufactured 1989-1991, and also have their own serial number ranges - 0001-0200 for bolt neck, 0001-0800 for set neck. Additionally, swamp ash specials mfg. 1997-1999 have their own range beginning with 00001.

***Source:* The PRS Guitar Book** *by Dave Burrluck, Balafon Books.*

PEAVEY

While more musicians may be aware of Peavey through the numerous high quality amplifiers and P.A. systems they build, the company has been producing solidbody guitars and basses since 1978. Peavey serial numbers exist more for the company's warranty program than an actual dating system. According to researcher Michael Wright, the earliest serial numbers had six digits; by 1978, the company switched to eight digits. Peavey can supply the shipping date (which is within a few weeks of actual production) for the more inquisitive.

Replacement manuals are generally available for Peavey products. For further information, contact Peavey Electronics through the Trademark Index located in the back of this book.

Information courtesy Michael Wright,* Guitar Stories, *Volume One.

RICKENBACKER

Rickenbacker offered a number of guitar models as well as lap steels prior to World War II, such as the **Ken Roberts Spanish** electric f-hole flattop (mid-1930s to 1940) and the **559** model archtop in the early 1940s. The company put production on hold during the war; in 1946, they began producing an **Electric Spanish** archtop. Serialization on early Rickenbacker models from 1931 to 1953 is unreliable, but models may be dated by patent information. This method should be used in conjunction with comparisons of parts, and design changes.

In 1953, Rickenbacker/Electro was purchased by Francis C. Hall. The **Combo 600** and **Combo 800** models debuted in 1954. From 1954 on, the serial number appears on the bridge or jackplate of the instrument. The Rickenbacker serial numbers during the 1950s have four to seven digits. The letter within the code indicates the type of instrument (Combo/guitar, bass, mandolin, etc), and the number after the letter indicates the year of production:

Example: X(X)B7XX (A bass from 1957)

1961 to 1986: In 1961, the serialization scheme changes. The new code has two-letter prefixes, followed by digits. The first letter prefix indicates the year; the second-letter indicates the month of production.

PREFIX	YEAR
A	1961
B	1962
C	1963
D	1964
E	1965
F	1966
G	1967
H	1968
I	1969
J	1970
K	1971
L	1972
M	1973
N	1974
O	1975
P	1976
Q	1977
R	1978
S	1979
T	1980
U	1981
V	1982
W	1983
X	1984
Y	1985
Z	1986

PREFIX	MONTH
A	January
B	February
C	March
D	April
E	May
F	June
G	July
H	August
I	September
J	October
K	November
L	December
M	January
N	February
P	March
Q	April

PREFIX	MONTH
R	May
S	June
T	July
U	August
V	September
W	October
X	November
Y	December

In 1987, the serialization was revised, again. The updated serial number code has a letter prefix (A to L) that still indicates month; the following digit that indicates the year:

DIGIT	YEAR
0	1987
1	1988
2	1989
3	1990
4	1991
5	1992
6	1993
7	1994
8	1995
9	1996
0	1997
1	1998

The following digits after the month/year digits are production (for example, *L2XXXX* would be an instrument built in December, 1989).

In 1999, the system was changed to a number-only system. The twodigits by themselves are the year, and the first two from the 4-5 set being the week it was made. Example: 0012345 - this instrument would have been made in the 12th week of 2000. Example: a new Ricky Model 620-12 with serial number 0119659 indicates an instrument built in the 19th week of 2001. 659 indicates the internal production number.

Information courtesy of Tommy Thomasson, Rickenbacker International Corporation.

TOM ANDERSON GUITARWORKS

Tom Anderson spent a number of years building necks and guitar bodies before producing completed guitars. Outside of custom-built specialties, 1987 was the first year that the volume began to resemble production numbers.

Serial numbers follow one of these two formats: 06-05-99 or 06-05-99A. Anderson's website www.andersonguitars.com, features a search engine that reports the specifications on every guitar Anderson has made. This is the best way to identify an Anderson guitar.

WASHBURN

The Washburn trademark was introduced by the Lyon & Healy company of Chicago, Illinois in 1864. While this trademark has changed hands a number of times, the historical records have not! Washburn suffered a fire in the 1920s that destoyed all records and paperwork that was on file; in the 1950s, another fire destroyed the accumulated files yet again.

When the trademark was revived yet again in 1964, the first production of Washburn acoustic guitars was in Japan. Washburn electric guitars debuted in 1979, and featured U.S. designs and Japanese production.

Production of Washburn guitars changed to Korea in the mid- to late 1980s; a number of U.S.-produced **Chicago Series** models were introduced in the late 1980s as well. Serial numbers from 1988 on use the first two digits of the instrument's serial number to indicate the year the instrument was produced (1988 = **88**XXX). This process works for most, but not all, of the instruments since then.

Washburn Limited Editions feature the year in the model name. For example, **D-95 LTD** is a Limited Edition introduced in 1995. No corresponding serialization information is available at this time.

Washburn information courtesy Dr. Duck's AxWax.

YAMAHA

Yamaha instruments were originally produced in Japan; production switched to Taiwan in the early 1980s. Instruments are currently produced in the U.S., Taiwan, and Indonesia. It is important to recognize that Yamaha uses two different serialization systems.

Yamaha electric guitars and basses have a letter/number (two letters followed by five numbers) code that indicates production date. The first two letters of the serial number indicate the year and month of production (the first letter indicates the year, the second letter indicates the month). Yamaha's coding system substitutes a letter for a number indicating year and month, thus:

CODE LETTER	MONTH or YEAR NUMBER
H	1
I	2
J	3
K	4
L	5
M	6
N	7
O	8
P	9
X	10
Y	11
Z	12

For example, an "H" in the first of two letters would be a "1," indicating the last digit of the year (1981 or 1991). An "H" in the second of two letters would also be a "1," indicating the first month (January). Like Hamer, the digits will cycle around every ten years.

After the two letter prefixes, five digits follow. The first two digits represent the day of the month, and the three digits indicate the production ranking for that day. For example:

NZ19218   December 19, 1987
                 (or 1997); #218.

The example's code should be properly broken down as N - Z - 27 - 19 - 218. The "N" in the first of the two letters would be a "7", indicating the last digit of the year (1987 or 1997). The "Z" in the second of the two letters would be a "12," indicating the twelfth month (December). The two-digit pair after the letters is the day of the month, the 19th. The final three digits indicate production ranking, therefore this imaginary guitar is the 218th instrument built that day.

Yamaha Acoustics and Acoustic Electrics contain eight-digit serial numbers. In this coding scheme, the first digit represents the last digit of the year (for example, 1987 = 7); the second and third numbers indicate the month (numbers 01 through 12); the fourth and fifth numbers will indicate the day of the month, and the final three digits will indicate the production ranking of the instrument.

This system works for most (but not all) Yamaha products. If a serial number doesn't fit the coding system, Yamaha offers internal research via their website (www.yamahaguitars.com) - just email them your request.

GUITAR REFERENCES

Maybe the best advice any guitar player/collector will ever get is "For every guitar you purchase, buy five guitar books." It's still a good rule of thumb. The guitar industry has been very fortunate in that many good reference works have been published within the last several decades. In terms of the major trademarks, it's pretty much over – most of the good books are already out there. All you have to do is buy 'em and read 'em. Some are even out of print, and have already become very collectible (expensive).

If you're a player, collector, or just kind of an all-around average guitar pervert, you gotta do your homework. And there have never been more ways to bone up on your chosen homework assignments. Even though the Web does a good job of performing many basic guitar information services, it's still not a book. It's also necessary that you subscribe to a few good magazines within your area (please refer to "Periodicals Listing").

The following titles represent a good cross sectional cut of those references that are outstanding in their field(s). Spending $300 annually to have these valuable books at your fingertips is the cheapest insurance policy you'll every buy. If you're serious about your guitars, this information could also save you thousands of dollars and a lot of bad attitude. So bone up or bail out! No whining either – it's a pretty cool homework assignment.

Most of the books listed below can be obtained through:

JK Lutherie
11115 Sand Run
Harrison, OH 45030
Phone: 800.344.8880
www.jklutherie.com
Guitar@jklutherie.com

JK Lutherie also attends many major guitar shows annually, and you may want to stop by the booth to either purchase or inquire about any new releases. Many video releases are also available, and can be found on their website.

Achard, Ken
The Fender Guitar, The Bold Strummer, Ltd., Westport CT, 1990

Achard, Ken
The History and Development of the American Guitar, The Bold Strummer, Ltd., Westport CT, 1990

Bacon, Tony (Editor), et al
Classic Guitars of the 50s, Miller Freeman, San Francisco, CA, 1996

Bacon, Tony (Editor), et al
Classic Guitars of the 60s, Miller Freeman, San Francisco, CA, 1997

Bacon, Tony
The History of the American Guitar, Friedman/Fairfax Publishers, New York, NY, 2001

Bacon, Tony, et al
The Classical Guitar - A Complete History, Outline Press Ltd./Miller Freeman, San Francisco, CA, 1997

Bacon, Tony
Electric Guitars - The Illustrated Encyclopedia, Thunder Bay Press/Advantage Publishers Group, San Diego, CA, 2000

Bacon, Tony
The Ultimate Guitar Book, Alfred A. Knopf, Inc., New York NY, 1991

Bacon, Tony
50 Years of the Gibson Les Paul, Backbear Books, San Francisco, CA, 2002

Bacon, Tony and Day, Paul, et al (Editors)
Guitar - A Complete Guide for the Player, Thunder Bay Press, San Diego, CA, 2002

Bacon, Tony and Day, Paul,
The Fender Book, GPI/Miller Freeman Inc., San Francisco CA, 1992

Bacon, Tony and Day, Paul
50 Years of Fender, Balafon Books, London, England, 2000

Bacon, Tony and Day, Paul,
The Gibson Les Paul Book, GPI/Miller Freeman Inc., San Francisco CA, 1993

Bacon, Tony and Day, Paul
The Gretsch Book, GPI/Miller Freeman Inc., San Francisco CA, 1996

Bacon, Tony and Day, Paul
The Guru's Guitar Guide, Track Record Publishing, London England, 1990

Bacon, Tony and Day, Paul
The Rickenbacker Book, GPI/Miller Freeman Inc., San Francisco CA, 1994

Bacon, Tony and Moorhouse, Barry
The Bass Book, GPI/Miller Freeman Inc., San Francisco CA, 1995

Bechtoldt, Paul
G&L: Leo's Legacy, Woof Associates, 1994

Bechtoldt, Paul and Tulloch, Doug
Guitars from Neptune - A Definitive Journey Into Danelectro Mania, JK Lutherie, Harrison OH, 1996

Benedetto, Robert
Making an Archtop Guitar - The Definitive Work on the Design and Construction of an Acoustic Archtop Guitar, Centerstream Publishing/Hal Leonard Corp, Anaheim Hills, CA, 1996

Bishop, Ian C.
The Gibson Guitar, The Bold Strummer, Ltd., Westport CT, 1990

Bishop, Ian C.
The Gibson Guitar From 1950 Vol. 2, The Bold Strummer, Ltd., Westport NY 1990

Blasquiz, Klaus
The Fender Bass, Hal Leonard Publishing Corp., Milwaukee WI, 1990

Briggs, Brinkman and Crocker
Guitars, Guitars, Guitars, All American Music Publishers, Neosho MO, 1988

Brozeman, Bob
The History and Artistry of National Resonator Instruments, Centerstream Publishing, Anaheim Hills CA, 1993

Burrluck, Dave
The PRS Guitar Book, Backbeat Books, San Francisco, CA, 2002

Carter, Walter
Epiphone, The Complete History, Hal Leonard Corporation, Milwaukee WI, 1995

Carter, Walter
Gibson Guitars, 100 Years of an American Icon, General Publishing, Inc., New York NY, 1994

Carter, Walter
The History of the Ovation Guitar, Hal Leonard Corporation, Milwaukee WI, 1996

Carter, Walter
The Martin Book, GPI/Miller Freeman Inc., San Francisco CA, 1995

Chapman, Richard
The Complete Guitarist, (Foreword by Les Paul), DK Publishing, New York, NY, 1993

Chapman, Richard
Guitar - Music, History, Players (Foreword by Eric Clapton), DK Publishing, New York, NY, 2000

Charle, Francois
The Story of Selmer Maccaferri Guitars, published by the author, Paris, France, 1999

Day, Paul
The Burns Book, The Bold Strummer, Ltd., Westport Connecticut, 1990

Denyer, Ralph
The Guitar Handbook, Alfred A. Knopf Inc., New York NY, 1982

Duchossoir, A.R.
Gibson Electrics, Hal Leonard Publishing Corp., Milwaukee WI, 1981

Duchossoir, A.R.
Gibson Electrics - The Classic Years, Hal Leonard Publishing Corp., Milwaukee WI, 1994

Duchossoir, A.R.
Guitar Identification, Hal Leonard Publishing Corp., Milwaukee WI, 1983

Duchossoir, A.R.
The Fender Stratocaster, Hal Leonard Publishing Corp., Milwaukee WI, 1989

Duchossoir, A.R.
The Fender Telecaster, Hal Leonard Publishing Corp., Milwaukee WI, 1991

Erlewine, Vinolpal and Whitford
Gibson's Fabulous Flat-Top Guitars, Miller Freeman Books, San Francisco CA, 1994

Evans, Tom and Mary Anne
Guitars from the Renaissance to Rock, Facts on File, New York NY, 1977

Fisch, Jim, and Fred, L.B.
Epiphone: The House of Stathopoulo, Amsco Publications (Music Sales Corporation), New York NY, 1996

Freeth, Nick and Alexander, Charles
The Acoustic Guitar, Courage Books, Philadelphia, PA, 1999

Freeth, Nick and Alexander, Charles
The Electric Guitar, Courage Books, Philadelphia, PA, 1999

Freeth, Nick and Alexander, Charles
The Guitar, Salamander Books, London, England, 2002

Fullerton, George
Guitar Legends, Centerstream Publishing, Fullerton CA, 1993

Giel, Kate, et al,
Ferrington Guitars, HarperCollins, New York NY, 1992

Giltrap, Gordon and Marten, Neville
The Hofner Guitar - A History, International Music Publications Limited, Essex England, 1993

Gjörde, Per
Pearls and Crazy Diamonds - Fifty Years of Burns Guitars 1952-2002, Addit Information AB, Göteborg, Sweden, 2001

Goudy, Rob
Electric Guitars, Schiffer Publishing, Atglen, PA, 1999

Green, Frank Wm.
The Custom Guitar Shop and Wayne Richard Charvel (What's In a Name?), Working Musician Publications, Sierra Madre, CA, 1999

Gruhn, George, and Carter, Walter
Acoustic Guitars and Other Fretted Instruments, Miller Freeman Inc., San Francisco CA, 1993

Gruhn, George, and Carter, Walter
Electric Guitars and Basses, GPI/Miller Freeman Inc., San Francisco CA, 1994

Gruhn, George, and Carter, Walter
Gruhn's Guide to Vintage Guitars, GPI/Miller Freeman Inc., San Francisco CA, 1991

Gruhn, George, and Carter, Walter
Gruhn's Guide to Vintage Guitars, GPI/Miller Freeman Inc., San Francisco CA, 1999

Hartman, Robert Carl
The Larsons' Creations, Guitars and Mandolins, Centerstream Publishing, Fullerton CA, 1995

Howe, Steve
The Steve Howe Guitar Collection, GPI/Miller Freeman, Inc., San Francisco CA, 1993

Huber, John
The Development of the Modern Guitar, The Bold Strummer, Ltd., Westport, CT, 1994

Ingram, Adrian
A Concise History of the Electric Guitar, Mel Bay Publications, Pacific, MO, 2001

Ingram, Adrian
The Gibson L5, Centerstram Publishing, Anaheim Hills, CA, 1997

Ingram, Adrian
The Gibson ES175, Music Maker Books, Cambs, England, 1994

Iwanade, Yasuhiko
The Beauty of the 'Burst, Rittor Music, Tokyo Japan, 1997

Iwanade, Yasuhiko
The Galaxy of Strats, Rittor Music, Tokyo Japan, 1998

Juan, Carlos
Collectables and Vintage, American Guitar Center, Stuttgart Germany, 1995

Lincoln, William A.
World Woods in Color, Linden Publishing Co. Inc. Fresno, CA, 1986

Longworth, Mike
Martin Guitars, a History, 4 Maples Press Inc., Minisink Hills PA, 1987

Meiners, Larry
Gibson Shipment Totals 1937-1979, Flying Vintage Publications, 2001

Meiners, Larry
Flying V - The Illustrated History of this Modernistic Guitar, Flying Vintage Publications, 2001

Minhinnett, Ray and Young, Bob
The Story of the Fender Stratocaster, Miller Freeman Books, San Francisco, CA, 1995

Moseley, Willie G.
Classic Guitars U.S.A., Centerstream Publishing, Fullerton CA, 1992

Moseley, Willie G.
Stellas and Stratocasters, Vintage Guitar Books, Bismarck ND, 1994

Moseley, Willie G.
Guitar People, Vintage Guitar Books, Bismarck ND, 1997

Moseley, Willie G. and Carson, Bill
Bill Carson - My Life and Times with Fender Musical Instruments, Hal Leonard Corp., Milwaukee, WI, 1998

Moust, Hans
The Guild Guitar Book, The Company and the Instruments, 1952-1977, Guitar Archives Publications, The Netherlands, 1995

Production, Maurice
Burst Gang, 1G Inc., Tokyo, Japan, 1999

Rich, Bill and Nielsen, Rick
Guitars of the Stars, Volume 1: Rick Nielsen, Gots Publishing Ltd., A Division of Rich Specialties, Inc., Rockford IL, 1993

Rittor Music,
Bizarre Guitars, Vol. 2, Japan, 1993

Rittor Music
Guitar Graphic, Vol. 1, Tokyo Japan, 1994

Rittor Music
Guitar Graphic, Vol. 2, Tokyo Japan, 1995

Rittor Music
Guitar Graphic, Vol. 3, Tokyo Japan, 1995

Rittor Music
Guitar Graphic, Vol. 4, Tokyo Japan, 1996

Rittor Music
Guitar Graphic, Vol. 5, Tokyo Japan, 1996

Rittor Music
Guitar Graphic, Vol. 6, Tokyo Japan, 1997

Rittor Music
Guitar Graphic, Vol. 7, Tokyo Japan, 1997

Rittor Music
Guitar Graphic, Vol. 8, Tokyo Japan, 1998

Roberts, Jim
How the Fender Bass Changed the World, Backbeat Books, San Francisco, CA, 2001

Sandberg, Larry
The Acoustic Guitar Guide, a cappella books, Pennington, NJ, 1991

Schmidt, Paul William
Acquired of the Angels: The lives and works of master guitar makers John D'Angelico and James L. D'Aquisto, The Scarecrow Press, Inc., Metuchen, NJ, 1991

Scott, Jay
'50s Cool: Kay Guitars, Seventh String Press, Hauppauge NY, 1992

Scott, Jay
The Guitars of the Fred Gretsch Company, Centerstream Publishing, Fullerton CA, 1992

Scott, Jay and Da Pra, Vic
'Burst 1958-'60 Sunburst Les Paul, Seventh String Press, Hauppauge NY, 1994

Smith, Richard R.
Fender - The Sound Heard 'Round the World, Garfish Publishing Company, Fullerton CA, 1995

Smith, Richard R.
Fender Custom Shop Guitar Gallery, Hal Leonard Corporation, Milwaukee WI, 1996

Smith, Richard R.
The History of Rickenbacker Guitars, Centerstream Publishing, Fullerton CA, 1989

Teagle, John
Washburn: Over One Hundred Years of Find Stringed Instruments, Music Sales Corp, New York NY, 1996

Teeter, Don E.
The Acoustic Guitar, University of Oklahoma Press, Oklahoma City, OK

Trynka, Paul (Editor)
The Electric Guitar - An Illustrated History, Chronicle Books, San Francisco, CA, 1993

Van Hoose, Thomas A.
The Gibson Super 400, Miller Freeman, Inc., San Francisco, 1991

Vose, Ken
Blue Guitar, Chronicle Books, San Francisco, CA, 1998

Wade, Graham
A Concise History of the Classic Guitar, Mel Bay Publications, Pacific, MO, 2001

Walker, Aidan
The Encyclopedia of Wood, Facts on File, New York, NY, 1989

Washburn, Jim and Johnston, Richard
Martin Guitars, Rodale Press, Emmaus, PA, 1997

Wheeler, Tom
American Guitars, HarperCollins Publishers, New York NY, 1990

Wheeler, Tom
The Guitar Book, A Handbook for Electric and Acoustic Guitarists, Harper and Row, New York NY, 1974

White, Forrest
Fender: The Inside Story, GPI/Miller Freeman Books, San Francisco CA, 1994

Wright, Michael,
Guitar Stories, Volume One, Vintage Guitar Books, Bismarck ND, 1995

Wright, Michael,
Guitar Stories, Volume Two, Vintage Guitar Books, Bismarck, ND, 2000

PERIODICALS LISTINGS

You've bought this book, so you're obviously interested in stringed instruments. Being knowledgeable about any subject is a good idea, and having the up-to-the-minute news is the best form of knowledge. We recommend the following publications for instrument information, collecting news, updates and show announcements, luthier and artist insights, and loads of other information that might interest

20th Century Guitar
135 Oser Avenue
Hauppauge, NY 11788
Phone: 631-273-1674,
Fax: 631-435-9057
Website: www.tcguitar.com
Email: tcguitar@tcguitar.com
Published monthly. 12 month subscription is $15.00 in the USA.

Acoustic Guitar
String Letter Publishing, Inc.
255 W. End Ave.
San Rafael, CA 94901
Phone: 415-485-6946,
Fax: 415-485-0831
Web site: www.acousticguitar.com
Published monthly. 12 month subscription is $32.95 in the USA.

Bass Guitar
149 5th Ave., 9th Floor
New York, NY 10010
Phone: 800-456-6441
Website: www.guitarworld.com
Published monthly. 6 month subscription is $16.97 in the USA.

Bass Player
Music Player Group
2800 Campus Drive
San Mateo, CA 94403
Phone: 650-513-4400
Web site: www.bassplayer.com
Published monthly. 12 month subscription is $29.95

Bassics
MI Media, LLC
21143 Hawthorne Blvd., Suite 508
Torrance, CA 90503
Phone: 310-782-8111
Email: bassicsrg@aol.com,
or lynngarant@aol.com
Website: www.bassics.com
Published bimonthly. Six issues/year subscription is $29.95. 12 issues/two years subscription is $54.95.

Downbeat
Maher Publications
102 N. Haven
Elmhurst, IL 60126-2932
Toll Free: 800-554-7470
Phone: 630-941-2030
Fax: 630-941-3210
Email: service@downbeat.com
Website: www.downbeat.com
Published monthly, 12 month subscription is $29.50, 24 month subscription is $54.50.

EQ
2800 Campus Drive
San Mateo, CA 94403
Phone: 888-256-5828,
Web site: www.eqmag.com
Email: eqmag@sfsdayton.com
Published monthly: $15.00 for 12 issues in the U.S.
Gitarre & Bass (Germany)
MM-Musik-Media-Verlag GmbH,
An Der Wachsfabrik 8, Koln, 50996 Germany
Phone: 011-39-2236-96217
Fax: 011-39-2236-96217-5
Web site: www1.gitarrebass.de/magazine
Published monthly.

Guitar Club (Italy)
Il Volo Srl
Via Brazzini 14
Milano, Italy

Guitar Digest
P.O. Box 66
The Plains, Ohio 45780
Phone: 740-797-3351
Web site: www.guitardigest.com
Published 6 times a year. A six issue subscription is $10.00 in the USA.

Guitar One
149 5th Ave., 9th Floor
New York, NY 10010
Phone: 800-456-6441
Website: www.guitarworld.com
Published monthly. 12 month subscription is $24.95 in the USA.

Guitar Player
Box 291807
Dayton, OH 45429
Phone: 937-853-2346
Email: guitarplayer@sfsdayton.com
Website: www.guitarplayer.com
Published monthly. 12 month subscription is $15.00 in the USA.

Guitar World
149 5th Ave., 9th Floor
New York, NY 10010
Phone: 800-456-6441
http://www.guitarworld.com
Web site: www.guitarworld.com
Published monthly. 12 month subscription is $19.95 in the USA.

Guitar World Acoustic
149 5th Ave., 9th Floor
New York, NY 10010
Phone: 800-456-6441
Website: www.guitarworld.com
Published bi-monthly. Six issue (one year) subscription is $21.97 in the USA.

Guitarist UK
Future Publishing
Published monthly. 13 month subscription is 84 euros in the USA
Web site: www.futurenet.com or www.guitarist.co.uk

JazzTimes
8737 Colesville Rd., 9th Floor
Silver Spring, MD 20910-3921
Phone: 301.588.4114
Fax: 301.588.5531
Web site: www.jazztimes.com
Email: info@jazztimes.com
Published 10 times/year. A one year subscription is $23.95 in the USA.

Just Jazz Guitar
P.O. Box 76053
Atlanta, Georgia 30358-1053
Phone: 404-250-9298
Fax: 404-250-9298
Web site: www.justjazzguitar.com
Published 4 times a year. A one year subscription is $40 in the USA.

MMR (Musical Merchandise Review)
Symphony Publishing
50 Brook Road
Needham, MA 02494
Published monthly. One year subscription is $32.00, two year subscription is $40.00.

Music Inc.
Maher Publications
102 N. Haven
Elmhurst, IL 60126-2932
Toll Free: 800-554-7470
Phone: 630-941-2030
Fax: 630-941-3210
Email: editor@musicincmag.com
Published Monthly except for April. One year subscription is $16.50, two year subscription is $26.00.

Music Trades, The
P.O. Box 432
80 West Street
Englewood, NJ 07631
Website: www.musictrades.com
Published montly. One year subscription is $16.00, two year subscription is $23.00.

Musician's Hotline
Heartland Communications Group
P.O. Box 1415 1003 Central Ave.
Fort Dodge, IA 50501
Toll free: 888-247-2009
Phone: 515-574-2264
Fax: 515-574-2217
Email: trent@musicianshotline.com
Website: www.musicianshotline.com
Published monthly. One year subscription is $14.95, two year subscription is $24.95.

Musico Pro
Music Maker Publications, Inc.
5412 Idylwild Trail, Suite 100
Boulder, Colorado 80301
Phone: 303-516-9118,
Fax: 303-516-9119
A music/gear magazine is published in Spanish (available in U.S., Argentine, Chile, Mexico, and Spain).
Published 12 times a year. Subscription is $19.95 in the USA.

Tonequest
Mounatinview Publishing LLC
P.O. Box 717
Decatur, GA 30030-0717
Phone: 877-629-8663
Email: tonequest1@aol.com
Website: www.tonequest.com
Published monthly. 12 issue subscription is $69.

Vintage Guitar Magazine
P.O. Box 7301
Bismarck, North Dakota 58507
Phone: 701-255-1197
Fax: 701-255-0250
Web site: www.vintageguitar.com
Published monthly. 12 month subscription is $24.95 in the USA.

Vintage News, The
Mandolin Brothers, Ltd.
629 Forest Ave.
Staten Island, NY 10310-2576
Phone: 718-981-3226
Fax: 718-816-4416
Email: mandolin@mandoweb.com
Website: www.mandoweb.com
Published bi-monthly. One year subscription (6 issues) is $20.00 in the USA.

In addition to the regular publications put out by these publishers, most offer Special Edition (i.e., yearly buyers' guides, new product reviews, market overviews, etc.) magazines that are released annually, or bi-annually. Please contact them directly for more information.

STRINGS

Another aspect of tone generation is Strings. How strings interact with the instrument and the player is another crucial portion of the overall "chain" of the sound produced. Several string companies offer different products for your guitar.

ADAMAS
Distributed by Kaman Music
P.O. Box 507
Bloomfield, CT 06002-0507
860-509-8888
www.kamanmusic.com

CONCERTISTE
Picato Musician Strings
Unit 24, Treorchy Ind. Est.
Treorchy Mid Glamorgan
United Kingdom CF42 6EJ
44.144.343.7928
Fax: 44.144.343.3624

J. D'ADDARIO
J. D'Addario & Co.
595 Smith Street
Farmingdale, NY 11735
800.323.2746
631.439.3300
Fax: 631.439.3333
strings@daddario.com
www.daddario.com

D'AQUISTO
P.O. Box 569
20 E. Industry Court
Deer Park, NY 11729
Phone: 631-586-4426
Fax: 631.586.4472
info@daquisto.com
www.daquisto.com

DEAN MARKLEY
3350 Scott Blvd. #45
Santa Clara, CA 95054
Toll Free: 800-800-1008
Phone: 408.988.2456
Fax: 408.988.0441
www.deanmarkley.com

DR STRINGS
7 Palisades Avenue
Emerson, NJ 07630
Phone: 201-599-0100
Fax: 201-599-0404
drstaff@drstrings.com
www.drstrings.com

ELIXIR STRINGS
W. L. Gore & Associates
201 Airport Rd.
Elkton, MD 21921
800.367.5533
elixirstrings@wlgore.com
www.elixirstrings.com

ERNIE BALL
151 Suburban Road
San Luis Obispo, CA 93401
Toll free: 800-543-2255
Fax: 800-577-3225
www.ernieball.com

EVERLY
Everly Music Company
2305 West Victory Blvd.
Burbank, CA 91506
Toll free: 888-438-3759
Phone: 818-842-1700
Fax: 818-842-5980
www.everlystrings.com

FENDER
Fender Musical Instruments Corp.
8860 East Chaparral Road Ste #100
Scottsdale AZ 85250
Phone: 480-596-9690
Fax: 480-367-5662
www.fender.com

GHS
G.H.S. Corporation
2813 Wilber Avenue
Battle Creek MI 49015
Toll free: 800-388-4447
Phone: 616-968-3351
strings@ghsstrings.com
www.ghsstrings.com

GIBSON
309 Plus Park Blvd
Nashville, TN 37217
toll free: 800-444-2766
phone: 615-871-4500
fax: 615-889-5509
service@gibson.com
www.gibson.com

JOHN PEARSE STRINGS
Breezy Ridge Instruments
P.O. Box 295
Center Valley PA 18034
Toll free: 800-750-3034
Fax: 610-691-3304
www.johnpearsestrings.com
jpinfo@aol.com

LABELLA
256 Broadway
Newburg , NY 12550
845-562-4400
Fax: 845-562-4491
www.labella.com
bellaon@msn.com

MARI
14 W. 71st Street
New York, NY 10023-4209
212-799-6781
Fax: 212-721-3932

MARTIN STRINGS
P.O. Box 329
510 Sycamore Street
Nazareth, PA 18064-0329
phone: 610-759-2837
fax: 610-759-5757
info@martinguitar.com
www.martinguitar.com

MAXIMA
57 Crooks Avenue
Clifton, NJ 07011
garpc@ix.netcom.com

PHANTOM STRINGS
80353 Qunicy Mayger Rd.
Clatskanie, OR 97016
Phone: 503-728-4825
Fax: 503-728-4979
www.phantomguitars.com

SABINE
NitroStasis Strings
13301 Highway 441
Alachua, FL 32615-8544
Phone: 386-418-2000
Fax: 386-418-2001
sabine@sabineinc.com
www.sabineinc.com

S.I.T. STRINGS
815 S. Broadway
Akron, OH 44311
Phone: 330-434-8010
sinfositstrings@aol.com

SNARLING DOGS STRINGS
P.O. Box 4241
Warren, NJ 07059
908-469-2828
Fax: 908-469-2882
customerservice@snarlingdogs.com
www.snarlingdogs.com

THOMASTIK-INFELD
P.O. Box 93
Northport, NY 11768
800-644-5268
www.thomastik-infeld.com
info@connollyandco.com

YAMAHA STRINGS
6600 Orangethorpe Avenue
Buena Park, CA 90620
Phone:714-522-9011
Fax: 714-739-2680

PICKUPS

Sometimes standard pickups do not serve justice on guitars. The good news is that there are several companies that specialize in pickups to find that ultimate sound..

KENT ARMSTRONG
Distributed by WD Music Products, Inc.
4070 Mayflower Road
Fort Myers, FL 33916
239-337-7575
941-337-4585
www.kentarmstrong.com
sales@wdmusicproducts.com
Exclusive Distributor for Kluson tuning
machines
Kent Armstrong - Europe
Rainbow Products
Unit 31, Old Surrenden Manor
Bethersden, Kent
TN26 3DL England
Mike@rainbowproducts.co.uk

BARCUS BERRY
Distributed by BBE Sound, Inc
5381 Production Drive
Huntington Beach, CA 92649
800.233.8346
714.897.6766
Fax: 714.896.0736

BARTOLINI
Bartolini Pickups and Electronics
2133 Research Drive #16
Livermore, CA 94550
510.443.1037
Fax: 510.449.7692

BENEDETTO
Benedetto Jazz Pickups
FMIC
8860 East Chaparral Road
Ste #100
Scottsdale, AZ 85250
Phone: 480-596-9690
Fax: 480-367-5662
benedetto@benedettoguitars.com
www.benedettoguitars.com

DEAN MARKLEY
Dean Markley Strings, Inc.
3350 Scott Blvd. #45
Santa Clara, CA 95054
800.800.1008
408.988.2456
Fax: 408.988.0441

DIMARZIO
Dimarzio, Inc.
1388 Richmond Terrace
Staten Island, NY 10310
800.221.6468
718.981.9286
Fax: 718.720.5296

SEYMOUR DUNCAN
5427 Hollister Avenue
Santa Barbara, CA
93111-2345
Phone: 805-964-9610
Fax: 805-964-9749
www.seymourducan.com

EMG
EMG. Inc.
P.O. Box 4394
Santa Rosa, CA 95402
707.525.9941
Fax: 707.575.7046
www.emginc.com

EPM
#6-399 South Edgeware Road
St. Thomas, Ontario
Canada N5P 4B8
Phone: 519-633-5195
Fax: 519-633-8314
info@epm-ltd.com
www.epm-ltd.com

FISHMAN
Fishman Transducers, Inc.
340 Fordham Road
Wilmington, MA 01887
Phone: 978-988-9199
Fax: 978-988-0770
www.fishman.com

LINDY FRALIN
Lindy Fralin Pickups
2015 W. Laburnum 2nd Floor
Richmond, VA 23227
Phone: 804-358-2699
Fax: 804-358-3431
www.fralinpickups.com

GROOVE TUBES LLC
1543 Truman St.
San Fernando, CA 91340
Phone: 818-361-4500
Fax: 818-365-9884
www.groovetubes.com

HIGHLANDER
Highlander Musical Audio Products
305 Glenwood Avenue
Ventura, CA 93003-4426
Phone: 805-658-1819
Fax: 805-658-6828

TOM HOLMES
P.O. Box 414
Joelton, TN 37080
615-876-3453

LACE MUSIC PRODUCTS
5561 Engineer Drive
Huntington Beach, CA 92649
Phone: 714-898-2776
Fax: 714-893-1045
www.lacemusic.com

WILLIAM LAWRENCE
Also KEYSTONE PICKUPS
William Lawrence Design Corp.
314 Taylor Street
Bethlehem, PA 18015
610.866.5211
Fax: 610.866.5495

L. R. BAGGS
483 N Frontage Road
Nipomo, CA 93444
Phone: 805-929-3545
Fax: 805-929-2043
Baggsco@LRBaggs.com
www.lrbaggs.com

PAN
Pan Electric
207 Rundlview Dr. N.E.
Calgary, AB Canada T1Y 1H7
403-285-8893
www.pan-electric.com
PASC123@telusplanet.net

RIO GRANDE PICKUPS
3526 East T.C. Jester Blvd.
Houston, TX 77018
713-957-0470
Fax: 713-957-3316
www.riograndepickups.com
sales@riograndepickups.com

SUNRISE
Sunrise Pickup Systems
8101 Orion Ave. #19
Van Nuys, CA 91406
818.785.3428
Fax: 818.785.9972
JimSunrise@earthlink.net
www.Sunrisepickups.com

VAN ZANDT
Distributed and Produced by VAN ZANDT
Pickups
205 Robinson Rd.
Combine, TX 75159
214.476.8844
Fax: 214.476.8844

KNOW YOUR WOODS!

Throughout the text of this book, readers may notice the different woods used in the construction of guitars and basses. In addition to wood types, we have also listed wood trade names as well (i.e., SmartWood, Certified Wood, Plywood, Wildwood, etc.). The following table is presented to help understand the names, family references, and many other common names that describe the woods used in guitar building. Without these woods, guitar building would be on a much lower plateau.

WOOD VARIETIES (SOFT & HARDWOOD) TRADENAMES, & RELATED INFORMATION

Common Name	Latin Name	Family	Other Names/Information
American Woods			
Alder	–	–	–
Ash	–	–	–
Cedar, Western Red	–	–	Typically harvested in California & Washington
Certified Wood	–	–	Term used by Smartwood Certified Forestry designating that
			the wood comes only from a certified forest.
Cherry	–	–	–
Deadwood	–	–	Stage following old wood, indigenous to a small area in South Dakota north of Rapid City.
Lyptus	–	–	Genetically grown eucalyptus hybrid (not SmartWood)
Madrone	Arbutus Menziessi	Ericaceae	–
Maple (generic)	Acer Macrophyllum	Aceraceae	–
Big Leaf Maple	–	–	–
Bird's-Eye Maple	–	–	Bird's-Eye, "dot-top," denoted by dark, small circular patterns, somewhat resembling bird's eyes.
Flame Maple	–	–	Flametop, denoted by discernible lines showing the dark and
			light contrast of the grain. Can be either wide or narrow.
Quilt Maple	–	–	Quilted, denoted by swirly, puffy, cloud-like patterns.
Red Birch	–	–	SmartWood
Rock Maple	Acer Saccharum	Aceraceae	Hard Maple, White Maple
	Good quality rock maple is straight grained, and almost white.		
Oak	—	—	Red or White Oak (mostly acoustic production)
Plywood	Cheapus Waytoomuchus	American Big Business	—
	Utilized in more recently mfg. instruments, allowing good overall tonal wood characteristics at a price point.		
SmartWood	Politicus Correctus	Treehuggers	Certified Wood
	The term SmartWood represents an organization called SmartWood Certified Forestry, run by the Rainforest Alliance, and governed by the Forest Stewardship Council. The SmartWood Certified Forestry program ensures that SmartWood is harvested only from certified managed forests that have been independently evaluated, ensuring that they meet internationally recognized environmental and socioeconomic standards.		
Spruce	—	—	Many variations
	The 3 main variations of American spruce are Sitka spruce, grown in the coastal region between Northern California & Alaska, Engelmann spruce is indigenous to the Rocky Mountain Range, including New Mexico, Idaho, and Montana, and Adirondack spruce, which comes from the Adirondack region in the eastern U.S. Other variations do exist.		
Sycamore	Acer Pseudoplatanus	Aceraceae	
Tonewood (universal term)			
	Generic term referring to any wood selected in the manufacturing process for tonal quality and performance. Tonewoods usually include maple, mahogany, rosewood, ebony, spruce, koa, cedar, walnut, etc.		
Walnut	Juglans Hindsii	Juglancaceae	California Walnut, Claro Walnut
Wildwood			
	Refers to Fender trademark for process utilizing German beech trees injected with dyes that have been cut into veneers and laminated to the top of the instrument, circa 1967–1970.		
South and Central American Woods			
Bocate	Cordia spp.	—	Mexican Rosewood
Brazilian Rosewood	Harvest Interuptus	Mucho Centavos	
	Brazilian rosewood was mostly discontinued after 1968, the last legal year of importation. Current legal mfg. requires C.I.T.E.S. certification beginning 1992. Since this now very controlled hardwood has achieved almost cult-like status, prices for instruments utilizing Brazilian rosewood (mostly back & sides) have skyrocketed - both on new and vintage instruments.		
Cocobola	Dalbergia Retusa	Leguminosae	Granadillo
Imbuia	—	—	—
	Indigenous in southern Brazil		
Mahogany	Swietinia Macrophylla	Meliaceae	—
Nato	—	—	—
	Utility Grade Mahogany, not as high grade as African or Indian mahogany.		
Purpleheart	Peltogne spp.	Leguminosae	Amaranth, Violetwood, Morado, Saka, Koroboreli, Tananeo, Pau Roxo
Tulipwood	Dalbergia Fructescens	Leguminosae	Jacaranda Rosa, Pinkwood, Pau Rosa
African Woods			
Bubinga	Guibouria Demusi	Leguminosae	African Rosewood
Cocobola	Microberlinia	Leguminosae	Zebrano, Zingana, Brazzavillensis, Allene, Ele, Amouk
Ebony	Diospryus Crassiflora	Ebenaceae	Gabon Ebony
	(African ebony is generally categorized by the country of orgin, i.e., Madagascar, etc.)		
Mahogany	—	—	—
South America			
Ovangkol	—	—	—
Pink Ivory	—	—	—
Sapele	—	—	—
Wenge	Millettia Laurentii	Leguminosae	Panga Panga
Zebrawood	—	—	—
European Woods			
Spruce	—	—	typically German Spruce
Indian Woods			
Ebony	Diospryus Ebenaceae	Ebenaceae	
Macassar Ebony	Diospryus Celebica	Ebenaceae	Striped Ebony
Indian Rosewood	Dalbergia Latifoloa	Leguminosae	Bombay Rosewood, Sissoo, Biti, Ervadi, Kalaruk
	(most currently manufactured guitars using rosewood are made from Indian rosewood - C.I.T.E.S. approval not needed)		
Vermillion	Pterocarpu Dalbergoides	Leguminosae	Paduak, Andaman Rosewood
Pacific Region Woods			
Koa	Acacia Koa	—	Australian Silky Oak
Lacewood	Carwellia Sublimis	Protaceae	Phillipine Mahogany, widely acclaimed for its
Mahogany	—	—	tonal characteristics.

(Wood information courtesy Mica Wickersham, Alembic, & S.P. Fjestad)

IDENTIFYING HOUSE BRANDS MUSICAL INSTRUMENTS

The phenomenon of large production companies producing House Brand instruments dates back to the late 1800s and early 1900s. A House Brand is defined as a trademark used by distributors, wholesalers, and retailers to represent their respective company instead of the manufacturer. These brands are found (for the most part) on budget instruments, although some models are currently sought after by players and collectors on the basis of playability, tone, or relative degree of "coolness" they project.

In the 1800s, many guitar manufacturers were located in New York and Philadelphia; by the early 1900s large guitar factories were centered in Chicago. The "Big Three" that evolved out of the early 1930s were Harmony, Kay, and Valco. Valco, producer of National and Supro instruments, produced the Airline House Brand as well as bodies and resonator parts that were sold to Harmony and Kay. However, the majority of House Brand instruments found today probably originated at either Harmony or Kay. On the East Coast, Danelectro was a large builder/supplier to Sears & Roebuck under Sears' Silvertone label (sometimes up to 85 percent of Danelectro's output).

Prior to World War II, Harmony and Kay sold straight to wholesalers like catalog houses and large distributors. In turn, these wholesalers would send their salesmen and "reps" out on the road to generate sales – no territories, no music store chains – just straight sales. Business was fierce, and companies used their own private labels to denote "their" product. House Brands were typically used as a marketing tool for distributors, wholesalers, and/or retailers to try to eliminate consumer shopping for the best price on popular makes and models of the time. How could you shop a trademark that didn't exist anywhere else? Tom Wheeler, in his book, *American Guitars*, quoted former Harmony president Charles A. Rubovits' recollection that the company built 57 private brands for the wholesalers – and sold over five million guitars.

An informative essay about House Brands and their place in the vintage guitar spectrum can be found in *Stellas & Stratocasters* (Vintage Guitar Books) by Willie G. Moseley, feature writer/columnist for *Vintage Guitar Magazine*. Moseley's commentary includes a listing of thirty-eight brands and their retailers/distributors, brief anecdotes about the major American manufacturers of budget instruments (Harmony, Kay, etc.) and photos of twenty-five American-made House Brand instruments.

Since writing that article, Moseley has advised the *Blue Book of Electric Guitars*: "I've come across a couple of other house brands in my travels; one example was a low-end, Stella-type variant with `Superior' sloppily screen-printed on its headstock. It was one of those cheap, beginner's instruments that were and still are at the nadir of American-made guitars, but so far I haven't been able to determine anything about its brand name...not that it matters too much!"

"It's my opinion, and I dare say the opinion of most vintage guitar enthusiasts, that a good rule of thumb concerning the collectibility of House Brands would be something along the lines of 'If it was a budget instrument then, it's proportionally a budget instrument now.' Regrettably, as the interest in vintage guitars continues to grow, some individuals and/or businesses tend to assume that simply because an instrument is 'old' and/or 'discontinued' and/or 'American-made', that automatically makes it a 'collector's item' and/or 'valuable.' That's certainly not the case, especially with House Brands. It's disheartening to walk into a pawn shop and see a Kay-made Silvertone archtop electric from the Sixties labeled as an 'antique' and priced at $499, when the instrument is worth no more than $100 in the vintage guitar market, and such incidents are apparently on the increase. And that's unfortunate for everybody."

The *Blue Book of Electric Guitars* is continuing to collect data and evaluate the collectibility and pricing on these House Brand instruments. Condition is a large factor in the pricing, as a thirty-to-forty year old guitar ordered from a catalog may have been used/abused by younger members of a household (to the detriment of the instrument). House Brand guitars may be antiques, they may be somewhat collectible, and they may be "classic pieces of Americana" (as one antique shop's sign declared), but they should still be relatively inexpensive when compared to the rest of the vintage guitar market. We believe Mr. Moseley to be correct in his C-note assessment of this aspect of the vintage market (at 80% to 90% condition); other music markets that service players and students may find pricing at a slightly wider range of $75 to $150 depending on other factors (playability, possessing an adjustable truss rod, appearance/"coolness" factor, a solid wood top versus plywood, veneer sides, additional parts, etc.) This is the bottom line: this book should help identify the brand/original company, give a few hints as to the quality and desirability, and a price range. The rest is up to you! We will continue to survey the market for pricing trends and "hot" models – further information will be included in upcoming editions of the *Blue Book of Electric Guitars*.

Blue Book of Electric Guitars

TRADEMARK INDEX

A BASSES
abasses@abasses.com
www.abasses.com

A.C.E. GUITARS
A division of The Poly-Tech Company
113 Crosby Rd. Unit 13
Dover, NH 03820
Phone: 603-742-1160
ppak@rcn.com
www.ace-guitars.com

ABYSS
535 N 13 ST
Forest City, IA 50436
Phone: 641 582 3718
kevin@abyssguitars.com
www.abyssguitars.com

ACACIA INSTRUMENTS
PO Box 162
Southampton, PA 18966
Phone: 215-953-9120
Fax: 215-953-8170
www.acaciainstruments.com

ADLER CUSTOM GUITARS
PO Box 553
Calimesa, CA 92320
Phone: 909-203-6549
www.adlerguitars.com

ALAMO GUITARS
3526 East T. C. Jester Road
Houston, TX 77018
Phone: 713-957-0470
Fax: 713-957-3316
sales@alamoguitars.com
www.alamoguitars.com

ALEMBIC
3005 Wiljan Court
Santa Rosa, CA 95407
Phone: 707-523-2611
Fax: 707-523-2935
alembic@alembic.com
www.alembic.com

ALLEN, ROB
511 East Gutierrez St #2
Santa Barbara, CA 93103
Phone: 805-965-9053
Fax: 805-965-9053
rob@roballenguitars.com
www.roballenguitars.com

ALVAREZ
Distributed by St. Louis Music
1400 Ferguson Ave.
St. Louis, MO 63133
Phone: 314-727-4512
www.alvarezgtr.com

AMBUSH CUSTOM BASSES
PO Box 16
Frederick, MD 21705-0016
Phone: 301-874-2177
www.ambushbass.com

AMERICAN ARCHTOP
RR#6 Box 6379B
Stroudsburg, PA 18360
Phone: 570-992-4956
dale@americanarchtop.com
www.americanarchtop.com

ANDERSEN STRINGED INSTRUMENTS
7811 Greenwood Ave. N.
Seattle, WA 98103
Phone: 206-782-8630
steve@AndersenGuitars.com
www.andersenguitars.com

ANDREAS C/O THOMASTIK-INFELD
Diehlgasse 27
1050 Vienna, Austria
info@thomastik-infeld.com
www.thomastik-infeld.com

ARCHER GUITARS
Dynamic Music Distributing Inc.
PO Box 27655
Milwaukee, WI 53227
Fax: 800-211-5570

ARIA/ARIA PRO II
A division of N.H.F. Musical Merchandise Inc.
9244 Commerce Highway
Pennsauken, NJ 08110
Toll free: 800-524-0441
Fax: 888-401-3051
www.ariausa.com

ARPEGGIO KORINA
Phone: 610-449-6900
arpeggio@rcn.com
www.arpkorina.com

ARTISTA
Distributed by Musicorp/MBT Hondo
Guitar Company
PO Box 30819
Charleston, SC 29417
Toll free: 800-845-1922
Phone: 843-763-9083
Fax: 843-763-9096

ASLIN DANE
Distributed by David Burns Musical
Instruments
Farmingdale, NY 11735
Phone: 631-777-5628
info@aslindane.com
www.aslindane.com

ASTURIAS
Distributed by J.T.G. of Nashville
5350 Hillsboro Road
Nashville, TN 37215
Phone: 615-665-8384
Fax: 615-665-9468

ATELIER Z
www.atelierz.co.jp/

ATLANSIA
atlansia@po.cnet.ne.jp
www.cnet.ne.jp/atlansia/

AUERSWALD
jerryauerswald@auerswald-instruments.com
www.auerswald-instruments.com/

AUSTIN
Distributed by St. Louis Music, Inc.
1400 Ferguson Ave.
St. Louis, MO 63133
Phone: 314-727-4512
Fax: 314-727-8929
www.austingtr.com

AW SHADOWS GUITARS
designer@awshadows.com
www.awshadows.com

AXL
Distributed by The Music Link
www.themusiclink.net

AXTRA
www.axtraguitars.com

AZOLA BASSES
PO Box 1519
Ramona, CA 92065
Phone: 760-789-8581
jill@azola.com
www.azola.com

B.C. RICH
A division of HHI
4940 Delhi Pike
Cincinnati, OH 45238
Toll free: 800-999-5558
Fax: 800-451-4944
saleswest@bcrich.com
www.bcrich.com

BSX BASS INC.
c/o Mr. Dino Fiumara 2256
Brodhead Road
Aliquippa, PA 15001
Phone: 724-378-8697
Fax: 724-378-4079
BsxBass@ccia.com
www.bsxbass.com

BACHMANN
Antholz, Italy
Phone: 39 (0)474 492 349
Fax: 39 (0)474 492 349
info@bachmann-guitars.com
www.bachman-guitars.com

BAKER
543 W. Batteravia Road Unit G
Santa Maria, CA 93455
Phone: 805-739-8990
Fax: 805-739-9063
www.bakerguitars.com

BAKER, JAMES R.
PO Box 398
Shoreham, NY 11786
Phone: 631-821-6935
jrbaker@optonline.net
www.geocities.com/bakerguitars/

BAKES GUITARS
687 E. Chicago St
Elgin, IL 60120
Phone: 847-931-0707
bakesguitars@aol.com

BARKER GUITARS LTD
117 S. Rockford Avenue
Rockford, IL 61104
Phone: 815-399-2929
Fax: 815-399-2930

BASSLINE
Krefeld, Germany
Phone: 02151 / 736496
bassline@t-online.de
www.bassline-bass.de/english/
index.htm

BELIGER GUITARS
PO Box 1175
Garden City, MI 48136
lemon@lemonjames.com
members.aol.com/foxeyaxe

BELSHE, JUSTIN
1605 Girard Ave.
San Marcos, TX 78666
justinbelsha@yahoo.com

BENAVENTE
Grants Pass, OR
Phone: 901-377-0088
chris@benaventeguitars.com
www.benaventeguitars.com

BENEDETTO, ROBERT
A Division of Fender Musical
Instrument Corporation
8860 E. Chaparral Road, Suite 100
Scottsdale, AZ 85250
Phone: 480-596-9690
www.benedettoguitars.com

BENEDICT GUITARS
888-256-2036
benedictguitar@uswest.net
www.users.uswest.net/~benedictguitar/

BILL LAWRENCE GUITAR COMPANY LLC
1785 Pomona Road Unit D
Corona, CA 92880
877-647-2651
Phone: 909-371-1494
Fax: 909-371-9191
becky@billlawrence.com
www.billlawrence.com

BISCAYNE
Distributed by Tropical Music
Corporation
6850 SW 81st Terrace
Miami, FL 33143
Phone: 305-740-7454
Fax: 305-740-7456
sales@tropicalmusic.com
www.tropicalmusic.com

BLACKHURST
blackhurst@blackhurst.com
www.blackhurst.com

BLACKSHEAR, TOM
17303 Springhill
San Antonio, TX 78232
Phone: 210-494-1141
tguitars@texas.net
tguitars.home.texas.net/

BLADE
4231 S. Natches Ct. Suite E.
Englewood, CO 80110
Toll free: 800-475-9006
Phone: 303-781-0990
Fax: 303-781-6465
www.bladeguitars.com

BLUE STAR GUITAR COMPANY
Distributed by Elderly Instruments
1100 North Washington
Lansing, MI 48906
Phone: 517-372-7890
Fax: 517-372-5155
web@elderly.com
www.elderly.com

BLUE STAR MUSIC
PO Box 493
177 Main Street
Lovingston, VA 22949
Phone: 804-263-6746

BORN TO ROCK
Toll free: 800-496-ROCK
Phone: 212-496-5342
71271.3051@compuserve.com
www.webcorp.com/btr/btr.htm

BRANDONI
Phone: 020-8908 2323
Fax: 020-8908 2323
roberto@brandonimu-
sic.freeserve.co.uk
www.brandoniguitars.co.uk

BRAWLEY GUITARS
27633 Commerce Center Drive
Temecula, CA 92590
Phone: 909-699-2428
Fax: 909-699-4171
keithwbrawley@cs.com
www.brawleyguitars.com

BRIAN EASTWOOD GUITARS
peter.williams@a-loss-for-words.co.uk
www.brianeastwoodguitars.co.uk

BRIAN MOORE CUSTOM GUITARS
60 Firemens Way
Poughkeepsie, NY 12603
Phone: 845-486-0744
Fax: 845-486-0745
info@brianmooreguitars.com
www.brianmooreguitars.com

BRIAN PAUL GUITARS
Phone: 214-761-3626
Fax: 972-250-0073
bripaul@airmail.net

BRUBAKER
250 Chartley Drive
Reisterstown, MD 21136 USA
Phone: 410-857-7600
Fax: 410-857-7622
info@brubakerguitars.com
www.brubakerguitars.com

BUNKER GUITARS
259313 Bk Bldg Hwy 101
Sequim, WA 98382
Phone: 360-417-6647
info@bunker-guitars.com
www.bunker-guitars.com/

BURNS USA/CODEL ENTERPRISES
Distributed by Codel Enterprises
PO Box 269
Bethel, CT 06801
Phone: 203-205-0056
Fax: 203-205-9062
www.burnsusa.com

BUSCARINO, JOHN
2348 Wide Horizon Drive
Franklin, NC 28734
Phone: 828-349-9867
Fax: 828-349-0558
John@Buscarino.com
www.buscarino.com

BYRD GUITAR COMPANY
strat110@yahoo.co.uk
www.jamesbyrd.com

C. HALL GUITARS
PO Box 6090
Pine Mountain Club, CA 93222
Phone: 661-242-9650
chall@challguitars.com
www.challguitars.com

CALLAHAM VINTAGE GUITARS
114 Tudor Drive
Winchester, VA 22603
Phone: 540-955-0294
callaham@callahamguitars.com
www.callahamguitars.com

CARMINE STREET GUITARS
42 Carmine St Fl 1
New York, NY 10014
Phone: 212-691-8400
www.kellyguitars.com

CARRUTHERS, JOHN
346 Sunset Avenue
Venice, CA 90291
Phone: 310-392-3910
Fax: 310-392-0389

CATALYST INSTRUMENTS USA
info@catalyst.nl
www.catalyst.nl

CELINDER
Gasvaerksvej 10 E 1656
Copenhagen V., Denmark
Phone: 45 331-8778
Fax: 45 331-8778
info@celinder.com
www.celinder.com

CHAPIN
PO Box 7401
San Jose, CA 95150
Phone: 408-295-6252
Fax: 408-295-6252
shades@chapinguitars.com
www.chapinguitars.com

CHAPPELL GUITARS
2619 Columbia Avenue
Richmond, CA 94804
Phone: 510-528-2904
Fax: 510-528-8310
sean@east-bay.com

CHARVEL
8860 E. Chaparral Road Suite 100
Scottsdale, AZ 85250-2618
Phone: 480-596-9690
Fax: 480-596-1384
www.charvelguitars.com

CHRIS LARKIN CUSTOM GUITARS
Castlegregory, County Kerry Ireland
Fax: +353 (0) 66 713 9330
chris@ChrisLarkinGuitars.com
www.chrislarkinguitars.com

CIMARRON GUITARS
538 Sherman Box 511
Ridgway, CO 81432
Phone: 970-626-4464
cimgit@cimarronguitars.com
www.cimarronguitars.com

CITRON
282 Chestnut Hill Road
Woodstock, NY 12498
Phone: 845-679-7138
Fax: 845-679-3221
harvey@citron-guitars.com
www.citron-guitars.com

CLEVINGER
553 Kenmore Ave.
Oakland, CA 94610
Phone: 510-444-2542
clevbass@comcast.net
www.clevinger.com

CLIFTON
South London, England
Phone: +44 (0)208 858 7795
Fax: +44 (0)208 858 7795
mo@cliftonbass.freeserve.co.uk
www.cliftonbasses.co.uk

CLOVER
Zum Wetterschacht 9
Recklinghausen, D-45659 Germany
Phone: 0049-2361 / 15881
Fax: 0049-2361 / 183473
clover@t-online.de
www.clover-guitars.com

COLLOPY
San Francisco, CA 94118
Phone: 415-221-2990
rcollopy@pacbell.net

COMINS GUITARS
PO Box 611
Willow Grove, PA 19090
Phone: 215-376-0595
bill@cominsguitars.com
www.cominsguitars.com

CONKLIN
PO Box 1394
Springfield, MO 65801
Phone: 417-886-3525
Fax: 417-886-2934
conklin@conklinguitars.com
www.conklinguitars.com

COOG INSTRUMENTS
147 Sacramento Ave
Santa Cruz, CA
Phone: 831-425-4933
ron@cooginstruments.com
www.cooginstruments.com

CORT
3451 W. Commercial Ave.
Northbrook, IL 60062
Phone: 847-498-6491
Fax: 847-498-5370
www.cort.com

CRATE
Also CRATE/ELECTRA Distributed by
St. Louis Music Inc.
1400 Ferguson Ave.
St. Louis, MO 63133
Phone: 314-727-4512

CURBOW
PO Box 309
24 Allen Lane
Morganton, GA 30560
Phone: 706-374-2873
Fax: 706-374-2530
greg@curbow.com
www.curbow.com

D'ANGELICO GUITARS OF AMERICA (VESTAX)
264 Rte. 537 E
Colts Neck, NJ 07722
Phone: 732-380-0995
Fax: 732-380-1303
info@dangelicoguitars.com
www.dangelicoguitars.com
Factory
1-18-6 Wakabayashi
Tokyo, Setagaya-ku
154-0023 Japan
Phone: 81-3-3412-7011
Fax: 81-3-3412-7013
info@vestax.co.jp

D'ANGELICO REPLICA
Working Musician
1760 Claridge Street
Arcadia, CA 91006
Phone: 626-355-5554

D'AQUISTO (CURRENT MFG.)
Distributed by Aria USA
1085 Thomas Busch Highway
Pennsauken, NJ 08110
Toll free: 800-524-0441
Fax: 856-663-0436
www.ariausa.com

D'LECO GUITARS
2000 NW 15th St
Oklahoma City, OK 73106
Phone: 405-524-0448
Fax: 405-524-0448
jamesdale@juno.com

D. C. HILDER BUILDER
2 Yorkshire Street N.
Guelph, Ontario N1H 5A5 Canada
Phone: 519 821-6030
Fax: 519 837-2268

DAISY ROCK
16320 Roscoe Blvd. Ste #100
Van Nuys, CA 91410-0003
1-877-693-2479
Fax: 1-800-632-1928
info@daisyrock.com
www.daisyrock.com

DALMEDO GUITARS
Phone: 01772-718907
dalmedoguitars@aol.com
www.dalmedoguitars.co.uk

DANELECTRO
PO Box 73010
San Clemente, CA 92673
Phone: 949-498-9854
Fax: 949-369-8500
info@danelectro.com
www.danelectro.com

DAVE KING GUITARS
4805 N. Borthwick Avenue
Portland, OR 97217
Phone: 503-282-0327
david@kingbass.com
www.kingbass.com

DAVIS J. THOMAS
3135 N. High St.
Columbus, OH 43202-1125
Phone: 614-263-0264
Fax: 614-447-0174
tom@jthomasdavis.com
www.jthomasdavis.com

DEAKON ROADS GUITARS
302F Wall Street
Saskatoon, Saskatchewan S7K 1N7
Canada
Phone: 306-244-3566
Fax: 306-244-4052
info@deakonroads.com
www.deakonroads.com

DEAN
15251 Roosevelt Blvd. Suite 206
Clearwater, FL 33760
Phone: 727-519-9669
www.deanguitars.com

DECAVA
PO Box 131
Stratford, CT 06497
888-661-0229
Phone: 203-377-0096
jrdecava@aol.com

DEERING BANJO COMPANY INC.
3733 Kenora Drive
Spring Valley, CA 91977-1829
Phone: 619-464-8252
Fax: 619-464-0833
info@deeringbanjos.com
www.deeringbanjos.com

DEVON GUITARS
1372 Lake Park Court
Pewaukee, WI 53072
Phone: 262-695-0218
devonjen@execpc.com
www.devonguitars.com

DI PINTO GUITARS
631 N. 2nd Street
Philadelphia, PA 19123 USA
Phone: 215-923-2353
Fax: 215-923-5899
www.dipintoguitars.com

DILLON GUITARS
Taos, NM
Phone: 505-758-1996
john@dillonguitars.com
dillonguitars.com/dg/dg.html

DINGWALL DESIGNER GUITARS
Box 9194
Saskatoon, Saskatchewan S7K 7E8
Phone: 306-242-6201
sales@dingwallguitars.com
www.dingwallguitars.com

DILLON GUITARS
Taos, NM
Phone: 505-758-1996
john@dillonguitars.com
dillonguitars.com/dg/dg.html

DINOSAUR
Distributed by Eleca International Inc.
21088 Commerce Point Drive
Walnut, CA 91789
Phone: 909-468-1382
Fax: 909-468-1652
info@eleca.com
www.elecaamps.com

DIPINTO
PO Box 29453
Philadelphia, PA 19125
Phone: 215-923-2353
Fax: 215-923-5899
info@dipintoguitars.com
www.dipintoguitars.com

DOBRO
A Division of Gibson/OMI
161 Opry Mills Drive
Nashville, TN 37214
Phone: 615-514-2200
www.gibson.com/products/bluegrass

DODGE
2120 Longview Drive
Tallahassee, FL 32303
Phone: 850-562-4331
rickdodge@dodgeguitars.com

DRAGONFLY
Made by Harry's Co. Inc.
info@harrysjp.com
www.harrysjp.com

DRISKILL GUITARS
2800 A Shamrock
Fort Worth, TX 76107
Phone: 817-336-0600
joe@driskillguitars.com
www.driskillguitars.com

DRIVE
Distributed by Switchmusic.com, Inc.
1900 S. Proforma Ave. Ste. F-2
Ontario, CA 91761
Phone: 909-947-8618
Fax: 909-947-8628
service@switchmusic.com
www.switchmusic.com

DUBREUILLE, PHILLIPE
25 Denmark Street 1st Floor
London, WC 2 H8NJ England
Phone: 00 44 777 633 2197
philgood@debreuille.com
www.dubreuille.com

DUESENBERG
Distributed by 3 Sons Specialized Music
info@duesenberg.de
www.duesenberg.de

ESP
10903 Vanowen St Unit A
North Hollywood, CA 91605
Toll free: 800-423-8388
Fax: 818-506-1378
www.espguitars.com

EYB GUITARS
Schillerstrasse 48
Leonberg, D-71229 Germany
Phone: 49 (0)7152 - 2 43 85
Fax: 49 (0)7152 - 2 43 99
mail@eyb-guitars.de
www.eyb-guitars.de

ECCLESHALL
Unit 2 Webber's Way
Darington, Totnes, Devon TQ9 6JY England
Phone: 011-44-1803-862364
Fax: 011-44-1803-868665
chris@eccleshallguitars.co.uk
www.eccleshallguitars.co.uk

ECHEVERRIA GUITARS
PO Box 50172
Tucson, AZ 85703-1172
Phone: 529-792-2136
Fax: 529-792-2136
echgtr@yahoo.com
www.echeverriaguitars.com

ED CLARK GUITARS, INC.
520A Hawkins Ave.
Ronkonkoma, NY 11779
Phone: 631-738-8181

EKO
info@ekoguitars.com
www.ekoguitars.com

ELECA
21088 Commerce Pointe Drive
Walnut, CA 91789
1-888-GO-ELECA
Phone: 909-468-1382
Fax: 909-468-1652
info@eleca.com
www.elecaamps.com

ELRICK
Phone: 386-517-6823
Fax: 386-439-4446
www.elrick.com

EMERY
Distributed by Resound Vintage Guitars
7438 Hwy 53
Britt, MN 55710
Phone: 218-741-9515

EMINENCE
Toll free: 800-741-3045
gelbass@aol.com
www.gelbass.com

EMPIRE GUITARS
220 N. Glendora Ave.
Glendora, CA 91741
Phone: 626-914-8082
Fax: 626-914-4287
gmw@deltanet.com
www.gmwguitars.com

ENCORE
Distributed by John Hornby Skewes & Co. Ltd.
Salem House Parkinson Approach Garforth
Leeds, Leeds United Kingdom
Phone: (+44) (0) 113 286 5381
Fax: (+44) (0) 113 286 8515
info@jhs.co.uk
www.jhs.co.uk

ENGLISH GUITARS
14586 Olive Vista Dr.
Jamul, CA 91935
Phone: 619-669-0833
Fax: 619-669-0833
englishguitars@email.com
www.englishguitars.com

EPIPHONE
A division of Gibson
645 Massman Drive
Nashville, TN 37210
Toll free: 800-444-2766
service@gibson.com
www.epiphone.com

ERLEWINE GUITARS
4402 Burnet Rd.
Austin, TX 78756
Fax: 512-371-1655
mark@erlewineguitars.com
www.erlewineguitars.com

ERNIE BALL/MUSIC MAN
Box 4117
San Luis Obispo, CA 93403
Toll free: 800-543-2255
Phone: 805-544-7726
Fax: 805-544-7275
ernieball@ernieball.com
www.ernieball.com

EUGEN
PO Box 1782 Nordnes
5816
Bergen, Norway
Phone: 47-55-23-28-60
Fax: 47-55-23-04-35
guitars@eugen.no
www.eugen.no

F BASS
16 McKinstry Street
Hamilton, Ontario L8L 6C1 Canada
Phone: 905-522-1582
Fax: 905-528-5667
info@fbass.com
www.fbass.com

FABREGUES BASSES
PO Box 364069
San Juan, PR 00936-4069
Phone: 787-753-7935
Fax: 787-759-9524
fabregues@viguiefilms.com
www.fabregues.com

FARNELL GUITARS
1009 Brooks St. Suite C
Ontario, CA 91762
Phone: 909-983-1741
Fax: 909-983-1742
www.farnellguitars.com

FENDER
8860 Chapparal Road Suite 100
Scottsdale, AZ 85250-2618
Phone: 480-596-9690
Fax: 480-367-5262
custserv@fenderusa.com
www.fender.com

FERNANDES
8163 Lankershim Blvd.
North Hollywood, CA 91605
Toll free: 800-318-8599
Fax: 818-252-6790
info@fernandesguitars.com
www.fernandesguitars.com

FICHTER
Postgasse 1
Waldems , D-65529 Germany
Phone: +49/ (0)6087 - 98 93 13
Fax: +49/ (0)6087 - 98 93 11
info@fichterbasses.com
www.fichterbasses.com

FIRST ACT
320 Needham Street
Newton, MA 02464
Phone: 781-453-2221
Fax: 781-453-2644
www.firstact.com

FISCHER FINE INSTRUMENTS
PMB B-2 621 SR9 NE
Lake Stevens, WA 98258
Phone: 425-335-4157
fischerguitars@ix.netcom.com
www.fischerguitars.com

FITZPATRICK JAZZ GUITARS
54 Enfield Avenue
Wickford, RI 02852
Phone: 401-294-4801

FLETCHER BROCK STRINGED INSTRUMENTS
1417 Boat Street
Seattle, WA 98105
Phone: 206-547-2279
tofletcher@yahoo.com

FLOYD ROSE
6855 176th Ave NE
Redmond, WA 98052
Phone: 425-883-9200
sales@floydrose.com
www.floydrose.com

FODERA
68 34th Street
Brooklyn, NY 11232
Phone: 718-832-3455
Fax: 718-832-3458
fodera@verizon.net
www.fodera.com

FONTANILLA, ALLAN
PO Box 31423
San Francisco, CA 94131
Phone: 415-642-9375
allan@fontinilla.com
www.fontanilla.com

FOSTER
Foster Guitar Manufacturing
76353 Eugene Wallace Road
Covington, LA 70435
888-317-4146
Phone: 985-892-9822
Fax: 985-871-7833
jimmy@fosterguitars.com
www.fosterguitars.com

FRAMUS
PO Box 10100 Gewerbegebiet
Wohlhausen
Markneukirchen, D-08258 Germany
Phone: 49-37422-555-0
Fax: 49-37422-55599
www.framus.com

FREDDY'S FRETS
866-204-4075
Phone: 905-384-0303
Fax: 905-384-0014
freddy@freddysfrets.com
www.freddysfrets.com

FRITZ BROTHERS GUITARS
Phone: 707-937-6060

FRUDUA GUITAR WORKS
info@frudua.com
www.fruduaguitars.it

FRYE
147 N. Broadway
Green Bay, WI 54303
Phone: 920-433-0722
www.fryeguitars.onbroadway.org/

FULLERTON
Distributed by NHF Musical
Merchandise Inc.
1085 Thomas Busch Highway
Pennsauken, NJ 08110
Phone: 856-663-8900
Fax: 856-663-0436
www.ariausa.com

FURY
902 Avenue J North
Saskatoon, Saskatchewan S7L 2L2
Canada
Phone: 306-244-4063
ussales@furyguitar.com
www.furyguitar.com

G & L
5381 Production Drive
Huntington Beach, CA 92649
Phone: 714-897-6766
Fax: 714-895-6728
info@glguitars.com
www.glguitars.com

G GOULD
1315 23rd Ave Suite 200A
San Francisco, CA 94122
Phone: 415-759-5199
Fax: 415-759-5399
geoff@ggould.com
www.ggould.com

GLF
Distributed by GLF Custom Shop
19817 Jackie Lane
Rogers, MN 55374
Phone: 763-428-8818
glfsmith@aol.com

GMP GUITARS
510 E. Arrow Hwy.
San Dimas, CA 91773
Phone: 909-592-5144
Fax: 909-599-0798
gmp@gmpguitars.com
www.gmpguitars.com

GR BASSES
12169 Kirkham Road Suite B
Poway, CA 92064
Phone: 858-637-8523
Fax: 760-761-0137
www.grbasses.com

GIBSON
Corporate Office
309 Plus Park Blvd
Nashville, TN 37217
Toll free: 800-444-2766
Phone: 615-871-4500
Fax: 615-889-5509
service@gibson.com
www.gibson.com
Gibson Acoustic
1894 Orville Way
Bozeman, MT 57915
Toll free: 800-426-2636
Phone: 406-587-4117
Fax: 406-587-9109
Gibson Custom, Art, &Historic
657 Massman Drive
Nashville, TN 37210-3781
Toll free: 800-444-2766
Fax: 615-871-9517
Gibson Nashville (USA Electric)
641 Massman Drive
Nashville, TN 37210
Phone: 615-871-9585
Gibson Europe BV
Clarissenhof 5C/4133 AB Vianen
Netherlands
Phone: +31-347-324010

GIFFIN GUITARS
Beavertone, OR
Phone: 503-643-7178
Fax: 503-643-7178
giffinguitars@usa.com
www.giffinguitars.com

GILCHRIST, STEPHEN
Distributed by Carmel Music
PO Box 2296
Carmel, CA 93921
Phone: 831-624-8078
Fax: 831-624-2066
info@carmelmusic.com
www.carmelmusic.com

GLORY
Room No. 1-202 Industrial Distribution
Center #129
Songhyun-Dong
Dong-Ku, Inchon Korea
Phone: 83-32-588-1675-7
Fax: 82-32-588-1678
glorym@chollian.net

GODIN
19420 Avenue Clark-Graham
Baie D Urfe, Quebec H9X 3R8
info@godinguitars.com
www.godinguitars.com

GORDON SMITH GUITARS
Partington, England
Phone: 0870 766 4028
info@gordonsmithguitars.com
www.gordonsmithguitars.com

GRAND
info@grandintl.com

GREENE & CAMPBELL GUITARS
P. O. Box 460
Westwood, MA 02090
Phone: 617-620-8153
Fax: 508-785-3577
sales@gcguitars.com
www.greeneandcampbellguitars.com

GRENDEL
Distributed by Matthews & Ryan
Musical Products, Inc.
68 34th Street
Brooklyn, NY 11232
Toll free: 800-248-4827
Phone: 718-832-6333
Fax: 718-832-5270
sales@matthewsandryan.com
www.matthewsandryan.com

GRETSCH
A division of FMIC
8860 East Chaparral Road,
Ste. 100
Scottsdale, AZ 85250-2618
Phone: 480-596-9690
Fax: 480-596-1384
www.gretschguitars.com

GROOVE TOOLS
PO Box 1394
Sprinfield, MO 65801
Phone: 417-886-3525
Fax: 417-886-2934
conklin@conkliguitars.com
www.conkliguitars.com

GROVES CUSTOM GUITARS
ggroves100@earthlink.net
home.earthlink.net/~ggroves100/

GROSH, DAN CUSTOM GUITARS
26818 Oak Ave. Suite F
Santa Clarita, CA 91351
Phone: 661-252-6716
Fax: 661-298-1103
sales@groshguitars.com
www.groshguitars.com

GRUGGETT GUITARS
Bakersfield, CA
guitars@gruggett.com
www.gruggett.com

GUILD
A division of FMIC
8860 East Chaparral Road,
Ste. 100
Scottsdale, AZ 85250-2618
Phone: 480-596-9690
Fax: 480-596-1384
www.guildguitars.com

GUITAR FACTORY
2816 Edgewater Dr.
Orlando, FL 32804
Toll free: 800-541-1070
Phone: 407-425-1070
www.theband2am.com/guitarfactory.html

GUITAR FARM
RR 1 Box 60
Sperryville, VA 22740
Phone: 540-987-9744
Fax: 640-987-9419

GUITAR SALON INTERNATIONAL
3100 Donald Douglas Loop North
Santa Monica, CA 90405
Phone: 310-399-2181
Fax: 310-396-9283

GUS GUITARS
Bewdley Old Heathfield
East Sussex, TN21 9BN England
Phone: 440-1435-863048
info@gusguitars.co.uk
www.gusguitars.co.uk

HAGSTROM
Distributed by AM&S
5304 Derry Ave. Suite C
Agoura Hills, CA 91301
Toll free: 800-994-4984
Fax: 800-431-3129
info@hagstromguitars.com
www.hagstromguitars.com

HALLMARK
PO Box 242
Greenbelt, MD 20768
info@hallmarkguitars.com
www.hallmarkguitars.com

HAMBURGUITAR
10188 Cupid's Dart Street
Las Vegas, NV 89123
Phone: 702-260-9777
hamburguitar@coam.net
www.hamburguitar.com

HAMER
Distributed by Kaman Music
PO Box 507
Bloomfield, CT 06002-0507
askus@hamerguitars.com
www.hamerguitars.com

HAMILTONE
Fort Wayne, IN
hamiltone@novan.com
www.novan.com/jimspage.htm

HAMMERTONE GUITARS
See F Bass

HANEWINCKEL GUITARS
10002 St. John Circle
Cypress, CA 90630
Phone: 714-484-2846
pete@hguitars.com
www.hanewinckelguitars.com/

HARMONIC DESIGN
325 Jefferson Street
Bakersfield, CA 93305
Phone: 661-321-0395
Fax: 661-322-2360
pickups@harmonicdesign.net
www.harmonicdesign.net

HARPERS
PO Box 2877
Apple Valley, CA 92307
Phone: 760-240-1792
Fax: 760-240-1792
harpergtrs@aol.com
members.aol.com/HARPERGTRS/

HARRISON CUSTOM GUITARS
Broad Lane Business Center
South Elmsall
Pontefract, West Yorks WF9 2JX
England
Phone: 0044 (0) 1977 642547
Fax: 0044 (0) 1977 645155
guy@wemakeguitars.com
www.wemakeguitars.com

HARTKE
Distributed by Samson Technologies
Corporation
PO Box 9031 575 Underhill Blvd.
New York, NY 11791-9031
1-800-328-2882
Phone: 516-364-2244
Fax: 516-364-3888
info@samsontech.com
www.samsontech.com

HEINS GUITARS
Hoogend 26 NL-8601 AE
Sneek, Netherlands
Phone: 31-515-423848
Fax: 31-515-423848
info@heinsguitars.nl
www.heinsguitars.nl

HEMBROOK
3703 Crownover
Austin, TX 78725-4705
Phone: 512-276-7439
www.hembrook.com

HERITAGE
Factory
225 Parsons Street
Kalamazoo, MI 49007
Phone: 269-385-5721
Fax: 269-385-3519
www.heritageguitar.com
Sales & Marketing by
Lasar Music Corporation
500 Wilson Pike Circle Suite 204
Brentwood, TN 37027
Phone: 615-377-4913
Fax: 615-377-4986

HEWETT GUITARS
22430 Gail Street
New Caney, TX 77357
Phone: 281-354-7894
guitar@wt.net
www.hewettguitars.com

HILL CUSTOM GUITARS
5350 Dobeckmum Road
Cleveland, OH 44102
Phone: 216-496-0994
jon@hillinstruments.com
www.hillguitars.com

HOFNER
Distributed by The Music Group
10949 Pendleton Street
Sun Valley, CA 91352
Phone: 818-252-6305
Fax: 818-252-6351
rob.olsen@musicgroup.com
www.musicgroup.com

HOHNER
Distributed by HSS
PO Box 15035
Richmond, VA 23227
Toll free: 800-446-6010
info@hohnerusa.com
www.hohnerusa.com

HOLST, STEPHEN
82722 Bear Creek Road
Creswell, OR 97426
Phone: 541-895-2362
sholst@pacinfo.com
www.pacinfo.com/~sholst/index.htm

HONDO
Distributed by MBT International
PO Box 30819
Charleston, SC 29417
Toll free: 800-641-6931
Phone: 843-763-9083
Fax: 843-763-9096
sales@mbtinternational.com
www.hondoguitars.com

HOPKINS GUITARS
97 Grandview Street
Penticton, British Columbia
V2A 4E5 Canada
Phone: 250-493-4318
www.hopkinsguitars.com

HOT LICKS
Distributed by Hotlicks Productions
4601 S.W. 128th Ave
Southwest Ranches, FL 33330
Toll free: 800-388-3008
Phone: 954-434-7070
Fax: 954-434-4757
hotlicks@hotlicks.com
www.hotlicks.com

HOYER
Distributed by Mario Pellarin
www.pellarin.de

HUBER, NIK
Borsigstr. 13
63110 Rodgau, Germany
Phone: 49 - (0) 61 06 - 77 21 66
Fax: +49 - (0) 61 06 - 77 21 67
info@nikhuber-guitars.com
www.nikhuber-guitars.com

IBANEZ
Distributed by Hoshino, Inc.
1726 Winchester Road
Bensalem, PA 19020
1-800-669-4226
Phone: 215-638-8670
Fax: 215-245-8583
www.ibanez.com

ITALIA
Distributed by LPD Music International
23575 Industrial Drive
Madison Heights, MI 48071
Phone: 248-585-9630
Fax: 248-585-7360
mail@lpdmusic.com
www.italiaguitars.com

J.B. PLAYER
Distributed by MBT International
PO Box 30819
Charleston, SC 29417
Phone: 843-763-9083
Fax: 843-763-9096
sales@mbtinternational.com
www.jbplayer.com

JP GUITARS
Formerly Pimentel Guitars
11917 150th St. Ct. E
Puyallup, WA 98374
Phone: 253-841-2954
Fax: 253-845-8357
sales@jpguitars.com
www.jpguitars.com

JACKSON
Distributed by FMIC
8860 E. Chaparral Road Suite 100
Scottsdale, AZ 85250-2618
Phone: 480-596-9690
Fax: 480-596-1384
www.jacksonguitars.com

JAROS CUSTOM GUTIARS
103 Mary Street
Rochester, PA 15074
Phone: 412-774-5615
www.jaroscustomguitars.com

JAY DEE
Phone: 0121 773 5711
john@jaydeeguitars.com
www.jaydeeguitars.com

Jay Turser
Distributed by Music Industries
Corporation
625 Locust Street #300
Garden City, NY 11530
Toll free: 800-431-6699
Phone: 516-794-1888
Fax: 516-794-4099
jay_turser@jayturser.com
www.jayturser.com

JEANNIE
292 Atherton Ave.
Pittsburg, CA 94565
Phone: 925-439-1447
pickguards@comcast.net
home.comcast.net/~pickguards/home.htm

JERRY JONES GUITARS
913 Church Street
Nashville, TN 37203
Phone: 615-255-0088
Fax: 615-255-7742
sales@jerryjonesguitars.com
www.jerryjonesguitars.com

JERZY DROZD
Barcelona, Spain
sales@jerzydrozdbasses.com
www.jerzydrozdbasses.com

JJ GUITARS
tony@jjguitars.com
www.jjguitars.com

JOHN BIRCH GUITARS
JC Business Services 220 Rutland Rd
West Bridgford, Nottingham NG2 5EB
England
Phone: (44) 0115 981 8523
Fax: 0115 846 9068
jc@johnbirchguitars.com
www.johnbirchguitars.com

JOHNSON
Distributed by The Music Link
PO Box 162
Brisbane, CA 94005
1-888-552-5465
Phone: 650-615-8991
Fax: 650-615-8997
feedback@themusiclink.net
www.themusiclink.com

JOHNSON'S EXTREMELY STRANGE MUSICAL INSTRUMENT COMPANY
119 W. Linden Ave.
Burbank, CA 91502
Phone: 818-955-8152
Fax: 818-955-8916
xstrange@earthlink.net
www.xstrange.com

JON KAMMERER GUITARS
222 Timea Street
Keokuk, IA 52632
Phone: 319-526-7651
Fax: 319-526-7649
kammguy1@interlinklc.net
www.jonkammererguitars.com

JORDAN GUITARS
2607 E 300 N.
Rankin, IL 60960
Phone: 217-397-2474

JUBAL GUITARS
326 S. Union Street
Olean, NY 14760
Phone: 716-372-7771

KALIL
132 S. Front Street
McComb, MS 39648
Phone: 601-249-3894
edekalil@aol.com
members.aol.com/edekalil/eddie.html

KAMAN MUSIC CORPORATION
PO Box 507
Bloomfield, CT 06002
Toll free: 800-647-2244
Phone: 860-509-8888
Fax: 860-509-8891
www.kamanmusic.com

KAY
Distributed by A.R. Musical
Enterprises, Inc.
9031 Technology Drive
Fishers, IN 46038
Toll free: 800-428-4807
Phone: 317-577-6999
Fax: 800-933-8207
Info@armusical.com
www.armusical.com

KELLET ALUMINUM GUITARS
415 Matthew Street
Santa Clara, CA 95050
Phone: 408-988-1910
Fax: 408-988-8606
anodize@pkselective.com
www.pkselective.com

KEN BEBENSEE GUITARS AND BASSES
29085A Highway 49
North San Juan, CA 95960
Phone: 530-292-0156
ken@kbguitars.com
www.kbguitars.com

KEN SMITH BASSES, LTD.
PO Box 199
Perkasie, PA 18944
Phone: 215-453-8887
Fax: 215-453-8084
support@kensmithbasses.com

KENDRICK
531 County Road 3300
Kempner, TX 76539-5755
Phone: 512-932-3130
Fax: 512-932-3135
kendrick@kendrick-amplifiers.com
kendrick-amplifiers.com

KENNETH LAWRENCE INSTRUMENTS
1055 Samoa Blvd.
Arcata, CA 95521
Phone: 707-822-2543
lawrence@reninet.com

KEVIN RYAN GUITARS
14211 Wiltshire Street
Westminster, CA 92683
Phone: 714-894-0590
Fax: 714-379-0944
ryanguitar@aol.com

KIMAXE
Distributed by Kenny & Michaels Co.
2425 S. Hill Street
Los Angeles, CA 90007
1-800-504-9831
Phone: 213-746-2848
Fax: 213-747-1161

KIMBARA
Distributed by FCN Music
Melody House Wealden Business Park
Farningham Road
Crowborough, E Sussex TN6 2JJ
England
Phone: 01892 603730
Fax: 01892 613220
info@fcnmusic.co.uk
www.fcnmusic.co.uk

KIMBERLY
Distributed by Kimex Trading
www.kimextrading.co.kr

KINAL
3239 East 52nd Ave.
Vancouver, BC V5S 1T9 Canada
Phone: 604-433-6544
guitar@istar.ca
www.kinal.com

KING, DAVID
4805 N. Borthwick Ave.
Portland, OR 97217
Phone: 503-282-0327
Fax: 503-282-0327
david@kingbass.com
www.kingbass.com

KLEIN ELECTRIC GUITARS
PO Box 247
Linden, CA 95236
Phone: 290-887-2651
Fax: 290-887-2651
kleinelectric@yahoo.com
www.kleinelectricguitars.com

KNUTSON LUTHIERY
Custom Guitar, Bass, and
Mandolin Works
PO Box 945
Forrestville, CA 95436
Phone: 707-887-2709

KOLL
2402 SE Belmont Street
Portland, OR 97214
Phone: 503-286-8938
saul@kollguitars.com
www.kollguitars.com

KONA
Distributed by M&M Merchandisers
1923 Bomar Ave.
Ft. Worth, TX 76103
Toll free: 800-687-0203
Phone: 817-339-1400
Fax: 817-335-2314
www.mmwholesale.com

KRAMER
Distributed by MusicYo.com
Fursdon Moreton
Hampstead
Devon, TQ13 8QT England
Phone: 44-647-70394
www.musicyo.com

KYDD
PO Box 2650
Upper Darby, PA 19082
Toll free: 800-622-KYDD
Phone: 800-622-KYDD

LTD
Distributed by ESP Guitar Company
10903 Vanowen St. Unit A
North Hollywood, CA 91605
Toll free: 800-423-8388
Fax: 818-506-1378
www.espguitars.com

LACE GUITARS
Distributed by Lace Music Products
5561 Engineer Drive
Huntington Beach, CA 92649
Phone: 714-898-2776
Fax: 714-893-1045
info@agi-lace.com
www.lacemusic.com

LADO
205 St. David Street
Lindsay, Ontario K9V 5K7 Canada
Phone: 705-328-2005
Fax: 705-328-0100
ladomusic@on.aibn.com
www.lado-guitars.com

LAKLAND
2044 N. Dominick
Chicago, IL 60614
Phone: 773-871-9637
Fax: 773-871-6675
dlakin@lakincorp.com
www.lakland.com

LAWRENCE, KENNETH
1055 Samoa Boulevard
Arcata, CA 95521
Phone: 707-822-2543
Fax: 707-822-8359
lawrence@reninet.com

LEDUC
1 place de l'église
Thionville, 57100 France
Phone: 33 (3) 82 53 16 16
Fax: 33 (3) 82 53 17 17
guitar@leduc.fr
www.leduc.fr/Gb/

LEGEND CUSTOM GUITARS
15 Durham Way
Dartmouth, NS B2V 1X1 Canada
Phone: 902-462-6292
contact@legendguitars.com
www.legendguitars.com

LIBERTY, GENE
PO Box 506
112 S. Bushnell Street
Sheridan, IL 60551
Phone: 815-496-9092
guitarfix@sannauk.com
www.guitarfix.com/index.htm

LINC, LUTHIER
1318 N. Monte Vista Ave. Suite 11
Upland, CA 91786
Phone: 909-931-0642
Fax: 909-931-0642
Guitars@LincLuthier.com
www.lincluthier.com

LINE 6
29901 Agoura Rd.
Agoura Hills, CA 91301-2513
Phone: 818-575-3600
Fax: 818-575-3601
internationalsales@line6.com
www.line6.com

LOWDEN
8 Glenford Way
Newtownards, BT23 4BX
United Kingdom
Phone: +44 (0) 28 9182 0542
Fax: +44 (0) 28 9182 0650
info@lowdenguitars.com
www.lowdenguitars.com
U.S. Distribution
14950 F.A.A Boulevard
Fort Worth, TX 76155
Toll free: 800-872-5856
Fax: 817-685-5699

LYRIC
56 E 53rd Place
Tulsa, OK 74105
Phone: 918-747-7380
lyric@wherever.com
www.southernphotography.com/lyric/

MDX
736 Cromwell Street
West Point, MS 39773
Phone: 662-494-8777
dwight@mdxguitars.net
www.mdxguitars.com

MJ GUITAR ENGINEERING
643 Martin Ave #2
Rohnert Park, CA 94928
Phone: 707-588-8075
mjguitar@aol.com
www.mjguitar.com

MTD
3 Lauren Court
Kingston, NY 12401
Phone: 845-246-0670
Fax: 845-246-1670
mike@mtdbass.com
www.mtdbass.com

MACDONALD, S.B. CUSTOM INSTRUMENTS
22 Fairmont Street
Huntington, NY 11743
Phone: 631-421-9056
guitardoc@customguitars.com
customguitars.com

MCCOLLUM GUITARS
PO Box 806
Colfax, CA 95713
Phone: 530-346-7657
mccollum@mccollumguitars.com
www.mccollumguitars.com

MCCURDY, RIC
19 Hudson St.
New York, NY 10013
Phone: 212-274-8352
Fax: 212-274-8352
info@mccurdyguitars.com
www.mccurdyguitars.com

MCGILL GUITARS
808 Kendall Drive
Nashville, TN 37209
Phone: 615-354-0070
conecaster@AOL.com
www.mcgillguitars.com

MCHUGH GUITARS
PO Box 2216
Northbrook, IL 60065-2216
Phone: 847-498-3319

MCINTURFF, TERRY C.
978 Chatham Church Road
Moncure, NC 27559
Phone: 919-542-5382
Fax: 919-552-0542
info@mcinturffguitars.com
www.mcinturffguitars.com

MCNAUGHT GUITARS
16382 Substation Road
Locust, NC 28097
Phone: 704-485-2787
Fax: 704-485-2806
davidmcnaught@mcnaughtguitars.com
www.mcnaughtguitars.com

MCSWAIN GUITARS
PO Box 1331
Burbank, CA 91507
Phone: 323-252-1393
Fax: 561-619-5937
stephen@mcswainguitars.com
www.mcswainguitars.com

MAGNUM GUITARS
3392 Sullivan Lake Rd.
Ione, WA 99139
Phone: 509-442-3078
info@magnumguitars.com
www.magnumguitars.com

MALDEN
10257 Santa Monica Blvd.
Los Angeles, CA 90067
Phone: 310-553-2214
sales@maldenguitars.com
www.maldenguitars.com

MANNE GUITARS
3630 Thompson Bridge Road Suite 15
PMB 110
Gainesville, GA 30506
Phone: 678-617-0520
info@atlantacustomguitars.com
www.manne.com
Factory
Via Paraiso 28
Schio, 36105 Italy
Phone: 0445 673872
Fax: 0445 512452
info@manne.com
www.manne.com

MANSON
The Ark 18 High Street
Crediton, Devon EX17 3AH England
Phone: +44 (0) 1363 773119
Fax: +44 (0) 1363 773119
andy@andymanson.co.uk
www.andymanson.co.uk/
Hugh Manson
Phone: 01363 775603
hugh@mansons.co.uk
www.andymanson.co.uk/
Sales
39 New Bridge Street
Exeter, Devon EX4 3AH England
Phone: 01392 496379
Fax: 01392 496335
sales@mansons.co.uk
www.andymanson.co.uk/

MAPSON, JAMES L.
3230 South Susan Street
Santa Ana, CA 92704
Phone: 714-754-6566
j.mapson@mapsoneng.com
www.mapsonguitars.com/

MARCHIONE
318 Hawthorne St.
Houston, TX 77006
Phone: 713 522 7221
marchioneguitars@yahoo.com
www.marchione.com

MARI BY REDIVIVUS
via Bava 32
Torino, 10124 Italy
Phone: +39 11 8171.667
Fax: +39 11 8172.309
info@maribyredivivus.it
www.maribyredivivus.it

MARLEAUX
U.S. Distribution
Phone: 212-334-8839
info@joeygmusic.com
www.marleaux-bass.de/
Factory
Zell way 20
Clausthal Zellerfeld, D-38678 Germany
Phone: +49 (0)5323 - 81747
Fax: +49 (0)5323 - 987137
marleaux@marleaux-bass.com
www.marleaux-bass.de/

MARTIN
510 Sycamore Street
PO Box 329
Nazareth, PA 18064-0329 USA
Phone: 610-759-2837
Fax: 610-759-5757
info@martinguitar.com
www.martinguitar.com

MASTER
info@master-guitars.com
www.master-guitars.com

MATON
6 Clarice Road Box Hill
Victoria, 3128 Australia
Phone: 61 3 9896 9500
Fax: 61 3 9896 9501
info@maton.com.au
www.maton.com.au

MAYORCA
Distributed by Tropical Music
Corporation
7091 N.W. 51st Street
Miami, FL 33166
Phone: 305-594-3909
Fax: 305-594-0786
www.tropicalmusic.com

MAXINE
Distributed by the Eternal Musical
Instrument Corp. Ltd.
xsma@embmusic.com
www.embmusic.com

MAXTONE
Distributed by the Renner
Piano Company
No.1 Sophia Road #01-09/10
Peace Centre, Singapore
Phone: +65 3370216
Fax: +65 3368396
support@renner.com.sg
www.renner.com.sg

MEGAS, TED
601 N.E. South Shore Road
Portland, OR 97211
Phone: 503-289-8788
Fax: 503-289-8789
ted@megasguitars.com
www.megasguitars.com

MELACON GUITARS
249 W. Main Street
Thibodaux, LA 70301
Phone: 504-447-4090
Fax: 504-447-4099

MELOBAR
PO Box 9501
Boise, ID 83707
866-650-6321
jfrost@melobar.com
www.melobar.com/

MENKEVICH GUITARS
624 Stetson Road
Elkins Park, PA 19027
Phone: 215-635-0694
Fax: 215-635-0694
michael@menkevich.com

MERCHANT BASS
208 West 29th Street Ste # 213
New York City, NY 10001
merchant@pipeline.com
www.merchantbass.com

MERMER
PO Box 782132
Sebastian, FL 32978
Phone: 772-388-0317
mermer@mermerguitars.com
www.mermerguitars.com

MESROBIAN
Salem, MA 01970
Phone: 978-740-6986
info@cmesrobian.com
mysite.verizon.net/vze2tx8u/

MICHAEL DOLAN CUSTOM GUITARS
3222 Airway Drive #4
Santa Rosa, CA 95403
Phone: 707-575-0654
mndolan@sbcglobal.net
www.dolanguitars.com

MESSENGER BASS
See Knuston Luthiery
PO Box 945
Forestville, CA 95436
Phone: 707-887-2709
john@messengerbass.com
www.messengerbass.com

METROPOLITAN
Distributed by Alamo Music Products
3526 East T.C. Jester Blvd.
Houston, TX 77018
Phone: 713-957-0470
Fax: 713-957-3316
sales@metropolitangutiars.com
www.metropolitanguitars.com

MICRO-FRETS
PO Box 4234
Frederick, MD 21705
Phone: 301-293-2500
Fax: 301-293-2929
paul@micro-frets.com
www.microfrets.com

MIDCO INTERNATIONAL
908 W. Fayette Avenue
Effingham, IL 62401
Toll free: 800-356-4326
Phone: 800-35-MIDCO
Fax: 800-700-7006

MIKE LULL
Mike Lull Custom Guitars
13240 NE 20th St. Suite #2
Bellevue, WA 98005
Phone: 425-643-8074
Fax: 425-746-5748
service@mikelull.com
www.mikelull.com

MILLER GUITARS
Sonnhöglstr. 7
Rossbach, D-94439 Germany
Phone: 08547-7508
Fax: 08547-7948
millerguitars@t-online.de
www.millerguitars.com

MINARIK GUITARS
Van Nuys, CA
Phone: 818-383-1254
minarikguitars@aol.com
www.minarikguitars.com

MIRAGE GUITAR WORKS
21605 Gunpowder Road
Manchester, MD 21102
mirageguitarwork@aol.com

MODULUS GUITARS
8 Digital Drive Suite 101
Novato, CA 94949
Phone: 415-884-2300
Fax: 415-884-2373
custserv@modulusguitars.com
www.modulusguitars.com

MOLL CUSTOM INSTRUMENTS
2304 E. Cardinal
Springfield, MO 65804
1-877-838-7348
billmoll@sbcglobal.net
www.mollinst.com

MONTELONE, JOHN
P.O Box 52
Islip, NY 11751
Phone: 631-277-3620
john@monteleone.net
www.monteleone.net

MOON GUITARS
web@moon-guitar.co.jp
www.moon-guitar.co.jp

MOONSTONE
PO Box 757
Eureka, CA 95502
Phone: 707-445-9045
steve@moonstoneguitars.com
www.moonstoneguitars.com

MORCH GUITARS
Voer Færgevej 104
Ørsted, DK-8950 Denmark
Phone: (+45) 86 48 89 23
Fax: (+45) 86 48 89 23
www.morch-guitars.dk

MORGAINE
Distributed by Salwender International
www.salwender.com

MORRIS
4476 Green Valley Road
Fairfield, CA 94585
Phone: 707-864-1442
Fax: 707-864-1209
moridairausa@att.net
www.morris-guitar.com

MORTORO, GARY
PO Box 161225
Miami, FL 33116-1225
Phone: 305-238-7947
Fax: 305-259-8745
mortorogtr@aol.com
www.mortoroguitars.com

MOSES GRAPHITE MUSICAL INSTRUMENTS
PO Box 10028
Eugene, OR 97440
Phone: 541-484-6068
Fax: 541-684-8579
info@mosesgraphite.com
www.mosesgraphite.com

MOURADIAN
1904 Massachusetts Ave
Cambridge, MA 02140
Phone: 617-547-7500
Fax: 978-374-8076
mguitars@aol.com

MUSICIAN SOUND DESIGN
Lindenstraße 32
Köln, 50674 Germany
Phone: 0449-221-240-96-14
Fax: 0449-221-240-96-15
kurandt@silvermachine.de
www.musiciansounddesign.com

MUSICVOX
877-Musicvx
Guitar@musicvox.com
www.musicvox.com

MYLES, CHRISTOPHER
PO Box 675
Silverton, CO 81433
Phone: 970-387-0185

9STEIN
111 Orchard Street
Yonkers, NY 10703
Phone: 914-376-4128

N.I.C.E GUITARS
www.niceguitars.com

NS DESIGN
134 Blackmeadow Road
Nobleboro, ME 04555
866-673-3744
Phone: 207-563-7705
Fax: 207-563-7701
sales@nedsteinberger.com
www.nedsteinberger.com

NYS
118 Black Creek Road
Middleburgh, NY 12122
Phone: 518-827-5965
Fax: 518-827-5965
c.hofschneider@earthlink.com.net

NAPOLITANO, ARTHUR
PO Box 0294
Allentown, NJ 08501
Phone: 609-259-8818
www.napolitanoguitar.home.att.net/

NEAL MOSER GUITARS
nmoser@comcast.net
www.nealmoser.com

NECHVILLE MUSICAL PRODUCTS
10021 Third Avenue S.
Bloomington, MN 55420
Phone: 952-888-9710
Fax: 952-888-4140

NEUSER
Horná 36
Modra , Slovakia
Phone: +421 33 647 4752
www.neuserbasses.com
Factory
Huvilarinne 9
Espoo, 027 30 Finland
Phone: +358 9 599 615
Fax: +358 9 599 615
basses@neuserbasses.com

NICKERSON
8 Easthampton Rd.
Northampton, MA 01060
Phone: 413-586-8521
nickersonguitars@hotmail.com
www.nickersonguitars.com

NOBLES, TONY
Precision Guitarworks 14 Brookside Dr.
Waverly, TX 78676

NORTH AMERICAN GUITARS
9200 Treasure Lane NE
St. Petersburg, FL 33702
Phone: 727-224-9550
americanguitars@aol.com
www.northamericanguitars.com

NORTON
103 East Main Street
Belgrade, MT 59714
Phone: 406-388-9191
Fax: 406-388-8282
sales@nortonguitars.com

NOVAX
920A Estabrook
San Leandro, CA 94577
Phone: 510-483-3599
bc@novaxguitars.com
www.novaxguitars.com

OLP
Officially Licensed Product
4940 Delhi Pike
Cincinnati, OH 45238
usa_sales@olpguitars.com
www.olpguitars.com

OSCAR SCHMIDT
Distributed by U.S. Music Corp.
444 E. Courtland St.
Mundelein, IL 60060
Phone: 847-949-0444
Fax: 847-949-8444
oscar@oscarschmidt.com
www.washburn.com

OTHON
8838 Greenback Lane
Orangevale, CA 95662-4019
Phone: 916-988-8533
Fax: 916-988-8533

OVATION
Distributed by Kaman Music Corp.
PO Box 507
Bloomfield, CT 06002-0507
Phone: 860-243-7105
Fax: 860-243-7287
info@ovationguitars.com
www.ovationguitars.com

OVERWATER BASSES
Overwater Design and Marketing
Atlas Works Nelson Street
Carlisle, CA2 5ND England
Phone: +44 (0) 1228 590591
Fax: +44 (0) 1228 590597
info@overwaterbasses.com
www.overwaterbasses.com

PALM GUITAR
PO Box 1135
Southbury, CT 06488
Phone: 203-264-1413
Fax: 203-264-1513
info@palmguitar.com
www.palmguitar.com

PALMER
Distributed by Tropical Music
Corporation
6850 S.W. 81 Terrace
Miami, FL 33143
Phone: 305-740-7454
Fax: 305-666-7625
Sales@tropicalmusic.com
www.tropicalmusic.com

PAO CHIA
Distributed by Guangzhou Bourgade
Musical Instruments Factory Co. Ltd.
www.paochia.com

PARKER
Distributed by U.S. Music Corp.
444 E. Courtland St.
Mundelein, IL 60060
toll free: 800-877-6863
support@parkerguitars.com
www.parkerguitars.com

PARKSONS
Distribute by Paxphil
#207 HYUNDAI BLDG. 982-4
YANGCHEON-KU
SEOUL, SHINWOL-DONG Korea
Phone: 82-2-2607-8283/4
Fax: 82-2-2607-8285
biech@paxphil.co.kr
www.paxphil.co.kr

PATRICK EGGLE GUITARS
63 Water Street
Birmingham, B3 1HN England
Phone: 0121 212 1989
Fax: 0121 212 1990
sales@patrickeggleguitars.com
www.patrickeggleguitars.com

PATTERSON GUITARS
1417 Iowa Ave West
Falcoln Heights, MN 55108
Phone: 651-647-5701
Fax: 651-647-5701

PAUL REED SMITH (PRS)
380 Log Canoe Circle
Stevensville, MD 21666
Phone: 410-643-9970
Fax: 410-643-9980
custserv@prsguitars.com
www.prsguitars.com

PAWAR GUITARS
28262 Chardon Road 132A
Willoughby Hills, OH 44092
Phone: 440-953-1999
Fax: 440-953-0183
dealerservice@pawarguitars.com
www.pawarguitars.com

PEAL
Distributed by Ye-II International
Company
Phone: (82-31) 879-3175
Fax: (82-31) 879-3389
yeilint@netsgo.com
www.guitar-peal.com

PEARL RIVER
wmk@pearlriverpiano.com
www.pearlriverpiano.com

PEAR DESIGN
1039 Serpentine Lane Suite E
Pleasanton, CA 94566
Phone: 925-462-2857
Fax: 925-462-2857
tom@peardesign.com
www.peardesign.com

PEAVEY
711 A Street
Meridian, MS 39301
Phone: 601-483-5365
Fax: 601-486-1278
customerservice@peavey.com
www.peavey.com

PEDULLA
PO Box 226
83 E. Water Street
Rockland, MA 02370 USA
Phone: 781-871-0073
Fax: 781-878-4028
christin@pedulla.com
www.pedulla.com

PEERLESS
prs@peerlessguitar.com
www.peerlessguitar.com

PENSA CLASSIC
Distributed by Rudy's Music Shop
169 West 48th St
New York, NY 10036
Phone: 212-391-1699
Fax: 212-768-3782

PERRON CUSTOM GUITARS
25471 CR 24
Elkhart, IN 45617
Phone: 219-875-3223
Fax: 219-875-3297
102377.1047@compuserve.com

PETE BACK GUITARS
8 Silver Street Reeth
Richmond, Yorkshire DL11 6SP
England
Phone: 01748 884887
guitarman@guitarmaker.co.uk
www.guitarmaker.co.uk/

PETILLO, PHILLIP J.
1206 Herbert Ave.
Ocean, NJ 07712-4035
Phone: 732-531-6338
Fax: 732-531-3045
Philluinc@aol.com
www.petilloguitars.com

PETROS
345 Co Rd CE
Kaukauna, WI 54130
Phone: 920-766-1295
petros@petrosguitars.com
www.petrosguitars.com

PHANTOM GUITAR WORKS
80353 Quincy Mayger Rd
Clatskanie, OR 97016
Phone: 503-728-4825
Fax: 503-728-4979
sales@phantomguitars.com
www.phantomguitars.com

PHIL
#141-3 Deungwon-Ri
Jori-Myun
Paju City, Kyunggi-do Korea
Phone: 031 941-5477
Fax: 031 941-7938

PHILIP KUBICKI
726 Bond Ave.
Santa Barbara, CA 93103
Phone: 805-963-6703
Fax: 805-963-0380
info@kubicki.com
www.kubicki.com

PICATO
Distributed bt Saga Musical Instruments
- see listing

PIGNOSE
3051 Coleman Street
Las Vegas, NV 89030
1-888-369-0824
Phone: 702-648-2444
Fax: 702-648-2440
HChatt@pignoseamps.com
www.pignose.com

PLAYMATE
Distributed by Dean and Armadillo
Enterprises
15251 Roosevelt Blvd. Suite 206
Clearwater, FL 33760
Phone: 727-519-9669
Fax: 727-519-9703
www.deanguitars.com

PREMIER
Premier Guitars & Amps Distributed by
the Entertainment Music Marketing
Corp.
770-9 Grand Blvd
Deer Park, NY 11729
Toll free: 800-345-6013
Phone: 516-243-0600
Fax: 516-243-0605

QUEST
Music Industries Corporation
99 Tulip Ave
New York , NY 11001
Toll free: 800-431-6699
Phone: 516-352-4110
Fax: 516-352-0754

RKS GUITARS
350 Conejo Ridge Ave.
Thousand Oaks, CA 91361
Phone: 805-370-5858
Fax: 805-370-1201
info@rksguitars.com
www.rksguitars.com

RWK GUITARS
PO Box 1068
Highland Park, IL 60035
bob@rwkguitars.com
www.rwkguitars.com

RALSTON
PO Box 138
Grant Town, WV 26574
Phone: 304-278-5645

RAINSONG
12604 NE 178th Street
Woodinville, WA 98072
Phone: 425-485-7551
Fax: 425-485-7274
webinquiry@rainsong.com
www.rainsong.com

RAMTRACK
24900 Capitol
Redford, MI 48239
Phone: 313-538-1200
Fax: 313-538-1255

RANSOM
15 Lafayette St
San Francisco, CA 94103
Phone: 415-864-3281

RAREBIRD
Distributed by Rarebird Guitar Labs
6406 Raleigh Street
Arvada, CO 80003
Phone: 303-657-0056
rarebruce@comcast.net
www.rarebirdguitars.com

RAT FINK GUITARS
Distributed by Lace Music Products
5561 Engineer Drive
Huntington Beach, CA 92649
Phone: 714-898-2776
Fax: 714-893-1045
info@agi-lace.com
www.ratfinkguitars.com

RAY RAMIREZ BASSES
20 Esmeralda Street
Humacao, P.R. 00791
Phone: 787-852-1476
Fax: 787-852-1476
rayramirezbasses@hotmail.com
www.rayramirezbasses.com

REDWING GUITARS
PO Box 125
St. Albans, Herts. AL1 1PX
United Kingdom
Phone: 1727-838-808
Fax: 1727-838-808
S.M.I.L.E.-@t-online.de

REITH GUITARS
12674 Esperanza Ct.
Castle Rock, CO 80108
Phone: 303-663-2015
Fax: 303-845-9297
info@reithguitars.com
www.reithguitars.com

RENAISSANCE GUITAR COMPANY
815 Almar Ave.
Santa Cruz, CA 95060
Phone: 831-460-9144
Fax: 931-469-9146
rick@renaissanceguitars.com
www.renaissanceguitars.com

RENDANO, V.J.
777 E. 82nd St.
Cleveland, OH 44103
Toll free: 800-321-4048
Phone: 800-321-4048
Fax: 216-432-3642

RESURRECTION GUITARS
845 Pop Tilton Place #8
Jensen Beach, FL 34957
Phone: 772-370-9789
info@resurrectionguitars.com
www.resurrectionguitars.com

REVEREND
27300 Gloede Unit D
Warren, MI 48088
Phone: 586-775-1025
sales@reverenddirect.com
www.reverenddirect.com

RIBBECKE, TOM
PO Box 2215
Healdsburg, CA 95448
Phone: 707-433-3778
ribguitar@aol.com
www.ribbecke.com

RICKENBACKER
3895 S. Main Street
Santa Ana, CA 92707
Phone: 714-545-5574
Fax: 714-754-0135
sales@rickenbacker.com
www.rickenbacker.com

RITTER BASS GUITARS
Bahnhofstr. 12
Wachenheim, 67157 Germany
Phone: +49 6322 9813-64
Fax: +49 6322 9813-65
webmaster@ritter-basses.com
www.ritter-basses.com

ROBIN GUITARS
3526 East T.C. Jester Blvd.
Houston, TX 77018
Phone: 713-957-0470
Fax: 713-957-3316
slaes@robinguitars.com
www.robinguitars.com

ROCKINGER
www.rockinger.com

ROGUE
Distributed by the Musician's Friend
www.musiciansfriend.com

ROLAND
PO Box 910921
5100 S. Eastern Ave.
Los Angeles, CA 90091-0921
Phone: 323-890-3700
Fax: 323-890-3701
www.rolandus.com

ROMAN, ED GUITARS
4305 S Industrial Rd
Las Vegas, NV 89103
Phone: 702-798-4995
www.edromanguitars.com

ROSCOE GUITARS
PO Box 5404
Greensboro, NC 27435
Phone: 336-274-8810
Fax: 336-275-4469
info@roscoeguitars.com
www.roscoeguitars.com

ROSEWOOD MUSIC
394 Lake Ave S.
Duluth, MN 55802
Phone: 218-720-6086

ROWAN CUSTOM GUITARS
809 Meadowgate Drive
Garland, TX 75040
Phone: 972-495-2413
mike1@rowanguitars.com
www.rowanguitars.com

S-101
Distributed by America Sejung Corporation
295 Brea Canyon Road
Walnut, CA 91789
Phone: 909-839-0757
Fax: 909-839-0713
sales@ascguitars.com
www.ascguitars.com

SMD
Distributed by Toys From The Attic
203 Mamaroneck Ave
White Plains, NY 10601
Phone: 914-421-0069
Fax: 914-328-3852
info@tfta.com
www.tfta.com

SSD
Distributed by Armadillo Enterprises
15251 Roosevelt Blvd #206
Clearwater, FL 33760
Toll free: 800-793-5273
Phone: 727-796-8868
Fax: 727-797-9448

SADOWSKY
20 Jay Street #5C
Brooklyn, NY 11201
Phone: 718-422-1123
Fax: 718-422-1120
roger@sadowsky.com
www.sadowsky.com

SAMICK
18521 Railroad Street
City of Industry, CA 91748
Toll free: 800-592-9393
info@samickguitar.com
www.samickguitar.com
Factory
424 Chongchon Dong
Pupyong-Gu, Inchon Korea
Phone: 82-32-453-3361-4
Fax: 82-32-453-3376-9
smi23@samick.co.kr
www.samickguitar.com

SANTA FE GUITARS
1412 Llano St.
Santa Fe, NM 87505
Phone: 505-988-4240

SCHACK BASSES
Hanauer StraBe 51
Hamersbach, 63546 Germany
Phone: +49-6185-1744
Fax: +49-6185-7959
www.schackbass.com

SCHAEFER GUITARS
4221 W. 4th Street
Duluth, MN 55807
Phone: 218-624-7231
ed@schaeferguitars.com

SCHARPACH GUITARS
Kuiperstraat 46
Duiven, 6921GM Netherlands
Phone: +31-316-264512
Fax: +31-497-540580
guitars@scharpach.com
www.scharparch.com

SCHECTER
Schecter Guitar Research
1840 Valpreda Street
Burbank, CA 91504
Toll free: 800-660-6621
Phone: 818-846-2700
Fax: 818-846-2727
www.schecterguitars.com

SCHULTE, C. ERIC
Beechwood Dr.
Malvern, PA 19355-1507
Phone: 610-644-9533

SELMER
The Selmer Co. Inc
PO Box 310
Elkhart, IN 46515
Toll free: 800-348-7426
Phone: 219-522-1675
www.selmer.com

SEVER
Cankarjev drevored 34 6310
Izola, Slovenia
Phone: 386/05/641-5130
Fax: 386/05/640-2076
sever@sever.si
www.sever.si

SHIFFLETT, CHARLES R.
124 7 Avenue SW
High River, Alberta T1V 1A2
Canada
Phone: 403-652-1526

SHINE
Distributed by Saein Musical Industrial
Co. LTD
www.saein.co.kr

SID JACOBS
3052 Lake Hollywood Drive
Los Angeles, CA 90068
Phone: 323-874-4110
Fax: 323-874-5408
sidjacobs@sidjacobs.com
sidjacobs.com

SIEGMUND
Tujunga, CA
Phone: 661-823-5453
Fax: 661-823-5453
chris@siegmundguitars.com
www.siegmundguitars.com

SIGGI GUTIARS
Schützenstr. 45 - D - 73110
Hattenhofen, Germany
Phone: 0049 (0)7164 / 130087
Fax: 0049 (0)7164 /130200
Siggi-Braun@t-online.de
www.siggiguitars.de

SIGMA
Distributed by the Martin Guitar Company - see listing.

SILVER CADET
Distributed by Ibanez USA - see listing.

SILVER STAR
Distributed by Un Sung Musical Instrument Co. LTD.
unsung@netsgo.com
www.unsung.co.kr

SILVERTONE
Distributed by Samick Music Corporation
18251 Railroad Street
City of Industry, CA 91748
Phone: 626-964-4700
Fax: 626-965-5224
guitars@samickmusic.com
www.samickguitar.com

SIMMONS GUITARS
3444 Hebron Road
Hendersonville, NC 28739
Phone: 828-967-8243
simmonsguitars@hotmail.com
www.simmonsguitars.com
Simpson, James
17 Spruce Circle
Westfield, MA 01085
Phone: 413-568-6654

SINGER
sggs@163.net
www.singercn.com

SLAMMER
Distributed by Kaman Music Corp.
PO Box 507
Bloomfield, CT 06002-0507
info@hamerguitars.com
www.kamanmusic.com

SMARTLIGHT
Distributed by Optek Music Systems
25 Indian Rock Road #415
Windham, NH 03087
Fax: 419-730-0810
questions@optekmusic.com
www.optekmusic.com

SPALT BASSES
1316 Manzanita St.
Los Angeles, CA 90027
Phone: 323-663-7652
info@spaltbasses.com
www.spaltbasses.com

SQUIER
Distributed by Fender Musical Instrument Corporation
8860 Chapparral Road Suite 100
Scottsdale, AZ 85250-2618
Phone: 480-596-9690
Fax: 480-367-5262
custserv@fenderusa.com
www.fender.com

SPECTOR
1450 Rt. 212
Saugerties, NY 12477
Fax: 401-539-8819
sales@spectorbass.com

ST. LOUIS MUSIC INC
1400 Ferguson Avenue
St. Louis, MO 63133
Toll free: 800-727-4512
Phone: 314-727-4512
Fax: 314-727-8929

STAGNITTO GUITARS
236 Vernon Avenue
Patterson, NJ 07503
Phone: 212-822-4533
Fax: 212-822-4503

STARFORCE
Distributed by Tropical Music Corporation
7091 N.W. 51st Street
Miami, FL 33166-5629
Phone: 305-594-3909
Fax: 305-594-0786

STARK
104 Gabriel Drive
Bakersfield, CA 93309
Phone: 661-861-8728
dave@starkguitars.com
www.starkguitars.com

STATUS
6a Commerce Way
Colchester
Essex, CO2 8HR England
Phone: +44 (0)1206 868150
Fax: +44 (0)1206 868160
mail@status-graphite.com
www.status-graphite.com

STAUFER
Daimlerstr. 10
Durnau, D-73105 Germany
Phone: +49(0)7164/800257
Fax: +49(0)7164/148536
staufer@planet-interkom.de
www.staufer-guitars.de

STEINBERGER
Distributed by Gibson
www.steinberger.com

STEVENS ELECTRICAL INSTRUMENTS
PO Box 1082
Alpine, TX 79831
Phone: 432-294-1389
Fax: 432-364-2487
acowboy@stevensguitars.com
stevensguitars.com

STEWART GUITAR COMPANY
PO Box 995
Swansboro, NC 28584
Phone: 910-326-3575
stewartguitars@ec.rr.com
www.stewartguitars.com

STICK ENTERPRISES, INC.
6011 Woodlake Ave.
Woodland Hills, CA 91367
Phone: 818-884-2001
Fax: 818-883-0668
stick@earthlink.net
www.stick.com

STUMP PREACHER GUITARS
12604 N.E. 178th Street
Woodinville, WA 98072
Phone: 425-402-1935
Fax: 206-706-8352
info@stumppreacher.com

SUKOP
Distributed by Sukop Electric Guitars
57 Crooks Avenue
Clifton, NJ 07011
Phone: 973-772-3333
Fax: 973-772-5410
info@sukop.com
www.sukop.com

SURINE BASSES
PO Box 6440
Denver, CO 80206
Phone: 303-388-3956
Fax: 303-388-3956
mail@surinebasses.com
www.surinebasses.com

SUZUKI
PO Box 261030
San Diego, CA 92196
Phone: 858-566-9710
www.suzuki.com

SWITCH
Distributed by Switchmusic.com, Inc.
1900 S. Proforma Suite F-2
Ontario, CA 91761
Phone: 909-947-8618
info@switchmusic.com
www.switchmusic.com

TDL GUITAR WORKS
Phone: 805-423-1672
Fax: 805-423-1672
tdlguitars@yahoo.com
www.tdlguitars.com

TV JONES GUITARS
PO Box 2802
Poulsbo, WA 98370
Phone: 360-779-4002
info@tvjones.com
www.tvjones.com

TALKOVICH, S., GUITARS
PO Box 98
Woodstock, GA 30188
Phone: 770-926-8876
talkgtr@aol.com
members.aol.com/talkgtr/

TANARA
Distributed by the Chesbro Music Company
327 Broadway
Idaho Falls, ID 83402
Phone: 208-522-8691
retailsales@chesbromusic.com
www.chesbromusicretail.com

TANGLEWOOD
Unit 6 Concorde Business Centre
Biggin Hill
Kent, TN16 3YN England
Fax: 01959 572267
emc@tanglewoodguitars.co.uk
www.tanglewoodguitars.co.uk/

TAUSCH HANDMADE GUITARS

Brunnenstrabe 25
Illertissen, 89257 Germany
Phone: 49(0) 7303 903883
Fax: 49(0) 7303 903884
tausch-guitars@nordschwaben.de
www.tausch-guitars.com

TEIGEN GUITARS

PO Box 990421
Naples, FL 34116
Phone: 239-455-5724
ross@teigenguitars.com
www.teigenguitars.com

TERRY ROGERS GUITARS

Phone: 931-879-4800
Fax: 931-879-4802
terryrogers@infoave.net
www.terryrogersguitars.com

TEUFFEL

Weissenhorner Strasse 13
Neu-Ulm/Holzschwang,
D-89233 Germany
Phone: +49 73 07 96 17 16
Fax: +49 73 07 96 17 19
mail@teuffel.com
www.teuffel.com

TEXARKANA

Distributed by V.J. Rendano Music
Company, Inc - see listing

THE PERFECT NOTE

Phone: 413-267-3392

THOMPSON, CARL

aaron@ctbasses.com
www.ctbasses.com

THUNDER BAY BASSES

Distributed by Sound Trek Distributors
U.S.A.
2119 W. Hillsborough Avenue
Tampa, FL 33603
888-466-TREk
Phone: 888-466-TREK

TICE, BOB

Robert Tice Luthier
HCR #1 Box 465
Sciota, PA 18354
Phone: 570-992-5695
Fax: 570-992-5695
luthier@enter.net

TIMELESS INSTRUMENTS

PO Box 51
Tugaske, Saskatchewan
S0H 4B0 Canada
1-888-884-2753
Fax: 306-759-2729
david@timelessinstruments.com
www.timelessinstrumnets.com

TIMM, JERRY

4512 47th Street S.E.
Auburn, WA 98092
Phone: 253-833-8667
Fax: 253-833-1820

TIMTONE

7742- 22nd St.
Grand Forks, British Columbia Canada
www.timtone.com
U.S. Distribution
P.O Box 193 19076 Hwy. 21 North
Danville , WA 99121
Phone: 250-442-5651
tim@timtone.com

TOBIAS

A Division of Gibson
PO Box 309
Conway, AR 72033
Toll free: 800-444-2766
www.tobiasbasses.com

TOM ANDERSON GUITARWORKS

2697 Lavery Court Unit 27
Newbury Park, CA 91320
Phone: 805-498-1747
Fax: 805-498-0878
aguitars@earthlink.net
www.andersonguitars.com

TOMKINS

Phone: (02) 9808-3313
Fax: (02) 9808-3313
tomkinsguitars@bigpond.com
www.users.bigpond.com/tomkinsguitars/

TOMMYHAWK

19 Rt. 10 Bldg 1, Ste. 3
Succasuanna, NJ 07876
Phone: 973-927-6711
tom@tombarthsmusicbox.com
www.tombarthsmusicbox.com

TONESMITH

19817 Jackie Lane
Rogers, MN 55374
Phone: 763-428-8907
Fax: 763-428-1535
www.tonesmith.com

TOTEM GUITARS

A division of TTR
1316 Manzanita Street
Los Angeles, CA 90027
Toll free: 800-328-0136
Phone: 323-663-7652
info@spaltinstruments.com
www.totemguitars.com

TRADEMARK STRINGED INSTRUMENTS

21 N. Shannon Ave.
Athens, OH 45701
trademarkguitar@hotmail.com
www.trademarkguitar.citymax.com

TRADITION GUITARS

PO Box 794
Tullahoma, TN 37388
Fax: 931-455-7434
traditionguitars@mindspring.com
www.traditionguitars.com

TRANSPERFORMANCE, LLC

Self-tuning Guitars
217 Racquette Dr Unit 8
Fort Collins, CO 80524
Phone: 970-482-9132
Fax: 970-482-8865
www.selftuning.com

TRAVELER

325 Alabama St #8
Redlands, CA 92373
Toll free: 800-476-1591
Phone: 909-307-2626
Fax: 909-307-2628
travel@travelerguitar.com
www.travelerguitar.com

TRAUGOTT, JEFF

2553 B Mission Street
Santa Cruz, CA 95060
Phone: 831-426-2313
Fax: 831-426-0187
jeff@traugottguitars.com
www.traugottguitars.com

TREKER

12334 South Pony Express Road
Draper, UT 84020
Phone: 435-623-5082
sales@trekerguitars.com
www.trekerguitars.com

TRIGGS GUITARS

Phone: 785-856-1131
jim@triggsguitars.com
www.triggsguitars.com

TRUSSART, JAMES

2658 Griffith Park Blvd. #262
Los Angeles, CA 90039-2520
Phone: 323-665-4405
jt@jamestrussart.com
www.jamestrussart.com

TUGGLE, ROD

208 Perry Avenue
Rossville, IL 60963
Phone: 217-748-6041

TURNER, RICK

See Renaissance Guitars

TYLER, JAMES

6166 Sepulveda Blvd.
Van Nuys, CA 91411
Phone: 818-901-0278
Fax: 818-901-0294
tylerguitars@tylerguitars.com
www.tylerguitars.com

TYM GUITARS

Phone: +61 7 3891 2185
tim@tymguitars.com.au
www.tymguitars.com.au

U.S. MASTERS GUITAR WORKS

2324 Pinehurst Drive Unit B
Middleton, WI 53562
877-716-6000
Phone: 608-836-5505
Fax: 608-836-6530
guitars@usmasters.com
www.usmasters.com

VF GUITARWORKS
Via Caravaggio 174/a
Napoli, Italy
info@vfguitars.com
www.vfguitars.com

VACCARO
1001 2nd Ave.
Asbury Park, NJ 07712
Phone: 732-774-8174
info@vaccaroguitars.com
www.grandcentralmusic.com/mall/vaccaro/

VANTAGE VANTEK
Distributed by Music Industries
Corporation
99 Tulip Avenue #101
Floral Park, NY 11001
Toll free: 800-431-6699
Phone: 516-352-4110
Fax: 516-352-0754
www.musicindustries.com

VALLEY ARTS
A Division of Gibson
309 Plus Park Blvd
Nashville, TN 37217
Toll free: 800-444-2766
Phone: 615-871-4500
Fax: 615-889-5509
service@gibson.com
www.gibson.com

VEILLETTE GUITARS
2628 Route 212
Woodstock, NY 12498
Phone: 845-679-6154
joe@veilletteguitars.com
www.veilletteguitars.com

VEKTOR ELECTRIC UPRIGHT
Marktstr. 5
Viersen, 41751 Germany
Phone: 049-(0)2162/53309
Fax: 049-(0)2162/45692
sven.gawron@arcor.de
www.vektor-bass.de

VELENO
PO Box 55268
St. Petersburg, FL 33732
Phone: 727-526-8656
velenoguitars@veleno.net
www.veleno.net

VENSON
Room 605 Dongyang Plaza #152
Gumgok-Dong
Pungdang-Gu
Sungnam-Shi, Kyonggi-Do 463-480
Korea
Phone: 82-31-713-3996/7
Fax: 82-31-713-5777
venson@unitel.co.kr
www.venson.co.kr

VERSOUL
Kutomotie 13 C
Helsinki, FIN-00380 Finland
Phone: + 358 9 565 1876
Fax: + 358 9 565 1876
kari.nieminen@versoul.com
www.versoul.com

VIGIER
Distributed by Salwender International
1147 W. Collins Ave.
Orange, CA 92867
Phone: 714-538-1285
uwe@salwender.com
www.vigierguitars.com

VINTAGE
Distributed by John Hornby Skewes
Salem House Parkinson Approach
Garforth
Leeds, LS25 2HR United Kingdom
Phone: (+44) (0) 113 286 5381
Fax: (+44) (0) 113 286 8515
webinfo@jhs.co.uk
www.jhs.co.uk

VINTIQUE
Box 12
Bergenfield, NJ 07621
Phone: 201-501-0337
jay@vintique.com
www.vintique.com

VOGEL GUITARS
La Pensa 4316
Quito, Ecuador
Phone: 5932-259-8457
Fax: 5486-259-5721
bob@vogelguitars.com
www.vogelguitars.com

VOGEL CUSTOM MADE GUITARS
Rheinstr.5
Rheinberg, 47495 Germany
Phone: +49 28 4316306
Fax: +49 28 43 959258
info@cmguitars.com
www.cmguitrs.com

W. PAUL GUITARS, INC.
Waukesha, WI
Phone: 262-544-6355
info@wpaulguitars.com
www.wpaulguitars.com/

WM GUITARS
121 B Arroyo Calabasas
Santa Fe, NM 87501
Phone: 505-995-8975
Fax: 505-995-8975
75032.3676@compuserve.com

WARR
572 Lotus Ave.
Thousand Oaks, CA 91360
Phone: 818-353-0025
Fax: 805-241-0568
warr@warrguitars.com
www.warrguitars.com

WARRIOR
93 Direct Connection Drive
Rossville, GA 30741
Phone: 706-891-3009
Fax: 706-891-3935
anointed@warriorinstruments.com
www.warriorinstruments.com

WARWICK
Distributed by Dana B. Goods
4054 Transport St Unit A.
Ventura, CA 93003
Toll free: 800-741-0109
Fax: 805-644-6332
www.warwick.de
  Factory
Distributed by Dana B. Goods
Gewerbegebiet Wohlhausen
Markneukirchen, Germany
Phone: 0049-037422-555-0
Fax: 0049-037422-555-99
info@warwick.sh.cn
www.warwick.de

WASHBURN
A Division of U.S. Music Corporation
444 East Courtland Street
Mundelein, IL 60060
Phone: 847-949-0444
Fax: 847-949-8444
washburn@washburn.com
www.washburn.com

WATERSTONE GUITARS
Phone: 615-500-6811
askwaterstone@waterstoneguitars.com.
www.waterstoneguitars.com

WAYNE
PO Box 583
Paradise, CA 95967
Phone: 530-872-5123
charvel@wayneguitars.com
www.wayneguitars.com

WECHTER GUITARS
PO Box 91 200 S. Gremps
Paw Paw, MI 49079
Phone: 269-657-3479
Fax: 269-657-5608
info@wechterguitars.com
www.wechterguitars.com

WILKINS GUITAR FINISHES
15734 Stagg St.
Van Nuys, CA 91406
Phone: 818-909-7310
Fax: 818-909-7439
pat@wilkinsguitars.com
www.wilkinsguitars.com

WITTMAN
691 Woodland Ave.
Williamsport, PA 17701
Phone: 570-327-1527
Fax: 570-321-0604
info@wittman-spins.com
www.wittman-spins.com

WRIGHT GUITAR TECHNOLOGY
4686-B Isabelle Street
Eugene, OR 97402
Phone: 541-343-0872
Fax: 541-343-0872
soloette@soloette.com
www.solette.com

WORLAND GUITARS
810 N. First Street
Rockford, IL 61107
Phone: 815-961-8854
www.worlandguitars.com

XOTIC
Distributed by Prosound
Communications Inc.
233 N. Maclay Ave. #403
San Fernando, CA 91340
Phone: 818-367-9593
Fax: 818-367-9593
info@prosoundcommunications.com
www.prosoundcommunications.com/
english/xotic/xotic_lineup.html

XTONE
Distributed by the ESP Guitar Company
10903 Vanowen St Unit A
North Hollywood, CA 91605
Toll free: 800-423-8388
Fax: 818-506-1378
www.espguitars.com

YAMAHA
Yamaha Corporation of America
6600 Orangethorpe Avenue
Buena Park, CA 90620
Toll free: 800-322-4322
Phone: 714-522-9011
Fax: 714-522-9587
www.yamahaguitars.com

YANUZIELLO, JOSEPH
Distributed by Elderly Instruments
1100 N. Washington
Lansing, MI 48906
Phone: 517-372-7890

YURIY
Phone: 909-902-1092
yfs64@inreach.com

ZETA
129 S. Rockford Dr.
Tempe, AZ 85281
Toll free: 800-622-6434
www.zetamusic.com

ZIMMERLY BASS GUITARS
PO Box 5498
Bayshore, NY 11706
Phone: 516-968-5523
zimmbasses@aol.com
members.aol.com/zimmbasses/
index.htm

ZION
2302 Atlantic Ave.
Raleigh, NC 27604
Phone: 919-754-9790
Fax: 919-754-8411
khoover@zionguitars.com
www.zionguitars.com

ZOLLA
8280 Clairemont Mesa Blvd. Suite 127
San Diego, CA 92111
Phone: 858-576-0017
Fax: 858-576-0017
zollaguits@hotmail.com
www.zollaguitars.com

ZON
780 Second Ave
Redwood City, CA 94063
Phone: 650-366-3516
Fax: 650-366-9996
customerservice@zonguitars.com
www.zonguitars.com

ZWIER, JACK
4381 BW
Vlissingen, Netherlands
Phone: 31 0 118-416668
Fax: 31 0 118-414068
zwier@zeelandnet.nl
www.zwiergitaarbouw.nl

INDEX

G

T

P.S.

OK crossword geniuses! So you think you're the Albert Einstein of guitar trivia? If so, please complete this puzzle and either mail or fax a copy of it to our office. If you're as good as you think you are, and all the answers are right, we'll give you a complimentary online subscription for a year! To qualify, you must also include your name, address, and email address. So get busy guitar perverts, and give us your best shot!

ACROSS:

2   Maybe most famous for the Boyd Tinsley signature model.
6   Models made by this company are broken down into the N.J. Series, Platinum Series, etc.
7   Typically found in the fingerboard.
10   Japanese guitar manufacturer.
12   See 3 down.
14   Company based in Meridian, MS.
15   Name used in the early 1980s when guitars were first produced in Japan.
17   Elite Bass manufacturer.
19   Joe Satriani and Steve Vai both have signature models from this trademark.
20   Company established in Fullerton, California.
21   Feature used to split a humbucker.
23   They have a model nicknamed the Light Show.
24   Most known for their Sensor pickups in Fender guitars.

DOWN:

1   Company started in the 1970s with the Standard and Sunburst models.
3   With 12 Across and 22 Down, they celebrated their 20th anniversary in 2005.
4   12 frets apart.
5   Popular guitar wood, often quilted or flamed.
8   See 16 Down.
9   Originally founded as a high-quality guitar and component part company.
11   Guitars produced under this name, as well as Silvertone.
13   Have produced hundreds of different guitar models since the 1970s.
15   They feature the Diamond Series.
16   The second name of his company after he sold 8 Down to Gibson.
18   Rumored to have once produced 50% of the world's guitars.
22   See 3 down.

Crypto Quiz

These are all guitar-related crypto quizzes. Each letter stands for another and each puzzle has a different code. If you think A=M, then it would equal that throughout the puzzle. For answers to these puzzles, please refer to our website, www.bluebookinc.com.

CLUE: O=B

XB D ODYS JUVG XVUY, ZIGGQ, DYS QGDS BUV MQUILGZ JUWQS ILGP

OG MUYZXSGVGS "LGDNP EGIDQ?"

CLUE: H=Y

WG W DBYSZ XLL QKUF FKL MLEF JWIJ KUAALFF TYWFUI QBYSZ NL, W

TYLXX HBY DBYSZ XUH W KUPL L.X.R.

CLUE: Z=A

AFTI RTG QRLZUUTY Z XOERZL RG FEQ PZL, FT YTPEYTY RG PZMM ER Z

JTIYTL.